SOCCERPLUS CAMPS

2001

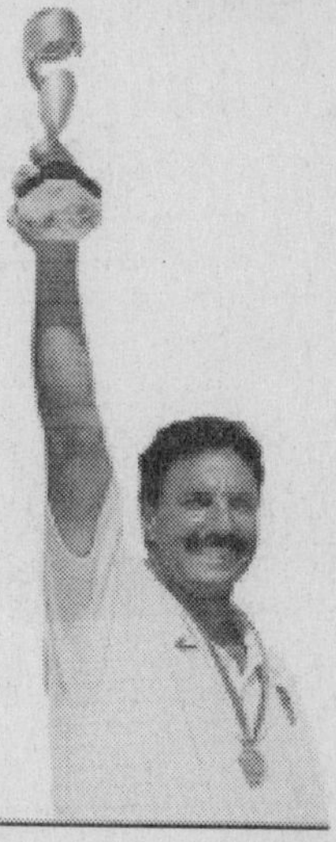

GOALKEEPER SCHOOL

FIELDPLAYER ACADEMY

Presented by SoccerPlus and Tony DiCicco, Head Coach of the 1996 USA Women s National Team Olympic Champions and 1999 World Cup Champions

Call for a FREE Brochure

1-800 KEEPER 1

www.soccerpluscamps.com

www.thesportsource.com
1-800-862-3092

What are professionals in the industry saying ...

"If you're serious about playing collegiate soccer, the Official Athletic College Guide is a must. It gives the student-athlete a competitive advantage in selecting the right college and obtaining athletic scholarships."

Schellas Hyndman, Head Coach - Men's Soccer Southern
Methodist University - Dallas, TX

"Thanks Charlie, for making women's soccer a vital part of THE SPORT SOURCE College Guide!"

April Heinrichs, Head Coach -
USA Womens National Team
Former Captain, U.S. Women's National Team

"Each year I counsel countless student-athletes and their parents. They want information on college programs and making the right choices. Without hesitation I refer them to the Official Athletic College Guide. What Charlie has done is to create a wonderful resource for the college bound athlete. I urge all to take advantage of this excellent book."

Tony DiCicco, Former Head Coach -
USA Women's National Team
Commissioner of the WUSA
Director of SoccerPlus Goalkeeper Schools

...about the Official Athletic College Guide: Soccer?

MATCHFIT™

ONLINE COLLEGE IDENTIFICATION SERVICE

Jump-start your own college search with MATCHFIT™ our new online college identification service offered exclusively at **www.thesportsource.com**. Confidentially enter personal biographical data including your G.P.A., class rank, and standardized test scores, along with information specific to the type of college or university you would like to attend. Your information is matched against our extensive database to identify ten (10) college programs which match your selection criteria. Then make changes to your data and re-run the search two (2) additional times.

The net effect is three (3) sets of ten (10) colleges and universities which are compatible with your requirements for a college athletic program. Any duplications further validate that particular program as one you will want to pursue. You may select any college or university and download information specific to that program directly to your PC. This includes both a general academic profile, and a detailed athletic profile with the coach's name, mailing address, office number, fax, e-mail address, and the college web address. MATCHFIT™ is available for $34.95 and can be ordered at **www.thesportsource.com** with a MasterCard, VISA, American Express, by E-check, or order by phone.

"PLAN FOR SUCCESS" COLLEGE SEMINARS

"PLAN FOR SUCCESS" - COLLEGE SEMINARS™ are conducted throughout the U.S. for teams, clubs, schools, and sports organizations. Our network of presenters include college coaches and experts within the field of collegiate athletics who will discuss in detail:

* *THE SPORT SOURCE™* "Action Plan for Success"
* What college coaches look for in a player
* NCAA / NAIA recruiting rules
* Evaluating colleges and athletic programs
* Writing resumes and cover letters
* Conducting campus visits
* Opportunities for obtaining a college athletic scholarship

"PLAN FOR SUCCESS" - COLLEGE SEMINARS™ are provided to your organizations For more information accross the United States call:

1-800-862-3092

website:http://www.thesportsource.com

2001
CLEMSON
Soccer Academy
Best Camp Value at 6 days, 5 nights
Residential Camps for young men
Directed by
Trevor Adair
Head Coach
Men's Soccer
Clemson University
Camp Dates 2001
Junior Elite Ages 10-13 June 22-24
Striker/ Goalkeeper Ages 20 & up June 22-24
Senior Elite Ages 14& up June 28-July 1
Advanced Ages 10 & up July 7-12
Advanced Ages 10 & up July 15-20
Advanced Ages 10 & up July 22-2
www.clemsonsocceracademy.com
email:info@clemsonsocceracademy.com
1-864-654-9300
105 Catawbah Rd. Clemson, SC 29631

I've LOST
my MAGIC BALL.
Please call me.
It Looks like this
SELECT
Some call it magic.
SELECT
www.selectsportamerica.com
The Official Match Ball For:
WUSA
CONCACAF
USFF
www.wusaleague.com
www.footballconfederation.com
www.futsal.com
SELECT

THE SPORT SOURCE®

AGREEMENT

I ________________________________ on this ________ day in __________ acknowledge and agree to take responsibility for my future and will commit the time, energy and resources necessary to find a college or university that will fit my academic, athletic, financial and geographic needs.

I understand that the task involved will enable me to obtain a college education and pursue my athletic endeavors.

The Official Guides To College Athletic Scholarship Programs
1845 Summit Ave ~ Suite 402~ Plano, Texas 75074 Toll Free: 1-800-862-3092
Telephone: 972-509-5707 Fax: 972-516-1754 Email: sports@thesportsource.com

PREFACE

THE SPORT SOURCE, INC. is pleased to present the ***Official Athletic College Guide: SOCCER.*** With over eleven years of assisting high school athletes in their pursuit of playing at the collegiate level, we continue to explore ways to improve our College Guides. They are the definitive guides to sports Colleges and sports Scholarships for Soccer, Baseball,Volleyball and Softball, functioning as both a reference handbook and self-promotional tool. Our commitment to providing the most current and comprehensive information available to our readers remains a priority!

The Official Athletic College Guides were created, in part, to allow college coaches an effective medium for disseminating information about their programs to high school athletes, their parents, youth and high school coaches, and guidance counselors. The information provided is systematically organized and packaged in the College Guides to provide concise, accurate, and timely data for the prospective student-athlete and his/her family. If fully utilized, it will assist your son or daughter in making the best choice to meet specific academic interests while continuing his/her athletic career. In addition, this publication will supplement the numerous other handbooks that offer more complete information regarding academics, on-campus facilities, and student lifestyles - publications that are available directly from the various colleges and universities.

The original premise for the College Guide was to provide a comprehensive reference tool to college and university academic and athletic programs. The idea was to provide individual profiles for each institution's academic and athletic environment. It became a starting from which student-athletes could begin to gauge the academic and athletic environment of colleges and universities of their interest. In effect, the College Guide became a barometer of various collegiate "climates." To this end, we consider our publications to be a tremendous success! We continue to get feedback from student-athletes currently enrolled in various colleges and universities who used the College Guide to assist them in choosing their particular school.

All of our publications have been well received by college coaches, parents and student athletes that have gone through the process of college selection. For the prospective student-athlete, one of the keys to communicating effectively with a college coach and university admissions counselor is to be able to converse intelligently about their athletic and academic programs. Accordingly, we have been advised that prospective players who have used our publications are submitting resumes and cover letters that are professional and comprehensive. Also, these players are better informed about a prospective college or university and its academic and athletic program.

The Official Athletic College Guide: WORKBOOK is another tool to use for your college research. The workbook can help you identify and select schools that meet a student's athletic and academic program needs. We believe this workbook is the perfect companion to our sport-specific guides to colleges and universities offering athletic/academic scholarships. The data compiled in this book was gathered through phone inquiries and detailed questionnaires mailed to college and university coaches throughout the United States.

As we continue to grow and expand, a few things have been learned about selecting the appropriate college. We have found that the college selection process for the student athlete becomes a two-fold issue. First, it is sometimes difficult to evaluate one's own ability as a player. All prospective student-athletes know where they would like to play, but the question becomes can they honestly be successful in that situation? Second, it becomes difficult to determine a university that will meet the specific academic needs of the individual student. Remember:: When you participate in athletics at the collegiate level, you are a student-athlete. This means that you are a student--first, and an athlete--second. This is the cornerstone of intercollegiate athletics. Therefore, there needs to be an interactive way that will allow the prospective student-athlete to find the right balance of both academics and athletics. This is why we have created the workbook. The workbook will allow student-athletes to assess not only a university's academic strengths, but also where they fit in to this competitive athletic and scholastic environment. This is a detailed and complete "Action - Plan for Success" that has been proven to work time and time again.

THE PUBLISHER

As founder of ***THE SPORT SOURCE, INC.***, Charlie Kadupski continues to annually compile, edit, and publish the *Official Athletic College Guides: SOCCER, BASEBALL, VOLLEYBALL and SOFTBALL.* Mr. Kadupski is a former collegiate soccer player having also played professionally with the San Jose Earthquakes, Houston Hurricanes, and Ft. Lauderdale Strikers of the North American Soccer League (NASL), the Los Angeles Lazers of the Major Indoor Soccer League (MISL), and the Dallas Americans of the American Soccer League (ASL). While at Hartwick College, he was an All-American selection in 1977 - the same year his college men's team won the NCAA Division I National Championship.

Charlie currently holds a USSF "A" License and serves on the United States Soccer Federation (USSF) National Coaching Staff and Editorial Board. He is also the full-time Coaching Director for the Storm Soccer Club in Plano, Texas.

ACKNOWLEDGMENTS

The 2001 Edition of the Official Athletic College Guides are dedicated to the memory of three men who have made a tremendous impact on the soccer community at large -- Ralph "Grif" Griffith, Mike Berticelli and Walt Chyzowych. Grif was committed to the growth of competitive youth Soccer in the North Dallas suburb of Plano, Texas where he was both a past president and founding member of Storm Soccer Club. Grif shared the vision of this publication in assisting young student-athletes in reaching their goals of participation in college athletics. His efforts helped to establish the Storm Junior-Senior Showcase, which annually attracts more than 200 college coaches and generates over $1,000,000 in scholarship opportunities for participating players. Grif also served on the Board of Directors for Plano Youth Soccer Association. His friendship and valuable contributions to the soccer community will be sorely missed. Both Walt Chyzowych and Mike Berticelli made lasting impressions in modern college soccer. They were both tireless ambassadors for the game and both had tremendous personality and charisma that will be truly missed.

Recognition: ***THE SPORT SOURCE™*** would like to thank all of the organizations who are committed to education and youth in sports.

Special acknowledgment for their help each year with the production of the ***Official Athletic College Guides and* WORKBOOKS.**

Editor & Publisher:
Charlie Kadupski

Edit Staff / Production:
Dave Barrett
Chad Blake
Tara Hewko
Heather Horne

Support & Marketing:
Lisa Lavelle
Aaron Spears
Pattie Moore

Technical Advisors:
Frank Pyle
Dustin Gove

Cover Art:
Tal Hollingsworth

Photography:
The Sport Source, Inc.
1845 Summit Ave - Suite 402
Plano, Texas 75074

Printing Company:
Brenda Cockrell
Dallas Offset, Inc.
2110 Panaromic Circle
Dallas, Texas 75212
(214) 630-8741

INTRODUCTION

Selecting the best college or university to meet your needs may seem like an enormous and intimidating task. The prospect of choosing one school over another may produce intense feelings of anxiety, panic, and even fear of making the wrong decision. But fear and panic are products of the unknown. There is no reason for this process to be overwhelming. By being organized and diligent, and surrounding yourself with the right resources and materials, you will be able to make an informed decision - a decision that you can truly feel good about!

Most people travel from the known to the unknown. The known is that you are a junior or senior in high school with a certain GPA and test scores. The unknown is, "Where am I going to college?" The task is not impossible. You will simply need to identify a school that offers the academic programs that best suit your needs, and a Soccer program that is compatible with your athletic ability. You may have as many as 20 schools on your initial list, but only target those schools where the minimum test scores and required GPA fit your own.

Use the College Guide extensively, but don't make it your only resource. Consult other reference materials. Ask questions of your parents, guidance counselors, coaches and other administrators at the colleges that interest you. Gather your information carefully; then examine your options. With regard to your own athletic and academic career, this may be the single biggest decision you will make to this point in your life. While it requires careful consideration, the process itself should never be a stumbling block, but rather a fun and exciting time to share with your parents in planning for your future. It does require a focused and concerted effort, however, a lack of follow-through may create roadblocks, forcing you to make unnecessary compromises in the type of school or sports program you may be seeking.

The process of identifying your interests and selecting the appropriate colleges should begin early. Your freshman year in high school is not too soon to begin the process. Those especially talented players will have less to worry about - the college coaches will be pursuing them. However, it is the greater majority of student-athletes who need to be prepared. As a prospective college player, it is critical that you do your research, and are identified by college coaches as early as possible. Your high school varsity soccer program and summer leagues are the best vehicles for college coaches to spot you as a prospective recruit. Olympic Development Programs, "All-Star," and college showcase events are also effective activities for personal recognition and identification by college coaches. Those student-athletes who make a conscious effort to evaluate college programs, and narrow those choices as they progress through their high school career, will have identified two to three solid choices by December of their senior year.

Most college coaches begin to identify student-athletes as high school juniors - your year to shine as both a player and a student. But even if you have delayed the process of selecting a college until your senior year, all hope is not lost. High school coaches who are well-connected will be able to pinpoint tournaments or showcase events where college coaches will be present. You must take the initiative to contact the coach at the school or schools that interest you by sending them your resume. Preface it with a personalized cover letter and be sure to mention your game schedule and the dates of any showcase events where you might be playing. In this situation, time is very critical - you will need to be seen quickly by college coaches in order for them to fairly evaluate your abilities before they make commitments to other players. (This topic is discussed further in the section titled The Student Athlete's Role in Choosing a College.)

Throughout the evaluation process, be advised that college coaches are selling their programs. They are going to tell you all the best things about their school and their team. Remember also, that college coaches are not just promoting their program to you, but to 25 or more other players as well. It is important to make sure the information you hear is accurate. If you do your homework, you won't overestimate your ability, or underestimate the competition for the position you wish to play. There may also be weaknesses and shortcomings in the program that you will be forced to identify on your own. If you make a mistake in your quest to join a high-profile program, you may end up riding the bench for four years or transferring to another school. This is the reason it is so very important to take an analytical approach to this process. Do your homework and be sure to do a thorough job.

As previously mentioned, one of the most critical steps in the recruitment process is your direct correspondence with the college coach. Because there are often coaching changes, it is highly recommended that you contact the college athletic department to verify the current coach and the correct spelling of the name before mailing any correspondence. Compose your resume and address a personalized cover letter directly to the soccer coach. Be sure to include specific information about the program - information contained in the academic and athletic profiles listed in the ***Official Athletic College Guide: Soccer***. Typically, the 1700+ profiles will also include information on the number of regional and national pool ODP players, and foreign players participating in the soccer program. If a team indicates that out of 20 players, they have 7 regional ODP players, 3 national ODP players, and 2 foreign players, you can assume this to be a very strong program. Other colleges may list 7 or 8 "walk-ons" on their roster. Assess your interests and ability accordingly.

***

The first step in the identification and evaluation process is to thoroughly explore this guide. It contains much of the information you will need to make an informed decision. Choosing the best avenue to continue your education and athletic development is not as hard as it really seems. We hope the ***Official Athletic College Guide: Soccer*** will assist you in making the right choice. We believe there is a program to fit everyone's needs. With proper research, you will find the program that is right for you.

Much success to you in the classroom and on the field of play!

Editor's Note: The following sections, **"THE COLLEGE IDENTIFICATION AND SELECTION PROCESS"** and **"THE STUDENT ATHLETE'S ROLE IN CHOOSING A COLLEGE"**, both have one goal; to prepare you, the prospective student athlete, for college athletics. Although similar in many ways, these methods have various distinctions that make them unique. They are all positive techniques. You are encouraged to examine them all and choose one or more methods that you feel will work for you.

THE SPORT SOURCE®

OFFICIAL ATHLETIC COLLEGE GUIDE: SOCCER

Table of Content

Editor's Note: The editor has tried to insure that both the academic and athletic information contained in this guide is up to date and accurate although subject to change. For that reason the reader should verify important information with the college or university admissions office or soccer coach.

THE SPORT SOURCE, INC.
1845 Summit Ave - Suite 402 ~Plano, TX 75075
E-mail: sports@thesportsource.com

WHAT DOES IT TAKE TO PLAY IN COLLEGE?

G. Guerrieri
Head Soccer Coach
Texas A&M University

The question of **"what does it takes for a player to compete as a college student-athlete?"** is constantly brought before me in my travels across the nation. The answer may be as broad and vague as the question.

In the Official Athletic College Guide you will find hundreds of athletic programs. Is there a program for you? **Yes**. Can you walk into any program and compete immediately? **No**.

To compete as a college soccer player, a student-athlete must be focused, dedicated, and opportunistic. However, to play college athletics you don't have to do it at the Division I level.

NCAA Division I is the most recognized level of college sports. There is also NCAA Division II, Division III, and NAIA. At all of these levels, players and coaches put in long hours all year to insure success and development. These hours (12 - 20 per week, depending on the team) are in addition to college classes, individual study, and social activities. The time commitment of a college soccer player is likened to a full-time job which thousands of players line up for every year.

Speed is the primary component that distinguishes a Division I player from Division II, Division III, and NAIA. The technical speed of a player is the ability to take control of the ball and do it in as few touches as possible and this is what separates the top Division I player from all others. The tactical speed is the ability to read and anticipate the flow of the game rather than just reacting to events as they happen. . The physical speed of a player is the most obvious. This is the ability of the player to get from one area of the field to another faster than his/her opponent. Depending on your relative speed in all of three of these areas, you should look for an appropriate level of play where you can compete with success.

College coaches receive letters and phone calls every week from high school players, coaches, and parents claiming that they have a player that can play at that school. The college coach's first question is always, **"Have you ever seen my team play?"** and **"Do you know what our level of play is like?"** Too often they don't. They have only seen youth and high school games and are not aware of the speed of play at the college level. The same could be said of college coaches pushing their players to the pro or international level; they don't always get a chance to truly see that game and naturally think that their most talented players can excel at that level without truly understanding what that level demands.

A quality college soccer player typically has a clear repertoire of attributes to bring to a college team. Here are examples of the capabilities of a typical Division I player.

FORWARDS

* Possess the physical speed necessary to break away from strong tenacious markers
* Able to hold and shield the ball with the head up while teammates move into support roles
* Show confidence and talent to take on 1, 2, 3 players en route to goal
* Comfortable and successful with both feet while under pressure
* Have superior physical fitness

MIDFIELDERS

* Have superior physical fitness level
* Physically strong and quick to avoid injury due to collision and physical play
* Possess the tactical ability to read and play within the tempo of the game
* Show the technical ability to play a controlled 1 and 2 touch game
* Able to play the ball from side to side as well as back to front of the team
* Can and will defend anytime the ball is lost
* Have the personality to play under pressure

DEFENDERS

* Possess the physical speed and strength to keep up with the nation's top strikers
* Have the grit and determination to play within a team's defensive system
* Show the technical ability to accurately play 40 yard passes to teammates and to control long passes from opponents
* Display the ability to win 50/50 challenges consistently
* Have the composure to play and create (not just destroy)

GOALKEEPERS

* Have the stature and physique that brings confidence to their teammates
* Have the strength and ability to win 50/50 balls and avoid injury
* Display the technical ability to make 100% of the saves in the middle two-thirds of goal and many of the bigger saves in the corner
* Possess the leadership and social skills to get along with players and lead his/hers defense
* Ability to distribute the ball safely in their own half of the field and penetrate the other team's half with long punts, throws, or drop kicks
* Willingness to work as hard in training as he/she does in games
* Display the tactical ability to play within the flow of the game

What does it take to play college soccer? The answer is "What do you want from your college experience?" If you have the technical, tactical, and physical tools to play at the Division I level, do you have the time and dedication? If you would sit the bence for a Division I team, wouldn't you be happier playing for a Division II, III, or NAIA program?

The college choice questions can be researched in the pages of this book. The answers to the questions ultimately lie in your abilities and aspirations.

In his 7 years at the helm of Aggie Soccer, head coach G. Guerrieri has put together a program that has consistently been ranked among the nation's elite. All together, A&M has a combined record of 99-26-3 (.785) overall and 24-4-0 (.857) in Big 12 competition. His overall career head coaching record, including non-NCAA I coaching wins, now stands at 173-64-6 (.724), while he stands fifth nationally among active women's Division I coaches with a record of 115-38-3 (.747). Prior to leading the Aggies, he was Head Men's and Women's Coach at Richland Junior College- NJCAA (1991-1993), Head Men's and Women's Coach at Hardin Simmons University- NCAA I , amd NAIA (1988-1990), Assistant Coach at the University of North Texas- NCAA I (1987-1988), Assistant Coach at Rollins College- NCAA II (1986), and a player and later Assistant Coach at the University of Tulsa - NCAA I (1981-1986).

WHAT DOES IT TAKE TO PLAY IN COLLEGE?

Anson Dorrance
Head Coach- Women's Soccer
University of North Carolina

I'm asked this question all the time: **"What do you look for in a player?"** It is almost an impossible question to answer. If I answer it in one way, I would be eliminating a whole group of players interested in me.

The way I answer the question is by telling the story about a Supreme Court Judge in Southern California who was asked to define pornography. He had to write a statute and he took twelve months trying to sort out an appropriated definition to pornography. After a whole year, this very intelligent man could not write the statute. So they asked him, "How do you know what pornography is? He said, "I know when I see it."

It's basically the same with players. I can tell you a player needs certain technical, tactical, physical and psychological levels, and yet I can find a player who has won either a world championship or gold medal who doesn't have a dimension that I'm saying you require. What you need is some kind of balance.

But rest assured, it is critical to be extraordinary in at least one area. Then you will have an impact, If you have world-class speed, you can have an impact. If you can out-head everybody in the world but can trap a ball farther than you kick it, you can have an impact. If you are a psychological rock, but have no tactical awareness, you can have an impact.

The great players, obviously, are extraordinary in more than one area, and the greatest players are extraordinary in all areas. It's based on a mix of all these different qualities. I would say the most important of all these qualities is your psychological strength, because the quality that separates winners is the ability to constantly reach down to find something deep inside them to make the commitment other people are not willing to make. With that in mind, here are the four dimensions that I believe are necessary.

PSYCHOLOGICAL

This is the capacity to be able to deal with all kinds of adversity. It is also the capacity to be so hard that in your duels with opposing players, you are not intimidated. In great duels, there are defining moments. There is the moment when you get a sense of the other person's hardness. It may be a physical risk issue or a fitness issue.

When you are competing, you measure your capacity to take physical risks, your capacity to push through pain threshold, and your capacity to not back down psychologically from someone. Those defining moments are constant in contact sports. If two players are running for the same destination, the one with the weaker psychological dimension is going to time it so he/she gets to the defined point late. In other words, he/she is going to time it so he/she misses the confrontation with the other player. That's the defining moment of that duel - who is going to slow down and who isn't.

PHYSICAL

A lot of this is inherited - your quickness, your speed, your agility, and your strength. But some of it can be developed. You can improve your quickness, your endurance and, to a certain extent, you can develop speed. The person who fills the physical dimension is the one who has an intelligent and consistent work ethic to improve all the physical qualities. Most people don't have the understanding that all these things work against each other.

For instance, the process of developing speed actually retards agility. If you are developing a good cardiovascular base, it actually hurts your speed development. If you are running 20 or 30 minutes over miles and miles, it actually detracts from your capacity to sprint. You need to develop a balance of all these qualities.

TECHNICAL

Speed of play is the critical element in a player's technical and eventually, tactical development. Speed of play is your ability to do things quickly with seamless effort. As you go from one level to the next technically, you are required to be able to do things so much faster - under pressure, do things with without time and space more efficiently. That's the ascension of your tactical growth.

TACTICAL

The tactical requirement actually has two parts. The first is being able to recognize what is happening on the field. The second is being able to make a decision that will help your team the most and hurt the other team the most. So your tactical requirements are having the awareness as to what is going on in the game by seeing it, then having the decision-making process to sort out what's best. And what is best is going to be determined by a lot of different factors - the field you are on, your match-up, time and space, etc.

What does it take to play college athletics? The answer is **"What do you want from your college experience?"** If you have the technical, tactical, and physical tools to play at the Division I level, do you have the time and dedication? If you would sit the bench for a Division I team, wouldn't you be happier playing for a Division II, III, or NAIA program?

The college choice questions can be researched in the pages of this book. The answers to questions ultimately lie in your abilities and aspirations.

Anson Dorrance, the highly successful head coach of the University of North Carolina women's Soccer team, has written a book sharing his philosophies, methods and insights into training champions. Dorrance's collegiate teams have won 16 NCAA championships. He also coached the U.S. Women's National Soccer Team in 1991 to the first-ever Women's World Cup Title. He is one of the most successful coaches in the World, and a much sought after motivational speaker. The University of North Carolina has won more NCAA championships than any other Division I women's program in any sport.

SELECTING A COLLEGE

YOUR FIRST CONSIDERATION MUST BE ACADEMIC

FIELDS OF STUDY
- Identify your general and specific interests
- Do you prefer a research institute or one committed to undergraduate studies?
- Do you prefer innovative programs or traditional, structured programs

COLLEGE SIZE
- Do you want a broad range of activities?(i.e., larger schools offer more)
- Do you require a broad range of courses or special ized training?
- Are graduate students acceptable as instructors in lower level course?
- Do you prefer a big name program?

LOCATION
- Would you like to be close to home?
- Do you prefer a rural or urban campus?
- Do you prefer a specific climate?
- Do you wish to play in a particular conference?

COLLEGE ENVIRONMENT
- Do you prefer a particular religious affiliation?
- Conservative or liberal environment?
- Coed or single-sex institution?
- Private or State University?
- Are sororities and fraternities important?

Identify up to 10 colleges that meet your individual needs

NOW CONSIDER THE SOCCER PROGRAM

IDENTIFY YOUR SKILLS
- What are your strengths? (Do you have speed,quickness, strength, etc.)
- Is your style compatible with the program you are interested in?
- What is your potential to contribute to the program and when?

IDENTIFY POTENTIAL COLLEGES
- Can you be competitive at the college's level of play?
- Competitiveness of schedule?
- Chance of making the team?
- Potential playing time in first year?
- Competence and personality of coach?

Identify 7-10 schools that meet your academic and athletic requirements

CONTACT SCHOOLS

COVER LETTER
Handwritten or typed

RESUME
Neatly typed and concise

CAMPUS VISIT:
Be prepared
Dress appropriately
Ask the right questions

KNOW THE RECRUITING RULES!

THE COLLEGE IDENTIFICATION AND SELECTION PROCESS

This chapter provides hints on how to make the selection process more manageable. There are many possible options, but if you are methodical, organized, and willing to spend the necessary time reviewing the available data, you will soon find that only a handful of schools offer exactly what you want. Your first task is to determine the type of college you wish to attend. If you follow the guidelines outlined in this chapter, you should be able to eliminate a great number of choices. In many cases, this process will allow you to better define your own wants, needs, and goals.

COLLEGE ACADEMIC LIFE

As a soccer player with proven skills, you are probably more interested in quality soccer programs than any other aspect of university life. Indeed, that is one of the main themes of the College Guide. **Nevertheless, your chances of making a career out of your soccer playing abilities are limited.** Even those who eventually find a place on a professional roster often find their careers can be very short-lived. The average professional soccer player retires in their late twenties and must rely on alternative skills to earn a living. This might seem a bleak picture to someone whose life revolves around the soccer field, but it is realistic. Put simply: professional soccer players are few; professional careers are many.

With this in mind, your search for the right university should revolve around **education first, and soccer second.** While your soccer skills will deteriorate with age, an education and the degree that seals it can open the door to new opportunities continuously.

Perhaps the most important aspect of university selection is flexibility. If you are reasonably sure you know what you want to study (engineering, for example), thoroughly research those institutions that offer the best programs. Compile a list of colleges maintaining quality engineering departments and compare their strong and weak points. Remember, however, that most students change majors at least once; some change many times before finding the right field. So be mindful not to lock yourself into a system that inhibits your ability to change and grow.

There are many different types of programs. Some, for example, stress traditional curriculum, basing studies on a liberal arts foundation. Others are better equipped to train students in particular trades, offering courses of study as diverse as finance and horticulture. To decide which is right for you, ask yourself a series of questions:

What are your main interests? In systematic fashion, list those subjects that interest you most. If you have many varied interests, look for schools with a comprehensive selection of programs. This will allow you to change majors freely without having to transfer to different colleges or universities.

Do you have one specific interest or skill? If so, look for schools specializing in that area, but keep in mind that if you do change majors you might be forced to transfer.

Do you prefer a faculty that is dedicated to teaching undergraduate courses? Institutions with large graduate populations are sometimes more committed to research than to teaching. Professors at those institutions generally have less time to spend on undergraduate activities outside the classroom. On the other hand, the ideas they do bring to the classroom represent current research.

THE COLLEGE IDENTIFICATION AND SELECTION PROCESS

Do you prefer more innovative programs? These programs offer unique opportunities such as overseas studies, cooperative work/study programs, and individually created majors stressing independent study.

Do you prefer a more structured traditional program? These programs are generally built around certain university core requirements which must be satisfied before a student embarks on a single major.

UNIVERSITY SIZE

You can eliminate many colleges and universities by determining the environment in which you feel most comfortable. In other words, do you prosper in larger classes or in a smaller, more personal atmosphere? To pick a school based primarily on its size, you will undoubtedly have to make some trade-offs. Large institutions generally have large classes. This often means that instruction is less personal and interaction among students and professors is limited. On the other hand, larger institutions usually offer more extracurricular activities and broader educational possibilities. Conversely, at small universities, classes tend to be smaller allowing students to more readily exchange ideas with professors and other students during class discussions. There are potential drawbacks though. Because the enrollment is small, the student population may be less diverse than at a larger college or university. Additionally, small schools do not have the resources necessary to offer a wide array of career options; therefore, the curriculum is usually more focused. If you do not know what you want to study, a small school might not be right for you. Ask yourself the following questions when determining the university size most appropriate for you:

What kind of environment exists at your high school? Are you more comfortable in large or small classes? Do you want to experience a different kind of environment or do you prefer to stick to what you already know?

Do you want to meet and interact with many of your classmates personally? This is more likely at a small school.

Is a wide range of activities outside the classroom important? If you answer yes, then a larger university may better suit your needs.

Would you like an academic program which offers specialized training in many fields, or one that focuses on a limited curriculum? Large universities obviously offer a wider range of courses. That, however, does not automatically ensure a better institution. Small universities can sometimes compensate for the lack of fields with more one-on-one instruction and better access to resources.

Are you concerned with the expertise of the faculty? Though the size of an institution does not determine faculty qualifications, there are some things you should research and consider. For example, at large universities, graduate students sometimes teach lower level courses. Though generally well-qualified, they do not have the experience or knowledge most professors possess.

Do you want to play soccer at a big-name university? Or, would you do better to target a smaller school where your chances to play might be better?

THE COLLEGE IDENTIFICATION AND SELECTION PROCESS

UNIVERSITY LOCATION

Another way to narrow your prospective list of schools is to determine geographically where you may want to spend the next four years. Some questions you should try to answer include:

Do you want to stay close to home or do you want the challenge of living far from your family in a distant environment?

Would you rather experience a rural or an urban campus? If you grew up in a small town, it may be beneficial for you to experience life in a big city for several years. On the contrary, if you are from a large city, can you see yourself adapting to a rural environment?

Do you prefer a particular climate? If you dislike cold weather, you might eliminate universities in the North and Northeast. On the other hand, you might want to consider those areas if you also enjoy winter recreational sports.

As a soccer player, do you prefer the competition a particular conference offers? Do the West Coast universities play a style more compatible with your skills? East Coast? North?

UNIVERSITY ENVIRONMENT

Each university or college offers a unique environment. Though hard to grasp from brochures and handbooks, each institution has distinct social, religious, and political attitudes. In order to better assess the information provided in printed materials, be sure to ask specific questions when speaking with college representatives.

Do you want to attend an institution with a particular religious affiliation?

Are you more comfortable in a conservative or liberal environment? You can gather insights about predominant political trends by reading campus newspapers, talking to university representatives, finding documentation written by faculty members, and asking questions of students when making campus visits.

Do you want to attend a university that considers fraternities and sororities important aspects of social life? Many soccer players consider their team an adequate substitute for organized social activities. Others might want a social life apart from their soccer team.

Do you prefer a coed or single sex institution?

Would you like to attend a private school or a public institution? Though private schools are generally more expensive, cost alone should not deter you from pursuing the university of your choice. Financial aid is available for many qualified applicants.

COLLEGE SOCCER

If you have followed the guidelines presented, you can now compile a preliminary list of schools based on academic, philosophical, social, and other prerequisites. Now you can start looking at college soccer programs.

Does the school have special academic counseling for athletes? This is very important because academic counselors who deal specifically with athletes can give you a slight edge. He or she can help you select the right courses and the best professors to allow you the flexibility you will need for training, games, and travel. Along the same lines, does the college have tutors available to athletes? If tutors are available, ask if they are free, or if you are required to pay for their services. Depending on your financial situation, it may make a difference, particularly if you are a marginal student. Also, are there required study sessions for athletes? These study sessions can be helpful in making sure you are devoting enough time to your studies. Many freshmen simply do not know how to budget their time.

How many players from the program have graduated and earned degrees in the last five years? This may give you an indication of the amount of emphasis a school puts on academics. Check to see what percentage of athletes graduate, and then weigh that against the percentage who graduate from the entire student body. Keep in mind that not all schools are alike, so strict comparisons of these numbers may sometimes be misleading.

What is the total number of players on athletic scholarship? Consider what effect this will have on your chances for a scholarship and on your playing time. There are other important questions to ask with regard to scholarships. What will the complete financial aid package include? Depending on how much need-based aid for which you will qualify, you may find a variety of sources comprising your total financial aid package. Grants-in-aid, loans, work study and other aid programs can be combined with scholarship money to meet your needs. You will need to know how to renew the scholarship each year there is no such thing as a four-year scholarship. It must be renewed every year. If you hear something about the renewal process you don't understand, ask for an explanation. You won't want to deal with surprises later on. Finally, you should determine what happens if you get injured and can't play for all, or part of a season.

How many games does a team play each year? You have to balance your desire to play as much soccer as possible with the realization that you can't get in over your head academically. Is there a fall season? A fall season is a good way to get into shape and make a determination about how much playing time you might see during your freshman and sophomore years.

How successful has the school's program been in recent years? Obviously, everybody wants to play for a winner. But the more successful a program is, the stronger the competition will be for playing time. The school's conference and playoff record can give yet another indication of its success. Is there a current upswing that indicates the program has turned the corner, or a down trend, indicating a turn for the worse?

Are you being recruited for a specific position? If so, find out who is ahead of you at that position. This can help determine your chances for playing time. If there are two sophomores ahead of you, there's a better chance of you being in the middle of the bench than in the middle of the line-up. Or, you may be asked to switch positions. Ask yourself honestly if you'll be happy moving to another position.

What kind of athletic facilities does the school have? Sure you're going to be a student, but you're also going to be an athlete. It's best to find out where you will be playing and training. Poor facilities may contribute to injuries, stifle development, or adversely affect your mental approach to the game. On the other hand, don't let a shiny new stadium color your judgment if you are not comfortable with the coaching staff.

Find out also if they have indoor training facilities. Does the program have a weight room and strength coach? Your physical development will play a major role in your success as a college player, and proper training facilities and professional coaching can help elevate your game to the next level. Find out what kind of in-season and off-season conditioning program you can expect.

Does the school offer a junior varsity soccer program? If so, how many players are on the junior varsity and varsity teams? If a junior varsity program is offered, find out if it is used as a feeder for the varsity, and if there is any movement to and from each program.

Who comprises the coaching staff? It is important to know who you will be "working for" during your college career. Find out if one specific coach will be working with players at your position, or if it will be the head coach.

Now that you have identified some of the things you want out of a soccer program, look at the list of schools you have already compiled for academic and other considerations. Try to find those schools among the university profiles listed in this guide. Are their soccer programs also compatible? If so, these are the schools you definitely want to pursue. If not, you might have to make some trade-offs. For example, can you adapt to a new position if a particular coach says you may have to switch?

If you are flexible, you can expand the list of schools that interest you. Remember, there are many quality schools with good soccer programs. Everyone should be able to find a number of match-ups that qualify for their final list.

At this point, attempt to identify up to ten colleges or universities that really interest you. Focus on these schools. The section on Admissions and Paying For College describe how to prepare information that will assist you with college admission requirements. Economic factors generally prohibit visiting all the campuses. Nevertheless, if you can afford the cost, visit as many schools and talk to as many coaches as you can. The section on The Importance of Campus Visits explains what the coach may be looking for, and how you can prepare yourself for this important meeting.

SUMMARY

It is important to remember that your final selection of a college or university should be based primarily on your educational needs. _The Official Athletic College Guide: Soccer_ does not describe individual academic programs in detail. For academic and other information, you should consult other handbooks devoted to that purpose by looking at individual college brochures, and consulting with parents, guidance counselors, current and former players, and college officials. Compile your list of schools from those resources. The soccer profiles in the College Guide should assist you in reducing the number of universities on your list to a more manageable size. Together with the school's complete academic profile you will be able to determine the right college to meet both your academic and athletic needs

THE STUDENT ATHLETES ROLE IN CHOOSING A COLLEGE

The diversity and abundance of opportunities for young men and women to participate in a college soccer program is overwhelming when considering the full range of classifications from NCAA Division I, II, III, NAIA, and NJCAA. To date there are 1700+ colleges and universities that sponsor Men's and Women's Soccer programs.

Each of these schools is unique in three key areas: academic programs, social and environmental factors, and athletic standards. The obvious result of any comprehensive search is that a positive match for the prepared and well-informed student-athlete does certainly exist.

The recommended process involves a focused effort in three areas. These are simply referred to as **THE THREE P's**.

I) BE PROACTIVE: Take a proactive approach to gathering information beginning the sophomore year. This should involve a system for prioritizing choices and a continuous evaluation of personal athletic and academic goals.

II) BE PERSISTENT: Once prioritized, be persistent in communicating your goals and personal interests to the program(s) of choice.

III) BE PREPARED: Prepare both athletically and academically to meet necessary eligibility and admission requirements.

THE WELL-INFORMED STUDENT ATHLETE

What are the variables to consider in selecting a college? The most frequent questions and discussion topics encountered may be generally categorized as academic, social, and athletic related. Essentially, the student-athlete should be attempting to set a variety of immediate and long-term goals for their own personal growth in each of these key areas. Matching a college opportunity to these goals is a vital step in achieving them.

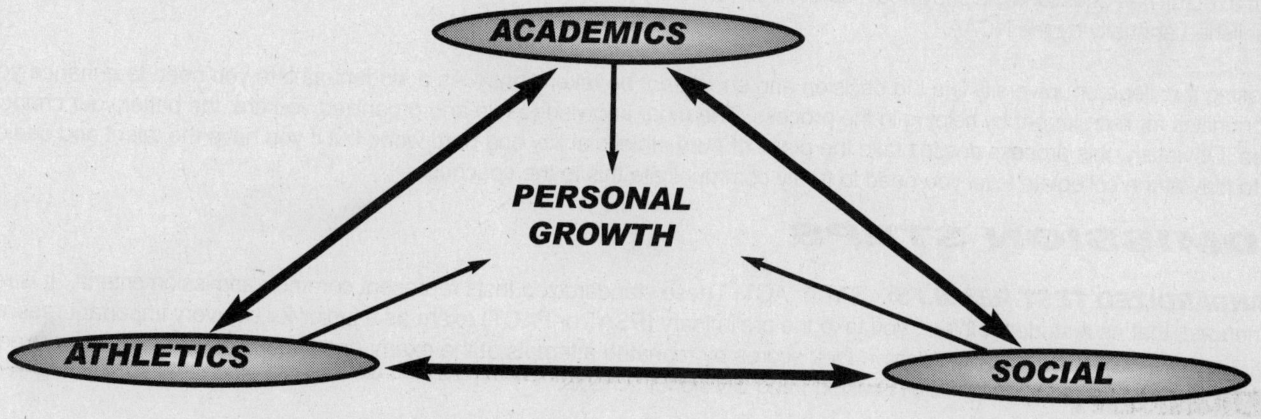

ESSENTIAL QUESTIONS TO CONSIDER

ACADEMICALLY...Will I have the desire, support, and ability to succeed here?

SOCIALLY...Will I be comfortable with my surroundings and able to grow as a person?

ATHLETICALLY...Will I contribute and become a better player?

THE STUDENT ATHLETE'S ROLE IN CHOOSING A COLLEGE

ACADEMIC ELIGIBILITY & ADMISSION REQUIREMENTS

Each Division (I, II, III) of the NCAA has some variability in eligibility requirements. The NAIA and NJCAA are significantly different from the NCAA. As well, the admissions requirements for various colleges and universities may be unique and vary greatly from one to another. However, it is possible to generally view the following items as essential elements for admission criteria to most colleges.

KNOW THE RECRUITING RULES

A recruit should know a few basic NCAA rules:

A college coach may not have off-campus contact with a recruit until July 1st after his junior year in high school.

A recruit may not practice with an NCAA Division I college team on a campus visit.

A player may not accept payments for playing for any club team.

A recruit should not accept any financial rewards for attending an institution outside the formal scholarship opportunities.

Recruitment must be by members of the institution's academic and athletic staff only.

Rules for NAIA and junior college associations are different. Therefore, the recruit should always seek advice directly from the association's governing body if something seems too good to be legal. Also, NCAA Division III rules vary from NCAA rules at other levels. If a recruit has questions, he/she should obtain a current copy of the NCAA Guide for the College-Bound Student-Athlete which is published annually by the NCAA.

Choosing a college or university is a big decision and should not be taken lightly. As a student-athlete you need to enhance your opportunities for recruitment by helping in the process. The more knowledgeable and organized you are, the better your chances will be. Obviously, this process doesn't take the place of pure athletic ability and hard work, but if you have the talent and dedication to play at the collegiate level you need to freely communicate this to the coaches.

ADMISSION STEPS

STANDARDIZED TEST RESULTS: (SAT or ACT) These standardized tests represent common admission criteria. It is recommended, that as a student-athlete, you take the preliminary (PSAT or PACT) exam as a junior for two very important reasons. One, students have a tendency to improve their scores by repeated attempts at the exam, and secondly, the exam is a prerequisite to an official campus visit to NCAA Division I and Division II schools.

PHOTOCOPIES OF UNOFFICIAL HIGH SCHOOL TRANSCRIPTS: Once you have established an open dialogue with a coaching staff, you should provide a copy of your academic history. Many athletic departments have access to qualified people who will analyze these transcripts and assess the probability of admission to the school well in advance of the official notification.

COLLEGE ELIGIBILITY REQUIREMENTS FOR THE STUDENT-ATHLETE

THE ADMISSIONS APPLICATION: This step must be completed during the first few months of the senior year. College coaches are not the admissions officials - the final decision for admission lies with a college official outside of the athletic department. In this regard, the soccer coaching staff is typically delighted when notified that a student-athlete has been responsible for completing the admission process on his own.

Be aware that in some cases an application may be "coded" by the athletic department in order to speed the process, or in some special cases to aid in the admission process. This is a specific question that should be asked of the coaching staff prior to making application.

ATHLETIC ELIGIBILITY REQUIREMENTS

This section is categorized separately because it is, in fact, a separate issue. While the athlete may be "admitted" to a college, this does not guarantee athletic eligibility - more rules to play by!

The NCAA has established a National Clearinghouse from which all decisions regarding an athlete's initial eligibility at an in-situation will be determined. If the athlete is not registered and certified through the Clearinghouse he or she will not be able to participate in Division I or Division II Soccer.

The key steps:

The key steps:

Freshman through Senior Year: Academic Requirements

1) Earn a minimum GPA of 2.5 on a 4.0 scale

2) Credit in at least 13 core academic courses, including:

4 years of English (3 years for Division II)
2 years of Math
2 years of Social Science
2 years of Science (minimum 1 lab science)
1 year additional English, Math Science
2 years additional any of above or foreign language

3) NCAA - Division I & II: Earn a summary score of at least 68 on the ACT or a combined score of 820 on the SAT. (Note: these scores may be higher based upon a sliding scale relative to the student's cumulative GPA.)

GPA	SAT	ACT SUM
2.5	820	68
2.0	1010	86

NCAA - Division III: Based on eligibility requirements set by the member institution and the college's participating athletic conference.

COLLEGE ELIGIBILITY REQUIREMENTS FOR THE STUDENT-ATHLETE

NAIA: Qualification criteria is based on any 2 of the 3 requirements outlined below.

1. A minimum GPA of 2.0 on a 4.0 scale
2. A combined score for the SAT of 860 or ACT of 18
3. Rank in the top 50% of high school graduating class

Junior Year: Registration with Clearinghouse

Immediately after the completion of the second semester the student-athlete should register with the Clearinghouse. This is accomplished by requesting a Clearinghouse "Student Release Form" from the high school counselor's office. The student should provide two copies of the form to the high school counselor for processing.

Senior Year: Verification of Standardized Test Scores

Verify that the standardized test scores and official transcripts have been sent to the Clearinghouse.

Finally, there are other valuable reference materials to aid in the student-athlete's pursuit of college playing opportunities. These publications will provide additional specific information:

NCAA RULES

NCAA Guide For The College-Bound Student-Athlete

National Collegiate Athletic Association

700 W. Washington Ave.
P.O. Box 6222
Indianapolis, Indiana 46206-6222
Phone: 317/917-6222 Fax: 317/917-6888
Website http://www.ncaa.org

NAIA RULES

NAIA Guide For The College-Bound Student

NAIA Headquarters

6120 South Yale, Suite 1450
Tulsa, OK 74136
Phone (918) 494-8828
Website http://www.naia.org

NCAA CLEARINGHOUSE

NCAA Clearinghouse

2255 North Dubuque Rd.
P.O. Box 4044
Iowa City, IA 52243-4404
Phone (319) 337-1492

ACADEMIC RATINGS OF COLLEGES

Gourman Report, Dr. Jack Gourman

Editor's Note: Please be aware that NCAA and NAIA rules and regulations regarding recruitment of high school athletes are under constant review. Annually request the current edition of the NCAA Guide for the College-Bound Student-Athlete and NAIA Guide For The College-Bound Student, but don't assume that you have definitive information - when in doubt, contact the NCAA or NAIA directly for clarification of any rules regarding recruiting practices.

COLLEGE EVALUATION TABLE

SELECTION FACTORS	1	2	3	4	5
SCHOOL NAMES					
ACADEMICS					
Academic Focus - Degree of Difficulty					
Academic Offering in Selected Major					
Size - Total Enrollment					
Athlete Tutoring					
Student-Athlete Support Service					
Quarter / Semester System					
Admissions - GPA Requirement					
Admissions - SAT/ACT Standard					
Coaches Academic "Perspective"					
Requirements for Selected Major					
Tuition (In-State)					
Tuition (Non-resident)					
ATHLETIC PROGRAM					
NCAA / NAIA Affiliation (i.e. Div I, II, III)					
Immediate Contribution / Playing Time					
Player Turnover (Number of Juniors/Seniors)					
Distribution of Scholarship Monies					
Coaching Staff Qualification					
Total Staff & Time Commitment					
Competitive Schedule					
Athletic Department Commitment					
Facilities					
Training Schedule (Traditional Season)					
Training Schedule (Fall / Non-Traditional season)					
Coaches Interest in Me?					
Team Atmosphere (Players Perspective)					
Travel Requirements					
Coach's Contacts to Higher Levels (All Star Teams)					
SOCIAL / ENVIRONMENT					
Metropolitan / City / Suburban / Rural					
Ethnic Diversity					
Cultural Environment					
Coed					
Fraternity / Sorority System					
Distance from Immediate Family					
Recreational Activities Available					
Campus Atmosphere					
Climate					
Team Social Atmosphere					
Employment Opportunities					
Totals (based on 1 to 5 - 5 being best) **Highest Total - Best Fit**					

COMMUNICATING WITH COLLEGE COACHES

NARROWING YOUR FOCUS

Student athletes should contact a number of colleges. There are many factors to be considered when choosing colleges: **location, size, public or private, academic difficulty, courses of study, cost, availability of academic and/or athletic scholarships, and opportunities for need based financial aid.** Added to these are factors regarding the Soccer program: level of play, competitiveness of the schedule, chance of making the team, and the competence and personality of the coach.

Once you have determined what your personal needs will be, some additional research is required. Obtain other college reference guides from a bookstore or a local library to assist you in your evaluation. Realistically, student-athletes should not expect to find a college that is tailor-made for them, but rather ones that provide a reasonable fit.

STEP I: WRITTEN COMMUNICATION

Having identified 7 - 10 schools of interest, entering your junior year of high school you should begin contacting the coaches for each program. Initially, this should be written communication that supplies the coaching staff with important information regarding you as a student-athlete.

CONTACTING THE SOCCER COACH

Take the time to prepare your resume and write a letter to each college coach. A personal cover letter is more effective than a generic version for all coaches. The cover letter should explain your expectations in terms of education, the Soccer program, financial need, and scholarship requirements. Be sure to request literature about the college, and specifically, the Soccer program. The cover letter should also be typed (although more recently, college coaches have given special consideration to neat handwritten letters) and, of course, have correct spelling and proper grammar.

Remember that the resume should be one typed page that presents only pertinent information. Coaches would rather read concise information about a player than page after page of trivia. If a player has a videotape it may be listed on the Resume, but should be sent only at the request of the coach. The resume should be sent to all the selected colleges and contain the following sections:

- A personal section with name, address, phone number, date of birth, height, weight, social security number, and high school graduation year.
- An academic section with high school name, address and phone number; grade point average and/or class rank and standardized test information (SAT, PSAT, ACT scores).
- An athletic section with a list of all Soccer teams on which the student athlete currently plays (high school, club, league, etc.), positions played, coaches names and team records. List any Soccer honors that have been received. This section should include any other sports that the athlete plays and any honors in those sports. Soccer camps recently attended are also helpful.
- A reference section with the names of 3 or 4 people who can accurately gauge the player's character and ability. In other words, those who are knowledgeable of the game and the player as a person. References' addresses and phone numbers are necessary.

STEP II: TELEPHONE CONTACT

The single key variable that separates a single student-athlete from all of the other solicitation letters received by a college coach is regular follow-up. Be sure to call once or twice each month after sending your resume and cover letter. The majority of letters received by college coaches are form letters mailed to numerous programs with the hope that some interest will be generated. **A specific letter followed by a telephone call indicates a sincere interest in a given program.**

The athlete should have a specific purpose in calling; most often it is to update the coaching staff on key games, tournaments, or other opportunities to see you compete. It is also an effective way to directly express interest in the program and to ask questions regarding information not readily available from published sources such as college brochures or the College Guide. Most coaches will be happy to answer questions that aid in the decision process, but may be less enthusiastic regarding information that is readily available from other sources, i.e. school size, degree programs, and athletic conference. Remember - direct conversation allows the coach and athlete to assess personalities and interest levels.

The well-prepared student-athlete will have assembled this information prior to the telephone call. NCAA rules permit high school athletes to call the coach without restrictions. However, be aware that a college coach may not call the student including returning messages until after July 1st following the completion of your junior year in high school.

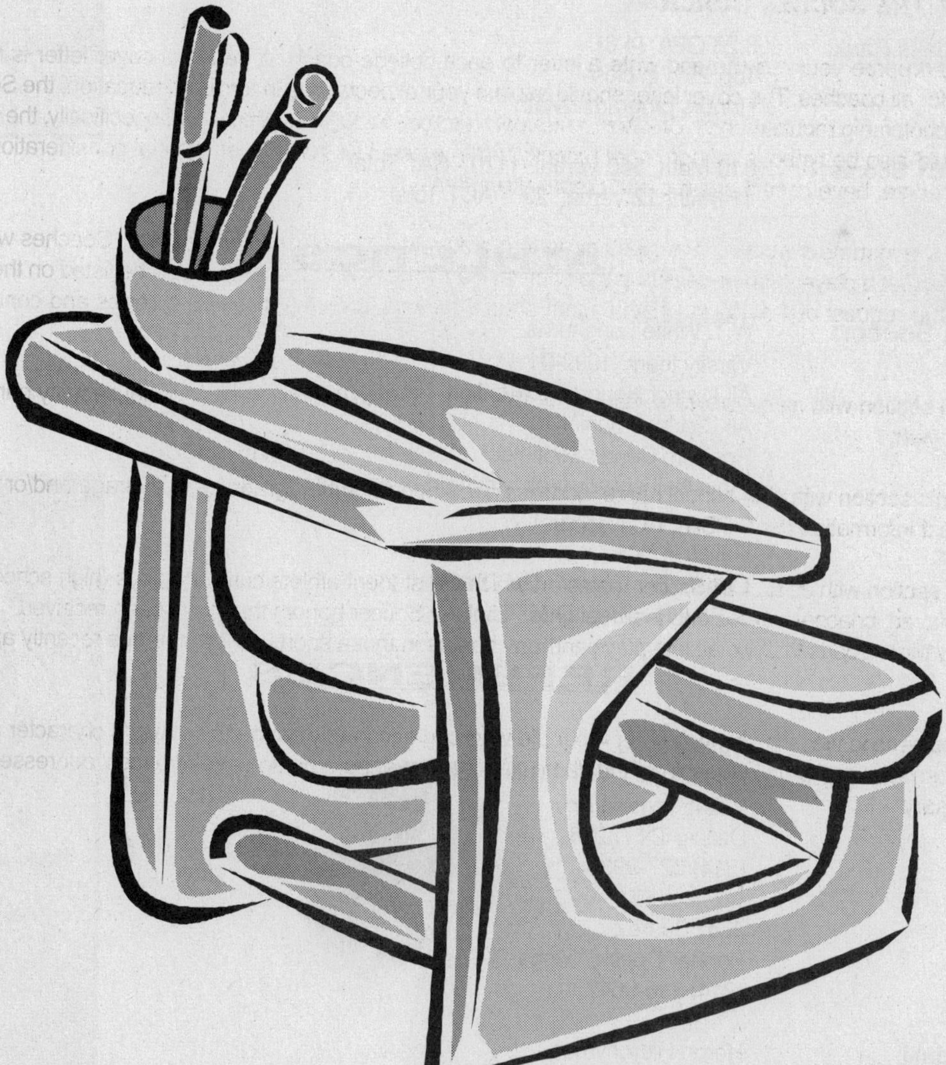

SAMPLE RESUME

YOUR NAME
Address
City, State Zip
Home Telephone
E-mail

Date of Birth: March 9, 1983
SSN: 446-29-1999
Height: 5' 6"
Weight: 125 lbs.

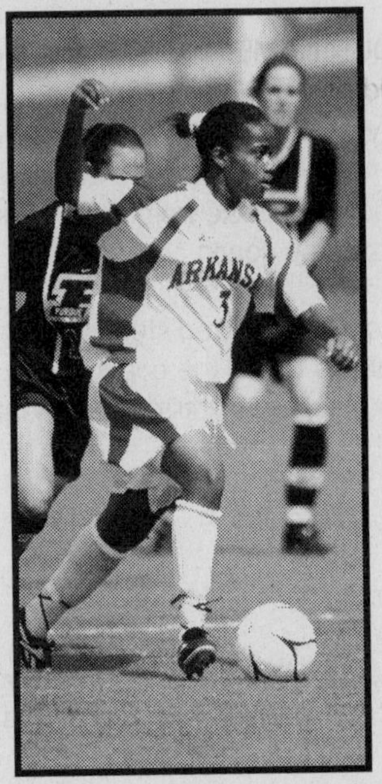

ACADEMICS

High School: W.T. White High School
1244 Forest Ln.
Dallas, TX 57228
(214) 385-5660

Graduation Date: Class of 2002

GPA/Class Rank: 3.28 GPA (4.0)
Top 25% in class
Honors program - Math

SAT/ACT Scores: 610 Math, 560 Verbal: 1170 - SAT Total
11 Math, 12 Verbal: 23 - ACT Total

ATHLETICS

High School Soccer: W.T. White Longhorns
Varsity team, 1999-01
All-District Honorable Mention - Sophomore
All-District - Junior
Position: Center Midfielder
Plays ball equally well with right or left foot

Soccer Club: Dallas Wings
Coach: Jim Turner / Bill Thacker
3-Time Regional ODP Pool

REFERENCES

Coaches: Chris Goode
Head coach, W.T. White High School
12345 Inwood Rd.
Dallas, TX 75228
(214) 827-9951

Judy Suarez
Former Coach, Wings
(214) 696-9642

Personal: Heron Hieronymus
Counselor
W.T. White High School
(214)385-5660

SAMPLE COVER LETTER

YOUR NAME
Address
City, State Zip
Home Telephone
E-mail Address

Date

Coach's Name
Women's/Men's Soccer Coach
Name of College
Address
City, State, Zip

Dear (Coach's Name):

Based on my research in preparation for choosing a college, (name of college) has both an excellent reputation, and the types of academic and athletic programs I hope to pursue after graduation from high school.

The enclosed resume details my academic standing and Soccer experience. I am currently a junior, with a GPA of ___ on a 4.0 scale, and taking college preparatory classes with an emphasis on (list core courses). The strength and variety of courses offered at (name of college) provide several degree plans of interest to me, although I have not yet decided on a specific major area of study.

More specifically, your Soccer program is of primary interest to me. I believe my skills and abilities would fit well into your program, and enable me to contribute to the success of the (team name) while continuing to develop my Soccer talents under your style of play.

I would like to pursue all available means for financial aid, and I believe my academic standing should qualify me for scholarship assistance.

Thank you for any consideration you can give me as a future (team name). Please send me information on your program, and any suggestions you may have on how best to prepare for attendance at (name of school) in the fall of (your graduation year).

Sincerely,

(Your Name)

Editor's Note: **The sample cover letter is for illustration purposes only. Please be original and write your own letter. College coaches tell us they have seen this one a few times and are likely to file it in the trash!**

CONDUCTING CAMPUS VISITS

To get the best feel for a college, it is best to plan a minimum of two visits to the campus - an initial visit and a second or "paid" visit. If this were to occur, you should plan an initial visit sometime in your junior year. The second visit would then occur during your senior year. Sometimes, because of distance or a late start in the college search process, this is not possible and the visits will have to be combined.

The initial visit is a way for you to get acquainted with the college and for the coaches and players to get acquainted with you - their recruit. Many athletes schedule a number of college visits on the same trip, as each visit will take only a short time. The initial visit should include a tour of the campus, an admissions interview (if available) and a talk with the soccer coach or a representative of the soccer program. As a student-athlete, you will need to call ahead and arrange interview times with the admissions department and the soccer coach.

Come prepared for both of these interviews, and be appropriately dressed since first impressions can mean a great deal. You should also have a list of specific questions to be asked of coaches, players, and college administrators. Coaches and admissions personnel are looking for individuals who have some substance. You should ask pertinent questions that fill in the gaps of your knowledge about the college and its soccer program.

Sample questions to ask the Soccer coach:

*What is the status of the returning team, including eligibility of players at the same position as the recruit?
*What are your chances of making the team and/or significant playing time as a freshman, sophomore, etc.?
*What is the availability and chances for a scholarship?
*What is the general practice schedule?
*How much time does soccer require?
*Does soccer interfere with a player's ability to complete academic work?
*How does the red-shirt program work?
*What are the coaches' goals for the team in the next four years?
*What equipment is provided for each player?

Many admissions department personnel will ask difficult questions that will require you to give thoughtful, unprepared responses. Think through your answers and give serious intuitive answers. Most of these questions will be about personal experiences so no preparation is required. It is helpful, however, to gain experience in an interview situation, be completely up-front with the coach and ask questions that will help you to better understand the level of commitment required for participation in the soccer program.

Most coaches will not bring up the subject of soccer scholarships unless asked, so find out what is available and what your own chances might be. As a recruit, be persistent but tactful in seeking answers to all your questions. The coach will want to get a feel for your personality - the type of player and competitor you are and may ask for your own assessment of personal strengths and weaknesses. The coach may also want to know where his program stands on the your list of colleges and universities, and information regarding other schools of interest. Be sure to answer these questions thoroughly and honestly.

The second visit, which can be a paid visit, should occur after you have narrowed your choices to a smaller number of schools. Paid visits can only be made after a student has started their senior year. Each student is allowed five paid visits by NCAA rules to different NCAA schools and only one paid visit per school. A visit would be considered "paid" if the soccer program provides anything free for the recruit (i.e., meals, lodging, etc.) The college may pay for transportation to and from the school and any expenses incurred during normal living arrangements as long as these expenses are not excessive. Paid visits can last up to 48 hours.

On the second visit the recruit will probably be staying with a varsity soccer team member. If this occurs, you are encouraged to go to class with the player to experience the full flavor of campus life, and get questions answered from a player's perspective. Be aware, however, that the coach will be observing you, so please act responsibly. At NCAA institutions, a recruit may not practice with the team while on a paid visit.

Editor's Note: If the two visits have to be combined, be ready to evaluate the college on a one-shot basis. Do as much as possible in this visit. Remember, you will spend almost four years of your life at your chosen college. An insightful visit limits the chances of making a mistake.

THE WORLD WIDE WEB AND YOUR COLLEGE SEARCH

ADVANTAGES OF THE INTERNET

With the low cost of computers and ease of Internet access almost anyone can now get "online", whether it be from your high school, home, public library, or the workplace. What previously was a medium for use only by computer enthusiasts has now become a medium for the masses. A simple message can easily be viewed by millions of people - almost instantly. That's a "reach" more powerful than any television network or metro newspaper could ever have dreamed about even 5 years ago. And that message could be your message!

This rapidly-evolving medium continues to open the door of opportunity to both student-athletes and college coaches alike. Taking a proactive approach to the recruiting process in today's marketplace means using all the tools current technology has to offer. Your ability to promote yourself to college coaches should not be limited to a well-written resume and personal cover letter. E-mail and personal Web sites have become an effective and viable means of communicating with busy college coaches caught balancing games and training sessions, a hectic travel and recruiting schedule, and their personal life. With a laptop computer and Internet access a coach can literally take his office with him. The net effect has been to stretch recruiting budgets and provide alternate means of locating and tracking potential recruits. A quick e-mail to or from a college coach shows genuine interest and opens the door for future direct contact either by telephone or in person.

Through extensive recruiting budgets, and both academic and athletic scholarships, colleges commit significant funds annually to the students and athletes they attract. To minimize these costs and to attract both the top students and top athletes, colleges and sports information directors have jumped into the Internet with both feet, making available vast resources. Realistically, they have only just begun to really explore the capacity of the Internet to help people learn and communicate about their programs. This new wealth of information has allowed student-athletes to explore how they match up with other scholarship candidates, and where playing opportunities may exist.

WHY YOU SHOULD HAVE YOUR OWN WEB SITE

As a result of recent technology developments, you can easily become part of this online community, have your own Web site, and explore the benefits of the Internet during the recruiting process. Your personal Web site will allow you to promote your abilities directly to coaches and college selection committees. Maintaining your site will provide a "fresh look" with new information and your accomplishments, including game highlights, honors, and personal stats. And you can manage this site on your own without depending on third party assistance - i.e. recruiting services or a Webmaster. You control the information being published and the timely release of updated information. Remember, the recruiting process represents a narrow window from your sophomore through senior year in high school. If playing college athletics remains your primary goal, you will want to create a chronological overview of your athletic career to assist college coaches in evaluating your abilities as both a player and student-athlete.

Your Web site can also be a powerful networking tool. Learn to use it effectively to interact with other people in your respective sport, such as your prep or club coach, and to assist you in creating your own online community. Having your information readily available will help others in promoting your abilities directly to various contacts at the collegiate level. To maximize your site's effectiveness, be sure to promote it through your personal e-mail account. (There are various providers who offer free e-mail accounts.) By building a private directory of your contacts, you can provide quick and effective notification of updates to your site.

Also encourage your team to build and maintain its own Web site. Information about the other players including the competitiveness and overall success of your team will all contribute to a college coach's evaluation of you as a player, and whether you are the "right fit" for his / her athletic program.

TIPS FOR DEVELOPING YOUR WEB SITE

Just like any good advertisement, your site must effectively convey your message to your target audience - in this case college coaches. Make it concise, well organized, and informative. Use your creativity to effectively communicate your message, and try to minimize the entertainment value associated with all the "gimmicky" shooting stars, fireballs, flashing signs, and scrolling message screens in more commercial sites.

THE WORLD WIDE WEB AND YOUR COLLEGE SEARCH

Treat your Web site as print medium. Lay it out like a news magazine and use color highlights, font styles, photographs, and subtle graphics to dress your page and not to dominate it. The college coaches will appreciate being able to quickly get the information they need, and are more likely to thoroughly read the material you present, if they are not being bombarded by technical enhancements.

WHAT SHOULD APPEAR ON YOUR WEB SITE

When building your site, it is of primary importance for you to provide as much information about yourself both as an athlete and student without jeopardizing your own right to privacy. Remember, anyone with a computer and Internet access will be able to log-on and visit your Web site. Although you will want to include a resume of your accomplishments, do not include your home address, telephone number, and social security number, which should not be a part of your biographical information on the Internet.

If you want to include a contact number, use your e-mail address or a third party telephone number such as a parent's work number or (with permission) that of your coach. While your most important personal contact will be directly with the college coach, if interested he / she will likely ask permission from your parents' before speaking with you, or leave a telephone number where you can call back. College coaches are recruiting you - not your parents, so be sure you take the time to speak with them personally and return their calls. As a quick overview your Web site should include the following:

Your name, city of residence, e-mail address, third party contact number, high school and its address, graduation year, GPA, class rank, standardized test scores, a listing of your extra-curricular activities, religious preference (if pertinent to your college search), accomplishments - both academically and athletically, other sports you participate in, current coaches -high school and club teams, won-loss records on those teams, current game schedule, any tournaments or showcase events you know you will be participating in, and personal references (again with permission only).

A current photograph - in your uniform works fine as long as your face is plainly visible!

Team photograph and action shot of yourself

In addition to the above, take time to describe some of your personal goals both on and off the field of play; possible degree plans; what you are looking for in a college environment - urban v. rural, larger v. smaller enrollment, on-campus v. off-campus housing, geographic location, climate, social aspects-fraternities/sororities, religious affiliation, etc.; and athletically - under what coaching style you best excel; your style of play; level of competition - NCAA Division I, II, III, NAIA, NCCAA, or NJCAA; and basically, anything a college coach and admissions department can use to evaluate you as a potential student-athlete for their college or university.

WHEN TO LAUNCH AND UPDATE YOUR WEB SITE

Your Web site is a personal snap shot of you as a student and potential college athlete. Much of the information you publish on your site will remain static (unchanged), however, any pertinent information including changes in your e-mail address and contact numbers, updated grades, standardized test scores, class rank, team and personal accomplishments, certain photographs, etc. should be updated. This information should be reviewed at least semi-annually beginning your sophomore year, and as available beginning your junior year in high school.

THE WORLD WIDE WEB AND YOUR COLLEGE SEARCH

PROMOTING YOURSELF AND YOUR WEB SITE

Identify the colleges you wish to target using one of the various student-athlete college handbooks currently available, or by directly visiting college Web sites on the Internet. Develop a Name & Address Book of college coaches capturing college Web sites and coaches e-mail addresses within the directory of your e-mail service. Prepare a more extensive resume with your home address, telephone numbers, birth date, and your Social Security Number along with a personal cover letter to be sent both e-mail and hard copy directly to college coaches beginning your sophomore year in high school. Be sure to include your Web address and do encourage the coaches to visit it periodically for updates. You will want to follow-up the initial distribution of resumes and cover letters with a personal phone call directly to the coach 7-10 days after it is sent. Remember, due to NCAA restrictions, college coaches may talk to you if they receive your call, but will not be able to return your telephone calls until after July 5th going into your senior year in high school.

Do not overlook the importance of hyper links to other Web sites. You will want to initiate link requests to your team or club for permission to link to their Web site. College coaches who are attracted to a particular team or club because of their reputation for competitiveness, or developing college level players in the past, may just "stumble" on your site. You will not want to miss-out on the opportunity to be "front and center" with your Web site if you fit their criteria as a player.

SUMMARY

From your Web site, coaches can view your player statistics, accomplishments, etc. and extend their recruiting efforts beyond the limits of their budgets. So what does this mean to you as a student-athlete? With only limited resources invested, you can systematically identify college programs, evaluate scholarship opportunities, review college admission requirements, view the campuses and athletic facilities, and create a personal profile to share with coaches both in the U.S. and around the world - all without ever leaving your desktop computer!

Editor's Note: These are merely guidelines and suggestions for using the Internet and building your own Web site. It is strongly recommended that any decision to build and maintain your own personal site be something that you discuss with your parents, coaches, and academic advisers. As well, you will need to refer to current collegiate recruiting guidelines with regard to use of the Internet and as outlined in the NCAA Guide For The College-Bound Student-Athlete - for more information call 913.339.1906, or visit their Web site at www.ncaa.org. Also, please refer to the NAIA Guide For the College-Bound Student - for more information call 918.494.8828, or visit their Web site at www.naia.org.

COLLEGE PLANNING CHECKLIST

Jul Aug Sep — SOPHOMORE YEAR

ACTIVITY	Date Planned	Date Scheduled	Date Completed
Student meeting with counselor			
Set academic plan for Junior year			
Check with counselor for PSAT & PACT registration deadline			
Purchase *Official Athletic College Guide*			
Obtain current *Guide for the College Bound Student Athlete* from NCAA			
Complete a practice admission application			
Set-up files - begin to assemble college information			
Do your homework			

NOTES

Oct Nov Dec — SOPHOMORE YEAR

ACTIVITY	Date Planned	Date Scheduled	Date Completed
Parent/Student meeting with counselor			
Verify PSAT & PACT test dates			
Use academic & CPN to write for admis-sions information for several schools			
Review progress with parents			
Attend College Night at high school - gather college information brochures			
Begin to identify 7-10 college programs			
Student meeting with coaches to evaluate athletic development			
Don't forget to study			

NOTES

Jan Feb Mar — SOPHOMORE YEAR

ACTIVITY	Date Planned	Date Scheduled	Date Completed
Review material in college file			
Continue requesting information			
Review progress with parents			
Become familiar with financial aid publications from counselor			
Begin to identify 7-10 college programs			
Perform on the field			

NOTES

Apr May Jun — SOPHOMORE YEAR

ACTIVITY	Date Planned	Date Scheduled	Date Completed
Parent/Student meeting with counselor to review goals-progress-interest			
Review progress with parents			
Begin a College Contact List			
Review academic progress			
Plan next year's academic program			
Begin investigating sources for financial aid			
Continue to update list of potential colleges			
Do your homework			

NOTES

COLLEGE PLANNING CHECKLIST

Jul Aug Sep — JUNIOR YEAR

ACTIVITY	Date Planned	Date Scheduled	Date Completed	NOTES
Student meeting with counselor				
Review academic plan for Junior year				
Check with counselor for Oct. & Nov. SAT & ACT registration deadlines				
Purchase **MATCHFIT** *Online Identification Service*				
Develop more selective college contact list-begin writing to college coaches				
Review Achievement Test results				
Purchase updated edition of the *Official Athletic College Guide*				
Relay event schedule to college coaches				

Oct Nov Dec — JUNIOR YEAR

ACTIVITY	Date Planned	Date Scheduled	Date Completed	NOTES
Review potential college list				
Verify & schedule SAT & ACT test dates				
Explore opportunities for college / high school joint enrollment credit				
Achievement Test given in Nov. nationally				
Verify December SAT registration deadline with counselor				
Visit College Nights / College Fairs				
Complete at least (2) two admission applications for practice only				
Get Letters of Recommendation/References				

Jan Feb Mar — JUNIOR YEAR

ACTIVITY	Date Planned	Date Scheduled	Date Completed	NOTES
Organize your personal portfolio				
Visit local colleges of different types & sizes				
Review Achievement Test results				
Check with counselor for re-test schedule pending on first testing results				
Develop your preferred college list				
Arrange for spring/summer visits & interviews at colleges from preferred college list				
Research internet for financial aid information				
Perform in the classroom and on the field				

Apr May Jun — JUNIOR YEAR

ACTIVITY	Date Planned	Date Scheduled	Date Completed	NOTES
Parent/Student meeting with counselor to review goals-progress-interest				
Take SAT and ACT				
Develop academic plan for senior year				
Achievement Test given in May				
Explore possibility of enrolling in AP courses during senior year for college credit				
Review admission applications questions & concerns with counselors				
Register with NCAA National Clearinghouse				

COLLEGE PLANNING CHECKLIST

Jul Aug Sep — SENIOR YEAR

ACTIVITY	Date Planned	Date Scheduled	Date Completed	NOTES
Finalize application essay topics				
Relay fall schedule to college coaches				
College coaches coaches can make contact & receive calls after Junior year after July 1				
Purchase *Official Athletic College Guide*				
Obtain current *Guide for the College Bound Student Athlete* from NCAA				
Parent/student meeting with counselor				
Verify SAT/ ACT retake schedule and registration dates				
Arrange for college visits & interviews				

Oct Nov Dec — SENIOR YEAR

ACTIVITY	Date Planned	Date Scheduled	Date Completed	NOTES
Update student-athlete portfolio				
Request referals from teachers/coaches				
Review application essays with teachers-parents for suggestions & proofing				
Get tax records to prepare financial aid forms				
If applying for early admissions, complete and send applications				
Obtain all financial aid forms(national & from schools)				
Narrow list to (5) five schools for possible admissions application				
Apply to at (3) three schools				
Inform counselor of applications sent				
National Letter of Intent Signing in November				
Achievement Test in November nationally				

Jan Feb Mar — SENIOR YEAR

ACTIVITY	Date Planned	Date Scheduled	Date Completed	NOTES
File financial Aid Forms ASAP after Jan. 1				
Final visits to schools where applied				
Make sure all applications have been sent				
Parent / student meeting with counselor to verify all transcript verification is complete				
Re-submit any necessary information				
Re-take SAT & ACT if necessary				
Decision Time - "Good Luck"				
National Letter of Intent Signing Day in Feb				

Apr May Jun — SENIOR YEAR

ACTIVITY	Date Planned	Date Scheduled	Date Completed	NOTES
Review acceptances and offers-choose college you wish to attend				
AP Examination given in May				
If put on waiting lists, contact college admissions officers & guidance counselor				
Submit necessary deposits to college chosen				
Notify college you have chosen to attend				
Notify colleges applied not attending				
Notify counselor of final choice and have final grades, proof of graduation,etc. sent				

APPLYING TO SELECTIVE COLLEGES:
The Admissions Committee

What makes applying to selective colleges and universities more of a challenge is that they are in fact selective; that is to say, they have many applicants to choose from and have therefore established selection criteria to determine worthy candidates. Students are not chosen solely on the basis of academic credentials, but also based on what the college is looking for in terms of filling academic and athletic programs. As a soccer player, you will not be evaluated like other candidates; your ability, as well as the needs of the team will be taken into careful consideration. Although the coach will have input, he will not have the authority to make the final decision regarding your admission request.

The matching approach to college admissions requires two basic steps: getting a realistic view of what is available, and an accurate assessment of your abilities. The number of selective colleges is small and can be defined easily by looking at any of the readily available guidebooks. Although definitions of "selective" may vary, most knowledgeable sources would say there are perhaps two hundred such institutions in the country. Of these, not all schools offer soccer programs, compete in NCAA Division I, offer scholarships or have strong winning traditions. The point is that by evaluating academic admission requirements and strength of the soccer program, you can separate institutions into categories and place them in a simple matrix or grid. (See page 15.) The programs more suitable to your abilities will appear with the higher accumulated values.

You can, and should, undertake a similar exercise for yourself looking at your academic achievements and standardized test scores, and rank them along with your soccer abilities. As an example, assign values for your SAT scores with a ranking from a high of 1600 = 10, to 1000 = 4 or a top 20% class ranking being worth an 8. Create similar values for playing on district or state level teams, all league and MVP honors, invitational opportunities, and so on through your senior year. You can then roughly determine where you stand. Keep in mind that there are relatively few institutions or individuals that score high in all areas. Just as it is very difficult to find institutions that have high academic standards and offer competitive soccer with a strong winning tradition, it is very difficult to find "blue chip" athletes that are similarly "blue chip" scholars. In fact, college administrators concede that there are only a limited number of gifted soccer players with superb academic credentials to fill the needs of their institutions. The resulting compromise is to balance academic standards with athletic abilities in order to find qualified student-athletes to fill college rosters. If your soccer abilities are stronger than your academics, try to match-up with those schools that are stronger in soccer than academics, and vice versa.

Once you have identified compatible colleges and universities, you can begin to eliminate schools from this list based on standard evaluation criteria - academic programs offered, distance from home, cost, and so on. This will further narrow your choices and give you an idea of where you might want to make initial contacts. Of course, while you are looking at colleges, coaches may be contacting you, which may continue to expand the number of colleges on your list.

Further elimination will occur by looking at particulars of your given situation - how much a college may want you to enroll, and whether your academic credentials deviate too far from their norm. In other words, are you as qualified as other applicants? If not, how far might an admissions committee be willing to compromise to get a talented soccer athlete?

COLLEGE ADMISSIONS

First, try to gauge your value to the soccer program. Keep in mind that not all institutions apply the same admission standards to their athletes as other students. Look at your position - what is the depth of the team at that position, and graduation year of the starters? Is their skill level far greater than yours? In short, do they need help, and do they need it right away? If the answer is clearly yes, an admissions committee may be likely to compromise on the academic side. However, there is a limit to how far they will go, even for a marquee player!

This "flexibility" can only be estimated, and the only truly reliable way to know is to ask the players. The coach should be willing to give you their phone numbers. If you have any questions, do not hesitate to contact them about their background and their experience academically on campus. Of course, be sure to ask how many hours they commit to their studies, so that you can fairly assess both their ability and willingness to work. If your credentials are well below key players, your chances are not good; if they are the same as average players, they are good; and if they are better than average players, your chances are excellent.

This should give you a pretty clear picture of your chances. Thus allowing you to direct your inquiries accordingly. Your chances for success will increase when your academic credentials are similiar to current players, and your soccer ability is within two years of making a contribution at your position. Be wary of long shots because they are just that and rarely pan out. Be aware, also, that any time you show a college both athletic and academic promise, you not only assure your chances of admission, but greatly increase your chances for a merit scholarship.

PRESENTING YOURSELF: The Application and Interview

How can you improve your chances at any selective institution? Present yourself well. It will not always be the difference, but it does make a difference and you want as much on your side as possible. You have only one, two, and possibly three bona fide opportunities to do this. The first, and most important, is the application itself; the second is a campus interview or visit that you initiate; the third is the campus visit that may be initiated by the athletic department, and for some selective schools, the fourth may be an interview with a review board. For all of these the basics are the same: you want to create the most positive impression that you can without giving up spontaneity or sincerity. Fake it and you will be found out - guaranteed!

The application should be organized, neat, complete, and returned early. The appearance cannot be over-emphasized. Admissions officers and committees will form an impression of you based on the application. Never send in anything that is not first rate. Make sure that all words are correctly spelled and use proper grammar. Be sure to type it, and think of it as a professional resume.

The same rules apply for personal meetings or interviews. Dress appropriately, neatly, and with good taste. Also, make sure that you are properly groomed. Being over-dressed is always better than being under-dressed, and take into account the appropriate style of clothes for the season and region of the country you will be visiting. Make your appointment well in advance and be on time. Better yet, be slightly early. If you are unavoidably detained, call and let the person know you will be late. A good rule of thumb is to prepare yourself as though your interview is with a potential employer. Do your homework on the school you are visiting and master the basic information to minimize dialogue about programs the institution does not have.

COLLEGE ADMISSIONS

Different individuals and institutions will conduct interviews in different ways, however, most selective institutions are interested in some very basic things: What interests you? How do you invest your time? With what results? What have you gained from this? Have you pursued any outside interests in depth, and have you been recognized by others for this effort? Can you ask intelligent questions? Can you respond intelligently to intuitive questions? The outcome will be to discern excellence, dedication, motivation and enthusiasm. Or to put it another way, they are designed to find out if you are as good in the classroom as you are on the field!

Above all, spend some time collecting your thoughts before the interview. Why are you interested in this particular college or university? What is important for your own personal growth? If you need to, write down your questions. Try to word them in a way that will reveal useful information. For example, ask how many of the classes during your freshman year will have less than 25 students. Ask whether specific classes are taught by tenured senior faculty. Ask how many soccer players graduated in the top third of their class and what the grade point average is for the soccer team. Be as particular and specific as possible. The more thorough you are, the more likely it is that you will be remembered in a positive way. And of course, keep in mind that although the interview will rarely get you crossed off the list; if done well, it will most certainly put you at or near the top.

IMPORTANT DIFFERENCES AMONG SELECTIVE INSTITUTIONS: The Six Categories

It is worthwhile to identify the various types of colleges and universities, and to learn more about their admissions criteria. **The six types of institutions are private colleges and universities (including the Ivy League), and state or public universities, the U.S. Service Academies, state and private military academies, and junior colleges.** While there are clearly differences among the various members within each group, understanding the common characteristics is beneficial to understanding the admissions process. As a group, the private selective colleges including the Ivy League have the most freedom in pursuing any type of mission that they choose, and almost total freedom in choosing whatever students they wish to admit to achieve that mission. This freedom is occasionally curbed by athletic league affiliations, but more generally is curbed by faculty review of the admissions activities, usually by setting higher academic standards as a part of the admission policy. Although it is extremely rare for faculty to be involved in selecting candidates, it does happen in some instances, and you need to be aware of this in researching schools.

Faculty members generally put more weight on academic indicators and objective test scores than admissions officers. Most admissions officers are very reluctant to admit athletes who are significantly less qualified academically than other candidates because of the negative opinion that will be formed. Be sure as well that your references include high school faculty can vouch for your character, integrity, and academic accomplishments.

The Ivy League is an association of private colleges comprising a specific athletic conference; it is the only athletic association founded on the premise that athletes should not be given scholarships. While this may be important if you are looking for an athletic scholarship, it has even more important ramifications for admissions. As an athletic conference, each member institution is required to report the academic qualifications of recruited athletes to other member institutions such that all athletes are within certain guidelines for the general population of admitted and enrolled students.

COLLEGE ADMISSIONS

Of all selective institutions, ***state*** and ***public colleges*** and **universities** will typically have lower academic admission standards for residents of their state; however, they often have higher standards for those out-of-state applicants. Applying to a selective university in your state always makes good sense. Applying to a public college or university out-of-state should be carefully evaluated since private selectives may be more generous in terms of admissions standards and financial aid. One way to gauge this is to look at the geographic composition of the members of the soccer team. If a large number of the players come from out-of-state you know that the admission committee has sufficient leeway to give you reasonable consideration; if the converse is true you may want to place your bets elsewhere. Remember, too, that the number of public selective institutions is rather small. This is due to the fact that, by their public nature, tuition and admission requirements must be affordable for residents, yet still attractive to qualified out-of-state applicants. For this reason, your residence may be as much a factor in determining your chance for admission as your credentials. View this, of course, in light of the geographic composition of the athletic teams as indicated above.

The U.S. Service Academies differ from the other groups in several important respects, not the least of which is the fact that they are free to those student athlete's who gain appointment. While the Ivy League offers no merit scholarships, although they are very generous with those demonstrating need, the service academies offer all appointees a merit scholarship. Of course, the hitch is that applicants must be sure they want the discipline and lifestyle that these institutions offer, and also willing to accept military service requirements after graduation. The other salient difference is that although these institutions are selective, they conduct their admissions business very differently from all the rest. Essentially, almost everyone who is admitted attends. As a result, the number of students admitted is very small compared to other institutions where (as a general rule) fewer than half of the admitted students will choose to enroll. Since the general admission procedures are readily available, there is no need to cover them here. Be sure, however, that you understand the singular nature of these institutions, the unique environment and curriculum, and the difficulty of transferring to another college or university later if you find it's not for you.

State and Private Military Academies have the same characteristics as other state and private colleges and universities for admissions and available financial aid, but offer similar discipline and lifestyle as the U.S. Service Academies without the mandatory military service requirements after graduation.

JUNIOR COLLEGES

There are many paths to follow ing your pursuit of higher education. A junior college is often a viable alternative to beginning a college education at a four-year school. A student-athlete may make a more comfortable transition to campus life in a smaller, friendlier and more familiar setting. The junior college also offers an Associate Degree for those who are seeking to gain employment after only two years of study.

Most junior colleges build a solid academic foundation for students who wish to move on to a four-year degree program and for those who have not fully applied themselves in previous settings. They allow students to acclimate themselves more slowly to the rigors of college life relieving some of the academic pressure by adding a personal touch that may not be found at larger universities. This does not mean, however, that they are less demanding than four-year institutions.

COLLEGE ADMISSIONS

Junior colleges almost always offer a smaller student-instructor ratio than that of a larger state school. And, because building the "academic foundation" is paramount, the junior college normally excels in support services. Resource rooms, tutoring, labs, mentoring programs, and academic counseling are staples of a junior college education.

When selecting a college, money may be a primary concern. Attending a nearby community college while living at home for the first year or two can significantly cut the cost of a four-year degree. The junior college offers a very affordable tuition that allows students and their parents some breathing room in the first two years. Moving away from home to attend a junior college offer the advantage of lower tuition, however housing, food and miscellaneous living expenses may match the costs for room and board while attending an in-state university.

Many junior college programs are serious about athletics, recognizing that they are valuable in the overall education of an individual. It is also widely recognized that through athletics an individual can increase his or her market value as a prospective student-athlete to a four-year school.

Junior college athletics are geared towards the continuation of skill development for an individual in a particular sport. Some athletes do not reach their full potential in high school. As in the academic areas, the junior college athletic program is also geared to improving the student's physical abilities. NJCAA intercollegiate athletic competition is very keen, with the various conference, district, regional and national play-offs and tournaments providing a great proving ground and barometer for student-athletes who want to pursue their sport at the NCAA Division I, II, and III levels, or in the NAIA.

Many student-athletes fall through the cracks of the recruiting process, while others are simply unable to make a decision about their future in education and athletics. For some, the financial situation is appealing; for others, the need to develop academically is a priority. These are all reasons that may best describe the cross section of student-athletes found in many junior colleges. Junior college affords them the opportunity to play soccer at the collegiate level. For the most part, these student-athletes continue their education and playing careers at four-year schools. Many are recruited from the junior college setting, and many receive scholarships. These are success stories that cannot be ignored or discounted.

SUMMARY

Evaluate yourself and selective institutions on two dimensions - athletic and academic, then match them as closely as possible. Apply early and try your best to leave a good first impression both on the application and during interviews or visits. Understand the differences that exist in the general grouping of selective institutions. Use this information to your advantage as you attempt to choose the best match possible.

Above all, do not get caught up thinking this is a "life or death" decision, or that, only one college could possibly be the "right" one for you. The fact is, if a college can provide the educational opportunities you want for your future and offer you an opportunity to play soccer, it is really hard to see how you can lose!

PAYING FOR COLLEGE

GORDON PECK
FORMER ASSOCIATE DEAN OF ADMISSIONS AND FINANCIAL AID
DAVIDSON COLLEGE

As you begin the important process of selecting a college, you and your parents will probably be influenced by the stated cost of each institution. Please do not be! At least, not at first.

Too many students rule out a college that may be well suited to meet their needs because of that college's apparent high price. They assume that a student must be from a low-income family in order to qualify for financial aid. They are unaware of student employment opportunities, creative payment plans, and low interest loans. Some have not turned over enough stones in search of competitive scholarships and restricted grants. Others are simply bewildered by the perceived complexities of the financial aid application process.

In the pages that follow, we will attempt to dispel these misconceptions and to provide you with the information you need to plan the financing of the most important investment you may make in your lifetime: your college education. We will focus on three general areas of assistance:

Need-Based Financial Aid
Non Need-Based Aid Including Merit Scholarships
Family Financial Planning

Need-based aid will receive the most attention because, as the foundation of most college financial aid programs, it provides the largest dollar volume of assistance. Before we guide you through the analysis, it is important that you accurately interpret the college price tag.

COLLEGE COSTS

No matter where you enroll, your expenses will include direct educational costs and living expenses. Financial aid assistance is generally determined by your school year budget using five categories:

Tuition And Fees
Room And Board
Books And Supplies
Personal Expenses (Clothing, Laundry, Medical, etc.)
Transportation

Typically the first category represents fixed costs payable directly to the college.

Room and board will be set by the college in the case of resident (on campus) students, but expenses may vary greatly for students living off campus.

Books, supplies, and personal expenses will vary with the student's academic program and personal spending habits.

Transportation costs for resident students are generally estimated on the basis of two round-trips home during the academic year while commuting students must estimate gasoline, parking and other related costs.

PAYING FOR COLLEGE

To be certain that you are comparing oranges with oranges when determining estimated college costs, we suggest that you use a chart similar to X1(below) to record actual and estimated costs in each category for each college you are considering. Be sure you are comparing costs for the same academic year. College A may be publishing 1998-99 costs while College B may be listing 1999-2000 costs.

X1 - ESTIMATING COLLEGE COSTS

Items of Expense	College A	College B	College C	College D
Tuition	______	______	______	______
Fees	______	______	______	______
Books/supplies	______	______	______	______
Room	______	______	______	______
Board	______	______	______	______
Personal expenses	______	______	______	______
Transportation	______	______	______	______
Other	______	______	______	______
TOTAL	______	______	______	______

Most colleges will provide estimates of costs in each category based on annual student surveys. Insist that the colleges you are considering provide these figures in updated form.

YOUR FAMILY CONTRIBUTION

Now that you have determined the estimated annual costs of your top choice of colleges, let us take a close look at how colleges determine your family's contribution toward college costs. Remember: do not rule out any college until you have analyzed all the possible means of reducing the real costs.

All colleges and government agencies expect you to pay something toward college expenses according to your family's financial strength. Most college financial aid offices will determine your family's ability to pay based on a standard financial aid "need analysis" system called Congressional Methodology. The analysis will examine your parents' income and assets as well as your own savings and summer earnings

You may assume that families with higher incomes will be expected to contribute more to college expenses, but the methodology also considers family assets (home equity, investments, savings) and family expenses. A family with six dependents and unusual medical expenses will be expected to contribute less than a family of three even though their annual income is similar.

In addition to the parent's contribution, you, the student, will be expected to contribute at least $700 towards your annual educational costs. The actual amount will depend on your earnings for the previous year and the savings you have been able to accumulate.

PAYING FOR COLLEGE

To the extent that each family's situation is unique, financial aid officers invite you to provide documentation which may substantiate unusual expenses or circumstances which cannot be adequately demonstrated on the FAF. Usually, high consumer debt may not be a legitimate basis for adjusting the results of the standard formula, but many other uncontrollable drains on income may be worth sharing with each aid office.

Table X2 provides an approximation of what many college, state, and private student aid programs will expect parents to pay at various income levels.

TABLE X2	ESTIMATED PARENTS CONTRIBUTION															
This chart of typical expected family contributions derives from Financial Aid Form (FAF)																
Net assets	$20000				$4000				$6000				$8000			
Family Size:	3	4	5	6	3	4	5	6	3	4	5	6	3	4	5	6
INCOME Before Taxes																
$8,000	0	0	0	0	0	0	0	0	0	0	0	0	314	0	0	0
12000	0	0	0	0	0	0	0	0	417	0	0	0	999	493	0	0
16000	266	0	0	0	562	72	0	0	1090	600	139	0	1618	1128	1284	130
20000	916	398	0	0	1176	687	228	0	1706	1215	756	236	2316	1750	916	784
24000	1567	1049	563	13	1804	1302	843	323	2430	1848	1371	851	3183	2481	1927	1379
28000	2296	1700	1214	663	2544	1947	1458	937	3317	2585	2025	1456	4265	3376	2686	2034
32000	3216	2471	1888	1314	3451	2709	2124	1552	4451	3517	2801	2133	5579	4533	3643	2813
36000	4388	3420	2688	2001	4636	3674	2935	2231	5764	4718	3800	2947	6892	5846	4866	3814
40000	5546	4616	3711	2824	5784	4864	3958	3061	6922	5992	5051	3972	8050	7120	6179	5068
44000	6621	5691	4276	3852	6869	5939	5076	4091	7997	7067	6204	5208	9125	8195	7332	6336
48000	7834	6895	6031	5035	8072	7143	6278	5283	9200	8271	7407	6411	10328	9399	8535	7539
52000	9027	8098	7234	6238	9276	8346	7482	6487	10404	9474	8610	7615	11532	10602	9738	8743
56000	1018	930111	8437	7442	10428	9549	8685	7690	11556	10677	9813	8818	12684	11805	10941	9946
60000	11252	0384	9583	8645	11500	10633	9831	8893	12620	11761	10959	10021	13756	12889	12087	11149

Figures on the chart are based on the following assumptions:

One Child In College
Only One Parent Working
No Unusual Financial Circumstances

Your actual circumstances could lead to an increase or decrease. Please use these figures as a general guide only.

Add a minimum student contribution of $700-$1000 to the parent contribution you derived from the table and you will have a rough estimate of the total family contribution you may be expected to pay at each of the colleges where you are accepted. Remember that the parents' contribution, as derived through the need analysis system, is a measure of the family's capacity to pay over time; it is not an amount that is expected to come solely from current income. While a few families may be able to provide the entire parent contribution from current income, most families use some combination of savings and borrowing to satisfy their share of the annual college costs. Supplemental loan programs, financing, and other options will be discussed later.

COLLEGE COST-FAMILY CONTRIBUTION = FINANCIAL AID ELIGIBILITY

Once your estimated family contribution has been determined, it should be subtracted from the total costs of the various colleges you are considering (remember, we are talking about need-base aid; "merit" aid is another matter). Because the majority of colleges will base their analysis on the same methodology, the expected family contribution will be about the same at each college.

Knowing the total college costs at the schools you are considering (Table X1) and knowing your estimated parents' contribution (Table X2), you are now able to begin the comparison of net costs of the colleges you are considering. For purposes of illustration, let us say that your family of six is supported on an income of $52,000 and that net assets are valued at $40,000. Using Table X2, you estimate that your parents' contribution would be $6,187. You then subtract that $6,187 and $1,000 (student contribution), a total family contribution of $7,187 from the total costs at colleges A, B, C and D as follows:

	COLLEGE A	COLLEGE B	COLLEGE C	COLLEGE D
Total Costs	$ 8,000	$12,000	$16,000	$20,000
Family Contribution	7,487	7,487	7,487	7,487
Aid Eligibility	513	4,513	8,513	12,813

As the various college financial aid offices use the standardized need analysis formula, family's annual contribution to your college costs should remain constant while your "need" or financial aid eligibility will vary with college costs. College D at $20,000 will be no less affordable than College A at $8,000 for the family used in this illustration. Knowing that the family contribution will be the same at Colleges A, B, C and D, this family can concentrate on important non-financial considerations in choosing the most appropriate college.

PACKAGING

After your financial aid eligibility is determined, the next task for the financial aid office is to determine which financial aid resources should be combined to form your financial aid "package". Packages may contain grants, scholarships, student loans, and campus employment. Sources of these may include federal and state funds, independent agencies, and college itself. Not all colleges are able to offer you a package that meets all of your financial need, and among those schools that do meet 100% of financial need, aid packages may vary greatly. To illustrate, look at three possible packages that might be offered to meet the $12,813 need of a student attending College D in the previous illustration.

	SHORTFALL PACKAGE	HIGH SELF-HELP	LOW SELF-HELP
Loan	$2,500	$3,000	$2,000
Job	1,500	1,500	800
State Grant	1,000	1,000	1,000
College Grant	1,000	7,313	9,013
Total	$6,000	$12,813	$12,813

The **"shortfall package"** provides $6,000 of financial aid but that amount falls $6,813 short of the calculated need. Most colleges will not offer you a package that falls so far short of your need unless your application materials arrive late or the institution simply has inadequate funds to provide full need for all its students. The "high self-help" package starts with a combination of loan and job (self-help) which totals $4,500 or 35% of the package. The "low self-help" package includes a total of $2,800 in self-help or 22% of the package, a more favorable package because the student's repayment and employment responsibilities are reduced. Both of these $12,813 packages meet 100% of the student's calculated need while holding the family contribution at $7,187.

You will be informed about your calculated need and the resulting financial aid package by way of an "award letter." Each college where you have been accepted for admission, applied for aid, and provided on-time financial aid application forms, will send you an "award letter" informing you of the amount and type of aid you will receive. This letter should reach you well before the deadline date for making your admissions deposit so that you will have time to compare packages and ask questions about your package.

NON-NEED BASED ASSISTANCE

In spite of our encouragement and your family's best efforts, the need analysis system may determine that you are not eligible for need-based financial aid, or perhaps your parents feel they cannot come up with all of the family contribution calculated by your top choice colleges. What then? There may still be hope in the form of grants-in-aid, merit scholarships, payment plans, alternative loan programs, and other creative financing options.

Grants and merit scholarships--As discussed earlier, many need-based financial aid packages will include grants or scholarships. Many colleges also offer gift aid (grants and scholarships) without regard to financial need to recognize outstanding accomplishments and potential in academics, performing arts, athletics, and other special talents. These special awards may be offered to no more than ten percent of the students at a particular college and may range in value from a hundred dollars to full cost.

Competition for these college-sponsored scholarships is keen and frequently requires a separate application. You should ask each college you are considering about the requirements and procedures that apply to merit scholarships at that institution. You should explore the possibility of scholarships and grants from private organizations. Your parents' employers, professional organizations, service organizations, churches, local PTA groups, veterans' organizations, charitable societies, and many other groups frequently provide aid for college-bound students. Begin your search for these private scholarships in your school's guidance library. Also check with the public library for such guides as "The College Blue Book: Scholarships, Fellowships, Grants and Loans or Financial Aid for Higher Education," Oreon Keesler, Editor.

Again, you might turn to individual college financial aid offices about outside sources of scholarships that have been used by their students in the past.

Alternative loan program--The loans referred to in our earlier discussion of packaging are subsidized student loans, available only to students who demonstrate need. These need-based loans are provided through the Perkins or Stafford loan programs, and they are generally included within a student's need-based package.

PAYING FOR COLLEGE

In this section, we want to make you aware of educational loan options available to parents and students who may not qualify for need- based aid or who may need assistance meeting the family contribution expected by the financial aid office.

At the federal level, Congress has authorized two programs: Parent Loans for Undergraduate Students (PLUS) and Supplemental Loans for Students (SLS). PLUS loans are available for parents of dependent students, and SLS loans are for independent students. Unlike the Perkins and Stafford loan programs, there is no in-school interest subsidy and very limited opportunity to postpone payments until after college. However, the programs offer interest rates and repayment advantages over most consumer loans.

Several alternative loan programs have been developed in the private sector over the past few years. Some are supported by nonprofit organizations such as The Education Resources Institute (TERI) in Boston, and Concern: Loans for Education in Washington, D.C. These loans offer high annual limits (as much as $25,000 annually) to credit-worthy families, plus options for postponing principal repayment while the student remains in school. Banks and other for-profit organizations also sponsor loan programs. Some of these arrangements establish a line of credit which families may draw against as needed for educational costs. Other loan plans may be tied to tuition payment plans.

Tuition payment plans--Some colleges, plus a number of private financial institutions provide payment plans which allow families to spread the cost of attending college over the entire school year. Such plans provide a budget-wise option to the traditional lump sum payment at the beginning of each semester. Generally, the only charge for such programs is an application fee, unless the program is combined with an educational loan. Organizations such as Academic Management Services of Pawtucket, RI and the Knight Tuition Payment Plan of Boston work closely with several colleges in arranging individual payment plans for families.

Other options--A number of other creative options are being developed to help families better plan and manage the costs of higher education. Federal agencies, state governments, colleges, financial institutions, and various consortia are involved in the creation of savings plans, prepayment plans, tuition guarantee plans, and other alternatives too numerous to mention here. Our advice is to gather all the facts you can through your guidance office from publications such as "The College Cost Book" published by The College Board and Peterson's, "The College Money Handbook," and especially from the financial aid offices at the colleges you are considering.

SCHEDULE FOR FINANCIAL AID APPLICANTS

Junior Year

As you investigate colleges, check each college's literature for financial aid application requirements, deadlines, and any special programs for which you may be eligible. When planning your college visits, try to set an appointment to see a financial aid officer. Be prepared with specific questions about application requirements, competitive scholarship programs, packaging policies, alternative loan programs, and other questions important to your family.

Senior Year

September - get a copy of "Meeting College Costs," a publication of the College Scholarship Service, available in most guidance offices. Use the charts in this handy guide to estimate your family contribution and financial needs.

PAYING FOR COLLEGE

December - get the FAF (Financial Aid Form), the SAAC (Student Aid Application for California) or the FFS (Family Financial Statement) from the guidance office. The form may not be submitted before January 1, but you should familiarize yourself with requested information and begin to gather the financial records you will need to complete the form.

January / February - complete and submit the FAF (or SAAC or FFS). Make a copy for your records before sending them. Complete other financial aid application materials and send them to the colleges to which you are applying. Make one last check for forms you may also need to submit to be considered for private scholarship programs or other outside aid. If you anticipate that you may not be eligible or receive enough need-based aid, you should complete your investigation of alternative loan programs and other sources of non-need based aid. Be sure to include college financial aid officers as you seek advice on these matters.

April/May - carefully compare the bottom line costs to your family from each of the colleges offering you financial aid. As you inform your first choice of colleges of your decision to attend, respond also to school's offer of financial aid. Be sure to let the other colleges know of your decision to attend the first choice college.

May/June - by now your family should have submitted copies of its federal tax returns, promissory notes for student loans and other required documents to the appropriate financial aid office. If suggested by your college, the Stafford loan application should be submitted at that time.

WHOM CAN I TRUST

While your high school coach and the college athletic recruiter may be very helpful and eager to assist you in the college search, it is important that you and your family maintain direct contact with the college financial aid offices. Do not send your financial aid application materials through the coach and do not rely on his or her interpretation of your eligibility for financial aid. Too many lost documents, missed deadlines, and misinterpreted financial aid packages have been attributed to well-meaning but unnecessary intercession by athletic recruiters.

While some high school officers may not have as much time or good information as you would like, they are still the best place to start when seeking financial aid advice. At a minimum, they can put valuable material into your hands and guide you to other people who can help. Financial aid officers at the college you are considering are probably in the best position to analyze your circumstances and lead you to the best sources of need-based and non need-based financial assistance.

Editors note:Some of the publications referred to earlier can provide you with excellent guidance as you contemplate the serious matter of financing your education.

PAYING FOR COLLEGE

FOREIGN STUDENTS

THE SPORT SOURCE, INC. has learned through its first ten years of publications that many student-athletes outside of the U.S. are using this College Guide. Because of this, we continue to include a brief outline of the steps necessary for international students to apply to schools in the U.S.

As an international applicant it is important to begin the process as early as possible. You should apply no later than 6 months prior to the semester in which you wish to begin your studies. You will need the extra time to obtain your official school records, arrange for the required examinations, forward bank verification of your financial resources, for your application to be reviewed, and to obtain your visa.

It is important to note that many U.S. colleges and universities require international students applying for undergraduate studies (bachelor's degree) to pay all expenses themselves. Many universities do not give scholarships or financial aid to international students seeking undergraduate studies.

REQUIREMENTS

International students usually are required to be proficient in the English language, and good students in their own countries before they will be considered for admission into a college in the U.S. Students usually should have 12 years of study in their own country, beginning at age six. The last four or five years should include the study of English, history, mathematics and science. Although each university may be different, this is a basic overview of what many universities require for application from international students:

An Application Form: Answer every question. Your principal or headmaster may also be asked to answer questions on the form. There may or may not be an application fee.
Financial Certification: The student or his/her parents must often submit proof that the family or sponsor can pay for the schooling. This amount can range anywhere from $14,000-$20,000 per year, including tuition, room, food, books, and other miscellaneous expenses. The university needs an official statement from a bank, employer, sponsor, or other official affidavit of support.
School Records: These are transcripts or certificates of satisfactory study. Records should include an English translation of the subjects the student has studied and grades the student has made in each subject. It is very important to explain the grading system of each school attended.
Test of English as a Foreign Language (TOEFL): This is usually required for all international students except those whose native language is English. Information about this test can be found at U.S. Embassies, Consulates, offices of the United States Information Services, or at schools in your home country.
Aptitude Tests (SAT/ACT): These tests, such as the Scholastic Aptitude Test (SAT) or American College Testing's (ACT) Assessment Program which measure verbal and mathematical ability are required for both international students and American students.

PAYING FOR COLLEGE

VISA

After you have been admitted and have submitted the financial certification information with bank statements, the university will send you a visa qualifying document. In most cases, you will be sent an I-20 Form which is used to get an F-l student visa. To get the visa, you will need to go to your nearest American Embassy or Consulate and show the following three items:

Your Passport
Your I-20
Your Current Financial Certification

Because you may be asked to prove your financial resources, you should retain certified copies of the original financial information that you are sending to U. S. colleges when applying.

If you already are in the United States, you will not need to get a new visa; you will receive a transfer, which will extend your time to the dates of the appropriate academic program. An I-20 will be sent for you to do your transfer.

PAYING FOR COLLEGE

IF YOU HAVE MORE TIME

If college is still several years away for you, your family has the advantage of planning and saving for your college education. Remember, colleges will consider the student and their family as the first and primary source of funds for education, and the bulk of financial aid awards will continue to be given on the basis of financial need. Therefore, it behooves you to do all you can in advance to painlessly provide the calculated family contribution when the time comes.

Educational financial planning can be complicated, but it is not as cumbersome as paying for college when there has been no planning at all. Start your savings plans knowing that college choices will be more numerous for those who have planned.

Government Organizations and web sites that may be helpful in the search for financial aid:

1. **Federal Student Aid Information Center**
   PO Box 84, Washington DC 20044, (800) 433-3234, 8 am- 8 pm EST,
   Funding Your Education (free publication) www.ed.gov/prog_info/SFA/FYE
   The Student Guide (free publication) www.ed.gov/prog_info/SFA/StudentGuide

2. **U.S. Department of Education, Office of Student Financial Assistance**
   400 Maryland Avenue, Washington, DC 20202, (800) USA-LEARN
   www.ed.gov/finaid.html

Helpful Publications:

1. **Best Buys in College Education by Lucia Solorzano**
   Barron's Educational Series, Inc., 250 Wireless Blvd., Hauppauge, NY 11788,
   (800) 645-3476, www.barronseduc.com

2. **Financial Aids for Higher Education by Judy K. Santamaria & Oreon Keeslar**
   McGraw-Hill Higher Education, P.O. Box 182605, Columbus, OH 43218,
   (800) 262-4729, www.mhhe.com

3. **College Money Handbook 2001**
   Peterson's Guides, 2200 Lenox Drive, Lawrenceville, NJ 08648,
   (800) 338-3282 ext. 5333, www.petersons.com

4. **Winning Money for College**
   Peterson's Guides, 2200 Lenox Drive, Lawrenceville, NJ 08648,
   (800) 338-3282 ext. 5333, www.petersons.com

5. **The Scholarship Book 2001: The Complete Guide to Private-Sector Scholarships, Fellowships, Grants, and Loans for the Undergraduate**
   Prentice Hall Press, P.O. Box 11075, Des Moines, IA 50336,
   (800) 947-7700, www.phdirect.com

MATCHING YOUR SKILLS TO THE PROGRAM THAT FITS YOUR NEEDS

matchfit[tm]

ONLINE COLLEGE IDENTIFICATION SERVICE

Jump-start your own college search with **MATCHFIT™** our new online college identification service offered exclusively at **www.thesportsource.com**. Confidentially enter personal biographical data including your G.P.A., class rank, and standardized test scores, along with information specific to the type of college or university you would like to attend. Your information is matched against our extensive database to identify ten (10) college programs which match your selection criteria. Then make changes to your data and re-run the search two (2) additional times.

The net effect is three (3) sets of ten (10) colleges and universities which are compatible with your requirements for a college athletic program. Any duplications further validate that particular program as one you will want to pursue. You may select any college or university and download information specific to that program directly to your PC. This includes both a general academic profile, and a detailed athletic profile with the coach's name, mailing address, office number, fax, e-mail address, and the college web address. **MATCHFIT™** is available **www.thesportsource.com**

AN ORGANIZED APPROACH TO "THE COLLEGE CHOICE"

The following pages represent a checklist for the prospective college athlete. Along with your parents, use these guidelines in assembling your college selection criteria beginning with your sophomore year. By using these guidelines as a planning tool you will have a road map that will keep you pointed in the right direction throughout the selection process.

A simple but complete analysis is critical to filtering the information that the student-athlete will discover as you begin to look at each program. The diagrams that follows is intended to help rank each variable that may be valuable in the decision-making process. As you begin to gather information from a variety of sources you should assign a ranking - numerical value for that specific variable.

www.thesportsource.com

evaluation

evaluating the college & soccer program

academic /athletic college profiles

alabama

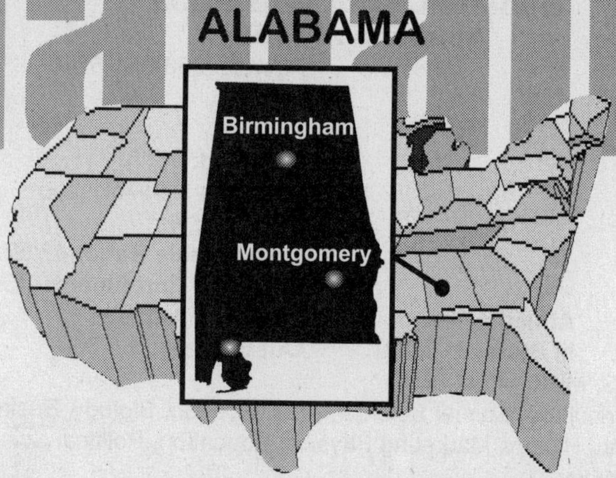

ALABAMA
Birmingham
Montgomery

Alabama A&M University

Academic Profile

Phone: (256)851-5245

Normal, AL 35762

Type: 4 Yr.,Public
Website: http://www.aamu.edu
SAT/ACT/GPA: 700/17
Student/Faculty Ratio: 17:1
Undergraduate Enrollment: 4,000
Scholarships/Academic: **Athletic:** Yes
Expenses by: Year **In State:** $ 5,000

Founded: 1875
Religion: Non-Affiliated
Housing: No
Male/Female Ratio: 48:52
Graduate Enrollment: 1,300
Financial Aid: Yes
Out of State: $ 6,700

Degrees Conferred: AA, AS, BA, MS, MBA, M.Ed., PHD
Programs of Study: Accounting, Agriculture, Animal Science, Art Education, Biology, Business Administration, Chemistry, Computer Science, English, History, Marketing Physical Education, Political Science, PreVeterinary, Psychology Telecommunications, Zoology

Men's Athletic Profile

P.O. Box 1597
Normal, AL 35762
Coach: Salah Yousif
Email: Not Available

NCAA I
Bulldogs/Maroon, White
Phone: 256-858-4001
Fax: (256) 851-5369

Estimated # of Men's Soccer Scholarships: None
Conference: SWAC
Camp or Clinic Dates: Not Available
Style of Play: We play both short & long ball.

Women's Athletic Profile

PO Bpx 1597
Normal, AL 35762
Coach: Frank Davies
Email: frank_davies@aamu.edu

NCAA I
Bulldogs/Maroon, White
Phone: (256) 858-8265
Fax: (256) 851-5369

Estimated # of Women's Soccer Scholarships: 7
Conference: SWAC
Program Profile: A new facility is currently being built and is scheduled to be ready for the 2001 season, with a seating capacity of 500-1000.
History: The program began in 2000.
Coaching: Coach Davies is entering his 2nd year with the Bulldogs.
Roster in State: 3 **Out of State:** 14 **Out of Country:** 1
ODP State: 0 **Regional:** 1 **National:** 0
Positions Needed: Midfield, Forward, Keeper
Camp or Clinic Dates: Late July, Early August. Call for details
Most Recent Record: 3-13-0
Schedule: Alabama, LSU, Murray State
Style of Play: We are building toward an indirect style of attack, and possession.

Auburn University
Academic Profile

Auburn, AL 36831-0351
Phone: 334-844-4080

Type: 4 Yr.,Public,Liberal Arts
Website: http://www.auburn.edu
SAT/ACT/GPA: 1100/24/3.2
Student/Faculty Ratio: 30:1
Undergraduate Enrollment: 22,000
Scholarships/Academic: Yes
Athletic: Yes
Expenses by: Year
In State: $ 7,935
Founded: 1856
Religion: Non-Affiliated
Housing: No
Male/Female Ratio: 55:45
Graduate Enrollment: N/A
Financial Aid: No
Out of State: $ 13,600
Specialty: Veterinary Medicine, Business, Education, Arts & Science
Degrees Conferred: BS, BA, MA, MS
Programs of Study: 150 areas of baccalaureate study including Agriculture, Agronomy, Animal, Production, Entomology, Horticulture, Architecture, Business, Marketing, Management, Engineering, Accounting

Women's Athletic Profile

P.O. Box 351
Auburn, AL 36831-0351
Coach: Karen Richter
Email: aubryer@mail.auburn.edu

NCAA I
Tigers/Navy, Orange, White
Phone: (334) 844-9773
Fax: (334) 844-4255

Estimated # of Women's Soccer Scholarships: None
Conference: Southeastern Conference (SEC)
Program Profile: The Auburn soccer stadium seats 2,000 with Bermuda grass surface. The playing season begins the first week in August and concludes with the SEC Tournament on November 2-5, 2000. The team will reconvene in January for conditioning and individual training. The 2001 Spring season runs from April 1- May 16
History: The Auburn Soccer program began in 1993 under Coach Steve Holeman. They posted a record of 7-6-3. Bill Wilkens guided the program for the following 5 years (1994-1998). Coach Karen Richter was named head coach on April 2, 1998. She lead the Tigers to a 6-12 record for the 1999 season.
Coaching: Head Coach Karen Richter. Formerly Head Coach at University of Central Florida. Matt Mott is the assistant coach. Formerly the assistant coach at University of Central Florida. Erin Aubry is also an assistant coach. Formerly a player at Northwestern University.
Roster in State: 5
Out of State: 19
Out of Country: 1
ODP State: 15
Regional: 2
National:
Walk-on/Other:
Graduation %:
Seniors on Team: 2
Positions Needed: Any
Camp or Clinic Dates: June 18-22, July 23-27
Most Recent Record: 6-12
Schedule: University of Florida, University of Kentucky, Vanderbilt, University of South Carolina, University of Arkansas, UNC-Charlotte
Style of Play: Auburn University Women's Soccer emphasizes building an attack through possession and good field shape. A zone defense throughout the field helps achieve this style of play.

Auburn University - Montgomery
Academic Profile

Montgomery, AL 36117
Phone: (800)227-2649

Type: 4 Yr.,Public,Liberal Arts
Website: http://www.aum.edu
Founded: 1967
Religion: Non-Affiliated

SAT/ACT/GPA: 860/18/2.0
Student/Faculty Ratio: 17:1
Undergraduate Enrollment: 5,500
Scholarships/Academic: Yes
Expenses by: Year
Athletic: Yes
In State: $ 5,500
Housing: Yes
Male/Female Ratio: 1:1
Graduate Enrollment: 1,000
Financial Aid: Yes
Out of State: $ 10,600
Degrees Conferred: BA, BS, MA, MS
Programs of Study: Accounting, Art, Biology, Business and Management, Chemistry, Communications, Computer Information Systems, Computer Science, Criminal Justice, Economics, Education, Environmental Biology, Finance, Graphic Art, Law Enforcement, Marine, Nursing, Social Science, Political Science, Psychology, Mathematics

Men's Athletic Profile

P.O. Box 244023
Montgomery, AL 36117
Coach: Matt Clark
Email: clarkma@hotmail.com

NAIA
Senators/Orange, White
Phone: (334) 244-3617
Fax: (334) 244-3886

Estimated # of Men's Soccer Scholarships:
Conference: Georgia-Alabama-Carolina Conference
Program Profile: We play a fall season. Our field is measures 75x120 yards, a Bermuda grass that seats 1,000. We have a Physical Education Complex, one varsity field and three practice fields.
History: Our program began 14 years ago and made two trips to NAIA National Tournaments.
Achievements: NAIA Midwest Region Coach of the Year in 1996 and American Midwest Conference Coach of the Year in 1996 & 1997.
Coaching: Matt Clark, Head Coach, was a former pro and assistant coaching director for Alabama. Sara Churchill, Assistant Coach, started at George Mason. She is a State ODP Coach and top club coach.
Style of Play: Patient and indirect - we like to attack out of the back and utilize the play of our flanks players.

Women's Athletic Profile

P.O. Box 244023
Montgomery, AL 36124-4023
Coach: Brett Teach
Email: Clarkma@hotmail.com

NAIA
Senators/Orange, White
Phone: (334) 244-3617
Fax: (334) 244-3886

Estimated # of Women's Soccer Scholarships: N/A
Conference: Georgia-Alabama-Carolina Conference
Program Profile: Play on 120 by 75 yard Bermuda grass field.
History: New program
Achievements: NAIA Midwest Region Coach of the Year in 1996, American Midwest Conference Coach of the Year in 1996 & 1997.

Birmingham Southern College

Academic Profile

Phone: (205) 226-4944

Birmingham, AL 35254

Type: 4 Yr.,Private,Liberal Arts
Website: http://www.bsc.edu
SAT/ACT/GPA: 26
Student/Faculty Ratio: 13:1
Undergraduate Enrollment: 1,150

Founded: 1856
Religion: Methodist
Housing: Yes
Male/Female Ratio: 46:54
Graduate Enrollment: 350

Scholarships/Academic: Yes
Athletic: Yes
Financial Aid: Yes
Expenses by: Year
In State: $ 20,886
Out of State: $ 20,886
Specialty: PreMed, PreLaw
Degrees Conferred: BA, BS, BF, BM, M.Ed.
Programs of Study: Accounting, Biology, Business, Chemistry, Computer, Economics, Education, English, Fine Arts, Graphic Design, Health, History, Information Science, International, Marketing, Math, Music, Philosophy, Political, Psychology, Social Science, Visual and Performing Arts

Men's Athletic Profile

900 Arkadelphia RD. BSC Box 549035
Birmingham, AL 35254
Coach: Preston Goldfarb
Email: pgoldfar@bsc.edu

NCAA I
Panthers/Black, Gold, White
Phone: (205) 226-4895
Fax: (205) 226-3059

Estimated # of Men's Soccer Scholarships: None
Conference: Tran South Conference
Program Profile: Play on beautiful, lighted grass field. 120x78. Two story press box with stadium seating 1000.
History: Our program began in 1983 with no scholarships. We were 1987,1989, and 1990 conference champions, 1993 District 27 champions, 1994-6th in the nation; 1995 Final four at NAIA National Tournament; 1996 runner-up NAIA National tournament; Received bids to 1997 and 1998 NAIA National Tournaments; 1999-Final Four NAIA National tournament 1999-Accepted as NCAA D-I member
Achievements: 1993 District Coach of the Year, 1995 Region Coach of the Year, 1996 Conference Coach of the Year, 1997 Conference and Region Coach of the Year, 1998 Conference Coach of the Year, 1999 Conference and Region Coach of the Year. 1995 Player of the Year, 1999 Player of the Year, 29 All-Americans, 35 Academic All-Americans, 10 Senior Bowl participants.
Coaching: Preston Goldfarb-Head Coach. Greg Vinson-Senior Assistant. Sean McBride and Todd Moon-Assistant Coaches.
Roster In State: 11
Out of State: 5
Out of Country: 5
Walk-on/Other:
Graduation %: N/A
Seniors on Team: 3
Camp or Clinic Dates: Not Available
Schedule: UAB, University of Central Florida, Memphis University, University of Missouri-Kansas City, Drury University, University of Louisville, Belmont University, Centenary, Georgia St.
Style of Play: We play a possession soccer.

Women's Athletic Profile

BSC, Box 549041
Birmingham, AL 35254
Coach: Keidane Mealpine
Email: letka@bsc.edu

NAIA/ NCAA I
Panthers/Black, Gold
Phone: (205) 226-4905
Fax: (205) 226-4931

Estimated # of Women's Soccer Scholarships: varies
Conference: Tran South Conference
History: The program began in 1995. 1999 second place finish in Tran South Conference Tournament with 21 loss to Berry College.
Achievements: We had 7 NAIA All-American Scholar Athletes, 1 honorable mention All-American, 1998-1999 Col-Coach of the Year for the Tran south Conference.
Coaching: Lorrin Etka Shepherd, Head Coach, 1985 graduate of University of Puget Sound; NSCAA National License. Sheldon Phillips - Assistant Coach.
Roster in State: 12
Out of State: 9
Out of Country: 3
Walk-on/Other:
Graduation %: 100%
Seniors on Team: 5
Camp or Clinic Dates: Not-Available
Most Recent Record: 11-7-2
Style of Play: Possession style of play.

Huntington College

Academic Profile

Phone: (800)763-0313

Montgomery, AL 36106

Type: 4 Yr.,Private,Liberal Arts
Website: http://www.huntingdon.edu
SAT/ACT/GPA: 920 combined/490 verbal/202.5
Student/Faculty Ratio: 9:1
Undergraduate Enrollment: 750
Scholarships/Academic: Yes
Athletic: No
Expenses by: Year
In State: $ 17,450
Specialty: Premed, Prelaw programs
Degrees Conferred: BS

Founded: 1854
Religion: Methodist
Housing: Yes
Male/Female Ratio: 1:2
Graduate Enrollment: N/A
Financial Aid: Yes
Out of State: $ 17,450

Programs of Study: Accounting, American Studies, Art, Biology, Business Administration, Chemistry, Computer Information Systems, Computer Science, Dance, Drama, Education, European Studies, Health Science, International Studies, Kinesiology, Mathematics, Music, Musical Theatre, Philosophy, Physical Education, Political Science, Psychology, Public Administration, Public Affairs, Public Policy, Religion, Social Science

Men's Athletic Profile

1500 E Fairview Avenue
Montgomery, AL 36106-2148
Coach: Todd S. Schilperoort
Email: tschilperoort@huntingdon.edu

NAIA
Hawks/Red, White
Phone: (334) 833-4565
Fax: (334) 833-4486

Estimated # of Men's Soccer Scholarships: None
Conference: Independent Conference
Program Profile: We play on Narrow Lane Field with a measurements of 120x75 Bermuda grass, located across from Ligon Dormitory and the President's House.
History: Our program began in 1982. Our team has captured conference championships and have been ranked in the Southeast Region. Program has produced All-Americans, All-Region and All-Conference players and has been ranked in the top ten nationally in team and individual scoring.
Achievements: We have 3 All-Americans in 1991, & 1992; 5 All-Area and All-District players in 1992; ranked 5th in South Region; 1 District Championship; 2 District Runner-up.
Coaching: Todd S. Schilperoort, Head Coach, holds a USSF "A License and NSCAA Advanced National Diploma. He is also a Director of Coaching for Alabama Youth Soccer Association. He played college soccer and some professional experience. Mark Johnson: - Assistant Coach. NSCAA National Diploma. Assistant to both men's and women's soccer programs
Roster In State: 5
Out of State: 12
Out of Country: 4
Walk-on/Other:
Graduation %: N/A
Seniors on Team: 6
Positions Needed: Striker, Midfield marking backs, Goalkeepers
Camp or Clinic Dates: Not Available
Most Recent Record: 14-4-1
Style of Play: We emphasize combination play and playing to maintain possession. Defend with a numbers behind the ball and counter against tougher opponents.

Women's Athletic Profile

1500 E Fairview Avenue
Montgomery, AL 36106
Coach: Michael Keating
Email: mkeating@huntingdon.edu

NAIA
LadyHawks/Red, White
Phone: (333) 833-4468
Fax: (334) 833-4486

Estimated # of Women's Soccer Scholarships: None
Conference: Southern States Conference
Program Profile: The Lady Hawks Soccer program employs a strong attacking mentality with no compromise in defending. Huntingdon plays on a natural grass surface that is located on campus across from the president's home. Last season we finished as the 19th ranked team in the country in NAIA soccer and came within one game from advancing to the NAIA National Tournament. We have produced numerous all-Americans including 3 last year and will look to place more each year.
History: Our first year was 1988 as a women's soccer team. We have had a rich history in NAIA soccer with three top twenty-five finishes in the NAIA over the last seven years. The program has produced a great number of all-region and all-American selections over the years.
Achievements: The Huntingdon college Lady hawks Soccer program has produced 20 All-American athlete's including 3-time recipient Goalkeeper Stephanie Upton and 29 Academic All-American's and presently hold a team grade point average of 3.48 for the 1999 team. We have won four conference titles and reached the NAIA Southeast Regional Final in 1998. We were also nationally ranked for 9-of-11 weeks that same season and placed two players on the NAIA Honorable mention All-America Team and placed four First-Team All-South Region players on the Regional Team.
Coaching: Michael Keating, Head Coach, is licensed by the United States Soccer Federation and also is a member of the National Soccer Coaches Association of America. Keating completed his playing career in 1992 after a short stint in the Universidad de Guadalajara professional system in Mexico and began his coaching career as an assistant coach at Center College. He moved into his position as an assistant for both men's and women's soccer at Huntingdon College before finally taking over the Lady Hawks.

Roster in State:	**Out of State:** 14	**Out of Country:** 2
ODP State: 1	**Regional:**	**National:** 1
Walk-on/Other:	**Graduation %:** 100%	**Seniors on Team:** 5

Positions Needed: central midfielder, sweeper, outside right mid
Camp or Clinic Dates: Not available
Most Recent Record: 10-9
Schedule: Berry College, William Wood College, William Carey College, Rollins College, University of Mobile Spring Hill College
Style of Play: Attacking style that incorporates combination play using central midfield and wide midfielder's to get up and down flank.

Jacksonville State University
Academic Profile

Jacksonville, AL 36265
Phone: (256) 782-5268

Type: 4 Yr.,Public		**Founded:** 1883
Website: http://www.jsu.edu		**Religion:** Non-Affiliated
SAT/ACT/GPA: 900/19/2.5		**Housing:** Yes
Student/Faculty Ratio: 22:1		**Male/Female Ratio:** 44:56
Undergraduate Enrollment: 6,477		**Graduate Enrollment:** 1,142
Scholarships/Academic: Yes	**Athletic:** Yes	**Financial Aid:** Yes
Expenses by: Year	**In State:** $ 5,720	**Out of State:** $ 7,960

Specialty: Education, Nursing, Criminal Justice
Degrees Conferred: BA, BS, BFA, BMU, MA, MS
Programs of Study: Art, Biology, Business, Chemistry, Communications, Computer Science, Drama, English, Exercise Science, Family & Consumer Science, Foreign Languages, General Studies, Geography, History, Mathematics, Music, Physics, Political Science, PreProfessional Programs, Psychology, Recreation Administration, Social Work, Sociology, Technology

Women's Athletic Profile

700 Pelham Rd N
Jacksonville, AL 36265
Coach: Lisa Howe
Email: lhowe@jsuscc,jsu.edu

NCAA I
Gamecocks/Red, White
Phone: (205) 782-5679
Fax: (205) 782-5527

Estimated # of Women's Soccer Scholarships: 12
Conference: Trans America Athletic Conference
Program Profile: Traditional Fall & Spring seasons, weather facilitates training outdoors year round; full size Bermuda field with lights, overseed with winter rye; 2500 capacity; weight room, training room, and locker room located in Pete Mathews Coliseum
History: The program began in 1995; first winning record was in 1998; 4th best record in conference in 1998; qualified for Conference Tournament in 1997 & 1999; 99-2nd best overall record in the conference..
Achievements: Produced 1 first team All-Conference player in 1997 - Andrea Poole; and second team in 1998;3 All-Tournament players. 1999-6 All-Conference players & TAAC coach of the year; goalkeeper ranked top 20 in shutouts-(11).
Coaching: Lisa Howe, Head Coach, graduate from Barry University in 1991 - NCAA Division II Champions in 1989. He coached Berry College, NAIA National Tournament in 1994. He holds "A" License, Alabama ODP Staff, Head Coach of U-83 Girls. Chris Adams, Assistant Coach, graduate of University of Georgia in 1998. He played at Presbyterian College and holds "B" License, Alabama ODP Staff and currently an assistant coach for '81 Boys.

Roster in State: 4	**Out of State:** 11	**Out of Country:** 6
ODP State: 3	**Regional:**	**National:**
Walk-on/Other:	**Graduation %:** 100%	**Seniors on Team:** 4

Positions Needed: Forwards, Center Midfield, Center Back, Goalkeeper
Most Recent Record: 12-4-5
Schedule: Central Florida, Auburn, Ole Miss, Mississippi State, Texas Christian, Jacksonville, South Alabama, Alabama-Birmingham, Georgia State
Style of Play: Excellent training habits; competitive; 4-4-2; zone defense; possession oriented; can play direct; usually exploit the flanks.

Spring Hill College

Academic Profile

Mobile, AL 36608

Phone: (800)742-6704

Type: 4 Yr.,Private,Liberal Arts		**Founded:** 1830
Website: http://www.shc.edu		**Religion:** Catholic- Jesuit
SAT/ACT/GPA: 1050/21/3.0		**Housing:** Yes
Student/Faculty Ratio: 14:1		**Male/Female Ratio:** 1:1
Undergraduate Enrollment: 1,000		**Graduate Enrollment:** 4,000
Scholarships/Academic: Yes	**Athletic:** Yes	**Financial Aid:** Yes
Expenses by: Semester	**In State:** $ 7,150	**Out of State:** $ 7,150

Specialty: Liberal Arts
Degrees Conferred: AS, BA, BS, MA, MS, MBA, M.Ed.
Programs of Study: Accounting, Advertising, Biology, Broadcasting, Business, Chemistry, Communications, Computer, Drama, Economics, Education, English, Environmental, Finance, Languages, General Science, History, Math, PreProfessional Programs, Religion, Theology

Men's Athletic Profile

4000 Dauphin Street
Mobile, AL 36608
Coach: Tom Condone
Email: tcondone@shc.edu

NAIA
Badgers/Purple, White
Phone: (334) 380-3491
Fax: (334) 460-2196

Estimated # of Men's Soccer Scholarships: Varies
Conference: Gulf Coast Athletic Conference
Program Profile: Our team plays at Dorn Field, with a seating capacity of 500 and has a grass field. We play 18 games and conference playoffs.
History: Our program started in 1990.
Coaching: Tom Condone is the Head Coach. Matt Convertino and Will Summer are the Assistant Coaches.
Style of Play: We play a 4-4-2; zonal defense and counter-attacking.

Women's Athletic Profile

4000 Dauphin Street
Mobile, AL 36608
Coach: John Mollaghan
Email: jmollaghan@shc.edu

NAIA
Lady Badgers/Purple, White
Phone: (334) 380-3491
Fax: (334) 460-2196

Estimated # of Women's Soccer Scholarships: None
Conference: Gulf Coast Athletic Conference
Program Profile: We play at Dorn Field which has natural grass and 500 seats. Our schedule includes 18 games and some conference playoff games.
History: The women's soccer program started in 1991.
Roster in State: 40% **Out of State:** 60% **Out of Country:** 1
Style of Play: 4-4-2; Zonal Defense; Counterattacking

Troy State University

Academic Profile

Troy, AL 36082
Phone: (334) 670-3926

Type: 4 Yr.,Public
Website: http://www.troyst.edu
SAT/ACT/GPA: 870+/18+/2.0
Student/Faculty Ratio: 21:1
Undergraduate Enrollment: 5,500
Scholarships/Academic: Yes **Athletic:** Yes
Expenses by: Year **In State:** $ 7,500
Founded: 1887
Religion: Non-Affiliated
Housing: Yes
Male/Female Ratio: 52:48
Graduate Enrollment: 1,500
Financial Aid: Yes
Out of State: $ 10,400
Degrees Conferred: Bachelors, Masters, Specialist
Programs of Study: Accounting, Art, Athletic Training, Biology, Chemistry, Computer Information Science, Criminal Justice, Economics, Education (Elementary & Secondary), English, Environmental Science, Finance, History, Journalism (Broadcast & Print), Management, Marketing, Nursing, Physical Science, Psychology, Rehabilitation, Social Science, Sociology, Sports Medicine, Sport & Fitness Management, Special Education, Social Work, Social Science, Sociology, Sport and Fitness Management, Studio Art

Women's Athletic Profile

Davis Fieldhouse, George Wallace Drive
Troy, AL 36082
Coach: Qasim Shiekh
Email: Qsheik8@hotmail.com

NCAA I
Trojans/Cardinal, Silver, Black
Phone: (334) 670-5652
Fax: (334) 670-3724

Estimated # of Women's Soccer Scholarships: None
Conference: TAAC
Program Profile: Play on grass field stadium with a new locker facilities.
History: The program began in 1997.
Coaching: Quasim Shiekh, Head Coach, was named head coach in the summer of 1999.
Style of Play: Defensively organized but attack-minded play.

University of Alabama
Academic Profile

Phone: (800) 933-2262

Tuscaloosa, AL 35487

Type: 4 Yr.,Public,Liberal Arts,Engineering
Website: http://www.ua.edu
SAT/ACT/GPA: 1010/20
Student/Faculty Ratio: 20:1
Undergraduate Enrollment: 15,000
Scholarships/Academic: Yes
Athletic: Yes
Expenses by: Year
In State: $ 7,420

Founded: 1831
Religion: Non-Affiliated
Housing: Yes
Male/Female Ratio: 1:1
Graduate Enrollment: 4,000
Financial Aid: Yes
Out of State: $ 11,300

Degrees Conferred: BA, BS, BM, MS, MBA, MD
Programs of Study: Accounting, Advertising, Athletic Training, Banking/Finance, Communications, Communication Disorders, Computer Science, Education, Engineering, English, Fashion Design, Foreign Languages, Journalism, Management, Marine Science, Marketing, Math, Medical

Women's Athletic Profile

P.O. Box 870393
Tuscaloosa, AL 35487
Coach: Don Staley
Email: dstaley@ia.ua.edu

NCAA I
Crimson Tide/Crimson, White
Phone: (205) 348-0143
Fax: (205) 348-9945

Estimated # of Women's Soccer Scholarships: 3
Conference: South Eastern Conference
Program Profile: We play on a natural, private facility for Women's Soccer only and our season is from August to December.
History: Our program began in 1994, when the SEC instituted soccer, Alabama has been the dominant team in the Conference's Western Division, winning the division crown three of the five years it has been awarded. The Crimson Tide has been ranked regionally and nationally, and made its first appearance in the NCAA Tournament in 1998.
Achievements: 1995, 1997 and 1998 SEC Western Division Champions; Don Staley 1994 and 1998 SEC Coach of the Year; 1998 Academic All-American, 1998 2 Freshman All-American.
Coaching: Don Staley, Head Coach, former head coach for both men's and women's programs at Radford (10 years), Big South Coach of the Year 1991 and 1993, three of his former players are now professional players and one Olympian. Karrei Miller - Assistant Coach, former assistant at University of South Carolina. Aaron Rodgers - Assistant Coach, former assistant at University of South Alabama.
Roster in State: 5
Out of State: 22
Out of Country: 1
Walk-on/Other:
Graduation %: 98
Seniors on Team: 5
Positions Needed: Goalkeeper, Striker, Utility
Camp or Clinic Dates: June 5-9, 12-16, 17-21
Most Recent Record: 6-14-0
Schedule: University of North Carolina, Vanderbilt University, University of Kentucky, University of Florida
Style of Play: Hoof and Gamble.

University of Alabama - Birmingham
Academic Profile

Phone: (205) 934-8066

Birmingham, AL 35294

Type: 4 Yr.,Public
Website: http://www.uab.edu

Founded: 1969
Religion: Non-Affiliated

SAT/ACT/GPA: 950/20/2.0
Student/Faculty Ratio: 17:1
Undergraduate Enrollment: 11,000
Scholarships/Academic: Yes
Expenses by: Year
Athletic: Yes
In State: $ 6,750
Housing: Yes
Male/Female Ratio: 45:55
Graduate Enrollment: 6,000
Financial Aid: Yes
Out of State: $ 9.750
Specialty: Business, Education, Engineering, Medicine, Research and Technology
Degrees Conferred: BA, BS, BFA, MA, MS, MBA, MEd, Ph D, Ed D, DDS, MD
Programs of Study: Over 70 degree programs available: Business, Education, Engineering, Health Sciences, Life Sciences, Social Science, Etc.

Men's Athletic Profile

Bartow Arena
Birmingham, AL 35294
Coach: Mike Getman
Email: mgetman@uab.edu

NCAA I
Blazers/Green, Gold, White
Phone: (205) 934-8066
Fax: (205) 975-6266

Estimated # of Men's Soccer Scholarships: 4
Conference: Conference USA
Program Profile: UBA is a top twenty-five program. We have a new stadium opened in 1998. We play in one of the best conferences and have one of the best schedules in the nation.
History: Our program began in 1979 and has grown tremendously in the last five years. We have been ranked in the top 25 each of the past four years.
Achievements: Conference Champions in 1994 and 1995. Coach of the Year in 1993 and 1995. Conference Freshman of the Year in 1993, 1994, and 1996. More All-Conference players than any other C-USA team each of the last two years. 5 players now playing in pro.
Coaching: Mike Getman, Head Coach, has coached or played in 4 Division Final Four. Has twice been named Conference Coach of the Year.
Camp or Clinic Dates: Not Available
Style of Play: The Blazers are a ball possession team that combines creativity with defensive discipline.

Women's Athletic Profile

617 S. 13th Street
Birmingham, AL 35294
Coach: Paul Harbin
Email: pharbin@uab.edu

NCAA I
Blazers/Green, Gold, White
Phone: (205) 934-4756
Fax: (205) 934-6266

Estimated # of Women's Soccer Scholarships: Fully Funded
Conference: Conference USA
Program Profile: The home field is West Campus Field. It is a Bermuda grass field equipped with lights. Year round program, very competitive schedule. New soccer stadium built in the fall of 1997 and has a seating capacity of 2000+.
History: The program began in 1996. In just 4 seasons of competition the Blazers have consistently been ranked in the top 10 teams in the Central Region.
Achievements: 2 Players have been named Central Region All-Americans, 5 Players named South Region Scholar Athlete All-Americans. 1999, player named 1st Team Academic All-American.
Coaching: Paul Harbin, Head Coach, is in his second season. He coached ten years in Division I, He has a USSF National License and a Master's degree in Sport Psychology. He is a State and Regional ODP Coach and a 1998 Region III Women's Select team coach. Todd Yelton is the Assistant Coach.
Roster in State: 3
Out of State: 15
Out of Country: 1
ODP State: 18
Regional:
National:
Walk-on/Other:
Graduation %: 100
Seniors on Team: 5
Positions Needed: ALL

Camp or Clinic Dates: July 10-14, July 16-21
Most Recent Record: 10-10-1
Schedule: North Carolina, Nebraska, Portland, Vanderbilt, Marquette, Washington, UNC Charlotte, Cincinnati, St. Louis, South Florida.
Style of Play: Creative, ball control oriented, all out attacking style combined with disciplined zonal man to man team defending.

University of Alabama - Huntsville

Academic Profile

Phone: (256) 824-6144

Huntsville, AL 35899

Type: 4 Yr.,Public,Liberal Arts,Engineering
Website: http://www.uah.edu
SAT/ACT/GPA: 840172.5
Student/Faculty Ratio: 20:1
Undergraduate Enrollment: 2,953
Scholarships/Academic: Yes
Athletic: Yes
Expenses by: Year
In State: $ 8,941
Founded: 1969
Religion: Non-Affiliated
Housing: Yes
Male/Female Ratio: 48/53
Graduate Enrollment: 1,500
Financial Aid: Yes
Out of State: $ 11,817
Specialty: Engineering, Business, Sciences
Degrees Conferred: BS, BA, MA, MS, Ph.D.
Programs of Study: Engineering: Electrical, Mechanical, Optical, Computer, Environmental, Civil, Aerospace; Business: Marketing, MIS, Accounting, Administration, Management, Finance; Nursing; Liberal Arts: Art, Communications, Education, English, Spanish, German, French, History, Music, Political Science, Philosophy, Psychology, Sociology; Sciences: Biology, Chemistry, Computer Science, Mathematics, Physics, Optical Science

Men's Athletic Profile

SH 205-G
Huntsville, AL 35899
Coach: Carlos Petersen
Email: petersc@uah.edu

NCAA II
Chargers/Blue, White
Phone: (256) 824-6144
Fax: (256) 824-7306

Estimated # of Men's Soccer Scholarships: Varies
Conference: Gulf South Conference
Program Profile: We are the only conference team to repeat Championships since it began in 1996. 3 of 4 seasons have been undefeated in conference play. We have represented GSC in NCAA Regional Tournament. Season is from August-November, January-April. Bermuda Game field with seating for 500. Currently one Gym/pool/weight room in 2001. We will have a second facility with two on campus practice fields.
History: NAIA 1973-1985 with 6 National Tournament Appearances, 8 Area titles. NCAA II 1986-present, 2 Conference Champions, Regional NCAA II appearance. Regional or National Ranked in past five years
Achievements: Two-time GSC Coach of the year, 100 wins in the past 9 years, One All-American, 10 All-South Region Players, 10 All-GSC Players, 25 players have gone on to play professional soccer in past 8 years.
Coaching: Carlos Petersen, Head Coach, holds a USSF "A" License and an Advanced National Diploma. Henri Pagi, Assistant Coach, was a former UAH stand-out and professional player. He is in his second year as assistant Coach.
Roster In State: 8
Out of State: 8
Out of Country: 4
ODP State: 10
Regional: 3
National: 5
Walk-on/Other:
Graduation %: 92
Seniors on Team: 5
Positions Needed: Striker, Midfielder, GK
Camp or Clinic Dates: June 3-23
Most Recent Record: 8—8—2

Schedule: St. Leo, Florida Southern, Monticello University, Christian Brother University, Lander College, Florida , Tech, Tampa University, Alabama A&M Div. I, Libscomb University Div. I, University of Alabama-, Birmingham Div. I
Style of Play: Quick one-two touch possession game, quick ball movement, counter attack soccer when can. We like quick, fast, technical players, with strong background in soccer at high levels with strong desire to win and disciplined work ethic.

University of Mobile

Academic Profile

Mobile, AL 36613-0220
Phone: (334) 675-5990

Type: 4 Yr.,Private,Liberal Arts
Website: http://www.umobile.edu
SAT/ACT/GPA: 19
Student/Faculty Ratio: 16:1
Undergraduate Enrollment: 1,707
Scholarships/Academic: Yes
Athletic: Yes
Expenses by: Year
In State: $ 12,060
Founded: 1961
Religion: Baptist
Housing: Yes
Male/Female Ratio: 6:1
Graduate Enrollment: 211
Financial Aid: Yes
Out of State: $ 12,060
Degrees Conferred: BS, BA, MS, MA, BSN, MSN, AA, AS
Programs of Study: The university offers a BA degree in the following areas: Arts, English, General Studies, Health, Physical Education and Recreation, History, Music, Political Science, Psychology, Religion, Social Science, Spanish, Sociology, and Theatre. The university offers a BS degree in the following areas: Accounting, Biology, Business Administration, Chemistry, Communications, Computer Information Systems, Early Childhood Education, Environmental Technology, General Studies, Health, Physical Education and Recreation, Marine Science, Mathematics, Music Education, Organizational Management, Psychology, Religion, Social Science and Sociology

Men's Athletic Profile

Box 13220
Mobile, AL 36663-0220
Coach: Peter Fuller
Email: Not Available

NAIA
Rams/Maroon, White
Phone: (205) 675-5990
Fax: (205) 675-5332

Estimated # of Men's Soccer Scholarships: None
Conference: Gulf Coast Athletic Conference

Women's Athletic Profile

P.O. Box 13220
Mobile, AL 36663-0220
Coach: Peter Fuller
Email: umsid@hotmail.com

NAIA
Lady Rams/Maroon, White
Phone: (334) 442-2363
Fax: (334) 442-2499

Estimated # of Women's Soccer Scholarships: Full-Partial
Conference: Gulf Coast Athletic Conference
Program Profile: Our home field has a measurements of 120x75 yards. We have a fall season on a natural Bermuda grass with a seating capacity of 1,500 and lights. Also year around program is conducted.
History: Our program started in 1991. 96 NAIA 2nd at Nationals, 1997 NAIA Champions, 1998 3rd at NAIA Nationals, 2000 National Tournament Regional Champions.
Achievements: Coach of the Year (92,94,95,96,97,98,99,2000), Regional Coach of the Year (96,97,98,2000), National Coach of the Year 1997, 40 plus All-Americans and 8 National Team Players and 10 players playing professionally.
Coaching: Peter Fuller Head Coach.
Roster in State: 3
Out of State: 25
Out of Country: 7

ODP State: 8 **Regional:** 2 **National:** 0
Walk-on/Other: 6 **Graduation %:** 90+ **Seniors on Team:** 4
Positions Needed: Looking at all potential recruits.
Most Recent Record: 15-8-1
Schedule: Linsey-Wilson, Auburn-Montgomery, William Carey, Life University, Lindenwood (MO)

University of Montevallo

Academic Profile

Montevallo, AL 35115
Phone: 205-665-6030

Type: 4 Yr.,Public,Liberal Arts
Founded: 1896
Website: http://www.montevallo.edu
Religion: Non-Affiliated
SAT/ACT/GPA: 850/18
Housing: Yes
Student/Faculty Ratio: 18:1
Male/Female Ratio: 1:2
Undergraduate Enrollment: 3,000
Graduate Enrollment: 500
Scholarships/Academic: Yes **Athletic:** Yes **Financial Aid:** Yes
Expenses by: Year **In State:** $ 4,980 **Out of State:** $ 7,480
Specialty: Education
Degrees Conferred: BA, BS, MEd
Programs of Study: Accounting, Banking & Finance, Broadcasting, Chemistry, Communications, Education, English, Fine Arts, French, Government, Health Science, History, Management, Marketing, Mathematics, Medical Technology, Music, Optometry, Photography, Political Science, PreDentistry, PreMed, PreLaw, Public Health, Social Science, Psychology, Spanish, Speech Pathology, Visual and Performing Arts

Men's Athletic Profile

Station 6600, Athletic Dept.
Montevallo, AL 35115
Coach: Rob King
Email: Not Available

NCAA II/NAIA
Falcons/Purple
Phone: (205) 665-6604
Fax: (205) 665-6586

Estimated # of Men's Soccer Scholarships: None
Conference: Gulf South Conference, NCAA Division II
Program Profile: The Falcons home field is natural grass.
History: Our program began in the Fall of 1994.
Style of Play: Attack minded - Possession game.

Women's Athletic Profile

Station 6600, Athletic Dept.
Montevallo, AL 35115
Coach: Rob King
Email: Not Available

NCAA II/NAIA
Falcons/Purple
Phone: (205) 665-6604
Fax: (205) 665-6586

Estimated # of Women's Soccer Scholarships: None
Conference: Gulf South Conference
Program Profile: The home games are played on natural grass field.
History: The women's program began intercollegiate in the fall of 1995.
Style of Play: Attack minded - possession game.

University of North Alabama

Academic Profile

Florence, AL 35632-0001

Phone: (256) 765-4221

Type: 4 Yr.,Public
Website: http://www.unanov.edu
SAT/ACT/GPA: 830 or higher18/2.0
Student/Faculty Ratio: 22:1
Undergraduate Enrollment: 5,000
Scholarships/Academic: Yes
Athletic: Yes
Expenses by: Year
In State: $ 6,608

Founded: 1830
Religion: Non-Affiliated
Housing: Yes
Male/Female Ratio: 42:58
Graduate Enrollment: 500
Financial Aid: Yes
Out of State: $ 8,744

Specialty: Business, Education, Nursing
Degrees Conferred: BA, BS, BFA, BAM, BGS, BM, BMMEd, BSEd., BSM, BSN, MA, MBA
Programs of Study: Art, Accounting, Banking/Finance, Biology, Broadcasting, Business, Chemistry, Communications, Criminal Justice, Economics, Education, English, Fine Arts, French, General Studies, Geography, German, Health and Physical Education, History, Home Economics, Information Science, Journalism, Management, Marketing, Mathematics, Physical Sciences, Psychology

Women's Athletic Profile

UNA Box 5071
Florence, AL 35632-0001
Coach: Aston Rhoden
Email: Arhoden@unanov.una.edu

NCAA II
Lions/Purple, Gold
Phone: (256) 765-4845
Fax: (256) 765-4685

Estimated # of Women's Soccer Scholarships: 5
Conference: Gulf South Conference
Program Profile: Program started in 1997. Soccer is played during the fall. Soccer field is measures 110x70 yards, lighted and grass. Program built on success in athletics, academic and community service.
History: Program started in 1996 as a club sport and moved quickly into the Gulf South conference in 1997. In the first season, the Lions advanced to the conference championship tournament with a 7-11 record. In the 1999 season, the Lions played their best record of 11-7-1 while advancing to the Gulf South Conference championship tournament. The program began in the fall 1998. Lost in the Gulf South Conference semi-final match in first year of competition.
Achievements: NCAA II, Most improved women's team for 1999-2000 season. Two Golf South Conference Championship tournament semi-final appearances. Highest finish of third Gulf South Conference. Highest regional rank of 7th in the NSCAA South Region (1999).
Coaching: Aston Rhoden, Head Coach, he holds USSF "A" License. He was named Jamaica Youth National player. Semi-professional player, collegiate soccer at University of Alabama-Huntsville, BS in Computer Science and Mathematics. Annie Klekamp, Graduate Assistant coach, NSCAA Diploma, collegiate soccer at John Carroll university, BS in Marketing
Roster in State: 7
Out of State: 14
Out of Country: 1
ODP State: 17
Regional: 0
National: 1
Walk-on/Other: 2
Graduation %:
Seniors on Team: 5
Positions Needed: ALL
Camp or Clinic Dates: TBA
Most Recent Record: 11-6-0
Schedule: Univ. of Tampa, Univ. of West Florida, Lincoln Memorial Univ. Univ. of Montevallo, Christian Brothers Univ.
Style of Play: We are a possession oriented team and usually play indirect. However, each year we make adjustments to our style of play based on the player's available.

University of South Alabama

Academic Profile

Phone:

Mobile, AL 36688

Type: 4 Yr.,Public,Liberal Arts
Website: http://www.usouthal.edu
SAT/ACT/GPA: 820/19
Student/Faculty Ratio: 14:1
Undergraduate Enrollment: 9,500
Scholarships/Academic: Yes
Athletic: Yes
Expenses by: Year
In State: $ 7,000
Founded: 1963
Religion: Non-Affiliated
Housing: Yes
Male/Female Ratio: 43:57
Graduate Enrollment: 3,000
Financial Aid: Yes
Out of State: $ 8,900
Degrees Conferred: Bachelors to Ph.D.
Programs of Study: College of Arts and Sciences, College of Business and Management Studies, College of Education, College of Engineering, School of Continuing Education and Special Programs, College of Allied Health Professions, College of Medicine, College of Nursing, School of Computer and Information Sciences

Women's Athletic Profile

1107 HPELS Buildings
Mobile, AL 36688
Coach: Mike Varga
Email: jaguarsoccer@hotmail.com

NCAA I
Jaguars/Red, White, Blue
Phone: (334) 414-8253
Fax: (334) 460-7297

Estimated # of Women's Soccer Scholarships: None
Conference: Big South Conference
Program Profile: USA has one of the top women's soccer programs in the southeast. In 1997, the Jaguars established a new NCAA record for the biggest turn-around in history, with a 15.5 game improvement from 1996 season (2-17) to the 1997 season (18-3-1). the Jags play on campus at the 500 seat "The Jags". surface is natural grass.
History: South Alabama started soccer in 1994 and since then has enjoyed much success, compiling winning seasons in four years of the first five years. In 1997, the Jags began a two-year associate membership in the Big South Conference after serving the three previous seasons an as Independent. USA went unbeaten during regular season league play (10-0) in 1997 & 1998. the Jags won the 1997 BSC Tourney Title and Advanced to their first NCAA Play-in contest, where the lost to UNC-Greensboro,
Achievements: We have Big South Conference Coach of the Year. Jag Hilla Rantala was a two-time All-Region performer and won Freshman All-America honors by Soccer Buzz.
Coaching: Mike Varga is the Head Coach. He is in his first season with the program. the former Lincoln Memorial Director of Soccer took over the Jaguar program in February 1999 after former three-year Coach Mark Francis left for University of Kansas. Doug Bracken is our Assistant Coach. He was a former coach of Union College. He was the top assistant to Coach Mike Varga from 1995-1997 at Lincoln Memorial.
Style of Play: We play a possession oriented with all players involved in attack and defense.

arizona

ARIZONA

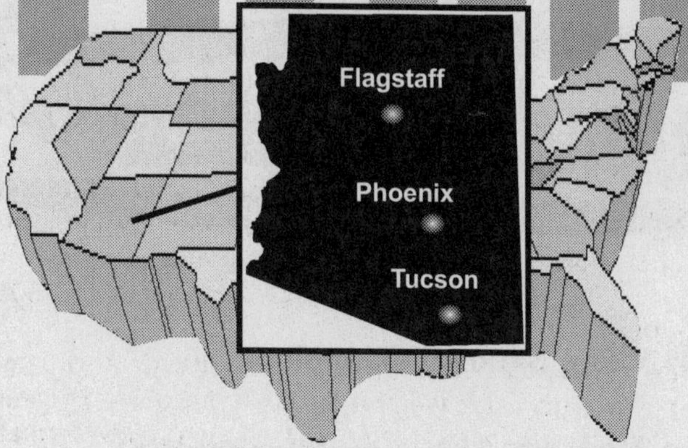

SCHOOL	CITY	AFFILIATION	PAGE
Arizona State University	Tempe	NCAA I	59
Grand Canyon University	Phoenix	NCAA II	59
Northern Arizona University	Flagstaff	NCAA I	60
Phoenix College	Phoenix	NJCAA	61
University of Arizona	Tucson	NCAA I	62
Yavapai College	Prescott	NJCAA	63

Arizona State University
Academic Profile

Tempe, AZ 85287-2505
Phone: 480-965-7788

Type: 4 Yr.,Public,Liberal Arts,Engineering
Founded: 1885
Website: http://www.asu.edu
Religion: Non-Affiliated
SAT/ACT/GPA: 930/22/3.0
Housing: Yes
Student/Faculty Ratio: 20:1
Male/Female Ratio: 38:62
Undergraduate Enrollment: 43,732
Graduate Enrollment: 100
Scholarships/Academic: Yes **Athletic:** Yes **Financial Aid:** Yes
Expenses by: Year **In State:** $ 11,000 **Out of State:** $ 17,000
Specialty: Business, Education, Nurses
Degrees Conferred: BS, BS, BM, BGS, BSN, MA, MBA, MEd
Programs of Study: Anthropology, Art, Broadcasting, Chemistry, Education, Music, Science, History, Geology, Economics, English, Geography, Humanities, Journalism, Math, Music, Philosophy, Political Science, Religious, Sociology

Women's Athletic Profile

ICA Building
Tempe, AZ 85287-2505
Coach: Ray Leone
Email: fbari@asu.edu

NCAA I
Sun Devils/Maroon, Gold
Phone: (480) 965-1715
Fax: (480) 965-7398

Estimated # of Women's Soccer Scholarships: 12
Conference: Pac-10 Conference
Program Profile: The Sun Devils home playing field is natural grass and stadium has a seating capacity of 1,050, which was newly renovated.
History: The program is its 6th year.
Achievements: Stacey Tulock was named Soccer Buzz All-American 2nd team, NFCAA All-American 2nd Team, Soccer Buzz All-West Region 1st team, NSCAA All-West and All-Conference 1st team, College Soccer.com All-American 3rd team. Patrice Fuelner was named Soccer Buzz West Region All-Freshman team. 2000 we had our 1st appearance in NCAA Tournament.
Coaching: Ray Leone is begininng his first year with the Sun Devils after a successful career at Clemson. Franco Bari is the Assistant Coach- 2nd season.
Roster in State: 5 **Out of State:** 15
ODP State: 2 **Regional:** 5 **National:** 1
Graduation %: N/A **Seniors on Team:** 7
Most Recent Record: 14-7-1
Schedule: Northern Arizona, Stanford, UCLA, USC, UMASS, Michigan, Colorado, Utah, Georgia, BYU
Style of Play: We play an aggressive with a lot of speed.

Grand Canyon University
Academic Profile

Phoenix, AZ 85287
Phone: 602-589-2885

Type: 4 Yr.,Private,Liberal Arts
Founded: 1949
Website: http://www.grand-canyon.edu
Religion: Southern Baptist
SAT/ACT/GPA: 1050/22/3.0
Housing: Yes
Student/Faculty Ratio: 17:1
Male/Female Ratio: 1:2
Undergraduate Enrollment: 1,594
Graduate Enrollment: 862

Scholarships/Academic: Yes **Athletic:** Yes **Financial Aid:** Yes
Expenses by: Year **In State:** $ 13,406 **Out of State:** $ 13,406
Specialty: Nursing, Education, Science
Degrees Conferred: BA, BS, BM, BGS, BSN, MA, MBA, MEd
Programs of Study: Accounting, Banking/Finance, Biology, Business, Chemistry, Communications, Criminal Justice, Economics, Education, English, Graphic Design, History, International Business, Management, Marketing, Mathematics, Music, Nursing, Religion, Speech, Science, Visual and Performing Arts

Men's Athletic Profile

3300 W Camelback Road
Phoenix, AZ 85017
Coach: Peter Draksin
Email: Not Available

NCAA II
Antelopes/Purple, White
Phone: (602) 589-2835
Fax: (602) 589-2529

Estimated # of Men's Soccer Scholarships: None
Conference: California Collegiate Athletic Association
Program Profile: Our team plays matches off campus at nearby recreation complex. Campus field is complete. Very competitive schedule in conference (CCAA)
History: Founded in 1985 and has been an independent until this past season.
Coaching: Peter Draksin, Head Coach , will enter his 5th season as head coach after serving as the program's assistant for 2 years.

Women's Athletic Profile

3300 W. Camelback
Phoenix, AZ 85017
Coach: Peter Duah
Email: Not Available

Phone: (602) 589-2009
Fax: (602) 965-2529

Did Not Return Profile

Northern Arizona University

Academic Profile

Phone: 520-523-6792

Flagstaff, AZ 86011

Type: 4 Yr.,Public
Website: http://www.nau.edu
SAT/ACT/GPA: 1040222.5
Student/Faculty Ratio: 22:1
Undergraduate Enrollment: 13,905

Founded: 1899
Religion: Non-Affiliated
Housing: Yes
Male/Female Ratio: 44:56
Graduate Enrollment: 6,059

Scholarships/Academic: Yes **Athletic:** Yes **Financial Aid:** Yes
Expenses by: Semester **In State:** $3,474 **Out of State:** $ 5,554
Specialty: Education, Engineering, Forestry, Hotel Management
Degrees Conferred: Bachelors, Masters, Doctorates
Programs of Study: College of Arts & Sciences, College of Business Administration, School of Communications, College of Ecosystem Science and Management, College of Engineering and Technology, Center for Excellence in Education, College of Professions, School of Hotel and Restaurant Management, Museum Faculty of Fine Art, School of Performing Arts, College of Social and Behavioral Sciences, Interdisciplinary Studies.

Women's Athletic Profile

P.O. Box 15400
Flagstaff, AZ 86011
Coach: Tracy Custer
Email: tracy.custer@nau.edu

NCAA I
Lumberjacks/Blue, Gold
Phone: (520) 523-2021
Fax: (502) 523-6793

Estimated # of Women's Soccer Scholarships: None
Conference: Big Sky Conference
Program Profile: The NAU soccer program plays its home matches at Lumberjack Stadium. It seats 3,000 people and is a natural grass surface. The soccer team also uses the Walkup Skydome (home to NAU football, basketball, and indoor track and field) for practices as well. Located within the Skydome is the 6, 500 square foot weight room facility utilized by all NAU athletes.
History: The NAU soccer program's inaugural season was 1997. Head Coach Tracy Custer has been at the helm all four seasons recording a 25-48-0 career record. The Jacks have reached the Big Sky Conference tournament the last three seasons and have advanced to the championship match the past two years.
Coaching: Head Coach Tracy Custer. Assistant Coach Sarah Comeaux.
Roster in State: 9 **Out of State:** 15 **Out of Country:** 0
ODP State: 14 **Regional:** 1 **National:** 0
Walk-on/Other: 0 **Graduation %:** **Seniors on Team:** 8
Positions Needed: ALL
Camp or Clinic Dates: July 22-27, 2001
Most Recent Record: 7-14-0
Schedule: Arizona State, Oklahoma, Ole Miss, Alabama, Montana, Cal Poly, Arizona
Style of Play: A very indirect style of play that is possession oriented.

Phoenix College

Academic Profile

Phoenix, AZ 85013-4234
Phone: (602) 285-7137

Type: 2 Yr.,Public
Website: http://pc.maricopa.edu
SAT/ACT/GPA: Recommend
Student/Faculty Ratio: 18/1
Undergraduate Enrollment: 12,000
Scholarships/Academic: Yes **Athletic:** Yes
Expenses by: Semester **In State:** $600
Specialty: General Studies
Degrees Conferred: AA, AGS, AAS
Founded: 1920
Religion: Non-Affiliated
Housing: No
Male/Female Ratio: 1:1
Graduate Enrollment: N/A
Financial Aid: Yes
Out of State: $3,500
Programs of Study: Certificates in EMT, Fire Sciences, Nursing, Dental Hygiene, Phlebotomy, Computers, Culinary Arts as well as two-year degrees in all listed. Above is only a sampling.

Men's Athletic Profile

1202 W Thomas Rd
Phoenix, AZ 85013
Coach: Brett Davis
Email: brett.davis@pcmail.maricopa.edu

NJCAA
Bears/Navy Blue, Gold
Phone: (602) 285-7665
Fax: (602) 285-7333

Estimated # of Men's Soccer Scholarships: Varies
Conference: Arizona Community College Athletic Association

Program Profile: Competitive in ACCAC (recognized as one of toughest conferences in the country) and NJCAA Region I. The Bears soccer program is part of a total program where education is emphasized above all. Advisement, tutoring, mentoring and academic monitoring provided to all athletes through the 'Student Athlete Scholastic Success'. Play in a 7,500 seating capacity stadium with natural grass.
History: Program began in 1991 and has made the playoffs nearly every year.
Achievements: 1994 ACCAC Player of the Year, 1995 ACAC Player of the Year, NJCAA All-Americans in 1994, 1995, 1996, 1997, and 2000. Excellent placement record of graduates including 4 year schools and several currently playing professionally both indoor and outdoor.
Coaching: Brett Davis is a USSF Nationally Licensed coach. Coach Davis is also a member of the Arizona State Coaching staff, Arizona State/USSF Licensing Instructor, State and Regional ODP Coach and has served as the AYSA Director of Coaching. Currently Coach Davis is the President of the 28,00 player AYSA. Coach Davis has guided the Bears since 1983 and work full-time on campus as the Assistant Athletic Director and Academic Advisor.
Positions Needed: All
Camp or Clinic Dates: Not Available
Most Recent Record: 16-5-1
Style of Play: Bear soccer emphasizes controlled rhythmic team play interspersed with individual improvisation. Supportive build-up with a quick striking attack and counter-attack, spreading opponents and penetrating with variety. Sportsmanship and class a premium!

Women's Athletic Profile

1202 W Thomas Rd
Phoenix, AZ 85013
Coach: Fred Jungemann
Email: Not Available

NJCAA
Bears/Navy Blue, Gold
Phone: (602) 285-7683
Fax: (602) 285-7333

Estimated # of Women's Soccer Scholarships: Varies
Conference: Arizona Community College Athletic Association
Program Profile: Competitive in the NJCAA Region (Program is entering its second year and is part of a total program where education is emphasized above all). Advisement, tutoring, mentoring, and academic monitoring is provided to all the athletes through the "Student Athlete Scholastic Soccer Program" (SASS). Play in a 7,500 seating capacity stadium with a natural grass.
History: First year of the program was in 1997. Bears have made playoff each year of their history.
Achievements: Made Region I Playoffs-first of the team's history.
Coaching: Fred Jungemann enters his third year at Phoenix College along with two year assistant Morgan Lee.
Camp or Clinic Dates: Not-Available
Most Recent Record: 12-8-1
Style of Play: High pressure defense with possession oriented attack.

University of Arizona

Academic Profile

Tucson, AZ 85721

Phone: 520-621-3237

Type: 4 Yr.,Public
Website: http//www.arizona.edu
SAT/ACT/GPA: 23
Student/Faculty Ratio: 19:1
Undergraduate Enrollment: 35,306
Scholarships/Academic: Yes
Athletic: Yes
Expenses by: Year
In State: $ 3,000

Founded: 1885
Religion: Non-Affiliated
Housing: No
Male/Female Ratio: 49:1
Graduate Enrollment: N/A
Financial Aid: Yes
Out of State: $ 8,600

Degrees Conferred: BA, BS, BFA, BM, MA, MBA, MFA, JD
Programs of Study: Accounting, Animal, Anthropology, Banking/Finance, Communications, Computer Engineering, Education, Horticulture, Languages, Journalism, Medical, PreProfessional Programs, Religion, Social Science, Speech

Women's Athletic Profile

Women's Soccer
Tucson, AZ 85721
Coach: Cathy Klein
Email: Not Available

NCAA I
Wildcats/Blue, Red
Phone: (520) 621-7771
Fax: (520) 621-2681

Estimated # of Women's Soccer Scholarships: None
Conference: Pacific-10
Program Profile: We have a natural grass field along with a year round program.
History: Program began in the fall of 1994.
Achievements: NCSC Coach of the Year 1991.
Style of Play: We deliberate in our attack and patient in defense.

Yavapai College

Academic Profile

Phone: (520) 776-2242

Prescott, AZ 86301

Type: 2 Yr.,Public
Website: http://www.yavapai.cc.az.us
SAT/ACT/GPA: Open
Student/Faculty Ratio: 19:1
Undergraduate Enrollment: 3,800
Scholarships/Academic: Yes
Athletic: Yes
Expenses by: Sem
In State: $2,750
Degrees Conferred: AA, AAS

Founded: 1969
Religion: Non-Affiliated
Housing: Yes
Male/Female Ratio: 3:5
Graduate Enrollment: N/A
Financial Aid: Yes
Out of State: $3,000

Programs of Study: 67 programs from A (Accounting) to Z (Zoology) with credits transferring to four-year institutions.

Men's Athletic Profile

1100 E Sheldon Street
Prescott, AZ 86301
Coach: Mike Pantalione
Email: philly@yavapai.cc.az.us

NJCAA
Roughriders/Dark Green, Gold
Phone: (520) 776-2242
Fax: (520) 776-2243

Estimated # of Men's Soccer Scholarships: 11
Conference: Arizona Athletic Conference
Program Profile: Our program is a part of a total education and is a very competitive. A tradition of excellence since its inception in 1989. Enthusiastically supported by the community (best junior college home attendance). Residence halls available on the Prescott Campus. Soccer profile video and media guide available upon request.
History: Program began in 1989. Ten-year overall record is 255-19-8. Ten consecutive plus 20 win seasons. Nationally-ranked every week this decade. Over 100 graduates from the 1990's on soccer scholarships at four-year schools.
Achievements: 1990 and 1992 NJCAA National Champions; 1991, 1994, 1995 & 1996 National Runner-Up; 1998 National Third Place; 1993 National Fourth Place; Arizona Conference, Regional and District Champions every year this decade; 23 All-Americans; 57 All-Region players; 1990, 1992 & 1997 National Coach of the Year; 1995 NSCAA & NISOA National Coaching Merit Award for professional and ethical behavior.
Coaching: Mike Pantalione, Head Coach, a tireless promoter of the sport. Pantalione holds an international and national coaching license. Best all-time winning percentage in men's college soccer (215-13-7 in ten years which is .930 in percentage). Capture the first three national titles with the school's initial recruiting class. Hugh Bell, Assistant Coach, is a 20-year high school and college coaching veteran.

Roster In State: 12
Out of State: 8
Out of Country: 2
ODP State: 0
Regional: 0
National: 0
Walk-on/Other: 0
Graduation %: 100
Seniors on Team: 0
Positions Needed: ALL
Camp or Clinic Dates: June, July
Most Recent Record: 22-3-0
Schedule: Conference regional district and national schedule
Style of Play: The Roughriders soccer team have built a reputation of playing a crisp game that emphasizes a balance passing attack, teamwork, and sportsmanship. An attacking style with a winning traditions!

arkansas

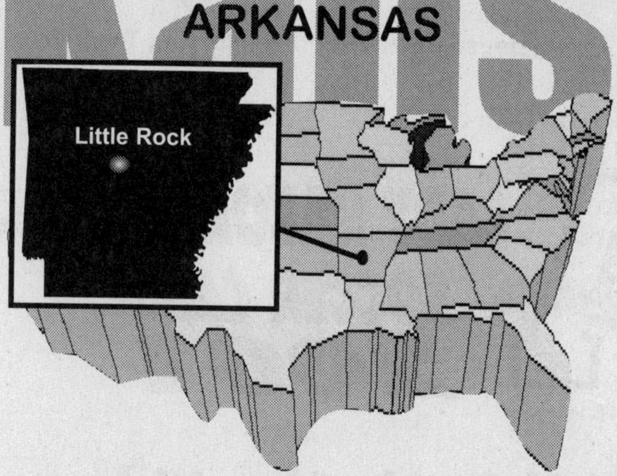

SCHOOL	CITY	AFFILIATION	PAGE
Harding University	Searcy	NCAA III	68
Hendrix College	Conway	NCAA III	68
John Brown University	Siloam Springs	NAIA	70
Ouachita Baptist College	Arkadelphia	NCAA II	70
University of Arkansas-Fayetteville	Fayetteville	NCAA I	71
University of Arkansas-Little Rock	Little Rock	NCAA I	72
University of Central Arkansas	Conway	NCAA II	73
University of the Ozarks	Clarksville	NCAA III	74

Harding University
Academic Profile

Phone: 501-279-4761

Searcy, AR 72149

Type: 4 Yr.,Private
Website: http://www.harding.edu
SAT/ACT/GPA: 1000/24
Student/Faculty Ratio: 18/1
Undergraduate Enrollment: 4500
Scholarships/Academic: Yes
Athletic: Yes
Expenses by: Year
In State: $11,000
Specialty: Liberal Arts
Founded: 1924
Religion: Church of Christ
Housing: Yes
Male/Female Ratio: 51/49
Graduate Enrollment: 200
Financial Aid: Yes
Out of State: $11,000
Degrees Conferred: AA, BA, BS, BFA, M
Programs of Study: Advertising, Art, Biblical, Biology, Business, Chemistry, Dietetics, Economics, Fashion, Finance, Journalism, PreProfessional Programs, Religious, Science, Speech, Special Education

Women's Athletic Profile

900 East Center
Searcy, AR 72169-0001
Coach: Terry Edwards
Email: tedwards@harding.edu

NCAA III
Lady Bison/Black, White, Gold
Phone: (501) 279-6284
Fax: (501) 279-4191

Estimated # of Women's Soccer Scholarships: 4.5
Conference: Gulf South Conference
Program Profile: 3rd year program, recruiting mostly from out of state. We have a field built specifically for our women's program, with lights. Average attendance at home games is 360. Season goes from mid-August to 1st week of November. The spring season includes participation in 2-3 tournaments in April. The field is all natural. We also have an indoor facility for rainy days.
History: The program began in 1998. 1st year record 6-9-1. 2nd year record 9-10-1
Achievements: Winner of 2 spring tournaments in 1st year of play.
Coaching: Terry L. Edwards, Head Coach. Steve Young, Assistant Coach for goalies. Ryan Singleton, Assistant coach for striker. Ronnie Harlow, Trainer.
Roster in State:
Out of State: 22
Out of Country:
ODP State: 6
Regional: 1
National:
Walk-on/Other:
Graduation %:
Seniors on Team: 3
Camp or Clinic Dates: Not Available
Most Recent Record: 9-10-1
Schedule: Barry University, West Florida, Lincoln Memorial, University of Arkansas-Little Rock, Northeastern, Oklahoma State, University of Missouri-ROUA, Alabama A&M, Arkansas State University
Style of Play: 4-4-2 with emphasis on ball control and containment of opponent. Heavy use of off-sides and shooting mid-fielders.

Hendrix College
Academic Profile

Phone: 800-277-9017

Conway, AR 72032

Type: 4 Yr.,Private,Liberal Arts
Website: http://www.hendrix.edu
SAT/ACT/GPA: Open
Student/Faculty Ratio: 13:1
Founded: 1876
Religion: United Methodist
Housing: Yes
Male/Female Ratio: 45:55

Undergraduate Enrollment: 1,047 **Graduate Enrollment:** 11
Scholarships/Academic: Yes **Athletic:** No **Financial Aid:** Yes
Expenses by: Year **In State:** $ 17,680 **Out of State:** $ 17,680
Specialty: Liberal Arts
Degrees Conferred: BA, Masters in Accounting
Programs of Study: Art, Biology, Chemistry, Computer Science, Business, Economics, Elementary Education, English, French, German, History, Interdisciplinary Studies, International Relations & Global Studies, Mathematics, Music, Philosophy, Philosophy & Religion, Physical Education, Physics, Politics, Psychology, Religion, Sociology, Spanish, Theater Arts, PreProfessional Programs: PreDentistry, PreEngineering, PreLaw, PreMedicine, PreMinistry, PrePharmacy, PrePhysical Therapy, PreVeterinary, PreSocial Work. Teacher Certification.

Men's Athletic Profile

1600 Washington Avenue
Conway, AR 72032
Coach: Glen Tourville
Email: tourville@hendrix.edu

NCAA III
Warriors/Orange, Black
Phone: (501) 450-3818
Fax: (501) 450-3805

Estimated # of Men's Soccer Scholarships: None
Conference: Southern Collegiate Athletic Association (SCAC)
Program Profile: 1998 newly constructed 80x120 natural grass soccer stadium, seats 1,500. Lighted practice facility inside soccer complex.
History: 1992 founded as a club team; 1998 will be the seventh season as a varsity sports.
Achievements: 1993-1994 All-SAAC 1st team - Kenny Jones and Joachim Schuller; Honorable Mention-Jeff Humiston, Rick Kennedy and David Rogers; 1994-1995 SCAC Honorable Mention - Jeremy Baler, Jeff Humiston, Rusty Roberts; 1995-1996 SCAC Honorable Mention - David Spiek; 1996-1997 All-SCAC 2nd team - Jeremy Baker.
Coaching: Glen Tourville, Head Coach, holds a US Soccer "A" License and NSCAA Advanced National Diploma; Head Coach (Age group) Region II ODP; professional coaching experience in the USISL in 1993.
Roster In State: 14 **Out of State:** 11 **Out of Country:**
ODP State: 2 **Regional:** **National:**
Walk-on/Other: **Graduation %:** N/A **Seniors on Team:** 1
Positions Needed: Goalkeeper
Camp or Clinic Dates: Not Available
Most Recent Record: 4-13-
Schedule: DePauw, Rhodes, Trinity, Wheaton
Style of Play: Ball possession with a heavy emphasis on playing rhythm. Very organized defensively; free flaming attacking play preferred.

Women's Athletic Profile

1600 Washington Avenue
Conway, AR 72032-3080
Coach: Glen Tourville
Email: tourville@hendrix.edu

NCAA III
Warriors/Orange, Black
Phone: (501) 450-1391
Fax: (501) 450-3805

Estimated # of Women's Soccer Scholarships: None
Conference: Southern Collegiate Athletic Conference
Program Profile: 1998 newly constructed 80x120 yards, natural grass soccer stadium that seats 1,500. Lighted practice facility adjacent to soccer stadium.
History: The program began competition in 1993 and entering its 6th year as a varsity sport.
Achievements: 1994-1995 All-SCAC Honorable Mention-Shana Haskins, Caroline Turpin; 1995-1996 NCAA Woman of the Year.
Coaching: Glen Tourville, Head Coach, US Soccer "A" License and NSCAA Advanced National Diploma; head age group Coach Region II ODP; Pre-professional coaching experience in the USISL in 1993.
Style of Play: Ball possession, well organized defensively; free flowing attacking play preferred.

John Brown University

Academic Profile

Siloam Springs, AR 72761

Phone: 877-528-4636

Type: 4 Yr.,Private,Liberal Arts
Website: http://www.jbu.edu
SAT/ACT/GPA: 900/40
Student/Faculty Ratio: 18:1
Undergraduate Enrollment: 1,200
Scholarships/Academic: Yes
Expenses by: Year

Athletic: Yes
In State: $ 13,510

Founded: 1919
Religion: Non-Affiliated
Housing: Yes
Male/Female Ratio: 45:55
Graduate Enrollment: N/A
Financial Aid: Yes
Out of State: $ 13,510

Degrees Conferred: BA, BS, BSE, BMus, AA, AS
Programs of Study: Accounting, Art, Biochemistry, Biology, Business Administration, Chemistry, Church Ministry, Construction Management, Elementary Education, Engineering, English, Environmental Science, History, Journalism, Mathematics, Medical Technology, Music, Physical Education, PreLaw, PreMed, Psychology, Sports Medicine

Men's Athletic Profile

2000 W University Street
Siloam Springs, AR 72761
Coach: Bob Gustavson
Email: Rgustavs@acc.jbu.edu

NAIA
Golden Eagles/Royal Blue, Gold
Phone: (501) 524-7321
Fax: (501) 524-7412

Estimated # of Men's Soccer Scholarships: 8
Conference: Sooner Athletic Conference
Program Profile: We a beautiful playing environment including raised alumni bleachers, electronics scoreboard, and public address system. We have an excellent student fan support.
History: Our program began in 1978 with an overall record of 214-137-35 including two National Championships (NCCAA). We have numerous post-season tournament appearances.
Achievements: We have 12 Coach of the Year Honors, 24 All-Americans and 8 Academic All-Americans.
Coaching: Bob Gustavson, Head Coach, is entering his 18th year as a head coach. He holds a USSF "A coaching license and was 1994 NAIA Senior Bowl West Squad Coach. He graduated from University of Connecticut in 1968.
Style of Play: Controlled; ball possession offense. Premium placed on ball possession in midfield and back thirds of the field. Shots on goal are encouraged from all field positions.

Ouachita Baptist University

Academic Profile

Arkadelphia, AR 71998-0001

Phone: 800-342-5628

Type: 4 Yr.,Private,
Website: Not Available
SAT/ACT/GPA: 950/23
Student/Faculty Ratio: 11:1
Undergraduate Enrollment: 1,604
Scholarships/Academic: Yes
Expenses by: Year

Athletic: Yes
In State: $ 10,620

Founded: 1886
Religion: Non-Affiliated
Housing: Yes
Male/Female Ratio: 48:52
Graduate Enrollment: N/A
Financial Aid: Yes
Out of State: $ 10,620

Degrees Conferred: BA, BS, BME, BM, M
Programs of Study: Accounting, Art, Biology, Business, Chemistry, Communications, Computer, Dietetics, Economics, Education, English, Languages, Health, History, Math, Medical, PreProfessional Programs, Speech

Women's Athletic Profile

Box 3718
Arkadelphia, AR 71998
Coach: Rod Spears
Email: spearsr@obc.edu

NCAA II
Tiger Soller/Purple, Gold
Phone: (870) 245-5187
Fax: (870) 245-5517

Estimated # of Women's Soccer Scholarships:
Conference: Lone Star Conference
Program Profile: Our field is a natural grass with a brand new goal post.
History: 1999 is our inaugural season. Our players get to play with each other for the first time. This will be a year for laying down a strong foundation.
Style of Play: We play a 4-4-2 formation. Our focus will be on establishing a strong defense and an opportunistic offense.

University of Arkansas - Fayetteville

Academic Profile

Fayetteville, AR 72701

Phone: (501) 575-2348

Type: 4 Yr.,Public
Website: http://www.uark.edu
SAT/ACT/GPA: 23/3.0
Student/Faculty Ratio: 15:1
Undergraduate Enrollment: 14,161
Scholarships/Academic: Yes
Expenses by: Year

Athletic: Yes
In State: $ 7,722

Founded: 1871
Religion: Non-Affiliated
Housing: Yes
Male/Female Ratio: 52:48
Graduate Enrollment: 2,600
Financial Aid: Yes
Out of State: $ 12,706

Specialty: Top Engineering program
Degrees Conferred: BS,BA,BFA,BM,BSBA, BSIM,BSPA, BSE, A-Architect, BSHES, BID
Programs of Study: Colleges - many programs of study within each Agricultural, Food & Life Sciences, Architecture, College of Arts & Sciences, Business, Education & Health Professions, Engineering, Law

Women's Athletic Profile

131 Barnhill Arena
Fayetteville, AR 72701
Coach: Alan Kirkup
Email: akirkup@comp.uark.edu

NCAA I
Razorbacks/Cardinal, White
Phone: (501) 575-2348
Fax: (501) 575-7501

Estimated # of Women's Soccer Scholarships: 3
Conference: Southeastern Conference (SEC)
Program Profile: Arkansas plays in the SEC Western Division against the likes of Alabama, Auburn, LSU, Ole Miss and Miss State. We play on Lady' Back Stadium which was the first soccer field dedicated solely to a women's soccer team. Lady 'Back field has 2,500 seats. The season runs from mid August through November. Lady 'Back Field is a natural grass field composed of Bermuda grass oversized with rye that stays green throughout the year.
History: Arkansas began play in 1986 and we were an independent NCAA Division I program until we joined the Southeastern Conference and the Conference adopted soccer in 1995. Since then, Arkansas has played in the SEC Western Division and won one Western Division Championship and made numerous trips to the Conference Championship Tournament. The Lady Razorbacks even played for the Tournament Title in 1986 against Florida. The Lady' Backs hosted the first conference televised game in 1996 and adopted lights to their field in 1997. Since the Lady' Backs began play on their home pitch of Lady' Back Field they have never had a losing record.
Achievements: 1996 Southeastern Conference Western Division Champions; 1993 SEC Player of the Year-Honey Marsh; 6 All-Conference Players earning nine honors; SEC Tournament MVP in 1993- Honey Marsh; 10 SEC All-

Tournament performances; 2 All-South and 3 All-Central Region Selections; 1999 Erin Sampson -SEC 2nd team; 4-1999 Academic Awards; 1996 SEC West Champs.
Coaching: Alan Kirkup, Head Coach, previously coached at University of Maryland and SMU. Julie Davis, Assistant Coach, was a women's coach at Miami of Ohio. Steve Oliver, Assistant Coach, is a former goalkeeper coach from the University of Maryland.
Roster in State: 3 **Out of State:** 18 **Out of Country:**
ODP State: 10 **Regional:** 4 **National:**
Walk-on/Other: **Graduation %:** **Seniors on Team:** 3
Positions Needed: Forward, Midfielder, Defender
Camp or Clinic Dates: June 11-15
Most Recent Record: 7-12-0
Schedule: San Diego, William and Mary, Florida, Georgia, Richmond, Baylor, SMU, Pepperdine, South Carolina, Tennessee
Style of Play: Play an attractive, entertaining soccer, try to win 5-4 than 1-0.

University of Arkansas - Little Rock

Academic Profile

Phone: 501-569-3127

Little Rock, AR 72204

Type: 4 Yr.,Public
Website: http://www.ualr.edu
SAT/ACT/GPA: 870/21/2.00
Student/Faculty Ratio: 16:1
Undergraduate Enrollment: 9,500
Scholarships/Academic: Yes **Athletic:** Yes
Expenses by: Year **In State:** $ 8,000
Founded: 1927
Religion: Non-Affiliated
Housing: Yes
Male/Female Ratio: 46:54
Graduate Enrollment: 2,500
Financial Aid: Yes
Out of State: $ 12,000
Specialty: Business, Engineering, PreMed, PreLaw, Information Tech
Degrees Conferred: BA, BS, MS, MA, M.Ed.
Programs of Study: Accounting, Advertising, Art, Biology, Business, Chemistry, Communicative Disorders, Computer, Construction, Criminal, Economics, Engineering, Finance, Geology, Health, Journalism, Science, Technology

Women's Athletic Profile

2801 S. University
Little Rock, AR 72204
Coach: Christopher Pratt
Email: capratt@ualr.edu

NCAA I
Trojans/Maroon, Silver
Phone: (501) 569-3452
Fax: (501) 569-3030

Estimated # of Women's Soccer Scholarships: 8
Conference: Sun Belt Conference
Program Profile: We have year-round strength and conditioning. We have excellent medical staff, a brand new weight room, natural grass field with a seating for 400. It is measures 80x120. In 2001-2002, will be a completion of a new soccer track stadium.
History: The program began as NAIA program in 1987 to 1991; 1991 to the present is member of NCAA I. We were member 1998 & 1999 Missouri Valley Conference and 2000 member of sun Belt Conference.
Achievements: We have had 8 All-conference players in the last two years.
Coaching: Christopher Pratt is our Head Coach. He is entering first year with the program and seventh year overall. He was a graduate of MacMurray College in 1994. Greg Hess is our Assistant Coach. He is entering second year with the program. He was a graduate of New Mexico in 1999. Emily Flansburgh is our Assistant Coach. He is entering first year with the program. He was a Nebraska Wesleyan graduate in 2000.
Roster in State: 1 **Out of State:** 19 **Out of Country:** 1
ODP State: 15 **Regional:** 2 **National:** 0

Walk-on/Other: 0 **Graduation %:** 85 **Seniors on Team:** 1
Positions Needed: Midfielder, Defenders
Camp or Clinic Dates: Early August & late May - 3 Goalkeeper Camps, 3
Most Recent Record: 4-15-0
Schedule: Nebraska, North Texas, Southern Alabama, Denver, FIU, Tulsa, South Mississippi
Style of Play: High intensity - high-pressure defense. Quick counter-attack offense.

University of Central Arkansas

Academic Profile

Conway, AR 72035
Phone: (501) 450-3258

Type: 4 Yr.,Public
Website: http://www.uca.edu
SAT/ACT/GPA: 890/17/3.0
Student/Faculty Ratio: 19:1
Undergraduate Enrollment: 9,000
Scholarships/Academic: Yes **Athletic:** Yes
Expenses by: Year **In State:** $ 6,638
Founded: 1907
Religion: Non-Affiliated
Housing: Yes
Male/Female Ratio: 2.3:1
Graduate Enrollment: 1,000
Financial Aid: Yes
Out of State: $ 7,136
Specialty: Liberal Arts, Physical Therapy, Teacher Education
Degrees Conferred: AA, AS. AAS, BA, BBA, BS, BSE, MA, MS, MSE, MSN, MM, Ph.D. (Physical Therapy)
Programs of Study: Athletic Training, Business, Communications, Education, Kinesiology (Physical Education), Liberal Arts, Music, Nursing, Occupational Therapy, Physical Therapy, Science, Speech(Language) Pathology

Men's Athletic Profile

P.O. Box 5004
Conway, AR 72035
Coach: Joel Harrison
Email: Not Available
NCAA II
Bears/White, Purple, Gray
Phone: (501) 328-0279
Fax: (501) 450-3151

Estimated # of Men's Soccer Scholarships: 6
Conference: Gulf South Conference
Program Profile: We have an excellent playing practice fields which are natural grass Bermuda. Stadium holds from 500-1,000 people.
History: First year of competition was in 1996-1997.
Achievements: First year team consisted of one player eligible for All-American Gulf South Conference team and made it.
Coaching: Joel Harrison, Head Coach, holds a USSF "A" License and a NSCAA Advanced National Diploma.
Style of Play: Attack-wings and forward attack. Midfield is primarily involved with the defenders. Midfielders also support the forwards. Defending two marking backs with a sweeper (pushes as far forward as possible), with sweeper/keeper support. Two defenders in the midfield front the defense.

Women's Athletic Profile

P.O. Box 5004
Conway, AR 72035
Coach: Hollie Harris
Email: hollien@mail.uca.edu
NCAA II
Lady Bears/Purple, Black, Grey
Phone: (501) 450-3258
Fax: (501) 450-3151

Estimated # of Women's Soccer Scholarships:
Conference: Gulf South Conference
Program Profile: We have a soccer complex with a soccer house adjacent to the fields. There are 3 fields and they are all natural grass. We have a concession area, a training facility and a seating capacity of 400.

History: Our program began in the Fall of 1997. We played a "club schedule" of 13 games and got a record of 8-5. We played a full schedule in 1998 as members of the Gulf South Conference. Our record is 6-11-0.
Achievements: 1 GSC Co-Freshman of the year, 1-GSC First Team in 1998; 3 All-Academic Players in 1998.
Coaching: Hollie Harris, Head Coach, has been our head coach for 3 years. Julie Del Giorno - Graduate Assistant Coach.
Style of Play: Direct attack play in the offensive third. Style stressing control and possession. Emphasis is strong technical skill development. Defensive: zone pressure with designated man-to-man marking back when appropriate.

University of the Ozarks

Academic Profile

Phone: 800-264-8636

Clarksville, AR 72830

Type: 4 Yr.,Private,Liberal Arts
Website: http://www.ozarks.edu
SAT/ACT/GPA: 800/18/2.0
Student/Faculty Ratio: 13:1
Undergraduate Enrollment: 600
Scholarships/Academic: Yes
Expenses by: Year

Athletic: No
In State: $ 11,740

Founded: 1834
Religion: Presbyterian
Housing: Yes
Male/Female Ratio: 49:51
Graduate Enrollment: N/A
Financial Aid: Yes
Out of State: $ 11,740

Degrees Conferred: BA, BS
Programs of Study: Accounting, Art, Business, Chemistry, General Studies, General Science, Education, English, Environmental Studies, History, Management, Marketing, Mathematics, Music, Physical Education, Physics, Psychology, Public Administration, Communications, Social Science, Theatre, Special Education, PreLaw, PreMed, Kinesiology, PreDentistry, PrePharmacy

Men's Athletic Profile

415 N College Ave.
Clarksville, AR 72830
Coach: Dave DeHart
Email: ddehart@ozark.edu

NCAA III
Eagles/Purple, Gold
Phone: (501) 979-1210
Fax: (501) 979-1330

Estimated # of Men's Soccer Scholarships: None
Conference: American Southwest Conference
Program Profile: Soccer only facility include Bermuda grass field, practice area and 2,000 seats stadium. They also have a field built in 1999. The team plays year around season.
History: Began in 1996. Regional ranking in 1998. ASC Championship finalist in 2000.
Achievements: Dave Dehart- 2000 ASC Coach of the Year, ASC East number one seed, ASC Championship finalist.
Coaching: Dave DeHart, the head coach, is entering his second season at Ozarks. He is from Northern California and holds and USSF "A" license. Jeremy Bernard, the assistant coach, is entering his first year and is from Utah.
Roster In State: 3
ODP State: 10
Walk-on/Other: 0

Out of State: 21
Regional: 1
Graduation %: 95

Out of Country: 1
National: 0
Seniors on Team: 8

Positions Needed: Defenders, Goalkeeper, Midfielder
Camp or Clinic Dates: TBA
Most Recent Record: 15-6-0
Schedule: East Texas Baptist Univ. Trinity Univ. Texas Lutheran Univ. Westminster College, Harding Univ. Mississippi College
Style of Play: Possession style of attack, pressure defense adapted to athletes abilities.

Women's Athletic Profile

415 N College Ave.
Clarksville, AR 72830
Coach: Andy Williamson
Email: awillia@ozarks.edu

NCAA III
Lady Eagles/Purple, Gold
Phone: (501) 979-1334
Fax: (501) 979-1330

Estimated # of Women's Soccer Scholarships: None
Conference: American Southwest Conference
Program Profile: Play on soccer only stadium that seats 500. Field is 120x70 Bermuda grass. Training facility has a measurements of 117x72, lighted field with a new lighted practice facility being built. Play a Fall and a Spring season.
History: Program began in 1996, the first recruiting class entered in 1998. First year with a full time Head Coach.
Coaching: First year as Head Coach of the Eagles
Roster in State: 3
Out of State: 10
Out of Country: 2
ODP State: 2
Regional:
National:
Walk-on/Other:
Graduation %:
Seniors on Team: 1
Positions Needed: GK, Forward, Central Midfield
Camp or Clinic Dates: TBA
Most Recent Record: 1-14-0
Schedule: Austin College, Webster Univ. Principia College, Mississippi College, Hendridge College, Rhodes College
Style of Play: Counter-attack but truly depends on personnel.

california

SCHOOL	CITY	AFFILIATION	PAGE
Azusa Pacific University	Azusa	NAIA	81
Biola University	La Mirada	NAIA	82
California Baptist University	Riverside	NAIA	83
California Institute of Technology	Pasadena	NCAA III	84
California Lutheran University	Thousand Oaks	NCAA III	85
California State-San Luis Obispo	San Luis Obispo	NCAA I	86
California State Poly U - Pomona	Pomona	NCAA II	87
Cal State University-Bakersfield	Bakersfield	NCAA	89
California State University - Chico	Chico	NCAA II	90
Cal State Univ - Dominguez Hills	Carson	NCAA II	91
Cal State University - Fresno	Fresno	NCAA I	92
Cal State University - Fullerton	Fullerton	NCAA I	94
Cal State University - Hayward	Hayward	NCAA II	95
Cal State University - Los Angeles	Los Angeles	NCAA II	96
Cal State University - Northridge	Northridge	NCAA I	97
Cal State University- Sacramento	Sacramento	NCAA I	98
Cal State Univ - San Bernardino	San Bernardino	NCAA II	99
Cal State University - Stanislaus	Turlock	NCAA II	100
Cañada College	Redwood City	NJCAA	101
Chapman University	Orange	NCAA III	102
Christian Heritage College	El Cajon	NAIA	103
Claremont - Mudd - Scripps	Claremont	NCAA III	104
College of Notre Dame	Belmont	NCAA II	105
Concordia University - California	Irvine	NAIA	105
De Anza College	Cupertino	CCC	106
Dominican College-California	San Rafael	NAIA	107
Fresno Pacific College	Fresno	NAIA	108
Hope International University	Fullerton	NAIA	109

SCHOOL	CITY	AFFILIATION	PAGE
Humboldt State University	Arcata	NCAA II	110
Long Beach State University	Long Beach	NCAA I	111
Loyola Marymount University	Los Angeles	NCAA I	111
Master's College	Santa Clarita	NAIA	113
Menlo College	Atherton	NCAA III	114
Mills College	Oakland	NCAA III	114
Occidental College	Los Angeles	NCAA III	115
Pepperdine University	Malibu	NCAA I	116
Point Loma Nazarene University	San Diego	NAIA	117
Pomona - Pitzer Colleges	Claremont	NCAA III	118
Saint Mary's College - California	Moraga	NCAA I	119
San Diego State University	San Diego	NCAA I	120
San Francisco State University	San Francisco	NCAA II	122
San Jose State University	San Jose	NCAA I	123
Santa Clara University	Santa Clara	NCAA I	124
Sonoma State University	Rohnert Park	NCAA II	126
Stanford University	Stanford	NCAA I	127
University of California - Berkeley	Berkeley	NCAA I	128
University of California - Davis	Davis	NCAA II	130
University of California - Irvine	Irvine	NCAA I	131
Univ of California - Los Angeles	Los Angeles	NCAA I	132
Univ of California - San Diego	La Jolla	NCAA III	134
Univ of California - Santa Barbara	Santa Barbara	NCAA I	134
Univ of California - Santa Cruz	Santa Cruz	NCAA III	136
University of La Verne	La Verne	NCAA III	137
University of Redlands	Redlands	NCAA III	138
University of San Diego	San Diego	NCAA I	139
University of San Francisco	San Francisco	NCAA I	140
University of the Pacific	Stockton	NCAA I	142
Vanguard U of S California	Costa Mesa	NAIA	143
Ventura College (Community)	Ventura	NJCAA	144
Westmont College	Santa Barbara	NAIA	144
Whittier College	Whittier	NCAA III	145

MESSAGE CSL PREMIER CHAIRMAN GARY SPARKS

The concept for the formation of the Coast Soccer Premier Leagues (CSL Premier League) is relatively simple: In order for truly great youth competition to become a reality, coaches, administrators, referees and players must all form a true partnership, each respecting the other, with a common goal of creating an atmosphere that will allow the players to do what they do best Play the Game.

The CSL Premier concept has been embraced by all those who participate in the CSL Premier League. Premier coaches have grasped the concept and are running with the ball. Games that need to be rescheduled due to recruiting trips are rescheduled between the respective coaches. Coaches control their sidelines. They take the responsibility to enforce Premier policy that referees, good or bad, are to be treated with respect and that all communication with a referee is to be between the coach and the referee.

The Referee Associations and their individual Premier referees have risen to the challenge as well and are working just as hard as the coaches to insure the games are won or lost on the field. Youth and Mentor Referees continue to provide a great surprise in their ability to grasp the significance of the Premier Leagues challenge and prove to be some of the best athletes on the field.

And CSL has committed to do its' part. CSL has leased two of the finest soccer complexes in Southern Calif. to host the Premier Games. CSL has created the Premier Magazine, the Premier League Website, fostered the development of Youth and Mentor Referees, and provide on site trainers to assist players to remain free from injury. And now, CSL introduces the CSL Premier League "Player Media Guide" in its' continuing efforts to promote the visibility of all CSL Premier League Players.

Each player has the ability to update their own home page at www.cslpremier.com as often as necessary to reflect their recent performances, both athletic and academic. We urge all coaches, scouts and recruiters to visit the Premier Games, watch our players and follow their careers. Coast Soccer League truly puts "The Best of the Best" on the pitch. The proof to this claim can clearly be demonstrated by the results of the 2000 MLS draft. Thirteen per cent (13%) of the 2000 draft consisted of CSL Players with six (6) out of twelve (12) first round selections coming from CSL.

This year, two (2) of our CSL Premier Leagues Champions, the So. Cal Blues Girls Under 16 and the Wolfpack Boys Under 18 made appearances at the Snicker's National Championship Finals. The So. Cal Blues took home the National Championship and the Wolfpack was a Finalist, losing a tough one in Shootouts. Excellent teams from excellent programs - that is what the CSL Premier Leagues is all about.

For every college coach who is planning a trip to our State, please do not hesitate to contact any member of the CSL Board of Directors or the CSL Premier Committee. We may easily be reached through the SCL Premier Website. We have made arrangements to accommodate you with our local sponsor hotels and will do everything possible to make your stay in Southern California enjoyable.

Very truly yours,

COAST SOCCER LEAGUE

By: **Gary L. Sparks**

Gary L. Sparks, CSL Premier Chairman

Golden Bear Soccer Camps For Boys 2001

Directed by
Head coach Kevin Grimes

Contact us now for a free brochure:

510-643-2267
calmsocc@uclink.berkeley.edu

Information & registration available online:

www.oski.org

Golden Bear Soccer Camps for Boys - directed by Head Coach Kevin Grimes

Advanced Players Camps
Resident and Commuter
June 24-28 Ages 11-19
July 8-12
July 28- August 1

Full Day Camps
June 25-29 Ages 9-18
July 9-13
July 30- August 3

Half Day Camps
June 25-29 Ages 5-11
July 9-13
July 30- August 3

Spring Break Camps
April 9-12 Ages 5-16
April 16-19

University of California at Berkeley
Intercollegiate Athletics & Recreational Sports

Azusa Pacific University

Academic Profile

Azusa, CA 91702
Phone: (626) 815-6000

Type: 4 Yr.,Private,Liberal Arts
Website: http://www.apu.edu
SAT/ACT/GPA: 920/18/2.5
Student/Faculty Ratio: 15:1
Undergraduate Enrollment: 2,500
Scholarships/Academic: Yes **Athletic:** Yes
Expenses by: Year **In State:** $ 18,000

Founded: 1899
Religion: Evangelical
Housing: Yes
Male/Female Ratio: 1:3
Graduate Enrollment: 2,400
Financial Aid: Yes
Out of State: $ 18,000

Degrees Conferred: 40+ undergraduate:18 Masters Degree; 3 Doctorates; CA Teaching Credentials
Programs of Study: Accounting, Applied Health, Art, Athletic Training, Biblical Studies, Biochemistry, Biology, Business Administration, Chemistry, Christian Ministries, Communications, Computer Science, English, Global Studies, History, International Business, Life Science, Liberal Studies, Mathematics, Marketing, Music, Nursing, Philosophy, Physical Education, Physics, Political Science, PreDentistry, PreEngineering, PreLaw, PreM.Ed., PreVeterinary, Psychology, Social Science, Social Work, Sociology, Spanish, Theology

Men's Athletic Profile

901 E Alosta Ave.
Azusa, CA 91702
Coach: Dr. Don Lawrence
Email: dlawrenc@apu.edu

NAIA
Cougars/Brick Red, Black
Phone: (626) 815-6000
Fax: (626) 812-3034

Estimated # of Men's Soccer Scholarships: 5.8
Conference: Golden State Athletic Conference
Program Profile: We are a member of NAIA Top 20 program that has placed 4 players in the professional ranks in the last three years. Cougar Stadium has 4,000 seats and is natural grass. Playing season starts from August 15-November 25th with a strong spring program. Most games are played at night.
History: Azusa Pacific University has produces a top NAIA twenty team in the past five years. The team has been in the Far West Regional Playoffs 8 out of the last 9 years. Our program began varsity play in 1972. Our team advanced to 1996 NAIA Championship Tourney, finished 1996 ranked #2 in NAIA, won Golden State Athletic Conference Championship in 1996 & 1997. Have won 77 games from 1994-1998.
Achievements: Head coach Don Lawrence has been honored as Far West coach of the Year twice in the last 6 years. They have won two titles and have been Far West Champions once. One player has been drafted by the MLS, one player is now playing for Necaxa in Mexico and two are playing for an A league team. 1997-1998 P.J. Brown - Defender was drafted by Colorado Rapids in 3rd round, 4 All-Americans this past season.
Coaching: Dr. Don Lawrence, Head Coach, came to Azusa Pacific in the Summer of 1973. He has been at the helm for the past 15 years. His overall record is 163-118-30 and his 17 career record is 176-133-32.He is the Dean of the Golden State Athletic Conference - that is the dean among soccer coaches. He is a winning soccer coach and is entering 15th season at the Cougars helm, also his 17th as a collegiate soccer coach. He began his coaching career in 1968 as the head soccer coach at Nyack College, where he also served five soccer team to the 1968 North Atlantic Christian College Championships. Sergio Hauptmann - Assistant Coach, former Brazilian professional coach. He is entering his 7th season. He was an NAIA All-American at Fresno Pacific College. Aaron Siefker, Assistant Coaches. Aaron Seifker is a graduate assistant who is in his first year of the Masters program. He is a 4 year player for Azusa, and helped lead the team to there best season with their best record over 4 years while playing for the cougars
Roster In State: 18 **Out of State:** 3 **Out of Country:** 1
ODP State: 4 **Regional:** 1 **National:**
Walk-on/Other: **Graduation %:** 93 **Seniors on Team:** 2
Positions needed: goalkeeper, right defender
Camp or Clinic Dates: No summer camp

Most Recent Record: 11-8-3
Schedule: Cal State Northridge, Westmont, Fresno Pacific, Cal Poly Pomona, Concordia, Graceland, Iowa
Style of Play: Possession; build-up. 3-5-2

Women's Athletic Profile

901 E Alosta Avenue
Azusa, CA 91702
Coach: Jason Surrell
Email: jsurrel@apu.edu

NAIA
Cougars/Brick Red, Grey
Phone: (626) 815-3852
Fax: (626) 815-5084

Estimated # of Women's Soccer Scholarships: N/A
Conference: Golden State Athletic Conference
Program Profile: Azusa Pacific plays in one of the finest small college facilities on the west cost. The hybrid athletic turf is perfect for high-speed teams. Azusa Pacific begins play in late August and continues its season through November. The schedule features approximately 20 regular season games. The roster is comprised of 20-25 players.
History: Azusa Pacific has been ranked in the NAIA top 25 for every poll over the past 3 seasons and has been in the top 5 for every poll of 1999 and 2000. The Cougars won the 1998 NAIA national championship and advanced to the final four in 2000. The program began in 1989.
Achievements: Christian Johnson was named NAIA Coach of the Year in 1998. Kendra Payne who ranks among the NAIA's all-time top 4 scorers, was the 1998 NAIA player of the year and is 3-time All-American.
Coaching:
Roster in State: 20 **Out of State:** 0 **Out of Country:** 0
Walk-on/Other: **Graduation %:** **Seniors on Team:** 6
Most Recent Record: 13-2-3
Schedule: Cal State Fullerton, Cal State Northridge, Sonoma State, Cal Poly Pomona, Westmont, Simon Fraser, Cal State Dominguez Hills.
Style of Play: Possession oriented with high pressure offense, man-to-man defense and build out of the back.

Biola University

Academic Profile

Phone: 800-652-4652

La Mirada, CA 90639

Type: 4 Yr.,Private,Liberal Arts
Website: http://www.biola.edu
SAT/ACT/GPA: Open
Student/Faculty Ratio: 18:1
Undergraduate Enrollment: 2,200
Scholarships/Academic: Yes
Expenses by: Year
Founded: 1908
Religion: Non-Denominational
Housing: Yes
Male/Female Ratio: 40:60
Graduate Enrollment: 1,100
Athletic: Yes
Financial Aid: Yes
In State: $ 22,924
Out of State: $ 22,924
Specialty: Liberal Arts
Degrees Conferred: BA, BS, Masters, Ph.D.
Programs of Study: Art, Biochemistry, Biological Science, Accounting, Computer Information Systems, Economics, Business Administration, Philosophy, Management, Marketing, Nursing, History, Humanities, Education, Sociology, Computer Science, Communications, Psychology

Men's Athletic Profile

13800 Biola Avenue
La Mirada, CA 90639
Coach: Matt Orr
Email: CoachMorr@aol.com

NAIA
Eagles/Red, White
Phone: (562) 944-0351x5933
Fax: (562) 903-4890

Estimated # of Men's Soccer Scholarships: 5 Variable
Conference: Golden State Athletic Conference
Program Profile: We have all season, one varsity field, scoreboard, three club fields, bleachers.
History: Program began in 1962. Several NAIA All-Americans; one NAIA Hall of Fame; active alumni program.
Achievements: 1986 Far west NCCAA Coach of the Year, 8 NAIA All-Americans, 18 NAIA All-District Awards, 10 All-GSAC Awards, 5 NAIA Far west All-Region, 12 NSCAA All-Far west Awards, 3 NAIA Academic All-Americans, 2 NSCAA All-Americans, 2 GSAC Team Sportsmanship Awards, 2 GSAC Team Academic All-League, 1986 - 2nd NCCAA Nationals, 1987 - NAIA District Champions National Participant, 1988 Runner-Up NAIA District 3.
Coaching: Matt Orr, Head Coach, is entering his thirteen season of coaching soccer here. He had a 10-10-0 record in 1998, while his overall record is 108-117-23. He played four years at Biola ending in 1968 when he was named NAIA All-District III 1st team and SCISA honorable mention. He is active in the youth soccer and baseball activities. Erik Schulz is the Assistant Coach. He played three years with the Eagles between 1989-1991. He scored 9 goals and had 7 assist. He was a two-time All-Far West and All-District honoree, as well as being named an honorable mention All-American in 1990. Paul Gizzi is the Assistant Coach. He played goalkeeper for Biola in 1974-1975. He was drafted by the Seattle Sounders of the professional NASI, where he played for two years. He also spent two years with the San Jose Earthquake. He is entering in third year with the program.
Style of Play: We play an attacking style of play.

Women's Athletic Profile

13800 Biola Avenue
La Mirada, CA 90639
Coach: Dave Christenson
Email: Not Available

NAIA
Eagles/Red, White
Phone: (562) 944-0351
Fax: (562) 903-4890

Estimated # of Women's Soccer Scholarships: varies
Conference: Golden State Athletic Conference
History: The program began in 1992. In 1999 we finished the season ranked in the top 25 in the nation.
Achievements: 1999- 6 Academic All-American, 4 All-Conference players, 1 All-Region, 1 All-American
Coaching: Dave Christenson - Head Coach. Darren Wren is Assistant Coach. Jayson Hummes is Goalkeeper Coach.
Roster in State: 5 **Out of State:** 5 **Out of Country:**
ODP State: 4 **Regional:** **National:**
Walk-on/Other: **Graduation %:** 100 **Seniors on Team:** 3
Positions Needed: Striker, Defenders, Midfielder
Camp or Clinic Dates: Not Available
Most Recent Record: 11-4-
Schedule: Cal State Fullerton, Grand Canyon University, Cal State Los Angeles, Westmont College, Azusa Pacific
Style of Play: Aggressive offensive attack.

California Baptist College

Academic Profile

Riverside, CA 92504
Phone: 877-228-8866

Type: 4 Yr.,Private,Liberal Arts
Founded: 1950
Website: http://www.calbaptist.edu
Religion: Southern Baptist
SAT/ACT/GPA: 870/20/2.3
Housing: Yes
Student/Faculty Ratio: 14:1
Male/Female Ratio: 50:50
Undergraduate Enrollment: 850
Graduate Enrollment: 45
Scholarships/Academic: Yes **Athletic:** Yes **Financial Aid:** Yes
Expenses by: Year **In State:** $ 15,000 **Out of State:** $ 15,000
Specialty: Education, Liberal Studies, Physical Education
Degrees Conferred: BA, BS, MS, BM

Programs of Study: Biology, Communications, Art, Business, Physical Education, Education, Liberal Arts, Religion, PreMed, PreNursing, PreDentistry, English, History, Psychology, Sociology

Men's Athletic Profile

8432 Magnolia Avenue
Riverside, CA 92504
Coach: Mike Sutherland
Email: Not Available
Estimated # of Men's Soccer Scholarships: None
Conference: Golden State Athletic Conference

NAIA
Lancers/Red, White, Blue
Phone: (714) 689-5771x318
Fax: (714) 351-1808

Women's Athletic Profile

8432 Magnolia Avenue
Riverside, CA 92504
Coach: Mike Sutherland
Email: Not Available

NAIA
Lady Lancers/Blue, White
Phone: (909) 343-4445
Fax: (909) 689-4754

Estimated # of Women's Soccer Scholarships: N/A
Conference: Golden State Athletic Conference
Program Profile: Have a brand new aquatics center as of Fall of 1998. CBU won the indoor tract National Title in 1998-1999 and won a National Title in men's volleyball in 1999
History: Program began in 1991 with a minimal funding. Marc Dale started the program with a record of 4-14-0 in the first year of the program, and now it has developed into a competitive program going 46-49-2 over their six years of existence. Mike Sutherland took over the program in Spring of 1998 and went to GSAC semi-finals in his first year.
Achievements: 2 All-Americans.
Coaching: Mike Sutherland, Head Coach, he was named CIF Southern Section High School Coach of the Year. He coached State ODP Olympic Development Team. He owns soccer Academy European Tour, Company. Jeff Tackett, Assistant Coach, is the owner of the California School of Goalkeeping. Mike Flemming, Assistant Coach, former CBU Athlete of the Year.
Style of Play: Attack system and style of play. Lots of team speed and physical. Attack quickly and get forward as soon as possible.

California Institute of Technology

Academic Profile

Pasadena, CA 91125

Phone: 800-568-8324

Type: 4 Yr.,Private,Engineering
Website: http://www.caltech.edu
SAT/ACT/GPA: Top 1%
Student/Faculty Ratio: 10:1
Undergraduate Enrollment: 800
Scholarships/Academic: Yes
Athletic: No
Expenses by: Year
In State: $ 25,000

Founded: 1891
Religion: Non-Affiliated
Housing: Yes
Male/Female Ratio: 3:1
Graduate Enrollment: 1,000
Financial Aid: Yes
Out of State: $ 25,000

Specialty: Engineering, Science, Mathematics
Degrees Conferred: BA, BS, MS, Ph.D.
Programs of Study: Aeronautical Engineering, Astronomy, Biology, Chemical Engineering, Chemistry, Civil Engineering, economics, Electrical Engineering, Engineering, Geochemistry, Geology, Geophysics, History, Literature, Mathematics, Mechanical Engineering, Physics, Planetary Science, Political Science, Seismology, Social Science, Space Science

Men's Athletic Profile

1201 E California Blvd./MC 1-2
Pasadena, CA 91125
Coach: Julie Tingle
Email: jtingle@cco.caltech.edu

NCAA III
Beavers/Blue, Orange, White
Phone: (626) 395-3260
Fax: (626) 584-0589

Estimated # of Men's Soccer Scholarships: None
Conference: Southern California Intercollegiate Athletic Conference

California Lutheran University

Academic Profile

Thousands Oaks, CA 91360

Phone: (877) 256-3678

Type: 4 Yr.,Private,Liberal Arts
Website: http://www.callutheran.edu
SAT/ACT/GPA: 1000/21/2.75
Student/Faculty Ratio: 15:1
Undergraduate Enrollment: 1,600
Scholarships/Academic: Yes
Athletic: No
Expenses by: Year
In State: $ 16,020

Founded: 1959
Religion: Lutheran
Housing: Yes
Male/Female Ratio: 45:55
Graduate Enrollment: 900
Financial Aid: Yes
Out of State: $ 16,020

Specialty: Biology, Business, Criminal Justice, Education, Psychology
Degrees Conferred: BA, BS, MA, MS
Programs of Study: Master of Business Education, Master of Public Administration, Master of Education, Master in Clinical Psychology, Master in Arts Education, Master of Science in Counseling and Guidance, Master of Special Education, Master in Marital and Family Therapy

Men's Athletic Profile

60 W Olsen Road
Thousand Oaks, CA 91360
Coach: Dan Kuntz
Email: kuntz@clunet.edu

NCAA III
Kingsmen/White, Purple, Gold
Phone: (805) 493-3855
Fax: (805) 493- 3860

Estimated # of Men's Soccer Scholarships: None
Conference: Southern California Intercollegiate Athletic Conference
Program Profile: We won SCIAC Champions in 1991, 1993, 1995, 1996, 1997 & 1998; Wet Region Champs in 1997; NCAA Bids in 1991, 1997 & 1998.
History: Our program began in 1974. The program is consistently one of the best in the Western United State and it is nationally recognized.
Achievements: SCIA Champions in 1991, 1993, 1995, 1996, 1997 & 1998; 12 All-Americans; 4 Scholar Athletes; 1 Clash MLS played goalkeeper.
Coaching: Dan E. Kuntz, Head Coach, holds a USSF "A" License. He was a semi-pro, ODP High school. Dan J. Kuntz, Assistant Coach, holds a USSF "A" License. He is a former pro-Atlanta Mexico City. Josh Parker, Assistant Coach, was an All-Far west player; captain CLM; Aaron Linder, University of California -Irvine, is our Goalkeeper Coach.
Roster In State: 10
Out of State: 12
Out of Country:
Walk-on/Other:
Graduation %: N/A
Seniors on Team: 5
Most Recent Record: 12-8
Schedule: Bethel, Lynnfield, Willamette, Concordia, Chapman University, Claremont-Mudd-Scripps
Style of Play: It depends on the talent of the athletes that come out each year.

Women's Athletic Profile

60 W Olsen Rd
Thousand Oaks, CA 91360
Coach: Dan Kuntz
Email: kuntz@clunet.edu

NCAA III
Regals/White, Purple, Gold
Phone: (805) 493-3855
Fax: (805) 493-3194

Estimated # of Women's Soccer Scholarships: None
Conference: (SCIAC) South California Intercollegiate Athletic Conference
Program Profile: Pride itself in having one of the most respected programs in the nation.
History: Our program began in 1989 in NAIA II and transitioned to NCAA III in 1991. It has been the most successful of any CLU athletics program in teams of SCIAC Championships.
Achievements: We earned 3 times Western Conference Region Coach of the Year and 9 times Conference Titles. We have had All-American player at least 1 every year and NSCAA Far West player at least one in 1992, 1993, 1995-1999.
Coaching: Dan Kuntz is our Head Coach. He has a USSF "A" License. He is a former professional player from Atlanta Mexico City. Nancy Moskowitz and Shannon Pennington are the Assistant Coaches. Aaron Linder is our Goalkeeping Coach.
Roster in State: 12 **Out of State:** 10 **Out of Country:** 0
ODP State: 5 **Regional:** 0 **National:** 0
Walk-on/Other: 0 **Graduation %:** 100 **Seniors on Team:** 5
Most Recent Record: 15-6-1
Schedule: Bethel of Minnesota, California State-Hayward, Linfield, Willamette, Azusa Pacific
Style of Play: It depends on the talent of the athletes that come out each year.

California Polytechnic State University - San Louis Obispo

Academic Profile

Phone: 805-756-2311

San Luis Obispo, CA 93405-2002

Type: 4 Yr.,Public,Liberal Arts
Website: http://www.calpoly.edu
SAT/ACT/GPA: 1000
Student/Faculty Ratio: 19:1
Undergraduate Enrollment: 15,540
Scholarships/Academic: Yes **Athletic:** Yes
Expenses by: Year **In State:** $ 7,542

Founded: 1901
Religion: Non-Affiliated
Housing: Yes
Male/Female Ratio: 58:42
Graduate Enrollment: 1,200
Financial Aid: Yes
Out of State:

Specialty: Agriculture, Architecture Business
Degrees Conferred: BA, BS, BLA, BAR, MA, MS, MBA, MCRP
Programs of Study: College of Agriculture (Business, Engineering, Systems Management, Science, Animal Science, Crop Science, Dairy/Food/Fruit Science, Forestry and Natural Resources, Nutritional, Horticulture, Plant Protection, Recreation, Soil Science), College of Architecture and Environmental Design (Engineering, Architecture, City and Regional Planning, Construction, Landscape), College of Business (Business Administration, Economics, Industrial Technology), College of Engineering (Aeronautical, Civil, Computer, Computer Science, Electrical, Engineering Science, Environmental, Industrial, Manufacturing, Materials, Mechanical), College of Liberal Arts (Applied Art and Design, English, Graphic Communication, History, Human Development, Journalism, Liberal Studies, Music, Philosophy, Political, Psychology, Social Science, Speech), College of Science and Mathematics (Biochemistry, Biological Sciences, Chemistry, Ecology and Systematic Biology, Math, Microbiology, Physical Education, Physical Science, Physics, Statistics)

Men's Athletic Profile

One Grand Avenue
San Luis Obispo, CA 93405-2002
Coach: Wolfgang Gartner
Email: Not Available

NCAA I
Mustangs/ Green, Gold
Phone: (805) 756-2905
Fax: (805) 756-2650

Estimated # of Men's Soccer Scholarships: None
Conference: Big West Conference
Program Profile: 1994 was the first year in Division I, scholarships available. The stadium seats 6,500 and has natural grass surface. Playing season begins in mid-August and concludes with playoffs in mid-November.
History: Program began in 1901.
Coaching: Wolfgang Gartner, Head Coach, was former professional.

Women's Athletic Profile

1 Grande Ave.
San Luis Obispo, CA 93407
Coach: Alex Crozier
Email: acrozier@calpoly.edu

NCAA I
Mustangs/Forest Green, White
Phone: (805) 756-2590
Fax: (805) 756-7601

Estimated # of Women's Soccer Scholarships: 12
Conference: Big West
Program Profile: Fairly new program that continues to grow. Home games are played at Mustang Stadium on natural turf. The football stadium holds 8,500 and is totally enclosed. Cal Poly focuses on Pacific Coast teams such as UCLA, Santa Clara and Portland as opponents.
History: Program began in 1992; finished first in CCAA 1992,1993; NCAA finals 1993, finished second; 1995 ranked ninth by Sagrin rating system, 21st in ISAA top 25. Big West Champion in 1999.
Achievements: Crozier named National Division II Coach of the Year in 1992 and 1993. Two All-Americans.
Coaching: Alex Cozier, Head Coach since 1992, two - time CCAA Coach of the Year; NCAA Coach of the Year in 1993, first and only women's coach at Cal Poly, led team to Division II Championships finals in 1993. P.J. Woolridge is the 1st year as Assistant Coach.
Roster in State: 27 **Out of State:** 0 **Out of Country:** 0
Walk-on/Other: **Graduation %:** 100 **Seniors on Team:** 7
Camp or Clinic Dates: June 25-29
Most Recent Record: 14-9-0
Schedule: Santa Clara, Fresno State, Dayton, Cincinnati, San Jose State, Butler
Style of Play: High pressure, attacking style of play with emphasis on possession.

California Polytechnic State University - Pomona

Academic Profile

Pomona, CA 91768
Phone: (909) 869-2810

Type: 4 Yr.,Public
Website: http://www.csupomona.edu
SAT/ACT/GPA: 820/68 sum/2.0
Student/Faculty Ratio: 18/1
Undergraduate Enrollment: 18,100
Founded: 1938
Religion: Non-Affiliated
Housing: Yes
Male/Female Ratio: 55:45
Graduate Enrollment: 2,000
Scholarships/Academic: Yes **Athletic:** Yes **Financial Aid:** Yes
Expenses by: Year **In State:** $9,000 **Out of State:** $14,000
Specialty: Engineering, Agriculture, Hotel/Restaurant Mgmt, Business
Degrees Conferred: BA, BS, BArch, MA, MS, MBA
Programs of Study: Accounting, Aerospace Engineering, Agricultural Biology, Agricultural Business Management, Apparel Merchandising, Architecture, Chemistry, Behavioral Science, Construction Engineering, Computer Engineering, Industrial Engineering, Horticulture, Marketing Management, Physics, Political Science, Sociology, Soil Science, Zoology

Men's Athletic Profile

3801 W Temple Avenue
Pomona, CA 91768
Coach: Ryan Heise
Email: rcheise@csupomona.edu

NCAA II
Broncos/Green & Gold
Phone: (909) 869-2821
Fax: (909) 869-2814

Estimated # of Men's Soccer Scholarships: 4.0
Conference: California Collegiate Athletic Association
Program Profile: Cal Poly Pomona competes in arguably one of the best NCAA D.II conferences in the nation the CCAA. CPP is a competitive program regionally and nationally athletically and academically. The soccer team competes in Kellogg Stadium. The playing season is Fall and off-season competition Occurs in the Spring.
History: Records indicate the men's soccer program began in 1983. CPP has one NCAA postseason appearance (98), one Coach of the Year honor and numerous All-CCAA Honorees.
Achievements: CCAA Coach of the Year; CCAA Regular Season Champions; 5 All-Far west members. Also 3 season of top 25 rankings.
Coaching: Ryan Heise is the interim Head Coach at this time. A search for a new coach will begin in Jan. 2001. Heise is a former student athlete in men's soccer at CPP earning All-CCAA three times. He has been an assistant coach the past four season.
Roster In State: 22
Out of State: 3
Out of Country: 2
Walk-on/Other: 0
Graduation %: 90+
Seniors on Team: 6
Positions Needed: F, GK, D
Camp or Clinic Dates: July, 2001
Most Recent Record: 8-8-3
Schedule: CS Dominguez Hills, UC San Diego, CS Bakersfield, Grand Canyon, AZ, Seattle Pacific, Sonoma State.

Women's Athletic Profile

3801 W Temple Avenue
Pomona, CA 91767
Coach: Ryan Heise
Email: rcheise@csupomona.edu

NCAA II
Broncos/Green and Gold
Phone: (909) 869-2821
Fax: (909) 869-2814

Estimated # of Women's Soccer Scholarships: 4.0
Conference: California Collegiate Athletic Association
Program Profile: Cal Poly Pomona competes in arguably one of the best NCAA DII conferences in the nation which is the CCAA. CPP is a competitive program regionally and nationally athletically and academically. The soccer team competes in Kellogg Stadium, named after the great cereal magnate William Kellogg. The playing season is fall and off-season competition occurs in the spring.
History: Cal Poly Pomona has one of the tope women's soccer programs in the nation. Records indicate the program began in 1083. CPP went to the 1999 NCAA Championship match finishing second in the nation. CPP has been a top 25 team the past three years. CPP has one national coach of the year (99), one national player of the year (99), two All-America Awards, two conference titles (91,99) and numerous All-CCAA honors.
Achievements: 2-conference titles, 7 coach of the Year awards, one NCAA DII player of the Year, 2 All-America.
Coaching: Ryan Heise is the interim Head Coach at this time. A search for a new coach will begin in January of 2001. He has been as assistant coach the past four season. CPP has had four consecutive winning season in M/W Soccer.
Roster in State: 24
Out of State: 0
Out of Country: 0
ODP State: 2
Regional: 2
National: 1
Walk-on/Other: 0
Graduation %: 90
Seniors on Team: 6
Positions Needed: F,MF,D
Camp or Clinic Dates: July 2001
Most Recent Record: 14-5-0
Schedule: UC San Diego, Sonoma State, CS Bakersfield, CS Dominguez Hills, Chico State, CS San Bernardino

California State University - Bakersfield

Academic Profile

Bakersfield, CA 93311-1099

Phone: (661) 664-2188

Type: 4 Yr.,Public,Liberal Arts
Website: http://www.csubak.edu
SAT/ACT/GPA: Sliding Scale
Student/Faculty Ratio: 17:1
Undergraduate Enrollment: 4,900
Scholarships/Academic: Yes
Expenses by: Year

Athletic: Yes
In State: $ 6,800

Founded: 1970
Religion: Non-Affiliated
Housing: Yes
Male/Female Ratio: 35:65
Graduate Enrollment: 1,000
Financial Aid: Yes
Out of State: $ 13,800

Specialty: Education, Business
Degrees Conferred: BA, BS, MA, MS, MBA
Programs of Study: Accounting, Agriculture, Anthropology, Banking & Finance, Biochemistry, Biology, Business Administration, Chemistry, Clinical Science, Communications, Computer Science, Criminal Justice, Economics, Education, English, Environmental Science, Fine Arts, Geology, History, Information Science, Land Resource Management, Management, Marketing, Math, Medical Technology, Nursing, Petroleum Engineering, Philosophy, Physics, Political Science, PreProfessional, Public Health, Religion, Social Science, Spanish

Men's Athletic Profile

9001 Stockdale Hwy.
Bakersfield, CA 93311-1099
Coach: Simon Tobin
Email: stobin@scbak.edu

NCAA II
Road Runners/Blue, Gold
Phone: (661) 664-2428
Fax: (661) 664-2378

Estimated # of Men's Soccer Scholarships: Up to 5
Conference: California Collegiate Athletic Association
Program Profile: CSUB is the CCA's most successful program of the 1990's with 4 CCAA and 1 NCAA title. Home field is the CSUB main soccer field, which has a seating capacity of 1,500. We play on natural grass under lights. Team attendance in August was over 900 per game.
History: Our program began in 1970. For a program which was just 15 games in its first 8 years, CSUB soccer has grown by leaps and bounds in the last 10 years under Simon Tobin. During his tenure, CSUB has earned four NCAA Appearances and three CCAA Titles, while producing eight All-Americans in the past five seasons.
Achievements: Simon Tobin was named four-time CCAA Coach of the Year and has had 8 All-Americans in the last seven years. Joe Nunos was named 1997 Player of the Year and was drafted by and played for the Metro Stars.
Coaching: Simon Tobin, Head Coach, owns a 152-79-22 record in 12 season as a men's coach. He has led CSUB to 5 NCAA Playoff Appearances in the pro's and 1 NCAA Title in 1997.
Style of Play: Exciting, fast attacking style, which emphasizes highly-skilled attackers and big strong physical defensive play.

Women's Athletic Profile

9001 Stockdale Hwy.
Bakersfield, CA 93311-1099
Coach: John Smith
Email: smith@csub.edu

NCAA
Road Runners/Blue, Gold
Phone: (661) 664-2407
Fax: (661) 664-2378

Estimated # of Women's Soccer Scholarships: N/A
Conference: California Collegiate Athletic Association
Program Profile: The home field is at the CSUB Activities Center, which has a capacity of 1,500. We play on natural grass under lights. The women's soccer games average attendance is 500 people.

History: The women's program started in 1996 and has never had a losing season. The team owns one 1st, one 2nd and one 3rd place in CCAA finishes.
Achievements: CCAA Coach of the Year four times.
Style of Play: Exciting, fast attacking style which emphasizes highly-skilled attackers and big, strong, physical defensive play.

California State University - Chico

Academic Profile

Chico, CA 95929
Phone: (530) 898-6470

Type: 4 Yr.,Public,Liberal Arts,Engineering
Website: http://www.csuchio.edu
SAT/ACT/GPA: TBA
Student/Faculty Ratio: 18:1
Undergraduate Enrollment: 13,600
Scholarships/Academic: Yes
Athletic: Yes
Expenses by: Year
In State: $ 5,250
Founded: 1887
Religion: Non-Affiliated
Housing: Yes
Male/Female Ratio: 49:51
Graduate Enrollment: 1,200
Financial Aid: Yes
Out of State: $ 7,030
Specialty: Business, Education, Communications, Engineering
Degrees Conferred: BS, MA
Programs of Study: Business, Education, Communication, Science, PreMed, Engineering, Art, Language, History, Accounting, Anthropology, Botany, Liberal Arts

Men's Athletic Profile

Men's Soccer Box 300 CSUC Athletics
Chico, CA 95928-0300
Coach: Mike O'Malley
Email:

NCAA Div. II
Wildcats/Red/White
Phone: (530)898-6810
Fax: (530)898-4699

Estimated # of Men's Soccer Scholarships:
Conference: California Collegiate Athletic Association
Program Profile: Great facility includes 120x75 natural grass field, with seating capacity of 1500. School has a rich and successful college soccer history, outstanding soccer stadium.
History: Our men's program began in 1963 and boasts 15 conference championships, 12 NCAA appearances and three final four appearances. Top 20 NCAA/Division II for 10 years.
Achievements: 8 seniors in College Senior Bowl, 7 All-Americans and several past and current professional players, several alumni are successful college, high school, and professional coaches. Several conference representations.
Coaching: Mike O'Malley, Career: 83-47-8, CSUC: 45-31-3
Roster In State: 18
Out of State: 8
Out of Country: 2
ODP State: 4
Regional:
National: 1
Walk-on/Other:
Graduation %:
Seniors on Team: 3
Positions Needed: All
Most Recent Record: 11-8-1
Schedule: Seattle Pacific University, Grand Canyon University, Cal Poly Pomona, UC Davis, St. Edwards University, Cal State Dominguez Hills, Incarnate Word, Sonoma State
Style of Play: Possession. All over the field. Build up attack. Aggressive, disciplined defense.

Women's Athletic Profile

Dept. Of Athletics
Chico, CA 95929
Coach: Prof. Bob Russ
Email: bruss@csuchico.edu

NCAA II
Wildcats/Red, White
Phone: (530) 898-6085
Fax: (530) 898-4699

Estimated # of Women's Soccer Scholarships: 6
Conference: CCAA
Program Profile: Women's Soccer is at its highest right now. We will be playing at a new stadium Sept. 2000.
History: Varsity program began in 1983; have been in the top 20 for 8 of these years; Many All-Americans.
Achievements: We have Conference Title 1992-1993 and 21 All-Americans.
Coaching: Prof. Bob Russ, Head Coach, 29 years in soccer, 17 years with women's soccer, founded CSU women's soccer team in 1972 as club sport which became varsity sport in 1984, NSCAA Advanced National Diploma, Masters degree, full-time professor, extensive international experience.
Roster in State: 16
Out of State: 4
Out of Country:
ODP State: 8
Regional: 4
National:
Walk-on/Other:
Graduation %: 97
Seniors on Team: 3
Positions Needed: All
Camp or Clinic Dates: Not-Available
Most Recent Record: 8-11-1
Schedule: Cal Poly, Dominguez Hills, Ft. Lewis College, Sonoma State, UC Davis
Style of Play: Ball control and emphasis on speed.

California State University - Dominguez Hills

Academic Profile

Carson, CA 90747
Phone: 310-243-3600

Type: 4 Yr.,Public,Liberal Arts
Founded: 1960
Website: http://www.csudh.edu
Religion: Non-Affiliated
SAT/ACT/GPA: 1200
Housing: Yes
Student/Faculty Ratio: 30:1
Male/Female Ratio: 1:2
Undergraduate Enrollment: 11,000
Graduate Enrollment: 1,500
Scholarships/Academic: Yes
Athletic: Yes
Financial Aid: Yes
Expenses by: Year
In State: $ 1,900
Out of State: $ Varies
Degrees Conferred: BS, MA
Programs of Study: Anthropology, Biology, Business Administration, Chemistry, Clinical Science, Communication, Computer Science, Economics, English, Fine Arts, French, Geology, Health Science, History, Human Services, Mathematics, Nursing, Physical Education, Physics, Political Science, Psychology

Men's Athletic Profile

1000 E Victoria St.
Carson, CA 90747
Coach: Joe Flanagan
Email: jflanagan@csvdh.edu

NCAA II
Toros/Cardinal, Gold
Phone: (310) 243-2221
Fax: (310) 516-4488

Estimated # of Men's Soccer Scholarships: None
Conference: California Collegiate Athletic Association
Program Profile: We play at a cozy field that has a capacity of 1,500. We compete in a three division alignment.
History: Our program began in 1978. We have won four CCAA crowns including the last two. We are also won our first ever NCAA II National Championship this year.
Achievements: 7 All-Americans including 3 this year; 1 National player of the year; coach Flanagan is CCAA Coach of the Year Honors twice.
Coaching: Joe Flanagan, Head Coach, is entering his fourth year. He was 1995 Coach of the Year and a1991 graduate of CSUSD. Jeff Tuttle and Sean Taketa - Assistant Coaches.
Roster In State: 21
Out of State: 0
Out of Country:
Walk-on/Other:
Graduation %: 80%
Seniors on Team: 8
Positions Needed: 6

Camp or Clinic Dates: Not Available
Most Recent Record: 23-1-1
Schedule: Seattle Pacific, CS Bakersfield, Sonoma State, Westmout College, UC Davis
Style of Play: Aggressive, Attack minded soccer

Women's Athletic Profile

1000 E Victoria
Carson, CA 90747
Coach: Karen Hanks
Email: khanks@csudh.edu

NCAA II
Toros/Cardinal, Gold
Phone: (310) 243-2837
Fax: (310) 516-4488

Estimated # of Women's Soccer Scholarships: N/A
Conference: California Collegiate Athletic Association
Program Profile: Natural grass field, seating for 600, post season seating for 2,000. Largest crowd ever was 1,500 for 1991 NCAA Division Women's National Championship game.
History: Program began in 1984.
Achievements: Head Coach Karen Hanks is the 8th winningest Coach in the NCAA II. She was named CCAA Coach of the year in 1996. Won conference titles in 1991, 92, 96, 97, 98.
Coaching: Head Coach is Karen Hanks and she is assisted by Heather Roland and Brandy Kahke.
Roster in State: 20
Out of State: 0
Out of Country: 0
ODP State: 0
Regional: 0
National: 0
Walk-on/Other: 0
Graduation %: 90%
Seniors on Team: 8
Positions Needed: All
Camp or Clinic Dates: Not-Available
Most Recent Record: 11-5-3
Schedule: UC San Diego, Sonoma State, C.S. Bakersfield, Azusa Pacific, Western Washington, U.C. Davis, Cal Polu Pomona
Style of Play: Possession and contain style of play. Emphasize tough defensive play.

California State University - Fresno

Academic Profile

Phone: (559) 278-8302

Fresno, CA 93740-7400

Type: 4 Yr.,Public
Founded: 1911
Website: http://www.csufresno.edu
Religion: Non-Affiliated
SAT/ACT/GPA: 900/3.0
Housing: Yes
Student/Faculty Ratio: 14:1
Male/Female Ratio: 2:3
Undergraduate Enrollment: 17,400
Graduate Enrollment: 3,345
Scholarships/Academic: Yes
Athletic: Yes
Financial Aid: Yes
Expenses by: Year
In State: $ 3,700
Out of State: $ 7,387
Specialty: Business, Agriculture
Degrees Conferred: BS, BA, 56 undergraduate programs, 41 graduate programs
Programs of Study: Architecture, PreMed, PreDental, Aerospace, Agricultural Business, Animal Science, Anthropology, Business, Kinesiology, Biology, Chemistry, Chicago Studies, Communications, Computer Science, Criminology, Dance, Ecology, Education, Engineering, Enology, Linguistics, Marine Science, Music, Philosophy, Physical Therapy, Sociology, Spanish, Speech Communications

Men's Athletic Profile

1620 E. Bulldog Lane
Fresno, CA 93740-7400
Coach: Dave Chesler
Email: davidch@csufresno.edu

NCAA I
Bulldogs/Red, Navy
Phone: (599) 278-4226
Fax: (599) 278-6363

Estimated # of Men's Soccer Scholarships: 1.5
Conference: MPSF
Program Profile: #1 attendance in the nation in 1998 and 1999. Home matches played in 41,000 seats Bulldog Stadium which is natural Bermuda grass surface. Has a three years old state-of-art strength and conditioning facility, new locker rooms and Bermuda 3-field training facility.
History: Program began in 1970 under head coach Bob Bereskin, ten years under his direction, placed first once in 1977, three top three finishes. From 1980-1990 under Jose Elgorriaga, had five first place finishes, placed in tip three all 11 years. From 91-96 under John Bluem, had three first place finishes, five top three finishes. Recently under Dave Chesler from 97-00 placed in top three all four years. We have had 12 conference titles.
Achievements: 12 Conference Champion titles; 15 NCAA appearances; 8 All-Americans; 3 GTE All-Americans; 3 ISAA/ adidas Academic All-Americans; 33 All-Far West Selections; 1 No. 1 MSL Draft pick; 22 All-MPSF Selections and many many others.
Coaching: Dave Chesler, Head Coach, US Soccer Federation National Staff, Region IV Head ODP Staff Coach, National "A" License. Paul Meehan, Assistant Coach, holds National "A License.
Roster In State: 21 **Out of State:** 1 **Out of Country:**
Walk-on/Other: **Graduation %:** N/A **Seniors on Team:** 5
Most Recent Record: 9-7-2
Schedule: Univ of Massachusettes, Hartford, Univ of San Fransico, Air Force, Denver, San Jose State
Style of Play: 4-4-2, attacking, pushing ball forward every possession, team-oriented, relying on every member to be a leader.

Women's Athletic Profile

1620 E. Bulldog Lane, MS27
Fresno, CA 93740
Coach: Peter Reynaud
Email: peterr@csufresno.edu

NCAA I
Bulldogs/Red, Blue, White
Phone: (559) 278-8302
Fax: (559) 278-6363

Estimated # of Women's Soccer Scholarships: 1.5
Conference: Western Athletic Conference
Program Profile: The women's soccer facilities included a locker room specifically for the soccer team. A 45,000- seat stadium with natural playing surface, one of the largest weight rooms in the country and practice fields for use by women's soccer only.
History: The program started in 1995 and has had the same head coach for all 5 years. The first team finished with a 9-11-1 record and the most recent team finished with a record of 13-4-2 marking a tremendous improvement and the program's second winning season. The program also made it into the NCAA college play-offs in the 1999 season.
Achievements: 1999-2000 Peter Reynaud WAC Coach of the Year; 1999-2000 FSU WAC Regular season champions; 3 1st team All-Conference Honors; 1999-2000 1st appearance in NCAA college play-offs.
Coaching: Peter Reynaud, Head Coach, graduate from Cal State-Hayward in 1975. He holds USSF "A" License Coach. He is U-18 California North ODP head coach. Won National Championship - NCAA Division II at Sonoma State in 1990. Stacy Welp, Assistant Coach, graduate of University of Tulsa in 1994. he holds USSF "A" License; staff coach for Region IV Olympic Development Program.
Roster in State: 24 **Out of State:** 1 **Out of Country:**
ODP State: 4 **Regional:** **National:**
Walk-on/Other: **Graduation %:** **Seniors on Team:** 2
Positions Needed: Forwards, Central Midfielders, Goalkeeper
Camp or Clinic Dates: June 26-29, July 10-13, August 1-4
Most Recent Record: 13-4-2
Schedule: UCLA, SMU, Colorado, Georgia, Auburn, California-Berkley, Tulsa, University of Pacific
Style of Play: It is a ball control - team oriented style emphasizing passing, combination plays and tenacious defense.

California State University - Fullerton

Academic Profile

Fullerton, CA 92834

Phone: (714) 278-3495

Type: 4 Yr.,Public,
Website: http://www.fullerton.edu
SAT/ACT/GPA: Sliding Scale
Student/Faculty Ratio: 19:1
Undergraduate Enrollment: 24,175
Scholarships/Academic: Yes **Athletic:** Yes
Expenses by: Year **In State:** $ 8,331

Founded: 1957
Religion: Non-Affiliated
Housing: Yes
Male/Female Ratio: 42:58
Graduate Enrollment: 4,000
Financial Aid: Yes
Out of State: $ 12,729

Specialty: Athletic Training, Communications, Business
Degrees Conferred: BA, BS, BFA, BM, MA, MS, MFA
Programs of Study: Seven Schools - Arts, Business Education/Economics, Communications, Engineering/Computer Sciences, Human Development/ Community Services, Humanities/Social Sciences, Natural Sciences and Mathematics

Men's Athletic Profile

800 N State College Blvd.
Fullerton, CA 92634
Coach: Al Mistri
Email: Not Available

NCAA I
Titans/Navy, Orange, White
Phone: (714) 278-3489
Fax: (714) 278-3425

Estimated # of Men's Soccer Scholarships: None
Conference: Mountain Pacific Soccer Federation Conference
Program Profile: National Top 20 program in the last several years with NCAA appearances in 1993 (semi-finals), 1994 (quarter-finals) and 1996 (second round). Home stadium has a 10,000 seating capacity with full-size soccer pitch with no running track nor intercollegiate football team. Drainage is the state of the art which means a very flat pitch. Outdoor play is year-round.
History: Program became Division I in 1975. All-time record at Division I is 238-165-41 including five trips to the NCAA playoffs where the record is 7-4-1. Currently have seven former players in the professional soccer in the United States.
Achievements: Advanced to the "Final Four" in 1993, losing to South Carolina, 1-0, minus leading score who was out with too many yellow cards. Have produced several All-Americans, most recently Sheldon Thomas in 1996 (2nd team) and Eddie Soto in 1994, and Olympian Mike Fox.
Coaching: Al Mistri, Head Coach, logged his 17th season in 1996 and has a record of 176-124-28. Native of Italy who received his "A" coaching license in 1976. As a high school coach helped develop Rick into one of the top US player in the world, and has seven recent Titans in the professional league in the US.
Style of Play: Ball control.

Women's Athletic Profile

P. O. Box 6810
Fullerton, CA 92834
Coach: Al Mistri
Email: akhosroshin@fullerton.edu

NCAA I
Titans/Navy, Orange, White
Phone: (714) 278-2267
Fax: (714) 278-3425

Estimated # of Women's Soccer Scholarships: None
Conference: Big West Conference
Program Profile: Our program has made huge strides in five years of existence. We play in a 10,000-seat soccer stadium with a full-sized pitch with no running track nor intercollegiate football team. We play outdoors and we play year-around.
History: The program began in 1993 and this will be the third year that we are recognized as a Big West Conference sport. In 1996, we were undefeated in regular season.

Achievements: 2 All-Americans in 1996: Dolores Browning and Michelle Rice (3rd team); 1997 Big West All-Conference;
Coaching: Al Mistr, Head Coach, has a 35-34-7 record in five years as the Titan's Women's Soccer Coach and a 176-124-28 mark in 16 season as a coach of men's team. As a high school coach, he helped develop Rick Davis into one of the top US players in the world and he currently has seven former male players in the US professional league.
Style of Play: Ball control.

California State University - Hayward

Academic Profile

Hayward, CA 94542
Phone: (510) 885-4805

Type: 4 Yr.,Public,Liberal Arts
Website: http://www.csuhayward.edu
SAT/ACT/GPA: 1300/30/2.0
Student/Faculty Ratio: 25:1
Undergraduate Enrollment: 10,000
Scholarships/Academic: Yes
Athletic: No
Expenses by: Year
In State: $ 5,500
Founded: 1957
Religion: Non-Affiliated
Housing: Yes
Male/Female Ratio: 40:60
Graduate Enrollment: 2,000
Financial Aid: Yes
Out of State: $ 8,750
Specialty: Liberal Arts, Business, Kinesiology, Physical Therapy
Degrees Conferred: BA, BS, MA, MS, MBA
Programs of Study: Biology, Business, Chemistry, Communications, Computer, Criminal, Dramatic Art, Ecology, Economics, English, Environmental, Ethnic, Management, Math, Nursing, Philosophy, Physical, Recreation, Statistics, Taxation

Men's Athletic Profile

25800 Carlos Bee Blvd.
Hayward, CA 94542
Coach: Jair Fy
Email: athletics@csuhayward.edu
NCAA II
Pioneers/Red, Black, White
Phone: (510) 885-4190
Fax: (510) 885-2282

Estimated # of Men's Soccer Scholarships: None
Conference: California Pacific Conference
Program Profile: Pioneer field has a natural grass and can hold up to 500 fans.
History: Program began in 1968. California State Hayward has captured eight Conference Championships and appeared in the NCAA Division II Final Four Championships in 1989.
Achievements: We have 2 Coach of the Year honors in the past three years and several players have received All-West Region while four athletes earned All-American recognition.
Coaching: Jair Fory, Head Coach, is entering his eight year with the program. Pablo Amador is the Assistant Coach, is entering his second season with the program.
Style of Play: Fast pace from goal-to-goal. Weak down opponents with fast pace match.

Women's Athletic Profile

25800 Carlos Bee Blvd.
Hayward, CA 94542
Coach: Lisa Best
Email: 1best@cjuhayward.edu
NCAA II
Pioneers/Red, Black, White
Phone: (510) 885-4190
Fax: (510) 885-2282
Estimated # of Women's Soccer Scholarships: None
Conference: Independent
Program Profile: The field is a natural grass and is located next to the softball field. The capacity of Pioneer Field is 400.
History: Placed 1st in Conference in 2000, 2nd in Conference 1999, and National Champions Div. III 1989

Achievements: 2000 Conference 1st Place, Lisa Best Coach of the Year for the California Pacific Conference 1999-2000.
Coaching: Lisa Best Head Coach and Rebecca Jumenez, Don Williams Assistant Coaches.
Roster in State: 22 **Out of State:** 0 **Out of Country:** 0
Walk-on/Other: **Graduation %:** **Seniors on Team:** 7
Positions Needed: Backs and Forwards
Most Recent Record: 9-8-0
Schedule: Hawaii Pacific, San Francisco State, Dominican College, California Lutheran Univ. Claremont Mudd Scripps
Style of Play: Possession, patient, emphasis on technical execution.

California State University - Los Angeles

Academic Profile

Phone: (323)343-3080

Los Angeles, CA 90032-8240

Type: 4 Yr.,Public
Founded: 1947
Website: http://www.calstatela.edu
Religion: Non-Affiliated
SAT/ACT/GPA: Varies2.0
Housing: Yes
Student/Faculty Ratio:
Male/Female Ratio: 39/61
Undergraduate Enrollment: 13,732
Graduate Enrollment: 5,797
Scholarships/Academic: Yes **Athletic:** Yes **Financial Aid:** Yes
Expenses by: Year **In State:** **Out of State:**
Specialty: Engineering, dance, elementary and secondary education
Degrees Conferred: BS, BA, MS, MA, Ph.D.
Programs of Study: 50 Academic departments and divisions. Liberal Arts, Physical Sciences, Social Sciences, Business, Education, Physical Education

Men's Athletic Profile

5151 State University Dr.
Los Angeles, CA 90032
Coach: Santo Rivas
Email: srivas2@calstatela.edu

NCAA II
Diablos/Black, Gold
Phone: (213) 343-3089
Fax: (213) 343-3199

Estimated # of Men's Soccer Scholarships: None
Conference: California Collegiate Athletic Association
Program Profile: Men's program has gone to the NCAA Tournament twice since 1992. Jess Owens Stadium features a natural grass surface and has a seating capacity of 5,000.
History: Men's program began in 1978.
Achievements: Won the CCAA Title in 1993 and had five All-Americans since 1981.
Coaching: Leonardo Cuellar is the Head Coach of both men's and women's soccer program. He is 96-67-16 at CSLA. Was a member of the 1972 Mexican Olympic Team. Was a Mexican National team member from 1973-1981. Named the 1977 MVP in the World Cup Tournament, also an All-Star Choice. Team captain of the 1980 San Diego (NASL) professional guard.
Style of Play: Fast, aggressive and strong defensively.

Women's Athletic Profile

5151 State University Dr.
Los Angeles, CA 90032
Coach: Leonardo Cuellar
Email: srivas2@calstatela.edu

NCAA II
Golden Eagles/Black, Gold
Phone: (323) 343-3089
Fax: (213) 343-3199

Estimated # of Women's Soccer Scholarships: None
Conference: California Collegiate Athletic Association
Program Profile: 1995 was the women's soccer program's first year. Owens's Stadium features a natural grass surface and has a seating capacity for 5,000 fans.
History: The women's program will mark its fourth season in 1998.
Achievements: None
Coaching: Leonardo Cuellar, Head Coach for both men's and women's soccer program. Was a member of a 1972 Mexican Olympic Team. Was a Mexican National Team from 1973 to 1981. Named the 1977 MVP in the World Cup Tournament, also an All-Star choice. Team captain of the 1980 San Diego (NASL) professional squad.

California State University - Northridge

Academic Profile

Northridge, CA 91330-8276
Phone: (818) 677-4512

Type: 4 Yr.,Public,Liberal Arts,Engineering
Website: http://www.csub.edu
SAT/ACT/GPA: Combo of GPA and SAT scores2.00 to 3.00
Student/Faculty Ratio: 21:1
Undergraduate Enrollment: 22,189
Scholarships/Academic: Yes
Athletic: Yes
Expenses by: Year
In State: $ 8,530
Founded: 1958
Religion: Non-Affiliated
Housing: Yes
Male/Female Ratio: 40:60
Graduate Enrollment: 5,464
Financial Aid: Yes
Out of State: $ 14,265
Specialty: Substantial programs in technological and professional fields
Degrees Conferred: BA, BS, BM, MA, MS, MBA
Programs of Study: Accounting, Anthropology, Astrophysics, Banking/Finance, Biochemistry, Biology, Broadcasting, Business, Chemistry, Computer, Criminology, Dietetics, Earth Science, Economics, Engineering, Mathematics, Music, Nursing, Physics, Radio and Television, Religion, Seismology, Etc.

Men's Athletic Profile

18111 Nordhoff Street
Northridge, CA 91330-8276
Coach: Terry Davila
Email: terry.davila@csun.edu
NCAA I
Matadors/Red, White, Black
Phone: (818) 677-2379
Fax: (818) 677-4762

Estimated # of Men's Soccer Scholarships: 6
Conference: Big West
Program Profile: We have plans for the construction for a new Soccer Stadium in 2002.
History: Program began in 1978. Made playoffs 7 straight years in Division II. 1994-1995 was the first losing season in the program's history.
Achievements: 6 All-Americans, Michael Pries-1999 US National Team U-23, Federico Arroyo- Independent Player of the Year, Academic All-American.
Coaching: Terry Davila-CSUN 1988-1991, Keith West-former professional-MPSF Player of the Year; 1995 - CSUN - 1992-1995, GK Coach - Tony Scalercio - former professional soccer player, Juan Flores - former professional soccer player - (CSUN - 1987).
Roster In State: 23
Out of State: 1
Out of Country: 0
ODP State: 5
Regional: 5
National: 1
Walk-on/Other: 5
Graduation %: 50
Seniors on Team: 2
Positions Needed: GK, Defenders, Forwards
Camp or Clinic Dates: Not Available
Most Recent Record: 6-12-0
Schedule: Tulsa, CS Fullerton, SW Missouri, San Jose State, Evansville, Oregon State
Style of Play: Our style allows the player to show their creative style of soccer. We try to penetrate the other team with control and a definite plan.

Women's Athletic Profile

18111 Nordhoff Street
Northridge, CA 91330-8276
Coach: Allison Lee
Email: aalis2811@csun.edu

NCAA I
Matadors/Red, White, Black
Phone: (818) 677-3208
Fax: (818) 677-4762

Estimated # of Women's Soccer Scholarships: None
Conference: Big West
Program Profile: NCAA Division I program. The home field is natural grass and seats 6,000.
History: Program began in 1995.
Roster in State: 23 **Out of State:** 1 **Out of Country:** 0
ODP State: 10 **Regional:** 2 **National:**
Walk-on/Other: **Graduation %:** **Seniors on Team:** 5
Positions Needed: Center-mid, Forward
Camp or Clinic Dates: June 19- August 25
Most Recent Record: 10-8-1
Schedule: Loyola Marymount, San Diego, Pepperdine, Air Force, Denver, Montana

California State University - Sacramento

Academic Profile

Sacramento, CA 95819-6099

Phone: (916) 278-6427

Type: 4 Yr.,Public,Liberal Arts
Website: http://www.csus.edu
SAT/ACT/GPA: Sliding Scale/2.5
Student/Faculty Ratio:
Undergraduate Enrollment: 22,000
Scholarships/Academic: Yes **Athletic:** Yes
Expenses by: Year **In State:** $ 7,500
Specialty: Many fields of study
Degrees Conferred: BA, BS, MBA, MS

Founded: 1947
Religion: Non-Affiliated
Housing: Yes
Male/Female Ratio:
Graduate Enrollment: N/A
Financial Aid: Yes
Out of State: $ 7,500

Programs of Study: Accounting, Anthropology, Art, Biochemistry, Biology, Business, Chemistry, Communication, Computer Science, Criminal Justice, Education, Finance, Engineering, Geography, Journalism, Nursing, Physics, Political Science, PreLaw, Philosophy, Microbiology, Public Administration

Men's Athletic Profile

6000 J Street
Sacramento, CA 95819-6099
Coach: Mike Linenberger
Email: Not Available

NCAA I
Hornets/Green, White, Navy
Phone: (916) 278-6769
Fax: (916) 278-5429

Estimated # of Men's Soccer Scholarships: 7
Conference: Mountain Pacific Sports Federation
Program Profile: Our home games are played on a natural grass field, which measures 115x75 yards with a seating capacity of 1,000. The team plays a year-round program.
History: Our program began in 1971. We went from Division II to Division I in 1991 and have been in the MPSF since 1992. Scholarship awarded in 1993.
Achievements: The team has had various All-Conference, All-Region, and All-Americans. Many All-Conference players, few All-Region players.
Roster In State: 20 **Out of State:** **Out of Country:** 2

ODP State: 8 **Regional:** 2 **National:** 1
Walk-on/Other: 2 **Graduation %:** 80 **Seniors on Team:** 4
Positions Needed: various
Camp or Clinic Dates: August
Most Recent Record: 4-14-0
Schedule: Santa Clara, Cal, Fresno, Air Force, Stanford, USF, MSD, San Jose State

California State University - San Bernardino

Academic Profile

San Bernardino, CA 92407
Phone: 909-880-3600

Type: 4 Yr.,Public
Founded: 1965
Website: http://www.csusb.edu
Religion: Non-Affiliated
SAT/ACT/GPA: 820+ varies w/GPA
Housing: Yes
Student/Faculty Ratio: 18:1
Male/Female Ratio: 40:60
Undergraduate Enrollment: 10,000
Graduate Enrollment: 3,059
Scholarships/Academic: Yes **Athletic:** Yes **Financial Aid:** Yes
Expenses by: Year **In State:** $ 7,943 **Out of State:** $ 13,847
Specialty: Education, Physical Education, Kinesiology, Business
Degrees Conferred: Bachelors, Master's
Programs of Study: Accounting, Afro-American Studies, American Studies, Anthropology, Art, Biochemistry, Biological Science, Business Administration, Chemistry, Child Psychology, Communications, Computer Science, Creative Writing, Criminal Justice, Dietetics, Economics, English, Environmental Studies, Finance, French, Geography, Geology, Graphic Art, Health Services Administration, Health Education, Health Science, History, Humanities, Human Development, Human Services, Information Science, Interdisciplinary Studies, Liberal Arts, Management, Management Information Systems, Marketing, Mathematics, Music, Natural Science, Nursing, Nutrition, Philosophy, Physical Education, Physics, Political Science, Psychology, Public Administration, Social Science, Spanish, Theatre, Vocational Education

Men's Athletic Profile

5500 University Parkway
San Bernardino, CA 92407
Coach: Christian Johnson
Email: Johnsonc@mail.csusb.edu

NCAA II
Coyotes/Sky Blue, Black
Phone: (909) 880-5017
Fax: (909) 880-5984

Estimated # of Men's Soccer Scholarships: Varies
Conference: California Collegiate Athletic Association
Program Profile: We moved from NCAA Division III to Division II in 1990; play on campus field grass stadium with a seating capacity of 1,000.
History: First of the program was in 1984; overall record is 141-103-21; NCAA Tournament Appearance in 1991.
Achievements: CCAA Champions first year of competition 1991; 3 times NCAA playoff entrant; Division II All - American 1993; Qualified for playoffs 1990; Division III Semi - Finalists 1987; 11 All - Far West players. NCAA Tournament in 1991, 6 All-Americans, and 4 professional players wherein one is MSL draft.
Coaching: Head Coach Johnson. Assistant Coach Noah kochman and GK Coach Brian Diamond
Roster In State: 14 **Out of State:** 6 **Out of Country:** 4
ODP State: 0 **Regional:** 0 **National:** 0
Walk-on/Other: 0 **Graduation %:** N/A **Seniors on Team:** 6
Most Recent Record: 1-18-1
Schedule: San Jose State, Fresno, Sonoma State, U.C. San Diego
Style of Play: Possession/ Attacking build out of the back.

Women's Athletic Profile

5500 University Pkwy
San Bernardino, CA 92407
Coach: Christian Johnson
Email: johnsonc@mail.csusb.edu

NCAA II
Coyotes/Sky Blue, Black
Phone: (909) 880-5017
Fax: (909) 880-5984

Estimated # of Women's Soccer Scholarships: N/A
Conference: California College Athletic Association
Program Profile: Moved from NCAA Division II in 1990; play on campus field; grass stadium seats 1,000.
History: The first year of the program was in 1988; moved from NCAA Division III to Division II in 1990.
Achievements: The team produced 3 All-American selections.
Coaching: Head Coach- Christian Johnson. Assistant Mary Jo Soufl
Roster in State: 22 **Out of State:** 0 **Out of Country:** 0
Walk-on/Other: **Graduation %:** **Seniors on Team:** 7
Camp or Clinic Dates: 1st week in August.
Most Recent Record: 12-8-0
Schedule: U.C. San Diego, Azusa Pacific Univ. Cal Poly Pomona, Sonoma State, C.S.U. Bakersfield
Style of Play: Possession, attacking build out of the back.

California State University - Stanislaus

Academic Profile

Phone: 209-667-3151

Turlock, CA 95382-0299

Type: 4 Yr.,Public,Liberal Arts
Website: http://www.lead.csustan.edu
SAT/ACT/GPA: 820
Student/Faculty Ratio: 18:1
Undergraduate Enrollment: 4,500
Scholarships/Academic: Yes **Athletic:** No
Expenses by: Year **In State:** $ 7,000

Founded: 1961
Religion: Non-Affiliated
Housing: No
Male/Female Ratio: 40:60
Graduate Enrollment: 1,500
Financial Aid: Yes
Out of State: $ 14,000

Degrees Conferred: BA, BS, MA, MS, MBA
Programs of Study: Accounting, Anthropology, Applied Mathematics, Art, Bilingual Education, Biology, Botany, Business, Chemistry, Communications, Computer Information Systems, Entomology, Criminal Justice, Environmental Studies, History, International Studies, Journalism, Liberal Arts, Physics, PreLaw, PreMed, PreVet, Spanish, Statistics, Theatre, Urban Studies

Men's Athletic Profile

801 W Monte Vista Avenue
Turlock, CA 95382-0299
Coach: Dave Siracusa
Email: DSiracusa@stan.csustan.edu

NCAA II
Warriors/Red, Gold
Phone: (209) 667-3802
Fax: (209) 667-3084

Estimated # of Men's Soccer Scholarships: None
Conference: NCAC

Women's Athletic Profile

801 W. Monte Vista Ave.
Turlock, CA 95382
Coach: Dave Siracusa
Email: Not Available

NCAA II

Phone: (209) 668-6768
Fax: (209) 668-6768

Did Not Return Profile

Cañada College
Academic Profile

Redwood City, CA 94061
Phone: (650) 306-3226

Type: 4 Yr.,Public
Website: http://www.smccd.net/accounts/canada
SAT/ACT/GPA: None
Student/Faculty Ratio: 15:1
Undergraduate Enrollment: 5,000
Scholarships/Academic: **Athletic:** No
Expenses by: Year **In State:** **Out of State:**
Degrees Conferred: AA
Programs of Study: Almost all areas of study available.

Founded: 1971
Religion: Non-Affiliated
Housing: Yes
Male/Female Ratio: 50:50
Graduate Enrollment: N/A
Financial Aid: Yes

Men's Athletic Profile

4200 Farm Hill Blvd.
Redwood City, CA 94061
Coach: Frank Mangiola
Email: Not Available

NJCAA
Colts/Green, Gold, White
Phone: (415) 306-3317
Fax: (415) 306- 3390

Estimated # of Men's Soccer Scholarships: None
Conference: Coast Conference
Program Profile: Our school is located between City of Woodside and Redwood City, thirty miles from San Francisco. The men's program is one of the best in the state soccer field and is 116x75 grass field in excellent shape. Training rooms, locker room is above the field.
History: There have been four head coaches all with winning tradition with two State Championships. Cañada had one of the top programs in California winning many Coast Conference Titles.
Achievements: It has had many All-Americans, All-Northern California, and All-Cost Conference Player of the Year, too many to list.
Coaching: Frank Mangiola, Head Coach, full-time head coach, holds "A" License, USSF Staff Coach, CYSAN Staff Coach and Region IV ODP Coach, record in 1996 was 20-21-1. Former professional coach with San Francisco Blackhawks in 1990-1992.
Style of Play: Our main goal is to develop players and prepares players to play at the next level. We strive to maintain possession of the ball, while attacking creatively, the system allows us to attack or defend as a total unit.

Women's Athletic Profile

4200 Farm Hill Boulevard
Redwood City, CA 94061
Coach: Frank Mangiola
Email: Not Available

NJCAA
Colts/Forest Green, Gold
Phone: (415) 306-3317
Fax: (415) 306-3390

Estimated # of Women's Soccer Scholarships: None
Conference: Coast Conference
Program Profile: Located in the heart of the Bay Area Peninsula which is five minutes from Stanford University. The soccer field is 118x75 yards. Has an excellent facilities.
History: The program began in 1963 and has won two State Championships in 1969 & 1971, and is always one of the top teams in the Coast Conference. Usually 1-2 in league and 1-2 in state.
Achievements: Coast Conference Champions in 1990 & 1996; Coach of the Year Honors in 1990, 1993, & 1996; (NSCAA All-Americans: Jim Ratters in 1990, Tony Alejandre in 1993, Chris Yantos in 1996 & Robert Collazzo in 1996).
Coaching: Frank Mangiola, Head Coach, full-time, USSF Staff Coach. CYSAN staff coach and Region IV ODP Staff Coach. Record in 1996 was 20-1-1, former professional coach with San Francisco Blackhawks in 1990-1992.

Style of Play: Dependent on personnel and situations. 4-4-2, 3-5-3 and 3-4-3, but overall like to play possession with a build up out of the back and a combination play. Short and long passes to switch point of attack. Tough defense, combination or man-to-man or zone.

Chapman University

Academic Profile

Orange, CA 92866
Phone: (714) 997-6815

Type: 4 Yr.,Private,Liberal Arts
Website: http://www.chapman.edu
SAT/ACT/GPA: 960/19/2.5
Student/Faculty Ratio: 15:1
Undergraduate Enrollment: 2,800
Scholarships/Academic: Yes
Athletic: No
Expenses by: Year
In State: $27,500
Founded: 1861
Religion: Disciples of Christ
Housing: Yes
Male/Female Ratio: N/A
Graduate Enrollment: 1,200
Financial Aid: Yes
Out of State: $27,500
Specialty: Business, Economics
Degrees Conferred: BA, BS, BFA, BM, MA, MS, MBA, MFA
Programs of Study: Accounting, American Studies, Art, Biology, Business and Economics, Communication, Criminal Justice, Education, Kinesiology, Languages, Liberal Studies, Music, Movement and Exercise Sciences, Nutrition, Philosophy, Psychology, Religion, Social Science, Sociology, Theatre & Dance

Men's Athletic Profile

One University Dr
Orange, CA 92866
Coach: Eddie Carrillo
Email: carrillo@chapman.edu

NCAA III
Panthers/Cardinal, Gray
Phone: (714) 997-6502
Fax: (714) 532-6010

Estimated # of Men's Soccer Scholarships: None
Conference: Independent
Program Profile: Our season is in the fall, our facilities are great, our field is natural grass with lights; our stadium seats about 1,000 people. Our program is successful and one of the most consistent in the west coast.
History: Our program began in 1984; we are consistently ranked in the top 5 in the west region and in 1997-1999 we were ranked in the top 25 in the Nation.
Achievements: We reached the NCAA tournament in 1999 for the first time in school history. We have had 9 All-Region selections in the past 4 years and 1 Academic All-American.
Coaching: Eddie Carrillo, Head Coach; Sal Lopez is the assistant coach and Pete Van DeVan is the Goalkeeper Coach.
Roster In State: 20
Out of State: 4
Out of Country:
ODP State: 2
Regional:
National:
Walk-on/Other:
Graduation %: 100
Seniors on Team: 1
Positions Needed: Forward, Goalkeeper
Camp or Clinic Dates: Not Available
Most Recent Record: 13-5-0
Schedule: Cal St. Fullerton, Azusa Pacific, Cal St. Los Angeles, Willamette, Cal Lutheran, Biola University
Style of Play: We like to play a medium paced soccer style. A combination of short to medium range passing. Everyone attacks and everyone defends. We are very active and intense defensively.

Women's Athletic Profile

One University Dr
Orange, CA 92866
Coach: Craig Bennett
Email: cbennett@chapman.edu

NCAA III
Panthers/Cardinal, Gray
Phone: (714) 628-7279
Fax: (714) 532-6010

Estimated # of Women's Soccer Scholarships: None
Conference: Independent
Program Profile: We have an excellent facility. Our field is natural grass, 75x115, with lights and seating for about 1,000 fans. 20-24 student athletes on roster, fall playing season with training camp beginning before Labor Day and the regular season ending the last week of October. Home games played in Ernie Champion Stadium on Campus.
History: Program began in 1984 as an NCAA Div. II program in the CCAA. The athletic department went to NCAA III in 1993. Since gone D.III the women's overall record is 100-47-7 and has reached the NCAA tournament the last 2 years. 1999 first round and 2000 third round.
Achievements: The panthers reached the NCAA tournament in 1999 for the first time in school history. We have 9 All-Region selections in the past four years and 1 Academic All-American.
Coaching: Head Coach Craig Bennett played at Chapman from 92-95. Jason Sorrell assistant. Coach.

Roster in State: 19	**Out of State:** 4	**Out of Country:** 0
ODP State: 2	**Regional:** 0	**National:** 0
Walk-on/Other: 0	**Graduation %:** 100	**Seniors on Team:** 8

Positions Needed: Forwards and defenders
Camp or Clinic Dates: June and July
Most Recent Record: 17-5-1
Schedule: Savannah College, Cal-Lutheran Univ. University of California-Santa Cruz, Univ. of Redlands, Biola Univ.
Style of Play: Solid team defense that starts by pressuring the backs, backs get into the attack, possession oriented out of the back and midfield.

Christian Heritage College

Academic Profile

El Cajon, CA 92019
Phone: 619-588-7747

Type: 4 Yr.,Private,Liberal Arts		**Founded:** 1970
Website: http://www.christianHeritage.edu		**Religion:** Baptist
SAT/ACT/GPA: 900/20/2.5		**Housing:** Yes
Student/Faculty Ratio: 15:1		**Male/Female Ratio:** 45:55
Undergraduate Enrollment: 630		**Graduate Enrollment:** N/A
Scholarships/Academic: Yes	**Athletic:** Yes	**Financial Aid:** Yes
Expenses by: Year	**In State:** $ 15,200	**Out of State:** $ 15,200

Specialty: Biblical Studies, Counseling, Teaching Education
Degrees Conferred: BA, BS
Programs of Study: Biblical Studies, Business, Clinical Psychology, Communications, Computer Information Systems, Economics, Education, Elementary Education, English, History, International Business, Management, Mathematics, Ministries, Music, Pastoral Studies, Physical Education, Psychology, Secondary Education, Social Science, Theology, Voice, Women's Studies

Men's Athletic Profile

2100 Greenfield Drive
El Cajon, CA 92019
Coach: Dave Merrifield
Email: Not Available

NAIA
Hawks/Blue, Gold
Phone: (619) 441-2200
Fax: (619) 440-0209

Estimated # of Men's Soccer Scholarships: None
Conference: NAIA, Far West Region
Program Profile: The Hawks play a regular Fall season, home field is on campus. Team plays indoor and Spring leagues.
History: Our program began in 1990.
Achievements: 4 NAIA All - Region players.

Coaching: Dave Merrifield, Head Coach, State Instructor for California, has coached 4 years at college level and 10 years at High School level; holds a USSF 'B' license.

Claremont - Mudd - Scripps College

Academic Profile

Claremont, CA 91711
Phone: (909) 607-3565

Type: 4 Yr.,Private,Liberal Arts,Engineering
Website: http://www.mckenna.edu - www.scrippscol.edu
SAT/ACT/GPA: 1300/4.0
Student/Faculty Ratio: 20:1
Undergraduate Enrollment: 900
Scholarships/Academic: Yes
Athletic: No
Expenses by: Year
In State: $ 28,000
Founded: 1946
Religion: Non-Affiliated
Housing: Yes
Male/Female Ratio: 60:40
Graduate Enrollment: N/A
Financial Aid: Yes
Out of State: $ 28,000
Specialty: Business, Engineering, History, Mathematics, Sciences
Degrees Conferred: BA, BS
Programs of Study: Business, Economics, English, Letters/Literature, Mathematics, Multi/Interdisciplinary Studies, Psychology, Sciences, Social Sciences

Men's Athletic Profile

500 E. 9th Street
Claremont, CA 91711
Coach: Louis Bilowitz
Email: louisbilowitz@mckenna.edu

NCAA III
Cardinal, Gold
Phone: 909-607-7471
Fax: 909-621-8848

Estimated # of Men's Soccer Scholarships: 0
Conference: SCIAC
Program Profile: 120x75 natural grass field. Stadium size of game field and a large practice field.
History: Program began in 1969
Coaching: Louis Bilowitz Head Coach finished his 3rd year with a record of 51-13-2. Two SCIAC Championships, Two Consecutive NCAA Western Regional finalists. Assistant Coach David Quesada former U.S. National player. GK Coach Kyle Bilowitz.
Roster In State: 12
Out of State: 12
Out of Country:
ODP State: 11
Regional: 2
National: 0
Walk-on/Other:
Graduation %: 100
Seniors on Team: 3
Positions Needed: Forward, MF, LMF, Marking Backs
Most Recent Record: 18-3-1
Schedule: Redlands, Cal-Lutheran, Pomona, Cal State-Los Angeles, Cal-State San Bernadino, Linfield, Puget Sound
Style of Play: Offense- Skilled, few touches, off the ball runs. Defense- Aggressive man marking with defenders also attacking.

Women's Athletic Profile

500 E 9th Street
Claremont, CA 91711
Coach: John Hall
Email: Not Available

NCAA III
Athena's/Black, White
Phone: (909) 621-8000
Fax: (909) 621-8336

Estimated # of Women's Soccer Scholarships: None
Conference: Southern California Intercollegiate Athletic Conference
Program Profile: 70X115 yard field is natural grass and one of the best in Southern California which is used only for soccer.

History: Program began in 1986.
Achievements: SCIAC Champions - 1987, 1988. Four times NSCAA 2nd team All - West Region.

College of Notre Dame

Academic Profile

Belmont, CA 94002-1997
Phone: (650) 508-3590

Type: 4 Yr.,Private,Liberal Arts
Website: http://www.cnd.edu
SAT/ACT/GPA: 790+/2.0
Student/Faculty Ratio: 14:1
Undergraduate Enrollment: 990
Scholarships/Academic: Yes **Athletic:** Yes
Expenses by: Year **In State:** $ 23,076
Founded: 1851
Religion: Roman Catholic
Housing: Yes
Male/Female Ratio: 30:70
Graduate Enrollment: 772
Financial Aid: Yes
Out of State: $ 23,076
Specialty: Liberal arts with career orientation
Degrees Conferred: BA, BS, BFA, MA, MS, MBA, MFA, M.Ed.
Programs of Study: Art, Biochemistry, Biology, Business Management, Communication, Computer Science, Economics, Education, Elementary Education, English, Environmental Studies, Finance, French, Graphic Art, History, Humanities, Human Services, Interior Design, International Business, Latin American Studies, Liberal Arts, Marketing, Music, Philosophy, Physical Science, PreDentistry, PreLaw, PreMed, Psychology, Religion, Secondary Education, Social Science, Sociology, Theatre, Voice

Men's Athletic Profile

1500 Ralston Avenue
Belmont, CA 94002
Coach: Gaspar Silveira
Email: Not Available

NCAA II
Argonauts/Gold, White, Blue
Phone: 650-508-3687
Fax: (415) 508-3691

Estimated # of Men's Soccer Scholarships: None
Conference: Northern California Athletic Conference
Program Profile: We have natural turf field. Play September through early November.
History: Program began in 1971.
Achievements:
Coaching: Joe Silveira, Head Coach, completed 5 seasons at college, strong coach and player, professional coaching experience with San Francisco Blackhawks and Salt Lake City Sting, played for San Jose State, San Jose Earthquakes and Jacksonville.

Concordia University - Irvine

Academic Profile

Irvine, CA 92612-3299
Phone: (949)854-8002

Type: 4 Yr.,Private,Liberal Arts
Website: http://www.cui.edu
SAT/ACT/GPA: 86018/2.5
Student/Faculty Ratio: 20/1
Undergraduate Enrollment: 950
Scholarships/Academic: Yes **Athletic:** Yes
Expenses by: Year **In State:** $21,000
Founded: 1972
Religion: Lutheran
Housing: Yes
Male/Female Ratio: 40/60
Graduate Enrollment: 250
Financial Aid: Yes
Out of State: $21,000
Specialty: Education and Business
Degrees Conferred: BA, Masters
Programs of Study: Art, Behavioral Science, Biology, Business Administration, Communications, Elementary Education, English, History, Mathematics, Music, Liberal Studies, PreLaw, Humanities, Religion, Psychology, Sports Management

Men's Athletic Profile

1530 Concordia
Irvine, CA 92715
Coach: TBA
Email: Not Available

NAIA
Eagles/Green, Gold
Phone: (714) 854-8002x432
Fax: (714) 854-6771

Estimated # of Men's Soccer Scholarships: None
Conference: GSAC

Women's Athletic Profile

1530 Concordia West
Irvine, CA 92612-3299
Coach: Kevin Macare
Email: Not Available

NAIA
Eagles/Green, White, Black
Phone: (714) 854-8002
Fax: (714) 854-6771

Estimated # of Women's Soccer Scholarships: None
Conference: Golden State Athletic Conference
Program Profile: Second year of the program and still in building phase, natural grass. Season is in the fall and conditions tend to be warm.
History: The program began in 1997. There is no history. In the first year of the program finished 1-17.
Coaching: Jeff Wells, Head Coach. Scott Wells - Assistant Coach. Both played NCAA Division I. Jeff previously coached at Central Washington and coached ODP in Eastern Washington and Northeastern California.
Style of Play: Short passing/possession; emphasized team. Defense with individual creativity on the offense.

De Anza College

Academic Profile

Cupertino, CA 95014

Phone: (408) 864-8745

Type: 2 Yr.,Public
Website: http://www.deanza.edu
SAT/ACT/GPA: None
Student/Faculty Ratio: 30:1
Undergraduate Enrollment: 22,000
Scholarships/Academic: Yes
Athletic: No
Expenses by: Year
In State: $ 4,000
Founded: 1967
Religion: Non-Affiliated
Housing: No
Male/Female Ratio: 48:52
Graduate Enrollment: N/A
Financial Aid: Yes
Out of State: $ 7,000
Specialty: Transfer, AA/As Degree, Guaranteed Admission, Job Training
Degrees Conferred: Associate of Arts, Associate of Sciences, Certificate Programs
Programs of Study: Over 100, from Administration of Justice to Zoology.

Men's Athletic Profile

21250 Stevens Creek Blvd.
Cupertino, CA 95014
Coach: Kulwant Singh
Email: cosing@aol.com

NJCAA
Dons/Cardinal, Gold
Phone: (408) 864-8745
Fax: (408) 864-5419

Estimated # of Men's Soccer Scholarships: None
Conference: Coast Conference

Program Profile: DeAnza College Men's soccer has established itself as arguably the best community college program in Northern California and one of the best in the state. In the 1990's, the team has been the Coast Conference Champion six times in State Final Four six times, and in 1994 & 1997, were the California State Champions. Our facilities are excellent. The soccer field measures 116 yardsx72 yards. Located in the heart of Silicon Valley.
History: The program began in 1971. There have only been three head coaches at Deanza: Bill Walker who has an overall record of 156-48-13 in eleven years, Cliff Draeger has an overall record of 104-34-17 in eight years and Kulwant Singh has an overall record of 158-19-21 in nine years.
Achievements: NSCAA Regional Coach of the Year in 1994. California Coaches Association Community College Coach of the Year in 1992 & 1998. Coast Conference Coach of the Year in 1991. California State Champions in 1994 & 1997. California State Semi-finalist in 1978, 1979, 1991, 1992, 1994, 1996, 1997 & 1998. Conference Champions in 1976, 1977, 1978, 1979, 1982, 1988, 1989, 1991, 1992, 1993, 1994, 1995 & 1997. All-Americans were Ralph Robertson, Justin Smith & Juan Ramos.
Coaching: Kulwant Singh, Head Coach, holds a National USSF 'A' License and NSCAA Premier License. He is a member of the California Youth Soccer Association (CYSA) and ODP Technical Director and Boy's ODP Chair, Region IV USYSA Staff Coach. Tom Vician, Assistant Coach, is a full-time faculty member, Ph.D. Mark Landefeld, Assistant Coach, holds a National "A" License.
Style of Play: If at all possible, we build from the back, go through the midfield and then go to goal. We play a variety of systems so players have a greater understanding of the game overall.

Women's Athletic Profile

21250 Stevens Creek Blvd.
Cupertino, CA 95014
Coach: Cheryl Owiesny
Email: Not Available

NJCAA
Dons/Maroon, Gold
Phone: (408) 864-8782
Fax: (408) 864-8751

Estimated # of Women's Soccer Scholarships: None
Conference: Coast Conference
Program Profile: DeAnza College is located in the Heart of the Silicon Valley. The soccer program is one of the best in the state. The field is 116 x 72 yards. Excellent facilities - great training room/team locker room situation. Season starts August 15 through November 15 approximately Thanksgiving. During the 2000 soccer season we finished with an overall record of 17-3-2. This placed us as the 3rd seed in the Northern California Community College playoffs. We were conference champions in the Coast conference.
History: Program began in 1989, State Champions in 1993 7 1994, been in play-offs every year since 1993.
Achievements: Have had All-Americans and many players transfer to a four-year programs and continue playing successfully.
Coaching: Cheryl Dwiesny - Head Coach.
Roster in State: 25
ODP State: 5
Walk-on/Other: 0
Positions Needed: ALL
Out of State: 2-3
Regional: 0
Graduation %: 90
Out of Country: 0
National: 0
Seniors on Team: 0
Most Recent Record: 17-3-2
Schedule: Scottsdale Community College Arizona, Santa Rosa Junior College, American River CC, Ohlone CC
Style of Play: DeAnza plays to win - whatever it takes. If at all possible the team will try to play an attacking style. We play different formation based on the players we have.

Dominican College
Academic Profile

San Rafael, CA 94901-8008
Phone: 888-323-6763

Type: 4 Yr.,Private,Liberal Arts
Website: http://www.dominican.edu
SAT/ACT/GPA: 810+
Student/Faculty Ratio: 6:1
Founded: 1890
Religion: Catholic
Housing: No
Male/Female Ratio: 23:77

Undergraduate Enrollment: 515
Graduate Enrollment: 284
Scholarships/Academic: Yes
Athletic: Yes
Financial Aid: Yes
Expenses by: Year
In State: $ 18,996
Out of State: $ 18,996
Degrees Conferred: BA, BS, BFA, MA, MS, MBA
Programs of Study: Contact school for programs of study.

Men's Athletic Profile

Did Not Return Profile

Women's Athletic Profile

Did Not Return Profile

Fresno Pacific University

Academic Profile

Phone: 559-453-2039

Fresno, CA 93702

Type: 4 Yr.,Private,Liberal Arts
Founded: 1944
Website: http://www.fresno.edu
Religion: Mennonite Brethren
SAT/ACT/GPA: 900/3.1
Housing: Yes
Student/Faculty Ratio: 14:1
Male/Female Ratio: 40:60
Undergraduate Enrollment: 800
Graduate Enrollment: 690
Scholarships/Academic: Yes
Athletic: Yes
Financial Aid: Yes
Expenses by: Year
In State: $ 14,665
Out of State: $ 14,665
Degrees Conferred: AA, BA, MA
Programs of Study: Accounting, Business & Management, Education, Communications, Computer Sciences, Mathematics, Social Sciences

Men's Athletic Profile

1717 Chesnut Ave.
Fresno, CA 93702
Coach: Marco Koolman
Email: Not Available

NAIA
Sunbirds/White, Blue, Rust
Phone: (209) 453-2085
Fax: (209) 453-2005

Estimated # of Men's Soccer Scholarships: None
Conference: Golden State Athletic Conference
Program Profile: Perennial contender for Region title, one of the best natural fields in the state, Steinert Field seats 1,000.
History: Program began in 1962.
Achievements: Original member of SCISA; went to NAIA National in 1983-1985, 1991; 1991-1992 Area player of the Year Honors; 1991, 1995 NAIA National Sr. Bowl participant.

Style of Play: We're a team that builds the attack from the back, utilizing our sweeper and outside defenders to bring the ball up to our midfielders and strikers. We push the ball well down the flanks and bring it across, creating many scoring opportunities for our team. We play a 3-4-3 system.

Hope International U (Pacific Christian C)

Academic Profile

Fullerton, CA 92831

Phone: (714) 879-3901

Type: 4 Yr.,Private
Website: http://www.hiu.edu
SAT/ACT/GPA: 890/18/2.00
Student/Faculty Ratio: 1:18
Undergraduate Enrollment: 598
Scholarships/Academic: Yes **Athletic:** Yes
Expenses by: Year **In State:** $ 14,965
Specialty: Christian Service

Founded: 1928
Religion: Independent Christian
Housing: Yes
Male/Female Ratio: 5:6
Graduate Enrollment: 178
Financial Aid: Yes
Out of State: $ 14,965

Degrees Conferred: AA, BA, BS, MA, MBA, MSM
Programs of Study: Biblical Studies, Biological Science, Business Administration, Church Ministry, Children's Ministry, Communications, Disability Ministry, Education, Health Science, Linguistics, Ministry of Older Adults, Mathematics, Music, Political Science, Social Science, Sports Ministry, Theatre Arts, Women's Ministry, Youth Ministry

Men's Athletic Profile

2500 E. Nutwood Ave.
Fullerton, CA 92831
Coach: David Nelson
Email: Not Available

NCCAA I/NAIA
Royals/Blue, Silver, White
Phone: (714) 879-3901
Fax: (714) 526-0231

Estimated # of Men's Soccer Scholarships: None
Conference: Independent

Women's Athletic Profile

2500 E. Nutwood
Fullerton, CA 92831
Coach: Josh Lee
Email:

NAIA
Royals/Blue, Silver, White
Phone: (714) 879-3901
Fax: (714) 681-7223

Estimated # of Women's Soccer Scholarships: 6
Conference: Golden State Athletic Conference
Program Profile: NAIA school that competes in the GSAC. Home games are played at Cal State Fullerton on natural grass.
History: Women's program began in August of 1996. It's still a relatively new program that has only competed for 4 years, only one of those years in the GSAC.
Achievements: 3 NCCAA All-Americans.
Coaching: Head Coach is Josh Lee
ODP State: 1
Seniors on Team: 3
Positions Needed: Goalie, midfield, defense
Most Recent Record: 1-8-1
Schedule: Azusa Pacific, Westmont, Cal Baptist, Biola, Concordia, Point Loma, Vanguard
Style of Play: Very young team, still trying to get everyone to mesh well. Determined, heart, and hard working.

Humboldt State University

Academic Profile

Phone: (707) 826-5941

Arcata, CA 95521-4757

Type: 4 Yr.,Public,Liberal Arts,Engineering
Website: http://www.humboldt.edu
SAT/ACT/GPA: 1000/3.0
Student/Faculty Ratio: 18:1
Undergraduate Enrollment: 6,535
Scholarships/Academic: Yes **Athletic:** Yes
Expenses by: Year **In State:** $ 8,500
Founded: 1913
Religion: Non-Affiliated
Housing: Yes
Male/Female Ratio: 50:50
Graduate Enrollment: 940
Financial Aid: Yes
Out of State: $ 13,500
Specialty: Biology, Forestry, Marine Biology, Natural Science
Degrees Conferred: BA, BS, MA, MS, MBA, MFA
Programs of Study: Business, Computer Science, Education, Environmental Engineering, Forestry, Kinesiology, Marine Biology, Natural Resources, Range Management, Psychology, Wildlife, plus a broad range of Liberal Arts programs.

Men's Athletic Profile

Department of Athletics
Arcata, CA 95521
Coach: Alan Exley
Email: aje2@axe.humboldt.edu

NCAA II
Lumberjacks/Green, Gold
Phone: (707) 826-5941
Fax: (707) 826-5446

Estimated # of Men's Soccer Scholarships: 5
Conference: Pacific West Conference
Program Profile: Competitive program at the Division 2 level, running both fall and spring seasons, one of the to fields on the West Coast, 115x74, grass surface, 1000 seating capacity, with an average attendance of 450.
History: Program started in 1970, NCAC Champions in 1994, National Ranking achieved seven of the last twelve seasons, traditionally in the top 5 programs in the west, NCAA 2.
Achievements: Produced five All-Americans, approx. 50 All-Far West Players, several players gone on to compete in Europe and at the Professional Level in the USA, Coach Exley, Far West Coach of the Year 1989.
Coaching: Alan Exley, Head Coach, USSF "A" License. Asst. Coach Duncan McMartin, USSF "A" License, Coach Lyle Wilks, Goalkeeper and conditioning coach.
Roster In State: 12 **Out of State:** 10 **Out of Country:** 1
ODP State: 5 **Regional:** 3 **National:** 0
Walk-on/Other: **Graduation %:** 95 **Seniors on Team:** 6
Positions Needed: Center Mids, Wing players
Camp or Clinic Dates: August 6-10, 2001
Most Recent Record: 11-5-3
Schedule: Seattle Pacific, Grand Canyon, UC Davis, CSU Bakersfield, Simon Frasier, Sonoma State
Style of Play: High pressure defense, quick counter-attacks via the flanks, numbers forward on both offense and defense.

Women's Athletic Profile

1 Harpst St.
Arcata, CA 95521
Coach: Kim Sutton
Email: ksb4@axe.humboldt.edu

NCAA II
Lumberjacks/Green, Gold
Phone: (707) 826-4129
Fax: (707) 826-5446

Estimated # of Women's Soccer Scholarships: N/A
Conference: Pacific West Conference

Program Profile: Our field is natural grass and measures 115' by 74'. We play in the fall. Our season goes from August 15th to the end of November. Attendance at our matches is between 200 to 800.
History: Our program began in 1995. We compiled a winning record in each season. We had an NCAA playoffs appearance in 1996. We were quarter finalists and ranked #6 in the Nation in 1996.Team GPA always exceeds 3.0.
Achievements: Coach of the Year 1998; Conference Champions 1998 and 1999; 9 All-West Region players, 4 Academic All-Conference; always ranked in the top six teams in the west region; NCAA playoff appearance in 1996-Quarterfinals finished ranked sixth in the country.
Coaching: Kim Sutton is our Head Coach and has been with us for 5 years. She holds and USSF "C" license, has coached 12 years of collegiate level, 5 Conference Championships, 2 Junior College State Runner-up Titles, Community College Coach of the Year, West Regional Coach of the Year, and Pacific West Coach of the Year in 1998.
Roster in State: 17
Out of State: 7
Out of Country: 0
ODP State: 4
Regional: 2
National: 0
Walk-on/Other: 0
Graduation %: 99
Seniors on Team: 4
Positions Needed: ALL
Camp or Clinic Dates: July 30- Aug 3rd
Most Recent Record: 6-12-1
Schedule: Sonoma State, Dominguez Hills, Seattle University, Bakersfield State, Pomona, Western Washington, UC Davis, UC San Diego
Style of Play: 3-4-3 system.

Long Beach State College

Academic Profile

Long Beach, CA 90808
Phone: 562-938-4205

Type: 4 Yr.,Public,Liberal Arts
Founded: 1949
Website: http://www.lbcc.cc.ca.us
Religion: Non-Affiliated
SAT/ACT/GPA: Open
Housing: Yes
Undergraduate Enrollment: 30,000
Graduate Enrollment: N/A
Scholarships/Academic: Yes
Athletic: Yes
Financial Aid: Yes
Expenses by: Year
In State: $ 8,000
Out of State: $ 10,000
Degrees Conferred: Bachelors, Masters
Programs of Study: Accounting, Advertising, Architectural, Art, Automotive, Aviation, Biology, Clothing/Textiles, Fashion Design/Technology, Flight Training, General Engineering, Horticulture, Insurance, Interior, Photography, Retail, Theatre, Travel/Tourism, Welding

Women's Athletic Profile

1250 N, Bellflower Blvd.
Long Beach, CA 90840
Coach: TBA
Email:
NCAA I
49ers/Black, Gold
Phone: (562) 985-1858
Fax: (562) 985-8197

Estimated # of Women's Soccer Scholarships: N/A
Conference: Big West Conference

Loyola Marymount University

Academic Profile

Los Angeles, CA 90045-8235
Phone: (310) 338-2700

Type: 4 Yr.,Private
Founded: 1911
Website: http://www.lmu.edu
Religion: Jesuit
SAT/ACT/GPA: 1000/3.0
Housing: Yes

Student/Faculty Ratio: 22:1
Male/Female Ratio: 1:4
Undergraduate Enrollment: 3,968
Graduate Enrollment: 1,155
Scholarships/Academic: Yes
Athletic: Yes
Financial Aid: Yes
Expenses by: Year
In State: $ 26,751
Out of State: $ 26,751
Specialty: Liberal Arts
Degrees Conferred: BA, BS, BBA, BSA, BSE, MA, MS, MBA, M.Ed., JD
Programs of Study: Accounting, Biochemistry, Biology, Business Administration, Civil Engineering, Communications, Dramatic Arts, Economics, Electrical Engineering, English, French, History, Humanities, Mathematics, Mechanical Engineering, Music, Philosophy, Physics, Political Science, Psychology, Religion, Social Science

Men's Athletic Profile

7900 Loyola Blvd.
Los Angeles, CA 90045
Coach: Paul Krumpe
Email: pkrumpe@lmumail.lmu.edu

NCAA I
Lions/Crimson, Navy Blue
Phone: 310-338-7640
Fax: 310-338-5915

Estimated # of Men's Soccer Scholarships: 9
Conference: West Coast Conference
Program Profile: We play on a fully enclosed Sullivan Field on LMU Campus situated in sunny Southern California.
History: Our program began in 1965.
Achievements: Paul Krumpe was named WCC Coach of the Year for 1999 season and 4 players were selected All-Conference. Three of the four were freshman: Andres Murriagui, Arturo Torres, Jeff Kovar.
Coaching: Paul Krump, Head Coach. Brian Irvin is our assistant coach. Jim San Martin is a volunteer coach along with Hooman Rahimizadeh and Jose Palomares.
Roster In State: 20
Out of State: 4
Out of Country: 0
ODP State: 8
Regional: 4
National: 1
Walk-on/Other:
Graduation %: N/A
Seniors on Team: 3
Positions Needed: All
Most Recent Record: 10-7-1
Schedule: Portland, Santa Clara, University of San Diego, UCLA, University of San Francisco, Gonzaga
Style of Play: Possession, but capable of direct and counter-attack 2 touch play. 11 players attack and 11 players defend.

Women's Athletic Profile

7900 Loyola Blvd.
Los Angeles, CA 90045-8235
Coach: Gregg Murphy
Email: gmurphy@lmu.edu

NCAA I
Lions/Navy Blue, Crimson
Phone: (310) 338-2795
Fax: (310) 338-5915

Estimated # of Women's Soccer Scholarships: 12
Conference: West Coast Conference
Program Profile: LMU competes in the West Coast Conference one of the most prestigious in the nation. Home games are played on campus at beautiful Sullivan Field, which is enclosed, has natural grass and seating capacity of 2000. Sullivan Field has been used as a training site for the 1994 World Cup, 1999 Women's World Cup, and numerous MLS teams.
History: First year of women's soccer at LMU was 1993. The all-time record stands at 67-73-12 (.460). The Lions have posted double-digit victory totals each of the past four seasons and nearly made the NCAA Tournament in 1997, 98 and 99. The Lions reached a No. 19 national ranking during the 1999 season. Perhaps the biggest win in program history came that season when LMU shut out ninth-ranked California 1-0.
Achievements: Goalkeeper Tracy Sharp was the first All-American in school history, earning honorable mention acclaim from College Soccer News in 1999. Sharp was also voted the West Coast Conference Defender of the Year Twice. The

Lions have had 31 All-Conference selections including defender Shari Nishikawa who became the first LMU player to earn All-WCC First Team honors as a freshman in 2000.
Coaching: All four coaches are in their fifth year with program. Under Murphy Loyola Marymount has enjoyed unprecedented success, finishing with a winning record each of the past four seasons including a school best 13-6-0 record in 1999. Before coming to LMU Murphy coached both men's and women's programs at Chapman College in Orange, CA in 1995 his women's team was ranked third in the West Region (NCAA DIII), while on the men's side in 1995 Chapman reached the D III Final Four. Murphy is a 1986 graduate of Chapman. Assistant Coach Michelle Myers was a standout player at Santa Clara in the mid-1980's and has head coaching experience at prep power Mater Dei High School in Santa Ana, CA.
Roster in State: 18
Out of State: 9
Out of Country: 0
ODP State: 5
Regional: 2
National: 2
Walk-on/Other:
Graduation %: 100
Seniors on Team: 5
Positions Needed: ALL
Camp or Clinic Dates: TBA
Most Recent Record: 12-6-1
Schedule: UCLA, Wake Forest, USC, Santa Clara, Portland, Michigan, Kentucky, Baylor, Univ. of San Diego
Style of Play: Possession oriented, everyone attacks and defends.

Master's College

Academic Profile

Santa Clarita, CA 91321
Phone: 800-568-6248

Type: 4 Yr.,Private,Liberal Arts
Founded: 1927
Website: http://www.masters.edu
Religion: Christian
SAT/ACT/GPA: 1000/20/2.5
Housing: Yes
Student/Faculty Ratio: 17:1
Male/Female Ratio: 47:53
Undergraduate Enrollment: 900
Graduate Enrollment: 280
Scholarships/Academic: Yes
Athletic: Yes
Financial Aid: Yes
Expenses by: Year
In State: $ 9,000
Out of State: $ 9,000
Specialty: Christian, Liberal Arts, Education
Degrees Conferred: BA, BS, MD in Biblical Counseling, Theology, Divinity
Programs of Study: Biblical Studies, Biological Science, Business Administration, Communications, English, History, Home Economics, Liberal Studies, Mathematics, Music, Natural Science, Physical Education, Political Studies

Men's Athletic Profile

21726 W Placerita Canyon
Santa Clarita, CA 91321
Coach: Jim Rickard
Email: Jandjrick@juno.com

NAIA
Mustangs/Royal, Gold, White
Phone: (805) 259-3540
Fax: (805) 254-6129

Estimated # of Men's Soccer Scholarships: 5
Conference: Independent
Program Profile: We play on a grass field that holds 1,000 seats. Our season runs from August through December.
History: We began in 1970 with an overall record of 287-228-40. Master's has been in the playoffs 10 years in a row and in region final 9 out of 10 years.
Achievements: NAIA Region Champs in 1990, 1991 & 1992; NCCAA National Champions in 1987, 1989 & 1993; NAIA Far West Region Independent Champions in 1989, 1991, 1992, 1993, 1994, 1995, 1997 & 1998.
Coaching: Jim Rickard, Head Coach, holds a USSF coaching license. He was a former college All-American and ODP while in high school. Our overall record of 108-61-12 is over 8 seasons. He has a BA Business, Master college graduate in 1990 and received MBA from California Lutheran University in 1999. Blake Gillen and Joel Murphy are Assistant Coaches.

Style of Play: Target offense, possession, work from the back.

Women's Athletic Profile

21726 W Placerita Canyon Rd
Santa Clarita, CA 91321
Coach: Jamie Lindvall
Email: Not Available

NAIA
Mustangs/Royal, Yellow
Phone: (805) 254-3540
Fax: (805) 254-6129

Estimated # of Women's Soccer Scholarships: None
Conference: Far Western Independent
Program Profile: Season is September through November. Play on a natural turf field, portable bleachers, locker rooms with showers, training room.
History: Program began fall 1992.
Style of Play: Defend our own defensive third with minimal use of long - ball.

Menlo College

Academic Profile

Phone: 800-556-3656

Atherton, CA 94027

Type: 4 Yr.,Private,Liberal Arts
Website: http://www.menlo.edu
SAT/ACT/GPA: 850/18/2.5
Student/Faculty Ratio: 15:1
Undergraduate Enrollment: 466
Scholarships/Academic: Yes
Athletic: No
Expenses by: Year
In State: $ 25,510
Founded: 1927
Religion: Non-Affiliated
Housing: Yes
Male/Female Ratio: 55:45
Graduate Enrollment: N/A
Financial Aid: Yes
Out of State: $ 25,510
Specialty: Management, Mass Communications
Degrees Conferred: BM, BMC, Liberal Arts
Programs of Study: Business Management, International Business, Environmental Resources Management, Management Information Systems, Media Studies, Media Management, Electronic Communications, Psychology, Humanities, International Policy and Planning or Environmental Policy and Planning

Men's Athletic Profile

1000 El Camino Real
Atherton, CA 94027
Coach: Len Renery
Email: Not Available

NCAA III
Oaks/Navy, White
Phone: (415) 688-3770
Fax: (415) 324-4937

Estimated # of Men's Soccer Scholarships: None
Conference: Independent
Program Profile: The Oaks have a full size natural grass field.
History: Program began in 1927. the program was discontinued in World War II and restarted in 1961.
Achievements: Won 11 Championships between 1970 and 1985. Produced 6 All - Americans; rated #1 Independent Team in the Far West 1962 and 1981.

Mills College

Academic Profile

Phone: 800-876-4557

Oakland, CA 94613

Type: 4 Yr.,Private
Website: http://www.mills.edu
Founded: 1852
Religion: Non-Affiliated

SAT/ACT/GPA: 940+
Student/Faculty Ratio: 11:1
Undergraduate Enrollment: 850
Scholarships/Academic: Yes **Athletic:** No
Expenses by: Year **In State:** $ 22,030
Degrees Conferred: BA, MA, MFA
Housing: No
Male/Female Ratio: Female
Graduate Enrollment: 300
Financial Aid: Yes
Out of State: $ 22,030
Programs of Study: American Studies, Anthropology, Art, Art History, Biochemistry, Biology, Education, Elementary Education, English, Environmental Science

Women's Athletic Profile

5000 Mac Arthur Blvd.
Oakland, CA 94613
Coach: Colette Bowler
Email: colehe@mills.edu

NCAA III
Cyclones/Navy, Gold
Phone: (510) 430-2395
Fax: (510) 430-2276

Estimated # of Women's Soccer Scholarships: None
Conference: CAL PAC/ NAIA
Program Profile: 8 Year old program every year team gets stronger. Finished 4th out of 8 teams, made playoffs. Field Best in the Bay Area with natural grass 120x80
History: Program began in 1993 Coach Colette Bowler Started the program.
Achievements: 2 All-CAL PAC Players, 4th place in CAL PAC
Coaching: Head Coach Colette Bowler played Div. I (Umass) for her college years. Colette is still very active with her own soccer skills. Coach Bowler loves soccer and wants others to love the sport and she welcomes all levels of skills to her team.
Roster in State: 12 **Out of State:** 6 **Out of Country:** 0
Walk-on/Other: **Graduation %:** 100 **Seniors on Team:** 4
Positions Needed: ALL
Camp or Clinic Dates: July/ Aug.
Most Recent Record: 6-8-0
Schedule: CSU-Hayward, Elms College, Dominican College
Style of Play: Possession develop from the back and play aggressive.

Occidental College
Academic Profile

Los Angeles, CA 90041
Phone: 800-527-6947

Type: 4 Yr.,Private,Liberal Arts
Website: http://www.oxy.edu
SAT/ACT/GPA: 1000
Student/Faculty Ratio: 12:1
Undergraduate Enrollment: 1,585
Scholarships/Academic: Yes **Athletic:** No
Expenses by: Year **In State:** $ 25,356
Founded: 1887
Religion: Non-Affiliated
Housing: No
Male/Female Ratio: 55%:45%
Graduate Enrollment: 50
Financial Aid: Yes
Out of State: $ 25,356
Degrees Conferred: BA, Graduate program: MA
Programs of Study: Anthropology, Art, Biology, Chemistry, Economics, Education, Engineering, Geology, History, International, Languages, Mathematics, Physical Fitness/Movement, Physics, Political, Religion, Seismology

Men's Athletic Profile

1600 Campus Road
Los Angeles, CA 90041
Coach: Costa Nicolaou
Email: Not Available

NCAA III
Tigers/Black, Orange
Phone: (213) 259-2983/2931
Fax: (213) 341-4993

Estimated # of Men's Soccer Scholarships: None
Conference: Southern California Independent Athletic Conference (SCIAC)
Program Profile: Our program is in the building process, having moved from the bottom of the conference tables to finished consistently in top half each year. Field recently revamped; 70x110 yards grass; training home of LA Galaxy of MSL. Recently US and Danish national teams trained for US Cup in 1997.
History: We have been in existence since early 1970's. Teams have been competitive at times and have done pretty well. At the time I (Costa Nicolaou) took the over program, team was in a slump.
Achievements: Numerous first and second team All-Conference pick over the years; All-Americans and Conference MVP"S as well as representation at USISL level for some players.
Coaching: Costa Nicolaou, Head Coach, USSF "A" License, South African Full Badge Coaching Credential, 17 years with a professional clubs in SA. Colm McFeely - Assistant Coach, FIFA coaching license, 17 year professional - Ireland, Australia, and Hong Kong. Glen Appels - Assistant Coach, USSF "C" License, UC Berkeley player, St. Francis High School Coach. Joe Begin - Goalkeeper Coach, former Cleveland Crunch and Canton Invaders Indoor Goalkeeper .
Style of Play: Depends on players available, but we try to play attacking soccer, mixing short and long passing, keeping possession and going to goal as often as possible.

Women's Athletic Profile

1600 Campus Rd
Los Angeles, CA 90041
Coach: Costa Nicolaou
Email: Not Available

NCAA III
Tigers/Black, Orange
Phone: (213) 259-2983
Fax: (213) 341-4993

Estimated # of Women's Soccer Scholarships: None
Conference: Southern California Intercollegiate Athletic Conference
Program Profile: Program is in the building process, having moved from bottom of the conference tables to finish consistently in the top half each year. Field recently revamped; 70x110 yards grass; training home of LA Galaxy of MLS. Recently the US and Danish national teams trained for US Cup 1997.
History: Began in the mid 1980's. Finished in the bottom or close to the bottom of respective conference tables. Coaching staff has worked hard to reverse this and have been successful so far.
Achievements: Erika Imhof (1991) SCIAC Conference MVP; All-Americans-Dawn Goodwin and Michelle Winscott in 1995. Numerous 1st and 2nd team All-Conference picks over the years. All-Americans and conference MVP's as well as representation at the USISL level for some players.
Coaching: Costa Nicolaou, Head Coach, holds USSF "A" License and South African Full Badge Coaching Credential, 17 years with professional clubs in SA. Colm McFeely - Assistant Coach, FIFA Coaching License, 17 years professional - Ireland, Australia, Hong Kong. Glen Appels - Assistant Coach, USSF "C" License, UC Berkeley player, St. Francis High School Coach. Joe Bergin - Goalkeeper Coach, former Cleveland Crunch and Canton Invaders Indoor Goalkeeper.
Style of Play: Depends on players available, but we try to play attacking soccer, mixing short and long passing, keeping possession and going to goal as often as possible.

Pepperdine University

Academic Profile

Malibu, CA 90263

Phone: (310) 456-4322

Type: 4 Yr.,Private,Liberal Arts
Website: http://www.pepperdine.edu
SAT/ACT/GPA: 1100
Student/Faculty Ratio: 13:1
Undergraduate Enrollment: 2,900
Scholarships/Academic: Yes
Athletic: Yes
Expenses by: Year
In State: $32,000
Specialty: Liberal Arts, Business, Professional Programs, Communications

Founded: 1937
Religion: Church of Christ
Housing: Yes
Male/Female Ratio: 42/58
Graduate Enrollment: 5,100
Financial Aid: Yes
Out of State: $32,000

Degrees Conferred: BA, BS, MBA, MA, JD, MS, Mdiv
Programs of Study: Business, Communication, Sports Medicine there are 36 total.

Women's Athletic Profile

24255 Pacific Coast Hwy.
Malibu, CA 90263
Coach: Tim Ward
Email: tward@pepperdine.edu

NCAA I
Lady Waves/Blue, Orange
Phone: (310) 456-4338
Fax: (310) 456-4322

Estimated # of Women's Soccer Scholarships: N/A
Conference: West Coast Conference
Program Profile: Home games are played on natural grass at Stotsenberg Field. It is a new field with scoreboard, bleachers and a locker room all overlooking the Pacific Ocean!.
History: We just finished our 6th season of existence! Three of the six seasons have finished with winning records (13-4 in 1994, 10-7-2 in 1995 and 12-8 in 1997). We compete in one of the toughest conference in the country in the WCC (Portland & Santa Clara). Our program is on the way up!!!
Achievements: 1997 2nd Place in WCC(tie with Santa Clara); Kristi DeVert-US Women's National Team in 1998-99; Jen Evans-First All-WCC three seasons; All-Far West in 1995; Jennifer Peterson-First Team All-WCC; NSCAA All-West 1996.
Coaching: Tim Ward, Head Coach. Kristy Walker - Assistant Coach (full-time); Josh Green - Goalkeeper Coach.
Style of Play: The style depends on the players! Ideally, we try to develop a team that knows when to possess the ball and who also knows when to be direct! We love skillful players! Ultimately, our team tends to be very tough mentally and very athletic!

Point Loma Nazarene College

Academic Profile

San Diego, CA 92106
Phone: (619) 849-2200

Type: 4 Yr.,Private,Liberal Arts
Website: http://www.ptloma.edu
SAT/ACT/GPA: Open
Student/Faculty Ratio: 18:1
Undergraduate Enrollment: 2,000
Scholarships/Academic: Yes
Athletic: Yes
Expenses by: Year
In State: $ 17,000
Specialty: Liberal Arts
Founded: 1902
Religion: Nazarene
Housing: Yes
Male/Female Ratio: 1:2
Graduate Enrollment: 400
Financial Aid: Yes
Out of State: $ 17,000
Degrees Conferred: BA, BSN, MA, MED, EDS
Programs of Study: Business and Management, Health Science, Home Economics, Letters/Literature, Multi/Interdisciplinary Studies, Social Science, Visual and Performing Arts

Men's Athletic Profile

3900 Lomaland Drive
San Diego, CA 92106
Coach: Tim Hall
Email: thall@ptloma.edu

NAIA
Crusaders/Green, Gold, Navy
Phone: (619) 849-2649
Fax: (619) 849-2769

Estimated # of Men's Soccer Scholarships: 7 Tuitions
Conference: Golden State Athletic Conference
Program Profile: Strong nationally ranked NAIA soccer program. We are located on the Pacific Ocean with a panoramic view of the Pacific. The field is natural grass with a seating capacity of 2,000. Located in the incredible San Diego, the climate is very good all year-round. Warmest it gets in the summer on the coast would be around the mid-70's. The facilities are some of the most beautiful you will find anywhere. The season runs from mid-August with training camp through mid-November.

History: Our program began in the early 1970's. Point Loma Nazarene University has always been a fairly competitive program up until the last three years where we have become nationally competitive and nationally ranked on a consistent basis.
Achievements: 1997 Coach of the Year for the GSAC Conference along with the 1997 Far West Coach of the Year Honors. Finished Runner-Up in the conference championships the last two years. Two All-Americans and a number of Conference and Far West Region players. The recruiting this past off-season has been the best ever.
Coaching: Tim Hall, Head Coach. Mark Keller, Goalkeeper Coach, named 1997 All-American keeper.
Style of Play: Systems vary - we play mainly a possession game. Depending on game situation and strengths of the athletes.

Women's Athletic Profile

3900 Lomaland Drive
San Diego, CA 92106
Coach: Mark Halpert
Email: Not Available

NAIA
Crusaders/Green, Gold
Phone: (619) 849-2557
Fax: (619) 849-2769

Estimated # of Women's Soccer Scholarships:
Conference: Golden State Athletic Conference
Program Profile: This is our first year as an intercollegiate team after one year as a club team. We have beautiful field over looking the ocean. We play on natural grass with a natural stadium effects as a result of the surrounding cliffs.
History: Our program began in 1998 with no money on short notice and had a tremendously successful first season playing .500. We were National Champions on our first game and losing only 3-1 to Azusa Pacific.
Coaching: Mark Halpert is the Head Coach. He holds a USSF "C" License. He was a former club coach for LaJolla Nomads and FC Bratz. He is also a former men's head coach at Point Loma in the mid 1980's.
Style of Play: We are very good defensively, with possession soccer. We try to play around and less direct against physically aggressive teams. Enjoy the ball and have fun winning.

Pomona - Pitzer Colleges

Academic Profile

Claremont, CA 91711

Phone: (909) 621-8427

Type: 4 Yr.,Private,Liberal Arts
Website: http://www.pomona.edu
SAT/ACT/GPA: Varies/3.0+
Student/Faculty Ratio: 10:1
Undergraduate Enrollment: 1,400
Scholarships/Academic: No
Athletic: No
Expenses by: Year
In State: $ 27,200
Specialty: Liberal Arts Colleges
Degrees Conferred: BA, BS

Founded: 1887
Religion: Non-Affiliated
Housing: Yes
Male/Female Ratio: 1:1
Graduate Enrollment: N/A
Financial Aid: Yes
Out of State: $ 27,200

Programs of Study: American Studies, Anthropology, Art, Asian Languages, Astronomy, Biology, Black Studies, Chemistry, Chicano Studies, Computer Science, Economics, Education, English, Geology, German and Russian, History, International Relations, Latin American Studies, Linguistics, Mathematics, Media Studies, Music, Neuroscience, Philosophy, Politics, Physical Education, Physics, Public Policy Analysis, Religious Studies, Romance Languages, Science, Technology and Society, Sociology, Theatre and Dance , Women's Studies

Men's Athletic Profile

Rains Ctr, 220 E 6th St.
Claremont, CA 91711
Coach: Bill Swartz
Email: wswartz@pomona.edu

NCAA III
Sagehens/Blue, Orange, White
Phone: 909/607-2771
Fax: (909) 621-8547

Estimated # of Men's Soccer Scholarships: None
Conference: Southern California Intercollegiate Athletic Conference
Program Profile: We have natural Bermuda grass playing surface in the finest athletic complex in the nation.
History: Our program began in 1960 with early success until 1980's which fell on hard times, now is very competitive.
Achievements: SCIA Champs in 1990, NSCAA All-American - Chris Davis; ISAA Academic All American was Dave Whidbee; 1990 Coach of the Year; 3 NCAA All-Far West players; 5 NSCAA/NCAA All-Far West in 1994.
Style of Play: Play out of the back through midfield coupled with counter attack.

Women's Athletic Profile

Rains Ctr - 220 E 6th St.
Claremont, CA 91711
Coach: Kristen Martin
Email: kmartini@pomona.edu

NCAA III
Sagehens/Blue, White
Phone: (909) 607-3719
Fax: (909) 621-8547

Estimated # of Women's Soccer Scholarships: None
Conference: Southern California Intercollegiate Athletic Conference
Program Profile: Home games are played on natural grass field called Strehne Field.
History: Program became a varsity sport in 1985 and has won four Conference Titles.
Achievements: 1 All-American. NSCAA West Region Coach of the Year
Roster in State: 6 **Out of State:** 14 **Out of Country:**
ODP State: 5 **Regional:** **National:**
Walk-on/Other: **Graduation %:** 99.5 **Seniors on Team:** 2
Positions Needed: Striker, GK, outside midfield
Camp or Clinic Dates: June 12-16, July 10-14
Most Recent Record: 7-11
Schedule: Trinity, UC Santa Cruz, California Lutheran, Chapman, St. Thomas, Redlands, University of La Verne

Saint Mary's College

Academic Profile

Moraga, CA 94575
Phone: (925) 631-4444

Type: 4 Yr.,Private,Liberal Arts
Website: http://www.stmarys-ca.edu
SAT/ACT/GPA: 1000/3.0
Student/Faculty Ratio: 20:1
Undergraduate Enrollment: 2,100
Scholarships/Academic: Yes **Athletic:** Yes
Expenses by: Year **In State:** $ 24,695
Specialty: Liberal Arts

Founded: 1863
Religion: Catholic
Housing: Yes
Male/Female Ratio: 45:56
Graduate Enrollment: 2,000
Financial Aid: Yes
Out of State: $ 24,695

Degrees Conferred: BA, BS, Nursing, MA, MS, MBA, M.Ed.
Programs of Study: Anthropology, Art, Biology, Business, Classical Languages, Chemistry, Communications, Economics, Engineering, Government, History, Mathematics, Nursing, Philosophy, Psychology, Sociology

Men's Athletic Profile

P.O. Box 5100
Moraga, CA 94575
Coach: Mark Talan
Email: msoccer@st.marys.ca.edu

NCAA I
Gaels/Red, Blue, White
Phone: (925) 631-4657
Fax: (925) 631-4405

Estimated # of Men's Soccer Scholarships: Varies
Conference: West Coast Conference

Program Profile: We are a member of the rugged West Coast Conference, which includes perennial NCAA Qualifiers San Diego and San Francisco. The College is unique in its rural, small college setting, because it is just 40 minutes away from San Francisco. Its newly constructed 'soccer only' field is short cut Bermuda of fast, perfectly level surface. SMC also features a stadium of full-dimension soccer field (117x72) with 3,500 capacity. It has a new stadium that has a capacity of 8,500. In 1999, we received $40,000,000 gift for new athletic aquatic second student recreation centers to be built within next few years.
History: Became Division I in 1978. Has four consecutive nine-win seasons from 1988-1991. Gaels were 8-9-2 overall in 1997. Finished 6-14-0 in 1998.
Achievements: Ranked in the NCAA Division I Top 20 in 1991 & 1997. Forward Gunda was 1990 & 1993 three-time 1st team All-WCC, Conference Offensive Player of the Year in 1991. Defender Ali John Utush was 1996 & 1998 was 1st team All-WCC, Conference Defensive Player of the Year in 1998; Midfielder Nick Marcum was named West Coast Conference Freshmen of the Year in 1998.
Coaching: Mark Talan, Head Coach, is entering his third year here. He was a SMC assistant for eight years. Tom Ginocchio, Assistant Coach, is entering his sixth year. Kevin Arthur, Assistant Coach, is entering his third year. Nate White, Assistant Coach, is entering his second year.
Style of Play: Solid one touch, two touch game; attacking the flanks.

Women's Athletic Profile

P.O. Box 5100
Moraga, CA 94575
Coach: Paul Ratcliffe
Email: pratclif@stmarys-ca.edu

NCAA I
Gaels/Blue, White
Phone: (925) 631-4415
Fax: (925) 631-4405

Estimated # of Women's Soccer Scholarships: 11
Conference: West Coast Conference
Program Profile: Our stadium is a full dimension field, Kentucky Blue Grass, fully enclosed; used for 1994 World Cup Training site for Sweden. Practice field is a full dimension (75X120 yd.), with short cut Bermuda grass, newly constructed. The program is consistently ranked nationally in Division I, Even though we are one of the smallest Division I schools. We have 18:1 student to teacher ratio.
History: Program began in spring of 1982 as NAIA and in 1987 became a NCAA Division I program.
Achievements: NAIA National Champs 1984 and 1986; NCAA Post-Season Qualifier 1988, 1994; Final 16 1994; Co-Coach of the Year 1999;
Coaching: Paul Ratcliffe has been our Head Coach since 1998. He graduated from UCLA in 1994. Sarah Miller is a graduate from UCLA class of 1999 and is our Assistant Coach and Daisy Rcaazco was a Mary's College Graduate of 1998.
Roster in State: 20 **Out of State:** 5 **Out of Country:**
Walk-on/Other: **Graduation %:** **Seniors on Team:** 5
Positions Needed: All
Camp or Clinic Dates: June July
Most Recent Record: 13-4-1
Schedule: Stanford, Fresno State, Oregon State, UC Irvine, Cal Poly, Santa Clara, Portland, University of San Diego, Loyola Marymount, San Jose State
Style of Play: Possession style with an emphasis on attacking as a unit.

San Diego State University

Academic Profile

San Diego, CA 92182-4328
Phone: (619) 594-5200

Type: 4 Yr.,Public
Website: http://www.sdsu.edu
SAT/ACT/GPA: 1058/22/3.48
Student/Faculty Ratio: 19:1
Undergraduate Enrollment: 25,800

Founded: 1897
Religion: Non-Affiliated
Housing: Yes
Male/Female Ratio: 49:51
Graduate Enrollment: 3,200

Scholarships/Academic: Yes **Athletic:** Yes **Financial Aid:** Yes
Expenses by: Year **In State:** $ 8,542 **Out of State:** $ 14,446
Specialty: Business, Engineering, Education
Degrees Conferred: BA, BS, MA, MS, MBA, MFA, Ph.D.
Programs of Study: Business Management, Computer Sciences, Education, Engineering, Exercise and Nutritional Sciences, Mathematics, Physical Therapy, Psychology, Telecommunications

Men's Athletic Profile

5500 Campanile Drive
San Diego, CA 92182-4324
Coach: Lev Kirshner
Email:

NCAA I
Aztecs/Scarlet, Black
Phone: (619) 594-0136
Fax: (619) 582-6541

Estimated # of Men's Soccer Scholarships: 4
Conference: Mountain Pacific Sports Federation
Program Profile: Opened new Sports Deck worth Approximately $18 million. Natural Surpale on top of 2 story Parking Garage. 1000 seat capacity. 2000 squad started 7-9 freshman and sophomores. First year Head Coach
History: 1987 NCAA National Runner-up. Ranked # 1 in nation 3 separate seasons. 7 NCAA play off appearances. Marcelo Balgoa, Eric Wynalda, Chris Sullivan all played at SDSU and were members of at least one World Cup Team. Kevin Crow also played at SDSU and was a 2 time Olympian.
Achievements: 1st season as Division I Head Coach.
Coaching: Lev Kirshner Head Coach, Matt Hall Former SDSU Goalkeeper is one of the Top 15 Goalkeepers in the country. Jason Annicgero All-American at Santa Clara Univ. Current Professional with S.D Flash are the assistant coaches.
Roster In State: 17 **Out of State:** 9 **Out of Country:** 1
ODP State: 10 **Regional:** 5 **National:** 2
Walk-on/Other: **Graduation %:** N/A **Seniors on Team:** 5
Positions Needed: Forward, Defender & Goalkeeper
Most Recent Record: 6-12-1
Schedule: Santa Clara, Univ. San Diego, Brown, UCLA, San Jose State, Gonzaga, Oregon State, CSU Fuleerton, Hofstra, Denver
Style of Play: We like to play a possession oriented style, but with purpose and direction. We like to compete and battle defensively, by staying organized and disciplined.

Women's Athletic Profile

5500 Campanile Dr.
San Diego, CA 92182-4324
Coach: Chuck Clegg
Email: clegg@mail.sdsu.edu

NCAA I
Aztecs/Scarlet, Black
Phone: (619) 594-3749
Fax: (619) 582-6541

Estimated # of Women's Soccer Scholarships: 12
Conference: Western Athletic Conference
Program Profile: New soccer field, academic support facilities, and $45 million athletic complex. Play a traditional fall and spring schedule (outdoor). ARCO Olympic and National team training complex in San Diego. Average team GPA: 2.86 (over 90% graduation rate).
History: Started program in 1989, WAC Champions in 1995, 1998, MWC Co Champs 1999, NCAA playoffs 1998, 1999.
Achievements: 1995, 98, 99 Conference Champions, 1998 sweet sixteen, 2 All-Americans, 2nd Coach in history of NCAA to have plauers play in the Men's and Women's World Cup.
Coaching: Chuck Clegg, Head Coach, US Soccer "A" License, English and Scottish coaching licenses, ODP Staff, NSCAA Region Eight representative; NSCAA ratings and Senior Bowl. Assistant Coach is Jill Young.
Roster in State: 14 **Out of State:** 5 **Out of Country:** 2
ODP State: 10 **Regional:** 5 **National:** 3
Walk-on/Other: **Graduation %:** 90+ **Seniors on Team:** 3

Positions Needed: 3
Camp or Clinic Dates: June, August
Most Recent Record: 15-7-0
Schedule: Duke, BYU, Santa Clara, Stanford, Cal, USC
Style of Play: Forward thinking with an emphasis on combining play and looking for quick attacks forward. Ball possession with playing it out of the back will be emphasized, being direct if playing against High pressure. Defensively will be a combination of a man-to-man and zone.

San Francisco State University

Academic Profile

Athletic Department Office 109
San Francisco, CA 94132

Phone: (415) 338-1100

Type: 4 Yr.,Public,
Website: http://www.sfsu.edu
SAT/ACT/GPA: 820/26+/2.0
Student/Faculty Ratio: 18:1
Undergraduate Enrollment: 19,000
Scholarships/Academic: Yes **Athletic:** Yes
Expenses by: Year **In State:** $ 8,500
Specialty: Business, Psychology, Sciences
Degrees Conferred: BA, BS, MA, MS, MBA

Founded: 1899
Religion: Non-Affiliated
Housing: Yes
Male/Female Ratio: 45:65
Graduate Enrollment: 6,000
Financial Aid: Yes
Out of State: $ 14,500

Programs of Study: Accounting, American Studies, Anthropology, Art, Astronomy, Biology, Broadcasting, Chemistry, Cinema, Communications, Computer Information Systems, Computer Science, Creative Writing, Dance, Ecology, Economics, Education, Engineering, Gerontology, Journalism, Management, Marketing, Mathematics, Music, Nursing, Philosophy, Political Science, Psychology, Social Science, Sociology, Physics

Men's Athletic Profile

1600 Holloway Avenue
San Francisco, CA 94132
Coach: Joseph Hunter
Email: hunterj@sfsu.edu

NCAA II
Gators/Purple, White
Phone: (415) 338-7571
Fax: (415) 338-1967

Estimated # of Men's Soccer Scholarships: Tuition Only (3)
Conference: California Collegiate Athletic Association
Program Profile: The Gators are a Division II, non-scholarship program. We play 20 matches, playing home games on a natural grass field (117x70 yards) with stadium renovations scheduled for 1998. Our season runs from August to November. Our team plays against the Top Far West and nationally ranked teams.
History: Our program began in 1939 and played in the Far West Conference until 1982 when they joined the NCAC. We had an excellent team in the 70's and 80's. Coach Hunter took over team from Jack Hyde, who coached the men for 18 seasons. SF State is set to be up and coming team of the 1990's.
Achievements: The Gators have had numerous All-Americans from 1938 to the present, consistently All-Conference and All-Far West players each season. Coach of the Year honors for the past coaches - Luis Sagastume, and Jack Hyde. Joseph Hunter was named Coach of the Year in 1998.
Coaching: Joseph Hunter, Head Coach, USSF "A" Coaching License, NSCAA License, BS in Physical Education and Biology, Master's in Sports Administration. USSF Regional Staff Coach and CYSA Staff Coach.
Style of Play: 3-4-3 system of play, emphasis on ball possession, high rate of ball circulation, zonal/man defensive arrangement, high fitness and technical level required - we play to win!

Women's Athletic Profile

1600 Holloway Ave.
San Francisco, CA 94602
Coach: Jack Hyde
Email: jhyde@sfsu.edu

NCAA II
Gators/Purple, White, Gold
Phone: (415) 338-1804
Fax: (415) 338-1967

Estimated # of Women's Soccer Scholarships: None
Conference: California Collegiate Athletic Association
Program Profile: We will have a new field in August of 2000, 120x75, natural grass and a capacity of 4,000.
History: Women's soccer program began in 1982.
Achievements: All Far West Players: 1983-84-85-87-88-89-90-91-95-98-99; Coach of the Year 1984 and 1987.
Coaching: Jack Hyde, Head Coach, NSCAA Staff Coach/Instructor, USSF 'A' license. Suzanne Sillet, Assistant Coach, graduated from University of California-Davis and played for four years. She holds a NSCAA National Coaching License. Kevin Walker is also an Assistant on his 1st year.

Roster in State: 21	**Out of State:** 0	**Out of Country:** 0
ODP State: 2	**Regional:**	**National:**
Walk-on/Other:	**Graduation %:** 85	**Seniors on Team:** 7

Positions Needed: All
Camp or Clinic Dates: Not Available
Most Recent Record: 11-8-0
Schedule: Cal Poly Pomona, Sonoma State, UC Davis, CSU Bakersfield, UC San Diego
Style of Play: Possession of the ball using the width of the field. High target player with overlapping wide midfielders. Programmed set plays, especially corner kicks. "Never give up" style on the field.

San Jose State University

Academic Profile

San Jose, CA 95192-0062
Phone: (408) 924-1291

Type: 4 Yr.,Public,Liberal Arts,Engineering		**Founded:** 1865
Website: http://www.spartnas.sjsu.edu		**Religion:** Non-Affiliated
SAT/ACT/GPA: 820/2.0		**Housing:** Yes
Student/Faculty Ratio: 30:1		**Male/Female Ratio:** 53:47
Undergraduate Enrollment: 19,000		**Graduate Enrollment:** 8,000
Scholarships/Academic: Yes	**Athletic:** Yes	**Financial Aid:** Yes
Expenses by: Year	**In State:** $ 15,000	**Out of State:** $ 21,000

Specialty: Business, Education, Communications, Engineering
Degrees Conferred: BA, BS, BFA, MA, MS, MBA, MFA
Programs of Study: Top 10 majors - Computer Science, Art & Design, Accounting, Management, Electrical Engineering, Management Information Systems, Computer Engineering, Psychology, Criminal Justice, Administration, Biology, Child Development

Men's Athletic Profile

1 Washington Square
San Jose, CA 95192
Coach: Gary St. Clair
Email: gstclair@email.sjsu.edu

NCAA I
Spartans/Blue, Gold, White
Phone: (408) 924-1261
Fax: (408) 924-1291

Estimated # of Men's Soccer Scholarships: TBA
Conference: Mountain Pacific Sports Federation
Program Profile: NCAA I program. Home facility-Spartan Stadium (30,476), natural grass. Fall season with conference playoffs.
History: First year of program-1927. SJSU has appeared in NCAA playoffs 13 times, last appearance in 2000. October 16, 2000- ranked #1 in NSCAA National ranking (second time in program's history team has been ranked number one in a poll).
Achievements: Won Mountain Pacific Sports Federation Championship in 2000. Has had 17 players named All-American (3 players named twice). Gary St.Clair named a regional Coach of the Year in 1994.
Coaching: Gary St. Clair head coach (11th season, San Jose State '76), Ron Smare assistant coach (11th season, San Jose State '77), Jake Kurrey, undergraduate assistant coach (1st year).

Roster In State: 29 **Out of State:** 1 **Out of Country:** 2
Walk-on/Other: **Graduation %:** N/A **Seniors on Team:** 7
Positions Needed: Keeper, Forward, Midfield
Camp or Clinic Dates: TBA
Most Recent Record: 20-1-1
Schedule: Stanford, USF, California, Santa Clara
Style of Play: Emphasis on attacking tactics. Combination play on ground into third of field.

Women's Athletic Profile

One Washington Square
San Jose, CA 95192
Coach: Tamie Grimes
Email: tamie10@pacbell.net

NCAA I
Spartans/Gold, White, Blue
Phone: (408) 924-1470
Fax: (408) 924-1290

Estimated # of Women's Soccer Scholarships: 12
Conference: WAC Conference
Program Profile: NCAA Division I program. Home facility-Spartan Stadium (30,476), natural grass. Fall playing with conference playoffs.
History: Program began in fall of 1995. Joined WAC in 1996
Achievements: Won WAC Tournament title and qualified for NCAA Tournament for first time in 2000. WAC Pacific Division Coach of the Year in 1996. Two players named to soccer Buzz All-West Second Team. One named to Soccer Buzz All-West first team.
Coaching: Tamie Grimes Head Coach, first year (Santa Clara). Was assistant coach at San Jose State for two seasons including one year as graduate assist. Coach. Orlando Cervantes assit. Coach, first year (San Jose State 99). First year as assit. Coach on women's team after two years as assist. Men's team. Wynne McIntosh, Nicole Leonard are assistant Coaches.
Roster in State: 21 **Out of State:** 3 **Out of Country:** 0
ODP State: 4 **Regional:** 1 **National:** 0
Walk-on/Other: 0 **Graduation %:** **Seniors on Team:** 7
Positions Needed: F, MF
Camp or Clinic Dates: TBA
Most Recent Record: 10-13-1
Schedule: Santa Clara, SMU, University. Of the Pacific, Cal Poly
Style of Play: A ball control style with emphasis on combination and attacking as a unit. Strong zone defense contributes greatly to attack.

Santa Clara University

Academic Profile

Santa Clara, CA 95053

Phone: (707) 864-7000

Type: 4 Yr.,Private,Liberal Arts,Engineering
Website: http://www.SantaClaraBroncos.com
SAT/ACT/GPA: 1210/3.5
Student/Faculty Ratio: 13:1
Undergraduate Enrollment: 4,200
Scholarships/Academic: Yes **Athletic:** Yes
Expenses by: Year **In State:** $ 25,713

Founded: 1851
Religion: Catholic-Jesuit
Housing: Yes
Male/Female Ratio: 50:50
Graduate Enrollment: 4,000
Financial Aid: Yes
Out of State: $ 25,713

Specialty: Liberal Arts, Business, Law
Degrees Conferred: BA, BS, MA, MS, MBA, Ph.D., JD
Programs of Study: Business and Management, Communications, Engineering, International, Letters/Literature, Multi/Interdisciplinary, PreProfessional Programs, Psychology, Social Sciences

Men's Athletic Profile

C/O Men's Soccer
Santa Clara, CA 95053
Coach: Mitch Murray
Email: Not Available

NCAA I
Broncos/Red, White
Phone: (408) 554-4003
Fax: (408) 554-6969

Estimated # of Men's Soccer Scholarships: None
Conference: West Coast Conference
Program Profile: Our games are played in Buck Shaw Stadium. The season is from September to December. There is natural grass training and game field (seats 6,000).
History: Program began in 1967.
Achievements: 1989 NCAA Co-Champs; 1990 NCAA Playoffs; 1990 World Collegiate Champs; 1991 World Collegiate Runner -up; 6th in 1993; 1995 - Final 8; ranked Top 10, NCAA Regional Finalist. 19 former SCU players have played professionally; 9 All - Americans; 4 Academic All - Americans; 1989, 1991 NCAA Coach of the Year; 1991 NCAA Finalist; 1994 WCC Champions.
Coaching: Mitch Murray, Head Coach, 10 years, holds licenses from USA, Germany and Canada, 1991 NCAA Coach of the Year, 1995 West Region Coach of the Year.
Style of Play: High work rate, pressure - type zonal defending, direct attack, successful.

Women's Athletic Profile

500 El Camino Real
Santa Clara, CA 95053
Coach: Jerry Smith
Email: rmanning@scu.edu

NCAA I
Broncos/Red, White
Phone: (408) 554-4624
Fax: (408) 554-5264

Estimated # of Women's Soccer Scholarships: Fully Funded
Conference: West Coast Conference
Program Profile: Play fall season August - December. Spring training February - May. Buck Shaw Stadium - lighted, 7,000 seating capacity, natural surface, official training site for a World Champion Brazilian National Team (May - July 1994). Ranked nationally in Top 5 for Division I.
History: Program began in 1980. Jerry has been the head coach since 1988. School hosted final four in 1996. Team competes against the top teams from across the country and has been recognized as one of the top teams in the West for over a decade. Women's soccer holds a unique place as the headlining sport on campus.
Achievements: 7 times in NCAA Final Four, 12 Consecutive Years in NCAA Playoffs, 12 Consecutive Years in Top 10, 4 WCC Champs, 17 All-Americans, 11 National Team Players, 2 National Players of the Year, 14 Players allocated or drafted into WUSA.
Coaching: Jerry Smith, Head Coach, led the team to the Final Four in 1989, 1990,1992, and the WCC Champions. He has been the head coach for 14 seasons. Assistants Rich Manning (3 seasons), Eric Yamamoto (10 seasons), Brandi Chastain (7 seasons)

Roster in State: 13	**Out of State:** 7	**Out of Country:** 0
ODP State: 2	**Regional:** 9	**National:** 4
Walk-on/Other: 5	**Graduation %:** 100	**Seniors on Team:** 6

Positions Needed: ALL
Camp or Clinic Dates: see web site
Most Recent Record: 16-7-1
Schedule: Florida State, Wake Forest, Notre Dame, California, Stanford, UCLA, Portland
Style of Play: Strong zone defense that also contributes greatly to the attack. Combines quick counter and build-up in their attack that creates many scoring opportunities.

Sonoma State University

Academic Profile

Rohnert Park, CA 94928

Phone: 707-664-2778

Type: 4 Yr.,Public
Website: http://www.sonoma.edu
SAT/ACT/GPA: 820/18
Student/Faculty Ratio: 20:1
Undergraduate Enrollment: 7,000
Scholarships/Academic: Yes
Athletic: Yes
Expenses by: Year
In State: $ 8,500
Degrees Conferred: BA, BS, MA, MS

Founded: 1960
Religion: Non-Affiliated
Housing: Yes
Male/Female Ratio: 40:60
Graduate Enrollment: 1,000
Financial Aid: No
Out of State: $ 14,900

Programs of Study: Accounting, Anthropology, Art, Banking/Finance, Biology, Botany, Cell Biology, Chemistry, Communications, Computer Science, Criminal Justice, Dance, Dramatic Arts, Economics, English, Geography, Geology, German, History, Marine Biology, Marketing, Math, Microbiology, Music, Nursing, Philosophy, Physics, Political Science, Psychology, Social Science

Men's Athletic Profile

1801 E Cotati Avenue
Rohnert Park, CA 94928
Coach: Marcus Ziemer
Email: marcus.ziemer@sonoma.edu

NCAA II
Cossacks/Navy, Blue, White
Phone: (707) 664-2614
Fax: (707) 664-4104

Estimated # of Men's Soccer Scholarships: None
Conference: Northern California Athletic Conference
Program Profile: Our home field is natural grass. Our program is very successful and is coached by one of the top coaches in the west.
Achievements: NCAC Champions 3 of the past 6 years; National Division II runner up in 1991; several All - American and All - Region players.
Coaching: Marcus Ziemer, Head Coach, former All - NCAC player for Sonoma State, 2 time NCAC Coach of the Year.
Style of Play: Aggressive, ball control, attacking offense.

Women's Athletic Profile

1801 E Cotati Avenue
Rohnert Park, CA 94928
Coach: John Gilson
Email: luke.oberkirch@sonoma.edu

NCAA II
Cossacks/Navy, Sky, White
Phone: (707) 664-2481
Fax: (707) 664-4104

Estimated # of Women's Soccer Scholarships: Varies
Conference: California Collegiate Athletic Association
Program Profile: Our team plays on natural grass field, enclosed field with seating for 1,500.
History: Program began in 1981. Within two years, SSU captured their first NCAC Championship and finished ranked 17th in the country. Since then, Sonoma State has been one of the dominant women's soccer programs in the division II. Conference Champions six consecutive years. National Champions in 1990. Six straight trips to the NCAA playoffs.
Achievements: Over 20 All-Americans since in the last 20 years; two former players playing professionally in Japan and over 20 years of coaching experience at all levels.
Coaching: Luke Oberkirch, Head Coach, former assistant to Peter Reynaud for five years, eleven years of coaching experience, 16 years of playing experience at all levels, head coach of the Olympic Development Program for girls U17, and coach of the Santa Rosa United Club since 1992. John Gilson is our Assistant Coach.

Roster in State: 15 **Out of State:** 3 **Out of Country:**
ODP State: 5 **Regional:** **National:**
Walk-on/Other: **Graduation %:** 100 **Seniors on Team:** 7
Positions Needed: Several
Camp or Clinic Dates: June 26-30, July 17-21, July 3-Aug. 4, Aug 7-10
Most Recent Record: 15-2-4
Style of Play: Possession oriented - emphasis on skill, attack from all positions; play a 3-4-3 formations.

Stanford University

Academic Profile

Ads
Stanford, CA 94305-6150
Phone: (650) 725-0736

Type: 4 Yr.,Private,Liberal Arts
Founded: 1891
Website: http://www.gostanford.com
Religion: Non-Affiliated
SAT/ACT/GPA: 1300+
Housing: Yes
Student/Faculty Ratio: 10:1
Male/Female Ratio: 55:45
Undergraduate Enrollment: 6,500
Graduate Enrollment: 6,500
Scholarships/Academic: Yes **Athletic:** Yes **Financial Aid:** Yes
Expenses by: Year **In State:** $ 31,599 **Out of State:** $ 31,599
Degrees Conferred: BA, BS, MA, MS, MBA, MFA, MEd, Ph.D., EdD
Programs of Study: African - American Studies, Anthropology, Art, Asian Languages, Biological Sciences, Chemistry, Classics, Communication, Comparative Literature, Computer Science, Drama, Earth Science, East Asian Studies, Economics, Engineering, English, Feminist Studies, French, German Studies, History, Human Biology, International Relations, Italian, Latin American Studies, Linguistics, Math, Music, Philosophy, Physics, Political Science, Psychology, Public Policy, Religion, Sociology, Spanish and Portuguese

Men's Athletic Profile

Arrillaga Family Sports Center
Stanford, CA 94305-6150
Coach: Bret Simon
Email: N/A

NCAA I
Cardinals/Cardinal, White
Phone: (650) 723-9375
Fax: (650) 725-8642

Estimated # of Men's Soccer Scholarships: Variable
Conference: PAC-10
Program Profile: The team plays at New Maloney Field which is one of the nicest mini-soccer stadiums in the country. It is situation at one end of a eucalyptus grove with a 116x76 yard natural Bermuda/rye grass field. It has seating for 1,800 spectators in modern concrete stands and also has a top of the range floodlighting system.
History: The program began back in 1911 when Harry Maloney was the coach. Current coach, Bobby Clark, is the 13th in a program that has made the NCAA Tournament on 11 occasions. The team has made the NCAA Tournament 3 consecutive years reaching the final in the 1998 season.
Achievements: 1998 we saw the team reach the College Cup Final only to lose a hard fought match to Indiana. That season saw All-American selections Jamie Clark and Simon Elliott both be drafted to the pros. for San Jose and Los Angeles respectively, and both featured as MLS Rookie of the year candidates. In 1999 season Andy Hemmerich was also drafted by the San Jose. This now totals 5 MLS Stanford players with Rhett Harty and Mark Semioli making up the number.
Coaching: Bret Simon, Head Coach, joined Stanford in 2001. He was with Creighton for the past 8 seasons. Brian Wiese is the Goalkeeper Coach and is entering his 5th year with us. Pieter Lehrer is also an Assistant Coach and will be entering his 2nd year.
Roster In State: 5 **Out of State:** 22 **Out of Country:** 2

ODP State: 24 **Regional:** 17 **National:** 8
Walk-on/Other: 3 **Graduation %:** 100 **Seniors on Team:** 7
Positions Needed: Goalkeeper, Central Defender, Midfielder, Forward
Camp or Clinic Dates: Last week in July
Most Recent Record: 12-4-3
Schedule: UCLA, Washington, California Berkeley, Indiana, Santa Clara, Seton Hall, Dartmouth, Cincinnati, Harvard, San Francisco.
Style of Play: We play a controlled pressing zonal style with emphasis on skilled technical players.

Women's Athletic Profile

Arrillaga Family Sports Center
Stanford, CA 94305-6150
Coach: Andy Nelson
Email:

NCAA I
Cardinal/Cardinal, White, Red
Phone: (650) 725-0757
Fax: (650) 725-8642

Estimated # of Women's Soccer Scholarships: varies
Conference: Pac-10 Conference
Program Profile: The team plays at New Maloney field which is one of the nicest mini-soccer stadiums in the country. It is situated at one end of a eucalyptus grove with a 116x76 yard natural Bermuda/rye grass field. It has seating for 1,800 spectators in modern concrete stands and also has a top of the range floodlighting system.
History: The Cardinal's rapid rise to the top of collegiate rankings began back in 1984 with the inception of the 1st Women's Soccer team. The Cardinals have racked up a 134-38-18 record in the 1990's, which ranks among the top10 in the nation. Stanford has also appeared in the tournament eight of the past nine years and has had 13 All-Americans, numerous US National team players and an Olympic Gold medallist. Current Coach Andy Nelson is the 5th Coach in Cardinal History.
Achievements: Stanford's Maloney field has been home to some of the greatest collegiate women's soccer players ever. Stanford's most famous star includes 4-time All-American, 1996 US Olympic team member, World Cup Champion and US National team Captain Julie Foudey. Other Stanford Standouts include, Sarah Rafarelli, Tess Fisher, Erin Martin, and Ronnie Fair.
Coaching: Head Coach Andy Nelson will build on the 1999 Pac-10 Championship team, bringing his success from the University of Pennsylvania to the farm. Nelson's team went undefeated at home in 1999, holding its opponents scoreless in seven home games and finished the season ranked No. 11 in the nation in shutouts and No. 12 in goals against average.
Roster in State: 12 **Out of State:** 12 **Out of Country:**
ODP State: **Regional:** 11 **National:** 7
Walk-on/Other: **Graduation %:** 100 **Seniors on Team:** 3
Positions Needed: Striker, Defenders, Center Midfield
Camp or Clinic Dates: July 15-20, July 22-27
Most Recent Record: 15-5-1
Schedule: Connecticut, Notre Dame, Santa Clara, UCLA, USC, Virginia, Wake Forest, Maryland, Hartford
Style of Play: As a very technical team we look to build possession at the right times and go forward quickly and with numbers. We play zoneally on defense.

University of California - Berkeley

Academic Profile

Ads
Berkeley, CA 94720

Phone: (510) 643-8100

Type: 4 Yr.,Public
Website: http://www.berkeley.edu
SAT/ACT/GPA: 600-710/3.89
Student/Faculty Ratio: 17:1

Founded: 1869
Religion: Non-Affiliated
Housing: Yes
Male/Female Ratio: 1:1

Undergraduate Enrollment: 14,578
Graduate Enrollment: 24,172
Scholarships/Academic: Yes
Athletic: Yes
Financial Aid: Yes
Expenses by: Year
In State: $ 14,598
Out of State: $ 24,172
Degrees Conferred: BA, BS, MA, MS, MBA, Ph.D., EdD, OD, JD
Programs of Study: Anthropology, Art, Architecture, Astronomy, BioEngineering, Biology, Business Administration, Chemistry, Communications, Computer Science, Earth Science, Economics, Engineering, Geology, Sociology, Political Science, Psychology, Physics

Men's Athletic Profile

140 Haas Pavilion #4422
Berkeley, CA 94720-4422
Coach: Kevin Grimes
Email: kgrimes@uclink.berkeley.edu

NCAA I
Golden Bears/Navy, Gold
Phone: (510) 642-5916
Fax: (510) 643-5344

Estimated # of Men's Soccer Scholarships: 6
Conference: PAC 5
Program Profile: A $3.5 million, 22,000-seat stadium with a state of the art, natural grass field and light is being developed. We play on a new grass field in Memorial Stadium. Check out our website www.caibears.com for the complete media guide to California Soccer.
History: Program began in 1912. 43-26-8 record for 1996-1999. Team Finished last season 30th in nation. 6 NCAA Tournament appearances.
Achievements: 1996 NCAA Tournament, 1996 MPSF Division Champions, 1996 Clemson Tournament Champions, 1996 USD Tournament Champions. Doug Brooks - 1996 National Freshman Goalkeeper of the Year Soccer America and Soccer News.
Coaching: Head Coach- Kevin Grimes. Assistant Coach- Brad Agoos. Goalkeeper Coach- Drew Leonard. Volunteer Coach- Todd Highley.
Roster In State: 20
Out of State: 5
Out of Country: 0
ODP State: 14
Regional: 6
National: 3
Walk-on/Other:
Graduation %: 98
Seniors on Team: 3
Positions Needed: Mid-fielders, and Forward
Camp or Clinic Dates: Spring Break 2001
Most Recent Record: 12-5-3
Schedule: Stanford, UCLA, Washington, Oregon State, UC-Irvine, Santa Clara, San Jose State, Loyola Marymount
Style of Play: Possession, short passing with a blend of controlled long passing, utilizing short passing game with quick combinations and attacking flair.

Women's Athletic Profile

2223 Fulton; 3rd Floor
Berkeley, CA 94720-4424
Coach: Kevin Boyd
Email: boydk@uclink4.berkeley.edu

NCAA I
Golden Bears/Blue, Gold
Phone: (510) 643-8100
Fax: (510) 643-2536

Estimated # of Women's Soccer Scholarships: None
Conference: Pacific 10 Conference
Program Profile: The track and field at Edwards Stadium is converted to a regulation 75 yard x 115 yard natural grass soccer field for the use of both men's team and women's team. The project which has a 3.3 million budget will require the removal of existing equipment and surface, installation of an extensive field drainage system and installation of the grass. The improvement plan will eventually include the addition of stadium lights to the facility, allowing for night matches and other field events. The construction of the regulation soccer facility will enable Cal to host an NCAA soccer event, a possibility that has been precluded in recent years due to the size and surface of Memorial Stadium, the Bears former home.
History: Thirteen-year program, 6 National Tournament Appearances, 3 Final Four Appearances. Finished 1996 ranked #25 in the post-season polls, #19 in Soccer America.

Achievements: One National Goalkeeper of the Year - Mary Harvey in 1986; 3 Women's World Cup team members (Joy Biefeld, Mary Harvey, and Brandi Chastain). Won Olympic Gold in 1996, won 1991 World Championship; 3 alumni (Joy Fayett, Brandi Chastain, and Mary Harvey), US National Team members.
Coaching: Kevin Boyd, Head Coach. Kathrine Roth - Assistant Coach. Duncan Lyon - Goalkeeper Coach.
Style of Play: Organized possession style attack and defensively high pressure on ball with all 11 players involved in attack and defense.

University of California - Davis

Academic Profile

Davis, CA 95616

Phone: (530) 752-2971

Type: 4 Yr.,Public,
Website: http://www.ucdavis.edu
SAT/ACT/GPA: 1000/3.4
Student/Faculty Ratio: 18:1
Undergraduate Enrollment: 19,500
Scholarships/Academic: Yes **Athletic:** Yes
Expenses by: Year **In State:** $ 10,988
Specialty: Premed, Prevet, Hard Sciences, Social Sciences
Degrees Conferred: All
Programs of Study: More than 100 undergraduate majors available.

Founded: 1906
Religion: Non-Affiliated
Housing: Yes
Male/Female Ratio: 48:52
Graduate Enrollment: 4,600
Financial Aid: Yes
Out of State: $ 20,372

Men's Athletic Profile

1 Shields Avenue
Davis, CA 95616
Coach: Dwayne Shaffer
Email: dlshaffer@ucdavis.edu

NCAA II
Aggies/Navy, Gold
Phone: (530) 752-8892
Fax: (530) 752-5099

Estimated # of Men's Soccer Scholarships:
Conference: California Collegiate Athletic Conference
Program Profile: We have an outstanding soccer stadium. Our field is Bermuda grass with a measurements of 118x74 yards. Stadium seating is for 1,200.
History: The program began in 1969. We always finish strong in the conference. 2 All-Americans; 10 All-Far West Region players in 7 season.
Achievements: Many All-Conference, All-Far West selections, several former players in A-League and Division pro league.
Coaching: Dwayne Shaffer, Head Coach, is entering his third year with the program. He served as a head coach at University of the Dayton in 1996. He was head assistant at Clemson for three years in 1993-1995. He is an ODP Region IV staff member and holds "A" License. Eric Mild is the Assistant Coach.
Style of Play: Play a 4-4-2 possession from the back.

Women's Athletic Profile

264 Hickey Gymnasium
Davis, CA 95616
Coach: Maryclaire Robinson
Email: mkrobinson@ucdavis.edu

NCAA II
Aggies/Navy, Gold
Phone: (530) 752-0735
Fax: (530) 752-6681

Estimated # of Women's Soccer Scholarships: None
Conference: CCAA
Program Profile: Our facilities include a natural grass stadium, stadium bleacher seating accommodating 1,200 spectators.

History: Our program began in 1987 and played in NCAC. Presently we have won NCAC Championships in '96 and are playing in the strongest NCAA Division II conference in the Nation.
Achievements: We have had numerous All-Conference players, NSCAA All-Americans, and NSCAA All-Region players
Coaching: Maryclaire Robinson, Head Coach, has coached several All-Americans and has been with us for 9 years, while Jim Burke has been with us for 6 years.
Roster in State: 22 **Out of State:** 2 **Out of Country:**
ODP State: 12 **Regional:** 4 **National:**
Walk-on/Other: 10 **Graduation %:** **Seniors on Team:** 3
Positions Needed: Unknown
Most Recent Record: 11-5-1
Schedule: Sonoma State, Cal Poly Pomona, CSU Dominguez Hills, Western Washington, UC San Diego, Chico State, UC Santa Cruz, CSU Bakersfield, San Francisco State
Style of Play: Fluid, attacking style with an emphasis on possession and building out of the back. Strong defensive system; zonal, man-to-man, combination. Good artistry, speed of play, and athleticism with teamwork emphasis.

University of California - Irvine

Academic Profile

Irvine, CA 92697-1075
Phone: (949) 824-6703

Type: 4 Yr.,Public,
Website: http://www.uci.edu
SAT/ACT/GPA: 1200/3.0
Student/Faculty Ratio: 19:1
Undergraduate Enrollment: 17,395
Founded: 1965
Religion: Non-Affiliated
Housing: Yes
Male/Female Ratio: 1:1
Graduate Enrollment: 2,373
Scholarships/Academic: Yes **Athletic:** Yes **Financial Aid:** Yes
Expenses by: Year **In State:** $ 10,109.50 **Out of State:** $ 19,093.50
Specialty: All subjects; Leading Research University
Degrees Conferred: BA, BS, BFA, MA, MS, MBA, Ph.D., MD
Programs of Study: Anthropology, Biological Sciences, Chemistry, Computer Science, Dance, Drama, Economics, Engineering, Fine Arts, Geography, Humanities, Mathematics, Music, Philosophy, Physical Science, Political Sciences, Psychology, Social Ecology, Social Sciences, Sociology

Men's Athletic Profile

UCI Athletics, Crawford Hall
Irvine, CA 92697
Coach: George Kuntz
Email: gekuntz@uci.edu
NCAA I
Anteaters/Blue, Gold
Phone: (714) 824-8158
Fax: (714) 824-8492

Estimated # of Men's Soccer Scholarships: 9
Conference: Mountain Pacific Sports Federation
Program Profile: We play on Anteater Stadium which is natural grass. Facilities are considered some of the nation's finest, multi-purpose facilities. Located on the UCI campus. Stadium features 1,000 seats and lights for the night games. The stadium which just underwent major renovations, has been transformed into a state-of-art track facility as well as a European open-air soccer field for day games. The track has a training site for numerous international Olympians.
History: Program began in 1984. 1994 was a successful season finishing third in the MPSF Pacific Division and upsetting #2 ranked UCLA; broke attendance records this season.
Achievements: MPSF Player of the Year; numerous All-Conference selections; First team All-Region; MPSF Coach of the Year. 1996 MPSF All-Federation Team honoree.

Coaching: George Kuntz, Head Coach, 4th season at UCI, USSF "A" License, NSCAA Advanced National Diploma, Assistant Technical Advisor for the FIFA 1994 World Cup, CYSA South State Director of Coaching. Chris Volk - Assistant Coach, played collegiate at San Diego State University from 1987 to 1991. Roger Dodge - Restricted Earning Coach, begins his first season with UCI. He was a midfielder and defender at Southern California College. Currently, he is coaching director for CYSA-South Division III and has a USSF "B" License.
Roster In State: 23 **Out of State:** 5 **Out of Country:** 1
ODP State: 12 **Regional:** 8 **National:** 0
Walk-on/Other: **Graduation %:** 100 **Seniors on Team:** 4
Positions Needed: goalkeepers, forwards
Camp or Clinic Dates: June25-28 July5-8 July10-14 July17-21 July24-28 July31-August4
Most Recent Record: 8-11-1
Schedule: UCLA, Washington, Cal State Fullerton, Univ. of Sand Diego, Loyola Marymount, UC Santa Barbara
Style of Play: Attacking style with an organized, aggressive defensive structure.

Women's Athletic Profile

Crawford Hall
Irvine, CA 92697
Coach: Marine Cano
Email: mcano@uci.edu

NCAA I
Anteaters/Blue, Gold
Phone: (949) 824-7432
Fax: (949) 824-8492

Estimated # of Women's Soccer Scholarships: 12
Conference: Big West Conference
Program Profile: Some of the nation's finest, multi-purpose facilities are located on the UCI campus. Anteater Field is a natural grass soccer stadium that features 2,500 seats and lights for night games. The stadium which just under-went major renovations, has been transformed into a state-of-the-art track facility as well as a European open-air soccer field for day games.
History: Program began in 1984. 1997 team captured its first conference championship, setting a school record of 15 wins, ending the season with a 15-7-0 record. Program has had a winning record of the past five years.
Achievements: Numerous All-Big West Conference selections, NSCAA All-Region, Academic All-American, Scholar-Athletes, Big West Players of the week.
Coaching: Marine Cano, Head Coach, is entering his seventh year with the program. He came to UCI after successful stint at Cal State Dominguez Hills, where he was the head men's and women's coach from 1984-1993. He served as the goalkeeping coach for the California in 1983-1984. As a goalkeeper, he was a member of the 1976 US National Team. He holds a USSF "A" license. Kristen Borland is our Assistant Coach and she holds a USSF "C" license.
Roster in State: 17 **Out of State:** 3 **Out of Country:** 0
ODP State: 5 **Regional:** 1 **National:** 0
Walk-on/Other: **Graduation %:** 100 **Seniors on Team:** 4
Positions Needed: Goalkeeper, Sweeper, Center Half, Forward
Camp or Clinic Dates: June 25-28 and July 5-8
Most Recent Record: 6-10-4
Schedule: USC, Cal Poly, University of San Diego, St. Mary's, Pacific, Pepperdine
Style of Play: Defensive, counter attacking style. Consistent wing play with every player offense and defense.

University of California - Los Angeles

Academic Profile

Ads
Los Angeles, CA 90024-0044

Phone:

Type: 4 Yr.,Public
Website: http://www.ucla.edu
SAT/ACT/GPA: 1000/21/3.0
Student/Faculty Ratio: 10:1
Undergraduate Enrollment: 23,000

Founded: 1919
Religion: Non-Affiliated
Housing: Yes
Male/Female Ratio: 1:1
Graduate Enrollment: 11,000

Scholarships/Academic: Yes **Athletic:** Yes **Financial Aid:** Yes
Expenses by: Year **In State:** $ 12,000 **Out of State:** $ 21,000
Specialty: Medical School, Business, Communications
Degrees Conferred: BA, BS, MA, MS, MBA
Programs of Study: Anthropology, Art, AstroPhysics, Biology, Classics, Computer, Cybernetics, Earth Science, English, Languages, Geology, GeoPhysics, History, International, Meteorology, Nursing, Religion, Seismology

Men's Athletic Profile

J.D. Morgan Ctr
Los Angeles, CA 90095-1639
Coach: Todd Saldaña
Email: Not Available

NCAA I
Bruins/Gold, Blue
Phone: (310) 825-8699
Fax: (310) 206-7047

Estimated # of Men's Soccer Scholarships: None
Conference: MPSF
Program Profile: UCLA North Athletic Field - capacity of 2,000.
History: Program began in 1937. Soccer was elevated to NCAA status at UCLA in 1967. UCLA soccer began with a British rugby coach Dennis Storer, along with 4 All - American Bruins, they not only gave the Bruins an international flavor, but helped build the foundation for one of the country's top intercollegiate programs. Storer, who divided his time coaching rugby, soccer , and teaching, won matches and guided the Bruins to 4 NCAA semifinal appearances. Twice his teams entered the NCAA final with unbeaten records only to lose their final game. In 1972, Storer obtained the services of a freshman midfielder - Siegfried Schmid - whose association with UCLA would perpetuate the winning tradition the Englishman had established. Storer resigned in 1974 and Terry Fisher assumed the reigns for 1 year. Fisher's replacement was Steve Gay. In 1980, Schmid became the fourth soccer coach.
Achievements: 16 All - Americans; 17 US 'A' National Team players, 8 freshman All - Americans; 30 All - Far West players, NCAA Champions 1985,1990; NCAA Semifinalist 1984, 1985, 1990, 1994.At the national team level, Bruin players past and present have represented the US in more than 800 games. In 1993, the Bruins, unranked by Soccer America in the preseason, rose as high as #2 in the national ranking. In each of the last 13 years, at least 1 UCLA player has earned 1st or 2nd team NSCAA All -American honors, and every Brun senior since 1983 has ended his season in the NCAA tournament.
Style of Play: A ball control style with emphasis on combination and attacking as a unit. Defense is a combination of zone and man-to-man.

Women's Athletic Profile

P.O. Box 24044
Los Angeles, CA 90024-0044
Coach: Jillian Ellis
Email: Not Available

NCAA I
Bruins/Blue, Gold
Phone: (310) 825-8699
Fax: (310) 825-8664

Estimated # of Women's Soccer Scholarships: None
Conference: PAC - 10 Conference
Program Profile: Spaulding Field is UCLA's home field. It seats a 1,000 (grass). The Bruins also play at El Camino College wherein stadium has 12,000 capacity and is grass. North Athletic Field has 1,500 capacity and is also a grass field.
History: The program will be beginning its sixth year at UCLA. In five years the program has recorded a 65-24-7. Started in 1993.
Achievements: Joy Fawcett was named 1997 Pacific Coach of the Year; 1997 Pacific 10 Champions (record was 9-0); All-Americans.
Style of Play: Possession based.

University of California - San Diego

Academic Profile

Phone: 619-534-4831

La Jolla, CA 92093

Type: 4 Yr.,Public,Liberal Arts
Website: http://www.ucsd.edu
SAT/ACT/GPA: Required
Student/Faculty Ratio: 22:1
Undergraduate Enrollment: 13,500
Scholarships/Academic: Yes
Expenses by: Year
Athletic: No
In State: $ 1,629
Founded: 1959
Religion: Non-Affiliated
Housing: Yes
Male/Female Ratio: 51:49
Graduate Enrollment: 3,500
Financial Aid: Yes
Out of State: $ 4,426
Degrees Conferred: BA, BS,MA,MS, MFA, MD
Programs of Study: Anthropology, Art, Biochemistry, Biology, BioPhysics, Communications, Computer Science, Dramatic Arts, Earth Science, Ecology, Engineering, English, Foreign Languages, Linguistics, Mathematics, Microbiology, Molecular Biology, Music, Philosophy, Physics, Physiology, Political Science, Psychology, Quantitative Methods, Religion, Social Science, Visual Performing Arts

Men's Athletic Profile

Intercollegiate Athletic 0905
La Jolla, CA 92093
Coach: Derek Armstrong
Email: Not Available

NCAA III
Tritons/Blue, Gold
Phone: (619) 534-4211
Fax: (619) 534-8172

Estimated # of Men's Soccer Scholarships: None
Conference: Independent

Women's Athletic Profile

9500 Gilman Drive
La Jolla, CA 92093
Coach: Brian McManus
Email: bmmcmanus@ucsd.edu

NCAA II
Tritons/Blue, Gold
Phone: (619) 534-8273
Fax: (619) 534-8172

Estimated # of Women's Soccer Scholarships: None
Conference: None
Program Profile: The program is in the transition to going Division II; we play on an all grass field which has a measurements of 75x115; we have lights and play most of our home games at night.
Achievements: NCAA Division III Champs in 1996, 1997, 1998, & 1989; Farwest Champions 9 times; NSCAA Coach of the Year in 1995, 1996, 2000.
Coaching: Brian McManus, Head Coach. Mike Nicholson - Assistant Coach.
Roster in State: 15
Out of State: 2
Out of Country:
ODP State: 6
Regional: 1
National:
Walk-on/Other:
Graduation %:
Seniors on Team: 15
Positions Needed: ALL
Style of Play: Attacking three at the back four in the midfield through with top.

University of California - Santa Barbara

Academic Profile

Phone: (805) 893-2200

Santa Barbara, CA 93106

Type: 4 Yr.,Public,Engineering
Website: http://www.gogauchos.ucsb.edu
Founded: 1909
Religion: Non-Affiliated

SAT/ACT/GPA: 1200/20/3.7
Student/Faculty Ratio: 20:1
Undergraduate Enrollment: 17,059
Scholarships/Academic: Yes
Expenses by: Year
Housing: Yes
Male/Female Ratio: 47:53
Graduate Enrollment: 2,304
Athletic: Yes
Financial Aid: Yes
In State: $ 13,700
Out of State: $ 23,274
Specialty: Engineering & Sciences, English & Languages, Drama, Music
Degrees Conferred: BA, BS, BFA, MA, MS, MFA, Ph.D.
Programs of Study: Anthropology, Art, Art History, BioChemistry, Biology, Chemistry, Composition, Computer Science, Criminal Justice, Dance, Dramatic Art, Ecology & Evolution, Engineering, Economics, Film, Film Studies, French, Geography, History, Literature, Mathematics, Music, Physics Philosophy, Physics, Pharmacology, Physiology, Political Science, Psychology, Religion

Men's Athletic Profile

UCSB Men's Soccer
Santa Barbara, CA 93106
Coach: Tim VomSteeg
Email: mensoccer@athletics.ucsb.edu

NCAA I
Gauchos/Blue, Gold, White
Phone: (805) 893-3473
Fax: (805) 893-7738

Estimated # of Men's Soccer Scholarships: 4.5
Conference: Big West
Program Profile: Harder Stadium has a 17,000 seating capacity with a natural turf. The team also has three practice fields.
History: Our program began in 1966. Last year the program completed the greatest turn-around in NCAA division one by winning 13 games.
Achievements: Numerous All-Conference, All-Far West, Scholar Athletes Awards, several former and current athletes play in the professional ranks. For Tim VomSteeg this will be his second season with the Gauchos. He received co-coach of the year inn MPSF 2000.
Roster In State: 22
Out of State: 1
Out of Country: 1
ODP State: 2
Regional: 2
National: 2
Walk-on/Other:
Graduation %: 95
Seniors on Team: 6
Positions Needed: Forwards, Attacking Midfielders
Camp or Clinic Dates: August 6-10
Most Recent Record: 13-7-0
Schedule: UCLA, Fullerton, UC Berkely, Kentucky, Fresno State, UNLV, San Jose State
Style of Play: Possess the ball on offense.

Women's Athletic Profile

Dept. of Intercollegiate Athletics
Santa Barbara, CA 93106
Coach: Paul Stumpf
Email: paul.stumpf@athletics.ucsb.edu

NCAA I
Gauchos/Blue, Gold
Phone: (805) 893-2715
Fax: (805) 893-8640

Estimated # of Women's Soccer Scholarships: 2.5
Conference: Big West
Program Profile: Harder Stadium is where all the games and the training task place. It is natural grass field and seats 17,000. Facility include soccer rooms under stadium.
History: Since its inception in 1983, the Gauchos have earned 7 NCAA post-season playoff berths. Five of those years advanced first round. Five Gauchos earned All-American Honors including US National I Team Member (Carin Jennings Gabarra). Gabarra held NCAA Division I record for career goals (102) and still holds record for career points.
Achievements: Big West Coach of the Year 1999. 5 All-Americans, 19 All Far West Selections, 7 NCAA D-I post-season appearances.
Coaching: Paul Stumpf is the Head Coach. Mike Friesen and Carolyn Weilman are the Assistant Coaches.
Roster in State: 26
Out of State: 2
Out of Country: 0
ODP State: 4
Regional: 0
National: 0

Walk-on/Other: **Graduation %:** **Seniors on Team:** 4
Positions Needed: Center Mid, Keeper, Center Defender, Striker
Camp or Clinic Dates: August 7-11
Most Recent Record: 9-9-1
Schedule: University of San Diego, US Naval Academy, University of Oklahoma, Fresno State, Cal Poly, University of San Francisco, Pepperdine, university of California-Irvine
Style of Play: We try to defend in groups and individually, change point of attack, get ball to forwards, and concentrate on fast speed of play.

University of California - Santa Cruz

Academic Profile

Santa Cruz, CA 95064
Phone: (831) 459-2531

Type: 4 Yr.,Public,Liberal Arts,Engineering
Website: http://www.ucsc.edu
SAT/ACT/GPA: 1000/3.4
Student/Faculty Ratio: 13:1
Undergraduate Enrollment: 10,000
Scholarships/Academic: Yes **Athletic:** No
Expenses by: Year **In State:** $ 14,598
Specialty: Natural Sciences, Engineering
Degrees Conferred: BA, BS, Masters, Doctoral
Programs of Study: Over 150 programs of study.

Founded: 1965
Religion: Non-Affiliated
Housing: Yes
Male/Female Ratio: 40:60
Graduate Enrollment: 1,000
Financial Aid: Yes
Out of State: $ 25,110

Men's Athletic Profile

1156 High Street
Santa Cruz, CA 95064
Coach: Paul Holocher
Email: holocher@cats.ucsc.edu

NCAA III
Banana Slugs/Navy Blue, Gold
Phone: (831) 459-3211
Fax: (831) 459-4070

Estimated # of Men's Soccer Scholarships: None
Conference: Independent
Program Profile: New Head Coach Paul Holocher is excited to develop a team of excellence. Fields overlook the City of Santa Cruz and the beaches of Monterey Bay. Twenty game season, training intensive and ambitious, the Banana Slugs are actively searching for dedicated, skilled, intelligent soccer player.
History: Our program began in 1986. Best record was in 1996 when the slug went 15-5.
Achievements: J. Clark was named All-American in 1989; W. Dodds was named All-American in 1988; M. Melander was named All-American in 1988; Thomas Chapin was named Division III Far West Coach of the Year in 1986.
Coaching: Paul Holocher, Head Coach, entering first year with the program. He is former professional player, having played in the MSL with San Jose Clash and in Europe. Sep Wolf, Assistant Coach, is currently playing professional in the A-League. They both are the founders of the Catalyst Soccer Club, a training club for youth players in Santa Cruz.
Style of Play: This team looks to attack and truly believes the best defense is excellent possession of the ball while still going forward with goal-scoring intent.

Women's Athletic Profile

1056 High Street
Santa Cruz, CA 95064
Coach: Paul Lester
Email: Socrslug@uscs

NCAA III
Banana Slugs/Blue, White
Phone: (408) 459-3362
Fax: (408) 459-4070

Estimated # of Women's Soccer Scholarships: None
Conference: Independent

Program Profile: Established program, excellent facilities, brand new soccer field over-looking Monterey Bay, new Olympic sized pool, season runs August - November. Looking to build the best soccer program in the nation.
History: Program began in 1989. NCAA program was a club team for the previous 10 years. Establishing a reputation as a strong Division III program in the Western Region.
Achievements:
Coaching: Paul Lester, Head Coach, third year, coached the Canada College of Redwood City women's soccer team, former assistant women's coach at Santa Clara University in 1994, and was a member of the San Jose Grizzlies' professional indoor team the same year. Shone Solis - Assistant Coach.
Style of Play: Simple, quick accurate passes with movement.

University of La Verne

Academic Profile

La Verne, CA 91750
Phone: 800-876-4858

Type: 4 Yr.,Private,Liberal Arts
Website: http://www.uv.edu
SAT/ACT/GPA: Open
Student/Faculty Ratio: 15:1
Undergraduate Enrollment: 1,100
Scholarships/Academic: Yes
Athletic: No
Expenses by: Year
In State: $ 18,100
Specialty: Business, Teacher
Degrees Conferred: BA, BS, MA, MS, MBA, EdD, JD
Founded: 1891
Religion: Non-Affiliated
Housing: Yes
Male/Female Ratio: 3:1
Graduate Enrollment: 3,000
Financial Aid: Yes
Out of State: $ 18,100
Programs of Study: Arts and Sciences, Athletic, Business Management, Communications, Computer, Economics, Engineering, Law, Physical, PreProfessional, Social Sciences, Teacher Preparation, Visual and Performing Arts

Men's Athletic Profile

1950 - 3rd Street
La Verne, CA 91750
Coach: Shayon Jalayer
Email: Not Available

NCAA III
Leopards/Forest Green, Orange
Phone: (909) 593-3511
Fax: (909) 596-9280

Estimated # of Men's Soccer Scholarships: None
Conference: SCIAC
Program Profile: We play a fall season, September through November. Home field is lighted for night games and practice; natural turf.
History: Program began in 1971. We had good teams in the mid-80's; the last 5 years the program has needed better players.
Achievements: 1987,1988 Conference - Champions; 1 All - American.
Style of Play: Ball control, short passes.

Women's Athletic Profile

1950 Third Street
La Verne, CA 91750
Coach: Wendy Zwissler
Email: Not Available

NCAA III
Leopards/Orange, Green
Phone: (909) 593-3511
Fax: (909) 596-9280

Estimated # of Women's Soccer Scholarships: None
Conference: Southern California Intercollegiate Athletic Conference
Program Profile: Natural grass fields with lights for practice and games. The Leos will place a strong emphasis on

mental preparation, national berth.
History: The program began in 1988. Full time staff hired in program's fifth year.
Achievements: 3 All-Conference 2nd team; 8 Far West All-Stars since 1994.
Coaching: Wendy Zwissler, Head Coach for six years.
Style of Play: Depends on the speed and the experience of the players.technique, teamwork, and tactics.

University of Redlands

Academic Profile

Redlands, CA 92373
Phone: (909) 793-2121

Type: 4 Yr.,Private,Liberal Arts
Founded: 1909
Website: http://www.redlands.edu
Religion: Non-Affiliated
SAT/ACT/GPA: 1100/19/3.2
Housing: Yes
Student/Faculty Ratio: 13:1
Male/Female Ratio: 56:44
Undergraduate Enrollment: 1,560
Graduate Enrollment: 500
Scholarships/Academic: Yes
Athletic: No
Financial Aid: Yes
Expenses by: Year
In State: $ 27,000
Out of State: $ 27,000
Specialty: Liberal Arts
Degrees Conferred: BS, BA
Programs of Study: Accounting, Art, History/Studio Art, Asian Studies, Biology, Business, Administration, Chemistry, Communicative Disorders, Computer Science, Creative Writing, Economics, English Literature, Environmental Studies, French, German, Government, History, International Relations, Latin American Studies, Math, Music, Philosophy, Physics, PreLaw, PreMed, Psychology, Race and Ethnic Studies, Religion, Sociology, Anthropology, Spanish, Theatre, Women's Studies, Interdisciplinary Minor

Men's Athletic Profile

1200 E. Colton Avenue
Redlands, CA 92373
Coach: Robert Becerra
Email: Ao'neil@jwper.edu.com

NCAA III
Bulldogs/Maroon, White
Phone: (909) 335-4004
Fax: (909) 335-4088

Estimated # of Men's Soccer Scholarships: None
Conference: SCIAC
Program Profile: Outstanding facility: Farquhar Field the Bulldogs play on a pitch that is 118 yards long and 78 yards wide, which allows the team emphasize possession-style soccer and physical fitness.
History: Men's program has been an intercollegiate team since 1968. The last three years we have placed no worse than third in our 8 team conference.
Achievements: Goalkeeper Eric Kenas ('00) was an All-American and played for the Riverside Elite team. Current forward Andy 0'Shay received All-American honors as a junior and leads this year's team in points with 28 (seven games to go this season)
Coaching: Rob Becerra is in his third year as head coach after working with the program for two years as the top assistant. He has made an impact on the program by creating an environment of success and hard work. He played for Cal State University San Bernardino and earned All-American honors as a goalkeeper.
Roster In State: 16
Out of State: 9
Out of Country: 0
ODP State: 6
Regional:
National:
Walk-on/Other: 19
Graduation %: 95
Seniors on Team: 2
Camp or Clinic Dates: Not Available
Most Recent Record: 10-2
Schedule: Cal Lutheran University, Claremont-Mudd-Scripps College, Pomona-Pitzer Colleges, Chapman University, Colorado College(tentative), Nebraska Wesleyan (tentative)

Women's Athletic Profile

1200 E. Coldon Ave.
Redlands, CA 92373
Coach: Suzette Soboti
Email: soboti@uor.edu

NCAA III
Bulldogs/Maroon, Grey
Phone: (909) 743-2121
Fax: (909) 335-4088

Estimated # of Women's Soccer Scholarships: None
Conference: SCIAC
Program Profile: We play on a newly built Farguhar Soccer Complex with a natural grass and seats 1,000. Our season is from August through November.
History: The women's soccer program began as a varsity sport in 1983. We play in the SCIAC Conference and have placed third in the conference in the last two years. We placed second in SCIAC last 2 years and as high as 4th in the West Region.
Achievements: We have had All-conference players in 1998 & 1999, Conference Player of the Year, 6 women were named to the All-Regional team in the past two years.
Coaching: Suzette Soboti is our Head Coach. She coached past two years with a record of 19-15-2. she came from nationally rank NJ Junior college. Deirdre Hamilton is our Assistant Coach.
Roster in State: 12
Out of State: 12
Out of Country: 0
ODP State: 13
Regional: 0
National: 0
Walk-on/Other: 0
Graduation %: 100
Seniors on Team: 2
Camp or Clinic Dates: Not Available
Most Recent Record: 9-9-0
Schedule: University Puget Sound, Willamette University, University of California-Santa Cruz, California Lutheran, Chapman, University of Laverne
Style of Play: We play possession style, which builds from the back and exploits the flanks.

University of San Diego

Academic Profile

San Diego, CA 92111
Phone: (619) 260-2306

Type: 4 Yr.,Private,
Website: http://www.acusd.edu
SAT/ACT/GPA: 1150/3.7
Student/Faculty Ratio: 15:1
Undergraduate Enrollment: 4,000
Scholarships/Academic: No
Athletic: No
Expenses by: Year
In State: $ 26,205
Founded: 1949
Religion: Roman Catholic
Housing: Yes
Male/Female Ratio: 45:55
Graduate Enrollment: 2,500
Financial Aid: Yes
Out of State: $ 26,205
Degrees Conferred: BA, BS, MA, MS, MFA, MEd, EdD, JD
Programs of Study: Accounting, Art, Biology, Business Administration, Chemistry, Communications, Computer Science, Diversified Liberal Arts, Broadcasting, Chemical Engineering, Economics, Electrical Engineering, English, Exercise & Sports Science, Geology, Health Education, Hispanic/Latin Studies, History, Humanities, Journalism, Mathematics, Music, Nursing, Ocean Studies, Pharmacy, Political Science, Psychology, Religious Studies, Sociology, Zoology

Men's Athletic Profile

5998 Alcala Park
San Diego, CA 92110
Coach: Séamus McFadden
Email: Not Available

NCAA I
Toreros/Col Blue, Navy, White
Phone: (619) 260-2305
Fax: (619) 292-0388

Estimated # of Men's Soccer Scholarships: None
Conference: West Coast Conference
Program Profile: We have two training fields and stadium for match play, with natural surface.
History: Program began in 1980.
Achievements: NCAA Championship appearance - 1992; 5 overall NCAA appearances 1990, 1992 - 1995.
Style of Play: Varies from year to year.

Women's Athletic Profile

5998 Alcala Park
San Diego, CA 92111
Coach: John Cossaboon
Email: Not Available

NCAA I
Lady Toreros/Navy, White
Phone: (619) 260-2306
Fax: (619) 260-5946

Estimated # of Women's Soccer Scholarships: 10
Conference: West Coast Conference
Program Profile: We have a great stadium that contains a 115 x 70 yards grass field. There is a separate grass training field next to the dorms. We have two weight facilities. We are very close to the most beautiful beaches in the world.
History: Our first year as a team was 1992. Here are our stats:1993 (8-8), (3-3 WCC); 1994 (8-11), (3-4 WCC); 1995 (10-6-1), (5-2 wcc); 1996 (14-6-1-), (5-2-1 wcc); Final 16, NCAA; 1997 (7-12-1) (4-3 wcc); 1998 (12-6-2-) (4-2-1 wcc); 1999 (16-5), (5-2 wcc) NCAA Div I playoffs, 2nd round.
Coaching: John Cossaboon - Head Coach. Ada Greenwood and Tommy Tait are Assistant Coaches.

Roster in State: 14	**Out of State:** 8	**Out of Country:**
ODP State: 7	**Regional:** 3	**National:**
Walk-on/Other:	**Graduation %:**	**Seniors on Team:** 6

Positions Needed: Center, Midfielder, Goalkeeper, Wide Back, Striker
Camp or Clinic Dates: June 25-29
Most Recent Record: 16-5
Schedule: Santa Clara, Portland, Brigham Young, University of California- Los Angeles, San Diego State University, Oregon, U.S. Air Force, Utah, Loyola Marymount University, UCLA, UNC Chapel Hill, CAL
Style of Play: Combination of building and directing; skill is a must; organized; a blend of individual attributes; fitness is a must; individuals must be decision makers; speed does not hurt!

University of San Francisco

Academic Profile

San Francisco, CA 94117-1080

Phone: (415) 422-6563

Type: 4 Yr.,Private,Liberal Arts		**Founded:** 1855
Website: http://www.usfca.edu		**Religion:** Catholic (Jesuit)
SAT/ACT/GPA: Yes		**Housing:** Yes
Student/Faculty Ratio: 18-25:1		**Male/Female Ratio:** 40:60
Undergraduate Enrollment: 5,000		**Graduate Enrollment:** 2,000
Scholarships/Academic: Yes	**Athletic:** Yes	**Financial Aid:** Yes
Expenses by: Year	**In State:** $ 26,348	**Out of State:** $ 26,348

Specialty: Business, International Business, Broadcasting, Nursing, Biology
Degrees Conferred: BS, MS, Ph.D.
Programs of Study: Biology, Business, Chemistry, Communications, Computer Economics, Environmental Science, English, History, Law , (MBA), Nursing, PrePhysical Therapy, Psychology, Sports Science, Exercise Sports Science, Communications

Men's Athletic Profile

2130 Fulton Street
San Francisco, CA 94117-1080
Coach: Eric Visser
Email: visser@usfca.edu

NCAA I
Dons/Green, Gold
Phone: (415) 422-2907
Fax: (415) 422-2510

Estimated # of Men's Soccer Scholarships: 9.9
Conference: West Coast Conference
Program Profile: We have 74x114 yards natural grass field with a seating capacity of 3,500. Has a flat - press box, and year-round use. Rich winning tradition NCAA I National 66, 75, 76,78, 80
History: Our program started in 1931. We have 10 straight Pacific Coast Titles 1948-58. We have 5 National NCAA Championships: 66-75,76-78-80. We have 25 Appearances in NCAA playoffs.
Achievements: 5 NCAA Championships, 33 West Coast Titles, 25 NCAA Playoffs. 1st team All-American in 1950, former National and Junior Championship in 1961, Amateur, Dewar Cup in 1975. Have a record of 44-20-4. Qualified for Final Four 9 times and 42 consecutive winning seasons.
Coaching: Eric Visser 1st year Head Coach, he was also head regional Olympic development Coach 95-97. Assistant Coach for men's national team under 20.
Roster In State: 7
Out of State: 10
Out of Country: 5
ODP State: 1
Regional: 0
National: 0
Walk-on/Other: 7
Graduation %: 95
Seniors on Team: 4
Positions Needed: Defenders
Camp or Clinic Dates: July 26-29, June 15-19, July 30-Aug 3
Most Recent Record: 8-10-2
Schedule: Xavier, Stanford, UCLA, Fresno, Portland, San Diego, San Jose State, Loyola
Style of Play: Creative, attacking with many combination and short passing.

Women's Athletic Profile

2130 Fulton St.
San Francisco, CA 94117-1080
Coach: Jean Paul Verhees
Email: childs@usfca.edu

NCAA I
Lady Dons/Green, Gold
Phone: (415) 422-2269
Fax: (415) 422-2856

Estimated # of Women's Soccer Scholarships: None
Conference: West Coast Conference
Program Profile: Natural grass soccer stadium that seats 4,500, European Style Media Boot. Facilities includes computerized scoreboard, lighted for night games, good fan support, excellent soccer climate, and full year training program. Play in Negoesco Stadium that seats 3,000. Playing season is in the mid-August to mid-November. The program continues to growth through the support of the University and the Athletic Department.
History: Established in 1983. Eleventh year, five winning season, very tough schedule, had a pre-season games in Japan in the summer of 1996. In 1991, Jean Paul Verhees took over the program as the head women's coach. Since 1992 throughout the 1996 season, Coach Verhees has had winning record.
Achievements: Jean Paul Verhees was named Western Region Coach of the Year in 1988; lead California Berkeley to third place in the NCAA finish; Director of Total Soccer Academy for Western Region.
Coaching: Jean Paul Verhees, Head Coach, USSF License, Regional Coach of the Year in 1987 & 1988 (West); two final appearances, finishing third with California Berkeley for eight years; three year All-American at Westmont College; four year professional NASL & ASL. Tina Childs - Assistant Coach, Washington State Masters in Sports Marketing. USSF "C" Licensed Coach, entering second season at USF.
Style of Play: Possession, being able to shift the field indirectly style of play. Technical athletes must be strong, accompanied with speed of thought, and must have a fury in the eyes to play tournament.

University of the Pacific

Academic Profile

Phone: (209) 926-2497

Stockton, CA 95211

Founded: 1851
Religion: Non-Affiliated
Housing: Yes
Male/Female Ratio: 43:57
Graduate Enrollment: 562
Financial Aid: Yes
Out of State: $ 25,485

Type: 4 Yr.,Private,Liberal Arts
Website: http://www.pacifictigers.com
SAT/ACT/GPA: No minimum
Student/Faculty Ratio: 13:6
Undergraduate Enrollment: 2,805
Scholarships/Academic: Yes **Athletic:** Yes
Expenses by: Year **In State:** $ 25,485
Specialty: Art & Sciences, Business, Education, Engineering, Nursing
Degrees Conferred: BA, BS, BFA, MA, MS, Ph.D., PharmD
Programs of Study: Accounting, Advertising, Athletic Training, Behavioral, Biology, Broadcasting, Business, Computer, Criminal, Engineering, Environmental Sciences, Finance, Geology, Linguistics, Ministries, Natural Science, Pharmacy, Spanish

Women's Athletic Profile

3601 Pacific Ave.
Stockton, CA 95211
Coach: Keith Coleman
Email: kcoleman@uop.edu

NCAA I
Tigers/Black, Orange
Phone: (209) 946-2129
Fax: (209) 946-2731

Estimated # of Women's Soccer Scholarships:
Conference: Big West Conference
Program Profile: Field is called Amos Alonzo Stagg Memorial Stadium, natural grass with 30,000 seating capacity. Playing season starts from August through November-December. Athletic training facilities, weight room, locker-rooms and academic center.
History: Pacific Soccer became varsity sports in 1994. Keith Coleman is in his seventh season with the Tigers. In 1998 Pacific went undefeated in Big West Conference play. Pacific defeated Cal 2-1 in the first round of the NCAA tournament in 1998, before falling to Santa Clara in second round; 1998 Big West Champions.
Achievements: Keith Coleman was named 1997 and 1998 Big West Coach of the Year, Natalie Dorr was named Big West Player of the Year. First Big West team to post an unbeaten conference record in 1998. Big West Champions in 1998.
Coaching: Keith Coleman, Head Coach, graduated from Cal Poly in 1991. He is entering seventh season . He was named Big West Coach of the Year. Michele Coleman, Assistant Coach, graduated from Chico State in 1991. She is entering seventh season with the program. Yvette Valdez, graduated from Pacific in 1997. She is entering fourth season with the program. She played as a goalkeeper for the Mexican National Women's Soccer Team.
Roster in State: 16 **Out of State:** 5 **Out of Country:** 1
ODP State: 13 **Regional:** 4 **National:** 0
Walk-on/Other: **Graduation %:** 100 **Seniors on Team:** 4
Positions Needed: ALL
Camp or Clinic Dates: June 18-22, July 9-13
Most Recent Record: 8-8-2
Schedule: Loyola Marymount Univ, Cal-Berkley, St. Mary's, Cal-Poly
Style of Play: Pacific plays a total team oriented attacking style. Emphasizing ball possession and ball controlled passing. Our goal is to play the highest quality of attacking soccer possible, where speed of play and ball possession are our top priorities.

Vanguard University of Southern Calif.(Southern California Coll.)

Academic Profile

Costa Mesa, CA 92626

Phone: (714) 556-3610

Type: 4 Yr.,Private,Liberal Arts
Website: http://www.vanguard.edu
SAT/ACT/GPA: 740+/18+/2.8
Student/Faculty Ratio: 16:1
Undergraduate Enrollment: 1,181
Scholarships/Academic: Yes
Expenses by: Year

Athletic: Yes
In State: $ 14,500

Founded: 1920
Religion: Assembly of God
Housing: Yes
Male/Female Ratio: 2:3
Graduate Enrollment: 134
Financial Aid: Yes
Out of State: $ 14,500

Specialty: Liberal Arts
Degrees Conferred: BA, MA, MS, MTS
Programs of Study: Accounting, Biology, Anthropology, Broadcasting, Chemistry, Communications, Education, English, Finance, Humanities, Journalism, Management, Marketing, Mathematics, Physical Education, PreLaw, PreMed, Social Science, Sociology, Theater

Men's Athletic Profile

55 Fair Drive
Costa Mesa, CA 92626
Coach: David McLeish
Email: DMcLeish@net999.com

NAIA
Lions/Navy, Gold
Phone: (714) 556-3610x218
Fax: (714) 668-6144

Estimated # of Men's Soccer Scholarships: 6.5 Tuition
Conference: Golden State Athletic Conference
Program Profile: We are a small Christian school with a natural grass field and a bleachers. We have a strong soccer tradition with a 3-2-2 against Division I school in the last four years.
History: Our program is in twenty-one years of existence; top three in the conference in the past ten years. 6 wins and 3 losses against strong Division I and Division II team in the past two years. Great community support.
Achievements: GSAC Runner-Up three times; 7 playoff bids in the past nine years.
Coaching: David McLeish, Head Coach, holds a USSF "A" License. He has 21 years high school experience and 20 years college experience. Cleon Jones and Miguel Lamotte are Assistant Coaches.
Style of Play: We are intelligent, skillful and fit.

Women's Athletic Profile

55 Fair Drive
Costa Mesa, CA 92626
Coach: Kerry Crooks
Email: Not Available

NAIA
Vanguards/Blue, Gold
Phone: (714) 556-3610
Fax: (714) 668-6144

Estimated # of Women's Soccer Scholarships: None
Conference: Golden State Athletic Conference
Program Profile: SCC is a four-year school and competes as a member of the Golden State Athletic Conference in the NAIA. We have a lighted home field that seats about 1,500. We offer competitive scholarships to qualified student-athletes. We at night on the lighted field and get excellent fan support for our growing program.
History: The 1994-1995 season was the second year as a varsity program. The Vanguards won six more games in the second year than in the first. Made first trip to the playoffs. We coming off consecutive winning seasons.
Achievements: Jamie Gardiner (F) named 1993-1994 Honorable Mention All-American scoring 17 goals in each of the first two seasons. 1995 Coach of the Year.
Style of Play: We emphasize starting with the defense first and playing tactically together which keeps many players around the ball. This allows us to counter attack quickly or build the ball up slowly and let our forwards create space up front.

Ventura College (Community)

Academic Profile

Phone: 661-763-7741

Ventura, CA 93003

Type: 2 Yr.
Website: http://www.vcccd.cc.ca.us
SAT/ACT/GPA: Open
Student/Faculty Ratio: 22:1
Undergraduate Enrollment: 11,381
Scholarships/Academic:
Athletic:
Expenses by:
In State:
Specialty:
Degrees Conferred:
Programs of Study: Contact school for programs of study.

Founded: 1925
Religion: Non-Affiliated
Housing: No
Male/Female Ratio: N/A
Graduate Enrollment: N/A
Financial Aid:
Out of State:

Women's Athletic Profile

4667 Telegraph
Ventura, CA 93003
Coach: Steve Hoffman
Email: stevehoffman@aol.com

NJCAA
Lady Pirates/Orange, Blue
Phone: (805) 654-6400
Fax: (805) 654-6328

Estimated # of Women's Soccer Scholarships: None
Conference: Western States Conference
Program Profile: We play in a grass field.
History: In 1996, our record was 41-3-5. In 1996, we were Western States Champions. In 1997, we were Western State Champions again
Achievements: 2 conference titles; 1 Coach of the Year ; 1 All-American
Coaching: Steve Hoffman, Head Coach.

Westmont College

Academic Profile

Phone: (805) 565-6221

Santa Barbara, CA 93108

Type: 4 Yr.,Private,Liberal Arts
Website: http://www.westmont.edu
SAT/ACT/GPA: 1200/3.0
Student/Faculty Ratio: 15:1
Undergraduate Enrollment: Yes
Scholarships/Academic: Yes
Athletic: Yes
Expenses by: Year
In State: $ 25,000
Specialty: Liberal Arts
Degrees Conferred: BS, BA
Programs of Study: Art, Biology, Business, Chemistry, Communications, Computer Science, Economics, Education, Engineering, English, French, History, Kinesiology, Mathematics, Music, Natural Sciences, Philosophy, Physics, Political Science, Psychology, Religious Studies, Social Science, Sociology, Spanish, Theatre Arts

Founded: 1937
Religion: Non-Denominational
Housing: Yes
Male/Female Ratio: 40:60
Graduate Enrollment: N/A
Financial Aid: Yes
Out of State: $ 25,000

Men's Athletic Profile

955 La Paz Rd
Santa Barbara, CA 93108
Coach: Dave Wolf
Email: wolf@westmont.edu

NAIA
Warriors/Maroon, White
Phone: (805) 565-6106
Fax: (805) 565-6221

Estimated # of Men's Soccer Scholarships: None
Conference: Golden State Athletic Conference
Program Profile: The Warrior's home field is a natural grass, and has a seating capacity of 2,000. We play a regular Fall season which is September 1 through December 1. Average year-round climate is 75 degree.
History: Our program began 32 years ago. The overall record is 415-175-60. 17 District Titles, 7 Area Titles, 2 Regional Titles and 13 National Tournament Appearances.
Achievements: Last year (1996) Far West Regional Champions in third consecutive time; Advanced to the National Tournament, and GSAC/Far West Player of the Year - Todd Emblem. Golden State Athletic Conference Champions nine of the last 11 years. Numerous All-American and Coach of the Year Awards.
Coaching: Dave Wolf, Head Coach, six years professional player. Randy Strawser - Assistant Coach. Ryan Sparve - Assistant Coach, All-Far West Goalkeeper at UCSB.
Style of Play: Possession.

Women's Athletic Profile

955 La Paz Road
Santa Barbara, CA 93108
Coach: Dr. Michael Giuliano
Email: giuliano@westmont.edu

NAIA
Warriors/Maroon, White
Phone: (805) 565-6134
Fax: (805) 565-6110

Estimated # of Women's Soccer Scholarships: 5
Conference: Golden State Athletic Conference
Program Profile: The players arrive in mid-August for a two-week early camp and the season ends with the NAIA National Tournament in late November. Home games are played on Carr Field on a grass surface, Practice is held on one of two auxiliary fields. We have one of the best fan following in NAIA which is about 500 per game. The team size is usually around 22 players.
History: Our program began in 1981. We were the National Champions in 1985 and 1999, Conference Champions 1999, 1997, 1995,1994, 1993.
Achievements: 21 All-Americans; 1999 Coach of the Year; 4 players were signed to 1999/2000 W-League contracts
Coaching: Dr. Michael Giuliano, Head Coach. He has a Ph.D. in Communications, an NSCAA Advanced National Diploma and twelve years as college head coach. His Westmont record is 110-33-8(eight years). Diane Strawser is assistant coach. She is in her 5th year here. And Jeff Ino is the Goalkeeper Coach.
Roster in State: 14
Out of State: 10
Out of Country:
ODP State: 10
Regional: 2
National:
Walk-on/Other:
Graduation %: 100
Seniors on Team: 6
Positions Needed: All
Camp or Clinic Dates: Not Available
Most Recent Record: 22-2-0
Schedule: Franklin Pierce, University Cal Santa Barbara, Trinity University, Azusa Pacific, Sonoma State, University of New Haven
Style of Play: We try to be the most deliberate, high pressure defensive team possible. Offensively, we determine style of play based on our personnel, to maximize their strength.

Whittier College

Academic Profile

Whittier, CA 90608

Phone:

Type: 4 Yr.,Private,Liberal Arts
Website: http://www.whittier.edu
SAT/ACT/GPA: 1100/21/3.0
Student/Faculty Ratio: 13:1
Undergraduate Enrollment: 1,300

Founded: 1887
Religion: Non-Affiliated
Housing: Yes
Male/Female Ratio: 50:50
Graduate Enrollment: 100

Scholarships/Academic: Yes **Athletic:** No **Financial Aid:** Yes
Expenses by: Year **In State:** $ 26,096 **Out of State:**
Specialty: Liberal Arts
Degrees Conferred: BA, BS, MA, MS, JD
Programs of Study: Anthropology, Art, Athletic Training, Biochemistry, Biology, Business & Management, Chemistry, Economics, Education, English, Fine Arts, French, Geology, History, International Studies, Liberal Arts, Literature, Mathematics, Modern Languages, Music, Philosophy, Physical Education, Physical Science, Physics, Political Science, PreDentistry, PreLaw, PreMed, PreVet, Psychology, Religion, Social Science, Spanish, Speech Pathology, Theatre

Men's Athletic Profile

13406 E Philadelphia St.
Whittier, CA 90601
Coach: Jim Cross
Email: klloyd@whittier.edu

NCAA III
Poets/Purple, Gold, White
Phone: 562-907-4872
Fax: 562-945-8024

Estimated # of Men's Soccer Scholarships: None
Conference: SCIAC
Program Profile: Our games are played on grass field under the lights.
Achievements: 2000- 2 All-Conference Selections.
Coaching: Jim Cross is the Head Coach.
Roster In State: 9 **Out of State:** 7 **Out of Country:** 6
Walk-on/Other: **Graduation %:** N/A **Seniors on Team:** 4
Positions Needed: Strikers
Camp or Clinic Dates: July 30- August 3
Most Recent Record: 3-17-0
Style of Play: Control play through the mid-field.

Women's Athletic Profile

13406 Philadelphia St.
Whittier, CA 90608
Coach: Kwame T. Lloyd
Email: klloyd@whittier.edu

NCAA III
Poets/Purple, Gold
Phone: (562) 907-4872
Fax: (562) 907-8024

Estimated # of Women's Soccer Scholarships: None
Conference: SCIAC
Program Profile: Home field is natural surface and lighted.
History: Program began in 1985.
Achievements: 2000- 4 All-Confernce Selections.
Coaching: Kwame T. Lloyd, Head Coach. Skelly Miller- Assistant Coach.
Roster in State: 8 **Out of State:** 9 **Out of Country:**
Walk-on/Other: **Graduation %:** N/A **Seniors on Team:** 3
Positions Needed: All
Camp or Clinic Dates: July 30- August 3
Most Recent Record: 2-17-0
Style of Play: Attacking!!!!

colorado

COLORADO

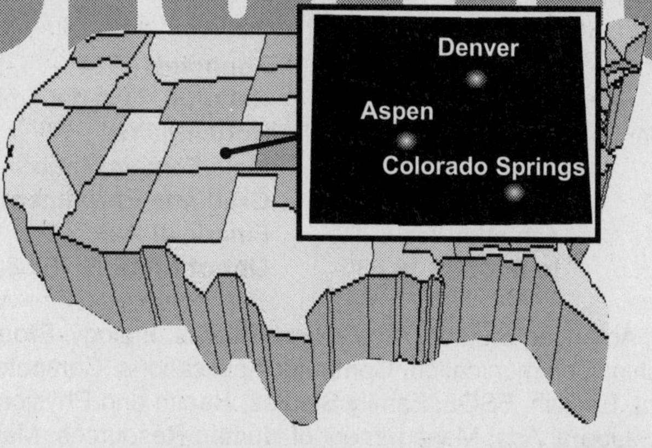

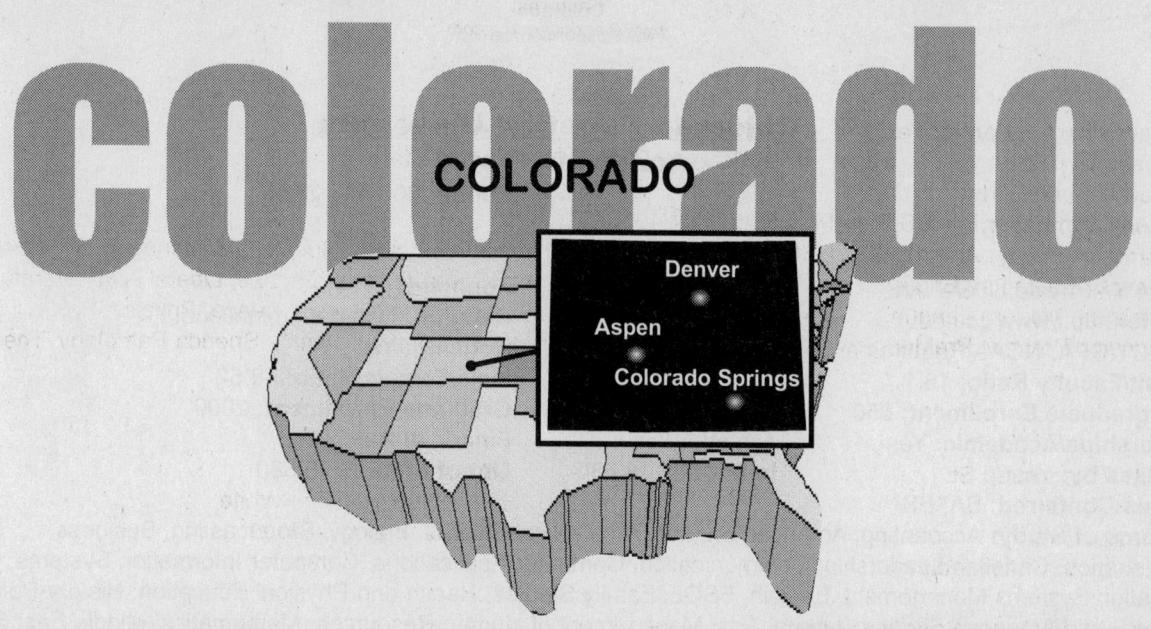

SCHOOL	CITY	AFFILIATION	PAGE
Colorado Christian University	Lakewood	NCAA II	148
Colorado College	Colorado Springs	NCAA III	148
Colorado School of Mines	Golden	NCAA II	150
Fort Lewis College	Durango	NCAA II	151
Mesa State College	Grand Junction	NCAA II	152
Metropolitan State College	Denver	NCAA II	153
Regis University	Denver	NCAA II	154
United States Air Force Academy	USAF Academy	NCAA I	156
University of Colorado - Boulder	Boulder	NCAA I	157
University of CO-Colorado Springs	Colorado Springs	NCAA II	158
University of Denver	Denver	NCAA I	159
University of Northern Colorado	Greeley	NCAA II	160
University of Southern Colorado	Pueblo	NCAA II	161

Colorado Christian University

Academic Profile

Phone: 800-443-2484

Lakewood, CO 80226

Type: 4 Yr.,Private,Liberal Arts
Website: http://www.ccu.edu
SAT/ACT/GPA: NCAA Requirements
Student/Faculty Ratio: 16:1
Undergraduate Enrollment: 850
Scholarships/Academic: Yes
Athletic: Yes
Expenses by: Year
In State: $ 15,680
Degrees Conferred: BA, BS

Founded: 1914
Religion: Non-denominational
Housing: Yes
Male/Female Ratio: 48:52
Graduate Enrollment: 2000
Financial Aid: Yes
Out of State: $ 15,680

Programs of Study: Accounting, American Studies, Art, Biblical Studies, Biology, Broadcasting, Business Administration, Christian Leadership, Communication, Computer Applications, Computer Information Systems, Computer Information Systems Management, English, ESOL, Family Studies, Health and Physical Education, History-Political Science, Latin American Studies, Liberal Arts, Management of Human Resources, Mathematics, Middle East Studies, Missions, Music, Organizational Management, Professional Counseling Certificate, Psychology, Russian Studies, Science, Youth Ministries

Men's Athletic Profile

180 S. Garrison St.
Lakewood, CO 80226
Coach: Gary E. Evans
Email: gevans@ccu.edu

NCAA II
Cougar, Blue & Gold
Phone: 303-963-3186
Fax: 303-963-3181

Estimated # of Men's Soccer Scholarships: 5.5
Conference: Rocky Mountain Athletic Conference
Program Profile: We have a competitive men and women's Division II program. We play in the largest conference at the Division II level. Both men and women are in conference and post-season play from August to November.
History: Our program began in 1989. We have a 62-142-14 record.
Achievements: Niall Murton - 1st Team All-Region 1996. Chris McClellan- GK 1st Team All-Conference, Brad Palik Second Team All-Conference, Gary M. Evans, Gabe Wilson and Eria Baliruno Def. RMAC Honorable Mention.
Coaching: Gary Evans, Head Coach, is an ex-professional with Liverpool FC England, the Edmonton Black Gold and the Cleveland Force. He is s a regional ODP coach and assistant director of coaching for Colorado Rush Soccer Club. Assistant Coach Brian Todd graduated from Denver University in 1999 All-Conference First Team member 2 years. Also played internationally with Athletes in Action.
Roster In State: 9
Out of State: 9
Out of Country: 3
ODP State: 2
Regional: 1
National: 1
Walk-on/Other:
Graduation %: 90
Seniors on Team: 2
Positions Needed: Striker, Sweeper, Outside MF, Fullbacks
Camp or Clinic Dates: June through July
Most Recent Record: 7-10-3
Schedule: Univ. of Denver, West Texas A&M Univ. Metro State College, Colorado School of Mines, Fort Lewis College.
Style of Play: Offensive minded possession from the back.

Women's Athletic Profile

180 S Garrison Street
Morrison, CO 80226
Coach: Gary Evans
Email: gevans@ccu.edu

NCAA II
Cougars/Blue/Gold
Phone: (303) 963-3186
Fax: (303) 963-3181

Estimated # of Women's Soccer Scholarships: 5.5
Conference: Rocky Mountain Athletic Conference
Program Profile: Competitive Division II program. We play in the largest conference at the D II level. We are in conference post-season play from August to November. Our spring season is from February to March. We play on a great flat natural surface. We can accommodate up to 500 people.
History: The program began in 1989. Our overall record is 65-95-13.
Achievements: Erin Brunelle was first team Regional All-American, First Team All-RMAC in 2000,1999, and 1998. Miranda Wagler was All-RMAC Second team in 2000 and 1999. Natalie Tafoya was All-RMAC Second Team in 1999.
Coaching: Gary Evans, Head Coach, is an ex-professional with Liverpool F.C.England. He played for Edmonton Black Gold and Cleveland Force. He is an "A" licensed coach, a regional ODP coach and an assistant director of coaching for the Colorado Rush Soccer Club.

Roster in State: 5	**Out of State:** 10	**Out of Country:**
ODP State: 4	**Regional:** 1	**National:**
Walk-on/Other: 3	**Graduation %:** 90	**Seniors on Team:** 1

Positions Needed: Strikers, Outside Midfielders, Central Defenders
Camp or Clinic Dates: June through July
Most Recent Record: 10-7-2
Schedule: Regis Univeristy, CW Post Long Island, Mesa State University, Metro State College, Midwestern State University, West Texas A&M University, University of Northern Colorado, University of Southern Colorado, National American University, Fort Lewis University.
Style of Play: Low pressure, possession, with quick attacking from the back.

Colorado College

Academic Profile

Colorado Springs, CO 80903
Phone: (719) 389-6000

Type: 4 Yr.,Private,Liberal Arts,		**Founded:** 1874
Website: http://www.cc.colorado.edu		**Religion:** Non-Affiliated
SAT/ACT/GPA: 1200-1350/25-30		**Housing:** Yes
Student/Faculty Ratio: 11:1		**Male/Female Ratio:** 42:58
Undergraduate Enrollment: 1,900		**Graduate Enrollment:** N/A
Scholarships/Academic: Yes	**Athletic:** Yes	**Financial Aid:** Yes
Expenses by: Year	**In State:** $ 27,390	**Out of State:** $ 27,390

Specialty: Sciences, Education
Degrees Conferred: BA, MAT
Programs of Study: Liberal Arts and Sciences

Men's Athletic Profile

14 E Cache La Poudre
Colorado Springs, CO 80903
Coach: Hst Richardson
Email: Not Available

NCAA III
Tigers/Black, Gold
Phone: (719) 389-6475
Fax: (719) 389-6873

Estimated # of Men's Soccer Scholarships: None
Conference: Rocky Mountain Intercollegiate Soccer League
Program Profile: We have a fall season; natural grass field at base of 14,14,110' Pikes Peak.
History: Operated as club program from 1950 to 1962, when it became a varsity program. Has competed in NCAA playoffs 10 times including a trip to the Division III semifinals in 1992, occasionally plays Division I teams (like Air Force Academy and University of New Mexico).
Achievements: Richardson has earned Regional Coach of the Year honors 4 times; team has won 6 league titles; 4 Division III All-Americans since 1986 including 1 two time selection; 3 players in last three years have signed professional contracts.

Coaching: Horst Richardson, Head Coach, enters his 35th season, has bachelor's and master's degrees from California - Riverside, as well as a Ph.D. (1975) from University of Connecticut, has serve on the District school board in Colorado Springs and owns a USSF 'A' coaching license.
Roster In State: 9 **Out of State:** 14 **Out of Country:** 2
Walk-on/Other: **Graduation %:** N/A **Seniors on Team:** 6
Positions Needed: All
Camp or Clinic Dates: Not Available
Most Recent Record: 9-9-0
Schedule: Coe, Whitman, George Fox, Linfield, Haverford, UC Santa Cruz
Style of Play: Attack oriented, shot passing, out of the back type play.

Women's Athletic Profile

14 E Cache La Poudre St.
Colorado Springs, CO 80903
Coach: Greg Ryan
Email: gryan@coloradocollege.edu

NCAA I
Tigers/Black, Gold
Phone: (719) 389-6492
Fax: (719) 389-6873

Estimated # of Women's Soccer Scholarships: 12
Conference: Independent
Program Profile: Play on Stewart Field which is natural grass and seating capacity is unknown. Facilities include weight room and locker room with tape viewing area.
History: Women's soccer at Colorado began in 1975 as a club team. Our program became varsity in 1978. In tournament every year from 1983-1991 and reached semi-finals in 1985, 1990 & 1991. Competed in championships match in 1986 & 1989.
Achievements: Has 14 All-Americans, 7 ISAA Adidas Scholar Athletes, 2000 Independent Coach of the Year.
Coaching: Greg Ryan, Head Coach, was named head coach the summer of 1999. He compiled 145-43-12 record as a collegiate head coach (108-32-7 in eight seasons at Wisconsin and 37-21-5 in three seasons at SMU). Ranked #8 all-time among active coaches in division I women's soccer. Led University of Wisconsin to 5 NCAA bids in his eight years there. He led SMU to Sweet 16 in 1997. Stephanie Porter, Assistant Coach.
Roster in State: 5 **Out of State:** 18 **Out of Country:** 0
ODP State: 15 **Regional:** 0 **National:** 0
Walk-on/Other: 0 **Graduation %:** 100 **Seniors on Team:** 5
Positions Needed: Finished Recruiting for 2001
Camp or Clinic Dates: June 3-7, June 10-14
Most Recent Record: 13-7-0
Schedule: Santa Clara, William & Mary, Harvard, Baylor, Montana, SMU
Style of Play: Possession style 4-4-2.

Colorado School of Mines

Academic Profile

Golden, CO 80401

Phone: 303-273-3220

Type: 4 Yr.,Public,Engineering
Website: http://www.gn.mines.colorado.edu
SAT/ACT/GPA: 1100/3.3
Student/Faculty Ratio: 25:1
Undergraduate Enrollment: 2,200
Scholarships/Academic: Yes **Athletic:** Yes
Expenses by: Year **In State:** $ 10,000

Founded: 1870
Religion: Non-Affiliated
Housing: Yes
Male/Female Ratio: 70:30
Graduate Enrollment: 800
Financial Aid: Yes
Out of State: $ 20,000

Specialty: Engineering, Math, Science, Computers
Degrees Conferred: BS, MS, MEng, Ph.D.
Programs of Study: Engineering (Chemical, Geological, Geophysical, Metallurgical/Materials, Mining, Petroleum), Chemistry, Economics, Mathematics, Physics

Men's Athletic Profile

1500 Illinois Street/Volk Gym
Golden, CO 80401
Coach: Frank Kohnelstein
Email: fkohleus@mines.edu

NCAA II
Orediggers/Navy, Silver, White
Phone: (303) 273-3369
Fax: (303) 273-3362

Estimated # of Men's Soccer Scholarships:
Conference: Rockie Mountain Conference
Program Profile: Our program is a year-round as far as school year with emphasis on developing players to their fullest. Team plays in natural grass stadium.
History: The program goes back to conference championships in the 1950's and includes 4 conference titles in the 1990's. A total of 11 conference titles.
Achievements: Frank has won two National Coach of the Year and three Regional along with 9 Conference Coach of the Year. Produced 22 all-Americans; 5 National Teams; Rhode Scholars and 14 drafted players.
Coaching: Frank Kohlenstein, Head Coach; was named twice National Coach of the Year and Regional Coach of the Year along with 9 Conference Coach of the Year. Kevin Frakes, Assistant Coach, former college and pro player. Rick Duessel, Assistant Coach, former high school and club coach. John Barone, Assistant coach, CSM assistant for five years.
Style of Play: The team plays an attractive attacking style of play. Trying to exploit the weakness of the opponents and take advantage of their own strengths.

Fort Lewis College

Academic Profile

Durango, CO 81301

Phone: (970) 247-7571

Type: 4 Yr.,Public,Liberal Arts
Website: http://www.fortlewis.edu
SAT/ACT/GPA: Sliding Scale
Student/Faculty Ratio: 23:1
Undergraduate Enrollment: 4,314
Scholarships/Academic: Yes **Athletic:** Yes
Expenses by: Year **In State:** $ 5,322
Specialty: Business School
Degrees Conferred: BA, BS

Founded: 1892
Religion: Non-Affiliated
Housing: Yes
Male/Female Ratio: 51:49
Graduate Enrollment: N/A
Financial Aid: Yes
Out of State: $ 11,744

Programs of Study: Agriculture, Anthropology, Art, Biology, Chemistry, Communications, Community Services, Computer Science Information Systems, Engineering, English, Forestry, French, General Sciences, Geography, Geology, German, Health, History, Humanities, International Studies, Japanese, Latin, Mathematics & Statistics, Music, Philosophy, Exercise Science, Physics, Physical Science, Political Science, Sociology, Southwest Studies, Spanish, Theatre, Women's Studies, Writing, Accounting, Agricultural Business, Business Administration, Economics, Engineering Management,Operation Management, Tourism & Resort Management, Teacher Education, Psychology

Men's Athletic Profile

1000 Rim Dr.
Durango, CO 81301
Coach: Jeremy Gunn
Email: gunn_j@fortlewis.edu

NCAA II
Skyhawks/Navy, Gold
Phone: (970) 247-7461
Fax: (970) 247-7655

Estimated # of Men's Soccer Scholarships: 6
Conference: Rocky Mountain Athletic Conference

Program Profile: We are a perennial Top 20 Division II program and conference champions Fort Lewis competes in the Rocky Mountain Athletic Conference. It plays at the FLC Soccer Field, which is a two-year old facility that holds nearly 1,000 fans for key contests. The FLC Soccer Field is a natural grass facility.
History: Fort Lewis fielded its first varsity soccer team in 1991. In its first eight seasons, the Skyhawks have posted a 78-60-8 record (.562) and won four league championships. The Skyhawks won Colorado Athletic Conference titles in 1993 & 1995, and Rocky Mountain Athletic Conference titles in 1997 & 1998. The team has cracked the NCAA II Top 20 six straight years and qualified for the NCAA playoffs the last two.
Achievements: Conference Champions in 1993, 1995, 1997 & 1998; All-Americans were Calum Robertson 1st team in 1997, Rich Hansen 1st team in 1998, Luc Cisna 2nd team in 1998; Academic All-American was Luc Cisna 1st team in 1998; League Player of the Year was Dio Cifuni in 1998; League Coach of the Year was Jeremy Fishbein in 1993, 1997 & 1998; Drafted players were Ruch Hansen by Milwaukee (indoor) and New Orleans (A-League) in 1999.
Coaching: Jeremy Gunn, Head Coach, was formerly assistant coach for men's and women's team at California State-Bakersfield. He helped their men to 1997 NCAA II National Champions. Chris Sletten is the Assistant Coach.

Roster In State: 15
Out of State: 7
Out of Country: 1
ODP State: 4
Regional: 1
National:
Walk-on/Other:
Graduation %: 90
Seniors on Team: 5
Positions Needed: Defenders/other
Camp or Clinic Dates: Last 3 weeks of July
Most Recent Record: 18-3-3
Schedule: CSU Bakersfield, University of New Mexico, West Texas, University of Southern Colorado, U.C. Colorado Springs
Style of Play: Fort Lewis features an attacking style with an emphasis on enjoyable, exciting and entertaining soccer.

Women's Athletic Profile

1000 Rim Drive
Durango, CO 81301-3999
Coach: Jaymee Stone
Email: stone_j@fortlewis.edu

NCAA II
Skyhawks/Navy, Gold
Phone: (970) 247-7640
Fax: (970) 247-7484

Estimated # of Women's Soccer Scholarships:
Conference: Rocky Mountain Athletic Conference
Program Profile: Fort Lewis competes in the Rocky Mountain Athletic Conference. The Skyhawks play at the FLC Soccer Field, which can seat up to 1,000 people. The FLC Soccer Field is a natural grass facility.
History: The Skyhawks have played five seasons at the varsity, NCAA II level. the team's first season was in 1994, when they went 3-10 overall. In five seasons, FLC's all-time record is 28-49-8 which is .376.
Achievements: The Skyhawks have had two-first team All-Great Plains Region players in five years: Kendra Keeley in 1995 and Danielle Ornelas in 1996 and one other (Carissa Bradford in 1998) was named to the All-Region second team.
Coaching: Jaymee Stone, Head Coach, begins third year at FLC. She has a career record of 12-21-4 in first two seasons. Damian Clarke, Assistant Coach.
Style of Play: Fort Lewis emphasizes possession building up through the back, and attacking and defending as a unit.

Mesa State College

Academic Profile

Phone: 800-982-6372

Grand Junction, CO 81501

Type: 4 Yr.,Public,Liberal Arts
Website: http://www.mesastate.edu
SAT/ACT/GPA: 880/19/2.5
Student/Faculty Ratio: 28:1
Undergraduate Enrollment: 4,500
Scholarships/Academic: Yes
Athletic: Yes

Founded: 1925
Religion: Non-Affiliated
Housing: Yes
Male/Female Ratio: 47:53
Graduate Enrollment: 50
Financial Aid: Yes

Expenses by: Year **In State:** $ 8,240 **Out of State:** $ 12,120
Specialty: Liberal Arts
Degrees Conferred: Cert, AS, BA, BS, MBA
Programs of Study: Accounting, Biological Science, Business, Communications, Computer, Criminal, Dramatic Arts, Economics, English, Fine Arts, Geology, History, Human Services, Management, Marketing, Parks/Recreation, Physics, Science, Social Science

Women's Athletic Profile

1175 Texas Avenue
Grand Junction, CO 81501
Coach: Jim Buchan
Email: jbuchan@mesastate.edu

NCAA II
Mavericks/Cardinal, White
Phone: (970) 248-1042
Fax: (970) 248-1980

Estimated # of Women's Soccer Scholarships: 20
Conference: Rocky Mountain Athletic Conference
Program Profile: Top 10, twice in last three years, Top 15 once in last four years, program only four years old. Playing season August 20th- Nov. 1 and playing surface is natural grass.
History: Our program began in 1996. On our second year, we won Conference and had a Player of the Year, a Freshman of the Year, a Coach of the Year, 2 All-Americans and 6 All-Region All-Americans. On our third year, our record was 10-1-1(a Conference record for most points). In 2000 record was 15-3 RMAC Regular Champions and ranked 13th in the nation.
Achievements: 3 Conference Championships; 2 Top Teams in the Country; 2 Regional Coach of the Year; 5 All-American Freshman; 6 All-Region All-American, Conference Coach of they Year.
Coaching: Jim Buchan, Head Coach, was Coach of the Year in 1996-1997 and in 1997-1998. He was Conference Coach of the Year in 1997-1998. He played professional soccer form 1978 to 1991. He was the goalkeeper for the Canada National Program.
Roster in State: 18 **Out of State:** 4 **Out of Country:** 1
ODP State: 10 **Regional:** 2 **National:** 0
Walk-on/Other: 0 **Graduation %:** 95 **Seniors on Team:** 3
Positions Needed: Sweeper, Defender
Camp or Clinic Dates: July 9-14, 16-20
Most Recent Record: 15-3-0
Schedule: Metro State, Regis Univ. Texas A&M Commerce, C.W Post Long Island, Texas Wesleyan, Univ. of Northern Colorado
Style of Play: Play from Back, 3-4-3 or 3-5-2

Metropolitan State College - Denver

Academic Profile

Campus 9
Denver, CO 80217-3362
Phone: 303-556-3058

Type: 4 Yr.,Public,
Website: http://www.mscd.edu
SAT/ACT/GPA: 820/18/2.5
Student/Faculty Ratio: 22:1
Undergraduate Enrollment: 17,500
Founded: 1963
Religion: Non-Affiliated
Housing: No
Male/Female Ratio: 1:1
Graduate Enrollment: N/A
Scholarships/Academic: Yes **Athletic:** Yes **Financial Aid:** Yes
Expenses by: Year **In State:** $ 7,250 **Out of State:** $ 12,450
Degrees Conferred: BA, BS, BFA
Programs of Study: Accounting, Anthropology, Art, Behavioral Science, Biology, Chemistry, Computer Information System, Computer Science, Criminalistics, Economics, English, Geography, Geology, Journalism, Land Use, Management, Marketing, Music, Philosophy, Physics, Political Science, Psychology, Public Administration, Social Work, Sociology, Spanish, Speech Communications, Theoretical Physics

Men's Athletic Profile

Campus Box 9, P.O. Box 173362
Denver, CO 80217-3362
Coach: Brian Crookham
Email: crrokhab@mscd.edu

NCAA II
Roadrunners/Burgundy, Navy
Phone: (303) 556-4875
Fax: (303) 556-2720

Estimated # of Men's Soccer Scholarships: 8.5
Conference: Rocky Mountain Athletic Conference
Program Profile: A $1 million field restoration was completed in the summer of 1997. We have a natural grass playing field with two practice fields. We play traditional and non-traditional playing seasons and we have an off-season weight program.
History: The program began in the mid 60's as a club program. We switched from NAIA to NCAA Division II in 1985.
Achievements: 11 Conference/District Titles in the last 25 years; 4 All-Americans, including Colorado Foxes Coach Lorne Donaldson.
Coaching: Brian Cookham, Head Coach, is in his third year here. He holds a USSF "B" License and has served in various capacities on ODP Staff.

Roster In State: 11 | **Out of State:** 12 | **Out of Country:** 2
ODP State: 12 | **Regional:** 3 | **National:** 1
Walk-on/Other: 0 | **Graduation %:** 90 | **Seniors on Team:** 4

Most Recent Record: 14-4-2
Schedule: Ft. Lewis, Colorado Mines, West Texas A & M, Incarnate Word, St. Edwards.
Style of Play: Prefer possession oriented game but will adjust style according to the personnel.

Women's Athletic Profile

Campus Box 9, P.O. Box 173362
Denver, CO 80217-3362
Coach: Ed Montojo
Email: Not Available

NCAA II
Roadrunners/Navy, Blue, White
Phone: (303) 556-4874
Fax: (303) 556-2720

Estimated # of Women's Soccer Scholarships: None
Conference: Colorado Athletic Conference
Program Profile: Grass field, 130x80 yards, newly remodeled indoor training facility. Play a traditional/non-traditional season, off-season weight training, and play a national schedule. Have been ranked in the NCAA II top twenty.
History: Began as a club sport in 1970's, played NAIA varsity status in 1981-1985, since 1986 has been at the NCAA II level.
Achievements: 1985 NAIA All-American; 1994 NCAA II All-American; 1994 Conference Player of the Year; 1992 Conference Champion; 8 NSCAA All-Region players.
Coaching: Ed Montojo, Head Coach, holds a USSF "B" License, former Colorado ODP Staff Coach. Saul Contreras - Assistant Coach, USSF "B License, former Colorado ODP Staff Coach.
Style of Play: Offensive - build up from the back, position switching, ball-control short passing. Defense-play a combination of man-to-man and zone.

Regis University
Academic Profile

Denver, CO 80221

Phone: 303-458-4900

Type: 4 Yr.,Private,Liberal Arts
Website: http://www.regis.edu
SAT/ACT/GPA: 1100/20/3.0
Student/Faculty Ratio: 15:1
Undergraduate Enrollment: 1,200

Founded: 1877
Religion: Roman Catholic
Housing: Yes
Male/Female Ratio: 45:55
Graduate Enrollment: 7,000

Scholarships/Academic: Yes **Athletic:** Yes **Financial Aid:** Yes
Expenses by: Year **In State:** $ 22,800 **Out of State:** $ 22,800
Specialty: Liberal Arts, Business, Preprofessional (Sciences)
Degrees Conferred: BA, BS, MBA, Nursing, Physical Therapy, MSL, MACL, MIS
Programs of Study: Business and Management, Communications, Life Sciences, Religion, Mathematics, Philosophy, Social Sciences, Theology

Men's Athletic Profile

3333 Regis Blvd.
Denver, CO 80221
Coach: Matt McDowell
Email: mmcdowel@regis.edu

NCAA II
Rangers/Navy Blue, Yellow
Phone: (303) 458-4359
Fax: (303) 964-5499

Estimated # of Men's Soccer Scholarships: 5.6
Conference: Rocky Mountain Athletic Conference
Program Profile: Professionally maintained match facility with a natural grass, adjacent training facility. 120x80 yards expertly maintained grass match facility with a seating capacity of 500, grass training facility. Strength of schedule rating top 5 in the region.
History: NAIA in 1960's, 1970' and 1980's. NCAA Division II in 1990-Coach Marchin Ward took over program in 1991.
Achievements: Coach of the Year in 1994; conference titles in 1994 7 1997; 6 Regional All-Americans; Top 25 National rankings in each of the last 6 years; NSCAA Team Academic Achievement Award for two years; 1998 finished 3rd in NCAA II and 15 for all men's soccer program.
Coaching: Amy Marchin-Ward, Head Coach, USSF License, NSCAA Advanced National Diploma, member of the NCAA Far West Region Selection Committee, member of NSCAA Regional Staff, ISAA Regional Rater, CAC Coach of the Year in 1994; Evergreen Junior Soccer Association in 1992-1993. Eric White, Assistant Coach.
Roster In State: 7 **Out of State:** 16 **Out of Country:** 2
ODP State: 5 **Regional:** 2 **National:**
Walk-on/Other: **Graduation %:** 95 **Seniors on Team:** 6
Positions Needed: Central and wide defenders
Most Recent Record: 3-15
Schedule: Ft. Lewis, W. Texas A&M, Midwestern (Texas), St. Edwards, Southern Colorado, St. Mary's, Texas Wesleyan, Metro State, Incarnate Word
Style of Play: Solid team defending leading to quick transition to an attractive attacking style. Where everyone attacks and everyone defends.

Women's Athletic Profile

3333 W Regis Blvd., F-20
Denver, CO 80221-1099
Coach: JB Belzer
Email: jbelzer@regis.edu

NCAA II
Rangers/Navy, Gold
Phone: (303) 458-4981
Fax: (303) 964-5486

Estimated # of Women's Soccer Scholarships: 6.3
Conference: Rocky Mountain Athletic Conference
Program Profile: Grass practice and game fields measure 120x80 yards located on campus. Both fields, beautifully maintained year-round. Full athletic training staff and facilities provided.
History: Program began in 1989. In 1994, we were NCAA Division II Runner-Up and 1996 NCAA Division II semi-finalist. In 1996, NCAA II National Semi-Finalist.
Achievements: Coach Belzer was named 1996 RMAC Coach of the Year; 1 NSCAA 1st team All-American; 3 NSCAA Regional All-Americans, 2 Umbro Select All-Stars, 1999 Regular Season Conference Champions.
Coaching: JB Belzer, Head Coach, holds a USSF "A" and a NSCAA Advanced National. Freddy Delgado - Assistant Coach, holds a USSF "C" and NSCAA National.
Roster in State: 9 **Out of State:** 10 **Out of Country:** 0

ODP State: 14 **Regional:** 5 **National:** 0
Walk-on/Other: 0 **Graduation %:** 98 **Seniors on Team:** 6
Positions Needed: forwards, Midfielders
Camp or Clinic Dates: July 15-20 individual camp, July 29-August 3 Team
Most Recent Record: 14-5-1
Schedule: Central Oklahoma, Angelo State, Incarnate Word, Midwestern, Metro State, Ft. Lewis, Mesa State
Style of Play: We play a high pressure zonal defending to create quick transition opportunities going forward. Emphasis on wing defenders and attacking up the flank, quick speed of play and 1 v 1 creativity.

United States Air Force Academy

Academic Profile

Suite 212
Colorado Springs, CO 80840-9500
Phone: (719) 333-2897

Type: 4 Yr.,Public,Engineering
Founded: 1954
Website: http://www.airforcesports.com
Religion: Non-Affiliated
SAT/ACT/GPA: 1140/25/3.0
Housing: Yes
Student/Faculty Ratio: 15:1
Male/Female Ratio: 85:15
Undergraduate Enrollment: 4,000
Graduate Enrollment: N/A
Scholarships/Academic: Yes **Athletic:** Yes **Financial Aid:** Yes
Expenses by: Year **In State:** $ 100% free **Out of State:** $ 100% free
Specialty: Sciences
Degrees Conferred: BS
Programs of Study: Has 27 academic majors, mostly Sciences, Languages (Foreign) and Political Science.

Men's Athletic Profile

2169 Field House Dr.
USAF Academy, CO 80840-9500
Coach: Lou Sagastume
Email: sagastumela.ahth@usafa.af.ml

NCAA I
Falcons/Blue, Silver
Phone: (719) 333- 2174
Fax: (719) 333-2819

Estimated # of Men's Soccer Scholarships: None
Conference: Western Athletic Conference (WAC)
Program Profile: We play in the Western Athletic Conference; season runs from August through November. New cadets - soccer stadium is grass surface and holds up to 2,000. Also has a junior varsity programs.
History: First year of soccer was 1956. Has gone 368-198-52 over the last forty-two years. Advanced to 10 NCAA Tournaments; had 7 first team All-Americans and won 9 Conference Championships.
Achievements: Advanced to 10 NCAA Tournament; 7 All-Americans; other top highlights include advancing to the Elite Eight in the 1993 NCAA Tournament and winning at least 10 games; 12 times in the last 18 years.
Coaching: Luis Sagastume, Head Coach, USSF "A" License and English "FA" Badge. He was a 1968 graduate of USF, led them to the National Championship, All-American, 1st round NASL draft pick. Major Paul Nowotny - Assistant Coach, USAFA in 1986. Captain Dave Hansen - Assistant Coach, USAFA in 1989.
Roster In State: 8 **Out of State:** 16 **Out of Country:**
ODP State: 20 **Regional:** 2 **National:** 1
Walk-on/Other: **Graduation %:** 100 **Seniors on Team:** 5
Positions Needed: sweeper, midfield, outside-mid
Camp or Clinic Dates: June 11-16; June 19-23; June 26-30 (commuters only)
Most Recent Record: 9-8-3
Schedule: Santa Clara, Wisconsin Madison, Davidson College, Fresno State, San Jose State, Denver University
Style of Play: Our team is a touch team that likes to mix the short ball with the long whenever necessary. We look for effectiveness mixed with flare. We enjoy playing attractive soccer regardless of the outcome. The system of play depends on the variety of the players.

Women's Athletic Profile

2169 Cadet Field House, Ste. 11
USAF Academy, CO 80840
Coach: Marty Buckley
Email: Not Available

NCAA I
Falcons/Blue, Silver, White
Phone: (719) 333-2201
Fax: (719) 333-2599

Estimated # of Women's Soccer Scholarships: None
Conference: Mountain West Conference
Program Profile: Stadium with natural grass field and has a seating capacity of 3,000.
History: 1996 was the first season at Division I after four years at Division II where the Falcons were ranked as high as #11 nationally in 1995 with a 14-3-2 record. The Falcons first season in WAC at Division I, they qualified for the conference post-season tournament.
Achievements: Head Coach Marty Buckley was Colorado Athletic Conference Coach of the Year in 1992. The Falcons had 1 first team All-American and 1 All-Region selection in 1995.
Coaching: Marty Buckley, Head Coach, holds USSF "A" License. He was a 1976 graduate of California State - Chico. He is entering his 8th season with the program. Served as men's assistant coach at AFA from 1986-1991. Captain Pat McKenna - Assistant Coach, (USAFA, in 1987), entering third year with the program. Captain Chris Cullen - Assistant Coach (USAFA in 1994), entering third year with the program.
Style of Play: Technical style of play. Short passing game that relies on high tech skills. Possession and discipline are critical.

University of Colorado

Academic Profile

Colorado Springs, CO 80933-7150
Phone: (719) 262-3679

Type: 4 Yr.,Public,
Website: http://www.uccs.edu
SAT/ACT/GPA: 850/18/3.4
Student/Faculty Ratio: 17:1
Undergraduate Enrollment: 6,000
Scholarships/Academic: Yes
Athletic: Yes
Expenses by: Year
In State: $ 7,800

Founded: 1965
Religion: Non-Affiliated
Housing: Yes
Male/Female Ratio: 2:3
Graduate Enrollment: 1,000
Financial Aid: Yes
Out of State: $ 14,600

Degrees Conferred: BA, BS, MA, MS, MBA, MPA, MEngineering, MBasic Science, BSN, MSN
Programs of Study: College of Business, College of Engineering and Applied Sciences, School of Education, College of Letters Arts and Sciences, Graduate School of Public Affairs

Men's Athletic Profile

1420 Austin Bluffs Parkway
Colorado Springs, CO 80933-7150
Coach: Eddy Karl Dietz
Email: edietz@mail.uccs.edu

NCAA II
The Gold/Blue, Gold
Phone: (719) 262-3448
Fax: (719) 262-3029

Estimated # of Men's Soccer Scholarships: None
Conference: Rocky Mountain Athletic Conference (RMAC)
Program Profile: UCCS is located in the north central of Colorado Springs at the foot of Austin Bluffs with a spectacular view of the Front Range of the Rockies. By the Fall of 1996, UCCS will add residential housing and a research park. Playing season is in September through November with home games being played on campus. Scholarships are extremely limited. Aid is restricted to federal guidelines based on income. Other scholarships are available through Financial Aid Department @ CU. Soccer program is getting stronger by the year. Four-Diamond Sport Complex; natural grass with a seating capacity of 1,500.

History: Our program began in 1986. Began as a club sport in 1988 and was elevated to varsity status in 1991. 1994/95 was a winning season (10-9-3). Program is steadily improving but has 50% player transfer ratio due to commuter campus status. In 1995 we replaced 7 starters from 1994 squad. 86-90 NAIA 6-57-1 record; 91-96 Division II-Eddie Dietz has a record of 50-54-14.
Achievements: 17 All-Conference players in the last three years, 5 All-Conference in 1993. Eddy Dietz - 1996 RMAC Coach of the Year; team ranked 18th in the Far West Region; team also ranked 20th in the Nation.
Coaching: Eddy Karl Dietz, Head Coach since 1991, USSF 'A' License, played professionally in the NASL, MISL, ASL, SISL, and NPSL, played at Colorado College and graduated with a degree in History, set several CC scoring records and was Regional All-Americans in four years, high coach at Liberty High School and led Them to a class 4A championship in 1990. Former Division I player, NASL, MISL player, Regional ODP staff coach.
Style of Play: Based on players on the program. Attacking with a high pressure.

University of Colorado - Boulder

Academic Profile

Boulder, CO 80309-0372
Phone: (303) 492-6141

Type: 4 Yr.,Public
Website: http://www.buffaloes.colorado.edu
SAT/ACT/GPA: 1080-1250/23-27/3.2-3.7
Student/Faculty Ratio: 14:1
Undergraduate Enrollment: 20,595
Scholarships/Academic: Yes **Athletic:** Yes
Expenses by: Year **In State:** $ 8,621
Specialty: Many
Founded: 1876
Religion: Non-Affiliated
Housing: Yes
Male/Female Ratio: 53:47
Graduate Enrollment: 4,530
Financial Aid: Yes
Out of State: $ 21,103
Degrees Conferred: BA, BS, BFA, MA, MS, MBA, MFA, Ph.D., EdD, PharmD
Programs of Study: All: Business, Communications, Environmental Design, Engineering, Journalism, Liberal Arts

Women's Athletic Profile

Campus Box 372
Boulder, CO 80309-0372
Coach: Austin Daniels
Email: klemer@moonshine.colorado.edu
NCAA I
Buffaloes/Silver, Gold, Black
Phone: (303) 492-0632
Fax: (303) 492-1709

Estimated # of Women's Soccer Scholarships: None
Conference: Big Twelve Conference
Program Profile: Program is entering its fourth season Division I. Has been able to schedule several Division I powerhouse, such as North Carolina, Maryland, Duke and BYU, as well as the Big Twelve opponents such Nebraska, Texas, A&M and Baylor. Games are played at Pleasant View Soccer Complex in Boulder, voted the Best College Soccer Pitch in 1997 (natural grass). There is no official capacity as there is no formal seating. New stadium slated for early 2000.
History: Our program started in 1996. Finished 6-10-1 overall and 3-6-1 in Big 12. in 1997, overall record of 6-12-0, 5-6-1 in Big 12. qualified for the 1997 Big 12 Tournament, where CU fell to Texas 1-0. Season included first win over a ranked opponent in beating No. 25 Baylor 3-2. in 1998, opened season against defending national champion North Carolina in front of state record 3,000 fans in 2-0 loss. UNC shut out in second half. Record was 5-12-3 overall, 2-6-2 in Big Twelve.
Achievements: In 1998, senior goalkeeper Sloane Cox (Burlington, Ontario) was named second team All-Big 12, the first All-Conference selection for Colorado. She also led the nation in total saves with 200.
Coaching: Austin Daniel, Head Coach, he was NSCAA Coach of the Year in 1989; Regional Coach of the Year in 1992. Two-time North Atlantic Conference Coach of the Year. Kim LeMere, Assistant Coach, three-time NSCAA All-American, four-time All-Region, Herman Trophy Finalist NAC Player of the Year in 1992; Soccer America MVP in 1991 and 1992.
Style of Play: Our passing style and use of midfielders.

University of Denver

Academic Profile

Phone: (303) 871-3944

Denver, CO 80208

Type: 4 Yr.,Private,
Website: http://www.du.edu
SAT/ACT/GPA: 610 U & M /273.4
Student/Faculty Ratio: 13:1
Undergraduate Enrollment: 3,000
Scholarships/Academic: Yes **Athletic:** Yes
Expenses by: Year **In State:** $ 25,000

Founded: 1864
Religion: Non-Affiliated
Housing: Yes
Male/Female Ratio: 48:52
Graduate Enrollment: 3,175
Financial Aid: Yes
Out of State: $ 25,000

Specialty: Business, Hotel & Restaurant Management, Science
Degrees Conferred: BA, BFA, BM, BSBA, MA, MBA, MFA, MS, MIM, MRCM, MSLA, MT, Ph.D., JD
Programs of Study: Art, Art History, Education, English, Finance, Finance-Marketing, Finance-Real Estate, General Business, Hotel/Restaurant & Tourism Management, Languages & Literature, History, Law, Management, Management Information Systems, Marketing, Music, Philosophy, Real Estate & Construction Management, Religious Studies, Statistics & Operations Research, Theatre, Pre-law, Pre-M.Ed.

Men's Athletic Profile

2201 E. Asbury Avenue
Denver, CO 80208
Coach: Chad Ashton
Email: cashton@du.edu

NCAA I
Pioneers/Red, Black, White
Phone: (303) 871-3923
Fax: (303) 871-3905

Estimated # of Men's Soccer Scholarships:
Conference: Mountain Pacific Sports Federation
Program Profile: We moved from Division II to Division I in the 1998-1999 season. We have a 20-game fall season and 5 dates in the spring season. We are entering MPSF in 1999-2000 season. A new grass field are in the future plans for a stadium as a part of a $ 60 million athletic facility.
History: The program began in 1960. We moved to Division I in 1998-1999 season and are entering MPSF in 1999-2000.
Achievements: Numerous players have been drafted into NPSL and A-League and many players and graduates are playing in USISL.
Coaching: Chad Ashton, Head Coach, is a UNC-Chapel Hill graduate. He played in NPSL, A-League, and MSL. Keith Tlemeyer is the Assistant Coach.

Women's Athletic Profile

2199 South University Blvd
Denver, CO 80208
Coach: Jeff Hooker
Email: jhooker@du.edu

NCAA I
Pioneers/Red, Black
Phone: (303) 871-3154
Fax: (303) 871-2800

Estimated # of Women's Soccer Scholarships: None
Conference: Sun Belt Conference
Program Profile: The University of Denver's new athletic facility has recently been completed. It includes state of the art strength and conditioning center, locker rooms, sport medicine facility, and a new soccer stadium with natural grass.
History: The University of Denver moved from Division II to Division I in 1998.
Achievements: Jeff Hooker 1993 and 1994 Coach of the Year; 1997 National Player of the Year-division II.
Coaching: Jeff Hooker, Head Coach, 1993 and 1994 Coach of the Year. Scott DeDycker and David Thomas are Assistant Coaches.

Roster in State: 11
Out of State: 11
Out of Country:
ODP State: 16
Regional: 5
National:
Walk-on/Other:
Graduation %: 100
Seniors on Team: 2
Positions Needed: Sweeper
Camp or Clinic Dates: Not Available
Most Recent Record: 9-9-1

University of Northern Colorado

Academic Profile

Greeley, CO 80639
Phone: (970) 351-1719

Type: 4 Yr.,Public,Liberal Arts
Founded: 1889
Website: http://www.uncBears.edu
Religion: Non-Affiliated
SAT/ACT/GPA: 1000/21/2.8
Housing: Yes
Student/Faculty Ratio: 30:1
Male/Female Ratio: 50:50
Undergraduate Enrollment: 10,000
Graduate Enrollment: 1,500
Scholarships/Academic: Yes
Athletic: Yes
Financial Aid: Yes
Expenses by: Year
In State: $ 7,649
Out of State: $ 14,679
Specialty: Business, Education, Nursing
Degrees Conferred: MA, MS, Ph.D., EdD, BA, BS, MM, MME
Programs of Study: Biology, Business, Communication Disorders, Dietetics, Earth Science, Economics, English, Geography, Gerontology, Health, History, Human Rehabilitation, Services, Interdisciplinary, Journalism, PreProfessional Programs, Psychology, Recreation, Visual Arts

Women's Athletic Profile

208K Butler-Hancock Hall
Greeley, CO 80639
Coach: Tim Barrera
Email: tim.barrera@unco.edu

NCAA II
Bears/Blue, Gold, White
Phone: (970) 351-1758
Fax: (970) 353-2018

Estimated # of Women's Soccer Scholarships: 2
Conference: North Central Conference
Program Profile: The home field is a natural grass, 70x120 yards, has a practice and game fields, weight training facilities-varsity and campus. Year-round training. Academic advising offered. Top 15 in the NCAA Division II for two years in a row.
History: Program began in 1979, participated in 1st ever national championship tourney in 1980 (placed 6th) have participated in 2 NCAA Tournaments, won at least 13 games in each of last 5 years, NCC Champions 3 of 5 years in conference.
Achievements: 3 NCC Championships, NCAA Tournament 1996, 1997, Coach of the Year 1999, 1 All-American 1999, 18 All-Region players 1995-1999, 4 All-NCC players 2000
Coaching: Tim Barrera Head Coach 2nd year at UNC (28-8), 8th year collegiate (88-52-3), Virginia Tech 86
Roster in State: 11
Out of State: 15
Out of Country: 0
ODP State: 6
Regional: 0
National: 0
Walk-on/Other:
Graduation %: 95
Seniors on Team: 5
Positions Needed: Midfielder, Defenders
Camp or Clinic Dates: Not Available
Most Recent Record: 13-5-0
Schedule: Nebraska-Omaha, Minnesota State-Mankato, Truman State, North Dakota State, Mesa State, Minnesota Duluth.
Style of Play: 4-3-3 Possession to get forward, high pressure zone.

University of Southern Colorado

Academic Profile

Pueblo, CO 81001-4901

Phone: 877-USC-WOLF

Type: 4 Yr.,Public
Website: http://www.uscolo.edu
SAT/ACT/GPA: 820/17
Student/Faculty Ratio: 17:1
Undergraduate Enrollment: 3,940
Scholarships/Academic: Yes **Athletic:** Yes
Expenses by: Year **In State:** $ 6,880

Founded: 1969
Religion: Non-Affiliated
Housing: Yes
Male/Female Ratio: 46:54
Graduate Enrollment: 130
Financial Aid: Yes
Out of State: $ 7,880

Degrees Conferred: BA, BS, MS, MBA
Programs of Study: Accounting, Art, Automotive Parts and Service Management, Biology, Business, Chemistry, Civil Engineering Technology, Computer Information Systems, Electrical Engineering, Electronic Engineering Technology, Computer Engineering, Elementary and Secondary Certification, English, Exercise Science, Athletic Training, Health Promotions, Foreign Languages, History, Industrial Engineering, Mass Communications, Mathematics, Mechanical Engineering, Music, Nursing, Political Science, PreProfessional Programs, Psychology, Recreation, Social Science, Sociology, Speech Communications

Men's Athletic Profile

2200 Bonforte Blvd.
Pueblo, CO 81001-4901
Coach: Roy Stanley
Email: stanley@uscolo.edu

NCAA II
Thunderwolves/Navy, Red
Phone: (719) 549-2793
Fax: (719) 549-2570

Estimated # of Men's Soccer Scholarships: 4-5
Conference: Rocky Mountain Athletic Conference (RMAC)
Program Profile: We have an excellent grass field, 115 x 75 yards, seating for 1,200. We play fall and spring schedule and conference championship. We have a soccer only locker room.
History: Our program began in 1990 and in each of the last two years has increased the winning percentage. We made the Rocky Mountain Athletic Conference Tournament in 1997 and set a school record for number of wins in 1998.
Achievements: Over the last 3 years we have had a record of 31-25. We have consistently have 3-4 players selected to the All-Conference team and 1-2 players selected to All-Region.
Coaching: Roy Stanley, Head Coach, holds a USSF 'A' license. Was RMAC 1000 Coach of the Year. Fred Flores and Kevin Smith Assistant Coaches, holds USSF "D" Licenses. Kevin is USCA four-year starter, two-year captain and holds a USSF "C" License.
Roster In State: 12 **Out of State:** 19 **Out of Country:** 0
ODP State: 8 **Regional:** 0 **National:** 0
Walk-on/Other: 0 **Graduation %:** 100 **Seniors on Team:** 6
Positions Needed: Defenders, Midfielders, Forwards
Camp or Clinic Dates: Not Available
Most Recent Record: 8-9-0
Schedule: Metro, Fort Lewis, Incarnate Word, Colorado School of Mines, St. Edwards, Midwestern State Univ.
Style of Play: Our players are skillful, committed individuals that understand the meaning of team play. Our main style is possession game with build-up from the back. However, our offense and defense will vary depending on players and conditions.

Women's Athletic Profile

2200 Bonforte Blvd.
Pueblo, CO 81001-4901
Coach: Roy Stanley
Email: stanley@uscolo.edu

NCAA II
Thunderwolves/Navy, Red
Phone: (719) 549-2793
Fax: (719) 549-2570

Estimated # of Women's Soccer Scholarships: 4-5
Conference: Rocky Mountain Athletic Conference (RMAC)
Program Profile: We have an excellent grass field, 115 x 75 yards, that seats 1,200. Fall and spring schedule, Conference Championships. Soccer only locker-room.
History: Our program began in 1994 and has been in the Top 3 in the Rocky Mountain Athletic Conference.
Achievements: Over the last 4 years we have had an overall record of 37-33. We consistently have 3-4 players selected to the All-Conference Team and 1-2 players selected to All-Region.
Coaching: Roy Stanley, Head Coach - USSF 'A' license, head coach at Division I Arkansas-Little Rock, assistant coach at Tulsa and Evansville, All-Ivy first Team at Princeton, Parade Magazine All-American, St. Louis University High School. Kevin Smith is our Assistant Coach.

Roster in State: 8	**Out of State:** 14	**Out of Country:** 0
ODP State: 6	**Regional:** 1	**National:** 0
Walk-on/Other: 0	**Graduation %:** 100	**Seniors on Team:** 3

Positions Needed: Defenders, Midfielders, Forwards
Camp or Clinic Dates:
Most Recent Record: 11-7-2
Schedule: Central Oklahoma, Metro, Mesa St. Regis Univ. West Texas A&M, Univ of Northern CO
Style of Play: Our players are skillful, committed individuals that understand the meaning of team play. Our main style is a possession game with build up. However our offense and defense will vary depending on players and conditions.

connecticut

CONNECTICUT

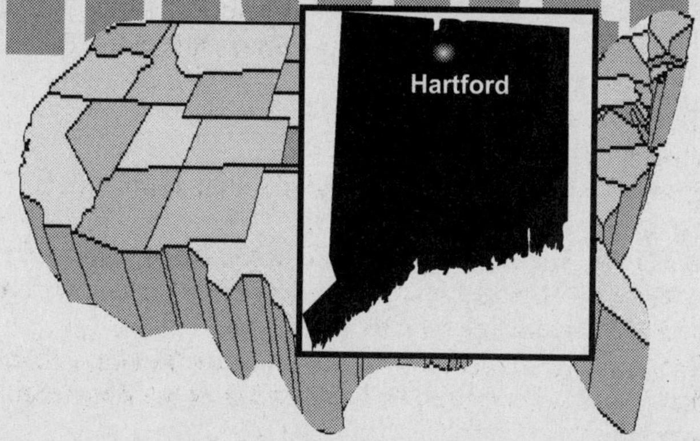

SCHOOL	CITY	AFFILIATION	PAGE
Albertus Magnus College	New Haven	NCAA III	165
Central Connecticut State Univ	New Britain	NCAA I	165
Connecticut College	New London	NCAA III	166
Eastern Connecticut State Univ	Willimantic	NCAA III	168
Fairfield University	Fairfield	NCAA I	169
Quinnipiac College	Hamden	NCAA II	170
Sacred Heart University	Fairfield	NCAA II	171
Southern Connecticut State Univ	New Haven	NCAA II	172
Teikyo Post University	Waterbury	NCAA II/NAIA	173
Trinity College - Connecticut	Hartford	NCAA III	174
United States Coast Guard Acad	New London	NCAA III	175
University of Bridgeport	Bridgeport	NCAA II	176
University of Connecticut	Storrs	NCAA I	177
University of Hartford	West Hartford	NCAA I	178
University of New Haven	West Haven	NCAA II	180
Wesleyan University	Middletown	NCAA III	181
Western Connecticut State U	Danbury	NCAA III	182
Yale University	New Haven	NCAA I	183

STAR GOALKEEPER
ACADEMY
THE BALL STOPS HERE
WWW.STARGOALKEEPER.COM
1-888-SGA-GOAL

Albertus Magnus College
Academic Profile

New Haven, CT 06511
Phone: 203-773-8501

Type: 4 Yr.,Private,Liberal Arts
Website: http://www.albertus.edu
SAT/ACT/GPA: Required
Student/Faculty Ratio: 15:1
Undergraduate Enrollment: 400+
Scholarships/Academic: Yes **Athletic:** No
Expenses by: Year **In State:** $ 20,000
Degrees Conferred: BA, MA
Founded: 1925
Religion: Catholic
Housing: Yes
Male/Female Ratio: 3:1
Graduate Enrollment: 100+
Financial Aid: Yes
Out of State: $ 20,000
Programs of Study: Accounting, Biology, Business and Management, Communications, Economics, Management/Administration, English, Finance, Fine Arts, Mathematics, History, Human Services, Philosophy, Political Science, PreLaw, PreMed, Psychology, Religion, Sociology

Men's Athletic Profile

700 Prospect Street
New Haven, CT 06511-1189
Coach: Gege Bedocs
Email: Not Available

NCAA III
Falcons/Royal, White
Phone: 203-773-8936
Fax: (203) 776-7533

Estimated # of Men's Soccer Scholarships: None
Conference: Great Northeast Athletic Conference
Program Profile: On-campus facilities include a regulation grass field, a electric scoreboard, a field house, and a pool.
History: Program began in 1990. 1996 GNAC Champions.
Achievements: 1996 Great Northeast Athletic Conference Champions.
Coaching: George Bedocs, Head Coach, NSCAA Advanced National Diploma, USFF "B" License, staff member of Connecticut ODP.
Style of Play: Build from the back, possession soccer.

Central Connecticut State University
Academic Profile

New Britain, CT 06050
Phone: 860-832-2258

Type: 4 Yr.,Public,Liberal Arts
Website: http://www.ccsu.ctsateu.edu
SAT/ACT/GPA: 930 combined SAT
Student/Faculty Ratio: 17:1
Undergraduate Enrollment: 9,551
Scholarships/Academic: Yes **Athletic:** Yes
Expenses by: Year **In State:** $ 4,457
Specialty: Education
Founded: 1849
Religion: Non-Affiliated
Housing: Yes
Male/Female Ratio: 45:55
Graduate Enrollment: 2,495
Financial Aid: Yes
Out of State: $ 7,196
Degrees Conferred: BS, BA, MA, MB, MS-Industrial Technical Management, Sixth Year Certificate
Programs of Study: Accounting, American Studies, Actuarial Science, Anthropology, Archaeology, Astronomy, Art, Biology, Computer Science, Business, Chemistry, Communication, Engineering, Math, General Studies

Men's Athletic Profile

1615 Stanley Street
New Britain, CT 06050
Coach: Shawn Green
Email: greens@mail.ccsu.edu

NCAA I
Blue Devils/Blue, White
Phone: (860) 832-3051
Fax: (860) 832-3754

Estimated # of Men's Soccer Scholarships: 9.9
Conference: NEC
Program Profile: The Blue Devils are two-time defending Conference Champions. We play in the fall which is our main season. We also play in the spring on a natural grass field.
History: Our program began in 1969.
Achievements: Under the guidance of Coach Green the Blue Devils have had numerous players awarded All-Conference, All-Region, and several have advanced to the professional ranks as members of the Connecticut Wolves. The team finished with a record of 15-6-2 in 1994 en route to winning the Conference Championship and qualifying for the NCAA Division I Championship play-offs for the first time.
Coaching: Shawn Green is our Head Coach. He holds NSCAA Advanced National coaching diploma, licensed in both the USSF and the English Football Association, the Director of Coaching for the National Soccer Coaches of America. Known as one of the winningest coaches in the past ten seasons.
Roster In State: 14 **Out of State:** 7 **Out of Country:** 4
ODP State: 0 **Regional:** 0 **National:** 0
Walk-on/Other: 0 **Graduation %:** N/A **Seniors on Team:** 4
Positions Needed: Forward, Midfield
Camp or Clinic Dates: Not Available
Most Recent Record: 1-16-1
Schedule: Univ. San Diego, UMBC, Hartford, St. Francis
Style of Play: Possession style.

Women's Athletic Profile

1615 Stanley Street
New Britain, CT 06050
Coach: Mick D'Arcy
Email: Darcym@ccsu.edu

NCAA I
Blue Devils/Royal Blue, White
Phone: (860) 832-3092
Fax: (860) 832-3754

Estimated # of Women's Soccer Scholarships:
Conference: Northeast Conference
Program Profile: A relatively young program, we quickly dominated the North East Conference by winning in 1997, 1998, and 1999. Our superb full-size natural grass field has a seating capacity of 1,000. We also have access to a new artificial grass stadium inclimate weather.
History: Our program began in 1995 and since has won three conference championships. We went to the NCAA tournament in 1998.
Achievements: 3 Conference Championships, Conference players of the Year. Jane McFarlane and Jackie Hadden are two of only three players to be selected All-Conference all four years. 3 All-Region Athletes.
Coaching: Head Coach Mick D'Arcy took over the program in 2000. He Previously spent four years as an Assistant Coach at University of Hartford. He is a USSF, UEFA NSCAA licensed Coach. Mick is also the National Director for Tony Dicicco's soccer plus camps. Assit Coach Jackie Hadden played four year at CCSU and graduated in 2000.
Roster in State: 10 **Out of State:** 6 **Out of Country:** 5
Walk-on/Other: **Graduation %:** **Seniors on Team:** 4
Camp or Clinic Dates: Not Available
Most Recent Record: 6-13-0
Schedule: University of Hartford, Boston College, Oregon, Boston University, Hoftra, Yale
Style of Play: Possession, attacking style of play is ideal. Adapt according to the strengths of personnel.

Connecticut College

Academic Profile

New London, CT 06320

Phone: (860) 439-2507

Type: 4 Yr.,Private,Liberal Arts
Website: http://www.camel.conncoll.edu

Founded: 1911
Religion: Non-Affiliated

SAT/ACT/GPA: Not required
Student/Faculty Ratio: 11:1
Undergraduate Enrollment: 1,700
Scholarships/Academic: No
Expenses by: Year
Specialty: Liberal Arts
Degrees Conferred: BA, MA
Athletic: No
In State: $ 28,475
Housing: Yes
Male/Female Ratio: 45:55
Graduate Enrollment: 100
Financial Aid: Yes
Out of State: $ 28,475
Programs of Study: Anthropology, Art, Art History, Asian Studies, Biochemistry, Biology, Botany, Chemistry, Chinese, Classics, Dance, Economics, European Studies, French, German, Hispanic Studies, History, Human Ecology, Interdisciplinary Studies, International Studies, Italian, Japanese, Marine Biology, Mathematics, Medieval Studies, Music, Philosophy, Physics, Political Science, Psychology, Religion, Russian, Sociology, Theatre, Urban Studies, Zoology

Men's Athletic Profile

270 Mohegan Avenue
New London, CT 06320
Coach: William Lessig
Email: wrles@conncoll.edu

NCAA III
Camels/Royal Blue, White
Phone: (860) 439-2200
Fax: (860) 439-2516

Estimated # of Men's Soccer Scholarships: None
Conference: NESCAC
Program Profile: Our team has three fields and are all grass.
History: Our program began in 1970.
Achievements: 8 All-Americans; 30 All-New England; 1 Olympian (Juan Gabarra in 1990); National Team; 1992 & 1996 ECAC New England Champions; NCAA Qualifier in 1995; 1997 NCAA Finalist.
Coaching: William Lessig, Head Coach, two times Olympian from Venezuela. Kyle Lessig - Assistant Coach, professional player.
Roster In State: 24
Out of State: 8
Out of Country: 16
ODP State: 5
Regional: 1
National:
Walk-on/Other:
Graduation %: 99
Seniors on Team: 1
Camp or Clinic Dates: August 7-14
Schedule: Williams, Middlebury, Amherst, Tufts, Bowdoin, Trinity
Style of Play: Possession with a h high demand on individual skills and technique. Sound understanding of small sided tactics. Passion for the game.

Women's Athletic Profile

270 Mohegan Avenue, Box 5531
New London, CT 06320
Coach: Ken Kline
Email: kakli@conncoll.edu

NCAA III
Camels/Royal, White
Phone: (860) 439-2567
Fax: (860) 439-2516

Estimated # of Women's Soccer Scholarships: None
Conference: New England Small College Athletic Conference
Program Profile: Natural field in center of campus overlooking Long Island Sound, 2 practice fields, fall season with off season fitness program.
History: Began in 1983, 13 winning seasons in last 15 years, ECAC New England Champions 1988, NCAA Elite Eight-1998, 10 post season tournaments in last 14 years.
Achievements: Has 7 All-American players, 18 All-Regional players, 3 players active in W-League (Boston Renegades, RI Stingray), ECAC Champions in 1988; NCAA Metro Region Champions in 1998.
Coaching: Ken Kline, Head Coach, USSF 'A' License and has a PhD. Winnie Bing Gnazza, Assistant Coach.
Roster in State: 3
Out of State: 21
Out of Country: 0
ODP State: 4
Regional: 1
National: 0

Walk-on/Other: 0 **Graduation %:** 100 **Seniors on Team:** 2
Positions Needed: ALL
Camp or Clinic Dates: July 9-13, July 16-20
Most Recent Record: 6-8-0
Schedule: Tufts, Middlebury, Williams, Bowdoin, Amherst, Wheaton
Style of Play: Ball control with emphasis on high level of skills and tactical abilities.

Eastern Connecticut State University

Academic Profile

Phone: 877-353-3278

Willimantic, CT 06226-2295

Type: 4 Yr.,Public,Liberal Arts,
Founded: 1889
Website: http://www.ecsu.ctstateu.edu
Religion: Non-Affiliated
SAT/ACT/GPA: 900/2.5
Housing: Yes
Student/Faculty Ratio: 17:1
Male/Female Ratio: 43:57
Undergraduate Enrollment: 4,335
Graduate Enrollment: 297
Scholarships/Academic: Yes **Athletic:** No **Financial Aid:** Yes
Expenses by: Year **In State:** $ 10,000 **Out of State:** $ 15,000
Specialty: Education
Degrees Conferred: AS, BA, BS, BGS, MS
Programs of Study: Accounting, Art, Biology, Business, Communications, Computer, Earth Science, Economics, Education, English, Environmental, History, Finance, Management, Microbiology, Sociology, Social Work

Men's Athletic Profile

83 Windham Street
Willimantic, CT 06226-2295
Coach: Frantz Innocent
Email: innocentf@ecsu.ctctateu.edu

NCAA III
Warriors/Blue, White
Phone: (860) 465-4334
Fax: (860) 465-4696

Estimated # of Men's Soccer Scholarships: None
Conference: ECAC, Little East Conference
Program Profile: Our soccer facility was constructed in 1992. It seats 1000 and is an all natural grass field. The team also plays indoor in winter and spring.
History: Program began in 1961. Post-season qualifier 1966-1975, 1977, 1992; National Tournaments 1968, 1969 & 1973; Conference Champion 1991, 1992; ECAC Championship 1994.
Achievements: Our Program began in 1961 and had back to back undefeated regular seasons in 1968 and 1969. From 1966 to 1975 we had 10 straight post season tournaments and 12 in all the history of the program. We also had 2 Little East titles in 1991 and 1992.
Coaching: Fantz Innocent, Head Coach, 9th year, Little East Conference Coach of the Year in 1991, 1992 and 1996.
Roster In State: 20 **Out of State:** 1 **Out of Country:** 0
Walk-on/Other: **Graduation %:** N/A **Seniors on Team:** 6
Positions Needed: All
Camp or Clinic Dates: Not Available
Most Recent Record: 8-9-2
Schedule: Plymouth State, Wheston, Trinity, Massachusetts State, West Connecticut, Keene State,
Style of Play: Build from the back - two touch ball control; put ball in the back of the net.

Women's Athletic Profile

83 Windham St.
Willimantic, CT 06226-2295
Coach: Chris D'Ambrosio
Email: cdambo@aol

NCAA III
Warriors/Blue, White
Phone: (860) 465-4334
Fax: (860) 465-4696

Estimated # of Women's Soccer Scholarships: None
Conference: Little East Conference, ECAC
Program Profile: Competitive Division III program that plays a 20 game schedule.
History: Program began in 1986.
Achievements: 1992 - programs had first All-American.
Style of Play: Control play with technical and tactical soundness. Players should be fit, physical and skilled. Utilize team speed throughout the field.

Fairfield University

Academic Profile

Fairfield, CT 06430-5195
Phone: (201) 254-4000

Type: 4 Yr.,Private,Liberal Arts
Website: http://www.fairfield.edu
SAT/ACT/GPA: 1100-1250/23-28/3.0
Student/Faculty Ratio: 13:1
Undergraduate Enrollment: 3,100
Scholarships/Academic: Yes
Athletic: Yes
Expenses by: Year
In State: $ 27,815
Degrees Conferred: BA, BS
Founded: 1942
Religion: Jesuit
Housing: Yes
Male/Female Ratio: 46:54
Graduate Enrollment: 900
Financial Aid: Yes
Out of State: $ 27,815
Programs of Study: Accounting, American Studies, Biology, Business, Chemistry, Communications, Computer Information Systems, Computer Science, Economics, Engineering, English, Family Health, Finance, History, Human Resources Management, International Business, International Taxation, International Studies, Management, Marketing, Mathematics, Mental Health, Modern Languages and Literature, Neuroscience, Philosophy, Physics Politics, Psychology, Religious Studies, Sociology and Anthropology, Visual and Performing Arts

Men's Athletic Profile

North Benson Road
Fairfield, CT 06430
Coach: Carl Rees
Email: creese@fair1.fairfield.edu

NCAA I
Stags/Red, White
Phone: (203) 254-4000
Fax: (203) 254-4270

Estimated # of Men's Soccer Scholarships: 2 Plus (9.9)
Conference: Metro Atlantic Athletic Conference
Program Profile: we are a fully funded program. Nationally competitive facilities and working budget. All games played on a flood lit grass field.
History: Our program is over 25 years old. Recently (three years ago), we upgraded our budget and scholarships to a fully funded program. 1998 record was 15-4-1 and top 25 national ranking during the 1998 season.
Achievements: Carl Reese was named 1998 New England Coach of the Year. We were 1998 regular season Conference Champions and had Top 25 national ranking. Lee Williams was drafted into the A-League (Toronto Lynx) in 1999.
Coaching: Carl Reese is our Head Coach. He graduated from Hartwick College in 1988. He was named 1998 New England Coach of the Year and MAAC Conference Coach of the Year. Jim McElderry, Assistant Coach, was a graduate of Fairfield in 1992.
Style of Play: Depends on personnel. Possession, attacking style is preferred. Stress organization, technique and the ability to play at speed.

Women's Athletic Profile

1073 North Benson Rd, Athletic Center
Fairfield, CT 06430-5195
Coach: Maria Piechocki
Email: mpiechoki@mail.fairfield.edu

NCAA I
Stags/Cardinal Red, White
Phone: (203) 254-4000
Fax: (203) 254-4130

Estimated # of Women's Soccer Scholarships: 2.2
Conference: Metro Atlantic Athletic Conference (MAAC)
Program Profile: We have a new athletic center that includes locker rooms, coaches offices, a weight room, a practice gym, an academic center and a training room. The center was built in 1998. We have natural grass training and game fields. We do have an Astroturf field but only use it occasionally.
History: Our first season was in 1993. We were MAAC Tournament Champions four times. We had 2 NCAA Tournament Appearances. We ranked #5 in the Northeast Regional Poll in Soccer Buzz in 1998. In 1998, we had the best record in the team's history: 18-2.
Achievements: Coach of the Year in 1997 and 1998; MAAC Regular Season Champions in 1993, 1994,1997 and 1998; MAAC Tournament Champions in 1993, 1995, 1997 and 1998; Ranked #5 in the Northeast in the1998 Soccer Buzz Regional Poll; Players on All-MAAC Teams, All-Northeast Teams and New England Teams; 1998 Freshman All-American Second Team. 2000 MAAC Conference Player of the Year.
Coaching: Maria Piechocki, Head Coach, graduated from Cal Davis in 1987. She has a USSF "A" License and an NSCAA Advanced National Diploma. She is an ENY ODP Coach and a Region I Staff Coach. Christan Dutchka- Boston Univ. 99, 1st year at Fairfield.

Roster in State: 5
Out of State: 21
Out of Country: 1
ODP State: 11
Regional: 1
National:
Walk-on/Other:
Graduation %: 100
Seniors on Team: 3
Positions Needed: GK, Striker
Camp or Clinic Dates: July 22-27
Most Recent Record: 10-10-2
Schedule: Boston Univ. Univ. of Rhode Island, Brown, Yale, Loyola (MD)
Style of Play: Passing, Possession oriented, and attacking.

Quinnipiac College

Academic Profile

Phone: (800) 462-1944

Hamden, CT 06518

Type: 4 Yr.,Private,Liberal Arts
Founded: 1929
Website: http://www.quinnipiac.edu
Religion: Non-Affiliated
SAT/ACT/GPA: 1070/3.0
Housing: Yes
Student/Faculty Ratio: 15:1
Male/Female Ratio: 1.25:0.8
Undergraduate Enrollment: 3,800
Graduate Enrollment: 2,000
Scholarships/Academic: Yes
Athletic: Yes
Financial Aid: Yes
Expenses by: Year
In State: $ 24,950
Out of State: $ 24,950
Specialty: Business, Communications, Health Science, Liberal Arts
Degrees Conferred: BA, BS, MS, MBA, MPS, MAT, ID, Associate in Court Education
Programs of Study: Accounting, BioChemistry, Computer Science, Diagnostic Imagery, Economics, English, Finance, Gerontology, Health Administration, History, Legal Studies, Management, Marketing, Mass Communications, Mathematics, Nursing, Occupational and Physical Therapy, Political Science, Psychology, Sociology, Spanish, VetTechnology, etc..

Men's Athletic Profile

275 Mount Carmel Ave.
Hamden, CT 06518
Coach: Vict Santos
Email: santos@quinnipiac.edu

NCAA II
Braves/Blue, Gold
Phone: 203- 582-5324
Fax: (203) 281-8716

Estimated # of Men's Soccer Scholarships: None
Conference: Northeast Conference
Program Profile: we play on a natural turf; competes against nationally ranked teams such as Southern Connecticut, New Hampshire, and Franklin Pierce. Advanced to the Northeast - 10 Championship three times in five years.

Women's Athletic Profile

275 Mount Carmel Ave.
Hamden, CT 06518
Coach: David Clarke
Email: dclarke@quinnipiac.edu

NCAA I
Braves/Blue, Gold
Phone: (203) 287-5315
Fax: (203) 281-8716

Estimated # of Women's Soccer Scholarships: 8
Conference: Northeast 10 Conference, ECAC
Program Profile: Quinnipiac University has a natural grass field, two practice fields, full athletic medicine staff, a new weight room and exercise facility. Plans have been approved to develop facility even more.
History: Our program began in 1987, and was a regional power in Division II level. The fall 2000 Season will be the second full season playing at the Division I level. Program is fully committed to establishing itself at the DI level in Connecticut and the region.
Achievements: Numerous awards at the DII level, but hoping to achieve the same level of success at the DI level. Lost in the conference final in 1999 and missed out on a trip to the NCAA's.
Coaching: Dave Clarke, Head Coach, on his second year holds a USSF "A" license, NSCAA Advanced National Diploma, Connecticut License Program Coordinator, Connecticut ODP, Region I Staff, Coach Windsor World Class U16 National Champions 1999, and Former player of Central Connecticut and the Connecticut Wolves.
Roster in State: 10 **Out of State:** 13 **Out of Country:**
ODP State: 14 **Regional:** 1 **National:**
Walk-on/Other: **Graduation %:** 100 **Seniors on Team:** 3
Positions Needed: Just looking for good quality players
Camp or Clinic Dates: Not Available
Most Recent Record: 16-5-0
Schedule: Boston University, Yale University, Rhode Island, Providence, Boston College, University of Connecticut, Hartford, St. Johns University, LIU
Style of Play: Not a prisoner to one style of play. Try to fit the system around the ability of the team. Teach players different formations to help them in specific game situations.

Sacred Heart University

Academic Profile

Fairfield, CT 06432
Phone: (203) 371-7999

Type: 4 Yr.,Private,Liberal Arts
Founded: 1963
Website: http://www.sacredheart.edu
Religion: Catholic
SAT/ACT/GPA: Competitive
Housing: Yes
Student/Faculty Ratio: 17:1
Male/Female Ratio: 50:50
Undergraduate Enrollment: 2,350
Graduate Enrollment: N/A
Scholarships/Academic: Yes **Athletic:** Yes **Financial Aid:** Yes
Expenses by: Year **In State:** $ 22,000 **Out of State:** $ 22,000
Degrees Conferred: AA, AS. BA, BS, MA, MS, MBA
Programs of Study: Business and Management, Business/Office and Marketing/Distribution, Communications, Computer Science, Health Sciences, Law, Letters/Literature, Social Sciences

Men's Athletic Profile

5151 Park Avenue
Fairfield, CT 06432
Coach: Joe McGuigan
Email: Not Available

NCAA II
Pioneers/Red, White
Phone: (203) 365-7604
Fax: (203)365-7696

Estimated # of Men's Soccer Scholarships: 1.5
Conference: Northeast Conference
Program Profile: Sacred Hear plays a 20 game, Fall schedule, weight training in Winter, Indoor Winter for two tournaments and Spring , three days a week practice for the three Spring games, program ends in April.
History: Sacred Heart is a member of the NECC, the toughest, Division II league in the nation.
Achievements: Div. III time Conference Coach in NECC. Graduated 2 All-Americans.
Coaching: Joe McGuigan, Head Coach, 1971 Pan-Am Team, 1972 US Olympic Team, 1971 All-American, captain for two and All-Star for one (1974).

Roster In State: 13
Out of State: 17
Out of Country: 2
ODP State: 5
Regional: 0
National: 0
Walk-on/Other: 0
Graduation %: N/A
Seniors on Team: 6
Positions Needed: Striker, Defenders
Camp or Clinic Dates: TBA
Most Recent Record: 1-12-4
Schedule: UMBC, Quininpiac, Dartmouth, CCSU, FDU, Holy Cross, St. Francis, Mt St Mary's, Monmouth, Robert Morris
Style of Play: What ever system I think can win.

Women's Athletic Profile

5151 Park Avenue
Fairfield, CT 06432-1000
Coach: Joe Barroso
Email: fallonj@Sacredheart.edu

NCAA II
Pioneers/Red, White
Phone: (203) 396-8123
Fax: (203) 365-7696

Estimated # of Women's Soccer Scholarships: None
Conference: New England Collegiate Conference
Program Profile: We are a new Division I program and we have outstanding facilities which include an Astroturf field.
History: The program is in its 8th year and will enter the NEC on the Division I level in 1999. We finished 8-8-1 in 1998.
Style of Play: Play the 4-4-2 with one of the 4 mid-fielders being free players, 2 marking backs, 1 defensive mid. Try to build out of the back with a lot of checking to the ball, creating and supporting each other.

Southern Connecticut State University

Academic Profile

Phone: (203) 392-5759

New Haven, CT 06515

Type: 4 Yr.,Public,Liberal Arts
Website: http://www.fastfeet.com
SAT/ACT/GPA: Required
Student/Faculty Ratio: 15:1
Undergraduate Enrollment: 5,500
Scholarships/Academic: Yes
Athletic: Yes
Expenses by: Year
In State: $ 9,500
Specialty: Liberal Arts
Degrees Conferred: BA, BS

Founded: 1893
Religion: Non-Affiliated
Housing: Yes
Male/Female Ratio: 1:5
Graduate Enrollment: 2,000
Financial Aid: Yes
Out of State: $ 9,500

Programs of Study: Art Education, Art History, BioChemistry, Biology, Business Administration, Chemistry, Computer Science, Corporate Communication, Earth Science, Economics, Elementary Education, English, Geography, Journalism, Liberal Studies, Mathematics, Nursing, Philosophy, Physical Education, Physics, Political Science, Psychology, Public Health, Social Work, Sociology, Special Education

Men's Athletic Profile

125 Wintergreen Avenue
New Haven, CT 06515
Coach: Tom Lang
Email: lang@scsud.ctstatee.edu

NCAA II
Owls/Blue, White
Phone: (203) 392-6018
Fax: (203) 392-6020

Estimated # of Men's Soccer Scholarships: Varies
Conference: NYCAC
Program Profile: Our program is ranked nationally with a 6,000 seat stadium that include lights and astro turf field. Playing season is in the fall and in the spring.
History: Our program began in 1968; has won 5 national championships in 1987, 1992, 1995 & 1998; 16 Final Four Appearances; 13 Conference Championships; 23 NCAA Playoff Appearances.
Achievements: Tom Lang was named 1998 division II Coach of the Year; 13 Conference Titles; 36 All-Americans; 111 All-Conference; 16 Senior Bowl Selections, 3 National Player of the Year; 1 Golden Boot Winner.
Coaching: Tom Lang, Head Coach, former player in NY-Cosmos, Atlanta Chiefs, Colorado Carabous; 21 years collegiate coach assistant, and won three National Championships; two-time former All-American. Chris Payne - Assistant Coach, Southern Alumni, 2 National Championships. Ken Polard and Phil Weddon, Assistant Coaches.
Style of Play: Possession style with an emphasis on creativity in attack and technical ability on the ball.

Women's Athletic Profile

125 Wintergreen Avenue
New Haven, CT 06515
Coach: Jim O'Brien
Email: coachob@hotmail.com

NCAA II
Owls/Navy, White, Sky
Phone: (203) 392-5759
Fax: (203) 392-6006

Estimated # of Women's Soccer Scholarships: $63,000/yr
Conference: Northeast 10
Program Profile: High Level of commitment, program only in fourth season. Will be playing on new field-turf synthetic surface.
History: Began in 1996 inaugural season, overall record 39-28-4. Produced several All-Regional, All-Conference players. 1999 1st time ranking in the Adidas NSCAA top 25. 1999 appearance in ECAC post-season tournament.
Achievements: Jim O'Brien 1999 NECC Coach of the Year, 4 All-New England, 1998 1 All-New England.
Coaching: Jim O'Brien 1999 Coach of the Year and Connecticut ODP U15 Head Coach. Assistant Coaches-Quinnipiac College All-American and Marc Kenney, former Head Women's Coach Tiekyo Post University for 3 years.

Roster in State: 16	**Out of State:** 3	**Out of Country:** 0
ODP State: 2	**Regional:** 0	**National:** 0
Walk-on/Other:	**Graduation %:** 100	**Seniors on Team:** 5

Positions Needed: Defenders
Camp or Clinic Dates: Not Available
Most Recent Record: 15-5-1
Schedule: Franklin Pierce, Merrimack, Stonehill, American International, Westchester, New Hampshire, UMASS-Lowell, St. Anselms, Pace.
Style of Play: Play a strict possession style of play. Building from the backs to the forwards. When able, quick counter attacks utilizing front players coming back for the ball.

Teikyo Post University

Academic Profile

Phone: (203) 596-4535

Waterburg, CT 06708

Type: 4 Yr.,Private,Liberal Arts
Website: http://www.teikyopost.edu

Founded: 1890
Religion: Non-Affiliated

SAT/ACT/GPA: 860/18/2.0
Student/Faculty Ratio: 14:1
Undergraduate Enrollment: 1,400
Scholarships/Academic: Yes **Athletic:** Yes
Expenses by: Year **In State:** $ 19,900
Housing: Yes
Male/Female Ratio: 40:60
Graduate Enrollment: N/A
Financial Aid: Yes
Out of State: $ 19,900
Specialty: International Business and Business Administration
Degrees Conferred: BA, BS, AA, AS
Programs of Study: Accounting, Art (minor), Criminal Justice, Early Childhood Education, English, Equine Management, Finance, General Studies, History, Computer Information Systems, International Business, Legal Assistant, Liberal Arts, Management, Management Information Systems, Marketing, Psychology, Sociology

Men's Athletic Profile

800 Country Club Rd
Waterbury, CT 06723-2540
Coach: Rick Bryant
Email: rbryant@teikyopost.edu

NCAA II, NAIA
Eagles/Green, White, Black
Phone: (203) 596-4568
Fax: (203) 596-4695

Estimated # of Men's Soccer Scholarships: 3
Conference: Central Atlantic Collegiate Conference
Program Profile: We have year-round program, playing outside whenever possible indoors due to necessity. Natural grass field which measures 120x80 yards.
History: 1986 transformed from NJCAA to NAIA; 1987 Regional Finalist; 1988 National Tournament; 1995, 1996, & 1997 NE Regional Championship Qualifiers; 1996 & 1997 CACC Champions. 1998 accepted NCAA II.
Achievements: 1996 Conference Player of the Year; All-Region ; 1997 Conference Player of the Year; All-Region; numerous Honorable Mention All-Americans. Three players involved with the A league.
Coaching: Rick Bryant, Head Coach, USSF "A License, formerly involved in the Massachusetts and Connecticut ODP. David Kelly, professional player in the A league, Connecticut Wolves, Captain.
Roster In State: 9 **Out of State:** 7 **Out of Country:** 7
ODP State: 5 **Regional:** 2 **National:** 2
Walk-on/Other: **Graduation %:** N/A **Seniors on Team:** 3
Positions Needed: Marking Backs and Goalkeepers
Camp or Clinic Dates: Preseason 8/20/2000
Most Recent Record: 9-13-
Schedule: Green Mt. College, Holy Family, University of New Haven, Stonehill College, Merrimack College, Bentley College
Style of Play: Coach according to talents of players within the team.

Trinity College - Connecticut

Academic Profile

Phone: 860-297-2180

Hartford, CT 06106

Type: 4 Yr.,Private,Liberal Arts
Website: http://www.trncoll.edu
SAT/ACT/GPA: 1200
Student/Faculty Ratio: 10:1
Undergraduate Enrollment: 2,088
Scholarships/Academic: Yes **Athletic:** No
Expenses by: Year **In State:** $ 32,130
Founded: 1823
Religion: Non-Affiliated
Housing: Yes
Male/Female Ratio: 51:49
Graduate Enrollment: 170
Financial Aid: Yes
Out of State: $ 32,130
Degrees Conferred: BA, BS, MA, MS
Programs of Study: American Studies, Anthropology, Art History, BioChemistry, Biology, Chemistry, Classics, Comparative Literature, Computer Science, Economics, Educational, Engineering, English, Fine Arts, Guided Studies, History, Interdisciplinary Science, International Studies, Jewish Studies, Legal Studies, Mathematics, Modern Languages, Music, Neuroscience, Political Science, Religion, Studio/Theatre, Women's Studies

Men's Athletic Profile

Ferris Athletic Center
Hartford, CT 06106
Coach: Ed Mighten
Email: Not Available

NCAA III
Bantams/Navy, Old Gold
Phone: (860) 297-2063
Fax: (860) 297-2892

Estimated # of Men's Soccer Scholarships: None
Conference: (NESCAC) New England Small College Athletic Conference
Program Profile: Trinity is a Division III program, Look for top scholar-athletes with the desire to play competitive soccer. The team plays on a natural grass field, playing 14 game competitive schedule.
History: The first varsity season began in 1936
Coaching: Ed Mighten, Head Coach eighth year,

Roster In State: 10
ODP State: 6
Walk-on/Other:
Out of State: 19
Regional:
Graduation %: N/A
Out of Country: 1
National:
Seniors on Team: 5

Camp or Clinic Dates: Not Available
Most Recent Record: 13-4
Style of Play: Play a balanced attack, focus on midfielders. Offense, strength and speed are key qualities we look for in athletes.

Women's Athletic Profile

300 Summit Street
Hartford, CT 06040
Coach: Michael Smith
Email: micheal.smith.3@exchange.trincoll.edu

NCAA III
Bantams/Blue, Gold, White
Phone: (860) 297-4263
Fax: (860) 297-2492

Estimated # of Women's Soccer Scholarships: None
Conference: (NESCAC) New England Small College Athletic Conference
Program Profile: Trinity plays on a natural grass field and is one of the nations top conferences. We play a very competitive 14 game, New England schedule. We look for top student-athletes who are very outgoing and possess exceptional technical skills, and love to attack.
History: The first year as varsity sport was in 1980.
Achievements: 1989 ECAC Division III New England Champions, 1994 ECAC Quarter-finalist.
Coaching: Micheal D. Smith, Head Coach, holds USSF "B" license, NSCAA Advanced National Diploma, and is the CT ODP Staff Coach.

Roster in State: 8
ODP State: 7
Walk-on/Other:
Out of State: 12
Regional:
Graduation %: 100
Out of Country:
National:
Seniors on Team: 3

Positions Needed: Goalkeeper, center mid, forward
Camp or Clinic Dates: Not Available
Most Recent Record: 4-8-1
Schedule: Williams, Amherst, Tufts, Middlebury, Bates, Bowdian
Style of Play: Combination of zone and man marking with quick transitions and explosive counters, with an aggressive attack minded attitude.

United States Coast Guard Academy

Academic Profile

New London, CT 06320

Phone: 800-883-8724

Type: 4 Yr.,Public,
Website: http://www.cga.edu

Founded: 1876
Religion: Non-Affiliated

SAT/ACT/GPA: None
Student/Faculty Ratio: 1:10
Undergraduate Enrollment: 900
Scholarships/Academic: None
Expenses by: Year
Athletic: None
In State: $ 4,158
Housing: Yes
Male/Female Ratio: 70:30
Graduate Enrollment: N/A
Financial Aid: None
Out of State: $ 12,676
Specialty: Federal Service Academy
Degrees Conferred: BS
Programs of Study: Business and Management, Computer Science, Engineering, Mathematics, Physical Sciences, Social Sciences

Men's Athletic Profile

15 Mohegan Avenue
New London, CT 06320
Coach: Ray Cieplik
Email: Not Available

NCAA III
Bears/Royal Blue, White
Phone: (860) 444-8603
Fax: (860) 444-8607

Estimated # of Men's Soccer Scholarships: None
Conference: New England Men's and Women's Athletic Conference (NEWMAC)
Program Profile: Division II program in seven time conference of strong New England small college programs. One Varsity game/practice field; one Junior Varsity practice field; stadium with lights in center of campus for football and soccer - four night games played at home.
History: Program began in 1940's, with war years of no soccer in early 50's; 22 straight years with winning record; several ECAC tournaments, NCAA bids; 1995 ECAC Champions.
Achievements: Conference Champions in 1993, 1994, 1995; 38 All-New England selections since 1970; 6 All-American selections.
Coaching: Ray Cieplik, Head Coach, full-time head coach, NSCAA Advanced National Diploma. He compiled a record of 234-148-33 since 1970. Four assistant coaches - full time faculty serving as a part-time assistants.
Style of Play: Fast-paced direct style mixed with a skillful short passing.

University of Bridgeport

Academic Profile

Bridgeport, CT 06601
Phone: (203) 576-4727

Type: 4 Yr.,Private,Liberal Arts,Engineering
Website: http://www.bridgeport.edu
SAT/ACT/GPA: 820/18
Student/Faculty Ratio: 13:1
Undergraduate Enrollment: 2,700
Scholarships/Academic: Yes
Expenses by: Year
Athletic: Yes
In State: $ 20,854
Founded: 1927
Religion: Non-Affiliated
Housing: Yes
Male/Female Ratio: 51:49
Graduate Enrollment: N/A
Financial Aid: Yes
Out of State: $ 20,854
Specialty: Education, Dental Hygiene
Degrees Conferred: All majors are fully accredited
Programs of Study: Accounting, Biology, Business, Computer Engineering, Education, Computer Science, Dental Hygiene, Fashion Merchandising, Finance, Graphic Design, Interior Design, Mass Communications, Social Science, PreVet, Marketing, Advertising, History, Psychology, Political Science, etc...

Men's Athletic Profile

120 Waldemere Avenue
Bridgeport, CT 06601
Coach: Brian s. Quinn
Email: BSQuinn@hotmail.com

NCAA II
Purple Knights/Purple, White
Phone: (203) 576-4727
Fax: (203) 576-4057

Estimated # of Men's Soccer Scholarships: 2-3
Conference: New England Collegiate Conference
Program Profile: Year round program 18-20 games in fall 5 in spring. Harvey Hubbell Gymnasium, Whekler Recreation Center, Seaside park. Home field is natural grass. comprehensive program designed to meet all players needs in areas of technique, tactics, and physical conditioning.
History: Program began in 1948. Program featured 3 legends coaching profession; John Mckeon, Joe Bean, and Fran Bacon. Reached National championship game in 1959 and National semi-finals in 1986.
Achievements: 16 All-Americans, players drafted, Coach of the Year, Regional Coach of the Year in 1995 and NECC Coach of the Year in 1997.
Coaching: Brian S. Quinn, Head Coach. Magnus Nilervd, Asst. Coach. Billy Gatti, Goalkeeper Coach. Elias Zurita, Asst. Coach
Walk-on/Other: **Graduation %:** **Seniors on Team:** 3
Positions Needed: LMF, L Back, C Back& Keeper, Midfield
Camp or Clinic Dates: Not Available
Most Recent Record: 7-10-1
Schedule: New Hampshire College, CW Post, Dowling College, Southampton College
Style of Play: Attractive possession style attack, very disciplined and organized on defense, but aggressive enough to win the ball and counter attack. high technical level players.

Women's Athletic Profile

120 Waldemere Avenue
Bridgeport, CT 06601
Coach: Magnus Nilerud
Email: nilen@prodigy.net

NCAA II
Purple Knights/Purple, White
Phone: (203) 576-4727
Fax: (203) 576-4057

Estimated # of Women's Soccer Scholarships: 12 Tuition
Conference: New England Collegiate Conference
Program Profile: Moving away from top nation Conference NECC, which will not operate in 2001, to top nation conference NYCAC. Field is natural grass, newly renovated indoor complex.
History: The program founded in the late 1980's.
Achievements: Regional Coach of the Year; All-Area; All-Leagues Players.
Coaching: Magnus Nilerud, Head Coach, and Brian Quinn, Assistant Coach, is our coaching staff.
Roster in State: 5 **Out of State:** 7 **Out of Country:** 7
Walk-on/Other: **Graduation %:** **Seniors on Team:** 6
Positions Needed: Goalkeeper, Forward
Camp or Clinic Dates: Not Available
Schedule: CW Post, Adelphi, New Haven, University of Massachusetts Lowell, St. Rose, Philadelphia University
Style of Play: Possession with quick attacking to goal.

University of Connecticut

Academic Profile

Ads
Storrs, CT 06269

Phone: (860) 486-4204

Type: 4 Yr.,Public,
Website: http://www.uconnhuskies.edu
SAT/ACT/GPA: 1100/2.0
Student/Faculty Ratio: 14:1
Undergraduate Enrollment: 11,216
Scholarships/Academic: Yes **Athletic:** Yes
Expenses by: Year **In State:** $ 11,216

Founded: 1881
Religion: Non-Affiliated
Housing: Yes
Male/Female Ratio: 48:52
Graduate Enrollment: 19,990
Financial Aid: Yes
Out of State: $ 19,990

Degrees Conferred: BA, BFA, BMS, General Studies
Programs of Study: Agriculture and Natural Science, Business Administration, Allied Health, Education, Engineering, Extended and Continuing Education, Family Studies, Fine Arts, General Studies, Honors Program, Liberal Arts & Sciences, Nursing, Pharmacy

Men's Athletic Profile

2095 Hillside Road, Box U-78
Storrs, CT 06269
Coach: Ray Reid
Email: deeley@athletics.edu

NCAA I
Huskies/Blue, White
Phone: (860) 486-4231
Fax: (860) 486-5568

Estimated # of Men's Soccer Scholarships: N/A
Conference: Big East Conference
Program Profile: We are a Division I program and member of the Big East Conference. Plays a traditional fall schedule and competition dates in the off-season. The Huskies play in Morrone Stadium on natural grass surface. Stadium capacity is 8,574 and field's dimensions are 75x120, the maximum for a collegiate soccer field.
History: Our program started in 1928 and has compiled an overall record of 551-383-72 over 70 years. Head Coach Ray Reid is the eight men's soccer coach. University of Connecticut won the National Title in 1981 under Head Coach Joe Marrone and was awarded the title in 1948 under Head Coach John Squires.
Achievements: The huskies have 3 National Titles; 19 NCAA Tournament Appearances; 26 All-Americans; 2 Major League Soccer draft picks; 64 All-New England performers; 5 Big East regular season titles; 3 Big East Tournament Championships; 6 Big East Player of the Year Awards; 4 Big East Coach of the Year Awards; Herman Trophy Winner in 1981; Herman Trophy runner-up in 1998.
Coaching: Ray Reid is our Head Coach. He holds a USSF "A" Licensed and was named three-time Division II National Coach of the Year. George Kiefer is our Assistant Coach. He holds USSF "A" Licensed. John Deeley is our Assistant Coach. He holds a USSF "C" Licensed.
Style of Play: Possession oriented team game.

Women's Athletic Profile

2111 Hillside Road
Storrs, CT 06269
Coach: Len Tsantiris
Email: fergie@athletics.ath.uconn.edu

NCAA I
Lady Huskies/Blue, White
Phone: (860) 486-4204
Fax: (860) 486-0525

Estimated # of Women's Soccer Scholarships: None
Conference: Big East
Program Profile: We play on a 8,500 seats soccer only stadium field. We are in Division I and fully-funded.
History: We began in 1979. Coach Tsantiris started here in 1981. We have had 17 straight NCAA appearances.
Achievements: NSCAA Division I National Coach of the Year in 1997; Division I Northeast Coach of the Year 1983,1987,1995,1996; Big East Conference Coach of the Year 1995; Coached 17 All-Americans Big East Coach of the Year 1998; NCAA Finalists in 1984,1990, 1997; NCAA Semi-Finalists 1982, 1983,1984, 1990, 1994 and 1997.
Coaching: Len Tsantiris, Head Coach, is in his 17th season. He has a USSF 'A' license and is recognized as one of the nation's leaders among women's soccer coaches. Karen Ferguson and George Kostelis are assistant coaches.
Style of Play: High-paced game, style depends upon strengths of players; style varies year to year.

University of Hartford

Academic Profile

Phone: 860-768-4296

West Hartford, CT 06117

Type: 4 Yr.,Private,Liberal Arts
Website: http://www.hartford.edu
SAT/ACT/GPA: 850+
Student/Faculty Ratio: 11:1
Undergraduate Enrollment: 5,230

Founded: 1877
Religion: Non-Affiliated
Housing: Yes
Male/Female Ratio: 49:50
Graduate Enrollment: 1,662

Scholarships/Academic: Yes **Athletic:** Yes **Financial Aid:** Yes
Expenses by: Year **In State:** $ 27,218 **Out of State:** $ 27,218
Degrees Conferred: AA, AS, AAS, BA, BS, BFA, MA, MS, MBA, MEd, D
Programs of Study: Accounting, Architecture, Audio Engineering, Business Administration, Business Accounting, BioEngineering, Biology, Chemistry, Communications, Computer Engineering , Dance, Drama, Drawing, Economics, Education, Engineering, History, Mathematics, Music, Nursing, Philosophy, Physics, Psychology, Public Administration, Respiratory Therapy, Women's Studies

Men's Athletic Profile

200 Bloomfield Avenue
West Hartford, CT 06117
Coach: Jim Evans
Email: Not Available

NCAA I
Hawks/Scarlet, White
Phone: (860) 768-4470
Fax: (860) 768-5047

Estimated # of Men's Soccer Scholarships: None
Conference: North Atlantic Conference
Program Profile: We have a lighted grass field with a seating capacity of 3,000.
History: Program began in 1957 in Division II. Began Division I in 1985. NCAA tournament second round, 1992, NCAA tournament first round 1991; two-time NAC Champions 1991,1992.
Achievements: Elvis Thomas: 2 time All-New England and 2 time All-NAC selection.
Coaching: Jim Evans is our Head Coach. He is in his 5th year at Hartford, 10th year as a head coach. former coach at Thomas College where he took them to three NAIA Finals, as well as assisting George Mason helping guide them to NCAA Regional Championship.
Style of Play: We play a possession oriented game that is based on the simple fundamentals of the game. We are very athletic and like to play at a fast pace that makes for exciting and attractive soccer. We like to be forward.

Women's Athletic Profile

200 Bloomfield Avenue
West Hartford, CT 06117
Coach: Ewa Bergsten
Email:

NCAA I
Hawks/Scarlet, White
Phone: (860) 768-4676
Fax: (860) 768-5047

Estimated # of Women's Soccer Scholarships: 3
Conference: America East Conference
Program Profile: The Hawks' home field is a natural grass and seats 2,500. Fall playing season.
History: Hartford has reached the NCAA Tournament 9 times. In 1999 Hartford went to the "Elite Eight" finishing ranked 7th Nationally. We have produced both National Team and Professional players.
Achievements: Hartford has reached the NCAA Tournament six times in 1989-1992, 1994-1995. The program has produced three National team members, 2 professional players, three Herman Trophy Nominees, and six All-Americans.
Coaching: 3rd year assistant coach Ewa Bergsten has been promoted to Head Coach.
Roster in State: 4 **Out of State:** 8 **Out of Country:** 8
ODP State: 4 **Regional:** 10 **National:** 6
Walk-on/Other: **Graduation %:** 90 **Seniors on Team:** 4
Positions Needed: All field positions
Camp or Clinic Dates: August 6-11
Most Recent Record: 18-5-2
Schedule: Santa Clara, Stanford, Virginia, Texas A&M, Florida, Harvard, Dartmouth, George Mason, Yale, Boston College
Style of Play: Ball control-possession oriented and attack out of the back.

University of New Haven

Academic Profile

West Haven, CT 06516

Phone: (203) 932-7027

Type: 4 Yr.,Private,Liberal Arts,Engineering
Website: http://www.newhaven.edu
SAT/ACT/GPA: 820/17
Student/Faculty Ratio: 14:1
Undergraduate Enrollment: 1,600
Scholarships/Academic: Yes
Athletic: Yes
Expenses by: Year
In State: $ 21,000
Specialty: Criminal Justice, Forensic Science
Degrees Conferred: AS, BA, BS, MA, MS, MBA, Ph.D.
Programs of Study: Contact school for programs of study.

Founded: 1920
Religion: Non-Affiliated
Housing: Yes
Male/Female Ratio: 7:5
Graduate Enrollment: 2,600
Financial Aid: Yes
Out of State: $ 21,000

Men's Athletic Profile

300 Orange Avenue
West Haven, CT 06516
Coach: Mark Lucas
Email: Not Available

NCAA II
Chargers/Blue, Gold
Phone: (203) 932-7027
Fax: (203) 932-7470

Estimated # of Men's Soccer Scholarships: 6
Conference: Independent
Program Profile: Top level D. II program. 19-20 game season with 5 top 10 ranked opponents. Technical team, plays possession. Multi-cultural team Americans, Isralis, Tabaga, Brazilian and African Players.
History: Program began in 1962. Made NCAA appearances, most recently in 1984. First winning season in 12 years in 1996. 3 ECAC included 1996 & 1997.
Achievements: 7 All-Americans, 2 NECC Titles, 8 NCAA appearances, 2 NAIA Appearances, 2 ECAC appearances, 1996 NECC Rookie of the Year. 1996 NECC & NEISL Coach of the Year.
Roster In State: 6
Out of State: 10
Out of Country: 8
ODP State: 2
Regional: 1
National: 0
Walk-on/Other: 0
Graduation %: 90
Seniors on Team: 3
Positions Needed: Forwards, Defenders
Camp or Clinic Dates: Not Available
Most Recent Record: 12-6-2
Schedule: Southern Ct. State, St. Anselms, CW Post, Concordia
Style of Play: Technical, possession attractive style and fast.

Women's Athletic Profile

300 Orange Avenue
West Haven, CT 06516
Coach: Daniel Bacon
Email: BelvoFC@aol.com

NCAA II
Chargers/Blue, Gold
Phone: (203) 932-7027
Fax: (203) 932-7470

Estimated # of Women's Soccer Scholarships:
Conference: New England Collegiate Conference, Eastern College Athletic Conference
Program Profile: New haven has a strong athletic tradition. Dodds Stadium has a full size natural grass field and seats 5,000. tough NECC and out of conference schedule.
History: Program will enter seventh year in the Fall of 1999. Returned to regional and national prominence in 1998. Enter 5th in New England and 25th in the nation.

Achievements: Dave Clarke was named NECC Coach of the Year in 1998; two players All-New England second team; NSCAA #26 Final Poll.
Coaching: Dave Clarke, Head Coach, entering third year with the program. He holds USSF "A" License, NSCAA Advanced National Diploma; CJSA Coaching License Coordinator, Connecticut ODP Staff Coach, Region I ODP Staff Coach, Windsor World Class Coach. He was a former player at Central Connecticut (NCAA I), Connecticut Wolves A-League.
Style of Play: Style suits the ability and capabilities of the players. Attack when we can, defend when we have to.

Wesleyan University
Academic Profile

Middletown, CT 06459
Phone: (860) 685-2690

Type: 4 Yr.,Private,Liberal Arts
Founded: 1831
Website: http://www.wesleyan.edu
Religion: Methodist
SAT/ACT/GPA: 1340
Housing: Yes
Student/Faculty Ratio: 11:1
Male/Female Ratio: 1:1
Undergraduate Enrollment: 2750
Graduate Enrollment: 300
Scholarships/Academic: Yes **Athletic:** No **Financial Aid:** Yes
Expenses by: Year **In State:** $ 32,000 **Out of State:** $ 32,000
Specialty: Premed, Psychology, Economics, Languages, Arts, Social Sciences
Degrees Conferred: BA, MA, Ph.D.
Programs of Study: Afro-American Studies, American Studies, Anthropology, Archaeological Studies, Art History, Astronomy, Biology, Classical Studies, Classical Civilization, Chemistry, College of Letters, College of Social Studies, Computer Science, Dance, Earth & Environmental Sciences, East Asian Studies, Economics, English, Film Studies, Government, History, Latin American Studies, Mathematics, Medieval Studies, Molecular Biology & BioChemistry, Music, Neuroscience & Behavior, Philosophy, Physics, Psychology, Religion, Romance Languages, Russian & Eastern Studies, Science in Society, Sociology, Studio Art, Theatre, Women's Studies

Men's Athletic Profile

161 Cross Street
Middletown, CT 06459
NCAA III
Cardinals/Red, Black
Coach: Geoffrey Wheeler
Phone: (860) 685-2898
Email: gwheeler@wesleyan.edu
Fax: (860) 685-2691
Estimated # of Men's Soccer Scholarships: None
Conference: New England Small College Athletic Conference
Program Profile: We are a highly competitive Division III program. We play on beautiful grass pitches both practice and game fields.
History: The program started as a varsity sport in 1924. Hugh McCurdy coached the first 39 years followed by Stan Plagenhad for two year, Don Long for one year and Terry Jackson for 31 years.
Achievements: 1991 record was 15-1; Top rated team in the Division II in NE; Coach of the Year in 1991; 2 ECAC Championship, 4 All-Americans.
Coaching: Geoffrey Wheeler, Head Coach, entering first year with the program.
Roster In State: 5 **Out of State:** 20 **Out of Country:**
Walk-on/Other: **Graduation %:** 98 **Seniors on Team:** 6
Positions Needed: Six
Camp or Clinic Dates: Not Available
Most Recent Record: 6-8
Schedule: Williams, Amherst, Middlebery, Trinity, Tufts, Springfield
Style of Play: 4-4-2 zoned defending. Attacking offensive play with everyone getting forward. Exciting and fun to watch.

Women's Athletic Profile

161 Cross Street
Middletown, CT 06459-2691
Coach: Holly Gutelius
Email: hgutelius@wesleyan.edu

NCAA III
Cardinals/Black, Red
Phone: (860) 685-2906
Fax: (860) 685-2691

Estimated # of Women's Soccer Scholarships: None
Conference: New England Small College Athletic Conference
Program Profile: The playing field is grass, and the field is located adjacent to the 10 year old Freedman Athletic Center which has an excellent indoor facility.
History: Program began in 1979. We won the ECACs in 1994.
Achievements: 1994 team posted best ever record of 12-4-1 and won ECAC New England Division III title. 2 First Team All-New England Strikers.
Coaching: This is Holly's first year as a soccer coach but her second year as a lacrosse coach.
Roster in State: 5
Out of State: 16
Out of Country:
Walk-on/Other:
Graduation %: 100
Seniors on Team: 2
Positions Needed: Goalkeeper, Midfielders
Camp or Clinic Dates: Not Available
Most Recent Record: 3-10
Schedule: Ambers, Williams, Wellesley, Middleburn, Colby, Trinity, Bowdoin, Springfield, Smith, Mt. Holyoke

Western Connecticut State University

Academic Profile

Danbury, CT 06810

Phone: (203) 837-9022

Type: 4 Yr.,Public,Liberal Arts
Website: http://www.ctstateu.edu
SAT/ACT/GPA: 900/17
Student/Faculty Ratio: 20:1
Undergraduate Enrollment: 1,500
Scholarships/Academic: Yes
Athletic: No
Expenses by: Year
In State: $ 9,904
Founded: 1903
Religion: Non-Affiliated
Housing: Yes
Male/Female Ratio: 50:50
Graduate Enrollment: 2,950
Financial Aid: Yes
Out of State: $ 15,413
Degrees Conferred: AS, BA, BS, MA, MS, MBA
Programs of Study: Accounting, American Studies, Art and Graphic Design, Astronomy, Biology, Business, Chemistry, Communications, Computer Science, Contract Major, Dramatic Arts, Earth Science, Economics, Elementary Education, English, Finance, Government, Health, History, Journalism, Justice and Law Administration, Law, Management, Marketing, Meteorology, Management Information Systems, Mathematics, Media, Music, Music Education, Nursing, Psychology, Political Science, School Professional, Secondary Education, Sociology & Anthropology, Social Work

Men's Athletic Profile

181 White Street
Danbury, CT 06810
Coach: Wayne Mones
Email: Not Available

NCAA III
Colonials/Blue, White
Phone: (203) 837-9057
Fax: (203) 837-9056

Estimated # of Men's Soccer Scholarships: None
Conference: Little East Conference
Program Profile: We have a new field house and soccer stadium, featuring lights, astro turf, exclusively for soccer. Has a seating capacity of 3,000, and field has a measurements of 120x80 yards. 20 game schedule which is the toughest in the New England.

History: Program began in 1960. Five straight tournament berths, 14+ wins for six consecutive seasons, made Final Eight in 1992.
Achievements: 1992 New England Coach of the Year; 3 All-Americans, 12 All-New England players.
Coaching: Wayne Moynes, Head Coach for eleven years, BS and MS, Certificate in Guidance, former UC player in 1973 & 1974, former Central Catholic High School Coach with a record of 165-75-24, his teams have won three conference championships.
Style of Play: Play to feet, build up style and on defense, we use various zonal defenses.

Women's Athletic Profile

181 White Street
Danbury, CT 06810
Coach: Joe Mingachos
Email: Mingachosj@wcou.ctstate.edu

NCAA III
Colonials/Blue, White
Phone: (203) 837-9020
Fax: (203) 837-9056

Estimated # of Women's Soccer Scholarships: None
Conference: Little East Conference
Program Profile: WCSU plays on a Astro Turf Stadium that seats 4,000 with lights and natural grass fields to practice on. We have a full time coach and are nationally ranked and in the top 5 in New England region. Head coach has been here for 3 years 2 NCATA tourney bids & 1 ECAC berth.
History: Our program became a varsity sport in 1994 and been nationally ranked the last 3 years and undefeated the last year. We have one 3 consecutive conference championships and have received 4 consecutive post season tournament bids. 2 ECAC & 2 NCAA
Achievements: Regional Coach of the Year in 1997; Conference Coach of the Year in 1999; Has compiled a 49-8-4 record in the last 3 years; 3 consecutive conference championships; 4 consecutive post season tournament bids; 1 All-American in 1997; varies regional honors for players.
Coaching: Joe Benitez, former player at Western-holds all time leading scoring record at Western. On stat for 3 years. Tina Fernandes former Western player. 2 time all regional performer at Western, just completed her 1st year on the staff. Everton McCatta, goalkeeper at Western, just completed 1st year on staff
Roster in State: 18 **Out of State:** 2 **Out of Country:**
Walk-on/Other: **Graduation %:** **Seniors on Team:** 5
Camp or Clinic Dates: Not Available
Most Recent Record: 17-1-2
Schedule: University of Scranton, Wheaton, Keene State, Wellesley, Plymouth State, Eastern Ct. St. University
Style of Play: We adjust to the players that we have on the team. We play to our strengths.

Yale University
Academic Profile

New Haven, CT 06520
Phone: 203-432-9300

Type: 4 Yr.,Private,Liberal Arts
Founded: 1701
Website: http://www.yale.edu
Religion: Non-Affiliated
SAT/ACT/GPA: Open
Housing: Yes
Student/Faculty Ratio: 5:1
Male/Female Ratio: 1:1
Undergraduate Enrollment: 5,200
Graduate Enrollment: 5,200
Scholarships/Academic: Yes **Athletic:** No **Financial Aid:** Yes
Expenses by: Year **In State:** $ 30,830 **Out of State:** $ 30,830
Degrees Conferred: BA, MA, Ph.D.., JD, M.Div, MD, BS, BLS
Programs of Study: African & African - American Studies, Anthropology, Astronomy & Physics, Chemistry, Chinese, Classics, Comparative Literature, Economics, Engineering, English, History, Judaic Studies, Latin American Studies, Mathematics, Organism Biology, Philosophy, Physics, Psychology, Religious Studies, Russian, Sociology, Theatre Studies, Women's Studies

Men's Athletic Profile

Men's Soccer Office, P.O. Box 208216
New Haven, CT 06520
Coach: Brian Tompkins
Email: brian.tompkins@yale.edu

NCAA I
Bulldogs/Blue, White
Phone: (203) 432-1495
Fax: (203) 432-7772

Estimated # of Men's Soccer Scholarships: None
Conference: Ivy League Conference
Program Profile: We play all home games at the Yale Soccer Lacrosse stadium. the stadium is bordered by picturesque row of pine trees and its seating capacity has been used for training for international teams as well as hosting the Special Olympic World Games. Season begins in late August and runs through mid-November. Seventeen regular season games per year.
History: Soccer program began at Yale in 1908. Ivy League play began in 1955. The school's all-time soccer record is 503-367-122.
Achievements: Have won 4 Ivy League Championships, and made 4 appearances in the NCAA Tournament, advancing to the quarterfinals in 1991. Yale has produced 10 first team All-Americans. Several Yale alumni are currently playing for teams in the A-League, including 1 draft in 1998.
Coaching: Brian Thompkins is our Head Coach. He is entering fourth year with a record of 21-11-2. A native of London, England, he has a USSF "A" license and is a member of Region I ODP staff coach. Former head coach at University of Wisconsin-Milwaukee, Tompkins has compiled a career coaching record of 111-52-13 in nine seasons. Dave Barrett - Assistant Coach, former goalkeeper at Wesleyan University. NSCAA Advanced National Diploma. State of Connecticut ODP Staff Coach. Chico Chacuria - Assistant Coach, native of Argentina, former player for US National Team. Member of the Soccer Hall of Fame. Long time member of Region I ODP Staff.

Roster In State: 2	**Out of State:** 22	**Out of Country:** 2
ODP State: 21	**Regional:** 6	**National:**
Walk-on/Other:	**Graduation %:** 100	**Seniors on Team:** 3

Positions Needed: various
Camp or Clinic Dates: Not Available
Most Recent Record: 13-5-1
Schedule: Harvard, Princeton, Brown, Penn, Carngll, Columbia, Penn, Connecticut, St. John's
Style of Play: Formation dependent upon personnel, usually a 3-5-2 or 4-4-2. Like to attack with a speed, especially featuring wide players and wing play. Will try to build from back and possess through the midfield.

Women's Athletic Profile

P.O. Box 208216
New Haven, CT 06520
Coach: Rudy Meredith
Email: Not Available

NCAA I
Eli, Bulldogs/Yale Blue, White
Phone: (203) 432-1492
Fax: (203) 432-7772

Estimated # of Women's Soccer Scholarships: None
Conference: Ivy League
Program Profile: Great stadium, 120 x 78 yards, lighted, three practice fields, grass, seats 3,000. Play strong in IVY Conference with three teams making NCAA's.
History: Program began in 1977.
Achievements: 1990 NSCAA Regional Coach of the Year, 1993, 1993, 1991 Ivy League Player of the Year; 1992 Ivy Champs, 16th in the country; ECAC finalist; 1993 and 1992 All-American, 1992 and 1991 II Regional All-American.
Coaching: Rudy Meredith, Head Coach.
Style of Play: We try to let the ball do the work, and play smart, controlled soccer.

delaware

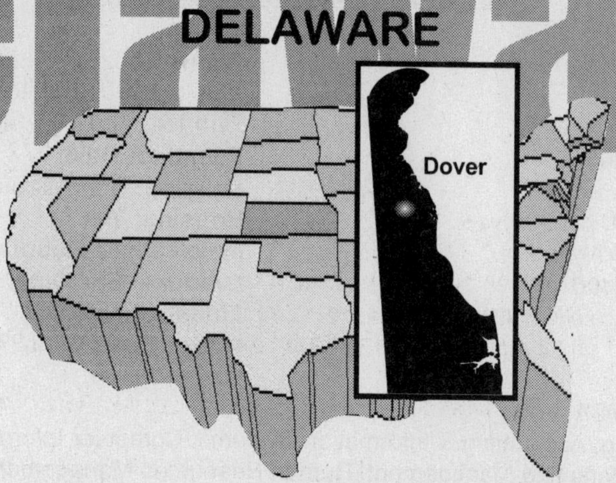

SCHOOL	CITY	AFFILIATION	PAGE
Goldey Beacom College	Wilmington	NCAA II	186
University of Delaware	Newark	NCAA I	187
Wesley College	Dover	NCAA III	188

Goldey - Beacom College

Academic Profile

Wilmington, DE 19808

Phone: (302) 998-8814

Type: 4 Yr.,Private,
Website: http://www.goldey.edu
SAT/ACT/GPA: 973
Student/Faculty Ratio: 26:1
Undergraduate Enrollment: 1,400
Scholarships/Academic: Yes
Expenses by: Year
Specialty: Business
Degrees Conferred: AS, BS, MBA

Athletic: Yes
In State: $ 13,370

Founded: 1886
Religion: Non-Affiliated
Housing: Yes
Male/Female Ratio: 40:60
Graduate Enrollment: 150
Financial Aid: Yes
Out of State: $ 13,370

Programs of Study: Accounting, Accounting & Information Systems, Computer Information Systems, Business Administration, Management, Marketing Management, Human Resources Management, Finance Management and International Business

Men's Athletic Profile

4701 Limestone Road
Wilmington, DE 19808
Coach: Mike Finizie
Email: finiziom@goldey.gbc.edu

NCAA II, NAIA
Lightning/Blue, Gold, White
Phone: (302) 225-6355
Fax: (302) 998-6823

Estimated # of Men's Soccer Scholarships: 4
Conference: CACC
Program Profile: Hold dual membership in the NAIN and NCAA. 110x70 natural grass field, seats 500.
History: Began in 1990 and have been in post season play each year since. Two time district champs.
Achievements: Two district titles and numerous conference all stars.
Coaching: Head Coach- mike Finizio, Assistant Coach- Mike Dickey
Roster In State: 5
ODP State: 5
Walk-on/Other:

Out of State: 5
Regional:
Graduation %: 90

Out of Country: 11
National:
Seniors on Team: 5

Positions Needed: Goalkeeper, forward
Camp or Clinic Dates: Not Available
Most Recent Record: 6-11-2
Schedule: Green Mountain, UDC, Richard Stockton, Holy Family, Tiekyo Post.
Style of Play: Ball control - build up from the defense to the midfield wings-passes to the center. Short passing game with a players having freedom to use individual skills in a team concept. Set plays are kept simple. Defend zone or close marking as needed. Counter Attack with speed.

Women's Athletic Profile

4701 Limestone Rd
Wilmington, DE 19808
Coach: Chris Morgan
Email: morganc@goldey.gbc.edu

NCAA II
Lighting, Navy, White & Gold
Phone: 302-225-6330
Fax: 302-998-6823

Estimated # of Women's Soccer Scholarships: Varies
Conference: Central Atlantic Collegiate Conference
Program Profile: We just finished our first season of intercollegiate competition. We are a dual member of the NCAA Division II and NAIA. Full NCAA Membership in 2003. We play on a 75x115 natural grass field. Our season consists of 10 Conference games and 8-10 non-conference games.

History: Fall of 2000 is the first season. We finished the year with an 8-7 record, and qualified for our conference play-offs. The team recorded 8 shutouts and only conceded 16 goals in 15 games. With 7 freshman starters returning, we look to improve next fall.
Coaching: Head Coach- Chris Morgan collegiate All-American and National Champion. Former Professional Player with 8 years of professional experience. 6 years coaching experience at Division I, director of youth soccer for 4 years.
Roster In State: 7 **Out of State:** 3 **Out of Country:** 6
ODP State: 4 **Regional:** **National:**
Walk-on/Other: 12 **Graduation %:** **Seniors on Team:** 1
Positions Needed: GK, Forward
Most Recent Record: 8-7-0
Schedule: Holy Family, Millersville, Philadelphia Univ, Teikyo Post Univ. Dominican College, Georgian Court College.
Style of Play: Defensive oriented, with counter attacking style.

University of Delaware
Academic Profile

Newark, DE 19716-2001
Phone: (302) 831-2000

Type: 4 Yr.,Public,Liberal Arts,Engineering
Founded: 1743
Website: http://www.udel.edu
Religion: Non-Affiliated
SAT/ACT/GPA: 1000/3.01
Housing: Yes
Student/Faculty Ratio: 15:1
Male/Female Ratio: 45:55
Undergraduate Enrollment: 15,000
Graduate Enrollment: 3,200
Scholarships/Academic: Yes **Athletic:** Yes **Financial Aid:** Yes
Expenses by: Year **In State:** $ 14,403 **Out of State:** $ 18,765
Degrees Conferred: BA, BS, BMAS, Engineering
Programs of Study: Agriculture, Anthropology, Apparel Design, Art, Athletics and Recreation, BioChemistry, Biology, BioTechnology, Business and Economics Accounting, Business Management, Chemistry, Communications, Computer Science, Criminal Justice, Dietetics, Economics, Education, Elementary Education, Engineering (Chemical, Civil, Electrical, Computer, Mechanical, Environmental), English, Entomology, Family and Consumer Services, Finance, Human Resources, Literature, Management, Marketing, Medical Technology, Nursing, Nutrition, Physical Education, Recreation/Park, Textiles and Clothing Merchandising

Men's Athletic Profile

610 S. College Avenue
Newark, DE 19716
Coach: Marc Samonisky
Email: marcsam@udel.edu

NCAA I
Fightin' Blue Hens/Blue, Gold
Phone: (302) 831-8603
Fax: (302) 831-4058

Estimated # of Men's Soccer Scholarships: Money Varies
Conference: America East Conference
Program Profile: Delaware plays its home games at 1,000-seat Delaware Min-Stadium, natural grass, lighting for practice only. Team has lockers at Delaware Fieldhouse which is located next to the 23,000-seat Delaware Stadium and 5,000-seat Bo Carpenter Center. Game field grass, artificial surface on campus.
History: Our men's soccer program was started in 1940 and the team advanced to NCAA regional in 1968 and 1970 and to ECAC Tournament in 1976. The team is one of the fastest rising programs in America East and one of the most competitive conferences in the nation in NCAA Division I (2 NCAA bids in 1996). The team advanced to the conference semi-finals in 1996.
Achievements: The team advanced to the NCAA Regional in 1968 and 1970, and to the ECAC Tournament in 1976. The team has had numerous All-Conference selections, numerous conference Academic Honor Roll recipients and 10 All-Americans.

Coaching: Marc Samonisky is our Head Coach. He has served the University of Delaware as a standout soccer and football player, as a long-time assistant coach, and just completed his sixth season as a head coach of the Blue Hens. He was named America East Coach of the Year in 1996 for leading team to a record of 9-8-1, and a conference semi-finals. "A" licensed coach in the US Soccer Federation of Mid-Atlantic Region rating committee (NSCAA Advanced Diploma).
Style of Play: We try to play according to our ability. We defend fairly well and are looking to possess the ball, get forward and score more goals.

Women's Athletic Profile

Delaware Fieldhouse
Newark, DE 19716
Coach: Scott Grzenda
Email: sag@udel.edu

NCAA I
Fighting' Blue Hens/Blue, Gold
Phone: (302) 831-4006
Fax: (302) 831-8653

Estimated # of Women's Soccer Scholarships: None
Conference: American East Conference
Program Profile: Natural grass facility to be completed in 2000; grass and turf practice facilities.
History: The program started in 1990 after a successful stint as a club sport team's seven-year record stands at 74-45-6. Team has finished as a runner-up in the America East (formerly North Atlantic Conference) in 1994, 1995, and 1996. The team continues to improve each season with a more challenging schedule.
Achievements: Scott Grzenda-America East Coach of the Year in 1993 and 1994; team has finished second in the America East in 1994, 1995, and 1996. M. Beth Hatt was named to the Umbro All-Region 1st team for three straight season this fall of 1996, numerous All-Conference and All-American award recipients.
Coaching: Scott Grzenda, Head Coach, has served as a head coach of Delaware program for each of its seven years, and has been a college coach ten years overall; FIFP licensed; ODP coach; assistant coaches are all experienced at the collegiate level. Mike Kienzart and Beth Hait - Assistant Coaches.
Style of Play: A commitment to attack and defend with eleven players.

Wesley College

Academic Profile

Dover, DE 19901

Phone: 800-937-5398

Type: 4 Yr.,Private,Liberal Arts
Website: http://www.wesley.edu
SAT/ACT/GPA: 900
Student/Faculty Ratio: 15:1
Undergraduate Enrollment: 800
Scholarships/Academic: Yes
Athletic: No
Expenses by: Year
In State: $ 16,000

Founded: 1873
Religion: Methodist
Housing: Yes
Male/Female Ratio: 50:50
Graduate Enrollment: 30
Financial Aid: Yes
Out of State: $ 16,000

Degrees Conferred: Baccalaureate, some new Masters Program
Programs of Study: Allied Health, Biology, Business and Management, Business/Office and Marketing/Distribution, Communications, Computer Sciences, Education, Environmental Science, Health Sciences, History, Law, Letters/Literature, Political Sciences

Men's Athletic Profile

120 N State Street
Dover, DE 19901
Coach: Steve Clark
Email: clarkst@marl.wesley.edu

NCAA III
Wolverines/Navy Blue, White
Phone: (302) 736-2557
Fax: (302) 736-0345

Estimated # of Men's Soccer Scholarships:
Conference: Pennsylvania Athletic Conference

Program Profile: Our team plays a fall and spring season. We play on a grass field. Our facilities include an indoor area and fitness center. Team travels - but overseas tour is every four years.
History: The program began in 1988. Steve Clark took it over in 1990. ECAC playoff 1993-1994 & 1994-1995. We only had one losing season in the nineties. The program is a strong regional team.
Achievements: One pro player on pro-contract; 2 All-Americans; Coach of the Year Honors; numerous tournament wins and regional rankings; 2 ECAC playoffs.
Coaching: Steve Clark, Head Coach since 1990, came from England. He holds an English FA Coaching License; was 1990 ECAC Coach of the Year and was on the 1994 NCAA Committee.
Style of Play: Exciting, attacking, keep the ball on the ground; hard work organization on defense.

Women's Athletic Profile

120 North State St.
Dover, DE 19901
Coach: Ed Muntz
Email: muntzed@mail.wesley.edu

NCAA III
Wolverines/Navy Blue, White
Phone: (302) 736-2516
Fax: (302) 736-0345

Estimated # of Women's Soccer Scholarships: None
Conference: Pennsylvania Athletic Conference
Program Profile: Facilities include grass field that measures 118x75 yards, indoor arena, fitness center; stadium capacity of a 2,000. Fall and spring seasons; also team travel in bus, overseas twice every four years.
History: Fall of 1995 was the first year of the program. Compiled a record of .520 in first three years.
Achievements: New program-winning record; independent program until 1998.
Coaching: Ed Muntz, Head Coach, Wesley graduate, all-time leading goal scorer on the men's team, ODP Coach for the Delaware Women's Soccer.
Roster in State: 3 **Out of State:** 23 **Out of Country:** 0
ODP State: 1 **Regional:** **National:**
Walk-on/Other: 2 **Graduation %:** 100 **Seniors on Team:** 1
Most Recent Record: 7-9-1
Schedule: Villa Julie College, Beaver College, York College
Style of Play: Exciting, attacking, keep the ball on the ground, hard work organization on defense.

district of columbia

DISTRICT OF COLUMBIA

SCHOOL	CITY	AFFILIATION	PAGE
American University	Washington	NCAA I	191
Catholic University of America	Washington	NCAA III	192
Gallaudet University	Washington	NCAA III	192
George Washington University	Washington	NCAA I	193
Georgetown University	Washington	NCAA I	194
Howard University	Washington	NCAA I	196
University of District of Columbia	Washington	NCAA II	197

American University

Academic Profile

Washington, DC 20016 — **Phone:** (202) 885-3031

Type: 4 Yr.,Private,Liberal Arts
Founded: 1893
Website: http://www.aueagles.edu
Religion: Methodist
SAT/ACT/GPA: 1200/3.4
Housing: Yes
Student/Faculty Ratio: 15:1
Male/Female Ratio: 2:3
Undergraduate Enrollment: 6,000
Graduate Enrollment: 5,000
Scholarships/Academic: Yes
Athletic: Yes
Financial Aid: Yes
Expenses by: Year
In State: $ 29,500
Out of State: $ 29,500
Specialty: Arts & Sciences, Communications, Public Affairs
Degrees Conferred: AA, BA, BS, BFA, MA, MS, MBA, MFA, Ph.D., JD, EdD
Programs of Study: Accounting, American Studies, Anthropology, Art History, Audio Technology, Biological Science, Business Administration, Chemistry, Communications, Computer Science, Economics, Education, Environmental Science, Fine Arts, Foreign Languages & Media, General Studies, Health, History, Interdisciplinary Studies, International Studies, Justice, Law, Liberal, Literature, Mathematics, Music, Performance Arts, Theater, Philosophy, Physics, Political Science, Psychology, Russian Studies, Secondary Education, Sociology, Spanish, Statistics, Studio Art

Men's Athletic Profile

4400 Massachusetts Avenue, NW
Washington, DC 20016-8005
Coach: Bob Jenkins
Email: winkler@american.edu

NCAA I
Eagles/Red, White, Blue
Phone: (202) 885-3044
Fax: (202) 885-3033

Estimated # of Men's Soccer Scholarships:
Conference: Colonial Athletic Association, CAA
Program Profile: Reeves Field is Bermuda grass with a measurements of 74x116. Our stadium has a capacity of 2,000. The team's playing season is in the fall against NCAA Division I.
History: The program began in 1949. NCAA Tournament in 1978, 1979, 1984; 1985 & 1997.
Achievements: Bob Jenkins was named 1997 CAA & Regional Coach of the Year; 1997 NCAA Quarterfinals-final ranking #5; numerous All-Americans including Antonio Otero with DC United, Seven players in A-League; 1985 Mike Brady Player of the Year; 1985 NCAA Finals; David Nahkid - New England Rev; John Diffley by Tama Bay Mutiny; Otero Olympic Team.
Coaching: Bob Jenkins, Head Coach, holds a USSF "A" License. He was a 1984 graduate of Duke. He coached 3 years as an Assistant at UVA. Todd West - Assistant Coach, is in his third year as an Assistant Coach; USSF "A" License; Virginia ODP State Staff Coach and a Braddock Road U17 Coach/Club.
Style of Play: Ball possession. Team build attack from the back through the midfield and forward.

Women's Athletic Profile

4400 Massachusetts Ave., NW
Washington, DC 20016
Coach: Colleen Corwell
Email: ccorwel@american.edu

NCAA I
Eagles/Red, White, Blue
Phone: (202) 885-3039
Fax: (202) 885-3033

Estimated # of Women's Soccer Scholarships: 2
Conference: Colonial Athletic Association
Program Profile: Home games are played on a natural grass soccer stadium. Featuring a World Class Bermuda playing surface.
History: The women's program began in 1990, and has been a varsity sport for five years.

Achievements: 2 players were named All-CAA 1st team; 2 players All-CAA 2nd team.
Colleen Corwell-Coach of the Year in 1996

Coaching: Colleen Corwell, Head Coach, enters her sixth year as a head coach at American University. She was named the 1995 Colonial Athletic Association Coach of the Year. She was a high school All-American soccer player at Severna Park High School. NSCAA National License. Coached Maryland's Olympic Development program, Director of Soccer Camp for Girls 8-18 in Columbia and Severna Park, Maryland, Washington, and Alexandria and McLean, Virginia.

Out of State: 21
ODP State: 18 **Regional:** 3
Most Recent Record: 8-10

Catholic University of America

Academic Profile

Washington, DC 20064
Phone: 202-319-5305

Type: 4 Yr.,Private,Liberal Arts,Engineering
Founded: 1887
Website: http://www.cua.edu
Religion: Catholic
SAT/ACT/GPA: 1100
Housing: Yes
Student/Faculty Ratio: 10:1
Male/Female Ratio: 47:53
Undergraduate Enrollment: 2,400
Graduate Enrollment: 2,800
Scholarships/Academic: Yes **Athletic:** No
Financial Aid: Yes
Expenses by: Year **In State:** $ 28,000
Out of State: $ 28,000
Degrees Conferred: BA, BS, BArch, MA, MS, MFA, Ph.D., EdD, JD, Mdiv
Programs of Study: Architecture and Planning, Arts and Sciences, Engineering, Music, Nursing and Philosophy

Men's Athletic Profile

620 Michigan Ave
Washington, DC 20064
Coach: Scott Racek
Email: racek@cua.edu

NCAA III
Cardinals/Black, Red
Phone: (202) 319-5287
Fax: (202) 319-6199

Estimated # of Men's Soccer Scholarships: None
Conference: Capital Athletic Conference

Women's Athletic Profile

620 Michigan Ave
Washington, DC 20064
Coach: Scott Racek
Email: Not Available

NCAA III
Cardinals/Red, Black
Phone: (202) 319-5287
Fax:

Estimated # of Women's Soccer Scholarships: None
Conference: Capital Athletic Conference

Gallaudet University

Academic Profile

Washington, DC 20002
Phone: (202)651-5603

Type: 4 Yr.,Private,Liberal Arts
Founded: 1864
Website: http://www.gallaudet.edu
Religion: Non-Affiliated

SAT/ACT/GPA: None
Student/Faculty Ratio: 1/3
Undergraduate Enrollment: 1,300
Scholarships/Academic: Yes
Athletic: No
Expenses by: Year
In State: $15,000
Housing: Yes
Male/Female Ratio: 7/10
Graduate Enrollment: 650
Financial Aid: Yes
Out of State: $15,000
Specialty: Deaf Education, Business, Computers, Biology, Mathematics
Degrees Conferred: AAS, BA, BS,MA, MS, MBA, M.Ed., Ph.D., EdD
Programs of Study: Accounting, Art History, BioChemistry, Biology, Business, Communications, Computer, Engineering, English, International Studies, Management, Math, Philosophy, Recreation, Deaf Studies, Social Science
***Contact school for more information

Men's Athletic Profile

800 Florida Avenue NE
Washington, DC 20002-3695
Coach: Kris Gould
Email: kris.gould@gallaudet.edu

NCAA III
Bison/Buff, Blue
Phone: (202) 651-5603
Fax: (202) 651-5274

Estimated # of Men's Soccer Scholarships: None
Conference: Capital Athletic Conference

George Washington University

Academic Profile

Washington, DC 20052
Phone: (202) 994-6650

Type: 4 Yr.,Private,Liberal Arts,Engineering
Website: http://www.gwu.edu
SAT/ACT/GPA: 1100/3.0
Student/Faculty Ratio: 17:1
Undergraduate Enrollment: 5,800
Scholarships/Academic: Yes
Athletic: Yes
Expenses by: Year
In State: $31,000
Founded: 1776
Religion: Non-Affiliated
Housing: Yes
Male/Female Ratio: 2:3
Graduate Enrollment: 10,000
Financial Aid: Yes
Out of State: $31,000
Specialty: Business, Engineering, Government
Degrees Conferred: 1184 Bachelors Degree conferred 1995-1996 foggy bottom campus.
Programs of Study: Accounting, Anthropology, Applied Mathematics, Archaeology, Arts, Biology, Business, Chemistry, Computer Science, Criminal Justice, Economics, Engineering, Psychology, General Studies

Men's Athletic Profile

Smith Center, 600 - 22nd St. NW
Washington, DC 20052
Coach: George Lidster
Email: Not Available

NCAA I
Colonials/Buff, Blue
Phone: (202) 994-6650
Fax: (202) 994-2713

Estimated # of Men's Soccer Scholarships: None
Conference: Atlantic 10 Conference
Program Profile: We play at South Riding Field with capacity of 5,000 and has natural grass.
Camp or Clinic Dates: Not Available
Most Recent Record: 5-12-2

Women's Athletic Profile

613 22nd St., NW
Washington, DC 20052
Coach: Tanya Vogel
Email: chippy0077@aol.com

NCAA I
Colonials/Buff, Blue
Phone: (202) 994-0152
Fax: (202) 994-2713

Estimated # of Women's Soccer Scholarships: 5
Conference: Atlantic 10 Conference
Program Profile: A brand new facility is being constructed. It will be ready for the season next fall and has the new Fieldturf surface.
History: 170-193-30 since program began in 1980.
Achievements: Our strongest teams were 1996 and 1997. The program has multiple Regional All-Americans, 1st and 2nd Team All-American players, 2 Umbro Senior All-Stars, GTE Academic All-American recipients, A-10 Rookie of the Year and Player of the Year.
Coaching: Tanya Vogel is Head Coach and is a 1996 graduate of George Washington University. She was 2 time captain and team MVP, A-10 Player of the Year in 1996. Brian Pensky is our Assistant Coach.
Roster in State: 7 **Out of State:** 14 **Out of Country:** 2
ODP State: 6 **Regional:** 1 **National:** 1
Walk-on/Other: 0 **Graduation %:** **Seniors on Team:** 2
Positions Needed: Goalkeeper, Forwards, Center-Midfield
Camp or Clinic Dates: Not Available
Most Recent Record: 5-14-0
Schedule: Maryland, Richmond, Dayton, Xavier, Umass, George Mason
Style of Play: Possession with emphasis on attacking quickly and organizing around the ball.

Georgetown University

Academic Profile

Washington, DC 20057
Phone: (202) 687-5414

Type: 4 Yr.,Private
Website: http://www.georgetown.ecu
SAT/ACT/GPA: 1200+
Student/Faculty Ratio: 12:1
Undergraduate Enrollment: 6,000
Scholarships/Academic: No **Athletic:** Yes
Expenses by: Year **In State:** $ 31,816

Founded: 1789
Religion: Jesuit
Housing: Yes
Male/Female Ratio: 49:51
Graduate Enrollment: 6,000
Financial Aid: Yes
Out of State: $ 31,816

Degrees Conferred: BA, BS, MA, MBA, Ph.D., MD, JD
Programs of Study: Accounting, Anthropology, Archeology, Arts, Biology, Business & Management, Communications, Computer Science, Criminal Justice, Geography, Engineering, Mathematics, Philosophy, Human Resources, Religion, Political Science, Medical Technology, Psychology

Men's Athletic Profile

Men's Soccer Office - Athletic Dept.
Washington, DC 20057
Coach: Keith Tabatznik
Email: Tabatznk@gunet.georgetown.edu

NCAA I
Hoyas/Blue, Gray
Phone: (202) 687-2364
Fax: (202) 687-3981

Estimated # of Men's Soccer Scholarships: None
Conference: Big East Conference
Program Profile: We play highly competitive schedule. Georgetown has two playing fields named Harbin Field. Sport Turf Managers Collegiate Soccer Field of the Year in 1998.

History: Although the program dates back to 1952, it has had unparalleled success over the last eleven years of culminating in 1994's first NCAA Tournament birth, Big East regular season championships and #9 rating in country. Then in 1997, Georgetown reached the NCAA Tournament for the second time and reached the Sweet 16.
Achievements: Keith Tabatznik was named Big East and South Atlantic Region Coach of the Year in 1994; 2 Scholar Athlete All-Americans; Chris Jugrs and Tim Keegan, Big East Championship; Big East Defense Player of the Year: Phil Wellington: #10 and #15 leading scorers in country: Ben McKnight and Raul Ferrer; 1999 All-American are Eric Kuello and is now playing in MLS.
Coaching: Keith Tabatznik is our Head Coach. He coached US Senior Amateur Team and coached in Olympic Festival. He holds Maryland and Regional ODP, USSF "A" License. Chad Lagerwey is our Assistant coach. He is a member of Maryland ODP Coach staff, USSF "C" License. Tom Graham is our Assistant Coach. He was a former pro-goalkeeper for the Jacksonville team of the old ASL, Maryland ODP.

Roster In State: 2	**Out of State:** 23	**Out of Country:** 3
ODP State: 18	**Regional:** 7	**National:** 2
Walk-on/Other: 5	**Graduation %:** 100	**Seniors on Team:** 5

Camp or Clinic Dates: July 17-21, 24-28
Most Recent Record: 11-9-1
Schedule: Connecticut, St. John's, Rutgers, William & Mary, Old Dominion, Richmond, West Virginia
Style of Play: Georgetown is an exciting , enthusiastic attacking team with a very high work rate; try to make the game enjoyable to watch and be a part of.

Women's Athletic Profile

37 & 'O' Streets, NW, McDonough Arena
Washington, DC 20057
Coach: Diane Drake
Email: draked@gunet.georgetown.edu

NCAA I
Hoyas/Navy Blue, Grey
Phone: (202) 687-7344
Fax: (202) 687-3981

Estimated # of Women's Soccer Scholarships: N/A
Conference: Big East Conference
Program Profile: Play on Bermuda grass, 120x73 yards field with 2,000-3,000 bleachers. Grass practice field, astro turf practice field, all on campus.
History: Program started in 1993 with an overall record of under former coach Leonel Popol was 38-55-3.
Achievements: Big East All-Rookie team were Barbara Niner in 1996, Liz Delgado in 1997, and Barbara Torres in 1998. 1997-1998 2nd team All-Big East was Liz Delgado.
Coaching: Diane Drake, Head Coach, BA from University of Dayton in 1993 and MS from LSU in 1996. Served as an assistant coach for five years at UNC-Greensboro, LSU, Wright State. USSF "A" License. In 1998 played for W-League National Champions, the Raleigh wings and in 1999 played for W-League Maryland Pride. David Nolan, Assistant Coach, NSCAA Advanced National License, former Seton Hall assistant coach. BS from Seton Hall in 1991, MBA in 1993. He is Director of Soccer Plus Academy for three years. He is a former assistant coach at Fairleigh Dickinson University.

Roster in State:	**Out of State:** 28	**Out of Country:**
ODP State: 17	**Regional:** 5	**National:** 1
Walk-on/Other: 6	**Graduation %:** 99	**Seniors on Team:** 6

Positions Needed: 5-6
Camp or Clinic Dates: July 9-14
Most Recent Record: 8-10-2
Schedule: Notre Dame, William & Mary, Boston College, University of Dayton, UCONN, JMU, Cal Berkley, Syracuse
Style of Play: Possession with purpose to free-up personality players one-to-one, patient building, but quick transitions. Zonal Defending, speed on flanks, one versus skill up top and enough savvy in all players to figure out during a match hour to adjust to opponents if need be.

Howard University

Academic Profile

Phone: 800-822-6363

Washington, DC 20059

Type: 4 Yr.,Private,Engineering
Website: http://www.howard.edu
SAT/ACT/GPA: 820/18
Student/Faculty Ratio: Not Available
Undergraduate Enrollment: 7,650
Scholarships/Academic: Yes **Athletic:** Yes
Expenses by: Year **In State:** $ 12,000
Specialty: Business

Founded: 1867
Religion: Non-Affiliated
Housing: No
Male/Female Ratio: 40:60
Graduate Enrollment: 3,050
Financial Aid: Yes
Out of State: $ 12,000

Degrees Conferred: BA, BS, BFA, BArch, BBA, BFA, BSW, MA, MS, ,BA, MFA, M.Ed., Ph.D., JD
Programs of Study: Accounting, Actuarial Science, Anthropology, Arabic, Architecture, Banking/Finance, Botany, Business Administration, Chemistry, Criminal Justice, Economics, Education, Engineering, History, Insurance, International Business & Relations, Marketing, MicroBiology, Occupational Therapy

Men's Athletic Profile

6th & Girard NW
Washington, DC 20059
Coach: Keith Tucker
Email: husoccer@howard.edu

NCAA I
Bison/Navy, White
Phone: (202) 806-7174
Fax: (202) 806-5961

Estimated # of Men's Soccer Scholarships: None
Conference: MEAC

Women's Athletic Profile

6th & Girard Sts. NW
Washington, DC 20059
Coach: Michelle Street
Email: mstreet@howard.edu

NCAA I
Bison/Navy Blue, White
Phone: (202) 806-7174
Fax: (202) 806-9090

Estimated # of Women's Soccer Scholarships: 4
Conference: Independent
Program Profile: The competitive season runs from August through November. The field is Astroturf.
History: The program began in 1995. Each year the team has improved its win tally and the talent of the recruiting classes. This season the team finished 8-10-1
Achievements: Last season as a member of the Big-South conference, Howard had 3 first-team All-Big South players, one Rookie-of-the-year, and one 2nd Team All-Big South selection.
Coaching:
Roster in State: 0 **Out of State:** 19 **Out of Country:** 1
ODP State: 3 **Regional:** **National:**
Walk-on/Other: **Graduation %:** **Seniors on Team:** 3
Positions Needed: center-midfielder, outside midfielder, defender
Camp or Clinic Dates: Not Available
Most Recent Record: 8-10-1
Style of Play: Possession, build up attack through passing and penetrate wings. Emphasis on attack. This season we played a 3-4-3. Last season we played a 4-4-2.

University of the District of Columbia

Academic Profile

Phone: 202-274-6110

Washington, DC 20008

Type: 4 Yr.,Public,Liberal Arts,Engineering
Website: http://www.udc.edu
SAT/ACT/GPA: Open
Student/Faculty Ratio: 14:1
Undergraduate Enrollment: 10,000
Scholarships/Academic: Yes **Athletic:** Yes
Expenses by: Year **In State:** $ 6,500
Degrees Conferred: BA, BS, MA, MS, MBA

Founded: 1976
Religion: Non-Affiliated
Housing: No
Male/Female Ratio: 42:58
Graduate Enrollment: 595
Financial Aid: Yes
Out of State: $ 9,000

Programs of Study: Accounting, Administration of Justice, Anthropology, Biology, Business Education & Management, Chemistry, Computer Science, Economics, Emergency Medical Services, Engineering, Environmental Science, Fire Science Administration, Marketing, Physical Education, Physics, Political Science, Sociology, Speech Pathology, Urban Studies

Men's Athletic Profile

4200 Connecticut Ave. NW
Washington, DC 20008
Coach: Osman Orlando
Email: Not Available

NCAA II
Firebirds/Red, Gold
Phone: (202) 274-5074
Fax: (202) 274-5065

Estimated # of Men's Soccer Scholarships: None
Conference: Independent
Program Profile: Much improved program over the last 4 years. Newly renovated field (1994) on campus, natural grass, official NCAA dimensions.
History: Program began in the early 80's, floundered for several years. Stability began in the late 80's under Orlando and has greatly improved in recent years.
Coaching: Osman Orlando, Head Coach, Kalpohim University (Ghana, 1964), former Olympian (1968 and 1973), conducts camps and has coached club and youth national teams.
Style of Play: Long ball, aggressive, up-tempo style.

florida

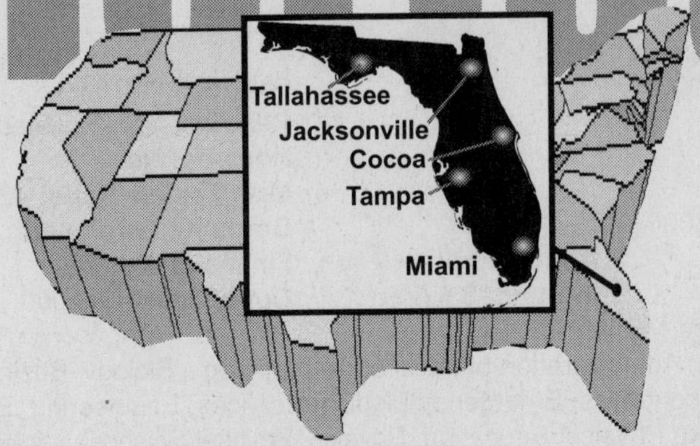

SCHOOL	CITY	AFFILIATION	PAGE
Barry University	Miami Shores	NCAA II	200
Eckerd College	St. Petersburg	NCAA II	201
Embry - Riddle University	Daytona Beach	NAIA	202
Flagler College	St. Augustine	NAIA	203
Florida Atlantic University	Boca Raton	NCAA I	204
Florida Institute of Technology	Melbourne	NCAA II	205
Florida International University	Miami	NCAA I	206
Florida Southern College	Lakeland	NCAA II	207
Florida State University	Tallahassee	NCAA I	209
Jacksonville University	Jacksonville	NCAA I	210
Lynn University	Boca Raton	NCAA II	211
Nova Southeastern University	Fort Lauderdale	NCAA II/NAIA	212
Palm Beach Atlantic College	West Palm Beach	NAIA	213
Rollins College	Winter Park	NCAA II	214
Saint Leo College	Saint Leo	NCAA II	215
Saint Thomas University	Miami	NAIA	216
Stetson University	DeLand	NCAA I	218
University of Central Florida	Orlando	NCAA I	219
University of Florida	Gainesville	NCAA I	220
University of Miami	Coral Gables	NCAA I	221
University of North Florida	Jacksonville	NCAA II	222
University of South Florida	Tampa	NCAA I	222
University of Tampa	Tampa	NCAA II	223
University of West Florida	Pensacola	NCAA II	225
Webber College	Babson Park	NAIA	226

SOCCER ACADEMY
The Soccer Academy
Where Players Train!
is open 52 weeks a year and offers the only full-time residency and summer camp, short-time (weekly) training programs designed from both an individual and a team perspective.
Full-Time Semesters
• September-May
Short-Time Weeks
Team Training
Summer Camp Specials
All Ages and Abilities Welcome
IMG Academies
Bollettieri Campus
800.872-6425 - 941.755.1000 - (f) 941.752.2531
5500 34th Street West - Bradenton, Florida 34210
www.academyzone.com
mysportsguru.com, the Soccer Academy's online home field, offers all of the Academy's training, skills, information and player development programs in the most exciting format and technology the Internet has to offer.
www.mysportsguru.com
mysportsguru.com
your exclusive online instructional connection to The Soccer Academy
© mysportsguru.com. All rights reserved.

Barry University

Academic Profile

Phone: 800-695-2279

Miami Shores, FL 33161

Type: 4 Yr.,Private
Website: http://www.2.barry.edu
SAT/ACT/GPA: 820
Student/Faculty Ratio: 12:1
Undergraduate Enrollment: 1,750
Scholarships/Academic: Yes **Athletic:** Yes
Expenses by: Year **In State:** $ 21,280

Founded: 1941
Religion: Catholic
Housing: Yes
Male/Female Ratio: 1:2
Graduate Enrollment: 5,500
Financial Aid: Yes
Out of State: $ 21,280

Specialty: Health Sciences, Business, Computer Science, Sports
Degrees Conferred: BA, BS, BFA, MA, MS, MBA, Ph.D., DPM
Programs of Study: Accounting, Biology, Business, Communications, Computer Science, Economics, Education, English, Exercise Science, Foreign Languages, History, Marketing, Mathematics, MedTech, Nuclear Medicine, Nursing, Occupational Therapy, Philosophy, Physical Education, Podiatry, Political Science, PreMed, PreVet, Psychology, Social Work, Sociology, Sports Management,
Theology

Men's Athletic Profile

11300 NE 2nd Avenue
Miami Shores, FL 33161
Coach: Steve McCrath
Email: smccrath@mail.barry.edu

NCAA II
Buccaneers/Red, Black, Silver
Phone: (305) 899-3560
Fax: (305) 899-3556

Estimated # of Men's Soccer Scholarships: 6.5
Conference: Sunshine State Conference
Program Profile: Our team plays on grass field with a measurements of 120x75. Playing season starts from August through December (Spring season from February through March). Stadium has a seating capacity of 1,000.
History: Our program began in 1984. Playoffs in 1985 & 1998; conference tri-champs in 1992 and member of NCAA II.
Achievements: Conference Coach of the Year in 1998; 1 All-South Americans three times.
Coaching: Steve McCrath is our Head Coach. He is entering first year the program. Troy Edwards, TJ Bean and Sergio Soriano are the Assistant Coaches.
Roster In State: 8 **Out of State:** 7 **Out of Country:** 10
ODP State: **Regional:** **National:** 1
Walk-on/Other: **Graduation %:** 90 **Seniors on Team:** 7
Positions Needed: N/A
Camp or Clinic Dates: Not Available
Most Recent Record: 14-3-3
Schedule: Seattle Pacific, S. Conn. St., Truman St., Lynn U., U. of Tampa

Women's Athletic Profile

11300 NE 2nd Avenue
Miami Shores, FL 33161-6695
Coach: Mike Neveu
Email: mneveu@mail.barry.edu

NCAA II
Buccaneers/Red, Black, Silver
Phone: (305) 899-3372
Fax: (305) 899-3556

Estimated # of Women's Soccer Scholarships: Varies
Conference: Sunshine State Conference
Program Profile: Two Bermuda grass playing fields (120x70), lighted game field surrounded by 1200 seat stadium,

lighted practice field perpendicular to game field. Site was used as host to six NCAA National Tournament Semifinals, hosted Brazilian Olympic team in training for 1996 Olympics, hosted many US men's and women's national teams, and in 1999, 2000 hosted Major League Soccer Spring Training.
History: Program began in 1984. There have been 13 NCAA appearances, 6 Final Four Appearances and 3 National Championships (1989, 1992, 1993). Overall team record since 1987 227-48-14. Only school to be ranked in NSCAA Top 10 since poll began in 1988, have finished the season in the NSCAA Top 5 in 11 of 13 years. Two Conference Titles (1999, 2000).
Achievements: Since 1984 2 National Players of the Year, 30 NSCAA All-Americans, 9 Academic All-Americans, 75 NSCAA All South Region Players, 30 NCAA All-Tournament Team Players. Since 1998 2 SSC Conference Players of the Year, 23 All-SSC Team Players, 2 Coach of the Year.
Coaching: Mike Neveu Head Coach- US Soccer "A" License, NCAA D.II women's soccer National Committee, NCAA South Regional Chairperson, overall record for 2 years 34-4-1. Assistant Coaches Amy Gray, Kyllene Carter and Sergio Soriano GK Coach.
Roster in State: 10 **Out of State:** 8 **Out of Country:** 4
ODP State: 6 **Regional:** 6 **National:** 3
Walk-on/Other: 7 **Graduation %:** 100 **Seniors on Team:** 7
Positions Needed: Forward, Midfield, defense, GK
Camp or Clinic Dates: Not Available
Most Recent Record: 18-1-0
Schedule: Lynn Univ. Texas A & M Commerce, Tampa, Christian Brothers, West Florida
Style of Play: European style of play, possession orientated, dangerous in the attack, balanced in the defense. Hard working team- High pressure defensively. Team has the ability to change style of play during game. Start of playing a 3-5-2 and can change to a 4-4-2 or 3-4-3 depending on the situation.

Eckerd College
Academic Profile

St. Petersburg, FL 33711
Phone: 800-456-9009

Type: 4 Yr.,Private,Liberal Arts
Founded: 1958
Website: http://www.eckerd.edu
Religion: Presbyterian
SAT/ACT/GPA: 1100/24/3.0
Housing: Yes
Student/Faculty Ratio: 14:1
Male/Female Ratio: 45:55
Undergraduate Enrollment: 1,500
Graduate Enrollment: N/A
Scholarships/Academic: Yes **Athletic:** Yes **Financial Aid:** Yes
Expenses by: Year **In State:** $ 22,500 **Out of State:** $ 22,500
Specialty: Business, Science, Medical
Degrees Conferred: BA, BS
Programs of Study: All areas of study (except physical education) including: Management, International Business, Marine Science/Biology, Political Science, Psychology, Human Resources, Chemistry, PreMed, PreLaw, PreVet

Men's Athletic Profile

4200 - 54th Avenue South
St. Petersburg, FL 33711
Coach: Jim DiNobile
Email: DiNobileJL@aol.com

NCAA II
Tritons/Red, White, Black
Phone: (727) 864-7697
Fax: (727) 864-8968

Estimated # of Men's Soccer Scholarships: Varies
Conference: Sunshine State Conference
Program Profile: We have a year-round program with intensive traditional and non-traditional seasons, plus an extensive summer camp program. The 120x75 yard beautiful Bermuda grass field with locker rooms is next to field. Our soccer program is for the complete student-athlete.

History: Our program began in 1973 as Division III and 1978 became Division II. The team has been regionally and nationally ranked with All-Conference, All-Region and All-American Selection.
Achievements: Several COY awards and some of the players have moved to play in a league.
Coaching: Jim DiNobile, Head Coach, holds a USSF "A" License. He is entering 16 years with the program. Stanley Urguhart and Roberto Lopez are the Assistant Coach.

Roster In State: 11	**Out of State:** 10	**Out of Country:** 4
ODP State: 8	**Regional:** 3	**National:**
Walk-on/Other:	**Graduation %:** 100	**Seniors on Team:** 3

Positions Needed: Forwards, Midfield
Camp or Clinic Dates: June, July, August
Most Recent Record: 9-8-0
Schedule: Barry, Lynn, Northern Tenn. State
Style of Play: Play a 4-3-3 Attack oriented and up tempo style.

Women's Athletic Profile

4200 54th Avenue, South
St. Petersburg, FL 33711
Coach: Siggi Nagele
Email: nagelesp@ocasun.eckerd.edu

NCAA II
Tritons/Red, White, Black
Phone: (727) 864-8251
Fax: (727) 864-8968

Estimated # of Women's Soccer Scholarships: 22 partials
Conference: Sunshine State Conference
Program Profile: Has risen to a top ranking in the south in just three years. Traditional playing season is August to November, non-traditional spring season that starts February to April. Beautiful Bermuda grass 120x80 yards. The program is year-round and competing. Two years old soccer facility, includes 120x80 yard Bermuda game field. Play national schedule.
History: The program was originated in 1996. Program has evolved into a conference and regional contender in just three years. Players committed to improving the program have elevated the level of play each year. A solid Foundation and tradition has been created.
Achievements: Each Year Produces All-South Players, All-Conference, Fall Commissioner's Honor Roll Members, NSCAA team academic award, All-South Region Scholar award. Karan Smith named Co-conference player of the year in 1999.
Coaching: Siggi Nagele, Head Coach, holds German "B" License, Director of Coaching at Chargers Soccer Club, former German youth player, ODP state and regional staff, former coach at Marshall University, played at Alderson-Broaddus College. Kevin Jones, Assistant Coach, South Africa, former Tampa Bay Rowdie player. He coached at University of South Florida and he was Director of Blackwatch Soccer Cup.

Roster in State: 9	**Out of State:** 14	**Out of Country:** 1
ODP State: 5	**Regional:** 3	**National:**
Walk-on/Other:	**Graduation %:** 100	**Seniors on Team:** 4

Positions Needed: Defender, Goalkeeper, Striker
Camp or Clinic Dates: 6/11-6/16, 7/3-7/7, 7/9-7/16, 7/23-7/28, 7/31-8/4
Most Recent Record: 9-7
Schedule: Barry University, Lynn University, West Florida, North Florida, Southern Connecticut, University of Tampa, Palm Beach Atlanta
Style of Play: Possession-oriented, looking for fast and technically sound players. Team-oriented play with emphasis on solid defending and quick counter attacks.

Embry - Riddle Aeronautical University

Academic Profile

Daytona Beach, FL 32114

Phone: 800-862-2416

Type: 4 Yr.,Private,Engineering
Website: http://www.erau.edu

Founded: 1925
Religion: Non-Affiliated

SAT/ACT/GPA: 1000/20/3.0
Housing: Yes
Student/Faculty Ratio: 14:1
Male/Female Ratio: 3:1
Undergraduate Enrollment: 4,400
Graduate Enrollment: N/A
Scholarships/Academic: Yes
Athletic: Yes
Financial Aid: Yes
Expenses by: Year
In State: $ 16,000
Out of State: $ 16,000
Specialty: Engineering
Degrees Conferred: Associate, Baccalaureate, Masters
Programs of Study: Aircraft Maintenance, Airway Science, Aviation Business Administration, Aviation Maintenance Technology, Professional Aeronautics, Aerospace Engineering, Aerospace Studies, Aviation Computer Science, Civil Engineering, Electrical Engineering, Engineering Physics

Men's Athletic Profile

600 S Clyde Morris Blvd.
Daytona Beach, FL 32114
Coach: David Gregson
Email: gregsond@cts.db.eraw.edu

NAIA
Eagles/Royal Blue, Gold
Phone: (904) 226-6653
Fax: (904) 226-6435

Estimated # of Men's Soccer Scholarships: None
Conference: Florida Sun Conference
Program Profile: Florida's weather permits a year-round play. Embry-Riddle had a new soccer field built in the fall of 1996. Stadium has a capacity of a 1,000 seats. Team plays on a natural Bermuda grass which measures 120x75 yards, and has a lights.
History: Program began in 1989. Present coach started in 1994.
Achievements: Coach of the Year in 1995; 1 All-American; 2 Academic All-Americans.
Coaching: David Gregson, Head Coach, has a USSF "A" License, is on ODP State Staff Coach, is a Florida NSCAA Regional Instructor, and was a former Division I player at Hartwick College. Joe De Palo - Assistant Coach, USSF "B" License, NSCAA Advanced National. Mike Cole - Soccer Plus Instructor.
Style of Play: Possession oriented, disciplined, counter-attacking when on at times semi-direct.

Women's Athletic Profile

600 south Clyde Morris Blvd.
Daytona Beach, FL 32114
Coach: Dan Blank
Email: blankd@cts.db.erau.edu

NAIA
Eagles/Royal Blue, Gold
Phone: (904) 226-4927
Fax: (904) 226-6435

Estimated # of Women's Soccer Scholarships:
Conference: Florida Sun Conference
Program Profile:
History: Our fist year of competition was in 1998.
Coaching: Dan Blank is the Head Coach. He has nine years of coaching college women. He led former team to 5 National Championship tournament. He holds a USSF and NSCAA Licensed. Nicole Roberts and Alison Smalling are the Assistant Coaches.
Style of Play: We are still a developing program

Flagler University

Academic Profile

St. Augustine, FL 32085
Phone: (904) 829-6481x252

Type: 4 Yr.,Private,Liberal Arts
Website: http://www.flagler.edu
Founded: 1968
Religion: Non-Affiliated

SAT/ACT/GPA: 1010/21/2.5
Student/Faculty Ratio: 20:1
Undergraduate Enrollment: 1,650
Scholarships/Academic: Yes
Athletic: Yes
Expenses by: Year
In State: $ 9,960
Specialty: Education, Business, Arts
Degrees Conferred: BA
Housing: Yes
Male/Female Ratio: 55:45
Graduate Enrollment: N/A
Financial Aid: Yes
Out of State: $ 9,960
Programs of Study: Accounting, Art, Art Education, Business Communications, Deaf Education, Drama, Elementary Education, English, History, Literature, Mathematics, Philosophy, Psychology, Secondary Education, Social Sciences, Spanish, Sport Management

Men's Athletic Profile

74 King Street
St. Augustine, FL 32084
Coach: John Lynch
Email: lynchj@flagler.edu

NAIA
Saints/Gold, Red
Phone: (904) 829-6481x254
Fax: (904) 810-2369

Estimated # of Men's Soccer Scholarships: None
Conference: Florida Sun Conference
Program Profile: The Saints play at Flagles Field, a full size 120 X75 field with Bermuda grass. We also have a large practice area. Facility is owned by the college.
History: Our program began in 1980. Tradition of success; numerous top 25 rankings. 1999 Regional runner-up.
Achievements: 15 All-Americans, 6 Academic All-Americans. 1982, 1983 Sportsmanship Trophy; 5 time District Coach of the Year. 2 time Conference Coach of the Year; 2 time State Coach of the Year; NAIA Top Twenty regularly (16th in 1995).
Coaching: John Lynch, Head Coach, entering second season with the program. Paul Tumaru - Assistant Coach, entering second season with the program
Roster In State: 10
Out of State: 7
Out of Country: 8
Walk-on/Other:
Graduation %: N/A
Seniors on Team: 7
Positions Needed: GK, Sweeper, Stopper, Center Midfield
Camp or Clinic Dates: June 25-30, July 30- Aug. 4
Most Recent Record: 10-10-
Style of Play: Fit and organized. Mix of passion and direct.

Florida Atlantic University

Academic Profile

Boca Raton, FL 33431-0991

Phone: (561) 297-3743

Type: 4 Yr.,Public,Liberal Arts,Engineering
Website: http://www.fau.edu
SAT/ACT/GPA: Sliding Scale
Student/Faculty Ratio: 20:1
Undergraduate Enrollment: 14,280
Scholarships/Academic: Yes
Athletic: Yes
Expenses by: Year
In State: $ 7,524
Specialty: Business, Education
Degrees Conferred: Bachelors, Masters, Specialist, Doctorate
Founded: 1961
Religion: Non-Affiliated
Housing: Yes
Male/Female Ratio: 60:40
Graduate Enrollment: 5,419
Financial Aid: Yes
Out of State: $ 14,149
Programs of Study: Accounting, Architecture, Art, Biology, Chemistry, Communications, Computer Engineering, Computer Information System, Computer Science, Counselor Education, Criminal Justice, Early Childhood Education, Economics, Electrical Engineering, English, Elementary Education, Exercise Science, Marketing, Mathematics, Music, Nursing, Ocean Engineering, Physical Therapy, Psychology, Social Work, Social Science, Women's Studies

Men's Athletic Profile

777 Glades Rd, P.O. Box 3091
Boca Raton, FL 33431
Coach: Kos Donev
Email: Not Available

NCAA I
Owls/Blue, Gray
Phone: (561) 367-3711
Fax: (561) 367-3963

Estimated # of Men's Soccer Scholarships:
Conference: Trans America Athletic Conference
Program Profile: Our facilities include two natural grass , lighted fields; three more waiting to be built. FAU plays in the Fall approximately ten games at home and at least one home tournament.
History: Program began in 1980, playing in NAIA until 1983, then moved to NCAA Division II in 1984. The Owls have been playing in NCAA Division I since 1983.
Achievements: State Coach of the Year 1989-1990; NCAA Top 20 1989; 3 named All-South Region.
Coaching: Kos Donev, Head Coach, has 22 years playing (amateur & college) experience and 12 years coaching.
Style of Play: Defensive.

Women's Athletic Profile

777 Glades Rd. PO Box 3091
Boca Raton, FL 33431-0991
Coach: Brian Dooley
Email: bdooley@fau.edu

NCAA I
Owls/Red, White, Navy Blue
Phone: (561) 267-3743
Fax: (561) 267-3963

Estimated # of Women's Soccer Scholarships: 6
Conference: Trans America Athletic Conference
Program Profile: 4 lighted practice fields of special blend Bermuda, Game field is immaculate, Stadium for seating 1000 is to be completed 2000-2001. Tom Oxley Athletic Center is opening Fall of 2000. New Facility for offices, lockers, meeting rooms, recruiting lounge, strength training, hydro-therapy, medical center, study hall and computer lab with 2 dozen computers for the student-athletes. Facility has hosted the US women's National Team and the US Men's National Team as well as the Norwegian women's National Team and the MLS Spring Training Camp. The USYSA ODP Regional Event has been hosted as well. south Florida weather allows for year-round outdoor training.
History: Program began in the early 90's and had the most successful season in 8 years in 99. Brian Dooley was hired just prior to the 99 season to head up a new commitment to the program by the administration. During his first year, the team qualified for the TAAC tournament for the first time in history.
Achievements: Three players on the 99 team were honored as All-Conference including the Conference player of the Year.
Coaching: Brian Dooley, Head Coach, entering first season in 1999. formerly head coach at Barry University. Assistant coach Tammy Mazza with one coach and volunteer assistant to be added.

Roster in State: 14 | **Out of State:** 7 | **Out of Country:** 3
ODP State: 7 | **Regional:** 0 | **National:**
Walk-on/Other: | **Graduation %:** | **Seniors on Team:** 9

Positions Needed: all positions will be graduating starters
Camp or Clinic Dates: 5/29-6/2, 6/5-6/9, 6/19-6/23, 6/26-6/30, 7/31-8/4
Most Recent Record: 5-8-1
Schedule: Central Florida, Florida International, Miami, Jacksonville, Georgia State
Style of Play: Attacking style with emphasis on possession. Man-zone combination

Florida Institute of Technology

Academic Profile

Phone: 800-888-4348

Melbourne, FL 32901

Type: 4 Yr.,Private,Engineering
Website: http://www.fit.edu

Founded: 1958
Religion: Non-Affiliated

SAT/ACT/GPA: 1050+
Student/Faculty Ratio: 14:1
Undergraduate Enrollment: 3,865
Scholarships/Academic: Yes **Athletic:** Yes
Expenses by: Year **In State:** $ 18,500
Housing: Yes
Male/Female Ratio: 67:33
Graduate Enrollment: 2,082
Financial Aid: Yes
Out of State: $ 18,500
Degrees Conferred: BA, BS, MS, MBA, M.Ed., Ph.D.
Programs of Study: Accounting, Aeronautical Engineering, Aeronautical Science, BioChemistry, Biological Science, Business Administration, Computer Science, Economics, Electrical Engineering, Fisheries, Management, Marine Biology, Marketing, Mathematics, Mechanical Engineering, MicroBiology, Physics, PreProfessional Courses, Science Education, Technical & Business Writing

Men's Athletic Profile

150 W University Blvd.
Melbourne, FL 32901
Coach: Kevin Johnson
Email: kjohnson@fit.edu
NCAA II
Panthers/Scarlet, Gray
Phone: 312-374-8064
Fax: 3219848529

Estimated # of Men's Soccer Scholarships: yes
Conference: Sunshine State Conference
Program Profile: We play on a lighted field adjacent to main campus with seating for 1700. Our season is all academic year.
History: Our season began in 1972 and we were NCAA region national tournament participants in 1987-1994.
Achievements: NCAA National Champions 1988, 1991: 7 All-Americans, Coach of the Year 1991; Sunshine State Conference Champions 1988-1993.
Coaching: Kevin Johnson is our new head coach and David Atkinson is our assistant coach.
Roster In State: 8 **Out of State:** 8 **Out of Country:** 8
ODP State: 5 **Regional:** **National:**
Walk-on/Other: **Graduation %:** N/A **Seniors on Team:** 4
Positions Needed: All
Camp or Clinic Dates: Not Available
Most Recent Record: 9-7-2
Schedule: Lynn University, Mercer University, Stetson University, University of Tampa, Barry University, Bollins College.
Style of Play: Possession, quick ball movement in midfield, and strong defensively.

Florida International University

Academic Profile

Phone: (305) 348-6155

Miami, FL 33199

Type: 4 Yr.,Public,
Website: http://www.fiu.edu
SAT/ACT/GPA: 1100
Student/Faculty Ratio: 18:1
Undergraduate Enrollment: 30,000
Scholarships/Academic: Yes **Athletic:** Yes
Expenses by: Year **In State:** $ 5,553
Founded: 1972
Religion: Non-Affiliated
Housing: Yes
Male/Female Ratio: 43:57
Graduate Enrollment: 6,677
Financial Aid: Yes
Out of State: $ 12,207
Specialty: Education, Hospitality
Degrees Conferred: BA, BS, MS, Ph.D.
Programs of Study: School of Architect, College of Arts & Sciences, School of Music, School of Computer Science, College of Business Administration, School of Accounting, College of Education, College of Engineering, College of Health Sciences, School of Hospitality Management, School of Journalism & Mass Communications, College of Urban and Public Affairs, School of Policy and Management, School of Social Work, PreProfessional Programs

Men's Athletic Profile

Golden Panther Arena
Miami, FL 33199
Coach: Karl Kremser
Email: Not Available

NCAA I
Golden Panthers/Blue, Yellow
Phone: (305) 348-2124
Fax: (305) 348-2963

Estimated # of Men's Soccer Scholarships: None
Conference: Trans American Athletic Conference
Program Profile: FIU and its soccer program have been associated with numerous national and international events down through the years. The natural grass surface of the University Park Soccer Field has been one of the main training facilities for the US National teams over the last several years. The field was also used by all the international squads in Miami for the Pele Cup.
Achievements: FIU was NCAA Division II National Champion in 1982 and 1984. Seven All-Americans have been part of the program since its inception in 1972. FIU has had more than a dozed All-Conference players and three Players' of the Year.
Coaching: Karl Kremser is our Head Coach. He has an 'A' license and has more than 20 years in the coaching profession. Kremser's may honors include being named State Coach of the year in 1980 and Southern Region Coach of the Year in 1985. He was also the TAAC Coach of the Year in 1991.
Style of Play: German Style.

Women's Athletic Profile

University Park Campus, 11200 SW 8th St
Miami, FL 33199
Coach: Everton Edwards
Email: eved008@aol.com

NCAA I
Golden Panthers/Blue, Gold
Phone: (305) 348-3411
Fax: (305) 348-2963

Estimated # of Women's Soccer Scholarships: 4
Conference: Trans America Athletic Conference
Program Profile: Home field is lighted, 120x75 yards of a natural grass. Playing season is in August to November and February to April. Has a seating for 1,500.
History: Began in 1985 - advanced to the second round of the NCAA Tournament in 1993.
Achievements: Edwards won the TAAC Coach of the Year honors after his team completed an 8-1-1 conference record. FIU has had two All-Americans: Catherine Liller in 1992-1993 and Sue-Moy Chin in 1993. Cindy Greenman was named TAAC Player of the Year and was an All-South Selection. Goalie Martine Materasso was a TAAC All-Conference second team.
Coaching: Everton Edwards, Head Coach, is the only coach the women's program has had. A former goalie on the men's team. He was named Coach of the Year by the TAAC (1996). Frankie Delgado is the Assistant Coach.
Roster in State: 8 **Out of State:** 8 **Out of Country:** 8
Walk-on/Other: **Graduation %:** 96 **Seniors on Team:** 5
Positions Needed: Defender, Mid, Forward
Camp or Clinic Dates: Not Available
Most Recent Record: 15-6-0
Schedule: Florida State, Miami (FL), North Texas, Denver, so far!!
Style of Play: Keep the ball moving in the ground whenever possible. Constantly switching the point of attack away from pressure through a series of short passes-except when crossing, shooting or exploiting an opening up top.

Florida Southern College

Academic Profile

Lakeland, FL 33801-5698

Phone: 800-274-4131

Type: 4 Yr.,Private,Liberal Arts
Website: http://www.flsouthern.edu

Founded: 1885
Religion: Methodist

SAT/ACT/GPA: 1000/23
Student/Faculty Ratio: 17:1
Undergraduate Enrollment: 1,800
Scholarships/Academic: Yes **Athletic:** Yes
Expenses by: Year **In State:** $ 17,930
Housing: Yes
Male/Female Ratio: 42:58
Graduate Enrollment: 100
Financial Aid: Yes
Out of State: $ 17,930
Degrees Conferred: BA, BS, MBA, Nursing
Programs of Study: Accounting, Art, Biology, Business, Chemistry, Citrus/Horticulture, Communications, Criminology, Economics, Education, English, History, Mathematics, Music, Natural Sciences, Physical Education, Physics, Political Science, Religion

Men's Athletic Profile

111 Lake Hollingsworth Drive
Lakeland, FL 33801-5698
Coach: Kris Pahl
Email: kpahl@flsouthern.edu
NCAA II
Moccasins/Red, White, Royal
Phone: (941) 680-4258
Fax: (941) 680-4122

Estimated # of Men's Soccer Scholarships: 6
Conference: Sunshine State Conference
Program Profile: We play on 110x75 yards Bermuda grass field on campus. Program competes in the tough Sunshine State Conference. Play spring exhibitions against MLS teams.
History: Program began in 1956.
Achievements: Kris Pahl - 1997 Sunshine State Conference Coach of the Year. 1997 had 5 All-South players; 1997 8 All-Conference players.
Coaching: Kris Pahl, Head Coach, USSF "A" coaching license, FYSA State Staff Coach since 1990, former goalkeeper, and has a MS Degree in Sports Management. Nine years FYSA State Staff. Tim Bussel - Assistant Coach, five years at FSC, former professional player.
Roster In State: 15 **Out of State:** 2 **Out of Country:** 5
ODP State: 1 **Regional:** **National:**
Walk-on/Other: **Graduation %:** 100 **Seniors on Team:** 3
Camp or Clinic Dates: Not Available
Most Recent Record: 13-5-2
Schedule: Lynn Univ., Barry Univ., Rollins College, Univ. of Tampa, USC Spartanburg, Presbyterian, Univ. Alabama at Huntsville
Style of Play: Strong defensive play with an emphasis on possession and build-up attack. the team plays with a high work rate and quick speed of play.

Women's Athletic Profile

111 Lake Hollingsworth Drive
Lakeland, FL 33801-5607
Coach: Chris Rizzieri
Email: crizzceri@flsouthern.edu
NCAA II
Moccasins/Scarlet, White
Phone: (863) 616-6455
Fax: (863) 680-4122

Estimated # of Women's Soccer Scholarships: 4
Conference: Sunshine State Conference
Program Profile: We play on a 112x72 Bermuda grass field, with non-permanent bleachers and can seat up to 1,500.
History: Our program is still very young having only begun in 1999.
Roster in State: 18 **Out of State:** 6 **Out of Country:** 1
Walk-on/Other: **Graduation %:** 99 **Seniors on Team:** 0
Positions Needed: Goalkeeper, Striker, Center-mid
Schedule: Lynn University, Barry University, University of Missouri- St. Louis, Eckerd College,
Style of Play: Direct and aggressive.

Florida State University

Academic Profile

Tallahassee, FL 32316

Phone: 850-644-6200

Type: 4 Yr.
Website: http://www.fsu.edu
SAT/ACT/GPA: 500/21
Student/Faculty Ratio: 20:1
Undergraduate Enrollment: 22,408
Scholarships/Academic:
Athletic:
Expenses by: Year
In State: $ 1,882+
Founded: 1857
Religion: Non-Affiliated
Housing: Yes
Male/Female Ratio: N/A
Graduate Enrollment: 7,856
Financial Aid: Yes
Out of State: $ 7,127+
Degrees Conferred: Bachelors Masters
Programs of Study: Accounting, Actuarial Science, Advertising, American Studies, Anthropology, Applied Mathematics, Archaeology, Art Education, Art/Fine Arts, Art History, BioChemistry, BioEngineering, Civil Engineering, Cell Biology, Clinical Psychology, Communications, Comparative Literature, Computer Science, Corrections, Creative Writing, Criminal Justice, Criminology, Dance, PreDentistry, Ecology, Economics, Education, Electrical Engineering Technology, Elementary Education, English, Environmental Engineering, Environmental Science, Environmental Studies, Fashion Design and Technology, Fashion Merchandising, Food Science, Health Education, History, Home Economics, Hotel and Restaurant Management, Humanities, Human Resources, Insurance, Interior Design, International Business, International Relations, Latin American, Law Enforcement, Police Science, Marine Biology, Liberal Arts, General Science, Molecular Biology, Music, Music Education

Women's Athletic Profile

Moore Athletic Center c/o Women's Soccer
Tallahassee, FL 32316-2195
Coach: Patrick Baker
Email: pdbaker@mailer.fsu.edu

NCAA I
Lady Seminoles/Garnet, Gold
Phone: (850) 644-7724
Fax: (850) 645-3201

Estimated # of Women's Soccer Scholarships: None
Conference: Atlantic Coast Conference
Program Profile: $3.5 million stadium that opened in March of 1999 with a seating for 2,000 people. The field is international 80x120 yards, fully lit, natural Bermuda grass field. Fall season that last from August through November, and spring season that last from February to April. The ACC Tournament is in the first week of November.
History: The program began in 1995 with a 4-14-1 season. In 1996, the program improved with a 12-7-1 season, including victories over NC-State and Clemson. Top twenty votes received in the 1996 season. In 1999 saw six of eleven weeks in Regional Top Ten.
Achievements: All-ACC 2nd team-Melissa Juhl; South East All-Stars included Melissa Juhl and Kasey McCall.
Coaching: Patrick Baker USSF "A" License, Head of Region III, Girls ODP, Former US U21 National Team Assistant, Current US U16 National Team Assistant Coach. Darren Ambrose USSF "A" license, Region III Coaching Staff. Lauren Cryan also assist.
Roster in State: 7
Out of State: 15
Out of Country: 3
ODP State: 10
Regional: 8
National: 1
Walk-on/Other:
Graduation %: 100
Seniors on Team: 6
Camp or Clinic Dates: June 10-14, 17-21, July 27-30
Most Recent Record: 9-10-1
Schedule: UNC, Florida, Santa Clara, Clemson, Virginia, Duke, Wake Forest, Portland
Style of Play: Come watch us play!

Jacksonville University

Academic Profile

Jacksonville, FL 32211

Phone: 800-225-2027

Type: 4 Yr.,Private,Liberal Arts
Website: http://www.junix.ju.edu
SAT/ACT/GPA: 1080/23
Student/Faculty Ratio: 14:1
Undergraduate Enrollment: 2,064
Scholarships/Academic: Yes
Athletic: Yes
Expenses by: Year
In State: $ 17,660
Specialty: Business, Education
Degrees Conferred: BA, BS, MAT
Founded: 1934
Religion: Non-Affiliated
Housing: Yes
Male/Female Ratio: 47:53
Graduate Enrollment: 352
Financial Aid: Yes
Out of State: $ 17,660
Programs of Study: Accounting, Art, Aviation Administration, Biology, Business, Chemistry, Computer, Economics, English, Finance, International Business, Geography, Management, Medical, Philosophy, PreProfessional Programs

Men's Athletic Profile

2800 University Blvd. North
Jacksonville, FL 32211-3394
Coach: Mike Johnson
Email: Not Available

NCAA I
Dolphins/Green, White
Phone: (904) 744-3950x7420
Fax: (904) 743-0067

Estimated # of Men's Soccer Scholarships: None
Conference: Sun Belt Conference
Program Profile: Our JU soccer program is a perennial Sun Belt power, including winning the 1995 championship. JU plays on a natural grass surface, and the local weather provides excellent year-round training opportunities.
History: Our program was started in the early 1950's and has continued to grow since. The program established itself upon joining the Sun Belt Conference, winning the championship in 1978. the program and players have grown because of the ability to schedule the best competition (ACC, Big Ten) over the years.
Achievements: Dennis Viollet - 1995 Sun Belt Conference Coach of the Year. Current Direct of Soccer, Aleks Mihailovicf - All-American for the Dolphins during his career from 1975-1978. Mihailovic was drafted by the NASL and played for that league as well as the Major Indoor Soccer League.
Style of Play: The team will play within the technical/tactical confines of the players on the squad. The coaching approach will be to play a quick-paced, build-up game where possession is most important.

Women's Athletic Profile

2800 University Blvd. N
Jacksonville, FL 32211-3394
Coach: Mike Johnson
Email: Not Available

NCAA I
Dolphins/Green, White
Phone: (904) 744-3950
Fax: (904) 743-0067

Estimated # of Women's Soccer Scholarships: N/A
Conference: Sun Belt
Program Profile: This is a new program which had its official start in the fall of 1995. 1996 was the first season with recruited athletes. Both a quality educational opportunity and the chance to build a growing Division I program from the ground up.
History: The women's soccer program played its first varsity season in 1995.
Style of Play: The team will play a work-up style, attempting to get all of the players involved in both attacking and defending. Playing with passion is a mandatory prerequisite.

Lynn University
Academic Profile

Boca Raton, FL 33431
Phone: 800-544-8035

Type: 4 Yr.,Private,Liberal Arts
Website: http://www.lynn.edu
SAT/ACT/GPA: 800/17
Student/Faculty Ratio: 12:1
Undergraduate Enrollment: 2,000
Scholarships/Academic: Yes
Athletic: Yes
Expenses by: Year
In State: $ 24,000
Specialty: Business

Founded: 1962
Religion: Non-Affiliated
Housing: Yes
Male/Female Ratio: 50:50
Graduate Enrollment:
Financial Aid: Yes
Out of State: $ 24,000

Degrees Conferred: AA, AS, BA, BS, MA, MPS
Programs of Study: Accounting, Aviation Management, Behavioral Science, Business & Management, Communications, Computer Science, Design, Education, Engineering, Fashion Marketing, Finance, Fine Arts, Health & Human Services, History, International Business, Management, Marketing, Parks/Recreation, Political Science, Protective Services, Psychology, Public Affairs, Social Sciences & more

Men's Athletic Profile

3601 N Military Trail
Boca Raton, FL 33431
Coach: Shaun Pendleton
Email: spendleton@lynn.edu

NCAA II
Knights/Royal, White
Phone: 561-237-7243
Fax: (407) 995-8135

Estimated # of Men's Soccer Scholarships: None
Conference: Sunshine State Conference
Program Profile: Lynn University has one of the top programs in the region that is filled with strong programs. The knights have an excellent natural grass field in a picturesque campus setting. Lynn plays the top teams in the region each year.
History: Lynn has been one of the top teams in the NAIA since the program began 11 years ago. LU won the NAIA Championship in 1987 and 1991, was defeated in the finals in sudden-death overtime in 1993, spoiling and otherwise undefeated season. LU was accepted into NCAA Division II in January 1994.
Achievements: Shau Pendleton coached the team to the NAIA National Championship in 1991. The Knights won the Area Championship in 1993 and had 6 players receive national honors. 3 players represented Lynn at the UMBRO Senior Bowl.
Coaching: Shaun Pendleton, Head Coach, 5th season, has been highly successful since coming to Lynn from West Virginia, co-director of the highly successful and popular Pine Tree Soccer Camp. Graduate of Akron in 1985, Masters in PE, played professionally with Sheffield United, Columbus Capitals and Memphis Storm.
Style of Play: Aggressive, attacking style.

Women's Athletic Profile

3601 North Military Trail
Boca Raton, FL 33431
Coach: Rocky Orezzoli
Email: rorezzoli@lyn.edu

NCAA II
Knights/Royal Blue, White
Phone: (561) 237-7244
Fax: (561) 237-7283

Estimated # of Women's Soccer Scholarships: 2-4
Conference: Sunshine State Conference
Program Profile: Lynn University is one of the top soccer programs at any level. The Knights have an excellent natural grass field in a picturesque setting on the southwest side of the campus. Lynn plays the top teams in the region each year.

History: Lynn has been one of the top teams in the NAIA since the program began 10 years ago. LU won the NAIA Championship in 1992 and lost in the final sudden-death overtime in 1993. LU was accepted as a member of the NCAA Division II in January 1994. NCAA Champs in 1998. Ranked #17 in Nation in 1999.
Achievements: 1992 NAIA Champions. 1991 appeared in the National Tournament in Boca Raton and lost to national champs. 4 players named All-Americans 1991. 1993 Area Champions, 5 All-Americans, 3 represented Lynn at the UMBRO Senior Bowl. 1998 2 All-Americans, 7 All-South Region. 1999 1 All-American, 4 All-South Region.
Coaching:
Roster in State: 3 **Out of State:** 9 **Out of Country:** 6
ODP State: 4 **Regional:** **National:**
Walk-on/Other: **Graduation %:** **Seniors on Team:** 3
Positions Needed: 4-5
Camp or Clinic Dates: Not Available
Most Recent Record: 11-4
Schedule: Barry University, Ashland University, Cal State Bakersfield, University of West Florida, C.W. Post, Lincoln Memorial
Style of Play: Possession style-a lot of players going forward.

Nova Southeastern University

Academic Profile

Phone: (954) 262-8264

Fort Lauderdale, FL 33314

Type: 4 Yr.,Private, **Founded:** 1964
Website: http://www.nova.edu **Religion:** Non-Affiliated
SAT/ACT/GPA: Open enrollment **Housing:** Yes
Student/Faculty Ratio: 13:1 **Male/Female Ratio:** 1:2
Undergraduate Enrollment: 4,207 **Graduate Enrollment:** 9,714
Scholarships/Academic: Yes **Athletic:** Yes **Financial Aid:** Yes
Expenses by: Year **In State:** $ 17,660 **Out of State:** $ 17,660
Degrees Conferred: BA, BS, MS, Ph.D., MBA, ID, DMD, DO
Programs of Study: Accounting, Administrative Studies, Applied Professional Studies, Business Administration, Computer Information Systems, Computer Science, Education, Elementary Education, Environmental Science, Business, Exceptional Legal Studies (PreLaw), General Studies, Hospitality Management, Humanities, Liberal Arts, Life Sciences (PreMedical), Ocean Studies, Physician's Assistant, Professional Management, Psychology, Science, Sports Wellness Business

Men's Athletic Profile

3301 College Avenue
Fort Lauderdale, FL 33314
Coach: Joe DePalo
Email: Depalog@hotmail.com

NCAA II, NAIA
Knights/Navy, White w/gold trim
Phone: (954) 475-7345
Fax: (954) 262-3926

Estimated # of Men's Soccer Scholarships: varies
Conference: Florida Sun Conference
Program Profile: We have three full fields, one field is lighted. Two unlighted fields are Olympic Size with the best grass. Season is combination of Division I, II and NAIA matches.
History: Team has rich tradition. Program began in 1984. Pinnacle of team was this National Championship appearance in 1988.
Achievements: Captured Florida Sun Conference Championship in 1995.
Coaching: Joe Depalo, USSF A License. 1 Florida Sun Conference Championship, 1 Regional Championship
Roster In State: 18 **Out of State:** 1 **Out of Country:** 3
Walk-on/Other: **Graduation %:** 90 **Seniors on Team:** 3

Positions Needed: Goalkeeper, Forward, Defender
Camp or Clinic Dates: July 17-21 July 24-28, 2000
Most Recent Record: 10-10-1
Schedule: Lindsay Wilson, Life, Barry, Lynn, West Florida
Style of Play: patient/methodical, Build up-Fast speed of play, Group oriented defense.

Women's Athletic Profile

3301 College Ave.
Fort Lauderdale, FL 33314
Coach: Mike Goodrich
Email: goodm@polaris.acast.nova.edu

NAIA
Knights/Navy, White w/gold trim
Phone: (954) 256-8270
Fax: (954) 476-8959

Estimated # of Women's Soccer Scholarships: None
Conference: Florida Sun Conference
Program Profile: There are three full fields with one being lighted. The two unlighted fields are Olympic size fields with the best grass. Our season is a combination of Division I, II and NAIA.
History: The team has been in existence for 2 years. In the first year the team won the Florida Sun Conference.
Achievements: Florida Sun Conference Title, Five players named to All-Conference first team, Player of the Year Florida Sun Conference.
Style of Play: The Nova team is young but very experienced. They play a short passing game with as much possession as opposing teams will allow. Conditioning is extremely important for any incoming player.

Palm Beach Atlantic College

Academic Profile

West Palm Beach, FL 33416-4708

Phone: 888-468-6722

Type: 4 Yr.,Private,Liberal Arts
Website: http://www.pbac.edu
SAT/ACT/GPA: 1000/24/3.0
Student/Faculty Ratio: 18:1
Undergraduate Enrollment: 1,800
Scholarships/Academic: Yes **Athletic:** Yes
Expenses by: Year **In State:** $ 15,000

Founded: 1968
Religion: Multi-denominational
Housing: Yes
Male/Female Ratio: 60:40
Graduate Enrollment: 400
Financial Aid: Yes
Out of State: $ 15,000

Specialty: Business, Education, Psychology, Music
Degrees Conferred: BA, BS, MS
Programs of Study: Accounting, Art, Biology, Business and Management, Communications, Computer Information System, Economics, Education, Elementary Education, English, Finance, International Business, Marine Biology, Marketing, Mathematics, Music, Physical Science, Political Science, PreDentistry, PreLaw, PreMed, Psychology, Religion

Men's Athletic Profile

P.O. Box 24708
West Palm Beach, FL 33416-4708
Coach: Juan Pablo Favero
Email: admit@pbac.edu

NAIA
Sailfish/Royal, White
Phone: (561) 803-2531
Fax: (561) 803-2532

Estimated # of Men's Soccer Scholarships: Varies
Conference: Florida Sun Conference
Program Profile: What is being built into a very strong program competing in the extremely competitive Florida Sun Conference. Play and practice in natural turf; beautiful weather for-year-round play. Green complex has a state-of-the-art weight room, locker rooms; 2,00 seat basketball arena and secondary gyms where indoor soccer may be played.

History: Our program began in 1978, started play in the NCCAA where the program was very successful and played in National Tournament. Joined the NAIA and Florida Sun Conference in 1991. Best finished is 4th in the regular season and reached the semi-finals of the tournament in 1995.
Achievements: Produced Academic All-American Athletes; have won NCAA Conference, and Regional Titles, and had one All-American Athlete
Coaching: Juan Pablo Favero, Head Coach, formerly played in PBA. He is assisted by a former PBA player. Jorge Castellanos and David Rezchley, Assistant Coaches.
Style of Play: Play a South American Style of Play. Moving the ball and to create the attack, but with a very solid defensive approach as well.

Women's Athletic Profile

901 S Flagler Dr., P. O. Box 24708
West Palm Beach, FL 33416-4708
Coach: John Webb
Email: PBACoach@acc.com

NAIA
Sailfish/Royal, White
Phone: (561) 803-2530
Fax: (561) 803-2532

Estimated # of Women's Soccer Scholarships: None
Conference: Florida Sun Conference
Program Profile: We play on Bermuda grass. Our fall season goes from August through November. We have a very young program that has only graduated 2 seniors. We play a variety of styles and pressure.
History: We have a young program which has made it to the playoffs every year in the last 5 years. We have and excellent 1999 recruiting class which propelled the team to the finals by beating the 9th ranked team in the Nation in semifinals.
Achievements: John Webb-1999 Conference Coach of the Year; 9 All-Conference Players; 1 Regional All-American; 1 All-American in the last 5 years.
Coaching: John Webb, Head Coach, is USSF licensed. He was 1998-1999 Coach of the Year. He started PBA women's soccer 5 years ago. David "Mo" Davis, Assistant Coach, was the leading striker for the PBA men's team before a knee injury. He was the head coach at Lake Worth High School. Chis Bean, Assistant Coach, is a 1997 graduate of PBA. He was midfielder for the men's soccer team. He is a former high school head coach.
Style of Play: We play a variety of styles and pressures. We are working on becoming more of a possession team, which likes to build as opposed to counter attacks.

Rollins College
Academic Profile

Phone: 407-823-3000

Winter Park, FL 32789

Type: 4 Yr.,Private,Liberal Arts
Website: http://www.rollins.edu
SAT/ACT/GPA: No minimum, 3.0
Student/Faculty Ratio: 12:1
Undergraduate Enrollment: 1,480
Scholarships/Academic: Yes
Expenses by: Year
Degrees Conferred: BA, BS

Athletic: Yes
In State: $ 28,042

Founded: 1885
Religion: Non-Affiliated
Housing: Yes
Male/Female Ratio: 40:60
Graduate Enrollment: 686
Financial Aid: Yes
Out of State: $ 28,042

Programs of Study: Anthropology, Art History, Art Studio, Biology, Chemistry, Classical Studies, Computer Science, Economics, Elementary Education, English, Environmental Studies, Foreign Languages, French, German, History, International Studies, International Relations, Latin American Affairs, Mathematics, Music, Philosophy, Physics, Politics, Psychology, Religious Studies, Sociology, Spanish, Theatre Arts

Men's Athletic Profile

1000 Holt Ave.
Winter Park, FL 32789
Coach: Keith Buckley
Email: kbuckley@rollins.edu

NCAA II
Tars/Blue, Gold
Phone: (407) 646-2513
Fax: (407) 646-1555

Estimated # of Men's Soccer Scholarships: 4
Conference: Sunshine State Conference
Program Profile: We are a nationally ranked program with outstanding facilities. We play on a superb field surface in a lighted stadium.
History: Our program is the oldest collegiate soccer program in Florida. It started in 1950; made nine NCAA Appearances and produced 7 All-Americans.
Achievements: Won Sunshine State Coach of the Year; 7 All-Americans; John Smith drafted in 1996 by Columbus Crew.
Coaching: Keith Buckley, Head Coach, holds a USSF "A" License, an Advanced NSCAA Diploma. He was a former professional player, spent six years at Rollins and was a World Cup Competition Manager. He was also a former professional soccer player at Albany. Joe Reynold - Assistant Coach.
Style of Play: We play a fast paced game that is very attacking. We try to put pressure on our opponents and use our team's speed.

Women's Athletic Profile

100 Holt Avenue
Winter Park, FL 32789
Coach: Leondra Dodge
Email:

Phone: (407) 646-2513
Fax: (407) 646-1555

Did Not Return Profile

Saint Leo College

Academic Profile

Saint Leo, FL 33574

Phone: (352) 588-8221

Type: 4 Yr.,Private,Liberal Arts
Website: http://www.saintleo.edu
SAT/ACT/GPA: 950/2.5
Student/Faculty Ratio: 16:1
Undergraduate Enrollment: 8,555
Scholarships/Academic: Yes
Athletic: Yes
Expenses by: Year
In State: $ 18,100
Specialty: Liberal Arts
Degrees Conferred: BA, Masters

Founded: 1889
Religion: Catholic
Housing: Yes
Male/Female Ratio: 1:1
Graduate Enrollment: 500
Financial Aid: Yes
Out of State: $ 18,100

Programs of Study: Accounting, American Studies, Banking & Finance, Biology, Business Administration, Business, Law, Chemistry, Communications, Computer Science, Criminology, Economics, Elementary Education, English, History, Hotel Restaurant, Human Resources, International Business, Management, Marketing, Political Science, PreDentistry, PreLaw, PreMed, Psychology, Public Administration, Religion, Social Science, Sports Management

Men's Athletic Profile

Box 6665, MC-2038
Saint Leo, FL 33574
Coach: Fran Reidy
Email: freidy@saintleo.edu

NCAA II
Monarchs/Green, White
Phone: (352) 588-8246
Fax: (352) 588-8290

Estimated # of Men's Soccer Scholarships: 5.0
Conference: Sunshine State Conference
Program Profile: Our program is nationally recognized in Division III that competes in the strong Sunshine State Conference. Play on Bermuda grass which measures 75x120 field with additional training area. Full Fall and Spring season with a climate for year-round development.
History: Our program began in 1968 as one of the first in Florida. Team finished in National ranking from 1996-1998. Program has posted winning record 7 of the last nine years.
Achievements: Coach Fran Reidy was named two-time Conference Coach of the Year, Sam Koleduk was named All-American in 19913-1994, Jon Akin was named All-American in 1996-1997, led the nation in scoring in 1996. Drafted first round in 1999 by A-League team.
Coaching: Fran Reidy, Head Coach, entering eleven years with the program. Serves as a school Athletic Director. On South Region Ranking Committee. NSCAA South Region Selection Committee. Tony Paris, Assistant Coach, English professional player for Ipswhich - "A" License Coach and State ODP Staff.
Style of Play: We will play a 4-3-3 with emphasis on attack. Three scorers should make this exciting team. Young team with a lot of depth.

Women's Athletic Profile

P.O. Box 6665 MC 2036
St. Leo, FL 33574
Coach: Fran Reidy
Email: fran.reidy@saintleo.edu

NCAA II
Lions/Forest Green, White
Phone: (352) 588-8221
Fax: (352) 588-8290

Estimated # of Women's Soccer Scholarships: 5
Conference: Sunshine State Conference
Program Profile: A consistent factor in the powerful sunshine state conference. Outstanding playing surface of Bermuda grass, 80x120. Florida weather allows for year round training. Great schedule year in and year out.
History: Winning record of six of the last seven years. Nationally ranked during each of the past five years.
Achievements: Nation's leading scorer-John Akin-1997-Akin was a 2 time All-American. Nation's second leading soccer scorer Sam Koleduh in 1993-Koleduh 2 time All-American. Coach named coach of the year twice.
Coaching: Fran Reidy-11 seasons, 100+ wins: also serves as athletic director. On NCAA national soccer committee. Tony Paris-asst.-"A" license-coach professional in Faroe Islands and played pro in England.
Greg Vallee-former SLU player.
Roster in State: 17 **Out of State:** 2 **Out of Country:** 3
Walk-on/Other: **Graduation %:** 55 **Seniors on Team:** 5
Positions Needed: Defender-2, 1mid, 1 forward
Camp or Clinic Dates: Not Available
Schedule: Lynn, Barry, USC-Spartanburg, Tampa, Presbyterian, Florida Southern, Rollins, West Florida, Montevallo, University of Alabama Huntsville
Style of Play: Entertaining!

Saint Thomas University

Academic Profile

Miami, FL 33054
Phone: (305) 628-6678

Type: 4 Yr.,Private,Liberal Arts
Website: http://www.stu.edu
SAT/ACT/GPA: 950/18/2.5
Student/Faculty Ratio: 15:1
Undergraduate Enrollment: 1,100
Scholarships/Academic: Yes **Athletic:** Yes
Expenses by: Year **In State:** $ 17,160
Specialty: Business Administration, Sports Administration

Founded: 1961
Religion: Catholic
Housing: Yes
Male/Female Ratio: 53:47
Graduate Enrollment: 2,500
Financial Aid: Yes
Out of State: $ 17,160

Degrees Conferred: BA, MA, MS, MBA
Programs of Study: Accounting, American Studies, Banking & Finance, Biology, Business Administration, Economics, Business Law, Chemistry, Communications, Computer Science, Criminal Justice, Elementary Education, History, Management, Marketing, Political Science, PreDentistry, PreLaw, PreMed, Psychology, Public Administration, Religion, Social Science, Sport Administration

Men's Athletic Profile

16400 NW 32nd Avenue
Miami, FL 33054
Coach: Ricardo Zambrano
Email: Not-Available

NAIA
Bobcats/N. Blue, Blue, White
Phone: (305) 628-6679
Fax: (305) 628-6790

Estimated # of Men's Soccer Scholarships: 6.5
Conference: Florida Sun Conference
Program Profile: Our facilities includes training room, weight room and locker room. Playing season starts from Fall which is August to November and spring February to April. Field is natural grass; stadium size seats 1,000.
History: Our program was suspended in 1987 and was reinstated in 1992.
Achievements: Coach of the Year in 1998; Conference Titles in 1993, 1997 & 1998; Third Team All-American Sheikh N' Dure in 1993; Honorable Mention All-American was David Gely in 1996; Honorable Mention All-American was Hendrick Dahlberg in 1998.
Coaching: Ricky Zambrano, Head Coach, takes over for Barry Kaplan after seven years. He served as an assistant for three years under Kaplan, and is a former player.

Roster In State: 40	**Out of State:** 6	**Out of Country:** 6
ODP State: 1	**Regional:** 1	**National:** 1
Walk-on/Other:	**Graduation %:** 95	**Seniors on Team:** 7

Positions Needed: All
Most Recent Record: 10-7-2
Schedule: Nova Southeastern, Barry University, Embry Riddle University, University of Tampa, Lindsey Wilson College
Style of Play: Possession game combine with a quick attack game.

Women's Athletic Profile

16400 NW 32nd Avenue
Miami, FL 33054
Coach: Tricia Dornisch
Email: N/A

NAIA
Bobcats/Navy, White
Phone: (305) 628-6678
Fax: (305) 628-6790

Estimated # of Women's Soccer Scholarships: None
Conference: Florida Sun Athletic Conference
Program Profile: The season starts August 14, 1999. It is a 24-week season plus playoffs. The field is natural Bermuda grass. Our practice field is next to the main field which has a 1,500 seating capacity. We will host the 1999-2000 NAIA Women's National Championships Tournament. Our most successful season ever was 1998 when we finished #9 in the nation.
History: Our program began in 1992 after a ten year hiatus. The team's record in 1995 was 7-10-3, in 1996 was 8-9-0, in 1997 was 15-7-1 and in 1998 17-7-0. We made National Tournament appearances in 1997 and 1998. We will be hosting the NAIA Women's National Championship Tournament in 1999-2000.
Achievements: The program has won the FSC regular season in 1996 and lost in the regional semi-final. Won 1997 FSC regular season. In 1997, we won the 1997 Regional and went to Nationals for the first time.
Style of Play: Aggressively attacking style with good transition offensively and defensively. applying high pressure all over the field and closing down any open routes toward our defense quickly. opponents and fans have said that it is exciting to watch STU play.

Stetson University

Academic Profile

Deland, FL 32720

Phone: (904) 822-8117

Type: 4 Yr.,Private,Liberal Arts
Website: http://www.stetson.edu
SAT/ACT/GPA: 1120/26/3.48
Student/Faculty Ratio: 11:1
Undergraduate Enrollment: 2,000
Scholarships/Academic: Yes **Athletic:** Yes
Expenses by: Year **In State:** $ 24,000
Founded: 1883
Religion: Non-Affiliated
Housing: Yes
Male/Female Ratio: 43:57
Graduate Enrollment: 300
Financial Aid: Yes
Out of State: $ 24,000
Specialty: Business, Liberal Arts, Music, Pre-Med, Pre-Law
Degrees Conferred: BA, BS, BEd, BM, MA, MS, MBA, M.Ed., Ph.D.
Programs of Study: Accounting, American Studies, Art, Biology, Business Administration, Chemistry, Communication Studies, Computer Science, Counseling, Economics, Education, English, Environmental Studies, Finance, Foreign Language, Geography, Geology, History, Humanities, Information Systems, Latin American Studies, Management, Marketing, Mathematics, Military Sciences, Philosophy, Physics, Political Science, Psychology, Religious Studies, Russian Studies, Sociology, Sports & Exercise Science, Sport Administration, Theatre

Men's Athletic Profile

421 N. Woodland Blvd., Unit 8378
DeLand, FL 32720
Coach: Sean Murphy
Email: smurphy@stetson.edu

NCAA I
Hatters/Forest Green, White
Phone: (904) 822-8122
Fax: (904) 822-8148

Estimated # of Men's Soccer Scholarships: 9.9
Conference: Trans America Athletic Conference
Program Profile: We play on a natural grass surface. Our new stadium plans to be completed ASAP. Season is in the fall and play in the spring is the maximum allowed by NCAA. Our newly constructed Wilson Athletic Center houses a student-athlete weight room and training facility, with a full-time conditioning specialist.
History: Started in 1957 and has been in NCAA Division I since 1971.
Achievements: 1998 TAAC Semi-finalists, Stian Tobiassen All-TAAC first team, NSCAA All-south; Mike Poole was named All-TAAC 3rd team; Scott Bower U-23 national team; project 40 players allocated by San Jose.
Coaching: Sean Murphy, Head Coach, is a native of Bristol, England. He was a former assistant coach at Clemson for five years. He holds USSF "A" License and is Head ODP State Coach. He was a former All-American Flagler, former pro with Hampton Rhodes & South Carolina Swamrocks. He has a Master's degree in Guidance and Counseling and is working on Ph.D.. Scott Calabrese, Assistant Coach, is a native of Newton, Ct. He was the former assistant coach for two years at Southern Wesleyan University, ODP Goalkeeper Coach, a former pro Rhode Island & South Carolina Swamrocks. He was a former All-Conference at Bryant College.
Style of Play: Possession oriented, attack with width, defend with compactness.

Women's Athletic Profile

421 N. Woodland Blvd. Unit 8359
DeLand, FL 32720
Coach: Bob Wilson
Email: bwilson@stetson.edu

NCAA I
Hatters/Forest Green, White
Phone: (904) 822-8139
Fax: (904) 822-8148

Estimated # of Women's Soccer Scholarships:
Conference: Trans American Athletic Conference

Program Profile: We are a Division I program that plays a very tough Division I schedule. Some of our past tough opponents include Florida, Florida State University, Georgia and Old Dominion. Our stadium has 1, 000 seats and the field is natural grass.
History: Our program started around 1993. We have cycled through both rich and lean years. The 1999 campaign promises to be our best ever.
Achievements: Many All-Conference players; Conference Player of the Week
Coaching: Bob Wilson, Head Coach, enters his fifth year as head coach. He has a USSF "B" license and an NSCAA National diploma. Vede Lally, Assistant Coach, enters his second year as assistant coach. He has a USSF "C" license.
Style of Play: Direct, possession-oriented.

University of Central Florida
Academic Profile

Orlando, FL 32816
Phone: 407-823-3000

Type: 4 Yr.,Public,Liberal Arts,Engineering
Founded: 1963
Website: http://www.ucf.edu
Religion: Non-Affiliated
SAT/ACT/GPA: 1050-2000/22-26/3.1-3.9
Housing: Yes
Student/Faculty Ratio: 16:1
Male/Female Ratio: 77:33
Undergraduate Enrollment: 23,729
Graduate Enrollment: 4,271
Scholarships/Academic: Yes **Athletic:** Yes **Financial Aid:** Yes
Expenses by: Year **In State:** $ 7,627 **Out of State:** $ 14,283
Specialty: Engineering, Business, Computer Science
Degrees Conferred: 73 Bachelors, 51 Masters, 3 Advanced Masters, 15 Doctorates
Programs of Study: Education, Health and Public Affairs, Biology, Communications, Visual Performing Arts, Psychology, Physical Therapy, Forensic Science, Social Work, Political Science, Criminal Justice, Public Administration.

Men's Athletic Profile

Men's Soccer Office
Orlando, FL 32816
Coach: Bob Winch
Email: Rwinch@pegasus.ccuct.edu

NCAA I
Golden Knights/Black, Gold
Phone: (407) 823-2262
Fax: (407) 823-5266

Estimated # of Men's Soccer Scholarships: 9.9
Conference: Trans America Athletic Conference
Program Profile: We have a Bermuda game field, 4 Bermuda training fields, stadium seats 1,500.
History: Program began in 1970. NCAA Division II Team until 1984. Moved to Division I in 1984.
Roster In State: 1 **Out of State:** 10 **Out of Country:** 7
Walk-on/Other: **Graduation %:** 100 **Seniors on Team:**
Positions Needed: Forwards
Camp or Clinic Dates: Not Available
Most Recent Record: 12-7-0
Schedule: Portland, San Diego, Jacksonville, RIU, UJF
Style of Play: Attack oriented style. Play forward as much as possible.

Women's Athletic Profile

P.O. Box 163555
Orlando, FL 32816
Coach: Amanda Cromwell
Email: acromwel@mail.ucf.edu

NCAA I
Golden Knights/Black, Gold
Phone: (407) 823-6345
Fax: (407) 823-5266

Estimated # of Women's Soccer Scholarships: 3
Conference: Trans America Athletic Conference

Program Profile: UCF Arena Field: Natural grass, full stadium lighting, bleacher seating is approx. 1,000, season from August-December, separate practice facilities with nearby locker rooms.
History: Program began in 1981 and was one of the founding teams on the NCAA. Played in the only AIWA National Championship and hosted the 1st NCAA Women's Soccer Championship in Orlando, Florida.
Achievements: NCAA Runner-Up (1982), NCAA Final Four (1982, 1987), NCAA Tournament (1982, 84, 87, 88, 91, 98, 99), TAAC Champions (1993, 94, 95, 96, 98, 99). All-Americans include Michelle Akers (1984, 86-88), Amy Jones (1995), Amy Allmann (1987), Kim Wyant (1985), Mary Varas (1983), Laura Dryden (1982), Michelle Sedita (1982), Pam Baughman (1981), Linda Gancitano (1981), Nancy Lay (1981). Olympian and World Cup Player Michelle Akers.
Coaching: Amanda Cromwell (24-14-2/2years at UCF) is a former Olympic and U.S. National Team Member. All-American at University of Virginia. Recently drafted by Washington of Women's Professional Soccer League. Matt Dillon (Asst. Coach), Donna Fishter (Goalkeeper Coach), Michelle Akers (Asst. Coach) Retired U.S. National Team, Olympics, All-American.

Roster in State: 15	**Out of State:** 12	**Out of Country:** 1
ODP State: 12	**Regional:**	**National:**
Walk-on/Other: 5	**Graduation %:** 100	**Seniors on Team:** 4

Positions Needed: Striker, Midfield, Goalkeeper
Camp or Clinic Dates: June 4-8, 10-14, 24-28 & July 22-26
Most Recent Record: 8-11-1
Schedule: Florida State, Miami-FL, Florida International, Jacksonville, Liberty, Pittsburgh
Style of Play: Control/possession on offense. Organized/tenacious on defense. Attractive/attacking soccer.

University of Florida

Academic Profile

Phone: (352) 375-4683

Gainesville, FL 32604

Type: 4 Yr.,Public		**Founded:** 1906
Website: http://www.uaa.ufl.edu		**Religion:** Non-Affiliated
SAT/ACT/GPA: 970/20/2.9		**Housing:** Yes
Student/Faculty Ratio: 17:1		**Male/Female Ratio:** 49:51
Undergraduate Enrollment: 31,329		**Graduate Enrollment:** 8,043
Scholarships/Academic: Yes	**Athletic:** Yes	**Financial Aid:** Yes
Expenses by: Year	**In State:** $ 9,372	**Out of State:** $ 16,028

Specialty: Business, Journalism, Architecture, Engineering, Education
Degrees Conferred: Bachelors, Master's, Doctoral
Programs of Study: Accounting, Advertising, Aerospace Engineering, Agricultural Business, Agricultural Economics, Agricultural Education, Agricultural Engineering, Agronomy, Soil and Crop Science, American Studies, Animal Science, Anthropology, Architecture, Art Education, Art/Fine Arts, Art History, Astronomy, Botany/Plant Science, Business Administration, Commerce, Management, Chemical Engineering, Chemistry, Civil Engineering, Classic, Computer Engineering, Computer Science, Conservation, Construction Management, Criminal Justice, Dairy Science, Dance, East Asian Studies, Ecology, Economics, Construction Management, English, Entomology, Health Science, Horticulture, Industrial Engineering, Insurance, Interior Design, Journalism, Management Information Systems, Mechanical Engineering, Microbiology, Music, Music Education, Natural Resources Management, Nuclear Engineering, Nursing, Nutrition, Occupational Therapy, Physician's Assistant Studies, Physics, Political Science, Psychology, Studio Art, Sociology

Women's Athletic Profile

P.O. Box 14485	**NCAA I**
Gainesville, FL 32604-2485	Gators/Orange, Blue
Coach: Becky Burleigh	**Phone:** (352) 375-4683
Email: WebAdmin@gators.uaa.ufl.edu/	**Fax:** (352) 373-1432

Estimated # of Women's Soccer Scholarships: Not Available
Conference: Southeastern Conference
Program Profile: The University of Florida women's soccer team is a fully funded program. The team has the use of two fields, one for practice and the other for matches- both are natural grass. The Percy Beard Stadium holds 4,500 people for home matches. The Gators finished second in the nation for average attendance in 1998. We have played host to NCAA matches the last three seasons and played host to the 1997 SEC Tournament. For most road matches, the team uses an athletic department plane that seats 35 .
History: Florida won its first NCAA team title in 1998 in only its fourth year of existence. We fielded our first soccer team in 1995 . Florida has won three consecutive Southeastern Conference tournament titles (1996-98) and has earned a berth in the NCAA tournament each of the last three seasons.
Achievements: Head Coach Becky Burleigh was named the 1998 National Coach of the Year by NSCAA, Adidas, College Soccer Weekly and Soccer Buzz; four Gators have seven NSCAA All-America honors; one player got the Honda Award for Soccer Female Player of the Year; One player is a member of the U.S.Women's National Team; 3 Southeastern Conference titles; 3 SEC Player of the Year awards.
Coaching: Becky Burleigh, Head Coach. Her overall record in three seasons here is 82-11-3. Her career record is 164-34-9. She has been coaching for nine years. Vic Campbell is Assistant Coach.
Style of Play: The Gators play a high pressure defending style, starting with the forwards. It is a flexible system of play, depending on talent year-to-year. University of Florida plays a possession-style offense.

University of Miami
Academic Profile

Coral Gables, FL 33124
Phone: 305-284-4323

Type: 4 Yr.,Private
Website: http://www.miami.edu
SAT/ACT/GPA: 1000/24
Student/Faculty Ratio: 8:1
Undergraduate Enrollment: 8,350
Scholarships/Academic: Yes
Athletic: Yes
Expenses by: Year
In State: $ 24,000
Founded: 1925
Religion: Non-Affiliated
Housing: Yes
Male/Female Ratio: 52:48
Graduate Enrollment: 5,200
Financial Aid: Yes
Out of State: $ 24,000
Degrees Conferred: BA, BS, MS, Ph.D., JD
Programs of Study: Aerospace Engineering, Afro-American Studies, American Studies, Anthropology, Audio Engineering, BioChemistry, Broadcasting, Caribbean Studies, Criminology, Foreign Languages, Latin American Studies, Photography, Real Estate, Renaissance Studies, *** Contact school admission office for more information on academic and admissions

Women's Athletic Profile

132 Ashe Building
Coral Gables, FL 33124-4616
Coach: Jim Blankenship
Email: admissions@admiss.ms.edu
NCAA I
Hurricanes/Green, Orange
Phone: (305) 284-4323
Fax: (305) 284-2507

Estimated # of Women's Soccer Scholarships: N/A
Conference: Independent
History: First year of university to have soccer program (1998).
Coaching: Jim Blankenship, Head Coach, accumulated a 199-37-8 record at Lynn University; coached 21 All-Americans and 40 Academic All-Americans; NAIA Coach of the Year in 1988, 1990, 1992, & 1998. Melissa Starman - Assistant Coach.

University of North Florida

Academic Profile

Phone: (904) 620-2897

Jacksonville, FL 32224

Type: 4 Yr.,Public,
Founded: 1972
Website: http://www.unf.edu
Religion: Non-Affiliated
SAT/ACT/GPA: 1000/21/3.0
Housing: Yes
Student/Faculty Ratio: 17:1
Male/Female Ratio: 58:32
Undergraduate Enrollment: 12,000
Graduate Enrollment: 2,000
Scholarships/Academic: Yes **Athletic:** Yes
Financial Aid: Yes
Expenses by: Year **In State:** $ 7,500
Out of State: $ 13,500
Specialty: Education, Health Sciences, Business
Degrees Conferred: BA, BFA, BS, BBA, BAE, MA, MS, MBA, MED, EdD
Programs of Study: College of Arts & Sciences, Business Administration, Computing Science & Engineering, College of Health, College of Education & Human Services

Men's Athletic Profile

4567 St. Johns Bluff Road South
Jacksonville, FL 32224-2645
Coach: Ray Bunch
Email: Not Available

NCAA II
Osprey/Navy, Gray
Phone: (904) 646-2948
Fax: (904) 646-2836

Estimated # of Men's Soccer Scholarships: None
Conference: Sunshine State Conference

Women's Athletic Profile

4567 St. Johns Bluff Rd S
Jacksonville, FL 32224
Coach: Mike Munch
Email: mmunch@unf.edu

NCAA III
Ospreys/Navy, Gray, White
Phone: (904) 620-1072
Fax: (904) 620-2836

Estimated # of Women's Soccer Scholarships: None
Conference: Peach Belt Athletic Conference
Program Profile: In 1999, we will be in our 4th year of the program. A soccer stadium is under construction and will open in 2000. It will have a natural grass field and 9,000 seats.
History: Third year of the program; 21-15-1 in two years; NSCAA Top 25 in nation in 1997; top 25 in south region.
Achievements: Two players-1998 All-Region; one player-1997 All-Region.
Coaching: Mike Munch, Head Coach, compiled a record of 27-20-5 in three years at Texas A&M-Commerce. Rodney Kenney, Assistant Coach, was a head women's soccer coach at Orange High School.
Style of Play: Depending on talents of players.

University of South Florida

Academic Profile

Phone: (813) 947-4149

Tampa, FL 33620

Type: 4 Yr.,Public,Liberal Arts
Founded: 1956
Website: http://www.usf.edu
Religion: Christian

SAT/ACT/GPA: 980/20/3.25
Housing: Yes
Student/Faculty Ratio: 13:1
Male/Female Ratio: 43:57
Undergraduate Enrollment: 34,000
Graduate Enrollment: 5,849
Scholarships/Academic: Yes
Athletic: Yes
Financial Aid: Yes
Expenses by: Year
In State: $ 7,792
Out of State: $ 19,785
Specialty: Education, Accounting, Engineering
Degrees Conferred: BA, BS, BFA, MA, MS, MBA, MFA, M.Ed., Ph.D., EdD, MD
Programs of Study: College of Arts & Science, College of Business Administration, College of Education, College of Engineering, Fine Arts, New College and College of Nursing

Men's Athletic Profile

4202 East Fowler Avenue
Tampa, FL 33620
Coach: John Hackwotch
Email: hackworth@admin.usf.edu

NCAA I
Bulls/Green, Gold
Phone: (813) 974-4149
Fax: (813) 974-4028

Estimated # of Men's Soccer Scholarships:
Conference: Conference USA
Program Profile: Site of Division I Championship in 1990-1991. Play on 120x75 yards, natural Bermuda grass, soccer-specific stadium which has a capacity of 4,000. Team plays in fall.
History: Our program began in 1965. our record in 34 seasons is 345-162-41. Won 14 Conference Championships, three in Conference USA and ten NCAA Tournaments (Elite Eight in 1997).
Achievements: John Hackworth was named 1998 Conference USA Coach of the Year; Jeff Cunningham was named 3rd team All-American in 1997, Mike Mekelberg was named Conference USA Player of the Year in 1996, Jeff Cunningham was named Conference USA Player of the Year in 1997, Brian Waltrip was named Conference USA Player of the Year, Jeff Cunningham was MLS Columbus (Crew) - 1996, 1997 & 1998 Conference USA Regular Season Champ; 1990 & 1998 Conference USA Tournament Champs.
Coaching: John Hackworth, Head Coach, entering 3rd year with the program. He has an overall record of 32-25-2. Kevin Johnson, Assistant Coach, entering third year with the program.
Roster In State: 20
Out of State: 4
Out of Country: 1
ODP State: 10
Regional: 8
National: 2
Walk-on/Other: 5
Graduation %: 80
Seniors on Team: 5
Positions Needed: Defenders & Forward
Camp or Clinic Dates: June 11-15, June 18-22, July 20-22
Most Recent Record: 10-9-0
Schedule: UNC-Chapel Hill, Duke Univ. St. Louis Univ. UNC-Charlotte, F.I.U, Marquette
Style of Play: An attacking, possession oriented style.

Women's Athletic Profile

4202 East Fowler Avenue
Tampa, FL 33620
Coach: Logan Fleck
Email: fleck2alan.usf.edu

NCAA I
Bulls/F.Green, White, Yellow
Phone: (813) 974-4026
Fax: (813) 974-4028

Estimated # of Women's Soccer Scholarships: None
Conference: Conference USA

University of Tampa
Academic Profile

Phone: 800-733-4773

Tampa, FL 33606

Type: 4 Yr.,Private,Liberal Arts
Founded: 1931
Website: http://www.utspartans@aol.com
Religion: Non-Affiliated

SAT/ACT/GPA: 950/21/2.8
Housing: Yes
Student/Faculty Ratio: 8:1
Male/Female Ratio: 45:55
Undergraduate Enrollment: 2,000
Graduate Enrollment: 450
Scholarships/Academic: Yes
Athletic: Yes
Financial Aid: Yes
Expenses by: Year
In State: $ 20,000
Out of State: $ 20,000
Specialty: Strong Business, Science, Criminology
Degrees Conferred: BA, BS, BFA, BMus, MBA
Programs of Study: Accounting, Biology, Banking/Finance, Biological Science, Chemistry, Communications, Creative Writing, Criminal Justice, Economics, Education, Fine Arts, Marketing, Mathematics, Medical Laboratory Technology, Nursing, Philosophy, Physics, Psychology, Social Science, Political Science

Men's Athletic Profile

401 W Kennedy Blvd. Box 1
Tampa, FL 33606-1490
Coach: Keith Fulk
Email: kfulk@alpha.utampa.edu

NCAA II
Spartans/White
Phone: (813) 253-6240x3407
Fax: (813) 253-6288

Estimated # of Men's Soccer Scholarships: 4
Conference: Sunshine State Conference
Program Profile: Natural grass playing field which ahs a seating capacity of 4500. One of the only school which has a covered grandstand in the country. Top 10 Division II program in the country who has a chance to win a national title every year.
History: Our program began in 1978, consistently in national Top Ten, #1 on several occasions. National Champions in 1991& 1994. 14 consecutive NCAA Tourney Appearances. NCAA National Runner-Up in 1983 & 1992. NCAA National Champions in 1981 & 1994. 17of 25 years on the NCAA tournament.
Achievements: 14 players currently in the pros; Conference Champions in 1982, 1983, 1984, 1986, 1987, 1990, 1992, 1994, 1995, 1996, & 1997. Regional Titles in 1981, 1983, 1987, 1992, 1994; National Champs in 1981, 1994; Coach of the Year in 1987, 1989, 1990, 1995, 1996; numerous All-Americans since 1981.
Coaching: Keith Fulk, Head Coach, "A" License, played professionally in Europe and US.
Roster In State: 12
Out of State: 5
Out of Country: 6
ODP State: 10
Regional: 2
National: 4
Walk-on/Other: 0
Graduation %: 100
Seniors on Team: 5
Positions Needed: Forward, Flank defenders, Right/Left Back.
Camp or Clinic Dates: June 11-15, June 18-22, June 25-29
Most Recent Record: 14-4-0
Schedule: Barry Univ. Lynn Univ. Southern Connecticut, Christian Brothers, Florida Southern, Stetson.
Style of Play: Exciting possession style of soccer.

Women's Athletic Profile

401 W. Kennedy Blvd.
Tampa, FL 33606-1450
Coach: Jay Entlich
Email: jentlich@alpha.utampa.edu

NCAA II
Spartans/Scarlet, Black
Phone: (813) 253-6240
Fax: (813) 253-6288

Estimated # of Women's Soccer Scholarships: 2.2
Conference: Sunshine State Conference
Program Profile: Will be entering our 3rd season in 2000. Peppin Rood Stadium has natural grass with a seating capacity of 4000. All three seasons have been winning seasons, play a top 20 schedule.
History: The program began in 1998 with a winning season. The team went 11-9 and then 11-9 and then this year was 12-8. The team is made up of 9 players from Florida and the rest from all parts of the country. We have one player from Sweden and we have the ability to train year round with the weather.

Achievements: We had the sunshine state freshman of the year in 1999, Tai Kirklin 1st team all conference in 1999 and 2000. Second team all conference Ginger Lynn in 2000. Second team All-South Ginger Lynn and Tai Kirklin in 2000.
Coaching: Jay Entlich is the Head Coach. USSF "A" License, Olympic Festival South Team Head Coach, U-14 Regional Team Assistant Team Coach for Region I, Regional Staff member since 1994, Head Coach Tampa Bay Heather.

Roster in State: 9	**Out of State:** 16	**Out of Country:** 1
ODP State: 5	**Regional:** 0	**National:** 0
Walk-on/Other: 1	**Graduation %:**	**Seniors on Team:** 0

Positions Needed: Goalkeeper and midfield
Camp or Clinic Dates: June 25- June 29, July 5-8, July 9-13
Most Recent Record: 12-8-0
Schedule: Barry, Lynn, North Florida, Southern Connecticut, Central Oklahoma
Style of Play: We play zonally in the back and try to possess the ball through the midfield. We play attack oriented soccer.

University of West Florida
Academic Profile

Phone: (850) 474-2000

Pensacola, FL 32514

Type: 4 Yr.,Public,Liberal Arts		**Founded:** 1967
Website: http://www.uswf.edu		**Religion:** Non-Affiliated
SAT/ACT/GPA: 900/21		**Housing:** Yes
Student/Faculty Ratio: 26:1		**Male/Female Ratio:** 45:55
Undergraduate Enrollment: 6,000		**Graduate Enrollment:** 2,000
Scholarships/Academic: Yes	**Athletic:** Yes	**Financial Aid:** Yes
Expenses by: Year	**In State:** $ 6,900	**Out of State:** $ 13,900

Specialty: Comprehensive
Degrees Conferred: AA, BA, BS, BFA, MA, MS, MBA
Programs of Study: Accounting, Advertising, Anthropology, Art, Biology, Broadcasting, Business, Chemistry, Communications, Computer Information System, Computer Science, Criminal Justice, Economics, Education, Engineering, English, Finance, French, History, Humanities, International Studies, Journalism, Marine Biology, Music, Natural Science, Physics, Political Science, Nursing, Physical Education, Physical Science, Religion, Social Science, Psychology

Men's Athletic Profile

11000 University Parkway	**NCAA II**
Pensacola, FL 32514-5750	Argonauts/R. Blue, Kelly Green
Coach: Bill Elliott	**Phone:** (850) 474-2584
Email: belliot@uwf.edu	**Fax:** (850) 474-3342

Estimated # of Men's Soccer Scholarships: varies
Conference: Gulf South Conference
Program Profile: The home stadium features a smooth, fast playing, Bermuda grass surface with good drainage, It is well lit, making night games and practice possible. The stadium seats approximately 1,500 specators.
History: West Florida has sponsored a varsity men's soccer program since 1987. The overall record is 116-101-20. The Argoanuts won the Gulf South Conference Championships in 1998 and advanced to the NCAA Division II South Regional. Three players off the 1998 squad signed professional contracts, including Division I leading scorer, John Stefansson.
Achievements: 2 Women's Conference titles; 1 National tournament; 1 Conference Coach of the Year; 1 South Region Coach of the Year; 1 All-American

Coaching: Bill Elliott, Head Coach, is entering his sixth year with the program. He was a graduate from Tennessee in 1991. Steve Hirayama is the Assistant Coach, graduated from Tennessee in 1994. Scottie Milton, Assistant Coach, graduated from Mobile in 1997. Steve Fitzgibbons, Goalkeeper Coach, graduated from Coastal Carolina in 1994.

Roster In State: 20 | **Out of State:** 6 | **Out of Country:** 0
ODP State: 2 | **Regional:** | **National:**
Walk-on/Other: 4 | **Graduation %:** N/A | **Seniors on Team:** 4

Camp or Clinic Dates: Late July , Early August
Most Recent Record: 13-7-1
Schedule: Tampa, Barry, Lynn, Christian Brother, Eckerd
Style of Play: A very short build up type of an attack. A lot play in the central midfield.

Women's Athletic Profile

11000 University Parkway
Pensacola, FL 32514-5750
Coach: Bill Elliott
Email: belliot @uwf.edu

NCAA II
Argonauts/R. Blue, Kelly Green
Phone: (850) 474-2584
Fax: (850) 474-3342

Estimated # of Women's Soccer Scholarships: Varies
Conference: Gulf South Conference
Program Profile: West Florida has sponsored a varsity women's soccer team since 1991. the overall record is 73-55-8. The Argonauts play on a lighted field enclosed by running track. The field is natural grass. The university also has two unlighted practice fields which can also be used for daylight games.
History: West Florida has advanced to the finals of the GSC Tournament each of the three years of the league's existence. Bill Elliot was named GSC Coach of the Year in 1996 and 1997. Last year, UWF was 6-0 in conference.
Achievements: Elliot's tenure at West Florida, he was the 1st coach to sweep the conference title. 1 men's conference title and 1 National Tournament berth. 2 Women's Conference title and 1 National Tournament berth. 1 conference Coach of the year and 1 South Region Coach of the Year.
Coaching: Bill Elliott, Head Coach, graduated from Tennessee in 1991. Assistant Coach, Scottie Milton was graduate from Mobile in 1997.

Roster in State: 20 | **Out of State:** 6 | **Out of Country:** 0
ODP State: 2 | **Regional:** 0 | **National:** 0
Walk-on/Other: 4 | **Graduation %:** N/A | **Seniors on Team:** 4

Positions Needed: Varies
Camp or Clinic Dates: Late July, Early August
Most Recent Record: 13-7-1
Schedule: Tampa, Barry, Lynn, Christian Brother, Eckerd
Style of Play: Short combination passing with strong midfield play and tight defensive marking.

Webber College
Academic Profile

Babson Park, FL 33827
Phone: 941-638-1431

Type: 4 Yr.,Private,
Website: http://www.webber.edu
SAT/ACT/GPA: 850/19
Student/Faculty Ratio: 17:1
Undergraduate Enrollment: 437
Scholarships/Academic: Yes | **Athletic:** Yes
Expenses by: Year | **In State:** $ 9,607

Founded: 1922
Religion: Non-Affiliated
Housing: Yes
Male/Female Ratio: 50:50
Graduate Enrollment: N/A
Financial Aid: Yes
Out of State: $ 9,607

Specialty: Business
Degrees Conferred: AA, BA in Business Administration
Programs of Study: Management, Marketing, Finance, Accounting, International Travel and Tourism, Hotel and Restaurant Management, Sports and Club Management

Men's Athletic Profile

1201 North Scenic Hwy.
Babson Park, FL 33827
Coach: Steve Warner
Email: warnersteve@hotmail.com

NAIA
Warriors/Green, Black, White
Phone: (941) 638-2947
Fax: (941) 638-2823

Estimated # of Men's Soccer Scholarships:
Conference: Florida Sun Conference, NAIA
Program Profile: The Webber Field is a natural grass that the size is 1,000. playing season runs from August through November - Fall and Spring - January to April. Strong international program; players all over the world including USA. Looking for a good academic and athletic players.
History: Program started in 1991. In 1995 Runner-Up in the Florida Sun Conference and third in 1996; 1996 Southeast Regional ranking. 1997-1999 Regional and National ranking.
Achievements: 3 NSCAA All-South, numerous All-Conference players, 2 players now playing first Division in Sweden.
Coaching: Steve Warner, Head Coach, USSF "C" coaching license, NSCAA Regional.
Camp or Clinic Dates: Not Available
Most Recent Record: 10-10
Schedule: Tampa, Cambry, Riddle, Rollings College
Style of Play: Zonal defense, ball control and shoot the flanks. Serve from the wings; like to play in the air to tall players.

Women's Athletic Profile

P.O. Box 56
Babson Park, FL 33827
Coach: Steve Warner
Email: Admissions @ Webber.edu

NAIA
Warriors/Green, White, Gold
Phone: (941) 638-2950
Fax: (941) 638-2915

Estimated # of Women's Soccer Scholarships: None
Conference: Florida Sun Conference
Program Profile: The Warriors' home field is a natural grass, and they have a full athletic facility. The playing season is a traditional fall and non-traditional spring season. Available also is an indoor facility.
History: The program began in 1995. The record for 1995 was 3-10, and in 1996 was 5-8-2. Third in the Sunshine State Conference.
Achievements: Two 1st team All-Conference players in 1995; 1996 Two All-South Region players; 1996 third place in the Florida Sun Conference; 1996 has two All-Conference 1st team; three All-Conference Honorable Mention; 1996 two All-Southern Region (NSCAA).
Style of Play: The style of play will depend upon the make-up of the squad.

georgia

GEORGIA

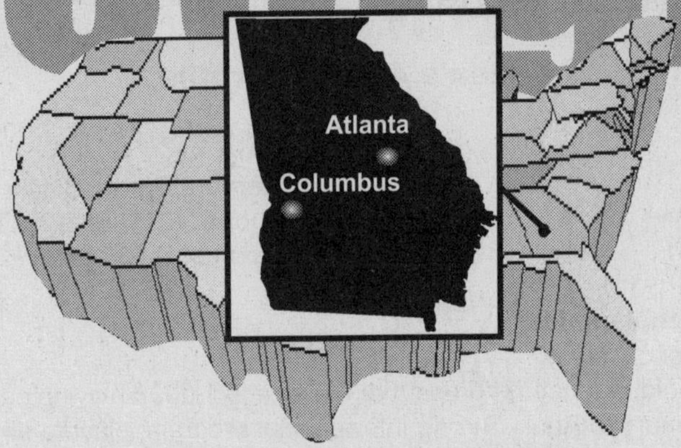

SCHOOL	CITY	AFFILIATION	PAGE
Agnes Scott College	Decatur	NCAA III	230
Andrew College	Cuthbert	NJCAA	230
Augusta State University	Augusta	NCAA II	231
Berry College	Mount Berry	NAIA	232
Brewton - Parker College	Mount Vernon	NAIA	234
Clayton State College	Morrow	NCAA II	235
Covenant College	Lookout Mountain	NAIA	236
Emory University	Atlanta	NCAA III	237
Georgia Southern University	Statesboro	NCAA I	238
Georgia State University	Atlanta	NCAA I	240
LaGrange College	LaGrange	NCAA III	241
Life College	Marietta	NAIA	242
Mercer University	Macon	NCAA I	243
N Georgia College & State Univ	Dahlonega	NAIA	244
Oglethorpe University	Atlanta	NCAA III	244
Piedmont College	Demorest	NAIA	246
Savannah College of Art & Design	Savannah	NCAA III	246
Thomas University	Thomasville	NAIA	247
University of Georgia	Athens	NCAA I	249
Wesleyan College	Macon	NCAA III	249

NIKE

Agnes Scott College

Academic Profile

Phone: (404)471-6285

Decatur, GA 30030

Type: 4 Yr.,Private,Liberal Arts
Website: http://www.agnescott.edu
SAT/ACT/GPA: 1090-130026-28
Student/Faculty Ratio: 10:1
Undergraduate Enrollment: 900
Scholarships/Academic: Yes
Athletic: No
Expenses by: Year
In State: $24,245.00
Founded: 1889
Religion: Presbyterian
Housing: Yes
Male/Female Ratio: Women
Graduate Enrollment: 25
Financial Aid: Yes
Out of State: $24,245.00
Specialty: Women's college - Liberal Arts, Sciences
Degrees Conferred: BA, Master of Arts in Teaching English
Programs of Study: Art, Astrophysics, BioChemistry, Biology, Chemistry, Classical Civilization, Classical Languages & Literature, Economics, Economics & Business, English, Literature & Creative Writing, French, German Studies, History, International Relations, Mathematics, Mathematics-Economics, Mathematics-Physics, Music, Philosophy, Physics, Theatre, Women's Studies. 28 Majors and 26 Minors.

Women's Athletic Profile

141 E College Avenue
Decatur, GA 30030
Coach: Laura LeDuc
Email: lleduc@agnesscott.edu

NCAA III
Scotties/Purple, White
Phone: (404) 471-6941
Fax: (404) 471-6099

Estimated # of Women's Soccer Scholarships: None
Conference: Independent
Program Profile: Young and building program on brink of NCAA Regional ranking in the South. Excellent facilities, 118x75 Bermuda grass field.
History: Joined NCAA in 1993. Program has improved dramatically since 1997. Several ODP players and players with extensive club experience have helped legitimize a once struggling program. Quality of schedule has improved significantly to include multiple contests with regionally ranked teams. Past 3 years records 6-11, 13-3, 8-6-1.
Achievements: Coach of the Year in 1991; Tennessee Region V; NAIA Academic All-American in 1992.
Coaching: Laura LeDuc Head Coach was a former 3 sport athlete at Emory University.
Roster in State: 6
Out of State: 14
Out of Country: 0
ODP State: 2
Regional: 0
National: 0
Walk-on/Other: 0
Graduation %: 100
Seniors on Team: 2
Positions Needed: Striker, Sweeper, Marking back, GK, Outside MF
Camp or Clinic Dates: June 1-23, June 26-30
Most Recent Record: 8-6-1
Schedule: Emory, Maryville, University of the South, Rhodes, Oglethorpe, Haverford, Carthage, Greensboro, Piedmont, Southeastern
Style of Play: Adaptive, prefers players who are able to play multiple positions.

Andrew College

Academic Profile

Phone: 800-664-4250

Cuthbert, GA 31740

Type: 2 Yr.,Private,Liberal Arts
Website: http://www.andrewcollege.edu
SAT/ACT/GPA: Varies
Student/Faculty Ratio: 12:1
Undergraduate Enrollment: 300
Scholarships/Academic: Yes
Athletic: Yes
Expenses by: Year
In State: $ 10,906
Founded: 1854
Religion: Methodist
Housing: Yes
Male/Female Ratio: 51:49
Graduate Enrollment: N/A
Financial Aid: Yes
Out of State: $ 10,906

Degrees Conferred: AA, AS, AM
Programs of Study: Communication Arts, History, Humanities, International Studies, Language and Literature, Photographic Arts, PreLaw, Preministry, Teaching, Theatre Arts, Visual Art, Biological Sciences, Business Administration, Education, Exercise Science, Golf Management, Health and Physical Science, Medical Technology, Occupational Therapy, Physical Sciences, Physical Therapy, Physician's Assistant, PreDentistry, PreForestry, PreMedicine, PreNursing, PrePharmacy, PreVet, Psychology

Men's Athletic Profile

413 College Street
Cuthbert, GA 31740
Coach: Chris J. Luppens, Jr.
Email: chrisluppens@andrewcollege.edu

NJCAA
Fighting Tigers/Blue, Gold
Phone: (912) 732-2080
Fax: (912) 732-2176

Estimated # of Men's Soccer Scholarships: 18
Conference: G.J.C.A.A. Region XVII
Program Profile: New complex, Bermuda grass field 115x73 separate practice field.
History: Our program began in 1977, 5th place in the Nation in 1989, 2nd place in 1991.
Achievements: Andrew College won the NJCAA Region XVII total 9 times, Southeast District twice and National Runner-up in 1992; 18 All-Americans; 1 NJCAA National Player of the Year.
Coaching: Chris J. Luppens, Jr., Head Coach.
Roster In State: 15 **Out of State:** 5 **Out of Country:** 4
Camp or Clinic Dates: Not Available
Schedule: Meridian, GA Perimeter, Young Harris, South GA, Lindsey Wilson JV
Style of Play: The emphasis is on ball control, possession soccer with quick counter- attacks. We work on speed of play with an eye toward the Dutch system of play.

Women's Athletic Profile

413 College Street
Cuthbert, GA 31740
Coach: Chris Luppens, Jr.
Email: chrisluppens@andrecollege.edu

NJCAA
Fighting Tigers/Blue, Gold
Phone: (912) 732-5932
Fax: (912) 732-2176

Estimated # of Women's Soccer Scholarships: 18
Conference: GJCAA
Program Profile: NJCAA Division I, Southeast District, Region XVII, a major varsity sport at Andrew; year round program; play on one of the top soccer fields in the GJCAA region. The program is new and growing
History: The program begin in 1984 and was dropped in 1990. It was reinstated in 1995 with a light schedule. The 1996 season was our first full scheduled season.

Augusta State University

Academic Profile

Augusta, GA 30904-2200

Phone: 800-341-4373

Type: 4 Yr.,Public
Website: http://www.aug.edu
SAT/ACT/GPA: Open
Student/Faculty Ratio: 19:1
Undergraduate Enrollment: 5,510
Scholarships/Academic: Yes **Athletic:** Yes
Expenses by: Year **In State:** $ 6,390

Founded: 1783
Religion: Non-Affiliated
Housing: No
Male/Female Ratio: 1:3
Graduate Enrollment: N/A
Financial Aid: Yes
Out of State: $ 11,610

Specialty: Member of the University System of Georgia
Degrees Conferred: Associate, Bachelor, Master, Specialist
Programs of Study: More than 50 programs of study.

Men's Athletic Profile

2500 Walton Way
Augusta, GA 30904
Coach: Ron Keller
Email: rkeller@aug.edu

NCAA II
Jaguars/Royal Blue, White
Phone: (706) 737-1632
Fax: (706) 667-4355

Estimated # of Men's Soccer Scholarships: 5
Conference: Peach Belt Athletic Conference
Program Profile: ASU practices and competes on natural playing fields with Bermuda grass that are maximum size according to NCAA regulations. They compete in both fall and spring seasons allowed by the NCAA with twenty games in the fall plus post-season action and an additional five dates in the spring. Men's soccer is one of eleven varsity sports offered at Augusta State University.
History: ASU began playing men's soccer in 1980 and has enjoyed twenty years of very successful teams in both NCAA Division I and II, making the transition in 1992 by joining the PBAC. ASU has had five head coaches in there twenty year history, with current head coach, Ron Keller, entering his fifth year at the helm of the program.
Achievements: 1998-99 Conference Runner-up & Tournament Runner-up, NSCAA national ranking #14. Two All-Americans, Five All-Region, Two Conf. Freshman of the Year, and Eleven All-Conference Selections in last four years under Head Coach, Ron Keller. Program has graduated all nineteen seniors in past four years. In the past four seasons, the program has posted twelve team records and four individual records in the history books.
Coaching: Ron Keller, Head Coach, is in his third season at ASU. He has compiled a record of 45-31-3. [.600] Highest winning percentage of any ASU coach in history of the program.

Roster In State: 14 | **Out of State:** 5 | **Out of Country:** 7
ODP State: 5 | **Regional:** 1 | **National:**
Walk-on/Other: | **Graduation %:** 100 | **Seniors on Team:** 5

Positions Needed: Left Midfield, Left Fullback, Striker, Sweeper, Midfielder
Camp or Clinic Dates: Not Available
Most Recent Record: 6-12-2
Schedule: Charleston Southern University, University of South Carolina-Spartanburg, Lander University, University of North Florida, Francis Marion University, Florida Southern University, Florida Tech. University, University of North Carolina-Pembroke, University of South Carolina-Aiken, Clayton State University
Style of Play: Although the Jaguars play a variety of different formations, they still balance everything around a very controlled possession style of play. A very proven style of play as the Jaguars were ranked in the top ten in the nation in both team offense and team defense in 1998 when they went 17-5-0.

Berry College

Academic Profile

Phone: (706) 236-1728

Mt. Berry, GA 30149

Type: 4 Yr.,Private,Liberal Arts
Website: http://www.berry.edu
SAT/ACT/GPA: 1000/22/3.0
Student/Faculty Ratio: 16:1
Undergraduate Enrollment: 1,800
Founded: 1902
Religion: Non-Denominational
Housing: Yes
Male/Female Ratio: 40:60
Graduate Enrollment: 200
Scholarships/Academic: Yes | **Athletic:** Yes | **Financial Aid:** Yes
Expenses by: Year | **In State:** $ 14,746 | **Out of State:** $ 14,746
Specialty: Business, Education
Degrees Conferred: BA,BM,BS, MA, MBA, Masters in Education, Education Specialist

Programs of Study: Accounting, Animal Science, Art, Art Education, Biochemistry, Biology, Business Administration, Chemistry, Child Development, Communications, Computer Science, Decision Science, Engineering, Early Childhood Education, Economics, English, Environmental Sciences, Finance, Health and PE, History, Horticulture, International Studies, Journalism, Management, Marketing, Mathematics, Middle-Grades Music, Physics, Political Science, Psychology, Religion, Philosophy, Pre-Professional Programs, Social Science, Sociology, Spanish, Theatre

Men's Athletic Profile

5015 Berry College
Mount Berry, GA 30149
Coach: Kurt Swanbeck
Email: kswanbeck@berry.edu

NAIA
Vikings/Blue, White
Phone: (706) 236-1728
Fax: (706) 236-1749

Estimated # of Men's Soccer Scholarships:
Conference: Tran South Conference
Program Profile: We have two 120 x 75 Bermuda fields. We play in the fall.
History: Our program began in 1962. Our program record was 356-206-42. We were in a national tournament in 1981. We have had 21 consecutive seasons qualifying for post-season.
Achievements: 23 All-Americans; 11 Conference Champions
Coaching: Kurt Swanbeck, Head Coach, USSF 'A' License, Advanced National Diploma. Richard Vardy and Matt Davenport - Assistant Coaches.
Style of Play: Attacking style with ball controlled offense.

Women's Athletic Profile

36 Berry College
Mount Berry, GA 30149
Coach: Lorenzo Canalis
Email: Lcanalis@berry.edu

NAIA
Vikings/Navy, Silver
Phone: (706) 236-1734
Fax: (706) 236-5497

Estimated # of Women's Soccer Scholarships: 10
Conference: Tran South Conference
Program Profile: We are consistently in the top 10 NAIA. We have two-full size playing fields, excellent equipment, training facilities, medical stand. the season is in the fall but training is year-round. We play a tough schedule of teams from the top 25 in NAIA and teams from NCAA Division I, II and III.
History: Our women's program began in 1986. Since the program began we have made the National Tournament nearly every year.
Achievements: 3 NAIA National Championships (1987, 90, 93); finished in top 3 nationally 7 times. 14 district or conference titles, 9 regional titles. 55 All-Americans, 14 All-America Scholar Athletes.
Coaching: Lorenzo Canalis, Head Coach, 6 seasons at Berry; 98-28-6 (highest winning % at Berry). 157-69-12 career record (20 years). 6 time Coach of The Year.

Roster in State: 14	**Out of State:** 11	**Out of Country:** 1
ODP State: 12	**Regional:** 1	**National:** 1
Walk-on/Other: 0	**Graduation %:** 100	**Seniors on Team:** 7

Positions Needed: Forwards, Midfielders
Camp or Clinic Dates: June, July
Most Recent Record: 13-7-1
Schedule: Mobile, Lindsey Wilson, VA Intermont, Brevard, William Carey, Union
Style of Play: Emphasis on possession, attacking with speed along sidelines, played a 3-5-2 in fall of 2000.

Brewton - Parker College

Academic Profile

Mt. Vernon, GA 30445
Phone: (912) 583-3277

Type: 4 Yr.,Private,Liberal Arts
Founded: 1904
Website: http://www.bpc.edu
Religion: Baptist
SAT/ACT/GPA: 860/18
Housing: Yes
Student/Faculty Ratio: 12:1
Male/Female Ratio: 2:3
Undergraduate Enrollment: 1,600
Graduate Enrollment: N/A
Scholarships/Academic: Yes **Athletic:** Yes **Financial Aid:** Yes
Expenses by: Year **In State:** $ 9,310 **Out of State:** $ 9,310
Degrees Conferred: BA, BS, Associates
Programs of Study: Accounting, Agricultural Business, Applied Art, Art, Biology, Business & Management, Chemistry, Computer Information System, Dental Services, Economics, Education, English, History, Marketing, Mathematics, Medical Assistant Technology, Music, Nursing, Political Science, Ministries, Physical Science, PreProfessionals, Psychology, Social Science

Men's Athletic Profile

Hwy. 280, Vidalia Rd
Mount Vernon, GA 30445-0197
Coach: Trei Mrison
Email: tmorrison@bpc.edu

NAIA
Wildcats/Navy, Orange
Phone: (912) 583-2241
Fax: (912) 583-4498

Estimated # of Men's Soccer Scholarships:
Conference: Georgia Athletic Conference
Program Profile: Our facilities include lighted, Bermuda Grass Fields.
History: Program began in 1992. The team placed 3rd in the District in 1992 and second in the District in 1993.
Achievements: Mike Mitchell has been named District 25 Coach of the Year in 1993.
Style of Play: We play an attacking style of play where we maintain possession while going forward as quickly as possible. We play high pressure defensively in each third of the field.

Women's Athletic Profile

Highway 280
Mount Vernon, GA 30445
Coach: Shela Fabri
Email: landarb@cybersouth.com

NAIA
Lady Barons/R. Blue, Orange
Phone: (912) 583-3277
Fax: (912) 583-4498

Estimated # of Women's Soccer Scholarships: N/A
Conference: Georgia Athletic Conference
Program Profile: We play in a Bermuda grass field that measures 116x78. We have a Bermuda training field, a beautiful weight room, a human performance laboratory and full size locker rooms that include a sauna.
History: The program began in 1993. In 1995, the Wildcats led all colleges in goals scored (161) and completed the season ranking fourth in the nation.
Achievements: 1996 Final Four, Southeast Regional Champions, Georgia Athletic Conference Champions. Southeast Regional Runner-Up; 5 All-Americans selections; 6 All-Region Players; Conference and Regional Players and Coach of the Year; Southeast Regional Runner-Up; 3 All-Americans Selections; Conference Player of the Year.
Style of Play: Creative style offense, off ball runs, high pressure defense on all thirds of the field.

Clayton College & State University

Academic Profile

Morrow, GA 30260
Phone: (770) 961-3500

Type: 4 Yr.,Public
Website: http://www.csc.clayton.edu
SAT/ACT/GPA: 430 (v); 400 (m)/ 18 (e), 16 (m)
Student/Faculty Ratio: 17:1
Undergraduate Enrollment: 4,500
Scholarships/Academic: Yes **Athletic:** Yes
Expenses by: Year **In State:** $ 8,143
Specialty: Information Technology
Degrees Conferred: AA, AS, AAS, BBA, BM, BSN, ASN, ASDH
Founded: 1969
Religion: Non-Affiliated
Housing: No
Male/Female Ratio: 1:3
Graduate Enrollment: N/A
Financial Aid: Yes
Out of State: $ 12,604

Programs of Study: Accounting, Art, Aviation Maintenance Technology, Avionics Technology, Architectural Design, Biology, Chemistry, Criminal Justice, Dentistry, Engineering, English, Forestry, General Business, General Science, Geology, Law, Management, Marketing, Mathematics, Medicine, Occupational Therapy, Office Administration, Pharmacy, Philosophy, Physics, Psychology, Secretarial Studies/Office Administration, Sociology, Urban Life

Men's Athletic Profile

5900 N. Lee Street
Morrow, GA 30260
Coach: John Rootes
Email: johnrootes@mail.clayton.edu

NCAA II
Lakers/Blue, Orange
Phone: (770) 860-2077
Fax: (770) 960-5127

Estimated # of Men's Soccer Scholarships: 8.5
Conference: Peach Belt Athletic Conference
Program Profile: Laker Field is an on-campus field, with a natural Bermuda grass surface and accommodates 500 spectators. The season is in the fall.
History: The program started in 1992 and has been competitive in the south region, one of the strongest regions in the nation.
Achievements: Has had 4 All-District, 4 All-Conference, 2 All-Tournament and 2 All-America selections over the years.
Coaching: John Rootes, Head Coach, is entering his first year with the program. Rich Webber is the Assistant Coach.

Women's Athletic Profile

5900 N. Lee Street
Morrow, GA 30260
Coach: T. O. Totty
Email: tottytotty@mail.clayton.edu

NCAA II
Lady Lakers/Blue, Orange
Phone: (770) 960-4261
Fax: (770) 960-5127

Estimated # of Women's Soccer Scholarships: N/A
Conference: Peach Belt Athletic Conference
Program Profile: We have one of the best soccer facilities in the Peach Belt Athletic Conference. Our game and practice fields are natural grass/ turf and are completely fenced in. The team plays fall and spring seasons. The regular size field has a seating capacity of approximately 2,000.
History: The Women's Soccer program was established in 1995. We made a transition from NAIA to NCAA II in 1997.
Achievements: The program has had several Academic Honorees including one All-American.
Coaching: T.O. Totty, Head Coach, was a member of the 1988 Nigerian National Team. As a three-time All-American, Totty led New Hampshire College to the 1989 NCAAII National Championship. He holds licenses with USFNCA and NECAA.
Roster in State: 16 **Out of State:** 4 **Out of Country:** 2

ODP State: 2 **Regional:** **National:**
Walk-on/Other: 2 **Graduation %:** **Seniors on Team:**
Positions Needed: All
Camp or Clinic Dates: June 12-16, 26-30, August 14-18
Most Recent Record: 6-11-1
Schedule: USC Aiken, Francis Marion, North Florida, Lander, USC Spartanburg, Montevallo, U. Alabama, North Alabama, Lenoir, Oglethorpe
Style of Play: A lot of ball possession and very little direct soccer.

Covenant College

Academic Profile

Phone: 888-451-2683

Lookout Mountain, GA 30750

Type: 4 Year, Private
Founded: 1955
Website: http://www.covenant.edu
Religion: Non-Affiliated
SAT/ACT/GPA: Open
Housing: Yes
Student/Faculty Ratio: 16:1
Male/Female Ratio: 58:42
Undergraduate Enrollment: N/A
Graduate Enrollment: N/A
Scholarships/Academic: Yes **Athletic:** Yes **Financial Aid:** Yes
Expenses by: Year **In State:** $22,060 **Out of State:** $22, 060
Degrees Conferred: Bachelor's
Programs of Study: Contact school for programs of study.

Men's Athletic Profile

14049 Scenic Highway
Lookout Mountain, GA 30750
Coach: Dr. Brian Crossman
Email: crossman@covenant.edu

NAIA
Scots/Blue, Gold
Phone: (706) 820-1560
Fax: (706) 820-2165

Estimated # of Men's Soccer Scholarships: Varies
Conference: Tennessee-Virginia Athletic Conference
Program Profile: We have an excellent facilities that include new Scotland yard. Our game field's dimension is 116 x 72 Bermuda grass with two training areas.
History: Our program started 31 years ago with numerous conference championships. We are consistent Top 20 team - NAIA in 1990's.
Achievements: Numerous team and individual awards.
Coaching: Brian Crossman, Head Coach, holds USSF 'A' license, a NSCAA Advanced National Diploma, and President of NAIA-Coaches (Soccer) Association. He compiled an overall record of 203-66-23. David Stanton, Assistant Coach.
Style of Play: Team possession and hard work.

Women's Athletic Profile

Rt. 1, Box 117
Lookout Mountain, GA 30750-9601
Coach: Mark Duble
Email: Not Available

NAIA
Lady Scots/Glue, Gold, White
Phone: (706) 820-1560
Fax: (706) 820-0672

Estimated # of Women's Soccer Scholarships: None
Conference: TVAC

Emory University
Academic Profile

Atlanta, GA 30322

Phone: 404-727-6036

Type: 4 Yr.,Private
Website: http://www.emory.edu
SAT/ACT/GPA: 1350/28/3.75
Student/Faculty Ratio: 24:1
Undergraduate Enrollment: 5,000
Scholarships/Academic: Yes
Athletic: No
Expenses by: Year
In State: $ 32,000
Founded: 1836
Religion: Methodist
Housing: Yes
Male/Female Ratio: 42:58
Graduate Enrollment: 6,000
Financial Aid: Yes
Out of State: $ 32,000
Specialty: PreLaw, PreMed, Business, Theology, Psychology
Degrees Conferred: BA, BS, MA, MS, MBA, MEd, Ph.D., MD, JD, Mdiv.
Programs of Study: African - American Studies, Anthropology, Art History, Asian Studies, Biology, Chemistry, Classical Civilization, Classical Studies, Classics, Computer Science, Creative Writing, Economics, Education Studies, English, Film Studies, French, French Cultural & Studies, German Studies, Greek History, International Studies, Judaic Languages & Literature, Latin, Literature, Mathematics, Medieval & Renaissance Studies, Music, Philosophy, Sociology, Spanish, Theatre Studies

Men's Athletic Profile

Woodruff PE Center
Atlanta, GA 30322
Coach: Mike Rubesch
Email: mrubesc@emory.edu

NCAA III
Eagles/Blue, Gold
Phone: (404) 727-0597
Fax: (404) 727-4989

Estimated # of Men's Soccer Scholarships:
Conference: University Athletic Association
Program Profile: Emory's program competes against the toughest teams in the South as a demanding UAA schedule that features travel to such places as New York City, Boston, Baltimore, Chicago, and St. Louis. The Eagles play at Woodruff P.E. Center's 1,000 seat stadium on natural grass. The season lasts from mid-August through early November, with a maximum of two hours of practice, six days a week.
History: Since its start in 1965, Emory's men's soccer program has won approximately 70 percent of its games. The Eagles have made several NCAA tournament appearances, including a trip to the national quarterfinals, with the most recent appearance in 1998. Within the conference, Emory has finished first or second nearly every year with multiple conference championships, the latest in 1998.
Achievements: Emory's success has resulted in numerous honors for its players. In the 80's and 90's the Eagles had 10 players recognized as All-Americans, 50 All-Region honorees and 70 All-Conference selection. The team enjoys success in the classroom with team GPAs typically around 3.4 Emory has been recognized several times by the NSCAA as an All-Academic Team. Emory coaches have been honored as regional and conference Coach of the Year.
Coaching: Mike Rubesch, Head Coach, USSF 'A' coaching license, has a winning percentage in excess of.680 at Emory, and is a staff coach for Georgia under 17.5 Olympic Development Team that placed four players on the 1994 U.S. Youth National Team.
Roster In State: 6
Out of State: 15
Out of Country: 0
ODP State: 5
Regional:
National:
Walk-on/Other:
Graduation %: N/A
Seniors on Team: 3
Camp or Clinic Dates: June 19-23; June 26-30
Most Recent Record: 12-2-3
Schedule: Washington, Greensboro, Trinity, Rochester, Maryville
Style of Play: Possession, creative attacking style.

Women's Athletic Profile

Woodruff PE Center
Atlanta, GA 30322
Coach: Michael Sabatelle
Email: msabate@emory.edu

NCAA III
Eagles/Blue, Gold
Phone: (404) 727-2839
Fax: (404) 727-4989

Estimated # of Women's Soccer Scholarships: None
Conference: University Athletic Association
Program Profile: Emory competes against the finest teams in the nation, as well as a demanding UAA schedule. Emory's schedule regularly includes travel to such sites as New York City, Boston, Los Angeles, Pittsburgh, Minneapolis, Cleveland, and St. Louis in 1997. The Eagles play at the Woodruff P.E. Center and its 1,000-seats stadium on a 120x75 yards natural grass surface.
History: Since its inception in 1986, Emory women's soccer program has grown to become a national power. Emory set the second longest unbeaten strike of 29 games in NCAA III Women's Soccer history. The teams overall record in 1998 and 1999 was 25-3-10.
Achievements: UAA Coach of the Year 1989, 1994, 1998; UAA Champion in 1994 and 1998; 5 NCAA Tournament appearances in last seven years; 7 All-Americans; 24 All-Region; 55 All-UAA players; 1 UAA Player of the Year; 2 Academic All-American; 1 NCAA Post-Graduate Scholar.
Coaching: Michael Sabatelle, Head Coach, holds a USSF 'A' License, is a NATA certified athletic trainer; and was the Georgia Girls Olympic Development Program Staff Coach for seven years. Compiled an overall record of 139-68-25 at Emory; Coach-Atlanta Classic W-League.

Roster in State: 5 **Out of State:** 20 **Out of Country:** 0
ODP State: 15 **Regional:** **National:**
Walk-on/Other: 10 **Graduation %:** 100 **Seniors on Team:** 4
Positions Needed: 4
Camp or Clinic Dates: July 17-21, 24-28
Most Recent Record: 11-2-4
Schedule: University of Chicago, University of Rochester, Washington University, Trinity University, NC Wesleyan
Style of Play: Creative attacking, passing, intelligent, aggressive and physically demanding, possession, counter attacks. Varied style based on player's strength, opponents style, field and environmental conditions.

Georgia Southern University

Academic Profile

Statesboro, GA 30460-8082
Phone: (912) 681-5391

Type: 4 Yr.,Public
Website: http://www.gasou.edu
SAT/ACT/GPA: 1000/2.5
Student/Faculty Ratio: 25:1
Undergraduate Enrollment: 12,000
Scholarships/Academic: Yes **Athletic:** Yes
Expenses by: Year **In State:** $ 7,200

Founded: 1906
Religion: Non-Affiliated
Housing: Yes
Male/Female Ratio: 45:55
Graduate Enrollment: 2,000
Financial Aid: Yes
Out of State: $ 12,560

Specialty: Business, Education, Technology
Degrees Conferred: BA, BS, BBA, BSEd, MA, MS, MEd, EdS, EdD
Programs of Study: Accounting, Biology, Broadcasting, Business, Chemistry, Civil Engineering, Communications, Computer Science, Counseling, Economics, Education, Electrical Engineering, English, Exercise Science, Food-Nutrition, Geology, German, Health, Physical Education, History, Industrial, Mathematics, International Studies, Journalism, Kinesiology, Journalism, Marketing, Mathematics, Nursing, Physics, Political Science, Public Relations, Recreation, Speech, Science, Sports Management, Sports Medicine, Sports Psychology

Men's Athletic Profile

P.O. Box 8082
Statesboro, GA 30460
Coach: Kevin Chambers
Email: kcham@gsaix2.u.gasou.edu

NCAA I
Eagles/Navy, White
Phone: (912) 871-1204
Fax: (912) 681-0095

Estimated # of Men's Soccer Scholarships: 5
Conference: Southern Conference
Program Profile: We play on 120 x 75 Bermuda turf game facility which has a seating capacity of 1000 spectators, located on campus. Academic enhancement facility.
History: The Eagles began in 1980 as Division I. 1980-1991 member of Trans America Athletic Conference (TAAC), 1992-present member of Southern Conference. 1997 ranked as high as #14 (Soccer America) during Regular Season.
Achievements: Kevin Chambers received Coach of the Year in 199.The team has had 6 All-Americans, 4 Academic All-Americans, and 4 drafted players.
Coaching: Kevin Chambers is our Head Coach. He is entering third season. He led the team Southern Conference Tournament Runner-up. Played at Georgia Southern University from 1988-1991. He was assistant coach at Georgia Southern University in 1992, 1994 and 1995. The assistant Coach is Jeremy Aven.

Roster In State: 17	**Out of State:** 8	**Out of Country:** 2
ODP State: 17	**Regional:** 5	**National:** 2
Walk-on/Other: 2	**Graduation %:** 85	**Seniors on Team:** 4

Positions Needed: Midfield
Camp or Clinic Dates: Not Available
Most Recent Record: 5-12-1
Schedule: Furman, UNC- Greensboro, North Carolina State, Liberty, Davidson, Virginia Tech
Style of Play: Attacking style of play out of the back; build the ball up through the back; strikers are targets and high pressure offensively.

Women's Athletic Profile

P.O. Box 8082
Statesboro, GA 30460
Coach: Tom Norton
Email: tnorton@gsums2.cc.gasa.edu

NCAA I
Lady Eagles/Navy, White
Phone: (912) 681-0270
Fax: (912) 681-0095

Estimated # of Women's Soccer Scholarships: 11
Conference: Southern Conference
Program Profile: Georgia Southern University is located in Stateboro, Georgia which is approximately one hour from the coast and Savannah. The current Eagle roster is made up of players from Georgia, Florida, South Carolina, Pennsylvania, England and Canada. Academically, the team is one of only five schools nation wide to receive Academic All-American four consecutive years. This past fall 2000 year, the team had it's best year ever with a 14-4 record. The team graduates four seniors and returns eight starters.
History: Our program started in 1993. Our overall record is88-64-3. We played in two Conference Championship games. We had two Conference Final Four appearances.
Achievements: 2 Conference Coach of the Year; 2 First Team Academic All-Americans; 8 Regional Academic All-Americans; Conference Leading Scorer 4 times
Coaching: Tom Norton, Head Coach, played four years at the University of South Carolina. He is a former high school All-American and has an NSCAA Advanced National Diploma.

Roster in State: 12	**Out of State:** 6	**Out of Country:** 8
ODP State: 18	**Regional:** 4	**National:** 0
Walk-on/Other: 0	**Graduation %:** 100	**Seniors on Team:** 4

Positions Needed: Strikers, Defenders
Camp or Clinic Dates: TBA

Most Recent Record: 14-5-0
Schedule: FIU, Furman, Greensboro, Jacksonville
Style of Play: Fast attacking style, ball possession, man marking.

Georgia State University
Academic Profile

Phone: (404) 651-3183

Atlanta, GA 30303

Type: 4 Yr.,Public,Liberal Arts
Founded: 1913
Website: http://www.gsu.com
Religion: Non-Affiliated
SAT/ACT/GPA: 830/18
Housing: Yes
Student/Faculty Ratio: 16:1
Male/Female Ratio: 40:60
Undergraduate Enrollment: 24,300
Graduate Enrollment: 24,300
Scholarships/Academic: Yes
Athletic: Yes
Financial Aid: Yes
Expenses by: Year
In State: $ 11,207
Out of State: $ 18,449
Specialty: Business, Education
Degrees Conferred: AA, AS, BA, BBA, BFA, BIS, BM, BS, BSEd, BSW, MAS, MAEd, MA, MAT, MBA, MBEd, M.Ed., MFA, MHA, MHP, MLM, MM, MPA
Programs of Study: Accounting, Actuarial Science, Anthropology, Arts, Business Administration, Biological Science, Chemistry, Computer Information Systems, Economics, Education, Exercise Science, Fine Arts, Geography, Health Nutrition, Interdisciplinary Studies, Music, Science, Science in Education, Social Work

Men's Athletic Profile

GSU Athletic Association Univ. Plaza
Atlanta, GA 30303
Coach: Kerem Daser
Email: athkud@langate.gsu.edu

NCAA I
Panthers, Red & Blue
Phone: 404-651-1210
Fax: 404-651-0842

Estimated # of Men's Soccer Scholarships: $110,000
Conference: TAAC
Program Profile: Our schedule consists of 20 games plus 5 out of season games as per NCAA rules. We play a very competitive schedule
History: Program began in 1968. 308-236-26 overall record. Won the TAAC Championship in 1983, 1986, 1987, 1997, 2000.
Achievements: 2 Conference Titles in 1997, 2000 in the last four years. 2000 TAAC Player of the Year, 2000 TAAC Coach of the Year. In 2000 we had 7 players named All-Conference.
Coaching: Kerem Daser Head Coach. Named 2000 TAAC Coach of the Year in his first year. Was an assistant coach from 1997-2000.
Roster In State: 22
Out of State: 2
Out of Country: 2
ODP State: 12
Regional: 5
National: 1
Walk-on/Other:
Graduation %: 70
Seniors on Team: 8
Positions Needed: Sweeper, Center Mid, Striker
Camp or Clinic Dates: July 26-30, August 2-6
Most Recent Record: 12-9-0
Schedule: UNC- Chapel Hill, UNC- Greensboro, UAB, Jacksonville Univ.
Style of Play: We look to possess the ball, we also try to get behind the defense with penetrating through balls. We like to put pressure on the opposing team by attacking aggressively.

Women's Athletic Profile

1 Park Place S, Ste. 840
Atlanta, GA 30303
Coach: Domenic Martelli
Email:

NCAA I
Panthers/Royal Blue, White
Phone: (404) 651-4631
Fax: (404) 651-0842

Estimated # of Women's Soccer Scholarships: Varies
Conference: Trans America Athletic Conference (TAAC)
Program Profile: Has 120x80 Bermuda turf field that seats 1,000 year-round commitment with traditional Fall season and Spring.
History: The first year of the program was in 1994; one Conference Championship in 1997; NCAA Tournament - lost to Connecticut 2-1 over-time in 1997; ranked #9 in southeast in 1997; #10 in Southeast in 1998 and had a record of 18-4-2 in 1997, 14-2-1 in 1998 and RPI 58th in the country in 1998.
Achievements: 20 All-Conference Players, 2 TAAC Tournament MVP's, 9 All-TAAC Tournament Team Players, 3 All-South Region Players, 29 All-TAAC Academic
Coaching: 1st year coach (Ohio State U. 89) MSCAA Advanced National Coaching License. Assit. Coach at West Point (NY) 7 years, state ODP Coach and Various camp and club experience. Assit. Louisville (00), 1st Year.

Roster in State: 20	**Out of State:** 2	**Out of Country:** 1
ODP State: 12	**Regional:** 2	**National:** 0
Walk-on/Other: 0	**Graduation %:**	**Seniors on Team:** 7

Positions Needed: GK, Forward
Camp or Clinic Dates: Not Available
Most Recent Record: 8-10-2
Schedule: Georgia, Jacksonville Univ. Colorado College, Air Force, Central Florida, Rutgers, College of Charleston
Style of Play: Utilize the strengths of all players- posses the ball working it out of the back playing a collective, compact defense and a dangerous penetrating offense.

LaGrange College
Academic Profile

La Grange, GA 30240

Phone: (706) 812-7330

Type: 4 Yr.,Private,Liberal Arts		**Founded:** 1861
Website: http://www.lgc.edu		**Religion:** Methodist
SAT/ACT/GPA: 860/16/2.0		**Housing:** Yes
Student/Faculty Ratio: 15:1		**Male/Female Ratio:** 1:3
Undergraduate Enrollment: 1,000		**Graduate Enrollment:** N/A
Scholarships/Academic: Yes	**Athletic:** No	**Financial Aid:** Yes
Expenses by: Year	**In State:** $ 15,500	**Out of State:** $ 15,500

Degrees Conferred: AA, BA, BS, BBA. MBA, M.Ed.
Programs of Study: Accounting, Arts, Biology, Business Administration, Chemistry, Computer Science, Criminal Justice, Economics, Education, English, History, International Business, Management, Mathematics, Nursing, Philosophy, Physical Education, Physical Science, Physics, PreProfessional Courses, Psychology, Radiological Technology, Religion, Social Work, Theatre

Women's Athletic Profile

601 Broad Street
LaGrange, GA 30240
Coach: Nathaniel Woodrow
Email: nwoodrow@lgc.edu

NCAA III
Panthers/Red, Black
Phone: (706) 882-8318
Fax: (706) 884-8350

Estimated # of Women's Soccer Scholarships: None
Conference: GIAC
Program Profile: A 5 year old million dollar soccer stadium, field is 120x80 with Bermuda grass, lights (all or most home games at night), seating for 800 people. We play 17 to 18 games a season plus conference tournament.
History: Program began in 1986, we travel all over the Southeast from Louisiana, Florida, Tennessee, to North Carolina. We have two more years of provisional status until we are fully NCAA III. Program started in the NAIA.
Achievements: Finished as high as Third in our old NAIA Conference, we have held 10 Academic All-Americans, 3 All-Region Players, 11 All-Conference. We've had one player lead the nation in every offensive category except for total goals scored she finished 2nd.
Coaching:

Roster in State: 10	**Out of State:** 4	**Out of Country:** 0
ODP State: 1	**Regional:**	**National:**
Walk-on/Other:	**Graduation %:** 100	**Seniors on Team:** 2

Positions Needed: Outside and Center Mids, Forwards
Most Recent Record: 3-14-0
Schedule: Mississippi College, Piedmont College, Maryville College

Life College

Academic Profile

Phone: 770-426-2884

Marietta, GA 30060

Type: 4 Yr.,Private,		**Founded:** 1974
Website: http://www.life.edu		**Religion:** Non-Affiliated
SAT/ACT/GPA: 850		**Housing:** Yes
Student/Faculty Ratio: 25:1		**Male/Female Ratio:** 3:1
Undergraduate Enrollment: 500		**Graduate Enrollment:** 4,000
Scholarships/Academic: Yes	**Athletic:** Yes	**Financial Aid:** Yes
Expenses by: Year	**In State:** $ 13,050	**Out of State:** $ 13,050

Specialty: Business, Chiropractic
Degrees Conferred: BS, MS, DC
Programs of Study: Business, Chiropractic, Nutrition, Sports Health Science

Men's Athletic Profile

1269 Barclay Circle	**NAIA**
Marietta, GA 30060	Running Eagles/Gold, Green
Coach: Graham Tutt	**Phone:** 1-800-543-3253
Email: Not Available	**Fax:** (770) 419-0331

Estimated # of Men's Soccer Scholarships: 15
Conference: Independent
Program Profile: We have a 4.5 million grass stadium that seats 3,500, is 115 x 75 yds, and the track surface is the same as the '96 Olympic track.
History: The program began in 1994 and we were the '97-'98 Regional champions
Achievements: We have had 6 All-Americans and were Coy SE Region 97-98.
Coaching: Luis Sibaja former under 20 Costa Rica National Team coach and is the technical advisor. Doug McMillian

Roster In State: 1	**Out of State:** 1	**Out of Country:** 20
ODP State: 1	**Regional:**	**National:**
Walk-on/Other:	**Graduation %:** 95	**Seniors on Team:** 6

Camp or Clinic Dates: Last 3 Weeks in June
Most Recent Record:
Schedule: Lindsey Wilson, Mobile, Illinois Springfield, Georgia Southern, William Carey, St. Thomas University, Nova University, Nova University, Berry College, Saint Gregory's, Embry Riddle.
Style of Play: South American/ European style of play. In order of importance is skill possession the physical.

Mercer University

Academic Profile

Macon, GA 31207
Phone: (912) 752-2994

Type: 4 Yr.,Private,Liberal Arts
Founded: 1833
Website: http://www.mercer.peachnet.edu
Religion: Baptist
SAT/ACT/GPA: 980/20
Housing: Yes
Student/Faculty Ratio: 12:1
Male/Female Ratio: 40:60
Undergraduate Enrollment: 2,800
Graduate Enrollment: 4,200
Scholarships/Academic: Yes **Athletic:** Yes **Financial Aid:** Yes
Expenses by: Year **In State:** $ 21,000 **Out of State:** $ 21,000
Specialty: Liberal Arts, Business, Economics, Engineering, Medical, Pharmacy
Degrees Conferred: BA, BS, BBA, BSEng, BM, BMEd, M.Ed., MBA, MTM, MSEng, MSM, MD
Programs of Study: Accounting, Art, Biology, Biomedical, Business, Chemistry, Communications, Computer Science, Economics, Education, Electrical and Mechanical Engineering, English, Environmental Science, Industrial, Management, Marketing, Medicine, Music, Natural Science, Philosophy, Physics, Political Science, Psychology, Special Education, Sociology, Spanish, Etc.

Men's Athletic Profile

1400 Coleman Avenue
Macon, GA 31207
Coach: Tom Melville
Email: melville_t@mercer.edu

NCAA I
Bears/Orange, Black, White
Phone: (912) 752-4011
Fax: (912) 752-2061

Estimated # of Men's Soccer Scholarships: 8
Conference: Trans America Athletic Conference
Program Profile: Division I program in strong conference (TAAC); Bermuda playing surface with enclosed game field, room for 3,000. Strong schedule; playing the full (NCAA) allowable games in the Fall and Spring.
History: Program is in its third decade and was one of the founder member of the TAAC 1992 Conference Champions. Melville has been rebuilding the program for the last two seasons. Only one senior in 1997-1998. A very young team.
Achievements: TAAC Champions in 1992; several drafted players - indoor were named Mike Potters and Hunter Goff; outdoor were named Dean Blain in 1999 and Patrick Horacius in 1999; Pascal Ocean was 1998 Canadian Olympic Team.
Coaching: Tom Melville is our Head Coach. He holds Irish FA, grade I licensed coach. He earned his BA from Olster Poly in 1984 and MSC from UNC-Chapel Hill in 1988.
Style of Play: Possession with high work rate; the system of play defends largely on the personnel available-usually 3-5-2.

Women's Athletic Profile

1400 Coleman Ave.
Macon, GA 31207
Coach: Jodie Smith
Email: smith_j@mercer.edu

NCAA I
Bears/Black, White, Orange
Phone: (478) 301-2060
Fax: (478) 301-3061

Estimated # of Women's Soccer Scholarships: 8
Conference: Trans America Athletic Conference (TAAC)
Program Profile: Bermuda grass field, 116 x 76 yards, in good conditions. Traditional fall season. Winter outdoors, spring is off-season program with weekend tournaments and conditioning programs.
History: Program began in 1995
Achievements: 1992 NCAA Woman of the Year - Debbie Chiolero. Mirela Ninic 2 time TAAC Player of the Year, 2000 Freshmen of the Year, and 3 time NCAA All-Academic Team (98,99,00)

Coaching: Career Record 72-53-7, 1997 TAAC Coach of the Year, Member NCAA Southeast Committee, Georgia Olympic Development Program.
Roster in State: 9 **Out of State:** 0 **Out of Country:** 8
ODP State: 5 **Regional:** 1 **National:** 1
Walk-on/Other: 0 **Graduation %:** 98 **Seniors on Team:** 1
Positions Needed: D, F, MF
Camp or Clinic Dates: Not Available
Most Recent Record: 5-12-1
Schedule: UCF, Auburn, Georgia, Southern Miss
Style of Play: Attack always, defend at all times.

North Georgia College

Academic Profile

Dahlonega, GA 30597
Phone: 800-498-9581

Type: 4 Yr.,Public,Liberal Arts **Founded:** 1873
Website: http://www.ngc.peachnet.edu **Religion:** Non-Affiliated
SAT/ACT/GPA: Required **Housing:** No
Student/Faculty Ratio: 22:1 **Male/Female Ratio:** 40:60
Undergraduate Enrollment: 2,500 **Graduate Enrollment:** 350
Scholarships/Academic: Yes **Athletic:** Yes **Financial Aid:** Yes
Expenses by: Year **In State:** $ 4,800 **Out of State:** $ 7,500
Specialty: Military
Degrees Conferred: AS, BA, BS, BBA, BSN, MS, M.Ed.
Programs of Study: Accounting, Art, Banking & Finance, Biology, Business Administration, Chemistry, Computer Science, Criminal Justice, Economics, Education, English, French, History, Management, Marketing, Mathematics, Music, Nursing, Physical Education, Physics, Political Science, PreProfessional Courses, Psychology, Recreation & Leisure, Secondary Education, Social Science, Special Education

Men's Athletic Profile

Department of Athletics
Dahlonega, GA 30597
Coach: Mark Howarth
Email: mhowarth@ngesu.edu

NAIA
Fightin Saints/Royal Blue, White
Phone: (706) 864-1549
Fax: (706) 864-1649

Estimated # of Men's Soccer Scholarships: 5 Full scholarships
Conference: Southeast Region, Georgia, Alabama, Carolina Conference
Program Profile: We have a roster of 23 players, separate soccer field and locker room facility, season is in the Fall, natural grass field.
History: Program began in 1967, joined NAIA in the late 70's. GAC District Champions in 1986.
Achievements: Coach of the Year in 1996, several players receiving GAC All-Conference.
Coaching: Mark Howarth, Head Coach, entering fifth year. He was a former assistant coach in 1987 (6-1), 18 years playing experience, GA State Amateur Select Team.
Style of Play: Changes with new players and loss of senior starter - control!!!

Oglethorpe University

Academic Profile

Atlanta, GA 30319
Phone: (404) 364-8414

Type: 4 Yr.,Private,Liberal Arts,Engineering **Founded:** 1835
Website: http://www.oglethorpe.edu **Religion:** Presbyterian

SAT/ACT/GPA: 1050/27/3.5
Housing: Yes
Student/Faculty Ratio: 17:1
Male/Female Ratio: 40:60
Undergraduate Enrollment: 1059
Graduate Enrollment: 122
Scholarships/Academic: Yes
Athletic: No
Financial Aid: Yes
Expenses by: Year
In State: $ 21,810
Out of State: $ 21,810
Specialty: Accounting, Education, Premed
Degrees Conferred: BA, BS, MA, MBA
Programs of Study: Biology, Business Administration, Communications, Education, Engineering, Political Science, PreLaw, PreMed, Psychology, Social Sciences

Men's Athletic Profile

4484 Peachtree Road, NE
Atlanta, GA 30319
Coach: Mike Lochstampf
Email: mlochstampfor@oglethorpe.edu
NCAA III
Stormy Petrels/Black, Gold
Phone: (404) 364-8416
Fax: (404) 364-8445

Estimated # of Men's Soccer Scholarships: None
Conference: Southern Collegiate Athletic Conference
Program Profile: We have a new Bermuda field that measures of 115x70 yards with separate practice facility. Stadium is seating for 1,000 with a sprinkler system. Season starts from September through November
History: Program began in 1975 as a club team, went to NAIA, Division III in 1989.
Achievements: The program produced 1 honorable Mention All-American; 2 Conference Player of the Year Nominations; numerous All-Region, All-Conference players.
Coaching: Mike Lochstampfor, Head Coach, fourth year, previously a Junior College coach for 2 years and as an assistant at top NAIA program. Two time All-American, and played overseas in high school with foreign club team. Will Lukon, Assistant Coach, entering four years of coaching. He was a 1994 graduate of Oglethorpe. He was named Conference Player of the Year two times, All-Conference four times, All-South four times. He holds USSF "B" License.
Walk-on/Other:
Graduation %: 95
Seniors on Team:
Style of Play: High pressure defense at midfield, quick counter-attack, quick switch on point of attack.

Women's Athletic Profile

4484 Peachtree Road, NE
Atlanta, GA 30319
Coach: Mike Lochstampfor
Email: mlochstampfor@oglethorpe.edu
NCAA III
Stormy Petrels/Black, Gold
Phone: (404) 364-8416
Fax: (404) 364-8445

Estimated # of Women's Soccer Scholarships: None
Conference: Southern Collegiate Athletic Conference
Program Profile: Has practice field and stadium which seats 1,000 and field is 115x70 Bermuda grass surface. Playing season runs from mid-august through first week of November.
History: Program began as a club team in 1987, achieved varsity status in 1989. When it joined the NCAA Division III; joined the Southern Collegiate Athletic conference in 1991.
Achievements: Academic All-Americans, numerous All-Conference players.
Coaching: Mike Lochstampfor, Head Coach, is entering his third year as head coach of the women at Oglethorpe and the Director of men's and women's soccer. Eighth year as a college coach; collegiate All-Americans and former player overseas; fourth year at Oglethorpe. Kristen Daly, Assistant Coach, responsible for goalkeeper. All conference player at Kean State, NJ.
Roster in State: 11
Out of State: 3
Out of Country: 0
Walk-on/Other:
Graduation %: 100
Seniors on Team: 5
Positions Needed: Forward, Goalkeeper
Camp or Clinic Dates: Not Available
Most Recent Record: 11-7-0
Schedule: Trinity, DePauw, Emory, Clayton State
Style of Play: Differs from one year to the next; depending on players.

Piedmont College

Academic Profile

Phone: 800-277-7020

Demorest, GA 30535

Type: 4 Yr.,Private,Liberal Arts
Website: http://www.piedmont.edu
SAT/ACT/GPA: 850/21+
Student/Faculty Ratio: 15:1
Undergraduate Enrollment: 700
Scholarships/Academic: Yes
Athletic: Yes
Expenses by: Year
In State: $ 9,800
Degrees Conferred: BA, BS

Founded: 1897
Religion: Congregationalist
Housing: Yes
Male/Female Ratio: 40:60
Graduate Enrollment: N/A
Financial Aid: Yes
Out of State: $ 9,800

Programs of Study: Accounting, Art, Art Administration, Biology, Business Administration, Chemistry, Computer Information System, Economics, Education, English, History, Management, Mathematics, Music, Psychology, Social Science, Theatre

Men's Athletic Profile

P.O. Box 10
Demorest, GA 30535
Coach: Jason P. Smith
Email: jpsmith@piedmont.edu

NAIA
Lions/Green, Gold
Phone: (706) 778-8500x351
Fax: (706) 776-2811

Estimated # of Men's Soccer Scholarships:
Conference: Georgia Athletic Conference
History: 1998-1999 will be seventh year of program's existence.
Achievements: Achievements include 1995 Conference Runner-Up; 1995-1996 Cumberland College's Hardee's Tournament Champions; 1995 Conference Coach of the Year; 8 players named All-Conference in History.

Women's Athletic Profile

P.O. Box 10
Demorest, GA 30535
Coach: Jason Smith
Email: jpsmith@piedmont.edu

NCAA III
Lady Lions/Green, Gold
Phone: (706) 778-3000
Fax: (706) 776-2811

Estimated # of Women's Soccer Scholarships: None
Conference: Great South Athletic Conference
Program Profile: We play our home games on a lighted natural field which will be extended to 120x75 yards in 2000. A new gym with new locker room facilities will also open in 2000.
History: The 2000 Season Will be the 8th season of the program.
Achievements: 3 time Conference Champions; 3 time Conference Runner-Up; 2 time Region Runner-Up; Cumberland College Invitational Champions; Birmingham Southern 1997 Invitational Champions; 30 players named to All-Conference teams; 13 named to All-Region; 2 Conference MVP's; 5 All-American Honorable Mentions

Savannah College of Art & Design

Academic Profile

Phone: (912) 238-2401

Savannah, GA 31401

Type: 4 Yr.,Private,
Website: http://www.scad.edu

Founded: 1978
Religion: Non-Affiliated

SAT/ACT/GPA: Varies/2.0
Student/Faculty Ratio: 20:1
Undergraduate Enrollment: 4,000
Scholarships/Academic: Yes **Athletic:** No
Expenses by: Year **In State:** $ 17,450
Specialty: Art & Design
Degrees Conferred: BFA, BArch, MArch, MFA, MA
Programs of Study: Architectural History, Architecture, Art History, Computer Art, Fashion, Fibers, Furniture, Graphic Design, Historic Preservation, Illustration, Industrial Design, Interior Design, Metal and Jewelry, Painting, Sequential Art, Photography, Video/Film

Housing: Yes
Male/Female Ratio: 50:50
Graduate Enrollment: 1,000
Financial Aid: Yes
Out of State: $ 17,450

Men's Athletic Profile

235 Habersham Street, P.O. Box 3146
Savannah, GA 31402-3146
Coach: Neil Cunningham
Email: info@scad.edu

NCAA III
Bees/Black, Yellow, White
Phone: (912) 238-2432
Fax: (912) 231-2367

Estimated # of Men's Soccer Scholarships: None
Conference: Independent
Program Profile: City of Savannah Chatham County Soccer Complex has an outdoor grass field and is regulation size with lights.
History: Our program started in 1990 with a 7-7-2 record in 1998.
Achievements: Alex Holland was named All-south in 1997.
Coaching: Neil Cunningham, Head Coach, has compiled an overall record of 21-24-2 in three years. Amy Alexander, Assistant Coach, has a Bachelor of Art and Marketing in 1997 at MacMurray College Jacksonville, Illinois. She is currently earning a second Bachelor's of Fine Art in Graphic Design.
Style of Play: Possession game, aggressive defense and passing game.

Women's Athletic Profile

235 Habersham Street
Savannah, GA 31402-3146
Coach: Neil Cunningham
Email: info@scad.edu

NCAA III
Lady Bees/Black, Yellow, White
Phone: (912) 238-2432
Fax: (912) 231-2367

Estimated # of Women's Soccer Scholarships: None
Conference: Independent
Program Profile: We play at the City of Savannah Chatham County Soccer Complex. It has an outdoor grass field that is regulation size and has lights.
History: Our program started in 1992. Our 1998 record was 15-3-1.
Achievements: All-South 1998 Verena Geisselmann
Coaching: Neil Cunningham, Head Coach. His career record is 37-25-2. He has been here four years. Amy Alexander is assistant coach. She has a B.S in Art and Marketing from MacMurray College. She is currently earning her second bachelor degree in Graphic Design.
Style of Play: Aggressive possession game; passing game.

Thomas College
Academic Profile

Thomasville, GA 31792

Phone: 912-226-1621

Type: 4 Yr.,Private,Liberal Arts
Website: http://www.thomascollege.edu

Founded: 1950
Religion: Non-Affiliated

SAT/ACT/GPA: 860
Housing: No
Student/Faculty Ratio: 15:1
Male/Female Ratio: 40:60
Undergraduate Enrollment: 700
Graduate Enrollment: Not Avai
Scholarships/Academic: Yes
Athletic: Yes
Financial Aid: Yes
Expenses by: Year
In State: $ 7,350
Out of State: $ 7,350
Specialty: Liberal Arts
Degrees Conferred: BS, BA, BM, BAS
Programs of Study: Anatomy, Business & Management, Computer Information Systems, Computer Science, Economics, Education, Environmental Science, Finance, Fine Arts, Health Services Administration, Human Development, Nursing, Physical Education, Physical Science, Social Science, Math, Military Science, History.

Men's Athletic Profile

1501 Millpond Road
Thomasville, GA 31792
Coach: Vincent Gill
Email: cgill@Thomascollege.edu

NAIA
Night Hawks/F. Green , White
Phone: (912) 226-1621
Fax: (912) 226-1653

Estimated # of Men's Soccer Scholarships: 10
Conference: NAIA Region XIII, Independent
Program Profile: On campus natural Bermuda grass field. Have access to three other top class fields; soccer fieldhouse on campus.
History: Our program began in 1994 and we have been to the NAIA Independent playoffs from 1997 to 2000.
Achievements: NAIA Southeast Regional Playoffs in 1997 & 1998; One NAIA All-American.
Coaching: Vincent Gill, Head Coach, UCD (Ireland in 1984), holds a USSF "C" License. Nicholas Mulligan is our Assistant Coach.
Roster In State: 10
Out of State: 9
Out of Country: 13
ODP State: 2
Regional:
National: 3
Walk-on/Other:
Graduation %: N/A
Seniors on Team: 6
Camp or Clinic Dates: June
Most Recent Record: 13-9
Schedule: Life University, Barry University, University of North Florida, St. Thomas, University of West Florida, University of Mobile
Style of Play: Possession with an attempt to get the ball forward as quickly as possible. Aggressive defense.

Women's Athletic Profile

1501 Millpond Road
Thomasville, GA 31792
Coach: Eric Faulconer
Email: efaul@tdo.infi.net

NAIA
Night Hawks/F. Green, White
Phone: (912) 226-1621
Fax: (912) 226-1653

Estimated # of Women's Soccer Scholarships: 5
Conference: Independent
Program Profile: Play on campus natural Bermuda grass field. Soccer fieldhouse on campus. Have access to three other top class fields.
History: Our program is very young having only begun in 1999.
Achievements: Two NAIA Region 13 Players of the Week in 1999.
Coaching: Eric Faulconer, Head Coach, was a men's coach at Thomas College in 1998. He was a former Deputy Commissioner of the Eastern Indoor Soccer League. BSI MPA-Florida State University.
Roster in State: 14
Out of State: 3
Out of Country: 5
ODP State:
Regional:
National:
Walk-on/Other:
Graduation %:
Seniors on Team: 0

Camp or Clinic Dates: Not Available
Most Recent Record: 9-7
Schedule: Troy State University, University of North Florida, University of West Florida, William Carey, St. Leo
Style of Play: Possession, High pressure and aggressive natured defense.

University of Georgia

Academic Profile

Ads
Athens, GA 30603

Phone: 706-542-2112

Type: 4 Yr.,Public
Website: http://www.sports.uga.edu
SAT/ACT/GPA: 1180/3.5
Student/Faculty Ratio: 20:1
Undergraduate Enrollment: 25,000
Scholarships/Academic: Yes
Athletic: Yes
Expenses by: Year
In State: $ 8,062

Founded: 1785
Religion: Non-Affiliated
Housing: Yes
Male/Female Ratio: 49:51
Graduate Enrollment: 5,000
Financial Aid: Yes
Out of State: $ 15,304

Degrees Conferred: Bachelors, Masters, Doctoral
Programs of Study: Agricultural Environmental Science, Art & Science, PreProfessional Programs, Business Administration, Education, Environmental Design, Family & Consumer Sciences, Forest Resources, Journalism and Mass Communications, Pharmacy, Social work, Veterinary Medicine

Women's Athletic Profile

P.O. Box 1472
Athens, GA 30603
Coach: Sue Patberg
Email: soccer @sports.uga.edu

NCAA I
Lady Bulldogs/Red, Black, White
Phone: (706) 542-1170
Fax: (706) 542-5224

Estimated # of Women's Soccer Scholarships: 12
Conference: Southeastern Conference (SEC)
Program Profile: Georgia plays its home matches at the UGA Soccer Stadium that seats 3,000 on Bermuda grass, 120x70, with a full practice field at the same complex. The complex opened in the fall of 1998 with a complete scoreboard and lights. The program also has a full athletic weight room. UGA will be hosting the 2000 SEC Tournament.
History: Georgia is in it sixth season of existence, participating in the NCAA Tournament in 1997 and 1998. The Bulldogs have averaged 13 wins per season since their inception. Georgia has ranked in the top 10 in attendance every year 1995, averaging 1500 fans in 1999.
Achievements: 10 SEC Players of the Week; 7 All-SEC players; 10 All-Southeast Region Players; 2 Freshman All-Americans and 2 All-Americans. 33 SEC Academic Honor Roll and have the high-test GPA on the UGA Campus.

Wesleyan College

Academic Profile

Phone: (912) 757-5260

Macon, GA 31210

Type: 4 Yr.,Private,Liberal Arts
Website: Not Available
SAT/ACT/GPA: 1000 + above/21/2.8+
Student/Faculty Ratio: 12:1
Undergraduate Enrollment: 600
Scholarships/Academic: Yes
Athletic: No
Expenses by: Year
In State: $ 22,900

Founded: 1836
Religion: Methodist
Housing: Yes
Male/Female Ratio: Women
Graduate Enrollment: N/A
Financial Aid: Yes
Out of State: $ 22,900

Degrees Conferred: BS, AB

Programs of Study: American Studies, Art History, Biology, Business Administration, Chemistry, Communications, Early Childhood Education, English, History, Interdisciplinary Studies, International Business , International Relations, Mathematics, Middle Grades Education, Philosophy, Political Science, Pre-Professional Courses, Psychology, Religion, Secondary Education, Sociology, Spanish, Studio Art

Women's Athletic Profile

4760 Forsyth Road
Macon, GA 31210
Coach: Robert Brund
Email: r.brund@post.Wesleyan-College.Edu

NCAA III
Pioneers/Purple, White
Phone: (912) 757-5253
Fax: (912) 757-2486

Estimated # of Women's Soccer Scholarships:
Conference: Not Available
Program Profile: We play at the $ 1.5 Matthews Athletic Center which has softball and soccer fields (natural grass), a tennis court, gyms and a fieldhouse. We have a quality program with great players and coaches. Our playing season goes form September 3rd until October 31st.
History: Our program began in 1990 and we were not successful until recently. We now have a full-time coach and we are beginning to compete at the level we would like to.
Coaching: Robert Brund, Head Coach, is entering second season of the program.
Style of Play: Quick 1 to 2 touch and very offensive- minded. Combination of Brazilian and Italian play.

hawaii

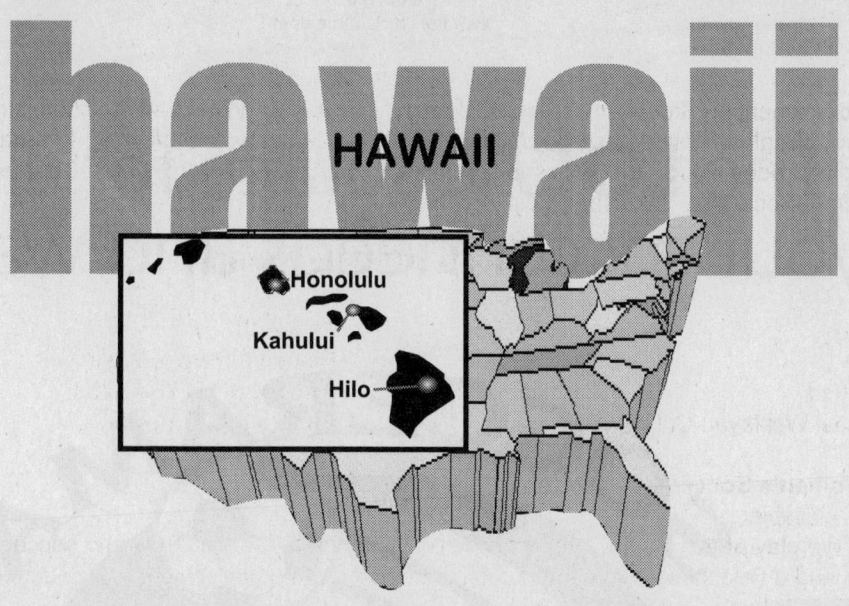

SCHOOL	CITY	AFFILIATION	PAGE
Brigham Young U-Hawaii	Laie	NCAA II	253
Hawaii Pacific University	Honolulu	NCAA II/NAIA	253
University of Hawaii	Honolulu	NCAA I	254

The **LOCAL** source for all of your soccer needs and wants.

TEAM BUSINESS is our specialty.
Stay local and save yourself the headache when the size, color or something goes wrong. We do all the running around for you!
Bring your quotes and we will either match it or tell you that we can't. Either way, you know you are getting the best deal!

NEW LOCATION!
More convenient! More parking!

930 Hauoli Street
Honolulu, HI 96826

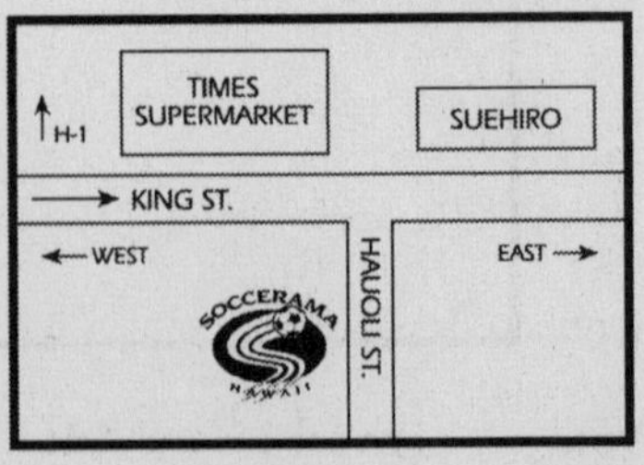

Brigham Young University - Hawaii

Academic Profile

Box 1937
Laie, HI 96762

Phone: 808-293-3738

Type: 4 Yr.,Private,Liberal Arts
Founded: 1955
Website: http://www.byuh.edu
Religion: Latter Day Saints
SAT/ACT/GPA: 830/17
Housing: Yes
Student/Faculty Ratio: 21:1
Male/Female Ratio: 39:61
Undergraduate Enrollment: 2,000
Graduate Enrollment: N/A
Scholarships/Academic: Yes **Athletic:** Yes **Financial Aid:** Yes
Expenses by: Year **In State:** $ Varies **Out of State:** $ Varies
Specialty: Emphasizes Liberal Arts with professional programs
Degrees Conferred: AA, AS, BA, BS, BFA, BSW
Programs of Study: Communications Studies, Theatre, Computer Science, Travel Management, Art, Art Education, English, English, Education, History, Music, Pacific Island Studies, Political Science, Psychology, Social Science Education, Accounting, Biological Science, Biology, Education, Business Education, Chemistry, Elementary Education, Hospitality and Tourism

Men's Athletic Profile

55-220 Kulanui Street
Laie, HI 96762
Coach: Bob Barry
Email: rbarry@iolani.honolulu.hi.us

NCAA II
Seasiders/Crimson, Gold, Gray
Phone: (808) 293-3764
Fax: (808) 293-3763

Estimated # of Men's Soccer Scholarships: N/A
Conference: Pacific West Conference
Program Profile: The Seasiders play on campus field which measures 72x120 at the foot of a beautiful Hawaiian mountain range and within walking distance from one of the many famous Hawaiian beaches.
History: BYUH is in its third season. After two straight season with losing records, the team is in high spirits with the announcement of Bob Harry as the new head coach, experienced players returning and new solid recruits.
Achievements: 1998-1second team MSCAA All-American & 2 Pac-West all conference first team selections
1998-1 All-Conference Academic team
1999-2 All-Conference second team selections & 3 All-Academic team selections
Coaching: Bob Barry is our Head Coach. He holds USSF "A" License and a NSCAA Advanced National Diploma. Steve Lewis is our Assistant Coach.
Roster In State: 21 **Out of State:** 17 **Out of Country:** 3
ODP State: 6 **Regional:** 3 **National:** 0
Walk-on/Other: **Graduation %:** 100 **Seniors on Team:** 4
Positions Needed: Goalkeeper & Striker
Camp or Clinic Dates: August 24-29
Most Recent Record: 7-6-1
Schedule: Seattle Pacific, Seattle Univ., Sonoma State, Western Washington, Humboldt State, Cal State-Dominguez Hills
Style of Play: High level of fitness, combination of man and zone marking. Possession game with a focus on flank play.

Hawaii Pacific University

Academic Profile

Phone: 800-669-4724

Honolulu, HI 96813

Type: 4 Yr.,Private,Liberal Arts
Founded: 1965
Website: http://www.hpu.edu
Religion: Non-Affiliated

SAT/ACT/GPA: 1000/22
Housing: Yes
Student/Faculty Ratio: 20:1
Male/Female Ratio: 55:45
Undergraduate Enrollment: 7,000
Graduate Enrollment: 1,000
Scholarships/Academic: Yes **Athletic:** Yes
Financial Aid: Yes
Expenses by: Year **In State:**
Out of State: $ 12,800
Degrees Conferred: AS, BA, BS, BSBA, BSCSci, MBA
Programs of Study: Accounting, American Studies, Anthropology, Applied Mathematics, Business Administration, Communications, Computer Information System, Computer Science, Criminal Justice, Economics, English, History, Humanities, Human Development, Human Resources, Management, Marketing, Nursing, Political Science, Psychology, Social Science, Tourism

Men's Athletic Profile

1060 Bishop Street
Honolulu, HI 96813
Coach: Frank Doyle
Email: Not Available
NCAA II/NAIA
Sea Warriors/Blue, Green
Phone: (808) 544-0221
Fax: (808) 521-7998

Estimated # of Men's Soccer Scholarships: N/A
Conference: Independent
Achievements: 1996 Far West Independent Champions; 1995 and 1996 All-American - Ce'sar Jube'.

Women's Athletic Profile

1060 Bishop St. Penthouse
Honolulu, HI 96813
Coach: Mark Kane
Email: Not Available
NCAA II/NAIA
Sea Warriors/Col Blue, Kelly
Phone: (808) 544-0221
Fax:

Did Not Return Profile

University of Hawaii - Manoa

Academic Profile

Phone: 800-823-9771

Honolulu, HI 96822

Type: 4 Yr.,Public
Founded: 1907
Website: http://www.hawaii.edu
Religion: Non-Affiliated
SAT/ACT/GPA: 430/20
Housing: Yes
Student/Faculty Ratio: 14:1
Male/Female Ratio: 43:57
Undergraduate Enrollment: 13,000
Graduate Enrollment: 5,500
Scholarships/Academic: Yes **Athletic:** Yes
Financial Aid: Yes
Expenses by: Year **In State:** $ 4,607
Out of State: $ 7,847
Degrees Conferred: Bachelors, Masters, Doctorate
Programs of Study: Accounting, Agricultural, Animal Anthropology, Architecture, Art, American Studies, Asian, Atmospheric, Biological, Botany, Business, Chemistry, Dental, Design, Economics, Entomology, Mathematics, Real Estate, Religion, Women's Studies

Women's Athletic Profile

1337 Lower Campus Road
Honolulu, HI 96822
Coach: Pinsoom Tenzing
Email: wmsoccer@hawaii.ed
NCAA I
Rainbow Wahines/Green, White
Phone: (808) 956-4525
Fax: (808) 956-9771

Estimated # of Women's Soccer Scholarships: 12
Conference: WAC
Program Profile: The Rainbows have built a solid program that looks to play attractive soccer. They will be playing at the beautiful New Waipio Peninsula Soccer Stadium on grass.
History: 1994-1995 was the first year as a varsity of the program.
Achievements: Amanda Paterson-1996 Goalkeeper- WAC 1st team; Denise Tsukada-Defender-WAC 2nd team.
Coaching: Pinsoom Tenzing, Head Coach, USSF "A" License. Kathy Carey - Assistant Coach, USSF "A" License. Derick Kato-Assistant Coach, USSF "D" License.

Roster in State: 14	**Out of State:** 12	**Out of Country:**
ODP State: 11	**Regional:** 1	**National:**
Walk-on/Other:	**Graduation %:** 95	**Seniors on Team:** 8

Positions Needed: Goalkeeper, Defenders, Midfielder, Striker
Camp or Clinic Dates: July 17-21
Most Recent Record: 12-7-1
Schedule: Cornell, St. Mary's, Fresno State, Southern Methodist, San Jose State
Style of Play: Looking to play the ball out of the back, working up the field.

idaho

IDAHO

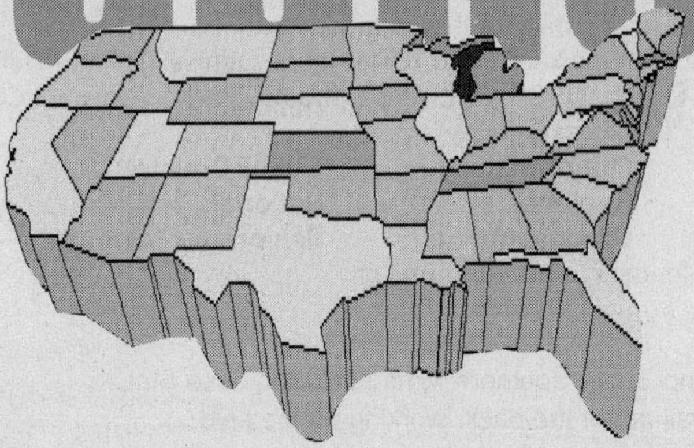

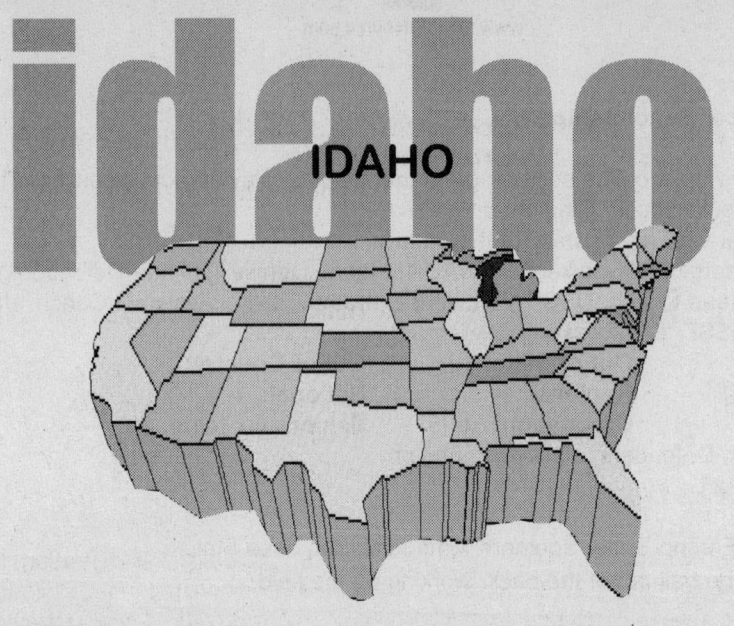

SCHOOL	CITY	AFFILIATION	PAGE
Albertson College - Idaho	Caldwell	NAIA	257
Boise State University	Boise	NCAA I	258
Idaho State University	Pocatello	NCAA I	258
North Idaho College	Coeur d' Alene	NJCAA	259
Northwest Nazarene University	Nampa	NAIA	260
University of Idaho	Moscow	NCAA I	261

Albertson College - Idaho

Academic Profile

Caldwell, ID 83605

Phone: 800-224-3246

Type: 4 Yr.,Private,Liberal Arts
Website: http://www.acofi.edu
SAT/ACT/GPA: 510/21
Student/Faculty Ratio: 12:1
Undergraduate Enrollment: 681
Scholarships/Academic: Yes **Athletic:** Yes
Expenses by: Year **In State:** $ 20,000

Founded: 1891
Religion: Non-Affiliated
Housing: Yes
Male/Female Ratio: 55:45
Graduate Enrollment: N/A
Financial Aid: Yes
Out of State: $ 14,100

Specialty: Liberal Arts, Preprofessional Programs
Degrees Conferred: BA, BS
Programs of Study: Accounting, Anthropology, Art, Biological Science, Business Administration, Chemistry, Computer Science, Economics, Elementary Education, English, French, History, Mathematics, Music, Philosophy, Physical Education, Physical Fitness/Exercise Science, Physics, Political Science, PreLaw, PreMed, Psychology, Religion, Science Education, Secondary Education, Social Science, Spanish, Sports Administration, Theatre

Men's Athletic Profile

2112 Cleveland Blvd.
Caldwell, ID 83605
Coach: John A. Calpin
Email: Not Available

NAIA
Coyotes/Purple, White
Phone: (208) 459-5857
Fax: (208) 459-5854

Estimated # of Men's Soccer Scholarships: None
Conference: PNW - Cascade Conference
Program Profile: Our playing field is natural grass which measures 120 by 70.
History: Program began in 1984.
Achievements: Conference Champions in 1989; Conference Coach of the Year in 1989; Conference Runner-up in 1997; 12 Academic All-Americans; 3 All-Americans.
Coaching: John A. Calpin, Head Coach, USSF 'B' License, full coaching badge England, Region IV ODP Staff Coach, NAIA District II Coach of the Year 1989. Bill Blazek - Assistant Coach.
Style of Play: Depends on talent of the players and what they show me and the situation in game.

Women's Athletic Profile

2112 Cleveland Blvd.
Caldwell, ID 83605
Coach: Bill Blazek
Email: Not Available

NAIA
Coyotes/Purple, Yellow, White
Phone: (208) 459-5857
Fax: (208) 459-5854

Estimated # of Women's Soccer Scholarships: None
Conference:
Program Profile: Playing season runs from August to November, games are played on grass field located on campus.
History: Program Began in 1991

Boise State University

Academic Profile

Phone: 800-824-7017

Boise, ID 83725

Type: 4 Yr.,Public
Founded: 1932
Website: http://www.broncosports.com
Religion: Non-Affiliated
SAT/ACT/GPA: 750+
Housing: No
Student/Faculty Ratio: 19:1
Male/Female Ratio: 46:54
Undergraduate Enrollment: 12,810
Graduate Enrollment: 1,444
Scholarships/Academic: Yes **Athletic:** Yes
Financial Aid: Yes
Expenses by: Year **In State:** $ 5,753
Out of State: $ 8,403
Degrees Conferred: AA, AS, BA, BS, BFA, MA, MS, MBA, MFA, AAS
Programs of Study: Contact school for programs of study.

Women's Athletic Profile

1910 University Drive
Boise, ID 83725
Coach: Steve Lucas
Email: slvcas@boisestate.edu

NCAA I
Broncos/Blue, Orange
Phone: (208) 426-1826
Fax: (208) 385-1778

Estimated # of Women's Soccer Scholarships: N/A
Conference: Big West Conference
History: Program started in 1998
Roster in State: 8 **Out of State:** 15 **Out of Country:**
Positions Needed: Forwards
Most Recent Record: 6-12
Schedule: Cal Poly, State, Montana, San Jose State, SMU, TCU

Idaho State University

Academic Profile

Phone: 208-282-2475

Pocatello, ID 83209

Type: 4 Yr.,Public
Founded: 1901
Website: http://www.isu.edu
Religion: Non-Affiliated
SAT/ACT/GPA: Open
Housing: No
Student/Faculty Ratio: 16:1
Male/Female Ratio: 48:52
Undergraduate Enrollment: 9,000
Graduate Enrollment: 2,000
Scholarships/Academic: Yes **Athletic:** Yes
Financial Aid: Yes
Expenses by: Year **In State:** $ 6,047
Out of State: $ 8,697
Degrees Conferred: AA, AS, BA, BS, BFA, MA, MS, MBA, MFA, M.Ed., Ph.D.
Programs of Study: Contact school for programs of study.

Women's Athletic Profile

Box 8173, holt Arena
Pocatello, ID 83209
Coach: Gordon Henderson
Email:

NCAA I
Bengals/Black, Orange
Phone: (208) 236-2771
Fax: (208) 236-4063

Estimated # of Women's Soccer Scholarships: N/A
Conference: Big Sky Conference

North Idaho College

Academic Profile

Coeur d'Alene, ID 83814
Phone: 208-769-3311

Type: 2 Yr.,Public,
Founded: 1933
Website: http://www.nic.edu
Religion: Non-Affiliated
SAT/ACT/GPA: Open Enrollment
Housing: No
Student/Faculty Ratio: 17/1
Male/Female Ratio: 45/55
Undergraduate Enrollment: 4,000
Graduate Enrollment: 0
Scholarships/Academic: Yes **Athletic:** Yes **Financial Aid:** Yes
Expenses by: Year **In State:** $6,796 **Out of State:** $8,944
Specialty: General Studies, Nursing
Degrees Conferred: Associate of Art, Associate of Applied Science
Programs of Study: General Studies, Applied Technology, Occupational Programs

Men's Athletic Profile

1000 W. Garden Ave.
Coeur d' Alene, ID 83814
Coach: Bill Eisenwinter
Email: bill_eisenwinter@nic.edu

NJCAA
Cardinals/Maroon, White
Phone: 208-769-5952
Fax: 208-769-7779

Estimated # of Men's Soccer Scholarships: 8
Conference: NWAACC
Program Profile: A new, highly successful program, campus located in Lake Coeur d' Alene with the Soccer field as a focal point in the middle of campus.
History: Program began in 2000, 14-5-2 in first year. The team placed 2nd om league and 3rd in conference Championships.
Achievements: Conference Championships-3rd place. 5 All-League Players.
Coaching: Head Coach- Bill Eisenwinter-USSF "A" Licensed, Region IV Olympic Development Program Regional Staff, former All-Mid East player. Dan Hogan- USSF "C" License, Dean Thompson- Goalkeeping Coach, USSF "C" License, former collegiate goalkeeper.
Roster In State: 24 **Out of State:** 2 **Out of Country:** 0
ODP State: 18 **Regional:** 1 **National:** 0
Walk-on/Other: 0 **Graduation %:** 100 **Seniors on Team:** 1 soph
Positions Needed: All
Camp or Clinic Dates: N/A
Most Recent Record: 14-5-2
Schedule: Edmonds, Spokane, Columbia Basin, Bellevue
Style of Play: Good team organization. Possession oriented, depends on ability, style, and make-up of players.

Women's Athletic Profile

1000 W. Garden Ave.
Coeur d' Alene, ID 83814
Coach: Bill Eisenwinter
Email: bill_eisenwinter@nic.edu

NJCAA
Cardinals/Maroon, White
Phone: (208) 769-5952
Fax: (208) 769-7779

Estimated # of Women's Soccer Scholarships: 8
Conference: NWAACC
Program Profile: A new, highly successful program, campus located in Lake Coeur d' Alene with the Soccer field as a focal point in the middle of campus.

History: Program began in 1999, 31-8-6 overall in 2 years. The team has made the Conference Championship in each of its 2 years of existence.
Achievements: Conference Runner-up in 2000. 12 All-League players in 2 years.
Coaching: Head Coach- Bill Eisenwinter-USSF "A" Licensed, Region IV Olympic Development Program Regional Staff, former All-Mid East player. Dan Hogan- USSF "C" License, Dean Thompson- Goalkeeping Coach, USSF "C" License, former collegiate goalkeeper.

Roster in State: 20	**Out of State:** 2	**Out of Country:** 0
ODP State: 12	**Regional:** 0	**National:** 0
Walk-on/Other: 0	**Graduation %:** 100	**Seniors on Team:** 7 soph.

Positions Needed: All
Camp or Clinic Dates: N/A
Most Recent Record: 16-4-2
Schedule: Edmonds, Spokane, Columbia Basin, Walla Walla
Style of Play: Good team organization. Possession oriented, depends on ability, style, and make-up of players.

Northwest Nazarene College

Academic Profile

Phone: 877-668-4968

Nampa, ID 83686

Type: 4 Yr.,Public,Liberal Arts		**Founded:** 1913
Website: http://www.nnc.edu		**Religion:** Nazarene
SAT/ACT/GPA: 870/18		**Housing:** Yes
Student/Faculty Ratio: 14:1		**Male/Female Ratio:** 1:1.3
Undergraduate Enrollment: 1096		**Graduate Enrollment:** 147
Scholarships/Academic: Yes	**Athletic:** Yes	**Financial Aid:** Yes
Expenses by: Year	**In State:** $ 16,725	**Out of State:** $ 16,725

Specialty: Education, Liberal Arts, Physical Therapy
Degrees Conferred: 3 Associate of Arts, 119 Bachelor of Arts, 39 Masters
Programs of Study: Accounting, Biology, Business Administration, Chemistry, Communications, Computer Information Systems, Computer Science, Elementary Education, Engineering, English, Finance, Fine Arts, History, Humanities, International Relations, Mathematics, Music, Philosophy, Physical Education, Physics, Political Science, PreDentistry, PreLaw, PreMed, PrePharmacy, Psychology, Recreation, Social Science, Social Work, Sociology, Sport Medicine

Men's Athletic Profile

623 Holly	**NAIA**
Nampa, ID 83686	Crusaders/Red, White
Coach: James Lang	**Phone:** (208) 887-3494
Email: jalang@hnu.edu	**Fax:** (208) 467-8396

Estimated # of Men's Soccer Scholarships: Varies
Conference: Cascade Collegiate Conference
Program Profile: NAIA season runs from August through November. Games are played on a natural grass field that measures 115x80 yards, with a seating capacity of 750. We expect to have students from Northwest and Intermountain area. Crusaders will be competing at the Pacific West-NCAA Division II.
History: Began in 1978. Overall record 103-112-12. In 1981, the Crusaders were District Soccer Champions. 1999 was the first winning season. We placed 2nd in Conference.
Achievements: Has consistently placed two players on the NAIA Scholar Athlete Team. 1981 team - District 2 Champs. Retired Head Coach Dr. Art Horwood is a member of NAIA District 2 Hall of Fame. 1977 and 1982 Mid-Central Conference Coach of the Year. 1983 - NCCAA National Coach of the Year, 1982 - NAIA District and Area Coach of the Year. NSCAA Advanced National Certificate.

Coaching: David Diehl, Head Coach, USSF "B" License, has received numerous Coach of the Year honors including the 1983 NCCAA National Coach of the Year.
Roster In State: 3 **Out of State:** 13 **Out of Country:**
Camp or Clinic Dates: July 1-August 4
Most Recent Record: 10-8-1
Schedule: Simon Fraser University, Seattle University, Western Washington University, Humboldt State University
Style of Play: We will play an aggressive attacking style of soccer, putting a lot of pressure on our opponents.

Women's Athletic Profile

623 Holly St.
Nampa, ID 83686
Coach: James Lang
Email: Not Available

NAIA
Crusaders/Red, White
Phone: (208) 887-3494
Fax: (208) 467-8396

Estimated # of Women's Soccer Scholarships: None
Conference: Cascade Collegiate
Program Profile: Crusaders will competing at the NAIA level. Players play on a natural grass field with 115x80 yards. We expect to have students from the Northwest and intermountain area.
History: 1997 Fall was the first season of the program.
Achievements: New program.
Coaching: Jim Lang, Head Coach, USSF "B" License. His last two high school teams finished first and third in the Idaho State Soccer Tournament.
Style of Play: We will play an aggressive attacking style of soccer, putting a lot of pressure on our opponents.

University of Idaho

Academic Profile

Moscow, ID 83844

Phone: (208) 885-0238

Type: 4 Yr.,Public
Website: http://www.uidaho.edu
SAT/ACT/GPA: 1070/23/2.0
Student/Faculty Ratio: 17:1
Undergraduate Enrollment: 8,128
Scholarships/Academic: Yes **Athletic:** Yes
Expenses by: Year **In State:** $ 9,750

Founded: 1887
Religion: Non-Affiliated
Housing: Yes
Male/Female Ratio: 7:5
Graduate Enrollment: 2,447
Financial Aid: Yes
Out of State: $ 15,750

Specialty: Agriculture, Art, Architecture, Business, Education, Engineering
Degrees Conferred: BA, BS, B of Dance, BFA, BGS, B of Land Arch., B of Music, BNS
Programs of Study: A wide variety of undergraduate programs and master's programs in 67 areas.

Women's Athletic Profile

Kibbie-ASUI Activity Center
Moscow, ID 83844-2302
Coach: Larry Foster
Email: lfoster@uidaho.edu

NCAA I
Vandals/Silver, Gold, Black
Phone: (208) 885-4804
Fax: (208) 882-2862

Estimated # of Women's Soccer Scholarships: 4-6
Conference: Big West Conference
Program Profile: We play at Guy Wicks Complex on natural grass - future plans include expansive of Kibbie Dove Facilities to include soccer complex with stadium.
History: The program began in 1998.

Achievements: 4 UI players were named to the 1999 Big West All-American Academic All-Conference team; the women's program was voted Idaho as one of the most improved 1999 Women's soccer programs. The Vandals placed in a six way tie for 15th based on the criteria.
Coaching: Larry Foster, Head Coach, was named PNWAC Coach of the Year in 1994, Central Washington Coach of the Year in 1997; had numerous All-Americans at Central Washington University. Steve Crum is the Assistant Coaches.

Roster in State: 5	**Out of State:** 21	**Out of Country:** 2
ODP State: 17	**Regional:** 1	**National:**
Walk-on/Other: 10	**Graduation %:** 100	**Seniors on Team:**

Positions Needed: 5
Camp or Clinic Dates: July 31-August 3
Most Recent Record: 9-8-2
Schedule: Cal Poly SLO, University of Washington, University of Oregon, Oregon State, Pacific, UCSB
Style of Play: Flexible play with many variations, but philosophically committed to attack.

illinois

ILLINOIS

SCHOOL	CITY	AFFILIATION	PAGE
Augustana College	Rock Island	NCAA III	265
Aurora University	Aurora	NCAA III	265
Belleville Area College	Belleville	NJCAA	267
Benedictine University	Lisle	NCAA III	267
Blackburn College	Carlinville	NCAA III	268
Bradley University	Peoria	NCAA I	269
Concordia University River Forest	River Forest	NCAA III	270
DePaul University	Chicago	NCAA I	271
Dominican University	River Forest	NAIA	272
Danville Area College	Danville	NJCAA	273
Eastern Illinois University	Charleston	NCAA I	274
Elmhurst College	Elmhurst	NCAA III	275
Eureka College	Eureka	NCAA III	276
Greenville College	Greenville	NCAA III	276
Illinois College	Jacksonville	NCAA III	277
Illinois State University	Normal	NCAA I	279
Illinois Wesleyan University	Bloomington	NCAA III	279
Judson College	Elgin	NAIA	280
Knox College	Galesburg	NCAA III	281
Lake Forest College	Lake Forest	NCAA III	283
Lewis University	Romeoville	NCAA II	284
Lincoln College	Lincoln	NJCAA	285
Loyola University - Chicago	Chicago	NCAA I	286
MacMurray University	Jacksonville	NCAA III	287
McKendree College	Lebanon	NAIA	288
Millikin University	Decatur	NCAA III	289
Monmouth College	Monmouth	NCAA III	290
North Central College	Naperville	NCAA III	291

SCHOOL	CITY	AFFILIATION	PAGE
North Park University	Chicago	NCAA III	293
Northern Illinois University	DeKalb	NCAA I	294
Northwestern University	Evanston	NCAA I	295
Olivet Nazarene University	Kankakee	NAIA	296
Principia College	Elsah	NCAA III	297
Quincy University	Quincy	NCAA I	299
Robert Morris College - Chicago	Chicago	NAIA	300
Robert Morris College - Springfield	Springfield	NAIA	301
Rockford College	Rockford	NCAA III	302
Sanagamon State University	Springfield	NAIA	303
Saint Xavier University	Chicago	NAIA	304
Southern Illinois University	Edwardsville	NCAA II	304
Trinity Christian College	Palos Heights	NAIA	305
Trinity International U	Deerfield	NAIA	307
University of Chicago	Chicago	NCAA III	308
University of IL - Chicago	Chicago	NCAA I	309
Univ of Illinois-Urbana-Campaign	Chamapaign	NCAA I	309
Western Illinois University	Macomb	NCAA I	310
Wheaton College - Illinois	Wheaton	NCAA III	311

Augustana College

Academic Profile

Rock Island, IL 61201
Phone: 309-794-7341

Type: 4 Yr.,Private,Liberal Arts
Website: http://www.augustana.edu
SAT/ACT/GPA: 24/3.2
Student/Faculty Ratio: 14:1
Undergraduate Enrollment: 1,150
Scholarships/Academic: Yes **Athletic:** No
Expenses by: Year **In State:** $ 22,224 **Out of State:** $ 22,224
Founded: 1860
Religion: Non-Affiliated
Housing: Yes
Male/Female Ratio: 45:55
Graduate Enrollment: N/A
Financial Aid: Yes
Specialty: Business, Sciences
Degrees Conferred: BA, B.Mus., BME
Programs of Study: Business and Management, Education, Health Science, Letters/Literature, Life Sciences, Psychology, Social Sciences

Men's Athletic Profile

639 - 38th Street
Rock Island, IL 61201
Coach: Bob Estabrook
Email: Not Available

NCAA III
Vikings/Blue, Gold
Phone: (309) 794-7000
Fax: (309) 794-7525

Estimated # of Men's Soccer Scholarships:
Conference: College Conference of Illinois and Wisconsin
Program Profile: We have a new natural turf field. Playing season runs from September through November.
History: Program began in 1981 - only 2 losing seniors in history.
Achievements: None
Coaching: Robert Estabrook, Head Coach.
Style of Play: Strong counter attack; physical aggressive defensive.

Women's Athletic Profile

3500 - 5th Avenue
Rock Island, IL 61201
Coach: Krisan Steiger
Email: Not Available

NCAA III
Vikings/Navy, Gold
Phone: (309) 794-7521
Fax: (309) 794-7525

Estimated # of Women's Soccer Scholarships: None
Conference: College conference of Illinois and Wisconsin

Aurora University

Academic Profile

Aurora, IL 60506
Phone: (630) 844- 4207

Type: 4 Yr.,Private,Liberal Arts
Website: http://www.aurora.edu
SAT/ACT/GPA: 900/19/2.0
Student/Faculty Ratio: 15:1
Undergraduate Enrollment: 2,700
Scholarships/Academic: Yes **Athletic:** No
Expenses by: Year **In State:** $ 17,200 **Out of State:** $ 17,200
Founded: 1893
Religion: Non-Denominational
Housing: Yes
Male/Female Ratio: 55:45
Graduate Enrollment: 1,000
Financial Aid: Yes

Specialty: Business, Education, Criminal Justice, Computer Science, Sports
Degrees Conferred: BA, BS, Masters
Programs of Study: Contact school for programs of study.

Men's Athletic Profile

347 S Gladstone Avenue
Aurora, IL 60506-4892
Coach: Oleg Vatchev
Email: Not Available

NCAA III
Spartans/Royal, White
Phone: (630) 844-5110
Fax: (630) 844-7809

Estimated # of Men's Soccer Scholarships:
Conference: NIIC
Program Profile: We have eleven varsity sports; 2,200 Thorton Gymnasium, 1,500 natural turf stadium with a Sports Information Center, training, weight, aerobic activities rooms, fitness center, racquetball courts.
History: Our program began in 1963; compiled a record of 218-240-28 overall; NAIA and Division III, past coaches were Rick Kilps, Fred Bornkaup, Chris Shinu, Glen Tourville. Member of Northern Illinois - Iowa Conference.
Achievements: 11 times NIIC Champions, the last was in 1997; 5 All-Americans, 7 professional players; Oleg Vatchwv was named Coach of the Year in 1997; 8 players All-Conference in 1997, Hernan Campuzano was named Player of the Year in 1997.
Coaching: Oleg Vatchev, Head Coach, USSF "A" License Coach. Illinois Youth Soccer Association - Olympic Development Program State Coach and Staff.
Style of Play: Zonal defending, possession with build-up out of the back, passing, combining, inter-classifying in and between the three functional lines.

Women's Athletic Profile

347 S Gladstone Avenue
Aurora, IL 60506-4892
Coach: Kanute Drugan
Email: kdrugan@aurora.edu

NCAA III
Spartans/Royal Blue, White
Phone: (630) 844-4207
Fax: (630) 830-1368

Estimated # of Women's Soccer Scholarships: Not Available
Conference: Northern Illinois - Iowa Conference (NIIC)
Program Profile: Nationally prominent women's soccer program ranked among top ten in its region in NCAA Division III. Draws top talent from eight states throughout Midwest. Has produced All-Americans, All-Region Players as well as Players of the Year within conference and region. Play aggressive, competitive schedule producing three consecutive conference champions. Practices and plays on superior quickly natural turf fields. Stadium seas 1,800. The Spartans are the first team ever to go 6-0 in conference play and currently hold a 10 game winning streak in conference. Of the 376 NCAA DIII women's soccer programs Aurora Univ. finished 15th in the nation in scoring in 1999 (75 goals in 20 games) and finished 19th in the nation in scoring in 2000 (83 goals in 22 games).
History: Entering his fifth year as head coach, Kanute Drugan will attempt to lead the Spartans to their fifth NIIC Conference Championship in the past six years. Aurora Univ. won conference championships in 1996, 1997, 1999 and 2000. Now in the eighth year of the women's soccer program, the team has steadily progressed from its first season in 1994 to its current status of national prominence.
Achievements: Kanute Drugan Head Coach record is 55-20-4 (.722) and includes three conference championships, three Coach of the Year, one NCAA All-American player (2nd team), three NCAA All-Region players and two NCAA Academic All-American. Also 25 NIIC All-Conference players, 3 NIIC Player of the Year.
Coaching: Head Coach- Kanute Drugan, Assistant Coaches- Michelle Wottreng, Kim Clark, Connie Sirota.

Roster in State: 14	**Out of State:** 10	**Out of Country:** 0
ODP State: 9	**Regional:** 3	**National:**
Walk-on/Other: 12	**Graduation %:** 100	**Seniors on Team:** 1

Positions Needed: 1 forward, 2 wings (outside mid), 2 marking backs

Most Recent Record: 16-6-0
Schedule: U. of Wisconsin-Eau Claire, U. of Chicago, St. Mary's College, U. of Wisconsin-Oshkosh, Illinois Wesleyan Univ. Mount St. Joseph's College, Lawrence Univ. Grinnell College, Lake Forest College
Style of Play: Aurora University utilizes a 4-4-2 marking man system. The style of play is attack oriented. The Spartans have scored 75 goals in 20 games (1999) and 83 goals in 22 games (2000). The Spartans are very aggressive and physical. They look for opportunities for 2V1 in both the attacking and defending ends of the field. The maintain their attack the Spartans emphasize possession using short and intermediate passes to move the ball through the midfield and to switch the point of attack.

Belleville Area College

Academic Profile

Belleville, IL 62221
Phone:

Type: 2 Yr.,Public
Founded: 1946
Website: http://www.bacnet.edu/index.htm
Religion: Non-Affiliated
SAT/ACT/GPA: Open
Housing: No
Student/Faculty Ratio: 30:1
Male/Female Ratio: 1:2
Undergraduate Enrollment: 22,000
Graduate Enrollment: N/A
Scholarships/Academic: Yes **Athletic:** Yes
Financial Aid: Yes
Expenses by: Semester **In State:** $ Varies
Out of State: $ Varies
Specialty: Transferable Programs
Degrees Conferred: AA, AS, AAS
Programs of Study: We have over 35 different transfer programs leading to a four-year degrees.

Men's Athletic Profile

2500 Carlyle Road
Belleville, IL 62221
Coach: Larry Petri
Email: Not Available

NJCAA
Dutchman/Royal, White
Phone: (618) 235-2700
Fax: (618) 235-1578

Estimated # of Men's Soccer Scholarships: 10
Conference: None
Program Profile: We have two fields for practice games. We have a highly competitive schedule and top training room. Our game schedule from August to November.
History: Our program began in 1974. We are always very competitive with other school in the state and local area. We've made two trips to the National Tournament and has been rated as high as #4 in the country.
Achievements: 4 All-Americans.
Coaching: Larry Petri, Head Coach, holds a USSF 'B' license and NSCAA Advanced National Diploma. He is a member of the State ODP staff. Chad L. Gnoul is the Assistant Coach.
Style of Play: Short passing game, built from the back and quick counter.

Benedictine University

Academic Profile

Lisle, IL 60532
Phone: 630-829-6300

Type: 4 Yr.,Private
Founded: 1887
Website: http://www.ben.edu
Religion: Roman Catholic
SAT/ACT/GPA: 21/2.0
Housing: Yes
Student/Faculty Ratio: 10:1
Male/Female Ratio: 48:52

Undergraduate Enrollment: 1,750
Graduate Enrollment: 900
Scholarships/Academic: Yes
Athletic: No
Financial Aid: Yes
Expenses by: Year
In State: $ 18,580
Out of State: $ 18,580
Specialty: Sciences, Business, Education
Degrees Conferred: 38 Undergraduates majors; 12 Graduate programs
Programs of Study: Accounting, Arts Administration, Biochemistry, Biology, Business and Economics, Chemistry, Clinical Laboratory Science, Communications Arts, Computer Science, Economics, Elementary Education, Engineering Science, English Languages & Literature, Environmental Science, Finance, Health Science, History, International Studies, Management & Organizational Behavior, Marketing, Mathematics, Molecular Biology, Music, Nutrition, Philosophy, Physics, Political Science, Sociology, Spanish, Special Education, Writing and Publishing

Men's Athletic Profile

5700 College Road
Lisle, IL 60532
Coach: Branton Joseph
Email: Not Available

NCAA III
Eagles/Red, White
Phone: (630) 829-6140
Fax: (630) 960-0899

Estimated # of Men's Soccer Scholarships: None
Conference: Northern Illinois Intercollegiate Conference
Program Profile: Facilities include 1 main soccer field and 3 practice fields. IBC hosted Spain's practice facilities for 1994 World Cup. Program ranked nationally in the Top 20 for the 4 years. Qualified for National tournament in 1993 and 1994.
History: Program began in 1985 by Paul Wardlaw.
Achievements: 1994 & 1991 NIIC Coach of the Year, 12 All-Midwest Players, 1992 State & Regional Coach of the Year.
Style of Play: Possession and slow build-up.

Women's Athletic Profile

5700 College Rd.
Lisle, IL 60532-0900
Coach: Mark Clynes
Email: Not Available

NCAA III
Eagles/Red, White
Phone: (913) 367-5340
Fax:

Estimated # of Women's Soccer Scholarships: None
Conference: Northern Illinois Intercollegiate Conference

Blackburn College

Academic Profile

Phone: 800-233-3550

Carlinville, IL 62626

Type: 4 Yr.,Private,Liberal Arts
Founded: 1837
Website: http://www.blackburn.edu
Religion: Presbyterian
SAT/ACT/GPA: 1000/21/3.0-4.0
Housing: Yes
Student/Faculty Ratio: 15:1
Male/Female Ratio: 1:1
Undergraduate Enrollment: 561
Graduate Enrollment: N/A
Scholarships/Academic: Yes
Athletic: No
Financial Aid: Yes
Expenses by: Year
In State: $ 11,120
Out of State: $ 11,120
Specialty: Education, Sciences
Degrees Conferred: BA, BS in Engineering & Applied Science, Preprofessional Programs
Programs of Study: Accounting, Art, Biology, Business Administration & Management, Chemistry, Computer Science, Elementary Education, Political Science, Psychology, Spanish, PreDentistry, PreEngineering, PreLaw, PreNursing, PreMedicine, PrePhysical Therapy, PreVet

Men's Athletic Profile

700 College Ave
Carlinville, IL 62626
Coach: Gene Baker
Email: Not Available

NCAA III
Beavers/Scarlet, Black
Phone: (217) 854-3231
Fax: (217) 854-9313

Estimated # of Men's Soccer Scholarships: N/A
Conference: St. Louis Intercollegiate Athletic Conference

Women's Athletic Profile

700 College Avenue
Carlinville, IL 62626
Coach: Elizabeth Koenn-Bollinger
Email: ekoen@mail.blackburn.edu

NCAA III
Beavers/Red, Black
Phone: (800) 233-3550
Fax: (217) 854-5520

Estimated # of Women's Soccer Scholarships: None
Conference: St. Louis Intercollegiate Athletic Conference
Program Profile: We have 1.5 practice fields and a game field made of natural turf. Our campus provides a weight room facility and the players have an option to use a local fitness center located 1/4 mile from campus in the off-season. Our athletes have the benefit of a full-time certified athletic trainer on staff along with an extensive amount of qualified student trainers. The playing season begins in mid to late August. Games begin in September and last through October. We attempt to participate in winter indoor tournaments and spring games as well.
History: Women's Soccer began in 1995 at Blackburn. Our record that year was 3-13-2. In 1996 we improved to a record of 9-11. In 1997, we dropped to a 6-13 overall record. In 1998, we dropped again to a 4-13-1 record. In 1999, we rebounded with a record of 8-9.
Coaching: Elizabeth Koenn, Head Coach, the only coach, played for Claremont-Mudd-Scripps joint athletic department in Claremont, CA. (NCAA Division III) in 1991, 1992, 1993; Awarded first team All-SCIAC each year and third team All-Western Region in 1992,1993.
Roster in State: 12 **Out of State:** 5 **Out of Country:** 0
ODP State: 1 **Regional:** 0 **National:** 0
Walk-on/Other: 0 **Graduation %:** 75 **Seniors on Team:** 2
Positions Needed: All Defensive
Camp or Clinic Dates: Not Available
Most Recent Record: 7-13-0
Schedule: Webster Univ. Principia College, Maryville University of St. Louis, Fontbonne College, Westminster College, Rose Hulman
Style of Play: We play a 4-4-2. As we've recruited better players over the last two years, we've been able to settle our game into more of a passing game as opposed to a "kick and run" game.

Bradley University

Academic Profile

1501 West Bradley Avenue
Peoria, IL 61625

Phone: (309) 677-3626

Type: 4 Yr.,Private,Liberal Arts
Website: http://www.bradley.edu
SAT/ACT/GPA: 1140/25
Student/Faculty Ratio: 15:1
Undergraduate Enrollment: 5,000
Scholarships/Academic: Yes **Athletic:** Yes
Expenses by: Year **In State:** $ 19,552

Founded: 1897
Religion: Non-Affiliated
Housing: Yes
Male/Female Ratio: 45:55
Graduate Enrollment: 1,000
Financial Aid: Yes
Out of State: $ 19,552

Degrees Conferred: BA, BS, MA, MS, MBA, MFA
Programs of Study: Business Administration, Communications and Fine Arts, Educational and Sciences, Engineering and Technology, Liberal Arts and Sciences

Men's Athletic Profile

1501 W Bradley Ave.
Peoria, IL 61625
Coach: Jim DeRose
Email: derose@bradley.edu

NCAA I
Braves/Red, White
Phone: (309) 677-2674
Fax: (309) 677-3626

Estimated # of Men's Soccer Scholarships: 8 total/ 1 available
Conference: Missouri Valley Conference
Program Profile: Bradley's Becker Park has 120x75 yards natural grass game field and an adjacent 20x75 yards natural grass practice field, with a stadium capacity of a 1,000.
History: We were a club sport from 1986 to 1988. We became a Division I program in 1988.
Achievements: 1998 team won the Missouri Valley Conference title, ranked #14 in "Soccer America" magazine and #20 according to the NSCAA poll. All-American (2nd team) Gavin Glinton; Academic All-American Dan Goldstein; College Soccer Weekly All-American Adam Gross; 3 players on the All-Midwest Team: Bryan Namoff, Stephen Wylie, and Gavin Glinton. 5 All-Conference team selections. Bradley also won the UNH Nike and Holiday Inn City Centre Classic tournaments.
Coaching: Jim DeRose, Head Coach, has been named MVC Coach of the in Year in 1996 and 1998 by the NSCAA and was named Midwest Coach of the Year in 1998. Assistant coach Chad Flanders holds a USSF "B" license and is a current member of the Region II ODP staff.
Roster In State: 13
Out of State: 20
Out of Country: 2
ODP State: 23
Regional: 6
National: 2
Walk-on/Other: 0
Graduation %: 100
Seniors on Team: 5
Positions Needed: 2 Midfielders, 4 Backs
Camp or Clinic Dates: July 16-20, 23-27
Most Recent Record: 10-10-0
Schedule: South Methodist, Southwest Missouri State, Creighton, Tulsa, Notre Dame, Evansville
Style of Play: Attacking and defending is viewed as a team's responsibility, with all players being able to fit into a variety of roles. Emphasis is placed on the team's ability to possess the ball, and play forward as quickly and effectively as possible.

Concordia University

Academic Profile

Phone:

Type: 4 Yr.,Public,
Website: http://www.csc.cc.il.us
SAT/ACT/GPA: Open
Student/Faculty Ratio: 12:1
Undergraduate Enrollment:
Scholarships/Academic: No
Athletic: No
Expenses by: Year
In State:
Degrees Conferred: N/A
Programs of Study: Please Call for more information

Founded:
Religion:
Housing: Yes
Male/Female Ratio: N/A
Graduate Enrollment: N/A
Financial Aid: Yes
Out of State:

Men's Athletic Profile

7400 Augusta
River Forest, ILL. 60305
Coach: Tony Pierce
Email: Piercet@curf.edu

NCAA III
Cougars/Maroon, Gold
Phone: 708-209-3569
Fax: 708-209-3154

Estimated # of Men's Soccer Scholarships:
Conference: Northern Illinois- Iowa Conference
Program Profile: We have a brand new stadium which seats 3,000 with a play surface of turf.
History: The 2000-2001 season was the first season ever for Concordia, both on the Men's and Women's side.
Coaching: Tony Pierce is USSF"B" licensed. He played 9 years in the NPSL.
Roster In State: 8 **Out of State:** 10 **Out of Country:** 2
ODP State: 3 **Regional:** 1 **National:**
Walk-on/Other: **Graduation %:** 100 **Seniors on Team:** 2
Positions Needed: Solid players
Style of Play: A possession game with an up tempo defense.

De Paul University

Academic Profile

Chicago, IL 60604
Phone: 800-433-7285

Type: 4 Yr.,Private,
Founded: 1898
Website: http://www.depaul.edu
Religion: Catholic
SAT/ACT/GPA: 1200/27
Housing: No
Student/Faculty Ratio: 16:1
Male/Female Ratio: 1:1
Undergraduate Enrollment: 6,839
Graduate Enrollment: 6,683
Scholarships/Academic: Yes **Athletic:** Yes **Financial Aid:** Yes
Expenses by: Year **In State:** $ 18,000 **Out of State:** $ 18,000
Degrees Conferred: BA, BS, BFA, BM, BSC, MA, MS, MBA, MFA, M.Ed., Ph.D., JD
Programs of Study: Accounting, Banking/Finance, Biology, Business Administration, Chemistry, Communications, Computer Science, Economics, Education, English, Environmental Science, French, Geography, International Relations, Management, Marketing, Mathematics, Medical Laboratory Technology, Music, Performing Arts, Philosophy, Physical Education, Physics, Political Science, Psychology, Religion, Social Science

Men's Athletic Profile

1011 W Belden Ave.
Chicago, IL 60614
Coach: Thomas Secco
Email: tsecco@wppost.depaul.edu

NCAA I
Blue Demons/Royal, Scarlet
Phone: (773) 325-7231
Fax: (312) 325-7529

Estimated # of Men's Soccer Scholarships: None
Conference: Great Midwest Conference

Women's Athletic Profile

1011 W Belden Ave.
Chicago, IL 60614
Coach: John Wilson
Email: lschinge@wppost.depaul.edu

NCAA I
Blue Demons/Red, White, Blue
Phone: (772) 325-7000
Fax: (773) 325-7212

Estimated # of Women's Soccer Scholarships: None
Conference: Conference USA
Program Profile: The women's soccer program will begin its first year as a varsity sport in 1997. The Blue Demons will be playing at the NCAA Division I level. play on natural grass field on campus; stadium site holds about 300 seats; playing season is traditional Fall season.
History: 1997-1998 was second year of the program.
Achievements: None due to new program.
Style of Play: Possession style of play, high pressure "D".

Dominican University (Rosary College)

Academic Profile

River Forest, IL 60305
Phone: (708) 366-2490

Type: 4 Yr.,Private,Liberal Arts
Website: http;//www.dom.edu
SAT/ACT/GPA: 950/20/2.5-4.0
Student/Faculty Ratio: 11:1
Undergraduate Enrollment: 1,100
Scholarships/Academic: Yes **Athletic:** No
Expenses by: Year **In State:** $ 19,260
Founded: 1901
Religion: Catholic
Housing: Yes
Male/Female Ratio: 37:63
Graduate Enrollment: 900
Financial Aid: Yes
Out of State: $ 19,260
Specialty: Psychology, Business, Accounting, Communications, English
Degrees Conferred: BA, BS, MA, MS
Programs of Study: Accounting, American Studies, Art, Arts & Media Management, Biology, Biology-Chemistry, Business Administration, Business-Writing, Chemistry, Communication Arts & Sciences, Computer Graphics, Computer Information Systems, Computer Science, Corporate Communications, Criminology, Economics, Education, Environmental Management, Environmental Science, Fashion, Fine & Performing Arts, Food Science, Food Service Management, French, German, Geography, Greek, Hebrew, History, International Business, International Relations and Diplomacy, International Studies, Italian, Latin, Linguistic, Mathematics, Mat & Computer Science, Medical Technology, Modern Languages, Spanish, Music, Natural Science, Nursing, Nutrition Sciences, Pastoral Ministry, Philosophy, Health and Physical Education, Physics, Political Science, Psychology, Religious Studies, Sociology

Men's Athletic Profile

7900 W Division Street
River Forest, IL 60305
Coach: Erick Baumann
Email: ebaumn@pmail.dom.edu

NAIA
Stars/Royal Blue, Black, White
Phone: (708) 488-5054
Fax: (708) 366-5095

Estimated # of Men's Soccer Scholarships:
Conference: Chicago Collegiate Athletic Conference
History: Program began in 1988 and has accumulated an record 100-68-9.
Achievements: Chicagoland Collegiate Athletic Conference Champions in 1998 & 1999; Oscar Alvarez All-American Honorable Mention in 1998 & 1999.
Coaching: Erick Baumann, Head Coach. Georgios Mihalopolous and Tim Musial - Assistant Coaches.
Style of Play: Attractive attacking style of play; team scored 101 goals in 22 games in 1997 season.

Women's Athletic Profile

7900 W. Division
River Forest, IL 60305
Coach: Joanna Fulton
Email: Jfulton@email.dom.edu

NCAA III/NAIA
Stars/Royal Blue, Black
Phone: (708) 524-6547
Fax: (708) 488-5095

Estimated # of Women's Soccer Scholarships: None
Conference: Chicagoland Collegiate Athletic Conference/ Northern Illinois Iowa Conference
Program Profile: We are beginning our fourth year into the program on a brand new field on the campus.
History: The Stars Women's Soccer program began in 1997.
Achievements: CCAC Conference Champs in 1998.
Coaching: Joanna Fulton is our new Head Coach making this fall her first season.
Roster in State: 13 **Out of State:** 5 **Out of Country:** 0
Walk-on/Other: **Graduation %:** 100 **Seniors on Team:** 3
Positions Needed: Goalkeeper, Midfielder, Defense
Camp or Clinic Dates: Not Available
Most Recent Record: 10-8-1
Schedule: Judson College, Trinity International University, St. Xavier University, St. Ambrose University, Clark College, Aurora University

Danville Area Community College

Academic Profile

Danville, IL 61832
Phone: (217) 443-8800

Type: 2 Yr.,Public
Founded: 1946
Website: http://www.dacc.ccil.us
Religion: Non-Affiliated
SAT/ACT/GPA: Open
Housing: No
Student/Faculty Ratio: 25:1
Male/Female Ratio: N/A
Undergraduate Enrollment: 2,662
Graduate Enrollment: N/A
Scholarships/Academic: **Athletic:** **Financial Aid:**
Expenses by: Credit hour **In State:** $44 **Out of State:** $176
Degrees Conferred: AA, AS
Programs of Study: Contact the Danville Area Community College Admissions Office

Men's Athletic Profile

2000 East Main Street
Danville, IL 61832
Coach: Mike Stone
Email: mstone@dacc.cc.il.us
NJCAA
Jaguars/Green & Gold
Phone: (217) 477-5733
Fax: (530) 323-6564

Estimated # of Men's Soccer Scholarships: 8
Conference: Central Collegiate Conference of Illinois
Program Profile: We were a first year program that had a few wins and showed good team chemistry. We will add scholarship and recruited athletes next year, to help take us to the next level. We play at the new prestigious Danville Area soccer complex, which grounds 8 full-size, 2 lighted and irrigated fields.
History: 1999 marked the new beginning of the DACC Men's Soccer Program. After a 20 year hiatus, 16 players helped start the program on the right foot. Mostly local, some of the players hadn't competed in awhile. With a few wins and some good team, we will add scholarships and recruited athletes to take us to the next level.
Achievements: We play a full fall season and shortened spring season (about 5 games).
Coaching: Coach Stone is in his second year of coaching with a twelve year history of coaching. 2nd year overall 10 years played division I college. 3 national coaching licenses.
Roster In State: 14 **Out of State:** 2 **Out of Country:** 1
Positions Needed: Goal, Defenders, Attackers
Camp or Clinic Dates: call 217-477-5733
Most Recent Record: —
Schedule: Belleville, Lewis & Clark, Purdue, Illinois, Valparaiso, Anderson
Style of Play: We currently have a strong counter-attack. Our goal is to increase our possessions game for next year.

Eastern Illinois University

Academic Profile

Charleston, IL 61920

Phone: 217-252-5711

Type: 4 Yr.,Public,Liberal Arts
Website: http://www.eiu.edu
SAT/ACT/GPA: 860/18
Student/Faculty Ratio: 17:1
Undergraduate Enrollment: 10,000
Scholarships/Academic: Yes
Athletic: Yes
Expenses by: Year
In State: $ 7,433
Specialty: Liberal Arts
Founded: 1895
Religion: Non-Affiliated
Housing: Yes
Male/Female Ratio: 40:60
Graduate Enrollment: 1,700
Financial Aid: Yes
Out of State: $ 11,951
Degrees Conferred: BA, BS, BM, BSR, BSEd, MA, MS, MBA
Programs of Study: Accounting, Administrative Information Systems, African-American Studies, Art, Anthropology, Biological Studies, Botany, Business Education, Career Occupations, Chemistry, Communication Disorders and Sciences, Computer Management

Men's Athletic Profile

1303 O'Brien Stadium
Charleston, IL 61920-3099
Coach: Tim McClements
Email: cftjm@eiu.edu

NCAA I
Panthers/Royal, White
Phone: (217) 581-6442
Fax: (217) 581-7192

Estimated # of Men's Soccer Scholarships: Yes
Conference: Missouri Valley Conference
Program Profile: We have on campus game and training facilities. Our game field is natural grass that measures 120x75.
History: The program began as NAIA team in 1963.
Achievements: NAIA National Champions in 1969; took 3rd and 2nd place in NCAA Division II in 1978 and 1979; finished 3rd in NCAA Division I in 1981; Missouri Valley Conference Tournament in 1997 & 1998; several All-Americans and current professional players.
Coaching: Tim McClements is our Head Coach. He is in his forth year. He holds USSF "A" License and played for Indiana University and Wheaton College. He is a former head coach at Baker University and former assistant coach at Northern Illinois University and Midwestern State University.
Roster In State: 14
Out of State: 13
Out of Country:
Walk-on/Other: 14
Graduation %: n/a
Seniors on Team: 6
Camp or Clinic Dates: June and July
Most Recent Record: 6-11-1
Schedule: SMU, Creighton, Southwest Missouri State, Bradley, Evansville, Tulsa, Vanderbilt
Style of Play: Team work is highly stress. Emphasis is placed on playing attractive and defensively sound soccer.

Women's Athletic Profile

O'Brien Stadium, Grant St.
Charleston, IL 61920
Coach: Stephen Ballard
Email: cfsjb@eiu.edu

NCAA I
Panthers/Royal Blue, Silver
Phone: (217) 581-7062
Fax: (217) 581-7192

Estimated # of Women's Soccer Scholarships: 12 in state 2 out
Conference: Missouri Valley Conference, OVC

Program Profile: Grass game field that has a measurements of 120x75, 2 full practice fields, on grid field, two gymnasiums and fieldhouse. Year-round program that includes weights.
History: 2000- OVC 15-4-1, regular season champions, OVC tournament runner-up. 1999- OVC 11-9-0 regular season champions, OVC tournament champions, 1998 MVC/OVC 10-7-1 4th reg. Season MVC, 2nd reg. Season OVC, MVC tournament quarterfinals.
Achievements: 2 regular season OVC Championships, 1 Ohio Valley Tournament Championship, 3 years NSCAA Team Academic Award for 3.0 or above, 2000 OVC Coach of the Year, 2000, 99, 98 OVC Player of the Year, 2000,1999 OVC Freshman of the Year. 19 OVC All-Conference Team, 7 OVC Tournament Team: 1 Tournament MVP, 3 All-Great Lakes Region Team, 15 MVC All-Conference, 6 MVC All-Tournament Team.
Coaching: Stephen Ballard, Head Coach, Carolina Conference and Region Coach of the Year honors (NAIA); North Carolina and Virginia ODP State coaching experience, "B" License Coach in 1989, seventeen years as a university coach. Ashley Rogers Assistant Coach.

Roster in State: 18	**Out of State:** 3	**Out of Country:** 1
ODP State: 6	**Regional:** 0	**National:** 0
Walk-on/Other: 0	**Graduation %:** 98	**Seniors on Team:** 2

Positions Needed: GK, Sweeper, Midfield, Forward
Camp or Clinic Dates: June 17-21, June 21-24, June 24-28, July 22-26
Most Recent Record: 15-4-1
Schedule: Univ. of Illinois, Univ. of Evansville, Univ. of Hawaii, Southwest Missouri State Univ. Eastern Michigan Univ. Illinois State Univ. Loyola-Chicago, Univ. of California-Northridge, Tennessee Tech Univ. DePaul Univ.
Style of Play: Attacking style from a 4-4-2, matching zonal defense.

Elmhurst College

Academic Profile

Elmhurst, IL 60126
Phone: (630) 617-3740

Type: 4 Yr.,Private,Liberal Arts		**Founded:** 1871
Website: http://www.elmhurts.edu		**Religion:** Church of Christ
SAT/ACT/GPA: 1000/21/2.75		**Housing:** Yes
Student/Faculty Ratio: 14:1		**Male/Female Ratio:** 1:2
Undergraduate Enrollment: 3,000		**Graduate Enrollment:** 52
Scholarships/Academic: Yes	**Athletic:** No	**Financial Aid:** Yes
Expenses by: Year	**In State:** $ 19,100	**Out of State:** $ 19,100

Specialty: Nursing, Education, Business (45 Majors)
Degrees Conferred: BA, BS
Programs of Study: Art, Biology, Business, Chemistry, Communications Arts, Computer Science & Information Systems, Economics, Education, English, Environmental Planning, Foreign Languages, Geography, History, Literature, Mathematics, Music, Nursing, Philosophy, Physical Education, Physics, Political Science, PreProfessional Programs, Psychology, Religion, Sociology, Theology, Urban Studies

Women's Athletic Profile

190 Prospect Avenue
Elmhurst, IL 60126
Coach: David DiTomasso
Email: davidd@elmhurst.edu

NCAA III
Blue Jays/Blue, White
Phone: (630) 617-3470
Fax: (630) 617-3726

Estimated # of Women's Soccer Scholarships: None
Conference: College Conference of Illinois and Wisconsin
Program Profile: Great 5th year program, new soccer stadium with practice facility. Field is natural grass that seats 1,200. Program is top notch with a new 3,000 sq. ft., fitness center which has 3,000 sq. ft.; weight training facility. Has one of the best sponsorship in the country. Players treated first class!!

History: The program began in 1997 and have had 3 winning seasons out of 4.
Achievements: Julie Sapp- Academic All-American
Coaching: David DiTomasso, Head Coach, NSCAA Premier License; ODP Staff Coach for four years, professional player for six years; A-League, 3rd Division Germany, coached at Division I (Wofford College) Level, Division III level and professional level (SC Shamrocks). He is a graduate of Jacksonville University, Florida. Mike Compisi, Assistant Coach, is a graduate from Yale University, and was a professional goalkeeper for five years; A-League. Everton McCalla is our Goalkeeper Coach and has just completed 1st year on staff. Tina Fernandes also just completed her first year on staff.
Roster in State: 18 **Out of State:** 2 **Out of Country:**
Walk-on/Other: **Graduation %:** **Seniors on Team:** 5
Most Recent Record: 17-1-2
Schedule: Wheaton, Keene State, Wellesley, Plymouth, Eastern Conn. State University, University of Scranton.
Style of Play: We adjust to the players that we have on the team. We play to our strengths.

Eureka College
Academic Profile

Phone: (309) 467-6350

Eureka, IL 61530

Type: 4 Yr.,Private,
Website: http://www.eureka.edu
SAT/ACT/GPA: 21avg
Student/Faculty Ratio: 12:1
Undergraduate Enrollment: 460
Scholarships/Academic: No **Athletic:** Yes
Expenses by: Year **In State:** $ 19,000
Degrees Conferred: BA, BS

Founded: 1855
Religion: Disciples of Christ
Housing: Yes
Male/Female Ratio: 49:51
Graduate Enrollment: N/A
Financial Aid: Yes
Out of State: $ 19,000

Programs of Study: Accounting, Biological, Business, Chemistry, Communications, Computer, Dramatics Arts, Economics, Education, English, Fine Arts, History, Management, Mathematics, Medical, Music, Philosophy, Physical Education, Physical Science, Psychology, Religion, Science Education, Social Science, Speech

Men's Athletic Profile

300 College Ave., P.O. Box 280
Eureka, IL 61530
Coach: Takis Paplomatas
Email: Not Available

NCAA III
Red Devils/Maroon, Gold
Phone: (309) 467-6370
Fax: (309) 467-6402

Estimated # of Men's Soccer Scholarships: None
Conference: NIIC
Coaching: Takis Paplomatas - Head Coach.

Greenville College
Academic Profile

Phone: 618-664-2800

Greenville, IL 62246

Type: 4 Yr.,Private,Liberal Arts
Website: http://www.greenville.edu
SAT/ACT/GPA: 20/2.0
Student/Faculty Ratio: 17:1
Undergraduate Enrollment: 1,100

Founded: 1892
Religion: Free Methodist
Housing: Yes
Male/Female Ratio: 40:60
Graduate Enrollment: 100

Scholarships/Academic: Yes **Athletic:** No **Financial Aid:** Yes
Expenses by: Year **In State:** $ 17,400 **Out of State:** $ 17,400
Specialty: Christian Liberal Arts
Degrees Conferred: BA, BS, MA
Programs of Study: Education, Christian Contemporary Music, PreMed, Business, Marketing, Management Information Systems, Computers, History, Political Science, Psychology, Sociology, Social Work, etc..

Men's Athletic Profile

315 E College Avenue
Greenville, IL 62246
Coach: Brian Reinhard
Email:

NCAA III
Panthers/Orange, Black
Phone: (618) 664-2800
Fax: (618) 664-1373

Estimated # of Men's Soccer Scholarships: non-scholarship
Conference: St. Louis Intercollegiate Athletic Conference
Program Profile: Greenville's Francis Field is one of the premier grass facilities in Southern Illinois. The men's soccer program is one of the most successful at the school and regularly draws 200-300 fans. We often have more fans at away games than the home team. Our season runs 10 weeks, from the 1st week of September until the middle of November. We participate in two away tournaments, this season traveling to Kansas and to Chicago.
History: Soccer at Greenville began in 1957. It's long-standing tradition is a hallmark of its current success. The fourth leading scorer in NAIA history is a Greenville alumni, Loren Aandahal who scored 39 goals in the 1973 season to lead the nation and tallied 103 career goals in just three seasons. Rodney Malone, of McPherson, Kansas, next year's captain, has already broken the school record for most career assists with 39.
Achievements: SLIAC Conference Champs in 1998 with 15-4-2 record; Coach of the Year; 6 players on All-Conference team; 2 players third team All-American.
Coaching: Head Coach, Brian Reinhard. Assistant Coach, Micheal Laughlin is a 1998 Greenville graduate who started all 4 years.
Roster In State: 12 **Out of State:** 14 **Out of Country:** 4
Walk-on/Other: **Graduation %:** 90 **Seniors on Team:** 4
Positions Needed: Sweeper, Stopper, Midfield, Forward
Most Recent Record: 12-9-1
Schedule: Webster University, Maryville, Westminister College, Principia College, Central Christian College, MacPherson College, Illinois Wesleyan, Fontbonne, Blackburn College
Style of Play: Building out of the back with tight, controlled passing, occasionally placing the ball into space behind the defense. Our style reflects a combination of players with experience playing in Ireland, England, and Argentina.

Women's Athletic Profile

315 E College Avenue
Greenville, IL 62246
Coach: Bob Johnson
Email: Not Available

NCAA III/NAIA
Panthers/Orange, Black
Phone: (618) 664-1840
Fax:

Estimated # of Women's Soccer Scholarships: None
Style of Play: Aggressive 4-4-2, build from the back, multiple-pass combination play, not a lot of long ball.

Illinois College

Academic Profile

Phone: (217) 245-3000

Jacksonville, IL 62650

Type: 4 Yr.,Private,Liberal Arts **Founded:** 1829
Website: http://www.ic.edu **Religion:** Presbyterian

SAT/ACT/GPA: 20
Student/Faculty Ratio: 15:1
Undergraduate Enrollment: 883
Scholarships/Academic: Yes **Athletic:** No
Expenses by: Year **In State:** $ 15,300
Degrees Conferred: BA, BS
Housing: Yes
Male/Female Ratio: 55:45
Graduate Enrollment: N/A
Financial Aid: Yes
Out of State: $ 15,300
Programs of Study: Accounting, Art, Art Management, Biology, Chemistry, Communications and Theatre, Computer Science, CytoTechnology and Medical Technology, Economics, Education, English, Fine Arts, French, German, History, Interdisciplinary Studies, International Studies, Management Information Systems, Music, Philosophy, Physical Education, Political Science, PreDental, PreEngineering, PreLegal, PreMedical, PreMinisterial, PreNursing, PreOccupational Therapy, PreOptometry, PrePharmacy, PrePhysical Therapy, PreVeterinary Medicine, Psychology, Religious Studies, Sociology, Special Education

Men's Athletic Profile

1101 W College Avenue
Jacksonville, IL 62650
Coach: John Mansholt
Email: Not Available

NCAA III
Blueboys/Navy, White
Phone: (217) 245-3400
Fax: (217) 245-3034

Estimated # of Men's Soccer Scholarships: None
Conference: Midwest Athletic Conference
Program Profile: In the Fall of 1997, we had a new practice goals and we will have a new scoreboard installed for the 1997 season. We have one game field and two practice fields with a natural turf. The playing season is from September through November.
History: Our program began in the Fall of 1985 under head coach Steve Bonner. He was succeeded by John Kelker in the 1989 season. Coach Kelker led IL to their best record in 1990 (9-7) and a conference titles. John Mansholt led IL to their second best record of 7-9-1 and a conference tourney appearances.
Achievements: 1990 Conference Title, 2 All-Midwest players - Seam Emerick and Kevin Peff; IC consistently places players on the first team All-Conference team, year in and year out.
Coaching: John Mansholt, Head Coach since 1992, played as a goalkeeper at Sangamon State University and University of North Carolina at Charlotte. Has a record of 4-10 in 1992, 7-9-1 in 1993, and 3-13 in 1994. Chuck Eguez - Assistant Coach, three years, played at Triton Junior College and Sangamon State.
Camp or Clinic Dates: Not Available
Style of Play: Solid, hard-nosed play. Strong touching all over the field. Ball control with everyone thinking offensively.

Women's Athletic Profile

1101 W College Avenue
Jacksonville, IL 62650
Coach: Brett Berry
Email: Not Available

NCAA III
Lady Blues/Navy Blue, White
Phone: (217) 245-3402
Fax: (217) 245-3398

Estimated # of Women's Soccer Scholarships: None
Conference: Midwest Conference
Program Profile: Women's soccer at Illinois College began in 1991 and has steadily grown into a competitive program. Spacious natural grass facilities for practice and games are located on campus. The program typically attracts about 8-10 new players each year, and most (if not all) are able to contribute at the varsity level. Several junior varsity are also scheduled each season.
History: The year-to-year improvement of the Illinois College women's soccer team reached a new peak in 1995 when the Lady Blues finished 8-8 overall and 4-6 in the South Division of the Midwest Conference. The team won only two varsity games during its first two varsity season, and team's success in the Midwest Conference reflects this improvement.

Achievements: Illinois College has had several of its women soccer players named to the All-Midwest Conference and Academic All-Midwest Conference teams.
Style of Play: Advocates a tight marking style of play that puts a great deal of responsibility in the hands and feet of the midfielders. Will give midfielders the option to make long runs and rely on well-conditioned defenders to cover wide open areas of the field. Program expects a great deal of dedication from athletes. Academics come ahead of athletics at Illinois College but sports play and important role in a campus that affords students the opportunity to compete extensively in the game they love.

Illinois State University

Academic Profile

Normal, IL 61790-2200
Phone: (309) 438-2181

Type: 4 Yr.,Public
Founded: 1857
Website: http://www.infosys.ilstu.edu
Religion: Non-Affiliated
SAT/ACT/GPA: 86018
Housing: Yes
Student/Faculty Ratio: 19-1
Male/Female Ratio: 59:41
Undergraduate Enrollment: 17,703
Graduate Enrollment: 2,578
Scholarships/Academic: Yes **Athletic:** Yes **Financial Aid:** Yes
Expenses by: Year **In State:** $9437 **Out of State:** $ 15,876
Specialty: Education, Business, Applied Science & Technology
Degrees Conferred: BA, BS, BM, B.Ed., BFA, BME, MS, MA
Programs of Study: Accounting, Business Information Systems, Agriculture Science, Computer Science, Graphic Design, Art, Business, Education, Chemistry, Biology, Criminal Justice, Economics, English, Dietetics, Fashion Merchandising, Foreign Languages, International Business, Broadcasting, Journalism, Math, Music, Physical Education, Philosophy, Nursing

Women's Athletic Profile

211 Horton Fieldhouse
Normal, IL 61790-7130
Coach: Pete Kowall
Email: parkwood@ilstu.edu

NCAA I
Redbirds/Red, Black, White
Phone: (309) 438-7074
Fax: (309) 438-3597

Estimated # of Women's Soccer Scholarships: varies
Conference: Missouri Valley
Program Profile: Our facilities include: a locker room, a weight room and an athletic training room. We play our games in a natural field surface.
History: Our program is four years old.
Achievements: 1998 Most Valuable Coach, Coach of the Year; 1998 and 1999 regular season Co-Champions;
Coaching: Pete Kowall, Head Coach. Jackie Billet is assistant coach.
Roster in State: 14 **Out of State:** 9 **Out of Country:** 3
Walk-on/Other: **Graduation %:** 85 **Seniors on Team:** 6
Camp or Clinic Dates: June 19-22 July 23-27
Most Recent Record: 14-2-2
Style of Play: Mixture of ball control and attacking type soccer.

Illinois Wesleyan University

Academic Profile

Bloomington, IL 61702-2900
Phone: (309) 556-3031

Type: 4 Yr.,Private,Liberal Arts
Founded: 1850
Website: http://www.iwu.edu
Religion: Methodist

SAT/ACT/GPA: 126027.8
Housing: Yes
Student/Faculty Ratio: 13:1
Male/Female Ratio: 43/57
Undergraduate Enrollment: 2,000
Graduate Enrollment: N/A
Scholarships/Academic: Yes **Athletic:** No
Financial Aid: Yes
Expenses by: Year **In State:** $ 25,560
Out of State: $ 25,560
Specialty: Premed, Business, Fine Arts, Nursing, Natural Science
Degrees Conferred: BA, BS, BFA, BSCompSci
Programs of Study: Accounting, Art, Biology, Business Administration, Chemistry, Computer Science, Economics, Political Science, Psychology, Religion, Risk Management & Financial Services, Sociology, Spanish, Theatre Arts

Men's Athletic Profile

P.O. Box 2900
Bloomington, IL 61702-2900
Coach: Tony Bankston
Email: bankston@titan.iwu.edu

NCAA III
Fighting Titans/F. Green, White
Phone: (309) 556-3031
Fax: (309) 556-3411

Estimated # of Men's Soccer Scholarships: None
Conference: College Conference of Illinois and Wisconsin
Program Profile: Our program is 13 years old. Our facilities are exceptional. Our outdoor stadium is all grass, 75 yards wide and 120 yards long, lighted and has a seating for 500. Our indoor facility provides option for eleven by eleven dimensions indoors. The season runs from August 20 to November 7 with off-season training January 7 to April 30.
History: The program began in 1986. The first eight years of the program the teams won only 22 games. They have won 21 games in the last 3 seasons under the third year coach, Tony Bankston.
Achievements: Tony Bankston was Coach of the Year in 1955 for the College Conference of Illinois and Wisconsin
Coaching: Tony Backston is the Head Coach. His staff consists of former players ranging from Division I to Division III of the NCAA.
Style of Play: Aggressive, 4-4-2, build from the back, multiple-pass combination play, and don't play a lot of long balls.

Women's Athletic Profile

P.O. Box 2900
Bloomington, IL 61702-2900
Coach: Steve Berry
Email: sberry@titan.iwu.edu

NCAA III
Fighting Titans/F. Green, Black
Phone: (309) 556-3031
Fax: (309) 556-3411

Estimated # of Women's Soccer Scholarships: None
Conference: College Conference of Illinois and Wisconsin
Program Profile: Our program is 13 years old. Our facilities are exceptional. Our outdoor stadium is all grass, 75 x 120 yards, lighted and seats 500. Our indoor facility provides an option for 11 x 11 dimension indoors. The season runs from August 20 to November 7. Our off-season training is from January 7 to April 30.
History: The varsity program began in 1994.
Achievements: Coach Bankston was the 1995 Conference Coach of the Year.

Judson College

Academic Profile

Phone: (847) 695-2500

Elgin, IL 60123

Type: 4 Yr.,Private
Founded: 1963
Website: http://www.judson-il.edu
Religion: Baptist
SAT/ACT/GPA: Open
Housing: Yes

Student/Faculty Ratio: 12:1
Male/Female Ratio: 1:4
Undergraduate Enrollment: 900
Graduate Enrollment: N/A
Scholarships/Academic: Yes **Athletic:** Yes **Financial Aid:** Yes
Expenses by: Sem **In State:** $ 9,000 **Out of State:** $ 9,000
Degrees Conferred: BA, BS
Programs of Study: Anthropology, Architecture, Art, Biblical Studies, Biology, Business, Chemistry, Communication Arts, Communications, Computer Science, Education, English, Graphic Design, History, International Business, Mathematics, Music, Physics, Political Science, PreNursing, Psychology, Science, Sociology, Sport Management, Teacher Education, Theatre, Youth Ministry

Men's Athletic Profile

1151 N State Street
Elgin, IL 60123
Coach: Steve Burke
Email: Not Available

NAIA
Eagles/Royal Blue, White
Phone: (847) 695-2500x3801
Fax: (847) 695-9252

Estimated # of Men's Soccer Scholarships: 18
Conference: Chicagoland Collegiate Athletic Conference
Program Profile: We have a great natural grass field with a new sprinkler system. We also have a new fitness center with weight rooms, locker rooms, etc.
History: The soccer program began at Judson College in 1970. We had the best college program in the country in the 90's. 8 of those 10 years the team had 20 or more wins along with 4 NCCAA National Championships.
Achievements: Northern Illinois Intercollegiate Conference Champions in 190, 1991, 1992, 1993, 1994, & 1995. Seven former players have made it to the pro's.
Coaching: Steve Burke, Head Coach, NSCAA Advanced National Diploma. Adrian Davis - Assistant Coach, English FA Badge. Coewer Coaching Coordinator of Illinois. Worked for English Premier Division team (Norwich City and Chelsea). Founder of School of Soccer, UK's #1 rated training camp. Josh Long - Junior Varsity Coach.
Roster In State: 10 **Out of State:** 3 **Out of Country:** 7
Walk-on/Other: **Graduation %:** 94 **Seniors on Team:** 3
Positions Needed: Goalkeeper, midfield
Camp or Clinic Dates: Not Available
Most Recent Record: 23-5
Schedule: UI Springfield, Dominican, Roberts Wesleyan, Mt. Vernon, Bethel
Style of Play: Hardworking, direct play.

Women's Athletic Profile

1151 N State Street
Elgin, IL 60123-1498
Coach: Marcelo Galvao
Email: Not Available

NAIA
Lady Eagles/Royal, White
Phone: (847) 695-2500
Fax: (847) 695-9252

Estimated # of Women's Soccer Scholarships: None
Conference: CCAC

Knox College

Academic Profile

Phone: (309) 341-7000

Galesburg, IL 61401

Type: 4 Yr.,Private,Liberal Arts
Founded: 1837
Website: http://www.knox.edu
Religion: Non-Affiliated
SAT/ACT/GPA: 1100/24
Housing: Yes

Student/Faculty Ratio: 12:1
Male/Female Ratio: 46:54
Undergraduate Enrollment: 1,195
Graduate Enrollment: N/A
Scholarships/Academic: Yes **Athletic:** No **Financial Aid:** Yes
Expenses by: Year **In State:** $ 24,150 **Out of State:** $ 24,150
Specialty: Liberal Arts
Degrees Conferred: BA, Bachelors Degree
Programs of Study: Accounting, American Studies, Anthropology, Art, Biology, Business, Chemistry, Classics, Computer Science, Economics, Education, English, French, German, History, Humanities, International Languages, Literature, Nursing/Medical Technology, Philosophy, Physics, PreProfessional Programs, Psychology, Social Science, Spanish, Studio Art, Theatre, Women's Studies

Men's Athletic Profile

2 E. South St.
Galesburg, IL 61401
Coach: Sean Jennings
Email: Not Available

NCAA III
Prairie Fire/Purple, Gold
Phone: (309) 341-7508
Fax: (309) 341-7718

Estimated # of Men's Soccer Scholarships: None
Conference: Midwest Conference
Program Profile: We are a competitive Division III soccer program drawing players from several different states and countries. Our emphasis is on developing the student/athlete to their fullest potential both athletically and academically. Thus, we want to attract athletes that are concerned with receiving a top-notch education from a quality Liberal Arts Institution. In addition, we want athletes who are confident in their ability to successfully take our program to the next level. Our season consists of 16 regular season games followed by a conference tournament, with the winner of the conference tournament automatically advancing to the National Tournament. We play on a beautiful grass field, and playing in front of our home crowd is a wonderful experience. Our typical season runs from late August to early November, with off-season workouts and scrimmages in the months of November through May.
History: We began as a club sport in 1966 and became a varsity sports in 1972.
Achievements: Midwest Conference Champion in 1973 and 1988.
Roster In State: 18 **Out of State:** 7 **Out of Country:** 3
ODP State: 0 **Regional:** 0 **National:** 0
Walk-on/Other: 0 **Graduation %:** 99 **Seniors on Team:** 6
Positions Needed: MF/F
Camp or Clinic Dates: Not Available
Most Recent Record: 5-10-1
Schedule: Ripon College, Lake Forest College, Augustana College, Illinois Wesleyan, Beloit College
Style of Play: We play a possession style game with emphasis on a high tempo defense. As long as we have the ball, we can control the game. Once possession is lost, our goal is to force our opponents into making turnovers due to high pressure and intense, physical defense. We want 11 players on offense, and 11 players on defense.

Women's Athletic Profile

2 E. South Street
Galesburg, IL 61401
Coach: Amy Fort
Email: afort@knox.edu

NCAA III
Prairie Fire/Purple, Gold
Phone: (309) 341-7484
Fax: (309) 341-7806

Estimated # of Women's Soccer Scholarships: None
Conference: Midwest Athletic Conference
Program Profile: We have become a force to be reckoned with in the Midwest Conference for women. We are looking forward to maintaining our position in the top of our conference. We play on a natural grass turf at Knox women's soccer field specifically designed for our program. We also have excellent practice fields including 6 practice goals and a soccer barn for bad weather.
History: The soccer program began in 1987. Our best record is 11-5-0 in 1995 and our second best is in 1990 with a 10-4-0 record. We also made the final four of Midwest Conference Tournament in 1995.

Achievements: Lloyd Brodnicki was a regional All-American and Megan Owens was in the top 10 leading scorer in the nation and top 10 leading assist person in the nation
Coaching: Amy Fort, Head Coach. She is a 1993 Grinnell College graduate. She is also head basketball coach. She is assistant professor of Sports Studies. She has a Master of Arts from Fairleigh Dickinson University. She has 4 years collegiate head coaching experience. She holds a National & Advanced National Diploma from NSCAA.
Roster in State: 16 **Out of State:** 15 **Out of Country:** 1
ODP State: 10 **Regional:** 5 **National:** 3
Walk-on/Other: **Graduation %:** 95 **Seniors on Team:** 6
Positions Needed: Goalkeeper, Midfield, Strikers
Camp or Clinic Dates: July 9-13
Most Recent Record: 5-10-0
Schedule: Grinnell College, Lawrence University, Aurora College, Principia College, Rockford College, Lake Forest College, St. Norbert College, Beloit College, Carroll College, Monmouth College
Style of Play: System of play 4-4-2, physical play expected, exercise aggressive finishing and midfield control, always emphasizing defensive tactics.

Lake Forest College

Academic Profile

Lake Forest, IL 60045
Phone: 800-828-4751

Type: 4 Yr.,Private,Liberal Arts
Founded: 1857
Website: http://www.lfc.edu
Religion: Non-Affiliated
SAT/ACT/GPA: None/25
Housing: Yes
Student/Faculty Ratio: 11:1
Male/Female Ratio: 50:50
Undergraduate Enrollment: 1,000
Graduate Enrollment: 200
Scholarships/Academic: Yes **Athletic:** No **Financial Aid:** Yes
Expenses by: Year **In State:** $ 23,600 **Out of State:** $ 23,600
Degrees Conferred: Bachelor of Arts/Science
Programs of Study: Art, Biology, Chemistry, German, History, Philosophy, Business, Spanish, French, Educational, Mathematics, Politics, PreMed, Sociology and Anthropology, Sciences, English, Computer Science, Communications

Men's Athletic Profile

555 Sheridan Road
Lake Forest, IL 60045
Coach: Ed Kositzki
Email: Not Available

NCAA III
Foresters/Red, White, Black
Phone: (847) 735-5285
Fax: (847) 735-6290

Estimated # of Men's Soccer Scholarships: None
Conference: Midwest Collegiate Athletic Conference
Program Profile: Natural turf on field surrounded by woods; beautiful campus.
Achievements: 11 Conference Championships in the last 20 years. NCAA National bid in 1981.
Coaching: Ed Kositzki, Head Coach, has an USSF 'A' license, NSCAA Advanced Certificate, and is the AYSO National Staff Coach.
Style of Play: Control game with explosive scoring transition; 4-4-2.

Women's Athletic Profile

555 N. Sheridan Rd.
Lake Forest, IL 60045
Coach: T.R. Bell
Email: tbell@lfc.edu

NCAA III
Foresters/Red, Black
Phone: (847) 735-6132
Fax: (847) 735-6290

Estimated # of Women's Soccer Scholarships: None
Conference: Midwest Conference
Program Profile: Top notch Division III title on the verge of a National Tournament birth, season runs from late August to mid-November. We have three natural grass soccer fields and a brand new weight room. We share our soccer facilities with the 1998 MLS Cup Champions, Chicago Fire.
History: The Women's Soccer program began in 1986 and has an overall record of 91-30-2. Coach bell has been coaching for three years. Last Conference Championship was in 1989.
Achievements: Won the regular season title in 1995, 1996, and 1998; Conference Champions in 1989; 12 All-Conference players in the past three years.
Coaching: T.R. Bell, Head Coach, in his fourth with the program. Graduate of Lake Forest College where he earned All-Conference honors as a starter on the men's team. Diane Kanney - Assistant Coach, third year. Works closely with the defense and goalkeeping. John Gallagher is also a Assistant Coach.

Roster in State: 5	**Out of State:** 17	**Out of Country:**
ODP State: 12	**Regional:** 5	**National:**
Walk-on/Other: 5	**Graduation %:** 95	**Seniors on Team:** 6

Positions Needed: Striker, Midfield, Goalkeeper
Camp or Clinic Dates: July 10-14, 17-21
Most Recent Record: 5-10-1
Schedule: University of Chicago, Aurora University, Grinnell College, Lawrence University, St. Norbert College, Beloit College, North Park University, North Central College, UW-Whitewater, Carroll College
Style of Play: We play a controlled passing game where every player is involved both defensively and offensively. We like to pressure our opponents into mistakes and then counter on those mistakes quickly.

Lewis University

Academic Profile

Romeoville, IL 60446

Phone: 800-897-9000

Type: 4 Yr.,Private,Liberal Arts		**Founded:** 1933
Website: http://www.lewisu.edu		**Religion:** Catholic
SAT/ACT/GPA: 700+/17+		**Housing:** Yes
Student/Faculty Ratio: 15:1		**Male/Female Ratio:** 50:50
Undergraduate Enrollment: 4,000		**Graduate Enrollment:** 1,000
Scholarships/Academic: Yes	**Athletic:** Yes	**Financial Aid:** Yes
Expenses by: Year	**In State:** $ 19,296	**Out of State:** $ 19,296

Specialty: Accounting, Aviation, Education, Nursing
Degrees Conferred: BA, BS, MBA, MSN, M Ed
Programs of Study: Accounting, Airway Science, Applied Science, Art, Athletic Training, Avionics, Biology, Broadcasting, Business Administration, Chemistry, Communications, Computer Science, Criminal Justice, Economics, Education, English, Finance, History, Journalism, Liberal Arts, Marketing, Mathematics, Music, Nursing, Philosophy, Physics, Political Science, Psychology, Religion, Sociology

Men's Athletic Profile

Route 53
Romeoville, IL 60446
Coach: Evan Fiffles
Email: Not Available

NCAA II
Flyers/Red, White
Phone: (815) 838-5495
Fax: (815) 836-5835

Estimated # of Men's Soccer Scholarships:
Conference: Great Lakes Valley Conference (GLVC)
Program Profile: NCAA Division II program; game field is 120x75 yards, watered, natural grass, seating for 500. Has two practice fields.
History: Program began in 1966; Conference record in the last six years is 49-6-2; ranked top 20 in nation in PAC of the last six years; 3 Region Conference Champs; 2 post-season Conference Champs.
Achievements: 1994 GLVC Champions, 1994 Coach of the Year, Conference Player of the Year in 1993 &1994 - Sean

Seaberg. Since Coach Fiffles has been here (three years) - 12 All-Conference players, 4 All-Midwest players, 1 NSCAA All-American. GLVC Coach of the Year in 1996.
Coaching: Evan Fiffles, Head Coach, USSF "A" License, Olympic Development U-17 Head Coach, Coaching School Staff Instructor, has compiled a three-year record of 39-19-6. Top 20 rankings.
Style of Play: Effective control soccer.

Women's Athletic Profile

Route 53
Romeoville, IL 60441
Coach: Mike Crowe
Email: Not Available

NCAA II
Flyers/Red, White
Phone: (815) 838-0500
Fax:

Estimated # of Women's Soccer Scholarships: None
Conference: Great Lakes Valley Conference
Program Profile: Finished 9th in 1994 poll.

Lincoln College
Academic Profile

Lincoln, IL 62656
Phone: 888-522-5228

Type: 2 Yr.,Private
Founded: 1865
Website: http://www.lincoln.mclean.il.us
Religion: Non-Affiliated
SAT/ACT/GPA: Varies
Housing: Yes
Student/Faculty Ratio: 13:1
Male/Female Ratio: 50:50
Undergraduate Enrollment: 610
Graduate Enrollment: N/A
Scholarships/Academic: Yes **Athletic:** Yes
Financial Aid: Yes
Expenses by: Year **In State:** $ 15,200
Out of State: $ 15,200
Degrees Conferred: Associates
Programs of Study: We are a geared to transfer to four-year colleges or universities. We do not offers majors - we offer courses in English, Math, Sciences, Business, Fine Arts, Political Science, Computers, Criminology

Men's Athletic Profile

300 Keokuk
Lincoln, IL 62656
Coach: Mark Howard
Email: Mhoward@lincolncollege.com

NJCAA
Lynx/Purple, White
Phone: (217) 732-3155
Fax: (217) 732-8859

Estimated # of Men's Soccer Scholarships: Varies
Conference: None
Program Profile: Lincoln College has a new 80 x 120 yd field. They have been nationally ranked for four years consecutively.
History: We play a very competitive schedule. We have sent many players to four-year level. We have been in the national polls for three years in a row now.
Achievements: 13 players have gone on to NCAA Division I schools since 1992, 2 currently professionals. Coach of the Year in 1995, 3rd year in a row when we were nationally ranked.
Coaching: Mark Howard, Head Coach, holds a USSF "B "License, Advanced National Diploma and is an Illinois State Coaches School Staff Instructor. He is in his 8th year as Lincoln College's Head Coach. He earned the NJCAA Region 24 Coach of the Year Award and coach of the year in 1997. Aaron Paskvan is the Assistant Coach, played at Lincoln College from 1991 to 1993 and he was a starter as well as a captain. He was a certified high school referee in Missouri. He is diver for the Lynx earning All-American honors.

Roster In State: 26 **Out of State:** 1 **Out of Country:** 0
ODP State: 3 **Regional:** **National:**
Walk-on/Other: **Graduation %:** 90 **Seniors on Team:** 9
Positions Needed: Forward, Mid, Defense, Goal Keeper
Camp or Clinic Dates: Not Available
Schedule: State Fair, College of Dupage, Belleville, State, Iowa Central, Cloud County

Loyola University - Chicago

Academic Profile

Phone: (773) 508-2560

Chicago, IL 60626

Type: 4 Yr.,Private,Liberal Arts **Founded:** 1870
Website: http://www.loyolaramblers.com **Religion:** Non-Affiliated
SAT/ACT/GPA: Open **Housing:** Yes
Student/Faculty Ratio: 13:1 **Male/Female Ratio:** 40:60
Undergraduate Enrollment: N/A **Graduate Enrollment:** N/A
Scholarships/Academic: Yes **Athletic:** Yes **Financial Aid:** Yes
Expenses by: Year **In State:** $ 25,000 **Out of State:** $ 25,000
Specialty: Jesuit Education, Law, Medical, Philosophy
Degrees Conferred: BA, BS, BSEd, BA (Classics), BBA, BSN, MA, MS, MBA, M.Ed., Ph.D., JD, MDiv, EdD, DMD
Programs of Study: Accounting, Anthropology, Art, Biology, Business & Management, Chemistry, Classics, Communications, Computer Information Systems, Computer Science, Criminal Justice, Economics, Elementary Education, English, French, German, Greek, History, Italian, Latin, Linguistics, Management Information Systems, Marketing, Mathematics, Music, Nursing, Philosophy, Physics, Political Science, PreDentistry, PreLaw, PreMed, PreVet, Psychology, Social Work, Sociology, Spanish, Special Education, Speech, Statistics, Theatre, Theology

Men's Athletic Profile

6525 N Sheridan Rd
Chicago, IL 60626
Coach: Ray O'Connell
Email: Not Available

NCAA I
Ramblers/Maroon, Gold
Phone: (773) 508-2570
Fax: (773) 508-3884

Estimated # of Men's Soccer Scholarships: None
Conference: Midwestern Collegiate Conference
Program Profile: New grass field and soccer facilities in 1996-1997 year.
History: Our program began in 1980; all-time record is 144-154-25.
Achievements: 1991 - O'Connell named MCC Coach of the Year, led 1991 team to their second place, finished in the MCC and a Top Ten ranking in the Midwest Region. Numerous first and second team All-Conference players, 2 Midwest Region players and several professionals.
Coaching: Ray O'Connell, Head Coach for 18 years, USSF "A" License, Division I Ethics Committee representative for the NCAA since 1988 and a member of the NCAA Men's Soccer Tournament Advisory Selection Committee.
Style of Play: An aggressive, attacking style of play.

Women's Athletic Profile

Alumni Gym 6525 N Sheridan Rd
Chicago, IL 60626
Coach: Brendan Eitz
Email: beitz@luc.edu

NCAA I
Ramblers/Maroon, Gold
Phone: (312) 508-2561
Fax: (312) 508-3884

Estimated # of Women's Soccer Scholarships: None
Conference: Midwestern Collegiate Conference
Program Profile: New grass field and soccer facilities for 1996-1997 year.
History: The program began in 1992 as Division I program; all time record in 16-57-3
Achievements: Two all-MICC players in the past 5 years.
Coaching: Brendan Eitz, Head Coach, former Loyola Men's soccer and track standout, licensed USSF coach. Allison Lester - Assistant Coach, former All-American for Notre Dame.

McMurray College

Academic Profile

Jacksonville, IL 62650
Phone: (217) 479-7211

Type: 4 Yr.,Private,Liberal Arts
Founded: 1846
Website: http://www.mac.edu
Religion: Methodist
SAT/ACT/GPA: 16/2.0
Housing: Yes
Student/Faculty Ratio: 12:1
Male/Female Ratio: 1:1
Undergraduate Enrollment: 650
Graduate Enrollment: N/A
Scholarships/Academic: Yes **Athletic:** No **Financial Aid:** Yes
Expenses by: Year **In State:** $ 8,500 **Out of State:** $ 8,500
Specialty: Preprofessional Programs
Degrees Conferred: BA, BS
Programs of Study: Accounting, Art, Biology, Business Administration, Chemistry, Computer Electronics, Computer Science, Criminal Justice, Deaf Studies: Teacher Education, Elementary Education, English, French, History, International Studies, Journalism, Learning Disabilities and Social Emotional Disorders, Management Information Systems, Marketing, Mathematics, Music, Nursing, PreMedicine, PreOccupation Therapy, PrePhysical Therapy, PreVet, Psychology, Religion, Secondary Education, Social Work, Spanish, Sports Management

Men's Athletic Profile

447 East College Avenue
Jacksonville, IL 62650
Coach: Bill Killen
Email: bkillen@mac.edu

NCAA III
Highlanders/Navy, Scarlet
Phone: (217) 479-7154
Fax: (217) 479-7147

Estimated # of Men's Soccer Scholarships: None
Conference: St. Louis Intercollegiate Athletic Association
Program Profile: Natural field in the middle of campus (focus on campus) which measures 120x80 yards. Natural seating along hill-side; electric scoreboard, and European Style Goals.
History: Program began in 1956, celebrated 40 years in 1996. 15 NCAA Tournament appearances: Final Four 2-times and Final Eight 1-time.
Achievements: Conference Champs several times (recently in 1997 season and conference playOff champs); Coach of the Year several times; several players drafted NPSL and NEISL.
Coaching: Bill Killen, Head Coach, USSF National 'A' license, FIFA International Youth License, USSF National Staff Coach over 20 years, former State Coach of several states, State and Regional ODP Coach. David Geffard - Student Assistant Coach.
Style of Play: Ball possession - play ball wide and get behind opposition defense. High intensity with a smooth transition from defense to attack.

Women's Athletic Profile

447 East College
Jacksonville, IL 62650-9982
Coach: Greg Walter
Email: coachgwalter@aol.com

NCAA III
Highlanders/Royal Blue, Scarlet
Phone: (217) 479-7211
Fax: (217) 479-7147

Estimated # of Women's Soccer Scholarships: None
Conference: St. Louis Intercollegiate Athletic Conference (SLIAC)
Program Profile: Our team plays in locations all across the mid-west in preparation for the conference season. Young program that is looking and building for the future.
History: Our program began in 1991. We have been competitive within the Conference. Our team reached the Tournament Championship game in 1998.
Coaching: Greg Walter Head Coach
Roster in State: 13 **Out of State:** 5 **Out of Country:**
Walk-on/Other: **Graduation %:** 99 **Seniors on Team:** 3
Positions Needed: ALL
Camp or Clinic Dates: Not Available
Most Recent Record: 4-13-0
Schedule: Webster, Principia, Mayville, Westminster, Blackburn, Fontbonne, Greenville
Style of Play: Aggressive to all balls.

McKendree College

Academic Profile

Phone: 800-232-7228

Lebanon, IL 62254

Type: 4 Yr.,Private,Liberal Arts
Founded: 1828
Website: http://www.mckendree.edu
Religion: United Methodist
SAT/ACT/GPA: 20/2.5
Housing: Yes
Student/Faculty Ratio: 14:1
Male/Female Ratio: 40:60
Undergraduate Enrollment: 1,883
Graduate Enrollment: N/A
Scholarships/Academic: Yes **Athletic:** Yes **Financial Aid:** Yes
Expenses by: Year **In State:** $ 16,100 **Out of State:** $ 16,100
Specialty: Business, Education, Computer Science
Degrees Conferred: BA, BS, BBA, BFA, BSEd, BSN
Programs of Study: Accounting, Art, Athletic Training, Biology, Business, Chemistry, Computer Science, Education, Economics/Finance, History, International Relations, Mathematics, Music, Management, Marketing, Medicine, Occupational Therapy, PreDentistry, PreLaw, PreMed, PreOptometry, PreVet, Sociology, Religious Studies, Speech Communications

Men's Athletic Profile

701 College Road
Lebanon, IL 62254
Coach: Tim Strange
Email: tstrange@atlas.mckendree.edu

NAIA
Bearcats/Purple, White
Phone: (618) 537-4411
Fax: (618) 537-6496

Estimated # of Men's Soccer Scholarships: 7.5
Conference: American Midwest Conference
Program Profile: We play on a grass field that seats 250 and measures 75x110. We also have a fitness center and locker rooms. We play a fall season.
History: Program began around 1970's; we have had 2 Regional Final Games in the last 4 years and have be rated as high as 17 in the nation and 4th in the nation in the 80's.
Achievements: Tim Henson - Midwest Regional Player of the Week and pro soccer indoor with St. Louis; Matt Craig - Midwest Regional Player of the Week; 1996 rated 17th in the nation; 1997 24th in the nation; Midwest Regional Appearance in 1997; 2 Regional Final Tournament games.
Coaching: Tim Strange, Head Coach, SLU four years soccer player, "F" State License. Tim Henson - Assistant Coach,

responsible for goalkeeping; Midwest Regional Team, EISL player draft. Jason Mathenia - Assistant Coach, EISL player draft.

Roster In State: 15 **Out of State:** 10 **Out of Country:** 4
ODP State: 8 **Regional:** 3 **National:**
Walk-on/Other: many **Graduation %:** 75 **Seniors on Team:** 8
Positions Needed: 2 Defenders, Sweeper, Stopper, Wing Midfield, Forward
Camp or Clinic Dates: Not Available
Most Recent Record: 12-10
Schedule: University of Illinois-Springfield, Quincy, University of Southern Indiana, Lindenwood, Columbia, Harris Stowe
Style of Play: Slow build target players; 4-4-2 or 3-5-2 attacking style.

Women's Athletic Profile

701 College Road
Lebanon, IL 62254
Coach: Tim Strange
Email: tstrange@atlas.mckendree.edu

NAIA
Bearcats/Purple, White
Phone: (618) 537-4481
Fax: (618) 537-6496

Estimated # of Women's Soccer Scholarships: 7.5
Conference: American Midwest Conference
Program Profile: We play on a natural grass field, known as Hypes Field and has 500 seats. Our field is 75 x 110.
History: The program began in 1994.
Achievements: We have had one All-American, Roxie Simpson and we made it to the finals of our Regional tournament.
Coaching: Tim Strange, Head Coach. Staci Dowdy and Tim Henson are Assistant Coaches.
Roster in State: 19 **Out of State:** 6 **Out of Country:** 0
ODP State: 7 **Regional:** 2 **National:**
Walk-on/Other: **Graduation %:** 80 **Seniors on Team:** 6
Positions Needed: Forward, Sweeper, Midfield
Camp or Clinic Dates: Not Available
Most Recent Record: 14-5-2
Schedule: Lindinwood, St. Ambrose, Graceland, Park University, University of Southern Indiana, William Woods
Style of Play: Attacking style, 4-4-2, ball wide, and target players.

Millikin University

Academic Profile

Phone:

Decatur, IL 62522

Type: 4 Yr.,Private **Founded:** 1901
Website: http://www.millikin.edu **Religion:** Presbyterian
SAT/ACT/GPA: 880+/21+ **Housing:** No
Student/Faculty Ratio: 15:1 **Male/Female Ratio:** 45:55
Undergraduate Enrollment: 1,840 **Graduate Enrollment:** N/A
Scholarships/Academic: Yes **Athletic:** No **Financial Aid:** Yes
Expenses by: Year **In State:** $ 15,800 **Out of State:** $ 15,800
Specialty: Nursing
Degrees Conferred: BA, BFA, BS, BSN, BMus
Programs of Study: Accounting, Agricultural Business, Automotive Technologies, Business Administration/Commerce/Management, Child Care, Criminal Justice, Drafting and Design, Legal Secretarial Studies, Liberal Arts, General Studies, Science

Men's Athletic Profile

1184 W Main Street
Decatur, IL 62522
Coach: Ryan Lakin
Email: rlakin@mail.millikin.edu

NCAA III
Big Blue/Blue, White
Phone: (217)-424-3607
Fax: (217) 424-6629

Estimated # of Men's Soccer Scholarships: None
Conference: CCIW
Program Profile: We play on a natural field at the moment but soon we will be playing in a stadium with brand new weight room, indoor track, and indoor playing surface. The field will be ready in 2001.
History: We have started a re-building of a tradition.
Achievements: Ryan Lakin CCIW Men's Coach of the Year 1998 and 1999.
Coaching: Ryan Lakin our Head Coach has a USSF "B" license and Tim Gira as the Assistant Coach with a USSF "D" license.
Roster In State: 20 **Out of State:** 1 **Out of Country:**
Walk-on/Other: **Graduation %:** 100 **Seniors on Team:** 4
Positions Needed: All
Camp or Clinic Dates: June 11-15
Most Recent Record: 11-4-2
Schedule: Wheaton College, Rockford College, IBC, Calvin College, Beloit College

Women's Athletic Profile

1184 W. Main
Decatur, IL 62522
Coach: Ryan Lakin
Email: rlakin@mail.millikin.edu

NCAA III
Big Blue/Blue, White
Phone: (217) 424-6344
Fax: (217) 420-6629

Estimated # of Women's Soccer Scholarships: None
Conference: CCIW
Program Profile: We will be getting a brand new stadium in fall of 2001, along with a new weight room, indoor track, and indoor playing surface.
History: We are going into our 4th year as a varsity program. We are looking for student athletes willing to contribute to building a tradition.
Coaching: Ryan Lakin is our Head Coach with a USSF "B" Nation License. Tim Gira is the Assistant Coach with a USSF "D" License.
Roster in State: 17 **Out of State:** 1 **Out of Country:**
Walk-on/Other: **Graduation %:** 100 **Seniors on Team:** 4
Positions Needed: All
Camp or Clinic Dates: June 11-15
Most Recent Record: 7-12
Schedule: Wheaton College, St. Ambrose, Elmhurst College, IBC, Rockford

Monmouth College

Academic Profile

Phone: (309)456-2322

Monmouth, IL 61462

Type: 4 Yr.,Private,Liberal Arts
Website: http://www.monm.edu
SAT/ACT/GPA: 18/2.5
Student/Faculty Ratio: 14:1
Founded: 1853
Religion: Presbyterian
Housing: Yes
Male/Female Ratio: 47:53

Undergraduate Enrollment: 1060
Graduate Enrollment: N/A
Scholarships/Academic: Yes
Athletic: No
Financial Aid: Yes
Expenses by: Year
In State: $26,550
Out of State:
Specialty: Liberal Arts
Degrees Conferred: BA
Programs of Study: Art, Biology, Chemistry, Classics, Communication/Theatre Arts, Education, English, Environmental Science, Government, History, Math/Computer Science, Modern Languages, Music, Philosophy, Physical Education, Physics, Political Economy & Commerce, Psychology, Sociology, Women's Studies

Men's Athletic Profile

700 E Broadway
Monmouth, IL 61462
Coach: Rue Carthew
Email: kathy@monm.edu

NCAA III
Fighting Scots/Crimson, White
Phone: (309) 457-2176
Fax: (309) 457-2168

Estimated # of Men's Soccer Scholarships: None
Conference: Midwest Athletic Conference, South Division
Program Profile: Matches are played at Peacock Memorial Athletic Park, a 1 year old facility. Playing surface is natural grass.
History: Program began in 1972.
Achievements: 31 All-conference selections.
Coaching: Rue Carthew, Head Coach; ten years professional club soccer player in England; hometown - Manchester, England.
Roster In State: 24
Out of State: 0
Out of Country: 0
Walk-on/Other:
Graduation %: N/A
Seniors on Team: 2
Most Recent Record: 7-8-1

Women's Athletic Profile

700 East Broadway
Monmouth, IL 61462
Coach: TBA
Email: kathy@monm.edu

NCAA III
Fighting Scots/Red, White
Phone: (309) 457-2176
Fax: (309) 457-2168

Estimated # of Women's Soccer Scholarships: None
Conference: Midwest Athletic Conference
Program Profile: Matches are played at 1 year old field at Peacock Memorial Athletic Park. Surface is natural grass
History: The varsity program began in 1994 with a record of 0-16. The 1995 record was 0-16, in 1996 record was 3-12-1.
Achievements: 1998 - first winning season. 8 All-Conference members.
Roster in State: 22
Out of State: 3
Out of Country: 0
Walk-on/Other:
Graduation %:
Seniors on Team: 12
Camp or Clinic Dates: Not Available
Most Recent Record: 5-11-0

North Central College

Academic Profile

Naperville, IL 60566
Phone: 630-637-5800

Type: 4 Yr.,Private,Liberal Arts
Founded: 1861
Website: http://www.noctrl.edu
Religion: Methodist

SAT/ACT/GPA: 820/20
Student/Faculty Ratio: 14:1
Undergraduate Enrollment: 1,300
Scholarships/Academic: Yes **Athletic:** No
Expenses by: Year **In State:** $ 16,326
Degrees Conferred: BA, BS, MA, MS, MBA
Housing: Yes
Male/Female Ratio: 52:48
Graduate Enrollment: 1,200
Financial Aid: Yes
Out of State: $ 16,326
Programs of Study: 36 Academic Majors, 6 Graduate Degrees; Business Management, Communications, Computer Sciences, Physical Sciences, Psychology, Social Sciences

Men's Athletic Profile

30 North Brainard
Naperville, IL 60566
Coach: Jason Hunter
Email: jahunter@noctrl.edu
NCAA III
Cardinals/Red, White
Phone: (630) 637-5516
Fax: (630) 637-5521

Estimated # of Men's Soccer Scholarships: None
Conference: College Conference of Illinois and Wisconsin
Program Profile: New 6000 seat stadium for conference games and tournaments, with 115x70 lights. We have a second field for non conference games. It has been newly sodded 110x65, and has team shelters, a score table, and a scoreboard.
History: Program since 1980. We expect this program to compete at the Regional and National level.
Achievements: Coach of the Year- Commonwealth Conference in 1998.
Coaching: Jason Hunter is the Head Coach.
Roster In State: 18 **Out of State:** 8 **Out of Country:** 0
ODP State: 12 **Regional:** 6 **National:** 2
Walk-on/Other: **Graduation %:** 90 **Seniors on Team:** 4
Positions Needed: Strikers, Mids
Camp or Clinic Dates: July 8-12
Schedule: Wheaton, Augustana, Carthage, Millikin, Lake Forest, Elmhurst
Style of Play: Possession style on the ground, we rule the air.

Women's Athletic Profile

30 N Brainard Street
Naperville, IL 60566
Coach: Jason Hunter
Email: jahunter@noctrl.edu
NCAA III
Cardinals/Red, White
Phone: (630) 637-5516
Fax: (630) 637-5521

Estimated # of Women's Soccer Scholarships: None
Conference: CCIW
Program Profile: New 7000 seat stadium for conference games and tournaments, with 115x70 lights. We have a second field for non conference games. It has been newly sodded 110x65, and has team shelters, a score table, and a scoreboard.
History: Program began in 1995.
Achievements: Coach of the Year- Commonweatlh Conference in 1998.
Coaching: Jason Hunter is the Head Coach.
Roster in State: 19 **Out of State:** 6 **Out of Country:** 0
ODP State: 14 **Regional:** 4 **National:** 1
Walk-on/Other: 0 **Graduation %:** N/A **Seniors on Team:** 3
Positions Needed: Keeper, Strikers
Camp or Clinic Dates: June 24-28
Schedule: Wheaton, Millikin, Lake Forest, Elmhurst, Illinois Wesleyan, Carthage, Augustana

Style of Play: Possession style on the ground, we rule the air.

North Park University
Academic Profile

Chicago, IL 60625
Phone: 800-888-6728

Type: 4 Yr.,Private,Liberal Arts
Website: http://www.northpark.com
SAT/ACT/GPA: 860/18/Upper 1/2
Student/Faculty Ratio: 15:1
Undergraduate Enrollment: 1,700
Scholarships/Academic: Yes
Athletic: No
Expenses by: Year
In State: $ 20,200
Degrees Conferred: 35
Founded: 1891
Religion: Evangelical Covenant
Housing: Yes
Male/Female Ratio: 45:55
Graduate Enrollment: 500
Financial Aid: Yes
Out of State:
Programs of Study: Accounting, Anthropology, Art, Biblical Studies, Biology, Business Administration, Chemistry, Clinical Laboratory, Science, Communication Arts, Constructed Majors, Economics, Education, English, Finance, General Science, History, International Business, Marketing, Math, Music, Nursing, Philosophy, PE, Physics, Politics and Government, Psychology, Social Studies, Sociology, Spanish, Sports Medicine, Swedish, Youth Ministry

Men's Athletic Profile

3225 W Foster Avenue
Chicago, IL 60625
Coach: John Born
Email: jborn@northpark.edu
NCAA III
Vikings/Royal, Gold
Phone: (773) 244-5771
Fax: (773) 244-4952

Estimated # of Men's Soccer Scholarships: None
Conference: Collegiate Conference of Illinois and Wisconsin
Program Profile: In June of 2000, unveiled $2.5 million soccer facility. The surface includes "Field turf" a synthetic grass blade that has been approved by FIFA. 2000 was a rebuilding year as team consistently started 7 freshmen. This was Coach Born's first recruiting class at North Park.
History: The program has been around since 1978. It has been mostly mediocre. Now with the arrival of Coach John Born and the new facility, the program has quickly risen. In his first year at NPU, the team was the 6th most improved team in the country. This past season they were regionally ranked for 5 weeks.
Achievements: Coach John Born 1996 Lake Michigan Coach of the Year.
Coaching: Coach John Born, 2nd year at NPU-6 total at college level. He has rebuilt 2 programs first at Milwaukee School of engineering where he inherited a team that won 3 in three seasons. His last 2 years there they won 24 games. At North Park, one year prior to his arrival the team won 1 game. In 2000 with one recruiting class the team won 10 games and was regionally ranked.
Roster In State: 6
Out of State: 11
Out of Country: 3
ODP State: 5
Regional: 0
National: 0
Walk-on/Other: 0
Graduation %: 93
Seniors on Team: 4
Positions Needed: Defense
Camp or Clinic Dates: Not Available
Most Recent Record: 10-7-0
Schedule: Wheaton, Puget Sound, Centre, UW-Whitewater, Hope, Millikin, Transylvania
Style of Play: Team oriented, building through the back-possession game.

Women's Athletic Profile

3225 W Foster Avenue
Chicago, IL 60625
Coach: Julie Lamm
Email: sbrunk@northpark.edu
NCAA III
Vikings/Royal Blue, Gold
Phone: (773) 244-6251
Fax: (773) 244-4952

Estimated # of Women's Soccer Scholarships:
Conference: College Conference of Illinois and Wisconsin
Program Profile: Field's measurement is 65x110 yards natural grass surface; training camp begins in August; season runs through November. Our women's team outdraw most of the other teams on campus, we get great for support. Gymnasium has been completely refurbished.
History: Program began in the Fall of 1994 with a record of 8-4. The team compiled a record of 9-6-1 in 1997 and 10-7-1 in 1996.
Achievements: Players on both of our teams have played with "all-star" team overseas. 1997 NCAA All-Academic Regional Selection was Alisa Bredenstien.
Style of Play: Dictated by new players each year. usually finesse-oriented, short game, stressing simplicity in attacking, going all out and finishing.

Northern Illinois University

Academic Profile

Phone: 773-583-4050

Dekalb, IL 60115

Type: 4 Yr.,Public,
Website: http://www.niu.edu
SAT/ACT/GPA: 22/3.0
Student/Faculty Ratio: 17:1
Undergraduate Enrollment: 15,781
Scholarships/Academic: Yes
Athletic: Yes
Expenses by: Year
In State: $ 11,300
Specialty: Business, Education
Degrees Conferred: BA, BS, BSBA
Founded: 1895
Religion: Non-Denominational
Housing: Yes
Male/Female Ratio: 45:55
Graduate Enrollment: 6,471
Financial Aid: Yes
Out of State: $ 13,730
Programs of Study: College of Business, College of Education, College of Engineering and Engineering Technology, College of Liberal Arts and Sciences, College of Professional Studies, College of Visual and Performing Arts

Men's Athletic Profile

224 Evans Field House
DeKalb, IL 60115
Coach: Frank Hovart
Email: fhovart@niu.edu

NCAA I
Huskies/Cardinal, Black
Phone: (815) 753-1372
Fax: (815) 753-7700

Estimated # of Men's Soccer Scholarships: 5
Conference: Mid-American Conference
Program Profile: We are in the top ten in the Midwest region. We have a 2,000 seating facility with natural grass, 2 practice fields.
History: The program began in 1960. Our 1973 team was a NCAA Qualifier; 1990 Midwest Coach of the Year; 1997 Nations #2 point man (52 pts); All-Americans in 1974, 19975, 1984, 1970, 19971, 19976, 1989, 1990 & 1991; Midwest rankings in top ten in 1998, 1997, 1994, 1993, 1991, 1990 & 1989.
Achievements: 1989 & 1990 Conference champs, Peter Mamons; 1974 & 1975 1st team All-American, Markus Roy in 1989 & 1991; 3-time Academic All-American; draft picks, Paul Wenson in 1976 by NASL, Peter Manos in 1976 by NASL, willy Roy, Jr. in 1991 by MLS, Markus Roy in 1992 by MSL and NPSL, and Karten Roy in 1992 by NPSL.
Coaching: William Roy, Head Coach, coached 1981-1984 Chicago Sting NASL Championships teams. Former All-Pro and US National Team Player. He was named US Hall of Fame and holds USSF National Coaching License. Karstein Roy, Assistant Coach, holds USSF National Coaching License, US Olympic Festival Participant, and Illinois ODP Staff Coach.
Style of Play: European Style of ball possession with offensive attacking.

Women's Athletic Profile

221 Evans Field House
DeKalb, IL 60115
Coach: Frank Horvat
Email: fhorvart@niu.edu

NCAA I
Huskies/Cardinal Red, Black
Phone: (815) 753-9535
Fax: (815) 753-9540

Estimated # of Women's Soccer Scholarships: None
Conference: Mid-American Conference
Program Profile: We have one of the best soccer facilities in the Midwest with a natural grass field that has a 115 yards x 75 yards with a 2,000 seating capacity.
History: Program began in 1993, finishing 7-10-0. Squad took next step forward in 1994, compiling 10-10-0 record, but breakthrough season came in 1995, when NIU went 11-6-2, finished year ranked ninth in the Great Lakes Region, and advanced to MCC semifinals. The 1995 unit defeated regional powers Evansville and Northwestern, both on the road, and tied defending Big East Champ, St. John's, while compiling unbeaten 8-0-2 home record.
Achievements: 1997 MAC Champions; Coach of the Year; MAC Player of the Year; 2 1st Team All-Americans.
Coaching: Frank Horvat, Head Coach since 1993 and was the Huskies first women's coach; as head coach of NIU Huskies , he led the team to a 10-10-0 record in only the program's second season. Derek Niepomnik - Assistant Coach.
Style of Play: Possessive through the midfield and then attack from the wings. We have a very technically sound midfield.

Northwestern University

Academic Profile

Evanston, IL 60208

Phone: 847-491-7271

Type: 4 Yr.,Private,Liberal Arts,Engineering
Website: http://www.nusports.com
SAT/ACT/GPA: Depends on school
Student/Faculty Ratio: 10:1
Undergraduate Enrollment: 7,600
Scholarships/Academic: No
Athletic: Yes
Expenses by: Year
In State: $ 30,000

Founded: 1851
Religion: Non-Affiliated
Housing: Yes
Male/Female Ratio: 49:51
Graduate Enrollment: 6,100
Financial Aid: Yes
Out of State: $ 30,000

Specialty: Engineering, Journalism, Biology, English, Mathematics
Degrees Conferred: BA, BS, MS, MA, Ph.D.
Programs of Study: African-American Studies, Anthropology, Applied Mathematics, Art, Art History, Asian Studies, Astronomy, Biological Science, Chemistry, Classic, English, Environmental Science, Computer Science, Dance, Economics, Engineering, Geography, Geological Science, History, International Studies, Italian, Journalism, Music, Music Education, Neuroscience, Philosophy, Physics, Political Science, Psychology, Religion, Secondary Education, Sociology, Theatre

Men's Athletic Profile

1501 Central Street
Evanston, IL 60208
Coach: Michael Kunert
Email: c-johnson6@northwestern.edu

NCAA I
Wildcats/Purple, White
Phone: (847) 491-7503
Fax: (847) 491-8818

Estimated # of Men's Soccer Scholarships:
Conference: Big 10 Conference
Program Profile: NU has a three year old complex that is hard to beat. Perfect playing surface with a view of the lake and the city of Chicago in the background. Sponsored fully by adidas and ready to become a serious program!!
History: Program started in 1980, first coach was Bob Kroha, Kunert became head coach in 1981.
Achievements: 15 All-Big 10 selections, 107 Academic Big Tens.
Coaching: Head Coach Mike Kunert. Assistant Coaches Mike Cornell and William Codd.

Roster In State: 8 **Out of State:** 6 **Out of Country:** 0
ODP State: 0 **Regional:** 0 **National:** 0
Walk-on/Other: 0 **Graduation %:** 100 **Seniors on Team:** 6
Camp or Clinic Dates: July 22- July 27
Most Recent Record: 0-17-1
Schedule: Indiana, Penn State, Ohio State, Michigan State, Michigan, Wisconsin, Marquette, UIC, Univ. of Wisc Milwaukee, Univ. of Wisc Green Bay
Style of Play: Very technical style 4-4-2, team mostly waits for counter attack opportunities.

Women's Athletic Profile

1501 Central Street
Evanston, IL 60208
Coach: Jenny Haigh
Email: nusoccer@aol.com

NCAA I
Wildcats/Purple, Black
Phone: (847) 467-3151
Fax: (847) 467-1406

Estimated # of Women's Soccer Scholarships:
Conference: Big Ten Conference
Program Profile: Fully-funded program, a two year old $3 million dollar complex (soccer/field hockey) adjacent to Lake Michigan, beautiful grass field with two adjacent fields.
History: Our program began in1994. In 1996 was third year of the program and won NCAA Tournament. 1997 was Big Ten Conference Finalist and in 1998 NCAA Sweet Sixteen and NSCAA ranked #14.
Achievements: Great Lakes Region Coach of the Year in 1996 & 1998; 15 All-Big Ten selections; Big Ten Rookie of the Year in 1996; Big Ten Player of the Year in 1998; 50 Academic All-Big Ten Selections and 6 All-Region selections.
Style of Play: "Make haste slowly" By: Lincoln

Olivet Nazarene University

Academic Profile

Phone: 800-648-1463

Kankakee, IL 60901

Type: 4 Yr.,Private,Liberal Arts **Founded:** 1907
Website: http://www.olivet.edu **Religion:** Nazarene
SAT/ACT/GPA: 18/2.0 **Housing:** Yes
Student/Faculty Ratio: 17:1 **Male/Female Ratio:** 43:57
Undergraduate Enrollment: 1,800 **Graduate Enrollment:** 600
Scholarships/Academic: Yes **Athletic:** Yes **Financial Aid:** Yes
Expenses by: Year **In State:** $ 16,424 **Out of State:** $ 16,424
Specialty: Business, Education
Degrees Conferred: BA, BS, MBA
Programs of Study: Accounting, Art, Athletic Training, Biblical Studies, Biology, Botany, Business Administration, Chemistry, Child Education, Christian Education, Church Music, Computer Science, Dietetics, Economics and Finance, Education, Engineering, English, Environmental Science, French, Fashion Merchandising, Geology, History, Mathematics, Medical Technology, Music, Nursing, Philosophy and Religion, Physical Education, Physical Science, Psychology, Religion, Romance Languages, Social Justice, Social Science, Social Work, Sociology, Spanish, Speech Communication, Theology, Zoology

Men's Athletic Profile

Box 592
Kankakee, IL 60901
Coach: Tom Knowles
Email: tknowles@olivet.edu

NAIA
Tigers/Purple, Gold
Phone: (815) 928-5141
Fax: (815) 939-7933

Estimated # of Men's Soccer Scholarships: N/A
Conference: CCAC
Program Profile: Facilities include outstanding natural turf field, new locker rooms and athletic complex. 20 game season. 1993 and 1994 best 2 seasons in the history of the team. Were 5-1 in conference play this year.
History: Program began at club level in 1977. Best Record ever in 1993, and 1994. Became a varsity sports in 1979.
Achievements: 2 NCCAA Academic All-Americans this year, 2 NAIA Academic All-Americans in 1998, 1 NCCAA 2nd team All-American in 1998.
Coaching: Larry C. Cary, Head Coach, entering thirteen years with the program. Chris Longtin - Assistant Coach.

Women's Athletic Profile

One University Ave
Bourbonnais, IL 60914
Coach: Bill Bahr
Email: bbahr@olivet.edu

NAIA
Tigers/Purple, Gold
Phone: (815) 928-5464
Fax: (815) 939-5068

Estimated # of Women's Soccer Scholarships: 5.5
Conference: CCAC
Program Profile: 2 game fields 120 x 80, 110 x 70, one 40 x 40 grid. 2 gymnasiums, turf room, 2 full weight rooms, 1 cardio room with the latest equipment, and 2 training rooms.
History: Program began in 1996 with Larry Cary as the Head Coach for both the men's and women's program. The women received its 1st full time coach in the fall of 1999 with Bill Bahr and its 1st part time coach in the winter of 2000.
Coaching: Head Coach- Bill Bahr. Assistant Coach- Justin Crew.
Roster in State: 9 **Out of State:** 14 **Out of Country:** 0
Walk-on/Other: **Graduation %:** 100 **Seniors on Team:** 5
Camp or Clinic Dates: Not Available
Most Recent Record: 4-13-1
Schedule: Trinity International, St. Francis, St. Xavier, Grace College, Robert Morris, Dominican
Style of Play: Play a possession style of soccer using either a 4-4-2 or 3-3-4.

Principia College

Academic Profile

Elsah, IL 62028
Phone: (618) 374-2131

Type: 4 Yr.,Private,Liberal Arts
Website: http://www.prin.edu
SAT/ACT/GPA: 910/2.0
Student/Faculty Ratio: 8:1
Undergraduate Enrollment: 550
Scholarships/Academic: Yes **Athletic:** No
Expenses by: Year **In State:** $ 21,500
Specialty: Liberal Arts
Degrees Conferred: BA, BS

Founded: 1898
Religion: Christian Science
Housing: Yes
Male/Female Ratio: 40:60
Graduate Enrollment: N/A
Financial Aid: Yes
Out of State: $ 21,500

Programs of Study: Liberal Arts and Sciences, Business and Education, Computer Science, Communications, Earth Science, Economics, Education, Engineering Science, Environmental Studies, Mass Communications, Philosophy, Physics, Religion, Political Science

Men's Athletic Profile

1 Maybeck Place
Elsah, IL 62028
Coach: Seth Johnson
Email: scj@prin.edu

NCAA III
Panthers/Blue, Gold
Phone: (618) 374-5025
Fax: (618) 374-5221

Estimated # of Men's Soccer Scholarships: None
Conference: St. Louis Intercollegiate Athletic Conference
Program Profile: We play on excellent facilities with natural turf and a seating capacity of 1,000. Fall is the main season, while spring season starts April & May and consists of five games.
History: Our program began as club in 1963. Varsity began in 1965. Original member of the NAIA; 1980 member of the NCAA Division III; member of the Prairei College Conference.
Achievements: Coach has won Conference of the Year; 10 Conference Titles; 1 All-American; 12 All-Midwest; two professional players.
Coaching: Seth Johnson, Head Coach at Principia since 1984, graduated from Williams in 1979, was an assistant coach at Williams from 1979 to 1983, Advanced National License with NSCAA, and National Soccer Coaches Association of America. Vitalis Atience, Assistant Coach.

Roster In State: 2	**Out of State:** 22	**Out of Country:** 4
Walk-on/Other:	**Graduation %:** 100	**Seniors on Team:** 3

Positions Needed: Back, Forward 4-5players
Camp or Clinic Dates: Not Available
Most Recent Record: 7-10-2
Schedule: Ohio Wesleyan Univ., Washington Univ., DePaul Univ., Kalamazoo College, Webster Univ.
Style of Play: Creative, attacking oriented, combine man-to-man and zone defense, set system to players; have played in recent years 4-4-2, 3-5-2 and 3-4-3 formations.

Women's Athletic Profile

1 Maybeck Place
Elsah, IL 62028
Coach: Lee Ellis
Email: lee@prin.edu

NCAA III
Panthers/Blue, White
Phone: (618) 374-5030
Fax: (618) 374-5221

Estimated # of Women's Soccer Scholarships: None
Conference: St. Louis Intercollegiate Athletic Conference
Program Profile: Nicole Hayashi was named Honorable Mention all-Conference, 1998 SLIA Newcomer of the Year Lauren Gaster. SLIAC Tournament Championships in 1991, 1993, 1994, 1995 & 1997, SLIAC Conference Championships in 1990, 1991, 1993, 1994 & 1995.
History: Principia formed the first small college women's soccer program in Illinois and one of the first in the country in 1983. Since 1991, and most recently in 1997, Principia has won five SLIAC conference Championships The team also won a record 26 straight conference games between 1993-1996.
Achievements: 1997 Coach of the Year (SLIAC); 1997 SLIAC Tournament Champions; 1997 NSCAA Team Academic Award (second year in a row). Junior, Nicole Gervais has been recognized twice as SLIAC Conference Player of the Year. 1997 and 1998. She was also voted Newcomer of the Year in 1997. Sophomore, Lauren Gaster received SLIAC Newcomer of the Year Honors in 1998
Lee Ellis, Head Coach has been awarded conference Coach of the Year honors in 1997-1999.
Coaching: Lee Ellis, Head Coach fifth year at the helm of Principia's program. He posted a career record of 49-27-4, won a SLIAC Tournament championship and twice received Coach of the Year Honors. His prior experience includes coaching stints at SUNY College of Technology and Utica College of Syracuse University. He holds an Advanced National soccer Coaching Diploma from the National Coaches Association of America. He also has an M.S. in Counseling Psychology and an M.B.A in Management. Jill Horton - Assistant Coach, responsible for Goalkeepers. She is entering her fourth season with the program. A graduate of Principia and a former varsity athlete.

Roster in State: 2	**Out of State:** 18	**Out of Country:**
Walk-on/Other:	**Graduation %:** 100	**Seniors on Team:**

Style of Play: Attacking, pressure defense - Fun! Full throttle attacking.

Quincy University

Academic Profile

Quincy, IL 62301

Phone: 217-228-5210

Type: 4 Yr.,Private,Liberal Arts
Website: http://www.quincy.edu
SAT/ACT/GPA: 950/20/2.0
Student/Faculty Ratio: 12:1
Undergraduate Enrollment: 1,300
Scholarships/Academic: Yes
Athletic: Yes
Expenses by: Year
In State: $ 18,300
Specialty: Business, Education
Degrees Conferred: BA, BS, MA, MBA

Founded: 1860
Religion: Catholic - Franciscan
Housing: Yes
Male/Female Ratio: 50:50
Graduate Enrollment: 150
Financial Aid: No
Out of State: $ 18,300

Programs of Study: Accounting, Art Biology, Business Administration, Chemistry, Communications, Computer Science, Education, English, Finance, History, Humanities, Human Resources, Information Science, International Studies, Management, Marketing, Mathematics, Medical Technology, Music, Music Business, Philosophy, Political Science, Psychology, Religious Education, Social Science, Special Education, Sports Management, Theology

Men's Athletic Profile

1800 College Avenue
Quincy, IL 62301
Coach: Jack Mackenzie
Email: mackeja@quincy.edu

NCAA I
Hawks/Brown, White
Phone: (217) 228-5591
Fax: (217) 228-5473

Estimated # of Men's Soccer Scholarships: None
Conference: Mid-Continent Conference
Program Profile: The North Campus Field is 120 x 70 yards with Blue Grass, lighting, and has a seating capacity of 2,000.
History: Since 1964, the Hawks have won 378 games and 2 NAIA National Championships. Entry in NCAA was in 1984.
Achievements: Coach Jack MacKenzie is a 4 time NAIA Coach of the Year and 1974 NSCAA National Coach of the Year. The Hawks have had 26 Pro-Draft Choices and 24 All-Americans.
Coaching: Jack MacKenzie, Head Coach, USSF License and a NSCAA Diploma.
Style of Play: LET GO GET 'EM . . . Defend Hard, attack quickly.

Women's Athletic Profile

1800 College Avenue
Quincy, IL 62301
Coach: Bill Postiglione
Email: Not Available

NCAA II
Lady Hawks/Brown, White
Phone: (217) 228-5290
Fax: (217) 228-5354

Estimated # of Women's Soccer Scholarships: None
Conference:
Program Profile: Program has been nationally ranked in the recent past. Play in the fall and home games are played at North Campus Soccer Complex which features a 120 x 70 grass field. The lighted stadium seats 2,500 and is one of the best in the Midwest.
History: Club sport 1980-82. Varsity status 1983. NAIA 1983-85. NCAA Sr. Women's Division 1986-87. NCAA

Division II 1988-present.
Achievements: NAIA Central Region Semi-finalist 1984. Region Finalist 1985. NCAA Division II national ranking in the final poll 1989, 1990. NAIA Central Region Coach of the YEAR 1985. Numerous All-Region players in NAIA and NCAA. 2 NCAA Division II All- American, several Academic All-Americans.
Coaching: Bill Postiglione, Head Coach, holds a NSCAA Advanced National Diploma. He has 12 years experience at the collegiate level.
Style of Play: Short passing game with place changing and over laps, midfield build-up, yet willing to by-pass the mid-field and play direct soccer to the forwards on occasions. Ability to play 4-3-3, 4-4-2 or 3-3-4 as indicated by opponent and game situation.

Robert Morris College - Chicago Campus

Academic Profile

Chicago, IL 60605
Phone: (312) 935-6815

Type: 4 Yr.,Private
Website: http://www.RMCIL.EDU
SAT/ACT/GPA: 18/2.0-4.0
Student/Faculty Ratio: 14:1
Undergraduate Enrollment: 3,600
Scholarships/Academic: Yes **Athletic:** Yes
Expenses by: Year **In State:** $ 14,000
Specialty: Business, Computer, Health Care, Graphic Design
Degrees Conferred: BBA, AAS
Programs of Study: Please call admissions.

Founded: 1913
Religion: Non-Affiliated
Housing: Yes
Male/Female Ratio: 1:1
Graduate Enrollment: 120
Financial Aid: Yes
Out of State: $ 14,000

Men's Athletic Profile

401 S. State Street
Chicago, IL 60605
Coach: Jerry Donovan
Email: Not Available

NAIA
Eagles/Maroon, Gold
Phone: (312) 836-4889
Fax: (312) 836-6270

Estimated # of Men's Soccer Scholarships: N/A
Conference: CCAC

Women's Athletic Profile

401 S. State Streer
Chicago, IL 60605
Coach: Kurt Melcher
Email: kmelcher@smtp.rmcil.edu

NAIA
Eagles/Maroon, Gold
Phone: (312) 935-6815
Fax: (312) 935-6804

Estimated # of Women's Soccer Scholarships:
Conference: Chicago Collegiate Athletic Conference
Program Profile: Our season is from August to November. We play at an NCAA Division I facility at the University of Illinois in Chicago. The stadium can accommodate from 750 to 1,500 people.
History: Our program is 5 years old. In 1998, our record was10-7-1 and we went to the CCAC Semi-Finals.
Achievements: 6 All-CCAC; 3 All-Americans.
Coaching: Kurt Melcher, Head Coach, is in his fourth year at RMC. He played at the University of Illinois at Chicago. He was captain four years, three-time team MVP and All-Conference. He played professionally in Europe. He was ODP Coach in Illinois. Tom Czop and Chris Ryan are assistant coaches.
Style of Play: Very good.

Robert Morris College-Springfield

Academic Profile

Springfield, IL 62704

Phone: (217) 529-4140

Type: 4 Yr.,Private
Website: http://www.rmcil.edu
SAT/ACT/GPA: 18/2.0
Student/Faculty Ratio: 12:1
Undergraduate Enrollment: 500
Scholarships/Academic: Yes
Athletic: Yes
Expenses by: YR
In State: $11,650

Founded: 1913
Religion: Non-Affiliated
Housing: No
Male/Female Ratio: 40:60
Graduate Enrollment: N/A
Financial Aid: Yes
Out of State: $11,650

Specialty: Business Administration, Computer Studies
Degrees Conferred: AA, BA
Programs of Study: Accounting, Computer Business Systems, Computer Aided Drafting, Computer Network Specialist, Computer Programming, Computer Systems Specialist, Health Information Technology, Medical Assistant, Paralegal

Men's Athletic Profile

3101 Montvale Drive
Springfield, IL 62704
Coach: Jerry Donovan
Email: jwdsoccer2@aol.com

NAIA
Eagles/Gold, Maroon
Phone: (217) 529-4140
Fax: (217) 793-4210

Estimated # of Men's Soccer Scholarships: 12
Conference: Independent
Program Profile: We use University of Illinois at Springfield that seats 3,500 stadium, lighted and has a measurements of 115x75 natural grass. One of the best facilities in the Mid-West. RMC facilities currently under construction.
History: Our program's inaugural season in 1999.
Achievements:
Coaching: Jerry Donovan, Head Coach, played at Forest Park CC in St. Louis Missouri. He graduated from University of Illinois-Springfield. He was a former assistant coach at Springfield College in Illinois and was a head coach at Lincoln Land Community College.
Style of Play: We play a tight aggressive marking. One and two touch with emphasis on off the ball movement. total team attacking and defending with emphasis on team-work and communications.

Women's Athletic Profile

3101 Montvale
Springfield, IL 62704
Coach: Jerry Donovan
Email: JWDSCCER@AOL.COM

NAIA
Eagles/Maroon,
Phone: (217) 793-2500
Fax: (217) 793-4210

Estimated # of Women's Soccer Scholarships: 12
Conference: Independent
Program Profile: New program; use University of Illinois-Springfield 3,500 seat stadium, measures 115x75 natural grass and is lighted. One of the best facilities in the mid-west. RMC facilities currently under construction.
History: Program's fist season was in 1999. Competes in National Small College Athletic Association.
Coaching: Jerry Donovan, Head Coach, played at Forest Park CC in St. Louis, Missouri and University of Illinois-Springfield. He holds USSF "C" License and former assistant coach at Springfield College in Illinois. He was a head coach at Lincoln Land Community College.
Roster in State: 18 **Out of State:** 0 **Out of Country:** 0

ODP State: 0 **Regional:** 0 **National:** 0
Walk-on/Other: **Graduation %:** 100 **Seniors on Team:** 8
Positions Needed: Goalkeeper, sweeper, striker
Camp or Clinic Dates: Not Available
Most Recent Record: 2-11
Schedule: Warren Wilson, Maryville, Milliken, Greenville, Illinois Wesleyan, Blackburn, Benedictine
Style of Play: Tight defensive marking one and two touch with emphasis on and off the ball movement. Total team attacking and defending with emphasis on team-work and communications.

Rockford College

Academic Profile

Rockford, IL 61108
Phone: (815) 226-4085

Type: 4 Yr.,Private
Founded: 1847
Website: http://www.rockford.edu
Religion: Non-Affiliated
SAT/ACT/GPA: 18/2.0, 2.5 (Transfers)
Housing: Yes
Student/Faculty Ratio: 14:1
Male/Female Ratio: 60:40
Undergraduate Enrollment: 775
Graduate Enrollment: 40
Scholarships/Academic: Yes **Athletic:** No **Financial Aid:** Yes
Expenses by: Year **In State:** $ 23,000 **Out of State:** $ 23,000
Specialty: General Education
Degrees Conferred: BA, BS, BSN, BFA, MBA, MAT
Programs of Study: Anthropology, Art, Biology, Business, Chemistry, Computer Science, Dance, Economics, English, French, German, History, Mathematics, Philosophy, Political Science, Psychology, Sociology, Spanish, Education, Physical Education, Athletic Training

Men's Athletic Profile

5050 E. State Street
Rockford, IL 61108
Coach: Louis Mateus
Email: Not Available

NCAA III
Regents/Purple, White
Phone: (815) 226-4085
Fax: (815) 226-4166

Estimated # of Men's Soccer Scholarships: None
Conference: Northern Illinois Intercollegiate Conference
Program Profile: Facilities include three practice fields, and a separate game field, (all in excellent condition)/ Program is year-round play, has indoor league and outdoor Spring seasons.
History: Program began in 1963.
Achievements: Regents earned NIIC Championship on 11 occasions and were 2 time qualifiers for the NCAA Tournament.

Women's Athletic Profile

5050 E. State
Rockford, IL 61108
Coach: Lee Carley
Email: lcarley@compuserve.com

NCAA III
Lady Regents/Purple, White
Phone: (815) 226-4188
Fax: (815) 623-9710

Estimated # of Women's Soccer Scholarships: None
Conference: Northern Illinois -Iowa Conference

Program Profile: The Regent Lions have three practice fields and a separate game field. We can play all year in our local indoor facility. Our fall season runs from late August through October.
History: Our program began in 1990. In the last three years, we have improved from 7-10-1 to 10-7-1 to 12-6-1.
Achievements: 1997 NIIC Conference Coach of the Year; 1998 NCAA Division III Scoring Leader
Coaching: Lee Carley, Head Coach, has been here since 1992. Robyn Serge is in his second year as assistant coach.
Roster in State: 10 **Out of State:** 10 **Out of Country:** 1
Walk-on/Other: **Graduation %:** 100 **Seniors on Team:** 1
Positions Needed: Defenders, Midfielders, Forwards
Camp or Clinic Dates: Not Available
Most Recent Record: 11-5-3
Schedule: Edgewood, Ill. Wesleyan, Aurora, UW Oshkosh, Maryville, Carthage
Style of Play: Changes from year to year and depending upon personnel.

Sangamon St. Univ.
Academic Profile

Phone:
Springfield, IL 62794-9243

Type: 2 Yr.,Public,Liberal Arts
Founded: 1969
Website: http://www.uis.edu
Religion: Non-Affiliated
SAT/ACT/GPA: Open
Housing: Yes
Student/Faculty Ratio: 17:1
Male/Female Ratio: 40:60
Undergraduate Enrollment: 2,388
Graduate Enrollment: 1,861
Scholarships/Academic: Yes **Athletic:** Yes **Financial Aid:** Yes
Expenses by: Year **In State:** $ 5,500 **Out of State:** $ 10,500
Specialty: Upper Division (some sophomores)
Degrees Conferred: BA, BBA, BSN, BSW, BS, MA, MBA, MPA
Programs of Study: Accounting, Biology, Business Administration, Chemistry, Clinical Laboratory Science, Communication, Computer Science, Criminal Justice, Economics, English, Health Services Administration, History, Labor Relations, Legal Studies, Management, Mathematics, Nursing, Political Science, Psychology, Sociology/Anthropology, Visual Arts

Men's Athletic Profile

Shepherd Road
Springfield, IL 62794-9243
Coach: Aydin Gonulsen
Email: Not Available

NAIA
Prairie Stars/Royal, White
Phone: (217) 786-6674
Fax: (217) 786-7280

Estimated # of Men's Soccer Scholarships: N/A
Conference: Independent
Program Profile: Facilities include lighted, grass field in stadium that seats 2,500. Also two grass athletic practice fields. Playing season runs from mid-August through November.
History: Started in 1977. Have made 13 National Tournament appearances. Have won 11 State/District Championships, 10 Area/Regional Championships. Current record is 300-96-27. Have never had a losing season.
Achievements: 3-time NAIA National Champs 1986, 88, 93. Third Place National Finish in 1987 and 1992. Coach of the Year 1980, and 1993. World Collegiate Runner - ups 1987. 4th place in 1989.
Coaching: Aydin Gonulsen, Head Coach, former All American At warren Wilson (1968), Started soccer in Springfield, only head coach at SSU, 1993 National Soccer Coaches Association of America Coach of the year.
Style of Play: Creative, attacking soccer with disciplined man - man marking.

Saint Xavier University

Academic Profile

Phone: 800-462-9288

Chicago, IL 60655

Type: 4 Yr.,Private,Liberal Arts
Website: http://www.sxu.edu
SAT/ACT/GPA: Required
Student/Faculty Ratio: 15:1
Undergraduate Enrollment: 2,400
Scholarships/Academic: Yes **Athletic:** Yes
Expenses by: Year **In State:** $ 15,000

Founded: 1846
Religion: Roman Catholic
Housing: No
Male/Female Ratio: 25:75
Graduate Enrollment: 1,400
Financial Aid: Yes
Out of State: $15,000

Degrees Conferred: BA, BS, MA, MS, MBA
Programs of Study: Accounting, Aeronautical Engineering, Banking & Finance, Biology, Chemical Engineering, Chemistry, Communications, Computer Science, Criminal Justice, Education, English, Fine Arts, French, History, International Business, Management, Philosophy, Political Science, International Business, Mathematics, PreDentistry, PreMed, PreLaw, PrePharmacy, Religion Social Science, Spanish, Speech Pathology

Men's Athletic Profile

3700 W 103rd Street
Chicago, IL 60655
Coach: Tim Donahue
Email: Not Available

NAIA
Cougars/Red, Gold
Phone: (773) 298-3000
Fax: (773) 298-3111

Estimated # of Men's Soccer Scholarships:
Conference: Chicagoland Collegiate Athletic Conference

Southern Illinois University - Edwardsville

Academic Profile

Phone: (618) 650-2000

Edwardsville, IL 62026

Type: 4 Yr.,Public
Website: http://www.siue.edu
SAT/ACT/GPA: Call for info.
Student/Faculty Ratio: 16/1
Undergraduate Enrollment: 9,313
Scholarships/Academic: Yes **Athletic:** Yes
Expenses by: Varies **In State:** $3,771.55

Founded: 1957
Religion: Non-Affiliated
Housing: Yes
Male/Female Ratio: 1/1.44
Graduate Enrollment: 2,564
Financial Aid: Yes
Out of State: $4,908.55

Degrees Conferred: Bachelor, master's and professional
Programs of Study: Anthropology, Art and Design, Biological Sciences, Computer Management and Information Systems, Chemistry, Economics, Education, English, Geography, Health, Mass Communications, Mathematics, Music, Nursing, Psychology, Physics, Political Science, Social Work, Sociology, Speech, Theatre,

Men's Athletic Profile

Box 1129
Edwardsville, IL 62026
Coach: Ed Huneke
Email: ehuneke@siue.edu

NCAA II
Cougars/Red, White
Phone: (618) 692-2866
Fax: (618) 692-3369

Estimated # of Men's Soccer Scholarships: TBA

Conference: Great Lakes Valley Conference
Program Profile: Ralph Korte Stadium/Bob Guelker Field is a natural grass field with approx. 4,000 seating capacity. The Stadium includes locker rooms, sky box and 1,000+ parking spaces. It is the site of IHSA Class A Boy's soccer tournament.
History: The program began in 1967 under the direction of Hall of Famer Bob Guelker. SIUE won the Division II National Championship in 1972 and the NCAA Division I Championship in 1979, being the only school to do so. Ed Huneke, who has been SIUE's Head Coach for 14 seasons, is only the second coach in the program's history.
Achievements: SIUE has an impressive list of All-Americans, Olympians, drafted players and such.
Coaching: Ed Huneke Head Coach

Roster In State: 12	**Out of State:** 10	**Out of Country:** 1
ODP State: 4	**Regional:** 1	**National:** 0
Walk-on/Other: 0	**Graduation %:** N/A	**Seniors on Team:** 6

Positions Needed: 1 Forward, 1 Midfielder, 1 Back, 1 GK
Camp or Clinic Dates: TBA
Most Recent Record: 11-7-2
Schedule: Lewis, Wisconsin-Parkside, Quincy, Christian Brothers, Truman State, Rockhurst, Missouri-Rolla
Style of Play: Possession with penetration. Organized and passionate on defense.

Women's Athletic Profile

Box 1129
Edwardsville, IL 62025
Coach: Brian Korbesmeyer
Email: bkorbes@siue.edu

NCAA II
Cougars/Red, White
Phone: (618) 650-3738
Fax: (618) 650-3369

Estimated # of Women's Soccer Scholarships: TBA
Conference: Great Lakes Valley Conference
Program Profile: Ralph Korte Stadium Bob Guelker Field is a natural grass field with approx. 4,000 seating capacity. The stadium includes locker rooms, sky box and 1,000 parking spaces. It is the site of IHSA Class A boy's soccer tournament.
History: Our program began in 1967. We won National Titles in 1972 and 1979. We have made numerous NCAA appearances. Coach Brian Korbesmeyer took over the program during the 1989 season and has posted a career record of 122-60-20, including three NCAA Tournament appearances.
Achievements: SIUE has attended the NCAA Tournament three times. The Cougars have been among the top three teams in the Great Lakes Valley Conference since joining the league in1995. Korbesmeyer named GLVC Coach of the Year in 1999.
Coaching: Brian Korbesmeyer, Head Coach, has been a coach for 23 years. His overall record is 109-53-17. He coached for 11 years at Lewis and Clark Community College and 4 years at SIUE. He was women's soccer head coach at SIUE. Bob Guion and Stacy Bundren are assistant coaches.

Roster in State: 11	**Out of State:** 9	**Out of Country:** 0
ODP State: 6	**Regional:** 1	**National:** 0
Walk-on/Other: 0	**Graduation %:**	**Seniors on Team:** 3

Positions Needed: ALL
Camp or Clinic Dates: Not Available
Most Recent Record: 13-4-3
Schedule: Northern Kentucky, Missouri- St. Louis, Southern Indiana, Wisconsin-Parkside, Indianapolis, Grand Valley State.
Style of Play: Attack with numbers and defend in numbers.

Trinity Christian College

Academic Profile

Palos Heights, IL 60463
Phone: (800) 748-0085

Type: 4 Yr.,Private,Liberal Arts
Founded: 1959

Website: http://www.trnty.edu
SAT/ACT/GPA: 1030/22/2.0
Student/Faculty Ratio: 12:1
Undergraduate Enrollment: 630
Scholarships/Academic: Yes **Athletic:** Yes
Expenses by: Year **In State:** $ 18,240
Religion: Non-Affiliated
Housing: No
Male/Female Ratio: 37:63
Graduate Enrollment: N/A
Financial Aid: Yes
Out of State: $ 18,240
Specialty: Business, Education, Nursing
Degrees Conferred: BA, BS
Programs of Study: Accounting, Banking & Finance, Biology, Chemistry, Communications, Computer Science, Education, English, Fine Arts, History, Marketing, Music, Nursing, Philosophy, PreDentistry, PreLaw, PreMed, Psychology, Religion, Social Science, Special Education

Men's Athletic Profile

6601 W College Drive
Palos Heights, IL 60463
Coach: David L. Ribbens
Email: dave.ribbens@trnty.edu

NAIA
Trolls/Navy, Blue, White
Phone: (708) 239-4781
Fax: (708) 396-7460

Estimated # of Men's Soccer Scholarships: 1.0
Conference: Chicagoland Collegiate Athletic Conference
Program Profile: Has a Fall season that consist of 20 games; Winter off-season, three teams compete in indoor soccer at Willy Roy's Soccer Dome in Dolton, IL; Spring season-use all 24 weeks allowed by NAIA. Lighted stadium for all home games. Great soccer atmosphere. Players coach and referee the youth soccer program sponsored by TCC. Has 1,200 kids play in the Fall and in the Winter leagues. Summer camps are offered by Head Coach Ribbens. European tours to Holland.
History: Our program began in the early 1960's. Have competed in the Chicagoland Collegiate Athletic Conference (CCAC) the last ten years.
Achievements: Coach David Ribbens was named three times Coach of the Year in the CCAC and in the NCCAA Region. Has 4 1st Team All-Americans in the NCCAA in the last four years.
Coaching: David Ribbens, Head Coach, 17 years coaching experience at TCC, committed Christians professional coach, and is a member of the NSCAA. He was named Regional Coach of the Year three times. Conference Soccer Chair for the past eight years. Jack Strong, Assistant Coach, TCC Alumni; former soccer player, coached HS State Champions in Wisconsin. Josh Lenarz, Keeper Coach, TCC Alumni, 1st team All-American, 4-year starter.
Style of Play: Short passing possession, build up from back line, creative attacking.

Women's Athletic Profile

6601 West College Drive
Palos Heights, IL 60463
Coach: Ed McNally
Email: ed.mcnally@trnty.edu

NAIA
Trolls/Blue, White
Phone: (708) 239-4783
Fax: (708) 396-7460

Estimated # of Women's Soccer Scholarships: N/A
Conference: CCAC
Program Profile: The program is 4 years old at the varsity level. Its overall record is 16-54-2. The season begins mid-August and runs through the end of October with post season tournament opportunities in both the NAIA and NCCAA. The team plays most of their games on a natural grass field in a stadium the holds 1300.
History: The program is 4 years old at the varsity level, beginning in 1996. Before that it competed on a club level. The overall record is 16-54-2 with most wins in a season at 7.
Coaching: Head Coach - Ed McNally
Roster in State: 7 **Out of State:** 11 **Out of Country:** 1
Walk-on/Other: **Graduation %:** 100 **Seniors on Team:** 7
Positions Needed: ALL
Most Recent Record: 5-13-0

Schedule: Saint Xavier, Trinity International, Robert Morris, Cardinal Stritch, Saint Francis

Trinity International University
Academic Profile

Deerfield, IL 60015
Phone: 800-822-3225

Type: 4 Yr.,Private,Liberal Arts
Founded: 1897
Website: http://www.trin.edu
Religion: Evangelical
SAT/ACT/GPA: 900/20
Housing: Yes
Student/Faculty Ratio: 17:1
Male/Female Ratio: 50:50
Undergraduate Enrollment: 850
Graduate Enrollment: 1,500
Scholarships/Academic: Yes
Athletic: Yes
Financial Aid: Yes
Expenses by: Year
In State: $ 17,800
Out of State: $ 17,800
Specialty: Business, Sports Medicine, Athletic Training, Education
Degrees Conferred: BA
Programs of Study: Biblical Studies, Biology, PreMed, Business Administration, Chemistry, Communications, Education, History, Music, English, Mathematics, Psychology, Sports and Wellness Management, Youth Ministry, Sports Medicine, Athletic Training

Men's Athletic Profile

2065 Half Day Road
Deerfield, IL 60015-1284
Coach: Patrick Gilliam
Email: pgilliam@trin.edu

NAIA
Trojans/R. Blue, White, Black
Phone: (847) 317-7094
Fax: (847) 317-8056

Estimated # of Men's Soccer Scholarships: 20
Conference: CCAC (Chicago Collegiate Athletic Conference)
Program Profile: The team has a fall season that starts from August through November. Leslie A. Frazier Field is natural grass with a 2,000 seating capacity. Has Junior Varsity squad with two part-time coaches in charge of duties there.
History: Our program existed since 1969; 1974 NCCAA National Champions; Coach Gilliam's MSOC record in three season is 34-21-3.
Achievements: In 1998 season produced 4 CCAC All-Conference Selections, 1 Scholar Athlete; 4 NCCAA All-Region Selections, 1 NCCAA Scholar Athlete.
Coaching: Pat Gilliam, Head Coach. Greg Hill, Jeff Perkins and Greg Trear, Assistant Coaches. All have played 4 years of intercollegiate soccer.
Style of Play: Possession style; build play from the back; zonal 4-4-2 defensive system.

Women's Athletic Profile

2065 Half Day Road
Deerfield, IL 60015
Coach: Patrick Gillianm
Email: pgilliam@trim.edu

NAIA, NCCAA
Trojans/R.Blue, White, Black
Phone: (847) 317-7094
Fax: (847) 317-8056

Estimated # of Women's Soccer Scholarships: 18
Conference: Chicagoland Collegiate Athletic Conference
Program Profile: Has fall season schedule that starts from August through November.
History: The program has been in existence since 1985; 5 consecutive 1st win seasons; 1998 NCCAA National Champions; Coach Gilliam's WSOC record for two seasons is 38-8-2. 4 year record is 75-17-4.
Achievements: CCAC Conference Champions in 1997,1998, 1999 NCCAA National Champions in 1998; 1998 Honors -

6 CCAC All-Conference Selections, 3 NCCAA Scholar Athletes, 3 NAIA Scholar Athletes, 5 NCCAA All-Region Selections, 2 NAIA All-Region Selections, NCCAA All-American Selections,4 NAIA All-American Selections.
Coaching: Patrick Gilliam, Head Coach, has two assistant coaches. They all have played four years of intercollegiate soccer.

Roster in State: 9 **Out of State:** 15 **Out of Country:** 0
ODP State: 3 **Regional:** 0 **National:** 0
Walk-on/Other: 0 **Graduation %:** 98 **Seniors on Team:** 0
Positions Needed: Forward, Midfield, GK
Camp or Clinic Dates: TBA
Most Recent Record: 15-5-2
Schedule: Xavier, Transylvania (KY), Virginia, Indiana Wesleyan, St. Ambrose (IA)
Style of Play: Possession style of play; build play from the back; zonal 4-4-2 defensive system. Keep ball on ground up wings then across.

University of Chicago

Academic Profile

Phone: (773) 702-7684

Chicago, IL 60637

Type: 4 Yr.,Private,Liberal Arts
Founded: 1892
Website: http://www.uchicago.edu
Religion: Non-Affiliated
SAT/ACT/GPA: 1100/25/3.5
Housing: Yes
Student/Faculty Ratio: 6:1
Male/Female Ratio: 56:44
Undergraduate Enrollment: 3,400
Graduate Enrollment: 6,000
Scholarships/Academic: Yes **Athletic:** No **Financial Aid:** Yes
Expenses by: Year **In State:** $ 33,200 **Out of State:** $ 33,200
Specialty: Economics, PreProfessional Programs, Social Sciences
Degrees Conferred: BA, BS, MA, MS, MBA, MFA, Ph.D., MD, JD
Programs of Study: Astronomy, Biology, Chemistry, Physics, Geology, Computer Science, Anthropology, English, History, Languages, Physical Science, Sociology, Law, Literature, Economics, PreMed, PreLaw

Men's Athletic Profile

5640 S University Avenue
Chicago, IL 60637
Coach: John O'Conn
Email: joconnor@midway.uchicago.edu

NCAA III
Maroons/Maroon, White
Phone: (773) 702-4660
Fax: (773) 702-6517

Estimated # of Men's Soccer Scholarships: N/A
Conference: University Athletic Association
Program Profile: We play on a 120x80 grass field with a separate practice areas, full-time professional and students trainers, indoor field house with a track, varsity weight room and spring season.
History: Our program began in 1946. We were independent until we joined MAC. In 1988 joined UAA and celebrated 60 years of soccer at UC in 1997.
Achievements: 1996 NCAA Division III Final Four, #5 Final National ranking; 1996 NSCAA UMBRO Coach of the Year; UMBRO All-Star game coach; 1996 & 1997 Regional All-Americans, All-UAA Performers.
Coaching: John O'Connor, Head Coach, is entering his fourth season with the program. In 1996, he was named NSCAA Coach of the Year. He holds a USSF "A" License and a NSCAA Advanced National Diploma. He was the assistant coach at Dartmouth College, under present New Zealand National Team Coach and former Scottish International Bobby Clark and 1994 Region I ODP Staff. David Fingerhut and Dawson Driscoll - Assistant Coaches.
Style of Play: Attacking, flat back four zonal system, combination of possession and direct play based on opponent's weakness and conditions of play. Encourage players to read the game and make correct decisions.

Women's Athletic Profile

5640 S University
Chicago, IL 60637
Coach: Amy Howley Reifert
Email: Not Available

NCAA III
Maroons/Maroon, White
Phone: (312) 702-4655
Fax: (312) 702-6517

Estimated # of Women's Soccer Scholarships: None
Conference: University Athletic Association

University of Illinois - Chicago

Academic Profile

Chicago, IL 60607
Phone: 312-996-4350

Type: 4 Yr.,Public,Liberal Arts,Engineering
Website: http://www.uic.edu
SAT/ACT/GPA: 21/3.0-3.5
Student/Faculty Ratio: 11:1
Undergraduate Enrollment: 16,500
Scholarships/Academic: Yes **Athletic:** Yes
Expenses by: Year **In State:** $ 12,145
Founded: 1982
Religion: Non-Affiliated
Housing: Yes
Male/Female Ratio: 46:54
Graduate Enrollment: 6,000
Financial Aid: Yes
Out of State: $ 18,421
Specialty: Medicine, Dentistry, Pharmacy, Kinesiology
Degrees Conferred: Bachelors, Masters, Doctoral
Programs of Study: Architecture, Medical, Business, Education, PreProfessional Programs

Men's Athletic Profile

P.O. Box 4348
Chicago, IL 60680
Coach: Sasha Begovic
Email: Not Available

NCAA I
Flames/Blue, Scarlet
Phone: (312) 996-6999
Fax: (312) 996-5882

Estimated # of Men's Soccer Scholarships: N/A
Conference: Midwestern

University of Illinois - Urbana/Champaign

Academic Profile

Urbana, IL 61801
Phone: (217) 333-0302

Type: 4 Yr.,Public
Website: http://www.uiuc.edu
SAT/ACT/GPA: 1150avg/25-29avg
Student/Faculty Ratio: 19:1
Undergraduate Enrollment: 27,452
Scholarships/Academic: Yes **Athletic:** Yes
Expenses by: Year **In State:** $ 10,186
Founded: 1867
Religion: Non-Affiliated
Housing: Yes
Male/Female Ratio: 1:1
Graduate Enrollment: 8,851
Financial Aid: Yes
Out of State: $ 17,002
Specialty: 8 Colleges and One Institution offer over 4,000 courses
Degrees Conferred: Undergraduate, Graduate and Professional Degrees available
Programs of Study: College of Agricultural, Consumer and Environmental Sciences, Applied Life Studies, College of Commerce and Business Administration, College of Communications, College of Education, College of Engineering, College of Fine and Applied Arts, College of Liberal Arts and Sciences. The University of Illinois has over 150 programs of study.

Women's Athletic Profile

1700 South 4th Street
Chamapaign, IL 61820
Coach: Tricia Taliaferro
Email: kcrabb@uiuc.edu

NCAA I
Fighting Illinois/orange and blue
Phone: (217) 333-0004
Fax: (217) 244-9759

Estimated # of Women's Soccer Scholarships: 12
Conference: Big Ten Conference
Program Profile: Compete in the prestigious BIG 10 Conference with a fully funded program; fall competition season and a spring season; locker room, weight room, separate practice and competition fields, both grass surfaces. Indoor turf facility; Academic services. Indoor facility completed 11/00 for winter and spring training.
History: Program started in spring of 1997. BIG 10 finishes for last four years. 1997 10th, 1998 8th, 1999 6th, 2000 4th. 2000 qualified for first NCAA Tournament losing in overtime to # 6 Penn State 1-0, in the 2nd round. Beat Xavier 2-0 in the first round. All 11 starters return in 2001.
Achievements: 2000 Fourth in the BIG 10 Conference. Beat Xavier 2-0 in the first round of NCAA Tournament. One 1st team BIG 10, 3 others 2nd team and 2 players 2000 BIG 10 tournament team.
Coaching: Tricia Taliaferro-Head Coach USSF "B" Licensed. Started program in 1997 3rd year as Head Coach played and graduated from Maryland. K.C. Crabb USSF "A" 2nd year as assistant, Missy Price 3rd year assistant coach.
Roster in State: 14 **Out of State:** 10 **Out of Country:** 1
ODP State: 8 **Regional:** 7 **National:** 1
Walk-on/Other: 8 **Graduation %:** **Seniors on Team:** 2
Positions Needed: multiple
Camp or Clinic Dates: June/July
Most Recent Record: 14-8-0
Schedule: Penn State, Michigan, Minnesota, Iowa State, Northwestern, Texas, Ohio State, Indiana, Purdue
Style of Play: Illinois is a team with amazing team speed. Illinois sets a fast tempo all over the field, using possession as a weapon to control pace and flow of play. A very possession oriented team.

Western Illinois University

Academic Profile

Phone: (309) 298-1190

Macomb, IL 61455

Type: 4 Yr.,Public
Website: http://www.wiu.edu
SAT/ACT/GPA: 1010/18
Student/Faculty Ratio: 14:1
Undergraduate Enrollment: 9,606
Scholarships/Academic: Yes **Athletic:** Yes
Expenses by: Year **In State:** $ 7,789

Founded: 1899
Religion: Non-Affiliated
Housing: Yes
Male/Female Ratio: 51:49
Graduate Enrollment: 2,509
Financial Aid: Yes
Out of State: $ 9,974

Specialty: Education, Criminal Justice, Business
Degrees Conferred: BA, BFA, BB, BS, BSEd, MS, MA
Programs of Study: Accounting, Agriculture, Art, BioChemistry, Communications, Computer Science, Education, Economics, Foreign Languages, Geography, Geology, Health Education, Physical Education, Industrial, Math, Marketing, Music, Philosophy, Physics, Political Science, Psychology, Recreation/Parks, Tourism, Sociology, Speed, Theatre

Men's Athletic Profile

203 Western Hall
Macomb, IL 61455
Coach: Eric Johnson
Email: ep -johnson@wiu.edu

NCAA I
Leathernecks/Purple, Gold
Phone: (309) 298-1954
Fax: (309) 298-1965

Estimated # of Men's Soccer Scholarships: 6
Conference: Mid-Continent Conference
Program Profile: Our home field is called John McKenzie Field with a seating capacity of 500. We have natural grass that measures of 120x80 and it is fenced.
History: Our program is 30 years old. The 29 years led by John McKenzie. Our record in 1979-1981 was 14-3, in 1984-1987 was 23-4 and in 1995 was 15-4-1.
Achievements: Has 7 Academic All-Americans; 7 All-Americans; 2 players in MSL (Teck & T. Soehn) Dave Coaches in MSL (Dallas).
Coaching: Eric Johnson, Head Coach, is entering his first season with the program. He has a USSF "A" License and is on the Illinois State ODP Staff (2nd year). Jevan Wuenzer - Assistant Coach, 1st year (all-District Goalkeeper at Baker University).
Style of Play: Possession.

Wheaton College - Illinois

Academic Profile

Phone: (630) 752-5047

Wheaton, IL 60187

Type: 4 Yr.,Private,Liberal Arts
Founded: 1860
Website: http://www.wheaton.edu
Religion: Interdenominational
SAT/ACT/GPA: 1340/30
Housing: Yes
Student/Faculty Ratio: 16:1
Male/Female Ratio: 1:1
Undergraduate Enrollment: 2,300
Graduate Enrollment: 350
Scholarships/Academic: Yes
Athletic: Yes
Financial Aid: Yes
Expenses by: Year
In State: $ 20,000
Out of State: $ 20,000
Degrees Conferred: BA, BS, BM, BMEd, MA, Ph.D.
Programs of Study: Ancient Languages, Archeology, Art, Biblical Studies, Biology, Business/Economics, Chemistry, Christian Education, Communications, Computer Science/Mathematics, Economics, Education, Environmental Science, French, Geological Studies, German, History, History/Social Science, Interdisciplinary Studies, Liberal Arts, Engineering,Nursing, Literature, Mathematics, Music (6 majors), Philosophy, Physical Education, Physical Science, Physics, Political Science, Psychology, Religious Studies, Sociology, Spanish

Men's Athletic Profile

501 College Avenue
Wheaton, IL 60187-5593
Coach: Joe Bean
Email: Not Available

NCAA III
Crusaders/Blue, Orange
Phone: (630) 752-5123
Fax: (630) 752-7007

Estimated # of Men's Soccer Scholarships: None
Conference: College Conference of Illinois and Wisconsin (CCIW)
Program Profile: Team practices at Lawson Field (natural grass) one block north of campus, and play games at East McCully Filed (natural grass), which is lighted for night games. Average attendance is 1,200. Soccer stadium seats 1,500 with one of the best natural grass playing fields in the nation.
History: Men's soccer began in 1935 and was coached by Jim McKetlin. Coach Bean is third winningest coach in college soccer history with 33-year record of 420-144-38 and 27-year record at Wheaton of 369-120-36. Wheaton has won six CCIW titles in last eight years and 20 conference titles (4 different conferences) since 1950. The 1984 team has played in NCAA playoffs in 21 of Bean's 27 years and has won its NCAA regional 11 times.
Achievements: Has 23 Conference Titles, 12 Regional Titles, NCAA III National Champs from 1997-1989; set national record with 66 matches unbeaten streak, 39 matches winning streak, Joe Bean was named 1997 NSCAA and CCIW Coach of the Year, All-Americans were Eric Brown and Rob Mouw.
Coaching: Joe Bean, Head Coach, third winningest coach in college history with 420-144-38 record in 34 years and 369-120-36 record in 27 years at Wheaton. Five-time CCIW Coach of the Year and 1984 National Coach of the. Past

President of NSCAA; Chair recipient of the NSCAA/NISOA Merit Awards for Sportsmanship and Integrity; editor and secretary of Midwestern Soccer News for 17 years; formerly coached at Quinnipiac (1962-1964); University of Bridgeport (1965-1968); and at Wheaton since 1969. Wheaton teams have appeared in NCAA playoffs 21 times in his 27 years and 26 times since 1962.
Style of Play: Possession style (rather than kick and run after); knock ball around and build up out of the back through the midfield; high pressure defense; a very sound technical team - stresses fundamental techniques like passing, trapping, heading. etc.

Women's Athletic Profile

501 E College Avenue
Wheaton, IL 60187
Coach: Peter Felske
Email: Pete.B.Felske@wheaton.edu

NCAA III
Crusaders/Royal Blue, Orange
Phone: (630) 665-1024
Fax: (630) 752-7007

Estimated # of Women's Soccer Scholarships: None
Conference: College Conference of Illinois & Wisconsin
Program Profile: Team practices at Lawson Field (natural grass) one block north of campus and plays its games at East McCully Field (natural grass) which is lighted for night games. Season lasts from mid-August pre-season workouts through mid-November, 20 game intercollegiate schedule against some of the best teams in Midwest - Also five game CCIW conference season. Stadium holds up to 2,000 fans, team plays mostly night games but some afternoon during week. Coach Pete Felske is part time at Wheaton and works full time in downtown Wheaton, easily reached.
History: Women's soccer began as club sport at Wheaton in 1987 and gained varsity status in 1988. Coach Felske is only coach in program history. Wheaton is 72-53-5 in Felske's eight years, with a best record of 14-5-1 in 1994. CCIW began conference sponsorship of women's soccer in 1995, and Wheaton was first-ever champion and freshman Katie Hawkins was named CCIW's first-ever women's soccer Player of the Year. From 1988-1994, Wheaton competed ad NCAA Division III independent.
Achievements: All-Americans - Jill Barber (1990 second team), Becky Fetzer (1993 first team). All-Region Jill Barber . The 1995 CICW Championship
Coaching: Pete Felske, Head Coach since 1987 when it began as club sport. Felske, a 1986 graduate of Wheaton College, played for 1984 Wheaton's Men's Soccer, national champion and was All-Midwest Region Player in 1986; active with summer soccer camps with Kopion Organization
Style of Play: Build out of back to center midfielders who distribute to forwards and create openings, solid defense with sweeper and stopper backs picking up top defensive assignments.

indiana

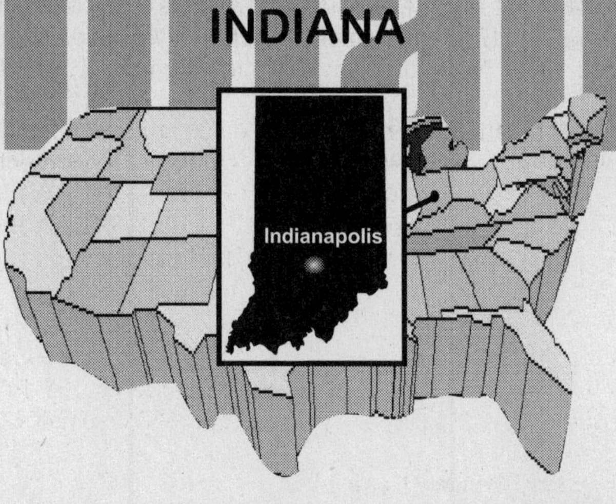

SCHOOL	CITY	AFFILIATION	PAGE
Anderson University	Anderson	NCAA III	316
Ball State University	Muncie	NCAA I	317
Bethel College	Mishawaka	NAIA	318
Butler University	Indianapolis	NCAA I	319
DePauw University	Greencastle	NCAA III	320
Earlham College	Richmond	NCAA III	322
Franklin College	Franklin	NCAA III	323
Goshen College	Goshen	NAIA	324
Grace College	Winona Lake	NAIA	325
Hanover College	Hanover	NCAA III	326
Huntington College	Huntington	NAIA	327
Indiana Institute of Technology	Fort Wayne	NAIA	328
Indiana State University	Terre Heute	NCAA I	329
Indiana University	Bloomington	NCAA I	330
Indiana University - Fort Wayne	Fort Wayne	NCAA II	331
Indiana University - Indy	Indianapolis	NCAA II	332
Indiana Wesleyan University	Marion	NAIA	333
Manchester College	North Manchester	NCAA III	334
Marian College	Indianapolis	NAIA	336
Purdue University	W. Lafayette	NCAA I	337
Purdue University Calumet	Hammond	NAIA	337
Rose-Hulman Institute of Tech.	Terre Haute	NCAA III	338
Saint Joseph's College - Indiana	Rensselaer	NCAA II	339
Saint Mary-of-the-Woods College	St.Mary-of-the-Woods	NSCAA	340
Taylor University	Upland	NAIA	341
Tri-State University	Angola	NAIA	342
University of Evansville	Evansville	NCAA I	343
University of Indianapolis	Indianapolis	NCAA II	344

SCHOOL	CITY	AFFILIATION	PAGE
University of Notre Dame	Notre Dame	NCAA I	346
University of Saint Francis	Fort Wayne	NAIA	347
University of Southern Indiana	Evansville	NCAA II	348
Valparaiso University	Valparaiso	NCAA I	349
Wabash College	Crawfordsville	NCAA III	350

Notre Dame
Girls Soccer Camp
• Home of the 1995
Women's Soccer National Champions
• 1999 NCAA Finalist
• Excellent Facilities
• Experienced Staff
Includes ND Players
• Located on the
Beautiful ND Campus
REGISTER NOW - LIMITED ENROLLMENT!
NOTRE DA
IRISH
6
For Free Brochure
Call (219) 631-8788

Anderson University

Academic Profile

Phone: 765-641-3043

Anderson, IN 46012-3462

Type: 4 Yr.,Private,Liberal Arts
Website: http://www.anderson.edu
SAT/ACT/GPA: 975+/21+
Student/Faculty Ratio: 15:1
Undergraduate Enrollment: 2,240
Scholarships/Academic: Yes **Athletic:** No
Expenses by: Year **In State:** $ 16,000
Founded: 1917
Religion: Church of God
Housing: Yes
Male/Female Ratio: 42:58
Graduate Enrollment: 400
Financial Aid: Yes
Out of State: $ 16,00
Specialty: Education, Liberal Arts, Theology
Degrees Conferred: AA, BA, BSN, MBA, MA, MDiv
Programs of Study: Athletic Training, Business/Marketing, Finance, Management, Accounting, Computer Science, Education, Health Sciences, Psychology, Social Sciences, Philosophy, Theology, Visual & Performing Arts, Music and Communications

Men's Athletic Profile

1100 E 5th Street
Anderson, IN 46012-3462
Coach: Scott Fridley
Email: sfridley@anderson.edu

NCAA III
Ravens/Orange, Black, White
Phone: (765) 641-4499
Fax: (765) 641-3857

Estimated # of Men's Soccer Scholarships: None
Conference: Heartland Collegiate Athletic Conference
Program Profile: Play on grass field, stadium seats 300; new up and coming program; starting to bring in quality players yearly. New focus on program last four years. 2000-01 renovating fields and the complex.
History: Program began in 1989. Up and coming program, very competitive with national programs and a high strength of schedule.
Achievements: 1999 Conference Runner-up, Conference Tournament Runner-up. 1999 4 All-conference players. 35 academic All Conference players, 2 National Academic All Americans.
Coaching: Head Coach- Scott Fridley 6th year. Assistant Coach- Brad Crumbacher.
Roster In State: 10 **Out of State:** 25 **Out of Country:** 0
ODP State: 5 **Regional:** 0 **National:** 0
Walk-on/Other: 1 **Graduation %:** 100 **Seniors on Team:** 6
Positions Needed: Sweeper, keeper, left midfielder, striker
Camp or Clinic Dates: July 16-20
Most Recent Record: 12-8-0
Schedule: Centre College, Wooster College, Mt. Union, Alma College, Ohio Northern University, Baldwin-Wallace, Earlham, Heidelberg, Otterbein, DePauw.
Style of Play: Depends on current players, high pressure, active backs, and patient play.

Women's Athletic Profile

1100 E Fifth Street
Anderson, IN 46012-3462
Coach: Scott Fridley
Email: sfridley@anderson.edu

NCAA III
Ravens/Black, Orange
Phone: (765) 641-4499
Fax: (765) 641-3857

Estimated # of Women's Soccer Scholarships: None
Conference: Heartland Collegiate Athletic Conference

Program Profile: We play on side by side grass fields with 300 seating. In 2000 we will be renovating fields and complex.
History: Our program began in 1989 and has had 3 coaches. We had 12 wins in 1999, and our up and coming program is competitive with National Programs, with a high strength schedule.
Achievements: 1999 Conference Runner-Up; Conference Tournament Runner-Up; 4 All-Conference players; 35 Academic All-Conference Players; 2 National Academic All-Americans
Coaching: Scott Fridley is our Head Coach and Assistant Coach is Brad Crumbacher.

Roster in State: 10	**Out of State:** 25	**Out of Country:** 0
ODP State: 5	**Regional:**	**National:**
Walk-on/Other: 1	**Graduation %:** 100	**Seniors on Team:** 6

Positions Needed: Goalkeeper, Sweeper, Left Halfback, Striker
Camp or Clinic Dates: July 16-20
Most Recent Record: 12-8-0
Schedule: Centre College, Wooster College, Mt. Union College, Alma College, Ohio Northern College, Baldwin-Wallace, Earlham College, Heidelberg College, Otterbein College, DePauw University
Style of Play: Depends on current players, but high pressure, active backs and patient play.

Ball State University

Academic Profile

Muncie, IN 47306-0949
Phone: (765) 285-1671

Type: 4 Yr.,Public		**Founded:** 1910
Website: http://www.bsu.edu		**Religion:** Non-Affiliated
SAT/ACT/GPA: 1150/24/3.0		**Housing:** Yes
Student/Faculty Ratio: 13:1		**Male/Female Ratio:** 50:50
Undergraduate Enrollment: 18,000		**Graduate Enrollment:** 2,000
Scholarships/Academic: Yes	**Athletic:** Yes	**Financial Aid:** Yes
Expenses by: Year	**In State:** $ 8,700	**Out of State:** $ 14,700

Specialty: Broad Liberal Arts & Sciences Curriculum
Degrees Conferred: BA, BS, BFA, MA, MS, Ph.D.
Programs of Study: Education, Exercise Science, Architecture, Business, Telecommunications, Arts, Psychology, etc..

Women's Athletic Profile

Intercollegiate Athletics, W. Soccer
Muncie, IN 47306
Coach: Ron Rainey
Email: rrainey@up.bsu.edu

NCAA I
Cardinals/Cardinal, White
Phone: (765) 285-2478
Fax: (765) 285-5123

Estimated # of Women's Soccer Scholarships: 9
Conference: Mid-American Conference
Program Profile: Gall State is a mid sized University where academic excellence is stressed, athletic success is achieved and a great social environment thrives. BSU Athletics is ranked 9th in the NCAA Div. 1 graduation rates and ranks 7th in the nation of GTE Academic All-Americans. We play on a full size natural grass field/ stadium.
History: Our first season began in the fall of 1999. BSU was on the unlucky end of 10 one goal games and forced its opponents into 4 double overtimes. This youthful team laid a solid foundation for many successful years to come.
Achievements:
Coaching: Ron Rainey, Head Coach, was named head coach in the summer of 1999. He also holds a USSF "A" coaching license. Sheri Huckleberry is our Assistant Coach.

Roster in State: 8	**Out of State:** 12	**Out of Country:**
ODP State: 10	**Regional:**	**National:**
Walk-on/Other:	**Graduation %:**	**Seniors on Team:** 0

Positions Needed: 5
Camp or Clinic Dates: Not Available
Most Recent Record: 1-17-1
Schedule: Illinois State, Eastern Michigan, Central Michigan, Miami (OH), Ohio University, Northern Illinois
Style of Play: A possession game where attacking creativity is emphasized.

Bethel College

Academic Profile

Mishawaka, IN 46545
Phone: 219-257-3339

Type: 4 Yr.,Private,Liberal Arts,Engineering
Founded: 1947
Website: http://www.bethel-in.edu
Religion: Missionary Church
SAT/ACT/GPA: 900/Open/2.0
Housing: Yes
Student/Faculty Ratio: 18:1
Male/Female Ratio: 34:66
Undergraduate Enrollment: 1,627
Graduate Enrollment: N/A
Scholarships/Academic: Yes **Athletic:** Yes
Financial Aid: Yes
Expenses by: Year **In State:** $ 17,050
Out of State: $ 17,050
Specialty: Education, Engineering, ASL
Degrees Conferred: AA, AND, BA, BSN, BS, MM, MBA
Programs of Study: Accounting, American Sign Languages, Art, Biblical Studies, Biology, Business Administration, Business Education, Chemistry, Christian Ministries, Communications, Drama, Elementary Education, PreDentistry, PreLaw, PreMedicine, Engineering, English, English Education, History, Interior Design, Liberal Arts, Mathematics, Music Education, Nursing, Psychology, Recreation Administration, Secondary Education, Science Education, Social Science, Sociology, Visual Communications

Men's Athletic Profile

1001 W McKinley Avenue
Mishawaka, IN 46545
Coach: Pete Mey
Email: moreyp@bethel-in.edu

NAIA
Pilots/Royal, White
Phone: (219) 257-2676
Fax: (219) 257-3385

Estimated # of Men's Soccer Scholarships: 4 Full
Conference: Mid-Central Conference
Program Profile: Our team plays on 80x120 natural turf stadium field with lights and separate practice facility. Has a national schedule.
History: Our program began in 1996 with a record of 2-13, in 1997 record was 5-12 and in 1998 record was 7-12.
Achievements: Has 4 players named to NCCAA All-Region in 1998, 2 players named All-Conference in 1998.
Style of Play: Disciplined possession game with room for individual flair and creativity.

Women's Athletic Profile

1001 W. McKinley Avenue
Mishawaka, IN 46545
Coach: Pete Morey
Email: moreyp@bethel-in.edu

NAIA
Pilots/Royal Blue, White
Phone: (219) 257-2676
Fax: (219) 257-3385

Estimated # of Women's Soccer Scholarships: 5 Partials
Conference: MCC
Program Profile: Facilities include one year old 120x80, floodlit game field, 110x70 practice field, women's soccer locker-room directly adjacent to field complex.

History: The program started in 1996. We have set school record for wins each year including 9-11 in 1999. NCCAA Regional Runner-Up in 1998 & 1999.
Achievements: In 1999, achievements include NSCAA College Team Academic Award, 1 NCCAA All-American, 1 NCCAA All-American, 1 NAIA Academic All-American, 5 NCCAA All-Region, 2 MCC All-Conference, 1 NCCAA Athlete of the week. In 1998 season, achievements were 1 NCCAA Scholar Athlete, 4 NCCAA All-Region, 2 MCC All-Conference, 1 NCCAA Athlete of the Week.
Coaching: Pete Morey is the Head Coach. He was a Bethel graduate and a former player for the Pilots. He holds NSCAA Diploma and member of Indiana ODP Staff Coach. Many years pf high school and club coaching experience. Christa Yearly is our Assistant Coach. She was a former player for Lady Pilots. Her career cut short due to knee injury. She holds USSF "E" Certificate.
Roster in State: 13 **Out of State:** 8 **Out of Country:** 1
ODP State: 3 **Regional:** 1 **National:** 0
Walk-on/Other: 0 **Graduation %:** 100 **Seniors on Team:** 3
Positions Needed: Best player available
Camp or Clinic Dates: July 17-20 (ages 8-14 only)
Most Recent Record: 9-11-2
Schedule: Indiana Wesleyan, St. Francis, Indiana State University, Malone, Grace, Taylor, Cornerstone
Style of Play: Disciplined, ball control, attacking soccer. We look to defend end-to-end in order to win possession ASAP. Our backs attack and our forwards defend. Building a tradition of strong goalkeeping.

Butler University

Academic Profile

Indianapolis, IN 46208
Phone: (800) 368-6852

Type: 4 Yr.,Private,Liberal Arts,Engineering
Founded: 1855
Website: http://www.butleruniversity.edu
Religion: Independent
SAT/ACT/GPA: 1000/3.0
Housing: Yes
Student/Faculty Ratio: 12:1
Male/Female Ratio: 40:60
Undergraduate Enrollment: 3,200
Graduate Enrollment: 800
Scholarships/Academic: Yes **Athletic:** Yes **Financial Aid:** Yes
Expenses by: Year **In State:** $ 23,000 **Out of State:** $ 23,000
Specialty: Pharmacy, Physician's Assistant, TV & Radio
Degrees Conferred: AA, AS, BA, BS, BFA, BM, BSHS, MA, MS, MBA, MM
Programs of Study: Accounting, Art, Biology, Business Administration, Chemistry, Composition, Computer Science, Dance, Economics, Education, Elementary Education, German, Journalism, History, Marketing, Management, Music, Mathematics, Philosophy, Religion, Political Science, Telecommunications, Sociology, Pharmacy, Psychology

Men's Athletic Profile

4600 Sunset Ave.
Indianapolis, IN 46208
Coach: Ian Martin
Email: imartin@butler.edu

NCAA I
Bulldogs/Blue, White, Silver
Phone: (317) 940-9922
Fax: (317) 940-6507

Estimated # of Men's Soccer Scholarships: 8.0
Conference: Midwestern Collegiate Conference
Program Profile: Ten year old program beginning to establish itself nationally. Three NCAA trips in five seasons, and two Sweet 16 appearances; have won three MCC tournament titles; two regular season crowns; tree players taken in MLS draft, including second round selections in 1999 and 2000 drafts; 16 pro players since 1992; two All-American selections in programs first 10 years; team finished 1998 season ranked No. 14 in NSCAA poll. We have two home fields: Varsity Field on campus, 1000 capacity; Kuntz Stadium off campus, 5000 capacity , lighted, both are natural grass surface.

History: Ten year old program beginning to establish itself nationally, two home fields(Varsity Field on campus, 1,000 capacity; Kuntz Stadium off campus, 5,000 capacity, lighted; both are natural grass surface)…
Achievements: three NCAA trips in five seasons, and two Sweet 16 appearances, won three MCC tournament titles, and two regular season crowns… three players taken in MLS draft, including second-round selections in 1999 and 2000 drafts… 16 pro players since 1992… two All-America selections in program's first 10 years… team finished 1998 season ranked No. 14 in NSCAA poll.
Coaching: Ian Martin is our Head Coach. He was a former professional player in the North American Soccer League, Major Indoor Soccer League and American Soccer League. Member of the Great Lakes Advisory Committee and is a part of the Region II Olympic Development Program. he was 1998 MCC Coach of the Year and led Butler to all three of its NCAA Tournaments Appearances. He is also a successful youth soccer coach within Carmel Cosmos system. He is head of a successful summer camp series at Butler. Joe Sochacki and Mark Newman - Assistant Coaches.
Roster In State: 5 **Out of State:** 17 **Out of Country:** 3
Walk-on/Other: **Graduation %:** 95 **Seniors on Team:**
Positions Needed: Center/Left Back, Left Mid, Defensive Mid, Forward, Goalkeeper
Camp or Clinic Dates: Weeks of June 12, 19 and 26; July 17, 24 and 31 (Day Camp 9-4, K-8)
Most Recent Record: 7-12-0
Schedule: UCLA, Portland, Duke, North Carolina State, Florida International, Creighton, Indiana, St. John's, William and Mary
Style of Play: Brazilian- short passing, possession game, attacking with numbers.

Women's Athletic Profile

4600 Sunset Avenue
Indianapolis, IN 46208
Coach: Woody Sherwood
Email: waherwood@butler.edu

NCAA I
Bulldogs/Navy, White
Phone: (317) 940-6496
Fax: (317) 940-9734

Estimated # of Women's Soccer Scholarships: 8.5
Conference: Midwestern Collegiate Conference
Program Profile: The Bulldogs play on a natural grass stadium that seats up to 6,000 fans.
History: Our program began in 1991. We have been National ranked in the top 25 '94, '95, '97, Conference finalist 6 years, 1996 Tournament Champions, 1999 regular season Co-Champions.
Achievements: We have had two All-American players in 1999 and 1994.
Coaching: Woody Sherwood is our Head Coach and Greg Miller is our Assistant Coach.
Roster in State: 8 **Out of State:** 15 **Out of Country:**
ODP State: 6 **Regional:** 5 **National:** 1
Walk-on/Other: **Graduation %:** 100 **Seniors on Team:** 3
Positions Needed: Defender, Midfielder
Camp or Clinic Dates: Not Available
Most Recent Record: 5-11-2
Schedule: Michigan, Kentucky, Cincinnati, Dayton, Indiana, Naval Academy, Xavier
Style of Play: Possession oriented, attractive, versatile, formations

De Pauw University

Academic Profile

Lilly Center
Greencastle, IN 46135

Phone: (800) 446-5295

Type: 4 Yr.,Private,Liberal Arts
Website: http://www.depauw.edu
SAT/ACT/GPA: 1180/25/3.3
Student/Faculty Ratio: 11:1
Undergraduate Enrollment: 2,100

Founded: 1837
Religion: Methodist
Housing: Yes
Male/Female Ratio: 45:55
Graduate Enrollment: N/A

Scholarships/Academic: Yes **Athletic:** No **Financial Aid:** Yes
Expenses by: Year **In State:** $ 25,810 **Out of State:** $ 25,810
Specialty: Business, Media, Music, Sciences; Honors and Fellows Programs
Degrees Conferred: Bachelor of Arts, Bachelor of Science, Bachelor of Music
Programs of Study: College of Liberal Arts, with a choice of 41 majors including: Biological Sciences, Chemistry, Communications, Economics, Education, Health and Physical Performance, International Studies, Management, Political Science, Psychology, etc. ; Also offers a School of Music with a choice of 5 majors.

Men's Athletic Profile

702 S College
Greencastle, IN 46135
Coach: S. Page Cotton
Email: pagecotton@depauw.edu

NCAA III
Tigers/Black, Gold
Phone: 765-658-4938
Fax: (765) 658-4964

Estimated # of Men's Soccer Scholarships: None
Conference: Southern Collegiate Athletic Conference
Program Profile: Outstanding soccer program. NCAA Tournament selection in 1993, 1994, 1998. Top Level facilities with natural grass, game field (120 X 75 yards.), training fields adjacent to game field, indoor facility, institution committed to academic/athletic excellence, team competes in the prestigious SCAC.
History: DePauw soccer began in 1996. Since 1984/85, the team has averaged more than 12 wins a season.
Achievements: Page Cotton has been named ICAC Coach of the Year 9 times; DePauw University completed ICAC play with an astonishing 56-0-0 record. He has coached numerous all Mid-East, an All-American and several players became professional. Four year graduation rate is 10%.
Coaching: S. Page Cotton, Head Coach, has directed the Tigers program for 30 seasons. His teams have a 294-149-26 record. He has seven ICAC Titles and participated in 7 NCAA Division III Tournaments. He was named ICAC Coach of the Year seven times and coached in 6 NCAA Tournaments. He also serves as athletic director. He is chairman of NSCAA games committee and has served on the Indiana ODP staff. Brian Jaworski is the Assistant Coach, has been here for eight seasons. He is former NSCAA All-American and has served on the Indiana ODP Staff.
Roster In State: 13 **Out of State:** 17 **Out of Country:**
ODP State: 9 **Regional:** 1 **National:**
Walk-on/Other: **Graduation %:** 100 **Seniors on Team:** 4
Positions Needed: All positions are open
Most Recent Record: 13-4-2
Schedule: Trinity University, Rhoades College, Ohio Wesleyan, Earlham College, Centre College, Sewanee, Wabash College
Style of Play: DePauw soccer attacks team with a short combination passing. Ball is constantly moving. Team relies on aggressive man-marking defense scheme. Likes to wear opponents down over course of 90 minutes; very hard team.

Women's Athletic Profile

Women's Soccer Office
Greencastle, IN 46135
Coach: John Carter
Email: jcarter@depauw.edu

NCAA III
Lady Tigers/Old Gold, Black
Phone: (800) 446-5295
Fax: (765) 658-4964

Estimated # of Women's Soccer Scholarships: None
Conference: Southern Collegiate Athletic Conference
Program Profile: 12 years varsity program; top 10 team in Great Lake Region past 9 years; finished 1999 as the 8th ranked team in the National Rankings. Participated in the NCAA III National Tournament 2 of the past 3 years; in 1999 advanced to the regional final in the NCAA national Tournament (Final Sixteen); plays one of the toughest schedules in the country; 18 game schedule; natural grass field, measures 120 x 75; practice field measures 120 x 75.

History: Began in 1988. Over the past 10 years the record is 115-57-8; never a losing record, ranked each year regionally, and has been nationally ranked finishing 1999 ranked 8th in final poll. NCAA III National Tournament participants 2 of last 3 years. SCAC conference record past 2 years 17-1-1. Conference champions in 1999 with a record of 9-0-0. Competes at the National level each year including a nationally recognized schedule.
Achievements: 1999: SCAC Conference Champs, SCAC player and coach of the year, 1 first Team All-American, 4 members of the Great Lakes All-Regional Team, 5 members of the SCAC All-Conference Team, Participated in the NCAA III National Championship reaching the Round of Sixteen, and finished the year ranked 8th in the country for NCAA III.
Coaching: Head Coach- John Carter: graduate of Earlham College 1986; Masters degree in Sports Management 1996; 10th year at DePauw with an overall record of 115-57-8. Holds a USSF "A" license; ODP Region II staff coach and state team coach for Indiana; Indiana Coaching Education Staff Coach; Former club coach for Club Carmel and Cincinnati Chiquita; Great Lakes Regional Ranking Committee Chair.

Roster in State: 5	**Out of State:** 17	**Out of Country:**
ODP State: 6	**Regional:**	**National:**
Walk-on/Other:	**Graduation %:** 100	**Seniors on Team:** 5

Positions Needed: Forwards, midfield, marking backs
Camp or Clinic Dates: July 9-13
Most Recent Record: 14-3-2
Schedule: Trinity, Ohio Wesleyan, Wheaton, University of Chicago, Denison, Earlham, Rhodes, University of the South.
Style of Play: Formation dependent on the personnel, attacking, fun, develop rhythm, possession, combination play, one-two touch soccer, building from the back, switching fields, creative/exciting play; high pressure defensively with a variation of zone and man marking; stresses creativity and flair on the pitch.

Earlham College

Academic Profile

Richmond, IN 47374
Phone: 800-327-5426

Type: 4 Yr.,Private,Liberal Arts		**Founded:** 1847
Website: http://www.earlham.edu		**Religion:** Society of Friends
SAT/ACT/GPA: 1210		**Housing:** Yes
Student/Faculty Ratio: 11:1		**Male/Female Ratio:** 46:54
Undergraduate Enrollment: 1,100		**Graduate Enrollment:** N/A
Scholarships/Academic: Yes	**Athletic:** No	**Financial Aid:** Yes
Expenses by: Year	**In State:** $ 25,066	**Out of State:** $ 25,066

Specialty: Liberal Arts, Education
Degrees Conferred: Bachelors
Programs of Study: Art, African/African-American Studies, Biology, Chemistry, Classics, Computer Science, Economics, Education, English, French, Geology, German, History, Human Development & Social Relations, International Studies, Japanese Studies, Philosophy, Physics, Astronomy, Politics, Psychology, Religion, Sociology, Anthropology, Spanish, Theatre Arts, Women's Studies

Men's Athletic Profile

801 National Road West
Richmond, IN 47374
Coach: Roy Messer
Email: messero@earlham.edu

NCAA III
Quakers/Maroon, White
Phone: (765) 983-1485
Fax: (765) 983-1446

Estimated # of Men's Soccer Scholarships: Financial Aid/Merit Scholarship
Conference: North Coast Athletic Conference
Program Profile: the Quakers play a 20-game schedule with home matches on natural grass. Charlie Matlock Field. Earlham home games are well attended by a boisterious knowledgeable crowd.

History: Our most successful program in Earlham athletic history, the men's soccer team has a 368-264-60 record for a .575 winning percentage since gaining varsity status in 1949.
Achievements: Roy Messer was named NCAC Coach of the Year in 1995 and 1997. Jamie Dick and Odeon Creamer were named NCAC's offensive and defensive Player of the Year. Jamie Pettingill was a 1998 3rd team All-American. Earlham was a 1998 NCAA Qualifier. four 1998 1st team Region players.
Coaching: Roy Messer, Head Coach, graduate of Wooster in 1970 and entering 19th year in coaching experience. Marc Colwell, Assistant Coach, graduate of Indiana in 1995, entering second year with the program.
Style of Play: Play through the midfield, zone block defending. Formation depends on strengths of players.

Women's Athletic Profile

801 National Road West
Richmond, IN 47374
Coach: Shane Meridith
Email: Not Available

NCAA III
Hustlin' Quakers/Maroon, Grey
Phone: (765) 983-1414
Fax: (765) 983-1446

Estimated # of Women's Soccer Scholarships: None
Conference: North Coast Athletic Conference
Program Profile: Competitive at Division III level. Play on some of the best fields in Indiana. Season begins August 19 and ends November 1.
History: Program began in 1988 and has become more successful every year.
Achievements: NCAA Division III affiliated North Coast Athletic Conference. 4 named to NCAC 3rd team, 2 named NCAA Honorable Mentions.
Coaching: Shane Meridith, Head Coach, entering fifth season with the program; graduate of Earlham, four - year varsity starter at Earlham (men's), member of three NAIA District Champs, 1987 All-Mideast, Indiana U-14 State ODP coach.
Style of Play: Play a 4-4-2 or 4-5-1formation; we are possession oriented.

Franklin College

Academic Profile

Franklin, IN 46131

Phone: 800-852-0232

Type: 4 Yr.,Private,Liberal Arts
Website: http://www.franklincoll.edu
SAT/ACT/GPA: 1000
Student/Faculty Ratio: 13:1
Undergraduate Enrollment: 900
Scholarships/Academic: Yes **Athletic:** No
Expenses by: Year **In State:** $ 18,000

Founded: 1834
Religion: Baptist
Housing: Yes
Male/Female Ratio: 45:55
Graduate Enrollment: N/A
Financial Aid: Yes
Out of State: $ 18,000

Specialty: Education, Business, Preprofessional, Athletic Training, Journalism
Degrees Conferred: BA, BS
Programs of Study: Franklin College offers major in a variety of traditional program, academic discipline as well as fields which uniquely blend the study of traditional liberal arts and sciences with PreProfessional preparation; 26 majors.

Men's Athletic Profile

501 E Monroe Street
Franklin, IN 46131
Coach: Bob Boucher
Email: boucher@franklincoll.edu

NCAA III
Grizzles/Navy Blue, Gold
Phone: (317) 738-8130
Fax: (317) 738-8248

Estimated # of Men's Soccer Scholarships: None
Conference: Heartland Collegiate Athletic Conference

Program Profile: Recently have taken over as head coach and rebuilding the program. Working for players that have the desire to continue to play and receive an excellent education; freshmen this time have an excellent chance of seeing playing time. Play a competitive schedules and are presently looking for players that can contribute immediately.
History: 1984 program has struggled from the beginning. Robert Boucher was the first full-time coach of the program.
Achievements: Produce 5 All-Regional All-American.
Coaching: Robert Boucher, Head Coach, has 23 years of coaching the college, university ranks; produced numerous All-Conference, All-Academic players, 5 Regional All-Americans, nationally and regionally ranked teams. Maurice Schilton, Assistant Coach.
Style of Play: Working towards a total game with fast counters attack. Aggressive total offense, defense oriented.

Women's Athletic Profile

501 E. Monroe St.
Franklin, IN 46131
Coach: Maurice Schilton
Email: boucher@franklincoll.edu

NCAA III
Grizzlies/Navy Blue, Gold
Phone: (317) 738-8130
Fax: (317) 738-8248

Estimated # of Women's Soccer Scholarships: None
Conference: Heartland Collegiate Athletic Conference
Program Profile: Our program is four years old. We look for players that can come in and contribute to our success immediately. Freshmen will also see a lot of playing time.
History: We play in the fall from late August through early November. Our field is 118 x 75 and has natural grass. We play in the Heartland Collegiate Athletic Conference. We play competitive schedules. We are looking for players that can contribute immediately.
Achievements: Numerous All-Conference, All-Academic players, 5 Regional All-Americans in the past 23 years of coaching

Goshen College
Academic Profile

Phone: 800-348-7422

Goshen, IN 46526

Type: 4 Yr.,Private,Liberal Arts
Website: http://www.goshen.edu
SAT/ACT/GPA: 920/19/2.0
Student/Faculty Ratio: 13:1
Undergraduate Enrollment: 1,000
Scholarships/Academic: Yes
Athletic: Yes
Expenses by: Year
In State: $ 16,920
Degrees Conferred: BA, BS

Founded: 1894
Religion: Mennonite
Housing: Yes
Male/Female Ratio: 45:55
Graduate Enrollment: N/A
Financial Aid: Yes
Out of State: $ 16,920

Programs of Study: Accounting, Anthropology, Architecture, Art, Art Therapy, Bible & Religion, Biblical Studies, Business, Business Administration, Chemical Engineering, Chemistry, Church Music, Coaching, Communications, Computer Science, Computer Systems, Data Processing, Early Childhood Education, Economics, Education, Elementary Education, English, Environmental Studies, Family Life, French, German, Graphics Design, Health & Safety, History, International Studies, Journalism, Mathematics, Medical Technology, Music, Music Performance, Music Researched, Natural Science, Nursing, Physical Studies, Physics, Political Science, PreEngineering, PreLaw, PreMed, PrePhysical Therapy, PreSeminary, PreVeterinary, Productions Crafts, Psychology, Recreational Leadership, Science, Social Studies, Social Work, Sociology, Spanish, Speech Communication, Sport Communication, Sport Management, Studio Art, TESOL, Theatre, Tropical Agriculture, Visual Arts, Women's Studies.

Men's Athletic Profile

1700 S Main Street
Goshen, IN 46526
Coach: Dwain Hartzler
Email: Not Available

NAIA
Maple Leafs/Navy, White
Phone: (219) 535-7492
Fax: (219) 535-7660

Estimated # of Men's Soccer Scholarships: N/A
Conference: Mid-Central Conference

Grace College
Academic Profile

Winona, IN 46590

Phone: 800-544-7223

Type: 4 Yr.,Private,Liberal Arts
Website: http://www.grace.edu
SAT/ACT/GPA: 920/19/2.0
Student/Faculty Ratio: 16:1
Undergraduate Enrollment: 777
Scholarships/Academic: Yes
Athletic: Yes
Expenses by: Year
In State: $ 14,988
Specialty: Education

Founded: 1948
Religion: Grace Brethren
Housing: Yes
Male/Female Ratio: 2:3
Graduate Enrollment: 35
Financial Aid: Yes
Out of State: $ 14,988

Degrees Conferred: BA, BS, BM, MS, AS
Programs of Study: Accounting, Art, Art Education, Biblical Studies, Biology, Biology Education, Business Administration, Business Education, Christian Ministries, Communication, Counseling, Criminal Justice, Education (Elementary, Secondary), English, English Education, French, French Education, General Science, German, German Education, Graphic Arts, International Business, Management Information Systems, Mathematics, Mathematics Education, Music Education, Music Management, Physical Education, Sports Broadcasting, Sport Journalism, Sports Management, Sports Medicine, Sports Psychology, Teaching Major, PreDentistry, PreLaw, PreMed, PrePharmacy, PrePhysical Therapy, Psychology, Russian, Science Education, Sociology, Spanish, Spanish Education, PreVeterinary Medicine

Men's Athletic Profile

200 Seminary Drive
Winona Lake, IN 46590
Coach: Roy Danielian
Email: danielg@grace.edu

NAIA
Lancers/Red, White, Black
Phone: (219) 372-5100x6002
Fax: (219) 372-5120

Estimated # of Men's Soccer Scholarships: 3
Conference: MCC
Program Profile: Beautiful natural grass field with scoreboard, bleachers, snack bar, equipment storage and team rooms and dugouts. Three additional practice fields available for training.
Program plays in a competitive conference and plays a full 18 game schedule and is a member in the NAIA & NCCAA Conferences.
History: Program was established in 1966. Grace College has won eight MCC conference championships since the program was established. In 2000, the Lancers finished second in the NCCAA Midwest Regional playoff.
Achievements:
Coaching: Roy Danielian completed his 1st year as the Head Coacj at Grace. He has 9 years experience as head coach at Western Baptist College in Salem, OR and 2 years as assistant Coach at Azusa Pacific University. Roy lead his 1996 Western Baptist team to a NCCAA D-I National Championship and won the 1995 and 1996 Cascade Collegiate Conference Championships. Danielian has collected 94 collegiate wins as a head coach in 10 years.

Roster In State: 10 **Out of State:** 15 **Out of Country:** 2
Walk-on/Other: 0 **Graduation %:** N/A **Seniors on Team:** 7
Positions Needed: Keeper, 3 defenders, 3 forwards
Camp or Clinic Dates: Not Available
Most Recent Record: 10-10-1
Schedule: Bethel, St. Francis, Taylor, Trinity Christian, Indiana Wesleyan, St. Joseph, Cedarville, Tri-State, Northland Baptist, Goshen College
Style of Play: Program is united and organized. Team players are unselfish and sacrificing. Lancers hustle and play hard but also play fair and by the rules. Our team's purpose is to glorify the Lord Jesus Christ in our attitudes and actions.

Women's Athletic Profile

200 Seminary Drive
Winona Lake, IN 46590
Coach: Mark Sproul
Email: Admissions@goshen.edu

NAIA
Maple Leafs/Purple, White
Phone: (219) 372-5224
Fax: (219) 535-7609

Estimated # of Women's Soccer Scholarships: None
Conference: Mid Central College Conference
Program Profile: Excellent facilities; lighted field with a seating capacity for 1,000; 8 full-sized fields on campus; college provides all equipment and laundry.
History: Program began in 1991. Building process began in earnest in 1993 with an arrival of a new coaches. Record has improved each of the past seasons.
Achievements: NAIA district 21 Champions. Numerous All-Conference selections.
Style of Play: Emphasize a solid defense and moving the ball quickly through the midfield. Want to emphasize use of the flanks and two-touch soccer in the middle third of the field. Offensively like to see combination play between strikers.

Hanover College

Academic Profile

Phone: (812) 866-7388

Hanover, IN 47243

Type: 4 Yr.,Private,Liberal Arts **Founded:** 1827
Website: http://www.hanover.edu **Religion:** Presbyterian
SAT/ACT/GPA: 1145/25/3.0 **Housing:** Yes
Student/Faculty Ratio: 11:1 **Male/Female Ratio:** 48:52
Undergraduate Enrollment: 1,050 **Graduate Enrollment:** Not Avai
Scholarships/Academic: Yes **Athletic:** No **Financial Aid:** Yes
Expenses by: Year **In State:** $ 15,000 **Out of State:** $ 15,000
Specialty: Not Available
Degrees Conferred: BA
Programs of Study: Anthropology, Biology, Broadcasting, Business Administration, Chemistry, Communications, Dramatic Arts, Economics, Education, English, Film Arts, French, Geology, German, History, International Relations, Management, Mathematics, Music, Philosophy, Physics, Political Science, PreDentistry, PreLaw, PreMed, Psychology, Religion, Social Science, Sociology, Spanish, Speech Pathology, Telecommunications, Theatre

Men's Athletic Profile

P.O. Box 890
Hanover, IN 47243
Coach: Jim Watts
Email: watts@hanover.edu

NCAA III
Panthers/Red, White, Blue
Phone: (812) 866-6819
Fax: (812) 866-6818

Estimated # of Men's Soccer Scholarships: None
Conference: Heartland Collegiate Athletic Conference
Program Profile: Home Field is the LS. Ayres Soccer Field which is grass surface.
History: Program began in 1991.
Achievements: 4 All-Conference players: Todd Smith, Stuart Cardon, Sam Rizk, and Todd Needham; 3 Academic All-Conference: Stuart Cardon, Sam Rizk, Joe Endress.

Women's Athletic Profile

P.O. Box 809
Hanover, IN 47243
Coach: Yin Lin Liu
Email: LinLiu@Hanover.edu

NCAA III
Panthers/Blue, White
Phone: (812) 866-7388
Fax: (812) 866-6818

Estimated # of Women's Soccer Scholarships:
Conference: Heartland Collegiate Athletic Conference
Program Profile: Has two soccer fields, one is for practice and one is for competition. Our team has a Fall playing season.
History: The women's soccer program has been together for 4 years.
Achievements: 7 All-Conference players in the last three years.
Coaching: Yi Lin Liu, Head Coach. David Johnson, Assistant Coach.
Roster in State: 13 **Out of State:** 8 **Out of Country:**
Walk-on/Other: **Graduation %:** **Seniors on Team:** 2
Positions Needed: Forwards, Midfielders
Camp or Clinic Dates: August
Most Recent Record: 8-8
Style of Play: 4-4-2 or 4-3-3

Huntington College
Academic Profile

Huntington, IN 46750
Phone: 219-356-6000

Type: 4 Yr.,Private,Liberal Arts
Website: http://www.huntcol.edu
SAT/ACT/GPA: 800/18
Student/Faculty Ratio: 12:1
Undergraduate Enrollment: 700
Scholarships/Academic: Yes **Athletic:** Yes **Financial Aid:** Yes
Expenses by: Year **In State:** $ 14,900 **Out of State:** $ 14,900
Founded: 1897
Religion: United Brethren
Housing: Yes
Male/Female Ratio: 49:51
Graduate Enrollment: 50
Degrees Conferred: AA, BA, BS, Masters
Programs of Study: Accounting, Arts, Biblical Studies, Biology, Broadcasting, Business Administration, Chemistry, Communications, Computer Science, Economics, Education, Elementary Education, English, Graphic Art, History, Management, Mathematics, Medical Technology, Ministries, Music, Natural Resources, Philosophy, Physical Education, Physical Fitness/Exercise Science, PreDentistry, PreEngineering, PreLaw, PreMed, PreVet, Psychology, Recreation & Leisure, Religion Science, Secondary Education, Sociology, Special Education, Theatre, Theology.

Men's Athletic Profile

2303 College Avenue
Huntington, IN 46750
Coach: N/A
Email: bmay@huntinton.edu

NAIA
Foresters/Red, Green
Phone: (219) 356-4212
Fax: (219) 356-4090

Estimated # of Men's Soccer Scholarships: 1.5
Conference: Mid-Central College Conference

Program Profile: Huntington College has an excellent facilities for all students. We have two playing grass fields and a top-notch training equipment and facilities.
History: Our men's program began in 1959 and has had many very successful teams.
Roster In State: 15 **Out of State:** 7 **Out of Country:**

Women's Athletic Profile

2303 College Avenue
Huntington, IN 46750
Coach: Jack Brady
Email: bmay@huntington.edu

NAIA
Foresters/Red, Green
Phone: (219) 359-4212
Fax: (219) 356-4090

Estimated # of Women's Soccer Scholarships: 1.5
Conference: Mid-Central College Conference
Program Profile: Huntington College has excellent facilities for all student athletes, including soccer players. Supported by a facility which allows for year-around play. HC offers top-notch training equipment and facilities. HC has two playing fields, both of which are natural grass.
History: The women's soccer at Huntington College is fairly new just beginning in 1997. The women's team continues to get big every year.
Roster in State: 15 **Out of State:** 7 **Out of Country:**
Walk-on/Other: **Graduation %:** **Seniors on Team:** 3
Camp or Clinic Dates: Not Available
Most Recent Record: 2-17
Style of Play: defense style of play.

Indiana Institute of Technology

Academic Profile

Fort Wayne, IN 46803
Phone: 219-422-5561

Type: 4 Yr.,Private,Engineering
Website: http://www.indtech.edu
SAT/ACT/GPA: Varies by majors
Student/Faculty Ratio: 21/1
Undergraduate Enrollment: 496
Scholarships/Academic: Yes **Athletic:** Yes
Expenses by: Year **In State:** 17,800
Specialty: Business & Engineering
Founded: 1930
Religion: Non-Affiliated
Housing: Yes
Male/Female Ratio: 3/1
Graduate Enrollment: N/A
Financial Aid: Yes
Out of State: N/A
Degrees Conferred: BS, Limited amount of Association Degrees
Programs of Study: Accounting, Computer Engineering, Computer Science, Electrical Engineering & Technology, Engineering & Management, Human Services, Marketing, Mechanical Engineering, Park & Recreations Management, Recreation Therapy, Sport Management, Technical & Business Writing

Men's Athletic Profile

1600 E Washington Blvd.
Fort Wayne, IN 46803
Coach: Martin Neuholf
Email: Not Available

NAIA
Warriors/Orange, Black
Phone: (219) 422-5561
Fax: (219) 422-7696

Estimated # of Men's Soccer Scholarships:
Conference: Wolverine - Hoosier Conference
Program Profile: Bill Armstrong Stadium - $4 million complex built in 1981, 74x117 yards, natural grass, has a seating capacity of 10,000, press seating for 100, has a photo decks and VIP lounge.

History: Program began in 1973. Overall record is 396-75-36; won NCAA Title in 1982, 1983, & 1988; appeared in 10 Final four; won Big Ten Titles in 1991, 1992, 1994 7 1995.
Achievements: Herman Trophy Winners: Angelo DiBernardo in 1978, Armando Betanooult in 1981, Ken Show in 1988 & 1990, and Brian Maisonneuve in 1994; MAC Player of the Year - Show in 1988 & 1990 and Todd Yeagley in 1994, NSCAA Coach of the Year - Jerry Yeagley in 1976, 1980, & 1994; 3 NCAA Titles, 4 Big Ten Titles and 38 All-Americans.
Style of Play: An attacking style that is pleasing to the eye.

Women's Athletic Profile

1600 E. Washington Blvd.
Ft. Wayne, IN 46803
Coach: David Allway
Email: allway@indtech.edu

NAIA
Warriors/Orange, Black
Phone: (219) 422-5561
Fax: (219) 422-7696

Estimated # of Women's Soccer Scholarships: 12
Conference: Wolverine-Hoosier Athletic Conference
Program Profile: 20 game varsity and 14 game reserve schedules. New fitness center being built for 2001-02.
History: 5 year old program with 2000-01 being the best year at 14-7, Regional Ranking and 4th place conference finish.
Coaching: Head coach is David Allway. The assistant coach is Karen McCormick.
Roster in State: 15 **Out of State:** 20 **Out of Country:** 1
ODP State: 7 **Regional:** 1 **National:**
Walk-on/Other: **Graduation %:** 100 **Seniors on Team:** 4
Positions Needed: All
Camp or Clinic Dates: Not Available
Most Recent Record: 14-7-0
Schedule: St. Francis, McKendree, Harris-Stowe, Judson College, Indiana Wesleyan, Madonna, Aquinas, Defiance, Siena Heights, Bethel
Style of Play: Team play depends on the players from year to year. Reserve team used to develop players for varsity.

Indiana State University

Academic Profile

Terre Haute, IN 47809
Phone: 800-742-0891

Type: 4 Yr.,Public
Founded: 1865
Website: http://www.indstate.edu
Religion: Non-Affiliated
SAT/ACT/GPA: 820/20
Housing: Yes
Student/Faculty Ratio: 20:1
Male/Female Ratio: 49:1
Undergraduate Enrollment: 11,870
Graduate Enrollment: 1,500
Scholarships/Academic: Yes **Athletic:** Yes **Financial Aid:** Yes
Expenses by: Year **In State:** $ 7,050 **Out of State:** $ 11,346
Degrees Conferred: AA, AS, AAS, BA, BS, BFA, MA, MS, MBA, MFA
Programs of Study: Accounting, Anthropology, Athletic, Banking/Finance, Biology, Business, Chemistry, Communications, Computer, Dietetics, Economics, Education, Engineering, English, Medical, Nursing, Office, Parks/Recreation, PreProfessional Programs, Religion, Safety, Textiles/Clothing, Urban Studies

Women's Athletic Profile

Women's Soccer Office
Terre Heute, IN 47809
Coach: Vernon Croft
Email: Vcroft@indstate.edu

NCAA I
Sycamores/R. Blue and White
Phone: (812) 237-7731
Fax: (812) 237-2913

Estimated # of Women's Soccer Scholarships: Varies
Conference: Missouri Valley

Program Profile: Second Year Program, two natural grass field 120-80, new locker rooms 2002, new weights room 2001.
History: Fall of 2000 will be first year
Achievements:
Coaching: Vernon Croft Head Coach NSCAA & USSF Licensed, former asst. at Southwest Missouri State, Current ODP staff Coach Director Indiana State Soccer School. Robie Dominguez Assit. Coach
Roster in State: 6 **Out of State:** 14 **Out of Country:** 0
ODP State: 7 **Regional:** 0 **National:** 0
Walk-on/Other: 0 **Graduation %:** 100 **Seniors on Team:** 2
Positions Needed: GK, Forward, Midfielders
Camp or Clinic Dates: June 4-8
Most Recent Record: 3-16-0
Schedule: Creighton University, Southwest Missouri State, Illinois State University, University of Evansville, Loyola University
Style of Play: Possession oriented with build up and combination play in advancing for one third to another. High pressure defending beginning with front runners.

Indiana University

Academic Profile

Ads
Bloomington, IN 47408-1590
Phone: (812) 855-3989

Type: 4 Yr.,Public
Website: http://www.athletics.indiana.edu
SAT/ACT/GPA: 800/19
Student/Faculty Ratio: N/A
Undergraduate Enrollment: 27,000
Founded: 1820
Religion: Non-Affiliated
Housing: Yes
Male/Female Ratio: 1:3
Graduate Enrollment: 6,500
Scholarships/Academic: Yes **Athletic:** Yes **Financial Aid:** Yes
Expenses by: Year **In State:** $ 12,332 **Out of State:** $ 20,948
Specialty: Business, Music, Journalism, Health, Physical Education and Recreation
Degrees Conferred: BA, BS, BFA, MBE, BSGS, AA, MA, MFA, MED, PH.D, OD, JD
Programs of Study: Over 850 degree programs offered including: Business, Criminal Justice, Education, Exercise Science, Music, Political Science, Psychology, Sports Marketing

Men's Athletic Profile

1001 E 17th St.
Bloomington, IN 47408-1590
Coach: Jerry Yeagley
Email: msoccer@indiana.edu
NCAA I
Hoosiers/Cream, Crimson
Phone: (812) 855-0051
Fax: (812) 855-9715

Estimated # of Men's Soccer Scholarships: N/A
Conference: Big Ten Conference
Program Profile: Top level Division I program. Bill Armstrong Stadium - $4 million complex built in 1981 that measures 75x117 yards natural grass with a seating capacity of 8,500, press seating for 250, has a photo decks and VIP Lounge. Mellencamp Pavilion - $6 million indoor facility with a full dimensions.
History: Indiana's men soccer program began in 1973 and have won a record tying five NCAA championships and have appeared in 13 Final Four. They have participated in 24 NCAA tournaments and have won eight Big Ten Championships.
Achievements: Jerry Yeagley has won a record five national coach of the year awards. The Hoosiers have won five NCAA titles and eight Big Ten Championships. Indiana has had 35 All-Americans, six Olympians and more than 60 professional players.
Coaching: Jerry Yeagley is our Head Coach. He is entering 25 years at Indiana University, 1995 first recipient of the Walt Chyzowych Award at 49th Annual NSCAA Convention, 1995 record of 14-6-4 with a berth in the NCAA

Tournament, NSCAA/Umbro Division I Coach of the Year in 1976, 1980, 1994. NSCAA Division Coach of the Year in 1976, 1980, & 1994. Joining him is Michael Fceiteg and John Trask.
Roster In State: 7 **Out of State:** 16 **Out of Country:** 0
Walk-on/Other: **Graduation %:** N/A **Seniors on Team:** 2
Camp or Clinic Dates: June 11-16, 18-23, July 9-14, 16-21
Most Recent Record: 21-3
Schedule: UCLA, Maryland, Penn State, Creighton, Stanford, Cal.-Berkley, Virginia
Style of Play: Possession and attack oriented.

Women's Athletic Profile

1001 E 17th Street
Bloomington, IN 47405
Coach:
Email: wsoccer@indiana.edu

NCAA I
Hoosiers/Red, White
Phone: (812) 855-0051
Fax: (812) 855-7150

Estimated # of Women's Soccer Scholarships: None
Conference: Big Ten Conference
Program Profile: Home games are played at Bill Armstrong Stadium which has a measurements of 118x75 yards. The main grandstand seats 8,000 and has a natural grass surface. There are several practice facilities including the Mellencamp indoor practice facility and a weight training facility in the Assembly Hall.
History: The women's soccer program began in 1993, and now is entering its fifth season. Big Ten champions in 1996.
Achievements: Big Ten Champions in 1996, ranked 17th in the nation in 1996; Merit Elzey - 1996 Regional All-American; 1996 All-Big Ten Selection; Soccer America Goalkeeper of the Week; Amy Frederich-All-Big Ten Selection in 1996; Abby Ryan - Soccer America Team of the Week.
Style of Play: Attractive.

Indiana University - PU/Fort Wayne

Academic Profile

Fort Wayne, IN 46805
Phone: (219) 481-6643

Type: 4 Yr.,Public,Liberal Arts,Engineering
Founded: 1973
Website: http://www.ipfw.indiana.edu
Religion: Non-Affiliated
SAT/ACT/GPA: 820/2.0
Housing: No
Student/Faculty Ratio: 22:1
Male/Female Ratio: 1:1
Undergraduate Enrollment: 11,000
Graduate Enrollment: N/A
Scholarships/Academic: Yes **Athletic:** Yes **Financial Aid:** Yes
Expenses by: Year **In State:** $ 6,100 **Out of State:** $ 12,100
Degrees Conferred: Associates, Bachelors, Masters
Programs of Study: We offer over 140 degrees.

Men's Athletic Profile

2101 Coliseum Blvd. East
Fort Wayne, IN 46805
Coach: Terry Stefankiewicz
Email: Not Available

NCAA II
Mastodons/Royal, White
Phone: (219) 481-6643
Fax: (219) 481-6880

Estimated # of Men's Soccer Scholarships: N/A
Conference: Great Lake Valley Conference
History: Program began in 1984.
Achievements: Third in the conference in 1984; 1985 second in the conference; 1986 8 All-Conference.
Coaching: Terry Stefankiewicz, Head Coach.

Camp or Clinic Dates: Not Available
Style of Play: Attractive with an open, attacking style. Develop the ball out of the back. High pressure combination man to man and zonal defending scheme, formation varies with a personnel.

Women's Athletic Profile

2101 Coliseum Blvd. East
Fort Wayne, IN 46805
Coach:
Email: Not Available

NCAA II
Mastadons/Royal, White
Phone: (219) 481-6643
Fax: (219) 481-6880

Estimated # of Women's Soccer Scholarships: None
Conference: Great Lake Valley Conference

Indiana University - Purdue University at Indianapolis

Academic Profile

Suite 105
Indianapolis, IN 46202

Phone: (317) 278-1823

Type: 4 Yr.,Public,Liberal Arts,Engineering
Website: http://www.iupui.edu
SAT/ACT/GPA: 840/18/2.0
Student/Faculty Ratio: 8:1
Undergraduate Enrollment: 21,000
Scholarships/Academic: Yes
Athletic: Yes
Expenses by: Year
In State: $ 6,952

Founded: 1969
Religion: Non-Affiliated
Housing: Yes
Male/Female Ratio: 55:45
Graduate Enrollment: 7,200
Financial Aid: Yes
Out of State: $ 12,438

Specialty: Liberal Arts, Engineering, Medical, Law, Education, Business
Degrees Conferred: AA, AS, AAS, BA, BS, BAE, BGS, BSE, BSEE, BSME, BSW, MA, MS, MBA
Programs of Study: Accounting, Anthropology, Art History, Banking and Finance, Biology, Business, Chemistry, City Planning, Communications, Computer Science & Technology, Economics, Education, Engineering, Engineering Technology, Marketing, Mathematics, Nursing, Philosophy, Physics, Political Science, Psychology, Telecommunications, Public Administration

Men's Athletic Profile

901 W New York Street Ste 105
Indianapolis, IN 46202-5193
Coach: Steve Franklin
Email: sfrankli@iupui.edu

NCAA II
Jaguars/Red, Gold, Black
Phone: (317) 278-1823
Fax: (317) 274-0609

Estimated # of Men's Soccer Scholarships: TBA
Conference: Mid-Continent Conference
Program Profile: IUPUI Carrol Track & Soccer Stadium seats 13,000. It is natural grass with lights and has hosted the 1998 US open Cup Championship and 1998 US Track & Field Championships. Pam Am Facilities are on campus. Notatarium Complex is site of US Olympic Trials for swimming and diving. Natural Institute for fitness and sport.
History: Our program began in 1987and competed in the NAIA and NCAA Division II through 1998. Numerous All-District, Regional and All-American honors.
Achievements: NAIA District 21 Champions in 1991 & 1993;5 former players playing professionally in USISL or A-League.
Coaching: Steve Franklin, Head Coach, has a USSF "A" License and NSCAA premier and Advanced National Diplomas. He is a state ODP Coach and Instructor for Coaching. Isang Jacobs is the Assistant Coach with a USSF "A" License and NSCAA Advanced National and Premier Diplomas. He is also an ODP Staff Coach. Todd Collan is our Assistant Coach. He holds a NSCAA All-Mideast Selection.

Style of Play: Attractive with an open attacking style of play. High pressure combination of man-to-man and zonal defending scheme.

Women's Athletic Profile

901 W New York Street
Indianapolis, IN 46202
Coach: Jean Delaski
Email: jdelaski@lupui.edu

NCAA I
Jaguars/Red, Gold
Phone: (317) 274-1447
Fax: (317) 274-0609

Estimated # of Women's Soccer Scholarships: 8
Conference: Mid-Continent Conference
Program Profile: Program will be in it's fourth year. We play our home games at the Michael A. Carroll Track and Field Stadium which seats 12,500 people. It is a natural grass field.
History: Program began in 1998 had a record of 6-13-1 in its 2nd year. 1999 1st year sanctioned by a conference the Jaguars went 4-14-1 and were 3rd in conference. 2000 they were 8-10-1 and ended the season 3rd in the conference for the 2nd time.
Achievements: Head Coach Jean Delaski named Mid-Con Coach of the Year. 2000 New Comer of the Year, 5 All-Conference team.
Coaching: Jean Delaski, Head Coach, USSF "B" License Coach; Indian Club and State ODP Coach. He played four years at Butler University a Division I program, played 4 consecutive years in the w-league, 1st two years with Jackson Calypso and the past 2 years with the Indiana Blaze.
Roster in State: 9 **Out of State:** 11 **Out of Country:** 1
ODP State: 14 **Regional:** 0 **National:** 0
Positions Needed: Backs, Midfielders
Camp or Clinic Dates: Not Available
Most Recent Record: 8-10-1
Schedule: Oakland, Eastern Michigan, Butler, Detroit Mercy, Oral Roberts
Style of Play: This past season the team played a 3-4-3 with high pressure.

Indiana Wesleyan University

Academic Profile

Marion, IN 46953
Phone: (765) 677-2318

Type: 4 Yr.,Private,Liberal Arts
Website: http://www.indwes.edu
SAT/ACT/GPA: 840/17/2.3
Student/Faculty Ratio: 17:1
Undergraduate Enrollment: 1,800
Founded: 1920
Religion: Wesleyan
Housing: Yes
Male/Female Ratio: 2:3
Graduate Enrollment: 125
Scholarships/Academic: Yes **Athletic:** Yes **Financial Aid:** Yes
Expenses by: Year **In State:** $ 16,340 **Out of State:** $ 16,340
Specialty: Education, Nursing, Psychology, Athletic Training, Sports Management
Degrees Conferred: AA, AS, BA, BS, MA, Master of Education, Master in Counseling and Ministerial Education, Master in Business Management and Community Health, MS, MBA
Programs of Study: Accounting, Art, Art Education, Athletic Training, Biology, Chemistry, Business Administration, Commercial Arts, Criminal Justice, Mathematics, Economics, Education, Physical Education, Social Science, Political Science, Nursing Education, Management, Marketing, Psychology, Social Studies, Sociology, Christian Ministry

Men's Athletic Profile

4201 S Washington St.
Marion, IN 46953
Coach: Freddie King, Jr.
Email: fking@indwes.edu

NAIA
Wildcats/Red, White
Phone: 765-677-2318
Fax: 765-677-2328

Estimated # of Men's Soccer Scholarships: N/A
Conference: Mid - Central Conference
Program Profile: Indiana Wesleyan University is home to one of the finest outdoor athletic facilities at the NAIA level. The soccer facilities include three fields, all 120 x 80 and kept in excellent condition by full-time maintenance staff. The game field is outstanding, well lighted and can seat over 1,000 fans. Also included are stylish covered dugouts, an elevated press box, a public address system and an easily accessible concession stand. A state-of-the-art field house and new physical education center will open in the fall of 1999.
History: Our program began in 1969 and was a mediocre program until 1992. Since 1992, we have compiled a 62-34-4 record and we have been ranked in the NAIA Top 20.
Achievements: Mid-Central Conference Champions: 1993,1994 and 1998;
NCCAA National Championships: 1992-8th, 1993-6th, 1995-4th, 1996-7th; 17 NCCAA All-Americans and 3 NAIA All-Americans since 1993; Mid-Central Conference Coach of the Year: 1996, 1998.
Coaching: Freddie King, Jr., Head Coach, is a former NAIA, NSCAA and NCCAA All-American selection as a player. He played three years of professional soccer in the USISL. His overall record at IWU is 59-45-7. He was Mid-Central Conference Coach of the Year in 1996. He is also the head of the local soccer club in Marion.
Style of Play: Attacking soccer that develops immediately from team's defensive concept. Quick counter attack through systematic passing (not kick and run) is always first option with possession buildup as second option. Midfield control of attack is overall goal.

Women's Athletic Profile

4201 S Washington Street
Marion, IN 46953
Coach: Joe Thomas
Email: jthoma@indwes.edu

NAIA
Wildcats/Red, White
Phone: (765) 677-2321
Fax: (765) 677-2328

Estimated # of Women's Soccer Scholarships: 3
Conference: Mid-Central Conference
Program Profile: We have a beautiful Kentucky blue grass playing field and separate practice facility for the women's team. The stadium seats about 1,000 spectators. IWU is a perennial conference and regional power. Last season we finished 9 in the NAIA final pole.
History: Our 8 year program has won 3 NCCAA National Championships and 3 Conference Championships.
Achievements: NCAA National Champions in 1999, 1997, 1996; MCC Conference Champions in 1999; Region 8 NAIA Champions in 1998; National NCAA Coach of the Year in 1999; MCC and Region 8 NAIA Coach of the Year in 1999; 4 NAIA All-Americans; Several All-Region; All-Conference Players.
Coaching: Joe Thomas, Head Coach, is in his first year as head coach. He was previously an assistant coach at John Brown University.

Roster in State: 3	**Out of State:** 21	**Out of Country:**
ODP State: 3	**Regional:** 1	**National:**
Walk-on/Other:	**Graduation %:** 100	**Seniors on Team:** 5

Positions Needed: Sweeper, Center-mid, Forward
Camp or Clinic Dates: Not Available
Most Recent Record: 21-4-0
Schedule: Lindsey Wilson, Trinity International, Siena Heights, St. Joseph's, Cumberland, St. Francis
Style of Play: Possession-oriented; ball control.

Manchester College

Academic Profile

Phone: (219) 982-5000

North Manchester, IN 46962

Type: 4 Yr.,Private,Liberal Arts
Website: http://www.manchester.edu
Founded: 1889
Religion: Brethren

SAT/ACT/GPA: Open
Student/Faculty Ratio: 14:1
Undergraduate Enrollment: 1,100
Scholarships/Academic: Yes **Athletic:** No
Expenses by: Year **In State:** $ 18,140+
Housing: Yes
Male/Female Ratio: 50:50
Graduate Enrollment: N/A
Financial Aid: Yes
Out of State: $ 18,140+
Specialty: Accounting, Education, Social Work
Degrees Conferred: BA, BS, Masters in Accounting
Programs of Study: Accounting, Art, Biology, Business, Chemistry, Computer Science, Economics, Communications, PreEngineering, Education-Elementary & Secondary, PreLaw, Music, Math, Physical Education, Political Science, History, PreMed, Psychology, Physics, Sociology, Social Work, Athletic Training, Peace Studies, Philosophy, English, Modern Languages, Criminal Justice

Men's Athletic Profile

604 College Ave.
North Manchester, IN 46962
Coach: David Good
Email: Not Available
NCAA III
Spartans/Black, Gold
Phone: (219) 982-5332
Fax: (219) 982-5291

Estimated # of Men's Soccer Scholarships: None
Conference: Heartland Collegiate Athletic Conference
Program Profile: We have two full-size natural grass field. We have a fall playing season with an informal spring season. Players run our indoor season.
History: Varsity program began in 1971. NAIA affiliated until 1989, NCAA Division III since 1989.
Achievements: NAIA District Champs in 1985; District Runner-Ups in 1994; NAIA District Coach of the Year in 1984 & 1985; 2 All-Americans; Conference Coach of the Year in 1998; numerous Academic All-Americans & NSCAA Scholar Athletes.
Coaching: David Good, Head Coach, spent 16 years at Manchester. He was an All-American midfielder whose team reached the NCAA Division III Final Four all four years and won the Championship in 1970. He was a two-time NAIA District Coach of the Year. He has a BA in Elizabethtown College. Dough Stahl, Assistant Coach, received his BA from Manchester College.
Roster In State: 14 **Out of State:** 8 **Out of Country:** 0
ODP State: 2 **Regional:** **National:**
Walk-on/Other: 20 **Graduation %:** N/A **Seniors on Team:** 4
Positions Needed: Goalkeeper, Forward, Defense, Midfield-All
Camp or Clinic Dates: Not Available
Most Recent Record: 10-10
Schedule: Earlham, Goshen, Ohio Northwestern, Anderson
Style of Play: Varies somewhat according to players; like to play a mixture of short passing, field switching, attacking ball.

Women's Athletic Profile

604 F college
North Manchester, IN 46962
Coach: Scott Stan
Email: jsstan@manchester.edu
NCAA III
Spartans/Black, Gold
Phone: (219) 982-5046
Fax: (219) 982-5032
Estimated # of Women's Soccer Scholarships: 0
Conference: Heartland
Program Profile: 3 soccer fields press box, natural grass, season sept. 1- early November, I'm new to the program as a 1st year coach.
History: The program began in 1994; finished third in the conference in 1996.
Achievements: I have a NSCAA Advanced National Diploma. This was my 1st year as a coach.
Coaching:

Roster in State: 19 **Out of State:** 1 **Out of Country:** 0
ODP State: 0 **Regional:** 0 **National:** 0
Walk-on/Other: **Graduation %:** 100 **Seniors on Team:** 1
Positions Needed: 2 forwards, 2 midfielders, 3 defenders
Camp or Clinic Dates: Not Available
Most Recent Record: 7-13-0
Schedule: Grace College, Anderson Univ. Transylvania College, Mt. St. Joseph, Hanover College, Alma College
Style of Play: 4-3-3 with a sweeper. Quick 1-2 touch passing out side backs join attack.

Marian College

Academic Profile

Phone: (317) 955-6116

Indianapolis, IN 46222

Type: 4 Yr.,Private,Liberal Arts
Founded: 1936
Website: http://www.marian.edu
Religion: Catholic
SAT/ACT/GPA: 860/18/2.3
Housing: Yes
Student/Faculty Ratio: 13:1
Male/Female Ratio: 2:3
Undergraduate Enrollment: 1,400
Graduate Enrollment: N/A
Scholarships/Academic: Yes **Athletic:** Yes **Financial Aid:** Yes
Expenses by: Year **In State:** $ 19,892 **Out of State:** $ 19,892
Specialty: Nursing, Education, Business & Finance
Degrees Conferred: AA, AS, BA, BS, BSN, AN
Programs of Study: Accounting, Art, Art History, Athletic Training, Biology, Business Administration, Chemistry, Coaching Endorsement, Computer Study, Economics, Elementary Education, Finance, Health & Safety, Interior Design, Liberal Arts, Nursing, Psychology, Philosophy, Religion, Sport Management, Sociology, Theatre, Theology

Men's Athletic Profile

3200 Cold Spring Road
Indianapolis, IN 46222
Coach: Ed Nirrengarten
Email: coached@compuserve.com

NAIA
Knights/Navy, Gold
Phone: (317) 955-6116
Fax: (317) 955-6401

Estimated # of Men's Soccer Scholarships: N/A
Conference: Mid-Central Conference
Program Profile: We have a small squad with no reserve team and a 25 man limit on the roster. We have a new 70 x 120 field on campus that has natural grass. We play 18 games in the fall and 4 scrimmages in the spring.
History: Our men's program began in 1992 with a record of 4-6. By 1995, our record was 16-4-1. In 1998, we won our first conference championship. We have had 15 All-conference players and 3 Mid-East All-Americans
Achievements: 1998 Conference Coach of the Year; 1998 Conference Champs; Honorable mention All-Americans 1994, 1995 and 1996
Coaching: Ed Nirrengarten, Head Coach, has coached 7 years here. His overall record is 54-39-5. His over 20 years high school, club and ODP record is 333-178-56. He holds a USSF and NJCAA national licenses. Assistant coach Matt Nirrengarten set an Indiana H.S. scoring record. He was 4 years college All-Conference including honorable mention All-American. He has played professionally and holds a NJCAA license.
Style of Play: Total team offense and defense. Had 14 players score last season. We like to control the ball and therefore tempo of the game but we will look for quick counter if it's on.

Women's Athletic Profile

3200 Cold Spring Rd.
Indianapolis, IN 46222
Coach: Kurt Guldner
Email: guldner@marian.edu

NAIA
Knights/Navy Blue, Gold
Phone: (317) 955-6310
Fax: (317) 955-6121

Estimated # of Women's Soccer Scholarships:
Conference: Mid-Central Conference
Program Profile: Second year of the program. On site fields as well as playing at Kuntz Field built for Pan Am Games and professional soccer tournament in Indy. It is natural grass.
History: Started Fall of 1998 from a small club team. First record was 2-11-1.
Coaching: Kurt Guldner, Head Coach, entering second year with the program. Josh Simpson, Assistant Coach.
Style of Play: Defensive minded and hard nosed physical play.

Purdue University Calumet

Academic Profile

Hammond, IN 46323
Phone: 219-989-2213

Type: 4 Yr.,Public,Liberal Arts
Founded: 1946
Website: http://www.calumet.purdue.edu
Religion: Non-Affiliated
SAT/ACT/GPA: 830+
Housing: Yes
Student/Faculty Ratio: 30:1
Male/Female Ratio: 50:50
Undergraduate Enrollment: 7,500
Graduate Enrollment: 800
Scholarships/Academic: Yes **Athletic:** Yes **Financial Aid:** Yes
Expenses by: Year **In State:** $ 4,000 **Out of State:** $ 7,000
Specialty: Engineering, Professional Studies
Degrees Conferred: AA, AS, BA, BS, BSCh, BSE, MA, MS
Programs of Study: Accounting, Banking & Finance, Biology, BioTechnology, Broadcasting, Chemistry, Communications, Computer Science, Computer Technology, Criminal Justice, Economics, Education, Electrical Engineering & Technology, English, French, German, History, Hotel/Restaurant Management, Industrial Engineering, Information Science, International Relations, Marketing, Mathematics, Mechanical Engineering & Technology, Medical Technology, MicroBiology, Nursing, Optometry, Philosophy, Physical Therapy, Physics, Political Science, PreDentistry, PreLaw, PreMed, PrePharmacy, PreVeterinary, Psychology, Social Science, Spanish, Zoology.

Men's Athletic Profile

2233 - 171st Street
Hammond, IN 46323
Coach: Oscar Gomez
Email: Not Available

NAIA
Lakers/Gold, Black
Phone: (219) 989-2290
Fax: (219) 989-2766

Estimated # of Men's Soccer Scholarships:
Conference: Chicagoland Collegiate Athletic Conference
Program Profile: Play conference schedule in the Fall. Excellent facilities which include team locker room and two grass fields.
History: Program began in 1945.
Coaching: Oscar Gomez, Head Coach.

Purdue University

Academic Profile

W. Lafayette, IN 47907
Phone: 765-494-1776

Type: 4 Yr.,Public
Founded: 1869
Website: http://www.purdue.edu
Religion: Non-Affiliated
SAT/ACT/GPA: Open
Housing: Yes
Student/Faculty Ratio: 13:1
Male/Female Ratio: 55:45
Undergraduate Enrollment: 28,000
Graduate Enrollment: 9,000

Scholarships/Academic: Yes **Athletic:** Yes **Financial Aid:** Yes
Expenses by: Year **In State:** $ 10,984 **Out of State:** $ 19,334
Degrees Conferred: BA, BS, Preprofessional programs
Programs of Study: All

Women's Athletic Profile

W. Mollen Kopf Ctr.
W. Lafayette, IN 47907-1790
Coach: Rob Klatte
Email: rlklatte@purdue.edu

NCAA I
Boilermakers/Old Gold, Black
Phone: (765) 496-3396
Fax: (765) 494-0554

Estimated # of Women's Soccer Scholarships: 3
Conference: Big Ten
Program Profile: 2001 season will be our programs 4th year of competition. We play and practice at a two field campus facility—each field with seating for 750 with press box and scoreboards and team dugouts. Playing surface is natural grass, 120 x 75. Year round training program, August - May. Winter training in an indoor Facility 120 x 70.
History: Program began in fall 1998 and record was 4-14. The 1999 season saw the record improve to 8-11 and the beginning of Big Ten Conference Play.
Achievements: Eight Big Ten Scholar Athletes, Soccer Buzz 1998 New Program Freshman of the Year.
Coaching: Rob Klatte is the Head Coach and he is assisted by Sue Moynihan and Rob Harrington.
Roster in State: 8 **Out of State:** 18 **Out of Country:** 0
ODP State: 8 **Regional:** 5 **National:** 0
Walk-on/Other: **Graduation %:** N/A **Seniors on Team:** 0
Positions Needed: All Field positions
Camp or Clinic Dates: Call 765-494-2445
Most Recent Record: 8-11-0
Schedule: Penn State, Michigan, SMU, Northwestern, Illinois, Oregon State, West Virginia, Minnesota, Ohio State.
Style of Play: Attacking, possession oriented with an allowance for creativity and flair. Athletic/Fitness based with zonal defending.

Rose - Human Institute of Technology

Academic Profile

Terre Haute, IN 47803

Phone: 800-248-7448

Type: 4 Yr.,Private,Engineering
Website: http://www.rose-hulman.edu
SAT/ACT/GPA: 550 M/ 500V SAT
Student/Faculty Ratio: 12:1
Undergraduate Enrollment: 1,500

Founded: 1874
Religion: Non-Affiliated
Housing: Yes
Male/Female Ratio: 4:1
Graduate Enrollment: 100

Scholarships/Academic: Yes **Athletic:** No **Financial Aid:** Yes
Expenses by: Year **In State:** $ 29,200 **Out of State:** $ 29,200
Specialty: Math, Science, Engineering
Degrees Conferred: BS, MS
Programs of Study: Civil Engineering, Computer Engineering, Electrical Engineering, Mechanical Engineering, Applied Optics, Chemistry, Computer Science, Economics, Mathematics, Physics

Men's Athletic Profile

5500 Wabash Avenue
Terre Haute, IN 47803
Coach: Greg Ruark
Email: gregory.k.ruark@rose-hulman.edu

NCAA III
Engineers/Red, White
Phone: (812) 877-8496
Fax: (812) 877-8407

Estimated # of Men's Soccer Scholarships: None
Conference: Southern Collegiate Athletic Conference
Program Profile: Rendel Field has a measurements of 74x118 yards natural grass. Renovated bleachers and press box, irrigation system with seating for 500. The practice fields are equipped with lights and are natural grass.
History: The men's soccer program began in 1979. Former member of College Athletic Conference. member of ICAC 1990-1997; southern collegiate Athletic Conference 1998-present; consistently top half finisher in the league.
Achievements: Coach of the Year in 1993; Academic All-American in 1990, All-Mideast in 1993 & 1995, 15 All-Conference performers since 1989; 20 Academic All-Conference members since 1991.
Coaching: Greg Ruark, Ball State 1981, Tom Baker Rose-Hulman 1992, head coach, since 1988, 16 years coaching veteran, NSCAA National Diploma recipient, academy program recipient. Tom Baker - Goalkeeping Specialist. Pat Goodwin - Assistant Coach, 1995 Rose-Hulman, Breck Schmidlkofer, Rose-Hulman 1995.
Roster In State: 10 **Out of State:** 25 **Out of Country:**
Walk-on/Other: **Graduation %:** 100 **Seniors on Team:** 6
Positions Needed: Defenders, Midfielders
Camp or Clinic Dates: Not Available
Most Recent Record: 6-12-0
Schedule: Calvin, Earlham, Wittenberg, DePauw University, Rhodes, Trinity(TX), Centre, Sewanee
Style of Play: 4-4-2, 4-4-3 short pass, possession style offense. High pressure defense from all field players.

Women's Athletic Profile

5500 Wabash Avenue
Terre Haute, IN 47803
Coach: Greg Ruark
Email: gregory.k.ruark@rose-hulman.edu

NCAA III
Engineers/Red, White
Phone: (812) 877-8496
Fax: (812) 877-8407

Estimated # of Women's Soccer Scholarships: None
Conference: Southern Collegiate Athletic Conference
Program Profile: Play on a grass field in 118x74 yards with a seating for 500. irrigation system; has 18-19 game fall season; practice field has lights.
History: Women's program will began in 1999.
Achievements: Coach of the Year 1993
Coaching: Greg Ruark, Head Coach, ten years at Rose-Hulman. Tom Baker - Goalkeeper Specialist, 1992 Rose-Hulman graduate. Pat Goodwin - Assistant Coach, 1995 Rose-Hulman graduate. Breck Schmidlkofer, 1995 Rose-Hulman graduate. Jenny Anklam, 1990 Stanford graduate.
Roster in State: 6 **Out of State:** 16 **Out of Country:**
Walk-on/Other: **Graduation %:** 100 **Seniors on Team:** 2
Positions Needed: goalkeepers, forwards
Camp or Clinic Dates: Not Available
Most Recent Record: 4-13-
Schedule: DePauw, Trinity (TX), University of the South, Centre College, Wittenberg, Rhodes
Style of Play: 4-4-2, man to man defending, short pass-possession oriented offense.

Saint Joseph's College - Indiana

Academic Profile

Phone: 800-447-8781

Rensselaer, IN 47978

Type: 4 Yr.,Private,Liberal Arts
Website: http://www.saintjoe.edu
SAT/ACT/GPA: Open
Student/Faculty Ratio: 14:1

Founded: 1891
Religion: Catholic
Housing: Yes
Male/Female Ratio: 50:50

Undergraduate Enrollment: 900-1000 **Graduate Enrollment:** N/A
Scholarships/Academic: Yes **Athletic:** Yes **Financial Aid:** Yes
Expenses by: Year **In State:** $ 18,380 **Out of State:** $ 18,380
Specialty: Business, Preprofessional Programs, Elementary Education
Degrees Conferred: AA, AS, BA, BS, BSN, MA
Programs of Study: Accounting, BioChemistry, Biology, Business Administration, Chemistry, Communications, Computer Information System, Computer Science, Economics, Education, Elementary Education, English, Human Services, Management, Music, Nursing, Philosophy, Physical Education, Social Science, Physics, Political Science, Humanities, Human Services, GeoPhysics, Psychology, Social Science

Men's Athletic Profile

P.O. Box 875
Rensselaer, IN 47978
Coach: Michael Singleton
Email: mikes@saintjoe.edu

NCAA II
Pumas/Maroon, White
Phone: (219) 866-6314
Fax: (219) 866-6140

Estimated # of Men's Soccer Scholarships: 5.5
Conference: Great Lakes Valley Conference
Program Profile: Program geared towards becoming a national power. Full size, grass field with lights and World Cup benches. Off-season speed & strength work-outs; spring season as well.
History: 1988 first year of program. Has a record of 99-69-7; has been to Final Four or NCAA Tournament.
Achievements: 1996 Regional and National Coach of the Year; 7 All-Region players; 1996 GLVC Conference Winners.
Coaching: Michael Singleton, Head Coach, was previously a Division I college player and product of Region I ODP system. He is a new coach geared towards making team a national power. Chuck Carmedy, Assistant Coach.
Style of Play: Short passing, attack style of play. Concentration on possession and moving forward from all positions.

Women's Athletic Profile

PO Box 875
Rensselaer, IN 47978
Coach: Camie Bechtold
Email: Not Available

NCAA II
Pumas/Purple, Cardinal Red
Phone: (219) 866-6335
Fax: (219) 866-6276

Estimated # of Women's Soccer Scholarships: 5.5
Conference: Great Lakes Valley Conference
Program Profile: Highest national ranking in 1999, which was 15. Traditionally in the top 20. Field is natural grass with a seating 1,500 and is international size.
History: Program began in 1988. We were Final Four finish in 1996 and NCAA Bid in 1997 and 2 Great Lakes Valley Conference Titles.
Achievements: We earned National Coach of the Year in 1996; Regional Coach of the Year in 1996-1997; GLVC Coach of the Year in 1996-1997; 4 All-Americans; 11 All-Region; 36 All-Academic All-Americans; 13 All-Conference.
Coaching: Camie Bechtold is our Head Coach. She is entering first year with the program.
Walk-on/Other: **Graduation %:** **Seniors on Team:** 4
Positions Needed: Sweeper, Outside midfielder
Camp or Clinic Dates: Not Available
Most Recent Record: 15-5-1
Style of Play: Possession oriented; fitness team.

Saint Mary-of-the-Woods College

Academic Profile

Phone: 812-535-5204

St.Mary-of-the-Woods, IN 47876

Type: 4 YearPrivateLiberal Arts **Founded:** 1840

Website: www.smwc.edu
SAT/ACT/GPA:
Student/Faculty Ratio: 1/12
Undergraduate Enrollment: 1100
Scholarships/Academic: Yes **Athletic:** Yes
Expenses by: Year **In State:** $20,400
Religion: Catholic
Housing: Yes
Male/Female Ratio: All Female
Graduate Enrollment:
Financial Aid: Yes
Out of State: $20,400
Programs of Study: Accounting, Art, Art Therapy, Business Administration, Biology, Computer Information Systems, Digital Media Communtication, Education, English, Equine Studies, French, Gerontology, History, Human Resources, Human Services, Humanties, Journalism, Management, Math, Marketing, Medical Technology, Not-for-Profit Management, Occupational Therapy, Paralegal Studies, Political Science, Pre-Med, Professional Writing, Psychology, Social Science, Spanish

Women's Athletic Profile

Saint Mary-of-the-Woods
St.Mary-of-the-Woods, IN 47876
Coach: Mike Aycock
Email: maycock@smwc.edu
NSCAA
Pomeroys/Navy, White
Phone: (812) 535-5204
Fax: (812) 535-5169

Estimated # of Women's Soccer Scholarships: 16 Partial
Conference: None
Program Profile: We play a fall season against a broad range of small college and university opponents. We have very good facilities, with a two-field complex, excellent irrigated natural bluegrass surface.
History: The program was begun in the fall of 2000. Some recruiting of scholarship athletes was accomplished. Many openings still exist as we build a competitive program.
Coaching: Head Coach Mike Aycock holds the USSF B and is a long time Indiana staff ODP coach. He has served as the men's coach at Indiana State University, Director of Coaching for his local club, and as both a boys' and girls' high school coach. He serves a number of summer camps. Assistant Coach Aaron Rhame is a recent graduate of Valparaiso University, where he earned All-Conference honors as a goalkeeper.
Roster in State: 14 **Out of State:** 3 **Out of Country:** 1
Positions Needed: Defender, midfielder, Keeper
Most Recent Record: 2-11-0
Schedule: Bethel, Anderson, Indiana Institute of Technology, Saint Joseph's, Hanover, Central Methodist
Style of Play: Since we are a new program, our style of play is still being formed. At this point we play a simple 4-4-2 and value ball possession. We often play through our strong midfielders, rather than over them.

Taylor University
Academic Profile

Upland, IN 46989
Phone: (765) 998-5376

Type: 4 Yr.,Private,Liberal Arts
Website: http://www.tayloru.edu
SAT/ACT/GPA: 1183/26/3.7
Student/Faculty Ratio: 17:1
Undergraduate Enrollment: 1,880+
Scholarships/Academic: Yes **Athletic:** Yes
Expenses by: Year **In State:** $ 19,748
Founded: 1846
Religion: Interdenominational
Housing: Yes
Male/Female Ratio: 47:53
Graduate Enrollment: N/A
Financial Aid: Yes
Out of State: $ 19,748
Specialty: Liberal Arts
Degrees Conferred: AA, BA, BS, BMEd
Programs of Study: 44 majors available plus PreProfessional programs in Medicine, Engineering, Law & Medical Technology

Men's Athletic Profile

236 W Reade Avenue
Upland, IN 46989-1001
Coach: Joe Lund
Email: jslund@tayloru.edu

NAIA
Trojans/Purple, Gold
Phone: (765) 998-5376
Fax: (765) 998-4930

Estimated # of Men's Soccer Scholarships: Varies
Conference: Mid-Central Conference
Program Profile: 5 year old soccer complex; natural turf; dugouts and bathrooms at the field; season runs through early part of November
History: Began in 1983; has grown to be one of the best small college programs in the state; have won or tied for conference title last four years.
Achievements: Joe Lund was named the MCC Coach of the Year in 1995; Taylor won the MCC in 1994 & 1995; Toby Bohl was named Honorable Mention All-American in 1994 & 1995; Matt Sarkela was Honorable Mention All-American in 1995.
Coaching: Joe Lund, Head Coach, since 1983 except for two seasons, a 1972 graduate of Graceland College, Lund earned his master's degree from Ball State in 1973. He completed in doctorate at Indiana University in 1981. In eleven years at the home of the Trojans, Lund has posted a 110-87-11 record. He is also an associate professor of Psychology at Taylor.
Walk-on/Other: **Graduation %:** 98 **Seniors on Team:** 4
Positions Needed: defenders; strikers; keepers
Camp or Clinic Dates: Not Available
Most Recent Record: 7-11
Schedule: Houghton, Earlham, Bethel
Style of Play: Short passing control style; offensive push from behind the ball; 4-4-2 typically; pressure on offense.

Tri-State University

Academic Profile

Angola, IN 46703

Phone: 800-347-4878

Type: 4 Yr.,Private
Website: http://www.tristate.edu
SAT/ACT/GPA: 800/19
Student/Faculty Ratio: 15:1
Undergraduate Enrollment: 1,200
Scholarships/Academic: Yes **Athletic:** Yes
Expenses by: Year **In State:** $ 9,000

Founded: 1884
Religion: Non-Affiliated
Housing: Yes
Male/Female Ratio: 3:3
Graduate Enrollment: N/A
Financial Aid: Yes
Out of State: $ 9,000

Specialty: Arts & Science, Engineering, Business
Degrees Conferred: AA, AS, BA, BS
Programs of Study: Arts and Sciences (Biology, Chemistry, Communications, Computer Science, Corporate English, Criminal Justice, Elementary Education, English, Environmental Science, General Studies, History, Individual Studies, Legal Administration, Mathematics, Physical Education, Physical Science, PreMedical, Psychology, Secondary Education, Social Science); Business (Accounting, Applied Management, Business and Arts, Computer Information Systems, General Studies, Management, Marketing, Office Administration); Engineering

Men's Athletic Profile

P.O. Box 307
Angola, IN 46703
Coach: Mike Ferrell
Email: ferrellm@tristate.edu

NAIA
Trojans/Blue, White
Phone: (219) 665-4294
Fax: (219) 665-4839

Did Not Return Profile

Women's Athletic Profile

1 University Avenue
Angola, IN 46703
Coach: Thomas Pawlick
Email: paqlikt@tristate.edu

NAIA
Thunder/Royal, White
Phone: (219) 665-4841
Fax: (219) 665-4839

Estimated # of Women's Soccer Scholarships: 6
Conference: Wolverine-Hoosier Athletic Conference
Program Profile: Well established regional power, pushing into national top area playing surface with press box and dugouts. Year-round program; game field and two practice fields are natural grass.
History: The program began in 1989, nationally ranked five out of nine years.
Achievements: WHAC Conference Champions in 1994; Coach of the Year in 1994; 4 All-Americans; 7 Academic All-Americans.
Coaching: Thomas Pawlik, Head Coach.

Roster in State: 4	**Out of State:** 18	**Out of Country:** 1
ODP State: 5	**Regional:** 1	**National:**
Walk-on/Other:	**Graduation %:** 100	**Seniors on Team:** 4

Positions Needed: Forward, Midfield
Camp or Clinic Dates: Not Available
Most Recent Record: 7-12-1
Schedule: St. Francis, Tiffin, Siena Heights, St. Ambrose, Aquinas
Style of Play: Control short passing game.

University of Evansville

Academic Profile

Evansville, IN 47722

Phone: 800-423-8633

Type: 4 Yr.,Private,Liberal Arts,Engineering		**Founded:** 1854
Website: http://www.evansville.edu		**Religion:** Methodist
SAT/ACT/GPA: No minimum		**Housing:** Yes
Student/Faculty Ratio: 13:1		**Male/Female Ratio:** 45:55
Undergraduate Enrollment: 2,600		**Graduate Enrollment:** 100
Scholarships/Academic: Yes	**Athletic:** Yes	**Financial Aid:** Yes
Expenses by: Year	**In State:** $ 10,600	**Out of State:** $ 10,600

Specialty: Physical Therapy, Theatre
Degrees Conferred: BA, BS, BFA, MSPT, MSHCM
Programs of Study: Over 80 degree programs - please visit our website.

Men's Athletic Profile

1800 Lincoln Avenue
Evansville, IN 47722
Coach: Fred Scmalz
Email: fs3@evansville.edu

NCAA I
Purple Aces/Purple, Orange
Phone: (800) 423-8633
Fax: (812) 479-2199

Estimated # of Men's Soccer Scholarships: 9.9
Conference: Missouri Valley Conference
Program Profile: 2000 is the first year that the Aces move into Arad McCutchan Stadium, which is located next tot he UE Fitness& Recreation Center with a seating capacity of 3,000 McCutchan Stadium gives the Aces one of the finest facilities in the country used exclusively for soccer.
History: Began in 1974; played in the NCAA Tournament 11 times in the last 10 years; has 2 trips to final Four; been

MVC Champions 6 times in the past 10 years.
Achievements: Produce 13 All-Americans, including 1989 Adin-Dassler; National Player of the Year was Rob Paterson; Produced All-Academic All-Americans, 1 professional player and one more All-American.
Coaching: Fred Schmalz, Head Coach, holds "A" License, ranked 3rd in wins amongst active coaches, 19th year at UE, national staff, Soccer American Coach of the Year in 1985; Region 11 Director of ODP. Jason Kittrup - Assistant Coach, "A" License, MEd, graduate of Brazilian Football Academy. Region II ODP Staff, author of Video "25 moves, 25 exercise".
Roster In State: 5 **Out of State:** 23 **Out of Country:** 7
ODP State: 7 **Regional:** 6 **National:** 2
Walk-on/Other: 4 **Graduation %:** N/A **Seniors on Team:** 3
Camp or Clinic Dates: June 25-30, July 24-28
Most Recent Record: 10-2-1
Schedule: Indiana University, Southern Methodist, Creighton, Southwest Missouri, Akron, Florida International
Style of Play: We are a possession-oriented team that can be dangerous going forward. Pretty organized defensively and pretty disciplined.

Women's Athletic Profile

1800 Lincoln Avenue
Evansville, IN 47722
Coach: Mick Lyon
Email: ml33@evansville.edu

NCAA I
Purple Aces/Purple, Orange
Phone: (812) 479-2084
Fax: (812) 479-2344

Estimated # of Women's Soccer Scholarships: 3
Conference: Missouri Valley Conference
Program Profile: In 2000, the Aces will be playing in a stadium that holds 3,000 people with on natural grass. Field dimensions are 120x75 yards with state of the art lighting.
History: The program began in 1993 and quickly made a name for itself. Since 1994, they have been in the championship game for the conference and have won 4 straight titles. In 1998 and in 1999, the team has participated in the NCAA tournament.
Achievements: We earned Coach of the Year three times, 3 Defensive Players of the Year three times, 4 Conference Players of the Year, 2 Conference Freshmen of the Year, 11 All-Region players, Conference Champions 4 times, NCAA Tournament twice.
Coaching: Mick Lyon is our Head Coach. He has ten years college coaching experience. He holds USSF "A" License. He was named All-American player and International player. Hilton Bashford is our Assistant Coach. He has 20 years of youth coaching experience. He holds USSF "A" License. Misty Long is our Goalkeeper Trainer and Second Assistant Coach. she holds USSF "A" License.
Roster in State: 7 **Out of State:** 12 **Out of Country:** 0
ODP State: 7 **Regional:** 2 **National:** 0
Walk-on/Other: 3 **Graduation %:** 100 **Seniors on Team:** 7
Camp or Clinic Dates: July 16-22, 2000
Most Recent Record: 10-10-2
Schedule: Dayton, Illinois, New Mexico, Illinois State, Cincinnati, Navy, Kentucky
Style of Play: Tough defense - attacking flair and play to win.

University of Indianapolis
Academic Profile

Phone: 800-232-8634

Indianapolis, IN 46227

Type: 4 Yr.,Private,Liberal Arts
Website: http://www.uindy.edu
SAT/ACT/GPA: 900/18/2.5

Founded: 1902
Religion: Methodist
Housing: Yes

Student/Faculty Ratio: 14:1
Male/Female Ratio: 45:55
Undergraduate Enrollment: 2,000
Graduate Enrollment: 1,500
Scholarships/Academic: Yes
Athletic: Yes
Financial Aid: Yes
Expenses by: Year
In State: $ 19,000
Out of State: $ 19,000
Specialty: Physical Therapy, Occupational Therapy, Education
Degrees Conferred: AA, AS, BA, BS, MA, MS, MBA
Programs of Study: Business, Education (Elementary & Secondary), Criminal Justice, Music, Art, Drama, Communications, Athletic Training, Health Science

Men's Athletic Profile

1400 E Hanna Avenue
Indianapolis, IN 46227-3697
Coach: Bob Kouril
Email: DrKouril@aol.com

NCAA II
Greyhounds/Maroon, White
Phone: (317) 788-6111
Fax: (317) 788-3472

Estimated # of Men's Soccer Scholarships: 6
Conference: Great Lakes Valley Conference
Program Profile: UI competes in the Great Lakes Valley Conference, one of the premier leagues in the NCAA II men's soccer. We play home matches at Key Stadium with a seating capacity of 5,500 and Kuntz Stadium, the site of the 1987 Pan American Soccer Games. Both fields are natural turf. Veteran soccer Coach Derek Brown became the men's coach in January of 1995, bringing the wealth of a professional and junior playing and coaching experience to UI.
History: Men's soccer began in 1981, progressing rapidly to an 11-5-2 record 3 seasons later in 1984. After a down period, the Greyhound posted the best 4-year record in school's history from 1990 to 1993 with an 8-7-2 mark in 1990, a 9-80 slate in 1991, 8-8 record in 1992, and 11-4 in 1993. The 1993 team set numerous school records including best record (.719), most goals (45), fewest goals against (24), most shutouts (5), longest winning streak (&).
Achievements: 2 X Third Place finish in Conference; 2 X Tournament Simi-Finalist; Several players All-Conference Athletic and Academic; Ranked 4th in Region in 1999.
Coaching: Bob Kouril is head Coach.
Roster In State: 10
Out of State: 6
Out of Country: 4
Positions Needed: All
Camp or Clinic Dates: Not Available
Most Recent Record: 11-9
Schedule: Truman State, Wisconsin-Parkside, Lewis, IPFW, Rockherst
Style of Play: Possession- Oriented; Attacking style.

Women's Athletic Profile

1400 E Hanna Avenue
Indianapolis, IN 46227
Coach: Chris Johnson
Email: cjohnson@undy.edu

NCAA II
Greyhounds/Crimson, Grey
Phone: (317) 788-3578
Fax: (317) 788-3472

Estimated # of Women's Soccer Scholarships: 6.5
Conference: Great Lakes Valley Conference
Program Profile: The Greyhounds plays on a grass playing field at St. Francis Soccer Complex.
History: 1995 was the first season of play for the women's varsity program. In 1999 we finished 3rd out of 12 in our Conference, which was a huge jump from 15th in 1997.
Achievements: 1 All-American; 4 All-Region.
Coaching: Chris Johnson, Head Coach, entering sixth year with the program. He holds USSF "A" License, Indiana ODP Staff Coach, Director of Coaching for Saint Francis Soccer Alliance. Robert McIntosh, Assistant Coach, he holds USSF "C" License and National Youth, Indiana ODP Staff Coach and Director of Coaching for Brownsburg Soccer Club.
Roster in State: 10
Out of State: 8
Out of Country: 1

ODP State: 5 **Regional:** 1 **National:**
Walk-on/Other: **Graduation %:** 100 **Seniors on Team:** 2
Positions Needed: Goalkeeper, Forward
Most Recent Record: 13-7
Schedule: Northern Kentucky, SIU-Edwardsville, Minnesota, Minnesota State, University of Southern Indiana, Truman State
Style of Play: 4-3-3 possession style of play.

University of Notre Dame
Academic Profile

Joyce Arena & Convocational Ctr
Notre Dame, IN 46556
Phone: 219-631-7505

Type: 4 Yr.,Private,Liberal Arts,Engineering
Founded: 1842
Website: http://www.und.com
Religion: Catholic
SAT/ACT/GPA: 1240 avg/3.5
Housing: Yes
Student/Faculty Ratio: 12:1
Male/Female Ratio: 53:47
Undergraduate Enrollment: 7,500
Graduate Enrollment: 3,000
Scholarships/Academic: Yes **Athletic:** Yes **Financial Aid:** Yes
Expenses by: Year **In State:** $ 27,000 **Out of State:** $ 27,000
Specialty: Business, Science
Degrees Conferred: BA, BS, BFA, MA, MS, MBA, MFA, Ph.D., JD
Programs of Study: Accounting, American Studies, Architecture, BioChemistry, Biological Sciences, Economics, Engineering (Aerospace, Civil, Computer, Electrical, Environmental, Mechanical) Finance, Government, History, Management Information Systems, Marketing, Mathematics, Philosophy, Physics, PreDental, PreMed, Theatre, Theology

Men's Athletic Profile

Soccer Office - Joyce Ctr
Notre Dame, IN 46556
Coach: Bobby Clark
Email: N/A

NCAA I
Fighting Irish/Navy, Gold, White
Phone: (219) 631-3376
Fax: (219) 631-9690

Estimated # of Men's Soccer Scholarships: 12
Conference: Big East Conference
Program Profile: Alumni Field gives the Irish one of the finest natural grass facilities in the Midwest. Alumni Field will be the home of the 2000 Big East Championships. The Irish have hosted many NCAA Championship games in the last five seasons at Alumni Field.
History: Our program began in 1988. In just 10 seasons, Notre Dame has become one of the premiere soccer programs in the nation.
Achievements: In 1999, National finalists, Big East Champions, 3 All-Americans, 4 finalists for the Missouri Athletic Club award, 3 finalist for the Hermann Award, Big East Defensive Player of the Year, Big East Coach of the Year, and many Big East All-Conference players.
Coaching: Bobby Clark, whose five seasons as coach at Stanford produced the most successful era in the history of Cardinal men's soccer, has been named men's soccer coach at the University of Notre Dame. Assistant Coaches are Amy Edwards and Barb Chura.
Roster In State: 2 **Out of State:** 20 **Out of Country:** 2
ODP State: **Regional:** 7 **National:** 7
Walk-on/Other: **Graduation %:** **Seniors on Team:** 4
Positions Needed: Defenders, Midfield, Forward
Most Recent Record: 21-4-1

Schedule: Santa Clara, Stanford, Penn State, Hartford, University of Connecticut, Michigan
Style of Play: Possess ional, build-up style. Want to also have the ability to counter attack efficiently when its on to do so. We look for soccer players who are technically gifted and who Laos possess physical dimensions of a top athlete.

Women's Athletic Profile

JACC
Notre Dame, IN 46556
Coach: Randy Waldrum
Email: Randy.Waldrum.1@nd.edu

NCAA I
Fighting Irish/Navy, Gold
Phone: (219) 631-8431
Fax: (219) 631-9690

Estimated # of Women's Soccer Scholarships:
Conference: Big East
Program Profile: We have a nationally ranked program, a natural grass stadium and a seating capacity for 5,000.
History: We started in 1988.
Achievements: 9 All-Americans; 1994 Runner-Up in Herman Trophy; four-time Coach of the Year; NCAA Runner-Up; 4 Conference titles; top rated recruited class 1992 and 1993; ranked #1 at end of 1994 season; 1993 Freshman of the Year; Big 12 Coach of the Year in 1998; 1998-99 Big 12 Conference Champions at Baylor University. Harmon Award winner Anne Makinen, Was ranked #1 team in the country lost to UNC in semi-finals.
Coaching: Randy Waldrum, Head Coach, is our new head coach. He has a USSF "A" License. He is a U.S. Soccer National Staff Coach. He was an assistant with the U-20 and U-18 U.S. National Teams. He was Big 12 Coach of the Year in 1998. Amy Edwards and Sue-Moy Chin are our assistant coaches.
Roster in State: 2 **Out of State:** 20 **Out of Country:** 2
ODP State: 4 **Regional:** 4 **National:** 3
Walk-on/Other: 0 **Graduation %:** 100 **Seniors on Team:** 5
Positions Needed: Defenders, Mid-Field
Camp or Clinic Dates: 1 week in June, 2 weeks in July
Most Recent Record: 23-1-1
Schedule: Santa Clara, Portland, Penn State, Connecticut, Stanford
Style of Play: Attacking play where individual creativity is encouraged. Speed and quickness are key to success of the team.

University of Saint Francis (St. Francis College)

Academic Profile

Phone: (219) 434-7476
Fort Wayne, IN 46808

Type: 4 Yr.,Private,Liberal Arts **Founded:** 1890
Website: http://www.sf.edu **Religion:** Catholic
SAT/ACT/GPA: 920/19/2.0 **Housing:** Yes
Student/Faculty Ratio: 18:1 **Male/Female Ratio:** 34:66
Undergraduate Enrollment: 1560 **Graduate Enrollment:** 420
Scholarships/Academic: Yes **Athletic:** Yes **Financial Aid:** Yes
Expenses by: Year **In State:** $ 15,000 **Out of State:** $ 15,000
Specialty: Arts, Business, Education, Nursing, Psychology, Social Work
Degrees Conferred: AA, AS, BA, BBA, BS in Education, BS in Nursing, MBA, MSEd, MS
Programs of Study: Accounting, Allied Health, American Studies, Art, Biology, Business Administration, Chemistry, Commercial Art, Communications, Education, English, Environmental Science, Fine Arts, Health and Safety, History, Human Resources, General Science, Medical Technology, Ministry, Nursing, PreLaw, PreMed, PreVet, Protective Services, Psychology, Radiography, Religious Studies, Social Science, Special Education

Men's Athletic Profile

2701 Spring Street
Fort Wayne, IN 46808
Coach: Mitch Ellisen
Email: mellisen@sf.edu

NAIA
Cougars/Royal, White
Phone: (219) 434-7559
Fax: (219) 434-7441

Estimated # of Men's Soccer Scholarships: N/A
Conference: Mid-Central Conference
Program Profile: A building program with a bright future. Natural grass field, soccer only. Playing season is in the Fall.
History: Our program is 25 years old.
Coaching: Mitch Ellisen, Head Coach, is entering his first year with the program. He holds a USSF "A" License and has a NSCAA Advanced National Diploma.
Style of Play: Possession, build, will counter team defense. Team is compact and organized.

Women's Athletic Profile

2701 Spring Street
Fort Wayne, IN 46808
Coach: Pamela Kalinoski
Email: kalinoskip@usfca.edu

NAIA
Lady Cougars/White, Blue
Phone: (415) 422-2269
Fax: (219) 434-7441

Estimated # of Women's Soccer Scholarships: 3
Conference: Mid-Central Conference
Program Profile: We play on a natural grass, 120x75, field in Coonon field.
History: Our program started in fall of 1995.
Achievements: 9 NAIA All-American; past 4 yrs MCC Player of the Year; 5 Academic All-Americans; 3 NSCAA National Team Academic awards; 2 Conference Championships in 4 years.
Coaching: Ken Nuber, Head Coach of both men's and women's programs, SFC second all-time goals 43; sixth all-time assists 16, second all-time points, most goals in a game 4, Fort Wayne High School Coach of the Year in 1993.

Roster in State: 20	**Out of State:** 4	**Out of Country:** 0
ODP State: 8	**Regional:** 1	**National:**
Walk-on/Other:	**Graduation %:** 100	**Seniors on Team:** 3

Positions Needed: Midfield, Forward
Camp or Clinic Dates: Not Available
Most Recent Record: 13-7
Style of Play: Possession style, attack out of back. Short passing game.

University of Southern Indiana

Academic Profile

Evansville, IN 47712

Phone: 800-467-1965

Type: 4 Yr.,Public		**Founded:** 1967
Website: http://www.usi.edu		**Religion:** Non-Affiliated
SAT/ACT/GPA: 17/2.0		**Housing:** Yes
Student/Faculty Ratio: 26:1		**Male/Female Ratio:** 1:5
Undergraduate Enrollment: 8,500		**Graduate Enrollment:** N/A
Scholarships/Academic: Yes	**Athletic:** Yes	**Financial Aid:** Yes
Expenses by: Year	**In State:** $ 6,000	**Out of State:** $ 12,000

Specialty: Education
Degrees Conferred: AA, BS, AS, BA, MA, MS, MBA
Programs of Study: Accounting, Business and Management, Science and Technology, PreMed, Allied Health, Communications, Education, Psychology, Social Science

Men's Athletic Profile

8600 University Blvd.
Evansville, IN 47712
Coach: Dan Hogan
Email: dhogannn@usi.edu

NCAA II
Screaming Eagles/Red, Blue
Phone: (812) 464-1946
Fax: (812) 465-7094

Estimated # of Men's Soccer Scholarships:
Conference: Great Lakes Valley Conference
Program Profile: Full size, soccer only field, bleachers, lights, and natural grass. Separate practice facility.
History: Program began in 1979. Eleven GLVC Tournament Championships. Participated in the NCAA I 1992-94. Overall record 206-170-23.
Achievements: This is coach Hogan's first year at USI. He was the former Head Coach at Columbia College the past 9 years.
Coaching: Head Coach is Dan Hogan and this is his first season with the Screaming Eagles.
Roster In State: 9 **Out of State:** 8 **Out of Country:** 0
ODP State: 3 **Regional:** **National:**
Positions Needed: All
Camp or Clinic Dates: Not Available
Most Recent Record: 4-12-1
Schedule: Rockhurst, Lewis, SIU Edwardsville, Indiana Purdue, University of Missouri at St. Louis, Quincy, Northern Kentucky, Wisconsin Parkside.
Style of Play: Based on the strengths and weaknesses of current players.

Women's Athletic Profile

8600 University Boulevard
Evansville, IN 47712
Coach: Bill Wilkins
Email: bwilkins@usi.edu

NCAA II
Screaming Eagles/Red, Blue
Phone: (812) 465-1041
Fax: (812) 465-7094

Estimated # of Women's Soccer Scholarships: None
Conference: Great Lakes Valley Conference
Program Profile: Field's size is 120 by 75; lighted; great playing surface; natural grass.
History: In two seasons of the program, has already been ranked in the top 25 nationally.
Achievements: Overall coaching record is 123-37-5; 4 Region Coach of the Year; 1992 NSCAA/UMBRO Regional Coach of the Year. 3 NJCAA National Appearances; 1 NCAA National Title.
Style of Play: Short passing - build-up possessions style. Attack and defend in numbers. High intensity, aggressive, and physical.

Valparaiso University

Academic Profile

Valparaiso, IN 46383

Phone: (219) 464-5011

Type: 4 Yr.,Private,Liberal Arts,Engineering
Website: http://www.valpo.edu
SAT/ACT/GPA: 1100+/21+/2.85
Student/Faculty Ratio: 12:1
Undergraduate Enrollment: 2,900
Scholarships/Academic: Yes **Athletic:** Yes
Expenses by: Year **In State:** $ 22,025

Founded: 1859
Religion: Lutheran
Housing: Yes
Male/Female Ratio: 46:54
Graduate Enrollment: 730
Financial Aid: Yes
Out of State: $ 22,025

Specialty: Engineering, Business, Law School
Degrees Conferred: AS, BA, BS, BSW, MA, M Ed, MM, MS, JD, ML

Programs of Study: Accounting, Art, Biology, Chemistry, Chinese & Japanese Studies, Civil Engineering, Communication, Computer Science, Criminology, Decision Science, Economics, Education, Electrical Engineering, English, Environmental Science, Finance, French, Geography, Geology, German, History, International Economics & Cultural Affairs, International Business, International Service, Management, Marketing, Mathematics, Mechanical Engineering, Meteorology, Music, Nursing, Philosophy, Physical Education, Athletic Training, Sports Management, Physics, Political Science, Psychology, Sociology, Spanish, Theatre/Television Arts, Theology

Men's Athletic Profile

ARC 175A
Valparaiso, IN 46383
Coach: Mis' Mrak
Email: mis.mrak@valpo.edu

NCAA I
Crusaders/Gold, Brown
Phone: (219) 464-5783
Fax: (219) 464-5762

Estimated # of Men's Soccer Scholarships:
Conference: Mid-Continent Conference
Program Profile: Top conference team, has three practice fields, game field, natural grass fall season August - November; spring season runs from March through May. The stadium has a seating capacity of 1,000 seats.
History: Began in 1983 as a non-scholarship Division I program. We have been phasing in scholarship over the last 3 years. Building program, close to achieving NCAA Tournament.
Achievements: Coach of the Year in 1997; Conference Champions in 1996; Divisional Conference Champions in 1997.
Coaching: Mis' Mrak, Head Coach, since 1991, former player and professional license coach.
Style of Play: Defense: Combination zonal man. Attack: Combination possession - direct system of play varies from year to year; use 3-5-2 or 3-4-3.

Women's Athletic Profile

Department of Athletics
Valparaiso, IN 46383
Coach: Stephen Anthony
Email: stephen.anthony@valpo.edu

NCAA I
Crusaders/Brown, Gold
Phone: (219) 464-5178
Fax: (219) 464-5762

Estimated # of Women's Soccer Scholarships: None
Conference: Missouri Valley Conference (Women's soccer only)
Program Profile: 70x115 yards game field natural grass, three 70x110 yards practice fields shared with men's soccer team.
History: The program began in 1993, and one scholarship, and with a record of 1-7; 1994 has one scholarship with a record of 2-17-1; 1995 has one scholarship with a record of 3-17; 1996 has four scholarships with a record of 2-18-1; 1997 has 6.6 scholarships.
Achievements: None
Style of Play: Possession style; indirect attacking utilizing more short passes. Zonal defending.

Wabash College

Academic Profile

Crawfordsville, IN 47933

Phone: 800-345-5385

Type: 4 Yr.,Private,Liberal Arts
Website: http://www.wabash.edu
SAT/ACT/GPA: 1100
Student/Faculty Ratio: 1:11
Undergraduate Enrollment: 850
Scholarships/Academic: Yes
Athletic: No
Expenses by: Year
In State: $ 24,000
Specialty: Pre-Professional Studies

Founded: 1832
Religion: Non-Affiliated
Housing: Yes
Male/Female Ratio: 100/0
Graduate Enrollment: N/A
Financial Aid: Yes
Out of State: $ 24,000

Degrees Conferred: BA, BS
Programs of Study: Biology, Chemistry, Mathematics & Computer Science, Physics, Humanities, Art, Music, Philosophy, Religion, Social Sciences, Economics, History, Political Science, Psychology, Teacher Education

Men's Athletic Profile

301 West Wabash Ave.
Crawfordsville, IN 47933-0352
Coach: Al Fye
Email: Not Available

NCAA III
Little Giants/Scarlet, White
Phone: (317) 361-6208
Fax: (317) 361-6447

Estimated # of Men's Soccer Scholarships: Academic/Financial Aid
Conference: North Coast Athletic Conference
Program Profile: Has a fall soccer season in a very competitive conference; avoid twenty week days because of missing classes.
History: Program began in 1967 (0-9), 13 winning seasons in 29 years, from 1986-1993 the team recorded a mark of 73-39-5.
Achievements: All-Conference, MVP's of conference; All-Mideast; Academic All-Conference; Academic All-American.
Coaching: Al Fye, Head Coach, graduate from Oral Roberts University in 1974, 12 year-record of 96-73-8, coached at Rogers State Junior College from 1979-1984 posting a record of 75-7-3.
Style of Play: Depends on individual's speed and skills.

IOWA

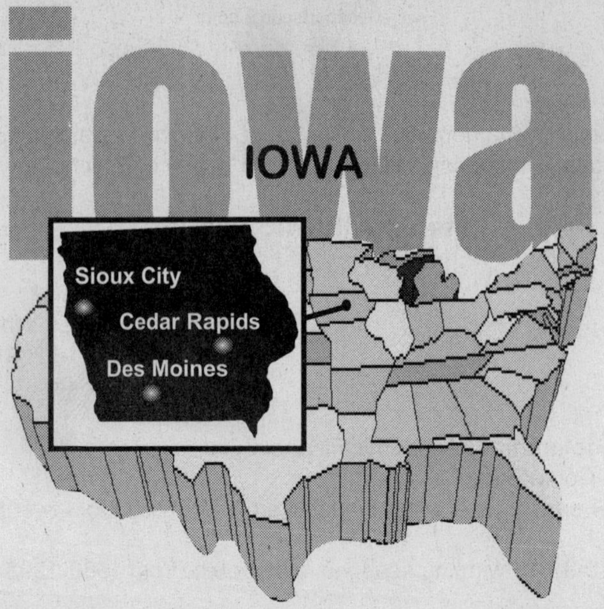

SCHOOL	CITY	AFFILIATION	PAGE
Briar Cliff College	Sioux City	NAIA	354
Buena Vista University	Storn Lake	NCAA III	355
Central College	Pella	NCAA III	356
Clarke College	Dubuque	NCAA III/NAIA	357
Coe College	Cedar Rapids	NCAA III	358
Cornell College	Mt. Vernon	NCAA III	359
Dordt College	Sioux Center	NAIA	360
Drake University	Des Moines	NCAA I	361
Graceland College	Lamoni	NAIA	362
Grand View College	Des Moines	NAIA	363
Grinnell College	Grinnell	NCAA III	365
Iowa State University	Ames	NCAA I	366
Iowa Wesleyan University	Mt. Pleasant	NAIA	366
Loras College	Dubuque	NCAA III	367
Luther College	Decorah	NCAA III	369
Marycrest International University	Davenport	NAIA	370
Mount Mercy College	Cedar Rapids	NAIA	371
Mount Saint Clare College	Clinton	NAIA	373
Saint Ambrose University	Davenport	NAIA	373
Simpson College	Indianola	NCAA III	375
University of Iowa	Iowa City	NCAA I	376
Upper Iowa University	Fayette	NCAA III	377
Wartburg College	Waverly	NCAA III	378
William Penn College	Oskaloosa	NCAA III	379

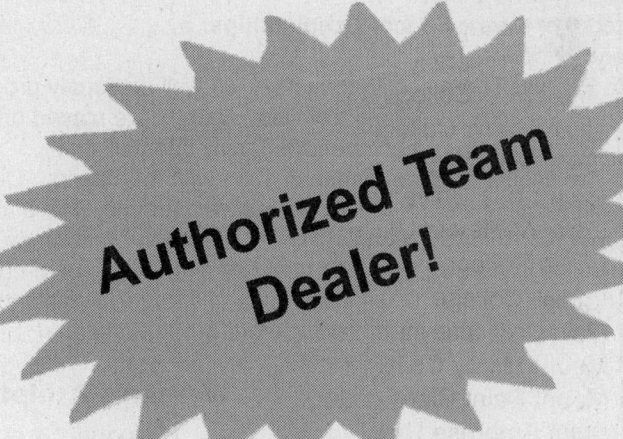

Briar Cliff College

Academic Profile

P. O. Box 2100
Sioux City, IA 51104-2100

Phone:

Type: 4 Yr.,Private,Liberal Arts
Founded: 1930
Website: http://www.briar-cliff.edu
Religion: Catholic
SAT/ACT/GPA: 890/19/2.25
Housing: Yes
Student/Faculty Ratio: 12:1
Male/Female Ratio: 1:3
Undergraduate Enrollment: 1,150
Graduate Enrollment: 600
Scholarships/Academic: Yes **Athletic:** Yes **Financial Aid:** Yes
Expenses by: Year **In State:** $ 16,578 **Out of State:** $ 16,578
Specialty: Liberal Arts
Degrees Conferred: BA, BS
Programs of Study: Majors: Accounting, Art, Biology, Business Administration, Chemistry, Computer Information Systems, Criminal Justice, Elementary Education, English, HPER, History, Human Resource Management, Mass Communications, Photography, Mathematics, Music, Nursing, Psychology, Secondary Education, Social Work, Sociology, Spanish, Theatre, Theology, Writing, PreProfessional Programs: Chiropractic, Church Ministry, Dentistry, Engineering, Law, Medical Technology, Medicine/Physician's Assistant, Occupational Therapy, Optometry, Pharmacy, Physical Therapy, Radiological Technology, Veterinary Medicine

Men's Athletic Profile

3303 Rebecca Street
Sioux City, IA 51104
Coach: Judy Guarneri
Email: guarneri@briar-cliff.edu

NAIA
Chargers/Blue, Gold
Phone: (712) 279-1617
Fax: (712) 276-1954

Estimated # of Men's Soccer Scholarships: 5
Conference: Independent
Program Profile: There is a junior varsity, as well as varsity program. Pre-season begins in late August. Practice is on a brand new, on campus natural turf field. Games are played on natural field located on campus behind the athletic building. The program is a competitive, family oriented one.
History: The soccer program began in 1991 with 14 players. Our numbers now range from 30 to 40. There has been a season with a losing record; more competitive overtime. Have made regional twice, post-season most years.
Achievements: 1996 Northern District Independent Conference Winner; 1994 Conference Champion.
Coaching: Judy Guarneri, Head Coach, has over 20 years of coaching club, high school and college level. Pat Herbst, Assistant Coach, holds a "C" License. Sean Finnegar, Assistant Coach, holds a "C" License
Style of Play: Controlled style of ball, short, quick passes.

Women's Athletic Profile

3303 Rebecca Street
Sioux City, IA 51104
Coach: Shawn Mansfield
Email: mansfields@briarcliff.edu

NAIA
Chargers/Blue, Gold
Phone: (712) 279-1617
Fax: (712) 276-1954

Estimated # of Women's Soccer Scholarships: N/A
Conference: Independent Conference
Program Profile: Our program began in 1993. We made post-season play the last two years. Our playing field is a natural turf and it located on campus behind our athletic facility. We have a full-size practice field that is also on campus. Pre-season starts in late August. Post season games are finished in November. This is a small school competitive program.
History: Our program began in 1993. We had some early building struggles. We are family oriented. We have become competitive.

Achievements: NAIA All-American Scholar Athlete one in 1995 and two in 1996.
Style of Play: Controlled play with short, quick, passes.

Buena Vista University
Academic Profile

Storm Lake, IA 50588

Phone:

Type: 4 Yr.,Private,Liberal Arts
Founded: 1891
Website: http://www.bvu.edu
Religion: Presbyterian
SAT/ACT/GPA: 1075/24
Housing: Yes
Student/Faculty Ratio: 15:1
Male/Female Ratio: 49:51
Undergraduate Enrollment: 1,250
Graduate Enrollment: 140
Scholarships/Academic: Yes
Athletic: No
Financial Aid: Yes
Expenses by: Year
In State: $ 20,393
Out of State: $ 20,393
Degrees Conferred: BA, BS
Programs of Study: 35 majors in the following schools: Communications & Arts, Business, Education, Science, Social Science, Philosophy & Religions

Men's Athletic Profile

610 W. 4th Street
Storn Lake, IA 50588
Coach: David Spataru
Email: spataprud@bvu.edu

NCAA III
Beavers/Navy, Gold
Phone: (800) 383-2821x2074
Fax: (712) 749-1460

Estimated # of Men's Soccer Scholarships: None
Conference: Iowa Intercollegiate Athletic Conference
Program Profile: We have a fall season. We will have a new facilities for fall of 2000.
History: Our program began in 1997 with a record of 3-7. Our 1998 record was 10-6-2.
Achievements: The men's team made conference playoffs in 1998 and finished 4th.
Coaching: David Spataru, our head coach, was a former player and coach in Europe and a former assistant Coach at University of San Francisco, head coach at Augustana College and Westfield State College.
Roster In State: 18
Out of State: 3
Out of Country: 4
ODP State: 4
Regional: 4
National:
Walk-on/Other:
Graduation %: 100
Seniors on Team: 4
Positions Needed: Defenders
Camp or Clinic Dates: July 3-7, 10-14 and June 26-30
Most Recent Record: 10-6-2
Schedule: Luther College, St Thomas, Simpson College, Nebraska Wesleyan
Style of Play: Varies

Women's Athletic Profile

610 W. 4th St.
Storm Lake, IA 50588
Coach: David Spataru
Email: spatarud@bvu.edu

NCAA III
Beavers/Navy, Gold
Phone: (800) 383-2821
Fax: (712) 749-1460

Estimated # of Women's Soccer Scholarships: None
Conference: Iowa Intercollegiate Athletic Conference
Program Profile: We have a new grass field.

History: Our program in 1997.
Coaching: David Spataru, former player and coach in Europe, is the head coach.
Roster in State: 18 **Out of State:** 3 **Out of Country:** 4
ODP State: 4 **Regional:** 4 **National:**
Walk-on/Other: **Graduation %:** 100 **Seniors on Team:** 4
Positions Needed: Defenders
Camp or Clinic Dates: July 3-7, 10-14, June 26-30
Most Recent Record: 1-16-0
Schedule: Luther College, St. Thomas, Simpson College, Nebraska Wesleyan
Style of Play: Varies

Central College

Academic Profile

Pella, IA 50219
Phone: (515) 678-5139

Type: 4 Yr.,Private,Liberal Arts
Founded: 1853
Website: http://www.central.edu
Religion: Reformed Church
SAT/ACT/GPA: Combination of test scores and class rank
Housing: Yes
Student/Faculty Ratio: 13:1
Male/Female Ratio: 45:55
Undergraduate Enrollment: 1,300
Graduate Enrollment: N/A
Scholarships/Academic: Yes **Athletic:** No **Financial Aid:** Yes
Expenses by: Year **In State:** $ 17,980 **Out of State:** $ 17,980
Specialty: Liberal Arts, Business, Education
Degrees Conferred: Many
Programs of Study: Accounting, Art, Biology, Business Management, Chemistry, Communications, Theatre, Computer Science, Economics, Elementary Education, French, English, German, History, International Management, Mathematics, Science, Music, Music Education, Philosophy, Anthropology, Spanish, Athletic Training

Men's Athletic Profile

812 University
Pella, IA 50219
Coach: Gary Laidlaw
Email: LaidlawG@Central.edu

NCAA III
Dutch/Red, White
Phone: (515) 628-7609
Fax: (515) 628-5356

Estimated # of Men's Soccer Scholarships: varies
Conference: Iowa Conference
Program Profile: New and growing program with a strong athletic tradition. It is 45 minutes from strong soccer area - Des Moines. Fully irrigated, full size pitch - immaculate condition.
History: Our program began in 1993, slowly progressed but now has finally named two separate full-time staff as head coaches (men's & women's). Largest recruiting class for upcoming 1998 season - new era!!
Achievements: Led by Nick Furlong - All-Conference 1st team - school's all-time leading scorer.
Coaching: Gary Laidlaw is our Head Coach. Alan Blasio is the Assistant Coach.

Women's Athletic Profile

812 University
Pella, IA 50219
Coach: Amy VanHeukelem
Email: vanheukelema@central.edu

NCAA III
Dutch/Red, White
Phone: (515) 628-7609
Fax: (515) 628-5356

Estimated # of Women's Soccer Scholarships: None
Conference: Iowa Conference

Program Profile: The games are played on natural grass at the Kuyper Athletic Complex (one of the largest and nicest pitches in the state). The Athletic complex also includes the Kuyper Fieldhouse which houses an indoor track as well as the Ron Schipper Fitness Center which includes a 7,000 sq. ft. strength and conditioning area. Central also has a full time strength/conditioning coach.
History: Our program began in 1994. In 1997 the team finished 7th in the IIAC with a 5th in the IIAC, in 1998 with a record of 8-8-1, and 1999 was the best season yet with a 12-8 overall record and 7-2 in conference play finishing them in 3rd in the IIAC.
Achievements: N/A
Coaching: Amy VanHeukelem was an All-State player in Colorado before going on to compete at Calvin College in Grand Rapids, MI. Coached High School in MI and CO and was an assistant coach at the University of Northern Colorado before coming to central. She also coaches the Iowa Olympic Development Program.
Roster in State: 11 **Out of State:** 5 **Out of Country:**
Walk-on/Other: **Graduation %:** 100 **Seniors on Team:** 3
Positions Needed: All
Camp or Clinic Dates: June 12-16
Most Recent Record: 12-8-0
Schedule: Simpson, University of Wisconsin-Osh Kosh, Luther, Cornell, Bethel, Grinnell

Clarke College

Academic Profile

Phone: (319) 588-6300
Dubuque, IA 52001

Type: 4 Yr.,Private,Liberal Arts **Founded:** 1843
Website: http://www.clarke.edu **Religion:** Catholic
SAT/ACT/GPA: 1000 +/21+/2.0-4.0 **Housing:** Yes
Student/Faculty Ratio: 12:1 **Male/Female Ratio:** 35:65
Undergraduate Enrollment: 1,279 **Graduate Enrollment:** 162
Scholarships/Academic: Yes **Athletic:** No **Financial Aid:** Yes
Expenses by: Year **In State:** $ 18,668 **Out of State:** $ 18,668
Degrees Conferred: AA, BA, BS, BFA, MA, BSN, MED, MS
Programs of Study: Accounting, Art, BioChemistry, Business and Management, Chemistry, Communications, Computer Information Systems, Computer Science, Economics, Education, Music, English, French, German, Journalism, Liberal Arts, Marketing, Mathematics, Medical Technology, Nursing, Philosophy, Physical Therapy, Political Science, PreLaw, PreMed, PreVet, Psychology, Public Relations, Religion, Social Science, Theatre

Men's Athletic Profile

1550 Clarke Drive
Dubuque, IA 52001
Coach: Patrick Herbst
Email: pherbst@ clarke.edu

NCAA III/NAIA
Crusaders/Navy, Gold
Phone: (319) 588-6760
Fax: (319) 588-6666

Estimated # of Men's Soccer Scholarships: None
Conference: Northern Illinois and Iowa Conference
Program Profile: competitive, rebuilding program, looking to overhaul current situation. natural grass on campus field, field is soccer use only.
History: Program began in 1984. NAIA & National Little College in 1984-1987, club status 1987-1992. Clarke restarted varsity soccer as an NCAA institution in 1992. Clarke became a member of the Northern Illinois Iowa Conference in 1996.
Achievements: 20 All-Conference players
Some All-Conference Academic performers
Coaching: Patrick Herbst Head Coach sine March 2000, Assistant Brian Henneger since fall 2000

Roster In State: 6 **Out of State:** 9 **Out of Country:** 2
Walk-on/Other: **Graduation %:** 90 **Seniors on Team:** 2
Camp or Clinic Dates: Not Available
Most Recent Record: —
Schedule: Dominican Univ. Rockford College, Loras College, North Central College, Mount St. Clare College
Style of Play: A ball control style with emphasis on attacking as a unit. Defense is a combination of man and zone.

Women's Athletic Profile

1550 Clarke Drive
Dubuque, IA 52001
Coach: Patrick Herbst
Email: pherbst@clarke.edu

NCAA III
Crusaders/Navy, Gold
Phone: (319) 588-6760
Fax: (319) 588-6666

Estimated # of Women's Soccer Scholarships: N/A
Conference: Northern Illinois & Iowa Conference
Program Profile: Natural turf field with a state of the art and water system. Field size is 110x55 yards and is among the best in the Midwestern States, all NAIA and NCAA III competition and matches, all roads within two hours of Dubuque. New $4.2 million athletic center opened April 7, 1994. Available indoor practice facility and for the winter. Fall season that runs from September one through November one with no stadium.
History: The program began in 1994. NAIA in 1994-1997. NCAA III in 1997. Clarke was conference championships in 1998.
Achievements: Several players NAYSD All-Midwest Classic; Squad and Academic All-Conference Squads. 1998 Conference Champs and 15 All-Conference Players.
Coaching: Patrick Herbst Head Coach sine March of 2000 and Brian Henneger who started in fall 2000
Roster in State: 5 **Out of State:** 8 **Out of Country:**
Walk-on/Other: **Graduation %:** **Seniors on Team:** 1
Positions Needed: Forwards, Midfield, Keeper
Camp or Clinic Dates: Not Available
Most Recent Record: 7-11-1
Schedule: Dominican Univ. Aurora Univ. Cornell College, Simpson College, Loras College.
Style of Play: A ball control style with emphasis on attaching as a unit. Defense is a combination of man and zone.

Coe College

Academic Profile

Phone: 319-399-8500

Cedar Rapids, IA 52402

Type: 4 Yr.,Private,Liberal Arts **Founded:** 1851
Website: http://www.coe.edu **Religion:** Presbyterian U.S.A.
SAT/ACT/GPA: 950/20/3.0 **Housing:** Yes
Student/Faculty Ratio: 12:1 **Male/Female Ratio:** 40:60
Undergraduate Enrollment: 1,100 **Graduate Enrollment:** 200
Scholarships/Academic: Yes **Athletic:** No **Financial Aid:** Yes
Expenses by: Year **In State:** $ 23,060 **Out of State:** $ 23,060
Degrees Conferred: BA, BS, Nursing
Programs of Study: Accounting, American Studies, Asian Studies, Biological Sciences, African-American Studies, Business Administration, Education, English, Environmental Science, French, German, History, Interdisciplinary Studies, Liberal Arts, Literature, Mathematics, Medical Technology, Molecular Biology, Music, Nursing, Philosophy, Physical Education, Physical Sciences, Physics, Political Science, PreLaw, PreVeterinary, Psychology, Religious Studies, Sciences, Social Science, Spanish, Speech, Theatre

Men's Athletic Profile

1220 1st Avenue NE
Cedar Rapids, IA 52402
Coach: Derek Pendergast
Email: o-athletics@coe.edu

NCAA III
Kohawks/Crimson, Gold
Phone: (319) 399-8852
Fax: (319) 399-8721

Estimated # of Men's Soccer Scholarships: None
Conference: Midwest Conference
Program Profile: We have an excellent program; play on natural grass in a 1,300-seat stadium.
History: Began in 1990.
Achievements: Finished second in the South Division Conference in 1995.

Women's Athletic Profile

1220 - First Ave. NE
Cedar Rapids, IA 52402
Coach: John Paul Besong
Email: mwu@coe.edu

NCAA III
Kohawks/Red, White
Phone: (319) 399-8599
Fax: (319) 399-8721

Estimated # of Women's Soccer Scholarships: None
Conference: IIAC
Program Profile: Playing season is in the fall; play on natural grass stadium field, outstanding athletic practice facility.
History: Started in the fall of 1989. moved from Midwest Athletic conference to Iowa Intercollegiate Athletic Conference in fall of 1997.
Achievements: Qualified for Midwest Athletic Conference Championships in 1993, 1994, & 1996; Iowa Intercollegiate Athletic Conference Champions in 1997.
Coaching: John Paul Besong, Head Coach, played for University of Minnesota Soccer Club and member of Cedar Rapids Comets; former soccer official. Mo Jahemi - Assistant Coach. Mickey Wu - Assistant Coach.
Style of Play: Team defense and offense. Simple wide-open attacking.

Cornell College

Academic Profile

Mt. Vernon, IA 52314-1098

Phone:

Type: 4 Yr.,Private,Liberal Arts
Website: http://www.cornell-iowa.edu
SAT/ACT/GPA: 1010/20/3.0-4.0
Student/Faculty Ratio: 14:1
Undergraduate Enrollment: 1,050
Scholarships/Academic: Yes **Athletic:** No
Expenses by: Year **In State:** $ 24,135

Founded: 1853
Religion: Non-Affiliated
Housing: Yes
Male/Female Ratio: 45:55
Graduate Enrollment: N/A
Financial Aid: Yes
Out of State: $ 24,135

Specialty: One Course -at-a -Time Curriculum
Degrees Conferred: BA, BSS, BM, BP
Programs of Study: Biology, Education, English, International Business, Politics, Psychology, Economics, PreProfessional Programs

Men's Athletic Profile

600- 1st St. W
Mt. Vernon, IA 52314-1098
Coach: Patrick Bourgeacq
Email: pbourgeacq@cornell-iowa.edu

NCAA III
Rams/Purple, White
Phone: (319) 895-4257
Fax: (319) 895-5895

Estimated # of Men's Soccer Scholarships: None
Conference: Iowa Intercollegiate Athletic Conference
Program Profile: We have two full-size grass soccer practice only fields. Game field is soccer only and top quality, as well as indoor facility. One course at a time format allows for interesting travel opportunities and class scheduling for in-season athletes. Switch to Iowa Conference is a big opportunity to advance the program.
History: Our program began in 1980.
Achievements: Conference Champions in 1984.
Style of Play: High pressure defense with a possession oriented attack.

Women's Athletic Profile

600 First St. W
Mount Vernon, IA 52314-1098
Coach: Steve Robertson/ Mike Robertso
Email: srobertson@cornell-iowa.edu

NCAA III
Rams/Purple, White
Phone: (319) 895-4151
Fax: (319) 895-5895

Estimated # of Women's Soccer Scholarships: None
Conference: Iowa Intercollegiate Athletic Conference
Program Profile: Has a 120x75 natural grass game field, a two full size 120x75 practice fields, an indoor playing surface which has a measurements of 48,000 ft. (100x80 yards), swimming pool, six lane 200 meter, indoor track, weight room, athletic training room, and 4 indoor tennis courts.
History: 2000 Regular Season Champions, Qualified for post-season competition in 1997, 1998, and 2000. IIAC Record of 27-6-1 in Four Years in Conference, Program began varsity competition in 1989.
Achievements: 1 All-Region Player (1998), 26 All-Conference Players in last 7 Seasons, 6 NSCAA Academic All-Region Players, 1997 IIAC Coach of the Year, 2000 IIAC Regular Season Champions, 1998 Player set NCAA Record for assists in a single game (6).
Coaching: Steve and Mike Robertson are in their seventh year at Cornell as co-head coaches. We operate with a philosophy that aims to compete against the toughest teams possible, which has resulted in one of the strongest Div.III schedules in the nation. Through demonstration, visualization and repetition we instruct our players on the intricate technical and tactical aspects of the games. We believe that ultimate success on the field can only be realized through intelligent team play.

Roster in State: 1
ODP State: 5
Walk-on/Other: 0
Out of State: 19
Regional: 0
Graduation %: 100
Out of Country: 1
National: 0
Seniors on Team: 1

Positions Needed: Forward, Center Midfield, Sweeper, GK
Camp or Clinic Dates: Not Available
Most Recent Record: 11-8-1
Schedule: Macalester, Washington Univ. Wheaton, St. Thomas, Claremont, Pomona-Pitzer, Simpson, Luther
Style of Play: At Cornell, players learn a style of soccer where backs attack, midfielders and forwards freely interchange position, possession is maintained and attacks are quick and decisive.

Dordt College

Academic Profile

Sioux Center, IA 51250

Phone: (712) 722-2273

Type: 4 Yr.,Private,Liberal Arts
Website: http://www.dordt.edu
SAT/ACT/GPA: 910/19/2.0 to 2.25
Student/Faculty Ratio: 14:1
Undergraduate Enrollment: 1,400
Scholarships/Academic: Yes
Expenses by: Year

Athletic: Yes
In State: $ 16,500

Founded: 1955
Religion: Christian Reformed
Housing: Yes
Male/Female Ratio: 45:54
Graduate Enrollment: 15
Financial Aid: Yes
Out of State: $ 16,500

Specialty: Elementary/Secondary Education, Social Work, Engineering, Business
Degrees Conferred: AA, BA, BS (Engineering), BSW (Social Work), MA
Programs of Study: Agriculture, Business/Office and Marketing/Distribution, Business and Management, Communications, Education, Letters/Literature, Life Sciences, Multi/Interdisciplinary Studies, Psychology, Social Sciences

Men's Athletic Profile

498 - 4th Ave. NE
Sioux Center, IA 51250
Coach: Dan Oppeneer
Email: doppenee@dordt.edu

NAIA
Defenders/Black, White, Gold
Phone: (712) 722-6305
Fax: (712) 722-6303

Estimated # of Men's Soccer Scholarships: 4 partial
Conference: Upper Midwest Athletic Conference
Program Profile: Strong program, 18-game schedule, playing season is in September through November, natural grass surface.
History: Program began in 1977.
Achievements: NAIA District Champs in 1981 & 1982. Conference Champions in 1990, 1991 & 1992; District Runner-Up in 1989, 1990, & 1991.
Roster In State: 12 **Out of State:** 8 **Out of Country:** 0
Walk-on/Other: **Graduation %:** 95 **Seniors on Team:** 3
Camp or Clinic Dates: Not Available
Most Recent Record: 2-14
Schedule: Park, National American , Huron, Nebraska Wesleyan, Hastings

Drake University
Academic Profile

Des Moines, IA 50311
Phone: (800) 44-DRAKE

Type: 4 Yr.,Private,Liberal Arts
Website: http://www.drake.edu
SAT/ACT/GPA: 970
Student/Faculty Ratio: 12:1
Undergraduate Enrollment: 3,000
Scholarships/Academic: Yes **Athletic:** Yes **Financial Aid:** Yes
Expenses by: Year **In State:** $ 20,970 **Out of State:** $ 20,950
Founded: 1881
Religion: Non-Affiliated
Housing: Yes
Male/Female Ratio: 42:58
Graduate Enrollment: 2,000
Specialty: Business, Journalism, Law School, Pharmacy
Degrees Conferred: BA, BS, BFA, BMus, BSBA, BSEd, BSN, BSPharm, MA, MS, MBA, MFA, M.Ed., EdD, PharmD
Programs of Study: Accounting, Advertising, Art, Art Education, Art History, Astronomy, Biology, Business Studies, Chemistry, Church Music, Computer Science, Cultural Studies, Early Childhood Education, English, Economics, Business Administration, Electronic Media, Elementary Education, German, Graphic Design, History, International Relations, Journalism, Latin American & Caribbean Area Studies, Military Science, Marine Science, Music, Music Education, Nursing, Painting, Pharmacy, Philosophy, Physics, Political Science, Psychology, Religion, Sociology, Spanish, Theatre Arts, Theatre Education, PreProfessional Programs

Men's Athletic Profile

2507 University Avenue
Des Moines, IA 50311-4505
Coach: Sean Holmes
Email: sean.holmes@drake.edu

NCAA I
Bulldogs/Blue, White
Phone: (800) 44DRAKE
Fax: (515) 271-2831

Estimated # of Men's Soccer Scholarships: None
Conference: Missouri Valley Conference
Program Profile: Our field is on campus with a seating for 150. We play on natural grass - dimensions are 120x80.
History: Our program started in 1985. Record to date is 99-102-16.
Achievements: Drake has had eight 1st team All-Conference winners, most recently, Brooks Biggers (defender) in 1995. The Bulldogs have also had one All-American. Ezra Hendrickson, who scored 43 goals in four seasons at Drake, earned third team All-American honors in 1993. Drake owns no conference titles but was second to NCAA qualifiers Creighton in 1994. Drake reached the conference tournament title match that year, losing to Creighton, 1-0.
Coaching: Sean Holmes, Head Coach, entering first season with the Bulldogs. He is the second head coach in program's history. Bill Koepper - Assistant Coach.
Style of Play: Possession - oriented with an attacking bias. Our style will be congruent with our player's abilities - we recruit technical athletes.

Graceland College

Academic Profile

Lamoni, IA 50140

Phone:

Type: 4 Yr.,Private,Liberal Arts
Website: http://www.graceland.edu
SAT/ACT/GPA: 960/22/2.0
Student/Faculty Ratio: 13:1
Undergraduate Enrollment: 1,100
Scholarships/Academic: Yes
Athletic: Yes
Expenses by: Year
In State: $ 16,340
Founded: 1895
Religion: Latter Day Saints
Housing: Yes
Male/Female Ratio: 50:50
Graduate Enrollment: N/A
Financial Aid: Yes
Out of State: $ 16,340
Degrees Conferred: BA, BSN, BS
Programs of Study: Accounting, Art, Athletic Training, Basic Science, Biology, Business Administration, Chemistry, Commercial Design, Communications, Computer Science, Economics, Education, English, French, German, Health, History, Human Services, Information Technology, International Studies, Liberal Studies, Literature, Mathematics, Music, Music Education, Nursing, Philosophy and Religion, Physical Education, PreDentistry, PreEngineering, PreLaw, PreMedicine, PreOptometry, Psychology, Publications Design, Recreation, Social Science, Sociology, Spanish, Speech, Theatre, Wellness Program Management,

Men's Athletic Profile

700 College Avenue
Lamoni, IA 50140
Coach: Ivan Joseph
Email: Not Available

NAIA
Yellowjackets/Blue, Gold
Phone: (515) 784-5117
Fax: (515) 784-5474

Estimated # of Men's Soccer Scholarships: N/A
Conference: Heart of America
Program Profile: Our seasons runs August through November for a schedule of 20 matches. Natural surface, indoor training facility, field size is 120x80 yards.
History: Program was a club sport for 15 years and was elevated to varsity status in 1988.
Achievements: 1994 District Champions, 4 All-Conference 1st team, 1 All-Conference 2nd team, 1 MVP All-Conference, Goalkeeper (Mike Lester) was selected All-American.
Style of Play: Match play based on midfield attack and defense. Passing ground game with a set restarts. Use of striking outside attacking midfield using attacking defenders in either a 4-4-2 or 3-5-2 field set.

Women's Athletic Profile

700 College Avenue
Lamoni, IA 50140
Coach: Mike Cullina
Email: cullina@graceland.edu

NAIA
Yellow Jackets/Blue, Gold
Phone: (800) 346-9208
Fax: (515) 784-5480

Estimated # of Women's Soccer Scholarships: 2.5
Conference: Heart of America Conference
Program Profile: Graceland plays a very competitive conference. Graceland's program is intense in nature, but allows academics to take priority. Graceland play at an on-campus field, The Bruce Jenner Sports Complex, with a natural grass, 120x75 yards, a scenic rolling hills backdrop. Play a 20 game regular season plus two friendlies versus foreign or bigger schools.
History: The program began as a varsity sport in 1993. The current head coach Mike Cullina began his stint at Graceland in 1998 and has led the team to its first back to back 10 win seasons in history and there first ever regional ranking. The 1996 team produced the school's first winning season 12-8.
Achievements: Graceland University has had 9 NAIA Academic All-Americans in the past three years. Iria Relvas graduates in 2000 with six school scoring records and three 1st team All-Conference honors. Jennifer Wheeler and Claudia Hryniewicz have each earned a 2nd team All-Conference honors. Tiffany Rasmussen - 1st team HAAC All-Conference. Melody Carroll - 2nd team HAAC All-Conference. Tasha Pettenozzo - 2nd team HAAC All-Conference.
Coaching: Mike Cullina, who enters his second season at the helm of Graceland University has a coaching record of 20-17-4 in two seasons with he Jackets and 33-31-5 in four seasons, overall. Coach Cullina has a USSF "A" License and NSCAA "advanced" Diploma and is on both the Olympic Development Region II and NSCAA staffs.

Roster in State: 4 **Out of State:** 10 **Out of Country:** 13
ODP State: 2 **Regional:** **National:**
Walk-on/Other: **Graduation %:** 100 **Seniors on Team:** 7

Positions Needed: looking for qualified players in all positions
Camp or Clinic Dates: June 11-16, 2000
Most Recent Record: 10-9-1
Schedule: Lindenwood University, Baker University, National American University, Benedictine College, William Woods College, McKendree College, Nebraska Wesleyan College, Friends University, Missouri Valley College, Northwest Missouri State University
Style of Play: We try and play the most attractive style of play that our abilities will allow. Several factors determine our style such as: Abilities, weather conditions, field conditions, and opponents. We try to establish a strong technical foundation with every player, and use a variety of tactical sets.

Grand View College

Academic Profile

Des Moines, IA 50316

Phone: (800) 444-6083

Type: 4 Yr.,Private,Liberal Arts
Website: http://www.gvc.edu
SAT/ACT/GPA: Open/2.0
Student/Faculty Ratio: 15:1
Undergraduate Enrollment: 1,400

Founded: 1896
Religion: Lutheran
Housing: Yes
Male/Female Ratio: 1:3
Graduate Enrollment: N/A

Scholarships/Academic: Yes **Athletic:** Yes **Financial Aid:** Yes
Expenses by: Year **In State:** $ 16,352 **Out of State:** $ 16,352
Specialty: Art, Education, Nursing
Degrees Conferred: AA, BA, BS
Programs of Study: Accounting, Applied Mathematics, Arts, Biology, Broadcasting, Business Administration, Chemistry, Commercial Art, Computer Information Systems, Computer Science, Creative and Performing Arts, Criminal Justice, Economics, Education, Elementary Education, English, History, International Business, Journalism, Music, Nursing, Philosophy, Physics, Political Science, PreLaw, PreMed, PreVet, Psychology, Radio and Television, Religion, Special Education, Visual Arts

Men's Athletic Profile

1200 Grandview Avenue
Des Moines, IA 50316
Coach: Blair Reid
Email: breid@gvc.edu

NAIA
Vikings/Red, White
Phone: (515) 263-2904
Fax: (515) 263-2882

Estimated # of Men's Soccer Scholarships: Amount Varies
Conference: Midwest Classic Conference
Program Profile: We play on natural field with a measurement of 110x72 yards. New field to be built in the year 2002. The team has a fall 18-20 game schedule plus conference tournament and 3-5 spring schedule. Indoor season at Johnston Soccer Complex that includes weight lifting program.
History: Began in 1983won 8 NAIA District 15 Championships, 2 MCC Conference Championships, 10 Regional Appearances, 2 NAIA Midwest Finalist.
Achievements: The program produced District Coach of the Year seven times; 8 All-Americans; 2 Academic All-American; Conference Coach of the Year two times; several players in NPSL, A-League and USISL, Coach of the Year (PDSL) in 19995 at Des Moines, Menace.
Coaching: Blair Reid, Head Coach, nine years at Dowling High School head varsity coach; 13 years at Grand View College; four years as a coach for the USISL Des Moines Menace in the PDSL; 1995 USISL Premier Coach of the Year.
Style of Play: For players to understand and react to situations correctly. To improve speed of thoughts, and physical play through that understanding. Improvement of techniques, skill and concept ional understanding and mental considerations.

Women's Athletic Profile

1200 Grandview Avenue
Des Moines, IA 50316
Coach: Vincent Stomirov
Email: vstoimirov@gvc.edu

NAIA
Vikings/Red, White
Phone: (515) 263-6159
Fax: (515) 263-2974

Estimated # of Women's Soccer Scholarships: varies
Conference: Midwest Classic Conference
Program Profile: We have a year around program. Our field is natural grass with dimensions of 115x75 yards. In the next year and a half we expect to have a new athletic complex with practice soccer fields.
History: We are a brand new program that just started in fall of 1998. We improve from 2-10-1 to 7-9-2. We finished 3rd in the conference in 1999 and reached semi-final of conference tournament.
Achievements: In the last three years we have had 3 All-Region 2nd team players, 1 1st team All-Conference, 4 2nd team All-Conference and 6 honorable mention. We also have 2 Academic All-Region and 8 Academic All-Conference.
Coaching: Ventsi Stoimirov is the Head Coach and Casey Mann is the Assistant Coach.

Roster in State: 15	**Out of State:** 5	**Out of Country:** 1
ODP State: 4	**Regional:**	**National:**
Walk-on/Other:	**Graduation %:** 95	**Seniors on Team:** 5

Positions Needed: Sweeper, Forward, Goalkeeper
Camp or Clinic Dates: Not Available
Most Recent Record: 7-9-2
Schedule: St. Ambrose University, Wayne State College, Simpson College
Style of Play: Our formation is 4-4-2. We have a combination of high and low pressure defense and possession or counter attacks offense, depending on the opponent, score, field and weather conditions. Emphasis on organized and disciplined teamwork where individual players one given the freedom of improvisation within the game plan.

Grinnell College

Academic Profile

Phone:

Grinnell, IA 50112

Type: 4 Yr.,Private,Liberal Arts
Website: http://www.grinnell.edu
SAT/ACT/GPA: 1250+/25+/3.5
Student/Faculty Ratio: 10:1
Undergraduate Enrollment: 1,300
Scholarships/Academic: Yes
Athletic: No
Expenses by: Year
In State: $ 23,860
Specialty: PreProfessional Programs
Degrees Conferred: BA

Founded: 1846
Religion: Non-Affiliated
Housing: Yes
Male/Female Ratio: 40:60
Graduate Enrollment: N/A
Financial Aid: Yes
Out of State: $ 23,860

Programs of Study: American Studies, Anthropology, Arts, Biology, Chemistry, Chinese, Classic, Computer Science, Economics, English, Education, French, General Science, German, History, Math, Music, Philosophy, Physical Education, Physics, Political Science, Psychology, Religious Studies, Russian, Sociology, Spanish, Theatre

Men's Athletic Profile

P.O. Box 805, Athletics
Grinnell, IA 50112
Coach: Jenny Wood
Email: wood@ac.grin.edu

NCAA III
Pioneers/Scarlet, Black
Phone: (515) 269-3820
Fax: (515) 269-3818

Estimated # of Men's Soccer Scholarships: None
Conference: Midwest Conference
Program Profile: Our season runs from mid-August to first week in November. Facilities includes two natural turf fields on campus. annually a top four team in our conference.
History: Our program began in 1963. Has an overall winning record, including three League Titles in the 1990's.
Achievements: three League Championships in the 90's.
Coaching: Jenny Wood, Head Coach, Grinnel in 1992. Assistant Coaches are TBA.
Style of Play: Possession and flank play. Play to the abilities of the personnel.

Women's Athletic Profile

Box 805 Athletics
Grinnell, IA 50112
Coach: Heather Benning
Email: benning@grinnell.edu

NCAA III
Pioneers/Scarlet, Black
Phone: (515) 269-4971
Fax: (515) 269-3818

Estimated # of Women's Soccer Scholarships: None
Conference: Midwest Conference
Program Profile: Consistently among the top four schools in the MWC. Outstanding natural turf field used solely by the women's program. Fall season with no spring competition. Non-Scholarship program.
History: Became varsity sport in 1987. Since then, became a regional top-ten team and one of the top teams in the Conference year in and year out. Only three losing seasons. Five Conference championships.
Achievements: Has 5 Conference Titles; 2 All-Central Region players; 1 All-American player. Midwest conference champions 91-94, 96, 99; three all-region players
Coaching: Heather Benning - Head Coach, Midwest Conference All-Conference player; completing masters work in Sport Psychology at the University of Iowa.

Roster in State: 4 **Out of State:** 20 **Out of Country:**
ODP State: 6 **Regional:** **National:**
Walk-on/Other: **Graduation %:** 100 **Seniors on Team:** 6
Positions Needed: ALL
Camp or Clinic Dates: Not Available
Most Recent Record: 14-3-1
Schedule: Gustavus Adolphus, Lawrence, Beloit, Simpson
Style of Play: Passing-possession game.

Iowa State University

Academic Profile

Phone:

Ames, IA 50014

Type: 4 Yr.,Public
Founded: 1858
Website: http://www.iastate.edu
Religion: Non-Affiliated
SAT/ACT/GPA: Open/3.0
Housing: Yes
Student/Faculty Ratio: 19:1
Male/Female Ratio: N/A
Undergraduate Enrollment: 24,726
Graduate Enrollment: N/A
Scholarships/Academic: Yes **Athletic:** Yes **Financial Aid:** Yes
Expenses by: Year **In State:** $ 10,000 **Out of State:** $ 16,280
Specialty: Science, Technology
Degrees Conferred: BA, BS, MS, MA, MFA, MEd, Ph.D.
Programs of Study: Accounting, Agriculture, Anthropology, Applied Art, Architecture, Arts, BioChemistry, BioPhysics, Botany, Broadcasting, Business and Management, Computer Science, Dietetics, Communications, City/Community/Regional Planning, Linguistic, Meteorology, MicroBiology, Russian, Sociology, Religion, Biology, Zoology, Social Work

Women's Athletic Profile

1800 South 4th Street
Ames, IA 50010
Coach: Stephanie Gabbert
Email: Ciklein@iastate.edu

NCAA I
Cyclones/Cardinal, Gold
Phone: (515) 294-5328
Fax: (515) 294-0125

Estimated # of Women's Soccer Scholarships: None
Conference: Big Twelve Conference
Program Profile: Program is going into its third year, we have an excellent facilities. Our field is a natural grass field. We also have an astro-turf to train on winter month.
History: Program is beginning its third year. Our program began in the fall of 1996.
Achievements: Cathy Klein was Big Twelve conference Co-coach of the Year in 1997; Qualified in only our second year for the Big Twelve Championships. Placed three players on All-Conference team.
Style of Play: The number one way to describe Iowa State is work ethic. We also stress a possession oriented game.

Iowa Wesleyan College

Academic Profile

Phone: (319) 385-6301

Mt. Pleasant, IA 52641

Type: 4 Yr.,Private,Liberal Arts
Founded: 1842
Website: http://www.iwc.edu
Religion: United Methodist
SAT/ACT/GPA: 980/18/2.0
Housing: Yes

Student/Faculty Ratio: 14:1
Male/Female Ratio: 50:50
Undergraduate Enrollment: 800
Graduate Enrollment: N/A
Scholarships/Academic: Yes
Athletic: Yes
Financial Aid: Yes
Expenses by: Year
In State: $ 16,950
Out of State: $ 16,950
Specialty: Real World Learning
Degrees Conferred: BA, BME, BSN, BS, BGS
Programs of Study: Accounting, Art, Biology, Business Administration, Business Computer Information Systems, Chemistry, Communications, Computer Science, Criminal Justice, Early Childhood Education, Elementary Education, English, Environmental Health, History, Political Science, International Business, Life Science, Mathematics, Music, Nursing, Physical Education, Psychology, Sociology, Sport Management

Men's Athletic Profile

601 N. Main Street
Mt. Pleasant, IA 52641
Coach: Michael Sheerin
Email: admitril@iwc.edu

NAIA
Tigers/Purple, White
Phone: (319) 385-6314
Fax: (319) 385-6384

Estimated # of Men's Soccer Scholarships: None
Conference: Midwest Classic Conference
Program Profile: We play at East Lake Park, which has five grass fields.
History: Our program is four years old.
Coaching: Michael Sheerin is the Head Coach. Gary Jellison is the Assistant Coach.
Style of Play: We play an aggressive style.

Women's Athletic Profile

601 N. Main Street
Mt. Pleasant, IA 52641
Coach: Michael Sheerin
Email: admitril@iwc.edu

NAIA
Tigers/Purple, White
Phone: (319) 385-6314
Fax: (319) 385-6384

Estimated # of Women's Soccer Scholarships: None
Conference: Midwest Classic Conference
Program Profile: We play at East Lake Park. We have five grass fields.
History: Our program is five years old. We were third in conference in 1998.
Achievements: Michael Sheerin was a Conference Coach of the Year in 1998.
Coaching: Michael Sheerin is the Head Coach. Gary Jellison is the Assistant Coach.
Style of Play: We play an aggressive style.

Loras College

Academic Profile

Phone: (319) 588-4975

Dubuque, IA 52004-0178

Type: 4 Yr.,Private,Liberal Arts
Founded: 1839
Website: http://www.loras.edu
Religion: Catholic
SAT/ACT/GPA: Open
Housing: Yes
Student/Faculty Ratio: 13:1
Male/Female Ratio: 50:50
Undergraduate Enrollment: 1,800
Graduate Enrollment: 200
Scholarships/Academic: Yes
Athletic: No
Financial Aid: Yes
Expenses by: Year
In State: $ 18,000
Out of State: $ 18,000
Specialty: Liberal Arts

Degrees Conferred: BA, BS, Masters
Programs of Study: Accounting, Art Education, Biology, Biological Research, Business, Chemistry, Classical Studies, Criminal Justice, Computer Science, Early Childhood Education, Economics, Elementary Education, Engineering, Physics, Finance, French, German, History, International Business, Journalism, Literature, Management, Management Information Systems, Marketing, Mathematics, Medicine Studies, Music, Parish Ministry, Philosophy, Physics, Physical Education, Sports Science, Sports Management, Psychology

Men's Athletic Profile

1450 Alta Vista, Box 178
Dubuque, IA 52004-0178
Coach: Dan Rothert
Email: drothert@loras.edu

NCAA III
DuHawks/Purple, Gold
Phone: (319) 588-4936
Fax: (319) 588-4975

Estimated # of Men's Soccer Scholarships: None
Conference: Iowa Intercollegiate Athletic Association
Program Profile: Our facilities include a picturesque natural grass field that is located on campus, a recreation center and a college fieldhouse with large weight room. Regular attendance is greater than 200.
History: Our program began in 1984. We have become one of the top teams in the IIAC and very competitive regionally. We play a very strong NCAA III schedule.
Achievements: Produced 3 All-conference in 1998; have had 2 players selected to All-Region in the last four years; 1 Academic All-American in 1996.
Coaching: Dan Rothert, Head Coach, was a four year starter at Loras College (1992-1995). He was named 1997 Mississippi Valley Coach of the Year in High School and 1998 Iowa Conference Women's Coach of the Year. He holds a USSF "B" License. He started as a head coach at Loras in 1998. He has previous experience as a women's assistant coach at Plattsburgh State in 1996 and a head coach at Dubuque Senior High School in 1996-1998. Troy Theile and Tiya Eggan are the Assistant Coaches.
Style of Play: Coach utilizes team's strengths. Possession style, but will play direct if opportunity presents itself and finishing components which have led to success.

Women's Athletic Profile

1450 Alta Vista
Dubuque, IA 52001
Coach: Dan Rothert
Email: drothert@loras.edu

NCAA III
Duhawks/Purple, Gold
Phone: (319) 588-4936
Fax: (319) 588-4975

Estimated # of Women's Soccer Scholarships: None
Conference: Iowa Intercollegiate Athletic Conference
Program Profile: Facilities: Own soccer field; playing is in the fall and in the spring; natural grass which measures 110 yards by 70 wide. Stadium has a capacity of 1,000.
History: The women's inaugural season was in 1995.
Achievements: 1998 Iowa Conference Coach of the Year. 9 All-IAC players in 3 years.
Coaching: Dan Rothert, Head Coach. He is our former assistant coach and was a 4 year starter at Loras from 1992 to 1995. He was 1998 Iowa Woman's Coach of the Year. He has a USSF "B" License. He was assistant women's coach at Plattsburg State in New York in 1996. Matt Klosterman is the assistant coach.

Roster in State: 5	**Out of State:** 18	**Out of Country:** 0
ODP State: 3	**Regional:**	**National:**
Walk-on/Other:	**Graduation %:** 100	**Seniors on Team:** 2

Positions Needed: All- we need to increase depth
Camp or Clinic Dates: Not Available
Most Recent Record: 11-8-1
Schedule: St. Ambrose, Luther, Simpson, Cornell, Nebraska Wesleyan, Augustana
Style of Play: Possession oriented with strong defensive principles. Also, not afraid to take risks.

Luther College

Academic Profile

Decorah, IA 52101

Phone: (319) 387-2000

Type: 4 Yr.,Private,Liberal Arts
Website: http://www.Luther.edu
SAT/ACT/GPA: Open
Student/Faculty Ratio: 14:1
Undergraduate Enrollment: 2,500
Scholarships/Academic: Yes
Expenses by: Year
Degrees Conferred: BA, BS

Founded: 1861
Religion: Lutheran
Housing: Yes
Male/Female Ratio: 40:60
Graduate Enrollment: N/A
Athletic: No
Financial Aid: Yes
In State: $ 21,100
Out of State: $ 21,100

Programs of Study: Accounting, Anthropology, Art, Biblical Languages, Biology, English, Chemistry, Communications, Computer Science, Economics, Elementary Education, History, Management, Mathematics, Music, Nursing, Philosophy, Physical Education, Physics, Political Science, Psychology, Religion, Social Work, Sociology, Spanish, Speech, Sports Management

Men's Athletic Profile

700 College Drive
Decorah, IA 52101-1045
Coach: Doug Mello
Email: Mellodou@Luther.edu

NCAA III
Norse/Royal Blue, White
Phone: (319) 387-2161
Fax: (319) 387-1228

Estimated # of Men's Soccer Scholarships: None
Conference: Iowa Intercollegiate Athletic Conference
Program Profile: Our top notch facilities include a soccer complex with a game stadium, three practice fields, plus a 80x80 grid with a portable goals. Year-round playing season of 22 games in the Fall, with an indoor tournament in the Winter and Spring practice schedule.
History: Ten years as varsity sport. NCAA Far West Top 10; Division III Top 25; NCAA Division III National Tournament 3 of the last 4 years; IIAC champs 1190 thru 1999; Average of 16 wins a season and numerous indoor tournament championships.
Achievements: Luther College has never lost an IIAC Match out of 63; they were the far west region champs in 1996. They were ranked as high as 8th in NCAA Division III; 14 All-Midwest players and have the IIAC MVP every year. Achievements also include 10 Academic All-American, 2 post-graduate scholars, IIAC Coach of the Year, Far West Coy, National Coy Candidate and USL National Coy in 1995.
Coaching: Doug Mello, Head Coach, NSCAA State of Iowa Coaching Director; ODP Region II Staff, Director of Luther College Soccer Camp, youngest coach to win 450 collegiate matches; coached in the USISL with Des Moines Menace and Sioux City Breeze; Head Coach of the Tallahassee Scorpion (Pro Indoor); NSCAA Regional and National Clinician; NCAA Division III National Rater; Master's in Counseling. Ian Collard is the Assistant Coach.
Roster In State: 12
Out of State: 12
Out of Country: 4
ODP State: 14
Regional: 2
National: 0
Walk-on/Other: 12
Graduation %: 100
Seniors on Team: 5
Positions Needed: Forwards, Midfielders and Defenders
Camp or Clinic Dates: July 23-28
Most Recent Record: 16-7-0
Schedule: Wheaton, Macalester, St Olaf, UW Oshkosh, UW Whitewater, Colorado
Style of Play: Dutch - Brazilian Style.

Women's Athletic Profile

700 College Drive
Decorah, IA 52101-1045
Coach: Doug Mello
Email: mellodoug@luther.edu

NCAA III
Norse/Royal Blue, White
Phone: (319) 387-2161
Fax: (319) 387-1228

Estimated # of Women's Soccer Scholarships: None
Conference: Iowa Intercollegiate Athletic Conference
Program Profile: We have top notch facilities that include a soccer complex with a game stadium, two practice fields and an 80x80 yards grid area with portable goals. We also have an indoor practice facility. We have a year-round playing season of twenty games in the fall and an indoor tournament during the winter.
History: Our program began in 1990. We are an NCAA Midwest top team and have won the IIAC championship three out of five years. We have an average of 14 wins a season and have numerous indoor tournament championships.
Achievements: Has 3 All-Americans, 5 Academic All-Americans; 8 All-Region players; IIAC MVP every year; IIAC COY; Umbro team Academic award.
Coaching: Doug Mello, Head Coach, is NSCAA State of Iowa Coaching Director. He is on the ODP Region II Staff and Director of the Luther College Soccer Camp. He was the youngest coach to win 450 collegiate matches. He coached in the USISL with Des Moines, Menace and Sioux City Breeze. He was the head coach of the Tallahassee Scorpions (pro-indoor). He has a new NSCAA premier Diploma, an NCAA Division III National Rates and a Master in Counseling. Mike Kim is Assistant Coach.

Roster in State: 12
Out of State: 12
Out of Country: 2
ODP State: 10
Regional: 2
National: 0
Walk-on/Other: 14
Graduation %: 100
Seniors on Team: 2
Positions Needed: Forwards, Midfield, Defenders
Camp or Clinic Dates: July 23-28
Most Recent Record: 14-7-2
Schedule: Gustavus, St. Olaf, UW Eau Claire, Simpson, Coe, Cornell
Style of Play: Dutch - Brazilian Style.

Marycrest International U(Teikyo)

Academic Profile

Phone:

Davenport, IA 52804

Type: 4 Yr.,Private,Liberal Arts
Founded: 1039
Website: http://www.mcrest.edu
Religion: Non-Affiliated
SAT/ACT/GPA: 840/20/2.3
Housing: Yes
Student/Faculty Ratio: 14:1
Male/Female Ratio: 1:1
Undergraduate Enrollment: 1,150
Graduate Enrollment: 100
Scholarships/Academic: Yes
Athletic: Yes
Financial Aid: Yes
Expenses by: Year
In State: $ 14,700
Out of State: $ 14,700
Specialty: Multi-media, Nursing, Education, Business
Degrees Conferred: BA, BS, BSN, BSW, MA, MS, BIB
Programs of Study: Accounting, American Language & Culture, Agriculture, Art, Biology, Business Administration, Chemistry/Biology, Communications, Computer Graphics, Computer Science, Early Childhood Education, Elementary Education, English, Environmental Management, Environmental Science, Food & Nutrition, Global Studies, Government, History, International Business, Mathematics, Liberal Arts, Multimedia, Musical Theatre, Nursing, PreLaw, PreMed, Psychology, Social Work, Spanish, Speech Communications/Theatre Education, Special Studies, Theatre Arts

Men's Athletic Profile

1607 W 12th Street
Davenport, IA 52804
Coach: Richard Markham
Email: Not Available

NAIA
Eagles/Royal, White
Phone: (319) 326-9561
Fax: (319) 326-9375

Estimated # of Men's Soccer Scholarships: None
Conference: Midwest Classic Conference (MCC)
Program Profile: We have a new soccer complex built in 1994, natural grass surface.
History: Program began in 1980, won NLCAA title in 1984.
Achievements: All-American selected in 1992, 1993 and 1994; advanced to Midwest Regional.

Women's Athletic Profile

1607 W 12th Street
Davenport, IA 52804
Coach: William Hudson
Email: whudson@mcrest.edu

NAIA
Marauding Eagles/Royal, White
Phone: (319) 326-9561
Fax: (319) 326-9375

Estimated # of Women's Soccer Scholarships: 15
Conference: Midwest Classic Conference (MCC)
Program Profile: Rebuilding after several coaching changes. Game field built in 1994, natural grass, seating for 300.
History: Program began in 1993. Conference Champions in 1996 and advanced to the Midwest regional.
Achievements:
Coaching: William Hudson is the Head Coach and is USSF licensed, a graduate of Bradley Univ. NCAA I. Erin Essy is the Assistant Coach and a graduate of Mt. St. Claire College. MCC Player of the Year 1997 & 1998.

Roster in State: 5	**Out of State:** 14	**Out of Country:** 1
ODP State: 4	**Regional:** 0	**National:** 0
Walk-on/Other:	**Graduation %:** 90	**Seniors on Team:** 0

Positions Needed: Goalkeeper and midfielder
Camp or Clinic Dates: Not Available
Schedule: Harris-Stowe, Graceland, St. Ambrose, Judson, Culver-Stockton
Style of Play: Play a possession game with aggressive tendencies in the attacking third. Formations most often use 3-4-3 or 4-3-3.

Mount Mercy College

Academic Profile

Cedar Rapids, IA 52402

Phone: (319) 363-1323

Type: 4 Yr.,Private,Liberal Arts		**Founded:** 1928
Website: http://www.mtmercy.edu		**Religion:** Roman Catholic
SAT/ACT/GPA: Open/18/2.5		**Housing:** Yes
Student/Faculty Ratio: 14/1		**Male/Female Ratio:** 1/3
Undergraduate Enrollment: 1350		**Graduate Enrollment:** N/A
Scholarships/Academic: Yes	**Athletic:** No	**Financial Aid:** Yes
Expenses by: Year	**In State:** $ 17,500	**Out of State:** $ 17,500

Specialty: Education, Criminal Justice, Health Careers
Degrees Conferred: BA, BS, BBA
Programs of Study: Art, Biology, Business Administration, Computer Information Systems, Computer Science, Criminal Justice Administration, Education, English, Health Services Administration, History, International Studies , Mathematics, Marketing, Medical Technician, Music, Nursing, Political Science, Psychology, Public Relations, Religion, Social Studies, Sociology, Speech Drama, Urban Studies

Men's Athletic Profile

1330 Elmhurst Drive, NE
Cedar Rapids, IA 52402
Coach: Amir Hadzic
Email: ahadzic@mmc.mtmercy.edu

NAIA
Mustangs/Blue, Gold
Phone: (319) 363-1323x1543
Fax: (319) 363-6341

Estimated # of Men's Soccer Scholarships: None
Conference: Midwest Classic Conference
Program Profile: Very strong program 1999- Final Four-Region VII.
History: Our program began in 1991, rough start big improvement in the last two years. Very young and talented (all players are freshmen and sophomore).
Achievements: We had 3 All-Conference and All-Region players last season.
Coaching: Amir Hadzic, Head Coach, was a professional player in Croatia and Bosnia ,Yugoslavia. He did a two years coaching school through the University of Sarajevo in which he learned more about all aspects of soccer from the best Yugoslavian and European soccer coaches. He held numbers of clinics in Iowa City and Cedar Rapids. Alen Kudumovic, Assistant Coach.

Roster In State: 5	**Out of State:** 14	**Out of Country:** 3
ODP State: 3	**Regional:** 1	**National:** 0
Walk-on/Other:	**Graduation %:** 95	**Seniors on Team:** 3

Positions Needed: All
Camp or Clinic Dates: June
Most Recent Record: 10-6-0
Schedule: Viterbo, St. Francis, Gran View, Carroll, North Central, Luther
Style of Play: We play 4-4-2 strong defense, solid ball control and powerful forwards. Depending on the team we are playing, we switch to 3-5-2 often.

Women's Athletic Profile

1330 Elmhurst Drive NE
Cedar Rapids, IA 52402
Coach: Amir Hadric
Email: ahadzic@mmc.mtmercy.edu

NAIA
Mustangs/Royal Blue, Gold
Phone: (319) 363-1323
Fax: (319) 363-6341

Estimated # of Women's Soccer Scholarships: none
Conference: Midwest Classic Conference
Program Profile: Playing season is in the fall on a natural grass field.
History: First year of the program was in 1999.
Achievements:
Coaching: Amir Hadric, Head Coach. Rebecca Humbert - Assistant Coach

Roster in State: 9	**Out of State:** 9	**Out of Country:** 0
ODP State: 2	**Regional:** 0	**National:** 0
Walk-on/Other:	**Graduation %:** 95	**Seniors on Team:** 3

Positions Needed: GK, 3 Defenders, 3 Midfielders, 3 Forwards
Camp or Clinic Dates: All June
Most Recent Record: 1-14-0
Schedule: Viterbo, St. Francis, Grand View, St. Ambrose, North Central, Dana
Style of Play: 3-5-2 or 4-4-2 Strong 1 to 1 defense with counter attacks usually carried by outside mids. Very fast and skillful forwards.

Mount Saint Clare College

Academic Profile

Clinton, IA 52732

Phone: 800-242-4153

Type: 4 Yr.,Private,Liberal Arts
Website: www.clare.edu
SAT/ACT/GPA: 860/18/2.0
Student/Faculty Ratio: 12:1
Undergraduate Enrollment: 625
Scholarships/Academic: Yes
Athletic: Yes
Expenses by: Year
In State: $18,620
Founded: 1918
Religion: Franciscan/Catholic
Housing: Yes
Male/Female Ratio: 1/1.5
Graduate Enrollment: N/A
Financial Aid: Yes
Out of State: $18,620
Specialty: Education, Business, Accounting
Degrees Conferred: AA, AAS, BA, BGS
Programs of Study: Accounting, Business Administration, Clinical CytoTechnology, Computer Information Systems, Elementary Education, Social Science, Liberal Arts, Fine Arts, Journalism, Music, Science, Social Science, PreLaw, PreMed, Precounseling, Arts, Biology, Chemistry, Computer Science, Early Childhood Education, Mathematics, Music, Philosophy, PreDentistry, Sociology, Speech Therapy, English as a second language

Men's Athletic Profile

400 N Bluff
Clinton, IA 52732
Coach: Ben John
Email: Not Available

NAIA
Mounties/Purple, Gold
Phone: (319) 242-4023
Fax: (319) 242-2003

Estimated # of Men's Soccer Scholarships:
Conference: Midwest Classic Conference
Program Profile: Our soccer field was renovated in 1995; natural turf with a measurement of 120x70 yards.
History: Our program in 1994.
Coaching: Ben John, Head Coach.

Women's Athletic Profile

400 N Bluff Blvd.
Clinton, IA 52732
Coach: Curt Lewis
Email: Not Available

NAIA
Mounties/Purple, Gold
Phone: (319) 242-4023
Fax: (319) 242-2003

Estimated # of Women's Soccer Scholarships: None
Conference: Midwest Classic Conference
Program Profile: Soccer field renovated in 1995; natural turf with a measurement of 120x70 yards.
History: Women's program began in 1995 and ended its first year with a 13-1 regular season record, 3-1 in conference (tied for first), and received an at-large bit to the NAIA Midwest Regional Tournament where the team lost in first round; finished 14-3 overall.

Saint Ambrose University

Academic Profile

Davenport, IA 52803

Phone: 319-333-6000

Type: 4 Yr.,Private,Liberal Arts
Website: http://www.sau.edu
Founded: 1882
Religion: Catholic

SAT/ACT/GPA: 950/21/2.4
Housing: Yes
Student/Faculty Ratio: 15:1
Male/Female Ratio: 42/58
Undergraduate Enrollment: 2114
Graduate Enrollment: 897
Scholarships/Academic: Yes **Athletic:** Yes **Financial Aid:** Yes
Expenses by: Year **In State:** $ 20,000 **Out of State:** $ 20,000
Specialty: Liberal Arts and Pre-Professional Career preparation
Degrees Conferred: BS, BA, MBA, MPT
Programs of Study: Business, Computer Science, Education, Social Work, Criminal Justice, History, Physical Therapy, Biology, Psychology, Accounting, Industrial Engineering, Mass Communications, Radio & TV, Special Education, Computer Networking

Men's Athletic Profile

518 W Locust Street
Davenport, IA 52803
Coach: Fr. Bud Grant
Email: bgrant@saunix.sau.edu

NAIA
Fighting Bees/Navy, White
Phone: (319) 333-6419
Fax: (319) 333-6243

Estimated # of Men's Soccer Scholarships: 15
Conference: Midwest Classic Conference
Program Profile: The Varsity has 20 games in season and 2 pre- season scrimmages with the season beginning in Augest and ending in November. We have grass games fields along with practice fields. We also have a JV program.
History: The Varsity program began in 1989. We generally finish 1-3 in our conference. In 1997 we were Conference Champions and we have never had a losing season.
Achievements: MCC Champions in 1997; Regional Qualifier; 2 players named All-American Honorable Mention in 1997; 2nd place MCC in 1998; Winning Season 1989-present.
Coaching: Fr. Bud Grant is our Head Coach with 2 assistants, 1 manager and 2 trainers.
Roster In State: 16 **Out of State:** 21 **Out of Country:** 6
Walk-on/Other: **Graduation %:** 100 **Seniors on Team:** 5
Positions Needed: 10-15
Camp or Clinic Dates: June 25-29
Most Recent Record: 12-10-0
Schedule: McKendree College, Grandview College, Judson, St. Francis, St. Xavier, Viterbo
Style of Play: Fast paced, control the middle, 2-3 touch and aggressive.

Women's Athletic Profile

518 W Locust St.
Davenport, IA 52803
Coach: Dr. Michael Orfitelli
Email: morfitei@sauniv.sau.edu

NAIA
Bees/Navy, White
Phone: (319) 333-6228
Fax: (319) 333-6239

Estimated # of Women's Soccer Scholarships: 10
Conference: Midwest Classic Conference
Program Profile: Program is in its 8th season. Facilities include game field at high school and use of city soccer park. Season starts August 15- November 20th.
History: The program will begin it's 8th season. We have had a winning season each year.
Achievements: Conference champs 5 of 7 years. Last 5 years played in Regional playoffs. 5 players of the Year in Conference. 2 players of the Year Regional. 8 players All-American HM. Coach of the Year 4 times.
Coaching: Dr. Michael Orfitelli, Head Coach, certified, former assistant for the National Championship team. three years as an assistant at Davis and Elkins; two years National Champ Boys. Mike Ortitelli, Jr. - Assistant Coaches and Laura Klutsayits is the Goalie Coach.
ODP State: 4 **Regional:** 0 **National:** 0

Walk-on/Other: 0 **Graduation %:** 95 **Seniors on Team:** 4
Positions Needed: Defense, Midfield
Most Recent Record: 15-3-2
Schedule: St. Xavier, Lindenwood, Western Illinois University, Cumberland, Baker University, Belhaven
Style of Play: Possession - more offensive minded; 4-3-3 or 4-4-2.

Simpson College

Academic Profile

Phone: (800) 362-2454

Indianola, IA 50125

Type: 4 Yr.,Private,Liberal Arts **Founded:** 1860
Website: http://www.simpson.edu **Religion:** Methodist
SAT/ACT/GPA: Contact Simpson Admissions Office **Housing:** Yes
Student/Faculty Ratio: 14:1 **Male/Female Ratio:** 1:1
Undergraduate Enrollment: 1,992 **Graduate Enrollment:** N/A
Scholarships/Academic: Yes **Athletic:** No **Financial Aid:** Yes
Expenses by: Year **In State:** $ 16,710 **Out of State:** $ 16,710
Specialty: Education, Music
Degrees Conferred: BA, BS
Programs of Study: Accounting, Art, Art with Commercial Design, Biology, Chemistry, Communication Studies, Computer Science, Computer Information Systems, Criminal Justice, Early Childhood Education, Economics, Elementary and Secondary Education, English, Environmental Science, French, German, History, International Management, Management, Mathematics, Medical Technology, Music, Music Education, Music Performance, Physical Education, Philosophy, Political Science, PreDentistry, PreEngineering, PreLaw, PreMed, PreNursing, PreOptometry, PrePhysical Therapy, PreTheology, PreVeterinary Medicine, Psychology, Russian Studies

Men's Athletic Profile

701 North E Street
Indianola, IA 50125
Coach: Aziz Haffar
Email: haffar@storm.simpson.edu

NCAA III
Storm/Red, Gold, Black
Phone: (515) 961-1643
Fax: (515) 961-1279

Estimated # of Men's Soccer Scholarships:
Conference: Iowa Intercollegiate Athletic Conference
Program Profile: Our facilities include a newly built natural grass with a measurements of 110x75 yards and a newly practice field with a measurements of 110x80 yards. Additional features that will be added this summer and will include a scoreboard, a public address system, and an additional fen way. We play a traditional fall season. Strength of schedule is a plus for any serious student-athletes.
History: Our program began in the fall of 1996 as junior varsity. Varsity play began in 1995 and has compiled a record of 46-30-8. In its four years, Simpson have ended up second three times and third in the conference once.
Achievements: Has 15 players 1st team named All-Conference selection for five years; 10 played 2nd team All-Conference selections for four years and 2 players named on the all NSCAA regional tea; 4 All-Academic.
Coaching: Aziz Haffar, Head Coach, holds a USSF "B" License, a NSCAA Advanced National Diploma and has a Master's Degree in Sport Coaching. He was a head high school coach at West Des Moines Valley from 1992 to the present. They were conference champs for five years in a row and 1996 & 1997 State High School champions, NSCAA/UMBRO rankings-spring 1995 (12th), in 1996 ranked 1. High school record at Valley is 118-11-3; overall high school record is 152-36-8. He is a three-year letter winner at Truman State University and formerly at Northeast Missouri.
Roster In State: 16 **Out of State:** 8 **Out of Country:** 10
ODP State: 3 **Regional:** **National:**
Walk-on/Other: **Graduation %:** 95 **Seniors on Team:** 4

Positions Needed: Forward, Outside Midfielders
Most Recent Record: 16-4-2
Schedule: Macalester, St Olaf, Gustavus Adolphus, Nebraska Wesleyan, St. Mary's University, Colorado College, St. Thomas College, Luther College, Grinnall College
Style of Play: Usually play a 4-4-2 and this varies from 3-5-2 or 4-3-3. Defense is a combination of zone and man-to-man, and prefer to play a possession and play out of the back utilizing sweeper and outside defenders to bring the ball up to the midfield and strike.

Women's Athletic Profile

701 North C Street
Indianola, IA 50125
Coach: Aziz Haffar
Email: haffar@storm.simpson.edu

NCAA III
Storm/Red, Gold
Phone: (515) 961-1643
Fax: (515) 961-1279

Estimated # of Women's Soccer Scholarships: None
Conference: Iowa Intercollegiate Athletic Conference
Program Profile: Our Facilities include a newly built natural grass field with measurements of 110x75. Additional features that will be added this summer will include a scoreboard, a public address system and an additional fence.
History: The program began play at the junior varsity level in the fall of 1995 and have compete on the varsity level the last four years. Have compiled a record of 54-28-5. Ranked 3rd, 4th and 5th respectively in conference. We were 1999 conference champions, broke school record of 20 wins and advanced into semi-final regional play.
Achievements: Has 12 1st team All-Conference selections, 7 2nd team All-Conference selections, 2 Conference MVPS and 2 All West Region All-Americans, 4 All-Americans.
Coaching: Aziz Haffar, Head Coach, holds USSF "B" license, NSCAA Advanced National Diploma, Masters Degree in Sports Coaching. He is high school coach at West Des Moines Valley from 1992 to the present, Conference Champions in six years in a row. He was 1996 & 1997 High School State Champions, high School NSCAA National rankings, spring 1995-ranked 8th, spring of 1997 ranked 7th. High school career record is 52-36-18. He was named High School Coach of the Year, High School NSCAA Midwest Coach of the Year. He was named two-time Conference Coach of the Year. Letter Winner at Truman State University (Formerly Northeast Missouri State University). JR Fernandes is our assistant coach, holding an USSF "A" license and have played professionally in brazil.
Roster in State: 16 **Out of State:** 4 **Out of Country:**
Walk-on/Other: **Graduation %:** 98 **Seniors on Team:** 4
Positions Needed: Forward, Goalkeeper, Midfield
Camp or Clinic Dates: June 18-25
Most Recent Record: 20-3-0
Schedule: Wisconsin Oskosh, Macalester, Coe, Luther, Augustana College, Grinnell College
Style of Play: Usually a 4-4-2 style. Defense is a combination of zone and man-to-man and prefer to play a possession style and play out of back utilizing sweeper and full backs to bring ball up to midfield and forwards.

University of Iowa
Academic Profile

Phone: (800) 553-4692

Iowa City, IA 52242

Type: 4 Yr.,Public
Website: http://www.uiowa.edu
SAT/ACT/GPA: 700/17
Student/Faculty Ratio: 17:1
Undergraduate Enrollment: 19,337
Founded: 1847
Religion: Non-Affiliated
Housing: Yes
Male/Female Ratio: 45:55
Graduate Enrollment: 9,368
Scholarships/Academic: Yes **Athletic:** Yes **Financial Aid:** Yes
Expenses by: Year **In State:** $ 7,368 **Out of State:** $ 14,810
Degrees Conferred: BA, BS, BFA, BLS, BM, BSN, MA, MBA, MFA, MD

Programs of Study: Accounting, Arts, Business Administration, Computer Science, Education, Engineering, Fine Arts, Health Administration, Jurisprudence, Law, Music, Nursing, Philosophy, Pharmacy, Physician Assistant, Science

Women's Athletic Profile

CHA 212 Soccer Office
Iowa City, IA 52242
Coach: Stephanie Gabbart
Email:

NCAA I
Hawkeye's/Black, Old Gold
Phone: (319) 335-9271
Fax:

Estimated # of Women's Soccer Scholarships: N/A
Conference: Big 10 Conference
Program Profile: We have natural grass practice and game fields. We have a new facility with indoor area to practice.
History: We started our program in 1997. We were ranked on of the best among first year programs.
Achievements: Coach Gubbert was Soccer Buzz Coach of the Year for first year program in 1997; 2 Academic All-Conference players.
Coaching: Coach Gabbert is on his 10th year Collegiate Coach and holds a USSF "A" License. The assistant coach Ian Rickerby is a 12th year Collegiate Coach and also holds a USSF "A" License. Our Goalie Coach is Wendy Scholz.
Roster in State: 5 **Out of State:** 20 **Out of Country:**
ODP State: **Regional:** 3 **National:**
Walk-on/Other: **Graduation %:** 100 **Seniors on Team:** 6
Positions Needed: Center Back, Center Mid, Fullback
Camp or Clinic Dates: Varies
Most Recent Record: 6-12-2
Schedule: Penn State, Northwestern, Michigan, Wisconsin, Minnesota, Indiana, Ohio State, Illinois
Style of Play: Very active on defense, possession game; use of midfield and width; find forwards' feet and penetrate.

Upper Iowa University

Academic Profile

Fayette, IA 52142
Phone: (319) 425-5285

Type: 4 Yr.,Private,Liberal Arts
Founded: 1857
Website: http://www.uiu.edu
Religion: Non-Affiliated
SAT/ACT/GPA: 760/17/2.0
Housing: Yes
Student/Faculty Ratio: 18:1
Male/Female Ratio: 3:1
Undergraduate Enrollment: 760
Graduate Enrollment: 17
Scholarships/Academic: Yes **Athletic:** No **Financial Aid:** Yes
Expenses by: Year **In State:** $ 15,000 **Out of State:** $ 15,000
Specialty: Conservation Management, Science, Business, Education
Degrees Conferred: BA, BS, Master of Business Leadership
Programs of Study: Accounting, American Studies, Applied Plant Science, Art, Art Administration, Athletic Training, Biology, Business Administration, Chemistry, Communications, Computer Conservation Management, Construction Management, Criminology, Education, Elementary Education, English, Financial Management, Fine Arts, Graphic Design, Health Care, Human Services, Life Science, Management Information Systems, Marketing, Mathematics, Music, Psychology, Physical Education, Public, Reading, Recreation, Science, Social Science, Sociology, Spanish, Sports Science, Wellness

Men's Athletic Profile

Box 1857
Fayette, IA 52142
Coach: Eric Diehl
Email: diehle@uiu.edu

NCAA III
Peacocks/Sky Blue, White
Phone: (319) 425-5369
Fax: (319) 425-5334

Estimated # of Men's Soccer Scholarships: None
Conference: Iowa Intercollegiate Athletic Conference (IIAC)
Program Profile: We play a fall traditional season. In the winter and in spring, we do a non-traditional season. We have a new soccer field complex that was completed in 1998. It has natural grass and 2 maximum NCAA size game fields.
History: We began in the Spring of 1997. We competed as a varsity sport in the Fall of 1997 and 1998.

Women's Athletic Profile

Box 1857
Fayette, IA 52142
Coach: Steve Reinhaieh
Email: Not Available

NCAA III
Peacocks/Sky Blue, White
Phone: (319) 425-5369
Fax: (319) 425-5334

Estimated # of Women's Soccer Scholarships: None
Conference: IIAC
Program Profile: We play a fall traditional season. We have a winter and spring non-traditional season. We have a new soccer field complex that was completed in 1998. It has natural grass and 2 maximum NCAA size game fields.
History: We began in spring of 1997. We competed as a varsity sport in the fall of 1997 and 1998.

Wartburg College

Academic Profile

Phone: (319) 352-8264

Waverly, IA 50677

Type: 4 Yr.,Private,Liberal Arts
Founded: 1852
Website: http://www.wartburg.edu
Religion: Lutheran
SAT/ACT/GPA: 19
Housing: Yes
Student/Faculty Ratio: 14:1
Male/Female Ratio: 647:893
Undergraduate Enrollment: 1,540
Graduate Enrollment: N/A
Scholarships/Academic: Yes **Athletic:** No **Financial Aid:** Yes
Expenses by: Year **In State:** $ 19,705 **Out of State:** $ 19,705
Specialty: Business Administration, Biology, Elementary Education, Music Edu.
Degrees Conferred: BA, B.Mus., BME, BAA, BAS
Programs of Study: Accounting, Art, BioChemistry, Biology, Business Administration, Business Management, Marketing, International Business, Finance, Chemistry, Communications, Arts, Broadcasting, Journalism, Public Relations, Design, Computer Information Systems, Computer Science, Economics, Education, Early Childhood Education, English, Fitness Management, History, International Relations, Mathematics, Modern Languages, French, German, Spanish, Music, Music Education, Music Ministry, Philosophy, Music Theory, Physical Education, Philosophy, Physics, Political Science, Psychology, Religion, Sociology, Law Enforcement, Occupational Therapy, Medical Technology

Men's Athletic Profile

222 9th St. NW
Waverly, IA 50677
Coach: Jim Conlon
Email: conlon@wartburg.edu

NCAA III
Knights/Black, Orange
Phone: (319) 352-8355
Fax: (319) 352-8528

Estimated # of Men's Soccer Scholarships: None
Conference: Iowa Intercollegiate Athletic Conference
Program Profile: Our facilities include one natural grass game field used soccer only. Playing season is in the Fall. Has 18-game season followed by a season end Conference Tournament. One game field, two practice fields, Lance De Complex for indoor play/practice, state of the art weight room.

History: Began in 1985. First men's soccer program in Iowa. Conference founded in 1980.
Achievements: None.
Roster In State: 11 **Out of State:** 8 **Out of Country:** 4
Walk-on/Other: **Graduation %:** 100 **Seniors on Team:** 3
Positions Needed: ALL
Camp or Clinic Dates: TBA
Most Recent Record: 2-12-1
Schedule: Simpson, Luther, Loras, Augsburg
Style of Play: Possession, Diamond 4 Defense and a aggressive keeper.

Women's Athletic Profile

222 9th St. NW
Waverly, IA 50677
Coach: Jim Conlon
Email: conlon@wartburg.edu

NCAA III
Knights/Black, Orange
Phone: (319) 352-8355
Fax: (319) 352-8528

Estimated # of Women's Soccer Scholarships: None
Conference: Iowa Athletic Conference
Program Profile: The program is 15 years old. Jim and Jason in their first year as coaches and are committed to making a dominate team. We have a championship field a training facility, an indoor multi-purpose training facility. Fields are natural grass with seating for 800. Fall season
History: 15 years old.
Achievements: None
Roster in State: 10 **Out of State:** 7 **Out of Country:** 0
Walk-on/Other: **Graduation %:** 100 **Seniors on Team:** 2
Positions Needed: ALL
Camp or Clinic Dates: TBA
Most Recent Record: 4-13-1
Schedule: Simpson, Luther, Cornell, Rockford, Augsburg
Style of Play: Possession, diamond 4 defense and a aggressive goalkeeper.

William Penn University

Academic Profile

Oskaloosa, IA 52577

Phone:

Type: 4 Yr.,Private,Liberal Arts
Website: http://www.wmpenn.edu
SAT/ACT/GPA: Open
Student/Faculty Ratio: 14:1
Undergraduate Enrollment: 1,300
Scholarships/Academic: Yes **Athletic:** No
Expenses by: Year **In State:** $ 16,150

Founded: 1873
Religion: Quaker
Housing: Yes
Male/Female Ratio: 2:1.5
Graduate Enrollment: N/A
Financial Aid: Yes
Out of State: $ 16,150

Specialty: Teacher Education, Industrial Technology
Degrees Conferred: BA, BS
Programs of Study: Industrial Technology, Teacher Education, Business, Computer Science, Physical Education, Communications, Accounting, Business Management, Biology, History, Psychology, Sociology, PreProfessional

Men's Athletic Profile

201 Trueblood Ave.
Oskaloosa, IA 52577
Coach: Bill Collman
Email: collmanb@wmpenn.edu

NCAA III
Statesmen/Navy, Gold
Phone: (515) 673-1021
Fax: (515) 673-1373

Estimated # of Men's Soccer Scholarships:
Conference: Iowa Intercollegiate Athletic Conference
Program Profile: This is the start of only the fourth year of varsity play. Our soccer field is part of a soccer complex with several fields for practice and for play (brand new!).
History: First year of varsity competition was in 1995.
Achievements:
Coaching: Bill Collman, Head Coach, had coached 4 All-Americans. He was named Coach of the Year at Blackburn College and won Prairie College Conference Title at Blackburn.
Roster In State: 4 **Out of State:** 13 **Out of Country:**
Walk-on/Other: **Graduation %:** 90 **Seniors on Team:** 5
Positions Needed: Goalie, Forwards
Camp or Clinic Dates: Not Available
Most Recent Record: 1-16
Schedule: Luther College, Augustana College, Simpson College, Loras College
Style of Play: We like to play an attacking style that penetrates the defense at every opportunity. We will play a short passing controlled game while looking for that offensive attack.

Women's Athletic Profile

201 Trueblood Avenue
Oskaloosa, IA 52577
Coach: Ammon Bennett
Email: Not Available

NCAA III
Lady Statemen/Navy, Gold
Phone: (515) 673-1081
Fax: (515) 673-1373

Estimated # of Women's Soccer Scholarships: None
Conference: Iowa Intercollegiate Athletic Conference
Program Profile: We are starting our 4th year of varsity soccer. Our soccer field is a part of a soccer complex with several fields for practice and play. They are brand new fields.
History: Fall of 1996 was the first year of varsity competition.
Achievements: 6 All-American players; Conference Coach of the Year; Conference Champion.
Style of Play: Short passing, ball control style of play; attack generated from the midfield.

kansas

KANSAS

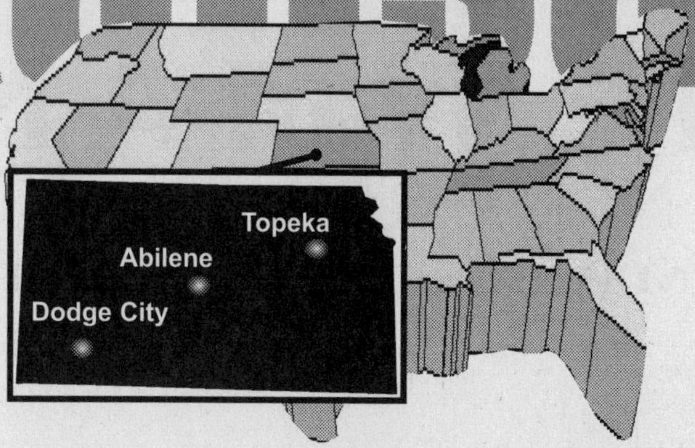

SCHOOL	CITY	AFFILIATION	PAGE
Baker University	Baldwin City	NAIA	383
Benedictine College	Atchison	NAIA	384
Bethany College	Lindsborg	NAIA	385
Bethel College	North Newton	NAIA	386
Friends University	Wichita	NAIA	388
McPherson College	McPherson	NAIA	389
Newman University	Wichita	NAIA	390
Ottawa University	Ottawa	NAIA	391
Saint Mary College	Leavenworth	NAIA	392
Southwestern College	Winfield	NAIA	393
Sterling College	Sterling	NAIA	394
Tabor College	Hillsboro	NCAA II/NAIA	395
University of Kansas	Lawrence	NCAA I	396

Baker University
Academic Profile

Baldwin City, KS 66006-0065
Phone: 800-873-4282

Type: 4 Yr.,Private,Liberal Arts,Engineering
Website: http://www.bakeru.edu
SAT/ACT/GPA: 1000/21/3.0
Student/Faculty Ratio: 14:1
Undergraduate Enrollment: 850
Scholarships/Academic: Yes
Athletic: Yes
Expenses by: Year
In State: $ 16,530
Founded: 1858
Religion: Non-Affiliated
Housing: Yes
Male/Female Ratio: 1:2
Graduate Enrollment: 1,800
Financial Aid: Yes
Out of State: $ 16,530
Specialty: Business, Liberal Arts
Degrees Conferred: BA, BS, BFA, BM, BE, BME, MS, MBA
Programs of Study: Accounting, Banking and Finance, Biology, Business, Chemistry, Communications, Computer Science, Economics, Education, English, Fine Arts, French, German, History, Languages, Life Science, Mathematics, Music, Philosophy, Physics, Political Science, PreDentistry, PreLaw, PreMed, Psychology, Religion, Sociology, Spanish, Physical Education

Men's Athletic Profile

P.O. Box 65
Baldwin City, KS 66006-0065
Coach: Ron Pulvers
Email: pulvers@harvey.baker.edu

NAIA
Wildcats/Orange, Navy, White
Phone: (785) 594-4551
Fax: (785) 594-8377

Estimated # of Men's Soccer Scholarships: 2.5
Conference: Heart of America Athletic Conference
Program Profile: We have a natural turf stadium soccer facility that measure 112x76 and seats 1,000. We also have two new full-sized training fields that measures 114x75 yards.
History: Our program began in 1986. NAIA top six in 1992, 1993, & 1998. Top 15 in1995, 1996 & 1997; 6 HAAC Titles, 2 District Titles, 8 times Midwest Region Finalist.
Achievements: 15 NAIA All-Americans; 2 Olympic Festival players (North team silver medal); 5 professional players (drafted 1st or 2nd round); 20 All-Midwest Region players, 6 HAAC Players of the Year; 38 All-Conference players; 10 Academic All-Americans.
Coaching: Ron Pulvers, Head Coach, holds a USSF "B" Licensed and has a NSCAA Advanced National Diploma. He is a Kansas State Boys Director of Coaching and Player Development. Jason Hopper, Assistant Coach.
Style of Play: Possession.

Women's Athletic Profile

P.O. Box 65
Baldwin City, KS 66006
Coach: Brandon Barkus
Email: barkus@harvey.bakeru.edu

NAIA
Wildcats/Black, White, Orange
Phone: (785) 594-8428
Fax: (785) 594-8377

Estimated # of Women's Soccer Scholarships: 4
Conference: Heart of America Athletic Conference
Program Profile: Playing season is Fall. Facilities include natural grass field. Both game and practice field are fenced in and capacity of 1,000.
History: Program started in 1989. Baker has produced 12 All-Americans and numerous All-Regions, All-Conference Players.
Achievements: 1996 Conference Champions.

Coaching: Brandon Barkus USSF "A" license, NSCAA Diploma and director of coaching of Olathe Soccer Club. KS State ODP coach 5 years.
Roster in State: 14 **Out of State:** 8 **Out of Country:** 0
Walk-on/Other: **Graduation %:** 100 **Seniors on Team:** 2
Camp or Clinic Dates: Not Available
Most Recent Record: 9-9-0
Schedule: Lindenwood Univ. College of St. Mary's, Huron Univ. Oklahoma City Univ. Park College, National American

Benedictine College

Academic Profile

Atchison, KS 66002
Phone: (913) 376-5340

Type: 4 Yr.,Private,Liberal Arts
Founded: 1858
Website: http://www.benedictine.edu
Religion: Catholic
SAT/ACT/GPA: 18/2.0/2.2
Housing: Yes
Student/Faculty Ratio: 14:1
Male/Female Ratio: 53:47
Undergraduate Enrollment: 1,200
Graduate Enrollment: N/A
Scholarships/Academic: Yes **Athletic:** Yes **Financial Aid:** Yes
Expenses by: Year **In State:** $ 16,200 **Out of State:** $ 16,200
Degrees Conferred: BA, BS
Programs of Study: Accounting, Astronomy, BioChemistry, Biology, Business, Chemistry, Computer Science, Economics, Education, English, French, Journalism, Physics, Natural Science, Sociology, Political Science, Religion, Philosophy, Technical Marketing

Men's Athletic Profile

1020 North 2nd Street
Atchison, KS 66002-1499
Coach: John Casey
Email: jcasey@benedictine.edu

NAIA
Ravens/Red, Black, White
Phone: (913) 367-5340x 2561
Fax: (913) 367-2564

Estimated # of Men's Soccer Scholarships: 24
Conference: Heart of America Athletic Conference
Program Profile: We play 18-20 regular season games, including 7 current opponents. We are ranked in the National Top 25.
History: Our program began in 1961. We were a club varsity in 1963. We have three Region Championships. We have seventeen District Championships and one post-season Conference Championship. We qualified for the playoffs for 31 years including 27 consecutive times.
Achievements: District Coach of the Year twice, Region Coach of the Year once, 14 All-Americans; 43 All-District players; 3 Conference titles out of 10 years.
Coaching: John Casey, Head Coach, is USSF "A" licensed. He is also a NSCAA member. He is entering eight years with the program. He was named two times District Coach of the Year in 1994 and Region Coach of the Year in 1983. Jim Schneider, assistant coach, is a 1990 graduate. He was an All-Region Goalkeeper. Nick Di Carlo is assistant coach.
Style of Play: Possession - target build up.

Women's Athletic Profile

1020 N 2nd Street
Atchison, KS 66002
Coach: Jim Schneiderhahn
Email: Not Available

NAIA
Ravens/Red, Black, White
Phone: (913) 367-5340
Fax: (913) 367-2564

Estimated # of Women's Soccer Scholarships: None
Conference: Heart of America (NAIA)
Program Profile: Natural grass 116 x 80, 2 gyms, mini bus for away games, weight room. The playing season is in the fall; strong academic record by team. Qualified for the region tournament 2 of last 3 years. Annually near the top of the conference standings.
History: Became varsity in 1989. Have gone from 2-12 in 1989 to 12-9 in 1994, second in the conference, on the edge of going to the Regional Tournament. Strong tradition of soccer exists at Benedictine, and women's program is building on the tradition built by the men's program.
Achievements: 1 NSCAA All-American; 3 NAIA Academic All-American Scholar Athletes; numerous All-Region; All-District; All-Conference players. Co-COY Heart of America Conference in 1995.
Coaching: Jim Schneiderhahn, 1st year head coach, 3 years as an assistant for the men's program, USSF "B" license. Set various goalkeeping records as a player at Benedictine. Kansas Olympic Development Program staff coach.
Roster in State: 10 **Out of State:** 17 **Out of Country:** 0
Walk-on/Other: **Graduation %:** **Seniors on Team:** 11
Positions Needed: Goalkeeper and forwards
Camp or Clinic Dates: Not Available
Most Recent Record: 11-9-0
Schedule: Lindenwood, Baker, Southern Nazarene, Park
Style of Play: Pressure up top, with strong defensive play, possession on offense creating many opportunities on goal.

Bethany College

Academic Profile

Lindsborg, KS 67456
Phone:

Type: 4 Yr.,Private,Liberal Arts,Engineering
Founded: 1881
Website: http://www.bethany.bethanylb.edu
Religion: Lutheran
SAT/ACT/GPA: 910/19/2.5
Housing: Yes
Student/Faculty Ratio: 13:1
Male/Female Ratio: 1:1
Undergraduate Enrollment: 650
Graduate Enrollment: N/A
Scholarships/Academic: Yes **Athletic:** Yes **Financial Aid:** Yes
Expenses by: Year **In State:** $ 15,105+ **Out of State:** $ 15,105+
Specialty: All Majors
Degrees Conferred: Bachelors
Programs of Study: Art, Communications, English, Music, Religion, Natural Science, Social Science, Biology, Chemistry, Computer Information Systems, Mathematics, Engineering, Economics, Elementary Education, Political Science, Psychology, Recreation, Sociology, Social Work, Physical Education

Men's Athletic Profile

421 N First St.
Lindsborg, KS 67456
Coach: Marc Gordon
Email: gordonu@bethany.bethanylb.edu

NAIA
Swedes/Blue, Gold
Phone: (785) 227-3380x8333
Fax: (785) 227-2021

Estimated # of Men's Soccer Scholarships: 7
Conference: Kansas Collegiate Athletic Conference (KCAC)
Program Profile: Bethany's home game field is a natural turf which measures 110x75 yards. We have an access to indoor facilities for seasonal weather changes. Full weight room and cardiovascular training area.
History: Our varsity program began in 1992. We have participated in post-season play 6 years out eight and have won the conference regular and post season in 1993.
Achievements: In 1993 and 1999 we received KCAC Coach of the Year. Also in 1993 were the KCAC Champions. We have had several All-Americans and in 1994 we ranked 4th in Region IV.

Coaching: Marc Gordon, Head Coach, USSF "B" License, NSCAA Advanced National Diploma, 1989 All-American, 1990-1992 Colorado Men's Open Regional Team.
Roster In State: 6 **Out of State:** 20 **Out of Country:** 1
ODP State: 7 **Regional:** 1 **National:**
Walk-on/Other: 2 **Graduation %:** 96 **Seniors on Team:** 4
Positions Needed: Strikers, Centermid, Center Defenders
Camp or Clinic Dates: Not Available
Most Recent Record: 12-7-3
Schedule: Newman University, University of Science and Art of Oklahoma, Kansas Wesleyan University, Hastings College, Friends University, St. Mary College
Style of Play: Emphasis on ball possession with speed getting forward quickly and maintaining possession in the attacking. Defensively we play a combination of high and low pressure.

Women's Athletic Profile

421 N First Street
Lindsborg, KS 67456
Coach: Todd Tucker
Email: tuckert@bethanylb.edu

NAIA
Terrible Swedes/Blue, Gold
Phone: 785) 227-3380
Fax: (785) 227-2021

Estimated # of Women's Soccer Scholarships:
Conference: KCAC
Program Profile: Natural practice/playing fields available indoor training facility for inclement weather. Season is from mid-August through mid-November with off-season weight and fitness programs.
History: Our program began in 1994 with one Conference Championship in 1998.
Achievements: Won KCAC Coach of the Year in 1998; KCAC Regular Season & Tourney Champs, 2 All-Americans in 1998.
Style of Play: Possession oriented team that is very structures behind the ball.

Bethel College

Academic Profile

Phone:

North Newton, KS 67117

Type: 4 Yr.,Private,Liberal Arts
Website: http://www.bethelks.edu
SAT/ACT/GPA: 19
Student/Faculty Ratio: 10:1
Undergraduate Enrollment: 600
Scholarships/Academic: Yes **Athletic:** Yes
Expenses by: Year **In State:** $ 15,870

Founded: 1887
Religion: Mennonite Church
Housing: Yes
Male/Female Ratio: 50:50
Graduate Enrollment: N/A
Financial Aid: Yes
Out of State: $ 15,870

Specialty: Strong in many areas: Liberal Arts, Education, Biology, Business
Degrees Conferred: BA, BS
Programs of Study: Accounting, Art, Bible and Religion, Biology, Business Administration, Chemistry, Communication Arts, Elementary Education, English, Fine Arts, German, Global Peace and Justice, Health Management and Human Ecology, History, History and Social Sciences, Mathematical Sciences, Music, Natural Sciences, Nursing, Physics, Psychology, Social Science, Social Work, Spanish, Political Science, International Development, Sociology, Special Education, Speech Communications, Theatre Arts

Men's Athletic Profile

300 E 27th
North Newton, KS 67117-0531
Coach: Gerry Sieber
Email: gsieber@bethelks.edu

NAIA
Threshers/Maroon, White
Phone: (316) 284-5297
Fax: (316) 284-5830

Estimated # of Men's Soccer Scholarships: Dollar limit per player
Conference: Kansas Collegiate Athletic Conference
Program Profile: Bethel College is a member of the NAIA and plays in the competitive KCAC. Our season is in the Fall with off-season conditioning and strength programs offered during the winter, spring, and summer. We christened a brand new soccer complex this fall (2000). We play on a natural grass (fescue) field which is in immaculate shape. A scoreboard and bleachers with seating for approximately 300 people add to the atmosphere of our games. Each team is also provided team dugouts for their bench area to sheild them from the elements and the crowd. Our practice facility is located adjacent to our game field and includes one regulation size field and two small fields.
History: Bethel has a long history of men's soccer. Soccer began as a club sport in the 1960's and early 1970's. The college added soccer as an official varsity sport in the fall of 1985 and recognized the program in the fall of 1988. The early years of the program were lean as the sport struggled to gain popularity and support. In the Spring of 1994 the current head coach, Gerry Sieber, was hired and the program has developed into one of the strongest in the KCAC.
Achievements: The Threshers have won 2 KCAC titles (1996 & 1998). Coach Sieber has been named KCAC Coach of the Year twice. He has won 312 College games. The team has been ranked nationally 5 times (NAIA). Seiber has coached two NAIA All-Americans.
Coaching: Gerry Sieber-has won 312 career college games, his teams have won numerous conference and regional championships, he has won Numerous Coach of the Year awards, and he was invited to an Olympic Team tryout as a player. Troy Fowler-played for the Threshers from 1988-91, serves as the team's goalkeeper coach, and also coaches youth teams. Matt Westerman-played for the Threshers for four years and is a semi-pro soccer player in Wichita.

Roster In State: 9	**Out of State:** 8	**Out of Country:** 2
ODP State: 2	**Regional:**	**National:**
Walk-on/Other:	**Graduation %:** 95	**Seniors on Team:** 3

Positions Needed: All
Camp or Clinic Dates: August 6-10, 2001
Most Recent Record: 7-9-1
Schedule: Newman, Hastings, Benedictine, William Jewell, Saint Mary, Kansas Wesleyan, Tabor, Bethany, Friends, Concordia
Style of Play: We play possession soccer, a good speed of play, with good defensive ball pressure. We are constantly looking for direct attacking possibilities.

Women's Athletic Profile

300 E 27th St.
North Newton, KS 67117-0531
Coach: Mark Yoder
Email: marco@bethelks.edu

NAIA
Threshers/Maroon, White
Phone: (316) 284-5297
Fax: (316) 284-5286

Estimated # of Women's Soccer Scholarships: None
Conference: Kansas Collegiate Athletic Conference (KCAC)
Program Profile: We have a Fall program and considered one of best weight training and athletic training in Kansas. We play approximately 18 regular season games. We have a new Bermuda grass field for 2000-2001 season. We are strong in academics and had an NSCAA Team Academic Award.
History: Our program began in 1985 and was dormant for about nine years. Since the arrival of Coach Gerry Sieber, our program has become one of the strongest in the area. We won conference 2 out of the past three years and ranked nationally several times in recent years. We advanced to semi-final round of Regional Tournament.
Achievements: We have numerous Conference and Regional Coach of the Year honors. We have 20 All-American players. 1999 graduate plays for semi-professional team in Wichita, Kansas (Blue Angels). We have several All-Conference. In 1996, we were 3rd leading scorer in nation; NAIA 33 goals was Jennifer Stipp.
Style of Play: Up tempo, possession but always looking for direct opportunities. Mostly high pressure with emphasis on fast speed of play and decision making.

Friends University

Academic Profile

Wichita, KS 67213

Phone:

Type: 4 Yr.,Private,Liberal Arts
Website: http://www.friends.edu
SAT/ACT/GPA: N/A/18
Student/Faculty Ratio: 15:1
Undergraduate Enrollment: 800
Scholarships/Academic: Yes **Athletic:** Yes
Expenses by: Year **In State:** $ 13,000
Founded: 1898
Religion: Non-Affiliated
Housing: yes
Male/Female Ratio: 48:52
Graduate Enrollment: 800
Financial Aid: Yes
Out of State: $ 13,000
Degrees Conferred: BA, BS, BFA, MA, MS, MBA
Programs of Study: Fine Arts & Business are strong areas of study. Management, Education, Psychology

Men's Athletic Profile

2100 University
Wichita, KS 67213
Coach: Bill Schilling
Email: Not Available

NAIA
Falcons/Red, Gray
Phone: (316) 264-9627
Fax: (316) 263-1092

Estimated # of Men's Soccer Scholarships: None
Conference: Kansas Collegiate Athletic Conference
Program Profile: The lighted stadium seats 4,000, is 120 x 75 with natural turf. 18 matches are played in two months.
History: Program began in the late 1980's and has a history of Conference Titles ever since.
Achievements: Conference Champions, KCAC Coach of the Year, Most Valuable Player of KCAC, and District 10 First Team Player all in 1982. Conference Titles were awarded in 1988, 1990, 1992.
Style of Play: Tenacious attack and defense. Man to man marking defensively, quick counter attack offensively with excellent offensive punch. Place changing and overlapping give and go offensively. Fitness is a must, for fast paced, physical play.

Women's Athletic Profile

2100 University
Wichita, KS 67203
Coach: Michael Budnowski
Email: mbudnowski@aol.com

NAIA
Lady Falcons/Red, Grey
Phone: (316) 268-7627
Fax: (316) 269-3818

Estimated # of Women's Soccer Scholarships: Varies
Conference: KCAC Kansas Collegiate Athletic Conference
Program Profile: Play in the football stadium, natural turf and is under lights. The lighted stadium seats 4,000 is 120x75 yards, with natural turf. 18 matches are played between August and November.
History: The program began in 1990. Seven consecutive district/conference championships beginning in 1990, qualified for regional play each year. Making three Regional Championship Finals. Numerous All-Conference, All-Region, and All-American players.
Achievements: Five-time District/conference Champions. 1st and 2nd team All-Americans in 1993 & 1994 (NAIA & NSCAA). At least four players on All-District/Conference Team each year. Qualified for Regional each year of the program's existence.
Coaching: Michael Budnowsk, Head Coach, two-time district Coach of the Year, former All-District player, State Select Coach for Kansas, USSF "C" License. Regional Coach of the Year.
Roster in State: 15 **Out of State:** 5 **Out of Country:** 0

ODP State: **Regional:** 1 **National:**
Walk-on/Other: **Graduation %:** 90 **Seniors on Team:** 1
Positions Needed: All
Camp or Clinic Dates: Call for details
Most Recent Record: 9-9-1
Schedule: College of St. Mary, Oklahoma City University, Southern Nazarene
Style of Play: Very German with emphasis on wing back play.

McPherson College
Academic Profile

McPherson, KS 67460 **Phone:** (316)241-0731

Type: 4 Yr.,Private,Liberal Arts **Founded:** 1887
Website: http://www.mcpherson.edu **Religion:** Brethren
SAT/ACT/GPA: 860182.25 **Housing:** Yes
Student/Faculty Ratio: 11.5/1 **Male/Female Ratio:** 1/1
Undergraduate Enrollment: 465 **Graduate Enrollment:** N/A
Scholarships/Academic: Yes **Athletic:** No **Financial Aid:** Yes
Expenses by: Year **In State:** $ 18,360 **Out of State:** $ 18,360
Specialty: Liberal Arts (General)
Degrees Conferred: BA, BS, AT (Associates degree of Technology)
Programs of Study: Nearly everything, especially since we have an interdisciplinary major where if we do not have specific major, you can combine classes from different areas to form that major. Contact admissions for complete list of majors....

Men's Athletic Profile

1600 E Euclid
McPherson, KS 67460
Coach: Dane Straight
Email: straighd@mcpherson.edu

NAIA
Bulldogs/Red, Black, White
Phone: (316) 241-0731
Fax: (316) 241-8443

Estimated # of Men's Soccer Scholarships:
Conference: Kansas Collegiate Athletics Conference (KCAC)
Program Profile: The 1999 season will be our first season on a new game field that has a dimension's of 120x75 yards. It is underground irrigated and should hold excellent shape. Our season runs from late August to mid-November. However, we play soccer year-round in a club format as well.
History: McPherson College began soccer in 1991. 1999 will be our ninth season. We have finished 2nd twice in our conference in 1995 & 1996. We have had numerous All-Conference players and a few All-Regional players. We were a young team this year starting 7 freshmen.
Achievements: 1999 NAIA All-American Scholar Athletes: Amanda Behnke, Nikki Unruh-Carey
Coaching: Dane Straight, 26, head coach since 1999, graduated from Bethany college in 1997 and was an Academic All American in 1995. Was invited to tryouts with Colorado Foxes in 1996. Prior coaching experience at Bethany college as an assistant for 3 years as well as coaching youth league teams in Salina area.
Roster In State: 5 **Out of State:** 15 **Out of Country:**
ODP State: 3 **Regional:** **National:**
Walk-on/Other: **Graduation %:** 100 **Seniors on Team:** 1
Positions Needed: Sweeper, Outside Midfielder
Camp or Clinic Dates: Not Available
Most Recent Record: 0-18

Schedule: Friends University, Bethany College, Bartlesville Wesleyan University, Southern Nazarene University, Bethel College, Tabor College
Style of Play: Play ball possession utilizing speed on the outsides and 1&2 touch combination passing to get forward. Play a 4-4-2 most of the time, but will push into a 3-5-2 with the right personnel.

Newman University
Academic Profile

Phone: 316-942-4291

Wichita, KS 67213

Type: 4 Yr.,Private,Liberal Arts
Founded: 1933
Website: http://www.newmanu.edu
Religion: Catholic
SAT/ACT/GPA: Open182.0
Housing: Yes
Student/Faculty Ratio: N/A
Male/Female Ratio: 1/2
Undergraduate Enrollment: 1967
Graduate Enrollment: N/A
Scholarships/Academic: Yes **Athletic:** Yes **Financial Aid:** Yes
Expenses by: Year **In State:** $14,098 **Out of State:** $14,098
Specialty: Nursing, Pre-med, Education, Business
Degrees Conferred: AS, BA, BS
Programs of Study: Accounting, Biology, Business Administration, Chemistry, Communications, Computer Science, CytoTechnology, Education, English, Fine Arts, Graphic Design, Health Science, History, Management, Marketing, Mathematics, Medical Laboratory Technology, Nursing, PreLaw, PreMed, Psychology, Religion, Social Science

Men's Athletic Profile

3100 McCormick Avenue
Wichita, KS 67213
Coach: Cliff Brown
Email: browncw@newman.edu

NAIA
Jets/Scarlet, Royal
Phone: 316-942-4291x197
Fax: (316) 942-4483

Estimated # of Men's Soccer Scholarships: Varies
Conference: Midlands Collegiate Athletic Conference
Program Profile: Natural grass, Soccer only, 120x75, seats 500, Lights in spring of 2001.
History: Program began in November of 1984, Coach Cliff Brown since 1988.
Achievements: District 10 Coach of the Year, 4 time Conference Coach of the Year, 3 time Region Coach of the Year, 6 time regular season conference champions, 4 time conference tournament champions, 3 time region champions, 3 National Tournament appearances, 2000 Quaterfinalist at National Tournament, 6 players played or playing professionally, 30+ All-Conference players.
Coaching: Cliff Brown, former NASL, MISL, AISA, NPSL, USISL goalkeeper, Jose Carranza: Newman grad 1998, Brian Cushing: Newman grad 1997, Wichita Wings Midfielder, Larry Inlow: Newman grad 1997, 3rd team All-American, Wichita Wings defender.
Roster In State: 11 **Out of State:** 4 **Out of Country:** 9
ODP State: 2 **Regional:** 1 **National:** 3
Walk-on/Other: **Graduation %:** N/A **Seniors on Team:** 7
Positions Needed: All
Camp or Clinic Dates: Not Available
Most Recent Record: 13-10-2
Schedule: Mobile, Life, Berry, William Carey, Columbia, National American, Oklahoma City, John Brown
Style of Play: Depends on the style of players recruited.

Women's Athletic Profile

3100 McCormick Avenue
Wichita, KS 67213
Coach: Cliff Brown
Email: Not Available

NAIA
Jets/Red, Blue
Phone: (800) 736-7585
Fax: (316) 942-4483

Estimated # of Women's Soccer Scholarships: None
Conference: Midlands Collegiate Athletic
Program Profile: Separate practice and game fields, both natural turf; seating for 500.
History: The program began in 1989 by Head Coach Cliff Brown.
Achievements: District 10 Coach of the Year in 1990; 1 All-American; 1992 Defensive Player of the Year; 1992 All-District 1st team; 3 1st team All-District.
Coaching: Cliff Brown, Head Coach at Newman since 1988, former professional (1978-1987 NASL, MISL and AISA), 1986 Head Coach at Ft. Waynes Flames AISA. Currently professional coach at Shreveport.
Style of Play: Attacking - high pressure

Ottawa University

Academic Profile

Ottawa, KS 66067

Phone:

Type: 4 Yr.,Private,Liberal Arts
Website: http://www.ottawa.edu
SAT/ACT/GPA: 18/2.5
Student/Faculty Ratio: 15:1
Undergraduate Enrollment: 500
Scholarships/Academic: Yes
Athletic: Yes
Expenses by: Year
In State: $ 14,100
Degrees Conferred: BA

Founded: 1865
Religion: American Baptist
Housing: Yes
Male/Female Ratio: 60:40
Graduate Enrollment: N/A
Financial Aid: Yes
Out of State: $ 14,100

Programs of Study: Art, Business Administration, Biology, PreMed, PreVet, PreDentistry, PreNursing, Chemistry, Communications, Education, English, History, Human Services, Management of Information Systems, Mathematics, Music, Physical Education, Political Science, Psychology, Religion, Sociology, Speech, Theatre

Men's Athletic Profile

1001 S Cedar Street
Ottawa, KS 66067
Coach: Tony Carbaugh
Email: tcar@ottawa.edu

NAIA
Braves/Black, Gold
Phone: (785) 242-5200
Fax: (785) 229-1015

Estimated # of Men's Soccer Scholarships: Varies
Conference: Kansas Collegiate Athletic Conference
Program Profile: Top quality, game only soccer field which is natural grass. Practice fields is lighted, and indoor facilities has a measurements of 40x34 yards. Has a terrific weight room.
History: Began in 1965. Highest ranking 3rd in 1971.
Achievements: 6th in the nation in 1969; 5th in the nation in 1970; 3rd in the nation in 1971; 1 All-American - Frank Lemp.
Coaching: Tony Carbaugh, Head Coach. Gary Dunda - Assistant Coach.
Style of Play: Ottawa team have a reputation for a clean, aggressive, attractive, possession-oriented soccer with a creative flair. Combination play and relentless attacking attitude is instilled in the players. Combine this with fundamental defender's principles and a combination to teamwork and you have Ottawa Soccer!!

Women's Athletic Profile

1001 S. Cedar Street, No.7
Ottawa, KS 66067
Coach: Matt Walberg
Email: tacr@ottawa.edu

NAIA
Braves/Black, Gold
Phone: (785) 242-5200
Fax: (785) 229-1015

Estimated # of Women's Soccer Scholarships: None
Conference: Kansas Collegiate Athletic Conference
Program Profile: We have a game-only field that is top quality and is made of natural grass. Our practice fields are lighted. Our indoor facilities are 40 x 35 yards. We have a terrific weight room.
Style of Play: Ottawa teams have a reputation for clean, aggressive, attractive, possession-oriented soccer with a creative flair, combination play and a relentless attacking attitude is instilled in the players. Combine this with fundamental defending principles and a commitment to teamwork, and you have Ottawa Soccer!

Saint Mary College

Academic Profile

Phone: (800) 752-7043

Leavenworth, KS 66048

Type: 4 Yr.,Private,Liberal Arts
Website: http://www.smcks.edu
SAT/ACT/GPA: 19/2.5
Student/Faculty Ratio: 11:1
Undergraduate Enrollment: 860
Scholarships/Academic: Yes
Athletic: Yes
Expenses by: Year
In State: $ 15,900

Founded: 1858
Religion: Roman Catholic
Housing: Yes
Male/Female Ratio: 1:2
Graduate Enrollment: 400 +
Financial Aid: Yes
Out of State: $ 15,900

Specialty: Pre-Med, Education, Fine Arts, Theatre
Degrees Conferred: AA, BA, BS, BMus, BSN
Programs of Study: Accounting, Biology, Business Administration, Chemistry, Computer Science, Criminal Justice, Dramatic Arts, Elementary Education, English, Fine Arts, History, Human Services, Languages, Management, Mathematics, Medical Technology, Music, Nursing, Performing Arts, Psychology, Public Affairs, Social Science, Spanish, Theology, Voice

Men's Athletic Profile

4100 S 4 St. Trafficway
Leavenworth, KS 66043
Coach: Jon Parry
Email: parryj@hub.smcks.edu

NAIA
Spires/Royal Blue, Gold
Phone: (913)758-6164
Fax: (913) 758-6140

Estimated # of Men's Soccer Scholarships: N/A
Conference: KCAC
Program Profile: Play on a natural grass, two soccer fields, one practice field, one match.
History: Our program began in 1992.
Achievements: 2000 KCAC Champions
Coaching: Jon Parry Head Coach, Asst. Blair Quinn
Roster In State: 9
Out of State: 9
Out of Country: 0
Walk-on/Other:
Graduation %: N/A
Seniors on Team: 3
Positions Needed: ALL
Most Recent Record: 13-6-2
Schedule: Columbia College, Newman Univ. Baker Univ. Park Univ. Hastings College, Avila College, William Woods
Style of Play: Fast paced, counter attacking style.

Women's Athletic Profile

4100 S 4 St.
Leavenworth, KS 66048
Coach: Jon Parry
Email: parryj@hub.smcks.edu

NAIA II
Spires/Royal Blue, Gold
Phone: (913) 758-6164
Fax: (913) 758-6140

Estimated # of Women's Soccer Scholarships: None
Conference: Kansas Collegiate Athletic Conference (KCAC)
Program Profile: Play on natural grass; has two soccer fields, one practice, one match field.
History: The program began in 1992.
Coaching: Head Coach- Jon Parry, Asst. Blair Quinn
Roster in State: 18 **Out of State:** 0 **Out of Country:** 0
Walk-on/Other: **Graduation %:** **Seniors on Team:** 3
Positions Needed: ALL
Camp or Clinic Dates: Not Available
Most Recent Record: 4-14-0
Schedule: Hastings College, Benedictine College, William Woods, Tabor College, Dana College, Bethany College

Southwestern College

Academic Profile

Winfield, KS 67156-2499

Phone: (316) 221-4150

Type: 4 Yr.,Private,Liberal Arts
Website: http://www.sckans.edu
SAT/ACT/GPA: 889/18/2.5
Student/Faculty Ratio: 13:1
Undergraduate Enrollment: 983
Scholarships/Academic: Yes **Athletic:** Yes
Expenses by: Year **In State:** $ 15,924
Specialty: Liberal Arts

Founded: 1885
Religion: Methodist
Housing: Yes
Male/Female Ratio: 50:50
Graduate Enrollment: 5
Financial Aid: Yes
Out of State: $ 15,924

Degrees Conferred: BA, BS, MA, M.Ed.
Programs of Study: Biology, Business Administration, Business and Computer Information Systems, Business Quality Management, Chemistry, Computer Science, Criminal Justice, Education, Elementary Education, English, Health and Physical Education, Sports Management, History, Human Resource Development, Modern Languages, Liberal Studies, Manufacturing Technology, Marine Biology, Mass Communication and Film, Mathematics, Music, Nursing, Philosophy & Religious Studies, Physics, Psychology, Theatre

Men's Athletic Profile

100 College Street
Winfield, KS 67156
Coach: Brockton R. Hickan
Email: brh33esckans.edu

NAIA
Moundbuilders/Purple, White
Phone: (316) 221-8383
Fax: (316) 229-2762

Estimated # of Men's Soccer Scholarships: Avg. $1,800/player
Conference: Kansas Collegiate Athletic Conference
Program Profile: We have lighted natural grass match field with a bleacher seats. Our practice field is natural grass. We have 1 regular and small sided practice fields, which are under construction for use in Fall of 2000. We have access to gymnasium, varsity weight room, training room with certified trainer and pool. Our season is in the fall.
History: Our program began in 1997 and has improved consistently. We expect to challenge every game and continue to improve in talent level, in depth and in experience with only 3 seniors in 1999.

Coaching: Brockton R. Hickan is the Head Coach, graduated from Southwest Baptist University in 1994. He holds NSCAA National Diploma. Dr. Andy Sheppard is the Assistant Coach.
Style of Play: We emphasis on possession play but will look to go direct when an opportunity present itself. Defense is our top priority and will use a high pressure to win the ball back. We strive to play attractively but will not lose focus on the result.

Women's Athletic Profile

100 College Street
Winfield, KS 67156
Coach: Brockton Hickan
Email: brh33@eskans.edu

NAIA
Moundbuilders/Purple, White
Phone: (316) 221-8383
Fax: (316) 229-2762

Estimated # of Women's Soccer Scholarships: N/A
Conference: Kansas Collegiate Athletic Conference
Program Profile: See men's profile.
History: See men's profile.
Achievements: Coach Brockton Hickan was named KCAC Coach of the Year in 1998.
Style of Play: We emphasis on possession play but will look to go direct an opportunity present itself. Defense is top priority and will use high pressure to win the ball back early. We strive to play attractively but will not love focus on the result.

Sterling College

Academic Profile

Sterling, KS 67579

Phone: 1-800-346-1017

Type: 4 Yr.,Private,Liberal Arts
Website: http://www.sterling.edu
SAT/ACT/GPA: 860/18/2.2
Student/Faculty Ratio: 14:1
Undergraduate Enrollment: 450
Scholarships/Academic: Yes
Athletic: Yes
Expenses by: Year
In State: $ 16,522
Specialty: Premed, Education, Business, Computers
Degrees Conferred: BA, BS

Founded: 1887
Religion: Presbyterian
Housing: Yes
Male/Female Ratio: 2.1:25
Graduate Enrollment: N/A
Financial Aid: Yes
Out of State: $ 16,522

Programs of Study: Art, Behavioral Science, Biology, Business Administration, Christian Education, Communications and Theatre Arts, Computer Information Technology, Elementary Education, English, History and Government, Mathematics, Music, Music Education, Physical Education and Health, Religion and Philosophy, Secondary Education Certification

Men's Athletic Profile

Broadway and Cooper
Sterling, KS 67579-0098
Coach: Justin Mris
Email: jmorris@sterling.edu

NAIA
Warriors/Navy, Silver, Red
Phone: (316) 278-4324
Fax: (316) 278-4319

Estimated # of Men's Soccer Scholarships: No full rides
Conference: Kansas Collegiate Athletic Conference
Program Profile: We play on grass field. It is a full World Cup field and has an adjacent practice field with a seating capacity of 500.
History: Program began in 1986.

Achievements: 2 Conference Champs, 97 Runner-up, Conference Runner-up, Conference Coach of the Year, 2 All-Americans on team.
Coaching: Justin Morris is the Head Coach. Karl Anderson is the Assistant Coach.
Roster In State: 10 **Out of State:** 9 **Out of Country:** 0
Walk-on/Other: **Graduation %:** N/A **Seniors on Team:** 4
Positions Needed: marking backs/forward
Camp or Clinic Dates: Not Available
Most Recent Record: 4-13
Schedule: Kansas Wesleyan University, Friends University, Bethany College, Tabor College, William Jewell, St.Mary's
Style of Play: Possession oriented, build out of the back, defense wins ball games.

Women's Athletic Profile

Broadway & Cooper
Sterling, KS 67579-0098
Coach: Juston Morris
Email: jmorris@sterling.edu

NAIA
Warriors/Red, Navy, Silver
Phone: (316) 278-4324
Fax: (316) 278-4319

Estimated # of Women's Soccer Scholarships: Varies
Conference: Kansas Collegiate Athletic Conference
Program Profile: We have a Full World Cup field that is natural grass and has 500 seats. We have a separate practice field.
History: Our program began in 1990 and we had 5 runner-up finishes. We have numerous All-Americans and All-Conference players.
Achievements: KCAC Coach of the Year, 5 runner up finishes, 3 All-Americans, Numerous All-Conference Players.
Coaching: Justin Morris is in his second season as head Coach
Roster in State: 9 **Out of State:** 10 **Out of Country:** 1
Walk-on/Other: **Graduation %:** 100 **Seniors on Team:** 0
Positions Needed: Midfield and Forwards
Most Recent Record: 4-13-1
Schedule: Dana College, Friends University, Tabor College, William Jewell, Bethany College, Concordia University.
Style of Play: Defense is the name of the game.

Tabor College

Academic Profile

Hillsboro, KS 67063

Phone: 800-822-6799

Type: 4 Yr.,Private,Liberal Arts
Website: http://www.tabor.edu
SAT/ACT/GPA: 860/18
Student/Faculty Ratio: 14:1
Undergraduate Enrollment: 500
Scholarships/Academic: Yes **Athletic:** Yes
Expenses by: Year **In State:** $ 16,090
Degrees Conferred: AA, BA, BS

Founded: 1908
Religion: Mennonite Brethren
Housing: Yes
Male/Female Ratio: 1.4:1
Graduate Enrollment: N/A
Financial Aid: Yes
Out of State: $ 16,090

Programs of Study: Accounting, Biology, Botany, Business Law, Business Administration, Chemistry, Communication, Computer Science, Economics, Education, History, Management, Marketing, Mathematics, Medical Technology, Philosophy, Physics, Religion, Psychology, Social Science

Men's Athletic Profile

400 S Jefferson Street
Hillsboro, KS 67063
Coach: Glenn Wiebe
Email: gwiebe@tabor.edu

NCAA II/NAIA
Bluejays/Royal Blue, Gold
Phone: (316) 947-3121
Fax: (316) 947-3789

Estimated # of Men's Soccer Scholarships: varies
Conference: Kansas Collegiate Athletic Conference, NCCAA
Program Profile: Facilities include 1 full size practice field, 1 full size game field with fescue Bermuda mix (watering system), 2-month season, 18-24 games including junior varsity , excellent institution and alumni support.
History: Our program started its intercollegiate soccer program in Kansas in 1959, several trips to NAIA. NCCAA National Tournaments, competitive program, part of Kansas Collegiate Athletic Conference.
Achievements: The team produced 2 All-Americans; 5 All-Americans Scholar Athletes, 7 All-Region and 42 All-Conference.
Coaching: Glenn Wiebe, Head Coach, was hired spring of 1995, has 13 years coaching experience. Joe Sechrist, Assistant Coach, entering three years at Tabor and has a nine years coaching experience.
Style of Play: Attacking-counter-attacking, 3-4-3 system.

University of Kansas
Academic Profile

Phone: (785) 864-3556

Lawrence, KS 66045

Type: 4 Yr.,Public
Website: http://www.ukas.edu
SAT/ACT/GPA: 1000+/20+/3.5
Student/Faculty Ratio: 20:1
Undergraduate Enrollment: 18,892
Scholarships/Academic: Yes
Athletic: Yes
Expenses by: Year
In State: $ 6,859
Founded: 1866
Religion: Non-Affiliated
Housing: Yes
Male/Female Ratio: 45:55
Graduate Enrollment: N/A
Financial Aid: Yes
Out of State: $ 13,462
Specialty: Law and Medicine
Degrees Conferred: BA, BGS, MA, MBA, MS
Programs of Study: Aerospace, Anthropology, Architecture, Art, Astronomy, Broadcasting, Business, Cellular Biology, Economics, Education, Engineering, Humanities, Illustration, Journalism, Languages, Linguistics, Mass Communications, Nursing, Pharmacy, Social Welfare, Theatre, Urban Design, Voice, Women's Studies

Women's Athletic Profile

275 Parrott
Lawrence, KS 66045
Coach: Mark Francis
Email: mfrancis@ukans.edu

NCAA I
Jayhawks/White, Blue, Red
Phone: (785) 864-3560
Fax: (785) 864-5670

Estimated # of Women's Soccer Scholarships: 4.5
Conference: Big 12 Conference
Program Profile: Located in Lawrence, Kansas. The Super Target Field is a natural full size field that holds 500. A new stadium is planned for completion for fall 2002. This stadium will hold 3000, and will house locker rooms, training rooms, soccer offices, as well as concessions.
History: The program began in 1995 with a total of a three head coach history. Mark Francis was hired in December 1999 to turn the program around. Francis came from South Alabama where he recorded the biggest turnaround in NCAA IA women's soccer history. Francis and the Jayhawks went undefeated in the 99 spring season, then recorded the best fall season in Kansas soccer history.
Achievements: 3 NSCAA Scholar Athlete All-American Regional team members.
Coaching: Head Coach- Mark Francis. Assistant Coaches- Kelly Miller, Donna Holyman.
Roster in State: 3
Out of State: 13
Out of Country: 7
ODP State: 20
Regional: 3
National: 3
Walk-on/Other:
Graduation %: 98
Seniors on Team: 7
Camp or Clinic Dates: July 23-27 and July 30-Aug 3
Schedule: Nebraska, Missouri, Texas A&M, Baylor, Illinois, UC Irvine
Style of Play: Build out of back and penetrate.

kentucky

KENTUCKY

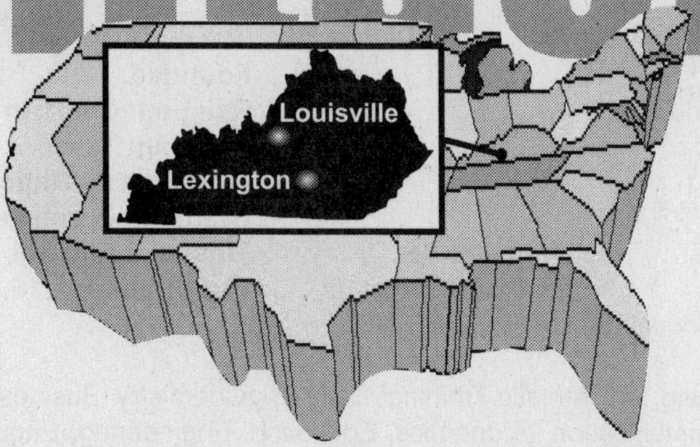

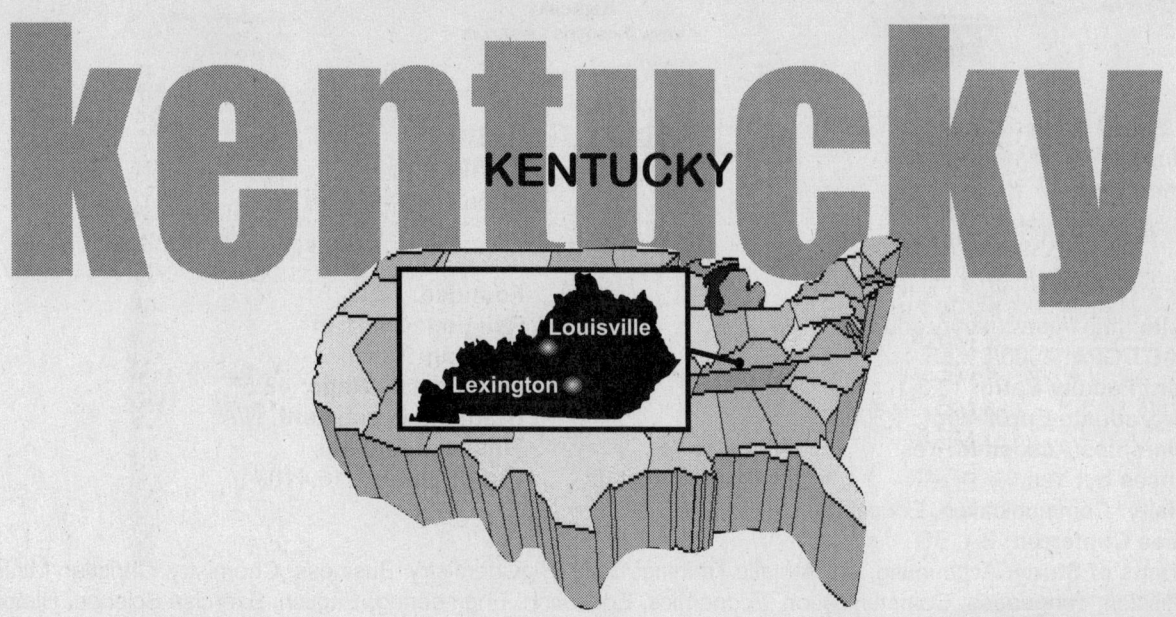

SCHOOL	CITY	AFFILIATION	PAGE
Asbury College	Wilmore	NAIA	398
Bellarmine College	Louisville	NCAA II	398
Berea College	Berea	NAIA	399
Brescia College	Owensboro	NAIA	400
Campbellsville College	Campbellsville	NAIA	401
Centre College	Danville	NCAA III	402
Cumberland University	Williamsburg	NAIA	403
Georgetown College	Georgetown	NAIA	404
Kentucky Wesleyan College	Owensboro	NCAA II	405
Lindsey Wilson College	Columbia	NAIA	406
Midway College	Midway	NAIA	408
Morehead State University	Morehead	NCAA I	408
Murray State University	Murray	NCAA I	409
Northern Kentucky University	Highland Heights	NCAA II	410
Thomas More College	Crestview Hills	NCAA III	411
Transylvania University	Lexington	NAIA	412
Union College	Barbourville	NAIA	414
University of Kentucky	Lexington	NCAA I	415
University of Louisville	Louisville	NCAA I	416
Western Kentucky University	Bowling Green	NCAA I	417

Asbury College

Academic Profile

Phone: 800-888-1818

Wilmore, KY 40390

Type: 4 Yr.,Private,Liberal Arts
Founded: 1890
Website: http://www.asbury.edu
Religion: Christian
SAT/ACT/GPA: 1000/21/2.5
Housing: Yes
Student/Faculty Ratio: 13.3:1
Male/Female Ratio: 43:57
Undergraduate Enrollment: 1,300
Graduate Enrollment: N/A
Scholarships/Academic: Yes **Athletic:** Yes **Financial Aid:** Yes
Expenses by: Year **In State:** $ 16,410 **Out of State:** $ 16,410
Specialty: Communication, Education
Degrees Conferred: BA, BS
Programs of Study: Accounting, Art, Athletic Training, Bible, BioChemistry, Business, Chemistry, Christian Ministries and Mission, Languages, Communication, Economics, Education, Engineering, English, Exercise Science, History, Journalism, Math, Music, Philosophy, Physical Education, PreMed, Psychology, Recreation, Social Work, Sociology, Theatre, Urban Studies

Men's Athletic Profile

1 Macklem Drive
Wilmore, KY 40390-1198
Coach: KJ Hill
Email: kjhill@asbury.edu

NAIA
Eagles/Purple, White
Phone: (606) 858-3511x 2471
Fax: (606) 858-3921

Estimated # of Men's Soccer Scholarships:
Conference: Kentucky Intercollegiate Athletic Conference
Program Profile: Natural turf field. Fall season, indoor season, and Spring practice. Has a seating capacity of 500 plus.
History: Program began in early 1970's. It was very successful throughout the 1970's. However, when NAIA school began offering athletic scholarship, we lost a competitive advantage. In recent years, we are improving and in 1994 we made it to the NCCAA National Tournament. We were runner-up to Lindsey Wilson in our conference.
Achievements: 1994 NCCAA District Champions, Charlie LeBoeuf was 1994-1996 NCCAA All-American, 1995-1996 NAIA All-Conference; Scott Shroyer was named 1994 NCCAA All-American; Rick Billings was named 1994 NCCAA All-American.

Bellarmine College

Academic Profile

Phone: 800-274-4723

Louisville, KY 40205

Type: 4 Yr.,Private,Liberal Arts
Founded: 1950
Website: http://www.bellarmine.edu
Religion: Catholic
SAT/ACT/GPA: 950/21/2.5
Housing: Yes
Student/Faculty Ratio: 14:1
Male/Female Ratio: 41:59
Undergraduate Enrollment: 1,250
Graduate Enrollment: 950
Scholarships/Academic: Yes **Athletic:** Yes **Financial Aid:** Yes
Expenses by: Year **In State:** $ 15,050 **Out of State:** $ 15,050
Degrees Conferred: BA, BS, BSN, MA, M.Ed., MAT, MBA, MLS
Programs of Study: Accounting, Art, Art Administration, Biology, Business Administration, Chemistry, Communication, Computer Engineering, Computer Science, Economics, Education, English, History, Mathematics, Music, Nursing, Philosophy, Political Science, Psychology, Sociology, Theology

Men's Athletic Profile

2001 Newburg Road
Louisville, KY 40205
Coach: Tim Chastonay
Email: Tchastonay@Bellarmine.edu

NCAA II
Knights/Scarlet and Silver
Phone: (502) 452-8043
Fax: (502) 452-8450

Estimated # of Men's Soccer Scholarships: Varies
Conference: Great Lakes Valley Conference
Program Profile: Division II program in a very competitive conference. Our team plays on natural grass field, which is one of our immediate attractions.
History: Varsity program began in 1973.
Achievements: Numerous ALL-GLVC players. Several All-Mideast players.
Coaching: Tim Chastonay, Head Coach, is entering his third season with the Knights program.
Roster In State: 10 **Out of State:** 15 **Out of Country:**
ODP State: 6 **Regional:** **National:**
Walk-on/Other: **Graduation %:** 98 **Seniors on Team:** 4
Most Recent Record: 9-11-0
Schedule: Lewis, Wisconsin-Parkside, SIU-Edwardsville, Quincy, Indianapolis, IUP-Fort-Wayne, Missouri-St. Louis.
Style of Play: Depends on players abilities and the level of competition.

Women's Athletic Profile

2001 Newburg Road
Louisville, KY 40205
Coach: Tim Chastonay
Email: Tchastonay@Bellarmine.edu

NCAA II
Lady Knights/Scarlet and Silver
Phone: (502) 452-8043
Fax: (502) 452-8450

Estimated # of Women's Soccer Scholarships: None
Conference: Great Lakes Valley Conference
Program Profile: We a Division II program in a very competitive conference. Our games played on a natural grass field.
History: The program began in 1988.
Achievements: Our program produced several All-Conference players.
Coaching: Tim Chastonay, Head Coach, is entering his second year at Bellarmine. He won a State Championships in 1996 at Lewisville Eastern High School and Niotis Cup (U-16 National Champions) with a club team in 1997. In 1996, was named Coach of the Year and Kentucky Youth Soccer Boys Coach of the Year. Chip Hayward is the Assistant Coach.
Roster in State: 13 **Out of State:** 10 **Out of Country:**
ODP State: 5 **Regional:** **National:**
Walk-on/Other: **Graduation %:** 98 **Seniors on Team:** 7
Camp or Clinic Dates: Not Available
Most Recent Record: 8-8-2
Schedule: Northern Kentucky University, SIU-Edwardsville, Transylvania University, University of Southern Indiana, Indianapolis University, St. Joseph's College
Style of Play: Depends on the players.

Berea College
Academic Profile

Berea, KY 40404

Phone: 800-326-5948

Type: 4 Yr.,Private,Liberal Arts
Website: http://www.berea.edu

Founded: 1855
Religion: Nonsectarian

SAT/ACT/GPA: 950/21
Housing: No
Student/Faculty Ratio: 14:1
Male/Female Ratio: 45:55
Undergraduate Enrollment: N/A
Graduate Enrollment: N/A
Scholarships/Academic: No
Athletic: No
Financial Aid: Yes
Expenses by: Year
In State: $ 7,000
Out of State: $ 7,000
Degrees Conferred: BA, BS
Programs of Study: Biblical Studies, Guidance, Ministries, Religious Education, Theology

Men's Athletic Profile

CPO 2287
Berea, KY 40403
Coach: David Vaughn
Email: swim@snapp.net

NAIA
Mountaineers/Royal, White
Phone: (606) 986-8604
Fax: (606) 986-7505

Estimated # of Men's Soccer Scholarships: Need Based
Conference: Kentucky Intercollegiate Athletic Conference
Program Profile: Have both practice and game facilities, new game field scheduled for 2000/2001. Natural grass. New $11 million Recreation facility with weight room, indoor track, pool and 2 gyms.
History: First Intercollegiate program in Kentucky, started in 1955. Originally composed of foreign players, now mostly Americans. Several NAIA District Championships.
Achievements: Honorable mention All-American 1990-1992, All Mid-East Team 1991, Academic All-American 1991, District 32 Champs 1986.
Coaching: David Vaughn, 15th year, USSF A license, formerly Kentucky ODP state coach, Region 2 Staff coach, Career Record 108-106-18.
Roster In State: 7
Out of State: 13
Out of Country: 5
Walk-on/Other:
Graduation %: 95
Seniors on Team: 6
Positions Needed: Goalkeeper and striker
Camp or Clinic Dates: Last week of July, first week of August
Most Recent Record: 9-6-1
Schedule: Transylvania, Georgetown, Bethel, Cumberland, Lipscomb, Union.
Style of Play: Equally balanced between attack and defense, usually 4-4-2 formation.

Women's Athletic Profile

W. CPO Box 2297
Berea, KY 40404
Coach: Marco A. Daros
Email: marcodaros@hotmail.com

NAIA
Mountaineers/Royal, White
Phone: (606) 986-9341
Fax: (606) 986-4506

Estimated # of Women's Soccer Scholarships: None
Conference: KISA

Brescia College

Academic Profile

Phone: 877-273-7242

Owensboro, KY 42301-3023

Type: 4 Yr.,Private,Liberal Arts
Founded: 1950
Website: http://www.brescia.edu
Religion: Catholic
SAT/ACT/GPA: Open
Housing: Yes
Student/Faculty Ratio: 15:1
Male/Female Ratio: 38:62

Undergraduate Enrollment: 760
Graduate Enrollment: 9
Scholarships/Academic: Yes
Athletic: Yes
Financial Aid: Yes
Expenses by: Year
In State: $ 11,849
Out of State: $ 11,849
Degrees Conferred: AA, AS, BA, BS, MS in Management
Programs of Study: Accounting, Art, Art Education, Biology, Business, Chemistry, English, General Studies, Graphic Design, History, Mathematics, PreProfessional Courses, Psychology, Social Studies, Sociology

Men's Athletic Profile

717 Frederica Street
Owensboro, KY 42301
Coach: Ossie Taylor
Email: ossiet@brescia.edu

NAIA
Bearcats/Blue, White
Phone: 270-686-4234
Fax: (502) 686-4317

Estimated # of Men's Soccer Scholarships:
Conference: Kentucky Intercollegiate Athletic Conference
Program Profile: Brescia is a relatively new program with a solid freshman nucleus. our home field is the main field at the 11 field Owensboro Soccer Complex. The field has lights, fantastic atmosphere and great fan support.
History: Program began in 1985 and has a school record of 79-103-10. This is a very young, aggressive, and growing program.
Achievements: 1989 NAIA District 32 Champs; 1990 NAIA District 32 Runner-up.; 12 NAIA District 32 selections; 5 NAIA Area 7 selections; 3 NAIA All-American Selections.

Campbellsville University

Academic Profile

Campbellsville, KY 42718
Phone:

Type: 4 Yr.,Private,Liberal Arts
Founded: 1906
Website: http://www.campbellsvil.edu
Religion: Baptist
SAT/ACT/GPA: 890/19
Housing: Yes
Student/Faculty Ratio: 16:1
Male/Female Ratio: 1:9
Undergraduate Enrollment: 1,530
Graduate Enrollment: 37
Scholarships/Academic: Yes
Athletic: Yes
Financial Aid: Yes
Expenses by: Year
In State: $ 11,700
Out of State: $ 11,700
Degrees Conferred: BA, BS, AA
Programs of Study: Accounting, Art, Athletic Training, Biology, Business Administration, Economics, Office Management, Chemistry, English, History, Journalism, Mathematics, PreProfessional Courses, Psychology, Social Work, Sociology, Sports Medicine/Exercise Science

Men's Athletic Profile

200 W College Street
Campbellsville, KY 42718
Coach: Marcos Alves
Email: Not Available

NAIA
Tigers/Maroon, White, Gray
Phone: (502) 465-8158
Fax: (502) 789-5257

Did Not Return Profile

Women's Athletic Profile

1 University Drive
Campbellsville, KY 42718
Coach: Dan Bailey
Email: danbailey@webtv.net

NAIA
Lady Tigers/Maroon, White
Phone: (502) 789-5179
Fax: (502) 789-5257

Estimated # of Women's Soccer Scholarships: None
Conference: Mid South Conference
Program Profile: We play at Powell Center, which has 1,800 seats.
History: We are in the 4th year of our program and in our 2nd year under a new head coach.
Achievements: 1997: 10 Academic All-Conference; 2 First Team All-Conference; Player of the Year.
Coaching: Dan Bailey-Head Coach.
Style of Play: 4-3-3 or 3-4-3, zonal defense, attack starts with outside backs.

Centre College

Academic Profile

Phone: 859-238-5493

Danville, KY 40422

Type: 4 Yr.,Private,Liberal Arts
Founded: 1819
Website: http://www.centre.edu
Religion: Presbyterian
SAT/ACT/GPA: 1150/25/3.0
Housing: Yes
Student/Faculty Ratio: 10/1
Male/Female Ratio: 1:1
Undergraduate Enrollment: 1,150
Graduate Enrollment: N/A
Scholarships/Academic: Yes **Athletic:** No **Financial Aid:** Yes
Expenses by: Year **In State:** $ 22,400 **Out of State:** $ 22,400
Specialty: Biology, Chemistry, Education, Pre Med, Pre Law
Degrees Conferred: BA, BS
Programs of Study: Art, Anthropology, BioChemistry, Molecular Biology, Biology, Chemistry, Chemical Physics, Classics, Economics, Elementary Education, English, French, German, Government, History, Mathematics, Music, Philosophy, Physics, PsychoBiology, Psychology, Religion, PreLaw, PreMed, Secondary Education

Men's Athletic Profile

600 W. Walnut St.
Danville, KY 40422
Coach: Brian Chafin
Email: chafin@centre.edu

NCAA III
Colonels/Gold, White
Phone: (859 238-5493
Fax: 859) 236-6081

Estimated # of Men's Soccer Scholarships:
Conference: SCAC
Program Profile: Winning over 75% of games, 2 full time coaches, attacking style of play, outstanding playing surface, seating areas, bermuda grass, NCAA top ten attendance, and year around training program with strength coach. Also spring non traditional season.
History: Varsity sport in 1984. 4 SCAC titles in the 90's, 3 consecutive NCAA playoff appearances (97,98,99), top 25 national rank in 1997, 98, 99, 2000 seasons. 1999 ranking of 5 in attendance playing NCAA D III top soccer conference. 1st NCAA team from KY to attend NCAA playoffs.
Achievements: Brian Chafin - 3 time SCAC Coach of the Year, 3 Conference titles in 5 years, 14 All-Region players, 3 All-American players, 3 players move on to A-League Teams.
Coaching: Brian Chafin Head Coach. NCCAA & USSF Certified. 29 years of collegiate coaching experience, 55 All Region players, 10 post season appearances, 6 All-Americans, NSCAA State Rep. KY Olympic Development Coaching Director, Regional Chair for the NCAA D III Championships Committee.
Roster In State: 18 **Out of State:** 13 **Out of Country:** 0
ODP State: 9 **Regional:** 2 **National:**
Walk-on/Other: **Graduation %:** 100 **Seniors on Team:** 11
Positions Needed: Outside mid, Center mid, Striker, Defender, GK
Camp or Clinic Dates: 3rd week in July
Most Recent Record: 15-4-0
Schedule: Trinity University, University of Chicago, Rhodes College, Depauw College
Style of Play: 4-4-2, 3-5-2, 3-4-3 possession style to get players forward to feet, drop to vision and play people in.

Women's Athletic Profile

600 West Walnut Street
Danville, KY 40422
Coach: Gina Nicoletti
Email: mailgina@centre.edu

NCAA III
Colonels/Gold, White
Phone: (606) 238-5253
Fax: (606) 236-6081

Estimated # of Women's Soccer Scholarships: None
Conference: Southern Collegiate Athletic Conference
Program Profile: Game field and full size practice field; natural grass. two weight rooms, aquatics, track, and gymnasiums.
History: The program moved into intercollegiate competition in 1991 and has been ranked in the Top Ten in the NCAA Division III South Region for three consecutive years.
Achievements: 4 All-Region Players, 15 All-Conference Players.
Coaching: Gina Nicoletti, Head Coach, five years at Centre, BS from Elon College, MS from Ithaca College, NAIA All-American at Elon, NSCAA National coaching license, USSF "C" License, ODP Coaching Staff. Shannon Jewell - Assistant Coach.
Roster in State: 12 **Out of State:** 8 **Out of Country:** 0
ODP State: 0 **Regional:** 0 **National:** 0
Walk-on/Other: 0 **Graduation %:** 95 **Seniors on Team:** 3
Camp or Clinic Dates: Not Available
Most Recent Record: 9-8-0
Style of Play: Possession style to utilize forward players.

Cumberland College

Academic Profile

Williamsburg, KY 40769
Phone: (606) 539-4241

Type: 4 Yr.,Private,Liberal Arts **Founded:** 1889
Website: http://www.cumber.edu **Religion:** Baptist
SAT/ACT/GPA: Sliding Scale/18/2.0 **Housing:** Yes
Student/Faculty Ratio: 16:1 **Male/Female Ratio:** 45:55
Undergraduate Enrollment: 1,416 **Graduate Enrollment:** 180
Scholarships/Academic: Yes **Athletic:** Yes **Financial Aid:** Yes
Expenses by: Year **In State:** $ 14,106 **Out of State:** $ 14,106
Specialty: Liberal Arts, Preprofessional Programs
Degrees Conferred: Bachelor - Arts, Science, Music, General Studies, M.Ed.
Programs of Study: Biological Sciences/Life Sciences, Computer and Information Sciences, Education, English Languages and Literature/Letters, Law and Legal Studies, Mathematics, Philosophy and Religion, Physical Sciences, Psychology, Social Sciences and History, Theological Studies and Religion Vocations, Visual and Performing Arts

Men's Athletic Profile

7988 College Station Dr.
Williamsburg, KY 40769
Coach: Rob Miller
Email: rmiller@cc.cumber.edu

NAIA
Indians/Maroon, White
Phone: (606) 539-4386
Fax: (606) 539-4459

Estimated # of Men's Soccer Scholarships: Varies
Conference: Mis-South Conference
Program Profile: We have a 20 game season. We play on a Bermuda grass field. We also have a practice field. Our season goes from August to November. Our indoor season goes from January to February. Our spring season is from March to April.

History: Our program began in 1992. We were conference champions in 1996 and 1998.
Achievements: 1996 Coach of the Year; 1998 Region Coach of the Year; 2 conference titles; 4 All-Americans. Several State ODP Players; 12 All-State Players; 1 US1SI Player; 2 U-20 National Team Players; 1 NCCAA National Tournament Appearances.
Coaching: Rob Miller, Head Coach, was Conference Coach of the Year in 1996 and 1998. He has a NSCAA Premier Diploma and an Advanced National Diploma. He was club coach for the SCK Blast and is a state ODP evaluator.
Style of Play: Often based on personnel. Tend to recruit technically sound players.

Women's Athletic Profile

7988 College Station Dr.
Williamsburg, KY 40769-1386
Coach: Lars Anderson
Email: landerss@cc.cumber.edu

NAIA
Indians/Maroon, White
Phone: (606) 539-4044
Fax: (606) 539-4467

Estimated # of Women's Soccer Scholarships: 12
Conference: Mid-South Conference
Program Profile: We have a 120 x 70 Bermuda grass field and a practice field. We play in the Mid-South Conference. Our season begins in August and ends in November and during the spring we play several indoor tournaments and a few outdoor 7 vs. 7 tournaments.
History: Our program began in 1993 and our overall record is 63-48-4.
Achievements: During the 1999 season we received Mid-South Conference Regular Season Champs, ranked 14th national, had 6 1st team All-Conference players, 2 All-Region players, 2 All-American players, 8 Academic All-Americans and Conference Coach of the year.
Coaching: Lars Anderson is the Head Coach and Tim Wolz is the Assistant Coach.
Roster in State: 6
Out of State: 12
Out of Country: 2
ODP State: 6
Regional:
National:
Walk-on/Other:
Graduation %: 90+
Seniors on Team: 9
Positions Needed: 1 Striker, 2 Midfielders, 1 Defender
Camp or Clinic Dates: July 9-14
Most Recent Record: 16-4-0
Schedule: Transylvania University, Berry College, Indiana Wesleyan University, Union College, Tusculum College, Lindsey Wilson College
Style of Play: We play a traditional 4-4-2, Much of our build up is done through the central midfielders. Halfbacks are very active in our attack along with forwards and an attacking midfielder. Defensively we play a straight up man marking system. Our goalkeeper must have solid foot skills as she will often be used as a sweeper-keeper.

Georgetown College

Academic Profile

Phone: 800-788-9985

Georgetown, KY 40324

Type: 4 Yr.,Private,Liberal Arts
Founded: 1829
Website: http://www.gtc.georgetown.ky.us
Religion: Baptist
SAT/ACT/GPA: 930/20
Housing: Yes
Student/Faculty Ratio: 10:1
Male/Female Ratio: 50:50
Undergraduate Enrollment: 1,200
Graduate Enrollment: 200
Scholarships/Academic: Yes
Athletic: Yes
Financial Aid: Yes
Expenses by: Year
In State: $ 5,432
Out of State: $ 5,432
Degrees Conferred: BA, BS, MA
Programs of Study: Accounting, American Studies, Biological Sciences, Business Administration, Chemistry, Economics, Elementary Education, Environmental Science, History, Marketing/Finance, Mathematics, Medical Technology, Philosophy, Physical Education, Physics, Political Science, PreProfessional Courses, Psychology, Sociology

Men's Athletic Profile

400 East College Street
Georgetown, KY 40324
Coach: Jim Tussey
Email: athletics@georgetowncollege.edu

NAIA
Tigers/Orange, White
Phone: (502) 863-8122
Fax: (502) 868-8892

Estimated # of Men's Soccer Scholarships: Valuable
Conference: Mid-South Region Conference
Program Profile: Member of NAIA and affiliated with Mid-South conference. We have a 500 seat complex and a 5,000 seats stadium for home games. Field is sport-grass and seasons runs from September through November.
History: Program has been going since early 1970's. Our records are not available prior to 1994. Since then, we have record of 68-44-6 and three titles in five years.
Achievements: Received Coach of the Year Award in 1994 & 1996. Won first conference in 1996. In the last three seasons combined 40-18-2. In 1996 won first regional appearances and won regional in 1995.
Coaching: Jim Tussey, Head Coach, Advanced National License, ODP Coach for five years straight, Coach of the Year in the conference in 1994 (KIAC), coach of select teams in the Lexington, Kentucky every Fall, currently team is Bluegrass United. NSCAA; 8 years select coach.
Style of Play: Fast speed of play, high pressure defensively.

Women's Athletic Profile

400 East College Street
Georgetown, KY 40324
Coach: Jim Tussey
Email: Not Available

NAIA
Tigers/Black, White, Orange
Phone: (502) 863-7044
Fax:

Estimated # of Women's Soccer Scholarships: Varies
Conference: Mid-South Conference
Program Profile: We are a member of NAIA and affiliated with Mid-South Conference. Have not been out of top three conference teams in five years. Our playing season runs from September through November. We a 500-seat field and 5,000-seat stadium used for home games. We play on sport-grass field.
History: The women achieved a strong status in its first season in 1994. Our overall record is 64-23-3.
Achievements: We have 3 Regular Season Conference Titles in five years.
Coaching: Jim Tussey, Head Coach. He coached four years in high school and was named 1994 Conference Coach of the Year. He graduated from Asbury college in 1986. Rick Underwood is the Assistant Coach, graduated from Mississippi College in 1970.
Roster in State: 25 | **Out of State:** 8 | **Out of Country:** 0
Walk-on/Other: | **Graduation %:** N/A | **Seniors on Team:** 6
Camp or Clinic Dates: Not Available
Most Recent Record: 14-4-0
Style of Play: Highly developed skills through training under pressure. Constantly changing the point of attack with all 10 players involved in attack. High pressure defense.

Kentucky Wesleyan College

Academic Profile

3000 Frederica St.
Owensboro, KY 42301

Phone: 800-999-0592

Type: 4 Yr.,Private,Liberal Arts
Website: http://www.kwc.edu
SAT/ACT/GPA: 800/19
Student/Faculty Ratio: 14:1

Founded: 1858
Religion: United Methodist
Housing: No
Male/Female Ratio: 50:50

Undergraduate Enrollment: 800
Graduate Enrollment: N/A
Scholarships/Academic: Yes
Athletic: Yes
Financial Aid: Yes
Expenses by: Year
In State: $ 13,250
Out of State: $ 13,250
Degrees Conferred: Associate in Nursing, BA, BS
Programs of Study: Business & Management, Communications, Education, Health Sciences, Life Sciences, Psychology, Social Sciences

Men's Athletic Profile

3000 Frederica Street
Owensboro, KY 42301
Coach: Scott Pulliam
Email: Not Available

NCAA II
Panthers/Purple, White
Phone: (502) 683-4795
Fax: (502) 926-3196

Estimated # of Men's Soccer Scholarships: None
Conference: Great Lakes Valley Conference
Program Profile: New coach from Ireland plans to rebuild the program and make it one of the most exciting and ambitious teams around. The potential is there for the program to achieve unlimited success and for a player to come in and make and immediate impact. The natural grass field adds to a beautiful campus.
History: Our men's program began in 1979.
Style of Play: We play with typical European passion. The style is influenced by Irish/English and other European style. it is exciting and direct with a lot of risk-taking. A program that suits the aggressive player.

Women's Athletic Profile

3000 Frederica Street
Owensboro, KY 42301
Coach: Larry Kirk
Email: Not Available

NCAA II
Panthers/Purple, White
Phone: (502) 683-4795
Fax: (502) 926-3196

Estimated # of Women's Soccer Scholarships: None
Conference: Great Lakes Valley Conference
Program Profile: Program offers quality soccer education. Play on grass field.
History: Program began in 1985.

Lindsey Wilson College

Academic Profile

Columbia, KY 42728

Phone: 270-384-2126

Type: 4 Yr.,Private,Liberal Arts
Founded: 1903
Website: http://www.lindsey.edu
Religion: Methodist
SAT/ACT/GPA: 860/18
Housing: Yes
Student/Faculty Ratio: 20:1
Male/Female Ratio: 60:40
Undergraduate Enrollment: 1,320
Graduate Enrollment: 50
Scholarships/Academic: Yes
Athletic: Yes
Financial Aid: Yes
Expenses by: Year
In State: $ 12,510
Out of State: $ 12,510
Degrees Conferred: AA, BA, BS, MA
Programs of Study: All Liberal Art types including: Business and Management, Computer Science, Education, and all Preprofessional Programs

Men's Athletic Profile

210 Lindsey Wilson Street
Columbia, KY 42728
Coach: Ray Wells
Email: wellsray@yahoo.com

NAIA
Raiders/Blue, White
Phone: (502) 384-8070
Fax: (502) 384-8078

Estimated # of Men's Soccer Scholarships: 12
Conference: Mid-South
Program Profile: New Stadium holds 1,000 spectators. Natural Bermuda grass, lighted.
History: 1999 NAIA National Champions, 1998 NAIA National Champions, 1996 NAIA National Champions, 1995 NAIA National Champions, 1994 NAIA Final Four, 1992 NAIA National Tournament, 1990 first year of program. National tournament record 6 years 17-3-3.
Achievements: 3 time coach of the year. 10 conference titles, seven players currently playing professionally. Coaching record 221-70-23.
Coaching: Ray Wells, Head Coach, professionally certified, has a record of 172-69-22. He was named Coach of the Year in 1995 & 1996. Willis Pooler - Assistant Coach, played at Lindsey Wilson. Drew Burwash goalkeeper coach, Youth National team for the USA. Former pro. Two time All-American at Lindsey Wilson

Roster In State: 4	**Out of State:** 2	**Out of Country:** 12
ODP State: 1	**Regional:**	**National:**
Walk-on/Other: 2	**Graduation %:** 80	**Seniors on Team:** 3

Positions Needed: midfield
Camp or Clinic Dates: Not Available
Most Recent Record: 24-1-1
Schedule: Mobile, Life, Ill-Springfield
Style of Play: 3-5-2 Attack oriented/ball possession/bring the ball out of the back.

Women's Athletic Profile

210 Lindsey Wilson Street
Columbia, KY 42728
Coach: Willis Pooler
Email: poolerw@lindsey.edu

NAIA
Lady Raiders/Royal, White
Phone: (502) 384-8174
Fax: (502) 384-8078

Estimated # of Women's Soccer Scholarships: 12
Conference: Mid-South
Program Profile: NAIA, Mid-South Conference, Region XI Nationally Ranked Top 10. 1000 seating capacity with lights and Natural Grass 110x74.
History: NAIA; KIAC South Region. Program began in 1992.
Achievements: 2 times Conference Coach of the Year; 1997 mid-South Region and NSCAA Regional Coach of the Year. 1 1st team All-American, 1 3rd team All-American; 29 All-Conference teams; 1997 Conference Champions; in the last four years ranked in Top 20.
Coaching: Willis Pooler 1st season 20-3-0.

Roster in State: 2	**Out of State:** 2	**Out of Country:** 16

Positions Needed: Varies
Camp or Clinic Dates: Not Available
Most Recent Record: 20-3-0
Schedule: Lindenwood, Mobile, Transylvania
Style of Play: Possession.

Midway College

Academic Profile

Phone: 800-755-0031

Midway, KY 40347-1120

Type: 4 Yr.,Private,Liberal Arts
Founded: 1847
Website: Not Available
Religion: Disciples of Christ
SAT/ACT/GPA: 860/18
Housing: Yes
Student/Faculty Ratio: 13:1
Male/Female Ratio: Women
Undergraduate Enrollment: 1,000
Graduate Enrollment: N/A
Scholarships/Academic: Yes
Athletic: Yes
Financial Aid: Yes
Expenses by: Year
In State: $ 12,260
Out of State: $ 12,260
Specialty: Nursing, Equestrian Studies
Degrees Conferred: 12 Degreed Programs
Programs of Study: Accounting, Biology, Business, Computer Information System, Early Childhood Education, Equine Studies, Liberal Studies, Nursing, Paralegal, Physical Therapy Assistant, Psychology, Teacher Education

Women's Athletic Profile

512 E Stephens Street
Midway, KY 40347-1120
Coach: Jean Kiernan
Email: jkiernan@midway.edu

NAIA
Eagles/Royal, White
Phone: (606) 846-5824
Fax: (606) 846-5754

Estimated # of Women's Soccer Scholarships: None
Conference: Kentucky Intercollegiate Athletic Conference
Program Profile: The Midway College soccer program competes against a scheduled featuring top twenty NAIA and NCAA institutions. Competitions are played on a 120x80 yards Bermuda grass surface from August through November.
History: Program was founded in 1992. Overall record is 86-19-5 in five seasons. Never fallen from the NAIA top twenty. Finished on the top ten for four of five seasons. Four consecutive KIAC Championships, two consecutive Mid-South Region Titles, two trips to the National Championships, nine All-Americans. Led national in scoring in 1993, and in shutouts in 1992.
Achievements: Five consecutive KIAC Titles; 2 Mid-South Region Titles; 2 NAIA National Tournament Appearances finishing fifth both; 10 All-Americans; 10 All-Regions; 14 All-Conferences; 2 Academic All-Americans; 3 KIAC Players of the Year.
Roster in State:
Out of State:
Out of Country: 1
Walk-on/Other:
Graduation %: 5
Seniors on Team: 99%
Positions Needed: All
Camp or Clinic Dates: June 18-21st
Most Recent Record: 10-10
Style of Play: A possession style focusing on combination play, high pressure, zonal defending and emphasis on attack.

Morehead State University

Academic Profile

Phone: (606) 783-2089

Morehead, KY 40351

Type: 4 Yr.,Public
Founded: 1923
Website: http://www.morehead-st.edu
Religion: Non-Affiliated
SAT/ACT/GPA: 14+
Housing: Yes
Student/Faculty Ratio: 18:1
Male/Female Ratio: 1:2

Undergraduate Enrollment: 6,734
Graduate Enrollment: 1,520
Scholarships/Academic: Yes
Athletic: Yes
Financial Aid: Yes
Expenses by: Year
In State: $ 4,858+
Out of State: $ 8,698+
Specialty: Education, Business, Communications, Nursing, PreLaw, PreVet
Degrees Conferred: AA, BA, BS,MA
Programs of Study: MSU offers 72 Undergraduate degree programs, including 15 Associate level degrees and 10 PreProfessional programs in four colleges-Business, Education, Behavioral Sciences, Humanities and Science and Technology and 21 academic departments. There are 24 graduate degree programs plus 2 graduate level non-degree programs designed especially for professional educators.

Women's Athletic Profile

Academic Athletic Center, #230
Morehead, KY 40351
Coach: Leslie Faber
Email: l.faber@morehead-st.edu

NCAA I
Eagles/Blue, Yellow
Phone: (606) 783-2589
Fax: (606) 783-5035

Estimated # of Women's Soccer Scholarships: 5
Conference: Ohio Valley Conference
Program Profile: Brand new facility Fall 2001-natural grass 120x80, season played from August to November
History: The program began in 1998.
Achievements: 2000 All OVC 2nd Team 2 Player, 2000 All OVC Honorable mention 2 player
Coaching: Leslie Faber - Head Coach 3rd year, also the senior women's administrator.
Roster in State: 7
Out of State: 10
Out of Country: 0
ODP State: 15
Regional: 0
National: 0
Walk-on/Other: 0
Graduation %: 100
Seniors on Team: 1
Positions Needed: 6
Most Recent Record: 9-10-1
Style of Play: Build from the back, Possession.

Murray State University

Academic Profile

Murray, KY 42071
Phone: 800-272-4678

Type: 4 Yr.,Public
Founded: 1922
Website: http://www.murraystate.edu
Religion: Non-Affiliated
SAT/ACT/GPA: 18
Housing: Yes
Student/Faculty Ratio: 16:1
Male/Female Ratio: 46:54
Undergraduate Enrollment: 7,350
Graduate Enrollment: 1,550
Scholarships/Academic: Yes
Athletic: Yes
Financial Aid: Yes
Expenses by: Year
In State: $ 6,450
Out of State: $ 6,450
Degrees Conferred: AA, AS, BA, BS, BFA, BSN, BSA, MA, MS
Programs of Study: Accounting, Art, Biology, Business, Chemistry, Engineering, Construction, Consumer Affairs, Dietetics, Earth Science, Finance, Manufacturing, Marketing, Music, Medical, Middle School, Occupational, Parks/Recreation Management, Education, Speech, Theatre, Vocational

Women's Athletic Profile

Women's Soccer Stewart Stadium
Murray, KY 42071
Coach: Mike Minielli
Email: mike.minielli@murraystate.edu

NCAA I
Racers/Navy, Gold
Phone: (270) 762-3136
Fax: (270) 762-6814

Estimated # of Women's Soccer Scholarships: 4
Conference: Ohio Valley
Program Profile: We play at a grass stadium which seats 1,000 fans.
History: The team began in 2000 with a records of 9-11-1
Achievements:
Coaching: Head coach Mike Minielle was 1996 Div II National Coach of the Year with a career record of 152-88-21. Rosa Dasilva, Jen Boone, and Matt Pack assist him.

Roster in State: 10	**Out of State:** 17	**Out of Country:** 0
ODP State: 13	**Regional:** 2	**National:**
Walk-on/Other:	**Graduation %:**	**Seniors on Team:** 1

Positions Needed: CM,SW,F
Camp or Clinic Dates: July 9-14
Most Recent Record: 9-11-1
Schedule: Alabama, Eastern Illinois, Tennesse Tech, Birmingham Southern, Sanford
Style of Play: 3-5-2 with pressure and numbers up.

Northern Kentucky University

Academic Profile

Highland Heights, KY 41099-7500
Phone: (606) 572-6372

Type: 4 Yr.,Public		**Founded:** 1968
Website: http://www.nku.edu		**Religion:** Non-Affiliated
SAT/ACT/GPA: 18		**Housing:** Yes
Student/Faculty Ratio: 12.5:1		**Male/Female Ratio:** 58:42
Undergraduate Enrollment: 12,489		**Graduate Enrollment:** 897
Scholarships/Academic: Yes	**Athletic:** Yes	**Financial Aid:** Yes
Expenses by: Year	**In State:** $ 6,432	**Out of State:** $ 10,272

Specialty: Broad scope of programs
Degrees Conferred: BA, BS, BFA, BMus, BMus Ed, BSN, BSW, MA, MBA, JD
Programs of Study: Accounting, Anthropology, Art Education, Biological Science, Business Education, Chemistry, English, Finance, Geology, Geography, Graphic Design, History, Journalism, Justice Studies, Management, Marketing, Mathematics, Philosophy, Physical Education, Physics, Psychology, Social Studies, Social Work, Sociology

Men's Athletic Profile

Nunn Drive - Regents Hall	**NCAA II**
Highland Heights, KY 41099-7500	Norse/Black, Gold, White
Coach: John Toebben	**Phone:** (606) 572-6314
Email: Not Available	**Fax:** (606) 572-5427

Estimated # of Men's Soccer Scholarships:
Conference: Great Lakes Valley Conference
Program Profile: Home games are played on a natural grass field with a capacity of 500.
History: Program began in 1980. Won three NAIA District 32 Championships, won four Great Lakes Valley Conference Championships.
Achievements: our team has produced 4 All-Americans, 19 All-Region performers, and since joining the GLVC in 1995, 43 All-Conference performers.
Coaching: John Toebben, Head Coach, named 1990 NSCAA All-Midwest Region Coach of the Year, 1192 and 1993 Great Lakes Valley Conference Coach of the Year.

Women's Athletic Profile

Nunn Drive, Regents Hall
Highland Heights, KY 41099-7500
Coach: Bob Sheeham
Email: nkusoccer@aol.com

NCAA II
Norse/Black, Gold
Phone: 513-688-1400
Fax: 513-688-1402

Estimated # of Women's Soccer Scholarships: 4.5
Conference: Great Lake Valley Conference
Program Profile: Our home field is at Town & Country Sports Complex. It has a 80x120 astro playing surface and a stadium that seats 3, 500. It has locker and meeting rooms.
History: The program began in 1997. We have won the Great Lakes Valley Conference 3 of the 4 years of competition. Finished 3rd in 1999 in NCAA Division II, finished 2nd in 2000 in NCAA D II.
Achievements: Coach Sheehan has been Coach of the Year in GLVC in 2 of last 3 years. Made national tournament the last 2 years, finishing 2nd last year. Won Conference tournament the last 3 years. 5 All-Americans.
Coaching: Bob Sheehan is the Head Coach. Record in last 3 years is 59-8-5 including 3 GLVC Championships and 2 final four appearances. Adam Meier GK Coach and has developed an All-American GK at NKU. Assistant Terry Gruelle who has a NSCAA Advanced National Diploma and USSF "C" License.
Roster In State: 5 **Out of State:** 15 **Out of Country:** 0
ODP State: 7 **Regional:** 0 **National:** 0
Walk-on/Other: 1 **Graduation %:** 100 **Seniors on Team:** 1
Positions Needed: Sweeper
Most Recent Record: 21-2-2
Schedule: Mercyhurst, Wheeling Jesuit, Southern Illinois-Edwardsville, University of Missouri-St. Louis
Style of Play: High pressure, quick transition and direct.

Thomas More College

Academic Profile

Crestview Hills, KY 41017
Phone: (606) 344-3332

Type: 4 Yr.,Private,Liberal Arts
Founded: 1921
Website: http://www.thomasmore.edu
Religion: Roman Catholic
SAT/ACT/GPA: 1010/20/80%
Housing: Yes
Student/Faculty Ratio: 12:1
Male/Female Ratio: 47:53
Undergraduate Enrollment: 1,350
Graduate Enrollment: 250
Scholarships/Academic: Yes **Athletic:** No **Financial Aid:** Yes
Expenses by: Year **In State:** $ 15,456 **Out of State:** $ 15,456
Degrees Conferred: BA, BS, BSN, BES, AA, AES
Programs of Study: Accountancy, Art, Art History, Biology, Business Administration, Chemistry, Computer Information Systems, Criminal Justice, Drama, Economics, Education, English, Exercise Science, Gerontology, History, International Studies, Mathematics, Medical Technology, Nursing, Philosophy, Physics, Political Sciences, PreLegal Studies, Psychology, Sociology, Spanish, Speech Communications, Theology, PreDental, PreEngineering, PreLaw, PreMedical, PreOccupational, Physical Therapy, PrePharmacy, PreVeterinary

Men's Athletic Profile

333 Thomas More Pkwy
Crestview Hills, KY 41017
Coach: Jeff Cummings
Email: jeff.cummings@thomasmore.edu

NCAA III
Rebels/Royal, White
Phone: (859)-344-4053
Fax: (606) 344-3632

Estimated # of Men's Soccer Scholarships: N/A
Program Profile: The Rebels play their home games on natural grass, 120 x 80 yard field.

Women's Athletic Profile

333 Thomas More Pkwy
Crestview Hills, KY 41017
Coach: Jeff Cummings
Email: jeff.cummings@thomasmore.edu

NCAA III
Saints/Blue, Grey
Phone: (606) 344-4053
Fax: (606) 344-3632

Estimated # of Women's Soccer Scholarships: None
Conference: Association of Mideast Colleges
Program Profile: Small Division III College, a very strong academic tradition. The program is geared towards the student/athletes, as academic loads are consistently considered as practice are planned. A new soccer facility will be ready for the Fall of 1998 season (on campus).
History: The program began in 1988. Record and top opponents that season (1996) are: 1990 record was 7-8-3 University of Louisville and University of Kentucky; 1992 record was 12-3-1 University of Louisville and University of Dayton; 1993 record was 11-7-1 University of Louisville and Lindsey Wilson; 1994 record was 11-7-0 Capital and Bellarmine; 1995 record was 6-10-2 Capital and Bellarmine; 1996 record was 8-8-1 Bellarmine and Wilmington; 1997 coming up Transylvania, Allegheny; 1998 not yet schedule. All Fall soccer.
Achievements: Only two losing season since 1990. We have ventured out to play some tough upper Division NCAA teams as well. The environment is very suited for the student who loves the game and does not want to sacrifice time for academic achievement in the process. We look forward to a challenging Fall (1997) and the development of our new soccer facility in 1998.
Style of Play: Balanced attack with the accent on the offensive. We try to develop athletes who are versatile enough to transcend from offense-defense or defense-offense and virtually change the complexion of any match at any time. We breed confidence in the athlete's mind set to achieve by believing. "If you believe - you will achieve"

Transylvania University

Academic Profile

Lexington, KY 40508

Phone: 800-872-6798

Type: 4 Yr.,Private,Liberal Arts
Website: http://www.transy.edu
SAT/ACT/GPA: 1000/22
Student/Faculty Ratio: 14:1
Undergraduate Enrollment: 1,027
Scholarships/Academic: Yes
Athletic: Yes
Expenses by: Year
In State: $ 17,950
Founded: 1780
Religion: Disciples of Christ
Housing: Yes
Male/Female Ratio: 3:4
Graduate Enrollment: N/A
Financial Aid: Yes
Out of State: $ 17,950
Specialty: Business
Degrees Conferred: BA
Programs of Study: Art, Biology, Business Administration, Chemistry, Computer Science, Drama, Economics, Elementary Education, English, French, History, Human Movement, Mathematics, Middle School Education, Music, Philosophy, Physical Education, Physics, Political Science, Psychology, Religion, Sociology, Sociology/Anthropology, Spanish

Men's Athletic Profile

300 N Broadway
Lexington, KY 40508
Coach: Parviz Zartoshty
Email: Not Available

NAIA
Pioneers/Crimson, White
Phone: (859)-281-3510
Fax: (606) 233-8638

Estimated # of Men's Soccer Scholarships: N/A
Conference: Independent

Program Profile: The season runs from late August until post season which reaches mid November. The team plays a limited spring season starting in April. The team has an outstanding 120x75 bermuda grass field, one of the best in the region.
History: First year for men's soccer at Transy was 1968. The Pioneers have qualified for post season play 13 of the last 16 years. We have 6 district titles, 2 Kentucky Intercollegiate Soccer Association crowns, and 3 NAIA area runner-up titles.
Achievements: 1991, Pioneers' won the NAIA District Championship and were runner up in Area Seven. Spiegel has led the Pioneers' to 12 post season appearances, six district titles, two Kentucky Intercollegiate Soccer Association Crowns, and three NAIA Area Runner-up titles.
Coaching: Head Coach, Parviz Zartoshty, has won 3 consecutive NAIA regional Coach of the Year awards. Zartoshty , a 1985 Transylvania graduate, is a former two-time Pioneer MVP. He is in his first season as the Transy men's coach after compiling a overall record of 81-22-2 and a 1999 NAIA National runner-up finish.

Roster In State: 26	**Out of State:** 4	**Out of Country:**
ODP State: 7	**Regional:**	**National:**
Walk-on/Other:	**Graduation %:** 91	**Seniors on Team:** 4

Positions Needed: Starting Goalkeeper, 5 Field players
Camp or Clinic Dates: Not Available
Most Recent Record: 15-3-1
Schedule: Marshall University, University Southern Indiana, Northern Kentucky, Centre, Trinity (TX), Southwestern, Bellarmine, Cumberland, Brescia, Georgetown.
Style of Play: Our players play total soccer. We do not have role players. Our defensive players will go on attack. Every player will learn to defend and attack from any position on the field. WE play a 4-4-2 style, but will change defending on our players strengths.

Women's Athletic Profile

300 North Broadway	**NAIA**
Lexington, KY 40508-1797	Pioneers/Crimson, White
Coach: Scott Scanlon	**Phone:** (859) 281-3510
Email: sscanlon@transy.edu	**Fax:**

Estimated # of Women's Soccer Scholarships: 0
Conference: Independent Conference
Program Profile: Transylvania's women have played at the highest level. The team plays its home games on Hall Field, an all Bermuda playing surface, which seats 400 and is lighted allowing for night games.
History: TU women's soccer program began in 1995. Our program is now recognized as one of the finest in the NAIA. Consistently ranked nationally. Overall record for the past 4 seasons (1996-1999) was 80-10-2.
Achievements: Regional champions 1997, 98, 1999. National tournament participant 1997, 1998, 1999. Best finish national runner-up 1999 (Record of 23-1). 1999 2 All-Americans Regional Player of the Year.
Coaching: Scott Scanlon is the Head Coach and holds USSF "D" License, BS Marketing 1985 from Northern Kentucky University. Scott served as an assistant coach for 5 years. The assistant coaches are Parviz Zartoshty and Marc Colwell.

Roster in State: 20	**Out of State:** 3	**Out of Country:** 0
Walk-on/Other:	**Graduation %:** 100	**Seniors on Team:** 7

Positions Needed: ALL
Most Recent Record: 23-1-0
Schedule: Berry College, Lindsey Wilson, Union College, Milligan, Centre College
Style of Play: Possession type game. Build from the back. We are a very aggressive, fast paced in the offensive third.

Union College
Academic Profile

Phone: 800-489-8646

Barbouville, KY 40906

Type: 4 Yr.,Private,Liberal Arts,Pre-Engineering
Founded: 1879
Website: http://www.unionky.edu
Religion: Methodist
SAT/ACT/GPA: 860/18/2.0
Housing: Yes
Student/Faculty Ratio: 13:1
Male/Female Ratio: 51:49
Undergraduate Enrollment: 700
Graduate Enrollment: 200
Scholarships/Academic: Yes **Athletic:** Yes **Financial Aid:** Yes
Expenses by: Year **In State:** $ 14,840 **Out of State:** $ 14,840
Specialty: Business, Education, Science Majors
Degrees Conferred: Bachelors, Masters
Programs of Study: Accounting, Athletic Training, Biology, Business, Business Education, Chemistry, Christian Education, Church Music, Criminal Justice, Drama, Early Elementary Education, English, Journalism, History, History & Political Science, Math, Middle Grades Education, Music, Music Education, Philosophy, Religion, Physical Education, Physics, Psychology, Religion, Science Education, Secondary Education, Sociology, Special Education.

Men's Athletic Profile

310 College St.
Barbourville, KY 40906
Coach: Helio D'Anna
Email: hdanna@unionky.edu

NAIA
Bulldogs/Orange, Black
Phone: (606) 546-4151
Fax: (606) 546-1286

Estimated # of Men's Soccer Scholarships: 10.5
Conference: Mid South Conference
Program Profile: We are a fully supported program with high profile players. Our season is in the fall, while our secondary season is in the spring which, is indoor and outdoor. Game field and practice field is Bermuda grass with a seating capacity of 300 people. Summer camp and pre-season camp in Brazil is every other year.
History: Our program began in 1979. The team was state champion three times through 1984. Our program was put on hold in 1984 and reinstated in 1992. Since then, the records were: 1992 was 3-12-1, 1993 record was 7-5-5, 1994 record was 10-10-0, 1995 record was 9-10-0, 1996 record was 10-7-2, and 1997 record was 15-2-1
Achievements: State Champions in 1979, 1980 & 19982; Conference Runner-Up in 1994; Conference Champions in 1997; Coach of the Year Conference in 1997; All-Americans - one in 1996, two in 1997 and two in 1998; drafted players: one in 1998; Conference Player of the Year in 1996 & 1997.
Coaching: Helio D'Anna, Head Coach, is certified in Brazil. He coached three countries and places camps every year in five different state including international camps. Roberto Brau, Assistant Coach, was a former All-New England, Honorable Mention All-American. He is a professional player, most recently as a captain or USISL with Vermont Vanguards and Voltage.
Style of Play: High pressure defense, fast paced attacking style when in possession, we attack quickly though not necessary. Throw long balls.

Women's Athletic Profile

310 College St.
Barbourville, KY 40906
Coach: Chris Kouns
Email: ckouns@unionky.edu

NAIA
Bulldogs/Orange, Black
Phone: (606) 546-1307
Fax: (606) 546-1286

Estimated # of Women's Soccer Scholarships: N/A
Conference: Mid - South Conference
Program Profile: We have a newly renovated complex that was completed in fall of 1999 and our locker facilities were completed in 2000. We play on a Bermuda sprigged field that seats about 500.
History: The program began in the fall of 1993 with 1999 being the best season ever. 15-9-0 breaking seven program records.
Achievements: MSC Tournament Champions 1999; Two All-Americans in 1999; 1 Conference player of the Year; Sectional Semi-Finalist in 1999; 6 players awarded All-Mid South Conference Honors in 1999; 2 All-South Selections in 1999; overall team GPA of 3.37.
Coaching: Chris Kouns has a USSF "B" license, NSCAA Advance National License, was the USYSA Women's Olympic Development Coach, director of coaching for Mountain Select Women's soccer Academy, USYSA coaching course instructor, 4 year letterman at NCAA Div II Mars Hill College, Academic All-American and GTE Cosida All-American Finalist.

Roster in State: 1	**Out of State:** 14	**Out of Country:** 4
ODP State: 4	**Regional:**	**National:**
Walk-on/Other: 2	**Graduation %:** 100	**Seniors on Team:**

Positions Needed: Goalkeeper, Flank Midfielder
Camp or Clinic Dates: July 21-26
Most Recent Record: 15-9-0
Schedule: UNC- Asheville, Transylvania University, Berry College, Lincoln Memorial University, Hawaii Pacific University
Style of Play: Very Attack oriented mentally expected from all players. Indirect style of play. Work ball from back but utilize all players to go forward. 1999 scored 96 goals and 77 assist and every player on the roster tallied a goal or assist.

University of Kentucky

Academic Profile

Lexington, KY 40506
Phone: 606-257-2000

Type: 4 Yr.,Public		**Founded:** 1865
Website: http://www.uky.edu		**Religion:** Non-Affiliated
SAT/ACT/GPA: NCAA Minimums		**Housing:** Yes
Student/Faculty Ratio: 20:1		**Male/Female Ratio:** 49:51
Undergraduate Enrollment: 30,000		**Graduate Enrollment:** N/A
Scholarships/Academic: Yes	**Athletic:** Yes	**Financial Aid:** Yes
Expenses by: Year	**In State:** $ Varies	**Out of State:** $ Varies

Degrees Conferred: BA, BS, BFA, MA, MS, MBA, MFA, M.Ed., Ph.D., EdD, JD
Programs of Study: Business/Office & Marketing/Distribution, Business & Management, Communications, Education, Engineering, Health Sciences, Social Sciences

Men's Athletic Profile

#1 Memorial Coliseum
Lexington, KY 40506
Coach: Ian Collins
Email: kentuckysoccer@yahoo.com

NCAA I
Wildcats/Blue, White
Phone: (859) 257-4059
Fax: (859) 323-3800

Estimated # of Men's Soccer Scholarships: Varies
Conference: Mid American Conference, SEC
Program Profile: The UK soccer complex opened in 1996 and houses a game field, full-sized practice field, locker rooms and training room. The field is a lighted international regulation-sized field of natural Bermuda grass with a modified sand base and in-ground irrigation system for drainage. Stadium holds about 1, 500 spectators, but with addt'l seating installed (including behind goals), can hold 3, 000. Season runs August to Dec.

History: A club sport for many years, it achieved varsity status on June 1, 1991. UK joined the Mid-American Conference in 1995, since the SEC does not sponsor men's soccer. The program won its 100th game by beating Louisville in the first game of 2000. The Cats have an overall record of 110-81-17.
Achievements: Ian Collins was named Mid-American Coach of the Year in 1997 and 1999, while being named Mideast Region COY in 1999. The Cats won the MAC tournament titles in 1999 and 2000. Won the MAC regular season crown for the first time in 2000. Ten players have been named All-Region 16 times. With 12 players named All-MAC 20 times. Have also had 2 players named MAC Newcomer of the Year.
Coaching: Ian Collins is our Head Coach. He holds USSF 'A' license. He has 12 years of NCAA Division I experience. Jeff Chaney and Tim Bennett are the Assistant Coaches.
Roster In State: 10 **Out of State:** 20 **Out of Country:** 2
Walk-on/Other: **Graduation %:** N/A **Seniors on Team:** 6
Positions Needed: ALL
Camp or Clinic Dates: Not Available
Most Recent Record: 11-9-2
Schedule: Indiana, Furman, Ohio State, FIU, Akron, Cincinnati
Style of Play: Pay a 4-4-2 formation.

Women's Athletic Profile

Memorial Coliseum
Lexington, KY 40506
Coach: Warren Lipka
Email: lipka@pop.uky.edu

NCAA I
Wild Cats/Blue, White
Phone: (859) 257-4911
Fax: (859) 323-4310

Estimated # of Women's Soccer Scholarships: None
Conference: South Eastern, Mid-American Conference
Program Profile: New soccer facility, 120x75 lighted field, 2,500 capacity, natural grass.
History: Nationally ranked program; 1995 record was 16-5-1; 1996 Conference Runner-Up; 1997 record was 12-7-2 second in the conference.
Roster in State: 3 **Out of State:** 23 **Out of Country:** 2
Walk-on/Other: **Graduation %:** **Seniors on Team:** 3
Camp or Clinic Dates: June 24-29, July 1-6, July 8-13
Most Recent Record: 15-6-0
Schedule: Southern Cal, Florida, Arizona State, Southern Methodist, Michigan, Vanderbilt, Michigan State.

University of Louisville

Academic Profile

Louisville, KY 40292
Phone: (800) 334-3635

Type: 4 Yr.,Public,Liberal Arts,Engineering
Founded: 1798
Website: http://www.louisville.edu
Religion: Non-Affiliated
SAT/ACT/GPA: 820/17/2.5
Housing: Yes
Student/Faculty Ratio: 19:1
Male/Female Ratio: 48:52
Undergraduate Enrollment: 20,857
Graduate Enrollment: 4,000
Scholarships/Academic: Yes **Athletic:** Yes **Financial Aid:** Yes
Expenses by: Year **In State:** $ 13,322 **Out of State:** $ 19,342
Specialty: Business, Research
Degrees Conferred: More than 17 Degrees in each of 11 colleges/schools
Programs of Study: Speed Scientific School, College of Arts & Sciences (Biology, Chemistry, English, ect..), College of Business and Public Administration, School of Allied Health Sciences, School of Dentistry, School of Education, Law & Medical School, Kent School of Social Work, School of Music, School of Nursing

Men's Athletic Profile

Men's Soccer, Student Activities Ctr
Louisville, KY 40292
Coach: Tony Colaveccia
Email: a cola 1@athena.louisville.edu

NCAA I
Cardinals/Red, Black, White
Phone: (502) 852-0105
Fax: (502) 852-0815

Estimated # of Men's Soccer Scholarships:
Conference: Conference USA
Program Profile: Cardinal Park is a new 3000 seat facility opening in August 2000.
History: Our soccer program is coming upon 20 years of Division I soccer. Our new conference has had as many as 3 top 25 teams.
Coaching: Head Coach-Tony Colavecchia. Assistant Coaches-Chad Harmon and Mike Keeney.
Roster In State: 5 **Out of State:** 16 **Out of Country:** 7
ODP State: 14 **Regional:** 4 **National:** 3
Walk-on/Other: **Graduation %:** 90 **Seniors on Team:** 3
Positions Needed: Defenders
Camp or Clinic Dates: 2 weeks in July
Most Recent Record: 9-11-0
Schedule: Indiana, St. Louis, Akron, UNC-Charlotte, Marquette, Evansville
Style of Play: An entertaining and hopefully a winning brand.

Women's Athletic Profile

Women's Soccer Coach, Sac Blvd.
Louisville, KY 40292
Coach: Karen Ferguson
Email: kferguson@louisville.edu

NCAA I
Cardinals/Red, White, Black
Phone:
Fax: (502) 852-0815

Estimated # of Women's Soccer Scholarships: 12
Conference: Conference USA
Program Profile: One of the top programs in the region. An Olympic size soccer complex is underway. Natural grass turf. Excellent training facilities. Fall playing season.
History: Started in 1985. Substantial improvement since 1992.
Achievements: Conference USA Co-Champions 1995-1996, Conference USA Coach of the Year 1995-1996, and All-Americans third team - Kristen Dowell.
Coaching: Karen Ferguson-Head Coach; Jennifer Mead- Assistant Coach; Carole Dutchka- Assistant Coach
Roster in State: 10 **Out of State:** 12 **Out of Country:** 1
ODP State: 12 **Regional:** 4 **National:**
Walk-on/Other: 3 **Graduation %:** **Seniors on Team:** 0
Camp or Clinic Dates: Not Available
Schedule: Ohio State, Dayton, Florida State, Evansville, St. Louis, Marquette, UNC- Charlotte
Style of Play: All attacking soccer. Short passes to stimulate the Brazilian style of play. A defensive mechanism with the European flair.

Western Kentucky University
Academic Profile

Phone: 270-745-2551

Bowling Green, KY 42101

Type: 4 Yr.,Public
Website: http://www.wku.edu
Founded: 1906
Religion: Non-Affiliated

SAT/ACT/GPA: 890/21
Student/Faculty Ratio: 20:1
Undergraduate Enrollment: 15,087
Scholarships/Academic: Yes **Athletic:** Yes
Expenses by: Year **In State:** $ 6,140
Specialty: Arts and Sciences
Degrees Conferred: BA, BS, BFA, MS, MA
Housing: Yes
Male/Female Ratio: 44:56
Graduate Enrollment: 2,067
Financial Aid: Yes
Out of State: $ 10,180
Programs of Study: Accounting, Advertising, Anthropology, BioChemistry, Biology, Botany, Communications, Computer Science, Creative Writing, Economics, Education, Engineering, Environmental Science, Finance, Fine Arts, Journalism, Liberal Arts, Library Science, Mathematics, Medical Technology, Physical Science, Religion, Social Science

Men's Athletic Profile

Athletic Department
Bowling Green, KY 42101
Coach: David Holmes
Email: dhomes@wtu.edu

NCAA I
Hilltoppers/Red, White
Phone: (270) 745-6068
Fax: (270) 745-3444

Estimated # of Men's Soccer Scholarships: None
Conference: Missouri Valley Conference
Program Profile: Play a strong regional and national schedule; WKU travel coast to coast to play the best possible NCAA Division I schedule. Natural grass field is located at the center of WKU's beautiful campus. Stadium has a seating capacity of 17,500 and is natural grass.
History: Program began in 1982. Ranked in Top 10 in Great Lakes Region in 1998, 1992, 1991, 1990, & 1989; Sun Belt Conference Champions in 1986.
Achievements: 1995 Sun Belt Conference regular season Co-Champions; 1 Academic All-American, 12 NSCAA All-Mideast Region players; 2 WKU Male Athlete of the Year awards, 1 Scholar Athletes of the Year Award, numerous Sun Belt Academic Honor Roll recipients (3.0GPA or above). 1986 Sunbelt Conference Coach of the Year, 1998 3rd place in MVC, and 1998-1999 WKY Team Academic Excellence Awards (Top Male Team - GPA). We were 1998 Sun Belt Conference Coach of the Year. In 1998, 3rd place in MVC and WKY team Academic Excellence Awards (Top Male Team GPA).
Coaching: David Holmes, Head Coach at WKU since 1984, holds a USSF "A" License, Region II Staff Coach and Sun Belt Conference Coach of the Year in 1985. Dale Helfrich, Assistant Coach, holds a USSf "B" License.
Style of Play: Dependent upon current group of players and their abilities. WKU has a very competitive reputation.

Women's Athletic Profile

Department of Athletics
Bowling Green, KY 42101
Coach: Jason Neidell
Email: jason.neidell@wku.edu

NCAA I
Hilltopers/Red, White
Phone: (270) 745-6563
Fax: (270) 745-6187

Estimated # of Women's Soccer Scholarships: Fully funded with 12 scholarships, 4 available
Conference: Sunbelt
Program Profile: Home games will be played at Creason Stadium which is a 115x75 yard natural grass field.
History: 2001 will the first season of competition.
Achievements:
Coaching: Jason Niedell joins the WKU staff after being the Assistant Coach at Tulsa University. David Neidell is the Assistant Coach.
Positions Needed: ALL
Camp or Clinic Dates: Call for details
Most Recent Record: N/A 1st Year Program
Schedule: North Texas, Florida International, Denver
Style of Play: Based on personel.

louisiana

LOUISIANA

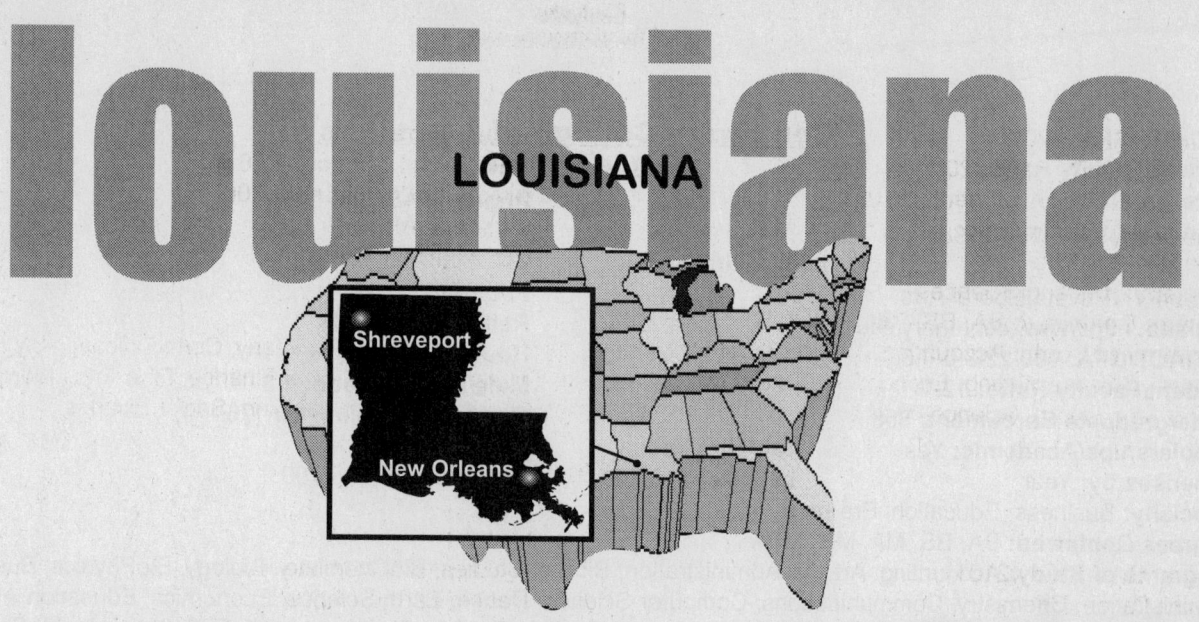

SCHOOL	CITY	AFFILIATION	PAGE
Centenary College of Louisiana	Shreveport	NCAA I	420
Louisiana State Univ-Baton Rouge	Baton Rouge	NCAA I	421
Loyola University - New Orleans	New Orleans	NAIA	422
McNeese State University	Lake Charles	NCAA I	422
Nicholls State University	Thibodaux	NCAA I	423
University of Louisiana, Monroe	Monroe	NCAA I	424
Northwestern State University	Natchitoches	NCAA I	424
Southeastern Louisiana University	Hammond	NCAA I	425
Tulane University	New Orleans	NCAA I	426
University of Louisiana-Lafayette	Lafayette	NCAA I	427

Centenary College of Louisiana

Academic Profile

Shreveport, LA 71134-1188

Phone: (318) 869-5165

Type: 4 Yr.,Private,Liberal Arts
Website: http://www.centenary.edu
SAT/ACT/GPA: 900/22/3.0-4.0
Student/Faculty Ratio: 12:1
Undergraduate Enrollment: 858
Scholarships/Academic: Yes **Athletic:** Yes
Expenses by: Year **In State:** $18,700
Founded: 1825
Religion: Methodist
Housing: Yes
Male/Female Ratio: 1/3
Graduate Enrollment: 175
Financial Aid: Yes
Out of State: $18,700
Specialty: Business, Education, Pre-med
Degrees Conferred: BA, BS, MA, MS, MBA
Programs of Study: Accounting, Art, Art Administration, Biblical Studies, BioChemistry, Biology, BioPhysics, Business Administration, Chemistry, Communications, Computer Science, Dance, Earth Science, Economics, Education, Elementary Education, Engineering and Applied Science, English, French, Geology, Health Education, Health Science, Physical Therapy, Physics, Political Science, PreDentistry, PreLaw, PreMed, PreVet, Psychology, Religion, Science Education, Secondary Education, Social Science, Spanish, Speech Pathology, Theatre, Voice

Men's Athletic Profile

P.O. Box 41188
Shreveport, LA 71134-1188
Coach: Jed Jones
Email: jdjones@centenary.edu

NCAA I
Gents/Maroon, White
Phone: (318) 869-5165
Fax: (318) 869-5145

Estimated # of Men's Soccer Scholarships: N/A
Conference: American South
Program Profile: The Gents play a full Division I schedule that normally lasts from early September to the early Nov. All the home matches are played at the Centenary Soccer Field which has a 500 seating capacity and recently added lights. The field is a 110 x 75 grass field.
History: Became NCAA I program in 1980 and soon developed into a highly respectable program in the late 1980's with several All-Conference, all-Midwestern Region, and All-American, All-Midwest Region, and All-American players.
Achievements: Coach Glenn Evens earned TAAC Coach of the Year honors from 1988-90 after the Gents captured 3 straight TAAC championships in those years. Many All-TAAC players and 2 All-Americans. Freshman Rogerio Lima named First Team All-Midwest 1994.
Coaching: Jed Jones is the Head Coach for the Gents. He holds a USSF "A" license and an International coaching license from the Football Association of Ireland. He is in his 4th year as head coach.
Roster In State: 4 **Out of State:** 23 **Out of Country:** 0
ODP State: **Regional:** **National:**
Walk-on/Other: **Graduation %:** N/A **Seniors on Team:** 3
Positions Needed: All
Camp or Clinic Dates: Last two weeks of July
Schedule: University of Missouri, University of Alabama-Birmingham, University of New Mexico, Oral Roberts, Texas Christian University, Central Florida, Florida Atlantic, Denver, Georgia Southern, Drury.
Style of Play: Possession style of play all over the field with high pressure defensively.

Women's Athletic Profile

P.O. Box 41188
Shreveport, LA 71134
Coach: Jed Jones
Email: jdjones@centenary.edu

NCAA I
Ladies/Maroon, White
Phone: (318) 869-5165
Fax: (318) 869-5145

Estimated # of Women's Soccer Scholarships: None
Conference: American South
Program Profile: The Ladies play a full Division I schedule that normally lasts from early September to early November. All home matches are played at the Centenary Soccer Field on campus. The field is natural grass, (110x75 yards), and has a capacity of a 500. Facilities include: soccer locker rooms, a training site, a head coach's office and assistant coaches offices. We play against southern states and Midwest states.
History: The Ladies program began in 1992. The Ladies have had 8 winning seasons out of 9.
Achievements: Glenn Evans TAAC Coach of the Year in 1983, 1988, 1989, 1990 (men) and 1994 (women). The Ladies have made four TAAC Championship appearances.
Coaching: Jed Jones is the Head Soccer Coach for the Centenary Ladies. He holds a USSF "A" Coaching license as well as the International Coaching License of the Football Association of Ireland. He is in his fourth year as head coach. Glenn Evans and Jaime Frias both assist in the Ladies program.

Roster in State: 4	**Out of State:** 19	**Out of Country:** 0
ODP State: 15	**Regional:** 5	**National:**
Walk-on/Other:	**Graduation %:** N/A	**Seniors on Team:** 8

Positions Needed: Forwards, Center Midfielders, Outside Midfielders
Camp or Clinic Dates: Last 2 weeks of July
Most Recent Record: 15-4-0
Schedule: North Texas, TCU, Mississippi State, SE Louisiana
Style of Play: Possession oriented. Building out of the back. We also attack with numbers and defend with numbers.

Louisiana State University - Baton Rouge

Academic Profile

Baton Rouge, LA 70894-5095
Phone: 225-578-1175

Type: 4 Yr.,Public		**Founded:** 1860
Website: http://www.sports.lsu.edu		**Religion:** All Denominations
SAT/ACT/GPA: 990/21/2.3		**Housing:** Yes
Student/Faculty Ratio: 40:1		**Male/Female Ratio:** 1:1.5
Undergraduate Enrollment: 24,773		**Graduate Enrollment:** 5,108
Scholarships/Academic: Yes	**Athletic:** Yes	**Financial Aid:** Yes
Expenses by: Year	**In State:** $ 4,584	**Out of State:** $ 8,784

Specialty: Agricultural & Mechanical
Degrees Conferred: BA, BS, BFA, B.Arch, BM, BME, MBA, M.Ed., Ph.D., JD
Programs of Study: Agriculture, Arts & Science, Basic Science, Business, Engineering, Mass Communications, Music, History, Physics, Political Science, Psychology, Criminology

Women's Athletic Profile

P.O. Box 25095
Baton Rouge, LA 70894-5095
Coach: George Fotopoulos
Email: gfotop1@lsu.edu

NCAA I
Tigers/Purple, Gold
Phone: (225) 388-8256
Fax: (225) 388-4066

Estimated # of Women's Soccer Scholarships: 14
Conference: Southeastern Conference
Program Profile: We are fairly new program with a lighted field, natural grass, 1,500 seat stadium, fall playing season, brand new 2,000 sq. feet locker room/ equipment room. We signed 15 girls for the 2,000 season.
History: We began in the fall of 1995 and this year with Fotopoulos is it 3rd coach. The program is headed towards a new era.
Achievements: 1 2nd Team All-SEC Winner; Academic All-SEC Nominees; Won Academic Award from NSCAA
Coaching: George Fotopoulos is our new Head Coach; Tracy Ward and Meredith Flaherty are the Assistant Coaches.

Roster in State: 16
Out of State: 15
Out of Country:
ODP State: 12
Regional: 12
National: 12
Walk-on/Other:
Graduation %: 100
Seniors on Team: 3
Positions Needed: Forward, Goalkeeper
Camp or Clinic Dates: June5-9, July10-14, 17-21
Most Recent Record: 4-15-1
Schedule: Tennessee, Kentucky, Vanderbilt, Alabama, Auburn, Georgia, Ole Miss, Oklahoma State, Troy State, Texas Tech
Style of Play: Counter-Attacking

Loyola University - New Orleans

Academic Profile

New Orleans
New Orleans, LA 70148-2135
Phone: (800) 4-LOYOLA

Type: 4 Yr.,Private,Liberal Arts
Founded: 1912
Website: http://www.loyno.edu
Religion: Catholic (Jesuit)
SAT/ACT/GPA: 1270/28/3.55
Housing: Yes
Student/Faculty Ratio: 12:1
Male/Female Ratio: 2:3
Undergraduate Enrollment: 3,500
Graduate Enrollment: 2,000
Scholarships/Academic: Yes
Athletic: No
Financial Aid: Yes
Expenses by: Year
In State: $ 21,577
Out of State: $ 21,577
Degrees Conferred: BA, BS, BFA, BM, BAM, BME, BMT
Programs of Study: College of Arts & Sciences, College of Business Administration, College of Music

Women's Athletic Profile

6363 St. Charles Ave, Box 21
New Orleans, LA 70118
Coach: Emmy Therrell
Email: admit@loyola.edu

NAIA
Wolfpack/Maroon, Gold
Phone: (504) 865-3137
Fax: (504) 865-3081

Estimated # of Women's Soccer Scholarships: None
Conference: Gulf Coast Athletic Conference
History: Program began in 1993.
Coaching: Emmy Therrell, Head Coach, NSCAA Advanced National license.

McNeese State University

Academic Profile

Phone: 337-475-5000
Lake Charles, LA 70609

Type: 4 Yr.,Public
Founded: 1939
Website: http://www.mcneese.edu
Religion: Non-Affiliated
SAT/ACT/GPA: 820/18
Housing: Yes
Student/Faculty Ratio: 24:1
Male/Female Ratio: 48:52
Undergraduate Enrollment: 6,000
Graduate Enrollment: 2,000
Scholarships/Academic: Yes
Athletic: Yes
Financial Aid: Yes
Expenses by: Year
In State: $ 4,800
Out of State: $ 9,800
Degrees Conferred: AA, AS, BA, BS, BM, BMEd, BSN, MS, MA
Programs of Study: College of Business, College of Engineering, College of Education, College of Science, College of Liberal Arts and the College of Nursing

Women's Athletic Profile

P.O. Box 91535
Lake Charles, LA 70609
Coach: Ryan Livengood
Email: plafosse@1aol.net

NCAA I
Cowgirls/Royal Blue, Gold
Phone: (318) 475-5216
Fax: (318) 475-5928

Estimated # of Women's Soccer Scholarships: None
Conference: Southland Conference
Program Profile: On campus natural grass training and game facilities. Our athletes utilize our newly renovated strength and conditioning facilities. We are currently building a new training facility for the care our athletes.
History: The program began in 1996 and we have improved our win-loss record in each of our first three seasons. We have competed twice in the Southland Conference championship Tournament.
Achievements: Has 10 players named to SLC All-Conference team in two years, 5 players named SLC All-Tournament in two years and one player in 1999 named to GTE Academic All-American District Team.
Style of Play: Adapt style of play to the characteristics of the team.

Nicholls State University
Academic Profile

Thibodaux, LA 70310
Phone: 1-504-NICHOLLS

Type: 4 Yr.,Public		**Founded:** 1948
Website: http://www.server.nich.edu		**Religion:** Non-Affiliated
SAT/ACT/GPA: None		**Housing:** Yes
Student/Faculty Ratio: 22:1		**Male/Female Ratio:** 1:1.66
Undergraduate Enrollment: 6,627		**Graduate Enrollment:** 791
Scholarships/Academic: Yes	**Athletic:** Yes	**Financial Aid:** Yes
Expenses by: Year	**In State:** $ 6,277	**Out of State:** $10,549

Degrees Conferred: AA, AS, BA, BS, MA, MBA
Programs of Study: Accounting, Agriculture, Arts, Biology, Business Administration, CardioPulmonary Care Science, Chemistry, Computer Science, Communicative Disorders, Computer Information Systems, Criminal Justice, Culinary Arts, CytoTechnology, Dietetics, Education, Finance, French, Government, History, Legal Assistant Studies, Management, Marketing, Mass Communication, Mathematics, Nursing, Psychology, Respiratory Therapy Science, Safety Technology, Sociology, Special Education

Women's Athletic Profile

Box 2032
Thibodaux, LA 70310
Coach: Roger Bimah
Email: ath-rb@mail.nich.edu

NCAA I
Lady Colonels/Red & White
Phone: (504) 448-4956
Fax: (504) 448-4924

Estimated # of Women's Soccer Scholarships: 7
Conference: South Land
Program Profile: Natural grass field and we play year round.
History: Begin in 1998, 1st conference tournament appearance. We have players from different parts of the country most with state ODP experience.
Achievements: 5 All-Conference Players in our short existence. 1st appearance in conference tournament.
Coaching: Roger Bimah Head Coach has 20 years experience USSA "A" License and NSCAA-Advanced Diploma.

Roster in State: 7	**Out of State:** 10	**Out of Country:** 1
ODP State: 6	**Regional:** 0	**National:** 0
Walk-on/Other: 0	**Graduation %:**	**Seniors on Team:** 1

Positions Needed: ALL
Most Recent Record: 2-16-0
Schedule: LSU, Univ. of Southern Mississippi, Stephan F. Austin
Style of Play: Possession oriented and zonal defense.

University of Louisiana-Monroe

Academic Profile

Phone: (318) 342-5090

Monroe, LA 71209

Type: 4 Yr.,Public,Liberal Arts
Founded: 1931
Website: http://www.nlu.edu
Religion: Non-Affiliated
SAT/ACT/GPA: Open Admission
Housing: Yes
Student/Faculty Ratio: 20:1
Male/Female Ratio: 1:1.5
Undergraduate Enrollment: 9,411
Graduate Enrollment: 1,116
Scholarships/Academic: Yes **Athletic:** Yes **Financial Aid:** Yes
Expenses by: Year **In State:** $ 2,805 **Out of State:** $ 5,217
Specialty: Health, Sciences, Business
Degrees Conferred: AA, AS, AGS, BA, BS, BFA, BM, BME, MA, MS, MBA
Programs of Study: Over 100 programs in five colleges - Business, Education, Liberal Arts, Pharmacy & Health Sciences, Pure & Applied Sciences

Women's Athletic Profile

Department of Athletics Stadium Drive
Monroe, LA 71209
Coach: Rena Richardson
Email: Not Available

NCAA I
Lady Indians/Card. Red, Gold
Phone: (318) 342-5090
Fax: (318) 342-5464

Estimated # of Women's Soccer Scholarships: 8
Conference: Southland
Program Profile: We play at a natural field stadium with capacity of 5,000.
History: Our program is fairly new having just begun in 1999.
Achievements: 2 2nd team All-Conference players.
Coaching: Rena Richardson, Head Coach, is head coach and Stacy Lamb is the assistant coach.
Roster in State: 4 **Out of State:** 18 **Out of Country:**
ODP State: 8 **Regional:** 5 **National:**
Positions Needed: All
Camp or Clinic Dates: July 17-21
Most Recent Record: 5-15-0
Schedule: Alabama, LSU, Southwest Texas State, Little Rock Arkansas, South Alabama, Arkansas State
Style of Play: Attacking style of play. High pressure. All over the field.

Northwestern State University - Louisiana

Academic Profile

Phone: (318) 357-4337

Natchitoches, LA 71497

Type: 4 Yr.,Public
Founded: 1922
Website: http://www.nsudemons.com
Religion: Non-Affiliated
SAT/ACT/GPA: 17
Housing: Yes
Student/Faculty Ratio: 17:1
Male/Female Ratio: 45:55
Undergraduate Enrollment: 9,000
Graduate Enrollment: 1,000

Scholarships/Academic: Yes **Athletic:** Yes **Financial Aid:** Yes
Expenses by: Year **In State:** $ 6,003 **Out of State:** $ 10,413
Specialty: Most majors and programs
Degrees Conferred: AA, AS, BA, BM, BS, MS, MFA
Programs of Study: Accounting, Advertising, Animal, Anthropology, Art, Biological Science, Botany, Broadcasting, Business, Dance, Early Childhood Education, Engineering, English, Fine Arts, History, Information, Journalism, Marketing, Management, Math, Medical, Music, Nursing, Personnel Management, Photography, Political Science, Physics, Psychology, Speech

Women's Athletic Profile

Prather Coliseum
Natchitoches, LA 71497
Coach: Jimmy Mitchell
Email: mandy@nsula.edu

NCAA I
Demons/Purple, Burnt Orange
Phone: (318) 357-4337
Fax: (318) 357-4515

Estimated # of Women's Soccer Scholarships: None
Conference: Southland Conference
Program Profile: This is our fourth year in Division I and we are a fully funded program. We have two natural grass fields. We were SLC tournament Champions in 1997.
History: Our program started in 1996. Our 1998 record was 9-9-2.
Achievements: Has three players named to SLC All-Tournament team in 1997; SLC Freshman of the Year - Steph O'Neil in 1997; Jimmy Mitchell Coach of the Year in 1996 and 1998.
Coaching: Jimmy Mitchell, Head Coach, is in his first year as head coach here. He led the 1998 Belmont Abbey to a Top 10 NCAA Division II ranking and to the National Quarterfinals. Kari LaRocco, Assistant Coach, is a graduate of Belmont Abbey.
Style of Play: Positional; attack from back; high pressure defensively.

Southeastern Louisiana University

Academic Profile

Phone: (504) 549-2253

Hammond, LA 70402

Type: 4 Yr.,Public
Founded: 1925
Website: http://www.selu.edu/athletics
Religion: Non-Affiliated
SAT/ACT/GPA: 830/17
Housing: Yes
Student/Faculty Ratio: 25:1
Male/Female Ratio: 38:62
Undergraduate Enrollment: 15,500
Graduate Enrollment: N/A
Scholarships/Academic: Yes **Athletic:** Yes **Financial Aid:** Yes
Expenses by: Year **In State:** $ 4,758 **Out of State:** $ 10,086
Specialty: Liberal Arts, Sciences, Professional Fields
Degrees Conferred: BA, BS, MA, MS
Programs of Study: Accounting, Biology, Business, Chemistry, Communication and Theatre, Computer Science, Counseling, Criminal Justice, Design Drafted Technology, Education, English, Finance, Foreign Languages, History, Industry Technology, Kinesiology, Literature, Management, Marketing, Mathematics, Music, Nursing, Physics, Political Science, Psychology, Sociology, Visual Arts

Women's Athletic Profile

SLU Box 10309
Hammond, LA 70402
Coach: Blake Hornbuckle
Email: bhornbuckle@selu.edu

NCAA I
Lady Lions/Green, Gold
Phone: (504) 549-2253
Fax: (504) 549-3495

Estimated # of Women's Soccer Scholarships:
Conference: Southland Conference
Program Profile: Reigning SC Champions. We play our home games on natural turf.
History: Program started in 1995. We won the SLC Tournament in 1998 and regular season in 1999.
Achievements: Coach of the year honors- Blake Hornbuckle- 1 Southland Conference- 2 All-Louisiana and 2 conference titles.
Coaching: Blake Hornbuckle, Head Coach, is entering his second year with the program. He lead the program to its best ever record in 1999 with 11 wins. He claimed his second conference title and was name Coach of the Year and All-Louisiana Coach of the Year for the second time.
Roster in State: 4 **Out of State:** 17 **Out of Country:** 3
ODP State: 12 **Regional:** 1 **National:** 1
Walk-on/Other: **Graduation %:** 100 **Seniors on Team:** 2
Positions Needed: Goalkeeper, Defenders, Forwards
Camp or Clinic Dates: June 25- 30
Most Recent Record: 11-4-5
Schedule: University of Houston, Louisiana State University, Mississippi State University, Tulane University, Southwest Texas, Centenary College, Memphis
Style of Play: Possession oriented and committing numbers into the attack while maintaining team shape.

Tulane University
Academic Profile

New Orleans, LA 70118-5681
Phone: (504) 865-5574

Type: 4 Yr.,Private
Founded: 1834
Website: http://www.tulane.edu
Religion: Non-denominational
SAT/ACT/GPA: 1200/27/Top 10%
Housing: Yes
Student/Faculty Ratio: 12:1
Male/Female Ratio: 50:50
Undergraduate Enrollment: 6,500
Graduate Enrollment: 4,800
Scholarships/Academic: Yes **Athletic:** Yes **Financial Aid:** Yes
Expenses by: Year **In State:** $ 31,343 **Out of State:** $ 31,343
Specialty: Architecture, Business, Engineering, Liberal Arts, Sciences
Degrees Conferred: BA, BS, Maters, Ph.D.
Programs of Study: School of Law, Medicine, Public Health, Tropical Medicine, Social Work, Engineering, Business, Architecture, Liberal Arts.

Women's Athletic Profile

James Wilson Center
New Orleans, LA 70118
Coach: Eliot Perkins
Email: eperkin@tulane.edu

NCAA I
Greenwave/Forest Green, Blue
Phone: (504) 865-5574
Fax: (504) 865-5512

Estimated # of Women's Soccer Scholarships:
Conference: Conference USA
Program Profile: Our program is in its 4th year and we have a new coach. We play at Seab Stadium, which has natural grass, 2,000 seats, an excellent weight room and is on campus.
History: Fall of 1996 was the first year of the program. This is the first four year soccer graduating class.
Coaching: Eliot Perkins, Head Coach, is heading into his first year. Melissa Mitchell and Eddie Pigford are Assistant Coaches.
Style of Play: High emphasis on possession and attack.

University of Louisiana-Lafayette
Academic Profile

Lafayette, LA 70506
Phone: 800-752-6553

Type: 4 yr,Public
Website: www.louisiana.edu
SAT/ACT/GPA: N/A/19/
Student/Faculty Ratio: N/A
Undergraduate Enrollment: 14,418
Scholarships/Academic: Need Based **Athletic:**
Expenses by: Year **In State:** $6,880
Specialty: Business
Degrees Conferred: 1,623 Bachelors, 60 Associates, Masters, Doctoral
Programs of Study: Check www.louisiana.edu for complete list

Founded: 1898
Religion: Non Affiliated
Housing: Yes
Male/Female Ratio: 44/56
Graduate Enrollment: 1,148
Financial Aid: Yes
Out of State: $12,112

Women's Athletic Profile

201 Reinhardt Drive
Lafayette, LA 70506
Coach: David Poggi
Email: coach.poggi@ragincajuns.com

NCAA I
Ragin Cajuns/Red, White
Phone: (337) 482-5165
Fax: (337) 482-5379

Estimated # of Women's Soccer Scholarships: 8
Conference: Sunbelt
History: Program began in 2000.
Achievements:
Coaching: David Poggi is the Head Coach and is Assisted by Adrian Boyle.
Roster in State: 16 **Out of State:** 1 **Out of Country:** 1
Walk-on/Other: **Graduation %:** N/A **Seniors on Team:** 2
Positions Needed: All
Camp or Clinic Dates: TBA
Most Recent Record: 2-14-0

maine

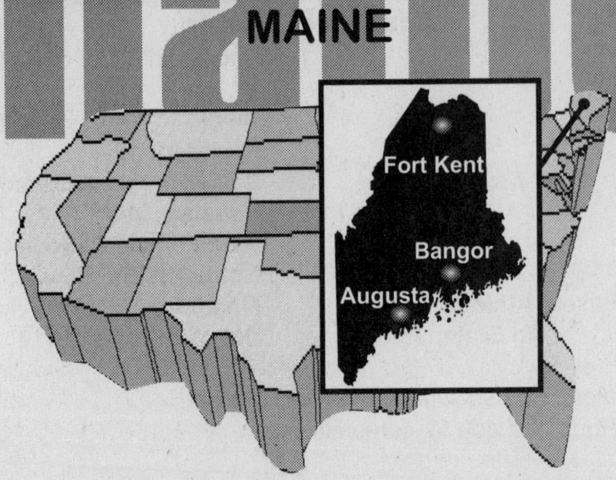

SCHOOL	CITY	AFFILIATION	PAGE
Bates College	Lewiston	NCAA III	429
Bowdoin College	Brunswick	NCAA III	430
Colby College	Waterville	NCAA III	431
Husson College	Bangor	NAIA	432
Maine Maritime Academy	Castine	NCAA III/NAIA	433
Saint Joseph's College - Maine	Standish	NCAA III	434
Thomas College	Waterville	NCAA III/NAIA	435
University of Maine	Orono	NCAA I	436
University of ME - Farmington	Farmington	NCAA III/NAIA	437
University of ME - Machias	Machias	NAIA	438
University of ME - Presque Isle	Presque Isle	NAIA	439
Univ of New England	Biddeford	NCAA III	440
University of Southern Maine	Gorham	NCAA III	441

Bates College
Academic Profile

Phone: 207-786-6000

Lewiston, ME 04240

Type: 4 Yr.,Private,Liberal Arts
Website: http://www.bates.edu
SAT/ACT/GPA: Optional/3.3
Student/Faculty Ratio: 11:1
Undergraduate Enrollment: 1,600
Scholarships/Academic: No **Athletic:** No
Expenses by: Year **In State:** $ 30,070
Specialty: Liberal Arts
Degrees Conferred: BA, BS

Founded: 1855
Religion: Non-Affiliated
Housing: Yes
Male/Female Ratio: 51:49
Graduate Enrollment: N/A
Financial Aid: Yes
Out of State: $ 31,070

Programs of Study: African Studies, American Studies, Anthropology, Art, BioChemistry, Biology, Chemistry, Chinese, Classics, Economics, English, Environmental Studies, French, Geology, German, History, Interdisciplinary Studies, Mathematics, Medieval Studies, Music, Philosophy, Physics, Political Science, Psychology, Religion, Russian, Social Science, Spanish, Speech, Theatre, Women's Studies

Men's Athletic Profile

Alumni Gym
Lewiston, ME 04240
Coach: Gege Purgavie
Email: gpurgavi@bates.edu

NCAA III
Bobcats/Garnet
Phone: (207) 786-6357
Fax: (207) 786-8232

Estimated # of Men's Soccer Scholarships:
Conference: NESCAC, ECAC
Program Profile: Play on one of the best soccer fields in New England, full size natural grass.
History: Program began in 1962.
Achievements: CBB Conference Champions in 1989.
Coaching: George Purgavie, Head Coach, has an USSF "A" license, a NSCAA Advanced National Diploma, is the MSYSA State Coaching Director and USYSA Regional Staff Coach.
Style of Play: Control!! We vary the type of pressure we apply. On attack we employ either a direct or indirect style based on relative strength and weaknesses of our team and opponents.

Women's Athletic Profile

Alumni Gym
Lewiston, ME 04240
Coach: Jim Murphy
Email: jmurphy@bates.edu

NCAA III
Bobcats/Garnet, White, Black
Phone: (207) 786-6369
Fax: (207) 786-8232

Estimated # of Women's Soccer Scholarships: None
Conference: New England Small College Athletic Conference
Program Profile: Play on grass surface that measures 120x75 yards. Program is highly competitive with a 14 game regular season schedule.
History: Program began in 1980.
Achievements: 5 All-Americans, 18 All- New England, Elite Eight of NCAA Tourney in 96, ECAC D.III Champions 86, 91, 98
Coaching: Jim Murphy, Head Coach.

Roster in State: 2 **Out of State:** 20 **Out of Country:** 0
Walk-on/Other: **Graduation %:** 100 **Seniors on Team:** 2
Positions Needed: Forwards, Midfield, Defenders
Camp or Clinic Dates: Not Available
Most Recent Record: 12-6-0
Schedule: Tufts, Williams, Bowdoin, Colby, Middlebury, Trinity, Wesleyan
Style of Play: Possession.

Bowdoin College
Academic Profile

Phone:

Brunswick, ME 04011

Type: 4 Yr.,Private,Liberal Arts
Founded: 1795
Website: http://www.bowdoin.edu
Religion: Non-Affiliated
SAT/ACT/GPA: No standarized tests required
Housing: Yes
Student/Faculty Ratio: 11:1
Male/Female Ratio: 50:50
Undergraduate Enrollment: 1,605
Graduate Enrollment: N/A
Scholarships/Academic: No **Athletic:** No **Financial Aid:** Yes
Expenses by: Year **In State:** $ 31,950 **Out of State:** $ 31,950
Degrees Conferred: BA
Programs of Study: Fine Arts, Archeology, Art History, Classics, English, French, German, History, Music, Philosophy, Religion, Romance, Russian, Spanish, Studio Art, Biology, Mathematics, BioChemistry, Chemistry, Physics, Natural Sciences, Geology, Computer Science, Chemical Physics, Physics, Sociology, African Studies, Asian Studies, Environmental Studies, Latin American

Men's Athletic Profile

Morrell Gym
Brunswick, ME 04011
Coach: Brian Ainscough
Email: bainscou@bowdoin.edu

NCAA III
Polar Bears/Black, White
Phone: (207) 725-3352
Fax: (207) 725-3019

Estimated # of Men's Soccer Scholarships:
Conference: ECAC, New England Conference
Program Profile: Full size grass fields for both games and practices. Season runs from September through November after the ECAC Tournament.
Achievements: ECAC Tournament Qualifiers in 1988 & 1990.
Style of Play: Well-disciplined, team oriented style of play.

Women's Athletic Profile

9000 College State Rd
Brunswick, ME 04011
Coach: John Cullen
Email: jcullen@bowdoin.edu

NCAA III
Polar Bears/Black, White
Phone: (207) 725-3721
Fax: (207) 725-3019

Estimated # of Women's Soccer Scholarships: None
Conference: NESCAC
Program Profile: We have a varsity and junior varsity program that practice and play games on natural grass fields with a stadium that seats 600.
History: The program began in 1977 and we have had 21 straight years of postseason competition and 5 straight years of NCAA bids.

Achievements: NE Coach of the Year '89 '92 '95; NSCAA National Coach of the Year 1992; 10 All-American selections; ECAC Champions 1992 and 1993
Coaching: John Cullen, Head Coach, named New England Coach of the Year in 1989 & 1995; 1992 National Coach of the Year; NSCAA Advanced National Diploma. Jessica Matzkin, Mya Mangawang, Lisa Petruccelli are Assistant Coaches.
Roster in State: 0 **Out of State:** 21 **Out of Country:** 1
ODP State: 9 **Regional:** 2 **National:**
Walk-on/Other: 7 **Graduation %:** 100 **Seniors on Team:** 7
Positions Needed: Midfield, Defenders
Camp or Clinic Dates: August 7-11
Most Recent Record: 13-3
Style of Play: Short passing game of control soccer with a high level of athletic skills.

Colby College

Academic Profile

Waterville, ME 04901
Phone: 800-723-3032

Type: 4 Yr.,Private,Liberal Arts **Founded:** 1813
Website: http://www.colby.edu **Religion:** Non-Affiliated
SAT/ACT/GPA: Open **Housing:** Yes
Student/Faculty Ratio: 11:1 **Male/Female Ratio:** 50:50
Undergraduate Enrollment: 1,800 **Graduate Enrollment:** N/A
Scholarships/Academic: No **Athletic:** No **Financial Aid:** Yes
Expenses by: Year **In State:** $ 30,420 **Out of State:** $ 30,420
Degrees Conferred: BA
Programs of Study: 45 Majors- largest English, Economics, Psychology, Government, Biology

Men's Athletic Profile

Mayflower Hill Drive
Waterville, ME 04901
Coach: Mark Serdjenian
Email: mrsedje@colby.edu
NCAA III
White Mules/Blue, Gray
Phone: (207) 872-3106
Fax: (207) 872-3076

Estimated # of Men's Soccer Scholarships:
Conference: NESCAC
Program Profile: Games are played on a natural grass field built in 1990 with in ground sprinkler.
History: 1959 was the inaugural season of the program; 1978 & 1993 ECAC Champions (16-1-1), semi-finalist in 1990, 1992, 1993 & 1994.
Achievements: ECAC Champions in 1978 & 1993; 6 Tournament Appearances in the 1990's.
Coaching: Mark Serdjenian, Head Coach, has been head coach since 1976 at Colby, is an associate NSCAA staff member; USSF "B" license and NSCAA Advanced National Diploma, 1990 New England Coach of the Year in 1990 and 1993; Maine College Coach of the Year. John Osbourne, Assistant Coach.
Style of Play: A very fit team that plays tough defense, with a legacy of superior goalkeeping. Crisp passing and dangerous in the attacking third, we've also won the Fair Play Award for New England in three of the past six years.

Women's Athletic Profile

Mayflower Hill Drive
Waterville, ME 04901
Coach: Jennifer Holsten
Email: jlholste@colby.edu
NCAA III
White Mules/Blue, Grey
Phone: (207) 872-3000
Fax: (207) 872-3420

Estimated # of Women's Soccer Scholarships: None
Conference: NESCAC
Program Profile: Has game field and practice field; varsity and junior varsity playing season starts from September 1 to mid-November. The team has posted five consecutive post-season appearances including National tournament births in 1997-1998.
History: Varsity since 1979. Since 1994, the team has made three consecutive post-season appearance including a trip to the Sweet Sixteen round of the 1997 Division III NCAA Tournament.
Achievements: Program has produced 3 All-New England players and 12 All-Maine Coach of the Year in 1997; Jenna DeSimone was named 1997 All-American; 5 Regional American since 1994, NCAA Tournament Sweet Sixteen Participant in 1997.
Coaching: Jennifer Holsten, Head Coach, NSCAA National Diploma & Advanced National Diploma. In six seasons at Colby, Coach Holsten has a 51-32-10 record.
Roster in State: 2 **Out of State:** 19 **Out of Country:**
ODP State: 11 **Regional:** 1 **National:**
Walk-on/Other: **Graduation %:** 100 **Seniors on Team:** 4
Camp or Clinic Dates: Not Available
Most Recent Record: 7-5-2
Schedule: Williams, Bowdoin, Amherst, Middlebury, Wheaton, Tufts, Connecticut College, Bates, Clark University, Trinity
Style of Play: Depends on personnel-varies year to year. Often a 4-4-2.

Husson College
Academic Profile

Phone:
Bangor, ME 04401

Type: 4 Yr.,Private, **Founded:** 1898
Website: http://www.husson.edu **Religion:** Non-Affiliated
SAT/ACT/GPA: 740+ **Housing:** Yes
Student/Faculty Ratio: 15:1 **Male/Female Ratio:** 40:60
Undergraduate Enrollment: 1,000 **Graduate Enrollment:** 200
Scholarships/Academic: Yes **Athletic:** No **Financial Aid:** Yes
Expenses by: Year **In State:** $ 14,000 **Out of State:** $ 14,000
Specialty: Business, Health
Degrees Conferred: AS, BS, MS
Programs of Study: Accounting, Banking & Finance, Business Administration, Computer Science, Court Reporting, Education, Management Information Systems, Marketing, Nursing, Physical Therapy, Personnel Management, Professional Studies, Secretarial Studies, Sport Management

Men's Athletic Profile

One College Circle
Bangor, ME 04401
Coach: Nate Benoit
Email: Not Available

NAIA
Braves/Green, White
Phone: (207) 941-7942
Fax: (207) 9731015

Estimated # of Men's Soccer Scholarships: None
Conference: Maine Athletic Conference
Program Profile: The Braves play on a natural grass field.
History: Our program began in 1959.
Achievements: In 1998 MAC Champions, 1999 MAC Champions and Joey Melanson received All-American in 1998.
Coaching: Nate Benoit is the head coach and Joey Melanson is the assistant coach.
Roster In State: 15 **Out of State:** 4 **Out of Country:** 2
Positions Needed: Forward, Center back, Centermid

Camp or Clinic Dates: Not Available
Most Recent Record: 12-7-1
Schedule: Mount Ida, Johnson St, Green Mountain, U-Maine Farmington, Bowdoin College, Notre Dame

Women's Athletic Profile

One College Circle
Bangor, ME 04401
Coach: Keith Bosley
Email: Not Available

NAIA
Lady Braves/Green, Gold
Phone: (207) 941-7017
Fax: (207) 941-7028

Estimated # of Women's Soccer Scholarships: None
Conference: Maine Athletic Conference
Program Profile: Natural grass field; playing season is in August through October.
History: The program began in 1989.
Achievements: 1994 NAIA All-American - Rochelle Gillis.
Style of Play: Passing - control.

Maine Maritime Academy

Academic Profile

Pleasant Street
Castine, ME 04420

Phone: 800-227-8465

Type: 4 Yr.,Public,Engineering
Founded: 1941
Website: http://www.state.me.us/maritime/mma.htm
Religion: Non-Affiliated
SAT/ACT/GPA: 1000+
Housing: No
Student/Faculty Ratio: 10:1
Male/Female Ratio: 70:30
Undergraduate Enrollment: 585
Graduate Enrollment: 35
Scholarships/Academic: Yes **Athletic:** No **Financial Aid:** Yes
Expenses by: Year **In State:** $ 8,750 **Out of State:** $ 9,750
Specialty: Engineering, Technological
Degrees Conferred: AS, BS, MS
Programs of Study: Business Administration, Engineering Technology, Management, Marine Engineering, Maritime Science, Oceanography, Marine Transportation, Boat Yard Management, Transportation Technology

Men's Athletic Profile

Pleasant Street
Castine, ME 04421
Coach: Mike Keller
Email: Not Available

NCAA III
Mariners/Blue, Gold
Phone: (207) 326-2484
Fax: (207) 326-2513

Estimated # of Men's Soccer Scholarships: None
Conference: ECAC, NCAA
Program Profile: Lighted field with a new turf playing surface, large field house for indoor training, fully equipped weight training facility.
History: First varsity season was in 1978. Overall record is 184-155-24.
Achievements: BC Voyov - 1992, 1993 All-Maine team.

Women's Athletic Profile

Pleasant Street
Castine, ME 04420
Coach: Mike Keller
Email: Not Available
Estimated # of Women's Soccer Scholarships: None
Conference: ECAC

NCAA III/NAIA
Mariners/Blue, Gold
Phone: (207) 326-2484
Fax: (207) 326-2513

Saint Joseph's College - Maine

Academic Profile

Standish, ME 04084

Phone: 800-338-7057

Type: 4 Yr.,Private,Liberal Arts
Website: http://www.sjcme.edu
SAT/ACT/GPA: Open
Student/Faculty Ratio: 16:1
Undergraduate Enrollment: 750
Scholarships/Academic: Yes **Athletic:** No
Expenses by: Year **In State:** $ 20,285

Founded: 1912
Religion: Roman Catholic
Housing: No
Male/Female Ratio: 60:40
Graduate Enrollment: N/A
Financial Aid: Yes
Out of State: $ 20,285

Specialty: Business Administration, Communications, Physical Education
Degrees Conferred: AS, BA,BS
Programs of Study: BioChemistry, Biology, Business Administration, Communications, Elementary Education, English, Environmental Science, History, Human Development, Mathematics, Natural Science, Nursing, Philosophy, Physical Education, Psychology, Radiology Technology, Theology, Sociology, PreProfessional (PreDental, PreLaw, PreMed, PreVet), Secondary Education. Honors Programs. Study Abroad.

Men's Athletic Profile

278 Whitebridge Rd
Standish, ME 04084
Coach: Bob Bourget
Email: bbourget@sjcme.edu

NCAA III
Monks/Royal, Red, White
Phone: (207) 893-7665
Fax: (207) 892-8074

Estimated # of Men's Soccer Scholarships: N/A
Conference: Maine Athletic Conference

Women's Athletic Profile

278 White's Bridge Rd
Standish, ME 04084
Coach: Camie Bechtold
Email: Not Available

NCAA III
Monks/Royal Blue, White
Phone: (207) 893-6672
Fax:

Estimated # of Women's Soccer Scholarships: None
Conference: Maine Athletic Conference
Program Profile: Captured Maine Athletic Conference Championship in 1996; final record is 12-6-2; play on a small stadium, natural grass which sits on shore of Sebego Lake.
History: This is the tenth year of the program; have captured five conference championships.
Achievements: Conference Championship in first year of coaching; two Academic All-Americans in 1996.
Style of Play: Aggressive style of play, usually with three forwards and three midfields. Attack oriented, constant movement. Like to double team ball defensively.

Thomas College
Academic Profile

Phone: 207-859-1111

Waterville, ME 04901

Type: 4 Yr.,Private
Founded: 1894
Website: http://www.thomas.edu
Religion: Non-Affiliated
SAT/ACT/GPA: For traditional students only - Freshmen
Housing: Yes
Student/Faculty Ratio: 16:1
Male/Female Ratio: 45:55
Undergraduate Enrollment: 775
Graduate Enrollment: 150
Scholarships/Academic: Yes **Athletic:** **Financial Aid:** Yes
Expenses by: Year **In State:** $ 16,800 **Out of State:** $ 16,800
Specialty: Business
Degrees Conferred: BS, MBA, MS
Programs of Study: Accounting, Accounting Information Systems, Business Teacher Education, Computer Information Systems, Banking & Investments, Environmental Management, International Business Studies, Management, Management Information System, Marketing Information Systems, Math/Computer Teacher Education, Retail Management, Sport Management

Men's Athletic Profile

180 West River Road
Waterville, ME 04901
Coach: Tim Robinson
Email: robinsonT@thomas.edu

NCAA III, NAIA
Terriers/Black, White, Red
Phone: (207) 873-0771
Fax: (207) 877-0114

Estimated # of Men's Soccer Scholarships: for leadership
Conference: Maine Athletic Conference
Program Profile: Has 17-game played in the Fall plus indoor soccer during the Winter and Spring. playing field is second to none and has a natural grass that measures 12x77 yards.
History: Program began in early 1960's.
Achievements: NAIA New England Champions in 1982, 1985 & 1988.
1999 NAIA All-American, Maine Athletic Conference Champs. 1999-2000, 1995-1996
Coaching: Tim Robinson- USSF "A", NSCAA Advanced National, & Premier (candidate)
Roster In State: 10 **Out of State:** 8 **Out of Country:** 1
Walk-on/Other: **Graduation %:** 90 **Seniors on Team:** 2
Positions Needed: Sweeper, Forward
Camp or Clinic Dates: Not Available
Most Recent Record: 12-7
Schedule: University of Maine-Farmington, University of Southern Maine, Colby College, Mt. Ida (Boston), Husson College (Banger Maine), Johnson State, UT
Style of Play: To score more goals than the opposition.

Women's Athletic Profile

180 West River Road
Waterville, ME 04330
Coach: Kelly Smith
Email: Smithk@thomas.edu

NAIA, NCAA III
Terriers/Black, Red, White
Phone: (207) 859-1314
Fax: (207) 859-1107

Estimated # of Women's Soccer Scholarships: None
Conference: Maine Athletic Conference

Program Profile: Beautiful, World Cup size field, Bermuda turf, two practice fields next to the game field, great soccer environment. Best natural field in the state.
History: Program began in 1987, Conference Champions in 1990, New England finalist in 1990.
Achievements: MAC Coach of the Year in 1995 & 1997; Honorable Mention All-American in 1997; Academic All-American in 1997; NSCAA All-Northeast in 1997.
Coaching: Kelly Smith, Head Coach, entering first season with the program.
Roster in State: 13 **Out of State:** 3 **Out of Country:** 0
Walk-on/Other: **Graduation %:** **Seniors on Team:** 2
Positions Needed: ALL
Camp or Clinic Dates: July-August
Most Recent Record: 3-14-0
Schedule: St. Joseph's College, Husson College, Notre Dame, Mt. Ida, Castleton, U. of Farmington, U. of Presque Isle, Lyndon State, Bay Path
Style of Play: Controlled, attack built from defensive third.

University of Maine
Academic Profile

Orono, ME 04469-5747
Phone: 207-581-1561

Type: 4 Yr.,Public,Liberal Arts,Engineering
Founded: 1865
Website: http://www.maine.edu
Religion: Non-Affiliated
SAT/ACT/GPA: Varies
Housing: Yes
Student/Faculty Ratio: 14:1
Male/Female Ratio: 50:50
Undergraduate Enrollment: 7,500
Graduate Enrollment: 2,000
Scholarships/Academic: Yes **Athletic:** Yes **Financial Aid:** Yes
Expenses by: Year **In State:** $ 9,681 **Out of State:** $ 16,551
Specialty: Various
Degrees Conferred: BA, BS, MA, MS, MBA, MEd, Ph.D., EdD, JD
Programs of Study: College of Arts & Humanities, College of Business Administration, College of Education, College of Engineering, College of Sciences, College of Social Behavioral Sciences, College of Natural Resources, Forestry & Agriculture

Men's Athletic Profile

5747 Memorial Gym
Orono, ME 04469-5747
Coach: Travers Evans
Email: N/A

NCAA I
Black Bears/Blue, White
Phone: (207) 581-3050
Fax: (207) 581-3474

Estimated # of Men's Soccer Scholarships: N/A
Conference: America East Conference
Program Profile: One of the top division I programs in New England. The University of Maine conducts a year-round program for men's soccer, with a competitive fall, winter and spring seasons. The team competes on a maximum size , natural surface field which measures 120x80 yards, that can accommodate spectators in both stadium bleachers and standing room.
History: Program began in 1963. The program is under its 8th head coach, and has compiled a record of 198-235-38 in 33 years of existence. 1995 marked the 13th consecutive winning season.
Achievements: The team earned the New England Intercollegiate Soccer League "Fair Play Award" in 1987 & 1988 for good sportsmanship and the 1988 North Atlantic Conference Championship. 1990 team included 4 All-New England Players.
Style of Play: Possession oriented.

Women's Athletic Profile

5747 Memorial Gym
Orono, ME 04469
Coach: Scott Atherley
Email: Not Available

NCAA I
Black Bears/Blue, White
Phone: (207) 581-1048
Fax: (207) 581-3297

Estimated # of Women's Soccer Scholarships: None
Conference: North Atlantic Conference

University of Maine - Farmington

Academic Profile

Phone: 207-778-7000

Farmington, ME 04938

Type: 4 Yr.,Public
Website: http://www.umf.maine.edu
SAT/ACT/GPA: Open
Student/Faculty Ratio: 15:1
Undergraduate Enrollment: 2,000
Scholarships/Academic: Yes
Athletic: No
Expenses by: Year
In State: $ 8,160

Founded: 1863
Religion: Non-Affiliated
Housing: Yes
Male/Female Ratio: 1:4
Graduate Enrollment: N/A
Financial Aid: Yes
Out of State: $ 12,930

Specialty: Liberal Arts, Education, Human Services
Degrees Conferred: BA, BS
Programs of Study: Education, Liberal Arts, Business and Economics, Health and Rehabilitation, Psychology, Social Sciences, Letters/Literature, Multi/Interdisciplinary Studies

Men's Athletic Profile

5 South Street
Farmington, ME 04938
Coach: Robert Leib
Email: Rbleib@maine.maine.edu

NCAA III/NAIA
Beavers/Maroon, White
Phone: (207) 778-7144
Fax: (207) 778-8177

Estimated # of Men's Soccer Scholarships:
Conference: Maine Athletic Conference
Program Profile: Has two natural grass playing fields (1 practice and I game field) with an electronic scoreboard. Playing season runs from September 1 through November 10.
History: Program began in late 50's and has became a respected program in Maine. Continually in the top first or 2nd in the conference for the past 15 years.
Achievements: 1995 3 Academic All-Americans, MAC Coach of the Year, 1994 MAC Champions.
Coaching: Robert Leib, Head Coach, entering 21 years of coaching soccer. Blake Johnson - Assistant Coach, entering two years with the program.
Style of Play: The "team play all over the place"; ball control with two touch passing.

Women's Athletic Profile

35 High Street
Farmington, ME 04938
Coach: Robert Leib
Email: RBLeib@Maine.Edu

NCAA III/NAIA
Beavers/Maroon, White
Phone: (207) 778-7144
Fax: (207) 778-8177

Estimated # of Women's Soccer Scholarships: None
Conference: Maine Athletic Conference

Program Profile: We have a competitive program and we have been Conference finalists for the last 5 years. We have 2 fields of natural grass. Our season is from September 3rd to October 30th and we have playoffs the first two weeks of November.
History: The women's program began in the 1980's, and we won the MAC Championship last year for the first time.
Achievements: Coach of the Year in 1982, 1986, 1991 and 1996. 8 All-Americans; 5 Academic All-Americans; 5 Conference Titles.
Coaching: Robert Leib, Head Coach, is entering three years with the program. Buch Muchaner, Assistant Coach, is entering eleven years with the Beavers. Niki Fulton is also Assistant Coach.
Style of Play: Team plays all over the field; Ball control with 2 touch passing.

University of Maine - Machias

Academic Profile

Machias, ME 04654
Phone:

Type: 4 Yr.,Public,Liberal Arts
Website: http://www.umm.maine.edu
SAT/ACT/GPA: 860/18/2.0
Student/Faculty Ratio: 16:1
Undergraduate Enrollment: 1,000
Scholarships/Academic: Yes **Athletic:** No
Expenses by: Year **In State:** $ 7,460
Founded: 1909
Religion: Non-Affiliated
Housing: Yes
Male/Female Ratio: 2:3
Graduate Enrollment: N/A
Financial Aid: Yes
Out of State: $ 11,760
Specialty: Marine Biology, Environmental Science, Business, Outdoor Recreation
Degrees Conferred: BA, BS, AA
Programs of Study: Elementary Education, Secondary Education, Business Education, Business Administration, English, Fine Arts, History, Behavioral Science, Recreation Management, Environmental Studies, Biology, Marine Biology

Men's Athletic Profile

9 O'Brien Avenue
Machias, ME 04654
Coach: Mark Hundhammer
Email: mhundham@acad.umm.maize.edu

NAIA
Clippers/Green, White, Purple
Phone: (207) 255-1387
Fax: (207) 255-4864

Estimated # of Men's Soccer Scholarships:
Conference: Maine Athletic Conference
Program Profile: In 1999 new natural field that has a measurements of 115x75 yards was built. In 1998 lights installed, includes several nights games, 80x50 yard training area and game field 600 with a seating capacity of 600.
History: Program began in 1975, is usually in the top 2 in the Conference, and the Final 4 in the Northeast Region.
Achievements: Produced 2 All-Regional players and 2 playing professional.
Coaching: Mark Hundhammer, Head Coach, NSCAA Advanced National Diploma. He is USSF "A" License candidate. Barry Studdard and Nicole Bemis, Assistant Coaches.
Style of Play: Attacking style of play patterned after the Dutch. Team plays a 3-4-3 with a possession play and a commitment from all players to attack and defend as a conservative unit.

Women's Athletic Profile

9 O'Brien Avenue
Machias, ME 04654
Coach: Mark Hundhammer
Email: mhundham@acad.umn.maine.edu

NAIA
Clippers/Green, White, Purple
Phone: (207) 255-1387
Fax: (207) 255-4864

Estimated # of Women's Soccer Scholarships: None
Conference: Maine Athletic Conference
Program Profile: We built a new field in 1999 that measures 115x75 yards. In 1998, lights were installed. We have an 80x50x40 yards training area. The seating capacity for the field is 600.
History: The program began in 1998. We are a very young program.
Achievements: Two All-Region Players; Two playing professionally
Coaching: Mark Hundhammer, Head Coach, holds an NSCAA Advanced National Diploma and is a USSF "A" License candidate. Barry Studdard and Nicole Bemis are Assistant Coaches.
Style of Play: Attacking style of play after the Dutch. Both teams play a 3-4-3 with a processional play and a commitment from all players to attack and defend as a competitive unit.

University of Maine - Presque Isle

Academic Profile

Phone: 207-768-9400

Presque Isle, ME 04769

Type: 4 Yr.,Public,Liberal Arts		**Founded:** 1903
Website: http://www.umpi.maine.edu		**Religion:** Non-Affiliated
SAT/ACT/GPA: 760		**Housing:** Yes
Student/Faculty Ratio: 12:1		**Male/Female Ratio:** 1:4
Undergraduate Enrollment: 1,500		**Graduate Enrollment:** N/A
Scholarships/Academic: Yes	**Athletic:** No	**Financial Aid:** Yes
Expenses by: Year	**In State:** $ 7,274	**Out of State:** $ 11,324

Specialty: Education, Physical Education, Teaching, Criminal Justice
Degrees Conferred: AA, AS, BA, BFA, BLS, BSW, Masters
Programs of Study: Accounting, Athletic Training, Art, Psychology, Sociology, Biology, Business, Communications, Criminal Justice, Elementary Education, English, Environmental Studies, Fine Arts, Fitness & Wellness, International Studies, Political Science, Liberal Studies, Mathematics, Physical Education, PreLaw, PreMed, Recreation & Leisure Services, Social Work

Men's Athletic Profile

181 Main Street	**NAIA**
Presque Isle, ME 04769	Owls/Blue, Gold
Coach: Alan Gordon	**Phone:** (207) 768-9473
Email: gordona@ polans.umpi.maine.edu	**Fax:** (207) 768-9476

Estimated # of Men's Soccer Scholarships:
Conference: Maine Athletic Conference
Program Profile: Play on one of the top three fields in the state. Season begins at the end of August and runs through November.
History: Program began in the early 60's.
Achievements: NCC Champs for ten years, NAIA District playoffs nine times.
Coaching: Alan Gordon, Head Coach, NAIA All-American as a player for the school in 1986, fifth year at UMPI, two-time Coach of the Year.

Roster In State: 20	**Out of State:** 2	**Out of Country:** 3
ODP State: 12	**Regional:**	**National:**
Walk-on/Other:	**Graduation %:** 80	**Seniors on Team:** 3

Positions Needed: goalie, forward, midfield
Camp or Clinic Dates: Not Available
Most Recent Record: 9-7

Schedule: Univ. Maine Farmington, Thomas College, Husson College, Mt. Allison Univ.(Canada), St. Joes, ME, Univ Maine, Fort Fent, Lyndon St. College, Notre Dame
Style of Play: Possession play generated by a strong defensive. Look to attack with speed and quickness off possession with target man.

Women's Athletic Profile

181 Main Street
Presque Isle, ME 04769-2888
Coach: Charles Hamel
Email: Not Available

NAIA
Owls/Royal, Gold
Phone: (207) 768-9421
Fax: (207) 768-9476

Estimated # of Women's Soccer Scholarships: None
Conference: Maine Athletic

University of New England

Academic Profile

Phone: 207-283-0171

Biddeford, ME 04005

Type: 4 Yr.,Private,Liberal Arts
Founded: 1953
Website: http://www.une.edu
Religion: Non-Affiliated
SAT/ACT/GPA: 900
Housing: No
Student/Faculty Ratio: 14:1
Male/Female Ratio: 15:85
Undergraduate Enrollment: 850
Graduate Enrollment: 550
Scholarships/Academic: Yes
Athletic: Yes
Financial Aid: Yes
Expenses by: Year
In State: $ 16,800
Out of State: $ 16,800
Specialty: Education
Degrees Conferred: AS, BA, BS, MS, Ph.D.
Programs of Study: Biology, BioMedical Science, Business Administration, Education, Environmental Science, Health Care Administration, Management, Marine Biology, Medical Laboratory Technology, Nursing, Occupational Therapy, Physical Therapy, PreDentistry, PreLaw, PreMed, PrePharmacy, Psychology, Sport Management

Men's Athletic Profile

11 Hills Beach Road
Biddeford, ME 04005
Coach: Douglas Biggs
Email: Not Available

NCAA III
Red Knights/Red, Gold
Phone: (207) 283-0171
Fax: (207) 284-0262

Estimated # of Men's Soccer Scholarships: n/a
Conference: Common Wealth Coast Conference
Program Profile: Facility is one of the better surfaces in New England, outstanding surface to play on. First weekend after labor day is when season starts. Play 16 game schedule.
History: Began around the 1950's.
Achievements: 4 All-Americans, 19 All-New England Players, Conference title in 1997.
Coaching: Doug Biggs Head Coach for 14 years at New England.
Roster In State: 8
Out of State: 12
Out of Country: 0
ODP State: 2
Regional: 2
National: 0
Walk-on/Other: 0
Graduation %: 95
Seniors on Team: 5
Positions Needed: ALL
Most Recent Record: 5-11-0
Schedule: Bowden College, Bates College, Colby College, Roger Williams College
Style of Play: Emphasis on technical play, control tempo and counter not giving the ball away. Build out of the back.

Women's Athletic Profile

11 Hills Beach Road
Biddeford, ME 04005
Coach: Douglas Biggs
Email: Not Available

NCAA III
Knights/Crimson, Ivory
Phone: (207) 283-0171
Fax: (207) 284-0262

Estimated # of Women's Soccer Scholarships: None
Conference: Maine Athletic
Program Profile: Facility is one of the better surfaces in New England, outstanding surface to play on. First weekend after labor day is when season starts. Play 16 game schedule.
History: Began around the 1950's
Achievements: Past 10 years record is 110-50-10. 4 regional tournaments, 4 Academic All-Americans, 10 NSCAA All-New England Players. 3 Conference Championships.
Coaching: Coach Biggs has been coaching the women for 10 years.
Roster in State: 4 **Out of State:** 16 **Out of Country:** 0
ODP State: 8-10 **Regional:** 0 **National:** 0
Walk-on/Other: 0 **Graduation %:** 95 **Seniors on Team:** 5
Positions Needed: GK, Back, Central Mid Fielders, Forwards
Camp or Clinic Dates: Not Available
Most Recent Record: 13-6-1
Schedule: Bowden College, Bates College, Colby College, Univ. of Southern Maine
Style of Play: Controlled, technical good ball possession and scored around 50+ goals.

University of Southern Maine

Academic Profile

Phone: (207) 780-5430

Gorham, ME 04038

Type: 4 Yr.,Public **Founded:** 1970
Website: http://www.usm.maine.edu **Religion:** Non-Affiliated
SAT/ACT/GPA: 950 & up **Housing:** Yes
Student/Faculty Ratio: 13/1 **Male/Female Ratio:** 40/60
Undergraduate Enrollment: 4,000 **Graduate Enrollment:** 1,800
Scholarships/Academic: Yes **Athletic:** No **Financial Aid:** Yes
Expenses by: Semester **In State:** $4461+ **Out of State:** $7806+
Degrees Conferred: AA, AS, BA, BS, MA, M.Ed.
Programs of Study: Applied Chemistry, Art, Biology, PreMed, PreVet, PreDental, Communications, Criminology, Economics, English, Environmental Science & Policy, French, Geography, Anthropology, Geology, History, Mathematics, Music, Philosophy, Physics, Political Science, Psychology, Social Work, Social Science, Sociology, Management, Computer Science, Engineering, Nursing

Men's Athletic Profile

37 College Ave.
Gorham, ME 04038
Coach: John Skelton
Email: Not Available

NCAA III
Huskies/Maroon, White, Navy
Phone: (207) 780-5430
Fax: (207) 780-5182

Estimated # of Men's Soccer Scholarships: None
Conference: Little East Conference
Program Profile: New field, natural turf; building a stadium environment; has 20 game fall schedule; full non-traditional Division III season indoor and outdoor.

History: Program began in 1957 and has a 51.0 all-time winning percentage.
Achievements: NAIA District Champions in 1976, 1979, 1980; Area Champion in 1979.
Coaching: John Skelton, Head Coach, USSF "A" License; 16 years head coach experience; third year at USM: Director of American Futures Soccer School, long time involvement in coaching, State ODP, varying ages; Director of Coaching at Mt. Washington Valley SC.
Style of Play: Rapidly improving team aims to build-up, control ball, work total team involvement offensively and defensively.

Women's Athletic Profile

37 College Ave.
Gorham, ME 04038
Coach: Steve Quinones
Email: mailquinones@usm.maine.edu

NCAA III
Huskies/Crimson, Navy, White
Phone: (207) 780-5328
Fax: (207) 780-5182

Estimated # of Women's Soccer Scholarships: None
Conference: Little East Conference
Program Profile: Sixteen year old program is second in quality only to the University of Maine (Division I) program. Project facilities improvement include 120x75 yards full regulation field in 1996, new field house with an indoor facilities in 1997. Fall season runs from August through November. Indoor and Spring programs. Play on a natural surfaces.
History: Since 1986, the program has matured gracefully, becoming the premier Division III state school. As the program developed, the University of Maine has adjusted its schedule so that it now plays the top Division III teams in New England. Last year's schedule included six teams from the top ten in /new England including number one Bowdoin. While the active seeking out-of-state players, the University is drawing some of the top players from Maine to keep competitive. Made post season in 2000, also set a record for most wins in a season (12).
Achievements: Three All New England Selections, 19 All-Conference Selections, 2 Conference "Player of the Year" Selections.
Coaching: Head Coach Steve Quinones has been with the program for 3 season, USYSA Region I GK Staff Coach, former professional soccer player. Graduated from Franklin Pierce College

Roster in State: 17	**Out of State:** 5	**Out of Country:** 0
ODP State: 2	**Regional:** 0	**National:** 0
Walk-on/Other: 0	**Graduation %:** 95	**Seniors on Team:** 7

Positions Needed: Midfield and Forward
Camp or Clinic Dates: July 8-12
Most Recent Record: 12-8-0
Schedule: Western Connecticut State Univ. Bowdoin College, Keene State College, Eastern Connecticut State Univ. Bates College, Colby College
Style of Play: We try to play a variety of styles and formations, but they all hinge on possession.

maryland

MARYLAND

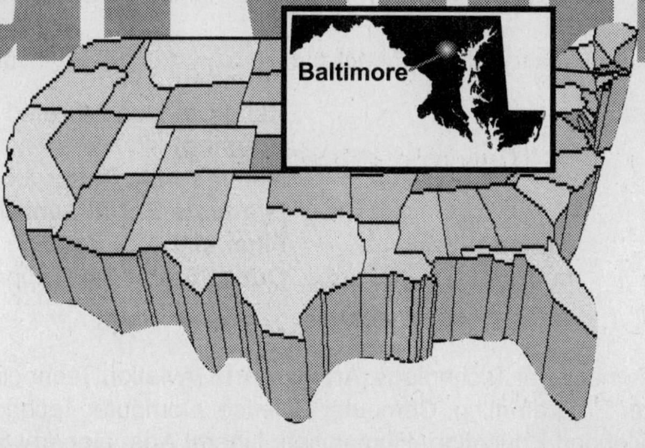

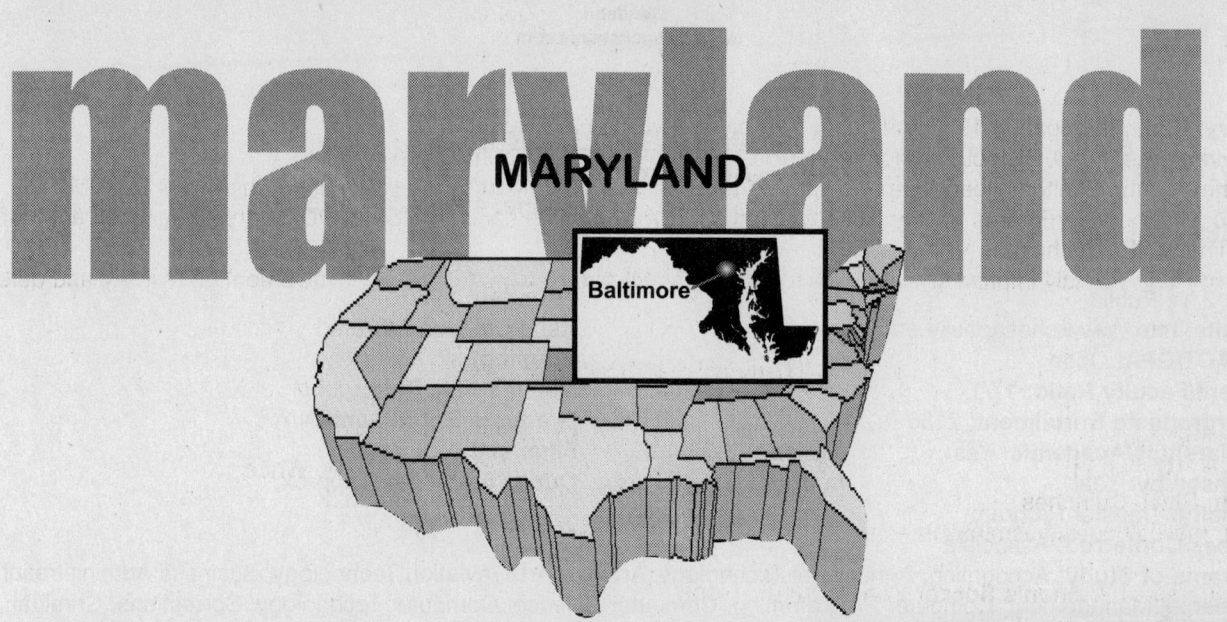

SCHOOL	CITY	AFFILIATION	PAGE
Chesapeake College	Wye Mills	NJCAA	444
College of Notre Dame - Maryland	Baltimore	NCAA III	444
Columbia Union College	Takoma Park	NCAA II/NAIA	445
Frostburg State University	Frostburg	NCAA III	446
Goucher College	Baltimore	NCAA III	447
Johns Hopkins University	Baltimore	NCAA III	449
Loyola College - Maryland	Balto	NCAA I	450
Mount Saint Mary's College	Emmitsburg	NCAA I	451
Saint Mary's College - Maryland	St. Mary's City	NCAA III	452
Salisbury State University	Salisbury	NCAA III	454
Towson University	Towson	NCAA I	455
United States Naval Academy	Annapolis	NCAA I	456
University of Maryland	College Park	NCAA I	458
Univ. of MD - Baltimore County	Bacto	NCAA I	459
Villa Julie College	Stevenson	NCAA III	460
Washington College	Chestertown	NCAA III	461
Western Maryland College	Westminster	NCAA III	462

Chesapeake College

Academic Profile

Phone: 410-822-5400x5750

Wye Mills, MD 21679

Type: 2 Yr.,Public
Founded: 1965
Website: http://www.chesapeake.edu
Religion: Non-Affiliated
SAT/ACT/GPA: Open
Housing: No
Student/Faculty Ratio: 17/1
Male/Female Ratio: 2.5/1
Undergraduate Enrollment: 2186
Graduate Enrollment: N/A
Scholarships/Academic: Yes **Athletic:** Yes **Financial Aid:** Yes
Expenses by: Year **In State:** $365 approx. **Out of State:** $429 approx.
Specialty: Transfer Program
Degrees Conferred: Associate
Programs of Study: Accounting, Agricultural Technology, Art/Fine Arts, Aviation Technology, Business Administration, Commerce, Management, Computer Programming, Computer Science, Computer Technology, Corrections, Criminal Justice, Data Processing, Early Childhood Education, Humanities, Liberal Arts, General Studies, General Studies, Mathematics, Physical Education, Music, Physical Science, Radiological, Office Management

Men's Athletic Profile

P.O. Box 8
Wye Mills, MD 21679
Coach: Todd Fuhrmann
Email: tlfuhr@aol.com

NJCAA
Skipjacks/Navy, Kelly Green
Phone: 410-822-5400x392
Fax: 410-927-5841

Estimated # of Men's Soccer Scholarships: Varies
Conference: MD Juco
Program Profile: Field is natural grass with dimensions of 120x80.
Roster In State: 13 **Out of State:** 0 **Out of Country:** 0
Walk-on/Other: **Graduation %:** N/A **Seniors on Team:** 5
Positions Needed: All
Camp or Clinic Dates: TBA
Most Recent Record: 3-12-0
Schedule: Prince George's Community College, Essex, Montgomery College, Dundalk, College of Southern Maryland, Catonsville
Style of Play: Direct!

College of Notre Dame - Maryland

Academic Profile

Phone:

Baltimore, MD 21210-2476

Type: 4 Yr.,Private,Liberal Arts
Founded: 1896
Website: http://www.ndm.edu
Religion: Catholic
SAT/ACT/GPA: 950
Housing: Yes
Student/Faculty Ratio: 15:1
Male/Female Ratio: Women
Undergraduate Enrollment: 650
Graduate Enrollment: N/A
Scholarships/Academic: Yes **Athletic:** No **Financial Aid:** Yes
Expenses by: Year **In State:** $ 16,000 **Out of State:** $ 16,000
Specialty: Education, Sciences
Degrees Conferred: BA, BS
Programs of Study: Art, Biology, Business, Chemistry, Classical Studies, Communication Arts, Computer Information Systems, Computer Science, Economics, Education, Engineering, English, History, Interdisciplinary Studies, Liberal Arts, Mathematics, PreProfessional Programs

Women's Athletic Profile

4701 N Charles Street
Baltimore, MD 21210
Coach: Jay Golomb
Email: jkgsoccer@home.com

NCAA III
Gators/Royal, White
Phone: (410) 532-5388
Fax: (410) 435-5796

Estimated # of Women's Soccer Scholarships: None
Conference: AWCC
Program Profile: We are in the process of building a top-quality program designed to be competitive at the national level. The team is built on hard work and an extremely tight-knit, supportive team atmosphere. We play and train on a beautiful 73x117 grass field with underground irrigation.
History: Program started in 1990. Was regionally ranked regularly from 1994-98, nationally ranked in 1995 and 1996. Since joining the AWCC in 1998, have been conference champions each year.
Achievements: AWCC Champions 1998, 1999, 2000. ECAC Champions 1995. 3 All-Americans, Amanda Laughton set school and conference records, and ranked 8th in the country, for goals and points scored in 2000.
Coaching: Jay Golomb is in his first year as Head Coach, after assisting for three years. He holds the NSCAA Advanced National Diploma and the USSF "C" License, is the Director of Coaching for the Baltimore Football Club, and has been a coach at all levels for 10 years. Laura Cool, a former GK for Notre Dame, serves as an assistant and GK Coach.
Roster in State: 16 **Out of State:** 1 **Out of Country:** 0
ODP State: 1 **Regional:** 0 **National:** 0
Walk-on/Other: **Graduation %:** **Seniors on Team:** 4
Camp or Clinic Dates: July 15-20, 22-27
Most Recent Record: 9-13-0
Schedule: Salisbury State, Johns Hopkins, Villa Julie, Western Maryland, Franklin & Marshall, Haverford, St. Mary's, Susquehanna, Randolph Macon, Wesley
Style of Play: We have a flexible system of play capable of adjusting to the strengths and weaknesses of our team and our opponents, based upon a possession-oriented attack and high pressure defending all over the field.

Columbia Union College

Academic Profile

Phone:

Takoma Park, MD 20912

Type: 4 Yr.,Private,Liberal Arts
Founded: 1904
Website: http://www.cuc.edu
Religion: 7th Day Adventist
SAT/ACT/GPA: Open
Housing: No
Student/Faculty Ratio: 14:1
Male/Female Ratio: 40:60
Undergraduate Enrollment: 950
Graduate Enrollment: N/A
Scholarships/Academic: Yes **Athletic:** Yes **Financial Aid:** Yes
Expenses by: Year **In State:** $ 13,500 **Out of State:** $ 13,500
Specialty: Business
Degrees Conferred: AA, BA, BS
Programs of Study: Accounting, Banking/Finance, BioChemistry, Broadcasting, Business Administration, Chemistry, Communications, Computer Science, Education, English, Health Science, History, Information Science, Journalism, Management, Mathematics, Medical Laboratory Technology, Music, Nursing, Personnel/Management, Physics, PreDentistry, PreLaw, PreMed, Psychology, Religion

Men's Athletic Profile

7600 Flower Avenue
Takoma Park, MD 20912
Coach: John Munoz
Email: Not Available

NCAA II/NAIA
Pioneers/Royal, White, Gold
Phone: (301) 891-4193

Fax: (301) 892-4026

Estimated # of Men's Soccer Scholarships: N/A
Conference: Keystone Conference

Frostburg State University

Academic Profile

Phone: 301-687-4201

Frostburg, MD 21532

Type: 4 Yr.,Public,Liberal Arts,Engineering
Website: http://www.fsu.umd.edu
SAT/ACT/GPA: Open
Student/Faculty Ratio: 17:1
Undergraduate Enrollment: 4,600
Scholarships/Academic: Yes
Athletic: No
Expenses by: Year
In State: $ 9,454

Founded: 1898
Religion: Non-Affiliated
Housing: Yes
Male/Female Ratio: 48:52
Graduate Enrollment: 800
Financial Aid: Yes
Out of State: $ 14, 012

Specialty: Education, Engineering, Environmental Sciences & Business
Degrees Conferred: BA, BS, BFA, B Ed , MA, MS, M Ed, MBA
Programs of Study: Art & Design, English, Foreign Languages and Literature, History, Mass Communications, Music, Philosophy, Speech Communications and Theatre, Business Administration, Accounting, Economics, Actuarial Science, Biology, Chemistry, PreMed, Computer Science, Earth Science, Electrical Engineering, Physics, Political Science, Psychology, Social Science, Social Work, Education, Early Childhood Education, Liberal Studies, Physical Education & Recreation

Men's Athletic Profile

112 Pullen Hall, 101 Braddock Rd.
Frostburg, MD 21532
Coach: Jay Hegeman
Email: jhegeman@frostburg.edu

NCAA III
Bobcats/Red, Black, White
Phone: (301) 687-3028
Fax: (301) 687-4207

Estimated # of Men's Soccer Scholarships: None
Conference: AMCC, Allegheny Mountain Collegiate Conference
Program Profile: We play on a picture perfect 115x75 yards grass field. We travel throughout the Mid-Atlantic and Northeast to compete with the best possible opposition. Games are televised regularly during the fall season and we also play a full non-traditional schedule in the spring.
History: Frostburg's soccer program dates back to the 1920's, completed records exist from 1937. The 1939 team won the Southeastern" championship with wind over Duke and High Point. More recently we have qualified for post-season 12 of the past 14 years. ECAC Champions in 1990 & 1992.
Achievements: Coach Hegeman was named AMCC Coach of the Year; 7 All-Conference player; 1 All-Regional All-American and 1 Academic All-American in 1998; 2 graduates playing in USL (Division III pro league); 7 All-Americans and 32 All-Region players since 1960.
Coaching: Jay Hegeman, Head Coach, NSCAA Advanced National Diploma, 1991 ESAC Coach of the Year, NCAA Division III Championship Tournament Selection Committee. Dave Morris - Assistant Coach. Rob DePaul - Assistant Coach.
Roster In State: 22
Out of State: 6
Out of Country: 0
Walk-on/Other:
Graduation %: N/A
Seniors on Team: 7

Positions Needed: fast, skilled, technically sound players
Camp or Clinic Dates: July24-28, July 31-August 4
Most Recent Record: 12-7
Schedule: Gettysburg, Richard Stockton, College of New Jersey, Bethany, Eastern Mennonite, Cabrini, Penn St. Behrend, Grove City, Washington & Jefferson, Shenandoah
Style of Play: Interchanging structure with an emphasis on possession and attacking flair. Practices stress technical skill and small group tactics.

Women's Athletic Profile

101 Braddock Road
Frostburg, MD 21532-1099
Coach: Carrie Lysick
Email: clysik@yahoo.com

NCAA III
Bobcats/Red, Black, White
Phone: (301) 687-3072
Fax: (301) 687-4780

Estimated # of Women's Soccer Scholarships: None
Conference: Allegheny Mountain Collegiate Conference
Program Profile: We play on a grass field which measures 70x115 yards.
History: The FSU women's soccer program is six years old.
Achievements: We have ECAC tournament in 1998. Amy Foute was a 1998 Freshman Regional All-American.
Coaching: Carrie Lysik is the Head Coach, is entering her second season with the program. Becky Keller is the Assistant Coach.

Roster in State: 20	**Out of State:** 13	**Out of Country:**
ODP State: 1	**Regional:**	**National:**
Walk-on/Other:	**Graduation %:**	**Seniors on Team:** 9

Positions Needed: 5
Camp or Clinic Dates: July 24-28 July 31- August 4
Most Recent Record: 11-10
Schedule: Salisbury State, Allegheny College, Eastern, St. Mary's
Style of Play: We are a possession oriented team. Play to feet and keep it simple. Confident that all players can play any position.

Goucher College

Academic Profile

Phone: 410-337-6385

Baltimore, MD 21204

Type: 4 Yr.,Private,Liberal Arts		**Founded:** 1885
Website: http://www.goucher.edu		**Religion:** Non-Denominational
SAT/ACT/GPA: 1170/3.0		**Housing:** Yes
Student/Faculty Ratio: 11/1		**Male/Female Ratio:** 31/69
Undergraduate Enrollment: 1,150		**Graduate Enrollment:** 725
Scholarships/Academic: Yes	**Athletic:** No	**Financial Aid:** Yes
Expenses by: Year	**In State:** $29,140	**Out of State:** $29,140

Specialty: Liberal Arts
Degrees Conferred: BS, BA, M.Ed.
Programs of Study: American Studies, Art, Business, Interdisciplinary, Chemistry, Cognitive Studies, Communications, Computer Science, Dance, Economics, Education, English, French, German, Historic Preservation, History, Interdisciplinary Studies, International and Intercultural Studies, International Relations, Management, Mathematics, Music, Peace Studies, Philosophy, Physics, Political Science, Psychology, Religion, Russian, Sociology, Sociology and Anthropology, Spanish, Special Education, Theatre, Women's Studies

Men's Athletic Profile

1021 Dulaney Valley Rd
Baltimore, MD 21204
Coach: Troy Snyder
Email: tsnyder@goucher.edu

NCAA III
Gophers/Royal, Gold
Phone: (410) 337-6381
Fax: (410) 337-6576

Estimated # of Men's Soccer Scholarships: None
Conference: Capital Athletic Conference
Program Profile: The program is on the cusp of breaking through in the Capital Athletic Conference. We have a great nucleus of freshman and sophomores whom make up our entire roster. The facilities are the best, a beautifully maintained natural grass field.
History: Our program began in 1991, we play in a very competitive conference. The team has had a strong history of playing a tough schedule.
Achievements: We have a tradition of placing a couple of players each year on the 1st and 2nd all conference team.
Coaching: Troy Snyder is the Head Coach and he is assisted by James Derse and Kert Mease.

Roster In State: 5	**Out of State:** 13	**Out of Country:** 0
ODP State: 2	**Regional:**	**National:**
Walk-on/Other:	**Graduation %:** 95	**Seniors on Team:** 2

Positions Needed: Keeper and Forwards
Camp or Clinic Dates: Not Available
Most Recent Record: 5-15-0
Schedule: John Hopkins, William Patterson, Mary Washington, Salisbury State, Dickenson, Washington and Lee.
Style of Play: Disciplined, controlled style of play.

Women's Athletic Profile

1021 Dulaney Valley Rd
Baltimore, MD 21204
Coach: Michele Hoffman
Email: mhoffman@goucher.edu

NCAA III
Gophers/Blue, Gold
Phone: (410) 337-6577
Fax: (410) 337-6185

Estimated # of Women's Soccer Scholarships: None
Conference: Capital Athletic Conference
Program Profile: Beldon Field opened in 1993; sodded, natural grass surface with an underground irrigation system. Has 120x75 yards field.
History: The program started in 1989. Team was 9-62-3 over the first five years; 30-20-2 over the past three years. 13th year of program in 2001.
Achievements: N/A
Coaching: Head Coach Michele Hoffman- former WVU Assistant, W.V ODP and club coach. Assistant Rick Nese former head coach of Keuka, national coaching and club coaching experience. Amy Miller is a graduate of Towson Univ.

Roster in State: 4	**Out of State:** 8	**Out of Country:** 0
ODP State: 3	**Regional:** 0	**National:** 0
Walk-on/Other: 0	**Graduation %:** 100	**Seniors on Team:** 1

Positions Needed: GK, Sweeper, Outside Mids
Camp or Clinic Dates: TBA
Most Recent Record: 4-15-0
Schedule: Salisbury, Mary Washington, Franklin & Marshall, Villa Julie, St. Mary's
Style of Play: Adapting our style each year as we build as a program, very dependant on our strengths on the field.

Johns Hopkins University
Academic Profile

Baltimore, MD 21218-2684

Phone: 410-516-8600

Type: 4 Yr.,Private,Liberal Arts,Engineering
Founded: 1876
Website: http://www.jhu.edu
Religion: Non-Affiliated
SAT/ACT/GPA: 1100avg/2.5
Housing: Yes
Student/Faculty Ratio: 10:1
Male/Female Ratio: 60:40
Undergraduate Enrollment: 3,600
Graduate Enrollment: 1,400
Scholarships/Academic: Yes **Athletic:** No
Financial Aid: Yes
Expenses by: Year **In State:** $ 32,000
Out of State: $ 32,000
Specialty: Natural Science, Engineering, English, History
Degrees Conferred: BA, BS, MA, MS, Ph.D., MD
Programs of Study: Arts and Sciences, Engineering (Biomedical, Chemical, Civil, Computer Science, Electrical, Computer, Mechanics, Geography, Environmental, Materials Science, Math, Mechanical), Anthropology, Behavioral Biology, Biology, BioPhysics, Chemistry, Classics, Cognitive Science, Comparative American Cultures, Earth and Planetary Science, East Asian Studies, Economics, English, Environmental Earth Sciences, History, Humanistic Studies, Math, Music, Natural Sciences, Neuroscience, Philosophy, Physics and Astronomy, Political Science, Psychology, Public Health, Social and Behavioral Sciences, Sociology, Writing Seminars

Men's Athletic Profile

3400 N Charles St.
Baltimore, MD 21218-2684
Coach: Matt Smith
Email: msmith@jhunix.hcf.jhu.edu

NCAA III
Blue Jays/Blue, Black
Phone: (410) 516-5099
Fax: (410) 516-5376

Estimated # of Men's Soccer Scholarships:
Conference: Centennial Conference
Program Profile: Play on an astro turf stadium; has 18 game season.
History: Program began in 1935. 1994 NCAA Finalist, 1995 ECAC Finalist, 1996 Centennial Conference Champions, NCAA Mid-Atlantic Semi-finalist.
Achievements: 1994 NCAA Finalist; 1996 & 1997 NCAA Mid-Atlantic Finalists; numerous All-Region; 1 All-American; 1997 Player drafted 3rd overall in 1st round.
Coaching: Matt Smith, Head Coach, was a two-time 1st team All-East Conference Pick and was selected to play in the Budweiser Senior Bowl. He was also a very successful in coaching in the Maryland Olympic Development, posting a sensational 74-8-6 record, and was recently named Director of Maryland ODP. Smith is also the director and founder of the Chesapeake Soccer Academy. Has a record of 56-16-4; NCAA Championship game in 1994; ECAC Championship in 1995; Centennial Championship in 1996. Winston Eil - Assistant Coach. Dan Warren - Goalkeeper Coach.
Style of Play: Very offensive, possession based systems.

Women's Athletic Profile

3400 North Charles St.
Baltimore, MD 21218
Coach: Leo Weil
Email: coachWeil@aol.com

NCAA III
Blue Jays/Columbia Blue, Black
Phone: (410) 516-7967
Fax: (410) 516-5376

Estimated # of Women's Soccer Scholarships: None
Conference: Centennial Conference

Program Profile: 8th year as a Varsity program, lighted astro turf field with a seating capacity of 3000, excellent facilities with year round locker rooms, and a new weight room.
History: The program began in 1992; gradual progress the first four years; very successful the last four years, 2 conference titles, 2 second place finishes, 2 trips to the NCAA's. Pre-season European trip in 1999 and will travel again summer of 2002.
Achievements: 1996 Maryland State Youth Soccer Association Girls Coach of the Year. Conference titles in 1996 and 1997. Eleven all Mid-Atlantic players. Team ranked 14th defensively in 1999, overall team ranked as high as 12th nationally and 2nd regionally.
Coaching: Head Coach- Leo Weil holds a National "C" license and has been a club coach for more than 20 years. He has been the coach of the Blue Jays since the beginning. Assistant Coach- Marty Brandwin; has assisted 7 years with the program and works closely with the goal keepers.

Roster in State: 2	**Out of State:** 23	**Out of Country:** 0
ODP State: 4	**Regional:** 0	**National:** 0
Walk-on/Other:	**Graduation %:** 100	**Seniors on Team:** 3

Positions Needed: ALL
Camp or Clinic Dates: Not Available
Most Recent Record: 15-5-2
Schedule: College of New Jersey, Mary Washington, Gettysburg, Muhlenberg, NYU, Elmhurst, Villa Julie.
Style of Play: Prefer short passing style, controlled game but adapt to how the other team is playing and their strengths and weaknesses.

Loyola College - Baltimore

Academic Profile

Phone: 800-221-9107

Baltimore, MD 21210-2699

Type: 4 Yr.,Private,Liberal Arts,Engineering		**Founded:** 1852
Website: http://www.loyola.edu		**Religion:** Catholic
SAT/ACT/GPA: 1200		**Housing:** Yes
Student/Faculty Ratio: 14:1		**Male/Female Ratio:** 43:57
Undergraduate Enrollment: N/A		**Graduate Enrollment:** N/A
Scholarships/Academic: Yes	**Athletic:** Yes	**Financial Aid:** Yes
Expenses by: Year	**In State:** $ 26,700	**Out of State:** $ 26,700

Specialty: Business, Science, Computer, Engineering
Degrees Conferred: BA, BS, BBA
Programs of Study: Accounting, Biology, Business Administration, Chemistry, Communications, Computer Science, Creative Writing, Economics, Electrical Engineering, Elementary Education, English, Finance, Fine Arts, French, Latin, Management, Marketing, Mathematics, Philosophy, Physics, Political Science, Psychology, Sociology, Pathology, Theology

Men's Athletic Profile

4501 North Charles St.	**NCAA I**
Balto, MD 21210	Greyhounds/Green, Gray, White
Coach: Bill Sento	**Phone:** (410) 617-2379
Email: Not-Available	**Fax:** (410) 617-5215

Estimated # of Men's Soccer Scholarships: 3.4
Conference: Metro Atlantic Athletic Conference
Program Profile: 1997 new natural field, first game US Penn State in September 1, 1997; playing season is in the fall and spring as well.
History: Our program began in 1940; won in 1976 Division II Champions - turned Division I in 1977 - 1986, 1987 NCAA Quarter Finalist, 1993 NCAA second round, MAAC Conference Champions in 1989, 1990, 1991, 1992, 1993, 1994, 1995, & 1996.

Achievements: 1986 NSCAA Regional Coach of the Year, All-Americans Eric Cox in 1973 second, 1974 first; Stan Koziol in 1986, 1987 and Joe Koziol in 1988 3rd. Zach Thornton in 1993 1st, 1993 3rd (Chicago MSL), Bill Harte drafted New England.
Coaching: Bill Sento, Head Coach, entering 19 season with the program. Mike Mason - Assistant Coach, entering 8 season with the Greyhounds. Bill Unek - Assistant Coach, entering third season.
Style of Play: Defender have the ability to get forward into attack and play primary central combination with each other and create spaces on side-center side act as target to penetrate and play ball ride. Zonal defensive tactics with pressure midfield pressure; our defense starts with our forwards.

Women's Athletic Profile

4501 N Charles Street
Baltimore, MD 21210
Coach: Joe Mallia
Email: jmallia@loyola.edu

NCAA I
Greyhounds/Green, White
Phone: (410) 617-5279
Fax: (410) 617-2008

Estimated # of Women's Soccer Scholarships: 11
Conference: Metro Atlantic Athletic Conference
Program Profile: A very competitive member of Mid-Atlantic Region. Ranked in the regional last year (1996) for the first time. Playing games at new grass field, natural and astro-turf.
History: Joined NCAA Division I in 1992. Has two conference championships, 3 runner-ups in the conference. Overall record is 71-37-12.
Achievements: Cara Mooney was three-time All-Mid-Atlantic Region selection; Amy Goetzinger was 2nd All-Mid-Atlantic; Kathleen Shields was 3rd All-Mid-Atlantic.
Coaching: Joe Mallia, Head Coach, entering first season with the program. Kiera Schaefenberger - Assistant Coach.
Roster in State: 4 **Out of State:** 17 **Out of Country:**
ODP State: 10 **Regional:** 4 **National:** 1
Walk-on/Other: 6 **Graduation %:** 100 **Seniors on Team:** 7
Positions Needed: Goalkeeper, Center defender, Centermid, Forward
Camp or Clinic Dates: July, August
Most Recent Record: 13-4-2
Schedule: University of Miami, Florida State, University of Maryland, Navy, Yale, Princeton, Old Dominion, Louisiana State, Fairfield
Style of Play: Indirect/ Possession. Attacking mentality and very organized defensively.

Mount Saint Mary's College - Maryland
Academic Profile

Emmitsburg, MD 21727
Phone: (301) 862-0320

Type: 4 Yr.,Private,Liberal Arts
Website: http://www.msmary.edu
SAT/ACT/GPA: 980-1150
Student/Faculty Ratio: 16:1
Undergraduate Enrollment: 1,400
Scholarships/Academic: Yes **Athletic:** Yes
Expenses by: Year **In State:** $ 21,135

Founded: 1808
Religion: Catholic
Housing: Yes
Male/Female Ratio: 47:53
Graduate Enrollment: 400
Financial Aid: Yes
Out of State: $ 21,135

Degrees Conferred: BA, BS, Graduate Degrees in Business
Programs of Study: Accounting, BioChemistry, Dramatic Arts, Economics, English, Fine Arts, History, Human Development, Languages, Literature, Mathematics, Music, Natural Science, Philosophy, Physics, Political Science, Psychology, Public Policy

Men's Athletic Profile

Route 15
Emmitsburg, MD 21727
Coach: Rob Ryerson
Email: ryersonsoccer@home.com

NCAA I
Mountaineers/Blue, White
Phone: 310-447-5383
Fax: (301) 447-5300

Estimated # of Men's Soccer Scholarships: 4.0
Conference: Northeast Conference
Program Profile: Competitive NCAA Division I team competes out of conference against nationally ranked opposition. The stadium is natural grass that seats 1,500 and has European style goals..
History: The Mountaineers program began in 1953. Their total record was 276- 315- 59. Their new coach is only the fifth in the history of the team.
Achievements: Mount St. Mary's College has had several All-Americans in the 1960's and 1970's.
Coaching: Rob Ryerson is the Head Coach and Simon Modkin is the Assistant Coach.

Roster In State: 14	**Out of State:** 7	**Out of Country:** 5
ODP State: 12	**Regional:** 4	**National:**
Walk-on/Other:	**Graduation %:** 100	**Seniors on Team:** 3

Camp or Clinic Dates: Not Available
Most Recent Record: 11-7-2
Schedule: Not Available
Style of Play: Possession oriented and extremely offensive minded with players emphasizing on creativity and discipline.

Women's Athletic Profile

Route 15
Emmitsburg, MD 21727
Coach:
Email: Ljohnsonsto@msmary.edu

NCAA I
The Mounts/Blue (Navy), White
Phone: (301) 447-3803
Fax: (301) 447-5300

Estimated # of Women's Soccer Scholarships: None
Conference: North East Conference
Program Profile: The team plays on a grass field that has a measurements of 120 yards long and 75 yards width.
History: 1992 was the first year of the program and member of the Northeast Conference. Has always been in the top half of the conference.
Achievements: Conference tournament in three years; All-Conference players.
Style of Play: Build a system around the players. quick to defend, look for counter attack, attack strong and fast with an eye on defense at all times.

St. Mary's College - Maryland
Academic Profile

Phone:

St. Mary's City, MD 20686

Type: 4 Yr.,Public,Liberal Arts		**Founded:** 1840
Website: http://www.smcm.edu		**Religion:** Non-Affiliated
SAT/ACT/GPA: 1100/21/3.0		**Housing:** Yes
Student/Faculty Ratio: 14:1		**Male/Female Ratio:** 40:60
Undergraduate Enrollment: 1,500		**Graduate Enrollment:** N/A
Scholarships/Academic: Yes	**Athletic:** No	**Financial Aid:** Yes
Expenses by: Year	**In State:** $ 13,144	**Out of State:** $ 17,844

Specialty: 31 Different majors
Degrees Conferred: BA
Programs of Study: Art, Dramatic Arts, English, Foreign Languages, Music, Anthropology, Sociology, Economics, History, Political Science, Education, Philosophy, Psychology, Religion, Biology, Chemistry, Mathematics, Computer Science, Physics, Interdisciplinary Majors, Cross Studies Majors

Men's Athletic Profile

Somerset Hall-Soccer Office
St. Mary's City, MD 20686
Coach: Eric Wagner
Email: erwagner@honors.smcm.edu

NCAA III
Seahawks/Navy, Old Gold
Phone: (301) 862-0321
Fax: (301) 862-0480

Estimated # of Men's Soccer Scholarships:
Conference: Capital Athletic Conference
Program Profile: We are regionally and nationally competitive NCAA Division III program. We offer the finest natural grass stadium field in the region, practice facilities, full-time coaching staff and athletic training staff, weight room, indoor center coming in spring of 2000, and full time equipment, laundry facilities and staff. St. Mary's is a rising program with a top level schedule and excellent academics and athletic environment.
History: The program began as a club team in late 1960's; joined NCAA Division III in late 1970's. Long history and tradition of support from community and alumni. Won conference championships in 1989, conference semi-finalist in 1993 & 1998. Have produced All-Region, All-Conference and professional players over the past dozen years.
Achievements: 1983 All-Region players; 1982-1983 Division II-III Maryland College Coach of the Year; 1993 professional player drafted in 1989 - CCAC Championships; 1989 All-Region players; 1998 USISL total for two players.
Coaching: Eric Wagner, Head Coach, is entering his third season with the program. He compiled a record of 18-17 in two years; BA at Connecticut College in 1988. He was a four-year letter-winner and a semi-professional soccer. He holds a NSCAA Advanced National Diploma. He was a former head coach at Southwestern University. He was a former assistant coach at Duke University and University of Notre Dame. He is an Olympic Development Staff Coach in South Texas, Indiana, and Maryland. Herb Gainey, Assistant Coach, holds a USSF and NSCAA Advanced Diplomas. He is NYSCAA Certification Director of Maryland District Development Program.
Style of Play: Ball possession; tenacious, adjustable defending, direct or indirect attacking style of play with emphasis on counter-attack; strong work ethic, commitment to player development in year-round program.

Women's Athletic Profile

18952 E. Fisher Road
St. Mary's City, MD 20686
Coach: Mark Mermelstein
Email: mamermelstein@honors.smcm.edu

NCAA III
Seahawks/Navy, White
Phone: (301) 862-0350
Fax: (301) 862-0480

Estimated # of Women's Soccer Scholarships: None
Conference: Capital Athletic Conference
Program Profile: The Seahawks play their home games on a Bermuda grass field, in a stadium that seats 1,400.
History: The women's program became as a club sport in 1983, and varsity program began in 1985. Has an overall record of 122-75-14.
Achievements: 2 All-Region players; 1 CAC Rookie-of-the-Year; Many All-Conference selections; CAC Coach of the Year 1991.
Coaching: Mark Mermelstein is the first full time Head Coach in the program's history. He was a former volunteer Asst. Coach at the University of the Pacific. Jackie Takacs has been our Asst. Coach for four years.
Camp or Clinic Dates: Not Available
Most Recent Record: 11-4-1
Schedule: Gettysburg, Mary Washington, Johns Hopkins, Salisbury State, Virginia Wesleyan
Style of Play: Pressure defensively; very attack.

Salisbury State University

Academic Profile

Phone:

Salisbury, MD 21801

Type: 4 Yr.,Public,Liberal Arts
Website: http://www.ssu.umd.edu
SAT/ACT/GPA: 980-1050
Student/Faculty Ratio: 17:1
Undergraduate Enrollment: 6,000
Scholarships/Academic: Yes
Athletic: No
Expenses by: Year
In State: $ 8,500
Founded: 1925
Religion: Non-Affiliated
Housing: Yes
Male/Female Ratio: 50:50
Graduate Enrollment: N/A
Financial Aid: Yes
Out of State: $ 13,000
Specialty: Business, Education
Degrees Conferred: BA, BS, BFA, BSN, BSW, MA, MS, MBA, MED
Programs of Study: Accounting, Biology, Broadcasting, Business Administration, Chemistry, Communications, Dramatic Arts, Earth Science, Economics, Education, English, Environmental Science, Fine Arts, French, History, Management, Marine Science, Marketing, Mathematics, PreLaw, PreMed, Psychology, Recreation, Social Science, Respiratory Therapy

Men's Athletic Profile

Department of Athletics
Salisbury, MD 21801
Coach: Gerry DiBartolo
Email: Not Available

NCAA III
Seagulls/Maroon, Gold
Phone: (410) 548-5338
Fax: (410) 546-2639

Estimated # of Men's Soccer Scholarships:
Conference: Eastern States Athletic Conference
Program Profile: Field is 120x75 yards, grass, irrigated field; excellent training staff. Emphasis on quality, travel experience. Fall and Spring season (practice), indoor training.
History: Program began in 1936. Highly competitive program with a difficult schedule.
Achievements: Conference Runner-Up in 1986 & 1991; Champs in 1987, numerous All-Region, 3 All-Conference in 1991.
Coaching: Gerry DiBartolo, Head Coach since 1979, Professor of Marketing.
Style of Play: 1-2 touch approach, control game. Strong defensive orientation, speed and control in attack, midfield build up, fitness oriented.

Women's Athletic Profile

1101 Camden Avenue
Salisbury, MD 21801
Coach: Jim Berkman
Email: jjberkman@ssu.edu

NCAA III
Sea Gulls/Maroon, Gold
Phone: (410) 543-6389
Fax: (410) 546-2639

Estimated # of Women's Soccer Scholarships: None
Conference: Capital Athletic Conference
Program Profile: Highly competitive, women have their own stadium, Bermuda grass surface and has 17 schedule. Four coaches/keeper coach. Excellent grass with a measurements of 120x75 yards and has a seating capacity of 500.
History: The program began in 1994. The Sea Gulls play a very competitive level of soccer. Has two conference championships and several All-Region players.
Achievements: 1994 Conference Coach of the Year; 1994 & 2000 Conference Champion. CAC Runner-Up in 1995, 1996, & 1997. Undefeated in regular season 2000, NCAA Southeast Regional Champs-
Elite 8 in 2000.

Coaching: Jim Berkman, Head Coach, coach for fourteen years, coach of the National Champions Lacrosse team in 1994 and 1995 at Salisbury State University (1991 National Coach of the Year). Scott Bowers - Assistant Coach/Keeper, former men's keeper at SSU. Wayne Gorrow - Assistant Coach.
Roster in State: 12 **Out of State:** 10 **Out of Country:** 0
Walk-on/Other: **Graduation %:** 100 **Seniors on Team:** 2
Positions Needed: GK, Forward, MB
Camp or Clinic Dates: Not Available
Most Recent Record: 20-1-2
Schedule: North Carolina Wesleyan, Richmond Stockton, Mary Washington, Rowan Univ. John Hopkins, Christopher Newport.
Style of Play: Pressure attacking team. Build out of the back 4-4-2 and encourage our backs to go forward at all times.

Towson University
Academic Profile

Towson, MD 21252-0001
Phone: (410) 830-3165

Type: 4 Yr.,Public,Liberal Arts
Founded: 1866
Website: http://www.towson.edu
Religion: Non-Affiliated
SAT/ACT/GPA: 1000/3.0
Housing: Yes
Student/Faculty Ratio: 17:1
Male/Female Ratio: 45:55
Undergraduate Enrollment: 12,614
Graduate Enrollment: 2,382
Scholarships/Academic: Yes **Athletic:** Yes **Financial Aid:** Yes
Expenses by: Year **In State:** $ 9,164 **Out of State:** $ 14,242
Specialty: Liberal Arts
Degrees Conferred: BA, BS, BFA, BM, MA, MS, MAT, MFA, M.Ed., MM
Programs of Study: Accounting, Art, Art Education, Biology, Business Administration, Chemistry, Communications, Computer Science, Dance, Early Childhood Education, Economics, Elementary Education, English, French, General Education, Geography, German, Health Science, Mass Communications, Physical Education, Physics, Political Science, Psychology, Social Science, Sociology

Men's Athletic Profile

Department of Athletics - Towson Center
Towson, MD 21252-7079
Coach: Frank Olszewski
Email: folszewski@towson.edu

NCAA I
Tigers/Gold, Black, White
Phone: (410) 830-3260
Fax: (410) 830-3748

Estimated # of Men's Soccer Scholarships: 1.5
Conference: America East Conference
Program Profile: Team h as been a Top Twenty, South Atlantic Region Top Ten, and Conference Regular Season Champion in the pas five years. Year round program ten former players currently playing professionally (three in Germany and one on the National Team of Finland). Stadium setting with a state of the art bermuda grass match facility, as well as a training facility with the same quality surface. The team has also been the recipient of the prestigious NSCAA Academic Achievement Award (entire team with a grade point average over 3.00). Team travels to Germany once every four years for preseason (has done so since 1984).
History: Our program began in 1921. The team is consistently a South Atlantic Top Ten program and were in the Top Twenty in 1995 and 1996. They also were America East Finalist in 1995, 1998, and 1999 and regular season champions 1998.
Achievements: We have Coach of the Year awards in 1989, 1995 & 1998; Conference Championships in 1989, 1990, 1991 & 1998. We were Tournament Runner-Up in 1984, 1985 & 1998. Forward Richie Miller was named All-American in 1998. We have 10 drafted players.

Coaching: Frank Olszewski, Head Coach, is entering his 18 years Division I coach. He holds a USSF "A" Licensed and member of Maryland ODP Head Coach Director. He is a member of Region I USYSA Staff. He is considered Towson University's winningest coach (100 victories). He played professionally at New York and with US Olympic Team. Pete Medd is our Assistant Coach. He plays USISL and NPSL professionally and the goalkeeper trainer is Craig Maki.

Roster In State: 12	**Out of State:** 9	**Out of Country:** 5
ODP State: 17	**Regional:** 10	**National:** 2
Walk-on/Other:	**Graduation %:** 96	**Seniors on Team:** 4

Positions Needed: Forward, Center Midfield, Defender
Camp or Clinic Dates: June 19-23, July 17-21
Most Recent Record: 11-4-4
Schedule: Boston University, Hartford, Richmond, Davidson, Drexel, Northeastern, Vermont, New Hampshire, Hofstra, Colgate
Style of Play: European - Continental; exact system dependent upon strengths of team and technically oriented. We play an attacking style balanced with tenacious pressure defense. Players must be versatile to attack or defend depending upon the situation. Players must be tactically sophisticated and continually striving to improve.

Women's Athletic Profile

8000 York Rd
Towson, MD 21252-0001
Coach: Leslie Kehrin
Email: wsherwood@towson.com

NCAA I
Tigers/Black, Gold, White
Phone: (410) 830-3165
Fax: (410) 830-3748

Estimated # of Women's Soccer Scholarships: None
Conference: America East Conference
Program Profile: Division I program in the America East Conference. We have a soccer stadium with Bermuda grass. It is 120x70 (approx.). The maintenance facility keep the field at tip top condition all year long.
History: The program began in 1991. the first winning season was in 1998 with Woody's first season as the head coach (14-6-1. In 1997 & 1998 season they were Conference Champs.
Achievements: The team won the Conference Champs in 1997 and Conference Runner-Up in 1998.
Coaching: Leslie Kehrin, Head Coach, was named head coach in the summer of 1999.. Natalie Rich is assistant coach.
Style of Play: We teach an attacking possession oriented system and adopt to several formations depending on our opponents and personnel.

United States Naval Academy
Academic Profile

Phone: 410-293-1561

Annapolis, MD 21402

Type: 4 Yr.,Public,Engineering		**Founded:** 1845
Website: http://www.nadn.navy.mil		**Religion:** Non-Affiliated
SAT/ACT/GPA: 1200/3.2		**Housing:** Yes
Student/Faculty Ratio: 20:1		**Male/Female Ratio:** 87:13
Undergraduate Enrollment: 4,000		**Graduate Enrollment:** N/A
Scholarships/Academic: Yes	**Athletic:** No	**Financial Aid:** No
Expenses by: Year	**In State:** Appointed	**Out of State:** Appointed

Specialty: Engineering, Math
Degrees Conferred: BS
Programs of Study: 9 Engineering majors, Math, Political Science, History, Economics, Oceanography, English, Chemistry, Physics

Men's Athletic Profile

Mac Donough Hall
Annapolis, MD 21402
Coach: Greg Myers
Email: myers@nadn.navy.mil

NCAA I
Midshipmen/Blue, Gold
Phone: (410) 293-5542
Fax: (410) 293-5264

Estimated # of Men's Soccer Scholarships: Unlimited
Conference: Patriot League Conference
Program Profile: Our Dewey Field is natural grass and seats approximately 3,000. It was named in honor of the "Admiral of the Navy" and Head of Manila Bay, George Dewey.
History: Our program started in 1921. Our current coach is only the third in school's history.
Achievements: We have numerous All-Americans, National Champs in 1965, NCAA Division I Champions, Conference Champions and NCAA Tournament (Numerous times).
Coaching: Greg Myers, Head Coach, has been 36 years in soccer. He holds a USSF "A" License. He was an assistant coach at William & Mary, Tuchmond, Navy and Canadian National Youth Team. He was a goalkeeper coach and an assistant coach at George Mason and Navy. He was a head coach in University of Hartford.
Style of Play: Depend on type of players we get (ideally we like to play continued and knock the ball around; keep possession).

Women's Athletic Profile

566 Brownson Road
Annapolis, MD 21402
Coach: Carin Gabarra
Email: gabarra@nadn.navy.mil

NCAA I
Lady Midshipmen/Navy, Gold
Phone: (410) 293-5562
Fax: (410) 293-5264

Estimated # of Women's Soccer Scholarships: Unlimited
Conference: Patriot League Conference
Program Profile: We play on a natural Bermuda field that measures 120 x 80 yards. We have great weight training and indoor facilities.
History: The program began in 1993, is consistently in League Playoffs and has an upgrade schedule every year. 1999: 14-8-0, 5-1 in conference play.
Achievements: 1997 Coach of the Year; Nine 1998 All-League; 1 Academic All-American; 2 GTE Regional All-Americans; 4 All-Region; 1998 Patriot League Regular Season Champions. Justine Fisher conference Player of the Year. Two members named to the 1st team all conference and four players named to the 2nd team all conference.
Coaching: Carin Gabarra, Head Coach, is a ten-year veteran of the US National Team and a member of the 1991 World Championship team. Her seven year overall record is 63-48-6. She is a 1996 Olympic Gold Medalist. Rob Blanck, Jim Cabarra and Amy Mills are Assistant Coaches..

Roster in State: 0	**Out of State:** 25	**Out of Country:**
ODP State: 10	**Regional:** 7	**National:** 1
Walk-on/Other:	**Graduation %:** 100	**Seniors on Team:** 3

Positions Needed: All
Camp or Clinic Dates: June 24-28, July 22-26
Most Recent Record: 14-8
Schedule: Colgate, Holy Cross, Army, Bucknell, Lafayette, Lehigh
Style of Play: Attack from all positions, styles vary and we teach all styles.

University of Maryland

Academic Profile

Phone:

College Park, MD 20741-0295

Type: 4 Yr.,Public,Liberal Arts
Website: http://www.umd.edu
SAT/ACT/GPA: 1200/23/3.6
Student/Faculty Ratio: 13:1
Undergraduate Enrollment: 21,224
Scholarships/Academic: Yes **Athletic:** Yes
Expenses by: Year **In State:** $ 11,349
Founded: 1856
Religion: Non-Affiliated
Housing: Yes
Male/Female Ratio: 1:1
Graduate Enrollment: 13,776
Financial Aid: Yes
Out of State: $ 17,871
Specialty: Everything
Degrees Conferred: BA, BS, BFS, MA, MS, MFA
Programs of Study: Within college of Agriculture & Natural Resources, School of Architecture, College of Arts & Humanities, College of Behavioral & Social Sciences, Smith School of Business, College of Computer, Mathematical & Physical Science, College of Education, Clark School of Engineering, College of Health and Human Performance, College of Journalism, College of Life Sciences, more...

Men's Athletic Profile

P.O. Box 295
College Park, MD 20742-0295
Coach: Sasho Cirovski
Email: Not Available

NCAA I
Terrapins/Red,White,Black,Gold
Phone: (301)314-7064
Fax: (301) 314-9094

Estimated # of Men's Soccer Scholarships: N/A
Conference: Atlantic Coast Conference
Program Profile: The University of Maryland men's soccer program possesses not just a rich history, but also embodies a bright future. The 4,000 seat stadium surrounds a sodded Bermuda grass playing field. Maryland also has a state-of-the-art practice field near the team's locker, training and weight room facilitates. The Terrapins' season stretches from competitive preseason exhibition to tournaments in August to the always challenging ACC and non conference schedule from September through November, and caps off with a post-season run through the end of November and beyond!
History: The Terrapin men's soccer program began in 1953. The Terps have taken 20 trips to the NCAA tournament, highlighted by a co-national championship in 1968, two runner-up finishes, and three semifinal trips. Maryland also captured the ACC tournament championship in 1996, and has won the ACC regular season crown 20 times.
Achievements: Maryland has accumulated 21 ACC titles since 1946and in 1968 were the co-national champion. The Terps have 20 NSCAA All-Americans in their history as well as two ACC coaches of the year. They also currently have 6 player in the MLS.
Coaching: Sasho Cirovski is our Head Coach and is going on eight years with Maryland. He holds USSF "A" License, NSCAA Advanced National Diploma, USYSA Region I and II ODP Staff Coach, National Staff Coach for the USSF and NSCAA. Assistant Coach for the US U-17 National Team. He is assisted by Jeff Rohrman, who has been with the team for six years
Roster In State: 2 **Out of State:** 17 **Out of Country:** 2
ODP State: 16 **Regional:** 9 **National:** 8
Walk-on/Other: 5 **Graduation %:** N/A **Seniors on Team:** 5
Positions Needed: All
Camp or Clinic Dates: July 5-9, July 12-16, July 24-28, June 28-30
Most Recent Record: 14-6-0

Schedule: Indiana, Virginia, Duke, South Carolina, Clemson, William and Mary, NC State, North Carolina, and Wake Forest
Style of Play: Attractive attacking, possession oriented organized and disciplined defensively.

Women's Athletic Profile

P.O. Box 295
College Park, MD 21044
Coach: Shannon Higgins-Cirovski
Email: kr83@umail.und.edu

NCAA I
Terrapins/Red, Black, Yellow
Phone: (301) 314-7034
Fax: (301) 405-0955

Estimated # of Women's Soccer Scholarships: 3
Conference: Atlantic Coast Conference
Program Profile: We play our games at a Bermuda grass stadium that seats up to 2,000 fans. We also have two practice fields, weight room, and lock room.
History: The program began in 1986. We have participated in NCAA Tournaments 5 times. We were 2nd in the ACC and 23 in the country.
Achievements: Numerous All-Americans and Regional All-Americans.
Coaching: Shannon Higgins-Cirovski, Head Coach, replaced Alan Kirkup in the summer of 1999.
Style of Play: We try to play as attractive play as we possibly can.

University of Maryland-Baltimore County

Academic Profile

Ads
Baltimore, MD 21228

Phone: (410) 455-3003

Type: 4 Yr.,Public,Liberal Arts,Engineering
Website: http://www.ab.umd.edu
SAT/ACT/GPA: 1100/2.5
Student/Faculty Ratio: 20:1
Undergraduate Enrollment: 10,000
Scholarships/Academic: Yes
Athletic: Yes
Expenses by: Year
In State: $ 10,000
Specialty: Sciences

Founded: 1966
Religion: Non-Affiliated
Housing: Yes
Male/Female Ratio: 45:55
Graduate Enrollment: 2,000
Financial Aid: Yes
Out of State: $ 14,000

Degrees Conferred: BA, BS, MA, MS, MFA, Ph.D.
Programs of Study: Art, BioChemistry, Biological Science, Chemistry, Computer Science, Economics, Engineering, Geography, Mathematics, Nursing, Philosophy, Physics, Political Science, Psychology, Social Work, Sociology, Theatre

Men's Athletic Profile

100 Hilltop Circle
Bacto, MD 21250
Coach: Pete Caringi
Email: caringiJ@umbc.edu

NCAA I
Retrievers/Black, Gold
Phone: (410) 455-3003
Fax: (410) 455-1159

Estimated # of Men's Soccer Scholarships: Varies
Conference: Northeast Conference
Program Profile: The facilities are some of the finest in the country. A 4,500 seat stadium with a lights along with a brand new soccer only grass stadium. The stadium host the Maryland Mania of the "A" League plus numerous All-Star and championship Games.
History: Our program was a power NCAA Division in the 1970's but now has made the National rankings along with a #11 National raking in 1999. We also have had a numerous amount of players continue their careers in professional soccer.

Achievements: Pete Caringi was named two-time National Coach of the Year, Judson Dieter and J.J. Kremer were members of the NPSL Becto Blant. Steve Zerchusen, Dave Andrewjewski and Bob Wagner were named All-Americans. Giuliano Celenza was named Conference Player of the Year in 1999 and while Ty Engramf was a #1 Draft Pick.
Coaching: Pete Caringi is our Head Coach. He holds "A" License. He was named two-time NSCAA National Coach of the Year. He coached APSL National Champions. He was a former two-time All-American at University of Baltimore, Maryland and all-time leading scorer (70 goals) (National Champions in 1975). Played for the Washington Diploma in 1978 and NJCAA Hall of Fame.
Roster In State: 15 **Out of State:** 7 **Out of Country:** 3
ODP State: 20 **Regional:** 8 **National:** 4
Walk-on/Other: **Graduation %:** 90 **Seniors on Team:** 10
Positions Needed: Forward, Midfield
Camp or Clinic Dates: June 19- July 28
Most Recent Record: 19-1-1
Schedule: Maryland, George Mason, Loyola (MD), Holy Cross, Howard, FDU
Style of Play: Very offensive oriented.

Women's Athletic Profile

1000 Hilltop Circle
Baltimore, MD 21250
Coach: Michelle Salmon
Email: msalmon09@aol.com

NCAA I
Retrievers/Black, Gold
Phone: (410) 455-2013
Fax: (410) 455-1536

Estimated # of Women's Soccer Scholarships: N/A
Conference: Northeast
Program Profile: A division I program that consistently contends for the conference title. We have 2 practice fields and artificial and grass stadiums. Both stadiums are 120x80 yards. We play mostly on the grass stadium field, but in case of bad weather we are able to swithch surfaces.
History: The program began in 1988. Won inaugural Big South Invitational Tournament at UMBC in 1992, played in the Big South Championship game in 1993, hosted league championships in 1993 and 1994.
Achievements: 1992 Big South Conference. 1998 Northeast Conference finalist.
Coaching: Michelle Salmon is the Head Coach and Diana Akin is the Assistant Coach.
Roster in State: 12 **Out of State:** 11 **Out of Country:** 1
ODP State: 24 **Regional:** 2 **National:** 0
Walk-on/Other: 3 **Graduation %:** 83 **Seniors on Team:** 4
Positions Needed: Not Available
Camp or Clinic Dates: June 25-29
Most Recent Record: 6-9-3
Schedule: Delaware, Villanova, Georgetown, Loyola, Monmouth, Central Connecticut, Qunnipiac, Long Island University
Style of Play: We like to possess the ball, building out of our back.

Villa Julie College

Academic Profile

Phone: 419-602-7280

Stevenson, MD 21153-0641

Type: 2/4YRPrivate,Liberal Arts
Website: http://www.vjc.edu
SAT/ACT/GPA: 900
Student/Faculty Ratio: 12:1
Undergraduate Enrollment: 2,000
Scholarships/Academic: Yes **Athletic:** No
Expenses by: Year **In State:** $ 15,530

Founded: 1947
Religion: Non-Affiliated
Housing: No
Male/Female Ratio: 30:70
Graduate Enrollment: 80
Financial Aid: Yes
Out of State: $ 15,530

Specialty: Off campus college-owned apartments available
Degrees Conferred: AA,AAS, BS,BA,MSATT
Programs of Study: Accounting, Administrative Science, Applied Mathematics, Art, Biology, BioTechnology, Business, Business Communication, Business Information Systems, Chemistry, Child Development, Computer Accounting, Computer Information Systems, Court Reporting, Early Childhood Education, Economics, Elementary Education, English Language and Literature, Environmental Technology, Finance, History, Interdisciplinary Studies, Liberal Arts & Technology: Computer, Liberal Arts & Technology: Science, Marketing, Medical Laboratory Technology, MicroBiology, Nursing, Paralegal Studies, PreDental, PreLaw, PreMedicine, PrePharmacy, PrePhysical Therapy, PreVeterinary, Psychology, Video/Film/Theater, Visual Communication Design, Writing

Men's Athletic Profile

1525 Green Spring Valley Rd
Stevenson, MD 21153
Coach: Kevin Cromwell
Email: Not Available

NCAA III
Mustangs/Green, White
Phone: 410-602-7165 (2165)
Fax: (410) 486-3552

Did Not Return Profile

Women's Athletic Profile

Greenspring Valley Road
Stevenson, MD 21153
Coach: Matt Biederman
Email: adm.matt@mail.vjc.edu

NCAA I
Mustangs/F.Green, White, Black
Phone:
Fax:

Estimated # of Women's Soccer Scholarships: None
Conference: Independent Conference
Program Profile: Soccer season is year-round with a traditional segment going from mid-August to November first, and non-traditional segment from February to early April. Field is a natural grass, 75x115 yards, surrounded by trees. A new gymnasium was completed November 1, 1997 which allow the program to go indoors, weight program, and use it for our indoor tournament.
History: The women's soccer program began in 1994 as a member of the NCAA Division III level.
Achievements: None
Coaching: Matthew Biedermann, Head Coach, holds his National Coaching Diploma from the NSCAA. Varsity soccer for four years at Pfeiffer, started NCAA Division III program at Villa Julie in 1994, Amateur Division - Maryland Soccer Association. He has been coaching women's soccer for the past nine years. He is also an Admission Counselor at Villa Julie College.
Style of Play: Knowledge, execution and communication are key components to the Mustang Soccer. A 4-4-2 and a 3-4-3 is used in most matches to create opportunities for overlapping runs while maintaining a sound, right marking, aggressive defense organization. A premium is placed on hard work and technical/tactical development.

Washington College

Academic Profile

Chestertown, MD 21620

Phone: (410) 778-7700

Type: 4 Yr.,Private,Liberal Arts,Engineering
Website: http://www.washcoll.edu
SAT/ACT/GPA: 1100
Student/Faculty Ratio: 12:1
Undergraduate Enrollment: 1,100
Scholarships/Academic: Yes **Athletic:** No

Founded: 1782
Religion: Non-Affiliated
Housing: Yes
Male/Female Ratio: 40:60
Graduate Enrollment: 100
Financial Aid: Yes

Expenses by: Year **In State:** $ 24,940 **Out of State:** $ 24,940
Degrees Conferred: BA, BS, MA
Programs of Study: American Studies, Anthropology, Art, Behavioral NeuroScience, Biology, Business Management, Chemistry, Creative Writing, Drama, Economics, English, Environmental Studies, French, German, History, Humanities, International Studies, Mathematics, Music, Philosophy, Physics, Political Science, Psychology, Sociology, Spanish, PreMed, PreLaw, Computer Science, Teacher Education

Men's Athletic Profile

300 Washington Ave.
Chestertown, MD 21620
Coach: Lin Outten
Email: lin.outten@washcoll.edu

NCAA III
Shoremen/Maroon, White
Phone: 410-778-7240
Fax: (410) 778-7741

Estimated # of Men's Soccer Scholarships: N/A
Conference: Centennial Conference
Program Profile: We play on a grass stadium which measures 120x70 with an only male fall sport.
History: In 31 seasons Hall of Fame Ed Athey compiled a record of 218-122-37. He coached 2 MAC Championships teams, 2 MAC Southern Division Champions, 4 Mason Dixon Conference Champions. Since 1947 Washington College has compiled an overall record of 302-262-58. Program was dominant in the 1950's, 1960's and 1970's and is resurgent in the 90's.
Achievements: We have several All-Conference and regional All-American selections every year.
Coaching: Lin Outten, Head Coach, is entering his third season here. He holds a USSF "A" License and was a former Old Dominion University. He was a Head Coach in Maryland and Virginia in the last four years.
Roster In State: 17 **Out of State:** 7 **Out of Country:** 2
ODP State: 3 **Regional:** **National:**
Walk-on/Other: **Graduation %:** 100 **Seniors on Team:** 3
Positions Needed: Goalkeeper, Forward, Central Midfield
Camp or Clinic Dates: June 19-23, 25-29
Most Recent Record: 9-9-0
Schedule: Gettysburg, Mary Washington, Salesbury State, Muhlenberg, John's Hopkins
Style of Play: We a play a skillful attacking soccer with strong possession. All 11 players defend hard.

Western Maryland College

Academic Profile

Phone: (800) 638-5005

Westminster, MD 21784

Type: 4 Yr.,Private,Liberal Arts **Founded:** 1867
Website: http://www.wmdc.edu **Religion:** Non-Affiliated
SAT/ACT/GPA: 1140/25/3.3 **Housing:** Yes
Student/Faculty Ratio: 13:1 **Male/Female Ratio:** 1:1
Undergraduate Enrollment: 1,500 **Graduate Enrollment:** 1,500
Scholarships/Academic: Yes **Athletic:** No **Financial Aid:** Yes
Expenses by: Year **In State:** $ 24,000 **Out of State:** $ 24,000
Specialty: Liberal Arts
Degrees Conferred: BA, BS, MA, MS
Programs of Study: Art, Art History, Biology, Business Administration, Chemistry, Communications, Economics, English, Exercise Science, Physical Education, French, German, History, Math, Music, Philosophy, Physics, Political Science, Psychology, Religious Studies, Social Work, Sociology, Spanish, Theatre Arts

Men's Athletic Profile

2 College Hill
Westminster, MD 21157-4390
Coach: John Plevyak
Email: Not Available

NCAA III
Green Terror/F.Green, Old Gold
Phone: (410) 857-2589
Fax: (410) 857-2729

Estimated # of Men's Soccer Scholarships: n/a
Conference: Centennial Athletic Conference
Program Profile: Playing season is in the Fall, indoor and Spring. Two fields, indoor facility, natural grass.
History: Our program is 85 years old.
Achievements: 2000 four players on All-Centennial Conference team, ranked # 10 in final Mid-Atlantic Regional Rankings. Finished season 5-0-1 set school record with 56 goals qualified as third seed in ECAC Post Season Tournament.

Roster In State: 8	**Out of State:** 14	**Out of Country:** 1
ODP State: 4	**Regional:** 0	**National:** 0
Walk-on/Other: 0	**Graduation %:** 100	**Seniors on Team:** 2

Positions Needed: GK, Center-Mid, Sweeper
Most Recent Record: 10-6-2
Schedule: John Hopkins, Drew, Frostburg, Gettysburg, Rutgers-Camden
Style of Play: Attacking style with emphasis on extreme defensive pressure than quick counter-attacks.

Women's Athletic Profile

2 College Hill
Westminster, MD 21157-4390
Coach: Scott Swanson
Email: scswanson1@aol.com

NCAA III
Green Terror/Green, Gold
Phone: (410) 386-4630
Fax: (410) 857-2586

Estimated # of Women's Soccer Scholarships: None
Conference: Centennial Athletic Conference
Program Profile: Playing fall season, practice and game fields are natural grass, indoor facilities for winter, new weight room. Member of 11-team Conference. All new practice and game facilities (sports turf grass on practice and game fields, weight rooms training rooms, etc..installed in 1997 when Baltimore Ravens made WMC their pre-season training site.
History: Program began in 1987.
Achievements: Finished in top three in the Conference 5 of the last 6 years. 7 All-American selections and 35 All-conference selections since 1993. 1999 season set records for total wins, conference wins, consecutive wins, shutouts and consecutive shutouts. WMC player selected as Conference Player of the Year in 1997 and 1999.
Coaching: Head coach Swansn is in his 6th year with the program, 3rd as head coach. 3 assistants, all WMC alums, Lynn Stone, Lynnae Stoehr-Kerr, and Julie Backof.

Roster in State: 16	**Out of State:** 5	**Out of Country:** 0
ODP State: 2	**Regional:** 0	**National:** 0
Walk-on/Other:	**Graduation %:** 95	**Seniors on Team:** 4

Positions Needed: ALL
Camp or Clinic Dates: Mid June to End of July
Most Recent Record: 11-5-0
Schedule: Gettysburg, Messiah, John Hopkins, Muhlenberg, Haverford, Franklin and Marshal, Ursinus, Ferrum
Style of Play: Offensive style is forward thinking and aggressive. Coach encourages individual creativity at all positions. Defensive style is tight and aggressive marking. "We want to get forward quickly as an organized unit and give ourselves a lot of opportunities to score goals."

massachusetts

MASSACHUSETTS

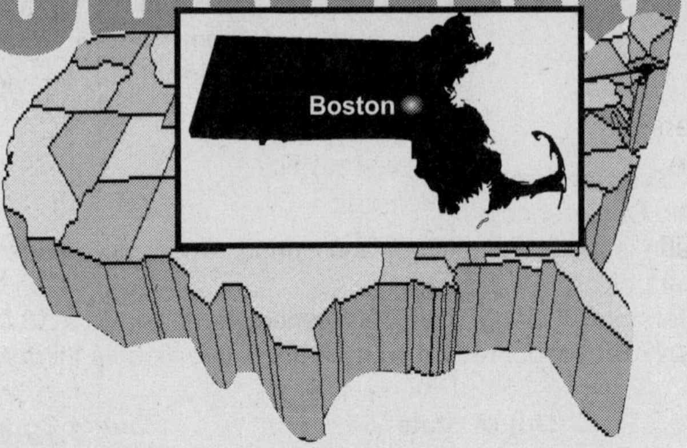

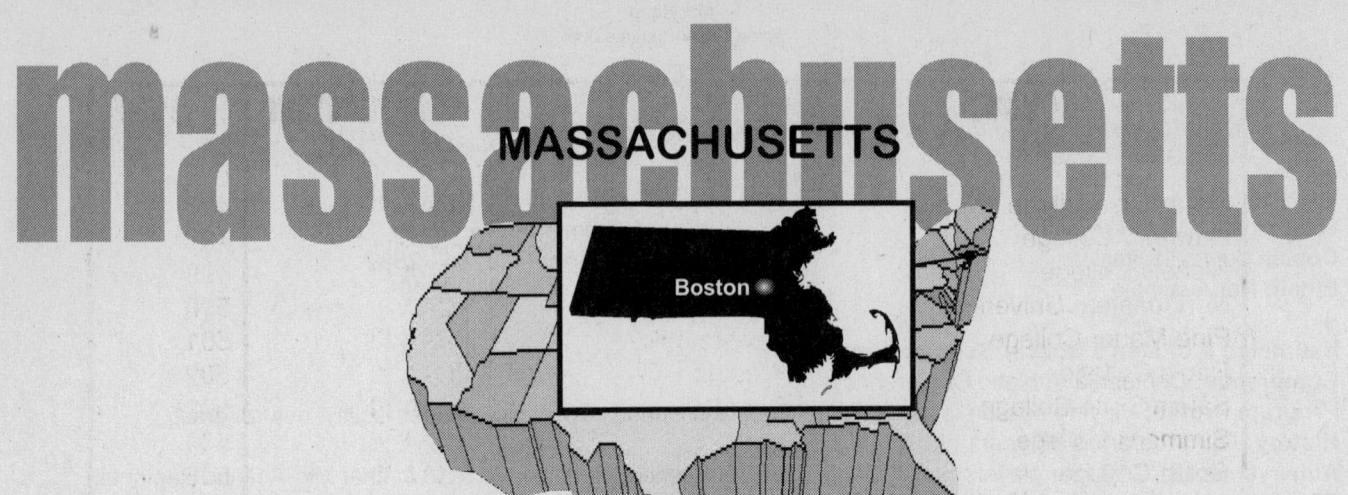

SCHOOL	CITY	AFFILIATION	PAGE
American International College	Springfield	NCAA II	467
Amherst College	Amherst	NCAA III	468
Anna Maria College	Paxton	NCAA III	469
Assumption College	Worcester	NCAA II	470
Babson College	Wellesley	NCAA III	471
Becker College	Leicester	NCAA III	472
Bentley College	Waltham	NCAA II	473
Boston College	Chestnut Hill	NCAA I	474
Boston University	Boston	NCAA I	475
Brandeis University	Waltham	NCAA III	477
Bridgewater State College	Bridgewater	NCAA III	478
Clark University	Worcester	NCAA III	479
College of the Holy Cross	Worcester	NCAA I	481
Curry College	Milton	NCAA III	482
Eastern Nazarene College	Quincy	NCAA III	483
Elms College	Chicopee	NCAA III	484
Emerson College	Boston	NCAA III	484
Endicott College	Beverly	NCAA III	486
Fitchburg State College	Fitchburg	NCAA III	487
Framingham State College	Framingham	NCAA III	488
Gordon College	Wenham	NCAA III	489
Harvard University	Boston	NCAA I	490
Lesley College	Cambridge	NCAA III	491
Mass College of Liberal Arts	North Adams	NCAA III	492
Mass Institute of Technology (MIT)	Cambridge	NCAA III	493
Massachusetts Maritime Academy	Buzzards Bay	NCAA III	494
Merrimack College	North Andover	NCAA II	495
Mount Holyoke College	South Hadley	NCAA III	497

SCHOOL	CITY	AFFILIATION	PAGE
Mount Ida College	Newton Centre	NCAA III	498
Newbury College	Brookline	NJCAA	499
Nichols College	Dudley	NCAA III	499
Northeastern University	Boston	NCAA I	500
Pine Manor College	Chestnut Hill	NCAA III	501
Regis College	Weston	NCAA III	502
Salem State College	Salem	NCAA III	502
Simmons College	Boston	NCAA III	504
Smith College	Northampton	NCAA III	505
Springfield College	Springfield	NCAA III	505
Stonehill College	North Easton	NCAA II	506
Suffolk University	Boston	NCAA III	507
Tufts University	Medford	NCAA III	508
Univ of Massachusetts - Amherst	Amherst	NCAA I	510
Univ of Massachusetts - Boston	Boston	NCAA III	511
Univ of Massachusetts-Dartmouth	North Dartmouth	NCAA III	512
Univ of Massachusetts - Lowell	Lowell	NCAA II	513
Wellesley College	Wellesley	NCAA III	514
Wentworth Inst of Tech	Boston	NCAA III	515
Western New England College	Springfield	NCAA III	515
Westfield State College	Westfield	NCAA III	517
Wheaton College	Norton	NCAA III	517
Williams College	Williamstown	NCAA III	519
Worcester Polytechnic Institute	Worcester	NCAA III	520
Worcester State College	Worcester	NCAA III	521

STAR GOALKEEPER ACADEMY

"Daniel Gaspar's goalkeeper training method and professional attitude are of the highest standards. His preparation of the Portuguese National Team, as well as Sporting Lisbon has been very impressive. He has demonstrated to have a positive impact in our journey towards the 1994 World Cup qualification process. Dan Gaspar is qualified to train." professional teams in any international arena.
Professor Carlos Queiroz, US Soccer Project 2010 Consultant, Portugal National Teams, Sporting Lisbon, J League Grampus Eight, MLS Metrostars, United Arab Emirates National and Olympic Team, FIFA Technical Staff, 89 & 91 Youth World Cup Champions

"I've watched Dan Gaspar in clinics across the country, and that in itself is a testament to his value. He is in constant demand. It is no surprise. He has excellent presence when he instructs, he is enthusiastic, knowledgeable and worthy of your attention."
Anson Dorrance, Women's National Team Coach, World Cup Champions, University of North Carolina NCAA National Champions,

"Having worked with goalkeepers form youth to top international level, Dan's knowledge, experience and enthusiasm continues to make SGA a fantastic place to train, play and grow."
Glenn Myernick, MLS Head Coach Colorado Rapids, US Soccer National Staff

"As an international and US National Team Keeper, It's important that I be associated with the highest in quality goalkeeper education. That is why I fully endorse SGA."
Brad Friedel, US National Team, Liverpool, MLS Columbus Crew, UCLA National Champion & All American, Herman Trophy Winner

"A great teacher/coach with unquestioned knowledge, unlimited enthusiasm and the experience to properly train his students. If your looking for these qualities in an instructor, then Dan Gaspar is your man."
Coach John Rennie, Duke University National Champions

"Dan is one of the nation's leaders and true professionals in the art of goalkeeping. I unequivocally recommend him to any coach or keeper who wants to gain real insight into what goalkeeping is all about."

"Dan Gaspar is one of the finest teachers and motivators of goalkeepers in America. His enthusiasm is contagious, and his sincere commitment to excellence is unquestionable."
Coach Mike Berticelli, University of Notre Dame, NSCAA National Director of Coaching

"Goalkeepers trained by Dan Gaspar reflect his passion and dedication for the game-one can be assured of that."
Coach Sigi Schmid, MLS LA Galaxy, US National Team U20 Coach, UCLA National Champions, US Soccer National Staff

"Dan's use of imagery and relentless study of the art of goalkeeping qualifies him as one of the top teachers, if not trailblazer's in today's game. Indeed, I am a better coach because of the innovations he has given to goalkeeping training."
Coach Cliff McGrath, Seattle Pacific University National Champions, NSCAA Hall of Fame

"SGA is won of the top training environments I've been privileged to watch and the results are incredible."
Coach Ray Reid, University of Connecticut, Southern Connecticut National Champions

"Dan Gaspar is a goalkeeper expert who creates a wonderful learning environment. Dan is without doubt one of the leading goalkeeping coaches in America today and I recommend him with no hesitation."
Coach Bobby Clark, Stanford University, Former Dartmouth Coach and Scottish National Team Keeper

American International College

Academic Profile

Phone: (413) 747-6546

Springfield, MA 01109

Type: 4 Yr.,Private,Liberal Arts
Founded: 1885
Website: http://www.aic.edu
Religion: Non-Affiliated
SAT/ACT/GPA: 900/20
Housing: Yes
Student/Faculty Ratio: 15:1
Male/Female Ratio: 55:45
Undergraduate Enrollment: 1,100
Graduate Enrollment: 900
Scholarships/Academic: Yes **Athletic:** Yes **Financial Aid:** Yes
Expenses by: Year **In State:** $ 20,206 **Out of State:** $ 20,206
Specialty: Education, International Business, Liberal Arts, Physical Therapy
Degrees Conferred: BA, BS, BSN, BSE, MBA
Programs of Study: Biology, Business, Chemistry, Communications, Criminal Justice, Education, Human Services, International Business, Nursing, Occupational Therapy, Psychology, Physical Therapy

Men's Athletic Profile

1000 State Street
Springfield, MA 01109
Coach: Fred Balbino
Email: Not Available

NCAA II
Yellow Jackets/Black, Gold
Phone: (413) 747-6596
Fax: (413) 731-5710

Estimated # of Men's Soccer Scholarships: None
Conference: Northeast 10 Conference
Program Profile: We are member of Division II. We play against South Connecticut and New Hampshire College). We play on natural grass pitch.
History: Traditionally, the soccer program has not been a strong. We've come along way and are excited about our future. In 1998 season, we have a record of 8-10 in tough conference and regional play.
Achievements: In 1998, Forward Jaime Marques was named Regional All-American.
Coaching: Fred Balbino is the Head Coach. He played at Westfield State College. Brian Graves is the Assistant Coach. He played at Elmira College. Andrew Boyea is the Goalkeeping Coach. He played at Northeastern University with New Hampshire Phantoms (Division III).
Style of Play: Blue collar work ethic; positive, hard working players.

Women's Athletic Profile

1000 State St.
Springfield, MA 01109-3189
Coach: Ciro Viviano
Email: Not Available

NCAA II
Yellow Jackets/Gold, White
Phone: (413) 747-6595
Fax: (413) 731-5710

Estimated # of Women's Soccer Scholarships: None
Conference: Northeast 10 Conference, ECAC,NCAA 11
Program Profile: Play on a grass field, 17 or 18 game schedule, Division I and II opponents. Has a seating capacity of a 2,500 (multi-purpose), and a stadium 1,500-seat gym. Nastilus Center has two soccer fields.
History: The program originated in 1985, it took three years to gain a winning record. Has been nationally ranked four out of ten years, including a 10th in the nation in 1989. Program now includes scholarship players and international players. Coach Carando is the only coach through 1996 (11 years), and has a record of 83-101-12. Highest National ranking 10th in 1989.
Achievements: Has 4 players named Regional All-Americans since 1989.
Style of Play: Indirect attack with speed ball possession.

Amherst College

Academic Profile

Amherst, MA 01002-5000
Phone: 413-542-2000

Type: 4 Yr.,Private,Liberal Arts
Founded: 1835
Website: http://www.amherst.edu
Religion: Non-Affiliated
SAT/ACT/GPA: 1200+
Housing: Yes
Student/Faculty Ratio: 10:1
Male/Female Ratio: 55:45
Undergraduate Enrollment: 1,600
Graduate Enrollment: N/A
Scholarships/Academic: No **Athletic:** No **Financial Aid:** Yes
Expenses by: Year **In State:** $ 30,000 **Out of State:** $ 30,000
Degrees Conferred: BA
Programs of Study: American Studies, Anthropology & Sociology, Asian Languages & Civilization, Astronomy, Biology, Black Studies, Chemistry Classics, Economics, English, European Studies, Fine Arts, Geology, German, History, LJST, Mathematics & Computer Science, Music Neuroscience, Philosophy, Physics, Political Science, Psychology, Religion, Romance

Men's Athletic Profile

Rm. 110 Alumni Gym
Amherst, MA 01007-5000
Coach: Peter Godding
Email: Not Available

NCAA III
Lord Jeffs/Purple, White
Phone: (413) 542-8117
Fax: (413) 542-2026

Estimated # of Men's Soccer Scholarships: N/A
Conference: NESCAC
Program Profile: Play a Fall season; home games are played on a natural grass field. The teams has been nationally ranked.
History: Program began in 1919.
Achievements: National Coach of the Year 1985 and 87. Regional Coach of the year in 1982, 85, 87, 93. Over 20 All - Americans.
Style of Play: Total Soccer - exciting entertaining, positive soccer.

Women's Athletic Profile

Box 2230 P.O. 5000
Amherst, MA 01002-5000
Coach: Michelle Morgan
Email: mcmorgan@amherst.edu

NCAA III
Jeffs/Purple, Black, White
Phone: (413) 542-2362
Fax: (413) 542-2026

Estimated # of Women's Soccer Scholarships: None
Conference: New England Small College Athletic Conference (NESCAC),ECAC
Program Profile: Home games are played on an excellent grass field. Amherst is a top Division III program in New England and is nationally ranked.
History: The program began in 1977, one of the first Division III programs in New England; historically competitive within context of excellent liberal arts education. Also had 5 consecutive NCAA Bids
Achievements: NE NSCAA Umbro Coach of the Year 1994, Kann Easar 1994 and NE All- American; Regional Coach of the Year three times. Many All-American and All-Academic Players.
Coaching: Michelle Morgan, Head Coach, NSCAA Advanced Diploma, Full professor, 19 years in Amherst.
Roster in State: 4 **Out of State:** 19 **Out of Country:** 0
ODP State: 4-6 **Regional:** 2-3 **National:**
Walk-on/Other: **Graduation %:** 100 **Seniors on Team:** 2

Positions Needed: Strikers, Midfielder
Camp or Clinic Dates: Not Available
Most Recent Record: 11-5-2
Schedule: Williams, Bates, Tufts, Clark
Style of Play: Build up soccer.

Anna Maria College

Academic Profile

Paxton, MA 01612
Phone:

Type: 4 Yr.,Private,Liberal Arts
Founded: 1946
Website: http://www.anna-maria.edu
Religion: Roman Catholic
SAT/ACT/GPA: 1000/2.8
Housing: Yes
Student/Faculty Ratio: 16:1
Male/Female Ratio: 60:40
Undergraduate Enrollment: 500
Graduate Enrollment: 1,100
Scholarships/Academic: Yes **Athletic:** No **Financial Aid:** Yes
Expenses by: Year **In State:** $ 18,250 **Out of State:** $ 17,000
Specialty: Criminal Justice, Education, Music Therapy, Art Therapy
Degrees Conferred: AA, AS, BA, BFA, BM, BBA, MA, MS, MBA
Programs of Study: Art, Biology, Natural Sciences, Business Administration, Criminal Justice, Education, Music, Music Therapy, Art Therapy, Psychology, Social Work, Paralegal Studies, English, History, Political Science

Men's Athletic Profile

Box 16, Athletics
Paxton, MA 01612
Coach: Dave Gentleman
Email: september3@email.msn.com

NCAA III
Amcats/Royal, White
Phone: 508-849-3225
Fax: (508) 849-3449

Estimated # of Men's Soccer Scholarships: None
Conference: Commonwealth Coast Conference, ECAC
Program Profile: The Amcats have 2 natural soccer fields.
History: Program began in 1978.
Style of Play: Aggressive offensive style with defense pressure in offensive end. Strong man defense with quick transitions to offense.

Women's Athletic Profile

Sunset Lane, Box A
Paxton, MA 01612
Coach: Joseph Brady
Email: jbrady@annamarie.edu

NCAA III
Amcats/Blue, White
Phone: (508) 849-3490
Fax: (508) 849-3449

Estimated # of Women's Soccer Scholarships: None
Conference: Commonwealth Coast
Program Profile: Women's Soccer program has been in existence for 10 years. We have become one of the top programs in the conference and New England. 2 grass fields used both for practice and games. Season from August to november with some off-season training.
History: Began in 1991 (1-8-1). Overall record 82-84-8, 44-34-1 - 10 years.
Achievements: 1997 - 17-4, Conference Champs, ECAC bid. 1998 - 13-7-1 - Conference runner-up, ECAC bid. 2000 - 15-6-1. 1997 Coach of the Year. Joseph Brady (conference) Heather Notidis - Conference Player of the Year 1997, 3rd team All-New England. Jess Haynes-Conference Rookie of the Year 1998.

Coaching: Head coach Joseph Brady, NSCAA National Diploma, Juventus Club girls coach. Marcy Henderson-Assistant coach- goalkeeper, 3 years. Servando Gac- Assistant Coach, 2 years.
Roster in State: 16 **Out of State:** 2 **Out of Country:** 0
ODP State: 3 **Regional:** 0 **National:** 0
Walk-on/Other: 0 **Graduation %:** 100 **Seniors on Team:** 5
Positions Needed: Keeper, Midfield
Camp or Clinic Dates: Not Available
Most Recent Record: 15-6-1
Schedule: Wheaton, Clark, Keene State, Babson, UNE, Endicott, Gordon
Style of Play: Play very simple, while being very patient. Build play from back through passes on the ground. Very little dribbling, high pressure on offense while playing hard for 90 minutes.

Assumption College
Academic Profile

Worcester, MA 01615-0005
Phone: 888-882-7786

Type: 4 Yr.,Private,Liberal Arts,Engineering **Founded:** 1904
Website: http://www.assumption.edu **Religion:** Catholic
SAT/ACT/GPA: 1000/26/3.0 **Housing:** Yes
Student/Faculty Ratio: 18:1 **Male/Female Ratio:** 1:4
Undergraduate Enrollment: 1,900 **Graduate Enrollment:** 450
Scholarships/Academic: Yes **Athletic:** No **Financial Aid:** Yes
Expenses by: Year **In State:** $ 22,000 **Out of State:** $ 22,000
Specialty: Liberal Arts, Communications
Degrees Conferred: BA, BS, MA, CAGS
Programs of Study: Accounting, Biology, Business, Management, Chemistry, Communications, Computer Science, Education English, Languages, Liberal Arts, Medical, Natural Science, Philosophy, Political Science, Rehabilitation Therapy, Religion, Romance Language

Men's Athletic Profile

500 Salisbury Street
Worcester, MA 01615
Coach: John Murphy
Email: smurphy@assumption.edu

NCAA II
Greyhounds/Royal Blue, White
Phone: (508) 767-7236
Fax: (508) 798-2568

Estimated # of Men's Soccer Scholarships: N/A
Conference: Northeast-10 Conference, ECAC
Program Profile: A program on the rise, Assumption just completed the most successful season in its 38 year history. An upgrade scheduling has complimented with modern facilities on campus. Rochalesum Field is one of the toughest playing venues in New England with its rambunctious crowds.
History: Program began in 1962.
Coaching: John Murphy, Head Coach, was a 1994 NSCAA Coach of the Year and a 1994 Colonial State Conference Coach of the Year. He holds a USSF "A" License, a NSCAA Advanced National Scottish Football "A" License and is a Region VI Staff Coach.
Style of Play: Direct with midfielders, looking up back and strikers. Attack the flanks, dangerous on set pieces. Zonal defending, high/low defensive looks, double down on flanks. Quick connecting team.

Women's Athletic Profile

500 Salisbury Street
Worcester, MA 01615-0005
Coach: John Murphy
Email: jgondek765@aol.com

NCAA II
Lady Greyhounds/R.Blue, White
Phone: (508) 767-7079
Fax: (508) 798-1053

Estimated # of Women's Soccer Scholarships: None
Conference: Northeast 10 Conference
Program Profile: Play a traditional fall-winter-spring season. Field is called Roschileau Field which is on campus and is a natural grass.
History: Program began in 1989, 1993 saw the first winning season in school's history with our first National Top 20 ranking, and semi-final appearance in the NE- 10 Tournament.
Achievements: 1997: ECAC Invitational first in school history; 2nd in conference in regular season; Conference Coach of the Year; NCAA Division II Coach of the Year for the Northwest Region.
Style of Play: Dutch possession, Brazilian counter-attacking.

Babson College
Academic Profile

Babson Park, MA 02157
Phone: 781-235-1200

Type: 4 Yr.,Private,Liberal Arts
Founded: 1919
Website: http://www.babson.edu
Religion: Non-Affiliated
SAT/ACT/GPA: Open
Housing: Yes
Student/Faculty Ratio: 20:1
Male/Female Ratio: 60:40
Undergraduate Enrollment: 1,600
Graduate Enrollment: 300
Scholarships/Academic: Yes **Athletic:** No **Financial Aid:** 60%
Expenses by: Year **In State:** $ 27,000 **Out of State:** $ 27,000
Specialty: Business
Degrees Conferred: BS, MBA
Programs of Study: Contact school for program of study.

Men's Athletic Profile

Babson Park
Wellesley, MA 02457
Coach: Jon Anderson
Email: Not Available
NCAA III
Beavers/Green, White
Phone: (781) 239-4250
Fax: (781) 239-5218

Estimated # of Men's Soccer Scholarships: 0
Conference: Newmac Conference
Program Profile: We play 18 regular season games in the fall and have encountered much post-season success. We have spring training and a winter workout schedule as well. Our facilities are top notch: many fields, even New England Revolution practice at Babson. A natural grass surface and no football programs allows from strong support from the student body.
History: Program began in 1967, and there was a great deal of success in the 70's to the 80's. Have always been competitive in New England since that period. Last season was one of rebuilding an we are looking forward to future success.
Achievements: NCAA titles in 1975, 79, 80. NCAA Final Four 1993. ECAC Champions 1997.
2 graduates currently playing professionally. Many All-Americans over the years.
Coaching: Head Coach- Jon Anderson, 14th season, Babson graduate 1975. Assistants- Bob Muscaro, Babson graduate 1986. Dave Decew, 1st year. Bill Lawler, 2nd year, Babson graduate 1997
Roster In State: 10 **Out of State:** 8 **Out of Country:** 1
ODP State: 4 **Regional:** 2 **National:**
Walk-on/Other: **Graduation %:** 100 **Seniors on Team:** 5
Positions Needed: All positions
Camp or Clinic Dates: Not Available
Most Recent Record: 6-10-2
Schedule: Williams, Amherst, Bowdoin, Wheaton, Colby, Brandeis, Springfield
Style of Play: Primarily use a ground attack and play to target forwards whom the outside midfielders can run off of. Very aggressive on defense and really stress the importance of winning 50/50 balls.

Women's Athletic Profile

Webster Ctr
Babson Park, MA 02457
Coach: Judy Blinstrub
Email: blinstrub@babson.edu
NCAA III
Beavers/Green, White
Phone: (781) 239-4418
Fax: (781) 239-5218
Estimated # of Women's Soccer Scholarships: None
Conference: NEWMAC
Program Profile: We have both types of field natural grass and Astroturf to play our matches on. We also have a new athletic complex.
History: The Women's Soccer program in 1982.
Achievements: Five Conference Champions; 5 times Conference Coach of the Year; All- American Honors; Many All-New England.
Coaching: Judy Blinstrub, Head Coach, entering 14 years with the program. Julie Tienken - Assistant Coach, Babson graduate in 1993. Gloria Gaiter - Assistant Coach, entering seven years with the program, Babson graduate in 1986. We also have 1 part time Assistant Coach.
Roster in State: **Out of State:** **Out of Country:** 1
Walk-on/Other: **Graduation %:** 100 **Seniors on Team:** 1
Positions Needed: Midfield, Strikers
Camp or Clinic Dates: Not Available
Most Recent Record: 8-9
Schedule: Bates, Bowdoin, Tufts, Wheaton, Clark, Wellesley
Style of Play: Give and go, skill work, and good team defense.

Becker College

Academic Profile

Phone:

Leicester, MA 01524

Type: 4 Yr.,Private
Founded: 1887
Website: http://www.beckercollege.edu
Religion: Non-Affiliated
SAT/ACT/GPA: Open/2.0
Housing: Yes
Student/Faculty Ratio: 15:1
Male/Female Ratio: 1:4
Undergraduate Enrollment: 1,030
Graduate Enrollment: N/A
Scholarships/Academic: Yes **Athletic:** No **Financial Aid:** Yes
Expenses by: Year **In State:** $ 18,000 **Out of State:** $ 18,000
Degrees Conferred: BS
Programs of Study: Accounting, Business Administration, Veterinary Science, Early Childhood Education, Elementary Education, Human Resources, Kinesiology, Legal Studies, Marketing, Psychology, Paralegal

Men's Athletic Profile

3 Paxton Street
Leicester, MA 01524
Coach: Gary Rudman
Email: hawkssocr@aol.com
NCAA III
Hawks/Royal, White, Scarlet
Phone: (508) 987-1375
Fax: (508) 892-8131

Estimated # of Men's Soccer Scholarships: None
Conference: North Atlantic Conference
Program Profile: Excellent natural grass field (115 x 70 yd.), equipped with scoreboard and underground sprinkler system.
History: NCAA member for two years.
Achievements: Three players named All-Conference including Player of the Year Honors.

Coaching: Gary Rudman is our Head Coach. Kevin Sloan is our Assistant Coach.
Roster In State: 14 **Out of State:** 6 **Out of Country:** 0
Walk-on/Other: **Graduation %:** N/A **Seniors on Team:** 3
Positions Needed: Goalkeeper and midfield
Camp or Clinic Dates: Not Available
Most Recent Record: 7-12-0
Schedule: Mount Ida, Lasell, Suffolk, Worcester State, Lyndon State, Southern Vermont, Nichols
Style of Play: Play 4-4-2 formation system.

Women's Athletic Profile

3 Paxton Street
Leicester, MA 01524
Coach: Ken Cameron
Email: Not Available

NCAA III
Hawks/Royal, White, Scarlet
Phone: (508) 791-9241
Fax: (508) 892-8131

Estimated # of Women's Soccer Scholarships: Not Available
Conference: North Atlantic Conference
Program Profile: The playing facilities consist of excellent natural grass game field that measures 115x70 yards, equipped with a sprinkler system and a scoreboard.
History: 1998 was first year in NCAA.
Achievements: Team was selected for MAIAW Tournament in 1998. New England Champs in 1988. We have four players named to All-Conference team.
Coaching: Ken Cameron is our Head Coach.
Roster in State: 12 **Out of State:** 6 **Out of Country:** 0
Walk-on/Other: **Graduation %:** **Seniors on Team:** 1
Positions Needed: Backs
Camp or Clinic Dates: Not Available
Most Recent Record: 10-8-0
Schedule: Nichols, University of Massachusetts - Boston, Wentworth, Lasell, Elms, Emerson, Lyndon State, New England College
Style of Play: We play 4-4-2 style.

Bentley College

Academic Profile

Phone: (781) 891-2256

Waltham, MA 02154-4705

Type: 4 Yr.,Private
Website: http://www.bentley.edu
SAT/ACT/GPA: 1100/3.0
Student/Faculty Ratio: 17:1
Undergraduate Enrollment: 3,293
Scholarships/Academic: Yes **Athletic:** Yes
Expenses by: Year **In State:** $ 25,855

Founded: 1917
Religion: Non-Affiliated
Housing: Yes
Male/Female Ratio: 53:47
Graduate Enrollment: 1,589
Financial Aid: Yes
Out of State: $ 25,855

Specialty: Business, Computer Technology
Degrees Conferred: BA, BS, MBA, MS
Programs of Study: Accounting, Accounting Information Systems, Business Communications, Business Economics, Computer Information Systems, Economics-Finance, English, Finance-Bank Management, Global Financial Analysis, History, International Business, International Culture and Economy, Liberal Arts, Management Information Systems, Managerial Economics, Marketing, Mathematical Sciences, Paralegal Studies, Philosophy, Self Design

Men's Athletic Profile

175 Forest St.
Waltham, MA 02154-4705
Coach: Peter Simonini
Email: moreinfo@bentley.edu

NCAA II
Falcons/Blue, Gold
Phone: (781) 891-2336
Fax: (781) 891-2648

Estimated # of Men's Soccer Scholarships:
Conference: Northeast 10 Conference
Program Profile: All home games are played at Bentley Athletic Field with a capacity of 3,100. Northeast opponents are American International College (AIC), Assumption College, Bryant College, LeMoyne College, Merrimack College, Saint Anselm College, St. Michaels and Stonehill College.
History: Our program began in 1972; made the NCAA Tournament in 1976; Northeast Regular Season Champs in 1983, 1991, 1992, 1993 & 1995; Northeast Playoff champs in 1992, 1993 & 1994.
Achievements: Conference Regular champs in 1983, 1991, 1992, 1993 & 1995; Conference tournament champs in 1992, 1993 & 1994. Simonini reached the 100 win plateau in 1995. Peter Simonini was named Northeast Coach of the Year in 1990, 1991 & 1993.
Coaching: Peter Simonini, Head Coach, entering twelve years; winningest coach in school's history, 1980 graduate of Plymouth State College, played professionally with the New England and Jacksonville Tea Men, 1983 American Soccer League MVP, was a two-time All-American goalie for Plymouth. Jim Murphy - Assistant Coach.
Style of Play: Play a 1 and 2 touch; 4-4-2 system.

Women's Athletic Profile

175 Forest Street
Waltham, MA 02154-4705
Coach: Lori Duran
Email: Not Available

NCAA II
Falcons/Blue, Gold
Phone: (781) 891-2451
Fax: (781) 891-2648

Estimated # of Women's Soccer Scholarships: None
Conference: Northeast 10 Conference
Program Profile: the playing season starts in early September and lasts until the Conference playoffs in November; play on turf field which seats 700.
History: The program began in 1991. Coach Avila has been at Bentley for all seven seasons and has compiled a 40-71-8 record.
Achievements: In six years, Bentley has had 2 All-Conference (first team) and 8 second team All-Conference players. Head Coach Julio Avila was the Northeast-10 Coach of the Year in 1995.
Style of Play: 4-4-2; defensively.

Boston College
Academic Profile

Chestnut Hill, MA 02167
Phone: 800-360-2522

Type: 4 Yr.,Private,Liberal Arts
Website: http://www.bc.edu
SAT/ACT/GPA: 1200/28/3.5
Student/Faculty Ratio: 15:1
Undergraduate Enrollment: 8,958
Scholarships/Academic: Yes
Athletic: Yes
Expenses by: Year
In State: $ 31, 010
Founded: 1863
Religion: Catholic
Housing: Yes
Male/Female Ratio: 48:52
Graduate Enrollment: 5,500
Financial Aid: Yes
Out of State: $ 31,010
Degrees Conferred: BA, BS, MA, MS, Ph.D.
Programs of Study: Arts & Sciences, Management, Nursing, Engineering

Men's Athletic Profile

411 Conte Forum
Chestnut Hill, MA 02467
Coach: Ed Kelly
Email: kellyeb@bc.edu

NCAA I
Eagles/Maroon, Gold
Phone: (617) 552-4085
Fax: (617) 552-4903

Estimated # of Men's Soccer Scholarships: 8
Conference: Big East Conference
Program Profile: New playing field (natural) on the Newton campus which measures 115x78.
Achievements: Last season we were the Big East Champions, Big East Coach of the Year, and Big East Goalkeeper and Offensive players of the Year.
Coaching: Our head coach is Ed Kelly and Zach Samol is the assistant coach.
Roster In State: 7 **Out of State:** 19 **Out of Country:** 8
ODP State: 8 **Regional:** 2 **National:** 1
Walk-on/Other: **Graduation %:** 100 **Seniors on Team:** 11
Positions Needed: Defenders
Camp or Clinic Dates: None
Most Recent Record: 12-7-1
Schedule: UCONN, Penn State, Ohio State, St. John's, Rutgers, Brown, Syracuse, Pittsburgh, Seton Hall

Women's Athletic Profile

Conte Forum 411H
Chestnut Hill, MA 02167
Coach: Allison Foley
Email: alison.foley@be.edu

NCAA I
Eagles/Maroon, White
Phone: (617) 552-3214
Fax: (617) 552-4930

Estimated # of Women's Soccer Scholarships: 12
Conference: Big East Conference
Program Profile: Games are played on multi-purpose athletic facility with a grass field for year-round training and play. Compete in traditional and non-traditional season with off-season program supervised as sanctioned by the NCAA. Competitive schedule and competitive Big East Conference play.
History: Program began in 1980. The Eagles made two NCAA Tournament appearances in the 80's.
Achievements: 1992, 1993 ECAC Post-season Tournament/All-New England players in the past decade. Big East Academic All-Stars in 1993 and 1994. 1999 New England Intercollegiate Soccer Association Coach of the Year.
Coaching:
Roster in State: 3 **Out of State:** 22 **Out of Country:** 0
ODP State: 7 **Regional:** 2 **National:** 1
Walk-on/Other: **Graduation %:** 98 **Seniors on Team:** 7
Positions Needed: Backs, GK
Camp or Clinic Dates: Not Available
Most Recent Record: 14-7-0
Schedule: Uconn, Syracuse, Miami, Dartmouth, James Madison
Style of Play: Total team soccer - aggressive offense and defense stressed in all parts of the field with an emphasis on technical and tactical development. Important that players develop as individual both on and off the field along with team growth.

Boston University

Academic Profile

Phone: (617) 353-2766

Boston, MA 02215

Type: 4 Yr.,Private,Liberal Arts,Engineering
Website: http://www.gobu.com

Founded: 1869
Religion: Non-Affiliated

SAT/ACT/GPA: 1200-1360/26-30/Top 25% **Housing:** Yes
Student/Faculty Ratio: 13:1 **Male/Female Ratio:** 40:60
Undergraduate Enrollment: 15,538 **Graduate Enrollment:** 7,500
Scholarships/Academic: Yes **Athletic:** Yes **Financial Aid:** Yes
Expenses by: Year **In State:** $ 31,018 **Out of State:** $ 31,018
Degrees Conferred: BA, BS, CAS, DDM, MA, MD, MS, Ph.D.. in Education,
Programs of Study: American Studies, Anthropology, Art History, Astronomy, Bilingual Education, Biochemistry, Biology, Chemistry, Computer Science, Earth Science, Economics, Environmental Science, French, German, Greek, History, Latin, Mathematics, Music, Psychology, Religion, Russian, Sociology, Urban Studies, Theatre Arts, Visual Arts

Men's Athletic Profile

285 Babcock Street
Boston, MA 02215
Coach: Neil Roberts
Email: neilrob@bu.edu
NCAA I
Terriers/Scarlet, White
Phone: (617) 353-2766
Fax: (617) 353-528
Estimated # of Men's Soccer Scholarships: 2.5
Conference: America East Conference
Program Profile: Nationally recognized program that combines technical training with strength & conditioning for overall development. Team plays home games on artificial turf & contains a mix of foreign & American players, which include 17 international level players and 15 professionals. Very comprehensive national schedule, with an automatic NCAA bid available from the conference. Traditionally one of the universities top academic teams.
History: Our program started in 1940. Since men II tournament appearances, 6 conference championships. Have advanced past the first round of the NCAA tournament five times. 1994 team went undefeated & was ranked #1 at tend of regular season.
Achievements: 3x New England coach of the year, 6 conference titles (5 straight from 93-97), 9 NCAA tournaments in 13 seasons, 19 All-Americans , One of the top 20 winning so in Division I in 1990's
Michael Emanuelo, Nigerian NH team.
Coaching: Neil Roberts, Head Coach, is a three-time NE Coach of the Year and has a USSF "A" License. Brian Quinn is assistant coach and has a USSF "A" License. Audy Fleming is assistant coach. Donny Neikkala is goalkeeper coach.
Roster In State: 2 **Out of State:** 12 **Out of Country:** 9
ODP State: 6 **Regional:** 4 **National:** 3
Walk-on/Other: **Graduation %:** 99 **Seniors on Team:** 3
Positions Needed: Marking Backs, Attacking MF, Flank MF
Camp or Clinic Dates: Not Available
Most Recent Record: 8-6-5
Schedule: Fairfield, Creighton, Syracuse, SW Missouri St., Cornell, Harvard, Connecticut, Hartford
Style of Play: Quick & exciting style that utilizes sound technique and athleticism. We play a skilled, possession oriented, attacking game that mixes in some direct play as well. Sound, organized team defense is a focal point of our program.

Women's Athletic Profile

285 Babcock Street
Boston, MA 02215
Coach: Nancy Feldman
Email: buwosoc@bu.edu
NCAA I
Terriers/Red, White
Phone: (617) 353-8456
Fax: (617) 353-5286

Estimated # of Women's Soccer Scholarships: Fully Funded
Conference: America East Conference

Program Profile: Boston University has an outstanding academic reputation, as well as an athletic program with a strong tradition. In addition, Boston is an exciting city, and when you combine all three, you have a very attractive package to appeal to recruits. The University is making a long-term commitment to women's soccer. The 1995 team carried 24 players with half being freshman. The starting line-up was 80% first-year players. Astroturf facility, play mid-August through November, indoor training February through March; outdoor season (non-traditional) mid-March through end of April.
History: Club program turned varsity in 1995; full fledge NAC team in 1996 (NAC turned America East); second place in America East Conference in 1997.
Achievements: 2000 America East Champions/ NCAA 2nd Round, Coach of the Year and Player of the Year. 1999 1 American East Player of the Year. 1997 America East Coach of the Year/NEWISA D.I
Coaching: Nancy Feldman, Head Coach (July 1, 1995), former head coach at Plymouth State College since 1990 (75-10-5 record at PSC), named New England Coach of the Year in 1991 and 1993, began her coaching career in 1986 at Smith College. She was named America East Conference Coach of the Year in 1997. Kelli Hurley Assistant Coach.

Roster in State: 9	**Out of State:** 17	**Out of Country:** 0
ODP State: 10	**Regional:** 3	**National:** 0
Walk-on/Other: 1	**Graduation %:** 97	**Seniors on Team:** 2

Positions Needed: Striker
Camp or Clinic Dates: TBA
Most Recent Record: 16-7-0
Schedule: BYU, Dartmouth, Harvard, Hartford, Boston College, Princeton
Style of Play: Possession orientated and build from the back.

Brandeis University

Academic Profile

Waltham, MA 02254-9110

Phone: 781-736-2000

Type: 4 Yr.,Private,Liberal Arts		**Founded:** 1948
Website: http://www.logos.cc.brandies.edu		**Religion:** Non-Sectarian
SAT/ACT/GPA: 1100+		**Housing:** Yes
Student/Faculty Ratio: 9:1		**Male/Female Ratio:** 50:50
Undergraduate Enrollment: 3,700		**Graduate Enrollment:** 973
Scholarships/Academic: Yes	**Athletic:** No	**Financial Aid:** Yes
Expenses by: Year	**In State:** $ 33,000	**Out of State:** $ 33,000

Specialty: Liberal Arts
Degrees Conferred: BA, MA, MFA, Ph.D.
Programs of Study: Anthropology, Art, Aviation Science, Biology, Business, Chemistry, Professional Chemistry, Communications Arts & Science, Computer Science, Early Childhood Education, Earth Science, Education, Economics, English, French, Geography, History, Management, Science, Mathematics, Music, Philosophy, Physical Education, Physics, Political Science, Psychology, Secondary Science, Social Work, Spanish, Special Education

Men's Athletic Profile

Gosman Center
Waltham, MA 02254-9110
Coach: Mike Coven
Email: Not Available

NCAA III
Judges/Blue, White
Phone: (781) 736-3638
Fax: (781) 736-3656

Estimated # of Men's Soccer Scholarships: n/a
Conference: University Athletic Association
Program Profile: Brandeis has on of the top NCAA Division III programs in the country. It has a top notch grass field and plays a competitive 18 game schedule in the fall and also plays indoors in the winter. Extensive travel in the UAA. Excellent natural turf stadium.

History: Traditionally Brandeis has been one of the top teams in the nation and in 1976 won the NCAA Division III Men's soccer championship. three years ago, Brandies won the ECAC Division III New England Championships and has advanced to the championship game last three years.
Achievements: Coach Mike Coven, has been a coach for 24 years, team won the NCAA division III title in 1976 and has also appeared two other times in the Final Four. Team has had 11 All-Americans, including Chris White last season, and has had a Goalie of the Year winner for all Divisions, National Runner-Up in 1981 and 1984. 2000 Selected to play in the ECAC Regional Tournament.
Coaching: Mike Coven, Head Coach, has been the head coach of the brandies soccer team for 24 years, he has won over 290 career games and has been honored as Coach of the Year several times.

Roster In State: 17	**Out of State:** 8	**Out of Country:** 01
ODP State: 12	**Regional:** 0	**National:** 1
Walk-on/Other: 0	**Graduation %:** 100	**Seniors on Team:** 5

Positions Needed: Mid fielders and Defenders
Camp or Clinic Dates: Not Available
Most Recent Record: 12-7-0
Schedule: Wheaton College, Univ. Rochester, Washington University (St. Louis) , Emory
Style of Play: Controlled style of play; ball feet, build-up wings, play total soccer.

Women's Athletic Profile

MS 007 Gorman Athletic Department	**NCAA III**
Waltham, MA 02254	Judges/Royal, White, Blue
Coach: Denise Dallamora	**Phone:** (781) 736-3644
Email: dallamora@brandeis.edu	**Fax:** (781) 736-3656

Estimated # of Women's Soccer Scholarships: None
Conference: University Athletic Association
Program Profile: Very competitive Division III program which allows for out of region play by airplane. Brand new $25 million dollar athletic facility which is also the home of the Boston Celtics.
History: Program began in 1980.
Achievements: 1990 New 8 all-conference Champions, ECAC 1986, 1987, 1990, 1991, 1993; NCAA 1988.
Coaching: Denise Dallamora, Head Coach, former NCAA Coach of the Year (NEWISA), UAA Conference Coach of the Year, New England Women's 8 Coach of the Year, Service Award NEWISA, letter of Commendation NSCAA.
Style of Play: Direct style of attack, high pressure defense in a 4-3-3 system. Attractive, controlled, enjoyable play, which allows players to improve skills and tactics that will hopefully produce further coaches for women's soccer.

Bridgewater State College

Academic Profile

Phone: 508-531-1200

Bridgewater, MA 02325

Type: 4 Yr.,Public,Liberal Arts		**Founded:** 1840
Website: http://www.bridgew.edu		**Religion:** Non-Affiliated
SAT/ACT/GPA: 850		**Housing:** yes
Student/Faculty Ratio: 17:1		**Male/Female Ratio:** 33:67
Undergraduate Enrollment: 5,700		**Graduate Enrollment:** 750
Scholarships/Academic: Yes	**Athletic:** No	**Financial Aid:** Yes
Expenses by: Year	**In State:** $ 7,983	**Out of State:** $ 12,077

Degrees Conferred: BA, BB, BSE, MA, MS, M.Ed. (31 degrees)
Programs of Study: Anthropology, Art, Aviation Science, Biology, Business, Chemistry, Professional Chemistry, Communications Art & Science, Early Childhood Education, Earth Science, Economics, Elementary Education, English, French, Geography, History, Management, Science, Mathematics, Music, Philosophy, Physical Education, Physics, Political Science, Psychology, Secondary Education

Men's Athletic Profile

Park Ave.
Bridgewater, MA 02325
Coach: Keith E. Clark
Email: Not Available

NCAA III
Bears/Red, White, Black
Phone: (508) 697-1352
Fax: (508) 697-1356

Estimated # of Men's Soccer Scholarships: None
Conference: Massachusetts State College Athletic Conference
Program Profile: The Bears will be playing their home games on natural grass Swenson Field. We have 2 grass fields to play on for both the men and the women.
History: Our program began in 1980, and has posted a great record of over 140 wins. The Bears have qualified for the post season play 4 times since 1989 and became member of ECAC in 1998.
Achievements: Won 1998 MASCAC Coach of the Year.
Coaching: Luis Reis, Head Coach, has a USSF National "B" Coaching license and NSCAA National Coaching Diploma, Mass. He was a Youth Soccer Association State Staff Instructor, Mass Massachusetts Boys U-18 ODP State Head Coach. Justin Ciccarelli is our Assistant Coach.
Style of Play: Suited to players, opponents and conditions in general. Possession and build-up, with zonal defending both low pressure and high pressure.

Women's Athletic Profile

Department of Athletics
Bridgewater, MA 02325
Coach: Andrea Zeigler
Email: Not Available

NCAA III
Bears/Crimson, White
Phone: (508) 531-1352
Fax: (508) 531-1356

Estimated # of Women's Soccer Scholarships: None
Conference: MASCAC
Program Profile: Member of MASCAC. Home games are played at Swenson Athletic Fields which is natural grass surface. Squad competes in the fall for its traditional season. The team also has a non-traditional season in the spring.
History: The women's varsity soccer program reached varsity status in 1987. BSC women's soccer has just completed its 14th season. Although the team has never competed in the NCAA post season, it has found success on the field. In its 3rd year of varsity status in 1989 the team had its best season with a 11-2-2 record.
Achievements: 1993, 1995 MASCAC Conference Champs under former head coach Tom McGuiness. Kate Feener, All-New Englan (1998).
Coaching: Head Coach-Andrea Zeigler. The assistants are Jennifer Monaghan and Heather Elliot. Mike O'Connor is the Volunteer assistant coach.
Roster in State: 15 **Out of State:** 4 **Out of Country:** 0
Walk-on/Other: **Graduation %:** N/A **Seniors on Team:** 2
Positions Needed: Keeper, Forward
Camp or Clinic Dates: Not Available
Most Recent Record: 9-9-0
Schedule: Bowdoin, Keene State, Framingham State, Plymouth State, Worcester State, Westfield State
Style of Play: 4-4-2, like to counter, good transition from Defense to Offense and back. Simple attacking patterns which will get more complex as the game progresses.

Clark University
Academic Profile

Worcester, MA 01610

Phone: 1-800-GO-CLARK

Type: 4 Yr.,Private,Liberal Arts
Website: http://www.clarku.edu

Founded: 1887
Religion: Non-Affiliated

SAT/ACT/GPA: 1150avg/25/3.2
Housing: Yes
Student/Faculty Ratio: 12/1
Male/Female Ratio: 41:59
Undergraduate Enrollment: 1925
Graduate Enrollment: 600
Scholarships/Academic: Yes
Athletic: No
Financial Aid: Yes
Expenses by: Year
In State: $28,500
Out of State: $28,500
Specialty: Geography, Psychology, Government, International Development
Degrees Conferred: BA, MA, Ph.D.
Programs of Study: Ancient Civilization, BioChemistry, Biology, Chemistry, Communication & Culture, Comparative Literature, Computer Science, Economics, Education, Engineering, English, Environmental Science & Policy, Foreign Languages, Geography, Government, History, International Development, Management, Mathematics & Computer Science, Philosophy, Physics, Psychology, Sociology, Visual & Performing Arts

Men's Athletic Profile

950 Main Street
Worcester, MA 01610
Coach: David Kulik
Email: dkulik@clarku.edu

NCAA III
Cougars/Red, White, Black
Phone: (508) 793-7636
Fax: (508) 793-7627

Estimated # of Men's Soccer Scholarships: Academic
Conference: NEWMAC
Program Profile: Grass game field 120x80, lights fir practice and home games. No football program, soccer is the main fall sport. Long tradition of success.
History: Program began in 1921, competed in ECAC and NCAA competitions in the 80's. Joined th NEWMAC Conference in 1998.
Achievements: NCAA Tournament Participant (1982-87), ECAC New England Champ (1984)
Coaching: David Kulik Yale 1988, USSF "A" License-NSCAA Advanced National, 3 years APSL FC Greater Boston Eagles Club Coach
Roster In State: 8
Out of State: 11
Out of Country: 3
ODP State: 9
Regional: 2
National:
Walk-on/Other:
Graduation %: 100
Seniors on Team: 7
Positions Needed: ALL
Camp or Clinic Dates: Not Available
Most Recent Record: 8-9-1
Schedule: Wheaton College, Babson College, Springfield College, Trinity College, Wesleyan Univ.
Style of Play: Attack with numbers. Send backs forward from the outside. 2 forwards that play in combination. High midfield work rate combined with excellent technical level.

Women's Athletic Profile

950 Main Street
Worcester, MA 01610
Coach: Thomas Skoglund
Email: tskoglund@clarku.edu

NCAA III
Cougars/Red, White
Phone: (508) 793-7729
Fax: (508) 793-7627

Estimated # of Women's Soccer Scholarships: None
Conference: New England Athletic Conference
Program Profile: Clark plays on a natural grass field that measures 120x75 yards. We have lights and play at night. There is a year-round training program, and we host an annual indoor tournament. The team has been a very successful in the last few years. Playing season is the fall. Has a winter training season.
History: The program started in 1985. Joined the NEWMAC Conference in 1998
Achievements: Undefeated in the 1998 season, NCAA Bid, ECAC Tournament (1986,1995,1996,1999)
Roster in State: 14
Out of State: 6
Out of Country: 0

Walk-on/Other: **Graduation %:** 100 **Seniors on Team:** 9
Positions Needed: ALL
Camp or Clinic Dates: Not Available
Most Recent Record: 11-7-0
Schedule: Wheaton College, Amherst College, Wellesley College, Keene State College
Style of Play: Possession Oriented

College of the Holy Cross

Academic Profile

Phone: (508) 793-2000
Worcester, MA 01610-2395

Type: 4 Yr.,Private,Liberal Arts **Founded:** 1843
Website: http://www.holycross.edu **Religion:** Catholic-Jesuit
SAT/ACT/GPA: 1250/3.5 **Housing:** Yes
Student/Faculty Ratio: 13:1 **Male/Female Ratio:** 50:50
Undergraduate Enrollment: 2,700 **Graduate Enrollment:** N/A
Scholarships/Academic: No **Athletic:** No **Financial Aid:** Yes
Expenses by: Year **In State:** $ 31,930 **Out of State:** $ 31,930
Specialty: Liberal Arts
Degrees Conferred: BA, BS
Programs of Study: Accounting, Biology, Chemistry, Classics, Computer, Economics, English, Education, Gerontology, History, International, Math, Peace Studies, PreProfessional Programs, Religious, Sociology, Theatre

Men's Athletic Profile

One College St.
Worcester, MA 01610-2395
Coach: Elvis A. Comrie
Email: ecomrie@holycross.edu

NCAA I
Crusaders/Purple, White
Phone: (508) 793-2726
Fax: (508) 793-2309

Estimated # of Men's Soccer Scholarships: none
Conference: Patriot League
Program Profile: We have two grass fields and brand new omni-turf field. Our varsity stadium is grass field. We are a Non-Scholarship program. NCAA I, Patriot League.
History: Began play in 1965. We have been in the Patriot League since 1990. Two-time Patriot League regular season champions and we have advanced to the league tournament 5 of the last 6 years.
Achievements: Coach of the Year in 1995; all-time winningest (A) HC played professionally for ten years; played national team; All-American; Soccer America Player of the Year in 1991; won NCAA Division I National Championships against University of Connecticut in 1981; Won North American National Championships; played for Mostpelliar France in 1987-1988.
Coaching: Elvis A. Comrie is our Head Coach, (Connecticut 1982), enters his 9th season at the Holy Cross soccer program. He was chosen as the Patriot League Coach of the Year, after guiding Holy Cross to the 1995 Patriot League regular season title. A collegiate standout, Comrie was selected as the Soccer America Player of the Year after helping the University of Connecticut to the 1979 National Championship. The assistant coach is Bryant Clark.
Roster In State: 4 **Out of State:** 27 **Out of Country:** 0
ODP State: 14 **Regional:** 2 **National:** 0
Walk-on/Other: 0 **Graduation %:** N/A **Seniors on Team:** 0
Positions Needed: All
Camp or Clinic Dates: July 9-14 Resident Camp, Day camps June 26-August 21st.
Most Recent Record: 9-4-4
Schedule: Howard, Fairfield, Harvard, Hartford, Navy, University of Baltimore County
Style of Play: Very technical, we play attractive attacking soccer. Zonal defense that is very organized.

Women's Athletic Profile

One College Street
Worcester, MA 01610-2395
Coach: Mary Curtis
Email: Not Available

NCAA I
Crusaders/Royal Purple, White
Phone: (508) 793-3624
Fax: (508) 793-2309

Estimated # of Women's Soccer Scholarships: None
Conference: Patriot League
Program Profile: Year-round program. Team Utilizes both astro-turf and natural grass practice fields. Players take part in off-season strength and conditioning program under the direction of strength coach. Spring season focuses on skill development with participation in several tournaments.
History: Program began in 1983. Joined Patriot League in 1990.
Achievements: Paula Russo, 1989 All-New England and 2nd team All-American. 3 consecutive winning seasons and 3rd post-season appearance at the ECAC women's soccer championship.
Coaching: Mary Curtis, Head Coach, entering the 7thth season, 1990 graduate of the University of Mass, completed in the 4 NCAA tournaments including 2 final Four berths and one appearance in the National Championship game, played both goalkeeper and forward for the Minute women, originally form Virginia, highly successful state and regal player during HS career.
Style of Play: Attack out of the back, using speed. Play zone defense, offense utilizes 3 attackers.

Curry College

Academic Profile

Milton, MA 02186

Phone:

Type: 4 Yr.,Private,Liberal Arts
Website: http://www.curry.edu
SAT/ACT/GPA: 800 - 1000/2.5-3.0
Student/Faculty Ratio: 12/1
Undergraduate Enrollment: 1,300
Scholarships/Academic: Yes
Athletic: No
Expenses by: Year
In State: $24,785
Degrees Conferred: BA, BS

Founded: 1879
Religion: Non-Affiliated
Housing: Yes
Male/Female Ratio: 1:1
Graduate Enrollment: 200
Financial Aid: Yes
Out of State: $24,785

Programs of Study: Biology, Business Management, Chemistry, Communications, Education, English, Environmental Science, Health Education, Nursing, Philosophy, Physics, Political & History, Psychology, Sociology/Criminal Justice, Visual Arts

Men's Athletic Profile

1071 Blue Hill Avenue
Milton, MA 02186
Coach: Brendan Donahue
Email: bdonahue@curry.edu

NCAA III
Colonels/Purple, White
Phone: (617) 333-2093
Fax: Not Available

Estimated # of Men's Soccer Scholarships: None
Conference: Commonwealth Coast Conference
Program Profile: Curry is a NCAA III program. We have a 120x65 yard (grass). Since taking the program over 2 years ago, we have instituted a year round program. We will train 3 times per week in the off season while following a weight training program.
History: Program began in 1978.
Achievements: 1995-Commonwealth Coast Conference Champions.
Coaching: Brendan Donahue-USSF- Licensed.

Roster In State: 12 **Out of State:** 8 **Out of Country:** 0
ODP State: 4 **Regional:** **National:**
Walk-on/Other: **Graduation %:** N/A **Seniors on Team:** N/A
Positions Needed: Keeper, Central Defender
Camp or Clinic Dates: Not Available
Most Recent Record: 7-10-1
Schedule: Roger Williams, UMASS-Dartmouth, Gordon, Colby-Sawyer, Wentworth, Mt. Ida
Style of Play: We will play a possession style of soccer based out of a 4-4-2 or 3-5-2.

Women's Athletic Profile

1071 Blue Hill Avenue
Milton, MA 02186
Coach: Danielle Ferrara
Email: dferrara@curry.edu

NCAA III
Colonels/Purple, White
Phone: (617) 333-2377
Fax: (617) 364-2027

Estimated # of Women's Soccer Scholarships: None
Conference: ECAC, MAIAW, Commonwealth Coast Conference
Program Profile: Natural field
History: Program began in 1979. NCAA Tournament qualifiers 86-87. State runners up 1995, State champs 84, 5 All-Americans, 2 Academic All-Americans, CCC Champs 1991-92.
Achievements: Graduate of Salem State College 1994; 4 year soccer NCAA Tournament qualifiers 1986, 1987. State runners-up 1995. State Champs 1984. 5 All-Americans, 2 Academic All-Americans. Commonwealth Coast conference Champs 1991,92. 11 CCC 1st Team, 7 CCC 2nd team.
Roster in State: 14 **Out of State:** 6 **Out of Country:**
Walk-on/Other: **Graduation %:** 100 **Seniors on Team:** 3
Positions Needed: Center mid, striker
Camp or Clinic Dates: Not Available
Schedule: University of New England, Gordon College, Ann-Marie, Roger Williams University.
Style of Play: Short passing, slow build up, mostly 4-3-3, and 4-4-2, fast and patient.

Eastern Nazarene College

Academic Profile

Quincy, MA 02170

Phone: 1-617-745-3639

Type: 4 Yr.,Private,Liberal Arts
Website: http://www.enc.edu
SAT/ACT/GPA: 960
Student/Faculty Ratio: 12:1
Undergraduate Enrollment: 646
Scholarships/Academic: Yes **Athletic:** No
Expenses by: Year **In State:** $18,612
Degrees Conferred: BA, BS, MA, MS
Programs of Study: For more information go to www.enc.edu

Founded: 1900
Religion: Nazarene
Housing: Yes
Male/Female Ratio: 45:55
Graduate Enrollment: 119
Financial Aid: Yes
Out of State: $18,612

Men's Athletic Profile

23 East Elm Avenue
Quincy, MA 02170-2999
Coach: David Cawthorne
Email: cawthord.edu

NCAA III
Crusaders/Red, White
Phone: (617) 745-3641
Fax: (617) 745-3640

Estimated # of Men's Soccer Scholarships: None
Conference: Commonwealth Coach Athletic Conference
Program Profile: Games are played at Bradley field which is a grass facility seating 750. Season consists of 18 games in Sept. - Oct. Off-season consists of indoor and weight training. All home games are televised on cable television.
History: Program began in 1963.
Coaching: David Cawthorne, Head Coach.
Style of Play: Build - up, attack wings, aggressive.

Elms College

Academic Profile

Phone:

, MA 01013-2839

Type: 4 Yr.,Private
Founded: 1928
Website: http://www.elms.edu
Religion: Catholic
SAT/ACT/GPA: 900+
Housing: No
Student/Faculty Ratio: 14:1
Male/Female Ratio: Women
Undergraduate Enrollment: 980
Graduate Enrollment: 180
Scholarships/Academic: Yes **Athletic:** No **Financial Aid:** Yes
Expenses by: Year **In State:** $17,000 **Out of State:** $ 17,000
Degrees Conferred: AA, BA
Programs of Study: Accounting, American Studies, Applied Art, Applied Mathematics, Art, Art Education, BioChemistry, Biology, BioMedical Science, Business Administration & Management, Chemistry, Commercial Art, Computer Science, Early Childhood Education, Education, Economics, English, French, Graphics Design, History, Mathematics, International Business, Liberal Arts, Marketing, Medical Laboratory Technology, Natural Science, Nursing, Philosophy, PreDentistry, PreLaw, PreMed, Social Science, Social Work, Sociology, Spanish, Speech, Pathology

Women's Athletic Profile

291 Springfield Street
Chicopee, MA 01013-2839
Coach: John Amaral
Email: Not Available

NCAA III
Blazers/Green, White
Phone: (413) 594-9474
Fax:

Estimated # of Women's Soccer Scholarships: None
Conference: ECAC, MAIAW
Program Profile: We play a 19 game competitive New England schedule. Elms opened a new athletic facility Sept. 1994.
History: Program began in 1986.
Coaching: John Amaral, Head Coach since 1994

Emerson College

Academic Profile

Phone: 617-824-8609

Boston, MA 02116

Type: 4 Yr.,Private,Liberal Arts
Founded: 1880
Website: http://www.emerson.edu
Religion: Independent
SAT/ACT/GPA: 1040-1240
Housing: Yes
Student/Faculty Ratio: 17:1
Male/Female Ratio: 45:55
Undergraduate Enrollment: 2,600
Graduate Enrollment: 1,000
Scholarships/Academic: Yes **Athletic:** No **Financial Aid:** Yes
Expenses by: Year **In State:** $ 27,620 **Out of State:**

Specialty: Communications, Performing Arts
Degrees Conferred: BA, BS, BFA, BLI, BM, BSSP, MA, MS, MFA, Ph.D.
Programs of Study: Advertising, Broadcasting, Communication Disorders, Communications, Creative Writing, Dance, Film Arts, Literature, PreLaw, Public Relations, Publishing, Radio & Television, Speech, Speech Pathology, Theatre

Men's Athletic Profile

100 Beacon Street
Boston, MA 02116
Coach: Graham Stafford
Email: emersonsoccer@aol.com

NCAA III
Lions/Gold, Purple
Phone: (617) 824-8498
Fax: (617) 824-8529

Estimated # of Men's Soccer Scholarships: None
Conference: Great Northeast Athletic Conference
Program Profile: Currently play on turf field at East Boston stadium (approx 3000 capacity) although a move to a grass location is possible for 2001. Boasts a 10,000 sq foot fitness center with impressive year round training opportunities. Professional fitness staff supplied by "Fit-Corp" provides top quality injury treatment, rehabilitation and training consultation. Fall GNAC and NCAA season supplemented by year round league play.
History: Program began in 1982 with Emerson being a charter member of the GNAC league. New coach has recently added great potential and ambition to the program.
Achievements: Conference finalists 1998.
Coaching: Graham Stafford just completed first season as head coach. Hails from London, England. BA HONS in teaching/coaching. Works as full time professional coach for a major private soccer company.
Roster In State: 5 **Out of State:** 13 **Out of Country:** 0
ODP State: 3 **Regional:** 0 **National:** 0
Walk-on/Other: 0 **Graduation %:** 100 **Seniors on Team:** 2
Positions Needed: Always open but specifically GK,MF
Camp or Clinic Dates: TBA
Most Recent Record: 6-10-0
Schedule: Norwich Univ (VT), Rivier (NH), Johnson and Wales (RI), Albertus Magnus (CT), Mount Ida (MA) Western New England (NH)
Style of Play: Adapted to squad strengths. Follows general principles of possession to unbalance opposition, counter attack and flank-play.

Women's Athletic Profile

100 Beacon Street
Boston, MA 02116
Coach: Kristen Parnell
Email: kristin_parnell@emerson.edu

NCAA III
Lions/Purple, Black, White
Phone: (617) 824-8905
Fax: (617) 824-8529

Estimated # of Women's Soccer Scholarships: None
Conference: Great Northeast Athletic Conference
Program Profile: 3rd year under Kristin Parnell. The team has improved every year, adding more games and harder competition. Pre-season 2000 is going to be held in the Netherlands at an Emerson owned castle.
History: The program began in 1988.
Achievements: 1998 team took 2nd in the GNAC playoffs. Also, invited to the Mass. Association for Intercollegiate Athletics for Women Post Season Tournament. 1999 team made the post season playoffs, but lost to the eventual conference champions.
Coaching: The head coach is a full time position, that is combined with Senior Women's Administrator. Playing experience- American International College 1992, Division II, Conference All Star and All New England. Assistant Coach- Michelle Duff, Played at Wesleyan University 1996.
Roster in State: 5 **Out of State:** 12 **Out of Country:**

ODP State: 2 **Regional:** **National:**
Walk-on/Other: **Graduation %:** 100 **Seniors on Team:** 5
Positions Needed: Forwards and defenders
Camp or Clinic Dates: Not Available
Most Recent Record: 9-10
Schedule: MIT, Norwich, Mt. Halyoke, Western New England, Simmon, St. Joseph's
Style of Play: Combination of diamond defense and flat defense, depending on the match up with other team. Offensively a great deal of high pressure, causing a large number of shots on goal.

Endicott College

Academic Profile

Beverly, MA 01915
Phone: (978) 232-2305

Type: 4 Yr.,Private
Founded: 1939
Website: http://www.endicott.edu
Religion: Non-Affiliated
SAT/ACT/GPA: Required for Admission
Housing: Yes
Student/Faculty Ratio: 13:1
Male/Female Ratio: 30:70
Undergraduate Enrollment: 1,200
Graduate Enrollment: 100
Scholarships/Academic: Yes **Athletic:** No **Financial Aid:** Yes
Expenses by: Year **In State:** $ 21,966 **Out of State:** $ 21,966
Specialty: Liberal & Preprofessional Programs, Required Internship
Degrees Conferred: BA, BS, M.Ed.
Programs of Study: Advertising, American Studies, Athletic Training, Business Administration, Communications, Creative Arts Therapy, Criminal Justice, Early Childhood Education, Elementary Education, Entrepreneurial Studies, Fine Arts, Visual Communications, Hotel/Restaurant/Travel/Administration, Interior Design, International Business, Liberal Studies, Management, Marketing, Nursing, Physical Education, Psychology, Sport Management, Physical Therapy Assistant

Men's Athletic Profile

376 Hale Street
Beverly, MA 01915
Coach: Mike Kersker
Email: Not Available

NCAA III
Power Gulls/Navy Blue, Green
Phone: (978) 232-2308
Fax: (978) 232-2600

Estimated # of Men's Soccer Scholarships: N/A
Conference: Commonwealth Coastal Conference
Program Profile: Training is at night under the lights. Playing season is in late August 23 through the beginning of November on natural grass field.
History: This is the sixth year of the program.
Achievements: 1997 GNAL Regular season Champions, and Coach of the Year; 1998 GNAL Conference Champion, Coach of the year, and CCC Semi-Finalist; one player 2nd team NSCAA All-Region team.
Coaching: Mike Kersker, Head Coach. Jared Scarpcei - Assistant Coach. Ryan Davis - Goalie Coach.
Roster In State: 15 **Out of State:** 10 **Out of Country:**
Walk-on/Other: **Graduation %:** 100 **Seniors on Team:** 7
Camp or Clinic Dates: July 31 - August 4
Most Recent Record: 8-12
Schedule: Salem State, Whenton (MA), Babson College, Brandeis College, Alfred University
Style of Play: Structure style towards strength of players.

Women's Athletic Profile

376 Hale Street
Beverly, MA 01915
Coach: Dina Gentile
Email: murphy@endicott.edu

NCAA III
Power Gulls/R. Blue, K. Green
Phone: (978) 232-2430
Fax: (978) 232-2600

Estimated # of Women's Soccer Scholarships: N/A
Conference: Commonwealth Coast Conference (CCC)
Program Profile: We play on a natural field, which has lights for night games. The team will start their inaugural season in the CCC where the champions receive an automatic bid to the NCAA tournament. In six years, the team record is 53-32-2.
History: Seventh year coach Dina Gentile returns a strong nucleus of veterans who have completed in several preseason and post season tournaments. We were 1997 Champions and 1998 second place the Great Northeast Athletic Conference. The Gulls begin a new quest for success in the CCC.
Achievements: Coach of the Year 1997-99, Conference Title 1997-99, All-New England Selections
Coaching: Dina Gentile, Head Coach, was named Coach of the Year in 1997. She is a 1992 graduate of Adelphi University.
Roster in State: 6 **Out of State:** 16 **Out of Country:** 0
ODP State: 10 **Regional:** 3 **National:**
Walk-on/Other: **Graduation %:** 100 **Seniors on Team:**
Camp or Clinic Dates: July 16-20, 2001
Most Recent Record: 12-5-2
Schedule: Keene State, Salem State, Univ. of New England
Style of Play: Solid defensive structure which is the spark for a quick attacking midfield and forward line. The team is built around precise passing and quick counter attacks.

Fitchburg State College

Academic Profile

Fitchburg, MA 01420

Phone:

Type: 4 Yr.,Public,Liberal Arts
Website: http://www.fsc.edu
SAT/ACT/GPA: 1090/2.0
Student/Faculty Ratio: 13:1
Undergraduate Enrollment: 2,700
Scholarships/Academic: Yes **Athletic:** No **Financial Aid:** Yes
Expenses by: Year **In State:** $ 8,400 **Out of State:** $ 14,450

Founded: 1894
Religion: Non-Affiliated
Housing: Yes
Male/Female Ratio: 45:55
Graduate Enrollment: 3,000

Specialty: Communications, Nursing, Education, Business
Degrees Conferred: BA, BS, BSEd, MA, MS, M.Ed.
Programs of Study: Biology, Business Administration, Clinical Laboratory Science, Communications, Computer Information Systems, Computer Science, Criminal Justice, Economics, Education, Secondary Education, English, Environmental Science, Fitness Management, General Studies, Geography, History, Human Services, Industrial Technology, Mathematics, Nursing, Political Science, Psychology, Sociology, Theatre, Undeclared

Men's Athletic Profile

160 Pearl Street
Fitchburg, MA 01420
Coach: Ken Min
Email: kmorin@fsc.edu

NCAA III
Falcons/Green, Gold
Phone: (978) 665-4683
Fax: (978) 665-3710

Estimated # of Men's Soccer Scholarships: None
Conference: MASCAC
Program Profile: Play a Rober Elliot Field, provides a beautiful Fall setting for soccer.
History:
Achievements: MASCAC title 1988 and earned automatic bid to NCAA tournament. All-Americans.

Women's Athletic Profile

160 Pearl Street
Fitchburg, MA 01420
Coach: Tom McGuinness
Email: TMACTOM@aol.com

NCAA III
Falcons/Green, White, Gold
Phone: (978) 665-4695
Fax: (508) 343-6833

Estimated # of Women's Soccer Scholarships: None
Conference: MASCAC

Framingham State College

Academic Profile

Framingham, MA 01701-9101

Phone:

Type: 4 Yr.,Public,Liberal Arts
Website: http://www.framingham.edu
SAT/ACT/GPA: 900
Student/Faculty Ratio: 17:1
Undergraduate Enrollment: 3,000
Scholarships/Academic: Yes
Athletic: No
Expenses by: Year
In State: $ 5,364
Specialty: Education
Degrees Conferred: BA, BS, MA, MS

Founded: 1839
Religion: Non-Affiliated
Housing: No
Male/Female Ratio: 1:3
Graduate Enrollment: 600
Financial Aid: Yes
Out of State: $ 9,412

Programs of Study: Accounting, Art, Biology, Business Administration, Chemistry, Communications, Computer Science, Construction Technology, Economics, Education, English, Environmental Science, Film Studies, Geography, Graphic Art, History, Human Services, Industrial Engineering, Literature, Management, Manufacturing Technology, Marketing, Mathematics, Medical Technology, Nursing, Photography, PreLaw, PreMed, Psychology, Sociology, Radio & Television, Special Education

Men's Athletic Profile

100 State Street
Framingham, MA 01701
Coach: John Ludgate
Email: Not Available

NCAA III
Rams/Black, Gold
Phone: (508) 626-4614
Fax: (508) 626-4069

Estimated # of Men's Soccer Scholarships: None
Conference: Massachusetts State Collegiate Athletic Conference
Program Profile: Play a full season which runs from Sept to Oct. The field is grass and seats 1,500
History: Program began in 1968.

Women's Athletic Profile

100 State Street
Framingham, MA 01701-9101
Coach: Sarah Behn
Email: bchncamp@aol.com

NCAA III
Rams/Black, Gold
Phone: (508) 626-4614
Fax: (508) 626-4069

Estimated # of Women's Soccer Scholarships: None
Conference: Massachusetts State College Athletic Conference
Program Profile: The home field is Maple Street Field which has natural grass and a capacity of 800.
History: The program began in 1982. IN 1999 we were the MASCAC Champions and made a NCAA Tournament Appearance.
Achievements: Jr. Nicole Abbott-Player of the Year 1998; Fr. Kristine O' Coin- Rookie of the Year and All-New England 1999; Sarah Behn Coach of the Year
Coaching:
Roster in State: 20
Walk-on/Other: **Graduation %:** 100
Camp or Clinic Dates: Not Available
Most Recent Record: 15-5
Schedule: Wheaton, Salem State

Gordon College

Academic Profile

Wenham, MA 01984
Phone:

Type: 4 Yr.,Private,Liberal Arts
Founded: 1889
Website: http://www.gordonc.edu
Religion: Non-Denominational
SAT/ACT/GPA: 1300
Housing: Yes
Student/Faculty Ratio: 14:1
Male/Female Ratio: 40:60
Undergraduate Enrollment: 1,500
Graduate Enrollment: N/A
Scholarships/Academic: Yes **Athletic:** No **Financial Aid:** No
Expenses by: Year **In State:** $ 21,000 **Out of State:** $ 21,000
Degrees Conferred: BA, BM, MEd
Programs of Study: Accounting, Allied Health, Biology, Business Administration, Chemistry, Communication Arts, Computer Science, Early Childhood Education, Economics, Elementary Education, English, French, International Affairs, Mathematics, Philosophy, Physics, Political Science, Psychology, Sociology, Social Work

Men's Athletic Profile

255 Grapevine Road
Wenham, MA 01984
Coach: Marc Whitehouse
Email: whitehouse@hope.Gordon.edu
NCAA III
Fighting Scots/Blue, White, Gold
Phone: (978) 927-2306
Fax: (978) 524-3000
Estimated # of Men's Soccer Scholarships: None
Conference: Commonwealth Coast Conference
Program Profile: Our field is natural grass with a measurements of 120x80 yards and located in the center of the campus. We built a new gym in 1996. Our program includes and varsity and a junior varsity team and our season is from September to Mid November.
History: The program began in 1960. In 1983 and 1984 we were in the NAIA finals and Runner-ups in the Conference Championships in 1999.
Achievements: Four Time Commonwealth Coast Conference Coach of the Year and three time Coach of the year for NAIA. The Scots also have had 7 All-Americans and 15 All-New England Players
Coaching: Marc Whitehouse is our Head Coach with Jason Martinez assisting him. Tom Card is the JV coach.
Roster In State: 7 **Out of State:** 11 **Out of Country:** 3
Walk-on/Other: **Graduation %:** 98 **Seniors on Team:** 4
Positions Needed: Striker, Keeper, Mid-field
Camp or Clinic Dates: July 17-21, 24-28
Most Recent Record: 14-7-0
Schedule: Babson, Brandeis, Wheaton, MA, Roger Williams, Salve Regina, Tufts University, Salem State
Style of Play: Strong defensively, attacking style from the wings.

Women's Athletic Profile

255 Grapevine Road
Wenham, MA 01984-1899
Coach: Rick Burns
Email: rburns@hope.gordon.edu

NCAA III
Fighting Scots/Blue, White, Gold
Phone: (508) 927-2306
Fax: (508) 524-3000

Estimated # of Women's Soccer Scholarships: None
Conference: Commonwealth Coast Conference, ECAC
Program Profile: Playing field is on quad in the center of a beautiful campus. Field is a natural turf.. Our playing season is in the fall. Has been to the NCAA Division III. Varsity and JV; September-mid November.
History: The program began in 1992 and has a record of 8-5-0, in 1993 has a record of 13-1-0, and in 1994 record was 16-3. 4 ECAC appearances, 2 time conference champions
Achievements: ECAC Tournament in third season; 1st All-American in 1994: Becky Craig, Senior Midfielder Third Team. 3 ECAC bids; 3 Conference titles, numerous All-New England Players. 4 time conference coach of the year. NAIA district 13 coach of the year. Minnesota Internally athletic conference coach of the year.
Coaching: Rick Burns is our Head Coach. He is entering first year at Gordon and has 18 years overall coaching experience. He compiled an overall record of 186-123-16. Assistant Coach is to be named.
Roster in State: 3 **Out of State:** 17 **Out of Country:** 0
Walk-on/Other: **Graduation %:** 99 **Seniors on Team:** 8
Positions Needed: keeper, defender, striker
Camp or Clinic Dates: July 17-21; July 24-28, 2000
Most Recent Record: 9-7-2
Schedule: MIT, Tufts, University of New England, Bates, Salem State
Style of Play: Possession

Harvard University

Academic Profile

Cambridge, MA 02138
Phone:

Type: 4 Yr.,Private,Liberal Arts
Founded: 1636
Website: http://www.harvard.edu
Religion: Non-Affiliated
SAT/ACT/GPA: Competitive
Housing: Yes
Student/Faculty Ratio: 11:1
Male/Female Ratio: 48:52
Undergraduate Enrollment: 6,400
Graduate Enrollment: N/A
Scholarships/Academic: Yes **Athletic:** No **Financial Aid:** Yes
Expenses by: Year **In State:** $ 33,000 **Out of State:** $ 33,000
Specialty: Liberal Arts, Premed
Degrees Conferred: All
Programs of Study: Biology, Economics, Government, BioChemistry, Computer Science, English, Psychology, Sociology, Anthropology, Philosophy, Social Studies, Chemistry, African American Studies, History and Literature, History of Science

Men's Athletic Profile

65 N. Harvard Street
Boston, MA 02163
Coach: John Kerr
Email: jkerr@fas.harvard.edu

NCAA I
Crimson/Crimson, Black, White
Phone: (617) 495-4549
Fax: (617) 496-3371

Estimated # of Men's Soccer Scholarships: Need Based
Conference: Ivy League Conference

Program Profile: The Crimson play a tough schedule including 5 teams who competed in the 2000 NCAA Playoffs. Ohiri field consists of a 120x75 natural grass pitch for matches and an additional one for practice.
History: On April 1, 1905, Harvard played in the first collegiate soccer game in history against Haverford College, NCAA semi-fianlist in 1986 and 1987.
Achievements: 11 Ivy league titles with the most recent in 1994 & 1996. Harvard's two 1997 Ivy League players of the year were both drafted into the MLS.
Coaching: John Kerr, Duke 1986 National Championship Team and Herman Trophy Winner 1986, played professionally in England and in the MLS.

Roster In State: 4	**Out of State:** 22	**Out of Country:** 2
ODP State: 8	**Regional:** 3	**National:**
Walk-on/Other:	**Graduation %:** 100	**Seniors on Team:** 3

Positions Needed: Forwards
Camp or Clinic Dates: Not Available
Most Recent Record: 7-9-1
Schedule: Stanford, Boston College, Brown, Dartmouth, Vermont, Yale
Style of Play: Possession, attacking style of play.

Women's Athletic Profile

Murr Center 65 Northharvard St.
Cambridge, MA 02138
Coach: Tim Wheaton
Email: twheaton@fas.harvard.edu

NCAA I
The Crimson/Crimson, White
Phone: (617) 495-3776
Fax: (617) 495-3371

Estimated # of Women's Soccer Scholarships: None
Conference: Ivy League
Program Profile: Play all home games on natural grass field, separate natural grass practice facilities. Players represent all areas of the country, most with state team level experience or higher.
History: We are one of the first women's Division I intercollegiate national championships. Traditionally one of the Top teams in New England. 7 times Ivy league Champions since 1978. We have qualified for the NCAA tournament 6 out of the last 7 years. We are presently ranked 18th in the Country.
Achievements: Head Coach Tim Wheaton finishes his 2000 season with a record of 134-69-19. In 1999 Tim was named Soccer Buzz National Coach of the Year and NSCAA/Adidas Northeast Region Coach of the Year. Tim has been the Head Coach at Harvard for 14 seasons. 2000 3 All-American.
Coaching: Tim Wheaton, Head Coach, holds a USSF Coaching license and NSCAA National License, USSF Region I coaching staff, Director, girls ODP for Mass.

Roster in State: 28	**Out of State:** 21	**Out of Country:** 0
ODP State: 4	**Regional:** 15	**National:** 4
Walk-on/Other: 5	**Graduation %:** 100	**Seniors on Team:** 5

Positions Needed: Defense, Forward
Most Recent Record: 12-8-0
Schedule: Penn State, Univ. of Connecticut, Dartmouth College, Univ. of Hartford, Boston Univ. Princeton
Style of Play: Dynamic, creative with numbers, and push to attack.

Lesley College
Academic Profile

Phone:

Cambridge, MA 02138

Type: 4 Yr.	**Founded:**
Website: http://www.lesley.edu	**Religion:** Non-Affiliated
SAT/ACT/GPA: Open	**Housing:** No
Student/Faculty Ratio:	**Male/Female Ratio:**

Undergraduate Enrollment: N/A **Graduate Enrollment:** N/A
Scholarships/Academic: **Athletic:** **Financial Aid:**
Expenses by: **In State:** **Out of State:**
Degrees Conferred:
Programs of Study: Contact school for programs of study.

Women's Athletic Profile

29 Everette St.
Cambridge, MA 02138
Coach: Irene Honnors
Email: svieina@mail.lesley.edu

NCAA III
Lynx/Forest Green, Gold
Phone: (617) 349-8498
Fax: (617) 349-8558

Estimated # of Women's Soccer Scholarships: None
Conference: North Atlantic Conference
Program Profile: We play our home games at Bunker Hill Community College on a natural grass field.
History: We have a new program that just began only 5 years ago.
Achievements: None
Coaching: Irene Honors is the Head Coach. This is her first coaching position. She has a strong knowledge of the game and was a varsity starter at University of Massachusetts at Dartmouth.
Roster in State: 7 **Out of State:** 7 **Out of Country:**
ODP State: 2 **Regional:** **National:**
Walk-on/Other: **Graduation %:** 95 **Seniors on Team:** 1
Positions Needed: Defense, Striker
Camp or Clinic Dates: Not Available
Most Recent Record: 0-14-0
Schedule: Suny Farmingdale, Eastern Nazarene, Notre Dame college, Bechen College, Lasell College, Mt. Ida College
Style of Play: Defense style this past season but looking for more offensive game this coming season. Very young team, mainly freshman and sophomores.

Massachusetts College (N Adams St. C)

Academic Profile

North Adams, MA 01247

Phone:

Type: 4 Yr.,Public,Liberal Arts **Founded:** 1894
Website: http://www.mcla.mass.edu **Religion:** Non-Affiliated
SAT/ACT/GPA: 1000/2.7 **Housing:** Yes
Student/Faculty Ratio: 14:1 **Male/Female Ratio:** 1:1
Undergraduate Enrollment: 1,500 **Graduate Enrollment:** 150
Scholarships/Academic: Yes **Athletic:** No **Financial Aid:** Yes
Expenses by: Year **In State:** $ 8,258 **Out of State:** $ 13,498
Specialty: Liberal Arts with professional program
Degrees Conferred: BA, BS, MEd
Programs of Study: Biology, Business Administration, Computer Science, Education, English, Communications, Fine and Performing Arts, History, Math, Philosophy, Physics, Psychology, Sociology

Men's Athletic Profile

375 Church Street
North Adams, MA 01201
Coach: Ron Shewcraft
Email: rshewcrh@mcla.mass.edu

NCAA III
Mohawks/Navy Blue, Gold
Phone: (413) 662-5354
Fax: (413) 662-5357

Estimated # of Men's Soccer Scholarships:
Conference: Massachusetts College State Conference
Program Profile: We are a NCAA Division III program, that is very competitive regionally and nationally. We have an outstanding playing facility, "men's soccer only" with a measurement of 120x75 and is a natural grass field. Facilities include a press box and an electronic scoreboard. We have a year-round playing and training schedule (fall, spring-outdoor and winter-indoor).
History: The program began in 1971; no losing season in 27 years in a row; 7 NCAA Tournament Appearances; 8 ECAC Tournament Appearances; Final Four NCAA division III in 1977.
Achievements: 22 players have been named All-Region, 2 All-Americans, and 3 have played professionally.
Coaching: Ron Shewcraft, Head Coach, is entering his twenty second year with the program. He compiled a record of 244-106-35. His squads have appeared in post-season play 10 times in 21 seasons. He was named New England Coach of the Year in 1978 & 1986. He had the NSCAA Advanced National Coaching License. Paul Cushion, Assistant Coach, is entering his fourth season with the program.
Style of Play: Will vary according to our own player's strength and abilities. Prefer to play through midfielder in attack. Will defend zonally or man markers based upon situation. Very competitive Division III team that can compete with Division II and mid level Division I teams.

Women's Athletic Profile

Athletics Office
North Adams, MA 01247
Coach: Chris Flint
Email: cflint@nasc.mass.edu

NCAA III
Mohawks/Blue, Gold
Phone: (413) 662-5355
Fax: (413) 662-5357

Estimated # of Women's Soccer Scholarships: None
Conference: Massachusetts State College Athletic Conference
Program Profile: The fall program is twelve weeks long and the spring program is ten weeks long. Play on a natural grass surface.
History: The program began in 1984.
Achievements: MASAC champions and post-season play in the ECAC Tournament in 1987, 1989, and 1994. ECAC Champions in 1987 and 1989. Kate Kelley named Adidas Division III Goalkeeper of the Year in 1994.
Coaching: Chris Flint, Head Coach, BA at Colby College, in 1992, MPE at Springfield College in 1995, NSCAA Nationals in 1997. Candace Casucci - Assistant Coach, BS at Roger Williams in 1993.
Style of Play: An attacking style, but also a possession oriented game. 4-3-3 or 3-5-2 formation.

Massachusetts Institute of Technology (MIT)

Academic Profile

Cambridge, MA 02139

Phone: 617-253-1000

Type: 4 Yr.,Private,Liberal Arts,Engineering
Website: http://www.web.mit.edu
SAT/ACT/GPA:
Student/Faculty Ratio: 4:1
Undergraduate Enrollment: 5,500
Scholarships/Academic: No **Athletic:** No
Expenses by: Year **In State:** $ 36,600

Founded: 1861
Religion: Non-Affiliated
Housing: Yes
Male/Female Ratio: 56:44
Graduate Enrollment: 4,000
Financial Aid: Yes
Out of State: $ 36,600

Specialty: Engineering, Science, Humanities, Social Sciences, Architecture
Degrees Conferred: BA, BS, MBA, MS, PhD
Programs of Study: Aero/Astro Engineering, Chemical Engineering, Civil Engineering, Environmental Engineering, Electrical Engineering, Mechanical Engineering, Nuclear Engineering, Computer Science, Biology, Chemistry, Mathematics, Physics, Anthropology, Asian Studies, Economics, Film, Foreign Languages, History, Literature, Music, Philosophy Political, Latin American Studies, Woman's Studies, Writing, Architectural Design, Building Technology, Visual Arts, Management, Information Technology, Operations Research, Finance and Marketing Research

Men's Athletic Profile

MIT Branch, PO Box D
Cambridge, MA 02139
Coach: Walter Alessi
Email: waalessi@mit.edu

NCAA III
Engineers, Beavers/Cardinal
Phone: (617) 258-5782
Fax: (617) 258-7343

Estimated # of Men's Soccer Scholarships: None
Conference: NEWMAC
Program Profile: The home field is a natural grass that seats 1,2000. for 1996 we have 15 lettermen returning. We need to improve our team defense and get more consistently play on the weekdays. We could use more depth in the goal and on the front line.
History: Our program began in 1921. In 1995 the team won the most games in the school's history (74 years), posted five shutouts, the most since 1986.
Achievements: 1991 Academic All-American, 3 All-League in 1994, 1 1st team All-League in 1994, 2 2nd team All-League in 1995, 1 NEC All-Star in 1990, ranked #7 in the South Central Region, #5 in the New England, and #9 in the Metro Region in 1995. Won 1995 first Annual Union Invitational Tournament.
Coaching: Walter Alessi, Head Coach, entering 24 years. John Paceni - Assistant Coach, entering third year. Matt Dietrich - Assistant Coach - entering third year.
Style of Play: Ball control with counters; in the last four years used the 3-5-2 alignment.

Women's Athletic Profile

MIT Box D
Cambridge, MA 02139
Coach: Melissa Hart
Email: Not Available

NCAA III
Beavers/Engineers/Cardinal
Phone: (617) 253-5006
Fax: (617) 258-7343

Estimated # of Women's Soccer Scholarships: None
Conference: NEWMAC
Program Profile: Competitive DIII soccer program in New England. Facilities include home grass stadium, as well as multiple grass practice soccer fields. Have artificial turf but only practice on it to prepare for away turf games.
History: Program began as club team in the early 80's. In 1986 got varsity status, has improved from a weak-average program to a very competitive Program. NEWMAC Conference of which MIT is part, is one of the strongest Women's soccer D III conferences in the Northeast.
Achievements: Each year there has been at least one player named to All-Conference honors. In NEWMAC the past two years there have been two.

Roster in State: 2	**Out of State:** 18	**Out of Country:** 2
ODP State: 4	**Regional:** 2	**National:**
Walk-on/Other:	**Graduation %:** 100	**Seniors on Team:** 3

Positions Needed: ALL
Camp or Clinic Dates: Not Available
Most Recent Record: 12-6-0
Schedule: Wheaton College (MA), Wellesley College, Springfield College, Clark Univ., Babson College, Gordon College.
Style of Play: Aggressive possession soccer. Utilize all players on the field to possess and control ball, attack can come from anywhere. Work to move ball around and change point of attack to exploit opponent's defense.

Massachusetts Maritime Academy

Academic Profile

Buzzards Bay, MA 02532

Phone:

Type: 4 Yr.,Public,Engineering
Website: Not Available

Founded: 1891
Religion: Non-Affiliated

SAT/ACT/GPA: Open
Housing: Yes
Student/Faculty Ratio: 14:1
Male/Female Ratio: 7:1
Undergraduate Enrollment: 750
Graduate Enrollment: N/A
Scholarships/Academic: Yes
Athletic: No
Financial Aid: Yes
Expenses by: Year
In State: $ 7,253
Out of State: $ 12,763
Specialty: Marine Engineering, Environmental Protection, Marine transportation
Degrees Conferred: BS
Programs of Study: Environment Protection, Facilities Engineering, Marine Engineering, Marine Safety, Marine Transportation

Men's Athletic Profile

101 Academy Dr.
Buzzards Bay, MA 02532
Coach: Greg Perry
Email: S.Thompson@mmm.edu
NCAA III
Buccaneers/Navy, Gold
Phone: (508) 830-5000
Fax: (508) 830-5056

Estimated # of Men's Soccer Scholarships: yes
Conference: Massachusetts State College Athletic Conference (MASCAC)
Program Profile: Games are played on natural grass, stadium field, season consists of 18 games.
History: 28th season
Achievements: 8 All-Conference players over the past seven years; Coach of the Year 1999.
Coaching: Greg Perry, Head Coach.
Roster In State: 10
Out of State: 8
Out of Country: 2
ODP State: 1
Regional:
National:
Walk-on/Other: 3
Graduation %: 100
Seniors on Team: 4
Positions Needed: Forwards, Backs
Camp or Clinic Dates: Not Available
Most Recent Record: 10-6-1
Schedule: Salem State, Westfield State, University of Massachusetts-Boston, Massachusetts College, University of Massachusetts-Dartmouth, Bridgewater State
Style of Play: Attack from the back.

Merrimack College
Academic Profile

North Andover, MA 01845
Phone: (978) 837-5345

Type: 4 Yr.,Private,Liberal Arts
Founded: 1947
Website: http://www.merrimack.edu
Religion: Catholic
SAT/ACT/GPA: 820/17
Housing: Yes
Student/Faculty Ratio: 14/1
Male/Female Ratio: 40/60
Undergraduate Enrollment: 2,200
Graduate Enrollment: N/A
Scholarships/Academic: Yes
Athletic: Yes
Financial Aid: Yes
Expenses by: Year
In State: $ 22,050
Out of State: $ 22,050
Specialty: Business, Science, Liberal Arts
Degrees Conferred: BA, BS, M.Ed.
Programs of Study: Liberal Arts (Communications, Economics, English, Fine Arts, French, History, Philosophy, Political Science, Psychology, Religion, Sociology, Spanish), Business Administration (Accounting, Finance, Business Economics, International Business, Management, Marketing), Sciences & Engineering (BioChemistry, Biology, Chemistry, Civil Engineering, Computer Science, Electrical Engineering, Environmental Science, Health Science, Math, Physics, Sport Medicine, Athletic Training, Exercise Physiology, PrePhysical Therapy)

Men's Athletic Profile

315 Turnpike Road
North Andover, MA 01845
Coach: Tony Martone
Email: Not Available

NCAA II
Warriors/Navy, Gold
Phone: (978) 837-4221
Fax: (978) 837-5079

Estimated # of Men's Soccer Scholarships: none
Conference: Northeast 10 Conference
Program Profile: The natural grass playing field has stadium seating for 1,000. There us a weight room and a cardio-vascular fitness training area. Merrimack has a lighted practice field and indoor facilities for off-season training.
History: Our program began in 1970 and has been led by 2 time Coach of the Year, Tony Martone, for the past 18 years. The program has won the regular season NE-10 conference twice and been to the NE-10 Conference Championship twice. The 2000 season was the beginning of a rebuilding period with 11 freshman and only 1 senior.
Achievements: The program has graduated a number of All American Academic and the E.C.A.C. Robbins Scholar-Athlete of the year in 1999. Our roster of graduating players include current and former professional athletes.
Coaching: Tony Martone, has been the head coach for Merrimack for 18 years. He was selected as "Coach of the year", two times in conference and once for region. He has coached professionally in ASL and USISL. Coaching includes many great area select and All-Star teams. Coach Martone is currently the Men's State Coach of Mass. He has played at the college, semi-pro, and pro-levels. Other accomplishments includes holding a USSF "A" License, NSCAA National Diploma; current Scout for New England Revelation for Major League Soccer.

Roster In State: 20	**Out of State:** 5	**Out of Country:** 0
ODP State: 9	**Regional:** 2	**National:** 0
Walk-on/Other: 0	**Graduation %:** 100	**Seniors on Team:** 1

Positions Needed: Keeper, Midfield, Forwards, Backs
Camp or Clinic Dates: None
Most Recent Record: 7-11-0
Schedule: Southern Connecticut, L.I.U. Southampton, New Hampshire College, Frankin Pierce, St. Anselm, New Haven and Concordia
Style of Play: The Merrimack Warriors play a very controlled game, keeping the ball on the ground and building up from the backfield.

Women's Athletic Profile

315 Turnpike Street
North Andover, MA 01845
Coach: Gabe Mejail
Email: gabe_mejail@bbns.org

NCAA II
Warriors/Navy Blue, Gold, White
Phone: (978) 837-4224
Fax: (978) 837-5079

Estimated # of Women's Soccer Scholarships: None
Conference: Northeast 10 Conference, ECAC
Program Profile: Play on natural grass field "stadium" that seats approximately 1,000. Traditional season is in the fall, also indoor in winter plus spring outdoors. There is a weight room and a cardiovascular fitness training area.
History: The program began in 1984 and have never had a losing season. Have won 8 regular season titles, 6 tournaments titles, 4 Runner-Ups, 9 times ECAC Selections, 2 times ECAC champs, 1996 NCAA Final Eight, ranked top 20 in nation this past six year. Merrimack has completed its 17th winning season in a row 2000. Have an all time record is 231-107-19.
Achievements: Has produced six times Conference Coach of the Year, four times NSCAA/New England Coach of the Year, 8 All-American players, 24 All-Region players, 43 All-Conference, 6 conference MVP's, 6 conference Defensive MVP's.

Coaching: Gabe Mejail, Head Coach, holds USSF "B" License, 20 years of coaching experience. She was born in Argentina with over 231career wins (top 10 nationally). She was named six times Conference Coach of the Year and four times NSCAA coach of the Year. Jason Miller, Assistant Coach, graduated from Babson College in 1993. Responsible with the goalkeeper. Her is a member of Final Four Babson Squad. Danielle Oullette, Assistant Coach, graduated from Merrimack in 1997. She is a former All-American, Spirit of Massachusetts Coach. Amy Heseltime, Assistant Coach, graduated from Providence in 1996. Current Boston Renegade's Captain.

Roster in State: 19	**Out of State:** 4	**Out of Country:** 1
ODP State: 4	**Regional:** 1	**National:** 0
Walk-on/Other:	**Graduation %:** 100	**Seniors on Team:** 4

Positions Needed: GK, Midfield, Forwards, Backs
Camp or Clinic Dates: Not Available
Most Recent Record: 16-5-0
Schedule: LIU C.W. Post, Bentley, Saint Rose, Franklin Pierce, American International, Southern Connecticut.
Style of Play: The team plays a 4-3-3 with emphasis on ball control and short passes. Key to the team's play is speed of execution. Defense is mostly played man to man.

Mount Holyoke College

Academic Profile

South Hadley, MA 01075
Phone: 413-538-2000

Type: 4 Yr.,Private,Liberal Arts		**Founded:** 1837
Website: http://www.mtholyoke.edu/athletics		**Religion:** Non-Affiliated
SAT/ACT/GPA: 1200/Top 10-15%		**Housing:** Yes
Student/Faculty Ratio: 10:1		**Male/Female Ratio:** Women
Undergraduate Enrollment: 1,980		**Graduate Enrollment:** N/A
Scholarships/Academic: Yes	**Athletic:** No	**Financial Aid:** Yes
Expenses by: Year	**In State:** $ 33,589	**Out of State:** $ 33,589

Specialty: Education, Liberal Arts, Pre-Law, Pre-Med
Degrees Conferred: BA
Programs of Study: African-American Studies, African Studies, Anthropology, Art History, Asian Studies, Astronomy, BioChemistry, Biology, Chemistry, Classical Languages, Computer Science, Dance, Economics, Education, English, European Studies, French, Geography, Geology, German, Greek, International Relations, Italian, Latin American Studies, Mathematics, Music, Philosophy, Physics, Political Science, PsychoBiology, Psychology, Religion, Romance, Social Science, Sociology & Anthropology

Women's Athletic Profile

College Street
South Hadley, MA 01075
Coach: Kristen Martini
Email: kmartini@mtholyoke.edu

NCAA III
Lyons/N. Blue, Columbia Blue
Phone: (413) 538-2112
Fax: (413) 538-2183

Estimated # of Women's Soccer Scholarships: None
Conference: NEW-8 Conference, ECAC
Program Profile: Young developing program. Fall season is from late Aug. to late Oct. with spring training. Newly renovated athletic complex. Mount Holyoke ranked by sports Illustrated for women # 1 athletic program in all-women's college category.
History: Soccer introduced to college 1925, NCAA competition began 1980's.
Achievements: 1999 Adidas Regional Coach of the Year
Coaching: Kris Martini Head Coach.

Roster in State: 9	**Out of State:** 11	**Out of Country:** 0
ODP State: 1	**Regional:**	**National:**

Walk-on/Other: **Graduation %:** 99 **Seniors on Team:** 2
Positions Needed: Striker, Central Midfielders
Camp or Clinic Dates: Not Available
Most Recent Record: 2-14
Schedule: Wheaton (MA), Ambers, Wellesley, Springfield, Connecticut, Clark.
Style of Play: Quick and possession based combination. Play out of 4-4-2 or 3-4-3.

Mount Ida College

Academic Profile

Phone: (617) 928-4500

Newton Centre, MA 02459

Type: 4 Yr.,Private,Liberal Arts **Founded:** 1899
Website: http://www.mountida.edu **Religion:** Non-Affiliated
SAT/ACT/GPA: None **Housing:** Yes
Student/Faculty Ratio: 9:1 **Male/Female Ratio:** 40:60
Undergraduate Enrollment: 1,800 **Graduate Enrollment:** N/A
Scholarships/Academic: Yes **Athletic:** No **Financial Aid:** Yes
Expenses by: Year **In State:** $ 23,186 **Out of State:** $ 23,186
Specialty: Various
Degrees Conferred: AA, AAA, AS, AAS, BS, BCS
Programs of Study: Business Early Education, Interior Design, Fashion Design, Graphic Design, Fashion Merchandising, Legal Studies, Liberal Arts, Communications, Management, Veterinary Technology, Equine Studies, Hotel/Restaurant Management, Criminal Justice

Men's Athletic Profile

777 Dedham Street
Newton Centre, MA 02459
Coach: Steve D'Arcy
Email: LBW200@aol.com

NCAA III
Mustangs/Forest Green
Phone: (617) 928-4576
Fax: (617) 928-4036

Estimated # of Men's Soccer Scholarships:
Conference: North Atlantic Conference
Program Profile: Our season extends from September through November. It is consists of 18 games and post-season play. We have a natural grass playing field.
History: Our program began in 1989-1998 as NJCAA Division I. We are now member of NCAA Division III
Achievements: NJCAA Region Coach of the Year in 1990, 1994 & 1997; College Region 7 District Champions in 1996, 1997 & 1998; Nationally ranked in the last seven years.
Coaching: Steve D'Arcy, Head Coach, was a former English ex-professional player and semi-professional coach in England. He was a Regional Coach of the Year in 1990, 1994, & 1997. Mike Haikal and Paul Kelleher are the Assistant Coaches.
Style of Play: Varies from year to year.

Women's Athletic Profile

777 Dedham Street
Newton Centre, MA 02159
Coach: Joseph Campbell
Email: Not Available

NJCAA
Mustangs/Green, White
Phone: (617) 969-7000
Fax: (617) 969-6993

Estimated # of Women's Soccer Scholarships:
Conference: Region 21

Program Profile: Play on a natural grass field on our Newton Campus (8 miles west of Boston). Season consists of 16-18 games from early September to mid November. We are starting to compete in indoor leagues in the off season and developing outdoor play in the spring.
History: Started in 1989
Achievements: New England Champs, Region XXI, 1992. Region Coach of the Year 1992. 7 First Team All New England Selection, 10 Second Team selections. Sara King, GK, NSCAA All-American 1991,1992, Academic All-American 1992.
Style of Play: 4-4-2 formation primarily with high pressure defense and an offensive attack we call the "Flex Your Head" approach. You have to see it to believe it.

Newbury College

Academic Profile

Phone: 617-730-7007

Brookline, MA 02146

Type: 2 Yr.,Private,Jr. College
Founded: 1962
Website: http://www.newbury.edu
Religion: Non-Affiliated
SAT/ACT/GPA: Open
Housing: Yes
Student/Faculty Ratio: 13:1
Male/Female Ratio: 45:55
Undergraduate Enrollment: 1,050
Graduate Enrollment: N/A
Scholarships/Academic: Yes **Athletic:** No **Financial Aid:** Yes
Expenses by: Year **In State:** $ 18,736 **Out of State:** $ 18,736
Degrees Conferred: Associate
Programs of Study: Accounting, Business Administration, Commerce, Management, Communications, Computer Information Systems, Computer Programming, Criminal Justice, Fashion Design, Graphic Arts, Interior Design, Marketing, Physical Therapy, Tourism

Men's Athletic Profile

129 Fisher Avenue
Brookline, MA 02146
Coach: Turi Lonero
Email: Not Available

NJCAA
Knights/Green, Gold
Phone: (617) 730-7091
Fax: (617) 730-7146

Estimated # of Men's Soccer Scholarships: N/A
Conference: Colonial State Conference

Nichols College

Academic Profile

Phone: (508) 213-2355

Dudley, MA 01571-5000

Type: 4 Yr.,Private,Liberal Arts
Founded: 1815
Website: http://www.nichols.edu
Religion: Non-Affiliated
SAT/ACT/GPA: 800
Housing: Yes
Student/Faculty Ratio: 15:1
Male/Female Ratio: 6:1
Undergraduate Enrollment: 800
Graduate Enrollment: 400
Scholarships/Academic: Yes **Athletic:** No **Financial Aid:** Yes
Expenses by: Year **In State:** $ 22,260 **Out of State:** $ 22,260
Specialty: Business, Education, Sport Management, Liberal Arts
Degrees Conferred: BS, BA (BS in Business & Public Administration), MBA
Programs of Study: Accounting, Finance, Economics, Real Estate, General Business, Management, Sport Management, MIS, Marketing, Liberal Arts, English, Secondary Education, Psychology

Men's Athletic Profile

P.O. Box 5000
Dudley, MA 01571
Coach: Mark Wagner
Email: Not Available

NCAA III
Bisons/Green, Black, White
Phone: (508) 943-8250
Fax: (508) 943-1560 x 102

Estimated # of Men's Soccer Scholarships: None
Conference: Commonwealth Coast Conference in 1995
Program Profile: Nichols just constructed a new soccer field this past summer. Men's and women's teams both use the field. excellent place to play and watch a soccer game. Has 18-game schedule. ECAC affiliated, growing athletic department.
History: Our program began in 1959. The Bison has an overall record of 233-278-51 (.455). First full-time coach this season. Recruiting will help a great deal.
Achievements: Nichols entered 1995 in a conference for the first time. The Bison had previously competed as an independent. They now compete in the Commonwealth Coast Conference.
Coaching: Mark Wagner is the new head coach and Sean Chenersut and Joe Appiah are the assistant coaches.
ODP State: 4 **Regional:** 2 **National:**
Walk-on/Other: **Graduation %:** N/A **Seniors on Team:** 5
Style of Play: Nichols plays a passing game out of the 3-5-2 system, tight defense and formation with a double stopper.

Women's Athletic Profile

Center Road P.O. Box 5000
Dudley, MA 01571-5000
Coach: Felicity Smith
Email: smithf@nichols.edu

NCAA III
Bison/Forest Green, White
Phone: (508) 213-2355
Fax: (508) 943-8250

Estimated # of Women's Soccer Scholarships: None
Conference: Commonwealth Coast Conference
Program Profile: We play in a natural grass field. We are building a new fieldhouse. We are also rebuilding our soccer program and made several improvements last season.
History: The program began in 1991 and the team's record is 76-51-4. Our best season was in 1994, when the team went 17-3.
Achievements: 1996 Conference Title (Commonwealth Coast Conference), Nichols has played in Conference Tournament three times: 1993 - Kendra Cestone All-American.
Style of Play: 4-3-3 composed, short, short long play.

Northeastern University

Academic Profile

Boston, MA 02115
Phone: (617) 373-3556

Type: 4 Yr.,Private,Liberal Arts
Founded: 1898
Website: http://www.northeastern.edu
Religion: Non-Affiliated
SAT/ACT/GPA: 1080/24/3.0
Housing: Yes
Student/Faculty Ratio: 14:1
Male/Female Ratio: 49:51
Undergraduate Enrollment: 11,978
Graduate Enrollment: 2,696
Scholarships/Academic: Yes **Athletic:** Yes **Financial Aid:** Yes
Expenses by: Year **In State:** $ Varies **Out of State:** $ Varies
Specialty: Physical Therapy, Engineering, Political Science, History
Degrees Conferred: Associate, Bachelor, Master, Doctoral Level
Programs of Study: Accounting, Anthropology, Art, Banking/Finance, Computer Technology, Biology, Broadcasting, Business, Chemistry, Communications, Computer Science, Criminal Justice, Economics, Education, Engineering, History, Human Services, Journalism, Marketing, Mathematics, Philosophy, Political Science, Public Administration, Physical Therapy

Men's Athletic Profile

219 Cabot
Boston, MA 02215
Coach: Ed Matz
Email: ematz@wheelock.edu

NCAA I
Huskies/Red, Black
Phone: (617) 373-4465
Fax: (617) 373-8988

Estimated # of Men's Soccer Scholarships: None
Conference: America East Conference
Program Profile: Facilities include an astro turf field. Has a 7,500-seat stadium.
History: Program began in 1984. Team record in 1996 is 12-5-2 and in 1995 is 11-5-2.
Achievements: NAC Coach of the Year in 1990; Bjoin Hansen - All-American, All-New England, Umbro Select Bowl; 7 All-New England selections for over the past four years.
Coaching: Ed Matz, Head Coach. Dennis Franczak - Assistant Coach. George Silva - Goalkeeping Coach.

Women's Athletic Profile

219 Cabot Center
Boston, MA 02115
Coach: Ed Metz
Email: Not Available

NCAA I
Huskies/Black, Red
Phone: (617) 373-4465
Fax: (617) 373-8988

Estimated # of Women's Soccer Scholarships: None
Conference: America East Conference
Program Profile: Division I program, looking to grow and attract quality student-athlete. Play on astro-turf field. Has a fall playing season.
History: The program began in July 1, 1996.
Style of Play: Emphasis on skill possession; try to build out of the back; depending on the personnel, on field and on opponents.

Pine Manor College

Academic Profile

Phone: 800-762-1357

Chestnut Hill, MA 02467

Type: 4 Yr.,Private,Liberal Arts
Website: http://www.pmc.edu
SAT/ACT/GPA: 800-900
Student/Faculty Ratio: 10:1
Undergraduate Enrollment: 320
Scholarships/Academic: Yes **Athletic:** No
Expenses by: Year **In State:** $ 10,000

Founded: 1911
Religion: Non-Affiliated
Housing: Yes
Male/Female Ratio: Women
Graduate Enrollment: N/A
Financial Aid: Yes
Out of State: $ 16,000

Specialty: 1007 Students participate in internships
Degrees Conferred: AA, AS, BA, M.Ed.
Programs of Study: Accounting, Allied Health, American Studies, Art History, Biology, BioTechnology, Broadcast, Business Management, Communications, Criminal Justice, Early Childhood Education, Economics, Elementary Education, English, Environmental Science, European Studies, International Business, International Systems, Liberal Arts, Management, Marine Studies, Marketing, Mass Communications, Museum Studies, Psychology, Social & Political Systems, Sociology, Visual Arts

Women's Athletic Profile

400 Heath Street
Chestnut Hill, MA 02167
Coach: Cyndy Falwell
Email: falwellc@pmc.edu

NCAA III
Gators/Green, White
Phone: (617) 731-7058
Fax: (617) 731-7199

Estimated # of Women's Soccer Scholarships: None
Conference: Great Northeast Athletic Conference
Program Profile: Hedley Field is a beautiful, natural turf field, has an electronic scoreboard, and is located on campus near the gym.
History: The program began in 1986 and was not competitive until Bill Kelly was hired as a full time soccer coach in 1994. Best season ever in 1995 with a 8-8-1 record. Also finished 5th in the GNAC. 1997 will promise to be a winning campaign for the young PMC team.
Style of Play: All out Attacking with overlapping midfielders. We use a striker system and emphasize playing the ball to the feet of our strikers. WE also stress good defense utilizing disciplined marking backs and a sweeper, but team defense is the key to our success in counter-attacking.

Regis College

Academic Profile

Phone: 781-768-7280

Weston, MA 02193-1571

Type: 4 Yr.,Private,Liberal Arts
Website: http://www.regiscollege.edu
SAT/ACT/GPA: 1000
Student/Faculty Ratio: 11:1
Undergraduate Enrollment: 850
Scholarships/Academic: Yes **Athletic:** No
Expenses by: Year **In State:** $ 23,600

Founded: 1927
Religion: Catholic
Housing: No
Male/Female Ratio: Women
Graduate Enrollment: 450
Financial Aid: Yes
Out of State: $ 23,600

Specialty: Sciences, Communication, Education, Fine Arts
Degrees Conferred: BA, BS, MS
Programs of Study: Art, Biology, BioChemistry, Business Administration, Chemistry, Classics, Communications, Education, Economics, English, French, German, History, Management, Mathematics, Political Science, Psychology, Social Science, Spanish, Women's Studies, Graphic Design

Women's Athletic Profile

235 Wellesley Street
Weston, MA 02193
Coach: Christina Contardo
Email: cherise.galasso@regiscollege.edu

NCAA III
Beacons/Cardinal
Phone: (781) 768-7383
Fax: (781) 768-8339

Estimated # of Women's Soccer Scholarships: None
Conference: Commonwealth Coast Conference
Program Profile: Pre-season the week before Labor Day; games start in the early Sept. and season concludes with the conference tournament in late Oct. Natural turf field.
History: Club program for 3 years. Became varsity sport in 1984.
Coaching: Cherise Galasso, Head Coach. Sean Oliver - Assistant Coach for two years. Kris Vander Plaat - Goalkeeper Coach, entering first year with the program.
Style of Play: Prefer to play a possession game with defending overlapping into offensive attack. Aggressive, physical, quick transition. Attack and defend as a team.

Salem State College

Academic Profile

Phone:

Salem, MA 01970-5353

Type: 4 Yr.,Public,Liberal Arts
Website: Not Available
SAT/ACT/GPA: 980/2.7

Founded: 1854
Religion: Non-Affiliated
Housing: Yes

Student/Faculty Ratio: 20:1
Male/Female Ratio: 45:55
Undergraduate Enrollment: 6,000
Graduate Enrollment: 4,000
Scholarships/Academic: Yes
Athletic: No
Financial Aid: Yes
Expenses by: Year
In State: $ 4,800
Out of State: $ 4,800
Specialty: Business, Nursing
Degrees Conferred: BA, BS, BFA, MS, MBA, M.Ed.
Programs of Study: Art, Aviation Science, Biology, Business Administration, Business Technology & Education, Cartography, Chemistry, Education, Communications, Computer & Information Studies, Criminal Justice, Economics, Educational Studies, English, Fire Science, General Studies, Geography, Geological Science, History, Mathematics, Music, Nursing, Office Management, Political Science, PreEngineering, Psychology, Social Work, Sociology, Sport/Fitness/Leisure Studies, Theatre Arts, Undeclared

Men's Athletic Profile

352 Lafayette Street
Salem, MA 01970-5353
Coach: Nicholas Padovani
Email: Not Available
NCAA III
Vikings/Blue, Orange
Phone: (978) 542-6589
Fax: (978) 542-2926

Estimated # of Men's Soccer Scholarships: None
Conference: MASCAC
Program Profile: Salem State has one of the best Division II programs in the nation. The stadium seats about 7,000 and has a great field with natural grass.
History: Program began in 1980, and the program has done well the past few years, and becoming one of the top 10 schools of the state. Our overall record is 301-51-34.
Achievements: NCAA Division III Final Four 3 times, an the Final Eight 5 times; 15 All-Americans players; New England Champs 5 times; Coach of the Year in 1985 & 1996.
Coaching: Nicholas Padovani, Head Coach, National Licenses. Assistant Coach is Sorin Balea and two 2 goalie Coaches.
Roster In State: 7
Out of State: 14
Out of Country: 4
ODP State: 2
Regional:
National:
Walk-on/Other:
Graduation %: 89
Seniors on Team: 2
Positions Needed: Goalie, Sweeper, Striker
Camp or Clinic Dates: June, July, August
Most Recent Record: 15-4-1
Schedule: Ferdonia, Keene State, Plymouth State, Roger Williams, Mass College, Westfield
Style of Play: Control, European, Develop Players

Women's Athletic Profile

352 Lafayette Street
Salem, MA 01970
Coach: Alvaro Ibanez
Email: alvaro.jbanez@salemstate.edu
NCAA III
Vikings/Orange, Navy
Phone: (978) 744-7349
Fax: (978) 542-2926

Estimated # of Women's Soccer Scholarships: None
Conference: MASCAC
Program Profile: Salem State uses a 1,500 seat, lighted, grass field. 90% of home games are under the lights. Additionally all athletic teams are housed in the O'Keefe Building, a modern athletic facility housing an Olympic size pool, full size basketball courts, a hockey rink, and a new age fitness center.
History: Women's soccer at SSC started in 1985. The program has see nothing but success in ten years. SSC has won 7 conference titles, received 3 NCAA bids and have been in the Division III Final Four 2 times.

Achievements: The team has had 7 All-Americans, 25 All-New England, and has never failed to place at least 5 players in the All-Conference teams. (at least a 3.4 GPA of better)
Roster in State: 14 **Out of State:** 4 **Out of Country:** 1
ODP State: 0 **Regional:** 0 **National:** 0
Walk-on/Other: 0 **Graduation %:** **Seniors on Team:** 3
Positions Needed: ALL
Camp or Clinic Dates: August
Most Recent Record: 7-7-3
Style of Play: We play a slow build up using all parts of the field. We emphasize switching points of attack and use a direct method of attack (North/South verses East/West). Although skill development is a point of emphasis, we push learning the game from the tactical viewpoint.

Simmons College
Academic Profile

Phone: (800) 345-8486
Boston, MA 02115

Type: 4 Yr.,Private,Liberal Arts **Founded:** 1899
Website: http://www.simmons.edu **Religion:** Nonsectarian
SAT/ACT/GPA: 480-570m, 510-610v **Housing:** Yes
Student/Faculty Ratio: 10:1 **Male/Female Ratio:** Female
Undergraduate Enrollment: 1,210 **Graduate Enrollment:** 2,191
Scholarships/Academic: Yes **Athletic:** No **Financial Aid:** Yes
Expenses by: Year **In State:** $ 28,680 **Out of State:** $ 28,680
Specialty: Physical Therapy
Degrees Conferred: BA, BS, MA, MS, MBA, Ph.D.
Programs of Study: Accounting, Arts, Arts Administration, Applied Music, BioChemistry, Chemistry, Chemistry/Pharmacy, Communications, Computer Science, East Asian Studies, Economics, Education, English, Environmental Science, Finance, Foreign Languages, Graphic Design, History, International Management, Management Information Systems, Mathematics, Music History, Nutrition, Nursing, Philosophy, Physical Therapy, Physics, Political Science, PreLaw, PsychoBiology, Psychology, Pubic Relations, Retail Management, Sociology, Women's Studies

Women's Athletic Profile

300 The Fenway **NCAA III**
Boston, MA 02115-5898 Lady Sharks/Blue, Gold
Coach: Chris Baker **Phone:** (617) 521-2000
Email: **Fax:** (617) 521-3190

Estimated # of Women's Soccer Scholarships: None
Conference: Great Northeast Athletic Conference
Program Profile: Simmons College competes as an NCAA III institution and is a member of the GNAC and ECAC. Scheduling includes up to 20 matches per year including some of the top teams in the northeast. The playing surface is natural grass. Off-season begins in early February and is not mandatory, but we compete in 3-5 tournaments each spring.
History: The program began in 1989. We went to the GNAC Championship games in 1995,1996,1997 and 1998. We were GNAC Champions in 1996 and 1998. Our overall record is 78-74-7. Since the inception of the GNAC, the conference record is 30-1-1. The program had four straight winnings seasons: 1995,1996,1997 and 1998. We had six straight non-losing seasons from 1994 to 1998. In 1998, the team finished 8th in the nation in average goals per game (4.26)
Achievements: 1998 Coach of the Year: Christopher Baker; 1995 and 1996 Coach of the Year: Maureen McCormack; 25 players have been named First Team All-Conference; 2 Conference Championships in 4 years.

Coaching: Christopher Baker, Head Coach. He was the 1997 assistant coach of the Indiana Blaze of the World League. He was also assistant coach at Butler University. He has a USSF B License. His B.S. in Exercise Science is from Bowling Green State University and his M.S. in Kinesiology is from Indiana University. He has competed as a player or a coach in over 20 countries including China, Soviet Union, Cuba, Nepal, Mexico and the countries of Europe.
Style of Play: The team focuses primarily on attacking principles utilizing a 3-4-3 formation; man-to-man marking in the back and high pressure defense in the attacking third. This approach has been highly successful with the team scoring 81 goals while allowing 27. This system is exciting for the players and spectators. Emphasis relates to overall performance as opposed to results and rankings.

Smith College

Academic Profile

Phone: (413) 585-2713

Northampton, MA 01063

Type: 4 Yr.,Private,Liberal Arts
Founded: 1880
Website: http://www.pmc.edu
Religion: Non-Affiliated
SAT/ACT/GPA: 1200+/3.5
Housing: Yes
Student/Faculty Ratio: 10:1
Male/Female Ratio: Women
Undergraduate Enrollment: 2,800
Graduate Enrollment: 100
Scholarships/Academic: Yes **Athletic:** No
Financial Aid: Yes
Expenses by: Year **In State:** $ 30,000
Out of State: $ 30,000
Specialty: Liberal Arts
Degrees Conferred: BA, MA, MS
Programs of Study: Almost everything available; Liberal Arts

Women's Athletic Profile

Ainsworth Gym
Northampton, MA 01063
Coach: Phil Nielsen
Email: mailto:pnielsen@smith.edu

NCAA III
Pioneers/Navy, White
Phone: (413) 585-3983
Fax: (413) 585-2712

Estimated # of Women's Soccer Scholarships: None
Conference: New England Women's 8
Program Profile: Has three grass field which has a seating capacity of a 1,000, complete indoor facility. Playing season is early August to early November (6 days a week); has a natural field.
History: The program began in 1978. Ranked 8th overall for most wins in Division I, II or III combined. Numerous conference, in-season and post-season championships.
Achievements: Tradition of All-Americans, All-Regional, All-Conference players.
Style of Play: Fast, lots of short passing, patterned attacks.

Springfield College

Academic Profile

Phone: (413) 748-3850

Springfield, MA 01109-3797

Type: 4 Yr.,Private
Founded: 1885
Website: http://www.spfldrol.edu
Religion: Non-Affiliated
SAT/ACT/GPA: Varies
Housing: Yes
Student/Faculty Ratio: 18:1
Male/Female Ratio: 50:50
Undergraduate Enrollment: 2,000
Graduate Enrollment: 600
Scholarships/Academic: No **Athletic:** No
Financial Aid: Yes
Expenses by: Year **In State:** $ 23,400
Out of State: $ 23,400

Specialty: PE Athletics Related
Degrees Conferred: BA, BS
Programs of Study: Art, Art Therapy, Training, Biology, Business, Chemistry, Computer Systems Management, Early Childhood Education, English, Environmental Studies, Gerontology, Health Service Administration, History, Human Services, Laboratory Science, Management, Mathematics, Medical Technology, Physical Education, Physical Therapy, Political Science, Psychology, Sociology

Men's Athletic Profile

263 Alden Street
Springfield, MA 01109-3797
Coach: Peter Haley
Email: peter-haley@spfldcol.edu

NCAA III
Pride/Maroon, White
Phone: (413) 748-3368
Fax: (413) 748-3537

Estimated # of Men's Soccer Scholarships:
Conference: New England Men's & Women's Conference
Program Profile: We have varsity and JV programs. V plays 18 games and JV plays 10 games. We have traditional and non-traditional seasons (about 10 weeks, 5 playing dates, training, lifting). Excellent facilities: grass game field, grass training field, synthetic training field, Olympic style weight facility, 2 indoor gyms.
History: 1995 will be 83rd collegiate season. The program began in1906. We currently have 30 plus graduates are coaching college soccer, close to 800 soccer alumnus, strong tradition of character and leadership.
Achievements: Conference Champs Division II in 1988 & 1989. All-Americans, and All-Regional players.
Coaching: Peter Haley, Head Coach, was 1989 New England Division II Coach of the Year. He begins his 15th season in the Fall of 1999. He holds a NSCAA Advanced National Diploma and a USSF "B" Coaching License. He is President of New England Intercollegiate Soccer League, a full time faculty member, an Assistant Professor of Physical Education and a Program (PE) Director. Jerry Block is the Assistant Coach.
Style of Play: A direct style of play that emphasizes quick play while focusing on individual and team concepts relating to defending and attacking. Looking for disciplined and committed players who have the ability to perform under pressure with a consistently good first touch, high work ethic and the desire to work hard academically.

Women's Athletic Profile

263 Alden Street
Springfield, MA 01109
Coach: John Gibson
Email: Not Available

NCAA III
Maroons/Maroon, White
Phone: (413) 748-3170
Fax: (413) 748-3855

Estimated # of Women's Soccer Scholarships: None
Conference: ECAC, Northeast 10 Conference

Stonehill College
Academic Profile

North Easton, MA 02356
Phone: 508-565-1000

Type: 4 Yr.,Private,Liberal Arts
Website: http://www.stonehill.edu
SAT/ACT/GPA: Open
Student/Faculty Ratio: 16:1
Undergraduate Enrollment: 2,000
Scholarships/Academic: Yes
Athletic: No
Expenses by: Year
In State: $ 24,000
Degrees Conferred: BA, BS, BSBA

Founded: 1948
Religion: Non-Affiliated
Housing: Yes
Male/Female Ratio: 42:58
Graduate Enrollment: N/A
Financial Aid: Yes
Out of State: $ 24,000

Programs of Study: American Studies, Communications, Criminal Justice, Economics, Education, Health Care Administration, History, International Studies, English, Mathematics, Philosophy, Political Science, Psychology, Public Administration, Religious, Sociology, Philosophy, Chemistry, Computer Science, Math-Computer, Medical Technology, Business Administration, Accounting, Finance, Marketing

Men's Athletic Profile

320 Washington Street
North Easton, MA 02357
Coach: Jason Tassinari
Email: jtassinari@stonehill.edu

NCAA II
Chieftains/Purple, White
Phone: (508) 565-1366
Fax: (508) 565-1460

Estimated # of Men's Soccer Scholarships:
Conference: NE-10 Conference
Program Profile: The Chieftains home field is on a natural grass surface at a stadium that can hold up to as many as 2000 fans. Not only do we have the large stadium but we also have two natural grass practice fields.
History: Stonehill College's men's soccer program began in 1963. In the past 10 years, Stonehill has captured 3 NE-10 championships and made several trips to the ECAC tournament.
Achievements: The Chieftains were conference champions in 1985,1990, and 1991.
Coaching: Jason Tassinari is the Head Coach and received coach of the year twice. The men's soccer staff includes 3 total coaches.

Roster In State: 15	**Out of State:** 10	**Out of Country:** 0
ODP State: 5	**Regional:** 2	**National:** 0
Walk-on/Other: 3	**Graduation %:** 100	**Seniors on Team:** 5

Positions Needed: Stopper, Central defenders, and Offensive central midfielders
Camp or Clinic Dates: Early July
Most Recent Record: 8-10-0
Schedule: South Connecticut State, Franklin Pierce, New Hampshire College, Tiekyo Post, St. Anselm, Merrimack, and Assumption
Style of Play: Individual and Team defending are the highest priority. We are a possession- oriented team that builds our attack out of the back and works hard to dispossess the opponent when possession is lost. When attacking, we attack up the flanks in numbers-up situations.

Women's Athletic Profile

320 Washington Street
North Easton, MA 02357
Coach: Jose Gomes
Email: Not Available

NCAA II
Chieftains/Purple, White
Phone: (508) 230-1384
Fax: (508) 238-9254

Estimated # of Women's Soccer Scholarships: None
Conference: Northeast 10 Conference
Program Profile: Facilities has a natural grass field.
History: Program began in 1982.
Achievements: Northeast - 10 Champions 1993, ECAC bids 1992-93.
Coaching: Jose Gomes, Head Coach, Coach of the year 1992-93
Style of Play: Control style of play, with focus on maintaining possession.

Suffolk University

Academic Profile

Phone: 617-573-8000

Boston, MA 02114

Type: 4 Yr.,Private,Liberal Arts,Engineering
Website: http://www.suffolk.edu

Founded: 1906
Religion: Non-Affiliated

SAT/ACT/GPA: 820+
Student/Faculty Ratio: 12:1
Undergraduate Enrollment: 3,126
Scholarships/Academic: Yes
Expenses by: Year
Specialty: Liberal arts, Business
Degrees Conferred: AA, AS, BA, BS, MS, MBA, M.Ed.
Programs of Study: Art & Design, Biology, Chemistry, Communications, Journalism, Computer Science, Economics, Education, Engineering, English, Government, History, Math, Medical Science, Modern Languages, Philosophy, Physics, Psychology, Sociology, Theatre, Accounting, PreDental, Business Administration, Finance, Management, Marketing, PreVet, PreLaw

Athletic: No
In State: $ 23,000

Housing: Yes
Male/Female Ratio: 45:55
Graduate Enrollment: 3,000
Financial Aid: Yes
Out of State: $ 23,000

Men's Athletic Profile

41 Temple Street
Boston, MA 02114
Coach: Andre Aycakian
Email: Not Available

NCAA III
Rams/Blue, White
Phone: (617) 573-8379
Fax: (617) 227-4935

Estimated # of Men's Soccer Scholarships: None
Conference: Great Northeast Athletic Conference
Program Profile: Developing into a strong New England team.
History: Program began in 1950, and was revived in 1983 after a 25 yr. hiatus. The program is become stronger each year.
Roster In State: 8
ODP State: 0
Walk-on/Other: 0
Out of State: 4
Regional: 0
Graduation %: 100
Out of Country: 4
National: 0
Seniors on Team: 1
Camp or Clinic Dates: Not Available
Most Recent Record: 4-11-0
Style of Play: We play a 3-2-3-2 system that emphasizes short passing and possession.

<u>Tufts University</u>
Academic Profile

Phone: (617) 627-3232

Medford, MA 02155

Type: 4 Yr.,Private,Liberal Arts,Engineering
Website: http://www.tufts.edu
SAT/ACT/GPA: 1100+/30+
Student/Faculty Ratio: 12:1
Undergraduate Enrollment: 4,500
Scholarships/Academic: No
Expenses by: Year
Specialty: International Relations, Premed, Engineering
Degrees Conferred: BA, BS, BSL, MA, ME, MS
Programs of Study: Biological and Physical Sciences, Education, Engineering, International Relations, Languages, Letters/Literature, Mathematics, Nutrition, PreLaw, PreMed, Psychology, Social Sciences, Visual and Performing Arts

Athletic: No
In State: $ 31,000

Founded: 1852
Religion: Non-Affiliated
Housing: Yes
Male/Female Ratio: 48:52
Graduate Enrollment: 500
Financial Aid: Yes
Out of State: $ 31,000

Men's Athletic Profile

The Soccer Office
Medford, MA 02155
Coach: Ralph Ferrigno
Email: lightsoc@aol.com

NCAA III
Jumbos/Sky Blue
Phone: (617) 627-5152
Fax: (617) 627-3614

Estimated # of Men's Soccer Scholarships:
Conference: New England Small College Athletic Conference
Program Profile: We are a top 20 Division III, five consecutive post-seasons. We have three outstanding full-size fields, 2 game and 1 practice, both are grass. We had a record crowd of 4,000 at 1994 NCAA Quarter Final (Division III record). We tour Great Britain every four years (1994, 1997 & 2000). We have played against pro-teams U-20 teams SULU as Aston Villa, Everton, Tranmere Rovers and Ca Diff City.
History: Our program began in 1946. 1967-1977 part of the program has been a sub. 500 program in the strongest Division III Conference in the country. That changed quite dramatically in the 90's with six post-season tournaments in nine years (Tufts University previously had only made post-season once). Tufts now has the foundation and potential for national success.
Achievements: 1994 NCAA New England Champions, NCAA Quarter Finals, 1996 NCAA New England Semi-finalist, 1998 ECAC Finalist, 1997 ECAC Semi-finalist, 1973, 1990 & 1995 ECAC Quarter-finalist. All-Americans were Gabe Gomez in 1976, Eric Anderson in 1994, Chris Vrias in 1996 & Matt Adler in 1997, Ralph Ferrigno was named NSCAA New England Coach of the Year in 1994.
Coaching: Ralph Ferrigno, Head Coach, holds a USSF "A" English and Welsh FA License. He was on the ODP Staff in 1986-1994. He is from Liverpool, England and was named NSCAA New England Coach of the Year. Matt Wainwright, Assistant Coach, came from Sueffield, England. He holds licensed with English FA. Rotueruam Schoolboys, Assistant Coach, junior with Westerfield. Bill Cardwell, Assistant Coach, came Belfast, North Ireland. He has a licensed with Northern Ireland FA. He is scout for Manchester united and played for Larne Town.
Style of Play: Take the game to the other team!! Very attack-originated.

Women's Athletic Profile

Athletics, Cousens Gym
Medford, MA 02155
Coach: Martha Whiting
Email: martha.whiting@tufts.edu

NCAA III
Jumbos/Brown, Blue
Phone: (617) 627-3232
Fax: (617) 627-3614

Estimated # of Women's Soccer Scholarships: None
Conference: New England Small College Athletic Conference
Program Profile: Tufts has both a varsity and a junior varsity team. Varsity plays a 14 game schedule. Field surface is a natural grass, stadium holds 1,200 fans. Student have access to one of the longest and best equipped fitness center in New England on campus within the Cousens Gym Complex.
History: Became a varsity sport in 1979 making it one of the first varsity soccer programs in the country. Coach Gehling has guided the Jumbos to 14 winning seasons in 16 years. Thirteen teams have gone to the playoffs, winning championships.
Achievements: Has 3 All-Americans, 13 All-New England Players, two-time New England Champions; 1996 Eastern Collegiate Conference Champions; 1985 & 1988 New England Intercollegiate Conference Soccer Champions. 2000 New England Div.III Champs, 2000 NCAA National Finalists.
Coaching: Head Coach Martha Whiting

Roster in State: 1	**Out of State:** 18	**Out of Country:** 0
ODP State: 5	**Regional:**	**National:**
Walk-on/Other:	**Graduation %:** 100	**Seniors on Team:** 3

Positions Needed: GK, Defender
Camp or Clinic Dates: Not Available
Most Recent Record: 18-4-1
Schedule: Middlebury, Bowdoin, Williams, Amherst, Bates, Colby
Style of Play: Flat back four. Possession with quick counters.

University of Massachusetts - Amherst

Academic Profile

Amherst, MA 01003
Phone: (413) 545-4343

Type: 4 Yr.,Public,Liberal Arts,Engineering
Founded: 1863
Website: http://www.umass.edu
Religion: Non-Affiliated
SAT/ACT/GPA: 950+
Housing: Yes
Student/Faculty Ratio: 18:1
Male/Female Ratio: 1:1
Undergraduate Enrollment: 18,000
Graduate Enrollment: 6,000
Scholarships/Academic: Yes **Athletic:** Yes **Financial Aid:** Yes
Expenses by: Year **In State:** $ 9,749 **Out of State:** $ 16,970
Specialty: Sport Management, Engineering, Business
Degrees Conferred: 6 Associates, 89 Bachelors, 68 Masters, Doctoral
Programs of Study: College of Natural Science & Mathematics, College of Humanities & Fine Arts, College of Social Behavioral Sciences, Education, College of Engineering, College of Food and Natural Resources, School of Nursing, Isenberg School of Management, School of Public Health Sciences

Men's Athletic Profile

Department of Athletics
Amherst, MA 01003
Coach: Sam Koch
Email: Not Available

NCAA I
Minutemen/Maroon, White
Phone: (413) 545-4341
Fax: (413) 545-3799

Estimated # of Men's Soccer Scholarships:
Conference: Atlantic 10 Conference
Program Profile: NCAA Division I program. Play on grass in soccer stadium that seats 3,000; the hill sits another 3,000.
History: Program began in the early 1930's.
Achievements: All-Americans, All-New England, 1994 A - 10 Conference Champs, 1991 New England Coach of the Year, and 1992-94. 1987 Pacific Coast Conference Coach of the Year in 1991; 1991 NE Coach of the Year; 1992 & 1994 Atlantic Coach of the Year; 1998 NE Soccer Hall of Fame inductee.
Coaching: Sam Koch is our Head Coach. He holds USSF "A" license, NSCAA Advanced National Diploma, All-American in 1988, coaching courses with Scottish, Brazilian, Canadian and English Soccer Associations. John Voight is our Assistant Coach. He played pro in England.
Roster In State: 10 **Out of State:** 16 **Out of Country:** 1
ODP State: **Regional:** 4 **National:** 1
Walk-on/Other: **Graduation %:** 100 **Seniors on Team:** 6
Positions Needed: Gk, Back, Det Mid, Forward
Camp or Clinic Dates: June 16-18, July 23-28
Most Recent Record: 13-7-0
Schedule: South Carolina, Brown, BU, Fresno State, URI, Hartford
Style of Play: One - Two touch passing team; short passing, high pressure defense. Will attack from any position and we all defend.

Women's Athletic Profile

222 Boyden Building
Amherst, MA 01003
Coach: Jim Rudy
Email: wsoccer@admin.umass.edu

NCAA I
Minute women/Maroon, White
Phone: (413) 545-4343
Fax: (413) 545-1404

Estimated # of Women's Soccer Scholarships: 12
Conference: Atlantic 10 Conference
Program Profile: Member of high level NCAA Division I program. Totman Field has a capacity of 1,500-1,750 and is natural grass field on University of Massachusetts campus. We are located in Western Massachusetts (hour and three quarters from Boston, 45 min from Hartford, CT)
History: The program is 17 years old with a total 326-95-27record, 175-28-9 is under Jim Rudy, NCAA tournament participants 15 out of the last 17 years; six Final Four Appearances; 13 Sweet 16 Appearances, NCAA Runner-Up in 1987. One of the first varsity level women's soccer programs in the country.
Achievements: Rudy was named three-time Atlantic 10 Conference Coach of the Year, one-time Northeast Regional Coach of the Year, four-time Atlantic 10 Champions for six years, five A-10 Players of the Year selections, 2 A-10 Rookie of the Year selections, 4 A-10 Tournament MVP selections,
40 A-10 All-Conference, 39 All-American, 13 NCAA All-Tournament, Missouri Athletic Club. Adidas GK of the Year, Hermann Trophy Award winner, 57 All-New England, 13 Academic All-American Selections.
Coaching: Jim Rudy, Head Coach overall record of 252-90-21, Umass record of 178-67-15, third all-time in NCAA history in coaching wins. Assistant coach yet to be determined.

Roster in State: 3	**Out of State:** 16	**Out of Country:** 1
ODP State: 11	**Regional:** 3	**National:** 1
Walk-on/Other:	**Graduation %:** 100	**Seniors on Team:** 2

Positions Needed: Midfield, GK
Camp or Clinic Dates: July 23-27, July 30- Aug.3
Most Recent Record: 11-7-1
Schedule: Uconn, Harvard, Richmond, Boston College, Georgia, Colorado College, Dayton, Xavier, Rhode Island, George Washington.
Style of Play: Skill and possession with a heavy accent on the quickness of play and the player, quick and athletic.

University of Massachusetts - Boston

Academic Profile

Boston, MA 02125
Phone: (617) 287-7000

Type: 4 Yr.,Public,		**Founded:** 1964
Website: http://www.umb.edu		**Religion:** Non-Affiliated
SAT/ACT/GPA: 1130/25/2.0		**Housing:** Yes
Student/Faculty Ratio: 15:1		**Male/Female Ratio:** 43:57
Undergraduate Enrollment: 9,482		**Graduate Enrollment:** 3,071
Scholarships/Academic: Yes	**Athletic:** No	**Financial Aid:** Yes
Expenses by: Year	**In State:** $ 6,994	**Out of State:** $ 6,994

Specialty: Multiple
Degrees Conferred: BA, BS, MA, MS, MBA, Doctorals
Programs of Study: Anthropology, Biology, Chemistry, Classics, Community Services, Computer Science, Criminal Justice, Dramatic Arts, Economics, Engineering, Physics, English, Fine Arts, French, Geography, German, Gerontology, Human Services, Law, Management, Mathematics, Music, Nursing, Philosophy, Physical Education, Political Science, Psychology, Social Science

Men's Athletic Profile

100 Morrisey Boulevard
Boston, MA 02072
Coach: Noel Cotterell
Email: Noel.Cotterell@umb.edu

NCAA III
Beacons/Royal Blue, White
Phone: (617) 287-5386
Fax: (617) 287-7840

Estimated # of Men's Soccer Scholarships: None
Conference: Little East Conference

Program Profile: Our playing season generally consists of a 20-game Fall season against strong regional competition. The home field is on-campus which is natural grass and also serves as a home field for the Bay State Games Tournament. Formal pre-season training begins in August. Student athletes are provided with a strength and conditioning coach, an exclusive weight room, an academic advisor and a sports psychologist. We are member of the Little East Conference, one of the top Division III Conference in the country.
History: Our program began in 1980 and has been competitive every year. Since 1989, when the Little East Conference began sponsoring men's soccer, the program has produced two Conference Players of the Year. Team was the only side from the Little East to reach the post-season in 1996.
Achievements: In 1996 Carlos Fernandes named third All-American, first-team All-New England and was unanimously selected as Little East Player of the Year. Charlie Keskinidis was a two-time Little East Player of the Year.
Coaching: Noel Cotterell, Head Coach, begins his 17th year. He was a standout goalkeeper at University of Massachusetts-Boston and graduated from the university in 1982. Carlos Fernandes, Assistant Coach, was an All-American sweeper at University of Massachusetts-Boston and was a unanimous selection as the Little East Player of the Year in 1996.
Roster In State: 20 **Out of State:** 6 **Out of Country:**
Camp or Clinic Dates: Not Available
Most Recent Record: 12-8-0
Style of Play: Smart, aggressive play in the midfield - working for the best possible opportunity on offense and fighting for possession on defense. Pressure on the ball in the midfield to force transition. 4-4-2

University of Massachusetts - Dartmouth

Academic Profile

North Dartmouth, MA 02747-2300
Phone: 509-999-8000

Type: 4 Yr.,Public,Engineering
Founded: 1895
Website: http://www.umassd.edu
Religion: Non-Affiliated
SAT/ACT/GPA: Required/2.0
Housing: Yes
Student/Faculty Ratio: 13:1
Male/Female Ratio: 52:48
Undergraduate Enrollment: 6,000
Graduate Enrollment: 725
Scholarships/Academic: Yes **Athletic:** No **Financial Aid:** Yes
Expenses by: Year **In State:** $ 9,943 **Out of State:** $ 16,805
Specialty: Business, Nursing, Arts & Sciences, Visual & Performing Arts
Degrees Conferred: 893 undergraduates, 169 graduates, 1 doctorate
Programs of Study: College of Art & Sciences: Biology, Chemistry, Computer Science, Economics, Education, English, French, German, History, Humanities & Social Sciences, Mathematics, Medical Laboratory, Psychology, Sociology, Political Science, Spanish, Accounting, Business Information, Engineering, Computer Engineering, Art History, Music, Painting

Men's Athletic Profile

Old Westport Rd
North Dartmouth, MA 02747-2300
Coach: Nial O'Donnell
Email: nodonnell@umassd.edu

NCAA III
Corsairs/Blue, Gold, White
Phone: (508) 999-8720
Fax: (508) 999-8730

Estimated # of Men's Soccer Scholarships: None
Conference: Little East Conference

Women's Athletic Profile

285 Old Westport Road
North Dartmouth, MA 02747-2300
Coach: Alex Silva
Email: asilva@umassd.edu

NCAA III
Corsairs/Blue, Gold, White
Phone: (508) 999-8720
Fax: (508) 999-8730

Estimated # of Women's Soccer Scholarships: None
Conference: NCAA Division III, Little East Conference
Program Profile: Play a fall season, with about 18 matches and 2 friendly matches. Home games on natural grass, and there are 1.5 practice fields.
History: Program began in 1990, ECAC's 1991-92, and NCAA 1993-present.
Achievements: Coach of the year awards, MVP awards, All-New England Awards, National Division finalist.
Style of Play: Aggressive on attack and defense.

University of Massachusetts - Lowell

Academic Profile

Lowell, MA 01854
Phone: 678-934-4000

Type: 4 Yr.,Public,Liberal Arts,Engineering
Founded: 1975
Website: http://www.uml.edu
Religion: Non-Affiliated
SAT/ACT/GPA: 960/3.0
Housing: Yes
Student/Faculty Ratio: 17:1
Male/Female Ratio: 42:58
Undergraduate Enrollment: 6,000
Graduate Enrollment: 2,700
Scholarships/Academic: Yes
Athletic: Yes
Financial Aid: Yes
Expenses by: Year
In State: $ 9,500
Out of State: $ 16,000
Specialty: Arts, Sciences, Engineering, Health Professions
Degrees Conferred: Bachelors, Masters, Doctorate
Programs of Study: Health Professions, Engineering, Management, Fine Arts, Arts and Sciences, Business, Communications, Computer Sciences, Education (graduate level only), Letters/Literature, Liberal Arts, Parks/Recreation, Psychology, Protective Services, Public Affairs, Social Sciences, Visual and Performing Arts

Men's Athletic Profile

One University Avenue
Lowell, MA 01854
Coach: Ted Priestly
Email: Edward_Priestly2uml.edu

NCAA II
River Hawks/Red, White, Blue
Phone: (978) 934-2317
Fax: (978) 934-2313

Estimated # of Men's Soccer Scholarships: varies
Conference: New England Collegiate Conference
Program Profile: We compete in the strongest Division II conference in the nation. Play on grass in lighted soccer complex, turf training facility coming in summer of 1999. Year-round program.
History: Our program established in 1949, ECAC Champions in 1980, 1997 was most successful season since 1982.
Achievements: 1980 Division II ECAC Champs. Michael Cancado 1998: member of Connecticut Wolves (A-League).
Coaching: Ted Priestly, Head Coach, is entering his first season with program. He has a NSCAA Advanced National Diploma and was with the Massachusetts Olympic Development program coaching staff in 1995-1998. He is entering his second year as a head coach at Lowell.
Roster In State: 6
Out of State: 14
Out of Country: 3
ODP State: 5
Regional: 1
National: 0
Walk-on/Other: 0
Graduation %: 100
Seniors on Team: 6
Positions Needed: All
Camp or Clinic Dates: July 31-August 4
Most Recent Record: 10-7-3
Schedule: Southern Connecticut, New Hampshire College, Franklin Pierce, St. Anselm, Holy Cross, Bentley, Concordia
Style of Play: Possession - oriented; attacking with numbers from all positions, immediate transition, organized high pressuring defense, with a high work rate.

Women's Athletic Profile

One University Avenue
Lowell, MA 01854
Coach: Ted Preistly
Email: edward_priestly@uml.edu

NCAA II
River Hawks/Red, White, Blue
Phone: (978) 934-2317
Fax: (978) 934-2313

Estimated # of Women's Soccer Scholarships: N/A
Conference: Northeast 10
Program Profile: The home field has a natural grass, lighted for night games and is located behind the gym on north campus. Playing season is a regular 18-19 game schedule in the fall and runs from September to November. Will have new facilities in 1999 season.
History: A five year club program began as a varsity in 1995 will start third season in 1992 (fall). Still growing into a very competitive conference.
Achievements: None Regional All-Americans; All-Conference players; All-Regional players.
Coaching: Ted Priestly is the Head Coach and Elie T. Monteiro is the Assistant Coach.

Roster in State: 13	**Out of State:** 4	**Out of Country:** 0
ODP State: 3	**Regional:**	**National:**
Walk-on/Other:	**Graduation %:** 100	**Seniors on Team:** 3

Positions Needed: Mids, Forwards
Camp or Clinic Dates: Not Available
Most Recent Record: 6-10-0
Schedule: Franklin Pierce, Southern Connecticut, Merrimack, Lemoyne, College of St. Rose
Style of Play: Possession oriented; attacking with numbers from all positions, immediated transition, organized high pressuring defense with high workrate.

Wellesley College

Academic Profile

Keohane Sports Center
Wellesley, MA 02481

Phone: (781) 283-2010

Type: 4 Yr.,Private,Liberal Arts		**Founded:** 1870
Website: http://www.wellesley.edu		**Religion:** Non-Affiliated
SAT/ACT/GPA: 1350 Average		**Housing:** Yes
Student/Faculty Ratio: 15:1		**Male/Female Ratio:** Women
Undergraduate Enrollment: 2,500		**Graduate Enrollment:** N/A
Scholarships/Academic: No	**Athletic:** No	**Financial Aid:** Need basis
Expenses by: Year	**In State:** $ 30,000	**Out of State:** $ 30,000

Specialty: Liberal Arts
Degrees Conferred: BA
Programs of Study: American Studies, Anthropology, Architecture, Art, Astronomy, Biological Science, Chemistry, Chinese, Computer Science, Economics, English, French, Geology, German, Greek, History, International Relations, Mathematics, Music, Philosophy, Physics, Political Science, Psychology, Religion, Russian, Sociology, Theatre

Women's Athletic Profile

106 Central St.
Wellesley, MA 02181
Coach: Anita Rodriguez
Email: edriscol@wellesley.edu

NCAA III
None/Blue, White
Phone: (781) 283-2012
Fax: (617) 283-3641

Estimated # of Women's Soccer Scholarships: None
Conference: New England Women's 8 (NEW 8), Seven Sisters

Program Profile: The twenty-year program at Wellesley is currently ranked #5 in New England and in 1996 had it most successful year, finishing the season with a 17-2-2 record. The facilities at Wellesley are first rate and the soccer field has a very short tight grass. All players are a former club and ODP standard, and the team has made the final of 11 of its last twelve tournament.
History: Program began in 1977 and was improved by the addition of a superb new soccer field in the 80's. Wellesley hired a full-time soccer coach in 1992 and has a major commitment to the soccer. Andy Nelson arrived in 1994 and has compiled a record of 35-17 5 record with ECAC final appearance in 1996, new 8 final appearance and two consecutive, seven sisters championships in 1995 & 1996. Team had best year ever in 1996.
Achievements: All-New England in 1993 - Lisa Janssen; All-New England in 1996 - Katie Knudsen and Sarah Hilgenberg; All-New England in 1996; EWISA New England Coach of the Year Division III - Andy Nelson in 1996; 1995-1996 Seven sisters Champions; 1996 ECAC Runner-Up, New 8 Runner-Up.
Style of Play: Attacking; passing style of play; zonal/team defense. Looking for fast technical players who are willing to learn a lot and play in a demanding team system geared towards maximizing the team's strength.

Wentworth Institute of Technology

Academic Profile

Boston, MA 02115
Phone: 617-442-9010

Type: 4 Yr.,Private,Engineering
Founded: 1925
Website: http://www.wit.edu
Religion: Non-Affiliated
SAT/ACT/GPA: 820
Housing: Yes
Student/Faculty Ratio: 19:1
Male/Female Ratio: 3:1
Undergraduate Enrollment: 2,800
Graduate Enrollment: N/A
Scholarships/Academic: Yes **Athletic:** No **Financial Aid:** Yes
Expenses by: Year **In State:** $ 16,000 **Out of State:** $ 16,000
Specialty: Architecture, Engineering, Construction Management
Degrees Conferred: AAS, BS, BArch
Programs of Study: Airway Science, Architecture, Building Construction Technology, Engineering, Computer Science, Construction Management, Interior Design, Mechanical Engineering, Technical Management

Men's Athletic Profile

550 Huntington Avenue
Boston, MA 02115
Coach: Bob Long
Email: athletics@wit.edu

NCAA III
Leopards/Black, Gold
Phone: (617) 989-4145
Fax: (617) 442-9081

Estimated # of Men's Soccer Scholarships: None
Conference: Commonwealth Coast Conference

Western New England College

Academic Profile

Springfield, MA 01119
Phone: (413) 782-1377

Type: 4 Yr.,Private,Liberal Arts,Engineering
Founded: 1919
Website: http://www.wnec.edu
Religion: Non-Affiliated
SAT/ACT/GPA: Varies by program of study
Housing: Yes
Student/Faculty Ratio: 17:1
Male/Female Ratio: 56/44
Undergraduate Enrollment: 1950 fulltime
Graduate Enrollment: 1,700
Scholarships/Academic: Yes **Athletic:** No **Financial Aid:** Yes
Expenses by: Year **In State:** $23,154 **Out of State:** $23,154

Specialty: Professional and Pre-Professional
Degrees Conferred: AA,BA, BS, MS, MBA, JD
Programs of Study: Accounting, American Studies, Biology, BioMedical Engineering, Chemistry, Computer Science, Criminal Justice, Economics, Electrical Engineering, English, Environmental Science, Finance, General Business, Government, History, International Business, Liberal Studies, Law and Conflict Resolution & Leadership, Management Studies & Manufacturing Management, Marketing, Marketing Communication Advertising, Mathematical Sciences, Mechanical Engineering, PrePharmacy, PrePhysician's Assistant, PreVeterinary, Social Work, Sociology, Sport Management

Men's Athletic Profile

1215 Wilbraham Road
Springfield, MA 01119
Coach: Erin Sullivan
Email: Not Available

NCAA III
Golden Bears/Blue, Gold
Phone: (413) 782-1792
Fax: (413) 796-2121

Estimated # of Men's Soccer Scholarships:
Conference: CAC
Program Profile: The Golden Bear play on the best grass field in New England.
History: Traditional, Strong, competitive program
Achievements: 4th in nation, 1975, NAIA National tournament
Style of Play: Versatile - adopt to layer's skill level. Like possession, encourage individual play, offensive minded.

Women's Athletic Profile

1215 Wilbraham Road
Springfield, MA 01119
Coach: Ron Dias
Email: Not Available

NCAA III
Lady Golden Bears/Royal, Gold
Phone: (413) 782-1632
Fax: (413) 796-2121

Estimated # of Women's Soccer Scholarships: None
Conference: Great Northeast Athletic Conference
Program Profile: We have a highly competitive Division II program. We play on a natural grass field that measures 120x75 (one of the best in region). Our season is from August to November. We have some winter indoor and short spring games.
History: Our program started in 1986. The last six years, our record is 79-39-2. Winning season last five out of six years.
Achievements: We were Conference Champions in 1996 & 1999; ECAC Champions in 1998 - NCAA first-round in 1999.
Coaching: Ron Diasis our Head Coach. He is entering his seventh season with the program. He compile an overall record of 79-39-2. Over 25 years coaching experience. His youth premier teams have won State Championships and competed at the Regional level. Assistant Coach WNEC men's Coach for three years. Assistant Coach Kate Brunelle was named 1999 Regional All-American.
Roster in State: 13 **Out of State:** 9 **Out of Country:** 0
Walk-on/Other: **Graduation %:** 90 **Seniors on Team:** 3
Positions Needed: All
Camp or Clinic Dates: July 10-14; 17-21
Most Recent Record: 14-8-2
Schedule: Williams College, Western Connecticut State University, Union College, Keene State College, Salem State College, Springfield College
Style of Play: Style of play depends on personnel available. We like to play a possession game and get everyone involved in offense and defense.

Westfield State College
Academic Profile

Phone: (413) 572-5405

Westfield, MA 01086-1630

Type: 4 Yr.,Public,Liberal Arts
Founded: 1839
Website: http://www.wsc.mass.edu
Religion: Non-Affiliated
SAT/ACT/GPA: 800/2.7
Housing: No
Student/Faculty Ratio: 18:1
Male/Female Ratio: 47:53
Undergraduate Enrollment: 3,100
Graduate Enrollment: 1,800
Scholarships/Academic: Yes **Athletic:** No **Financial Aid:** Yes
Expenses by: Year **In State:** $ 7,148 **Out of State:** $ 13,468
Specialty: Business, Criminal Justice, Education, Mass Communications
Degrees Conferred: BA, BS, BSE, MA, MS, M.Ed.
Programs of Study: Biology, Business Administration, Chemistry, Communications, Computer Science, Criminal Justice, Economics, Education, English, Fine Arts, French, Geology, Geography, History, Information Science, Management, Mathematics, Music, Political Science, Psychology, Social Science, Spanish, Special Education, Urban Studies

Men's Athletic Profile

577 Western Avenue
Westfield, MA 01086
Coach: Paul Whalley
Email: phw@wca.com

NCAA III
Owls/Blue, White
Phone: (413) 568-5509
Fax: (413) 568-5509

Estimated # of Men's Soccer Scholarships: None
Conference: MASCAS
Program Profile: Highly respected program. Play on astro-turf field which has a seating capacity of 4,000. Has 17 game schedule in fall.
History: Our program began in 1984 - 4 New England State Titles; 7 Conference titles; 6 NCAA Tournaments and 7 ECAC Tournaments.
Achievements: Conference coach of the Year in 1997.

Women's Athletic Profile

Western Avenue
Westfield, MA 01085
Coach: Heather Boisvere
Email: Not Available

NCAA III
Owls/Blue, White
Phone: (413) 572-5405
Fax: (413) 572-5477

Estimated # of Women's Soccer Scholarships: None
Conference: MSCAC, ECAC

Wheaton College - Massachusetts
Academic Profile

Phone: 508-286-8200

Norton, MA 02766

Type: 4 Yr.,Private,Liberal Arts
Founded: 1834
Website: http://www.weatonma.edu
Religion: Non-Affiliated
SAT/ACT/GPA: None/2.5
Housing: Yes
Student/Faculty Ratio: 13:1
Male/Female Ratio: 1:2

Undergraduate Enrollment: 1,400 **Graduate Enrollment:** N/A
Scholarships/Academic: Yes **Athletic:** No **Financial Aid:** Yes
Expenses by: Year **In State:** $ 28,460 **Out of State:** $ 28,460
Degrees Conferred: BA, BS
Programs of Study: American Studies, Anthropology, Art History, BioChemistry, Biology, Chemistry, Economics, Mathematics, Music, Philosophy, Physics, Social Psychology, Sociology, International Relations, Political Science, Computer Science, Religion

Men's Athletic Profile

E Main St.
Norton, MA 02766
Coach: Matt Cushing
Email: mcushing@wheatonma.edu

NCAA III
Lyons/Blue, White
Phone: (508) 286-3996
Fax: (508) 285-8273

Estimated # of Men's Soccer Scholarships: None
Conference: NEW MAC
Program Profile: The team play at Keef Field, the training site of Nigerian National team World Cup in 1994. The field measures 78 x 118 is natural grass and seats 1,000. For winter play there is an indoor field measuring 58 x 100. The Lyons have a 20 game season with 5 out of season dates. The game attendance is one of the best in New England.
History: Our program began in 1989. Since Coach Cushing's arrival in 1994, Wheaton has had a 86-24-11 record and has gone to The Post Season the last eight years.
Achievements: Cushing NEISL Coy 1996, NEWMAC Coy 1997, NEWMAC champions, ECAC champions 1998, NCAA New England semifinalist 1997, 5 All-Americans, 12 All New Englands NEWMAC player of the year in 1998 and 1999.
Coaching: Matt Cushing, Head Coach (Massachusetts 1988), is in his 6th year. He has an NSCAA Advanced National Diploma. He holds a USSF "B" License. He was an assistant coach at Rutgers, Lafayette the NEISL Coach of the Year in 1997 and New MAC Coach of the Year.
Roster In State: 9 **Out of State:** 18 **Out of Country:** 0
ODP State: 15 **Regional:** 3 **National:**
Walk-on/Other: **Graduation %:** 100 **Seniors on Team:** 6
Positions Needed: Backs and Goalkeeper
Camp or Clinic Dates: Not Available
Most Recent Record: 12-6-1
Schedule: Amherst, Brandeis, Plymouth State, Keene State, Babson, Springfield, Coastguard
Style of Play: Possession oriented attack. Going forward at opportune times. Defending with eleven players. system at play will be adopted to player's ability and opponents.

Women's Athletic Profile

E. Main Street
Norton, MA 02766
Coach: Luis Reis
Email: lreis@wheatonma.edu

NCAA III
Lyons/Royal Blue, White
Phone: (508) 286-3997
Fax: (508) 286-8273

Estimated # of Women's Soccer Scholarships: None
Conference: New England Women's & Men's Athletic Conference
Program Profile: We play on Elm Field, which measures 110x70, gorgeous grass field and is surrounded by trees located in the woods (beautiful New England Fall setting environment). Our $12 million Evelyn Danzing Has Athletic Center has indoor playing facility, which measures 90x55 and 8 lane pool.
History: Our program began in the late 1970's. The college hired its first full-time coach, Luie Reis in 1997. A major commitment to the women's soccer program. The program has had the best years in the program's history in 1997 & 1998 (13-2 and 13-7-0 record). We ranked as high as 5th in 1998. We finished season with 7th placed in New England in 1998. In 1999 we ranked 1st in the New England Final Regular Season Pole, and ranked 7th in the Country in the Division III Final National Pole.

Achievements: We were Conference Champions in 1995 & 1997; ECAC Regional Tournament in 1997m & 1998 (semi-finalist in 1998). Christina Mirrione was a 4-time All-New England Regional player and was drafted by the New Hampshire Lady Phantoms W-League in 1998. Coach Luis Reis was 1 of five coaches nominated for NE Region Coach of the Year in 1998. NEWMAC Conference Rookie of the Year in 1999. New England Regional Tournament 1999 Champions.
Coaching: Luis Reis is the Head Coach, is entering his third year, holds a USSF "A" License and NSCAA "Premier" Licensed Coach. He was USYSA Region ODP Staff Coach and Massachusetts U17 Girl's ODP State Team Head Coach for two years (1998& 1999). He is currently Massachusetts Youth Soccer Association State Staff Instructor (1994-present). He was FC Greater Boston Bocts U20 Women Head Coach (USYA National Finalist in 1996). He was a former professional player at Boston Storm (USISL in 1994-1995), which is in 1989 went NCAA Division II Final Four. He graduated from California State University-Hayward in 1991. Bryan Medeirds and Lodian Condon are the Assistant Coaches.

Roster in State: 12 | **Out of State:** 13 | **Out of Country:**
ODP State: 10 | **Regional:** 1 | **National:**
Walk-on/Other: | **Graduation %:** 100 | **Seniors on Team:** 4

Positions Needed: All
Camp or Clinic Dates: July 10-14, 17-21
Most Recent Record: 23-2-0
Schedule: Wellesley College, Western Connecticut State College, Clark University, Colby College, Connecticut College, Keene State College, Plymouth State College, Babson College, Anna Maria College, Framingham State College, Springfield College, Smith College
Style of Play: We use various formations like 3-4-5, 4-4-2, 4-3-3, 3-5-2, 4-5-1 and 5-4-1. Zonal back and defending or man-to-man marking. Possession-oriented with short passing game or direct long accurate driven balls over the top or attack through the flanks with dangerous crosses. Score more goals than the opponents.

Williams College

Academic Profile

Williamstown, MA 01267 | **Phone:** 413-597-3131

Type: 4 Yr.,Private,Liberal Arts | **Founded:** 1793
Website: http://www.williams.edu | **Religion:** Non-Affiliated
SAT/ACT/GPA: Open | **Housing:** Yes
Student/Faculty Ratio: 11:1 | **Male/Female Ratio:** 51:49
Undergraduate Enrollment: 2,000 | **Graduate Enrollment:** N/A
Scholarships/Academic: Yes | **Athletic:** No | **Financial Aid:** Yes
Expenses by: Sem | **In State:** $ 16,000 | **Out of State:** $ 16,000
Degrees Conferred: BA, MA
Programs of Study: African & Middle Eastern Studies, Afro-American Studies, American Studies, Anthropology & Sociology, Art History, Art Studio, Asian Studies, Astronomy, AstroPhysics, BioChemistry, Biology, Chemistry, Classics, Computer Science, Economics, English, Environmental Studies, GeoScience, German History, History of Science, Linguistic, Literacy Studies, Mathematics, Music, NeuroScience, Philosophy, Physics, Political Science, Political Economy, Psychology, Religion, Russian, Science & Technology Studies, Theatre, Women's Studies

Men's Athletic Profile

Men's Soccer, Williams College | **NCAA III**
Williamstown, MA 01267 | Ephs/Purple, White
Coach: Mike Russo | **Phone:** (413) 597-3329
Email: t.michael.russo@williams.edu | **Fax:** (413) 597-4272

Estimated # of Men's Soccer Scholarships:
Conference: NESCAC

Program Profile: Williams has one of the best soccer facilities. Its fields are impeccably manicured grass surfaces. One game field has a measurements of 120x80 yards and is used exclusively for matches. There are two practice fields, which are grass. We have one of the best Division III schedules in New England. We use the most modern training methods. In the recent years, the program has developed into one of the strongest in the country. Our playing season runs from September through November.
History: Our program began in 1922. The record since Russo's arrival in 1979 is 140-57-20 (.645).
Achievements: Mike Russo was named 4 time Coach of the Year; 25 All-Americans; 1998 NCAA Semi-finalist; 1995 NCAA National Champion; 1993 NCAA second place.
Coaching: Mike Russo, Head Coach since 1979, holds a USSF coaching license. He completed the coaching course held by Dutch National Staff in Zeist, Holland and on two different occasions, held soccer clinics at the Department of Defense Schools in Germany. He was selected New England division III Coach of the Year in 1984, 1987, 1988, 1993, & 1995. Tom Demeo and Eric Watson are the Assistant Coaches.
Style of Play: Attacking style with zonal defending.

Women's Athletic Profile

Spring St.
Williamstown, MA 01267
Coach: Lisa Melendy
Email: lisa.m.melendy@williams.edu

NCAA III
Ephs/Purple, Gold
Phone: (413) 597-2477
Fax: (413) 597-4272

Estimated # of Women's Soccer Scholarships: None
Conference: NESCAC
Program Profile: One practice and one game field, both natural grass. Playing season is in the fall of both varsity and junior varsity.
History: The varsity program began in 1978. In 1989 NIAC Champions, 1990 ECAC Champions, 1992 ECAC Runner-Up; 1993, 1994, 1995 and 1996 NCAA Tournament appearances.
Achievements: 1991 and 1992 NSCAA New England Coach of the Year, NCAA Appearances in 1993 and 1994, ECAC Champions in 1990, Finalist in 1993; 10 All-Americans; 22 all-New England.
Coaching: Lisa Melendy, Head Coach, Smith College undergraduate, received MS at UM-Amherst, in eleventh year as a head coach at Williams, holds NSCAA Advanced National and National Diploma. Ron Hansen - Assistant coach.
Style of Play: An aggressive offense which stresses quick play and short passes to create dangerous scoring opportunities.

Worcester Polytechnic Institute

Academic Profile

Worcester, MA 01602
Phone: 508-831-5000

Type: 4 Yr.,Private,Liberal Arts
Website: http://www.wpi.edu
SAT/ACT/GPA: 890/2.7
Student/Faculty Ratio: 12:1
Undergraduate Enrollment: 2,600
Scholarships/Academic: Yes
Athletic: No
Expenses by: Year
In State: $ 27,592
Specialty: Liberal Arts
Founded: 1874
Religion: Non-Affiliated
Housing: Yes
Male/Female Ratio: 80:20
Graduate Enrollment: 800
Financial Aid: Yes
Out of State: $ 27,592
Degrees Conferred: BS, BA, BS in Education
Programs of Study: Engineering: BioMedical, Civil, Chemical, Electrical, Fire Protection, Industrial, Mechanical, Manufacturing, Materials, Sciences, BioChemistry, Chemistry, Computer Science, Math, Physics, Humanities, Management, Interdisciplinary Studies

Women's Athletic Profile

100 Institute Road
Worcester, MA 01609
Coach: Stephanie Carlson
Email: Not Available

NCAA III
Engineers/Crimson, Grey
Phone: (508) 831-5975
Fax: (508) 831-5775

Estimated # of Women's Soccer Scholarships: None
Conference: NEW-8
Program Profile: The Engineers playing field is a synthetic turf field (Omni turf), and is lighted for night games. We play a traditional Fall Season.
History: Program began in 1987, began varsity in 1995.
Style of Play: Good, hard soccer.

Worcester State College

Academic Profile

Worcester, MA 01602-2597

Phone:

Type: 4 Yr.,Public
Website: http://www.mass.edu
SAT/ACT/GPA: 820/2.7
Student/Faculty Ratio: 16:1
Undergraduate Enrollment: 4,800
Scholarships/Academic: Yes **Athletic:** No
Expenses by: Year **In State:** $ 6,900
Founded: 1874
Religion: Non-Affiliated
Housing: Yes
Male/Female Ratio: 1:3
Graduate Enrollment: 3,200
Financial Aid: Yes
Out of State: $ 6,900
Specialty: Business, Education, Physics
Degrees Conferred: BA, BS
Programs of Study: Biology, BioTechnology, Business Administration, Chemistry, Communications, Communications Disorders, Computer Science, Economics, Early Childhood Education, Elementary Education, English, Engineering Transfer Program, French, Geography, Health Studies, History, Mathematics, Nursing, Natural Science, Occupational Therapy, Physics, Psychology, Sociology, Spanish, Urban Studies

Men's Athletic Profile

486 Chaldler Street
Worcester, MA 01602
Coach: Tony Conte
Email: tconte@worchester.edu

NCAA III
Lancers/Blue, Gold
Phone: (508) 929-8034
Fax: (508) 929-8184

Estimated # of Men's Soccer Scholarships: None
Conference: MASCAC
Program Profile: The team plays on an astro-turf field with a capacity of 2,200 equipped with a press box and score-board. 20 game fall schedule.
History: Program started in 1968.
Achievements: Tony Conte was named Coach of the Year; Rookie of the Year in 1998 was Casey Hynes, 2 1st team All-Stars MASCAC.
Coaching: Tony Conte is the Head Coach, 4th year. Mario Prata, Assistant Coach, second year.
Roster In State: 20 **Out of State:** 3 **Out of Country:** 1
Walk-on/Other: **Graduation %:** N/A **Seniors on Team:** 6
Positions Needed: Goalkeeper, defensemen, forwards
Most Recent Record: 10-7
Schedule: Salem State, Clark, WPI, Mass Dartmouth, Endicott, Mass College

Style of Play: European Style; create space, play 2-4-4-1 set-up, very aggressive.

Women's Athletic Profile

486 Chandler Street
Worcester, MA 01602-2597
Coach: Tony Marriel
Email: amarriel@aol.com

NCAA III
Lancers/Royal Blue, Gold
Phone: (508) 752-3479
Fax: (508) 929-8184

Estimated # of Women's Soccer Scholarships: None
Conference: Massachusetts State College Conference
Program Profile: Fall season. Playing field is Astroturf and has a seating capacity of 2,200 and has press boxes as well as a scoreboard.
History: Varsity women's soccer began in 1991. Competes in the tough Massachusetts State College Conference. Team was 12-4-2 in 1998 and played in the ECAC Tournament.
Achievements: Kim Miller was the 1998 MASCAC Coach of the Year.
Coaching: Tony Marriel-Head Coach- 2000.
Roster in State: 20 **Out of State:** 0 **Out of Country:** 0
Walk-on/Other: **Graduation %:** **Seniors on Team:** 1
Positions Needed: Goalkeeper
Camp or Clinic Dates: Not Available
Most Recent Record: 11-5-2
Schedule: Worcester State, Salem State, Wheaton College, Anna Marie College, Endicott College, Bridgewater State College
Style of Play: 4-4-2 system with a 80% of possession and 20% on finishing and attacking system from the back.

michigan

MICHIGAN

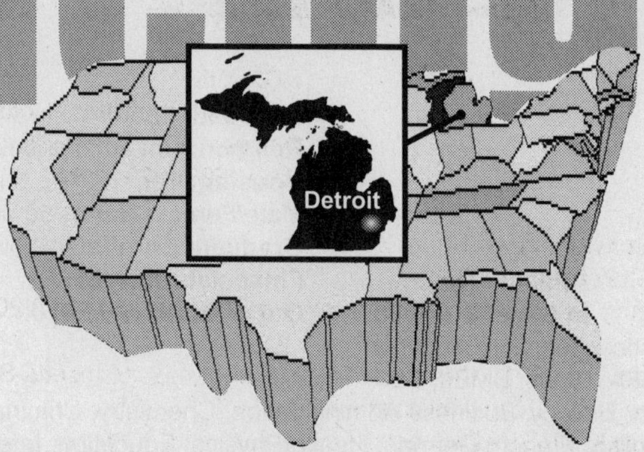

SCHOOL	CITY	AFFILIATION	PAGE
Adrian College	Adrian	NCAA III	524
Albion College	Albion	NCAA III	525
Alma College	Alma	NCAA III	525
Aquinas College	Grand Rapids	NAIA	527
Calvin College	Grand Rapids	NCAA III	528
Central Michigan University	Mt. Pleasant	NCAA I	529
Concordia College - Ann Arbor	Ann Arbor	NAIA	530
Cornerstone College	Grand Rapids	NAIA	531
Eastern Michigan University	Ypsilanti	NCAA I	532
Hillsdale College	Hillsdale	NCAA II	533
Hope College	Holland	NCAA III	535
Kalamazoo College	Kalamazoo	NCAA III	536
Kellogg Community College	Battle Creek	NJCAA	537
Madonna University	Livonia	NAIA	538
Michigan State University	E. Lansing	NCAA I	539
Northern Michigan University	Marquette	NCAA II	540
Northwood University	Midland	NCAA II	541
Oakland University	Rochester	NCAA I	542
Olivet College	Olivet	NCAA III	543
Siena Heights College	Adrian	NAIA	544
Spring Arbor College	Spring Arbor	NAIA	545
University of Detroit Mercy	Detroit	NCAA I	546
University of Michigan	Ann Arbor	NCAA I	547
Western Michigan University	Kalamazoo	NCAA I	549

Adrian College
Academic Profile

Phone:

Adrian, MI 49221-2575

Type: 4 Yr.,Private,Liberal Arts
Website: http://www.adrian.edu
SAT/ACT/GPA: 900/18/2.5
Student/Faculty Ratio: 16:1
Undergraduate Enrollment: 1,100
Scholarships/Academic: Yes **Athletic:** No
Expenses by: Year **In State:** $ 17,950
Founded: 1859
Religion: United Methodist
Housing: Yes
Male/Female Ratio: 50:50
Graduate Enrollment: N/A
Financial Aid: Yes
Out of State: $ 17,950
Specialty: Accounting, Criminal Justice, Teacher Education
Degrees Conferred: AA, BS, BA, BFA, BMus, BMEd, BB
Programs of Study: Accounting, Art, Biology, Business Administration, Chemistry, Criminal Justice, Communication Arts, Earth Science, Economics, English, French, German, Health/Physical Education, International Business, Math, Music, Philosophy, Religion, Sociology, Teacher Education, Medical Technology, Political Science, PreLaw, PreMed, PreDentistry

Men's Athletic Profile

110 S. Madison St.
Adrian, MI 49221
Coach: TBA
Email:

NCAA III
Bulldogs, Black & Gold
Phone: 517-266-2571
Fax:

Estimated # of Men's Soccer Scholarships:
Conference: Michigan Intercollegiate Athletic Assoc. (MIAA)
Program Profile: Adrian plays in the tough MIAA. The Bulldogs have a 120x75 yards natural grass field and a 100x65 natural grass practice field.
History: Program began in 1980.
Roster In State: 18 **Out of State:** 2 **Out of Country:** 1
Walk-on/Other: **Graduation %:** **Seniors on Team:** 6
Most Recent Record: 3-14
Schedule: Kalamazoo College, Alma College, Hope College, Calvin College

Women's Athletic Profile

110 S. Madison St.
Adrian, MI 49221
Coach: Rick Gutierrez
Email: rgutierrez@adrian.edu

NCAA III
Bulldogs, Black & Gold
Phone: 517-264-3990
Fax:

Estimated # of Women's Soccer Scholarships:
Conference: Michigan Intercollegiate Athletic Assoc. (MIAA)
Program Profile: Adrian plays in the tough MIAA. The Bulldogs have a 120x75 yards natural grass field. The field will feature a new scoreboard for 1999. Practice takes place on women's practice field with a measurements of 100x65 yds.
History: The program began in 1988.
Coaching: Rick Gutierrez, Head Coach, entering third year as a head coach.
Roster In State: 13 **Out of State:** 4 **Out of Country:** 1
Walk-on/Other: **Graduation %:** 100 **Seniors on Team:** 2
Most Recent Record: 3-17-0
Schedule: Albion College, Kalamazoo College, Calvin College, Olivet College
Style of Play: Coach favors an attacking, high pressure style of play. The type of players on the team dictates the style to be used.

Albion College
Academic Profile

Phone: (517) 629-1000

Albion, MI 49224

Type: 4 Yr.,Private,Liberal Arts
Founded: 1835
Website: http://www.albion.edu
Religion: United Methodist
SAT/ACT/GPA: V-540-640, Math-530-640/22-283.0
Housing: Yes
Student/Faculty Ratio: 19:1
Male/Female Ratio: 1:1
Undergraduate Enrollment: 1,450
Graduate Enrollment: N/A
Scholarships/Academic: Yes **Athletic:** No **Financial Aid:** Yes
Expenses by: Year **In State:** $ 23,000 **Out of State:** $ 23,000
Specialty: Business, Pre-medicine
Degrees Conferred: BA, BFA
Programs of Study: Accounting, Anthropology, Art, Biology, Business and Management, Chemistry, Communications, Economics, Education, English, Geology, history, Letters/Literature, Life Sciences, Mathematics, Music, Philosophy, Physical Education, Physics, Political Science, Psychology, Religious Studies, Social Science, Speech, Theatre

Men's Athletic Profile

611 E Porter Street
Albion, MI 49224
Coach: Aaron Smith
Email: Not Available

NCAA III
Britons/Purple, Gold
Phone: (517) 629-1000
Fax: (517) 629-0281

Estimated # of Men's Soccer Scholarships:
Conference: Michigan Intercollegiate Athletic Association
Program Profile: Game, practice and training facilities all in same complex and are natural grass.
History: Program began in 1967. Play in nation's oldest league (MIAA).
Achievements: Regional All - Americans in 1992, 1993.
Coaching: Aaron Smith, Head Coach, 3rd year , holds USSF 'A' coaching license. Region Staff ODP Coach.
Style of Play: Style of play dictated by players level of play and opponent.

Women's Athletic Profile

611 East Porter Street
Albion, MI 49224
Coach: Jerry Block
Email: Not Available

NCAA III
Britons/Purple, Gold
Phone: (517) 629-0452
Fax: (517) 629-1648

Estimated # of Women's Soccer Scholarships: None
Conference: Michigan Intercollegiate Athletic Conference
Program Profile: The Briton's has 18 games conference tournament on a natural field. Stadium has a capacity of 1,000.
History: Program began in 1988.
Achievements: Produced one All-American.

Alma College
Academic Profile

Phone: (517) 463-7017

Alma, MI 48801

Type: 4 Yr.,Private,Liberal Arts
Founded: 1888
Website: http://www.alma.edu
Religion: Presbyterian
SAT/ACT/GPA: 1030/22/3.0
Housing: Yes

Student/Faculty Ratio: 14:1
Male/Female Ratio: 45:55
Undergraduate Enrollment: 1,400
Graduate Enrollment: N/A
Scholarships/Academic: Yes **Athletic:** No **Financial Aid:** Yes
Expenses by: Year **In State:** $ 21,000 **Out of State:** $ 21,000
Specialty: Business, Education, Exercise & Health Science, Pre-Med
Degrees Conferred: BA, BS, Bachelor of Fine Arts, Bachelor of Music
Programs of Study: Accounting, Art, BioChemistry, Business Management, Chemistry, Communications, Computer Science, Corporate Fitness, Ecology, Economics, Elementary Education, English, Environmental Studies, Exercise Science, Foreign Languages, Graphic Design, Health Science, History, Humanities, International Business, Journalism, Liberal Arts, Literature, Mathematics, Modern Languages, Music, Philosophy, Physics, Political Science, PreDensity, PreEngineering, PreLaw, PreMed, Psychology, Public Health, Religion, Sociology, Sport Medicine, Theater

Men's Athletic Profile

614 W Superior Street
Alma, MI 48801
Coach: Scott Frey
Email: frey@alma.edu

NCAA III
Scots/Maroon, White
Phone: (517) 463-7352
Fax: (517) 463-7018

Estimated # of Men's Soccer Scholarships:
Conference: Michigan Intercollegiate Athletic Association
Program Profile: Play on a natural grass; playing season is the fall.
History: In 1997 we won our first MIAA Conference Championship. Was selected to compete in the NCAA Tournament. Finished the year ranked #14.
1999 Regional Champions
1999 NCAA Final Four
Achievements: Our team produced 3 All- Americans, won MIAA Champions in 1997 & 1999, 3 NCAA III Tournament bids.
Coaching: Scott Frey, Head Coach, USSF "B" License, Advanced National Diploma, in his third season he has taken a team which never finished better than 10-7 and fourth in the conference, to a 12-4-1 record, second place in the conference.
Roster In State: 16 **Out of State:** **Out of Country:**
ODP State: 1 **Regional:** **National:**
Walk-on/Other: **Graduation %:** N/A **Seniors on Team:** 7
Positions Needed: Keeper
Camp or Clinic Dates: Not Available
Most Recent Record: 16-5-2
Schedule: Otterbein, Calvin, Kalamazoo, Hope
Style of Play: Possession through combinations with an attitude to attack.

Women's Athletic Profile

614 W Superior Street
Alma, MI 48801
Coach: Tammy Anderson or
Email: Not Available

NCAA III
Scots/Maroon, Cream
Phone: (517) 463-7279
Fax: (517) 463-7277

Estimated # of Women's Soccer Scholarships: None
Conference: Michigan Intercollegiate Athletic Association
Roster in State: 15 **Out of State:** 2 **Out of Country:**
Positions Needed: All
Camp or Clinic Dates: Not Available
Most Recent Record: 5-12-1
Style of Play: 4-4-2 or 4-4-3 team possession and built on the attack. Play indirect.

Aquinas College
Academic Profile

Phone: 616-459-8281x3101

Grand Rapids, MI 49506

Type: 4 Yr.,Private,Liberal Arts
Founded: 1922
Website: http://www.aquinas.edu
Religion: Catholic-Dominican
SAT/ACT/GPA: Open/18Top 1/2 of class
Housing: Yes
Student/Faculty Ratio: 14/1
Male/Female Ratio: 37/63
Undergraduate Enrollment: 2100
Graduate Enrollment: 600
Scholarships/Academic: Yes **Athletic:** Yes **Financial Aid:** Yes
Expenses by: Year **In State:** $14,034 **Out of State:** $14,034
Specialty: Liberal Arts
Degrees Conferred: AA, AS, BA, BS, BFA, M
Programs of Study: Accounting, Art, Art History, Athletic Training, Biology, Business, Chemistry, Commercial Art, Communications, Computer Information Systems, Ecology, Economics, Education, English, Environmental Science, French, Geography, German, Gerontology, Graphic Art, History, Interior Design, International Business, Liberal Arts, Mathematics, Medical Laboratory Technology, Music, Nuclear Medical Technology, Philosophy, Science, PreDentistry, PreEngineering, PreLaw, PreMed, PreVet, Psychology, Religion, Science, Social Science, Spanish

Men's Athletic Profile

1607 Robinson Road SE
Grand Rapids, MI 49506-1741
Coach: Abraham Shearer
Email: arshearer@aol.com

NAIA
Saints/Red, White
Phone: (616) 459-8281
Fax: (616) 732-4548

Estimated # of Men's Soccer Scholarships: 4
Conference: Wolverine-Hoosier Athletic Conference
Program Profile: Preseason trip in early August followed by a twenty game and two scrimmages fall season. Field is natural grass located in the middle of 107-acre wooded campus. The program is well funded by the administration and strongly supported by students, faculty and alumni.
History: This fall program will be on its 25th years. It's been a varsity sport for 24 years. The program began 1975. 1999 was the best year in the history of the school as the team finished 19-3-2, won a conference championship, the conference tournament championship, and finished the season ranked #17 in the Country.
Achievements: WHAC 1999 Champions and WHAC Tournament Champions. 2000 WHCA Champions, 6 All-Americans in the 90's, and 1999 Conference coach of the year.
Coaching: Abraham Shearer Head Coach. He holds NSCAA National Diploma and works full time as a soccer director for soccer now! Camps and clinics.
Roster In State: 12 **Out of State:** 8 **Out of Country:**
ODP State: 2 **Regional:** **National:**
Walk-on/Other: **Graduation %:** 85 **Seniors on Team:** 3
Positions Needed: Forwards
Camp or Clinic Dates:
Most Recent Record: 16-2-3
Schedule: Bethel, Roberts Wesleyan, Harris Stowe, Walsh, Siena Heights, Madonna, Kalamazoo College, Calvin College, Hope College, Alma College.
Style of Play: All players have a strong commitment to defensive principles. Attacks are made from the back through overlapping runs.

Women's Athletic Profile

1607 Robinson Road, SE
Grand Rapids, MI 49506
Coach: Shannon Bessette
Email: bessesha@aquinas.edu

NAIA
Saints/Red, White
Phone: (616) 459-8281
Fax: (616) 732-4548

Estimated # of Women's Soccer Scholarships: 39,000
Conference: Wolverine-Hoosier Athletic Conference
Program Profile: Aquinas has one of the largest regulation fields in Michigan, located on campus, natural grass. the playing season is September to October; post-season through November.
History: Program began in 1992.
Achievements: 10 All - American; 3 All - Region; 6 All - Conference Academic; ranked 4th - 1992, 1993, 1994 and 3rd in 1995; 1995-.500 average and a player named NAIA Player of the Week in October.
Coaching: Shannon Bessette, Head Coach, 1995 WHAC Coach of the year. Assistant Coach Jaimie Watson.
Roster in State: 22 **Out of State:** 2 **Out of Country:** 0
Walk-on/Other: **Graduation %:** 85 **Seniors on Team:** 4
Positions Needed: 10
Camp or Clinic Dates: Not Available
Most Recent Record: 12-8-2
Schedule: Madonna Univ. Calvin College, Hillsdale College, St. Francis Univ.
Style of Play: Team oriented, controlled; we love to switch fields, make the other team run; majority of scoring off of crosses and striker breakaways of long, well executed through passes.

Calvin College

Academic Profile

Phone: (616) 957-6606

Grand Rapids, MI 49546

Type: 4 Yr.,Private,Liberal Arts
Founded: 1876
Website: http://www.calvin.edu
Religion: Reformed Church
SAT/ACT/GPA: 470v 470m/ 2020/2.5
Housing: Yes
Student/Faculty Ratio: 17:1
Male/Female Ratio: 44:56
Undergraduate Enrollment: 4,086
Graduate Enrollment: 42
Scholarships/Academic: Yes **Athletic:** No **Financial Aid:** Yes
Expenses by: Year **In State:** $ 18,500 **Out of State:** $ 18,500
Specialty: Business, Communications, Education, Engineering, Sciences
Degrees Conferred: BA, BS, BSA, M Ed
Programs of Study: Accounting, BioChemistry, Biology, Business Administration, Christian Ministry, Communications, Computer Science, Criminal Justice, Economics, Education, Film Studies, French, Geography, Geology, German, History, Mathematics, Medical Technology, Music, Natural Science, Nursing, Sociology, Social Science, Telecommunications

Men's Athletic Profile

3201 Burton SE
Grand Rapids, MI 49546
Coach: Dave Ver Merris
Email: dvermerr@calvin.edu

NCAA III
Knights/Maroon, Gold
Phone: (616) 957-6606
Fax: (616) 957-6777

Estimated # of Men's Soccer Scholarships: 0
Conference: Michigan Intercollegiate Athletic Association
Program Profile: Facilities include one game field which is natural turf that measurements of 70x120 and has a seating capacity of 500 and a three full size practice fields which is natural turf. The program includes and varsity and a junior varsity.

History: Our program began in 1959. Over the years we have received won 14 league championships and have made 4 NCAA D-3 appearances.
Achievements:
Coaching: Dave Vermerris, Head Coach, has thirty years high school experience and one in college level and Casey Ter Haar as the assistant coach.
Roster In State: 10 **Out of State:** 10 **Out of Country:**
Walk-on/Other: **Graduation %:** 90 **Seniors on Team:** 3
Positions Needed: midfield
Camp or Clinic Dates: Not Available
Most Recent Record: 16-3-1
Schedule: Not Completed
Style of Play: Play with a fast-pace and ball control.

Women's Athletic Profile

3201 Burton Street, SE
Grand Rapids, MI 49546
Coach: Dr. Deb Bakker
Email: dbakker@calvin.edu

NCAA III
Knights/Maroon, Gold
Phone: (616) 957-6222
Fax: (616) 957-6060

Estimated # of Women's Soccer Scholarships: None
Conference: Michigan Intercollegiate Athletic Association (MIAA)
Program Profile: Has a full length practice fields which is all natural grass. Has a 1,500 seats soccer stadium which is all grass field. Also home to the local professional soccer team Grand Rapids Explosion. Stadium is located on campus. Has twenty game season that runs from September through November against Division II, Division III and NAIA schools.
History: The program began in 1988. Program has a total won-loss record of 116-36-4 for winning percentage of .756. Team has won MIAA Titles in 1995 and 1996, and has won-loss record of 33-3-2 over the last two years.
Achievements: Conference Champions in 1995, 1996 & 1997; Tara Dyk was named All-American in 1996 & 1997; Amber Wiersma All-American in 1997.
Coaching: Dr. Deb Bakker, Head Coach, fourth year, career record is 33-3-2. He was a 1982 graduate of Calvin, Masters at Western Michigan, Ph.D. at Indiana University. Ted Terhaar - Assistant Coach, a 1975 graduate of Calvin, four year member of Calvin varsity soccer (1972-1975), head girl's soccer coach at Jenison Huigh School in the Spring.
Style of Play: Short passing game. Very aggressive offensively and defensively.

Central Michigan University

Academic Profile

Mount Pleasant, MI 48859

Phone: 517-774-4000

Type: 4 Yr.,Public **Founded:** 1892
Website: http://www.cmichi.edu **Religion:** Non-Affiliated
SAT/ACT/GPA: NCAA minimums **Housing:** Yes
Student/Faculty Ratio: 17:1 **Male/Female Ratio:** 1:1
Undergraduate Enrollment: 17,000 **Graduate Enrollment:** 4,000
Scholarships/Academic: Yes **Athletic:** Yes **Financial Aid:** Yes
Expenses by: Year **In State:** $ 21,500 **Out of State:** $ 21,500
Specialty: Education, Business
Degrees Conferred: BA, BS, BFA, BAA, BSBA, MA, MS
Programs of Study: Numerous Majors offered in each of these areas: Business Administration, Communications, Health-Related Programs, Human Services, Liberal Arts, Fine Arts, PreProfessional Programs, Science and Technology, Elementary Education, Secondary Education, Special Education

Women's Athletic Profile

208 IAC
Mt. Pleasant, MI 48859
Coach: Mark Salisbury
Email: nicole.bartkus@cmich.edu

NCAA I
Chippewas/Maroon, Gold
Phone: (517) 774-1123
Fax: (517) 774-1946

Estimated # of Women's Soccer Scholarships: 11
Conference: MAC
Program Profile: Brand new soccer stadium complex; 2 adjacent practice fields. Brand new full-sized indoor training complex.
Coaching: Mark Salisbury, Head Coach. Nicole Bartkus, Assistant Coach.

Roster in State: 22	**Out of State:** 6	**Out of Country:** 1
ODP State: 12	**Regional:** 5	**National:** 1
Walk-on/Other: 10	**Graduation %:** 100	**Seniors on Team:** 2

Camp or Clinic Dates: Not Available
Most Recent Record: 14-6-1

Concordia College - Ann Arbor

Academic Profile

Phone: (734)995-7342

Ann Harbor, MI 48105

Type: 4 Yr.,Private,Liberal Arts		**Founded:** 1963
Website: http://www.ccaa.edu		**Religion:** Lutheran
SAT/ACT/GPA: 20/2.5		**Housing:** Yes
Student/Faculty Ratio: 12:1		**Male/Female Ratio:** 60:40
Undergraduate Enrollment: 550		**Graduate Enrollment:** N/A
Scholarships/Academic: Yes	**Athletic:** Yes	**Financial Aid:** Yes
Expenses by: Year	**In State:** $ 20,200	**Out of State:** $ 20,200

Specialty: Education, Business, Art, Music, Psychology, English
Degrees Conferred: BA
Programs of Study: Art, Biblical Languages, Biology, Business Administration, Communications, Elementary Education, English, General Science, History, Political Science, Mathematics, Music, Church Music, Physical Education, Psychology, Religious Studies, Social Studies, Sociology, Sports Management

Men's Athletic Profile

4090 Geddes Road
Ann Arbor, MI 48105
Coach: Lloyd Ankle
Email: anklel@ccaa.edu

NAIA
Cardinals/Red, White
Phone: (313) 995-7342
Fax: (313) 995-4610

Estimated # of Men's Soccer Scholarships: N/A
Conference: WHAC

Women's Athletic Profile

4090 Geddes Rd.
Ann Arbor, MI 48105
Coach: David Tapping
Email: DevTapp1@aol.com

NAIA
Cardinals/Red, White
Phone: (734) 995-4607
Fax: (734) 995-4883

Estimated # of Women's Soccer Scholarships: 7
Conference: WHAC
Program Profile: We Start our training two weeks before classes begin in August. This year we are going out of state to train for one week. We will be in a tournament in September. Our soccer stadium natural grass, press box, and play 20 games. We are looking to be a very competitive in this coming year.
History: We are only a 4 year program, David Tapping is in his 2nd year as coach and has been doing recruiting, something that has never been done for the school until this year. We have 4 All-State (high- school) players coming back.
Achievements: Since we are literally starting from scratch we have had 4 players make All-Conference in 4 years. We also have 4 All-State High School players.
Coaching: Dave Tapping has a National "C" license and is our Head Coach.
Roster in State: 9 **Out of State:** 4 **Out of Country:** 6
Walk-on/Other: **Graduation %:** 95 **Seniors on Team:** 2
Positions Needed: All positions are open
Camp or Clinic Dates: July 31-August 3
Most Recent Record: 1-15
Schedule: Ferris State University, Aquinas College, Madonna University, Sienna Heights University, Spring Arbor College
Style of Play: Style of play is defense first, then counter attacks off defense. Possession soccer.

Cornerstone College

Academic Profile

Grand Rapids, MI 49505
Phone:

Type: 4 Yr.,Private,Liberal Arts **Founded:** 1941
Website: http://www.cornerstone.edu **Religion:** Regular Baptist
SAT/ACT/GPA: 850/18 **Housing:** Yes
Student/Faculty Ratio: 17:1 **Male/Female Ratio:** 45:55
Undergraduate Enrollment: 1,100 **Graduate Enrollment:** 115
Scholarships/Academic: Yes **Athletic:** Yes **Financial Aid:** Yes
Expenses by: Year **In State:** $ 15,118 **Out of State:** $ 15,118
Specialty: Liberal Arts, Business, Education
Degrees Conferred: AAS, BA, MDiv
Programs of Study: Bible, Business, Marketing, Business Administration, Education, PreMed, Predental, PreVet, Life Sciences, Psychology, Social Sciences, Letters/Literature, Philosophy, Physical Education, Religion, Theology, Visual & Performing Arts

Men's Athletic Profile

1001 East Beltline Avenue, NE
Grand Rapids, MI 49525
Coach: Mark Bell
Email: Mbell@cornerstone.edu

NAIA
Golden Eagles/Navy, Gold
Phone: (616) 222-1425
Fax: (616) 222-1542

Estimated # of Men's Soccer Scholarships: 6-8
Conference: Wolverine - Hoosier Athletic Conference
Program Profile: Play on a great grass field that has a seating capacity of 1,500 with a bleachers. A new 14 million dollar Athletic Facility with state of the art training room, underwater dunk tank, and a pro style locker room.
History: Program began in 1968; went to NCAA National Tournament 6 times in last 12 years. Daff Dresser is an All-American and Kern Matthews is a two time All-American Honorable Mention.
Achievements: The Eagles won the WHAL conference in 1993. Jeff Dressar is an All-American- all time leading scorer for C.U., Kern Matthews two time All-American Honorable Mention; and a number of Academic All-Americans. Jeff currently plays for Indiana A-league and 4 players play for USL- West Michigan Explosion(DDSC)

Coaching: Mark Ball has a BS in Exercise Science, which he is currently working on getting his masters in. He was the All-Conference player at Wheaton College('79-'82). He worked as the Asst. coach for North Park University in IL and University of MA at Boston; he also was head coach for U17 boys club Forest Hills Soccer Club and Asst. coach for West Michigan Explosion of PDSC. Matt Slemp is the Asst. coach who was All-Conference player at North Park University.

Roster In State: 18 **Out of State:** 4 **Out of Country:** 2
ODP State: 2 **Regional:** **National:** 1
Walk-on/Other: **Graduation %:** 100 **Seniors on Team:** 6
Positions Needed: Sweeper, Midfield, and Forward
Camp or Clinic Dates: June 19
Most Recent Record: 10-7-3
Schedule: Aquinas, Madonna, Westmont, Bethel, Kalamazoo College, Tri-State, Siena Heights
Style of Play: Possession, and physical defense.

Women's Athletic Profile

1001 East Beltline NE
Grand Rapids, MI 49525
Coach: Randy and Dianne Strawser
Email: stevethomas@cornerstone.edu

NAIA
Golden Eagles/Navy, Gold
Phone: (616) 222-1413
Fax: (616) 222-1542

Estimated # of Women's Soccer Scholarships: N/A
Conference: Wolverine-Hoosier Athletic Conference
Program Profile: This is our third year as a varsity program. We an 8,000 capacity soccer stadium. Our field is natural grass and we have a fall season. We have indoor training schedule and spring training scrimmages.
History: Our program began as a club team in 1996. Our first year record was 11-9-1. This is our second year as a varsity team.
Achievements: Steve Thomas was WHAC Coach of the Year in 1998. Freshman Grace Sohlden was WHAC Player of the Year-2nd Team Great Lakes Region in 1998. Sophomore Rachel Althoff was two-time All-WHAC and Freshman Jess Berryman named All-WHAC First Team in 1998.
Style of Play: We play a possession soccer, love to attack, will play direct style to speed up front. We like to work the ball out of the back.

Eastern Michigan University

Academic Profile

Phone: (734) 487-0291

Ypsilanti, MI 48197

Type: 4 Yr.,Public **Founded:** 1849
Website: http://www.emich.edu **Religion:** Non-Affiliated
SAT/ACT/GPA: Sliding Scale/21/3.0 **Housing:** Yes
Student/Faculty Ratio: 20:1 **Male/Female Ratio:** 1:4
Undergraduate Enrollment: 25,000 **Graduate Enrollment:** 10,000
Scholarships/Academic: Yes **Athletic:** Yes **Financial Aid:** Yes
Expenses by: Year **In State:** $ 8,825 **Out of State:** $ 13,878
Specialty: Education, Business
Degrees Conferred: BA, BS, BFA, BAE, BBA, BBE, BMP, MA, MS, MBA, MFA
Programs of Study: Accounting, Advertising, Anthropology, Aviation, Banking/Finance, BioChemistry, Biology, Chemistry, Broadcasting, Communications, Computer Science, Criminal Justice, Design, Dramatic Arts, Earth Science, Economics, Education, English, Geography, Geology, Management, Marketing, MicroBiology, Music, Nursing, Physics, Political Science, Psychology, Social Science

Men's Athletic Profile

200 Bowen Field House
Ypsilanti, MI 48197
Coach: Brian Tinnion
Email: Scott.Hall@emich.edu

NCAA I
Eagles/Green, White
Phone: (734) 487-2144
Fax: (734) 487-4568

Estimated # of Men's Soccer Scholarships: 5
Conference: Mid-America Conference
History: Won its first ever regular season in the Mid-American Conference game with a 3-1 victory over Western Michigan, and MAC Tournament game, in a convincing 4-1 win over perennial favorite Miami, OH.
Achievements: Has seven players earned post-season honors: MAC Freshman of the Year - George Tomasso (GK); All-MAC George Tomasso and Vesa Virtanen; All-MAC (1st team) - Tim McCarley; Academic All-MAC (Honorable Mention) - Scott Elmy, Brandon Podolski, and Vesa Virtanen.
Coaching: Brian Tinnion is our Head Coach.

Women's Athletic Profile

200 Bowen Field House
Ypsilanti, MI 48197
Coach: Scott Hall
Email: Scott.Hall@emich.edu

NCAA I
Eagles/Green, White
Phone: (734) 487-2144
Fax: (734) 487-4568

Estimated # of Women's Soccer Scholarships: 12
Conference: Mid-American Conference
Program Profile: 5 year old program. We play on natural grass field 110x80 and train year around.
History: 1994-2000 finished top 4 for past 6 years in MAC. 1999 NCAA Tournament 1st round.
Achievements: 1 All-American, 3 Great Lakes Region Players, 12 MAC 1st Team. 1 Coach of the Year for Conference in 1999
Coaching: Scott Hall is the Head Coach.1999 coach of the year. MAC Conference & tournament champions. NCAA Qualifier. Paul Tinnion is Assistant Coach.

Roster in State: 15	**Out of State:** 10	**Out of Country:** 0
ODP State: 15	**Regional:** 5	**National:** 0
Walk-on/Other: 5	**Graduation %:**	**Seniors on Team:** 4

Positions Needed: Forwards, Center Midfield
Camp or Clinic Dates: Not Available
Most Recent Record: 11-7-2
Schedule: Michigan State, Oakland Univ. Miami of Ohio, Central Michigan
Style of Play: Possession, attacking style of play.

Hillsdale College

Academic Profile

Hillsdale, MI 49242

Phone: (517) 437-7341

Type: 4 Yr.,Private,Liberal Arts		**Founded:** 1844
Website: http://www.hillsdale.edu		**Religion:** Non-Affiliated
SAT/ACT/GPA: 1200/26/3.5		**Housing:** Yes
Student/Faculty Ratio: 11:1		**Male/Female Ratio:** 1:1
Undergraduate Enrollment: 1,200		**Graduate Enrollment:** N/A
Scholarships/Academic: Yes	**Athletic:** Yes	**Financial Aid:** Yes
Expenses by: Year	**In State:** $ 19,090	**Out of State:** $ 19,090

Degrees Conferred: BA, BS
Programs of Study: Accounting, Art, Biology, Business Administration, Chemistry, Classical Studies, Early Childhood Education, Economics, Education, Elementary Education, English, French, German, History, Mathematics, Music, Philosophy, Physical Education, Physics, Political Science, Psychology, Religion, Sociology, Spanish, Theatre and Speech

Men's Athletic Profile

201 Oak Street
Hillsdale, MI 49242
Coach: Roy Bonny
Email: roy.bonny@hillsdale.edu

NCAA II
Chargers/Royal Blue, White
Phone: (517) 437-7341x3163
Fax: (517) 437-0014

Estimated # of Men's Soccer Scholarships: Varies
Conference: GLIAC
Program Profile: Hillsdale College Men's soccer plays on a natural grass field near the George Roche Sports Complex. The sports complex houses Jesse Philips Arena and a weight room. They compete in a traditional fall season and a limited spring season.
History: The program was a varsity sport in the fall of 1998. It has made steady progress, finishing this season with a 6-11 overall record. It was the best mark in the programs three years of existence.
Coaching: Roy Bonny just finished his second season as the head coach of the Charger program. He is also a part of the Olympic Development Program and state instructional staff. Dave Dilanni is in first season with the Chargers.
Roster In State: 12
Out of State: 5
Out of Country: 0
ODP State: 5
Regional: 1
National: 0
Walk-on/Other: 0
Graduation %: 100
Seniors on Team: 2
Camp or Clinic Dates: Not Available
Most Recent Record: 6-11-0
Schedule: Mercyhurst, Ashland, Wisconsin-Parkside, Lewis, Findlay

Women's Athletic Profile

201 Oak Street
Hillsdale, MI 49242
Coach: Roy Bonny
Email: roy.bonny@hillsdale.edu

NCAA II
Chargers/White, Blue
Phone: (517) 437-7341
Fax: (517) 437-0014

Estimated # of Women's Soccer Scholarships: Varies
Conference: Great Lakes Intercollegiate Athletic Conference
Program Profile: Hillsdale College Women's soccer plays on a natural grass field near the George Roche Sports Complex. The sports complex houses Jesse Philips Arena and a weight room. They compete in a traditional fall season and a limited spring season.
History: The program was instituted as a varsity sport in the fall of 1998. It made huge strides in its second season, collecting 8 wins, and set a standard for future success.
Achievements: NSCAA Team Ethics Gold Award in 1999
Coaching: Roy Bonny just finished his second season as the Head Coach. He is also a part of Olympic Development Program and state instructional staff in Michigan. Dave Dilanni is in his first season with the Charger program.
Roster in State: 9
Out of State: 6
Out of Country: 0
ODP State: 2
Regional: 1
National: 0
Walk-on/Other: 0
Graduation %: 100
Seniors on Team: 1
Positions Needed: Available
Camp or Clinic Dates: Not Available
Most Recent Record: 7-11-0
Schedule: Mercyhurst, Ashland, Findlay, Grand Valley State, Gannon, Lewis, Ferris State.

Hope College

Academic Profile

Phone: 616-395-7060

Holland, MI 49422

Type: 4 Yr.,Private,Liberal Arts
Founded: 1866
Website: http://www.hope.edu
Religion: Christian
SAT/ACT/GPA: Open
Housing: Yes
Student/Faculty Ratio: 13:1
Male/Female Ratio: 45:55
Undergraduate Enrollment: 2,900
Graduate Enrollment: N/A
Scholarships/Academic: Yes **Athletic:** No **Financial Aid:** Yes
Expenses by: Year **In State:** $ 19,874 **Out of State:** $ 19,874
Specialty: Sciences
Degrees Conferred: BA, BS
Programs of Study: Liberal Arts with concentrated study in 39 academic areas including Business and Management, Letters/Literature, Life Sciences, Physical Sciences, Psychology, Social Sciences

Men's Athletic Profile

P.O. Box 9000
Holland, MI 49422
Coach: Steve Smith
Email: Not Available

NCAA III
Flying Dutchmen/Orange, Blue
Phone: (616) 395-7569
Fax: (616) 395-7175

Estimated # of Men's Soccer Scholarships: None
Conference: Michigan Intercollegiate Athletic Association
Program Profile: Hope competes in the MIAA perennially contending or obtaining the conference title. “A commitment to excellence,” is our theme. We have had many division III appearances. The college has two natural grass fields and a recently constructed field house which provides modern locker-rooms and training room.
History: Program began in 1966. Hope has competed in the MIAA since 1970.
Achievements: Conference Champions - 1970, 1972, 1977, 1980-81, 1992, 1994; NCAA playoffs 3 times; 3 All - Americans . Coach of the Year NSCAA Mideast 1994
Coaching: Steve Smith, Head Coach, 7th year, played 4 years ant Grand Rapids Baptist State, assisted at Manchester College in 1988 & 1989, received doctorate degree in motor development from Michigan State.
Roster In State: 20 **Out of State:** 7 **Out of Country:** 0
Walk-on/Other: **Graduation %:** 98 **Seniors on Team:** 2
Positions Needed: Forwards
Camp or Clinic Dates: July 9-14, July 18-21
Most Recent Record: 13-6-1
Schedule: Wheaton, Ohio Wesleyan, Alma
Style of Play: Physical and tactically smart team. Most often use a 4-3-3, depending on personnel. Uses the entire field.

Women's Athletic Profile

168 E. 13th ST.
Holland, MI 49422
Coach: Leigh Sears
Email: sears@hope.edu

NCAA III
Flying Dutch/Orange, Blue
Phone: (616) 395-7850
Fax: (616) 395-7275

Estimated # of Women's Soccer Scholarships: None
Conference: Michigan Intercollegiate Athletic Association
Program Profile: Has two well-organized playing fields with a full service fieldhouse adjacent. Tough schedule each year. We practice hard, but focus on having fun.

History: Fall of 1998 the program will in its 10th year. Top 3 team in the conference every year.
Style of Play: High pressure, strong attacking team; high work rate and tough defensively. Controlled style of play.

Kalamazoo College
Academic Profile

Kalamazoo, MI 49006
Phone: (616) 337-7000

Type: 4 Yr.,Private,Liberal Arts
Founded: 1833
Website: http://www.kzoo.edu
Religion:
SAT/ACT/GPA: 1280/
Housing: Yes
Student/Faculty Ratio: 13/1
Male/Female Ratio: 43/57
Undergraduate Enrollment: 1,322
Graduate Enrollment: N/A
Scholarships/Academic: Yes **Athletic:** No
Financial Aid: Yes
Expenses by: Year **In State:** $25,725
Out of State: $25,725
Degrees Conferred: BA
Programs of Study: 24 Majors, 30 concentrations & special programs including Anthropology, Biology, Business Administration, Chemistry, Computer Science, Dramatic Arts, Economics, English, Fine Arts, French, German, Health Science, History, Management, Mathematics, Music, Philosophy, Physics, Political Science, PreDental, PreLaw, PreMed, Psychology, Religion, Secondary Education, Social Science, Spanish

Men's Athletic Profile

1200 Academy Street
Kalamazoo, MI 49006
Coach: Hardy Fuchs
Email: fusch@kzoo.edu

NCAA III
Hornets/Orange, Black
Phone: (616) 337-7048
Fax: (616) 337-5740

Estimated # of Men's Soccer Scholarships: None
Conference: Michigan Intercollegiate Athletic Association
Program Profile: We play on a natural grass field. Our playing season is in the Fall. We have very competitive program.
History: Program began in 1970; 8 MIAA Titles since 1985.
Achievements: Coach of the Year; Great Lakes Region in 1988; 8 All-Americans since 1985.
Coaching: Hardy Fuchs, Head Coach, is entering his 28th season with the program. He led the Hornets to eight Michigan Intercollegiate Athletic Association Championships (seven of the last 13) and four NCAA Division III playoffs appearances. His overall record is 272-115-34, including a 200-61-20 mark versus MIAA opponents over the last 14 years. He was named NCAA Division III Coach of the Year for the Great Lakes Region. He holds a soccer license "B" from the German Soccer Federation and a United States Soccer Federation "A" License.
Style of Play: Possession soccer with an attacking style.

Women's Athletic Profile

1200 Academy Street
Kalamazoo, MI 49006
Coach: Phil Nielsen
Email: molby@excite.com

NCAA III
Hornets/Orange, Black, White
Phone: (616) 337-7088
Fax: (616) 337-7401

Estimated # of Women's Soccer Scholarships: None
Conference: Michigan Intercollegiate Athletic Association (MIAA)
Program Profile: Games are played on natural grass fields. Nine games are played before school year begins.
History: Program began in 1981. We have an all-time record of 231-67-20.

Achievements: MIAA Champions 1999, 1998, 1989-1994; NCAA Participant 1999, 1998, 1997, 1991, 1990, 1988; MIAA MVP 1999, 1998, 1993, 1992, 1991, 1990, 1989; 10 All-Americans since 1986.
Coaching: Head Coach, Phil Nielson, is on his 3rd season and Assistant Coach, Susie Anderson, is in her 2nd season.
Roster in State: 18 **Out of State:** 1 **Out of Country:**
ODP State: 5 **Regional:** 2 **National:**
Walk-on/Other: **Graduation %:** 100 **Seniors on Team:** 6
Positions Needed: Forward, Midfield, Defense
Camp or Clinic Dates: Not Available
Most Recent Record: 16-3
Schedule: Western Michigan University, University of Detroit Mercy, Wheaton College, John Carroll University, Ohio Northern University, Calvin College
Style of Play: Possession game with high pressure. 3-5-2 with a sweeper and two marking backs, 3 central midfielders, and 2 outside midfielders.

Kellogg Community College

Academic Profile

Phone: 616-965-3931

Battle Creek, MI 49017

Type: 2 Yr.,Public,Jr. College **Founded:** 1956
Website: http://www.kellogg.cc.mi.us **Religion:** Non-Affiliated
SAT/ACT/GPA: Open **Housing:** No
Student/Faculty Ratio: 19/1 **Male/Female Ratio:** 1/3
Undergraduate Enrollment: 11,000 **Graduate Enrollment:** N/A
Scholarships/Academic: Yes **Athletic:** Yes **Financial Aid:** Yes
Expenses by: Year **In State:** $2600 **Out of State:** $4700
Specialty: Allied Health, Industrial Trades, Law Enforcement
Degrees Conferred: Associates
Programs of Study: Accounting, Anthropology, Art, Administration, Automotive, Banking/Finance, Biological, Broadcasting, Business, Chemistry, Communications, Corrections, Criminal, Dental, Drafting/Design Technology, Education, Engineering, Fire Science, Food Services, Gerontology, History, Legal, Machine/Tool Technology, Office Management, Paralegal, Pharmacy, Philosophy, Retail, Robotics, Science, Speech, Technical Writing, Theatre

Men's Athletic Profile

450 North Ave
Battle Creek, MI 49017
Coach: Michael C. Nunn
Email: nunnm@kellogg.cc.mi.us

NJCAA
Bruins/Royal, Silver
Phone: 616-965-4137x2836
Fax: 616-962-7370

Estimated # of Men's Soccer Scholarships: 8
Conference: Michigan Community College Athletic Association
Program Profile: We play end of August through November. 18-20 games against established Michigan and Ohio Community College programs; as well as 4-year College JV programs. Home games are played on a natural grass field with full bleachers and lights.
History: Our first Varsity year was 1996.
Achievements: MCCAA League Championship in 1999. Second place by a 1/2 game in 2000. 1996 Jared Bahr was Second Team All-American. Ranked as high as 20th place Nationally in 2000 polls. KCC placed 21st in the fianl poll in 2000.
Coaching: Head Coach: Michael Nunn- Eight years of coaching at KCC- 3 years Club, 3 years Varsity D-III (Non-scholarship), 2 years Varsity D-I. 30-9 record at the D-I level. He has coached over 20 years at various levels of soccer. Assistant coach: Andy McCormack-was All-State Plaer at Marshall High School. Played college soccer at KCC. Was a captain, leader in assists, strong influence on others. Assistant coach: Charles Pratt-certified referee-years of coaching with youth.

Roster In State: 15 **Out of State:** 1 **Out of Country:** 1
Walk-on/Other: **Graduation %:** N/A **Seniors on Team:** 7
Positions Needed: Keeper, Defender, Midfield
Camp or Clinic Dates: June 25-28-Girl Scouts Soccer, July 30-Aug. 3-Girls, Aug 6-10 boys
Most Recent Record: 15-4-0
Schedule: Schoolcraft College, Macomb CC, Lakeland CC, Cuyahoga CC, Cincinnati State Tech, Owens CC, Calvin College JV, Delta CC, Indiana Tech JV
Style of Play: Modified 4-4-2 with both an attach and a defensive midfielder. We play an aggressive man-to-man with constant pressure on the ball.

Madonna University

Academic Profile

Livonia, MI 48150
Phone:

Type: 4 Yr.,Private,Liberal Arts
Founded: 1947
Website: http://www.munet.edu
Religion: Catholic
SAT/ACT/GPA: 18/2.8
Housing: Yes
Student/Faculty Ratio: 18:1
Male/Female Ratio: 1:4
Undergraduate Enrollment: 4,000
Graduate Enrollment: Varies
Scholarships/Academic: Yes **Athletic:** Yes **Financial Aid:** Yes
Expenses by: Year **In State:** $ 9,500 **Out of State:** $ 9,500
Specialty: Education, Nursing, Criminal Justice, Business
Degrees Conferred: Bachelors, Master
Programs of Study: Criminal Justice, Sign Languages Studies, Nursing, Business & Education, Social Work, Sociology, Fire Science, Athletic Training, Art, Applied Science, Chemistry, English, Journalism, Hospice Care, History, Mental Health, Communications

Men's Athletic Profile

36600 Schoolcraft Rd
Livonia, MI 48150
Coach: Peter Alexander
Email: alexander@smtp.munet.edu

NAIA
Crusaders/Blue, Gold, White
Phone: (734) 432-5607
Fax: (734) 432-5611

Estimated # of Men's Soccer Scholarships: 2.5
Conference: Wolverine Hoosier Athletic Conference
Program Profile: Both our practice and game fields are natural grass and located on campus. We have four full-size goals, two quick goals, two 8x6 goals and an assortment of many goals.
Our stadium has 1,500 seats.
History: Our program began in 1994 with a 2-6 season. In 1995, we finished 9-10. Since then, through 1998, we have a 49-18 record with back-to-back conference championships in 1997 & 1998. In 1998, we were ranked as high as 10th in the nation finishing the season ranked 21st with an overall record of 20-3.
Achievements: 1995 Great Lakes Sectional Coach of the Year; 1998 WHAC Coach of the Year and Player of the Year; 1998 we had 6 All-Conference; 31 1st team All-Region.
Coaching: Peter Alexander, Head Coach, holds a USSF "A" License and National Youth License. He currently runs a youth program out of the Canton Soccer Club and owns and directs World Class soccer camps and clinics. Rick Larson, Assistant Coach, has a USSF "B" License and has won 3 state championships with his Bishop Foley Girls High School Team.
Style of Play: Strong defensively, quick attacking style. Used 3-5-2 system in previous season. Finished in the top 20 in goals per game and lowest goals against.

Women's Athletic Profile

36600 Schoolcraft
Livonia, MI 48150-1173
Coach: Rick Larson
Email: larson@smtp.munet.edu

NAIA
Lady Crusaders/Gold, White
Phone: (734) 432-5882
Fax: (734) 432-5611

Estimated # of Women's Soccer Scholarships:
Conference: Wolverine-Hosier Athletic Conference
Program Profile: Natural grass field on campus with a measurements on 110x65. three years old playing facility extremely well kept. Playing season is from August 16th to November.
History: Program began in 1998. Getting off the ground was a challenge. Now with key players in place and a solid foundation the future of our program is promising following the four year old men's program. Our goals are to reach the national tournament within four years.
Achievements: 2 All-Conference players, 1 All-Region player.
Coaching: Rick Larson, Head Coach, he holds USSF "B" License. ODP State team head coach. Bob Stohl and Kari Watson, Assistant Coaches.
Style of Play: Early in our program, we experimented with a few systems. Our personnel being the greatest decider what system we will play in 1999. We will try to use our strong midfielders to control tempo and make the best use of our explosive speed wide and up front.

Michigan State University
Academic Profile

East Lansing, MI 48824
Phone: 517-355-1855

Type: 4 Yr.,Public
Founded: 1855
Website: http://www.msu.edu
Religion: Non-Affiliated
SAT/ACT/GPA: 1120/24
Housing: Yes
Student/Faculty Ratio: 25:1
Male/Female Ratio: 48:52
Undergraduate Enrollment: 31,000
Graduate Enrollment: 9,000
Scholarships/Academic: Yes **Athletic:** Yes **Financial Aid:** Yes
Expenses by: Year **In State:** $ 17,320 **Out of State:** $ 31,450
Degrees Conferred: AA, BA, BS, MS, Ph.D., AAS
Programs of Study: Agriculture and Natural Resources, Arts and Letters, Business, Communication, Arts and Science, Education, Engineering, Human Ecology/Medicine, Natural Science, Nursing, Osteophathe Medicine, Social Science, Veterinary Medicine

Men's Athletic Profile

404 Jenison Field House
E. Lansing, MI 48824
Coach: Joe Baum
Email: baum@msu.edu

NCAA I
Spartans/Green, White
Phone: (517) 355-8493
Fax: (517) 432-1047

Estimated # of Men's Soccer Scholarships: 9.9
Conference: Big Ten Conference
Program Profile: Scholarship amount vary; play on old grass college field which has a seating capacity of a 5,000. Sponsored by Adidas. MSU plays a tough BIG TEN schedule Top ranked Midwest programs and one out of region tournament. MSU has state of the art lockeroom, training room and weight room facilities.
History: Became varsity sport in 1958. NCAA co-champions in 1964& 1965. 1996 finished second in Big Ten Conference.

Achievements: Joe Baum - Big Ten Coach of the Year in 2000 & 1996; Reid Frederichs (GK) - Big Ten Player of the Year in 1996. 3 frist team All-Big Ten, 3 2nd team All-Big Ten.
Coaching: Joe Baum, Head Coach, 21 years as a head coach at MSU, USSF "A" License, has a record of 230-179-37. Goalkeeper on 1967 & 1968, NCAA Co-Champions team at MSU. Steve Schad - Assistant Coach, 1982 MSU graduate, played for Coach Baum in 1979 & 1980, was five years assistant coach.
Asst. Damon Rensing-played at MSU 93-96 Holds a NSCAR "national" license
Roster In State: 20 **Out of State:** 5 **Out of Country:** 1
ODP State: 13 **Regional:** 7 **National:** 1
Walk-on/Other: 5 **Graduation %:** N/A **Seniors on Team:** 6
Positions Needed: Sweeper, Defender, Midfield, Forward
Camp or Clinic Dates: Not Available
Most Recent Record: 11-6-2
Schedule: Indiana, Univ. of San Diego, Penn St. UNLV, Ohio State, Univ. of Wisconsin, Oakland
Style of Play: Traditional 4-4-2 emphasis on possession and quick counter attacks. Encourages attack out of the back especially wing backs.

Women's Athletic Profile

404 Jenison Field House
East Lansing, MI 48824
Coach: Tom Saxton
Email: ath52@msu.edu

NCAA I
Spartans/Dark Green, White
Phone: (517) 353-3152
Fax: (517) 432-1047

Estimated # of Women's Soccer Scholarships: None
Conference: Big Ten Conference
Program Profile: Play on 120x75 yards natural grass field that seats 2,000.
History: Program began in 1986.
Achievements: 1994 big Ten Conference Regular Season champs; 1994 Big Ten Conference Coach of the Year.
Coaching: Tom Saxton, Head Coach. Tammy Anderson - Assistant Coach.
Style of Play: Indirect style of game.

Northern Michigan University

Academic Profile

Marquette, MI 49855
Phone: (906) 227-2105

Type: 4 Yr.,Public,Liberal Arts
Founded: 1899
Website: http://www.nmu.edu
Religion: Non-Affiliated
SAT/ACT/GPA: 900/19/2.25
Housing: Yes
Student/Faculty Ratio: 20:1
Male/Female Ratio: 1:1
Undergraduate Enrollment: 8,186
Graduate Enrollment: 1,200
Scholarships/Academic: Yes **Athletic:** Yes **Financial Aid:** Yes
Expenses by: Year **In State:** $ 8,186 **Out of State:** $ 10,622
Specialty: Education
Degrees Conferred: Baccalaureate, Associate, Certificate, Diploma
Programs of Study: Accounting, Art, Biology, Broadcasting, Business, Chemistry, Computer Programming, Criminal Justice, Elementary Education, English, French, Geography, Health, Liberal Arts, Math, Nursing, Physical Education, Psychology, Public Relations, Social Work, Sociology, Sport Medicine, Theatre, Water Science, Zoology, and many others..

Women's Athletic Profile

1401 Presque Isle Avenue
Marquette, MI 49855
Coach: John Peppler
Email: Not Available

NCAA II
Wildcats/F. Green, Old Gold
Phone: (906) 227-2139
Fax: (906) 227-2492

Estimated # of Women's Soccer Scholarships: None
Conference: Great Lakes Intercollegiate Athletic Conference
Program Profile: Pre-season begins in mid-August, non-conference begins during the first week of September. Conference play begins in late September. The pitch is grass, 80x120 yards, we also have an indoor stadium (turf) that has a seating capacity of 8,000.
History: The program began in 1996. The program is growing in prominence. NMU soccer will soon reach the highest in competitiveness as other women's sport at NMU. The University is committed to advancing women's soccer to a national prominence.
Achievements: Not-established-first year was in 1996. Placed one year on All-GLIAC Team - Kim Phelps.
Coaching: John Peppler, Head Coach, third year at NCAA. Milton Braga, Rio Janeko Brazil - Assistant Coaches. Six-time Brazil National Team. Merideth Ammons - GA, Milwaukee, WI, All-American at UW-Milwaukee
Style of Play: Solid defense, need scoring.

Northwood University

Academic Profile

Midland, MI 48460-2398

Phone: (800) 457-7878

Type: 4 Yr.,Private
Website: http://www.northwood.edu
SAT/ACT/GPA: 820/68/2.0
Student/Faculty Ratio: 24:1
Undergraduate Enrollment: 1,700
Scholarships/Academic: Yes
Athletic: Yes
Expenses by: Year
In State: $ 17,659

Founded: 1960
Religion: Non-Affiliated
Housing: Yes
Male/Female Ratio: 55:45
Graduate Enrollment: 207
Financial Aid: Yes
Out of State: $ 17,659

Specialty: Business, Computer, Computer Science
Degrees Conferred: AA, BBA, MBA
Programs of Study: Accounting, Advertising, Automotive After-Market Management, Automotive Marketing and Management, Banking and Finance/Management, Business Management, Computer Information Management, Economics & Management, Fashion Marketing & Merchandising, Health Care Management, Hotel Restaurant and Resort Management, International Business and Management

Women's Athletic Profile

4000 Whiting Dr
Midland, MI 48640
Coach: Doug Carter
Email: Not Available

NCAA II
Timberwolves/Col. Blue, White
Phone: (517) 837-4759
Fax: (517) 837-4484

Estimated # of Women's Soccer Scholarships: 5
Conference: Great Lakes Intercollegiate Athletic Conference
Program Profile: Northwood has a six year women's soccer program. It includes a natural grass playing field which covers 120x80 in area. Training takes place in the Bennett Sport Center, and presently on one practice field with a new practice field ready for fall 2000.
History: The program began in 1994 with a winning season. Struggling over the next few years, Northwood was without a winning record until 1998 season when the Timberwolves finished 10-7. They improved that mark to a school record breaking 13-6 mark this past fall.

Achievements: 1999 ranked 3rd Regional, 27th National; 1999 Freshman of the Year, Margart Humiecki.
Coaching: Doug Carter, Head Coach, will be with us for his second year and Michael Tetreault, Assistant Coach, for his first year here at Northwood.
Walk-on/Other: **Graduation %:** **Seniors on Team:** 1
Positions Needed: Goalkeeper, Fullback, Midfielder, Forward
Camp or Clinic Dates: Not Available
Most Recent Record: 13-6-0
Schedule: Mercyhurst College, Ashland University, Wheeling Jesuit University, University of Indianapolis, Gannon University, Grace College
Style of Play: Very direct play focus on high defensive pressure on the ball. Used a 3-5-2 formation for majority of 1999, now with right personnel, should be able to play more possession, working a more attacking, faster 4-4-2, that should play down on the flanks.

Oakland University
Academic Profile

Rochester, MI 48309-4401
Phone: (248) 370-3190

Type: 4 Yr.,Public,Liberal Arts,Engineering
Founded: 1957
Website: http://www.acs.oakland.edu
Religion: Non-Affiliated
SAT/ACT/GPA: 23/2.5
Housing: Yes
Student/Faculty Ratio: 19:1
Male/Female Ratio: 35:65
Undergraduate Enrollment: 14,000
Graduate Enrollment: N/A
Scholarships/Academic: Yes **Athletic:** Yes **Financial Aid:** Yes
Expenses by: Year **In State:** $ 8,000 **Out of State:** $ 14,000
Specialty: Broad base academic offering
Degrees Conferred: Bachelors, Master, Doctorate
Programs of Study: Accounting, Anatomy, Anthropology, Art, History, BioChemistry, Biology, Business, Chemistry, Communications, Computer Science, CytoTechnology, Economics, Education, Engineering, Environmental Science, Finance, French, German, Journalism, Mathematics, Marketing, Medical Laboratory, Music, Nursing, Philosophy, Physical Therapy, Physics, Political Science, Psychology, Toxicology, PreLaw, PreMed, PreDentistry

Men's Athletic Profile

Athletic Department
Rochester, MI 48309-4401
Coach: Gary Parsons
Email: parsons@oakland.edu

NCAA I
Golden Grizzlies/Gold, Black
Phone: (248) 370-3190
Fax: (248) 370-4056

Estimated # of Men's Soccer Scholarships: 9.9
Conference: Mid-Continent Conference
Program Profile: Former perennial NCAA Division II Top Ten program, moved to Division I for 1999. Facilities include $39,000,000 Recreational/Athletic Center, 1,000-seat soccer stadium with a grass surface that measures 120x70 yards, and indoor soccer facility.
History: Program began in 1973. Selected 14 times to the NCAA National Championships. There has never been a losing season in the history of the program. Seven times National Semi-finalist and three time National Finalist.
Achievements: Coach of the Year, Mideast Region five times; Central Region Champions five times; 11 All-Americans; 38 All-Regain players. Has been in the NCAA playoffs 14 seasons, 7 semi-final appearances, 3 appearances in the National Championship Final.
Coaching: Gary Parsons, Head Coach, this is his 20th seasons. He has a USSF “A” License and has been to the NCAA playoffs 13 times. Region II ODP Staff, 20 years head coach at OU. He was named Regional Coach of the Year five times. Steve Sergeant - Assistant Coach, 17 years professional with Everten FC and NASL Detroit Express, Region II ODP Staff, 9 years assistant coach at OU.

Roster In State: 7 **Out of State:** 2 **Out of Country:** 9
ODP State: 6 **Regional:** 3 **National:**
Walk-on/Other: **Graduation %:** N/A **Seniors on Team:**
Positions Needed: Center back, Center Midfielder, Striker
Camp or Clinic Dates: Not Available
Most Recent Record: 11-6-2
Schedule: University of San Diego, Akron, Gonzaga, Cincinnati, Ohio State, Butler, Marquette
Style of Play: Zonal Defense.

Women's Athletic Profile

Athletic Department
Rochester, MI 48309-4401
Coach: Nick O'Shea
Email: nkoshea@oakland.edu

NCAA I
Lady Pioneers/Black, Gold
Phone: (248) 370-4009
Fax: (248) 370-4056

Estimated # of Women's Soccer Scholarships: 3
Conference: Mid-continent Conference
Program Profile: 2001 will be the 8th season of Oakland University's soccer program. The playing season begins in August and ends in November. OU has a natural grass stadium size field which will be new in 2001. The off season last from February-April and is played on the indoor soccer dome.
History: Oakland University began women's soccer in 1994 and went DI in 1998. OU captured the Mid-Continent Conference Tournament in 2000. Oakland women's soccer also won the title of Mid-Con Champions in both 1999 and 2000.
Achievements: 2 All-Americans, Conference Coach of the Year (1999) Nick O'Shea, Conference Champions 3 years (1996,99,2000) and several All-Region Players.
Coaching: Nick O'Shea, Head Coach (7th season) USSF "A" licensed, head age group Coach for Region II. ODP Overseas Michigan ODP, ranked 6th among Division I winningest active coaches that have been at the DI level less than 5 years. Assistant Coach- Michele Brach (1st season) University of Michigan (1999)
Roster in State: 12 **Out of State:** 0 **Out of Country:** 11
Walk-on/Other: **Graduation %:** **Seniors on Team:** 3
Positions Needed: Mid and defender
Camp or Clinic Dates: July 15-19, July 29-Aug. 2
Most Recent Record: 12-5-1
Schedule: Univ. of Michigan, Univ. of Wisconsin, Univ. of Southern California, Michigan State Univ., Marquette Univ.
Style of Play: Aggressive, attacking, thoughtful play.

Olivet College

Academic Profile

Phone:

Olivet, MI 49076

Type: 4 Yr.,Private,Liberal Arts **Founded:** 1844
Website: http://www.olivetnet.edu **Religion:** UCC
SAT/ACT/GPA: 18 **Housing:** Yes
Student/Faculty Ratio: 12:1 **Male/Female Ratio:** 6:4
Undergraduate Enrollment: 850 **Graduate Enrollment:** 75
Scholarships/Academic: Yes **Athletic:** No **Financial Aid:** Yes
Expenses by: Year **In State:** $ 17,710 **Out of State:** $ 17,710
Degrees Conferred: BA
Programs of Study: Education, Insurance and Business Administration are the most popular. Typical Liberal Arts Institution curriculum offering general academic program including Business and Management, Communications, Education, Liberal Art Education, Psychology and Sociology, Visual/Performing Arts

Men's Athletic Profile

300 S Main St., Athletics
Olivet, MI 49076
Coach: Doug Booth
Email: Not Available

NCAA III
Comets/Red, White
Phone: (616) 749-7156
Fax: (616) 749-7229

Estimated # of Men's Soccer Scholarships: None
Conference: Michigan Intercollegiate Athletic Association

Women's Athletic Profile

320 S Main
Olivet, MI 49076
Coach: Hans Morgan
Email: hmorgan@olivetcollege.edu

NCAA III
Comets/Red, White
Phone: (616) 749-7155
Fax: (616) 749-7229

Estimated # of Women's Soccer Scholarships: None
Conference: Michigan Intercollegiate Athletic Association
Program Profile: Olivet College has recently completed a new athletic facility with new soccer field. The field and the facility are state-of-the-art. The women's soccer team plays a full NCAA DIII schedule in the fall. In the off season the team participates in a strength and conditioning program along with spring "non-traditional" schedule.
History: The program began in 1989. The overall record is 63-126-10 (.34). In 1998, Olivet College won the MIAA Tournament and advanced to the NCAA Tournament. 2000 was the 1st season under new Coach Hans Morgan. The team went 7-6-1 (.54), which is already the highest winning percentage of any Coach in Olivet College History.
Achievements: 1998 MIAA Tournament Champions, 1998 NCAA Tournament Appearance
Coaching: Head Coach Hans Morgran, Assit. Coach -TBA
Roster in State: 11 **Out of State:** 4 **Out of Country:** 4
ODP State: 5 **Regional:** 0 **National:** 0
Walk-on/Other: 0 **Graduation %:** **Seniors on Team:** 2
Positions Needed: ALL
Camp or Clinic Dates: Not Available
Most Recent Record: 7-6-1
Schedule: Kalamazoo College, Calvin. College, Hope College, Albion College, Penn St. Behrend College.

Siena Heights University

Academic Profile

Phone: (517) 264-7873

Adrian, MI 49221

Type: 4 Yr.,Private,Liberal Arts
Founded: 1919
Website: http://www.sienahts.com
Religion: Dominican
SAT/ACT/GPA: 22/2.5
Housing: Yes
Student/Faculty Ratio: 14:1
Male/Female Ratio: 55:45
Undergraduate Enrollment: 1,100
Graduate Enrollment: 200
Scholarships/Academic: Yes **Athletic:** Yes **Financial Aid:** Yes
Expenses by: Year **In State:** $ 16,190 **Out of State:** $ 16,190
Specialty: A wide variety of academic majors
Degrees Conferred: AA, BA, AFA, BFA, BS, BAS, AS
Programs of Study: Accounting, American Studies, Art, Biology, Business Administration, Management, Marketing, Chemistry, Child Development, Computer Information Systems, Hospitality Management, Human Services, Criminal Justice, Gerontology, Psychology, Public Administration, Music, PreLaw, Philosophy, PreEngineering, PreDentistry

Men's Athletic Profile

1247 E Siena Heights Drive
Adrian, MI 49221
Coach: Aldo Zid
Email: azid@sinahts.edu

NAIA
Saints/Navy, Gold, White
Phone: (517) 264-7873
Fax: (517) 264-7737

Estimated # of Men's Soccer Scholarships: 5
Conference: Wolverine - Hoosier Athletic Conference
Program Profile: We have a very competitive program and a nicely manicured and well maintained surface field. We play a fall season.
History: We began in 1985. Our program has a strong tradition of winning, having played in the National Tournament, Regional Finals and Conference Finals, numerous conference titles, Regional and National.
Achievements: District Titles, Regional and National tourney appearances.
Coaching: Aldo Zid, Head Coach, holds a USSF National License. He has Coach of the Year Awards, Conference Championships, Regional experience as ODP Coach, premier level coaches experience, seven years at the college level as well as college playing experience. He was a former Regional Coach of the Year (New England Region) and has coached of several Conference Championship Teams. 1995-1997 Coach of Conference Champs; 1997 Conference Coach of the Year. Scott Oliver is the Assistant Coach.
Style of Play: Possession team - short passing through triangulation and a build up from the back.

Women's Athletic Profile

1247 E Siena Heights Drive
Adrian, MI 49121
Coach: Aldo Zid
Email: azid@sienahts.edu

NAIA
Saints/Royal, White
Phone: (517) 264-7873
Fax: (517) 264-7737

Estimated # of Women's Soccer Scholarships:
Conference: Wolverine-Hoister Conference
Program Profile: The team plays on natural grass field which is nicely manicured and well maintained surface.
History: The program began in 1986.
Achievements: Won 1993, 1994, 1995, & 1997 Conference Titles, Regional Final Four, National Runner-Ups.
Coaching: Aldo Zid, Head Coach, USSF National License, Coach of the Year Awards, Conference Championships, ODP Regional and Premier Level coaching experience. Former Regional Coach of the Year (New England Region), coach of several conference championships. 1995-1997 Coach of Conference Champs; 1997 Conference Coach of the Year. John Mallon, Assistant Coach.
Style of Play: System varies, generally play to feet and play wide through build-up.

Spring Arbor College

Academic Profile

Spring Arbor, MI 49283

Phone: (517) 750-1200

Type: 4 Yr.,Private,Liberal Arts
Website: http://www.admin.arbor.edu
SAT/ACT/GPA: 20
Student/Faculty Ratio: 25:1
Undergraduate Enrollment: 1,900
Scholarships/Academic: Yes
Athletic: Yes
Expenses by: Year
In State: $ 15,310
Specialty: Education, Communication
Degrees Conferred: Bachelors, Associate

Founded: 1873
Religion: Free Methodist
Housing: Yes
Male/Female Ratio: 1:3
Graduate Enrollment: 800
Financial Aid: Yes
Out of State: $ 15,310

Programs of Study: Exercise Sports, PreMed, Communications, Education, Christian Ministries, Psychology, Biology, Music, Arts, Chemistry, English, BioChemistry, French, Spanish, Geography, History, Greek, Math, Philosophy, Political Science, Religion, Social Work, Sociology, Speech, Urban Studies, Accounting, Business

Men's Athletic Profile

106 Main Street
Spring Arbor, MI 49283
Coach: Anil Joseph
Email: anilj@admin.arbor.edu

NAIA
Cougars/Blue, Gold
Phone: 517-524-8917
Fax: (517) 750-2745

Did Not Return Profile

Women's Athletic Profile

106 E Main Street
Spring Arbor, MI 49283
Coach: Lyle Wensley
Email: Not Available

NAIA
Cougars/Navy, Gold
Phone: (517) 750-6510
Fax: (517) 750-2745

Estimated # of Women's Soccer Scholarships: None
Conference: Wolverine-Hoosier Conference

University of Detroit Mercy

Academic Profile

Phone: 313-993-1245

Detroit, MI 48219-0900

Type: 4 Yr.,Private,Liberal Arts
Website: http://www.uomercy.edu
SAT/ACT/GPA: 870+/20+
Student/Faculty Ratio: 18:1
Undergraduate Enrollment: 8,000
Scholarships/Academic: Yes **Athletic:** Yes
Expenses by: Year **In State:** $ 20,322

Founded: 1877
Religion: Jesuit
Housing: Yes
Male/Female Ratio: 44:56
Graduate Enrollment: N/A
Financial Aid: Yes
Out of State: $ 20,322

Specialty: Science
Degrees Conferred: ASBA, BS, BCE, BEE, BFA, MA, MS, DMD
Programs of Study: Accounting, Architecture, Biology, Nursing, Business, Chemistry, Engineering, Communications Studies, Computer Information Systems, Counseling, Computer Science, Economics, Education, Criminal Justice, Counseling, English, Health Services, History, Math, Philosophy, Physics, Political Science, Psychology, Dentistry, Religious Studies, Social Work, Sociology, Sports Medicine, Theatre

Men's Athletic Profile

4001 W McNichols Ave.
Detroit, MI 48219-0900
Coach: Morris Lupenec
Email: corderudm@aol.com

NCAA I
Titans/Red, White
Phone: (313) 993-1739
Fax: (313) 993-2449

Estimated # of Men's Soccer Scholarships: 9.9
Conference: Midwestern Collegiate Conference
Program Profile: Playing and practice field both on campus, both natural grass, we play 7-8 home games per season, as well as two pre-season tournament.

History: Program began in 1987, current coach Morris Lupenec took over in 1993 and has only 3 losing seasons since. Team has won the conference championship twice, been to the conference tournament championship four times, and has on NCAA appearance (1996), all under current head coach.
Achievements: 2 time coach of the year, two conference players of the year, numerous All-Region selections, two conference titles. Last player drafter (1999) in first round of NPSC.
Coaching: Morris Lupenec, Head Coach, continues to prove himself as one of the top soccer coaches in the region. With his playing and coaching knowledge and love of the game, he has the belief that he can get the Titans to the same position that he did in 1996-the MCC Tournament Championship and a second berth in the NCAA Tournament. Steve Corder, Assistant Coach, 1998 graduate and a member of the Titan's men's soccer program. He came to UDM in 1994 from one of the top high school teams in the state at DeLaSalle. Also a member of the highly respected Vandar II Club program, where he earned All-Catholic League honors as a senior. He be responsible for many duties both on the sidelines as well as in the office. his responsibilities include making travel arrangements, overseeing practices and conditioning as well as a various administrative duties, ensuring the things runs smoothly for the team both on the road and at home. While fulfilling his coaching responsibilities, he will begin pursuing a law degree at UDM's Law School.

Roster In State: 19	**Out of State:** 4	**Out of Country:** 2
ODP State: 8	**Regional:**	**National:**
Walk-on/Other:	**Graduation %:** 80	**Seniors on Team:** 4

Camp or Clinic Dates: Not Available
Most Recent Record: 7-12
Schedule: San Francisco, Bowling Green, Butler, University of Michigan, Oregon State, Loyola Marymont, Sacramento State, Drury, Valparaiso
Style of Play: Up-tempo, fast-paced, high scoring.

Women's Athletic Profile

4001 W McNichols Ave.	**NCAA I**
Detroit, MI 48219-0900	Titans/Red, White, Navy Blue
Coach: Mike Lupenec	**Phone:** (313) 993-1739
Email: Not Available	**Fax:** (313) 993-1765

Estimated # of Women's Soccer Scholarships: None
Conference: Midwestern Collegiate Conference

<u>University of Michigan - Ann Arbor</u>
Academic Profile

Phone: (734) 764-7433

Ann Arbor, MI 48109-2201

Type: 4 Yr.,Public,Liberal Arts,Engineering		**Founded:** 1817
Website: http://www.mgoblue.com		**Religion:** Non-Affiliated
SAT/ACT/GPA: 1030+		**Housing:** Yes
Student/Faculty Ratio: 15:1		**Male/Female Ratio:** 1.2:1
Undergraduate Enrollment: 36,450		**Graduate Enrollment:** 14,000
Scholarships/Academic: Yes	**Athletic:** Yes	**Financial Aid:** Yes
Expenses by: Year	**In State:** $ 9,559	**Out of State:** $ 19,881

Specialty: Architecture, Nursing
Degrees Conferred: AB, BS, BFA, BBA, BMus, BSN, MA, MS, MBA, MFA, Ph.D., MD, JD
Programs of Study: Accounting, Anthropology, Art, Architecture, Astronomy, Atmospheric/Oceanic Studies, Biblical, Biology, Botany, Business, Chemistry, Computer, Dentistry, Design, Economics, Education, Engineering, Geology, History, Kinesiology, Literature, Management, Mathematics, Medieval, Movement, Music, Natural Resources, Nursing, Oceanography, Pharmacy, Philosophy

Men's Athletic Profile

1000 S. State St.
Ann Arbor, MI 48109
Coach: Steve Burns
Email: burnss@umich.edu

NCAA I
Wolverines/Maize and Blue
Phone: 734-615-4546
Fax: 734-647-7825

Estimated # of Men's Soccer Scholarships: Full Funding
Conference: Big Ten Conference
Program Profile: Fully funded start-up program in 2000 season. Temporary grass practice and game facility on campus. New multi-million dollar grass game and practice facility will be ready in fall of 2002.
History: 2000 Inaugural Season!
Achievements: Club program since 1946 with multiple national titles
Coaching: Steve Burns-Head Coach, "A" License; Graduate of the University of Michigan in '89; Master's Degree in Kinesiology; Region II ODP Staff coach; Former player and coach in the USISL; Former coach of the U-M men's soccer club (8 years)
Walt Barrett-Assistant coach, "B" License; Michigan ODP Staff Coach, Former Asst. coach at Eastern Michigan.
Assistant Coach-Ernie Yarborough. Former A-League professional keeper. Former goalkeeper coach at Indiana University, 97-99.

Roster In State: 18 **Out of State:** 7 **Out of Country:** 0
ODP State: 12 **Regional:** 5 **National:** 2
Walk-on/Other: **Graduation %:** 100 **Seniors on Team:** 8

Positions Needed: Central Mid, Wide Mid, Forward
Camp or Clinic Dates: July 22-26, July 29-August 2
Most Recent Record: 6-10-0
Schedule: Indiana, Penn State, Ohio State, Michigan State, Oakland, Dayton, Illinois-Chicago, Evansville
Style of Play: Players Ultimately dictate the style of play. Emphasis on possession with attack in the flanks and a pressing defense.

Women's Athletic Profile

1000 S. State St.
Ann Arbor, MI 48109-2201
Coach: Debbie Belkin
Email: dbelk@umich.edu

NCAA I
Wolverines/Maize, Blue
Phone: (734) 647-4530
Fax: (734) 764-3221

Estimated # of Women's Soccer Scholarships: varies
Conference: Big Ten Conference
Program Profile: The Michigan soccer field is an natural grass field with seating for 3000. Team locker room, training room and meeting room are located on site. The field is 6 years old and the building is 4 years old.
History: The Michigan Soccer Program began play as a varsity sport in 1994. In the six years of its existence, the Wolverines have accumulated a 77-42-9 record. It has already established itself as a regional power, winning the Big Ten Tournament in 1997 and 1999. The Wolverines have started to establish themselves nationally, qualifying for the NCAA Tournament in each of the past three years.
Achievements: The made Big Ten Tournament champions in 1997 and NCAA Tournament Participant in 1997, 1998 and 1999.
Coaching: Debbie Belkin, Head Coach, USSF "A" License. She named Michigan's first women's varsity soccer head coach on December 13,1993, 1997 Great Lakes Region Coach of the Year, 1993 MAAC Coach of the Year at Fairfield University. She is a member of the 1991 United Women's World Championships team. US National Team Member in 1986-1991. She was named three-time All-American at Massachusetts and she played in the NCAA National Championship Final Four for four seasons. Inducted in to the University of Massachusetts of Hall of Fame in 19999 and Massachusetts Soccer Hall of Fame in 19999. Member of Soccer America All-Decade (1980's) Team and MVP Squad in 1986 and 1987.

Roster in State: 8 | **Out of State:** 18 | **Out of Country:** 0
ODP State: 16 | **Regional:** 10 | **National:** 4
Walk-on/Other: | **Graduation %:** | **Seniors on Team:** 4
Positions Needed: Midfield, Forwards, Goalkeeper, Defender
Camp or Clinic Dates: June 26-30, July 23-27
Most Recent Record: 17-6-1
Schedule: Notre Dame, Penn State, Southern California, Minnesota, Missouri, Illinois, Ohio State, Arizona State, Indiana, Washington
Style of Play: The style of play could be characterized as that of a possession orientated type. It is an attacking style that has finesses with an aggressiveness that gets inline. It combines various player strengths to play an exciting style of soccer.

Western Michigan University
Academic Profile

Kalamazoo, MI 49008
Phone: 616-387-1000

Type: 4 Yr.,Public,
Founded: 1903
Website: http://www.wmich.edu
Religion: Non-Affiliated
SAT/ACT/GPA: 900/18/2.5
Housing: Yes
Student/Faculty Ratio: N/A
Male/Female Ratio: 60:40
Undergraduate Enrollment: 23,000
Graduate Enrollment: 5,000
Scholarships/Academic: Yes | **Athletic:** Yes | **Financial Aid:** Yes
Expenses by: Year | **In State:** $ Varies | **Out of State:** $ Varies
Specialty: Business, Engineering, Education
Degrees Conferred: BA, BS, BFA, MA, MS, MFA, Ph.D.
Programs of Study: Business and Management, Business/Office and Marketing/Distribution, Communications, Education, Engineering, Parks/Recreation, Protective Services, Public Affairs, Fine Arts, Health & Human Services

Men's Athletic Profile

217 Red Fieldhouse
Kalamazoo, MI 49008
Coach: Chris Karwoski
Email: karwoski@wmich.edu

NCAA I
Broncos/Black, Gold, White
Phone: (616) 387-3059
Fax: (616) 387-3668

Estimated # of Men's Soccer Scholarships: 6.0
Conference: Mid-American Conference
Program Profile: Has grass training area; grass practice field and grass game field which measures 74x112 yards.
History: Program began in 1971 and has developed over the years to be contender in the Mid-American Conference.(6-29-4)
Achievements: 5 All-Mid-Americans Conference players, 7 MAC All-Academic Team players, 11 All-Mideast, 3 All-Academic Region team players, 18 named Academic All-American since 1990.
Coaching: Chris Karwoski, Head Coach, entering second season with the program.
Roster In State: 14 | **Out of State:** 12 | **Out of Country:** 2
ODP State: 4 | **Regional:** 3 | **National:** 2
Walk-on/Other: | **Graduation %:** 90 | **Seniors on Team:** 3
Positions Needed: Forward, Attacking Center Midfield, Defense
Camp or Clinic Dates: Not Available
Schedule: Akron, Oakland, Kentucky, Michigan State, Bowling Green, University of Michigan
Style of Play: Variable to players in program; attack oriented. Zonal defending. 3-4-2 Build out of back. 3-5-2 Aggressive Defensively.

Women's Athletic Profile

217 Read Fieldhouse
Kalamazoo, MI 49008
Coach: Mike Haines
Email: michael.haines@wmich.edu

NCAA I
Broncos/Brown, Gold, Black
Phone: (616) 387-3059
Fax: (616) 387-3668

Estimated # of Women's Soccer Scholarships: None
Conference: Mid - American Conference

minnesota

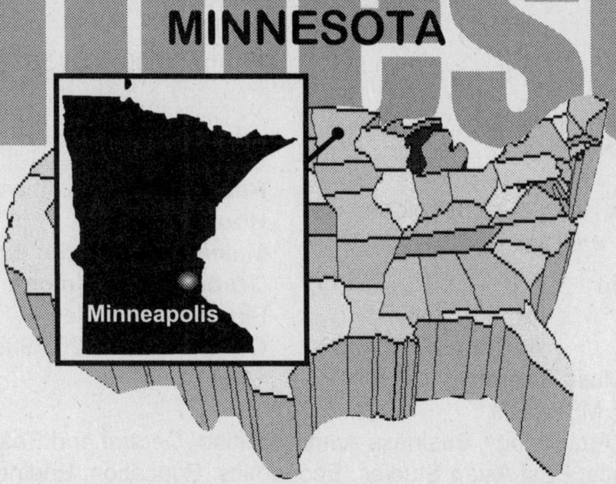
MINNESOTA
Minneapolis

Augsburg College
Academic Profile

Phone: (800) 788-5678

Minneapolis, MN 55454

Type: 4 Yr.,Private,Liberal Arts
Website: http://www.augsburg.edu
SAT/ACT/GPA: 950/20
Student/Faculty Ratio: 14:1
Undergraduate Enrollment: 1,550
Scholarships/Academic: Yes **Athletic:** No
Expenses by: Year **In State:** $ 20,490
Founded: 1869
Religion: ELCA Lutheran
Housing: Yes
Male/Female Ratio: 49:51
Graduate Enrollment: 1,292
Financial Aid: Yes
Out of State: $ 20,490.
Specialty: Business, Education, Music Therapy
Degrees Conferred: BA, BS, MA, MSW, BM
Programs of Study: Accounting, Art, Biology, Business Administration, Central and East European Studies, Chemistry, Communications, Computer Science, East Asian Studies, Economics, Education, Engineering, English, Health Education, History, International Relations, Management Information Systems, Mathematics, Metro-Urban Studies, Modern Languages, Music, Nordic Area Studies, Nursing, Philosophy, Physical Education, Physician's Assistant, Physics, Political Science, Psychology, Religion, Russian, Social Work, Sociology, Theatre Arts, Trans-Disciplinary Women's Studies

Men's Athletic Profile

2211 Riverside Ave. S
Minneapolis, MN 55454
Coach: Mike Navarre
Email: navarre@augsburg.edu

NCAA III
Auggies/Maroon, White
Phone: (612) 330-1623
Fax: (612) 330-1382

Estimated # of Men's Soccer Scholarships: N/A
Conference: Minnesota Intercollegiate Athletic Conference (MIAC)
Program Profile: Facilities: Anderson-Nelson Field, Astro-turf, 2,000 capacity. Season: Fall, 18 regular season contests (MIAC/non-conference).
History: Program began in 1968. MIAC Titles and NAIA tournament berths in 1973, 1974, 1975, and 1980. Overall record since 1973 is 161-222-34.
Achievements: 3 MIAC Championships, Academic Excellence, several NAIA playoffs berths. 35 All-MIAC players since 1974.
Coaching: head Coach, Mike Novarre, is entering his second season. 1992 graduate of the University of Wisconsin-Madison. Received BA Honors in Sociology and Psychology. 1999 received a MA in Sport Psychology at the University of North Carolina- Chapel Hill, where he was The Corad-Ast. for the UNC women's team. 1997-1999 head boy's and Ast. Girls varsity coach at Madison Edgewood H.S., Madison WI. from 1995-1997. USSF "B" license and NSCAA Adu. National Diploma. Assistant Coaches are Chris Martinelle, Jim Stone, and Ride Tungoch.
Roster In State: 15 **Out of State:** 5 **Out of Country:** 7
ODP State: 3 **Regional:** 1 **National:**
Walk-on/Other: **Graduation %:** 100 **Seniors on Team:** 3
Positions Needed: Forwards, Goalkeeper, MF
Camp or Clinic Dates: Macalester, St. Olaf, Madison Edgewood, Gustavos Adolphus, St. Thomas
Most Recent Record: 3-13
Schedule: Macalester, St. Olaf, Madison Edgewood, Gustavos Adolphus, Concordia, St. Thomas
Style of Play: High Pressure, Direct attacking style.

Women's Athletic Profile

2211 Riverside Ave. S
Minneapolis, MN 55454
Coach: Mike Navarre
Email: navarre@augsburg.edu

NCAA III
Auggies/Maroon, Grey
Phone: (612) 330-1623
Fax: (612) 330-1382

Estimated # of Women's Soccer Scholarships: None
Conference: Minnesota Intercollegiate Athletic Conference
Program Profile: Facilities: Anderson Nelson field (Astro-turf, 2,000 capacity). Season: Fall, 18-regular-season contests (MIAC/non-conference).
History: The varsity program began in 1986. highest MIAC finishes have been fifth (three times), overall record in school history is 79-129-12; 34-14-4 since 1995.
Achievements: MIAC Coach of the Year in 1995 (Scott Hansing), 2 All-Americans; 5 All-West Region; 26 All- MIAC players; 1 MIAC Player of the Year (Astrid Larssen).
Coaching: Head Coach Mike Navarre has been with Auggies for 2 years, in that time the program is getting stronger went from a record of 2-15 to a record of 7-10-1 and started 7 freshman. Was the grad assistant at North Carolina.

Roster in State: 13
Out of State: 4
Out of Country: 0
ODP State: 5
Regional: 0
National: 0
Walk-on/Other:
Graduation %: 100
Seniors on Team: 3

Positions Needed: Forwards, Midfielder, Defenders
Camp or Clinic Dates: August
Most Recent Record: 7-10-1
Schedule: Macalster College, St. Thomas, Grinnell, Edgewood, St. Benedictine.
Style of Play: High pressure attacking will play a 3 front next season.

Bethel College

Academic Profile

St. Paul, MN 55112

Phone: (651) 638-6400

Type: 4 Yr.,Private,Liberal Arts
Founded: 1947
Website: http://www.bethel.edu
Religion: Baptist
SAT/ACT/GPA:
Housing: Yes
Student/Faculty Ratio:
Male/Female Ratio:
Undergraduate Enrollment: 2,456
Graduate Enrollment: N/A
Scholarships/Academic: Yes
Athletic: No
Financial Aid: Yes
Expenses by: Year
In State: $21,560
Out of State: $21,560
Specialty: Education, Sciences, Business
Degrees Conferred: BA, BS, BAEd, M.Ed.
Programs of Study: Has 67 different areas of study within 58 majors.

Men's Athletic Profile

3900 Bethel Drive
St. Paul, MN 55112-6999
Coach: Mark Leigh
Email: Not Available

NCAA III
Royals/Royal Blue, Gold
Phone: (612) 638-6351
Fax: (612) 638-6001

Estimated # of Men's Soccer Scholarships: None
Conference: Minnesota Intercollegiate Athletic Conference
Program Profile: Varsity and Junior Varsity teams. Fall season, and a new game field (75 x 115 yards). Play an 18 game schedule.

History: Program began in 1960's.
Achievements: Ranked Top 10 West NCAA Division III pole for 6 weeks in 1994. Conference Champs 1982.

Women's Athletic Profile

3900 Bethel Drive
St. Paul, MN 55112-6999
Coach: Scott Krohn
Email: scott-krohn@bethel.edu

NCAA III
Royals/Blue, Gold
Phone: (651) 638-8522
Fax: (651) 635-8645

Estimated # of Women's Soccer Scholarships: N/A
Conference: Minnesota Intercollegiate Athletic Conference
Program Profile: Our women's soccer program is above all, else a unique combination of faith and soccer. We are quickly becoming a very competitive team in our conference which is traditionally sends 3 or 4 teams to the national tournament. Our program more than anything else, hides to change lives as we are unified in faith and committed to excellence.
History: We are a relatively new program, starting as a club team in 1993. This will be our sixth year as a varsity team, and through the development of our junior varsity program, we are quickly becoming a very competitive team at the Division III.
Achievements: Had All-MIAC 1999 Player
Coaching: Scott Krohn- section IV coach of the year 1999 (high school) coached 5 years at Irondale High School (girl program). Assistant Kari Nokken former MIAC player at Concordia Moorehead, All MIAC, MVP 3 times and captain
Roster in State: 12 **Out of State:** 6 **Out of Country:**
Walk-on/Other: **Graduation %:** **Seniors on Team:** 3
Positions Needed: All
Camp or Clinic Dates: 3rd week of August
Schedule: Macalester, Gustavas Adolfus, St. Thomas, St. Benedict
Style of Play: Based on ball possession, short passing style and good individual skills needed.

Carleton College

Academic Profile

Phone:

Northfield, MN 55057

Type: 4 Yr.,Private,Liberal Arts
Website: http://www.carleton.edu
SAT/ACT/GPA: 25
Student/Faculty Ratio: 11:1
Undergraduate Enrollment: 1,800
Scholarships/Academic: N/A **Athletic:** No
Expenses by: Year **In State:** $ 26,950
Specialty: Liberal Arts
Degrees Conferred: BA

Founded: 1866
Religion: Non-Affiliated
Housing: Yes
Male/Female Ratio: 50:50
Graduate Enrollment: N/A
Financial Aid: Yes
Out of State: $ 26,950

Programs of Study: African/African-American Studies, American Studies, Art & Art History, Asian Languages, Asian Studies, Biology, Chemistry, Classical Languages, Studies in Dance, East Asian Studies, Economics, Educational, Studies, English, ENTS, French, Geology, German, History, Latin American Studies, Math and Computer Science, Medieval Studies, Music, Philosophy, Physics and Astronomy, Political Science, Psychology, Religion, Russian, Sociology, Anthropology, Spanish, Theatre Arts, Women's Studies

Men's Athletic Profile

One North College Street
Northfield, MN 55057
Coach: Bob Carlson
Email: rcarlson@carleton.edu

NCAA III
Knights/Navy, Blue
Phone: (507)646-5840
Fax: (507) 646-7040

Estimated # of Men's Soccer Scholarships: n/a
Conference: Minnesota Intercollegiate Athletic Conference
Program Profile: Carleton College soccer is about academic and athletic excellence. Scholar-athletes at one of the finest undergraduate colleges in the country compete in a highly competitive and successful soccer program. Our soccer players have received honors both on and off the field including our '00 captain earning a prestigious Rhodes Scholarship. Our schedule includes the well-respected Minnesota Intercollegiate Athletic Conference as well as nationally ranked opponents. Trips in the past three years included matches in Texas, Colorado and California. Given our academic reputation, the wealth of opportunities available beyond soccer and the potential for leadership positions after graduation, several recruits have chosen Carleton over Division I programs. Carleton was honored by the Nationals Soccer Coaches Association of America with the Team Academic Award and Maintained the highest team Grade Point Average in Division III men's soccer in 1999. Home matches are played on picturesque Bell Field. Fans sit on top a gently sloping hill overlooking the 120x75 yard soccer only pitch. Carleton has consistently been ranked in the top ten in the West Region and finished a 10-6-2 in 2000.
History: Our program began in early 1980's.
Achievements: 2000 Rhodes Scholar, Numerous All-Midwest performers, Academic All-Region Teams, NSCAA College Team Academic Award.
Coaching: Bob Carlson, Head Coach.

Roster In State: 2	**Out of State:** 24	**Out of Country:** 1
ODP State: 8	**Regional:** 1	**National:** 0
Walk-on/Other: 0	**Graduation %:** 100	**Seniors on Team:** 2

Positions Needed:
Camp or Clinic Dates: Not Available
Most Recent Record: 10-6-2
Schedule: Gustavus, Maclaster, St. Olaf, Nebraska Wesleyan, Simpson, St. John's, Marian, Ripon
Style of Play: Carleton's coaching staff recognizes that soccer is a player's game and encourages players to display individual skill and flair. We take a "total football" approach to our intelligent attack-oriented style.

Women's Athletic Profile

One North College Street
Northfield, MN 55057
Coach: Bo Conroy
Email: bconroy@carleton.edu

NCAA III
Athenas/Maize, Blue
Phone: (507) 646-4484
Fax: (507) 663-5550

Estimated # of Women's Soccer Scholarships: None
Conference: MIAC

College of Saint Benedict

Academic Profile

St. Joseph, MN 56374

Phone: (320) 363-5873

Type: 4 Yr.,Public,Liberal Arts		**Founded:** 1913
Website: http://www.csbsju.edu		**Religion:** Catholic
SAT/ACT/GPA: Open		**Housing:** Yes
Student/Faculty Ratio: 13:1		**Male/Female Ratio:** All Female
Undergraduate Enrollment: 1,940		**Graduate Enrollment:** N/A
Scholarships/Academic: Yes	**Athletic:** No	**Financial Aid:** Yes
Expenses by: Year	**In State:** $ 21,466	**Out of State:** $21,466

Specialty: Nursing, Medical Technology
Degrees Conferred: BA, BS in Nursing and MEdical Technology

Programs of Study: Accounting, Allied Health, Art, Biology, Business and Management, Chemistry, Classics, Communications, Computer Science, Dietetics, Economics, Elementary Education, English, Forestry, French, German, Government, History, Humanities, Latin, Liberal Studies, Management, Math, Medical Technology, Ministries, Music, Natural Science, Nursing, Nutrition, Occupational Therapy, Peace Studies, Pharmacy, Philosophy, Physical Therapy, Physics, Political Science, PreDentistry, PreEngineering, PreLaw, PreMed, PreVet, Psychology, Religion, Social Science, Social Work, Sociology, Spanish, Theatre, Theology, Teacher Education

Women's Athletic Profile

37 S. College Avenue
Saint Joseph, MN 56374
Coach: Bill Kelly
Email: bkelly@csbsju.edu

NCAA III
Blazers/Red, Black
Phone: (320) 363-5873
Fax: (320) 363-6098

Estimated # of Women's Soccer Scholarships: None
Conference: Minnesota Intercollegiate Athletic Conference
Program Profile: We have varsity and junior varsity teams. Our pre-season typically begins last week in August and practices are 4-6 pm. We travel to distance opponents takes place on weekends.
History: Our program began in 1983, competing in the Minnesota Intercollegiate Athletic Conference. Winning the conference once in 1991, and making the national playoffs three times (1990, 1997 & 1998). Overall record since 1983 is 140-111-17
Achievements: We were 1990 NCAA Regional Champs - Final Four. Kathy Yarnott was named All-American. We were 1991 Minnesota Intercollegiate Athletic Conference Champs and Colleen Neary was named All-American. We were 1998 NCAA "Sweet Sixteen" and Lisad Grefe was named All-American.
Coaching: Bill Kelly is our Head Coach. He has been with the program since 1996. TJ Henderickson, Assistant Coach at St. Ben's since 2000, resource coach with O.D.P and Minnesota State Select. Dave Wilke, Goalie Coach since 1996, former German Semi-Professional and Lis Grefe Assit. Coach sine 2000 was former St. Ben's All-American
Roster in State: 22 **Out of State:** 1 **Out of Country:** 0
ODP State: 6 **Regional:** 3 **National:**
Walk-on/Other: **Graduation %:** 99 **Seniors on Team:** 5
Positions Needed: Sweeper, Outside Midfielder, Forward, Goalkeeper
Camp or Clinic Dates: June 11-15 and June 18-22
Most Recent Record: 13-3-1
Schedule: Macalester College, University of St. Thomas, Gustavus Adolphus College, University of Chicago
Style of Play: Attacking style based on strong midfield play and 1 vs. 1 talent up front. We emphasize disciplined individual and team defending. We utilize both 4-4-2 and 4-3-3 formations. Overall, we combine direct and indirect styles to create a dynamic and up tempo attack.

College of Saint Catherine

Academic Profile

Phone: (651) 690-8850

St. Paul, MN 55105

Type: 4 Yr.,Private,Liberal Arts
Website: http://www.stkate.edu
SAT/ACT/GPA: 820+/19/2.0
Student/Faculty Ratio: 14:1
Undergraduate Enrollment: 2,470
Scholarships/Academic: Yes **Athletic:** No
Expenses by: Year **In State:** $ 19,000

Founded: 1905
Religion: Catholic
Housing: Yes
Male/Female Ratio: Women
Graduate Enrollment: 589
Financial Aid: Yes
Out of State: $ 19,000

Specialty: Health Care
Degrees Conferred: Associate Degree and certificate programs in Health care
Programs of Study: Accounting, Art, Biology, Business Administration, Chemistry, Communications, Computer Science, Economics, Education, English, History, Hotel/Restaurant Management, International Business, Journalism, Management, Marketing, Mathematics, Medical Laboratory Technology, Music, Nursing, Pharmacy

Women's Athletic Profile

2004 Randolph Avenue
St. Paul, MN 55105
Coach: Chris Galbraith
Email: csgalbraith@stkate.edu

NCAA III
Wildcats/Purple, White, Gold
Phone: (651) 779-8068
Fax: (651) 690-8790

Estimated # of Women's Soccer Scholarships: None
Conference: MIAC
Program Profile: The Wildcats are a Division III non-scholarships program. We will play between 16-20 games a season. Our new field on campus is to be completed for the 2001 season. We have a state of the art fitness center.
History: The program started August 1999. The team is growing but is improving rapidly. The over all record of the wildcats is 19-7-4.
Achievements: The whole women's soccer team was named Athletes of the week at the school; Upper IA tournament champions and Mindy Daugarty Tournament MVC
Coaching: Chris Galbraith, Head Coach, USSF "C" Coaching License, NSCAA member, BS in Corp Fitness, Sports Medicine and Health Education and ODP Coaching Staff. He played semi-pro indoor and played Division I and II college soccer, club coach at Bloomington Soccer Club. Madge Makowski, Assistant Coach, responsible for the goalkeeper. He is also the assistant athletic trainer and a youth coach.

Roster in State: 14	**Out of State:** 8	**Out of Country:** 1
ODP State: 3	**Regional:** 2	**National:**
Walk-on/Other:	**Graduation %:** 100	**Seniors on Team:** 4

Positions Needed: Goalkeeper, Defender, Midfield
Camp or Clinic Dates: Not Available
Most Recent Record: 19-7-4
Schedule: Macalester, UW Riverfalls, Wisconsin Lutheran, UM Morris
Style of Play: Hard working and Aggressive all players encourage to attack when needed. The entire team sets tempo of the game. Team focus on offence and defense and we use varies systems of play.

College of Saint Scholastica

Academic Profile

Duluth, MN 55811

Phone: (218) 723-6000

Type: 4 Yr.,Private,Liberal Arts		**Founded:** 1912
Website: http://www.css.edu		**Religion:** Roman Catholic
SAT/ACT/GPA: Open		**Housing:** Yes
Student/Faculty Ratio: 16:1		**Male/Female Ratio:** 30:70
Undergraduate Enrollment: 1,200		**Graduate Enrollment:** 720
Scholarships/Academic: Yes	**Athletic:** No	**Financial Aid:** Yes
Expenses by: Year	**In State:** $ 15,420	**Out of State:** $ 15,420

Specialty: Health Sciences
Degrees Conferred: BA, BS, BSN, MSN, MA, MS
Programs of Study: Accounting, American Indian Studies, Art, Biology, Broadcasting, Business Administration, Chemistry, Communications, Computer Science, Clinical Laboratory Science, Economics, Education, English, History, Hotel/Restaurant Management, International Business, Journalism, Management, Marketing, Mathematics, Medical Laboratory Technology, Music, Nursing, Pharmacy, Photography, Physical Therapy, PreDentistry, PreLaw, PreMed, Psychology, Religion, Social Science, Theatre Art

Men's Athletic Profile

1200 Kenwood Avenue
Duluth, MN 55811
Coach: Nic Bacigalupo
Email: Not Available

NCAA III
Saints/Black, Blue, White
Phone: (218) 723-6603
Fax: (218) 723-6290

Estimated # of Men's Soccer Scholarships: None
Conference: Upper Midwest Athletic Conference
Program Profile: Playing season Aug. 15-Nov.15 (20 games + Play-offs) Natural grass field overlooking Lake Superior.
History: Program began in 1978
Achievements: Conference Champs 1984, 1985, 1987. NLCAA National Champs 1988, 5 NLCAA All-Americans, 7 NAIA All-District, NCAA Northern District Champs 1988. Cane named NLCAA Coach of the Year 1988.
Coaching: 7 years as Head coach, prior to that 3 yrs as an Asst. coach. 2x NCAA Small College Runner-up. As a coach, he has won the UMAC Championship 3 of the 5 years of existence. He has been Coach of the Year 3 times as well. Dave Reyelts (2 years as Assistant Coach) is a former Saint and 3 time 1st team All-Conference Goalie.
Roster In State: 22 **Out of State:** 2 **Out of Country:**
ODP State: 6 **Regional:** 2 **National:**
Positions Needed: Center Midfield, Outside Defense
Camp or Clinic Dates: August 7-12
Most Recent Record: 12-10
Schedule: Mt. Senario, University of Mary, Gustavus College, Northland College, St. Thomas University, Dordt College
Style of Play: Organized, calculated team defense. Patient countering that stresses opportunistic, imaginative attacking style and tactical systems reflect skills of players.

Women's Athletic Profile

1200 Kenwood Avenue
Duluth, MN 55811
Coach: Dave Reyelts
Email: dreyelts@css.edu

NAIA
Saints/Royal Blue, Gold
Phone: (218) 723-6603
Fax: (218) 723-5958

Estimated # of Women's Soccer Scholarships: 0
Conference: UMAC (Upper Midwest Athletic Conference)
Program Profile: We play a full schedule (20 games) on a natural surface on campus field. We play in the Six team upper Midwest Athletic Conference. We also are Region III of the NAIA.
History: Program instituted in 1990.
Achievements: In the 11 year history, the Saints have had 4 Conference Championships a number of Academic All-Americans, and 3 Coach of the Year.
Coaching: Head Coach Dave Reyelts 2nd season. Was a 3 year starter GK at St. Scholastica. Dave is also assistant Softball coach and assistant Athletic Director.
Roster in State: 14 **Out of State:** 4 **Out of Country:** 0
Walk-on/Other: **Graduation %:** 100 **Seniors on Team:** 3
Positions Needed: GK, Forward, Mid, Full-backs, Sweeper
Camp or Clinic Dates: Not Available
Most Recent Record: 6-15-0
Schedule: Gustavas College, Huron Univ. Brian Cliff, Minnesota-Duluth, Northwestern College, Bethany Univ.
Style of Play: We try to control the ball, building our attack from the back of our defense. We generally play a 4-4-2.

Concordia College - Moorhead

Academic Profile

Moorhead, MN 56562
Phone: (218) 299-4434

Type: 4 Yr.,Private,Liberal Arts
Website: http://www.cord.edu
SAT/ACT/GPA: 900+/20+
Student/Faculty Ratio: 15:1
Undergraduate Enrollment: 2,800
Scholarships/Academic: Yes **Athletic:** No

Founded: 1891
Religion: Lutheran
Housing: Yes
Male/Female Ratio: 1:2
Graduate Enrollment: N/A
Financial Aid: Yes

Expenses by: Year **In State:** $ 17,100 **Out of State:** $ 17,100
Specialty: Education, Music, Sciences
Degrees Conferred: BA, BS
Programs of Study: Accounting, Advertising, Art, Biology, Broadcasting, Business & Management, Chemistry, Classic, Communications, Computer Science, Creative Writing, Criminal Justice, Music, History, Humanities, Physical Education, Mathematics, Nursing, Political Science, Philosophy, Political Science, Religion, Social Work, Sociology

Men's Athletic Profile

901 South 8th Street
Moorhead, MN 56562
Coach: Jim Cella
Email: cella@cord.edu

NCAA III
Cobbers/Maroon, Gold
Phone: (218) 299-4162
Fax: (218) 299-4189

Estimated # of Men's Soccer Scholarships:
Conference: Minnesota Intercollegiate Athletic Conference
Program Profile: Concordia men's soccer program relies on the complete student-athlete. In 1996 the team had 18 players with at least a 3.0 GPA. The team carries this onto the field where they have won the past two conference titles.
History: Our soccer program began in 1987. Jim Cella took over in 1992 and the team won the MIAC title in 1995 and 1996. We advanced to the NCAA Regional Final in 1996.
Achievements: MIAL Conference Champions in 1995 & 1996. Jim Cella - Coach of the Year in 1993 & 1995; 3 All-Region players in 1995 and 2 in 1996. West Region Runner-up in 1996
Coaching: Jim Cella, Head Coach.
Style of Play: A very aggressive, total team play with all eleven players making contributions. A combined passing/individualistic attack that creates many scoring opportunities.

Women's Athletic Profile

901 South 8th Street
Moorhead, MN 56562
Coach: Jim Cella
Email: cella@cord.edu

NCAA III
Lady Cobbers/Maroon, Gold
Phone: (218) 299-3194
Fax: (218) 299-4189

Estimated # of Women's Soccer Scholarships: None
Conference: Minnesota Intercollegiate Athletic
History: Program began in 1982.
Roster in State: 9 **Out of State:** 9 **Out of Country:** 0
ODP State: 0 **Regional:** 2 **National:** 0
Walk-on/Other: 0 **Graduation %:** 100 **Seniors on Team:** 2
Positions Needed: ALL
Most Recent Record: 8-8-0
Schedule: Macalester, Gustavus, St. Ben's, St. Thomas, MSU-Moorhead, Carleton
Style of Play: Concordia plays a team orientated passing style of soccer. The emphasis is on developing the complete soccer player and allowing that player to shine in our system. We are very cognizant about having a unified team both on and off the field.

Concordia University - Saint Paul

Academic Profile

Phone:

St. Paul, MN 55104

Type: 4 Yr.,Private,Liberal Arts **Founded:** 1893
Website: http://www.csp.edu **Religion:** Lutheran

SAT/ACT/GPA: 17+
Student/Faculty Ratio: 17:1
Undergraduate Enrollment: 1,200
Scholarships/Academic: Yes
Athletic: No
Expenses by: Year
In State: $ 13,700
Degrees Conferred: AA, BA, MA
Housing: No
Male/Female Ratio: 45:55
Graduate Enrollment: 4
Financial Aid: Yes
Out of State: $ 13,700
Programs of Study: Accounting, Banking & Finance, Biblical Languages, Biology, Business Administration, Economics, Education, English, Environmental Science, Fine Arts, History, Languages, Literature, Management, Marketing, Mathematics, Music, Natural Science, Physical Science, PreLaw, PreMed, Psychology, Religion, Religious Education, Social Science, Speech Science

Men's Athletic Profile

275 North Syndicate
St. Paul, MN 55104
Coach: Scott Zachman
Email: doherty@luther.csp.edu

NAIA
Comets/Royal, Old Gold
Phone: (651) 641-8726
Fax: (612) 641-8787

Estimated # of Men's Soccer Scholarships: N/A
Conference: Upper Midwest Athletic Conference

Gustavus Adolphus College

Academic Profile

St. Peter, MN 56083

Phone: 507-933-8000

Type: 4 Yr.,Private,Liberal Arts
Website: http://www.gac.edu
SAT/ACT/GPA: 1100/27/3.6
Student/Faculty Ratio: 13:1
Undergraduate Enrollment: 2,300
Scholarships/Academic: Yes
Athletic: No
Expenses by: Year
In State: $ 21,800
Founded: 1862
Religion: ELCA (Lutheran)
Housing: Yes
Male/Female Ratio: 45:55
Graduate Enrollment: N/A
Financial Aid: Yes
Out of State: $ 21,800
Specialty: Bachelor of Arts in 40 majors, Liberal Arts, PreProfessional Programs
Degrees Conferred: BA
Programs of Study: Accounting, Art, Athletic Training, Biology, Chemistry, Classics, Communications, Computer Science, Criminal Justice, Economics, Education, English, Environmental Studies, General Sciences, Geography, Geology, Health and Fitness, History, International Management, Management, Mathematics, Music, Nursing, Philosophy, Physical Education and Health, Physics, Physical Science, Political Science, Psychology, Religion, Sociology/Anthropology, Speech, Theatre. PreProfessional Programs: Actuarial Science, Architecture, Arts Administration, Church Vocations, Dentistry, Engineering, Law, Medicine, Ministry, Occupational Therapy, Optometry, Pharmacy, Physical Therapy, Veterinary Medicine

Men's Athletic Profile

800 W College Street
St. Peter, MN 56082
Coach: Larry Zelenz
Email: lzelenz@gac.edu

NCAA III
Gusties/Gold, Black
Phone: (507) 933-7699
Fax: (507) 933-8412

Estimated # of Men's Soccer Scholarships: None
Conference: Minnesota Intercollegiate Athletic Conference
Program Profile: Full size natural turf surface with an underground sprinkler system for game field. Ample practice facilities, $12 million dollar Lund Athletic Complex.

History: Our program began in 1969. Since then there have been eight conference championship appearances in both NAIA and NCAA Tournaments.
Achievements: 9 Regional All-Americans; 2 All-Americans, and numerous All-Conference. Coach Zelenz was two-time Conference Coach of the Year, one-time Regional Coach of the Year.
Coaching: Larry Zelenz, Head Coach, is on his fifteenth year with the team.
Roster In State: 28 **Out of State:** 8 **Out of Country:**
ODP State: 6 **Regional:** 1 **National:**
Walk-on/Other: **Graduation %:** 100 **Seniors on Team:** 8
Positions Needed: Midfield, Forward
Camp or Clinic Dates: Not Available
Most Recent Record: 9-8-1
Schedule: Macalister, Colorado College, St. Olaf, St. Johns, Nebraska Wesleyan,, Luther
Style of Play: Will vary depending on personnel but generally combination play and ball control. Strong man to man team defense.

Women's Athletic Profile

800 W. College Avenue
St. Peter, MN 56082
Coach: Mike Stehlik
Email: mstehlik@gac.edu

NCAA III
Golden Gusties/Black, Gold
Phone: (507) 933-7619
Fax: (507) 933-8412

Estimated # of Women's Soccer Scholarships: None
Conference: Minnesota Intercollegiate Athletic Conference (MIAC)
Program Profile: Excellent grass field and practice fields, very competitive conference.
History: The program started in 1984; 5 times Conference Champs; 5 times NCAA Tournaments.
Achievements: MIAC Coach of the Year 1993; MIAC Champions in 1986, 1993, 1994, 1995, & 1996; 6 All-Americans in 1990; Regional Coach of the Year in 1995.
Coaching: Mike Stehlik, Head Coach since 1990, winningest coach in the team's history.
Roster in State: 22 **Out of State:** 3 **Out of Country:** 0
ODP State: 3 **Regional:** 0 **National:** 0
Walk-on/Other: 0 **Graduation %:** 100 **Seniors on Team:** 5
Camp or Clinic Dates: July 8-12
Most Recent Record: 14-4-0
Schedule: Wheaton (IL), UW Stevens Point, Chicago, Macalester, St. Benedict, St. Thomas
Style of Play: We play to win, but we have a lot of fun along the way.

Hamline University
Academic Profile

St. Paul, MN 55104

Phone: 651-523-2800

Type: 4 Yr.,Private,Liberal Arts **Founded:** 1854
Website: http://www.hamlin.edu **Religion:** Methodist
SAT/ACT/GPA: Open **Housing:** Yes
Student/Faculty Ratio: 13:1 **Male/Female Ratio:** 37:63
Undergraduate Enrollment: 1,709 **Graduate Enrollment:** 1,282
Scholarships/Academic: Yes **Athletic:** No **Financial Aid:** Yes
Expenses by: Year **In State:** $ 21,941 **Out of State:** $ 21,941
Specialty: Preprofessional Programs
Degrees Conferred: BA, MAPA, MFA, MAEd, JD, LLM, DPA, EdD
Programs of Study: Anthropology, Art, Art History, Biology, Chemistry, Communication Studies, Criminal Justice, East Asian Studies, Economics, Environmental Studies, International Studies, Latin American Studies, Legal Studies, Management, Mathematics, Musical Studies, Philosophy, Physical Education, Physics, Political Science, Psychology, Religion, Russian, Social Studies, Sociology, Spanish, Theater Arts, Urban Studies, Woman's Studies

Men's Athletic Profile

1536 Hewitt Avenue
St. Paul, MN 55104
Coach: Andy Coutts
Email: acoutts@ gw.hamline.edu

NCAA III
Pipers/Red, White
Phone: 651-523-2036
Fax: 651-523-3075

Estimated # of Men's Soccer Scholarships: 0
Conference: Minnesota Intercollegiate Athletic Conference (MIAC)
Program Profile: Paterson field, a state of the are natural grass field with the same innovative turf system as the soccer fields at the 2000 Sydney Olympic games
History: Young and growing program.
Achievements:
Coaching: Andy Coutts is our head coach.
Roster In State: 15 **Out of State:** 9 **Out of Country:** 1
Walk-on/Other: **Graduation %:** N/A **Seniors on Team:** 3
Positions Needed: All
Camp or Clinic Dates: Not Available
Most Recent Record: 3-11-3
Schedule: Macalester, St. Olaf, Colorado College, Gustavus Adolphus, St. John's, Carleton
Style of Play: Flexible, possession.

Women's Athletic Profile

1536 Hewitt Avenue
St. Paul, MN 55104
Coach: Sheryl Raithel
Email: sraithel@gw.hamline.edu

NCAA III
Pipers/Red, White
Phone: (651) 523-2065
Fax: (651) 523-2390

Estimated # of Women's Soccer Scholarships: None
Conference: MIAC, NCAA Division III
Program Profile: Games are played on natural grass in the Hutton Stadium. Hutton Stadium seats approximately 2,000 people. Practices are held on nearby recreational field.
History: HU had its inaugural season in 1991 and has been improving ever since.
Achievements: 6 All-Conference Honorable mention players; 1 All-Conference 1st team player; numerous Academic All-Conference Players.
Coaching: Sheryl Raithel is the Head Coach and Sean Brazil is the Assistant Coach.
Roster in State: 13 **Out of State:** 4 **Out of Country:**
Walk-on/Other: **Graduation %:** 100 **Seniors on Team:** 2
Positions Needed: Strikers, Midfield
Camp or Clinic Dates: June 19-23
Most Recent Record: 5-14
Schedule: Macalaster, Gustavus, Northern University, University of Minnesota, Bemidji State
Style of Play: Possession and short passes style of play.

Macalester College

Academic Profile

Phone: (651) 696-6467

St. Paul, MN 55102

Type: 4 Yr.,Private,Liberal Arts
Website: http://www.macalester.edu
SAT/ACT/GPA: 1000/26/3.4

Founded: 1885
Religion: Presbyterian
Housing: Yes

Student/Faculty Ratio: 10:1 **Male/Female Ratio:** 45:55
Undergraduate Enrollment: 1,700 **Graduate Enrollment:** N/A
Scholarships/Academic: Yes **Athletic:** No **Financial Aid:** Yes
Expenses by: Year **In State:** $ 25,394 **Out of State:** $ 25,394
Specialty: Liberal Arts
Degrees Conferred: BA, BS
Programs of Study: Anthropology, Art, Biology, Chemistry, Classics, Communication Studies, Computer Science, Dance, Dramatic Arts, East Asian Studies, Economics, Education, English, Environmental Studies, French, Geography, Geology, German, History, Humanities, Individually Designed Major, International Studies, Japan Studies, Latin American Studies, Legal Studies, Linguistics, Mathematics, Music, NeuroScience, Philosophy, Physics, Political Science, Psychology, Religious Studies, Russian, Russian/Central and Eastern European Studies, Sociology, Spanish, Urban Studies, Women's Studies

Men's Athletic Profile

1600 Grand Avenue
St. Paul, MN 55105
Coach: John Leaney
Email: leaney@macalester.edu

NCAA III
Scots/Orange, Royal Blue
Phone: (651) 696-6737
Fax: (651) 696-6328

Estimated # of Men's Soccer Scholarships: None
Conference: Minnesota Intercollegiate Athletic Conference
Program Profile: Nationally competitive program playing in a first class stadium. Grass field has a measurements of 110x75. Very popular sport on campus with a great fan support.
History: Our program is one of the oldest in the country (Kali Annan - Secreatry General of UN played in 1961). Our team qualified for NCAA Championships last three years with two conference championships and two regional championships last two years. Currently we are on a 32 game conference winning streak.
Achievements: Our Head coach has received 4 conference COY and 3 COY west region awards. We have had 5 All-Americans and 4 professional players.
Coaching: John Leaney, Head Coach since 1987, English Coaching License, MIAC Coach of the Year three times in ten years (1987, 1988, & 1990), West Region Coach of the Year in 1982 & 1992.Lan Barker is our new Assistant Coach along with John Curits who both are Directors of MYSA and David Wonder, who is our goalkeeper coach.
Roster In State: 2 **Out of State:** 10 **Out of Country:** 5
ODP State: 12 **Regional:** **National:**
Walk-on/Other: **Graduation %:** 100 **Seniors on Team:** 9
Positions Needed: Defenders
Camp or Clinic Dates: Not Available
Most Recent Record: 14-3-2
Schedule: Wheaton, Richard Stockton, Rowan, Colorado College, Nebraska Wesleyan, St Olaf, Luther, Bethel, St. Johns, Simpson
Style of Play: Attacking style; we always score the most goals in our league.

Women's Athletic Profile

1600 Grand Avenue
St. Paul, MN 55105
Coach: John Leaney
Email: leaney@macalester.edu

NCAA III
Scots/Royal Blue, Orange
Phone: (651) 696-6737
Fax: (651) 696-6328

Estimated # of Women's Soccer Scholarships: None
Conference: Minnesota Intercollegiate Athletic Conference
Program Profile: Nationally ranked program for the last ten years. Ranked 8th on the all time list for play off victories. Outstanding facility of 110x75 yards grass field in a 4,000 seat stadium. Undefeated at home for nearly four years.

History: The varsity soccer program began in 1983. Since then they have won the conference and regional championships 3 straight years; NCAA tournament 8 times in 11 years; National champs in 1998 and National finalist in 1999.
Achievements: 10 All-Americans; 1 National Player of the Year; 1 player invited to the draft; and conference champions 4 times.
Coaching: John Leaney, Head Coach, has received National COY in1998, Conference COY 5 times, Region COY 4 times. Steve Bellis is the Assistant Coach and Dave Wonder is the Goalkeeper Coach.
Roster in State: 5 **Out of State:** 13 **Out of Country:** 2
ODP State: 12 **Regional:** 1 **National:**
Walk-on/Other: **Graduation %:** 100 **Seniors on Team:** 8
Positions Needed: Goalkeeper, Defender
Camp or Clinic Dates: Not Available
Most Recent Record: 20-3-0
Schedule: Washington University, University of Chicago, UW Stevens Point, St. Benedict, Gustavus, St. Thomas, St. Mary's
Style of Play: Controlled ball to feet. High goal scoring and disciplined defense.

Minnesota State University (Mankato State U)

Academic Profile

Mankato, MN 56002
Phone: (507) 389-2673

Type: 4 Yr.,Public,Liberal Arts **Founded:** 1868
Website: http://www.makato.msus.edu **Religion:** Non-Affiliated
SAT/ACT/GPA: 960/23 **Housing:** Yes
Student/Faculty Ratio: 20:1 **Male/Female Ratio:** 50:50
Undergraduate Enrollment: 12,000 **Graduate Enrollment:** 3,000
Scholarships/Academic: Yes **Athletic:** Yes **Financial Aid:** Yes
Expenses by: Year **In State:** $ 6,119 **Out of State:** $ 9,319
Specialty: Accredited Business Program, top Nursing program, Elementary Education
Degrees Conferred: BA, BS, MS
Programs of Study: Over 150 degree programs: Business College including Marketing, Management, Accounting, Insurance; Education College including both Elementary and Secondary Education; Speech Pathology, Accredited undergraduates Athletic Training Program, PreMed, PreDental, PrePhysical Therapy, as well as all common Liberal Arts degree as English, History, Psychology, Sociology, etc..

Women's Athletic Profile

HC 123
Mankato, MN 56001-8400
Coach: Christine Miskec
Email: christine_miskec@ms1.mankato.msus.edu

NCAA II
Mavericks/Purple, Gold, Black
Phone: (507) 389-2671
Fax: (507) 389-2904

Estimated # of Women's Soccer Scholarships: 4
Conference: North Central Conference
Program Profile: MSU is a fully-funded, NCAA D-II program. We are beginning our 6th season of competition in fall of 2000. We play on a 120x75 yard enclosed natural grass field with permanent bleachers that seat 500.
History: The program began in fall of 1995 under Mitchell Van Atta. Chris Miskec took over in 1996. In 1997 finished 8-9-1, 2-1 in conference; in 1998 10-6 in, 2-1 conference; 1st place in 1999 10-8-1 and 4th in conference.
Achievements: 1998 we were the Conference Champions. We have had 1 Conference MVP, 1 Conference Freshman of the Year, and 5 All-Region players.
Coaching: Christine Miskec, Head Coach, Master's in Physical and Sports, "C" License holder in spring of 1998. Graduate assistant new every two years. Courtney Longua is our Assistant Coach.
Roster in State: 18 **Out of State:** 11 **Out of Country:**

ODP State: 10 **Regional:** 3 **National:**
Walk-on/Other: **Graduation %:** 100 **Seniors on Team:** 5
Positions Needed: Central Defenders, Midfielders
Camp or Clinic Dates: Not Available
Most Recent Record: 10-8-1
Schedule: University of Northern KY, North Dakota State University, University of Northern Colorado, St. Joseph of Indiana, University of Indianapolis, University of Minnesota, Winona State University, Truman State, Rockhurst University
Style of Play: Attempt to us the outside of the field to our advantage. Possession of ball and quick changes in field positions.

Moorhead State University

Academic Profile

Phone:

Moorhead, MN 56563

Type: 4 Yr.,Public,Liberal Arts **Founded:** 1889
Website: http://www.moorhead.msus.edu **Religion:** Non-Affiliated
SAT/ACT/GPA: 21 **Housing:** Yes
Student/Faculty Ratio: 18:1 **Male/Female Ratio:** 40:60
Undergraduate Enrollment: 6,000 **Graduate Enrollment:** 800
Scholarships/Academic: Yes **Athletic:** Yes **Financial Aid:** Yes
Expenses by: Year **In State:** $ 5,800 **Out of State:** $ 8,500
Specialty: Business, Education, Biology, Communications
Degrees Conferred: AA, AS, BA, BS, BFA, MA, MS, MBA
Programs of Study: Accounting, Anthropology, Advertising, Arts, Biology, Broadcasting, Chemistry, Communications, Computer Information Systems, Computer Science, Criminal Justice, Earth Science, Education, Economics, Finance, Fine Arts, Journalism, Marketing, Mathematics, Nursing, Physical Education, Political Science, Social Science, Physics, PreLaw, PreMed, Psychology, Therapy, Social Science

Women's Athletic Profile

1107 7th Avenue
Moorhead, MN 56563
Coach: Eric Swanbert
Email: swanbeck@mnstate.edu

NCAA II
Dragons/Red, White, Black
Phone: (218) 236-2320
Fax: (218) 299-5825

Estimated # of Women's Soccer Scholarships: Not Available
Conference: Northern Sun Intercollegiate Conference
Program Profile: The Dragons have a new field which is natural grass with a measurements of 115x75 yards. They also have a separate practice field, both are located on campus. The game field is designated for women's soccer only. 2 weight rooms, field house, Indoor/outdoor track, staff of physical therapist, exercise physiologist and team doctors.
History: The new program began in 1995 with a record of 5-11-1, in 1996 was 12-4-2, NSIC Champion, 7-0 conference record.
Achievements: 1999 Coach of the Year
Coaching: Eric Swanbeck is the head coach and he is assisted by Eric Singer.
Roster in State: 4 **Out of State:** 9 **Out of Country:** 0
ODP State: 10 **Regional:** **National:**
Walk-on/Other: **Graduation %:** 95 **Seniors on Team:** 0
Positions Needed: Forwards, Mids, Keeper
Camp or Clinic Dates: August 6-10, 2001
Most Recent Record: 7-9-2
Schedule: North Dakota State, Winona State, MSU Duluth, University of North Dakota, Wayne State, Northern Michigan
Style of Play: First look to counter attack quickly - if that is not on, then work through midfield keeping the ball on the ground.

Northwestern College

Academic Profile

St. Paul, MN 55113

Phone:

Type: 4 Yr.,Private,Liberal Arts
Website: http://www.nwc.edu
SAT/ACT/GPA: Open enrollment
Student/Faculty Ratio: 15:1
Undergraduate Enrollment: 1,350
Scholarships/Academic: Yes **Athletic:** No
Expenses by: Year **In State:** $ 18,690

Founded: 1902
Religion: Non-Denominational
Housing: Yes
Male/Female Ratio: 1:3
Graduate Enrollment: N/A
Financial Aid: Yes
Out of State: $ 18,690

Degrees Conferred: BA, BS, AA
Programs of Study: Accounting, Adult/Continuing Education, Agriculture, Art, Bible Studies, Broadcasting, Business & Management, Communications, Computer Information Systems, Education, Elementary Education, English, Finance, Fine Arts, Graphic Arts, Human Resources, International Business, Journalism, Liberal Arts, Literature, Marketing, Mathematics, Ministries, Music, Physical Education, PreEngineering, Psychology, Science, Social Science, Theatre, Theology

Men's Athletic Profile

3003 Snelling Ave. N
St. Paul, MN 55113
Coach: Dr. Ripley Smith
Email: lrs@ncoll.edu

NAIA
Eagles/Purple, White
Phone: (651) 631-5581
Fax: (651) 631-5124

Estimated # of Men's Soccer Scholarships: None
Conference: UMAC - Upper Midwest Athletic Conference
Program Profile: We have a new locker-room, training room and weight room facility in 1997. Our outdoor game facilities are some of the best in Twin Cities. Our season has approximately 13 games. We, also have 20 games with 6 conference opponents, rounded out with non-conference games. Our stadium seats 2,000 people.
History: Our program began in 1972 when college purchased a new site in suburb of Minneapolis and St. Paul. We a member of NCCAA and NSCAA in early years, which was NCCAA District Champions in 1986. We joined or formed UMAC in early 1990's and NAIA in 1995. We have finished on top 3 in UMAC each year.
Achievements: We had 2 Academic All-Americans in 1996 & 1997.
Coaching: Dr. Ripley Smith, Head Coach, has over ten years collegiate and high school coaching experience. Greg Wheaton is the Assistant Coach. He is entering his fourth year Division I player at Liberty University. He played professionally on Bolivia and on MS Thunder Development Team.
Style of Play: We are sophisticated. We build out of the back and up the wings styles. The style emphasis possession and movement from all players. We emphasis fitness and developing individual ball skills.

Saint Cloud State University

Academic Profile

St. Cloud, MN 56301

Phone: (320) 255-3041

Type: 4 Yr.,Public,Liberal Arts
Website: http://www.stcloudstate.edu
SAT/ACT/GPA: 1000/25
Student/Faculty Ratio: 15:1
Undergraduate Enrollment: 1500
Scholarships/Academic: Yes **Athletic:** Yes
Expenses by: Year **In State:** $ 6,000

Founded: 1869
Religion: Non-Affiliated
Housing: Yes
Male/Female Ratio: 46:53
Graduate Enrollment: 2500
Financial Aid: Yes
Out of State: $ 8.400

Degrees Conferred: BA, BS
Programs of Study: Accounting, Advertising, Anthropology, Arts, Banking/Finance, Biological Science, Broadcasting, Business Administration, Chemistry, Earth Science, Elective Studies, Geography, International Business & Relations, Journalism, PreProfessional Programs, Psychology, *** contact school for more information.

Women's Athletic Profile

721 Fourth Ave
St. Cloud, MN 56301
Coach: Stephanie McGuinness
Email: smcguinness@stcloudstate.edu

NCAA II
Huskies/Red, Black
Phone: (612) 255-2143
Fax: (612) 203-6146

Estimated # of Women's Soccer Scholarships: 5
Conference: North Central Conference
Program Profile: 6 year program, play on 80x115 yd natural grass surface which is overlooking Mississippi River.
History: Soccer obtained varsity status in the Spring of 1994 and began competition in September of 1994. Finished 4th in Conference in 1999 and 5th in 2000.
Achievements: Finished 4th in conference in 1999 and 5th in 2000. 2000 1 All-Central Region Player, 3 All-Central Region Players in 1995 & 1996.
Coaching: Stephanie McGuinness is the Head Coach she has a Master degree, holds National Diploma from NSCAA and "D" License from USSF. There is always a Goalkeeper Coach.

Roster In State: 13	**Out of State:** 7	**Out of Country:** 0
ODP State: 1	**Regional:** 0	**National:** 0
Walk-on/Other: 0	**Graduation %:** 100	**Seniors on Team:** 3

Positions Needed: Strikers, Defenders
Most Recent Record: 9-9
Schedule: Minnesota State, Nebraska, Northern Colorado, North Dakota State, Missouri, Southwest Missouri State, Rockhurst, Univ. of Minnesota
Style of Play: Offensive minded team with emphasis on possession soccer and exploited weakness of opponents defense. Usually play a 4-3-3 system with exception to current personnel.

Saint John's University - Minnesota

Academic Profile

Collegeville, MN 56321

Phone:

Type: 4 Yr.,Private,Liberal Arts		**Founded:** 1858
Website: http://www.csbsju.edu		**Religion:** Roman Catholic
SAT/ACT/GPA: 1000/2.8		**Housing:** Yes
Student/Faculty Ratio: 12:1		**Male/Female Ratio:** 100:0
Undergraduate Enrollment: 1,750		**Graduate Enrollment:** N/A
Scholarships/Academic: Yes	**Athletic:** No	**Financial Aid:** Yes
Expenses by: Year	**In State:** $ 20,000	**Out of State:** $ 20,000

Degrees Conferred: BA, BS
Programs of Study: Accounting, Art, Biology, Chemistry, Classics, Communications, Computer Science, Economics, Elementary Education, English, French, German, Government, History, Humanities, Liberal Studies, Management, Mathematics, Medical Technology, Medieval Studies, Music, Natural Science, Nursing, Nutrition, Peace Studies, Philosophy, Physics, Psychology, Social Science, Social Work, Sociology, Spanish, Theatre, Theology, PreProfessional

Men's Athletic Profile

Athletic Department
Collegeville, MN 56321
Coach: Pat Haws
Email: Phaws@csbsju.edu

NCAA III
Johnnies/Red, Blue
Phone: (320) 363-2758
Fax: (320) 363-3130

Estimated # of Men's Soccer Scholarships: None
Conference: MIAC
Program Profile: A quality Division III program with a long and rich tradition of soccer excellence. Natural turf field, covered benches to protect players during bad weather, play a competitive schedule that features travel sites around the country, and competes in conference. Play in the fall in one of the most beautiful college in the US.
History: Program began in 1967 with an excellent history of national caliber soccer.
Achievements: Six Conference Titles; 12 top three finishes in conference play in the past 20 seasons.
Coaching: Pat Haws, Head Coach; 20 years at SJU.
Style of Play: Up-tempo offense that centers around solid defensive play. We strive to make fast transition, which has been a trademark of our program.

Saint Mary's University - Minnesota

Academic Profile

Phone: (507) 457-1583

Winona, MN 55987

Type: 4 Yr.,Private,Liberal Arts
Founded: 1912
Website: http://www.smumn.edu
Religion: Catholic
SAT/ACT/GPA: 21/3.1
Housing: Yes
Student/Faculty Ratio: 13:1
Male/Female Ratio: 50:50
Undergraduate Enrollment: 1,300
Graduate Enrollment: 100
Scholarships/Academic: Yes
Athletic: No
Financial Aid: Yes
Expenses by: Year
In State: $ 18,000
Out of State: $ 18,000
Specialty: Education, Business, Psychology
Degrees Conferred: BA, BS
Programs of Study: Accounting, Art, Graphic Design, Art Studio, Biology, Chemistry, Computer Science, Criminal Justice, Electronic Publishing, Elementary Education, English Education, French, History, Life Science, Marketing, Mathematics, Mathematics Education, Music Merchandising, Philosophy, Physics, Political Science, Social Science, Sociology, Theatre, Theatre Education, Theology, PreProfessional Programs

Men's Athletic Profile

700 Terrace Heights
Winona, MN 55987-1309
Coach: Brad Hauter
Email: bhauter@smumn.edu

NCAA III
Cardinals/Red, White, Navy
Phone: (507) 457-6957
Fax: (507) 457-1439

Estimated # of Men's Soccer Scholarships: None
Conference: Minnesota Intercollegiate Athletic Conference
Program Profile: We have a great facilities and successful program. The team plays on grass field. Our program is one of the top ones in the region.
History: Began in 1972. Coming off best 6 years in school history.
Achievements: Our team produced 1 All-American, 10 All-Conference players and 2 All-Area players.
Coaching: 1 All-American, and 3 players had pro tryouts.
Roster In State: 6
Out of State: 19
Out of Country: 0
ODP State: 10
Regional: 2
National:
Walk-on/Other:
Graduation %: 100
Seniors on Team: 3
Positions Needed: Forwards, Defenders
Camp or Clinic Dates: July 8-12
Most Recent Record: 9-8-1
Schedule: Macalester, Simpson, Gustuvus, St. Olaf, St. John's, St. Thomas
Style of Play: Possession based.

Women's Athletic Profile

700 Terrace Heights-#49
Winona, MN 55987
Coach: Dan Blank
Email: dblank@smumn.edu

NCAA III
Cardinals/Red, White
Phone: (507) 457-1583
Fax: (507) 457-1439

Estimated # of Women's Soccer Scholarships: None
Conference: Minnesota Intercollegiate Athletic Conference (MIAC)
Program Profile: Three full-sized fields with a natural grass surface; play August 24 through early November. Fields are within walking distance from dorms. Soccer is the top sport in the Fall since there is no football program.
History: Program began in 1982 and has won MIAC Title seven of last ten years. Also received seven of nine NCAA post-season bids. We have had the same Head Coach for the past 18 years.
Achievements: 15 All-Americans (7 1st team, 1 2nd team and 3 3rd team). 1986 and 1987 NCAA Regional Coach of the Year. 1994 MIAC Coach of the Year; NCAA Regional bid, 1st team All-American: Katie Kortsch.
Coaching: Dan Blank, Head Coach, 16 years, won seven Conference Championships, selected to the NCAA Tournament seven out of nine years, Regional Coach of the Year in 1986 and 1987; MIAC Coach of the Year in 1987, 1991, and 1994. Overall record at St. Mary's University is 175-58-11. Jeff Halberg and Kate Manor, Assistant Coaches.
Style of Play: Adjust to team's personnel, controlled and build-up with an emphasis on attack - forward and number of backs.

Saint Olaf College

Academic Profile

Northfield, MN 55057

Phone:

Type: 4 Yr.,Private
Website: http://www.stolaf.edu
SAT/ACT/GPA: 25
Student/Faculty Ratio: 11:1
Undergraduate Enrollment: 2,888
Scholarships/Academic: Yes
Athletic: No
Expenses by: Year
In State: $ 15,000

Founded: 1874
Religion: Lutheran
Housing: Yes
Male/Female Ratio: 2.4:3
Graduate Enrollment: N/A
Financial Aid: Yes
Out of State: $ 15,000

Degrees Conferred: BA, BS, BM
Programs of Study: Art, Art History, Asian Studies, Biology, Chemistry, Classic, Dance, Economics, English, Fine Arts, French, Mathematics, Music, Nursing, Physical Education, Physics, Political Science, Philosophy, PreLaw, PreMed, PreDentistry, Religion, Psychology, Social Studies, Social Work

Men's Athletic Profile

1520 St. Olaf Avenue
Northfield, MN 55057
Coach: Kurt Anderson
Email: anderk@stolaf.edu

NCAA III
Oles/Old Gold, Black
Phone: (507) 646-3253
Fax: (507) 646-3572

Estimated # of Men's Soccer Scholarships: None
Conference: Minnesota Intercollegiate Athletic Conference
Program Profile: The home field seats 500, has natural grass pitch (76 x 110 yards), earthen bowl field. Program also has four practice fields, modern weight room and training facilities. The team plays a Fall season (September through October).
History: After 27 years of Ole soccer, we experienced our first losing season in 1995.
Achievements: Conference titles in 1992 and 1984.
Coaching: Kurt Anderson, Head Coach, more than 100 victories after 15 years as a coach, holds a national coaches license with the USSF, graduated from Augustana College, holds MS in Physical Education from Drake University, oversees the coaching certification program at St. Olaf.

Women's Athletic Profile

1520 St. Olaf Ave.
Northfield, MN 55057
Coach: Judy Stromayer
Email: stromayer@stolaf.edu

NCAA III
Oles/Old Gold, Black
Phone: (507) 646-3989
Fax: (507) 646-3572

Estimated # of Women's Soccer Scholarships: None
Conference: Minnesota Intercollegiate Athletic Conference
Program Profile: Great Bowl game field, four additional practice fields natural grass excellent. Conference and competition is nationally recognized.
History: The program began in 1981-1982 and had only three seasons below 500 since then. Long tradition of soccer excellence.
Achievements: Miranda Swanson - 1st team All-West Region. Beth Williams - 2nd and 3rd team All-West. All-Regional players, All-Conference.
Coaching: Judy Stromayer, Head Coach, debuted in 1994 with a record of 11-7 and a fifth place finish in the MIAC. Prior to St. Olaf, she coached Westminster College (Fulton, MO), has a degree in Geology from Denison University and a MS in Sports Management from Indiana University. Has two assistant coaches and one goalkeeper coach.
Style of Play: Possession ball with quick strike capabilities, excellent defense and defense transition, solid skill levels.

Southwest State University

Academic Profile

Marshall, MN 56258
Phone: (507) 537-7021

Type: 4 Yr.,Public,Liberal Arts
Founded: 1967
Website: http://www.southwest.com
Religion: Non-Affiliated
SAT/ACT/GPA: 21/2.5
Housing: Yes
Student/Faculty Ratio: 18:1
Male/Female Ratio: 40:60
Undergraduate Enrollment: 3,000
Graduate Enrollment: 300
Scholarships/Academic: Yes **Athletic:** Yes **Financial Aid:** Yes
Expenses by: Year **In State:** $ 6,966 **Out of State:** $ 10,284
Specialty: Liberal Arts
Degrees Conferred: BA, BS, AS, MA, M.Ed.
Programs of Study: Accounting, AgriBusiness Management, Agronomy, Anthropology, Applied Technology, Art, Art Education, Art Graphic, Biology, Biology Education, Business Administration, International Business, Management, Chemistry, Chemistry Education, Computer Science, Criminal Justice, Early Childhood Education, Elementary Education, English Education, History, Literature, Marketing, Mathematics, Teaching, Music, Music Education, Philosophy, Physical Education, Physical Science, Political Science, Psychology, Radio & TV, Restaurant Administration, Sociology, Spanish, Speech Communications, Secondary Education, Theatre Arts, Graduate Programs (Master of Science in Education, Master of Science in Business Management), PreProfessional Programs

Women's Athletic Profile

1501 State Street
Marshall, MN 56258
Coach: Jill McCartney
Email: jillmc@southwest.msus.edu

NCAA II
Mustangs/Brown, Gold
Phone: (507) 537-7256
Fax: (507) 537-6578

Estimated # of Women's Soccer Scholarships: 2
Conference: Northern Sun Intercollegiate Conference

Program Profile: The Mustang Soccer team gets together for pre-season in mid-august, which leads directly into our 18-20 game regular season. In late October, the team competes in the NSIC championship tournament. Mustang Soccer players participate in weight training, conditioning, individual skills work during the winter & then reconvene for a non-traditional spring season. The soccer field is 120x74 yards, natural grass. The locker room has been newly renovated, and indoor facilities include the spacious R/A facility, the PE gym, wight room, pool, and sports medicine center.
History: Mustang Soccer started in 1996 and has improved each year with a record of 1-13, 6-11-1 and 7-11. The program was first coached by Jen Zebroski in the 1996 & 1997 seasons. She was succeeded by Jill McCartney in 1998. In 1999, the team had its first winning season and finished 3rd in the NSIC conference tournament.
Achievements: In 1999, two player made All-conference and two were named Honorable mention. Three players were recognized on the NSIC All-Academic Team, and coach McCartney was honored with coach of the year.
Coaching: Jill McCartney, Head Coach, will be in her second year as a head coach. A 1988 graduate from the University of North Carolina at Chapel Hill, she was the head coach at Marquette University from 1993-1994 and was an assistant coach at the university of Arizona from 1994-1996. Natalie Rhodes, Assistant Coach, entering her second year as an assistant coach. She graduated from the University of Minnesota in 1993 and played semi-pro soccer in men's league in Japan. Judy Gettner, Graduate Assistant Coach, from Tucson, Arizona, will join the coaching staff in 1999 as a graduate assistant coach.

Roster in State: 12	**Out of State:** 10	**Out of Country:**
ODP State: 5	**Regional:**	**National:**
Walk-on/Other:	**Graduation %:**	**Seniors on Team:** 4

Positions Needed: Defender, Forward
Camp or Clinic Dates: Not Available
Most Recent Record: 11-9-1
Schedule: Northern Kentucky, Missouri-Rolla, Minnesota State-Mankato, UM-Duluth, Winona State, St. Cloud State
Style of Play: Fast, controlled build up through flanks. High risk in attacking 3rd-emphasis on creating scoring opportunities. Defensively, we play pressure -cover-balance-so not strictly man-to-man or zone. We tend to use medium to high pressure all over the field defensively.

University of Minnesota - Twin Cities

Academic Profile

Minneapolis, MN 55455-0101
Phone: 800-752-1000

Type: 4 Yr.,Public		**Founded:** 1851
Website: http://www.umn.edu		**Religion:** Non-Affiliated
SAT/ACT/GPA: Sliding Scale		**Housing:** Yes
Student/Faculty Ratio: 25:1		**Male/Female Ratio:** 1:1
Undergraduate Enrollment: 24,000		**Graduate Enrollment:** 14,000
Scholarships/Academic: Yes	**Athletic:** Yes	**Financial Aid:** Yes
Expenses by: Year	**In State:** $ 9,719	**Out of State:** $ 17,680

Degrees Conferred: BA, BS, MA, MS, MBA, DMD, JD
Programs of Study: Liberal Arts, PreMed, Medical/Dental, Veterinary Med., Agriculture, Management, Engineering, Forestry, Teaching, Pharmacy, Physical Therapy, Kinesiology, Housing Design, Social Work, Nutrition, Biology, and over 200 undergraduates.

Women's Athletic Profile

516 15th Avenue SE
Minneapolis, MN 55455
Coach: Barbara Wickstrand
Email: mnsoccer00@yahoo.com

NCAA I
Golden Gophers/Maroon, Gold
Phone: (612) 626-7381
Fax: (612) 626-0020

Estimated # of Women's Soccer Scholarships: 3
Conference: Big Ten Conference

Program Profile: Brand new 2.4 million dollar soccer facility with club room, lockerooms and workout equipment. Lights on practice and game field, natural grass 120x75 and seats 1000 fans.
History: Program began in 1993. Big 10 Champions 1995, 97. NCAA post season 5 out of last 6 years. Advancing to second rounds 1997,98,99. #1 in attendance in Big Ten 1999 and 2000, #1 in Region in 1999.
Achievements: Big 10 Championships in 1995 and 1997; Big 10 Coach of the Year in 1995 and 1997; NSCAA/Umbaro All-American Jennifer McElmury 1997 (1st team) 1995 and 1996 (2nd team); Big 10 Player of the Year 1995 Jennifer Walek; 1996 and 1997 Jennifer McElmury; Big 10 Newcomer of thy Year 1994 Jennifer McElmury; 1997 Laurie Seidl Big 10 Goalkeeper of the Year 1997 Dana Larson.
Roster in State: 1 **Out of State:** 12 **Out of Country:** 2
ODP State: 20 **Regional:** 3 **National:** 1
Walk-on/Other: 3 **Graduation %:** **Seniors on Team:** 3
Positions Needed: 5
Camp or Clinic Dates: June 18-22, July 23-27, 2001
Most Recent Record: 8-10-1
Schedule: BYU, Nebraska, Penn State, Michigan, Illinois, Wisconsin
Style of Play: Possession oriented with quick transition from defehse to offense using a 3-4-3 formation.

University of Minnesota - Duluth

Academic Profile

Phone: (218) 726-8000

Duluth, MN 55812

Type: 4 Yr.,Public,Liberal Arts **Founded:** 1947
Website: http://www.umn.edu **Religion:** Non-Affiliated
SAT/ACT/GPA: 820/19 **Housing:** Yes
Student/Faculty Ratio: 19:1 **Male/Female Ratio:** 52:48
Undergraduate Enrollment: 7,100 **Graduate Enrollment:** 310
Scholarships/Academic: Yes **Athletic:** Yes **Financial Aid:** Yes
Expenses by: Year **In State:** $ 9,868 **Out of State:** $ 17,848
Specialty: Business, Education, Engineering
Degrees Conferred: AA, AS, BA, BS, BAA, BAS, BM, MA, MS, MBA
Programs of Study: Accounting, American Studies, Anthropology, Applied Sciences, Biological Science, Business Administration, Chemistry, Communications, Computer, Criminology, Dramatic Arts, Early Childhood Education, Earth Science, Economics, Education, Engineering, English, Fine Arts, Geography, Geology, History, Liberal Arts, Mathematics, Music, Philosophy, Physics, Political Science, Psychology, Speech, Women's Studies

Women's Athletic Profile

10 University Drive
Duluth, MN 55806
Coach: Greg Cane
Email:

NCAA II
Bulldogs/Maroon, Gold
Phone: (218) 726-6229
Fax: (218) 726-6529

Did Not Return Profile

University of Minnesota - Morris

Academic Profile

Phone: 320-589-2211

Morris, MN 56267

Type: 4 Yr.,Public,Liberal Arts **Founded:** 1959
Website: http://www.mrs.umn.edu **Religion:** Non-Affiliated
SAT/ACT/GPA: 820/17min **Housing:** No

Student/Faculty Ratio: 15:1
Male/Female Ratio: 45:55
Undergraduate Enrollment: 1,933
Graduate Enrollment: N/A
Scholarships/Academic: Yes
Athletic: No
Financial Aid: Yes
Expenses by: Year
In State: $ 8,000
Out of State: $ 15,000
Degrees Conferred: BA
Programs of Study: Contact school for program of study.

Women's Athletic Profile

PE Center
Morris, MN 56267
Coach: Christian Devrie
Email: devriesc@mrs.umn.edu

NCAA II
Cougars/Maroon, Gold
Phone: (320) 589-6422
Fax: (320) 589-6422

Did Not Return Profile

University of Saint Thomas

Academic Profile

St. Paul, MN 55105
Phone: 651-962-5000

Type: 4 Yr.,Private,Liberal Arts
Founded: 1885
Website: http://www.stthomas.edu
Religion: Catholic
SAT/ACT/GPA: 800/20
Housing: No
Student/Faculty Ratio: 17:1
Male/Female Ratio: 50:50
Undergraduate Enrollment: 5,000
Graduate Enrollment: 5,000
Scholarships/Academic: Yes
Athletic: No
Financial Aid: Yes
Expenses by: Year
In State: $ 16,800
Out of State: $ 16,800
Degrees Conferred: BA, MA, MS, MBA, EdD, Mdiv
Programs of Study: Accounting, Advertising, Art History, Asian Studies, Banking & Finance, Biology, Broadcasting, Business Administration, Chemistry, Communications, Computer Science, Criminal Justice, Dramatic, Arts, Education, English, French, Geography, Geology, German, History, International Business, Journalism, Latin, Literature, Management, Marketing, Mathematics, Music, Philosophy, Psychology, Public Relations, Public Administration, Russian, Social Science, Spanish, Speech, Telecommunications, Theology, Urban Studies

Men's Athletic Profile

2115 Summit Avenue
St. Paul, MN 55105
Coach: Denzil Lue
Email: deNe@hotmail.com

NCAA III
Tommies/Purple, Gray
Phone: (612) 962-5923
Fax: (612) 962-5910

Estimated # of Men's Soccer Scholarships: None
Conference: Minnesota Intercollegiate Athletic Conference
Program Profile: We are a non-scholarship, Division III program with a solid coaching staff. Strong team chemistry. Strong team chemistry, strong academic. We have 20 varsity and 20 junior varsity players. We have grass soccer field, practice August 23. First game September 4-5 16 game Regular Season schedule. One tournament each year in Colorado California or Texas.
History: Our program began in 1968. Coach Denzil Lue compiled a record of 191-105-43 with a two losing seasons since UST owns winning records in all-time series versus all 10 MAC foes.
Achievements: In 1993-1994 our Goalie Joe Warren is now on Minnesota Thunder. Coach Denzil Lue was named Coach of the Year in 1991 & 1985. We have 4 UST players named Conference MVP Awards in 1985, 1987, 1993 & 1994.

Coaching: Denzil Lue is the Head Coach, compiled a record of 191-105-43. He has 20 years of coaching experience and led the team to 4 NCAA play-offs berth. Stan Marza is the Assistant Coach is entering his 17 years with the program. Aaron Macke is the Assistant Coach, is entering third year with the program. Yousseff Darbaki is the Assistant Coach, is entering six years with the program.
Style of Play: We are aggressive but smart team. Good athletes playing together in team concept.

Women's Athletic Profile

2115 Summit Ave
St. Paul, MN 55105
Coach: Colleen Carry
Email: cdcarey@stthomas.edu

NCAA III
Tommies/Purple, Grey
Phone: (612) 962-5900
Fax: (612) 962-5910

Estimated # of Women's Soccer Scholarships: None
Conference: Minnesota Intercollegiate Athletic
Program Profile: The season is played during the fall season. Our field is located on our south campus and is played on a natural field.
History: Our program began in 1995, and we have reached NCAA playoffs five times.
Achievements: 3 All-Americans; 34 First Team All-Conference selections
Coaching: Colleen Carey is the Head Coach and Katie Storey is the Assistant Coach.
Roster in State: 15 **Out of State:** 2 **Out of Country:**
Walk-on/Other: **Graduation %:** 100 **Seniors on Team:** 6
Positions Needed: All
Camp or Clinic Dates: Not Available
Most Recent Record: 10-7-1
Schedule: Macalester, University of Chicago, Wisc. Steven's Point, Gustavus, St. Benedict, Cornell
Style of Play: We play a possession style of play. We attack from every where and switch from a zonal defense to a marking defense depending on opponent.

mississippi

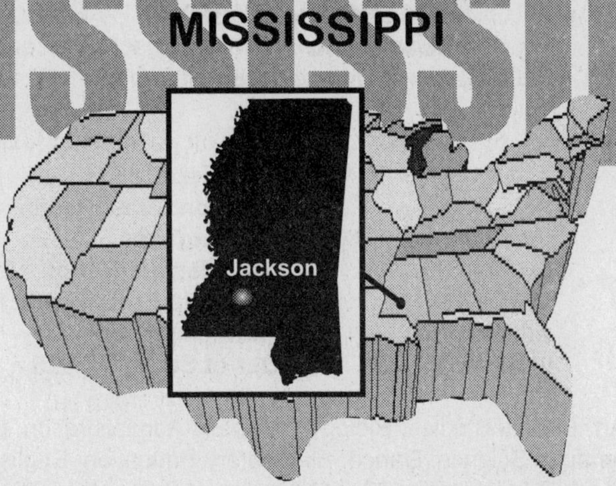

SCHOOL	CITY	AFFILIATION	PAGE
Belhaven College	Jackson	NAIA	576
Itwamba Community College	Fulton	NJCAA	577
Millsaps College	Jackson	NCAA III	577
Mississippi College	Clinton	NCAA III	579
Mississippi State University	Starkville	NCAA I	580
University of Southern Mississippi	Hattiesburg	NCAA I	581
William Carey College	Gulfport	NAIA	582

Belhaven College

Academic Profile

Phone:

Jackson, MS 39202

Type: 4 Yr.,Private,Liberal Arts
Website: http://www.belhaven.edu
SAT/ACT/GPA: 960/20/2.0
Student/Faculty Ratio: 18:1
Undergraduate Enrollment: 1,300
Scholarships/Academic: Yes
Athletic: Yes
Expenses by: Year
In State: $ 7,025
Founded: 1883
Religion: Presbyterian
Housing: Yes
Male/Female Ratio: 1:2.5
Graduate Enrollment: 100
Financial Aid: Yes
Out of State: $ 7,025
Degrees Conferred: BA, BS, BM
Programs of Study: Accounting, Art, Biblical Studies, Biology, Business Administration, Chemistry, Combined Science, Computer Information Systems, Computer Science, Dance, Elementary Education, English, History, Humanities, Mathematics, Music, Philosophy, Sports Administration, Sports Medicine, Sports Ministry, PreLaw, PreMed, Psychology

Men's Athletic Profile

1500 Peachtree St.
Jackson, MS 39202
Coach: Neal Kaspar
Email: nkaspar@belhaven.edu

NAIA
Blazers/F. Green, Vegas Gold
Phone: (601) 965-7013
Fax: (601) 965-7025

Estimated # of Men's Soccer Scholarships: None
Conference: Gulf Coast Athletic Conference
Program Profile: The Blazers home field is the 'Bowl' with natural grass, and hillside seating. They play a regular Fall season, September to November. The field is on campus and is also the site for campus events.
History: Our program began as a club sport in 1970. Moved to a full NAIA Division I in 1980. Appeared in first NAIA National tournament in 1982. Our program is the most successful of any college in Mississippi (in terms of conference, region, and national championships).
Achievements: 1992 - NAIA National Champions; 1991, 1993 NAIA Semifinalists; 22 All - American Honors since 1982; 6 appearances in NAIA National tournaments; 6 District 30 Championships; 4 Area Seven Championships; 1994 ISAA Player of the Year; 1992 NAIA Coach of the Year; 1982,1992 NAIA Tournament Most Valuable Players.
Coaching: Neal Kaspar is the Head Coach.

Women's Athletic Profile

1500 Peachtree Street
Jackson, MS 39202
Coach: David Dixon
Email: ddixon@belhaven.edu

NAIA
Blazers/Green, Gold
Phone: (601) 968-8708
Fax: (601) 965-7025

Estimated # of Women's Soccer Scholarships: varies
Conference: Independent
Program Profile: The team plays a 18 game fall season and has an off-season fitness and training program. We have a state of the art weight/training facility. We will be playing on a brand new Bermuda grass field.
History: Our program began in 1997.
Achievements: We have had 9 All-Conference players in three years, NAIA region player of the week and 1 Academic All-American.
Coaching: This will be David Dixon's second year here previously being at Roberts Wesleyan College in Rochester, NY. He was a former professional player and college All-American.
Roster in State: 4
Out of State: 11
Out of Country: 0

ODP State: 7 **Regional:** **National:**
Walk-on/Other: **Graduation %:** 100 **Seniors on Team:** 4
Positions Needed: Forward, Defender, Goalkeeper
Camp or Clinic Dates: Not Available
Most Recent Record: 12-8-0
Schedule: William Carey, Mobile, National American, Birmingham-Southern, Berry, Houghton, Roberts Wesleyan
Style of Play: We play a direct style attacking down the flanks with wide midfielders or outside back. Defensively we try to pressure hard and are tough and aggressive.

Itawamba Community College

Academic Profile

Fulton, MS 38843
Phone: 662-862-8124

Type: 2 Yr.,Public,Jr. College
Founded: 1947
Website: http://www.icc.cc.ms.us
Religion: Non-Affiliated
SAT/ACT/GPA: Must Take ACT
Housing: Yes
Student/Faculty Ratio: N/A
Male/Female Ratio: N/A
Undergraduate Enrollment: 3000
Graduate Enrollment: N/A
Scholarships/Academic: Yes **Athletic:** Yes **Financial Aid:** Yes
Expenses by: Year **In State:** $1,750 **Out of State:** $2,575
Degrees Conferred: Associates
Programs of Study: Accounting, Agricultural Business, Art Education, Art/Fine Arts, Biology, Biological Science, Business Administration, Commerce, Management, Chemistry, Child Care/Child and Family Studies, Child Psychology, Child Development, Computer Science, Computer Technologies, Data Processing

Men's Athletic Profile

602 West Hill Street
Fulton, MS 38843
Coach: Matthew C. Convertino
Email: mcconvertino@icc.cc.ms.us

NJCAA
Indians/Blue, Red, White
Phone: 662-862-8124
Fax:

Estimated # of Men's Soccer Scholarships: 18
Conference: MACJC
Program Profile: NJCAA D-I program that plays on a bermuda grass field measuring 120x75.
History: Our program began in 1998.
Achievements: 2000 MACJC Finalist, finished #2 in the state, lost in NJCAA Region 23 Semi-Finals.
Coaching: Matthew Convertino is our head coach.
Roster In State: 21 **Out of State:** 1 **Out of Country:** 0
ODP State: 12 **Regional:** **National:**
Walk-on/Other: **Graduation %:** **Seniors on Team:** 10
Positions Needed: All
Most Recent Record: 12-4-1
Schedule: Meridian CC, Hinds CC, Gulf Coast CC
Style of Play: Depends on players.

Millsaps College

Academic Profile

Jackson, MS 39210
Phone: (601) 974-1198

Type: 4 Yr.,Private,Liberal Arts
Founded: 1890
Website: http://www.millsaps.edu
Religion: United Methodist

SAT/ACT/GPA: 1100/21/2.5
Housing: Yes
Student/Faculty Ratio: 15:1
Male/Female Ratio: 49:51
Undergraduate Enrollment: 1,200
Graduate Enrollment: 250
Scholarships/Academic: Yes **Athletic:** No **Financial Aid:** Yes
Expenses by: Year **In State:** $21,000 **Out of State:** $21,000
Specialty: Business, Education, Liberal Arts, Premed
Degrees Conferred: BA, BS, BBA, BMus, MBA, MA, MLS, BLS
Programs of Study: Accounting, Biology, Business Administration, Chemistry, Classics, Computer Science, Dramatic Arts, Economics, Elementary Education, English, Fine Arts, French, Geology, History, Management, Mathematics, Music, Philosophy, Physics, Political Science, Psychology, Religion, Science Education, Social Science, Spanish

Men's Athletic Profile

1701 N State Street
Jackson, MS 39210
Coach: William Lytton
Email: Lyttonwd@okra.millsaps.edu

NCAA III
Majors/Purple, White, Black
Phone: (601) 974-1198
Fax: (601) 974-1209

Estimated # of Men's Soccer Scholarships:
Conference: Southern Collegiate Athletic Conference
Program Profile: Stadium seating for 750; 118 x93 natural turf field; playing season mid August- end of October; Style of play is classical possession, build out of back, numbers in attack, zonal defense
History: Program began in 1982; All-time record 122-163-21, 1999 season 9-10; SCAC finish 5th.
Achievements: 1982 NAIA Runner-up Coach of the Year, 1986 Florida College Coach of the Year, five All-Americans, five players to go on to play pro.
Coaching: William Lytton, Head Coach, was named 1982 Runner-up National Coach of the Year NAIA, 1986 Florida College Coach of the Year and 1986 Sunshine State Conference Coach of the Year. He coached 1986 SS Conference Champions - St. Thomas University and 1982 NAIA 3rd place.
Roster In State: 7 **Out of State:** 14 **Out of Country:**
Walk-on/Other: **Graduation %:** 98 **Seniors on Team:** 5
Camp or Clinic Dates: July 9-14, 2000
Most Recent Record: 9-10
Schedule: Trinity, Rhodes, DePauw, Centre, Sewanee, Huntington, Southwestern, East Texas Baptist, letourneau, Oglethorpe.
Style of Play: Possession, build out of the back through midfield to get numbers in the attack. Emphasis on techniques and tactics.

Women's Athletic Profile

1701 N State Street
Jackson, MS 39210
Coach: William Lytton
Email: lyttond@okra.millsaps.edu

NCAA III
Lady Majors/Purple, White
Phone: (601) 974-1198
Fax: (601) 974-1209

Estimated # of Women's Soccer Scholarships: None
Conference: Southern Collegiate Athletic Conference
Program Profile: The team plays on 115x70 natural grass field; fall season, stadium size has 750 capacity.
History: Program began in 1986.
Achievements: William Lytton 1982 runner-up National Coach of the Year-NAIA; 1986 Florida College Coach of the Year; 1986 Sunshine State Conference Coach of the Year; 1986 SS conference Champions - St. Thomas University; 1982 NAIA 3rd place.

Coaching: William Lytton, Head Coach, 1982 Runner-Up National Coach of the Year. Sergio Moura Duarte, Assistant Coach (Brazil).
Style of Play: Indirect style of play, build out of the back through midfield, numbers in the attack including at least one defender in every attack; exciting attacking style.

Mississippi College
Academic Profile

Clinton, MS 39058
Phone: (601) 925-3000

Type: 4 Yr.,Private,Liberal Arts
Founded: 1826
Website: http://www.mc.edu
Religion: Southern Baptist
SAT/ACT/GPA: 870/18
Housing: No
Student/Faculty Ratio: 20:1
Male/Female Ratio: N/A
Undergraduate Enrollment: 2,500
Graduate Enrollment: 1,000
Scholarships/Academic: Yes **Athletic:** No **Financial Aid:** Yes
Expenses by: Year **In State:** $12,998 **Out of State:** $12,998
Degrees Conferred: BS, BA, MA
Programs of Study: Accounting, Administration of Justice, Art, Biology, Business Administration, Chemistry, Christian Studies, Communications, Computer Science, Counseling, English, Foreign Languages, Geography, Paralegal, Mathematics, Music, Nursing, Physics, PreMed, Psychology, Sociology, Teacher Education

Men's Athletic Profile

Box 1018
Clinton, MS 39058
Coach: Dr. Merle Wm. Ziegler
Email: mziegler@mc.edu

NCAA III
Choctaws/Navy Blue, Old Gold
Phone: (601) 925-3456
Fax: (601) 925-3953

Estimated # of Men's Soccer Scholarships:
Conference: American Southwest Conference
Program Profile: The college has brand new practice and game fields. The season begins in September and concludes in early or mid November. Mississippi College has outstanding athletic and recreational facilities for its athletes and the general student body as a whole.
History: Mississippi College has been a member of the American Southwest Conference for the past two years. The men's soccer program began as a club them in the 1970's. It became a varsity sport in 1998 competing in the American Southwest Conference. The Choctaws qualified for the ASC Final Four Tournament in its first year in the conference and narrowly missed being in the Final Four Tournament in 1999.
Achievements: In the past two years the Choctaw's have placed seven players on the ASC All Conference teams as well as eight on the ASC All-Academic Team. IN 1999, Mitch Peters was named to the NSCAA All-South team.
Coaching: Dr. Ziegler grew up in Bolivia, South America and has coached the Choctaws since 1994. Previously he coached youth select and ODP teams in Virginia and Mississippi. He is also a full Professor in the Department of Communication.
Roster In State: 22 **Out of State:** 3 **Out of Country:** 0
ODP State: 0 **Regional:** 0 **National:** 0
Walk-on/Other: **Graduation %:** 100 **Seniors on Team:** 5
Positions Needed: Keeper, Midfield, Marking Back
Most Recent Record: 7-8-1
Schedule: University of the South, East Texas Baptist University, Letourneau, Belhaven College, Austin College, Oglethorpe, Louisiana College, Univ. of the Ozarks, Milsaps College
Style of Play: We play a short passing game which focuses on maintaining possession. However, we will adapt that overall philosophy depending on the skills of the individual's on our team and the type of opponent we are up against.

Women's Athletic Profile

P.O. Box 4049
Clinton, MS 39056
Coach: Darryl Longabaugh
Email: longabau@mc.edu

NCAA III
Lady Choctaws/Navy, Old Gold
Phone: (601) 925-3892
Fax: (601) 925-3344

Estimated # of Women's Soccer Scholarships: None
Conference: American Southwest Conference
Program Profile: We two natural soccer only fields, which measures 75x110, state of the art, weight room and we have our own strength coach.
History: Our program began in 1997 with a 5-6 record. In 1998 season, we went 6-6-4 and in 1999 season, we were 12-6-1 finishing second.
Achievements: We have had 2 Conference Freshman of the Year awards, 6 All-Conference players, 1 Conference Player of the Year, Conference Coach of the Year in 1998 & 1999.
Coaching: Darryl Longabaugh is our Head Coach. Jana Carter is our Assistant Coach.

Roster in State: 15 **Out of State:** 3 **Out of Country:** 0
ODP State: 6 **Regional:** 2 **National:** 0
Walk-on/Other: 0 **Graduation %:** 100 **Seniors on Team:** 2

Positions Needed: Goalkeeper, Midfielder
Camp or Clinic Dates: Not Available
Most Recent Record: 12-6-1
Schedule: Huntingdon College, Austin College, East Texas Baptist University, Hollins College, Sweet Briar College, Millsaps College
Style of Play: Depends on players, like to control the ball; strong defense. We have 11 shutouts in 1999.

Mississippi State University

Academic Profile

Phone: 662-325-3076

Mississippi State, MS 39762

Type: 4 Yr.,Public,Liberal Arts,Engineering
Founded: 1878
Website: http://www.msstate.edu
Religion: Non-Affiliated
SAT/ACT/GPA: Call for information
Housing: Yes
Student/Faculty Ratio: 15/1
Male/Female Ratio: 55:45
Undergraduate Enrollment: 10,818
Graduate Enrollment: 2,946
Scholarships/Academic: Yes **Athletic:** Yes **Financial Aid:** Yes
Expenses by: Year **In State:** $4,358 **Out of State:** $6,332
Specialty: Engineering, Veterinarian Medicine
Degrees Conferred: BA, BBA, BFA, BGS, BS, BLA, BPA, MA, MS, MAM, MBA
Programs of Study: Accounting, Agriculture, Anthropology, Biology, Business and Management, Chemistry, Communications, Computer, Education, Engineering, English, Finance, Management, Sciences, Technology

Women's Athletic Profile

P.O. Box 5327
Starkville, MS 39762
Coach: Neil McGuire
Email: bulldogsoccer@athletics.msstate.edu

NCAA I
Bulldogs/Maroon, White
Phone: (601) 325-0718
Fax: (601) 325-9051

Estimated # of Women's Soccer Scholarships: 2.0
Conference: Southeastern Conference

Program Profile: High quality playing field, 120x75 yards. Bermuda tift hybrid surface. Natural amphitheatre-like surroundings. Compete in a very strong SEC. Will continue to develop highly competitive NCAA Division I program with a talented players from throughout the country. Grandstand holds 500-750 fans; lights to be added July 2000.
History: 2000 record of 8-11-1
Coaching: Neil McGuire Head Coach, Assistant Jennie Alther, and Scott Eloke.
Roster in State: 7 **Out of State:** 19 **Out of Country:** 1
ODP State: 0 **Regional:** 0 **National:** 1
Walk-on/Other: 3 **Graduation %:** **Seniors on Team:** 7
Positions Needed: Defenders, Midfield
Camp or Clinic Dates: June 10-14, June 18-21
Most Recent Record: 8-11-1
Schedule: Florida, Vanderbilt, Kentucky, South Carolina, Mississippi, Arkansas, L.S.U, Alabama, Auburn
Style of Play: Possession and low pressure

University of Southern Mississippi

Academic Profile

Phone: (601) 266-6220

Hattiesburg, MS 39406-5017

Type: 4 Yr.,Public,Liberal Arts **Founded:** 1910
Website: http://www.usm.edu **Religion:** Non-Affiliated
SAT/ACT/GPA: 870/18/2.0-2.5 **Housing:** Yes
Student/Faculty Ratio: 18:1 **Male/Female Ratio:** N/A
Undergraduate Enrollment: 11,000 **Graduate Enrollment:** 2,000
Scholarships/Academic: No **Athletic:** Yes **Financial Aid:** No
Expenses by: Year **In State:** $ 5,580 **Out of State:** $ 8,475
Specialty: Education, Technology, Liberal Arts
Degrees Conferred: Bachelors, Masters, Doctoral
Programs of Study: Accounting, Advertising, American Studies, Anthropology, Architecture, Art, Biology, Business Administration, Chemistry, Community Services, Computer Engineering, Computer Science, Computer Technologies, Economics, Education, Film Studies, Management, Music, Music Education, Nursing, Pathology, Physical Education, Real Estate, Science Education, Speech

Women's Athletic Profile

Box 5017 **NCAA I**
Hattiesburg, MS 39406-5017 Lady Golden Eagles/Black, Gold
Coach: John Mollaghan **Phone:** (601) 266-5017
Email: john.mollaghan@usm.edu **Fax:** (601) 266-6595

Estimated # of Women's Soccer Scholarships: 12
Conference: Conference USA
Program Profile: Strong C-USA soccer program. Have own soccer complex 1/2 mile off campus, full size natural field. Can hold 2,000 spectators. Playing season runs Mid August-November.
History: Program is going into its 4th yr. Last season, we had a record of 10-9-1. Overall record is 25-21-2 (.521) Conference tournament record of 1-1. (.500)
ranked in top 10 All-America first year programs
Achievements: 1999 conference semi final. 1st no.8 seed to beat a no.1 seed in tournament history.
2 members C-USA freshmen team.
3rd team all conference
Coaching: John Molbghan-USSF"C"liscence, NSCAA national diploma 4rth year at program. ODP State coach Ged O'Connor-NSCAA Certified Goalkeeper Coach. 2nd year on staff ODP State coach
Roster in State: 3 **Out of State:** 17 **Out of Country:** 5

Walk-on/Other: **Graduation %:** **Seniors on Team:** 5
Positions Needed: looking for athletes to strengthen the squad
Camp or Clinic Dates: June 4-9, 11-15-18-22
Most Recent Record: 10-9-1
Schedule: Marquette University, UAB, South Florida, Ole Miss, Alabama University, Houston University UNC Charlotte, St. Louis University, Cincinnati University, Tulane
Style of Play: Tough, physical team that is capable of a good passing game. The team style is decided around the ability of the team and opponents and changes as needed.

William Carey College on th Coast

Academic Profile

Gulfport, MS 39507
Phone:

Type: 4 Yr.,Private,Liberal Arts
Founded: 1906
Website: Not Available
Religion: Baptist
SAT/ACT/GPA: 18+
Housing: Yes
Student/Faculty Ratio: 13:1
Male/Female Ratio: 1:1
Undergraduate Enrollment: 2,200
Graduate Enrollment: 200
Scholarships/Academic: Yes **Athletic:** Yes **Financial Aid:** Yes
Expenses by: Year **In State:** $ 7,500 **Out of State:** $ 7,500
Degrees Conferred: BS, BA, BFA, BSN, BM, MBA, M Ed
Programs of Study: Business, Education, Art, Nursing, English, History, Math, Psychology, Biology

Men's Athletic Profile

9119 Victoria Circle
Gulfport, MS 39503
Coach: Doug Stovall
Email: dsrstovall@aol.com

NAIA
Crusaders/Red, Black
Phone: (228) 897-7144
Fax: (228) 897-7131

Estimated # of Men's Soccer Scholarships: Varies
Conference: Gulf Coast Athletic Association
Program Profile: Our playing season is in the fall and in the spring. We play on a natural grass field.
History: Program began in 1986; made five trips to National tournament; Final Four in 1997.
Achievements: Coach of the Year five times; Conference Titles five times; All-Americans - 14 players; players drafted - 1.
Coaching: Doug Stovall, Head Coach, was the former ODP State Coach for Mississippi. He holds a USSF "B" license and spent twelve years collegiate head coach. Chris Pryor and Chris Kennie are the Assistant Coaches.
Roster In State: 1 **Out of State:** 30 **Out of Country:** 12
ODP State: 0 **Regional:** 2 **National:** 0
Walk-on/Other: 0 **Graduation %:** 86 **Seniors on Team:** 4
Positions Needed: ALL
Camp or Clinic Dates: Not Available
Most Recent Record: 11-7-1
Schedule: Movile University, Life University, Auburn, Flagler, Marris, Lindenwood
Style of Play: 4-4-2 formation; direct work the flank. One and two touch.

Women's Athletic Profile

1856 Beach Drive
Gulfport, MS 39507
Coach: Doug Stovall
Email: dsrstovall@aol.com

NAIA
Crusaders/Red, Black
Phone: (228) 897-7144
Fax: (228) 897-7138

Estimated # of Women's Soccer Scholarships: varies
Conference: Gulf Coast Athletic Conference, Southwest Region
Program Profile: Our program is very competitive at the small college level against other top NAIA programs. We play on natural grass field, which school is located directly across from the Gulf of Mexico. A very beautiful location.
History: The program began in 1990-1991.
Achievements: In the past four years, the team has had 22 All-Region and 6 All-Americans. Our team has had 12 Academic All-Americans. Our 1995 team was ranked #6 in the nation, while our 1998 team ranked 23rd in the nation.

Roster in State: 6	**Out of State:** 8	**Out of Country:** 5
ODP State: 1	**Regional:** 0	**National:** 0
Walk-on/Other: 0	**Graduation %:** 86	**Seniors on Team:** 1

Positions Needed: ALL
Most Recent Record: 14-5-0
Schedule: St. Gregory's Univ. Lindenwood Univ. Univ. of Mobile, Barry College

missouri

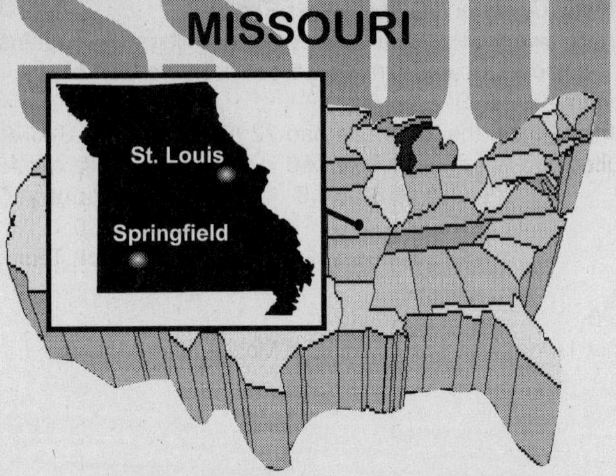
MISSOURI
St. Louis
Springfield

SCHOOL	CITY	AFFILIATION	PAGE
Webster University	St. Louis	NCAA III	617
Westminster College	Fulton	NCAA III	618
William Jewell College	Liberty	NAIA	619
William Woods U	Fulton	NAIA	620

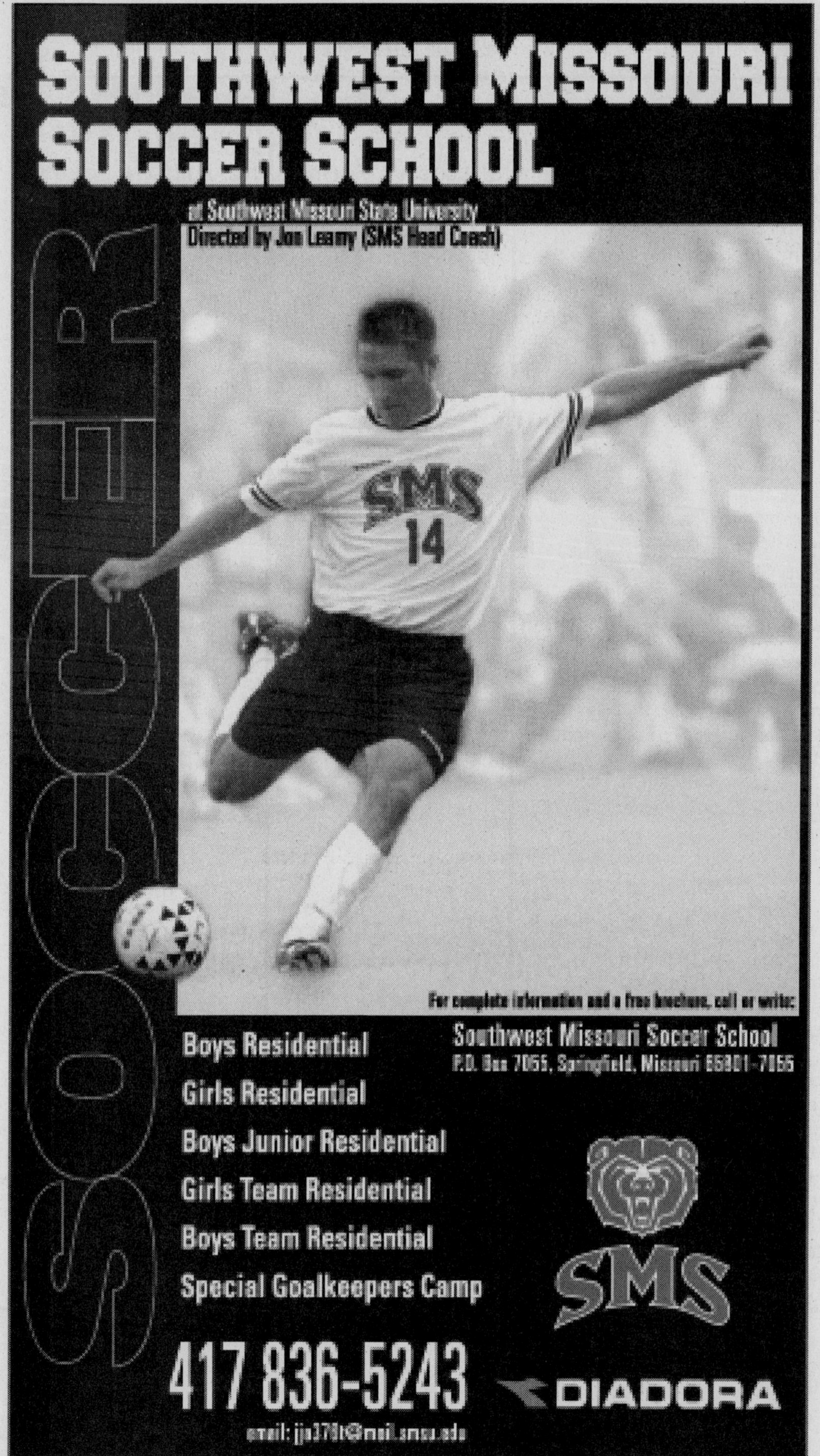
SOUTHWEST MISSOURI
SOCCER SCHOOL
at Southwest Missouri State University
Directed by Jon Leamy (SMS Head Coach)
SOCCER
SMS 14
For complete information and a free brochure, call or write:
Southwest Missouri Soccer School
Boys Residential
Girls Residential
Boys Junior Residential
Girls Team Residential
Boys Team Residential
Special Goalkeepers Camp
SMS
417 836-5243
DIADORA

Avila College

Academic Profile

Kansas City, MO 64145
Phone: (816) 942-8400

Type: 4 Yr.,Private,Liberal Arts
Founded: 1916
Website: http://www.avila.edu
Religion: Catholic
SAT/ACT/GPA: 22/3.2
Housing: Yes
Student/Faculty Ratio: 13:1
Male/Female Ratio: 40:60
Undergraduate Enrollment: 1,200
Graduate Enrollment: 200
Scholarships/Academic: Yes **Athletic:** Yes **Financial Aid:** Yes
Expenses by: Year **In State:** $ 16,010 **Out of State:** $ 16,010
Specialty: Nursing, Education, Radiological Technology, Communications
Degrees Conferred: BA, BS, BSBA, BSN, BSMT, BSW, BFA, MS, MBA
Programs of Study: Art, Communication, English, General Studies, History, Mathematics, Music, Natural Sciences, Political Sciences, Psychology, Sociology, Theatre, Theology, Etc.

Men's Athletic Profile

11901 Wornall Road
Kansas City, MO 64145
Coach: Patrick Phillips
Email: Not Available

NAIA
Eagles/Purple, Gold
Phone: (816) 942-8400x 2417
Fax: (816) 942-3362

Estimated # of Men's Soccer Scholarships: 24
Conference: Midlands Collegiate Athletic Conference
Program Profile: We have a practice field on the west side of campus. We also have an All-Sports Complex that is accompanied by the men's playing field.
History: Our men's soccer program originated in 1977. It was started with 11 freshmen and two transfer students and reached district playoffs. In 1982, the team was ranked number one in the NAIA winning the Division IV championship.
Achievements: NAIA All-Americans.
Coaching: Patrick Phillips is Head Coach. Rob Fenton and Ken McDonald are the Assistant Coaches.

Women's Athletic Profile

11901 Wornall Road
Kansas City, MO 64145
Coach: Jeff Randolph
Email: Randolphjj@mail.Avila.edu

NAIA
Eagles/Gold, Purple
Phone: (816) 501-2400
Fax: (816) 942-3362

Estimated # of Women's Soccer Scholarships: 30
Conference: Heart of America Conference
Program Profile: Varsity and junior varsity teams. building a strong stadium of tough competition in Midwest region. Playing season is mid-August to early November.
History: Program began in 1994. Coach Randolph has been the longest-tenured coach, arriving for 1997 season. Moved to Heart of America Athletic Conference in 2000.
Achievements: In 1998 season set 7 new school records, including best season. Numerous MCAC Conference honors.
Coaching: Jeff Randolph, Head Coach, entering second season with the program.
Roster in State: 20 **Out of State:** 6 **Out of Country:** 0
ODP State: 9 **Regional:** **National:**
Walk-on/Other: **Graduation %:** 90 **Seniors on Team:** 3

Positions Needed: Goalkeeper, Mid-fielder
Camp or Clinic Dates: Not Available
Most Recent Record: 7-8-1
Schedule: Lindenwood Univ. Baker Univ. Benedictine Univ.
Style of Play: Offensive-oriented. controlled passing game Dutch style. Physical play, yet, we still remember this soccer is a game and is supposed to be fun.

Central Methodist College

Academic Profile

Phone: (660) 248-6348

Fayette, MO 65248

Type: 4 Yr.,Private,Liberal Arts
Founded: 1852
Website: http://www.cmc.edu
Religion: Methodist
SAT/ACT/GPA: 1840/18/2.0
Housing: Yes
Student/Faculty Ratio: 14:1
Male/Female Ratio: 2:1
Undergraduate Enrollment: 1161
Graduate Enrollment: 30
Scholarships/Academic: Yes **Athletic:** Yes **Financial Aid:** Yes
Expenses by: Year **In State:** $ 15,490 **Out of State:** $ 15,490
Specialty: Education, Nursing, Pre-professional (Law and Medicine)
Degrees Conferred: AA, AS, BA, BS, BSEd, BSN, BM, BMEd, B Music
Programs of Study: Accounting, Athletic Training, Biology, Business Administration, Chemistry, Communications, Community Services, Computer Science, Criminal Justice, Dramatic Arts, Economics, Education, English, Environmental Science, French, German, History, Languages, Management, Mathematics, Music, Music History, Nursing, Philosophy, Physical Science, Political Science, PreLaw, Psychology, Recreation Administration Management, Religion, Social Science

Men's Athletic Profile

411 Central Methodist Square
Fayette, MO 65248
Coach: Mozaffar Rahmatpanah
Email: mrahmat@cmc.edu

NAIA
Eagles/Green, Black
Phone: (816) 248-3391
Fax: (816) 248-1632

Estimated # of Men's Soccer Scholarships: 25
Conference: Heart of America
Program Profile: Excellent program for student/athlete who likes to play and learn the game from a professional coaching staff.. Natural grass pitch.
History: program start in 1971.
Roster In State: 26 **Out of State:** 4 **Out of Country:**
Walk-on/Other: **Graduation %:** 90 **Seniors on Team:** 5
Positions Needed: Forwards, Defenders
Camp or Clinic Dates: Not Available
Most Recent Record: 9-6-2
Schedule: Ball possession, short passes or much as possible, very aggressive.

Women's Athletic Profile

411 Central Methodist Square
Fayette, MO 65248
Coach: Pat Reardon
Email: preardon@cmc.edu

NAIA
Eagles/Green, Black, White
Phone: (660) 248-6348
Fax: (660) 248-1632

Estimated # of Women's Soccer Scholarships: 2.5
Conference: Heart of America Athletic Conference
Program Profile: Excellent program for the student athlete who likes to play and learn from the professional coaching staff. A young program with completely redone playing field, natural grass, practice area, new bleachers and lighted practice field.
History: Program began in 1987. The Eagles had a coaching change in 1992.
Achievements: The team produced 8 Academic All-Americans and finished in top half of conference the past four years. Has several All-Conference players since the start of the program.
Coaching: Pat Reardon, Head Coach, joined the staff as assistant in 1990 after completing 4 years as a starter for Central Methodist, career leader in goals at Central, team Captain for two years. Nicole Vieth is the Assistant Coach.

Roster in State: 18	**Out of State:** 4	**Out of Country:** 0
ODP State: 5	**Regional:** 2	**National:**
Walk-on/Other:	**Graduation %:**	**Seniors on Team:** 2

Positions Needed: Goal Keeper, Forward, Defender
Camp or Clinic Dates: Not Available
Most Recent Record: 5-13-0
Schedule: Linden Wood, St. Xavier, McKendree, Nebraska Wesleyan, Bethel College
Style of Play: Very aggressive style of play. Part man and part zone defense style.

Central Missouri State University

Academic Profile

Warrensburg, MO 64093
Phone: 800-729-2678

Type: 4 Yr.,Public,Liberal Arts		**Founded:** 1871
Website: http://www.cmsu.edu		**Religion:** Non-Affiliated
SAT/ACT/GPA: 20		**Housing:** Yes
Student/Faculty Ratio: 20:1		**Male/Female Ratio:** 47:53
Undergraduate Enrollment: 9,500		**Graduate Enrollment:** 1,500
Scholarships/Academic: Yes	**Athletic:** Yes	**Financial Aid:** Yes
Expenses by: Year	**In State:** $ 7,200	**Out of State:** $ 10,050

Specialty: Education, Criminal Justice, State Mission in Technology
Degrees Conferred: AS, AA, BA, BS, BFA, BM, BME, BSBA, MA, MS, MBA, MEd
Programs of Study: Accounting, Actuarial Science and Mathematics, Agriculture, Art, Anthropology, Asian Studies, Power Technology, Biology, Broadcasting, Business, Chemistry, Coaching, Computer Information Systems, Criminal Justice, Education, Engineering, English, Fashion, Fitness/Wellness, Languages, Graphic Arts, History, Hotel Administration, International Studies, Music, Nursing, Medical Technology, Photography, Political Science, etc, Also, Law, Medicine, Physical Therapy, etc..Please call for more

Women's Athletic Profile

500 Washington Street
Warrensburg, MO 64093
Coach: Al Iantorno
Email: Iantorno@cmsul.cmsu.edu

NCAA II
Lady Jennies/Cardinal, Black
Phone: (660) 543-4187
Fax: (660) 543-8034

Estimated # of Women's Soccer Scholarships: Partial Scholarships
Conference: MIAA
Program Profile: Very strong program. Winning seasons the last three years. Team ranked defensively fall of 98. Field is Bermuda grass.
History: Program began in the Fall of 95. Winning seasons the last three years.
Achievements: Team very strong defensively. Fall of 1998 the team was ranked 4th nationally, and 2nd in shut-outs. The team is also very strong academically with several team members on the honor roll. Team G.P.A. is just over a 3.0 with three individuals achieving a 4.0 in the fall of 1999.

Coaching: Al Iantorno, Head Coach, has a USSF "B" License and an NSCAA Diploma. He has a doctorate in education. Assistant coach Karen Hibdom has a masters degree. Style of coaching is a combination of direct and indirect soccer.

Roster in State: 12	**Out of State:** 8	**Out of Country:** 2
ODP State: 10	**Regional:** 2	**National:**
Walk-on/Other:	**Graduation %:** 81.5	**Seniors on Team:** 2

Positions Needed: Mid-field, forward, goalkeeper
Most Recent Record: 10-8
Schedule: Northern Colorado, North Dakota State, northern Kentucky, Truman State, Drury, Southwest Missouri State, Winona State, Rockhurst College, UNO
Style of Play: Combination of direct and indirect soccer. Very aggressive in defense. Ball possession in middle of field, and quick crosses and counter attacks. Physical fitness extremely important. Size of players a plus.

Columbia College

Academic Profile

Columbia, MO 65216
Phone: (573) 875-7414

Type: 4 Yr.,Private,Liberal Arts		**Founded:** 1851
Website: http://www.ccis.edu		**Religion:** Disciples of Christ
SAT/ACT/GPA: 18/2.0		**Housing:** Yes
Student/Faculty Ratio: 14:1		**Male/Female Ratio:** 1:3
Undergraduate Enrollment: 1,500		**Graduate Enrollment:** 50
Scholarships/Academic: Yes	**Athletic:** Yes	**Financial Aid:** Yes
Expenses by: Year	**In State:** $ 14,394	**Out of State:** $ 14,394

Specialty: Business Administration, Criminal Justice, Education
Degrees Conferred: AA, BA, BS, MBA
Programs of Study: Accounting, Art History, Biology, Business Administration, Ceramics, Chemistry, Computer Science, Criminal Justice, Education, English, Environmental Studies, Finance, Geology, Graphic Design, Sports Medicine, Social Work, All-Pre-Areas, Political Science

Men's Athletic Profile

1001 Rogers Street
Columbia, MO 65216
Coach: John Klein
Email: jdklein@email.ccis.edu

NAIA
Cougars/Navy Blue, Silver
Phone: (573) 875-7413
Fax: (573) 875-7415

Estimated # of Men's Soccer Scholarships: 9
Conference: American Midwest Conference
Program Profile: We play at Marrin Owens Stadium that has natural grass and capacity of 1,500.
History: The Men's Soccer program began in 1971. We were in the Top 20 of NAIA in 1996, 1998, and 1999 and Top 10 in 1998 and 1999.
Achievements: Won Conference Coach of the Year in 1992, 1994 & 1998; Conference Champs in 1994, 1996 & 1998; Conference Tournament Champions; in 1998 has 5 Academic All-Americans 10 overall; NSCAA team Academic Award; 1 All-American.
Coaching: John Klein is our Head Coach.

Roster In State: 10	**Out of State:** 6	**Out of Country:** 5
Walk-on/Other:	**Graduation %:** 98	**Seniors on Team:** 2

Camp or Clinic Dates: Not Available
Most Recent Record: 20-5

Schedule: Truman State, Rockhurst University, Lindenwood University, Dominican, Baker University, McKendree University, Park University, University of Illinois, Newman University, Benedictine College
Style of Play: Depends on players and size of field playing on.

Culver - Stockton College

Academic Profile

Canton, MO 63435

Phone:

Type: 4 Yr.,Private,Liberal Arts
Website: http://www.culver.edu
SAT/ACT/GPA: 23/3.0
Student/Faculty Ratio: 1:16
Undergraduate Enrollment: 908
Scholarships/Academic: Yes
Athletic: Yes
Expenses by: Year
In State: $ 14,670
Founded: 1853
Religion: Non-Affiliated
Housing: Yes
Male/Female Ratio: 1:3
Graduate Enrollment: N/A
Financial Aid: Yes
Out of State: $ 14,670
Specialty: Business, Education
Degrees Conferred: BA, BS, BFA, BME, BSN
Programs of Study: Art, Biology, Accounting, Business & Management, Chemistry, Communications, Computer Information Systems, Computer Science, Criminal Justice, Education, Foreign Languages, Health Science, History, Marketing, Mathematics, Music, Nursing, Philosophy, Political Science, Engineering, PreProfessional Programs, Psychology, Religion, Psychology, Religion, Social Science, Theatre & Drama

Men's Athletic Profile

One College Hill
Canton, MO 63435
Coach: Bill Schneider
Email: wschneider@culver.edu

NAIA
Wildcats/Royal, White
Phone: (217) 231-6391
Fax: (217) 231-6442

Estimated # of Men's Soccer Scholarships: 5
Conference: Heart of America Athletic Conference (HAAC)
Program Profile: We are building new soccer complex with natural grass. We play a 20 game schedule.
History: 1988 was the inaugural season of the program. In 1998, our record was 11-6-2. We have 5 graduating seniors.
Achievements: 1998 Luke Schneider 1st team HAAC, MVP, HAAC, All-Region NSCAA; second team honorable Mention All-American NAIA
Coaching: Bill Schnieder, Head Coach, has been with us since the inception of the program. Matt Longo - Assistant Coach.
Style of Play: Controlled and physical.

Drury University

Academic Profile

Springfield, MO 65802

Phone: (417) 873-7449

Type: 4 Yr.,Private,Liberal Arts
Website: http://www.drury.edu
SAT/ACT/GPA: 21
Student/Faculty Ratio: 12:1
Undergraduate Enrollment: 1,400
Scholarships/Academic: Yes
Athletic: Yes
Expenses by: Year
In State: $ 15,500
Founded: 1873
Religion: Church of Christ
Housing: Yes
Male/Female Ratio: 53:47
Graduate Enrollment: 300
Financial Aid: Yes
Out of State: $ 15,500

Specialty: Liberal Arts
Degrees Conferred: BA, BS BArch, BM, BME, BSN, AS, MBA, M.Ed.
Programs of Study: Liberal Arts, Business, Education, Architecture, Communications, PreLaw, PreMedicine, Accounting, Environmental Studies, Criminology, Exercise and Sports Science, English, Political Science, Art

Men's Athletic Profile

900 N. Benton
Springfield, MO 65802
Coach: John Senkosky
Email: jsenkonsk@drury.edu

NCAA I
Panthers/Scarlet, Gray
Phone: (417) 873-7449
Fax: (417) 873-7581

Estimated # of Men's Soccer Scholarships: 9.9
Conference: Western Athletic Conference
Program Profile: A NCAA Division II program associated with an academically prestigious school. The program enjoys strong support from the school and community. Outstanding facilities include a lighted, natural grass field with a seating of 500+, locker rooms, fitness center, and separate practice field. Play on 120x75 yards bermuda field with lighting and surrounded by a track. Has a seating capacity of 1,000.
History:
Achievements: Two times NSCAA Midwest Coach of the Year, NAIA District Coach of the Year.
Coaching: John Senkosky, Head Coach, has a USSF 'A' license; over 16 years coaching experience and 2-time Midwest Coach of the Year.

Roster In State: 13	**Out of State:** 9	**Out of Country:** 0
ODP State: 8	**Regional:**	**National:**
Walk-on/Other:	**Graduation %:** 100	**Seniors on Team:** 4

Positions Needed: Midfielders, Defenders, Forwards
Most Recent Record: 8-12-0
Schedule: SMU, Tulsa, Bradley, Michigan, Missouri-Kansas City, Oral Roberts, Drake, New Mexico, Western Illinois, Detroit
Style of Play: Possession with attack oriented style of play. We give the players the freedom to express themselves on field. We also stress the values of in individual creativity , hard work, an team unity.

Women's Athletic Profile

900 N. Benton Avenue
Springfield, MO 65802
Coach: Named in 2001
Email: jporter@drury.edu

NCAA I
Panthers/Red, Black
Phone: (417) 873-7897
Fax: (417) 873-7510

Estimated # of Women's Soccer Scholarships:
Conference: Missouri Valley
Program Profile: We are an academically prestigious school that will become Division I in the fall of 1999. We play in a lighted, natural grass field with a seating capacity for 750 people.
History: The program began in 1990, moved to Division II in 1993 and will become Division I in the fall of 1999. We will be eligible for championship play.
Achievements: 2 All-Region NSCAA Players in 1995 & 1996; Nationally ranked in Division II.
Coaching:

Roster in State: 14	**Out of State:** 7	**Out of Country:** 1
ODP State: 0	**Regional:** 0	**National:** 0
Walk-on/Other: 0	**Graduation %:** 100	**Seniors on Team:** 6

Positions Needed: 4
Camp or Clinic Dates: Not Available

Most Recent Record: 6-12-1
Schedule: Missouri Univ. Kansas Univ. Illinois State Univ. University of Evansville, Tulsa Univ. Creighton Univ. SMS Univ.
Style of Play: A ball control style with emphasis on combination play and attacking as a unit. Defense is a combination of zone and man to man.

Fontbonne College

Academic Profile

St. Louis, MO 63108
Phone: (314) 889-1444

Type: 4 Yr.,Private,Liberal Arts
Founded: 1914
Website: http://www.fontbonne.edu
Religion: Catholic
SAT/ACT/GPA: 21/2.5 or above
Housing: Yes
Student/Faculty Ratio: 14:1
Male/Female Ratio: 1:2
Undergraduate Enrollment: 1,400
Graduate Enrollment: 600
Scholarships/Academic: Yes
Athletic: No
Financial Aid: Yes
Expenses by: Year
In State: $ 16,000
Out of State: $ 16,000
Specialty: Deaf Education
Degrees Conferred: BS, BA, Masters, Ph.D.
Programs of Study: Applied Mathematics, Art, Biology, Broadcasting, Business, Communication Disorders, Computer Science, Deaf Education, Dietetics, Drawing, English, Fashion, Painting, Sculpture, Special Education, Studio Major, Mathematics, Human Services

Men's Athletic Profile

6800 Wydown Blvd.
St. Louis, MO 63105
Coach: Brian Hoener
Email: rsteiner@fontbonne.edu

NCAA III
Griffins/Purple, Gold
Phone: (314) 889-4534
Fax: (314) 889-1451

Estimated # of Men's Soccer Scholarships: None
Conference: St. Louis Intercollegiate Athletic Conference
Program Profile: Play games at St. Louis Soccer Park which is used by the National Team.
History: Our program began in 1980 and won national title for small school in 1986. joined NAIA in 1987 and NCAA Division III in 1990.
Achievements: District & Area Coach of the Year 1987 and 1990. Conference Champs 1988.
Style of Play: Ball possession, attacking from the back. Defensive in nature. Very disciplined.

Women's Athletic Profile

6800 Wydown Blvd.
St. Louis, MO 63105-3043
Coach: Scott Hager
Email: rstriner@fontbonne.edu

NCAA III
Griffins/Purple, Gold, White
Phone: (314) 889-4535
Fax: (314) 889-4507

Estimated # of Women's Soccer Scholarships: None
Conference: St. Louis Intercollegiate Athletic Conference
Program Profile: Our Home field is St. Louis Soccer Park, which has natural grass.
History: Our program began in 1994 and we have been Conference Champions twice. We won an SLIAC Post-Season Tournament Championship.
Achievements: 1996 won the SLIAC Tournament /Championship over Maryville 1-0; 1996 record was 15-3-3.
Coaching: Head Coach Scott Hager former player at Missouri Valley. Assistant Coach Jamie Sanchez.

Roster in State: 17 **Out of State:** 3 **Out of Country:** 0
Walk-on/Other: 0 **Graduation %:** **Seniors on Team:** 2
Positions Needed: ALL
Camp or Clinic Dates: Not Available
Most Recent Record: 7-12-1
Schedule: Washington Univ. Webster Univ. Maryville Univ. Greensboro College
Style of Play: Attacking using wings. Deadly on restarts.

Harris - Stowe State College

Academic Profile

Phone: (314) 340-3530

St. Louis, MO 63103

Type: 4 Yr.,Public
Founded: 1857
Website: http://www.hssc.edu
Religion: Non-Affiliated
SAT/ACT/GPA: 21
Housing: N
Student/Faculty Ratio: 15:1
Male/Female Ratio: 2:3
Undergraduate Enrollment: 1,700
Graduate Enrollment: N/A
Scholarships/Academic: Yes **Athletic:** Yes **Financial Aid:** Yes
Expenses by: Year **In State:** **Out of State:**
Specialty: Education and Business
Degrees Conferred: BS, BA, CJ, Urban Education
Programs of Study: Business Administration, Criminal Justice, Early Childhood, Elementary Education, Secondary Education, Urban Education, Interdisciplinary Study.

Men's Athletic Profile

3026 Laclede Avenue
St. Louis, MO 63103
Coach: Dennis Currier
Email: Currierd@hssc.edu

NAIA
Hornets/Black, White, Gold
Phone: (314) 340-3304
Fax: (314) 340-3555

Estimated # of Men's Soccer Scholarships: 12
Conference: American Midwest Conference
Program Profile: We have been a nationally ranked program for the past three years. We have been to the national tournament the past two years. We have a varsity team with no junior varsity. We carry 25 field players and 3 keepers. Play on 120x80 grass field. New field being built for 2001 as well as a new gymnasium.
History: Program began in the 1960's. It thrived in the 60's and 70's before it started to take a turn for the worse. In early 1990's, the program was re-built and for the past 5 years has been very successful with a 188-43-2 record.
Achievements: 1998 Midwest Region Coach of the Year, 1996 and 1997 American Midwest Conference Coach of the Year, 1996 and 1997 American Midwest Conference Title, 1997 American Midwest Conference Sectional Title, 8 All-Americans since 1992, 1998 Midwest Regional Champs, NAIA National Rankings in 1996, 1997 & 1998, Represented Midwest Region at 1998 National Tournament, one player drafted in 1999.
Coaching: Dennis Currier, Head Coach is in his 5th season. He was named AMC Coach of the Year 1996 and led the Hornets to their 1st ever AMC Championships. Brian Adams is the Assistant Coach. Matt Dowling is the Goalie Coach.
Roster In State: 7 **Out of State:** 20 **Out of Country:** 15
Most Recent Record: 22-3-0
Schedule: William Carey, Illinois Springfield College, Columbia College, Lindenwood, Mckendree College, Park, John Brown, Graceland, Oklahoma City University
Style of Play: 4-4-2; Very fast team with excellent flanks. Work ball outside and link front two runners very well. Emphasize defense on entire field.

Women's Athletic Profile

3026 Laclede Avenue
St. Louis, MO 63103
Coach: Richard (Rock) Rone
Email: Roner@hssc.edu

NAIA
Hornets/Brown, Gold
Phone: (314) 644-4492
Fax: (314) 340-5762

Estimated # of Women's Soccer Scholarships: 10
Conference: American Midwest Conference
Program Profile: We play in a natural grass field. Our women's program will have a new natural grass field in the year 2000. Within a year, we will have a new gymnasium including locker-rooms, a training room and a full gym with indoor facilities next to the new women's field.
History: Our program began in the fall of 1995. Our first year record was 3-12-1. Our record was 8-12-1 in 1996 and 13-7-1 in 1997 .
Achievements: None above "All-Region Team"; Several All-Conference players; Several "Academic All-Conference " players. 1999 First year we had All-American recognition for one of our student athletes.
Coaching: Richard (Rock) Rone, Head Coach, is entering his second year with the program. Vince Becker is the Assistant Coach.

Roster in State: 15	**Out of State:** 1	**Out of Country:**
ODP State: 2	**Regional:**	**National:**
Walk-on/Other:	**Graduation %:** 95	**Seniors on Team:** 3

Positions Needed: Goalie, Forward
Camp or Clinic Dates: Not Available
Most Recent Record: 11-6
Schedule: Lindenwood University, William Woods University, Missouri Baptist College, Pack C-University, McKendree College
Style of Play: Target up top and play ball positions in back.

Lincoln University

Academic Profile

820 Chestnut, Rm 142
Jefferson City, MO 65101-3500

Phone: 573-681-5342

Type: 4 Yr.,Public		**Founded:** 1866
Website: www.lincolnu.edu		**Religion:** Non-Affiliated
SAT/ACT/GPA: 820/18		**Housing:** Yes
Student/Faculty Ratio: 18:1		**Male/Female Ratio:** 40:60
Undergraduate Enrollment: 3,500		**Graduate Enrollment:** 1000
Scholarships/Academic: Yes	**Athletic:** Yes	**Financial Aid:** Yes
Expenses by: Year	**In State:** $ 6,734	**Out of State:** $ 9,158

Specialty: Education, Nursing Science
Degrees Conferred: AA, AAS, BA, BS, MA, MBA, Ed
Programs of Study: Accounting, Agriculture, Art, Biology, Business, Chemistry, Computer Information Systems, Computer Science, Criminal Justice, Economics, Electrical/Electronic Technology, Marketing, Mathematics, Mechanical Design Technology, Music Education, Nursing, Philosophy, Physical Education, Physics, Political Science, Psychology, Public Administration, Social Science, Sociology, Special Education

Men's Athletic Profile

820 Chestnut Street
Jefferson City, MO 65101-3500
Coach: Kirby Keth
Email: kethk@lincolnu.edu

NCAA II
Blue Tiger/Navy Blue
Phone: (573) 681-5337
Fax: (314) 681-5998

Estimated # of Men's Soccer Scholarships:
Conference: Heartland
Program Profile: Practice field; game field, grass, 60 X 120 (football field). play a Fall season. Since the program started, the team has improved academically and athletically; Soccer is growing fast - it's the number one sport in Lincoln's future.
History: Began as a club sport in 1990 and became a Division II varsity program in 1991. Record at 600% over the past 11 years. A major transaction of the soccer program has occurred with Kriby keth taking over the program. New Field under construction Dec. 2000 at the campus. Second year of recruiting at hand.
Achievements:
Coaching: Kirby Keth Head Coach 2nd Year. Raymound Clarke and Craig Tyrell are the assistants.
Roster In State: 8 **Out of State:** 0 **Out of Country:** 14
ODP State: 0 **Regional:** 0 **National:** 0
Walk-on/Other: 0 **Graduation %:** N/A **Seniors on Team:** 3
Positions Needed: Mids, Backs, Strikers, GK
Camp or Clinic Dates: TBA
Most Recent Record: 2-12-0
Schedule: Truman State Univ. SIU-Edwardsville, St. Marys, Rockhurst College
Style of Play: Aggressive attacking style of play, like to control midfield.

Lindenwood College
Academic Profile

Phone:

St. Charles, MO 63301

Type: 4 Yr.,Private,Liberal Arts
Founded: 1827
Website: http://www.lindenwood.edu
Religion: Presbyterian
SAT/ACT/GPA: 860/18/2.0
Housing: Yes
Student/Faculty Ratio: 20:1
Male/Female Ratio: 50:50
Undergraduate Enrollment: 9,500
Graduate Enrollment: N/A
Scholarships/Academic: Yes **Athletic:** No **Financial Aid:** Yes
Expenses by: Year **In State:** $ 16,000 **Out of State:** $ 16,000
Specialty: Communications, Education, Sports Management
Degrees Conferred: BA, BS, MA, MS, MBA, MPA
Programs of Study: Accounting, Art, Art History, Biology, Business, Chemistry, Computer Science, Corporate Communications, Criminal Justice, Early Childhood Education, Elementary Education, Fashion Marketing, French, History, Human Resources, Management, Marketing, Mass Communications, Mathematics, Physical Education, Political Science, Psychology, Public Administration, Secondary Education, Sociology, Special Education, Theatre, PreLaw, PreMed, PreVet

Men's Athletic Profile

209 S Kings Highway
St. Charles, MO 63301
Coach: Carl Hutter, Jr.
Email: Not Available

NAIA
Lions/Gold, Black
Phone: (314) 949-4939
Fax: (314) 949-4910

Estimated # of Men's Soccer Scholarships: unlimited
Conference: Heart of America Conference
Program Profile: We are a usually top 20 nationally ranked team. We have varsity and development teams. Our 5,000 seat stadium has the latest top of the market artificial field surface, which plays as well or better than grass, causing less injury to your body. It has a measurement of 118x75. We have a grass field for training with a top line fitness center.
History: Our program began in mid-1970's and we have had many top teams from 1989 to the present. Our athlete are from Metro St. Louis area and from all over US and abroad. We are blessed with good people who can play and are intent on winning.

Achievements: Numerous Coach of the Year; Conference Titles, All-Americans 7-8; 1-3 and HM drafted - NPSL Eastern League and one Free-agent MLS try-out with KCWIZ in 1999; A-League opportunity in Arizona - 3rd Division.
Coaching: Carl H. Hutter Jr., Head Coach, has 17 years college level experience as well as club teams. John Guffey, Assistant Coach, has spent 18 years coaching college level, NCAA and NAIA club teams.
Style of Play: Build-up ball possession - finding targets with lots of support around back, and second, third and fourth runners to open spaces away from the ball on the flanks and behind defense. Work very hard on transition to get forward and to win ball back. Attack and defend with numbers. Style varies and depends on players during given year.

Women's Athletic Profile

209 S Kings Highway
St. Charles, MO 63301
Coach: Kevin Kilcullin
Email: kkilcull@lindenwood.edu

NAIA
Lady Lyons/Black, Gold, White
Phone: (636) 916-8251
Fax: (314) 949-4910

Estimated # of Women's Soccer Scholarships: 12
Conference: Heart of America Athletic Conference
Program Profile: One of the top women's program in the St. Louie Metro area. Season of competition is in fall. We have a new artificial playing surface called Astro Play. Our stadium size is 5,000 with fitness center and performance arena.
History: Our program began in 1985 and has been to the National tournament 9 out of 15 years.
Achievements: 3 COY Honors in HAAC Conference; 3 Conference Title; 2 Regional Championships; 2 COY for Region; 2 National Appearance in 1998 and 1999; numerous All-Americans and Academic All-Americans.
Coaching: Kevin J. Kilcullin is the Head Coach. He has over 14 years of camp experience. He graduated from Rockhurst College and has an overall record of 54-10-6, which never out of top 20 ranking. Dan O'Keepe is the Assistant Coach. He graduated from SIU-Edwardsville. He played professional soccer for over five years and has an over 20 years of camp experience. He currently coaches the Scott Gallagher Organization. Kelley Bowen is on her 1st year as our Assistant Coach.
Roster in State: 11 **Out of State:** 5 **Out of Country:** 6
ODP State: **Regional:** **National:** 4
Walk-on/Other: **Graduation %:** 100 **Seniors on Team:** 5
Positions Needed: All
Camp or Clinic Dates: Not Available
Most Recent Record: 20-4-0
Style of Play: Attack with 10 players with a very simple and direct approach with 1,2, or 3 touch system of moving the ball. Defend with all 11 players behind the ball and then go on the attack.

Maryville University - Saint Louis

Academic Profile

St. Louis, MO 63141

Phone:

Type: 4 Yr.,Private
Website: http://www.maryvillestl.edu
SAT/ACT/GPA: 950/20
Student/Faculty Ratio: 17:1
Undergraduate Enrollment: 1,300
Scholarships/Academic: Yes **Athletic:** No
Expenses by: Year **In State:** $ 16,300

Founded: 1872
Religion: Non-Affiliated
Housing: Yes
Male/Female Ratio: 1:3
Graduate Enrollment: 400
Financial Aid: Yes
Out of State: $ 16,300

Degrees Conferred: BA, BS, BFA
Programs of Study: Art (Studio & International Design), Business, Communications, Education, History, English, Nursing, Physical Therapy, Occ. Therapy, Music, Psychology, Accounting, Management, Business Administration, Biology, Chemistry, Science

Men's Athletic Profile

13550 Conway Road
St. Louis, MO 63141
Coach: Eric Delabar
Email: Not Available

NCAA III
Saints/Red, White
Phone: (314) 529-9313
Fax: (314) 549-9947

Estimated # of Men's Soccer Scholarships: None
Conference: St. Louis Intercollegiate Athletic Conference
Program Profile: Winningest program in SLIAC history. Three - time conference tournament champions. Over twelve All-Midwest selections. Natural grass (all) underground sprinkler system. Nice facilities in beautiful safe area.
History: Began in 1977 as NCAA Division III and still is. SLIAC was formed in 1991.
Achievements: Conference Coach of the Year 1993 & 1994, Midwest COY in 1993, 3 Conference Region Season Titles and 3 Conference Tournament Titles.
Coaching: John Renaud, Head Coach, at Maryville 12 years, 1980 graduate from Quincy, 1st team All-Illinois, 1993 Division III Midwest Coach of the Year. 3 time National Champions (NAIA); All-Midwest selection 1979. Has a record of 137-99-22 from 1984 to present. Randy Behnen - Assistant Coach, 1990 graduate of Maryville University. Mike Muschick - Assistant Coach.
Style of Play: Ball control.

Women's Athletic Profile

13550 Conway Road
St. Louis, MO 63141-7299
Coach: Eric Delabar
Email: delabar@maryville.edu

NCAA III
Saints/Red, White
Phone: (314) 529-9313
Fax: (314) 529-9947

Estimated # of Women's Soccer Scholarships: None
Conference: St. Louis Intercollegiate Athletic Conference (SLIAC)
Program Profile: Team plays on soccer-only field. Playing surface is 75 x 120 yards and natural grass. Field sits at the bottom of a hill just outside the residence halls.
History: Coach Eric second year at MU and we dropped to a 13-7. We were third in our conference, but are looking to rebound next year. We finished my first year at MU with a 15-3-1 record and lost in the second round of the D. III play-offs.
Achievements: Conference Coach of the Year in 1999, won conference season title and conference tournament title in 1999.
Coaching: Eric Delabar Head Coach, Jill Miller Assistant Coach.
Roster in State: 22 **Out of State:** 1 **Out of Country:** 0
Walk-on/Other: 0 **Graduation %:** 100 **Seniors on Team:** 3
Positions Needed: GK, Striker
Camp or Clinic Dates: June 9-15, June 16-22, June 23-29, July 7-13
Most Recent Record: 13-7-0
Schedule: Washington Univ. Principia College, Webster Univ. Hardin-Simmons, Illinois Wesleyan.
Style of Play: Possession style with a build up out of the back. Emphasis on wing play, crosses, and movement off the ball.

Missouri Baptist College

Academic Profile

Phone: 314-434-1115

St. Louis, MO 63141

Type: 4 Yr.,Private,Liberal Arts
Website: http://www.mobap.edu

Founded: 1950
Religion: Southern Baptist

SAT/ACT/GPA: 840/18/2.0
Housing: Yes
Student/Faculty Ratio: 18:1
Male/Female Ratio: 40:60
Undergraduate Enrollment: 2,300
Graduate Enrollment: 500
Scholarships/Academic: Yes **Athletic:** Yes **Financial Aid:** Yes
Expenses by: Year **In State:** $ 13,590 **Out of State:** $ 13,590
Specialty: Business, Education, Music
Degrees Conferred: AA, AS, BA, BS, BSEd, BSN
Programs of Study: Accounting, Behavioral Science, Biblical Studies, Biology, Business Administration, Chemistry, Communications, Computer Information Systems, Computer Science, Management, Mathematics, Military Science, Music, Natural Science, Nursing, Philosophy, Physical Education, PreDental, PreLaw, PreMed, PreVet, Psychology, Religion, Secondary Education, Social Science, Theology

Men's Athletic Profile

One College Park
St. Louis, MO 63141
Coach: Juan Fablo Favero
Email: Not Available

NAIA
Spartans/Blue, White, Black
Phone: (314) 434-1115
Fax: (314) 434-7596

Estimated # of Men's Soccer Scholarships: 8
Conference: American Midwest Conference
Program Profile: Competing in the high level America Midwest Conference. Play games at the St. Louis Soccer Park. Season played from August to November with a spring season in March.
Coaching: Juan Pablo Favero, Head Coach, takes over the program and will bring the experience of rebuilding a program originally from Buenoss Aines, Argentina. Favero played at Marist College (Division I) and at Palm Beach Atlantic College where he coached and rebuilt the men's program.
Roster In State: 5 **Out of State:** 0 **Out of Country:** 13
ODP State: 1 **Regional:** **National:**
Walk-on/Other: **Graduation %:** N/A **Seniors on Team:** 1
Positions Needed: All
Camp or Clinic Dates: Not Available
Most Recent Record: 15-5-1
Schedule: Harris-Stowe State, William Carey, Union, Columbia, Wiiliam Woods, Lambuth, McKendree, Palm Beach Atlantic, Culver-Stockton
Style of Play: Like to keep the ball on the ground and to keep possession of the ball. Strong defensive effort, a must from all athletes, and very good tactical and technical abilities required of player.

Women's Athletic Profile

One College Park Drive
St. Louis, MO 63141-8698
Coach: Juan Pablo Favero
Email: Not Available

NAIA
Lady Spartans/R. Blue, Black
Phone: (314) 434-1115
Fax: (314) 434-7596

Estimated # of Women's Soccer Scholarships: 8
Conference: American Midwest Conference
Program Profile: Competing in the District America Midwest Conference, games played at the St. Louis Soccer Park. Season played for August to November when March spring season.
Achievements: Regular Season Conference Champions in 1997; 1st team All-American was Carrie Overmoeller in 1997; several other 2nd team All-Americans and Honorable Mention All-Americans.
Coaching: Juan Pablo Favero, Head Coach, entering first season as women's collegiate coach. Originally from Buenos Aires, Argentina. He came to the state on a soccer scholarship where he played at Division I men's college of New York and at Palm Beach Atlantic College where he also coached and rebuilt the men's program.

Roster in State: 9 **Out of State:** 6 **Out of Country:** 3
ODP State: 3 **Regional:** 1 **National:** 0
Walk-on/Other: 0 **Graduation %:** **Seniors on Team:** 2
Positions Needed: Keeper, Defenders, Midfielders, and Strikers
Camp or Clinic Dates: Not Available
Most Recent Record: 9-8-2
Schedule: Palm Beach Atlantic College, McKendree College, William Carey Univ. William Woods Univ. Bethel College, Lamuth Univ. Harris-Stowe State College, Southwest Baptist Univ. Montreat College, Culver-Stockton College.
Style of Play: Like to keep ball on the ground and thus keeping possession of the ball. A strong defensive effort is a must from all athletes. Very good tactical and technical abilities required of all players.

Missouri Southern State College

Academic Profile

Joplin, MO 64801
Phone: (417) 625-9573

Type: 4 Yr.,Public, **Founded:** 1937
Website: http://www.mssc.ecu **Religion:** Non-Affiliated
SAT/ACT/GPA: 18 **Housing:** Yes
Student/Faculty Ratio: 25:1 **Male/Female Ratio:** 4:5
Undergraduate Enrollment: 5,400 **Graduate Enrollment:** N/A
Scholarships/Academic: Yes **Athletic:** Yes **Financial Aid:** Yes
Expenses by: Year **In State:** $ 6,427 **Out of State:** $ 8,843
Degrees Conferred: AA, AS, AAS, BA, BS, BSBA, BSE, BGS
Programs of Study: Accounting, Biology, Broadcasting, Business Administration, Chemistry, Computer Science, Criminal Justice, Dramatic Arts, Economics, Education, Fine Arts, History, Management, Mathematics, Music, Nursing, Physics, PreDentistry, PreMed, Social Science

Men's Athletic Profile

3950 E Newman Road
Joplin, MO 64801-1595
Coach: Geoff Vandeusen
Email: Vandeusen-G@mail.mssc.edu

NCAA II
Lions/Green, Gold
Phone: (417) 625-3014
Fax: (417) 625-9397

Estimated # of Men's Soccer Scholarships: None
Conference: Independent
Program Profile: Grass field, 75 x 120, 5 practice fields. Fall and Spring practices and games.
History: Program began in 1972. MSSC soccer has been very competitive over the years. Originally a club sport, soccer first was an NAIA sport and in 1988 became NCAA Division II sport. 1995 saw the Lions go 11-6-1.
Achievements: Numerous All-Conference players, and some All-Americans in the past. MIAA Coach of the Year 1996.
Roster In State: 13 **Out of State:** 13 **Out of Country:** 3
ODP State: 0 **Regional:** 0 **National:** 0
Walk-on/Other: 0 **Graduation %:** 72 **Seniors on Team:** 4
Positions Needed: ALL
Camp or Clinic Dates: Not Available
Most Recent Record: 6-10-0
Schedule: Rock Hurst, Central Arkansas, Truman State, SIU-E, Univ. Missouri-St. Louis, Quincy, St. Joseph
Style of Play: Depends on players.

Women's Athletic Profile

3950 East Newman Rd
Jouplin, MO 64801-1595
Coach: Geoff VanDeusen
Email:

NCAA II
Lady Lions/Green, Yellow
Phone: (417) 625-3014
Fax:

Estimated # of Women's Soccer Scholarships:
Conference: Mid-America Intercollegiate Athletic Association.
Program Profile: Home field is Bodon Field which is located on campus, it has a seating capacity of 250.
Achievements: 2000 Coach of the Year, 6 voted to All-Conference Team.
Coaching:
Roster in State: 11 **Out of State:** 10 **Out of Country:** 0
ODP State: 6 **Regional:** 0 **National:** 0
Positions Needed: ALL
Most Recent Record: 5-11-0
Schedule: Truman State, South Illinois-Edwardsville, SW State, Rockhurst
Style of Play: Depends on players.

Missouri Valley College

Academic Profile

Phone: (660) 831-4000

Marshall, MO 65340

Type: 4 Yr.,Private,Liberal Arts **Founded:** 1889
Website: http://www.murlin.com/~webfx/mvc/ **Religion:** Presbyterian
SAT/ACT/GPA: 800/18/2.0 **Housing:** Yes
Student/Faculty Ratio: 10:1 **Male/Female Ratio:** 3:1
Undergraduate Enrollment: 1,300 **Graduate Enrollment:** 50
Scholarships/Academic: Yes **Athletic:** Yes **Financial Aid:** Yes
Expenses by: Year **In State:** $ 17,000 **Out of State:** $ 17,000
Degrees Conferred: AA, BA, BS, Master of Arts
Programs of Study: Accounting, Actuarial Sciences, Agribusiness, Alcohol & Drug Studies, Art, Biology, Business Administration, Computer Information Systems, Criminal Justice, Economics, Elementary Education, English, Exercise Science, General Studies, History, Human Services Agency Management, Mass Communications, Mathematics, Physical Education, Political Science, Public Administration, Psychology, Recreation Administration, Religious, Social Studies Education, Sociology, Speech Communications, Theatre, PreProfessional Programs

Men's Athletic Profile

500 East College
Marshall, MO 65340
Coach: Lance Welker
Email: Not Available

NAIA
Vikings/Purple, Orange
Phone: (660) 831-4217
Fax: (660) 831-4039

Estimated # of Men's Soccer Scholarships: 12
Conference: Heart of America Athletic Conference
Program Profile: A full size practice field right next to game field used only for soccer. Game field has natural grass and seats 350. Fall season - September through November.
Style of Play: We play a creative, attacking and entertaining style of play.

Women's Athletic Profile

500 E College Street
Marshall, MO 65340
Coach: Gary Dunda
Email: dundag@moval.edu

NAIA
Vikings/Orange, Purple
Phone: (660) 831-4114
Fax: (660) 831-4038

Estimated # of Women's Soccer Scholarships: 12
Conference: Heart of America Athletic Conference

Program Profile: We play on natural grass field that measures 120x75. We play a fall season schedule.
History: Our program began in 1985.
Achievements: HAAC Conference Champs 1991, 1992, 1993; National Runner-up 1991, 6 All-Americans, 2 All-Regions, 6 All-Districts and 13 All-Conference players.
Coaching: Gary Dunda is the Head Coach. He is entering his first season with Missouri Valley College. He played his college soccer at Messiah College and graduated in 1997. He then was the Assistant Coach at Messiah in 1998. Coach Dunda then moved to Ottawa University, where he served as both the men's and women's Assistant Coach in 1999. His is assisted by Tim Linhart at Missouri Valley University.

Roster in State: 7	**Out of State:** 10	**Out of Country:** 1
ODP State: 5	**Regional:** 4	**National:**
Walk-on/Other:	**Graduation %:**	**Seniors on Team:** 7

Camp or Clinic Dates: Not Available
Most Recent Record: 10-9-1
Schedule: Lindenwood University, Baker University, Harris Stowe, Kansas Newman, Benedictine
Style of Play: We play a creative, attacking style of soccer, with strong defensive principles.

Northwest Missouri State University

Academic Profile

Phone: (660) 562-1562

Maryville, MO 64468

Type: 4 Yr.,Public		**Founded:** 1905
Website: http://www.nwmissouri.edu		**Religion:** Non-Affiliated
SAT/ACT/GPA: 860/21/2.0		**Housing:** Yes
Student/Faculty Ratio: 27:1		**Male/Female Ratio:** 45:55
Undergraduate Enrollment: 5,300		**Graduate Enrollment:** 700
Scholarships/Academic: Yes	**Athletic:** Yes	**Financial Aid:** Yes
Expenses by: Year	**In State:** $ 7,077	**Out of State:** $ 9,207

Specialty: Education
Degrees Conferred: BS, BA, MA, MS, BFA, MFA, BMT, BSF, MBA
Programs of Study: Accounting, Agricultural, Banking/Finance, Botany, Broadcasting, Early Childhood, Computer Earth Science, Economics, History, Horticulture, Humanities, Journalism, Philosophy, PreProfessional Programs, Science, Special Education, Speech, Zoology

Women's Athletic Profile

800 University Drive	**NCAA II**
Maryville, MO 64468	Bearcats/Green, White
Coach: Joann M. Wolf	**Phone:** (660) 562-1302
Email: jmwolf@mail.nwmissouri.edu	**Fax:** (660) 562-1483

Estimated # of Women's Soccer Scholarships: 7.4
Conference: MidAmerican Intercollegiate Athletic Assoc.
Program Profile: Northwest Missouri will be playing on a brand new natural grass field on campus with scoreboard, dimensions of 120x80 yards and seating of 250. We also have a certified trainer assigned to the soccer team for the entire season.
History: Our program began in 1999 and ended they year with a 7-7-1 recorded. The first year we had no scholarships but this year have added 7.4.
Achievements: In 1999 we received 1 first team All-Conference, second team All-Conference, and one honorable mention All-Conference.
Coaching: Our Head Coach is Joann Wolf. She was a 10 year head coach of collegiate level, has a NSCAA advanced National Diploma and a Master Degree in education. Our Assistant Coach is TBA.

Roster in State: 9	**Out of State:** 13	**Out of Country:** 0

ODP State: 2 **Regional:** 0 **National:** 0
Walk-on/Other: 0 **Graduation %:** 100 **Seniors on Team:** 4
Positions Needed: GK, Sweeper, Mid, FWD
Camp or Clinic Dates: Not Available
Most Recent Record: 7-11-0
Schedule: SIU-Edwardsville, Truman State University, Quincy University, University of Nebraska-Omaha, University of Central Oklahoma, Rockhurst University, University of Missouri-Rolla
Style of Play: Possession style of play build up from the back; depending on the opponent. Basic individual skills stressed with a great deal of movement off the ball. Our system is a 3-5-2- or 4-4-2.

Park University

Academic Profile

Phone:

Parkville, MO 64152

Type: 4 Yr.,Private,Liberal Arts **Founded:** 1875
Website: http://www.park.edu **Religion:** Non-Affiliated
SAT/ACT/GPA: 840/20/2.0 **Housing:** Yes
Student/Faculty Ratio: 9:1 **Male/Female Ratio:** 60:40
Undergraduate Enrollment: 17,000 **Graduate Enrollment:** 1,000
Scholarships/Academic: Yes **Athletic:** Yes **Financial Aid:** Yes
Expenses by: Year **In State:** $ 9,400 **Out of State:** $ 9,400
Specialty: Liberal Arts, Sports Medicine
Degrees Conferred: BA, BS, AA, AS, MBA, M.Ed., M.Rel
Programs of Study: Physical Therapy, Sports Medicine, Management, Elementary Education, Secondary Education, International Business, Accounting, Math, English, Art

Men's Athletic Profile

8700 NW River Park Drive
Parkville, MO 64152-3795
Coach: Roger Bongaerts
Email: Parksoccer@aol.com

NAIA
Pirates/Gold, Maroon
Phone: (816) 741-2000x6437
Fax: (816) 741-4911

Estimated # of Men's Soccer Scholarships: 6
Conference: NAIA Independent
Program Profile: We have a new stadium that has a seating capacity of 2,000, with lights and sprinkler system. We have three practice fields, all natural grass. We have 12 month soccer and our season runs from August through November. We also have indoor soccer.
History: Our program began in 1983. We have had a NAIA National Tournament appearance, AMC Conference Champions in 1992 and are NAIA ranked in the top 25.
Achievements: 3 players drafted to MLS; 2 players to international leagues; 10+ players drafted into NPSL; NAIA Academic All-Americans; AMC Conference Champions; NAIA top 25.
Coaching: Roger Bongaerts is the Head Coach, came Netherlands. He was named CAC and northeast Coach of the Year in 1997. He coached Adidas Summer League and Adidas ESP, He was a former pro player. Efren Shimlis is the Assistant Coach, was a graduate of Park in 1996. He was named All-American and was a former pro player, which was NPSL Champs in 1996.
Roster In State: 10 **Out of State:** 6 **Out of Country:** 12
ODP State: 6 **Regional:** 6 **National:** 2
Walk-on/Other: **Graduation %:** 100 **Seniors on Team:** 6
Positions Needed: Goalkeeper, Outside Midfield
Camp or Clinic Dates: July
Most Recent Record: 10-7-1

Schedule: Lindsey Wilson College, Harris Stowe State College, Columbia College, National American University, Baker University, Newman University
Style of Play: Possession oriented with aggressive attacking and pressure defense.

Women's Athletic Profile

8700 NW River Park Drive
Parkville, MO 64152-3795
Coach: James Hemingway, MSS
Email: yecats72@hotmail.com

NAIA
Pirates/Black, Yellow, White
Phone: (816) 741-2000
Fax: (816) 741-4911

Estimated # of Women's Soccer Scholarships:
Conference: American Midwest Conference
Program Profile: Completed 1 million game stadium, natural grass, lights that seats 2,500 soccer dedicated. Has three practice facilities, all natural grass; 1998 undefeated in AMC with 7-0 record (regular and post-season).
History: Started in 1985.
Achievements: Won Conference Titles numerous, Dozen of All-Americans and few players playing professionally (overseas).
Coaching: James Hemingway, Head Coach, was a 1998 W-League National Champion Coach; 1993 National Champion Collegiate Player; 1994 & 1995 National Finals, 1999 Adidas ESP Staff Coach. Scott Bowen - established the girls soccer at Fayetteville High School (Fayetteville, AR) State Champions.
Style of Play: Play an aggressive, organized soccer based on attacking play.

Rockhurst University

Academic Profile

Kansas City, MO 64110

Phone: (816) 501-4141

Type: 4 Yr.,Private,Liberal Arts
Website: http://www.rockhurst.edu
SAT/ACT/GPA: 20+/2.5
Student/Faculty Ratio: 14:1
Undergraduate Enrollment: 1,000
Scholarships/Academic: Yes
Athletic: Yes
Expenses by: Year
In State: $ 18,650
Founded: 1910
Religion: Catholic/Jesuit
Housing: Yes
Male/Female Ratio: 45:55
Graduate Enrollment: 1,400
Financial Aid: Yes
Out of State: $ 18,650
Specialty: Business
Degrees Conferred: BA, BS, BA Elem. Ed, BSBA, BSN, MS, MBA
Programs of Study: Business, Communications, Computer Science, Chemistry, Education, English, Human Relations, Marketing, Mathematics, Nursing, Occupational Therapy, Physical Therapy, PreDental, PreLaw, PreMedical, Psychology, Science, Spanish

Men's Athletic Profile

1100 Rockhurst Road
Kansas City, MO 64110
Coach: Dr. Anthony Tocco
Email: Not Available

NCAA II
Hawks/Blue, White
Phone: (816) 926-4141
Fax: (816) 926-4119

Estimated # of Men's Soccer Scholarships:
Conference: Independent
Program Profile: Games are played in the Fall on natural turf.
History: Program began in 1964.
Style of Play: Aggressive!

Women's Athletic Profile

1100 Rockhurst Road
Kansas City, MO 64110
Coach: Greg Herdlick
Email: Not Available

NCAA/NAIA
Hawks/Blue, White
Phone: (816) 501-4141
Fax: (816) 501-4119

Estimated # of Women's Soccer Scholarships: None
Conference: Independent Conference
Program Profile: Top #5 in the NAIA, natural grass, has 4,000 seats.
History: 1991 to the present; last two seasons, top ten in the NAIA.
Achievements: 1997 Coach of the Year in Midwest Region.
Style of Play: 4-4-2 diamond, attack on offense.

Saint Louis University

Academic Profile

Phone: 314-977-3266

St. Louis, MO 63103

Type: 4 Yr.,Private
Website: http://www.slu.edu
SAT/ACT/GPA: 1165/20-27/average last year
Student/Faculty Ratio: 15/1
Undergraduate Enrollment: 6,889
Scholarships/Academic: Yes
Athletic: Yes
Expenses by: Year
In State: $ 17,000+

Founded: 1818
Religion: Jesuit
Housing: Yes
Male/Female Ratio: 44/56
Graduate Enrollment: 3,111
Financial Aid: Yes
Out of State: $ 17,000+

Specialty: Business, Law, Medicine, and Aeronautics
Degrees Conferred: BA, BS, MA, MS, MBA, Ph.D., Ed, JD
Programs of Study: Arts & Sciences, Law, Medicine, Philosophy & Letters, Business and Administration, Nursing, Social Services, Engineering & Aviation, Allied Health Professions, Public Health, Professional Studies, 23 Doctoral Degrees, 40 Master Degrees

Men's Athletic Profile

3672 W Pine Mall
St. Louis, MO 63108
Coach: Dan Donigan
Email: donigand@slu.edu

NCAA I
Billikens/Blue, White
Phone: (314) 977-3266
Fax: (314) 977-3178

Estimated # of Men's Soccer Scholarships: Flexible
Conference: Conference USA
Program Profile: Newly renovated Robt. R. Hermann Stadium state-of-the-art natural grass surface. St Louis has won a record 10 NCAA Men's Soccer National Championships. Billikens have qualified for 38 of 41 NCAA Tournaments. St. Louis has won or tied for the Conference USA regular season title each of the past 4 years and twice has won the post-season tournament.
History: 1959 began, 10 NCAA national Championships, played in 38 out of 401 NCAA tournaments.
Achievements: Over 40 All-Americans. Billikens currently have 4 players in MLS and a wide variety playing at various levels on indoor and outdoor professionally. Have had a first-team Academic All-American for 4 straight seasons.
Coaching: Head Coach,Dan Donigan,"A" license.
Roster In State: 14
Out of State: 12
Out of Country: 0
Walk-on/Other:
Graduation %: 100
Seniors on Team: 3
Positions Needed: Wide mid, left defender
Camp or Clinic Dates: June 18-22, June 25-29, June 23-27

Most Recent Record: 13-3-2
Schedule: SMU, SMSU, UAB, Rutgers, St. John's, Cal-Berkley, USF, UNC Charlotte
Style of Play: Possession- attacking.

Women's Athletic Profile

3672 W. Pine Street
St. Louis, MO 63108
Coach: Tim Champion
Email: Not Available

NCAA I
Billikens/Blue, White
Phone: (314) 977-3271
Fax: (314) 977-3178

Estimated # of Women's Soccer Scholarships: None
Conference: Conference USA
Program Profile: Saint Louis University plays in a 7,000 seat soccer stadium with a natural grass field and with dimensions of 120x75.
History: Saint Louis is entering its 5th year. The program has a four year record of 44-26-9 including a 14-3-3 record in 1999.
Achievements: Conference Champions 1999; Conference Coach of the Year 1999; Soccer Buzz Mionest Coach of the Year 1999; 2 players on 1999 NSCAA All-Midwest 1st team; 2 players on Academic All-Region team 1999; 1 player GTE All-District player 1999.
Coaching: Tim Champion is our Head Coach and Janet Oberle and Jay Zaber are the Assistant Coaches.
Roster in State: 15 **Out of State:** 15 **Out of Country:** 0
ODP State: **Regional:** 4 **National:** 2
Walk-on/Other: **Graduation %:** 100 **Seniors on Team:** 6
Camp or Clinic Dates: Not Available
Most Recent Record: 14-3-3
Schedule: SMU, Marquette, Wisconsin, Iowa, UNC Charlotte, Evansville
Style of Play: We try to keep possession of the ball and move it. We try to get all players involved in our attack without giving up the defensive parts of the game.

Southeast Missouri State University

Academic Profile

Cape Girardeau, MO 63701
Phone: 573-651-2000

Type: 4 Yr.,Public
Website: http://www.semo.edu
SAT/ACT/GPA: 990/21
Student/Faculty Ratio: 17:1
Undergraduate Enrollment: 6,409
Scholarships/Academic: Yes **Athletic:** Yes **Financial Aid:** Yes
Expenses by: Year **In State:** $ 4,704+ **Out of State:** $ 6,552
Founded: 1873
Religion: Non-Affiliated
Housing: No
Male/Female Ratio: 44:56
Graduate Enrollment: 721
Degrees Conferred: AA, AAS, BA, BS, BGS, BSBA, BSEd, BSM, MA, MS
Programs of Study: Accounting, Advertising, Animal, Art, Banking/Finance, Biological, Business, Chemistry, Computer, Dietetics, Earth Science, Engineering, Nursing, Parks/Recreation, etc..

Women's Athletic Profile

#1 University Plaza
Cape Giradeau, MO 63701
Coach: Heather Nelson
Email:

NCAA I
Indians/Red, White
Phone: (573) 651-2227
Fax: (573) 651-2959

Did Not Return Profile

Southwest Baptist University

Academic Profile

Phone: 417-328-1739

Bolivar, MO 65613

Type: 4 Yr.,Private,
Founded: 1878
Website: http://www.sbuniv.edu
Religion: Southern Baptist
SAT/ACT/GPA: Not Available
Housing: Yes
Student/Faculty Ratio: 17/1
Male/Female Ratio: N/A
Undergraduate Enrollment: 2,000
Graduate Enrollment: 1,000
Scholarships/Academic: Yes **Athletic:** Yes **Financial Aid:** Yes
Expenses by: Year **In State:** $13,000 **Out of State:** $13,000
Specialty: Education, Business and Physical Therapy
Degrees Conferred: BA, BBA, BS, MED, MBA, MS
Programs of Study: College of Education & Social Sciences, College of Science & Mathematics, College of Business, College of Music, Arts & Letters, College of Christian Studies

Men's Athletic Profile

1600 University Avenue
Bolivar, MO 65613
Coach: Donald Thompson
Email: dthompson@sbuniv.edu

NCAA II
Bearcats/Purple, White
Phone: (417) 328-1739
Fax: (417) 328-2009

Estimated # of Men's Soccer Scholarships: 1.5
Conference: Independent
Program Profile: We have a fescue and Bermuda field surface. It is measures 120x72 yards and has a seating capacity of 250.
History: Our program began in 1993.
Achievements:
Coaching: Donald Thompson is the Head Coach.
Roster In State: 16 **Out of State:** 4 **Out of Country:** 0
Walk-on/Other: **Graduation %:** N/A **Seniors on Team:** 2
Positions Needed: GK, Midfield, Sweeper
Camp or Clinic Dates: TBA
Most Recent Record: 8-11-0
Schedule: Truman State, Missouri-Rolla, Southern Illinois, University of Central Arkansas, John Brown, Rockhurst
Style of Play: Zonal, high pressure defense and quick counter attack.

Women's Athletic Profile

1600 S Springfield
Bolivar, MO 65613
Coach: Donald Thompson
Email: dthompson@sbuniv.edu

NCAA II
Bearcats/Purple, White
Phone: (417) 328-1739
Fax: (417) 328-2009

Estimated # of Women's Soccer Scholarships: 3.0
Conference: Mid-America Intercollegiate Athletic Association
Program Profile: We play on natural turf. We play a Fall season and our facilities include locker-room, weights in and out of season.
History: 1993 when program began as a varsity NCAA Division II sport.
1994-1995 gained varsity/ NCAA status

Achievements: In 1999 season, we have had 4 players to the Academic All-Conference team, 2 2nd-team All-Conference players and 1 honorable mention player.
Coaching: Donald Thompson is our Head Coach. Amy Stockton is our Assistant Coach.
Roster in State: 7 **Out of State:** 9 **Out of Country:** 0
ODP State: 0 **Regional:** 0 **National:** 0
Walk-on/Other: 0 **Graduation %:** **Seniors on Team:** 1
Positions Needed: Goal Keeper, Forward, Midfield, Def.
Camp or Clinic Dates: TBA
Most Recent Record: 4-14-2
Schedule: Truman State University, University of Missouri Rolla, Harding Univ. Central MO State
Style of Play: Zonal defending, quick counter attack and high pressure defense.

Southwest Missouri State University

Academic Profile

Ads
Springfield, MO 65804-0089
Phone: (417) 836-8384

Type: 4 Yr.,Public, **Founded:** 1905
Website: http://www.smsu.edu **Religion:** Non-Affiliated
SAT/ACT/GPA: sliding scale **Housing:** Yes
Student/Faculty Ratio: 16:1 **Male/Female Ratio:** 5:6
Undergraduate Enrollment: 14,067 **Graduate Enrollment:** 2,727
Scholarships/Academic: Yes **Athletic:** Yes **Financial Aid:** Yes
Expenses by: Year **In State:** $ 7,700 **Out of State:** $ 10,730
Specialty: Public Affairs
Degrees Conferred: BA, BS, BFA, BSEd, BSN, BSW, Macc, MA, MS, MBA, MSEd
Programs of Study: Accounting, Administrative Office Systems, Agriculture, Agronomy, Animal Science, Biology, Business Education, Cartography, Communications, Computer Science, Construction Technology, Elementary Education, Economics, Geography, Geology, Education, Management, Marketing, Mathematics, Music, Nursing, Philosophy, Physical Education, Physics, Political Science, Religion, Psychology, Social Work, Teacher Education

Men's Athletic Profile

901 S National Ave.
Springfield, MO 65804-0089
Coach: Jon Leamy
Email: jhl928t@mail.smsu.edu

NCAA I
Bears/Maroon, White
Phone: (417) 836-5243
Fax: (417) 836-8475

Estimated # of Men's Soccer Scholarships: 3-4
Conference: Missouri Valley Conference
Program Profile: SMSU competes in highly competitive Missouri Valley Conference. Team play both a traditional fall season and non-traditional spring season. Heavy emphasis is placed on attracting the serious minded student-athlete. home field is Cooper Sports complex, natural grass surface, seats 1,000 spectators. New Bermuda grass practice facility. Program is sponsored by DIADORA.
History: Program began in 1981. Overall record for the last five years is an impressive 64-28-5.
Achievements: Four consecutive seasons of twelve or more wins. 1997 NCAA Tournament Appearances; MVC Champions in 1997, Runner-Up in 1998; NSCAA Team Academic Award in 1997 & 1998; 3 Academic All-Americans; numerous All-Midwest and All-MVC players; Jon Leamy was 1995 & 1997 MVC Coach of the Year; 1997 NSCAA Midwest Coach of the Year; 8 players were drafted over the past three years (EISL, NPSL, A-League, MSL).
Coaching: Jon Leamy, Head Coach, 8th season, NSCAA Advanced Diploma USSF "B" License, Ireland FA coaching badge, Midwest ODP Staff. Jeremy Alumbaugh, Assistant Coach, entering fourth season with the program. NSCAA National Diploma, USSF "C" License. Neil Anderson - goalkeeping coach, entering second season with the program, USSF License.

Roster In State: 14 **Out of State:** 14 **Out of Country:**
ODP State: 12 **Regional:** 10 **National:** 3
Walk-on/Other: 3 **Graduation %:** 100 **Seniors on Team:** 7
Camp or Clinic Dates: July 16-21
Most Recent Record: 17-1-3
Schedule: Saint Louis, Creighton, Washington, Brown, Penn State, Ohio State, Yale
Style of Play: Team's style of play is based on a solid defense and ball possession in getting forward in the attack.

Women's Athletic Profile

901 S National Ave.
Springfield, MO 65804-0089
Coach: Rob Brewer
Email: WomenSoccer@mail.SMSU.edu

NCAA I
Lady Bears/Maroon, White
Phone: (417) 836-6654
Fax: (417) 836-8475

Estimated # of Women's Soccer Scholarships: Varies
Conference: Missouri Valley Conference
Program Profile: We play a traditional season plus a fall-spring season with matches and training. Matches are played on natural surface and practices on a new Bermuda field. We compete in the Missouri Valley Conference which has an automatic bid.
History: Our program began in 1996 and we have competed in the MVC semi-finals every year.
Achievements: Our team produced 6 All-Conference players in 1996, 5 All-Conference players in 1998. 2000 NCAA playoffs, Won MVC Conference in 2000. 1 player selected to All-Region, 1999 2 All-Region. 5 All-Conference team, 1 All-Freshman team.
Coaching: Rob Brewer, Head Coach, is entering his sixth season with the program. He holds a USSF "B" License and is a member of the NCAA Central Region Committee. He was Regional Coach of the Year twice and his team won the NAIA Regional Championship in 1992 while at Elon College. Vernon Croft, Assistant Coach, is entering his fourth season. He is USSF licensed and has an NSCAA Advanced National Diploma. .
Roster in State: 12 **Out of State:** 12 **Out of Country:** 0
ODP State: 15 **Regional:** 0 **National:** 0
Walk-on/Other: 0 **Graduation %:** 99 **Seniors on Team:** 4
Positions Needed: ALL
Camp or Clinic Dates: TBA
Most Recent Record: 12-11-1
Schedule: SMU, Baylor, Oklahoma, St. Louis
Style of Play: Develop attack through possession out of the back and defend with high pressure beginning with forwards.

Stephens College
Academic Profile

Phone: 800-876-7207

Columbia, MO 65215

Type: 4 Yr.,Private,Liberal Arts **Founded:** 1833
Website: http://www.stephens.edu **Religion:** Non-Affiliated
SAT/ACT/GPA: Open **Housing:** Yes
Student/Faculty Ratio: 11:1 **Male/Female Ratio:** 1:34
Undergraduate Enrollment: 550 **Graduate Enrollment:** 36
Scholarships/Academic: Yes **Athletic:** No **Financial Aid:** Yes
Expenses by: Year **In State:** $ 19,000 **Out of State:** $ 19,000
Specialty: Education, Sciences, Theatre, Dance
Degrees Conferred: AA, AS, BA, BS

Programs of Study: Biology, Business Administration, English, International Studies, Mathematical Sciences, Philosophy, Social Sciences, Psychology, Creative Writing, Dance, Fashion Design, Theatre Arts, Accounting, Health Sciences, Early Childhood Education, Elementary Education, Environmental Science, Equestrian, Business Management, Marketing, Mass Communications, Student-initiated Majors

Women's Athletic Profile

1200 East Broadway
Columbia, MO 65215
Coach: Lori Towle
Email: ltowle@w.c.stephens.edu

NCAA III
Stars/Maroon, Gold
Phone: (573) 442-2211
Fax: (573) 876-7160

Estimated # of Women's Soccer Scholarships: None
Conference: None
Program Profile: Stephens Lake & Gold Course is the location of the NCAA Regulation soccer field. Pre-season begins in mid-August with play extending to the end of October. competition is against both NCAA Division
History: The soccer program began in the Fall of 1993. The hiring of a full-time coach occurred in 1998, giving athletics the support it needs to be more competitive recruit, scout, etc...
Achievements:
Coaching: Lori Towle, Head Coach, received Bachelor's Degree and played soccer and basketball at the University of Southern Maine. She was an assistant coach for two years of women's basketball and soccer (national championship appearances in basketball). She received Master's Degree in Sport Management from the United States Sports Academy. Currently Head Coach of soccer, basketball and tennis at Stephens College.
Style of Play: With one year of recruiting, the team is improving its level of play. Looking to be very competitive by the year 2000. The team has moved from a defensive-minded structure to an offensive-minded structure and has made large improvements with experience.

Truman State U (Northeast MO St. U)

Academic Profile

100 E. Normal
Kirksville, MO 63501-4221

Phone: (660) 785-4468

Type: 4 Yr.,Public,Liberal Arts
Website: http://www.truman.edu
SAT/ACT/GPA: 1000/22/3.0
Student/Faculty Ratio: 16:1
Undergraduate Enrollment: 6,300
Scholarships/Academic: Yes
Athletic: Yes
Expenses by: Year
In State: $ 8,400
Founded: 1867
Religion: Non-Affiliated
Housing: Yes
Male/Female Ratio: 45:55
Graduate Enrollment: 250
Financial Aid: Yes
Out of State: $ 11,016
Specialty: Liberal Arts and Sciences
Degrees Conferred: BA, BS, BFA, MAE, MA, MS, MBA
Programs of Study: Accounting, Agricultural Science, Anthropology, Art, Art History, Business, Biology, Chemistry, Communication, Computer Science, Economics, Education, English, French, German, Health and Exercise Science, History, Journalism, Justice Systems, Mathematics, Music, Nursing, Performance, Philosophy, Physics, Political Science, PreDental

Men's Athletic Profile

100 East Normal
Kirksville, MO 63501
Coach: Alf Bilbao
Email: Dsweeney@truman.edu

NCAA II
Bulldogs/Purple, White
Phone: (816) 785-4168
Fax: (816) 785-4189

Estimated # of Men's Soccer Scholarships: N/A
Conference: MIAA
Program Profile: Has an excellent facilities; year-round training program.
History: 1979 first year. Playoff contender each year; NCAA Final Four in 1997.
Achievements: Coach of the Year MIAA in 1995, 1996, & 1997; playoffs 1993, 1995, & 1997; Conference Champions in 1993 - 1997 inclusive.

Women's Athletic Profile

Pershing Building 213, 100 East Normal
Kirksville, MO 63501-4221
Coach: Mike Cannon
Email: mcannon@truman.edu

NCAA II
Bulldogs/Purple, White
Phone: (660) 785-4463
Fax: (660) 785-4189

Estimated # of Women's Soccer Scholarships: TBA
Conference: Mid-America Intercollegiate Athletics Association
Program Profile: Truman Soccer Park, game pitch has a measurements of 120x75, natural grass, press box, seating capacity of 500, film tower. Adjoining practice field located inside fenced park which measures 120x70. Year-round training in the Fall that starts mid-August through November/December. Main season which has 20 matches in the Spring starts from February through April with an exhibition season. Also, season has five playing dates of competition.
History: First year of the program was in 1984; 1987 was the first winning season; 1998 was the first national ranking (12th); 1989 was the first All-Region selection and #5th national ranking; 1995 had a record of 12-4-1, 1996 was #4 ranking (12-3-5), 1997 first national Tournament trip, made it to national quarterfinals, 1st All-American selection; #6 Final National Ranking in 1999; 1st year as a conference sport (MIAA). 7 consecutive winning season (1994-2000).
Achievements: Back to Back Conference Titles (1999, 2000), 2 Conference MVP (1999, 2000), 25 All-Conference Selections (1999, 2000), 34 All-Region Selection (1987, 2000), 1 All-American (1997).
Coaching: Mike Cannon, Head Coach, six years as a head coach at Truman, overall record is 91-44-13. He was named fist All-American and 1st Academic All-American selections. He was an assistant coach for Truman men in 1992. He was with the Truman Soccer from 1988-1991, USISL All-Star in 1996 and played two seasons for Des Moines, Menace (PDSL-USISL). 1999, 2000 Conference Coach of the Year.
Roster in State: 13 **Out of State:** 11 **Out of Country:** 0
ODP State: 0 **Regional:** 0 **National:** 0
Walk-on/Other: 0 **Graduation %:** 95 **Seniors on Team:** 3
Positions Needed: GK, FW, Wing MF, Def, C-Mid
Camp or Clinic Dates: TBA
Most Recent Record: 15-4-0
Schedule: Minnesota-Duluth, Minnesota State-Mankato, Northern Colorado, Nebraska-Omaha, Winona State, North Dakota State, Rockurst
Style of Play: Possession oriented, skill oriented, attack and defend as a unit.

University of Missouri - Columbia
Academic Profile

Columbia, MO 65211
Phone: (573) 882-3894

Type: 4 Yr.,Public,Liberal Arts
Founded: 1839
Website: http://www.mutigers.edu
Religion: Non-Affiliated
SAT/ACT/GPA: 700 Min/25.8/2.0
Housing: Yes
Student/Faculty Ratio: 19:1
Male/Female Ratio: 47:53
Undergraduate Enrollment: 17,346
Graduate Enrollment: 5,154
Scholarships/Academic: Yes **Athletic:** Yes **Financial Aid:** Yes
Expenses by: Year **In State:** $ 9,368 **Out of State:** $ 16,524
Degrees Conferred: BA, BS, BFA, AB, BSEd, BGS, BSN, BJ, BM, MA, MS, MFA, BSW, MBA, BES

Programs of Study: College of Agriculture, Food and Natural Resources, School of Natural Resources, College of Arts & Sciences, School of Fine Arts, College of Business and Public Administration, School of Accounting, College of Education, College of Engineering, College of Human Environmental Sciences, School of Social Work, School of Nursing, School of Journalism, School of Law, School of Medicine, School of Health Related Problems

Women's Athletic Profile

Hearnes Center
Columbia, MO 65205
Coach: Bryan Blitz
Email: blitzb@missouri.edu

NCAA I
Tigers/Old Gold, Black
Phone: (573) 884-7914
Fax: (573) 882-4720

Estimated # of Women's Soccer Scholarships: None
Conference: Big 12 Conference
Program Profile: The Mizzou Tigers are entering their fifth year of collegiate competition backed by seven returning starters, including All-American forward Nikki Thole, and 12 returning letter winners. The Tigers play in the Audrey J. Walton Track-Soccer Stadium that seats 2,500 fans. The 74 x 118 yard field is natural grass.
History: Missouri initiated the women's soccer program in 1996. Since that time, Mizzou has posted a 38-43-2 all-time record making drastic improvements each year. In their inaugural season, the Tigers went 6-14 and went on to boost their 1997 record to 7-12. Missouri saw its first winning season in 1998 when the Tigers went 11-9-1. Mizzou achieved another milestone in 1999 when they finished the year with a 14-8-1 season record and earned birth in the NCAA first round where they lost to Marquette (2-3).
Achievements: Coach Blitz prepped the Butler University women's program through its first five years and led the program to a top-25 ranking. He was named the Midwest Collegiate Conference Coach of the Year after leading Butler through an undefeated conference season in 1995. He also received an invitation to coach the U.S. Women's National Team. Nikki Thole was honored as a 1999 All-American by the NSCAA, College Soccer Online and Soccer Buzz. As a junior she was also tabbed the Soccer Buzz Central Region Offensive Player of the Year and was named to the NSCAA all-central region first team and the Soccer Buzz all-central first team. In the Big 12 Conference, Thole was a first team all-conference and an all-tournament pick as a sophomore and junior. Thole was also named a third-team freshman All-American by Soccer American in 1997.
Coaching: Bryan Blitz, Head Coach, USSF "A" License, Irish Coaching Badge, MBA at Butler University. Julie Krisanic - Assistant/Goalkeeper Coach, NJCAA All-American, USSF "C" License. Jen Haigh is in her first year with the MU program. Previous to her Missouri appointment, Haigh served as an assistant coach at Arizona State University from 1997-1999. She helped with Sundevils to a program best 13-6 record last year. Haigh made strides as a recruiter for ASU and was nationally recognized for compiling some of the nation's best athletes under the Arizona State program. Dave Collie enters his second season under Blitz, and his third overall with the Tigers. Collie works as Mizzou's goalkeeper coach. He helped Tiger goalie Jackie Adamec earn Big 12 all-tournament honors and set Missouri records with 131 saves. Prior to Mizzou, Collie was the goalkeepers coach at Seneca College and William Woods University.

Roster in State: 10	**Out of State:** 13	**Out of Country:** 0
ODP State: 16	**Regional:** 5	**National:** 1
Walk-on/Other:	**Graduation %:** 100	**Seniors on Team:** 5

Positions Needed: Defenders, Midfielders, Forwards
Camp or Clinic Dates: June 2001
Most Recent Record: 14-8-1
Schedule: University of Nebraska, University of Michigan, Texas A&M, Wake Forest, Cal, Baylor
Style of Play: Exciting, attacking soccer, possession oriented, with a creative flare.

University of Missouri - Kansas City
Academic Profile

Kansas City, MO 64110
Phone: (816) 235-1036

Type: 4 Yr.,Public,Liberal Arts
Founded: 1963
Website: http://www.umkc.edu
Religion: Non-Affiliated
SAT/ACT/GPA: 850/24
Housing: Yes
Student/Faculty Ratio: 14:1
Male/Female Ratio: 2:3
Undergraduate Enrollment: 6,108
Graduate Enrollment: 4,502
Scholarships/Academic: Yes **Athletic:** Yes **Financial Aid:** Yes
Expenses by: Year **In State:** $ 11,000 **Out of State:** $ 16,000
Specialty: Medicine, Dentistry
Degrees Conferred: BA, BS, BFA, MA, MS, MBA, Ph.D., JD, PharmD, MD, DMD
Programs of Study: Accounting, Arts & Science, Business Administration & Management, Communications, Dentistry, Education, Engineering, English, Law, Law Enforcement & Correction, Mathematics, Medicine, Music, Nursing, Performing Arts, Pharmacy, Psychology, Social Sciences

Men's Athletic Profile

5100 Rockhill Road
Kansas City, MO 64110-2499
Coach: Rick Benben
Email: schlichtingf@umkc.edu

NCAA I
Kangaroos/Blue, Gold
Phone: (816) 235-5469
Fax: (816) 235-1035

Estimated # of Men's Soccer Scholarships: 9.9
Conference: Mid-Continent Conference
Program Profile: Has new stadium that has seating capacity of 2,000. Field dimension is 110 X 70 yards of natural grass. Playing season is in the fall.
History: Our program in 1987. We played in Conference Tournament in the past five years and was a Runner-Up in 1998.
Achievements: 1996 Coach of the Year, 2 All-Midwest team members; 1 Conference Titles (West Division); 4 drafted players.
Coaching: Rick Benben, Head Coach, played in 1972, where won National Champs as a goalkeeper. Team won National Champs in 1979 while he was an assistant coach. He was an assistant coach and Director of Player Personnel for the Kansas city Comets (MISL) in 1982-1984 and became a Head Coach of Kansas City Comets (MISL) in 1984-1987. Fred Schlichting is the Assistant Coach, was a graduate of Notre dame in 1995. Chris Snitko is the Assistant Coach, was graduated from UCLA and currently with Kansas City Wizards.
Style of Play: Depends on players.

University of Missouri - Rolla
Academic Profile

Rolla, MO 65409-0740
Phone: 573-341-4111

Type: 4 Yr.,Public,Liberal Arts,Engineering
Founded: 1870
Website: http://www.umr.edu
Religion: Non-Affiliated
SAT/ACT/GPA: 24
Housing: Yes
Student/Faculty Ratio: 8:1
Male/Female Ratio: 3:1

Undergraduate Enrollment: 4,800 **Graduate Enrollment:** 800
Scholarships/Academic: Yes **Athletic:** Yes **Financial Aid:** Yes
Expenses by: Year **In State:** $ 7,400 **Out of State:** $ 13,400
Specialty: Engineering
Degrees Conferred: BA, BS, MS, Ph.D.
Programs of Study: Art, English, History, Psychology, Philosophy, PreLaw, Engineering, Aerospace, Management, Chemical, Civil Engineering, Computer, Electrical, Theatre, Metallurgic, Management, Mechanical, Ceramic, Mining, Nuclear, Petroleum, Physics, Chemistry, Biological Science, PreMed, Computer Science, Management System, Economics

Men's Athletic Profile

1870 Miner Circle
Rolla, MO 65409-4880
Coach: Dawson L. Driscoll
Email: ddriscol@umr.edu

NCAA II
Miners/Gold, White
Phone: (573) 341-4102
Fax: (573) 341-4880

Estimated # of Men's Soccer Scholarships: 4
Conference: Midwest Intercollegiate Athletic Association
Program Profile: Lighted game and practice field; natural grass indoor practice facility.
History: Program began in 1972. The miners have been ranked in the Top Ten in the Central Region several years.
Achievements: MIAA Conference Champions in 1997; 1998 Regional ranking.
Coaching: Dawson Driscoll, Head Coach. Matt Long and Lori Douglas are the assistant coaches.
Roster In State: 8 **Out of State:** 12 **Out of Country:** 2
ODP State: 10 **Regional:** 3 **National:**
Walk-on/Other: **Graduation %:** 98 **Seniors on Team:** 6
Positions Needed: Forwards
Most Recent Record: 11-5-1
Schedule: Truman State, Rockhurst, S Indiana University, S Illinois, University of Missouri, Quincy
Style of Play: Aggressive - attacking style of play.

Women's Athletic Profile

1870 Miner Circle
Rolla, MO 65409-0740
Coach: Dawson Driscoll
Email: ddriscol@ume.edu

NCAA II
Lady Miners/Gold, White
Phone: (573) 341-4102
Fax: (573) 341-4880

Estimated # of Women's Soccer Scholarships: 4
Conference: Midwest Intercollegiate Athletic Association
Program Profile: We have a lighted game and practice field. We also have a natural grass indoor practice facility.
History: The program started in 1984 and is 11 years old.
Achievements: Ranked #24 in the Nation in 1997. MIAA Coach of the Year in 1998.
Coaching: Dawson Driscoll, Head Coach. Jesus Rodriguez, Assistant Coach, is responsible with the goalkeeper.
Roster in State: 10 **Out of State:** 10 **Out of Country:** 2
ODP State: 8 **Regional:** 1 **National:**
Walk-on/Other: **Graduation %:** 98 **Seniors on Team:** 3
Positions Needed: Forwards
Most Recent Record: 10-7-1
Schedule: Truman State, Rockhurst, S Indiana University, S Illinois-Edwardsville, University of Missouri- St Louis, Quincy
Style of Play: The team plays an aggressive attacking style.

University of Missouri - Saint Louis

Academic Profile

St. Louis, MO 63121

Phone: 314-516-5000

Type: 4 Yr.,Public
Website: http://www.umsl.edu
SAT/ACT/GPA: 24
Student/Faculty Ratio: 14:1
Undergraduate Enrollment: 12,844
Scholarships/Academic: Yes **Athletic:** Yes
Expenses by: Year **In State:** $ 7,545

Founded: 1963
Religion: Non-Affiliated
Housing: Yes
Male/Female Ratio: 50:50
Graduate Enrollment: 2,732
Financial Aid: Yes
Out of State: $ 13,500

Degrees Conferred: BA, NS, MA, MS, MEd, MBA, Ph.D., BFA, BGS, BM, BSBA, BSEd, BSN, BSPA, BSW,, MPPA, MSN, EdD, OD
Programs of Study: Anthropology, Art History, Biology, Business Administration, Chemistry, Communication, Computer Science, Criminal Justice, Economics, Education, English, French, German, History, Management, Mathematics, Music, Nursing, Philosophy, Physics, Political Science, Psychology, Public Administration, Social Science, Spanish, Special Education

Men's Athletic Profile

8001 Natural Bridge
St. Louis, MO 63121
Coach: Hannibal Najjar
Email: Not Available

NCAA II
Rivermen/Red, Gold
Phone: (314) 516-4661
Fax: (314) 553-5503

Estimated # of Men's Soccer Scholarships: N/A
Conference: Missouri Intercollegiate Conference

Women's Athletic Profile

8001 Natural Bridge RD.
St. Louis, MO 63121
Coach: Beth Goetz
Email: marygoetz@emsl.edu

NCAA II
Riverwomen/Red, Gold
Phone: (314) 516-5646
Fax: (314) 516-5503

Estimated # of Women's Soccer Scholarships: approx 4
Conference: Great Lakes Valley Conference
Program Profile: Playing season runs from mid-August through November, spring season, natural grass stadium that seats 1,350.
History: The program began in 1981, finished in nation's top 25 schools; 12 of the past 15 years; 2000 will be fifth year in the Great Lakes Valley Conference.
Achievements: Produced 11 All-Americans; reached the Final Four twice.
Coaching: Beth Goetz, Head Coach, is entering her fourth year as a head coach after serving as an assistant. Graduate from Clemson University. Assistant Coach, Daniel Brizard, is entering his third season having played collegiate at Berry College.
Roster in State: 15 **Out of State:** 7 **Out of Country:**
Walk-on/Other: **Graduation %:** **Seniors on Team:** 5
Positions Needed: Defenders
Camp or Clinic Dates: Not Available
Most Recent Record: 7-13-0
Schedule: Northern Kentucky, Southern Illinois at Edwardsville, Southern Indiana, University of Tampa, Truman State, Indianapolis

Washington University-St. Louis

Academic Profile

Phone: (314) 935-4713

St. Louis, MO 63130-4899

Type: 4 Yr.,Private,Liberal Arts,Engineering
Founded: 1853
Website: http://www.bearsports.wustl.edu
Religion: Non-Affiliated
SAT/ACT/GPA: 1300+/27+
Housing: Yes
Student/Faculty Ratio: 1:15-17
Male/Female Ratio: 1:1
Undergraduate Enrollment: 5,452
Graduate Enrollment: 5,700
Scholarships/Academic: Yes **Athletic:** No **Financial Aid:** Yes
Expenses by: Year **In State:** $ 33,000 **Out of State:** $ 33,000
Specialty: 3,100 undergraduates in Arts & Sciences, 1,030 undergrad Engineering
Degrees Conferred: BS, BA, MS
Programs of Study: Consistently ranked in the top 20 universities in America. Business, Engineering, Biological Sciences, PreMed, PreLaw, Education

Men's Athletic Profile

One Brookings Drive
St. Louis, MO 63130
Coach: Joe Clarke
Email: joec@athletics.wustl.edu

NCAA III
Battling Bears/Red, Green
Phone: (314) 935-5174
Fax: (314) 935-5545

Estimated # of Men's Soccer Scholarships: None
Conference: University Athletic Association (UAA)
Program Profile: Play a 20 game schedule, includes air travel in the Midwest, East, and California. Field is 120 x 72 yards, natural grass, and seats 3,500.
History: Program began in 1959. Since 1978 the team has qualified for the NCAA Division III post-season tournament 13 times, has been a three time NCAA Finalist 1975, 1985, 1987. In 1995 - NCAA South Central Region Champions, NCAA Division III National Quarter-finalist, ranked as high as #5 in National Division III Poll, and won regional Coaching Staff of the Year.
Achievements: Numerous All-Conference, All-Region, Coaches of the Year.
Coaching: Joe Clarke, Head Coach.
Style of Play: Possession, everyone attacks, everyone defends.

Women's Athletic Profile

1 Brookings Dr.
St. Louis, MO 63130
Coach: Doug Hippler
Email: skchuds@umslvma-umsl.edu

NCAA III
Bears/Red, White
Phone: (314) 935-4706
Fax: (314) 935-5545

Estimated # of Women's Soccer Scholarships: None
Conference: University Athletic Association Conference
Program Profile: Games played on Francis Field which was used for 1904 Olympics and 1994 Sports Festival (natural turf). Conference is unique; made up of other research universities: Brandeis, Rochester, New York University, Carnegie Mellon, Case Western, Emory, and Chicago. Needs for the next recruiting class is keeper and attacking center midfield.
History: The program began in 1989. Ranked in the Top Twenty for three years. Overall record is134-66-13.
Achievements: UAA Coach of the Year in 1990 & 1995; Conference Champions in 1995; NCAA Tournament in 1995; Top Twenty in 1995; players have been advanced All-Conference, All-Regions and All-American.

Coaching: Doug Hippler, Head Coach, has an Advanced National Coaching Diploma and is beginning his tenth season with an overall record of 134-66-13. Assistant Coaches - Harry Keough (Sixth year) and Kathleen Kerry (Sixth year). Soccer Hall of Fame: Harry Keough.

Roster in State: 3 | **Out of State:** 17 | **Out of Country:** 0
ODP State: 0 | **Regional:** 0 | **National:** 0
Walk-on/Other: 0 | **Graduation %:** 100 | **Seniors on Team:** 4
Positions Needed: GK, Backs, MF, Forwards
Camp or Clinic Dates: Not Available
Most Recent Record: 13-5-0
Schedule: Emory, NYU, Rochester, Chicago, Brandis
Style of Play: Control, short passing team. Utilize all field players in the offense. Very sound defensively. Players are very versatile.

Webster University
Academic Profile

St. Louis, MO 63119 | **Phone:** (314) 968-7191

Type: 4 Yr.,Private,Liberal Arts | **Founded:** 1915
Website: http://www.websteruniv.edu | **Religion:** Non-Affiliated
SAT/ACT/GPA: 1000/22/2.5 | **Housing:** Yes
Student/Faculty Ratio: 15:1 | **Male/Female Ratio:** 40:60
Undergraduate Enrollment: 1,800 | **Graduate Enrollment:** 2,500
Scholarships/Academic: Yes | **Athletic:** No | **Financial Aid:** Yes
Expenses by: Year | **In State:** $ 18,460 | **Out of State:** $ 18,460
Specialty: Business, Communication, Education
Degrees Conferred: BA, BFA, BS, BM, MA, MBA, MM, MT
Programs of Study: Accounting, Advertising, Art, Behavioral & Social Science, Biology, Business, Business Administration, Computer Science, Dance, Education, English, Film, Foreign Languages, History, Journalism, Marketing, Mathematics, Media Communications, Music, Political Science, Public Relations, Science

Men's Athletic Profile

470 E Lockwood | **NCAA III**
St. Louis, MO 63119 | Gorlok/Navy, Gold
Coach: LUIGI SCIRE | **Phone:** 314.968.6900
Email: Not Available | **Fax:** (314) 968-7115

Estimated # of Men's Soccer Scholarships: None
Conference: St. Louis Intercollegiate Athletic Conference
Program Profile: Top Ten program in the South Central Region. Travel to some of the largest metropolitan areas in the Midwest and South. Home games are played at St. Louis Soccer Park. Field surface is grass and astro turf.
History: Program began in 1984.
Achievements: Midwest Regional All-Americans 1986, 1988, 1989, 1993, and 1994.
Style of Play: Disciplined passing game, hard working, physical team.

Women's Athletic Profile

470 E. Lockwood | **NCAA III**
St. Louis, MO 63123 | Gorloks/Navy, Gold
Coach: Luigi Scire | **Phone:** (314) 968-7191
Email: scirela@webste.edu | **Fax:** (314) 968-7115

Estimated # of Women's Soccer Scholarships: None
Conference: St. Louis Intercollegiate Athletic Conference
Program Profile: NCAA Division III program that has 20 game Division III schedule. Facilities and games are played at the Anheuser-Busch Soccer complex on natural grass.
History: Fall of 1999 will be our first season.
Coaching: Luigi Scire, Head Coach, he was named NSCAA Academic All-American in 1987. He has eleven years experience as an assistant coach at Webster University. Patty Kelly, Assistant Coach, was named Division II All-American. She was five years assistant coach at Missouri Baptist. Mike Hutchison, Assistant Coach, he was NSCAA All-Midwest player in 1988 and 1990.
Style of Play: We play a 4-4-2 system.

Westminster College

Academic Profile

Fulton, MO 65251
Phone: 573-642-3361

Type: 4 Yr.,Private,Liberal Arts
Website: http://www.westminster-mo.edu
SAT/ACT/GPA: Yes
Student/Faculty Ratio: 12:1
Undergraduate Enrollment: 700
Scholarships/Academic: Yes
Athletic: No
Expenses by: Year
In State: $ 17,190
Degrees Conferred: BS, BA
Founded: 1851
Religion: Presbyterian
Housing: Yes
Male/Female Ratio: 6:4
Graduate Enrollment: N/A
Financial Aid: Yes
Out of State: $ 17,190
Programs of Study: Accounting, Advertising, Art, Biology, Business Administration, Business Communications, Chemistry, Classic, Economics, Education, English, French, History, Mathematics, Philosophy, Physical Education, Physics, Political Science, PreLaw, PreMed, Psychology, Religion, Sport Medicine

Men's Athletic Profile

501 Westminster Avenue
Fulton, MO 65251
Coach: Joel Wallace
Email: wallacj@jaynet.wcmo.edu

NCAA III
Bluejays/Blue, White
Phone: (573) 592-1200
Fax: (573) 592-1366

Estimated # of Men's Soccer Scholarships: None
Conference: St. Louis Intercollegiate Athletic Conference.
Program Profile: Young team, play a Fall season.
History: First played intercollegiate men's soccer in 1967 although soccer was a club sport before that time. Jaime Vargas is the sixth coach in the history of program.
Achievements: Coach of the Year 1996. Sophomore goalkeeper - 2nd team, first team as freshman.
Style of Play: European, short passing style.

Women's Athletic Profile

501 Westminster Avenue
Fulton, MO 65251
Coach: Ralph Aubuchon
Email: aubuchr@jaynet.wcmo.edu

NCAA III
Blue Jays/Blue, White
Phone: (573) 592-1200
Fax: (573) 592-1366

Estimated # of Women's Soccer Scholarships: None
Conference: St. Louis Intercollegiate Athletic Conference (SLIAC)

Program Profile: The team plays and practices on a natural surface and is awaiting the completion of the new on-campus facility. Young team; playing season is in the fall, and has a 17-match schedule.
History: Westminster first played women's intercollegiate soccer in 1987.
Achievements: Five members of the 1995 squad received All-Conference Honors. Sophomore Goalkeeper - 2nd team, 1st team as a freshman.

William Jewell College

Academic Profile

Liberty, MO 64068
Phone: 816-781-7700

Type: 4 Yr.,Private,Liberal Arts
Founded: 1849
Website: http://www.jewell.edu
Religion: Baptist
SAT/ACT/GPA: Open
Housing: Yes
Student/Faculty Ratio: 15:1
Male/Female Ratio: 1:3
Undergraduate Enrollment: 1,200
Graduate Enrollment: N/A
Scholarships/Academic: Yes
Athletic: Yes
Financial Aid: Yes
Expenses by: Year
In State: $ 17,400
Out of State: $ 17,400
Degrees Conferred: BA, BS
Programs of Study: Art, Biology, British Studies, Business Administration & Economics, Accounting, Chemistry, Communications, Speech/Theatre, Education, English, History, Languages, Mathematics, Computer Science, Music, Nursing, Oxbridge Honors Program, Philosophy, Physics, Political Science, Psychology, Religion, Sociology

Men's Athletic Profile

500 College Hill
Liberty, MO 64068-9988
Coach: Mike Hendershot
Email: hendershot@william.jewell.edu

NAIA
Cardinals/Red, White
Phone: (816) 781-7700
Fax: (816) 415-5029

Estimated # of Men's Soccer Scholarships: 4
Conference: Heart of America Conference
Program Profile: We have four natural field, which are considered the best field in the region. The seating capacity is about 2000. Our playing season is in the fall.
History: Our program began in 1970's.
Coaching: Mike Hendershot is the Head Coach. Chad Jolley is the Assistant Coach.
Roster In State: 10
Out of State: 20
Out of Country: 2
ODP State: 8
Regional: 3
National:
Walk-on/Other:
Graduation %: 95
Seniors on Team: 6
Positions Needed: All
Camp or Clinic Dates: June 12-18 July 2-16,30
Most Recent Record: 5-12
Schedule: Lindenwood, Harris-stowe, Park, Mckendree
Style of Play: Controlled, short quick passes and high pressure defense.

Women's Athletic Profile

500 College Hill
Liberty, MO 64068-1896
Coach: Chris Cissell
Email: cissell@william.jewell.edu

NAIA
Cardinals/Black, White, Red
Phone: (816) 781-7700
Fax: (816) 415-5029

Estimated # of Women's Soccer Scholarships: 2
Conference: Heart of America Conference

Program Profile: Program is in its 2nd year under the leadership of full time Coach Chris Cissell. Jewell has made a huge commitment to Soccer and has built a first class soccer facility.
History: The program began in 1990.
Coaching: Chris Cissell, Head Coach.
Roster in State: 12 **Out of State:** 8 **Out of Country:** 0
ODP State: 12 **Regional:** 2 **National:** 0
Walk-on/Other: **Graduation %:** 100 **Seniors on Team:** 1
Positions Needed: Marking Backs, Goalkeeper, Outside Midfielders
Camp or Clinic Dates: June 12- August 4
Most Recent Record: 2-15-1
Schedule: Baker, Benedictine, Mckendree, Harris-Stowe, Graceland, Missouri Valley, Hannibal LaGrange, Simpson, Avila.
Style of Play: Possession Soccer. Good, skillful build-up, controlled passes. Play in triangles. Hard working dedicated team ready to make an impact in the Heart of America Athletic Conference and NAIA Region V play.

William Woods University

Academic Profile

Phone: (573) 592-4340

Fulton, MO 65251

Type: 4 Yr.,Private,Liberal Arts **Founded:** 1870
Website: http://www.wmwoods.edu **Religion:** Disciples of Christ
SAT/ACT/GPA: Open **Housing:** Yes
Student/Faculty Ratio: 13:1 **Male/Female Ratio:** Women
Undergraduate Enrollment: 700 **Graduate Enrollment:** 300
Scholarships/Academic: Yes **Athletic:** Yes **Financial Aid:** Yes
Expenses by: Year **In State:** $ 16,000 **Out of State:** $ 16,000
Specialty: Liberal arts - Education, Business Administrations, Fine Arts
Degrees Conferred: BA, BA, BFA
Programs of Study: Accounting, Biology, Business Administration, Chemistry, Commercial Art, Communications, Computer Science, Deaf Interpreter, Design, Early Childhood Education, Economics, English, Equestrian Science, Fashion Merchandising, Fine Arts, French, Geography, German, History, Interior Design, Management, Marketing, Mathematics, Military Science, Music, Philosophy, Physics, Political Science, PreLaw, PreMed, Psychology, Religion, Secondary Education, Social Science, Spanish, Special Education, Speech, Visual & Performing Arts

Men's Athletic Profile

200 W. 12th Street
Fulton, MO 65251
Coach: Dan Palmer
Email: dpalmeer@williamwoods.edu

NAIA
Owls/Green, White, Maroon
Phone: (573) 592-1156
Fax: (573) 592-4386

Estimated # of Men's Soccer Scholarships: N/A
Conference: American Midwest Conference

Women's Athletic Profile

200 W 12th Street
Fulton, MO 65251
Coach: Dan Palmer
Email: dpalmer@iris.wmwoods.edu

NAIA
Owls/Forest Green, White
Phone: (573) 592-1156
Fax: (573) 445-5747

Estimated # of Women's Soccer Scholarships: 3
Conference: American Midwest Conference

Program Profile: NAIA program. Excellent natural grass playing surface, located on campus, a 120 x 70 yard playing field. 20+ match Fall season with a limited Spring Season.
History: Program began in 1989. Program has improved from 4-14-1 to 16-5 in last four years under Coach Palmer. 5 First team All-Conference selections in 1999 and 3 All-American selections in last two years.

Roster in State: 6	**Out of State:** 14	**Out of Country:** 3
ODP State: 5	**Regional:**	**National:**
Walk-on/Other:	**Graduation %:** 100	**Seniors on Team:** 7

Positions Needed: Goalkeeper, Striker, Wing Midfield
Most Recent Record: 16-5
Schedule: Oklahoma City University, Lindenwood University, Central Missouri State University, McKonaree College, Auburn University at Montgomery, Baker University, Hannibal LaGrange-College, University of Missouri-Rolla, Harris-Stowe State College, Park University
Style of Play: Pressure defense and attacking.

montana

MONTANA

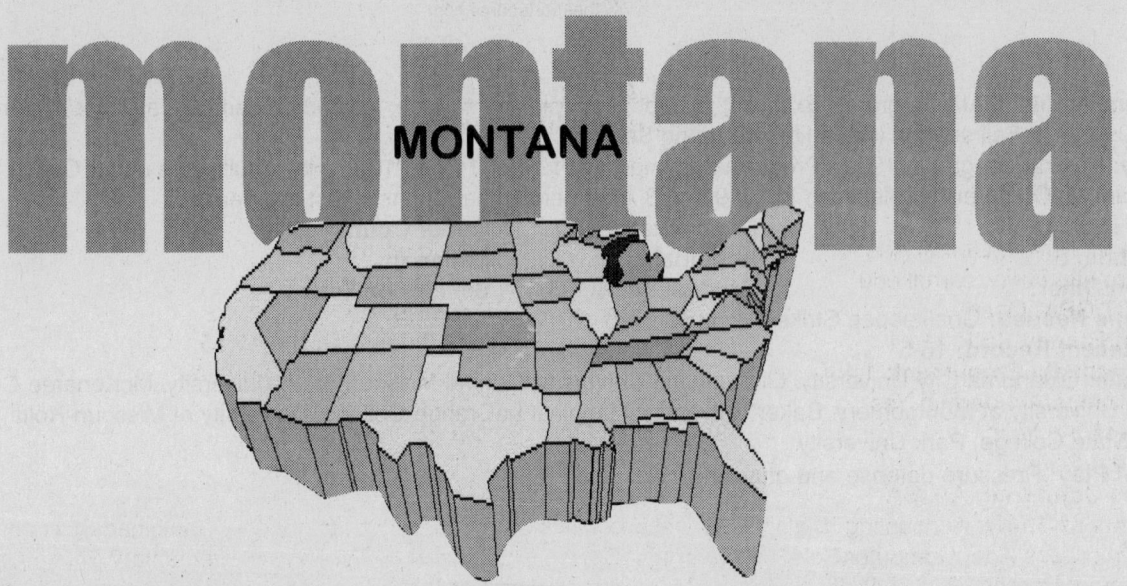

SCHOOL	CITY	AFFILIATION	PAGE
Carroll College	Helena	NAIA	623
Montana State University-Billings	Billings	NAIA	623
University of Montana	Missoula	NCAA I	624

Carroll College
Academic Profile

Phone: 800-992-3648

Helena, MT 59625

Type: 4 Yr.,Private,Liberal Arts
Website: http://www.carroll.edu
SAT/ACT/GPA: Open
Student/Faculty Ratio: 14:1
Undergraduate Enrollment: 1,400
Scholarships/Academic: Yes
Athletic: Yes
Expenses by: Year
In State: $ 12,750
Specialty: Science
Degrees Conferred: AA, BA
Founded: 1909
Religion: Catholic
Housing: No
Male/Female Ratio: 45:55
Graduate Enrollment: N/A
Financial Aid: Yes
Out of State: $ 12,750

Programs of Study: Accounting, Biology, Business Administration, Classical Languages, Combined Science, Communications Arts, Computer Science, Computer Software Engineering, Economics, Elementary Education, Engineering, English, English/Writing, French, Mathematics, Medical Technology, Nursing, Occupational Therapy, Philosophy, Physical Therapy, Physical Education, Political Science, Psychology, Public Administration, Public Relations, Social Science, Social Work, Sociology, Spanish

Women's Athletic Profile

1601 North Benton Ave
Helena, MT 59625
Coach: Jim Dushin
Email: Not Available

Phone: (406) 447-4480
Fax: (406) 447-4955

Did Not Return Profile

Montana State University-Billings
Academic Profile

Phone: 406-657-2011

Billings, MT 59101

Type: 4 Yr.
Website: http://www.msubillings.edu
SAT/ACT/GPA: Open
Student/Faculty Ratio: 20:1
Undergraduate Enrollment: 3,624
Scholarships/Academic:
Athletic:
Expenses by:
In State:
Degrees Conferred: Masters, Bachelors
Founded: 1927
Religion: Non-Affiliated
Housing: No
Male/Female Ratio: N/A
Graduate Enrollment: N/A
Financial Aid:
Out of State:

Programs of Study: Accounting, Art Education, Art/Fine Arts, Automotive Technology, Biology, Biological Science, Computer Information Systems, Human Services, Practical Nursing, Reading, Education, Music, Sociology

Women's Athletic Profile

1500 North 30th
Billings, MT 59101
Coach: Carlos Arce
Email: Not Available

NAIA
Lady Yellowjackets/Blue, Gold
Phone: (406) 657-2399
Fax:

Estimated # of Women's Soccer Scholarships: None
Conference: Pacific West Conference

University of Montana

Academic Profile

Athletics
Missoula, MT 59812-1291

Phone: (406) 243-2760

Type: 4 Yr.,Public,Liberal Arts
Website: http://www.umt.edu
SAT/ACT/GPA: 1030/22/2.5
Student/Faculty Ratio: 19:1
Undergraduate Enrollment: 9,000
Scholarships/Academic: Yes **Athletic:** Yes
Expenses by: Year **In State:** $ 8,500

Founded: 1892
Religion: Non-Affiliated
Housing: Yes
Male/Female Ratio: 50:50
Graduate Enrollment: 2,000
Financial Aid: Yes
Out of State: $ 13,500

Specialty: Business, Education, Forestry, Physical Therapy, Sports Medicine
Degrees Conferred: BA, BS
Programs of Study: Arts & Sciences, Business Administration, Education, Fine Arts, Forestry, Honors College, Journalism, Law, Pharmacy

Women's Athletic Profile

Athletics - Adam's Field House
Missoula, MT 59812
Coach: Betsy Duerksen
Email: Not Available

NCAA I
Grizzlies/Maroon/Silver
Phone: (406) 243-2760
Fax: (406) 243-6859

Estimated # of Women's Soccer Scholarships:
Conference: Big Sky Conference
Program Profile: We play in a new natural grass stadium with a seating capacity for 1,000. We have a newly renovated athletic facility that includes a weight room, an indoor sport court and an athletic training room.
History: 1998 record: 15-5-1. 1999 record: 12-5-1. Invited to the National Tournament for the first time in program history. Program began in 1994. 1999 Big Sky Conference Champions.
Achievements: Big Sky Conference Champions in 1997; 2 Academic All-Americans in 1997 and 1998; NAIA Coach of the Year- National-NSCAA in 1993; 3 players in Semi-pro West League. Conference Champions in1999. Two Scholar athlete All-Americans in 1999. Three All-West players in 1999.
Coaching: Betsy Duerksen, Head Coach. Her record here is 77-34-3. She was NAIA National Coach of the Year in 1993. She was a four-year All-American player at Boston College. She was Boston College Athlete of the 1980's Decade. Erik Oman is Assistant Coach. Previously, he was goalkeeper for the Colorado Foxes.
Roster in State: 5 **Out of State:** 21 **Out of Country:** 0
ODP State: 4 **Regional:** 3 **National:** 1
Walk-on/Other: 19 **Graduation %:** 98 **Seniors on Team:** 5
Positions Needed: Outside Mids, Center Mids, Goalkeeper
Camp or Clinic Dates: July 23-28
Most Recent Record: 12-5-1
Schedule: Minnesota, Northwestern, Cal-Poly, BYU, Utah, Colorado College
Style of Play: Athletic, good team speed, hard working, try to play a possession game.

nebraska

NEBRASKA

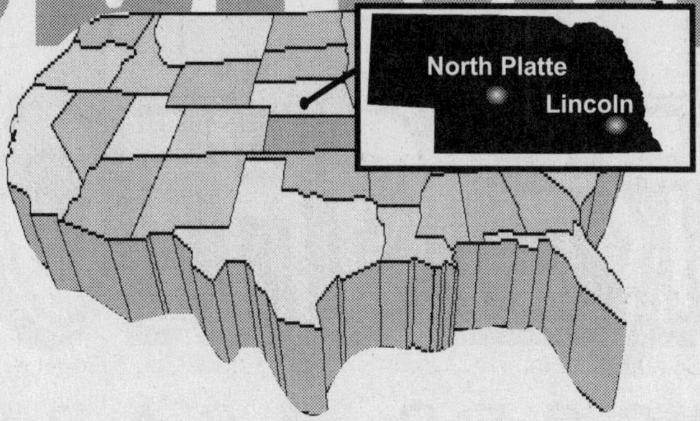

SCHOOL	CITY	AFFILIATION	PAGE
Bellevue College	Bellevue	NAIA	627
College of St. Mary	Omaha	NAIA	627
Creighton University	Omaha	NCAA I	628
Concordia College - Nebraska	Seward	NAIA	629
Dana College	Blair	NAIA	631
Doane College	Crete	NIAC	631
Hastings College	Hasting	NAIA	633
Midland Lutheran College	Freemont	NAIA	634
Nebraska Wesleyan University	Lincoln	NCAA III	635
University of Nebraska - Lincoln	Lincoln	NCAA I	636
University of Nebraska - Omaha	Omaha	NCAA II	637
Wayne State College	Wayne	NAIA	638
York College - Nebraska	York	NAIA	639

Bellevue University
Academic Profile

Phone: (402) 293-3783

Bellevue, NE 68005

Type: 4 Yr.,Private,Liberal Arts
Founded: 1966
Website: http://www.bellevue.edu
Religion: Non-Affiliated
SAT/ACT/GPA: 870/18/2.0
Housing: Yes
Student/Faculty Ratio: 13:1
Male/Female Ratio: 54:46
Undergraduate Enrollment: 3,000
Graduate Enrollment: 1,100
Scholarships/Academic: Yes **Athletic:** Yes
Financial Aid: Yes
Expenses by: Year **In State:** $ 6,640
Out of State: $ 6,640
Specialty: Business & Professional Education, Liberal Arts
Degrees Conferred: BA,BS,MA,MS
Programs of Study: Accounting, Art History, Art Management, Biology, Business Administration, Chemical Dependency, Communication Arts, Computer Information Systems, Economics, English, Environmental Science, Geology, History, International Studies, Mathematics, Physical Education, Political Science, PreMed, PreNursing, PrePhysical Therapy, Psychology, Social Science, Sociology, Spanish, Sports Management, Studio Art, Urban Studies, Women's Studies

Men's Athletic Profile

1000 Galvin Rd. South
Bellevue, NE 68005-3098
Coach: Dan Holstein
Email: Not Available

NAIA
Bruins/Purple, Gold
Phone: (402) 293-3781
Fax: (402) 293-2086

Did Not Return Profile

Women's Athletic Profile

1000 Galvin Rd. South
Bellevue, NE 68005-3098
Coach: Sterling Nabours
Email: Not Available

NAIA
Bruins/Purple, Gold, White
Phone: (402) 293-3781
Fax: (402) 293-2086

Did Not Return Profile

College of Saint Mary
Academic Profile

Phone:

Omaha, NE 68124

Type: 4 Yr.,Private,Liberal Arts
Founded: 1923
Website: http://www.csm.edu
Religion: Catholic
SAT/ACT/GPA: Open
Housing: No
Student/Faculty Ratio:
Male/Female Ratio:
Undergraduate Enrollment: N/A
Graduate Enrollment: N/A
Scholarships/Academic: Yes **Athletic:** Yes
Financial Aid: Yes
Expenses by: Year **In State:** $ 14,194
Out of State: $ 14,194
Degrees Conferred: AA, AS, BA, BS
Programs of Study: Contact school for programs of study.

Women's Athletic Profile

1901 South 72nd Street
Omaha, NE 68124
Coach: Phil Comstock
Email: Not Available
Phone: (402) 399-2359
Fax: (402) 399-2341

Did Not Return Profile

Creighton University

Academic Profile

Phone: (402) 280-2703

Omaha, NE 68178

Type: 4 Yr.,Private,Liberal Arts
Founded: 1878
Website: http://www.creighton.edu
Religion: Catholic Jesuit
SAT/ACT/GPA: 700/17/2.0
Housing: Yes
Student/Faculty Ratio: 14:1
Male/Female Ratio: 1:1.08
Undergraduate Enrollment: 4,000
Graduate Enrollment: 2,000
Scholarships/Academic: Yes **Athletic:** Yes **Financial Aid:** Yes
Expenses by: Year **In State:** $ 18,584 **Out of State:** $ 18,584
Specialty: Preprofessional School, Business
Degrees Conferred: AA, AS, BA, BS, BFA, MA, MS, MBA, Ph.D., DMD, MD
Programs of Study: American Studies, Art Administration, Applied Computer Studies, Atmospheric Science, Biology, Chemistry, Classical Civilization, Communication, Computer Science, Economics, Education, English, Environmental Science, Exercise Science, French, German, Graphic Design, Greek, Health Administration, History, International Studies, Journalism, Medical Physics, Ministry, Music, Pharmacy, Philosophy, Political Science, Theatre, Theology, Physics, Political Science, Psychology, Secondary Education, Social Work, Sociology, Spanish, Theology

Men's Athletic Profile

2500 California Plaza
Omaha, NE 68178
Coach: Bob Warming
Email: bwarming@creighton.edu

NCAA I
Bluejays/Blue, White
Phone: (402) 280-5785
Fax: (402) 280-5596

Estimated # of Men's Soccer Scholarships: 2-3
Conference: Missouri Valley Conference
Program Profile: Creighton plays at well-known Tranquility Park, a beautiful community stadium with a capacity of over 5,000. Some of the largest and most vocal crowds in the country make for a great home field advantage.
History: The Creighton Soccer program was reinstated in 1990. during the 1990's the team has made the NCAA Tournament seven consecutive years and has finished in the national Top 10 for the last three season in a row.
Achievements: Winner of the Missouri Valley Conference Regular Season and/or conference tournament seven consecutive years. Numerous conference All-Stars and All-American, 4 MLS striker this year and many other in the A-League and NPSL. Extremely high graduation rate. 1997 National Player of the Year.
Coaching: Bob Warming, Head Coach, holds a USSF National "A" Coaching License. Jim Paulz, Assistant Coach and Techniques Assistance. Bruce Erickson, Assistant Coach and Goalkeeper Director. Matt Stomson, Assistant Coach and Recruiting Coordinator.
Roster In State: 6 **Out of State:** 20 **Out of Country:** 1
ODP State: 22 **Regional:** 10 **National:** 6
Walk-on/Other: **Graduation %:** 95 **Seniors on Team:** 5
Positions Needed: Defense, Midfield, Forward

Camp or Clinic Dates: July 30-August3 August 5-9
Most Recent Record: 11-5-2
Schedule: Penn State, SMU, Ohio State, Southwest Missouri, Harvard, Oregon State, Hartford
Style of Play: Attack oriented from all areas on the field. Technically and tactically clean and emphasis on speed of play.

Women's Athletic Profile

2500 California Plaza
Omaha, NE 68178
Coach: Bruce Erickson
Email: ericuson@creighton.edu

NCAA I
Blue Jays/Blue, White
Phone: (402) 280-5553
Fax: (402) 280-5596

Estimated # of Women's Soccer Scholarships: 3
Conference: Missouri Valley Conference
Program Profile: We have a competitive Division I program with good facilities. We play at an off-campus stadium with a natural grass and 3,500 seats. We did a $2 million upgrade to the locker rooms, weight room, training room and Academic Learning Center. Building a new stadium on campus in the next 2-3 years is a priority.
History: The program began in 1989.We have 8 winning seasons with a current record of 102-71-8. We have been members of the Missouri Valley Conference since 1996 and placed 2nd in post-season tournament. Conference tournament winner gets an NCAA bid. We have placed in the top 3 each year of the tournament and in 1998 we had a National Player of the Week and an All-American, Jessica Powers.
Achievements: 1996 Missouri Valley second place; several All-conference players; NSCAA team Academic Award in 1996 & 1997. 1 All-American
Coaching: Bruce Erickson is Head Coach. He is entering his first season with the program. NSCAA Advanced National Diploma, NSCAA Goalkeeper Diploma. He was named Coach of the Year and ODP staff coach for five years. Heather Cairns is the Assistant Coach. He holds a USSF "B" License and Advanced National Diploma. He is ODP Coach for five for five years.

Roster in State: 7	**Out of State:** 18	**Out of Country:**
ODP State: 3	**Regional:** 1	**National:**
Walk-on/Other: 1	**Graduation %:** 100	**Seniors on Team:** 5

Positions Needed: All
Camp or Clinic Dates: June 24-28 July dates TBA
Most Recent Record: 7-13-1
Schedule: Evansville, Illinois State, UAB, St. Louis, Oklahoma State, Southwest Missouri State, Pepperdine, Colorado College, Loyola Marymount, UW-Milwaukee
Style of Play: Possession oriented, play aggressive attacking style, and disciplined man marking as well as zone defense.

Concordia College - Nebraska

Academic Profile

Phone: (402) 643-7328
Seward, NE 68434

Type: 4 Yr.,Private,Liberal Arts		**Founded:** 1894
Website: http://www.cune.edu		**Religion:** Lutheran Church
SAT/ACT/GPA: 890/18/2.0		**Housing:** Yes
Student/Faculty Ratio: 13:1		**Male/Female Ratio:** 44:56
Undergraduate Enrollment: 1,110		**Graduate Enrollment:** 90
Scholarships/Academic: Yes	**Athletic:** Yes	**Financial Aid:** Yes
Expenses by: Sem	**In State:** $ 7,898	**Out of State:** $ 7,898
Specialty: Education, Liberal Arts		

Degrees Conferred: BA, BSEd, MAEd
Programs of Study: Business, Commercial Art, Computer Science, Director of Christian Education, Law, Medicine and other Health Careers, PreProfessional Programs in Engineering, Social Work, PreSeminary, Teacher Education, other Liberal Arts Fields

Men's Athletic Profile

800 North Columbia
Seward, NE 68434
Coach: Bill Schranz
Email: bschranz@seward.cone.edu

NAIA
Bulldogs/Navy, White
Phone: (800)535-5494 x-7363
Fax: (402) 643-3966

Estimated # of Men's Soccer Scholarships: 7
Conference: Great Plains Athletic Conference
Program Profile: Academics and Christian commitment are priorities. Players are committed to developing techniques and physical abilities year round. New lighted stadium completed in 1992 with natural surface 120x75 field.
History: Our program began in the 1970 and has been a varsity since the early 1980's. A young squad in 1996, 18 of the 21 players Fr. and So. (6-9-2).
Achievements: Various All-American Honors, All-American Scholor Athletes, All-Conference Honors, Bernie Ochoa named 2000 GPAC Co-Player of the Year and to the NAIA Region 4 Team.
Coaching: Bill Schranz Head Coach 20 years experience. Coaching youth through college national coaching license.
Roster In State: 11 **Out of State:** 9 **Out of Country:** 0
Walk-on/Other: 0 **Graduation %:** 100 **Seniors on Team:** 2
Positions Needed: ALL
Camp or Clinic Dates: Not Available
Most Recent Record: 12-7-0
Schedule: National American, Hastings, Nebraska Wesleyan, Parks (MO)
Style of Play: Depends on personnel and their abilities.

Women's Athletic Profile

800 N. Columbia Ave
Seward, NE 68434
Coach: Bill Schranz
Email: bschranz@seward.cune.edu

NAIA
Bulldogs/Navy, White
Phone: (800) 535-5494
Fax: (402) 643-3966

Estimated # of Women's Soccer Scholarships: 15
Conference: Great Plains Athletic Association
Program Profile: Academics and Christian commitment are priorities. Players are committed to developing techniques and physical abilities year round. New lighted stadium completed in 1997 with a 120x75 natural surface field.
History: Program made its beginning in 1995.
Achievements: All-American Scholar athlete honors, All-Conference honors
Coaching: Bill Schranz, Head Coach, 20 years experience coaching youth through college. National coaching license. Assistant: Janet Myers, Head Coach at Norris High School.
Roster in State: 3 **Out of State:** 14 **Out of Country:** 0
Walk-on/Other: **Graduation %:** 100 **Seniors on Team:** 7
Positions Needed: All
Camp or Clinic Dates: Not Available
Most Recent Record: 7-12-0
Schedule: Parks, Hastings, National American, Nebraska Wesleyan
Style of Play: Varied, depends on personnel.

Dana College

Academic Profile

Phone: (402) 426-7272

Blair, NE 68008

Type: 4 Yr.,Private,Liberal Arts
Website: http://www.acad2.dana.edu
SAT/ACT/GPA: 18/2.5
Student/Faculty Ratio: 13:1
Undergraduate Enrollment: 600
Scholarships/Academic: Yes **Athletic:** Yes
Expenses by: Year **In State:** $ 16,800
Degrees Conferred: BA, BS
Programs of Study: Contact school for program of study.

Founded: 1884
Religion: Lutheran
Housing: Yes
Male/Female Ratio: 60:40
Graduate Enrollment: N/A
Financial Aid: Yes
Out of State: $ 16,800

Women's Athletic Profile

2848 College Drive
Blair, NE 68008
Coach: Todd Wick
Email: twick@acad2.dana.edu

NAIA
Vikings/Scarlet, White
Phone: (402) 426-7367
Fax: (402) 426-7299

Estimated # of Women's Soccer Scholarships: None
Conference: Nebraska Iowa Athletic Conference
Program Profile: In just 5 years, Dana has developed into a quality program. We have a stadium field that measures 120 x 75 yards. We have a new practice field that will be finished by the year 2000.
History: Our program began in 1996. We are in our 5th year. Dana College has solid fundamental players. We finished 2nd in Conference and we have a promising future.
Achievements: 4 Coach of the Year; ODP Coach; Regional Coach of the Year.
Coaching: Todd Wick, Head Coach, was a four time high school Coach of the Year.. Mariann Andersen is the Assistant Coach.
Walk-on/Other: **Graduation %:** 100 **Seniors on Team:** 5
Positions Needed: All
Camp or Clinic Dates: Not Available
Most Recent Record: 17-4-0
Style of Play: We play quickly out of the back looking for solid possession in the midfield, with a creative flair. Our forwards are risk takers . Our players are looking for a lot of shots.

Doane College

Academic Profile

Phone:

Crete, NE 68333

Type: 4 Yr.,Private,Liberal Arts
Website: http://www.doane.edu
SAT/ACT/GPA: NAIA eligibility required/2.0
Student/Faculty Ratio: 15:1
Undergraduate Enrollment: 915
Scholarships/Academic: Yes **Athletic:** Yes
Expenses by: Year **In State:** $ 14,420

Founded: 1872
Religion: Church of Christ
Housing: Yes
Male/Female Ratio: 1:1
Graduate Enrollment: 200
Financial Aid: Yes
Out of State: $ 14,420

Specialty: Education, Business
Degrees Conferred: BA, BS, M
Programs of Study: Accounting, Biological Science, Business Administration, Chemistry, Communications, Computer Science, Elementary Education, English, Environmental Science, German, Human Services, International Studies, Management, Philosophy, Physical Science, Political Science, Psychology, Public Administration, Science, Social Science, Special Education

Men's Athletic Profile

1014 Boswell Avenue
Crete, NE 68333
Coach: Marty Shields
Email: mlshields@hotmail.com

NIAC
Tigers/Orange, Black
Phone: (402) 826-8622
Fax: (402) 826-8647

Estimated # of Men's Soccer Scholarships: 10
Conference: GPAC
Program Profile: The Doane Soccer program is a NAIA II school that plays in the Great Plains Athletic Conference. There are 9 men's soccer programs. The Tigers play a full 20 game schedule with home games having the luxiary of 2 game fields. "The Den" soccer complex is a grass field 75yd x120yd and "Simon Field" is the field turf Football field that has lights and seating of 2000.
History: Doane College began varsity soccer in 1996. The program has made steady improvement during the 5 years of exsistance. The past 2 years have been above 500 win/loss percentage while improving the quality of opponents. The program plays in region IV of the NAIA. 2000 Doane Tigers were runners up in the conference tourney, getting beat in OT of the conference final.
Achievements: Runners-up in the conference tournament 2000, Academic All-Americans the past 2 seasons, Conference chairman 1999.
Coaching: Marty Shields Head Men's Coach, Eliot Siegman Assistant Head Coach, Greg Jarosik Student Assistant Coach.

Roster In State: 14	**Out of State:** 10	**Out of Country:** 0
ODP State: 15	**Regional:** 3	**National:** 0
Walk-on/Other:	**Graduation %:** 80	**Seniors on Team:** 7

Positions Needed: Sweeper, Stopper, GK, outside MF
Camp or Clinic Dates: June 6-9, 2000
Most Recent Record: 12-10-0
Schedule: Baker Univ. (KS), Park Univ. (MO), Hastings College (NE), Missouri Baptist College (MO), Huron Univ. Benedictine College (KS), McKendree College (IL), Nebraska Wesleyan (NE), St. Mary's College (KS) Friends Univ (KS)
Style of Play: Aggressive attacking with fast attacking players. We play ball on ground with one/two touch feet to feet passes. Our team is attempting to develop an improved "build up" to go along with our counter attack.

Women's Athletic Profile

1014 Boswell Avenue
Crete, NE 68333
Coach: Elliot Siegman
Email: esiegman@doane.edu

NAIA
Tigers/Orange, Black
Phone: (402) 826-8622
Fax: (402) 826-8600

Estimated # of Women's Soccer Scholarships: 10
Conference: Great Plains Athletic Conference (GPAC)
Program Profile: Excellent field conditions, natural grass with a measurements of 120x75 fenced in field with soccer scoreboard. New astro-turf field being constructed in 1500-seat stadium.
History: Our program began in 1996 and has improved and become stronger with player participation from 5 different states.

Achievements: We earned Coach of the Year in 1997. We have had All-American Scholar Athlete in 1999, numerous All-Region players and NIAC Player of the Year in 1999.
Coaching: Elliot Siegman is our Head Coach. Marty Shields is our Assistant Coach.
Roster in State: 9 **Out of State:** 7 **Out of Country:** 0
ODP State: 2 **Regional:** 0 **National:** 0
Walk-on/Other: 0 **Graduation %:** 95 **Seniors on Team:**
Positions Needed: Goalkeeper, Midfielder, Sweeper
Camp or Clinic Dates: Not Available
Most Recent Record: 12-10-0
Schedule: University of Mobile, William Carey College, College of St. Mary, Benedictine college, Friends University, Nebraska Wesleyan, Hasting College, Dordt College
Style of Play: We defend and attack as a team. We use combination play off-short and long pass combinations. We believe in using the pass to set up the dribble.

Hastings College
Academic Profile

Hasting, NE 68901
Phone:

Type: 4 Yr.,Private,Liberal Arts **Founded:** 1882
Website: http://www.hasting.com **Religion:** Presbyterian
SAT/ACT/GPA: 20/2.0 **Housing:** Yes
Student/Faculty Ratio: 13:1 **Male/Female Ratio:** 1.5:1
Undergraduate Enrollment: 1,100 **Graduate Enrollment:** N/A
Scholarships/Academic: Yes **Athletic:** Yes **Financial Aid:** No
Expenses by: Year **In State:** $ 17,004 **Out of State:** $ 17,004
Degrees Conferred: BA, MA, BM, MAT
Programs of Study: Contact school for program of study.

Men's Athletic Profile

7th and Turner Avenue
Hasting, NE 68901
Coach: Chris Kranje
Email: ckranje@hasting.edu

NAIA
Broncos/Red, White
Phone: 402-461-7707
Fax: (402) 461-7489

Estimated # of Men's Soccer Scholarships: 5
Conference: Great Plains Athletic Conference
Program Profile: The Broncos will begin there season in the fall and play have an 18 game schedule. We will be playing in a new stadium that will be ready in the fall. The stadium will seat 3,000 and is a turf field.
History: The program began in 1996. By 1997 the team had won the regular season conference title. In 1998 the qualified for the post season and in 1999 we qualified for the Region IV tournament for the first time ever.
Achievements: In 1997 we were the conference champions. We have 6 All-Conference players since 1996 and 2 All-American Honorable Mentions in 1998. We also were the Region IV Qualifier.
Coaching: Geoff VanDeusen, Head Coach, graduated from Western Illinois University, NCAA Division I. He was an assistant at Western Illinois University for two years. Chris Kranjc - Assistant Coach.
Style of Play: Possession and 4-4-2 style of play.

Women's Athletic Profile

800 Turner Avenue
Hasting, NE 68902
Coach: Dale Behrens
Email: dbehrens@hastings.edu

NAIA
Broncos/Red, White
Phone: (402) 461-7339
Fax: (402) 461-7490

Estimated # of Women's Soccer Scholarships: 8
Conference: Great Plains Athletic Conference
Program Profile: Play home games on field turf in a stadium, the field is 75x115. Practice on the stadium field turf and nearby natural grass field. Eighteen regular season games plus post-season tournaments. Off season indoor schedule and limited number of spring scrimmages.
History: 1996- First year of program. Finished 2nd in the conference and conference tournament. Record 11-6. 1997- Finished 3rd in the conference and conference tournament. Record 9-9-1, 1998 Finished 2nd in the conference and conference tournament. Record 15-5. 1999 Finished 2nd in the conference and 1st in the conference tournament, played in regional tournament, record 12-9. 2000- Finished 1st in the conference, 1st in the conference tournament, lost in the finals of the regional tournament. Record 18-4.
Achievements: 1996- one NAIA Academic All-American. 1999- four NAIA Academic All-Americans, Conference Coach of the Year. 2000- five NAIA Academic All-Americans, Conference Coach of the Year.
Coaching: Dale Behrens, Head Coach. Chris Page, Assistant Coach.
Roster in State: 17 **Out of State:** 7 **Out of Country:** 0
Walk-on/Other: 0 **Graduation %:** **Seniors on Team:** 8
Positions Needed: GK, Center Midfielders, Forwards
Camp or Clinic Dates: Not Available
Most Recent Record: 18-4-0
Schedule: College of St. Mary (NE), Huron Univ. Nebraska Wesleyan Univ. Park College, Univ. of Mary, Dordt College, Friends Univ. Bethany College, Dana College.
Style of Play: Possession-oriented and build from the back. Use the flat-back four defense.

Midland Lutheran College

Academic Profile

Fremont, NE 68025
Phone:

Type: 4 Yr.,Private,Liberal Arts
Founded: 1883
Website: http://www.mlc.edu
Religion: Lutheran
SAT/ACT/GPA: Top half
Housing: No
Student/Faculty Ratio: 18:1
Male/Female Ratio: 2:3
Undergraduate Enrollment: 1,025
Graduate Enrollment: N/A
Scholarships/Academic: Yes **Athletic:** Yes **Financial Aid:** Yes
Expenses by: Year **In State:** $ 14,000 **Out of State:** $ 14,000
Degrees Conferred: AA, BA, BS, BBA, BSN
Programs of Study: Contact school for program of study.

Women's Athletic Profile

900 N. Clarkson Street
Freemont, NE 68025
Coach: Ron Lau
Email: Not Available

NAIA
Warriors/Black, Orange
Phone: (402) 721-5480
Fax: (402) 721-9406

Estimated # of Women's Soccer Scholarships: None
Conference: Nebraska-Iowa Intercollegiate Conference
Program Profile: Beginning our fourth year of a women's program. We have a practice field near campus and a very nice soccer complex for our games on natural grass. It is a Fall sport beginning mid-August for pre-season, games and conference tournament through the first week in November.
History: The program began in the Fall of 1995 as a club team. It remained a club team in 1996. then in 1997 it became a varsity sport.
Achievements: Two Academic All-Americans each year for the last 3 years. Coach Lau holds a national coaching certificate.

Coaching: Ron Lau, Head Coach, entering four years with the program. He coached for eight years at Fremont High girls soccer team. and holds National Coaching Certificate. He began and coached Fremont Soccer Club 12 years ago.

Roster in State: 17 **Out of State:** 4 **Out of Country:** 0
ODP State: 0 **Regional:** 0 **National:** 0
Walk-on/Other: **Graduation %:** 100 **Seniors on Team:** 0
Positions Needed: ALL
Camp or Clinic Dates: Not Available
Most Recent Record: 3-14
Schedule: Nebraska Wesleyan, Doane, Hastings, Dordt, York
Style of Play: We play a 4-4-2 or 4-3-3 system. I like to try to get in as many players as the rules permit.

Nebraska Wesleyan University

Academic Profile

Lincoln, NE 68504
Phone: (402)466-2371

Type: 4 Yr.,Private,Liberal Arts **Founded:** 1887
Website: http://www.nebwesleyan.edu **Religion:** United Methodist
SAT/ACT/GPA: **Housing:** Yes
Student/Faculty Ratio: 14:1 **Male/Female Ratio:** 41/59
Undergraduate Enrollment: 1,682 **Graduate Enrollment:** N/A
Scholarships/Academic: Yes **Athletic:** No **Financial Aid:** Yes
Expenses by: Year **In State:** $16,716 **Out of State:** $16,716
Degrees Conferred: BA, BS
Programs of Study: Full Liberal Arts and PreProfessional Curriculum; Applied Music, Art, Biology, BioChemistry, Business Administration, Business Psychology, Business, Sociology, Chemistry, Communications, Computer Science, Economics, Elementary Education, English, French, German, Health/Physical Science, History, International Business, Mathematics, Music, Physics, Political Science, Psychology, Physical Education, Philosophy, Sport Management

Men's Athletic Profile

5000 St. Paul Ave.
Lincoln, NE 68504-2796
Coach: John Carlson
Email: JPC@nebrwesleyan.edu

NCAA III
Plainsmen/Yellow, Brown
Phone: (402) 465-7516
Fax: (402) 465-2170

Estimated # of Men's Soccer Scholarships:
Conference: Great Plains Athletic Conference
Program Profile: The Plainsmen play in the 5,000 seat, multi-purpose Abel Stadium on the Nebraska Wesleyan campus. It features a natural grass surface and was constructed in 1986.
History: Program began in 1993 with over 55 wins in the last three years; 19-0 in 1999 and 20-2 record in 1998.
Achievements: The team has received all of the following in the past few years: "COY", Anore Watts, NIAC Player of the year, 7 1st team All-American Players, Watts, GTE Academic All-American and Regional team.
Roster In State: 24 **Out of State:** 1 **Out of Country:** 0
ODP State: 22 **Regional:** 2 **National:**
Walk-on/Other: **Graduation %:** 95 **Seniors on Team:** 4
Positions Needed: Midfielder, Forwards
Camp or Clinic Dates: Not Available
Most Recent Record: 19-0-0
Schedule: MaCallister, Gustauus, Simpson College, St. Johns University, Concovnia College, Hasting College
Style of Play: Aggressive, attacking. style of players: love the play.

Women's Athletic Profile

5000 St. Paul Ave.
Lincoln, NE 68504-2796
Coach: Brett Rosenberger
Email: Not Available

NCAA III
Plainswomen/Yellow, Brown
Phone: (402) 465-2372
Fax: (402) 465-2170

Estimated # of Women's Soccer Scholarships: None
Conference: Nebraska-Iowa Athletic Conference
Program Profile: The fall of 1998 will mark the fifth season of the NWU women's soccer. We practice and play on a natural grass with a games in the Abel Stadium, which seats for 2,000. The college practice season is played in the fall, along with all non-traditional schedule in the Spring semester.
History: The program began in the fall of 1993. The cumulative four years record of the program is 55-22-1 with a total of four winning seasons and two NAIA Top Twenty finishes. NIAC Conference Champion in 1996, the first year of conference play. Highest team grade point average (3.53) of any collegiate team in the nation in 1995-1996. Won two Team Athletic Awards of MVP from the NSCAA in 1993 and 1996.
Achievements: 5 NAIA All-Americans; 9 NAIA Scholar Athletes All-Americans; 7 All-Conference Players in 1996, the first year of conference play. Doug Williamson, NIAC Coach of the Year in 1996; NSCAA Team Ethic Awards of Merit in 1993 and 1996.
Style of Play: Aggressive attacking style combining both indirect and direct style of play, with a strong ball or hold. Defensively we will use combination of one-on-one marking and zone depending on the opponent. Can play high and low pressure defense.

University of Nebraska - Lincoln

Academic Profile

Phone: 402-672-7211

Lincoln, NE 68588-0243

Type: 4 Yr.,Public,Liberal Arts,Engineering
Website: http://www.huskerwebcast.com
SAT/ACT/GPA: 850/20/2.0
Student/Faculty Ratio: 17:1
Undergraduate Enrollment: 25,000
Scholarships/Academic: Yes **Athletic:** Yes
Expenses by: Year **In State:** $ 6,812

Founded: 1869
Religion: Non-Affiliated
Housing: Yes
Male/Female Ratio: 54:46
Graduate Enrollment: 5,100
Financial Aid: Yes
Out of State: $ 10,585

Specialty: Agriculture, Education, Journalism
Degrees Conferred: AS, BA, BFA, BS, BBA, BJ, BSAE, BSBSE, MBA
Programs of Study: Office of admissions: 1410 Q Street, P.O. Box 880417
Lincoln, NE 68588-0417
Phone: 402-472-2023 or 800-742-8800

Women's Athletic Profile

1410 Q Street, P.O. Box 880417
Lincoln, NE 68588-0243
Coach: John Walker
Email: jwalker@huskey.unl.edu

NCAA I
Cornhuskers/Scarlet, Cream
Phone: (402) 472-0456
Fax: (402) 472-0455

Estimated # of Women's Soccer Scholarships: 12
Conference: Big 12 Conference
Program Profile: Nebraska has placed itself among the top programs in the nation by advancing to four consecutive NCAA Sweet 16's, including Elite Eight appearances in 1996 and 1999. The Huskers have also finished each of the last four years ranked in the final NSCAA Top 10, including a 22-1-2 record and final No.5 ranking in 1999. The Huskers average 1,529 fans at the Abbott Sports Complex in 1999. NU plays on natural grass with a seating capacity of 2,500.

History: The program is entering its seventh season in 2000 with a 104-22-3 record overall. The Huskers have won three Big 12 Tournaments titles and two Big 12 regular-season championships. Six Huskers have earned nine NSCAA All-American awards the last four seasons. Coach Walker was the NSCAA National and Central Region Coach in 1996. He was also the Central Region Coach of the Year in 1999, to go along with Big 12 Coach of the Year honors. He was also the Big 12 Coach of the Year in 1996.
Achievements: 4 NCAA Tournaments, 4 Sweet 16s, 2 Elite Eights, 4 Straight NSCAA Top 10 Final Rankings, 1996 Coach of the Year; 1996/1999 Central Coach of the Year; 1996/1999 Big 12 Coach of the Year; 9 All-American Awards; 24 First team All-Big 12 Awards; 3 Big 12 Tournaments Titles; 2 Big 12 Regular Season titles; 6 World Cup Participants.
Coaching: John Walker, Head Coach, holds USSF 'A' license, 1 of only 2 Canadians to hold a Canadian 'A' license, Canadian National Staff Coach, Nebraska ODP State Coach. Queens University, 1987), 65-17 (six seasons at Nebraska), 103-45-18 (nine seasons career). Marty Everding - Assistant Coach, (Queens) six seasons at Megan Bechtold (Creighton) five seasons.

Roster in State: 3	**Out of State:** 22	**Out of Country:** 7
ODP State: 15	**Regional:** 10	**National:** 2
Walk-on/Other:	**Graduation %:** 100	**Seniors on Team:** 4

Camp or Clinic Dates: July 16-20, June 26-29, 12-15, July 24-27
Most Recent Record: 22-1-2
Schedule: Florida, Connecticut, Texas A&M, Baylor, Missouri, Texas, Dartmouth, Minnesota
Style of Play: Heavy emphasis on possession, fitness and dominance in the air. Players are encouraged to take risks in the attacking third and to win the ball back early.

University of Nebraska - Omaha

Academic Profile

Phone: 402-554-2800

Lincoln, NE 68588

Type: 4 Yr.,Public		**Founded:** 1908
Website: http://www.unomaha.edu		**Religion:** Non-Affiliated
SAT/ACT/GPA: 21avg		**Housing:** No
Student/Faculty Ratio: 30:1		**Male/Female Ratio:** 48:52
Undergraduate Enrollment: 13,300		**Graduate Enrollment:** 2,588
Scholarships/Academic: Yes	**Athletic:** Yes	**Financial Aid:** Yes
Expenses by: Year	**In State:** $ 2,500	**Out of State:** $ 5,500

Degrees Conferred: AS, BA, BS, BFA, BBA, BGS
Programs of Study: Contact school for program of study.

Women's Athletic Profile

6001 Dodge Street, Athletics Offices
Omaha, NE 68182
Coach: Don Klosterman
Email: don_kloskerman@unomaha.edu

NCAA II
Mavericks/Red, Black
Phone: (402) 554-4962
Fax: (402) 554-2555

Estimated # of Women's Soccer Scholarships: 3-4
Conference: North Central Conference
Program Profile: We have a new facilities this year including academic study room, 8,000 sq ft. weight room, state of the art athletic training facility, new locker room and on campus field that will hold up to 2,000.
History: This program is very new starting only in 1999. It finish 3rd in the conference.
Achievements:
Coaching: Don Klosterman is the Head Coach. He is entering 20 years of coaching at all levels - Division I, men's, NAIA men's and Boy's High School. He holds a US "A" License and NSCAA Advanced Diploma. Tanya Frank is the full-time Assistant Coach. He was a former All-American at Nebraska. He played on Canadian World Cup Team in 1999.

Roster in State: 14 **Out of State:** 4 **Out of Country:** 0
ODP State: 12 **Regional:** 0 **National:**
Walk-on/Other: **Graduation %:** **Seniors on Team:** 3
Positions Needed: Midfield, Striker
Camp or Clinic Dates: Not Available
Most Recent Record: 14-5-0
Schedule: Northern Colorado, Truman State, SIU-E, North Dakota State, Minnesota State, Northern Iowa
Style of Play: 3-4-3 very attack oriented. We scored over 60 goals in 1999.

Wayne State College

Academic Profile

Wayne, NE 68787
Phone:

Type: 4 Yr.,Public
Founded: 1910
Website: http://www.wsc.edu
Religion: Non-Affiliated
SAT/ACT/GPA: Open Admission2.0
Housing: Yes
Student/Faculty Ratio: 17:1
Male/Female Ratio: 44:56
Undergraduate Enrollment: 13,300
Graduate Enrollment: 725
Scholarships/Academic: Yes **Athletic:** Yes **Financial Aid:** Yes
Expenses by: Year **In State:** $ 5,733 **Out of State:** $ 7,518
Specialty: Education, Business
Degrees Conferred: BA, BS, BFA, MA, MS, MBA
Programs of Study: Art, Business, Chemistry, Computers, Computer Science, Criminal Justice, Early Childhood, English, Exercise Science, Family & Consumer Sciences, Food Services, Geography, History, Counseling, Industrial Tech, Life Sciences, Mass Communications, Math, Modern Languages, Music, Political Science, Psychology, Social Sciences, Sociology, Speech Communications, Sports Management, Technology, Theatre and many major inside of these broad subject.

Women's Athletic Profile

1111 Main Street
Wayne, NE 68787
Coach: Justin S. Cole
Email: jcole@wscgate.wsc.edu

NAIA
Wildcats/Black, Gold
Phone: (402) 375-7506
Fax: (402) 375-7120

Estimated # of Women's Soccer Scholarships: 2.5
Conference: Northern Sun Intercollegiate Conference
Program Profile: We are finishing our second season as a varsity sport. We play games during the fall season on the WSC soccer field of natural grass. We do a condition and workout in the off-season. We play a limited schedule in the spring. We are enthusiastic about the future as we are gaining support of the athletic department, school and community. Led NSIC in attendance during the 2000 season.
History: Our first season was in 1997. Our record in 1998-1999 was 6-5. 2000 18-4-1, 17-2-0 in NSIC (3rd reg. Season and conference tournament runner up) 7th in the Central Region Final Rankings.
Achievements: 2000 NSIC Runner-up, NSIC Coach of the Year in 2000.
Coaching: Justin Cole, Head Coach, is finishing his third season as head coach of the Wildcats. Cole took a team that was winless in their inaugural campaign to a 6-5 in just one year. Cole has a full-year now to recruit and further build the foundation he has began. Cole was a keeper and defender during his playing days. He lived in the Netherlands for four years.
Roster in State: 16 **Out of State:** 7 **Out of Country:** 0
ODP State: 0 **Regional:** 0 **National:** 0
Walk-on/Other: 0 **Graduation %:** 90-95 **Seniors on Team:** 1
Positions Needed: Forward, Midfiled, Defender

Camp or Clinic Dates: Not Available
Most Recent Record: 18-4-1
Schedule: Nebraska-Omaha, Minnesota-Duluth, Southwest State, South Dakota
Style of Play: Aggressive and opportunistic offense (14th in D.II in 99 and 11th in the nation in 2000) completed with a high-pressure defense.

York College

Academic Profile

Phone:

York, NE 68467

Type: 4 Yr.,Private,Liberal Arts
Founded: 1890
Website: hhtp://www.york.edu
Religion: Church of Christ
SAT/ACT/GPA: 820/18
Housing: Yes
Student/Faculty Ratio: 12:1
Male/Female Ratio: 1.4:1
Undergraduate Enrollment: 505
Graduate Enrollment: N/A
Scholarships/Academic: Yes **Athletic:** Yes
Financial Aid: Yes
Expenses by: Year **In State:** $ 11,300
Out of State: $ 11,300
Specialty: Education, Bible Studies, Business
Degrees Conferred: Associates, Bachelors
Programs of Study: Education, Business Administration, Bible Studies, Psychology, General Sciences, Accounting, Finance, Management, Human Resources Management, Communications, English, Liberal Arts

Men's Athletic Profile

912 Kiplinger Ave.
York, NE 68467
Coach: Chris Luther
Email: cluther@york.edu

NAIA
Panthers/Royal, Blue
Phone: (402) 363-5635
Fax: (402) 363-5738

Estimated # of Men's Soccer Scholarships: N/A
Conference: MCAC
Program Profile: We play on a natural grass in a stadium that has a seating capacity of 1,000. It is located on campus.
History: The Panthers have above a 75% winning percentage since 1989. York offers a quality program which started in Mid-1970's.
Achievements: Won National Small College Tournament in 1990 & 1992.

Women's Athletic Profile

912 Kiplinger Avenue
York, NE 68467
Coach: Kim McDaniel
Email: Not Available

NAIA
Panthers/Royal, Blue
Phone: (402) 362-5601
Fax: (402) 362-5738

Estimated # of Women's Soccer Scholarships: None
Conference: Midland Classic Athletic Conference
Program Profile: We play on a natural grass that seats a 1,000. It is located on campus.
History: None
Achievements: None
Coaching: Kim McDaniel, Head Coach, played at Oklahoma Christian All-District, All-Region, Honorable Mention All-American.

nevada

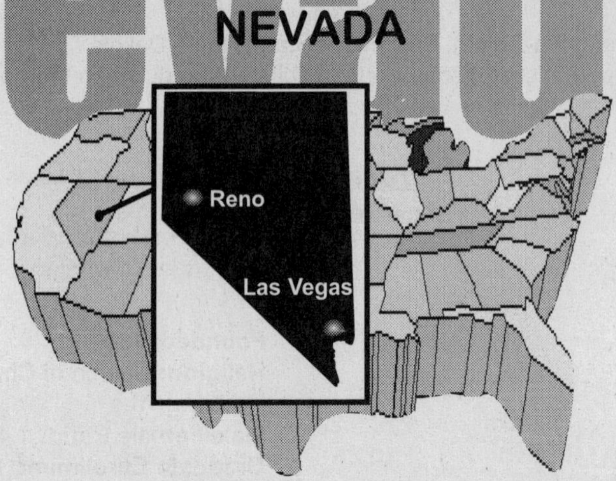

SCHOOL	CITY	AFFILIATION	PAGE
University of Nevada - Las Vegas	Las Vegas	NCAA I	641

University of Nevada - Las Vegas

Academic Profile

Phone:

Las Vegas, NV 89154

Type: 4 Yr.,Public
Website: http://www.unly.edu
SAT/ACT/GPA: 820/18
Student/Faculty Ratio: 25;1
Undergraduate Enrollment: 14,350
Scholarships/Academic: Yes
Athletic: Yes
Financial Aid: Yes
Expenses by: Year
In State: $ 7,000
Out of State: $ 12,000
Founded: 1957
Religion: Non-Affiliated
Housing: No
Male/Female Ratio: 46:54
Graduate Enrollment: 5,350
Specialty:
Degrees Conferred: BA, BS, BFA, BArch, MA, MS, MBA, MFA, M.Ed., Ph.D.
Programs of Study: Accounting, Anthropology, Applied Mathematics, Architecture, Art, Biochemistry, Biology, Botany, Management, Comparative Literature, Geography, Geology, Industrial, Insurance, Linguistics, Recreation, Romance Languages, Travel, Zoology

Men's Athletic Profile

4505 Maryland Pkwy
Las Vegas, NV 89154
Coach: Barry Barto
Email: dconnelly@ccmail.nevada.edu

NCAA I
Rebels/Scarlet, Gray
Phone: (702) 895-4175
Fax: (702) 895-0989

Estimated # of Men's Soccer Scholarships: None
Conference: Mountain Pacific Sports Federation
Program Profile: Season lasts from the end of August to the first week in December. Games are mostly on Friday & Sunday. We travel all over the U.S. UNLV is the only soccer program with soccer only building; locker rooms, training room, equipment room, located next to 2,500 seat stadium.
History: Program began in 1974. Barto is the 3rd coach and the program has had only 1 losing season since 1982.
Achievements: Advanced to NCAA Tourney 5 times, last one in 1988; 2 All - Americans; 3 conference titles; 1985 NCAA West Regional Final.
Coaching: Barry Barto, Head Coach, 22nd year coaching, 16th at UNLV, 6 years at Philadelphia Textile, produced 11 All - Americans, has made 11 NCAA Tournament appearances, advanced to 2 Final Fours, 1972 runner-up NASL Rookie of the Year, Captain of US National Team-1974 and 1975.
Style of Play: Fast pace attacking style of play where we dictate the tempo and the action. Everyone needs to work hard and leave it all on the playing field. A style similar to Brazil with lots of goals and solid defense.

Women's Athletic Profile

4505 Maryland Parkway
Las Vegas, NV 89154
Coach: Dan Abdalls
Email: abdalld1@nevada.edu

NCAA I
Rebels/Scarlet, Grey
Phone: (702) 895-4176
Fax: (702) 895-1686

Estimated # of Women's Soccer Scholarships: 4
Conference: Mountain West Conference
Program Profile: A young driven program committed to competing at the highest level of women's college soccer. Peter Johann Memorial field is generally regarded as one of the top college soccer facilities in the west and boasts seating for approx. 2500 with a tremendous natural grass pitch, a press box, Locke room and lights for evening matches.
History: 2000 will be the third season for women's soccer at UNLV. The previous two seasons have produced a solid foundation with very respectable records and also include being ranked third in the nation for first year programs in 1998.

Achievements: 1998 WAC Freshman of the Year.
1998 Nationally ranked 3rd for 1st year programs.
Coaching: Head Coach Abdalla is a former UNLV soccer standout still posting many records at the University. 2000 will be his first as head coach coming off a three year professional soccer career. Assistant coach Maren Hendershot was a two-time All-American Striker at Brigham Young University and is entering her first year on the UNLV staff.

Roster in State: 10	**Out of State:** 14	**Out of Country:** 0
ODP State: 14	**Regional:** 2	**National:** 0
Walk-on/Other:	**Graduation %:** N/A	**Seniors on Team:** 3

Positions Needed: All, but emphasis on defenders
Camp or Clinic Dates: Not Available
Most Recent Record: 7-11-1
Schedule: Arizona State, BYU, San Diego State, Utah, Loyola Marymount
Style of Play: Very possession oriented, while attacking from the back with numbers. Physically strong and tenacious defensively.

new hampshire

NEW HAMPSHIRE

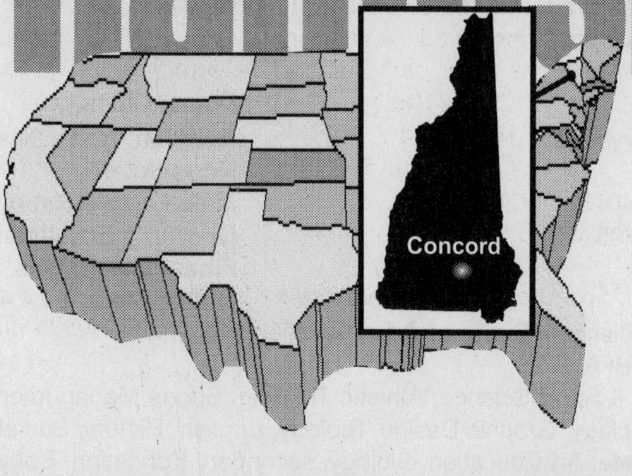

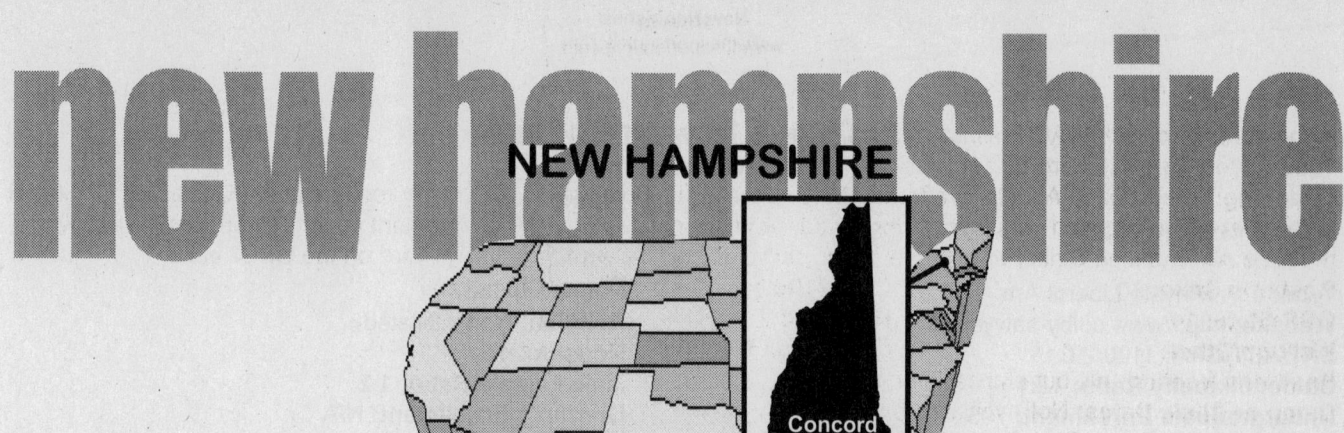

SCHOOL	CITY	AFFILIATION	PAGE
Colby - Sawyer College	New London	NCAA III	644
Daniel Webster College	Nashua	NCAA III	645
Dartmouth College	Hanover	NCAA I	646
Franklin Pierce College	Rindge	NCAA II	647
Keene State College	Keene	NCAA II	649
New England College	Henniker	NCAA III	650
New Hampshire College	Manchester	NCAA II	651
Notre Dame College	Manchester	NAIA	652
Plymouth State College	Plymouth	NCAA III	653
Rivier College	Nashua	NCAA III	654
Saint Anselm College	Manchester	NCAA II	655
Univ of New Hampshire	Durham	NCAA I	656

Colby - Sawyer College

Academic Profile

Phone:

New London, NH 03257

Type: 4 Yr.,Private,Liberal Arts
Founded: 1837
Website: http://www.colby-sawyer.edu
Religion: Non-Affiliated
SAT/ACT/GPA: 1100/2.0
Housing: Yes
Student/Faculty Ratio: 12:1
Male/Female Ratio: 1:2
Undergraduate Enrollment: 793
Graduate Enrollment: N/A
Scholarships/Academic: Yes **Athletic:** No
Financial Aid: Yes
Expenses by: Year **In State:** $ 24,400 **Out of State:** $ 24,400
Specialty: Exercise & Sport Sciences, Business Administration, Nursing
Degrees Conferred: BA, BS, BFA, AAS
Programs of Study: Exercise & Sport Science, Athletic Training, Sports Management, Exercise Science, Communications Study, Psychology, Graphic Design, Biology, English, History, Society and Culture, Art, Nursing, Child Development, Teacher Certificate, Art Education, Biology Secondary Education, Early Childhood Education, English Secondary Education, Social Science, Secondary Education

Men's Athletic Profile

100 Main Street
New London, NH 03257
Coach: Peter Steese
Email: psteese@Colby-Sawyer.edu

NCAA III
Chargers/R. Blue, White, Black
Phone: (603) 526-3611
Fax: (603) 526-3435

Estimated # of Men's Soccer Scholarships: None
Conference: Commonwealth Coast Conference
Program Profile: Our program is considered among top 15 in New England. In addition to being a member of Commonwealth Coast Conference, Colby Sawyer is also a member of the ECAC. Mercer Field is a natural grass surface measuring 120x75 yards. It is serves as home game field, along with an addition of a new game field on newly developed 45 acres. Its season is conducted in accordance with NCAA guidelines.
History: Our program began in 1990 with an overall record of 87-69-21. We had Conference Tournament record of 6-3-1. We received votes for one of the top ten in New England in 1997. Our 1998 opponents included 6 regionally ranked and nationally ranked teams.
Achievements: We had 3 NEISL Senior All-Star Game, 1 CCC Player of the Year, 2 CCC Senior Scholar Athlete, 7 First team All-CCC, 4 second team All-CCC, Regular Season Champs, Conference Champs Tournament, 1 Professional Player and 1 ECAC Award of Valor Winner.
Coaching: Peter Steese, Head Coach since 1990. He is NCAA Premier License and a USSF "B" License. He is semi-professional player and NCAA Division I player. He is New Hampshire ODP Staff and Director of Unitor Soccer School. he is also, a Chair NEISL Honors Committee and CCC-NCAA Liason. Kris Galuzzo is the Assistant Coach.
Style of Play: Combination Play.

Women's Athletic Profile

100 Main Street
New London, NH 03257
Coach: Jill Donavan
Email: jdonovan@colby-swayer.edu

NCAA III
Chargers/Royal, White
Phone: (603) 526-3605
Fax: (603) 526-3435

Estimated # of Women's Soccer Scholarships: None
Conference: Commonwealth Coast Conference

Program Profile: We play at Mercer Field which has a seating capacity of 350 and has natural grass. We are a competitive Division III soccer program. We play 13 conference teams and 5 non-conference teams. Playing season runs from the end of August through mid-November. Have added a new field for 2000 season.
History: Our program began in 1980. We have consistently been a very competitive women's program.
Achievements: 1 NEWISA Sr. All-Star; Several Regional All-Americans
Roster in State: 3 **Out of State:** 20 **Out of Country:** 0
Walk-on/Other: **Graduation %:** **Seniors on Team:** 4
Positions Needed: ALL
Camp or Clinic Dates: Not Available
Most Recent Record: 9-9-1
Schedule: Middlebury, Plymouth State, Univ. of New England, Anna Maria College
Style of Play: Strong defensive team, cohesive team.

Daniel Webster College

Academic Profile

Nashua, NH 06063-1300
Phone: (800) 325-6876

Type: 4 Yr.,Private
Founded: 1965
Website: http://www.dwc.edu
Religion: Non-Affiliated
SAT/ACT/GPA: 1050
Housing: Yes
Student/Faculty Ratio: 14:1
Male/Female Ratio: 4:1
Undergraduate Enrollment: 450
Graduate Enrollment: N/A
Scholarships/Academic: Yes **Athletic:** No
Financial Aid: Yes
Expenses by: Year **In State:** $ 22,083
Out of State: $ 22,083
Specialty: Aviation, Business, Computer Science, Engineering
Degrees Conferred: BS
Programs of Study: Air Traffic Control, Aviation Management, Aviation Flight Operations, Business and Management, Computer Science, Computer Systems, Engineering, Engineering Science, Flight Operations, Sports Management

Men's Athletic Profile

20 University Drive
Nashua, NH 03063-1300
Coach: Corlton Simmond
Email: simmond@dwc.edu

NCAA III
Eagles/Blue, White
Phone: (603) 577-6497
Fax: (603) 577-6001

Estimated # of Men's Soccer Scholarships: None
Conference: Great Northeast Athletic Conference
Program Profile: Greatly improving program that is competitive with some of the top teams in Division III in New England. The Daniel Webster Soccer Field is one of the best in New England. The weather is Nashua in the fall is perfect for soccer.
History: Program began in 1965.
Style of Play: Attacking and aggressive, very offensive minded.

Women's Athletic Profile

20 University Drive
Nashua, NH 03063-1300
Coach: Jim Lipocky
Email: lipocky@dwc.edu

NCAA III
Eagles/Navy, White, Red
Phone: (603) 577-6495
Fax: (603) 577-6001

Estimated # of Women's Soccer Scholarships: None
Conference: Great Northeast Athletic Conference
Program Profile: We are growing and improving program that is going through a youth movement. Our program competes in the GNAC and has a tough conference schedule. Our team plays on a large, natural grass field located on the beautiful fifty acre campus.
History: Our program began in 1994.
Achievements: Sheryl Ayre was selected as Rookie of the Week in 1998.
Coaching: Jim Lipocky is our Head Coach. He coached previously at Felician College (Lodi, New Jersey) and has extensive experience in the premier soccer programs in the Northeast, Ohio. Coach Lipocky holds a USSF "C" License and a NSCAA National Diploma.
Style of Play: Our style of play is built around the athletes. Coach encourages individual to play good.

Dartmouth College

Academic Profile

Hanover, NH 03755
Phone: (603) 646-3529

Type: 4 Yr.,Private,Liberal Arts,Engineering
Website: http://www.dartmouth.edu
SAT/ACT/GPA: 1100+
Student/Faculty Ratio: 12:1
Undergraduate Enrollment: 4,200
Scholarships/Academic: No
Athletic: No
Expenses by: Year
In State: $ 31,722
Founded: 1769
Religion: Non-Affiliated
Housing: Yes
Male/Female Ratio: 50:50
Graduate Enrollment: 1,260
Financial Aid: Yes
Out of State: $ 31,722
Degrees Conferred: BA, MA, MS, MBA, Ph.D., MD
Programs of Study: Anthropology, Art, Asian, BioChemistry and Molecular Biology, Biology, BioPhysical, Chemistry, Classical Archaeology, Classics, Cognitive, Comparative Literature, Computer Science, Drama, Economics, Engineering, English, Earth Science, Environmental, Genetics, Geography, Government, Mathematics, Music, Philosophy, Physics, Psychology, Religion, Sociology, Spanish, Women's Studies

Men's Athletic Profile

6083 Alumni Gym
Hanover, NH 03755
Coach: Fran O'Leary
Email: Dartmouth.soccer@dartmouth.edu

NCAA I
Big Green/Green, White
Phone: (603) 646-3545
Fax: (603) 646-3348

Estimated # of Men's Soccer Scholarships:
Conference: Ivy League Conference
Program Profile: Chase Field is 116 x 75 and has natural grass. It has a seating capacity of 3,500. The Soccer Complex includes four full-sized practice fields. Our playing season runs from early September to mid-November. We play 17 regular season games. Off-season, we have training including weight-training, ball work and conditioning.
History: Our program began in 1914. Since 1988, we have won three Ivy League titles and advanced to the NCAA tournament 2nd round three times in the 1990's. This includes quarter-final appearances in 1990 and 1992.
Achievements: Dartmouth has won four Ivy League titles and made six NCAA Tournament Appearances. The program has produced 18 All-Americans including; Matt Nyman 1999 Tampa Bay, and 1998 All-American Bob Neyer, who was also the only Ivy League player drafted in the 1999 MLS draft.
Coaching: Fran O'Leary is our Head Coach. He is in his fifth year after compiling standout records at Elmira College in New York and Kenyon College in Ohio. His Kenyon Team in 1993 was ranked #I in Division III for much of the year and earned an NCAA Tournament semi-final berth. He is certified in the USA and in Ireland. Chris Cheney- Assistant Coach and B.J. Graig- Assistant Coach.
Roster In State: 1
Out of State: 18
Out of Country: 2
ODP State: 10
Regional: 6
National: 1

Walk-on/Other: **Graduation %:** 95 **Seniors on Team:** 6
Positions Needed: All
Camp or Clinic Dates: July 30- August f4
Most Recent Record: 3-9-4
Schedule: Stanford, Brown, Princeton, Yale, UNC- Chapel hill, UNC- Greensboro, Harvard, BU
Style of Play: Dartmouth defends zonal and plays in a 4-4-2 formation.

Women's Athletic Profile

6083 Alumni Gymnasium
Hanover, NH 03755
Coach: Erica Walsh
Email: erica.walsh@dartmouth.edu

NCAA I
Big Green/Green, White
Phone: (603) 646-2178
Fax: (603) 646-3348

Estimated # of Women's Soccer Scholarships: None
Conference: Ivy League
Program Profile: Excellent athletic facilities - five full size grass fields, game fields, game field is 78 x 115 yards, indoor facility, turf. Locker rooms with training room attached, full-time athletic trainer. Stadium holds 3,000 - 4,000. Playing season is September - November and off-season. 2000 overall record 14-5-0, ranked #16 in National Polls. Ivy Champions advanced to 3rd round of 2000 NCAA Tournament.
History: Varsity began in 1979. 1994 - fourth in Northeast Region, 14th in country. Second year in a row to be in Top 20, and win a NCAA Tournament bid. Overall record 176-144-2, 6 NCAA Appearance, and 4 time Ivy league championships including 2000.
Achievements: 1993 - second Ivy Title in past three years. 6 All-Ivy first team 1994, 9 All-Ivy 1993, 6 in 1992, 7 in 1991. 3 All-New England 1994, 2 in 1993 & 1992, 2 in 1990-1991. 1 Academic All-American 1994,1993,1992, 1 in 1989. New England Coach of the Year 1992, nominated for COY New England 1991.
Coaching: Head Coach: Erica Walsh 1st season 14-5-0. Assistant Coaches Ben Landis and Michelle Horbaly.
Roster in State: 1 **Out of State:** 25 **Out of Country:** 0
ODP State: 18 **Regional:** 10 **National:** 1
Walk-on/Other: 0 **Graduation %:** 100 **Seniors on Team:** 7
Positions Needed: F, M, B, GK
Camp or Clinic Dates: July 29-August 3
Most Recent Record: 14-5-0
Schedule: Stanford, Santa Clara, Uconn, Boston College, Boston University, Hartford, Syracuse, Harvard, Princeton, Brown
Style of Play: We utilize our kid's intelligence to play in different systems of play and styles of play that best exemplify our player's talents while exposing our opponents weaknesses.

Franklin Pierce College

Academic Profile

Rindge, NH 03461

Phone:

Type: 4 Yr.,Private,Liberal Arts **Founded:** 1962
Website: http://www.fpc.edu **Religion:** Non-Affiliated
SAT/ACT/GPA: 900 **Housing:** Yes
Student/Faculty Ratio: 20:1 **Male/Female Ratio:** 50:50
Undergraduate Enrollment: 1,495 **Graduate Enrollment:** 150
Scholarships/Academic: Yes **Athletic:** Yes **Financial Aid:** Yes
Expenses by: Year **In State:** $ 23,875 **Out of State:** $ 23,875
Specialty: Liberal Arts
Degrees Conferred: BA, BS, MBA
Programs of Study: 28 majors - 5 Divisions: Humanities, Behavioral Sciences, Natural Science, Business Administration, Visual and Performing Arts

Men's Athletic Profile

P.O. Box 60, College Road
Rindge, NH 03461
Coach:
Email:

NCAA II
Ravens/Crimson, Gray
Phone: (603) 899-4087
Fax: (603) 899-4328

Estimated # of Men's Soccer Scholarships: 3
Conference: Northeast 10
Program Profile: Our pre-season starts in mid-August with a full 20 game schedule. We have a cyrstal rielo grass field which measures 120x75 yards. Our season ends mid-November. We also have a limited spring season.
History: Our program began in 1965. Team has made eight straight National Tournaments. Program has been ranked in the top 10 nationally every year.
Achievements: NCAA II Regional Coach of the Year, 11 straight All-Americans, 39 All-Americans, 8 All-Conference Scoring Champions, 6 Academic All-Americans, and 17 professional players.
Coaching: Tod Silegy, Head Coach, is in his 20th season and holds both NSCAA National and Advanced National Diplomas. Suleyman Doenmeg, John Mitchell and Rich Rollins are the Assistant Coaches.
Roster In State: 1 **Out of State:** 26 **Out of Country:** 11
ODP State: 1 **Regional:** **National:**
Walk-on/Other: **Graduation %:** 92% **Seniors on Team:** 5
Positions Needed: Defense, Midfield
Camp or Clinic Dates: July 9-14, July 23-27
Most Recent Record: 14-6-0
Schedule: So. Connecticut, New Hampshire College, Southampton, Merrimack, IUPU-Fort Wayne, New Haven, Bentley
Style of Play: Semidirect, but very attacking.

Women's Athletic Profile

College Road, P.O. Box 60
Rindge, NH 03461
Coach: Jeff Bailey
Email: baileyj@fpc.edu

NCAA II
Ravens/Crimson, Grey
Phone: (603) 899-4072
Fax: (603) 899-4328

Estimated # of Women's Soccer Scholarships: 5
Conference: New England Collegiate Conference (NECC); Northeast 10 Conference
Program Profile: Play at the highest NCAA Division II level. Train all year including a weight program and indoor soccer. Games are played on natural grass.
History: 1986, Competed as an independent until 1994, when the NECC recognized women's soccer and awarded a conference championship. FPC has not lost to a regional opponent since November 5, 1991. FBC won the 1994, 1995, 1996 and 1997 NCAA Division II Championships. FPC has advanced to seven straight NCAA Tournament semifinals. FPC has defeated 104 straight New England Opponents.
Achievements: NCAA Champions in 1994, 1995, 1996, 1997; NECC Champions same years; 12 All-Americans; 3 NCAA Players of the Year; Jeff Bailey named New England Region Coach of the Year in 1998.
Coaching: Elie Monteiro, third year, Jamie William, second year, Paulina Miettinen, first year.
Roster in State: 1 **Out of State:** 18 **Out of Country:** 7
ODP State: 3 **Regional:** **National:**
Walk-on/Other: **Graduation %:** 100% **Seniors on Team:** 5
Positions Needed: Forward, Defense
Camp or Clinic Dates: Not Available
Most Recent Record: 21-1-0
Schedule: Bloomsburg, Lock Haven, St. Anselm, Merrimack, American International, New Hampshire College

Keene State College

Academic Profile

Phone:

Keene, NH 03435-0002

Type: 4 Yr.,Public,Liberal Arts
Founded: 1909
Website: http://www.keene.edu
Religion: Non-Affiliated
SAT/ACT/GPA: 1000/2.5
Housing: Yes
Student/Faculty Ratio: 21:1
Male/Female Ratio: 2:3
Undergraduate Enrollment: 3,900
Graduate Enrollment: 500
Scholarships/Academic: Yes **Athletic:** No **Financial Aid:** Yes
Expenses by: Year **In State:** $ 10,434 **Out of State:** $ 15,744
Specialty:
Degrees Conferred: Associates, Bachelors, Masters
Programs of Study: American Studies, Biology, Chemistry, Computer Science, Dietetics, Dramatic Arts, Education, English, Environmental Science, Fine Arts, Geography, History, Industrial Technology, Journalism, Mathematics, Music, Music Performance, Political Science, Psychology, Safety Management, Social Science, Spanish, Special Education, Sports Management, Sports Medicine

Men's Athletic Profile

229 Main Street
Keene, NH 03435-0002
Coach: Ron Butcher
Email: Not Available

NCAA II
Owls/Red, White
Phone: 603-358-2805
Fax: (603) 358-2888

Estimated # of Men's Soccer Scholarships: None
Conference: New England Collegiate Conference
Program Profile: Top New England Division II program that is looking to return to post-season tournament. Owls play a highly competitive schedule in the New England Collegiate Conference. Keene State plays at Owl stadium, a lighted omni-turf facility.
History: A program that dates back to the 1948 season, the Keene State soccer team is rich in tradition. Current KSC coach Run Butcher, who has directed the Owls to 17 post-season tournaments in his 26 year tenure, coached his 500th game at Keene State this past year.
Achievements: Over the years, Keene State has had its share of All-American, All-Region and All-New England Players. This past season back Erik Foley was named to the All-New England team and selected to play in the New England Senior game.
Coaching: Ron Butcher, Head Coach since 1970, USSF licensed coach she is second all-time in wins in New England.

Women's Athletic Profile

229 Main Street
Keene, NH 03431
Coach: Denise Lyons
Email: dlyons@keene.edu

NCAA III
Owls/Red, White
Phone: (603) 358-2852
Fax: (603) 358-2888

Estimated # of Women's Soccer Scholarships: None
Conference: Little East Conference
Program Profile: We have a brand new soccer grass field which will have lights for the fall 2001 and all our home games will be played on it. There will be a seating capacity of 2000.
History: Soccer program began in 1981.
Achievements: Coach of the Year in 1996 for the New England Women's Intercollegiate Soccer Association ; 1997 Little East Coach of the Year; 6 NSCAA All-Americans; several conference titles in NECC Division II.

Coaching: Denise Lyons, , Head Coach, fifth season as head coach. Lyons played for the Irish National Team before embarking on her career at Keene State. She was named to four All-New England teams and received All-American honors while leading her team to four post season tournaments, including two trips to the NCAA Division II Nationals. She has two part-time assistant.

Roster in State: 9 | **Out of State:** 12 | **Out of Country:** 1
ODP State: 6 | **Regional:** 0 | **National:** 0
Walk-on/Other: 0 | **Graduation %:** 98 | **Seniors on Team:** 3

Positions Needed: Always looking for good players
Camp or Clinic Dates: Last 3 weeks in July, 1st week in August.
Most Recent Record: 12-7-3
Schedule: Oneonta (NY), Western (CT), Middlebury (UT), University of Rochester (NY), Wheaton (MA), Clark Univ. (MA)
Style of Play: Very finesse one and two touch soccer.

New England College

Academic Profile

Henniker, NH 03242
Phone:

Type: 4 Yr.,Private,Liberal Arts
Founded: 1946
Website: http://www.nec.edu
Religion: Non-Affiliated
SAT/ACT/GPA: Optional
Housing: Yes
Student/Faculty Ratio: 16:1
Male/Female Ratio: 53:47
Undergraduate Enrollment: 700
Graduate Enrollment: N/A
Scholarships/Academic: Yes | **Athletic:** No | **Financial Aid:** Yes
Expenses by: Year | **In State:** $ 20,706 | **Out of State:** $ 20,076
Degrees Conferred: AA, BA, BS, MA, MS
Programs of Study: Art, Biology, Business Administration, Communications, Education, Environmental Science Kinesiology, Philosophy, Political Science, Psychology, Sociology, Theatre

Men's Athletic Profile

24 Bridge Street
Henniker, NH 03242
Coach: John Skelton
Email: jskelton@nec1.neo.edu

NCAA III
Pilgrims/Red, White, Blue
Phone: (603) 428-2406
Fax: (603) 428-6023

Estimated # of Men's Soccer Scholarships: None
Conference: Commonwealth Coast Conference
Program Profile: Natural turf field. Season is from August to November with 16 regular season games, two to three tournament games. Every three years team takes pre-season trip to England.
History: 20 plus years with NAIA until the mid 1980's. Now NCAA Division III.
Achievements: 1989 Commonwealth Coast Conference Champions; 1990 and 1991 Runner-up.
Coaching: John Skelton 1st year Head Coach

Roster In State: 6 | **Out of State:** 14 | **Out of Country:** 2
ODP State: 6 | **Regional:** 1 | **National:**
Walk-on/Other: 2 | **Graduation %:** 95% | **Seniors on Team:** 3

Positions Needed: quality players in all positions
Camp or Clinic Dates: Not Available
Most Recent Record: 6-10-1
Schedule: Colby-Sawyer, Salve Regina, Gordon, Roger Williams, University of New England
Style of Play: Young team looking to become more technical and build up more in attack. will defend whit high pressure.

Women's Athletic Profile

23 Bridge Street
Henniker, NH 03242
Coach: Jason Hunter
Email: jhunter@nec1.nec.edu

NCAA III
Pilgrims/Red, White, Blue
Phone: (603) 428-2263
Fax: (603) 428-6023

Estimated # of Women's Soccer Scholarships: None
Conference: Commonwealth Coast Conference
Program Profile: Play on natural grass surface. Season runs from September - early November.
History: The program began in 1986.
Achievements: Jason Hunter CCC Coach of the Year in 1998.
Coaching: Jason Hunter is on his 3rd season as Head Coach and Mike Foley is our Assistant Coach.
Roster in State: 3 **Out of State:** 19 **Out of Country:** 0
ODP State: 4 **Regional:** 1 **National:**
Walk-on/Other: 2 **Graduation %:** 95% **Seniors on Team:** 5
Positions Needed: All
Camp or Clinic Dates: Not Available
Most Recent Record: 10-8
Schedule: Colby-Sawyer, Nicholas, Anna Maria, Endicott, Salve Regina, Whitworth
Style of Play: Up beat and high pressure defense.

New Hampshire College

Academic Profile

Ads
Manchester, NH 03106

Phone:

Type: 4 Yr.,Private,Liberal Arts
Website: http://www.nhc.edu
SAT/ACT/GPA: 820/20/2.8
Student/Faculty Ratio: 15:1
Undergraduate Enrollment: 1,500
Founded: 1932
Religion: Non-Affiliated
Housing: Yes
Male/Female Ratio: 1:1
Graduate Enrollment: 300
Scholarships/Academic: Yes **Athletic:** Yes **Financial Aid:** Yes
Expenses by: Year **In State:** $ 19,500 **Out of State:** $ 19,500
Specialty: Business
Degrees Conferred: AS, AAS, BS, MS, MBA
Programs of Study: Business Administration, Business Studies, Communications, Computer Science, Economics, English, Finance, Hotel/Restaurant Management, Liberal Arts, Marketing, PreLaw, Psychology, Social Science, Sports Management, System Analysis, Teacher Education

Men's Athletic Profile

2500 North River Rd
Manchester, NH 03106-1045
Coach: Tom Poitras
Email: peitrath@nhc.edu

NCAA II
Penmen/Blue, Gold
Phone: (603) 645-9627
Fax: (603) 645-9686

Estimated # of Men's Soccer Scholarships: 8
Conference: New England Collegiate Conference
Program Profile: Top 10 NCAA program, has one lighted game field, natural surface, years round program with a fall season in the winter and training in the spring.
History: Program began in 1965; in 1989 NCAA Division II National Champs; 8 NCAA Appearances.
Achievements: The program made 8 NCAA Appearances; Tom Poitras was named 1996 NECC Coach of the Year.

Coaching: Tom Poitras, Head Coach, USSF "A" License, ODP Coach, Region I staff member, has professional playing experience in 1996 NECC Coach of the Year. Dave Anderson, Assistant Coach.
Style of Play: Defensive marked, possession, quick play, organization in defense and attack with creativity in final third.

Women's Athletic Profile

2500 N River Road
Manchester, NH 03106-1045
Coach: Terry M. Prouty
Email: proutyte@nhc.edu

NCAA II
Penmen/Navy, Gold
Phone: (603) 645-9641
Fax: (603) 645-9686

Estimated # of Women's Soccer Scholarships: None
Conference: NECC
Program Profile: We are member of NCAA Division II, one of the best facilities in New England. Our soccer pitch is sweet grass and flat. It is professionally kept. We play a fall ball.
History: Our former coach was Peter Tufts from 1982-1998. Terry Prouty became a head coach in May of 1999. Our program has 15 consecutive winning seasons and 12 ECAC Tournaments bids, ECAC title in 1984, 1985, 1988, 1989, 1991, 1994 & 1996; NCAA Regional in 1997.
Achievements: We have 23 NSCAA All-Region players and 3 All-American players.
Coaching: Terry M. Prouty is our Head Coach. He coached at Daniel Webster College. He was a former assistant coach at Keene State College. He was an assistant coach and a player at Amateur Professional Team Lady Phantoms out of New Hampshire. Deb Robitaille and Hillary Gikchel are the Assistant Coaches.
Style of Play: The Lady Penmen's Style of Play will be possession and two touch soccer.

Notre Dame College

Academic Profile

Manchester, NH 03104-2299

Phone:

Type: 4 Yr.,Private
Website: http://www.notredme.edu
SAT/ACT/GPA: Open
Student/Faculty Ratio: 15:1
Undergraduate Enrollment: 800
Scholarships/Academic: Yes **Athletic:** Yes
Expenses by: Year **In State:** $ 22,000

Founded: 1950
Religion: Catholic
Housing: Yes
Male/Female Ratio: 1:3
Graduate Enrollment: 500
Financial Aid: Yes
Out of State: $ 22,000

Specialty: Education, Physical Therapy
Degrees Conferred: AA, BS, BA, MA, M.ED.
Programs of Study: Elementary Education, PreLaw, Biology, Physical Therapy, Physician's Assistant, History, English, Management, Psychology, Legal Studies

Men's Athletic Profile

2321 Elm Street
Manchester, NH 03104-2299
Coach: Sean Wisbey
Email: Not Available

NAIA
Saints/Royal, White
Phone: (603) 669-4298
Fax: (603) 644-8316

Estimated # of Men's Soccer Scholarships:
Conference: Mayflower Conference
Program Profile: Facilities includes two lighted, grass fields.
History: Began in 1992. The overall record is 24-21-4.
Achievements: 5 All-New England, 2 NAIA All-Region, numerous All-Conference.

Women's Athletic Profile

2321 Elm Street
Manchester, NH 03104
Coach: Eric Swanbeck
Email: Not Available

NAIA
Saints/Royal Blue, White
Phone: (603) 669-5500
Fax: (603) 669-6968

Estimated # of Women's Soccer Scholarships:
Conference: Mayflower Conference
Program Profile: Two grass fields which is lighted for night games (not college owned). Beautifully-kept fields. Facilities include stadium with 300 seating capacity. Playing season is in the fall which has 20 games.
History: The program began in 1993; overall record is 40-38-2. Qualified for the NAIA playoffs in 1993 and 1995; two NAIA All-Northeast Region selections. Solid NAIA program where just starting to reach its potential.
Achievements: Conference Coach of the Year; 1 All-American, 1 Academic All-American, 5 All-Region and 15 All-Conference.
Coaching: Eric Swanbeck, Head Coach. Assistant coach is TBA.
Style of Play: Prefers controlled passing styles, but depend on type of players.

Plymouth State College

Academic Profile

Phone: (603) 535-2778

Plymouth, NH 03264

Type: 4 Yr.,Public,Liberal Arts
Website: http://www.plymouth.edu
SAT/ACT/GPA: 850/2.0
Student/Faculty Ratio: 19:1
Undergraduate Enrollment: 3,500
Scholarships/Academic: Yes **Athletic:** No
Expenses by: Year **In State:** $ 9,554
Founded: 1871
Religion: Non-Affiliated
Housing: Yes
Male/Female Ratio: 50:50
Graduate Enrollment: 500
Financial Aid: Yes
Out of State: $ 14,854
Specialty: Business, Education
Degrees Conferred: 80 academic majors & 50 minors offered
Programs of Study: Actuarial Science, Athletic Training, Business and Management, Computer Science, Education, Health & Physical Education, Liberal Arts, Meteorology, Parks/Recreations, Protective Sciences, Psychology, Public Affairs, Social Sciences, Visual & Performing Arts

Men's Athletic Profile

MSC #52, 17 High Street
Plymouth, NH 03264
Coach: Keith Byrnes
Email: S.Griffin@oz.plymouth.edu

NCAA III
Panthers/F. Green, Black, White
Phone: (603) 535-2516
Fax: (603) 535-2758

Estimated # of Men's Soccer Scholarships: None
Conference: Little East Conference, ECAC
Program Profile: Natural grass field that has a measurements of 120x75; lights, stadium has 1,000-20 game regular season schedule with conference championships and end of season. Year-round training program with complete spring season five games; large spacious indoor field house-spacious practice facilities.
History: 1957 was first year with the program; 15 NCAA Tournament Appearances; % ECAC Tournament Appearances (402-178-62); one final Four Appearances NCAA Division III.

Achievements: Head Coach Shawn Griffin was named 1998 New England Region Coach of the Year (NSCAA), Little East Coach of the Year four times (1993, 1995, 1997 & 1998); LEC team champions in 1989, 1993, 1996, 1997 & 1998; several players drafted by USISL and GAISL which is indoor league; players drafted in old NASL League ACSO; 18 All-Americans; 6 Senior Bowl Participants; 38 All-New England Players.
Style of Play: Creative - technical players - attacking style of play. Pressurizing zonal defending - like players that are hard tacklers. Possession/attacking style of soccer.

Women's Athletic Profile

PE Center
Plymouth, NH 03264
Coach: Rebecca Lisack
Email: rlisack@mail.plymouth.edu

NCAA III
Panthers/Green, White
Phone: (603) 535-2732
Fax: (603) 535-2758

Estimated # of Women's Soccer Scholarships: None
Conference: Little East Conference, ECAC, NCAA III
Program Profile: Our stadium is Panther Field, natural grass, bleachers and a press box.
History: Program began in 1978. Nine straight NCAA appearances from 1985 to 1994. Our team has had only one losing season.
Achievements: 1993 National Player of the Year - M.B. Pawlick, 1995 ECAC New England Champions; numerous All-Americans.
Style of Play: Build up using speed, passing and ball movement.

Rivier College

Academic Profile

Phone: (800) 44-RIVIER

Nashua, NH 03060-5086

Type: 4 Yr.,Private,Liberal Arts
Website: http://www.rivier.edu
SAT/ACT/GPA: Required/B-avg.
Student/Faculty Ratio: 18:1
Undergraduate Enrollment: 1,600
Scholarships/Academic: Yes
Athletic: No
Expenses by: Year
In State: $ 20,680
Specialty: Comprehensive

Founded: 1933
Religion: Roman Catholic
Housing: Yes
Male/Female Ratio: 1:4
Graduate Enrollment: 1,100
Financial Aid: Yes
Out of State: $ 20,680

Degrees Conferred: AA, AS, BA, BS, BFA, MA, MAT, MSN
Programs of Study: Art, Accounting, Art Education, Athletic Training, Biology, Biology Education, Business Administration, Business Information Systems, Chemistry, Chemistry Education, Communications, Computer Science, Early Childhood Education, Elementary and Secondary Education, Special Education, English, English Education, Exercise Physiology, French, Graphic Design, History, Human Development, Illustration, Law & Government, Liberal Arts, Management, Mathematics, Math Education, Modern Languages, Nursing, Photography & Digital Imaging

Men's Athletic Profile

420 South Main Street
Nashua, NH 03060-5086
Coach: Scott Thomas
Email: sthomas@rivier.edu

NCAA III
Raiders/Blue, Gray
Phone: (603) 888-1311
Fax: (603) 888-3975

Estimated # of Men's Soccer Scholarships:
Conference: GNAC, ECAC
Program Profile: Fifth year in 1998; Conference Champions in 1997. Has a natural field, beautiful new field which is three years old. Playing season is in the fall that starts in August and ends in November.

History: Our program began in 1994 with a record of 17-1-2 in 1996; GVAC Conference Champions in 1997.
Achievements: Scott Thomas was named three-time GNAC Coach of the Year; GNAC Champions in 1998.
Coaching: Scott Thomas, Head Coach. Matt Nugett - Assistant Coach.
Style of Play: Possession out of the back.

Women's Athletic Profile

420 S Main Street
Nashua, NH 03060-5086
Coach: Scott Thomas
Email: sthomas@rivier.edu

NCAA III/NAIA
Raiders/Blue, Grey
Phone: (603) 888-1311
Fax: (603) 888-3975

Estimated # of Women's Soccer Scholarships: None
Conference: Great Northeast Athletic Conference-ECAC
Program Profile: Relatively a new program. Beautiful natural turf-high or hilly on the college campus. The field is three years old. Playing season is in the fall which is in August through November.
History: The program began in 1994. The 1996 record was 8-10.
Achievements:
Coaching: Scott Thomas, Head Coach, Advanced National Diploma.
Style of Play: Possession - build up style out of the back.

Saint Anselm College

Academic Profile

Manchester, NH 03102-1310

Phone: (603) 656-6014

Type: 4 Yr.,Private,Liberal Arts
Website: http://www.anselm.edu
SAT/ACT/GPA: 1000
Student/Faculty Ratio: 17:1
Undergraduate Enrollment: 2,000
Scholarships/Academic: Yes **Athletic:** No
Expenses by: Year **In State:** $ 22,530

Founded: 1889
Religion: Catholic-Benedictine
Housing: Yes
Male/Female Ratio: 40:60
Graduate Enrollment: N/A
Financial Aid: Yes
Out of State: $ 22,530

Specialty: Nursing, Business, Criminal Justice
Degrees Conferred: BA, BSN
Programs of Study: Biology, Business & Management, Chemistry, Computers, Criminal Justice, Economics, Education, Engineering, English, Health Sciences, History, Languages, Liberal Arts, Life Sciences, Mathematics, Nursing, Parks/Recreation, Political Science, Protective Services, Psychology, Public Affairs, Social Sciences and many others.

Men's Athletic Profile

100 St. Anselm Drive
Manchester, NH 03102
Coach: Edward Cannon
Email: ecannon@anselm.edu

NCAA II
Hawks/Royal, White
Phone: (603) 641-7800
Fax: (603) 641-7172

Estimated # of Men's Soccer Scholarships: N/A
Conference: Northeast 10 Conference

Women's Athletic Profile

100 Saint Anselm Drive
Manchester, NH 03102
Coach: Heather Doucette
Email: Not Available

NCAA II
Hawks/Navy Blue, White
Phone: (603) 641-7000
Fax: (603) 641-7172

Estimated # of Women's Soccer Scholarships: None
Conference: Northeast 10 Conference
Program Profile: Average eleven wins per year over the last four years; plays at Cofran Field which has a seating capacity of 510; natural grass. Season runs from September 1 through November 15 (average); ranked #15 at end of 1997 season in NCAA Division II; played nationally ranked teams in 1997.
History: The first year of the program was in 1984. NE-10 Championship in 1991, all-time record is 101-96-24; all-time NE-10 record is 57-24-13.
Achievements: 1994 NE-10 Conference Regular Season Champions; WCAC semi-finalist, I 1st team All-American, 3 All-NE Region players, 2 All-New England players, 1991 NE-10 Conference Champions, NSCAA New England Region Coach of the Year. Heather Doucette Northeast 10; NEWISA Coach of the Year in 1995.
Coaching: Heather Doucette, Head Coach, was named Northeast Coach of the Year in 1995. Alicia Coffee is the Assistant Coach.

University of New Hampshire

Academic Profile

Durham, NH 03824
Phone: (603) 862-3822

Type: 4 Yr.,Public,
Founded: 1923
Website: http://www.geocities.com
Religion: Non-Affiliated
SAT/ACT/GPA: 1150
Housing: Yes
Student/Faculty Ratio: 14:1
Male/Female Ratio: 43:57
Undergraduate Enrollment: 10,000
Graduate Enrollment: 1,500
Scholarships/Academic: Yes
Athletic: Yes
Financial Aid: Yes
Expenses by: Year
In State: $ 11,400
Out of State: $ 20,900
Specialty: Business, Engineering, Athletic Training, Environmental Sciences
Degrees Conferred: AA, Bachelors, Masters, Doctorate Degree
Programs of Study: Business Administration, Psychology, Biology, Communications, Criminal Justice, Engineering, English, Kinesiology, Liberal Arts, Life Science, Music and Arts, Nursing, Occupational Therapy, Political Science

Men's Athletic Profile

UNH Field House -Room 161
Durham, NH 03824
Coach: Rob Thompson
Email: robt@hopper.unh.edu

NCAA I
Wildcats/Blue, White
Phone: (603) 862-3211
Fax: (603) 862-4069

Estimated # of Men's Soccer Scholarships: N/A
Conference: America East Conference
Program Profile: We play on a natural grass field which measures 120x70. Our playing season is in the fall and in the spring. We have national recruiting.
History: We have made three National rankings in the last five years, 5 Top 10 Regional rankings, 2 All-Americans, 6 All-New England and one Conference Player of the Year.
Achievements: 1995 America East Co-Champs, Mike Veneto was named two times All-American in 1994 & 1995; Willy Schweitzer (NH Panthoms USISL), Ross Sandler (Worcester Wildfire - A-League), David Francisco - Sporting Lisbon Reserve (Portugal). Mike Keena was 2-time All-New England and was drafted by Philadelphia Kixx.
Coaching: Rob Thompson, Head Coach, holds a USSF 'A' license. He is NSCAA State Director and Region I ODP Staff Coach. John Cirillo, Assistant Coach, graduated from UNH in 1996. Willy Schweitzer (UNH in 1996) and Brint Shone (Maine 1993) are Assistant Coaches.
Style of Play: Varies from year to year; 3-5-2; 4-4-2. Zone and man-to-man; possession build-up; combination possession and build-up and direct play.

Women's Athletic Profile

145 Main St.
Durham, NH 03824-3510
Coach: Michael Jackson
Email: klmartin@cisunix.unh.edu

NCAA I
Wildcats/Blue, White
Phone: (603) 862-3822
Fax: (201) 585-5405

Estimated # of Women's Soccer Scholarships: None
Conference: American East Conference
Program Profile: Lewis field has natural grass playing surface. Season runs from the end of August until mid November.
History: Program began in 1995, 1st coach Marjorie Anderson 1985-94. Mike Jackson 1995-present. As of 1998 overall record of 117-122-17.
Achievements: 1998 Coach of the Year, 1998 American East Runner-Up, All-American Goalkeeper Maja Hansen in 1995.
Coaching: Mike Jackson is in his 6th season at UNH. 1998 Coach of the Year. Assistant Coach at UCONN from 1990-1994. Prior to that, girls varsity soccer coach at East Hampton High School. Kelly Martin- 6th season at UNH as assistant coach. Graduated of University of Vermont. Played for Sheffield Hallam United and Boston Renegades,

Roster in State: 6	**Out of State:** 18	**Out of Country:** 2
ODP State: 15	**Regional:**	**National:**
Walk-on/Other:	**Graduation %:**	**Seniors on Team:** 7

Positions Needed: ALL
Camp or Clinic Dates: July 16-20
Most Recent Record: 6-10-2
Schedule: University of Hartford, Dartmouth, Boston College, Indiana
Style of Play: Combination possession and direct attack. Team defense which initiates the offense.

new jersey

NEW JERSEY

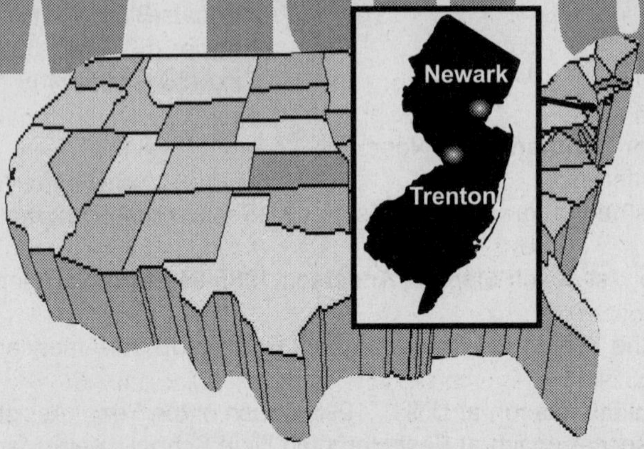

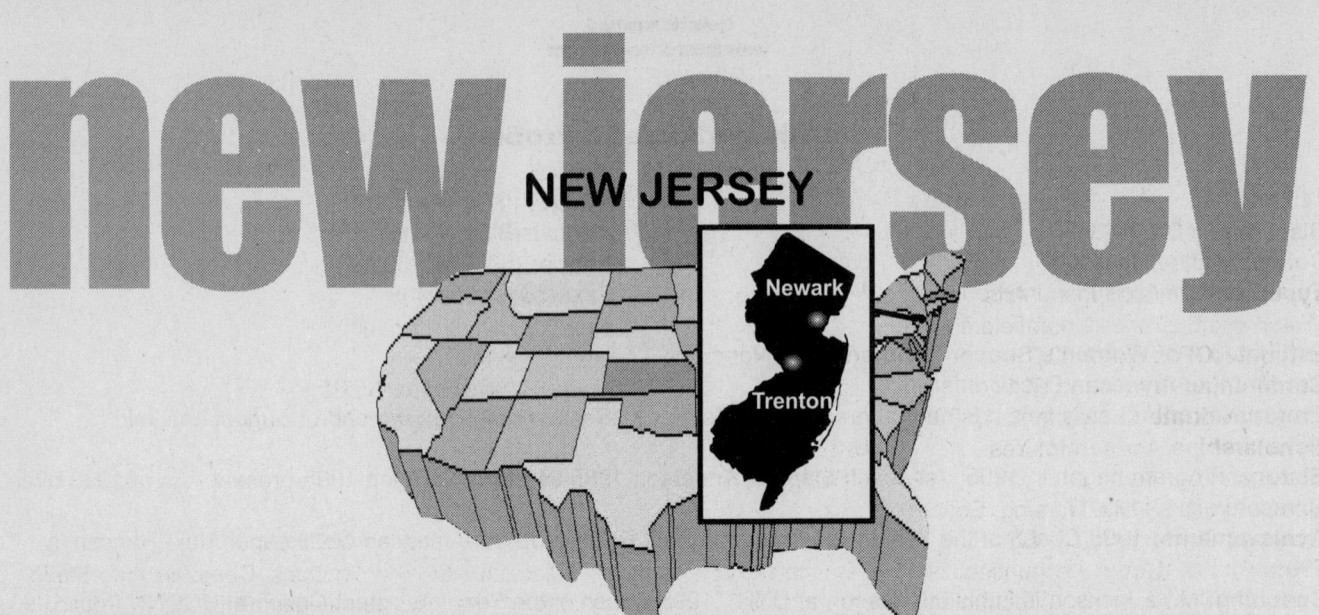

SCHOOL	CITY	AFFILIATION	PAGE
Bloomfield College	Bloomfield	NCAA II/NAIA	659
Caldwell College	Caldwell	NAIA II/NAIA	659
Centenary College	Hackettstown	NCAA III/NSCAA	660
College of New Jersey	Ewing	NCAA III	661
Drew University	Madison	NCAA III	663
Fairleigh Dickinson University	Madison	NCAA III	664
Fairleigh Dickinson Univ-Teaneck	Teaneck	NCAA I	665
Georgian Court College	Lakewood	NAIA	666
Kean University	Union	NCAA III	667
Monmouth University	West Long Branch	NCAA I	668
Montclair State College	Upper Montclair	NCAA III	669
New Jersey City University	Jersey City	NCAA III	670
New Jersey Institute of Tech.	Newark	NCAA III	672
Princeton University	Princeton	NCAA I	672
Ramapo College of New Jersey	Mahwah	NCAA III	673
Richard Stockton College	Pomona	NCAA III	675
Rider University	Lawrenceville	NCAA I	676
Rowan University	Glassboro	NCAA III	676
Rutgers - State University of NJ	Piscataway	NCAA I	678
Rutgers University - Camden	Camden	NCAA III	679
Rutgers University - Newark	Newark	NCAA III	680
Saint Peter's College	Jersey City	NCAA I	680
Seton Hall University	South Orange	NCAA I	681
Stevens Institute of Technology	Hoboken	NCAA III	683
William Paterson University	Wayne	NCAA III	684

Bloomfield College
Academic Profile

Bloomfield, NJ 07003
Phone: (973) 748-9000

Type: 4 Yr.,Private,Liberal Arts
Website: http://www.bloomfield.edu
SAT/ACT/GPA: 860/18/2.0
Student/Faculty Ratio: 17:1
Undergraduate Enrollment: 1,900
Scholarships/Academic: Yes **Athletic:** Yes
Expenses by: Year **In State:** $ 15,500
Founded: 1868
Religion: Presbyterian
Housing: Yes
Male/Female Ratio: 35:65
Graduate Enrollment: N/A
Financial Aid: Yes
Out of State: $ 15,500
Specialty: Business, Nursing, Education
Degrees Conferred: BA, BS
Programs of Study: Accounting, Biology, Business Administration, Chemistry, Communications, Computer Information Systems, Creative Arts & Technology, Criminal Justice, Economics, English, History, Humanities, Philosophy, Political Science, Psychology, Religion, Sociology

Men's Athletic Profile

467 Franklin Street
Bloomfield, NJ 07003
Coach: Doug Moore
Email: socson@aol.com

NCAA II/NAIA
Deacons/Maroon, Gold
Phone: (973) 748-9000x365
Fax: (973) 743-3998

Estimated # of Men's Soccer Scholarships: 2 Full-toal of 8
Conference: Central Atlantic Collegiate Conference
Program Profile: Has had six major injuries that contributed a poor season last year. The team should strong this year. Our team plays on natural grass field.
History: Traditionally a very strong team. In place for over thirty years of playing soccer.
Achievements: Our program produced 6 All-Americans, many Conference titles, National Tournament NAIA in 1995.
Style of Play: International Style of Play since 16 members of the team were born outside of the US.

Women's Athletic Profile

467 Franklin Street
Bloomfield, NJ 07003
Coach: Efrain Borjess
Email: Not Available

NAIA
Lady Deacons/Maroon, Gold
Phone: (973) 748-9000
Fax: (973) 743-3998

Did Not Return Profile

Caldwell College
Academic Profile

Caldwell, NJ 07006
Phone: (973) 618-3321

Type: 4 Yr.,Private,Liberal Arts
Website: http://www.caldwell.edu
SAT/ACT/GPA: 1000/2.75
Student/Faculty Ratio: 12:1
Undergraduate Enrollment: 1,700
Scholarships/Academic: Yes **Athletic:** Yes
Founded: 1956
Religion: Catholic
Housing: Yes
Male/Female Ratio: 45:55
Graduate Enrollment: 250
Financial Aid: Yes

Expenses by: Year **In State:** $ 18,200 **Out of State:** $ 18,200
Specialty: Education, Business, Communications, Criminal Justice
Degrees Conferred: BA, BFA, BS, MA
Programs of Study: Accounting, Art, Biology, Business Administration, Chemistry, Communication Arts, Computer Science, Computer Information System, Criminal Justice, Education, English, Fine Arts, French, History, International Business Management, Marketing, Mathematics, Medical Technology, Music, Political Science, Psychology, Religious Studies, Social Studies, Sociology, Spanish

Men's Athletic Profile

9 Ryerson Avenue
Caldwell, NJ 07006
Coach: William McGrath
Email: bmcgrath@caldwell.edu

NAIA II, NAIA
Cougars/Scarlet, White, Gold
Phone: (973) 618-3260
Fax: (973) 618-3370

Estimated # of Men's Soccer Scholarships: varies
Conference: Central Athletic Collegiate Conference
Program Profile: We have a new recreation center, campus parking and road system.
History: Program began in 1991; won conference In 1993; Conference Finalist (Tournament) in 1993, 1995 & 1997.
Achievements: Emmett Idzahl was drafted and playing Division III (South Jersey Riptide). Numerous Awards Winners.
Coaching: William McGrath, Head Coach, entering 5th year with the program.
Roster In State: 15 **Out of State:** 1 **Out of Country:**
Walk-on/Other: **Graduation %:** 100 **Seniors on Team:** 4
Positions Needed: Forwards, Fallbacks
Camp or Clinic Dates: July and August
Most Recent Record: 8-9-1
Schedule: LIU Southampton, Kutztown, NYACK, Holy Family, Teikyo Post, Felician, Dominican

Centenary College - New Jersey

Academic Profile

Hackettstown, NJ 07840

Phone: (908) 852-1400

Type: 4 Yr.,Private,Liberal Arts
Website: http://www.centenarycollege.edu
SAT/ACT/GPA: 850/18/2.3
Student/Faculty Ratio: 13:1
Undergraduate Enrollment: 750
Scholarships/Academic: Yes **Athletic:** No
Expenses by: Year **In State:** $ 19,870

Founded: 1867
Religion: United Methodist
Housing: Yes
Male/Female Ratio: 40:60
Graduate Enrollment: 40
Financial Aid: Yes
Out of State: $ 19,870

Specialty: Business, Education, Equine Studies
Degrees Conferred: AA, AS, BA, BS
Programs of Study: Accounting, Applied Mathematics, Art, Business Administration, Commercial Art, Communication, Computer Information Systems, Early Childhood Education, Education, Elementary Education, English, Equestrian Studies, Fashion Design/Technology, Fashion Merchandising, Graphical & Art Design, History, Interior Design, International Studies, Liberal Arts, Marketing, Merchandising, Mathematics, Political Science, Psychology, Radio/Television, Secondary Education, Special Education, Social & Behavioral Sciences, Sports Management, Teacher Aide, Textile/Clothing

Men's Athletic Profile

400 Jefferson Street
Hackettstown, NJ 07840
Coach: Steve Widdowson
Email: athletics@centenarycollege.edu

NCAA III/NSCAA
Cyclones/Royal Blue, White
Phone: (908) 852-1400 x2198
Fax: (908) 813-8295

Estimated # of Men's Soccer Scholarships: 0
Conference: None
Program Profile: 3 grass fields, game field with spectator seating. Regular season goes from August to November. Spring Season goes from February to March.
History: Program began participating as an NCAA Div. III program in 1996. The program has seen tremendous growth, especially recently. Majority of the team is recruited from New Jersey. Along with a few international players.
Achievements: NSCAA National Champions in 1995.
One players selected as NSCAA All-American in 1999.
Coaching: Steve Widdowson, Head Coach, graduated from Rutgers in 1998.

Roster In State: 17	**Out of State:** 3	**Out of Country:** 0
ODP State: 0	**Regional:** 0	**National:** 0
Walk-on/Other:	**Graduation %:** N/A	**Seniors on Team:** 4

Positions Needed: Forward and Midfield
Camp or Clinic Dates: Not Available
Most Recent Record: 14-6-1
Schedule: East Stroudsburg University, Muttlenberg College, Dominican College, Hunter College, Vasser College, Manhattanville College
Style of Play: Game is played in an English Style. Fast paced with plenty of ball movement. Encouraged to pass the ball. Team is organized and enthusiastic. Play with limited touches, quick decision making and aggression.

Women's Athletic Profile

400 Jefferson Street
Hackettstown, NJ 07840
Coach: Kevin Davies
Email: athletics@centenarycollege.edu

NCAA III
Cyclones/Royal, White
Phone: (908) 852-1400
Fax: (908) 813-8295

Estimated # of Women's Soccer Scholarships: None
Conference: Women's Intercollegiate Athletic Conference, ECAC, NSCAA
Program Profile: Our program has 3 fields (2 practice, 1 game field) and they are all grass with 120 seats. Fall season goes from early September to the end of October. Short spring season usually takes place mid February to beginning of April.
History: Our program began in 1993.
Achievements: Coach of the Year for the Conference in 2000, 1st team All-Conference player, 1 All-American Player.
Coaching: Head Coach Kevin Davies just completed his second season. His two year record is 14-19-1. His assistant coach Melissa Loder was a former player.

ODP State: 1	**Regional:**	**National:**
Walk-on/Other:	**Graduation %:**	**Seniors on Team:** 2

Camp or Clinic Dates: TBA
Most Recent Record: 10-9-0
Schedule: Drew Univ. William Patterson, Kean Univ.
Style of Play: We tried to be attack-minded as much as we could, however the way we play also depended on our opposition. Next season will depend on the personnel I bring in as my recruiting class.

College of New Jersey

Academic Profile

Phone: 609-771-2230

Ewing, NJ 08628-0718

Type: 4 Yr.,Public,Liberal Arts
Website: www.tcnj.edu
SAT/ACT/GPA: 1200/87th percentile
Student/Faculty Ratio: 12/1

Founded: 1855
Religion: Non-Affiliated
Housing: Yes
Male/Female Ratio: 45/55

Undergraduate Enrollment: 5400 **Graduate Enrollment:** N/A
Scholarships/Academic: Yes **Athletic:** No **Financial Aid:** Yes
Expenses by: Year **In State:** $12,015 **Out of State:** $15,332
Degrees Conferred: BA, BS, BFA, BSN, MA, MD
Programs of Study: Childhood Education, Economics, Education, Engineering Science, Health & Physical Education, Music, Nursing, Philosophy, Physics, Political Science, Psychology, Secondary Education, Sociology, Special Education for the developmentally Handicapped, Technology Education

Men's Athletic Profile

P.O. Box 7718
Ewing, NJ 08628-0718
Coach: George Nazario
Email: nazariog@tcnj.edu

NCAA III
Lions/Blue, Gold
Phone: (609) 771-244
Fax: (609) 637-5133

Estimated # of Men's Soccer Scholarships: 0
Conference: New Jersey Athletic Conference
Program Profile: Play in 6,000 seat Lions Stadium, which is lighted Astroturf field, also includes two-level press box, grandstand, concession stand, and restroom facilities.
History: Program began in 1950.
Achievements: 1991 NCAA III Runner-up, 1994 3rd place, 1995 5th place, 1996 NCAA III Champion, 1997 Runner-up.
Coaching: George Nazario, Head Coach, 1991 graduate of Seton Hall University, experience as both a player and a coach, former assistant for 3 years at Seton Hall, served as a graduate intern within the Pirate Sports Information Office, selected as a member of the Puerto Rico National Soccer team 1992, former member of US National Amateur team 1987-1990, currently serving as athletic director of the Union Lancers Youth Club.
Camp or Clinic Dates: Not Available
Most Recent Record: 14-7-0

Women's Athletic Profile

P.O. Box 7718, 2000 Pennington Rd.
Ewing, NJ 08628-0718
Coach: Joe Russo
Email: jrusso@tcnj.edu

NCAA III
Lions/Blue, Gold
Phone: (609) 771-3155
Fax: (609) 637-5133

Estimated # of Women's Soccer Scholarships: None
Conference: NJAC
Program Profile: Lions Stadium - seats 6,000, Astro-turf surface, lighted for night games, two-level press box, grandstand, concession stand, and restroom facilities.
History: Program began in 1990. Two first place finishes, Two second place finishes, one Third place finish. Goals for TCNJ 53, Goals allowed by TCNJ 15. 2 finishes as National Runner-up.
Achievements: 10 All-Americans, 3 National Titles, Player of the Year, Academic All-Americans
Coaching: Joe Russo, Head Coach, since 1989, 1976 graduate from Ewing HS, earned his NSCAA National Advanced Diploma, BS in Physical Education and Social Studies from Alderson Broaddus College, voted 1991 and 1992 NJ College Division women's soccer Coach of the Year by the NJCSCA; 1992 NSCAA/Umbro Northeast Coach of the Year.
Roster in State: 23 **Out of State:** 0 **Out of Country:** 0
Walk-on/Other: **Graduation %:** 100 **Seniors on Team:** 7
Camp or Clinic Dates: Not Available
Most Recent Record: 20-1-0

Drew University

Academic Profile

Madison, NJ 07940

Phone: 973-408-3000

Type: 4 Yr.,Private,Liberal Arts
Website: http://www.drew.edu
SAT/ACT/GPA: 1100
Student/Faculty Ratio: 10:1
Undergraduate Enrollment: 1,318
Scholarships/Academic: Yes **Athletic:** No
Expenses by: Year **In State:** $ 19,128

Founded: 1867
Religion: United Methodist
Housing: yes
Male/Female Ratio: 40:60
Graduate Enrollment: 1,336
Financial Aid: Yes
Out of State: $ 19,128

Degrees Conferred: BA, BS, MA, Ph.D.
Programs of Study: American Studies, Anthropology, Art, Behavioral Sciences, Biology, Chemistry, Computer Science, Economics, English, French, German, Mathematics, Music, Philosophy, Physics, Political Science, Psychology, Religion.

Men's Athletic Profile

36 Madison Avenue
Madison, NJ 07940
Coach: Lenny Armuth
Email: Larmuth@Drew.edu

NCAA III
Rangers/Forest, Navy
Phone: (973) 408-3135
Fax: (973) 408-3574

Estimated # of Men's Soccer Scholarships: None
Conference: Middle Atlantic State Collegiate Athletic Conference
Program Profile: Drew received new astro-turf this year, which was manufactures by Politan Sportbelagsysteme and selected by the athletic department members as the best surface available to meet their needs. The polypropylene carpet is one-inch high and is expected to last at least eight years.
History: The men's soccer program was established in 1954. The Drew Rangers return 9 starters from last year's 15-5 Freedom League Championship team, which earned its second consecutive NCAA post season bid. Coach Lenny Armuth has the luxury of returning both forwards, whom were voted First team Freedom league All-Stars.
Achievements: 76 MAC All-Stars. 32 MAC Academic Team, 18 Regional Al-Americans, 1 All-American, 6 Mac League Titles, 2 MAC Conference titles, 5 NCAA Tournament Appearances.
Coaching: Lenny Armuth, Head Coach, holds a USSF "A" License. He was a former assistant coach at Rutgers University, an ODP Coach and a professional player. He has ten years college coaching experience.
Style of Play: We play a possession style with a lot of players going forward. A lot of wing plays.

Women's Athletic Profile

36 Madison Avenue
Madison, NJ 07940
Coach: Christa Racine
Email: cracine@drew.edu

NCAA III
Rangers/Navy, Forest
Phone: (973) 408-3650
Fax: (973) 408-3014

Estimated # of Women's Soccer Scholarships: None
Conference: Middle Atlantic States Collegiate Athletic Conference
Program Profile: We play on an astro-turf field and lighted stadium with a seating capacity of 2,000.
History: Our program was started in 1987. Overall record under Coach Racine is 97-43-11
Achievements: Freedom Conference Championship participant past six years, NCAA tournament 1997, 6 All-Region Players
Coaching: Christa Racine, Head Coach, holds USSF "A" License. She was named Conference Coach of the Year two times. Emily Regie is the Assistant Coach.

Roster in State: 12 **Out of State:** 13 **Out of Country:** 0
ODP State: 2 **Regional:** **National:**
Walk-on/Other: **Graduation %:** 100 **Seniors on Team:** 7
Most Recent Record: 12-8-2
Schedule: Montclair State Univ. William Paterson, Univ. of Scranton, Elizabethtown College, Richard Stockton, Western Connecticut.

Fairleigh Dickinson University - Madison

Academic Profile

Madison, NJ 07940
Phone: 973-443-8500

Type: 4 Yr.,Private,Liberal Arts
Founded: 1958
Website: http://www.fdu.edu
Religion: Non-Affiliated
SAT/ACT/GPA: 1000
Housing: Yes
Student/Faculty Ratio: 30:1
Male/Female Ratio: 1:3
Undergraduate Enrollment: 2,200
Graduate Enrollment: 1,200
Scholarships/Academic: Yes **Athletic:** No **Financial Aid:** Yes
Expenses by: Year **In State:** $ 21,110 **Out of State:** $ 21,110
Specialty: Business, Education, Psychology, 5-year quest program
Degrees Conferred: BA, BS, MA, MAT, MBA, MS, MPA, DMD
Programs of Study: Accounting, Biology, Business Management, Chemistry, Clinical Laboratory Science, Computer Science, Economics, Electronic Filmmaking & Digital Video Design, English Languages & Literature, Finance, Fine Arts, French Languages & Literature, History, Hotel/Restaurant Management, Humanities, Marine Biology, Marketing, Mathematics, Medical Technology, Philosophy, Political Science, Psychology, Radiological Technology, Sociology

Men's Athletic Profile

283 Madison Avenue
Madison, NJ 07940
Coach: Tom McLoughlin
Email: Not Available

NCAA III
Jersey Devils/Blue, Black
Phone: (973) 443-8827
Fax:

Estimated # of Men's Soccer Scholarships: N/A
Conference: Mid-Atlantic Conference
Program Profile: Large grass field that is used only for soccer during the season on beautiful campus. The New York Giants use the facilities during summer. Brand new Athletic Center was completed September 1995.
History: Program began in 1963. Program has improved the past 3 seasons after 4 poor seasons in the 80's.
Achievements:
Coaching: Tom McLoughlin, Head Coach, graduated from St. Joseph's in Belfast, Ireland. The teams he has coached have a history of steady improvement. He holds a USSF 'B' license and played and coached in Ireland and the US.
Roster In State: 20 **Out of State:** 6 **Out of Country:**
Walk-on/Other: **Graduation %:** 90 **Seniors on Team:** 6
Positions Needed: All
Camp or Clinic Dates: August
Schedule: Drew, Clairmont, Stevens, Ramapo, Lycoming, Wilkes, Misericordia, Scranton
Style of Play: Depends on type of players.

Women's Athletic Profile

285 Madison Avenue
Madison, NJ 07940
Coach: Renee D. Montana
Email: montana@mailbox.fdu.edu

NCAA III
Devils/FDU- Blue, Black, White
Phone: (973) 443-8943
Fax: (973) 443-8796

Estimated # of Women's Soccer Scholarships: None
Conference: Middle Atlantic Conference
Program Profile: We have a beautiful 5-year old facility with an indoor pool, a fully-stocked weight room, a separate free weight room, a cardio theater section, an indoor track (1/8 mile) and a full sized gymnasium which can be divided into three sections. We play on a natural grass field. The program is demanding off-season as well as in-season. We have a year round commitment to bringing success to the program. We have a family atmosphere through common goals and good work ethics.
History: Our program was started in 1993 by Roger Bonnegarts. Each year, we show great promise and improvement. In 1998, the Devils marked their 1st winning season with a record of 10 wins and 8 losses under the new head coach Renee Montana. Coach Montana joined the Devils in April of 1998 starting a winning tradition and dedication to success within the program.
Achievements: 2000 Co-Coach of the Year in Mid-Atlantic Conference. 1999 Co-Rookie of the Year MAC, 2000 1st All-Mac Player and 2nd Team All-Mac Player.
Coaching: Renee Montana, Head Coach, is a native of Long Island and attended Lenoire- Rhyne College in North Carolina where she achieved All-Conference honors for 4 straight years. She finished her career as the 5th goal scorer in the history of the program She worked as a professional trainer for the Soccer Excellence. Andy Pappas, Assistant Coach, is a native of New Jersey and attended Rowan as a standout athlete winning many Championships during his time on the soccer team. Gina Lazaro, Assistant Coach, is a native of Denville, New Jersey. She was All-American Goalkeeper and attended LIU-Southampton.

Roster in State: 19	**Out of State:** 4	**Out of Country:** 0
ODP State: 5	**Regional:** 0	**National:** 0
Walk-on/Other: 0	**Graduation %:** 100	**Seniors on Team:** 5

Positions Needed: Defenders, Central Midfielder, GK
Camp or Clinic Dates: Not Available
Most Recent Record: 9-8-1
Schedule: Scranton Univ. Drew Univ. Montclair State Univ. Lebanon Valley, Misericordia, William Patterson
Style of Play: Possession style of play work the ball down flanks look for early cross. Indirect constant switching of fields look to play wide. Redirect inside box. Defensive sweeper aggressive on attack.

Fairleigh Dickinson University - Teaneck

Academic Profile

Phone: 201-692-2000

Teaneck, NJ 07666

Type: 4 Yr.,Private,Liberal Arts		**Founded:** 1942
Website: http://www.fdu.edu		**Religion:** Non-Affiliated
SAT/ACT/GPA: 900+		**Housing:** Yes
Student/Faculty Ratio: 15:1		**Male/Female Ratio:** 50:50
Undergraduate Enrollment: 4,000		**Graduate Enrollment:** N/A
Scholarships/Academic: Yes	**Athletic:** Yes	**Financial Aid:** Yes
Expenses by: Year	**In State:** $ 19,858	**Out of State:** $ 19,858

Degrees Conferred: BS, BA
Programs of Study: Accounting, Arts, Biology, Business Management, Chemistry, Economics, English Language & Literature, Finance, History, International Studies, Marine Biology, Marketing, Mathematics, Philosophy, Psychology, Science, Sociology, PreProfessional Courses

Men's Athletic Profile

1000 River Road, H400A
Teaneck, NJ 07666
Coach: Seth Roland
Email: Not Available

NCAA I
Knights/FDU Blue, White, Black
Phone: (201) 692-2247
Fax: (201) 692-9361

Estimated # of Men's Soccer Scholarships: None
Conference: Northeast 10 Conference
Program Profile: The Knights play at University Field on the Teaneck side of the campus overlooking the Hackensack River. The stadium capacity is 3,000. The field has natural grass. The Knights are a Division I program and are one of the most successful in the East Conference.
History: Intercollegiate soccer began in the 1950's, because their is no football at the Teaneck-Hackensack campus, soccer is the main sport in the fall.
Achievements: The Knights have had numerous players earn post-season honors and play professionally; 3 All -NEC players; 2 All - Region; 3 All - Region Academic; 1 NEC Player of the Year.
Style of Play: We play an aggressive counterattacking style of play that hopes to take advantage of our opponents mistakes. Our defense is always looking to strike quickly with long balls to our midfield and forwards, off turnovers.

Women's Athletic Profile

1000 River Road, H400A
Teaneck, NJ 07666
Coach: PETER GAGLIOTI
Email: gaglioti@mailbox.fdu.edu

NCAA I
Knights/Blue, White
Phone: (201)-692-2007
Fax: N/A

Estimated # of Women's Soccer Scholarships: N/A
Conference: NEC
Program Profile: Our program is entering its 2nd season of competition.
History: We started in 2000.
Coaching: Veteran soccer coach Peter Gaglioti leads a team of first-year varsity athletes onto the soccer pitch this fall as Fairleigh Dickinson University's 16th intercollegiate sport.
Roster in State: 7 **Out of State**: 5 **Out of Country**: 1
Most Recent Record: 2-16-1
Schedule: Temple, Howard, Drexel, Rider

Georgian Court College

Academic Profile

Lakewood, NJ 08701

Phone:

Type: 4 Yr.,Private,Liberal Arts
Website: http://www.georgian.edu
SAT/ACT/GPA: 860
Student/Faculty Ratio: 12:1
Undergraduate Enrollment: 1,013
Scholarships/Academic: Yes **Athletic:** Yes
Expenses by: Year **In State:** $ 15,676

Founded: 1908
Religion: Catholic
Housing: Yes
Male/Female Ratio: 0:100
Graduate Enrollment: 712
Financial Aid: Yes
Out of State: $ 15,676

Degrees Conferred: 348 Bachelor's, 113 Master's
Programs of Study: Accounting, Arts, BioChemistry, Biology, Business Administration, Chemistry, Elementary Education, English, French, History, Humanities, Mathematics, Music, Physics, PreDentistry, PreLaw, PreMed, Psychology, Religion, Special Education

Women's Athletic Profile

900 Lakewood Avenue
Lakewood, NJ 08701-2697
Coach: Mike Lyons
Email: Not Available

NAIA
Lions/Blue, Gold
Phone: (732) 364-2200
Fax: (732) 901-7151

Estimated # of Women's Soccer Scholarships: None

Conference: Central Atlantic Collegiate Conference
Program Profile: The program has two fields, practice area, soccer tennis and pendulum natural gas. Season runs from August through November.
History: Program began in 1988, constantly ranked in the country (top 10) for the last six years. final Four Appearances; 1997 National Championships.
Achievements: Has 10 All-Americans, in the past three years however, CACC Conference Titles (8 in row); Regional Championships in 1997.
Style of Play: Attacking style based on possession, initiative and aggression, a zone defense with a high pressure in all area's of the field.

Kean College of New Jersey

Academic Profile

Phone: 908-527-2000

Union, NJ 07083

Type: 4 Yr.,Public,Liberal Arts
Founded: 1855
Website: http://www.kean.edu
Religion: Non-Affiliated
SAT/ACT/GPA: 950+/2.0
Housing: Yes
Student/Faculty Ratio: 18:1
Male/Female Ratio: 1:4
Undergraduate Enrollment: 4,000
Graduate Enrollment: 5,000
Scholarships/Academic: Yes
Athletic: No
Financial Aid: Yes
Expenses by: Year
In State: $ 10,908
Out of State: $ 12,090
Specialty: Education
Degrees Conferred: BA, BS, BFA, BSN, BSW, MA, MS
Programs of Study: School of Business, Government & Technology, School of Liberal Arts, School of Natural Science, Nursing, Mathematics, School of Education

Men's Athletic Profile

1000 Morris Ave.
Union, NJ 07083
Coach: Tony Ochrimenko
Email: tkoaturbo@kean.edu

NCAA III
Cougars/Navy, White
Phone: (908) 527-2936
Fax: (908) 354-9423

Estimated # of Men's Soccer Scholarships: None
Conference: New Jersey Athletic Conference
Program Profile: The home field is natural grass, 80 X 120 yd., seats 1,200, a press box, scoreboard, and a underground water system, fence enclosure. The playing season runs from August to November, and nontraditional season runs from February to April.
History: 1960 was the first year of the program. In 1984 we were in the NCAA final four. IN 1992 we were National Champions. We were the NJAC Champions for 8 years and we are always ranked nationally and regionally.
Achievements: Regional Coach of the Year in 1997 and 1998; 8 NJAC Titles; Many professional players.
Coaching: Tony Ochrimenko, Head Coach, USSF 'A' license, 22nd season, 17 winning seasons in 21 years of coaching including 12 straight, 1974 graduate of Kean, BA in Urban & Outdoor Recreation from Kean.
Roster In State: 15
Out of State: 1
Out of Country: 2
ODP State: 2
Regional: 1
National: 0
Walk-on/Other:
Graduation %: 85
Seniors on Team: 5
Positions Needed: Goalkeeper, Striker, Center Midfield
Camp or Clinic Dates: July 24-28, July 31-August 4, August 7-11
Most Recent Record: 14-6-2
Schedule: Ohio Wesleyan University, Rowan University, College of New Jersey, New York University, Richard Stockton College
Style of Play: Possession, ball control, attacks from the back four, alternating quick transition and attack with speed of play.

Women's Athletic Profile

1000 Morris Ave
Union, NJ 07083
Coach: Brian Doherty
Email: seaclub@prodigy.net

NCAA III
Cougars/Royal Blue, Silver
Phone: (908) 527-3031
Fax: (908) 354-9423

Estimated # of Women's Soccer Scholarships: None
Conference: New Jersey Athletic
Program Profile: Kean has its own natural grass, and turf surface soccer complex for the men's and women's teams consisting of 3 practice fields and a separate game field. This past year the University mad the addition of a turf stadium. This allows for preparation of whatever surface an opponent may have.
History: Kean competes in one of the top conferences in the nation and has consistently been one of the top programs in Division III. The Cougars have had 9 winning seasons since the program began in 1984 and has made the post season 8 times.
Achievements: Kean has had 2 All -Americans, including 28 year old Ireland native, Noelle Meeke, who was honored this past year. Meeke had 31 goals, 11 assists and 73 points.
Coaching: Bryan Doherty, Head Coach, is a nationally licensed coach. he has been coaching for over 10 years at the high school and college level. In 1999, his first with the program, he led the team to their first Post Season Appearance in 3 years.
Roster in State: 28 **Out of State:** 2 **Out of Country:** 1
Walk-on/Other: **Graduation %:** **Seniors on Team:** 1
Positions Needed: Midfielder, Defense
Camp or Clinic Dates: Not Available
Most Recent Record: 9-8
Schedule: College of New Jersey, Rowan, Stockton, William Patterson, Scranton, Montclair, Drew, Elizabeth Town, Villa Julie, Wilkes
Style of Play: Ball possession attacking out of the back. Flexibility in formations 3-5-2, 4-4-3, 3-4-3.

Monmouth University - New Jersey

Academic Profile

West Long Branch, NJ 07764
Phone: 732-571-3400

Type: 4 Yr.,Private,Liberal Arts
Website: http://www.monmouth.edu
SAT/ACT/GPA: 1050/3.0
Student/Faculty Ratio: 18:1
Undergraduate Enrollment: 3,200
Scholarships/Academic: Yes **Athletic:** Yes
Expenses by: Year **In State:** $ 21,000
Founded: 1955
Religion: Non-Affiliated
Housing: Yes
Male/Female Ratio: 44:56
Graduate Enrollment: 2,000
Financial Aid: Yes
Out of State: $ 21,000
Specialty: Comprehensive
Degrees Conferred: AA, BA, BS, MA, MS, MBA, MEd, Liberal Arts
Programs of Study: Arts, Business & Management, Computer Science, Chemistry, Communications, Education, Health Science, Criminal Justice, Multi/Interdisciplinary Studies, Psychology, Social Sciences, English, Special Education, Foreign Languages, English

Men's Athletic Profile

Cedar Avenue
West Long Branch, NJ 07764
Coach: Shannon Poser
Email: sposer@mondec.monmouth.edu

NCAA I
Hawks/Blue, White
Phone: (732) 263-5150
Fax: (732) 571-3535

Estimated # of Men's Soccer Scholarships: None
Conference: Northeast Conference
Program Profile: NCAA Division I program that plays in the Northeast Conference. The team plays on a sodded field. Players enjoy the natural grass field that measures 75x115 yards. The stadium consist of 3,500 seats.
History: Program began in 1958. Northeast Champions in 1990 and 1993. Tournament Champions in 1991, qualified for NEC 5 out of last 8 years (top four teams qualify).
Achievements: Conference Title in 1991, Regional All-Americans: Jim Adams, Cox Cockwood, Joni Kallionipn, and PJ Farrell.
Coaching: Shannon Poser is our Head Coach. He is entering first season with the program.
Style of Play: Attacking with a possession of ball.

Women's Athletic Profile

Cedar Avenue
West Long Branch, NJ 07764
Coach: Krissy Jeremiah
Email: kjeremia@monmouth.edu

NCAA I
Hawks/Royal Blue, White
Phone: (732) 571-4410
Fax: (732) 571-3535

Estimated # of Women's Soccer Scholarships: 2
Conference: Northeast Conference
Program Profile: We have a year around program that is played on a grass field that seats 1,000.
History: Program began in 1985; competitive Division I program. NEC Champions in 1995 and 1996.
Achievements: 1999 Coach of the Year; 1997 7 All-Conference players; NSCAA Team Academic Award.
Coaching: Krissy Jeremiah, Head Coach, holds USSF "A" License, named college All-American. Ron Autenrieth, Assistant Coach, has ten years ODP coaching experience.

Roster in State: 17	**Out of State:** 6	**Out of Country:**
ODP State: 10	**Regional:**	**National:**
Walk-on/Other:	**Graduation %:** 90	**Seniors on Team:** 4

Positions Needed: All
Camp or Clinic Dates: July 28
Most Recent Record: 10-6-2
Schedule: University of Pennsylvania, Seton Hall, Old Dominion, St. John's
Style of Play: Attacking possession oriented.

Montclair State University

Academic Profile

Upper Montclair, NJ 07043

Phone: (973) 655-7830

Type: 4 Yr.,Public		**Founded:** 1908
Website: http://www.montclair.edu		**Religion:** Non-Affiliated
SAT/ACT/GPA: 1200		**Housing:** Yes
Student/Faculty Ratio: 30:1		**Male/Female Ratio:** 14:1
Undergraduate Enrollment: 10,000		**Graduate Enrollment:** 3,500
Scholarships/Academic: Yes	**Athletic:** No	**Financial Aid:** Yes
Expenses by: Year	**In State:** $ 5,000	**Out of State:** $ 5,000

Specialty: Teaching University
Degrees Conferred: School of Business, School of Arts, College of Humanities, Social Sciences
Programs of Study: Has 43 undergraduate majors, 30 graduate majors, Aging Doctor Program, all school of Business, Arts, Humanities, Sciences, and Math Education

Men's Athletic Profile

Normal Ave.
Upper Montclair, NJ 07043
Coach: Rob Chesney
Email: Not Available

NCAA III
Red Hawks/Scarlet, White
Phone: (201) 655-7594
Fax: (201) 655-5390

Estimated # of Men's Soccer Scholarships: N/A
Conference: New Jersey Athletic Conference
History: Our program began in 1958. MSU soccer's greatest successes have come in the last 9 years.
Achievements: 1989 Conference Championship; 4 Coach of the Year Honors; 2 Player of the Year Honors in 10 years; NCAA Tournament; ECAC Championship 2 times; 18 Regional All -Americans; 5 All - Americans in 6 years in 11 years.
Coaching: Rob Chesney, Head Coach, 2 time first team Regional All - American, NJ Player of the Year, Masters Degree, 2 time Coach of the Year; Winningest Soccer Coach ever at MSU in only 6 years.

Roster In State: 25	**Out of State:** 2	**Out of Country:** 2
ODP State: 8	**Regional:** 1	**National:**
Walk-on/Other:	**Graduation %:** 90	**Seniors on Team:** 2

Schedule: Methodist College, Maryville College, Rowan College, College of New Jersey, Stockton College, Kean College, U.S. Merchant Marine Academy, N.C. Wesleyan, York College
Style of Play: Very organized, excellent work rate, 100% effort. Allow players to be creative offensively, will attack with numbers. Defensively the team is very structured and disciplined. All players must work and defend hard.

Women's Athletic Profile

Normal Avenue
Upper Montclair, NJ 07043
Coach: Eileen Blair
Email: Not Available

NCAA III
Red Hawks/Red, White
Phone: (201) 655-5234
Fax: (201) 655-5390

Estimated # of Women's Soccer Scholarships: None
Conference: ECAC, NJAC

New Jersey City University (Jersey City State C)

Academic Profile

Phone: (201) 200-3317

Jersey City, NJ 07305-1597

Type: 4 Yr.,Public,Liberal Arts		**Founded:** 1929
Website: http://www.njcu.edu		**Religion:** Non-Affiliated
SAT/ACT/GPA: 480-V, 480-M		**Housing:** Yes
Student/Faculty Ratio: 17:1		**Male/Female Ratio:** 48:52
Undergraduate Enrollment: 5,200		**Graduate Enrollment:** 1,800
Scholarships/Academic: Yes	**Athletic:** No	**Financial Aid:** Yes
Expenses by: Year	**In State:** $ 8,042	**Out of State:** $ 9,332

Specialty: Comprehensive college with liberal arts and professional programs
Degrees Conferred: BA, BS, BFA, BSN, MA, MS
Programs of Study: Accounting, Biology, Chemistry, Communications, Computer Science, CIS, Economics, English, History, Justice Studies, Management, Marketing, Music, Elementary Education, Music Education, Special Education, Social Work, Sociology, Art History, Art Education, Psychology, Film Studies, and more

Men's Athletic Profile

2039 Kennedy Blvd.
Jersey City, NJ 07305
Coach: Kevin East
Email: Not Available

NCAA III
Gothic Knights/Forest, Gold
Phone: (201) 200-3209
Fax: (201) 200-2365

Estimated # of Men's Soccer Scholarships: None
Conference: New Jersey Athletic Conference
Program Profile: We play on a natural grass field with a measurements of 115x75 yards. We have two practice fields. Our playing season runs from August to November then a short season in spring for a non-traditional season and indoor turf field 7 a-side. Our field is located next to ocean bay. Facilities include weight room, pool and lockers.
History: Our program began in 1958.
Achievements: The program produced 2 Conference Titles; 2 Regional All-American in 1998; 4 All-Conference players in 1998. 4 in 99' (3 were named 1st team)/ 1 scholar-Athlete in 99'
Coaching: Kevin East, Head Coach, holds a USSF "B" Licensed. He played six years in pro and first season here as a head coach was in 1998 and has had program's first winning season since 1985. He was with New York and New Jersey Metro Stars as a player for the part of 1998 season (MLS). Alex Malaga, Assistant Coach, was the assistant coach of the NJ Stallions (USISL). He is an NJ ODP Coach and played pro for Tigers in Mexico.

Roster In State: 20	**Out of State:** 0	**Out of Country:** 1
ODP State: 5	**Regional:** 0	**National:** 0
Walk-on/Other: 2	**Graduation %:** 100	**Seniors on Team:** 2

Positions Needed: Forward, Midfield, Defender, Goalkeeper
Camp or Clinic Dates: Not Available
Most Recent Record: 9-10-1
Schedule: Christopher Newport Univ., Rowan Univ., Kean Univ., college of New Jersey, Ramapo College, Richard Stockton College, Montclair University
Style of Play: Possession style of play.

Women's Athletic Profile

2039 Kennedy Blvd.
Jersey City, NJ 07305
Coach: Janice Cavuto
Email: Not Available

NCAA III
Gothic Knights/Green, Gold
Phone: (201) 200-3210
Fax: (201) 200-2365

Estimated # of Women's Soccer Scholarships: None
Conference: NJAC (New Jersey Athletic Conference)
Program Profile: McNuity Field located at Thomas M. Gerrity Athletic Complex with a natural grass. It is ten minutes outside New York City. It has a brand new athletic center. Top conferences in the country.
History: Women's program started in 1993. Team has had some problems with numbers of coaches. The 1997 new coach, new (positive) outlook, will start a winning tradition. College and soccer program have a bright future.
Achievements: 1st time 2 players received All-Conference Honorable Mention; 3 Rookie of the Week; 2 1st team All-WIAC Selections for 1999; 3 2nd team All-WIAC Selections for 1999.
Coaching: Janice Cavuto is our Head Coach.

Roster in State: 10	**Out of State:** 3	**Out of Country:**
Walk-on/Other:	**Graduation %:**	**Seniors on Team:** 1

Positions Needed: All- Goalkeeper a must!!
Camp or Clinic Dates: August 24-31
Most Recent Record: 1-14
Schedule: College of New Jersey, Rowan, William Paterson, Montclair, Kean

New Jersey Institute of Technology

Academic Profile

Newark, NJ 07102

Phone: 973-596-3000

Type: 4 Yr.,Public,Engineering
Founded: 1881
Website: http://www.njit.edu
Religion: Non-Affiliated
SAT/ACT/GPA: required
Housing: Yes
Student/Faculty Ratio: 14;1
Male/Female Ratio: 82:18
Undergraduate Enrollment: 3,400
Graduate Enrollment: 2,500
Scholarships/Academic: Yes **Athletic:** No **Financial Aid:** Yes
Expenses by: Year **In State:** $ 11,200 **Out of State:** $ 15,800
Degrees Conferred: BA, BS, BArch, BSCE, BSChemE, BSEE, BSET, BSME, MA, MArch, MS, Ph.D.
Programs of Study: Actuarial Sciences, Architecture, Chemical Engineering, Chemistry, Civil Engineering, Computer Science, Mathematics, Physics, Science, Technology & Society, Statistics

Men's Athletic Profile

University Heights
Newark, NJ 07102
Coach: Ricky Hill
Email: Not Available

NCAA III
Highlanders/White, Red
Phone: (201) 596-3633
Fax: (201) 596-8440

Estimated # of Men's Soccer Scholarships: N/A
Conference: Independent Athletic, Skyline, ECAC
Program Profile: Lubetkin Field is a natural grass surface with lights and a 1,000 seat capacity bleacher. Playing season is from late August to early November.
History: Program began in 1952.
Achievements: 1960 NAIA Championship; 1994 IAC Champions; 17 All -Americans; 3 NCAA tournament appearances.
Style of Play: Possession of the ball with an emphasis on off ball movement. Interchanging positions, all players must know how to attack and defend.

Princeton University

Academic Profile

Princeton, NJ 08544

Phone: 609-258-9026

Type: 4 Yr.,Private,Liberal Arts,Engineering
Founded: 1746
Website: http://www.princeton.edu
Religion: Non-Affiliated
SAT/ACT/GPA: 1260+/27+
Housing: Yes
Student/Faculty Ratio: 5:1
Male/Female Ratio: 58:42
Undergraduate Enrollment: 4,524
Graduate Enrollment: 1,770
Scholarships/Academic: Yes **Athletic:** No **Financial Aid:** Yes
Expenses by: Year **In State:** $ 30,000 **Out of State:** $ 30,000
Degrees Conferred: BA, BS, MA, Ph.D.
Programs of Study: Aeronautical Engineering, Anthropology, Archeology, Architectural Engineering, Computer Engineering, Asian Studies, AstroPhysics, Biology, Chemistry, Computer Science, Economics, Fine Arts, Geology, History, International Relations, Math, Music, Philosophy, Physics, Political Science, Psychology, Religion, Social Science

Men's Athletic Profile

Jadwin Gymnasium
Princeton, NJ 08540
Coach: Jim Barlow
Email: Not Available

NCAA I
Tigers/Orange, Black
Phone: (609) 258-4977
Fax: (609) 258-2490

Estimated # of Men's Soccer Scholarships: None
Conference: Ivy League Conference
Program Profile: We play in the Ivy League, which we won last season. Our home field is Lourie-Love Field, which is a natural grass surface.
History: All-Time record is 503-367-114 (578,93 seasons). Our first game was versus the Merion Cricket Club on November 10, 1906, which we one 3-0. Princeton has won five Ivy League Championships and appeared in five NCAA tournaments.
Coaching: Head Coach- Jim Barlow
Roster In State: 5 **Out of State:** 22 **Out of Country:** 2
Walk-on/Other: **Graduation %:** N/A **Seniors on Team:** 6
Camp or Clinic Dates: Not Available
Most Recent Record: 7-5-1

Women's Athletic Profile

Dillon Gym
Princeton, NJ 08544
Coach: Julie Shackford
Email: jcs@princeton.edu

NCAA I
Tigers/Black, Orange, White
Phone: (609) 258-5092
Fax: (609) 258-2490

Estimated # of Women's Soccer Scholarships:
Conference: Ivy League Conference
Program Profile: Lourie-Love Field is grass, enclosed by fenced, and surrounded by bleachers. Natural grass and has a seating capacity of 1,500.
History: 1980 was the inception of the program.
Achievements: 5 NCAA Tournament berths; several All-Americans.
Coaching: Julie Shackford, Head Coach, three-time All-American at College of Mary and William, four times All-Region, holds USSF "A" License, Region I ODP Staff Coach. Ron Celestin - Assistant Coach, graduated from the NAIA National Champion in 1994 in WV-Wesleyan, played semi-pro in New Jersey. Coaches various team in central New Jersey area. Dodie Calavecchio - Assistant Coach. Mike Calise, Assistant Coach.
Roster in State: 3 **Out of State:** 22 **Out of Country:** 2
ODP State: 22 **Regional:** 8 **National:** 2
Walk-on/Other: **Graduation %:** 100 **Seniors on Team:** 7
Camp or Clinic Dates: August 1-5
Most Recent Record: 12-5-1
Schedule: Harvard, Yale, Boston University, Richmond, George Washington, Dartmouth

Ramapo College of New Jersey

Academic Profile

Mahwah, NJ 07430

Phone:

Type: 4 Yr.,Public,Liberal Arts
Website: http://www.ramapo.edu
SAT/ACT/GPA: 1150/85
Student/Faculty Ratio: 15:1
Undergraduate Enrollment: 4,533

Founded: 1969
Religion: Non-Affiliated
Housing: Yes
Male/Female Ratio: 49:51
Graduate Enrollment: N/A

Scholarships/Academic: Yes **Athletic:** No **Financial Aid:** Yes
Expenses by: Year **In State:** $ 7,658 **Out of State:** $ 9,658
Degrees Conferred: BA, BS
Programs of Study: Accounting, American Studies, BioChemistry, Biology, Business Administration, Management, Marketing, Chemistry, Clinical Laboratory Science, Communications, Arts, Graphic Design, Journalism, Public Communications, Radio/Television, Writing, Computer Science, Contemporary Arts, Economics, Environmental Science, Environmental Studies, History, Fine Arts, Information Systems, Literature, Law and Society, Mathematics, Metropolitan Studies, Nursing, Physics, Political Science, Social Work, Sociology, Anthropology, Philosophy, Psychology, Elementary Education, Women's Studies, Sociology

Men's Athletic Profile

505 Ramapo Valley Road
Mahwah, NJ 07430
Coach: Peppe Pinton
Email: ppinton@ramapo.edu

NCAA III
Roadrunners/Scarlet, Gold
Phone: (201) 684-7065
Fax: (201) 684-7958

Estimated # of Men's Soccer Scholarships: N/A
Conference: ECAC
Program Profile: Our main soccer field has a seating capacity of 800, and a natural grass surface, tennis courts, locker rooms, training rooms, meeting rooms, and weight rooms. We play a Fall season.
History: Began in 1985, the program has a short history but an outstanding winning record during the last six years. Were ECAC Champions and in the NCAA Tournament.
Achievements: We have had players win the All Mid-Atlantic, All-State, Player of the year, All-American, and All-Conference 1st Team. We have also had players go on to play professional.
Coaching: Peppe Pinton, Head Coach, formerly executive with the New York Cosmos, assisted by Santiago Formoso, a former player with the New York Cosmos.
Roster In State: 27 **Out of State:** 3 **Out of Country:** 2
ODP State: 4 **Regional:** 1 **National:**
Walk-on/Other: **Graduation %:** 97 **Seniors on Team:** 4
Positions Needed: Forward, Mid-Field
Camp or Clinic Dates: July 10- August 21
Most Recent Record: 14-3-2
Schedule: Rowan, Stockton, Drew, College of NJ, Kean
Style of Play: Traditional 4-4- system, a passing style of soccer.

Women's Athletic Profile

505 Ramapo Valley Road
Mahwah, NJ 07430-1680
Coach: Arnold Ramirez, Jr.
Email: Not Available

NCAA III
Roadrunners/Red, White
Phone: (201) 684-7076
Fax: (201) 684-7958

Estimated # of Women's Soccer Scholarships: None
Conference: New Jersey Athletic Conference (NJAC), ECAC
Program Profile: We have a young program and our facilities are excellent. Our stadium has 2,000 seats and our natural grass field measures 120 x 75.
History: Our program began in 1993. After a rebuilding year last season, this year looks to be promising with ten returning players and some promising young recruits.
Achievements: None
Coaching: Arnold Ramierz, Jr, Head Coach, is our new coach. He is a licensed coach and a former coach from Long Island University. He coached the men's team for 20 years. His all-time record is 259-189-33.
Style of Play: Short passing game; ball possession; technical playing.

Richard Stockton State College

Academic Profile

Jim Leeds Road
Pomona, NJ 08240

Phone: (609) 652-4875

Type: 4 Yr.,Public,Liberal Arts
Founded: 1969
Website: http://www.stockton.edu
Religion: Non-Affiliated
SAT/ACT/GPA: 1140/24/top 20%
Housing: Yes
Student/Faculty Ratio: 20:1
Male/Female Ratio: 43:57
Undergraduate Enrollment: 6,000
Graduate Enrollment: 200
Scholarships/Academic: Yes **Athletic:** No **Financial Aid:** Yes
Expenses by: Year **In State:** $ 9,300 **Out of State:** $ 11,200
Degrees Conferred: BA, BS, Master's in Business, Nursing, Physical Therapy
Programs of Study: Business, Marine Biology, Computer Science, Nursing, Public Health, Speech, Pathology/Audiology, Criminal Justice, Economics, Political Science, Psychology, Social Work, Sociology, Anthropology, Art, Latin, English, French, Biological Science, Earth Science, Elementary, Mathematics, Music, Physical Science, Social Studies, Spanish

Men's Athletic Profile

P.O. Box 195
Pomona, NJ 08240
Coach: Jeff Haines
Email: jeffreyhaines@stockton.edu

NCAA III
Ospreys/Black, White
Phone: (609) 652-4873
Fax: (609) 748-5541

Estimated # of Men's Soccer Scholarships: None
Conference: New Jersey Athletic Conference
Program Profile: $ 2.5 million soccer complex featuring three grass playing fields with grandstands seating 2,000 spectators with lights.
History: Four of the last five years we have received an NCAA Bid; 1996 NJAC Conference Champs.
Achievements: Produced 2 NCAA1st team All-Americans; 1996 NJAC Conference champs; 6 players playing professionally (NPSL, Argentina 1st Division.
Coaching: Jeff Haines, Head Coach. Joe Elmer and Don Norton - Assistant Coaches.
Style of Play: Very physical defensive mind set countering off of opponent's errors. If counter isn't possible very deliberate possession style of play. (Up tempo or direct). Great team unity and school spirited.

Women's Athletic Profile

Jim Leeds Road
Pomona, NJ 08240
Coach: Roy Wilkins
Email: Not Available

NCAA III
Ospreys/Black, White
Phone: (609) 652-4874
Fax: (609) 748-1557

Estimated # of Women's Soccer Scholarships: None
Conference: New Jersey Athletic Conference
History: Program became varsity in 1989.
Achievements: ECAC Finalist for the past 3 years; ECAC Champion, 1993.
Coaching: Roy Wilkins, Head Coach, ODP State Select U-17 Girls coach for NJ, PA State Staff coach.
Style of Play: High pressure, attacking style. Scored 140 goals in the last 2 seasons allowing only 20. 3-4-3.

Rider University
Academic Profile

Phone: 800-257-9026

Lawrenceville, NJ 08648

Type: 4 Yr.,Private,Liberal Arts
Founded: 1865
Website: http://www.rider.edu
Religion: Non-Affiliated
SAT/ACT/GPA: 960/18/2.4
Housing: Yes
Student/Faculty Ratio: 1:19
Male/Female Ratio: 1:1
Undergraduate Enrollment: 2,900
Graduate Enrollment: 750
Scholarships/Academic: Yes **Athletic:** Yes **Financial Aid:** Yes
Expenses by: Year **In State:** $ 23,000 **Out of State:** $ 23,000
Specialty: Business, Education, Liberal Arts
Degrees Conferred: BA, BS, MA, MBA
Programs of Study: Business (11 majors), Communications, Computer Sciences, Liberal Arts, PreLaw, PreMed, Psychology, Sociology, Teacher Education

Men's Athletic Profile

2083 Lawrenceville Road
Lawrenceville, NJ 08648
Coach: Russ Fager
Email: Foger@rider.edu

NCAA I
Broncs/Cranberry, White
Phone: (609) 896-5319
Fax: (609) 895-5744

Estimated # of Men's Soccer Scholarships:
Conference: MAAC
Program Profile: Field is natural grass with a small stadium. Playing season is in the fall with some travel while spring has 5 dates schedule. Team technical, hardworking family atmosphere.
Achievements: MAAC Champions in 1997-1998 and 1998 -1999; NEC Champions in 1992-1993; Regional Coach of the Year in 1997; NJ Coach of the Year in 1992, 1996 & 1997.
Coaching: Russ Fager is our Head Coach. He holds USSF 'A' license. He was an ODP Coach for 8 years, ODP Director for 2 years and Club Coach State Staff Coach. Nick Juengert is our Assistant Coach.
Style of Play: Ball control, short passing.

Women's Athletic Profile

2083 Lawrenceville Rd.
Lawrenceville, NJ 08648-3099
Coach: PeggyMatthews
Email: Not Available

Phone: (609) 895-5054
Fax: (609) 896-0341

Estimated # of Women's Soccer Scholarships: None
Conference: MAAC
Coaching: Peggy Graham-Matthews, Head Coach, was named head coach summer of 1999.

Rowan University
Academic Profile

Phone: (609) 256-4684

Glassboro, NJ 08028

Type: 4 Yr.,Public,Liberal Arts
Founded: 1923
Website: http://www.rowan.edu
Religion: Non-Affiliated

SAT/ACT/GPA: Average:1,000-1,300
Housing: Yes
Student/Faculty Ratio: 16:1
Male/Female Ratio: 40:60
Undergraduate Enrollment: 9,480
Graduate Enrollment: N/A
Scholarships/Academic: Yes **Athletic:** No **Financial Aid:** Yes
Expenses by: Year **In State:** $ 5,021 **Out of State:** $ 6,731
Degrees Conferred: BA, BS, MA, MS, MBA
Programs of Study: Art, Biological Science, Chemistry, Communications, Computer Science, Economics, Elementary Education, English, Engineering, Geography, Health & Physical Education, History, Law/Justice, Liberal Studies, Mathematics, Music, Physical Science, Physics, Political Science, Psychology, School Nursing, Sociology, Spanish, Theatre

Men's Athletic Profile

201 Mullica Hill Road
Glassboro, NJ 08028
Coach: Dan Gilmore
Email: sportsinfo@rowan.edu

NCAA III
Profs/Brown, Gold
Phone: (609) 256-4684
Fax: (609) 256-4916

Estimated # of Men's Soccer Scholarships: None
Conference: New Jersey Athletic Conference
Program Profile: One of the top teams in the Division III; won the 1990 Division III Championship. Home field is a lighted stadium with a natural grass field that measures 120x75 yards, and has a seating capacity of 1,500 plus. Has a new scoreboard and a press box for media and video taping.
History: Our program began in 1956. The program has had only two coaches in its history: Sam Porch, Jr. and Dan Gilmore. In 23 seasons, Gilmore has a record of 361-87-36 and a winning percentage of .783. Rowan has won the national championship in 1981 and 1990. The Profs also finished second in 1979 and third in 1980, 1985 and 1998. Rowan has advanced to the NCAA Tournament 19 times. The Profs have a 24-16-2 overall record.
Achievements: Goalkeeper Michael Oehmann First Team All-American in 1995 and Third Team in 1994 and NJAC Goalkeeper of the Year 1992 through 1995.
Coaching: Dan Gilmore, Head Coach, is in his 24th season. His record at Rowan is 361-87-36. He is a 1974 graduate of Plymouth with a BS in Health and PE. He received his master's from Eastern Illinois.
Style of Play: High pressure, short passing, controlled, build out of the back, attack in numbers.

Women's Athletic Profile

201 Mullica Hill Rd
Glassboro, NJ 08028
Coach: Scott Leacott
Email: leacott@rowan.edu

NCAA III
Profs/Brown, Gold
Phone: (856) 256-4694
Fax: (856) 256-4916

Estimated # of Women's Soccer Scholarships: None
Conference: New Jersey Athletic Conference
Program Profile: Home field is lighted stadium with a natural grass field that measures 75x120 yards and seats 1,500. We have a new scoreboard and a press box for media and video taping.
History: Our program began in 1995 and in five seasons the team has posted a 60-22-5 record. In 1990, Rowan made its first NCAA Tournament appearance and defeated Beaver College, 1-0 in the first round. The Profs also established school records for wins in a season 17 and most consecutive games with out lose 12.
Achievements: 5 NJAC All-Conference first team; 12 NJAC All-Conference second team; 4 NJAC All-Conference honorable mentions.
Coaching: Head Coach Scott Leacott earned a bachelor's degree in marketing from Rowan in 1998. He was also the Assist Coach of the men's soccer from 1996-1998. To assist him are Karen Little and Michele McGowan.
Roster in State: 25 **Out of State:** 1 **Out of Country:**
ODP State: 1 **Regional:** **National:**
Walk-on/Other: **Graduation %:** 100 **Seniors on Team:** 7
Positions Needed: Defenders, Midfielders

Camp or Clinic Dates: last two weeks of June and second week of August
Most Recent Record: 17-3-2
Schedule: The College of New Jersey, William Paterson, Richard Stockton, Elizabethtown, Scranton, Green Mountain
Style of Play: High pressure; short passing; controlled; build out of the back; attack in numbers.

Rutgers - State University of NJ

Academic Profile

Piscataway, NJ 08854
Phone: (732) 445-4206

Type: 4 Yr.,Public,Liberal Arts,Engineering
Founded: 1766
Website: http://www.rutgers.edu
Religion: Diverse
SAT/ACT/GPA: 1100
Housing: Yes
Student/Faculty Ratio: 15:1
Male/Female Ratio: 46:54
Undergraduate Enrollment: 35,712
Graduate Enrollment: 9,500
Scholarships/Academic: Yes **Athletic:** Yes **Financial Aid:** Yes
Expenses by: Year **In State:** $ 12,000 **Out of State:** $ 17,000
Specialty: Pharmacy, Environmental, Business
Degrees Conferred: BA, BS, MA, Ph.D.
Programs of Study: Accounting, Agricultural and Animal Sciences, Arts, Biology, Business & Management, Communications, Criminal Justice, Dance, Education, Engineering, English Environmental/Exercise Science, Journalism, Languages, Libaral Arts, Life Sciences, Mathematics Nursing, Physical Education, Physics, PreMed, Psychology, Social Sciences, Political Science, Theater Arts, Women's Studies

Men's Athletic Profile

Rutgers Soccer Office
Piscataway, NJ 08855-1373
Coach: Bob Reasso
Email: rusoccer@rci.rutgers.edu

NCAA I
Scarlet Knights/Red, Black
Phone: (732) 445-4206
Fax: (732) 445-5589

Estimated # of Men's Soccer Scholarships: N/A
Conference: Big East Conference
Program Profile: We have a top 20 program in the U.S. We have an outstanding playing facility. It has natural grass, Phillips lighting, 4 practice fields. We have an indoor facility with outstanding weight training. We have an Elite-Addidas sponsored program.
History: Our program began in 1938. Bob Reasso's program began in 1981. He was A-10 Coach of the Year 4 times. He was Mid Atlantic Coach of the Year 4 times. He was undefeated during the regular season in 1983 with a record of 17-0-2.
Achievements: 1990 Coach of the Year; 24 Big East Champions; A-10 Championship 4 times; 11 All-Americans; 10 NCAA Appearances; 30 professional players; many National Team players; 3 Final Four Appearances
Coaching: Bob Reasso, Head Coach, holds a USSF 'A' license.
Roster In State: 70% **Out of State:** 20% **Out of Country:** 10%
ODP State: All **Regional:** Most **National:** 6
Walk-on/Other: **Graduation %:** 95 **Seniors on Team:**
Camp or Clinic Dates: July 16-20, July 30-Aug 3
Most Recent Record:
Schedule: Duke, Indiana, St. Louis, North Carolina, St. John, University of Connecticut, California State, Georgetown

Women's Athletic Profile

83 Rockafelier Road
Piscataway, NJ 08854-8053
Coach: Charlie Duccilli
Email: chasduc@rci.rutgers.edu

NCAA I
Scarlet Knights/Scarlet, Black
Phone: (732) 445-4073
Fax: (732) 445-4690

Estimated # of Women's Soccer Scholarships: N/A
Conference: Big East Conference
Program Profile: We play in a fully-lighted stadium that has 5,000 seats and a natural turf field . We have an indoor full-field training facility. We play a traditional fall season and a non-traditional spring season. We have one of the top thirty programs in the country that is fully-funded and staffed.
History: We became a varsity program in 1984. We made an NCAA Tournament appearance in 1987. We have 3 consecutive ECAC Championships in 1990, 1991 and 1992. We are a member of the Big East Conference and finished third in 1995 and 1996.
Achievements: 17 in the Nation and 3rd in the Big East Conference; New Jersey Coach of the Year four times; Eastern Collegiate Athletic Conference Champions in 1990, 1991 and 1992; Saskia Webber- 1992 MAC Adidas Goalkeeper of the Year; 1992 All-America All-Americans; 5 Regional All-Americans.
Coaching: Charlie Ducilli, Head Coach, is the first and only head coach of the 13 year program. He has a USSF "A" License and was a former professional player in the NASL and ASL. He had coaching stints with US Olympic Festival and the US Region Teams. He is the Director of the State ODP Program. Julie Vetack, Assistant Coach, has a coaching license and is a former Rutgers standout player. She has US Regional experience and was a New Jersey State Coach.
Style of Play: Patterned after highest women's level play within individual and team's skill, tactics, and athletic talents.

Rutgers University - Camden

Academic Profile

Camden, NJ 08102
Phone: 856-225-6133

Type: 4 Yr.,Public,Liberal Arts
Founded: 1927
Website: http://www.camden-www.rutgers.edu
Religion: Non-Affiliated
SAT/ACT/GPA: 1030
Housing: Yes
Student/Faculty Ratio: 15:1
Male/Female Ratio: 1:1
Undergraduate Enrollment: 3,455
Graduate Enrollment: 1,587
Scholarships/Academic: Yes **Athletic:** No **Financial Aid:** Yes
Expenses by: Year **In State:** $ 6,105 **Out of State:** $ 10,986
Specialty: Liberal Arts
Degrees Conferred: BA, BS, MA, MS, MSW
Programs of Study: Bachelor of Arts: Afro-American Studies, Art, Biology, Chemistry, Computer Science, Criminal Justice, Economics, English, French, German, History, Student-Proposed Major, Mathematics, Music, Philosophy, Political Science, Psychology, General Studies, Social Work, Sociology, Spanish, Theatre Arts, Urban Studies; Bachelor of Science: BioMedical Technology, Nursing

Men's Athletic Profile

3rd & Linden Streets
Camden, NJ 08102
Coach: Greg Ogden
Email: mballard@crab.rutgers.edu

NCAA III
Pioneers/Scarlet, Black
Phone: (609) 225-6198
Fax: (609) 225-6024

Estimated # of Men's Soccer Scholarships: None
Conference: ECAC, NJAC

Women's Athletic Profile

3rd & Linden
Camden, NJ 08102
Coach: Brian Sheehan
Email: Not Available
Did Not Return Profile

Phone: (609) 225-6193
Fax: (609) 225-6193

Rutgers University - Newark

Academic Profile

Phone:

Newark, NJ 07102

Type: 4 Yr.,Public,Liberal Arts,Engineering
Founded: 1766
Website: http://www.rutger.edu/newark
Religion: Non-Affiliated
SAT/ACT/GPA: Open
Housing: Yes
Student/Faculty Ratio: 12:1
Male/Female Ratio: 46:54
Undergraduate Enrollment: 6,000
Graduate Enrollment: 3,500
Scholarships/Academic: Yes **Athletic:** No
Financial Aid: Yes
Expenses by: Year **In State:** $ 7,500
Out of State: $ 11,000
Degrees Conferred: BA, BS
Programs of Study: Business, Marketing, Management, Computer Science, Literature, Education, Criminal Justice, Mathematics, PreLaw, Engineering, Psychology, PreMed, Social Sciences

Men's Athletic Profile

42 Warren St.
Newark, NJ 07102
Coach: Eddie Ballas
Email: Not Available

NCAA III
Raiders/Scarlet
Phone: 201-944-1822
Fax: (201) 648-1431

Estimated # of Men's Soccer Scholarships: N/A
Conference: NJAC

Saint Peter's College

Academic Profile

Phone:

Jersey City, NJ 07306

Type: 4 Yr.,Private,Liberal Arts
Founded: 1872
Website: http://www.spc.edu
Religion: Roman Catholic
SAT/ACT/GPA: Varies
Housing: Yes
Student/Faculty Ratio: 12:1
Male/Female Ratio: 55:45
Undergraduate Enrollment: 2,900
Graduate Enrollment: 800
Scholarships/Academic: Yes **Athletic:** Yes
Financial Aid: Yes
Expenses by: Sem **In State:** $ 10,500
Out of State: $ 10,500
Specialty: Business, Education, Sociology, Accounting, Communications
Degrees Conferred: MBA, MA, MS, BA, BS, AA, AAS
Programs of Study: Accounting, American Studies, Art History, Biological, Chemistry, Biology, Business Management, Chemistry, Clinical Laboratory, Medical Technology, Toxicology, Computer Science, Economics, Mathematics, Elementary Education, English, History, Marketing, Management, Political Science, Philosophy, Physics, Psychology, Sociology, Theology

Men's Athletic Profile

2641 Kennedy Blvd.
Jersey City, NJ 07306
Coach: Cesar Markovic
Email: markovicacademy@aol.com

NCAA I
Peacocks/Blue, White
Phone: (201) 915-9068
Fax: (201) 915-9102

Estimated # of Men's Soccer Scholarships: 7
Conference: MAAC
Program Profile: Facilities include a grass game field as well as separate grass training field and a bubble structure indoor field.
History: Program began over 20 years ago.
Coaching: Head Coach Cesar Markovic holds USSF "A" License. Had been an Assistant coach with the long Island rough riders. New York State ODP Coach presently. Jack Stefanowski is the Assistant Coach.
Roster In State: 6 **Out of State:** 15 **Out of Country:** 0
ODP State: 0 **Regional:** 0 **National:** 0
Walk-on/Other: 0 **Graduation %:** N/A **Seniors on Team:** 5
Camp or Clinic Dates: Not Available
Most Recent Record: 2-16-0
Schedule: University of Connecticut, Seton Hall, Fairfield, Holy Cross, Bucknell
Style of Play: Attack minded ball control style utilizing highly technical players.

Women's Athletic Profile

2641 Kennedy Blvd.
Jersey City, NJ 07306
Coach: Erin Fitzgerald
Email: parker_j@spcvxa.spc.edu

NCAA I
Peahens/Peacock Blue, White
Phone: (201) 915-9108
Fax: (201) 915-9102

Estimated # of Women's Soccer Scholarships:
Conference: Metro Atlantic Athletic Conference
Program Profile: Young but successful Division I program competing in the MAAC Conference. Qualify new grass playing surface on game and practice areas. Both fall and spring season (non-traditional).
History: Have won at least 10 games each of the past three seasons. 1996 MAAC Regular Season Champions. Young, but successful past. Program began in 1992.
Achievements: Won three-time National Soccer Coaches Association of America Academic Awards Winners (one of only eight Division I programs). Won 1996 MAAC Regular Season Title. One Academic All-American nominee. Nicole Tracey C'1997 and Liz Kelly in C'1997, hold the MAAC all-time career records for total points, goals and assists. More academic All-MAC selections over the past four years than any other school.
Style of Play: Entertaining play involving 11 players attacking and 11 players defending. Like to go forward trying to create scoring opportunities. Zonal group defending. Possession oriented. the modern attacking game with group defending responsibilities.

Seton Hall University

Academic Profile

Phone: (973) 275-9498

South Orange, NJ 07079

Type: 4 Yr.,Private,Liberal Arts **Founded:** 1856
Website: http://www.shu.edu **Religion:** Catholic
SAT/ACT/GPA: All factors are considered **Housing:** Yes
Student/Faculty Ratio: 14/1 **Male/Female Ratio:** 46/54
Undergraduate Enrollment: 4,700 **Graduate Enrollment:** 6,000
Scholarships/Academic: Yes **Athletic:** Yes **Financial Aid:** Yes
Expenses by: Year **In State:** $26,187 **Out of State:** $26,187
Degrees Conferred: BA, BS, MS, MA, Ph.D., EdD
Programs of Study: 40 majors at the undergraduate level, as well as many minors, certificates and special programs that includes: Business, Arts, Sciences, Nursing, Education, Theology, Law, Medical Education

Men's Athletic Profile

400 S Orange Avenue
South Orange, NJ 07079
Coach: Manfred Schellscheidt
Email: athletics@shu.edu

NCAA I
Pirates/Blue, White
Phone: (973) 761-9693
Fax: (973) 761-9675

Estimated # of Men's Soccer Scholarships: 3-4
Conference: Big East Conference
Program Profile: A member of the completive BIG EAST Conference, the Seton Hall soccer program plays 17-18 games in the traditional fall season. The athletes also participate in a competitive training program in the spring that features several tournaments. Seton Hall plays all of its home games at Owen T. Carroll Field, a 1,800 seat stadium with a natural grass surface that is located on campus. A varsity weight room and field house are also available to the athletes for off season training.
History: One of the most successful programs in the Northeast, the Seton Hall soccer program dates back to 1928. Seton Hall, which began play in the BIG EAST Conference in 1982, has qualified for the league's tournament 14 times, second only to Connecticut. The program has compiled 15 winning campaigns in the last 16 years. Seton Hall has won four BIG EAST Championships and has qualified for the NCAA Championship six times during that period.
Achievements: Seton Hall has had 13 All-Americans Selections in it soccer history. Additionally, 41 players have been selected to the All-Region squad. Head Coach Manfred Schellscheidt was selected as BIG EAST Coach of the Year in 1995 and 1998. Eight players have been selected BIG EAST Player of the Year. Seton Hall has won the BIG EAST Championship in 1986, 1987, 1988 and 1991. The program annually ranks among the top academic teams in the conference as 13 players were named to the BIG EAST Academic All-Star Team in 1999 after earning a 3.0 GPA or better.
Coaching: Manfred Schellscheidt Head Coach recently completed his 13th season as head men's soccer coach of Seton Hall. Schellscheidt has guided the Pirates to 12 winning campaigns in his 13 seasons. He has also let Seton Hall to two BIG EAST Championships, four NCAA Tournament berths and 6 conference title game appearances. The first coach in the United States to earn an "A-1" license, Schellscheidt has compiled a 144-86-21 record over the past 13 seasons. Schellscheidt, who was inducted into the United States Soccer Hall of Fame, was selected to the "Collegiate All-Coaches Team' By Soccer America. During his career, he has coached the 1984 United States Olympic Team and two editions of the U.S. Pan American Games team, along with numerous youth national squads.

Roster In State: 8	**Out of State:** 11	**Out of Country:** 4
ODP State: 5	**Regional:** 1	**National:** 0
Walk-on/Other: 3	**Graduation %:** 95	**Seniors on Team:** 4

Positions Needed: Forwards, Midfielders
Camp or Clinic Dates: Not Available
Most Recent Record: 13-7-0
Schedule: Connecticut, St. John's Rutgers, Notre Dame, Pittsburgh, Boston College, Georgetown, West Virginia, Princeton, Syracuse
Style of Play: Team plays ball-control style of soccer, utilizing three backs, five midfielders and two forwards. Focus is on generating scoring opportunities on offense. Seton Hall led the Conference in scoring in 2000.

Women's Athletic Profile

400 S Orange Avenue
South Orange, NJ 07079
Coach: Betty Ann Kempf
Email: kempfeli@shu.edu

NCAA I
Pirates/Blue, Silver, Black
Phone: (973) 761-9777
Fax: (973) 275-2064

Estimated # of Women's Soccer Scholarships: N/A
Conference: Big East Conference
Program Profile: G Stadium is natural grass with a seating capacity for 2,000, year-round program. Consist of a conditioning, a weight training facility, and an individual player development.
History: Our program began in 1994; we have made a progression to number three in the Big East have beaten #2 ranked Notre Dame and ranked #17 in the country.

Achievements: Big East Conference Coach of the Year in 1997, NJ Coach of the Year in 1997 & 1998; Big East Tournament in 1997-1998; Stacey Nagle Academic All-American, Kelly Smith All-American.
Coaching: Betty Ann Kempf, Head Coach. Jim Harrison - Assistant Coach. Chris McDonald - Assistant Coach. Kelly Smith-full time All-American, leading scorer in NCAA-2x, 3x Big East player of the year England National Team
Roster in State: 6 **Out of State:** 15 **Out of Country:** 3
ODP State: 12 **Regional:** 4 **National:** 2
Walk-on/Other: 6 **Graduation %:** 100 **Seniors on Team:** 5
Positions Needed: all
Camp or Clinic Dates: Not Available
Most Recent Record: 11-7
Schedule: Notre Dame, Connecticut, William & Mary, George Mason, Princeton
Style of Play: We play a style that compliments our players strength and weaknesses.

Stevens Institute of Technology

Academic Profile

Hoboken, NJ 07030
Phone: (201) 216-5691

Type: 4 Yr.,Private,Engineering **Founded:** 1870
Website: http://www.stevens.tech **Religion:** Non-affiliated
SAT/ACT/GPA: Required **Housing:** Yes
Student/Faculty Ratio: 9:1 **Male/Female Ratio:** 78:22
Undergraduate Enrollment: 1,533 **Graduate Enrollment:** 1,934
Scholarships/Academic: Yes **Athletic:** No **Financial Aid:** Yes
Expenses by: Year **In State:** $ 29,400 **Out of State:** $ 29,400
Specialty: Engineering, Applied Science, Computer Science, Preprofessional
Degrees Conferred: BA, BE, BS, M Eng, MS, ME, MIM, MTM, Ph D
Programs of Study: B.A. in English, and American Literature, History, Philosophy; B.E. in Chemical, Civil, Computer, Electrical, Environmental Materials and Mechanical Engineering, Engineering Management and Engineering Physics; B.S. in Applied Physics, Chemical Biology, Chemistry, Computer Science and Mathematical Sciences; Pre-Professional Programs in Pre-Dental, Pre-Law and Pre-Med. Accelerated programs, too.

Men's Athletic Profile

Castle Point Station
Hoboken, NJ 07030
Coach: Nick Mykulak
Email: Not Available
NCAA III
Ducks/Red, White
Phone: (201) 216-5689
Fax: (201) 216-8244

Estimated # of Men's Soccer Scholarships: N/A
Conference: Skyline Conference
Program Profile: Natural grass field with a lights. Play a very competitive Division III schedule. Recently opened a new $14 million Athletic Center which include an indoor astro turf training center.
History: Soccer has been played at Stevens for over 100 years.
Achievements: NJ College Coach of the Year in 1993; Conference Coach of the Year in 1993 & 1996; 1 All-American in 1996.
Coaching: Nick Mykulak, Head Coach, who holds a USSF "A" License, John Joseph, Associate Coach, played striker at Wake Forest, Matt Wall , Assistant Coach, was captain of the St. Bonaventure team, played midfield.
Roster In State: 6 **Out of State:** 12 **Out of Country:**
ODP State: 1 **Regional:** 3 **National:**
Walk-on/Other: **Graduation %:** 100 **Seniors on Team:** 9
Positions Needed: Goalkeeper, Sweeper, Striker
Camp or Clinic Dates: August 7-11, 14-18
Most Recent Record: 7-11-1

Schedule: Drew, Kean University, Vassar, Manhattaville, Trinity
Style of Play: Control style, working the ball from the defense to either the midfielders or forwards depending on the pressure. Create scoring opportunities by going wide and serving ball across the pitch.

Women's Athletic Profile

Castle Point on Hudson
Hoboken, NJ 07030
Coach: Sarah Raslowsky
Email: Not Available

NCAA III
Ducks/Cardinal, White, Black
Phone: (201) 216-8087
Fax: (201) 216-8244

Estimated # of Women's Soccer Scholarships: None
Conference: Women's Intercollegiate Athletic Conference
Program Profile: Stevens soccer is played on a large natural turf field with lights. We start pre-season training at the end of August; the regular season ends in late October.
History: Program started in 1992. Recruiting is done on a national level.
Achievements: WIAC Champions: '98, '99. WIAC Coach of the Year: '96, '98, '99. Career Record: 30-26-2
Coaching: Sarah Raslowsky, Head Coach, graduated from Brown University in 1985. She played two years in Brown. She was an assistant coach at Stevens. In 1996 she took over as the head coach here. She got her National Diploma in 1991. She got her Advanced National Diploma in 1999. Her coaching record is: 30-6-2.
Roster in State: 5 **Out of State:** 15 **Out of Country:** 0
Walk-on/Other: **Graduation %:** 100 **Seniors on Team:** 3
Positions Needed: All
Camp or Clinic Dates: Not Available
Most Recent Record: 9-10-1
Schedule: Montclair State, Kean, SUNY-New Platz, Mt. St. Mary, Marymount, St. Joe's-LI, Ramapo, Rutgers-Camden
Style of Play: Style imprinted depends on the team's composition any given year.

William Paterson University

Academic Profile

Wayne, NJ 07470

Phone:

Type: 4 Yr.,Public
Website: http://www.wpunj.edu
SAT/ACT/GPA: 1100
Student/Faculty Ratio: 1:28
Undergraduate Enrollment: 9,800
Scholarships/Academic: Yes **Athletic:** No
Expenses by: Year **In State:** $ 9,200

Founded: 1855
Religion: Non-Affiliated
Housing: Yes
Male/Female Ratio: 45:55
Graduate Enrollment: 2,400
Financial Aid: Yes
Out of State: $ 10,800

Specialty: Business, Biology, Athletic Training, Education, Music
Degrees Conferred: BA, BS, BFA, MA, MS, MBA, MEd
Programs of Study: Business and Management, Communications, Health Sciences, Psychology, Social Sciences, Teacher Education, Visual and Performing Arts

Men's Athletic Profile

300 Pompton Road
Wayne, NJ 07470
Coach: Brian Woods
Email: woods@nebula.wlpaterson.edu

NCAA III
Pioneers/Black, Orange
Phone: (973) 720-3120
Fax: (973) 720-3017

Estimated # of Men's Soccer Scholarships: None

Conference: New Jersey Athletic Conference
Program Profile: We have a new lighted, natural grass field with a measurements of 120x72 yards and has a seating capacity of 1,500. It has a new locker rooms and practice facility.
History: Our program began in 1945. We are always competitive and considered one of the premier programs in the region and the nation.
Achievements: Coach of the Year in New Jersey and NJAC in 1995; 7 All-American players since 1991; 3 players playing in the USISL.
Coaching: Brian Woods, Head Coach, holds a USSF "B" License. He was an Advanced National Head Coach for seven year at WPC. He was a Head Coach of New Jersey Stallions W-League (USL), and ODP Coach.
Style of Play: Strong man to man defense with an English attacking style of with a speed and direct to the box.

Women's Athletic Profile

300 Pompton Road
Wayne, NJ 07470
Coach: Keith Woods
Email: woodsk@wponj.edu

NCAA III
Pioneers/Black, Orange
Phone: (973) 720-3010
Fax: (201) 595-3017

Estimated # of Women's Soccer Scholarships: None
Conference: New Jersey Athletic Conference
Program Profile: Twenty-game regular season. Home games are played on a new natural grass which lighted with 2,000 seats stadium. New practice facilities are being constructed, new locker rooms. Play a traditional fall season and Spring season. Students are expected to condition on their own during the summer months.
History: The program began in 1994. We are consistently ranked in the top 10 of the region. Ranked in the country since 1997.
Achievements: NCAA Tournament participant in 1997 and 1998; 1998 New Jersey Athletic Conference Champions; 1999 NJAC runner-up; 18 All-Conference players; 6 All-Region players; 1 first team All-American since 1994; Conference Coach of the Year in 1997 and 1998.
Coaching: Keith Woods is the Head Coach. Justin Renna and Kathy Sincam are Assistant Coaches and Amy Seja is the Goalkeeper Coach.

Roster in State: 17	**Out of State:** 1	**Out of Country:**
ODP State: 7	**Regional:**	**National:**
Walk-on/Other:	**Graduation %:** 85	**Seniors on Team:** 4

Positions Needed: All
Camp or Clinic Dates: Not Available
Most Recent Record: 15-4-0
Schedule: College of New Jersey, Mary Washington College, Rowan University, Lynchburg College, Richard Stockton College, Scranton University
Style of Play: A "total soccer" style that looks to attack by getting numbers forward as a unit as well as numbers behind the ball to defend.

new mexico

NEW MEXICO

SCHOOL	CITY	AFFILIATION	PAGE
College of the Southwest	Hobbs	NAIA	687
New Mexico Highlands	Las Vegas	NCAA II	687
University of New Mexico	Albuquerque	NCAA I	688

College of the Southwest

Academic Profile

Phone:

Hobbs, NM 88240

Type: 4 Yr.,Private,Liberal Arts
Founded: 1962
Website: http://www.csw.edu
Religion: Non-Denominational
SAT/ACT/GPA: 910/19/2.5
Housing: Yes
Student/Faculty Ratio: 13:1
Male/Female Ratio: 1:2
Undergraduate Enrollment: 577
Graduate Enrollment: 108
Scholarships/Academic: Yes **Athletic:** Yes **Financial Aid:** Yes
Expenses by: Year **In State:** $ 4,338 **Out of State:** $ 4,338
Specialty: Teacher Education, Business
Degrees Conferred: BA, BS, BBA, MSE
Programs of Study: Accounting, Athletic Training, Biology, Business, Education, English, Fine Arts, History, Human Relations, Mathematics, Natural Science, Psychology, Social Science, Counseling

Women's Athletic Profile

6610 Lovington Hwy.
Hobbs, NM 88240
Coach: Jason Jones
Email: jjones@csw.edu

NAIA
Mustangs/Navy, White
Phone: (505) 392-6561
Fax: (505) 392-6006

Estimated # of Women's Soccer Scholarships: Partial
Conference: Red River Conference
Program Profile: We play on natural grass surface. Our field is a 110 yards in length by 75 yards wide. Our season begins in late August and finishes in Mid-November. We play both a fall and spring season.
History: Program began in 1987. Nationally ranked in 1992. Regionally ranked as high as second in Region VI in 1999. Ranked as high as 37th in the country during the 1999 season.
Achievements: 1 All-American, 4 Academic All-Americans and 4 All-Sectional Selections.
Coaching: Jason Jones, Head Coach, entering his 4th season as the Mustangs' coach. Jason holds a USSF "B" license and an Advanced National Diploma from the NSCAA.
Roster in State: 5 **Out of State:** 12 **Out of Country:** 0
Walk-on/Other: **Graduation %:** **Seniors on Team:** 5
Positions Needed: MF, D, GK
Camp or Clinic Dates: May 6-7, June 23-24, July 24-26
Most Recent Record: 11-6-0
Schedule: Oklahoma City, Oklahoma Christian, Northwood, Incarnate Word, St. Mary's, St. Gregory's
Style of Play: We play a possession style of soccer and like to use our defenders in our attack when it is on.

New Mexico Highlands University

Academic Profile

Phone: 505-425-7511

Las Vegas, NM 87701

Type: 4 Yr.,Public,Liberal Arts
Founded: 1893
Website: Not Available
Religion: Non-Affiliated
SAT/ACT/GPA: NCAA Minimum
Housing: No
Student/Faculty Ratio: 17:1
Male/Female Ratio: 42:58
Undergraduate Enrollment: 2,250
Graduate Enrollment: 821
Scholarships/Academic: Yes **Athletic:** Yes **Financial Aid:** Yes
Expenses by: Year **In State:** $ 4,776 **Out of State:** $ 9,474

Degrees Conferred: BA, BS, MA, MS, MBA, MEd, MSW
Programs of Study: Accounting, Biological Sciences, Business Administration, Computer Technology, Environmental Sciences, History, Journalism, Management Information Systems, Marketing, Mathematics, Physical Fitness & Movements, Political Science, PreProfessional Programs, Psychology, Radio & Television Technology, Recreation & Leisure Service, Social Science, Technical Education, Travel & Tourism

Women's Athletic Profile

P.O. Box 9000
Las Vegas, NM 87701-9000
Coach: Gregory Rusk
Email: RuskGregory@nmhu.edu

NCAA II
Cowgirls/Purple, White
Phone: (505) 426-2019
Fax: (505) 426-2014

Estimated # of Women's Soccer Scholarships: 4
Conference: Rocky Mountain Athletic Conference
Program Profile: Fully funded NCAA II women's soccer team in the RMAC. Team home games are played in the newly renovated Perkins Stadium. The natural turf field measures 118x65 yards and is surrounded by an eight lane urethane track and stadium seating 5000.
History: Our program started in 1996 as a member of RMAC.
Achievements: The team routinely places one or two players on the RMAC 1st team. 1999 we had Rookie of the year and All-RMAC 1st team.
Coaching: Gregory M. Rusk is the Head Coach. He holds a USSF "A" License and NSCAA Advanced National Diploma. The assistant coach is Enrique Serrano.
Roster in State: 18 **Out of State:** 3 **Out of Country:** 0
ODP State: 7 **Regional:** 0 **National:** 0
Walk-on/Other: **Graduation %:** **Seniors on Team:** 3
Positions Needed: GOALKEEPER, Central defender, Outside midfield
Camp or Clinic Dates: Not Available
Most Recent Record: 5-12-0
Schedule: Metro State College of Denver, Regis University, West Texas A&M University, Mesa State college, university of Northern Colorado, Ft. Lewis College
Style of Play: We play a fast paced passing game and a high pressure defense.

University of New Mexico
Academic Profile

Phone: 505-277-0111

Albuquerque, NM 87131

Type: 4 Yr.,Public,Engineering
Founded: 1887
Website: http://www.unm.edu
Religion: Non-Affiliated
SAT/ACT/GPA: 850/2.25
Housing: Yes
Student/Faculty Ratio: 19:1
Male/Female Ratio: 45:55
Undergraduate Enrollment: 23,700
Graduate Enrollment: 3,500
Scholarships/Academic: Yes **Athletic:** Yes **Financial Aid:** Yes
Expenses by: Year **In State:** $ 6,945 **Out of State:** $ 13,165
Degrees Conferred: BS, MS, MS, Ph.D.
Programs of Study: Over 170 accredited disciplines; Accounting, Anthropology, Architecture, Art, Art Education, Art History, BioChemistry, Biology, Business Computer Systems, Business Education, Engineering, Communications, Computer Science, Creative Writing, Criminology, Dance, Earth Science, Elementary Education, Economics, Music, Nursing, Pharmacy, Philosophy, Physical Education, Physical Therapy, Sociology

Men's Athletic Profile

Athletic Bldg, South Campus
Albuquerque, NM 87131
Coach: Klaus Weber
Email: Not Available

NCAA I
Lobos/Cherry, Silver
Phone: (505) 277-5244
Fax: (505) 277-5941

Estimated # of Men's Soccer Scholarships: N/A
Conference: Mountain Pacific Sports Federation
Program Profile: We have a new 10,000 sq. ft. weight/training facility. The team plays in the fall, but they do have a small spring schedule. All home matches are played at University Stadium which has a capacity of 30,646 and its surface is natural grass.
History: Our varsity program is 14 years old. The programs first year was 1983.
Achievements: 1992 MPSF Coach of the Year; 2 All -Federation 1st team for the MPSF; 1 2nd Team All - American; 2 on West Regional Team; All - American Scholar Athlete; 1994 - 14-6-0 record, 2nd in MPSF with 5-2 record (a game behind UCLA).
Coaching: Klaus Weber, Head Coach, 11th season, native of Switzerland, USSF 'B' license, 1972 graduate of Keene State.
Style of Play: Modern 'total' soccer - Offensive oriented.

Women's Athletic Profile

Johnson Center
Albuquerque, NM 87131
Coach: TBA
Email: jdsoccer@unm.edu

NCAA I
Lobos/Cherry, Silver
Phone: (505) 277-4358
Fax: (505) 277-5941

Estimated # of Women's Soccer Scholarships: 12
Conference: Mountain West Athletic Conference.
Program Profile: Home games are played at UNM Soccer/Track Complex with a seating capacity of 5,000 that just built in 1996. Play on a natural two full-sized fields which has a 10,000 square foot weight room and a 10,000 square foot training room. Has a 5,000 seat natural grass stadium.
History: Entering 9th year. WAC 2nd place division finish; 5th ranked in the NSCAA school region; 36th ranking in National Sagarin Competition. Have two 2nd place finishes in the WAC, overall program record entering the 2000 season was 63-64-7
Achievements: 1 All-American; 2 UMBRO Select All-Star; 2 Academic All-American; 3 NSCAA team Academic Awards. 2 players from youth national team.

Roster in State: 7	**Out of State:** 12	**Out of Country:** 2
ODP State: 17	**Regional:** 6	**National:** 2
Walk-on/Other:	**Graduation %:** 100	**Seniors on Team:** 3

Positions Needed: Forwards, Center Midfield
Schedule: Syracuse, SMU, Colorado College, BYU, Utah
Style of Play: Possession build from back and use speed on flanks.

new york

NEW YORK

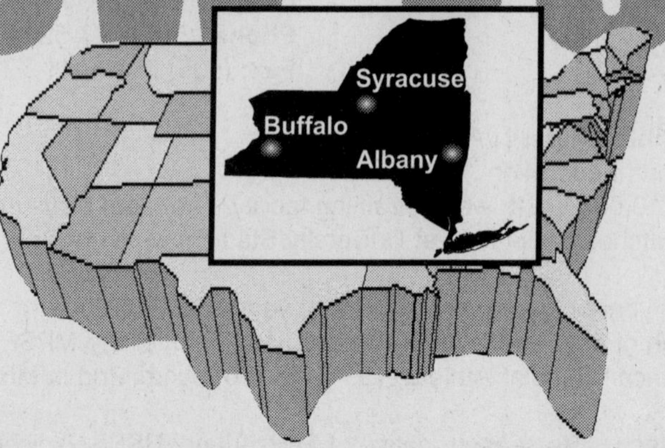

SCHOOL	CITY	AFFILIATION	PAGE
Adelphi University	Garden City	NCAA I	693
Alfred University	Alfred	NCAA III	694
Bard College	Annandale-on-Hudson	NCAA III	695
Buffalo State College	Buffalo	NCAA III	696
Canisius College	Buffalo	NCAA I	698
City College of New York	New York	NCAA III	699
Clarkson University	Potsdam	NCAA III	700
Colgate University	Hamilton	NCAA I	701
College of Mount Saint Vincent	Bronx	NCAA III	702
College of Saint Rose	Albany	NCAA II	703
College of Staten Island - CUNY	Staten Island	NCAA III	704
Columbia University	New York	NCAA I	705
Concordia College - New York	Bronxville	NCAA II	706
Cornell University	Ithaca	NCAA I	706
Dominican College	Orangeburg	NAIA	707
Dowling College	Oakdale	NCAA II	708
Elmira College	Elmira	NCAA III	709
Fordham University	Bronx	NCAA I	710
Hamilton College	Clinton	NCAA III	711
Hartwick College	Oneonta	NCAA I	712
Hilbert College	Hamburg	NCAA III/NAIA	714
Hobart College	Geneva	NCAA III	715
Hofstra University	Hempstead	NCAA I	716
Houghton College	Houghton	NAIA	717
Hunter College	New York	NCAA III	718
Iona College	New Rochelle	NCAA I	719
Ithaca College	Ithaca	NCAA III	720
Keuka College	Keuka Park	NCAA III	722

SCHOOL	CITY	AFFILIATION	PAGE
Le Moyne College	Syracuse	NCAA II	723
Long Island University - Brooklyn	Brooklyn	NCAA I	724
Long Island University - C.W. Post	Brookville	NCAA II	725
Long Island Univ- Southampton	Southampton	NCAA II	726
Manhattan College	Riverdale	NCAA I	727
Manhattanville College	Purchase	NCAA III	728
Marist College	Poughkeepsie	NCAA I	730
Medgar Evers College	Brooklyn	NCAA III	731
Molloy College	Rockville Ctr.	NCAA II	732
Mount Saint Mary College	Newburgh	NCAA III	733
Nazareth College	Rochester	NCAA III	734
New York Institute of Technology	Old Westbury	NCAA II	735
New York University	New York	NCAA III	736
Niagara University	Niagara Falls	NCAA I	737
Nyack College	Nyack	NCAA II/NAIA	738
Pace University	Pleasantville	NCAA II	740
Polytechnic University	Brooklyn	NCAA III	740
Pratt Institute	Brooklyn	NCAA III	741
Rensselaer Polytechnic Institute	Troy	NCAA III	742
Roberts Wesleyan College	Rochester	NCAA II/NAIA	743
Rochester Institute of Technology	Rochester	NCAA III	745
Russell Sage College	Troy	NCAA III	746
Saint Bonaventure University	St. Bonaventure	NCAA I	746
Saint Francis College - New York	Brooklyn	NCAA I	748
Saint John Fisher College	Rochester	NCAA III	748
Saint John's University	Jamaica	NCAA I	749
Saint Joseph's College - New York	Patchogue	NCAA III/NAIA	750
Saint Lawrence University	Canton	NCAA III	751
Saint Thomas Aquinas College	Sparkill	NAIA	752
Siena College	Loudonville	NCAA I	753
Skidmore College	Saratoga Springs	NCAA III	754
SUNY - Binghamton	Binghamton	NCAA II	755
State University of NY- Brockport	Brockport	NCAA III	757
SUNY - Buffalo College	Buffalo	NCAA III	758
SUNYC - Cortland	Cortland	NCAA III	759
SUNYC - Fredonia	Fredonia	NCAA III	760
Geneseo State University	Geneseo	NCAA III	761
SUNY - New Paltz	New Paltz	NCAA III	763
SUNYC - Old Westbury	Old Westbury	NCAA III	764
SUNYC - Oneonta	Oneonta	NCAA I	765
SUNYC - Oswego	Oswego	NCAA III	766
SUNYC - Plattsburgh	Plattsburgh	NCAA III	767

SCHOOL	CITY	AFFILIATION	PAGE
SUNYC - Potsdam	Potsdam	NCAA III	768
SUNY - Stony Brook	Stony Brook	NCAA I	769
SUNY Maritime College	Bronx	NCAA III	771
Syracuse University	Syracuse	NCAA I	771
University at Albany	Albany	NCAA I	773
University of Rochester	Rochester	NCAA III	774
Utica College - Syracuse	Utica	NCAA III	775
Union College - New York	Schenectady	NCAA III	777
US Merchant Marine Academy	Kings Point	NCAA III	778
United States Military Academy	West Point	NCAA I	779
Vassar College	Poughkeepsie	NCAA III	780
Wagner College	Staten Island	NCAA I	781
Wells College	Aurora	NCAA III	782
York College - CUNY	Queens	NCAA III	782

Adelphi University

Academic Profile

Phone: 516-877-3000

Garden City, NY 11530

Type: 4 Yr.,Private,Liberal Arts
Founded: 1896
Website: http://www.adelphi.edu
Religion: Non-Affiliated
SAT/ACT/GPA: 900
Housing: Yes
Student/Faculty Ratio: 12:1
Male/Female Ratio: 1:1.3
Undergraduate Enrollment: 4,100
Graduate Enrollment: 2,000
Scholarships/Academic: Yes
Athletic: Yes
Financial Aid: Yes
Expenses by: Year
In State: $ 19,200
Out of State: $ 19,200
Degrees Conferred: Varied
Programs of Study: Business and Management, Communications, Education, Health Sciences, Life Sciences, Multi/Interdisciplinary Studies, Nursing, Physical Education, Psychology, Social Sciences

Men's Athletic Profile

1 South Ave, Woodruff Hall
Garden City, NY 11530
Coach: Bob Montgomery
Email: montgomery@adelphi.edu

NCAA I
Panthers/Black, Gold
Phone: (516) 877-4234
Fax: (516) 877-4237

Estimated # of Men's Soccer Scholarships: 3
Conference: Atlantic Soccer Conference
Program Profile: Adelphi men's soccer is a Division I program that competes in the Atlantic Soccer Conference. Games are played at Stiles Field (2,800 capacity). The team is comprised of players from the Metro New York area and international students.
History: Inaugural season in 1953. Competed in NCAA's in 1968, 72, 73, 74, 75, 77, 87, 88, 89, 90, 91, 92. Adelphi won the Division II National Championship in 1975.
Achievements: Montgomery was New York Region Coach of the Year in 1987 and 1991. Former players played MLS, MISL, ASL and A League. Chris Armas and Mike Windischmann- U.S. National Team Members.
Coaching: Bob Montgomery, Head Coach USSF "B" license, USYSA East Staff Coach in 1985-present, 1988 Senior Bowl Coach, 1990 Senior Bowl players. Tom Ruane and Ronan Wiseman- Assistant Coaches.
Roster In State: 24
Out of State: 0
Out of Country: 10
ODP State: 3
Regional: 3
National:
Walk-on/Other:
Graduation %: 88
Seniors on Team: 5
Positions Needed: Striker and Defender
Camp or Clinic Dates: Not Available
Most Recent Record: 10-9-0
Schedule: St. John's, Columbia, Princeton, Florida International, Hartwick, Stony Brook
Style of Play: Ball possession on offense, zonal defending.

Women's Athletic Profile

1 South Ave, Woodruff Hall
Garden City, NY 11530
Coach: Rich Ilsley
Email: ilsley@adephi.edu

NCAA II
Panthers/Black, Gold
Phone: (516) 877-4233
Fax: (516) 877-4237

Estimated # of Women's Soccer Scholarships: 5
Conference: New York Collegiate Athletic Conference

Program Profile: Adelphi women's soccer is a Division II program that competes in the New York Collegiate Athletic Conference. The home games are played at Stiles Field (2,800 capacity), a 120x70 natural turf field. The team is comprised of players from the Metro New York area and the Southwest.
History: Inaugural season in 1982. The Panthers won the 1983, 1984, 1985, 1993 ECAC Championship and finished second in the 1992 NCAA tournament. Adelphi has reached the NCAA tournament six times overall. The Panthers have a 212-109-24 all-time record.
Achievements: ilsley was the 1986 National Coach of the Year at Nassau Community College. He was the Regional Coach of the Year from 1991-93 at Adelphi and NYCAC Coach of the Year in 1996, 1997 and 1999. The Panthers won NYCAC Championships in 1996 and 1997. Isley, who completed his 10th season began coaching at Adelphi in 1990.
Coaching: Rich Ilsley, Head Coach, has led the team to two NYCAC Championships.

Roster in State: 17	**Out of State:** 4	**Out of Country:** 0
ODP State: 4	**Regional:**	**National:**
Walk-on/Other:	**Graduation %:** 94	**Seniors on Team:** 3

Positions Needed: Defense, Forward
Camp or Clinic Dates: Not Available
Most Recent Record: 13-6-2
Schedule: Lock Haven, Bloomsburg, C.W. Post, East Stroudsburg, West Chester, Philadelphia
Style of Play: High pressure with emphasis on attacking with numbers.

Alfred University

Academic Profile

Alfred, NY 14802
Phone: (607) 871-2115

Type: 4 Yr.,Public,Liberal Arts,Engineering		**Founded:** 1836
Website: http://www.alfred.edu		**Religion:** Non-Affiliated
SAT/ACT/GPA: v500-600, m510-620/24-28		**Housing:** Yes
Student/Faculty Ratio: 12:1		**Male/Female Ratio:** 49:51
Undergraduate Enrollment: 2,000		**Graduate Enrollment:** 500
Scholarships/Academic: Yes	**Athletic:** No	**Financial Aid:** Yes
Expenses by: Year	**In State:** $ 26,248	**Out of State:** $ 26,248

Specialty: Art, Athletics Training, Business, Education, Engineering, Sciences
Degrees Conferred: BA, BS, BFA, MA, MBA, MPS,MS, MFA, MSE, Ph.D., DPsy
Programs of Study: Engineering & Professionals Studies, Business, Art & Science, Ceramics, Art & Design, Environmental Studies, Performing Arts, Computer Science, Criminal Justice, Sport Medicine, Mechanical Engineering, Chemistry, Accounting

Men's Athletic Profile

1 Saxon Dr.	**NCAA III**
Alfred, NY 14802	Saxons/Purple, Gold
Coach: Ken Hassler	**Phone:** (607) 871-2899
Email: fhassler@alfred.edu	**Fax:** (607) 871-2712

Estimated # of Men's Soccer Scholarships: None
Conference: Independent
Program Profile: Has a year-round program; playing 20 game in fall and 6 in spring. Facilities include lighted 5,000 seat, astro-turf stadium, lighted practice field with a 3,000 seats, and indoor training.
History: Program began in1965 and since that time Alfred University has received numerous Conference, Regional and National Honors. Post season appearances six seasons, numerous All-American and Academic All-American selections.
Achievements: All-Americans in 1982 & 1983 - Charlie Gilje, 1983 Scott Taylor, 1988 Martxel Mariscal; Academic All-American - 1992 Neil Howard; 18 Regional All-Americans since 1982; NCAA Regional tournament in 1988, and ECAC Champions in 1984, 1987, & 1990.

Coaching: Ken Hassler, Head Coach, 7th year at Alfred, State Coach for New York West ODP for five years, nine years as a head coach at college level. Scott Retnouk - Assistant Coach, entering second with the program.
Style of Play: High paced attacking soccer focusing on quick penetrating play through intelligent possession, switching the point of attack, and smart off ball movement. A dangerous offensive style is complimented by team oriented defensive intensity design to overwhelm opponents.

Women's Athletic Profile

McLane Center
Alfred, NY 14802-1205
Coach: Pat Codispoti
Email: codispoti@alfred.edu

NCAA III
Saxons/Purple, Gold
Phone: (607) 871-2896
Fax: (607) 871-2712

Estimated # of Women's Soccer Scholarships: None
Conference: Empire 8 Conference
Program Profile: The Saxons play on Merril Field: Omni turf (installed in 1987), seats 5,000.
History: The program began in 1980; 1986 NYSCWAA consolation championship, 1988 NSAA tournament berth, 1989 ECAC Champions; 1986-1989, 1991, 1994 NYSWCAA tournament berth.
Achievements: Northeast Regional All-American team - 1988 Andrea Hynes, Denise Friendly, 1989 Andrea Hynes, Carolyn Clark; 1994 Melissa Meczwor. NSYWCAA All-State - 1988 Andrea Hynes, Denise Friendly, Carolyn Clark. EAA All-Conference - 1990 Diane Morell, 1991 Daine Morell, Julie Duggan, Jeni-lynn Wetzel. EAA Rookie of the Year - 1990 Jeni Wetzel.
Coaching: Pat Codispoti, Head Coach, is leading into her 13th season with a career record of 81-73 16 after posting a 7-7-3 mark in 1994 campaign. A graduate of Brockport State, coached Saxons to their first ever NCAA Division II tournament appearance in 1988, 1989 the team went 11-6-2 and earned the ECAC Division II Mid-Atlantic Championship, coached at nearby high school before coming to UA, compiling a 107-46-11 record.

Roster in State: 14	**Out of State:** 7	**Out of Country:**
ODP State: 10	**Regional:**	**National:**
Walk-on/Other:	**Graduation %:** 100	**Seniors on Team:** 5

Camp or Clinic Dates: Not Available
Most Recent Record: 7-8-1
Schedule: Ithaca, Vassar, RPI, Nazareth, Hartwick, Elmira
Style of Play: Short passing game with overlapping runs.

Bard College
Academic Profile

Stevenson Gymnasium
Annandale-on-Hudson, NY 12504-5000

Phone: (914) 758-7531

Type: 4 Yr.,Private,Liberal Arts
Website: http://www.bard.edu
SAT/ACT/GPA: Not required, but very competitive
Student/Faculty Ratio: 9:1
Undergraduate Enrollment: 1,100

Founded: 1860
Religion: Nonsectarian
Housing: Yes
Male/Female Ratio: 48:52
Graduate Enrollment: 200

Scholarships/Academic: Yes	**Athletic:** No	**Financial Aid:** Yes
Expenses by: Year	**In State:** $ 31,220	**Out of State:** $ 31,220

Specialty: Film, Arts, Social Sciences, Prelaw
Degrees Conferred: BA, MA, MFA
Programs of Study: Anthropology, Economics, History, Philosophy, Political Studies, Psychology, Religion, Sociology, Arts, Photography, Environmental Science, Biochemistry, Biology, Ecology, Mathematics, Chemistry, Natural Science, Studio Art

Men's Athletic Profile

Athletics Men's Soccer
Annandale-on-Hudson, NY 12504
Coach: Scott Swere
Email: Not Available

NCAA III
Blazers/Red, White, Black
Phone: (914) 758-7530
Fax: (914) 758-7530

Estimated # of Men's Soccer Scholarships:
Conference: Independent Athletic Conference
Program Profile: Field is 120x75 yards set in the mountains, a large gymnasium with all facilities including squash courts. NCAA Division III; Metro Region; Memorial Field, it is all grass.
History: Program began C Div. III level in 1992; Competitive at conference level.
Achievements: None
Style of Play: Possession oriented with a strong emphasis of getting forward. "Direct possession".

Women's Athletic Profile

Stevenson Gymnasium
Annandale, NY 12504
Coach: Matthew Cunniff
Email: Not Available

NCAA III
Blazers/Red, Black, White
Phone: (914) 758-7531
Fax: (914) 758-7530

Estimated # of Women's Soccer Scholarships: None
Conference: Independent Athletic
Program Profile: Memorial Field - adjacent to Stevenson Gymnasium.
History: Began in the early 1960's, recently affiliated with the IAC; first year champions
Achievements: IAC - Artie Gribbins Coach of the Year and Rosanna Reff (Jr. Captain) Player of the Year
Style of Play: Cooperative, competitive; looking for skilled players; commitment.

Buffalo State College

Academic Profile

Phone: (716) 878-6533

Buffalo, NY 14222

Type: 4 Yr.,Public
Founded: 1871
Website: http://www.buffalostate.edu
Religion: Non-Affiliated
SAT/ACT/GPA: No Minimum/2.0
Housing: Yes
Student/Faculty Ratio: 12:1
Male/Female Ratio: 40:60
Undergraduate Enrollment: 9,173
Graduate Enrollment: 1,850
Scholarships/Academic: Yes
Athletic: No
Financial Aid: Yes
Expenses by: Year
In State: $ 4,990
Out of State: $ 14,385
Specialty: Education, Communications, Broadcasting
Degrees Conferred: BA, BS, BFA, BSEd, BT, MA, MS, MPS, MSEd
Programs of Study: Art, Business, Economics, Technology, Communications, Humanities, Languages, Education, Health Sciences, Natural Sciences and Mathematics, Social Sciences, Special and Interdisciplinary Programs

Men's Athletic Profile

1300 Elmwood Avenue
Buffalo, NY 14222
Coach: Anthony Massop
Email: Not Available

NCAA III
Bengals/Black, Orange
Phone: (716) 878-6721
Fax: (716) 878-3401

Estimated # of Men's Soccer Scholarships: None
Conference: SUNYAC
Program Profile: A competitive NCAA Division III program. Our Coyer Field is a natural Kentucky Blue grass playing surface. The season stretches from late August (3 weeks) to early November (conference playoffs). The Bengals also have a state of the art practice facility on campus.
History: The program began in 1935 and is entering its 62st season of competition (the Bengals did not field a team in 1941, 1993, 1994 & 1995). The Bengals State's best season was in 1967 when the team finished 12-1-1
Achievements: Buffalo State has the most All-Americans to date of all Soccer teams in the SUNYAC conference (22) and numerous All-Conference, All-State players named to those teams. A Buffalo State player was named SUNYAC MVP in 1980, 1983 & 1984. A Buffalo State player was named Academic SUNYAC MVP 3 years in a row 1997, 1998, 1999. Buffalo State had the SUNYAC Coach of the Year in 1980, 1982 and Coach Anthony Massop in 1998.
Coaching: Head Coach- Anthony Massop. Assistant Coach- Tim Kronenwetter.

Roster In State: 16	**Out of State:** 1	**Out of Country:** 2
ODP State: 2	**Regional:**	**National:**
Walk-on/Other: 2	**Graduation %:** 95	**Seniors on Team:** 2

Positions Needed: All
Most Recent Record: 9-10-
Schedule: Fredonia, Plattsburg, Nazareth, Roberts Wesleyan College, Cortland, Greensboro, Brockport
Style of Play: We play an attacking style, both offensively and defensively. We have a passionate Latin and African flavor, coupled with a rugged defense.

Women's Athletic Profile

1300 Elmwood Ave.
Buffalo, NY 14222
Coach: Rudy Pompert
Email: rudolfpompert@netscape.net

NCAA III
Bengals/Black, Orange, White
Phone: (716) 878-6631
Fax: (716) 878-3401

Estimated # of Women's Soccer Scholarships: None
Conference: SUNYAC
Program Profile: We have a fast rising soccer program since the arrival of the new head coach in 1997. We have highly professional facilities with natural grass and a 3,000+-seat stadium. Having fun is as important as winning.
History: The first year of women's soccer at Buffalo State was in 1981 when the team posted an 8-6 record. In the last five seasons, the team have won a total of 12 games. Buffalo State was a charter member of the SUNYAC in 1983, and reached the Conference Title game in 1984. Our all-time record is 96-193-13.
Achievements: None
Coaching: Rudy Pompert, Head Coach, former pro soccer player from the Netherlands goalie with National University Team (University in 1991 and 1993. He is USISL W-League team with Buffalo Phillies.

Roster in State: 17	**Out of State:** 1	**Out of Country:**
ODP State:	**Regional:** 7	**National:**
Walk-on/Other: 11	**Graduation %:**	**Seniors on Team:** 4

Positions Needed: Goalkeeper, Forwards
Camp or Clinic Dates: July 17-21, 10-14
Most Recent Record: 6-10-1
Schedule: Cortland, Oneonta, Houghton, Plattsburgh, Roberts Wesleyan, Geneva
Style of Play: We always play with three forwards, and depending on the opponent with three or four defenders. It is our goal to play on the half of the opponent. Our intention is to score goal than the opponent not to get less goals against our opponent.

Canisius College
Academic Profile

Buffalo, NY 14208
Phone: 716-883-7000

Type: 4 Yr.,Private,Liberal Arts
Website: http://www.canisius.edu
SAT/ACT/GPA: 950/2.5
Student/Faculty Ratio: 17:1
Undergraduate Enrollment: 3,000
Scholarships/Academic: Yes **Athletic:** Yes
Expenses by: Year **In State:** $ 21,000
Founded: 1870
Religion: Jesuit
Housing: Yes
Male/Female Ratio: 1:1
Graduate Enrollment: 500
Financial Aid: Yes
Out of State: $ 21,000
Specialty: Business, Education
Degrees Conferred: BS, BA, MBA, PA, MPA, MS, MSEd
Programs of Study: Accounting, Anthropology, Art, Athletic, Banking/Finance, Biology, Business, Chemistry, Economics, International, Languages, Management, Marketing, Medical, Religion, Social Science, Urban, Women's Studies

Men's Athletic Profile

2001 Main Street
Buffalo, NY 14208
Coach: Dave Kreger
Email: kreger@canisius.edu

NCAA I
Griffins/Blue, Gold
Phone: (716) 888-2897
Fax: (716) 888-3174

Estimated # of Men's Soccer Scholarships: 7
Conference: Metro Atlantic Athletic Conference
Program Profile: Play on an grass astro turf covered, lighted field that seats 1,000. A very competitive Division I schedule with an annual trips to Metro-New York and part of the Midwest and south.
History: Our program began in 1996. Won regular season MAAC title in 1996 for the first time ever.
Achievements: 1996 Regular Season; MAAC Champions. 2 All-Americans, 4 drafted players professional.
Coaching: David Kreger, Head Coach. Brian Cribbs, Assistant Coach.
Style of Play: Possession oriented attacking style.

Women's Athletic Profile

2001 Main Street
Buffalo, NY 14208
Coach: Carlos Obiano
Email: Not Available

NCAA I
Golden Griffins/Blue, Gold
Phone: (716) 888-2899
Fax: (716) 888-2980

Estimated # of Women's Soccer Scholarships: None
Conference: Metro Atlantic Athletic Conference
Program Profile: Astro turf on-campus facility, lighted, stadium seats 1,000.
History: The program began varsity play in 1981 and joined the MAAC in 1992; semi-finals in 1992; Championship in 1994; career record of 105-120-9; 6 winning seasons.
Achievements: Two-time MAAC Player of the Year - Stacey Wagenseil.
Coaching: Carlos Obiano, Head Coach, is entering his sixth season. Member of the US Soccer Federation, the National Soccer Coaches of America, and the English Association of Football Coaches and Teachers.
Style of Play: Dynamic, offensive-minded, aggressive and direct style of play.

City College of New York

Academic Profile

Phone: 212-850-7000

New York, NY 10031

Type: 4 Yr.,Public,Engineering
Founded: 1847
Website: http://www.cuny.edu
Religion: Non-Affiliated
SAT/ACT/GPA: 1020/80
Housing: No
Student/Faculty Ratio: 16:1
Male/Female Ratio: 45:55
Undergraduate Enrollment: 5,000
Graduate Enrollment: 2,000
Scholarships/Academic: No
Athletic: No
Financial Aid: Yes
Expenses by: Year
In State: $c3,200
Out of State: $ 6,800
Specialty: Engineering, Liberal Arts, Education, Social Sciences
Degrees Conferred: BA, BS
Programs of Study: Atmospheric Sciences, Computer Engineering, Electrical Engineering, Humanities, Marine Engineering, Marine Transportation & Business, Mechanical Engineering, Meteorology, Naval Architecture, Oceanography

Men's Athletic Profile

138th Street at Convent Avenue
New York, NY 10031
Coach: Ray D'Argenio
Email: Not Available

NCAA III
Beavers/Lavender, Black
Phone: (212) 650-8228
Fax: (212) 650-8230

Estimated # of Men's Soccer Scholarships: n/a
Conference: CUNY-AC, ECAC
Program Profile: A $6.8 million sport complex completed in 1993. It seats 2,000, has an astro turf and lighting system.
History: Won Conference championship 8 out of the last ten years. Eleven years are on conference All-Star team in 1992 including MVP Rookie of the Year. Back to back Championship in 1991 and 1992.
Roster In State: 20
Out of State: 0
Out of Country: 0
ODP State: 0
Regional: 0
National: 0
Walk-on/Other: 0
Graduation %: 90
Seniors on Team: 1
Positions Needed: Forwards
Camp or Clinic Dates: Not Available
Most Recent Record: 11-5-1
Schedule: Kean, York, N.Y
Style of Play: Defensive oriented.

Women's Athletic Profile

138 St. Convent Ave. Athletic Dep.
New York, NY 10031
Coach: TBA
Email:

NCAA III
Beavers/Lavender & Black
Phone: (212) 650-8228
Fax: (212) 650-8230

Estimated # of Women's Soccer Scholarships: n/a
Conference: none
Program Profile: Astroturf field, 1,500 seating capacity.
History: 2 year varsity program. 1-115 record
Achievements: Won first varsity game this season 7-0 against Mount Saint Vincent College.
Coaching: TBA
Roster in State: 20
Out of State: 0
Out of Country: 0
ODP State: 0
Regional: 0
National: 0

Walk-on/Other: 0 **Graduation %:** 90 **Seniors on Team:** 0
Positions Needed: ALL
Most Recent Record: 1-7-0
Schedule: New Jersey City University, Bloomfield, St. Elizabeth, Mt. St. Mary, Rutgers-Newark
Style of Play: Defensive oriented.

Clarkson University

Academic Profile

Potsdam, NY 13699-5830
Phone: 315-268-6622

Type: 4 Yr.,Private,Engineering
Founded: 1896
Website: http://www.clarkson.edu
Religion: Non-Affiliated
SAT/ACT/GPA: Not available
Housing: Yes
Student/Faculty Ratio: 16/1
Male/Female Ratio: 3/2
Undergraduate Enrollment: 2,581
Graduate Enrollment: 321
Scholarships/Academic: Yes **Athletic:** No **Financial Aid:** Yes
Expenses by: Year **In State:** $28,781 **Out of State:** $28,781
Specialty: Engineering and Management
Degrees Conferred: BS, MBA, MA
Programs of Study: Biological Science, Business, Communications and the Arts, Computer and Physical Science, Engineering & Environmental Design, Health Professions, Social Sciences, Physical Therapy

Men's Athletic Profile

Box 5830
Potsdam, NY 13699
Coach: Willi H. Steinrotter
Email: Mnsoccer@clarkson.edu

NCAA III
Golden Knights/Green, Gold
Phone: (315) 268-7983
Fax: (315) 268-7613

Estimated # of Men's Soccer Scholarships: 0
Conference: Upstate Collegiate Athletic Association (UCAA)
Program Profile: We have two grass field that measures 120x80 yards, sodded game field, winning program.
History: The program began in 1953. We've had four times NSCAA Tournament Appearances, 2 NCAA showings in the last five years; round of 16 in 1998 and made the final four in 1993.
Achievements: Willi Steinrotter named Coach of the Year (NSCAA Northeast Regional and EAA in 1993), Seven All-Americans, 44 All-NYS Players, 138 All-League All-Stars.
Coaching: Willi H. Steinrotter, Head Coach, was the 1993 EAAC Coach of the Year. He was the 1993 NSCAA New York Regional Coach of the Year.. He is winningest coach in Clarkson soccer history.
Roster In State: 20 **Out of State:** 9 **Out of Country:** 1
ODP State: **Regional:** **National:**
Walk-on/Other: **Graduation %:** 99 **Seniors on Team:** 2
Positions Needed: Forward, Goal
Camp or Clinic Dates: Not Available
Most Recent Record: 4-12-0
Schedule: St. Lawrence, Hamilton, Plattsburgh, Nazareth, RIT, Ithaca
Style of Play: Ball Control, offensively opportunisitc.

Women's Athletic Profile

Box 5830, Alumni Gym
Potsdam, NY 13699-5830
Coach: TBA
Email: TBA

NCAA III
Golden Knights/Green, Gold
Phone: (315) 268-6622
Fax: (315) 268-7613

Estimated # of Women's Soccer Scholarships: None
Conference: Upstate Collegiate Athletic Association, ECAC
Program Profile: We play in a competitive Division III program. We have both practice and game fields and they have natural grass. Our fall season goes from August to November. Our post-season begins after that.
History: Our program started in 1983. In 17 years, our program has developed into a very competitive program in one of the top Division III Conferences in the nation. ECAC Playoff Appearances (1991,92), NYSWCAA tr. (1992)
Achievements: 25 League All-Stars, three GTE Academic All-Americans
Roster in State: 16 **Out of State:** 5 **Out of Country:** 0
Walk-on/Other: **Graduation %:** 99 **Seniors on Team:** 2
Positions Needed: Forwards
Camp or Clinic Dates: n/a
Most Recent Record: 3-15-0
Schedule: St. Lawrence, Union, Ithaca, Rensselaer, Oswego
Style of Play: Ball control, Offensively opportunistic.

Colgate University
Academic Profile

Phone: (315) 228-7969

Hamilton, NY 13346

Type: 4 Yr.,Private,Liberal Arts **Founded:** 1819
Website: http://www.colgate.edu **Religion:** Non-Affiliated
SAT/ACT/GPA: 1250/27/3.5 **Housing:** Yes
Student/Faculty Ratio: 11:1 **Male/Female Ratio:** 49:51
Undergraduate Enrollment: 2,750 **Graduate Enrollment:** N/A
Scholarships/Academic: Yes **Athletic:** No **Financial Aid:** Yes
Expenses by: Year **In State:** $ 31,000 **Out of State:** $ 31,000
Specialty: Liberal Arts, Business, English, Political Science, Science
Degrees Conferred: BA, MA
Programs of Study: 49 majors and opportunities for individualized majors; 24 faculty led off-campus study groups. Student/faculty collaborative research projects.

Men's Athletic Profile

13 Oak Drive
Hamilton, NY 13346
Coach: Mike Doherty
Email: mdoherty@mail.colgate.edu

NCAA I
Red Raiders/Maroon, White,
Phone: (315) 228-7574
Fax: (315) 228-7925

Estimated # of Men's Soccer Scholarships: None
Conference: Patriot League Conference
Program Profile: We have an all year-round program. Our facility includes Van Doren Field, which is natural grass with lights and seating for 2,500. Our indoor facility, Sanford Fieldhouse is used for winter training. We have a full weight training facility, astro turf facility and Tylers Field, which off season practices are on.
History: The soccer program at Colgate began in 1920. Numerous All-Americans, All-Region and All-League players have been through the program. Nationally rated in 1994 and 1998. The league record is 40-15-5 since the inception of the Patriot League in 1990.
Achievements: Patriot League Coach of the Year in 1992; NSCAA NY State Regional Coach of the Year in 1992 & 1994; Coach Lanzera was named National Coach of the Year in 1992; Conference Titles in 1992 & 1997; 8 All-Americans; 28 Regional All-Americans; 25 All-League Players; players that went to pro: Bobby Newman in 1996 with New York Fever A-League, Jeff Lipman in 1998 with Connecticut Wolves-A-League; Dave MacKenzie in 1978 with Baltimore Blast (MISL), and Jeff Standish in 1992 with Virginia Royals - USISL.

Coaching: Mike Doherty is our Head Coach. He is entering 15 years in coaching. His Alma Mater is Binghamton. His career record is 116-111-27. He was named Regional Coach of the Year; Patriot League Coach of the Year in 1992. Erik Ronning, Assistant Coach, is entering his third season with the program. His Alma mater is Colgate College and graduated in 1997.
Style of Play: Dependent on personnel available.

Women's Athletic Profile

13 Oak Drive
Hamilton, NY 13346
Coach: Kathy Brawn
Email: kbrawn@mail.colgate.edu

NCAA I
Red Raiders/Maroon, Gray
Phone: (315) 228-7762
Fax: (315) 228-7925

Estimated # of Women's Soccer Scholarships: 0
Conference: Patriot League
Program Profile: NCAA II women's soccer program competing in the Patriot League. Lighted Van Doran field, with a natural grass surface and a capacity of 2500, is the home of the women's soccer team. Other facilities include Reid Athletic Center, William Brian Little Fitness Center, Sanford Field House indoor and an outdoor astroturf facility known as Tyler's field.
History: After 19 seasons as a varsity program, the Colgate Women's soccer program posted a 220-114-20 record. Colgate has posted winning records in 17 of the 19 seasons.
Achievements: 9 Patriot League Championships in the League's 11 year history, 3 ECAC Championships, 3 NCAA Tournament appearances, Northeast Region Coach of the Year in 1994, Patriot League Coach of the Year in 1993 and 1994, 1 All-American, 10 All-Northeast Regional All-Americans.
Coaching: Kathy Brawn, Head Coach, has been our head coach for 10 years. Her career record is 131-58-13. She previously coached in Princeton, Yale and Cornell. She has also coached at camps and clinics all around the country. Assistant Coach and former Red Raider Jen Hughes completed her 1st season behind the bench. Maureen Smyth and Tim Amass are the Athletic Trainers.

Roster in State: 10	**Out of State:** 14	**Out of Country:** 0
ODP State: 24	**Regional:** 1	**National:** 0
Walk-on/Other: 0	**Graduation %:** 100	**Seniors on Team:** 7

Positions Needed: All
Camp or Clinic Dates: Call for information
Most Recent Record: 11-9-0
Schedule: West Virginia, NC State, Boston University, UCONN
Style of Play: High Pressure, attacking style of play.

College of Mount Saint Vincent

Academic Profile

Riverdale, NY 10471

Phone: (718) 405-3200

Type: 4 Yr.,Private,Liberal Arts		**Founded:** 1847
Website: http://www.cmsv.edu		**Religion:** Catholic
SAT/ACT/GPA: 1000/2.75		**Housing:** No
Student/Faculty Ratio: 12:1		**Male/Female Ratio:** 1:4
Undergraduate Enrollment: 1,350		**Graduate Enrollment:** 150
Scholarships/Academic: Yes	**Athletic:** No	**Financial Aid:** Yes
Expenses by: Year	**In State:** $ 17,100	**Out of State:** $ 21,950

Degrees Conferred: AA, BA, BS, MS, AAS
Programs of Study: Allied Health Studies, Biology, Business Administration, Chemistry, Computer Science, Economics, Education, English, Exercise and Athletic Training, Fine Arts, French, Health Education, History, International Studies, Liberal Arts, Management, Mathematics, Nursing, Peace Studies, Philosophy, Physics, PreDentistry, PreLaw, PreMed, Psychology, Religious Studies, Social Science, Spanish, Urban Studies

Men's Athletic Profile

Riverdale Avenue & 263rd Street
Bronx, NY 10471-1093
Coach: John Konstantiandis
Email: Not Available

NCAA III
Dolphins/Gold, Royal, White
Phone: (718) 405-3410
Fax: (718) 549-0915

Estimated # of Men's Soccer Scholarships: N/A
Conference: ECAC, Skyline Conference

Women's Athletic Profile

6301 Riverdale Avenue
Riverdale, NY 10471
Coach: Matt Strong
Email: Not Available

NCAA III
Dolphins/Gold, Royal, White
Phone: (718) 405-3410
Fax: (718) 549-0915

Estimated # of Women's Soccer Scholarships: None
Conference: ECAC

College of Saint Rose

Academic Profile

Albany, NY 12203

Phone:

Type: 4 Yr.,Private,Liberal Arts
Website: http://www.strose.edu
SAT/ACT/GPA: 920+/3.0
Student/Faculty Ratio: 17:1
Undergraduate Enrollment: 1,950
Scholarships/Academic: Yes **Athletic:** Yes
Expenses by: Year **In State:** $ 11,968

Founded: 1920
Religion: Independent
Housing: Yes
Male/Female Ratio: 27:73
Graduate Enrollment: 1,400
Financial Aid: Yes
Out of State: $ 11,968

Degrees Conferred: Numerous undergraduate and graduate
Programs of Study: Accounting, American Studies, Art Education, BioChemistry, Biology, Business Administration, Chemistry, Communication Disorders, Communications, Computer Information Systems, Elementary Education, English, Graphic Design, History, Political Science, Religious Studies, Mathematics, Medical Technology, Music, Music Education, Psychology, Religious Studies, Secondary Education, Social Work, Sociology, Sociology/Criminal Justice, Spanish, Special Education, Studio Arts, Studio Music

Men's Athletic Profile

432 Western Avenue
Albany, NY 12203
Coach: P.J. Motsiff
Email: Not Available

NCAA II
Golden Knights/Black, Gold
Phone: (518) 454-2043
Fax: (518) 458-5457

Estimated # of Men's Soccer Scholarships: 5
Conference: New York Collegiate Athletic Conference
Program Profile: Bleecker Stadium is a natural grass field that seats 2,000. We play a traditional season that runs from late August through November. Our non-traditional season runs from December through April.
History: Our program started in 1985. We are in the process of rebuilding.
Achievements: NAIA post-season play twice; 19 All-Conference, 6 All-Region players, 1 All-American, 1 Academic All-American, 3 Academic All-State, 1 Conference Scholar Athlete of the Year.
Coaching: P.J Motsiff is the Head Coach, is entering in his second year with the program.

Women's Athletic Profile

432 Western Avenue
Albany, NY 12203
Coach: Laurie Darling-Gutheil
Email: Not Available

NCAA II
Golden Knights/Gold, White
Phone: (518) 454-2042
Fax: (518) 458-5457

Estimated # of Women's Soccer Scholarships: None
Conference: New York Collegiate Athletic Conference
Program Profile: Saint Rose play's at city-owned Bleecker Stadium. It's a 2,500 seat lighted facility with natural grass.
History: Program began in 1986 and competed in the NAIA and has since risen to the NCAA II level. The 2000 regular season record of 11-5-1 is the best at the school since going 11-4-2 in 1993.
Achievements: 2000 season NE-10 Final Four, post conference tournament, 2000 season ranked fourth out of 15 teams at conclusion. Tied defending national champions 2-2 Franklin Pierce in double overtime. 2000 season will earn an ECAC post season conference bid.
Coaching: In the fifth season under Coach Laurie Darling-Gutheil the program has achieved its most wins ever at 12. It is moving towards earning a top 20 designation in the NCAA after being ranked 4th in the NE-10 conference at the conclusion of the 2000 season.
Roster in State: 20 **Out of State:** 3 **Out of Country:** 0
ODP State: 10 **Regional:** 1 **National:**
Walk-on/Other: **Graduation %:** **Seniors on Team:** 5
Positions Needed: forwards, midfielders, backs, Goalie
Camp or Clinic Dates: August 2001
Most Recent Record: 11-5-1
Schedule: Southern Connecticut State, Franklin Pierce College, Merrimack College, American International College, Bentley College, Stonehill College, LeMoyne College
Style of Play: Direct attacking style with possess ional passing. High pressure defense with zonal defending scheme.

College of Staten Island

Academic Profile

Phone: 718-982-2000

Staten Island, NY 10314

Type: 4 Yr.,Public,
Founded: 1976
Website: http://www.csi.cuny.edu
Religion: Non-Affiliated
SAT/ACT/GPA: 1020 up/80 and better
Housing: None
Student/Faculty Ratio: 19:1
Male/Female Ratio: 1:1.5
Undergraduate Enrollment: 10,674
Graduate Enrollment: 1,522
Scholarships/Academic: Yes **Athletic:** No **Financial Aid:** Yes
Expenses by: Year **In State:** $ Varies **Out of State:** $ Varies
Specialty: All fields
Degrees Conferred: Associates, Bachelor's in Arts and Science, Master's
Programs of Study: Accounting, American Studies, Anthropology, BioChemistry, Biology, Business Administration, Chemistry, Communications, Computer Science, Dramatic Arts, Economics, Education, Engineering, English, Film Arts, Fine Arts, History, International Studies, Languages, Political Science, Psychology, Social Science, Spanish, Women's Studies

Men's Athletic Profile

2800 Victory Blvd.
Staten Island, NY 10314
Coach: Carlo Tramontozzi
Email: Not Available

NCAA III
Dolphins/Maroon, Blue
Phone: (718) 982-3162
Fax: (718) 447-2746

Estimated # of Men's Soccer Scholarships: None
Conference: CUNYAC, Skyline

Columbia University
Academic Profile

Phone: (212) 854-7772

New York, NY 10027

Type: 4 Yr.,Private,Liberal Arts,Engineering
Founded: 1754
Website: http://www.columbia.edu
Religion: Non-Affiliated
SAT/ACT/GPA: 1100/26/Top 20%
Housing: Yes
Student/Faculty Ratio: 7:1
Male/Female Ratio: 49:51
Undergraduate Enrollment: 4,500
Graduate Enrollment: 17,000
Scholarships/Academic: No
Athletic: No
Financial Aid: Yes
Expenses by: Year
In State: $ 31,000
Out of State: $ 31,000
Degrees Conferred: BA, BS, BE
Programs of Study: Just about everything.

Men's Athletic Profile

116th & Broadway
New York, NY 10027
Coach: Dieter Ficken
Email: dwf1@columbia.edu

NCAA I
Lions/Blue, White
Phone: (212) 854-5436
Fax: (212) 854-8168

Estimated # of Men's Soccer Scholarships: None
Conference: Ivy League Conference

Women's Athletic Profile

116th St. & Broadway
New York, NY 10027
Coach: Kevin McCarthy
Email: jkm28@columbia.edu

NCAA I
Lions/Columbia Blue
Phone: (212) 854-4559
Fax: (212) 854-7397

Estimated # of Women's Soccer Scholarships: Ivy League
Conference: Ivy League
Program Profile: The Columbia Soccer Stadium that seats 3,500 is one of the largest in the nation for women's soccer.
History: Program began in 1986.
Achievements: Columbia has received a post season bid to the E.C.A.C. Tournament twice in the past three seasons and has been ranked in the top ten of the Northeast region for three consecutive years. In 1998, we finished 6th nationally in defense.
Coaching: Kevin McCarthy, Head Coach.
Roster in State: 5
Out of State: 15
Out of Country: 1
ODP State: 15
Regional: 5
National: 1
Walk-on/Other: 0
Graduation %: 100
Seniors on Team: 3
Camp or Clinic Dates: Not Available
Most Recent Record: 5-10-2
Schedule: Harvard, Princeton, Dartmouth
Style of Play: Style is determined by the personality of our players and their strengths.

Concordia College - New York

Academic Profile

Phone:

Bronxville, NY 10708

Type: 4 Yr.,Private,Liberal Arts
Website: http://www.ccri.cc.ri.us
SAT/ACT/GPA: No minimum
Student/Faculty Ratio: 10:1
Undergraduate Enrollment: 600
Scholarships/Academic: Yes
Athletic: Yes
Expenses by: Year
In State: $ 18,340
Founded: 1881
Religion: Lutheran
Housing: Yes
Male/Female Ratio: 41:58
Graduate Enrollment: N/A
Financial Aid: Yes
Out of State: $ 18,340
Specialty: Education, Business, Music, Social Work
Degrees Conferred: BA, BS, B.Mus.
Programs of Study: Behavioral Science, Biology, Business Administration, Church Music, Education, English, Environmental Science, History, Interdisciplinary Studies, Mathematics, Music Education, Social Work

Men's Athletic Profile

171 White Plains Road
Bronxville, NY 10708
Coach: Dan Fisher
Email: Not Available

NCAA II
Clippers/Blue, Gold
Phone: (914) 337-9300x2444
Fax: (914) 395-4500

Estimated # of Men's Soccer Scholarships: N/A
Conference: New York Collegiate Conference
Program Profile: Grass field, totally enclosed, seating for 1,500.
History: Program began in 1975, moved from the NAIA to NCAA II in 1985.
Achievements: ECAC Champions in 1981 & 1992; 2 All-State in 1988, 1989, 1990 7 1992; Region Coach of the Year in 1992, NAIA Regional Champs in 1982; 4 All-Conference in 1988 & 1989; 1 Academic All-American; 1 All-American in 1990.

Women's Athletic Profile

171 White Plains Road
Bronxville, NY 10708
Coach: Laurence Piturro
Email: Not Available

NCAA II
Clippers/Blue, Gold
Phone: (914) 337-9300
Fax: (914) 395-4500

Estimated # of Women's Soccer Scholarships: None
Conference: NYCC

Cornell University

Academic Profile

Phone: (607) 255-4762

Ithaca, NY 14853

Type: 4 Yr.,Private,Liberal Arts,Engineering
Website: http://www.cornell.edu
SAT/ACT/GPA: Varies around 1300; Top 10%
Student/Faculty Ratio: 12:1
Undergraduate Enrollment: 13,300
Founded: 1865
Religion: Non-Affiliated
Housing: Yes
Male/Female Ratio: 52:48
Graduate Enrollment: 5,134

Scholarships/Academic: No **Athletic:** No **Financial Aid:** Yes
Expenses by: Year **In State:** $ 19,000 **Out of State:** $ 30,000
Specialty: 7 Specialized diverse colleges on campus
Degrees Conferred: BA, BS, BFA, BA in Architecture, MA, MS, MFA
Programs of Study: Major programs in seven undergraduate colleges: Agriculture & Life Sciences; Art & Architecture Planning ; Arts & Sciences; Engineering; Hotel Administration; Human Ecology; Industrial and Labor Relations

Men's Athletic Profile

Teagle Hall, Campus Rd.
Ithaca, NY 14853
Coach: Bryan Scales
Email: bs38@cornell.edu

NCAA I
Big Red/Red, White
Phone: (607) 255-1312
Fax: (607) 255-2969

Estimated # of Men's Soccer Scholarships:
Conference: Ivy League Conference
Program Profile: Play on natural grass stadium with a seating capacity of 1,800, lighted and was built in 1997.
History: Our program began in 1908.
Achievements: Ivy League Champions in 1975, 1977, & 1995; 14 All-Americans; 10 NCAA Tournaments (most recent was in 1996).
Coaching: Brian Scales is our Head Coach. He graduated from Hartwick in 1991. Robert Elliot is our Assistant Coach. He graduated from Cornell 1997.
Style of Play: Indirect style of play.

Women's Athletic Profile

Teagle Hall Campus Rd
Ithaca, NY 14853
Coach: Berhane Andeberhan
Email: ba22@cornell.edu

NCAA I
Big Red/Red, White
Phone: (607) 255-4762
Fax: (607) 255-2969

Estimated # of Women's Soccer Scholarships:
Conference: Ivy Conference
Program Profile: Has a new soccer track complex with seating for 1,600 spectators and has lighting with grass. Has a 8,000 square feet weight training and conditioning facility for athletes. Has indoor turf facility which measures 60x60 yards and indoor tract for conditioning. All practice and game facilities located on central part of campus.

Dominican College

Academic Profile

Orangeburg, NY 10962-1299

Phone: (914) 398-3008

Type: 4 Yr.,Private,Liberal Arts **Founded:** 1952
Website: http://www.dc.edu **Religion:** Catholic
SAT/ACT/GPA: 1000 Average **Housing:** Yes
Student/Faculty Ratio: 12:1 **Male/Female Ratio:** 1:3
Undergraduate Enrollment: 1,850 **Graduate Enrollment:** 1,000
Scholarships/Academic: Yes **Athletic:** Yes **Financial Aid:** Yes
Expenses by: Semester **In State:** $ 20,000 **Out of State:** $ 20,000
Specialty: Athletic Training, Business Administration, Computers, Education, Etc.
Degrees Conferred: AA, BA, BS, BSN, BSW
Programs of Study: Athletic Training, Biology, Business Administration, Computers, Elementary Education, English, Financial Management, History, Humanities, Nursing, Occupational Therapy, Physical Therapy, Psychology, Special Education

Men's Athletic Profile

470 Western Highway
Orangeburg, NY 10962-1299
Coach: John Cassidy
Email: Not Available

NAIA
Chargers/Red, Black
Phone: (914) 398-3008
Fax: (914) 359-2313

Estimated # of Men's Soccer Scholarships: N/A
Conference: Central Atlantic Collegiate Conference
Program Profile: Strong program, plays team from the entire East Coast including Division I.
History: Program began in 1974, joined NAIA in 1980. District Champs in 1983 & 1989.
Achievements: CACC Champs in 1989 & 1983; 23 All-District, 5 All-Americans.

Women's Athletic Profile

470 Western Highway
Orangeburg, NY 10962
Coach: Lou Fratello
Email: Not Available

NCAA II, NAIA
Chargers/Red, Black
Phone: (914) 398-3009
Fax: (914) 358-3042

Estimated # of Women's Soccer Scholarships:
Conference: CACC
Program Profile: It is a strong program that plays teams from entire East Coast. Made it to the nationals.
History: Our program started in 1990; became Northeast Regional Champs and played in Nationals in 1998.
Coaching: Lou Fratello, Head Coach, entering first year with the program.

Dowling College

Academic Profile

Phone: (800) Dowling
Oakdale, NY 11769

Type: 4 Yr.,Private,Liberal Arts
Founded: 1955
Website: http://www.dowling.edu
Religion: Non-Affiliated
SAT/ACT/GPA: NCAA Div II Requirements
Housing: Yes
Student/Faculty Ratio: 15:1
Male/Female Ratio: 1:3
Undergraduate Enrollment: 4,000
Graduate Enrollment: 1,000
Scholarships/Academic: Yes **Athletic:** Yes
Financial Aid: Yes
Expenses by: Semester **In State:** $ 5,000
Out of State: $ 5,000
Specialty: Aviation, Business, Education
Degrees Conferred: BA, BS, MBA, MS, Ph D in Education
Programs of Study: Accounting, Aero, Airway Science, Arts, Biology, Computer Information Systems, Computer Science, Economics, Education, Elementary Education, English, Finance, History, Humanities, Management, Marketing, Mathematics, Music, Natural Science, Political Science, Psychology, Romance, Languages, Social Science, Special Education, Speech, Drama Arts, Travel and Tourism, Visual Arts

Men's Athletic Profile

Idle Hour Blvd.
Oakdale, NY 11769
Coach: John V. DiRico
Email: jvrd@aol.com

NCAA II
Golden Lions/Blue, Gold
Phone: (516) 244-3315
Fax: (516) 244-3317

Estimated # of Men's Soccer Scholarships: N/A
Conference: New York Collegiate Athletic Conference

Program Profile: We have a new state-of-the-art stadium with a capacity of 2,000. We will have it in place for the 2000 season.
History: We were in the NAIA Final Four in 1981. We have been in the NCAA Division II from 1983 to the present. We have a New York Collegiate Athletic Association affiliation.
Achievements: NYCAC Coach of the Year in 1995 and 1998; NYCAC Champions in 1995,1996,1997,1998; NCAA Tournament in 1996, 1997, 1998; NCAA Tournament Quarterfinals in 1996.
Coaching: John DiRico, Head Coach, has a USSF "B" License. He is a State ODP Staff Coach. Nick Iadanza, Kjetil Soyland and Lou Maia are assistant coaches. John Urbam is goalkeeper coach.
Style of Play: Attack oriented, ball possession play built upon a strong ability to defend in all parts of the field.

Elmira College

Academic Profile

Elmira, NY 14901
Phone: (607) 735-1800

Type: 4 Yr.,Private,Liberal Arts
Founded: 1855
Website: http://www.elmira.edu.com
Religion: Non-Affiliated
SAT/ACT/GPA: Open
Housing: Yes
Student/Faculty Ratio: 12:1
Male/Female Ratio: 2:3
Undergraduate Enrollment: 1,150
Graduate Enrollment: 400
Scholarships/Academic: Yes **Athletic:** No **Financial Aid:** Yes
Expenses by: Year **In State:** $ 26,956 **Out of State:** $ 26,956
Specialty: Liberal Arts Education
Degrees Conferred: AA, AS,BA, BS, MSE
Programs of Study: Accounting, American Studies, Anthropology, Art, Art History, Biology, BioChemistry, Business Administration, Chemistry, Classical Studies, Computer Information Systems, Criminal Justice, Economics, Elementary Education, English Literature, Environmental Studies, Foreign Languages, History, Human Services, Liberal Arts, Marketing, Mathematics, Medical Technology, Music, Nursing, Philosophy & Religion, Political Science, PreDentistry, PreLaw, Psychology, Social Science, Sociology

Men's Athletic Profile

One Park Place
Elmira, NY 14901
Coach: Brandon Banman
Email: bbowman@elmira.edu

NCAA III
Soaring Eagles/Purple, Gold
Phone: (607) 735-1980
Fax: (607) 735-1717

Estimated # of Men's Soccer Scholarships: None
Conference: Empire Eight
Program Profile: Natural Grass, enclosed with an Ivy fence, on campus.
History: 1978-1979 was first Varsity Season.
Achievements: 14 Regional All-Americans in the past nine years; 4 players have gone on to play pro.
Camp or Clinic Dates: Not Available
Most Recent Record: 11-8-0
Schedule: Ithaca, St. Lawrence, U of Rochester, Clarkson, Nazareth, Houghton

Women's Athletic Profile

One Park Place
Elmira, NY 14901
Coach: Shawn Ferris
Email: sferris@elmira.edu

NCAA III
Soaring Eagles/Purple, Gold
Phone: (607) 735-1973
Fax: (607) 735-1717

Estimated # of Women's Soccer Scholarships: None
Conference: Empire Eight Athletic Association
Program Profile: Emerson Hall- gym, fitness center, locker rooms, pool, staff offices, racquetball courts, training room. Murray Athletic center- 2 practice fields outdoor- 1 with lights, 2 indoor gyms. Campus field is a grass field for home contests and measures 110x70.
History: Our program started in 1984.
Achievements: 1994- NYSWCAA 2nd. 1997- 2nd round NCAA tournament. 1998- ECAC Tournament 2nd.
Coaching: Head Coach is Shawn Ferris. Heather Orman and Vanessa Alderman are the Assistant coaches.
Roster in State: 14 **Out of State:** 10 **Out of Country:** 0
ODP State: 7 **Regional:** 0 **National:** 0
Walk-on/Other: 0 **Graduation %:** **Seniors on Team:** 3
Camp or Clinic Dates: Call for info.
Most Recent Record: 7-8-1
Schedule: Scranton, Nazareth, Framingham State, Ithaca, Cortland
Style of Play: Attacking, combination direct, indirect possession to go forward. High pressure defensively.

Fordham University

Academic Profile

Bronx, NY 10458
Phone: (718) 817-4412

Type: 4 Yr.,Private,Liberal Arts
Founded: 1841
Website: http://www.fordham.edu
Religion: Jesuit
SAT/ACT/GPA: 1000/3.0
Housing: Yes
Student/Faculty Ratio: 27:1
Male/Female Ratio: 45:55
Undergraduate Enrollment: 6,275
Graduate Enrollment: 5,000
Scholarships/Academic: Yes **Athletic:** Yes **Financial Aid:** Yes
Expenses by: Year **In State:** $ 28,200 **Out of State:** $ 28,200
Specialty: Prelaw, Premed, Business, Theatre, Arts, Sciences
Degrees Conferred: Bachelors, Masters, Doctoral, Professional
Programs of Study: American Studies, Anthropology, Art, Biology, Broadcasting, Business, Chemistry, Economics, Journalism, Medieval, Peace, Public, Theology, Urban, Women's Studies

Men's Athletic Profile

441 E Fordham Rd
Bronx, NY 10458
Coach: Frank Schnur
Email: Not Available

NCAA I
Rams/Maroon, White
Phone: (718) 817-4269
Fax: (718) 817-4244

Estimated # of Men's Soccer Scholarships: None
Conference: Atlantic 10 Conference
Program Profile: Natural grass game field located in the middle of campus. Pre-season is in August, Fall season; Spring off-season training and tournaments. Great visibility and fan support.
Coaching: Frank Schnur is our Head Coach.

Women's Athletic Profile

441 E Fordham Rd
Bronx, NY 10458
Coach: Ness Selmani
Email: nessluma@aol.com

NCAA I
Rams/Maroon
Phone: (718) 817-4267
Fax: (718) 817-5588

Estimated # of Women's Soccer Scholarships: 2
Conference: Atlantic Ten Conference
Program Profile: Playing season is from September till November; we play on natural grass.
History: The program began in 1993. Spent eight years as a club program. In 1996 team made its first winning season with 8-6-3 record and made it to the Atlantic 10, losing to eventual champion against University of Dayton.
Achievements: Christine Geves was 2nd team All-Atlantic 10 in 1997 and Meghan Rogers was 2nd team All-Atlantic 10 in 1998.
Coaching: Ness Selmani, Head Coach, holds a USSF "A" coaching license since 1982, Coach State team, semi pro teams, Director of Coaching for Cosmopolitan Junior League, USSF Staff Coach.
Roster in State: 14 **Out of State:** 8 **Out of Country:**
ODP State: 8 **Regional:** 2 **National:**
Walk-on/Other: **Graduation %:** 100 **Seniors on Team:** 2
Positions Needed: Midfielders
Camp or Clinic Dates: Not Available
Most Recent Record: —
Schedule: Dayton, Xavier, URI, University of Massachusetts, Columbia, Hofstra, St. Bonaventure, St. John's
Style of Play: Possession game with pressure and skill.

Hamilton College

Academic Profile

Clinton, NY 13323
Phone: (315) 859-4421

Type: 4 Yr.,Private,Liberal Arts **Founded:** 1812
Website: http://www.hamilton.edu **Religion:** Non-Affiliated
SAT/ACT/GPA: 1220/30 **Housing:** Yes
Student/Faculty Ratio: 10:1 **Male/Female Ratio:** 51:48
Undergraduate Enrollment: 1,700 **Graduate Enrollment:** N/A
Scholarships/Academic: Yes **Athletic:** No **Financial Aid:** Yes
Expenses by: Year **In State:** $ 32,000 **Out of State:** $ 32,000
Specialty: Liberal Arts
Degrees Conferred: BA
Programs of Study: Anthropology, Arts, Biochemistry, Biology, Chemistry, Classics, Comparative Literature, Computer Science, Creative Writing, Economics, English, French, Geology, German, Greek, History, International Studies, Latin, Linguistic, Literature, Mathematics, Modern Languages, Molecular Biology, Music, Philosophy, Physics, Political Science, Psychology, Public Affairs, Religion, Sociology, Spanish, Theatre

Men's Athletic Profile

198 College Hill Road
Clinton, NY 13323
Coach: Perry Nizzi
Email: p.nizzi@hotmail.edu

NCAA III
Continentals/Buff, Blue
Phone: (315) 859-4756
Fax: (315) 859-4117

Estimated # of Men's Soccer Scholarships: N/A
Conference: ECAC, NESCAC
Program Profile: Play on turf field from September through October.
History:
Achievements: 2000 UCAA Conference Champion- 1st NCAA apperance, 2000 UCAA Div. III Elite Eight, 6 All-Conference Players, 2000 Coach of the Year.
Coaching: Head Coach Perry Nizzi. Coach Nizzi was 8 time Regional Coach of the Year and 2 time ASCAA National COY. Assistant Coaches Mike Fornina and Donny Dutchet
Roster In State: 22 **Out of State:** 11 **Out of Country:** 3

ODP State: 15 **Regional:** 10 **National:** 0
Walk-on/Other: 0 **Graduation %:** N/A **Seniors on Team:** 4
Positions Needed: Backs, Midfield, GK
Camp or Clinic Dates: July 8-13
Most Recent Record: 11-4-2
Schedule: Middlebury, St. Lawrence, Williams, Skidmore, Nazareth, Clarkson, RPI, Hobart, Union, Vassar
Style of Play: Controlled.

Women's Athletic Profile

198 College Hill Road
Clinton, NY 13323
Coach: Melissa Egeny
Email: meging@homilton.edu

NCAA III
Continentals/Blue, Buff
Phone: (315) 859-4643
Fax: (315) 859-4535

Estimated # of Women's Soccer Scholarships: None
Conference: New England Small College Athletic Conference (NESCAC)
Program Profile: Natural field, seasons runs from September through November. Schedule is composed both nationally and regionally ranked teams. Program is up and coming.
History: Program began in 1979.
Achievements: 3 appearances in state post-season (NYSWCAA) tournament in the last nine years (1986, 1987 & 1988).

Hartwick College

Academic Profile

Oneonta, NY 13820

Phone:

Type: 4 Yr.,Private,Liberal Arts
Website: http://www.hartwick.edu
SAT/ACT/GPA: Open
Student/Faculty Ratio: 13:1
Undergraduate Enrollment: 1,200
Scholarships/Academic: Yes **Athletic:** Yes
Expenses by: Sem **In State:** $ 14,000
Specialty: Business, Liberal Arts
Degrees Conferred: BA, BS

Founded: 1797
Religion: Non-Affiliated
Housing: Yes
Male/Female Ratio: 50:50
Graduate Enrollment: N/A
Financial Aid: Yes
Out of State: $ 14,000

Programs of Study: Accounting, Anthropology, Arts, BioChemistry, Biology, Business Administration, Chemistry, Computer Science, Economics, English, French, Geology, German, History, Information Science, Management, Mathematics, Medical Technology, Music, Nursing, Philosophy, Physics, Political Science, PreLaw, PreMed, PreVet, Psychology, Religion, Sociology, Spanish, Theatre

Men's Athletic Profile

Binder PE Building, West Street
Oneonta, NY 13820
Coach: Jim Lennox
Email: soccermen@hartwick.edu

NCAA I
Hawks/Blue & White
Phone: (607) 431-4712
Fax: (607) 431-4720

Estimated # of Men's Soccer Scholarships: N/A
Conference: Atlantic Soccer Conference
Program Profile: Hartwick is a NCAA I program with a 45 year history. Hawks have been in the NCAA tournament 22 times. They play on Elmore field, which is natural grass and has seating for nearly 3,000 fans. Hartwick plays in the Atlantic Soccer Conference and has 19+ games per season.

History: Program began in 1956 and has had 39 winning seasons in the last 42 years. Hartwick won the NCAA championship in 1977, defeating San Francisco 2-1. Hartwick has been to the NCAA Final 4 seven times. The Hawks rank in the top 10 with 36 career NCAA wins.
Achievements: Jim Lennox- 1977 and 1984 Soccer America Coach of the Year. 1985 NSCAA Coach of the Year. 25 All-Americans.
Coaching: Jim Lennox, head coach, 25 years, 297-149-40. Gregory Moss-Brown, entering 5th year as an assistant. Mark Snell is entering his 3rd year as an assistant.

Roster In State: 3	**Out of State:** 13	**Out of Country:** 11
ODP State: 14	**Regional:** 3	**National:** 1
Walk-on/Other:	**Graduation %:** N/A	**Seniors on Team:** 6

Positions Needed: Forward, Defenders, Goalkeeper
Camp or Clinic Dates: 2 weeks in July
Most Recent Record: 11-8-1
Schedule: University of Conn., Penn State, Florida International, Virginia Commonwealth, Princeton, Cornell University, Columbia University, Fairfield University, Adelphi University, Syracuse University
Style of Play: A mix style of play. If can't penetrate keep it.

Women's Athletic Profile

Binder PE Centre
Oneonta, NY 13820
Coach: Ray Nause
Email: nauser@hartwick.edu

NCAA III
Hawks/Royal Blue, White
Phone: (607) 431-4728
Fax: (607) 431-4020

Estimated # of Women's Soccer Scholarships: None
Conference: Empire Eight, New York State Women's Collegiate Athletic Association
Program Profile: Schedule runs from early September to early November; students arrive in mid-August for pre-season work-outs. Home games at natural grass called Elmore Field, also home to the Hartwicks Division I men's program (field size is 120x75 yards with a capacity of 3,000 surrounded by 8-lane all-weather track). National Soccer Hall of Fame within a mile of campus. We also have three training fields and one turf field available.
History: The program initiated in 1980. The team has posted winning records in 15 to 20 seasons as will as being selected for 12 post-season appearances. Our post-season appearances include five NCAA Division III tournaments, four ECAC Championship tournaments, and three NYSWCAA tournaments.
Achievements: Hartwick has had seven players recognized as All-Americans, four recognized as Academic All-Americans and a player recognized as 1985 ISAA Goalkeeper of the Year. The team has also been recognized with the 1998-1999 NSCAA Team Academic Award.
Coaching: Ray Nausa enters his second season as head women's soccer coach at Hartwich College and his tenth season as a collegiate head coach during the Fall of 2000. He holds a USSF 'B' license, a NSCAA Advanced National Diploma and the NSCAA Goalkeeping Level I Certificate.

Roster in State: 6	**Out of State:** 8	**Out of Country:** 0
ODP State: 5	**Regional:** 0	**National:** 0
Walk-on/Other: 0	**Graduation %:**	**Seniors on Team:** 2

Positions Needed: Forwards, Defenders
Camp or Clinic Dates: 2 weeks in July
Most Recent Record: 5-13-0
Schedule: Ithaca, RIT, Nazareth, Oneonta State.
Style of Play: We adopt the style of play each year that is best suited to the blend of strengths that the current group of players bring to the program.

Hilbert College
Academic Profile

Hamburg, NY 14075

Phone: (716) 649-7900

Type: 4 Yr.,Private,Liberal Arts
Website: http://www.hilbert.edu
SAT/ACT/GPA: Open
Student/Faculty Ratio: 10:1
Undergraduate Enrollment: 950
Scholarships/Academic: Yes **Athletic:** No
Expenses by: Year **In State:** $ 10,000

Founded: 1957
Religion: Franciscan
Housing: Yes
Male/Female Ratio: 306:345
Graduate Enrollment: N/A
Financial Aid: Yes
Out of State: $ 10,000

Specialty: Criminal Justice, Economics, Crime Investigation
Degrees Conferred: BA, BS, AAS, AA, AS
Programs of Study: Accounting, Business Administration, Criminal Justice, English, Human Services, Paralegal Studies, Psychology, Banking, Liberal Arts, Management Information Systems, Economics

Men's Athletic Profile

5200 S Park Avenue
Hamburg, NY 14075
Coach: Andrew Crawfd
Email: Not Available

NCAA III/NAIA
Hawks/Blue, Silver, White
Phone: (716) 649-7900x333
Fax: (716) 649-6429

Estimated # of Men's Soccer Scholarships: None
Conference: Eastern States Athletic Conference
Program Profile: Home games are played on campus; play a Fall season.
History: Hilbert College was a Junior College until 1992, when it joined the NCAA Division III program.

Women's Athletic Profile

5200 S Park Avenue
Hamburg, NY 14075
Coach: Mark Malikowski
Email: Not Available

NCAA III
Lady Hawks/Blue, White
Phone: (716) 649-7900
Fax: (716) 649-6429

Estimated # of Women's Soccer Scholarships: None
Conference: ECAC
Program Profile: The 1996-1997 season marked our debut into our newly created Eastern State Athletic Conference. Games are played on a natural grass field located behind Hafner Recreation Center.
History: We became a member of the NCAA Division III in 1992. Prior to that, we belonged to the NJCAA.
Achievements: None
Coaching: Mark Malikowski, Head Coach, was a four year Division I varsity player. He was a U-17 New York State Champion Player. He has an NSCAA National Diploma and a USSF "B" License.
Style of Play: Emphasis on ball control - slow methodical build-up from the keeper to the backs through the midfield and then to the forwards. Emphasis on possession.

Hobart and William Smith Colleges

Academic Profile

Geneva, NY 14456

Phone:

Type: 4 Yr.,Private,Liberal Arts
Website: http://www.hws.edu
SAT/ACT/GPA: None
Student/Faculty Ratio: 13/1
Undergraduate Enrollment: 1,800
Scholarships/Academic: Yes **Athletic:** No
Expenses by: Year **In State:** $31,224
Specialty: Liberal Arts
Degrees Conferred: BA, BS

Founded: 1822
Religion: Non-Affiliated
Housing: Yes
Male/Female Ratio:
Graduate Enrollment: none
Financial Aid: Yes
Out of State: $31,224

Programs of Study: Art, BioChemistry, Chemistry, Classics, Comparative Literature, Computer Information Science, Economics, English, Environmental Studies, French, Geoscience, German, Greek, History, Mathematics, Music, Philosophy, Physics, Political Science, Psychology, Religious, Women's Studies, Urban Studies

Men's Athletic Profile

Bristol Gymnasium
Geneva, NY 14456
Coach: Willi Steinrotter, Sr.
Email: Not Available

NCAA III
Statesmen/Orange, Navy
Phone: (315) 781-3565
Fax: (315) 781-3570

Estimated # of Men's Soccer Scholarships: N/A
Conference: UCAA
Program Profile: Fall season schedule has 18 game, and practice is in the Spring. Play on a grass field (Alumni Field). Travel to Germany every four years.
History: Program began in 1981- present under Coach Steinrotter, 1992 NCAA appearances,. number one in the nation
Achievements: Coach Steinrotter was named 1992 NCAA National Coach of the Year.
Coaching: Willi Steinrotter, Head Coach, USSF "A" coaching license, played professionally, 1992 Coach of the Year, well known ski instructor, has his own family owned ski area.
Style of Play: High work-rate, emphasis on fitness, and the attacking style is with high pressure.

Women's Athletic Profile

Hamilton Street
Geneva, NY 14456
Coach: Aliceann Wilber
Email: Not Available

NCAA III
Herons/Dark Green, White
Phone: (315) 781-3500
Fax: (315) 781-3503

Estimated # of Women's Soccer Scholarships: None
Conference: Empire Athletic Association, NYSWCAA
Program Profile: Natural grass with a fieldhouse for off-season training. Two programs; Varsity and Junior Varsity. Varsity plays a very demanding Division III schedule and is consistently nationally ranked.
History: Program began in 1980.
Achievements: 1987 Division II Finalist, 1988 Division III National Champions, 1993 NCAA Semi-Finals; since 1987 - 34 Regional All-Americas, 14 NSCAA All-American, 7 Adidas Academic All-Americans.
Coaching: Aliceann Wilber, Head Coach, NSCAA Coach of the Year in 1987, 1988, 1989, & 1991; NSCAA Regional Coach of the Year in 1993; NCAA Division Women's Chair (National) in 1988-1993.
Style of Play: Controlled, attacking style of play; high pressure defense.

Hofstra University

Academic Profile

Phone: (516) 463-6758

Heampstead, NY 11550

Type: 4 Yr.,Private,Liberal Arts
Website: http://www.hofstra.edu
SAT/ACT/GPA: 1100/23/3.0
Student/Faculty Ratio: 13:1
Undergraduate Enrollment: 8,000
Scholarships/Academic: Yes **Athletic:** Yes
Expenses by: Year **In State:** $ 22,000
Founded: 1932
Religion: Non-Affiliated
Housing: Yes
Male/Female Ratio: 47:53
Graduate Enrollment: 4,000
Financial Aid: Yes
Out of State: $ 22,000
Specialty: Education, Business
Degrees Conferred: AAS, BA, BS, BFA, BBA, BE, BSE, Ph.D., JD, MS, MA, MBA
Programs of Study: American Studies, Anthropology, Art History, Asian Studies, Biology, Chemistry, Communications, Comparative Literature & Languages, Computer Science, Drama & Dance, Economics, Engineering, English, Fine Arts, French, Geology, History, Humanities, International Affairs, Mathematics, Military Science, Music, Philosophy, Physics, Political Science, Psychology, Religious Studies, Sociology

Men's Athletic Profile

Hempstead Turnpike
Hempstead, NY 11550-1090
Coach: Richard Nuttall
Email: Not Available

NCAA I
Flying Dutchmen/Gold, Blue
Phone: (516) 463-6762
Fax: (516) 463-5033

Estimated # of Men's Soccer Scholarships: None
Conference: North Atlantic Conference
Program Profile: The home playing field is natural grass, and is enclosed by a fence. The team is sponsored by Umbro.
History: Our program began in 1954. The Flying Dutchmen have had nine different coaches, and an overall record of 242-391-60 for 42 years.
Achievements: Won East Coast Conference in 1985.
Coaching: Richard Nuttall is our Head coach. He is entering ninth year as a head soccer coach. He was named 1993 East Coast Conference Coach of the Year. He played professionally with Leeds United and Stroke City in England, English FA Coaching Certificate.
Style of Play: Attack minded, direct tough tackling.

Women's Athletic Profile

212 Stadium Building
Hempstead, NY 11549
Coach: JoAnne Russell
Email: athjer@hofstra.edu

NCAA I
Flying Dutch/Gold, White, Royal
Phone: (516) 463-6960
Fax: (516) 463-4860

Estimated # of Women's Soccer Scholarships: 11
Conference: America East Conference, Affiliated with CAA (2003)
Program Profile: Relatively young Division I program. Plays in the fall on a natural grass field. Players have access to the state of the art weight room. play in a soccer rich area; long Island has numerous youth leagues which provide a strong fan base.
History: The program began as a club team in 1992. Went to Division I in 1993. Had a record of 16-2-1 in 1994, and advancing to the ECAC Quarterfinals. 2000 lost to Hartford in playoffs 1-0.
Achievements: Coach of the Year-America East 1999, 1-Regional All-American, 2 Irish National Team Members, 1 drafted to New York Power, 2 play in W League.

Coaching: JoAnne Russell, Head Coach, named 1994 Nassau County Sports Commission Coach of the Year. Enters her 10th year as a head coach of the Hofstra University women's soccer program. She served as a coached in the East Meadow Soccer Club, and player-coach of the Long Island Women's Soccer club champions in 1982 and 1983. Also coached the Long Island Women's Open Tournament at the New York Empire State Games, winning a silver medal in 1992 and 1994, and a bronze in 1993. Simon Riddlough - Assistant Coach, fifth season as an assistant coach at Hofstra University. He was an All-New York Region performer in 1993 and 1994, and an All-East Coast Conference pick in 1993. He was also a member of the All-Region Academic Squad. Grad Assist. Coach- Jason Beehler. Volunteer Coach- David Willems.

Roster in State: 14 **Out of State:** 9 **Out of Country:** 6
ODP State: 8 **Regional:** 1 **National:** 2
Walk-on/Other: 11 **Graduation %:** 100 **Seniors on Team:** 7
Positions Needed: GK, Sweeper, C.Mid, 2 Forwards
Camp or Clinic Dates: Not Available
Most Recent Record: 12-5-2
Schedule: Hartford, Boston Univ. O.D.U, Florida International, West Virginia, JMU, George Mason, William & Mary.
Style of Play: We like to play a possession game with a direct and positive approach. A full pressure defense.

Houghton College
Academic Profile

Phone: 800-777-2556

Houghton, NY 14744-0128

Type: 4 Yr.,Private,Liberal Arts **Founded:** 1886
Website: http://www.houghton.edu **Religion:** Non-Affiliated
SAT/ACT/GPA: 1170/3.4 **Housing:** Yes
Student/Faculty Ratio: 15:1 **Male/Female Ratio:** 1:1.8
Undergraduate Enrollment: 1,250 **Graduate Enrollment:** Not Avai
Scholarships/Academic: Yes **Athletic:** Yes **Financial Aid:** Yes
Expenses by: Year **In State:** $19,000 **Out of State:** $19,000
Specialty: Liberal Arts
Degrees Conferred: BA, BS
Programs of Study: Accounting, Art, Bible, Biology, Business, Chemistry, Christian Ministry, Communications, Computer Science, Elementary Education, English, French, History, International Studies, Mathematics, Music, Philosophy, Physical Education, Physics, Political Science, PreMental, PreMed , PreVet, Psychology, Recreation, Religion, Sociology, Spanish,

Men's Athletic Profile

One Willard Avenue
Houghton, NY 14744-0128
Coach: Dwight Hnibrook
Email: dhornibrook@houghton.edu

NAIA
Highlanders/Purple, Gold
Phone: (800) 777-2566x489
Fax: (716) 567-9365

Estimated # of Men's Soccer Scholarships: 5
Conference: Northeast Atlantic Conference
Program Profile: We have an outstanding facilities, including lit practice and game field. We have a high quality grass playing surface with 1,500 seat grant stand.
History: For 35 years, Houghton has had a highly regarded soccer tradition. Bringing players from all over the world to Western New York the past four years. Our record is 62-22-6.
Achievements: We won KECC Coach of the Year in 1995, Conference and Regional Champions in 1995 & 1996. We have produced several All-Americans during this span.

Coaching: Dwight Hornibrook, Head Coach, is entering his fifth season with the program. He was a National Team's Staff Coach in Canada in 1987-1994. He was involved with 1994 World Cup Team and in 1987 U-17 National Team. He played and coached pro-soccer in Canada. Also, National American Scout for Middlesbrough FC and an English Premier League

Roster In State: 16 **Out of State:** 8 **Out of Country:** 2
ODP State: 7 **Regional:** 2 **National:**
Walk-on/Other: 2 **Graduation %:** 100 **Seniors on Team:** 5
Positions Needed: Striker, Midfielder, Back, Goalkeeper
Camp or Clinic Dates: July 23-28 and July 30-August 4
Most Recent Record: 18-3-1
Schedule: Milligan College, Green Mountain College, Gannon University, Belhaven College, Roberts Wesleyan College, St. Joseph's College
Style of Play: We want to possess the ball but are able to change to a more direct style if needed. We will play zonal defending in midfielder and three at the back with a Sweeper.

Women's Athletic Profile

1 Willard Avenue
Houghton, NY 14744
Coach: David Lewis
Email: david.lewis@houghton.edu

NAIA
Highlanders/Purple, Gold
Phone: (716) 567-9548
Fax: (716) 567-9225

Estimated # of Women's Soccer Scholarships: Varies
Conference: American Mideast Conference
Program Profile: Has a new lighted game which has a maximum size. Two new practice and game fields that are natural grass, with a seating capacity of 1,200. Excellent facilities.
History: Began in 1981, both varsity and Junior varsity and sports ministry emphasis.
Achievements: 8 Consecutive Conference Title in 1993-2000, Northeast Region Finalist or Semi-Finalist in 1993-1997; 17 NAIA All-Americans; NSCAA UMBRO East Region Coach of the Year in 1997. Coach Lewis was named NSCAA/Umbro 1997 Senior College Women's NAIA Coach of the Year; NSCAA/Adidas 1998 Senior College Women's NAIA Coach of the Year; Team has 6 consecutive Conference Championships in 1993-1998; nationally ranked #6 in 1998, #8 in 1997; 16 NAIA All-Americans over the past six years. Overall record past 6 seasons 105-13-2 (.883)
Coaching: David Lewis, Head Coach, NSCAA Advanced Licensed, USSF License, former collegiate All-American player, former player with Athlete in Action, Conference Coach of the Year, camp and clinic clinician, international experience with Missionary Athletes International. Compiled a record of 148-43-5 and former All-American player.
Roster in State: 15 **Out of State:** 10 **Out of Country:** 2
ODP State: 7 **Regional:** 4 **National:** 0
Walk-on/Other: 0 **Graduation %:** 100 **Seniors on Team:** 5
Positions Needed: Defender, Midfielder, Striker, GK
Camp or Clinic Dates: July, Aug.3 and Aug. 5-10
Most Recent Record: 19-2-0
Schedule: Tiffin Univ. Seton Hill College, Roberts Wesleyan College, Malone College, Cedarville College, Mount Vernon Nazarene Univ.
Style of Play: Possession style, emphasis on sound fundamentals.

Hunter College

Academic Profile

Phone:

New York, NY 10021

Type: 4 Yr.,Public,Liberal Arts
Website: http://www.hunter.cuny.edu
SAT/ACT/GPA: Open

Founded: 1870
Religion: Non-Affiliated
Housing: Yes

Student/Faculty Ratio: 17:1
Male/Female Ratio: 3:1
Undergraduate Enrollment: 14,100
Graduate Enrollment: 4,300
Scholarships/Academic: Yes
Athletic: No
Financial Aid: Yes
Expenses by: Year
In State: $ 5,672
Out of State: $ 9,272
Specialty: Education, Nursing, Liberal Arts
Degrees Conferred: BA, BS, BFA, MA, MS, MFA, M.Ed.
Programs of Study: Numerous fields of study.

Men's Athletic Profile

695 Park Avenue
New York, NY 10021
Coach: John Benintendo
Email: Not Available

NCAA III
Hawks/Purple, Gold
Phone: (212) 650-3901
Fax: 212-772-4739

Estimated # of Men's Soccer Scholarships: None
Conference: CUNYAC
Program Profile: Hunter College features a highly competitive NCAA III men's soccer team that is one of the top programs in the New York City area each year. The Hawks compete every fall for championships in the CUNYAC in addition to taking on numerous suburban, upstate, and regional foes. The team plays its home games at Riverbank State Park on New York's Upper West Side.
History: Program began in approximately 1953. Cumulative record since 1980 adds up to 152-167-28. Since 1995, we are 61-40-8. Team has enjoyed winning seasons in 5 of last 6 years and 9 out of the last 16. The Hawks have won 3 CUNYAC tournament championships, 6 regular season titles, and 1 ECAC crown. The team has played in 4 ECAC tournaments and 1 NCAA tournament.
Achievements: NCAA III tournament bid in 1999. ECAC tournament bids 1973, 87, 95, 98. ECAC Champions 1973. CUNYAC tournament champions 1995, 97, 99. CUNYAC regular season champions 1987, 95, 96, 97, 98, 99.
Coaching: Head Coach: John Benintendo (3-14-2 overall since 2000). Assistant coach: Salvador Brianes.
Roster In State: 7
Out of State: 1
Out of Country: 15
Walk-on/Other:
Graduation %: 85
Seniors on Team: 2
Positions Needed: All
Camp or Clinic Dates: Not Available
Most Recent Record: 3-14-2
Schedule: Rowan, Kean, New Jersey City, NYU, Centenary, SJC-Patchogue, Farmingdale State, CCNY, Medgar Evers, York
Style of Play: Fast paced, skill reliant, and exciting!

Iona College
Academic Profile

New Rochelle, NY 10801
Phone: (914) 633-2315

Type: 4 Yr.,Private,Liberal Arts
Founded: 1940
Website: http://www.iona.edu
Religion: Catholic
SAT/ACT/GPA: 820
Housing: Yes
Student/Faculty Ratio: 12:1
Male/Female Ratio: 1:1
Undergraduate Enrollment: 6,000
Graduate Enrollment: 1,000
Scholarships/Academic: Yes
Athletic: Yes
Financial Aid: Yes
Expenses by: Year
In State: $ 23,000
Out of State: $ 23,000
Specialty: Liberal Arts, Business
Degrees Conferred: AA, AAS, BA, BS, MA, MS, MBA, M.Ed.
Programs of Study: Accounting, BioChemistry, Biology, Chemistry, Computer and Information Science, Business, Education, PrePhysical Therapy, Communications, Psychology, Teacher Education, Computer Science, Law, Math, Health Science

Men's Athletic Profile

715 North Avenue
New Rochelle, NY 10801
Coach: Mike Jacobs
Email: Not-Available

NCAA I
Gaels/Black Gold, White
Phone: (914) 633-2315
Fax: (914) 633-2662

Estimated # of Men's Soccer Scholarships: N/A
Conference: Metro Atlantic Athletic Conference (MAAC)
Program Profile: Iona College is one to the up and coming programs in Division I. No program has risen in the RPI like Iowa over the last three years. The Gaels have both an artificial turf and a natural grass playing facility.
History: The program started in 1981. It reached the MAAC Conference finals in 1995. We set school records for overall wins (12) in 1997 and conference wins (6).
Achievements: Bobby Herodes was named MAAC Coach of the Year in 1995; Stefan Miglioranzi was named MAAC Rookie of the Year in 1995; All-New York Region in 1995; Rhet Mitchell was All-Academic MAAC in 1994 & 1995; All-New York Region in 1995; Academic All-American in 1995.
Coaching: Mike Jacobs is our Head Coach. He is regarded as one of the top young coaches in the country. Before working at Iona, Jacobs had stints with both the Long Island Rough Riders (A-League) and No. Jersey Imperials (D-III Pro) as an assistant. He also has worked on staff with Region One and Eastern New York Olympic Development Programs.
Style of Play: Our team plays a very direct style of play offensively, constantly looking to go forward at a high pace. Defensively, we play a high pressure system, trying to cause turn-over in our attacking third.

Women's Athletic Profile

714 North Avenue
New Rochelle, NY 10801-1890
Coach: Dwayne Roberts
Email: droberts@iona.edu

NCAA I
Gaels/Maroon, Gold
Phone: (914) 633-2131
Fax: (914) 633-2662

Estimated # of Women's Soccer Scholarships: None
Conference: Metro Atlantic Athletic Conference (MAAC)
Program Profile: Rebuilding program, astro-turf field; fall season, stadium size is consists of 1,000 seats.
History: Program began in 1989. MAAC Champions in 1992.
Achievements: 1992 MAAC Champions, had players named to 1993 Northeast Region All-America second team, All-MAAC Conference Team.
Coaching: Dwayne Roberts, Head Coach. Chris Lynn - Assistant Coach. Mike Demakis - Strength and Conditioning Coach.
Style of Play: We play an attractive style of soccer building out of the back; possession oriented. However, will go forward at speed with a numbers when available. Both defending in all areas of the field and intelligent tactical decision making with and without the balls is also emphasized.

Ithaca College

Academic Profile

Ithaca, NY 14850

Phone: 607-274-3011

Type: 4 Yr.,Private,Liberal Arts
Website: http://www.ithaca.edu
SAT/ACT/GPA: None
Student/Faculty Ratio: 12:1
Undergraduate Enrollment: 5,600
Scholarships/Academic: Yes **Athletic:** No

Founded: 1892
Religion: Non-Affiliated
Housing: Yes
Male/Female Ratio: 47:53
Graduate Enrollment: 200
Financial Aid: Yes

Expenses by: Year **In State:** $ 19,849 **Out of State:** $ 19,849
Degrees Conferred: BA, BS,' BFA, BM, MS, MM
Programs of Study: Accounting, Finance, Human Resources Management, International Business, Management and Marketing, Corporate Communications, Film, Photography, Arts, Journalism, Media Studies, Telecommunications, Health Services, Athletic Training, Exercise Science, Clinical Science, Physical Therapy, Community Health Education, Health & Physical Education, Health Information Management, Physical Education Teacher, Recreation, Anthropology, Applied Psychology, Musical Theatre, Computer Science, Sociology, Spanish, Music, Religion

Men's Athletic Profile

953 Danby Road
Ithaca, NY 14850
Coach: Andy Byrne
Email: Not Available
NCAA III
Bombers/Blue, Gold
Phone: (607) 274-3337
Fax: (607) 274-1667

Estimated # of Men's Soccer Scholarships: N/A
Conference: Independent
Program Profile: Ithaca College men's soccer is a very competitive program in Upstate New York. The Bombers competes against a tough regional schedule every year. Ithaca practices and plays (at home) on a natural grass surface located at the top of the campus. Ithaca begins pre-season workouts the last week in August and can play through November. The field seats about 500. There are Spring workouts.
History: Men's soccer has been a varsity sport at Ithaca College for 63 years. Its first year of existence was in 1932 and since then the Bombers have posted a 366-266-58 record for an impressive .573 winning percentage. Amazingly enough, there have only been eight head coaches at Ithaca in the history of the sport, including the current boss who is the all-time winningest coach in school annuals (126-60-19). In the Fall of 1995 advanced to the NCAA Division III quarterfinals for the first time in the history of the program.
Achievements: NCAA Division III playoff participant (1965, 1979, 1980, 1985, 1987, 1989, 1990, 1991, 7 1995). Conference Champions in 1979, 1982, 1980, & 1991; a total of eight All-American athletes, including two-time recipient Sandor Szabo, who scored 80 goals and 180 points in just 33 games back in the mid 1960's.
Coaching: Andy Byrne, Head Coach, enters his 14th season at Ithaca College this coming Fall and has produced 11 consecutive winning seasons at Ithaca. From 1985 through 1993 the Bombers made post-season appearances. He is a 1975 graduate of Plymouth State.
Style of Play: Heavy emphasis on skill, encourage players to take on defenders and play with flair.

Women's Athletic Profile

953 Danby Road
Ithaca, NY 14850
Coach: Mindy Quigg
Email: Not Available
NCAA III
Bombers/Blue, Gold
Phone: (607) 274-3180
Fax: (607) 274-1667

Estimated # of Women's Soccer Scholarships: None
Conference: Independent
Program Profile: Ithaca College women's soccer is a very young competitive program in Upstate New York. Bombers practice and play (at home) on a natural grass surface located at the top of the campus. Ithaca begins pre-season workouts during the last week in August, and depending on playoffs, can play through November. The field seats about 500. There are Spring workouts.
History: 1981 was Ithaca's first season as a varsity sport. They have had nothing short of winning record in each of its 15 varsity seasons. From 1987-1994, Ithaca made eight straight appearances in the NCAA Division III playoffs and captured national championships in 1990 and 1991. Ithaca's overall record is 196-57-36 for an outstanding .741 winning percentage.

Achievements: NCAA division III Champs in 1990 & 1991; NCAA Division III playoffs in 1987-1994; Empire Athletic Association Champions in 1992 & 1994; New York State Women's Collegiate Athletic Association (NYSWCAA) Champions in 1983, 1986, 1988, 1989, 1991, 1992, 1993, & 1994; at least one 1 All-American player each year since 1985. A total of 12 All-American athlete in the program's history.
Coaching: Mindy Quigg, Head Coach, entering fourth year, record of 25-9-7 as Bomber Mentor. Quigg replaced the program's all-time winningest coach, Patrick Farmer (110-17-23), who is now at Penn Stte. Jeff Long - Assistant Coach, entering 11th year, head men's lacrosse coach in the Spring.
Style of Play: Player is oriented instead of specific system. Aggressive defensively all over the field. Small group decision making stressed over the system of play. High fitness level. Competitive at all levels of play. Forward looking team on offense.

Keuka College

Academic Profile

Phone:

Keuka Park, NY 14478

Type: 4 Yr.,Private,Liberal Arts
Founded: 1890
Website: http://www.keuka.edu
Religion: American Baptist
SAT/ACT/GPA: 1040
Housing: Yes
Student/Faculty Ratio: 11:1
Male/Female Ratio: 1:5
Undergraduate Enrollment: 1,000
Graduate Enrollment: N/A
Scholarships/Academic: Yes **Athletic:** No **Financial Aid:** Yes
Expenses by: Year **In State:** $ 19,063 **Out of State:** $ 19,063
Specialty: Occupational Therapy, Education, Business, Nursing
Degrees Conferred: BA, BS, Pre-Professional
Programs of Study: Occupational Therapy, Unified Education, Special Education, Secondary Education, Elementary Education, Business, Marketing, Nursing, Advertising, Hotel Resource Management: We are a liberal arts school.

Men's Athletic Profile

Men's Soccer Office
Keuka Park, NY 14478
Coach: Al Louks
Email: aloucks@mail.keuka.edu

NCAA III
Warriors/Forest Green, Gold
Phone: (315) 536-4411
Fax: (315) 536-5380

Estimated # of Men's Soccer Scholarships: None
Conference: Independent
Program Profile: We are a competitive NCAA II program looking to move into the tournament within the next three years. Our fall season is usually 13-15 weeks long and balance of our 21 weeks is used in the spring. including 5 playing dates. We play on a beautiful 120x75 natural surface.
History: Our 1999 season will be our tenth anniversary of men's soccer. We will be very young and look forward to making playoff very soon.
Coaching: Al Loucks, Head Coach, is the all-time winningest coach in Keuka's history. Formerly to Keuka women's team to 4 ECAC Final Fours. Shawn Beldue, Assistant Coach, will continue to be our goalkeeper coach. Joe Sabbour will be the Warriors' assistant coach.
Style of Play: We like to play high pressure defense. We play flat as often as possible. We attack with a possession involving all eleven players.

Women's Athletic Profile

Keuka College
Keuka Park, NY 14478
Coach: Paul Bonus
Email: pbonus@mail.keuka.edu

NCAA III
Warriors/Green, Gold
Phone: (315) 531-5619
Fax: (315) 279-5315

Estimated # of Women's Soccer Scholarships: None
Conference: ECAC
Program Profile: We are a small school that provides a very competitive program. We play in one of the toughest regions of college soccer in New York State. We play between 16-18 regular season games including a short spring season.
History: The Keuka women's soccer program has been very successful in the 1990's. Except for 2 years, the program has made it to the post season. We are looking forward to it again real soon. Over all record for 16 years is 166-111-17.
Achievements: Several Region All-Americans, 1999 ECAC Semi Finals, NYSWCAA 1st round.
Coaching: Paul Bonus, Head Coach, two year record of 21-16-0. Also NYSW ODP Coach.
Roster in State: 21 **Out of State:** 0 **Out of Country:** 0
ODP State: 4 **Regional:** 0 **National:** 0
Walk-on/Other: 0 **Graduation %:** 95 **Seniors on Team:** 4
Positions Needed: GK, Outside Mid, Forwards
Camp or Clinic Dates: June 25-29
Most Recent Record: 10-8-0
Schedule: Cortland State, RPI, RIT, Elmira
Style of Play: We would like to play a very technical game. We will play with high pressure all over. We will attack with possession and numbers.

Le Moyne College
Academic Profile

Syracuse, NY 13214
Phone: 315-445-4100

Type: 4 Yr.,Private,Liberal Arts **Founded:** 1946
Website: http://www.lemoyne.edu **Religion:** Jesuit
SAT/ACT/GPA: 1000+ **Housing:** Yes
Student/Faculty Ratio: 13:1 **Male/Female Ratio:** 47:53
Undergraduate Enrollment: 1,800 **Graduate Enrollment:** N/A
Scholarships/Academic: Yes **Athletic:** Yes **Financial Aid:** Yes
Expenses by: Year **In State:** $ 11,700 **Out of State:** $ 11,700
Degrees Conferred: BA, BS, MBA
Programs of Study: Business and Management, Education, Letters/Literature, Life Science, Psychology, Social Science, Accounting, Biology, Chemistry, Computer Science, Economics, History, Industrial Relations, Mathematics, Physics, Philosophy, Political Science, Psychology

Men's Athletic Profile

Springfield Rd
Syracuse, NY 13214
Coach: Carlos Villarreal
Email: Not Available

NCAA II
Dolphins/Old Gold, Forest
Phone: (315) 445-4422
Fax: (315) 445-4678

Estimated # of Men's Soccer Scholarships: None
Conference: Northeast 10 Conference
Program Profile: Field has a measurements of 72x120 yards grass. Facilities includes a press box, and a visible scoreboard.
History: ECAC Division II finals in 1994.
Achievements: None
Coaching: Carlos Villarreal, Head Coach, had a record of 124-44-13 in nine seasons of high school coaching, played professionally in Peru.
Style of Play: Progressive shot.

Women's Athletic Profile

Springfield Rd
Syracuse, NY 13214
Coach: Patty Kloidt
Email: Bertha55@aol.com

NCAA II
Dolphins/Green, Gold
Phone: (315) 445-4713
Fax: (315) 445-4678

Estimated # of Women's Soccer Scholarships: None
Conference: Northeast 10 Conference
Program Profile: Our playing field maximum size is 72x120 yards all natural grass. Facilities include a press box and a visible scoreboard.
History: The first season of the program was in 1980; ECAC tournament participants in 1992 & 1993.
Achievements: Several All-Americans over the last ten year, Regional Awards Winners, and a Conference Weekly Stars.
Coaching: Patty Kloidt, Head Coach, begins her first season in the fall.
Style of Play: Progressive, shots.

Long Island University - Brooklyn Campus

Academic Profile

Brooklyn, NY 11201

Phone: 718-488-1011

Type: 4 Yr.,Private,Liberal Arts
Website: http://www.liu.edu
SAT/ACT/GPA: 820/17
Student/Faculty Ratio: 14:1
Undergraduate Enrollment: 6,300
Scholarships/Academic: Yes **Athletic:** Yes
Expenses by: Year **In State:** $ 23,100

Founded: 1926
Religion: Non-Sectarian
Housing: No
Male/Female Ratio: 45:55
Graduate Enrollment: 2,800
Financial Aid: Yes
Out of State: $ 23,100

Specialty: Health Professions, Media Arts, Education
Degrees Conferred: BA, BS, AA, MBA, Ph.D.
Programs of Study: Biology, Communications, Journalism, Art, Jazz Studies, Dance, Nursing, Physical Therapy, Respiratory Therapy, Occupational Therapy, Athletic Training, Physician's Assistant, Pharmacy, Elementary Education, Secondary Education, Physical Education, Modern Languages, English, Speech, Social Work, Anthropology, Accounting, Business Management, Computer Science, United Nations, PreLaw, Political Science

Men's Athletic Profile

One University Plaza
Brooklyn, NY 11201
Coach: T.J. Kostecky
Email: gfox@hornet.liu.edu

NCAA I
Blackbirds/Blue, White
Phone: (718) 488-1530
Fax: (718) 488-1669

Estimated # of Men's Soccer Scholarships: 9
Conference: Northeast Conference
Program Profile: The home game field has a natural grass surface.
History: The program began in 1933. LIU has appeared in 12 NCAA Tournaments. Arnold Ramirez is LIU's 11th coach.
Achievements: 26 All-Americans, won 2 ECAC Championships in 1976 & 1979. Coach Ramirez has taken the Blackbirds to 4 NCAA Tournaments in his 17 years as a coach, the last time being in 1986.
Coaching: T. J. Kostecky, Head Coach, became the new head coach in March of 1998. John Ramirez and Chris Lawrence are the Assistant Coaches.
Style of Play: Continental Style - controlled, possession soccer with mix of long and short passing.

Women's Athletic Profile

1 University Plaza
Brooklyn, NY 11201
Coach: Glenn Crooks
Email: gcrooks@liu.edu

NCAA I
Blackbirds/Blue, White
Phone: (718) 488-3496
Fax: (718) 780-1669

Estimated # of Women's Soccer Scholarships: varies
Conference: Northeast Conference
Program Profile: We have year-round training with an outdoor, lighted, natural grass field. We recruit top student-athletes both nationally and internationally.
History: In just three years of existence we won Northeast Conference Championship and qualified for NCAA tournament. The program began in fall of 1997 and finished with a 1-16-1 record. Over the years it has continued to grow and in 1999 the record was 11-9-2.
Achievements: 1999 Northeast Conference Champions; defeated SW Texas State in NCAA Play; ranked 3rd Academically out of 262 Division 1 programs.
Coaching: Glenn Crooks, Head Coach, is a 1980 Georgia graduate. He was a former Metro Atlantic Athletic Conference Coach of the Year while at St. Peter's College. Tracy Farrell, Assistant Coach, is a 1991graduate of Trenton State University. He is responsible for the goalkeeper. Kurt Scotland, Graduate Assistant, recently signed a professional contract in Trinidad.
Roster in State: 3 **Out of State:** 17 **Out of Country:** 3
ODP State: 11 **Regional:** **National:**
Walk-on/Other: **Graduation %:** **Seniors on Team:** 3
Positions Needed: Defenders, Forwards
Camp or Clinic Dates: Not Available
Most Recent Record: 11-9-2
Schedule: University of Arizona, University of Massachusetts, Fairfield, St. John's, Hofstra, Central Connecticut, Quinnipiac, St. Joseph's, LaSalle, Northern Arizona
Style of Play: All players are encouraged to participate in the attack at the appropriate time. There is a demand on all players to defend as a team, both zonal and man-marking.

Long Island University - CW Post Campus

Academic Profile

Phone: (516)299-3856

Brookville, NY 11548

Type: 4 Yr.,Private,Liberal Arts
Website: http://www.cwpost.liunet.edu
SAT/ACT/GPA: 840/2.0
Student/Faculty Ratio: 16:1
Undergraduate Enrollment: 4,500
Scholarships/Academic: Yes **Athletic:** Yes
Expenses by: Year **In State:** $ 21,000

Founded: 1954
Religion: Non-Affiliated
Housing: Yes
Male/Female Ratio: 38:62
Graduate Enrollment: 3,600
Financial Aid: Yes
Out of State: $ 21,000

Specialty: Business, Criminal Justice, Education
Degrees Conferred: AA, BA, Bs, BFA, Ma, MS, MBA, MFA, D
Programs of Study: Acting, Art, Biology, Broadcasting, Business, Chemistry, English, Environmental, Interdisciplinary, International, Mathematics, Molecular Biology, PreProfessional Programs, Public, Radiological, Teachers of Special Education/Speech/Hearing Handicapped

Men's Athletic Profile

Northern Blvd.
Brookville, NY 11548
Coach: Bill EASTEADT
Email: Not Available

NCAA II
Pioneers/Green, White
Phone: (516) 299-3856
Fax: (516) 626-0150

Estimated # of Men's Soccer Scholarships: None
Conference: New York Collegiate Athletic Conference
Program Profile: We have been to the NCAA playoffs two out of the last three years, finished seventh in the National Division II Poll in both 1993 and 1994. Field has a measurement of 120x80 yards grass - beautiful. Probably one of the finest soccer facilities in the state.
History: NCAA Quarterfinals yin 1987 & 1993. Moved to a new field in 1978 that has a measurement of 12x80 yards.
Achievements: 3 All-Americans, won NYCAC Regional coach of the Year in 1993.
Style of Play: We have a big beautiful grass field so we have a very exciting and attacking style of play. In the last three seasons we have scored over 60 goals in each game.

Women's Athletic Profile

720 Northern Blvd.
Brookville, NY 11548
Coach: Bob Blitz
Email: Not Available

NCAA II
Pioneers/Green, Gold
Phone: (516) 299-3856
Fax: (516) 299-3155

Estimated # of Women's Soccer Scholarships:
Conference: New York Collegiate Athletic Conference
Program Profile: Program is in sixth year of existence. Play on grass field, separate practice fields. Playing season is in the Fall & in the Spring.
History: The program initiated in 1994; overall record is 54-37-5. In 1998 season record was 14-6-1 and won NYCAC Champions; NCAA Division II Quarter-finalist and ranked #13 in the nation.
Achievements: 1998 NYCAC Coach of the Year and 1998 NYCAC Champions.
Coaching: Bob Blitz, Head Coach, Brooklyn College in 1993. Gerry Lucey - Assistant Coach, C.W. Post in 1994, Division II All-American. Shiela Verbeck, Assistant Coach, graduated from CW Post in 1999. Manull Caron, Assistant Coach.
Style of Play: Possession game; attack from flanks, quick play through midfielder. Man to man defend; 4-4-2 with sweeper and strong emphasis on fitness.

Long Island University - Southampton College

Academic Profile

Southampton, NY 11968

Phone:

Type: 4 Yr.,Private
Website: http://www.southampton.liunet.edu
SAT/ACT/GPA: 900+/80+
Student/Faculty Ratio: 20:1
Undergraduate Enrollment: 1,350
Scholarships/Academic: Yes **Athletic:** Yes
Expenses by: Year **In State:** $ 23,000
Specialty: Marine Science
Degrees Conferred: BA, BS, MS
Programs of Study: Marine Biology, Education, Business, Communications, Arts

Founded: 1962
Religion: Non-Affiliated
Housing: Yes
Male/Female Ratio: 4:6
Graduate Enrollment: 300
Financial Aid: Yes
Out of State: $ 23,000

Men's Athletic Profile

239 Montauk Highway
Southampton, NY 11968
Coach: Ed Goodhines
Email: Not Available

NCAA II
Colonials/Blue, Gold
Phone: (516) 287-8388
Fax: (516) 287-8188

Estimated # of Men's Soccer Scholarships: 2
Conference: New York Collegiate Athletic Conference
Program Profile: Grass stadium that has a seating capacity of 500. Field measures 118x70 yards. Game field and practice are both grass.
History: Our program ranked in the Top 20 nationally four out of the last five years. Ranked as high as 3rd in 1998. ECAC Champs in 1994 and 1995. Won Division II NCAA championship in 1999.
Achievements: Produced 1998 1st team All-American. 1999 Northeast Coach of the year, 1999 NYCAC coach of the year. 1999 NYCAC champs undefeated 8-0. 1st and 3rd team All-American in 1999. Had a 1st team All-Academic All-American in 1999.
Coaching: Ed Goodhines, Head Coach, started in 1993 to the present. State Certification, Regional License. He was a graduate of Southampton in 1983. Mark Dawson - Assistant Coach, started in 1995 to the present. He was a Southampton graduate in 1994.
Roster In State: 6 **Out of State:** 5 **Out of Country:** 9
ODP State: 5 **Regional:** **National:**
Walk-on/Other: **Graduation %:** 85 **Seniors on Team:** 4
Positions Needed: Goalie, Defender, Midfield
Camp or Clinic Dates: August 6-10
Most Recent Record: 17-1-2
Schedule: Southern Connecticut, Dowling, C.W. Post, E. Stroudsburg, Concordia, Gannon
Style of Play: Strong defensively, countering team.

Women's Athletic Profile

239 Montauk Hwy.
Southampton, NY 11968
Coach: Mark Dawson
Email: Not Available

NCAA II
Colonials/Blue, Gold
Phone: (516) 287-8386
Fax: (516) 287-3898

Estimated # of Women's Soccer Scholarships: None
Conference: New York Collegiate Athletic Conference
Program Profile: The home field is a natural grass that has a seating capacity of 500. Field has a measurements of 118x70 yards.
History: The Colonials were ranked in the Top Ten nationally from 1989-1992.
Achievements: 3 All-Americans, 9 All-Region, ECAC Champs in 1990, Runner-Up in 1991.

Manhattan College
Academic Profile

Phone: (718) 862-7227

Riverdale, NY 10471

Type: 4 Yr.,Private,Liberal Arts,Engineering
Website: http://www.mancol.edu
SAT/ACT/GPA: 1000/23
Student/Faculty Ratio: 13:1
Undergraduate Enrollment: 3,200
Scholarships/Academic: Yes **Athletic:** No

Founded: 1853
Religion: Roman Catholic
Housing: Yes
Male/Female Ratio: 55:45
Graduate Enrollment: 1,000
Financial Aid: Yes

Expenses by: Year **In State:** $ 23,450 **Out of State:** $ 23,450
Specialty: Business, Education, Science
Degrees Conferred: BA, BS, MA, MBA, Ph.D.
Programs of Study: Liberal Arts with freshman Perceptional and portfolio systems.

Men's Athletic Profile

4513 Manhattan College Pkwy
Riverdale, NY 10471
Coach: Dan Lazo
Email: jbernste@manhattan.edu

NCAA I
Jaspers/Kelly Green, White
Phone: (718) 862-7227
Fax: (718) 543-8802

Estimated # of Men's Soccer Scholarships: None
Conference: Metro Atlantic Athletic Conference
Program Profile: Mid-Major NCAA Division I program. We have a 1,500-seat stadium (Gaelic Park) with a natural grass.
History: Our men's soccer program began in 1967-1968.
Achievements: Metro Atlantic Athletic Conference Championship Finalist in 1994.
Coaching: Danny Lazo is our Head Coach. He earned undergraduate degree in Management in 1982 and a Master's Degree in Finance in 1985 at St. John's University. Former assistant coach at St. John's and former head coach at Chaminade High School in Mineola, New York.

Women's Athletic Profile

Manhattan College Pkwy
Riverdale, NY 10471
Coach: John Sanchez
Email: Not Available

NCAA I
Lady Jaspers/K. Green, White
Phone: (718) 862-7843
Fax: (718) 862-8020

Estimated # of Women's Soccer Scholarships: None
Conference: Metro Atlantic Athletic Conference
Program Profile: Manhattan's home field has natural grass and 2,000 seats. The Jaspers are a NCAA Division I program.
History: Our Division I program began with the 1991 season. Our overall record is 55-72-9.
Achievements: 1993 - Rookie of the Year, MAAC Scoring leader, MAAC All-First Team and NSCAA Umbro Second Team All-American Northeast Region was Emily Rogie. 1995 - All-MAAC 1st team was Jen Mclaughlin. 1993 GTE Academic All-American was Lisa Margiotta.
Coaching: John Sanchez, Head Coach. He holds a United States Soccer Federation License "B" and an NSCAA Advanced License. He is the head coach for the Olympic Development Program of Eastern New York. He coached the Empire State Games.
Style of Play: Offensive minded 3-4-3, high pressure. Want offensive players that can "take on" defenders one versus one.

Manhattanville College

Academic Profile

Phone: 914-694-2200

Purchase, NY 10577

Type: 4 Yr.,Private,Liberal Arts
Website: http://www.mville.edu
SAT/ACT/GPA: 1000
Student/Faculty Ratio: 10:1
Undergraduate Enrollment: 1,100

Founded: 1841
Religion: Sacred Heart
Housing: Yes
Male/Female Ratio: 1:2
Graduate Enrollment: 800

Scholarships/Academic: Yes **Athletic:** No **Financial Aid:** Yes
Expenses by: Year **In State:** $ 25,000 **Out of State:** $ 25,000
Specialty: Business
Degrees Conferred: BA, BS, MA, MAT, MFA
Programs of Study: Business Management, Chemistry, Computer Science, Design, Dramatic Arts, Economics, Education, English, Environmental Science, Finance, Philosophy, Photography, Physics, Political Science, PreDentistry, PreLaw, PreMed, Psychology, Sociology

Men's Athletic Profile

2900 Purchase St.
Purchase, NY 10577
Coach: Peter Schachter
Email: pschacter@email.msa.com

NCAA III
Valiants/Red, White
Phone: (914) 323-5280
Fax: (914) 323-5130

Estimated # of Men's Soccer Scholarships:
Conference: Skyline Athletic Conference, ECAC
Program Profile: Competitive Division III program, looking to advance to national tournament. Field being made into soccer specific site; natural grass with a measurement of 74x110 yards. Bleachers for 500, scoreboard; team benches with shelters, and host site for USISL Premier Development Team in summer. Opportunities for advanced players to train and compete with this team.
History: Program was founded in 1974. Best season was in 1992 when team finished 11-9.
Achievements: Marlon Nurse was named Regional Division III All-American in 1988.
Coaching: Peter Schachter, Head Coach, BA from Brandets University, MS from University of Leicester (England); Advanced National Diploma, NSCAA; (member of 1976 NCAA Division III, National Championship Team). John O'Sullivan - Assistant Coach, BA from Bethany College, two-time National Runner-Up NCAA Division III.
Style of Play: Versatile, practices built on two-touch ball to feet foundation. flexible 4-4-2 with mobility and technical strength to maintain effectiveness.

Women's Athletic Profile

2900 Purchase Street
Purchase, NY 10577
Coach: UB McCaffrey
Email: mccaffreye@mville.edu

NCAA III
The Valiants/Valiant Red, White
Phone: (914) 323-7275
Fax: (914) 323-5130

Estimated # of Women's Soccer Scholarships: None
Conference: Skyline
Program Profile: We play at a centrally located grass field and with seating for 300-500. We play against Division II and Division III colleges. In the spring, we conduct a popular youth soccer clinic. We have a full-time NATA-certified athletic trainer. Our Health Center has two orthopedic physicians on duty, a training room and a fitness and wellness center.
History: The program is back at a competitive level. After a few down years, the team was in contention for a post-season spot late in the season. With several top recruits committed to the school, the program is looking forward to the Fall season.
Achievements: In 1999 we received Skyline COY and Skyline Conference Champs.
Coaching: Our Head Coach is a graduate of Manhattenville who posted the teams best record in 15 years with in her 1st season and our assistant coach coaches at the NY State level and has a extensive soccer background with more than 15 years of coaching.
Roster in State: 12 **Out of State:** 12 **Out of Country:** 1
ODP State: 7 **Regional:** **National:**
Walk-on/Other: **Graduation %:** 100 **Seniors on Team:** 2
Positions Needed: Defenders, Midfield, Forward

Camp or Clinic Dates: July 24-28
Most Recent Record: 9-6-1
Schedule: Trinity College (CT), Western Connecticut State, SUNY-Cortland, Elmira college, NYU, Vassar College
Style of Play: Use all 11 players offensively and defensively.

Marist College

Academic Profile

Poughkeepsie, NY 12601
Phone: 845-575-3000

Type: 4 Yr.,Private,Liberal Arts
Founded: 1946
Website: http://www.marist.edu
Religion: Catholic
SAT/ACT/GPA: 1000+/23/85%
Housing: Yes
Student/Faculty Ratio: 15:1
Male/Female Ratio: 55:45
Undergraduate Enrollment: 3,200
Graduate Enrollment: 500
Scholarships/Academic: Yes **Athletic:** Yes **Financial Aid:** Yes
Expenses by: Year **In State:** $ 19,000 **Out of State:** $ 19,000
Specialty: Education, Communications, Business, Fashion
Degrees Conferred: BA, BS, MA, MS, MFA, MBA
Programs of Study: Accounting, American Studies, BioChemistry, Biology, Business Administration, Chemistry, Communications, Computer Science, Criminal Justice, Economics, Education, Fashion Design, Film Arts, History, Journalism, Management, Mathematics, Medical Laboratory Technology, Political Science, Psychology, Social Science

Men's Athletic Profile

North Road,
Poughkeepsie, NY 12601
Coach: Bobby Herodes
Email: Not Available

NCAA I
Red Foxes/Red, Black, White
Phone: (914) 575-3000 x 2529
Fax: (914) 452-7028

Estimated # of Men's Soccer Scholarships: None
Conference: ECAC, Metro Atlantic
Program Profile: Has 18-game regular season schedule includes the Likes of Farleigh Dickinson, CW-Post, St. John's, Martwick, Loyola, Adelphi & University of Connecticut. Scholarship are available, Kelme sponsorship, enjoyed best record of 8-5 in the last five years. In 1996, soccer only (grass) field in Hudson River, off-season includes five-game in February-May.
History: Began in 1963; 1976, 1978 & 1980 reached Regional of NCAA Division II, elevated to Division I in 1984. 10-6-4 record in 1992 include season ending win over St. John's #2 national rank. Move from Northeast conference into the MAAC last 1997.
Achievements: Sean Scott was named 1992 All-Northeast Conference, All-New York State, David Siepp - 1995 All-American, MVP National Tourney, NJCAA Champs Merkimer CC (NY), Josh Thomas - 1995 All-Region, National NJCAA Champs, Merkimer Comm. Coll. (NY), Mike Schilling - 1996 Regional & National Poll, 1996 NEC Newcomer Team, #6 New York State ranking in 1992, #9 New York State ranking in 1996.
Coaching: Bobby Herodes is our Head Coach. He holds NSCAA "B" License, NSCAA All-American (SUNY, Morrisville). He was named 1995 MAAC Coach of the Year. George Dianwi is our Assistant Coach. He was named All-Conference, All-New York State, while at Ithaca College in 1987 at Empire State Games. Andy Fleming - Coach. He was a former Marist captain. He holds NSCAA "C" Licensed.
Style of Play: Uses three front runners (Forwards) offensive oriented and physical style of play. Play a built up style on the ground from the midfield. Preferred intense players with a strong work ethic.

Women's Athletic Profile

290 North Road
Poughkeepsie, NY 12601
Coach: Megan McGonagle
Email: megan.mcgonagle@marist.edu

NCAA I
Red Foxes/Red, White
Phone: (845) 575-3000
Fax: (845) 575-3322

Estimated # of Women's Soccer Scholarships: N/A
Conference: MAAC
Program Profile: Program finished it's sixth season in NCAA DI, 4th year in the MAAC, natural grass-2 practice fields, 1 game field. Playing season 8/12-10/29, Spring Season- Feb through April
History: Program finished it's 6th year in 2000 season and 4th year in MAAC Conference
Achievements: Made Conference semi-finals 3 out of 4 years.
Roster in State: 11 **Out of State:** 14 **Out of Country:** 0
ODP State: 17 **Regional:** **National:**
Walk-on/Other: 8 **Graduation %:** 100 **Seniors on Team:** 3
Positions Needed: Forwards
Camp or Clinic Dates: July 16-27, July 23-24
Most Recent Record: 8-8-1
Schedule: Bucknell, Hofstra, Lafayette, Providence, Villanova, Holy Cross, Loyola
Style of Play: Knock and move, build from the back, play to feet.

Medgar Evers College

Academic Profile

Brooklyn, NY 11225-2201
Phone:

Type: 4 Yr.,Public,
Founded: 1969
Website: Not Available
Religion: Non-Affiliated
SAT/ACT/GPA: Not Required
Housing: No
Student/Faculty Ratio: 21:1
Male/Female Ratio: 25:75
Undergraduate Enrollment: 5,200
Graduate Enrollment: N/A
Scholarships/Academic: No **Athletic:** No **Financial Aid:** Yes
Expenses by: Year **In State:** $ 2,200 **Out of State:** $ 2,800
Degrees Conferred: AA, AS, AAS, BA, BS
Programs of Study: Contact school for program of study.

Men's Athletic Profile

1150 Carroll Street
Brooklyn, NY 11225
Coach: Stanley Harmon
Email: roy@mec.cuny.edu

NCAA III
Cougars/Red, White
Phone: (718) 270-6071
Fax: (718) 270-6198

Estimated # of Men's Soccer Scholarships: None
Conference: CUNYAC
Program Profile: Our home games are played at Brooklyn College which is Astroturf.
History: Medgar Evers College has never won the CUNYAC Soccer Tournament but has been in the finals in 1997, 1996, and 1994. MEC won the ECAC Championships in 1999.
Achievements: 1997 Stanley Harmon CUNYAC Coach of the Year
Roster In State: 13 **Out of State:** 1 **Out of Country:** 6
Walk-on/Other: **Graduation %:** N/A **Seniors on Team:** 3
Camp or Clinic Dates: Not Available
Most Recent Record: 8-9-1
Schedule: Rowan, St. Joseph's, Hunter, Staten Island, Centenary, Plattsburgh

Molloy College

Academic Profile

Phone:

Rockville center, NY 11570

Type: 4 Yr.,Private,Liberal Arts
Website: http://www.molloy.edu
SAT/ACT/GPA: 900
Student/Faculty Ratio: 11:1
Undergraduate Enrollment: 2,000
Scholarships/Academic: Yes **Athletic:** Yes
Expenses by: Year **In State:** $ 10,600
Founded: 1955
Religion: Catholic
Housing: Yes
Male/Female Ratio: 23:77
Graduate Enrollment: 300
Financial Aid: Yes
Out of State: $ 10,600
Specialty: Medical, Education
Degrees Conferred: AA, BA, MS, MA, AS, BS
Programs of Study: Accounting, Art, Biology, Business Management, Cardio-Respiratory Sciences, Communications, Computer Science, English, French, Gerontology, History, Interdisciplinary Studies, International Peace & Justice, Mathematics, Music, Nursing, Philosophy, Political Science, Psychology, Social Work, Sociology, Theology, Preparation for Teaching Certification in Secondary, Elementary and Special Education

Men's Athletic Profile

100 Hempstead Avenue
Rockville Ctr., NY 11570
Coach: Doug Baylis
Email: Not Available

NCAA II
Lions/Maroon, White
Phone: (516) 678-5000
Fax: (516) 256-2231

Estimated # of Men's Soccer Scholarships: 6
Conference: NYCAC
Program Profile: Play on a natural field on campus.
History: Started in 1996 – we joined the NYCAC in 1997.
Achievements: We had 1st second team All-Conference player.
Coaching: Tougher standards/ better skilled players looking to improve level of recruited players- opportunity for young players to play and improve.
Roster in State: 18 **Out of State:** 2 **Out of Country:** 2
Walk-on/Other: **Graduatiion %:** 90 **Seniors on Team:** 2
Positions Needed: All
Most Recent Record: 5-14-1
Schedule: Dowling, Southampton, C.W. Post, Concordia, Felician, Teikyo Post
Style of Play: Aggressive defensive pressure/ offensive ball movement creative attack down flanks-overlapping full-backs.

Women's Athletic Profile

1000 Hempstead Avenue
Rockville Centre, NY 11570
Coach: Neil Graham
Email: Neilgrm@aol.com

NCAA II
Lions/Maroon, White
Phone: (516) 256-2207
Fax: (516) 256-2231

Estimated # of Women's Soccer Scholarships: None
Conference: New York State Collegiate Athletic Conference

Program Profile: Adequate facilities - the field is natural surface on campus. The team plays a traditional playing season.
History: The program began in 1995; have never had a losing season.
Achievements: None
Coaching: Neil Graham, Head Coach, pro in England, co-owner of NOGA Soccer Camps. NSCAA Advanced National License and FA Prelim. Sheila Kelly - Assistant Coach, 9th all-time NCAA goal scorer.
Roster in State: 14 **Out of State:** **Out of Country:**
Walk-on/Other: **Graduation %:** **Seniors on Team:** 3
Positions Needed: Not Available
Camp or Clinic Dates: Not Available
Most Recent Record: 6-11-1
Schedule: Queens, Holy Family, Mercy, St. Rose, Southampton
Style of Play: Short passing, possession when possible. Everyone defend each 1/3 of the field.

Mount Saint Mary College - New York

Academic Profile

Newburgh, NY 12550
Phone:

Type: 4 Yr.,Private,Liberal Arts
Founded: 1960
Website: http://www.msmc.edu
Religion: Catholic
SAT/ACT/GPA: 950/18
Housing: Yes
Student/Faculty Ratio: 16:1
Male/Female Ratio: 1:2.5
Undergraduate Enrollment: 1,900
Graduate Enrollment: 400
Scholarships/Academic: Yes **Athletic:** No **Financial Aid:** Yes
Expenses by: Year **In State:** $ 14,730 **Out of State:** $ 14,730
Degrees Conferred: BA, BS, BSN, MBA, MSEd, MSM
Programs of Study: Accounting, Biology, Business Management/Administration, Chemistry, Communications, Computer Science, Elementary Education, English, Political Science, International Studies, Mathematics, Medical Technology, Nursing, PreDentistry, Social Science, Sociology, Theatre

Men's Athletic Profile

330 Powell Avenue
Newburgh, NY 12550
Coach: Chris Knittel
Email: Not Available

NCAA III
Knights/Royal Blue, Gold
Phone: (914) 569-3594
Fax: (914) 569-3589

Estimated # of Men's Soccer Scholarships: N/A
Conference: Skyline Conference
Program Profile: Games are played on lighted, natural surface field in Cronamer Hill Park which seats approximately 2,000 fans; newly field house. The schedule consist of 17-game plus two tournaments.
History: Program began in 1986 in the NAIA and has moved to NCAA Division III, ECAC. The team has a record of 13-6 in 1990 best year of the program
Coaching: Chris Knittel, Head Coach, was named head coach in summer of 1999.
Style of Play: Ball control.

Women's Athletic Profile

330 Powell Ave.
Newburgh, NY 12550
Coach: Eileen Allesendrino
Email: Not Available

NCAA III
Knights/Royal Blue, Gold
Phone: (914) 569-3594
Fax: (914) 569-3589

Estimated # of Women's Soccer Scholarships: None
Conference: None
Program Profile: We have an off campus field with lights. Seating capacity is 500, game schedule is in the fall. Night games due the fact the field has a lights.
History: The program began in 1992. Have won at least ten games every season. Two conference championships in 1993 and 1994. Won the WIAC two years in a row.
Achievements: 1993 Coach of the Year.
Coaching: Eileen Allesendrino, Head Coach.
Style of Play: Ball control.

Nazareth College - Rochester

Academic Profile

Rochester, NY 14618-3790
Phone: 800-462-3949

Type: 4 Yr.,Private,Liberal Arts
Website: http://www.nax.edu
SAT/ACT/GPA: 1120/24/85
Student/Faculty Ratio: 13:1
Undergraduate Enrollment: 1,800
Scholarships/Academic: Yes **Athletic:** No
Expenses by: Year **In State:** $ 21,500
Founded: 1924
Religion: Non-Affiliated
Housing: No
Male/Female Ratio: 1:3
Graduate Enrollment: 1,000
Financial Aid: Yes
Out of State: $ 21,500
Specialty: Physical Therapy, Business, Education
Degrees Conferred: BA, BS, BSE, MBA, MS Education, MS
Programs of Study: Business Administration, Accounting, Physical Therapy, Education, Speech & Languages, Pathology, Political Science, Environmental Science, Social Work, PreMed, PreVet, Predental

Men's Athletic Profile

4245 East Avenue
Rochester, NY 14618
Coach: Doug May
Email: djmay@naz.edu
NCAA III
Golden Flyers/Purple, Gold
Phone: (716) 389-2191
Fax: (716) 389-2839

Estimated # of Men's Soccer Scholarships: None
Conference: Independent
Program Profile: The Golden Flyers home playing field is a natural grass that has a measurements of 120x75 yards, and has a seating capacity of 5,000.
History: Program initiated 1980. Up and coming program.
Achievements: 1989 NCAA Coach of the Year Division III; Regional Coach of the Year in 1984, 1988, 1989 & 1992; 5 All-Americans; 8 Conference Titles while second RIT.
Coaching: Doug May, Head Coach, USSF "A" License, NCAA Advanced Licensed, Instructor/Staff Coach for NSCAA. Scott Wilson - Assistant Coach, played at RIT, played and leading score on team that played for national championship.
Style of Play: Build-up; combination play backs getting into attack, hard work, ball movement with mobile players who love the game.

Women's Athletic Profile

4245 East Avenue
Rochester, NY 14618
Coach: Gail Mann
Email: gemann@naz.edu
NCAA III
Golden Flyers/Purple, Gold
Phone: (716) 389-2813
Fax: (716) 389-2839

Estimated # of Women's Soccer Scholarships: None
Conference: Eastern Collegiate Athletic Conference, NYSWCAA, Empire Athletic Association
Program Profile: The Golden Flyers game field is natural grass which measures 110x80 yards, and seats 2,000. We are a nationally ranked program for the past 3 years. We have a year around program.
History: Program began in 1983. Our coach started here in 1993 and has a record of 59-16-4. We have two NCAA appearances.
Achievements: 1996 NYS Coach of the Year; 1997 Division III Regional Coach of the year; 18 All-State; 9 All-Region; 1 All-American
Coaching: Gail Mann, Head Coach, played four years at Cortland in 1983-1986 in Division I.
Style of Play: 3-5-2 formation, try to create 'numbers up' situation at all times both defense and offense. Short-short-long style; play the ball to feet.

New York Institute of Technology

Academic Profile

Phone:

Old Westbury, NY 11568-800

Type: 4 Yr.,Private,Liberal Arts,Engineering
Founded: 1955
Website: http://www.nyit.edu
Religion: Non-Affiliated
SAT/ACT/GPA: NCAA Requirements
Housing: No
Student/Faculty Ratio: 18:1
Male/Female Ratio: 6:4
Undergraduate Enrollment: 6,000
Graduate Enrollment: 4,000
Scholarships/Academic: Yes **Athletic:** Yes **Financial Aid:** Yes
Expenses by: Year **In State:** $ 21,000 **Out of State:** $ 21,000
Specialty: Liberal Arts & Science
Degrees Conferred: AAS, BA, BS, BFA, BArch, MA, MS, MFA, DO
Programs of Study: Accounting, Advertising, Architectural Technology, Architecture, Art, Biology, Business & Management, Chemistry, Communications, Computer Information Systems, Computer Science, Economics, Education, Electrical Engineering & Technology, Mathematics, Political Science

Men's Athletic Profile

P.O. Box 8000
Old Westbury, NY 11568-8000
Coach: Gus Constantine
Email: guscon@aol.com

NCAA II
Bears/Navy, White, Gold
Phone: (516) 686-7626
Fax: (516) 626-0750

Estimated # of Men's Soccer Scholarships: 8
Conference: NYACA
Program Profile: The field is natural grass and the stadium has a seating capacity of 2,000. The playing season schedule is an extremely competitive Division II schedule.
History: Have been associated with NCAA and have been to the NCAA playoffs and Final Four in 1985, ECAC Champions in 1988 and undefeated Champions of the SSC.
Achievements: In 1985, NYIT reached Final Four of Division I, NCAA Championships, consistent ECAC and Conference Champions.
Coaching: Gus Constantine, Head Coach, has been a collegiate coach for 20 seasons. He was a former Official North American Soccer League (18 years) Olympic and World Cup Soccer Referee. Andreas Tauros - Assistant Coach.
Roster In State: 12 **Out of State:** 5 **Out of Country:** 3
ODP State: 3 **Regional:** **National:**
Walk-on/Other: 2 **Graduation %:** N/A **Seniors on Team:** 5
Positions Needed: Striker, Defender, Goalkeeper

Camp or Clinic Dates: Not Available
Most Recent Record: 12-6-1
Schedule: Dowling, Post, West Chester, Slippery Rock, Mercyhurst
Style of Play: Whole team attacks; whole team defends.

Women's Athletic Profile

P.O. Box 8000
Old Westbury, NY 11568
Coach: Tessa Payne
Email: tessanyitsoccer@aol.com

NCAA II
Lady Bears/Blue, Gold
Phone: (516) 686-7627
Fax: (516) 626-0750

Estimated # of Women's Soccer Scholarships: 7
Conference: NYCAC
Program Profile: Our program is located at Old Westbury campus, small squad mostly local players. Grass stadium field located on-campus close to gymnasium and fieldhouse.
History: Our program started in 1994, current head coach has been with the program since 1996, making yearly developments in building a relatively new and young program. Gaining recognition in the NYCAC Conference.
Coaching: Tessa Payne is our Head Coach. He has been a head coach since 1996, a graduate from Hofstra university in 1994 with a degree in Physical Education, director and staff coach for Naga Soccer, Long Island Junior Select Coach. Licenses include English FA License, NSCAA National and Advanced National Awards. Aidan Lyons and Kristen Kastrines are the Assistant Coaches.
Roster in State: 14 **Out of State:** 2 **Out of Country:** 2
Walk-on/Other: **Graduation %:** 0 **Seniors on Team:** 4
Positions Needed: Center Midfielder, Full Backs
Camp or Clinic Dates: Not Available
Most Recent Record: 6-11-0
Schedule: CW Post New York, Adelphi University, West Chester University, Slippery Rock University, Philadelphia university

New York University

Academic Profile

Phone: (212) 998-1212
New York, NY 10012

Type: 4 Yr.,Private,Liberal Arts
Founded: 1831
Website: http://www.nyu.edu
Religion: Non-Affiliated
SAT/ACT/GPA: Required/3.6
Housing: Yes
Student/Faculty Ratio: 13:1
Male/Female Ratio: Not Available
Undergraduate Enrollment: 17,673
Graduate Enrollment: 19,406
Scholarships/Academic: Yes **Athletic:** No **Financial Aid:** Yes
Expenses by: Year **In State:** $ 33,582 **Out of State:** $ 33,582
Specialty: Business, Law, Performing Arts, Premed
Degrees Conferred: Associate, Bachelor's, Certificate, Diploma, Doctoral, First Pre-Professional, Master's, Post-Doctoral Certificate, Post-Master's Certificate
Programs of Study: Accounting, Acting, Africans Studies, Anthropology, Biology, Chemistry, Cinema Studies, Classical Civilization, Communication Studies, Comparative Literature, Computer Science, Dance, Dramatic Literature, Dramatic Writing, Early Childhood Education, East Asian Studies, Economics, English Literature, English Education, European Studies, Film/Television, Finance, Fine Arts, French, History, Hotel/Tourism Management, Individualized Major, Information Systems, Journalism/Mass Communication, Latin American Studies, Linguistics and Languages, Management and Organizational Behavior, Marketing, Mathematics, Metropolitan Studies, Music Education, Music/Business/Technology, Neural Science, Nursing, Nutrition and Food Studies, Philosophy, Politics, Psychology, Religious Studies, Social Work, Sociology, Special Education, Speech and Hearing Handicap Education, Sports Management and Marketing-Recreation and Leisure Studies, Studio Art

Men's Athletic Profile

181 Mercer Street
New York, NY 10012
Coach: Joe Behan
Email: jmb1184@nyu.edu

NCAA III
Bobcats/Violet, White
Phone: (212) 998-2072
Fax: (212) 995-4105

Estimated # of Men's Soccer Scholarships: N/A
Conference: University Athletic Association
Program Profile: Home field is a turf; Cole Fieldhouse, a member of the UAA, and play a Fall and Spring season.
History: Program began in 1924. Pro's - Shep Messing, Joey Fink.
Achievements: All-Americans and professionals: Shep Messing Joey Finl.
Coaching: Joe Behan, Head Coach, since 1995, originally from Ireland, three-time league All-Star, coached New York Irish and New York Irish Shamrock.
Style of Play: International Style.

Women's Athletic Profile

181 Mercer Street
New York, NY 10012
Coach: John Clement
Email: jmc17@is7.nyu.edu

NCAA III
Violets/Violet, White
Phone: (212) 998-2041
Fax: (212) 995-4105

Estimated # of Women's Soccer Scholarships: None
Conference: University Athletic Association
Program Profile: We play both a traditional fall and a non-tradition spring season. We have a year around fitness program including a demanding summer workout. We have a field at Riverbank State Park in New York City which measures 120 x 70 and has an artificial surface.
History: Our varsity program is in its 5th year.
Achievements: 1997 one All-UAA Selection; 1998 two All-UAA players. 1999 3 All-UAA players, 1 Adidas All-Region player, 1999 Jon Clement UAA Coach or the year; 1999 2 All-UAA players; 1999 1 Adidas All-Region Player; 1999 Jon Clement UAA Coach of the Year.
Coaching: John Clement is head coach and has a USSF license. He is a former ODP Staff Coach from Greenwich Connecticut High School. He was coach and staff coach for the Yankee Premier Women's Club.
Walk-on/Other: **Graduation %:** 100 **Seniors on Team:**
Most Recent Record: 7-8-3
Style of Play: We play to feet but with an attacking emphasis; usually zonal; defending system designed around the strengths of our players; we need athletic technicians; players who love the game will do well.

Niagara University

Academic Profile

Niagara, NY 14109-2009
Phone: (716) 286-8600

Type: 4 Yr.,Private,Liberal Arts
Website: http://www.niagara.edu
SAT/ACT/GPA: 1000
Student/Faculty Ratio: 16:1
Undergraduate Enrollment: 2,400+
Scholarships/Academic: Yes **Athletic:** Yes
Expenses by: Year **In State:** $19,290
Specialty: Travel & Tourism

Founded: 1856
Religion: Catholic/Vincentian
Housing: Yes
Male/Female Ratio: 42:58
Graduate Enrollment: 600
Financial Aid: Yes
Out of State: $19,290

Degrees Conferred: BA, BS
Programs of Study: Accounting, Biology, Business, Chemistry, Commerce, Criminal Justice, Education, English, French, History, Hotel/Restaurant Administration, Inclusion Elementary & Special Education, Mathematics, Nursing, Philosophy, Social Work, Travel/Tourism

Men's Athletic Profile

Lewiston Road
Niagara Falls, NY 14109
Coach: Tim Smith
Email: Not Available

NCAA I
Purple Eagles/Purple, Black
Phone: (716) 286-8661
Fax: (716) 286-8609

Estimated # of Men's Soccer Scholarships: None
Conference: Metro Atlantic Athletic Conference
Program Profile: Has one game field, and two practice fields.
History: Our program began in 1969.
Achievements: Paul James was named 1996 MAAC Coach of the Year; 1996 3 MAAC first team All-Conference players: Craig Donaghue, Gary McGurdan, and Guillermo Rodger.
Style of Play: Contingent on player personal - ideally 3-5-2 short passing build-up.

Women's Athletic Profile

P. O. Box 2009
Niagara University, NY 14109-2009
Coach: Peter Veltri
Email: pveltri@niagara.edu

NCAA I
Purple Eagles/Purple, White
Phone: (716) 286-8600
Fax: (716) 286-8609

Estimated # of Women's Soccer Scholarships: None
Conference: Metro Atlantic Athletic Conference
Program Profile: We are an NCAA Division I program that plays in the Metro Atlantic Athletic Conference. We play on campus on a natural grass field.
History: The program began in 1983, and we have had several outstanding seasons.
Achievements: Coach of the Year (MAAC) 1999
Coaching: Peter Veltri is Head Coach.
Roster in State: 14 **Out of State:** 3 **Out of Country:** 7
ODP State: 10 **Regional:** 1 **National:**
Walk-on/Other: **Graduation %:** 100 **Seniors on Team:** 4
Camp or Clinic Dates: Not Available
Most Recent Record: 8-10-0
Schedule: Temple Univ. Lehigh, Lafayette, Buffalo Univ.
Style of Play: Depends on the player's personnel; ideally 3-5-2 short passing build-up.

Nyack College

Academic Profile

Nyack, NY 10960

Phone:

Type: 4 Yr.,Private,Liberal Arts
Website: http://www.nyackcollege.du
SAT/ACT/GPA: 860/18/2.0
Student/Faculty Ratio: 10:1
Undergraduate Enrollment: 790
Scholarships/Academic: Yes **Athletic:** Yes

Founded: 1886
Religion: Christian
Housing: Yes
Male/Female Ratio: 3.5:5
Graduate Enrollment: 300
Financial Aid: Yes

Expenses by: Year **In State:** $ 18,440 **Out of State:** $ 18,440
Degrees Conferred: BA, BS
Programs of Study: Biblical Studies, Business & Economics, Christian Studies, Communication, Education, English, History, Humanities, Management, Math, Ministries, Missions, Music, Music Theory & Composition, Natural Science, Performing Arts, Philosophy, Psychology, Religion, Religious Education, Religious Music, Secondary Education, Social Science, Voice, Youth Ministry

Men's Athletic Profile

1 South Blvd.
Nyack, NY 10960
Coach: Keith Davie
Email: daviek@nyack.edu

NCAA II/NAIA
Purple Pride/Purple, Gold
Phone: (914) 358-1710
Fax: (914) 353-2147

Estimated # of Men's Soccer Scholarships: 11
Conference: Central Atlantic Collegiate Conference
Program Profile: The program is thirty years old; first year provisional NCAA Division II program. We have a brand new soccer field with the measurements of 115x72 natural grass. Our stadium has a seating capacity for 200.
History: Our program began in 1960-1961; all-time winningest coach was Bill Galipaulti; all-time leadership scorer is Ken Brock.
Achievements: Coach Keith Davie was named 1997 CACC Coach of the Year; 1998 Honorable Mention All-American was Sophomore Jason Rollins.
Coaching: Keith Davie, Head Coach, holds a national Diploma from NSCAA. He was a two-time Honorable Mention All-American selection and seven years coaching experience at the high school and college level. He spent two years at Houghton College and compiled a record of 35-41-4 in three years at Nyack. Andrew Brokopp, Assistant Coach, is responsible with for goalkeeper.
Style of Play: Attempts to emulate Dutch Style of free movement. Tends to play a 3-5-2 or a 3-2-2-3.

Women's Athletic Profile

1 South Boulevard
Nyack, NY 10960
Coach: Randy Bowman
Email: bowman@Nyack.edu

NAIA II, NAIA
Purple Pride/Purple, Gold
Phone: (845) 358-1710
Fax: (845) 353-2147

Estimated # of Women's Soccer Scholarships: open
Conference: Central Atlantic Collegiate Conference
Program Profile: We have an outdoor field,120x85, with natural grass and about 900 seats for our fans. Indoor facilities pending permits estimated date is 2001 and that will include an indoor turf field.
Achievements: All-Americans: 1998 Priscilla Deager, 1999 Debbie Vanderplaat, 2000 Sarah Butler
Coaching: Randy Bowman is going into his second season as head coach. Rangy played soccer in Africa. He has been working with both the men's and women's programs at Nyack for the last 6 years. Andy Brokopp is our goalkeeper coach.

Roster in State: 4	**Out of State:** 13	**Out of Country:** 2
ODP State: 3	**Regional:**	**National:**
Walk-on/Other:	**Graduation %:**	**Seniors on Team:** 4

Positions Needed: Sweeper, Goalkeeper, Defenders
Camp or Clinic Dates: August 16
Most Recent Record: 8-5-2
Schedule: Houghton College, Green Mount College, Roberts Wesleyan, Georgian Court College, Dominican College, Holly Family College
Style of Play: Attacking possession with composure and technical speed. " Soccer is game it has to be fun"

Pace University
Academic Profile

Phone:

Pleasantville, NY 10570

Type: 4 Yr.,Private
Founded: 1963
Website: http://www.pace.edu
Religion: Non-Affiliated
SAT/ACT/GPA: 900
Housing: Yes
Student/Faculty Ratio: 21:1
Male/Female Ratio: 1:2
Undergraduate Enrollment: 3,500
Graduate Enrollment: N/A
Scholarships/Academic: Yes **Athletic:** Yes **Financial Aid:** Yes
Expenses by: Year **In State:** $ 21,000 **Out of State:** $ 21,000
Specialty: Business
Degrees Conferred: AA, AS, AAS, BA, BS, BBA, BFA, LLM, MBA, MSN
Programs of Study: Business and Management, Equestrian Science, Communications, BioEngineering and BioMedical, Engineering, International Studies, Psychology, Social Sciences

Women's Athletic Profile

861 Bedford Rs-Athletics Field House
Pleasantville, NY 10570
NCAA II
Setters/Navy, Gold
Coach: Mike Winn
Phone: (914) 923-2904
Email: mwinn@pace.edu
Fax: (914) 923-2895

Estimated # of Women's Soccer Scholarships: N/A
Conference: Northeast 10
Program Profile: Program is in its 3rd year of existence; soccer field at Briarcliff, NY campus; natural grass; season starts with non-conference games usually out of state; no bleachers, grass hill for spectators to enjoy games at.
History: Began in 1998 with first year of conference play in 1999.
Coaching: Head Coach-Mike Winn, Assistant Coach is Tanya Yavarow.
Roster in State: 13 **Out of State:** 9 **Out of Country:** 0
Walk-on/Other: 0 **Graduation %:** N/A **Seniors on Team:** 4
Positions Needed: GK, F
Camp or Clinic Dates: July 16-20, 22-27 2001
Most Recent Record: 4-16-0
Schedule: Franklin Pierce, Merrimack, Southern Connecticut, American International, Barry University

Polytechnic University
Academic Profile

Phone: 800-POLYTECH

Brooklyn, NY 11201

Type: 4 Yr.,Private,Engineering
Founded: 1854
Website: http://www.poly.edu
Religion: All
SAT/ACT/GPA: Open
Housing: Yes
Student/Faculty Ratio: 18:1
Male/Female Ratio: 7:1
Undergraduate Enrollment: 1,200
Graduate Enrollment: 1,000
Scholarships/Academic: Yes **Athletic:** No **Financial Aid:** Yes
Expenses by: Year **In State:** $ 18,000 **Out of State:** $ 18,000
Specialty: Engineering, Computer Science & Engineering, Humanities
Degrees Conferred: BS, Masters, Ph.D.
Programs of Study: Mechanical Engineering, Electrical Engineering, Civil Engineering, Computer Science, Computer Engineering, Technical Writing, Chemical Engineering, Pure Science, Humanities

Men's Athletic Profile

333 Jay Street
Brooklyn, NY 11201
Coach: Lou Zinser
Email: athletic@poly.edu

NCAA III
Blue Jays/Blue, Gray
Phone: (718) 637-5900
Fax: (718) 637-5959

Estimated # of Men's Soccer Scholarships: N/A
Conference: Independent
Program Profile: Fall sport playing September through October; facilities - Farmingdale New York, natural turf.
History: Program began in 1972.
Achievements: Won eight consecutive games in 1990 for the first time in the school's history and missed the ECAC tournament by one vote.
Coaching: Lou Zinser, Head Coach, the program's only coach, former member of a National Junior College Championship team, played on Baltimore University team that placed third in the NCAA Division I.
Style of Play: Open - run and gun.

Pratt Institute

Academic Profile

Brooklyn, NY 11205

Phone:

Type: 4 Yr.,Private,Engineering
Website: http://www.pratt.edu
SAT/ACT/GPA: Open
Student/Faculty Ratio: 9:1
Undergraduate Enrollment: 2,900
Scholarships/Academic: Yes
Athletic: No
Expenses by: Year
In State:
Founded: 1888
Religion: Non-Affiliated
Housing: Yes
Male/Female Ratio: 1:1
Graduate Enrollment: 600
Financial Aid: Yes
Out of State:
Specialty: Art Design, Architecture
Degrees Conferred: AA, AS, BA, BS, MA, MS
Programs of Study: Adult/Continuing Education, Architecture, Arts, Art History, Ceramic Art, City/Community/Regional Planning, Commercial Art, Computer Graphics, Construction Management, Fashion Design, Fashion Merchandising, Film Studies, Fine Arts, Graphic Art, Interdisciplinary Studies, Interior Design, Photography

Men's Athletic Profile

200 Willoughby Avenue
Brooklyn, NY 11205
Coach: Richard Griffiths
Email: Not Available

NCAA III
Cannoneers/Gold, Black
Phone: (718) 636-3774
Fax: (718) 636-3785

Estimated # of Men's Soccer Scholarships: N/A
Conference: Hudson Valley Conference
Program Profile: Seasons starts from September through late October. Play a natural grass field.
History: Our program began in 1989.

Women's Athletic Profile

200 Willoughby Ave.
Brooklyn, NY 11205
Coach: Ian Williams
Email: Not Available

NCAA III
Cannoneers/Gold, Black
Phone: (718) 636-3774
Fax: (718) 636-3785

Estimated # of Women's Soccer Scholarships: None
Conference: Hudson Valley Conference
Program Profile: Playing season runs from early September through late October. Has a natural grass field.
History: The women's program began in 1996

Rensselaer Polytechnic Institute (RPI)

Academic Profile

Troy, NY 12180
Phone: 518-276-6000

Type: 4 Yr.,Private,Liberal Arts,Engineering
Founded: 1824
Website: http://www.rpi.edu
Religion: Non-Affiliated
SAT/ACT/GPA: 1090+28
Housing: Yes
Student/Faculty Ratio: 11:1
Male/Female Ratio: 80:20
Undergraduate Enrollment: 5,000
Graduate Enrollment: 2,400
Scholarships/Academic: Yes **Athletic:** Yes **Financial Aid:** Yes
Expenses by: Year **In State:** $ 28,000 **Out of State:** $ 28,000
Specialty: Engineering, Science, Management
Degrees Conferred: BS, BArch, MS, MBA, MFA, Ph.D.
Programs of Study: Aeronautical Engineering, Architecture, Biology, BioMedical Engineering, Chemical Engineering, Chemistry, Engineering, Computer Science, Economics, Geology, Interdisciplinary Studies, Management, Mathematics, Philosophy, Physics, PreDentistry, PreLaw, PreMed, Psychology, Science Technology

Men's Athletic Profile

110 - 8th Street
Troy, NY 12180
Coach: Aldo Nardiello
Email: nardia@rpi.edu

NCAA III
Redhawks/Red, White
Phone: (518) 276-6182
Fax: (518) 276-8997

Estimated # of Men's Soccer Scholarships: n/a
Conference: UCAA, ECAC
Program Profile: UCAA has been one of the toughest Division III conference in the country, proudace the 1999 National Conference Champions Play on a natural grass. Ned Harkness Field; $2.4 million astro turf field.
History: Program started in 1986.
Achievements: Rensselaer has won 8 ICAC titles and has produced 20 All-Americans and numerous ICAC All-Stars. Won USA Championship in 1996, Award 3 consecutive bids in late 1990's. Constantly Rank Regional.
Coaching: Aldo Nardiello, Head Coach, Howie Charbonneau, Patrick Udeh, Jason - Assistant Coaches.
Roster In State: 19 **Out of State:** 8 **Out of Country:** 1
ODP State: 7 **Regional:** 0 **National:** 0
Walk-on/Other: 0 **Graduation %:** 98 **Seniors on Team:** 1
Positions Needed: Always room for good players
Camp or Clinic Dates: Aug.
Most Recent Record: 6-8-1
Schedule: St. Lawerence, Hamilton College, Plattsburgh, NYU, Vassar
Style of Play: We coach players to become technically proficient and develop a tactical understanding for the game. We work hard to regain possession of the ball and encourage and attacking style of play.

Women's Athletic Profile

110 - 8th Street
Troy, NY 12180
Coach: Aldo Nardiello
Email: nardia@rpi.edu

NCAA III
Redhawks/Red, White
Phone: (518) 276-6182
Fax: (518) 276-8997

Estimated # of Women's Soccer Scholarships: None
Conference: UCAA, ECAC
Program Profile: Playing season runs from August through November. Indoor spring soccer. Astro truf and grass field.
History: Program began in 1985.
Achievements: Several league All-Stars. Conference title in 1996, Post-season last 3 years in a row, Women's New York State tournament, 2 All-Americans in 2000.
Coaching: Aldo Nadiello, Head Coach. , Jim Townsend a Jason Ranundo GK coach- Assistant Coaches.
Roster in State: 17 **Out of State:** 9 **Out of Country:** 0
ODP State: 7 **Regional:** 0 **National:** 0
Walk-on/Other: 0 **Graduation %:** 100 **Seniors on Team:** 4
Positions Needed: Always looking for good players.
Camp or Clinic Dates: Aug.
Most Recent Record: 12-4-0
Schedule: St. Lawrence, Union, NYU, Vassar, William Smith
Style of Play: Highly technical, skill orientated, and ball possession style of play.

Roberts Wesleyan College

Academic Profile

Rochester, NY 14624
Phone:

Type: 4 Yr.,Private,Liberal Arts
Founded: 1866
Website: http://www.roberts.edu
Religion: Free Methodist
SAT/ACT/GPA: 860/18/2.0
Housing: Yes
Student/Faculty Ratio: 14:1
Male/Female Ratio: 1:2
Undergraduate Enrollment: 1,200
Graduate Enrollment: 300
Scholarships/Academic: Yes **Athletic:** Yes **Financial Aid:** Yes
Expenses by: Year **In State:** $ 17,458 **Out of State:** $ 17,458
Specialty: Christian Liberal Arts Education
Degrees Conferred: AS, BA, BS, M.Ed., MSW
Programs of Study: Accounting, Art, Biology, Business Administration, Chemistry, Computer Science, Criminal Justice, Chemistry, Communications, Education, Engineering, Fine Arts, Gerontology, Mathematics, Music, Physical Science, Physics, PreMed, Psychology, Religion, Philosophy, Social Work, Sociology, Contemporary Ministries, History, Humanities, Math, Music, Nursing, Physics, Religion, Sociology

Men's Athletic Profile

2301 Westside Drive
Rochester, NY 14624
Coach: Greg Gidman
Email: gidmang@roberts.edu

NCAA II/NAIA
Raiders/Red, White
Phone: (716) 594-6514
Fax: (716) 594-6580

Estimated # of Men's Soccer Scholarships: Varies
Conference: NAIA Region IX
Program Profile: Robert Wesleyan has an established 1st team and has initiated a full second team in the fall of 2000. The facilities both indoor and outdoor are excellent with a building project of a new natural grass stadium seating 1500 to be completed in the fall of 2001, the indoor facility houses a pool, weight room, rehab center, and 65x45 yard gym and indoor track. Roberts Wesleyan is the Official training for the A-league's Rochester Rhinos. The raiders run a full-year program with extensive travel.
History: Robert Wesleyan entered the NAIA in 1956. The team has competed in the NAIA National Tournament 3 times in 1967, 1978 & 1998. The team also competed in the NCCAA Division National I Tournament 2 times in 1984 & 1991. the team has boasted numerous All-Americans, All-Region and All-Conference players. The 1998-1999 team set the school record for wins in a season (19-5-1 and goals against average of .70. Currently the Raiders are dually affiliated with the NCAA II.

Achievements: Roberts Wesleyan attended the 1998 NAIA National Tournament as the 12th seed in the country and again returned in 1999 as the 7th seed in the Nation. The teams boasts international players such as the TNTS U23 goalie Richard Goddard, and has had several players play in the A-league such as Leon Minott and Howard Allen. Coach Greg Gidman has received the NCCAA National Coach of the Year in 1998 and NAIA Regional and NSCAA Mid-East Coach of the Year in 1999.
Coaching: Coach Greg Gidman attended Houghton College where he was both an NAIA and NCCAA All-American and later at the Univ. of Victoria, BC was an academic All-Canadian. He holds his NCCP leve 2 license, coaches the U-83 New York State West ODP team, and had a short Professional career in the Canadian Soccer League. Coach Gidman has a Masters in Sport Administration and BS in physical education. Assistant Coach Derek May competed on an NCCAA National Championship Team in 1986 and attended the NAIA National Tournament in 1987. Coach May has a Masters Degree in School Psychology. Coach Todd Miner has attended three NAIA National Tournaments as a player and work closely with player development and recruiting.

Roster In State: 8	**Out of State:** 6	**Out of Country:** 6
ODP State: 0	**Regional:** 1	**National:** 2
Walk-on/Other:	**Graduation %:** 95	**Seniors on Team:** 4

Positions Needed: Sweeper, Defender, Goalkeeper
Camp or Clinic Dates: August 7-11
Most Recent Record: 16-4-1
Schedule: Lindsey Wilson, University of Mobile, Simon Frasier, Seattle university, University of Victoria, BC, Tiffin, Houghton, Rio Grande
Style of Play: Defensively sound giving up less than .75 goals per game over the last two years. Movement of ball through midfield on the ground but never fearful of sending the attack forward quickly.

Women's Athletic Profile

2301 Westside Drive
Rochester, NY 14624
Coach: Mark Palma
Email: palmam@roberts.edu

NAIA
Raiders/Red, White, Black
Phone: (716) 594-6507
Fax: (716) 594-6580

Estimated # of Women's Soccer Scholarships: 4
Conference: American Mideast Conference
Program Profile: Roberts Women's Soccer plays a highly competitive schedule. The team plays on a well maintained grass field with two fall size practice fields. A stadium is schedule for completion in 2002.
History: The program began in 1985 under Head Coach Cindy Aymo in the NCCAA. Head Coach Mark Palma took over in 1994. The team is in the NAIA and the team's record under Coach Palma is 84-57-6. The team competed in the NCCAA National Tournament in 1995,96,97 and in 2000.
Achievements: Mark Palma Conference Coach of the Year in 1998 and 1999; NAIA Regional Finalists in 1999; Each year since the beginning the team has had Academic All-Americans; 1 NAIA and NCCAA All-American.
Coaching: Mark Palma is the Head Coach who has been with the Raiders for seven years, and before that coached high school for 13 years. The assistant coaches are Josh Hinman and Julie Redband.

Roster in State: 17	**Out of State:** 1	**Out of Country:** 0
ODP State: 1	**Regional:** 0	**National:** 0
Walk-on/Other: 2	**Graduation %:** 100	**Seniors on Team:** 8

Positions Needed: GK, Striker, Midfielder
Camp or Clinic Dates: July, August
Most Recent Record: 13-8-1
Schedule: Houghton, Tiffin, Malone, Cedarville, Mt. Vernon Nazarene, Seton Hill
Style of Play: We play a creative controlled type of play, in recent years attacking hard down the flanks.

Rochester Institute of Technology

Academic Profile

Phone: 716-475-6700

Rochester, NY 14623

Type: 4 Yr.,Private
Founded: 1829
Website: http://www.rit.edu
Religion: Non-Affiliated
SAT/ACT/GPA: Open
Housing: Yes
Student/Faculty Ratio: 12/1
Male/Female Ratio: N/A
Undergraduate Enrollment: 11,300
Graduate Enrollment: 2200
Scholarships/Academic: Yes **Athletic:** No **Financial Aid:** Yes
Expenses by: Year **In State:** $25,989 **Out of State:** $25,989
Degrees Conferred: AAS, AS, BS, BA, BFA, MS, MA, MGA, MST, Ph.D.
Programs of Study: Applied Science & Technology (Computer Science, Food, Hotel & Travel Management, Packing Science, Engineering Technology, Industrial Technology), Business, Engineering, Imaging Arts & Sciences (School for American Craftsmen, School of Arts and Design, School of Printing Management Services, Center for Imaging Science), Liberal Arts, Science and the National Technical Institute for the Deaf

Men's Athletic Profile

51 Lomb Memorial Dr.
Rochester, NY 14623
Coach: Bill Garno
Email: Not Available

NCAA III
Tigers/Orange, White
Phone: (716) 475-2618
Fax: (716) 475-6510

Estimated # of Men's Soccer Scholarships: N/A
Conference: Independent Conference
Program Profile: Nationally known program, no American football, new field, stadium with lights. The field is a natural grass and the stadium has a seating capacity of 2,000.
History: Program began in 1960, has received national recognition for the past several years.
Achievements: National Coach of the Year in 1989; Conference Coach of the Year in 1983-present; Conference Champions in the last eight years; Regional Coach of the Year in 1982, 1984, 1987, & 1989; 11 NCAA Tournament Appearances; 1988 Finalist four times Semi-Finalist in 1992 and 1995, ECAC Champions.
Coaching: Bill Garno, Head Coach, third season as a head coach of the Tigers, four years as an assistant at the University of Rochester; played for Predecessor. Doug May from 1983-1986, played four NCAA Tournaments in North Carolina in 1984 Final Four has 59-8-6 record while player at RM.

Women's Athletic Profile

51 Lomb Memorial Dr.-George H. Clark Gym
Rochester, NY 14626
Coach: Tom Natalie
Email: TFNATL@RIT.EDU

NCAA III
Tigers/Burnt Umber, Orange
Phone: (716) 475-7373
Fax: (716) 475-5675

Estimated # of Women's Soccer Scholarships: None
Conference: Empire Athletic Association, NYSWCAA, ECAC
Program Profile: The RIT women's soccer participates in the NCAA Division III and the ECAC. The team plays @ RIT field on a natural surface field. The program has been around since in 1982.
History: 1982 was the first year of the program. The program most victories came in 1990 with 1.5; 1990 was the season that saw the team go a 15-5-1, their best season record. The overall team record is 112-1434-19.

Achievements: RIT has played in 2 NYSWCAA Championships; 2 players have been named All-New York State, 3 named NYSWCAA All-Tournament, 8 named All-Empire Athletic Association.
Coaching: Tom Natalie, Head Coach, entering his third year with the program. Dan Schoniker, Assistant Coach.
Style of Play: At RIT we have been playing a possession type game with emphasis on defense. This is evolving into a more attacking style as we upgrade our roster with better athletes. In summary, we try to best utilize the talents that the team possess on a year to year basis.

Russell Sage College

Academic Profile

Phone: 518-244-2000

Troy, NY 12180

Type: 4 Yr.,Private,Liberal Arts
Founded: 1916
Website: http://www.sage.edu
Religion: Non-Affiliated
SAT/ACT/GPA: 1050/2.75
Housing: Yes
Student/Faculty Ratio: 12:1
Male/Female Ratio: Women
Undergraduate Enrollment: 1,038
Graduate Enrollment: N/A
Scholarships/Academic: Yes **Athletic:** No **Financial Aid:** Yes
Expenses by: Year **In State:** $ 21,580 **Out of State:** $ 21,580
Specialty: Physical, Creative Arts & Occupational Therapy, Theatre
Degrees Conferred: BA, BS, MS
Programs of Study: Offers more than 30 Bachelor's Degrees to women. Art Management, Communications, Biology, Computer Science, Computer Information Systems, Math, Medical Technology, Economics, Criminal Justice, Marketing, Political Science, Psychology

Women's Athletic Profile

Robison Athletic and Recreation Ctr
Troy, NY 12180
Coach: Ray Nause
Email: nauser@sage.edu

NCAA III
Gators/Dark Green, White
Phone: (518) 244-2283
Fax: (518) 270-3107

Estimated # of Women's Soccer Scholarships: None
Conference: New York State Women's Collegiate Athletic Association
Program Profile: Team competes in both a fall (16-18 matches) and a spring season (3-5 tournaments). A weight training program is incorporated. Team utilizes a 120x70 yards natural turf field.
History: Program initiated in fall of 1988.
Achievements: 1993 NSCAA Division III All-Northeast team - Kelley Richer, 1992 NYSWCAA Scholar Athlete-Wendy Kuhn, 1997-1998 and 1995-1996 NSCAA Team Academic Award Winner; 1996, 1997 & 1998 NSCAA team Ethics Award of Merit Recipient.
Coaching: Ray Nause, Head Coach, has coached soccer at the collegiate level for eleven years including eight season as a head coach. He holds the United States Soccer Federation "B" License, the NSCAA National and National Diploma. Sherry Domagala, Assistant Coach.
Style of Play: Style of play matched to player's talents each year.

Saint Bonaventure University

Academic Profile

Phone:

St. Bonaventure, NY 14778

Type: 4 Yr.,Private,Liberal Arts
Founded: 1858
Website: http://www.cs.sbu.edu
Religion: Catholic
SAT/ACT/GPA: Open
Housing: Yes

Student/Faculty Ratio: 16:1 **Male/Female Ratio:** 50:50
Undergraduate Enrollment: N/A **Graduate Enrollment:** N/A
Scholarships/Academic: Yes **Athletic:** Yes **Financial Aid:** Yes
Expenses by: Year **In State:** $ 19,600 **Out of State:** $ 19,600
Degrees Conferred: BA, BS, BSEd, MA, MBA, MS, MSEd
Programs of Study: Biology, BioChemistry, Environmental Science, Accounting, Finance, Management Science, Marketing, Economics, Math & Business Administration, JMC, Computer Science, Elementary Education, Physical Education, French, Spanish, Latin, Medical Technology, English, Philosophy, Math, Physics, Chemistry, Political Science, Psychology, Social Science, Social Studies, History, Sociology, Visual Arts, Art Teacher, Interdisciplinary Studies

Men's Athletic Profile

P.O. Box 6
St. Bonaventure, NY 14778
Coach: Bill Brady
Email: wbrady@sbu.edu

NCAA I
Bonnies/Brown, White, Gold
Phone: (716) 375-2642
Fax: (716) 375-2383

Estimated # of Men's Soccer Scholarships: 2.5
Conference: Atlantic 10 Conference
Program Profile: Our facilities include a natural grass field that measures 120x75 yards, game and practice fields, and 1,500 seats. We also have a weight room with full-time strength coach and an academic support center with 2 part-time staff members.
History: Began in 1962. Was a Division III school until the late eighties. 1999, Bonaventure qualified for the A-10 Conference tourney first time in school history. Top 4 team qualify out of 12 teams.
Achievements: Coach Brady is in his second year with the program. Justin Evans (1998) drafted 16th overall by the San Jose Earthquakes-1999 draft. He currently plays with the Pittsburgh Riverhounds of the A-League.
Roster In State: 6 **Out of State:** 10 **Out of Country:** 5
ODP State: 10 **Regional:** 3 **National:** 2
Walk-on/Other: 3 **Graduation %:** 99 **Seniors on Team:** 3
Positions Needed: GK, Outside Midfielders
Camp or Clinic Dates: Not Available
Most Recent Record: 6-12-0
Style of Play: Attacking style of play, fast and furious in aiming for goals. "Maturity will be a key for us. Our season may ride on how we respond to those early matches". Possession with a purpose.

Women's Athletic Profile

Women's Soccer Office
St. Bonaventure, NY 14778
Coach: Geoff Bennett
Email: gbennett@SBU.edu

NCAA I
Bonnies/Brown, Gold
Phone: (716) 375-2286
Fax: (716) 375-2280

Estimated # of Women's Soccer Scholarships: None
Conference: Atlantic 10 Conference
Program Profile: Year-round program - facilities include fenced in grass field (120x75), permanent scoreboard, benched shields, 2 practice fields. Game field capacity of 1,000 people.
History: Program began in 1981. compiled a record of 95-90-7 record over the last 10 ten years.
Achievements: Numerous All-Conference and All-Region Awards; 1996 3rd team freshman All-American.
Coaching: Geoff Bennett, Head Coach, graduated from Hartwick College. Todd Hofford - Assistant Coach, graduated Hartwick College. Joanne Storms, graduated from St. Bonaveture.
Style of Play: possession orientated game which revolves around fast, technical players.

Saint Francis College - New York

Academic Profile

Phone:

Brooklyn, NY 11201

Type: 4 Yr.,Private,Liberal Arts
Founded: 1884
Website: http://www.stfranciscollege.edu
Religion: Franciscan Brothers
SAT/ACT/GPA: 820/18
Housing: No
Student/Faculty Ratio: 24:1
Male/Female Ratio: 45:55
Undergraduate Enrollment: 2,300
Graduate Enrollment: N/A
Scholarships/Academic: Yes **Athletic:** Yes
Financial Aid: Yes
Expenses by: Year **In State:** $ 8,000
Out of State: $ 8,000
Degrees Conferred: AS, AAS, BA, Bs
Programs of Study: Accounting, Aviation Management, Biology, BioMedical Science, Broadcasting, Business Administration, Communications, Computer Information Systems, Computer Science, Criminal Justice, Economics, Elementary Education, English, Film Studies, Finance, Health Services, History, Interdisciplinary Studies, Liberal Arts, Management, Marketing, Mathematics, Medical Technology Physical Education, Political Science, PreDentistry, PreLaw, PreMed, Psychology, Secondary Education, Social Science, Special Education

Men's Athletic Profile

180 Remson Street
Brooklyn, NY 11201
Coach: Sam Carrington
Email: jwhoffman@usa.net

NCAA I
Terriers/Red, Blue
Phone: 718-489-5489
Fax: (718) 522-1274

Estimated # of Men's Soccer Scholarships: None
Conference: Northeast Conference

Saint John Fisher College

Academic Profile

Phone: (716) 385-8309

Rochester, NY 14618

Type: 4 Yr.,Private,Liberal Arts
Founded: 1948
Website: http://www.sjfc.edu
Religion: Roman Catholic
SAT/ACT/GPA: 1050/22/8.5
Housing: Yes
Student/Faculty Ratio: 15:1
Male/Female Ratio: 45:55
Undergraduate Enrollment: 1,500
Graduate Enrollment: 386
Scholarships/Academic: Yes **Athletic:** No
Financial Aid: Yes
Expenses by: Year **In State:** $ 19,290
Out of State: $ 19,290
Specialty: Liberal Arts, Accounting, Education, Business
Degrees Conferred: BA, BS, MBA
Programs of Study: Accounting, Biology, Chemistry, Communications, Computer Science, Economics, English, French, German, History, Interdisciplinary Studies, International Studies, Italian, Mathematics, Philosophy, Physics, Political Science, Psychology, Sociology, Spanish

Men's Athletic Profile

3690 East Avenue
Rochester, NY 14618
Coach: Rob Searl
Email: Not Available

NCAA III
Cardinals/Cardinal Red, White
Phone: (716) 385-8459
Fax: (716) 3857-7308

Estimated # of Men's Soccer Scholarships: N/A
Conference: ECAC
Program Profile: Team plays on a natural turf field with a seating capacity of 500. Has an indoor facility and 45x70 yards playing surface.
History: Program started in 1968. 1996 record is 13-4-1.
Achievements: 2 All-New York State players in 1996.
Coaching: Rob Searl, Head Coach, 18 years, USSF "B" License. Steve Smith - Assistant Coach, eight years college coach, USSF "A" Licensed. Mike McMahon - Assistant Coach, five years college coach, NSCAA National Licensed.
Style of Play: Whatever takes to win!!!

Women's Athletic Profile

3690 East Avenue
Rochester, NY 14618
Coach: Jill McCabe
Email: Not Available

NCAA III
Cardinals/Cardinal, Gold
Phone: (716) 385-8309
Fax:

Estimated # of Women's Soccer Scholarships: None
Conference: Independent, ECAC, NYSWCAA

Saint John's University - New York

Academic Profile

Jamaica, NY 11439

Phone: (718) 990-6161

Type: 4 Yr.,Private,Liberal Arts
Website: http://www.stjohns.edu
SAT/ACT/GPA: 1000/21/80
Student/Faculty Ratio: 15:1
Undergraduate Enrollment: 12,000
Scholarships/Academic: Yes
Athletic: Yes
Expenses by: Year
In State: $ 23,000

Founded: 1875
Religion: Vincentian
Housing: Yes
Male/Female Ratio: 45:55
Graduate Enrollment: 3,000
Financial Aid: Yes
Out of State: $ 23,000

Specialty: Business, Law, Pharmacy, Health, Sports Medicine
Degrees Conferred: BA, BS, BFA, MA, MBA, MS
Programs of Study: Accounting, American Studies, Anthropology, Banking and Finance, Biology, Broadcasting, Business, Chemistry, Communications, Computer Science, Criminal Justice, Economics, Education, English, Environmental Science, Fine Arts, Journalism, Management, Marketing, Mathematics, Nursing, Pharmacy, Philosophy, Physical Education Physics, Political Science, Psychology, Religion, Social Science, Toxicology

Men's Athletic Profile

8000 Utopia Pkwy
Jamaica, NY 11439
Coach: David Masur
Email: Not Available

NCAA I
Red Storm/Red, White
Phone: (718) 990-6197
Fax: (718) 990-2197

Estimated # of Men's Soccer Scholarships: None
Conference: Big East Conference
Program Profile: We are building a new soccer stadium on campus.
History: NCAA Division I championships; 5 Big East Title for eight years; 6 Big East Championships.
Achievements: 1996 Men's Coach of the Year Division I was Dave Masur; NCAA Division I Champs in 1996; Big East Regular Season Champs in 1992, 1993, 1996 & 1997; Big East tournament Champs in 1992, 1993, 1994, 1995 & 1998.

Coaching: David Masur is Head Coach. He was named 1996 Men's Coach of the Year. John Diffley is the Assistant Coach.
Roster In State: 18 **Out of State:** 5 **Out of Country:** 2
Camp or Clinic Dates: July 10-14, July 17-21, July 31-August 4

Women's Athletic Profile

8000 Utopia Pkwy.
Jamaica, NY 11439
Coach: Ian Stone
Email: stonei@st.john's.edu

NCAA I
Red Storm/Red, White
Phone: (718) 990-6163
Fax: (718) 990-2099

Estimated # of Women's Soccer Scholarships: 12
Conference: Big East Conference
Program Profile: At present we have an Astroturf surface but have proposed a grass stadium for the fall of 2001. The new stadium will be enclosed with seating 3,000 plus. We play a traditional season plus an intense spring season.
History: Our program began in 1987. Our all time record is 95-101-18.
Achievements: Won Big East Tournament in 1994; Numerous Big East All-American members; player on Big East All Second Team in 1997; Member of Big East Rookie team in 1997; two players All-Northeast team in 1994
Coaching: Our coaching staff includes Ian Stone, Wayne Fortino, and Cristin Burtis.
Roster in State: 13 **Out of State:** 10 **Out of Country:** 1
ODP State: 12 **Regional:** 3 **National:**
Walk-on/Other: **Graduation %:** 100 **Seniors on Team:** 6
Positions Needed: All
Camp or Clinic Dates: Summer 2001
Most Recent Record: 10-6-3
Schedule: Notre Dame, University of Connecticut, Syracuse, Boston College, West Virginia, Miami
Style of Play: Short passing, possession style based on intensity, high work rate. Positive, aggressive style of defense.

Saint Joseph's College - New York

Academic Profile

Patchogue, NY 11772-2603

Phone:

Type: 4 Yr.,Private,Liberal Arts **Founded:** 1916
Website: Not Available **Religion:** Catholic
SAT/ACT/GPA: 980/80 **Housing:** No
Student/Faculty Ratio: 20:1 **Male/Female Ratio:** 40:60
Undergraduate Enrollment: 2,400 **Graduate Enrollment:** 100
Scholarships/Academic: Yes **Athletic:** No **Financial Aid:** Yes
Expenses by: Sem **In State:** $ 4,300 **Out of State:** $ 4,300
Specialty: Liberal Arts
Degrees Conferred: BA, BS
Programs of Study: Accounting, Biology, Business Administration, Child Study, Classics, Computer Science, Education, English, Fine Arts, History, Human Relations, Mathematics, Modern Languages, Philosophy, Physical Education, Physical Sciences, Recreation, Religious Studies, Social Science, Psychology, Religious Studies, Social Science, Speech Communications, Interdisciplinary Courses, Sociology

Men's Athletic Profile

155 Roe Blvd.
Patchogue, NY 11772-2603
Coach: Gary Smith
Email: eaglecoach@erds.com

NCAA III
Golden Eagles/Navy Blue, Gold
Phone: (516) 447-3351
Fax: (516) 447-3347

Estimated # of Men's Soccer Scholarships: N/A
Conference: Hudson Valley Men's Athletic Conference
Program Profile: The program is moving from the NAIA to NCAA Division III. Our We have an irrigated home field,. There are no dorms but off campus housing is available.
History: Our program began in 1986. The overall record is 149-83-8 and our winning percentage is .642.
Achievements: Conference Champions in 1991, 1995, 1996, & 1997; Won 9 Tournament Titles in past eleven years.
Coaching: Gary Smith, Head Coach, won his 100th game at SJC in 1994 (9th year) .He was NAIA Coach of the Year in 1991 and he got the NISOA Soccer Officials Sportsmanship Award in 1992. His total career record is 344-240-47 in 35 years of coaching.
Style of Play: Short pass. Possession. Defensive pressure.

Women's Athletic Profile

155 Roe Blvd.
Patchogue, NY 11772
Coach: Gary Smith
Email: Not Available

NCAA III/NAIA
Golden Eagles/Navy, Gold
Phone: (516) 447-3291
Fax: (516) 654-1782

Did Not Return Profile

Saint Lawrence University

Academic Profile

Canton, NY 13617

Phone: 315-229-5011

Type: 4 Yr.,Private,Liberal Arts
Website: http://www.stlawu.edu
SAT/ACT/GPA: Open
Student/Faculty Ratio: 12:1
Undergraduate Enrollment: 1,950
Scholarships/Academic: Yes
Expenses by: Year

Athletic: No
In State: $ 28,815

Founded: 1856
Religion: Non-Affiliated
Housing: Yes
Male/Female Ratio: 1:1
Graduate Enrollment: 100
Financial Aid: Yes
Out of State: $ 28,815

Specialty: Preprofessional Programs, Environmental Science, many others
Degrees Conferred: BA, BS, MA, MS, MEd
Programs of Study: African Studies, Anthropology, Art, Asian Studies, Biology, BioPhysics, Canadian Studies, Chemistry, Computer Science, Creative Writing, Ecology, Economics, Engineering, English, Environmental Science, Fine Arts, French, Geology, Geophysics, German, Government, History, Literature, Mathematics, Modern Languages, Music, Philosophy, Physical Education, Physics, Political Science, Psychology, Recreation & Leisure, Religion, Romance Languages, Speech, Social Sciences, Spanish, Theatre

Men's Athletic Profile

Augsbury Ctr, Leigh Street
Canton, NY 13617
Coach: Bob Durocher
Email: bdur@music.st.lawrence.edu

NCAA III
Saints/Scarlet, Brown
Phone: (315) 229-5870
Fax: (315) 229-5589

Estimated # of Men's Soccer Scholarships: All Academic
Conference: Upstate Collegiate Athletic Association
Program Profile: We are NCAA 21 weeks during the school year. We have three natural grass fields. One is 120x80 yards and game only. We have a grass 120 x 80 practice field. We have a 120 x 80 Astroturf practice field. We have a 120 x 60 grid field that is lighted. We have a 60x40 indoor artificial turf field.

History: Our program began in 1963. We have 12 Conference Championships. We got 7 ECAC tournament selections. We were NCAA Tournament selections in 1976, 1981, 1995 and 1996.
Achievements: 12 Conference Titles in three of the last four years; four times Conference Coach of the Year; 7 All-Americans three in the last 2 years; 5 players professional in the last three years; 25 Regional All-Americans during the last 9 years;5 trips to NCAA Tournament; NCAA Final Eight in 1998; MLS draft pick Chicago Fire 1999; ECAC Tournament selection 7 times.
Coaching: Bob Durocher, Head Coach, has been here 9 years. He got Conference Coach of the Year 5 times. He was 1998 Northeast Regional Coach of the Year. His last 6 years record is 67-21-12. He has an NSCAA advanced diploma. Mike Toshack, goalkeeper coach, has been here 5 years. He was a Canadian Olympic goalkeeper assistant coach and scout. Martin Noe, assistant academic coach, has been here 3 years. Calin Lennon -Recruiting Coach.
Style of Play: Attacking style of play, but still possession based. Total soccer-backs attack, interchange of positions. We allow our technical players to be creative.

Women's Athletic Profile

Augsbury Center, Park Street
Canton, NY 13617
Coach: Deb Biche
Email: dbiche@stlawu.edu

NCAA III
Lady Saints/Scarlet, Brown
Phone: (315) 229-5790
Fax: (315) 379-5589

Estimated # of Women's Soccer Scholarships: None
Conference: EAA, ECAC
Program Profile: Play season games on outdoor field. Astro-turf fieldhouse for practice and the indoor season.
History: Program began in 1978 and has been successful since its inception.
Achievements: Won State Championship in 1990, number state Tournament appearances and 2 Appearances in the NCAA Tournament.
Style of Play: Short passing, ball control team. Excellent defense - high intensity.

Saint Thomas Aquinas College

Academic Profile

Sparkill, NY 10976-1050

Phone:

Type: 4 Yr.,Private
Founded: 1952
Website: http://www.stac.edu
Religion: Non-Affiliated
SAT/ACT/GPA: 830+
Housing: No
Student/Faculty Ratio: 18;1
Male/Female Ratio: 50;50
Undergraduate Enrollment: 1,400
Graduate Enrollment: 40
Scholarships/Academic: Yes **Athletic:** Yes **Financial Aid:** Yes
Expenses by: Year **In State:** $ 15,000 **Out of State:** $ 15,000
Degrees Conferred: BA, BS, MEd
Programs of Study: Accounting, Applied Art, Applied Mathematics, Business Administration, Communications, Computer Information Systems, Criminal Justice, Education, Engineering, English, Finance, Fine Arts, History, Humanities, Journalism, Mathematics, Medical Laboratory Technology, Modern Languages, Natural Science, PreMed, Psychology, Recreation & Leisure, Religion Romance, Social Science, Spanish, Speech Education

Men's Athletic Profile

125 Route 340
Sparkill, NY 10976-1050
Coach: Thomas Delehanty
Email: Not Available

NAIA
Spartans/Maroon, Gold
Phone: (914) 398-4053
Fax: (914) 359-8136

Estimated # of Men's Soccer Scholarships: N/A
Conference: CACC
Program Profile: New playing field currently under construction.
History: Program began in 1994.
Achievements: Frank Fuchs - Head Coach.

Women's Athletic Profile

125 Route 340
Sparkill, NY 10976
Coach: John J. Crapanzano
Email: Not Available

NAIA
Lady Spartans/Maroon, Gold
Phone: (914) 398-4058
Fax: (914) 359-8136

Estimated # of Women's Soccer Scholarships: None
Conference: CACC
Program Profile: The Lady Spartans play a competitive league. They play a Fall season that runs from August through November. The school has a new playing field.
History: Program in began in 1992 and became a varsity sport in 1993.

Siena College

Academic Profile

Loudonville, NY 12211-1462
Phone: (518) 583-2450

Type: 4 Yr.,Private,Liberal Arts
Website: http://www.siena.edu
SAT/ACT/GPA: 1000/80
Student/Faculty Ratio: 16:1
Undergraduate Enrollment: 2,700
Scholarships/Academic: Yes
Athletic: Yes
Expenses by: Year
In State: $ 21,100
Founded: 1937
Religion: Franciscan
Housing: Yes
Male/Female Ratio: 47:53
Graduate Enrollment: N/A
Financial Aid: Yes
Out of State: $ 21,100
Specialty: Biology, Business
Degrees Conferred: BA, BS, MBA
Programs of Study: Accounting, American Studies, Biology, Chemistry, Computer Science, Economics, English, Environmental Studies, Finance, French, History, Marketing/Management, Mathematics, Physics, Political Science, Religious Studies, Social Work, Sociology, Spanish, Undecided Arts

Men's Athletic Profile

515 Loudon Road
Loudonville, NY 12211-1462
Coach: Charlie Curto
Email: Not Available

NCAA I
Saints/Green, Gold
Phone: (518) 786-5042
Fax: (518) 783-2992

Estimated # of Men's Soccer Scholarships: None
Conference: Metro Atlantic Athletic Conference (MAAC)
Program Profile: Program undergoing growth and increase emphasis. Conference has automatic NCAA bid.
History: Program began in 1974, entered MAAC in 1989.
Achievements: 5 players since 1983 named Division I All-Area and All-New York State.
Coaching: Charlie Curto is our Head Coach. He is entering 14th season. He was a 1979 Sienna graduate, where he played soccer for two seasons. He played with New York Eagles in ASL and he was a former head coach for the New York Kick of the NPSL.
Style of Play: Aggressive, defensive - minded.

Women's Athletic Profile

515 London Road
Loudonville, NY 12211-1462
Coach: Steve Karbowski
Email: skarbowski@siena.edu

NCAA I
Saints/Green, Gold
Phone: (518) 786-5042
Fax: (518) 783-2992

Estimated # of Women's Soccer Scholarships: 6
Conference: Metro Atlantic Athletic Conference
Program Profile: Here at Siena we have a natural grass field, modern gym, indoor track, and a full time conditioning coach.
History: Our program began in 1980 and entered the MAAC conference in 1991. We have had 4 tournament appearances in 1993, 1995, 1996, and 1997; in 1996 we were the conference finalist.
Coaching: Steve Karbowski is not only our head women's coach, he is our men's assistant coach. Katie Terrenzio and Lori Perillo assists him.
Roster in State: 19 **Out of State:** 9 **Out of Country:**
ODP State: 6 **Regional:** **National:**
Walk-on/Other: **Graduation %:** **Seniors on Team:** 5
Positions Needed: Goalkeeper, Striker
Camp or Clinic Dates: July 10-14, 17-21
Most Recent Record: 3-11-2
Schedule: St. John's, Army, Providence, Northeastern, Temple, Holy Cross, Lafayette
Style of Play: Possession.

Skidmore College

Academic Profile

Saratoga Springs, NY 12866

Phone: (518) 580-5000

Type: 4 Yr.,Private,Liberal Arts
Website: http://www.skidmore.edu
SAT/ACT/GPA: Median combined SAT 1100+
Student/Faculty Ratio: 10:1
Undergraduate Enrollment: 2,200
Scholarships/Academic: Yes **Athletic:** No **Financial Aid:** Yes
Expenses by: Year **In State:** $ 28243+ **Out of State:** $ 28243+
Degrees Conferred: BA, BS
Programs of Study: All traditional Liberal Arts majors and Business, Social Work, Exercise Science, and Elementary Education

Founded: 1911
Religion: Presbyterian
Housing: Yes
Male/Female Ratio: 2:3
Graduate Enrollment: N/A

Men's Athletic Profile

North Broadway
Saratoga Springs, NY 12866-1632
Coach: Ron McEachen
Email: jhuckle@skidmore.edu

NCAA III
Thoroughbreds/Gold, Green
Phone: (518) 580-5381
Fax: (518) 580-5396

Estimated # of Men's Soccer Scholarships: None
Conference: Upstate Collegiate Athletic Association
Program Profile: Facilities include 1,500 seat stadium built for soccer, lacrosse and field hockey, Stadia turf surface which measures 122x90. Playing field measures 120x75, with an addition two grass training fields that measure 120x75 and 100x60. Excellent site for the on the ground ball control style played at Skidmore.

History: Varsity program began in 1982, formed Upstate Collegiate Athletic Association in 1996 - Top Division III, Men's Soccer Conference, nationally ranked teams in 1998.
Achievements: Goalkeeper 1996 1st team All-American; NCAA, UCAA Coach of the Year in 1994. Top conference finish - 4th in 1996, 4 NSCAA New York All-Region players.

Roster In State: 4	**Out of State:** 20	**Out of Country:**
ODP State: 2	**Regional:**	**National:**
Walk-on/Other:	**Graduation %:** 98	**Seniors on Team:** 5

Positions Needed: Central Defender, Central Midfield
Camp or Clinic Dates: Not Available
Most Recent Record: 8-6-3
Schedule: St. Lawrence University, Renselaer, Hamilton, Vassar, Hobart, Union, Clarkson, Middlebury, Manhattanville
Style of Play: A tenacious defense with a ball control offense. Very potent on attack, scoring 35 goals in the final 8 games of the season. We emphasize running at opponent defense form the flank position and built our attack around that.

Women's Athletic Profile

Physical Education & Dance Dept.	**NCAA III**
Saratoga Springs, NY 12866-1632	Thoroughbreds/Green, White
Coach: Terry Corcoran	**Phone:** (518) 584-5000
Email: tcorcora@skidmore.edu	**Fax:** (518) 581-7421

Estimated # of Women's Soccer Scholarships: None
Conference: Upstate Collegiate Athletic Association
Program Profile: Stadium: Turf field that has a measurement of 120x75 yards, bleacher seating for 1,600. The
History: The program is eight years old (1980), State play team eight of the last nine years, NCAA tournament team in 1994, ranked nationally in 1994 (third in the nation), in 1995 (11th in the nation).
Achievements: New York State Coach of the Year in 1994, 2 Regional All-Americans; most recent All-Americans 1 in 1996 and 1 in 1997.
Style of Play: Ground ball, attack from the back, forward, diagonal balls in the offensive third. Straight marking in t/he defensive end. Control.

SUNY - Binghamton University

Academic Profile

Phone: (607) 777-6838

Binghamton, NY 13904

Type: 4 Yr.,Public,		**Founded:** 1946
Website: http://www.binghamton.edu		**Religion:** Non-Affiliated
SAT/ACT/GPA: 1207/92.2		**Housing:** Yes
Student/Faculty Ratio: 13:1		**Male/Female Ratio:** 1:1.2
Undergraduate Enrollment: 9,460		**Graduate Enrollment:** 2,696
Scholarships/Academic: Yes	**Athletic:** Yes	**Financial Aid:** Yes
Expenses by: Year	**In State:** $ 9,637	**Out of State:** $ 14,537

Degrees Conferred: BA, BS, BFA, MA, MS, MFA, M.Ed., Ph.D.
Programs of Study: Accounting, American Studies, Anthropology, Art, Art History, BioChemistry, Biology, Business & Management, Chemistry, Classics, Comparative Literature, Computer Science, Creative Writing, Ecology, Economics, Engineering, English, Environmental Studies, Film Studies, French, Geography, Geology, Geophysics, German, History, Liberal Arts, Life Sciences, Literature, Mathematics, Nursing, Philosophy, Physical Education, Political Science, PreDentistry, PreLaw, PreMed, PreVet, Psychology, Social Science, Theatre

Men's Athletic Profile

P.O. Box 6000
Binghamton, NY 13902
Coach: Hristos Dimitriou
Email: hdimitri@bingamton.edu

NCAA II
Colonials/Dark Green , White
Phone: 607-777-4571
Fax: 607-777-4597

Estimated # of Men's Soccer Scholarships: N/A
Conference: New England Collegiate Conference
Program Profile: Binghamton is in its second year of a three year transition to division I competition. In 2000-02, the Bearcats will be a "countable" division I competitor and will face 15 opponents at the highest level of NCAA competition. BU competes during the fall season on one of three natural field surfaces.
History: The program is 72-53-7 under head coach Dimitrou. Since its inception in 1960, BU's men's soccer teams have accrued on overall record of 336-198-53 (.629 winning percentage). The Bearcats have made nine appearances in the NCAA tournament, 12 times in the ECAC championship (crowned champion three times), and have won six conference championships. Only three times in 23 years did BU have a losing record versus conference opponents.
Achievements: Binghamton boasts seven All-Americans in its 40 year history. Dimitriou was named State University of New York Coach of the Year for guiding the team to a 12-6-1 record and an NCAA tournament berth.
Coaching: Dimitriou's teams have earned post-season berths five times in his seven years as head coach. Before embarking on his illustrious coaching career, Dimitriou captained Rodiakos, A First Division team in his native Rhodes, Greece. The team won consecutive promotional championships in the Third and Second Divisions. Has coached in NYS West Olympic Developmental Program and holds an NSCAA premier National Diploma and a USSF "A" coaching license.
Roster In State: 26 **Out of State:** **Out of Country:**
Walk-on/Other: **Graduation %:** N/A **Seniors on Team:** 8
Camp or Clinic Dates: Not Available
Most Recent Record: 10-7-1
Schedule: Florida International, Hartwick, Philadelphia University, Adelphi, Colgate, University of Massachusetts, Hartford, Howard, Oneonta, Manhattan
Style of Play: Indirect with emphasis on possession.

Women's Athletic Profile

P.O. Box 600
Binghamton, NY 13902
Coach: Jeff Leightman
Email: jleight@binghamton.edu

NCAA I
Bearcats/Forest Green
Phone: (607) 777-6439
Fax: (607) 777-2495

Estimated # of Women's Soccer Scholarships: 7.5
Conference: New England College Conference
Program Profile: We have 4 natural grass practice fields and a 2,000 seat natural grass stadium. Construction is being done on a new 26.5 Athletic Fieldhouse.
History: Program began in 1985; ranked Top 20 in Division III 6 out of the last 7 years.
Achievements: 3 national All-Americans; 28 Regional All-Americans; 74 All-Conference players; 3 Academic All-Americans; 6 Conference Championships; 17 Postseason Tournament Invitations; 2 Coach of the Year Honors; 2 USISL W- League Players.
Coaching: Jeff Leightman, Head Coach.
Roster in State: 21 **Out of State:** 2 **Out of Country:**
Walk-on/Other: **Graduation %:** 99 **Seniors on Team:** 3
Positions Needed: All
Camp or Clinic Dates: Not Available

Most Recent Record: 13-6-1
Schedule: Duke University, St. John's University, Western Michigan University, St. Joseph University, US Naval Academy, College of Holy Cross, St. Bonaventure
Style of Play: Attacking style 3-4-3 commitment to scoring lots of goals, most of play on surface to feet.

State University of New York College - Brockport

Academic Profile

Brockport, NY 14420-2915
Phone: 716-395-2211

Type: 4 Yr.,Public
Founded: 1840
Website: http://www.brockport.edu
Religion: Non-Affiliated
SAT/ACT/GPA: 1000/20/3.0
Housing: Yes
Student/Faculty Ratio: 21:1
Male/Female Ratio: 44:56
Undergraduate Enrollment: 7,691
Graduate Enrollment: 1,890
Scholarships/Academic: No **Athletic:** No **Financial Aid:** Yes
Expenses by: Year **In State:** $ 9,840 **Out of State:** $ 14,740
Specialty: Physical Education
Degrees Conferred: All
Programs of Study: Accounting, African-American Studies, Anthropology, Art History, Art Studio, Art for Children, Biological Science, Business Administration, Chemistry, Communications, Computer Science, Criminal Justice, Dance, Earth Science, Engineering, Economics, English, Environment & Forest, French, Geology, Health Science, History, International Business & Economics, International Studies, Journalism, Liberal Studies, Mathematics, Medical Technology, Meteorology, Nursing, Philosophy, Physical Education, Physics, Political Science, Psychology, Social Work, Sociology, Spanish, Theatre, Water Resources

Men's Athletic Profile

350 New Campus Drive
Brockport, NY 14420
Coach: Gary LaPietra
Email: glapietr@brockport.edu

NCAA III
Golden Eagles/Green, Gold
Phone: (716) 395-5448
Fax: (716) 395-2160

Estimated # of Men's Soccer Scholarships: None
Conference: State University of New York Athletic Conference (SUNYAC)
Program Profile: All home games are played on a natural grass surface. The regular season extends from mid-August to early November, and non-traditional season is in the Spring.
History: Our program began in 1938 and nine coaches have coached since that time. Huntley Parker coached the team from 1946-1970 and in 1995, the team was Co-National Champions with Penn State. The 1974 team won the NCAA Division III title under Coach Walt Kapezuk.
Achievements: 22 All-Americans, 2 National Champions in 1955 & 1974; 11 trips to the NCAA Division III Championships, 9 SUNYAC Titles, 106 All-New York State Selections.
Coaching: Gary LaPietra, Head Coach, second year, prior coaching experience includes nine years as a head varsity boys coach at Aquinas Institute and coaching youth leagues in the Rochester area.
Style of Play: Total team offense and total team defense and can play either a 4-4-2 or 4-3-3 formation.

Women's Athletic Profile

350 New Campus Drive
Brockport, NY 14420
Coach: Joan Schockow
Email: Not Available

NCAA III
Golden Eagles/Green, Gold
Phone: (716) 395-5350
Fax: (716) 395-2160

Estimated # of Women's Soccer Scholarships: None
Conference: SUNYAC

Program Profile: All home games are played on a natural grass surface. Regular season extends from mid-August to early November and non-traditional season is in the Spring.
History: The program began in 1983 and has had two other coaches besides current Head Coach Joan Schockow. The program's overall record is 113-89-10, and since Schockow took over in 1988, the team has made the SUNYAC tournament twice, won the 1995 NYSWCAA tournament, and were finalist at the 1995 ECAC Mid-Atlantic Championships.
Achievements: 1995 NYSWCAA Champions, 1995 ECAC Tournament Runner-Up, 2 All-SUNYAC Selections, 9 All-NYSWCAA Tournament Selections, 4 All-Northeast Selections, 2 SUNYAC Coach of the Year honors.
Coaching: Joan Schockow, Head Coach, ninth season, overall record is 71-58-8, school's all-time most winningest women's soccer coach, four-time All-American goalkeeper at SUNY Cortland and has been named SUNYAC Coach of the Year on two occasions.
Style of Play: Short passing, building up from the back. Total team defense and total offense.

State University of New York College - Buffalo

Academic Profile

Buffalo, NY 14222-1095
Phone: (716) 878-5420

Type: 4 Yr.,Public,Liberal Arts,Engineering
Founded: 1871
Website: http://www.ubathletics.buffalo.edu
Religion: Non-Affiliated
SAT/ACT/GPA: 900/20/2.0
Housing: Yes
Student/Faculty Ratio: 12:1
Male/Female Ratio: 3:5
Undergraduate Enrollment: 11,000
Graduate Enrollment: 4,000
Scholarships/Academic: Yes **Athletic:** No
Financial Aid: Yes
Expenses by: Semester **In State:** $ 3,550
Out of State: $ 6,000
Specialty: Art-related Fields, Broadcasting, Education
Degrees Conferred: BA, BS
Programs of Study: Anthropology, Art, Biology, Broadcasting, Business, Chemistry, Communications, Computer Information Systems, Criminal Justice, Design, Dietetics, Earth Sciences, Economics, Engineering, Education, English, Fashion, Forensic Chemistry, Geography Health & Wellness, History, Hospitality, Humanities, Journalism, Mathematics, Music, Philosophy, Photography, Physics, Political Science, Psychology, Social Work, Speech Language, Pathology, Theatre, Urban Regional Analysis & Planning

Men's Athletic Profile

1300 Elmwood Avenue-Houston Gym
Buffalo, NY 14222-1095
Coach: Anthony Massop
Email: Canlam@webt.com

NCAA III
Bengal/Black, Orange
Phone: (716) 878-5420
Fax: (716) 878-3401

Estimated # of Men's Soccer Scholarships: None
Conference: SUNYAC
Program Profile: Has a varsity team only. Houston Gym and Sports Arena seats 5,000. Playing season is the Fall and in the Spring. playing field is called Coyer Field that seats 3,500 and measures 120x65. Practice field is also natural turf.
History: Our program began in 1957. Our program is the most successful college soccer program ever in our conference and Western New York. Returned to play-offs in 1998 after 15 years lay-off. Program has been steadily improving in the past three seasons and is looking to be in contention for the conference title in the years to come.
Achievements: 1998 SUNYAC Coach of the Year, 5 Titles, many All-American players in the past.
Coaching: Anthony Massop, Head Coach. Nick Demarsh and Rich Paige, Assistant Coaches. Chris Hershey, Goalkeeper Coach.
Style of Play: Play out of the back, counter-attacking, rugged style of defense with strong goalkeeping. Latin flair in the midfield and strong strikers to hold the ball up top.

Women's Athletic Profile

55 Alumni Arena
Buffalo, NY 14260-5000
Coach: Jean-A. Tassy
Email: tassy@acsu.buffalo.edu

NCAA I
Bulls/Royal Blue, White
Phone: (716) 645-6664
Fax: (716) 645-3756

Estimated # of Women's Soccer Scholarships: None
Conference: Mid-American Conference
Program Profile: The University of Buffalo volleyball team plays all its home games at RAC Field, which is fully lighted for evening games and has 1,000 seats. It is a natural grass field.
History: Our program was elevated to varsity status in 1982, after two seasons as a club sport.
Achievements: Nora Bender named 1st team All-SUNYAC and second team All-New York State selection; 1987 Big Four Title, 1988 ranked number one in the Northeast Region and sixth nationally in Division II, 1990 ranked 14th nationally and third in the Northeast.
Coaching: Jean-A. Tassy, Head Coach, has coached here since August 1, 1995. She was drafted by the North American Soccer League's Toronto Metros in 1971 and played professionally in Canada and New York City. She coached at Niagara for seven years and was the men's coach at Buffalo State from 1982 to 1988. She was SUNYAC Coach of the Year in 1982, was inducted into the Buffalo State Athletic Hall of Fame in 1988 and coached the Western New York Empire State Games. Meagan Dougherty, Assistant Coach, is entering her fifth season. She has club experience and played for the nationally known Coach Anson Dorrance. Jeff Hoerner is Assistant Coach.
Style of Play: Possession, team speed, creative ball movement, team attack and team defense.

State University of New York College - Cortland

Academic Profile

Cortland, NY 13045

Phone: 607-753-2011

Type: 4 Yr.,Public,Liberal Arts
Website: http://www.Cortland.edu
SAT/ACT/GPA: 1000/85
Student/Faculty Ratio: 20:1
Undergraduate Enrollment: 5,500
Scholarships/Academic: Yes
Athletic: No
Expenses by: Year
In State: $ 9,944
Founded: 1868
Religion: Non-Affiliated
Housing: Yes
Male/Female Ratio: 45:55
Graduate Enrollment: 2,000
Financial Aid: Yes
Out of State: $ 14,844
Specialty: Education, Biology, PE, Sports Management
Degrees Conferred: BS, BA, BSE, MA, MSE
Programs of Study: Elementary & Secondary Education, Physical Education, Athletic Training, Art, Biology, Business, Chemistry, Communications, Economics, English, PreEnvironmental Science, Health Science, History, Math, Political Science, Psychology, Recreation, Philosophy, Sociology, Speech & Hearing Science, Sports Management, Exercise Science, Spanish, French, PreDental, PreLaw, PreMedicine

Men's Athletic Profile

P.O. Box 2000
Cortland, NY 13045
Coach: Mike Middleton
Email: middletonm@cortland.edu

NCAA III
Red Dragons/Red, White
Phone: (607) 753-4958
Fax: (607) 753-4929

Estimated # of Men's Soccer Scholarships: None
Conference: SUNYAC
Program Profile: A grass field, fenced in stadium with a press box, an equipment room, lights, and an underground watering system. Also has two full size practice fields with lights. Stadium has a seating capacity of 2,000.

History: Program began in 1937. Team posted a remarkable record of 191 victories, 94 losses and 23 ties during the tenure of 35 years. T. Fred Halloway is a legendary head coach of the Cortland State soccer team. He established a legacy of excellence, inspiration and tradition. Today remains the standard by which Cortland athletes (past and present), continue to measures themselves and their accomplishments.
Achievements: NCAA Tournament in 1990, 1991, 1992 and 1993; SUNYAC Champs in 1990, 1991, and 1993; ECAC in 1995; 27 All-American; 4 players drafted by professional organization (3 in 1978, 1 in 1982); NSCAA - Annual Honor Award in 1958; 20 All-Americans.
Style of Play: Direct possession.

Women's Athletic Profile

P.O. Box 2000
Cortland, NY 13045
Coach: Janine Corning
Email: corning@cortland.edu

NCAA III
Red Dragons/Red, White, Black
Phone: (607) 753-5715
Fax: (607) 753-4929

Estimated # of Women's Soccer Scholarships: None
Conference: SUNYAC
Program Profile: Prof Holloway Stadium is lighted, has natural grass and seats 2,000. The Cortland program placed second nationally out of 400 colleges in the 1997-98 Sears Directors' Cup for Division III. Our program emphasizes total development of student-athletes, including a competitive playing environment and achievement of academic excellence.
History: Our program began in 1978. In 1980 de defeated UCLA to win the first ever U.S.National Women's Soccer Championship. We were National Champions in 1980 and 1992. In 1982, the University of North Carolina at Chapel Hill lost back to back to Cortland. We qualified for NCAA tournaments 13 consecutive years and a total of 15 years. The most recent was in 1998.
Achievements: All-Americans - 21 for a combined 43 All-American awards; Conference titles 7 years; Consecutive games without a loss: 25 in 1991; Consecutive wins-20 in 1990; Most Shutouts - 18 in 1990 (25 games)
Coaching: Janine Corning, Head Coach, has a NSCAA Advanced Diploma and a U.S.Soccer "B" coaching license. Cortland is a 3 time All-American and was captain of the 1992 National Championship team NCAA Tournament "Offensive MVP". He has a Master of Science degree in Physical Education with a concentration in teaching and coaching. Hershey Strosberg is Assistant Coach. He was Eastern N.Y. upstate girls coaching coordinator and a Region I staff member. He has an NSCAA Advanced & U.S. Soccer "A" license. He is completing his Masters in Physical Education.
Style of Play: Zonal defense foundation with emphasis on attacking and getting ball forward early. Balance of possession and direct style of play.

State University of New York College - Fredonia

Academic Profile

Fredonia, NY 14063
Phone: 716-673-3111

Type: 4 Yr.,Public,Liberal Arts
Founded: 1826
Website: http://www.cs.fredonia.edu
Religion: Non-Affiliated
SAT/ACT/GPA: 1000/3.0
Housing: Yes
Student/Faculty Ratio: 20:1
Male/Female Ratio: 42:58
Undergraduate Enrollment: 4,591
Graduate Enrollment: 218
Scholarships/Academic: Yes **Athletic:** No **Financial Aid:** Yes
Expenses by: Year **In State:** $ 9,990 **Out of State:** $ 14,895
Specialty: Education, Music
Degrees Conferred: BA, BS, BFA, BM, MA, MS, Post-Master's Certificate
Programs of Study: Accounting, Art, Biology, Business Administration, Chemistry, Communications, Computer Information Science, Cooperative Agriculture, Cooperative Engineering, Earth Science, Economics, (Elementary and Secondary) Education, English, French, GeoSciences, Health Service Administration, History, Industrial Management, Interdisciplinary Studies, Mathematics, Medical Technology, Music, Philosophy, Physics, Political Science, Psychology, Recombinant Gene Technology, Social Work, Sociology, Sound Recording, Spanish, Speech and Hearing Handicapped, Theatre Arts

Men's Athletic Profile

Dods Hall
Fredonia, NY 14063
Coach: P.J. Gondek
Email: Patrick.Gondek@fredonia.edu

NCAA III
Blue Devils/Royal Blue, White
Phone: (716) 673-3366
Fax: (716) 673-3136

Estimated # of Men's Soccer Scholarships: N/A
Conference: SUNYAC, ECAC
Program Profile: We are a Division III program that includes nine conference (SUNYAC) and 11 non-conference games each season. Field is a natural turf. Playing season runs from first of September to first week of November. Fredonia host annual Sheraton Harbor front Tournament Labor Day weekend.
History: Began in 1959. Fredonia won NAIA district and area championships in 1972 & 1975; SUNY Western Conference Championship in 1977; Sunyac Championships in 1984, 1986, 1987, & 1995; ECAC Upstate New York Championship in 1981 and NCAA New York regional championship in 1985 & 1986.
Achievements: 4 SUNYAC Coach of the Year Award Winners; 103 All-Conference players; 56 All-New York State players; 5 SUNYAC Players of the Year; 6 All-Americans.
Style of Play: Although the Blue Devils are a highly disciplined and cohesive team, they are also aggressively competitive. Relying on a strong defensive style of play, the team is equality effective at home or on the road.

Women's Athletic Profile

50 Dods Hall
Fredonia, NY 14063
Coach: Jen Goff
Email: goff@fredonia.edu

NCAA III
Blue Devils/Blue, White
Phone: (716) 673-3279
Fax: (716) 673-3624

Estimated # of Women's Soccer Scholarships: None
Conference: SUNYAC, NYSWCAA, ECAC
Program Profile: Our seasons begins in late August and ends in early November. The women's team has their own practice field and share a separate game field with the men. Both fields are grass. A comprehensive off-season begins in February and ends in April. A large fieldhouse with an artificial surface is used for indoor approximately 5 indoor or outdoor tournaments are played.
History: The program began in 1986.
Achievements: Chelsea Kampas was named All-SUNYAC in 1996, Kelly Boyd was named All-SUNYAC team in 1996, Shannon Fox was named All-SUNYAC in 1999.
Coaching: Jen Goff is our Head Coach since 1999. She is a 1995 graduate of SUNY - Plattsburgh and received her Masters Degree in Physical Education from Springfield College in 1999. She has served as the Assistant Varsity Coach at SUNY-Plattsburgh for the 1995-1996 season. From 1996-1999, she was the head junior varsity and assistant varsity coach at Springfield College. she holds an advanced National Diploma from the National Soccer Coaches Association of America.
Roster in State: 21 **Out of State:** 1 **Out of Country:** 0
Walk-on/Other: **Graduation %:** 100 **Seniors on Team:**
Camp or Clinic Dates: TBA
Style of Play: Team adjust style of play depending on personnel and opponents.

State University of New York College - Geneseo

Academic Profile

Phone: 716-245-5571

Geneseo, NY 14454

Type: 4 Yr.,Public,Liberal Arts
Website: http://www.geneseo.edu
Founded: 1871
Religion: Non-Affiliated

SAT/ACT/GPA: 1200
Housing: Yes
Student/Faculty Ratio: 20:1
Male/Female Ratio: 34:66
Undergraduate Enrollment: 5,000
Graduate Enrollment: 200
Scholarships/Academic: Yes
Athletic: No
Financial Aid: Yes
Expenses by: Year
In State: $ 8,500
Out of State: $ 11,500
Specialty: Arts & Sciences
Degrees Conferred: BA, BS, BSEd, MA, MS, M.Ed.
Programs of Study: Business, Accounting, Economics, Management, Education, Art & Science, Computer, Pharmacy, Chemistry, Literature, Communication, Sociology, Art Studio, English, French, Optometry, Law, Physics, Biology

Men's Athletic Profile

1 College Circle
Geneseo, NY 14454
Coach: Michael Mooney
Email: monney@geneseo.edu
NCAA III
Knights/Navy, White
Phone: (716) 245-5343
Fax: (716) 245-5347

Estimated # of Men's Soccer Scholarships: None
Conference: SUNYAC, ECAC
Program Profile: Fall schedule consist of 19 games. Spring season is a combination of indoor and outdoor. Games are played on a natural turf field; has a practice area, competition pitch. Non-traditional spring season.
History: Our program began in 1947. Overall record from 1947 to 1999 is 302-331-51.
Achievements: Coach of the Year in 1989 & 1997; ECAC Co-Champs in 1997-1998; 3 All-Americans and 79 All-State players.
Coaching: Michael Mooney, Head Coach, received his BS from University of Buffalo in 1983 and his MS from Canisius College in 1985. Nick Valentino is the Assistant Coach.
Roster In State: 23
Out of State: 1
Out of Country: 1
ODP State: 3
Regional: 1
National:
Walk-on/Other:
Graduation %: 100
Seniors on Team: 7
Positions Needed: Goalkeeper, Defender, Attack, Mid
Camp or Clinic Dates: Not Available
Most Recent Record: 14-7-0
Schedule: Ithaca, Plattsburgh, St. Lawerence University, Fredonia, University of Rochester, Cortland, RIT, Elmira
Style of Play: Short ball, one-two-touch, overlap, balls on the deck. South American Style preferred.

Women's Athletic Profile

1 College Circle
Geneseo, NY 14454
Coach: Sue Behme
Email: Not Available
NCAA III
Lady Knights/Royal, White
Phone: (716) 245-5342
Fax: (716) 245-5347

Estimated # of Women's Soccer Scholarships: None
Conference: State Univ. of New York Athletic Conference (SUNYAC)/NYSWCAA
Program Profile: Competitive Division III program; one game field and two practice fields both natural turf.
History: Program began in 1981; 1994 Division III Final Four; six years first place in SUNYAC Champs; four years first place in ECAC Champs; three years in NCAA playoffs.
Achievements: 3 Conference titles in the last three years, 3 trips to the NCAA, 1 NCAA Final Four Appearances in 1994; 1993 All-American - Betsy Balling; 1994 All-American - Paula Fischer.
Coaching: Sue Behme, Head Coach, BSE at Cortland in 1993. Tracy Cass - Assistant Coach, BS Education at Nazareth in 1990.
Style of Play: One-two-touch short passing game.

State University of New York College - New Paltz

Academic Profile

Phone: 888-639-7589

New Paltz, NY 12561-2499

Type: 4 Yr.,Public,Liberal Arts,Engineering
Founded: 1828
Website: http://www.newpaltz.edu
Religion: Non-Affiliated
SAT/ACT/GPA: 1000/22/3.0
Housing: Yes
Student/Faculty Ratio: 19:1
Male/Female Ratio: 2:3
Undergraduate Enrollment: 4,986
Graduate Enrollment: 1,606
Scholarships/Academic: Yes **Athletic:** No **Financial Aid:** Yes
Expenses by: Year **In State:** $ 9,914 **Out of State:** $ 14,814
Specialty: Comprehensive Regional University
Degrees Conferred: BA, BS, BFA, BSE, BS Ed., MA, MS, MFA, MS Ed., MAT, MST, CAS
Programs of Study: Accounting, Art, Biology, Business, Chemistry, Communication Disorders, Computer Engineering, Computer Science, Elementary Education, Electrical Engineering, English, Foreign Languages, Geology, History, International Relations, Journalism, Mathematics, Media, Medical Program (7 Year), Music Therapy, Political Science, Physics, Psychology, Sociology, Special Education

Men's Athletic Profile

75 South Manheim Blvd.
New Paltz, NY 12561
Coach: Stuart Robinson
Email: robinsos@npvm.newpaltz.edu

NCAA III
Hawks/R. Blue, Burnt Orange
Phone: (914) 257-3908
Fax: (914) 257-3920

Estimated # of Men's Soccer Scholarships: N/A
Conference: State University of New York Athletic Conference
Program Profile: New Paltz competes in the highly competitive SUNYAC, with the conference winner annually receiving an automatic bid to the NCAA division II tournament. Alumni field will be undergoing a refurbishment for the 2000 season, with improved drainage, sod and leveling of the playing surface.
History: At one time during the mid 1960's New Paltz was a regional power. It is not clear as to when the program actually started.
Achievements: Stuart Robinsons; 1996 SUNYAC men's soccer Coach of the Year; won 1965 NCAA Atlantic Regional; won 1996 SUNYAC Championships.
Coaching: Stuart Robinson, Head Coach, coached at the collegiate level for over ten years. He was named 1996 SUNYAC Coach of the Year. He graduate from Williams College in 1983. He previously coached at Vassar College.
Roster In State: 22 **Out of State:** 1 **Out of Country:** 1
ODP State: 4 **Regional:** **National:**
Walk-on/Other: **Graduation %:** 90 **Seniors on Team:** 2
Positions Needed: F, MF, D, GK
Camp or Clinic Dates: 7/24-8/3
Most Recent Record: 3-13-3
Schedule: Plattsburgh, Fredonia, Rensselaer, Geneseo, Elmira, Penn. State-Behrend, Rowan
Style of Play: A high-pressure unit that is zonal, marking defense, plays to feet, changing point of attack.

Women's Athletic Profile

75 S. Manheim Blvd.
New Paltz, NY 12561-2499
Coach: Colleen Bruley
Email: bruleyc@lan.newpaltz.edu

NCAA III
Lady Hawks/Blue, Burnt Orange
Phone: (914) 257-3918
Fax: (914) 257-3920

Estimated # of Women's Soccer Scholarships: None
Conference: SUNYAC
Program Profile: We play anywhere from 18-20 games per season that include all of the State University of the SUNY-AC Conference. We will be playing on a new $70,000 soccer field next season and we are very excited about the future of Women's Soccer here at New Paltz. We are very competitive and serious program, while at the same time we concentrate very strongly on the academic side as well.
History: New Paltz women's soccer has been growing tremendously over the past four years. In the past, the program had not been taken serious by the players of the coaching staff. Throughout the past four years, myself, my staff and the players have worked very hard to change that attitude. We are now thought of as a contender in our conference which had never really happened before.
Achievements: We are a growing program that has been very successful over the past 2 years. In 1999 we went to our Conference Championship as well as the ECAC Conference Championship. This past season has been a rebuilding season but we hope to be back at the top of the SUNYAC Conference next season. We have had many All-Conference team members as well as an All-Northeast American last season.
Coaching: Colleen Bruley, Head Coach, entering first year with the program. She is a 1991 Plattsburgh graduate and previously coached at the University of Albany (Division I), also she played professionally in England as a goalkeeper. Laura Neander Assistant Coach.

Roster in State: 19	**Out of State:** 1	**Out of Country:** 1
ODP State: 5	**Regional:** 2	**National:** 0
Walk-on/Other: 0	**Graduation %:** 98	**Seniors on Team:** 3

Positions Needed: Forward, Midfield, Defender, GK
Camp or Clinic Dates: Not Available
Most Recent Record: 5-13-0
Schedule: Oneonta State, Union College, St. Lawrence, Cortland, Rensselaer, Vassar, Brockport
Style of Play: We like to play a passing game in which we work the ball quickly out of the back. We also like to try to change to point of attack quickly using quick short and long passes. Over the past two years we have played a 4-4-2, last year using a flat back 4, and this year switching back to a stopper sweeper.

State University of New York College - Old Westbury

Academic Profile

Phone:

Old Westbury, NY 11568

Type: 4 Yr.,Public		**Founded:** 1968
Website: http://www.oldwestbury.edu		**Religion:** Non-Affiliated
SAT/ACT/GPA: 800		**Housing:** No
Student/Faculty Ratio: 25:1		**Male/Female Ratio:** 45:55
Undergraduate Enrollment: 3,800		**Graduate Enrollment:** 800
Scholarships/Academic: No	**Athletic:** No	**Financial Aid:** Yes
Expenses by: Year	**In State:** $ 7,600	**Out of State:** $ 11,900

Degrees Conferred: BA, BS
Programs of Study: Business, Accounting, Economics, Management, Education, Arts & Sciences, American Studies, Anthropology, Applied Physics, Art History, Art Studio, BioChemistry, Biology, BioPhysics, Chemistry, Communications, Comparative Literate, Computer

Men's Athletic Profile

Rt. 107
Old Westbury, NY 11568
Coach: Patrick Hne
Email: Not Available

NCAA III
Panthers/Green, White
Phone: (516) 876-3244
Fax: (516) 876-3230

Estimated # of Men's Soccer Scholarships: N/A
Conference: Independent

Program Profile: Division III; playing season is in the Fall on a natural turf.
History: Program began in 1968.

Women's Athletic Profile

Clark Ctr Bldg, Box 210
Old Westbury, NY 11568
Coach: TBA
Email: Not Available

NCAA III
Panthers/Green, White
Phone: (516) 876-3241
Fax: (516) 876-3209

Estimated # of Women's Soccer Scholarships: None
Conference: Independent

State University of New York College - Oneonta

Academic Profile

Phone: 607-436-2531

Oneonta, NY 13820

Type: 4 Yr.,Public,Liberal Arts,Engineering
Founded: 1889
Website: http://www.oneonta.edu
Religion: Non-Affiliated
SAT/ACT/GPA: 1000/21/85
Housing: Yes
Student/Faculty Ratio: 21:1
Male/Female Ratio: 2:3
Undergraduate Enrollment: 5,500
Graduate Enrollment: 250
Scholarships/Academic: Yes **Athletic:** No **Financial Aid:** Yes
Expenses by: Year **In State:** $ 9,600 **Out of State:** $ 14,500
Specialty: Education, Business, Sciences, Dietetics, Communications
Degrees Conferred: BS, BA, BBA, MA, MS, MST
Programs of Study: Accounting, Adulthood and Aging Studies, African and Latino Studies, Anthropology, Art History, Art Studio, Biology, Dietetics, Earth Science, Food & Business, French, Geography, Geology, History, Home Economics, Hospitality Management, Human Ecology, International Studies, Mathematics, Meteorology

Men's Athletic Profile

Chase PE Building
Oneonta, NY 13820
Coach: TBA
Email: byrneiji@oneonta.edu

NCAA I
Red Dragons/Red
Phone: (607) 436-2102
Fax: (607) 436-3088

Estimated # of Men's Soccer Scholarships: 5.5
Conference: Independent
Program Profile: Completion of a brand new $12 million fieldhouse, scheduled to open in fall of 1999. Red Dragon field being revamped. Scheduled to re-open for 2000 season. Currently play @ Oneonta is Hall of Fame Lush . Facilities include four fields and a stadium; play a division one, independent schedule.
History: Program began in 1955. 1972 NCAA National Runner-Up; 1995 University renewed commitment to the soccer program by adding scholarship to the program in 1997.
Achievements: Has 2 final Fours; Herman Trophy winner Farruk Quarashi.
Style of Play: European Style of Play.

Women's Athletic Profile

Upper West Street
Oneonta, NY 13820
Coach: Tracey Ranieri
Email: raniertm@oneonta.edu

NCAA III
Red Dragons/Red, White, Black
Phone: (607) 436-2446
Fax: (607) 436-3088

Estimated # of Women's Soccer Scholarships: None
Conference: SUNYAC, NYSWCAA
Program Profile: 2001 Will bring a state of the art natural grass soccer stadium, along with a soccer practice field. National Soccer Hall of Fame campus is three miles away.
History: The program began in 1986. Recently team has been ranked nationally and regionally. Strong Division III program playing top teams in region and out of state.
Achievements: 1999 Coach of the Year SUNYAC Conference, Conference Champions 1997,1999 and 2000. Five regional All-Americans in the past four years.
Coaching: Tracey and David Ranieri - both Head Coach. Married, they coach together and create a family atmosphere. Tracey is a High School and College All-American, David is a former Division I player. Both have NCCAA Advanced Diplomas.

Roster in State: 22	**Out of State:** 2	**Out of Country:**
ODP State: 5	**Regional:** 1	**National:**
Walk-on/Other:	**Graduation %:** 100	**Seniors on Team:** 1

Positions Needed: Keeper and Midfield
Schedule: William Smith NY, Ithaca NY, Cortland NY, Geneseo NY, Clark. Mass. Southampton NY, Brockport NY, Plattsburgh NY, New York University, Hamilton NY,
Style of Play: Controlled, short passing style with speed and discipline. Like to use flank players to service balls into the box. Pressure defending, quick counter-attack.

State University of New York College - Oswego

Academic Profile

Oswego, NY 13126
Phone: (315) 341-4280

Type: 4 Yr.,Public,Liberal Arts		**Founded:** 1861
Website: http://www.oswego.edu		**Religion:** Non-Affiliated
SAT/ACT/GPA: 1050/87		**Housing:** Yes
Student/Faculty Ratio: 21:1		**Male/Female Ratio:** 47:53
Undergraduate Enrollment: 6,100		**Graduate Enrollment:** 1.000
Scholarships/Academic: Yes	**Athletic:** No	**Financial Aid:** Yes
Expenses by: Year	**In State:** $10,300	**Out of State:** $15,200

Specialty: Arts & Science, Business, Education
Degrees Conferred: BA, BS, MA, MS, M.Ed., CAS, MBA, MAT, MBA
Programs of Study: Over 40 majors with in 3 schools: School of Education, School of Business, School of Arts and Sciences

Men's Athletic Profile

Laker Hall Route 104
Oswego, NY 13126
Coach: Ken Peterson
Email: kpeterson@oswego.edu

NCAA III
Lady Lakers/White, Green
Phone: 315-312-4142
Fax: 325-312-6397

Estimated # of Men's Soccer Scholarships: n/a
Conference: State University of New York Athletic Conference
Program Profile: The Oswego State men's soccer program competes in the fall at the South Athletic Fields Complex. We play on a grass field 120x80 with seating capacity 250.
History: Program began in 1986.
Achievements: Ken Peterson-SUNYAC Coach of the Year in 1987, 1988 and 1993; Robert Thole- All-American in 1961.
Coaching: Ken Peterson is Head Coach. He has coached the men's team for thirty-four years and has been Head Coach of both programs since 1997. The two assistants have been in the program for five years.

Roster In State: 21 **Out of State:** 0 **Out of Country:** 0
ODP State: 6 **Regional:** 0 **National:** 0
Walk-on/Other: 0 **Graduation %:** 95-100 **Seniors on Team:** 7
Positions Needed: Team needs 5 solid field players
Camp or Clinic Dates: Not Available
Most Recent Record: 11-8-1
Schedule: Oneonta, Cortland, Geneseo, Ithaca, Hamilton, Mulenburg Tournament, St. Lawrence
Style of Play: Combination of indirect and direct with heavy emphasis on possession. (We like to go to the Goal).

Women's Athletic Profile

Laker Hall
Oswego, NY 13126
Coach: Ken Peterson
Email: kpeterson@oswego.edu

NCAA III
Lady Lakers/White, Green
Phone: (315) 341-4142
Fax: (315) 341-6397

Estimated # of Women's Soccer Scholarships: None
Conference: State University of New York Athletic Conference
Program Profile: The Oswego State women's soccer program competes in the fall at the South Athletic Fields Complex. We play on a grass field 120x80 with seating capacity 250.
History: Program began in 1986. We have gone to post season play twelve consecutive years competing in one of three tournaments: NYS Women's II, ECAC Tournament, and SUNYAC Conference Championship.
Achievements: Ken Peterson-SUNYAC Coach of the Year in 1987, 1988 and 1993
Coaching: Ken Peterson is Head Coach. He has coached the women's team for thirty-four years and has been Head Coach of both programs since 1997. The two assistants have been in the program for five years.
Roster in State: 21 **Out of State:** 0 **Out of Country:** 0
Walk-on/Other: **Graduation %:** 98 **Seniors on Team:**
Positions Needed: Team needs 5 solid field players
Camp or Clinic Dates: Not Available
Most Recent Record: 11-8-1
Schedule: Oneonta, Cortland, Geneseo, Ithaca, Hamilton, Mulenburg Tournament, St. Lawrence
Style of Play: Combination of indirect and direct with heavy emphasis on possession. (We like to go to the Goal)

State University of New York College - Plattsburgh

Academic Profile

Plattsburgh, NY 12901
Phone: 518-564-2000

Type: 4 Yr.,Public,Liberal Arts
Website: http://www.plattsburgh.edu
SAT/ACT/GPA: 1000/22/"B"
Student/Faculty Ratio: 18:1
Undergraduate Enrollment: 5,400
Scholarships/Academic: Yes **Athletic:** No **Financial Aid:** Yes
Expenses by: Year **In State:** $ 8,445 **Out of State:** $ 13,345
Founded: 1889
Religion: Non-Affiliated
Housing: Yes
Male/Female Ratio: 43:57
Graduate Enrollment: N/A
Specialty: Liberal Arts & Science, Business, Professional Studies
Degrees Conferred: BA, BS, MEd, MST, Cas, MA, MSEd
Programs of Study: Accounting, Anthropology, Art, Biology, Business Administration, Business Economics, Canadian Studies, Cellular BioChemistry, Chemistry, Child Care Management, Child/Family Services, Communications Disorders, Communications, Radio/TV/Speech, Computer Science, Criminal Justice, Economics, Elementary Education, Engineering, English, Environmental Science, Food-Nutrition, French, Geography, Geology, History, Hotel & Restaurant and Tourism Management, Mathematics, Nursing, Political Science, PreLaw, PreMed, Psychology, Secondary Education, Social Work, Spanish, Theatre

Men's Athletic Profile

101 Broad Street
Plattsburgh, NY 12901
Coach: Chris Waterbury
Email: Not Available

NCAA III
Cardinals/Cardinal, White
Phone: (518) 564-4142
Fax: (518) 564-4155

Estimated # of Men's Soccer Scholarships: N/A
Conference: SUNYAC

Women's Athletic Profile

101 Broad St.
Plattsburgh, NY 12901
Coach: Karen Wiley Waterbury
Email: Karen.waterbury@plattsburgh.edu

NCAA III
Cardinals/Red, White
Phone: (518) 564-4141
Fax: (518) 564-4155

Estimated # of Women's Soccer Scholarships: None
Conference: SUNYAC, ECAC, NCAA
Program Profile: We play both a traditional and a non-traditional season. We have one 75 x 110 game field, four practice fields and three indoor facilities.
History: We have made 9 consecutive post-season appearances. We made a 1995 NCAA Tournament appearance. In 1996, we were NYSWCAA Champions. In 1999, we were Conference Champions (12-0) and ECAC Champions
Achievements: 1995, 1999 Coach of the Year; 1999 Conference Champions (12-0); 1999 Conference Player of the Year; Rookie of the Year; 1999 ECAC Champions
Coaching: Karen Wiley Waterbury, Head Coach, has an NSCAA Advanced National License and an "A" License. She took the Premiere Course for National and Advanced National diploma. She coached the NSCAA. We have two assistant coaches and one goalkeeper coach.
Style of Play: 4-4-2. High pressure defense. (Man to man)

State University of New York College - Potsdam

Academic Profile

Potsdam, NY 13676-2294

Phone: (315) 267-2313

Type: 4 Yr.,Public,Liberal Arts
Website: http://www.potsdam.edu
SAT/ACT/GPA: 960/20
Student/Faculty Ratio: 18:1
Undergraduate Enrollment: 3,475
Scholarships/Academic: Yes **Athletic:** No
Expenses by: Year **In State:** $ 9,700

Founded: 1816
Religion: Non-Affiliated
Housing: No
Male/Female Ratio: 2:3
Graduate Enrollment: 525
Financial Aid: Yes
Out of State: $ 9,575

Specialty: Mathematics, Music Education, Teacher Education
Degrees Conferred: BA, BS, MA, MST
Programs of Study: Art, Anthropology, Biology, Chemistry, Communication, Computer Science, Dance, Dramatic Arts, Education, English, Fine Arts, Geology, History, Mathematics, Music, Physics, Political Science, Photography, Science

Men's Athletic Profile

Pierrepont
Potsdam, NY 13676-2316
Coach: Joseph Vaadi
Email: Vaadiis@potsdam.edu

NCAA III
Bears/Maroon, Gray
Phone: (315) 267-2313
Fax: (315) 267-2316

Estimated # of Men's Soccer Scholarships: N/A
Conference: SUNYAC
Program Profile: Our program is rebuilding. We have two new natural full-sized fields with a capacity for 1,000 spectators. The playing season is in the fall and goes from August to November. Our spring season is from April to May.
History: Our program began in 1962. We have only 2 winning seasons and 1 All-American. We have many SUNYAC players but a poor
winning record. We are rebuilding our program and playing a tough schedule. We have young soccer players who will have ample opportunity to play soccer while getting a good education.
Achievements: Fred Raymond Goalkeeper was named All-American
Joe Knox was named All-American
Coaching: Joseph Vaadi, Head Coach. Dan Rose is assistant coach. We have a very young and enthusiastic staff. We are trying a lot of new things! We have a former All-American forward on staff that is looking to pass on his knowledge. He also played professionally in Baltimore. We have an All-Conference defender on staff that is looking to pass on his knowledge.

Roster In State: 22	**Out of State:** 1	**Out of Country:** 1
ODP State: 13	**Regional:** 1	**National:**
Walk-on/Other:	**Graduation %:** 100	**Seniors on Team:** 5

Positions Needed: Midfield/Backs
Camp or Clinic Dates: Not Available
Most Recent Record: 4-13
Schedule: St. Lawrence, Plattsburgh, Fredonia, Wilkes, Geneseo, Clarkson, Brockport, Cortland
Style of Play: Very aggressive and defensive- oriented. Looking to open up play more!

Women's Athletic Profile

Maxcy Hall
Potsdam, NY 13676
Coach: Mike Kazmierczak
Email: michales@potsdam.edu

NCAA III
Bears/Maroon, Grey
Phone: (315) 267-2322
Fax: (315) 267-2316

Estimated # of Women's Soccer Scholarships: None
Conference: SUNYAC- State University of NY Athletic Conference
Program Profile: Natural grass surface stadium field.
History: Inception in 1987. Winningest season was in 1996-1997.

Roster in State: 20	**Out of State:** 0	**Out of Country:** 0
ODP State: 0	**Regional:** 0	**National:** 0
Walk-on/Other: 0	**Graduation %:** 95	**Seniors on Team:** 3

Positions Needed: GK, Stopper, Centermid, Sweeper
Camp or Clinic Dates: Not Available
Most Recent Record: 4-12-0
Schedule: SUNY-Brockport, St. Lawrence, SUNY-Oswego
Style of Play: 4-4-2, 4-3-3.

State University of New York College - Stony Brook

Academic Profile

Phone: 631-632-6868

Stony Brook, NY 11794-3500

Type: 4 Yr.,Public,Liberal Arts		**Founded:** 1959
Website: http://www.sunysb.edu		**Religion:** Non-Affiliated
SAT/ACT/GPA: For athletes 80 avg/900		**Housing:** Yes
Student/Faculty Ratio: 20:1		**Male/Female Ratio:** 50:50
Undergraduate Enrollment: 12,500		**Graduate Enrollment:** 5,500
Scholarships/Academic: Yes	**Athletic:** Yes	**Financial Aid:** Yes

Expenses by: Year **In State:** $ 12,657 **Out of State:** $ 17,575
Specialty: Medicine, Engineering, Business
Degrees Conferred: BA, BS
Programs of Study: Biological Science, Communications and the Arts, Computer & Physical Science, Education, Engineering & Environmental Design, Exercise Science, Health Profession, Physical Therapy, Social Science

Men's Athletic Profile

USB Sports Complex, Men's Soccer
Stony Brook, NY 11794-3500
Coach: Scott Dean
Email: sdean@ccmail.sunysb.edu

NCAA I
Seawolves/White, Red
Phone: (516) 632-7203
Fax: (516) 632-7122

Estimated # of Men's Soccer Scholarships: 7
Conference: Independent
Program Profile: The team has outstanding facility, 2 enclosed practice fields. A new 3,000 seats soccer stadium underway. We have a Plexiglas bench covers. We play on natural grass field with a measurements of 120x80 yards. We play an 18 match and 2 scrimmages. Fall season with a complete off-season. outstanding varsity weight room.
History: A new program in Division I ranks as of 1999. The program was a Division III program for 23 years, Division II program for four years.
Achievements: Coach of the Year in 1998-1999 for the New England Collegiate Conference.
Coaching: Scott Dean, Head Coach, entering two years at Stony Brook. NECC Coach of the Year in second year. He holds USSF "A" License coach. Director of Coaching for Connecticut and Long Island, New York for MLS cams and clinic. State staff member in Connecticut and Rhode Island for the USSF. George Dacos, Assistant Coach, holds an NSCAA Advanced National Diploma.
Style of Play: We are very possession oriented. Build up out of the back and through the midfield, attacking with numbers.

Women's Athletic Profile

USB Sports Complex
Stony Brook, NY 11794-3500
Coach: Sue Ryan
Email: sryan@notes.cc.sunyob.edu

Seawolves/Scarlet/White
Phone: (516) 631-7126
Fax: (516) 632-7122

Estimated # of Women's Soccer Scholarships: None
Conference: Independent
Program Profile: We have top-notch facilities including a soccer complex which has a grass field that measures 125' X 74'. We have a regular season in the fall and a full secondary season on the spring.
History: Our program is in its 16th year with the last 10 being at the Division I level. We are coming off our best year in Division I and are entering our 3rd year receiving scholarships.
Achievements: NSCAA-All-American-Nancy Zimmer; Scholar Athlete All-American - Noreen Heilignestadt; NSCAA All-Northeast Lisa Shaffer,Michele Turchiano, Kim Canada, Erica Keller; NSCAA and USSF Coach of the Year - 1998 - Sue Ryan
Coaching: Sue Ryan, Head Coach, is on her 14th year as head coach. Her record is 104-128-19. She was 1998 NSCAA and USSF Coach of the Year. Eric Teepe, assistant coach, is in her 5th year. Kim Brown, assistant coach, is on her 1st year.
Style of Play: Possession type of game, but in a way letting the players dictate what style they are best suited for.

State University of New York Maritime College

Academic Profile

Phone: 718-409-7200

Bronx, NY 10465

Type: 4 Yr.,Public,Engineering
Founded: 1874
Website: Not Available
Religion: Non-Affiliated
SAT/ACT/GPA: 990+
Housing: No
Student/Faculty Ratio: 15:1
Male/Female Ratio: 90:10
Undergraduate Enrollment: 725
Graduate Enrollment: 190
Scholarships/Academic: Yes **Athletic:** No **Financial Aid:** Yes
Expenses by: Year **In State:** $ 11,000 **Out of State:** $ 11,000
Specialty: Naval Architecture
Degrees Conferred: BS, MS
Programs of Study: Afro-American Studies, Anthropology, Architecture, Asian Studies, BioChemistry, Biology, Business Administration, Chemical Engineering, Chemistry, Civil Engineering, Classics, Communications, Computer Science, Creative Writing, Dance, Earth Science, Economics, Education, Electrical Engineering, English, French, Geography, Geology, German, Management, Marine Science, Mathematics, Music, Nursing, Philosophy, Physics, Political Science, PreDentistry, PreLaw, PreMed, Psychology, Social Science, Spanish, Speech, Speech Pathology, Visual & Performing Arts

Men's Athletic Profile

6 Pennywise Ave
Bronx, NY 10465
Coach: John Kakavas
Email: Not Available

NCAA III
Privateers/Navy, White
Phone: (718) 409-7331
Fax: (718) 409-7404

Estimated # of Men's Soccer Scholarships: None
Conference: Skyline
Program Profile: Natural grass field.
Roster In State: 16 **Out of State:** 8 **Out of Country:**
Walk-on/Other: **Graduation %:** 96 **Seniors on Team:** 3
Positions Needed: Forward
Camp or Clinic Dates: Not Available
Most Recent Record: 3-12-1
Schedule: Kings Point, St. Joseph's, Manhattanville, Coast Guard, Centenarry, Stevens Tech, Rutgers-Newark, Old Westbury, Mount St. Mary

Syracuse University

Academic Profile

Phone: (315) 443-5859

Syracuse, NY 13244-5020

Type: 4 Yr.,Private,Liberal Arts,Engineering
Founded: 1870
Website: http://www.sur/edu
Religion: Non-Affiliated
SAT/ACT/GPA: Depends on applicant
Housing: Yes
Student/Faculty Ratio: 11:1
Male/Female Ratio: 49:51
Undergraduate Enrollment: 10,400
Graduate Enrollment: 4,200

Scholarships/Academic: Yes **Athletic:** Yes **Financial Aid:** Yes
Expenses by: Year **In State:** $ 19,360 **Out of State:**
Specialty: Liberal Arts, Communications, Education, Engineering, etc.
Degrees Conferred: BA, BS, BFA, BArch, MA, MS, MBA, MFA, Ph.D., JD, EdD
Programs of Study: Architecture, Arts and Sciences, Education, Engineering and Computer Science, Human Development, Information Studies, Management, Public Communications, Nursing, Social Work, Visual and Performing Arts, 200+ Majors

Men's Athletic Profile

Manley Field House
Syracuse, NY 13244-5020
Coach: Dean Foti
Email: Not Available

NCAA I
Orangemen/Orange, Blue
Phone: (315) 443-3025
Fax: (315) 443-2076

Estimated # of Men's Soccer Scholarships: None
Conference: Big East Conference
Program Profile: Our soccer program is first-class in every respect. SU facilities are second to none including a push grass practice field, two astro turf practice field, a state-of-the-art weight room and the Carrier Dome for year-round training. A new chapter in SU soccer begins in 1996 when the Orangemen move to their new home field. Reaffirming SU's commitment to providing its student-athletes with the best facilities in the country the Orangemen move from the artificial surface of the Carrier Dome to a brand new natural grass soccer stadium. The lighted 120x75 yards soccer only complex located adjacent to Manley Field House will be the new home to the Orangemen and bring to a close successful 16-year era in the Carrier Dome. SU competes in the Big East Conference and annually maintains a difficult schedule. In 1996 Rutgers, Notre Dame and West Virginia were added to the conference elevating the Big East from a good soccer conference to one of the premier soccer conferences in the nation. The new members joined Boston College, Connecticut, Georgetown, Pittsburgh, Providence, St., John's Seton Hall and Villanova to round out SU's conference schedule. regional powers Hartwick, Cornell, Army and Adelphi along with the new season ending eight team Big East Conference Tournament complete a schedule that annually pits the Orangemen against the best teams in the country.
History: Program began in 1920, with James Paisley as the first head coach of the team. In 1922 No games were played. Lawrence Lee became the new head coach in 1923. He coached until 1926. In 1927 Arthur Horrocks became head coach. He coached until 1952, but 1943, 1944, 1945, and 1951 no games were played. 1953 to 1960 the Orangemen went through three other coaches and then in 1961 the Syracuse soccer was discontinued. The program began again in 1970 with Joe Sayer has the head coach, and there has been five other coaches since 1971. Then in 1991 Dean Foti began coaching the Orangemen and is currently the head coach now.
Achievements: 4 All-American 1st team - Vincent Black in 1932 & 1933, John McEwan in 1932, Bill Nelson in 1952, 1982 All-American third team - Joe Papaleo in 1982, Homere Breton in 1984, Jim Garrant in 1986, Greg Kolodziey in 1986; 6 All-New York State Honorable Mentions; 12 All-New York State 1st team; 7 All-New York State second team; Big East Tournament Champs in 1982 & 1985; Runner-Up in 1983 and 1986, NCAA Tournament Participant in 1984.
Coaching: Dean Foti, Head Coach, five years at Syracuse, 1983 graduate of Syracuse, played for SU in 1979-1982, previously assistant coach at Maryland for six years, Masters in PE in 1985, USSF "A" License, NSCAA Advanced National Diploma. Angelo Panzetta - Assistant Coach, played professionally, 1990 BS from RIT. Ed Schmitt - Assistant Coach, works with goalkeepers, high school and college coaching experience, USSF "A" License.

Women's Athletic Profile

Manley Field House
Syracuse, NY 13244-5020
Coach: April Kater
Email: askater@syr.edu

NCAA I
Orange women/Orange, Blue
Phone: (315) 443-5859
Fax: (315) 443-1534

Estimated # of Women's Soccer Scholarships: 11.4
Conference: Big East Conference

Program Profile: We have a 1,500 seat grass soccer stadium, academic services, weight room, team locker room, sports medicine facilities and equipment room - all located in Manley Field Arena. Also, 2 grass practice fields, 2 astro-turf practice fields and track. Most of these facilities are only three years old, the others have been expanded or redone.
History: The program started in 1996; first season was in 1996 with a record of 10-6-1 and became top 10 ranking in Northeast Region, second season was in 1997 with a record of 14-6-0 and became Top 5 ranking in Northeast Region, third season was in 1998 with a record of 14-7-1 and made second round of the NCAA Tournament Big East Tournament Semi-finals. 2000 14-7 Big East Semifinal Appearance Ranked Top 6 in Northeast Region.
Achievements: The team produced 3 Regional All-Americans, numerous All-Big East Academic Honors, 2 1st team Big East members, and 2 All-Rookie Big East members.
Coaching: April Kater, Head Coach, university of Massachusetts graduate. She served as an assistant coach at West Virginia Wesleyan college and university of Massachusetts which she led the team to NCAA Final Four in 1993. Maren Rojas is Assistant Coach.

Roster in State: 6	**Out of State:** 18	**Out of Country:** 0
ODP State: 12	**Regional:** 9	**National:**
Walk-on/Other:	**Graduation %:** 100	**Seniors on Team:** 4

Positions Needed: ALL
Camp or Clinic Dates: July 29th, August 2
Most Recent Record: 14-7-0
Schedule: Notre Dame, UCONN, Richmond, Illinois, BC, Miami
Style of Play: Depends on strengths and weaknesses of particular program each year and of each opponent. Overall a very attacking style team out of the back and midfield, but like to possess the ball and pick apart opponents with solid possession.

University at Albany
Academic Profile

Albay, NY 12222
Phone: (518) 442-4391

Type: 4 Yr.,Public,Liberal Arts		**Founded:** 1896
Website: http://www.Albany.edu		**Religion:** Non-Affiliated
SAT/ACT/GPA: 1000/80 or above		**Housing:** Yes
Student/Faculty Ratio: 17:1		**Male/Female Ratio:** 52:48
Undergraduate Enrollment: 10,000		**Graduate Enrollment:** N/A
Scholarships/Academic: Yes	**Athletic:** Yes	**Financial Aid:** Yes
Expenses by: Year	**In State:** $ 10,681	**Out of State:** $ 15,581

Specialty: Business, Criminal Justice, Education
Degrees Conferred: BA, BS, MA, MS, MEd, Ph.D.
Programs of Study: Accounting, Afro-American Studies, Ancient Civilization, Anthropology, Archaeology, Biochemistry, Biology, Business Administration, Caribbean Studies, Chemistry, Chinese, Communications, Computer Science, Criminal Justice, Economics, Education, English, Fine Arts, French, Geography, Geology, German, Greek, History, Human Biology, Music, Philosophy, Physics, Political Science, PreDentistry, PreLaw, PreMed, Psychology, Religion, Russian, Social Science, Spanish

Men's Athletic Profile

1400 Washington Ave.
Albany, NY 12222
Coach: Johan Aarnio
Email: jaarnio@uamail.albany.edu

NCAA I
Great Danes/Purple, Gold
Phone: (518) 442-3065
Fax: (518) 442-3013

Estimated # of Men's Soccer Scholarships: N/A
Conference: New England Collegiate Conference

Program Profile: Excellent natural grass playing field with a capacity of 1500. Aug 15-Nov.15 playing season for 20 games. First year in Division I conference 2000-01. Record 8-7-3
History: Celebrated 50th soccer anniversary.
Achievements: NCAA Tournament appearances in 1973, 1975, 1978, & 1994. ECAC Upstate New York Champions in 1989 & 1992; 2 All-Americans in the past four years and several All-State players.
Coaching: Head Coach Johan Aarnio first year at Albany posted a winning season. Prior experience includes approx. 20 years professional coaching in most US and Canadian leagues. Involved in 6 US national professional championships. USSF "A" Licensed. Adam Clinton assitant coach USSF"A" Licensed former coach at Hudson Valley CC and Adirondak CC. Bernie Watt GK Coach one of the best in the US.
Roster In State: 16
Out of State: 4
Out of Country: 2
ODP State: 20
Regional: 6
National: 2
Walk-on/Other: 4
Graduation %: 99
Seniors on Team: 5
Positions Needed: Strikers, Midfield
Camp or Clinic Dates: Not Available
Most Recent Record: 8-7-3
Schedule: University of San Diego, Florida International Univ. Stoney Brook, San Diego State, Hartwick
Style of Play: Possession play with mature attacking.

Women's Athletic Profile

1400 Washington, PE 307
Albany, NY 12222
Coach: Joanna Tomasino
Email: tomasino@uamail.albany
NCAA I
Great Danes/Purple, Gold
Phone: (518) 442-3043
Fax: (518) 442-3031

Estimated # of Women's Soccer Scholarships:
Conference: Independent, ECAC
Program Profile: Has great fields and good staff. Becoming better and better.
History: Began late 80's at Division III; 1995 moved to Division II; moved to Division I in 1999.
Achievements: 1989 Cheryl Hensen named Northeast Regional All-American.
Roster in State: 20
Out of State: 5
Out of Country:
ODP State: 12
Regional:
National:
Walk-on/Other:
Graduation %:
Seniors on Team: 2
Camp or Clinic Dates: Not Available
Style of Play: possession oriented and creative.

University of Rochester

Academic Profile

Phone: 716-275-2121

Rochester, NY 14627

Type: 4 Yr.,Private,Liberal Arts,Engineering
Founded: 1850
Website: http://www.rochester.edu
Religion: Non-Affiliated
SAT/ACT/GPA: 1190
Housing: Yes
Student/Faculty Ratio: 9:1
Male/Female Ratio: 50:50
Undergraduate Enrollment: 3,000
Graduate Enrollment: 3,000
Scholarships/Academic: Yes
Athletic: No
Financial Aid: Yes
Expenses by: Year
In State: $ 30,000
Out of State: $ 30,000
Degrees Conferred: BA, BS, MA, MS, Ph.D., EdD
Programs of Study: Anthropology, Applied Mathematics, Art, Astronomy, BioChemistry, Biology, Chemistry, Classic, Computer Science, Earth Science, Economics, Engineering, English, Environmental Science, French, Geology, German, Health Science, History, Mathematics, Music, Natural Science, Nursing, Philosophy, Physics, Political Science, Psychology, Religion, Science, Spanish

Men's Athletic Profile

Alumni Gym
Rochester, NY 14627
Coach: Mike Pilger
Email: mikep@sport.rochester.edu

NCAA III
Yellowjackets/Navy, Gold
Phone: (716) 275-5630
Fax: (716) 461-5081

Estimated # of Men's Soccer Scholarships: N/A
Conference: University Athletic Association
Program Profile: Facilities include 5,000-seat, lighted astroturf stadium. Frequent air travel for out of state games. Excellent indoor training facility. We have in one of the toughest Division III schedules which is one of the best leagues in the country.
History: 7 post sseason appearences in the last 10 years; only undeafeated team in the leagues history1997
Achievements: National Coach of the Year 1990; Regional Coach of the Year '90, '95; 6 conference titles in lasst 15 years; 3 drafted players; many all region and all american players
Coaching: Mike Pilger, Head Coach.
Roster In State: 11 **Out of State:** 14 **Out of Country:**
ODP State: 14 **Regional:** 5 **National:**
Walk-on/Other: **Graduation %:** 100 **Seniors on Team:** 5
Positions Needed: defenders
Camp or Clinic Dates: July 30 - Augest 3, Augest 6-10
Most Recent Record: 14-3-1
Schedule: St. Lawrence, Washington U, Emory, Rit, Ithaca, Nazareth,Carnegie Mellon, Chicago
Style of Play: Doesn't stay the same, sometimes direct often possesion, balls to feet, etc..

Women's Athletic Profile

Alumni Gym
Rochester, NY 14627
Coach: Terry Gurnett
Email: tgurnett@sports.rochester.edu

NCAA III
Yellow Jackets/Blue, Gold
Phone: (716) 275-6698
Fax: (716) 473-5739

Estimated # of Women's Soccer Scholarships: None
Conference: University Athletic Association Conference
Program Profile: The home games are played at Fauver Stadium which is artificial turf with a seating capacity of 5,000.
History: 1979 program began; overall record in 21 years of Coach Terry Gurnett is 259-71-34.
Achievements: 1997 UAA Coach of the Year; won National Championships in 1986 & 1987; second in 1990 while finished 8th in 1997; 24 All-Americans; 18 consecutive years in top 20; 8 Conference Titles; 1980's Coach of the Year. 14 former players coaching in college.
Coaching: Terry Gurnett, Head Coach, holds NSCAA Advanced License, 20 years experience, two-time All-American, ten years as an assistant coach, "B" License. He was named Coach of the Year in 1997. Jill McCabe - Assistant Coach, entering 12th year with the program. Betsy Balling - Assistant Coach, entering third year with the program.
Style of Play: Control, possession, attacking style.

Utica College - Syracuse University

Academic Profile

Utica, NY 13502

Phone:

Type: 4 Yr.,Private,Liberal Arts
Website: http://www.ucsu.edu
SAT/ACT/GPA: Not required
Student/Faculty Ratio: 10:1

Founded: 1947
Religion: Non-Affiliated
Housing: Yes
Male/Female Ratio: 40:60

Undergraduate Enrollment: 2,300 **Graduate Enrollment:** N/A
Scholarships/Academic: Yes **Athletic:** No **Financial Aid:** Yes
Expenses by: Year **In State:** $ 15,414 **Out of State:** $ 15,414
Specialty: Physical Therapy & Occupational Therapy
Degrees Conferred: BA, BS
Programs of Study: Liberal Arts, specialize in Occupational Therapy, Physical Therapy & Therapeutic Recreation

Men's Athletic Profile

1600 Burrstone Road
Utica, NY 13502-4892
Coach: Tim Nelson
Email: tnelson@utica.ucsu.edu

NCAA III
Pioneers/Blue, Orange
Phone: (315) 792-3706
Fax: (315) 792-3211

Estimated # of Men's Soccer Scholarships: N/A
Conference: Empire 8 Athletic Association
Program Profile: Grass playing field with bleachers on one side that seats 500, two grass practice fields. Play a very competitive schedule.
History: Our program began in 1941. Men's soccer was not a varsity sport here from 1951-1960. It is has been a varsity since 1961.
Achievements:
Coaching: Tim Nelson is the head coach and Daviusz Panol is the assistant coach.
Roster In State: 11 **Out of State:** 3 **Out of Country:**
ODP State: 3 **Regional:** **National:**
Walk-on/Other: **Graduation %:** N/A **Seniors on Team:** 2
Positions Needed: Defenders, Midfielders
Camp or Clinic Dates: July 24-28
Schedule: Ithaca College, Elmira College, Nazareth College, Hobart College, Hamilton College, RIT
Style of Play: European.

Women's Athletic Profile

1600 Burrstone Road
Utica, NY 13502-4892
Coach: Kate Stoehr
Email: kstoehr@utica.ucsu.edu

NCAA III
Pioneers/Navy, Orange
Phone: (315) 792-3182
Fax: (315) 792-3211

Estimated # of Women's Soccer Scholarships: None
Conference: Empire Eight Athletic Conference
Program Profile: We are a competitive Division III program. We are member of the Empire Eight Athletic Conference. Our playing surface is a natural grass field but turf facilities will be available.
History: Our program began in 1986 and has been building and improving each year. We earned a NYSWCAA Tournament berths in 1992 and advanced to the semi-finals.
Achievements: Erin Gilmore was named EAA second-team All-Star in 1999 season. Kate Stoehr was named Empire Eight Co-Coach of the Year in 1999.
Coaching: Kate Stoehr is our Head Coach. She was a 1998 Hartwick graduate. Tina Hogan is our Assistant Coach. She was a Hartwick graduate in 1999.
Roster in State: 12 **Out of State:** 3 **Out of Country:** 0
Walk-on/Other: **Graduation %:** 100 **Seniors on Team:** 4
Camp or Clinic Dates: Not Available
Most Recent Record: 5-8-0
Schedule: Nazarene, Ithaca, Hartwick, RIT, Elmira, St. John Fisher, Alfred
Style of Play: Varies according to where our strength is.

Union College - New York

Academic Profile

Phone:

Schenectady, NY 12308

Type: 4 Yr.,Private,Liberal Arts,Engineering
Founded: 1795
Website: http://www.union.edu
Religion: Non-Affiliated
SAT/ACT/GPA: 1260/3.3
Housing: No
Student/Faculty Ratio: 11:1
Male/Female Ratio: 1:1
Undergraduate Enrollment: 2,000
Graduate Enrollment: 100
Scholarships/Academic: Yes **Athletic:** No **Financial Aid:** Yes
Expenses by: Year **In State:** $ 30,000 **Out of State:** $ 30,000
Degrees Conferred: BA, BS, MS, MA
Programs of Study: Anthropology, Art History, BioChemistry, Biological Science, Chemistry, Engineering, Computer Science, Dance, Economics, English, Environmental Studies, Geology, History, Mathematics, Music, Philosophy, Political Science, Psychology, Sociology, Fine Arts, Theatre

Men's Athletic Profile

Alumni Gym
Schenectady, NY 12308-3162
Coach: Jeff Guinn
Email: guinnj@union.edu

NCAA III
Dutchmen/Garnet, White
Phone: (518) 388-6287
Fax: (518) 388-6695

Estimated # of Men's Soccer Scholarships: N/A
Conference: UCAA
Program Profile: Program is its 50th season, playing facilities includes 120x75 natural grass field, astro-turf (lighted) facility for game preparation, early spring training.
History: In 1948 was first year of varsity soccer.
Achievements: Has 6 NCAA Tournament Appearances, 7 ECAC Tournament bids, 3 All-Americans.
Coaching: Jeff Guinn, Head Coach, holds a USSF "A" License and was a former Brown University assistant coach. He is a professional player of APSL, NPSL, USISL. FJ Zwickbauer - Assistant Coach, USSF "B" License, former pro player, APSL, NPSL, USISL. Steve Freeman, Assistance Coach.
Style of Play: Possession - direct style organized pressure defending.

Women's Athletic Profile

Alumni Gym
Schenectady, NY 12308
Coach: Brian Speck
Email: speckb@idol.uwon.edu

NCAA III
Dutchwomen/Maroon, White
Phone: (518) 388-6191
Fax: (518) 388-6695

Estimated # of Women's Soccer Scholarships: None
Conference: UCAA Upstate Collegiate Athletic Assoc.
Program Profile: The team plays a 15-game schedule, with three possible post-season tournaments - NY States, ECAC, NCAA. Games and practices are played on a natural grass and artificial turf.
History: Union College's women's soccer program began in 1982. IN 1998 we won the UCAA title and in 1999 we won the state tournament.
Achievements: Coach of the Year; NY State Regional Coach of the Year.
Coaching: Brian Speck is the Head Coach and Yon Struble is the Assistant Coach.
Roster in State: 8 **Out of State:** 18 **Out of Country:**
ODP State: 5 **Regional:** 2 **National:**
Walk-on/Other: **Graduation %:** 100 **Seniors on Team:** 2

Positions Needed: Forward, Defender
Camp or Clinic Dates: July 24-28, August 7-11
Most Recent Record: 16-3-1
Schedule: William Smith, Nazareth, Rochester, RPI, Skidmore, St. Lawrence
Style of Play: A short-short-long controlled passing game with an aggressive attacking approach to goal by any position on the field. An individual's creativity and decision making enhances much of the team's style of play each individual year.

United States Merchant Marine Academy
Academic Profile

Kings Point, NY 11024
Phone: 516-773-5000

Type: 4 Yr.,Public,Engineering
Founded: 1943
Website: http://www.usmma.edu
Religion: Non-Affiliated
SAT/ACT/GPA: 1050/21
Housing: Yes
Student/Faculty Ratio: 12:1
Male/Female Ratio: 9:1
Undergraduate Enrollment: 950
Graduate Enrollment: N/A
Scholarships/Academic: No
Athletic: No
Financial Aid: No
Expenses by: Year
In State: $ Free
Out of State: $ Free
Specialty: Engineering, Business
Degrees Conferred: BS
Programs of Study: Engineering and Business. One of five federal service academics. Students can major in Engineering or Business and may enter any branch of the services as an active duty officer or serve in the naval reserve (2 weeks a year).

Men's Athletic Profile

O'Hara Hall
Kings Point, NY 11024
Coach: Michael Smolens
Email: mike -smolen@usyma.edu

NCAA III
Mariners/Blue, Gray
Phone: (516) 773-5321
Fax: (516) 773-5469

Estimated # of Men's Soccer Scholarships: Tuition Free School
Conference: Skyline Conference, ECAC
Program Profile: We are a top Division III program with NCAA traditional and non-traditional seasons. We have one natural grass match field, one grass field, and one astro-turf field.
History: Our program started in 1952. Ranked in Top 20 of NCAA in 1998. Have received post-season bids in seven of the last eight seasons. Conference Champions for the last three of the four seasons.
Achievements: Conference Champions in 1998, 1997, 1996, 1994, 1992, & 1990; Aaron Moore was named Player of the Year; Lawina Lucas was named Player of the year in 1998; Michael Smolens was named Coach of the Year in 1998, 1997, 1996, 1995, 1993 & 1991.
Coaching: Michael Smolens, Head Coach, graduated from Springfield College in 1984. He holds a USSF "B" NSCAA Advanced National. John Fitzgerald, Assistant Coach, graduated from SUNY-Farmingdale in 1985. He holds a USSF "A" License. 1997 W-League National Champions.
Roster In State: 6
Out of State: 20
Out of Country:
ODP State: 7
Regional: 1
National:
Walk-on/Other:
Graduation %: 100
Seniors on Team: 8
Positions Needed: 10
Most Recent Record: 9-2
Schedule: College of New Jersey, Kean College, Montclair State, Drew, Western Connecticut, Coast Guards, Springfield college, Vassar.
Style of Play: Build up and possession. Play to feet with good technical.

United States Military Academy
Academic Profile

West Point, NY 10996
Phone: (914) 938-6528

Type: 4 Yr.,Public,Liberal Arts,Engineering
Founded: 1802
Website: http://www.usma.edu
Religion: Non-Affiliated
SAT/ACT/GPA: 1200/Top 10%
Housing: Yes
Student/Faculty Ratio: 10:1
Male/Female Ratio: 4:1
Undergraduate Enrollment: 4,000
Graduate Enrollment: N/A
Scholarships/Academic: Yes **Athletic:** No
Financial Aid: Yes
Expenses by: Year **In State:** $ Free
Out of State: $ Free
Specialty: Military Academy-engineering, Science, Computer Science
Degrees Conferred: BS
Programs of Study: Behavioral Science, Engineering, Foreign Languages, General Management, Letter/Literature, Life Sciences, Mathematical Science, Military Science, Physical Science, Social Science

Men's Athletic Profile

Odia, USMA - Bldg 639
West Point, NY 10996
Coach: Joe Chiavaro
Email: Not-Available

NCAA I
Black Knights/Black, Gold, Gray
Phone: (914) 938-2463
Fax: (914) 938-7061

Estimated # of Men's Soccer Scholarships: None
Conference: Patriot League Conference
Program Profile: Our playing field is a natural grass and has a measurements of 120x75 yards.
History:
Achievements: 1 Regional All-American in 1997; Patriot League Champs in 1991, 1993, & 1996; NCAA Tournament in 1996.
Coaching: Joe Chiavaro is our Head Coach. Tony Martelli & Paul Gannon are the Assistant Coaches.
Style of Play: Depends upon the players in the program.

Women's Athletic Profile

Bldg 639, Howard Rd
West Point, NY 10996
Coach: Gene Ventriglia
Email: Not Available

NCAA I
Lady Cadets/Black, Gold, Grey
Phone: (914) 938-4826
Fax: (914) 446-2556

Estimated # of Women's Soccer Scholarships: None
Conference: Patriot League
Program Profile: Home field is Clinton Field; natural grass with lights (most games for W/M are played under lights). Electronic scoreboard; seating is approximately 2,000. High level of player development.
History: Program joined the varsity ranks in 1986. A school record was set in 1993 of 20-1-1.
Achievements: Army captured Patriot League title in 1993, while reaching championship finals all four years. Five players selected for All-American honors, 3 for Division I honor. In 1995 Freshman Holly Pedley ranked nationally in scoring in the Fall and was the most recent Lady Knight to achieved the honor of being named to the Umbro National Soccer Coaches Association of America; 2nd team All-American. Coach Ventriglia named for league coaching honors in 1991 and 1992.
Coaching: Gene Ventriglia, Head Coach, was named three-time All-American, 1987 Pan American Team Member, 1968 US Olympic Team Member; led Lady Knights into the national (18th) regional (4th in the Northeast) ranking in 1993 following a record-setting campaign and also earned 100th career victory.
Style of Play: Ball possession style - building from the back-looking for counter attack and using the 4-4-2 or 3-4-3 system.

Vassar College

Academic Profile

P. O. Box 259
Poughkeepsie, NY 12604
Phone: (845)437-7450

Type: 4 Yr.,Private,Liberal Arts
Website: http://www.vassar.edu
SAT/ACT/GPA: 1200283.5
Student/Faculty Ratio: 11:1
Undergraduate Enrollment: 2,400
Scholarships/Academic: No
Athletic: No
Expenses by: Year
In State: $ 30,000
Specialty: Liberal Arts
Degrees Conferred: BA, BS
Founded: 1861
Religion: Non-Affiliated
Housing: Yes
Male/Female Ratio: 40:60
Graduate Enrollment: N/A
Financial Aid: Need Based
Out of State: $ 30,000
Programs of Study: African Studies, American Studies, Anthropology, Art Education, Asian Studies, BioChemistry, Biology, Chemistry, Computer Science, Dramatic Arts, Economics, Elementary Education, Engineering, English, Film Arts, Fine Arts, Foreign Language, Geography, Geology, International Studies, Mathematics, Music, Philosophy, Physics, Political Science, PreLaw, PreMed, PsychoBiology, Psychology

Men's Athletic Profile

Box 259
Poughkeepsie, NY 12601
Coach: Chris Parsons
Email: Chaparsons@vassar.edu
NCAA III
Brewers/Burgundy, Gray
Phone: (914) 437-5343
Fax: (914) 437-7033

Estimated # of Men's Soccer Scholarships: None
Conference: Upstate Collegiate Athletic Association
Program Profile: Vassar College has a highly competitive Division III soccer program. The Brewers play a competitive, non-traditional, and indoor season. Our plans for the future to build a new facility, tentative opening date is set for Fall on 1998. Our schedule includes nationally and regionally ranked teams. We toured UK during Spring of 1996.
History: Our Brewers soccer team has been in the Top Ten regionally for the past six years. We have appeared in the ECAC four of the last six years, ECAC Champions in 1990 and 1994.
Achievements: 6 ECAC Appearances, 2 ECAC Champions, numerous regional All-Americans.
Coaching: Head Coach, Chris Parsons, NSCAA Advanced National Diploma, Collegiate All-American, MS Sports Management, University of Massachusetts 1990.
Roster In State: 6
Out of State: 19
Out of Country: 0
Walk-on/Other:
Graduation %: 100
Seniors on Team: 4
Positions Needed: Strikers
Camp or Clinic Dates: June
Most Recent Record: 5-4-2
Schedule: St. Lawrence, Clarkson, RIP, Union Hamilton, USMMA, Ithaca
Style of Play: We generally play out of a 4-4-2 looking to create width and scoring opportunity.

Women's Athletic Profile

Box 259 Raymond Avenue
Poughkeepsie, NY 12604
Coach: Dick Sipperly
Email: risipperly@vassar.edu
NCAA III
Brewers/Burgundy, Grey
Phone: (914) 437-7456
Fax: (914) 437-7033

Estimated # of Women's Soccer Scholarships: None
Conference: ECAC, NYSWCAA

Program Profile: A young but talented team that plays a very competitive schedule throughout New York, New Jersey, and Nebraska. Play on natural grass, and plans for new facility and stadium by the fall of 2000.
History: Vassar joined NCAA in 1981, but has regained new height since the arrival of Coach Sipperly in 1994.
Achievements: Won the 1997 Mid-Atlantic ; ECAC Championships. Ali Dorris, class 1999 wins NYSWCAA - Soccer Player of the Year.
Coaching: Dick Sipperly, Head Coach. Norm Riker - Assistant Coach, have been together for five years. Both hold National and Advanced NSCAA Diplomas.
Roster in State: 3 **Out of State:** 19 **Out of Country:**
Walk-on/Other: **Graduation %:** 100 **Seniors on Team:** 6
Positions Needed: All
Camp or Clinic Dates: Not Available
Most Recent Record: 8-6-0
Style of Play: Our dangerous and opportunistic forwards are well supported as we look to build our attack from the back.

Wagner College

Academic Profile

Phone:

Staten Island, NY 10301

Type: 4 Yr.,Private,Liberal Arts **Founded:** 1883
Website: http://www.wagner.edu **Religion:** Lutheran
SAT/ACT/GPA: 1000/18/3.0 **Housing:** No
Student/Faculty Ratio: 12:1 **Male/Female Ratio:** 50:50
Undergraduate Enrollment: 1,800 **Graduate Enrollment:** 400
Scholarships/Academic: Yes **Athletic:** Yes **Financial Aid:** Yes
Expenses by: Year **In State:** $ 24,000 **Out of State:** $ 24,000
Specialty: Liberal Arts
Degrees Conferred: BA, BS, MS, MA
Programs of Study: Accounting, Anthropology, Arts Administration, Banking/Finance, Biology, Business Administration, Chemistry, Computer Science, Criminal Justice, Education, English, Mathematics, Music, Physics, Physician's Assistant, Psychology, Theatre

Women's Athletic Profile

1 Campus Road **NCAA I**
Staten Island, NY 10301 Seahawks/Green, White
Coach: Philip Fluhr **Phone:** (718) 390-3156
Email: haszletselect@yahoo.com **Fax:**

Estimated # of Women's Soccer Scholarships: 4
Conference: Northeast Conference
Program Profile: We are a growing program building skills and tactical and decision making skills for possession play. We had a very strong recruiting year and expect to place in the top four with in the year.
History: The program began in 1994and has grown slowly. We are entering our second year with Phil Fluhr program and consistency of an excellent program is already evident.
Achievements: Dana Honcharuk is the third ranked goalkeeper and Phil Fluhr has received CACC Coach of the Year and NE NAIA Coach of the Year in 1998. Jen Spadafino was player of the Year.
Coaching: Philip Fluhr, Head Coach, formerly the head coach at Dominican College. Bill Abrams and Pam Ambrams are our Assistant Coaches.
Roster in State: 12 **Out of State:** 16 **Out of Country:**
ODP State: 15 **Regional:** 3 **National:**
Walk-on/Other: **Graduation %:** 89 **Seniors on Team:** 2

Positions Needed: Fast Halfbacks and Strikers
Most Recent Record: 4-12
Style of Play: Possession play with use of the field. Determined ball winning and pressure on ball as a means of beginning attack.

Wells College
Academic Profile

Aurora, NY 13026
Phone: 315-364-3266

Type: 4 Yr.,Private,Liberal Arts
Founded: 1868
Website: http://www.wells.edu
Religion: Non-Affiliated
SAT/ACT/GPA: 900
Housing: Yes
Student/Faculty Ratio: 8:1
Male/Female Ratio: Women
Undergraduate Enrollment: 400
Graduate Enrollment: N/A
Scholarships/Academic: Yes **Athletic:** No **Financial Aid:** Yes
Expenses by: Year **In State:** $ 23,300 **Out of State:** $ 23,300
Degrees Conferred: BA
Programs of Study: Languages, Letters/Literate, Life Sciences, Psychology, Social Science, Visual & Performance Arts, Western European Studies

Women's Athletic Profile

Department of Athletics
Aurora, NY 13026
Coach: Chris Perkins
Email: cperkins@wells.edu
NCAA III
Express/Red, White, Black
Phone: (315) 364-3409
Fax: (315) 364-3227

Estimated # of Women's Soccer Scholarships: None
Conference: NYSWCAA
Program Profile: Strong 17-game schedule in the tough New York region. Host of a small college tournament with out-of-state opponents each year. Soccer only facilities, no competition with other teams on the same field.
History: Program began in 1978.
Achievements:
Coaching: Chris Perkins, Head coach, entering fifth year at Wells, former assistant women's coach at SUNY-Cortland, NSCAA National Diploma, certified to teach the State Diploma course to youth coaches.
Style of Play: Controlled short passing game.

York College - The City University of New York
Academic Profile

Queens, NY 11451
Phone:

Type: 4 Yr.,Public,Liberal Arts
Founded: 1930
Website: http://www.york.edu
Religion: Non-Affiliated
SAT/ACT/GPA: 900+
Housing: No
Student/Faculty Ratio: 12:1
Male/Female Ratio: 1:2
Undergraduate Enrollment: 6,300
Graduate Enrollment: N/A
Scholarships/Academic: No **Athletic:** No **Financial Aid:** Yes
Expenses by: Year **In State:** $ 6,000 **Out of State:** $ 7,400
Specialty: Health & Education
Degrees Conferred: BA, BS

Programs of Study: Health Education, Communications, Health, Gerontology, Physical Therapy, Environmental Sciences, Nursing, PreMed, Education, Physical Education

Men's Athletic Profile

94-20 Guy Brewer Blvd.
Queens, NY 11451
Coach: Richard Packard
Email: Not Available

NCAA III
Cardinals/White, Red
Phone: (718) 262-5115
Fax: (718) 262-5216

Estimated # of Men's Soccer Scholarships: None
Conference: CUNYAC, ECAC
Program Profile: Team plays 15-game during the regular season. Opponents are from same conference and from the NY/NJ Metro area. The schedule includes one or two Division II teams. The Cardinals have their own playing field which astro turf, with a seating capacity of about 1,500. The facility is five years old and includes a track.
Achievements: CUNYAC Champions in 1990 & 1994.
Style of Play: Pressing in the midfield, and quick attacks. Long passing and fast forward.

north carolina

NORTH CAROLINA

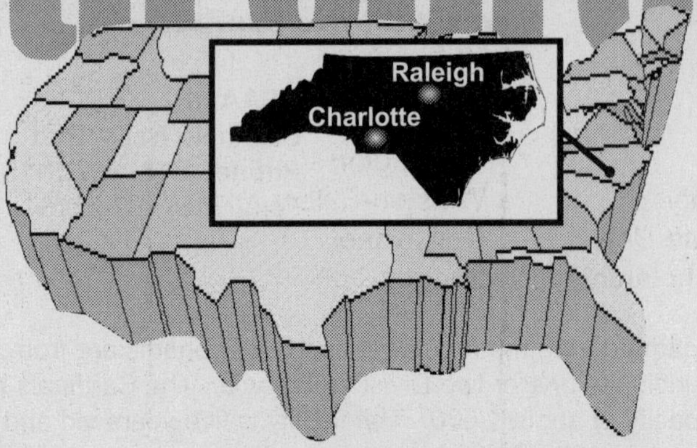

SCHOOL	CITY	AFFILIATION	PAGE
Appalachian State University	Boone	NCAA I	791
Barton College	Wilson	NCAA II	792
Belmont Abbey College	Belmont	NCAA II	793
Campbell University	Buies Creek	NCAA I	794
Catawba College	Salisbury	NCAA II	796
Chowan College	Murfreesboro	NCAA III	797
Davidson College	Davidson	NCAA I	798
Duke University	Durham	NCAA I	800
East Carolina University	Greenville	NCAA I	801
Elon College	Elon College	NCAA I	804
Gardner - Webb University	Boiling Springs	NCAA I	804
Greensboro College	Greensboro	NCAA III	805
Guilford College	Greensboro	NCAA III	806
High Point University	High Point	NCAA I	807
Lees - McRae College	Banner Elk	NCAA II	808
Lenoir - Rhyne College	Hickory	NCAA II	810
Mars Hill College	Mars Hill	NCAA II	811
Meredith College	Raleigh	NCAA III	812
Methodist College	Fayetteville	NCAA III	813
Montreat College	Montreat	NAIA	814
Mount Olive College	Mount Olive	NCAA II	815
North Carolina State University	Raleigh	NCAA I	816
North Carolina Wesleyan College	Rocky Mount	NCAA III	818
Pfeiffer University	Misenheimer	NCAA II	819
Queens College	Charlotte	NCAA II	820
Saint Andrews Presbyterian	Laurinburg	NCAA II	821
UNC - Asheville	Asheville	NCAA I	823
UNC - Chapel Hill	Chapel Hill	NCAA I	824

SCHOOL	CITY	AFFILIATION	PAGE
UNC-Charlotte	Charlotte	NCAA I	825
UNC-Greensboro	Greensboro	NCAA I	826
UNC-Pembroke	Pembroke	NCAA II	828
UNC-Wilmington	Wilmington	NCAA I	829
Wake Forest University	Winston-Salem	NCAA I	830
Western Carolina State Univ	Cullowhee	NCAA I	831
Wingate University	Wingate	NCAA II	831

Come join the *WOLFPACK* this summer for Soccer Camp!

We are gearing up for another summer of exciting soccer!

Coach George Tarantini, a former professional player and accomplished coach will be directing the camp for his thirteenth year. His goal is to share his vast knowledge of soccer with you personally! Coach Tarantini has proven that he has a remarkable ability to take a player and help him reach his full potential. Here is your chance to benefit from this!

The camp staffs have included players such as: Tab Ramos, 1990 and 1994 World Cup Team member; Henry Guiterrez, US National Team and Two-time ACC Player of the Year; and Dario Brose, 1992 Olympic Team Member and Three Time All-American.

All of these individuals are former NC State soccer players who benefited from George Tarantini's style of coaching.

NC State Soccer School Day Camp:

Two (2) Sessions
Ages 5 to 12 years old

NC State Soccer School:

Intensive Overnight Camp
Two (2) Sessions
Ages 11 to 18 years old

For a free brochure write or call:
NC State Soccer School
P.O. Box 5697· Raleigh, NC 27650
Phone: (919) 851-1627
Web-site: www.gopack.com
e-mail: george_tarantini@ncsu.edu

NC STATE

Summer 2001

UNC Charlotte soccer academies

boys-(704) 547-3991

Head Coach: John Tart

"Our program has proven to be successfull in developing and improving soccer skills of camp participants. It is my personal goal to ensure that each player has the opportunity for wonderful camp experience. I personally gaurantee that the organization and enthusiasm that go into the college program also go into the camp."

Residential Academy
Goal Keeper Academy
Advanced Academy
Full Day Academy

girls-(704) 547-3984

Head Coach: Neil Roberts

"The UNC Charlotte Girl's Soccer Camp staff is made up of current ant and former college coaches and players as well as current high school club coaches. All of our staff is dedicated to helping improve the campers skills through individual instructions and match play. Each camper will receive a written evaluation of her performance during camp."

Residential I
Residential II
Full Day Camp
Half Day Camp

PUMA® **Call about TEAM DISCOUNTS!!!**

Come be a part of the Country's Premier Girls' Soccer Camp

KWIKGOAL

North Carolina Girls' Soccer Camp

"Where Champions are Trained"

Call: Toll-Free 1-800-394-1223 (24 hours a day)

North Carolina Girls' Soccer Camp
P.O. Box 4933
Chapel Hill, N.C. 27515

Website: www.ncgsc.com

Appalachian State University

Academic Profile

Ads
Boone, NC 28608

Phone: (828) 262-2000

Type: 4 Yr.,Public,Liberal Arts
Website: http://www.AppState.edu
SAT/ACT/GPA: 1100/25/3.5
Student/Faculty Ratio: 16:1
Undergraduate Enrollment: 11,300
Scholarships/Academic: Yes **Athletic:** Yes
Expenses by: Year **In State:** $ 5,313

Founded: 1899
Religion: Non-Affiliated
Housing: Yes
Male/Female Ratio: 49:51
Graduate Enrollment: 1,000
Financial Aid: Yes
Out of State: $ 12,583

Specialty: Comprehensive- 5 Colleges
Degrees Conferred: BA, BS, MA, M.Ed., Education Specialist, Doctoral
Programs of Study: Over 170 majors to choose from in all areas of study including Arts and Science, Business and Management, Education, Fine and Applied Arts, Music, Natural Sciences, Parks/Recreation, Protective Services, Public Affairs, Psychology, Social Sciences, and over 300 majors

Men's Athletic Profile

Owens Field House
Boone, NC 28608
Coach: Aidan Heaney
Email: heaneyaj@appstate.edu

NCAA I
Mountaineers/Black, Gold
Phone: (828) 626-6747
Fax: (828) 626-2556

Estimated # of Men's Soccer Scholarships: N/A
Conference: Southern Conference
Program Profile: We have a competitive national schedule. A new natural turf stadium being developed.
History: Our program began in 1965 and has been a member of the Southern Conference since 1971.
Achievements: 2000 SoCon Player of the Year and 2000 SoCon Coach of the year.
Coaching: Aidan Heaney is our Head Coach. Bryan Cunningham, Assistant Coach, is entering his second year with the program.
Walk-on/Other: **Graduation %:** 100 **Seniors on Team:**
Schedule: James Madison, George Mason, Furman, Clemson, UNC Greensboro, Davidson, College of Charleston, Campbell
Style of Play: Attack-oriented style, looking to build out of the back. High pressure once ball is turned over. Disciplined approach, but we like players to express themselves.

Women's Athletic Profile

Owens Field House
Boone, NC 28608
Coach: Ben Popoola
Email: popoolabo@appstate.edu

NCAA I
Mountaineers/Black, Gold
Phone: (828) 262-2563
Fax: (828) 262-2556

Estimated # of Women's Soccer Scholarships: 5.5
Conference: Southern Conference
Program Profile: Our main season is the fall. We are currently play home games on astro-turf in a stadium, which seats 10,000+. We have a new natural turf stadium scheduled to open in near future.
History: Our program began in 1994-1995. This is our 4th year under Coach Ben Popoola. We compete in Southern Conference, which has an automatic bid to the NCAA National Tournament.
Achievements: Popoola 1st year he set school records for wins in a single season (7), home wins (4), road wins (6), league victories in a single season (3).

Coaching: Ben Popoola is the Head Coach. He played on Nigerian National Team and Olympic Team. He attended Clemson University and played professionally in the US. He has compiled a winning record. He holds a coaching license.

Roster in State: 7 **Out of State:** 13 **Out of Country:** 2
ODP State: 8 **Regional:** 0 **National:** 0
Walk-on/Other: 0 **Graduation %:** 100 **Seniors on Team:** 4
Positions Needed: Forward, Defense
Camp or Clinic Dates: June 23-27, July 28-Aug 1
Most Recent Record: 7-11-2
Schedule: Furman, Georgia Southern, Charleston, UNC-Greensboro, Wafford, Elon, Morehead State, Liberty
Style of Play: Build-up from the back, ball on the ground, good passing style.

Barton College

Academic Profile

Phone: (252) 399-6552

Wilson, NC 27893

Type: 4 Yr.,Private,Liberal Arts
Founded: 1902
Website: http://www.barton.edu
Religion: Disciples of Christ
SAT/ACT/GPA: 820/17/2.0
Housing: Yes
Student/Faculty Ratio: 20:1
Male/Female Ratio: 1:2
Undergraduate Enrollment: 1,500
Graduate Enrollment: N/A
Scholarships/Academic: Yes **Athletic:** Yes **Financial Aid:** Yes
Expenses by: Year **In State:** $ 14,726 **Out of State:** $ 14,726
Specialty: Liberal Arts
Degrees Conferred: BA, BS, BFA, BLS
Programs of Study: Accounting, Art, Art Education, Biology, Business Administration, Chemistry, Computer Information Systems, Communications, Criminal Justice, Economics, Education, English, Environmental Science, French, Hispanic Studies, History, Management of Human Resources, Music, Nursing, Psychology, Religion, Sports Management, Studio Art, Writing, Sports Medicine

Men's Athletic Profile

Barton College, Box 5000
Wilson, NC 27893
Coach: Gary W. Hall
Email: ghall@barton.edu

NCAA II
Bulldogs/Royal Blue, White
Phone: (252) 399-6517
Fax: (252) 399-6516

Estimated # of Men's Soccer Scholarships: 3.5
Conference: Carolinas-Virginia Athletic Conference (CVAC)
Program Profile: The game field is 120x75 with Bermuda grass and an automatic irrigation system. The training field is beside the game field.. The game field was the site for the 1997 and 1998 CVAC Tournament and will be the host site again in 2000.
History: The program began in 1972 and has produced 9 championship teams in those 28 seasons. The program's overall record is 240-222-27. All 32 of the players recruited into the program by the current coach who have completed their eligibility at Barton will have graduated by the end of the 2000-01 academic year. Of those 32 student-athletes, 20 have been named to the Dean's list.
Achievements: Since 1991 the program has produced 2 All-Americans, 4 Academic All-Americans, 2 Coach of the Year Awards, 3 Conference Player of the Year Award, and 2 Professional players.
Coaching: Head Coach Gary W. Hall, who also serves as the Director of Athletics, is entering his 12th season at Barton. His career record is 141-114-22 and he has won three Coach of the Year Awards. He is ranked 23rd Nationally for career wins by active NCAA II Coaches. He is also a former assistant at Wake Forest University.
Roster In State: 14 **Out of State:** 8 **Out of Country:** 1

ODP State: 9 **Regional:** 0 **National:** 0
Walk-on/Other: **Graduation %:** 100 **Seniors on Team:** 5
Positions Needed: All
Camp or Clinic Dates: July 10-14, and 17-21
Most Recent Record: 11-7-0
Schedule: Schedule is not finalized
Style of Play: Tight man marking in defending half in an effort to not concede balls played straight forward, countering to goal with speed while numbers and space are advantageous, quickness and two-touch ball movement.

Women's Athletic Profile

College Station
Wilson, NC 27893
Coach: Todd Bailess
Email: Not Available

NCAA II
Bulldogs/Blue, White
Phone: (252) 399-6518
Fax: (252) 399-6516

Estimated # of Women's Soccer Scholarships: None
Conference: Carolina - Virginia Athletic Conference
Program Profile: The team plays on a natural grass field which measures 120x75 yards with a seating capacity of 500; excellent weight training facilities.
History: The program began in 1994.
Achievements: Has 2 All-Conference players in 1996; 6 All-Conference players in 1997 and 2 players chosen All-Region in 1998.
Coaching: Todd Bailess, gradute of Barton '98, played professionally for the United Soccer League's Carolina Dynamo, will begin 2nd season with Barton in 2001.
Roster in State: 9 **Out of State:** 13 **Out of Country:** 0
ODP State: 5 **Regional:** 1 **National:**
Walk-on/Other: **Graduation %:** 100 **Seniors on Team:** 4
Positions Needed: All
Camp or Clinic Dates: July 9-13 / 16-20
Most Recent Record: 9-9-0
Schedule: Francis Marion, Wingate, Belmont Abbey, Lees Mcrae, Longwood, Pfeiffer
Style of Play: The team play a possession style. Lots of ball and player movement; Zonal defense.

Belmont Abbey College

Academic Profile

Phone: 704-825-6809

Belmont, NC 28012

Type: 4 Yr.,Private,Liberal Arts
Website: http://www.bac.edu.com
SAT/ACT/GPA: 850//2.5
Student/Faculty Ratio: 20/1
Undergraduate Enrollment: 995
Scholarships/Academic: Yes **Athletic:** Yes
Expenses by: Year **In State:** $ 16,160
Specialty: Education, Business
Degrees Conferred: BA, BS

Founded: 1876
Religion:
Housing: Yes
Male/Female Ratio: 50/50
Graduate Enrollment: N/A
Financial Aid: Yes
Out of State: $ 17,600

Programs of Study: Accounting, Biological Sciences, Business Administration, Chemistry, Computer Information Systems, Economics, Education, Elementary Education, English, History, Management, Mathematics, Medical Technology, Philosophy, Political Science, PreDentistry, PreLaw, PreMed, Psychology, Recreation & Leisure, Recreation Therapy, Secondary Education, Social Science, Sports Administration, Theology

Men's Athletic Profile

100 Belmont - Mt. Holly Rd
Belmont, NC 28012
Coach: Paul Stahlschmidt
Email: soccer@crusader.bac.edu

NCAA II
Crusaders/Red, White
Phone: (704) 825-6806
Fax: (704) 825-6570

Estimated # of Men's Soccer Scholarships: Varies
Conference: Carolinas-Virginia Athletic Conference
Program Profile: We play on alumni field Bermuda grass with a seating capacity of 1,000. Financial aid available including athletic, academic and work-study.
History: Our program began in 1957. We have several coaches, including current coach, which named Conference Coach of the Year. We are Conference Champions for 5 years.
Achievements: Carolinas-Virginia Athletic Conference Champions 1995; 5 All-Conference 1995. We were CVAC Co-Champions in 1997 and 2nd in CVAC in 1998.
Coaching: Paul Stahlschmidt, Head Coach, is entering his second season with the program. Tatum Bergue is our Assistant Coach.
Style of Play: Disciplined style of play.

Women's Athletic Profile

100 Belmont - Mt. Holly Rd
Belmont, NC 28012
Coach: Scot Wieland
Email: scotabbey@hotmail.com

NCAA II
Crusaders/Red, White
Phone: (704) 825-6243
Fax: (704) 825-6570

Estimated # of Women's Soccer Scholarships: 3.5
Conference: Carolinas-Virginia Athletic Conference
Program Profile: Field-Natural 1994 2-112, 1995 4-12, 1996 13-8, 1997 13-7, 1998 20-4, 1999 20-3
coach of the year 96,98,99
98, 99 CVAC Title, CVAC tournament champion, NCAA Division II quarter finalist
Venetta Wilson 1st team All-American 98, 99
Amanda Euge, Angela Placona 2nd team All-American
History: 1999 team GPA 3.1. 1999 # 7 post season national ranking NCAA division II
Achievements: 1999 coach of the year. 5 1st team all conference players. 5 1st team all south east region.
3 all Americans
Coaching: Scot Wieland Head women's soccer USSF/NSCAA license
Roster in State: 6 **Out of State:** 16 **Out of Country:**
Walk-on/Other: **Graduation %:** 100 **Seniors on Team:** 4
Camp or Clinic Dates: June 19-23 July 10-14
Most Recent Record: 20-3
Schedule: Presbyterian College, Francis Marion, North Florida, Catawba, Longwood

Campbell University

Academic Profile

Phone: (910) 893-1333

Buies Creek, NC 27506

Type: 4 Yr.,Private,Liberal Arts
Website: http://www.campbell.edu
SAT/ACT/GPA: 850/17/2.5
Student/Faculty Ratio: 18:1
Undergraduate Enrollment: 2,100

Founded: 1887
Religion: Southern Baptist
Housing: Yes
Male/Female Ratio: 1:2
Graduate Enrollment: 900

Scholarships/Academic: Yes **Athletic:** Yes **Financial Aid:** Yes
Expenses by: Year **In State:** $ 14,500 **Out of State:** $ 14,500
Specialty: Business, Education, Law, Pharmacy
Degrees Conferred: BA, BS, MSC, MBA, Pharmacy, Law, Education
Programs of Study: Accounting, Applied Science, Art, Biology, Business Administration, Chemistry, Computer Information Systems, Drama, Economics, Elementary Education, English, Journalism, Mass Communications, Mathematics, Music, Philosophy, Physical Education, PreLaw, PreMedicine, Psychology, Religion, Social Science, Sports Management

Men's Athletic Profile

P.O. Box 10
Buies Creek, NC 27506
Coach: Derrick Leeson
Email: leeson@mailcenter.campbell.edu

NCAA I
Fighting Camels/Orange, Black
Phone: (910) 893-1333
Fax: (910) 893-1330

Estimated # of Men's Soccer Scholarships: 7.5
Conference: Trans America Athletic Conference
Program Profile: We have a stadium and practice field with Bermuda grass and irrigation. The stadium has 2,000 seats.
History: Our program started in 1963. Campbell University first competed at the NCAA Division I from NAIA in 1977.
Achievements: 5th in 1968 NAIA Tournament; 3rd in 1970 NAIA Tournament; 6th at 1975 NAIA Tournament; Big South Champions in 1984, 1985, 1991 and 1992; Big South Runner-up 1986,1989 and 1993; TAAC Runner-up in 1995 and 1996.
Coaching: Derrick Leeson, Head Coach, was National Champion with West Virginia Wesleyan 4 times: two as a coach and two as a player. He was Coach of the Year in 1989 and 1990. In 1993, he was South Coach of the Year and Big South Coach of the Year. He was TAAC Coach of the Year in 1995 and 1997. Marco melo is assistant coach. Andrew McCarthy is goalkeeper coach.
Style of Play: We like to have the possession of the ball. We like to pass the ball using the midfield players and defend with everybody.

Women's Athletic Profile

P.O. Box 10
Buies Creek, NC 27506
Coach: Patrick Ferguson
Email: ferguson@mailcenter.campbell.edu

NCAA I
Camels/Orange, Black
Phone: (910) 893-1324
Fax: (910) 893-1330

Estimated # of Women's Soccer Scholarships: 9
Conference: Trans American Athletic Conference
Program Profile: We play in a natural Bermuda grass field which measures 120x75 and has a seating capacity of 2,000. We have a new practice field that is specifically for the women's program. Our paying season is in the fall.
History: The program began in 1992. We became members of the TAAC in 1994. Big South Conference Champions, TAAC runners-up.
Achievements: 1993 Big South Conference champions; 1995 TAAC Conference Runner-Up; 1995 Top 10 Regional Ranking.
Roster in State: 10 **Out of State:** 10 **Out of Country:** 1
ODP State: 5 **Regional:** 0 **National:** 0
Walk-on/Other: 0 **Graduation %:** 80 **Seniors on Team:** 2
Camp or Clinic Dates: July 8-12
Most Recent Record: 4-12-1
Schedule: Jacksonville Univ. NC State, Central Florida, Liberty, Virginia Commonwealth, East Carolina
Style of Play: Direct.

Catawba College

Academic Profile

Ads
Salisbury, NC 28144

Phone: 800-CATAWBA

Type: 4 Yr.,Private,Liberal Arts
Founded: 1851
Website: http://www.catawba.edu
Religion: Church of Christ
SAT/ACT/GPA: 800 min/2.8
Housing: Yes
Student/Faculty Ratio: 15:1
Male/Female Ratio: 50:50
Undergraduate Enrollment: 1,200
Graduate Enrollment: 100
Scholarships/Academic: Yes **Athletic:** Yes **Financial Aid:** Yes
Expenses by: Year **In State:** $ 16,784 **Out of State:** $ 16,784
Degrees Conferred: BA, BS, M Ed
Programs of Study: Accounting, Biology, Business and Management, Chemistry, Communications, Computer Science, Education, English, French, History, Law, Mathematics, Medical Technology, Philosophy, Political Science, PreProfessional, Psychology, Religion, Social Sciences, Sport Medicine

Men's Athletic Profile

2300 West Innes Street
Salisbury, NC 28144-2488
Coach: Craig Turnbull
Email: cturnbul@catawba.edu

NCAA II
Indians/Navy Blue, White
Phone: (704) 637-4348
Fax: (704) 637-5705

Estimated # of Men's Soccer Scholarships: 4
Conference: South Atlantic Conference
Program Profile: NCAA Division II program. One of the top small colleges in the nation. Situated in the heart of North Carolina. Three Bermuda grass fields; lighted match filed, stadium seats 1000 people.
History: Our program began in 1975 and reached NAIA finals in 1990 and 1991. Ranked #6 in South NCAA Division II. Three consecutive conference championships in 1996, 1997, and 1998. Six Conference Championships in the past ten years.
Achievements: Since assuming coaching responsibilities in 1998, Coach Turmbull has won conference championships, has had three All-South honors, one Conference Player of the Year, and six All-Conference seconds. To date, three players remain with professional clubs.
Coaching: Craig Turnbull, Head Coach, is in his third year at Catawba. He holds a NSCAA National Diploma; NC ODP staff coach; Rowan Rige Director of Coaching; played collegiately at ECU.
Roster In State: 4 **Out of State:** 19 **Out of Country:** 2
ODP State: 2 **Regional:** **National:** 2
Walk-on/Other: **Graduation %:** **Seniors on Team:** 5
Positions Needed: Strikers, Midfielders
Camp or Clinic Dates: June 18-22, June 25-29, July 16-20
Schedule: Wingate University, Presbyterian College, Eckerd College, Lynn University, Clayton State, Lander University
Style of Play: Possession oriented. Indirect style with build out of the back and through the midfield (4-4-2).

Women's Athletic Profile

2300 W Innes Street
Salisbury, NC 28144
Coach: Kevin Dempsey
Email: Kdempsey@catawba.edu

NCAA II
Indians/Navy, White
Phone: (704) 637-4324
Fax: (704) 637-5705

Estimated # of Women's Soccer Scholarships: N/A
Conference: South Atlantic Conference

Program Profile: Has three full-sized Bermuda field with lighted stadium and has a seating capacity of 1,000. Situated in the Heart of the ACC and consistently competes against Division I program.
History: Program began in 1990; 1 NAIA District 26 against Division I playoff appearance; 1997 NCAA Quarterfinals; 1SAC Title; 3 SAC Tournament Titles, consistently ranked in Top 20 in nation; 1997 Final Ranking of #14
Achievements: District playoffs in 1991; 2 All-Americans in 1996; 3 All-South in 1996; 3 1st team All-Conference in 1996, 1 2nd team All-Conference in 1996; 1996 Freshman of the Year; 7 current USISL - W players. Consistently ranked in Top 20 in the nation.
Coaching: Kevin Dempsey, Head Coach, NSCAA Advanced National Diploma, NSCAA State Course Staff, North Carolina ODP Staff, Director of Coaching for Rowan Rage Soccer Club. Played collegiate at UMBC and Catawba. Member of the Regional ODP Staff.

Roster in State: 4	**Out of State:** 16	**Out of Country:** 0
ODP State: 6	**Regional:** 0	**National:** 0
Walk-on/Other: 0	**Graduation %:** 98	**Seniors on Team:** 3

Positions Needed: the best players possible
Camp or Clinic Dates: June 3-7, 10-14, July 22-26
Most Recent Record: 11-7-0
Schedule: Barry, University of North Florida, Presbyterian College, Belmont Abbey, Tusculum, Pfeiffer, Longwood
Style of Play: Indirect style - attacking through the midfield.

Chowan College

Academic Profile

Phone: (252) 398-4499

Murfreesboro, NC 27855

Type: 4 Yr.,Private,Liberal Arts		**Founded:** 1848
Website: http://www.chowan.edu		**Religion:** Baptist
SAT/ACT/GPA: 900192.0		**Housing:** Yes
Student/Faculty Ratio: 12:1		**Male/Female Ratio:** 58/42
Undergraduate Enrollment: 780		**Graduate Enrollment:** N/A
Scholarships/Academic: Yes	**Athletic:** No	**Financial Aid:** Yes
Expenses by: Year	**In State:** $ 17,000	**Out of State:** $17,000

Specialty: Liberal Arts; Graphic Communications
Degrees Conferred: Bachelor of Science and Arts
Programs of Study: Art-Graphic Design, Studio Art; Biology-Allied Health/Laboratory Technology, Environmental Science, General Biology; Business Administration-Accounting, Computer Information Systems, Marketing, Small Business Management, General Business Administration, Communications, Criminal Justice, Drama, Elementary Education, English; Music-Church Music, Conducting, Performance; Physical Education, Athletic Training, Sport Management, Sport Science, Teacher Education; Physical Science-Chemistry, Physics; PreProfessional Programs-PreNursing, PreOptometry, PrePharmacy, PrePhysical Therapy, PreVet, PreMed; Religion

Men's Athletic Profile

P.O. Box 1848	**NCAA III**
Murfreesboro, NC 27855	Braves/Blue, White
Coach: Micheal Lias	**Phone:** (919) 398-6323
Email: Not Available	**Fax:** (919) 398-1390

Estimated # of Men's Soccer Scholarships: N/A
Conference: Dixie
Program Profile: Field-natural
History: Our program began in 1992.
Achievements: NSCA C.SCS certified (head coach)

Coaching: Jon Lindsay, Head Coach, 1994 graduate of Radford University, BA of Science in Health and Physical Education, coaching experience of two years as an assistant at Radford, two years assistant coach at Radford HS, a 77% career winning record.
Style of Play: Prepare for every aspect of each game, be intense, have fun!

Women's Athletic Profile

200 Jones Dr
Murfreesboro, NC 27855
Coach: Pam Kocher Brown
Email: brownp@chowan.edu

NCAA III
Braves/Columbia Blue, White
Phone: (252) 398-6433
Fax: (252) 398-1390

Estimated # of Women's Soccer Scholarships: None
Conference: Independent
Program Profile: Play on grass field with a primary fall season; we are currently build a new stadium and we do play a non traditional spring season.
History: Program began in 1993; current coach with program since 1995. We just added a full-time coach to assist with recruiting, practice and game-day coaching.
Achievements: In 1999 we received Hood College Tournament MVP, 3 All-Tournament team, Chowan College Tournament MVP, and 2 Chowan College All-Tournament team, and school record 37 goals in 1999.
Coaching: Pam Kocher Brown, Head Coach, since 1995. Stuart Horne just joined the coaching staff with a USSF "D" license. Chirrs Brown and Jody Preiche are also assistant coaches.
Roster in State: 2
Out of State: 8
Out of Country:
ODP State: 2
Regional:
National:
Walk-on/Other:
Graduation %:
Seniors on Team: 1
Positions Needed: Goalkeeper
Camp or Clinic Dates: Not available
Most Recent Record: 4-11
Schedule: Methodist, Christopher Newport University, Shenandoah College, Meredith College
Style of Play: Possession game, team oriented attack and defense.

Davidson College
Academic Profile

Phone: 740-894-2000

Davidson, NC 28036

Type: 4 Yr.,Private,Liberal Arts
Founded: 1837
Website: http://www.davidson.edu
Religion: Presbyterian
SAT/ACT/GPA: 1380/28/3.8
Housing: Yes
Student/Faculty Ratio: 10.7:1
Male/Female Ratio: 1:1
Undergraduate Enrollment: 1,600
Graduate Enrollment: N/A
Scholarships/Academic: Yes
Athletic: Yes
Financial Aid: Yes
Expenses by: Year
In State: $ 28,000
Out of State: $ 28,000
Specialty: Preprofessional Programs
Degrees Conferred: BA, BS
Programs of Study: Anthropology, Art, Biology, Chemistry, Classical Studies, Economics, English, French, German/Russian, Mathematics, Music, Philosophy, Physics, Political Science, Psychology, Religion, Sociology, Spanish, Theatre

Men's Athletic Profile

P.O. Box 1750, Athletics
Davidson, NC 28036
Coach: Charlie Slagle
Email: chslagle@davidson.edu

NCAA I
Wildcats/Black, Red, White
Phone: (704) 892-2345
Fax: (704) 892-2556

Estimated # of Men's Soccer Scholarships: 2.0
Conference: Southern Conference
Program Profile: Primary season is in the fall which consists of 20 game schedule against NCAA Division I opponents; "non-traditional" season in spring that last for two and half months. Field has a measurements of 120x75 yards Bermuda Stadium with a lights, 2 Bermuda practice fields with a measurement of 115x70 Bermuda game field without lights.
History: Our program founded in 1950, since 1980 program has posted winning percentage of .500 in ten of 18 years under Charlie Slagle, 1992 NCAA Division I Soccer Final Four.
Achievements: Charlie Slagle - Southern Coach of the Year 1981, 1983, 1985, 1987, 1992, 1994; NCAA Division I Coach of the Year 1992; Bob Ukrop - Adi Dassler Memorial Award 1992, All-American, first team 1992, second team 1990; Jim Kelly - second team 1987; Claude Finney - first team 1960; Tracy Hawjubs - Academic All-American 1989; Regional All-South - Rob Ukrop 1990, 1992, Peter Cobb 1990, Jim Kelly 1987; Bill Jeffrey Award - Charlie Slagle 1993; Conference Player of the Year - Robert Clark 1995, John Sampers 1994, Rob Ukrop 1992, Jim Kelly 1987. Charlie Slagle is acting cheer of the NCAA Division I Coaches Committee; David Bucker - Southern Conference Freshmen of the Year in 1997.NSCAA All-American
Coaching: Charlie Slagle is our Head Coach. He is entering his 21st season. He holds a USSF 'A' license and NSCAA Advanced National Diploma. He is a NCAA South Region Tournament Selection Committee and in NSCAA regional ranking committee. NCAA-Men's and Women's Soccer Rules Committee. Jon Wright is our Assistant Coach. He is entering his 10th season and was a 1981 NC ODP State Coach. He holds a "A" License and NSCAA Advanced National Diploma. NSCAA-Chairman of Championships Subcommittee of Division I Coaches committee

Roster In State: 6	**Out of State:** 24	**Out of Country:** 0
ODP State: 13	**Regional:** 3	**National:** 1
Walk-on/Other: 4	**Graduation %:** 100	**Seniors on Team:** 6

Most Recent Record: 10-11-1
Schedule: North Carolina, South Carolina, Wake Forest, Clemson, Furman, Richmond, Air Force Academy, UNC-Charlotte, Naval Academy
Style of Play: Possession oriented on offense, hard-working zonal trapping defense.

Women's Athletic Profile

P.O. Box 1750
Davidson, NC 28036
Coach: Kevin Hundley
Email: kehundle@davidson.edu

NCAA I
Wildcats/Red, Black
Phone: (704) 892-2818
Fax: (704) 892-2556

Estimated # of Women's Soccer Scholarships: 1
Conference: Southern Conference
Program Profile: We have two game fields including one 6,000-seat, lighted soccer stadium and additional practice fields. The fields are all natural grass for year-round playing.
History: Our program began in 1989. We have an overall record of 73-81-12 and three Southern Conference Championships. We have been seven seasons under Head Coach Kevin Hundley.
Achievements: Southern Conference Champions in 1994 & 1996; Tournament Champions in 1994, 1995, & 1996; 1 Division I All-South Region team selection in 1994 & 1995; Southern Conference Player of the Year in 1994 & 1996; Coach Slagle is acting Chair of the NCAA Division I Coaches Committee; Coach Slagle has been coaching 20 years. Ginny Dye-Academic All-American
Coaching: Kevin Hundley, Head Coach, has a USSF 'A' license. He compiled an overall record of 63-66-10. He graduated from Middlebury College. Ileana Moschas, Assistant Coach, graduate Wofford in 1998. Heidi Slaymaker, Assistant Coach, graduate of university of British Columbia in 1996.

Roster in State: 2	**Out of State:** 24	**Out of Country:**
ODP State: 13	**Regional:**	**National:**
Walk-on/Other: 13	**Graduation %:** 100	**Seniors on Team:** 8

Positions Needed: GK, and field players
Camp or Clinic Dates: June 24-28, 2000-freshmen through senior girls

Most Recent Record: 12-8-3
Schedule: Duke, Wake Forest, Harvard, South Carolina, NC State, UNC Charlotte, Furman, UNC Greensboro
Style of Play: Tight marking in midfield and back; quick to play to front players who lay balls back to midfield or turn to take defenders on; all midfielders get involved with attack by overlapping or running through.

Duke University

Academic Profile

Durham, NC 27708-0555
Phone:

Type: 4 Yr.,Private,Liberal Arts
Founded: 1838
Website: http://www.duke.edu
Religion: United Methodist
SAT/ACT/GPA: 1200/28/3.5
Housing: Yes
Student/Faculty Ratio: 11:1
Male/Female Ratio: 55:45
Undergraduate Enrollment: 5,800
Graduate Enrollment: 3,000
Scholarships/Academic: Yes **Athletic:** Yes **Financial Aid:** Yes
Expenses by: Year **In State:** $ 31,000 **Out of State:** $ 31,000
Degrees Conferred: BA, BS, MA, MS, MBA, D, MD, JD, Mdiv
Programs of Study: Engineering, Letters/Literature, Life Sciences, Psychology, Social Science, PreMed, Arts & Art History, Chemistry, Sociology, Philosophy, Economics, International Studies

Men's Athletic Profile

Box 90555
Durham, NC 27706
Coach: John Rennie
Email: Jrennie@acpub.duk.edu

NCAA I
Blue Devils/Blue, White
Phone: (919) 684-5180
Fax: (919) 681-7866

Estimated # of Men's Soccer Scholarships: None
Conference: ACC
Program Profile: Host's Adidas/Met Life Soccer Classic in September. Hosted 1995 ACC Tournament. Play on natural grass field with a seating capacity of 6,000.
History: In the final 'Soccer America' the team was ranked # 6 in 1994. 4 Final Four Appearances; 2 in the 90's (192 & 1995); National Champions in 1986; Final Ranking #10 in 1997.
Achievements: The team has 4 Herman Award winners, 9 NCAA Tournament appearances, and were in the NCAA Final Four 3 times in past 10 years. National Champs in 1986.
Coaching: John Rennie is our Head Coach. He is entering 20 seasons, USSF 'A' license, member of USSF National Coaching Staff. He was named Coach of the Year in 1997.John Barrett is assistant coach as of 1999.
Style of Play: Play a 3-5-2 with a zonal defenses' tactics. Looking to counter back. turn-over - otherwise possession build-up exploiting other team's weakness.

Women's Athletic Profile

Cameron Indoor Stadium Box 90555
Durham, NC 27708
Coach: Bill Hempen
Email: bhempen@duke.edu

NCAA I
Blue Devils, Blue & White
Phone: 919-681-3456
Fax: 919-681-7866

Estimated # of Women's Soccer Scholarships:
Conference: Atlantic Coast Conference (ACC)
Program Profile: Fully funded program. Has grass stadium that seats 6,000 fans and has a measurements of 75x120 yards. New athletic weight room to open in July of 1999. Playing season starts from August through December with a spring season that starts February to April. Hosted 2000 ACC Championships.

History: Program began in 1988 and went to final NCAA game. 1994 regular season ACC Champion, been to NCAA Tournament eight years. Bill Hempen is the only coach of this program.
Achievements: Won ACC Coach of the Year in 1992, 1994 & 1997; 1992 National Coach of the Year; 3 National U-21 players; 7 All-Americans, 1 ACC Rookie of the Year and 3 players taken in pro draft.
Coaching: Bill Hempen, Head Coach, he's been coaching for 12 years. Carla Overbeck - Assistant Coach, was an Olympic Medallist, World Cup Champion and captain of National Team. Sue-Moy Chin also Assistant Coach.
Roster In State: 5 **Out of State:** 20 **Out of Country:** 1
ODP State: 24 **Regional:** 12 **National:** 2
Walk-on/Other: **Graduation %:** 100 **Seniors on Team:** 5
Positions Needed: All
Camp or Clinic Dates: 6/22-26/01, 6/28/01-7/02/01
Most Recent Record: 14-8-1
Schedule: UNC-Chapel Hill, Penn State, Virginia, Clemson, Florida State, Wake Forest, Univ. of San Diego, Vanderbilt, Missouri, Maryland
Style of Play: Our style of play is dictated by personnel available.

East Carolina University

Academic Profile

Greenville, NC 27858
Phone: 252-328-6131

Type: 4 Yr.,Public **Founded:** 1907
Website: http://www.ecu.edu **Religion:** Non-Affiliated
SAT/ACT/GPA: Varies **Housing:** Yes
Student/Faculty Ratio: 25:1 **Male/Female Ratio:** 50:50
Undergraduate Enrollment: 15,000 **Graduate Enrollment:** 2,000
Scholarships/Academic: Yes **Athletic:** Yes **Financial Aid:** Yes
Expenses by: Year **In State:** $ 6,200 **Out of State:** $ 13,200
Specialty: Education, Business, Exercise Science, Art
Degrees Conferred: BA, BS, BFA, BM, BSA, BSBA, BSBE, MA, MS, MBA, MFA, MEd, Ph.D.
Programs of Study: Offers 106 undergraduate and 92 graduate majors in the Schools of Allied Health Sciences, Art, Arts/Sciences, Business, Education, Health and Human Performance, Human Environmental Sciences, Industry/Technology, Music, Nursing, Social Work

Men's Athletic Profile

104 Scales Field House, Rm. 105
Greenville, NC 27858
Coach: Devin O'Neill
Email: oneill@mail.ecu.edu

NCAA I
Pirates/Purple, Gold
Phone: (252) 328-4626
Fax: (252) 328-4647

Estimated # of Men's Soccer Scholarships: 8.5
Conference: Colonial Athletic Association (CAA)
Program Profile: ECU plays a full year of soccer within the guidelines of the NCAA. The game field is a nice Bermuda grass surface in Bunting Stadium, which seats 500. the training facility is right next to the game field and is lighted.
History: Soccer started here at ECU in 1965. Since this time there has been 14 different head soccer coaches.
Achievements: Several ECU players have received All-CAA Conference first and second recognition.
Coaching: Devin O'Neill is our Head Coach. He comes to ECU after successful assistant coaching at Lafayette College, Fresno State, and most recently Ohio State University. This is his first head coaching assignment and has obtained his USSF "A" Licensed and the NSCAA Advanced National Diploma. Coach O'Neill brings a wealth of soccer knowledge to the Pirate soccer program.
Roster In State: 14 **Out of State:** 11 **Out of Country:**
Most Recent Record: 3-12-1

Schedule: North Carolina State, St. Louis, UAB, South Florida, UNC-Charlotte, Cincinnati
Style of Play: Changes year to year based on strengths of personnel.

Women's Athletic Profile

Scales Fieldhouse
Greenville, NC 27858-4353
Coach: Rob Donnenwirth
Email: donnenwirth@mail.ecu.edu

NCAA I
Pirates/Purple, White, Gold
Phone: (252) 328-4672
Fax: (252) 328-4647

Estimated # of Women's Soccer Scholarships: 7
Conference: Colonial Athletic Association
Program Profile: Our program is in its 4th year. We play on a natural grass facility that seats 1,000. In 1999, we will be in our 6th season with NCAA I status.
History: Our women's program began its fourth year of varsity status in 1997. Our 1995 record was 3-17-0. Our 1996 record was 7-11-2. Our 1997 record was 10-10-0. 40 wins in the last 4 years and rank 10th in the South Region in 1999.
Achievements: Coach Roberts - CVAC Coach of the Year in 1993. 1997 CAA Coach of the Year.
Roster in State: 7 **Out of State:** 17 **Out of Country:** 0
Walk-on/Other: 0 **Graduation %:** 100 **Seniors on Team:** 4
Camp or Clinic Dates: June 23-27
Most Recent Record: 10-7-2
Schedule: Maryland, Richmond, Marquette, St. Louis, Charlotte, TCU, Houston, Tulane.
Style of Play: Varies according to individual players strengths and weaknesses.

Elon College

Academic Profile

Elon College, NC 27244

Phone: 800-334-8448

Type: 4 Yr.,Private,Liberal Arts
Website: http://www.elon.edu
SAT/ACT/GPA: 1090/3.2
Student/Faculty Ratio: 16:1
Undergraduate Enrollment: 3,800
Scholarships/Academic: Yes **Athletic:** Yes
Expenses by: Year **In State:** $ 17,446

Founded: 1889
Religion: Church of Christ
Housing: Yes
Male/Female Ratio: 45:55
Graduate Enrollment: 300
Financial Aid: Yes
Out of State: $ 17,446

Specialty: Liberal Arts, Career-oriented majors & graduate programs
Degrees Conferred: AB, BFA, BS, MED, MBA, MPT
Programs of Study: Accounting, Art, Biology, Business, Chemistry, Communications, Computer Science, Dance, Economics, Education, English, Sport Medicine, History, Human Services, Math, Medical Technology, Music, Physics, Religion, Social Science, Theatre, Health Education, Environmental Science, Leisure Sport Management, Journalism, Philosophy, Sociology, Political Science

Men's Athletic Profile

2500 Campus Box
Elon College, NC 27244
Coach: Mike Reilly
Email: reillym@elon.edu

NCAA I
Phoenix/Garnet, Old Gold
Phone: (336) 584-2319
Fax: (336) 538-2686

Estimated # of Men's Soccer Scholarships: 6
Conference: Big South Atlantic Conference

Program Profile: New Bermuda field 2000 (stadium completion 2001). 1999 1st full year of Div. I.
History: Program began in 1974. NAIA beginnings-District Champs 1985. NCAA Div. II 1989-98 South Atlantic Conference. NCAA Div. I 1999-present Big South.
Achievements: 3 All-Americans. 1985 NSCAA Region 10 Coach of the Year- while at Spartanburg Methodist College-JUCO-I. 1993-Old Dominion Athletic Conference Coach of the Year- Hampden-Sydney Div. III.
Coaching: Mike Reilly, Head Coach (enters 5th year at Elon). 17th overall, USSF "A" license, NC ODP Staff Coach. Jamie Guyan-3rd yr., Brian Neiberline-2nd yr.

Roster In State: 3	**Out of State:** 22	**Out of Country:** 0
ODP State: 3	**Regional:** 2	**National:**
Walk-on/Other:	**Graduation %:** 100	**Seniors on Team:** 2

Positions Needed: Goalkeeper-Forward
Camp or Clinic Dates: 6/25-6/29/2000
Most Recent Record: 3-14-0
Schedule: Virginia, UNC-Chapel Hill, Furman, UNC-Charlotte, NC State, Liberty, Coastal Carolina, Radford
Style of Play: 3-5-2,4-4-2, indirect, use of wing defenders in attack. Man to man defense with zonal principles. Some straight zonal defending.

Women's Athletic Profile

Campus Box 2500
Elon College, NC 27244
Coach: Paul Webster
Email: websterp@elon.edu

NCAA I
Phoenix/Maroon, White
Phone: (336) 278-6745
Fax: (336) 278-6767

Estimated # of Women's Soccer Scholarships: 6.75
Conference: Big South Conference
Program Profile: Rudd Field opened in the fall of 2000. Main grandstand will open fall 2001. Surface is Bermuda Grass. On going renovations to Koury Field house will be complete by fall 2001 and will include sports medicine facilities and home and visiting team locker rooms.
History: We began in 1986, appeared in 1992 NAIA National Tournament and won 6 of 7 South Atlantic Conference season titles as a Division II school. We just completed our second year in the transition to Division I. We will be eligible for conference play in 1999. Won the 2000 Big South Conference Regular Season Title. The program's overall record is 157-90-6.
Achievements: SAC Champions in 1990, 1991, & 1995; SAC Co-Champions in 1992, 1993 & 1996; Food Lion SAC Tournament Champions in 1991 & 1992; NAIA National Tournament in 1992; 15 All-Americans, most recent was Ginger Staulcup in 1995. Paul Webster was voted SAC Coach of the Year in 1995 and NSCAA Division II South Region Coach of the Year in 1996.
Coaching: Paul Webster, Head Coach, is entering his sixth year at Elon College with a record of 56-47-7. He holds both USSF and NSCAA Diplomas. He has a BS from the University of Florida in 1989 and a MAT from Queens College in 1996. He served two seasons as assistant coach for the Charlotte Speed of the USISL W-League. Justin Bryant is assistant coach.

Roster in State: 1	**Out of State:** 26	**Out of Country:** 0
ODP State: 18	**Regional:** 0	**National:** 0
Walk-on/Other: 9	**Graduation %:** 100	**Seniors on Team:** 5

Positions Needed: GK, Defender, Midfield, Forward
Camp or Clinic Dates: June 24-28
Most Recent Record: 8-11-0
Schedule: Furman, Davidson, North Carolina State, East Carolina Univ.
Style of Play: Plays an attractive, attacking style with an emphasis on possession. All players are involved in both attacking and defending. Many systems are incorporated and requires all players to be of a high technical ability.

Gardner - Webb University

Academic Profile

Phone: 704-406-2361

Boiling Spring, NC 28017

Type: 4 Yr.,Private,Liberal Arts
Website: http://www.gardner-webb.edu
SAT/ACT/GPA: 850/17/2.4
Student/Faculty Ratio: 16:1
Undergraduate Enrollment: 2,369
Scholarships/Academic: Yes
Athletic: Yes
Expenses by: Year
In State: $ 16,010

Founded: 1905
Religion: Baptist
Housing: Yes
Male/Female Ratio: 37:62
Graduate Enrollment: 551
Financial Aid: Yes
Out of State: $ 16,010

Specialty: Liberal Arts
Degrees Conferred: BA, BS, BSN, AA in Nursing, MA, MD, MBA
Programs of Study: American Sign Languages, Communication Studies, English, French, History, Journalism, Music, Political Science, Religious Studies, Sacred Music, Social Sciences, Sociology, Spanish, Theatre, Accounting, Athletic Training, Biology, Business Administration, Chemistry, Computer Science, Mathematics, Elementary Education, Health Education, International Business, Nursing, Management, Information System, Mathematics, Medical Technology, Middle Grades, Education, Physical Education, Pschology, Sport Management, Agency Counseling, Business, Divinity, Elementary Education, English Education, Middle Grades Eduction, Physical Education, School Counseling, School Ad.

Men's Athletic Profile

Campus Box 237
Boiling Springs, NC 28017
Coach: Tony Setzer
Email: tsetzer@gardner-webb.edu

NCAA I
Running Bulldogs/Scarlet
Phone: (704) 434-4350
Fax: (704) 434-4739

Estimated # of Men's Soccer Scholarships: 9.9
Conference: Independent
Program Profile: The team plays on the Erne Varsity Stadium, which holds 1,500 people. They play from August to November. Our soccer program has a very strong background.
History: Program began in 1987. Moved to NCAA Division II in 1993. Has been very competitive over the past ten years. The program finished third two-time and twice in the conference with four appearances in the tournament finals.
Achievements: 1990 SAC Player of the Year, 1990 Coach of the Year, 4 All-Americans, 10 Academic All-Americans, 1st Union Scholar Athlete. 3 first Union South Atlantic Conference Award Winners, 2 SCA Player of the Year. 1 Freshman of the Year, 18 - 1st Team All-Conference, 24 - 2nd Team All-Americans.
Coaching: Tony Setzer, Head Coach,USSF 'A' license, BS 1986 From Lander College, Masters in Education in 1988 from the Citadel. Athletic Director.
Roster In State: 11
Out of State: 16
Out of Country: 4
ODP State: 4
Regional: 1
National:
Walk-on/Other:
Graduation %: 98
Seniors on Team: 2
Positions Needed: Defenders, Midfielders
Camp or Clinic Dates: July 23-28
Schedule: The Citadel, UNC-Asheville, Liberty University, NC State University, Virginia Tech
Style of Play: Build from the back and play through the midfield. Defend with high pressure zone man system. Play a 3-5-2 system.

Women's Athletic Profile

PO Box 877
Boiling Springs, NC 28017
Coach: Kevin Mounce
Email:

NCAA I-A
Runnin' Bulldogs/Black, Scarlet
Phone: (704) 406-4353
Fax: (704) 406-3503

Estimated # of Women's Soccer Scholarships: N/A
Conference: Independent
Program Profile: The team plays on the Varsity Field, which holds 1500 people. They play from August to November. Soccer has a very strong background.
History: Program began in 1990.
Achievements: Numerous All-Conference and All-Region players.
Roster in State: 6 **Out of State:** 11 **Out of Country:** 2
Schedule: Morehead State University, Marshall, Coastal Carolina, Tennessee Tech

Greensboro College

Academic Profile

Greensboro, NC 27358
Phone: (336) 272-7102

Type: 4 Yr.,Private,Liberal Arts
Founded: 1838
Website: http://www.gborocollege.edu
Religion: Methodist
SAT/ACT/GPA: 800/2.0
Housing: Yes
Student/Faculty Ratio: 15:1
Male/Female Ratio: 55:45
Undergraduate Enrollment: 1,000
Graduate Enrollment: N/A
Scholarships/Academic: Yes **Athletic:** No **Financial Aid:** Yes
Expenses by: Year **In State:** $ 16,500 **Out of State:** $ 16,500
Specialty: Business, Education
Degrees Conferred: BA, BS
Programs of Study: Accounting, Biological Science, Business Administration, Chemistry, Elementary Education, English, French, History, Interdisciplinary Studies, Liberal Arts, Management, Mathematics, Medical Laboratory Technology, Music, Physical Education, Political Science, PreDentistry, PreLaw, PreMed, PreVet, Psychology, Radiological Technology, Religion, Secondary Education, Spanish, Special Education, Sports Medicine, Theatre

Men's Athletic Profile

815 West Market Street
Greensboro, NC 27401-1875
Coach: Darren Powell
Email: dpowell@gborocollege.edu

NCAA III
The Pride/Green, White, Black
Phone: (336) 272-7102x260
Fax: (336) 230-9707

Estimated # of Men's Soccer Scholarships: None
Conference: Dixie Intercollegiate Athletic Conference
Program Profile: Nationally competitive NCAA Division III team. Game field on campus, Bermuda grass, 500 seats down one side. Fall traditional season, spring non-traditional season.
History: 1972 was the first year of our program. We have three Dixie Conference Champions, two NCAA Runner-Up in 1989 & 1998 and 8 NCAA Appearances in nine years. Coach Duerall holds a record of 218-162-21.
Achievements: Coach Darren Powell has won Conference and All-Region Coach of the Year in 1998. Steve Allison has won Conference in 1992, 1994, 1996-1997, and Coach of The Year. The program has had 5 All-Americans, 16 All-Region players, 50 All-Conference players, 4 players in active USL 3 professional leagues.
Coaching: Darren Powell is the Head Coach. Bob Rosairio, Dan Collins, and Kent Bighinatti are the Assistant Coaches.
Roster In State: 14 **Out of State:** 12 **Out of Country:** 4
ODP State: 5 **Regional:** 1 **National:**
Walk-on/Other: **Graduation %:** 75 **Seniors on Team:** 2
Positions Needed: Forward
Camp or Clinic Dates: Not Available
Most Recent Record: 15-4-1

Schedule: Christopher Newport, Hampden-Sydney, Cabrini, Salisbury State, Messiah, Mary Washington, Emory, Virginia Wesleyan, Roanoke, Methodist
Style of Play: We play 4-4-2 or 3-5-2 formation. We play a passing game at pace always looking to attack and score goals.

Women's Athletic Profile

815 West Market Street
Greensboro, NC 27401-1875
Coach: Doug Shank
Email: dshank@gborocollege.edu

NCAA III
Pride/Green, White
Phone: (336) 272-7102
Fax: (336) 203-9707

Estimated # of Women's Soccer Scholarships: None
Conference: Dixie Intercollegiate Athletic Conference
Program Profile: A programon the rise. Committed to developing players who have the desire to take their game to the next level. Natural grass surface; 120x80; traditional and non-traditional seasons. Filed seating capacity 2,000. Bleacher and Grass seating available.
History: Program began in 1990. 1999 5-11. 2000 5-8-3.
Achievements: 25 players- All-Conference. 3 players- All-South Region. 1 player- All-American. 2 players- Regional Scholar All-Americans.
Coaching: Doug Shank is our head coach and he is assisted by Mike Lackemacher.
Roster in State: 8 **Out of State:** 8 **Out of Country:** 0
ODP State: 5 **Regional:** 0 **National:** 0
Walk-on/Other: 0 **Graduation %:** 100 **Seniors on Team:** 0
Positions Needed: All
Camp or Clinic Dates: Not Available
Most Recent Record: 8-10-0
Schedule: Methodist College, Christopher Newport, North Carolina Wesleyan, Redlands, Maryville, Randolph Macon, Montclair State, William Patterson, Virginia Wesleyan
Style of Play: Aggressive, attacking oriented style of play. Play an indirect, possession oriented theme with purpose of scoring goals. Defensively, utilize team zonal concepts. Primary formation is a 3-4-3 but will vay to others if needed.

Guilford College

Academic Profile

Greensboro, NC 27410

Phone: (336) 316-2161

Type: 4 Yr.,Private,Liberal Arts
Website: http://www.guilford.edu
SAT/ACT/GPA: 900/20
Student/Faculty Ratio: 12:1
Undergraduate Enrollment: 1,200
Scholarships/Academic: Yes **Athletic:** No
Expenses by: Year **In State:** $ 21,000
Degrees Conferred: BA, BS

Founded: 1837
Religion: Non-Affiliated
Housing: Yes
Male/Female Ratio: 1:1
Graduate Enrollment: N/A
Financial Aid: Yes
Out of State: $ 21,000

Programs of Study: Biology, Business & Management, Chemistry, Criminal Justice, Dentistry, Education, History, Justice & Policy, Law, Letters/Literature, Liberal Arts, Management, Medicine, Parks/Recreation, Philosophy, Physical Education, Physics, Psychology, Public Affairs, Sport Management, Sport Medicine, Social Sciences

Men's Athletic Profile

5800 W Friendly Avenue
Greensboro, NC 27410
Coach: Liam Behrens
Email: dwalters@guilford.edu

NCAA III
Quakers/Maroon, White
Phone: (910) 316-2875
Fax: (910) 316-2873

Estimated # of Men's Soccer Scholarships:
Conference: Old Dominion Athletic Conference
Program Profile: Best facility in league. Natural grass surface, 120 x 75 game and practice field. Has two regulation soccer field and two practice field.
History: Program began in 1963. Moved to NCAA Division III and Old Dominion Athletic Conference in 1991.
Coaching: Liam Behrens, Head Coach, graduate of Virginia Commonwealth in 1988, former pro players with a five years pro experience.
Style of Play: Ball possession with building out of the back.

Women's Athletic Profile

5800 West Friendly Avenue
Greensboro, NC 27410
Coach: Forrest Collier
Email: Not Available

NCAA III
Quakers/Crimson, Grey
Phone: (910) 316-2197
Fax: (910) 316-2953

Estimated # of Women's Soccer Scholarships: None
Conference: Old Dominion Athletic Conference
Program Profile: Natural field; one of the largest and nicest in the ODAC Conference: very strong athletic training program and support staff; warmer weather with nay competitive schools in the area.

High Point University

Academic Profile

High Point, NC 27262

Phone: 800-345-6993

Type: 4 Yr.,Private,Liberal Arts
Website: http://www.highpoint.edu
SAT/ACT/GPA: 1130
Student/Faculty Ratio: 16:1
Undergraduate Enrollment: 2,500
Scholarships/Academic: Yes
Athletic: Yes
Expenses by: Year
In State: $ 15,680
Founded: 1924
Religion: United Methodist
Housing: Yes
Male/Female Ratio: 45:55
Graduate Enrollment: 300
Financial Aid: Yes
Out of State: $ 17,280
Specialty: Well rounded Liberal Arts
Degrees Conferred: BA, BS, MBA
Programs of Study: Art, Elementary Education, English, French, History, Human Relations, International Studies, Education, Special Education, Philosophy, Religion, Sociology, Spanish, Theatre Arts, Political Science, Accounting, Biology, Business Administration, Chemistry, Computer Information Systems, Exercise, Forestry, Business-all areas, Mathematics, Physical Education, Psychology, Sports Management, Sports Medicine, etc..

Men's Athletic Profile

University Station/Montlieu Ave.
High Point, NC 27262
Coach: Peter Broadley
Email: pbroadley@acme.highpoint.edu

NCAA I
Panthers/Purple, White, Black
Phone: (336) 841-4607
Fax: (336) 841-9182

Estimated # of Men's Soccer Scholarships: 6
Conference: Big South Conference
Program Profile: First year of Division I program - full Division I schedule playing ACC and Southern Conference teams. Bermuda turf practice fields and stadium has a capacity of 2,000 seats.
History: Program is very strong NAIA and NCAA Division II program. Previously one of the top small college programs in the Carolinas. School is increasing in size and is now NCAA Division I

Achievements: Coach Peter Broadley 2 Division National Championships, NAIA National Finalist, 5 Conference Championships, 5 Conference and South Regional Coach of the Year Awards, 7 All-Americans and 9 professional USISL.
Coaching: Peter Broadley, Head Coach, NSCAA National Academy Staff Member, South Region and NC ODP Staff Coach, USSF "B" License, English, Preliminary License, NSCAA Advanced National Diploma. Jeff Gephart, Assistant Coach, entering four years of coaching collegiate players, athletic trainer at Georgetown, William and Mary and Davidson College.
Style of Play: Attacking style of play, good team speed, tough to beat, and tight defensively.

Women's Athletic Profile

Dept. of Athletics, 833 Montlieu Ave
High Point, NC 27262
Coach: Tracie Foels
Email: tfoels@highpoint.edu

NCAA I
Panthers/Purple, White
Phone: (336) 841-4573
Fax: (336) 841-9182

Estimated # of Women's Soccer Scholarships: Varies
Conference: Big South Conference
Program Profile: Division I program competing in Big South Conference, 6000 seat Albion Mills Soccer Stadium 120x80 Bermuda pitch with lights, Bermuda practice fields, traditional and nontraditional training and matches (Fall & Spring)
History: New Division I program previously competed in Division II CIAC and CVAC. Program began in 1993.
Achievements: All Conference (D I) 6, Academic All-Conference 2, All Conference Tournament Team 3, NCAA Women of the year 1.
Coaching:

Roster in State: 1	**Out of State:** 21	**Out of Country:** 1
ODP State: 4	**Regional:** 2	**National:** 0
Walk-on/Other: 0	**Graduation %:** 100	**Seniors on Team:** 2

Camp or Clinic Dates: Not Available
Most Recent Record: 4-11-2
Schedule: NC State Univ. Jacksonville Univ. Davidson College, UNC Wilmington, East Carolina Univ. Campbell Univ. Tennessee Tech Univ. Elon College, Radford Univ. Liberty Univ.
Style of Play: Possession, attacking style of play.

Lees - McRae College

Academic Profile

Phone: (828) 898-8725

Banner Elk, NC 28604

Type: 4 Yr.,Private,Liberal Arts		**Founded:** 1900
Website: http://www.lmc.edu		**Religion:** Presbyterian
SAT/ACT/GPA:		**Housing:** Yes
Student/Faculty Ratio: 14:1		**Male/Female Ratio:** N/A
Undergraduate Enrollment: N/A		**Graduate Enrollment:** N/A
Scholarships/Academic: Yes	**Athletic:** Yes	**Financial Aid:** Yes
Expenses by: Year	**In State:** $15,400	**Out of State:** $15,400

Degrees Conferred: BA, BS
Programs of Study: Art, Biology, Naturalist, Pre-Health Professional, Science Education, Sports Medicine, Business Administration, Computer Information Systems, Criminal Justice, Dance, Education, English (Communication & Literature), History, Interdisciplinary Studies, International Studies, Mathematics, Military Science, Music, Musical Theatre, Physical Education, Psychology, Reading, Religious Studies, Social Studies, Sociology, Theatre Arts

Men's Athletic Profile

P.O. Box 128
Banner Elk, NC 28604
Coach: Jeremy Tittle
Email: tittle@lmc.edu

NCAA II
Bobcats/Forest Green, Gold
Phone: (704) 898-8725
Fax: (704) 898-8742

Estimated # of Men's Soccer Scholarships: 3.5 Total scholarships
Conference: Carolinas-Virginia Athletic Conference
Program Profile: Top Division II men's program. Features 4 natural grass practice fields and 120x76 yards game field with a seating capacity of 750. The season is year-round indoor and outdoor training with a full spring schedule.
History: Program began in 1986 competing in the NJCAA until 1990; NAIA in 1991-1995; NCAA Division III-present.
Achievements: 1998: CVAC Player of the Year was Mark McShea; CVAC Tournament MVP; CVAC Tournament Champions; ranked 9th in South Region as high as 7th nationally in scoring. In the past four years the program has broken almost all school records and has produced an All-Region, 8 All-CVAC, 8 Academic All-CVAC, and 3 Academic All-Americans; over 50 players named to Dean's List across the past 8 semesters, maintaining almost a 3.0 team GPA. Roy Lassiter, MLS and National Team player, was an All-American in 1989.
Coaching: Jeremy Tittle, Head Coach, entering five years with the program, CVAC Coach of the Year in 1998; NSCAA National Diploma, MS Kinesiology, former assistant at Midwestern State University. Ralph McGuinness, Assistant Coach, entering first year, played for the Armed Forces and Junior Level in Scotland.
Roster In State: 5 **Out of State:** 16 **Out of Country:** 4
Walk-on/Other: **Graduation %:** 85 **Seniors on Team:** 6
Positions Needed: All
Camp or Clinic Dates: Not Available
Most Recent Record: 13-10-
Schedule: Queens, Belmont-Abbey, Pfeiffer, Barton, Clayton College, Tusulum, Mars Hill
Style of Play: Blend of possession and quick transition counter-attack. Man-to-man and zonal defensive principles are combined with ability to apply high and low pressure.

Women's Athletic Profile

P.O. Box 128
Banner Elk, NC 28604
Coach: Ried Estus
Email: estus@lmc.edu

NCAA II
Bobcats/Green, Gold, White
Phone: (828) 898-8903
Fax: (828) 898-8742

Estimated # of Women's Soccer Scholarships: 3.5
Conference: Carolinas - Virginia Conference
Program Profile: Lees-McRae College offers a very competitive soccer program. We won the CVAC Championship for the 2000-2001 season. There are 4 practice fields and the match field. They are natural grass surface. The game field is one of the best in the conference measuring 120x78 yards.
History: Program began as a Junior College in 1987.
Achievements: 2000 Conference Champions; 7 All-Americans
Coaching: Head Coach: Ried Estus 14th season. Asst. Coach: Tracey Leipold 4th season.
Roster in State: 4 **Out of State:** 20 **Out of Country:** 1
Camp or Clinic Dates: Not Available
Most Recent Record: 17-6-0
Schedule: north Florida, Francis Marion, Belmont-Abbey, Pfeiffer University, Longwood College, Barton College

Lenoire - Rhyne College

Academic Profile

Hickory, NC 28603

Phone:

Type: 4 Yr.,Private,Liberal Arts
Website: http://www.lrc.edu
SAT/ACT/GPA: 900/18
Student/Faculty Ratio: 11:1
Undergraduate Enrollment: 1,633
Scholarships/Academic: Yes **Athletic:** Yes
Expenses by: Year **In State:** $ 17,000

Founded: 1891
Religion: Lutheran
Housing: Yes
Male/Female Ratio: 60:40
Graduate Enrollment: N/A
Financial Aid: Yes
Out of State: $ 18,500

Degrees Conferred: BA, BS, BME, MA, Education & Counseling
Programs of Study: Accounting, Anthropology, Art, Astronomy, Biology, Business, Chemistry, Classics, Computer Science, Dance, Drama, Earth Science, Education, Environmental Studies, Geography, Sport Studies, Mathematics, Military Science, Nursing, Office Science, Sociology, Social Science

Men's Athletic Profile

P.O. Box 7356
Hickory, NC 28603
Coach: Kevin Demers
Email: demersk@lrc.edu

NCAA II
Bears/Black, White, Red
Phone: (828) 328-7137
Fax: (828) 328-7399

Estimated # of Men's Soccer Scholarships:
Conference: South Atlantic Conference
Program Profile: Our programs has its home field on campus. Highlight is a beautiful 1,000 capacity football only grass field. We regularly get 5,000 spectators. The game and practice fields are Bermuda grass. Playing season is in the fall.
History: We began soccer in 1984. The program began to take off in 1987 with the arrival of Coach Tom Melville. He served until the 1995 season when Coach Kevin Demers began his tenure. We moved from NAIA to NCAA Division II in 1993.
Achievements: Produced 1 SAC Championship; 25 All-Conference players; 2 All-Americans.
Coaching: Kevin Demers, Head Coach, is in his fourth season and is a graduate of Hope College. In 1994, he received a Master's degree from Western Michigan University. He holds a USSF 'B' license, along with the National and Advanced National Diploma from the NSCAA. Pursuing 'A' license in June 1997. Jason Ondriezek is our Assistant Coach and Bobby Graham is our Volunteer Assistant Coach.
Style of Play: Defensively organized looking to possess the ball and go forward whenever possible.

Women's Athletic Profile

Campus Box 7356
Hickory, NC 28603
Coach: Will Beddingfield
Email: beddingfieldw@lrc.edu

NCAA II
Bears/Red, Black
Phone: (828) 328-7169
Fax: (828) 328-7399

Estimated # of Women's Soccer Scholarships: Varies
Conference: South Atlantic Conference
Program Profile: A highly competitive year-round program that plays one of the toughest schedules in the entire region. Focus is on academic performance while developing you as a soccer player while playing other nationally competitive

teams. Daily high competitive training sessions, emphasis is on possession style of attack, and zonal defending. A new $8 million addition to the gym, $250,000 with 2000 seat soccer stadium will be started on in 2000. Demanding spring training season includes weight, fitness, and outdoor training and matches against NCAA DI schools to enhance players development.

History: Program began in 1990 and has been extremely competitive ever since it's inception. Has an overall record of 85-70-9 playing a nationally competitive schedule year after year.

Achievements: One All-American; numerous All-Region players; numerous All-Conference and Academic All-Conference players as well.

Coaching: Will Beddingfield- NSCAA premier diploma, nine years of head coaching experience. Has coached both men and women at the collegiate and professional levels, has coached and played in a national championship game. Currently coaches for the Carolina Dynamo Soccer club.

Roster in State: 14 **Out of State:** 10 **Out of Country:** 0
ODP State: 3 **Regional:** **National:**
Walk-on/Other: 4 **Graduation %:** 100 **Seniors on Team:** 3
Positions Needed: Striker, Outside Midfield, Sweeper, Marking Back
Camp or Clinic Dates: July 22-27, 2001
Most Recent Record: 7-12-0
Schedule: Catawba College, Pfeiffer Univ. Francis Marion Univ. University of North Florida, Longwood College
Style of Play: We play a possession oriented style of soccer focusing on high pressure zonal defending. We always play with 3 frontrunners and focus on team attacking and defending shape. Our intense style during games is fostered in our challenging training sessions and year-round program.

Mars Hill College
Academic Profile

Mars Hill, NC 28754
Phone: (330) 672-2121

Type: 4 Yr.,Private,Liberal Arts
Founded: 1856
Website: http://www.mhc.edu
Religion: Baptist
SAT/ACT/GPA: 820/2.5
Housing: Yes
Student/Faculty Ratio: 13:1
Male/Female Ratio: 52:48
Undergraduate Enrollment: 1,200
Graduate Enrollment: N/A
Scholarships/Academic: Yes **Athletic:** Yes **Financial Aid:** Yes
Expenses by: Year **In State:** $ 12,700 **Out of State:** $ 12,700
Specialty: Numerous
Degrees Conferred: BA, BS, BM, BSM, BFA
Programs of Study: Business Administration & Economics, Business/Office and Marketing/Distribution, Education, Fine Arts, Health, Humanities, Life Science, Natural Science & Mathematics, Physical Education & Recreation, Social Behavioral Sciences, Sport Medicine

Men's Athletic Profile

P.O. Box 666 B
Mars Hill, NC 28754
Coach: Mr. Kelly Findlay
Email: kfindley@mhc.edu

NCAA II
Lions/Royal Blue, Gold
Phone: 828-639-1227-
Fax: 8286891521

Estimated # of Men's Soccer Scholarships: varies
Conference: South Atlantic Conference
Program Profile: We have a natural grass playing field surrounded by the Blue Ridge Mountains. Facilities include press box, locker rooms, separate practice facility.
History: Program began collegiately play in 1985.
Achievements: South Atlantic Conference Tournament Champs in 1997. 2 All-Americans, 2 Professional players 20 All-Region 35 All-Conference, conference tournament champs, 2x conference champs, NCAA top 25 players

Coaching: Mr. Kelly findley, six years professional experience. 3x NAIA All-American, 2x NSCAA All-American, USSF "A" License, NSCAA advanced national diploma

Roster In State: 3 **Out of State:** 16 **Out of Country:** 2
ODP State: 9 **Regional:** 1 **National:**
Walk-on/Other: **Graduation %:** 80 **Seniors on Team:** 1
Positions Needed: All
Camp or Clinic Dates: Not Available
Most Recent Record: 7-14-0
Style of Play: Possession oriented and generate attack from the back.

Women's Athletic Profile

100 Athletic St
Mars Hill, NC 28754
Coach: David Bennett
Email: dbennett@mhc.edu

NCAA II
Lady Lions/Blue, White
Phone: (828) 689-1171
Fax: (828) 689-1501

Estimated # of Women's Soccer Scholarships: 3.5
Conference: South Atlantic Conference (SAC)
Program Profile: We have a fully equipped training room and team training. Our home field is a natural grass and lights. It measures 68 x 118. It has a seating capacity of 500. Our season is in the fall with an abbreviated spring season.
History: Our first season was in 1992. Our team has posted a better record each year since its inception including the 10-6-2 record in 1996. In 1997 we ranked 23rd in the nation Division II and from 1996 to 1998 3 consecutive top ten regional ranking.
Achievements: 1997 Coach of the Year; 6 All-region players; 1997 national ranking 23rd.
Coaching: Dave Bennett, Head Coach, has been with us since inception of the program. In 1997 he was SAC Coach of the Year. He holds a USSF and NSCAA National license.
Roster in State: 5 **Out of State:** 15 **Out of Country:**
ODP State: 3 **Regional:** **National:**
Walk-on/Other: **Graduation %:** 80 **Seniors on Team:** 3
Positions Needed: Defenders, Midfielders, Forwards
Camp or Clinic Dates: Not Available
Most Recent Record: 6-12-0
Schedule: UNC-Asheville, Presbyterian College, Catawba College, Fransis Marion University
Style of Play: Possession oriented-quick counter attack, semi-zonal defense.

Meredith College

Academic Profile

Phone:

Raleigh, NC 27607-5298

Type: 4 Yr.,Private,Liberal Arts
Website: http://www.meredith.edu
SAT/ACT/GPA: 800
Student/Faculty Ratio: 17:1
Undergraduate Enrollment: 2,000
Scholarships/Academic: Yes **Athletic:** No
Expenses by: Year **In State:** $ 14,090
Specialty: Liberal Arts

Founded: 1891
Religion: Historically Baptist
Housing: Yes
Male/Female Ratio: Women
Graduate Enrollment: 800
Financial Aid: Yes
Out of State: $ 14,090

Degrees Conferred: BA, BS, BMus, MBA, M.Ed., Master of Health Administration
Programs of Study: Accounting, American Civilization, Art, Biology, Business, Chemistry, Communications, Computer Science, Criminal Justice, Dance, Economics, Education, English, Fashion Merchandising, French, Health Science, History, Home Economics, International Business International Studies, Management, Mathematics, Medical Technology, Music, Nutrition, Political Science, PreDentistry, PreLaw, PreMed, PreVet, Psychology, Religion, Social Work, Theatre

Women's Athletic Profile

3800 Hillsborough Street
Raleigh, NC 27607-5298
Coach: Glad Bugariu
Email: Not Available

NCAA III
Angels/Maroon, Grey
Phone: (919) 760-2250
Fax: (919) 760-2341

Estimated # of Women's Soccer Scholarships: None
Conference: Independent Conference
Program Profile: Facilities include a new 120x85 yards, Bermuda grass soccer field. Year-round training program. State-of-the-art weight room, Spring soccer, and several indoor tournaments.
History: Program began in 1993 and has improved every year from a record of 8-8-1 in 1997 to 11-5-2 in 1999.
Achievements: Jessica Brooks holds 2 NCAA records, single season scoring, NCAA All-Time leader in scoring in all Divisions. Scottie Eustis 1st Team Academic All-American.
Coaching: Glad Bugariu, Head Coach, USSF "B" license NSCAA National Diploma, former Head Coach Women's Soccer and Men's Asst. at Louisburg College, former all region player with Brevard College and Emory and Henry College. Played in Romanian 4th Division with Solmii Sibiu.
Roster in State: 10 **Out of State:** 5 **Out of Country:**
Walk-on/Other: **Graduation %:** **Seniors on Team:** 4
Camp or Clinic Dates: Not Available
Most Recent Record: 11-5-2
Schedule: University of the South, Methodist College, NC Wesleyan College, Greensboro College, Washington and Lee
Style of Play: Dictated by the type of players available.

Methodist College

Academic Profile

Phone: (910) 630-7182

Fayetteville, NC 28311

Type: 4 Yr.,Private,Liberal Arts
Website: http://www.methodist.edu
SAT/ACT/GPA: 800/2.0
Student/Faculty Ratio: 17:1
Undergraduate Enrollment: 1,700
Scholarships/Academic: Yes **Athletic:** No
Expenses by: Year **In State:** $ 16,000
Specialty: Business
Degrees Conferred: BS, BA

Founded: 1954
Religion: United Methodist
Housing: Yes
Male/Female Ratio: 2:1
Graduate Enrollment: N/A
Financial Aid: Yes
Out of State: $ 16,000

Programs of Study: Business and Management, Education, Criminal Justice, Sports Medicine, Physician's Assistant, Physical Education, Sports Management, Social Work, Art, Theatre, Communications, Accounting, Professional Golf Management, Professional Tennis Management, Music, Foreign Languages, Marketing, Mathematics

Men's Athletic Profile

5400 Ramsey Street
Fayetteville, NC 28311
Coach: Adrian Blewitt
Email: ablewitt@earthlink.net

NCAA III
Monarchs/Green, Gold
Phone: (910) 630-7097
Fax: (910) 630-7676

Estimated # of Men's Soccer Scholarships: N/A
Conference: Dixie Intercollegiate Athletic Conference
Program Profile: We have a fenced in, 120 x 76 yards, Bermuda grass complex. Locker rooms, press box and coaches office make it one of the best facilities in the country.
History: Our program began in the 1950's.
Style of Play: Attractive, attacking soccer.

Women's Athletic Profile

5400 Ramsey Street
Fayetteville, NC 28311
Coach: Bobby Graham
Email: bgraham@methodist.edu

NCAA III
Monarchs/Gold, Green
Phone: (910) 630-7096
Fax: (910) 488-7676

Estimated # of Women's Soccer Scholarships: None
Conference: Dixie Intercollegiate Athletic Conference (DIAC)
Program Profile: Brilliant natural grass soccer complex. The offices and lockers are by the fields. Described by Soccer Jr. Magazine as "one of the best places to watch college soccer".
History: Program began in 1985. Has four NCAA Division III finalist, four appearances in the Final Four, and the 1996 National Finalist, Conference Champions nine times.
Achievements: 21 All-Americans, 31 All-South Selections and 9 Academic All-Americans. NCAA Tournament 1986,87,89,90,93,94, and 1995. South Regional Champions NCAA Final Four, Conference Champions (DIXIE) and no players drafted as of yet.
Coaching: Bobby Graham, Head Coach as of 1999. 1988 graduate of Methodist College.
Roster in State: 9 **Out of State:** 8 **Out of Country:** 0
ODP State: 0 **Regional:** 0 **National:** 0
Walk-on/Other: 0 **Graduation %:** 100 **Seniors on Team:** 1
Positions Needed: I would like to be deep in every position.
Camp or Clinic Dates: Not Available
Most Recent Record: 10-7-2
Schedule: NC Wesleyan College, Christopher Newport Univ. University of the South, Oglethrope University, Savannah College of Art and Design.
Style of Play: Aggressive and in your face.

Montreat College

Academic Profile

Montreat, NC 28757
Phone: (828) 669-8011

Type: 4 Yr.,Private,Liberal Arts
Founded: 1916
Website: http://www.montreat.edu
Religion: Presbyterian
SAT/ACT/GPA: 860/18/2-3
Housing: Yes
Student/Faculty Ratio: 12:1
Male/Female Ratio: 50:50
Undergraduate Enrollment: 500
Graduate Enrollment: N/A
Scholarships/Academic: Yes **Athletic:** Yes **Financial Aid:** Yes
Expenses by: Year **In State:** $ 15,272 **Out of State:** $ 15,272
Specialty: Outdoor Education, Business
Degrees Conferred: BA, BS
Programs of Study: Accounting, Bible Studies, Business and Management, Ecology, Economics, English, Environmental Studies, History, Human Services, Liberal Arts, Mathematics, Missionary Studies, Religion, Secondary Education, Social Sciences

Men's Athletic Profile

P.O. Box 1267
Montreat, NC 28757
Coach: David Ballenger
Email: dballenger@montreat.edu

NAIA
Cavaliers/Blue, White
Phone: (704) 669-8011x3410
Fax: (704) 669-8014

Estimated # of Men's Soccer Scholarships: N/A
Conference: Tennessee-Virginia Athletic Conference (TVAC)
Program Profile: Year-round program - competitive fall season; indoor season; spring season. Outdoor facility includes natural grass field.
History: Began in 1968; 1996 record is 6-11-1.
Coaching: David Ballenger, Head Coach, holds a USSF 'A' license, has a NSCAA Advanced National Diploma, and is a former USISL player.
Style of Play: Possession - 1/2 touch; high pressure zonal defense.

Women's Athletic Profile

P.O. Box 1267
Montreat, NC 28757
Coach: Michael White
Email: mwhite@montreat.edu

NAIA
Cavaliers/Navy, White, Gold
Phone: (704) 669-8011
Fax: (704) 669-9554

Estimated # of Women's Soccer Scholarships: N/A
Conference: Tennessee-Virginia Athletic Conference
Program Profile: Year-round play - competitive fall season, indoor season, spring season, outdoor facility, natural grass.
History: Our program began in 1995 with a record of 6-5-1, and lost the first match in the playoffs. Our 1996 record was 10-8.
Coaching: Michael White, Head Coach, became head coach in 1998 and has a USSF "B" License. David Ballenger, Assistant Coach, has a USSF "A" license and an NSCAA Advanced National Diploma. He is a former USISL player.
Style of Play: Possession - 1/2 touch; high pressure zonal defense.

Mount Olive College

Academic Profile

Phone: (919) 658-5056

Mount Olive, NC 28365

Type: 4 Yr.,Private,Liberal Arts
Founded: 1951
Website: http://www.mountolivetrojans.com
Religion: Free-will Baptist
SAT/ACT/GPA: 820/18/2.5
Housing: Yes
Student/Faculty Ratio: 15:1
Male/Female Ratio: 2:1
Undergraduate Enrollment: 1,600
Graduate Enrollment: N/A
Scholarships/Academic: Yes **Athletic:** Yes
Financial Aid: Yes
Expenses by: Year **In State:** $ 12,810
Out of State: $ 12,810
Specialty: Liberal Arts, Sciences, Business, Criminal Justice, English, Math
Degrees Conferred: BA, BS, BAS
Programs of Study: Arts, Biology, English, Communications, English with Secondary School Education, Fine Arts, General Studies, History, Music, Psychology, Recreation & Leisure Studies, Business Administration, Church Ministries, Criminal Justice, Math, PreMed, PreVet, PreDental, Pharmacy

Men's Athletic Profile

634 Henderson St.
Mount Olive, NC 28365
Coach: Philmore George
Email: moc.soccer@hotmail.com

NCAA II
Trojans/Green, White, Black
Phone: (919) 658-5056
Fax: (919) 658-1753

Estimated # of Men's Soccer Scholarships:
Conference: Carolina-Virginia Athletic Conference (CVAC)

Program Profile: The Trojans is a small NCAA Division III team made up of players having the opportunity to still play, while obtaining a quality education from a small school atmosphere. Facilities include excellent outdoor and indoor facilities. Our playing fields is natural grass.
History: We started in 1995. We moved from NAIA to NCAA in 1995.
Achievements: 1994 second in conference tournament; 1996 third in the regular season and second in the conference tournament.
Coaching: Philmore George, Head Coach, has a FA preliminary coaching license. He trained with professional clubs in England and played semi-pro. He is a 4 time All-American. He played with the Bandits in the USISL. Our Assistant Coach, Keith London, played for the Guyana National team at the Junior and senior level. He was a member of NJCAA championship.
Style of Play: A combination of the Dutch system, using players effectively in small group situations to building cohesion along flair like Brazil, to be creative in one on one opportunity, all combined with hard work.

Women's Athletic Profile

634 Henderson St.
Mount Olive, NC 28365
Coach: Philmore George
Email: moc_soccer@hotmail.com

NCAA II
Trojans/Green, White
Phone: (919) 658-5056
Fax: (919) 658-1753

Estimated # of Women's Soccer Scholarships: None
Conference: Carolinas Virginia Athletic Conference (CVAC)
Program Profile: The Trojans is a small NCAA Division III team made up of players having an opportunity to still play while obtaining a quality education from a small school atmosphere. Facilities are excellent outdoor and indoor facility. We have a new field in 1997.
History: The program will going into the fifth season and has been building gradually.
Achievements: None
Coaching: Philmore George, Head Coach, four-year All-American at Tiffin University, attended graduate school at Marshall University and assisted with the men's team. He also founded and coached the first women's club team there, and earned the English Football Association Coaching Badge. Trained with five professional clubs in England, play semi-pro, four-time All-American, played with Lexington Bandits in the USISL. Has two assistant coaches and two managers.
Style of Play: Work to keep the ball and look for opportunities wherever they may arise.

North Carolina State University

Academic Profile

Ads
Raleigh, NC 27659

Phone: (919) 515-3013

Type: 4 Yr.,Public,Engineering
Website: http://www.ncsu.edu
SAT/ACT/GPA: Varies
Student/Faculty Ratio: 13:1
Undergraduate Enrollment: 18,700
Scholarships/Academic: Yes **Athletic:** Yes
Expenses by: Year **In State:** $ 4.085
Specialty: Engineering and Textiles
Degrees Conferred: Various

Founded: 1887
Religion: Non-Affiliated
Housing: Yes
Male/Female Ratio: 58:42
Graduate Enrollment: 8,900
Financial Aid: Yes
Out of State: $ 14,296

Programs of Study: Agriculture & Life Sciences, Design, Education, Engineering, Forest Resources, Humanities, Management, Mathematics, Physical Sciences, Psychology, Social Science, Textiles

Men's Athletic Profile

Box 8501
Raleigh, NC 27695
Coach: Gege Tarantini
Email: george-taratini@ncsu.edu

NCAA I
Wolfpack/Red, White
Phone: (919) 515-3013
Fax: (919) 515-1904

Estimated # of Men's Soccer Scholarships: N/A
Conference: Atlantic Coast Conference
Program Profile: Method Road Stadium seats 5,000 and is a natural grass playing surface (Bermuda Grass) with a measurements of 120x80 yards. North Carolina State plays from August until November. We have a locker rooms, new weight rooms and 3 training fields.
History: We began in 1950 with Eric DeGroat as a Head Coach. There have been 7 head coaches, never finished lower than sixth in conference before 1996. Our overall record from 1950 to 1998 is 364-268-55 and conference record is 75-143-23.
Achievements: George Tarantini was named ACC Coach of the Year in 1992 & 1994; 7 ACC Atlantic Players of the Year, Atlantic Coast Conference Tournament Champions in 1990; 57 All-ACC players; 11 All-Americans; 19 players in pro-soccer.
Coaching: George Tarantini is the Head Coach. Kurt Sokolowski is the Assistant Coach.
Style of Play: Southern American Style; aggressive, attacking tempo.

Women's Athletic Profile

Box 8501
Raleigh, NC 27695-8501
Coach: Laura Kerrigan
Email: laura_kerrigan@ncsu.edu

NCAA I
Wolfpack/Red, White
Phone: (919) 515-3476
Fax: (919) 515-5443

Estimated # of Women's Soccer Scholarships: 12
Conference: Atlantic Coast Conference
Program Profile: Our home field is Method Road Stadium, which has an exceptional playing surface. It has been the host field for the 1990 and 1993 ACC women's soccer tournaments. We have access to two fully-equipped weight rooms supervised by professional strength training coaches. Our training room facility is equipped with a superb Sports Medicine and training staff headed by Charlie Rozanski.
History: NC State began its women's soccer program in 1984 and almost immediately became a contender for the national championship. In all, the Wolfpack has eleven NCAA appearances, including two trips to the Final Four, and eight trips to the Final Eight.
Achievements: 5 WUSA drafted and allocated players, 23 Athletic & Academic All Americans, 1 National Coach of the Year.
Coaching: Laura Kerrigan, Head Coach, is a former Wolfpack, an ISAA and an Academic All-American. Betsy Anderson and Lindsay Cobb and Megan Jeidy are the Assistant Coaches.

Roster in State: 6	**Out of State:** 18	**Out of Country:** 2
ODP State: 14	**Regional:** 4	**National:** 2
Walk-on/Other:	**Graduation %:** 100	**Seniors on Team:** 3

Camp or Clinic Dates: July 18-22 and July 24-28 2001
Most Recent Record: 10-6-3
Schedule: UNC Chapel Hill, Clemson, University of Virginia, Duke, Wake Forest, Florida State, Maryland, Tennessee, Brown
Style of Play: Possession/ indirect.

North Carolina Wesleyan College

Academic Profile

Rocky Mount, NC 27804

Phone: (252) 985-5209

Type: 4 Yr.,Private,Liberal Arts
Website: http://www.ncwc.edu
SAT/ACT/GPA: 850/2.0
Student/Faculty Ratio: 1:13
Undergraduate Enrollment: 1,000
Scholarships/Academic: Yes **Athletic:** No
Expenses by: Year **In State:** $ 14,000
Founded: 1956
Religion: Methodist
Housing: Yes
Male/Female Ratio: 1:1
Graduate Enrollment: N/A
Financial Aid: Yes
Out of State: $ 14,000
Degrees Conferred: BA, BS
Programs of Study: Accounting, Biology, Business Administration, Chemistry, Computer Information Systems, Elementary Education, English, Environmental Science, Food Services and Hotel Management, History, Justice Studies, Mathematics, Middle Grades Education, Philosophy-Religious Studies, Physical Education, Political Science, Psychology, Religious Studies, Secondary Education Certification, Sociology-Anthropology, Theatre

Men's Athletic Profile

3400 North Wesleyan Blvd.
Rocky Mount, NC 27804
Coach: Greg Vogel
Email: gvogel@ncwc.edu

NCAA III
Battling Bishops/R. Blue, Gold
Phone: (252) 985-5209
Fax: (252) 985-5252

Estimated # of Men's Soccer Scholarships: N/A
Conference: Dixie Intercollegiate Athletic Conference
Program Profile: We play on 120x80 bermuda surface. one of the best in the nation with a seating capacity of 2,000. We, also have two practice fields.
History: This program has a strong tradition and is currently making a push to becoming one of the strongest teams in the south. In 1998, we were Top ten in South Region.
Achievements: We have 3 Conference Titles, 15 All-American players and 2 pro players.
Coaching: Greg Vogel, Head Coach, is entering his second season, was a former professional player with overseas experience in Greek 2nd Division. He has seven years college coaching experience.
Style of Play: Strong attacking possession. Solid defense team shape. Creativity in the attacking 1/3 and strong transitional awareness.

Women's Athletic Profile

3400 N Wesleyan Boulevard
Rocky Mountain, NC 27804
Coach: Kelly Walters
Email: kwalters@ncwc.edu

NCAA III
Battling Bishops/R. Blue, Gold
Phone: (252) 985-5215
Fax: (252) 985-5252

Estimated # of Women's Soccer Scholarships: None
Conference: Dixie Intercollegiate Athletic Conference
Program Profile: Year-round program, one of the top Division III program in the country. field considered one of the best in any division. Bermuda "tifton" grass that has a seating capacity of 1,200 with a scoreboard, fenced in and will have light in the year 2001.
History: The program began in 1983.
Achievements: The program produced 25 All-South players; 6 All-American; 1994 Division Player of the Year; 84 All-Dixie Conference players. We have been the Conference Champions the past 2 seasons. We have finished in the top 25 in NCAA III the past 2 years. Last season we lost to the defending National Champs 1-0 in overtime.

Coaching: Entering 3rd season at her alma mater. NSCAA National Diploma. North Carolina U-13 east ODP girls coach. Conference Coach of the Year past 2 seasons.
Roster in State: 3 **Out of State:** 14 **Out of Country:** 0
ODP State: 6 **Regional:** **National:**
Walk-on/Other: **Graduation %:** 100 **Seniors on Team:** 1
Positions Needed: Mids, Forward, Keeper
Camp or Clinic Dates: Call for information
Most Recent Record: 16-4-1
Style of Play: Team devoted itself to an attacking style with an emphasis on possession. Team defense is also stressed where everyone defends and everyone attacks. The team is committed to each other to accomplish their goals.

Pfieffer University

Academic Profile

Misenheimer, NC 28109
Phone: 800-338-2060

Type: 4 Yr.,Private,Liberal Arts
Founded: 1885
Website: http://www.pfeiffer.edu
Religion: Methodist
SAT/ACT/GPA: 820/17/2.0
Housing: Yes
Student/Faculty Ratio: 15:1
Male/Female Ratio: 1:1
Undergraduate Enrollment: 800
Graduate Enrollment: 600
Scholarships/Academic: Yes **Athletic:** Yes **Financial Aid:** Yes
Expenses by: Year **In State:** $ 15,211 **Out of State:** $ 15,211
Specialty: Business, Athletic Training, Sports Medicine
Degrees Conferred: BA, BS, MBA, Masters
Programs of Study: Accounting, Arts Administration, Biology, Business Administration, Chemistry, Economics, Elementary Education, Law, Journalism, Engineering, Sociology, Sport Management, Sport Medicine, Psychology, Physical Education History, Mathematics

Men's Athletic Profile

P.O. Box 960
Misenheimer, NC 28109
Coach: Chris Neal
Email: coachneal@aol.com

NCAA II
Falcons/Black, Gold
Phone: (704) 463-1360
Fax: (704) 463-5051

Estimated # of Men's Soccer Scholarships: 3.5
Conference: Carolinas-Virginia Athletic Conference
Program Profile: The home field is Bermuda grass, 12 x 78 yards and seats 500. We also have a natural Bermuda training field. We play on Mercer Athletic Complex. Program is sponsored by Puma.
History: the first year of the program was in 1958. We joined NCAA Division II in 1996.
Achievements: 1997 Regular Season Conference Champions; 1998 ranked #13 by NSCAA; 1997 NSCAA All-American was Matt Harmer.
Coaching: Chris Neal, Head Coach, is entering his second year with the program. He compiled a record of 12-6-1. He graduated from University of North Carolina-Wilmington in 1995 and Augustana State University in 1998.
Style of Play: Team is knowledgeable and competent in various systems of play. Build attack from the back. Defending fluctuates from zonal to aggressive man marking system.

Women's Athletic Profile

P.O. Box 960, Hwy. 52
Misenheimer, NC 28109
Coach: Chad Miller
Email: cmiller@pfeiffer.edu

NCAA II
Lady Falcons/Gold, Black
Phone: (704) 463-1360
Fax: (704) 463-5051

Estimated # of Women's Soccer Scholarships: 3.5
Conference: Carolinas-Virginia Athletic Conference
Program Profile: We are a young program with the desire to get better and earn respect. We are only losing 1 starter from '99. Tough conference and regional schedule. We play on NE Liftko field with natural grass and 500 seating capacity.
History: This program began in 1993, a very young program. Of course the program struggled the first four years, we have had four coaches in four years. In the 1999 season we had a turnaround finishing 3rd in conference and 2nd in the CVAC Tournament.
Achievements: 2 players 2nd team All-Conference, 3 players All Tournament team
Coaching: Chad Miller, Head Coach, and Steve Brdarski, Assistant Coach, but have a USSF license
Roster in State: 7 **Out of State:** 24 **Out of Country:** 1
ODP State: 7 **Regional:** **National:**
Walk-on/Other: 4 **Graduation %:** 100 **Seniors on Team:** 5
Positions Needed: Defense, Forwards, Midfielders
Camp or Clinic Dates: May 29-June2
Most Recent Record: 12-7-2
Schedule: Belmont Abbey College, Longwood College, North Florida University, USC Spartanburg University, Francis Marion University, Catawba College, Queens College, High Point University
Style of Play: Possession - build out of the back in our 4-4-2 or 3-4-3 formation. Still building a style of play into team. Excellent when play as in ground not as good as in the air. Man marking, played in 1997. Team vastly improved in 1997.

Queens College

Academic Profile

Phone:
Charlotte, NC 28274

Type: 4 Yr.,Private,Liberal Arts **Founded:** 1857
Website: Not Available **Religion:** Presbyterian
SAT/ACT/GPA: 970-1160/20-26/3.1 **Housing:** Yes
Student/Faculty Ratio: 13:1 **Male/Female Ratio:** 1:2
Undergraduate Enrollment: 1600 **Graduate Enrollment:** N/A
Scholarships/Academic: Yes **Athletic:** Yes **Financial Aid:** Yes
Expenses by: Year **In State:** $ 18,580 **Out of State:** $ 18,580
Degrees Conferred: BS, BA, BM, BSN, MBA, MAT, MA
Programs of Study: Accounting, American Studies, Art, BioChemistry, Biology, Business Administration, Communications, Education, English, Drama, Foreign Languages, History, Mathematics, Music, Nursing, Philosophy, Political Science, Psychology, Religion; Can be combined with over 50 concentrations.

Men's Athletic Profile

1900 Selwyn Avenue
Charlotte, NC 28274
Coach: Fred Nchi
Email: norchif@queens.edu

NCAA II
Royals/Royal Blue
Phone: (704) 337-2530
Fax: (704) 337-2237

Estimated # of Men's Soccer Scholarships:
Conference: Carolinas-Virginia Athletic Conference
Program Profile: Play on 118 x 74 yard Bermuda Field. Has 17 game Fall season plus conference tournament. Has 5 games during Spring season.
History: Program began in 1990. Team and coach record in 1990-1999 is 124-50-8. Fred Norchi is the head coach since its inception. Team never has a losing season. Ranked Top 25 Division II five years out of nine years.

Achievements: 1991 National Shoot-out record, 14 shutouts in 17 games; 1994 Fred Norchi, NCAA II South Region Coach of the Year. Entered CVA Conference in 1995; won conference tournament in 1995, and 1996. CVAC Player of the Year 1995 - Bill Kennedy; CVAC Player of the Year - Kevin Yearick; 1st team All-American - Bill Kennedy, 1996; Fred Norchi - CVAC Coach of the Year, 1996. The 1999 season; All-Americans Jeff Yearick, Travis Bobb, Fred Norchi was Southeast Region Coach of the Year, CVAC Coach of the Year. We were NCAA Quarterfinalists. Finished the season ranked 7th in the nation, 1st in Southeast.
Coaching: Fred Norchi, Head Coach, holds a USSF 'A' license and a M.E.D. Physical Education. Ben Graham, Assistant Coach, BS in Business Administration form College of Charleston
Walk-on/Other: **Graduation %:** Excellent **Seniors on Team:** 6
Camp or Clinic Dates: June 5-9, June 26-30, July 31- August 4
Most Recent Record: 18-4-0
Schedule: USC Spartanburg, Lander, Wingate. University of North Florida, Francis Marion, Rollins
Style of Play: Short passing game primarily. Over 3 goals per game average in 1995. Man on man defense with sweeper, 4-4-2 system. Looks for defensive stability first and then attack on a strong base.

Women's Athletic Profile

1900 Selwyn Avenue
Charlotte, NC 28274
Coach: Jonathan W Brabson
Email: brabsonj@queens.edu

NCAA II
Royals/Blue, White
Phone: (704) 337-2540
Fax: (704) 337-2237

Estimated # of Women's Soccer Scholarships: 3.5
Conference: Carolina - Virginia Athletic Conference
Program Profile: Our home playing field is solid Bermuda grass, 120 x 75 yards, in great condition. Our playing season is in the fall with 16-games and playoffs combined with a Spring Season.
History: Our program began in 1989.
Achievements: We have produced numerous All-Conference, Conference Players of the Year, All-South players, and 1 All-American
Coaching: Johnathan W. Brabson, Head Coach, has an Advanced National diploma from NSCAA
Roster in State: 4 **Out of State:** 9 **Out of Country:**
Walk-on/Other: **Graduation %:** 99 **Seniors on Team:** 1
Positions Needed: Goalkeeper, Forwards, Defense
Camp or Clinic Dates: Not Available
Schedule: Presbyterian College, Belmont Abbey College, Catawba College, Lynn University, Barry University, Francis Marion University, Longwood College
Style of Play: 4-4-2 system, very technical short passing game. Man-to Man defense with sweeper. All positions attack and defend. Hard working very disciplined team that has a good chemistry with each other.

Saint Andrews Presbyterian College

Academic Profile

Laurinburg, NC 28352

Phone: 800-763-0198

Type: 4 Yr.,Private,Liberal Arts
Website: http://www.sapc.edu
SAT/ACT/GPA: 820/17/2.0
Student/Faculty Ratio: 12:1
Undergraduate Enrollment: 600
Scholarships/Academic: Yes **Athletic:** Yes
Expenses by: Year **In State:** $ 18,500
Degrees Conferred: BA, BS

Founded: 1958
Religion: Presbyterian
Housing: Yes
Male/Female Ratio: 2:1
Graduate Enrollment: N/A
Financial Aid: Yes
Out of State: $ 18,500

Programs of Study: Art, BioChemistry, Biology, Business, Chemistry, Communications, Theatre, Creative Writing, Education, English, Environmental Science, History, International Business, Math, Math Computer Science, Music, Philosophy, Physical Education, Sports Management, Politics, Psychology, Religious Studies, Sports Medicine, Accounting, Dentistry, Engineering, Law, Medicine, Equine Studies

Men's Athletic Profile

1700 Dogwood Mile
Laurinburg, NC 28352
Coach: Lance Watkins
Email: watkins@tartans.sapc.edu

NCAA II
Knights/Royal Blue, White
Phone: (910) 277-5428
Fax: (910) 277-5272

Estimated # of Men's Soccer Scholarships: .5
Conference: Carolinas-Virginia Athletic Conference
Program Profile: We play fall playing season, with a non-traditional season consisting of practice and weight training. The game facility is a natural grass field enclosed in ropes with an unlimited capacity. The facility also includes a natural grass practice field.
History: The program began in the early 1960's competing at the Division III level. It then moved to NAIA status and now competes at the NCAA Division II level in the CVAC Conference.
Achievements: One Conference Title; 3 All-Americans
Coaching: Lance Watkins is the Head Coach.
Roster In State: 3 **Out of State:** 17 **Out of Country:** 1
ODP State: 3 **Regional:** **National:**
Walk-on/Other: **Graduation %:** N/A **Seniors on Team:** 1
Positions Needed: Goalkeeper, Midfield, Defense
Camp or Clinic Dates: Not Available
Most Recent Record: 6-12-1
Schedule: Queens College, Belmont Abbey College, Barton College, Lees-McRae College, Catawba College, UNC-Pembroke
Style of Play: Controlled, possession style of play.

Women's Athletic Profile

1700 Dogwood Mile
Laurinburg, NC 28352
Coach: Stevan Hernandez
Email: hernandez@tartan.sapc.edu

NCAA II
Knights/Royal, White, Black
Phone: (910) 277-5274
Fax: (910) 277-5272

Estimated # of Women's Soccer Scholarships: 3.5
Conference: CVAC
Program Profile: NCAA-II, one game field with natural surroundings, 3 practice fields, sand soccer facility.
History: Re-Started the program in the fall of 1999.
Coaching: Stevan Hernandez is the Head coach and Liz Bowden is the Assistant.
Roster in State: 2 **Out of State:** 15 **Out of Country:** 1
ODP State: 2 **Regional:** **National:**
Walk-on/Other: **Graduation %:** 75 **Seniors on Team:** 2
Positions Needed: Center Mid, Stopper, Sweeper
Camp or Clinic Dates: TBA
Most Recent Record: 3-13-0
Schedule: Pfeiffer, Belmont Abbey, Lees McRae, Longwood, Wingate, Queens, Barton, Erskine
Style of Play: Aggressive, high pressure attacking style.

University of North Carolina - Asheville

Academic Profile

Asheville, NC 28804

Phone: (828) 251-6386

Type: 4 Yr.,Public,Liberal Arts
Founded: 1927
Website: http://www.cs.unca.edu
Religion: Non-Affiliated
SAT/ACT/GPA: 1000/20/3.0
Housing: Yes
Student/Faculty Ratio: 19:1
Male/Female Ratio: 47:53
Undergraduate Enrollment: 3,000
Graduate Enrollment: N/A
Scholarships/Academic: Yes **Athletic:** Yes **Financial Aid:** Yes
Expenses by: Year **In State:** $ 6,603 **Out of State:** $ 13,086
Specialty: Meteorology, Business, Computer Science, Psychology
Degrees Conferred: BA, BS, BFA, M
Programs of Study: Accounting, Actuarial Science, Applied Mathematics, Art, Atmospheric Science, Biology, Business and Management, Chemistry, Classics, Communications, Computer Information Systems, Computer Science, Economics, Education, English, Environmental Science, Finance, French, German, Greek, Health Services, History, Latin, Literature, Marketing, Mathematics, Music, Philosophy, Physics, Political Science, Psychology, Social Science, Spanish, Theatre

Men's Athletic Profile

One University Heights
Asheville, NC 28804
Coach: Steve Coruish
Email: scoruish@unca.edu

NCAA I
Bulldogs/Royal Blue, White
Phone: (828) 251-6938
Fax: (828) 251-6386

Estimated # of Men's Soccer Scholarships: 6
Conference: Big South Conference
Program Profile: Facilities include lighted training field and 120 x 75 game field. Mid level Division I in Arguaby the toughest region in the country. The program always looks to add nationally ranked non-conference opponents.
History: Started in NCAA D. I in 1986. Been a member of Big South Conference since inception and has developed into being a very competitive member.
Achievements: NCAA District Championship game 1981. Big South Semi-finals 1988-1991. 1995 Coach of the Year.
Coaching: Steve Cornish is our Head Coach. He holds USSF 'A', FA licenses, and he is ODP Regional coach.
Roster In State: 18 **Out of State:** 6 **Out of Country:** 0
ODP State: 7 **Regional:** 3 **National:** 0
Walk-on/Other: 0 **Graduation %:** 100 **Seniors on Team:** 6
Positions Needed: 2 Defenders, Forwards
Camp or Clinic Dates: Not Available
Most Recent Record: 8-11-0
Schedule: North Carolina, Kentucky, Liberty
Style of Play: Varies depending on personnel and opponent.

Women's Athletic Profile

1 University Heights
Asheville, NC 28804
Coach: Michele Cornish
Email: Not Available

NCAA I
Bulldogs/Royal, White
Phone: (704) 251-6459
Fax: (704) 251-6386

Estimated # of Women's Soccer Scholarships: None
Conference: Big South

University of North Carolina - Chapel Hill

Academic Profile

Ads
Chapel Hill, NC 27515

Phone:

Type: 4 Yr.,Public,Liberal Arts
Website: http://www.ga.unc.edu
SAT/ACT/GPA:
Student/Faculty Ratio: 10:1
Undergraduate Enrollment: 18,000
Scholarships/Academic: Yes **Athletic:** Yes
Expenses by: Year **In State:** $ 7,000
Specialty: Liberal Arts

Founded: 1792
Religion: Non-Affiliated
Housing: Yes
Male/Female Ratio: 40:60
Graduate Enrollment: 7,000
Financial Aid: Yes
Out of State: $ 17,000

Degrees Conferred: Bachelors, Masters, Doctoral, Professional Degree
Programs of Study: African Studies, American Studies, Art, Astronomy, History, BioStatistics, Biology, Dental, Economics, Engineering, Geology, Geography, Health, Math, Recreation, Political, Physical, Physics, Sociology, Religious

Men's Athletic Profile

P.O. Box 2126, Men's Soccer UNC, CB#8600
Chapel Hill, NC 27514
Coach: Elmar Bolowich
Email: oweiss@uncaa.unc.edu

NCAA I
Tar Heels/Carolina Blue, White
Phone: (919) 962-0466
Fax: (919) 962-4038

Estimated # of Men's Soccer Scholarships: 9.9
Conference: Atlantic Coast Conference
Program Profile: One of the top men's soccer programs in the country. The best proving ground for future professional players. Facilities are state of the art: 6600 square feet soccer center with offices, locker rooms, team meeting room, conference room, laundry facility. 5700 capacity Fetzer Field (natural grass), 4 field training facility, Academic Support Center, Weight training room.
History: Program began in 1947. Produced several impact players for Major League Soccer and 4 full US National Team members as well as several Olympians.
Achievements: 19 All-Americans, 85 All-South Selections, 99 All-ACC Selections, 2 ACC Championships (1987 & 2000), 1 Final Four appearance, Finished regular season ranked #1 in 2000. ACC Coach of the Year (2000), ACC Player of the Year (2000).
Coaching: Elmar Bolowich, Head Coach, has been with our program from 1989 to the present. He took over the program as only the fourth coach in school history in 1989. He holds a USSF 'A' license, holds a USSF ODP Staff Coach.
Roster In State: 17 **Out of State:** 8 **Out of Country:** 1
ODP State: 25 **Regional:** 14 **National:** 10
Walk-on/Other: 1 **Graduation %:** **Seniors on Team:** 5
Positions Needed: 2 Defenders, 2 Midfielders, GK
Camp or Clinic Dates: Ages 10-13 June 16-19, 21-24. Ages 14-18 July 12-16, 17-21
Most Recent Record: 21-2-0
Schedule: St. Louis, Virginia, Duke, Maryland, Clemson, Wake Forest, William & Mary, South Forlida, Old Dominion, Cincinnati.
Style of Play: Possession oriented style that highlights our strengths and minimizes our weaknesses. Attack minded at all times, relentless defending is expected from all players, system of play varies due to own players and opponents abilities in order to maximize our own fortunes, most used systems are 3-5-2, 3-4-3, 4-3-3.

Women's Athletic Profile

P. O. Box 2126
Chapel Hill, NC 27515
Coach: Anson Dorrance
Email: ducar@uncaa.unc.edu

NCAA I
Tarheels/Carolina Blue
Phone: (919) 962-4100
Fax: (919) 962-4038

Estimated # of Women's Soccer Scholarships: 12
Conference: Atlantic Coast Conference
Program Profile: We are the country's elite women's soccer program. We have won 14 of 16 National Championships. Our stadium has a 6,000 seating capacity. The stadium has a grass field and is in the middle of the campus. We have a majestic two story soccer facility with a state-of-the-art office, a team meeting room, a locker room complex and a football fieldhouse. A rigorous player development oriented training, with year around training.
History: Our program begun in 1979 and has pioneered Soccer of America. We have seven out of the sixteen Olympic gold medallists. 1st program in the South to offer scholarships. Has been to every Final Four held since 1981. Numerous Players of the Year, Collegiate Coaches, and National Team Coaches and World Cup Stars.
Achievements: Won 13 of 14 Conference Championships including last 12 in a row, won 14 of 16 National Championships, produced 62 All-Americans, Ten National Players of the Year, 8 players on 99 World Cup Team, 6 players on 2000 Olympic Team, Anson Dorrance Coach of the Year Twice.
Coaching: Anson Dorrance, Head Coach, led the USA to a World Championship in 1991. He was USSF and NSCAA National Staff Coach. He has a USSF "A" License, is a charter member of the NCAA Women's Soccer Committee and is the NCAA Rules Chairman. Assistant Coaches Bill Palladino who was SE Region Coach of the Year, Coach of 2 time National Champion. Chris Ducar- Goalkeeper coach and recruiting coordinator.

Roster in State: 11 | **Out of State:** 17 | **Out of Country:** 0
ODP State: 14 | **Regional:** 14 | **National:** 11
Walk-on/Other: | **Graduation %:** 100 | **Seniors on Team:** 9

Camp or Clinic Dates: Not Available
Most Recent Record: 485-22-11
Schedule: Texas A & M, Virginia, Duke, Clemson
Style of Play: Relentless high pressure attacking style with a full commitment of each player to go forward at every opportunity even at the sacrifice or risk of being scored on. Total support and encouragement for the one to one artist and the creative player like alumnae Mia Hamm, Kristine Lilly and Tisha Venturini. Fast, high paced combination of ball possession passing game and "1 V 1". Attack supported by a team shape of semi flat back 3-4-3 with a high goalkeeper that can read the game and use her feet.

University of North Carolina - Charlotte

Academic Profile

Charlotte, NC 28223

Phone:

Type: 4 Yr.,Public,Liberal Arts,Engineering
Website: http://www.uncc.edu
SAT/ACT/GPA: 1030/18/3.0
Student/Faculty Ratio: 16:1
Undergraduate Enrollment: 13,770

Founded: 1946
Religion: Non-Affiliated
Housing: Yes
Male/Female Ratio: 45:55
Graduate Enrollment: 2,670

Scholarships/Academic: Yes | **Athletic:** Yes | **Financial Aid:** Yes
Expenses by: Year | **In State:** $ 3,119 | **Out of State:** $ 6,754

Specialty: Architecture, Engineering, Business, Education, Nursing
Degrees Conferred: AS, AA, BArch, BSBA, BSEE, BET, BSME, BSN, BSW, MS
Programs of Study: Accounting, African Studies, Anthropology, Architecture, Biological Science, Business Administration, Chemistry, Civil Engineering, Computer Science, Criminal Justice, Dance, Dramatic Arts, Economics, Electrical Engineering, Elementary Education, Engineering Technology, English, Fine Arts, French, Geography, German, History, Human Services, Management, Mathematics, Mechanical Engineering, Music, Nursing, Political Science, Philosophy, Physics, Psychology, Religion, Social Science

Men's Athletic Profile

9201 University City Blvd.
Charlotte, NC 28223
Coach: John Tart
Email: mensoccer@uncc.edu

NCAA I
49ers/Green, White
Phone: (704) 547-3988
Fax: (704) 547-3991

Estimated # of Men's Soccer Scholarships: 9.9
Conference: Conference USA
Program Profile: The home field is the Erwin Belk Track and Field Center (Tans-America Field). It has a natural surface, is Olympic size and seats approximately 4,000 (permanent) and 9,000 (temporary). Facility opened in April of 1996.
History: Our program began in 1976. 1983 Sun Belt Champions, 1988 Sun Belt East Champion, 11988 Sun Belt East Champion, 1992 and 1994 Metro Champions in 1991, 1992, 1994, 1996 & 1997 NCAA. 1996 NCAA Final Four.
Achievements: Gabe Garcia, Mac Cozier, John Busch, Ben Berry - NSCAA All-Americans, 3 MLS Players, 4 A-League Players, 3 USISL Players, 6 All-South Region players, 7 Conference USA All-Conference in 1998; 1 Conference USA Coach of the Year honors.
Coaching: John Tart, Head Coach, started coaching from 1995 to the present. Former head coach at Furman University in 1982 to 1994. He was named 1991 South Region Coach of the Year and 1993 NCAA Tournament four times Southern Coach of the Year, 1996 Conference USA Coach of the Year.
Style of Play: Attacking oriented style with emphasis on possession through short and long passes. Variation of medium to high pressure defensively.

Women's Athletic Profile

9201 University City Blvd.
Charlotte, NC 28223
Coach: Maureen McDonough
Email: nroberts@email.uncc.edu

NCAA I
49ers/Green, White
Phone: (704) 547-3984
Fax: (704) 547-3991

Estimated # of Women's Soccer Scholarships:
Conference: Conference USA
Program Profile: Play on a Bermuda grass with 118x70 yards; stadium. Newly built coaches' offices, locker room and soccer stadium. Fully lit practice and game field. Has a 4,000 seats stadium. Playing season is in the fall.
History: We are going into our eighth year for women's soccer.
Achievements: 1999 and 1998 Conference USA Players of the Year has come from UNC Charlotte
Coaching: Neil Roberts is the Head Coach and Maureen McDounough is the Assistant Coach.

Roster in State: 12
Out of State: 12
Out of Country:
ODP State: 20
Regional: 4
National:
Walk-on/Other:
Graduation %: 95
Seniors on Team: 4

Positions Needed: All
Camp or Clinic Dates: June 18-22, June 26-29 and July 23-27
Most Recent Record: 13-7-2
Schedule: Wake Forest, Duke, Marquette, NC State, St. Louis, Furman
Style of Play: Varies according to player's abilities.

University of North Carolina at Greensboro

Academic Profile

322 HHP Building
Greensboro, NC 27412-0001

Phone: 336-334-5000

Type: 4 Yr.,Public,Liberal Arts
Website: http://www.uncg.edu

Founded: 1891
Religion: Non-Affiliated

SAT/ACT/GPA: Floating scale
Housing: Yes
Student/Faculty Ratio: 14:1
Male/Female Ratio: 35:65
Undergraduate Enrollment: 12,000
Graduate Enrollment: 2,500
Scholarships/Academic: Yes
Athletic: Yes
Financial Aid: Yes
Expenses by: Year
In State: $ 6,000
Out of State: $ 14,500
Degrees Conferred: BA, BS, BFA, MA, MS, MFA, MEd, Ph.D., EdD
Programs of Study: UNCG is organized into the Graduate School, The College of Arts and Sciences and six Professional Schools: The Joseph M. Bryan School of Business and Economics, School of Education, School of Health and Human Performance, School of Human Environmental Sciences, School of Music, School of Nursing

Men's Athletic Profile

1000 Spring Garden St., Athletic Dept.
Greensboro, NC 27402
Coach: Jack Poland
Email: jspoland@uncg.edu

NCAA I
Spartans/Navy, Gold, White
Phone: (336) 334-4474
Fax: (336) 334-4063

Estimated # of Men's Soccer Scholarships: 10
Conference: Big South Conference
Program Profile: Spartans have the State's best playing facility which was completed in 1991. It contains 3,450 seats, has TV quality lighting and a state of the art scoreboard. Hosted NCAA National Championship 97-98. Bermuda grass.
History: Inaugural season 1988 Div II 88-90; Div I 91-present; 8 of 11 seasons top 25 in nation; 96 and 97 "at large" bid to NCAA's; 98 automatic bid as Southern Conference Champions; 97 advanced to second round with 3-1, OT win over Duke
Achievements: 2 time Conference coach of the year. 4 time Conference coach of the year. 6 time Conference Champions. 2 All-American (1 Division II; 1 Division I).
Coaching: Susie Williams USSF "C"; played UNCG 93-95. Jim Wain USSF "A"; played professionally in California. Dana Tilley USSF "C"; played UNCG 94-97.
Roster In State: 11
Out of State: 14
Out of Country:
ODP State:
Regional:
National: 3
Walk-on/Other:
Graduation %: N/A
Seniors on Team: 1
Positions Needed: Forwards, Attacking Midfield, Speed
Most Recent Record: 13-9-1
Schedule: Duke, William & Mary, Wake Forest, South Carolina, Richmond, George Mason, NC State, UNC Charlotte, James Madison, Furman
Style of Play: controlled possession; flank speed.

Women's Athletic Profile

1000 Spring Gorden St.
Greensboro, NC 27402-6168
Coach: TBA
Email:

NCAA I
Spartans/Blue, Gold
Phone: (336) 334-4474
Fax: (336) 334-4063

Estimated # of Women's Soccer Scholarships: $40,000
Conference: Southern Conference
Program Profile: 5,000-seat stadium, Bermuda pitch, hosting the 1997 and the 1998 NCAA Women's Division I Final Four. Ranked 14th final season NSCAA Poll in 1996, first round NCAA Tournament in 1996, nationally ranked all polls in 1996 every week except one.
History: The program began in 1988, twelve years ago. Joined Division I in 1991. Jack Poland is the head coach since the beginning of the program.
Achievements: 1996 - Ali Lord - 3rd team All-American; 4 straight Big South Conference Titles. Never lost a regular season in the Big South Conference match. Moved to Southern Conference in the Fall of 1997. Two Southern Conference Championships and NCAA appearances in 1996 and 1998 and advanced to the Round of Sixteen in 1997.

Roster in State: 9 **Out of State:** 14 **Out of Country:** 3
ODP State: 0 **Regional:** 2 **National:** 1
Walk-on/Other: 4 **Graduation %:** 100 **Seniors on Team:** 3
Positions Needed: Forwards
Camp or Clinic Dates: June 26-30, 2000
Most Recent Record: 14-8-1
Schedule: Wake Forest, South Carolina, Richmond, Vanderbilt, George Mason, NC State, Duke, James Madison.
Style of Play: Dependent on Personnel.

University of North Carolina at Pembroke

Academic Profile

Phone: 800-949-UNCP

Pembroke, NC 28372-1510

Type: 4 Yr.,Public,Liberal Arts **Founded:** 1887
Website: http://www.uncp.edu **Religion:** Non-Affiliated
SAT/ACT/GPA: 820 **Housing:** Yes
Student/Faculty Ratio: 16:1 **Male/Female Ratio:** 45:55
Undergraduate Enrollment: 2,900 **Graduate Enrollment:** 250
Scholarships/Academic: Yes **Athletic:** Yes **Financial Aid:** Yes
Expenses by: Year **In State:** $ 5,000 **Out of State:** $ 12,00
Specialty: More than 50 majors
Degrees Conferred: BA, BS, BSN, BSW, BM, MA, MS, MBA, M.Ed.
Programs of Study: American Indian Studies, Art, Business, Business Administration, Accounting, Chemistry, English, Education, Theatre Arts, Elementary Education, Middle School Education, Special Education, Physical Education, Recruiting Management, Athletic Training, Community Health, History, Social Science Education, Mass Communications, Journalism, Broadcasting, Math, Math Education, Computer Science, Music, Music Education, Philosophy & Religion, Political Science, PreLaw, Public Administration, International Studies, Psychology, Sociology, Criminal Justice, Social Work

Men's Athletic Profile

Soccer Office, Box 1510 UNCP
Pembroke, NC 28372-1510
Coach: Mike Schaefer
Email: schaeffer@sassette.uncp.edu

NCAA II
Lady Braves/Black, Gold
Phone: 910-521-6342
Fax: 910-521-6540

Estimated # of Men's Soccer Scholarships: Various amounts
Conference: Peach Belt Atlantic Conference
Program Profile: We are an NCAA Division II program and play in a very competitive conference. We ranked nationally for 7 weeks in 1998. We play on a natural grass field that has 300 seats. We will be opening a new lighted game field in 2001.
History: Our program started in 1964. We have been an NCAA program for four years. We have been in the Peach Belt Atlantic Conference for seven years. Our best finish was in 1996 when we placed 2nd. Also in 1998 we were ranked national.
Achievements: 1998 Carolinas Atlantic Conference Coach of the Year; Peach Belt Atlantic Conference Coach of the Year in 1993 and 1996; 2 Players in USC D3 League at present and 1 All-American.
Coaching: Mike Schaeferis our Head Coach. He started his 20th season with the team in 1999.
Roster In State: 21 **Out of State:** 1 **Out of Country:** 5
ODP State: 1 **Regional:** 0 **National:** 0
Walk-on/Other: 0 **Graduation %:** 90 **Seniors on Team:** 2
Most Recent Record: 2-16-0
Schedule: Wingate, USE Spartanburg, U. North Florida
Style of Play: Mixture of possession and counter attack. Man-to-man (pick up) defensively.

University of North Carolina - Wilmington

Academic Profile

Phone: 910-962-3000

Wilmington, NC 28403-3297

Type: 4 Yr.,Public,Liberal Arts
Founded: 1947
Website: http://www.uncwil.edu
Religion: Non-Affiliated
SAT/ACT/GPA: 1100/3.0
Housing: Yes
Student/Faculty Ratio: 16:1
Male/Female Ratio: 41:59
Undergraduate Enrollment: 9,000
Graduate Enrollment: 600
Scholarships/Academic: Yes **Athletic:** Yes **Financial Aid:** Yes
Expenses by: Year **In State:** $ 7,500 **Out of State:** $ 14,600
Specialty: Marine Biology
Degrees Conferred: BA, BS, MA, M.Ed., MAT, MFA
Programs of Study: Anthropology, Art, Biology, Chemistry, Communications, Criminal Justice, Economics, Elementary Education, English, Environmental Studies, French, Geology, History, Mathematics, Music, Music Education, Parks & Recreation Management, Philosophy & Religion, Physical Education, Physics, Political Science, Psychology, Social Science, Secondary Education, Sociology, Spanish, Special Education, Account, Chemistry, Computer Science, Economics, Finance, Geology, Marine Biology, Marketing, Mathematics, Physics

Men's Athletic Profile

601 S College Road
Wilmington, NC 28403-3297
Coach: Keith Cammidge
Email: cammidgek@uncwil.edu

NCAA I
Seahawks/Navy, Gold, Green
Phone: (910) 962-3044
Fax: (910) 962-3002

Estimated # of Men's Soccer Scholarships: None
Conference: Colonial Athletic Association
Program Profile: Brooks Field Soccer Stadium has recently been renovated over the summer. Now it features a full size regulation playing field, two practice fields, expanded seating, irrigation system, and lights for night games. In the near future we are planning on enclosing the seating area, a press box will be constructed and other additions will be added.
History: Program began in 1965 through 1975 as NAIA, 1976 to present NCAA Division I.
Achievements: Ranked 3rd in Southern Regional Soccer Poll in 1980, Ranked 20th in the nation on 1980, and NAIA All-American 1975.
Coaching: Keith Cammidge is our Head Coach. He is entering 3rd season and holds USSF 'A' license FA coaching Badge.

Women's Athletic Profile

601 South College Road
Wilmington, NC 28403-3297
Coach: Paul Cairney
Email: cairneyp@uncwil.edu

NCAA I
Seahawks/Teal, Gold, Navy
Phone: (910) 962-3932
Fax: (910) 962-3686

Estimated # of Women's Soccer Scholarships: will vary
Conference: Colonial Athletic Association
Program Profile: We have state of the art and lighted Bermuda playing field with two Bermuda practice fields. Brooks Soccer Stadium seats 3,000. Great home support; averaging 400 per game. UNCN's athletes have highest graduation rates in the UNC system. UNCN team gpa, 3.12 overall. UNC Wilmington's marine Biology program is ranked 5th best in the world, completed $17.5 million marine science research center in 1999. Also have a strength and conditioning coach for women's soccer.

History: The program began as a club in 1994. From 1995 to the present, we have a Division I varsity team. We have made steady progress every year and are now a very competitive Division I program. We started 8 freshmen in 1998. Last three seasons (11-9-2) (10-10-1) (11-7-1) Winning program with unlimited potential. In 2000 our record was 8-12-1 our young program has made progress, however we need to keep getting better.
Achievements: 1997 was our first winning season: 11-9-1; in 1998, we upset #1 seed at the CAA Tournament 3-2 in overtime; we lost 2-0 in semifinals. 1999-2000 team GPA was 3.20, the team is Academic All-Americans.
Coaching: Paul Cairney, Head Coach, is a SFA licensed coach. He has been head coach for 4 years. Scott Schweitter is a USSF "A" licensed coach. He is goalkeeper coach and currently plays in USISL with Wilmington Hammerheads. Tammy De Cesare is Assistant Coach. Former head coach at DIV III Hamline University.
Roster in State: 12 **Out of State:** 11 **Out of Country:** 0
ODP State: 9 **Regional:** 3 **National:** 0
Walk-on/Other: **Graduation %:** 100 **Seniors on Team:** 3
Positions Needed: ALL
Camp or Clinic Dates: June 25-29; July 28-Aug 1
Most Recent Record: 8-12-0
Schedule: William and Mary, George Mason, James Madison, Richmond, NC State, Old Dominion
Style of Play: A winning style!!

Wake Forest University

Academic Profile

Box 7348
Winston - Salem, NC 27109-7265
Phone: 336-758-5255

Type: 4 Yr.,Private,Liberal Arts
Founded: 1834
Website: http://www.wfu.edu
Religion: Non-Affiliated
SAT/ACT/GPA: 1270/29
Housing: Yes
Student/Faculty Ratio: 11.4:1
Male/Female Ratio: 1:1
Undergraduate Enrollment: 3,841
Graduate Enrollment: 2,226
Scholarships/Academic: Yes **Athletic:** Yes **Financial Aid:** Yes
Expenses by: Year **In State:** $ 26,700 **Out of State:** $ 26,700
Specialty: Preparation for graduate and professional education
Degrees Conferred: BA, BS, MA, MS, MBA, MEd, Ph.D., MD, JD.
Programs of Study: Anthropology, Art History, Studio Art, Chemistry, Classical Studies, Communications, Economics, English, French, German, Greek, History, Latin, Music, Philosophy, Physics, Politics, Psychology, Religion, Russians, Sociology, Spanish, Theatre, Biology, Computer Science, Health & Exercise Science, Mathematical Economics, Mathematics, Elementary Education, Education, Dentistry, Engineering, Forestry, Environmental Studies, Medieval Technology, Physician's Assistant, Business, Analytical Finance, Professional Accountancy

Men's Athletic Profile

Box 7348
Winston-Salem, NC 27109-7265
Coach: Jay Vidovich
Email: Not Available
NCAA I
Demon Deacons/Black, Gold
Phone: 336-758-5783
Fax: 336-758-6090

Estimated # of Men's Soccer Scholarships: None
Conference: Atlantic Coast Conference (ACC)
Program Profile: Training and competition during the Fall and Spring. Demanding schedule against ACC and other top 20 soccer programs. Wake Forest is nationally recognized for its standard of excellence in both academics and athletics. Wake Forest is just completing the construction of a lighted 4,000 seat soccer complex.
History: Program began in 1981.
Achievements: Numerous All-Americans, All-Conference, All-South,. 7 players have represented the USA in international competition.
Coaching: Jay Vidovich is our Head Coach. He holds USSF 'A' license, NSCAA Advanced National Diploma.
Style of Play: Wake Forest plays an efficient attacking style of soccer.

Women's Athletic Profile

P.O. Box 7265
Winston-Salem, NC 27109
Coach: Tony da Luz
Email: Not Available

NCAA I
Demon Deacons/Gold, Black
Phone: (910) 759-5616
Fax: (910) 759-6090

Did Not Return Profile

Western Carolina University

Academic Profile

Cullowhee, NC 28723

Phone: 828-227-7211

Type: 4 Yr.,Public
Founded: 1889
Website: http://www.wcu.edu
Religion: Non-Affiliated
SAT/ACT/GPA: 850avg
Housing: Yes
Student/Faculty Ratio: 17:1
Male/Female Ratio: 49:51
Undergraduate Enrollment: 5,685
Graduate Enrollment: 866
Scholarships/Academic: Yes **Athletic:** Yes **Financial Aid:** Yes
Expenses by: Year **In State:** $ 4,250 **Out of State:** $ 10,700
Degrees Conferred: BA, BFA, BS, BSBA, BSN, MBA, MA, MS
Programs of Study: 90 programs leading to bachelors degree and 70+ programs leading to maters degree.

Women's Athletic Profile

Ramsey Center
Cullowhee, NC 28723
Coach: Debbie Hensley
Email: wcucoach@aol.com

NCAA I
Catamounts/Purple, Gold
Phone: (828) 227-2337
Fax: (828) 227-7688

Estimated # of Women's Soccer Scholarships:
Conference: Southern Conference
Program Profile: In the process of building a 3, 000 seat soccer stadium with Bermuda Grass.
History: First season was 1999. We qualified for the Southern Conference Tournament and had a winning record of 10-9-1. Our second season of 2000 we went 11-8-2 and advanced to the semi-finals of the SC tourney.
Achievements: We have had 2 All-Southern Conference Players. The National Freshman of the Year for new programs in 1999, and 2 All-National team players for first year programs in 1999.
Coaching:
Roster in State: 13 **Out of State:** 6 **Out of Country:** 0
ODP State: 9 **Regional:** 0 **National:** 0
Positions Needed: ALL
Camp or Clinic Dates: TBA
Most Recent Record: 11-8-2
Schedule: Forman, Davidson, UNC-Greensboro, Georgia Southern
Style of Play: Fast paced, possession oriented and physical.

Wingate University

Academic Profile

Wingate University
Wingate, NC 28174

Phone: 800-755-5550

Type: 4 Yr.,Private,Liberal Arts
Founded: 1895
Website: http://www.wingate.edu
Religion: Baptist

SAT/ACT/GPA: 850+
Housing: Yes
Student/Faculty Ratio: 15:1
Male/Female Ratio: 1:3
Undergraduate Enrollment: 1,400
Graduate Enrollment: 150
Scholarships/Academic: Yes **Athletic:** Yes **Financial Aid:** Yes
Expenses by: Year **In State:** $ 16,000 **Out of State:** $ 16,000
Specialty: Education, Business, Sports Medicine, Pre-Professional
Degrees Conferred: AA, AS, BA, BS, MBA
Programs of Study: Accounting, Biology, Business & Management, Chemistry, Communications, Computer Information Systems, Economics, Education, English, Fine Arts, Journalism, Liberal Arts, Mathematics, Music, Parks Management, PreEngineering, PreLaw, PreMed, PreVet, Religion, Social Science, Speech, Sports Medicine, Telecommunications

Men's Athletic Profile

Box 2510
Wingate, NC 28174
Coach: Gary Hamill
Email: hamill@wingate.edu

NCAA II
Bulldogs/Navy, Gold
Phone: 704-233-8175
Fax: (704) 233-8169

Estimated # of Men's Soccer Scholarships: N/A
Conference: South Atlantic Conference
Program Profile: Competitive and nationally ranked program; excellent training facilities, Sports Medicine program. Playing season is in the Fall. Field is a natural Bermuda grass with an unlimited capacity stadium.
History: Program began in 1982. Competed in Carolina Conference until 1989, then moved to the SAC.
Achievements: Coach Hamil was named National Coach of the Year Award in 1993; South Region Coach of the Year Award in 1993; SAC Coach of the Year in 1993. Mark (GK), SAC Player of the Year, 1994 All-South 1st team selection; All-American Awards in 1994 - Sean Balles; All-South 1st team selection in 1994, 1995, & 1996. Ron Ladimir was named All-South 1st team in 1996; All-American Awards in 1996, Conference Champions in 1994.
Style of Play: Defensively controlled game ball with a high-pressure offense especially down the flanks.

Women's Athletic Profile

P.O. Box 157
Wingate, NC 28174
Coach: Geri-Lyn Dubay
Email: gdubay@wingate.edu

NCAA II
Bulldogs/Navy, Old Gold
Phone: (704) 233-8166
Fax: (704) 233-8170

Estimated # of Women's Soccer Scholarships: yes
Conference: South Athletic Conference (SAC)
Program Profile: Playing season is mid-August to late October with the indoor season running from February to March. Facilities include grass field.
History: Program began in 1992.
Style of Play: Deliberate, ball control, emphasis on control of midfield, creative in the offensive third.

north dakota

NORTH DAKOTA

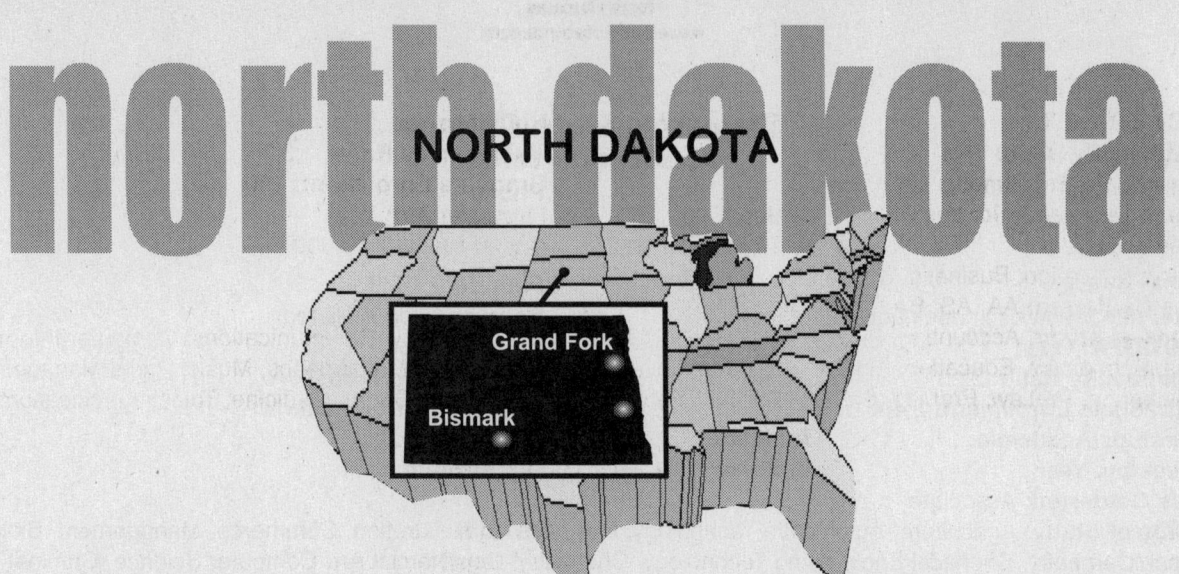

SCHOOL	CITY	AFFILIATION	PAGE
Bismarck State College	Bismarck	NCAA II	834
Jamestown College	Jamestown	NAIA	835
North Dakota State University	Fargo	NCAA II	835
University of Mary	Bismarck	NAIA	836

Bismarck State College

Academic Profile

Phone:

Bismarck, ND 58501

Type: 2 Yr.,Public
Website: http://www.bsc.nodak.edu
SAT/ACT/GPA: Open
Student/Faculty Ratio: 22:1
Undergraduate Enrollment: 2,406
Scholarships/Academic: **Athletic:**
Expenses by: Year **In State:**
Founded: 1939
Religion: Non-Affiliated
Housing: No
Male/Female Ratio: N/A
Graduate Enrollment: N/A
Financial Aid:
Out of State:
Degrees Conferred: Associate
Programs of Study: Agriculture, Automotive Technology, Business Administration, Commerce, Management, Biology, Biological, Carpentry, Chemical Engineering Technology, Chemistry, Commercial Art, Computer Science, Criminal Justice, Education, Electrical/Electronics Technology, Elementary Education, Energy Management, English, Farm/Ranch Management, Health Education, Journalism, Management, Public Administration, Physical education, Political Science, Psychology, Retail Management, Welding Technology

Men's Athletic Profile

P.O.Box 5576 - Bentson Bunker Fieldhouse
Fargo, ND 58105-5576
Coach: Matt Townsend
Email: townsend@badlands.nodak.edu

NCAA II
Bison/Yellow, Green
Phone: 701-231-9471
Fax: 701-231-8872

Estimated # of Men's Soccer Scholarships: 6
Conference: North Central Conference
Program Profile: Compete in the NCC, one of the toughest conferences in the country. All games are played at Ellig Sports Complex, a natural grass stadium located on campus, Team participates in a year-round strength training program under guidance of strength coach.
History: Division II North Central Region final in 1999. Team has won two NSCAA Team Academic Awards- most recently in 1999.
Achievements: NCC Coach of the Year 1998, 1999; NSCAA Division II All-American- Lisa Leach 1999; NSCAA Division II All-North Central Region, Lisa Leach, Mandi Miller, Nicole Vanden Bos.
Coaching: Matt Townsend, head Coach, is in his second year, 25-8-3 record, NSCAA Advanced National Diploma Canadian Soccer Association "C" License, Bachelor of Physical Education at University of Alberta- 1989, Master of Business Administration at St. Mary's University- 1995. Assistant Coach, Dan Dougherty, has a USSF "C" license.
Roster In State: 2 **Out of State:** 17 **Out of Country:** 1
ODP State: 10 **Regional:** 1 **National:** 1
Walk-on/Other: 9 **Graduation %:** 70 **Seniors on Team:** 8
Positions Needed: Striker, Midfielder, Sweeper
Camp or Clinic Dates: July 16-21, July 30-August 2
Most Recent Record: 14-3-2
Schedule: UNC, Minnesota State-Mankato, Truman State University, Central Missouri State, University of Nebraska-Omaha, Rockherst College, University of Minnesota- Duluth, Winona State University
Style of Play: A possession-based style of play that emphasizes an aggressive attitude towards shooting combined with a quick mobile defense and solid goalkeeping. All players are encouraged to push forward.

Jamestown College

Academic Profile

Phone: (701) 252-3467

Jamestown, ND 58402

Type: 4 Yr.,Private,Liberal Arts
Founded: 1883
Website: http://www.acc.jc.edu
Religion: Presbyterian
SAT/ACT/GPA: 850/18/2.5
Housing: Yes
Student/Faculty Ratio: 17:1
Male/Female Ratio: 1:1
Undergraduate Enrollment: 1,100
Graduate Enrollment: N/A
Scholarships/Academic: Yes **Athletic:** Yes
Financial Aid: Yes
Expenses by: Year **In State:** $ 11,050
Out of State: $ 11050
Specialty: Accounting, Business, Criminal Justice, Education, Biology
Degrees Conferred: Bachelors (4-year)
Programs of Study: Accounting, Business Administration, Criminal Justice, Biology, BioChemistry, Chemistry, Clinical Laboratory Science, Communications, Computer Science, Education, Elementary and Secondary, English, Fine Arts, History-Political Sciences, Management Information Science, Mathematics, Music, Nursing, Physical Education, Psychology, Radiological Technology, Religion, Philosophy

Women's Athletic Profile

P.O. Box 6088
Jamestown, ND 58402
Coach: Donavan Gibson
Email: Not Available

NAIA
Jimmies/Black, Orange
Phone: (701) 237-8982
Fax: (701) 237-8022

Estimated # of Women's Soccer Scholarships: None
Conference: NDCAC

North Dakota State University - Fargo

Academic Profile

Phone:

Fargo, ND 58105

Type: 4 Yr.,Public,Liberal Arts
Founded: 1890
Website: http://www.ndsu.nodak.edu
Religion: Non-Affiliated
SAT/ACT/GPA: 21/2.5
Housing: Yes
Student/Faculty Ratio: 19:1
Male/Female Ratio: 60:40
Undergraduate Enrollment: 9,626
Graduate Enrollment: N/A
Scholarships/Academic: Yes **Athletic:** Yes
Financial Aid: Yes
Expenses by: Year **In State:** $ 6,027
Out of State: $ 10,003
Specialty: Agriculture, Liberal Arts, Engineering
Degrees Conferred: BA, BS, MA, MS, Ph.D.
Programs of Study: College of Agriculture, College of Business Administration, College of Engineering & Architecture, College of Human Development & Education, College of Arts, Humanities & Social Sciences, College of Pharmacy, College of Science & Mathematics, College of University Studies

Women's Athletic Profile

P.O Box 5576 Bentson Bunker Fieldhouse
Fargo, ND 58105
Coach: Matt Townsend
Email: matt.townsend@ndsu.nodak.edu

NCAA II
Bison/Green, Yellow
Phone: (701) 231-9471
Fax: (701) 231-6540

Estimated # of Women's Soccer Scholarships: 5
Conference: North Central Conference
Program Profile: Young program that is slowly building a reputation in Division II. Competes at the Ellig Sports Complex, a 6,000-seat natural grass facility located on the NDSU campus. Competes during the Fall season.
History: Women's soccer began at NDSU in the Fall of 1995. The Bison earned a share of their first North Central Conference Title this past Fall with a 2-1 mark in conference play and 11-5-1 overall record. NDSU finished the 1997 season with a 7-11 record in 1997 in its third season play. The 1996 season saw the Bison set a school record for wins with 14 as they completed the campaign with a 14-3 record. The inaugural season of women's soccer resulted in a 6-8 mark for the NDSU soccer team. The record for the Bison in the last three years is 36-15-4.
Achievements: Matt Townsend NCC Coach of the Year 1998, 1999. NSCAA Central Region Coach of the Year 1999. Lisa Leach NSCAA 2nd Team All-American 1999. 1999 NCAA D.II Central Region Playoff Participant.
Coaching: Matt Townsend - Head Coach.3rd with program, NSCAA, Canadian Soccer Association "C" License, Charter Member of Canadian Professional Coaches Association.
Roster in State: 1 **Out of State:** 18 **Out of Country:** 1
ODP State: 8 **Regional:** 1 **National:** 1
Walk-on/Other: 9 **Graduation %:** 75 **Seniors on Team:** 8
Positions Needed: Defender, GK
Camp or Clinic Dates: July 15-19
Most Recent Record: 11-7-1
Schedule: MSU-Mankato, Northern Colorado, Nebraska-Omaha, North Dakota, Truman State, Central Missouri State, UM-Duluth, Winona State, St. Cloud State.
Style of Play: We play a possession style of play where we look to penetrate as early as possible. Play with a traditional sweeper.

University of Mary
Academic Profile

Phone: (701) 255-7500

Bismarck, ND 58504

Type: 4 Yr.,Private, **Founded:** 1955
Website: http://www.umary.edu **Religion:** Catholic Benedictine
SAT/ACT/GPA: 870/18/2.5 **Housing:** No
Student/Faculty Ratio: 18:1 **Male/Female Ratio:** 42:58
Undergraduate Enrollment: 2,049 **Graduate Enrollment:** 318
Scholarships/Academic: Yes **Athletic:** Yes **Financial Aid:** Yes
Expenses by: Year **In State:** $ 11,700 **Out of State:** $ 11,700
Specialty: Business, Education, Medical Fields
Degrees Conferred: AA, BA, BS, M
Programs of Study: Accounting, Addiction Counseling, Athletic Training, Biology, Business Administration, Business Communications, Clinical Laboratory Science, Communications, Computer Information Systems, Early Childhood Education, English, Mathematics, Science, Music, Nursing, Occupational Therapy, Pastoral Ministry, Physical Education, Psychology, Radiological Technology, Respiratory Care, Social & Behavioral Science, Social Work, Special Education, PreProfessional Programs, Management

Men's Athletic Profile

7500 University Drive
Bismarck, ND 58504
Coach: Bill Ashby
Email: Not Available

NAIA
Marauders/Blue, Orange
Phone: (701) 255-7500
Fax: (701) 255-7687

Estimated # of Men's Soccer Scholarships: 8
Conference: NDCAC
Program Profile: A natural grass stadium with a seating capacity of 3000.

History: Team began in 1995 and has been ranked in the NAIA top 25 for the past two seasons. Ranked 1st in the Great Plains Region and finished 1999 with a record of 16-6-0. The team led the nation in goal scoring with 102 goals in 22 games.
Achievements: Coach Ashby named the Great Plains Coach of the Year. Richard Duffy was named a 3rd team All-American. Jason Huber and Lance Kalbere were named Honorable Mention All-Americans.
Coaching: Head Coach- Bill Ashby. Assistant Coach- Brock Thompson.

Roster In State: 15	**Out of State:** 10	**Out of Country:** 5
ODP State: 4	**Regional:** 0	**National:** 0
Walk-on/Other:	**Graduation %:** 100	**Seniors on Team:** 5

Positions Needed: ALL, Goal scorers always welcome
Camp or Clinic Dates: Not Available
Most Recent Record: 16-6-0
Schedule: Kansas Newman, Mt. Senario, Master, National American
Style of Play: Possession style of play. Risk taking to score goals. Attack and defend with numbers.

SCHOOL	CITY	AFFILIATION	PAGE
Ashland University	Ashland	NCAA II	842
Baldwin - Wallace College	Berea	NCAA III	843
Bluffton College	Bluffton	NCAA III	844
Bowling Green State University	Bowling Green	NCAA I	845
Capital University	Columbus	NCAA III	846
Case Western Reserve University	Cleveland	NCAA III	847
Cedarville College	Cedarville	NAIA	848
Cleveland State University	Cleveland	NCAA I	849
College of Wooster	Wooster	NCAA III	850
Defiance College	Defiance	NCAA III	851
Denison University	Granville	NCAA III	853
Heidelberg College	Tiffin	NCAA III	854
Hiram College	Hiram	NCAA III	855
John Carroll University	University Heights	NCAA III	856
Kenyon College	Gambier	NCAA III	858
Lake Erie College	Painesville	NCAA III	859
Malone College	Canton	NAIA	860
Marietta College	Marietta	NCAA III	861
Mount Union College	Alliance	NCAA III	862
Mount Vernon Nazarene College	Mount Vernon	NAIA	863
Muskingum College	New Concord	NCAA III	864
Notre Dame College	Cleveland	NAIA	865
Oberlin College	Oberlin	NCAA III	866
Ohio Dominican College	Columbus	NAIA	867
Ohio Northern University	Ada	NCAA III	868
Ohio State University	Columbus	NCAA I	869
Ohio University	Athens	NCAA I	870
Ohio Wesleyan University	Delaware	NCAA III	871

SCHOOL	CITY	AFFILIATION	PAGE
Otterbein College	Westerville	NCAA III	873
Shawnee State University	Portsmouth	NAIA	874
Tiffin University	Tiffin	NCAA II/NAIA	875
University of Akron	Akron	NCAA I	876
University of Cincinnati	Cincinnati	NCAA I	877
University of Dayton	Dayton	NCAA I	878
University of Findlay	Findlay	NCAA I	880
University of Rio Grande	Rio Grande	NAIA	881
University of Toledo	Toledo	NCAA I	881
Walsh University	N. Canton	NAIA	882
Wilmington College	Wilmington	NCAA III	883
Wittenberg University	Springfield	NCAA III	884
Wright State University	Dayton	NCAA I	886
Xavier University	Cincinnati	NCAA I	887
Youngstown State University	Youngstown	NCAA I	888

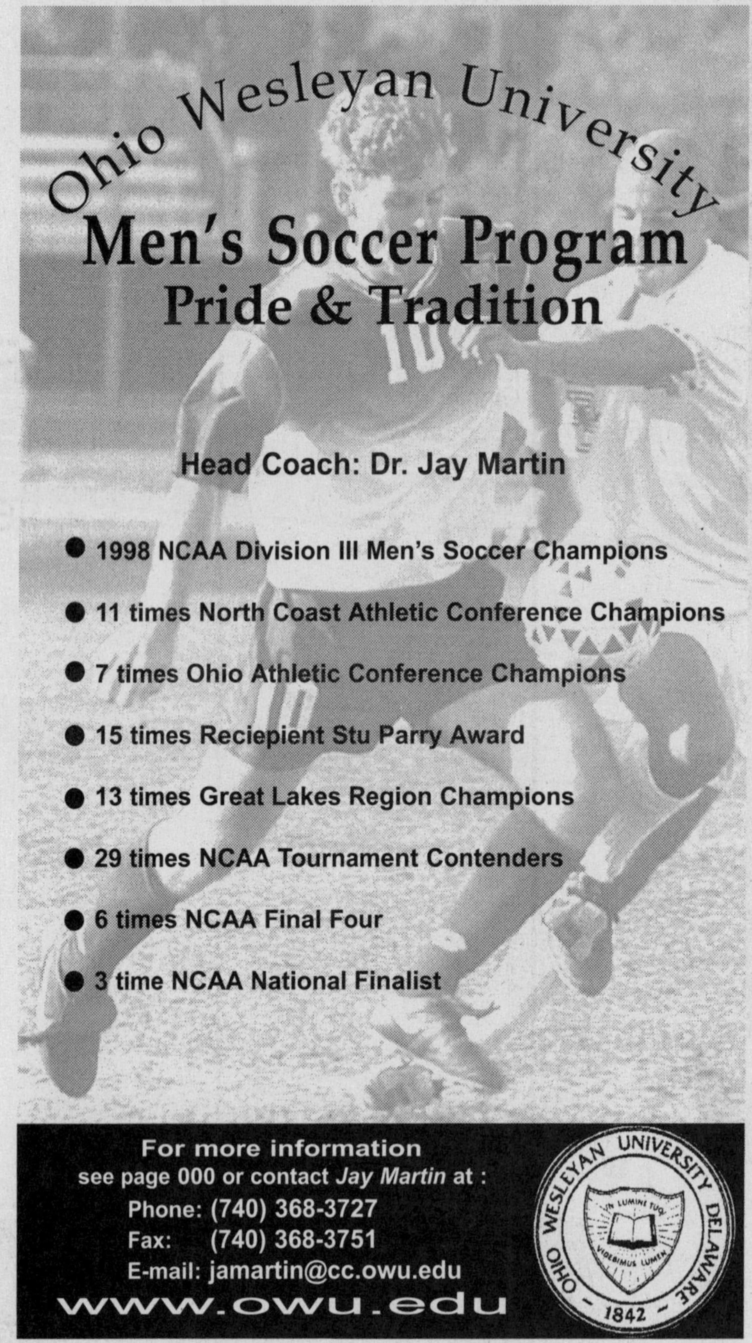
Ohio Wesleyan University
Men's Soccer Program
Pride & Tradition
Head Coach: Dr. Jay Martin
1998 NCAA Division III Men's Soccer Champions
11 times North Coast Athletic Conference Champions
7 times Ohio Athletic Conference Champions
15 times Reciepient Stu Parry Award
13 times Great Lakes Region Champions
29 times NCAA Tournament Contenders
6 times NCAA Final Four
3 time NCAA National Finalist
For more information
see page 000 or contact *Jay Martin* at :
Phone: (740) 368-3727
Fax: (740) 368-3751
E-mail: jamartin@cc.owu.edu
www.owu.edu
OHIO WESLEYAN UNIVERSITY DELAWARE
IN LUMINE TUO VIDEBIMUS LUMEN
1842

Ryan's Soccer
Supporting the Soccer Player
From
Youth League to College
Visit Our Two Ohio Locations!
Ryan's Soccer
817 Bethel Rd
Columbus, OH 43214
(614) 459-5425
Ryan's Soccer
1729 Brice Rd
Reynoldsburg, OH 43068
(614) 856-0450

Ashland University
Academic Profile

Ashland, OH 44805
Phone: 419-289-4142

Type: 4 Yr.,Private,Liberal Arts
Website: http://www.ashland.edu
SAT/ACT/GPA: 870/18/2.5
Student/Faculty Ratio: 14:1
Undergraduate Enrollment: 2,000
Scholarships/Academic: Yes
Athletic: Yes
Expenses by: Year
In State: $ 19,366
Founded: 1878
Religion: Brethren Church
Housing: Yes
Male/Female Ratio: 41:59
Graduate Enrollment: 3,000
Financial Aid: Yes
Out of State: $ 19,366
Specialty: Business, Education
Degrees Conferred: BA, BS, M.Ed., MBA
Programs of Study: Art, Biology, Business Administration, Chemistry, Communications, Computer Science, Criminal Justice, Economics, English, Foreign Languages, Geology, History, Journalism, Math, Music, Nursing, Philosophy, Physical Science, Education, Physics, Political Science, Psychology, Radio/Television, Recreation, Religion, Social Work, Sociology, Speech, Theatre, Athletic Administration

Men's Athletic Profile

401 College Avenue
Ashland, OH 44805
Coach: Brad Evans
Email: soccer@ashland.edu

NCAA II
Eagles/Purple, White
Phone: (419) 289-5466
Fax: (419) 289-5468

Estimated # of Men's Soccer Scholarships: Varies
Conference: Great Lakes Intercollegiate Athletics Conference
Program Profile: We have a competitive year-round program. Our program's philosophy is based on competition. Everything that is done is ranked and record. From one to one to two versus two to distance/sprint training. There is always a winner and a loser, usually a penalty for the loser. Play on one of the best fields in Ohio, natural surface with a measurements of 110x70 yards.
History: Our program began in 1995. Prior to that it was a club team. 1995 team record is 13-6-0; 1996 record was 7-11-0; 1997 record was 5-11-1, and 1998 record was 11-7-0.
Achievements: Damian Willoughby was drafted by EISL in 1997.
Coaching: Brad Evans, Head Coach, holds a "B" License, a youth coaching license and is an ODP Coach. He started in 1996 as a Head Coach and is a graduate of College of Wooster in 1992. Erie Bell, Assistant Coach, is a graduate of College of Wooster.
Most Recent Record: 12-5-0
Style of Play: Hard working team, plays quickly through the thirds.

Women's Athletic Profile

401 College Avenue, Kates Gym
Ashland, OH 44805
Coach: Brad Evans
Email: soccer@ashland.edu

NCAA II
Eagles/Purple, White
Phone: (419) 289-5466
Fax: (419) 289-5468

Estimated # of Women's Soccer Scholarships: Varies
Conference: Great Lakes Intercollegiate Athletics Conference
Program Profile: We have a competitive, year-around program. Our program's philosophy is based on competition. Everything that is done is ranked and recorded. We have distance and sprint training. We play on one of the best fields in Ohio. It has a natural surface and measures 110 x 70.

History: Our program began in 1995. We compiled a record of 13-6-0 in their first season. The year 1995 marked the inaugural season as we were established as a new NCAA Division II team . Our 1996 record was 8-11-0. Our 1997 record was 12-7-0. Our 1998 record was 17-3-2. In 1997,98,99, 00 GLIAC Champion. 19997,98,99,00 NCAA Tournament. 1998 NCAA Div.II Final Four

Achievements: Brad Evans 1997-98 Great Lakes Region Coach of the Year; 1997 GLIAC Coach of the Year; 1997-1998 GLIAC Championship; 1998 team advanced to Division II NCAA semi-finals; Kristy Ritchie named to 1998 NSCAA All-American Team.

Coaching: Brad Evans, Head Coach, started here in 1996. He holds a "B" License and a youth coaching license. He was ODP Coach. He graduated from College of Wooster in 1992. He was 1997 and 1998 Great Lakes Region Coach of the Year. He was 1997 Great Lakes Intercollegiate Athletic Conference Coach of the Year. Eric Bell is assistant coach. He graduated from College of Wooster in 1992.

Roster in State: 26 **Out of State:** 1 **Out of Country:** 0
ODP State: 8 **Regional:** 2 **National:** 0
Walk-on/Other: 0 **Graduation %:** **Seniors on Team:** 5
Positions Needed: ALL
Camp or Clinic Dates: Not Available
Most Recent Record: 14-4-0
Schedule: Lynn Univ. Mercy Hurst College, Gannon.
Style of Play: Play a 4-3-3.

Baldwin - Wallace College

Academic Profile

Phone: 440-826-2325

Berea, OH 44017

Type: 4 Yr.,Private,Liberal Arts **Founded:** 1845
Website: http://www.balwinw.edu **Religion:** Methodist
SAT/ACT/GPA: 1050/21/3.0 **Housing:** Yes
Student/Faculty Ratio: 14:1 **Male/Female Ratio:** 40:60
Undergraduate Enrollment: 2,800 **Graduate Enrollment:** 600
Scholarships/Academic: Yes **Athletic:** No **Financial Aid:** Yes
Expenses by: Year **In State:** $ 20,000 **Out of State:** $ 20,000
Degrees Conferred: BA, BS, BM, BME, MBA, MAEd
Programs of Study: Accounting, Banking/Finance, Biology, Business Administration, Chemistry, Communications, Computer Science, Dance, Earth Science, Education, Geology, Health, Marketing, Mathematics, Medical Laboratory, Physical Education, Psychology, Sports Management, Sociology, Sports Medicine

Men's Athletic Profile

275 Eastland Road
Berea, OH 44017-2088
Coach: Thom Clark
Email: Not Available

NCAA III
Yellow Jackets/Black, Yellow
Phone: (440) 826-2222
Fax: (440) 826-2129

Estimated # of Men's Soccer Scholarships: N/A
Conference: Ohio Athletic Conference
Program Profile: Play on Finnie stadium, a stadium turf surface that seats 8,100 and has a natural grass field.
Coaching: Thom Clark, Head Coach, was an assistant coach here until he became head coach in the summer of 1999.

Women's Athletic Profile

275 Eastland Road
Berea, OH 44017
Coach: Kelly Gray
Email: Not Available

NCAA III
Yellow Jackets/Brown, Gold
Phone: (216) 826-2222
Fax:

Estimated # of Women's Soccer Scholarships: None
Conference: Ohio Athletic Conference
Program Profile: Top of the line training facilities, practice field (natural grass) and play on astro turf in the stadium.
History: The program began in 1969, full varsity program.
Style of Play: Play ball out of the back. Controlled but fast game.

Bluffton College

Academic Profile

Bluffton, OH 45817
Phone: (419) 358-3000

Type: 4 Yr.,Private,Liberal Arts
Website: http://www.bluffton.edu
SAT/ACT/GPA: 920/19/2.3
Student/Faculty Ratio: 15:1
Undergraduate Enrollment: 981
Scholarships/Academic: Yes
Athletic: No
Expenses by: Year
In State: $ 17,496
Founded: 1899
Religion: Mennonite
Housing: Yes
Male/Female Ratio: 45:55
Graduate Enrollment: 19
Financial Aid: Yes
Out of State: $ 17,496
Degrees Conferred: BA, BS, BM, MA
Programs of Study: Accounting, Apparel/Textile Merchandising & Design, Art, Biology, Business, Chemistry, Child Development, Communications, Computer Science, Criminal Justice, Dietetics, Economics, Early Childhood Education, English, Family & Consumer Science, Food & Nutrition, Health, History, Humanities, Mathematics, Middle Childhood Education, Music, Physical Education, Psychology, Recreational Management, Religion, Social Work, Young Adult Education, Youth Ministries

Men's Athletic Profile

280 W College Avenue
Bluffton, OH 45817
Coach: Randy Keeler
Email: keeler@bluffton.edu
NCAA III
Beavers/Royal Purple, White
Phone: (419) 358-0806
Fax: (419) 358-3070

Estimated # of Men's Soccer Scholarships: None
Conference: Heartland Collegiate Athletic Conference
Program Profile: Bluffton College plays in the Sears Athletic Complex on a natural grass surface.
History: Our program began in 1968.
Coaching: Randy Keeler is our Head Coach. Andy Kirkland is our Assistant Coach.
Roster In State: 14
Out of State: 4
Out of Country: 4
Walk-on/Other:
Graduation %: N/A
Seniors on Team: 1
Positions Needed: All
Camp or Clinic Dates: Not Available
Most Recent Record: 4-13-1
Schedule: Hillsdale, Ohio Northern, Oberlin, Anderson, Franklin, Hanover
Style of Play: Positive and encouraging and competitive in our league.

Women's Athletic Profile

280 W College Avenue
Bluffton, OH 45817
Coach: Rick Fee
Email: feer@bluffton.edu
NCAA III
Beavers/Purple, White
Phone: (419) 358-1057
Fax: (419) 358-3070

Estimated # of Women's Soccer Scholarships: None
Conference: Heartland Collegiate Athletic Conference

Program Profile: The Beavers play a 16 game schedule on a natural grass field at Emery Sears Athletic Complex.
History: Began competition in 1990 and the program is growing each year.
Achievements: Last season Bluffton won 8 matches, the best single-season win total in the 11 season of BC women's soccer.
Coaching: Rick Fee, Head Coach, 1995 AMC Coach of the Year. Assistant Coach Crystal Bennett
Roster in State: 14 **Out of State:** 4 **Out of Country:** 0
Positions Needed: ALL
Camp or Clinic Dates: Not Available
Most Recent Record: 3-14-0
Schedule: Indian Tech, Heidelberg, Anderson, Mount St. Joseph, Hanover, Capital.
Style of Play: Players have an opportunity to play and help a building team.

Bowling Green State University

Academic Profile

Bowling Green, OH 43403
Phone: (419) 372-2401

Type: 4 Yr.,Public
Founded: 1910
Website: http://www.bgsu.edu
Religion: Non-Affiliated
SAT/ACT/GPA: Varies/Varies
Housing: Yes
Student/Faculty Ratio: 18:1
Male/Female Ratio: 40:60
Undergraduate Enrollment: 14,000
Graduate Enrollment: 4,000
Scholarships/Academic: Yes **Athletic:** Yes **Financial Aid:** Yes
Expenses by: Year **In State:** $ 10,600 **Out of State:** $ 15,600
Specialty: Education & Business along with 16 other majors
Degrees Conferred: AA, Bachelors, Masters
Programs of Study: Accounting, Apparel Merchandising & Production Development, Applied Health Science, Art, Biological Sciences, Chemistry, Child & Family Community Service, Computer Science, Criminal Justice, Economics, English, Exercise Specialist, Finance, Hospitality Management, Human Movement Science, Human Resource Management, Information Systems Auditing, International Business, Interpersonal Communications, Journalism, Management Information Systems, Marketing, Mathematics, Music, Nursing, Philosophy, Photography, Physical Therapy, Physics, Political Science, Popular Culture, PreLaw, PreMed, PreOccupational Therapy, Psychology, Recreation & Tourism, Social Work, Sports Management, Teacher Preparation, Early Childhood Education, Special Education, Physical Education, Telecommunications, Visual Communications

Men's Athletic Profile

Perry Stadium
Bowling Green, OH 43403
Coach: Mel Mahler
Email: soccer@bgnet.bgsu.edu

NCAA I
Falcons/Orange, Brown
Phone: (419) 372-7072
Fax: (419) 372-6015

Estimated # of Men's Soccer Scholarships: 5.5
Conference: Mid-American Conference
Program Profile: Our team plays at Mickey Cochrane Field that has a measurements of 120x75 and is natural grass.
History: Our program began as a club in 1962 and became a varsity program in 1965. Our overall record is 302-173-42 in 33 years. We have won the NCAA tournament six times in 1972, 1973, 1992, 1995, 1996 & 1997.
Achievements: Won MAC Tournament Champs in 1995, 1996 & 1997; 8 All-Americans, 22 players drafted, 1 project 40 - Vallow, 2 players at NDSL, 1 at MLS - Klein and 1 A-League in the past three years.
Coaching: Mel Mahler, Head Coach, is entering fifth year with the program. He has coached 12 years with a record of 62-20-3 which, is .717 percent. Rob Martela, Assistant Coach, is entering his first year with the program. Chris Prezemienieckle, Assistant Coach, entering first year.

Women's Athletic Profile

Stadium East
Bowling Green, OH 43403
Coach: Andy Richards
Email: arich@bgnet.bgsu.edu

NCAA I
Falcons/Orange, Brown
Phone: (419) 372-9602
Fax: (419) 372-9422

Estimated # of Women's Soccer Scholarships: 12
Conference: Mid-American Conference
Program Profile: Home field Mickey Cochrane Field (natural), seats 1500+, hosts men's ODP Region II camp for the last 15 years. Practice on 2 full fields and one small field, also indoor field house, 90 yd turf room and 200 meter indoor track.
History: First year 1997, All-time record: 19-34-4. All-time MAC record: 7-17-4, Mac Tournament appearances: 1 (1998)
Achievements: 4 Players who were OCSA All-Ohio
Coaching: Head Coach Andy Richards, Asst. women's soccer coach at Oregon State for five years, first year at Bowling Green. Asst. Coach is Ashlee Orr- first year at Bowling Green, played at Ohio State (1999)

Roster in State: 19 | **Out of State:** 6 | **Out of Country:** 0
ODP State: 10 | **Regional:** 2 | **National:** 0
Walk-on/Other: | **Graduation %:** | **Seniors on Team:** 7

Positions Needed: Midfield, Forward
Most Recent Record: 6-6-0
Schedule: Miami (Ohio), Michigan State, Ohio State,, Wright State, Eastern Michigan, Western Michigan, Buffalo
Style of Play: Controlled possession, composed finishing, aggressive attacking play from wide positions, building attacks from defense. Practices and games are conducted in a positive learning environment.

Capital University

Academic Profile

Phone: (614) 236-6918

Columbus, OH 43209

Type: 4 Yr.,Private,Liberal Arts
Website: http://www.capital.edu
SAT/ACT/GPA: 870/17
Student/Faculty Ratio: 14:1
Undergraduate Enrollment: 1,900

Founded: 1830
Religion: Lutheran
Housing: Yes
Male/Female Ratio: N/A
Graduate Enrollment: 1,900

Scholarships/Academic: Yes | **Athletic:** No | **Financial Aid:** Yes
Expenses by: Year | **In State:** $ 18,500 | **Out of State:** $ 18,500

Degrees Conferred: BA, BFA, General Studies, Social Work, Music, Nursing
Programs of Study: Accounting, Art, Art Education, Art Therapy, Biology, Business, Chemistry, Communications, Computer Science, Criminology, Economics, Education, Elementary Education, English, Finance, French, Health Education, Liberal Arts, Management, Marketing, Math, Music, Nursing, Philosophy, Physical Education, Political Science, PreDentistry, PreLaw, PreMed, Psychology, Public Administration, Social Science

Men's Athletic Profile

2199 E Main Street
Columbus, OH 43209
Coach: Dwight Burgess
Email: drburgess@mail.com

NCAA III
Crusaders/Purple, White
Phone: 614-236-6375
Fax: (614) 236-6820

Estimated # of Men's Soccer Scholarships: N/A
Conference: Ohio Athletic Conference

Women's Athletic Profile

2199 E Main Street
Columbus, OH 43209
Coach: Jodi Stranges
Email: jstrange@law.capital.edu

NCAA III
Crusaders/Purple, White
Phone: (614) 236-6203
Fax: (614) 236-6178

Estimated # of Women's Soccer Scholarships: None
Conference: Ohio Athletic Conference
Program Profile: We are awaiting the construction of the new Capital Center, Athletic Complex, but at the moment we are playing on a natural grass field with bleachers that seat 75.
History: The program began in 1991. Our OAC all time record is 49-26-5 and all time record of 101-59-10. OAC Tournament Champions in 199 and 1st NCAA BID in 1999.
Achievements: OAC Coach of the Year 1997 and 1999: Brian Arnold; NCAA Tournament first time in 1999; OAC Champions for regular season and conference title in 1998 and 1999; Joey Hayes: 3 time 1st team All-OAC, 2 time POY OAC-offense, 2 time All-Region; Katie Sutliff: 3 time 1st team All-OAC, 2 time POY OAC-defense, 2 time All-Region
Coaching: Jodie Stranges, Women's Head Coach, is four time All-Big Ten at Ohio State, All-American at Ohio State and Ambassador SC, Trainer/ Instructor.
Roster in State: 9 **Out of State:** **Out of Country:**
ODP State: 4 **Regional:** **National:**
Walk-on/Other: **Graduation %:** 100% **Seniors on Team:** 6
Positions Needed: Goalkeeper, Defense, Midfield, Forward
Camp or Clinic Dates: June 26-30, July 10-14
Most Recent Record: 15-5-1
Schedule: North Carolina Wesleyan, Wittenberg, John Carroll, Ohio Northern, Heidelberg, Wilmington
Style of Play: Build out of the back; possess in the offensive third; very attack oriented; looking to get to end line to create scoring opportunities.

Case Western Reserve University

Academic Profile

Cleveland, OH 44106-7223

Phone: (216) 368-0322

Type: 4 Yr.,Private,Engineering
Website: http://www.cwru.edu
SAT/ACT/GPA: 1250/27
Student/Faculty Ratio: 8:1
Undergraduate Enrollment: 3,600

Founded: 1967
Religion: Non-Affiliated
Housing: Yes
Male/Female Ratio: 59:41
Graduate Enrollment: 6,300

Scholarships/Academic: Yes **Athletic:** No **Financial Aid:** Yes
Expenses by: Year **In State:** $ 24,666 **Out of State:** $ 24,666
Specialty: Engineering, Nursing, Premed, Biology, Chemistry, Management
Degrees Conferred: BA, BA
Programs of Study: Accounting, Art, BioChemistry, Biology, Chemistry, Communications, Computer Science, Economics, Engineering, English, French, German, History, Literature, Management, Math, Music, Natural Sciences, Nursing, Nutrition, Physics, Political Science, Sociology, Theatre, Women's Studies

Men's Athletic Profile

10900 Euclid Avenue
Cleveland, OH 44106
Coach: Jerry Harbak
Email: Not Available

NCAA III
Spartans/Blue, White
Phone: (800) 220-7813
Fax: (216) 368-2422

Estimated # of Men's Soccer Scholarships: N/A
Conference: North Coast Athletic Conf., University Athletic Ass. NCAA II
Program Profile: Field is all grass that measures 100x75 yards with a seating capacity of a 200. Has a separate locker room for only soccer. Has two full-time groundskeepers.
History: Program began in 1951. There have been numerous Conference Championships.
Achievements: Our program went to the conference two times.
Coaching: Jerry Harbak is our Head Coach. He is the only men's soccer coach in Case Western Reserve University history. The skipper of twenty-nine years has guided the program since its inaugural season in 1971. He has been with the university since his graduation from Case Western Reserve University in 1967. He spent time with local club teams, clinics and getting involved with the National Soccer Coaches Association. He earned All-President's Athletic Conference and All-city honors in basketball as a senior and was a team captain and MVP that same year.
Style of Play: High pressure, long ball, quick attack, and strong defense.

Women's Athletic Profile

10900 Euclid Avenue
Cleveland, OH 44106
Coach: Emily Donovan
Email: ekdo@po.cwru.edu

NCAA III
Spartans/Royal Blue, White
Phone: (800) 220-7866
Fax: (216) 368-5475

Estimated # of Women's Soccer Scholarships: None
Conference: University Athletic Assoc.
Program Profile: Playing season starts one week before school begins (although off-season and summer workouts are required) and ends roughly at the end of October. We have a natural surface game field. Stadium seats 200 people. The program is in a stage of rebirth currently, with a very young team. There is tremendous potential for freshman to contribute to the team.
History: Program started in 1984; used to be in 2 conferences - UAA and NCAC. Beginning in 1999 season UAA is sole conference
Achievements: 2000- Two players named to All-Association. 2000-Four players named to Academic All-Association team.
Roster in State: 9 **Out of State:** 5 **Out of Country:** 0
Walk-on/Other: **Graduation %:** 100 **Seniors on Team:** 3
Positions Needed: We need depth in all positions, Defense,GK
Camp or Clinic Dates: Not Available
Most Recent Record: 9-8-1
Schedule: Emory, University of Chicago, University of Rochester, Washington University(MO), New York University, Carnegie Mellon, Brandeis, Wooster (OH)
Style of Play: Team works on the passing game working it up front from the back. Look to get crosses off in the box with runners there to meet them. Emphasis placed on conditioning.

Cedarville College
Academic Profile

Phone:

Type: 2 Yr.
Founded:
Website: http://www.dcccd.edu/cvc/cvc
Religion: Non-Affiliated
SAT/ACT/GPA: Open
Housing: No
Student/Faculty Ratio:
Male/Female Ratio:
Undergraduate Enrollment: N/A
Graduate Enrollment: N/A
Scholarships/Academic: **Athletic:** **Financial Aid:**
Expenses by: **In State:** **Out of State:**
Specialty:
Degrees Conferred:
Programs of Study: Contact school for programs of study.

Men's Athletic Profile

P.O. Box 601
Cedarville, OH 45314
Coach: Roger Swigart
Email: swigart@cedarville.edu

NAIA
Yellow Jackets/Royal, Gold
Phone: (937) 766-3247
Fax: (937) 766-5556

Estimated # of Men's Soccer Scholarships: N/A
Conference: American Mideast Conference
Program Profile: Some of the best facilities in Ohio. Has two new field sin 1999 which is natural grass. Just built 75 X 120 yd, natural grass game field with irrigation system installed. The program features a strong NAIA and NCAA Division III schedule plus excellent game and practice facilities.
History: Program began in 1963. Has an overall record of 297-245-40.
Achievements: 12 Conference Championships; 5 NAIA 1st team All-Americans, 2 professional players, 18 NCCAA All-Americans, 3 NAIA Hall of Fame Inductees.
Coaching: Head Coach Swigart 4th season. He was a four year starter with the Yellow Jackets, he has traveled all over the world playing soccer.
In State: 8 **Out of State:** 19
Walk-on/Other: 0 **Graduation %:** 98 **Seniors on Team:** 6
Most Recent Record: 9-9-2
Camp or Clinic Dates: July 30-August 3, 2001
Style of Play: Possession - attacking style of play with a emphasis on defense.

Women's Athletic Profile

Box 601 251 N. Main St.
Cedarville, OH 45314
Coach: John McGillivray
Email: McGilliv@cedarville.edu

NAIA
Yellow Jackets/Blue, Yellow
Phone: (937) 766-7757
Fax: (937) 766-5556

Estimated # of Women's Soccer Scholarships: 1-3
Conference: American Mideast Conference
Program Profile: Three natural grass fields 120 x 75 with underground irrigation and drainage. Two fields with electronic scoreboards. Main game field has a seating capacity of 1000.
History: 1997- 4-7-1 and qualified for post-season play. 1998 8-9-2 and qualified for post-season play. 1999 5-9-0.
Achievements: The program has had 4 National Christian College Athletic Association All-Americans.
Coaching: Head Coach- John McGillivray 1998-present. Men's head coach 1974-1997, 215 wins, 8 conference championships, 6 National Tournament appearances.
Roster in State: 2 **Out of State:** 24 **Out of Country:** 0
Walk-on/Other: **Graduation %:** 100% **Seniors on Team:** 3
Positions Needed: Goalkeeper, midfield, striker
Camp or Clinic Dates: June 19-23
Most Recent Record: 5-9-0
Schedule: Taylor U., Otterbein College, Tiffin, Seton Hill, Malone, Geneva, Wittenberg, Walsh
Style of Play: Short passing combinations with an emphasis on possession and encouraging players to move off the ball to create numerical superiority offensively.

Cleveland State University

Academic Profile

Cleveland, OH 44115

Phone:

Type: 4 Yr.,Public,Liberal Arts,Engineering
Website: http://www.csuohio.edu

Founded: 1964
Religion: Non-Affiliated

SAT/ACT/GPA: 820/68/2.0
Housing: Yes
Student/Faculty Ratio: 27:1
Male/Female Ratio: 46:54
Undergraduate Enrollment: 11,000+
Graduate Enrollment: 5,000
Scholarships/Academic: Yes **Athletic:** Yes **Financial Aid:** Yes
Expenses by: Year **In State:** $ 8,848 **Out of State:** $ 12,448
Specialty: Engineering, Prelaw, Business
Degrees Conferred: BA, BS
Programs of Study: College of Arts and Sciences, College of Business Administration, College of Education, College of Engineering, Graduate Degrees, College of Law

Men's Athletic Profile

2451 Euclid Avenue, Rm. 324
Cleveland, OH 44115
Coach: Pete Curtis
Email: p.curtis@csuohio.edu

NCAA I
Vikings/Forest Green, White
Phone: (216) 687-4810
Fax: (216) 687-9242

Estimated # of Men's Soccer Scholarships: 7
Conference: Midwestern Collegiate Conference
Program Profile: CSU has a strong soccer tradition with a history of All-America and All-Region recognition. Team's home field is Krenzler stadium, a 2000 seat facility that boasts a beautiful natural grass playing surface, top quality lighting, on-site locker rooms, and an on-site training facility. It is one of the top collegiate facilities in the nation.
History: Program began in 1954 as the Fenn College Foxes. In 1964, the Cleveland State era began and in the late 70's and through the 1980's, CSU was ranked consistently in the top nationally (Division I).
Achievements: Coach curtis is entering his first season at the helm of the Vikings program, having previously led the University of Charleston to National Prominence in NCAA Division II. His 1999 team reached the national semi-final, was ranked #3 nationally and #1 regionally. We outscored opponents 112-10, featured 3 All-Americans, 4 All-Region players, and 1st team All-Conference selections. he team won the conference regular-season and tournament title, and coach Curtis was named both conference and Great Lakes regional coach of the year.
Coaching: Brian Doyle, Head Coach, was named Coach of the Year. Andrew Marson is the Assistant Coach. He was former All-Conference when he was a player. Andy Carl is the Recruiting Coordinator. He was named All-Conference when he was a player.
Roster In State: 10 **Out of State:** 4 **Out of Country:** 9
ODP State: 10 **Regional:** 5 **National:** 1
Walk-on/Other: **Graduation %:** N/A **Seniors on Team:** 6
Camp or Clinic Dates: Not Available
Most Recent Record: 2-14-2
Schedule: Notre Dame, Ohio State, Akron, Butler, Michigan, Michigan State, Wisconsin-Milwaukee, Marshall, Illinois-Chicago, Loyola
Style of Play: Dynamic pass and move style centered around solid defense and explosive offense.

College of Wooster

Academic Profile

Wooster, OH 44691
Phone: (330) 263-2349

Type: 4 Yr.,Public,Liberal Arts
Founded: 1866
Website: http://www.wooster.edu
Religion: Presbyterian
SAT/ACT/GPA: 1000/22/3.2
Housing: Yes
Student/Faculty Ratio: 12:1
Male/Female Ratio: 48:52
Undergraduate Enrollment: 1,800
Graduate Enrollment: N/A
Scholarships/Academic: Yes **Athletic:** No **Financial Aid:** Yes
Expenses by: Year **In State:** $ 25,000 **Out of State:** $ 25,000
Specialty: Liberal Arts & Sciences
Degrees Conferred: BA, BMusic, BSEd., BS

Programs of Study: Art, BioChemistry, Biology, Black Studies, Business Economics, Chemistry, Chinese, Communications Studies, Communications Sciences & Disorders, Computer Science, English, Geology, International Relations, Math, Music, Physics, Political Science, Psychology, Religious Studies, Sociology & Anthropology, Theatre, Women's Studies, etc..

Men's Athletic Profile

Armington PE Ctr
Wooster, OH 44691
Coach: Graham Ford
Email: gford@wooster.edu

NCAA III
Fighting Scots/Black, Old Gold
Phone: (330) 263-2348
Fax: (330) 263-2537

Estimated # of Men's Soccer Scholarships: None
Conference: North Coast Athletic Conference
Program Profile: Homes games are played on beautiful, natural grass surface, seats 1,000.
History: Our program began in 1963. The Scots' best season was 1989.
Achievements: Has qualified for the NCAA Tournament 11 different times; 7 players earned All - American honors.

Women's Athletic Profile

Beall Avenue
Wooster, OH 44691
Coach: David Brown
Email: dvbrown@wooster.edu

NCAA III
Fighting Scots/Black, Gold
Phone: (330) 263-2503
Fax: (330) 263-2537

Estimated # of Women's Soccer Scholarships: None
Conference: North Coast Athletic Conference
Program Profile: Wooster is very competitive program that stresses academics as well as athletics. It is the kind of school that gives you the best of both worlds. The field is great with a separate practice field, both of which are on campus.
History: Our women's program became varsity in 1985. Since then we have won our Conference four times and been to national three times. Our head coach has just finished his 8th season with Wooster.
Achievements: David Brown has been the NCAC Coach of the Year three times and Great Lakes Region Coach of the Tear twice. We have won the conference four times and been to nationals three times. We have also had 3 All-Americans in the 1990's.
Coaching: David Brown, Head Coach, entering Nine years with the program; former Division I college and professional player, NSCAA National Diploma, played at Cleveland State, has a Master's Degree in Exercise Physiology. Michelle Keldsen Assistant coach a graduated from Ashland Univ.

Roster in State: 12	**Out of State:** 12	**Out of Country:** 0
ODP State: 6	**Regional:** 0	**National:** 0
Walk-on/Other: 0	**Graduation %:** 100	**Seniors on Team:** 4

Positions Needed: ALL
Camp or Clinic Dates: July 8-12, 15-19
Most Recent Record: 10-7-0
Schedule: Ohio Wesleyan, Denison, Allegheny, Penn State Behrend, Wilmington, Malone
Style of Play: Passing, building, high pressure defense.

Defiance College

Academic Profile

Phone:

Defiance, OH 43512

Type: 4 Yr.,Private,Liberal Arts
Website: http://www.defiance.edu

Founded: 1850
Religion: Church of Christ

SAT/ACT/GPA: 700/18/2.0
Housing: Yes
Student/Faculty Ratio: 13:1
Male/Female Ratio: 1:1
Undergraduate Enrollment: 1,000
Graduate Enrollment: 50
Scholarships/Academic: Yes
Athletic: No
Financial Aid: Yes
Expenses by: Year
In State: $ 17,870
Out of State: $ 17,870
Degrees Conferred: AA, BS, BA, MA, MBA
Programs of Study: Accounting, Arts, Arts & Humanities, Biology, Business Administration, Christian Education, Communication Arts, Criminal Justice, Design Graphics, Early Childhood Education, Finance, History, Human Resources Management, Information Technology, Marketing, Mathematics, Natural Science, Middle Childhood Education, Multi-Age in Health, Physical Education & Visual Arts, Psychology, Sports Medicine, Sports Management

Men's Athletic Profile

701 North Clinton St.
Defiance, OH 43512
Coach: Mike Selim
Email: mselim@defiance.edu

NCAA III
Yellow Jackets/Purple, Gold
Phone: (419) 783-2588
Fax: (419) 783-2369

Estimated # of Men's Soccer Scholarships: None
Conference: Heartland Collegiate Atlantic Conference
Program Profile: The men's soccer program at Defiance College is in the beginning stages. The Yellow Jackets play at Matthew Winsper Field which is only 5 years old. It is a natural grass facility.
History: The first year for men's soccer at Defiance College was 1989.
Coaching: Head coach Mike Selim is currently in his 5th season with Defiance College. Coach Selim is serving in his 3rd season as men's head coach.
Roster In State: 13
Out of State: 1
Out of Country: 0
Walk-on/Other:
Graduation %: N/A
Seniors on Team: 4
Camp or Clinic Dates: Not Available
Most Recent Record: 0-12-
Schedule: Cedarville University, Adrian College, Olivet College, Ohio Northern, Franklin College.
Style of Play: 4-4-3, possession control.

Women's Athletic Profile

701 N Clinton Street
Defiance, OH 43512
Coach: Tim Rickabaugh
Email: trickabaugh@defiance.edu

NCAA III
Lady Jackets/Purple, Gold
Phone: (419) 783-2346
Fax: (419) 783-2369

Estimated # of Women's Soccer Scholarships: None
Conference: Heartland Collegiate American Association
Program Profile: The women's soccer program of defiance college is in the middle of their 7th season. The Lady Jackets play at Matthew Winsper Kushel Memorial Field which is only 5 years old. It is a natural grass facility
History: First year 1994. The Lady Jackets are in their 7th season of intercollegiate competition. This year they are off best start in school history with a 6 and 6 record.
Achievements:
Coaching: Head coach Tim Rickabaugh is currently in this 3rd season at Defiance College. This season he has the Lady Jackets to their best start in school history with a 6 and 6 record.
Roster in State: 10
Out of State: 6
Out of Country: 0
Walk-on/Other:
Graduation %: 90
Seniors on Team: 0
Most Recent Record: 6-6-
Schedule: Kenyon College, Bethel College, Thomas More College, College of Mount St. Joseph.
Style of Play: Emphasizes transition, solid defense.

Denison University
Academic Profile

Granville, OH 43023

Phone: (740) 578-5735

Type: 4 Yr.,Private,Liberal Arts
Founded: 1831
Website: http://www.denison.edu
Religion: Non-Affiliated
SAT/ACT/GPA: 1060/22/3.0
Housing: Yes
Student/Faculty Ratio: 11:1
Male/Female Ratio: 1:1
Undergraduate Enrollment: 1,900
Graduate Enrollment: N/A
Scholarships/Academic: Yes
Athletic: No
Financial Aid: Yes
Expenses by: Year
In State: $ 27,450
Out of State: $ 27,450
Specialty: Biology, Pre-Med
Degrees Conferred: BS, BA, B. Fine Arts
Programs of Study: Art, Biology, Black Studies, Chemistry, Cinema, Classical Studies, Communications, Computer Science, Dance, International Studies, Latin American, Mathematics, Music, Philosophy, Physical Education, Physics, Political Science, Psychology, Religion, Sociology, Anthropology, Spanish, Speech, Theatre

Men's Athletic Profile

Box M
Granville, OH 43023
Coach: Rob Russo
Email: Russo@denison.edu

NCAA III
Big Red/Red, White
Phone: (740) 587-5735
Fax: (740) 587-6362

Estimated # of Men's Soccer Scholarships: None
Conference: North Coast Athletic Conference
Program Profile: Game facility includes 75 by 120 which is lighted, natural grass and has a seating capacity for 1,000. Full year program has Fall, Winter and Spring training.
History: Est. as a varsity sport in 1979 (The first in the State of Ohio).
Achievements: 1985 National Coach of the Year, 13 All-Americans, and 3 National Players of the Year.
Coaching: Rob Russo, Head Coach, entering first year with the program. He is entering 20th season coaching collegiate level. He was named National Coach of the Year, 2 times Peach Belt Conference Coach of the Year. Taken teams to the NCAA Tournament eleven times. He holds USSF "A"License. Mike Caravana, Assistant Coach, coached eight season (head coach) at Denison. Stepped down to devote time to lacrosse as the head coach.
Style of Play: 4-4-2 looking for fast skilled players that can play short and long passes depending upon opposition.

Women's Athletic Profile

Physical Education - Athletic Department
Granville, OH 43023
Coach: Gail Murphy
Email: murphyg@denison.edu

NCAA III
Big Red/Red, White
Phone: (740) 587-5728
Fax: (740) 587-6362

Estimated # of Women's Soccer Scholarships: None
Conference: North Coast Athletic Conference
Program Profile: We are a regionally and nationally ranked program. Our main season is in the fall and we have a short spring season. We have a women's soccer practice field. Our game field is natural grass, is lighted and measures 120x78 yards with stadium seating.
History: Our program began in 1979. We have won 5 Conference Championships and made 6 NCAA appearances. We were in the 1999 NCAA Tournament Round of 16 and Southeast Region Runner-up, 1999 NSCAA/Adidas Post Tournament Poll Ranked 17th in the Nation.

Achievements: 1999 Ranked 17th in nation, 2nd in Great Lakes Region; I NSCAA All-American; 4 NSCAA All-Region Players, 7 NCAC All-Conference Players, Conference Newcomer of the Year; Gail Murphy named 1999 Great Lakes Regional Coach of the Year and Ohio Collegiate Soccer Association Coach of the Year.
Coaching: Gail Murphy, Head Coach, has a sixteen years head coaching experience. Her 2 year record at Denison is 32-6-3. Her career record is 162-60-14. She was the 1998 NSCAA Regional Coach of the Year and 1997 Ohio Collegiate Soccer Association Coach of the Year. Mike Lentz is the Assistant Coach and this is his 2nd year at Denison.
Roster in State: 14 **Out of State:** 12 **Out of Country:** 0
ODP State: 10 **Regional:** 2 **National:**
Walk-on/Other: **Graduation %:** 100% **Seniors on Team:** 2
Positions Needed: All
Camp or Clinic Dates: Not Available
Most Recent Record: 18-2-
Schedule: Ithaca College, DePauw University, Wilmington College, Mary Washington College, Ohio Wesleyan University, The College of Wooster, Allegheny College
Style of Play: Possession soccer that builds from the back.

Heidelberg College

Academic Profile

Phone:

Tiffin, OH 44883

Type: 4 Yr.,Private,Liberal Arts **Founded:** 1849
Website: http://www.heidelburg.edu **Religion:** Church of Christ
SAT/ACT/GPA: 900/17/2.4 **Housing:** Yes
Student/Faculty Ratio: 14:1 **Male/Female Ratio:** 50:50
Undergraduate Enrollment: 1,200 **Graduate Enrollment:** 400
Scholarships/Academic: Yes **Athletic:** No **Financial Aid:** No
Expenses by: Year **In State:** $ 21,000 **Out of State:** $ 21,000
Specialty: Teacher Education, Preprofessional Law & Medicine, Music
Degrees Conferred: BA, BSC
Programs of Study: 35 majors in all fields including: Accounting, Allied Health, Anthropology, Business & Management, Biology, Chemistry, Communications, Computer Science, Education, English, French, Health Science, Philosophy, Physical Science, PreMed, Psychology, Social Science, Sport Medicine, Zoology

Men's Athletic Profile

310 E Market Street
Tiffin, OH 44883
Coach: John Hall
Email: jhall@heidelberg.edu

NCAA III
Berg/Black, Red, Orange
Phone: (419) 448-2381
Fax: (419) 448-2025

Estimated # of Men's Soccer Scholarships: 0
Conference: Ohio Athletic Conference
Program Profile: Excellent game field, 2 full size practice fields and a 60x40 grid area for GK training. We are a program committed to excelling on the game field and in the classroom.
History: Varsity program began in 1989.
Achievements: Conference Champion 5 times, Nationally ranked in the top 20 in 1996 and Regionally ranked top 25 each year.
Coaching: John Hall 1998-present. Record at school 30-23-1. NSCAA and English F.A. coaching liscenses.
Roster In State: 15 **Out of State:** 6 **Out of Country:** 0
Walk-on/Other: **Graduation %:** 90% **Seniors on Team:** 3
Positions Needed: Full Backs, Flank Midfield, Goalscorers
Camp or Clinic Dates: Not Available

Most Recent Record: 11-5-1
Schedule: Ohio Wesleyan, Kalamazoo, Penn St. Behrend, Wilmington, Wittenberg, College of Wooster, John Carroll
Style of Play: Play to ability of the players on the team.

Women's Athletic Profile

310 E Market Street
Tiffin, OH 44883
Coach: John Hall
Email: jhall@heidelberg.edu

NCAA III
Student Princes/Red, Black
Phone: (419) 448-2381
Fax: (419) 448-2025

Estimated # of Women's Soccer Scholarships: None
Conference: Ohio Athletic Conference (OAC)
Program Profile: Heidelberg College is one of the premiere programs of the Ohio Athletic Conference. The program competes at Mayer Field, a natural grass stadium located on campus. The soccer facility in the center of campus on the edge of Rock Creek has seating capacity of 300, but can hold up 3,000 spectators. The soccer field combines with the outdoor track and softball facilities to make-up the Mayer field collection. The Berg women's soccer program is one of 19 varsity sports offered at Heidelberg, and boasts of the best winning percentage of all. The Berg plays a traditional fall season.
History: One of the top programs in the conference. The Berg has been a fixture at the top of the conference standing and tournament finishes. Heidelberg has participated in eight of the OAC's nine post season tournaments and won it five times with an astounding 10-3 mark. The Berg won Five OAC regular season titles, during the decade of the 90's the club won an OAC record 26 games in a row. The program has compiled a overall record of 160-75-6.
Achievements: The program has won seven OAC titles in the 14 years that the conference has sponsored the sport. 3 times have had coach of the year, Defensive players of the year, Offensive players of the year, 16 players honored a total of 34 times as first-team All-OAC selection.
Coaching: John Hall has Heidelberg College soccer on the verge of returning The Berg to the top of OAC standing. Coach Hall is entering 5th season as head coach.
Roster in State: 14 **Out of State:** 5 **Out of Country:** 0
Walk-on/Other: **Graduation %:** **Seniors on Team:** 3
Camp or Clinic Dates: Not Available
Most Recent Record: 11-5-1
Schedule: Ohio Wesleyan Univ. Kalamazoo College, Penn St. Behrend, Wilmington College, College of Wooster, John Carroll Univ.
Style of Play: Play to ability of the players on the team.

Hiram College

Academic Profile

Phone:

Hiram, OH 44234

Type: 4 Yr.,Private,Liberal Arts
Founded: 1850
Website: http://www.hiram.edu
Religion: Disciples of Christ
SAT/ACT/GPA: Selective
Housing: Yes
Student/Faculty Ratio: 12:1
Male/Female Ratio: 1:1
Undergraduate Enrollment: 1,000
Graduate Enrollment: N/A
Scholarships/Academic: Yes **Athletic:** No **Financial Aid:** Yes
Expenses by: Year **In State:** $ 23,000 **Out of State:** $ 23,000
Specialty: Sciences, Business, Computers
Degrees Conferred: BA
Programs of Study: Art, Art History, Biology, Chemistry, Classical Studies, Communications, Comparative Studies, Computer Science, Economics, Elementary Education, English, Environmental Studies, French, German, History, International Economics & Management, Management, Mathematics, Music, Philosophy, Physics, Political Science, Psychology, Religion Studies, Sociology, Spanish, Theatre Arts, Exercise and Sport Science, Photography, Health Care

Men's Athletic Profile

Box 177
Hiram, OH 44234-1777
Coach: Reid Ayers
Email: ayersrp@hiram.edu

NCAA III
Terriers/Light Blue, Navy, Red
Phone: (330) 569-5350
Fax: (330) 569-5392

Estimated # of Men's Soccer Scholarships: None
Conference: North Coast Athletic Conference
Program Profile: Play on 110x75 yards natural grass surface located in northwest corner of athletic facility. Goalkeeper sand pit located in lower half of athletic facility. Small group training in lower half of the athletic facility. The season will begin on the first date the NCAA allows and will run until through the beginning of November (2 Pre-season games, 18 regular season games and the OAC Tournament).
History: Program began in 1959. Have won 5 of last 6 conference championships.
Achievements: All - American and numerous All - Region players.
Coaching: Reid Ayer, Head Coach, is entering his first season with the program. USSF Staff Instructor and Ohio-North Olympic Development Staff Coach.
Graduation %: 90%

Women's Athletic Profile

Athletic Department
Hiram, OH 44234-1777
Coach: Nicole Barbuto
Email: barbutona@hiram.edu

NCAA III
Terriers/Col Blue, Red, White
Phone: (330) 569-5968
Fax: (330) 569-5392

Estimated # of Women's Soccer Scholarships: None
Conference: North Coast Athletic Conference
Program Profile: 80 X 120, natural turf field in wooded location, 2 practice fields indoor field house.
History: Program began in 1989 as club team, became a varsity sport in 1991.
Achievements: 7 Academic All - Conference; 2 All - Conference.
Style of Play: Attacking game, with a strong defensive posture, 4-4-2, 3-5-2.

John Carroll University

Academic Profile

Phone:

University Heights, OH 44118

Type: 4 Yr.,Private,Liberal Arts
Website: http://www.jcu.edu
SAT/ACT/GPA: Based on a broad range of criteria.2.85
Student/Faculty Ratio: 16:1
Undergraduate Enrollment: 500
Scholarships/Academic: Yes **Athletic:** No
Expenses by: Year **In State:** $ 21,900

Founded: 1886
Religion: Jesuit (Catholic)
Housing: Yes
Male/Female Ratio: 49:51
Graduate Enrollment: 900
Financial Aid: Yes
Out of State: $ 21,900

Specialty: Business, Communications
Degrees Conferred: BA, BS, MBA, MS, MA
Programs of Study: Biology, Chemistry, Computer Science, Engineering, Physics, Mathematics, Physics, Psychology, PreDental, PreLaw, PreMedicine, PreVeterinary, Communications, Economics, History, Political Science, Sociology, Education, French, German, Greek, Latin, Spanish, Art History, English, Humanities, Philosophy, Religious Studies, Worlds Literature, Accounting, Business Logistics, Economics, Finance, Management, Marketing

Men's Athletic Profile

20700 North Park Blvd.
University Heights, OH 44118
Coach: Ali Kazemaini
Email: skearney@jcu.edu

NCAA III
Blue Streaks/Navy Blue, Gold
Phone: (216) 397-3041
Fax: (216) 397-3043

Estimated # of Men's Soccer Scholarships: None
Conference: Ohio Athletic Conference
Program Profile: Men's and Women's teams share a 1/2 field natural grass practice area. The game field is next ot the practice area. Game field is natural grass 116x73. The game field is in a great area of campus, with beautiful clock tower in the background behind one of the goals. A ne field will be built in three years.
History: Program began in 1964. Since moving to the OAC conference in 1989, John Carroll has had the most consistent program in the conference. The Blue Streaks have had only one losing season, and one season in which it did not finish in the top 4 of the conference. We have won 5 regular season championships and 2 conference tournament championships. The team has qualified for the OAC tournament in 8 of the 9 years of the tournament. The 2000 team was the first to qualify for the NCAA tournament by winning the OAC Tournament and finishing with a 13-3-2 record. Overall record is 253-195-41.
Achievements: NSCAA/Umbro All-American- Drue Carney 1985/ 9 All-Mideast Region. 2000 OAC coach of the Year.
Coaching: Ali Kazemaini overall record of 107-50-10 in 10 years. 5 conference titles-2 tournament champions-1NCAA appearance. Former All-American at Cleveland State University and member of the 1984 Olympic team. Was named Rookie of the Year in the MISL in 1984. Besides his duties at JCU, Ali is the director of the Mentor Soccer Club and Director of Soccer Operations at Lost Nation Sports Park.

Roster In State: 19	**Out of State:** 7	**Out of Country:** 0
ODP State: 6	**Regional:**	**National:**
Walk-on/Other:	**Graduation %:** 100%	**Seniors on Team:** 6

Positions Needed: Sweeper, Forward
Camp or Clinic Dates: Not Available
Most Recent Record: 13-3-2
Schedule: Ohio Wesleyan, Wilmington, Ohio Northern, Heidelberg, Otterbein, Denison, Alma
Style of Play: Possession-Build form the back.

Women's Athletic Profile

20700 North Park Blvd.
University Heights, OH 44118-4581
Coach: Tracy Blasius
Email: admissions@JCVAXA.edu

NCAA III
Blue Streaks/Blue, Gold
Phone: (216) 397-4527
Fax: (216) 397-3093

Estimated # of Women's Soccer Scholarships: None
Conference: Ohio Athletic Conference
Program Profile: Will begins 10th season in 1998, play in a 3,500-seat Wasmer Field Stadium on astro turf, just built a natural grass field. Season runs from August through November. Facilities includes indoor pool, weight room and cardiovascular center.
History: Program began in 1989 and will be in its 10th season in 1998. Hired full-time head coach in 1996. Team is 53-68-8 through 8 seasons.
Achievements: Danille Slusa named Academic All-American. 1997 Recipient of the NSCAA team Academic Award.
Coaching: Tracy Blasius, Head Coach.
Style of Play: Play a possession soccer, very aggressive defensively. 4-4-2 or 4-3-3 depending on the situations, aggressive, controlled passing game.

Kenyon College
Academic Profile

Gambier, OH 43022
Phone: (740) 427-5000

Type: 4 Yr.,Private,Liberal Arts
Founded: 1824
Website: http://www.kenyon.edu
Religion: Non-Denominational
SAT/ACT/GPA: 1100/25+/3.5
Housing: Yes
Student/Faculty Ratio: 10:1
Male/Female Ratio: 44:56
Undergraduate Enrollment: 1,500
Graduate Enrollment: N/A
Scholarships/Academic: Yes **Athletic:** No **Financial Aid:** Yes
Expenses by: Year **In State:** $ 27,800 **Out of State:** $ 27,800
Specialty: Education, Liberal Arts
Degrees Conferred: BA, BS
Programs of Study: Anthropology, Art, Biology, Chemistry, Classics, Dance & Drama, Economics, English, History, Mathematics, French, German, Spanish, Literature, Music, Philosophy, Physics, Political Science, Psychology, Religion, International Studies, Molecular Biology, African Studies, Neuroscience, American Studies, Law and Society

Men's Athletic Profile

Duff St./Wertheimer Gym
Gambier, OH 43022
Coach: Des Lawless
Email: lawlessd@kenyon.edu

NCAA III
Lords/Purple, White
Phone: (740) 427-5564
Fax: (740) 427-5464

Estimated # of Men's Soccer Scholarships: None
Conference: North Coast Athletic Conference
Program Profile: We have highly competitive program playing in the NCAC. We have a tremendous playing surface, a full sized field, plus a quality practice field mini-stadium that holds 1,000. We have two playing seasons-fall runs from August through November and spring from March through May. We normally carry 22-24, cutting about 30 players in the pre-season - cut to 22-24.
History: Our program began in 1957. Kenyon, over the last twelve years, has consistently been involved in the NCAA playoffs, reaching the Final Four in 1993 and Runner-Up in 1996. The team plays in the prestigious NCAC Conference competing against the best in the country.
Achievements: We regularly have been national runner-ups and have12 All-Americans in the history of the program.
Coaching: Des Lawless, Head Coach, hold a USSF "A" License and a NSCAA A/Premier License. Dallas Pulliam is the Assistant Coach.
Roster In State: 4 **Out of State:** 16 **Out of Country:** 2
ODP State: 10 **Regional:** 2 **National:** 1
Walk-on/Other: 7 **Graduation %:** 96% **Seniors on Team:** 2
Most Recent Record: 6-12-2
Schedule: Ohio Wesleyan, Otterbein College, Heidelberg College, Wilmington College, College of Wooster, Allegheny College
Style of Play: Style will always depend upon the type of players in the squad. Basic style of play is 4-4-2, possession out of the back with the emphasis an attack.

Women's Athletic Profile

Wertheimer Fieldhouse
Gambier, OH 43022
Coach: Jen Scanlon
Email: scanlonj@kenyon.edu

NCAA III
Ladies/Purple, White
Phone: (740) 427-5796
Fax: (740) 427-5402

Estimated # of Women's Soccer Scholarships: None
Conference: North Coast Athletic Conference
Program Profile: The program's focus is to become competitive on a regional and national level. New indoor facilities is expected at Kenyon within three years. Our outdoor facilties are some of the best in the region.
History: The program began in 1984. We have moderate success in the mid '90's. 2000 was the first year with a full-time coach.
Achievements: NCAC Players of the Year '86, '87, '94, '96, '00; All-Region Players '92, '94, '95.
Coaching: This is Jen Scanlon's first year with Kenyon but her fourth year as a Head Coach.
Roster in State: 4 **Out of State:** 24 **Out of Country:**
ODP State: 4 **Regional:** **National:**
Walk-on/Other: **Graduation %:** 100% **Seniors on Team:** 8
Positions Needed: Forward, Defenders
Most Recent Record: 9-8-
Schedule: Ohio Wesleyan, Kalamazoo, Albion, Allegheny, Wilmington, Centre
Style of Play: possession.

Lake Erie College

Academic Profile

Phone:

Painesville, OH 44077

Type: 4 Yr.,Private,Liberal Arts **Founded:** 1856
Website: http://www.lakeerie.edu **Religion:** Non-Affiliated
SAT/ACT/GPA: 850/18/2.0 **Housing:** Yes
Student/Faculty Ratio: 16:1 **Male/Female Ratio:** 1:2
Undergraduate Enrollment: 600 **Graduate Enrollment:** 100
Scholarships/Academic: Yes **Athletic:** No **Financial Aid:** Yes
Expenses by: Year **In State:** $ 17,270 **Out of State:** $ 17,270
Specialty: Equestrian
Degrees Conferred: BA, BS, BFA, M.Ed., MBA
Programs of Study: Accounting, Biology, Business Administration, Chemistry, Communications, English, Elementary Education, Environmental Management, Fine Arts, Health Care, Mathematics, Music, PreDental, PreLaw, PreMed, Psychology, Social Sciences

Men's Athletic Profile

391 W Washington St. **NCAA III**
Painesville, OH 44077 Storm/Forest Green, White
Coach: John C. Stewart **Phone:** (440) 639-7863
Email: jstewart@lakeerie.edu **Fax:** (440) 639-7862

Estimated # of Men's Soccer Scholarships: N/A
Conference: Alleghany Mountain Collegiate Conference
Program Profile: Play on natural turf field, used exclusively for men's and women's soccer at the college, located on campus. We offer a short spring season.
History: Our program was started in 1994 and continues to develop rapidly. 1999 saw a much stronger schedule for a team starting 9 sophomores that compiled an 8-12 record.
Achievements: 1 All-Conference player in 1999.
Coaching: John C. Stewart, Head Coach, started both men's and women's program at Lake Erie College in 1994 and 1993. He holds a USSF National Coaching License and was named Lake Erie College staff Member of the Year in 1996.
Style of Play: The program stresses team unity, friendship, "family atmosphere", team work, collective effort, and fun. Possession play, short passing on the ground. Controlled build-up from the defending third and rapid penetration into the attacking third.

Women's Athletic Profile

391 W. Washington St.
Painesville, OH 44077
Coach: John C. Stewart
Email: jstewart@lakeerie.edu

NCAA III
Storm/Forest Green, White
Phone: (440) 639-7863
Fax: (440) 639-7862

Estimated # of Women's Soccer Scholarships: None
Conference: Allegheny Mountain Collegiate Conference
Program Profile: We have a natural turf field used exclusively for men's and women's soccer at the college. It is located on campus. LEC offers a short spring season. The program stresses team unity, friendship, team-work, collective effort and a family atmosphere and fun.
History: Our program started in 1993 and this year posted its first winning season with a record of 13-6, with a team comprised mostly freshman (8 starters).
Achievements: Produced 3 All-Conference players all freshmen in 1999.
Coaching: John C. Stewart, Head Coach, started both men's and women's soccer programs at Lake Erie College in 1994 and 1993 respectively. He was named Lake Erie College Staff Member of the Year in 1996.
Style of Play: Possession play, short passing on the ground. Controlled build up from the defending third and rapid penetration into attacking third.

Malone College

Academic Profile

Phone:

Canton, OH 44709

Type: 4 Yr.,Private,Liberal Arts
Website: http://www.malone.edu
SAT/ACT/GPA: 870/25/2.5
Student/Faculty Ratio: 14:1
Undergraduate Enrollment: 1,968
Scholarships/Academic: Yes
Athletic: Yes
Expenses by: Year
In State: $ 16,900
Degrees Conferred: BA, BS, MA

Founded: 1892
Religion: Evangelical Friends
Housing: Yes
Male/Female Ratio: 36:64
Graduate Enrollment: 262
Financial Aid: Yes
Out of State: $ 16,900

Programs of Study: Accounting, Art, Art Education, Bible, Biology, Business Administration, Chemistry, Commercial , Communication Arts, Computer Science, Education, Sports, Elementary Education, Psychology, Social Science, Internal Affairs, Law & Society, Liberal Arts, Management, Mathematics, Music, Nursing, Physical Education, Sport Medicine, Social Studies, Sport Science, Theology, PreMed, PrePharmacy, PrePhysical Therapy

Men's Athletic Profile

515 25th Street N. W
Canton, OH 44709
Coach: Mike Russ
Email: seberly@malone.edu

NAIA
Pioneers/Red, White
Phone: (330) 471-8295
Fax: (330) 471-8298

Estimated # of Men's Soccer Scholarships: N/A
Conference: American Mideast Conference
Program Profile: Play on a natural grass field in the center of campus. Year-round program with a Fall season competition. Schedules includes NAIA and NCAA Division III top 20 teams.
History: Program began in 1966. The past eight years participated in NCCAA National tournament 7 consecutive years; play championship game twice.
Achievements: 5 NSCAA Umbro All-Americans, 24 NCCAA All-Americans; numerous NAIA All-Mideast and Conference 1st team honors; numerous Academic All-Americans. Conference Coach of the Year Sherman Eberly.
Style of Play: Attacking style of play. building out of back through midfield. Everyone involved in attack and defense.

Women's Athletic Profile

515 25th Street N. W
Canton, OH 44709
Coach: Todd Clark
Email:

Phone:
Fax:

Did Not Return Profile

Marietta College
Academic Profile

Marietta, OH 45750

Phone:

Type: 4 Yr.,Private,Liberal Arts
Website: http://www.marietta.edu
SAT/ACT/GPA: 1000/20/2.5
Student/Faculty Ratio: 12:1
Undergraduate Enrollment: 1,200
Scholarships/Academic: Yes **Athletic:** No
Expenses by: Year **In State:** $ 22,000

Founded: 1835
Religion: Non-Affiliated
Housing: Yes
Male/Female Ratio: 50:50
Graduate Enrollment: 200
Financial Aid: Yes
Out of State: $ 22,000

Specialty: Education, Sports Medicine, Petroleum Engineering
Degrees Conferred: BA, BS, MA
Programs of Study: Computer Science, Engineering, Business, Sport Medicine, Accounting, Advertising, Athletic Training, Biology, Chemistry, Communications, Education, Marketing, Mathematics, Music, Philosophy, Geology, Political Science, Physics, Psychology, Religion

Men's Athletic Profile

215 5th Street
Marietta, OH 45750
Coach: Patrick J. Holguin
Email: Not-Available

NCAA III
Pioneers/Blue, White
Phone: (740) 376-4672
Fax: (740) 376-4674

Estimated # of Men's Soccer Scholarships: None
Conference: Ohio Athletic Conference
Program Profile: We have a natural grass field, and a 500-seat soccer stadium. We will play twenty games this season.
History: The program began in 1967.
Achievements: 1984 Conference Champions; 2 All-Conference player in 1996; 1 All-Ohio player in 1996.
Coaching: Patrick Holguin, Head Coach, is in his second year with the program.
Style of Play: Possession style; high pressure.

Women's Athletic Profile

215 Fifth Street
Marietta, OH 45750
Coach: Patrick Holguin
Email: holguinp@marietta.edu

NCAA III
Pioneers/Blue, White
Phone: (740) 376-4672
Fax: (614) 376-4674

Estimated # of Women's Soccer Scholarships: None
Conference: Ohio Athletic Conference
Program Profile: Play in the Fall on an open grass field (in the process of building a stadium). The Pioneers are a young team - in the process of building a strong program.

History: Program began in 1985.
Achievements: 1989 OAC Champions. Each year at least 1 player receives conference honors. 1 player on All - Ohio team.
Style of Play: Quick transitions, very creative with many runs out of the back. Strong defense.

Mount Union College

Academic Profile

Phone:

Alliance, OH 44601

Type: 4 Yr.,Private,Liberal Arts
Founded: 1846
Website: http://www.muc.edu
Religion: Methodist
SAT/ACT/GPA: 850/18/2.2
Housing: Yes
Student/Faculty Ratio: 16:1
Male/Female Ratio: 60:40
Undergraduate Enrollment: 1,850
Graduate Enrollment: N/A
Scholarships/Academic: Yes **Athletic:** No **Financial Aid:** Yes
Expenses by: Year **In State:** $ 20,160 **Out of State:** $ 20,160
Specialty: Business, Education
Degrees Conferred: BA, BS
Programs of Study: Accounting, American Studies, Art, Biology, Business Administration, Chemistry, Communications, Computer Science, CytoTechnology, Economics, Education, Geology, Mathematics, Medical Technology, Philosophy, Physical Education, Physics & Astronomy, Sport Management, Sport Medicine

Men's Athletic Profile

1972 Clarke Ave.
Alliance, OH 44601
Coach: Josh Eaton
Email: eatonua@muc.edu

NCAA III
Raiders/Purple, White
Phone: (330) 823-4792
Fax: (330) 823-2399

Estimated # of Men's Soccer Scholarships: None
Conference: Ohio Athletic Conference
Program Profile: Has a varsity and junior varsity program; stadium seats 500-1,000, press-booth, videotape facilities, fenced in field that measures 120x75 yards. Season begins in September and ends in November. Pre-season last week in August. International trip every three years.
History: Club program began in 1961, became varsity status in 1967. Overall record is 214-156-27, four times Conference Champions. Never finished lower than 5th (ten team league).
Achievements: Conference Champions in 1974, 1983, 1984, 1986 & 1998; 3 All-Americans, 15 All-Region, 31 All-Ohio, 62 All-Conference, 2 NCAA Tournament Appearances; overall program win in percentage is .529 (236-208-36 record).
Coaching: Josh Eaton, Head Coach, NSCAA Advanced National Diploma, USSF "B" License; 11 years as a head coach. Graduate from SUNY - Cortland in 1984. Phil Cratty, Assistant Coach, junior varsity head coach, graduate of Hope College in 1993. Horlando Manay, Varsity Assistant Coach, trained and played in Ecuador.
Style of Play: Control play, variety of formations.

Women's Athletic Profile

1972 Clarke Avenue
Alliance, OH 44601
Coach: Patrick Ferguson
Email: ferguspj@muc.edu

NCAA III
Purple Raiders/Purple, White
Phone: (330) 823-4667
Fax: (330) 823-2399

Estimated # of Women's Soccer Scholarships: None
Conference: Ohio Athletic Conference
Program Profile: Natural grass facility that measures 120 x 75 and a full size practice field. Soccer Facility only that has a press box.

History: Soccer had its inaugural season in 1987-1988. In 1988, we were Conference Champions. In 1995, we were Conference Runner-Up. In 1996, we were Conference Champions and Tournament Champions in 1996. In 1997 and 1998, we finished 500 in Conference.
Achievements: 2 time conference champs and 2 time conference runner-up.
Coaching: Patrick Ferguson is the Head coach and is on the ODP staff, holds a USSF "B" license, NSCAA Premier Diploma, Technical Director and Director of Coaching for Successful club programs. Former Professional trainer in Houston, TX. Staff Coach at Notre Dame and University of Texas Soccer Camps.

Roster in State: 18	**Out of State:** 5	**Out of Country:** 0
ODP State: 5	**Regional:** 0	**National:** 0
Walk-on/Other:	**Graduation %:** 100%	**Seniors on Team:** 3

Positions Needed: Midfield and Forwards
Camp or Clinic Dates: Not Available
Most Recent Record: 9-9-0
Schedule: Capital, Wooster, Denison, Allegheny
Style of Play: Direct style of play with an emphasis on counter attack and meaningful possession play.

Mount Vernon Nazarene College

Academic Profile

Phone: (740) 397-9000

Mount Vernon, OH 43050

Type: 4 Yr.,Private,Liberal Arts		**Founded:** 1964
Website: http://www.mvnc.edu		**Religion:** Nazarene
SAT/ACT/GPA: 18/2.5		**Housing:** Yes
Student/Faculty Ratio: 17:1		**Male/Female Ratio:** 40:60
Undergraduate Enrollment: 1,800		**Graduate Enrollment:** 100
Scholarships/Academic: Yes	**Athletic:** Yes	**Financial Aid:** Yes
Expenses by: Year	**In State:** $ 14,630	**Out of State:** $ 14,630

Specialty: Education, Religion, Business
Degrees Conferred: BA, BS, Associates, Masters
Programs of Study: Accounting, Applied Art, Art, Biblical Studies, BioChemistry, Biology, Broadcasting, Business, Chemistry, Communications, Computer Science & Technology, Criminal Justice, Early Childhood Education, Education, Elementary Education, English, Health Science, History, Human Services, Liberal Arts, Literature, Management, Marketing, Mathematics, Medical Technology, Modern Languages, Music, Nursing, Philosophy, Physical Education, PreDentistry, PreLaw, PreMed, PreVet, Psychology, Religion, Science, Secondary Education, Social Sciences, Spanish, Special Education, Sports Administration, Sports Medicine, Theatre, Theology

Men's Athletic Profile

800 Martinsburg Road	**NAIA**
Mount Vernon, OH 43050	Cougars/Blue, Green
Coach: Paul Furey	**Phone:** (614) 397-6862
Email: pfurey@mvnc.edu	**Fax:** (614) 397-2769

Estimated # of Men's Soccer Scholarships: 3
Conference: American Mideast Conference
Program Profile: Record setting seasons the past 3 years in program's 20 year history. Top rated playing facility- one of the best playing surfaces nationally. The past 3 seasons, won 50 matches including a 2nd and 3rd place finish at the NCCAA National Tournament.
History: Program began 16 years ago. It has been the most successful the past 4 years.
Achievements: Furey named COY in conference in 1997, twice named Regional COY in the NCCAA. Cougars had two NAIA All-Americans in 1999- Josh Robson, Matt Salisburg
Coaching: Paul Furey, Head Coach, entering his 8th year at MVNC, 12 years coaching experience, NSCAA National Diploma, winningest coach in the MVNC soccer history.

Roster In State: 17	**Out of State:** 3	**Out of Country:** 1

Walk-on/Other: **Graduation %:** N/A **Seniors on Team:** 4
Camp or Clinic Dates: July 10-14
Most Recent Record: 17-5-2
Schedule: Lindsey Wilson (ky), Tiffin University, Rio Grande University, Roberts Wesleyan College, Judson College, Walsh University, Kenyon College, Nyack College
Style of Play: Hard working and dedicated; team play; like to attack. Play hard and clean; earn the respect of the opponent, officials and spectators.

Muskingum College
Academic Profile

New Concord, OH 43762
Phone: (740) 826-8320

Type: 4 Yr.,Private,Liberal Arts
Founded: 1837
Website: http://www.muskingum.edu
Religion: Presbyterian Church
SAT/ACT/GPA: 100/20/2.5
Housing: Yes
Student/Faculty Ratio: 15:1
Male/Female Ratio: 1:1
Undergraduate Enrollment: 1,300
Graduate Enrollment: 1,000
Scholarships/Academic: Yes **Athletic:** No **Financial Aid:** Yes
Expenses by: Year **In State:** $ 16,690 **Out of State:** $ 16,690
Specialty: Liberal Arts
Degrees Conferred: BA, BS
Programs of Study: Accounting, American Studies, Art, Biology, Business, Chemistry, Christian Education, Computer Science, Earth Science, Economics, Elementary Education, English, Environmental Science, French, Geology, German, History, Humanities, International Affairs, Journalism, Math, Music, Philosophy, Physical Education, Physics, Political Science, PreDentistry, PreMed, PreEngineering, PreLaw, PrePhysical Therapy

Men's Athletic Profile

163 Stormont St.
New Concord, OH 43762
Coach: Jim George
Email: jgeorge@muskingum.edu

NCAA III
Fighting Muskies/Blk, Magenta
Phone: (740) 826-8025
Fax: (740) 826-8026

Estimated # of Men's Soccer Scholarships: None
Conference: Ohio Athletic Conference
Program Profile: 2000 season will be first season played in new facility-120x75 game field and separate practice field-all natural grass.
History: Program began in 1969-by Jim Theiser current NSCAA Executive Vice President
Program gained varsity status in 1970.
Achievements: 1 All-American; 1 Academic All-American; 52 All-Conference selections; 21 Academic All-Conference Selections; 3 Conference Players of Year selections; one Ohio Player of the Year
Coaching: Jim George, Head Coach, NSCAA National Diploma, BSBM in 1987 at Northern University, MSPE in 1997 at Ohio University.
Goalkeeper Coach- Jon Pwell, form Muskingum player 2 time all-conference selection
Roster In State: 15 **Out of State:** 6 **Out of Country:** 1
ODP State: 2 **Regional:** 1 **National:** 0
Walk-on/Other: **Graduation %:** 85% **Seniors on Team:** 4
Positions Needed: forwards, inside midfielders, sweepers
Camp or Clinic Dates: Not Available
Most Recent Record: 6-12—
Schedule: Otterbein College, Heidelberg College, Wilmingtion College, Denison University, College of Wooster, Denison University, Grove City College, Case Western Reserve University, Washington & Jefferson College, Wittenberg University

Style of Play: European style-possession, with a high work rate, tight marking and a hard tackling team-more skill than physical 4-4-2 system-both zonal and man marking systems used
Similar to German and Dutch styles.

Women's Athletic Profile

163 Stormont St.
New Concord, OH 43762
Coach: Mary Beth Lengefeld
Email: marybeth@muskingum.edu

NCAA III
Fighting Muskies/Black, Red
Phone: (740) 826-8319
Fax: (740) 826-8300

Estimated # of Women's Soccer Scholarships: None
Conference: Ohio Athletic Conference
Program Profile: The home field is 118 x 75 yards, has natural grass, a scoreboard and is separate from the football field. Our playing season runs from September 1 through October 30. We have a energetic, determined, disciplined, fun, family-like program.
History: Our program began in 1987. We gained stability in 1996. Our best seasons were 1992, 1996 and 1997. We hired a new coach in 1996. Our best record was in 1998 and in 2000 a new field location.
Achievements: 1998 NSCAA Team Ethics Award of Merit (no yellow or red cards); 1997-98 NSCAA Team Academic Award; Several individual awards received in and out of our conference.
Coaching: Mary Beth Lengefeld, Head Coach, started in 1996. She has a USSF "B" License. In 1995, she was an assistant coach at Wright State University. She was captain at Wright State. She is a 1993 Academic All-American, a Scholar-Athlete and an MVP. She was an ODP coach for ten years. She played for the Cleveland Eclipse W League. She has a BA in Psychology and an MA in Student Affairs.
Roster in State: 15 **Out of State:** 3 **Out of Country:** 0
ODP State: 1 **Regional:** 0 **National:** 0
Walk-on/Other: 0 **Graduation %:** 100 **Seniors on Team:** 3
Positions Needed: ALL
Camp or Clinic Dates: Not Available
Most Recent Record: 7-8-1
Schedule: Wilmington, John Carroll, Capital, Wooster, Ohio Northern, Heidelberg, St. Vincent
Style of Play: 100% Hustle, high pressure, high work rate, counter attack and the systems used are 4-3-3, 4-4-2, 5-3-2.

Notre Dame College - Ohio

Academic Profile

Cleveland, OH 44121
Phone:

Type: 4 Yr.,Private
Website: http://www.ndc.edu
SAT/ACT/GPA: 720+
Student/Faculty Ratio: 11:1
Undergraduate Enrollment: 865
Scholarships/Academic: Yes **Athletic:** No **Financial Aid:** Yes
Expenses by: Year **In State:** $ 12,240 **Out of State:** $ 12,240
Founded: 1922
Religion: Catholic
Housing: No
Male/Female Ratio: Women
Graduate Enrollment: 9
Specialty:
Degrees Conferred: Bachelors, Masters, Associates
Programs of Study: Accounting, Communications, Education, English, History, Psychology, Spanish, Theology, Biology, Chemistry, Mathematics, Public Relations, Ministry

Men's Athletic Profile

4545 College Road
Cleveland, OH 44121
Coach: Michael McBride
Email: mmcbride@ndc.edu

NAIA
Blue Falcons/Blue and Gold
Phone: 216-381-1680x419
Fax: 216-381-1779

Estimated # of Men's Soccer Scholarships: Not Available
Conference: American Mideast Conference
Program Profile: Our home field is located on campus and is natural grass surface that measures 120x68.
History: Play begins in 2001.
Achievements:
Coaching: Micheal McBride is the head coach of the Blue Falcons.
Positions Needed: ALL
Schedule: Walsh, Roberts Wesleyan, Rio Grande, Tiffin University, Ohio Dominican, Houghton
Style of Play: Open Attacking/passing game, with zonal defending.

Women's Athletic Profile

4545 College RD
Cleveland, OH 44121
Coach: Phil Cratty
Email: paratty@ndc.edu

NAIA
Blue Falcons/Blue & Gold
Phone: (216) 381-1680
Fax: (216) 381-1779

Estimated # of Women's Soccer Scholarships:
Conference: American Mideast
Program Profile: Play on natural grass field with lockerooms and other facilities located Nearby.
History: Began 1995.
Coaching: Phil Cratty Head Coach and former Pro. Player and College All-American 3 times.
Roster in State: 13 **Out of State:** 0 **Out of Country:** 1
ODP State: 3 **Regional:** 1 **National:** 0
Walk-on/Other: 0 **Graduation %:** 100 **Seniors on Team:** 2
Positions Needed: 8
Camp or Clinic Dates: TBA
Most Recent Record: 4-16-0
Schedule: Tiffin, Houghton, Walsh, Malone, Cedarville, John Carroll
Style of Play: We play a strong attacking game. Strength comes from our midfield up to two target players. Flat back defense as well.

Oberlin College

Academic Profile

Phone:

Oberlin, OH 44074

Type: 4 Yr.,Private,Liberal Arts
Founded: 1833
Website: http://www.oberlin.edu
Religion: Non-Affiliated
SAT/ACT/GPA: No cut-off
Housing: Yes
Student/Faculty Ratio: 12:1
Male/Female Ratio: 2:3
Undergraduate Enrollment: 2,950
Graduate Enrollment: N/A
Scholarships/Academic: Yes **Athletic:** No **Financial Aid:** Yes
Expenses by: Year **In State:** $ 31,017 **Out of State:** $ 31,017
Specialty: Music, Science

Degrees Conferred: BA
Programs of Study: Anthropology, Archaeology, Astronomy, Biochemistry, Biology, Chemistry, Computer Science, Creative Writing, Arts, Economics, Fine Arts, Geology, Law, Literature, Mathematics, Music, Education, Philosophy, Physics, Political Science, Psychology, Social Science

Men's Athletic Profile

200 Woodland Avenue
Oberlin, OH 44074
Coach: Blake New
Email: N/A

NCAA III
Yeomen/Crimson, Gold
Phone: (440) 775-8500
Fax: (440) 775-8957

Estimated # of Men's Soccer Scholarships: None
Conference: North Coast Athletic Conference
Program Profile: Varsity and reserve teams play on excellent grass field. Start pre-season on late August and last game is in early November. Take a trip during fall break to a different of country for two years. Positive reinforcement and constructive criticism coaching style.
History: Program began in 1930.
Achievements: All - American 1988; 2 Academic All - Americans, 1985, 1988; Coach of the Year, 1987, 1988.
Style of Play: One and two touch "Dutch Style" of play.

Women's Athletic Profile

200 Woodland Avenue
Oberlin, OH 44074
Coach: Jane Wildman
Email: jane.wildman@oberlin.edu

NCAA III
Yeowomen/Maroon, White
Phone: (440) 775-8509
Fax: (440) 775-8957

Estimated # of Women's Soccer Scholarships: None
Conference: North Coast Athletic Conference
Program Profile: Women's program has a separate training field, natural turf playing field. Fall season starts in September 1 through November 1. Has an excellent facilities.
History: The program began in 1982.
Achievements: Regional All-American, NCAC Coach of the Year in 1989.
Style of Play: Ball possession; aggressive attacking style; total team defense; prefer the 4-4-2.

Ohio Dominican College

Academic Profile

Phone:

Columbus, OH 43219

Type: 4 Yr.,Private,Liberal Arts
Website: http://www.odc.edu
SAT/ACT/GPA: 800/22/2.5
Student/Faculty Ratio: 16:1
Undergraduate Enrollment: 1,977
Scholarships/Academic: Yes
Athletic: Yes
Expenses by: Year
In State: $ 14,070
Specialty: Education

Founded: 1911
Religion: Roman Catholic
Housing: Yes
Male/Female Ratio: 40:60
Graduate Enrollment: N/A
Financial Aid: Yes
Out of State:

Degrees Conferred: BS, BA
Programs of Study: Accounting, Art, Biology, Business Administration, Business Administration with Fashion Merchandising Concentration, Chemistry, Communication Arts, Computer Science, Criminal Justice, Economics, Elementary Education, International Business, Mathematics, Philosophy, Political Science, Political Science With Environmental Issues Concentration, Psychology, Public Relations, Social Sciences, Social Work, Sociology, Spanish, Special Education, Teaching English to Speakers of Other Languages, Theology, Visual Communications

Men's Athletic Profile

1216 Sunbury Road
Columbus, OH 43219
Coach: Dr. David Mor
Email: denhard@odc.edu

NAIA
Panthers/Black, Gold, White
Phone: (614) 251-4577
Fax: (614) 252-2556

Estimated # of Men's Soccer Scholarships: N/A
Conference: American Mideast Conference
Program Profile: 1997 Mid-Ohio conference regular season champions. 1997 was the first season for the new soccer field, Panther Field (fenced in facility with a scoreboard).
History: First ever conference championship last season (1997). since David Mor came to Ohio Dominican he guided the squad to their first ever winning season (14-5 in 1996); the Panthers are 31-10 the last two seasons.
Achievements: 1997 Mid-Ohio Conference Champs; Senior David Florius - 1996 NSCAA and UMBRO All-American; All-Mid-East and MOC leading scorer. 1997 NSCAA and UMBRO All-American MOC Offensive Player of the Year.
Coaching: Dr. David Mor, Head Coach, former pro, played 8 years in the Israeli First Division, played in the ASL for 3 seasons, 'A' level coaching license from Israel coaching school, NSCAA Advanced National license, was assistant at Capital University, begins 4th season at ODC. Ush Shreli - Assistant Coach.
Style of Play: Very creative and disciplined soccer.

Ohio Northern University

Academic Profile

Phone: (419) 772-2558

Ada, OH 45810

Type: 4 Yr.,Private,Liberal Arts,Engineering
Founded: 1871
Website: http://www.onu.edu
Religion: Methodist
SAT/ACT/GPA: 21+
Housing: Yes
Student/Faculty Ratio: 13:1
Male/Female Ratio: 54:46
Undergraduate Enrollment: 3,000
Graduate Enrollment: 400
Scholarships/Academic: Yes **Athletic:** No **Financial Aid:** Yes
Expenses by: Year **In State:** $ 25,680 **Out of State:** $ 25,680
Specialty: Engineering, Pharmacy, Business, Arts & Sciences
Degrees Conferred: BS, BA, BFA
Programs of Study: Arts & Science, Business, Education, Engineering, Health Science, Law, Pharmacy

Men's Athletic Profile

Sports Center
Ada, OH 45810
Coach: Brent Ridenour
Email: b-ridenour@onu.edu

NCAA III
Polar Bears/Orange, Black
Phone: (419) 772-2558
Fax: (419) 772-2470

Estimated # of Men's Soccer Scholarships: None
Conference: Ohio Athletic Conference
History: Program began in 1975.
Coaching: Brent Ridenour, Head Coach, entering second season with the program.
ODP State: 6 **Regional:** 1 **National:**
Walk-on/Other: **Graduation %:** 100% **Seniors on Team:** 4
Positions Needed: ALL
Camp or Clinic Dates: June-July
Most Recent Record: 10-9-1
Schedule: Ohio Wesleyan, Calvin, Alma, Anderson, Otterbein, Heidelberg, John Carroll, Wilmington
Style of Play: Possession oriented, attacking style.

Women's Athletic Profile

Sports Center
Ada, OH 45810
Coach: Jeff Coleman
Email: Not Available

NCAA III
Lady Polar Bears/Orange, Black
Phone: (419) 772-1497
Fax: (419) 772-2470

Estimated # of Women's Soccer Scholarships: None
Conference: Ohio Athletic Conference
Program Profile: The Ohio Northern women's soccer program is one of the top programs in the Ohio Athletic Conference. The Lady Polar Bears play one of the best schedules in the region and have finished in the upper division of the ten-team OAC six consecutive seasons. All grass playing field-one of the best in the state for Division III. Playing season is in the Fall.
History: 9th year of the program and has posted six straight winning seasons and has qualified for the four-team OAC Tournament all three years of its existence.
Achievements: Won Conference Champions in 1991. Erin Happ - OAC (Ohio Athletic Conference) Defensive Player of the Year.
Coaching: Jeff Coleman, Head Coach, record of 33-23-4 in his five years at the helm. The team has a record of 17-8-2 in OAC during that time. Bent Rodeman - Assistant Coach, former player for Carlon Invaders of the Major Indoor League.
Style of Play: 4-4-2; ball control possession.

Ohio State University

Academic Profile

Columbus, OH 43210

Phone:

Type: 4 Yr.,Public,Liberal Arts
Website: http://www.acs.ohio-state.edu
SAT/ACT/GPA: 1000/23
Student/Faculty Ratio: 14:1
Undergraduate Enrollment: 36,000
Scholarships/Academic: Yes **Athletic:** Yes
Expenses by: Year **In State:** $ 12,570

Founded: 1870
Religion: Non-Affiliated
Housing: Yes
Male/Female Ratio: 1:1
Graduate Enrollment: 10,000
Financial Aid: Yes
Out of State: $ 20,138

Specialty: Business, Engineering, Fine Arts, Medical Fields, Science
Degrees Conferred: BA, BS, MS, MA, Ph.D.
Programs of Study: The Ohio State University, with an enrollment of 36,000, is the second-largest university in the nation in terms of student population. OSU offers 25 different colleges in which to get a degree. Undergraduate degree majors: 176; Master's degree majors: 122; Doctorate degree majors: 98. Number of classes: 10,444.

Men's Athletic Profile

2491 Olentangy River Road Woody Hays A.C
Columbus, OH 43210
Coach: John Bluem
Email: bluem.1@osu.edu

NCAA I
Buckeyes/Scarlet, Gray
Phone: (614) 292-3139
Fax: (614) 292-9195

Estimated # of Men's Soccer Scholarships: 9.9
Conference: Big Ten Conference
Program Profile: The Buckeyes will at the brand new Jesse Owens Track and Soccer Complex this season. The grass field will play host to an OSU team that has won 30 games the past two seasons. Under Head Coach John Bluem, who took over in 1997, Ohio State has finished second in the Big Ten two years in a row.

History: Ohio State soccer began in 1953 and we have compiled a record of 269-335-66. (.450) Current Coach John Bluem is the ninth head coach in the program's history. He led OSU to its highest Big Tan finish in 1997 (second). That team also won 11 games, second to the team that has won the most wins in school history.
Achievements: Big Ten Co-Coach of the Year in 1999 - John Bluem; Big Ten Coach of the Year in 1992- Gary Avedikian; All-Big Ten selection- 17; Big Ten Freshman of the Year 1999 - John Tomaino; Big Ten Freshman of the Year in 1998- John Monebrake.
Coaching: John Bluem, Head Coach. His overall record here is 116-51-17 (.677). He coached at Fresno State from 1991 to 1996 where his overall record was 86-27-12 (.736). Kevin Posey, and Frank Speth are Assistant Coaches.
Roster In State: 8 **Out of State:** 18 **Out of Country:**
ODP State: 3 **Regional:** 3 **National:** 3
Walk-on/Other: **Graduation %:** N/A **Seniors on Team:** 5
Positions Needed: Sweeper, Stopper
Camp or Clinic Dates: Residential Camp July 16-21
Most Recent Record: 11-8-0
Schedule: Indiana, Penn State, Akron, Oakland, Cincinnati, Bowling Green, Kentucky, UNLV, VCU, Charleston
Style of Play: Defense is organized around man-to-man with a zones used on and off. Offense is fast break controlled build-up based on where we recover ball and shape of the opponent at the time.

Women's Athletic Profile

1950 Cannon Dr., S.W. Stadium
Columbus, OH 43210
Coach: Lori Walker
Email: womenssoccer@osu.edu

NCAA I
Buckeyes/Scarlet, Grey
Phone: (614) 292-8482
Fax: (614) 292-8480

Estimated # of Women's Soccer Scholarships: Not Available
Conference: Big Ten Conference
Program Profile: Ohio State home matches are played in a state of the art Jesse Owens track and soccer complex, which features a grandstand and concourse level, working press box, visiting and official looker rooms, and concession stands. The stadium will house a NCAA regulation natural grass pitch dimension of 116x75 yards.
History: The Ohio State Women's Soccer Program began in 1993. Our current overall record is 77-73-7 and our conference tournament record is 3-5-0. Lori Walker took over the program 4years ago and entering her fifth year as OSU Women's Soccer Head Coach. In the 1998 Big Ten Tournament, the Buckeyes placed second while upsetting the second and third seed in the tournament. The Bucks are looking forward to an impressive 2001 season.
Achievements: All-American - Jodi Stranges (1996)
All-Great Lakes Region -Jodi Stranges (1995-97), Jennifer Plante (1995), Bree Blakely (1996), Becky Borchers (1998). Big Ten Awards - Big Ten Freshman of the Year- Jennifer Plante (1955); All-Big Ten Selections - 1st Team-Bree Blakely (1994-96), Jennifer Plante (1995), Jodi Stranges (1995-97), Becky Borchers (1998); 2nd Team- Nicole Morris (1994-96), Jodi Stanges (1994), Lisa Suttmiller (1994), Tiffany Tisdale (1994).
Coaching: Lori Walker, Head Coach, is in her 5th year. She has a U.S.Soccer A" License. Croft Young, assistant coach, is in his 5th year. He has a U.S. Soccer "B" License. Erin Taylor, Assistant Coach, is in her 3rd year. She has a NSCAA National Diploma.
Style of Play: OSU plays an indirect style in which we build out of the back through our midfield and then into the attacking third of the field. We play simple out of the back and use a combination play through the midfield into the attacking third.

Ohio University
Academic Profile

Phone:

Athens, OH 45701

Type: 4 Yr.,Public,Liberal Arts
Website: http://www.ohiobobcats.com
SAT/ACT/GPA: Very Selective

Founded: 1804
Religion: Non-Affiliated
Housing: Yes

Student/Faculty Ratio: 21:1
Male/Female Ratio: 20:1
Undergraduate Enrollment: 16,000
Graduate Enrollment: 3,000
Scholarships/Academic: Yes **Athletic:** Yes **Financial Aid:** Yes
Expenses by: Year **In State:** $ 14.600 **Out of State:** $ 14.600
Specialty: Journalism, Communications, Physical Therapy, Education, Athletic Trng
Degrees Conferred: AA, AS, BA, BS, BSC, MA, MS, MBA, MFA
Programs of Study: Accounting, Advertising, Airway Sciences, Anthropology, Broadcasting, Chemical Engineering, Civil Engineering, Communications, Criminal Justice, Economics, Engineering Technology, Food Science, Geography, Languages, Marketing, Mathematics, Microbiology

Women's Athletic Profile

Convocation Center - Soccer
Athens, OH 45701-2979
Coach: Stacy Strauss
Email:

NCAA I
Bobcats/Hunter Green, White
Phone: (740) 593-2990
Fax: (740) 593-2420

Estimated # of Women's Soccer Scholarships: 12
Conference: Mid-American Conference
Program Profile: 4th year NCAA I program. home field is Natural grass. 1998 MAC Champions.
History: 1997 first year. MAC runner-up, 1998 MAC Champions, 1999 MAC Tournament Runner-up.
Coaching: Stacy Strauss is the Head Coach.
Roster in State: 22 **Out of State:** 2 **Out of Country:**
ODP State: 20 **Regional:** **National:**
Walk-on/Other: **Graduation %:** **Seniors on Team:** 9
Positions Needed: ALL
Style of Play: Attack with a purpose, defend in an organized fashion, quick transition, high paced.

Ohio Wesleyan University

Academic Profile

Phone:

Delaware, OH 43015

Type: 4 Yr.,Private,Liberal Arts
Founded: 1842
Website: http://www.owu.edu
Religion: Methodist
SAT/ACT/GPA: 525 V, 573 M/25
Housing: Yes
Student/Faculty Ratio: 14:1
Male/Female Ratio: 49:51
Undergraduate Enrollment: 1,850
Graduate Enrollment: N/A
Scholarships/Academic: Yes **Athletic:** No **Financial Aid:** Yes
Expenses by: Year **In State:** $ 27,210 **Out of State:** $ 27,210
Specialty:
Degrees Conferred: BA, BFA, BM
Programs of Study: Botany - Microbiology, Chemistry, Economics, Education, English, Fine Arts, Geography, Geology, History, Humanities - Classics, Journalism, Mathematical Science, Modern Foreign Languages, Music, Philosophy, Physical Education, Physics, Politics & Government, Psychology, Religion, Sociology, Anthropology, Theatre & Dance, Zoology

Men's Athletic Profile

Edwards Gym
Delaware, OH 43015
Coach: Jay Martin
Email: jmartin@cc.cwu.edu

NCAA III
Battling Bishops/Red, Black,
Phone: (740) 368-3727
Fax: (740) 368-3751

Estimated # of Men's Soccer Scholarships: None
Conference: North Coast Athletic Conference
Program Profile: Roy Rike Field has a natural grass surface. Its dimension's is 120x80. New stands were installed in 1998 with a capacity of nearly 2,000. A new building complex will be finished before the fall of 1999 season. The 1998 Division III Final Four was hosted by Ohio Wesleyan at the Roy Rike Soccer Complex.
History: Our men's soccer program began in 1953. OWU holds NCAA records in: most NCAA Appearances, most NCAA wins, best NCAA winning percentage and, most consecutive NCAA Appearances; former players have gone on to play professionally indoor, A-League, MLS, and in Europe. Our spring schedules consists of mostly Division I teams.
Achievements: OWU has won the OAC or NCAC Conference Titles 16 times since 1971, Greak Lakes Regional Champs 12 times, participated in the NCAA Tournament 28 times, Final Four 6 times and National Finals 3 times, winning the National Championships in 1998. Jay Martin was National Coach of the Year in 1991 & 1998.
Coaching: Jay Martin, Head Coach, took Ohio Wesleyan to the NCAA Tournament 20 of 22 years as a coach. He is a past-president of the NSCAA and twice named National Coach of the Year. He also takes the team to Germany every three years. Nick Theslof, Assistant Coach, captained at UCLA to the NCAA Division I Championships in 1997, played for PSU Eindoven in Holland, the US U-21 National Team and the Columbus Crew.
Style of Play: Short-pass possession style. Attack down the flanks, high pressure defense, physical and fast brand of soccer.

Women's Athletic Profile

Edwards Gym, Sandusky Street
Delaware, OH 43015
Coach: Bob Barnes
Email: rcbarnes@cc.owu.edu

NCAA III
Battling Bishops/Red, Black
Phone: (740) 368-3757
Fax: (740) 368-3751

Estimated # of Women's Soccer Scholarships: None
Conference: North Coast Athletic Conference
Program Profile: One of the top in Great Lakes Region, nationally ranked for the past 3 seasons. Facilities are outstanding have held NCAA tournament past two seasons. Men's team hosted national championship in 98. Grass field, maximum dimensions, men's and women's locker rooms. Season start in the first of Sept. and runs through the end of October. NCAA tournament runs through the middle of November. Non-traditional season runs from Feb. through April.
History: Our program began in 1984. We were Conference Champions in 1989, 1990 and 1995. We were Conference runner-up in 1991,1992, 1993 and 1998. 16 year record: 174-85-21 (only 3 losing seasons).
Achievements: Conference Champs, 1989, 1990; #1 ranking, 1989, 1990; Regional rankings, 1989-1994; National ranking 1990-1992; Division III playoffs, 1991, 1992; NCAC Coach of the Year 1987; OCSA Coach of the Year in Ohio 1988, 1989; 7 Regional All - Americans; 1st National All - American 1990; 2 Regional All - Americans 1991; 1st Team National All - American 1991, 1992; 2 Regional All - Americans 1993, 1994. Also Coach of The Year 1999, 2 All-Americans in 1999 in four seasons 58-14-1 record.
Coaching: Bob Barnes Head Coach, Billy Thompson 2nd season was former member of Columbus Crew, MLS, Brett Barber 1st season as goalkeeper coach.

Roster in State: 16	**Out of State:** 10	**Out of Country:** 1
ODP State: 2	**Regional:** 2	**National:**
Walk-on/Other:	**Graduation %:** 100	**Seniors on Team:** 4

Positions Needed: 2 defenders, midfielder, forward
Camp or Clinic Dates: July 22-26 (ages10-14) July 29-Aug.2 (high school)
Most Recent Record: 9-3-1
Schedule: Wheaton, Ill, DePauw, Denison, Wilmington, Nazareth, NY, Allegheny
Style of Play: 4-3-3 high pressure defense with ball control offense.

Otterbein College
Academic Profile

Westerville, OH 43081

Phone:

Type: 4 Yr.,Private,Liberal Arts
Website: http://www.otterbein.edu
SAT/ACT/GPA: 820+/20+
Student/Faculty Ratio: 13:1
Undergraduate Enrollment: 2,397
Scholarships/Academic: Yes
Athletic: No
Expenses by: Year
In State: $ 19,053
Specialty:

Founded: 1847
Religion: Methodist
Housing: Yes
Male/Female Ratio: 43:57
Graduate Enrollment: 93
Financial Aid: Yes
Out of State: $ 19,053

Degrees Conferred: BA, BS, BFA, M.Ed.
Programs of Study: Accounting, Art, Business Administration, Broadcasting, Chemistry, Communications, Education, Computer Science, Dance, Economics, Engineering, English, French, Health Education, History, Individualized Degree, International Studies, Journalism, Life Science, Mathematics, Music, Nursing, Philosophy, Physical Education, Physics/Astronomy, Political Science, PreDentistry, PreLaw, PreMed, PrePhysical Therapy, PreVet, Psychology, Public Relations, Religion, Sociology, Spanish, Sports Medicine, Theatre, Visual Arts

Men's Athletic Profile

Rike Center
Westerville, OH 43081
Coach: Gerry D'Arcy
Email: gdarcy@otterbein.edu

NCAA III
Cardinals/Tan, maroon
Phone: (614) 823-3524
Fax: (614) 823-1966

Estimated # of Men's Soccer Scholarships: Many Academic
Conference: Ohio Athletic Conference
Program Profile: finished 5th in the Nation in 1999. Play in Ohio Athletic Conference. We field a varsity and a J.V. program. In ground watering system in 2000 can improve and already very good field. Hosted NCAA Regional Championship in 1999.
History: Program began in 1983. 6 OAC Championships, 3 NCAA Berths.
Achievements: Ohio Athletic Conference Champs 1997, 1998, and 1999; 2 All-American Awards; numerous All-Mid East and All-Ohio awards; 10 of 1st x1 players made All-Conference in 1999. Ohio Team of the Year and Player of the Year in 1999. Numerous Coach of the Year awards.
Coaching: Gerry D'Arcy, Head Coach, is a District, State, and Regional Coach for USYSA and is an 'A' licensed and Staff Coach for USSF. Brendon Hrabhsa, Assistant Coach.
Roster In State: 26
Out of State: 10
Out of Country: 2
ODP State: 15
Regional: 5
National:
Walk-on/Other:
Graduation %: 95%
Seniors on Team: 4
Positions Needed: Various
Camp or Clinic Dates: late June
Most Recent Record: 19-1-1
Schedule: Ohio Wesleyan, Alma, Wisconsin-Oshkosh, Wilmington, John Carroll, Wittenberg, Heidelberg
Style of Play: Attack with 6, Defend with8. Very tempo: short back/ long ball, depending on personnel. Disciplined and organized, with or without the ball. Adventurous in attack.

Women's Athletic Profile

Rike Center
Westerville, OH 43081
Coach: Brandon Koons
Email: bkoons@otterbein.edu

NCAA III
Cardinals/Tan, Cardinal
Phone: (614) 823-3529
Fax: (614) 823-1966

Estimated # of Women's Soccer Scholarships: None
Conference: Ohio Athletic Conference (OAC)
Program Profile: Competitive program in strong conference, with the largest field in the OAC (natural grass, 80X110 yards, bleacher seating for spectators). Season is September through October.
History: Varsity competition began in 1987. The Ohio Athletic Conference has a long history of supporting varsity sports for women.
Achievements: Several All-Conference platters, including 4 in 1999.
Coaching:
Roster in State: 23 **Out of State:** 2 **Out of Country:**
ODP State: 3 **Regional:** **National:**
Walk-on/Other: **Graduation %:** **Seniors on Team:** 1
Positions Needed: All
Camp or Clinic Dates: Not Available
Most Recent Record: 9-8-1
Schedule: Wilmington, Capital, Ohio Northern, John Carrol Malone
Style of Play: Quick, attacking, possession game with individual flair encouraged. Premium on intelligent, aggressive players.

Shawnee State University

Academic Profile

Phone: (800) 959-2778

Portsmouth, OH 45662-4344

Type: 4 Yr.,Public
Founded: 1986
Website: http://www.shawnee.edu
Religion: Non-Affiliated
SAT/ACT/GPA: Open Admission
Housing: Yes
Student/Faculty Ratio: 15:1
Male/Female Ratio: 40:60
Undergraduate Enrollment: 3,500
Graduate Enrollment: N/A
Scholarships/Academic: Yes **Athletic:** Yes
Financial Aid: Yes
Expenses by: Quarter **In State:** $ 7,609
Out of State: $ 9,952
Specialty: Athletic Training, Plastic and Computer Engineering
Degrees Conferred: BA, BS, BFA
Programs of Study: Accounting, Applied Mathematics, Arts, Biology, Business Administration, Computer Science, Computer Technology, Dentistry, Education, Elementary Education, English, Finance, Fine Arts, Humanities, Liberal Arts, Management, Mathematics, Medical Laboratory Technology, Natural Science, Nursing, Occupational Therapy, Physical Education, Physical Science, Physical Therapy, Plastic Technology, PreLaw, PreMed, PreVet, Radiological Technology, Real Estate, Respiratory, Therapy, Science, Social Science

Men's Athletic Profile

940 Second Street
Portsmouth, OH 45662-4344
Coach: Lee Lord
Email: llord@shewanee.edu

NAIA
Bears/Blue, Gray
Phone: (740) 355-2528
Fax: (740) 355-2381

Estimated # of Men's Soccer Scholarships: N/A
Conference: American Mideast Conference
Program Profile: Play on a field that has a size of 120x780 natural grass.
Coaching: Lee Lord, Head Coach, is entering his second season with the program. His 1998 record was 3-15-1. Brenton Cole, Assistant Coach, is entering his first year with the program after playing at SSU for four years as a starter.
Style of Play: We try to play a possession game, based on a zone defense and controlled attack from a 4-43-3 style. Try to push the attack whenever it is advantageous.

Tiffin University
Academic Profile

Phone: (419) 448-3453

Tiffin, OH 44883

Type: 4 Yr.,Private,Liberal Arts
Founded: 1888
Website: http://www.tiffin.edu
Religion: Non-Affiliated
SAT/ACT/GPA: 860/18/2.0
Housing: Yes
Student/Faculty Ratio: 12:1
Male/Female Ratio: 3:1
Undergraduate Enrollment: 1,200
Graduate Enrollment: 120
Scholarships/Academic: Yes **Athletic:** Yes **Financial Aid:** Yes
Expenses by: Year **In State:** $ 800 **Out of State:** $ 800
Specialty: Business, Criminal Justice, Liberal Arts
Degrees Conferred: BA, BBA, BCJ, ABA
Programs of Study: Liberal Studies in Humanities, Liberal Studies in Social Sciences, Accounting, Finance, Hospitality Management, Information Studies, Sports Management, Health Care Management, Hotel & Restaurant Management, International Business, Marketing, Criminal Justice, Corrections, Forensic Psychology, Law Enforcement

Men's Athletic Profile

155 Miami Street
Tiffin, OH 44883
Coach: Ian Day
Email: lday@tiffin.edu

NCAA II/NAIA
Dragons/Green, Gold
Phone: (419) 448-3452
Fax: (419) 443-5007

Estimated # of Men's Soccer Scholarships: 6
Conference: American Mideast Conference
Program Profile: Our program is 16 year olds and currently rebuilding. We play at Tiffin University Athletic fields, which is natural turf and has a seating capacity for 500. The season runs from September to November.
History: We started in 1983. We won conference title in 1984 and won the next 9 in a row. We only have one losing season in program's history.
Achievements: The program produced 10 Conference Titles, Coach of the year in 1985, 1990-1992 & 1995; Runner-up for National Coach of the Year in 1988; 28 All-Americans.
Coaching: Ian Day, Head Coach, holds a NSCAA Advanced National Diploma. He was Coach of the Year for all NAIA/NCAA Division III teams in 1988 and Mideast Coach of the Year 5 times. Rudy Brownell is the Assistant Coach.
Roster In State: 18 **Out of State:** 3 **Out of Country:** 6
ODP State: 4 **Regional:** **National:**
Walk-on/Other: **Graduation %:** 700% **Seniors on Team:** 4
Positions Needed: Defender
Camp or Clinic Dates: Team Camp July 29-30
Most Recent Record: 19-3-1
Schedule: Rio Grande, Houghton, Roberts Wesleyan, Walsh, Ashland, Findlay
Style of Play: Strong offense with an aggressive defense.

Women's Athletic Profile

155 Miami Street
Tiffin, OH 44883
Coach: Jimmy Walker
Email: jwalker@tiffin.edu

NACAA II/NAIA
Dragons/Green, Gold
Phone: (419) 448-3290
Fax: (419) 443-5007

Estimated # of Women's Soccer Scholarships: 5
Conference: American Mideast

Program Profile: We have a new multi million dollar facility that has natural grass. We have a varsity and junior varsity programs. We are competitive in state and region. We have a 12 month program that includes indoor and outdoor soccer.
History: We began in 1991 and have been varsity since then. After rebuilding the program, Tiffin University has won back-to-back AMC titles and have shattered most team records over the last two years.
Achievements: 1998 and 1999 AMC champs; Walker Coach of the Year both years he coached here; top-ranked in the region; Elizabeth Wead was AMC player of the year in 1999.
Coaching: James Walker, Head Coach, has an English Prelim license. Rudy Brownell, Assistant Coach, has a USSF license.
Roster in State: 24 **Out of State:** 5 **Out of Country:** 4
ODP State: 6 **Regional:** **National:**
Walk-on/Other: **Graduation %:** 95% **Seniors on Team:** 1
Positions Needed: Defenders
Camp or Clinic Dates: July 29-30
Most Recent Record: 16-4-0
Schedule: Ashland, Findley, Ohio Wesleyan, W Virginia Wesleyan, St. Francis, Houghton
Style of Play: Fast-paced offense with smothering defense.

University of Akron
Academic Profile

Phone:

Akron, OH 44325-5201

Type: 4 Yr.,Public **Founded:** 1870
Website: http://www.uakron.edu **Religion:** Non-Affiliated
SAT/ACT/GPA: Varies **Housing:** Yes
Student/Faculty Ratio: 20:1 **Male/Female Ratio:** 1:1
Undergraduate Enrollment: 20,037 **Graduate Enrollment:** 3,568
Scholarships/Academic: Yes **Athletic:** Yes **Financial Aid:** Yes
Expenses by: Year **In State:** $ 8,317 **Out of State:** $ 14,167
Specialty: Engineering
Degrees Conferred: AA, AS, BA, BS, BFA, MA, MS, MBA
Programs of Study: Accounting, Art, Advertising, Biology, Business Administration, Chemistry, Classics, Communications, Communicative Disorder, Computer Science, Construction Technology, CytoTechnology, Dance, Economics, Elementary Education, Engineering, English, Finance, Geography, Geology, History, Humanities, Management, Marketing, Mathematics, Medical Science, Psychology, Music, Nursing, Philosophy, Political Science, Physical Education, Physics, Social Science, Social Work, Sociology, Special Education.

Men's Athletic Profile

302 E. Buchtel Mall
Akron, OH 44325
Coach: Ken Lolla
Email: lolla@uakron.edu

NCAA I
Zips/Blue, Gold
Phone: (330) 972-7990
Fax: (330) 972-6463

Estimated # of Men's Soccer Scholarships: N/A
Conference: Mid-American College Conference
Program Profile: We are one of the top four programs in the Midwest. We play on a lighted, natural grass field, called Lee Jackson Field, with a seating capacity for 2,500. We have a very competitive schedule.
History: Our program began in 1955. We made the Mid-American Conference for three years and our overall conference record is 11-5-2. We have a tradition of strong teams, and have appeared in NCAA Soccer Championship competition. Original coach and a founder is Stu Parry.
Achievements: Conference titles ;1991 Mid-Continent in 1993, 1995 & 1997 ; Mid-American in 1986 NCAA Finalist; 32 All-Americans; 26 players in the pros (1969 to the present); 1997 3 District IV Academic All-Americans.

Coaching: Ken Lolla, Head Coach, was two-time MAC Coach of the Year. He played professionally for the Canton Invaders of the National Professional Soccer League in 1984-1988. He was named Carolina's Conference Coach of the Year in 1990. He was a high school All-American pick in 1980. NSCAA - NAIA Coach of the Year Honors and Mid-American Conference Coach of the Year. Herb Haller - Assistant Coach, Indiana in 1988. Brian Stock - Assistant Coach, joined Akron in 1995.
Style of Play: Emphasis on possession, attacking style.

Women's Athletic Profile

JAR-Arena 75
Akron, OH 44325-5201
Coach: Catherine Byrne
Email: cbyrne@uakron.edu

NCAA I
Zips/Blue & Yellow
Phone: (330) 972-2167
Fax: (330) 972-6463

Estimated # of Women's Soccer Scholarships: 10
Conference: Mid-American Conference (MAC)
Program Profile: 1st year program, playing field 120x75 on campus with lights and has a seating capacity of 4,000. Training facilities include Olympic sized indoor pool, weight room is one of the largest in Ohio/Midwest.
History: Will begin in 2001
Coaching: Head Coach Catherine Byrne. Assistant Coach Keith Closson.
Schedule: Miami Univ. Buffalo, BGSU, Robert Morris, Ohio Univ.

University of Cincinnati
Academic Profile

Phone:

Cincinnati, OH 45221-0021

Type: 4 Yr.,Public,Liberal Arts,Engineering
Founded: 1819
Website: http://www.uc.edu
Religion: All-Denomination
SAT/ACT/GPA: 1054/22
Housing: Yes
Student/Faculty Ratio: 20:1
Male/Female Ratio: 47:53
Undergraduate Enrollment: 17,833
Graduate Enrollment: 4,422
Scholarships/Academic: Yes **Athletic:** Yes **Financial Aid:** Yes
Expenses by: Year **In State:** $12,129 **Out of State:** $12,129
Specialty: Architecture, Education, Engineering, Interior Design, Medicine
Degrees Conferred: 500 undergraduates, Master's, Doctoral Degree
Programs of Study: African American Studies, Anthropology, Asian Studies, Biological Sciences, Biology, Chemistry, Classical Civilization Classics, Communications, Comparative Literature, Computer Science, Earth Science, Economics, English Literature, Environmental Science, French, Geography, Geology, German, History, International Affairs, Judaic Studies, Latin American Studies, Linguistics, Mathematics, Philosophy Physics, Political Science, Psychology, Sociology, Spanish

Men's Athletic Profile

P.O. Box 210021
Cincinnati, OH 45221
Coach: Jeff Cook
Email: coojf@email.uc.edu

NCAA I
Bearcats/Red, Black, White
Phone: (513) 556-1100
Fax: (513) 556-1105

Estimated # of Men's Soccer Scholarships: N/A
Conference: Conference USA

Program Profile: Play on natural grass field with a lights, seats about 600-800. We had a turf practice field. Season runs from mid-August to late November.
History: Program began in 1973, entering fourth year in Conference USA. Second year as a full time program. Overall record is 209-208-26.
Achievements: 1997 Conference USA Coach of the Year; 2 players in the Eastern Indoor Soccer League.
Coaching: Jeff Cook is our Head Coach. He has a USSF "A" License, NSCAA Advanced National Diploma, Region I Staff Coach for Olympian Development Team, Liason for Nigeria National Team during M-V Cup in 1994. He also spent two years as assistant coach at Dartmouth, three years as a head coach at Wheaton College, MA. Bill Brady - Assistant Coach. Darryn Fiske - Strength Coach.

Women's Athletic Profile

P.O. Box 0021, Women's Soccer
Cincinnati, OH 45221-0091
Coach: Meridy Glenn
Email: meridy.glenn@uc.edu

NCAA I
Bearcats/Red, White, Black
Phone: (513) 556-0567
Fax: (513) 556-2209

Estimated # of Women's Soccer Scholarships: None
Conference: Conference USA
Program Profile: We have a new facility that includes lights and sport turf.
History: Our women's soccer program started in 1980. We have had three coaches: Janet Lines, John McNamara and Meridy Glenn.
Achievements: Top half of C-USA competitively, 4 NCAA appearances, 3 Conference Championships
Coaching: Meridy Glenn, Head Coach, has a USSF 'A' license. She was a former Region II & Ohio - South State ODP Coach. She is Bearcat Soccer Director. She was a NSCAA Convention Clinician in 1990 and in the NCAA Women's Championship committee (Sept 1994). Shannon Jewell is assistant coach.
Roster in State: 21 **Out of State:** 4 **Out of Country:**
ODP State: 6 **Regional:** 3 **National:**
Walk-on/Other: 2 **Graduation %:** 90% **Seniors on Team:** 7
Positions Needed: Goalkeeper, Central players
Camp or Clinic Dates: July
Most Recent Record: 8-10-1
Style of Play: Athletic, good speed, balanced and very good goalkeeping.

University of Dayton

Academic Profile

Phone: (937) 229-2492
Dayton, OH 45469-1220

Type: 4 Yr.,Private
Founded: 1850
Website: http://www.udayton.edu
Religion: Catholic (Marianist)
SAT/ACT/GPA: 1110/22
Housing: Yes
Student/Faculty Ratio: 14.5:1
Male/Female Ratio: 49:51
Undergraduate Enrollment: 6,000
Graduate Enrollment: 3,000
Scholarships/Academic: Yes **Athletic:** Yes **Financial Aid:** Yes
Expenses by: Year **In State:** $ 19,840 **Out of State:** $ 19,840
Specialty: Comprehensive Studies
Degrees Conferred: BS, MS, Doctorate
Programs of Study: Administration Studies, Biology, BioChemistry, Chemistry, Communications, Computer Information Systems, Computer Science, Criminal Justice, Economics, English, Environmental Biology, Environmental Geology, Geology, History, International Studies, Languages, Math, Music, Philosophy, Physical Science, Physics, Physics Computer Science, Political Science, PreLaw, PreMed, PreDental, Psychology, International Business, Management, Marketing, Health & Sport Science, Teacher Education, Engineering, Electrical, Manufacturing, Mechanical

Men's Athletic Profile

300 College Park
Dayton, OH 45469
Coach: Jim Launder
Email: launder@yar.udayton.edu

NCAA I
Flyers/Red, Blue
Phone: (937) 229-4411
Fax: (937) 224-4461

Estimated # of Men's Soccer Scholarships: N/A
Conference: Atlantic 10 Conference
Program Profile: Our game field is on campus with a seating capacity of a 1,200 and a natural grass field that measures 110x73 yards. We have two on campus dedicated soccer fields, and an indoor training facility with a dimensions of 80x50 yards.
History: Our program began in 1956 and joined Atlantic 10 in 1995.
Achievements: 1997 Atlantic 10 Championships; 1989 Atlantic 10 Championship; 1995 Jim Launder named National College Soccer Coach of the Year.
Coaching: Jim Launder, Head Coach, was a Big Ten Coach of the Year in 1991 & 1995. He was NSCAA Regional Coach of the Year in 1989, 1981 & 1995, NSCAA National Coach of the Year in 1995 and NCAA I National Champion at UW. Dave Schureck is the Assistant Coach.
Style of Play: Aggressive possession - play to penetrate or hold the ball in the opponent's half and win back as soon as possible.

Women's Athletic Profile

300 College Park
Dayton, OH 45469-1220
Coach: Mike Tucker
Email: tucker@yar.udayton.edu

NCAA I
Flyers/Red, Blue
Phone: (937) 229-4459
Fax: (937) 229-4461

Estimated # of Women's Soccer Scholarships: 9.75
Conference: Atlantic 10 Conference
Program Profile: The team plays a traditional fall & non-traditional spring seasons. This is the 15th year of varsity soccer. Also, starting junior varsity team in 1999. Field is natural grass that measures 112x75 yards. Balltan Field on campus with capacity of 3,000 and presently building a new soccer stadium to open in 2000. Has two practice field on campus.
History: The program started in 1984; playing an independent schedule. We joined the MCC in 1987-1988 and played until joining the Great Midwest in 1992-1993, where we played until the 1995-1996 season. In 1995-1996, we joined the Atlantic 10 Conference, where we are currently affiliated.
Achievements: Coach Mike Tucker named the OCSCA 1996 Division I Coach of the Year, won a Regular Season Championships in 1996 & 1998, Atlantic 10 Tourney Championship in 1996, produced numerous Regional All-Americans including 2 in 1998. Missy Gregg, a freshman, was named All-American in 1999.
Coaching: Mike Tucker, Head Coach, fifth year, five years as an assistant coach at University of Dayton, Staff Coach at Ohio South Olympic Development Program, and former coach of Cardinals, South Carolina. Compiled 22-18-1 record in two years as a head coach. He was named in 1996 Coach of the Year. Greg Sheen is spending his second year at UD. He formerly was director of coaching for TopHat soccer club in Georgia; he also played professionally in Europe and with the Atlanta Attack. George Demetriades is the Assistant Coach of five years after having been with the men's team for four years.

Roster in State: 14	**Out of State:** 4	**Out of Country:** 0
ODP State: 4	**Regional:** 5	**National:** 1
Walk-on/Other:	**Graduation %:** 100%	**Seniors on Team:** 3

Positions Needed: Striker, Midfielder, Defender
Most Recent Record: 18-5-0
Schedule: Michigan, Oakland, Xavier, University of Massachusetts, Air Force, Cincinnati, Michigan State
Style of Play: Possession, get forward early if it creates numbers up; attack with 11, defend with 11. we run a 4-4-2.

University of Findlay

Academic Profile

Phone: (352) 375-4683

Findlay, OH 45840

Type: 4 Yr.,Private,Liberal Arts
Founded: 1882
Website: http://www.findlay.edu
Religion: Church of God
SAT/ACT/GPA: 740/18/2.0
Housing: Yes
Student/Faculty Ratio: 17:1
Male/Female Ratio: 1:1
Undergraduate Enrollment: 3,200
Graduate Enrollment: 400
Scholarships/Academic: Yes **Athletic:** Yes
Financial Aid: Yes
Expenses by: Year **In State:** $ 19,238
Out of State: $ 19,238
Degrees Conferred: AA, BA, BS, MBA
Programs of Study: Agriculture, Bilingual Education, Business and Management, Environmental and Hazardous Material Management, Equestrian Studies, Education, Health Science, PreMed, PreVet, Social Sciences

Men's Athletic Profile

1000 North Main Street
Findlay, OH 45840
Coach: Andy Smyth
Email: Smyth@Lucy.findlay.edu

NCAA I
Oilers/Orange, Black
Phone: (800) 548-0932
Fax: (419) 424-4618

Estimated # of Men's Soccer Scholarships:
Conference: Great Lakes Intercollegiate Athletic Conference
Program Profile: We have separate game and practice fields consistently of a natural surface. Fall and spring seasons.
History: Our program began in 1980. Our men's team has made the playoffs for five times.
Achievements: We have 2 Academic All-American players.
Coaching: Andy Smyth, Head Coach, holds a USSF "A" License, NSCAA Advanced National Diploma and FA England Preliminary Badge. Mark Steinmetz and Devin Kent are Assistant Coaches.
Style of Play: Mid to low pressure defense and indirect short passing offense.

Women's Athletic Profile

1000 North Main Street
Findlay, OH 45840
Coach: Andy Smyth
Email: Smyth@Lucy.Findlay.edu

NCAA II/NAIA
Oilers/Orange, Black
Phone: (800) 548-0932
Fax: (419) 424-4618

Estimated # of Women's Soccer Scholarships:
Conference: Great Lakes Intercollegiate Athletic Conference
Program Profile: We play and new grass field.
History: Our program in 1986. Our team made the National Tournament 4 times (NAIA in 1994 & 1997).
Achievements: Numerous All-Americans and NAIA Scholar Athletes; Regional Champions in 1994, 1995, & 1996; NAIA National Tournament Participants in 1994, 1995 & 1996.
Coaching: Andy Smyth, Head Coach, holds a USSF "A" License, NSCAA Advanced National Diploma, FA (England) Preliminary Badge.
Style of Play: High pressure defense, indirect short passing offensively.

University of Rio Grande
Academic Profile

Phone:

Rio Grande, OH 45674

Type: 4 Yr.,Private,Liberal Arts
Website: http://www.rio.edu
SAT/ACT/GPA: 820/18
Student/Faculty Ratio: 20:1
Undergraduate Enrollment: 2,000
Scholarships/Academic: Yes **Athletic:** Yes
Expenses by: Year **In State:** $ 10,100
Founded: 1876
Religion: Non-Affiliated
Housing: Yes
Male/Female Ratio: 50:50
Graduate Enrollment: 150
Financial Aid: Yes
Out of State: $ 10,500
Specialty:
Degrees Conferred: AA, AS, AAS, BS, M.Ed.
Programs of Study: Accounting, Art, BioChemistry, Biology, Business & Management, Chemistry, Communications, Computer Science, Economics, Education, English, Finance, Health Sciences, Communications, Computer Science, Economics, Education, International Business, Liberal Arts, Mathematics, Music, Nursing, Physical Fitness/Exercise Science, Physical Science, Physics, PreMed, Psychology, Social Science, Special Education, Theatre

Men's Athletic Profile

UPO 879
Rio Grande, OH 45674
Coach: Scott Morrissey
Email: Not Available
NAIA
Redmen/Red, White
Phone: (614) 245-5353
Fax: (614) 245-7555

Estimated # of Men's Soccer Scholarships: N/A
Conference: Mid-Ohio Conference
Program Profile: Season is from August - November. Preseason training, 20 game schedule. Off-season training (indoor & outdoor), weight training program. 2 fields, 1 game field, beautiful location.
History: Rio Grande men's soccer hired its first full-time coach in 1990.
Achievements: Conference Coach of the year 1990, 1 All - American, 1 Academic All - American, 4 All - Mid East, 6 All - District.
Coaching: Scott C Morrissey, Head Coach, NSCAA National Diploma, 1989 graduate of Tiffin, 2 time All - American, 1988 Senior Bowl participant, various camps attended, hosts soccer camps on campus.
Style of Play: Build up, 1-2 combinations. Direct in the final third of the field. Team play will also be decided by players style and how they blend together.

University of Toledo
Academic Profile

Phone: (419) 530-2072

Toledo, OH 43606

Type: 4 Yr.,Public,Liberal Arts
Website: http://www.utoledo.edu
SAT/ACT/GPA: 900/18
Student/Faculty Ratio: 23:1
Undergraduate Enrollment: 20,000
Scholarships/Academic: Yes **Athletic:** Yes
Expenses by: Year **In State:** $ 11,000
Founded: 1867
Religion: Non-Affiliated
Housing: Yes
Male/Female Ratio: 51:49
Graduate Enrollment: 2,000
Financial Aid: Yes
Out of State: $ 16,000
Specialty: Engineering, Education, Business, Law, Nursing, Pharmacy
Degrees Conferred: BA, BS, MA, MS, MBA, MBA, JD, Nursing
Programs of Study: Arts & Sciences, Business Administration, Education and Allied Professions, Engineering, Law, Pharmacy, University College, Community and Technical College. 150 undergraduate majors, more than 50 graduate and doctoral degrees.

Women's Athletic Profile

2801 W Bancroft St.
Toledo, OH 43606
Coach: R.J. Anderson
Email: randers@pop3.utoledo.edu

NCAA I
Rockets/Midnight Blue, Gold
Phone: (419) 530-3448
Fax: (419) 530-3953

Estimated # of Women's Soccer Scholarships: None
Conference: Mid - America Conference (MAC)
Program Profile: Facilities include a 120x75 natural grass playing field and a separate practice field.
History: Our program began in 1995. Toledo has a varsity and developmental (junior varsity) team maintaining a roster total of 35 players.
Achievements: Mandy Delbrideg - All-Ohio 1st team in 1996; Jamie Appelton - Paramount Academic Award; Molly Skeen, Angela Sapienza - Paramount Academic Award. Shauna Cotterell ('00) - 3rd team Great Lakes All-American.
Coaching: R.J. Anderson, Head Coach, first year, over 35 years of soccer experience at the national and international level as a coach, official , and a professional player.
Roster in State: 18 **Out of State:** 15 **Out of Country:** 6
Walk-on/Other: **Graduation %:** **Seniors on Team:** 3
Positions Needed: midfield, defense
Camp or Clinic Dates: Not Available
Most Recent Record: 9-8-0
Style of Play: Normally play a 4-4-2. Short, short, long. We look to play direct if available.

Walsh University

Academic Profile

Phone:

N. Canton, OH 44720

Type: 4 Yr.,Private,Liberal Arts
Founded: 1959
Website: http://www.walsh.edu
Religion: Catholic
SAT/ACT/GPA: 860/18/2.0
Housing: Yes
Student/Faculty Ratio: 20:1
Male/Female Ratio: 1:1
Undergraduate Enrollment: 1,350
Graduate Enrollment: 200
Scholarships/Academic: Yes **Athletic:** Yes **Financial Aid:** Yes
Expenses by: Year **In State:** $ 17,000 **Out of State:** $ 17,000
Specialty: Business, Nursing, Physical Therapy, Education
Degrees Conferred: Assn., BA, BS, MA
Programs of Study: General Liberal Arts, Business, Nursing, Education, PreDental, PreMed, PreOptical, PreVet, PreLaw, Physical Therapy, PreNatural Resources, International Studies, Communications, Computer Science, English, History, Mathematics, Sociology, Psychology, Philosophy, Theology

Men's Athletic Profile

2020 Easton Street, NW
N. Canton, OH 44720-3396
Coach: Tim Mead
Email: t.mead@walsh.edu

NAIA
Cavaliers/Maroon, Gold
Phone: (330) 490-7013
Fax: (330) 490-7038

Estimated # of Men's Soccer Scholarships: 2.5
Conference: American Mideast Conference
Program Profile: Play all year round; indoor starts from January and February; spring-outdoor starts from March and April. Play on 120x75 yards natural playing field; 100x60 natural practice field.
History: Program began in 1971. Won Mid-Ohio Conference in 1977, 1981, 1987, 1993, and 1994; qualified or NAIA National Tournament in 1993 with a record of 21-4 (best ever). 17-5-2 in 1994. Qualified for playoffs that last 10 years. 1999 11-6-1 8-3 in AMC 3rd place.

Achievements: Tim Mead was named Coach of the Year in 1993, 1992, 1990, 1987 & 1983; COY - Ohio in 1993; All-Americans: Per Tunestaw in 1987 & 1988, Ron Mendel in 1990 & 1991, Mario Gigauti in 1993, and Joe Urbanick in 1993. 8 All-Americans. M.O.C. Champions 1993 & 1994. NAIA National tournament 1993, qualified for post-season play 13 consecutive years.
Coaching: Tim Mead, Head Coach, NSCAA Advanced National in 1989; has 17 years of coaching experience with a record of 205-125-22; Conference Coach of the Year in 1983, 1987, 1990, 1992, 1993 & 1994. Ron Mendel, Assistant Coach, Ph.D. degree, Exercise Physiology at Kent State. He was named two-time All-American at Walh University in 1990 & 1991. Mike McBride, Assistant Coach, was named All-American in 1998.
Michael McBride-NSCAA National Diploma 1999, 2x All-Conference players for Walsh

Roster In State: 18	**Out of State:** 2	**Out of Country:** 2
ODP State: 7	**Regional:** 2	**National:**
Walk-on/Other:	**Graduation %:** 100%	**Seniors on Team:** 5

Positions Needed: GK, Midfield (Center), Outside backs
Camp or Clinic Dates: last 2 weeks of July
Most Recent Record: 11-6-1
Schedule: Roberts Wesleyan, Rio Grande, Houghton, Tiffin, Ashland, Ohio Wesleyan, Aquinas, Michigan
Style of Play: Possession - short, short, short, long.

Women's Athletic Profile

2020 Easton St., NW	**NAIA**
North Canton, OH 44720-3396	Cavaliers/Maroon, Gold
Coach: Jack Heim	**Phone:** (330) 490-7022
Email: jheim@alex.walsh.edu	**Fax:** (330) 490-7038

Estimated # of Women's Soccer Scholarships: 1+
Conference: Mid Ohio Conference
Program Profile: Competitive League and NAIA Region. We have grass field built in 1995. We have 20 game fall schedule.
History: Our program began in 1988. We were qualified for post-season tournaments 8 times.
Achievements: Allison Davis was named 2-time All-American in 1991 & 1992. We have had 14 Academic All-Americans and 9 Regional All-Americans.
Coaching: Jack Heim is our Head Coach. He is entering ninth year with the program. He has 14 years college coaching experience. He holds NSCAA National Diploma, Ohio Northern U18 ODP Coach from 1988-1996.

Roster in State: 20	**Out of State:** 1	**Out of Country:** 0
Walk-on/Other:	**Graduation %:** 99.9%	**Seniors on Team:** 7

Positions Needed: Center Midfielder, Sweeper
Most Recent Record: 6-10-1
Schedule: Houghton College, Tiffin University, Indiana Wesleyan University, College of Wooster, Ohio northern University, Malone College, Roberts Wesleyan College, Seton Hill College
Style of Play: Ball control, short passing, lot of motion and aggressive defense.

Wilmington College - Ohio

Academic Profile

	Phone:
Wilmington, OH 45177	

Type: 4 Yr.,Private,Liberal Arts		**Founded:** 1870
Website: http://www.wilmington.edu		**Religion:** Non-Affiliated
SAT/ACT/GPA: 850/20		**Housing:** Yes
Student/Faculty Ratio: 17:1		**Male/Female Ratio:** 50:50
Undergraduate Enrollment: 1,100		**Graduate Enrollment:** N/A
Scholarships/Academic: Yes	**Athletic:** No	**Financial Aid:** Yes
Expenses by: Year	**In State:** $ 18,500	**Out of State:** $ 18,500

Specialty: Education, Athletic Training, Sports Management, Business
Degrees Conferred: BA, BS
Programs of Study: Accounting, Agricultural, Art, Athletic Training, Biology, Business Administration, Chemistry, Communications Arts, Computer Information Science, History, Computer Science, Criminal Justice, Elementary & Secondary Education, English, History, Mathematics, Physical Education, Psychology, Religion & Philosophy, Social & Political Studies, Social Work, Spanish, Sports Management, Theatre, PreLaw, PreMedicine, PreVet Science

Men's Athletic Profile

Box 1205, Wilmington College
Wilmington, OH 45177
Coach: Bud Lewis
Email: bad_lewis@wilmington.edu

NCAA III
Quakers/Forest Green, White
Phone: (937) 382-6661
Fax: (937) 382-8560

Estimated # of Men's Soccer Scholarships: None
Conference: Heartland Collegiate Athletic Conference
Program Profile: We have one of the top NCAA Division III program in the country. We had 22 consecutive winning seasons and 7 national tournament appearances. We play on a 120x75 natural grass, lighted soccer stadium. We've had four consecutive conference championships.
History: Our program was initiated in 1960 and competed in the NAIA until 1991. Coach Bud Lewis, started in 1975 to the present and has established the national reputation of the program. They play a national recognized schedule and are consistently ranked in the top 25 NCAA Division III rankings.
Achievements: Coach Bud Lewis, has been recognized as NSCAA Regional Coach of the Year 6 times and one of nine Division III coaches to record over 300 wins. Has had 21 NSCAA All-American selections. Steve Spirk, Greg Ayers, Greg Segureh and Chris Wanamaker were drafted and played professionally.
Coaching: Bud Lewis, Head Coach, holds a NSCAA Advanced National USSF "B" License, is on the ODP State Staff and Director of Midwest Soccer Academy. His coaching record is 311 wins, 122 losses, and 21 ties. Jim Adams, Assistant Coach, was a seven year NPSL veteran goalkeeper and NSCAA, All-American at Monmouth.
Style of Play: Very creative, ball possession indirect attacking. High technical and tactical capability. Blue colors defending mentality.

Women's Athletic Profile

Pyle Ctr, Box 1246
Wilmington, OH 45177
Coach: Steve Spirk
Email: Not Available

NCAA III
Lady Quakers/Green, White
Phone: (937) 382-6661
Fax: (937) 382-7077

Estimated # of Women's Soccer Scholarships: None
Conference: Association of Mideast Colleges
Program Profile: Best facilities of any small college in Ohio. Play elite Division III colleges. Season runs from September - November.
History: Program began in 1982.
Achievements: NAIA 3rd in nation 1986; 1987 Regional runner-up; 1993 American Mideast Conference Champs; All - Region 3rd team players.
Coaching: Steve Spirk, Head Coach, NSCAA National Diploma, AMC Conference and All - Ohio Coach of the Year.
Style of Play: 4-4-2; high pressure.

Wittenberg University

Academic Profile

Phone: (800) 677-7558

Springfield, OH 45501

Type: 4 Yr.,Private,Liberal Arts
Website: http://www.wittenberg.edu

Founded: 1845
Religion: Lutheran

SAT/ACT/GPA: 1160/25/3.5
Student/Faculty Ratio: 14:1
Undergraduate Enrollment: 2,100
Scholarships/Academic: Yes **Athletic:** No
Expenses by: Year **In State:** $ 26,112
Housing: Yes
Male/Female Ratio: 1:1
Graduate Enrollment: N/A
Financial Aid: Yes
Out of State: $ 26,112
Specialty: Undergraduate liberal arts
Degrees Conferred: BA, B.Mus., BME, BEA
Programs of Study: American Studies, Art, Biology, Chemistry, Computer Science, East Asian Studies, Economics, Education, English, French, Geography, Geology, German, History, Management, Mathematics, Music, Philosophy, Physics, Political Science, Psychology, Religion, Russian Area Studies, Sociology, Spanish, Theatre-Dance

Men's Athletic Profile

P.O. Box 720
Springfield, OH 45501
Coach: Dr. Steve Dawson
Email: sdawson@wittenberg.edu
NCAA III
Tigers/Red, White
Phone: (937) 327-6450
Fax: (937) 327-6428

Estimated # of Men's Soccer Scholarships: None
Conference: North Coast Athletic Conference
Program Profile: Facilities include grass field, 120 X 75, and 2 practice fields.
History: Program began in 1966; OAC Conference until 1989 then into NCAC.
Achievements: Coach of the Year NCAC in 1991, 1992, & 1993; team made NCAA playoffs in 1991, 1992, 1993, & 1996; OAC Champs in 1984, NCAC Champs in 1993, numerous All-Americans, 4 players USISL.
Coaching: Steve Dawson, Head Coach, FA Badge, USSF Badge, Advanced National Diploma, USSF "A" License. Chris Brown - Assistant Coach, UEFA "A" License, USSF "A" License.
Style of Play: Use whole field on attack, aggressive but-disciplined on defense, get players forward.

Women's Athletic Profile

P.O. Box 720
Springfield, OH 45501
Coach: Fran Kulas
Email: fkulas@wittenberg.edu
NCAA III
Tigers/Red, White
Phone: (937) 327-6496
Fax: (937) 327-6428

Estimated # of Women's Soccer Scholarships: None
Conference: North Coast Athletic Conference
Program Profile: We have varsity program that compete in the extremely competitive NCAC Conference. We have excellent playing and practice facilities (grass). Our 2000 season will consist of 17 regular season matches with post-season conference tournament.
History: Our program began in 1986.
Achievements: We have has 2 All - Americans in 1995; NCAC Defensive Player of the Year in 1995; Offensive Player of the Year in 1995; 1st team All - American in 1995; 2nd team All - American in 1995.
Coaching: Fran Kulas is our Head Coach. He was graduate of the University of Delaware. He has served as an assistant coach at the University of Delaware and with the Delaware Wizards (USL professional) and Delaware Genies (USL W-I league). He has been the Head Coach of Girls ODP teams in both Delaware and Ohio. He coached the Al Dupont girls high school team to the 1999 State Championship and ranking and a ranking of 5th nationally.
Roster in State: 15 **Out of State:** 11 **Out of Country:** 1
ODP State: 9 **Regional:** 1 **National:** 0
Walk-on/Other: 0 **Graduation %:** **Seniors on Team:** 6
Positions Needed: Goalkeeper, Attacking Midfielder, Forward
Camp or Clinic Dates: July 24-28; July 31-August 4
Most Recent Record: 7-11-1
Schedule: DePauw, Ohio Wesleyan, Denison, Capital, Earlham, Wooster
Style of Play: Creative, attacking minded and entertaining.

Wright State University

Academic Profile

Dayton, OH 45435

Phone: (937) 775-2368

Type: 4 Yr.,Public,Liberal Arts,Engineering
Website: http://www.wright.edu
SAT/ACT/GPA: General/2.0
Student/Faculty Ratio: 20:1
Undergraduate Enrollment: 12,000
Scholarships/Academic: Yes
Athletic: Yes
Expenses by: Year
In State: $ 9,365
Specialty: 107 Degrees
Founded: 1964
Religion: Non-Affiliated
Housing: Yes
Male/Female Ratio: 1:1.3
Graduate Enrollment: 3,000
Financial Aid: Yes
Out of State: $ 13,295
Degrees Conferred: BA, BS, BBA, MA, MD, MS
Programs of Study: Accounting, Biology, Business Administration, Communications, Computer Science, Education, Engineering, Health Science, History, Mathematics, Philosophy, Physical Education, Physical Sciences, Social Sciences

Men's Athletic Profile

3640 Colonel Glenn Hwy.
Dayton, OH 45435
Coach: Hylton Dayes
Email: hdayes@wright.edu

NCAA I
Raiders/Hunter Green, Gold
Phone: (937) 775-3014
Fax: (937) 775-2368

Estimated # of Men's Soccer Scholarships:
Conference: Midwestern Collegiate Conference
Program Profile: The team plays on alumni field which has lights and is natural grass field. It has a seating capacity of 1,000. Playing season is in the fall.
History: Our program is in existing since 1968, record is 247-151-50 for 25 years.
Achievements: 7 All-Americans; several All-Ohioans, several All-Conference players.
Coaching: Hylton Dayes, Head Coach, NSCAA National Staff, four-time All-American; former professional player and assistant coach at James Madison University from 1994-1996. Mike Tracy, Assistant Coach (WSU). John Mers, Assistant Coach, Youth National Goalkeeper, professional player, Region II goalkeeper trainer, USSF Licensed Coach.
Style of Play: The team plays a 4-4-2 possession build-up.

Women's Athletic Profile

3640 Colonel Glenn Avenue
Dayton, OH 45435
Coach: Scott Rodgers
Email: Not Available

NCAA I
Raiders/Forest Green, Gold
Phone: (937) 775-2771
Fax: (937) 775-2368

Estimated # of Women's Soccer Scholarships: None
Conference: Midwestern Collegiate Conference
Program Profile: We are in the Midwest Collegiate Conference. Our field has natural grass and measures 120 x 76. We have 2,000+ stadium seats. Our stadium was rebuilt and it now has a new playing surface and lights.
History: The program began in 1985 . We joined Division I in 1987.We had six straight winning seasons and ranked in the Top Ten in the Central Region in 1990 & 1991.
Achievements: We were MCC Tournament Champions, 1999 MCC Regular Season Champions and 1995 MCC Tournament Champions, 1998 & 1999 NCAA Tournament Appearance and MCC Coach of the Year in 1999.
Coaching: Scott Rodgers is our Head Coach. He holds USSF "A" License. He is entering third year with the program. Kevin Arcuri is our Assistant Coach. He holds USSF "A" License. He is entering third year with the program. John Mers is our Assistant Coach. He holds USSf "C" License. He is entering third year with the program.

Roster in State: 19
Out of State: 6
Out of Country: 1
ODP State: 7
Regional: 2
National: 0
Walk-on/Other: 0
Graduation %: 2000
Seniors on Team:

Camp or Clinic Dates: July 16-20
Most Recent Record: 11-8-1
Schedule: Dayton, Butler, Milwaukee, Michigan State, Air Force, Evansville, Miami
Style of Play: Attacking!!! Multiple systems (depends upon players available).

Xavier University

Academic Profile

Cincinnati, OH 45207 | **Phone:**

Type: 4 Yr.,Private,Liberal Arts | **Founded:** 1831
Website: http://www.xu.edu | **Religion:** Jesuit
SAT/ACT/GPA: 900+/20+ | **Housing:** yes
Student/Faculty Ratio: 16:1 | **Male/Female Ratio:** 46:54
Undergraduate Enrollment: 3,500 | **Graduate Enrollment:** 2,000
Scholarships/Academic: Yes | **Athletic:** Yes | **Financial Aid:** Yes
Expenses by: Year | **In State:** $ 18,500 | **Out of State:** $ 18,500
Degrees Conferred: BA, BS, AA, BFA, BSBA, BSN
Programs of Study: Over 50 majors including: Allied Health, Business & Management, Communications, Education, Health Sciences, Letters/Literature, Psychology, Social Sciences

Men's Athletic Profile

3800 Victory Pkwy
Cincinnati, OH 45207-6114
Coach: Jack Hermans
Email: hermans@xavier.xu.edu

NCAA I
Musketeers/N Blue, Gray, White
Phone: (513) 745-3879
Fax: (513) 745-2835

Estimated # of Men's Soccer Scholarships: N/A
Conference: Atlantic-10 Conference
Program Profile: A very competitive Division I. Has a very good playing field which is natural grass. Year-round commitment program. Stadium holds 1,500 people. Stadium is called Cocoran Field located on campus and is natural grass.
History: Program began in 1974 and became part of the MCC in 1987. Became part of the Atlantic 10 Conference in 1995. Hermans has been coaching at Xavier for six years. He has compiled a record of 67-81-12.
Achievements: In 1992, Jack Hermans was named MCC Coach of the Year; drafted players were Doug Teggre by the National Professional Soccer League, Chris Stamper by the USISL League and Mike Crosby by the USISLA-League called up to MLS Columbus Crew for try-out.
Coaching: Jack Hermans, Head Coach, USSF 'A' license, Director of Soccer Unlimited Soccer Camp, Dutch Full Badge, State Coach Ohio South, USSF Coaching Instructor. He was named MCC Coach of the Year in 1992. Brad Ruzzo and Chris Combs, Assistant Coaches.
Style of Play: Possession oriented, attractive and hopefully effective.

Women's Athletic Profile

3800 Victory Parkway
Cincinnati, OH 45207
Coach: Dr. Ron Quinn
Email: quinnr@xu.edu

NCAA I
Musketeers/Navy, White
Phone: (513) 745-1084
Fax: (513) 745-4291

Estimated # of Women's Soccer Scholarships: None
Conference: Atlantic 10 Conference
Program Profile: Play on a new natural grass lighted stadium with a measurements of 75x120 yards.

History: The program began in 1985.
Achievements: 1995 Athletic 10 Runner-Up.
Coaching: Dr. Ron Quinn, Head Coach, Associate Professor Director of Health, Physical Education and Sport Studies, USSF "A" coaching license, National Staff, authored "The Peak Performance: Soccer Games for Player Development". Assistant Coach is Carrie Taylor who holds a USSF"A" license.
Roster in State: 16 **Out of State:** 8 **Out of Country:** 0
Walk-on/Other: **Graduation %:** 100% **Seniors on Team:** 13
Camp or Clinic Dates: Not Available
Most Recent Record: 13-8-0
Schedule: Indiana, Kentucky, U-Mass, Loyola Marymount, Dayton.
Style of Play: Multiple formation used, attacking and possession play.

Youngstown State University

Academic Profile

Youngstown, OH 44555
Phone: (330) 742-1920

Type: 4 Yr.,Public
Founded: 1906
Website: http://www.ysu.edu
Religion: Non-Affiliated
SAT/ACT/GPA: 860/18/2.5
Housing: Yes
Student/Faculty Ratio: 20:1
Male/Female Ratio: 45:55
Undergraduate Enrollment: 12,324
Graduate Enrollment: 1,050
Scholarships/Academic: Yes **Athletic:** Yes **Financial Aid:** Yes
Expenses by: Year **In State:** $ Varies **Out of State:** $ Varies
Specialty: Health & Human Service, Education, Business, Nursing, Criminal Justice
Degrees Conferred: AA, BA, MS, Ph.D.
Programs of Study: 34 majors in College of Health & Human Services, 40 majors in College of Arts & Sciences, 20 majors in College of Business, 6 majors in College of Education, 15 majors in College of Engineering, 10 majors in College of Fine Arts & Performing Arts

Women's Athletic Profile

One University Plaza
Youngstown, OH 44555
Coach: Elizabeth Bartley
Email: Not Available

NCAA I
Penguins/Red, White
Phone: (330) 742-3629
Fax: (330) 742-2968

Estimated # of Women's Soccer Scholarships: N/A
Conference: Mid-Continent Conference
Program Profile: We are a competitive NCAA I program. We have a fall season schedule comprised of Ohio and Regional opponents. Our facility is Stambaugh Stadium which has artificial surface and a 20,384 capacity. We also have a natural grass training facility.
History: Our program began in 1996 and our overall record is 14-39-0.
Achievements: 1998 Missy Laforet-Second Team All-Ohio; 1998 Christine Handte-Nation's Division I leader in saves per game.
Coaching: Elizabeth Bartley, Head Coach is a 1993 graduate from Beloit College. She is the former coach from St. Xavier University, where they were Chicagoland Conference Champions in 1997 and Finalists in 1998. Brian Stock, Assistant Coach, is a 1995 graduate from the University of Akron. He led Akron to the Mid-American Conference Title in 1997.
Style of Play: 4-4-2 with a lot of motion; building up from the midfield to the attacking 1/3 and using the backs with overlapping runs and looking for far post runners.

oklahoma

OKLAHOMA

SCHOOL	CITY	AFFILIATION	PAGE
Bartlesville Wesleyan College	Bartlesville	NAIA	891
East Central University	Ada	NCAA II	892
Northeastern State University	Tahlequah	NCAA II	893
Northern Oklahoma College-Enid	Enid	NJCAA	894
Oklahoma Christian University	Oklahoma City	NAIA	895
Oklahoma City University	Oklahoma City	NAIA	896
Oklahoma State University	Stillwater	NCAA I	897
Oral Roberts University	Tulsa	NCAA I	898
St. Gregory's University	Shawnee	NAIA	899
Southern Nazarene University	Bethany	NAIA	900
Southwestern Oklahoma State	Weatherford	NCAA II	901
University of Central Oklahoma	Edmond	NCAA II	902
University of Oklahoma	Norman	NCAA I	903
U of Science & Arts of Oklahoma	Chickasha	NAIA	904
University of Tulsa	Tulsa	NCAA I	906

Bartlesville Wesleyan College

Academic Profile

Phone: (800) 468-6292

Bartlesville, OK 74006

Type: 4 Yr.,Private,Liberal Arts
Founded: 1909
Website: http://www.bwc.edu
Religion: Wesleyan
SAT/ACT/GPA: 860/18/2.0
Housing: Yes
Student/Faculty Ratio: 14:1
Male/Female Ratio: 38:62
Undergraduate Enrollment: 600
Graduate Enrollment: N/A
Scholarships/Academic: Yes
Athletic: Yes
Financial Aid: Yes
Expenses by: Year
In State: $ 13,400
Out of State: $ 13,400
Specialty: Business, Education, Nursing
Degrees Conferred: AA, AS, BS, BA
Programs of Study: Accounting, Applied Computer Information System, Behavioral Sciences, Biology, Business Administration, Business Education, Chemistry, Church Music, Communications Arts, Computer Science, Cross-Cultural, Ministry, Elementary Education, English, English Education, Exercise Science, General Science, History, Political Science, LBA, MHR, Mathematics, Music Education, Nursing, Pastoral Ministry, Physical Education, PreMedicine, PrePhysical Education Therapy

Men's Athletic Profile

2201 Silver Lake Road
Bartlesville, OK 74006-6299
Coach: Eric Mills
Email: emills@bwc.edu

NAIA
Eagles/Red, White, Blue
Phone: (800) 468-6292
Fax: (918) 335-6229

Estimated # of Men's Soccer Scholarships: Varies
Conference: Midlands Collegiate Athletic Conference
Program Profile: BWC Men's Soccer has been a very successful program over the years. We play a fall season on a 73x120 bermuda field.
Achievements: Produced 36 All-Americans and 12 Academic All-Americans. We made the NAIA National Tournament in 1997.
Coaching: Eric Mills, Head Coach, is entering his second year at BWC. He graduated from BWC in 1992 and was a three-year captain and four-year starter for the Eagles. After graduating from BWC, he coached for the Charlotte Eagles Soccer Club directing the U-19 Boys program and International Tours. He also played for four years for the Charlotte Eagles of the USL.
Style of Play: A strong possession game playing the ball out of the back with an emphasis on quick counter-attacks.

Women's Athletic Profile

2201 Silverlake Rd
Bartlesville, OK 74006
Coach: Curt Cloud
Email: ddjarmola@bwc.edu

NAIA
Lady Eagles/Red, White, Navy
Phone: (918) 333-6250
Fax: (918) 335-6244

Estimated # of Women's Soccer Scholarships: N/A
Conference: Midlands Collegiate Athletic Conference
Program Profile: The home games are played on natural turf, 75 X 120 yards. The Eagles have one of the finest fields in Oklahoma that seats 450. Playing season is from September to November.
History: The program began in 1992. We were in NCCAA and in NAIA from the beginning. Our overall record is 44-51-3. The team has had 4 winning seasons in the past 4 years. BWC has won NCCAA Central Region in 1998 and 1997 and advanced to the NCCAA Final Four in 1998 and Elite Eight in 1997. In 1995,1996,1997 and 1998, BWC qualified for the NAIA playoffs, losing each time in the first round of the playoffs. In 1998, BWC's record was 13-4-0.

Achievements: 9 All-Americans, 7 Academic All-Americans, 6 NAIA All-Conference players, 20 NCCAA All-Region players, 2 NCCAA All-Tournament players; 1997 and 1998 NSCAA Sportsmanship and Ethics Award for fairplay; 100% graduation rate and team overall GPA is 3.11.
Coaching: D.Darek Jarmola, Head Coach, is in his 5th season at BWC. He is a native of Poland where he played for KS Gwardia Kozalin. He played for FC Esso Zurich before a knee injury. He has coached high school, club and college teams in Kentucky, Georgia and Oklahoma. He coached Andrew College into the NJCAA Championship Game in 1992. He coached BWC to the NAIA finals in 1997. His overall coaching record is `131-44-7. His record at BWC is 62-30-4.
Style of Play: Possession oriented attacking soccer. We look to develop patience and discipline in our attack with short possession passing out of the back, deep overlaps by marking backs occur often. If we have an attack we take it, but we don't force it.

East Central University

Academic Profile

Ada, OK 74820
Phone: 580-332-8000

Type: 4 Yr.,Public
Founded: 1909
Website: http://www.ecok.edu
Religion: Non-Affiliated
SAT/ACT/GPA: 19avg
Housing: Yes
Student/Faculty Ratio: 24:1
Male/Female Ratio: 45:55
Undergraduate Enrollment: 4,200
Graduate Enrollment: 650
Scholarships/Academic: Yes **Athletic:** Yes **Financial Aid:** Yes
Expenses by: Year **In State:** $ 4,583 **Out of State:** $ 7,231
Degrees Conferred: BS, BA, BSE, BSW, MED, MS
Programs of Study: Accounting, Art, Biology, Business Administration, Cartography, Chemistry, Criminal Justice, Education, English, Environmental Science, Health, History, Human Resources, Legal Studies, Mass Communications, Mathematics, Music, Nursing, Physics, Political Science, Psychology, Social Work, Sociology, Speech

Women's Athletic Profile

East 14th Street
Ada, OK 74820
Coach: Heather Beam
Email: hbeam@mailclerk.ecok.edu

NCAA II
Tigers/Black, Orange, White
Phone: (580) 332-8000
Fax: (580) 332-8361

Estimated # of Women's Soccer Scholarships: None
Conference: Lone Star Conference
Program Profile: We have a new natural turf field and new locker room facilities are scheduled to be completed in the fall of 2001. We play a fall season of 20 games. We also play a spring tournament.
History: Our program began in 1997.
Achievements: Numerous All-Conference and All-Conference Academic selections.
Coaching: Heather Beam, Head Coach. Riley Bailey is Assistant Coach.
Roster in State: 10 **Out of State:** 8 **Out of Country:** 1
ODP State: 6 **Regional:** **National:**
Walk-on/Other: **Graduation %:** **Seniors on Team:** 5
Positions Needed: All
Camp or Clinic Dates: Not Available
Most Recent Record: 11-7
Schedule: Midwestern State, Texas A&M-Commerce, Southern Colorado, Incarnate Word, Regis

Northeastern State University

Academic Profile

Phone: 918-456-5511

Tahlequah, OK 74464

Type: 4 Yr.,Public,
Founded: 1851
Website: http://www.nsuok.edu
Religion: Non-Affiliated
SAT/ACT/GPA: 19+
Housing: Yes
Student/Faculty Ratio: 20:1
Male/Female Ratio: 40:60
Undergraduate Enrollment: 7,500
Graduate Enrollment: 1,800
Scholarships/Academic: Yes **Athletic:** Yes
Financial Aid: Yes
Expenses by: Year **In State:** $ 53.50/hr
Out of State: $ 127/hr
Degrees Conferred: BS, BA, BFA, MA, MS, MBA, OD
Programs of Study: Mathematics, Science, Nursing, Biology, Chemistry, Computer Science, Medical Technology, Nursing, Physics, Geography, History, Native American Studies, Political Science, Psychology, Sociology, Allied Health Administration, Criminal Justice, Social Work, Accounting, Business Administration, Business Education, Marketing, Finance, Management, Art, English, Mass Communications, Music

Men's Athletic Profile

600 N Grand Ave.
Tahlequah, OK 74464-2399
Coach: Charlie Mitchell
Email: Not Available

NCAA II
Redmen/Green, White
Phone: (918) 458-2071
Fax: (918) 458-2339

Estimated # of Men's Soccer Scholarships: None
Conference: Lone Star Conference
Program Profile: NSU soccer facility is considered one of the best in region. Fieldhouse consists of two dressing areas, weight room, training room, 1,000 seat bleachers, all natural turf.
History: NSU soccer began in 1981 as first state-funded institution in Oklahoma to offer varsity soccer. Last three years, NSU has compiled a record of 37-17-1 and twice finished as a Sectional Runner-u
Achievements: 2 District Championships; 2 Sectional Runner-up titles; numerous All-District players and Academic All-Americans.
Coaching: Charlie Mitchell, Head Coach, has brought a new level of soccer at NSU. Mitchell is a former player/coach for several professional soccer teams. Dan Deloache and Lee Quiett - Assistant Coaches, both of whom are professors in the NSU College of Education, have been with the program since it began in 1981.
Roster In State: 14 **Out of State:** 3 **Out of Country:** 5
Walk-on/Other: **Graduation %:** N/A **Seniors on Team:** 4
Positions Needed: All
Camp or Clinic Dates: Not Available
Most Recent Record: 10-8
Schedule: West Texas A&M, St. Gregory's, Oral Roberts, Central Arkansas, Oklahoma City University, Midwestern State University
Style of Play: Style of play is dictated by utilizing talents of recruited athletes and quality of competition - Diversified Style.

Women's Athletic Profile

600 N Grand Ave.
Tahlequah, OK 74464-2399
Coach: Charlie Mitchell
Email: Not Available

NCAA II
Lady Reds/Green, White
Phone: (918) 458-2071
Fax: (918) 458-2339

Estimated # of Women's Soccer Scholarships: None
Conference: Lone Star Conference
Program Profile: NSU soccer facility is considered one of the best in region. Fieldhouse consists of two dressing areas, weight room, training room, 1,000 seat bleaches, all natural turf.
History: Program began in 1996 and has improved dramatically. won four games first year and had 9-10-1 record in 1997. Won 6 Conference game last year and qualified for LCS Tournament both years.
Achievements: 3 Academic All-Conference selections in 1997.
Coaching: Charlie Mitchell, Head Coach, has brought a new level of soccer to NSU. Mitchell is a former player/coach for several professional soccer teams, including the New York Cosmos where he played with the legendary Pele.
Style of Play: Style of play is dictated by utilizing talents of recruited athletes and quality of competition-Diversified Style.

Northern Oklahoma College-Enid Campus

Academic Profile

Phone: 580-548-2208

Enid, OK 73701

Type: 2 YearPublic
Founded: 1901
Website:
Religion:
SAT/ACT/GPA:
Housing: Y
Student/Faculty Ratio: 20/1
Male/Female Ratio: 50/50
Undergraduate Enrollment: 1000
Graduate Enrollment:
Scholarships/Academic: Yes
Athletic: Yes
Financial Aid: Yes
Expenses by: Year
In State: $4959
Out of State: $6984
Degrees Conferred: Associate
Programs of Study: Early Education, Secondary Education, Social Science, General Studies, Nursing, Business Administration

Women's Athletic Profile

100 South University Avenue
Enid, OK 73701
Coach: Mark Persson
Email: nocsoeermp@hotmail.com

NJCAA
Jets/Red,Black,Silver
Phone: (580) 548-2395
Fax: (580) 548-2218

Estimated # of Women's Soccer Scholarships: Varies
Conference: Region II
Program Profile: 2001-2002 will be the second year of the program. 110x75 yard natural grass playing surface. Traditional fall playing season with a 20 game schedule.
History: The women's soccer program at the Enid campus began in 2000-01.
Achievements: SAC Coach of the Year 1997.
Coaching: Mark Persson-Head Soccer Coach. Repeat All-American at Southern Nazarene University. Head Coach at Phillips University from 1994-97.
Roster in State: 10
Out of State: 1
Out of Country: 2
ODP State: 2
Regional: 0
National: 0
Walk-on/Other: 4
Graduation %: 100
Seniors on Team: 1
Positions Needed: ALL
Most Recent Record: 12-5-0
Schedule: SNU, Southwestern Oklahoma State, Newman Univ. Richland College-Dallas
Style of Play: Man to man defensive marking in the midfield and back. Attack through the midfield with emphasis on ball possession.

Oklahoma Christian University

Academic Profile

Oklahoma City, OK 73136-1100

Phone:

Type: 4 Yr.,Private,Liberal Arts
Founded: 1950
Website: http://www.oc.edu
Religion: Church of Christ
SAT/ACT/GPA: None
Housing: Yes
Student/Faculty Ratio: 17:1
Male/Female Ratio: 51:49
Undergraduate Enrollment: 1,600
Graduate Enrollment: 30
Scholarships/Academic: Yes **Athletic:** Yes
Financial Aid: Yes
Expenses by: Year **In State:** $ 13,300
Out of State: $ 13,300
Specialty: Business, Education, Engineering
Degrees Conferred: BA, BS, BSE, BSEE, BSME, BBE, BFA, BME, MA
Programs of Study: Art & Design, Behavioral & Social Science, Biblical Studies, Business, Communications, Education, Language & Literature, Music, Science & Engineering

Men's Athletic Profile

P.O. Box 11000
Oklahoma City, OK 73136-1100
Coach: Eric Thornhill
Email: eric.thornhill@oc.edu

NAIA
Eagles/Maroon, White
Phone: (405) 425-5356
Fax: (405) 425-5351

Estimated # of Men's Soccer Scholarships: 10
Conference: Sooner Athletic Conference
Program Profile: We play on a lighted grass field with a concession stand. It has a seating capacity of 2,000. We play a fall season and our spring season consists of several scrimmages with 1 or 2 tournaments.
History: Our overall all-time record is 36-65-2. We have not gone to NAIA tournaments. We have 4 out of 6 years of post-season play. Our last post-season opponent was Southern Nazarene University. We lost in the first round district in 1998.
Achievements: Jon Goad received Coach of the Year Honors in 1998. All-American player was Kevin Arledge second team in 1992, All-American Honorable Mention were Smith in 1996, Eric Thornhill in 1996, Lee Edgerton in 1996 and Sam Winterbotham in 1998; Player of the Year honors were Kevin Arledge-district 9 in 1990 and 1992; Drafted Players were Scott Wallace, Lee Edgerton and Eric Thornhill.
Style of Play: Attack slowly from the back in an effort to get as many players forward as possible. Defend intelligently, and counter-attack when opportunities are there. Possession through passing on the ground, 4-4-2 formation with a zoning defending. Try to emulate a more Latin American approach.

Women's Athletic Profile

P.O. Box 11000
Oklahoma City, OK 73136-1100
Coach: Adam Basic
Email:

NAIA
Lady Eagles/Maroon, White
Phone: (405) 425-5356
Fax: (405) 425-5351

Estimated # of Women's Soccer Scholarships:
Conference: Sooner Athletic Conference
Program Profile: We play in a lighted grass field that has a concession stand and 2,000 seats. Our games are in the fall. The spring season consists of several scrimmages and 1 or 2 tournaments.
History: Our first year was 1993. Our overall record is 36-65-2. We have not been to any NAIA Tournaments. We have been in post-season play 4 of the last 6 years. Southern Nazarene University was our last post-season opponent. We lost in the first round in district in 1998.
Achievements: Nathan Shotts was Coach of the Year in 1993.
Style of Play: Possession through passing on the ground, 4-4-2 formation with zonal defending. Try to emulate a more Latin American approach.

Oklahoma City University

Academic Profile

Phone: (405)521-5165

Oklahoma City, OK 73106

Type: 4 Yr.,Private,Liberal Arts
Founded: 1904
Website: http://www.okcu.edu
Religion: Methodist
SAT/ACT/GPA:
Housing: Yes
Student/Faculty Ratio: 8-1
Male/Female Ratio: 35-65
Undergraduate Enrollment: 1,700
Graduate Enrollment: 2,300
Scholarships/Academic: Yes **Athletic:** Yes **Financial Aid:** Yes
Expenses by: Year **In State:** $13,000 **Out of State:** $13,000
Degrees Conferred: BA, BS
Programs of Study: Accounting, Advertising Asian Studies, Banking & Finance, Biology, Broadcasting, Business Administration, Chemistry, Communications, Computer Science, Criminal Justice, Dance, Dramatic Arts, Economics, Education, Fine Arts, Journalism, Law Enforcement, Management, Marketing, Mathematics, Nursing, Political Science, Social Science

Men's Athletic Profile

2501 N. Blackwelder
Oklahoma City, OK 73106
Coach: Brian Harvey
Email: bmartin@okcu.edu

NAIA
Stars/Blue, White
Phone: (405) 521-5165
Fax: (405) 521-5816

Estimated # of Men's Soccer Scholarships: TBA
Conference: Sooner Athletic Conference
Program Profile: Natural grass. Play in the fall and in the spring. Fall is the major season of the program. Men qualified for regional play last two seasons.
History: The men's program began in 1986, only missed conference championship once. One losing season in history, the men have a lifetime record of 223-97
Achievements: District 9 Champions in 1990, 1991, & 1995; Runner-Up in 1987, 1988, 1989, 1993, & 1994; NAIA Champions Quarterfinalist in 1991; 10 NAIA All-Americans, and 4 NAIA Scholar Athletes.
Coaching: Brian Harvey, Head Coach, former professional player and coach, English FA Badge, FIFA Badge, USSF "B" License. Billy Martin - Assistant Coach, former OCU player.
Roster In State: 11 **Out of State:** 7 **Out of Country:** 6
Walk-on/Other: **Graduation %:** 85 **Seniors on Team:** 7
Camp or Clinic Dates: May through August
Most Recent Record: 13-7-0
Schedule: Harris Stowe, William Carey, Centenary, St. Gregory's
Style of Play: Control soccer; we have an International and US mix which makes a good brand of soccer. On good day we try to play soccer and on bad day we try to play soccer.

Women's Athletic Profile

2501 N Blackwelder
Oklahoma City, OK 73106
Coach: Brian Harvey
Email: bmartin@okcu.edu

NAIA
Stars/Blue, White
Phone: (405) 521-5165
Fax: (405) 521-5816

Estimated # of Women's Soccer Scholarships: TBA
Conference: Sooner Athletic Conference
Program Profile: Women's program undefeated in last 39 regular season games, qualified for NAIA National Tournament the past two seasons. Undefeated in conference play last two seasons.

History: Program began in 1994. Have won at least 12 games in every season. 116-30 lifetime record.
Achievements: NAIA Region VI Women's Coach of the Year in 1999. Likely winner for women in 2000. Arkansas-Oklahoma Coach of the Year in 1996 and District 9 Coach of the Year in 1991.
Coaching: Brian Harvey, Head Coach, former professional player and coach, English FA Badge, FIFA Badge, USSF 'B' license.
Roster in State: 17 **Out of State:** 1 **Out of Country:** 0
Walk-on/Other: **Graduation %:** 85 **Seniors on Team:** 2
Camp or Clinic Dates: May through August
Most Recent Record: 20-0-1
Schedule: Southern Nazarene, Centenary, Lindenwood, Park College
Style of Play: Control soccer, we have an US and international mix which makes a good brand of soccer. On good day we try to play soccer and on a bad day we try to play soccer still.

Oklahoma State University

Academic Profile

Phone: (541) 346-5410

Stillwater, OK 74078

Type: 4 Yr.,Public **Founded:** 1890
Website: http://www.okstate.com **Religion:** Non-Affiliated
SAT/ACT/GPA: 1010/22/3.0 **Housing:** Yes
Student/Faculty Ratio: 24:1 **Male/Female Ratio:** 52:48
Undergraduate Enrollment: 20,000 **Graduate Enrollment:** 4,200
Scholarships/Academic: Yes **Athletic:** Yes **Financial Aid:** Yes
Expenses by: Year **In State:** $ 7,980 **Out of State:** $ 11,730
Specialty: Engineering, Business, Agriculture, etc..
Degrees Conferred: BA, BS, BED, Masters, Doctorate
Programs of Study: Engineering, Agriculture, Education, Fire Protection & Safety Technology, Hotel & Restaurant Administration, Physical Education, Nutritional Sciences, Geography, Geology, Journalism & Broadcasting, Political Science, PreVet, PreMed, PreLaw, Music Education, Accounting, Economics, Finance, Management, Marketing, International Business, Computer Science, Management Information Systems, Chemistry, Biology…

Women's Athletic Profile

104 Droke Track Complex
Stillwater, OK 74078
Coach: Karen Hancock
Email: horstma@okstate.edu

NCAA I
Cowgirls/Orange, Black
Phone: (405) 744-5603
Fax: (405) 744-3785

Estimated # of Women's Soccer Scholarships: 3.5
Conference: Big Twelve Conference
Program Profile: We play on a 115 x 75 year Bermuda grass field. The field has lights for night games and seats approximately 1,000 and soon we will be adding a press box.
History: Our program began in 1996 and our over-all record is 31-38-6.
Achievements: Oklahoma State University was ranked by top soccer magazine as one of the best start up programs in 1996.
Coaching: Karen Hancock, Head Coach, is a 1990 Tulsa graduate. She has a USSF "A" License and is in the ODP Staff. Colin Carmaichael, Assistant Coach, is a 1993 South Alabama graduate. He has a USSF "A" License and is on the ODP Region III Staff. Christy Barringer, Goalkeeper Coach, is a 1995 Vanderbilt graduate.
Roster in State: 12 **Out of State:** 5 **Out of Country:** 5
ODP State: 12 **Regional:** 2 **National:**
Walk-on/Other: 8 **Graduation %:** 100 **Seniors on Team:** 1
Positions Needed: Forward, Midfield, Defense

Camp or Clinic Dates: June 18-22
Most Recent Record: 5-14-0
Schedule: Nebraska, Texas A&M, Missouri, Texas, Baylor, Alabama
Style of Play: Players must have a high work rate and are expected to get up and down the field as a unit. Like to play an attractive passing style with creative players.

Oral Roberts University

Academic Profile

Tulsa, OK 74171
Phone: 800-678-8876

Type: 4 Yr.,Private,
Founded: 1963
Website: http://www.oru.com
Religion: Non-Affiliated
SAT/ACT/GPA: Open
Housing: Yes
Student/Faculty Ratio: 25:1
Male/Female Ratio: 1:4
Undergraduate Enrollment: 4,500
Graduate Enrollment: 800
Scholarships/Academic: Yes
Athletic: Yes
Financial Aid: Yes
Expenses by: Year
In State: $ 16,125
Out of State: $ 16,125
Degrees Conferred: BA, BS, BSE, MA
Programs of Study: All

Men's Athletic Profile

7777 S Lewis Avenue
Tulsa, OK 74171
Coach: Stephen Hayes
Email: Not Available

NCAA I
Golden Eagles/Gold,Blue, White
Phone: (918) 495-6830
Fax: (918) 495-7123

Estimated # of Men's Soccer Scholarships: N/A
Conference: Mid-Continent Conference
Program Profile: ORU soccer complex is a natural grass with a seating capacity of a 500.
History: Started in 1967-1974 then restarted 1988 to present.
Achievements: None

Women's Athletic Profile

7777 S Lewis Avenue
Tulsa, OK 74171
Coach: Kyle Cussen
Email: sbra2581@stu.oru.edu

NCAA I
Golden Eagles/Gold, Navy
Phone: (918) 495-6830
Fax: (918) 495-6788

Estimated # of Women's Soccer Scholarships:
Conference: Mid-Continent Conference
Program Profile: Entering 6th program, built new field with a new grass, lights and locker room. Has small stadium that holds 2,000 seats.
History: Our program began in 1992; has had great soccer the last three years ending all three years with winning records. in 1998 we had a record of 12-6.
Achievements: Produced a Academic All-American, and 1 Regional All-American.
Coaching: Kyle Cussen, Head Coach, entering second season with the program. Scott Branan - Assistant Coach and Goalkeeper Trainer.
Style of Play: Tough work ethic, play direct to front runners feet. Play a 4-4-2 with two marking backs, one point man upfront.

Saint Gregory's University

Academic Profile

Shawnee, OK 74804

Phone: (888) 784-7347

Type: 4 Yr.,Private,
Website: http://www.sgc.edu
SAT/ACT/GPA: 18/2.0
Student/Faculty Ratio: 12:1
Undergraduate Enrollment: 850
Scholarships/Academic: Yes
Athletic: Yes
Expenses by: Year
In State: $ 12,000
Specialty: Liberal Arts
Degrees Conferred: A to Z
Programs of Study: A through Z
Founded: 1878
Religion: Catholic
Housing: Yes
Male/Female Ratio: 1:1
Graduate Enrollment: 50
Financial Aid: Yes
Out of State: $ 12,000

Men's Athletic Profile

1900 W. McArther Drive
Shawnee, OK 74801
Coach: Duane Cummings
Email: ddcummings@sgc.edu

NAIA
Cavaliers/Red, Navy Blue
Phone: (888) 784-7347x184
Fax: (405) 878-5198

Estimated # of Men's Soccer Scholarships: 12
Conference: Sooner Athletic Conference
Program Profile: The program has a fall season, winter indoor, spring exhibitions. We have a full varsity and junior varsity program. Our field is Bermuda grass with a measurements of 120x80 yards, plus practice fields. It has a seating capacity of 1,000. Exhibitions include Notre Dame and Tulsa University.
History: Our program started in 1996 as a two-year school. 1997 team was a NJCAA National Runner-Up. Our 1998 record was 15-5-1, where we lost in a shoot-out at the conference championship.
Achievements: Team's GPA is 3.25; 2 All-American players; 2 Foreign National Team Players. We have quailified for the NAIA National Tournament the past 2 Seasons.
Coaching: Duane Cummings, Head Coach, coached USISL for OKC Warriors and OKC Slickers. He has won championships in club, semi-pro and high school.
Roster In State: 18
Out of State: 11
Out of Country: 11
Walk-on/Other:
Graduation %: 100
Seniors on Team: 5
Positions Needed: Keeper, Defender, Forward
Camp or Clinic Dates: Call for information.
Most Recent Record: 20-3-1
Schedule: Oklahoma City University, Mobile, Lindsey Wilson, Southern Nazarene, Park University
Style of Play: Varies with player's available. We play the style that lends itself to the level and talent of the players we have.

Women's Athletic Profile

1900 W. McArthur Drive
Shawnee, OK 74801
Coach: Kara Lowery
Email: kdlowery@sgc.edu

NAIA
Cavaliers/Red, Navy, White
Phone: (405) 878-5242
Fax: (405) 878-5198

Estimated # of Women's Soccer Scholarships: 12
Conference: Sooner Athletic Conference
Program Profile: A year-round program; fall season; indoor winter; spring exhibitions. Bermuda Field with has a measurements of 120x80 yards. Varsity and Junior Varsity programs. Qualified for the 2000 Regional Tournament.

History: The program started in 1995 as a Junior College men and women went to NJCAA Regional. 1996 four year university woman NSCAA National Champs.
Achievements: Won Small College National Championship in 1997; 2 NSCAA All-Americans.
Coaching: Kara Lowery is the head coach and is a former assistant coach at the University of Central Oklahoma. Kara was a 4-year starter at Southern Nazarene University.
Roster in State: 8 **Out of State:** 6 **Out of Country:** 4
Walk-on/Other: **Graduation %:** 100 **Seniors on Team:** 4
Positions Needed: All
Camp or Clinic Dates: Call for details
Most Recent Record: 7-10-2
Schedule: Oklahoma City University, Southern Nazarene, Oklahoma Christian, Northwood, Baker, USAO, East Central
Style of Play: Very organized; more than one system of play; possession with a purpose; pro-active.

Southern Nazarene University

Academic Profile

Bethany, OK 73008
Phone: 405-791-6324

Type: 4 Yr.,Private,Liberal Arts
Website: http://www.snu.edu
SAT/ACT/GPA: 19
Student/Faculty Ratio: 17:1
Undergraduate Enrollment: 1,950+
Founded: 1899
Religion: Nazarene
Housing: Yes
Male/Female Ratio: 2:1
Graduate Enrollment: N/A
Scholarships/Academic: Yes **Athletic:** Yes **Financial Aid:** Yes
Expenses by: Year **In State:** $ 12,888 **Out of State:** $ 12,888
Degrees Conferred: BS, Masters
Programs of Study: Over 70 different fields of undergraduate degree options. It also offers eight convenient graduate degree programs. Has two renowned adult studies programs

Men's Athletic Profile

6729 NW 39th Expressway
Bethany, OK 73008
Coach: Mucio de Macedo
Email: mmacedo@smu.edu

NAIA
Crimson Storm/Crimson, White
Phone: (405) 491-6629
Fax: (405) 491-6387

Estimated # of Men's Soccer Scholarships: N/A
Conference: Sooner Athletic Conference
Program Profile: Christ centered program, one of the oldest and best established NAIA Soccer program in the state with numerous All-Americans and Academic All-Americans. Has two playing fields, one is 70x110 yards and is lighted, the other is 75x120 yards which is made up of Arizona Bermuda grass, an extra practice field which measures 75x120 yards and also made up of Arizona Bermuda Grass.
History: Our program is the first program in the state. Nationally recognized and consistently ranked programs. Made three trips to National Tournament finishing 3rd both times. Program is its 20th year of history.
Achievements: NAIA Conference Champions in nine running years in 1981 to 1989 and 1993; Regional champions in 1982, 1987 & 1989 post-season 18 out of 20; Terry Woodberry, first US Olympic team, Mike Cook drafted by Colorado Comets, Kyle Robertson K. Attack and other semi-pro players.
Coaching: Mucio de Macedo, Head Coach. Jason Ciszmadia, Assistant Coach.
Roster In State: 9 **Out of State:** 7 **Out of Country:** 5
ODP State: 9 **Regional:** 4 **National:**
Walk-on/Other: **Graduation %:** 99 **Seniors on Team:** 4
Positions Needed: Goalkeepers, Full Backs, Forwards
Camp or Clinic Dates: June 5-9, June 12-16, June 19-23, July 16-21

Most Recent Record: 5-13-
Schedule: Saint Gregory's, OCU, Lindenwood, Park Co, Benedictine Co, JBU, Oklahoma Christian, ORU, USAO, Southwestern State
Style of Play: Very indirect style of play, controlling the game throughout the midfield with short passes and changing the point of attack.

Women's Athletic Profile

6729 NW. 39TH Exp. Way
Bethany, OK 73008
Coach: Patty Avalos
Email: pavalos@snu.edu

NAIA
Crimson Storm/Crimson, White
Phone: (405) 717-6238
Fax: (405) 491-6387

Estimated # of Women's Soccer Scholarships: 6
Conference: Sooner Athletic Conference
Program Profile: Our program is Christ-centered. We are one of the oldest and best established NAIA soccer programs in the state. We have had numerous All-Americans and Academic All-Americans. We have two playing fields: one is 70 x 110 yards and is lighted and the other field is 75 x 120 yards. We have Arizona Bermuda grass and an extra practice field that is 75 x 120 and it also has Arizona Bermuda grass. We play a fall season with winter indoor and spring exhibition.
History: Began in 1993 with undefeated regular season. We were one of the first programs in the state with 30 men and women. We have a nationally recognized and a consistently ranked program. The women's soccer team took 2 trips to the National Tournaments and finished 3rd both times. The women's team has 6 years of history.
Achievements: Undefeated in the 1993 regular season: 13-0; Conference Champions all 6 years of existence (1992-1998); Regional Champions in 1995 and 1996; National Tournament Final Four in 1995 and several All-American players, All-Region, and National player of the week.
Coaching: Head Coach Patty Avalos graduate from SNU. Four time All-American national assist. Leader in 1996. Patty started the program here at SNU in 1993 and is determined to see it's continued success.
Roster in State: 12 **Out of State:** 4 **Out of Country:** 0
Walk-on/Other: **Graduation %:** 100 **Seniors on Team:** 5
Positions Needed: All positions
Most Recent Record: 12-4-2
Schedule: Oklahoma City Univ. Harding Univ. St. Gregory's Univ. Northeastern State Univ. Oklahoma Christian
Style of Play: Extremely controlled, team is allowed to make adjustments as they see fit on the field. Ball position and building from the back with center mids controlling the tempo of game.

Southwestern Oklahoma State University

Academic Profile

Phone: 580-774-3068

Type: 4 Yr., Public
Website:http://www.swosu.edu
SAT/ACT/GPA: 940/20/ 2.7
Student/Faculty Ratio: 19/1
Undergraduate Enrollment: 4600
Scholarships/Academic: Y **Athletic:** Y

Founded: 1901
Religion: Non-Affiliated
Housing: Yes
Male/Female Ratio: 45/55
Graduate Enrollment: 258
Financial Aid: Y

Specialty: Pharmacy and Education
Degrees Conferred: BA, BBA, MM, M.Mus
Programs of Study: Southwestern is composed of 5 schools which are further divided into various departments. The schools include: Arts & Science, Business, Education, Health Science and Graduate School

Men's Athletic Profile

100 Campus Dr
Weatherford, OK 73096
Coach: Jim Loomis
Email: loomisj@swosu.edu

NCAA II
Bulldogs/Navy, White
Phone: 580-774-3100
Fax: 580-774-3102

Estimated # of Men's Soccer Scholarships: Unknown
Conference: Lone Star
Program Profile: Milam Stadium, natural grass with a seating capacity of 8,500.
History: 1999 was first season for the men's program. Record was 8-9.
Coaching: Head Coach - Jim Loomis. Assistant Coach - Ryan Featherstone.
Roster In State: 23 **Out of State:** 6 **Out of Country:** 1
Walk-on/Other: **Graduation %:** **Seniors on Team:** 2
Positions Needed: ALL
Most Recent Record: 8-9-0
Style of Play: Aggressive defensively, attacking offensive, organized and with numbers, very fit and quick players.

Women's Athletic Profile

100 Campus Drive
Weatherford, OK 73096
Coach: Scott Hume
Email: humes@swosu.edu

NCAA II
Bulldogs/Navy, White
Phone: (580) 774-3782
Fax: (580) 774-7131

Estimated # of Women's Soccer Scholarships: 1
Conference: Lone Star Conference
Program Profile: Games are played in Milam Stadium that has a seating capacity of 5,000. Our field is natural and field usage shared with men's and football team.
History: The program began August of 1998. Comprised predominately of local kids who had not competed at higher competitive level. Although we did not win a game this year, we showed marked improvement.
Coaching: Head Coach- Scott Hume. Assistant Coach- Richard Stoneman
Roster in State: 14 **Out of State:** 5 **Out of Country:** 1
ODP State: 2 **Regional:** **National:**
Walk-on/Other: **Graduation %:** 100 **Seniors on Team:** 2
Positions Needed: All field positions
Most Recent Record: 2-17
Schedule: St. Edwards, Texas A&M Commerce, University of Central Oklahoma, Midwestern State, West Texas A&M, Texas Wesleyan, St. Mary's, Northeastern State, Angelo State.
Style of Play: Aggressive 3-4-3.

University of Central Oklahoma

Academic Profile

Edmond, OK 73034

Phone: (405) 974-2148

Type: 4 Yr.,Public,Liberal Arts
Website: http://www.ucok.edu
SAT/ACT/GPA: 910/19/2.7
Student/Faculty Ratio: 23:1
Undergraduate Enrollment: 14,500
Scholarships/Academic: Yes **Athletic:** Yes
Expenses by: Year **In State:** $ 4,800

Founded: 1890
Religion: Non-Affiliated
Housing: Yes
Male/Female Ratio: 1:2
Graduate Enrollment: N/A
Financial Aid: Yes
Out of State: $ 4,200

Specialty: Business, Sciences, Psychology, Education
Degrees Conferred: BA, BS, MA, MS, MBA, MED
Programs of Study: Accounting, Actuarial Science, Advertising, Applied Mathematics, Art, Art Education, Economics, Business Economics, Criminal Justice, Construction Technology, Design, Journalism, Reading Education, Nutrition, Philosophy, Photography, Graphic Arts, Food Service

Women's Athletic Profile

100 N. University Drive
Edmond, OK 73034
Coach: Mike Cook
Email: mcook@ucok.edu

NCAA II
Bronchos/Royal Blue, Gold
Phone: (405) 974-2136
Fax: (405) 974-3820

Estimated # of Women's Soccer Scholarships: 5
Conference: Lone Star Conference
Program Profile: We play on Bermuda grass that has a measurements of 74x116, on campus. We try to play a position style game where all players play roles both offensively and defensively. We like hard working coach able players who give 100% doing whatever is needed of them.
History: Our program began in 1998 and in two years has a record of 24-14-1. We were ranked as high as 10th in the nation in 1999 in just our second season. We had both the offensive and Freshman Players of the Year in the conference in 1999.
Achievements: We won both the Spectrum and Ionet Classic in 1999. We had the offensive and Freshman of the Year players in the conference in 1999. We lead the conference in almost every statistical category.
Coaching: Mike Cook is our Head Coach. He started the program at UCO after starting the program at perennial NAIA power Southern Nazarene. Two NAIA National Appearances finishing third. Three times SW Regional Coach of the Year and four times Sooner Conference Coach of the Year. He compiled an overall record of 112-36-2. He was a former professional player with national coaching license. Kara Lowery is our Assistant Coach. She was a 4 year starter at perennial NAIA power Southern Nazarene. She was a captain and 4 year All-Conference, All-Region and Honorable Mention All-American.
Roster in State: 19
Out of State: 6
Out of Country: 2
ODP State: 16
Regional: 3
National: 0
Walk-on/Other: 6
Graduation %: 100
Seniors on Team: 5
Positions Needed: Good all around players
Camp or Clinic Dates: June 5-9; June 19-23; August 7-11
Most Recent Record: 13-5-1
Schedule: Oral Roberts, Arkansas State, Metro State, Rockhurst, Midwestern, Lees-McRae, Incarnate Word, Regis, Texas A&M Commerce, West Texas A&M
Style of Play: Position style with all players required to play both sides of the ball.

University of Oklahoma
Academic Profile

Norman, OK 73019-0201
Phone:

Type: 4 Yr.,Public,Liberal Arts,Engineering
Website: http://www.ou.edu
SAT/ACT/GPA: 1030/22/3.0
Student/Faculty Ratio: 21:1
Undergraduate Enrollment: 16,000
Scholarships/Academic: Yes
Athletic: Yes
Financial Aid: Yes
Expenses by: Year
In State: $ 7,568
Out of State: $ 11,349
Founded: 1890
Religion: Non-Affiliated
Housing: Yes
Male/Female Ratio: 1.1:1
Graduate Enrollment: 8,000

Specialty: Health Sports Science, Engineering, Liberal Arts
Degrees Conferred: 200 Master's and Doctoral
Programs of Study: Business, Meteorology, Education, Engineering, Fine Arts, GeoSciences, Architecture, Psychology, Marketing, Music, Political Science, Science Education, Journalism, Linguistics, Drama, Dance, Botany, Zoology, Economics, Physics, Sociology, Social Work, Special Education

Women's Athletic Profile

151 W. Brooks E-16
Norman, OK 73019-0201
Coach: Randy Evans
Email: evanss@ou.edu

NCAA I
Sooners/Crimson, Cream
Phone: (405) 325-8296
Fax: (405) 325-7632

Estimated # of Women's Soccer Scholarships: 12
Conference: Big Twelve Conference
Program Profile: Just completed phase I of the new $ 3 million soccer facility, which included state of the art game field and lighting system. Phase two will include a stadium with 2000 seats with locker rooms, restrooms, concessions, laundry training rooms and meeting rooms.
History: The program began in 1996. Coach Evans led the team to its first winning season in 2000 in his second year at the Helm. The 2000 season was highlighted by making the Big 12 tournament giving the #2 Nebraska squad its only regular season loss and beating Texas 2-0 twice.
Achievements: Coach Evans was named Big 12 and Central Region Coach of the Year in 2000.
Coaching: Randy Evans, Head Coach. Matt Granstrand is assistant coach.
Roster in State: 13 **Out of State:** 11 **Out of Country:** 0
ODP State: 20 **Regional:** 6 **National:** 0
Walk-on/Other: 0 **Graduation %:** 100 **Seniors on Team:** 3
Positions Needed: Midfielders, Forwards
Camp or Clinic Dates: June 16-20
Most Recent Record: 10-9-1
Schedule: Nebraska, Texas A & M, SMU, Texas, Missouri, Baylor
Style of Play: A possession style with an effective counter attacking ability, every player is required to have good skills.

University of Science and Arts of Oklahoma

Academic Profile

Chickasha, OK 73018
Phone: (405) 222-2830

Type: 4 Yr.,Public,Liberal Arts
Website: http://www.usao.edu
SAT/ACT/GPA: 19
Student/Faculty Ratio: 16:1
Undergraduate Enrollment: 1,740
Founded: 1908
Religion: Non-Affiliated
Housing: Yes
Male/Female Ratio: 1:3
Graduate Enrollment: N/A
Scholarships/Academic: Yes **Athletic:** Yes **Financial Aid:** Yes
Expenses by: Year **In State:** $ 4,968 **Out of State:** $ 7,128
Degrees Conferred: Over 26 degrees
Programs of Study: Accounting, Art Education, Fine Arts, Biology, Biological Science, Business Economics, Business Education, Music, Music Education, Data Processing, Political Science, English, History, Psychology, Theatre

Men's Athletic Profile

P.O. Box 82345
Chickasha, OK 73018
Coach: Jimmy Hampton
Email: fachamptonJ@usao.edu

NAIA
Drovers/Green, Gold
Phone: (405) 574-1358
Fax: (405) 522-1220

Estimated # of Men's Soccer Scholarships: 2.5
Conference: Sooner Athletic Conference
Program Profile: The Drovers play on a natural grass surface located on campus. Practices are held on an adjacent field with regulation size goals. Players have access to indoor swimming pool, tennis courts and a fitness center that allows players to use both cardiovascular and strength training equipment. Regular playing season starts from August 21 through November 20 and Spring season starts from January 18th through May 1st.
History: This is our 4th year.
Achievements: Has 2 Academic All-Americans, 3 All-Conference players and 1 Honorable Mention All-American. 2x Red River Athletic Conference Champions.
Coaching: Jimmy Hampton, Head Coach, USSF National "A" License and ODP Staff Coach. He was a Club Coach of Norman Celtic U-84 which is three-time State Champs, 9 Girls Coach OSFC, 9 National Indoor Champs, Chickasha High School Coach, three times State Champs.

Roster In State: 19	**Out of State:** 1	**Out of Country:** 9
ODP State: 13	**Regional:** 6	**National:** 3
Walk-on/Other:	**Graduation %:** N/A	**Seniors on Team:** 3

Positions Needed: Goalkeeper, forward, defender
Most Recent Record: 11-9
Schedule: St. Gregory's, Oklahoma City, John Brown, Oklahoma Christian, Southern Nazarene
Style of Play: Solid defense that looks to join the attack when available. Quick Midfield that moves the ball well. Overall; physical, aggressive soccer that looks to attack or counterattack when available.

Women's Athletic Profile

P.O. Box 82345
Chickasha, OK 73018
Coach: Jimmy Hampton
Email: fachamptonj@usao.ed

NAIA
Dovers/Green, Gold
Phone: (405) 574-1358
Fax: (405) 574-1220

Estimated # of Women's Soccer Scholarships: 3.5
Conference: Sooner Athletic Conference (SAC)
Program Profile: The lady Dovers play on a new grass field which measures 70x110 and is located on campus. Our practice field is adjacent to the game field equipped with full size goals. Players have access to an indoor pool, tennis courts, and a fitness center.
History: The program began in 1998 and is going into there 4th season. In two season the Lady Dovers have competed as a Southwest Region Independent. The first season the lady Dovers qualified for the post season and in their second year narrowly missed the final playoff spot.
Achievements: In 1999 and 1998 the Dovers have been recognized for post season honors and have had 3 in all All-Sectional Southwest Independent team. One All-Region, one All-Region honorable mention, one academic All-American.
Coaching: Head Coach Jimmy Hampton is assisted by former USAO Dover players: Dave Kunitz, Juan Carlos, Garcie and Mauricio Garcio.

Roster in State: 15	**Out of State:** 2	**Out of Country:** 2
ODP State: 5	**Regional:** 0	**National:** 0
Walk-on/Other: 0	**Graduation %:**	**Seniors on Team:** 1

Positions Needed: Center Midfield, Sticker
Most Recent Record: 9-11-0
Schedule: Oklahoma City University, St. Gregory's University, Midwestern State University, Oklahoma Christian, Southern Nazarene University, John Brown University.
Style of Play: Low key tempo that favors ball control and smart players. Defense is very physical but is also able to move the ball forward. Strong forwards look to attack whenever possible. English influenced.

University of Tulsa

Academic Profile

Phone: (918) 631-2000

Tulsa, OK 74104-3189

Type: 4 Yr.,Private,Liberal Arts,Engineering
Website: http://www.utulsa.edu
SAT/ACT/GPA: 1215/25/3.7
Student/Faculty Ratio: 12:1
Undergraduate Enrollment: 3,300
Scholarships/Academic: Yes **Athletic:** Yes
Expenses by: Year **In State:** $ 21,230
Founded: 1894
Religion: Methodist
Housing: Yes
Male/Female Ratio: 48:52
Graduate Enrollment: 1,000
Financial Aid: Yes
Out of State: $ 21,230
Specialty: Liberal Arts, Engineering, Business
Degrees Conferred: BA, BS, BFA, MA, MS, MBA, MFA
Programs of Study: Anthropology, Arts, Biological Science, Computer Information Systems, Chemistry, Computer Science, Economics, Education, Electrical Engineering, Engineering, Finance, History, Management, Mathematics, Philosophy, Political Science

Men's Athletic Profile

600 S College Avenue
Tulsa, OK 74104
Coach: Tom McIntosh
Email: thomas-mcintosh@utulsa.edu

NCAA I
Golden Hurricane/Gold, Blue
Phone: (918) 631-3789
Fax: (918) 631-2127

Estimated # of Men's Soccer Scholarships: 9
Conference: Missouri Valley Conference
Program Profile: 2001 will be first season on new on-campus natural grass field. Construction is underway for a new stadium field for 2002 season.
History: Our program began in 1980. 1997 WAC Conference Tournament Finals, 1998 WAC Conference Tournament Finals.
Achievements: 1991 All-American - Frank Velez; Kevin Cronk - Academic All-American and MVC Goalkeeper of the Year; Randy Waldrum - MVC Coach of the Year; Jimmy Dowell - MVC Player of the Year in 1994. WAC Freshman of the Year in 1996 (Robbie Arristdemo); 3 All-WAC players in 1997 and Midwest Region All-American in 1997 (Demivary Bradshaw). 2000 3 players on All-MVC Newcomer team.
Coaching: Tom McIntosh, Head Coach, entering his 7th season, 1989-1991 assistant coach at TU, 1987-1988 TU soccer captain, played for Tulsa Renegades of Southwest Outdoor Soccer League. Overall record of 61-47-6 at Tulsa. Brian Riggs assistant coach enterning 2nd season.
Roster In State: 6 **Out of State:** 18 **Out of Country:** 2
ODP State: 10 **Regional:** 4 **National:** 1
Walk-on/Other: 4 **Graduation %:** 99 **Seniors on Team:** 4
Positions Needed: ALL
Camp or Clinic Dates: June, July
Most Recent Record: 10-7-2
Schedule: Creighton, SMU, Yale, Brown, Santa Clara, Southwest Missouri State, Bradley, UNLV, Eastern Illinois.
Style of Play: Possession oriented, encourage players to attack which staying organized and balanced.

Women's Athletic Profile

600 S College Avenue
Tulsa, OK 74104
Coach: Damon Gore
Email: D-Gore@utulsa.edu

NCAA I
Golden Hurricanes/Gold, Royal
Phone: (918) 631-3836
Fax: (918) 631-2127

Estimated # of Women's Soccer Scholarships: N/A
Conference: Western Athletic Conference
Program Profile: we have a fall and spring season; we play on a natural grass field. We will have a new stadium in the Fall of 2000.
History: Program began in 1987 with 8 winning season in the past ten years. We experienced our 100th win in the 1997 season.
Achievements: 10 Regional All-Americans; 3 Olympics Festival Players; 2 Regional Coach of the Year Awards; 4 All-Tournament Conference players.
Coaching: Damon Gore, Head Coach, was named head coach in the summer of 1999. He was a former assistant coach at Alabama and University of Tulsa.
Style of Play: Attack oriented, get many players involved in the attack, very disciplined and organized.

oregon

OREGON

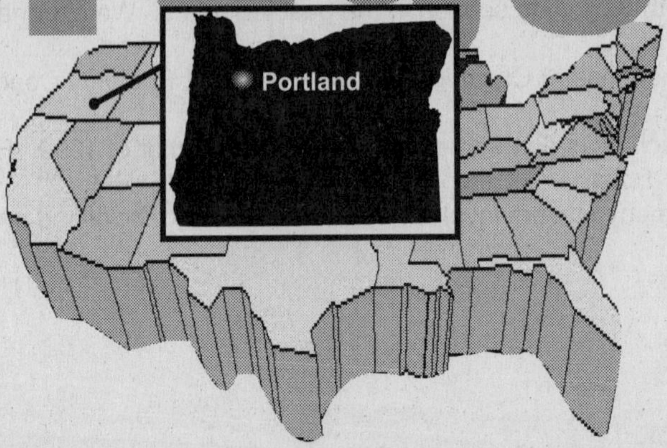

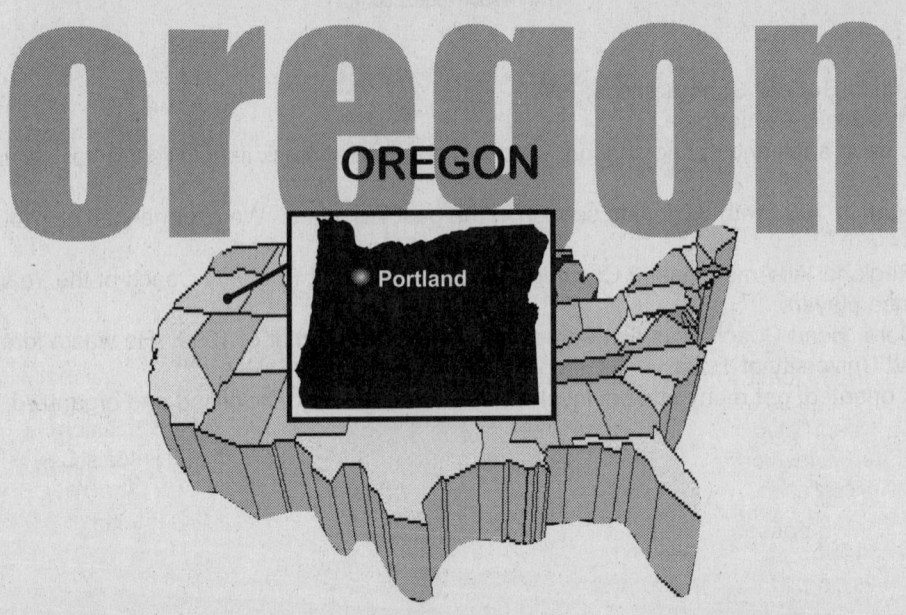

SCHOOL	CITY	AFFILIATION	PAGE
Cascade College	Portland	NCCAA/NAIA	909
Concordia University - Portland	Portland	NAIA	909
George Fox University	Newberg	NCAA III	911
Linfield College	McMinnville	NCAA III	912
Oregon State University	Corvallis	NCAA I	913
Pacific University	Forest Grove	NCAA III/NAIA	914
Portland State University	Portland	NCAA I	915
Southern Oregon University	Ashland	NAIA	916
University of Oregon	Eugene	NCAA I	916
University of Portland	Portland	NCAA I	917
Warner Pacific College	Portland	NAIA	918
Western Baptist College	Salem	NAIA	919
Willamette University	Salem	NCAA III	920

Cascade College
Academic Profile

Phone:

Portland, OR 97216

Type: 4 Yr.,Private,Liberal Arts
Website: http://www.cascade.edu
SAT/ACT/GPA: Open Admission
Student/Faculty Ratio: 17:1
Undergraduate Enrollment: 309
Scholarships/Academic: Yes **Athletic:** Yes
Expenses by: Year **In State:** $ 12,000
Specialty: Bible Studies
Degrees Conferred: Bachelors
Programs of Study: Bible, Ministry, Business, Education, Environmental Science, Psychology, Interdisciplinary Studies

Founded: 1994
Religion: Christian
Housing: Yes
Male/Female Ratio: 50:50
Graduate Enrollment: N/A
Financial Aid: Yes
Out of State: $ 12,000

Men's Athletic Profile

9101 E. Burnside Street
Portland, OR 97216
Coach: Ben Langford
Email: blangford@cascade.edu

NAIA
Thunderbirds/Green, Black
Phone: (503)257-1219
Fax: 503-257-1222

History: The program began in 1994-95.
Coaching: Our Head Coach is Ben Langford who is a graduate and 4 year starter at Oklahoma Christian.
Graduation %: 100% **Number of Seniors:** 3
Positions Needed: All
Most Recent Record: 6-11
Schedule: Chico State, Linfield College, and Concordia

Women's Athletic Profile

9101 Burnside Street
Portland, OR 97216
Coach: Ben Langford
Email:

NCCAA/NAIA
Thunderbirds/Green, White
Phone: (503) 255-7060
Fax: (503) 255-1222

Did Not Return Profile

Concordia University
Academic Profile

Phone: 503-280-8501

Portland, OR 97211

Type: 4 Yr.,Private,Liberal Arts
Website: http://www.cu-portland.edu
SAT/ACT/GPA: 480v/18/2.5
Student/Faculty Ratio: 20/1
Undergraduate Enrollment: 935
Scholarships/Academic: Yes **Athletic:** Yes
Expenses by: Year **In State:** $ 21,000

Founded: 1905
Religion: Lutheran
Housing: Yes
Male/Female Ratio: 40:60
Graduate Enrollment: 105
Financial Aid: Yes
Out of State: $ 21,000

Specialty: Education, Business
Degrees Conferred: BA, BS, MEd
Programs of Study: College of Arts & Science, College of Business, College of Education, College of Health & Social Sciences, College of Theological Studies

Men's Athletic Profile

2811 NE Holman Street
Portland, OR 97211
Coach: Dan Birkey
Email: dbirkey@cu-portland.edu

NAIA
Cavaliers/Navy, White
Phone: (503) 280-8551
Fax: (503) 280-8591

Estimated # of Men's Soccer Scholarships: 3
Conference: Cascade Collegiate Conference
Program Profile: Play on a natural grass field with a measurements of 76x118 yards; pitch located in the center of campus. The team room and training room are next to the field, scoreboard, PA system, well attended by students facility.
History: Program began in 1988. Won first NAIA District Championship 1992, rated in Top 20 in 1991, 1992, 1993, 1994 and 1995. Several NAIA championships and post-season play in 1990-1995. Good team work concept and an earnest passion for the game.
Achievements: CU program has been to post-season play seven of the past ten years. Placed in NAIA top 20 five of last ten years. CU players have been drafted into CISL, USISL, & ESL.
Coaching: Dan Birkey, Head Coach, came CU in 1988 and has received numerous Coach of the Year Awards, coached professionally in the USISL pro division. He is a professor in Kinesiology. Jason Moore and Estavan DelGadillo are the assistant coaches.
Roster In State: 7 **Out of State:** 15 **Out of Country:** 1
ODP State: 5 **Regional:** **National:**
Walk-on/Other: **Graduation %:** N/A **Seniors on Team:** 6
Camp or Clinic Dates: Not Available
Most Recent Record: 13-8-0
Schedule: Simon Fraser Univ., Seattle Univ. Westmont, Azusa Pacific, Univ. of British Columbia, Univ. of Victoria
Style of Play: Balanced attack with quick transitional play, pressure defense team with athletic players with attentiveness and high work in training sessions.

Women's Athletic Profile

2811 NE Holman St.
Portland, OR 97211
Coach: Grant Landy
Email: glandy@cu-portland.edu

NAIA
Cavaliers/Navy, White
Phone: (503) 280-8141
Fax: (503) 280-8143

Estimated # of Women's Soccer Scholarships: 3.0
Conference: Cascade Collegiate Conference
Program Profile: We play on a natural grass field with measurements of 74 x 115. We play a fall season and a spring season and during the winter we have an updated weight room for winter strengthen and conditioning. One of the Top 25 NAIA programs.
History: We began playing intercollegiate in 1995. 53-22-4 since 1997 (4 seasons)
Achievements: 1997, 1998, 2000 Coach of the Year, 1996, 98, 2000 conference champions, 1998-2000 Regional Tournament, 4 NAIA All-Americans, 16-4-1 record in 2000, and 2000 Regional Coach of the Year.
Coaching: Grant Landy, Head Coach, graduated from Cal Poly San Luis Obispo in 1991. He was named 1997 and 1998 Conference Coach of the Year. Kim Street (Portland State 1999) Goalkeeping Coach.
Roster in State: 6 **Out of State:** 15 **Out of Country:** 0
ODP State: 3 **Regional:** **National:**

Walk-on/Other: 3 **Graduation %:** 80 **Seniors on Team:** 3
Positions Needed: ALL
Camp or Clinic Dates: Last week in July, first week August
Most Recent Record: 16-4-1
Schedule: Simon Fraser, Seattle University, Cal-Baptist, Point Loma Nazarene, Western Baptist College
Style of Play: Possession, build from the back and wing attack.

George Fox University

Academic Profile

Newberg, OR 97132
Phone:

Type: 4 Yr.,Private,Liberal Arts
Founded: 1891
Website: http://www.georgefox.edu
Religion: Quaker (Friends)
SAT/ACT/GPA: Formula
Housing: Yes
Student/Faculty Ratio: 15:1
Male/Female Ratio: 40:60
Undergraduate Enrollment: 1,350
Graduate Enrollment: 700
Scholarships/Academic: Yes **Athletic:** No **Financial Aid:** Yes
Expenses by: Year **In State:** $ 22,315 **Out of State:** $ 22,315
Degrees Conferred: BA, BS, MA, MAT, MEd, M.Div, Ed.D. Psy D
Programs of Study: Accounting, Applied Science, Art, Biblical Studies, Biology, Business & Economics, Chemistry, Christian Ministries, Cognitive Science, Communication Arts, Communication Media/Broadcast, Computer & Information Science, Elementary Education, Engineering, Family & Consumer Science, Health & Human Performance, History, Interdisciplinary Studies, International Studies, Mathematics, Music, Philosophy, Psychology, Religion , Social Work, Sociology, Spanish, Writing & Literature

Men's Athletic Profile

414 N Meridian Street
Newberg, OR 97132
Coach: Manfred Tschan
Email: mtschan@georgefox.edu

NCAA III/NAIA
Bruins/Navy, Gold
Phone: (503) 538-8383
Fax: (503) 537-3834

Estimated # of Men's Soccer Scholarships: None
Conference: Northwest Conference
Program Profile: The Bruins have 2.5 soccer fields with natural grass and a 'Soccer Only' grass field. Soccer is the main Fall sport and cable television broadcasts the home games. The new field was built in 1988.
History: Program began in 1984.
Achievements: Christian College National Champions 1988, 1990; NAIA District Champions 1990, 1993; Area Champions 1993; NAIA National Tournament 1993; 1995-96 Conference Champs; NCIC Champs; Post-season playoffs (Conference tournament 2nd); 1995-96: Co-Rookie of the Year, Most Improved, Most Inspirational, Offensive Player of the Year, Co-Defensive Player of the Year, Most Valuable Player.
Coaching: Manfred Tschan, Head Coach.
Roster In State: 23\14 **Out of State:** 9 **Out of Country:**
ODP State: 2 **Regional:** **National:**
Walk-on/Other: **Graduation %:** N/A **Seniors on Team:** 13
Positions Needed: Goalkeeper, Striker
Camp or Clinic Dates: Not Available
Most Recent Record: 6-12
Schedule: Colorado College, Chapman, Puget Sound, Willamette, Whitworth.

Women's Athletic Profile

414 N Meridian Street
Newberg, OR 97132
Coach: Byron Shenk
Email: bshenk@georgefox.edu

NCAA III
Bruins/Blue, Gold
Phone: (503) 554-2912
Fax: (503) 537-3864

Estimated # of Women's Soccer Scholarships: None
Conference: Northwest Conference of Independent Colleges
Program Profile: The home game field is a natural grass. Playing season starts in August 24; national championships.
History: The program began in 1991. The record for 1994 was 9-3-3; in 1995-1996 NAIA record was 6-9-2. Finish in the conference fifth out of seven teams in the NCIC. Overall record is 93-73-11
Achievements: 3 Time Coach of the Year. 2 time Far West Coach of the Year. 3 Academic All-Americans, 2 All-Americans.
Coaching: Byron Shenk, Head Coach, USSCA A&B Licensed, 27 years of coaching men and women; Conference Coach of the Year. Tim Tsohantaridis - Assistant Coach. Todd Williams - Goalkeeper Coach.

Roster in State: 13	**Out of State:** 6	**Out of Country:** 0
ODP State: 0	**Regional:** 0	**National:** 0
Walk-on/Other: 0	**Graduation %:** 92	**Seniors on Team:** 3

Positions Needed: GK, Defender, 2 Midfield, Forward
Camp or Clinic Dates: Not Available
Most Recent Record: 14-5-0
Schedule: Willamette Univ. Univ Puget's Sound, Univl Cal- Santa Cruz, Cal State-Hayward, Whitworth
Style of Play: Ball control offense; pressure defense.

Linfield College

Academic Profile

Phone: 503-434-2200

McMinnville, OR 97128-6894

Type: 4 Yr.,Private,Liberal Arts		**Founded:** 1849
Website: http://www.linfield.edu		**Religion:** Baptist
SAT/ACT/GPA: 900/2.8		**Housing:** Yes
Student/Faculty Ratio: 17:1		**Male/Female Ratio:** 45:55
Undergraduate Enrollment: 1,600		**Graduate Enrollment:** N/A
Scholarships/Academic: Yes	**Athletic:** No	**Financial Aid:** Yes
Expenses by: Year	**In State:** $ 26,000	**Out of State:** $ 26,000

Specialty: Business, Education, Communications, Physical Education
Degrees Conferred: BA, BS, M.Ed.
Programs of Study: Accounting, Anthropology, Art, Biology, Botany, Business, Chemistry, Communications, Computer Science, Creative Writing, Earth Science, Ecology, Economics, Education, English, Finance, French, German, Health Education, History, Humanities, Information Science, International Business, Japanese, Journalism, Liberal Arts, Management, Mathematics, Medical Technology, Modern Languages, Music, Natural Science, Nursing, Philosophy, Physical Education, Physics, Political Science, PreDentistry, PreLaw, PreMed, PreVet, Psychology, Public Relations, Radio & Televisions, Religion Science, Sociology, Spanish, Theatre

Men's Athletic Profile

900 S Baker Street
McMinnville, OR 97128-6894
Coach: Steve Simmons
Email: ssimmons@linfield.edu

NCAA III
Wildcats/Purple, Red
Phone: (503) 434-2528
Fax: (503) 434-2453

Estimated # of Men's Soccer Scholarships: None
Conference: Northwest Conference of Independent Colleges
Roster In State: 7 **Out of State:** 16 **Out of Country:** 1
Walk-on/Other: **Graduation %:** 100 **Seniors on Team:** 3
Most Recent Record: 12-8-1

Women's Athletic Profile

900 S Baker Avenue
McMinnville, OR 97128-6894
Coach: Steve Simmons
Email: ssimmons@linfield.edu

NCAA III
Wildcats/Red, Purple
Phone: (503) 434-2528
Fax: (503) 434-2453

Estimated # of Women's Soccer Scholarships: None
Conference: Northwest Conference of Independent Colleges
Roster in State: 8 **Out of State:** 16 **Out of Country:** 1
Walk-on/Other: **Graduation %:** 100 **Seniors on Team:** 4
Camp or Clinic Dates: Not Available
Most Recent Record: 4-15-0

Oregon State University

Academic Profile

Corvallis, OR 97331

Phone: 541-737-4411

Type: 4 Yr.,Public,
Website: http://www.osu.orst.edu
SAT/ACT/GPA: 970/23/3.06
Student/Faculty Ratio: 16:1
Undergraduate Enrollment: 13,400
Scholarships/Academic: Yes **Athletic:** Yes
Expenses by: Year **In State:** $10,115

Founded: 1868
Religion: Non-Affiliated
Housing: Yes
Male/Female Ratio: 54:46
Graduate Enrollment: 2,600
Financial Aid: Yes
Out of State: $19,565

Degrees Conferred: BA, BS, BFA, MA, MS, MAIS, MAT, Ph.D.
Programs of Study: Business, Engineering, Forestry, Health and Human Performance, Home Economics and Education, Liberal Arts, Pharmacy, Science, Anthropology, American Studies, History, Geology, Computer Science, Geography, MicroBiology, Mathematics, Music, Natural Resources, Physics, Philosophy, Political Science, Poultry Science, Psychology, Sociology, Social Sciences, Pharmacy

Men's Athletic Profile

Rm. 103 - Gill Coliseum
Corvallis, OR 97331
Coach: Dana Tayl
Email: not available

NCAA I
Beavers/Orange, Black
Phone: (541) 737-7489
Fax: (541) 737-3072

Estimated # of Men's Soccer Scholarships: Not Available
Conference: Pacific 10
Program Profile: Oregon State plays its home contests at Paul Lorenz Field at Valley Stadium. The field is natural grass with a sand base. The 2000 season began September 1 and ended November 12. The Beavers played 19 contests, eight of which were PAC-10 conference matches. Valley Stadium has a capacity of approximatley 1500.
History: OSU has an overall record of 109-112-14 since the program began in 1988 under coach Jimmy Conway. Dana Taylor is the second coach in the history of the program, having taken over in 1999. In league games, OSU is 30-42-6. The Beavers have competed in the Norhtwest Collegiate Soccer Conference beginning in 1988, and in the Mountain Pacific Sports Federation through 19999 before joining the PAC-10.

Achievements: OSU claimed the NWCSC title in 1990, Jimmy Conway Coach of the Year MPSF 1995, Conway-Coach of the Year NWCSC 1990, Rick Kempf NWCSC Player of the year 1990.
Coaching: Dana Taylor, Head Coach, entering 2nd year of the program. coach at Creighton University. He is been coaching for 7 years in Division I. Graduate of Gordon College. Kevin O'Brien, Assistant Coach, entering 2nd year, came from Creighton University. Three years assistant coach at Creighton. Played at College of Charleston.
Roster In State: 9 **Out of State:** 19 **Out of Country:** 2
ODP State: 18 **Regional:** 9 **National:** 5
Walk-on/Other: 0 **Graduation %:** N/A **Seniors on Team:** 4
Positions Needed: Forwards
Camp or Clinic Dates: July 22-27
Most Recent Record: 7-11-1
Schedule: UCCH, Stanford, Washington, Santa Clara, Creighton, University of Portland, University of San Francisco, San Diego State, Gonzaga, Cal-Berkeley
Style of Play: Quick, technical speed of play emphasis.

Women's Athletic Profile

Gill Coliseum
Corvallis, OR 97331
Coach: Steve Fannah
Email: atccmail@ors.edu

NCAA I
Beavers/Black, White, Orange
Phone: (541) 737-7489
Fax: (541) 737-4002

Estimated # of Women's Soccer Scholarships: None
Conference: Mountain Pacific Conference
Program Profile: Fall playing season, and played on a nice new, natural grass soccer field with a seating capacity of a 2,500. A ten years program in 1997.
History: Program has been going for its nine years.
Achievements: Coach Jimmy Conway won Coach of the Year three times; drafted players into indoor teams.
Style of Play: Fast play; like to have team who is technical strong.

Pacific University

Academic Profile

Forest Grove, OR 97116
Phone: 503-357-6151

Type: 4 Yr.,Private,Liberal Arts **Founded:** 1842
Website: http://www.pacifcu.edu **Religion:** Non-Affiliated
SAT/ACT/GPA: 1000/20 **Housing:** Yes
Student/Faculty Ratio: 14:1 **Male/Female Ratio:** 60:40
Undergraduate Enrollment: 1,100 **Graduate Enrollment:** 1,000
Scholarships/Academic: Yes **Athletic:** No **Financial Aid:** Yes
Expenses by: Year **In State:** $ 21,000 **Out of State:** $ 21,000
Specialty: Liberal Arts
Degrees Conferred: BA, BS, MA, MS
Programs of Study: Accounting, Banking & Finance, Biology, Business Administration, Chemistry, Computer Science Creative Writing, Dramatic Arts, Economics, Elementary Education, Exercise Science, French, German, History, Humanities, Japanese, Literature, Management, Marketing, Mathematics, Music, Philosophy, Physical Education, Physics, Political Science, Psychology, Science, Social Science, Sociology, Spanish

Men's Athletic Profile

2043 College Way
Forest Grove, OR 97116
Coach: Jim Brazeau
Email: Not Available

NCAA III/NAIA
Boxers/Red, Black, White
Phone: (503) 357-6151
Fax: (503) 359-2209

Estimated # of Men's Soccer Scholarships: None
Conference: Northwest Conference of Independent Colleges
Program Profile: Wonderful, small college environment for college soccer. Played in the climate of Northwest, the field is located directly on campus, in fact behind one residence hall. If a player misses the goal on the high side, the ball could wind up in somebody's dorm room.
Achievements: 1994 NCIC Conference Champions, 1994 NCIC Coach of the Year.
Coaching: Jeff Enquist, Head Coach, 5th year, led team to one conference championship, played NCAA Division I at UNLV, and Oregon State.
Style of Play: Offensively very direst with strong build-up out of the back four.

Women's Athletic Profile

2043 College Way
Forest Grove, OR 97116
Coach: Tim Copeland
Email: Not Available

NCAA III/NAIA
Boxers/Red, Black, White
Phone: (503) 357-6151
Fax: (503) 359-2209

Estimated # of Women's Soccer Scholarships: None
Conference: Northwest Conference of Independent Colleges

Portland State University

Academic Profile

Portland, OR 97207

Phone: 503-725-3000

Type: 4 Yr.,Public,Liberal Arts
Website: http://www.vinkings.pdx.edu
SAT/ACT/GPA: 700/18+
Student/Faculty Ratio: 20:1
Undergraduate Enrollment: 12,000
Scholarships/Academic: Yes **Athletic:** Yes
Expenses by: Year **In State:** $ 8,000

Founded: 1924
Religion: Non-Affiliated
Housing: No
Male/Female Ratio: 50:50
Graduate Enrollment: 2,000
Financial Aid: Yes
Out of State: $ 14,000

Degrees Conferred: BA, BS, MA, MS, MBA, MFA, MED, Ph.D., EdH
Programs of Study: Arts, Business and Management, Business/Office and Marketing/Distribution, Communications, Education, Engineering, General Studies, Letters/Literature, PreMed, Psychology, Social Science, Social Science, Social Work, Teacher Education

Women's Athletic Profile

P.O. Box 751
Portland, OR 97207
Coach: Dana Kusjanovic
Email: kusjand@mail.pdx.edu

NCAA I
Vikings/Forest Green, White
Phone: (503) 725-5632
Fax: (503) 725-5610

Estimated # of Women's Soccer Scholarships: None
Conference: Big Sky Conference
Program Profile: great synthetic practice field in the heart of campus. Beautiful urban location. Progressive academic programming.

History: Seven Years old. Young team with great potential.
Achievements: 1993 & 1994 NSCAA Regional Coach of the Year; 1997 - Jen Bruno was Big Sky All-League selection. NCC Conference coach of the year 1996 and 1997.
Coaching:

Roster in State: 12	**Out of State:** 13	**Out of Country:**
ODP State: 20	**Regional:**	**National:**
Walk-on/Other:	**Graduation %:**	**Seniors on Team:** 3

Camp or Clinic Dates: Not Available
Most Recent Record: 5-13
Schedule: San Jose St., Oregon St., Montana, Colorado College, Texas Tech, Cal State Northridge
Style of Play: Attack; oriented play looking to get forward and score at all costs, keep professional. Offensive strengths and strong tackles and speed, heart and determination.

Southern Oregon University

Academic Profile

Phone: 541-552-7672

Ashland, OR 97520

Type: 4 Yr.,Private		**Founded:** 1883
Website: http://www.sou.edu		**Religion:** Non-Affiliated
SAT/ACT/GPA:		**Housing:** Y
Student/Faculty Ratio:		**Male/Female Ratio:** 43/57
Undergraduate Enrollment: 5500		**Graduate Enrollment:** 300
Scholarships/Academic: Yes	**Athletic:** Yes	**Financial Aid:** Yes
Expenses by: Year	**In State:** $3,198	**Out of State:** $9,402

Programs of Study: Contact school for programs of study.

Women's Athletic Profile

1250 Sisiyou Blvd.
Ashland, OR 97520
Coach: Jose Chavez
Email: chavezj@sou.edu

NAIA
Raiders/Red, Black
Phone: (541) 552-7672
Fax: (541) 552-6543

Estimated # of Women's Soccer Scholarships: 2
Conference: Cascade
Program Profile: We are a NAIA program with an on campus natural grass facility. 2000 was our first intercollegiate season.
History: Program began in 2000. 6-9 overall and 5-5 in conference play.
Achievements: 5 conference All-Stars in 2000.
Coaching: Jose Chavez is our Head Coach and Rael Hirning is the assistant.

Roster in State: 14	**Out of State:** 3	**Out of Country:** 1
Walk-on/Other:	**Graduation %:** N/A	**Seniors on Team:** 2

Positions Needed: Forward, defense
Camp or Clinic Dates: N/A
Most Recent Record: 6-9-0
Schedule: Simon Fraser, Concordia, Western Baptist, Hawaii Pacific, Southern Indiana

University of Oregon

Academic Profile

Phone: (541) 346-5410

Eugene, OR 97401

Type: 4 Yr.,Public,Liberal Arts	**Founded:** 1876
Website: http://www.uoregon.edu	**Religion:** Non-Affiliated

SAT/ACT/GPA: 1,000+/3.0
Housing: Yes
Student/Faculty Ratio: 19:1
Male/Female Ratio: 1:1
Undergraduate Enrollment: 13,000
Graduate Enrollment: 4,200
Scholarships/Academic: Yes
Athletic: Yes
Financial Aid: Yes
Expenses by: Term
In State: $ 3,721
Out of State: $ 6,538
Specialty: Liberal Arts, Social Sciences
Degrees Conferred: BA, BS, BFA, MA, MS, MBA, MFA, Ph.D., JD, EdD
Programs of Study: Visual & Performing Arts, Parks/Recreation, Protective Services, Public Affairs, Business & Management, Communications, Letter/Literature, Music, Psychology, Social Sciences, Teacher Education

Women's Athletic Profile

2727 Leo Harris Pkwy
Eugene, OR 97401-8835
Coach: Bill Steffen
Email: steffen@oregon.uoregon.edu

NCAA I
Ducks/Green, Gold, White
Phone: (541) 346-5506
Fax: (541) 346-2244

Estimated # of Women's Soccer Scholarships: None
Conference: PAC - 10 Conference
Program Profile: We have a rising program. We are capable of competing with anyone. Our field is among the best playing surfaces in the country. We have a 140 x 70 yard indoor training facility. We have one of the toughest schedules in the country.
History: Our program began in 1996 and has developed rapidly. We attained our first Regional ranking in 1998. We defeated regionally ranked UNCG in the opening weekend of 1998.
Achievements: Lead PAC 10 in All-Academic Selections; PAC 10 Player of the Week; Soccer America Team of the Week Player; 3 NSCAA All-West Academic Players; NSCAA Academic Athlete Award (11th highest GPA).
Coaching: Bill Steffen, Head Coach, is a former UNC assistant coach and is completing Ph.D. in Sport Psychology. He is a former pro player and NSCAA National Staff Coach. Keri Sanchez is assistant coach She is a former UWC player, national team player and a former pro player (Japan).
Style of Play: Positive possession, quick rhythm, skillful, athletic.

University of Portland

Academic Profile

Phone: 503-943-7911

Portland, OR 97203

Type: 4 Yr.,Private,Liberal Arts,Engineering
Founded: 1901
Website: http://www.up.edu
Religion: Roman Catholic
SAT/ACT/GPA: Individually evaluated3.5
Housing: Yes
Student/Faculty Ratio: 15:1
Male/Female Ratio: 45:55
Undergraduate Enrollment: 2,155
Graduate Enrollment: 247
Scholarships/Academic: Yes
Athletic: Yes
Financial Aid: Yes
Expenses by: Year
In State: $ 22,000
Out of State: $ 22,000
Specialty: Arts & Sciences, Business, Nursing, Education, Engineering
Degrees Conferred: BA, BS, BBA, Masters
Programs of Study: Business and Management, Communications, Education, Engineering, Health Science, Life Science, Social Science

Men's Athletic Profile

5000 North Willamette Boulevard
Portland, OR 97203
Coach: Clive Charles
Email: Not-Available

NCAA I
Pilots/Purple, White
Phone: (503) 943-7117
Fax: (503) 943-8082

Estimated # of Men's Soccer Scholarships: 4.9
Conference: West Coast Conference
Program Profile: Our field is natural grass with a seating capacity of a 5,000. We have a soccer only facility, and a fully funded soccer program.
History: The program began in 1977. Clive Charles took over in 1986. School all-time record is 244-123-40.
Achievements: 7 NCAA berths in the last nine years; 2 Final Four Appearances in 1988 and 1995; Coach of the Year in 1988; Far West Region WCC; WCC Titles in 1988, 1989, 1990 & 1992; Final Four in 1988 & 1885. All-Americans: Scott Benedictine-1988, Kasey Keller-1983, 1990, & 1991, Leone Cti-1989, Allan Clarke.
Coaching: Clive Charles, Head Coach, serves as an Assistant Coach of the US National Team, Olympic Team Coach and holds an "A" License. Bill Erwin, Assistant Coach, also holds an "A" License. Garreth Smith, Paul Gouldsbrough, Nyla Sbucky, Shannon McMillan are also Assistant Coaches.

Roster In State: 4	**Out of State:** 20	**Out of Country:** 1
ODP State: 19	**Regional:** 9	**National:** 7
Walk-on/Other: 3	**Graduation %:** 96.5	**Seniors on Team:** 6

Camp or Clinic Dates: Mid June , Last week in Aug.
Most Recent Record: 10-7-2
Schedule: Indiana, Stanford, University of Washington
Style of Play: Entertaining, attacking style of play.

Women's Athletic Profile

5000 N Willamette Blvd.
Portland, OR 97203
Coach: Clive Charles
Email: Not Available

NCAA I
Pilots/Purple, White
Phone: (503) 943-7117
Fax: (903) 943-8082

Estimated # of Women's Soccer Scholarships:
Conference: West Coast Conference
Program Profile: We are a traditionally strong program situated on a bluff overlooking the Willamette River. The Pilots play in what is considered one of the nation's finest soccer facilities - Merlo Field (5,000 capacity). The playing surface is natural grass which has a dimensions of 120x75 yards. Our fall season runs from August through December. We also have a spring season.
History: The program began in 1980. Clive Charles took over in 1989 and his all-time record is 202-85-27. We have been to the NCAA playoffs five straight. We have three Final Four appearances in the last three years (1994, 1995 & 1996). We were a Finalist in 1995.
Achievements: Shannon McMillan Heramn-MAC I; Tiffany Millvett, Shannon McMillan, Justi Baungandt and Erin Tahey - All-Americans; Clive Charles 1990 NCSC; Far West Region in 1992, 1993 & 1995; WCC Coach of the Year in 1993, 1994 & 1995.
Coaching: Clive Charles, Head Coach, is in his seventh year in Portland. He is native of London and is a 7 years veteran of pro soccer in English 1st Division and NASL. He is the Assistant Coach of US National Team Olympic Team. He holds an "A" License. Bill Irwin, Assistant Coach, has an "A" License. Nyla Stuckey, Garrett Smith, Paul Gouldibrough and Shannon MacMillan are assistant coaches.
Style of Play: Attractive attacking soccer.

Warner Pacific College

Academic Profile

Phone: 503-517-1000

Portland, OR 97215-4026

Type: 4 Yr.
Website: http://www.warnerpacific.edu
SAT/ACT/GPA: Open

Founded:
Religion: Non-Affiliated
Housing: No

Student/Faculty Ratio:
Male/Female Ratio:
Undergraduate Enrollment: N/A
Graduate Enrollment: N/A
Scholarships/Academic:
Athletic:
Financial Aid:
Expenses by:
In State:
Out of State:
Specialty:
Degrees Conferred:
Programs of Study: Contact school for programs of study.

Men's Athletic Profile

2219 SE 68th Avenue
Portland, OR 97215
Coach: Bernie Fagan
Phone: (503) 517-1000
Email: Not Available
Fax:

Did Not Return Profile

Western Baptist College

Academic Profile

Salem, OR 97301
Phone: 503-581-8600

Type: 4 Yr.,Private,Liberal Arts
Founded: 1939
Website: http://www.wbc.edu
Religion: Independent Baptist
SAT/ACT/GPA: 800
Housing: Yes
Student/Faculty Ratio: 17:1
Male/Female Ratio: 1:2
Undergraduate Enrollment: 5,720
Graduate Enrollment: N/A
Scholarships/Academic: Yes
Athletic: Yes
Financial Aid: Yes
Expenses by: Year
In State: $ 17,570
Out of State: $ 17,000
Degrees Conferred: AA, BA, BS
Programs of Study: Accounting, Bible Studies, Community Services, Education, Elementary Education, English, Family Studies, Finance, Humanities, Human Performances, Interdisciplinary Studies, Liberal Arts, Management & Communications, Mathematics, Ministries, Music, PreLaw, PreNursing, Psychology, Recreation & Leisure, Religious Education, Religion, Social Science, Theology

Men's Athletic Profile

5000 Deer Park Drive, SE
Salem, OR 97301
Coach: Doug Roberts
Email: Athletics@wbc.edu

NAIA
Warriors/Royal Blue, Gold
Phone: 503-315-2947
Fax: (503) 315-2947

Estimated # of Men's Soccer Scholarships: None
Conference: Cascade Collegiate Conference, NCCAA Div. I, NAIA
Program Profile: Western Baptist provides a quality soccer program within a Christian college setting. The soccer field measures 115 X 80 yd. and is nestled in a beautiful fur tree setting. The playing surface is natural grass and is noted as one of the finest fields in the Northwest.
History: Program began in 1976. It has duel memberships with the NAIA and NCCAA District I (National Christian College Assoc. of America).
Achievements: 1995 Cascade Champions and finalist in NCCAA National Tournament in Cleveland (TN).
Style of Play: The coach stresses fair play (1995 Cascade Conference Sportsmanship Award) and positive team attitude. Integration of a Christian life style and athletic excellence is the team's goal. Watch the Warriors move forward in the Northwest ranking of the NAIA.

Women's Athletic Profile

5000 Deer Park Drive SE
Salem, OR 97301
Coach: Marty Ziesemer
Email: mziesemer@wbc.edu

NAIA
Warriors/Blue, White
Phone: (503) 375-7115
Fax: (503) 585-4316

Estimated # of Women's Soccer Scholarships: 5
Conference: Cascade Collegiate Conference
Program Profile: Chance for two season tournaments. The home field is a natural grass, 80x115 yards. Has a Certified Athletic Trainer, 20-game schedule in the fall. Spring practice-winter indoor facility. Student-athlete must have relationship with Jesus to enroll in the school or must be a Christian.
History: Started in 1993. Last 5 years the women's teams has qualified for playoffs including being in the NAIA Region I tournament the last two years. The team was the Cascade Conference Champions in 1999 and second place finish in 1998 and 2000. The last two season also the team qualify and finished runner-up in the NCCAA National Tournament.
Achievements: 1998 Cascade Conference Coach of the Year. 2000 NCCAA National Coach of the Year. Several players have been at least Honorable Mention All-American in the NAIA and in 2000 we had a player awarded the NCCAA National Player of the Year.
Coaching: Marty Ziesemer, Head Coach, four-year college letterwinner, was an assistant for men's program that won the conference. NSCAA National Diploma. Entering 4th year with the program.
Roster in State: 4 **Out of State:** 17 **Out of Country:** 0
Walk-on/Other: **Graduation %:** **Seniors on Team:** 5
Camp or Clinic Dates: Not Available
Most Recent Record: 13-11-2
Schedule: Concordia, Simon Fraser, Seattle, George Fox, Northwest Nazarene

Willamette University

Academic Profile

Phone: 303-370-6300

Salem, OR 97301

Type: 4 Yr.,Private,Liberal Arts
Founded: 1842
Website: http://www.willamette.edu
Religion: Methodist
SAT/ACT/GPA: 1250/27/3.8
Housing: Yes
Student/Faculty Ratio: 13:1
Male/Female Ratio: 40:60
Undergraduate Enrollment: 1,700
Graduate Enrollment: 700
Scholarships/Academic: Yes **Athletic:** No **Financial Aid:** Yes
Expenses by: Year **In State:** $ 21,700 **Out of State:** $ 21,700
Degrees Conferred: BA, BS, BM
Programs of Study: American Studies, Art, Biology, Business Administration, Economics, Chemistry, Comparative Literature, Computer Science, English, Environmental Science, French, German, History, Humanities, International Studies, Japanese Studies, Math, Music, Philosophy, Physics, Psychology, Religion Studies, Media Studies, Spanish, Theatre

Men's Athletic Profile

900 State Street
Salem, OR 97301
Coach: Jim Tursi
Email: jtursi@tursissoccer.com

NCAA III
Bearcats/Maroon, White
Phone: (503) 370-6657
Fax: 503-297-0219

Estimated # of Men's Soccer Scholarships: None
Conference: Northwest Conference
Program Profile: We have the best soccer facility in district/conference. It is natural grass, seats 1,000 and is located

on campus. We have a as traditional fall season.
History: The program was upgraded to intercollegiate sport in 1981.
Achievements: Ranked nationally in 1982,1987-1988, 1990-1992;District Coach of the Year 1982; NCIC Coach of the Year 1990; 2 All - NAIA West Coast Players; 47 All - District, All - Conference players; 1 Academic All - American; District Champions 1982, 1991.
Coaching: Jim Tursi is the Head Coach. Mike Greer and Steve Storlie are the assistant coaches.

Roster In State: 10	**Out of State:** 10	**Out of Country:** 0
ODP State: 10	**Regional:**	**National:**
Walk-on/Other:	**Graduation %:** 95	**Seniors on Team:** 3

Camp or Clinic Dates: Not Available
Schedule: Linfield, University of Puget Sound, Pacific University, Hawaii Pacific, BYU Hawaii, Whitworth
Style of Play: 4-4-2 build from back, play to 2 forwards.

Women's Athletic Profile

900 State Street
Salem, OR 97301
Coach: Jim Tursi
Email: jtursi@tursissoccer.com

NCAA III
Bearcats/Maroon, White
Phone: (503) 370-6657
Fax: (503) 297-0219

Estimated # of Women's Soccer Scholarships: None
Conference: Northwest Conference
Program Profile: The Bearcats play a traditional Fall season. The home games are played on 72 X 110 yd field which seats 500-800 and a separate training area.
History: Program began in 1981.
Achievements: 7 out of 8 conference titles, NCAA postseason tournament 8 years in a row, NCAA final four 1998, 8 All-Americans.
Coaching: Jim Tursi - Head Coach. Mike Greer & Steve Storlie Assistant Coaches.

Roster in State: 10	**Out of State:** 10	**Out of Country:** 0
ODP State: 10	**Regional:** 0	**National:** 0
Walk-on/Other: 0	**Graduation %:** 95	**Seniors on Team:** 4

Positions Needed: Goalkeeper, Center Midfield
Camp or Clinic Dates: Not Available
Most Recent Record: 19-3-1
Schedule: University of Puget Sound, George Fox, Whitworth, University of Hawaii, Hawaii Pacific, Pacific Univ.
Style of Play: 4-4-2: Build attack from back, using two strikers as target players.

pennsylvania

PENNSYLVANIA

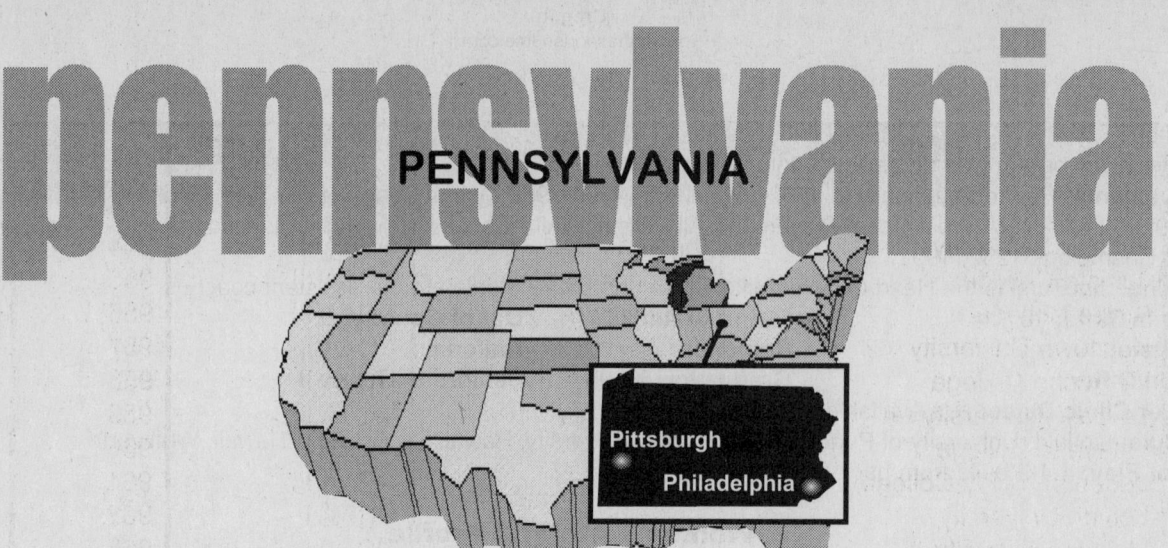

SCHOOL	CITY	AFFILIATION	PAGE
Albright College	Reading	NCAA III	925
Allegheny College	Meadville	NCAA III	926
Alvernia College	Reading	NCAA III	927
Arcadia Univ. (Beaver College)	Glenside	NCAA III	928
Bloomsburg University	Bloomsburg	NCAA II	929
Bryn Mawr College	Bryn Mawr	NCAA III	930
Bucknell University	Lewisburg	NCAA I	931
Cabrini College	Radnor	NCAA III	932
California University	California	NCAA II	933
Carnegie Mellon University	Pittsburgh	NCAA III	934
Chatham College	Pittsburgh	NCAA III/NAIA	935
College Misericordia	Dallas	NCAA III	935
Delaware Valley College	Doylestown	NCAA III	937
DeSales University	Center Valley	NCAA III	937
Dickinson College	Carlisle	NCAA III	939
Drexel University	Philadelphia	NCAA I	940
Duquesne University	Pittsburgh	NCAA I	941
East Stroudsburg University	East Stroudsburg	NCAA II	942
Eastern College	St. David's	NCAA III	943
Elizabethtown College	Elizabethtown	NCAA III	944
Franklin and Marshall College	Lancaster	NCAA III	945
Gannon University	Erie	NCAA II	946
Geneva College	Beaver Falls	NAIA	947
Gettysburg College	Gettysburg	NCAA III	948
Grove City College	Grove City	NCAA III	950
Gwynedd - Mercy College	Gwynedd Valley	NCAA III	951
Haverford College	Haverford	NCAA III	952
Holy Family College	Philadelphia	NCAA II	953

SCHOOL	CITY	AFFILIATION	PAGE
Indiana University	Indiana	NCAA II	954
Juniata College	Huntingdon	NCAA III	955
King's College	Wilkes-Barre	NCAA III	956
Kutztown University	Kutztown	NCAA II	957
La Roche College	Pittsburgh	NCAA II	958
La Salle University	Philadelphia	NCAA I	959
Lafayette College	Easton	NCAA I	960
Lebanon Valley College	Annville	NCAA III	961
Lehigh University	Bethlehem	NCAA I	962
Lincoln University	Lincoln University	NCAA III	963
Lock Haven University	Lock Haven	NCAA II	964
Lycoming College	Williamsport	NCAA III	965
Mercyhurst College	Erie	NCAA II	966
Messiah College	Grantham	NCAA III	968
Millersville University	Millersville	NCAA II	969
Moravian College	Bethlehem	NCAA III	970
Muhlenberg College	Allentown	NCAA III	971
Pennsylvania State University	University Park	NCAA I	972
Penn State University - Erie	Erie	NCAA III	973
Philadelphia College of T&S	Philadelphia	NCAA I	974
Point Park College	Pittsburgh	NAIA	976
Robert Morris College	Moon Township	NCAA I	976
Saint Francis College	Loretto	NCAA I	977
Saint Joseph's University	Philadelphia	NCAA I	979
Saint Vincent College	Latrobe	NAIA	980
Seton Hill College	Greensburg	NAIA	981
Shippensburg University	Chambersburg	NCAA II	981
Slippery Rock University	Slippery Rock	NCAA II	983
Susquehanna University	Selinsgrove	NCAA III	984
Swarthmore College	Swarthmore	NCAA III	985
Temple University	Philadelphia	NCAA I	986
Theil College	Greenville	NCAA III	987
University of Pennsylvania	Philadelphia	NCAA I	987
University of Pittsburgh	Pittsburgh	NCAA I	989
University of Pittsburgh - Bradford	Bradford	NCAA III	990
UP - Greensburg	Greensburg	NCAA III	991
PU - Johnstown	Johnstown	NCAA II	991
University of Scranton	Scranton	NCAA III	992
Ursinus College	Collegeville	NCAA III	993
Villanova University	Villanova	NCAA I	994
Washington and Jefferson	Washington	NCAA III	995
Waynesburg College	Waynesburg	NCAA III	996

SCHOOL	CITY	AFFILIATION	PAGE
West Chester University	West Chester	NCAA II	997
Westminster College	New Wilmington	NCAA II	999
Widener University	Chester	NCAA III	999
Wilkes University	Wilkes-Barre	NCAA III	1000
York College - Pennsylvania	York	NCAA III	1001

Albright College
Academic Profile

N. 13th Street
Reading, PA 19612

Phone:

Type: 4 Yr.,Private,Liberal Arts
Website: http://www.albright.edu
SAT/ACT/GPA: Open
Student/Faculty Ratio: 12:1
Undergraduate Enrollment: 1,100
Scholarships/Academic: Yes **Athletic:** No
Expenses by: Year **In State:** $ 24,502

Founded: 1856
Religion: Methodist
Housing: Yes
Male/Female Ratio: 48:52
Graduate Enrollment: N/A
Financial Aid: Yes
Out of State: $ 20,000

Specialty: Education, Dentistry, Law, Medicine, Finance
Degrees Conferred: BA, BS
Programs of Study: Accounting, Biology, Business, Chemistry, Computer, Economics, Education, Education, English, Environmental, Family Studies, Fine Arts, French, German, History, Management, Marketing, Math, Medical, Nutrition, Philosophy, Physics, Political Science

Men's Athletic Profile

P.O. Box 15234
Reading, PA 19612-5234
Coach: Dale Witmer
Email: athletics@alb.edu

NCAA III
Lions/Red, Black, White
Phone: 610-921-7840
Fax: (610) 921-7566

Estimated # of Men's Soccer Scholarships: N/A
Conference: Middle Atlantic Conference
Program Profile: The team plays on a natural surface field.
History: Our program began in 1976 and has struggled to make up ground on more established programs.
Coaching: Dale Witmer, Head Coach, is entering his first year with the program. He holds a USSF National "B" License. john Sweeney - Assistant Coach, holds Albright College record for games played, saves in a game season and career.
Style of Play: Possession, with varies formations; 3-5-2, 4-4-2 and the flat back 4.

Women's Athletic Profile

P.O. Box 15234
Reading, PA 19612-5234
Coach: Harry Kline
Email: hwkline@mail.ptd.net

NCAA III
Lions/Red, White
Phone: (610) 921-7535
Fax: (610) 921-7566

Estimated # of Women's Soccer Scholarships: None
Conference: Middle Atlantic Conference
Program Profile: We have a fall season. We have approximately 18 games. We play on a natural grass and we play non-traditional spring indoor season.
History: In 1997, our program became varsity conference team. We were Commonwealth League of MAC.
Coaching: Harry W. Kline is the Head Coach. He holds an "A" License. He was a Penn State Varsity Scholarships Player. He has 35 years of coaching experience including NCAA Division II. Michele Kline is our Assistant Coach. She holds a "D" License. she has 11 years of experience and founder of Country Girls Soccer Association at Roanoke, Virginia.
Style of Play: We play a short passing game.

Allegheny College

Academic Profile

Meadville, PA 16335

Phone: 814-332-3100

Type: 4 Yr.,Private
Website: http://www.alleg.edu
SAT/ACT/GPA: 500
Student/Faculty Ratio: 14.5:1
Undergraduate Enrollment: 1,900
Scholarships/Academic: Yes **Athletic:** No
Expenses by: Year **In State:** $ 24,860

Founded: 1815
Religion: Methodist
Housing: Yes
Male/Female Ratio: 47:53
Graduate Enrollment: N/A
Financial Aid: Yes
Out of State: $ 24,860

Specialty: Preprofessional Programs
Degrees Conferred: BS, BA
Programs of Study: Art, Biology, Chemistry, Computer Science, Communication Arts, Economics, English, Environmental Studies, French, Geology, German, History, International Studies, Mathematics, Music, Neuroscience, Philosophy, Physics, Political Science, Psychology, Religious Studies, Russian, Spanish, Theatre, Women's Studies

Men's Athletic Profile

520 N. Main Street, Box 5
Meadville, PA 16335
Coach: Paul Hogan
Email: phogan@administration.allegheny.edu

NCAA III
Gators/Navy Blue, Gold
Phone: (814) 332-5208
Fax: (814) 337-1217

Estimated # of Men's Soccer Scholarships:
Conference: North Coast Athletic Conference
Program Profile: We have a20 game season with tournament. We have a separate game and practice fields with a measurements of 75x120 yards. Our locker and full training facilities are at fields. In off season, we do weight training, have supervised training sessions, and play the maximum allowed number of springs games.
History: Our program began in 1935 and has played every year since. Allegheny was a member of the Presidents Athletic Conference for 23 years and in 1984 became a charter member of the North Coast Athletic Conference. Allegheny has had All-Americans, Academic All-Americans, as well as All-Region and All-Conference players.
Achievements: The program produced 5 All-Americans; 46 All-Conference players; 3 GTE Academic All-American; 1997 & 1998 Conference Newcomer of the Year Awards.
Coaching: Paul Hogan is the Head Coach. Karel Jelik is the Assistant Coach.
Style of Play: Flat back four, zonal defense, build from back and possession top ten.

Women's Athletic Profile

520 N. Main Street
Meadville, PA 16335
Coach: Jeff Groff
Email: jgroff@alleg.edu

NCAA III
Gators/Navy Blue, Gold
Phone: (814) 332-2811
Fax: (814) 337-1217

Estimated # of Women's Soccer Scholarships: None
Conference: North Coast Athletic Conference (NCAC)
Program Profile: We have 20 game season with tournaments. We have a separate game and practice field, which is grass and measures 75x120 yards. We have locker and full training facilitates at fields; off season supervised work-outs including indoor league participation.
History: Our varsity program began in 1985. Our overall record was 179-95-19. Our conference record was 86-30-8. We were Conference Champions five times; several times in top 10 regional rankings.

Achievements: We have had 12 All-American players, 32 All-Region players, and 88 All-Conference players. We were Conference Champions in 1985, 1986, 1987, 1988 & 1989. Our 1997 school record for wins was 18.
Coaching: Jeff Groff is our Head Coach, also our Athletic Director. Christina Alonzo is our Assistant Coach. Jack Steiger is our Assistant Coach as well as Strength Coach.
Roster in State: 11 **Out of State:** 13 **Out of Country:** 0
ODP State: 5 **Regional:** 2 **National:** 0
Walk-on/Other: 0 **Graduation %:** 96 **Seniors on Team:** 4
Positions Needed: Backs, Midfielder
Camp or Clinic Dates: Not Available
Most Recent Record: 15-5-2
Schedule: Ohio Wesleyan, Denison, Wooster, Earlham, Edinboro, John Carroll, Carnegie Mellon
Style of Play: We play a 4-4-2 formation. Primarily man-to-man marking. Building from back-possession soccer.

Alvernia College

Academic Profile

Phone:

Reading, PA 19067

Type: 4 Yr.,Private, **Founded:** 1959
Website: http://www.alvernia.edu **Religion:** Catholic-Franciscan
SAT/ACT/GPA: None **Housing:** Yes
Student/Faculty Ratio: 12:1 **Male/Female Ratio:** 35:36
Undergraduate Enrollment: 800 **Graduate Enrollment:** 800
Scholarships/Academic: Yes **Athletic:** No **Financial Aid:** Yes
Expenses by: Year **In State:** $ 16,210 **Out of State:** $ 16,210
Specialty: Criminal Justice, Physical Therapy, Education, Nursing
Degrees Conferred: BA, BSN, BS, MBA
Programs of Study: Accounting, Addictions Studies, Banking/Finance, Biology, Business, Chemistry, Communications, Computer, Criminal Justice, Education, English, Health, History, Math, Medical, Nursing, Optometry, Philosophy, Political Science, PreProfessional Programs, Psychology, Religion, Science, Secondary Education, Social Science, Spanish, Theology

Men's Athletic Profile

400 St. Bernardine St.
Reading, PA 19607-1799
Coach: Adams Hertz
Email: hertzed@alvernia.edu

NCAA III
Crusaders/Maroon, Gold
Phone: (610) 796- 8374
Fax: (610) 796- 8349

Estimated # of Men's Soccer Scholarships: N/A
Conference: Penna Athletic Conference , ECAC
Program Profile: The fourth year of the program- new grass field with 20 game season; indoor facilities.
History: Our program is 42 years as an NCAA program.
Coaching: Adam Hertz, Head Coach. Dan Hartzman - Assistant Coach.
Style of Play: Prefer possession, 4-4-2; aggressive marking and ball movement.

Women's Athletic Profile

400 Saint Bernadine St.
Reading, PA 19607-1799
Coach: Rachel Hoffman
Email: keenewe@alvernia.edu

NCAA III
Crusaders/Maroon, Gold
Phone: (610) 796-8309
Fax: (610) 796-8349

Estimated # of Women's Soccer Scholarships: None
Conference: Penna Athletic Conference, ECAC
Program Profile: We are in the second year of our program. We have new soccer and gym facilities. Our outdoor field is a full size field. We have new women's locker rooms.
History: 1997 was the first year of the program.
Style of Play: Our women's soccer team has a very tight bond and they play as a team. They are aggressive and determined to win.

Arcadia University (Beaver College)

Academic Profile

Phone: 215-572-2100

Glenside, PA 19038-3295

Type: 4 Yr.,Private,Liberal Arts
Founded: 1853
Website: http://www.beaver.ed
Religion: Presbyterian
SAT/ACT/GPA: Open
Housing: Yes
Student/Faculty Ratio: 13:1
Male/Female Ratio: 30:70
Undergraduate Enrollment: 1,200
Graduate Enrollment: 1,090
Scholarships/Academic: Yes **Athletic:** No **Financial Aid:** Yes
Expenses by: Year **In State:** $ 20,990 **Out of State:** $ 20,990
Degrees Conferred: BA, BS, BFA
Programs of Study: Accounting, Art, Art Education, Fine Arts, Biology, Business Administration, Management, Marketing, Chemistry, Communications, Computer Science, Education, Mathematics, Engineering, Optometry, Philosophy, Physical Therapy, Political Science

Men's Athletic Profile

450 S Easton Rd
Glenside, PA 19038-3295
Coach: Tom Carlin
Email: wink@beaver.edu

NCAA III
Scarlet Knights/Scarlet, Gray
Phone: (215) 572-2976
Fax: (215) 572-2159

Estimated # of Men's Soccer Scholarships: N/A
Conference: Pennsylvania Athletic Conference
Program Profile: NCAA Division III team, players are from some of the best high school programs, and club program in the area.
History: 1993 was the school's first year of the NCAA participation
Achievements: 4 All-Conference Players
Style of Play: Play a team oriented game stressing the fundamentals. Everybody works; patience and discipline will go along way for this young program.

Women's Athletic Profile

450 S Easton Road
Glenside, PA 19038-3295
Coach: Art Goon
Email: agoon@mc3.edu

NCAA III
Scarlet Knights/Scarlet, Grey
Phone: (215) 572-2982
Fax: (215) 572-4049

Estimated # of Women's Soccer Scholarships: N/A
Conference: Pennsylvania Athletic Conference
Program Profile: A state-of-the-art complex, Kuch Center houses, a six-lane swimming pool, indoor track, basketball and volley ball courts and aerobic and dance studios, fitness center, sauna and whirlpool. Natural grass soccer field.
History: Became an NCAA Division III program in 1991 and joined the Pennsylvania Athletic Conference in 1992.

Achievements: Several All-PAC players in its short history as an NCAA program. Coach Art Goon was named PAC Coach of the Year; in 1997 - 3 1st team All-Conference players; 11 PAC All-Academic players; 1 NSCAA All-Mid Atlantic player.
Coaching: Art Goon, Head Coach, former head coach at Rutgers Newark, SUNY-New Paltz, Tennessee-Chattanooga and Tennessee Wesleyan (13 years.); former All-Conference and All-NAIA District Player of the Year; named Conference and NAIA District Coach of the Year three times; guided teams to the TISA, NAIA, SUNYAC and ECAC Championship Tournament, second year at Beaver College. Ed Henry - Assistant Coach. Kelly Ann Coughlin - Assistant Coach. Jean Marie Andrews - goalkeeper Coach.
Walk-on/Other: **Graduation %:** 94.8 **Seniors on Team:** 4
Positions Needed: GK, MF, F
Camp or Clinic Dates: Not Available
Most Recent Record: 14-6-1
Schedule: Richard Stockton, Lynchburg College, Drew Univ. Rowan Univ.
Style of Play: 4-4-2 Build from the back, overlapping support on offense from mid-field, like to play high pressure on offensive third.

Bloomsburg University

Academic Profile

Bloomsburg, PA 17815
Phone: 570-389-4000

Type: 4 Yr.,Public
Founded: 1856
Website: http://www.bloomu.edu
Religion: Non-Affiliated
SAT/ACT/GPA: Require
Housing: Yes
Student/Faculty Ratio: 18:1
Male/Female Ratio: 40:60
Undergraduate Enrollment: 7,000
Graduate Enrollment: 650
Scholarships/Academic: Yes **Athletic:** Yes **Financial Aid:** Yes
Expenses by: Year **In State:** $ 7,712 **Out of State:** $ 12,910
Specialty: Education, Business, Preprofessional Programs
Degrees Conferred: BA, BS
Programs of Study: PrePhysical Therapy, PreMed, Education, Business, PreLaw, PreDental, PreVet, PreProfessional Art, Biology, Chemistry, Communications, Criminal Justice, Economics, Geography, History, Humanities, Arts & Sciences, Physics, Psychology, Physics, Sociology, Spanish, Theatre Arts, German, Exercise Science, English, Criminal Justice

Men's Athletic Profile

Nelson Field House
Bloomsburg, PA 17815
Coach: Paul Payne
Email: ppayne@bloomu.edu

NCAA II
Huskies/Maroon, White
Phone: (717) 389-4381
Fax: (717) 389-2099

Estimated # of Men's Soccer Scholarships: N/A
Conference: Pennsylvania State Athletic Conference
Program Profile: Has indoor facilities and three full-size grass fields.
History: Program started in 1975. 1993 - PSAC playoffs; 1996 PSAC Runner-Up.
Achievements: 1995 - 3 Mid-Atlantic All-Americans; 1996 - 3 Mid-Atlantic All-Americans; 1996 Conference Player and Freshman of the Year.
Coaching: John O'Leary, Head Coach, NSCAA Advanced National Diploma, FA Prelim Badge, Director NSCAA Recreation Diploma, NCAA Central Region Advisory Committee, player at Reading Racie USISL professional league. Mark Waite - Assistant Coach, Academic All-American, All-American, FA Prelim, professional player Hampton Rhoads USISL.
Style of Play: Attacking, possession orientated, emphasis on all played being comfortable on the ball and help work-out both offensively and defensively.

Women's Athletic Profile

Nelson Field House
Bloomsburg, PA 17815
Coach: Sandy Dickson
Email: sdickson@bloomu.edu

NCAA II
Huskies/Maroon, White
Phone: (570) 389-4162
Fax: (570) 389-2099

Estimated # of Women's Soccer Scholarships: None
Conference: Pennsylvania State Athletic Conference (PSAC)
Program Profile: We were 1998 PSAC Champions and our 1998 record was 16-1-4. We were in the NCAA Final Sixteen. Our 1998 NSCAA national final ranking was #5.
History: Our program started in 1990. We were PSAC Champions in 1996 and 1998. In 1996, we were in the NCAA Quarterfinals. In 1998, we were NCAA Final Sixteen. In 1998, we were National Final #5 ranking.
Achievements: 13 All-Americans; 1996, 1998 PSAC Champions; All-Region (25) players.
Coaching: Sandy Dickson, Head Coach, was as assistant in 1995 &1997.
Style of Play: Possession, high pressure, quick transitions game.

Bryn Mawr College

Academic Profile

Phone: 610-526-5000

Bryn Mawr, PA 19010

Type: 4 Yr.,Private,Liberal Arts
Website: http://www.brynmawr.edu
SAT/ACT/GPA: 1150+
Student/Faculty Ratio: 9:1
Undergraduate Enrollment: 1,100
Scholarships/Academic: No **Athletic:** No
Expenses by: Year **In State:** $ 26,000

Founded: 1885
Religion: Non-Affiliated
Housing: Yes
Male/Female Ratio: Women
Graduate Enrollment: N/A
Financial Aid: Yes
Out of State: $ 26,000

Degrees Conferred: AB, MA, Ph.D.
Programs of Study: African Studies, Anthropology, Archeology, Art History, Asian Studies, Astronomy, BioChemistry, Biology, Chemistry, Classical Languages, Computer Science, Economics, English, Fine Arts, French, Geology, German, Greek, History, International Economics, Italian, Latin, Literature, Math, Music, NeuroScience, Peace Studies, Philosophy, Physics, Political Science, Psychology, Romance Languages, Russian, Social Science, Spanish, Urban Studies

Women's Athletic Profile

101 N. Merion Avenue
Bryn Mawr, PA 19010
Coach: Kathleen Miller
Email: @brynmawr.edu

NCAA III
Mawrter/Yellow, White
Phone: (610) 526-7348
Fax: (610) 526-7347

Estimated # of Women's Soccer Scholarships: None
Conference: Centennial Conference
Program Profile: Natural turf, 18-20 game fall season.
History: Began in 1984.
Coaching: Kathleen Miller, Head Coach, graduate of Temple in 1990, All-American lacrosse player and member of a n defeated national championship team

Bucknell University

Academic Profile

Lewisburg, PA 17837

Phone: 570-577-2000

Type: 4 Yr.,Private,Liberal Arts,Engineering
Website: http://www.bucknell.edu
SAT/ACT/GPA: Required
Student/Faculty Ratio: 12.5:1
Undergraduate Enrollment: 3,200
Scholarships/Academic: No
Athletic: No
Expenses by: Year
In State: $ 29,800
Specialty: Engineering, Sciences
Degrees Conferred: BA, BS

Founded: 1846
Religion: Non-Affiliated
Housing: No
Male/Female Ratio: 52:48
Graduate Enrollment: 200
Financial Aid: Yes
Out of State: $ Varies

Programs of Study: Accounting, Animal, Anthropology, Art, BioChemistry, Biology, Business and Management, Computer, Environmental, Engineering, Religion, Social Sciences, Statistics, Theatre, Women's Studies

Men's Athletic Profile

Men's Soccer Office, Fieldhouse
Lewisburg, PA 17837
Coach: Brendan Nash
Email: bnash@bucknell.edu

NCAA I
Bison/Orange, Blue
Phone: (570) 577-3083
Fax: 570-577-1660

Estimated # of Men's Soccer Scholarships: 0
Conference: Patriot League
Program Profile: Team consists of 20-25 members that play about a 20 game season in the fall. Outdoor is on natural grass field which is located on the campus that contains seating for approximately 300 and a grassy hill which holds a large number of fans relax and enjoy the games. Bucknell competes in the 8 team Patriot League with the regular season champion hosting a post season tournament.
History: Started in 1929; Overall record 358-404-70.
Achievements: NCAA tournament qualifications 1974,75,76. Coach of the year awards, Player of the Year awards, and 1994 Mid - Atlantic Region Adidas Scholar Athlete Team
Coaching: Brendan Nash is the Head Coach. Mike Jacobson and Steve Pokorny are the assistant coaches.
Roster In State: 2
Out of State: 22
Out of Country: 0
ODP State: 13
Regional: 2
National:
Walk-on/Other: 3
Graduation %: 100
Seniors on Team: 4
Camp or Clinic Dates: July 15-19 and July 22-26 (High School Boys)
Most Recent Record: 9-9-2
Schedule: Penn State, Old Dominion, William & Mary, American, Pittsburgh
Style of Play: 4-4-2 with sweeper and stopper. 1-2 touch possession.

Women's Athletic Profile

Women's Soccer Office, Fieldhouse
Lewisburg, PA 17837
Coach: Chrissy Findlay
Email: cfindlay@bucknell.edu

NCAA I
Bison/Navy, Orange
Phone: (570) 577-1772
Fax: (570) 524-1660

Estimated # of Women's Soccer Scholarships: None
Conference: Patriot League Conference

Program Profile: Our home playing field has natural grass and lights. Facilities include a practice field, a 7-a-side field, a locker room, a weight room pool and indoor and outdoor tracks. Sponsored by Adidas. Fall season. Year round training program with conditioning, weight training, and functional training with competitions in the spring as well. We are building a new athletic complex in spring of '01.
History: Our program began in 1990. We advanced to P.L. Tournament 7 out of 10 years.
Achievements: 2 Academic All-Americans; 1 Regional All-American; 1 Coach of the Year for P.L.; 4 players in "W" league.
Coaching: Chrissy Findlay-Head Coach.

Roster in State: 4	**Out of State:** 21	**Out of Country:**
ODP State: 20	**Regional:**	**National:**
Walk-on/Other:	**Graduation %:** 98	**Seniors on Team:** 1

Positions Needed: Outside Midfielder, Stopper, Sweeper
Camp or Clinic Dates: July 29- August 2
Most Recent Record: 8-8-1
Schedule: Navy, Colgate, Penn, Villanova, Army, St. Job
Style of Play: zone defense all over field; Quick transitional team; short passing possession play.

Cabrini College

Academic Profile

Radnor, PA 19087

Phone:

Type: 4 Yr.,Private,Liberal Arts		**Founded:** 1957
Website: http://www.cabrini.edu		**Religion:** Non-Affiliated
SAT/ACT/GPA: Open		**Housing:** Yes
Student/Faculty Ratio: 18:1		**Male/Female Ratio:** 1:3
Undergraduate Enrollment: 850		**Graduate Enrollment:** N/A
Scholarships/Academic: Yes	**Athletic:** No	**Financial Aid:** Yes
Expenses by: Year	**In State:** $ 16,950	**Out of State:** $ 16,950

Specialty: Communications, Business
Degrees Conferred: BA, BS, M.Ed.
Programs of Study: Contact school for program of study.

Men's Athletic Profile

610 King of Prussia Rd
Radnor, PA 19087
Coach: Doug Meder
Email: Not Available

NCAA III
Cavaliers/Royal Blue, White
Phone: (610) 902-8387
Fax: (610) 902-8385

Estimated # of Men's Soccer Scholarships: None
Conference: Pennsylvania Athletic Conference
History: Program begin in 1980. P.A.C. Champions in 1993, 1994 and 1995.

Women's Athletic Profile

610 King of Prussia Rd
Radnor, PA 19087
Coach: Diane Pierangeli
Email: Not Available

NCAA III
Lady Cavs/Royal, White
Phone: (610) 902-8386
Fax:

Estimated # of Women's Soccer Scholarships: None
Conference: PAC

California University - Pennsylvania

Academic Profile

California, PA 15419

Phone: 724-938-4000

Type: 4 Yr.,Public,Liberal Arts
Website: http://www.cup.edu
SAT/ACT/GPA: 910/20/2.5
Student/Faculty Ratio: 20:1
Undergraduate Enrollment: 5,000
Scholarships/Academic: Yes **Athletic:** Yes
Expenses by: Year **In State:** $ 4,450
Founded: 1847
Religion: Non-Affiliated
Housing: Yes
Male/Female Ratio: 50:50
Graduate Enrollment: 1,000
Financial Aid: Yes
Out of State: $ 7,750
Specialty: Education, Science & Technology, Liberal Arts
Degrees Conferred: BA, BS, MA, MEd
Programs of Study: Liberal Arts, Education, Science and Technology, Human Services

Men's Athletic Profile

250 University Avenue
California, PA 15419
Coach: Dennis Laskey
Email: laskey@cup.edu

NCAA II
Vulcans/Red, Black
Phone: (412) 938-5793
Fax: (412) 938-5849

Estimated # of Men's Soccer Scholarships: None
Conference: Pennsylvania State Athletic Conference
Program Profile: Division II, facilities include 5 soccer natural grass game fields, 3 practice fields, 2 indoor facilities, and athlete's training room.
History: Program began in 1984.
Achievements: Has 14 Regional All-Americans.
Coaching: Dennis Laskey, Head Coach, USSF "A" License, NSCAA Advanced National Diploma. He has five assistant coaches.
Style of Play: Flexible to the capabilities of the players.

Women's Athletic Profile

250 University Avenue
California, PA 15419
Coach: Dennis Laskey
Email: laskey@cup.edu

NCAA II
Vulcans/Red, Black
Phone: (412) 938-5793
Fax: (412) 938-5849

Estimated # of Women's Soccer Scholarships: None
Conference: Pennsylvania State Athletic Conference
Program Profile: Has five soccer fields which are all natural surface.
History: Program began in 1991.
Achievements: 14 Regional All-Americans.
Coaching: Dennis Laskey, Head Coach, holds a USSF "A" license and a NSCAA Advanced National Diploma. He has five assistant coaches.
Style of Play: Flexible to the capabilities of the players.

Carnegie Mellon University

Academic Profile

Pittsburgh, PA 15213-3890

Phone: 412-268-2000

Type: 4 Yr.,Private,Liberal Arts,Engineering
Website: http://www.cmu.edu
SAT/ACT/GPA: 1300/30
Student/Faculty Ratio: 9:1
Undergraduate Enrollment: 4,800
Scholarships/Academic: Yes
Athletic: No
Expenses by: Year
In State: $ 30,095
Founded: 1900
Religion: Non-Affiliated
Housing: Yes
Male/Female Ratio: 2:1
Graduate Enrollment: 2,700
Financial Aid: Yes
Out of State: $ 30,095
Specialty: Engineering, Math, Science
Degrees Conferred: BA, BS, MA, MS, Ph.D.
Programs of Study: Chemical Engineering, Civil Engineering, Electrical Engineering, Computer Engineering, Material Engineering, Mechanical Engineering, Fine Arts, Liberal Arts, Humanities, Science, Computer Science, Business Administration, Math

Men's Athletic Profile

5000 Forbes Avenue
Pittsburgh, PA 15213
Coach: Nick Gaudioso
Email: Not Available

NCAA III
Tartans/Cardinal, Gray, White
Phone: (412) 268-2217
Fax: (412) 268-3099

Estimated # of Men's Soccer Scholarships: None
Conference: University Athletic Association
Program Profile: Home games are played at Gesling Stadium, a 4,000 seats facility that has lights and omni-turf field; stadium opened in Fall of 1990. The University Athletic Association is generally regarded as the nation's premier NCAA Division II Soccer Conference.
History: Program began in 1940. Joined UAAA 10 years ago.
Achievements: 3 All-Americans during Gaudioso's tenure; team made its first NCAA appearance last year losing to Muhlenberg in a shoot out in the first round; have recorded 13 straight winning seasons.
Coaching: Nick Gaudioso, Head Coach, 20 year career, 14 CMU career highlights include 13 straight winning seasons, 1992 UAA Coach of the Year, and the school's first conference title in 1984, USSF 'A' license, 1977 graduate of Maine(BA in Physical Education), played midfielders for the Bears.
Style of Play: European Style attacking — up tempo with ball played on the ground due to homefield's fast astro-turf. Playing balls out of back.

Women's Athletic Profile

5000 Forbes Ave., Women's Soccer
Pittsburgh, PA 15213
Coach: Heather Kendra
Email: hkendra@andrew.cmu.edu

NCAA III
Tartans/Cardinal, Gray, White
Phone: (412) 268-2187
Fax: (412) 268-3099

Estimated # of Women's Soccer Scholarships: None
Conference: University Athletic Association
Program Profile: Has new turf (1999) field/stadium, grass practice area, stadium seats 6,000. Located just five miles from downtown Pittsburgh. Athletic department only weight room.
History: The program began in 1991. Joined UAA in 1992; finished 1994 with 13-3-2 record with 4-1-1 conference record. Overall record is 42-21-4 in four seasons.

Achievements: 1 All-Conference in 1992, 4 All-Conference in 1993, 4 All-Conference in 1994, 1 NSCAA All-Region in 1993, 2 NSCAA All-Region in 1994, 1 NSCAA All-American 1st team in 1994. in 1998 season, we finished 5th in the UAA.
Coaching: Heather Kendra, Head Coach, is entering her first season at CMU (1998-1999). She is previously the assistant coach at Washington and Lee University. She holds NSCAA National Diploma; BS from Plymouth State in 1996 and MA from University of North Carolina in 1998. Deb Yost is Assistant Coach.
Roster in State: 2 **Out of State:** 18 **Out of Country:**
Walk-on/Other: **Graduation %:** 100 **Seniors on Team:** 2
Positions Needed: GK
Most Recent Record: 6-8-2
Schedule: University of Chicago, Emory University, John Hopkins, Washington University, University of Rochester, Washington and Lee University
Style of Play: Quick and controlled passing style of play.

Chatham College
Academic Profile

Pittsburgh, PA 15232
Phone: (800) 837-1290

Type: 4 Yr.,Private,Liberal Arts
Founded: 1869
Website: http://www.chatham.edu
Religion: Non-Affiliated
SAT/ACT/GPA: 1100avg/3.0-avg
Housing: Yes
Student/Faculty Ratio: 12:1
Male/Female Ratio: 100%-F
Undergraduate Enrollment: 522
Graduate Enrollment: 331
Scholarships/Academic: Yes **Athletic:** No **Financial Aid:** Yes
Expenses by: Year **In State:** $ 23,508 **Out of State:** $ 23,508
Specialty: Liberal Arts - Psychology, English, Communications
Degrees Conferred: BA, BS
Programs of Study: Accounting, Administration of Justice, Arts Management, Behavioral NeuroScience, BioChemistry, Biology, Chemistry, Communications, Cyber Communications, Economics, English, English and Dramatic, Literature, Entrepreneurial Management, Environmental Science, and Studies, French, Global Policy Studies, Graphic Design, History, International Business, Marketing, Math, Music, Philosophy and Religion, Political Science, Psychology, Spanish, Theatre, Women's Studies

Women's Athletic Profile

Woodland Road
Pittsburgh, PA 15232
Coach: Tim Meszar
Email: Not Available

NCAA III/NAIA
Purple, White
Phone: (412) 365-1265
Fax: (412) 365-1620

Estimated # of Women's Soccer Scholarships: None
Conference:
Program Profile: Strong, young, and inexperienced team and are looking for quality student-athletes to come to make an impact in our team.
History: Started in 1995 (was first full season, FALL)

College Misericordia
Academic Profile

Dallas, PA 18612
Phone: (570) 674-6492

Type: 4 Yr.,Private,Liberal Arts
Founded: 1924
Website: http://www.miseri.edu
Religion: Catholic

SAT/ACT/GPA: Varies with the major
Housing: Yes
Student/Faculty Ratio: 14:1
Male/Female Ratio: 35:65
Undergraduate Enrollment: 1,200
Graduate Enrollment: N/A
Scholarships/Academic: Yes
Athletic: No
Financial Aid: Yes
Expenses by: Year
In State: $ 22,190
Out of State: $ 22,190
Degrees Conferred: BS, BA, MS
Programs of Study: Accounting, Biology, Business Administration, Computer Science, Early Childhood, Elementary Education, English, History, Humanities, Management, Marketing, Mathematics, Medical Laboratory Technology, Natural Science, Nursing, Physical Therapy, PreDentistry, PreLaw, PreMed, Social Science

Men's Athletic Profile

301 Lake Street
Dallas, PA 18612
Coach: Paul Van Hooydonk
Email: pvanhooy@miseri.edu

NCAA III
Cougars/Royal, Gold
Phone: 570-674-6492
Fax: 570-674-5785

Estimated # of Men's Soccer Scholarships: NA
Conference: ECAC, Pennsylvania Athletic Conference
Program Profile: We play a 20-game traditional fall season and a spring non-traditional season. Our field measures 120 x 75 , has natural grass and a 500 person capacity. We are in the Division III Atlantic Region.
History: Our program started in 1990.
Achievements: 2 Pennsylvania Athletic Conference Championships in 1996 and 1997; 1 Regional All-American (twice named); PAC Coach of the Year in 1996
Coaching: Paul Van Hooydonk, Head Coach. Scott Crispell is assistant coach.
Style of Play: Attack oriented with three front runners, high pressure defense, possession offense.

Women's Athletic Profile

301 Lake Street
Dallas, PA 18612
Coach: Mark Stauffer
Email: scrispel@miseri.edu

NCAA III
Cougars/Blue, Gold
Phone: (570) 674-6492
Fax: (570) 674-3024

Estimated # of Women's Soccer Scholarships: None
Conference: Pennsylvania Athletic Conference, ECAC
Program Profile: Play a 20-game traditional Fall season; Spring non-traditional season. Has 120x75 yards natural grass field with a seating capacity of 500.
History: Program is 7 years old. Recorded first winning season in 1994. Conference championship play began in 1994.
Achievements: 1995-1996 and 1996-1997 PAC Conference Titles; 1997-1998 and 1998-1999 PAC runner-ups; All-Metro player selections; All- Mid-Atlantic players selections. PAC Runner-up in 1999.
Coaching: Mark Stauffer is in his 1st season as head coach in 2001. He is a former standout player and assistant men's coach at Misericordia.
Roster in State: 9
Out of State: 11
Out of Country: 0
Walk-on/Other:
Graduation %: 95
Seniors on Team: 7
Positions Needed: All
Camp or Clinic Dates: Not Available
Most Recent Record: 12-5-3
Schedule: Scranton, Beaver, Cabrini
Style of Play: Attack oriented with three front runners. High pressure defense, possession offense.

Delaware Valley College

Academic Profile

Doylestown, PA 18901

Phone: (215) 230-2963

Type: 4 Yr.,Private,
Website: http://www.devalcol.edu
SAT/ACT/GPA: 900/2.5
Student/Faculty Ratio: 15:1
Undergraduate Enrollment: 1,400
Scholarships/Academic: Yes **Athletic:** No
Expenses by: Year **In State:** $ 21,250

Founded: 1896
Religion: Jewish
Housing: Yes
Male/Female Ratio: 40:60
Graduate Enrollment: N/A
Financial Aid: Yes
Out of State: $ 21,250

Specialty: Agricultural, Biology, Chemistry, Environmental Science
Degrees Conferred: BA, BS
Programs of Study: Marketing, Management, Criminal Justice, Business Administration, Accounting, Management Information Systems, Computer Information Systems, Biology, Micro BioTech, Environmental Biology, Animal Biology, Plant Biology, Chemistry, Mathematics, English, Secondary Education, PreVeterinary Medicine, PreMedicine, PreDental Medicine, PreOptometry, AgriBusiness, Agronomy, Animal Science, Dairy Science, Food Science, Horticulture, Ornamental Hort, Environmental Design

Men's Athletic Profile

700 E Butler Ave.
Doylestown, PA 18901
Coach: Kalman Csapo
Email: admitme@devalcol.edu

NCAA III
Aggies/F. Green, Gold, White
Phone: (800) 2DELUNL
Fax: (215) 230-2963

Estimated # of Men's Soccer Scholarships: None
Conference: Middle Atlantic Conference
Program Profile: Soccer is played and natural grass. Has 18 game regular season with off-season training.
History: Our men's soccer program has existed since 1976. The best season came in 1993 when the team finished with a record of 8-6-4. School record for wins is 4-game winning streak and an 8-game unbeaten streak (5-0-3) that had the team at 30 days without suffering a loss. Has a recent history of being a competitive team. Future looks bright.
Style of Play: Ball position with opportunistic scoring.

Women's Athletic Profile

700 E Butler Avenue
Doylestown, PA 18901
Coach: Kevin Doherty
Email: Not Available

NCAA III
Aggies/Forest Green, Gold
Phone: (215) 489-2240
Fax: (215) 230-2963

Estimated # of Women's Soccer Scholarships: None
Conference: Middle Atlantic Conference, Freedom League
History: Program began in 1994.
Achievements: NSCAA / Umbro Mid-Atlantic Region 2nd team
Coaching: Kevin Doherty, Head Coach, and assistant coach for the men's

De Sales University

Academic Profile

Center Valley, PA 18034

Phone: (610) 282-1100x 1204

Type: 4 Yr.,Private,Liberal Arts
Website: http://www.desales.edu

Founded: 1964
Religion: Catholic

SAT/ACT/GPA: N/A
Student/Faculty Ratio: 17/1
Undergraduate Enrollment: 1,200
Scholarships/Academic: Yes
Athletic: No
Expenses by: Year
In State: $ 18,200
Housing: Yes
Male/Female Ratio: 1/1.5
Graduate Enrollment: 1,000
Financial Aid: Yes
Out of State: $ 18,200
Specialty: Nursing School and Physician Assistant Program
Degrees Conferred: BA, BS
Programs of Study: Accounting, Biology, Communications, Chemistry, Computer Science, Creative Writing, Criminal Justice, Dance, Elementary Education, English, Environmental Studies, Finance, History, Human Resources Management, Legal Studies, Liberal Studies, Management, Management of Information Technology, Marketing, Marriage and Family Studies, Math, Nursing, Philosophy, Physician's Assistant, Political Science, Physical Education, Social Work, Spanish, Sport Management, Theatre, Theology, TV/Film, PreProfessional Programs

Men's Athletic Profile

2755 Station Avenue
Center Valley, PA 18034-9568
Coach: George Crampton
Email: gwc@desales.edu
NCAA III
Bulldogs/Blue, Red
Phone: (610) 282-1100x1635
Fax: (610) 282-2279

Estimated # of Men's Soccer Scholarships: None
Conference: MAC - Freedom League Conference
Program Profile: Full size soccer field with natural grass turf. Seats up to 200 people, with viewing capacity of more than 1,000.
History: Program began in 1969 and has a record of 174-285-40 in 32 years.
Achievements: Won Pennsylvania Athletic Conference Regular Season title in 1996. Became the first team in the PAC history to not allow a goal in regular-season conference play.. Eastern State Athletic Conference champions in 1988. NAIA district 19 Champion in 1984, 1987, and 1988.
Coaching: George Crampton 2 time All-American, NJCAA National Champion. Plays professionally with the Reading Rage D-3. Holds a NSCAA Distingushed National Coaching Diploma.
Roster In State: 15
Out of State: 6
Out of Country: 0
Walk-on/Other:
Graduation %: 100
Seniors on Team: 1
Camp or Clinic Dates: 3rd week in June and 1st 2 weeks in August
Most Recent Record: 7-11-2
Schedule: SUNY Cortland, Ithaca, William Patterson, Drew, Wilkes, Beaver College
Style of Play: Play a 4-4-2 with a sweeper or a 4-3-3 with a sweeper.

Women's Athletic Profile

2755 Station Avenue
Center Valley, PA 18034-9568
Coach: David Yob
Email: AcwsocYob@MSN.com
NCAA III
Bulldogs/Navy, Red
Phone: (610) 282-1100
Fax: (610) 282-2279

Estimated # of Women's Soccer Scholarships: None
Conference: Middle Atlantic Conference
Program Profile: We have 2 natural grass fields. We have a new Recreation Center. Our playing season is from August to October. We play some off-season indoor and outdoor soccer.
History: Our program began in 1996. Dave Barnes was head coach in 1996 and his record was 2-12-0. Dave Yob has been head coach for two years. In 1997, his record was 2-13-1. In 1998, his record was 5-14-1. In five years overall record is 27-57-3
Achievements: Dave Yob- Coach of the Year in 1994 for Women's Intercollegiate Athletic Conference while at Centenary College in New Jersey. Coach of the Year in 2000 in MAC Freedom Conference

Roster in State: 14 **Out of State:** 10 **Out of Country:** 0
Walk-on/Other: **Graduation %:** 100 **Seniors on Team:** 1
Camp or Clinic Dates: Not Available
Most Recent Record: 9-8-1
Style of Play: Utilize 4-3-3 but will adapt to what is best for personnel.

Dickinson College

Academic Profile

Carlisle, PA 17013
Phone: 717-243-5121

Type: 4 Yr.,Private,Liberal Arts
Founded: 1773
Website: http://www.dickinson.edu
Religion: United Methodist
SAT/ACT/GPA: Not Required
Housing: Yes
Student/Faculty Ratio: 10:1
Male/Female Ratio: N/A
Undergraduate Enrollment: 1,950
Graduate Enrollment: N/A
Scholarships/Academic: Yes **Athletic:** No **Financial Aid:** Yes
Expenses by: Year **In State:** $ 26,260 **Out of State:** $ 26,260
Specialty: Study Abroad Program
Degrees Conferred: BA, BS
Programs of Study: 31 majors including American Studies, Anthropology, Asian Studies, Biology, Chemistry, Computer Science, Dramatic Arts, Economics, English, Fine Arts, Foreign Languages, French, Geology, German, Greek, History, Humanities, International Studies, Latin, Mathematics, Music, Natural Sciences, Philosophy, Physics, Political Science, Psychology, Religion, Russian, Russian & Soviet Area Studies, Social Sciences, Spanish

Men's Athletic Profile

P.O. Box 1773
Carlisle, PA 17013
Coach: Mark Brown
Email: brownma@dickinson.edu

NCAA III
Red Devils/Red, White
Phone: (717) 245-1320
Fax: (717) 245-1441

Estimated # of Men's Soccer Scholarships: N/A
Conference: Centennial Conference
Program Profile: Full size natural grass fields with an additional training field. Regular season runs from early September through the end of Oct. Excellent athletic training facilities.
History: Established program in 1929. Played consistently since 1964.
Achievements: 3 ECAC South Region championships.
Style of Play: Ball control, and possession.

Women's Athletic Profile

P.O. Box 1773
Carlisle, PA 17013
Coach: Shellee Copley
Email: Not Available

NCAA III
Red Devils/Red, White
Phone: (717) 245-1320
Fax: (717) 245-1441

Estimated # of Women's Soccer Scholarships: None
Conference: Centennial
Program Profile: Full-size natural grass field with additional training field. Reg. season runs from early Sept. to the end of Oct. Excellent athletic facilities.
History: Established in 1984.
Style of Play: Strong Defensive play with an improving offense.

Drexel University

Academic Profile

Phone: 800-2-DREXEL

Phile, PA 19104

Type: 4 Yr.,Private,
Founded: 1891
Website: http://www.drexel.edu
Religion: Non-Affiliated
SAT/ACT/GPA: Varies
Housing: None
Student/Faculty Ratio: 13:1
Male/Female Ratio: 65:35
Undergraduate Enrollment: 5,300
Graduate Enrollment: 2,900
Scholarships/Academic: Yes **Athletic:** Yes **Financial Aid:** Yes
Expenses by: Year **In State:** $ 25,000 **Out of State:** $ 25,000
Specialty: Technical and Co-op Education
Degrees Conferred: Bachelors, Masters, Doctoral
Programs of Study: Accounting, Architecture, Atmospheric Sciences, Biology, Business & Management, Chemistry, Communications, Computer Information Systems, Computer Science, Construction Management, Economics, Education, Engineering, Environmental Science, Graphic Art, Humanities, Interior Design, International Business, Literature, Management Information System, Marketing, Mathematics, Music, Natural Science, Nutrition, Operation Research, Philosophy, Photography, Physical Science, Physics, Political Science, PreVet, Psychology, Science, Science Education, Social Science, Sociology, Technical Writing

Men's Athletic Profile

32nd and Chestnut Streets
Philadelphia, PA 19104
Coach: Lew Meehl
Email: Not Available

NCAA I
Dragons/Navy, Gold
Phone: (215) 895-1936
Fax: (215) 895-2037

Estimated # of Men's Soccer Scholarships: 2.5
Conference: American East Conference
Program Profile: Division I program with indoor, artificial turf and natural grass practice facilities; games practice facilities; game field surface is grass (one of the best in the area), seating capacity of 1,500 located 10 blocks from main part of the campus. Play a tough regional schedule that includes all six Philadelphia Division I
History: Started in 1947. Play in the North Atlantic Conference past few years, Won the Philadelphia Soccer Seven Title in 1994.
Achievements: Coach of the Year '93; Regional Coach of the Year '89; Conference Champions 1998; several All-Americans; Local Conference Titles- Soccer 7;
Coaching: Lew Meehl is our Head Coach. He holds USSF 'A' License, National Staff over 10 years. He was named 5-time PSS Coach of the Year. Woddy Hartman is an Assistant Coach and was a professional Goalkeeper and holds a USSF "A" License and Rick Tompkins played at Penn State and also holds a USSF "A" License.
Roster In State: 21 **Out of State:** 5 **Out of Country:** 3
ODP State: 12 **Regional:** **National:**
Walk-on/Other: 4 **Graduation %:** 98 **Seniors on Team:** 4
Positions Needed: Forward, Midfielder, 2 Defenders
Camp or Clinic Dates: Not Available
Most Recent Record: 13-6-2
Schedule: George Manson, Boston University, Towson State, Hartford, Seton, Hofstra
Style of Play: Attack: Possession. Defensively: Combination of zonal and man to man.

Women's Athletic Profile

3141 Chestnut Street
Philadelphia, PA 19104
Coach: Ray Goon
Email: Not Available

NCAA I
Dragons/Navy, Blue
Phone: (215) 590-8945
Fax: (215) 590-8848

Estimated # of Women's Soccer Scholarships: None
Conference: North Atlantic Conference, Philadelphia Soccer 7

Duquesne University
Academic Profile

Pittsburgh, PA 15282
Phone: 412-396-6000

Type: 4 Yr.,Private,
Founded: 1878
Website: http://www.duq.edu
Religion: Catholic
SAT/ACT/GPA: Open
Housing: Yes
Student/Faculty Ratio: 15:1
Male/Female Ratio: 40:60
Undergraduate Enrollment: 8,000
Graduate Enrollment: 1,500
Scholarships/Academic: Yes **Athletic:** Yes **Financial Aid:** Yes
Expenses by: Year **In State:** $ 21,000 **Out of State:** $ 21,000
Degrees Conferred: BA, BS, MA, MS, MPT, MSLP, Ph.D.
Programs of Study: Business, Education, Nursing, Health Sciences, Pharmacy, PreMed, Liberal Arts

Men's Athletic Profile

600 Forbes Ave., Palumbo Center
Pittsburgh, PA 15282
Coach: Shelly Heisey
Email: heisey@duq.edu

NCAA I
Dukes/Blue, Red, White
Phone: (412) 396-5241
Fax: (412) 396-6210

Estimated # of Men's Soccer Scholarships: 8
Conference: Atlantic 10 Conference
Program Profile: The sport was added in 1994-1995 competing at the club level and was elevated to NCAA Division I. Play for the 1995 fall season. Stadium has a 5,000 capacity and has an excellent athletic facilities, winter training full-field bubble which is indoor.
History: Our program began as a club team in 1994. Became Division I in 1995 to the present and became affiliated with Atlantic 10 Conference.
Achievements: Produced All-Conference players; 4 Academic All-Conference players.
Coaching: Shelly Heisey, Head Coach, is entering her first season with the program. She was a graduate of Boston College in 1991. Brooke Lang is the Assistant Coach, was a graduate from St. Bonaventure. Heather Border is the Assistant Coach, was a graduate of Duquesne University in 1998.
Style of Play: We try to play the game.

Women's Athletic Profile

A.J. Palumbo Ctr, 600 Forbes Ave
Pittsburgh, PA 15282
Coach: Shelly Saba
Email: sabas@duq.edu

NCAA I
Lady Dukes/Royal, White, Red
Phone: (412) 396-5241
Fax: (412) 396-6560

Estimated # of Women's Soccer Scholarships: 8
Conference: Atlantic - 10
Program Profile: Duquesne is a Division I program that competes in the Atlantic 10 Conference. The Dukes compete on campus at Arthur J. Rooney Athletic Field, a lighted Astroturf stadium which seats 4,500 spectators
History: Soccer was added at the club level at Duquesne in 1994 and elevated to Division 1 status beginning in 1995. Coach Saba has been with the program since the beginning in 1994. Duquesne has a 42-55-11 overall record and a 18-39-7 mark in the highly competitive Atlantic 10 conference.
Achievements: Duquesne has produced a Rookie of the Year (2000), has had five All-Conference awards, six Academic All-Conference awards, a first team GTE (now Verizon) Academic All-America citations. Academically,

Duquesne has posted the highest team grad point average in the Nation among DI programs in 1998 and 1999 as announced each Spring by the NSCAA.
Coaching: Head Coach Shelly Saba, Assistant Coach Brooke, Graduate Assistant Coach Colleen Mulhair.
Roster in State: 10 **Out of State:** 12 **Out of Country:** 0
ODP State: 15 **Regional:** 2 **National:** 0
Walk-on/Other: **Graduation %:** **Seniors on Team:** 4
Positions Needed: All
Camp or Clinic Dates: TBA
Most Recent Record: 4-14-1
Schedule: West Virginia, St. John's, Dayton, Xavier, Massachusetts, Central Michigan
Style of Play: Possession oriented, like to attack out of the back. Formation depends on players ability team's abilities.

East Stroudsburg University

Academic Profile

Phone: 570-422-3211

East Stroudsburg, PA 18301

Type: 4 Yr.,Public,Liberal Arts **Founded:** 1893
Website: http://www.esu.edu **Religion:** Non-Affiliated
SAT/ACT/GPA: 1000 **Housing:** Yes
Student/Faculty Ratio: 21:1 **Male/Female Ratio:** 3:5
Undergraduate Enrollment: 4,800 **Graduate Enrollment:** 600
Scholarships/Academic: Yes **Athletic:** No **Financial Aid:** Yes
Expenses by: Year **In State:** $ 3,900 **Out of State:** $ 5,600
Specialty: Computer Science, Business, Education, Sport Medicine
Degrees Conferred: AS, BA, BS, BFA, MA, MS, MEd
Programs of Study: Business, Education, Letters/Literature, Life Science, Social Science

Men's Athletic Profile

Koehler Field House
East Stroudsburg, PA 18301
Coach: Jerry Sheska
Email: jsheska@esu.edu

NCAA II
Warriors/Red, Black
Phone: (717) 422-3303
Fax: (717) 422-3306

Estimated # of Men's Soccer Scholarships: N/A
Conference: Pennsylvania State Athletic Conference
Program Profile: Year round program; grass field 116x75.
History: Program began in 1930.
Achievements: Jason Petronis - 1995 and 1996 Division II Goalkeeper of the Year. Mike Finger - 3 times 1st Team All-American, Draft Pick of Colorado Rapids. 9 players presently playing Pro Soccer.
Coaching: Jerry Sheska, Head Coach, USSF 'A' license, coached professionally in the ASL, in 15th year, four time Pennsylvania Coach of the Year, four-time Mid-Atlantic Coach of the Year. Former Pro Coach.
Style of Play: Ball possession.

Women's Athletic Profile

Koehler Fieldhouse
East Stroudsburg, PA 18301
Coach: Derek Arneud
Email: dareaud@po-box.esu.edu

NCAA II
Warriors/Red, Black
Phone: (570) 422-3648
Fax: (717) 422-3306

Estimated # of Women's Soccer Scholarships: None
Conference: Pennsylvania State Athletic Conference

Program Profile: Year - round program, grass field 116 x 75 yards.
History: Program began in 1930.
Achievements: 5 NCAA bids, 5 PA Conference Championships, All-Americans, over 10 players have signed professional contracts since 1989, National Team player.
Coaching: Derek Arneud, Head Coach, was a former player of ESU. James Allison - Assistant Coach, was a former star forward for the men's soccer team in ESU.

Eastern College

Academic Profile

St. Davids, PA 19087
Phone: (610) 341-1736

Type: 4 Yr.,Private,Liberal Arts
Founded: 1932
Website: http://www.eastern.edu
Religion: Baptist, Christian
SAT/ACT/GPA: Varies
Housing: Yes
Student/Faculty Ratio: 14:1
Male/Female Ratio: 1:2
Undergraduate Enrollment: 1,000
Graduate Enrollment: 1,000
Scholarships/Academic: Yes **Athletic:** No **Financial Aid:** Yes
Expenses by: Year **In State:** $ 19,600 **Out of State:** $ 19,600
Specialty: Sciences, Education, Business
Degrees Conferred: BA, BS
Programs of Study: Art History, Astronomy, Biblical Studies, Biology, Business Administration, Chemistry, Communications, Elementary Education, Health & Physical Education, History, Mathematics, Medical Technology, Music, Nursing, Philosophy, Political Science, Psychology, Social Work, Sociology

Men's Athletic Profile

1300 Eagle Rd.
St. Davids, PA 19087-3696
Coach: Mark Wagner
Email: mwagner@eastern.edu

NCAA III
Eagles/Maroon, Gray
Phone: (610) 341-5030
Fax: (610) 341-1317

Estimated # of Men's Soccer Scholarships: N/A
Conference: Pennsylvania Athletic Conference
Program Profile: Eastern's program starts with a foundation in Jesus Christ and a very strong commitment in soccer. Eastern plays on natural pitch of 120X75 yards. The regular season starts the third week in August and ends on the first week of November with playoffs.
History: Eastern College soccer started over 30 years ago as a competitor in the NAIA. Over the past four years Eastern has changed its affiliation to the NCAA and is now poised to compete regionally on the Division III level. Forming tradition is important to Eastern. The program has gone on trips (Colorado, Texas and this year California) in the past few years.
Achievements: 1998 Nations leading scorer; 1998 PAC Player of the Year; Rookie of the Year; 1998 Coach of the Year; 1992 PAC Champs; 1997 PAC Finalist - NCAA tournament; 1998 PAC Finalist.
Coaching: Mark Wagner, Head Coach, is entering his second season with the program. He is Olympic Development Coach, NSCAA National Advanced Coaching License and Irish and Czchoslovakton Coaching Schools.
Style of Play: High pressure, match-up zone, combined within a fast-paced, possession-oriented attacking style.

Women's Athletic Profile

1300 Eagle Rd.
St. David's, PA 19087-3696
Coach: Penny Spahr
Email: pspahr@eastern.edu

NCAA III
Eagles/Maroon, White, Gold
Phone: (610) 225-5065
Fax: (610) 341-1317

Estimated # of Women's Soccer Scholarships: None
Conference: PAC (Pennsylvania Athletic Conference
Program Profile: The Eagles play on a natural grass field, size 120x80 yards, and their playing season is a regular fall season that runs from August through November 1st, indoor season: four tournaments and two Spring warm up.
History: The program began in 1992. Young team, very talented, and in a healthy soccer area. The Tri-State area feeds the program well. Has grown into a competitive Division III. We will certainly give you a realistic, honest picture of where we have come from, where we are headed, and your part in making it happen.
Achievements: Penny Spahr is the first Head Coach to receive Coach of the Year; Player of the Year; 5 All-Conference in 1999, First Rookie of the Year in 1998.
Coaching: Penny Spahr is entering her second year as Head Coach and served one year as an assistant. Assistant Coach Jim Beatty brings goalkeeping experience to his position.
Walk-on/Other: **Graduation %:** 100 **Seniors on Team:** 5
Positions Needed: Defense, Goalkeeper, Midfield
Most Recent Record: 13-5-1
Schedule: Mary Washington, Rowan University, Elizabethtown, Ursinus
Style of Play: Strong defense. Fitness is a must. Ability to work within a team is a must.

Elizabethtown College

Academic Profile

Phone: (717) 361-1533

Elizabethtown, PA 17022-2298

Type: 4 Yr.,Private,Liberal Arts
Founded: 1899
Website: http://www.etown.edu
Religion: Church of Brethren
SAT/ACT/GPA: 1000 +
Housing: Yes
Student/Faculty Ratio: 18:1
Male/Female Ratio: 1:3
Undergraduate Enrollment: 1,500
Graduate Enrollment: N/A
Scholarships/Academic: Yes **Athletic:** No
Financial Aid: Yes
Expenses by: Year **In State:** $ 22,000
Out of State: $ 22,000
Specialty: Occupational Therapy, Education, Communications
Degrees Conferred: BA, BS
Programs of Study: Accounting, Anthropology, BioChemistry, Biology, Business Administration, Chemical Physics, Chemistry, Chemistry Management, Communications, Computer Engineering, Computer Science, Early Childhood Education, Economics, Education, Engineering, English, Environmental Science, History, Industrial Engineering, International Business, Mathematics, Medical Technology, Modern Languages, Music, Music Education, Music Therapy, Philosophy, Physics, Political Philosophy, Political Science, Mathematics, Social Studies, Social Work, Sociology

Men's Athletic Profile

One Alpha Drive
Elizabethtown, PA 17022
Coach: Arthur "Skip" Roderick
Email: roderiad@etown.edu

NCAA III
Blue Jays/Blue, Gray
Phone: (717) 361-1144
Fax: (717) 361-1148

Estimated # of Men's Soccer Scholarships:
Conference: Middle Atlantic Conference Commonwealth League
Program Profile: One of the premier Division III programs in nation; top level facilities.
History: Began in 1937.
Achievements: Skip Roderick voted MAC League Section Coach of the Year in 1989, 1994, & 1986; voted Regional Coach of the Year in 1985, 1987, 1990, 1992, 1996; 21 NCAA Tournament Appearances, 1989 National Champions; 17 MAC Championships; 29 All-Americans.

Coaching: Arthur "Skip" Roderick, Head Coach, USSF 'A' license, played professionally in the MISL, MASL and Ireland, 1974 graduate of Elizabethtown, Coach of the Year awards. Mark Brown, Chris Bair, Scott Fedezko, & Doug Perras - Assistant Coaches.
Style of Play: Attacking, free flowing soccer that stresses passing and possession. midfield controls the game with reliance on the ground skills and speed.

Women's Athletic Profile

One Alpha Drive
Elizabethtown, PA 17022-2298
Coach: Barry Dohner
Email: dohnerbm@etown.edu

NCAA III
Blue Jays/Blue, Grey
Phone: (717) 361-1462
Fax: (717) 361-1488

Estimated # of Women's Soccer Scholarships: None
Conference: Middle Atlantic Conference
Program Profile: We were nationally ranked Division III program (Top 25), excellent full-size facilities and stadium. We play natural grass (site of NCAA Division III Dinal Four in 1997). We have Fall season sport.
History: Our program began in 1988. It has had only two losing seasons, participated in Middle Atlantic Conference Playoffs in 1995, 1996, 1997, 1998 & 1999. middle Atlantic Conference Champions in 1996 & 1998, MAC Runner-Up in 1997 & 1999, Middle Atlantic Region Champs in 1997, NCAA Division III National Semi-finalist in 1997.
Achievements: We were 1996-1997 Middle Atlantic Conference - Commonwealth League Coach of the Year, 1996 & 1997 Mid-Atlantic Region Coach of the Year and 1997 NSCAA/UMBRO Division III National Coach of the Year. We have had 2 players have received All-American players.
Coaching: Barry Dohner is our Head Coach. He is entering seven years with the program. He was coach of a boys team at Milton Hershey High School. John Kluba, Assistant Coach. Henrik Madsen, Assistant Coach. Mike Logan, Assistant Coach.
Roster in State: 12 **Out of State:** 10 **Out of Country:** 0
Walk-on/Other: **Graduation %:** 99 **Seniors on Team:** 8
Positions Needed: Keepers, Forwards, Midfielders
Camp or Clinic Dates: Not Available
Most Recent Record: 15-7-1
Schedule: College of New Jersey, Wellesley, Western Connecticut, William Smith, Rowan, West Chester
Style of Play: Short passing, possession oriented style, building the attack and allowing players to go forward into the attack. Allowing players the freedom and creativity.

Franklin and Marshall College

Academic Profile

Lancaster, PA 17604-4440

Phone: (717) 291-4102

Type: 4 Yr.,Private,Liberal Arts
Website: http://www.fandm.edu
SAT/ACT/GPA: Open
Student/Faculty Ratio: 11:1
Undergraduate Enrollment: 1,804
Founded: 1787
Religion: Non-Affiliated
Housing: Yes
Male/Female Ratio: 51:49
Graduate Enrollment: N/A
Scholarships/Academic: Yes **Athletic:** No **Financial Aid:** Yes
Expenses by: Year **In State:** $ 28,564 **Out of State:** $ 28,564
Specialty: Preprofessional Programs, Business
Degrees Conferred: BA, BS
Programs of Study: Anthropology, Art, Art History, Asian Studies, Astronomy, Biology, Business Administration, Chemistry, Classics, Computer Science, Dance, Economics, English, Environmental Science, Film, French, GeoScience, German, Government, Hebrew, History, Mathematics, Music, Philosophy, Psychology, Religion, Russian, Sociology, Spanish, Theatre

Men's Athletic Profile

P.O. Box 3003
Lancaster, PA 17604
Coach: Andy Woolley
Email: Not Available

NCAA III
Diplomats/Navy, Blue
Phone: (717) 291-4103
Fax: (717) 399-4440

Estimated # of Men's Soccer Scholarships: N/A
Conference: Centennial Conference
Program Profile: Well established program; fall season has 16-18 games. Has a natural grass surface field.
History: Our program began in 1926; has a winning percentage of 51.3% (371-352-62). won the National Champions in 1952.
Achievements: All-Americans, All-Conference players,
Style of Play: Possession; short passing ball control building out of the back.

Women's Athletic Profile

P.O. Box 3003
Lancaster, PA 17604-3003
Coach: Steve O' Day
Email: s_oday@fandm.edu

NCAA III
Diplomats/Blue, White
Phone: (717) 399-4546
Fax: (717) 399-4440

Estimated # of Women's Soccer Scholarships: None
Conference: Centennial Conference
Program Profile: Natural grass full-sized field which measures 120x75 yards. Women's soccer is one of the most successful programs at F and M. Baker Campus, located at the west of the main campus, contains 3 wall - manicured soccer fields; two practice a one maximum size game field. There is a grid area for technical and tactical training and a kickboard for individual shooting practice.
History: Program began in fall of 1980. Team recorded consecutive 10 win seasons in 1996 & 1997 - only 2nd time in team history. Had school record and conference All-Stars in 1997.
Achievements: 1989 graduate Beth Byrne was leading scorer in collegiate soccer history with 110 career goals (including 10 in 1 game at Wilkes in 1988).
Coaching: Steve O'Day, Head Coach. Lee Richardson - Assistant Coach (class of 1998).
Style of Play: Defensive style of play. Prefer quick, smart player with high kill level who can complete in competitive new conference.

Gannon University

Academic Profile

Erie, PA 16541-0001

Phone: 800-GANNON-U

Type: 4 Yr.,Private,Liberal Arts
Website: http://www.gannon.edu
SAT/ACT/GPA: 980/21/3.0
Student/Faculty Ratio: 13:1
Undergraduate Enrollment: 2,600
Scholarships/Academic: Yes
Expenses by: Year

Athletic: Yes
In State: $ 19,500

Founded: 1925
Religion: Roman Catholic
Housing: Yes
Male/Female Ratio: 1:5
Graduate Enrollment: 650
Financial Aid: Yes
Out of State: $ 19,500

Specialty: Engineering, Business, Education, Health Sciences
Degrees Conferred: Associates, BS, Master's, Pre-Professional

Programs of Study: Offers 62 Bachelor's degrees, 10 PreProfessional Programs, 11 Associate's degrees, 16 Master's degrees through five academic areas: Business Administration, Education, Health Sciences, Humanities and Science, Engineering. The programs include: Accounting, Business, Economics, Finance, Industrial Distribution, International Business, Management, Marketing, Anthropology, Arts and Humanities, Communications, Criminal Justice, English, Languages, History, Human Services, Liberal Arts, Mental Health, PreMed, PreDentistry, PrePharmacy, PreOptometry, PreVet Medicine, Science, Early Childhood, Elementary/Second Education, Nursing, Medical, Dietetics, Special Education, Mortuary Science, Paralegal, Philosophy, Political Science, PreLaw, PreMortuary, Social Work/Science, Theology, etc.

Men's Athletic Profile

109 University Square
Erie, PA 16541-0001
Coach: Rob Van Rheenen
Email: vanheenaol@mail.gannon.edu

NCAA II
Golden Knights/Maroon, Gold
Phone: (814) 871-5810
Fax: (814) 871-7794

Estimated # of Men's Soccer Scholarships: N/A
Conference: GLIAC
Program Profile: Our team plays at Family First Sports Park.
History: Final four appearances 1989,90,93. the program started in 1968.
Achievements: All-Americans, Players of the Year, professional players, Coach of the year awards
Coaching: Rob Van Rheenen, Head Coach, entering his first season with program. Brad Dean - Assistant Coach. Nick Enami - Assistant Coach.
Style of Play: We play a passing game and controlled game.

Women's Athletic Profile

109 University Square
Erie, PA 16541
Coach: Rob Van Rheenen
Email:

NCAA II
Knights/Maroon, White
Phone: (814) 871-5810
Fax: (814) 871-7794

Estimated # of Women's Soccer Scholarships: 7
Conference: Great Lakes Intercollegiate Athletic Conference
Program Profile: We have a new stadium being built. For now however we play on natural grass field at Family First Sport Park.
History: The program began in 1987.
Achievements: 1997 3 All-Americans; 1998 3 All-Americans; 1999 2 All-Americans;
Coaching: Rob Van Rheenen is our Head Coach and Jim Nestor assist him.
Roster in State: 9 **Out of State:** 11 **Out of Country:**
ODP State: 3 **Regional:** **National:**
Walk-on/Other: **Graduation %:** 90 **Seniors on Team:** 8
Positions Needed: All
Most Recent Record: 12-7
Schedule: Ashland, Mercyhurst, Wheeling Jesuit, West Virginia Wesleyan, Slippery Rock, Lock Haven
Style of Play: Indirect style of play and building more styles of play.

Geneva College

Academic Profile

Beaver Falls, PA 15010

Phone: 724-846-5100

Type: 4 Yr.,Private
Website: http://www.geneva.edu

Founded: 1848
Religion: Christian

SAT/ACT/GPA: 21
Housing: Yes
Student/Faculty Ratio: 18:1
Male/Female Ratio: 45:55
Undergraduate Enrollment: 1,500
Graduate Enrollment: 70
Scholarships/Academic: Yes **Athletic:** Yes
Financial Aid: Yes
Expenses by: Year **In State:** $ 16,284
Out of State: $ 16,284
Degrees Conferred: AS, BA, BS, MA
Programs of Study: Accounting, Applied Mathematics, Bible Studies, Biology, Broadcasting, Business Administration, Computer Science, Education, Electrical Engineering, Elementary Education, English, Guidance, History, Human Resources, Industrial Engineering, Medical Technology, Ministries, Music, Philosophy, Physics, Political Science, PreMed, Psychology, Radio & Television, Science, Secondary Education, Spanish, Speech, Speech Pathology

Men's Athletic Profile

3200 College Avenue
Beaver Falls, PA 15010
Coach: David Murray
Email: dbmurray@geneva.edu

NAIA
Tornadoes/Gold, White
Phone: (412) 847-5226
Fax: (412) 847-5001

Estimated # of Men's Soccer Scholarships: None
Conference: Mid-Ohio Conference
Program Profile: Soccer is very popular, large crowds of 200-800 attend. Natural grass field
History: Began in 1972, 2 NCCAA National playoffs; NCCAA National Champs in 1994.
Achievements: All-Americans, District Coach of the Year - 1996 & 1990 Conference Champs in 1996, NAIA Top 20 in 1997.
Coaching: David Murray, Head Coach, played in Europe and South America, on the coaching staff of Division II pro team in Arequipa, Peru.
Style of Play: Brazilian Style; indirect.

Women's Athletic Profile

3200 College Ave.
Beaver Falls, PA 15010
Coach: Kristin Steffey
Email: Not Available

NAIA
Golden Tornadoes/Gold, Black
Phone: (412) 847-6552
Fax: (412) 847-5001

Estimated # of Women's Soccer Scholarships: None
Conference: American Mideast Conference
Program Profile: Has a brand new natural grass soccer field with stadium and lights; separate practice facilities.
History: Program began in 1984.
Achievements: Finished 4th in the East Region, 1987 - 88. Top 12 nationally with several players named to All - East tournament team and several named NAIA Scholar Athletes.
Coaching: Kristin Steffey, Head Coach.
Style of Play: Aggressive, quick attacks and lot of ball movement.

Gettysburg College

Academic Profile

Phone: 717-337-6400

Gettysburg, PA 17325

Type: 4 Yr.,Private,Liberal Arts
Founded: 1832
Website: http://www.gettysburg.edu
Religion: Lutheran
SAT/ACT/GPA: 1090-1260
Housing: Yes
Student/Faculty Ratio: 11.5/1
Male/Female Ratio: 48/52

Undergraduate Enrollment: 2,300 **Graduate Enrollment:** N/A
Scholarships/Academic: Yes **Athletic:** No **Financial Aid:** Yes
Expenses by: Year **In State:** $30,821 **Out of State:** $30,821
Degrees Conferred: BA, BS
Programs of Study: Anthropology, Sociology, Art, Art History, BioChemistry, Biology, Chemistry, Classical Studies, Computer Science, Economics, English, French, German, Greek, Health and Exercise Sciences, Latin, History, Management, Mathematics, Music, Music Education, Philosophy, Physics, Political Science, Psychology, Sociology, Spanish, Theatre Arts Women's Studies

Men's Athletic Profile

300 North Washington
Gettysburg, PA 17325
Coach: David Wright
Email: dwright@gettysburg.edu

NCAA III
Bullets/Orange, Blue
Phone: (717) 337-6407
Fax: (717) 337-6528

Estimated # of Men's Soccer Scholarships: None
Conference: Centennial Conference
Program Profile: Natural grass field: 120x75 yards. Hauser Field House for indoor play: 64x45 yards. Out of season wieght training; spring (non-traditional) season.
History: Gettysburg College fielded its first soccer team in the autumn of 1930, and has since compiled a 411-398-76 record through 68 seasons (there were no games in 1943 & 1944). Current Head Coach Dave Wright is the 10th Bullet coach, and the program's all-time winningest coach with a record of 188-80-21.
Achievements: Dave Wright, who has a record of 188-80-21 with the Bullets over 15 years, has been named the Middle Atlantic Region D-III Coach of the Year 3 times by the NSCAA (1991, 93, 97). Under Wright's guidance, Gettysburg has gone to the NCAA's 6 times (1992, 93, 95, 97, 98, 99) and won the Centennial Conference Championship twice (1993, 1999). The Bullets have also gone to the Eastern College Athletic Conference championship tournament 4 times, winning the ECAC title in 1991 and 2000.
Coaching: David Wright, Head Coach, Cortland State '82: 188-80-21 overall through 15 seasons. Ken Corbran and James Reigel are the assistant coaches.
Roster In State: 9 **Out of State:** 19 **Out of Country:** 0
Walk-on/Other: **Graduation %:** 100 **Seniors on Team:** 5
Camp or Clinic Dates: June 24-28, 2001
Most Recent Record: 14-5-1
Schedule: Messiah, Johns Hopkins, Muhlenberg, Elizabethtown, Frostburg State, Haverford
Style of Play: Short passing, deliberate, build-out-of-back style. Zonal defending.

Women's Athletic Profile

300 North Washington Street
Gettysburg, PA 17325
Coach: Todd Wawrousek
Email: twawrous@gettysburg.edu

NCAA III
Bullets/Orange, Blue
Phone: (717) 337-6460
Fax: (717) 337-6528

Estimated # of Women's Soccer Scholarships: None
Conference: Centennial Conference
Program Profile: Natural grass field 120x75 yards (three grass training grounds, 1 grass match field). Hauser Field house for indoor play 65x45 yards. Highly competitive schedule, squad competes in the Middle Atlantic Region.
History: Gettysburg's first women's soccer team took to the pitch in the fall of 1988, but it was two years later when Head Coach Todd Wawrousek took the program under his guidance that Gettysburg women's soccer was really born. The Bullets who have a 115-75-9 all time record are 108-64-7 under Wawrousek. As only the second Head Coach in the history of the program, Wawrousek has fielded five NCAA tournament teams and four centennial Conference Championship teams.

Achievements: Head Coach Todd Wawrousek has taken the Bullets to six post-season tournament, including five NCAA Division II playoffs. (1999, 98, 97, 94, 93). In 1993, 1994 and 1998 he was named the Mid-Atlantic Region Division III women's coach of the year. The Bullets have also won four Centennial Conference titles.
Coaching: Head Coach Todd Wawrousek, Millersville (12th season), Assistant Coach Tom Bachman, West Chester (11th season)
Roster in State: 7 **Out of State:** 20 **Out of Country:** 0
ODP State: 3 **Regional:** 0 **National:** 0
Walk-on/Other: 0 **Graduation %:** 95 **Seniors on Team:** 6
Positions Needed: ALL
Most Recent Record: 9-5-2
Schedule: College of New Jersey, William Smith, Mary Washington, Elizabethtown, Johns Hopkins
Style of Play: Attacking combination play.

Grove City College

Academic Profile

Phone: (724) 458-2129

Grove City, PA 16127

Type: 4 Yr.,Private,Liberal Arts **Founded:** 1876
Website: http://www.gcc.edu **Religion:** Non-Affiliated
SAT/ACT/GPA: 1110/26/3.7 **Housing:** Yes
Student/Faculty Ratio: N/A **Male/Female Ratio:** 1:1
Undergraduate Enrollment: 2,200 **Graduate Enrollment:** 20
Scholarships/Academic: Yes **Athletic:** No **Financial Aid:** Yes
Expenses by: Year **In State:** $ 10,600 **Out of State:** $ 10,600
Specialty: Accounting, Business, Computers, Education, Engineering Music
Degrees Conferred: BA, BS, BMus, BSME, BSEE
Programs of Study: Electrical & Mechanical Engineering, Elementary & Secondary Education: All Areas - Business, Economics, International Management, PreProfessional Programs, Natural Science, Mathematics & Computer Systems, Humanities and Social Sciences, Music

Men's Athletic Profile

100 Campus Drive
Grove City, PA 16127
Coach: Melissa Lamie
Email: Mdlamie@gcc.edu

NCAA III
Wolverines/Crimson, White
Phone: (724) 458-2122
Fax: (724) 458-3855

Estimated # of Men's Soccer Scholarships: None
Conference: President's Athletic Conference, WPISC
Program Profile: 8 year old program. 3 grass practice fields. 2 full grass game field, fall season
History: Program began in 1938, with no matches during war time. The program enjoys five undefeated seasons.
Achievements: 4x coach of the year, 3 conference titles.
Coaching: Head Coach 7th year, 4x coach of Year, undergrad at Calvin college-All MIAA player there, Masters from Northern Colorado.
Roster In State: 10 **Out of State:** 11 **Out of Country:**
Walk-on/Other: **Graduation %:** 100 **Seniors on Team:** 1
Positions Needed: All
Camp or Clinic Dates: Not Available
Most Recent Record: 8-10-1
Schedule: Carnegie Melon, Penn State, Allegheny
Style of Play: ball possession, passing game, defend and attack with all 10 field players.

Women's Athletic Profile

100 Campus Drive
Grove City, PA 16127
Coach: Melissa Lamie
Email: mdlamie@gcc.edu

NCAA III
Wolverines/Crimson, White
Phone: (724) 458-2128
Fax: (724) 458-3855

Estimated # of Women's Soccer Scholarships: None
Conference: Presidents' Athletic Conference
Program Profile: Natural grass practice and game fields.
History: The program began in 1992 with a record of 3-9-3; Coach Lamie has a record of 74-74-6 in 9 seasons and 39-6 in conference play.
Achievements: 4 conference titles and 5 Coach of the Year Awards.
Coaching: Melissa Lamie, Head Coach, Alma mater-Calvin College in 1992, 8 years at Grove City and has won 4 conference titles and 5 Coach of the Year Awards.
Roster in State: 11 **Out of State:** 12 **Out of Country:** 0
Walk-on/Other: **Graduation %:** 100 **Seniors on Team:** 4
Camp or Clinic Dates: Not Available
Most Recent Record: 14-6-0
Schedule: Penn State-Behrend, Allegheny, John Carroll, Hope, Westminster, Carnegie Mellon
Style of Play: Ball control, team possession, combination man-zone defense.

Gwynedd Mercy College

Academic Profile

Gwynedd Valley, PA 19437

Phone: (215) 641-5574

Type: 4 Yr.,Private
Website: http://www.gmc.edu
SAT/ACT/GPA: 900
Student/Faculty Ratio: 13:1
Undergraduate Enrollment: 2,100
Scholarships/Academic: Yes **Athletic:** No **Financial Aid:** Yes
Expenses by: Year **In State:** $ 20,100 **Out of State:** $ 20,100
Specialty: All majors
Degrees Conferred: Associate, BA, BS, Masters
Programs of Study: Biology, Biological Science, Secondary Education, English, Communications, Literature, PreLaw, History, Math, Psychology, Sociology, Accounting, Business Administration, Finance, Health Administration, Marketing, Business Education, Elementary Education, Early Childhood Education, Special Education, Special Elementary Education, Nursing, Medical Technology, Respiratory Care, Radiation Therapy

Founded: 1948
Religion: Catholic
Housing: Yes
Male/Female Ratio: 1:20
Graduate Enrollment: 300

Men's Athletic Profile

Sumneytown Pike
Gwynedd Valley, PA 19437
Coach: Marty Stanton
Email: Not Available

NCAA III
Griffins/Red, Gold
Phone: (215) 641-5574
Fax: (215) 542-4683

Estimated # of Men's Soccer Scholarships:
Conference: Pennsylvania Athletic Conference (PAC)
Program Profile: This is a very young program that offers immediate opportunities to play. The team plays a Fall season in a strong Division III conference. The home games are played on natural turf.

History: Program began in 1994 and completed its inaugural season with 1-10 record.
Achievements: N/A
Coaching: Dave McNamara, Head Coach, former varsity player at Villanova University.

Haverford College

Academic Profile

Haverford, PA 19041
Phone: 610-896-1000

Type: 4 Yr.,Private,Liberal Arts
Founded: 1833
Website: http://www.haverford.edu
Religion: Non-Affiliated
SAT/ACT/GPA: 1200+
Housing: Yes
Student/Faculty Ratio: 11:1
Male/Female Ratio: 50:50
Undergraduate Enrollment: 1,200
Graduate Enrollment: N/A
Scholarships/Academic: No
Athletic: No
Financial Aid: Yes
Expenses by: Year
In State: $ 29,520
Out of State: $ 29,520
Degrees Conferred: BA, BS
Programs of Study: Archaeology, Astronomy, Biology, Chemistry, Classics, Comparative Literature, East Asian Studies, Economics, English, Fine Arts, French, Geology, German, History, History of Art, Mathematics, Music, Philosophy, Physics, Political Science, Psychology, Religion, Russian, Sociology, Anthropology

Men's Athletic Profile

370 Lancaster Avenue
Haverford, PA 19041
Coach: Joe Amorim
Email: jamorim@haverford.edu

NCAA III
Fords, Redwave/Scarlet, Black
Phone: (610) 896-1117
Fax: (610) 896-1224

Estimated # of Men's Soccer Scholarships: N/A
Conference: Centennial Conference
Program Profile: Program has Varsity and JV teams. Facility includes full size, natural turf field.
History: Program began in 1901. Played 1,080 games; gained 611 victories, most in the nation.
Achievements: Several Conference Championships, most recently 1988. Numerous Divisional Championships; many Regional and National All-Americans.
Coaching: Joe Amorim, Head Coach, has a USSF 'A' license.
Style of Play: Modern.

Women's Athletic Profile

370 Lancaster Avenue
Haverford, PA 19041-1392
Coach: Wendy Smith
Email: w1smith@hartford.edu

NCAA III
Red Wave/Fords/Red, Black
Phone: (610) 896-1307
Fax: (610) 896-4220

Estimated # of Women's Soccer Scholarships: None
Conference: Centennial Conference
Program Profile: Enjoy playing on a grass field.
History: Became a varsity program in 1985.
Achievements: 4 Regional All-Americans; 1999 Centennial Conference Champions
Coaching: Wendy Smith, Head Coach.
Roster in State: 7
Out of State: 38
Out of Country:
Walk-on/Other:
Graduation %: 100
Seniors on Team: 5
Positions Needed: All

Most Recent Record: 8-9-1
Schedule: College of New Jersey, Gettysburg, John Hopkins, Richard Stockton, William Patterson, Messiah, Lynchburg
Style of Play: Possession through short passing with a short and long pass and penetrate to opponent's defense.

Holy Family College

Academic Profile

Phone:

Philadelphia, PA 19114

Type: 4 Yr.,Private,Liberal Arts
Founded: 1954
Website: http://www.hfc.edu
Religion: Catholic
SAT/ACT/GPA: 830+
Housing: No
Student/Faculty Ratio: 13:1
Male/Female Ratio: 25:75
Undergraduate Enrollment: 2,200
Graduate Enrollment: 375
Scholarships/Academic: Yes **Athletic:** Yes **Financial Aid:** Yes
Expenses by: Year **In State:** $ 8,700 **Out of State:** $ 8,700
Specialty: Nursing, Commuter College
Degrees Conferred: AA, BA, BS, BSN
Programs of Study: Accounting, BioChemistry, Biology, Business Administration, Chemistry, Communications, Criminal Justice, Early Childhood Education, Economics, Elementary Education, English, Fine Arts, Foreign Languages, French, History, Information Science, International Business, Management, Marketing, Mathematics, Medical Laboratory Technology, Nursing, Philosophy, PreDentistry, PreLaw, PreMed, Psychology, Religion, Science Education, Social Science, Spanish, Special Education

Men's Athletic Profile

Grant 8 Frankford Ave
Philadelphia, PA 19114
Coach: John Amurim
Email: Athletics@hfc.edu

NCAA II
Tigers/Blue, White
Phone: (215) 637-7700
Fax: (215) 637-6675

Estimated # of Men's Soccer Scholarships: Varies
Conference: Central Atlantic Collegiate Program
Program Profile: We are a Division II program that has a natural playing surface field that is 120x80. We have a new athletic facility with weight traning ect.
History: Began in 1986. Have won 2 Conference Championship and participated in several regional tournament's
Achievements: 4 All-Americans at NAIA level.
Coaching: Head Coach John Amurim former two time All-American and former pro-player. Also has a USSF "A" License.
Roster In State: 21 **Out of State:** 1 **Out of Country:** 0
ODP State: 10 **Regional:** 0 **National:** 0
Walk-on/Other: 2 **Graduation %:** 95 **Seniors on Team:** 5
Positions Needed: Midfielders, Strickers, Keeper
Camp or Clinic Dates: August 3-9
Most Recent Record: 11-9-2
Schedule: West Chester, Millersville, Teikyo-Post, Shippensburg, Goldey-Beacom
Style of Play: We play a possession build up style with the goal to penetrate in numbers. Combination and flank play.

Women's Athletic Profile

Grant & Frankfort Street
Philadelphia, PA 19114
Coach: Joe Mikolajewski
Email: mrybicki@hfc.edu

NAIA
Tigers/Copenhagen Blue
Phone: (215) 637-7000
Fax: (215) 637-6675

Estimated # of Women's Soccer Scholarships: 7
Conference: Central Atlantic
History: Instituted 1996- overall record 59-19. 1999-16-4-CACC Champions.
Achievements: 2 Honorable Mention All-Americans.

Roster in State: 18	**Out of State:** 0	**Out of Country:** 0
ODP State: 5	**Regional:** 0	**National:** 0
Walk-on/Other: 0	**Graduation %:**	**Seniors on Team:** 2

Positions Needed: 2
Most Recent Record: 16-4-0
Schedule: West Chester, Greorgian Court, Philadelphia University, Kutztown, Shippenburg, Dominican
Style of Play: A one-two touch direct style of play.

Indiana University - Pennsylvania

Academic Profile

Indiana, PA 15701
Phone: 724-357-2217

Type: 4 Yr.,Public,Liberal Arts		**Founded:** 1875
Website: http://www.iup.edu		**Religion:** Non-Affiliated
SAT/ACT/GPA: 950/2.7		**Housing:** No
Student/Faculty Ratio: 16:1		**Male/Female Ratio:** 4:5
Undergraduate Enrollment: 12,000		**Graduate Enrollment:** 1,800
Scholarships/Academic: Yes	**Athletic:** Yes	**Financial Aid:** Yes
Expenses by: Year	**In State:** $ 8,366	**Out of State:** $ 12,866

Degrees Conferred: BA, BS, BFA, BSEd, BSN
Programs of Study: Business, Criminology, Consumer Services, Elementary & Secondary Education, Fine Arts, Food & Nutrition, Health & Physical Education, Home Economics, Medical Technology, Nursing, Respiratory Therapy, Safety Management, Art & Sciences, Computer Science, Accounting, Music

Women's Athletic Profile

107 Memorial Fieldhouse	**NCAA II**
Indiana, PA 15701	Indians/Crimson, Grey
Coach: Eric Bell	**Phone:** (724) 357-6245
Email: ebell@grove.iup	**Fax:** (724) 357-7804

Estimated # of Women's Soccer Scholarships:
Conference: Pennsylvania State Athletic Conference (PSAC)
Program Profile: The home field is natural grass. Our facilities include: three weight rooms and a 8,000 seats stadium. We play 16 to 18 games per season.
History: The program began in 1993. We won the PSAC Champions in 1995.
Achievements: 1995 Conference Champions; 28 varsity wins in 2 seasons; All - Americans, Conference Player of the Year - 1994 -1995; All - Conference 1994 - 1995
Coaching: Head Coach Eric Bell

Roster in State: 19	**Out of State:** 5	**Out of Country:** 0
ODP State: 2	**Regional:** 0	**National:** 0
Walk-on/Other: 0	**Graduation %:** 100	**Seniors on Team:** 0

Positions Needed: ALL
Camp or Clinic Dates: June 11-15
Most Recent Record: 7-10-0
Schedule: Lock Haven, Bloomsburg, Slippery Rock, Adelphi, CW Post, West Chester, Millersville
Style of Play: We play a very attacking style (4-3-3).

Juniata College

Academic Profile

Phone: (814) 641-3510

Huntington, PA 16652-2119

Type: 4 Yr.,Private,Liberal Arts
Founded: 1876
Website: http://www.juniata.edu
Religion: Brethren
SAT/ACT/GPA: 1130
Housing: Yes
Student/Faculty Ratio: 13:1
Male/Female Ratio: 45:55
Undergraduate Enrollment: 1,250
Graduate Enrollment: N/A
Scholarships/Academic: Yes **Athletic:** No **Financial Aid:** Yes
Expenses by: Year **In State:** $ 22,200 **Out of State:** $ 22,200
Specialty: Sciences, Prehealth
Degrees Conferred: BA, BS
Programs of Study: Business, Education, PreHealth, Psychology, Sciences, Social Work

Men's Athletic Profile

18th & Moore St.
Huntingdon, PA 16652-2119
Coach: Scott P. McKenzie
Email: mckenzs@juniata.edu

NCAA III
Eagles/Yale Blue, Old Gold
Phone: (814) 641-3503
Fax: (814) 641-3508

Estimated # of Men's Soccer Scholarships: N/A
Conference: Middle Atlantic Conference, Commonwealth League
Program Profile: Growing program with dedicated coach. Play in strong soccer conference. Intimate setting for soccer at College Field (grass) on campus.
History: Began in 1979.
Coaching: Head Coach Scott Mckenzie is first year coach. Coached for 8 years at Southern Vermont College.
Roster In State: 20 **Out of State:** 4 **Out of Country:** 3
Walk-on/Other: 0 **Graduation %:** N/A **Seniors on Team:** 5
Positions Needed: ALL
Camp or Clinic Dates: TBA
Most Recent Record: 5-13-0
Schedule: Messiah College, Lebanon Valley College, Moravian College
Style of Play: Attacking.

Women's Athletic Profile

1700 Moore St.
Huntingdon, PA 16652-2119
Coach: Scott P. McKenzie
Email: mckenzs@juniata.edu

NCAA III
Eagles/Yale Blue, Old Gold
Phone: (814) 641-3503
Fax: (814) 641-3508

Estimated # of Women's Soccer Scholarships: None
Conference: Middle Atlantic Conference, Commonwealth League
Program Profile: Our season is 18 games long and commences in late Aug. and ends in early Nov. ending with both conference and NCAA tournament play. The facilities and equipment are top notch.
History: Began as a varsity sport in the Fall of 1994.
Coaching: Head Coach Scott McKenzie first year at Juniata was at Southern Vermont College for 8 years.
Roster in State: 13 **Out of State:** 4 **Out of Country:** 3
Walk-on/Other: 0 **Graduation %:** **Seniors on Team:** 1
Positions Needed: ALL

Camp or Clinic Dates: TBA
Most Recent Record: 4-12-0
Schedule: Elizabethtown College, Lebanon Valley, Messiah College, Moravian College.
Style of Play: Attacking.

King's College - Pennsylvania

Academic Profile

Wilkes Barre, PA 18711
Phone: (570) 826-5900

Type: 4 Yr.,Private,Liberal Arts
Founded: 1946
Website: http://www.kings.edu
Religion: Roman Catholic
SAT/ACT/GPA: Average 1050
Housing: Yes
Student/Faculty Ratio: 14:1
Male/Female Ratio: 50:50
Undergraduate Enrollment: 1,700
Graduate Enrollment: 100
Scholarships/Academic: Yes **Athletic:** No **Financial Aid:** Yes
Expenses by: Year **In State:** $ 21,000 **Out of State:** $ 21,000
Specialty: Education, Accounting, Business, Sports Medicine, Physician's Asst.
Degrees Conferred: BA, BS, MA
Programs of Study: Education, Biology, Psychology, Business, Accounting, Sports Medicine, Physician's Assistant, Computer Information Systems, Sociology, Physics, Chemistry, Math, Computer Science, Human Resources, Gerontology, Criminal Justice, Communications, BioMedical Technology, English, PreLaw, PreMed, International Business, Health Administration

Men's Athletic Profile

133 N. River St.
Wilkes-Barre, PA 18711
Coach: Paul Kennedy
Email: Not Available

NCAA III
Monarchs/Red, Gold
Phone: (717) 826-5855
Fax: (717) 826-5937

Estimated # of Men's Soccer Scholarships: N/A
Conference: Middle Atlantic Conference
Program Profile: Play home games at newly constructed Monarch Fields, grass includes 13,000 sq. ft. fieldhouse. complex is three years old. Complex includes fields for football, men and women soccer, field hockey, softball, baseball
History: Program competes in the MAC.

Women's Athletic Profile

133 N. River Street
Wilkes-Barre, PA 18711
Coach: Matt Yelton
Email: mbyelton@king.edu

NCAA III
Lady Monarchs/Red, Gold
Phone: (423) 652-4704
Fax: (717) 826-5937

Estimated # of Women's Soccer Scholarships: None
Conference: Middle Atlantic Conference
Program Profile: Program will enter 3rd year as NCAA varsity sport in 1995. Play games at the newly built Monarch Fields, a older natural grass facility; includes use of a 13,000 sq. ft. fieldhouse. Complex houses football, m/w soccer, field hockey., baseball and soccer fields.
History: Started in 1992 and played one year as JV level sport before gaining admission to NCAA and Mid-Atlantic Conference in 1993.
Achievements: MAC All-Star Team player in 1993.
Style of Play: Depends on the strength and weakness of the team at hand.

Kutztown University

Academic Profile

Room 219
Kutztown, PA 19530

Phone: (610) 683-4060

Type: 4 Yr.,Public,Liberal Arts
Founded: 1866
Website: http://www.kutztown.edu
Religion: Non-Affiliated
SAT/ACT/GPA: 1050 Avg.
Housing: Yes
Student/Faculty Ratio: 8:1
Male/Female Ratio: 1/1.5
Undergraduate Enrollment: 6,000
Graduate Enrollment: N/A
Scholarships/Academic: Yes **Athletic:** Yes **Financial Aid:** Yes
Expenses by: Year **In State:** $ 8,000 **Out of State:** $ 13,000
Specialty: Visual & Performing Arts, Business, Education
Degrees Conferred: BA, BFA, BS, BSBA, Education, Engineering
Programs of Study: Accounting, Anthropology, Biology, Chemistry, Communications, Computer & Information Science, Criminal Justice, Economics, Education, English, Environmental Science, Geography, Geology, Management, Mathematics, Marketing, Music, Nursing, Philosophy, Physics, Political Science, Psychology, Sociology

Men's Athletic Profile

Keystone Hall 208
Kutztown, PA 19530
Coach: Otto Ormosi
Email: ormosi@kutztown.edu

NCAA II
Golden Bears/Maroon, Gold
Phone: (610) 683-1517
Fax: (610) 683-1379

Estimated # of Men's Soccer Scholarships: N/A
Conference: Pennsylvania State Athletic Conference (PSAC)
Program Profile: Collegiate regulation size field, natural grass, electrical score board, field used for soccer matches only; excellent facilities. Compete in tough PSAC Conference with top Div. II teams.
History: Program began in 1971. Competed in Division III until 1984 then moved to Division II.
Achievements: Regional 1997 NSCAA Jouniour College Coach of the Year, NJSCA Coach of the Year, Reagon II Coach of the Year.
Coaching: Our Head Coach is Otto Ormosi. Assistant Coach, Mathew Hahn, works mostly with the goal keepeers on the team.
Roster In State: 17 **Out of State:** 4 **Out of Country:** 1
Walk-on/Other: **Graduation %:** 100 **Seniors on Team:** 2
Positions Needed: Backs, MF, GK
Camp or Clinic Dates: July 30- Aug. 3, 2000
Most Recent Record: 18-2
Schedule: LIU Southampton, Dowling, C.W. Post
Style of Play: Possession with attack from the flanks. Basic fundamental soccer.

Women's Athletic Profile

Keystone Hall, Room 219
Kutztown, PA 19530
Coach: Jeff Schellenberger
Email: Not Available

NCAA II
Golden Bears/Maroon, Gold
Phone: (610) 683-1522
Fax: (610) 683-1379

Estimated # of Women's Soccer Scholarships: None
Conference: Pennsylvania State Athletic Conference

Program Profile: A young and growing program looking for great student-athletes. Two great fields, two-month season, off-season training, three year old field house. Natural playing field with a measurements of 120x75 yards located on campus. Compete in the tough PSAC Conference with the top Division teams.
History: The program began in 1981. Entering the second year in the Penn State Athletic Conference.
Achievements: 2 All-Conference players.

La Roche College

Academic Profile

Phone: 412-536-1270

Pittsburgh, PA 15237

Type: 4 Yr.,Private,Liberal Arts
Founded: 1863
Website: http://www.La Roche.edu
Religion: Catholic
SAT/ACT/GPA: Varies
Housing: Yes
Student/Faculty Ratio: 20:1
Male/Female Ratio: 40:60
Undergraduate Enrollment: 1,500
Graduate Enrollment: 350
Scholarships/Academic: Yes
Athletic: No
Financial Aid: Yes
Expenses by: Year
In State: $ 15,000
Out of State: $ 15,000
Specialty: Graphic & Interior Design
Degrees Conferred: BA, BS, MS
Programs of Study: Accounting, Applied Art, Art, Applied Mathematics, Astronomy, Biology, Business Administration, Chemistry, Commercial Art, Communications, Computer Information Systems, Creative Writing, Earth Science, Education, English, Environmental Science, Finance, Graphic Art, History, Human Services, Interior Design, International Business, Journalism, Literature, Management, Mathematics, Medical Technology, Natural Science, Nursing, PreDentistry, PreLaw, PreMed, PreVet, Psychology, Public Relations, Radiological Technology, Religion, Respiratory Therapy, Secondary Education, Social Work, Sociology, Technical Writing

Men's Athletic Profile

9000 Babcock Blvd.
Pittsburgh, PA 15237
Coach: Weston Hawley
Email: hawleyw1@laroche.edu

NCAA II
Red Hawks/Red, White
Phone: (412) 367-9275
Fax: (412) 536-1001

Estimated # of Men's Soccer Scholarships: None
Conference: Allegheny Mountain Conference

Women's Athletic Profile

9000 Babcock Boulevard
Pittsburgh, PA 15237
Coach: Miguel Lozano
Email: Not Available

NCAA III
Red Hawks/Red, White
Phone: (412) 536-1016
Fax: (412) 536-1012

Estimated # of Women's Soccer Scholarships: None
Conference: AMCC
Coaching: Miguel Lozano is our Head Coach. He was named AMCC Coach of the Year in 1998.
Roster in State: 20
Out of State: 2
Out of Country: 0
ODP State: 1
Regional: 0
National: 0
Walk-on/Other: 0
Graduation %:
Seniors on Team: 4
Most Recent Record: 15-3-2

La Salle University

Academic Profile

1900 W. Olney Avenue
Philadelphia, PA 19141-1199

Phone: (215) 951-1727

Type: 4 Yr.,Private,Liberal Arts
Website: http://www.lasalle.edu
SAT/ACT/GPA: 1000 +/Required
Student/Faculty Ratio: 16:1
Undergraduate Enrollment: 3,000
Scholarships/Academic: Yes **Athletic:** Yes
Expenses by: Sem **In State:** $ 11,175
Founded: 1863
Religion: Christian Brothers
Housing: Yes
Male/Female Ratio: 46:54
Graduate Enrollment: 1,500
Financial Aid: Yes
Out of State: $ 11,175
Specialty: Comprehensive University
Degrees Conferred: AA, AS, BA, BS, BSN, MBA
Programs of Study: Art History, Asian Studies, Biology, Chemistry, BioChemistry, Communications, Computer Science, Criminal Justice, Digital Arts, Economics, Education, English, Environmental Science, Fine Arts, Foreign Languages, Geology, History, Religion, Sociology, Accounting, Finance, Law, Management

Men's Athletic Profile

1900 W Olney Avenue
Philadelphia, PA 19141
Coach: Pat Farrell
Email: athletics@lasalle.edu

NCAA I
Explorers/Blue, Gold
Phone: (215) 951-1993
Fax: (215) 951-1694

Estimated # of Men's Soccer Scholarships: None
Conference: Atlantic 10 Conference
Program Profile: Regional program in the Mid-Atlantic area. McCarthy Stadium is the top grass facility in the area with a seating capacity of 7,500.
History: Our program began in 1949. We are qualified for Atlantic 10 Tournament for the last two years and joined Atlantic 10 in 1995. Our career record is 302-344-59.
Achievements: Pat Farrell was named 1996 Atlantic 10 Coach of the Year, 1994 Midwestern Collegiate Conference and Philadelphia Soccer Seven Coach of the Year. Cesidio Colasante third team was named All-American, three-time Conference Player of the Year and three-time PSS Player of the Year.
Coaching: Pat Farrell is our Head Coach. He is entering his 13th season with the program. He holds a USSF 'A' license and compiled a record of 107-94-16 in eleven seasons. Jim Coleman - Assistant Coach, is entering his 13th season with the program. Bob Wilkinson - Assistant Coach, is entering 8th season with the program.

Women's Athletic Profile

1900 W Olney Ave, Box 805
Philadelphia, PA 19141
Coach: Jennine Calhoun
Email: calhoun@lasalle.edu

NCAA I
Explorers/Blue, Gold
Phone: (215) 951-1516
Fax: (215) 951-1694

Estimated # of Women's Soccer Scholarships: None
Conference: Atlantic 10 Conference
Program Profile: Games are played on natural grass field stadium, with seating for 7,500. Play around 18 games with the season.
History: Program began in 1986. Joined Atlantic 10 Conference in 1995.
Style of Play: Strong defensively, opportunistic.

Lafayette College
Academic Profile

Phone: (610) 330-5470

Easton, PA 18042

Type: 4 Yr.,Private,Liberal Arts,Engineering
Website: http://www.lafayette.edu
SAT/ACT/GPA: 1150-1330
Student/Faculty Ratio: 11:1
Undergraduate Enrollment: 2179
Scholarships/Academic: Yes
Expenses by: Year
Founded: 1826
Religion: Non-Affiliated
Housing: Yes
Male/Female Ratio: 1:1
Graduate Enrollment: 0
Athletic: Need
In State: $31,771
Financial Aid: Yes
Out of State: $31,711
Specialty: Liberal arts and Engineering
Degrees Conferred: MBA, MBS
Programs of Study: Engineering, International Studies, Economics & Business, Government & Law, Liberal Arts, History, Literature

Men's Athletic Profile

AP Kirby Field House
Easton, PA 18042-1772
Coach: Tim Lenahan
Email: lenahant@lafayette.edu

NCAA I
Leopards/Maroon, White
Phone: (610) 330-5495
Fax: (610) 330-5702

Estimated # of Men's Soccer Scholarships: Academic Need Based
Conference: Patriot League Conference
Program Profile: Beautiful school with high academic standards. Great soccer facility, 2000 seats, lighted. 120x75, bench shields, and soccer locker room. Combination of academics and soccer rarely matched at the national level.
History: Program began in the early 1900's. Three League Championships in the 1980's as part of the East Coast Conference. Lafayette Men's soccer evolved as the team of the 90's in the Patriot League winning four championships including back to back titles in 94,95 and 98,99. No other team has won back to back titles in league history. Only team to win consecutive championships and qualify for NSCAA Team Academic Award. Patriot League now rated as the 11th best conference in Division 1 soccer.
Achievements: East Coast Conference Champions in 1985, 1987, 1988. Patriot League Championship 1994, 1995, 1998, 1999. NCAA Tournament 1995, 1998. NCAA Play-In 1994, 1995, 1998, 1999. Regional All-Americans 1985-1998. All-American 1995.
Coaching: Tim Lenahan, Head Coach, M.A. Rider University, B.S. Richard Stockton College, USSF "A" License, NSCAA Premier Diploma, NJAC Coach of the Year 1990, 93, 96. Patriot League Coach of the Year 1998, NSCAA Mid-Atlantic Coach of the Year 1998. Fernando Barboto, Asst. Coach, BA Montclair State, Head Women's Coach Mont Clair State 1993-1997, Professional Player New Jersey Imperials 1994-98. Advanced National Diploma, NSCAA All-American 1992. Dennis Bohn, BA Columbia University, Asst. Coach Columbia University, 1998 Professional Player South Jersey Barons, 1997-98.
Roster In State: 5
Out of State: 20
Out of Country: 2
ODP State: 20
Regional:
National:
Walk-on/Other: 2
Graduation %: 100
Seniors on Team: 5
Positions Needed: Defenders, midfield, forward
Camp or Clinic Dates: July 22-26
Most Recent Record: 8-8-3
Schedule: Yale, Brown, Richmond, Penn, Lehigh
Style of Play: 4-4-2, possession in the back, change point of attack, look for combination in the box and get after it when the opportunity comes. No team defends as hard as we do. Team first, unselfish play, championships are the primary focus.

Women's Athletic Profile

108 Alumni Gym
Easton, PA 18042-1772
Coach: Wayne Miller
Email: millerw@lafayette.edu

NCAA I
Leopards/Maroon, White
Phone: (610) 250-5458
Fax: (610) 330-5702

Estimated # of Women's Soccer Scholarships: None
Conference: Patriot League Conference
Program Profile: Year-round program which boast a grass game field (115x75 yard) with a stadium which holds 1,500 people. Practice facilities include two grass fields and a 50x60 yards "grid" area.
History: Program began in 1990 and is a member of the Patriot League. The schedule is competitive and is composed of teams from the Mid-Atlantic Region.
Achievements: Heide Caruso - 1991 Patriot League Offensive Player of the Year; three-time member of All-Patriot 1st team; 1993 Adidas Scholar-Athlete Soccer All-American.

Roster in State: 14	**Out of State:** 15	**Out of Country:** 1
ODP State: 20	**Regional:**	**National:**
Walk-on/Other:	**Graduation %:** 100	**Seniors on Team:** 3

Positions Needed: Forwards
Camp or Clinic Dates: call soccer office 610-330-5458
Most Recent Record: 7-9-1
Schedule: Army, Brown, Colgate, Navy, Bucknell, Holy Cross

Lebanon Valley College

Academic Profile

Annville, PA 17003

Phone: 717-867-6100

Type: 4 Yr.,Private		**Founded:** 1866
Website: http://www.cuc.edu		**Religion:** Non-Affiliated
SAT/ACT/GPA: Required		**Housing:** Yes
Student/Faculty Ratio: 15:1		**Male/Female Ratio:** 50:50
Undergraduate Enrollment: 1,670		**Graduate Enrollment:** N/A
Scholarships/Academic: Yes	**Athletic:** No	**Financial Aid:** Yes
Expenses by: Year	**In State:** $ 16,630	**Out of State:** $ 16,630

Specialty: Biology, Education, Sciences
Degrees Conferred: AA, AS, BA, BS, BM, MBA
Programs of Study: Contact school for program of study.

Men's Athletic Profile

101 N College Ave.
Annville, PA 17003
Coach: Mark Pulisic
Email: pulisic@lvc.edu

NCAA III
Flying Dutchmen/Blue, Red
Phone: (717) 867-6267
Fax: (717) 867-6019

Estimated # of Men's Soccer Scholarships: None
Conference: Middle Atlantic Conference
Program Profile: We have a brand new soccer stadium for men and women's natural surface.
History: The program began in 1974, now rebuilding .
Achievements: A record of 10-8 in 1999.
Coaching: Mark Pulisic, Head Coach, holds a USSF 'A' license. He played professionally for 8 years. He played in former Yugoslavia and graduate of George Mason University. John Forster is the Assistant Coach.

Roster In State: 20 **Out of State:** 3 **Out of Country:**
Camp or Clinic Dates: Not Available
Most Recent Record: 10-8
Style of Play: Depends on the type of players, however, enjoys playing short - balls, and possession, strong in the back, attack quickly when offensive third. Very fit team - running for 90 minutes.

Women's Athletic Profile

101 N. College Avenue
Annville, PA 17003
Coach: Mark Pulisic
Email: pulisic@luc.edu

NCAA III
Flying Dutchmen/Blue, Red
Phone: (717) 867-6267
Fax: (717) 867-6019

Estimated # of Women's Soccer Scholarships: None
Conference: Middle Atlantic Conference
Program Profile: Only five year made tremendous strides over past 2 years brand new state of the art natural grass stadium seats 500 brand new locker room, weight room. All athletic facilities are 2 yrs old.
History: Began in 96 went from 3-15 to 14-5 this year. Made Eciac Middle Atlantic semi-final in 2000.
Coaching: Mark Pulisic - Head Coach. John Forster is Assistant Coach.
Roster in State: 15 **Out of State:** 5 **Out of Country:** 0
Walk-on/Other: **Graduation %:** 100 **Seniors on Team:** 4
Camp or Clinic Dates: June 27, July 7, Aug.2
Most Recent Record: 13-5-1
Schedule: Elizabeth Town, Messiah, Moravian, Franklin and Marshall, Susquehanna Univ.

Lehigh University

Academic Profile

Phone: (610) 758-6111

Bethlehem, PA 18015-3187

Type: 4 Yr.,Private,Liberal Arts,Engineering **Founded:** 1865
Website: http://www.lehigh.edu **Religion:** Non-Affiliated
SAT/ACT/GPA: Very competitive **Housing:** Yes
Student/Faculty Ratio: 14:1 **Male/Female Ratio:** 65:35
Undergraduate Enrollment: 4,400 **Graduate Enrollment:** 2,000
Scholarships/Academic: Yes **Athletic:** Yes **Financial Aid:** Yes
Expenses by: Year **In State:** $ 30,000 **Out of State:** $ 30,000
Degrees Conferred: BA, BS, MS, MBA, M.Ed., Ph.D., EdD
Programs of Study: Accounting, American Studies, Anthropology, Architecture, Art, Biology, Business & Economics, Chemistry, Classics, Computer Science, East Asian Studies, Economics, Electrical Engineering, Engineering, Engineering & Applied Science, English, French, Geology, GeoPhysics, International Careers, International Relations, Journalism, Mathematics, Molecular Biology, Music, Natural Science, Philosophy, Physics, PreDental, PreMed Russian Studies, Science Writing

Men's Athletic Profile

641 Taylor Street
Bethlehem, PA 18015-3187
Coach: Dean Koski
Email: dksoccer@lehigh.edu

NCAA I
Mountain Hawks/Brown, White
Phone: (610) 758-5355
Fax: (610) 758-6629

Estimated # of Men's Soccer Scholarships: N/A
Conference: Patriot League

Program Profile: Murray H. Goodman Campus has a capacity of 1,000; natural grass game field; natural grass practice field.
History: Program is 83 years old. Compiled a record of 11-6-2 in 1997; Patriot League Finalist; had a record of 9-6-2 in 1996.
Achievements: 1997 Patriot League Coach of the Year; 2 Regional All-Americans in 1997 & 1996; 3 players have signed professional contract in the past two years.
Coaching: Dean Koski, Head Coach, USSF 'A' license, NSCAA Advanced National Diploma, England FA Preliminary and International Diplomas, ODP New Jersey State Coach (1988-92), ODP Penn. State Coach (1996). Mark Swartz and Mike O'Connell, Assistant Coaches.
Style of Play: 4-4-2 flat back, zonal system; possession oriented.

Women's Athletic Profile

641 Taylor Street
Bethlehem, PA 18015
Coach: Julie Leonhardt
Email: wsoccer@lehigh.edu

NCAA I
Mountain Hawks/Brown, White
Phone: (610) 758-4346
Fax: (610) 758-6629

Estimated # of Women's Soccer Scholarships: varies
Conference: Patriot League Conference
Program Profile: The Murray H. Goodman Athletic Complex has over 600 acres. We play a fall season. We have natural grass training and match fields. A natural grass soccer stadium will be built in the year 2000. Play a regional schedule against many regionally ranked teams...building a new soccer stadium...play on grass...emphasize strongly academic and athletic achievement.
History: Our program began in 1991 under Alison Moxey. Made conference semi-finals in 1994. We are members of the Patriot League.
Achievements: Dia Johnson was named All-American in 1995; numerous All-League members.
Coaching: Coach Leonhardt has been at Lehigh since 1997. Prior to that she was an Assistant Coach at Ohio State University from 1995-1997 and an Assistant coach at the University of New Hampshire from 1990-1995. She has been actively involved with the Olympic Development Program as a state coach since 1992 and is currently working with the EPA state program. In 1998, she was named to the ODP Region I staff. Coach Leonhardt currently holds her NSCAA National, Advanced National, and Premier coaching licenses. She also holds her USSF "B" license as well. Coach Leonhardt received her Bachelor's degree in English from the University of New Hampshire in 1991 and then received her Master's degree in Sports Psychology from UNH in 1997.

Roster in State: 7	**Out of State:** 12	**Out of Country:**
ODP State: 16	**Regional:**	**National:**
Walk-on/Other:	**Graduation %:** 100	**Seniors on Team:** 3

Most Recent Record: 7-9-1
Schedule: Princeton, Pennsylvania, Villanova, Delaware, Navy, Colgate, Army, Towson, Temple
Style of Play: We play with an attacking mentality. If the conditions and personnel are right we may play with a three front. We also use a zonal system of play whether or not is with 3 or 4 in the back.

Lincoln University

Academic Profile

Phone: 610-932-8300

, PA 19352

Type: 4 Yr.,Public,Liberal Arts		**Founded:** 1854
Website: http://www.lincoln.edu		**Religion:** Non-Affiliated
SAT/ACT/GPA: 800		**Housing:** Yes
Student/Faculty Ratio: 12:1		**Male/Female Ratio:** 40:60
Undergraduate Enrollment: 1,270		**Graduate Enrollment:** 200
Scholarships/Academic: Yes	**Athletic:** No	**Financial Aid:** Yes

Expenses by: Year **In State:** $ 7,000 **Out of State:** $ 9,000
Specialty: Sciences
Degrees Conferred: BA, BS, M
Programs of Study: Accounting, Actuarial Science, Anthropology, Banking & Finance, Biology, Business Administration, Chemistry, Computer Science, Criminal Justice, Economics, Education, English, French, History, Human Services, International Relations, Journalism, Management, Mathematics, Medical Technology, Music, Nursing, Philosophy, Physical Education, Physics, Political Science, PreDental, PreEngineering, PreLaw, PreMed, PreVet, Psychology, Public Affairs, Recreation & Leisure, Recreation Therapy, Religion, Russian Work, Sociology, Spanish

Men's Athletic Profile

Route 1
Lincoln University, PA 19352
Coach: Robert Bryars
Email: Not Available

NCAA III
Lions/Orange, Blue
Phone: (610) 932-8300
Fax: (610) 932-0815

Estimated # of Men's Soccer Scholarships: None
Conference: ESAC
Program Profile: Great Tradition, tough schedule, fun entertainment in which to play. Natural grass, picturesque field, always successful.
History: Program began in 1938.
Achievements: 3 NCAA Championships, PSAC champs over ten times, many All-Americans
Schedule:
Style of Play: Like to play the ball out of the back. Keep the ball on the ground and look for interplay between midfield and forwards.

<u>Lock Haven University</u>

Academic Profile

Phone: 570-893-2011

Lock Haven, PA 17745

Type: 4 Yr.,Public,Liberal Arts
Website: http://www.lhup.edu
SAT/ACT/GPA: 950/2.5
Student/Faculty Ratio: 17:1
Undergraduate Enrollment: 3,500
Scholarships/Academic: Yes **Athletic:** Yes **Financial Aid:** Yes
Expenses by: Year **In State:** $ 8,248 **Out of State:** $ 11,604
Founded: 1870
Religion: Non-Affiliated
Housing: Yes
Male/Female Ratio: 55:45
Graduate Enrollment: 200
Specialty: Education, Sports Medicine, Biology, Computer Science
Degrees Conferred: BA, BS, BFA, MA
Programs of Study: Early Childhood Education, Elementary Education, Secondary Education, Physical Education, Special Education, Recreation, English, History, Sociology, Psychology, Sports Medicine, Health Science, Mathematics, Art, Music, Communications, Management Science, Accounting, Computer Science, Biology, Environmental Biology, Geology, Chemistry, Physics, Fitness Management, Leisure, Commercial Management, Outdoor Management, Earth & Space Science

Men's Athletic Profile

Thomas Fieldhouse
Lock Haven, PA 17745
Coach: Rob Eaton
Email: reaton@eagle.lhup.edu

NCAA II
Bald Eagles/Maroon, White
Phone: (570)893-2192
Fax: (717) 893-2414

Estimated # of Men's Soccer Scholarships:
Conference: Pennsylvania State Athletic Conference
Program Profile: Great tradition, quality players and coaches, tough schedule, large crowd. Has natural grass field - foreign tours - 13 players on the program. Top 20 Division II team. Has a quality facilities.
History: Program began in 1938; 3 National Championships; 14 State Titles in the last 25 years; 469 total wins.
Achievements: 14 All-Americans and 11 players in pro's.
Coaching: Rob Eaton, Head Coach LHU Alumni '88 All-American.
Style of Play: Controlled possession with quick attacks. Sensible defense.

Women's Athletic Profile

Thomas Fieldhouse
Lock Haven, PA 17745
Coach: Peter Campbell
Email: pcampbel@cardinal.lhup.edu

NCAA II
Lady Eagles/Crimson, White
Phone: (570) 893-2459
Fax: (717) 893-2414

Estimated # of Women's Soccer Scholarships: 6
Conference: Pennsylvania State Athletic Conference (PSAC)
Program Profile: We have a natural grass field, 8 practice fields, an Astroturf field if needed, and we play a fall traditional season.
History: Our program is only six years old and in the top 20 of the country for 1996, 1997, and 1999. In 1999 we ranked 5th in the country and were the PSAC and NSCAA Northeast Regional Champions.
Achievements: 1999 PSAC and NSCAA Northeast Regional Champions; 1999 5th in the country; 1999 1 first team All-Americans; 5 Regional Team Players; 5 All-Conference players; NSCAA Northeast Regional and PSAC Coach of the Year in 1999.
Coaching: Peter Campbell is the Head Soccer Coach and Tracy Cross is the Assistant Coach.

Roster in State: 18	**Out of State:** 3	**Out of Country:** 1
ODP State: 11	**Regional:** 5	**National:** 1
Walk-on/Other: 7	**Graduation %:** 100	**Seniors on Team:** 3

Positions Needed: Goalkeeper, Sweeper, Center-mid, Forward
Camp or Clinic Dates: Last week in July
Most Recent Record: 15-4-1
Schedule: CW Post, Bloomsburg, Mercyhurst, Slippery Rock, West Virginia Wesleyan, Adelphi, West Chester
Style of Play: Possession.

Lycoming College

Academic Profile

Phone: 570-321-4000

Williamsport, PA 17701

Type: 4 Yr.,Private,Liberal Arts		**Founded:** 1812
Website: http://www.lycoming.edu		**Religion:** Methodist
SAT/ACT/GPA: 900+		**Housing:** Yes
Student/Faculty Ratio: 14:1		**Male/Female Ratio:** 50:50
Undergraduate Enrollment: 1,400		**Graduate Enrollment:** N/A
Scholarships/Academic: Yes	**Athletic:** No	**Financial Aid:** Yes
Expenses by: Year	**In State:** $ 21,700	**Out of State:** $ 21,700

Specialty: Liberal Arts
Degrees Conferred: BA, BS
Programs of Study: Accounting, Actuarial Mathematics, American Studies, Art History, Art Studio, Astronomy, Biology, Business Administration, Chemistry, Communications, Computer Science, Criminal Justice, Economics, Education, English, French, German, History, International Studies, Mathematics, Music, Near East Culture & Archaeology, Nursing, Philosophy, Physics, Political Science, Psychology, Religion, Sociology-Anthropology, Spanish, Theatre

Men's Athletic Profile

700 College Place
Williamsport, PA 17701-5192
Coach: Scott Kennell
Email: shafer@lycoming.edu

NCAA III
Warriors/Blue, Gold
Phone: (570) 321-4308
Fax: (570) 321-4158

Estimated # of Men's Soccer Scholarships: None
Conference: Middle Atlantic Conference: Freedom League
Program Profile: Top Mid-Atlantic Region Team. Back to back league champions. Several regional All-Americans in recent years. Quality year round program with foreign tours. Natural grass field with a capacity for a large number of crowds. Playing season runs from September to November in NCAA Division III competition.
History: Our men's soccer program began in 1957. Has made great strides over the years by capturing MAC Freedom League titles and reaching the Regional Recognition in the NCAA ranking.
Achievements: 1994, 1995 MAC Freedom League Champion. 6 Regional All-Americans in the last three years. Several All-Americans and All-Region Players over the last four years.
Coaching: Jack Shafer, Head Coach, entering fourth year with the program. NSCAA National Advanced Diploma, 1994 Division III National Champion Coach, 5 years experience as assistant at Washington College and Bethany College. Played professionally in the USISL with the Delaware Wizards. He compiled a record of 32-2-2.
Style of Play: Possession indirect.

Women's Athletic Profile

700 College Pl
Williamsport, PA 17701-5192
Coach: Katherine Roberts
Email: shafer@lycoming.edu

NCAA III
Warriors/Blue, Gold
Phone: (570) 321-4308
Fax: (570) 321-4158

Estimated # of Women's Soccer Scholarships: None
Conference: Middle Atlantic Conference; Freedom League
Program Profile: Has a practice and game facilities located at the Person Field Complex. women's soccer is housed in the Robert L. Shangri Athletic Stadium in their own personal locker room.
History: Fifth year program that has begun to establish itself as a winning team and strong, building program in the Middle Atlantic Conference. Have had marked success over in 1997 with a record of 11-6 an din 1998 with a record of 9-5-2; breaking many school and individual records.
Achievements: 1997 MAC Coach of the Year.
Coaching: Jack Shafer, Head Coach, entering fourth season with the program. He graduated from Bethany in 1992.
Style of Play: Possession and indirect style of play.

Mercyhurst College

Academic Profile

Phone: (814) 824-2227

Erie, PA 16546

Type: 4 Yr.,Private,Liberal Arts
Website: http://www.mercyhurst.edu
SAT/ACT/GPA: 900/18/2.5
Student/Faculty Ratio: 18:1
Undergraduate Enrollment: 2700
Scholarships/Academic: Yes
Athletic: Yes
Expenses by: Year
In State: $ 18,555
Founded: 1926
Religion: Catholic
Housing: Yes
Male/Female Ratio: 54:46
Graduate Enrollment: N/A
Financial Aid: Yes
Out of State: $ 18,555

Specialty: Arts, Business, Criminal Justice, Sports Medicine, Anthropology
Degrees Conferred: BA, BS, BM, MS
Programs of Study: Accounting, Archeology, Art, Biology, Business, Chemistry, Computer Systems, Communications, Criminal Justice, Dance, Dietetics, Education, Fashion Merchandising, Graphic Design, Graphic Design, History, Hotel and Restaurant Management, Mathematics, Music, Philosophy, Political Science, Psychology, Religious Studies, Sociology, Sports Management, Sports Medicine

Men's Athletic Profile

501 E 38th Street
Erie, PA 16546
Coach: John Melody
Email: melodyjohn@hotmail.com

NCAA II
Lakers/Blue, Green, White
Phone: (814) 824-2128
Fax: (814) 824-2591

Estimated # of Men's Soccer Scholarships: yes
Conference: Great Lakes Intercollegiate Athletic Conference
Program Profile: We play on a grass field, stadium on campus, practice off campus at a soccer complex with 22 fields.
History: Our program began in 1977,and have been to four Final Four tournaments. Our 1999 season record was 13-5-1 and were the conference champions.
Achievements: John Melody was named conference coach of the year 8 times, Regional coach of the year twice and, we have had 9 All-Americans over the years
Coaching: John Melody, Head Coach, is an Alumni of Mercyhurst College. Yvonne Parker, Assistant Coach, is a graduate of Mercyhurst in 1993.Darren Murray, Assistant Coach, is also an Alumni, 1997.
Roster In State: 4 **Out of State:** 16 **Out of Country:** 9
ODP State: 10 **Regional:** 5 **National:**
Walk-on/Other: **Graduation %:** 100 **Seniors on Team:** 2
Positions Needed: Good Players
Camp or Clinic Dates: Not Available
Most Recent Record: 13-5-1
Schedule: Truman State, W.V. Wesleyan, Dowling, LIU Southampton, C.W. Post
Style of Play: Varies depending on opponents.

Women's Athletic Profile

501 East 38th St.
Erie, PA 16546
Coach: John Melody
Email: melodyjohn@hotmail.com

NCAA II
Lakers/Blue, Green, White
Phone: (814) 824-2128
Fax: (814) 824-2591

Estimated # of Women's Soccer Scholarships: yes
Conference: Great Lakes Intercollegiate Athletic Conference
Program Profile: We play on a natural grass field. A new stadium is being built on campus for the 1999 season. It is being sponsored by Umbro.
History: Our women's program began in 1987. We have been to 4 Final Four Tournaments. Our 1999 record 16-6-0 made it to the quarter finals NCAA play-offs.
Achievements: John Melody was named 1998 Conference Coach of the Year for men and women; 8 All-Americans over the years; Claire Scarlon played professional in Japan during 1996-97
Coaching: John Melody, Head Coach, is an alumni of Mercyhurst College. He has an English FA License. Richard Shelton, assistant coach, is a 1994 graduate of Mercyhurst.. Yvonne Parker, assistant coach, is a 1933 graduate of Mercyhurst.
Roster in State: 5 **Out of State:** 18 **Out of Country:** 2
ODP State: 11 **Regional:** 4 **National:**
Walk-on/Other: **Graduation %:** 100 **Seniors on Team:** 3

Positions Needed: good players
Camp or Clinic Dates: Not Available
Most Recent Record: 16-6-0
Schedule: Ashland, Northern Kentucky, WV Wesleyan, Lock Haven, Wheeling Jesuit, Bloomsburg University
Style of Play: Varies with opponent's style.

Messiah College

Academic Profile

Grantham, PA 17027
Phone: (717) 766-2511

Type: 4 Yr.,Private,Liberal Arts
Website: http://www.messiah.edu
SAT/ACT/GPA: 1000/3.0
Student/Faculty Ratio: 15:1
Undergraduate Enrollment: 2,700
Scholarships/Academic: Yes **Athletic:** No
Expenses by: Year **In State:** $22,000

Founded: 1909
Religion: Christian Liberal Arts
Housing: Yes
Male/Female Ratio: 45/55
Graduate Enrollment: N/A
Financial Aid: Yes
Out of State: $22,000

Specialty: Christian Liberal Arts & Applied Sciences
Degrees Conferred: BA, BS, BSN&E
Programs of Study: Accounting, Art, Art History, Bible, BioChemistry, Biology, Broadcasting, Telecommunications & Mass Media, Business Administration, Business Information Systems, Chemistry, Christian Ministries, Civil Engineering, Communications, Computer Science, Economics, Education, Health & Physical Education, Mechanical and Electrical Engineering, English, Environmental Studies International Business, Journalism, Marketing, Mathematics, Music, Nursing, Nutrition & Dietetics, Philosophy, Physics, Political Science, Psychology, Recreation, Religion, Social Work, Sociology, Spanish, Sport & Exercise Science, Sports Medicine, Theatre, Therapeutic Recreation

Men's Athletic Profile

1 College Ave.
Grantham, PA 17027
Coach: Dave Brandt
Email: Dbrandt@messiah.edu

NCAA III
Falcons/Royal Blue, White
Phone: (717)766-2511 x.2690
Fax: (717) 691-6044

Estimated # of Men's Soccer Scholarships: N/A
Conference: MAC
Program Profile: Consistently Top 20 in Division III. Outstanding natural grass plying field, stadium capacity of 1,500, lighted for night games. Extend trips (Europe every 3 yrs.)
History: Program began in 1967, NAIA. Moved to the NCAA Division III in 1982. 2 national championships in NCCAA, 2 Final Four appearances in NCAA Division III.
Achievements: NCAA National Coach of the Year in 1986, NCAA Regional coach of the Year in 1983,86,88; MAC Champions in 1992,95, NSCAA Ethics Award.
Style of Play: An electric style of play. Try to adjust style to team talent. Mixture of direct and indirect.

Women's Athletic Profile

1 College Ave.
Grantham, PA 17027
Coach: Scott Frey
Email: sfrey@messiah.edu

NCAA III
Falcons/Royal, White
Phone: (717) 796-5359
Fax: (717) 691-6044

Estimated # of Women's Soccer Scholarships: None
Conference: Middle Atlantic Conference

Program Profile: The Falcons have an excellent game stadium. Natural grass, lighted and seats 1500. Practice field is natural grass.
History: Began in 1988, and has improved each year. 1992 nationally ranked
Achievements: 1999 Men's Coach of the Year, Great Lakes Region, 2000 Commonwealth Conference Champions, 2000 NCAA Tournament.
Roster in State: 12 **Out of State:** 12 **Out of Country:** 0
Walk-on/Other: **Graduation %:** **Seniors on Team:** 2
Camp or Clinic Dates: Not Available
Most Recent Record: 17-3-0
Schedule: Wheaton, Stockton, Scranton

Millersville University - Pennsylvania

Academic Profile

Millersville, PA 17551
Phone: 717-872-3824

Type: 4 Yr.,Public **Founded:** 1855
Website: http://www.millersville.edu **Religion:** Non-Affiliated
SAT/ACT/GPA: Open **Housing:** Yes
Student/Faculty Ratio: 17/1 **Male/Female Ratio:** 45/55
Undergraduate Enrollment: 5,300 **Graduate Enrollment:** 2,200
Scholarships/Academic: Yes **Athletic:** Yes **Financial Aid:** Yes
Expenses by: Year **In State:** $10,234 **Out of State:** $ 15,922
Specialty: Education, Arts and Sciences
Degrees Conferred: BA, BS, BSEd, BFA, BSN, MA, MS, MEd
Programs of Study: Art, Biology, Business Administration, Chemistry, Computer Science, Education Foundation, Elementary & Early Childhood Education, English, Foreign Languages, Geography, History, Psychology, Sociology, Anthropology, Special Education

Men's Athletic Profile

P.O. Box 1002
Millersville, PA 17551
Coach: Bob Charles
Email: rcharles@marauder.millersu.edu

NCAA II
Marauders/Black, White
Phone: (717) 872-3491
Fax: (717) 871-2244

Estimated # of Men's Soccer Scholarships: N/A
Conference: Pennsylvania State Athletic Conference
Program Profile: We have a grass lighted field, with state of the art computerized irrigation system. Field's dimension is 120x80 yards.
History: Started in 1960; we had 4 coaches John Haser who compiled 60-68; Gene Wise compiled 64-65; Al Wooley compiled 66-85, and Bob Charles 86-to the present. The program has recorded 238 wins, 271 losses and 49 ties.
Achievements: Bob Charles was named PSAC Coach of the Year in 1988, 1990 & 1998; Bill John was named All-American in 1991.
Coaching: Bob Charles, Head Coach, Advanced National Diploma. George Crampton - Assistant Coach, entering three years with the program.
Roster In State: 21 **Out of State:** 6 **Out of Country:** 1
Walk-on/Other: **Graduation %:** N/A **Seniors on Team:** 6
Positions Needed: Forward, Keeper, back
Most Recent Record: 7-9-4
Schedule: East Stroudsburg, Dowling, C.W. Post, Concordia, Bloomsburg, California (PA)
Style of Play: Transition.

Women's Athletic Profile

P.O. Box 1002
Millersville, PA 17551-0302
Coach: Trevor Hershey
Email: trevor.hershey@millersville.edu

NCAA II
Marauders/Black, Gold
Phone: (717) 871-2350
Fax: (717) 871-2200

Estimated # of Women's Soccer Scholarships: 3
Conference: Pennsylvania State Athletic Conference
Program Profile: Young up and coming program with a great future and winning attitude. Wonderful environment for student-athletes to excel in all areas. Natural grass field - Biemesderfer Field Complex (500). Has a new natural grass field with lights, in ground water system and motivated team and staff. Looking for talented players to compliment the program. Playing season is in the fall.
History: Program became a varsity sport in 1994. The 1999 record was 10-8-1.
Achievements: NSCAA College Team Academic Award 1998-1999; Jen Yoder All-PSAC Player.
Coaching: Trevor Hershey, Head Coach, NSCAA National Diploma, USSF "B" License, EPYSA ODP Coach U-19, professional playing experience. Assistant men's coach at Millersville in 1991-1993 (32-16-9), member of the Capital City Spartans of the Atlantic Professional Soccer League. Linda Lee Hershey - Assistant Coach, two years Regional All-American, three years playing experience in the USWISL>
Roster in State: 19 **Out of State:** 4 **Out of Country:** 0
Walk-on/Other: **Graduation %:** 100 **Seniors on Team:** 5
Positions Needed: Forward, Back
Most Recent Record: 8-8-0
Schedule: Lock Haven, CW Post, WV Wesleyan, West Chester, Bloomsbury, IUP
Style of Play: Attack minded game based on technical skills and ball-possession approach.

Moravian College

Academic Profile

Bethlehem, PA 18018

Phone: (610) 861-3940

Type: 4 Yr.,Private,Liberal Arts
Website: http://www.moravian.edu
SAT/ACT/GPA: 1000
Student/Faculty Ratio: 12:1
Undergraduate Enrollment: 1,300
Scholarships/Academic: No **Athletic:** Yes
Expenses by: Sem **In State:** $ 11,500

Founded: 1742
Religion: Non-Affiliated
Housing: Yes
Male/Female Ratio: 50:50
Graduate Enrollment: N/A
Financial Aid: Yes
Out of State: $ 11,500

Degrees Conferred: BA, BS, B.Mus.
Programs of Study: Business, Accounting, Biology, Economics, Chemistry, Physics, PreMed, PreDentistry, PreVet, Nursing, Psychology, Sociology, Political Science, Religion, Art, Music, Elementary Education, Secondary Education, English, Journalism, Spanish, French, German, Classics, History, Computer Science, Allied Health, Engineering, Co-op, Mathematics, Philosophy, Natural Resource Management

Men's Athletic Profile

1200 Main Street
Bethlehem, PA 18018
Coach: Eric Lambinus
Email: Not Available

NCAA III
Greyhounds/Navy, White
Phone: (610) 861-3913
Fax: (610) 861-3940

Estimated # of Men's Soccer Scholarships:
Conference: Middle Atlantic Conference (MAC)

Program Profile: Play on full-size natural grass surface, 75X60 yards. Has indoor facility, and a 21 week (year-round) program.
History: Program began in 1963. Record in 1996 is 8-10-1, in 1995 is 12-7-0, and 1994 is 9-9-0.
Achievements: Several first team All-MAC Conference selectees, several All-Mid-Atlantic Regional team selectees.
Style of Play: Possession oriented with emphasis on constantly attacking. Entertaining style with emphasis on individual development.

Women's Athletic Profile

1200 Main Street
Bethlehem, PA 18018
Coach: Eric Lambinus
Email: Not Available

NCAA III
Greyhounds/Nay, White
Phone: (610) 861-3913
Fax: (610) 861-3940

Estimated # of Women's Soccer Scholarships: N/A
Conference: Middle Atlantic Conference, ECAC
Program Profile: Has a full-sized natural grass surface; twenty-one week (year-round) program. Indoor training facility has a measurements of 75x60 yards.
History: Program began In 1994.

Muhlenberg College
Academic Profile

Allentown, PA 18104

Phone: 484-664-3100

Type: 4 Yr.,Private,Liberal Arts
Website: http://www.muhlberg.edu
SAT/ACT/GPA: 1150+
Student/Faculty Ratio: 25:1
Undergraduate Enrollment: 1,900
Scholarships/Academic: Yes
Athletic: No
Expenses by: Year
In State: $ 26,000
Founded: 1848
Religion: Non-Affiliated
Housing: Yes
Male/Female Ratio: 50:50
Graduate Enrollment: N/A
Financial Aid: Yes
Out of State: $ 26,000
Specialty: Preprofessional Programs, Entrepreneurial Studies
Degrees Conferred: BA, BS
Programs of Study: Accounting, American Studies, Art, BioChemistry, Biology, Business Administration, Chemistry, Classics, Communication Studies, Computer Science, Economics, English, Environmental Science, French, German, Greek, History, Human Resources Administration, Information's Science, International Studies, Latin, Mathematics, Music, Natural Science, Philosophy, Philosophy/Political Thought, Physical Science, Physics, Political Science, Political Economy, PreLaw, PreMed, PreMinistry, Psychology, Religion, Russian Studies, Social Science, Social Work, Sociology, Spanish, Theatre Arts

Men's Athletic Profile

2400 Chew St./Soccer Office
Allentown, PA 18104
Coach: Jeff Tipping
Email: jc.tipping@muhlenberg.edu

NCAA III
Mules/Cardinal, Gray
Phone: (610) 821-3383
Fax: (610) 821-3537

Estimated # of Men's Soccer Scholarships: N/A
Conference: Centennial Conference
Program Profile: We have a $ 750,000 new lighted grass field, which seats 1,500. We have a brand new practice field.
History: Our program began in 1957; 1970-1976 was nationally ranked; 1986-1999 nationally ranked; Conference Champs in 1972, 1989, 1994, 1995, 1997; NCAA Appearances in 1972, 1973, 1990, 1991, 1992, 1994, 1995, 1996 & 1997; ECAC Champs in 1994, 1995 & 1988.

Achievements: Produced 7 All-Americans since 1989; ; Regional Coach of the Year in 1989, 1994, & 1995. Conference Champs - 60.
Coaching: Jeff Tipping, Head Coach, holds a USSF 'A' license. He is NSCAA Director of Coaching and Regional Coach of the Year. Jeff Person - Assistant Coach. Dave Weit-man and Stan Cadwallader - Assistant Coaches.
Style of Play: 4-4-2; zone defense, play through midfield.

Women's Athletic Profile

2400 Chew Street
Allentown, PA 18104
Coach: Leslie Benintend
Email: beninten@muhlenberg.edu

NCAA III
Mules/Cardinal, Grey
Phone: (484) 664-3382
Fax:

Estimated # of Women's Soccer Scholarships: None
Conference: Centennial Conference
Program Profile: Has a full-sized natural grass surface; twenty-one week (year-round) program. Indoor training facility has a measurements of 75x60 yards.
History: The program is only 8 years old.
Achievements: 1999 ECAC Champions.
Coaching: Leslie Benintend is our Head Coach and Brian Kelly is our Assistant Coach.
Roster in State: 10 **Out of State:** 10 **Out of Country:**
Walk-on/Other: **Graduation %:** 100 **Seniors on Team:** 2
Camp or Clinic Dates: Not Available
Most Recent Record: 14-6-1
Schedule: Rowan, Scranton, Drew, Messiah, Gettysburg, John Hopkins
Style of Play: Possession oriented while always looking to attack. Entertaining style; emphasized individual development.

Pennsylvania State University (Penn State)

Academic Profile

Phone: (814) 863-7474

University Park, PA 16802

Type: 4 Yr.,Public,Liberal Arts,Engineering
Founded: 1855
Website: http://www.psu.edu
Religion: Non-Affiliated
SAT/ACT/GPA: 1200/25-30/3.42 avg.
Housing: Yes
Student/Faculty Ratio: 16:1
Male/Female Ratio: 55:45
Undergraduate Enrollment: 36,000
Graduate Enrollment: 4,000
Scholarships/Academic: Yes **Athletic:** Yes **Financial Aid:** Yes
Expenses by: Year **In State:** $ 11,170 **Out of State:** $ 17,986
Specialty: Engineering, Teaching, Science, Agriculture
Degrees Conferred: Baccalaureate, Masters, Doctoral, Post-Docs
Programs of Study: We have all colleges on the university park campus including: Agriculture, Architecture, Business and Management, Communications, Education, Engineering, Health Sciences, Liberal Arts, Social Sciences

Men's Athletic Profile

148 Bryce Jordan Center
University Park, PA 16802
Coach: Barry Gorman
Email: soccer@psu.edu

NCAA I
Nittany Lions/Blue, White
Phone: (814) 863-7477
Fax: (814) 865-8149

Estimated # of Men's Soccer Scholarships: 9.9
Conference: Big Ten Conference

Program Profile: We play in the very competitive Big Ten Conference. Our schedule includes not only the Big Ten schools but also a demanding out of conference schedule. The 1999 season ended with a record of 19-4-1 with three of our losses to national champions Indiana. We earned a birth in the 1999 NCAA tournament and advanced to the national quarterfinals. The home field is 3,500 seat, natural grass, Jeffrey Field.
History: 2000 begins Penn State's 90th year of varsity soccer competition.
Achievements: Coach Gorman was awarded the Mid Atlantic Region Coach of the year for 1999. We also had a player , Junior Ricardo Villar, honored as 1st Team All-America.
Coaching: Barry Gorman, Head Coach, is entering his 14th season with the program. In addition to his duties with Penn State, Coach Gorman is also heavily involved with the Olympic Development Program and is a national staff coach with the National Soccer Coaches Association of America. Assistant Coach Kevin Doyle is starting his second season with the Nittany Lions. Coach Doyle is also involved with the NSCAA and is a goalkeeper coach with the U.S. Soccer Federation.

Roster In State: 11	**Out of State:** 10	**Out of Country:** 4
ODP State: 24	**Regional:** 10	**National:** 2
Walk-on/Other: 4	**Graduation %:** 99	**Seniors on Team:** 4

Positions Needed: Midfield, Forward
Camp or Clinic Dates: July 16-20 and July 22-26
Most Recent Record: 19-4-1
Schedule: Indiana, Ohio State, South Carolina, VCU, Kentucky, Cincinnati, Akron, Seton Hall
Style of Play: Possession- oriented attacking soccer. On good days we play good soccer. On bad days, we try to play good soccer.

Women's Athletic Profile

148B Bryce Jordan Center
University Park, PA 16802
Coach: TBA
Email:

NCAA I
Nittany Lions/Navy, White
Phone: (814) 863-5372
Fax: (814) 865-8149

Estimated # of Women's Soccer Scholarships: 12
Conference: Big Ten Conference
Program Profile: Penn State plays in the Big Ten Conference of the NCAA Division I. Home games are played on Jeffery Field, a natural grass stadium that holds 3,500.
History: Our program began in 1994 and has produced four straight NCAA Tournament teams and four straight teams ranked in the Top 25 in the nation. Penn State has five year record of 80 wins - 27 losses and 6 ties while consistently playing one of the most difficult schedule in the country.
Achievements: Big Ten Champions (1998, 1999, 2000), Big Ten Tournament Champions (1998, 2000), NCAA Tournament Final 8 (1998, 2000), NCAA Tournament Final 4 (1999)

Roster in State: 12	**Out of State:** 14	**Out of Country:** 1
ODP State: 13	**Regional:** 8	**National:** 6
Walk-on/Other:	**Graduation %:** 100	**Seniors on Team:** 6

Most Recent Record: 22-3-1
Schedule: UNC, Uconn, Texas A&M, Harvard, Wisconsin, Michigan
Style of Play: Solid defense unit with excellent depth and variety at midfield; excellent speed up front and at the marking backs. Look for combination play and the ability to build through the midfield with several opportunities to take advantage of transition play and serve some penetrating balls to forwards.

Pennsylvania State University - Erie, Bherend College

Academic Profile

Erie, PA 16563

Phone:

Type: 4 Yr.,Public,Liberal Arts,Engineering
Website: http://www.pserie.psu.edu

Founded: 1947
Religion: Non-Affiliated

SAT/ACT/GPA: 1150/3.3
Student/Faculty Ratio: 17:1
Undergraduate Enrollment: 3,600
Scholarships/Academic: Yes **Athletic:** No
Expenses by: Year **In State:** $ 11,000
Housing: Yes
Male/Female Ratio: 6:4
Graduate Enrollment: 300
Financial Aid: Yes
Out of State: $ 11,000
Specialty: Plastic Engineering, Management Information Systems
Degrees Conferred: BA, BS, MBA
Programs of Study: 25 baccalaureate. Programs Including Business (Economics, Management, Accounting, Management Information System), Biology, Chemistry, Communications, Engineering, Mathematics, Political Science, Psychology, Sciences, Social Science

Men's Athletic Profile

5091 Station Road
Erie, PA 16563
Coach: Dan Perritano
Email: Not Available

NCAA III
Lions/Red, White, Blue
Phone: (814) 898-6163
Fax: (814) 898-6013

Estimated # of Men's Soccer Scholarships: N/A
Conference: Western Pennsylvania Intercollegiate Soccer Conference
Program Profile: 18 game schedule, fall season, very competitive NCAA Division III Schedule.
History: Program began in 1959. Post Season playoffs in 1977, 1978. Won NAIA District 18 Championship 1978.
Achievements: District Titles 1978, All-Americans (national, regional), Coach of the Year.
Style of Play: Depends on personnel.

Women's Athletic Profile

Station Road
Erie, PA 16563-0400
Coach: Dan Perritano
Email: Not Available

NCAA III
Lions/Blue, White
Phone: (814) 898-6296
Fax:

Estimated # of Women's Soccer Scholarships: None
Conference: Eastern College Athletic Conference
Program Profile: Games are played on a natural grass which seats for 400. Team plays 14-game Fall schedule.
History: 1994-1995 was the first season as varsity program. As a club team finished 6-0 in 1994-1995.
Achievements: None
Coaching: Dan Perritano, Head Coach, Masters in Counseling from Springfield.
Style of Play: Possession.

Philadelphia College of Textiles & Science

Academic Profile

Philadelphia, PA 19144
Phone: (215) 951-2700

Type: 4 Yr.,Private
Website: http://www.philacol.edu
SAT/ACT/GPA: 980/68/2.5
Student/Faculty Ratio: 14:1
Undergraduate Enrollment: 2,014
Scholarships/Academic: Yes **Athletic:** Yes
Expenses by: Year **In State:** $21,094
Founded: 1884
Religion: Non-Affiliated
Housing: No
Male/Female Ratio: 42:58
Graduate Enrollment: 890
Financial Aid: Yes
Out of State: $21,094

Degrees Conferred: AS, BS, MS, MBA
Programs of Study: Accounting, Applied Economics, Applied Mathematics, Architectural Studies, BioChemistry, Business and Science, Chemistry, Computer Science, Environmental Science, Fashion Apparel Management, Fashion Design, Fashion Merchandising, Finance, Graphic Design, Human Resources Management, Industrial Design Management, Interior Design, International Business, Marketing, Physician Assistant, Textile Design, Psychology

Men's Athletic Profile

School House Ln. & Henry Ave.
Philadelphia, PA 19144
Coach: John Dunlop
Email: bittlek@PhilaU.edu

NCAA I
Rams/Maroon, White
Phone: (215) 951-2725
Fax: (215) 951-2775

Estimated # of Men's Soccer Scholarships: 9
Conference: Philadelphia Soccer 7 Conference
Program Profile: We have a great soccer tradition. We play in a field of grass that is in great condition.
History: Program began in 1953. We have 20 All-Americans. We were a two-time Division I Final Four participant. Out all time record is 410-200-58. The former Head Coach Barry Barto is Head Coach at UNLV.
Achievements: 1996 Philadelphia Soccer Seven Champions; Dunlop named Coach of the Year; Former Textile stand-outs Leon Creary and Peter Pappas of Philadelphia Kixx; 1999 graduate Patrick Morris named 2nd Team All-American; First-round draft pick of Kixx.
Coaching: John Dunlop, Head Coach, has been coaching for three years. He earned a Coach of the Year Award in 1996.

Roster In State: 10	**Out of State:** 1	**Out of Country:** 4
ODP State: 7	**Regional:**	**National:**
Walk-on/Other: 4	**Graduation %:** 92	**Seniors on Team:** 7

Positions Needed: Mid-Fielders, Defenders
Camp or Clinic Dates: August 7-11
Most Recent Record: 8-10-1
Schedule: James Madison, Florida International, Hartwick, Lafayette, Drexel, Howard, Rider, Oneonta, Aldephi
Style of Play: 4-4-2 and 3-5-2. Nice passing game with possession.

Women's Athletic Profile

Schoolhouse Ln & Henry Ave.
Philadelphia, PA 19144-5497
Coach: George Dunbar
Email: bericht@PhilaU.edu

NCAA II
Lady Rams/Maroon, Grey
Phone: (215) 951-2739
Fax: (215) 951-2859

Estimated # of Women's Soccer Scholarships:
Conference: New York Athletic Conference (NYAC)
Program Profile: Home field is Ravenhill Field (seating capacity of 1000 and natural grass).
History: Program began in 1991 and has compiled an overall mark of 95-67-7.
Achievements: Diana Trzaska was an All-American in 1995, scoring 65 points.
Coaching: George Dunbar is the Head Coach. Marj Nece and Peg Hogan are the assistant coaches.

Roster in State: 9	**Out of State:** 15	**Out of Country:** 0
Walk-on/Other:	**Graduation %:**	**Seniors on Team:** 2

Positions Needed: Sweeper, Center Mid, forward
Camp or Clinic Dates: Not Available
Most Recent Record: 12-6-1
Schedule: Lock Haven, Bloomsburg, East Stroudsburg, Adelphi, LIU-CW Post, Drexel
Style of Play: Play a possession style of soccer. Play balls to feet and create opportunities to penetrate. Geared towards attractive style and finesse play.

Point Park College

Academic Profile

Phone: 412-392-3997

Pittsburgh, PA 15222

Type: 4 Yr.,Private,
Website: http://www.ppc.edu
SAT/ACT/GPA: 850/18/2.5
Student/Faculty Ratio: 36/1
Undergraduate Enrollment: 2,557
Scholarships/Academic: Yes
Athletic: Yes
Expenses by: Year
In State: $19,314
Founded: 1960
Religion: Non-Affiliated
Housing: Yes
Male/Female Ratio: 40/60
Graduate Enrollment: 285
Financial Aid: Yes
Out of State: $19,314
Specialty: Best known for our Theatre arts and Journalism programs.
Degrees Conferred: AA, AS, BA, BS, BFA, MA, MBA
Programs of Study: Accounting, Advertising, Allied Health, Applied Arts, Applied Corporate Communication, Behavioral Science, Broadcast, Business Management, Biological Sciences, Criminal Justice, Dance, Education, Engineering Technology, English, Environmental Health, Film & Video Production, Funeral Services, General Studies, Health Services, History, Human Resources Management, Information Technology, International Studies, Journalism, Legal Studies, Liberal Arts, Marketing Communications, Mass Communication, Political Science, Psychology, Public Administration, Theatre Arts

Men's Athletic Profile

201 Wood Street
Pittsburgh, PA 15222
Coach: Oli Theodorsson
Email: Not Available

NAIA
Pioneers/Green, Gold, White
Phone: (412) 392-3844
Fax: (412) 391-1980

Estimated # of Men's Soccer Scholarships: None
Conference: Independent

Robert Morris College

Academic Profile

Phone:

Moon Township, PA 15108-1189

Type: 4 Yr.,Private,Liberal Arts
Website: http://www.robert-morris.edu
SAT/ACT/GPA: 950/21
Student/Faculty Ratio: 15:1
Undergraduate Enrollment: 3,500
Scholarships/Academic: Yes
Athletic: Yes
Expenses by: Year
In State: $ 12,628
Founded: 1921
Religion: Non-Affiliated
Housing: Yes
Male/Female Ratio: 50:50
Graduate Enrollment: 1,500
Financial Aid: Yes
Out of State: $ 12,628
Specialty: Business Administration, Sport Management, Accounting, Communications
Degrees Conferred: BA, BS, BAS, MS, MBA
Programs of Study: Business Administration, Accounting, Administrative Management, Communication Management, Computer Information Systems, Economics, Finance, Health Services, Management, Marketing, Sport Management, Transportation, Arts, Secondary Teacher Certification

Men's Athletic Profile

881 Narrows Run Road
Moon Township, PA 15108
Coach: William A Denniston
Email: dennisto@robert-morris.edu

NCAA I
Colonials/Navy Blue, White
Phone: (412)262-8446
Fax: (412) 262-8557

Estimated # of Men's Soccer Scholarships: None
Conference: Northeast Conference
Program Profile: Has 2 NCAA Tournament in the last 4 years; 4 NEC regular season titles in the last 5 years; 1 National Top 20 rankings in 2 of the last 3 years. Stadium is grass and has seating capacity of 1,000.
History: Program dates back to 1979. Team began competing in the NEC in 1988, made first-ever league tournament in 1991, won its first-ever NEC regular season title in 1992, first-ever NEC tournament championship in 1993, first squad (aside from basketball) to qualify for the NCAA tournament with back-to-back appearances in 1993-1994, program was consistently ranked nationally during the entire 1995 season.
Achievements: Coach Kowalski - NEC Coach of the Year 1992,1995. Striker Troy Fabiono - NEC Player of the Year in 1993. Goalkeeper - Doug Petras, Sweeper - Clint Wisniewki - All-Mid-Atlantic Region for Intercollegiate Soccer Association of America in 1993. Wisniewski, midfielder; David Moxon - All-Region in 1994, midfielder Chris Hultguist -- All-Region in 1995. NEC Champions in 1993-1994, regular season Champions in 1992, 1994-1995. Musa Shannon 1997(drafted indoor/outdoor).
Coaching: Bill Denniston, Head Men's Coach.
Style of Play: Up tempo, ball control.

Women's Athletic Profile

881 Narrows Run Road
Moon Township, PA 15108
Coach: Libbie Tobin
Email: tobin@robert-morris.edu

NCAA I
Colonials/Navy Blue, White
Phone: (412) 262-8631
Fax: (412) 262-8557

Estimated # of Women's Soccer Scholarships: N/A
Conference: Northeastern Conference
Program Profile: An NCAA Division I program at the mid-major level with a traditional late August to late October playing schedule. Home field is North Athletic Complex, located on campus and considered one of the finest natural turf facilities for soccer in the region complex seats 1, 000 comfortably adjacent to complex are dressing rooms, concessions, restrooms. Complex also has working press box for media/sports information.
History: The RMC women's program began in 1992 and is 28-121-2 in its nine years of existence. The team finished 7-11 in 2000. Nickname is "Colonials". Coaching staff is comprised of one full time, one part-time coach. Program has yet to win a conference championship in its history.
Achievements: Over the years, several Colonials have achieved first and second team All-Northeast Conference status, but nobody has been drafted, All-American or Coach of the Year.
Coaching: Libbie Tobin, Head Coach. Assistant Coach Matt Thompson.
Roster in State: 12 **Out of State:** 10 **Out of Country:** 0
Walk-on/Other: 0 **Graduation %:** 90 **Seniors on Team:** 4
Positions Needed: ALL
Camp or Clinic Dates: June 2000
Most Recent Record: 7-11-0
Schedule: Pittsburgh, Villanova, Binghamton, Kent State, Duquesne, Quinnipiac, Maryland-Baltimore County
Style of Play: A 4-4-2 system with a zonal defensive trap.

Saint Francis College - Pennsylvania

Academic Profile

Loretto, PA 15940
Phone: (814) 472-3100

Type: 4 Yr.,Private,Liberal Arts
Website: http://www.sfcpa.edu
SAT/ACT/GPA: 900/2.9
Student/Faculty Ratio: 15:1
Undergraduate Enrollment: 1,280

Founded: 1847
Religion: Franciscan 3rd Order
Housing: Yes
Male/Female Ratio: 1:2
Graduate Enrollment: 800

Scholarships/Academic: Yes **Athletic:** Yes **Financial Aid:** Yes
Expenses by: Year **In State:** $ 21,517 **Out of State:** $ 21,517
Specialty: Engineering
Degrees Conferred: BA, BS, BSW, MA, MBA, M.Ed., MPT, MMT, MMS
Programs of Study: Business Administration, Humanities, Health Sciences, Social Sciences, Natural & Applied Science, PreProfessional Programs

Men's Athletic Profile

Loretto Dr.
Loretto, PA 15940
Coach: Fernando Barboto
Email: fbarboto@sfcpa.edu

NCAA I
Red Flash/Red, White
Phone: (814) 472-3288
Fax: (814) 472-3209

Estimated # of Men's Soccer Scholarships: 6.0
Conference: Northeast Conference
Program Profile: Division I small school, play on grass facility 80x120. The facility has a press box, bench shields, score board, fenced in field with room for more than 1,000 fans.
History: Program started in 1982.
Achievements:
Coaching: Head Coach Barboto is in his 1st year. Assistant Coach Barry Bimbi holds every offensive record at Saint Francis he also hold a USSF "B" License. Assistant Coach Joe Spagola is he GK coach he holds a USSF "C" License.
Roster In State: 10 **Out of State:** 5 **Out of Country:** 6
ODP State: 5 **Regional:** 0 **National:** 0
Walk-on/Other: 0 **Graduation %:** 89 **Seniors on Team:** 3
Positions Needed: Good Players, backs-left footed, MF, Strikers.
Camp or Clinic Dates: Not Available
Most Recent Record: 5-9-3
Schedule: St. John's Univ. Pittsburgh, Univ. of Memphis, Univ. of North Carolina-Charlotte, UMBC, FDU, Bucknell
Style of Play: Play to our strengths, defend like warriors, possession with a purpose.

Women's Athletic Profile

P.O. Box 600 - Stokes Building
Loretto, PA 15940-0600
Coach: Michael Coll
Email: mcoll@sfcpa.edu

NCAA I
Red Flash/Red, White
Phone: (814) 472-3104
Fax: (814) 472-3209

Estimated # of Women's Soccer Scholarships: 6
Conference: Northeast Conference
Program Profile: Stadium: Stokes soccer complex (grass, 3500 seating capacity).
History: The program began in 1986
Achievements: Team finished 3rd in Conference in 2000.
Coaching: Michael Coll, Head Coach, 4 year starter at Penn State, 3 year Penn State Assistant Coach, Irish Youth National Team.
Roster in State: 10 **Out of State:** 16 **Out of Country:** 5
ODP State: 5 **Regional:** **National:**
Walk-on/Other: **Graduation %:** 98 **Seniors on Team:** 5
Positions Needed: Keeper, Striker, Center Mid, Left Back
Camp or Clinic Dates: Not Available
Most Recent Record: 9-10-0
Schedule: Virginia Commonwealth, Old Dominion, Navy, Bucknell, Quinnipiac, Monmouth, Long Island
Style of Play: We are a possession team.

Saint Joseph's University

Academic Profile

Philadelphia, PA 19131

Phone: 610-660-1000

Type: 4 Yr.,Private,Liberal Arts
Website: http://www.sju.edu
SAT/ACT/GPA: Varies
Student/Faculty Ratio: 20:1
Undergraduate Enrollment: 3,000
Scholarships/Academic: Yes
Athletic: Yes
Expenses by: Year
In State: $ 24,725

Founded: 1851
Religion: Catholic (Jesuit)
Housing: Yes
Male/Female Ratio: 49:51
Graduate Enrollment: N/A
Financial Aid: Yes
Out of State: $ 24,725

Specialty: Also strong college of Business
Degrees Conferred: BS, BA, MS, MA, MBA
Programs of Study: Accounting, Banking & Finance, Biology, Business Administration, Chemistry, Computer Science, Criminal Justice, Economics, Elementary Education, English, Fine Arts, Food Marketing, French, German, Health Care, History, Humanities, Human Services, Psychology, Information Science, International Relations, Labor Studies, Management, Marketing, Mathematics, Philosophy, Physics, Political Science, Psychology, Public Administration, Religion, Secondary Education, Social Science, Spanish

Men's Athletic Profile

5600 City Ave.
Philadelphia, PA 19131
Coach: Tom Turner
Email: Not Available

NCAA I
Hawks/Crimson, Gray
Phone: (610) 660-1707
Fax: (610) 660-1716

Estimated # of Men's Soccer Scholarships: None
Conference: Atlantic 10 Conference
Program Profile: A small university competing against the powers of the Atlantic 10, also competes in the Philadelphia Soccer Seven against the 6 other Division I schools in the Philadelphia area.
History: Program began in 1958.
Achievements: N/A
Coaching: Tom Turner is our Head Coach. He was a 4-yr starter St. Joseph's during its period of glory which included 2 NCAA bids. Previously coached at La Salle HS for 10 years.
Style of Play: An aggressive one-touch team that allows individual expression at time. We employ the 4-4-2 most of the time, but we can adapt if necessary.

Women's Athletic Profile

5600 City Avenue
Philadelphia, PA 19131
Coach: John Byford
Email: Not Available

NCAA I
Hawks/Crimson, Grey
Phone: (610) 660-3367
Fax: (610) 660-1724

Estimated # of Women's Soccer Scholarships: 4
Conference: Atlantic 10 Conference
Program Profile: SJU women's soccer plays in the fall season. Their home field is Finnesey Field and is Astroturf. Capacity is 1000
History: The women's soccer program began in 1996 and have had three winning season in five years. Overall record is 40-46-4
Achievements: Ellen Stenrud was Mid-Atlantic honoree in 1997, Several All-Conference Players.

Coaching: John Byford spent four years playing soccer professionally with the Leyton Orient Club in England. He has received honors from the Southeastern Pennsylvania Girls High School Coaches Association, National Soccer Coaches Association of America and the English Football Association.
Roster in State: 13 **Out of State:** 8 **Out of Country:** 0
ODP State: 8 **Regional:** **National:**
Walk-on/Other: **Graduation %:** 100 **Seniors on Team:** 6
Positions Needed: Forward, Midfield, Central Defender
Camp or Clinic Dates: TBA
Most Recent Record: 4-13-0
Schedule: Xavier, Dayton, Massachusetts, Richmond, Pennsylvania, Delaware, Rhode Island
Style of Play: Possession style of play.

Saint Vincent College

Academic Profile

Phone: (724) 539-9761

Latrobe, PA 15650-2690

Type: 4 Yr.,Private,Liberal Arts **Founded:** 1846
Website: http://www.stvincent.edu **Religion:** Catholic
SAT/ACT/GPA: Vary **Housing:** Yes
Student/Faculty Ratio: 12:1 **Male/Female Ratio:** 52:48
Undergraduate Enrollment: 1,250 **Graduate Enrollment:** N/A
Scholarships/Academic: Yes **Athletic:** Yes **Financial Aid:** No
Expenses by: Year **In State:** $ 19,800 **Out of State:** $ 19,800
Specialty: Preprofessional Programs - Business, Law, Medicine, Sciences
Degrees Conferred: 250
Programs of Study: Anthropology, Art, Biology, BioChemistry, Business Administration, Chemistry, Communications, Computing & Information Sciences, Economics, Education Certification, Engineering, English, Environmental Sciences, Family & Consumer Sciences, Fine Arts, History, Liberal Arts, Mathematics, Medical Technology, Modern & Classics Languages, Music, Music Performance, Philosophy, Physics, Political Science, Psychology, Public Policy, Religious Education, Social Work, Sociology, Theatre

Men's Athletic Profile

300 Fraser Purchase Road
Latrobe, PA 15650-2690
Coach: Keith Harmon
Email: kharmon@stvincent.edu

NAIA
Bearcats/Green, Gold
Phone: (412) 539-9761
Fax: (412) 206-6674

Estimated # of Men's Soccer Scholarships: None
Conference: WPIS Conference, Keystone-Empire Conference

Women's Athletic Profile

300 Fraser Purchase Rd
Latrobe, PA 15650-2690
Coach: Gary Butkovich
Email: Not Available

NAIA
Bearcats/Green, White
Phone: (412) 539-9761
Fax: (412) 532-5050

Estimated # of Women's Soccer Scholarships: None
Conference: Keystone-Empire Collegiate Conference NAIA
Program Profile: Highlight sport in the fall, natural grass with a measurements of 120x80 yards. Field set in the center of the campus near main entrance. Play competitive; 18 game schedule of NAIA-NCAA Division II & III teams.

History: 1997 would be third full year of the program that has showed steady progress, ranked fifth in the Northeast Region of the NAIA six of eleven weeks in the last season (1996).
Achievements: No championships or All-American in the first two years, but freshmen and sophomores were nominated for Regional All-American. Freshman Forward - Amy Krahe made 14 goals, 10 ast. and Sophomore Becca May made 7 goals and 5 ast.
Coaching: Gary Butkovich, Head Coach, 21st years as a coach, ten high school boys, seven college men, three college women, seven years ODP and two years women ODP PA, West.
Style of Play: Style of play varies from year to year to best utilize the talent on the team.

Seton Hill College

Academic Profile

Phone: 724-834-2200

Greensburg, PA 15601

Type: 4 Yr.,Private,Liberal Arts
Founded: 1926
Website: http://www.setonhill.edu
Religion: Catholic
SAT/ACT/GPA: 860
Housing: Yes
Student/Faculty Ratio: 13:1
Male/Female Ratio: Female
Undergraduate Enrollment: N/A
Graduate Enrollment: N/A
Scholarships/Academic: Yes **Athletic:** Yes
Financial Aid: Yes
Expenses by: Year **In State:** $ 18,200
Out of State: $ 18,200
Specialty: Education, Business Management, Accounting
Degrees Conferred: BA, BS, BFA, BMus, BSMEdTech
Programs of Study: Accounting, Art, Art Therapy, Banking/Finance, BioChemistry, Biology, Business Administration, Chemistry, Communications, Computer Science, Design, Dramatics Arts, Economics, Education, English, Fine Arts, Food Production, French, History, International Business, Journalism, Management, Marketing, Mathematics, Medical Laboratory, Technology, Music, Nursing, Personnel Management, Philosophy, Photography, Physics, Political Science, PreLaw, PreMed, Psychology, Religion, Theatre

Women's Athletic Profile

Seton Hill Drive
Greensburg, PA 15601
Coach: John Fogle
Email: Not Available

NAIA
Spirit/Scarlet, Gold
Phone: (412) 838-4259
Fax: (412) 830-1296

Estimated # of Women's Soccer Scholarships: None
Conference: Mid-Ohio Conference
Program Profile: Play on a natural grass field. Team has 17 game schedule.
History: The program began in 1987 - rearing 100 win mark.
Achievements: 3 All-Americans; 3 Academic All-Americans, 10 All-Region players, 10 All-Conference players.
Coaching: John Fogle, Head Coach, graduated from Broaddus in 1973, All-American South in 1972.
Style of Play: Build-up from the defense, use all players.

Shippensburg University

Academic Profile

Phone: 717-477-7447

Chambersburg, PA 17257

Type: 4 Yr.,Public,Liberal Arts
Founded: 1871
Website: http://www.ship.edu
Religion: Non-Affiliated
SAT/ACT/GPA: Open
Housing: Yes

Student/Faculty Ratio: 20:1 **Male/Female Ratio:** 1:1
Undergraduate Enrollment: 5,600 **Graduate Enrollment:** 1,000
Scholarships/Academic: Yes **Athletic:** Yes **Financial Aid:** Yes
Expenses by: Year **In State:** $ 8,358 **Out of State:** $ 13,714
Degrees Conferred: BA, BS, BSBA, Minors and Pre-Professional Options
Programs of Study: Art, Biology, Medical Technology, Chemistry, Communications/Journalism, English, French, Geography, Earth & Space Science, Public Administration, History, Mathematics, Mathematics/Computer Science, Physics, Applied Physics, Psychology, Sociology, Speech Communication, Accounting, Business Education, Office Administration, Management, Marketing, Criminal Justice, Social Work, Elementary Education, PreLaw, PreMed, PreDentistry, PrePharmacy

Men's Athletic Profile

1871 Old Main Drive
Chambersburg, PA 17257
Coach: Guy Furfaro
Email: gtfurf@ship.edu

NCAA II
Red Raiders/Red, Blue
Phone: (717) 532-1740
Fax: (717) 530- 4045

Estimated # of Men's Soccer Scholarships: 4 Partial
Conference: Pennsylvania State Athletic Conference
Program Profile: We are a competitive NCAA II program belonging to one of the nation's top NCAA Conferences. With a capacity of up to 2,000, David See Field is a natural turf soccer field measuring 120x75 yards and is a part of the 50 acre athletic facility.
History: Our program began in 1962. Ship has been consistently one of the strongest team in the PSAC.
Achievements: PSAC Champions in 1979 (tie) & 1975; PSAC Eastern Division Champions in 1970 (tie), 1971, 1972 (tie), 1975 & 1978. Tom Hotham - All-American in 1985 & 1987, Adidas Scholar Athlete in 1986; All-Conference - Chris Hayburn in 1992; Chris McCaffrey in 1993; Trevor Law in 1995, Jared Smith and Joe Geist in 1995 second team. PSAC 1st team Steve Hixon - Regional All-American.
Coaching: Gur Furfaro, Head Coach, is entering his third year with the program. He was graduated from Phila Textile in 1989 and named All-American when he played with Baltimore Blast in 1989-1990. Penn Jersey of the APSL in 1990. Chris Goetter, Assistant Coach, is entering his second year with Shippensburg. He graduated from Shippensburg in 1996. He was a former captain and team MVP in his senior year.
Style of Play: A mix of indirect and direct style of attack. A mix of low and high pressure defense.

Women's Athletic Profile

1871 Old Main Drive
Shippensburg, PA 17257
Coach: Guy Furfaro
Email: gtfurf@ship.edu

NCAA II
Lady Raiders/Red, Blue
Phone: (717) 532-1740
Fax: (717) 530-4045

Estimated # of Women's Soccer Scholarships:
Conference: PSAC
Program Profile: Competitive NCAA Division II program belonging to one of the nation's top NCAA Conferences. With a capacity of up to 2,000, David See Field is a natural turf soccer field measuring 12075 yards, and is part of the 50 acre athletic facility.
History: The program began in 1994 and received votes for top 25 in 1997.
Achievements: Sara Kane-Grimes and Lisa Dambelta received 2nd team regional All-Americans in 1998.
Coaching: Guy Furfaro, Head Coach, entering third year with Shippensburg, graduated from Phila Textile in 1989, All-American and drafted by Baltimore Blast in 1989-1990. Penn Jersey of the APSL in 1990. Chris Goetter, Assistant Coach, second year at Shippensburg, graduated from Shippensburg College in 1996. He was a captain and team MVP in his senior year.
Style of Play: A sound mix of indirect and direct style of attack. A mix of low and high pressure defense.

Slippery Rock University of Pennsylvania
Academic Profile

Soccer Office
Slippery Rock, PA 16057-1326
Phone: (724) 738-2946

Type: 4 Yr.,Public,Liberal Arts
Founded: 1889
Website: http://www.sru.edu
Religion: Non-Affiliated
SAT/ACT/GPA: 950/2.5
Housing: Yes
Student/Faculty Ratio: 25:1
Male/Female Ratio: 60:40
Undergraduate Enrollment: 7,500
Graduate Enrollment: 750
Scholarships/Academic: Yes **Athletic:** Yes **Financial Aid:** Yes
Expenses by: Year **In State:** $ 8,470 **Out of State:** $ 13,822
Specialty: Education, Sports Medicine, Physical Education
Degrees Conferred: BA, BS, MA, MBA, Doctorate in Physical Therapy
Programs of Study: Accounting, Anthropology, Art, Athletic Training, Biology, Business Administration, Chemistry, Communications, Community Health, Computer Science, CytoTechnology, Dance, Economics, Elementary Education, English, Environmental Education, Environmental Science, Environmental Studies, Exercise Science, Finance, French, Geography, Geology, German, Gerontology, Health Education, History, International Business, Management, Marketing, Mathematics, Medical Technology, Music, Music Education, Music Therapy, Nursing, Park and Resource Management, Physics, Political Science, PreDental, PreEngineering, PreLaw, Secondary Education, Sociology, Spanish, Special Education, Sports Management, Theatre, Therapeutic Recreation, Undeclared

Men's Athletic Profile

102 Morrow Field House
Slippery Rock, PA 16057
Coach: Neen Herlihy
Email: noreen.herlihy@sru.edu

NCAA II
Rockets/Green, White
Phone: (724) 738-2946
Fax: (724) 738-2626

Estimated # of Men's Soccer Scholarships: Varies
Conference: Pennsylvania State Athletic Association
Program Profile: We have ten practice fields, all natural including game field. Our playing season lasts from September through November.
History: Established in 1928 with a strong tradition in Pennsylvania.
Achievements: Many Coach of the Year Awards; Conference Titles, All-Americans; two players drafted by English 2nd Division professional team.
Coaching: Noreen Herlihy, Head Coach, was a former Trish National Team Player and named 3 times Collegiate All-American. Anthony Calrke is the Assistant Coach. Erin Gilroy is the Goalkeeper Coach.
Style of Play: Attack minded team that works hard on defense. Good passing team with an emphasis on individual flare. Currently a vary young team and needs players for the 1997-1998 season.

Women's Athletic Profile

201 Morrow Field House
Slippery Rock, PA 16057
Coach: Noreen Herlihy
Email: Noreen.Herlihy@sru.edu

NCAA II
Rockets/Green, White
Phone: (724) 738-2946
Fax: (724) 738-2297

Estimated # of Women's Soccer Scholarships: varies
Conference: Pennsylvania State Athletic Conference
Program Profile: We have six soccer fields, all natural.
History: Our program was established in 1993. We finish 24th in the Nation with a record of 13-4.
Achievements: 1996 Coach of the Year; 6 All-Region; 7 All Conference; 1 All-American 2 players played for Irish National Team.

Coaching: Noreen Herlihy, Head Coach, is a former member of the Irish Women's National Team and was in European Championship competition. She is a three-time collegiate All-American, an Academic All-American and a former assistant at Mercyhurst College. Anthony Clarke is Assistant Coach. Erin Gilroy is Goalkeeper Coach.

Roster in State: 13 **Out of State:** 8 **Out of Country:** 3
ODP State: 5 **Regional:** 2 **National:** 2
Walk-on/Other: **Graduation %:** **Seniors on Team:** 3
Positions Needed: Defense, midfield, forward *Goalkeeper
Camp or Clinic Dates: July 9-13
Most Recent Record: 13-4
Schedule: Lock Haven, Mercyhurst, CW Post, West Chester, Bloomsburg, WV Wesleyan
Style of Play: Attacking style of play, play a lot to feet, very dangerous on set pieces.

Susquehanna University

Academic Profile

Selinsgrove, PA 17870-1001
Phone: (570)372-4273

Type: 4 Yr.,Private,Liberal Arts
Founded: 1858
Website: http://www.susqu.edu
Religion: Evangelical Lutheran
SAT/ACT/GPA:
Housing: Yes
Student/Faculty Ratio: 14:1
Male/Female Ratio: 750:900
Undergraduate Enrollment: 1,650
Graduate Enrollment: N/A
Scholarships/Academic: Yes **Athletic:** No **Financial Aid:** Yes
Expenses by: Year **In State:** $ 26,200 **Out of State:**
Specialty: Quality, personalized Liberal Arts and Professional Preparation
Degrees Conferred: Associates, Bachelors
Programs of Study: The School of Art & Science offers Biochemistry, Biology, Chemistry, Classics, Computer Science, Economics, Elementary Education, English, Environmental Science, French, GeoScience, German, Greek, History, Information Systems, International Studies, Latin, Mathematics, Philosophy, Physics, Political Science, Psychology, Religion, Sociology, And Spanish. The School of Fine Arts offers Art, Art History, Communications & Theatre Arts, Music, Church Music, Music Education, And Music Performance. The Sigmund Wels School of Business offers Accounting, Business Administration, and Economics.

Men's Athletic Profile

514 University Ave.
Selinsgrove, PA 17870-1001
Coach: Jim Findlay
Email: Not Available

NCAA III
Crusaders/Orange, Maroon
Phone: (717) 372-4277
Fax: (717) 372-2758

Estimated # of Men's Soccer Scholarships: N/A
Conference: Middle Atlantic Conference, Commonwealth League
Program Profile: Men's soccer program plays on one of two natural grass playing fields. The game field has a capacity of approximately 500. They play a fall season, although they also have a limited (5 games) non-traditional season in the spring.
History: Although the program has been around since before 1959, records officially began in 1959. Play in the strongest NCAA Division III leagues — now the MAC Commonwealth League — with such national powers as Elizabethtown and Messiah.
Achievements: Coach of the Year
Style of Play: A defensive fundamentalist. He really stresses discipline and skills development. His teams are always fundamentally sound and well conditioned.

Women's Athletic Profile

514 University Avenue
Selinsgrove, PA 17870-1001
Coach: Jim Findlay
Email: Not Available

NCAA III
Crusaders/Orange, Maroon
Phone: (717) 372-4033
Fax: (717) 372-4048

Estimated # of Women's Soccer Scholarships: None
Conference: Middle Atlantic Conference, Commonwealth League
Program Profile: The team plays at one of two natural grass playing fields with an approximate capacity of 500. The play a reg. fall season.
History: Program started in 1994 and was officially registered as a club in 1992.

Swarthmore College

Academic Profile

Swarthmore, PA 19081

Phone: 610-328-8000

Type: 4 Yr.,Private,Liberal Arts
Founded: 1864
Website: http://www.swarthmore.edu
Religion: Quaker
SAT/ACT/GPA: 1250/21
Housing: Yes
Student/Faculty Ratio: 10:1
Male/Female Ratio: 1:1
Undergraduate Enrollment: 1,350
Graduate Enrollment: N/A
Scholarships/Academic: Yes **Athletic:** No **Financial Aid:** Yes
Expenses by: Year **In State:** $ 25,900 **Out of State:** $ 25,900
Degrees Conferred: BA, BS
Programs of Study: Art, Art History, Asian Studies, Astronomy, AstroPhysics, Biology, Black Studies, Chemistry, Classics, Computer Science, Economics, Education, Engineering, English, Literature, History, International Relations, Mathematics, Medieval Studies, Modern Languages & Literature, Music & Dance, Philosophy, Physics, Political Science, Psychology, Public Policy, Religion, Sociology & Anthropology, Special Major, Theatre Studies, Women's Studies

Men's Athletic Profile

500 College Ave.
Swarthmore, PA 19081
Coach: Don Norton
Email: Not Available

NCAA III
Garnet/Garnet, White
Phone: (610) 328-8218
Fax: (610) 328-7798

Estimated # of Men's Soccer Scholarships: N/A
Conference: Centennial Conference
Program Profile: Complete against Top Division III and local Division I and II teams. 11 miles southwest of Philadelphia. Best among liberal arts colleges in the country.
History: Program began in 1915
Achievements: 3 - time division champs in the 80's. Southeast Division Champs of MAC and made NCAA division III tournament.
Style of Play: Emphasis on technique.

Women's Athletic Profile

500 College Ave.
Swarthmore, PA 19081
Coach: Amy Brunner
Email: abrunne1@swarthmore.edu

NCAA III
Garnet Tide/Garnet
Phone: (610) 328-8210
Fax: (610) 328-7798

Estimated # of Women's Soccer Scholarships: None
Conference: Centennial Conference
Program Profile: A young developing program in regards to plyers. Facilities include 3 fields and a 40x40 yard grid which shared with and women's team. New weight room/fitness facility and an indoor tract. Fall playing season with indoor and spring practices tournaments. Fields are all natural grass.
History: Our program began in 1982. We joined Centennial Conference in 1992. Coach Brunne is beginning second year as full time coach this fall 2000.
Achievements: We have had conference player recognition.
Coaching: Amy Brunne is our Head Coach. She is entering her second year with the program. She was named Division III All-American Goalkeeper at Bates College. Assistant Coach Merry Lubkin is hoping to come back this fall. Stellar high school career in New Jersey and was assisted at Penn State.
Roster in State: 1 **Out of State:** 20 **Out of Country:** 1
Walk-on/Other: **Graduation %:** 100 **Seniors on Team:** 3
Positions Needed: Midfielder, Forward, Goalkeeper
Camp or Clinic Dates: Not Available
Most Recent Record: 7-12-0
Schedule: Gettysburg, Muhlenberg, Johns Hopkins, Western Maryland, Haverford, NYU
Style of Play: Short passing, very contained players.

Temple University

Academic Profile

Phone: (215) 204-7445
Philadelphia, PA 19122

Type: 4 Yr.,Public, **Founded:** 1884
Website: http://www.temple.edu **Religion:** Non-Affiliated
SAT/ACT/GPA: 950/2.75 **Housing:** Yes
Student/Faculty Ratio: 25:1 **Male/Female Ratio:** 48:52
Undergraduate Enrollment: 18,000 **Graduate Enrollment:** 11,000
Scholarships/Academic: Yes **Athletic:** Yes **Financial Aid:** Yes
Expenses by: Year **In State:** $ 8,357 **Out of State:** $ 13,927
Specialty: Medical, 12 undergraduate schools with several majors
Degrees Conferred: AAS, BA, BS, BBA, BFA, BArch, BSN, BSEE, MA, MS, MBA, Ph.D., JD
Programs of Study: Allied Health Professions: Tyler School of Arts, Business & Management, Communications, & Theatre, Education, Engineering, Health, Physical Education, Recreation & Dance, Ester Boyer College of Music, Pharmacy, Social Administration, Architecture, Landscape Architecture and Horticulture

Men's Athletic Profile

1900 N Broad Street
Philadelphia, PA 19122
Coach: David MacWilliams
Email: Not Available

NCAA I
Owls/Cherry, White
Phone: (215) 204-7447
Fax: (215) 204-7770

Estimated # of Men's Soccer Scholarships: None
Conference: Atlantic 10 Conference, Philadelphia Soccer 7

Women's Athletic Profile

Broad & Montgomery Avenues
Philadelphia, PA 19122
Coach: Seamus McWillia
Email: maghera@aol.com

NCAA I
Owls/Cherry, White
Phone: (215) 204-6668
Fax: (215) 204-7499

Estimated # of Women's Soccer Scholarships: None
Conference: Atlantic 10 Conference
Program Profile: Teams play at Temple Stadium on outskirts of the city; natural grass field, seats 20,000 plus. The team plays in the fall with 11 conference games and 10 non-conference games.
History: Began in 1991.
Coaching: Seamus McWilliams, Head Coach, is entering his fourth season at Haverford College in Penn. as a head coach, also volunteered as an assistant coach for Temple in 1993.
Style of Play: Depends on the personnel.

Thiel College

Academic Profile

Greenville, PA 16125-2181
Phone:

Type: 4 Yr.,Private,Liberal Arts
Founded: 1866
Website: http://www.theil.edu
Religion: Lutheran
SAT/ACT/GPA: Required
Housing: Yes
Student/Faculty Ratio: 12:1
Male/Female Ratio: 48:52
Undergraduate Enrollment: 1,000
Graduate Enrollment: N/A
Scholarships/Academic: Yes **Athletic:** No
Financial Aid: Yes
Expenses by: Year **In State:** $ 17,080
Out of State: $ 17,080
Degrees Conferred: BA, BSN, AA
Programs of Study: Allied Health, Art, Biology, Business Administration, Accounting, Economics, Chemistry, Communication Arts & Science, Education, Engineering, English, Environmental Science, Geography, Geology, Spanish, Nursing, Philosophy, Political Science, Psychology, Religion, PreProfessional Programs

Men's Athletic Profile

75 College Avenue
Greenville, PA 16125
Coach: Bryan Williams
Email: bwilliam@thiel.edu

NCAA III
Tomcats/Navy, Gold
Phone: 724.589.2869
Fax: (412) 589-2021

Did Not Return Profile

Women's Athletic Profile

75 College Avenue
Greenville, PA 16125
Coach: Bryan Williams
Email: Not Available

NCAA III
Tomcats/Blue, Gold
Phone: (412) 589-2165
Fax: (412) 589-2021

Estimated # of Women's Soccer Scholarships: None
Conference: President's Athletic Conference

University of Pennsylvania

Academic Profile

Philadelphia, PA 19104-6376
Phone: (215) 898-7507

Type: 4 Yr.,Private,Liberal Arts,Engineering
Founded: 1740
Website: http://www.upenn.edu
Religion: Non-Affiliated
SAT/ACT/GPA: 1200/Top 10%
Housing: Yes

Student/Faculty Ratio: 7:1
Male/Female Ratio: 50:50
Undergraduate Enrollment: 10,000
Graduate Enrollment: 8,000
Scholarships/Academic: Yes **Athletic:** No **Financial Aid:** Yes
Expenses by: Year **In State:** $ 31,664 **Out of State:** $ 31,664
Specialty: Business, Engineering, Liberal Arts, Nursing
Degrees Conferred: BA, BS, Various Master's and Ph.D. Programs
Programs of Study: Accounting, Anthropology, BioChemistry, BioEngineering, Chemistry, Communications, Computer Science, Economics, English, Environmental Studies, Finance, Fine Arts, Geology, History, Latin American Studies, Management, Marketing

Men's Athletic Profile

235 S 33rd Street
Philadelphia, PA 19104-6322
Coach: Rudy Fuller
Email: bfuller@pobox.upenn.edu

NCAA I
Quakers/Navy, Burgundy, White
Phone: (215) 898-4815
Fax: (215) 573-6030

Estimated # of Men's Soccer Scholarships: None
Conference: Ivy League Conference
Program Profile: The Quaker plays a seventeen games regular season against top rated Division I programs. They play their game as on Thodes Field which is a beautiful grass surface located next to the Schuylkill River.
History: Our first inaugural season as a varsity sport was in 1910.
Achievements: Produced 19 All-Americans since 1953.
Coaching: Rudy Fuller is our Head Coach. He is entering second season with the program. Jon Pascale is our Assistant Coach.
Style of Play: Organized balanced zonal defense. An attack focused around possession and numbers.

Women's Athletic Profile

235 S. 33rd Street
Philadelphia, PA 19104
Coach: Darren Ambrose
Email:

NCAA I
Lady Quakers/Red, Blue
Phone: (215) 898-2923
Fax: (215) 573-6030

Estimated # of Women's Soccer Scholarships: need based
Conference: Ivy League Conference
Program Profile: We play in a highly competitive Division I Ivy League. Our season runs from August through November. We have a two month spring season. Our facilities include a natural grass field that measures 115x75, indoor facility and 2 weight rooms.
History: Our program began in 1991. We were the ECAC Champions in 1998, 1999 Ivy League Runner-Up, NCAA tournament appearance, and have had winning seasons the past three.
Achievements: In 1999 we had 3 All-Ivy League selections, 1 All-Mid Atlantic Region, and in 1998 2 All-Ivy League selections and 1 All-Mid Atlantic Region.
Coaching: University of Pennsylvania's Head Coach is Darren Ambrose, who holds a USSF "A" license and Assistant Coach Scott Morganroth holds a USSF "B" license.
Roster in State: 4 **Out of State:** 24 **Out of Country:** 0
ODP State: 15 **Regional:** 4 **National:**
Walk-on/Other: 2 **Graduation %:** 99 **Seniors on Team:** 7
Positions Needed: Goalkeeper, Midfield, Defender, Forward
Camp or Clinic Dates: August 13-17
Most Recent Record: 13-4-1
Schedule: Harvard, Princeton, William and Mary, Richmond, George Mason, Dartmouth, Yale
Style of Play: Possession, build up from the back, direct when appropriate. Everyone on the team must be able to defend and attack.

University of Pittsburgh

Academic Profile

Pittsburgh, PA 15260

Phone:

Type: 4 Yr.,Public,Liberal Arts,Engineering
Website: http://www.pitt.edu
SAT/ACT/GPA: 1230/24
Student/Faculty Ratio: 14:1
Undergraduate Enrollment: 14,200
Scholarships/Academic: Yes **Athletic:** Yes
Expenses by: Year **In State:** $ 12,588

Founded: 1787
Religion: Non-Affiliated
Housing: Yes
Male/Female Ratio: 48:52
Graduate Enrollment: 9,075
Financial Aid: Yes
Out of State: $ 19,622

Degrees Conferred: BA, BS, BSE, MA, MS, MBA, MEd, MENG, Ph.D., EdP, PsyD
Programs of Study: Biological Science, Business, Communications and the Arts, Computer and Physical Science, Education, Engineering and Environmental Design, Health Profession, Social Science. Over 90 majors offered.

Men's Athletic Profile

516 Stadium, Soccer Office
Pittsburgh, PA 15213
Coach: Joseph Luxbacher
Email: Not Available

NCAA I
Panthers/Blue, Gold
Phone: (412) 648-8217
Fax: (412) 648-8940

Estimated # of Men's Soccer Scholarships: None
Conference: Big East Conference
Program Profile: Home field is Pitt Football Stadium (turf), lighted, seats 52,000 fans. Varsity sports weight room, full size indoor sports complex, grass practice field. A new stadium is being built.
History: Soccer began play in 1953, Pitt Stadium has been team's home for 36 years.
Achievements: Coach of the Year in BIG EAST 2 times
Coaching: Joseph Luxbacher is our Head Coach. Kirk Brodos and Brian Retzlof are the Assistant Coaches.
Roster In State: 10 **Out of State:** 13 **Out of Country:** 0
ODP State: 0 **Regional:** 0 **National:** 0
Walk-on/Other: 0 **Graduation %:** 99 **Seniors on Team:** 6
Camp or Clinic Dates: June, July
Most Recent Record: 13-4-0
Schedule: Uconn, Boston College, George Town
Style of Play: Possession Midfield, attacking forward, marking defenders. Team zonal defense philosophy.

Women's Athletic Profile

P.O. Box 7436
Pittsburgh, PA 152130436
Coach: Roland Sturk
Email: rmsy@pitt.edu

NCAA I
Panthers/Navy, Old Gold
Phone: (412) 648-8232
Fax: (412) 648-8248

Estimated # of Women's Soccer Scholarships: N/A
Conference: Big East Conference
Program Profile: Playing season is year-round. Play both on turf and grass field. The stadium (56,000), includes indoor and outdoor training facilities.
History: The program began from scratch in 1996. First year of competition in Big East Conference in 1997 was placed 10th.
Achievements: None to date at Pittsburgh.

Coaching: Roland Sturk, Head Coach, USSF "A" License; Scottish FA, Intro "A" certificate; Brusa certificate; Region 4 age-group head coach; Director PA, West State ODP; Region I assistant ODP Coach. Nicole Bartrus - Assistant Coach, USSF "B" license, State ODP Coach. Erik Ingram - goalkeeper Coach, holds USSF "B" License.
Style of Play: Latin/Dutch Style; tendency to build from through midfield, heavy possession orientation; zonal marking with sweeper; like players with an individual creativity.

University of Pittsburgh - Bradford

Academic Profile

Bradford, PA 16701-2898

Phone: (814) 362-7500

Type: 4 Yr.,Public,Liberal Arts
Website: http://www.upb.pitt.edu
SAT/ACT/GPA: 950/20/2.0
Student/Faculty Ratio: 14:1
Undergraduate Enrollment: 1,400
Scholarships/Academic: Yes
Athletic: No
Expenses by: Year
In State: $ 10,535
Founded: 1963
Religion: Non-Affiliated
Housing: Yes
Male/Female Ratio: 40:60
Graduate Enrollment: N/A
Financial Aid: Yes
Out of State: $ 10,535
Degrees Conferred: BA, BS
Programs of Study: Accounting, Actuarial Science, Administration of Justice, American Studies, Anthropology, Biology, Business, Chemistry, Communications, Computer Science, Electrical, Industrial, Manufacturing, Mechanical, English, Environmental Geology, Gerontology, History, Human Relations, International Business, International Studies, Marketing, Mathematics, Nursing, Physical Science, Physical Therapy Preparation, Political Science, PreDental, PreLaw, PreMed, Psychology, Public Relations, Radio & Television, Secondary Education, Social Sciences, Sociology, Sport & Recreation Management, Sports Medicine/Athletic Training, Writing

Men's Athletic Profile

300 Campus Drive
Bradford, PA 16701-2898
Coach: Peter R. Butler
Email: pr68+@pitt.edu

NCAA III/NAIA
Panthers/Blue, Gold
Phone: (814) 362-7537
Fax: (814) 362-7503

Estimated # of Men's Soccer Scholarships: N/A
Conference: Allegheny Mountain Conference (AMCC)
Program Profile: Natural field adjacent to gym, and student housing. Bleachers that will fit 100 fans. Playing season is from Aug. through Nov.
History: Program began in 1982. Pitt-Bradford has had 3 coaches in that time; J. Michael Stuckart (1982-1987), Derek Clysdale (1988) and Peter R. Butler (1989-present).
Achievements: 1989 District Coach of the Year (NAIA).
Coaching: Peter R. Butler, Head Coach. Bob Jimerland - Assistant Coach.

Women's Athletic Profile

300 Campus Drive
Bradford, PA 16701-2898
Coach: Peter R. Butler
Email: pr68+@pitt.edu

NCAA III
Panthers/Blue, White
Phone: (814) 362-7537
Fax: (814) 362-7503

Estimated # of Women's Soccer Scholarships: None
Conference: Allegheny Mountain Conference
Program Profile: Natural field adjacent to the gym, and the student housing. No stadium; only bleachers that will accommodate about 100 people.

History: Our program began in 1995.
Coaching: Peter R. Butler, Head Coach, NSCAA Advanced National Diploma, played professionally in England. Kathy Greenwallt - Assistant Coach.
Style of Play: Relies on break away most of the time. Plays a 4-4-2.

University o Pittsburgh at Greensburg

Academic Profile

Phone: 724-836-9880

Greensburg, PA 15601-5898

Type: 4 Yr.,Public
Website: http://www.pitt.edu
SAT/ACT/GPA: 900
Student/Faculty Ratio: 18:1
Undergraduate Enrollment: 1,500
Scholarships/Academic: Yes
Athletic: No
Expenses by: Year
In State: $ 10,354
Founded: 1963
Religion: Non-Affiliated
Housing: Yes
Male/Female Ratio: 45:55
Graduate Enrollment: N/A
Financial Aid: Yes
Out of State: $ 17,118
Degrees Conferred: BA, BS
Programs of Study: American Studies, Biology, Environmental Science, Accounting, Management, Communications, Criminology, English, Literature, English Writing, Humanities, Information Science, Mathematics, Natural Science, Political Science, Mathematics, Natural Science, Political Science, Psychology, Social Science, PreDental, PreLaw, PreMedicine, PrePhysical Therapy

Men's Athletic Profile

1050 Mt. Pleasant Road
Greensburg, PA 15601-5898
Coach: Ted Wawrzyniak
Email: tedewawrzyniak@cs.com

NCAA III
Bobcats/Blue, Gold
Phone: (724) 864-6993
Fax: (724) 864-3351

Estimated # of Men's Soccer Scholarships: N/A
Conference: Allegheny Mountain Collegiate Conference
Program Profile: We presently have one practice and one game field with bleachers. Our soccer complex adjoins the gym and training facility indoor . Our game field has a measurement of 115x75 yards and natural grass. Soccer is the premier fall sport.
History: Our program began in Fall of 1998 with a 7-9-0 overall record and 2-3-0 in conference, scoring 32 goals starting 8 freshmen, 2 sophomores, 1 junior. UPG qualified for conference playoffs in first year of competition.
Achievements:
Coaching: Ted Wawrzyniak, Head Coach, is entering his second season. He holds a USSF License and was a highly successful amateur and youth coach at Western Pennsylvania. He lead his masters Amateur Squad Norwin to its 1998 US Championship. John Curley, Assistant Coach, hold a USSF License. He was a former player at the University of Pittsburgh.
Schedule: CMU, Frostburg, Allegheny, Penn State-Behrend
Style of Play: High pressure defense. One and two touch passing involving all players. High level of fitness for players.

University of Pittsburgh, The - Johnstown

Academic Profile

Phone:

Type: 4 Yr.,Public,Liberal Arts,Engineering
Website: http://www.pitt.edu
Founded: 1927
Religion: Non-Affiliated

SAT/ACT/GPA: 900
Housing: Yes
Student/Faculty Ratio: 20:1
Male/Female Ratio: 1:1
Undergraduate Enrollment: 3,000
Graduate Enrollment: N/A
Scholarships/Academic: Yes
Athletic: Yes
Financial Aid: Yes
Expenses by: Year
In State: $ 9,300
Out of State: $ 15,000
Degrees Conferred: BA, BS, M.Ed.
Programs of Study: Accounting, Biology, Business & Management, Chemistry, Communications, Computer Science, Creative Writing, Ecology, Economics, Education, Engineering, English, Finance, Geography, Geology, History, Humanities, Journalism, Literature, Mathematics, Medical Laboratory Technology, Natural Science, Political Science, PreDental, PreLaw, PreMed, PreVet, Psychology, Respiratory Therapy, Social Science, Theatre

Men's Athletic Profile

450 Schoolhouse Rd
Johnstown, PA 15904
Coach: Bob Rukavina
Email: Not Available

NCAA II
Mountain Cats/Blue, Gold
Phone: (814) 269-2000
Fax: (814) 269-2026

Estimated # of Men's Soccer Scholarships: None
Conference: Western PA IC
History: Program began in 1967.

University of Scranton

Academic Profile

Phone: 570-941-7400

Scranton, PA 18510

Type: 4 Yr.,Private,
Founded: 1888
Website: http://www.uofs.edu
Religion: Jesuit
SAT/ACT/GPA: Open
Housing: Yes
Student/Faculty Ratio: 17:1
Male/Female Ratio: 45:55
Undergraduate Enrollment: 3,200
Graduate Enrollment: 250
Scholarships/Academic: Yes
Athletic: No
Financial Aid: Yes
Expenses by: Year
In State: $ 23,000
Out of State: $ 23,000
Degrees Conferred: AA, AS, BA, BS, MA, MS, MBA
Programs of Study: Accounting, Advertising, BioChemistry, Biology, BioPhysics, Broadcasting, Business, Chemistry, Classics, Communications, Computer Information System, Computer Science, Criminal Justice, Economics, Education, Engineering, English, Finance, French, German, Gerontology, History, Journalism, Marketing, Mathematics, Political Science, PreLaw, PreMed, PreVet, Psychology, Religion, Social Science, Theology

Men's Athletic Profile

Linden Street
Scranton, PA 18510-4650
Coach: Steve Klingman
Email: Not Available

NCAA III
Royals/Purple, White
Phone: (717) 941-6191
Fax: (717) 941-4223

Estimated # of Men's Soccer Scholarships: N/A
Conference: Middle Atlantic Conference
Program Profile: On-campus astro turf field constructed in Summer '97 - off campus grass facility. Play a maximum 20 match Fall Schedule - 5 match Spring Schedule
History: Program started in 1968 - 8 Mid-Atlantic Conference Championships; 13 NCAA Division II tourney appearances; 2 National Championship appearances; 2 additional Final Four appearances; over 75 All-Conference selections; 30 Regional selections; 10 Division III All-Americans selections in the history of program.

Women's Athletic Profile

Linden Street
Scranton, PA 18510
Coach: Matthew Pivirotto
Email: klingmanS1@uofs.edu

NCAA III
Lady Royals/Purple, White
Phone: (570) 941-6191
Fax: (717) 941-4223

Estimated # of Women's Soccer Scholarships: None
Conference: Middle Atlantic Conference
Program Profile: We have artificial playing field, however University of Scranton just purchased 100 acres of land off campus to develop into athletic facility, which will include 2 game fields for soccer and 2 training fields, baseball, softball, 2 field hockey, 2 lacrosse, track, etc...
History: Our program began in 1969 - on over 375 games in 30 year history of the program. Received 13 NCAA Division III Tournament berths, reached the Division III National Championships 2 times, the Final Four4 times, won the Middle Atlantic Conference Championships 8 times, reached the MAC playoffs 21 times over the past 25 seasons. Produced 10 NSCAA Division III All-Americans, 38 All-Region selections and over 75 All-Middle Atlantic Conference Selections.
Achievements: We have had 39 players earned All-Conference, 10 All-Region and 4 All-Americans.
Coaching: Matt Pivirotto is our Head Coach. He is entering his second year with the program. He was a four-time All-Conference and 3-time Middle Atlantic Region selection as a player at Lycoming College. He was selected as the Middle Atlantic Conference Most Valuable Player as a senior at Lycoming. He earned the NSCAA National Coaching Diploma during the summer of 1999. Kevin Davy is our Graduate Assistant Coach (Lock Haven graduate from England.
Roster in State: 10 **Out of State:** 15 **Out of Country:** 2
Walk-on/Other: **Graduation %:** 100 **Seniors on Team:** 8
Positions Needed: All positions are open
Camp or Clinic Dates: Day Camps - not set as of this date
Most Recent Record: 4-15-0
Schedule: Elizabethtown, Rowan, Kean, Drew, Franklin & Marshall

Ursinus College

Academic Profile

Collegeville, PA 19426

Phone:

Type: 4 Yr.,Private,Liberal Arts
Website: http://www.ursinus.edu
SAT/ACT/GPA: 1200
Student/Faculty Ratio: 12:1
Undergraduate Enrollment: 1,200
Scholarships/Academic: Yes **Athletic:** No
Expenses by: Year **In State:** $ 24,400
Degrees Conferred: BA, BS

Founded: 1869
Religion: Church of Christ
Housing: Yes
Male/Female Ratio: 50:50
Graduate Enrollment: N/A
Financial Aid: Yes
Out of State: $ 24,400

Programs of Study: Biology, Chemistry, Economics & Business, Exercise & Sports Science, English, History, Politics, International Relations, Psychology, French, German, Spanish, Japanese, Philosophy, Religion, Computer Science, Mathematics, Physics, PreMed, PreLaw, Education, PreEngineering

Men's Athletic Profile

Main Street
Collegeville, PA 19426
Coach: Ed Jackson
Email: Not Available

NCAA III
Bears/Red, Gold, Black
Phone: (610) 489-4111x2251
Fax: (610) 486-0627

Estimated # of Men's Soccer Scholarships: N/A
Conference: Centennial Conference

Women's Athletic Profile

P.O. Box 1000
Collegeville, PA 19426
Coach: Bill Bonewitz
Email: bbonewitz@ursinus.edu

NCAA III
Bears/Red, Gold, Black
Phone: (610) 409-3000
Fax: (610) 409-3620

Estimated # of Women's Soccer Scholarships: None
Conference: Centennial Conference
Program Profile: The Bears play on a natural field,120x75 yards with underground watering system set in natural amphitheatre style. Our practice facilities are separate lighted fields for the evening practices. We also have new field house and locker room facilities. Our season runs from Labor Day to November 1st.
History: The soccer program began in 1996.
Achievements:
Coaching: Bill Bonewitz is entering his 7th year at Ursinus College; 2 years as the men's Assistant Coach and 4 years as the women's Head Coach. Prior to UC he coached for 12 years for EPYSA Premier Level.
Roster in State: 13 **Out of State:** 11 **Out of Country:**
ODP State: 14 **Regional:** 3 **National:**
Walk-on/Other: **Graduation %:** 100 **Seniors on Team:** 5
Positions Needed: Outsides Flanks, Defenders
Camp or Clinic Dates: Not Available
Most Recent Record: 6-12-0
Schedule: John Hopkins, Gettysburg, Muhlenberg, Rowan, Millersville, Plattsburg State
Style of Play: Possession and pressure.

Villanova University
Academic Profile

Phone: (610) 519-4135

Villanova, PA 19085

Type: 4 Yr.,Private,Engineering
Founded: 1847
Website: http://www.villanova.com
Religion: Catholic-Augustinian
SAT/ACT/GPA: 1180-1340/27-29/3.46-3.91
Housing: Yes
Student/Faculty Ratio: 13:1
Male/Female Ratio: 1:1
Undergraduate Enrollment: 6,039
Graduate Enrollment: 3,623
Scholarships/Academic: Yes **Athletic:** Yes **Financial Aid:** Yes
Expenses by: Year **In State:** $ 28,120 **Out of State:** $ 28,120
Specialty: Commerce & Finance, Engineering, Liberal Arts & Sciences, Nursing
Degrees Conferred: AA, AS, BA, BS, MA, MS, MBA, Ph.D., JD
Programs of Study: Art History, Astronomy, Classical Studies, Communications, Computer Science, Criminal Justice, Economics, Education, Engineering, English, Finance, French, Geography, German, History, Honors Program, Humanities, Human Services, Interdisciplinary Studies, International Business, Liberal Arts, Marketing, Meteorology, Military Science, Natural Science, Naval Science, Nursing, Philosophy, Physics, Political Science, PreDental, PreLaw, PreMed, PreVet, Psychology, Religion, Social Science, Spanish, Special Education

Men's Athletic Profile

800 E Lancaster Avenue
Villanova, PA 19085
Coach: Larry Sullivan
Email: larry.sullivan@villanova.edu

NCAA I
Wildcats/Blue, White
Phone: (610) 519-7266
Fax: (610) 519-7987

Estimated # of Men's Soccer Scholarships: None
Conference: Big East & Philadelphia 7 Conference

Women's Athletic Profile

800 E Lancaster Avenue
Villanova, PA 19085
Coach: Ann Clifton
Email: aclifton@email.vill.edu

NCAA I
Lady Wildcats/Navy Blue, White
Phone: (610) 519-4135
Fax: (610) 519-5387

Estimated # of Women's Soccer Scholarships: 12
Conference: Big East Conference
Program Profile: We play on a brand new soccer only stadium built in 1999, with two grass fields and stadium seating for 3,000. In 2000 the Villanova will open a new Locker room facility with own training, laundry room and soccer specific weight room/ cardio room on site. In addition, a new Press Room attacked to the locker room.
History: The program in 1984. The team has reached the Post Season Big East Tournament for the past six years. The team finished the 1999 season with a 14 win and 8 losses record. During the season the team won the Cape Cod classic Tournament and the ECAC Post Season Tournament.
Achievements: The team has had several Regional All-Americans and All big East Performers. The 1999 Post Season Honors had Sophomore Janel Schillig winning the First Team All-Big East and being named as the Big East Goalkeeper of the Year.
Coaching: The program has had only 3 Head Coaches. Currently entering her fourth season as Head Coach of the Wildcats is Ann Clifton. Her Assistant Coach is Paul Royal. During the 2000 season the team will have second Assistant Beth McCaffery as a Recruiting coordinator and special events director. Beth was a second team All-Big East Performer for the Wildcats in 1997.

Roster in State: 7	**Out of State:** 16	**Out of Country:**
ODP State: 20	**Regional:** 9	**National:** 2
Walk-on/Other:	**Graduation %:** 100	**Seniors on Team:** 2

Positions Needed: Forwards, Defenders, Midfielders
Camp or Clinic Dates: July 16-20
Most Recent Record: 14-8-0
Schedule: Notre Dame, University of Connecticut, Syracuse, Coalgate, Princeton
Style of Play: Possession oriented with the ability to attack with a flair. Each player is encouraged to use the special talents to help the team to success. Team is very important with the focus on individual growth as a player.

Washington and Jefferson College

Academic Profile

Washington, PA 15301

Phone: (724) 223-5251

Type: 4 Yr.,Private,Liberal Arts		**Founded:** 1787
Website: http://www.washjeff.edu		**Religion:** Presbyterian
SAT/ACT/GPA: 1000/20/Upper 1/3		**Housing:** Yes
Student/Faculty Ratio: 12:1		**Male/Female Ratio:** 50:50
Undergraduate Enrollment: 1,200		**Graduate Enrollment:** N/A
Scholarships/Academic: Yes	**Athletic:** No	**Financial Aid:** Yes
Expenses by: Year	**In State:** $23,950	**Out of State:** $23,950

Specialty: Pre-Med, Pre-Law, Business
Degrees Conferred: BA, Liberal Arts College
Programs of Study: Accounting, Art, Biology, Business Administration, Chemistry, Economics, Education, English, French, German, History, Human Resources Management, Physics, Philosophy, Political Science, Psychology, Sociology, PreLaw, PreMed, PreDentistry,

Men's Athletic Profile

60 S Lincoln St.
Washington, PA 15301
Coach: Ian McDonald
Email: Imcdonald@washjeff.edu

NCAA III
Presidents/Red, Black
Phone: (724) 223-5261
Fax: (724) 223-5271

Estimated # of Men's Soccer Scholarships: N/A
Conference: President's Athletic Conference (PAC)
Program Profile: Our home games are played about a mile off campus. We have four natural grass fields. The playing season is the last week of August through the first week of November. This does not include post-season play.
History: Our program is eight years old.
Achievements: Start since 1991: Conference Coach of the Year 1994; 1 two-time GTE Academic All-American, 1 Conference MVP, 1 Conference Co-MVP, 30 All-Conference team selections, 1 two-time Regional Academic All-Americans, ECAC South Regional 19 host.
Coaching: Ian McDonald, Head Coach, is a native of England and a graduate of Davis-Elkins College. He is a 1st team Division II All-American, WV All-Conference Selection, All-South Region, Players of the Year 1983, Conference MVP 1985, member of indoor SR Bowl All-East team, former Pro player with the Pittsburgh Stingers (CISL) and a PA West ODP Staff Coach. He has an Advanced National Diploma and is USSF Certified, Med ESU.
Style of Play: European Style of Play.

Women's Athletic Profile

60 S Lincoln Street
Washington, PA 15301
Coach: Anita Rodriguez
Email: Cmedwig@WashJeff.Edu

NCAA III
Presidents/Red, Black (White)
Phone: (412) 223-5251
Fax: (412) 223-5271

Estimated # of Women's Soccer Scholarships: None
Conference: Presidents' Athletic Conference
Program Profile: Home games are played about a mile off campus. We have four natural grass fields. The playing season is the last week of August through the first week of November. This does not include the post-season play.
History: Our program is 8 years old.
Achievements: Every year several players are elected to All-Conference.
Style of Play: Play 4-4-2 formation.

Waynesburg College

Academic Profile

Phone:

Waynesburg, PA 15370

Type: 4 Yr.,Private,Liberal Arts
Website: http://www.waynesburg.edu
SAT/ACT/GPA: Open
Student/Faculty Ratio: 16:1
Undergraduate Enrollment: 1,133
Scholarships/Academic: Yes **Athletic:** No
Expenses by: Year **In State:** $ 15,400

Founded: 1849
Religion: Presbyterian
Housing: No
Male/Female Ratio: 47:53
Graduate Enrollment: N/A
Financial Aid: Yes
Out of State: $ 15,400

Degrees Conferred: AA, AS, BA, BSN, BSBA
Programs of Study: Accounting, Advertising, Art, Biology, Business Administration, Chemistry, Commercial Art, Computer Science, Criminal Justice, Economics, Electronic Media, Elementary Education, English, Finance, Health Care, History, Literature, Management, Marketing, Mathematics, Medical Laboratory Technology, Nursing, Political Science, PreDental, PreLaw, PreMed, Professional Writing, Psychology, Public Administration, Secondary Education, Social Science, Sociology, Sport Broadcasting & Information, Sport Medicine, Visual Communications

Men's Athletic Profile

51 West College Drive
Waynesburg, PA 15370
Coach: Jim Balach
Email: Not Available

NCAA III
Yellow Jackets/Orange, Black
Phone: 412-884-8283
Fax: 724-852-4122

Estimated # of Men's Soccer Scholarships: N/A
Conference: President's Athletic
Program Profile: Play a fall season. The field is natural turf, and has a seating capacity of 2,500.
History: Our program began in 1990.
Coaching: Jim Balach is our head coach.
Camp or Clinic Dates: Not Available
Most Recent Record: 7-13
Style of Play: Depends on the personnel.

Women's Athletic Profile

51 W College Street
Waynesburg, PA 15370
Coach: Ken Alberta
Email: kalberta@waynesburg.edu

NCAA III
Yellow Jackets/Black, Orange
Phone: (724) 852-3306
Fax: (724) 852-4122

Estimated # of Women's Soccer Scholarships: None
Conference: President's Athletic Conference
Program Profile: Our facilities include separate game and practice fields of natural surface. We have a fieldhouse at the stadium. We have an electronic scoreboard. We start to play on August 17th. We have a 20 game schedule. We provide players with all the equipment. This includes travel warm-ups, sweat shorts, t-shirts, travel bag, etc.
History: Our program began in 1990. We placed second in conference 4 times. We were 1998 PAC Champions, and 5th seed ECAC Mid-Atlantic Region. We play several NAIA and Division II institutions.
Achievements: Coach of the Year 1998; 40 All-PAC players; 3 PAC MVP's; 2 Freshman Player of the Year; 4 Players nominated for Regional All-American; 1998 PAC Champions; Top two scores in conference in 1997, 1998.
Coaching: Ken Alberta, Head Coach, 4 years college, 5 years regional men's league selected and travel team play. Assistant Coach - Division III National Pro-Italy, numerous cam appearances.
Style of Play: 4-4-2.

West Chester University

Academic Profile

West Chester, PA 19383

Phone:

Type: 4 Yr.,Public
Website: http://www.wcupa.edu
SAT/ACT/GPA: 840+
Student/Faculty Ratio: 19:1
Undergraduate Enrollment: 9,400
Scholarships/Academic: Yes **Athletic:** Yes
Expenses by: Year **In State:** $ 8,000
Degrees Conferred: AA, AS, BA, BS, BFA, MS, MBA, M.Ed.

Founded: 1871
Religion: Non-Affiliated
Housing: No
Male/Female Ratio: 39:61
Graduate Enrollment: 1,900
Financial Aid: Yes
Out of State: $ 11,900

Programs of Study: Accounting, Biology, Astronomy, Anthropology, Athletic Training, BioChemistry, Biological Science, Business, Cell Biology, Chemistry, Communications, Computer Science, Computer Information Systems, Creative Writing, Criminal Justice, Ecology, Earth Science, Education, English, Fine Arts, Forensic Studies, GeoChemistry, International Studies, Liberal Arts, Marketing, Mathematics, MicroBiology, Music, Natural Science, Nursing, Philosophy, Physical Education, Physics, Political Science, PreDental, PreLaw, PreMed, PreVet, Psychology, Public Health, Religion, Science, Social Science, Space Science, Spanish, Special Education, Speech, Speech Pathology, Speech Therapy, Sports Medicine, Theatre

Men's Athletic Profile

220 Sturzebecker Health Science Center
West Chester, PA 19383
Coach: Kendall Walkes
Email: kwalkes@wcupa.edu

NCAA II
Golden Rams/Purple, Gold
Phone: (610) 436-2221
Fax: (610) 436-1020

Estimated # of Men's Soccer Scholarships: 2.5
Conference: Pennsylvania State Athletic Conference
Program Profile: Highly competitive Division II program with approximately 25 % of match played against Division I. 2 max. dimension playing fields plus an additional practice facilities. Traditional fall season is played with full compliment of matches. Winter season runs from Jan. to March the spring seasons runs April to early may
History: Began in 1927, WCU has won 3 national titles, the last of which was in 1961. At this time there were no separation by division. WCU's most famous soccer alumnus is Gerry Yeagley, Coach of Indiana Univ.
Achievements: Several All-Americans; regional All-Americans; Coach of the year in 1991; several players participating in the lower professional divisions.
Coaching: Kendall Walkes, Head Coach, former international player form Trinidad and Tobago with over 50 caps, former U-23 National team Coach, was an outstanding player at Davis and Elkins, FIFA, English FA and NSCAA coaching qualifications

Roster In State: 23	**Out of State:** 3	**Out of Country:** 1
ODP State: 4	**Regional:** 0	**National:** 0
Walk-on/Other: 0	**Graduation %:** 95	**Seniors on Team:** 4

Positions Needed: Sweeper, Center-Mid, Striker
Camp or Clinic Dates: July 8-12
Most Recent Record: 11-9-0
Schedule: East Stroudsburg Univ. Dowling College, L.I.U Southampton, West Virginia Wesleyan College, Concordia College, NY
Style of Play: Attacking Style, fluid, skill oriented.

Women's Athletic Profile

South Campus Fieldhouse
West Chester, PA 19383
Coach: Jessica Reynolds
Email: jreynolds@wcupa.edu

NCAA II
Golden Rams/Purple, Gold
Phone: (610) 436-2221
Fax: (610) 436-1020

Estimated # of Women's Soccer Scholarships: None
Conference: Pennsylvania State Athletic Conference
Program Profile: Division II, approximately 25 percent of matches played against Division I. 2 maximum dimension playing fields plus additional practice facilities. Traditional Fall season is played with a full compliment of matches. Winter season runs Jan - March. Spring season runs April - early May.
History: Program began at varsity level in 1992.
Achievements: Several All-Americans, innumerable Regional All-Americans. Coach Walkes was PSAC Coach of the Year 1992.
Style of Play: Attacking, fluid, skill oriented, speed.

Westminster College - Pennsylvania

Academic Profile

New Wilmington, PA 16172

Phone:

Type: 4 Yr.,Private,Liberal Arts,Engineering
Website: http://www.westminster.edu
SAT/ACT/GPA: 840/23/2.5
Student/Faculty Ratio: 14:1
Undergraduate Enrollment: 1,700
Scholarships/Academic: Yes **Athletic:** Yes
Expenses by: Year **In State:** $ 20,000
Founded: 1852
Religion: Presbyterian
Housing: Yes
Male/Female Ratio: 1:6
Graduate Enrollment: 100
Financial Aid: Yes
Out of State: $ 20,000
Specialty: Preprofessional Programs, Business, Education
Degrees Conferred: BA, BS, B.Mus., MBA, M.Ed., MS
Programs of Study: Accounting, Art, Biology, Broadcasting, Communication, Business Administration, Chemistry, Computer Information System, Computer Science, Economics, Elementary Education, Environmental Science, Management, Political Science, Religion, Philosophy, Physics, PreLaw, PreMed, Psychology

Men's Athletic Profile

South Market Street
New Wilmington, PA 16172
Coach: Girish Thakar
Email: thakaras@westminster.edu

NCAA II
Titans/Navy Blue, White
Phone: (412) 946-7316
Fax: (412) 946-7021

Estimated # of Men's Soccer Scholarships: 1-9
Conference: Great Lakes Conference
Program Profile: We have an indoor facilities, an indoor gym for soccer, and a fitness center for off-season work-out.
History: Our program is only eleven years old. New to the NCAA, 1989 NAIA District 18 Champions; NAIA playoffs; new full-time coach in 1999. We are rebuilding the program with very good players. We have small squad and a strong schedule. We became a Division II program in 1998.
Achievements: All-Conference players were Jim Matheus and Richard Argelski; 1998 Academic All-East was Jim Matheus; All-Region and All-American player was Ryan Matheus.
Coaching: Girish Thakar, Head Coach, is entering his first year with the program. She was the former head coach at Slippery Rock University for five years. She has an English FA Badge and a NSCAA Advanced Diploma. He has coached College Youth and semi-pro player for ten years.
Style of Play: Attack-minded team, allows players to express themselves. Enjoyable to play and watch.

Widener University

Academic Profile

Chester, PA 19013-5792

Phone: 610-499-4126

Type: 4 Yr.,Private,Liberal Arts
Website: http://www.widener.edu
SAT/ACT/GPA: 800/18
Student/Faculty Ratio: 12:1
Undergraduate Enrollment: 2,400
Scholarships/Academic: Yes **Athletic:** No
Expenses by: Year **In State:** $ 21,800
Founded: 1821
Religion: Non-Affiliated
Housing: Yes
Male/Female Ratio: 1:1.2
Graduate Enrollment: 2,100
Financial Aid: Yes
Out of State: $ 21,800
Degrees Conferred: AAS, BA, BS, MA, MS, MBA, MED, EdD, JD
Programs of Study: Business Administration, Engineering, Hospitality Management, Nursing, Human Services, Arts & Science, School of Law, Criminal Justice, Communications Studies, Physical Therapy, Physics, Psychology, Biology, Chemistry, Computer Science, Mathematics, Education, Economics

Men's Athletic Profile

1 University Place
Chester, PA 19013
Coach: Fred Dohrmann
Email: Not Available

NCAA III
Pioneers/Col Blue, Gold
Phone: (610) 499-4450
Fax: (610) 499-4481

Estimated # of Men's Soccer Scholarships: None
Conference: Middle Atlantic Conference
Program Profile: 30-21-3 in the past 3 seasons. ECAC Conference playoffs in 1999. Competitive, high profile schedule and team.
History: Program Began in 1969.
Achievements: 1987 qualified for ECAC tournament; Coach of the Year in 1998.
Coaching: Fred Dohrmann, Head Coach and a USSF 'A' license.
Roster In State: 20 **Out of State:** 9 **Out of Country:** 4
Walk-on/Other: **Graduation %:** 90 **Seniors on Team:** 5
Camp or Clinic Dates: Not Available
Most Recent Record: 13-7-1
Schedule: Elizabethtown, Messiah

Women's Athletic Profile

One University Place
Chester, PA 19013-5792
Coach: Jack Shafer
Email: Jack.L.Shafer@widener.edu

NCAA III
Pioneers/Columbia Blue, Gold
Phone: (610) 499-4437
Fax: (610) 499-4481

Estimated # of Women's Soccer Scholarships: None
Conference: Middle Atlantic Conference: Commonwealth League
Program Profile: This is fifth year program at a very competitive level. The program's goal is to move forward in the conference and the region. The team plays on a grass field located at the center of the Widener University campus.
History: Our soccer program began in 1995. The women's soccer program is looking forward to moving forward in the conference and region this coming year.
Achievements: Reached Commonwealth League Championship in 1995 and Middle Atlantic Conference semi finals in 1995 and 1996.
Coaching: Jack Shafer, Head Coach, was the former men's and women's coach at Lycomming College in 1996-1999. He also was the former Assistant Men's Coach at Bethany College from 1994-1995, 1994 NCAA National Champions and NSCAA Regional Staff Coach.
Seniors on Team: 3
Positions Needed: Center Midfield, Backs, Forward
Camp or Clinic Dates: Not Available
Schedule: Susquehanna University, Elizabethtown College, Messiah College, Moravian College, Lebanon Valley College, Albright College, Juniata College, University of Scranton
Style of Play: Work out of the back, taking advantage of a strong defense. Three on the top, penetrate, using skill-speed and quickness.

Wilkes University

Academic Profile

Phone: 570-408-5000

Wilkes - Barre, PA 18766

Type: 4 Yr.,Private,Liberal Arts,Engineering
Website: http://www.wilkes.edu
SAT/ACT/GPA: 950

Founded: 1933
Religion: Non-Affiliated
Housing: Yes

Student/Faculty Ratio: 13:1
Male/Female Ratio: 1:1
Undergraduate Enrollment: 1,780
Graduate Enrollment: N/A
Scholarships/Academic: Yes
Athletic: No
Financial Aid: Yes
Expenses by: Year
In State: $ 19,000
Out of State: $ 19,000
Degrees Conferred: BA, BS, MS, MA, Ph.D.
Programs of Study: Business & Management, Communication, Engineering, Health Sciences, Life Sciences, Psychology, Social Sciences

Men's Athletic Profile

274 S. Franklin
Wilkes-Barre, PA 18766
Coach: Philip Wingert
Email: Not Available

NCAA III
Colonels/Navy, Gold
Phone: (717) 408-4020
Fax: (717) 823-9470

Estimated # of Men's Soccer Scholarships: N/A
Conference: Middle Atlantic Conference
Program Profile: The Colonels play on a natural grass field and have a brand new Munson Fieldhouse.

Women's Athletic Profile

274 S. Franklin
Wilkes-Barre, PA 18766
Coach: Melissa Elwell
Email: Not Available

NCAA III
Lady Colonels/Navy, Gold
Phone: (717) 831-4031
Fax: (717) 823-9470

Estimated # of Women's Soccer Scholarships: None
Conference: Middle Atlantic Conference
Program Profile:
History: The program began in 1988. First full-time head coach in the school's history.
Achievements: 3rd team Regional All-American - Lance Labbe.
Style of Play: Possession - short passing and zonal marking.

York College - Pennsylvania

Academic Profile

York, PA 17405-7199
Phone: 717-846-7788

Type: 4 Yr.,Private,Liberal Arts,Engineering
Founded: 1941
Website: http://www.ycp.edu
Religion: Non-Affiliated
SAT/ACT/GPA: 970/21
Housing: Yes
Student/Faculty Ratio: 18:1
Male/Female Ratio: 40:60
Undergraduate Enrollment: 3,300
Graduate Enrollment: N/A
Scholarships/Academic: Yes
Athletic: No
Financial Aid: Yes
Expenses by: Year
In State: $ 9,980
Out of State: $ 9,980
Degrees Conferred: BA, BS
Programs of Study: Contact school for program of study.

Men's Athletic Profile

Wolf Gym Country Club Road
York, PA 17405
Coach: Mark Ludwig
Email: mludwig@ycp.edu

NCAA III
Spartans/Green, White
Phone: (717) 815-1919
Fax: (717) 849-1626

Estimated # of Men's Soccer Scholarships: 0
Conference: CAC
Program Profile: We play in the South region. Next fall we will be playing in 2 tournaments at Christopher Newport and Methodist College. Our home field is located on Campus.
History: Our program began in 1968.
Achievements: Three 1st team all conference players.
Coaching: This is Coach Ludwig 2nd year. The overall team record 22-18-2.

Roster In State: 11	**Out of State:** 5	**Out of Country:** 0
ODP State: 2	**Regional:** 5	**National:**
Walk-on/Other:	**Graduation %:** 100	**Seniors on Team:** 7

Positions Needed: All
Camp or Clinic Dates: Team July 28-August 1st and August 1-5 Individual July 8-12
Most Recent Record: 14-6-1
Schedule: Christopher Newport , Gettysburg, Mary Washington, Salisbury State, Ramapo
Style of Play: Try to play possession attacking with numbers forward. Play 3-5-2 or 4-3-3 play it out wide and get cross in through central players.

Women's Athletic Profile

Country Club Road
York, PA 17405-7199
Coach: Vicki Sterner
Email: vsterner@ycp.edu

NCAA III
Spartans/Kelly Green, White
Phone: (717) 815-1517
Fax: (717) 792-0015

Estimated # of Women's Soccer Scholarships: None
Conference: Capital Athletic Conference
Program Profile: We play in the fall on a natural grass field with plans in five year time frame to renovate entire area with a new stadium.
History: Women's first season was in the fall of 1996 as a varsity sport. Our record for the first season was 3-14-0. With each incoming freshman class we feel we can build a program that is competitive with other Division III School.
Achievements: in 1997 Erin Burke and Justine Rice selected for 2nd team All-conference. in 1998 Caitlin McCracken was selected 1st team All-Conference goalkeeper, Erin Burke was 2nd team All-Conference.
Coaching: Vicki Sterner, Head Coach, 11 years coaching experience. High school coach, Coach of the Year in YIAA League 3in 1995. Keystone game coach, U-16 Club Coach, CPYSL Select Coach. Brent Kling - Assistant Coach, seven years as an assistant high school coach.
Style of Play: We play a 4-4-2 with a possessing style. We like to bring the ball down the flanks and finish with a cross.

rhode island

RHODE ISLAND

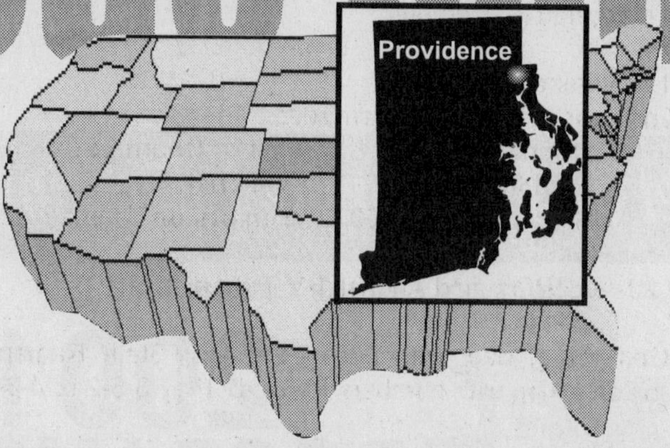

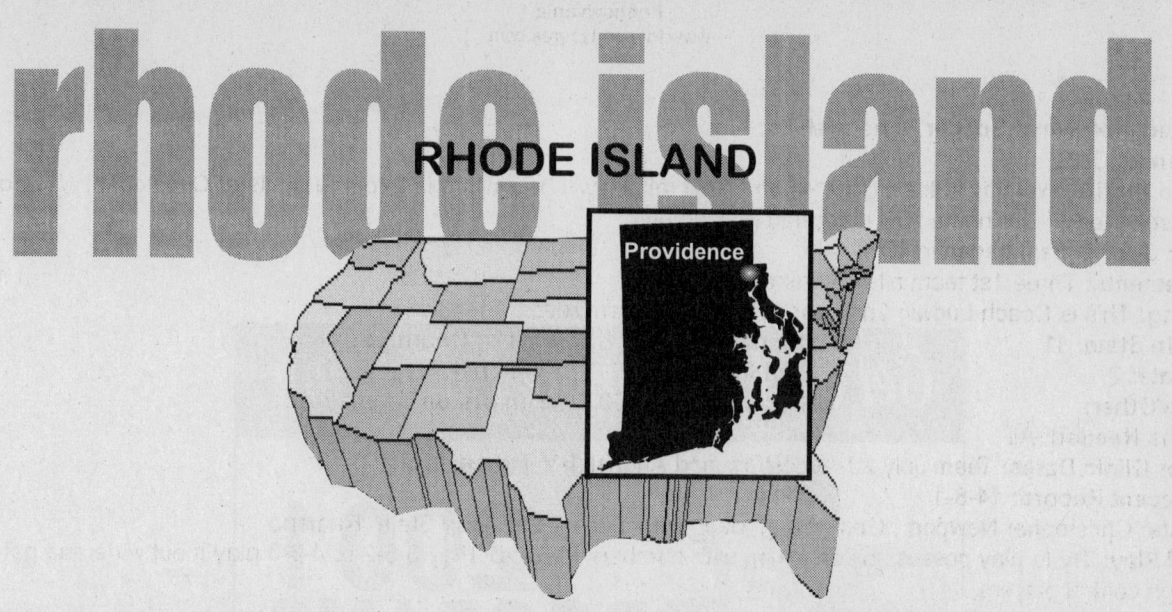

SCHOOL	CITY	AFFILIATION	PAGE
Brown University	Providence	NCAA I	1005
Bryant College	Smithfield	NCAA II	1006
Johnson & Wales University	Providence	NCAA III	1007
Providence College	Providence	NCAA I	1008
Rhode Island College	Providence	NCAA III	1009
Roger Williams University	Bristol	NCAA III	1010
Salve Regina University	Newport	NCAA III	1011
University of Rhode Island	Kingston	NCAA I	1013

Get an Ivy League Education
2000 Ivy League Champions
SUBMIT Sports Source Ad for $15.00 DISCOUNT
2001 PROGRAMS
Mike Noonan's
BROWN SOCCER CAMP
Tricolore
adidas
Elite 100 Week
(residential)
High School Jr & Sr.
All 1999 and 2000 camps sold out by May sign up early!
Boys Select Week
(residential) Ages 10-18
adidas
Official Supplier
For information: 401/863-2910
www.brownBEARS.com

Brown University

Academic Profile

Pizzitola Sports Center
Providence, RI 02912

Phone: (401) 863-2910

Type: 4 Yr.,Private,Liberal Arts,Engineering
Website: http://www.brownbears.com
SAT/ACT/GPA: 580-680v, 640-750m
Student/Faculty Ratio: 8:1
Undergraduate Enrollment: 5,500
Scholarships/Academic: Yes **Athletic:** No
Expenses by: Year **In State:** $ 26,000

Founded: 1764
Religion: Non-Affiliated
Housing: Yes
Male/Female Ratio: 1:1
Graduate Enrollment: 1,600
Financial Aid: Yes
Out of State: $ 26,000

Specialty: No specific course requirement outside of concentration
Degrees Conferred: BS, BA, MA, MS, MFA, Ph.D., MD
Programs of Study: Art, Behavioral Science, Biology, BioMedical Sciences, BioPhysics, Chemistry, Cognitive Science, Comparative Literature, Creative Writing, Electrical, Materials, Computer, Geology, GeoPhysics, NeuroScience, Religion, Theatre, Women's Studies

Men's Athletic Profile

P.O. Box 1932
Providence, RI 02912
Coach: Michael Noonan
Email: Michael_Noonan@Brown.edu

NCAA I
Bears/Red, Brown, White
Phone: (401) 863-2910
Fax: (401) 863-1436

Estimated # of Men's Soccer Scholarships:
Conference: Ivy League Conference
Program Profile: The home field is a natural grass. We have lights for night games and a seating capacity of 3,000. The Athletic Center has an astro turf and a roof. It is ideal for preparation in bad weather. There are excellent indoor facilities.
History: Our program has had only five coaches since its inception in 1926.
Achievements: 22 All-Americans, 4 Final Four, 8 Final Eight, NCAA Appearances, Ivy Champions; Herman Award Winner: Steve Rabolusky.
Coaching: Michael Noonan, Head Coach, is in his second year. He holds a USSF "A" License and a NSCAA Advanced National Diploma. He is a NSCAA Staff Coach. Brian Young, Jamie Smith ,assistant coaches, both hold Advanced National Diplomas.
Style of Play: Possession and direct offensive style with an organized collective defense. Positive possession.

Women's Athletic Profile

Box 1932
Providence, RI 02912
Coach: Phil Pincince
Email: Not Available

NCAA I
Bears/Cardinal, Brown, White
Phone: (401) 863-1952
Fax: (401) 863-1436

Estimated # of Women's Soccer Scholarships: None
Conference: Ivy League
Program Profile: Grass enclosed field, 115 x 72 yards with seating for 3,000.
History: Program began in 1977.
Achievements: 1994 Ivy Champions, 10 All-Americans, 92 All-Ivy League players.
Coaching: Phil Pincince, Head Coach, USSF 'A' license, NSCAA Advance National License,
Style of Play: Adaptive, according to the players talents.

Bryant College

Academic Profile

Phone: 401-232-6000

Smithfield, RI 02917-1284

Type: 4 Yr.,Private,Liberal Arts
Founded: 1863
Website: http://www.bryant.edu
Religion: Non-Affiliated
SAT/ACT/GPA: 820
Housing: Yes
Student/Faculty Ratio: 20:1
Male/Female Ratio: 1:1
Undergraduate Enrollment: 2,300
Graduate Enrollment: 700
Scholarships/Academic: Yes **Athletic:** Yes
Financial Aid: Yes
Expenses by: Year **In State:** $ 18,500 **Out of State:** $ 18,500
Specialty: Business
Degrees Conferred: AS, BA, BS, MS, MBA
Programs of Study: Accounting, Actuarial Science, Business Administration, Communications, Computer Information System, Economics, English, Finance, History, Information Science, International Studies, Management, Marketing

Men's Athletic Profile

1150 Douglas Pike
Smithfield, RI 02917
Coach: Seamus Purcell
Email: Not Available

NCAA II
Bulldogs/Black, Gold
Phone: (401) 232-6354
Fax: (401) 232-6361

Estimated # of Men's Soccer Scholarships:
Conference: Northeast 10 Conference
Program Profile: Play a fall schedule against top Northeast Division II teams. Facilities are state of the art (Patriot Prep Camp), with a natural grass field that is best in the northeast. Play two indoor tournaments and a light spring season.
Coaching: Seamus Purcell, Head Coach, former All-American at Providence College.
Style of Play: High pressure, offensive off defense.

Women's Athletic Profile

1150 Douglas Pike
Smithfield, RI 02917
Coach: Chris Flint
Email: cflint@bryant.edu

NCAA II
Bulldogs/Black, Gold
Phone: (401) 232-6511
Fax: (401) 232-6361

Estimated # of Women's Soccer Scholarships: None
Conference: Northeast 10 Conference
Program Profile: Program is young (new coach and young team), 3 grass fields (2 practice), 3500 seat stadium, indoor facility for 5 a side games.
History: Began in 1979
Achievements: First year Coach
Coaching: Chris Flint Head Coach, 1 year as Assit. At Springfield College DII men's program. 4 yr Head Coach DIII (M.C.L.A.), 1 yr Head DII (Bryant College), NSCAA Advanced national diploma. Jim Moore is assit. Coach with 6 years experience.
Roster in State: 3 **Out of State:** 21 **Out of Country:** 0
ODP State: 5 **Regional:** 0 **National:** 0
Walk-on/Other: 0 **Graduation %:** 100 **Seniors on Team:** 4
Positions Needed: CMF, Flank Mid, GK, FWD
Camp or Clinic Dates: TBA

Most Recent Record: 3-13-0
Schedule: Franklin Pierce, Merrimack College, Stonehill College, College of St. Rose, Lemoyne
Style of Play: Possession, build from the back.

Johnson & Wales University

Academic Profile

Providence, RI 02903
Phone: (800) 342-5598 x1614

Type: 4 Yr.,Private
Founded: 1914
Website: http://www.jwu.edu
Religion: Non-Affiliated
SAT/ACT/GPA: None/2.3 or higher
Housing: Yes
Student/Faculty Ratio: 1:25
Male/Female Ratio: 51:49
Undergraduate Enrollment: 7,500
Graduate Enrollment: 2,000
Scholarships/Academic: Yes **Athletic:** No **Financial Aid:** Yes
Expenses by: Year **In State:** $ 18,000 **Out of State:** $ 18,000
Specialty: Hospitality, Culinary Arts, Criminal Justice, Business
Degrees Conferred: As, BS, MS, MBA, Ph.D.
Programs of Study: Culinary Arts, Business, Criminal Justice, Hospitality, Marketing/Accounting Technology, Recreation/Leisure Management, Hotel/Restaurant Management, Travel & Tourism,

Men's Athletic Profile

8 Abbott Park Place
Providence, RI 02903
Coach: Gregg Miller
Email: gmiller@jwu.edu

NCAA III
Wildcats/Red, Gold
Phone: 401-598-1614
Fax: (401) 598-1601

Estimated # of Men's Soccer Scholarships: N/A
Conference: Great Northeast Athletic Conference
Program Profile: Our home field is Pierce Memorial stadium. It has 5,000 seats and natural grass. Indoor facility is on campus. Full boards with recessed goals (160 X 80 yards.). Season September through November, pre-season camp begins August 20th with strong emphasis on academic achievement.
History: Began in 1991 (club) became NCAA in 1994. Won Conference in 1993, and 1995. Runner-Up in 1998. Semi-Finalist in 1996, 1997, 1999.
Achievements: SNEAC Champions 1993; GNAC Champions 1995.
Coaching: Gregg Miller, Head Coach, is a JWU graduate. He has coached here since 1991. He played semi-professionally.
Roster In State: 1 **Out of State:** 21 **Out of Country:** 3
ODP State: 3 **Regional:** 1 **National:**
Walk-on/Other: **Graduation %:** 100 **Seniors on Team:** 5
Positions Needed: Striker, Central Midfield
Most Recent Record: 8-8-1
Schedule: Connecticut College, U-Mass Dartmouth, Rhode Island College, U-Mass Boston, Norwich University
Style of Play: Emphasis on wide play, passing and movement, hard work. Style of play will reflect the players abilities and strengths.

Women's Athletic Profile

8 Abbott Park Place
Providence, RI 02860
Coach: Chris Guay
Email: cguay@jwu.edu

NCAA III
Wildcats/Red, Black
Phone: (401) 598-1608
Fax: (401) 598-1601

Estimated # of Women's Soccer Scholarships: None
Conference: Great Northeast Athletic Conference
Program Profile: Games played at Pierce Stadium (E Providence, RI home of the RI Stingrays) New on-campus field complex to be completed in 2002 (1 game field and 2 practice field and 2 practice fields)
History: 1996: 3-13 (first year NCAA) 1997: 3-14, 1998: 9-10, 1999: 12-6-2 (first GNAC tournament appearance) 2000: 18-2-2 (GNAC regular season champs, GNAC Tournament Champs, first NCAA Tournament appearance).
Achievements: 1999 GNAC Coach of the Year, 4 players All-Conference, 2000 GNAC Coach of the Year, GNAC Player of the Year, GNAC Rookie of the Year, 7 players All-Conference.
Coaching: Chris Guay, Head Coach, Advanced National Diploma. He is entering six years at Division II school. He took over JWU in August of 1998. Luis Faria, Assistant coach, National Diploma. He is also six years at Division II before coming over to Johnson & Wales College. He coached RI ODP for six years and various club levels.

Roster in State: 0	**Out of State:** 20	**Out of Country:** 0
ODP State: 2	**Regional:**	**National:**
Walk-on/Other:	**Graduation %:** 99	**Seniors on Team:** 2

Positions Needed: All
Most Recent Record: 18-2-2
Schedule: Wheaton College (MA), Johns Hopkins Univ. Framingham State College, Salem State College
Style of Play: Attacking soccer with organized high pressure defending. Modeled after the Dutch.

Providence College

Academic Profile

Phone: 401-865-1000

Providence, RI 02918

Type: 4 Yr.,Private,Liberal Arts		**Founded:** 1917
Website: http://www.providence.edu		**Religion:** Catholic (Dominican)
SAT/ACT/GPA: 1200		**Housing:** Yes
Student/Faculty Ratio: 13:1		**Male/Female Ratio:** 4:5
Undergraduate Enrollment: 3,800		**Graduate Enrollment:** N/A
Scholarships/Academic: Yes	**Athletic:** Yes	**Financial Aid:** Yes
Expenses by: $24,600	**In State:**	**Out of State:** $ 24,600

Degrees Conferred: BA, BS, MBA, MA, MS
Programs of Study: Accountancy, African Studies, American Studies, Anthropology, Art, Asian Studies, Biology, Chemistry, Computer Science, Economics, Education, Engineering, English, Finance, Health Services, History, Humanities, Latin American Studies, Management, Marketing, Mathematics, Modern Languages, Music, Philosophy, Political Science, Psychology, Social Science, Social Work, Sociology, Theatre Arts, Theology

Men's Athletic Profile

River Avenue	**NCAA I**
Providence, RI 02918	Friars/Black, White
Coach: Brian Ainscough	**Phone:** (401) 865-2005
Email: Not Available	**Fax:** (401) 865-1231

Estimated # of Men's Soccer Scholarships: N/A
Conference: Big East Conference
History: Program began in 1968.
Achievements: 2 All-Americans
Coaching: Brian Ainscough is our Head Coach.

Women's Athletic Profile

549 River Avenue
Providence, RI 02918
Coach: Tracy Kerr
Email: tkerr@providence.edu

NCAA I
Black & White
Phone: 401-865-2032
Fax: 401-865-1231

Estimated # of Women's Soccer Scholarships: 4
Conference: Big East
Program Profile: Play on campus natural grass field; playing season is in the fall.
History: Woman's program began in 1983. Won first-ever Big East Championship and advanced to the Big East tournament, 1992 graduate of the University of Hartford, assisted one year at Yale after graduation.
Achievements: 1993 NCAA Tournament; 1993 Big East Champions; Jen Mead was named All-New England; Northeast All-American, Honda Award; Kerry Lyons - All-New England, Northeast All-American.
Coaching: Tracy Kerr-Senior All-American and 4 time Regional All-American at University of Virginia. Played in England and US Women's League. English Coaching badge and USSF "B" License.
Roster In State: 1 **Out of State:** 20 **Out of Country:**
ODP State: 10 **Regional:** 3 **National:**
Walk-on/Other: 1 **Graduation %:** 100 **Seniors on Team:** 5
Positions Needed: All
Most Recent Record: 7-11-1
Schedule: Univ. of Conn, Boston College, Brown, Notre Dame, Yale

Rhode Island College

Academic Profile

Phone: 401-456-8000

Providence, RI 02908

Type: 4 Yr.,Public,Liberal Arts
Founded: 1854
Website: http://www.rhodeislandcollege.edu
Religion: Non-Affiliated
SAT/ACT/GPA: Required
Housing: Yes
Student/Faculty Ratio: 15:1
Male/Female Ratio: 33:67
Undergraduate Enrollment: 6,873
Graduate Enrollment: 1,810
Scholarships/Academic: Yes **Athletic:** No **Financial Aid:** Yes
Expenses by: Year **In State:** $ 9,500 **Out of State:** $ 14,400
Specialty: Education
Degrees Conferred: BA, BS, BFA, BM, BSN, BSW, MA, MS, MEd
Programs of Study: Accounting, Biology, Chemistry, Music, Science, Computer Science, CIS, Economics, English, History, Justice Studies, Management, Marketing, Music, Elementary Education, Music Education, Special Education, Nursing, Physical Education, Psychology, Secondary Education, Social Work, Sociology, Art History, Art Education, Film Studies

Men's Athletic Profile

600 Mt. Pleasant Avenue
Providence, RI 02908
Coach: Len Mercurio
Email: lmercurio@ric.edu

NCAA III
Anchormen/Gold, Burgundy
Phone: (401) 456-8251
Fax: (401) 456-8514

Estimated # of Men's Soccer Scholarships: None
Conference: Little East Conference (ECAC)
Program Profile: RIC has its own field, the Rhode Island College/Track & Field Complex, directly on campus. It is natural grass and has seats for 1,500 people.

History: 1959 was the first season RIC began playing men's soccer. The program was strong in the early 70's and with second-year Head Coach, Len Mercurio, the Anchormen are on the rise once again. After enduring losing seasons for five consecutive years, in 1992-1996, RIC has posted ten wins in 1997 and 1998. Compiled a record of 242-331-63 in 42 seasons and have qualified for post-season action in 2000.
Achievements: RIC has been competitve in the Little East Conference. 2 2nd team All-LEC in 2000. Goalkeeper first team All-LEC
Coaching: Len Mercurio, Head Coach, took over the program in the Fall of 1998. He is an Legend in Rhode Island a member of the Hall of Fame, Mercurio still holds the school record for the most career goals and played professionally for 3 yrs (1981-83). He was also the Head Coach at Bryant College from 1991-93.
Roster In State: 25 **Out of State:** 0 **Out of Country:** 0
Walk-on/Other: **Graduation %:** N/A **Seniors on Team:** 6
Positions Needed: Forward, Midfield, back
Camp or Clinic Dates: Not Available
Most Recent Record: 10-9-1
Schedule: Plymouth State, Keene State, Umass-Darthmouth, Eastern Connecticut
Style of Play: Defensively minded, ball control, look to capitalize on opponent's mistake.

Women's Athletic Profile

600 Mt Pleasant Avenue
Providence, RI 02908
Coach: Nicole Barber
Email: nbarber@ric.edu

NCAA III
Anchorwomen/Gold, Burgundy
Phone: (401) 456-8252
Fax: (401) 456-8514

Estimated # of Women's Soccer Scholarships: None
Conference: Little East Conference
Program Profile: We play at the RIC Soccer/Track and Field Complex. It has a natural field with a seating capacity for 1,500 and is located on campus. It is a two year old complex and it is a state-of-the-art facility.
History: Our soccer team has been a varsity sport since 1995. RIC has continued to improve and is on the verge of becoming one of the top teams in the Little East Conference. Qualified for it's first ever post season berth in 2000. The programs All-time record is 40-58-4
Achievements: Jill Lozeau was named Second Team All-Conference as a midfielder in 1997. Joan Hecler was named Second Team All-Conference in 1996.
Coaching: Nicole Barber, Head Coach, is the only women's soccer coach that Rhode Island College has ever had. The players and program have continued to develop under her guidance. This past season, RIC finished the season with a 7-11-1 record. However, ten of the squad's 11 losses were by one goal. At Brown University, she played women's soccer, ice hockey and softball during her career.
Style of Play: Coach Barber's team relies on an "all-around" team game. The players must play as a unit and complement each other. The team looks to control the ball and take advantage of scoring opportunities at all times.

Roger Williams University

Academic Profile

Bristol, RI 02809

Phone:

Type: 4 Yr.,Private,Liberal Arts,Engineering
Website: http://www.rwu.edu
SAT/ACT/GPA: 1050
Student/Faculty Ratio: 20:1
Undergraduate Enrollment: 2,100
Scholarships/Academic: Yes **Athletic:** No
Expenses by: Year **In State:** $ 22,000
Specialty: Law School, Architecture

Founded: 1956
Religion: Non-Affiliated
Housing: Yes
Male/Female Ratio: 56:44
Graduate Enrollment: 465
Financial Aid: Yes
Out of State: $ 22,000

Degrees Conferred: BA, BS, BFA, B-Arch, Juris Doctor
Programs of Study: Art & Science, Architecture, Business, Engineering, Law

Men's Athletic Profile

One Old Ferry Road
Bristol, RI 02809
Coach: Jim Cook
Email: smithra@uwplatt.edu
NCAA III
Hawks/Royal, Gold
Phone: (401) 254-3091
Fax: (401) 254-3535
Estimated # of Men's Soccer Scholarships: None
Conference: Commonwealth Coast Conference, ECAC
Program Profile: Always top of the conference. Has three grass fields and has a natural grass playing field. Athletic facilities available. Has 20 game schedule and two tournaments.
History: Always in top 4 of conference; 60% win percentage over the last years. Began in 1st year.
Achievements: ranked #1 in state (out of 17)-1998
ranked #7 in region (out of 50)-1998
Brian Hagen-All-American-1998
Coaching: Jim Cook, Head Coach, USSF License, Advanced National (NSCAA); 25 years coaching experience. Dave Demello - Assistant Coach, USSF License, professional player (USISL), five years coaching experience.
Roster In State: 11 **Out of State:** 16 **Out of Country:**
ODP State: 3 **Regional:** **National:**
Walk-on/Other: **Graduation %:** N/A **Seniors on Team:** 2
Positions Needed: All
Camp or Clinic Dates: June 2000
Most Recent Record: 14-3-2
Schedule: Wheaton College, St. Olaf College, Washington University, Luther College, UW-Oshkosh, UW-Whitewater, University of Chicago, Augustana College
Style of Play: Direct, transitional, high pressing.

Women's Athletic Profile

One Old Ferry Road
Bristol, RI 02809
Coach: Frank Kowalik
Email: Not Available
NCAA III
Hawks/Blue, White, Gold
Phone: (401) 254-3500
Fax: (401) 254-3480

Estimated # of Women's Soccer Scholarships: None
Conference: Commonwealth Coast Conference
Program Profile: Top women's program at RWV.
History: Program began in 1991.
Style of Play: Finesse, pass-oriented, short passing, quick attack type of game. We keep the ball on the ground.

Salve Regina University

Academic Profile

Newport, RI 02840
Phone:

Type: 4 Yr.,Private,Liberal Arts
Website: http://www.salve.edu
SAT/ACT/GPA: Varies in ratio to academical performance
Student/Faculty Ratio: 16:1
Undergraduate Enrollment: 1,377
Scholarships/Academic: Yes **Athletic:** No
Founded: 1947
Religion: Catholic
Housing: Yes
Male/Female Ratio: 1:2
Graduate Enrollment: 515
Financial Aid: Yes

Expenses by: Year **In State:** $ 21,900 **Out of State:**
Degrees Conferred: Associates, Bachelors, Masters
Programs of Study: Accounting, Administration of Justice, American Studies, Art, Biology and BioMedical Sciences, Business Administration, Chemistry, CytoTechnology, Early Childhood Education, Economics, Elementary Education, English, French, History, Mathematical Science, Medical Technology, Nursing, Philosophy, Politics, PreLaw, PreMed, Psychology, Religious Studies, Secondary Education, Social Work, Sociology

Men's Athletic Profile

100 Ochre Point Avenue
Newport, RI 02840
Coach: Keith J. Cory
Email: coryk@salve.edu

NCAA III
Seahawks/Navy, White, Kelly
Phone: (401) 341-2273
Fax: (401) 341-2907

Estimated # of Men's Soccer Scholarships: 6
Conference: Commonwealth Coast Conference.
Program Profile: Play on a natural grass field.
History: Program began in 1978.
Achievements: Conference Coach of the Year, 1998 Conference Champions, 1997 Conference Champions, Regional top ten ranking 1998, 1997, 1996.
Coaching: Keith J. Cory, Head Coach, holds NSCAA Advanced National License.
Roster In State: 2 **Out of State:** 20 **Out of Country:** 0
ODP State: 15 **Regional:** 2 **National:**
Walk-on/Other: **Graduation %:** 90 **Seniors on Team:** 5
Positions Needed: Striker, sweeper, Midfield
Camp or Clinic Dates: Not Available
Most Recent Record: 10-10-2
Schedule: Wheaton College, Trinity College, Babson College, Connecticut College, West Connecticut State College,
Style of Play: Ball control, Dutch; 3-5-2.

Women's Athletic Profile

100 Ochre Point Ave.
Newport, RI 02840
Coach: Lisa Yenush
Email: yenush1@salve.edu

NCAA III
Seahawks/Navy, White
Phone: (401) 314-2247
Fax: (401) 314-2907

Estimated # of Women's Soccer Scholarships: None
Conference: Commonwealth Coast Conference
History: Program began in 1978.
Achievements: 1990 Conference Champs.
Roster in State: 0 **Out of State:** 21 **Out of Country:** 0
Walk-on/Other: **Graduation %:** 100 **Seniors on Team:**
Positions Needed: Forwards, Midfielders
Camp or Clinic Dates: Not Available
Most Recent Record: 6-13-1
Style of Play: We strive to play possession style of play. We alternate between the basic formations of 4-3-3 and 4-4-2. Our objective is to maintain ball control and dictate the speed of play.

University of Rhode Island

Academic Profile

Kingston, RI 02881
Phone: (701) 874-5231

Type: 4 Yr.,Public,Liberal Arts,Engineering
Founded: 1892
Website: http://www.uri.edu
Religion: Non-Affiliated
SAT/ACT/GPA: 1000/24+/2.5
Housing: Yes
Student/Faculty Ratio: 16:1
Male/Female Ratio: 44:56
Undergraduate Enrollment: 10,000
Graduate Enrollment: 3,000
Scholarships/Academic: Yes **Athletic:** Yes **Financial Aid:** Yes
Expenses by: Year **In State:** $ 11,582 **Out of State:** $ 19,586
Specialty: Engineering, Ocean Sciences
Degrees Conferred: BA, BS
Programs of Study: Arts & Science, Business Administration, Engineering, Human Science and Services, Nursing, Pharmacy, Resource Development, Finance, Accounting, Chemistry, Economics, Computer, History, Mechanical, Music, Electrical, Political Science

Men's Athletic Profile

3 Keaney Road-Suite 1
Kingston, RI 02881-0810
Coach: Ed Bradley
Email: jprim@uri.edu

NCAA I
Rams/Blue, White
Phone: (401) 874-2560
Fax: (401) 874-5354

Estimated # of Men's Soccer Scholarships: 9.9
Conference: Atlantic 10 Conference
Program Profile: We were Very competitive in Atlantic 10 in 1995 & 1996. We were Atlantic 10 Champs and had NCAA Berth, ranked as high as 4th in the country. We have 2 practice fields and soccer complex with lights.
History: The program began in 1963. UNR has made the tournament Tourney five times and has had 10 All-Americans.
Achievements: Produced Atlantic 10 Coach of the Year in 1995; NAISL, Regional Coach of the Year; back to back titles in 1995 & 1996; 4 All-Americans; 10 players in professional soccer; 3 players in MSL in the last three years.
Coaching: Ed Bradley, Head Coach, is in his tenth season with the program. He holds a NSCAA Advanced National Diploma and a USSF "A" License. He was named Coach of the Year in 1995. Jay Primiano, Assistant Coach, holds a USSF "A" License and a NSCAA Advanced National Diploma. John Rosendes is the Restricted Earnings Coach.
Roster In State: 6 **Out of State:** 21 **Out of Country:** 7
ODP State: 13 **Regional:** **National:** 6
Walk-on/Other: **Graduation %:** 99.9 **Seniors on Team:** 7
Positions Needed: Goalkeeper, Defense
Camp or Clinic Dates: July 16-20
Most Recent Record: 17-4-1
Schedule: Washington University, Portland University, Dayton University, James Madison University, George University, University of Massachusetts, Brown University
Style of Play: Possession, offense, high pressure defensive.

Women's Athletic Profile

303 Keaney Rd. Suite 1
Kingston, RI 02881
Coach: Shelley Smith
Email: saddison@uri.edu

NCAA I
Rams/Light Blue, Navy Blue
Phone: (401) 874-5233
Fax: (401) 874-5354

Estimated # of Women's Soccer Scholarships: 2
Conference: Atlantic 10 Conference
Program Profile: Fully-funded program with two full-time coaches. Ample practice play facilities, new stadium being constructed on site, new state of the art, lighting, natural grass with 1,500 seats.
History: 1984 was first year of the program as a varsity. increase in funding when hiring Coach Smith in 1997. Record in 1998 was 12-6-1, greatest turn-round in history of the conference.
Achievements: Coach Shelley Smith was named Coach of the Year in the Atlantic 10 Conference. Shannon Kittlson was named Rookie of the Year, 12 Atlantic 10 All-Conference.
Coaching: Shelley A. Smith, Head Coaches, hired in 1997. She served as an assistant coach at Dartmouth College in 1995-1997. Regional All-American at the University of Vermont in 1993. Assistant Coach Greg Brinn and Chrissy McCann
Roster in State: 3 **Out of State:** 22 **Out of Country:** 1
Seniors on Team: 3
Most Recent Record: 15-3-1
Style of Play: Play a possessive and attacking style.

south carolina

SOUTH CAROLINA

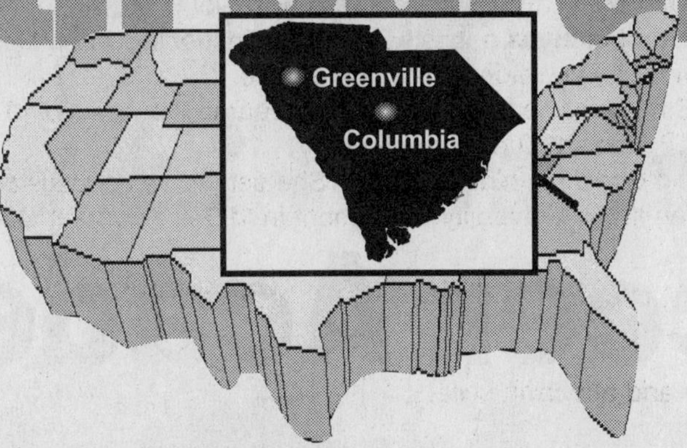

SCHOOL	CITY	AFFILIATION	PAGE
Anderson College	Anderson	NCAA II	1019
Charleston Southern University	Charleston	NCAA I	1020
Citadel	Charleston	NCAA I	1021
Clemson University	Clemson	NCAA I	1022
Coastal Carolina University	Myrtle Beach	NCAA I	1023
Coker College	Hartsville	NCAA II	1023
College of Charleston	Charleston	NCAA I	1025
Erskine College	Due West	NCAA II	1026
Francis Marion University	Florence	NCAA II	1027
Furman University	Greenville	NCAA I	1029
Lander University	Greenwood	NCAA II	1030
Limestone College	Gaffney	NCAA II	1031
Newberry College	Newberry	NCAA II	1032
Presbyterian College	Clinton	NCAA II	1033
Southern Wesleyan University	Central	NAIA	1035
Spartanburg Methodist College	Spartanburg	NJCAA	1036
University of South Carolina	Columbia	NCAA I	1038
USC - Aiken	Aiken	NCAA II	1037
USC - Spartanburg	Spartanburg	NCAA II	1039
Winthrop University	Rock Hill	NCAA I	1040
Wofford College	Spartanburg	NCAA I	1041

Best Camp Value
at 6 days, 5 nights
2001
CLEMSON
Soccer Academy
Residential
Camps
for young men
Directed by
Trevor Adair
Head Coach
Men's Soccer
Clemson University
Camp Dates 2001
Junior Elite Ages 10-13 June 22-24
Striker/ Goalkeeper Ages 10 & up June 22-24
Senior Elite Ages 14& up June 28-July 1
Advanced Ages 10 & up July 7-12
Advanced Ages 10 & up July 15-20
Advanced Ages 10 & up July 22-27
www.clemsonsocceracademy.com
email:info@clemsonsocceracademy.com
1-864-654-9300
105 Catawbah Rd. Clemson, SC 29631

Anderson College

Academic Profile

Anderson, SC 29621

Phone: (864) 231-2000

Type: 4 Yr.,Private,Liberal Arts
Founded: 1911
Website: http://www.anderson-college.edu
Religion: Baptist
SAT/ACT/GPA: 1000/not available/3.0
Housing: Yes
Student/Faculty Ratio: 14:1
Male/Female Ratio: 40:60
Undergraduate Enrollment: 1400
Graduate Enrollment: n/a
Scholarships/Academic: Yes **Athletic:** Yes **Financial Aid:** Yes
Expenses by: Year **In State:** $ 16,400 **Out of State:** $ 16,400
Specialty: Music, Art, Education
Degrees Conferred: AA, BA, BS
Programs of Study: Art, Biology, Business, Communications, Education, English, Fashion, Finances, General Studio, Graphic Art, History, Human Services & Resources, Interior Design, Journalism, Liberal Studies, Literature, Management, Marketing, Medical Technology, Music, Painting and Drawing , Physical Education, Psychology, Religion, Speech, Theatre

Men's Athletic Profile

316 Boulevard
Anderson, SC 29621
Coach: Chris Pearson
Email:

NCAA II
Trojans/Black, Gold
Phone: (864) 231-2034
Fax: (803) 231-5601

Estimated # of Men's Soccer Scholarships: N/A
Conference: Carolina-Virginia Athletic Conference
Program Profile: We are a young division II program that is getting better every year. We play a fast hard tackling brand of soccer that is exciting to watch. We have a great facility; we just got a face lift that makes the facility look real good. We play in the fall and the spring trying to get as many games as it is possible. The field is natural turf without a stadium. But we still get nice size crowds.
History: We were a Junior College until 1995. We have been a member of the CVAC since 1998.
Coaching: Chris Pearson, Head Coach.
Walk-on/Other: **Graduation %:** N/A **Seniors on Team:** 2
Positions Needed: All
Camp or Clinic Dates: Not Available
Most Recent Record: 2-15-0
Schedule: Pfeiffer, Barton
Style of Play: Hard nose attack speed in the defense; exciting to watch and to play. Built with slow build up and composure on the ball. Defensively, we will not be scared to tackle the ball.

Women's Athletic Profile

316 Boulevard
Anderson, SC 29621
Coach: Bailey Woods
Email:

NCAA II
Trojans/Black, Gold
Phone: (864) 231-2012
Fax: (864) 231-5601

Estimated # of Women's Soccer Scholarships:
Conference: Carolinas - Virginia Athletic Conference
Program Profile: We play pre-season, usually starts second week in August. Games start around the first of September and finish up round the end of October. The soccer field is natural turf and is NCAA regulation size. Have alumni bleachers for fans.

History: As a Junior College, Anderson women's team won the Region Championship and qualified for the National Tournament in 1991, 1992, 1993. We won the National Championship at the NCAA in 1995 and we became dual members (NCAA II/NAIA). We played post-season in 1996 & 1997. In 1999, we became official member of CVAC.
Achievements: Coach of the Year 1990,1991, 1992, 1993.
Seniors on Team: 3
Positions Needed: Open
Most Recent Record: 3-14-0
Schedule: Pfeiffer, Barton

Charleston Southern University

Academic Profile

9200 University Boulevard
Charleston, SC 29423-8087

Phone:

Type: 4 Yr.,Private,Liberal Arts
Founded: 1964
Website: http://www.csuniv.edu
Religion: Southern Baptist
SAT/ACT/GPA: NCAA Standard
Housing: Yes
Student/Faculty Ratio: 14:1
Male/Female Ratio: 50:50
Undergraduate Enrollment: 2,500
Graduate Enrollment: 500
Scholarships/Academic: Yes **Athletic:** Yes **Financial Aid:** Yes
Expenses by: Year **In State:** $ 13,516 **Out of State:** $ 13,516
Degrees Conferred: BA, BS, M Ed, MS
Programs of Study: Accounting, Biology, Botany, Business, Chemistry, Communications, Criminal Justice, Fine Arts, Economics, Education, English, Geology, History, Liberal Arts, Management, Mathematics, Microbiology, Music, Nursing, Political Science, Psychology, Religion

Men's Athletic Profile

P.O. Box 118087
Charleston, SC 29423-8087
Coach: Daniel Allen
Email: Not Available

NCAA I
Buccaneers/Blue, Gold
Phone: (843) 863-7067
Fax: (843) 863-7695

Estimated # of Men's Soccer Scholarships: None
Conference: Big South Conference
Program Profile: Play on a natural Bermuda grass surface with a measurements of 110x75 yards. Has an irrigation and drainage system in the middle of campus. Soccer stadium facility holds about 2,200 people.
History: Program began at varsity level in 1978.
Achievements: 6 players drafted and played in the "USISL" of "A-League". 1997 Big South Champions; NCAA Tournament Participant.
Coaching: Daniel Allen is our Head Coach. Tony Sikkala is our Assistant Coach.
Style of Play: Total soccer.

Women's Athletic Profile

9200 University Blvd.
Charleston, SC 29423-8087
Coach: Eric Terrill
Email: Eterrill@csuniv.edu

NCAA I
Buccaneers/Gold, Blue, White
Phone: (843) 863-7931
Fax: (843) 803-7695

Estimated # of Women's Soccer Scholarships: 7
Conference: Big South Conference
Program Profile: Seven years old program; play on natural grass stadium; playing season runs from August to November; fieldhouse include weight room, pool, gym and training room.

History: Program began in 1993 and had a record of 12-5-1; in 1994 record was 12-8-0; in 1995 record was 8-11-0; in 1996 record was 11-8-0 and in 1997 record was 5-13-1.
Achievements: Coach of the Year in 1993; 25 All-Conference players; 2 All-Americans; 1 Player of the Year; 16 All-Tournament players, 2 Rookie of the Year.
Coaching: Eric Terrill, Head Coach, Michigan State in 1987.

Roster in State: 8	**Out of State:** 10	**Out of Country:** 0
ODP State: 14	**Regional:** 0	**National:** 0
Walk-on/Other: 0	**Graduation %:** 90	**Seniors on Team:** 6

Positions Needed: GK, 2 Defenders, 2 Midfield, Forward
Camp or Clinic Dates: Not Available
Most Recent Record: 7-9-3
Schedule: Texas-El Paso, Univ. of Wilmington, Radford
Style of Play: 4-4-2 or 4-3-3 direction key off striker and runs 360 degree zone defense.

Citadel

Academic Profile

Phone:

Charleston, SC 29409

Type: 4 Yr.,Public,Liberal Arts		**Founded:** 1842
Website: http://www.citadel.edu		**Religion:** Non-Affiliated
SAT/ACT/GPA: 920/20/2.0		**Housing:** Yes
Student/Faculty Ratio: 17:1		**Male/Female Ratio:** 40:1
Undergraduate Enrollment: 1,641		**Graduate Enrollment:** N/A
Scholarships/Academic: Yes	**Athletic:** Yes	**Financial Aid:** Yes
Expenses by: Year	**In State:** $ 8,410	**Out of State:** $ 18,500

Specialty: The Military College of South Carolina
Degrees Conferred: BA, BS
Programs of Study: Biology, Business Administration, Chemistry, Civil Engineering, Computer Science, Education, Electrical Engineering, English, French, German, Health and PE, History, Mathematics, Physics, Political Science, Psychology, Spanish

Men's Athletic Profile

171 Moultrie Street
Charleston, SC 29409
Coach: Joel Christy
Email: Not Available

NCAA I
Bulldogs/Citadel (sky) Blue
Phone: (843) 953-5902
Fax: (843) 953-5058

Estimated # of Men's Soccer Scholarships: None
Conference: Southern Conference.
Program Profile: Natural turf; field located on the Ashley River.
History: Began as a club in 1970, varsity in 1975. First Alumnus (1989), Joel Christy became head coach of the program in the Fall of 1995.
Achievements: Southern Conference tournament runner-up 1988,1990. 7 players named All-South.
Coaching: Joel Christy, Head Coach, 1995 was the first year as head coach, previous two years served as the assistant coach, Advanced NSCAA National Coaching Diploma.
Style of Play: We play an attractive style in which we build from the back, stress possession and utilization of the field' with.

Clemson University
Academic Profile

Phone: 864-656-3311

Clemson, SC 29633

Type: 4 Yr.,Public,
Website: http://www.clemson.edu
SAT/ACT/GPA: Avg. 1172/3.7
Student/Faculty Ratio: 17/1
Undergraduate Enrollment: 12,710
Scholarships/Academic: Yes **Athletic:** Yes
Expenses by: Year **In State:** $8,642
Founded: 1889
Religion: Non-Affiliated
Housing: Yes
Male/Female Ratio: 54/46
Graduate Enrollment: 3,800
Financial Aid: Yes
Out of State: $14,836
Specialty: Agricultural
Degrees Conferred: BS, BA, Masters, Ph.D.
Programs of Study: 70 fields of study in 5 colleges: Agriculture, Forestry and Life Sciences; Architecture' Arts and Humanities; Business and Public Affairs; Engineering and Science; Health , Education and Human Development

Men's Athletic Profile

P.O. Box 31
Clemson, SC 29633-0031
Coach: Trev Adair
Email: tbrambl@clemson.edu

NCAA I
Tigers/Orange, Purple
Phone: (864) 656-1944
Fax: (864) 656-7324

Estimated # of Men's Soccer Scholarships: TBA
Conference: Atlantic Coast Conference
Program Profile: One of the finest soccer stadiums in America, seats 10,000. Also has one of the best practice facilities and weight rooms in America. The fields have natural grass playing surface.
History: Program began in 1967. National Champions in 1984 & 1987.
Achievements: 12 ACC Championships, 2 National Championships, 6 Final Four appearances, 1987 Hermann Trophy - Bruce Murray, 13 All-Americans, 12 ACC Players of the Year, 24 Professionals.
Coaching: Trevor Adair is our Head Coach. He is entering fifth year at Clemson. He holds USSF National Staff Coach, Region I Staff Coach, USSF 'A' license and Northern Ireland Preliminary Badge. Todd Bramble is our Assistant Coach. He holds "A" License. Andy McMahon is our Assistant Coach. He holds "B" License.

Women's Athletic Profile

P.O. Box 31
Clemson, SC 29633
Coach: TBA
Email: Check Web Site

NCAA I
Lady Tigers/Orange, Blue
Phone: (864) 656-1970
Fax: (864) 656-7324

Estimated # of Women's Soccer Scholarships:
Conference: Atlantic Coast Conference (ACC)
Program Profile: Clemson offers a top notch strength training facility with 14,000 square feet. Student-athlete enrichment: Vicker Hall has 28 tutorial rooms, 11 classrooms, and 75 personal computers. The nation's finest facilities available to student-athletes. Riggs field: Bermuda grass, 6500 seat grandstand with 2000 additional bleacher seating.
History: Clemson has fielded a women's soccer team since 1994. Clemson has been selected to the NCAA tournament each season while making 2 Elite Eight appearances in addition to a Sweet 16 appearance in 1998. The lady tigers have played in the ACC Tournament finals in 2 seasons.
Achievements: Sara Burkett-All-American 1997, 1998. Numerous All-ACC and All-South Selections.
Roster in State: 4 **Out of State:** 19 **Out of Country:** 0

ODP State: 21 **Regional:** 13 **National:** 4
Walk-on/Other: 2 **Graduation %:** 100 **Seniors on Team:** 3
Positions Needed: ALL
Camp or Clinic Dates: June 15-17, June 18-22, July 12-15, Aug 3-5
Most Recent Record: 19-3-1
Schedule: UNC-Chapel Hill, Florida, UCLA, Virginia, Wake Forest, Maryland, Richmond, Duke
Style of Play: "Possession" We combine throughout the field to get to goal.

Coastal Carolina University

Academic Profile

Phone:

Myrtle Beach, SC 29578

Type: 4 Yr.,Public,Liberal Arts
Founded: 1954
Website: http://www.coastal.edu
Religion: Non-Affiliated
SAT/ACT/GPA: 900/20/2.5
Housing: Yes
Student/Faculty Ratio: 17:1
Male/Female Ratio: 1:2
Undergraduate Enrollment: 4,500
Graduate Enrollment: 500
Scholarships/Academic: Yes **Athletic:** Yes **Financial Aid:** Yes
Expenses by: Year **In State:** $ 8,020 **Out of State:** $ 13,240
Specialty: Business, Marine Sciences
Degrees Conferred: BA, BS, MED, MBA
Programs of Study: Accounting, Finance, Management, Marketing, Elementary Education, Physical Education, Secondary Education, Biology, Chemistry, Computer Science, Marine Science, Mathematics, Sociology, Psychology, Art Studio, Dramatic Arts, English, History, Political Science

Men's Athletic Profile

P.O. Box 261954
Myrtle Beach, SC 29528-6054
Coach: Shaun Docking
Email: sdocking@coastal.edu

NCAA I
Chanticleers/Teal, White
Phone: (843) 349-2803
Fax: (843) 349-2893

Estimated # of Men's Soccer Scholarships: 9.9
Conference: Big South Conference
Program Profile: We have 7 Bermuda turf water system fields, a 6,000-seat lighted stadium field, an Olympic size swimming pool, a state of the art weight room and "the beach" is only seven miles away.
History: Our program is 17 years of existence with an overall record of 197-130-18.
Achievements: Coach Shaun Docking, was named Big South Coach of the Year; 2 NCAA Tournament; 5 Big South Conference Championships; 1 All-American; 10 Regional All-Americans; 2 Big-South Player of the Year; 20 players now playing in the pros.
Coaching: Shaun Docking is our Head Coach. He is entering his second season with the program. He holds a USSF "A" License and a NSCAA Advanced License. He is Director of Coaching at South Carolina ODP. He was named Big South Conference Coach of the Year. Dermont Mcrane is the Assistant Coach, holds a FA Prelim License.
Style of Play: Possession, oriented.

Coker College

Academic Profile

Phone:

Hartsville, SC 29550

Type: 4 Yr.,Private,Liberal Arts
Founded: 1908
Website: http://www.coker.edu
Religion: Non-Affiliated

SAT/ACT/GPA: 850/17/2.5
Housing: Yes
Student/Faculty Ratio: 10:1
Male/Female Ratio: 47:53
Undergraduate Enrollment: 900
Graduate Enrollment: N/A
Scholarships/Academic: Yes
Athletic: Yes
Financial Aid: Yes
Expenses by: Year
In State: $ 19,000
Out of State: $ 19,000
Specialty: Preprofessional Programs, Divinity
Degrees Conferred: BA, BS, BME
Programs of Study: Art, Biology, Chemistry, Communication, Business, Communications, Dance, Drama, Education, English, History, Political Science, Physical Education, Music, Graphic Design, Photography, French, Psychology, Mathematics, Computer Science, Sociology, Spanish, Religion, Accounting, International Studies, Criminology, Theatre, Political Science, Exercise Science, Medical Technology

Men's Athletic Profile

300 E College Avenue
Hartsville, SC 29550
Coach: Chris Dax
Email: cdax@pascal.coker.edu

NCAA II
Cobras/Navy, Gold
Phone: (843) 383-8165
Fax: (843) 383-8167

Estimated # of Men's Soccer Scholarships:
Conference: Carolina-Virginia Athletic Conference
Program Profile: Bermuda grass, lighted field, irrigation system on field. Within an eleven team conferences, we fight through out the season to qualify for the eight team conference playoffs in 17 years the program has been around.
History: Tim Greggs founded men's soccer program in 1980, current Athletic Director. Coker competed in NAIA through 1994 and is now affiliated with NCAA II.
Achievements: Mike Wallace - one-time All-American and Senior Bowl participants; 5 All-South players; All-Region; All-District; All-Conference; All-American in 1989 - Sheldon Brthaite' Academic All-American in 1989-1990 - Patrick Brooks' NAIA Senior Bowl participants: Mike Wallace in 1989, Pedro Papadopoulos in 1991.
Coaching: Chris Dax, Head Coach, NCAA Licensed, USSF certified, BS in Physiology at Michigan State University in 1992, MA in Psychology at Washington College in 1996. Mike Kinnalyy - Assistant Coach, NSCAA License, previous coach at St. Mary College, New York, NCAA III - currently coaches Hartsville High School in the Spring.
Style of Play: Strong defensive principles, indirect style but primarily dependent on the player's abilities and strength.

Women's Athletic Profile

300 E College Avenue
Hartsville, SC 29550
Coach: Rohan Naraine
Email: rohan.naraine@coker.edu

NCAA II
Cobras/Navy, Gold, White
Phone: (843) 383-8168
Fax: (843) 383-8167

Estimated # of Women's Soccer Scholarships: 2.5
Conference: Carolina-Virginias Athletic Conference
Program Profile: Coker plays year round and competes in a strong fall (12) team Conference with nationally ranked teams. Only 8 teams make the CUAC Conference Tournament. Most home games are played under the lights on our beautiful Bermuda grass field that measures 120 x 75 yards. Coker is comprised of players from South Carolina and 10 other states. We have a great soccer atmosphere to play in.
History: The first women's soccer program began in 1987. Coach Tim Griggs started the program. Coach Rohan O. Naraine took over the program in 1998. Coach Griggs is now the full time Athletic Director.
Achievements: 3 CVAC Conference titles, 3 All-Americans, 4 SR Bowl Players, 15 AU South Players, 12 All-Conference Players, 3 NSCAA Academic All-American Players, 10 NSCAA All-South Academic Players.

Coaching: Rohan Naraine, Head Coach, has an NSCAA National diploma and a FIFA Olympic Solidarity coaching diploma. He is a South Carolina ODP State coach. He was in the Guyana South America National Coaching Staff. He was in the men's and women's national teams. He coached at Beaufort Academy from 1990 to 1998 where he won 8 private school state championships. He went to school in London, England. He is a 1986 graduate from N.C.Wesleyan. Steve Berzins, Assistant Coach, has an NSCAA diploma. He was a NECSA club coach.

Roster in State: 11 **Out of State:** 11 **Out of Country:** 0
ODP State: 3 **Regional:** 0 **National:** 0
Walk-on/Other: 2 **Graduation %:** 100 **Seniors on Team:** 2
Positions Needed: ALL
Camp or Clinic Dates: July 30-Aug 3
Most Recent Record: 7-11-0
Schedule: Belmont Abbey, Lees McRae, Longwood, Queens, Wingate, Barton, Pfieffer, Limestone, Erskine, Anderson.
Style of Play: (4-4-2) 3-4-3) Attacking soccer possession play with quick counterattacking style. Very strong aggressive defensive style with all players attacking when we win the ball. A very disciplined team who works hard together as a team.

College of Charleston

Academic Profile

Phone: (843) 953-5583

Charleston, SC 29424

Type: 4 Yr.,Public,Liberal Arts,Engineering **Founded:** 1770
Website: http://www.cofc.edu **Religion:** Non-Affiliated
SAT/ACT/GPA: 1130/25/3.1 **Housing:** Yes
Student/Faculty Ratio: 19:1 **Male/Female Ratio:** 3:1
Undergraduate Enrollment: 11,000 **Graduate Enrollment:** 1,500
Scholarships/Academic: Yes **Athletic:** Yes **Financial Aid:** Yes
Expenses by: Year **In State:** $ 7,290 **Out of State:** $ 10,780
Specialty: Very Broad
Degrees Conferred: BA, BS, MA, MS, MED
Programs of Study: Accounting, Anthropology, Art, BioChemistry, Biology, Business and Management, Chemistry, Classics, Communications, Computer Information Systems, Computer Science, Economics, Education, Elementary Education, English, French, Geology, German, Greek, History, Marine Biology, Mathematics, Music, Nursing, Optometry, Philosophy, Physical Education, Physics, Podiatry, Political Science, PreDentistry ,PreMed, Psychology, Social Science, Spanish, Special Education, Theatre, Urban Studies, Veterinary Studies

Men's Athletic Profile

30 George Street
Charleston, SC 29424
Coach: Ralph Lundy
Email: peacock@cofc.edu

NCAA I
Cougars/Maroon, Silver
Phone: (843) 953-8253
Fax: (843) 953-8296

Estimated # of Men's Soccer Scholarships: None
Conference: Southern Conference
Program Profile: New stadium ready to play in 1999 and will have 2,000 seats which is located at Patriot Point overlooking the ocean.
History: Participated in Division I since 1991. Won TAAC 5 straight years, finished 3rd in Southern Conference last year. Went to NCAA Final in 1994 before losing to UCLA in overtime. Participated in NCAA Tournament four of the past six years.
Achievements: Coach Ralph Lundy was named TAAC Coach of the Year in 1993 & 1994; TAAC Champion in 1993 & 1994; Jr. Rashad Miller was US U-23 National Team; 2nd team All-TAAC.

Coaching: Ralph Lundy, Head Coach, in his 23rd year, 11th at Charlestone. He compile a record is 262-141-25 overall. 131-70-12 at Charleston. He has been named South Carolina Coach of the Year three times, he has won 7 District and 3 NAIA Tournament Appearances. He also coach 18 All-Americans and 8 National Team members. Jeff Peacock - Assistant Coach. Todd Siedel - Administration. Jeremy Ransom and Paul Suarez, Assistant Coaches.
Style of Play: High pressure - defense oriented.

Women's Athletic Profile

30 George Street
Charleston, SC 29424
Coach: Ronnie Covelskie
Email: hillrc@admin.cofc.edu

NCAA I
Cougars/Maroon, White
Phone: (843) 953-5583
Fax: (843) 953-8296

Estimated # of Women's Soccer Scholarships: 7
Conference: Southern Conference
Program Profile: The Cougars' play on an incredibly picturesque field; one entire side has a sunset view of the ocean. Playing season is in the fall; member of NCAA Division I; home field is called Patriot Point which is natural grass. We have a new stadium and locker room facilities.
History: The program started in 1993.
Achievements: Coach of the Year in 1995, All-Conference Players, Conference players of the week, All-Region Players, Academic All-Region Players.
Coaching: Ronnie Coveleskie, Head Coach.
Roster in State: 2
Out of State: 20
Out of Country: 1
ODP State: 15
Regional: 1
Walk-on/Other: 0
Seniors on Team: 3
Positions Needed: forwards and midfielders
Camp or Clinic Dates: June
Most Recent Record: 4-12-2
Schedule: Univ. of Georgia, Auburn, NC State, Furman, Davidson, East Tenn State, Georgia State

Erskine College

Academic Profile

Due West, SC 29639

Phone:

Type: 4 Yr.,Private,Liberal Arts
Website: http://www.erskine.edu
SAT/ACT/GPA: Required
Student/Faculty Ratio: 13:1
Undergraduate Enrollment: N/A
Scholarships/Academic: Yes
Athletic: Yes
Expenses by: Year
In State: $ 19,762
Founded: 1839
Religion: Non-Affiliated
Housing: Yes
Male/Female Ratio: 1:3
Graduate Enrollment: N/A
Financial Aid: Yes
Out of State:
Specialty: Sciences, Business, Education
Degrees Conferred: BA, BS
Programs of Study: Accounting, Athletic Training, Behavioral Science, Biblical Studies, Biology, Business and Management, Chemistry, Early Childhood Education, Elementary Education, English, French, History, Mathematics, Music, Music Education, Natural Science, Physical Education, Physics, Psychology, Religion, Spanish, Special Education, Sports Administration

Men's Athletic Profile

Soccer Office
Due West, SC 29639
Coach: Billy Lesesne
Email: Not Available

NCAA II
Flying Fleet/Maroon, Gold
Phone: (864) 379-8859
Fax: (864) 379-3164

Estimated # of Men's Soccer Scholarships: N/A
Conference: Independent
Program Profile: Huggins Field has a Bermuda playing surface, 120 x 70. Faire Media Center is located on playing site.
History: Program began in 1966
Achievements: 13 District 6 NAIA titles, 7 area titles, 21 NAIA All-Americans.
Coaching: Billy Lesesne, Head Coach, former All-American and All-South player at Erskine, served as Assistant Coach at College of Charleston, member of South Carolina ODP staff and State Coach for 1976 boys.
Style of Play: Attack based on the priority of ball possession. Style of play adjusted to maximize ability of players. Premium placed on hard work and technical development.

Women's Athletic Profile

P.O. Box 338
Due West, SC 29639
Coach: Brad McCarty
Email: mccarty@erskine.edu

NCAA II
Flying Fleet/Maroon, White
Phone: (864) 379-8706
Fax: (864) 379-2197

Estimated # of Women's Soccer Scholarships: 3
Conference: Carolinas-Virginia Athletic
Program Profile: The Women's soccer programs at Erskine College is well-founded and is given widespread support across the campus. The team plays on Higgins Field, a 120x75 lighted Bermuda grass field that provides excellent seating of approx. 500 with a press box and scoreboard. The women's soccer team has their own locker room, a three year agreement with Umbro, and is able to offer athletic scholarships.
History: Erskine College has had a long tradition of a successful women's soccer program, dating back to it's inaugural season in 1984. The women's soccer team earned Erskine it's highest national finish ever, losing 1-0 to Berry College in the 1987 NAIA Championship game. Sine 1992, Erskine has been a member of NCAA Division II, after previously participating under the auspices of the South Carolina Intercollegiate Athletic Association (SCIAA), (SIAA), (NAIA). 1995 became a member of NCAA DII conference which has 12 members.
Achievements: 2000-Three All-Conference Players, 1997- Conference Champions, 1987-National Runner-up
Coaching: Brad McCarty, is in his first year as Head Women's Soccer Coach. Brad has been the head coach and physical education instructor at Hesston College for the past six years. Coaching his team to two regional play-off appearance. He played four season for the Charlotte Eagles a USL professional team. Assistant Jodi McCarty she brings a strong background in soccer. Jodi was an integral part of the women's soccer team at Messiah and was named First-Team All-Mid Atlantic Conference all four years of competition.
Roster in State: 5 **Out of State:** 14 **Out of Country:** 0
ODP State: 7 **Regional:** 1
Graduation %: 82 **Seniors on Team:** 7
Positions Needed: Midfield, Defenders, Goalkeeper
Most Recent Record: 10-7-1
Schedule: Presbyterian College, Belmont Abbey College, Longwood Univ. Queens College, Lees McRae, Pfeiffer College, Lander Univ. Barton College.
Style of Play: We play with a combination of direct and indirect play that balances possession with an attacking style of soccer. We play with an aggressive attitude on the field, and look to win the 50/50 balls in the midfield. Last, we emphasize team unity and the importance of recognizing the effectiveness of a collective group.

Francis Marion University
Academic Profile

Florence, SC 29501
Phone: (843) 661-1237

Type: 4 Yr.,Public,Liberal Arts
Website: http://www.fmarion.edu
Founded: 1970
Religion: Non-Affiliated

SAT/ACT/GPA: 940/2.2
Housing: Yes
Student/Faculty Ratio: 18:1
Male/Female Ratio: 45:55
Undergraduate Enrollment: 3,400
Graduate Enrollment: 600
Scholarships/Academic: Yes
Athletic: Yes
Financial Aid: Yes
Expenses by: Year
In State: $ 7,420
Out of State: $ 10,800
Specialty: Comprehensive University
Degrees Conferred: BA, BS, BBA, BGS and Graduate Degrees in Business Administration Education and Psychology
Programs of Study: Accounting, Art, Art Education, Biology, Business Administration, Economics, Chemistry, Computer Science, Education, English, Finance, Health Physics, History, International Studies Management, Marketing, Mass Communications, Math, Medical Technology, Physics, Political Science, Psychology, Sociology, Spanish, Theatre Arts, Visual Arts, PreDental, PreEngineering, PreLaw, PreMedical, PreNursing, PrePharmacy, PreVeterinary

Men's Athletic Profile

P.O. Box 100547
Florence, SC 29501-0547
Coach: Murray Hartzler
Email: Mhartzler@Fmarion.edu

NCAA II
Patriots/Red, White, Blue
Phone: (803) 661-1231
Fax: (803) 661-4645

Estimated # of Men's Soccer Scholarships: Varies
Conference: Peach Belt Athletic Conference
Program Profile: Natural grass service which measures 120x70 yards and is Bermuda. Enclosed stadium can seat 1000. Play a fall schedule and spring exhibition schedule.
History: Our program began in 1975.
Achievements: The team produced 2 All-Americans, one in 1997 and one in 1998; 1 player signed professionally in 1998; three All-Conference players, two All-Region players in 1998. 1998 Regional Coach of the Year, have had six All-Region players. Coach Hartzler is the All-time most winning coach in school history. Team has improved in record every year since 1994
Coaching: Murray Hartzler, Head Coach, named four times Coach of the Year and named once Regional Coach of the Year. He holds Advanced National Diploma, NSCAA and USS Coaching License. Assistant Coach-Martin Beall.
Roster In State: 12
Out of State: 7
Out of Country: 2
ODP State: 10
Regional: 2
National: 0
Walk-on/Other: 0
Graduation %: 70
Seniors on Team: 4
Positions Needed: Forward, Midfield
Camp or Clinic Dates: June 11-15, July 30-August 3
Most Recent Record: 17-3-1
Schedule: USC Spartanburg, Clayton State, North Florida, Lander, Wingate, Queens
Style of Play: Zone defense in the back. Creativity and attack at speed in front half- possession out of the back.

Women's Athletic Profile

P.O. Box 100547
Florence, SC 29501
Coach: Murray Hartzler
Email: Mhartzler@fmarion.edu

NCAA II
Lady Patriots/Royal, White, Blue
Phone: (843) 661-1237
Fax: (843) 661-4645

Estimated # of Women's Soccer Scholarships: Varies
Conference: Peach Belt Athletic Conference
Program Profile: The Patriots play on a Bermuda grass field that measures 120 x 70 and has 500 seats. We play a spring season addition to the traditional fall season.

Furman University

Academic Profile

Greenville, SC 29613

Phone: 864-294-2000

Type: 4 Yr.,Private,Liberal Arts
Website: http://www.furman.edu
SAT/ACT/GPA: Open
Student/Faculty Ratio: 12:1
Undergraduate Enrollment: 2,500
Scholarships/Academic: Yes
Athletic: Yes
Expenses by: Year
In State: $ 22,000

Founded: 1820
Religion: Non-Affiliated
Housing: Yes
Male/Female Ratio: 49:51
Graduate Enrollment: 250
Financial Aid: Yes
Out of State: $ 22,000

Degrees Conferred: BA, BM, BGS, BS, MAEd, MSChem
Programs of Study: Art, Asian Studies, Biology, Chemistry, Classics, Communications, Computer Science, Drama, Earth & Environment Science, Economics, Business, Education, Engineering, English, Health & Exercise Science, History, Business, Education, Engineering Modern Languages, Music, Philosophy, Physics, Political Sciences, PreMed, PreLaw, Psychology, Religion, Sociology, Women's Studies

Men's Athletic Profile

3300 Poinsett Highway
Greenville, SC 29613
Coach: Doug Allison
Email: doug.allison@furman.edu

NCAA I
Paladins/Purple, White, Black
Phone: (864) 294-2011
Fax: (864) 294-3059

Estimated # of Men's Soccer Scholarships: 0
Conference: Southern Conference
Program Profile: New stadium built in 1995 - Eugene E Stone III Soccer Stadium - has 3,000 seats, press box, lights, and natural grass.
History: Our program began in 1967 with an all-time record of 279-226-41. We have only had 4 Coaches in the history of the program.
Achievements: 3 trips to NCAA Tournament; Coach of the Year in 1995,1996,1999; NSCAA Coach of the Year 1999; Conference titles; All-Americans
Coaching: Doug Allison, Head Coach, USSF 'A' license, NSCAA Advanced National license, former 4 years assistant at South Carolina, 2 years assistant at North Carolina, earned Master's in PE, Recreation and Sports Science, played 4 years at South Carolina. Bret Boulware and Ryan Higginbotham - Assistant Coaches.
Roster In State: 1
Out of State: 25
Out of Country: 3
ODP State: 6
Regional: 10
National: 5
Walk-on/Other: 0
Graduation %: N/A
Seniors on Team: 2
Positions Needed: Goalkeeper, Central Mid, Forward, Defender
Camp or Clinic Dates: July 2-6, 9-13
Most Recent Record: 21-2-1
Schedule: Clemson, South Carolina, UAB, Brown, CS Fullerton, South Florida, UNC Greensboro, Bowling Green, College of Charleston, Davidson
Style of Play: 4-4-2 Winger style.

Women's Athletic Profile

330 Poinseh Highway
Greenville, SC 2961-5510
Coach: Brian Lee
Email: brian.lee@furman.edu

NCAA I
Paladins, Purple, Black & White
Phone: 864-294-2053
Fax: 864-294-3059

Estimated # of Women's Soccer Scholarships: 6.5
Conference: Southern Conference
Program Profile: 3,000 seating capacity at Stone Stadium. Bermuda practice and playing surface. NCAA I program play in the Southern Conference.
History: The program began in 1994. In 1995 the team with the Southern Conference Champions. In 1996 the team finished third in the conference. The 1997 record was 12-6-2 and in 1998 record was 13-8-0, 1999 20-3-0, and in 2000 20-3-0.
Achievements: Southern Conference Champion in 1995, 1999, 2000. 3 NSCAA All-Americans, 7 NSCAA All-Southeast selection, 2 Southern Conference Player of the Year, 34 All-Southern Conference Players, 4 time Southern Coach of the Year.
Coaching: Brian Lee, Head Coach, graduate from Furman in 1993. He was named Southern Conference Coach of the Year in 1995 & 1998. Assistant Coaches Laura Wise and Andrew Burr.
Roster In State: 2
Out of State: 20
Out of Country: 0
ODP State: 21
Regional: 6
National: 0
Walk-on/Other:
Graduation %: 100
Seniors on Team: 4
Positions Needed: D, M, F, GK
Camp or Clinic Dates: June 29-July 3
Most Recent Record: 20-3-0
Schedule: Baylor, Vanerbilt, SMU, Arizona State, Clemson, UNC-Greensboro, UNC-Charlotte
Style of Play: Attacking oriented possession.

Lander University

Academic Profile

Greenwood, SC 29649
Phone:

Type: 4 Yr.,Public,Liberal Arts,Engineering
Founded: 1872
Website: http://www.lander.edu
Religion: Non-Affiliated
SAT/ACT/GPA: 840
Housing: Yes
Student/Faculty Ratio: 16:1
Male/Female Ratio: 40:60
Undergraduate Enrollment: 2,700
Graduate Enrollment: 300
Scholarships/Academic: Yes
Athletic: Yes
Financial Aid: Yes
Expenses by: Year
In State: $ 7,200
Out of State: $ 10,000
Degrees Conferred: BA, BS, M.Ed., MBA
Programs of Study: Biology, Business Administration, Chemistry, Computer Science, Elementary Education, Engineering, English, Health Care, Management, History, Mass Communications & Theatre, Mathematics, Allied Health, Music, Nursing, Physical Education, Political Science, Psychology, Sociology, Criminal Justice, PreLaw, PreMed, PrePharmacy, PreOptometry

Men's Athletic Profile

Athletic Department
Greenwood, SC 29649
Coach: Van Tayl
Email: vtaylor@lander.edu

NCAA II
Senators/Royal Blue, Gold
Phone: (864) 388-8291
Fax: (864) 388-8889

Estimated # of Men's Soccer Scholarships: 7
Conference: Peach Belt Athletic Conference
Program Profile: Play on a natural Bermuda grass field which measures 120x80 yards. Physical Education and Exercise Science Complex consists of: 6 racquetball courts, 3 auxiliary gyms, Olympic size pool, weight training center, indoor running track, dance studio, human performance lab and multi-purpose rooms.
History: Program began in 1980. Celebrating 20 years in 1999; NCAA Division II since 1991, NAIA in 1980-1990, NAIA District champions in 1987, 1990 & 1991; career record is 199-82-11; 70% winning percentage.

Achievements: PBAC Conference Champions in 1991, 1993, 1995 & 1996; PBAC Tournament Champions in 1991 & 1996; NCAA Tournament in 1996, Stilian Shiskov - 3 time All-American and currently plays for Atlanta Silverbacks A League.
Coaching: Van Taylor, Head Coach, 13 years at Lander; USSF "A" License, BS in Physical Education, Masters in Education. George Snyder - Assistant Coach, USSF "A" License, USSF National Youth License, UEF "A" License SCYSA Director of Coaching.
Roster In State: 12 **Out of State:** 13 **Out of Country:** 8
Walk-on/Other: **Graduation %:** 89 **Seniors on Team:** 5
Positions Needed: Goalkeeper, Defenders
Camp or Clinic Dates: June 19-23, July 2-7, July 9-14
Most Recent Record: 12-7-1
Schedule: USC Spartanburg, Francis Marion, North Florida, Alabama Huntsville, Wingate, Queens, Presbyterian, Clayton State, Augusta State, Tusculum
Style of Play: Attacking style, 3-5-2 system of play.

Women's Athletic Profile

CPO 6016
Greenwood, SC 29649
Coach: George Sugden
Email: gsugden@lander.edu

NCAA II
Lady Senators/Royal Blue, Gold
Phone: (864) 388-8896
Fax: (864) 388-8889

Estimated # of Women's Soccer Scholarships: 4.5
Conference: Peach Belt Athletic Conference
Program Profile: Fenced in game field (125x80), pressbox, bleachers, natural turf. Our season is in the Fall but we also have a Spring season for six weeks. Superb athletic training facilities and have our own trainer.
History: We are 3 years old and our records have been 1st year 1-14, 2nd 9-8-1, and 3rd 7-10-0
Coaching: George Sugden is Head Coach.
Roster in State: 20 **Out of State:** 5
ODP State: 12
Graduation %: 100 **Seniors on Team:** 2
Positions Needed: GK, Sweeper, Strikers
Camp or Clinic Dates: July
Most Recent Record: 7-10-0
Schedule: U. North Florida, Francis Marion, Presbyterian College, Tusculum, Lees McRae, Wingate, Mars Hill, USC-Spartanburg, USC-Aiken.
Style of Play: Possession on the floor, zonal defending, system varies 3-4-3, 4-4-2, 3-5-2 are what we used the year depending on opponents.

Limestone College
Academic Profile

Gaffney, SC 29340
Phone:

Type: 4 Yr.,Private,Liberal Arts
Website: Not Available
SAT/ACT/GPA: 800/18
Student/Faculty Ratio: 11:1
Undergraduate Enrollment: 500
Scholarships/Academic: Yes **Athletic:** Yes
Expenses by: Year **In State:** $ 12,500
Degrees Conferred: BA, BS

Founded: 1845
Religion: Non-Affiliated
Housing: Yes
Male/Female Ratio: 55:45
Graduate Enrollment: N/A
Financial Aid: Yes
Out of State: $ 12,500

Programs of Study: Applied Art, Art, Biology, Business Administration, Computer Science, Early Childhood Education, Education, Elementary Education, English, Guidance, History, Humanities, Liberal Arts, Management, Math, Music, Physical Education, PreDentistry, PreLaw, PreMed, Psychology, Science, Social Work

Men's Athletic Profile

1115 College Drive
Gaffney, SC 29340
Coach:
Email: Not Available

NCAA II
Saints/Blue, Gold, White
Phone: (864) 488-4568
Fax: (864) 487-8706

Estimated # of Men's Soccer Scholarships: None
Conference: Carolinas-Virginia Athletic Conference
Program Profile: Both practice and game fields, natural grass, own locker rooms, play year round.
History: Program began in 1985.
Achievements: 4 Palmetto State All-Conference and District 6 1990. 6 All-District 1992. Coach Cerino - District Coach of the Year in 1992.
Style of Play: Slow build up.

Women's Athletic Profile

1115 College Drive
Gaffney, SC 29340
Coach: TBA
Email: Not Available

NCAA II
Saints/Royal Blue, Gold
Phone: (864) 488-8350
Fax: (864) 902-0174

Estimated # of Women's Soccer Scholarships: 3.5
Conference: Carolina Virginia Athletic Conference
Program Profile: Program has both practice and game fields with our own locker rooms. Young Division II program, play in the Limestone Field, natural grass. Traditional season as well as tournament off season.
History: Program began in 1993. 1997 record: 10-7. 1998 6-9-1, 1999 6-10
Achievements: Four All-Conference players, 2 All-Americans.
Roster in State: 2 **Out of State:** 18
Seniors on Team: 3
Positions Needed: Midfield, forward, sweeper
Camp or Clinic Dates: June 15-19
Most Recent Record: 6-10-
Schedule: Belmont Abbey, Longwood, Queens, Barton, Pfieffer.
Style of Play: Proactive, "Total Football".

Newberry College

Academic Profile

Newberry, SC 29108
Phone: (803) 321-5164

Type: 4 Yr.,Private,Liberal Arts
Website: http://www.newberry.edu
SAT/ACT/GPA: 850/20/2.5
Student/Faculty Ratio: 12:1
Undergraduate Enrollment: 744
Scholarships/Academic: Yes **Athletic:** Yes
Expenses by: Year **In State:** $ 17,962

Founded: 1856
Religion: Evangelical Lutheran
Housing: Yes
Male/Female Ratio: 52:48
Graduate Enrollment: N/A
Financial Aid: Yes
Out of State: $ 17,962

Specialty: Education, Business Administration, Communications
Degrees Conferred: BA, BM, BME, BS
Programs of Study: Art, Athletic Training, Biology, Chemistry, Veterinary Technology, Accounting, Economics, Business Administration, Computer Science, Communications, Elementary Education (Special Education, Learning Disabilities), English, French, German, Spanish, History, Music Literature, Music Theory, Music Education, Performance, Physical Education, PE/Leisure Services, Sports Management, Teacher Certification

Men's Athletic Profile

2100 College Street
Newberry, SC 29108
Coach: Bobby Ladimir
Email: Bladimir@newberry.edu

NCAA II
Indians/Scarlet, Gray
Phone: (803) 321-5155
Fax: (803) 321-5169

Estimated # of Men's Soccer Scholarships: N/A
Conference: South Atlantic Conference
History: Program began in 1995.
Achievements: 1999 Freshman of the Year
Roster In State: 8 **Out of State:** 12 **Out of Country:** 1
Walk-on/Other: **Graduation %:** 100 **Seniors on Team:** 1
Positions Needed: All
Most Recent Record: 4-16
Schedule: Wingate University, Presbyterian College, Lander University, St. Leo College, Augusta St. University, Tusculum College

Women's Athletic Profile

2100 College Street
Newberry, SC 29108
Coach: Cory Hundley
Email: chundley@newberry.edu

NCAA II
Lady Indians/Red, White
Phone: (803) 321-5164
Fax: (803) 321-5169

Estimated # of Women's Soccer Scholarships: None
Conference: South Atlantic Conference
Program Profile: We are entering our 5th year of our coaching transitional stage of redevelopment. We have on-campus facilities that include: a locker room, a game field and a separate practice field and Bermuda grass surface. We play a fall schedule.
History: We began in 1995 and did not have much success in the first 3 years. There was a coaching change in April of 1998. Under coach Reyes, we have had the most wins of first conference wins, most goals scored and least goals allowed. The upcoming season squad will include six seniors and six freshmen.
Achievements: 1997 All-Conference; 1998 First Team All-Conference; Freshman of the Year; All-Region Second Team.
Style of Play: We played very direct last season due to weakness in central midfield. However, we hope to be a bit more possession-oriented this year. Possibly, we will play a 4-4-2 or 3-4-3. low pressure zonal defense.

Presbyterian College
Academic Profile

Clinton, SC 29325-2994

Phone: (864) 833-8538

Type: 4 Yr.,Private,Liberal Arts
Website: http://www.presby.edu

Founded: 1880
Religion: Presbyterian Church

SAT/ACT/GPA: 1000/3.0
Housing: Yes
Student/Faculty Ratio: 14:1
Male/Female Ratio: 1:1.5
Undergraduate Enrollment: 1,100
Graduate Enrollment: N/A
Scholarships/Academic: Yes **Athletic:** Yes **Financial Aid:** Yes
Expenses by: Year **In State:** $ 22,000 **Out of State:** $ 22,000
Specialty: Business, Education, Pre-Medical, Pre-Law, Sciences
Degrees Conferred: BS, BA
Programs of Study: Accounting, Chemistry, Computer Science, Economics, Elementary Education, Engineering, English, Fine Arts, History, Mathematics, Music, PreDental, PreLaw, PreMedical, PreVeterinary, Physics, Political Science, Psychology, Religion, Philosophy, Social Science, Sociology, Theatre Arts, Visual Arts

Men's Athletic Profile

105 Ashland Ave
Clinton, SC 29325
Coach: Bret Boulware
Email: bboulwar@presby.edu

NCAA II
Blue Hose/Garnet, Blue
Phone: (864) 833-8255
Fax: (864) 833-8323

Estimated # of Men's Soccer Scholarships: 3
Conference: SAC 8
Program Profile: Nationally ranked D-II program for the 90's, brand new $880,000 lighted stadium with brick encased seating. Traditional fall season.
History: Program began in 1978.
Achievements: Numerous SAC tournament appearances. All-Americans & All-South, All-Conference.
Coaching: Bret Boulware is our Head coach and Wes Kirk is the assistant.
Roster In State: 5 **Out of State:** 17 **Out of Country:** 0
ODP State: 8 **Regional:** 2 **National:**
Walk-on/Other: **Graduation %:** 100 **Seniors on Team:** 11
Positions Needed: All postions sought
Camp or Clinic Dates: Overnight, July 22-26 (co-ed)
Most Recent Record: 12-5-2
Schedule: Francis Marion, Clayton, USC-Spartanburg, Lander, Wingate, Augusta State, University of North Florida
Style of Play: 4-4-2.

Women's Athletic Profile

105 Ashland Avenue
Clinton, SC 29325-2994
Coach: Brian Purcell
Email: bpurcell@presby.edu

NCAA II
Blue Hose/Garnet, Royal Blue
Phone: (864) 833-8327
Fax: (864) 833-8323

Estimated # of Women's Soccer Scholarships: 2.5
Conference: South Atlantic Conference
Program Profile: Nationally competitive Division II program. Brand new state of the art stadium w/900 seating capacity, Bermuda grass surface among the best in Div. II
History: Program began in 1989. Coach Purcell has been head coach since the inception. All-time record of program is 148-67-8
Achievements: Very successful program with 6 Conference Championships, 4 National Tournament Appearances, 7 All-Americans, Conference Coach of the Year 6 times, Regional Coach of the Year 4 times, National Coach of the Year in 1994.
Coaching: Brian Purcell, Head Coach, since the program began in 1989, USSF "B" license, three-time Conference Coach of the Year, 1994 National Coach of the Year, Master's in Sports Management; Region III ODP Staff Coach, SC State Team Coach, MSS from US Sport Academy.

Roster in State: 10
Out of State: 14
Out of Country: 0
ODP State: 11
Regional: 0
National: 0
Walk-on/Other: 0
Graduation %: 100
Seniors on Team: 6
Positions Needed: ALL
Camp or Clinic Dates: July 22-26
Most Recent Record: 13-5-1
Schedule: Francis Marion, Tusculum, Catawba, Longwood, Belmont Abbey, Carson-Newman
Style of Play: Possession oriented, very strong defensively and a tradition of strong Goal Keeping.

Southern Wesleyan University

Academic Profile

Central, SC 29630
Phone: (864) 644-5302

Type: 4 Yr.,Private,Liberal Arts
Founded: 1906
Website: http://www.swu.edu
Religion: Wesleyan
SAT/ACT/GPA: 85018/
Housing: Yes
Student/Faculty Ratio: 14/1
Male/Female Ratio: 46/54
Undergraduate Enrollment: 570
Graduate Enrollment: 700
Scholarships/Academic: Yes
Athletic: Yes
Financial Aid: Yes
Expenses by: Year
In State: $ 16,800
Out of State: $ 16,800
Specialty: Bible, Business, Education
Degrees Conferred: BS, BA
Programs of Study: Accounting, Biblical Studies, Biology, Business Administration, Chemistry, Education, Elementary Education, English, History, Liberal Arts, Mathematics, Medical Technology, Ministries, Music, Music Education, Nursing, Physical Education, Psychology, Religion, Social Science, Special Education, Theology

Men's Athletic Profile

907 Wesleyan Drive
Central, SC 29630
Coach: Claudio Arias
Email: carias@swu.edu
NAIA
Warriors/Royal, Gold
Phone: 864-644-5302
Fax: 864-644-5903
Estimated # of Men's Soccer Scholarships: 5
Conference: GACC
Program Profile: We have one playing field with natural turf and unlimited seating on grassy bank. Spring practice, indoor tournaments and play during Winter.
History: 27 year old program.
Achievements: 5 players in 1991 District VI All-District team.
Coaching: 1st official season for Head Coach Claudio Arias. Joey Johnson and Paddy Deakins are the Assistant Coaches.
Roster In State: 1
Out of State: 13
Out of Country: 0
ODP State: 5
Regional:
National:
Walk-on/Other:
Graduation %: N/A
Seniors on Team: 3
Positions Needed: GK, Defenders, Forwards
Camp or Clinic Dates: Not Available
Schedule: USC-Aiken, AUM, Brewton-Parker, Coker College, Thomas College, North Georgia.

Women's Athletic Profile

907 Wesleyan Drive
Central, SC 29630
Coach: Claudio Arias
Email: carias@swu.edu
NAIA
Warriors/Gold, Royal
Phone: (864) 644-5302
Fax: (864) 644-5903

Estimated # of Women's Soccer Scholarships: 5
Conference: GACC
Program Profile: 1 playing field (120x65), 1 practice field, Bermuda grass.
History: Entering our 5th year.
Coaching: This is the first official year for Coach Arias.
Roster in State: 1 **Out of State:** 13 **Out of Country:** 0
ODP State: 5
Seniors on Team: 3
Positions Needed: GK, Defenders, Forwards
Schedule: USC-Aiken, AUM, Brewton-Parker, Coker College, Thomas College, North Georgia

Spartanburg Methodist College

Academic Profile

Spartanburg, SC 29301
Phone: 864-857-4000

Type: 2 Yr.,Private,Jr. College
Founded: 1919
Website: http://www.smcsc.edu
Religion: Methodist
SAT/ACT/GPA: 760/15
Housing: Yes
Student/Faculty Ratio: 16:1
Male/Female Ratio: 50:50
Undergraduate Enrollment: 1,000
Graduate Enrollment: N/A
Scholarships/Academic: Yes **Athletic:** Yes **Financial Aid:** Yes
Expenses by: Year **In State:** $ 11,720 **Out of State:** $ 11,720
Specialty: Jr. College
Degrees Conferred: AS, AA, ACJ
Programs of Study: Business, Education, Criminal Justice, Law Enforcement, Liberal Arts, Office Management, Social Science, Science

Men's Athletic Profile

1200 Textile Road
Spartanburg, SC 29301
Coach: Dan Kenneally
Email: kennea@smcsc.edu
NJCAA
Pioneers/Red, White
Phone: (864) 587-4270
Fax: (864) 587-4265
Estimated # of Men's Soccer Scholarships: 18
Conference: NJCAA
Program Profile: Play on a grass field that measures 118x68 yards. Ranked in the top 20 nationally
History: National Champs in 1994. Regular season Region X 6 out of the last 10 years. Region X Champion playoff 5 out of the last 10 years.
Achievements: 2 time Coach of the Year, 10 All-Americans; and Conference Regional in 1995 & 1997.
Coaching: Dan Kenneally, Head Coach.
Roster In State: 13 **Out of State:** 10 **Out of Country:** 3
ODP State: 10 **Regional:** 1 **National:** 1
Walk-on/Other: 0 **Graduation %:** 90 **Seniors on Team:** 16
Positions Needed: Forwards
Camp or Clinic Dates: Not Available
Most Recent Record: 10-9-1
Schedule: Meridian, Young Harris, George Perimeter, South Georgia, Louisburg
Style of Play: 3-5-2, 4-4-2 depending on opponent. Possession and attacking.

Women's Athletic Profile

1200 Textile Road
Spartanburg, SC 29301
Coach: Dan Kenneally
Email: kenneed@smcsc.edu

NJCAA
Pioneers/Royal, Blue, White
Phone: (864) 587-4270
Fax: (864) 587-4265

Estimated # of Women's Soccer Scholarships: 18
Conference: NJCAA
Program Profile: Field 120x70 Bermuda grass sits in a natural valley to make it like a stadium. Ranked in the top 10 for women.
History: Won National Champion in 1994; South District Champs six times; Conference District four times; Region Champs four times. Region Champs 1999.
Achievements: Coach of the Year in 1995; Conference Regional in 1995-1997; 15 All-Americans.
Coaching: Dan Kenneally, Head Coach.
Roster in State: 12 **Out of State:** 4 **Out of Country:** 3
ODP State: 3
Graduation %: 90 **Seniors on Team:** 12
Positions Needed: Forwards
Most Recent Record: 5-10-2
Schedule: Young Harris, Louisburg, Truet McConnel
Style of Play: 4-4-2 or 3-5-2 depending on opponent. Possession attacking style of play.

University of South Carolina - Aiken

Academic Profile

Phone: (803) 641-3717

Aiken, SC 29801

Type: 4 Yr.,Public,Liberal Arts,Engineering
Website: http://www.usca.sc.edu
SAT/ACT/GPA: 820
Student/Faculty Ratio: 12:1
Undergraduate Enrollment: 3,300
Founded: 1961
Religion: Non-Affiliated
Housing: Yes
Male/Female Ratio: 35:65
Graduate Enrollment: 500
Scholarships/Academic: Yes **Athletic:** Yes **Financial Aid:** Yes
Expenses by: Year **In State:** $ 6,000 **Out of State:** $ 10,000
Specialty: Nursing
Degrees Conferred: 4 years Baccalaureate Degrees
Programs of Study: Accounting, Banking/Finance, Biology, Business, Chemistry, Computer Science, Criminal Justice, Education, English, History, Marketing, Mathematics, Nursing, Physical Education, Political Science, Psychology, Social Science

Men's Athletic Profile

471 University Parkway
Aiken, SC 29801
Coach: Ike Ofoje
Email: ikeo@aiken.sc.edu

NCAA II
Pacers/Cardinal, White
Phone: (803) 641-3717
Fax: (803) 641-3441

Estimated # of Men's Soccer Scholarships: N/A
Conference: Peach Belt Athletic Conference
Coaching: Ike Ofoje, Head Coach, two-time 1st team All-American at New Hampshire College, MA at Marshall University, WV; USSF "A" License, Junior and Senior National Team Player (Nigeria).

Women's Athletic Profile

471 University Parkway
Aiken, SC 29803
Coach: Ike Ofoje
Email: ikeo@aiken.sc.edu

NCAA II
Pacers/Cardinal, White
Phone: (803) 641-3717
Fax: (803) 641-3441

Estimated # of Women's Soccer Scholarships:
Conference: Peach Belt Conference
Program Profile: Women's Soccer team began it's first year in the Peach Belt Conference. Soccer field is comprised of natural grass under lights.
History: Program began in 1997.
Coaching: Ike Ofoje, Head Coach. Assistant Coach Carol Lach
Roster in State: 0 **Out of State:** 13 **Out of Country:** 4
Seniors on Team: 2
Positions Needed: ALL
Most Recent Record: 12-8-1
Schedule: Francis Marion, Univ. of North Florida, Lincoln Memorial Univ. Lenoir Rhyne, Tusculum College, Alabama-Huntsville.

University of South Carolina-Columbia

Academic Profile

Ads
Columbia, SC 29033

Phone: 803-777-7000

Type: 4 Yr.,Public
Website: http://www.uscsports.com
SAT/ACT/GPA: 1000/3.0
Student/Faculty Ratio: 17:1
Undergraduate Enrollment: 16,000
Scholarships/Academic: Yes **Athletic:** Yes
Expenses by: Year **In State:** $ 8,378
Specialty: International Business, Journalism
Degrees Conferred: 100 different bachelor degrees
Programs of Study: 70 fields of study.

Founded: 1801
Religion: Non-Affiliated
Housing: Yes
Male/Female Ratio: 46:54
Graduate Enrollment: 10,000
Financial Aid: Yes
Out of State: $ 14,232

Men's Athletic Profile

1300 Rosewood Drive
Columbia, SC 29208
Coach: Mark Berson
Email: richard@uscround.sc.ad.edu

NCAA I
Gamecocks/Garnet, Black
Phone: (803) 777-7901
Fax: (803) 777-2967

Estimated # of Men's Soccer Scholarships: None
Conference: Southeastern Conference
Program Profile: Stadium which is lighted is called Eugene E. Stone. Excellent facilities, brand new soccer only state of the art stadium completed in 1996. Attendance ranks in the top 10 in the nation annually, 2 Bermuda practice field. Seating capacity of 5,700.
History: Started in 1978; six straight NCAA Tournament Appearances in 1985-1990; 13 Appearances overall; 12 of the last 14 seasons; final in 1993 and Final Four in 1998 and 1993; South Region Titles in 1985 & 1986; NCAA Quarterfinal in 1985, 1988, 1989 7 1993.
Achievements: National Soccer Coaches Association/Metropolitan Life Coach of the Year in the South in 1984, 1985, 1988 & 1995; All-Americans: Doug Allison in 1987, Tommy Loeber in 1990, Charles Acedo in 1988, Marty Baltzegar in 19887, Chris Faklaris in 1993, Rob Smith in 1994, Clark Brisson in 1989, Clint Mathis in 1995-1997, Henry ring in 1998.

Coaching: Mark Berson, Head Coach, 21 years, USSF 'A' License, USSF National Staff Coach; USSF National Team Coaching Staff, former Region III Assistant Coach; SCYSA State Coach, and Three-time South Region Coach of the Year. Dave Golan - Assistant Coach, three years as an assistant coach . Richard Rowell - Assistant Coach, four years as an assistant coach. US National License - SC ODP Coach.
Style of Play: The team play a 4-4-2 formation and attacking soccer.

Women's Athletic Profile

1300 Rosewood Drive
Columbia, SC 29033
Coach: TBA
Email: Not Available

NCAA I
Lady Gamecocks/Garnet, Black
Phone: (803) 777-7869
Fax: (803) 777-0964

Estimated # of Women's Soccer Scholarships: N/A
Conference: Southeastern Conference
Program Profile: Has a practice and indoor facilities (astro turf), game field, and graveyard. Eugene Stone III Stadium built in 1996 which has a seating capacity of 6,000.
History: Fourth year of the program in 1998. 1995 was the first season has a record of 7-10-2, and 1996 was the second season that has a record of 8-10-2.
Achievements: Debbie Smith - 2nd team All-SEC in 1995, 1st team SEC in 1996. Eleven players All-Americans, SEC Academic.
Positions Needed: All
Camp or Clinic Dates: Not Available
Most Recent Record: 4-16-0
Style of Play: High intensity: Systematic combination play, and direct but with a possession

University of South Carolina - Spartanburg

Academic Profile

Spartanburg, SC 29303

Phone:

Type: 4 Yr.,Public
Website: http://www.uscs.sc.edu
SAT/ACT/GPA: Varies
Student/Faculty Ratio: 16:1
Undergraduate Enrollment: 3,800
Scholarships/Academic: Yes
Athletic: Yes
Financial Aid: Yes
Expenses by: Year
In State: $ 7,540
Out of State: $ 12,000

Founded: 1967
Religion: Non-Affiliated
Housing: Yes
Male/Female Ratio: 40:60
Graduate Enrollment: N/A

Degrees Conferred: AA, AS, BA, BS, MA, MS
Programs of Study: More than 30 Fields of Study in Liberal Arts, Sciences, Business Administration, Nursing and Teacher Education, plus Associate Degree in Nursing. Master's degree programs are offered in Early Childhood Education and Elementary Education. Other graduate courses are offered at USCS through the Graduate Regional Studies program of the USCS system.

Men's Athletic Profile

800 University Way
Spartanburg, SC 29303
Coach: Greg Hooks
Email: ghooks@uscs.edu

NCAA II
Rifles/Green, Black, White
Phone: (864) 503-5117
Fax: (864) 503-5130

Estimated # of Men's Soccer Scholarships: 9
Conference: Peach Belt Athletic Conference

Program Profile: 287 games won in 19 year history; in the last seven years: 6 PBAC Tournament Championships and 4 PBAC Titles; made seven of eight appearances in NCAA Men's Soccer Championships; have won eight NCAA Tournament games.; host of two National Championships, reaching the Championship Match twice; 3,000 capacity size stadium (Rifle Field), Bermuda grass.
History: Our program began in 1979-1980 in the NAIA and became a member of the NCAA in 1990-1991.
Achievements: Frank Kohlenstein was Coach of the Year honors 1983, 1984 in NAIA, NSCAA; NAIA District 6 Coach of the Year 1983, 1981; NSCAA Division II South Region Coach of the Year 1998, 1997. Greg Hooks was 1992 PBAC Coach of the Year 1998, 1997. 20 All-Americans, 4 GTE All-Americans, 4 Confer
Coaching: Greg Hooks, Head Coach, has found success at every stop in his career. He has a 33-11-3 in three seasons at the junior college level. At the University of Charleston, West Virginia, he has a 54-19-3 in four seasons. Those teams won two conference titles and were ranked as high as #4 in the nation. The Rifles have advanced to the NCAA Tournament in three of those four seasons, including two trips to the championships game. He holds the two highest coaching degrees available in the US. Jeff Negalha is Assistant Coach.
Roster In State: 5 **Out of State:** 5 **Out of Country:** 15
Walk-on/Other: **Graduation %:** N/A **Seniors on Team:** 4
Positions Needed: Forwards, Goalkeeper
Most Recent Record: 12-3-3

Winthrop University
Academic Profile

Phone: (803) 323-2129 ext. 6249

Rock Hill, SC 29733

Type: 4 Yr.,Public,Liberal Arts **Founded:** 1886
Website: http://www.winthrop.edu **Religion:** Non-Affiliated
SAT/ACT/GPA: 850/2.75 **Housing:** Yes
Student/Faculty Ratio: 17:1 **Male/Female Ratio:** 35:65
Undergraduate Enrollment: 4,500 **Graduate Enrollment:** 1,000
Scholarships/Academic: Yes **Athletic:** Yes **Financial Aid:** Yes
Expenses by: Year **In State:** $ 7,850 **Out of State:** $ 11,068
Specialty: Business, Education, Visual and Performing Arts
Degrees Conferred: BA, BS, BFA, MA, MS, MBA, MFA, MEd
Programs of Study: Art History, Biology, Business Administration, Business Education, Chemistry, Computer Science, Dance, Distributive Education, Early Childhood Education, Education, Elementary Education, English, Fine Arts, History, Home Economics, Interior Design, International Marketing, Mass Communications, Mathematics, Medical Technology, Modern Languages, Music, Music Education, Philosophy & Religion, Physical Education, Political Science, Psychology, Science Communications, Social Work, Sociology, Special Education, Speech, Theatre

Men's Athletic Profile

Soccer Office
Rock Hill, SC 29733
Coach: Rich Posipanko
Email: posipaukor@winthrop.edu

NCAA I
Eagles/Garnet, Gold
Phone: (803) 323-2129
Fax: (803) 323-2433

Estimated # of Men's Soccer Scholarships: N/A
Conference: Big South Conference
Program Profile: Excellent facilities. New soccer facility in 1996 from NFL Carolina Panthers.
History: Program began in 1975. Placed second in Big South with a record of 13-5-1 in 1994
Achievements: Coach of the Year 1984, 1986, 1987, 1991
Coaching: Rich Posipanko is our Head Coach. He holds USSF 'A' license.
Roster In State: 2 **Out of State:** 24 **Out of Country:** 12
ODP State: 8 **Regional:** 3 **National:** 1
Walk-on/Other: **Graduation %:** 100 **Seniors on Team:** 4
Camp or Clinic Dates: Not Available
Schedule: Clemson, UNC-Charlotte, North Carolina, South Carolina, Davidson

Wofford College

Academic Profile

Phone: 864-597-4000

Spartanburg, SC 29303

Type: 4 Yr.,Private,Liberal Arts
Website: http://www.wofford.edu
SAT/ACT/GPA: 1100/3.0
Student/Faculty Ratio: 9:1
Undergraduate Enrollment: 1,100
Scholarships/Academic: Yes **Athletic:** Yes
Expenses by: Year **In State:** $ 21,500
Specialty: Sciences
Degrees Conferred: BA, BS

Founded: 1854
Religion: Methodist
Housing: Yes
Male/Female Ratio: 52:48
Graduate Enrollment: N/A
Financial Aid: Yes
Out of State: $ 21,500

Programs of Study: Accounting, Art History, Biology, Chemistry, Computer Science, Economics, Finance, English, French, German, Government, History, Humanities, Math, Philosophy, Physics, Psychology, Religion, Sociology, Spanish

Men's Athletic Profile

429 North Church Street
Spartanburg, SC 29303
Coach: John Blair
Email: blairji@wofford.edu

NCAA I
Terriers/Old Gold, Back
Phone: (864) 597-4125
Fax: (864) 597-4112

Estimated # of Men's Soccer Scholarships: 2+
Conference: Southern Conference
Program Profile: New 120x75 lighted soccer only stadium. Natural grass that seats 3,000. Campus is summer training camp for NFL's Carolina Panthers.
History: Program began in 1977 as an NAIA and now Division I. Playing in Iowa Southern Conference.
Achievements: 23 All-Region Players.
Coaching: John Blair, Head Coach, is entering his 14th season as the head coach at Wofford College. He holds a USSF License and has been a member of South Carolina ODP Staff for 14 years along with the South Carolina ODP State coach for four years.
Style of Play: Build - up from the back with a combination passes; attractive short and long pass combination to create goal scoring opportunities. Possession plus attacking from build-up.

Women's Athletic Profile

429 N Church Street
Spartanburg, SC 29303-3663
Coach: Amy Burns
Email: burnsam@wofford.edu

NCAA I
Terriers/Gold, Black
Phone: (864) 597-4100
Fax: (864) 597-4124

Estimated # of Women's Soccer Scholarships:
Conference: Southern Conference
Program Profile: Has a locker room for men's and women's team, a machine, and a free weight rooms, a training room, racquetball courts, an aerobic dance studio, an administrative and coaches' offices with a meeting room. Recently renovated Snyder Field which consists of 2,250 seat is the home of the Wofford Soccer.
History: Program began in 1994 playing in the NCAA Division II (record was 7-7); 1995 Division I (record was 2-16); 1996 record was 11-5-2; 1997 record was 12-7-3; 2nd place in Southern Conference Regular Season and Playoffs.
Achievements: Ileona Moschos - 1996 All-South Goalkeeper; Bridgid Meadow - All-Southern Conference.
Style of Play: Controlled, aggressive - lots of pressure on the ball. Would like to play out of the back with a fast, skilled players who have remarkable first touch.

south dakota

SOUTH DAKOTA

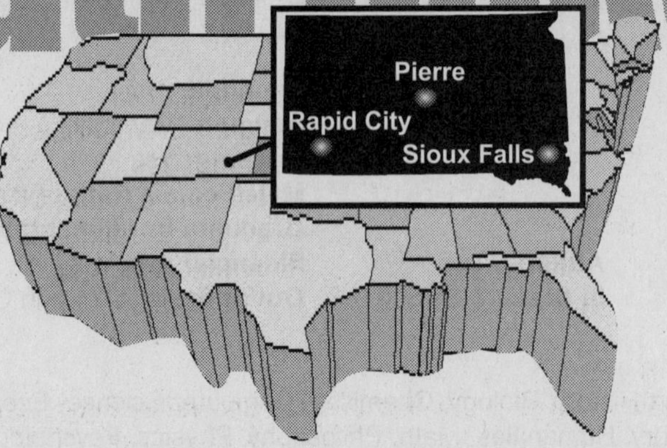

SCHOOL	CITY	AFFILIATION	PAGE
Huron University	Huron	NAIA	1043
Mount Marty College	Yankton	NAIA	1044
National American University	Rapid City	NAIA	1045
University of Sioux Falls	Sioux Falls	NAIA	1046

Huron University
Academic Profile

Phone:

Huron, SD 57350

Type: 4 Yr.,Private,Liberal Arts
Founded: 1883
Website: http://www.huron.edu
Religion: Non-Affiliated
SAT/ACT/GPA: 870/18/2.0
Housing: Yes
Student/Faculty Ratio: 15:1
Male/Female Ratio: 65:35
Undergraduate Enrollment: 600
Graduate Enrollment: 70
Scholarships/Academic: Yes **Athletic:** Yes **Financial Aid:** Yes
Expenses by: Year **In State:** $ 13,250 **Out of State:** $ 13,250
Specialty: Liberal Arts
Degrees Conferred: AA, AS, BA, BS, MBA
Programs of Study: Physical Education, Nursing, Criminal Justice, Secondary Education, Elementary Education, Business Administration, Psychology

Men's Athletic Profile

333 9th Street SW
Huron, SD 57350
Coach: Brad Smith
Email: bsmith@basec.net

NAIA
Eagles/Burgundy, White
Phone: (800) 710-7159
Fax: (605) 352-7421

Estimated # of Men's Soccer Scholarships: Varies
Conference: DAC 10
Program Profile: We have a brand new six-field complex with each field measuring 120x80 yards. Lights are scheduled for spring 2000, program enters it's third year as a varsity program and should now be in position to compete for post season play. We like to play hard defense and possession offense. Speed is our biggest asset.
History: 1998 3-14-1, 1999 7-8-1. During this time there have been 3 All-Americans and 10 NAIA All-American scholar-athletes.
Coaching: Brad Smith enters his 22nd year as a collegiate coach with a 202-157-28 record. He has numerous coach of the year honors and several conference and district and region championships. He has coached 24 All-Americans.
Roster In State: 1 **Out of State:** 24 **Out of Country:** 1
Walk-on/Other: **Graduation %:** 95 **Seniors on Team:** 2
Positions Needed: Defenders are a Top Priority
Camp or Clinic Dates: Not Available
Most Recent Record: 7-8-1
Schedule: National, Mary, Newman, Briar Cliff, Viterbo, Bellvue
Style of Play: High pressure defense - possession offense.

Women's Athletic Profile

333 9th St. SW
Huron, SD 57350
Coach: L. Dale Roden
Email: droden@huron.edu

NAIA
Screaming Eagles/Burgundy
Phone: (605) 352-8721
Fax: (605) 352-7421

Estimated # of Women's Soccer Scholarships:
Conference: Great Plains Independent Section
Program Profile: Full 20 game schedule, six field (120x80) game complex with lights. Separate practice facilities available.
History: Program began in 1998 with an accumulative record of 23-16-2.

Achievements: Advanced to the playoffs during both years of competition as a varsity program. Have produced numerous All-Independent and section players, 4 All-Region players, 3 NAIA, NSCAA All-Americans and 6 academic All-Americans

Coaching: L. Dale Roden, Head Coach, has an NSCAA Advanced National Diploma. He has two sectional championships, one regional championship and a career mark of 63-41-6. Robert Talley is Assistant Coach and Goalkeeper Coach.

Roster in State: 5 **Out of State:** 20 **Out of Country:**
Walk-on/Other: **Graduation %:** 100 **Seniors on Team:** 7
Positions Needed: C mid, moving back, sweeper, strikers
Camp or Clinic Dates: Not Available
Most Recent Record: 13-7
Schedule: National-American University, College of St. Mary, Baker, Bellevue, University of Mary
Style of Play: Play possession while building to attack - formations and style may chance do to by the personnel and/or by the opponent.

Mount Marty College

Academic Profile

Phone: 605-668-1268

Yankton, SD 57078

Type: 4 Yr.,Private,Liberal Arts **Founded:** 1936
Website: http://www.mtmc.edu **Religion:** Catholic
SAT/ACT/GPA: 17 & up **Housing:** Yes
Student/Faculty Ratio: 1/15 **Male/Female Ratio:** 1/2
Undergraduate Enrollment: N/A **Graduate Enrollment:** N/A
Scholarships/Academic: Yes **Athletic:** Yes **Financial Aid:** Yes
Expenses by: Year **In State:** $19,000 **Out of State:** $19,000
Degrees Conferred: AA, AS, BA, BS, BSEd, MED
Programs of Study: Accounting, Athletic Training, Behavioral Science, Biology, Biological Science, Business Administration, Commerce, Management, Chemistry, Communications, Computer Science, Criminal Justice, PreDentistry, Elementary Education, Music, Music Education, Nursing, Radiological Technology

Men's Athletic Profile

1105 W. 8th St
Yankton, SD 57078
Coach: Chris Pfau
Email: cpfau@mtmc.edu

NAIA
Lancers/Navy, Gold
Phone: 605-668-1268
Fax: 605-668-1357

Estimated # of Men's Soccer Scholarships: 5-8
Conference: Great Plains Athletic Conference
Program Profile: Brand new program in the fall of 2000, we are in the process of building a new soccer field which should be ready in the spring of 2001. It will be natural grass surface that measures 110x85.
History: We started our first year in the fall of 2000. We finished our first year 1-14 and we had three players named to Conference Honorable Mention Team.
Achievements: 3 playes received Honorable mention All-Conference.
Coaching: Chris Pfau is our Head Coach.
Roster In State: 4 **Out of State:** 8 **Out of Country:** 0
ODP State: 2 **Regional:** 0 **National:** 0
Walk-on/Other: 0 **Graduation %:** N/A **Seniors on Team:** 0
Positions Needed: All
Camp or Clinic Dates: Call for details
Most Recent Record: 1-14-0

Schedule: University of Mary, Nebraska Wesleyan, Hastings, Huron, Baker
Style of Play: Possessive with a purpose. I give a structure and give options within the structure to give the players freedom to play.

National American University

Academic Profile

Phone: (800) 843-8892

Rajpit City, SD 57701

Type: 4Private
Founded: 1941
Website: http://www.national.edu
Religion: Great Plains
SAT/ACT/GPA: Open
Housing: Yes
Student/Faculty Ratio: 15:1
Male/Female Ratio: 60:40
Undergraduate Enrollment: 750
Graduate Enrollment: N/A
Scholarships/Academic: Yes **Athletic:** Yes **Financial Aid:** Yes
Expenses by: Year **In State:** $13,470 **Out of State:** $13,470
Specialty: Business, Computer Information Systems, Athletic Training, Sport Mgmt.
Degrees Conferred: BA
Programs of Study: Accounting, Athletic Training, Business Administration, Computer Information Systems, Computer Technology, Financial Management, International Business, Management Information Systems, Occupational Therapy, Paralegal Studies, Veterinary Technician, Web Developer/Web Master Microsoft Certification

Men's Athletic Profile

321 Kansas City Street
Rapid City, SD 57709
Coach: Wulf Dieter Koch
Email: wkoch@rc.national.edu

NAIA
Mavericks/Royal, White, Red
Phone: (605) 394-4825
Fax: (605) 394-4971

Estimated # of Men's Soccer Scholarships: varies
Conference: Independent
Program Profile: Strong Program, participant in the 1998 NAIA National Tournament, 5 consecutive play-off runs; home field is called Omaha Field which is natural grass and lighted. Playing season starts from August 27 through October 23.
History: Our program started in 1995, Regional Runner-Up in 1997, Regional champions (Great Plains), NAIA National Tournament Participant.1998 NAIA National Tournament participant, 5 consecutive Play-off appearances.
Achievements: Coach Wulf Dieter Koch was named NAIA & NSCAA Great Plains Regional Coach of the Year in 1998 & 1997, 1998 Great Plains Region Sectional Champs, 1997 Regional Runner-Up, 1998 Regional Champs, 4 All-Region players and 1 All-American in 1997, 4 All-Region players and 1 All-American player in 1998, 3 Academic All-Americans in 1998, NSCAA Team Academic Award in 1998.
Coaching: Wuld Dieter Koch is our Head Coach. He holds USSF "B" License and NSCAA Advanced National Diploma. Angelo Abraham is our Assistant Coach. He holds USSF "C" License. Jeff Simpson is our Assistant Coach. He holds NSCAA National Diploma. Brian Pritts and Scott Dixon are the Goalkeeper Coaches.
Roster In State: 3 **Out of State:** 5 **Out of Country:** 10
ODP State: 6 **Regional:** **National:**
Walk-on/Other: **Graduation %:** 90 **Seniors on Team:** 4
Positions Needed: goalkeepers, forwards
Camp or Clinic Dates: June 5-10, June 12-16
Most Recent Record: 13-6-2
Schedule: Mt. Senario College, St. Gregory's University, Life University, Baker University, Park University, University of Mary, Bellevue, Colorado Christian
Style of Play: We play a 3-5-2 system, ball control with midfield. Very technical; very passionate.

Women's Athletic Profile

321 Kansas City Street
Rapid City, SD 57701
Coach: Luis Usera
Email: Luisu@rc.national.edu

NAIA
Mavericks/Red, White, Blue
Phone: (605) 394-4834
Fax: (605) 394-4871

Estimated # of Women's Soccer Scholarships:
Conference: Independent
Program Profile: We play on Omaha Field, natural grass, with lights.
History: NAU began women's soccer in 1996. The team went 13-4 overall. In 1998-1999 the Lady Mavericks finished the year at 17-4-1 winning the Independent Sectional Championships. Great Plains Regional Championship. An appearance at the NAIA National Tournament and a final season poll ranking. NAU #17 starting line-up held 9 freshmen and 2 sophomores.
Achievements: 3 All-Americans; Regional Coach of the Year in 1998 and 1999; Region III Champion; 1999 Region III Champions; Region III and IV Champions.
Coaching: Luis Usera, Head Coach, holds a USSF "A" License. Waleska Bucene, Strength and Conditioning Coach. Sao Paulo Bramil and Bill Ensporn, Assistant Coaches.
Roster in State: 5 **Out of State:** 5 **Out of Country:** 8
ODP State: 6 **Regional:** **National:** 1
Walk-on/Other: **Graduation %:** 90 **Seniors on Team:** 7
Positions Needed: Defenders, Midfield
Camp or Clinic Dates: June 5-10, 12-16
Most Recent Record: 16-9
Schedule: William Carey, Bell Haven, Colorado Christian, Park University, University of Mary, Seattle University
Style of Play: 4-4-2, extremely technical ball control.

University of Sioux Falls

Academic Profile

Sioux Falls, SD 57105
Phone: (605) 331-6600

Type: 4 Yr.,Private,Liberal Arts
Founded: 1883
Website: http://www.thecoo.edu
Religion: American Baptist
SAT/ACT/GPA: 19+/2.0+
Housing: Yes
Student/Faculty Ratio: 14:1
Male/Female Ratio: 45:55
Undergraduate Enrollment: 1,039
Graduate Enrollment: N/A
Scholarships/Academic: Yes **Athletic:** Yes **Financial Aid:** Yes
Expenses by: Year **In State:** $ 15,200 **Out of State:** $ 15,200
Specialty: Business, Education
Degrees Conferred: AA, BA, BS, MBA, M Ed
Programs of Study: Art, Biology, Business Administration, Chemistry, Computer Science, Education, English, Exercise Science, History, Political Science, Mass Communication, Mathematics, Music Psychology, Religious Studies, Social Science, Social Work, Sociology, Speech, Radiologic Technology, Theatre, Wellness

Men's Athletic Profile

1101 West 22nd Street
Sioux Falls, SD 57105
Coach: Brockton Hickam
Email: brhickam@usiouxfalls.edu

NAIA
Cougars/Purple, White
Phone: (605) 331-6597
Fax: (605) 331-6615

Estimated # of Men's Soccer Scholarships: 6
Conference: SDIC

Program Profile: Plays a fall schedule and games are played at Yankton Trails which is a facility with 16 fields and lights. There is a varsity weight room, athletic trainers etc..
History: The program is in its 5th year.
Coaching: Head Coach Brockton Hickam has a NSCAA National Diploma. Assistant Coaches Eric Couilino and Mat Kludt.

Roster In State: 11	**Out of State:** 7	**Out of Country:** 0
ODP State: 5	**Regional:** 0	**National:** 0
Walk-on/Other: 0	**Graduation %:** N/A	**Seniors on Team:** 3

Positions Needed: ALL
Most Recent Record: 5-11-0
Schedule: Hastings, Dordt, Midland Luthern, Northwestern
Style of Play: Possession oriented with Dutch style. Like to be an intelligent, skillful side that will defend early and physically, look to go direct upon winning the ball but have the intelligence to play possession when the direct attack is not on.

Women's Athletic Profile

1101 West 22nd Street
Sioux Falls, SD 57105
Coach: Brockton Hickam
Email: brhickam@usiouxfalls.edu

NAIA
Cougars/Purple, White
Phone: (605) 331-6597
Fax: (605) 331-6615

Estimated # of Women's Soccer Scholarships: 6
Conference: Great Plains Athletic Conference
Program Profile: USF soccer is a varsity program and plays a fall schedule. The Cougars play at a facility with 16 fields, lights making evening games possible. Multiple practice fields, varsity weight room, athletic training staff, etc.
History: USF soccer finished its 5th year.
Coaching: Brockton Hickam- NSCAA National Diploma. Eric Gilano 1999 All-American Defender at Bethany College. Matt Kludt- USSF "C" liences.

Roster in State: 10	**Out of State:** 6	**Out of Country:** 0
Walk-on/Other:	**Graduation %:**	**Seniors on Team:** 2

Positions Needed: ALL
Camp or Clinic Dates: Not Available
Most Recent Record: 2-14-0
Schedule: Hasting, Dordt, Dana, Concordia, Mt. Marty, Northwestern
Style of Play: Possession oriented with Dutch style. Like to be an intelligent, skillful side that will defend early and physically, look to go direct upon winning the ball but have the intelligence to play possession when the direct attack is not on.

tennessee

TENNESSEE

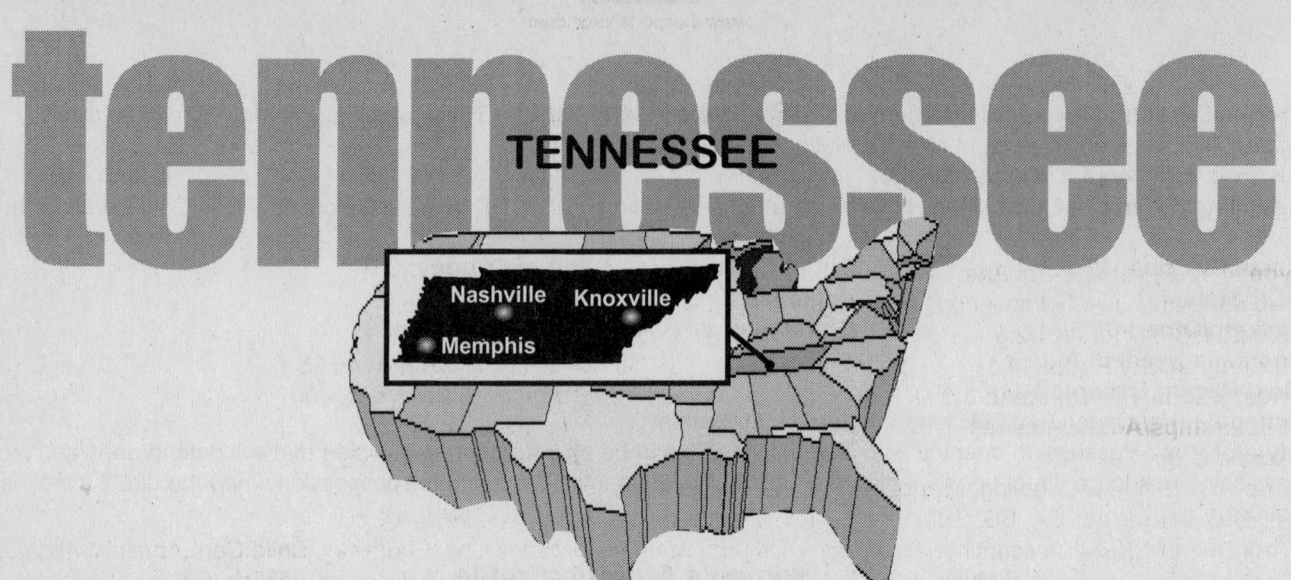

SCHOOL	CITY	AFFILIATION	PAGE
Belmont University	Nashville	NCAA I	1049
Bethel College	McKenzie	NAIA	1050
Bryan College	Dayton	NAIA	1050
Carson - Newman College	Jefferson City	NCAA II	1052
Christian Brothers University	Memphis	NCAA II	1053
Cumberland University	Lebanon	NAIA	1054
East Tennessee State University	James City	NCAA I	1055
King College	Bristol	NAIA	1056
Lambuth University	Jackson	NCAA II/NAIA	1057
Lee University	Cleveland	NAIA	1059
Lincoln Memorial University	Harrogate	NCAA II	1060
Martin Methodist College	Pulaski	NAIA	1061
Maryville College	Maryville	NCAA III	1062
Milligan College	Milligan College	NAIA	1063
Rhodes College	Memphis	NCAA III	1065
Tennessee Wesleyan College	Athens	NAIA	1066
Tusculum College	Greenville	NCAA II	1067
Union University	Jackson	NCCAA/NAIA	1068
University of Memphis	Memphis	NCAA I	1070
Univ of Tennessee-Chattanooga	Chattanooga	NCAA I	1071
University of Tennessee- Knoxville	Knoxville	NCAA I	1072
University of Tennessee-Martin	Martin	NCAA I	1073
University of the South	Sewanee	NCAA III	1074
Vanderbilt University	Nashville	NCAA I	1075

Belmont University

Academic Profile

Phone:

Nashville, TN 37221

Type: 4 Yr.,Private,Liberal Arts
Founded: 1951
Website: http://www.belmont.edu
Religion: Christian
SAT/ACT/GPA: 1000/21/2.5
Housing: Yes
Student/Faculty Ratio: 14:1
Male/Female Ratio: 45:55
Undergraduate Enrollment: 3,000
Graduate Enrollment: 400
Scholarships/Academic: Yes **Athletic:** Yes **Financial Aid:** Yes
Expenses by: Year **In State:** $ 15,500 **Out of State:** $ 15,500
Specialty: Business, Nursing, Music, Education, Humanities
Degrees Conferred: BA, BS, BBA, BM, BMEd, BSN, BFA, MA, MSN, MS, MBA, MEd
Programs of Study: Accounting, Art, Biology, Communications, Broadcasting, Chemistry, Child Care Administration, Church Music, Commercial Music, Computer Science, Economics, Elementary Education, English, Exercise Science, Finance, French, Graphic Design, Health, History, Hospitality Management, Marketing, Mathematics, Medical Technology, Music, Music Business, Physical Education, Physics, Political Science, Nursing, Philosophy, Psychology, Religion, Science, Social Work, Spanish, Studio Art, Theatre & Dance

Men's Athletic Profile

1900 Belmont Blvd.
Nashville, TN 37221
Coach: Earle Davidson
Email: davidsone@mail.belmont.edu

NCAA I
Bruins/Red, White, Navy
Phone: (615) 460-6134
Fax: (615) 460-5584

Estimated # of Men's Soccer Scholarships: 7.5
Conference: To be determined
Program Profile: Growing Division I program with a strong schedule. Games are played at Whitten Field, a regulation size natural turf field with seating for approximately 1000 fans. The team plays 18-20 games in the fall and also participates in the spring.
History: Program began as NAIA in 1991m made conference semifinals in 1995. Began transition to Division I in 1996. Completed transition in 1999.
Achievements: NAIA - TCAC Player of the Year, 21 All-Conference performers, and 2 Academic All-Americans.
Roster In State: 7 **Out of State:** 6 **Out of Country:** 5
ODP State: 17 **Regional:** 1 **National:**
Walk-on/Other: **Graduation %:** **Seniors on Team:** 1
Positions Needed: Goalkeepers, Defenders
Camp or Clinic Dates: Not Available
Schedule: Furman, Creighton, SMU, SMS, Evansville
Style of Play: Possession oriented with an emphasis on technical ability.

Women's Athletic Profile

1900 Belmont University
Nashville, TN 37212
Coach: Sterling Nabours
Email: nabours@mail.belmont.edu

NCAA I
Bruins/Navy, Red, White
Phone: (615) 460-6013
Fax: (615) 460-5584

Estimated # of Women's Soccer Scholarships: 8
Conference: TAAC
History: Program just completed 4th year. First year of conference affiliation last year with Missouri valley, next year the whole school joins the TAAC for 2001 competition.

Roster in State: 5 **Out of State:** 14 **Out of Country:** 0
ODP State: 6 **Regional:** 1 **National:** 0
Walk-on/Other: 0 **Graduation %:** 100 **Seniors on Team:** 6
Positions Needed: 8
Camp or Clinic Dates: Not Available
Most Recent Record: 6-15-0
Schedule: Jacksonville Univ. Univ of Central Florida, Florida Atlantic Univ. Georgia State, Creighton Univ.
Style of Play: Attack Oriented with ball control.

Bethel College

Academic Profile

Phone:

McKenzie, TN 38201

Type: 4 Yr.,Private, **Founded:** 1842
Website: http://www.bethel-college.edu **Religion:** Presbyterian
SAT/ACT/GPA: 14+ **Housing:** No
Student/Faculty Ratio: 15:1 **Male/Female Ratio:** 43:57
Undergraduate Enrollment: 420 **Graduate Enrollment:** 40
Scholarships/Academic: Yes **Athletic:** Yes **Financial Aid:** Yes
Expenses by: Year **In State:** $ 9,400 **Out of State:** $ 9,400
Degrees Conferred: AA, BA, BS, MA, MED
Programs of Study: Accounting, Applied Mathematics, Biological Science, Business Administration, Chemistry, Elementary Education, English, Health Education, History, Music, Physical Education, Psychology, Religion, Social Science

Men's Athletic Profile

College Drive
McKenzie, TN 38201
Coach: TBA **Phone:** 901-352-4000
Email: Not Available **Fax:**

Did Not Return Profile

Women's Athletic Profile

Coach: Misty Schmitz **Phone:**
Email: **Fax:**

Did Not Return Profile

Bryan College

Academic Profile

Phone:

Dayton, TN 37321

Type: 4 Yr.,Private,Liberal Arts **Founded:** 1930
Website: http://www.bryan.edu **Religion:** Inter-denominational
SAT/ACT/GPA: 860/18/2.5 **Housing:** Yes
Student/Faculty Ratio: 14:1 **Male/Female Ratio:** 45:55
Undergraduate Enrollment: 500 **Graduate Enrollment:** N/A

Scholarships/Academic: Yes **Athletic:** Yes **Financial Aid:** Yes
Expenses by: Year **In State:** $ 15,150 **Out of State:** $ 15,150
Degrees Conferred: AA, AS, BA, BS
Programs of Study: Bible, Biology, Business, Christian Education, Communications, English, History, Liberal Arts, Elementary Education, Mathematics, Music, Exercise Science, Physical Education, Psychology

Men's Athletic Profile

Box 7000
Dayton, TN 37321-7000
Coach: Dr. Sanford Zensen
Email: zensensa@bryannrt.edu

NAIA
Lions/Red, Gold
Phone: (615) 775-1255
Fax: (615) 775-7255

Estimated # of Men's Soccer Scholarships: N/A
Conference: Tennessee-Virginia Athletic Conference
Program Profile: Competitive program, field is natural grass with a measurements of 120 by 75 yards.
History: Program began in 1960; 3 National NCCAA Titles; 8 NCCAA Regional Titles; 1 Tennessee Virginia Athletic Conference Titles in 1996; 1996 NSIS Regional Tournament Appearance.
Achievements: 3 NCCAA Coach of the Year; 1 National Coach of the Year (NCCAA Division I); 10 NCCAA All-Americans; 2 NAIA All-South; All-Americans.
Coaching: Dr. Sanford Zensen, Head Coach, 18 years coaching, NSCAA National Diploma. He has two assistant coaches.
Style of Play: Short pass; possession; build from the back.

Women's Athletic Profile

Box 7000
Dayton, TN 37321
Coach: Marc Neddo
Email: neddoma@bryan.edu

NAIA
Lions/Red, Black
Phone: (423) 775-7235
Fax: (423) 775-7330

Estimated # of Women's Soccer Scholarships: 3.5
Conference: Appalachian Athletic Conference
Program Profile: 6th year program in a very competitive conference, international players members of their respective national teams. Natural grass field with lights. Full size practice field. Season runs from mid-August to end of October/early November. Christian College, not just in name only.
History: Program began in 1996. Coach Neddo has been coaching since the inception.
Achievements: No Conference titles. Southern region All-American, NSCAA academic All-Americans, national player of the week in 1999 and 2000.
Coaching: Mark Neddo, Head Coach. He has a USSF National "C" License. He was born and raised in France. He has over 20 years of playing and coaching experience in the U.S. and overseas.
Roster in State: 5 **Out of State:** 10 **Out of Country:** 1
ODP State: 1 **Regional:** 1 **National:** 0
Walk-on/Other: 0 **Graduation %:** 90 **Seniors on Team:** 2
Positions Needed: Forwards, Midfielders
Camp or Clinic Dates: Not Available
Most Recent Record: 6-11-1
Schedule: Virginia Intermont, Brevard, Milligan College, King College
Style of Play: Very purposeful, short passing game looking for long passes. Key is firs touch with a purpose. Aggressive on 50-50 balls. Intelligent players sought. System of play is adapted to players, NOT vice versa, thus it varies.

Carson - Newman College

Academic Profile

Phone: (423) 471-3424

Jefferson City, TN 37760

Type: 4 Yr.,Private,Liberal Arts
Founded: 1851
Website: http://www.cn.edu
Religion: Southern Baptist
SAT/ACT/GPA: 880/21
Housing: Yes
Student/Faculty Ratio: 13:1
Male/Female Ratio: 1:1
Undergraduate Enrollment: 2,000
Graduate Enrollment: 200
Scholarships/Academic: Yes
Athletic: Yes
Financial Aid: Yes
Expenses by: Year
In State: $ 14,480
Out of State: $ 14,480
Specialty: Medical Science, Business, Education, Nursing
Degrees Conferred: AA, BA, BS, MA, M.Ed.
Programs of Study: All Sciences, Humanities, Mathematics, Art, Athletic Training, Nursing, Business, PreMed, PreLaw, Communication Arts, Computer Science, Education, English, Family and Consumer Services, Foreign Languages, General Studies, History, Human Studies, Math, Music, Natural and Physical Science

Men's Athletic Profile

2130 S. Branner Avenue, Holt Fieldhouse
Jefferson City, TN 37760
Coach: Allen Vital
Email: avital@cn.edu

NCAA II
Eagles, Blue & Orange
Phone: 865-471-3520
Fax: 865-471-3514

Estimated # of Men's Soccer Scholarships: 4
Conference: South Atlantic Conference
Program Profile: Field is natural Bermuda grass which measures 120x75 yards. Team lockers are located in one of the finest athletic facilities in the country.
History: Program began in 1985. In 1995 season the Eagles had best overall record and conference record in team's history.
Achievements: Stephen Jones was the first CN Coach to be named SAC Coach of the Year. The 2000 season brought many accolades the Eagles way. For the first time in the school's history the team won the regular season conference championship. Along with this accomplishment, vital was named Coach of the Year and 7 of CN's players were named All-Conference. 2 All-Southeast in 2000, 1 SAC-Scholar Athlete of the Year.
Coaching: Allen Vital has posted a 36-35-2 overall record in his five seasons as Head Coach of the Eagles. Before coming to CN, Vital spent three years as the Coordinator of Special Student Activities and soccer Coach Walters State Community College. He holds an Advance National Coaching License and has several years of coaching experience with the East Tennessee Soccer Federation. Vital, himself was a soccer standout at Tusculum College.
Roster In State: 3
Out of State: 6
Out of Country: 13
ODP State: 2
Regional: 5
National: 15
Walk-on/Other:
Graduation %: 100
Seniors on Team: 7
Positions Needed: All
Camp or Clinic Dates: TBA
Most Recent Record: 12-7
Schedule: Francis-Marion, Radford Univ. Rollins College, USC-Spartanburg
Style of Play: Ball oriented defense.

Women's Athletic Profile

2130 S. Branner Ave. Holt Fieldhouse
Jefferson City, TN 37760
Coach: Derek Greene
Email: dgreene@cn.edu

NCAA II
Eagles, Blue & Orange
Phone: 865-471-3395
Fax: 865-471-3514

Estimated # of Women's Soccer Scholarships: 4
Conference: South Atlantic Conference
Program Profile: McCowan Field is the home of Carson-Newman soccer program. The newly renovated stadium will now seat 500. The Lady Eagles have the luxury of playing on a Bermuda field.
History: The women's soccer program was started in 1991 on the Carson-Newman campus. Since the program was started there have only been three head coaches.
Achievements: This season saw the Lady Eagles with their best ever finish in the conference. The program has seen numerous girls named to the All-Conference teams as well as NCAA All-District and All-South/Southeast region. 80% of the girls are named to the SAC Commissioners honor roll each semester.
Coaching: Derek Greene has posted a 23-28-5 overall record in his 3 years as Head Coach of the Lady Eagles. Greene was not only a soccer stand out in high school, but during his collegiate years as well. While playing at the University of Tennessee he began his coaching career. He has been heavily involved in the TN Olympic Development program. Currently he is coaching a team that boasts four Region III team players as well as one National Player. He holds his NSCAA Advance National Diploma and has served as an instructor in TN on behalf of the U.S. Soccer Federation.

Roster In State: 7	**Out of State:** 12	**Out of Country:** 1
ODP State: 7	**Regional:** 5	**National:** 2
Walk-on/Other: 2	**Graduation %:** 100	**Seniors on Team:** 4

Positions Needed: All
Camp or Clinic Dates: TBA
Most Recent Record: 8-10-1
Schedule: East Tennessee State, Anderson, USC-Spartanburg, Rollins, Tusculum, Wingate
Style of Play: Possession oriented team who likes to pick the other team apart by playing together. Every player must have solid skill and an extremely competitive personality. Good team chemistry and attacking in numbers are also team traits.

Christian Brothers University

Academic Profile

Phone: (901) 321-3371

Memphis, TN 38104

Type: 4 Yr.,Private,Liberal Arts,Engineering		**Founded:** 1871
Website: http://www.cbu.edu		**Religion:** Non-Affiliated
SAT/ACT/GPA: 1000/22/3.0		**Housing:** Yes
Student/Faculty Ratio: 15:1		**Male/Female Ratio:** 52:48
Undergraduate Enrollment: 1,200		**Graduate Enrollment:** 3,000
Scholarships/Academic: Yes	**Athletic:** Yes	**Financial Aid:** Yes
Expenses by: Year	**In State:** $ 17,400	**Out of State:** $ 17,400

Specialty: Business, Education, Engineering, Sciences
Degrees Conferred: Bachelors, Masters
Programs of Study: Biology, Business Administration, Accounting, Chemical Engineering, Chemistry, Computer Science, Economics-Finance, Engineering, English, History, Human Development, Liberal Studies, Management, Marketing, Mathematics, Natural Science, Psychology, Physics, Religion, Telecommunications

Men's Athletic Profile

650 E Parkway, So.	**NCAA II**
Memphis, TN 38104	Buccaneers/Red, White
Coach: Gareth O'Sullivan	**Phone:** (901) 321-3377
Email: gosullivan@cbu.edu	**Fax:** (901) 321-3570

Estimated # of Men's Soccer Scholarships: 4.5
Conference: Gulf South Conference

Program Profile: The team plays on natural grass with a measurements of 120x80 yards and has a seating capacity for 500. The season starts in August and ends in November.
History: Started in 1985 as an NAIA program.
Achievements: The team produced several draftees and several All-Americans. 2000 Conference Champs, NCAA Tournament Bid. 2000 Coach of the Year.
Coaching: Gareth O'Sullivan is the Head Coach. Assistant Coach Toni Carbognani

Roster In State: 6	**Out of State:** 12	**Out of Country:** 7
ODP State: 5	**Regional:** 3	**National:** 0
Walk-on/Other: 0	**Graduation %:** 98	**Seniors on Team:** 3

Positions Needed: GK, F, MF
Camp or Clinic Dates: July 11-15
Most Recent Record: 16-5-0
Schedule: Barry University, Lynn Univ. Truman State, Univ. of Tampa, Univ. of Memphis, Southern illinois
Style of Play: Possession, balls played to feet.

Women's Athletic Profile

650 E Parkway South
Memphis, TN 38104
Coach: Gareth O'Sullivan
Email: gosulliv@cbu.edu

NCAA II
Lady Bucs/Red, White
Phone: (901) 321-3377
Fax: (901) 321-3570

Estimated # of Women's Soccer Scholarships: 3.0
Conference: Gulf South Conference
Program Profile: We play a fall season on a natural grass, 120 x 80 yards, game field which has 500 seats. Our season goes from August to November.
History: Our program began in 1992. We were NAIA District Champions and TNAV Athletic Conference Champions. We were in the Gulf South Final Four the first year that we were in the conference.
Achievements: TCAC third place; 1992 District 24 Semi-finalist; 1994 TCAC regular season tied first place, 1994 TCAC/TVAC Conference Champs, TVAC/TCAC Collegiate Coach of the Year. 2000 Conference Champs, 2000 Coach of the Year.
Coaching: Gareth O'Sullivan, Head Coach. Assistant Coach Jody Orellana

Roster in State: 10	**Out of State:** 6	**Out of Country:** 5
ODP State: 7	**Regional:** 3	**National:** 0
Walk-on/Other: 0	**Graduation %:** 98	**Seniors on Team:** 5

Positions Needed: GK, MF, F
Camp or Clinic Dates: July 11-15
Most Recent Record: 17-3-0
Schedule: Barry Univ. Lynn Univ. Truman State, Univ. of Tampa, Univ. of Memphis
Style of Play: Possession, balls played to feet.

Cumberland University

Academic Profile

Phone:

Type: 4 Yr.,Private,Liberal Arts		**Founded:** 1842
Website: http://www.cumberland.edu		**Religion:** Non-Affiliated
SAT/ACT/GPA: 850/18/2.0		**Housing:** Yes
Student/Faculty Ratio: 12:1		**Male/Female Ratio:** 60:40
Undergraduate Enrollment: 1,206		**Graduate Enrollment:** 177
Scholarships/Academic: Yes	**Athletic:** Yes	**Financial Aid:** Yes
Expenses by: Year	**In State:** $ 12,800	**Out of State:** $ 12,800

Specialty: Education, Business, Nursing
Degrees Conferred: Associates, Bachelors, Masters
Programs of Study: Art, Biology, Chemistry, Criminal Justice, Education, English, History, Mathematics, Natural Science, Psychology, Social Science, Sociology, Business Administration & Economics, Nursing, Education, Physical Education & Fine Arts, Graduate Studies (Arts in Education, Science, Business Administration), Psychology

Men's Athletic Profile

One Cumberland Square
Lebanon, TN 37087
Coach: Anthony Winter
Email: Awinter@Camberland.edu

NAIA
Bulldogs/Maroon, White
Phone: (615) 444-2562 x1116
Fax: (615) 444-2569

Estimated # of Men's Soccer Scholarships: N/A
Conference: Mid South Conference
Program Profile: We play a Fall season. We have a stadium field with natural grass, and separate practice facilities.
History: We are a long established male program. We are annual conference title contenders. We are ready to break into national rankings.
Achievements: Several All-Conference and Region players.
Coaching: Head Coach is Anthony Winter.
Roster In State: 9 **Out of State:** 6 **Out of Country:** 6
Walk-on/Other: **Graduation %:** 90 **Seniors on Team:** 3
Camp or Clinic Dates: Not Available
Schedule: Lindsey Wilson, Lipscomb University, Lee University, Union College, Lambuth University, Lagrange College, N. Greenville
Style of Play: Fast, Fluent, European Style of soccer.

Women's Athletic Profile

One Cumberland Square
Lebanon, TN 37087
Coach: Anthony Winter
Email: awinter@cumberland.edu

NAIA
Bulldogs/Maroon, Grey
Phone: (615) 444-2562
Fax: (615) 444-2569

Estimated # of Women's Soccer Scholarships: None
Conference: Mid South Conference
Program Profile: We have a Stadium field with natural grass and separate practice facilities.
History: We are on 4th year into the program and are already conference contenders and ready to break into national rankings.
Achievements: The bulldogs have had several All Conference and Region players
Coaching:
Roster in State: 6 **Out of State:** 9 **Out of Country:** 6
Walk-on/Other: **Graduation %:** 90 **Seniors on Team:** 2
Camp or Clinic Dates: Not Available
Schedule: Lindsey Wilson, Lipscomb University, Union College, Lambuth University, Lagrange College, N. Greenville
Style of Play: Fast, Fluent, European style soccer.

East Tennessee State University

Academic Profile

Phone: (423) 439-4259

Johnson City, TN 37614

Type: 4 Yr.,Public
Website: http://www.etsu.edu

Founded: 1909
Religion: Non-Affiliated

SAT/ACT/GPA: NCAA Requirements
Student/Faculty Ratio: 20:1
Undergraduate Enrollment: 12,000
Scholarships/Academic: Yes
Expenses by: Year
Specialty: Education, Medical School
Degrees Conferred: BS, MA
Programs of Study: All
Athletic: Yes
In State: $ 6,482
Housing: Yes
Male/Female Ratio: 1:3
Graduate Enrollment: 1,000
Financial Aid: Yes
Out of State: $ 11,308

Women's Athletic Profile

Box 70707
James City, TN 37614
Coach: Heather P. Herson
Email: hersonha@etsu.edu

NCAA I
Buccaneers/Blue, Gold
Phone: (423) 439-4294
Fax: (423) 439-5294

Estimated # of Women's Soccer Scholarships: Varies
Conference: Southern Conference
Program Profile: We play on Liberty Bell Soccer Complex, which seats 500 spectators. It is Bermuda grass stadium with weight room and has 7,200 square foot facility. Our Memorial Center seats for spectator for football and basketball. We have an indoor stadium with astro-turf Bucs.
History: Our program began in 1997 Improve each year. A committed team in 200 who broke 6 records in 2000 season.
Coaching: Heather Herson Head Coach also a member of NSCAA advance national diploma.
Roster in State: 8
Out of State: 12
Out of Country: 0
ODP State: 10
Regional: 4
National:
Walk-on/Other: 2
Graduation %:
Seniors on Team: 4
Camp or Clinic Dates: Not Available
Most Recent Record: 6-12-0
Schedule: UNCG, Furman Univ. Davidson College, Wofford
Style of Play: We play a possession game and defend, attack as a unit.

King College
Academic Profile

Bristol, TN 37620
Phone:

Type: 4 Yr.,Private,Liberal Arts
Website: http://www.king.edu
SAT/ACT/GPA: 950+21+
Student/Faculty Ratio: 14:1
Undergraduate Enrollment: 600
Scholarships/Academic: Yes
Expenses by: Year
Athletic: Yes
In State: $ 14,600
Founded: 1867
Religion: Presbyterian
Housing: Yes
Male/Female Ratio: 50:50
Graduate Enrollment: N/A
Financial Aid: Yes
Out of State: $ 14,600
Specialty: Premed, Humanities, Economics, Business
Degrees Conferred: BA, BS
Programs of Study: PreProfessional Programs, PreMedicine, Health Sciences, Dentistry, Engineering, Law, Pharmaceutical Science, Physical and Occupational Therapy, Veterinary Medicine, Ministry, American Studies, Mathematics, Behavioral Science, Bible & Religion, Biology, Chemistry, Computer Information Systems, Computer Science, Economics and Business Administration, Education, English, Fine Arts, French, History, Medical Technology, Modern Languages, Physics, Political Science, Psychology, Spanish

Men's Athletic Profile

1350 King College Road
Bristol, TN 37620
Coach: Matt Lavinder
Email: tmlavind@king.edu

NAIA
Tornado/Navy, White
Phone: (423) 652-4815
Fax: (423) 652-4815

Estimated # of Men's Soccer Scholarships: 8
Conference: Tennessee Virginia Athletic Conference
Program Profile: The King Soccer Program seeks student-athletes with character and integrity to continue a rich tradition. In addition to success on the field, players are expected to make a positive impact on the campus and community. Players benefit from year-round training program and Bermuda game field. Absence of football team makes soccer the primary fall spectators sport.
History: Program began in the 1950's and continue to have a diverse mix of International and American players. King boasts a strong tradition of soccer within a Christian environment.
Achievements: The program produced a number of All-Americans and Academic All-Americans. More importantly, numerous King's player have graduated and become leaders in their communities.
Coaching: Matt Lavinder, Head Coach, is entering his first year with the USSF "A" License candidate, former Division I assistant. He was named All-American, 1st team All-conference, and leading scorer each of four years at King. He earned a Master's of Divinity of Duke University and teaches in the history department at King. Phil McNamara is the Assistant Coach.
Style of Play: High intensity zonal defense and creative attacking that implements indirect and direct styles. Multinational make-up brings about dynamic's style.

Women's Athletic Profile

1350 King College Rd.
Bristol, TN 37620
Coach: Matt Yeltisen
Email: Not Available

NAIA
Tornado/Blue, Red, White
Phone: (423) 652-4704
Fax: (423) 652-6041

Estimated # of Women's Soccer Scholarships: None
Conference: TVAC
Program Profile: Facilities include brand new stadium for fall of 2000 with Bermuda grass surface. 1000 seat seating capacity. Field is lighted as well as Bermuda grass practice field.
History: 1996
Achievements: Conference runner-up in 1999. 2 Academic All-Americans
Coaching: Mathew Yelton, head coach

Roster in State: 3	**Out of State:** 19	**Out of Country:** 4
ODP State: 3	**Regional:**	**National:**
Walk-on/Other: 1	**Graduation %:** 100	**Seniors on Team:** 6

Positions Needed: Defenders-Midfielders
Camp or Clinic Dates: June 5-9 and June 12-16
Most Recent Record: 8-9-3
Schedule: Tennessee Tech, Milligan College, Brevard College, Carson-Newman College, Tusculum College, Cumberland College

Lambuth University
Academic Profile

Phone:

Jackson, TN 38301

Type: 4 Yr.,Private,Liberal Arts
Website: http://www.lambuth.edu

Founded: 1843
Religion: Methodist

SAT/ACT/GPA: 930/20/2.5
Housing: Yes
Student/Faculty Ratio: 13:1
Male/Female Ratio: 50:50
Undergraduate Enrollment: 1,250
Graduate Enrollment: N/A
Scholarships/Academic: Yes
Athletic: Yes
Financial Aid: Yes
Expenses by: Year
In State: $ 18,808
Out of State: $ 18,808
Specialty: Liberal Arts
Degrees Conferred: BA, BS
Programs of Study: Accounting, Applied Arts, Art, Biblical Studies, Biology, Broadcasting, Business and Management, Business Administration, Chemistry, Communications, Computer Science, Computer Information Systems, Economics, Education, Elementary Education, English, Fashion, Merchandising, History, Human Ecology, Interior Design, International Relations, Management, Marketing, Mathematics, Modern Languages, Music, Nutrition, Philosophy, Physical Education, Physical Science, Physics, Political Science, Pre-Professional Programs, Psychology, Recreation/Athletic Training, Religion, Science, Secondary Education, Social Science, Sociology, Spanish, Special Education, Speech Pathology, Speech Therapy, Theatre, Visual Art

Men's Athletic Profile

705 Lambuth Blvd.
Jackson, TN 38301
Coach: Chris Przemieniecki
Email: przemien@lambuth.edu

NAIA
Eagles/Navy, White
Phone: (901) 425-3302
Fax: (901) 425-3333

Estimated # of Men's Soccer Scholarships: varies
Conference: Mid-South
Program Profile: Our games are played on a 120x70 field with natural grass.
History: Program began in 1992.
Achievements: Mid-South Tournament Champions 1997, 1998, 1999; TCAC Champions 1994, 1995; 3 All-Americans; 3 Conference players of the Year; 15 All-Conference; 8 All-Region.
Roster In State:
Out of State:
Out of Country: 4
Walk-on/Other:
Graduation %: 100
Seniors on Team: 4
Positions Needed: Gk, F, M, D
Camp or Clinic Dates: Not Available
Most Recent Record: 10-11-1
Schedule: Lindsey Wilson College, Birmingham Southern, Union College

Women's Athletic Profile

705 Lambuth Blvd., Box 474
Jackson, TN 38301
Coach: Tina Conley
Email: Not Available

NCAA II/NAIA
Eagles/Navy, White
Phone: (901) 425-3392
Fax: (901) 423-1990

Estimated # of Women's Soccer Scholarships: None
Conference: Mid-South
Program Profile: Full size Bermuda field; Fall season and a 20-game schedule, indoor tournaments during Winter; Spring season is limited to a few games and tournaments.
History: The program began in 1991.
Achievements: 1995 - NAIA All-Mid South (3)
Style of Play: Possession - we play a controlled game of possession and keep away. We usually play two forwards, four midfielders and four backs. I expect players to have sound technical and tactical skills to play a high level of soccer. I look for players who love the game and want to always become better.

Lee University

Academic Profile

Cleveland, TN 37311

Phone: 1-800-LEE-9930

Type: 4 Yr.,Private,Liberal Arts
Website: http://www.leeuniversity.edu
SAT/ACT/GPA: 860/18
Student/Faculty Ratio: 19:1
Undergraduate Enrollment: 2,652
Scholarships/Academic: Yes **Athletic:** Yes
Expenses by: Year **In State:** $ 9,600

Founded: 1918
Religion: Church of God
Housing: Yes
Male/Female Ratio: 49:51
Graduate Enrollment: N/A
Financial Aid: Yes
Out of State: $ 9,600

Specialty: Music, Pre-Med, Religion, Education
Degrees Conferred: BA, BS
Programs of Study: Behavioral & Social Sciences, Education, Business, Bible and Christian Ministries, Language Arts, Accounting, Education, Elementary and Secondary Education, Physical Education, Secretarial & Related Programs

Men's Athletic Profile

1120 N Ocoee Street
Cleveland, TN 37320-3450
Coach: Dr. John Bratcher
Email: jbratcher@leeuniversity.edu

NAIA
Flames/Maroon, White
Phone: (423) 614-8444
Fax: (423) 614-8443

Estimated # of Men's Soccer Scholarships: Varies
Conference: Tran South Conference
Program Profile: Has 20 game full season; lighted field with a 750 seating, World Cup Style team shelters and press box Bermuda Pitch.
History: 1987 program began as a club; in 1988 the program became varsity team.
Achievements: TVAC Champ in 1995; TranSouth Runner-up in 1997; NCAA National Runner-up in 1997; 6 NAIA All-Americans, 1997 team GPA was 3.248. Several Coach of the Year honors.
Coaching: Dr. John Bratcher, Head Coach since 1989, ten seasons at Lee; former head coach at Grand Rapids Baptist, 1 NAIA District Coach of the Year award; TVAC Co-Coach of the Year; two-time NCCAA National Coach of the Year, 8-time NCCAA District Coach of the Year, NSCAA National Diploma, NSCAA and TSSA Instructor. Manny Sanchez, Assistant Coach, USSF A license-NSCAA Advanced National Premier License.
Roster In State: 7 **Out of State:** 9 **Out of Country:** 7
ODP State: 2 **Regional:** **National:**
Walk-on/Other: **Graduation %:** 90+ **Seniors on Team:** 4
Positions Needed: Keeper, Midfield
Camp or Clinic Dates: Not Available
Most Recent Record: 13-4-1
Schedule: Birmingham Southern, Gardner Webb, Berry, Union, Cumberland, Covenant, Martin Methodist
Style of Play: Quick play with 1-2 touch possession.

Women's Athletic Profile

1120 N. Ocoet
Cleveland, TN 37311
Coach: Henry Moyo
Email: hmoyo@leeuniversity.edu

NAIA
Lady Flames/Maroon, White
Phone: (423) 614-8158
Fax: (423) 614-8443

Estimated # of Women's Soccer Scholarships: 6
Conference: Tran South Conference
Program Profile: We play in a Bermuda pitch, lighted field that seats 570+. We also have World Cup style soccer shelters and a press box.

History: Our program began in 1991.
Achievements: NCCAA Region Champion 1999, Produced 2, 3-time All-Americans, All-Tournament Players, Drafted Jamaican National Team Players.
Coaching: Henry Moyo, Head Coach, has an English FA Preliminary License. He is a former professional goalkeeper and played at Zimbabwe , Botswana and Germany. He was an assistant coach for three seasons at Lee University.
Roster in State: 3 **Out of State:** 14 **Out of Country:** 2
ODP State: 0 **Regional:** 3 **National:** 0
Walk-on/Other: 3 **Graduation %:** 100 **Seniors on Team:** 3
Positions Needed: Defenders, Midfielders
Camp or Clinic Dates: Not Available
Most Recent Record: 11-7-0
Schedule: Berry College, Michigan College
Style of Play: 4-4-2 or 3-5-2

Lincoln Memorial University

Academic Profile

Harrogate, TN 37752
Phone: (423) 869-6245

Type: 4 Yr.,Private,Liberal Arts **Founded:** 1897
Website: http://www.lmunet.edu **Religion:** Non-Affiliated
SAT/ACT/GPA: 21-26/2.3 **Housing:** Yes
Student/Faculty Ratio: 13:1 **Male/Female Ratio:** 1:3
Undergraduate Enrollment: 1,300 **Graduate Enrollment:** 650
Scholarships/Academic: Yes **Athletic:** Yes **Financial Aid:** Yes
Expenses by: Year **In State:** $ 12,620 **Out of State:** $ 21,620
Degrees Conferred: Associate, Bachelor's, Master's, Education Specialist
Programs of Study: Accounting, Art, Athletic Training, Business, Biology, Chemistry, Communications Arts, Economics, English, Environmental Science, General Business, Health History, Humanities, Management, Marketing, Math, Medical Technology, Nursing, Physical Education, Psychology, Social Work, Veterinary Science, Wild Life and other PreProfessional Degrees

Men's Athletic Profile

Cumberland Gap Parkway
Harrogate, TN 37752
Coach: Jeff Winterberger
Email: athletics@centuryinter.net

NCAA II
Railsplitters/Blue, White
Phone: (423) 869-6245
Fax: (423) 869-6382

Estimated # of Men's Soccer Scholarships: 8.5
Conference: Gulf South Conference
Program Profile: Les Gibbs Field is a Bermuda surface. Tex Turner Arena has a locker room and weight training equipment. Training is year-round.
History: Program began in 1987 as NAIA program, moved to NCAA Division II in 1991. Mike Varga is the winningest coach in the program's history. Numerous All-Conference selections.
Achievements: Numerous All-Conference selections.
Coaching: Jeff Winterberger, Head Coach. Brad Wigand and Dave Swaney, Assistant Coaches.
Style of Play: Very technical, skillful soccer, getting numbers into attack and defense. Build from the back, possession.

Women's Athletic Profile

Cumberland Gap Parkway
Harrogate, TN 37752
Coach: Jeff Winterberger
Email: athletics@centuryinter.net

NCAA II
Lay Railsplitters/Blue, Grey
Phone: (423) 869-6245
Fax: (423) 869-6382

Estimated # of Women's Soccer Scholarships:
Conference: Gulf South Conference
Program Profile: Home matches are played on Les Gibbs Field in the middle of campus. The field measures 120x70 yards and has Bermuda grass. We play a very competitive Division II schedule and have a year-around training program.
History: The program began in 1994 as a NCAA Division II, and in three seasons our record is 34-20-3. The Lady Railsplitters are ranked as high as #10 in the country. They were 1997 Conference Champions with a record of 14-3-2. They have had 48 wins in the last 3 years.
Achievements: 1996 Regular Season Conference Champions; 1996 Conference Coach of the Year-Erin Alexander; 4 All-Central Region Players; 1997 Conference Champions.
Coaching: Jeff Winterberger, Head Coach, has played professionally in the United States. Dave Swaney and Brad Wigard are assistant coaches.
Style of Play: Very skillful, play to feet & work combinations. Very attack oriented.

Martin Methodist College

Academic Profile

Pulaski, TN 38478
Phone:

Type: 2 Yr.,Private,Jr. College
Website: http://www.martinmethodist.edu
SAT/ACT/GPA: 860/18
Student/Faculty Ratio: 13:1
Undergraduate Enrollment: 500
Scholarships/Academic: Yes **Athletic:** Yes
Expenses by: Year **In State:** $ 9,585
Founded: 1870
Religion: United Methodist
Housing: Yes
Male/Female Ratio: 49:51
Graduate Enrollment: N/A
Financial Aid: Yes
Out of State: $ 9,585
Specialty: Jr. College
Degrees Conferred: Associate
Programs of Study: Business, Elementary Education, Church Vocations, Human Services

Men's Athletic Profile

433 W Madison Street
Pulaski, TN 38478
Coach: Paschal Dunne
Email: p4611280@hotmail.com
NAIA
Indians/Red, White
Phone: (615) 363-9807
Fax: (615) 363-9832

Estimated # of Men's Soccer Scholarships:
Conference: Tran South Athletic Conference
Program Profile: In 1999 we developed a new soccer facility. The field is Bermuda grass 120 X 77 1/2 yards. Excellent training and playing facilities.
History: Our program began in 1990. 1993-1994 National Champions NSCAA (Small Colleges 1993). Became a four year program in 1995 (NAIA).
Achievements: Record 1999-00 11-5 & Conference Semi-Finalist; 1998-99 14-4 & Conference Finalist; First winning season since becoming a four year college was 1995. Six All-Conference players, two All-Region, two A League/ MLS Drafted players in the last two years.
Coaching: Paschal Dunne, Head Coach, Dublin Ireland. 3rd season with the program. over 70% winning record the past two seasons. David Farmer, Assistant Coach, Leicester England.
Camp or Clinic Dates: June 12-16 and July 10-14
Schedule: Birmingham Southern, AL, Life University, GA, Berry College, GA, Xavier University, Montevallo University, AL, Auburn Montgomery, AL, Union University, TN
Style of Play: A very dynamic team. High technical and tactical competence.

Women's Athletic Profile

433 West Madison Street
Pulaski, TN 38478
Coach: Frank Davies
Email: Not Available

NAIA
Indians/Red, White
Phone: (615) 363-9807
Fax: (615) 363-9832

Estimated # of Women's Soccer Scholarships: None
Conference: Tran South Athletic Conference
Program Profile: The home field is natural grass, 118 x 70 yards. Excellent training facilities with well equipped gym and medical personnel.
History: The women's program began its first season in 1996.

Maryville College

Academic Profile

Maryville, TN 37805

Phone:

Type: 4 Yr.,Private,Liberal Arts
Website: http://www.maryvillecollege.edu
SAT/ACT/GPA: 900/21/3.0
Student/Faculty Ratio: 14:1
Undergraduate Enrollment: 950
Scholarships/Academic: Yes **Athletic:** No
Expenses by: Year **In State:** $ 20,415

Founded: 1819
Religion: Presbyterian
Housing: Yes
Male/Female Ratio: 2.5:1
Graduate Enrollment: N/A
Financial Aid: Yes
Out of State: $ 20,415

Specialty: Liberal Arts
Degrees Conferred: BA, BS, BM
Programs of Study: Art Education, Biology, Business Administration, Chemistry, Computer Science, Economics, Education, English, Fine Arts, Health Science, History, International Relations, Journalism, Management, Mathematics, Music, Music Education, Nursing, Physical Therapy, Political Science, PreDental, PreEngineering, PreLaw, PreMed, Psychology, Religion, Science Education, Secondary Education, Social Science, Spanish, Speech

Men's Athletic Profile

502 E. Lamar Alexander Parkway
Maryville, TN 37804
Coach: Pepe Fernandez
Email: fernande@maryvillecollege.edu

NCAA III
Scots/Garnet, Orange
Phone: (423) 981-8284
Fax: (423) 981-8285

Estimated # of Men's Soccer Scholarships: None
Conference: Independent
Program Profile: the field is measures 120x75 yards grass. Stadium that seats 500 due to be completed in June of 1999. Bermuda grass practice field adjacent to game field due to be completed in August of 1999.
History: Program began in 1981. Best seasons were 1995 & 1996. Made the NCAA Tournament both season (15-4 in 1995 and 13-4 in 1996). Coach Fernandez has been here for 10 seasons.
Achievements: Nationally ranked several times, consistently ranked in the top 10 in the South - NCAA Tournament Appearances in 1995 & 1996; 2 All-Americans, 30+ players named All-South, several players in the A-League and USISL.
Coaching: Pepe Fernandez, Head Coach, entering ten years with the program and compiled a record of 119-56-9. He was a former NAIA All-American, holds NSCAA Advanced National Diploma, on the ODP staff, TSSA Coaching instructor. John LaCava, Assistant Coach. Grant Kelly, Goalkeeper Coach.
Style of Play: Style of play is dictated by personnel. We prepare a wide-open offensive style featuring short passing with strong team defense.

Women's Athletic Profile

502 E. Lamar Alexander Parkway
Maryville, TN 37804
Coach: Pepe Fernandez
Email: fernandez@maryvillecollege.edu

NCAA III
Scots/Garnet, Orange
Phone: (865) 981-8000
Fax: (423) 981-8285

Estimated # of Women's Soccer Scholarships: None
Conference: Independent
Program Profile: Game field is 120x75 Bermuda grass. Bermuda grass practice field adjacent to the game field due to be completed August of 1999. Stadium with 500 person capacity completed June of 1999.
History: Our program began in 1998. One losing season in the program's history. Best record was 15-3 (nationally ranked #20) in 1992. Coach Fernandez has been here 8 seasons with 90-45-4 record.
Achievements: Consistently ranked in the Top 10 in the South; nationally ranked several times; 1 All-American; 9 players named All-South.
Coaching: Pepe Fernandez, Head Coach. John LaCava, Assistant Coach. Grant Kelly, Goalkeeper Coach.
Style of Play: Style of play is dedicated by personnel. We prefer a wide open offensive style featuring short passing with strong team defense.

Milligan College

Academic Profile

Milligan College, TN 37682

Phone:

Type: 4 Yr.,Private,Liberal Arts
Website: http://www.milligan.edu
SAT/ACT/GPA: 900+/20+
Student/Faculty Ratio: 15:1
Undergraduate Enrollment: 900
Scholarships/Academic: Yes **Athletic:** Yes
Expenses by: Year **In State:** $ 15,880
Specialty: Liberal Arts
Degrees Conferred: AS, BA, BS, MED, MOT

Founded: 1881
Religion: Christian Church
Housing: Yes
Male/Female Ratio: 40:60
Graduate Enrollment: 100
Financial Aid: Yes
Out of State: $ 15,880

Programs of Study: Accounting, Advertising, Art, Biblical Studies, Biology, Broadcasting, Business Administration, Chemistry, Communications, Computer Science, Education, Health Music, Religious Science, English, General Engineering, History, Humanities, Human Services, Liberal Arts, Management, Mathematics, Ministries, Music, Nursing, PreDental, PreMed, PreVet, Psychology, Radio & Television, Religion, Science, Social Work, Sociology, Theatre

Men's Athletic Profile

P.O. Box 9
Milligan College, TN 37682
Coach: John Garvilla
Email: soccer@milligan.edu

NAIA
Buffaloes/Black, White
Phone: (423) 461-8469
Fax: (423) 461-8470

Estimated # of Men's Soccer Scholarships: 12
Conference: TVAC
Program Profile: Facilities include two lighted Bermuda fields with a measurements of 120x75 yards and has a seating capacity of 1,000, 2 electronic scoreboards, indoor facility - 3 inches thick turf with dashboards. Program has year-round training with extensive indoor season 3-4 tournaments. The program also consists of junior varsity team with 14 matches. Junior Varsity was undefeated in 1998.
History: 1978 was the inception of the program. The last 3 years marked the 1st appearance in the playoffs with the team appearing in the Championship each time.

Achievements: TVAC Champions in 1999 and made it to the Region 12 finals; 5 Academic All-American; 3 All-American.
Coaching: John Garvilla, Head Coach, is entering his 8th year of college coaching, his fourth year as a head coach, and his second year at Milligan College. He compiled an overall record of 80-58-5. He played semi-pro for Falmouth and collegiate at Winthrop University. Marty Shirly, Assistant Coach, three times MVP at Milligan. Jeff Johnson, Assistant Coach was named USL All-Star team. Joey Johnson, Assistant Coach, pro player in USL and Boliva. Hans Hobson, Assistant Coach, played collegiate at Emory and Henry University.
Roster In State: 6 **Out of State:** 27 **Out of Country:** 3
ODP State: 6 **Regional:** 0 **National:** 2
Walk-on/Other: **Graduation %:** **Seniors on Team:** 5
Positions Needed: 2 Midfield, 1 Defender, Goalkeeper
Camp or Clinic Dates: July 16-21
Most Recent Record: 19-2
Schedule: Barry University, Berry College, Lindsey Wilson College, Florida Southern University, Brevard College, Lincoln Memorial University, Transylvania University, Houghton College, Less McRae College, Auburn Montgomery University
Style of Play: Depends on personnel. Preference is to play possession build up with quick counter attack. Defensively low pressure and zone.

Women's Athletic Profile

P.O. Box 9, Soccer Office
Milligan College, TN 37682
Coach: John Garvilla
Email: soccer@milligan.edu

NAIA
Buffaloes/Black, White
Phone: (423) 461-8469
Fax: (423) 461-8470

Estimated # of Women's Soccer Scholarships: 12
Conference: Tennessee-Virginia Athletic Conference
Program Profile: Facilities include 2 lighted Bermuda fields which measures 120x75 yards. It has a seating capacity of 1,000 and two electronic scoreboards. Indoor facility includes turf 3 inches thick with dashboards. Program has a year-round training and extensive indoor season with 3-4 tournaments. The program also consists of a junior team.
History: 1997 was the inception of the program. The team captured its first TVAC Championships in just two years with a 7-0 win over Tennessee Wesleyan. The team has been undefeated in conference play the last two years.
Achievements: 1998 and 1999 TVAC Champions; Coach of the Year 1998 and 1999; Team led nation in scoring in 1999 with 110 goals; Mercy Akide led the nation scoring 42 and 15 assist; 9 All-Region players; 5 All-American. Mercy Akide is a FIFA World All-Star and has also played in 3 World Cups and is playing in the 2000 Olympics.
Coaching: John Garvilla, Head Coach, is entering his 9th year in college coaching, his fourth as a head coach and second at Milligan. his overall record is 80-58-5. John played semi-pro Falmouth and collegiate at Winthrop University. Marty Shirley, Assistant Coach, three times MVP at Milligan. John Migbrese is the goalkeeper coach and he played at Georgia Southern University. Hans Hobson played for Emory and Henry College.
Roster in State: 8 **Out of State:** 21 **Out of Country:** 11
ODP State: 2 **Regional:** 1 **National:** 5
Walk-on/Other: **Graduation %:** 85 **Seniors on Team:** 4
Positions Needed: Goalkeeper, Defenders, Midfielder, Striker
Camp or Clinic Dates: July 16-21
Most Recent Record: 12-9-1
Schedule: Barry University, Coasted Carolina University, Florida Southern University, Catawba College, Echerd College, Houghton College, Lincoln Memorial University, Brevard College, Mars Hill College, Bryan College
Style of Play: Dependent on personnel. Prefer is to play possession build up with quick counter attack. Defensively low pressure and zone.

Rhodes College
Academic Profile

Memphis, TN 38112
Phone: 901-843-3000

Type: 4 Yr.,Private,Liberal Arts
Website: http://www.rhodes.edu
SAT/ACT/GPA: 1100/25/3.0
Student/Faculty Ratio: 12:1
Undergraduate Enrollment: 1,450
Scholarships/Academic: Yes **Athletic:** No
Expenses by: Year **In State:** $ 23,528
Founded: 1848
Religion: Presbyterian, USA
Housing: Yes
Male/Female Ratio: 45:55
Graduate Enrollment: 10
Financial Aid: Yes
Out of State: $ 23,528
Specialty: Business, Pre-professional programs
Degrees Conferred: BA, BS
Programs of Study: Art, Biology, Chemistry, English, History, Business & Management, International Studies, Philosophy, Political Science, Psychology, Religion

Men's Athletic Profile

2000 North Parkway
Memphis, TN 38112
Coach: Andy Marcinko
Email: marcinko@rhodes.edu
NCAA III
Lynx/Red, Black
Phone: (901) 834-3948
Fax: (901) 843-3749

Estimated # of Men's Soccer Scholarships: 0
Conference: Southern Collegiate Athletic Conference
Program Profile: Has 20-game fall season, five-game spring season, 120x80 yards Tifton Bermuda grass, soccer-only stadium with 750 seating capacity. Practice field has a 53,000 sq. ft. gymnasium plus $22 million athletic facility opened last fall of 1996; 1,800 sq. ft. training room, state of the art, resistive exercise equipment.
History: Program began in 1985, with a commitment to become nationally competitive in 1991. Since 1992, Lynx have won two conference championships and have had two NCAA Tournament Appearances in 1994-1995, including national rankings in 1994 and 1995.
Achievements: Since 1991 3 SCAC Champions, 5 Runner-up. 4 NCAA Tournament Appearance, top 25 ranking since 1994. Coach of the Year 1991, 93, 95, 98. 3 All-Americans, 9 All-region selections.
Coaching: Andy Marcinko, Head Coach, USSF "A" License, NSCAA Advanced National , Brazilian Football Academy Diploma, Irish FA Diploma, Tennessee ODP State staff, BS in Biology, and MS in Exercise Physiology. Assistant coach is Scott Quick.
Roster In State: 4 **Out of State:** 24 **Out of Country:** 0
ODP State: 14 **Regional:** 3 **National:** 0
Walk-on/Other: 1 **Graduation %:** 100 **Seniors on Team:** 9
Positions Needed: Forwards, Mid-Fielders, Keeper
Camp or Clinic Dates: Not Available
Most Recent Record: 14-3-0
Schedule: Trinity, DePauw, Chicago, Washington University, Wheaton, Colorado College
Style of Play: Possession oriented, 11 Attack, 11 Defend. Training must be fun to be effective.

Women's Athletic Profile

2000 North Parkway
Memphis, TN 38112
Coach: Laura Whiteley
Email: Whiteley@rhodes.edu
NCAA III
Lynx/Red, Black
Phone: (901) 843-3452
Fax: (901) 843-3749

Estimated # of Women's Soccer Scholarships: None
Conference: Southern Collegiate Athletic Conference
Program Profile: 20-game fall season, five-game spring season. 120x80 yards of Tifton Bermuda grass, soccer only stadium with a 750 seating capacity, $22 million athletic facility opened in 1996 with state-of-the-art training room, resistive exercise equipment, etc...
History: Program began in 1985, with a commitment to become nationally competitive in 1991. National ranking in 1994 and 1995, top finisher in conference since 1991. Record of 115-46-6(1191-1999).
Achievements: 7 All-Region players; 25+ All-Conference players. NSCAA All-Academic Team Award, 1995-1998.
Coaching: Laura Whiteley, Head Coach. USSF "B" License, NSCAA Advanced National Diploma. Entering 2nd year at Rhodes in fall of 2000. Former assistant coach at Western Michigan University.

Roster in State: 2	**Out of State:** 18	**Out of Country:** 0
ODP State: 2	**Regional:**	**National:**
Walk-on/Other:	**Graduation %:** 100	**Seniors on Team:** 4

Positions Needed: ALL
Camp or Clinic Dates: TBA
Most Recent Record: 4-13-2
Schedule: Trinity, DePauw, University of the South, Southwestern University, Emory, Mt. St. Joseph, Wilmington College, Ohio Northern, Agnes Scott
Style of Play: Dependant on the players we have in our program. Preference toward an attack-oriented possession game, with lots of players going forward from all positions.

Tennessee Wesleyan College

Academic Profile

Phone:

Athens, TN 37303

Type: 4 Yr.,Private,Liberal Arts		**Founded:** 1857
Website: Not Available		**Religion:** Methodist
SAT/ACT/GPA: 880/18		**Housing:** Yes
Student/Faculty Ratio: 14:1		**Male/Female Ratio:** 1:2
Undergraduate Enrollment: 800		**Graduate Enrollment:** N/A
Scholarships/Academic: Yes	**Athletic:** Yes	**Financial Aid:** Yes
Expenses by: Year	**In State:** $ 11,630	**Out of State:** $ 11,630

Degrees Conferred: BA, BS
Programs of Study: Athletic Training, Biology, Business Administration, Chemistry, Church Vocations, English, General Science, Health & Physical Education, Exercise Science, History, Human Learning, Human Services, Interdisciplinary Studies, Mathematics, Behavioral Science, English, History, PreSeminary Psychology

Men's Athletic Profile

P.O. Box 40
Athens, TN 37371
Coach: Sean Clanton
Email: clanton@tnwc.edu

NAIA
Bulldogs/Blue, Gold, White
Phone: (423) 745-5225
Fax: (423) 744-9968

Estimated # of Men's Soccer Scholarships: 8
Conference: Tennessee-Virginia Athletic Conference
Program Profile: Our field is 120 x 65 yards with a mixture of Bermuda and Zoysia. The hill overlooking our game field will soon be cut into a natural stadium with a 1,000 seats. We have a full-time trainer on staff with a complete training room, a practice field, weights, scoreboard, press box, and stadium, which seats approx. 500. Playing season is in the fall that runs from August to November.
History: Our TVAC is the second largest NAIA Conference in the nation. The program has been around for more than 20 years.

Achievements: Won 9 Conference Titles; 7 District Titles; 4 trips to South Regional Finals; 6 All-Americans; 5 All-South; 35 All-Conference players; 37 All-District players.
Coaching: Sean Clanton, Head Coach, graduated from TWC with a BA in History. He holds a NSCAA National Diploma. Sean Asburn is the Assistant Coach. Kevin Trobaugh is the Student Assistant.
Style of Play: Direct and fast with some Latin fair in attack.

Women's Athletic Profile

P.O. Box 40
Athens, TN 37371
Coach: Sean Clanton
Email: clantons@tnwc.edu

NAIA
Bulldogs/Royal, Blue, White
Phone: (423) 745-7504
Fax: (423) 744-9968

Estimated # of Women's Soccer Scholarships: None
Conference: Tennessee-Virginia Athletic Conference
Program Profile: Game field is 120 x 65 yards with mixture of Bermuda and Zoysia. The hill overlooking our game field will be cut out into a natural stadium. We have a full time trainer on staff with a complete training room. We also have a practice field, weights and aerobics at our disposal. Stadium has approximately 500 seats.
History: The TVAC is the second largest NAIA Conference in the nation. The program is ten years old.
Achievements: 1997 TVAC Coach of the Year; 5 Conference Titles
Coaching: Sean Clanton, Head Coach. Sean Ashburn - Assistant Coach. Kevin Trobaugh - Student Assistant Coach.
Style of Play: Indirect, ball control, able to quick counter.

Tusculum College

Academic Profile

P.O. Box 5074
Greenville, TN 37743

Phone: (423) 636-7328

Type: 4 Yr.,Private,Liberal Arts
Website: http://www.tusculum.edu
SAT/ACT/GPA: 920/18/2.0
Student/Faculty Ratio: 14:1
Undergraduate Enrollment: 1200
Scholarships/Academic: Yes
Athletic: Yes
Expenses by: Year
In State: $ 17,025
Founded: 1794
Religion: Presbyterian
Housing: Yes
Male/Female Ratio: 1:1
Graduate Enrollment: 200
Financial Aid: Yes
Out of State: $ 17,025
Specialty: Civic Arts, Education, Biology
Degrees Conferred: BS, BA, MA, M.Ed.
Programs of Study: Biology, Computer Information Systems, Computer Science, English, Mass Media, Environmental Science, History, Management, Mathematics, Medical PreProfessional, Medical Technology, Museum Studies, Physical Education, Psychology, Visual Arts, Teaching-Licensure Programs

Men's Athletic Profile

P.O. Box 5062
Greenville, TN 37743
Coach: Tony Castainca
Email: tcastain@tusculum.edu

NCAA II
Pioneers/Orange, Black, White
Phone: (423) 636-7496
Fax: (423) 798-1636

Estimated # of Men's Soccer Scholarships: Varied
Conference: South Atlantic Conference
Program Profile: Play on international size field - Pioneer Field which is Bermuda grass with a seating capacity of 3,500. Play on 120x80 yards field. In Fall 2000 will have an indoor athletic practice facility.

History: Program began in 1960's. NAIA District 24 Champions in 1983, 1991, 1992 and 1993. Conference appearances from 1990 to 1995. 1996 NCAA and Independent NAIA Mid-South Region (Sectional).
Achievements: 1991, 1992, 1993 Tennessee- Virginia Athletic Conference Champions; 1991, 1992, NAIA District 24 Champions; 1999 South Atlantic Conference Tournament Champions. Coach Castainca was named TVAC Coach of the Year 4 times, and NAIA District 24 Coach of the Year twice.
Coaching: Tony Castainca, Head Coach, 15 years experience at high school and college level. David Crickmar, Assistant Coach.
Roster In State: 8 **Out of State:** 12 **Out of Country:** 7
Walk-on/Other: **Graduation %:** N/A **Seniors on Team:** 2
Positions Needed: Striker, Central Offender, Mid Fielder
Camp or Clinic Dates: Not Available
Most Recent Record: 10-9-2
Schedule: Francis Marion University, Wingate University, Presbyterian, L.M.U., Alabama Huntsville, Carson- Newman
Style of Play: 4-2-4, aggressive style attacking, midfield and outside backs overlapping.

Women's Athletic Profile

P.O. Box 5019
Greeneville, TN 37743
Coach: Mike Joy
Email: jmaddox10@hotmail.com

NCAA II
Pioneers/Orange, Black
Phone: (423) 636-7321
Fax: (423) 798-1636

Estimated # of Women's Soccer Scholarships:
Conference: South Atlantic Conference
Program Profile: We traveled to Hawaii to play three matches. We have a 120x80 Bermuda grass lighted soccer stadium that seats 5,000 with press box and concessions.
History: Our program began in 1990. I took over the program in 1997 and have taken a program that was 2-13-1 in 1996 to a 10 win season in 1997 and 13 wins, which is most wins college history. This year we finished 13-7-2, 7th in the NCAA II South Region.
Achievements: Tusculum TVAC Conference Championship in 1991. We now participate in the NCAA Division II South Atlantic Conference (SAC). 2000 South Atlantic Conference regular season Champions and Tournament Champions 22nd in the Nation with a record of 19-3-0.
Coaching: Mike Joy, Head Coach, started the program in University of Kentucky and Midway College in Kentucky; led teams to two national championship appearances in 1994 & 1995; named 2 Mid-South Region NSCAA Coach of the Year Awards and 4 times Conference Coach of the Year. Jessica Maddox - Assistant Coach, former players at Midway College. Jenny Steirle, Graduate Assistant Coach.
Roster in State: 2 **Out of State:** 26 **Out of Country:** 0
ODP State: 16 **Regional:** 2 **National:**
Walk-on/Other: **Graduation %:** 100 **Seniors on Team:** 4
Positions Needed: Midfield, Wing, Defender, Striker
Camp or Clinic Dates: June 11-15, July 16-20
Most Recent Record: 19-3-0
Schedule: North Florida, Presbyterian, Pfeiffer, Wingate
Style of Play: Attacking-direct, defending-zonal and man to man.

Union University
Academic Profile

Jackson, TN 38305

Phone: (901)668-1818

Type: 4 Yr.,Private,Liberal Arts
Website: http://www.uu.edu
SAT/ACT/GPA: 930202.5

Founded: 1823
Religion: Southern Baptist
Housing: Yes

Student/Faculty Ratio: 12:1
Male/Female Ratio:
Undergraduate Enrollment: 2100
Graduate Enrollment: 400
Scholarships/Academic: Yes
Athletic: Yes
Financial Aid: Yes
Expenses by: Year
In State: $15,570
Out of State: $15,570
Specialty: Christian Liberal Arts University
Degrees Conferred: BA, BM, BS, MBA, M Ed
Programs of Study: Accounting, Biology, Chemistry, Communications, Computer, Economics, Education, English, French, History, Journalism, Marketing, Mathematics, Medical, Ministries, Music, Nursing, Sports Marketing & Management, Sports Medicine, Physics, PreProfessional Programs, Psychology, Religion, Social Science, Spanish

Men's Athletic Profile

1050 Union University Drive
Jackson, TN 38305
Coach: Dr. Darin White
Email: dwhite@uu.edu

NCCAA/NAIA
Bulldogs/Red, White
Phone: (901) 661-5108
Fax: (901) 661-5366

Estimated # of Men's Soccer Scholarships: 6
Conference: Tran South Conference
Program Profile: We have a year-round program that includes 18 games in the fall season, winter indoor tournaments, spring six sided tournaments, and summer tours of Brazil and Europe. We are a part of the very competitive Tran South Conference that includes three Top 25 programs. We are also part of the National Christian College Athletic Association (NCCAA). over 100 Christian schools from around the country annually hold a national championships soccer tournament that we compete in.
History: This past year has been a historic one for the Union University Men's Soccer Teams. The Bulldogs achieved their national ranking when College Soccer Weekly ranked the team #1 in the country for two weeks in September. In addition, the team achieved the longest winning streak in school history with 11 straight victories. The teams defense was ranked 9th nationally, only allowing 1.16 goals against average. The Bulldogs finished the year as the #3 seed in the NCCAA National Championship tournament in Orlando, FL.
Achievements: Coach White received NCCAA Mid-East Regional Coach of the Year in 1999. Also in 1999 3 players were named to the NCCAA All-American Team, 2 players named to the Tran South team and 4 players participated on their country's national team(Canada, Zambia, Australia, and Guatemala)
Coaching: Dr. Darin White, Head Coach, was an Olympic Development player in high school, played varsity soccer for Birmingham Southern College, where he won the Top Defensive Player, and Most Determination Awards. In addition, the Union Soccer Program has three Assistant Coaches - Russ White, James Huggins, and Dr. Toni Chiareli (Goalkeeper Coach). Russ White is the father of the head coach and brings several decades of successful coaching experience at the highest level to the program. On numerous occasions his teams has won the top national honor.
Roster In State: 5
Out of State: 15
Out of Country: 8
ODP State: 10
Regional: 2
National: 5
Walk-on/Other:
Graduation %: 100
Seniors on Team: 2
Positions Needed: Goalkeeper and Defense
Camp or Clinic Dates: Not Available
Most Recent Record: 14-5-0
Schedule: Birmingham- Southern College, Berry College, Bethel University (Indiana), David Lipscomb, William, Carey
Style of Play: Exciting, speed - oriented attack style offense. Man-making, 1-2-1 defensive set-up.

Women's Athletic Profile

1050 Union University Drive
Jackson, TN 38305
Coach: Darin W. White
Email: Not Available

NCCAA/NAIA
Bulldogs/Red, White
Phone: (901) 661-5108
Fax: (901) 661-5366

Estimated # of Women's Soccer Scholarships: None
Conference: Tran South Conference

Program Profile: We have a year-round program that includes 18 game fall season, winter indoor tournaments, spring six sided tournaments, and summer tours of Brazil and Europe. We are part of the very competitive Tran South Conference that includes three Top 25 programs. We are also part of the National Christian College Athletic Association (NCCAA). Over 100 Christian schools from around the country annually hold a national championship soccer tournament that we compete in.
History: The program began in 1994; highlights includes game against numerous SEC schools with victories against Auburn University, Southern University, etc..
Coaching: Darin W. White, Head Coach, was an Olympic Development player in high school, played varsity soccer for Birmingham Southern College where he won the Top Defensive Player and Most Determination awards, and had the opportunity to play professionally in Europe. In addition, the Union Soccer Programs has two assistant Coaches - Coach Russ White and Dr. James Huggins. Russ White is the father of the head coach and brings several decades of successful coaching experience at the highest level to the program. On numerous occasions his teams have won the top national honor.
Style of Play: Exciting, speed-oriented attack style offense. Man-marking, 1-2-1 defensive set-up.

University of Memphis
Academic Profile

Phone: (901) 678-3570

Memphis, TN 38152

Type: 4 Yr.,Public
Founded: 1912
Website: http://www.memphis.edu
Religion: Non-Affiliated
SAT/ACT/GPA: 19
Housing: Yes
Student/Faculty Ratio: 18:1
Male/Female Ratio: 1:1.38
Undergraduate Enrollment: 11,656
Graduate Enrollment: 8,444
Scholarships/Academic: Yes **Athletic:** Yes **Financial Aid:** Yes
Expenses by: Semester **In State:** $ 3,390 **Out of State:** $ 5,826
Specialty: Business, Education
Degrees Conferred: BA, BS, MA, MS, Ph.D., EdD
Programs of Study: Accounting, Anthropology, Applied Mathematics, Art, Biology, Business & Management, Chemistry, Communications, Computer Science, Criminal Justice, Education, Economics, Geography, Geology, History, Journalism, Liberal Arts, Medical Technology, Marketing, Psychology, Physics, Physical Education, Political Science

Men's Athletic Profile

Athletic Office Building Room 207
Memphis, TN 38152
Coach: Richie Grant
Email: rjgrant@memphis.edu

NCAA I
Tigers/Blue, Gray
Phone: (901) 678-4141
Fax: (901) 678-5952

Estimated # of Men's Soccer Scholarships: 2.5
Conference: Conference USA
Program Profile: The University of Memphis will play its home games at the Mike Rose Soccer Complex. The stadium will include 2,600 seats, numerous concession stands, restroom facilities, TV compliant lighting, locker rooms, PA system, and adequate parking. The playing surface is a Mississippi select Hybrid Bermuda and will play at approx. 120x78. Future plans call for skyboxes, jumbo TV, on site restaurant and retail store.
History: Program established in 1982. The Tigers have amassed 11 winning seasons, including an NCAA appearance in 1983, Memphis also won the Great Midwest Conference Tournament in 1983. Memphis played in the nationally televised 1998 C-USA Final. The 14 wins in the 2000 season is the most wins since the program was established in 1982.
Achievements: 1992 Great Midwest regular season title, 1993 Great Midwest Tournament Championships. 1993 NCAA Tournament appearance, 1998 C-USA Finalist. Player drafted to A-League. Richie Grant C-USA Coach of the Year.
Coaching: Richie Grant- Head Coach, Ryan Shea, Troy Norwood, Paul Conway are the Assistant Coaches.
Roster In State: 11 **Out of State:** 12 **Out of Country:** 5

ODP State: 10 **Regional:** 4 **National:** 2
Walk-on/Other: 0 **Graduation %:** 85 **Seniors on Team:** 5
Positions Needed: Center Fullback, Center Midfield, Left Midfield, Forward
Camp or Clinic Dates: Not Available
Most Recent Record: 14-6-0
Schedule: SMU, Creighton, Saint Louis, UAB, South Florida, UNC Charlotte, Cincinnati, Louisville, Marquette
Style of Play: At the University of Memphis we coach our players to do the simple things well. We focus on positive possession allowing us to attack and penetrate our opposition. We defend as a squad forcing our opponents to play predictable.

Women's Athletic Profile

207 Athletic Office Building.
Memphis, TN 38152-3730
Coach: Richie Grant
Email: rgrant@memphis.edu

NCAA I
Tigers/Blue, Gray
Phone: (901) 678-4141
Fax: (901) 678-5952

Estimated # of Women's Soccer Scholarships: 2.5
Conference: Conference USA
Program Profile: Enthusiastic growing program that plays on 120x70 yard Bermuda grass, on campus facility. Echles field is lit and seats 1,000 plus plenty of additional areas for fan seating. Athletes have access to 10,500 sq. ft training facility 60x40 indoor facility and an all athletics facilities.
History: Program established in 1982. The tigers have amassed ten winning seasons in that time, including NCAA appearance in 1983. The university of Memphis also won the Great Midwest Conference Tournament that season. Played in the televised 1998 Conference USA Final.
Achievements: 1942 Great Midwest Regular Season; 1993 Great Midwest Tournament Champions 1993 NCAA Appearance; 1998 Conference USA Finals.
Brian Covey drafted to Tennessee Rhythm (a league) 2000.
Coaching: Richie Grant is the University of Memphis' head coach. Ryan Shea I the asst. coach. Troy Norwood is the Goalkeeper coach.
Roster in State: 11 **Out of State:** 12 **Out of Country:** 5
ODP State: 10 **Regional:** 4 **National:** 2
Walk-on/Other: **Graduation %:** 85 **Seniors on Team:** 5
Positions Needed: Center Fullback, Midfield, Left Midfield, Forward
Most Recent Record: 14-6-0
Schedule: SMU, Creighton, Saint Louis, UAB, South Florida, UNC Charlotte, Cincinnati, Louisville, Marquette
Style of Play: At the University of Memphis we coach our players to do the simple things well. We focus on positive possession allowing us to attack and penetrate our opposition. We defend as a squad forcing our opponents to play predictable.

University of Tennessee - Chattanooga

Academic Profile

Chattanooga, TN 37403-2598
Phone: 423-755-4111

Type: 4 Yr.,Public **Founded:** 1886
Website: http://www.utc.edu **Religion:** Non-Affiliated
SAT/ACT/GPA: 750+/2.75 **Housing:** Yes
Student/Faculty Ratio: 19:1 **Male/Female Ratio:** 45:55
Undergraduate Enrollment: 2,126 **Graduate Enrollment:** 1,275
Scholarships/Academic: Yes **Athletic:** Yes **Financial Aid:** Yes
Expenses by: Year **In State:** $ 7,323 **Out of State:** $ 11,505
Degrees Conferred: BA, BS, BFA, MA, MS, MBA, M.Ed.

Programs of Study: Business and Management, Business/Office & Marketing/Distribution, Computer Science, Engineering, Health Science, Psychology, Social Science, System Analysis, Teacher Education

Women's Athletic Profile

615 McCallie Ave.
Chattanooga, TN 37415
Coach: JD Kyzer
Email: jd-kyzer@utc.edu

NCAA I
Mocs/Blue, Gold
Phone: (423) 755-5302
Fax: (423) 755-2160

Estimated # of Women's Soccer Scholarships: 5
Conference: Southern Conference, NCAA Division 1
Program Profile: Our program is still under development after first four years. We hired Coach JD Kyzer in March to lead the program in a more competitive direction. Our practice facility is Chamberbin Field former home of football team. We play our home games on natural grass, Finley Stadium, with 20,000 seating.
History: The program began in 1996 and won six matches in the first three years before winning five in 1999. Linda Whitehead was the first coach in school history. We showed great improvement in 1999 with five wins and two ties. Last season we lost our seven games by two goals or less. We have 11 overall in program history.
Achievements: None
Coaching: JD Kyzer is in his first season after spending the past five years as the Head Coach at Queens College in Charlotte, NC. Kyzer compiled a 60-27-3 record as the Head Coach of women's program. Assistant Coach Cory Hundley is in her first season also.
Roster in State: 7 **Out of State:** 8 **Out of Country:** 3
ODP State: 6 **Regional:** 2 **National:**
Walk-on/Other: **Graduation %:** 90 **Seniors on Team:** 5
Positions Needed: Goalkeeper, Midfielders
Camp or Clinic Dates: Not Available
Most Recent Record: 5-12-2
Schedule: Furman, Mississippi State, Davidson, College of Charleston, Indiana State, Tennessee Tech
Style of Play: Offensively will look to attack and push the ball forward. Defensively will play a player on player style with double teams on the ball to force the action. Defense is our strong suit.

University of Tennessee - Knoxville

Academic Profile

Knoxville, TN 37996-3110
Phone: 865-974-1000

Type: 4 Yr.,Public,Engineering
Founded: 1794
Website: http://www.utk.edu
Religion: Non-Affiliated
SAT/ACT/GPA: 21/2.0
Housing: Yes
Student/Faculty Ratio: 17:1
Male/Female Ratio: 51:49
Undergraduate Enrollment: 14,000
Graduate Enrollment: 4,500
Scholarships/Academic: Yes **Athletic:** Yes **Financial Aid:** Yes
Expenses by: Year **In State:** $ 6,659 **Out of State:** $ 11,715
Specialty: Engineering, Business Administration, Nursing
Degrees Conferred: Numerous majors nationally-ranked
Programs of Study: Accounting, Advertising, Aerospace Engineering, Animal Science, Anthropology, Architecture, Biological Science, Broadcasting, Chemical Engineering, Chemistry, Computer Science, Education, Exercise Science, Finance, Forestry, Journalism, Logistics Transportation, Management, Marketing, Nursing, Political Science, Psychology, Public Administration, Religious Studies, Speech Pathology, Statistics, Sports

Women's Athletic Profile

117 Stokely, Athletics Center
Knoxville, TN 37996
Coach: Angela Kelly
Email: akelly@utk.edu

NCAA I
Lady Volunteers/Orange, White
Phone: (865) 974-7496
Fax: (865) 974-8914

Estimated # of Women's Soccer Scholarships: 12
Conference: Southeastern Conference
Program Profile: Play on two fields which measure 120x75 Bermuda grass. Stadium has a seating capacity of 1,500. SEC Conference member and fully funded program.
History: Our program is three years old - 1996 was inaugural season with a record of 6-13-1. Qualified for Conference Tournament. In 1997 our record was 11-8 and in 1998 our record was 12-8 and qualified for Conference Tournament.
Achievements: We were #6 in attendance in 1998 (937 per game). In our 1998 season we had 2 players All-South & All-SEC.
Coaching: Angela Kelly begins her first full year as Head Coach with the fall 2000 season. Angela is joined by former teammate Sarah Dacey and Goalkeeper Coach John Cone.
Roster in State: 5 **Out of State:** 17 **Out of Country:** 2
Walk-on/Other: **Graduation %:** 100 **Seniors on Team:** 6
Positions Needed: Goalkeeper, Forward
Camp or Clinic Dates: July 9-16, 13-20
Most Recent Record: 8-11-1
Schedule: North Carolina, Florida, Kentucky, Georgia, George Mason, Vanderbilt
Style of Play: High pressure defensively and we look to attack quickly with good numbers. And most of all look to play exciting attack-minded soccer.

University of Tennessee - Martin

Academic Profile

Phone: 901-587-7000
Martin, TN 38238

Type: 4 Yr.,Public
Founded: 1927
Website: http://www.utm.edu
Religion: Non-Affiliated
SAT/ACT/GPA: 910/19/2.25
Housing: Yes
Student/Faculty Ratio: 20:1
Male/Female Ratio: 45:55
Undergraduate Enrollment: 5,400
Graduate Enrollment: 400
Scholarships/Academic: Yes **Athletic:** Yes **Financial Aid:** Yes
Expenses by: Year **In State:** $ 6,538 **Out of State:** $ 11,364
Degrees Conferred: BA, BS, MBUs, MEd, MH
Programs of Study: Agricultural, Animal, Biological, Broadcasting, Chemistry, Civil Engineering, Criminal Justice, Dental Science, Earth Space, Economics, Finance, GeoScience, History, Management, Parks/Recreation, Pharmacy, PreProfessional Programs

Women's Athletic Profile

Coach: Nathan Pifer
Phone: (901) 587-7931

Did Not Return Profile

University of the South

Academic Profile

Phone: 615-322-7311

Sewanee, TN 37383

Type: 4 Yr.,Private,Liberal Arts
Founded: 1858
Website: http://www.sewanee.edu
Religion: Episcopal
SAT/ACT/GPA: 1160/25/3.53
Housing: Yes
Student/Faculty Ratio: 10:1
Male/Female Ratio: 48:52
Undergraduate Enrollment: 1,300
Graduate Enrollment: N/A
Scholarships/Academic: Yes **Athletic:** No **Financial Aid:** Yes
Expenses by: Year **In State:** $ 23,380 **Out of State:** $ 23,380
Degrees Conferred: BA, BS
Programs of Study: American Studies, Anthropology, Art History, Biology, Chemistry, Computer Literature, Computer Science, Comparative Literature, Economics, English, Fine Arts, French, Geology, German, German Studies, Greek, History, Latin, Mathematics, Mathematics and Computer Science, Medieval Studies, Music, Natural Resources, Emphasis on Forestry, Philosophy, Physics, Political Science, Psychology, Religion, Russian, Russian Area Studies, Social Science, Foreign Language, Spanish, Theatre Arts, Third World Studies

Men's Athletic Profile

735 University Ave.
Sewanee, TN 37383
Coach: Matt Kern
Email: mkern@sewanee.edu

NCAA III
Tigers/White, Purple
Phone: (931) 598-1582
Fax: (931) 598-1673

Estimated # of Men's Soccer Scholarships:
Conference: Southern Collegiate Athletic Conference (SCAC)
Program Profile: Nationally Ranked in NCAA III the last three years. Finished the 2000 season 16-3-0 ranked #20 in the Nation. Play in the SCAC which was the top rated NCAA III men's soccer conference in the country during 2000. Play on natural grass with a capacity 1,000 soccer only stadium.
History: Began in 1968 33 years. All time record is 266-250-34
Achievements: 23 All-South Players, 39 All-Conference Players, 2000 SCAC Player of the Year, 2000 SCAC Coach of the Year.
Coaching: Matt Kern, Head Coach, is in his 10th season here. He received his Bachelor's degree in Elementary Education at Hartwick in 1988. He was a former assistant at Springfield College and holds a NSCAA Advanced National Diploma. He was a four-year starter on teams which reached the NCAA playoffs, including two Final Four Appearances. Assistant Coach Rafe Mauran.
Roster In State: 8 **Out of State:** 17 **Out of Country:** 0
ODP State: 12 **Regional:** 2 **National:** 0
Walk-on/Other: 0 **Graduation %:** **Seniors on Team:** 5
Positions Needed: Central Def, Central MF, Forward
Most Recent Record: 16-3-0
Schedule: Trinity, Chicago, DePauw, Rhodes, Centre, Washington Univ. Webster
Style of Play: Zonal defending, quick transition play and combination play in the final 3rd.

Women's Athletic Profile

735 University Ave.
Sewanee, TN 37375
Coach: Margot Burns
Email: mburns@sewanee.edu

NCAA III
Tigers/Purple, White
Phone: (931) 598-1545
Fax: (423) 598-1145

Estimated # of Women's Soccer Scholarships: None
Conference: Southern Collegiate Athletic
History: Program began in 1988. Joined SCAC in 1991 allowing for post-season tournament play.

Vanderbilt University

Academic Profile

Jess Neely Drive
Nashville, TN 37212

Phone:

Type: 4 Yr.,Private,Liberal Arts,Engineering
Founded: 1873
Website: http://www.vanderbilt.edu
Religion: Non-Affiliated
SAT/ACT/GPA: 1150/28
Housing: Yes
Student/Faculty Ratio: 8:1
Male/Female Ratio: 50:50
Undergraduate Enrollment: 5,800
Graduate Enrollment: 4,200
Scholarships/Academic: Yes **Athletic:** Yes **Financial Aid:** Yes
Expenses by: Year **In State:** $ 32,022 **Out of State:** $ 32,022
Degrees Conferred: BA, BS, MA, MS, MBA, MED, Ph.D., MD, JD
Programs of Study: Education, Engineering, Human Development, Letters/Literature, Liberal Arts & Sciences, Life Sciences, Mathematics, Music, Psychology, Social Sciences plus a full range of graduate and professional degree

Men's Athletic Profile

Box 120158
Nashville, TN 37212
Coach: Randy Johnson
Email: randallb.johnson@vanderbilt.edu

NCAA I
Commodores/Black, Gold
Phone: (615) 343-8098
Fax: (615) 343-8123

Estimated # of Men's Soccer Scholarships: 1/3
Conference: Missouri Valley Conference
Program Profile: New stadium with lights and Bermuda grass playing surface. Adjacent athletic department contains weight room, training room, academic center and cafeteria for the athletes. Separate practice field.
History: Began as a club in 1965. Varsity status in 1978; joined the Missouri Valley Conference in 1997.
Achievements: Tony Kuhn was named 1996 & 1997 All-American, also he played with Chicago Fire of the MLS in 1998. one playing professionally in Japan and one just drafted into A-League; Coach Randy Johnson was named 1996 Conference Coach of the Year.
Coaching: Randy Johnson, Head Coach, 26 years, he holds "A" license and Advanced National Diploma. He was named 1996 Conference Coach of the Year. Robert Acunto, Assistant coach, entering two years with the program. He holds "A" License and Advanced National Diploma.
Style of Play: Possession offense and advanced zonal defending.

Women's Athletic Profile

P.O. Box 120158
Nashville, TN 37212
Coach: Randy Johnson
Email:

NCAA I
Commodores/Black, Gold
Phone: (615) 343-8099
Fax: (615) 343-8123

Estimated # of Women's Soccer Scholarships: 2
Conference: Southeastern Conference

Program Profile: We have newly renovated and expanded athletic facilities that include a first class Bermuda grass playing field, new lights, stadium seating and two scoreboards. Our facilities include an Olympic sport weight room, 2 training rooms, an academic center with a computer lab and 2 training table meal program.
History: Our program began in 1995. We were SEC Champions in 1993 and 1994. We were Division Champions in 1995 and 1997. We won the NCAA Tournament in 1994 and 1998. In 1998, our final season ranking was 17th.
Achievements: 1998 1st Team All-American- Asta Helgadottir; 4 All-Region players: Asta Helgadottir, Laura Koerner, Valle Vanholz and Lauren Whitt; SEC Coach of the Year in 1993 and 1997.
Style of Play: We play a possession game with a creative exciting attack and an aggressive defense. Also, we have the ability to play a multiple number of formations and positions.

texas

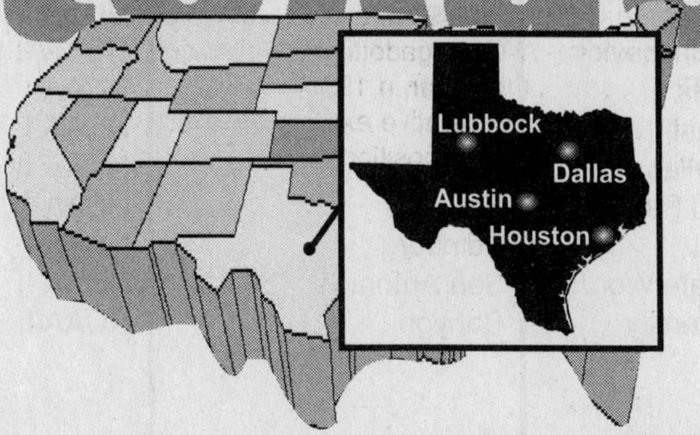

SCHOOL	CITY	AFFILIATION	PAGE
Angelo State University	San Angelo	NCAA II	1083
Austin College	Sherman	NCAA III	1083
Baylor University	Waco	NCAA I	1085
Concordia University - Austin	Austin	NAIA	1086
Dallas Baptist University	Dallas	NCAA II/NAIA	1087
East Texas Baptist	Marshall	NCAA II	1088
Hardin - Simmons University	Abilene	NCAA III	1089
Hill Junior College	Hillsboro	NJCAA	1090
Jarvis Christian College	Hawkins	NCAA II	1091
LeTourneau University	Longview	NCAA III	1092
Midwestern State University	Wichita Falls	NCAA II	1093
Mountian View College	Dallas	NJCAA	1094
Richland College	Dallas	NJCAA	1094
Saint Edward's University	Austin	NCAA II	1096
Saint Mary's University	San Antonio	NCAA II	1097
Schreiner College	Kerrville	NCAA III	1098
Southern Methodist University	Dallas	NCAA I	1099
Southwestern University	Georgetown	NCAA III	1100
Stephen F. Austin	Nacogdoches	NCAA I	1102
Texas A & M University	College Station	NCAA I	1103
Texas A &M University-Commerce	Commerce	NCAA II	1103
Texas Christian University	Fort Worth	NCAA I	1104
Texas Lutheran College	Seguin	NCAA II/NAIA	1105
Texas Tech University	Lubbock	NCAA I	1106
Texas Wesleyan University	Fort Worth	NCAA II	1107
Trinity University	San Antonio	NCAA III	1108
Tyler Junior College	Tyler	NJCAA	1109
University of Dallas	Irving	NCAA III	1110

SCHOOL	CITY	AFFILIATION	PAGE
University of Houston	Houston	NCAA I	1111
University of Mary Hardin-Baylor	Belton	NCAA II	1112
University of North Texas	Denton	NCAA I	1113
University of Texas - Austin	Austin	NCAA I	1114
University of Texas - Dallas	Richardson	NCAA III	1115
University of Texas of El Paso	El Paso	NCAA I	1116
UT - Pan American	Edinburg	NCAA I	1117
University of the Incarnate Word	San Antonio	NCAA II	1117
West Texas A & M University	Canyon	NCAA II	1119

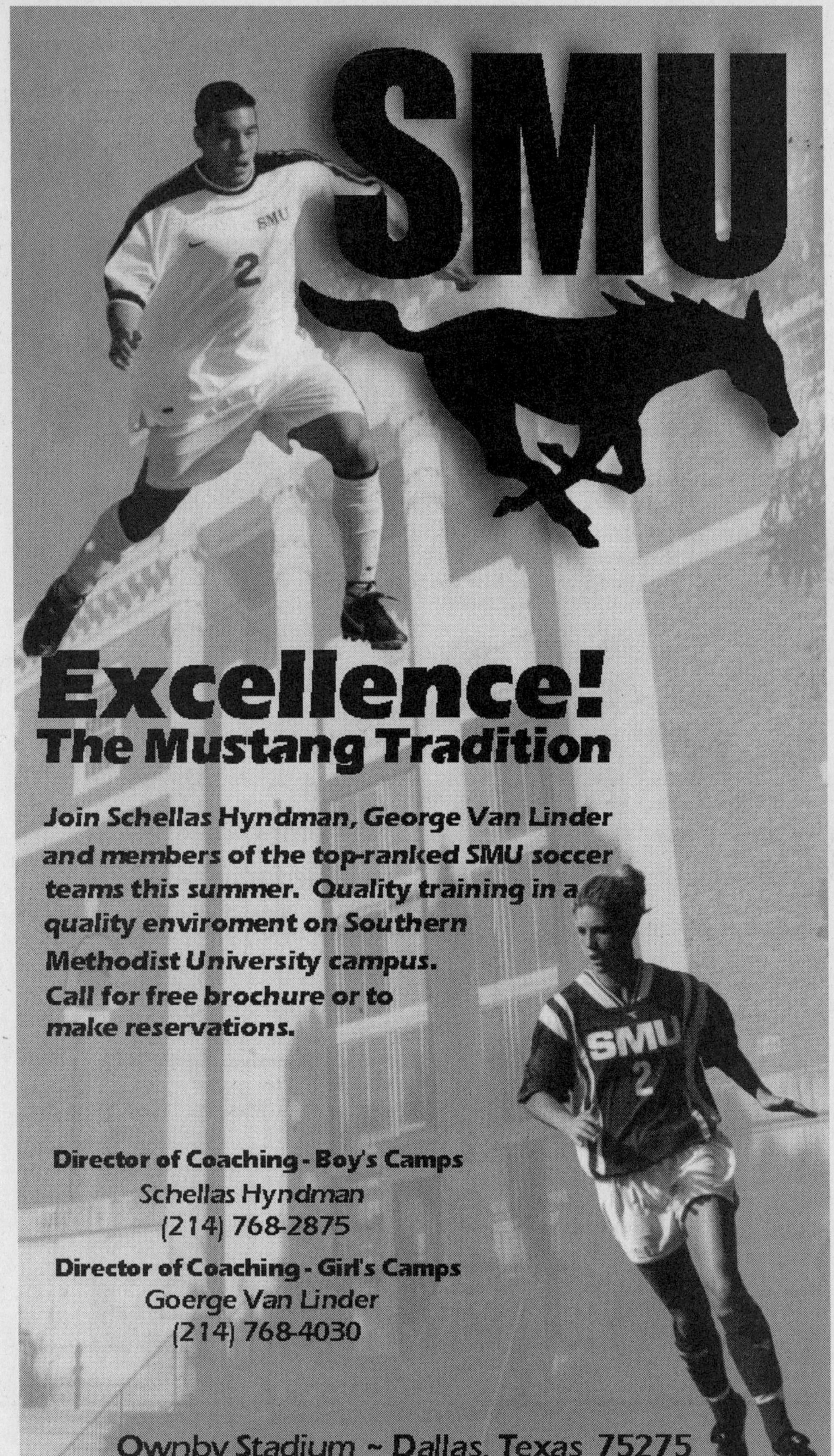
SMU
Excellence!
The Mustang Tradition
Join Schellas Hyndman, George Van Linder and members of the top-ranked SMU soccer teams this summer. Quality training in a quality enviroment on Southern Methodist University campus.
Call for free brochure or to make reservations.
Director of Coaching - Boy's Camps
Schellas Hyndman
(214) 768-2875
Director of Coaching - Girl's Camps
Goerge Van Linder
(214) 768-4030
Ownby Stadium ~ Dallas, Texas 75275

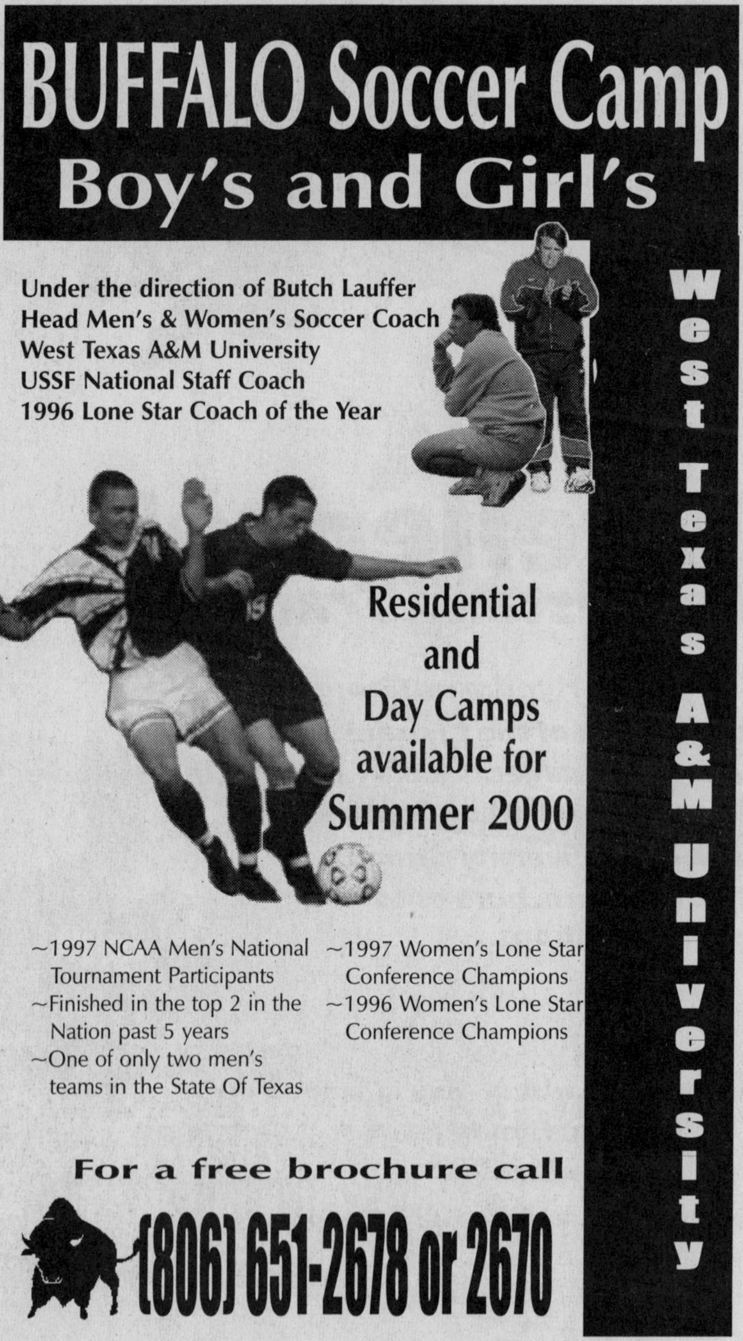
BUFFALO Soccer Camp
Boy's and Girl's
Under the direction of Butch Lauffer
Head Men's & Women's Soccer Coach
West Texas A&M University
USSF National Staff Coach
1996 Lone Star Coach of the Year
Residential
and
Day Camps
available for
Summer 2000
~1997 NCAA Men's National Tournament Participants
~Finished in the top 2 in the Nation past 5 years
~One of only two men's teams in the State Of Texas
~1997 Women's Lone Star Conference Champions
~1996 Women's Lone Star Conference Champions
For a free brochure call
(806) 651-2678 or 2670
West Texas A&M University

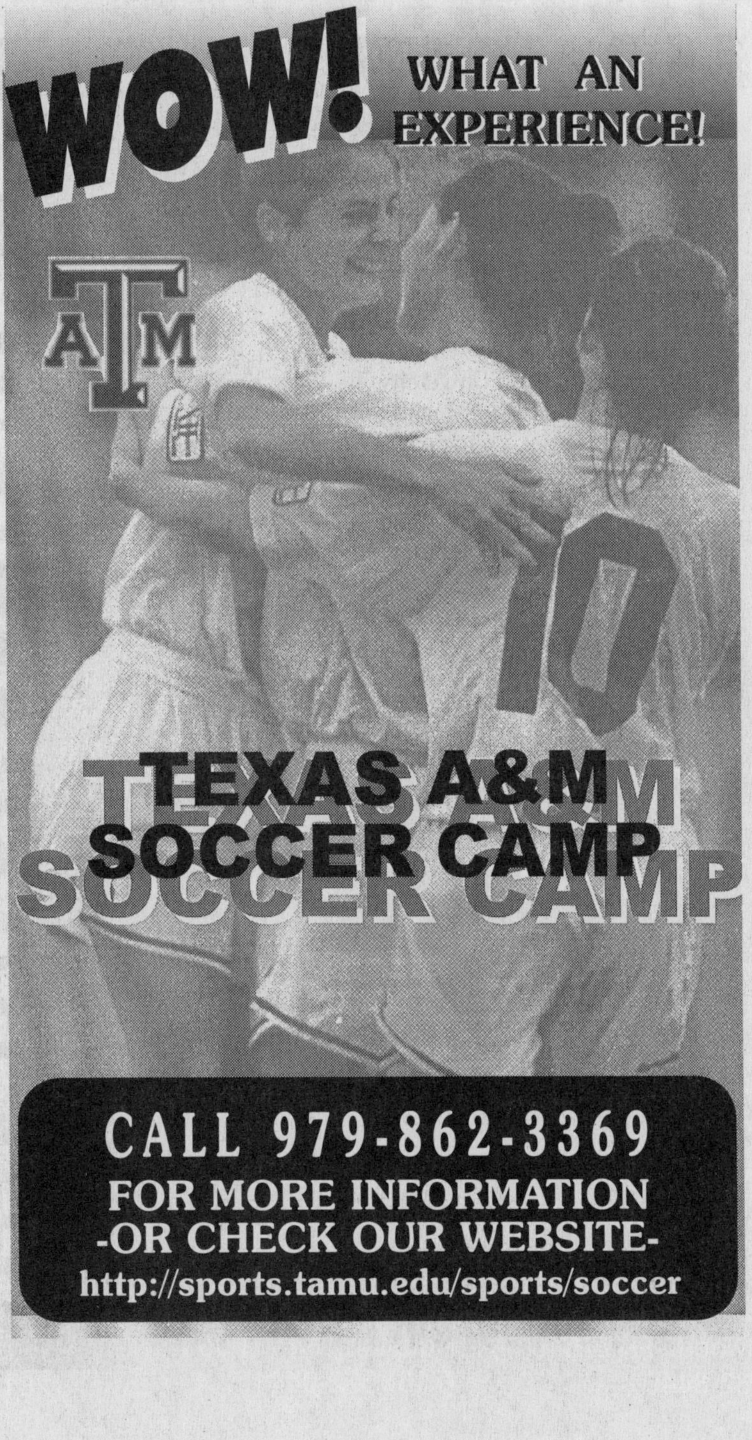
WOW! WHAT AN EXPERIENCE!
TEXAS A&M SOCCER CAMP
CALL 979-862-3369
FOR MORE INFORMATION
-OR CHECK OUR WEBSITE-
http://sports.tamu.edu/sports/soccer

www.soccer4all.com
...for all
your soccer needs!
1306 FM 1092-Ste 101
Missouri City, TX 77459
(281) 499-6665
104D S. Friendswood Dr.
Friendswood, TX 77546
(281) 482-8440
4423 Kingwood Drive
Kingwood, TX 77339
(281) 361-4434
2413 Rice Blvd.
Houston, TX 77005
(713) 522-0441
6700C Louetta Rd.
Spring, TX 77379
(281) 367-7890
16211 Clay Road
Houston, TX 77084
(281) 861-7744

Angelo State University
Academic Profile

Phone: (915) 942-2185

San Angelo, TX 76909

Type: 4 Yr.,Public,
Founded: 1928
Website: http://www.angelo.edu
Religion: Non-Affiliated
SAT/ACT/GPA: 700 min
Housing: Yes
Student/Faculty Ratio: 24:1
Male/Female Ratio: 50:50
Undergraduate Enrollment: 6,500
Graduate Enrollment: 2,000
Scholarships/Academic: Yes **Athletic:** Yes **Financial Aid:** Yes
Expenses by: Year **In State:** $ 6,700 **Out of State:** $ 12,000
Degrees Conferred: AA, AS, BA, BS, BBA, BM, BSN, Masters
Programs of Study: Accounting, Animal Science, Biology, Business Administration, Chemistry, Computer Science, Economics, Education, English, Finance, French, Geology, German, History, Journalism, Kinesiology, Management, Marketing, Mathematics, Music, Nursing, Physics, Psychology, Sociology, Spanish

Women's Athletic Profile

ASU Station Box 10914
San Angelo, TX 76909
Coach: Tom Brown
Email: tom.brown@angelo.edu

NCAA II
Rambelles/Royal Blue, Gold
Phone: (915) 942-2264
Fax: (915) 942-2270

Estimated # of Women's Soccer Scholarships: 3
Conference: Lone Star Conference
Program Profile: We play in a 75 x 120 natural grass field that is exclusively for women's soccer. Our program has a full spring season.
History: Our program began in 1995. Head Coach Tom Brown took over the program in 1997. Our team is an original member of the Lone Star Conference.
Achievements: Lone Star Player of the Year in 1997; Freshman of the Year in 1998; 1997-1999 we have had 4 first team, five second team, and five honorable mention All-Conference Selections; Several All Region and All- Conference Academic Selections
Coaching: Tom Brown, Head Coach, has an "A" License. He is an ODP state staff coach and an ODP Regional Staff Coach. Eric Alonzo, assistant coach, has "B" License and is an ODP state staff coach.
Roster in State: 24 **Out of State:** **Out of Country:** 2
Walk-on/Other: **Graduation %:** 100 **Seniors on Team:**
Positions Needed: Forward, Midfield
Camp or Clinic Dates: Not Available
Most Recent Record: 5-11-1
Schedule: Mesa State College, Midwestern State University, West Texas A&M, Southern Colorado University, St. Mary's University, University of Incarnate Word
Style of Play: Play a high intensity, indirect, ball possession style of play.

Austin College
Academic Profile

Phone: 903-813-2000

Sherman, TX 75092

Type: 4 Yr.,Private,Liberal Arts
Founded: 1849
Website: http://www.austinc.edu
Religion: Presbyterian
SAT/ACT/GPA: 1000+/22/3.0
Housing: Yes
Student/Faculty Ratio: 15:1
Male/Female Ratio: 50:50

Undergraduate Enrollment: 1,200
Graduate Enrollment: 20
Scholarships/Academic: Yes
Athletic: No
Financial Aid: Yes
Expenses by: Year
In State: $ 20,000
Out of State: $ 20,000
Specialty: Sciences, PreMed
Degrees Conferred: BA, MAT
Programs of Study: American Studies, Art, BioChemistry (as an interdisciplinary major using Special Program Option), Biology, Business Administration, Chemistry, Classics, Communication Arts (Speech-Theatre-Media), Computer Science (as an interdisciplinary major using Special Program Option), Economics, English, French, German, History, International Studies, Latin, Latin American Studies, Mathematics, Music, Philosophy, Physical Education, Physics, Political Science, Psychology, Religion, Sociology, Spanish, Teacher Education (Austin Teacher Program - graduate level only)

Men's Athletic Profile

900 N Grand Avenue
Sherman, TX 75090
Coach: Truett Cates
Email: tcates@austin.edu

NCAA III
Kangaroos/Crimson, Gold
Phone: (903) 813-2255
Fax: (903) 813-3196

Estimated # of Men's Soccer Scholarships: None
Conference: American Southwest Conference
Program Profile: Soccer facility is measure 115x80 yards, natural grass field for soccer only.
History: Program began in 1975, member of NCAA Division III since 19997, American Southwest Conference since 1996; ASC champions in 1996 & 1997.
Achievements: NAIA National playoffs in 1991-1995.
Coaching: Truett Cates, Head Coach, started coaching in 1989. He previously was a club player and a coach in Texas and Germany.
Style of Play: Dynamic; attack from all position.

Women's Athletic Profile

900 N. Grand Avenue
Sherman, TX 75090
Coach: Paul Burns
Email: pburns@austin.edu

NCAA III
Kangaroos/Maroon, White
Phone: (903) 813-2290
Fax: (903) 813-3196

Estimated # of Women's Soccer Scholarships: None
Conference: American Southwestern Conference
Program Profile: We play at an exclusive soccer-use-only field that measures 80 x 115 and has Bermuda grass. We have on campus facilities and dorms. We are located less than one hour north of Dallas.
History: Our program started in 1996 and our record that year was 8-10-1. In 1997, our record was 11-7-1. In 1998, our record was 12-7-1.
Achievements: Runner-up in ASC in 1997-1998; 11 All-Conference players in 1998; 9 Academic All-Conference players in 1971; 7 Academic All-Conference players in 1997; ASC Player of the Year.
Coaching: Paul Burns, Head Coach, started in 1996, he coached in many states within the USA and UK. He is an ODP North Texas Staff Coach and has USSF, NSCAA and English FA Licenses. He got his BA with honors in England. He has a Master's in Sports Psychology from the University of Missouri-Columbia. There is one Assistant Coach and one Graduate Assistant on staff.
Style of Play: Our style of play depends on the “strengths” of the team.

Baylor University
Academic Profile

Waco, TX 76711

Phone: (254) 710-3039

Type: 4 Yr.,Private,Liberal Arts
Founded: 1845
Website: http://www.baylor.edu
Religion: Baptist
SAT/ACT/GPA: 1100
Housing: Yes
Student/Faculty Ratio: 18:1
Male/Female Ratio: 45:55
Undergraduate Enrollment: 12,500
Graduate Enrollment: 2,500
Scholarships/Academic: Yes **Athletic:** Yes **Financial Aid:** Yes
Expenses by: Year **In State:** $ 15,500 **Out of State:** $ 15,500
Specialty: Education, Business, Premed, Prelaw
Degrees Conferred: BA, BS, BFA, BBA, BME, BSAC, BSN, MA, MS, MBA, Ph.D., JD
Programs of Study: College of Arts & Sciences, Engineering & Computer Science, Education, PreMed, PreLaw, Business

Women's Athletic Profile

150 Bear Run, Athletic Department
Waco, TX 76711
Coach: Nick Cowell
Email: Nick_Cowell@baylor.edu

NCAA I
Bears/Green, Gold
Phone: (254) 710-3090
Fax: (254) 710-1019

Estimated # of Women's Soccer Scholarships: 4
Conference: Big 12 Conference
Program Profile: We have brand new 3,000-seat lighted stadium on the banks of the Brazos River. We also have a new soccer locker room, meeting rooms, and offices at the stadium. The field is natural Bermuda grass.
History: Our program began only a few years ago in 1996. In 1998 we were the Big XII Champions and in 1998 and 1999 we made NCAA Tournament.
Achievements: In 1998 Big XII Conference Champions, and we have 3 All-Americans and 5 All-Central Region players and Big XII and Academic All Big XII Honors.
Coaching: Nick Cowell - Head Coach. NSCAA Advanced Diploma, South Region U-19 Girls Regional Coach, BA (Honors) at University of Birmingham (England), M.Ed at Cleveland State University. NSCAA National Instructor, NCAA Division III Coach of the Year 1992, 1993, 1995 and 1996. Rebecca Hornbacher is Assistant Coach.
Roster in State: 12 **Out of State:** 12 **Out of Country:** 1
ODP State: 12 **Regional:** 6 **National:** 2
Walk-on/Other: 5 **Graduation %:** 100 **Seniors on Team:** 5
Positions Needed: Goalkeeper, 2 Defenders, Midfield, Forward
Camp or Clinic Dates: Last two weeks in July
Most Recent Record: 14-7-1
Schedule: UCLA, USC, Nebraska, SMU, Texas A&M, Texas, Missouri, San Diego, Arizona State
Style of Play: Balance between playing quickly through midfield and tenacious attack at all cost mentality. Team expected to apply high defensive pressure.

Concordia University - Austin

Academic Profile

Austin, TX 78705

Phone:

Type: 4 Yr.,Private,Liberal Arts
Website: http://www.concordia.edu
SAT/ACT/GPA: 1080/19/3.0 or 4.0
Student/Faculty Ratio: 12:1
Undergraduate Enrollment: 800
Scholarships/Academic: Yes
Athletic: No
Expenses by: Year
In State: $ 14,200

Founded: 1926
Religion: Lutheran
Housing: Yes
Male/Female Ratio: 1:3
Graduate Enrollment: N/A
Financial Aid: Yes
Out of State: $ 14,200

Degrees Conferred: Bachelors, Masters in Education
Programs of Study: Behavioral Science, Biology, Business Administration, Business Management, Church Music/Conducting, Church, Music/Organ, Communications, Computer Science, Early Childhood Education, Elementary Education, Secondary Education, English, Environmental Sciences, History, Liberal Arts, Mexican-American Studies, PreDental, PreLaw, PreMed, PreSeminar, Spanish

Men's Athletic Profile

3400 IH 35 North
Austin, TX 78705
Coach: Graham Hutton
Email: Not Available

NAIA
Tornados/Purple, White
Phone: (512) 486-1263
Fax: (512) 512-4365

Estimated # of Men's Soccer Scholarships: N/A
Conference: Heart of Texas Conference
Program Profile: We have a grass practice facility. We play our home games on a FIFA World Size Stowherd Field which all natural grass.
History: Our program started in 1995 we had wins in 1996. the program improved to 8 wins, 1 tie 10 loses; 1997 lost a lot of players and Luis Cantu took over the coaching when the program is 2-2-15.
Style of Play: Control South American Style; build from the back, create over own offensive opportunities.

Women's Athletic Profile

3400 N, I.H. 35
Austin, TX 78705
Coach: Graham Hutton
Email: Not Available

NAIA II
Tornados/Purple, White
Phone: (512) 452-7661
Fax: (512) 459-8517

Estimated # of Women's Soccer Scholarships: None
Conference: Heart of Texas Conference
Program Profile: We have a grass practice facility. We play our home games on a FIFA World Size Stanford Field which is all natural grass.
History: Program started in 1995; we had wins in 1996; the program improved to 8 wins, tied 10 losses; 1997 lost lot of players and Luis Cantu took over the coaching and two wins, 2 ties and 15 losses.
Achievements: None, He hold a FIFA coaching license from Brazil. played pro in Mexico for four and half years with CD. Victoria Carre Canichos.
Style of Play: Control South American Style; build from the back; create our own offensive opportunities.

Dallas Baptist University

Academic Profile

Dallas, TX 75211

Phone: 214-333-7100

Type: 4 Yr.,Private,Liberal Arts
Website: http://www.dbu.edu
SAT/ACT/GPA: 910/19/2.0
Student/Faculty Ratio: 19/1
Undergraduate Enrollment: 3,190
Scholarships/Academic: Yes
Athletic: Yes
Expenses by: Semester
In State: $6,149.57
Founded: 1898
Religion: Southern Baptist
Housing: Yes
Male/Female Ratio: 38/62
Graduate Enrollment: 842
Financial Aid: Yes
Out of State: $ 6,149.57
Degrees Conferred: BA, BS, MBA, MED, MLA
Programs of Study: Accounting, Allied Health, Aviation Management, Banking & Finance, Biblical Studies, Biology, Broadcasting, Communications, Computer Science, Criminal Justice, Dramatic Arts, Economics, English, Fine Arts, History, Marketing, Mathematics, Music, Music Performance, Nursing, Pastoral Studies, Physical Education, Political Science, Psychology, Real Estate, Religious Education, Social Science

Men's Athletic Profile

3000 Mountain Creek Parkway
Dallas, TX 75116
Coach: David J. Grannis
Email: davidg@dbu.edu

NCAA II/NAIA
Patriots/Red, White, Navy
Phone: (214) 333-5325
Fax: (214) 333-5306

Estimated # of Men's Soccer Scholarships: 0
Conference: Independent Conference
Program Profile: Program Goal: To organize and operate a championship caliber NCAA II soccer program that glorifies God and makes Disciples. It is our goal to develop servant leaders that use college soccer and its competitive atmosphere to exercise Christ-like characteristics. The field is natural grass and was new in 1996. In 2000 over 50% of our games were D-II competition.
History: Program began in 1992. Tn 1998 the team was 9-10 and went to the playoffs. In 1999 the team was 9-9-. In 2000 the team went 4-12.
Achievements: Playoff appearances in 1998 and 1999.
Coaching: Davis Grannis, Head Coach, holds a NSCAA Advanced National Diploma. Michelle Nolan is the Student Assistant.
Roster In State: 17
Out of State: 1
Out of Country: 3
ODP State: 1
Regional:
National:
Walk-on/Other:
Graduation %: N/A
Seniors on Team: 4
Positions Needed: All
Camp or Clinic Dates: Not Available
Most Recent Record: 9-9-0
Schedule: Midwestern State, St. Mary's, Texas Wesleyan, Arkansas State, NW Oklahoma State, College of the Southwest
Style of Play: We generally play a 3-4-3.

Women's Athletic Profile

3000 Mount Creek Parkway
Dallas, TX 75211
Coach: David Granniss
Email: davidg@dbu.edu

NCAA II, NAIA I
Patriots/Red, White, Navy
Phone: (214) 333-5325
Fax: (214) 333-5306

Estimated # of Women's Soccer Scholarships: 6
Conference: Independent

Program Profile: Program Goal: To organize and operate a championship caliber NCAA D. II soccer program that glorifies God and Makes Disciples. It is our goal to develop servant leaders that use college soccer and its competitive atmosphere to exercise Christ like characteristics. The field is natural grass (115x72) and was new in 1996. In 2000 over 50% of our games were Division II Competition.
History: Program began in 1996 record: 1996 0-15, 1997 9-11-1, 1998 15-7-1, 1999 11-7, 2000 9-9 Playoffs in both 1998 and 2000. Won sectional playoffs in 1998.
Achievements: Playoffs in both 1998 and 2000. Won sectional playoffs in 1998 GTE All-American in 1998. Four players elected to All-Sectional team in 1998. Four players nominated to All-Sectional team in 2000.
Coaching: David Granniss is the head coach, student assistant Michelle Nolan
Roster in State: 17 **Out of State:** 1
ODP State: 1
Seniors on Team: 8
Positions Needed: ALL
Camp or Clinic Dates: Not Available
Most Recent Record: 4-12-0
Schedule: St. Mary's Univ. Ouachita Baptist, Harding Univ. Texas Wesleyan, SW Oklahoma State, Univ of Central Missouri, Midwestern State, Le Tourneau
Style of Play: We generally play with 3 fields, 4 midfielders, and 3 forwards.

East Texas Baptist

Academic Profile

Marshall, TX 75670
Phone: (903) 935-7963

Type: 4 Yr.,Private,Liberal Arts
Founded: 1917
Website: http://www.etbu.edu
Religion: Baptist
SAT/ACT/GPA: 860/18
Housing: Yes
Student/Faculty Ratio: 16:1
Male/Female Ratio: 40:60
Undergraduate Enrollment: 1,200+
Graduate Enrollment: 1,400
Scholarships/Academic: Yes **Athletic:** No **Financial Aid:** Yes
Expenses by: Year **In State:** $ 11,500 **Out of State:** $ 11,500
Degrees Conferred: BA, BS, BAS, BSN, BBA, BSE, BM, AA, ABA, AAS
Programs of Study: Behavioral Science, Christian Ministry, English, History, Music, Psychology, Sociology, Spanish, Speech, Communications, Theatre Arts, Accounting, Biology, Business Administration, Chemistry, Computer Information System, Kinesiology, Mathematics, Medical Technology, Nursing

Men's Athletic Profile

1209 N Grove Street
Marshall, TX 75670
Coach: Jose Alonzo
Email: Jalonzo@ETBU.EDU

NCAA II
Tigers/Royal, Gold
Phone: (903) 935-7963x282
Fax: (903) 935-0162

Estimated # of Men's Soccer Scholarships: N/A
Conference: American Southwest Conference
Program Profile: Our tome games are played on a lighted, Bermuda grass field on campus, which measures 120x80 yards. Our team has use of the $3.5 million Dean Healthplax, which has a state of the art training and rehabilitation center.
History: We began in 1994 with walk on players and played first full schedule against sanctioned teams in 1995 - went 19-3 and won conference. We belonged to Heart of Texas Conference in 1996 and 1997, compiling a 16-5 and 15-4 records. Our best season was in 1998 with a 22-1-2 record. We have made post-season playoffs every year since 1994. Our overall record is 72-13-2.

Achievements: 1995 Big State Conference Champions; 1995 Big State Conference Coach of the Year; 1996 & 1999 Heart of Texas Conference North Zone Champions; 1998 Southeast Region Runner-Up and #4 ranks NAIA Team in nation in the 1998 final rankings; NCCAA National Champions, NCCAA Regional Coach of the Year, NAIA Sectional Coach of the Year, NAIA All-American Honorable Mention player in 1995, Several All-Conference players, 2 NAIA All-American Honorable Mentions players in 1997, second team NAIA All-American in 1998 and 1 Honorable Mention NAIA All-American, 2 NCCAA All-American in 1998, NCCAA National Tournament MVP, 2 ETBU graduate in 1998 are playing professional.
Coaching: Jose Alonzo, Head Coach, joined ETBU in 1994. He is a native of Honduras Central America. He enters his 6th season with an overall record of 73-13-2. David Collins is the Assistant Coach.
Style of Play: Develop the ball out of the back with finesse and creativity. Mix Latin American with European Style - possession and ball control are imperative.

Hardin - Simmons University

Academic Profile

Abilene, TX 79698-6050
Phone: 800-568-2692

Type: 4 Yr.,Private,Liberal Arts
Founded: 1891
Website: http://www.hsutx.edu
Religion: Baptist
SAT/ACT/GPA: 990/21/"c" average
Housing: Yes
Student/Faculty Ratio: 17:1
Male/Female Ratio: 5:8
Undergraduate Enrollment: 2200
Graduate Enrollment: 300
Scholarships/Academic: Yes **Athletic:** No **Financial Aid:** Yes
Expenses by: Year **In State:** $13,000 **Out of State:** $13,000
Degrees Conferred: AS, BA, BS, BFA, BMus, BSN, MA, MBA, MED
Programs of Study: Accounting, Banking/Finance, Biology, Business Administration, Chemistry, Communications, Computer Science, Criminal Justice, Education, English, Fine Arts, History, Marketing, Math, Medical Laboratory, Nursing, Philosophy, Physical Education, Physical Therapy, Physics, Political Science, PreDentistry, PreLaw, PreMed, Religion, Social Science

Men's Athletic Profile

HSU Box 16185
Abilene, TX 79698
Coach: Kevin Wardlaw
Email: kwardlaw@hsutx.edu
NCAA III
Cowboys/Purple, Gold
Phone: (915) 670-1469
Fax: (915) 670-1572

Estimated # of Men's Soccer Scholarships: N/A
Conference: American Southwest Conference
Program Profile: Bermuda grass practice and game fields. Games are played on 120 X 75 yard field in a 4,000 seat lighted stadium.
History: Our program began in 1975. Was a NCAA Div I program until 1990, and then made the move to Div III.
Achievements: Several All-Americans while still in the NCAA Div I. Several Academic All-Americans and numerous All-Region and All-Conference awards in Div III. 1998 and 1999 American Southwest Conference Champs. 5 players playing in the United Soccer Leagues.
Coaching: Kevin Wardlaw, Head Coach. 1999 was first year as head Coach. Former ODP goalkeeping director; holds advanced National License form NSCAA; founder and director of Attack the Skills Soccer Camps; ODP player evaluator. Lao Munoz and Brad Bankhead are the Assistant Coaches.
Roster In State: 19 **Out of State:** 7 **Out of Country:** 1
ODP State: 9 **Regional:** 2 **National:**
Walk-on/Other: **Graduation %:** 100 **Seniors on Team:** 4
Positions Needed: Forward, Goalkeeper, Outside Backs
Camp or Clinic Dates: June 17-21, July 1-5 (2001)

Most Recent Record: 13-6
Schedule: Trinity, UT Dallas, Webster (St. Louis, MO), Illinois Wesleyan, Southwestern, Rhodes
Style of Play: Possession oriented with an understanding of when to commit numbers forward. Stubborn, hard-nosed defending with a relentless commitment to shutting the opponent out.

Women's Athletic Profile

HSU Box 16185
Abilene, TX 79698
Coach: Marcus Wood
Email: mwood@hsutx.edu

NCAA III
Cowgirls/Purple, Gold, White
Phone: (915) 670-5834
Fax: (915) 670-1572

Estimated # of Women's Soccer Scholarships: None
Conference: American Southwest Conference
Program Profile: Hsu women's soccer are two-time conference champions and play in 5,000-seat Shelton Stadium which is natural grass with lighted field.
History: We have won four straight American Southwest Conference Titles and advanced to the Sweet 16 of the NCAA Division III National Tournament in 1999.
Achievements: American Southwest Conference Champion 4 of the last five years. Appearance in NCAA Sweet 16 in 1999. Ranked 6th in the NSCAA south region in 2000. Eight players on the All-Conference team. Conference Player of the Year. 6 Conference Players of the week.
Coaching: Marcus Wood Head Coach, He holds a NSCAA Advanced National Diploma. 2nd All-Time leading scorer at Olivet Nazarene University.
Roster in State: 21 **Out of State:** 1 **Out of Country:** 0
Walk-on/Other: **Graduation %:** 95 **Seniors on Team:** 6
Positions Needed: ALL
Camp or Clinic Dates: June 17-21, July 1-5
Most Recent Record: 14-3-2
Schedule: Trinity, UT Dallas, Austin College, Maryville, Southwestern, Savannah College of Art & Design
Style of Play: Possession style soccer emphasizing combination play. Tenacious defending. Technical and physical speed are very important.

Hill Junior College

Academic Profile

Hillsboro, TX 76645

Phone:

Type: 2 Yr.,Public,Jr. College
Website: http://www.hillcollege.hill-college.cc.tx.us
SAT/ACT/GPA: Open
Student/Faculty Ratio: 25:1
Undergraduate Enrollment: 2,200
Scholarships/Academic: None **Athletic:** Yes
Expenses by: Year **In State:** $ 4,200
Degrees Conferred: Associate

Founded: 1923
Religion: Non-Affiliated
Housing: No
Male/Female Ratio: 40:60
Graduate Enrollment: N/A
Financial Aid: Yes
Out of State: $ 4,600

Programs of Study: Accounting, Agriculture, Animal Science, Applied Art, Art, Automotive Technology, Banking/Finance, Behavioral Science, Biological Science, Botany, Business Administration, Chemistry, Commercial Art, Communications, Computer Science, Cosmetology, Criminal Justice, Drafting/Design, Economics, Education, Electrical/Electronics Technology, Engineering and Applied Science, Engineering Science, & Technology, English, Farm/Ranch Management, Geography, Health Science, History, Horticulture, Humanities, Journalism, Law Enforcement, Liberal Arts, Machine/Tool Technology, Mathematics, Music, Music Education, Music Therapy, Nursing, Photography, Physical Education, Physical Science, Physics, Political Science, Practical Nursing, PreEngineering, Psychology, Public Affairs, Real Estate, Robotics, Science, Social Science, Speech, Theatre, Welding

Women's Athletic Profile

112 Lamar Drive
Hillsboro, TX 76645
Coach: Atanas Arsov
Email: Not Available

NJCAA
Rebels/Red, White
Phone: (254) 582-2555
Fax: (254) 582-7591

Estimated # of Women's Soccer Scholarships: 18
Conference: north Texas Junior College Athletic Conference
Program Profile: Hill College has a progressive soccer program with a nice facility. Our season starts in August and finishes at the end of the National Tournament which is at the end of November. The field is natural grass.
History: In 1992 the soccer program was started at Hill College. The team wasn't doing very well, but after each year the program was in progress.
Achievements: IN 1996 Hill College advanced to the Regional Tournament.
Coaching: Atanas Arsov is our Head Coach.
Roster in State: 15 **Out of State:** 7
Graduation %: 60 **Seniors on Team:** 0
Positions Needed: Goalkeeper, Defense, Midfield, Offense
Style of Play: Offensive style of play with a very well organize team work.

Jarvis Christian College

Academic Profile

Hawkins, TX 75765

Phone:

Type: 4 Yr.,Private,Liberal Arts
Website: http://www.jarvis.edu
SAT/ACT/GPA: 800+/18+/2.0
Student/Faculty Ratio: 15:1
Undergraduate Enrollment: 500
Scholarships/Academic: Yes **Athletic:** Yes
Expenses by: Year **In State:** $ 9,235

Founded: 1913
Religion: Disciples of Christ
Housing: No
Male/Female Ratio: 38:62
Graduate Enrollment: N/A
Financial Aid: Yes
Out of State: $ 9,235

Specialty: Business Administration, Computer Info Systems, Teacher Certification
Degrees Conferred: BA, BS, BBA, Bachelor of Computer Information Systems
Programs of Study: Biology, Business Administration, Chemistry, Computer Information Systems, Criminal Justice, English, Generic Special Education, History, Human Performance, Interdisciplinary Studies in Education, Mathematics, Music, Reading, Religion. Sociology, Speech, Texas Teacher Certification (Biology, Business Administration, Chemistry, English, Special Education, History, Human Performance, Mathematics, Music, Reading) Joint Degree Programs in Nursing, Mass Communications and Engineering.

Men's Athletic Profile

P.O. Box 1470
Hawkins, TX 75765
Coach: Brian Cooper
Email: Not Available

NCAA II
Bulldogs/Gold, Royal Blue
Phone: (903) 769-0416
Fax: (903) 769-1282

Estimated # of Men's Soccer Scholarships: ½ Scholarships
Conference: Red River
Program Profile: Medium size multipurpose gym with large Basketball/Volleyball court, large size swimming pool, a small upstairs auxillary gym. Our soccer field is natural grass.
History: 1992
Roster in State: 7 **Out of State:** 7 **Out of Country:** 7

Positions Needed: Striker
Most Recent Record: 0-9
Schedule: S.W. Assemblies of God, Huston Tillison, Wiley College
Style of Play: Defensive minded team, with the bulk of players back in defense of goal.

Le Tourneau University

Academic Profile

Longview, TX 75607
Phone: 800-759-8811

Type: 4 Yr.,Private,Liberal Arts,Engineering
Founded: 1948
Website: http://www.letu.edu
Religion: Non-Denominational
SAT/ACT/GPA: 1050/21/2.8
Housing: Yes
Student/Faculty Ratio: 10:1
Male/Female Ratio: 17:1
Undergraduate Enrollment: 850
Graduate Enrollment: N/A
Scholarships/Academic: Yes
Athletic: No
Financial Aid: Yes
Expenses by: Year
In State: $ 16,00
Out of State: $ 16,000
Specialty: Engineering & Aviation
Degrees Conferred: BS, BA
Programs of Study: Engineering, Aviation, Liberal Arts, Natural Science, Business Administration: Nearly 40 associates and bachelors programs.

Men's Athletic Profile

P.O. Box 7001
Longview, TX 75607
Coach: Steve Barrett
Email: stevebarrett1@juno.com

NCAA III
Yellow Jackets/Gold, Blue
Phone: (903) 233-3374
Fax: (903) 233-3822

Estimated # of Men's Soccer Scholarships: None
Conference: American Southwest Conference
Program Profile: The varsity natural grass field has a measurements of 110x78 yards and seats 600. Has 2 full size practice fields and one is lighted.
History: Program began in 1976, overall record is 194-223-18; in the past three seasons compiled a 46-22-2 record.
Achievements: Numerous NAIA Academic All-Americans, NAIA All-Americans; 2 players played professionally in 1998.
Coaching: Steve Barrett, Head Coach, entering seventh year. While at LeTourneau he compiled a record of 78-5-1, and overall record is 91-68-5. He played and coached soccer in his native England and America for over thirty years. Played collegiately at Liberty University and received his Masters at Virginia Tech.
Style of Play: Direct style, high and low pressure defending.

Women's Athletic Profile

2100 S.Mobberly
Longview, TX 75607
Coach: Pedro Blanco
Email: Blancop@letu.edu

NCAA III
Yellow Jackets/Royal Blue, Gold
Phone: (903) 233-3531
Fax: (903) 233-3822

Estimated # of Women's Soccer Scholarships: None
Conference: South West American Conference
Program Profile: 3 Light soccer fields, one main light soccer field
History: 3 year
Achievements: 1992 north west conference
Coaching: Pedro Blanco

Roster in State: 8 **Out of State:** 5 **Out of Country:** 2
Walk-on/Other: **Graduation %:** 100 **Seniors on Team:** 8
Camp or Clinic Dates: June/July
Most Recent Record: 6-6
Style of Play: Possession style of play and we are selective in playing the long ball.

Midwestern State University

Academic Profile

Phone: 940-397-4000

Wichita Falls, TX 76308

Type: 4 Yr.,Public,Liberal Arts **Founded:** 1922
Website: http://www.mwsu.edu **Religion:** Non-Affiliated
SAT/ACT/GPA: 860/19 **Housing:** Yes
Student/Faculty Ratio: 20:1 **Male/Female Ratio:** 1:2
Undergraduate Enrollment: 5,500 **Graduate Enrollment:** 500
Scholarships/Academic: Yes **Athletic:** Yes **Financial Aid:** Yes
Expenses by: Year **In State:** $ 5,620 **Out of State:** $ 9,905
Degrees Conferred: AAS, BA, BAAS, BBA, BS, BSW, BSIS, BSDH, BM, BSN, MA, MBA, ME, MS, MSK, MSN
Programs of Study: Accounting, Art, Art & Theatre, Applied Arts & Science, Biology, Business, Computer Information Systems, Chemical Technology, Chemistry, Computer Science, Criminal Justice, Economics, Marketing, Mass Communications, Mathematics, Medical Technology, Nursing, Political Science, Psychology, Social Work, Sociology

Men's Athletic Profile

3410 Taft Blvd.
Wichita Falls, TX 76308-2099
Coach: Dough Elder
Email: msusoccer<soccer@nexus.mwsu.edu

NCAA II
Indians/Maroon, Gold
Phone: (940) 689-4772
Fax: (940) 691-8129

Estimated # of Men's Soccer Scholarships: N/A
Conference: Lone Star Conference
Program Profile: Well manicured Bermuda grass field with a 200 seat stadium. Playing season runs from August through November and Midwestern is a nationally known soccer team.
History: Program began in 1972. Midwestern has qualified for the NAIA National Tournament 16 years in a row with four final appearances. The program is now moving into the NCAA Div. II which will be a new exciting chapter for MSU soccer
Achievements: District Coach of the Year in 1991-1994; Southwest Region Coach of the Year in 1987, 1990, 1993, 1995, & 1996; 11 All-American players.
Style of Play: Possession working it out of the back.

Women's Athletic Profile

3410 Taft Boulevard
Wichita Falls, TX 76308-2099
Coach: Jeff Trimble
Email: Not Available

NCAA II
Indians/Maroon, Gold
Phone: (940) 689-4772
Fax: (940) 691-8129

Estimated # of Women's Soccer Scholarships: None
Conference: Lone Star Conference
Program Profile: NCAA Division II fully-funded program with a 3,000-seat natural turf stadium. We have one of the finest university facilities in the country. We have started a strong program by being the first Lone Star Conference Champions.

History: The women's soccer program began in 1995. Qualified for the playoffs both years. In 1996 record was 15-6-1, MSU became the first NCAA Division II Star Conference Champions.
Achievements: Midwestern State has only women's varsity soccer for two years and already claims the Lone Star NCAA Division II Conference Championship; 5 All-Conference payers; 1 Freshman of the Year and 1 Honorable Mention All-American.
Style of Play: Controlled finesse passing style of play. We control the ball out of the back and pass the ball through the midfield in order to build numbers into the attack.

Mountain View College

Academic Profile

Phone:

Type:
Website: http://www.mvc.dcccd.edu
SAT/ACT/GPA: Open
Student/Faculty Ratio:
Undergraduate Enrollment: N/A
Scholarships/Academic: **Athletic:**
Expenses by: **In State:**
Specialty:
Degrees Conferred:
Programs of Study: Contact school for programs of study.
Founded:
Religion: Non-Affiliated
Housing: No
Male/Female Ratio:
Graduate Enrollment: N/A
Financial Aid:
Out of State:

Men's Athletic Profile

4849 W. Illinois
Dallas, TX 75211
Coach: Tony Falcon
Email: txf6451@dcccd.edu

NJCAA
Lions/Blue, White
Phone: 214-860-8791
Fax: 214-860-8573

Estimated # of Men's Soccer Scholarships: 0
Conference: NJCAA
Program Profile: 1st year varsity program; on campus soccer field (110x80 yards), all natural grass.
History: 1st year varsity program; club soccer for 5 years.
Achievements: Players recruited to 4-year schools and 2 players recruited to play professionally.
Coaching: Head Coach is Tony Falcon.
Roster In State: 20 **Out of State:** 0 **Out of Country:** 0
ODP State: 3 **Regional:** **National:**
Walk-on/Other: **Graduation %:** 75 **Seniors on Team:** 11
Positions Needed: Forwards, Outside Mids
Schedule: Richland College, Bacone College, San Jacinto, Northern Oklahoma College, Tyler
Style of Play: 5-3-2; outside backs attacking & compacting the defensive 3rd.

Richland College

Academic Profile

Phone: 972-238-6106

Dallas, TX 75243

Type: 2 Yr.,Public,
Website: http://www.rlc.edu
SAT/ACT/GPA: None
Student/Faculty Ratio: 30:1
Undergraduate Enrollment: 12,000
Founded: 1972
Religion: Non-Affiliated
Housing: No
Male/Female Ratio: 46:54
Graduate Enrollment: N/A

Scholarships/Academic: Yes **Athletic:** No **Financial Aid:** Yes
Expenses by: Year **In State:** $ 251-$441 **Out of State:** $ 843
Specialty: Junior College
Degrees Conferred: Associates
Programs of Study: Accounting, Advertising, Agriculture, American Studies, Anthropology, Architecture, Art, Biological Sciences, Botany, Business Administration, Chemistry, Computer Science, Dance, Drama, Economics, Engineering, English, Entomology, Finance, Fine Arts, Geography, Geology, Health Sciences, History, Interior Design, Journalism, Legal Science, Liberal Arts, Life Sciences, Management, Marine Biology, Marketing, Mathematics, Management, Medical Technology, MicroBiology, Music, Nursing, Pharmacy, Philosophy, PhotoJournalism, Physical Education, Physical Science, Physical Therapy, Pathology, Political Science, Psychology, Telecommunications, Theatre, Zoology

Men's Athletic Profile

12800 Abrams Road
Dallas, TX 75243-2199
Coach: Sean Wley
Email: skw8450@dcccd.edu

NJCAA
Thunderducks/F. Green, Purple
Phone: (972) 238-6243
Fax: (972) 238-3736

Estimated # of Men's Soccer Scholarships: N/A
Conference: NJCAA
Program Profile: Consistently in the national ranking year in and out. Top soccer complex is the top in Texas with eleven fields in which four were lighted, with Bermuda pitch. our playing season is in the Fall and we have a Spring off-season training program .
History: Our program began in 1993.
Achievements: NJCAA Regional Champions in 1988, 1990, 1991, 1992, 1993, 1994, and 1995. NJCAA District Runner-Up in 1990, 1991, 1992, 1993, 1994, and 1995. Regional Champions in 1996 & 1997; District Runner-Up in 1996 & 1997; ranked 2nd in NJCAA pro Division I in the Poll.
Coaching: Sean Worley, Head Coach, holds a USSF "A" License and is the NTSSA Staff Coach and ODP Coach. He was a former assistant coach at DeAnza College, CA.
Roster In State: 20 **Out of State:** 1 **Out of Country:** 3
Walk-on/Other: **Graduation %:** N/A **Seniors on Team:** 8
Positions Needed: Top caliber players
Camp or Clinic Dates: Not Available
Most Recent Record: 14-3-4
Schedule: Meridian, Cloud County, San Jancento, Lincoln, State Fair, Tyler, Johnson County
Style of Play: Style depends on the caliber of players recruited each year.

Women's Athletic Profile

12800 Abrams Road
Dallas, TX 75243-2199
Coach: Sean Worley
Email: kcrabb3257@aol.com

NJCAA
Thunderducks/F. Green, Purple
Phone: (972) 238-6243
Fax: (972) 238-3736

Estimated # of Women's Soccer Scholarships: N/A
Conference: Region V - NJCAA
Program Profile: Consistently National ranked. Soccer complex is the top in Texas with 11 fields, 4 lighted, with Bermuda pitch. Our playing season is in the fall; we have of spring off-season training program. Richland is non-scholarship program competing against NJCAA, NAIA and NCAA schools.
History: Program began in 1989 as a club sport. Has been a varsity since 1992.
Achievements: NJCAA Regional Champs in 1992, 1993 & 1994; National Final Four Appearance in 1994; Regional Champion in 1997.

Saint Edward's University

Academic Profile

Austin, TX 78704
Phone: (512) 448-8480

Type: 4 Yr.,Public,Liberal Arts
Founded: 1885
Website: http://www.stedwards.edu
Religion: Catholic
SAT/ACT/GPA: 950/19/Top 1/2
Housing: Yes
Student/Faculty Ratio: 16:1
Male/Female Ratio: 40:60
Undergraduate Enrollment: 1,986
Graduate Enrollment: 640
Scholarships/Academic: Yes **Athletic:** Yes
Financial Aid: Yes
Expenses by: Year **In State:** $ 16,198
Out of State: $ 16,198
Specialty: Liberal Arts, Value Based Education with emphasis on learning
Degrees Conferred: BA, BS, BBA, MA, MBA
Programs of Study: Accounting, Art, BioChemistry, Biology, Business & Management, Chemistry, Communications, Computer Information Systems, Computer Science, Creative Writing, English, Finance, Criminal Justice, Economics, Education, Elementary Education, English, History, Mathematics, Management, Marketing, Philosophy, Photography, Physical Education, Political Science, PreDentistry, PreLaw , Psychology, Religion, Secondary Education, Soil Science

Men's Athletic Profile

3001 South Congress Avenue
Austin, TX 78704
Coach: Mike Smith
Email: michaels@stedwards.admin.edu

NCAA II
Hilltoppers/Navy Blue, Gold
Phone: (512) 448-8507
Fax: (512) 416-5834

Estimated # of Men's Soccer Scholarships: 7.6
Conference: New Conference being formed
Program Profile: We are a member of the NCAA Division II. Our 1998 record of 12-4-5 was versus primarily Division opponents. We have two playing grass fields that measure 120x75. Our game field seats approximately 700.
History: Our program began in 1985. Since 1990: Conference Tourney Finals 8 of 9 years. Regular season conference champions in 1993, Conference Tourney Champs in 1994 & 1998; Regional Tourney (NAIA) in 1992, 1993, 1994 & 1998.
Achievements: Conference Champs in 1993, Conference Tourney Champs in 1994 & 1998; Regional Tourney in 1992, 1993, 1994 & 1998; 8 NAIA All-Americans since 1990; HOTC Coach of the Year in 1994; NAIA District Coach of the Year in 1990 & 1992.
Coaching: Mike Smith, Head Coach, is entering his twelve years with the program. He holds a USSF National Coaching License, has been coaching nine years at St. Edward's Coach of the Year in 1990 & 1992 and has 18 years coaching at all levels. Bill Bullock is our Assistant Coach.
Style of Play: Extremely possession oriented on attack. Only occasionally direct. Defense typically man-to-man in defense/mid 1/3.

Women's Athletic Profile

3001 S Congress Avenue
Austin, TX 78704
Coach: Erin Lynch
Email: erin1@admin.stedwards.edu

NCAA II
Lady Hilltoppers/Navy, Gold
Phone: (512) 428-1052
Fax: (512) 416-5834

Estimated # of Women's Soccer Scholarships: 7.5
Conference: Heartland Conference
Program Profile: We have 120x75 grass game and practice fields with seating for approximately 200. We play 20 games in the fall season and have 5 scrimmages in the spring. In 1998, our record in the NCAA Division II was 10-7-1.

History: The program began in 1990. We were in the Conference Finals four times. We played in a Regional Tournament in 1994.
Achievements: 4 NAIA All-Americans in 1990's; Regional Tournament Appearance in 1994
Coaching: Erin Lynch, Head Coach, she got a BS from the University of Massachusetts at Amherst in 1997. She is a 3 time NCAA Division I All-American and an Academic All-American. She is also a 2 time Atlantic 10 Conference Player of the Year and has 2 years Club and ODP coaching experience. Assistant Coaches will be announced.
Roster in State: 15 **Out of State:** 2
Seniors on Team: 1
Positions Needed: All
Camp or Clinic Dates: July 24-28 and July 31-4
Most Recent Record: 7-10-1
Schedule: Texas A&M Commerce, West Texas A&M, Metropolitan State, University of Central Oklahoma, Colorado Christian, Midwestern State, Incarnate Word
Style of Play: Balanced combination of possession oriented build up and occasional direct play.

Saint Mary's University - Texas

Academic Profile

San Antonio, TX 78228
Phone: (210) 436-3528

Type: 4 Yr.,Private,Liberal Arts,Engineering
Founded: 1852
Website: http://www.stmarytx.edu
Religion: Catholic
SAT/ACT/GPA: 950/22
Housing: Yes
Student/Faculty Ratio: 17:1
Male/Female Ratio: 45:55
Undergraduate Enrollment: 2,600
Graduate Enrollment: 1,522
Scholarships/Academic: Yes **Athletic:** Yes **Financial Aid:** Yes
Expenses by: Sem **In State:** $ 8,000 **Out of State:** $ 8,000
Specialty: Biology, Business, Engineering, Computer Science
Degrees Conferred: BA, BS, BAS, BBA, MA, MS, MBA, Ph.D., JD
Programs of Study: Accounting, Banking/Finance, Biology, Chemistry, Business Education, Business Administration, Communications, Computer Engineering, Computer Science, Criminal Justice, Earth Science, Economics, Education, International Relations, Management, Marketing, Mathematics, Music, Philosophy, Physics, Political Science, Psychology, Social Sciences

Men's Athletic Profile

One Camino Santa Maria
San Antonio, TX 78228
Coach: Brad O'Kelley
Email: bradokelley@aol.com

NCAA II
Rattlers/Royal, Gold
Phone: (210) 436-3248
Fax: (210) 436-3040

Estimated # of Men's Soccer Scholarships: 4
Conference: Heartland Conference
Program Profile: Has four fields, three practice, and one game; lighted practice field and all natural grass. Soccer complex holds about 1,000.
History: Began as a club in 1969; 1997 Heart of Texas Conference champions; nationally ranked top 20 - goals scored and goals allowed.
Achievements: Conference Champions 1997 Men and Women 4 out of 5 All-Americans last 4 years.
Roster In State: 20 **Out of State:** 6 **Out of Country:** 2
ODP State: 12 **Regional:** 2 **National:** 1
Walk-on/Other: 0 **Graduation %:** 96 **Seniors on Team:** 3
Positions Needed: GK, F, MF, DF
Most Recent Record: 3-15-0
Schedule: West Texas A&M, Incarnate Word Univ. St. Edwards Univ. Truman State, Midwestern State Univ. Texas Wesleyan Univ.

Women's Athletic Profile

One Camino Santa Maria
San Antonio, TX 78228-8508
Coach: Brad O'Kelley
Email: bradokelley@aol.com

NCAA II
Rattlers/Royal, Gold
Phone: (210) 436-3248
Fax: (210) 436-3040

Estimated # of Women's Soccer Scholarships: 6
Conference: Heart of Texas Conference
Program Profile: Game field is 110x70 yards, with an additional practice field. Has three fields, all grass; game field is in excellent condition and has a lighted training facility. Varsity field seats 1,000
History: Program as a club in 1978, and became a varsity sport in 1991. 1 Conference Championship in 1997; Regional Tournament in 1997.
Achievements: Lance Noble was named Coach of the Year in 1997; 1 Conference Title; 2 All-American in 1997,1998. Program Nationally ranked in 1996,97 and 1998
Coaching: Lance Noble, Head Coach, USSF "A" License, NSCAA Advanced National, Irish International Diploma, KNUB Dutch Certification (Obtained in Amsterdam, Holland in 1995), South Texas Coaching Development and Olympic Development (ODP). Chris Sharp and Mark Embley - Assistant Coaches.
Roster in State: 24 **Out of State:** 2 **Out of Country:** 0
ODP State: 9 **Regional:** 1 **National:** 0
Walk-on/Other: 0 **Graduation %:** 94 **Seniors on Team:** 3
Positions Needed: GK, Sweeper, Forward
Camp or Clinic Dates: Mid June, Mid July
Most Recent Record: 4-11-2
Schedule: West Texas A & M, Univ. of Central Oklahoma,
Style of Play: Possession , slow build-up, indirect style, controlled counter attack: 11 attack, 11 defend; many chances off of set-plays.

Schreiner College
Academic Profile

Kerrville, TX 78028
Phone: (830)896-5411

Type: 4 Yr.,Private,Liberal Arts **Founded:** 1923
Website: http://www.athletics.schreiner.edu **Religion:** Presbyterian
SAT/ACT/GPA: Rolling admission **Housing:** Yes
Student/Faculty Ratio: 14:1 **Male/Female Ratio:**
Undergraduate Enrollment: 675 **Graduate Enrollment:** 125
Scholarships/Academic: Yes **Athletic:** No **Financial Aid:** Yes
Expenses by: Year **In State:** N/A **Out of State:** N/A
Specialty: Education
Degrees Conferred: BA, BS, BBA, BGS, M.Ed.
Programs of Study: Accounting, Art Education, BioChemistry, Biology, Business Administration, Chemistry, Communications, Computer Studies, Engineering (312 Program), English, Exercise Science, Finance, Fine Arts, French, German, Graphic Design, History, Humanities, Legal Studies, Management, Marketing, Mathematics, Philosophy, Religion, Studio At, Teaching Certification

Men's Athletic Profile

2100 Memorial Blvd.
Kerrville, TX 78028
Coach: David Hoffmann
Email: scsoccer11@aol.com

NCAA III
Mountaineers/Maroon, White
Phone: (830) 792-7289
Fax: (830) 792-7483

Estimated # of Men's Soccer Scholarships: None
Conference: American Southwest Conference
Program Profile: Game and practice facilities; natural grass (Bermuda); fall season; spring off-season; limited games.
History: Program founded eight years ago. The varsity program began in 1988. Competed as an independent NAIA as of June 1998 Division I School. Will begin competition in NCAA Division III American Southwest Conference.
Achievements: In 1997-1998 has 9 Academic All-Americans; 6 All-Division Players; 5 All-Conference; 1 Conference MVP; Sectional Finalist, NSCAA Team Academic Award.
Coaching: David Hoffmann, Head Coach.
Style of Play: Adjust to personnel, but ball control with total attacking style typically.

Women's Athletic Profile

CMB 5905 2100 Memorial Boulevard
Kerrville, TX 78028-5697
Coach: David Hoffmann
Email: scsoccer11@aol.com

NCAA III
Mountainers/Maroon, White
Phone: (830) 792-7293
Fax: (830) 792-7483

Estimated # of Women's Soccer Scholarships: None
Conference: American Southwest Conference
Program Profile: Fourth year of the program 3-11-2 overall with a bid to NAIA Sectionals. Natural grass game and practice fields located between gym and surrounding hills. Fall playing season; newly upgraded weight room, tennis center, racquetball courts that has a driving range within 50 yards of soccer facilities.
History: Program will field its first team in the fall of 1997. Will begin competing in the NCAA Division III, American Southwest Conference.
Achievements: Highest GPA in the nation for all varsity soccer programs (August 3.27). 1 Academic All-American.
Coaching: Coach David Hoffmann started the women's program four years ago. Is also the Men's Head Coach.
Roster in State: 16
Out of State: 0
Out of Country: 0
ODP State: 1
Regional:
National:
Walk-on/Other: 2
Graduation %: 100
Seniors on Team: 1
Positions Needed: Forwards, midfielders
Camp or Clinic Dates: Not Available
Most Recent Record: 3-11-2
Schedule: UT-Dallas, Hardin-Simmons, Dallas Baptist, College of the Southwest, University of Dallas.
Style of Play: Adjust to personnel.

Southern Methodist University

Academic Profile

Dallas, TX 75275-0216
Phone: 214-768-2000

Type: 4 Yr.,Private,Liberal Arts,Engineering
Founded: 1911
Website: http://www.smumustangs.com/
Religion: Methodist
SAT/ACT/GPA: 1000/25
Housing: Yes
Student/Faculty Ratio: 20:1
Male/Female Ratio: 50:50
Undergraduate Enrollment: 5,000
Graduate Enrollment: 4,500
Scholarships/Academic: Yes
Athletic: Yes
Financial Aid: Yes
Expenses by: Year
In State: $ 21,000
Out of State: $ 21,000
Degrees Conferred: BA, BS, BFA, MA, MS, MBA, MFA, Ph.D., JD, MDiv
Programs of Study: 68 majors offered in four schools: School of Humanities & Sciences, School of Business, Arts, Engineering and Applied Science.

Men's Athletic Profile

5990 Airline Road
Dallas, TX 75275
Coach: Schellas Hyndman
Email: shyndman@mail.smu.edu

NCAA I
Mustangs/Blue, Red
Phone: (214) 768-2875
Fax: (214) 768-2255

Estimated # of Men's Soccer Scholarships: 1 1/2
Conference: Western Athletic Conference
Program Profile: Program is 14 years in the NCAA playoffs, eight years reaching NCAA Quarter Finals. Westcott Field is a natural grass, training site for 1994 World Cup, the team is sponsored by Nike.
History: Program began in 1975. Coach Hyndman is the second coach in the school's history.
Achievements: 24 professional players, Midwest Coach of the Year 3 times; 1981 NSCAA Coach of the Year, Dallas All-Sports Coach of the Year; numerous All-Americans.
Coaching: Schellas Hyndman, Head Coach, coach for 21 years. Holds license in Brazil and England, NSCAA National Staff, USSF "A" License.
Style of Play: Control-possession built from the back; attacking third go to goal. Team defense and shape is very important. Good team structure.

Women's Athletic Profile

5800 Ownby Drive
Dallas, TX 75275
Coach: George Van Linder
Email: Not Available

NCAA I
Lady Mustangs/Royal, Blue
Phone: (214) 768-4030
Fax: (214) 768-2255

Estimated # of Women's Soccer Scholarships: None
Conference: Western Athletic Conference
Program Profile: Play home games on Wescott Field natural grass field which seats a 4,500. August - December became a lighted facility.
History: The program began in 1986. Compiled an all-time record of 176-64-12; reached 1995 NCAA Final Four; best record of 23-1-1 in 1995; 5 NAIA Appearances; top 20 team.
Achievements: Won 2 Conference Titles (SWC & WAC); 3 Coach of the Year titles; 7 All-American honors; 13 players named All-Region; 3 players of the Year honors; 19 All-Conference honors.
Style of Play: Quick possession play with an emphasis on a quick offensive and defensive transition.

Southwestern University

Academic Profile

Phone: (512) 863-1532

Georgetown, TX 78626-0770

Type: 4 Yr.,Private,Liberal Arts
Website: http://www.southwestern.edu
SAT/ACT/GPA: 1100/24
Student/Faculty Ratio: 11:1
Undergraduate Enrollment: 1,270
Scholarships/Academic: Yes **Athletic:** No
Expenses by: Year **In State:** $ 20,000

Founded: 1848
Religion: Methodist
Housing: Yes
Male/Female Ratio: 47:53
Graduate Enrollment: N/A
Financial Aid: No
Out of State: $ 20,000

Specialty: Biology, Business, Engineering, Premed
Degrees Conferred: BS, BA, BFA, BM
Programs of Study: Accounting, American Studies, Animal Behavior, Art, Biology, Business, Chemistry, Child Study & Language Development, Communications, Computer Science, Economics, English, French, German, History, International Studies, Kinesiology, Mathematics, Music, Philosophy, Physical Science, Physics, Political Science, Psychology, Religion, Sociology, Theatre

Men's Athletic Profile

Robertson Center- P.O. Box 770
Georgetown, TX 78628-0770
Coach: Don Gregory
Email: gregoryd@southwestern.edu

NCAA III
Pirates/Black, Gold, White
Phone: (512) 863-1532
Fax: (512) 863-1393

Estimated # of Men's Soccer Scholarships: N/A
Conference: Southern Collegiate Athletic Conference (SCAC)
Program Profile: Varsity team with a roster of 29 in the Fall of 1999. Two new fields in the Fall of 2000- Both 115X75 Bermuda. New lighted stadium (118X75) will be added in 2 years. 20 match Fall season, 5 matches in the Spring.
History: 1999- first winning record (11-8) ever in school history. The program has been NCAA for 7 years.
Achievements: The program has competed in the NCAA for the past seven years. We had the first winning record in the program's history in 1999 (11-8). We are a team on the rise.
Coaching: Don Gregory, Head Coach, has 18 years head coaching experience, holds a USSF "B" License and STYSA Staff Coach. Assistant Coach, Malek Ben- Musa graduated form McMurray College in 1990.

Roster In State: 28	**Out of State:** 1	**Out of Country:**
ODP State: 10	**Regional:** 2	**National:**
Walk-on/Other:	**Graduation %:** 100	**Seniors on Team:** 4

Positions Needed: Left Flank, Goal Keeper
Camp or Clinic Dates: Not Available
Most Recent Record: 11-8-0
Schedule: Trinity University, Rhodes, University of the South, Colorado College, Stephen's Institute (NJ), Transylvania, Belhaven College, West Texas A&M (DII)
Style of Play: Go to class first, then have a passion for playing hard in the world's greatest game. Have fun playing hard.

Women's Athletic Profile

P.O. Box 770
Georgetown, TX 78627
Coach: Jack Flatau
Email: flatauj@southwestern.edu

NCAA III
Pirates/Black, Gold
Phone: (512) 863-1531
Fax: (512) 863-1393

Estimated # of Women's Soccer Scholarships: None
Conference: Southern Collegiate Athletic Conference (SCAC)
Program Profile: We have two natural grass fields (120x78 yards). Our new athletic facility includes two gymnasiums, a wood running track, a weight room (all cybex), a pool and a tennis complex. New facility with soccer field house in near future.
History: Our program gained varsity status in the fall of 1993. We joined the SCAC Conference in the fall of 1994.
Achievements: In five years of existence, our program has had 28 All-Conference players, 3 All- Region 3 All-American and one Conference Coach of the Year.
Coaching: Jack Flatau, Head Coach, 4th year at SU. He has 21years head coaching experience. He has a USSF "A" License and was an ODP staff coach. Glen Holzer, assistant coach, is in his Fifth year with the program. He was in the ODP state staff and a director of coaching at Georgetown.
Allen Fincher is in his 1st year former J.V. Grad, All-SCAC Conference player.

Roster in State: 22	**Out of State:** 3	**Out of Country:** 0
ODP State: 8	**Regional:**	**National:**
Walk-on/Other:	**Graduation %:** 100	**Seniors on Team:** 4

Positions Needed: ALL, GK particular
Camp or Clinic Dates: Not Available
Most Recent Record: 8-8-1
Schedule: Trinity, Univ. of Mic-Stevens Point, Emory, DePauw, Roanoke, Transylvania
Style of Play: Style of play is dictated by the players' strengths and weaknesses. Organize defensive shape and technically flexible.

Stephen F. Austin State University

Academic Profile

Ads
Nacogdoches, TX 75962

Phone: 936-468-2011

Type: 4 Yr.,Public
Founded: 1923
Website: http://www.stfasu.edu
Religion: Non-Affiliated
SAT/ACT/GPA: 1010/21/3.0
Housing: Yes
Student/Faculty Ratio: 20:1
Male/Female Ratio: 45:55
Undergraduate Enrollment: 12,132
Graduate Enrollment: N/A
Scholarships/Academic: Yes **Athletic:** Yes **Financial Aid:** Yes
Expenses by: Year **In State:** $ 2,427.50 **Out of State:** $ 8,817.50
Specialty: Education
Degrees Conferred: Various bachelors degrees, masters degrees, and doctorate Forestry
Programs of Study: Agriculture, Art, Biology, Chemistry, Communications, Computer Information Systems, Computer Science, Criminal Justice, Economics, English, Environmental Science, French, Geography, Gerontology, Health Science, Hearing Impaired, History, Horticulture, Humanities, Kinesiology, Management, Marketing, Mathematics, Medical Technology, Physics, Political Science, Psychology, Public Administration, Sociology, Spanish, Speech, Theatre

Women's Athletic Profile

P. O. Box 13010
Nacogdoches, TX 75961
Coach: Lance Noble
Email: howtsoc@hotmail.com

NCAA I
Lady Jacks/Purple, Scarlet
Phone: (409) 468-4467
Fax: (409) 468-4580

Estimated # of Women's Soccer Scholarships: 11
Conference: South Land Conference
Program Profile: The program is in its 6th season as a NCAA Div I. The Lady Jacks play their home matches on an Astroturf field at Homer Bryce Stadium,120x64, which seats 1,700. The lady's have their own strength and conditioning Coach four soccer and train during the season and off season at the weight room Wellness Center.
History: Our program in 1995 and our overall record is 38-38-13 in five years.
Achievements: 2 back to back Southland Conference Titles in 1997 and 1998. 18 1st team All-Conference players and 2 1st team All-Region players.
Coaching: Tony Howard, Head Coach, he holds a USSF "B" license and played a professional goalkeeper for Canton Invaders and Miami Freedom. He has won 5 Conference titles at the NCAA and NAIA level and taken two teams to the NCCAA Final Four National Championships. He also coached Miami Christian College Men's Soccer and ODP Goalkeeper Coach for North Texas Youth Soccer. Our assistant coach is Mike Cedeno.
Roster in State: 20 **Out of State:** 4 **Out of Country:** 2
ODP State: 9 **Regional:** 2 **National:**
Walk-on/Other: 4 **Graduation %:** 96 **Seniors on Team:** 2
Positions Needed: All
Camp or Clinic Dates: June
Most Recent Record: 7-9-3
Schedule: University of San Francisco, San Jose State University, Texas A&M, Southern Methodist, University of Houston, University of Texas in El Paso, University of North Texas, University of Arkansas
Style of Play: Relentless defense with great depth and flexibility at midfield and front. Very speedy and fit team. Lots of combination play building through the midfield. Involves all with opportunity to get to goal. High pressure putting many balls into the "mixer" for scoring opportunities. Fast high paced energy with lots of possession and man to man play.

Texas A & M University - College Station

Academic Profile

College Station, TX 77842-3017

Phone: (979) 845-1051

Type: 4 Yr.,Public,Liberal Arts
Founded: 1876
Website: http://www.sports.tamu.edu
Religion: Non-Affiliated
SAT/ACT/GPA: 920/19/2.5
Housing: Yes
Student/Faculty Ratio: 18:1
Male/Female Ratio: 55:45
Undergraduate Enrollment: 43,000
Graduate Enrollment: 6,774
Scholarships/Academic: Yes **Athletic:** Yes **Financial Aid:** Yes
Expenses by: Year **In State:** $ 7,725 **Out of State:** $ 14,145
Specialty: Business Adm., Engineering, Science, Veterinary Medicine, Med
Degrees Conferred: BA, BS, MA, MS, MBA, MD
Programs of Study: 138 fields of undergraduate study; 152 masters, 102 doctoral degrees.

Women's Athletic Profile

John Koldus Bldg. Rm. 225
College Station, TX 77843-3017
Coach: G. Guerrieri
Email: g@athletics.tamu.edu

NCAA I
Aggies/Maroon, White, White
Phone: (979) 862-4248
Fax: (979) 862-1791

Estimated # of Women's Soccer Scholarships: None
Conference: Big 12 Conference
Program Profile: Our stadium has a seating capacity of 2,400. Playing season runs from August through December. We play on natural Tiffany Bermuda grass.
History: Our program began in 1993 to the present. Our record in 1993 was 15-3-1, in 1994 was 15-2-2, in 1995 was 18-6-0, in 1996 was 19-4-0, in 1997 was 18-3-0 and in 1998 was 14-8-0. We were big Twelve Regular Season and Tournament Champs in 1997, NCAA tournament in 1995-1998.
Achievements: G. Guerrie was Big Twelve Coach of the Year in 1997. Bryn Ballack was named All-American in 1996 & 1997. Diana Rowe in 1996, Freshman All-American - Clare Elliott - Melanie Wilson and Bryn Blalack nominations for the MAC and Herman Trophy. Participated with women's National Team. National team pool members Amber Childers U-18, Jessica Martin U-18 Martha More member of the Mexican National Team that competed in the 1999 World Cup.
Coaching: G. Guerrieri is the Head Coach. He holds NSCAA Advanced Natural Diploma. Phil Stephenson, Head Coach, was former head coach at Methodist College. National A License. Robin Conter is Assistant Coach. Hr is a member of US National Team Pool. Winner of 3 natural championships at UNC.
Style of Play: Sophisticated possession style. We attack couple with tenacious defense.

Texas A & M University - Commerce

Academic Profile

Commerce, TX 75429-3011

Phone:

Type: 4 Yr.,Public
Founded: 1889
Website: http://www.estu.edu
Religion: Non-Affiliated
SAT/ACT/GPA: 900/20/2.0
Housing: Yes
Student/Faculty Ratio: 17:1
Male/Female Ratio: 44:56
Undergraduate Enrollment: 4,800
Graduate Enrollment: 3,000
Scholarships/Academic: Yes **Athletic:** Yes **Financial Aid:** Yes
Expenses by: Sem **In State:** $ 4,000 **Out of State:** $ 7,350

Specialty: Education, Business, Psychology, Fine Arts, Sciences
Degrees Conferred: BA, BS, BFA, MA, MS, MBA, MFA, M.Ed., Ph.D., EdD
Programs of Study: Education, Business, Psychology, Fine Arts, Technology, Agriculture, Accounting, Animal Science, Arts, Communications, Computer Information Systems, Criminal Justice, Earth Science, Economics, Computer Science, English, Finance, Geography, Geology, Management, Mathematics, Marketing, Music, Psychology, Social Work, Social Science, Theatre

Women's Athletic Profile

P.O. Box 3011
Commerce, TX 75429-3011
Coach: Neil Piper
Email: Neil_Piper@tamu-commerce.edu

NCAA II
Lions/Navy, Gold
Phone: (903) 886-5571
Fax: (903) 886-5365

Estimated # of Women's Soccer Scholarships: 6
Conference: Lone Star Conference
Program Profile: Our roster team is consists of 22 players; facilities include locker-room, equipment room, field which called Smith Field and is natural grass and has a measurements of 115x75. Playing season is the Fall.
History: Our program started in 1995 and our overall record is 56-30-6. 1999 record was 16-4-1 and were "Elite Eight" Participants and finished the 1999 season ranked 6th in the nation by the NSCAA.
Achievements: 1999 Lone Star regular season and Conference Tournament champions. Lone Star Coach of the Year. Six players named to the Midwest Regional Team.
Coaching: Neil Piper, Head Coach, he holds NSCAA National Diploma. He has a college soccer experience at Penn State University and pro soccer and training experience with Kansas City Wizards (MLS) and Wichita Wings (NPSL). 1999 Lone Star Conference Coach of the Year. Assistant Coach is Erik Forrest.
Roster in State: 16 **Out of State:** 4 **Out of Country:** 0
ODP State: 2 **Regional:** 2 **National:** 2
Walk-on/Other: **Graduation %:** 100 **Seniors on Team:** 4
Positions Needed: Defense and goalkeeper
Camp or Clinic Dates: Not Available
Most Recent Record: 16-4-1
Schedule: Incarnate Word, Midwestern, Central Oklahoma, Metro State, Mesa State, Fort Lewis, West Texas A&M.
Style of Play: Very direct. Use of speed on the wings. Strong in the air.

Texas Christian University

Academic Profile

Phone: (800) 828-3764

Fort Worth, TX 76129

Type: 4 Yr.,Private,Liberal Arts
Website: http://www.tcu.edu
SAT/ACT/GPA: 1010/22/3.0
Student/Faculty Ratio: 14:1
Undergraduate Enrollment: 5,500
Scholarships/Academic: Yes **Athletic:** Yes
Expenses by: Year **In State:** $ 14,700

Founded: 1873
Religion: Disciples of Christ
Housing: Yes
Male/Female Ratio: 43:57
Graduate Enrollment: 1,500
Financial Aid: Yes
Out of State: $ 14,700

Specialty: Business, Education, Sciences
Degrees Conferred: BA, BS, BFA, BBA, B.Mus., BMEd, BSN, MA, MS, MFA, MED, Ph.D.
Programs of Study: Art, Business, Communications, Computer Science, Criminal Justice, Dance, Education, Engineering, Journalism, Kinesiology, Languages, Marketing, Music, Nursing, Nutrition & Dietetics, Physical Education, PreLaw, PreMed, Radio/Television Film, Speech Communication

Men's Athletic Profile

TCU Box 2976000
Fort Worth, TX 76129
Coach: David Rubinson
Email: d.rubinson@tcu.edu
NCAA I
Horned Frogs/Purple, White
Phone: (817) 257-7096
Fax: (817) 257-7964
Estimated # of Men's Soccer Scholarships: N/A
Conference: Western Athletic Conference
Program Profile: Has soccer facilities to be opened for the 1999 season. The new TCU Soccer Complex is projected to have 1,250 seats and is natural grass facility.
History: Program began in 1981. Won several SWC League Championships in the 70's. Competed as a Division I independent until moving into WAC in 1996.
Coaching: David Rubinson, Head Coach (TCU in 1977), four-time All-SWC as a player for TCU, became head coach in 1981. He compiled 117-208-24 in 18 seasons. Blake Amos and Jay Fitzgerald - Assistant Coaches.
Style of Play: Ball possession - attack in numbers; defend in numbers.

Women's Athletic Profile

TCU Box 297600
Fort Worth, TX 76129
Coach: David Rubinson
Email: d.rubinson@tcu.edu
NCAA I
Horned Frogs/Purple, White
Phone: (817) 257-7096
Fax: (817) 257-7787

Estimated # of Women's Soccer Scholarships: 12
Conference: Western Athletic Conference
Program Profile: New soccer facilities will open for the 1999 season. The new TCU soccer complex is projected to have 1,000 seats and a natural grass field.
History: The program began in 1986, posting a 8-8-2 record in first season of competition. We competed in the Southwest Conference during 1995. We moved to WAC in 1996 and began offering scholarships for the first time. Our all-time record is 107-125-14.
Achievements: 1997 WAC Co-coach of the Year.
Coaching: David Rubinson, Head Coach (TCU in 1977), began the women's program in 1986. Coach Rubinson is head coach for the men's program as well. Blake Amos, Jay Fritzgerald, and Christine Keeley are Assistant Coaches.
Roster in State: 12 **Out of State:** 11 **Out of Country:**
ODP State: 20 **Regional:** 5 **National:** 1
Walk-on/Other: **Graduation %:** 100 **Seniors on Team:** 5
Positions Needed: FWD, OMF, GK
Camp or Clinic Dates: June 17-22, 24-29, July-TBA
Most Recent Record: 10-9-1
Schedule: SMU, Marquette, Oklahoma, Pepperdine, St. Louis, UAB
Style of Play: Very possession oriented, with focus on technique and patience.

Texas Lutheran College

Academic Profile

Seguin, TX 78155
Phone:

Type: 4 Yr.,Private,Liberal Arts
Website: http://www.txlutheran.edu
SAT/ACT/GPA: 900/19/2.0
Student/Faculty Ratio: 14:1
Undergraduate Enrollment: 1,500
Scholarships/Academic: Yes **Athletic:** No
Founded: 1891
Religion: Lutheran
Housing: Yes
Male/Female Ratio: 2:3
Graduate Enrollment: N/A
Financial Aid: Yes

Expenses by: Year **In State:** $ 14,042 **Out of State:** $ 14,042
Specialty: Business, Kinesiology, Pre-Professional
Degrees Conferred: BBA, BA, BS
Programs of Study: Accounting, Applied Science, Arts, Biology, Business Administration, Chemistry, Communication Studies, Computer Science, Early Childhood Education, Economics, English, German, History, International Studies, Kinesiology, Management Information Systems, Mathematics, MultiDisciplinary Studies, Music, Philosophy, Physical Education, Physics, Political Science, PreDental, PreMed, PreVet, Psychology, Public History, Social Science, Spanish, Theology, Social Work, Theatre

Men's Athletic Profile

1000 W Court Street
Seguin, TX 78155
Coach: Mike Alderson
Email: malderson -m@txlutheran.edu

NCAA III/NAIA
Bulldogs/Black, Gold
Phone: (830) 372-6577
Fax: (830) 372-8135

Estimated # of Men's Soccer Scholarships: None
Conference: American Southwest Conference
Program Profile: The team travels to Colorado to maintain a tough Division schedule. We have a new natural grass field with 1,000 capacity.
History: The program began in 1983, winning a District IV Championship in 1988 and finishing runner-up in 1989.
Achievements: District IV Champions in 1988; 7 All-Conference selections.
Coaching: Mike Alderson, Head Coach, has a FA coaching badge (England), BA (honors) 1993, University of Birmingham-England. He previously was an assistant coach at Trinity University and was a South Texas ODP State Coach. Xavier Holauin is the Assistant Coach/Goalkeeper Coach.
Style of Play: 4-4-2; aggressive ball movement, quick passing and early services. Man to man defense at the back, zonal in midfield and forwards.

Women's Athletic Profile

1000 W Court Street
Seguin, TX 78155-5999
Coach: Mike Alderson
Email: Not Available

NCAA II/NAIA
Lady Bulldogs/Black, Gold
Phone: (830) 372-6577
Fax: (210) 372-8135

Estimated # of Women's Soccer Scholarships: None
Coaching: Mike Alderson, Head Coach. He has an NSCAA Advanced National Diploma and an English F.A. Coaching Badge. He is also South Texas ODP State Coach.
Style of Play: 4-4-2, Combination of quick passing and direct style encouraged in attack; zonal defensive system.

Texas Tech University
Academic Profile

Ads
Lubbock, TX 79409-3021

Phone: (806) 742-3355

Type: 4 Yr.,Public,Engineering
Founded: 1929
Website: http://www.ttu.edu
Religion: Non-Affiliated
SAT/ACT/GPA: 1270/29/Depends on SAT/ACT scores
Housing: Yes
Student/Faculty Ratio: 18:1
Male/Female Ratio: 1.5:1
Undergraduate Enrollment: 18,136
Graduate Enrollment: 3,315
Scholarships/Academic: Yes **Athletic:** Yes
Financial Aid: Yes
Expenses by: Year **In State:** $ 7,340 **Out of State:** $ 13,700
Specialty: Engineering, Law School, Medical School, Agriculture

Degrees Conferred: Bachelors, Masters, Doctorate
Programs of Study: Architecture, Business Administration, Chemistry, Communication Studies, Dietetics, Electrical Engineering, Elementary Education, Exercise and Sports Science, Family Studies, German, Human Development, Journalism, Secondary Education, Theatre Arts

Women's Athletic Profile

Box 43021
Lubbock, TX 79409-3021
Coach: Felix Oskam
Email: F.Oskam@ttu.edu

NCAA I
Red Raiders/Black, Red
Phone: (806) 742-3355
Fax: (806) 742-0200

Estimated # of Women's Soccer Scholarships:
Conference: Big Twelve Conference
Program Profile: Game field is natural grass inside a track which seats 2,000 with scoreboard and sound system.
History: Began varsity play in 1994 with former Head Coach Diane Nichols. In fall of 1997 Felix Oskam took over the program over the three years she was at Tech Coach Nichols compiled a record of 36-20-3.
Achievements: Began varsity play in 1994 under Diane Nichols. In the fall of 1997 Felex Oskam took over the program. One big 12 All-Conference team and one All-Central region team.
Coaching: Felix Oskam, Head Coach, started since 1997, holds USSF "A" License, NTSSA Staff Coach, Regional Staff Coach, former player at University of North Texas. Barbara Chura, Assistant Coach, holds USSF "B" License, NTSSA Staff Coach, former player and captain at the University of Connecticut. David Bucciero, Assistant Coach, holds USSF "B" License, NTSSA Staff Coach, former goalkeeper at James Madison University.

Roster in State: 12	**Out of State:** 8	**Out of Country:**
ODP State: 10	**Regional:** 2	**National:**
Walk-on/Other:	**Graduation %:** 100	**Seniors on Team:** 4

Positions Needed: Every position
Camp or Clinic Dates: June 5-9 and June 18-22
Most Recent Record: 8-11-1
Schedule: Portland, Nebraska, Texas A&M, Missouri, Baylor, Texas, North Texas, TCU, Iowa's State
Style of Play: Possession, emphasis on attacking, transition play with zonal defense.

Texas Wesleyan University

Academic Profile

Fort Worth, TX 76105

Phone:

Type: 4 Yr.,Private		**Founded:** 1890
Website: http://www.txwesleyan.edu		**Religion:** Methodist
SAT/ACT/GPA: 820/18/3.0		**Housing:** Yes
Student/Faculty Ratio: 14:1		**Male/Female Ratio:** 38:62
Undergraduate Enrollment: 2,106		**Graduate Enrollment:** 980
Scholarships/Academic: Yes	**Athletic:** Yes	**Financial Aid:** Yes
Expenses by: Year	**In State:** $ 13,750	**Out of State:** $ 13,750

Specialty: Business, Education
Degrees Conferred: BA, BS, BME, BBA, MBA, MAT, ME, MHS, DJ
Programs of Study: Accounting, Business Administration, Finance, Management, Marketing, Sports Management, Business Education, Business Psychology, Mass Communication, Human Learning & Development, Exercise & Sport Studies, Psychology, Reading, Bilingual Education, Art, Music, Theatre Arts, Biology, Chemistry, English, Computer Science, Spanish, History, Mathematics, Political Science, Religion

Men's Athletic Profile

1201 Wesleyan Street
Fort Worth, TX 76105-1536
Coach: Kenneth Medina
Email: medinak@txwes.edu

NCAA II
Rams/Royal, Gold
Phone: 817-531-7556
Fax: 817-531-4208

Estimated # of Men's Soccer Scholarships: None
Conference: Heart of Texas Conference
Program Profile: We have a brand new natural grass field.
History: Program began in 1989 and has had 5 years playoff appearances.
Achievements: 2 All-Americans.
Coaching: Kenneth Medina, Head Coach, has been a player and a coach in the North Texas area all of his life. Along with his duties at Texas Wesleyan, he is also a staff coach with the Dallas Texans. Mark Medina - Assistant Coach.
Style of Play: Play to what the game demands.

Trinity University

Academic Profile

Phone: (210) 999-8274

San Antonio, TX 78212

Type: 4 Yr.,Private,Liberal Arts
Website: http://www.trinity.edu
SAT/ACT/GPA: 1276/3.7
Student/Faculty Ratio: 11:1
Undergraduate Enrollment: 2,298
Scholarships/Academic: Yes **Athletic:** No
Expenses by: Year **In State:** $ 23,000

Founded: 1869
Religion: Presbyterian
Housing: Yes
Male/Female Ratio: 49:51
Graduate Enrollment: N/A
Financial Aid: Yes
Out of State: $ 23,000

Specialty: Liberal Arts, Education
Degrees Conferred: Bachelors, Masters
Programs of Study: Accounting, Ancient Mediterranean Studies, Anthropology, Art, Art History, BioChemistry, Biology, Business Administration, Chemistry, Chinese, Classical Studies, Communications, Computer Science, Drama, Economics, Education, Engineering, English, French, GeoScience, German, Greek, History, International Studies, Latin, Mathematics, Music, Philosophy, Physics, Political Science, Psychology, Religion, Russian, Sociology, Spanish, Speech, Urban Studies

Men's Athletic Profile

715 Stadium Drive
San Antonio, TX 78212
Coach: Paul McGinlay
Email: pmginla@trinity.edu

NCAA III
Tigers/Maroon, White
Phone: (210) 999-8222
Fax: (210) 999-8292

Estimated # of Men's Soccer Scholarships: None
Conference: Southern Collegiate Athletic Conference
Program Profile: Fly five times a year to maintain Division III national schedule. Stadium has floodlights, natural grass and is considered one of the best surfaces in the south.
History: Full-time program began in 1991, although the program started in 1963; ranked in top 20 in the country in 1995, 1996, & 1997.

Achievements: SCAC champions four times since 1991; numerous 1st team All-Conference selection; 4 All-Americans since 1994; Jaime Ramirez in MLS draft.
Coaching: Paul McGinlay, Head Coach, USSF "A" license and a NSCAA Advanced National Diploma, Regional Clinician, US Soccer, and NSCAA, South Texas ODP State Coach, Region II Regional ODP Coach, Board Member of NSCAA.
Style of Play: Play 4-4-2 or 3-5-2 depending on personnel. Speed (technical and physical) is very important.

Women's Athletic Profile

715 Stadium Drive
San Antonio, TX 78212
Coach: Greg Ashton
Email: ncowell@trinity.edu

NCAA III
Tigers/Maroon
Phone: (210) 999-8222
Fax: (210) 999-8292

Estimated # of Women's Soccer Scholarships: None
Conference: Southern Collegiate Athletic Conference (SCAC)
Program Profile: Season runs from September through November; state of the art athletic facilities include two gyms, racquetball, indoor pool, weight room, dance studio and excellent rooms. Play on natural field stadium that seats 1,500.
History: This is the oldest varsity program in Texas. joined SCAC in 1991; won consecutive conference championships from 1992 to the present; NCAA tournament Appearances in 1992, 1993, 1995, 1996, 1997 & 1998.
Achievements: The team produced 6 All-American players, 6-time Player of the Week in SCAC, 4-time SCAC Coach of the Year, 2 Scholar Athlete All-Americans
Style of Play: The team play an oriented attack. The players individual assets fit into a strong team concept. Attack from all areas of the field.

Tyler Junior College

Academic Profile

Tyler, TX 75711

Phone:

Type: 2 Yr.,Public,Jr. College
Website: http://www.tyler.cc.tx.us
SAT/ACT/GPA: None
Student/Faculty Ratio: 25:1
Undergraduate Enrollment: 7,800
Scholarships/Academic: Yes **Athletic:** Yes
Expenses by: Year **In State:** $ 4,200
Degrees Conferred: AA, AS

Founded: 1926
Religion: Non-Affiliated
Housing: Yes
Male/Female Ratio: 3:4
Graduate Enrollment: N/A
Financial Aid: Yes
Out of State: $ 4,500

Programs of Study: Business Management, Commercial Art, Computer Science, Criminal Justice, Electronics Technology, Emergency Medical Technology, Graphics Arts, Medical Laboratory Technician, MicroComputer Service, Horticulture Science, Radiological Technology, Computer Information System

Men's Athletic Profile

P.O. Box 9020
Tyler, TX 75711
Coach: Peter E. Jones
Email: pjon@tjc.tyler.cc.tx.us

NJCAA
Apaches/Black, Gold
Phone: (903) 510-2445
Fax: (903) 510-2708

Estimated # of Men's Soccer Scholarships: 18 Tuition only
Conference: Mid-Southwest
Program Profile: Consistently in the national ranking, four times participant in the NJCAA National Men's Division I Tournament; most of the NJCAA National Men's Division I Tournament in 2000-2001; two lighted 75x120 yards Bermuda grass fields with seating for 1,200 called Pat Hartley Field.

History: Soccer began as a club program in 1990. In seven seasons made three appearances at NSCAA Maine Division I National Tournament. Consistently comprehensive in top 20.
Achievements: NJCAA Regional Champions in 1990, 1991, 1992, 1993, 1995, 1996 & 1998; NJCAA District Champions in 1991, 1995, 1996 & 1998; NJCAA National Final Eight Tournament in 1991, 1995, 1996 & 1998; 12 All-Americans; 5 Academic All-Americans; numerous All-South; All-West players; four professional players.
Coaching: Peter E. Jones, Head Coach, NSCAA National Diploma in 1993; beginning 8th season as a head coach at TJC, five-time Region 14 Coach of the Year; 1995 NSCAA/Umbro South Coach of the Year; 1995 NSCAA/Umbro Division I NJCAA Coach of the Year. Rob Nicholson, Assistant Coach.
Style of Play: Depends on student-athlete's profile/skills but generally a fast, short passing game of attack and tight defensive marking.

University of Dallas
Academic Profile

Irving, TX 75062
Phone: 972-721-5000

Type: 4 Yr.,Private,Liberal Arts
Founded: 1910
Website: http://www.udallas.edu
Religion: Catholic
SAT/ACT/GPA: Individually evaluated
Housing: Yes
Student/Faculty Ratio: 11:1
Male/Female Ratio: 2:3
Undergraduate Enrollment: 1,180
Graduate Enrollment: N/A
Scholarships/Academic: Yes **Athletic:** No **Financial Aid:** Yes
Expenses by: Year **In State:** $ 16,576 **Out of State:** $ 16,576
Specialty: Liberal Arts
Degrees Conferred: BA, BS, MA, MS, PhD, MBA, MFA, MH, etc..
Programs of Study: English, History, Art, Drama, Biology, Chemistry, Theology, Politics, Business, Engineering, Physics, Economics, Music, Spanish, German, French, Modern Languages, Mathematics, Journalism, Religious & Pastoral Studies, Management

Men's Athletic Profile

1845 E Northgate Drive
Irving, TX 75062
Coach: Kenny Jones
Email: kjones61@juno.com

NCAA III
Crusaders/Navy, White
Phone: (972) 721-4026
Fax: (972) 721-5208

Estimated # of Men's Soccer Scholarships: N/A
Conference: American Southwest Conference
Program Profile: NCAA Division III American Southwest Conference. Play on grass field; has 20-game season. Schedule is in the Fall and tournament play is in the Spring.
History: Program played NCAA Division III for the first season in 1994. 1995 will be the last year for dual membership in NCAA and NAIA; the team will be playing only in NCAA Division III after 1995.
Achievements: 1 Academic All-American; Joe Weinpel - All-Conference selection and Conference MVP; Runner-Up, Academic All-American; Jerome Bear Schoch - Honorable Mention All-Conference; Kyle Francis- Freshman Player of the Year.
Coaching: Kenny Jones, Head Coach, entering second season with the program. Eleazar Jedsen and Kenny Mars are Assistant Coaches.
Positions Needed: Outside Mids, Forwards Defenders
Style of Play: Aggressive in final third.

Women's Athletic Profile

1845 E Northgate Drive
Irving, TX 75080
Coach: Stefani Papageorge Webb
Email: spwebb@acad.udallas.edu

NCAA III
Crusaders/Navy, White
Phone: (972) 721-5188
Fax: (972) 721-5208

Estimated # of Women's Soccer Scholarships: None
Conference: American Southwest Conference
Program Profile: We play on a natural grass field and play a traditional season.
History: Program began in the Fall of 1995, NCAA Division III American Southwest Conference.
Achievements: The Crusaders finished #4 in the country in scoring offense.
Coaching: Stefani Papageorge Webb, Head Coach. Kenny Marrs, Elezar Jepson, and Kenny Jones, Assistant Coaches.
Roster in State: 13 **Out of State:** 10 **Out of Country:** 1
ODP State: 5 **Regional:** **National:**
Positions Needed: Forwards, Defenders, Goalkeeper
Camp or Clinic Dates: June 17-21
Most Recent Record: 11-6-0
Schedule: Hardin- Simons, Austin College University of Texas at Dallas, Concordia- Wisconsin, Hendrix College, Mary Hardin Baylor
Style of Play: Creative Possession.

University of Houston

Academic Profile

Phone: (713) 743-9474

Houston, TX 77204

Type: 4 Yr.,Public,
Website: http://www.uh.edu
SAT/ACT/GPA: 920-1180/19-26
Student/Faculty Ratio:
Undergraduate Enrollment: 31,000
Scholarships/Academic: Yes **Athletic:** Yes **Financial Aid:** Yes
Expenses by: Year **In State:** $ 2,339 **Out of State:** $ 8,779
Founded: 1927
Religion: Non-Affiliated
Housing: Yes
Male/Female Ratio:
Graduate Enrollment: N/A
Degrees Conferred: BA, BS, Master of Arts, Science
Programs of Study: Architecture, Environmental Design, Accounting, Finance, MIS, Marketing, Education, Kinesiology, Engineering, Hotel & Restaurant Management, Art, Communications Disorder, English, History, Foreign Languages (4), Music, Radio & Television, Theatre, Speech Communications, Biology, Chemistry, Computer Science, Geology, GeoPhysics, Math, Physics, PreOptometry, PrePharmacy, Anthropology, Economics, Psychology, Human Development and Family Studies, Information System Technology

Women's Athletic Profile

3100 Cullen
Houston, TX 77204-6742
Coach: Chris Huston
Email: chuston@bayou.uh.edu

NCAA I
Lady Cougars/Red, White
Phone: (713) 743-9377
Fax: (713) 743-9411

Estimated # of Women's Soccer Scholarships: 5
Conference: Conference USA
Program Profile: Program started in 1998. Home games in 1998, 1999 were played at O'Quinn Field at Robertson Stadium. Track and Soccer complex under construction to be ready by spring of 2000. Robertson stadium has 33,000 seating capacity and has a grass field. The new complex has a seating capacity of 3,500 and has a grass field.

History: Program began in 1998.
Achievements: Recognized as the #1 ranked new program in the nation by Soccer Buzz online magazine. The Cougars were selected over the 17 other first year programs. 4 Lady Cougars were selected to Conference USA All-Conference teams. Soccer Buzz voted Head Coach Chris Huston as National Coach of the Year.
Coaching: Head Coach - Chris Huston is entering his 3rd season with the Cougars and he is a graduate of the University of North Carolina, 1992. The assistant coaches are Bill Solberg, a Marquette graduate, and Joe Kirt, a Wisconsin-Oshkosh graduate.
Roster in State: 17 **Out of State:** 0 **Out of Country:** 1
ODP State: 3 **Regional:** **National:**
Walk-on/Other: **Graduation %:** N/A **Seniors on Team:** 1
Positions Needed: Defenders
Most Recent Record: 11-8-0
Schedule: Marquette, Cincinnati, SMU, Texas, South Florida, UNC-Charlotte
Style of Play: Possession; skillful; speed; aggressive; good work ethic.

University of Mary Hardin - Baylor

Academic Profile

Phone: 254-295-2599

Belton, TX 76513

Type: 4 Yr.,Public,Liberal Arts **Founded:** 1845
Website: http://www.umhb.edu **Religion:** Southern Baptist
SAT/ACT/GPA: 900/19/Top half of senior class **Housing:** Yes
Student/Faculty Ratio: 20:1 **Male/Female Ratio:** 40:60
Undergraduate Enrollment: 2,479 **Graduate Enrollment:** 200
Scholarships/Academic: Yes **Athletic:** No **Financial Aid:** Yes
Expenses by: Year **In State:** $ 12,000 **Out of State:** $ 12,000
Specialty: Nursing
Degrees Conferred: BA, BS, BBA, BFA, BM, BSN, MBA, MED
Programs of Study: Accounting, Art, Business Administration, Biology, Chemistry, Computer Information Systems, Computer Science, Economics, English, History, Finance, Mathematics, Management, Marketing, Medical Technology, Music Education, Nursing, Physical Education, Political Science, Psychology, Religion Social Work, Sociology, Spanish, Speech

Men's Athletic Profile

900 College St Box 8010 **NCAA II**
Belton, TX 76513 Crusaders/Purple, Gold
Coach: David Plunk **Phone:** 254-295-4488
Email: dplunk@umhb.edu **Fax:** 254-2954614

Estimated # of Men's Soccer Scholarships: None
Conference: American Southwest Conference
Program Profile: We contain one game and one practice field, both 117x75 yds. Game field seating capacity is 400. We put strong emphasis on academics, off season work, and community involvement. Fall season with 3-4 scrimmages in spring.
History: Program existence is 13 years. Several All-Conference player in NAIA; Two professional players. We have made the sectional play-off tournament in each of last 2 years.
Achievements: Last 2 years we have produced 3 1st team All-Conference, 6 second team, and seven honorable mention players. Two Academic All-Conference players.
Coaching: Overall record-22-32-2, coaching since 1997, MVP 1990-91 from Hardin-Simmons University, 1st team All-Conference, TIAA, "C" coaching license; trained under J. Valdecentos
Asst. Coach Red Betis, Spain
Roster In State: 22 **Out of State:** 0 **Out of Country:** 0

ODP State: 6 **Regional:** 1 **National:** 0
Walk-on/Other: 4 **Graduation %:** 84 **Seniors on Team:** 3
Positions Needed: Forward, Goalkeeper, Center Midfield
Most Recent Record: 7-11-0
Schedule: UT Dallas, ETBU, Hardin-Simmons, Texas Lutheran, Belhaven
Style of Play: Gurca Style of Play, which is 3-4-3 and 3-5-2. Strong defensive scheme with use of direct attacking with fast, strong forwards.

Women's Athletic Profile

900 College Street
Belton, TX 76513
Coach: Marcia Oliveira
Email: moliveira@umhb.edu

NCAA III
Crusaders/Purple, White, Gold
Phone: (254) 295-4215
Fax: (254) 295-4614

Estimated # of Women's Soccer Scholarships: None
Conference: American Southwest Conference
Program Profile: This is program started in 1998 and got a new coach in 1999. It is growing strongly and fast. The new coach has played soccer in Brazil and her coaching philosophy combines the best of South America and European styles. The school has two soccer field of natural grass (Bermuda), and play all the home games in one of the fields designed exclusively for games.
Achievements: The program has produced first and second conference teams named players. Both athletically and academically.
Coaching: Head coach, student assistant, athletic trainer.
Roster in State: 21 **Out of State:** 0 **Out of Country:** 0
ODP State: 1 **Regional:** 2 **National:**
Walk-on/Other: **Graduation %:** **Seniors on Team:** 1
Positions Needed: Goalie(2), Defenders(2), Midfielders(2), Forward
Camp or Clinic Dates: June 25-29,2001
Most Recent Record: 5-12-1
Schedule: Hardin Simmons University, University of Texas-Dallas, University of Dallas, Austin College, East Texas Baptist University.
Style of Play: Brazilian soccer school philosophy, with strong attack and European defending style.

University of North Texas

Academic Profile

Phone: 940-565-2000

Denton, TX 76203

Type: 4 Yr.,Public **Founded:** 1890
Website: http://www.unt.edu **Religion:** Non-Affiliated
SAT/ACT/GPA: 820/18 **Housing:** Yes
Student/Faculty Ratio: 19:1 **Male/Female Ratio:** 50:50
Undergraduate Enrollment: 19,200 **Graduate Enrollment:** 6,600
Scholarships/Academic: Yes **Athletic:** Yes **Financial Aid:** Yes
Expenses by: Year **In State:** $ 6,800 **Out of State:** $ 12,900
Specialty: Art, Business, Music, Education, Accounting, Broadcasting
Degrees Conferred: BA, BS, BFA, BM, BSEd, MA, MS, MBA, MFA, M.Ed., Ph.D., EdD
Programs of Study: Accounting, Advertising, Anthropology, Art, Banking & Finance, BioChemistry, Biology, Broadcasting, Business, Chemistry, Communications, Computer Science, Criminal Justice, Dance, Earth Science, Economics, Education, Geography, Journalism, Mathematics, Music, Management, Marketing, Philosophy, Physics, Political Science, Social Science

Women's Athletic Profile

P.O. Box 13917
Denton, TX 76203
Coach: John Hedlund
Email: Not Available

NCAA I
Eagles/Forest, White, Navy
Phone: (817) 565-3669
Fax: (817) 565-3470

Estimated # of Women's Soccer Scholarships: None
Conference: Big West Conference
Program Profile: We have a grass field with lights that measures 120 x 75. We play a very competitive schedule. We play in the Big West Conference and travel to the west coast two to three times.
History: Our program began in the Fall of 1995. In just 4 years, our overall record was 48-24-3.
Achievements: We have the highest regional ranking. In 1998, we ranked 5th in the Central Region National Rankings. In 1998 we got two All-Americans; Five All-Region, Nine All-Conference, Five Big West Player of the Week.
Coaching: John Hedlund, Head Coach, started the program in 1995. His overall record is 48-24-3. He played 10 years professionally in which six years were with the Dallas Sidekicks when they won Championships in 1986 to 1993. He is a member of the 1984 U.S. Olympic team and a two-time All-American at Midwestern State University.
Style of Play: Team speed is a must, possession oriented, short build-up out of the back and always looking to attack.

University of Texas

Academic Profile

Austin, TX 78705

Phone:

Type: 4 Yr.,Public,Liberal Arts,Engineering
Website: http://www.utexas.edu
SAT/ACT/GPA: Sliding Scale
Student/Faculty Ratio: 50:50
Undergraduate Enrollment: 35,106
Scholarships/Academic: Yes **Athletic:** Yes
Expenses by: Year **In State:** $ 13,000+

Founded: 1883
Religion: Non-Affiliated
Housing: Yes
Male/Female Ratio: 51:49
Graduate Enrollment: 11,780
Financial Aid: Yes
Out of State: $ 18,000+

Specialty: One of the nation's top research, Engineering & Business Universities
Degrees Conferred: BA, BS, MA, MS
Programs of Study: See www.utexas.edu

Women's Athletic Profile

Bellmont Hall 324
Austin, TX 78712
Coach: Chris Petrucelli
Email: Cpetrucelli@athletics.utex.edu

NCAA I
Longhorns/Burnt Orange
Phone: (512) 471-3624
Fax: (512) 232-4160

Estimated # of Women's Soccer Scholarships: None
Conference: Big 12 Conference
Program Profile: Top notch program, most challenging schedule; one of the best facilities in the country. Has a brand new 20,000 seat soccer and track stadium.
History: 1994 as a full varsity; has competed against the best and ranked in the top 25 teams this past two years.
Achievements: Coach Pibulvech has taken two programs to 7 Final Four Appearances including a second place finishes, all 4 programs built from ground ups and raked in Top 25.
Coaching: Chris Petrucelli, Head Coach, he was named two-time National Coach of the Year. Tony Carasso and Jen Renola, Assistant Coaches.
Style of Play: Creative, possession and team attacking scheme; build up with mobility and indirect plays.

University of Texas - Dallas

Academic Profile

Phone: 972-883-2111

Richardson, TX 75083-0688

Type: 4 Yr.,Public,Engineering
Founded: 1969
Website: http://www.utdallas.edu
Religion: Non-Affiliated
SAT/ACT/GPA: 1140/24Top 25%
Housing: Yes
Student/Faculty Ratio: 22:1
Male/Female Ratio: 50:50
Undergraduate Enrollment: 4,500
Graduate Enrollment: 4,500
Scholarships/Academic: Yes **Athletic:** No **Financial Aid:** Yes
Expenses by: Year **In State:** $ 3,300+ **Out of State:** $ 4,000+
Specialty: Electrical Engineering, Computer Science, Biology
Degrees Conferred: Bachelors, Masters, Doctorate
Programs of Study: Electrical Engineering, Computer Science, Mathematics, Biology, PreMed, Business Administration, Psychology, NeuroScience, Accounting, Government, Politics, Teacher Certification, Chemistry, History, Speech Languages, Pathology, Audiology, GeoScience, Geography, Economics, Finance, Arts & Humanities, Art & Performance

Men's Athletic Profile

P.O. Box 830688
Richardson, TX 75083-0688
Coach: Jack Peel
Email: jpeel@utdallas.edu

NCAA III
Comets/Green, Orange, White
Phone: (972) 883-4062
Fax: (972) 882-2026

Estimated # of Men's Soccer Scholarships: n/a
Conference: American Southwest Conference
Program Profile: Men's soccer team will begin its4th year of NCAA III competition in the Fall of 2000. They are the defending west division champions in the ASC. They compete on a natural grass field with 500 seat stadium bleachers and team bench cover. 8 field soccer complex.
History: NAIA in 1994 to 1997. Became a member of NCAA III in 1998.
Achievements: Sectional play offs NAIA in 1995, 96, 97. ASC Conference play offs in 1998, 1999. Conference Coach of the Year in 1998,1999. MVP of Conference, Freshman of the Year in Conference.
Coaching: Jack Peel, Head Coach, holds USSF "A" License. Scott Turner and Jeromy Morse are the Assistant Coaches.
Roster In State: 24 **Out of State:** 3 **Out of Country:** 0
ODP State: 4 **Regional:** 1 **National:** 1
Walk-on/Other: 0 **Graduation %:** 86 **Seniors on Team:** 3
Camp or Clinic Dates: June 4, 11, 18
Most Recent Record: 13-5-0
Schedule: UC Santa Cruz, Cal. St. Hayword, Hardin Simmons, Maryville Univ.
Style of Play: We play 4-4-2, zonal defense counter attacking style with the ability to build out of the back when needed.

Women's Athletic Profile

Box 830688, AB 10
Richardson, TX 75083-0688
Coach: John Antonisse
Email: john@utdallas.edu

NCAA III
Comets/Green, White
Phone: (972) 883-4061
Fax: (972) 883-2026

Estimated # of Women's Soccer Scholarships: None
Conference: American Southwest Conference

Program Profile: We have top-notch soccer facilities. Six lighted fields, covered player bench area, the stadium field is 75x120 and has a 500 seat bleacher system. We have a new athletic facility with a 5,000 square foot weight room. Probably one of the finest facilities in the Southwest.
History: Program began in 1994 with a part-time coach. 1998 is the first year with a full-time coach. With a full time coach the women's soccer program has flourished. The last two season we have record of 28-8-1.
Achievements: 1999-2000 ASC Coach of the Year; ASC West Division Champion; 9 All-Conference players; ASC Freshman of the Year.
Coaching: John Antonisse, Head Coach. He has a USSF "A" Advanced National License. Lisa Tomasell and Tom Hart are the assistant coaches.
Roster in State: 22 **Out of State:** 1 **Out of Country:**
Walk-on/Other: **Graduation %:** 95 **Seniors on Team:** 2
Positions Needed: Forwards and Midfielders
Camp or Clinic Dates: June 4-8, 11-15, 18-22
Most Recent Record: 13-4-1
Schedule: Trinity University, Hardin-Simmons University, Southwestern University, Austin College, University of Dallas, St. Gregory's University, Northwood University
Style of Play: Organized defensively with fast paced counter attack, direct style.

University of Texas - El Paso

Academic Profile

Phone: 915-747-5000

El Paso, TX 79968-0579

Type: 4 Yr.,Public
Founded: 1914
Website: http://www.utep.edu
Religion: Non-Affiliated
SAT/ACT/GPA: 920 min
Housing: Yes
Student/Faculty Ratio: 24:1
Male/Female Ratio: 46:54
Undergraduate Enrollment: 15,393
Graduate Enrollment: 2,233
Scholarships/Academic: Yes **Athletic:** Yes **Financial Aid:** Yes
Expenses by: Year **In State:** $ 7,368 **Out of State:** $ 13,788
Degrees Conferred: BA, BS, BFA, MA, MS, MBA, M.Ed., Ph.D.
Programs of Study: 52 undergraduate; 60 master's degree choices.

Women's Athletic Profile

500 W. University Ave.
El Paso, TX 79968-0579
Coach: TBA
Email:

NCAA I
Miners/Blue, White, Orange
Phone: (915) 747-5872
Fax: (915) 747-5162

Estimated # of Women's Soccer Scholarships: 6
Conference: Western Athletic Conference
Program Profile: UTEP Soccer started play in the fall of 1996 as a fully-funded Division I program in the Western Athletic Conference. Charlie Davis Park was built for the program and is regard as one of the top soccer facilities in the Southwest. the playing surface is flat, fast and wide. the seating holds about 1,500 fans and overlooks the Franklin Mountain Range which provides for a very scenic background.
History: UTEP soccer began in 1996 finishing one game sly of the conference playoffs. That year UTEP soccer produced the Mountains Division Freshman of the Year for the WAC and a first team All-WAC player. By 1997, into the second year of the program, UTEP had a .500 record, won two tournaments best a regionally ranked team, set a record for goals scored in a game (20) and had another 1st team All-WAC player.
Achievements: 1998 Mt-Div.Coach of the Year, 1998 Mt-Div Co-Champions, 1998 Freshman of the Year, 6 All-Wac, 1 drafted pro-player.
Roster in State: 11 **Out of State:** 13 **Out of Country:** 7

ODP State: 7 **Regional:** 2 **National:** 1
Walk-on/Other: **Graduation %:** 100 **Seniors on Team:** 4
Positions Needed: 8
Camp or Clinic Dates: June 1-6
Most Recent Record: 8-12-0
Schedule: SMU, Fresno State, Texas Tech, LSU, Colorado College, San Jose St.
Style of Play: Fast, physical, like to knock the ball around.

University of Texas - Pan American

Academic Profile

Phone: (956) 316-7007

Edinburg, TX 78539

Type: 4 Yr.,Public
Founded: 1927
Website: http://www.panam.edu/athletics
Religion: Non-Affiliated
SAT/ACT/GPA: 930/20/1.5
Housing: Yes
Student/Faculty Ratio: 20:1
Male/Female Ratio: 1:1
Undergraduate Enrollment: 11,500
Graduate Enrollment: 2,500
Scholarships/Academic: Yes **Athletic:** Yes **Financial Aid:** Yes
Expenses by: Year **In State:** $ 3,358 **Out of State:** $ 6,381
Specialty: Education, International Business
Degrees Conferred: BA, BS, BFA, BSN, Masters
Programs of Study: College of Arts and Humanities, College of Business Administration, College of Education, College of Heath Sciences and Human Services, College of Science and Engineering, College of Social and Behavioral Sciences.

Men's Athletic Profile

1201 W University Drive
Edinburg, TX 78539
Coach: Miguel Paredes
Email: Not Available

NCAA I
Broncs/Forest Green
Phone: (210) 381-2221
Fax: (210) 381-2398

Estimated # of Men's Soccer Scholarships: N/A
Conference: Sun Belt Conference

University of the Incarnate Word

Academic Profile

Phone:

San Antonio, TX 78209

Type: 4 Yr.,Private
Founded: 1881
Website: http://www.viwtx.edu
Religion: Catholic
SAT/ACT/GPA: 960/18/2.5
Housing: Yes
Student/Faculty Ratio: 15:1
Male/Female Ratio: 1:3
Undergraduate Enrollment: 2,500
Graduate Enrollment: 684
Scholarships/Academic: Yes **Athletic:** Yes **Financial Aid:** Yes
Expenses by: Year **In State:** $ 15,060 **Out of State:** $ 15,060
Specialty: Nursing, Business
Degrees Conferred: BA, BS, MA, MS, MBA, MED
Programs of Study: 40 undergraduate degrees in Applied Arts, Business Administration, Education, Fine Arts, Humanities, Social Sciences, Natural Science, Mathematics, Nursing, and PreProfessional Studies

Men's Athletic Profile

4301 Broadway
San Antonio, TX 78209
Coach: Jeremy Fishbein
Email: jeremyf@universe.uiwtx.edu

NCAA II
Crusaders/Black, Red
Phone: (210) 841-7396
Fax: (210) 805-3574

Estimated # of Men's Soccer Scholarships: 3
Conference: Heart of Texas Conference
Program Profile: Our goal is to compete for a National Title. Lighted, Bermuda grass game field which seats 1500. Two full size training fields. No Football team. Play outdoors year round. Athletic Department has a strength coach, and we have year round condition and weight programs. Spring matches vs. professional teams. Three coaches, all with professional playing experience. Fly twice in 2000. National caliber schedule.
History: Program in its 15th year. 12 winning seasons in the past 13 years. Eight former players currently playing professionally.
Achievements: Western Region Coach of the Year in 1993; 3 times Conference Coach of the Year; 7 All-Americans and 8 players currently in pro's.
Coaching: Head coach, Jeremy Fishbein. Assistant coaches, Dennis Bryan, current captain of Austin Lone Stars Professional Soccer Club (USISL), Kam Momeni, former USISL player.

Roster In State: 14 | **Out of State:** 7 | **Out of Country:** 2
ODP State: 8 | **Regional:** 3 | **National:** 0
Walk-on/Other: | **Graduation %:** N/A | **Seniors on Team:** 4

Schedule: Seattle Pacific, California Bakersfield, Fort Lewis College, Midwestern, St. Edwards, West Texas, Southern Colorado.
Style of Play: Attacking, highly technical with interchange of positions. Looking for athletic, attack orientated players with desire, dedication and tenacity.

Women's Athletic Profile

4301 Broadway
San Antonio, TX 78209
Coach: Tina Patterson
Email: tpatterson@universe.uiwtx.edu

NCAA II
Crusaders/Red, Black, White
Phone: (210) 829-3941
Fax: (210) 829-3574

Estimated # of Women's Soccer Scholarships: 9.9
Conference: Heartland
Program Profile: Six years as a varsity sport, won conference/district all six years, field is on campus and is schedule to get lights over summer, natural grass that seats 500.
History: Club sport in 1989, varsity in 1990. Won conference/district titles. Went to nationals in 1994. Nationally ranked five years; 6 All-Americans for the last two years, six-year record of 61-27-4.
Achievements: Team's GPA is 3.2, GTE Academic All-American, 11 NAIA Academic All-Americans, 3 NSCAA Academic All-Americans, 7 Regional Academic All-Americans, 30 Conference Academic All-Americans, 4 All-Americans, 7 All-Regional, 28 All-Conference, 4-5 Conference MVP, 4-5 Freshmen of the Year, 4-5 Coach of the Year, and 1 Region Coach of the Year.
Coaching: Tina Patterson, Head Coach, is a graduate of Texas A & M with a bachelor's degree in Kinesiology. Played on 1984 North Carolina-Chapel Hill team which won NCAA title. Played on gold medal in 1986 US Olympic Festival team. Two-year record as IWC head coach is 21-12-2. The 1994 team won conference and regional titles to advance to the nationals.

Roster in State: 21 | **Out of State:** | **Out of Country:**
ODP State: 5 | **Regional:** 1 | **National:**
Walk-on/Other: | **Graduation %:** 90 | **Seniors on Team:** 2

Positions Needed: Forward

Camp or Clinic Dates: June- July
Most Recent Record: 16-4-1
Schedule: Colorado, Missouri, Midwestern, West Texas A&M, East Texas A&M Commerce, St. Mary's, TX Wesleyan, Oklahoma
Style of Play: Strong midfield and defense. Take the offensive opportunities when available.

West Texas A & M University

Academic Profile

Canyon, TX 79016
Phone: (806) 651-2695

Type: 4 Yr.,Public,Liberal Arts
Founded: 1910
Website: http://www.wtamu.edu
Religion: Non-Affiliated
SAT/ACT/GPA: 950/21
Housing: Yes
Student/Faculty Ratio: 24:1
Male/Female Ratio: N/A
Undergraduate Enrollment: 5,200
Graduate Enrollment: 1,300
Scholarships/Academic: Yes
Athletic: Yes
Financial Aid: Yes
Expenses by: Year
In State: $ 3,000
Out of State: $ 6,458
Degrees Conferred: BA, BS, BFA, MA, MBA, MFA, MED
Programs of Study: Agribusiness, Agriculture, Biology, Chemistry, Accounting, Communications, Computer/Information Science, Education, English, Finance, History, Marketing, Music, Nursing, PreLaw, PreMed, Psychology, Biology, Chemistry, Physics

Men's Athletic Profile

Box 49
Canyon, TX 79016
Coach: Butch Lauffer
Email: Not Available

NCAA II
Buffaloes/Maroon, White
Phone: (806) 651-2678
Fax: (806) 651-2688

Estimated # of Men's Soccer Scholarships: None
Conference: Independent Conference
Program Profile: Good locker room which is close to the field. The field has 117x67 yards, natural grass with a seating capacity of a 1,500. Fall season. Has three fields one for game and two for practice.
History: Initial season was 1991-1992; the record for 1996 was 12-4-0, finishing the season ranking 13th in the nation in the Final Poll and 3rd in the West Region. Six years record of 73-31-9; ranked in top 20 nationally last four years.
Achievements: 1997 National Tournament; Academic All-Americans; many All-Midwest selections; 5 top twenty national ranking.
Coaching: Butch Lauffer, Head Coach, USSF "A" License, Irish FA Full Badge, Football Association of Ireland Full Badge, English Prelim Badge, Advanced National License, Author of two soccer coaching books, record at WTAMU is 46-26-4. Troy Farrar - Assistant coach, USSF "C" License.
Style of Play: Zonal defending, possession play.

Women's Athletic Profile

WTAMU BOX 49
Canyon, TX 79016
Coach: Robert "Butch" Lauffer
Email: Not Available

NCAA II
Buffalos/Maroon, White
Phone: (806) 656-2678
Fax: (806) 656-2688

Estimated # of Women's Soccer Scholarships: None
Conference: Lone Star Conference

Program Profile: Natural grass field with a measurements 117x67 yards, two practice fields, good locker room, and nice facilities. Stadium has a seating capacity of 1,500.
History: The program began in 1996, and first season become Lone Star Conference Champions, Final Ranking of fifth in the Great Plains, ranked in the Top 25 for three weeks, 1996 record was 12-4.
Achievements: Lone Star Conference Coach of the Year in 1996. Regular Season Lone Star Conference Champions in 1996. Two All-Conference players in 1996.
Coaching: Butch Lauffer, Head Coach, USSF "A" License, Irish FA Full Badge, Football Association of Ireland Full Badge, English Prelim Badge, Advanced National License, Author of two soccer coaching books. Troy Farrar - Assistant Coach, USSF "C" License. Liz Schaper - Assistant Coach, "C" License.
Style of Play: Zonal defending; professional play.

SCHOOL	CITY	AFFILIATION	PAGE
Brigham Young University	Provo	NCAA I	1122
University of Utah	Salt Lake City	NCAA I	1123
Utah State University	Logan	NCAA I	1123
Weber State University	Ogden	NCAA I	1124
Westminster C - SLC	Salt Lake City	NAIA	1125

Brigham Young University
Academic Profile

Phone: (801) 378-8732

Provo, UT 84602

Type: 4 Yr.,Private
Website: http://www.byu.edu
SAT/ACT/GPA: 26/3.3
Student/Faculty Ratio: 20:1
Undergraduate Enrollment: 29,000
Scholarships/Academic: Yes **Athletic:** Yes
Expenses by: Year **In State:** $ 7,000

Founded: 1882
Religion: Non-Affiliated
Housing: Yes
Male/Female Ratio: 48:52
Graduate Enrollment: 4,000
Financial Aid: Yes
Out of State: $ 7,000

Degrees Conferred: BA, BS, MA, MS, EDD, Ph.D., JD
Programs of Study: Accounting, Advertising, Agriculture, Animal, Anthropology, Banking/Finance, Biology, Botany, Broadcasting, Manufacturing, Medical, Cartography, Ceramic, Engineering, Clothing/Textiles, Geography, Entomology, Fashion, Food, Humanities, International, Nursing, Nutrition, Philosophy, Psychology, Natural Resources, Special Education, Speech, Sports Medicine

Men's Athletic Profile

P.O. Box 22241
Provo, UT 84602-2241
Coach: Lee Gibbons
Email: Not Available

NCAA I
Cougars/Royal Blue, White
Phone: (801) 378-3334
Fax: (801) 378-3520

Estimated # of Men's Soccer Scholarships: N/A
Conference: WAC

Women's Athletic Profile

248 Smith Field House
Provo, UT 84602-2241
Coach: Jennifer Rockwood
Email: jrockwood@byu.edu

NCAA I
Cougars/Blue, White
Phone: (801) 378-8732
Fax: (801) 378-5756

Estimated # of Women's Soccer Scholarships: 12
Conference: Mountain West Conference
Program Profile: Top 25 National Ranking past four years, Top facilities including training and weight rooms. On campus game field that is exclusive to the soccer program and has a seating capacity of 2,500.
History: 3 NCAA appearances. 1st year NCAA was 1995 and finished 11-8-1. 1996 22-1 ranked 17th and were the Mountain West Conference Champions. 19997 19-4, NSCAA ranking 22nd and NCAA ranked 17th. 1998 20-5 NSCAA ranking 13th and NCAA ranked 9th. 1999 21-4, Conference champions, NSCAA ranking 20th and NCAA 17th.
Achievements: Our All-American players were Shauna Bohbock in 1997 & 1998 and Maven Hendershot in 1998, all NCAA third team. Jennifer Rockwood was named WAC Coach of the Year and Soccer Buzz West Region Coach of the Year in 1996.
Coaching: Jennifer Rockwood, Head Coach, was named WAC Coach of the Year and Soccer Buzz West Region Coach of the Year in 1996. Chris Watkins and Brian Jolley are our assistant coaches.
Roster in State: 16 **Out of State:** 12 **Out of Country:**
ODP State: 18 **Regional:** 3 **National:** 1
Walk-on/Other: **Graduation %:** 95 **Seniors on Team:** 6
Positions Needed: Goal Scorer, Goal Keeper
Camp or Clinic Dates: July 3-7, 24-28, August 1-4

Most Recent Record: 21-4
Schedule: Nebraska, Portland, Virginia, Wake Forest, USC, Minnesota, Northwestern, Washington, San Diego State, Tennessee.
Style of Play: Attacking/ Possess ional play out of the back and side to side.

University of Utah
Academic Profile

Salt Lake City, UT 84112
Phone: 801-581-7200

Type: 4 Yr.,Public
Founded: 1850
Website: http://www.utah.edu
Religion: Non-Affiliated
SAT/ACT/GPA: 24
Housing: Yes
Student/Faculty Ratio: 21:1
Male/Female Ratio: 55:45
Undergraduate Enrollment: 19,635
Graduate Enrollment: 4,823
Scholarships/Academic: Yes **Athletic:** Yes **Financial Aid:** Yes
Expenses by: Year **In State:** $ 8,861 **Out of State:** $14,401
Specialty: Business & Medical Related Sciences
Degrees Conferred: BA, BS, MS, MBA, MFA
Programs of Study: Architecture, Business, Education, Engineering, Fine Arts, Health, Humanities, Law, Medicine, Miners & Earth Sciences, Nursing, Pharmacy, Science, Social & Behavioral Science, Social Work

Women's Athletic Profile

1825 E. South Campus Drive
Salt Lake City, UT 84112
Coach: Amy Freeman Winslow
Email: awinslow@huntsman.utah.edu

NCAA I
Utes/Red, White
Phone: (801) 585-7250
Fax: (801) 585-6453

Estimated # of Women's Soccer Scholarships: N/A
Conference: Mountain West Conference
Program Profile: Natural field which has a measurements of 115x75 yards, also a 10,000sq. ft. 2 weight rooms are available, training rooms used by athletes, and average attendance is 800 out of a population of a 2,000.
History: Began program in 1995. Team has matured into a regional contender that had its best season (12-7) in Fall of 1998 with its first-ever regional ranking. Playing its most difficult schedule to date as five teams advanced to the NCAA Tournament. Academics is highly emphasized as 19 out of 25 Fall 1998 players made the Honor Roll.
Achievements: Coach of the Year in Mountain West Conference 1999, Co-Champs of MWC 1999, 2nd place in MWC 2000,
Coaching: Amy Freeman Winslow, Head Coach, was named Mountain Division Coach of the Year (WAC Conference Award). Assit. Coach Jim Winslow
Roster in State: 17 **Out of State:** 8 **Out of Country:** 0
ODP State: 18 **Regional:** 7 **National:** 1
Camp or Clinic Dates: June 25-29, 2001
Most Recent Record: 13-7-1
Schedule: Arizona State, BYU, Marquette, Montana, Kentucky, Portland, Boston Univ.
Style of Play: Extremely athletic team that plays quickly in transition. Strength is in the air especially on corner kicks.

Utah State University
Academic Profile

Logan, UT 84322-1600
Phone: 435-797-1000

Type: 4 Yr.,Public
Founded: 1888
Website: http://www.usu.edu
Religion: Non-Affiliated

SAT/ACT/GPA: Sliding Scale
Housing: Yes
Student/Faculty Ratio: 22:1
Male/Female Ratio: 53:47
Undergraduate Enrollment: 16,500
Graduate Enrollment: 4,500
Scholarships/Academic: Yes
Athletic: Yes
Financial Aid: Yes
Expenses by: Year
In State: $ 6,975
Out of State: $ 11,415
Degrees Conferred: BA, BS, BFA, MA, MS, MBA, MFA, M.Ed., Ph.D., EdD, AAS
Programs of Study: Agriculture, Business, Education, Engineering, Family Life, Humanities, Arts and Social Sciences, Natural Resources, and Science

Women's Athletic Profile

Harris Athletic Center
Logan, UT 84322-7400
Coach: Stacey Enos
Email: sallyb@cc.usu.edu

NCAA I
Aggies/Navy, White
Phone: (801) 797-0900
Fax: (801) 797-1837

Estimated # of Women's Soccer Scholarships: None
Conference: Big West Conference
Program Profile: Facilities include a natural grass soccer field located on campus with a seating capacity of 500. Season is from August to November.
History: Program began in the Fall of 1996.
Achievements: None - new program.
Coaching: Stacey Enos, Head Coach, former Division I player at University of North Carolina, four year starter, 1985 All-American, NCAA National Championship team in 1982, 1983 and 1984. Member of US Women's National Team in 1985-1987.
Style of Play: Possess ional, and ball control.

Weber State University

Academic Profile

Phone: 801-626-6000

Ogden, UT 84408-2701

Type: 4 Yr.,Public
Founded: 1875
Website: http://www.weber.edu
Religion: Non-Affiliated
SAT/ACT/GPA: Open
Housing: No
Student/Faculty Ratio: 17:1
Male/Female Ratio: 59:41
Undergraduate Enrollment: 1,732
Graduate Enrollment: 518
Scholarships/Academic: Yes
Athletic: No
Financial Aid: Yes
Expenses by: Year
In State: $ 17,826
Out of State: $ 17,826
Degrees Conferred: BA, BS, MA, MS
Programs of Study: Accounting, Art, Aviation, Biology, Business, Chemistry, Communications, Computer Science, Economics, Education, Engineering, English, Finance, History, Human Resource Management, Information Resource Management, International Business, Management, Marketing, Mathematics, Nursing, Philosophy, Physics, Political Studies, PreDental, PreLaw, PreMedical, Psychology, Social Sciences, Sociology

Women's Athletic Profile

2706 University Circle
Ogden, UT 84408-2706
Coach: Lynn Kofoed
Email: Lkofoed@weber.edu

NCAA I
Wildcats/Purple, White
Phone: (801) 626-7291
Fax: (801) 626-8962

Estimated # of Women's Soccer Scholarships: 12
Conference: Big Sky Conference

Program Profile: We play natural grass, which measures 115x75 fields. Our playing season starts August-December.
History: 1996/1997 was first year of the program in Division I with a record of 7-7-2. In 1997-1998, we were place Big Sky Conference 16-5-1. In 1998-1999, we were Big Sky Conference Champs with a record of 17-3-0.
Achievements: We were 1997 & 1998 Coach of the Yea, Big sky Conference, 1998 Big Sky Conference Champions. We have had 2 All-West Region players in 1998, 1 Freshmen All-West Team 3rd-team and 1 Freshman All-American 3rd-team in 1998.
Coaching: Lynn Kofoed is our Head Coach. Tom Vudhivadhana is our Co-Head Coach. Rick Talamantez is our Assistant Coach.
Roster in State: 23 **Out of State:** 2 **Out of Country:** 0
ODP State: 5 **Regional:** 0 **National:** 0
Walk-on/Other: 0 **Graduation %:** 99 **Seniors on Team:** 3
Positions Needed: Keeper, Forward, Sweeper
Most Recent Record: 4-12-2
Schedule: BYU, Fresno State, University of Montana, University of Utah, Pacific
Style of Play: Technically oriented and defensive-minded. Attack from all positions. Players must be versatile and able to play a variety of positions and formations. Technical control emphasized not a "run and gun" program. Soccer that is beautiful to watch.

Westminster College - Salt Lake City

Academic Profile

Salt Lake City, UT 84105
Phone: (800) 748-4753

Type: 4 Yr.,Private
Founded: 1875
Website: http://www.wcslc.edu
Religion: Presbyterian
SAT/ACT/GPA: 950+
Housing: No
Student/Faculty Ratio: 18:1
Male/Female Ratio: 35:65
Undergraduate Enrollment: 1,760
Graduate Enrollment: 400
Scholarships/Academic: Yes **Athletic:** No **Financial Aid:** Yes
Expenses by: Year **In State:** $ 13,200 **Out of State:** $ 13,200
Specialty: Liberal Arts Core with Professional Programs
Degrees Conferred: BA, BS, BSN, MBA
Programs of Study: Accounting, Aviation Management, Biology, Business Administration, Chemistry, Communications, Computer Science, Dramatic Arts, Early Childhood, Economics, Elementary Education, English, Fine Arts, History, Human Development, Management, Marketing, Mathematics, Nursing, Philosophy, Physics, Psychology, Secondary Education, Social Science

Men's Athletic Profile

1840 S 1300 East
Salt Lake City, UT 84105
Coach: Chris Dorich
Email: Not Available

NAIA
Parsons/Purple, Gold
Phone: (801) 594-3785
Fax: (801) 466-6916

Estimated # of Men's Soccer Scholarships: N/A
Conference: RMISL

vermont

VERMONT

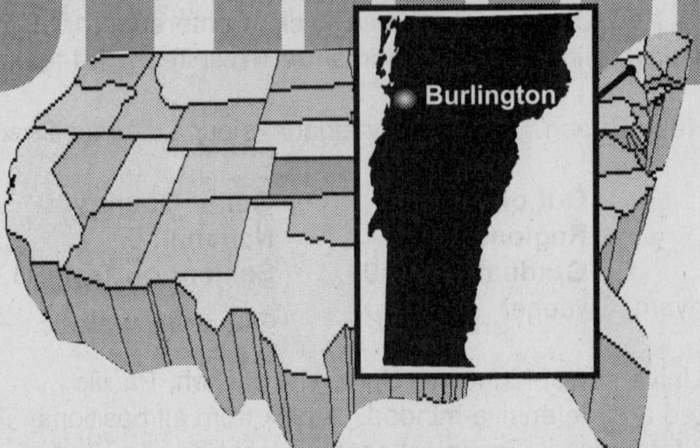

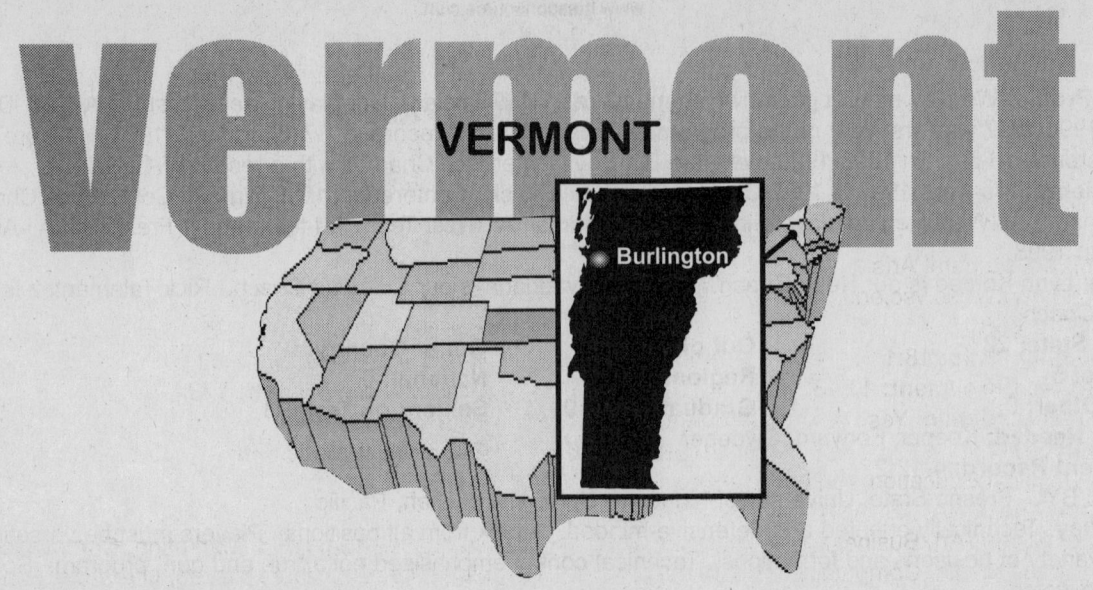

SCHOOL	CITY	AFFILIATION	PAGE
Castleton State College	Castleton	NCAA III	1127
College of Saint Joseph	Rutland	NAIA	1128
Green Mountain College	Poultney	NAIA	1129
Johnson State College	Johnson	NCAA III	1130
Lyndon State College	Lyndonville	NAIA	1131
Middlebury College	Middlebury	NCAA III	1132
Norwich University	Northfield	NCAA III	1133
Saint Michael's College	Colchester	NCAA II	1135
Southern Vermont College	Bennington	NCAA III/NAIA	1136
University of Vermont	Burlington	NCAA I	1137

Castleton State College

Academic Profile

Phone: 802-468-5611

Castleton, VT 05735

Type: 4 Yr.,Public,Liberal Arts
Founded: 1787
Website: http://www.csc.vsc.edu
Religion: Non-Affiliated
SAT/ACT/GPA: 860/18
Housing: Yes
Student/Faculty Ratio: 18:1
Male/Female Ratio: 48:52
Undergraduate Enrollment: 1,543
Graduate Enrollment: 193
Scholarships/Academic: Yes **Athletic:** No **Financial Aid:** Yes
Expenses by: Year **In State:** $ 8,946+ **Out of State:** $ 13,458+
Specialty: Physical Education, Athletic Training
Degrees Conferred: AA, AS, ASN, BA, BS, BSW, MA
Programs of Study: Art, Business Administration, Accounting, Finance, Management, Marketing, Communications, Journalism, Mass Media, Computer Information Systems, Criminal Justice, Education, History, Literature, Math, Music, Biology, Geology, General Science, Physical Education, Psychology, Social Work, Sociology, Theatre Arts

Men's Athletic Profile

Glenbrook Gymnasium
Castleton, VT 05735
Coach: Chris O'Brian
Email: msoccer@castleton.edu

NCAA III
Spartans/Green, White
Phone: (802) 468-1369
Fax: (802) 468-2189

Estimated # of Men's Soccer Scholarships: None
Conference: Mayflower Conference
Program Profile: Castleton plays on a natural grass turf at Alumni Field.
History: Program began in 1959, post season 27 out of 37 years, played in 3 national championships.
Achievements: 1995 Mayflower Conference Champions, 16th consecutive Post Season appearance.
Style of Play: Man defense, quick counter if on, patient and ball possession if not.

Women's Athletic Profile

Glenbrook Gym
Castleton, VT 05735
Coach: James Tyson
Email: wsoccer@castleton.edu

NCAA III
Spartans/Dark Green, White
Phone: (802) 468-1369
Fax: (802) 468-2189

Estimated # of Women's Soccer Scholarships: None
Conference: Mayflower Conference
Program Profile: The home field is a natural grass, and the playing season runs from August (pre-season) to November. Two gym facilities used for indoor in the off-season and additional workouts. Olympic size pool used for team workouts, and a fitness center used for off-season workouts.
Achievements: Beth Stelmak - NAIA Academic All-American in two years; Darcy Riggs - NAIA Academic All-American in one year; Christina Damato - NAIA District 5 team.
Style of Play: Aggressive, clean style, shoot at any time the opportunity arise, use speed as much as possible, try to control the midfield, and work the ball out of the back.

College of Saint Joseph - Vermont

Academic Profile

Phone:

Rutland, VT 05701

Type: 4 Yr.,Private,
Website: http://www.csj.edu
SAT/ACT/GPA: Varies
Student/Faculty Ratio: 12:1
Undergraduate Enrollment: 500
Scholarships/Academic: Yes **Athletic:** Yes
Expenses by: Year **In State:** $ 15,000

Founded: 1954
Religion: Catholic
Housing: Yes
Male/Female Ratio: 1:1
Graduate Enrollment: 200
Financial Aid: Yes
Out of State: $ 15,000

Degrees Conferred: AA, AS, BA, BS, M.Ed.
Programs of Study: 21 Majors: Business Education, Human Services, and Arts & Sciences. Graduate Programs in Education and Counseling Psychology.

Men's Athletic Profile

71 Clement Road
Rutland, VT 05701
Coach: E.J. Bishop
Email: Not Available

NAIA
Fighting Saints/R. Blue, White
Phone: (802) 773-5900
Fax: (802) 773-5900x3

Estimated # of Men's Soccer Scholarships: None
Conference: Mayflower Conference
Program Profile: A very competitive NAIA program in the Mayflower Conference. Play against nationally ranked teams.
Roster In State: 4 **Out of State:** 12 **Out of Country:** 1
Walk-on/Other: **Graduation %:** N/A **Seniors on Team:** 2
Positions Needed: All
Schedule: Green Mountain College, Dominican College, St. Rose, Skidmore, Middlebury
Style of Play: Fast and physical.

Women's Athletic Profile

71 Clement Road
Rutland, VT 05701
Coach: Karl Roemer
Email: Not Available

NAIA
Fighting Saints/Blue, White
Phone: (802) 773-5900
Fax: (802) 773-5900

Estimated # of Women's Soccer Scholarships: None
Conference: Mayflower Conference
Program Profile: New program in 2000.
History: Started as a club sports and projected to be intercollegiate in 1999.
Achievements: Will be fielding 1st team ever in 2000
Schedule: Green Mountain College, Lyndon State, Johnson State, Castleton State, Atlantic Union

Green Mountain College
Academic Profile

Phone: (802) 287-8238

Poultney, VT 05764

Type: 4 Yr.,Private,Liberal Arts
Founded: 1834
Website: http://www.greenmtn.edu
Religion: United Methodist
SAT/ACT/GPA: 1000/20/2.8
Housing: Yes
Student/Faculty Ratio: 20:1
Male/Female Ratio: 49:51
Undergraduate Enrollment: 596
Graduate Enrollment: N/A
Scholarships/Academic: Yes **Athletic:** Yes **Financial Aid:** Yes
Expenses by: Year **In State:** $ 21,270 **Out of State:**
Specialty: Business, Education, Recreation, Environmental Studies
Degrees Conferred: BS, BA, BFA
Programs of Study: Accounting, Adventure Recreation, Arts, Behavioral Science, Business Management, Communications, History, Liberal Arts, PreLaw, PreArchitecture, Leisure Resource, Environmental Studies

Men's Athletic Profile

One College Circle
Poultney, VT 05764-1199
Coach: Chris Gilme
Email: athletic@greenmtn.edu

NCAA, NAIA
Eagles/Green, Gold
Phone: (802) 287-8238
Fax: (802) 287-8099

Estimated # of Men's Soccer Scholarships: 3
Conference: Mayflower Conference
Program Profile: Has one game field, three practice fields, plays winter indoor while spring play outdoors. Enjoy playing on a natural grass field. Play a fall schedule on natural grass field indoor.
History: Program started in 1979. We joined NAIA in 1984; played in the NAIA National in 1991, 1992, 1997, 1998, 1999; 5 Mayflower Conference players of the Year; 3 NAIA Regional Players of the Year.
Achievements: 1996 NSCAA National Coach of the Year; 3 time NIAI Regional Coach of the Year; 5 time Mayflower Conference Coach of the Year; several 1st Tea, NAIA All-Americans; Several 1sr Team NAIA Academic All-Americans.
Coaching: Chris Gilmore, Head Coach for 18 years, overall record 222-113-23, named Coach of the Year in the Mayflower Conference NAIA District 5 in 1991 & 1992; NAIA men's National Coach of the Year in 1996; Umbra Northeast Region Coach of the Year in 1996; Mayflower Coach of the Year in 1996. Assistant Coach, Tim Davis.
Roster In State: 3 **Out of State:** 12 **Out of Country:** 11
Walk-on/Other: **Graduation %:** 65 **Seniors on Team:** 3
Positions Needed: Defender, Goalkeeper, midfield
Camp or Clinic Dates: July 16-21, 2000 & July 23-28, 2000
Schedule: Franklin Pierce College, St Anselm's, Bentley, America International, Bryant, Roberts Wesleyan, Teiyko Post, Nyack College.
Style of Play: Possession with strong attacking offensive middle team.

Women's Athletic Profile

16 College St., Box 46
Poultney, VT 05764-1199
Coach: Tim Dempsey
Email: Not Available

NAIA
Eagles/Green, Gold
Phone: (802) 287-9313
Fax: (802) 287-9313

Estimated # of Women's Soccer Scholarships: None
Conference: Mayflower Conference
Program Profile: Highly competitive; ranked in the Top 10 in the country. Year-round program with an emphasis on Fall season. Grass surface for both the stadium field and the practice facility. Coach looking for student-athletes who take pride in doing well both on the field and in the classroom. Play a very competitive schedule for the size of the school.
History: Has had one losing season since the program began in 1982. Finished the 1987 season undefeated and ranked #1 in the NAIA (lost in the regional finals). Have won twelve Mayflower Conference Championship in 14 years, two Northeast Regional championship, and participated in two NAIA National Championship Tournaments. Career win-loss record program.
Achievements: Coach Dempsey (1989-present) career record at GMC is 108-51-6; Conference Coach of the Year five times; Regional Coach of the Year two times; 40 All-Conference players; 24 All-Region players; 18 All-American players; 6 All-American Scholar players.
Coaching: Tim Dempsey, Head Coach, 11 years at GMC. Graduate of Glassboro State (now Rowan College of New Jersey). Captain for three years and 1981 National Championship in the NCAA Division III, 17 years of Summer Camp Counselor, USSF "C" License.
Roster in State: 0 **Out of State:** 20 **Out of Country:** 4
ODP State: 5 **Regional:** **National:**
Walk-on/Other: **Graduation %:** 95 **Seniors on Team:** 3
Positions Needed: Goalkeeper, Forwards
Camp or Clinic Dates: Not Available
Most Recent Record: 18-4-2
Schedule: St. Anselm's College, Rowan University, Plymouth State, Houghton College, Roberts Wesleyan College
Style of Play: Short passing style that emphasis good technical skills. Will play long "over the top" if opposition makes us. Use a combination zone man-to-man defensive marking system. Will play either a 4-4-2 or a 4-3-3. Coach stresses that players need to be two way players capable of playing both offense and defense during games.

Johnson State College

Academic Profile

Phone:

Johnson, VT 05656

Type: 4 Yr.,Public,Liberal Arts
Founded: 1828
Website: http://www.jsc.vsc.edu
Religion: Non-Affiliated
SAT/ACT/GPA: 800
Housing: No
Student/Faculty Ratio: 19:1
Male/Female Ratio: 55:45
Undergraduate Enrollment: 1,675
Graduate Enrollment: 90
Scholarships/Academic: Yes **Athletic:** No **Financial Aid:** Yes
Expenses by: Year **In State:** $ 8,800 **Out of State:** $ 13,000
Degrees Conferred: AA, AS, BA, BS, BFA, MA
Programs of Study: Accounting, Anthropology, Arts, Behavioral Science, Biology, Business Administration, Creative Writing, Early Childhood Education, Ecology, Education, Elementary Education, English, Environmental Science, Health Science, History, Hotel/Restaurant Management, Humanities, Information Science, Journalism, Liberal Arts, Management, Management Information Systems, Marketing, Mathematics, Music, Physical Education, Political Science, Psychology, Sports Science, Technical Writing, Theatre

Men's Athletic Profile

RR 2, Box 75
Johnson, VT 05656
Coach: Brian Buczek
Email: Not Available

NCAA III
Badgers/Green, White, Blue
Phone: (802) 635-2356x285
Fax: (802) 635-9745

Estimated # of Men's Soccer Scholarships: None
Conference: Mayflower Conference

Women's Athletic Profile

RR 2, Box 75
Johnson, VT 05656
Coach: Mark Kalet
Email: Not Available

NCAA III
Badgers/Green, Blue, White
Phone: (802) 635-2356
Fax: (802) 635-9745

Estimated # of Women's Soccer Scholarships: None
Conference: Mayflower Conference
Program Profile: We have an indoor gymnasium playing area, a natural grass field, no stadium, and beautiful setting.
History: Program began in 1984. Ranked #1, #2 in NAIA New England 1987/1988 seasons.
Achievements: 1990 All-American, NAIA All-Districts, Mayflower Conference, District 5 Runner-ups.

Lyndon State College

Academic Profile

Lyndonville, VT 05851

Phone:

Type: 4 Yr.,Public,Liberal Arts
Website: http://www.lsc.vsc.edu
SAT/ACT/GPA: 800+
Student/Faculty Ratio: 17:1
Undergraduate Enrollment: 1,100
Scholarships/Academic: Yes
Athletic: No
Expenses by: Year
In State: $ 9,000

Founded: 1911
Religion: Non-Affiliated
Housing: No
Male/Female Ratio: 55:45
Graduate Enrollment: 70
Financial Aid: Yes
Out of State: $ 12,900

Degrees Conferred: AA, AS, BA, BS, MEd
Programs of Study: Accounting, Atmospheric Science, Behavioral Science, Biology, Business Administration, Communications, Computer Science, Education, English, Environmental Science, Humanities, Interdisciplinary Studies, Journalism, Liberal Arts, Management, Mathematics, Meteorology, Natural Science, Parks, Physical Education, Psychology, Radio & Television, Recreation & Leisure, Social Science, Spanish, Special Education, Sports Management

Men's Athletic Profile

Vail Hill
Lyndonville, VT 05851
Coach: Skip Pound
Email: pounds@mail.lsc.vsc.edu

NAIA
Hornets/Green, White, Gold
Phone: (802)-626-6477
Fax: (802) 626-9770

Estimated # of Men's Soccer Scholarships: None
Conference: Mayflower Conference
Program Profile: One of the strongest teams in District 5. Beautiful grass field.
Achievements: Conference Champs 2 years. Conference, District NSCAA Coach of the Year (New England) 1989.
Coaching: Skip Pound, Head Coach, 15-plus years experience, named District & Regional Coach of the Year 1990.
Style of Play: Aggressive and creative, often change formation and player's roles within the game.

Women's Athletic Profile

P.O. Box 1503
Lyndonville, VT 05851
Coach: Tonya Davis
Email: tdavis@togther.net

NAIA
Hornets/Green, Gold
Phone: (802) 626-4833
Fax: (802) 626-9770

Estimated # of Women's Soccer Scholarships: None
Conference: Mayflower
Program Profile: We have two fields with a Fall schedule of August to October and an indoor season in the Spring.

Middlebury College
Academic Profile

Phone: (802) 443-5410

Middlebury, VT 05753

Type: 4 Yr.,Private,Liberal Arts
Founded: 1800
Website: http://www.middlebury.edu
Religion: Non-Affiliated
SAT/ACT/GPA: 1300/29/5.1
Housing: Yes
Student/Faculty Ratio: 11:1
Male/Female Ratio: 50:50
Undergraduate Enrollment: 2,200
Graduate Enrollment: 200
Scholarships/Academic: Yes
Athletic: No
Financial Aid: Yes
Expenses by: Year
In State: $ 30,475
Out of State: $ 30,475
Specialty: Liberal Arts
Degrees Conferred: BA, BS
Programs of Study: American Civilization, American Literature, Art, Biology, Chemistry & BioChemistry, Chinese, Classical Studies, Computer Science, Dance, Economics, English, Environmental Science, Film, French, Geography, Geology, German, History, International Studies, International Studies, Italian, Japanese, Literary Studies, Mathematics, Molecular Biology & BioChemistry, Music, Philosophy, Physics, Political Science, PreLaw, PreMed, Psychology, Religion, Russian, Sociology-Anthropology, Spanish, Studio Art, Theatre-Dance & Film/Video, Women's Studies

Men's Athletic Profile

Memorial Field House
Middlebury, VT 05753
Coach: David Saward
Email: Not Available

NCAA III
Panthers/Navy Blue
Phone: (802) 443-5000x5410
Fax: (802) 443-0259

Estimated # of Men's Soccer Scholarships: None
Conference: NESCAC, ECAC
Program Profile: Middlebury has on of the finest soccer facilities in New England. We can boast 6 full size grass with separate game fields for the men and the women. The game field is 120 X 80 yards and has one of the finest surfaces in the region, plus one of the more spectacular views.
History: Soccer program began at Middlebury in 1953 and has grown to be of the premier Division III programs in New England and the country.
Achievements: 1983 NESCAC Champions, 1986 ECAC Champions, 1987 Fair Play Award; NEISL Service Award, 1994 NCAA Tournament Team, ECAC Tournament 7 out of previous 9 seasons.
Coaching: David Seward, Head Coach, FA Prelim Badge, NSCAA National Certificate, Canadian 'B' license, Vermont State Coach.
Roster In State: 3
Out of State: 19
Out of Country: 1
ODP State: 12
Regional: 1
National:
Walk-on/Other:
Graduation %: 100
Seniors on Team: 4
Camp or Clinic Dates: July
Most Recent Record: 13-2-2
Schedule: Williams, Amherst, Colby, Bates, Wesleyan, Bowdoin, Tufts, Trinity (CT), Conn College, Hamilton
Style of Play: Combination of possession play with an emphasis put on attacking with numbers. Attractive attacking soccer is encouraged, with an emphasis on quality passing.

Women's Athletic Profile

Memorial Field House
Middlebury, VT 05753
Coach: Diane R. Boettcher
Email: dboettch@middlebury.edu

NCAA III
Panthers/Navy
Phone: (802) 443-5410
Fax: (802) 443-2073

Estimated # of Women's Soccer Scholarships: None
Conference: NESCAC
Program Profile: One of the strongest programs (Division III) in New England. Have a beautiful practice field, grid area and small sided proactive area and new game field in perfect condition.
History: Among the nations oldest programs, Middlebury began varsity competition in 1979 after several years at the club level. Initially a training sport for skiers, the program moved into national prominence in 1997. Under the present Head Coach, the team looks to find a consistent place among the nations top teams.
Achievements: Captured the inaugural NESCAC Championship in 2000, NESCAC Player of the Year 2000, 5 All-NESCAC 2000, NESCAC Coach of the Year 2000, 2 All-Americans, Numerous All-New England, 4 time NSCAA Team Academic Award (3.34 GPA)
Coaching: Diane R. Boettcher, Head Coach, holds Royal Dutch (KNVB), US Soccer Federation and NSCAA Certifications. she serves on the California youth soccer Association-North Coaching Staff and formerly served as the State Coach of the Maine Affiliate of US Soccer. Michelyne Pinard, Assistant Coach, is a recent Dartmouth graduate where she played both soccer and hockey. Jeffrey Brown is a University of Vermont Hall of Fame inductee.

Roster in State: 2	**Out of State:** 19	**Out of Country:**
ODP State: 8	**Regional:**	**National:**
Walk-on/Other:	**Graduation %:** 100	**Seniors on Team:** 3

Positions Needed: Goalkeeper, 4 Field Players
Camp or Clinic Dates: Not Available
Most Recent Record: 15-2-0
Schedule: Tufts, Bowdoin, Amherst, Bates, Williams, Keene State, Colby
Style of Play: The team's possession style melds distinct regional variations of players from across the US. Players are encouraged to use technical flair for game impact. Team uses a channeling collective defending scheme with a mobile goalkeeper.

Norwich University

Academic Profile

Northfield, VT 05663
Phone: 802-828-8500

Type: 4 Yr.,Private,Engineering		**Founded:** 1819
Website: http://www.norwich.edu		**Religion:** Non-Affiliated
SAT/ACT/GPA: Open		**Housing:** Yes
Student/Faculty Ratio: 14:1		**Male/Female Ratio:** 3:1
Undergraduate Enrollment: N/A		**Graduate Enrollment:** N/A
Scholarships/Academic:	**Athletic:**	**Financial Aid:**
Expenses by: Year	**In State:** $ 22,100	**Out of State:** $ 22,100

Specialty: Architecture, Engineering, Physical Education, Sports Medicine
Degrees Conferred: BA, BS, MS, MA
Programs of Study: Communications, English, History, International Studies, Liberal Studies, Peace War Diplomacy, Political Science, Psychology, Accounting, Architecture, Biology, BioMedical Technology, Chemistry, Civil Engineering, Computer Information Systems, Computer Science, Economics, Engineering, Environmental Science, Geology, Management, Mathematics, Mechanical Engineering, Nursing, Physical Education, Physics, Sports Medicine

Men's Athletic Profile

Andrew's Hall
Northfield, VT 05663
Coach: Rob Friske
Email: robertf@norwich.edu

NCAA III
Cadets/Maroon, Vegas Gold
Phone: (802) 485-2240
Fax: (802) 485-2234

Estimated # of Men's Soccer Scholarships: None
Conference: Great Northeast Athletic Conference
Program Profile: We have an indoor facility, 2 outdoor practice fields, 1 game field, 4 pair full-size goals, 2 pair indoor goals, jugs and natural field. We play a traditional and non-traditional season.
History: The program began in 1957.
Achievements: Coach of the Year, Coach Friske; 7 players made All-Conference, Conference Championships.
Coaching: Rob Friske, Head Coach, has BS Business Management, a MS in Athletic Administration. He holds a NSCAA National Diploma. He is an ODP Coach in Duecta Indoor Soccer League, on the faculty and staff council and club coach. Keith Byrnes is the Assistant Coach.
Roster In State: 4 **Out of State:** 19 **Out of Country:** 4
ODP State: 7 **Regional:** **National:**
Walk-on/Other: **Graduation %:** 98 **Seniors on Team:** 4
Positions Needed: 10
Camp or Clinic Dates: August
Most Recent Record: 17-4-0
Schedule: United State Coast Guard, Middlebury, Plattsburgh
Style of Play: Possession play, physical, and well disciplined.

Women's Athletic Profile

65 S. Main Street
Northfield, VT 05663
Coach: Stephen Looke
Email: slooke@norwich.edu

NCAA III
Cadets/Maroon, Gold
Phone: (802) 485-2241
Fax: (802) 485-2161

Estimated # of Women's Soccer Scholarships: None
Conference: Independent Conference
Program Profile: Home field is called Howard Field with a capacity of 500; indoor field house has 50,000 sq. ft. synthetic based. Playing season starts August through October with a spring training.
History: 1985 the program began with an overall record of 88-85-10; 1993 GNC Champs; 1994 Semi-finals GNC.
Achievements: 1991 New England Coach of the Year; 1993 NEWAC Conference Champions; 5 All New England players over the past two years.
Coaching: Stephen Looked, Head Coach, has over 500 winning record, been had coach since 1985; graduate of NU in 1976; Coach of the Year NEWISA in 1991; he has a best record of 12-6.
Roster in State: 1 **Out of State:** 18 **Out of Country:** 1
ODP State: 8 **Regional:** 1 **National:**
Walk-on/Other: **Graduation %:** 100 **Seniors on Team:** 2
Positions Needed: All
Most Recent Record: 9-6-1
Schedule: Bates, Wheaton, Middlebury, Green Mountain College, Western New England College, Simmons
Style of Play: Possession , controlled-disciplined defense with free wheeling attack.

Saint Michael's College

Academic Profile

Phone: (802) 654-3000

Colchester, VT 05439

Type: 4 Yr.,Private,Liberal Arts
Founded: 1904
Website: http://www.smcvt.edu
Religion: Catholic
SAT/ACT/GPA: 1000+
Housing: Yes
Student/Faculty Ratio: 14:1
Male/Female Ratio: 50:50
Undergraduate Enrollment: 1,700
Graduate Enrollment: 200
Scholarships/Academic: Yes **Athletic:** Yes **Financial Aid:** Yes
Expenses by: Year **In State:** $ 23,400 **Out of State:** $ 23,400
Specialty: Liberal Arts
Degrees Conferred: BA, BS, MA, MS, MED
Programs of Study: Accounting, American Studies, BioChemistry, Biology, Business Administration, Chemistry, Computer Science, East Asian Studies, Economics, Elementary Education, Engineering, English, Environmental Science, Fine Arts, French, History, International Business Journalism, Philosophy, Political Science, Psychology, Religious Studies, Sociology, Spanish, Theatre Arts

Men's Athletic Profile

Winooski Park
Colchester, VT 05439
Coach: Tim Kaleita
Email: tkaleita@smcvt.edu

NCAA II
Knights/Purple, Gold
Phone: (802) 654-2693
Fax: (802) 654-2497

Estimated # of Men's Soccer Scholarships:
Conference: Northeast 10 Conference, ECAC
Program Profile: Play a Fall season on excellent, new, natural grass field which has a measurements of 120x80 yards. We are a very competitive Division II team comprised of American players. The NE-10 Conference is a very competitive. Has an indoor facility.
History: Our program began in 1960's, with the best season having a record of 13-3-1.
Achievements: Several NEISL All-Stars, All-New England, All-League, Regional Coach of the Year in 1986.
Roster In State: 1 **Out of State:** 22 **Out of Country:** 0
ODP State: 6 **Regional:** 0 **National:** 0
Walk-on/Other: 0 **Graduation %:** 100 **Seniors on Team:** 4
Positions Needed: ALL
Most Recent Record: 7-9-2
Schedule: Southern Conn. State, New Hampshire College, Franklin Pierce College, St. Anselm, Middlebury College.
Style of Play: Possession and attacking.

Women's Athletic Profile

Winooski Park
Colchester, VT 05439
Coach: Marcel Choquette
Email: Not Available

NCAA II
Lady Knights/Purple, Gold
Phone: (802) 654-2903
Fax: (802) 654-2592

Estimated # of Women's Soccer Scholarships: None
Conference: Northeast 10 Conference
Program Profile: Natural grass fields; one of the best in New England.
History: Program began in 1982 with a turn around in 1989. The team has been in the Northeast Western Conference playoffs since 1989.

Achievements: Saint Ambroise was New England Coach of the Year in 1989. 2All-Americans.
Style of Play: International style of play. A lot of passing, very pleasant soccer to watch.

Southern Vermont College
Academic Profile

Bennington, VT 05201
Phone:

Type: 4 Yr.,Private,Liberal Arts
Founded: 1926
Website: Not Available
Religion: Non-Affiliated
SAT/ACT/GPA: None
Housing: Yes
Student/Faculty Ratio: 16:1
Male/Female Ratio: 1:1
Undergraduate Enrollment: 641
Graduate Enrollment: N/A
Scholarships/Academic: No **Athletic:** No
Financial Aid: Yes
Expenses by: Year **In State:** $ 16,100
Out of State: $ 16,100
Specialty: Criminal Justice, Environmental Studies
Degrees Conferred: AA, BA, BS, AS, AND
Programs of Study: Accounting, Business Management, Communications, Criminal Justice, Child Development, Child Care Management, English, Environmental Studies, Gerontology, Hospitality/Resort Management, Nursing, Liberal Arts, Private Security Management, Social Work

Men's Athletic Profile

Monument Avenue Extension
Bennington, VT 05201
Coach: Tony Kasulinous
Email: Not Available

NCAA III/NAIA
Mountaineers/F. Green, White
Phone: (802) 447-7289
Fax: (802) 442-5529

Estimated # of Men's Soccer Scholarships: None
Conference: Eastern College Athletic Conference (ECAC)
Program Profile: The team competes on the natural turf, Bill Epstein Athletic Field located on campus. The team plays approximately 17 matches and participates in weekend tournaments. The team is also active in training and competitions during the Winter (indoor soccer) and Spring.
History: Our program was started in 1978.
Achievements: Colonial States Conference Champions 1993, & 1991, MVP in Conference 1993 & 1991, Conference Scholar-Athlete recognized in 1992, 1993, NAIA All-American 1987.

Women's Athletic Profile

Monument Avenue
Bennington, VT 05201
Coach: Scott McKenzie
Email: Not Available

NCAA III/NAIA
Mountaineers/Green, Gold
Phone: (802) 447-4671
Fax: (802) 447-4695

Estimated # of Women's Soccer Scholarships:
Conference: Eastern College Athletic Conference (ECAC)
Program Profile: Traditional fall competition against regionally and nationally ranked opponents. Play all home games at the Bill Epstien field grass. Competitive program with a room for first year players to make an impact.
History: Program began competition in 1988. Current head coach has been with the program since 1992. Record for the past three seasons: 10-7 in 1994, 6-9-2 in 1995, and 10-6-1 in 1996.
Achievements: 1993 Colonials State Conference Champions.
Coaching: Scott McKenzie, Head Coach, National Diploma, NSCAA, played goalkeeper at both SUNY-Brockport and SUNY-New Plattsburg, and has coached soccer for the past five years at the collegiate, high school and club level.
Style of Play: Attacking style of play. The team has an ability through the midfield or over the top.

University of Vermont
Academic Profile

Burlington, VT 05401

Phone: 802-656-3131

Type: 4 Yr.,Public,Liberal Arts
Founded: 1791
Website: http://www.uvm.edu
Religion: Non-Affiliated
SAT/ACT/GPA: Open
Housing: Yes
Student/Faculty Ratio: 15:1
Male/Female Ratio: 48:52
Undergraduate Enrollment: 7,514
Graduate Enrollment: 1,208
Scholarships/Academic: Yes **Athletic:** Yes **Financial Aid:** Yes
Expenses by: Year **In State:** $ 15222 **Out of State:** $ 26,094
Specialty: Eight Academic Schools
Degrees Conferred: AS, BA, BS, MA, MS, MBA, MED, Ph.D., MD
Programs of Study: Animal Science, Anthropology, International Studies, Art Education, Art History, Art Studio, Asian Studies, BioChemical Studies, Biological Studies, Biology, Botany, Business, Canadian Studies, Chemistry, Civil Engineering, Classical Civilization, Communications, Computer Science, Communications, Dental Hygiene, Dietetics, Economics, Elementary Education, English, Languages, Mathematics, Mechanical Engineering, Music, Natural Resources, Nursing, Nutrition, Physical Education, Physical Therapy, Forestry, Political Science, Theatre

Men's Athletic Profile

Patrick Gymnasium
Burlington, VT 05405
Coach: Roy Patton
Email: rpatton@zoo.uvm.edu

NCAA I
Catamounts/Green, Gold, White
Phone: (802) 656-7694
Fax: (802) 656-0949

Estimated # of Men's Soccer Scholarships: 7
Conference: America East Conference
Program Profile: The UVM men' s soccer team plays in the American East conference which includes teams from the Northeast Region. The season takes place during the months of August through November. The teams play on a top class natural surface in a stadium of 5,000 seats.
History: The UVM soccer program has a proud history starting in 1964. It has been a Division I institution from the beginning and it has been developing successful student athletes that have dedicated themselves to high standards on and off the pitch.
Achievements: Head Coach Roy Patton was selected coach of the year in the conference in 1997. UVM won the conference in 1989,90,91 and qualified for the conference tournament in 92,93, 97. UVM qualified for the NCAA tournament in 89, 90 and went to the elite 8 in 89.
Coaching: Roy Patton is our Head Coach. he was a former head coach at University of South Alabama, USSF "A" License, NSCAA Advanced National Diploma, Irish FA Badge, USSF Regional Coach. Roberto Beall - Assistant Coach, former professional player; currently captain of Vermont Voltage in USISL.
Roster In State: 4 **Out of State:** 21 **Out of Country:** 5
ODP State: 11 **Regional:** 2 **National:**
Walk-on/Other: **Graduation %:** 100 **Seniors on Team:** 5
Positions Needed: Defender, Striker
Camp or Clinic Dates: June 20-24, June 26-30, July 30-August3, August 7-11
Most Recent Record: 10-7-1
Schedule: Penn St., Boston U., Hofstra U., Towson St., Dartmouth, Air Force, New Mexico, Harvard
Style of Play: UVM plays an attacking style of play with emphasis on quick transition and a high pressure defense.

Women's Athletic Profile

Patrick Gymnasium
Burlington, VT 05405
Coach: Jodi Kenyon
Email: jkenyon@zoo.uvm.edu

NCAA I
Catamounts/Green, Gold
Phone: (802) 656-7740
Fax: (802) 656-0949

Estimated # of Women's Soccer Scholarships: None
Conference: America East Conference
Program Profile: The University of Vermont provides a comprehensive, competitive and equitable program of varsity sports for the students. Stress is places on fostering the pursuit of academic excellence and community enrichment. The facilities are top-notch both indoor and outdoor. Soccer program has 3 natural grass surfaces, with a 73x120 yd game field. A new $13 million indoor complex just finished completion and offers a variety of conditioning and exercise avenues. Our stadium is capable of holding 2,000 spectators. The team participates in a year-round program with the primary season in the fall and a non-traditional season in the spring.
History: women's soccer has been a varsity sport at UVM for 24 years, competing in 23 seasons to date. The program played its inaugural season in 1976 and has had just six different coaching changes. The overall record of the program is 205-146-28. The team competes in the very competitive America East conference.
Achievements: The women's team has accomplished many things in its 24 years of existence. There have been 3 All-Americans, ISAA/ADIDAS National Goalkeeper of the year, 15-All-Conference Award winners, 3 players inducted into the UVM Hall of Fame, 1 Conference Rookie of the year, 40 players named the conference academic honor roll in the last 2 seasons, 3 conference tournament appearances, 2 post season appearances.
Coaching: Jodi Kenyon, Head Coach, is a former Academic All-American at Adelphi. He served as an assistant for Adelphi and Harvard University. He has a class "B" coaching license (USSF) and an Advanced National Diploma (NSCAA). He served four years as a coach of U-17 ODP ENYYSA. Wendy Elles, assistant coach, graduated from Gettysburg in 1996.

Roster in State: 6	**Out of State:** 18	**Out of Country:**
ODP State: 12	**Regional:** 5	**National:**
Walk-on/Other: 5	**Graduation %:**	**Seniors on Team:** 5

Positions Needed: Goalkeeper, Defenders, Forward
Camp or Clinic Dates: 7/23-28
Most Recent Record: 5-13
Schedule: Hartford, Harvard, Dartmouth, Boston University, Davidson College, Colgate, ARMY, Cornell, Indiana, Delaware
Style of Play: We play a very possessive style with build up out of the back and penetration on the flanks and thought midfield. Most of our goals are scored from through balls and shots inside the penalty box. We use all of our players in the attack.

virginia

VIRGINIA

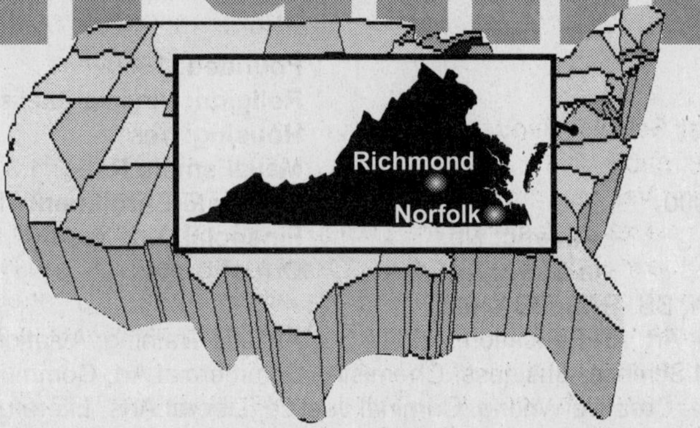

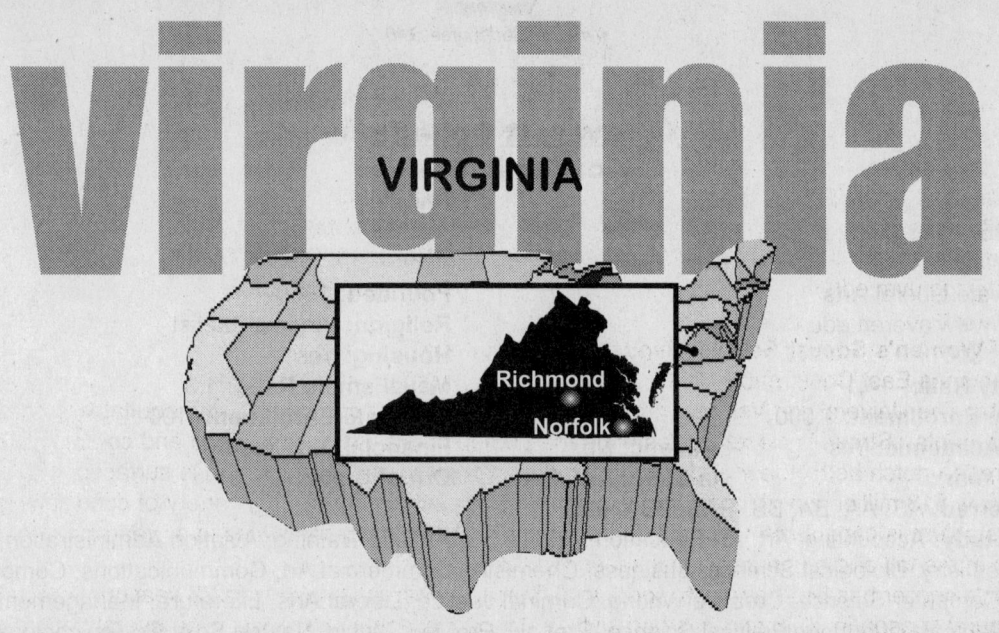

SCHOOL	CITY	AFFILIATION	PAGE
Averett College	Danville	NCAA III	1140
Bluefield College	Bluefield	NAIA	1140
Bridgewater College	Bridgewater	NCAA III	1141
Christopher Newport University	Newport News	NCAA III	1142
College of William and Mary	Williamsburg	NCAA I	1143
Eastern Mennonite College	Harrisonburg	NCAA III	1144
Emory and Henry College	Emory	NCAA III	1145
Ferrum College	Ferrum	NCAA III	1146
George Mason University	Fairfax	NCAA I	1148
Hampden - Sydney College	Hampden-Sydney	NCAA III	1149
Hollins College	Roanoke	NCAA III	1150
James Madison University	Harrisonburg	NCAA I	1150
Liberty University	Lynchburg	NCAA I	1152
Longwood College	Farmville	NCAA II	1153
Lynchburg College	Lynchburg	NCAA III	1154
Mary Baldwin College	Staunton	NCAA III	1156
Mary Washington College	Fredericksburg	NCAA III	1156
Marymount University	Arlington	NCAA III	1157
Old Dominion University	Norfolk	NCAA I	1159
Radford University	Radford	NCAA I	1160
Randolph - Macon College	Ashland	NCAA III	1161
Roanoke College	Salem	NCAA III	1162
Shenandoah University	Winchester	NCAA III	1164
Sweet Briar College	Sweet Briar	NCAA III	1165
University of Richmond	Richmond	NCAA I	1166
University of Virginia	Charlottesville	NCAA I	1167
Virginia Commonwealth University	Richmond	NCAA I	1168
Virginia Military Institute	Lexington	NCAA I	1169
Virginia Tech	Blacksburg	NCAA I	1170
Virginia Wesleyan College	Norfolk	NCAA III	1171
Washington and Lee University	Lexington	NCAA III	1173

Averett College

Academic Profile

Phone:

Danville, VA 24541

Type: 4 Yr.,Private,Liberal Arts
Website: http://www.averett.edu
SAT/ACT/GPA: 800
Student/Faculty Ratio: 14:1
Undergraduate Enrollment: 1,000
Scholarships/Academic: Yes **Athletic:** No
Expenses by: Year **In State:** $ 16,800
Founded: 1859
Religion: Virginia Baptist
Housing: Yes
Male/Female Ratio: 1:3
Graduate Enrollment: 100
Financial Aid: Yes
Out of State:
Degrees Conferred: AS, AA, BA, BS, BAS, BBA, MAT
Programs of Study: Accounting, Art, Art Education, Art History, Athletic Training, Aviation Administration, Biblical Studies, BioChemistry, Biological Science, Business, Chemistry, Commercial Art, Communications, Computer Programming, Computer Science, Creative Writing, Criminal Justice, Liberal Arts, Literature, Management, Marketing, Mathematics, Medical Laboratory, Political Science, PreLaw, PreMed, Music, Natural Science, Psychology, Public Administration, Social Science, Sports Administration, Sports Medicine

Men's Athletic Profile

420 W Main Street
Danville, VA 24541
Coach: Jim Gourlay
Email: Not Available

NCAA III
Cougars/Navy, Gold
Phone: (804) 791-5749
Fax: (804) 791-5740

Estimated # of Men's Soccer Scholarships: None
Conference: Dixie Conference
Program Profile: Play on a natural grass that measures 120x80 yards.
History: Program began in 1970.
Coaching: Jim Gourlay, Head Coach.
Style of Play: Varies, depending on opponent.

Women's Athletic Profile

420 W Main Street
Danville, VA 24541
Coach: Brian Mateer
Email: Not Available

NCAA III
Cougars/Navy, Gold
Phone: (804) 791-5749
Fax: (804) 791-5740

Estimated # of Women's Soccer Scholarships: None
Conference: Dixie Conference
Program Profile: Our home playing field is a natural grass with a measurements of 120x80 yards.
History: The program began in 1992. Since then the overall record is 5-39-0.
Achievements: None
Style of Play: Varies, depends on opponents.

Bluefield College

Academic Profile

Phone:

Bluefield, VA 24605

Type: 4 Yr.,Private,Liberal Arts
Website: http://www.bluefield.edu
Founded: 1919
Religion: Baptist

SAT/ACT/GPA: 860/18/2.0
Housing: Yes
Student/Faculty Ratio: 27:1
Male/Female Ratio: 1;1
Undergraduate Enrollment: 725
Graduate Enrollment: N/A
Scholarships/Academic: Yes
Athletic: Yes
Financial Aid: Yes
Expenses by: Year
In State: $ 12,700
Out of State: $ 12,700
Specialty:
Degrees Conferred: Baccalaureate and Associate Degrees
Programs of Study: Allied Health, Administration of Justice, Biology, Business Administration, Chemistry, Christian Ministry, Communication Arts Criminal Justice, Drama, Education, English, Fine Arts, Health, History, Human Resources, Interdisciplinary Studies, Mathematics, Music, Organizational Management and Development, Physical Education, Psychology, Recreation, Religion and Philosophy, Humanities, Science, Social Sciences

Men's Athletic Profile

3000 College Drive
Bluefield, VA 24605
Coach: John Lynch
Email: admissions@mail.bluefield.edu

NAIA
Rams/Blue, White
Phone: (540) 326-4477
Fax: (540) 326-4288

Estimated # of Men's Soccer Scholarships: N/A
Conference: Tennessee Virginia Athletic Conference (TVAC)
Program Profile: The team plays on East River Soccer Complex which is a natural grass field. It is located off campus. Fall is our main season. In spring season , we have 4 or 5 tournaments.
History: Our program began in 1991. We won TVAC regular season in 1996 and have hosted playoff tournament. Our 1996 record was 12-6 (5-1 in conference play).
Achievements: We were conference champions in 1996-97; LOTY 1996; 1 Honorable mention All—American Gary Ricketts (MVP Conference); 5 Regional 1st Team members; All-Conference players in last 3 years.
Coaching: John Lynch, Head Coach, currently in his third year. He came from Ireland and holds a Football Association of Ireland (FIA) Coaching Badge. He was 2 time Academic All-American at Green Mountain College and Coach of the Year in 1996 TVAC.
Style of Play: We play a possession game. We like to get the fullback on the ball from the goalkeeper and work through the midfield. 4-4-2 system more often than not.

Bridgewater College

Academic Profile

Bridgewater, VA 22812
Phone: (540) 828-5756

Type: 4 Yr.,Private,Liberal Arts
Founded: 1880
Website: http://www.bridgewater.edu
Religion: Brethren
SAT/ACT/GPA: 900
Housing: Yes
Student/Faculty Ratio: 15:1
Male/Female Ratio: 45:55
Undergraduate Enrollment: 1,050
Graduate Enrollment: N/A
Scholarships/Academic: Yes
Athletic: No
Financial Aid: Yes
Expenses by: Year
In State: $ 19,980
Out of State: $ 19,980
Specialty: Business, PreLaw, PreMed, PreVet
Degrees Conferred: BA, BS
Programs of Study: Accounting, Art, Athletic Training, Biological Science, Business Administration, Chemistry, Computer Science, Early Childhood Education, Economics, Elementary Education, English, French, German, Health Science, History, International Studies, Management, Mathematics, Medical Technology, Music, Music Education, Philosophy, Physical Education, Physical Science, Physics, Political Science, PreDental, PreLaw, PreMed, PreVet, Psychology, Religion, Science, Secondary Education, Social Science

Men's Athletic Profile

402 E College Street
Bridgewater, VA 22812
Coach: Ian Spooner
Email: ispooner@bridgewater.edu

NCAA III
Eagles/Crimson, Vegas Gold
Phone: (540) 828-5756
Fax: (54) 828-5484

Estimated # of Men's Soccer Scholarships: N/A
Conference: Old Dominion Athletic Conference
Program Profile: Play on 70x120 field that seats 750 people.
History: Our program began in 1992; 1999 was first year under Head Coach Ian Spooner.
Achievements: Many All-Conference players.
Coaching: Ian Spooner, Head Coach, holds NSCAA Advanced National and Premier Diplomas as well as English FA Badge. He played professionally in England and United States. He is also a State ODP Coach.
Style of Play: Style and formations depends on type of personnel available, but mostly attacking with possession.

Women's Athletic Profile

402 E. College Street
Bridgewater, VA 22812
Coach: Andrea Zeigler
Email: ispooner@bridgewater.edu

NCAA III
Eagles/Crimson, Vegas Gold
Phone: (508) 531-1352
Fax: (540) 828-5484

Estimated # of Women's Soccer Scholarships: None
Conference: Old Dominion Athletic Conference
Program Profile: An all-year program with main season in the fall. Excellent facilities with a new field proposed that measures 70x120 and seats 750. New program in 1999.
History: 1999 was the first full varsity season and looking to be a winning team immediately
Achievements: Not Available
Style of Play: Style and formation will depend on type of players available mostly attacking with possession.

Christopher Newport University

Academic Profile

Phone: 757-594-7000

Newport News, VA 23606

Type: 4 Yr.,Public,Liberal Arts
Website: http://www.cnu.edu
SAT/ACT/GPA: Open
Student/Faculty Ratio:
Undergraduate Enrollment: N/A
Scholarships/Academic: Yes
Athletic: No
Expenses by: Year
In State: $ 8,424
Degrees Conferred: BA, BS, MS, M Ed
Founded: 1960
Religion: Non-Affiliated
Housing: Yes
Male/Female Ratio:
Graduate Enrollment: N/A
Financial Aid: Yes
Out of State: $ 13,374
Programs of Study: Teaching Education, Marketing & Business, Fine & Performing Arts, etc..

Men's Athletic Profile

1 University Place
Newport News, VA 23606
Coach: Steve Shaw
Email: sshaw@edu.com

NCAA III
Captains/Royal, Silver
Phone: (757) 594-7383
Fax: (757) 594-7876

Estimated # of Men's Soccer Scholarships: 0
Conference: Dixie Conference

Program Profile: A very competitive, varsity only, all Bermuda grass field with an underground irrigation. Fenced in complex with a practice fields and a new stadium seats.
History: Program began in 1974 and received tournament bid in 1986.
Achievements: 5th year as Head coach- coach of the year in 1999, 2000. We finished 13th in the Nation in 1999 and made it to the Elite Eight in the 2000 NCAA National Tournament.
Coaching: Steve Shaw is our head coach and he is assisted by Brian Schwab and Steve Sachs.

Roster In State: 22	**Out of State:** 1	**Out of Country:** 2
ODP State: 8	**Regional:** 1	**National:**
Walk-on/Other:	**Graduation %:** N/A	**Seniors on Team:** 4

Positions Needed: Keeper, Defender
Camp or Clinic Dates: August 6-10, 2001
Most Recent Record: 18-3-1
Schedule: Messiah, Greensboro, Salisbury State, Emory, Virginia Wesleyan, Roanoke, Mary Washington.
Style of Play: Possession, counter attack, 4-4-2.

Women's Athletic Profile

One University Place
Newport News, VA 23606
Coach: Melissa Mitchell
Email: mitchell@cnu.edu

NCAA III
Lady Captains/Royal, Silver
Phone: (757) 594-7381
Fax: (757) 594-7839

Estimated # of Women's Soccer Scholarships: None
Conference: Dixie Conference
Program Profile: We have a fall playing season. We have full regulation Bermuda grass in our stadium. The stadium has stands. We hosted an NCAA Division I play-off game last year.
History: Our program stated in 1997 and it is going into its third year.
Achievements: 2 All-Americans; 3-4 All-Conference every year; NCAA appearance in 1986; two players All-South Atlantic
Style of Play: Counter attacking team.

College of William and Mary

Academic Profile

Williamburg, VA 23185
Phone: 757-221-4000

Type: 4 Yr.,Public		**Founded:** 1693
Website: http://www.wm.edu		**Religion:** Non-Affiliated
SAT/ACT/GPA: Open		**Housing:** Yes
Student/Faculty Ratio: 12:1		**Male/Female Ratio:** N/A
Undergraduate Enrollment: 5,500		**Graduate Enrollment:** 2,200
Scholarships/Academic:	**Athletic:**	**Financial Aid:**
Expenses by: Year	**In State:** $ 9,91+	**Out of State:** $ 20,874+

Degrees Conferred: BA, BSC, BBA
Programs of Study: American Studies, Anthropology, Art Administration, Art History, Biology, Business, Chemistry, Computer Science, Economics, English, Geology, Kinesiology, Mathematics, Music, Philosophy, Physics, Psychology, Public Policy, Religion, Sociology, Theatre

Men's Athletic Profile

P.O. Box 399
Williamsburg, VA 23187
Coach: Al Albert
Email: afalbe@mail.wm.edu

NCAA I
Tribe/Green, Gold
Phone: (757) 221-3385
Fax: (757 221-3412

Estimated # of Men's Soccer Scholarships: None
Conference: CAA
Program Profile: Lighted astro turf soccer stadium located on campus which seats 2,200.
History: Our program is 30 years old with 25 consecutive winning seasons and 5 consecutive NCAA Bids.
Achievements: 4 time CAA Coach of the Year; 7 All-Americans; 3 MLS players
Coaching: Al Albert is our Head Coach for 26 years. He holds USSF "A" license; FA Full Badge, was a US Maccabiah Coach in 1981 & 1985.
Roster In State: 20 **Out of State:** 6 **Out of Country:** 2
ODP State: 20 **Regional:** 6 **National:** 2
Walk-on/Other: **Graduation %:** 90 **Seniors on Team:** 5
Camp or Clinic Dates: July 9-13, 16-20
Most Recent Record: 14-7-2
Schedule: UVA, Maryland, UNC, FIU, Butler, Princeton, Georgetown, VCU, JMU, UNC-G
Style of Play: Control.

Women's Athletic Profile

P.O. Box 399
Williamsburg, VA 23185
Coach: John Daly
Email: jbdaly@wm.edu

NCAA I
Tribe/Green, White, Yellow
Phone: (757) 221-3387
Fax: (757) 221-3412

Estimated # of Women's Soccer Scholarships: Varies
Conference: Colonial Athletic Association
Program Profile: Playing fields include Barksdale Field (Bermuda Grass) and Busch Field (Astroturf stadium-holds 2,200 0.
History: The program began in 1981. Coach Daly took over the program in 1987. Has taken team to NCAA Tournament 13 times, including 9 years in a row. The Tribe has been nationally ranked 18 consecutive seasons among the country's' top 20 programs. 16 NCAA Tournament appearances (3rd highest in the nation).
Achievements: John Daly was All-CAA Coach of the Year in 1993, 94, 99; Mid-Atlantic Coach of the Year four times in 1989, 1990, 1992 & 1997; CAA titles 7 of the last 8 years; 10 players have earned 22 All-Americans honors, 4 players drafted to WUSA
Coaching: John Daly, Head Coach, 14 years as Head Coach at W&M, Compiled a record of 205-76-12. Lindsay Nohl, former player, Jay Cooney is the Goalkeeper coach.
Roster in State: 12 **Out of State:** 13 **Out of Country:** 2
ODP State: 17 **Regional:** 8 **National:** 2
Walk-on/Other: **Graduation %:** 98 **Seniors on Team:** 1
Positions Needed: Keeper, defender, midfield, forward
Camp or Clinic Dates: July 1-5, July 22-26, July 29- Aug 2
Most Recent Record: 15-6-0
Schedule: UCLA, UCONN, Virginia, Richmond, Maryland, Wisconsin, George Mason, James Madison
Style of Play: Varied.

Eastern Mennonite University

Academic Profile

Harrisonburg, VA 22802
Phone: (540) 432-4440

Type: 4 Yr.,Private,Liberal Arts
Website: http://www.emu.edu
SAT/ACT/GPA: 880/19/2.0
Student/Faculty Ratio: 15:1
Undergraduate Enrollment: 950

Founded: 1917
Religion: Non-Affiliated
Housing: Yes
Male/Female Ratio: 40:60
Graduate Enrollment: 350

Scholarships/Academic: Yes **Athletic:** No **Financial Aid:** Yes
Expenses by: Year **In State:** $ 19,030 **Out of State:** $ 19,030
Specialty: Education, Biology, Business, Education, Nursing
Degrees Conferred: BA, BS, Masters in Business, Education ant Theology
Programs of Study: Accounting, Biology, Business and Management, Chemistry, Computer Science, Education, Health Sciences, Psychology, Letters/Literature, Life Sciences, Multi/Interdisciplinary Studies, Nursing, Philosophy, PreMed, Protective Services, Public Affairs, Religion, Theology

Men's Athletic Profile

1200 Park Road
Harrisonburg, VA 22801
Coach: Roger E. Mast
Email: mastre@emu.edu

NCAA III
Royals/Royal, White
Phone: (540) 432-4437
Fax: (703) 432-4443

Estimated # of Men's Soccer Scholarships: None
Conference: Old Dominion Athletic Conference
Program Profile: Home field is Bomberger Field constructed in 1991; irrigate grass. Also train on lighted omni turf field. Year-round program. Competitive program in the south Atlantic Region.
History: Our program began in 1965. Compete in the Old Dominion Athletic Conference and Virginia Intercollegiate Soccer Association.
Achievements: NCCAA National Tournament in 1982, 1983, & 1988; 2 NSCAA All-Americans; 10 NSCAA All-South Atlantic Regional All-Americans; 10 NCAA All-Americans; 12 NCCAA All-District All-Americans.
Coaching: Roger E. Mast, Head Coach since 1991, played at EMU from 1980-1984; 43-33-2 record at EMU; 53-32-9 high school record prior to joining the university; holds NSCAA Advanced National Diploma and MS in Health 7 Physical Education from the University of West Chester.
Style of Play: Play to maintain possession of the ball, going to goal whenever the opportunity present itself.

Emory and Henry College

Academic Profile

Emory, VA 24327
Phone: 540-944-4121

Type: 4 Yr.,Private,Liberal Arts
Founded: 1836
Website: http://www.emory-henry.emory.va.us
Religion: Non-Affiliated
SAT/ACT/GPA: 930/19/2.5
Housing: Yes
Student/Faculty Ratio: 12:1
Male/Female Ratio: 1:1
Undergraduate Enrollment: 1,000
Graduate Enrollment: N/A
Scholarships/Academic: Yes **Athletic:** No **Financial Aid:** Yes
Expenses by: Year **In State:** $ 17,800 **Out of State:** $ 17,800
Degrees Conferred: BS, BA, BED, MA
Programs of Study: Accounting, Anthropology, Applied Mathematics, Art, Art Education, Biology, Business, Chemistry, Classics, Communications, Computer Information Systems, Computer Science, Creative Writing, Economics, Education, English, French, Geography, German, History, Human Services, Liberal Arts, Music, Philosophy, Physical Education, Physics, Political Science, PreLaw, PreMed, PreVet, Sociology, Sports Medicine

Men's Athletic Profile

P.O. Box 4
Emory, VA 24327
Coach: Neal Bland
Email: nabland@ehc.edu

NCAA III
Wasps/Navy, White, Gold
Phone: (540) 944-6831
Fax: (540) 944-3673

Estimated # of Men's Soccer Scholarships: N/A
Conference: Old Dominion Athletic Conference
Program Profile: Game field with Bermuda grass and sprinkler system. completely enclosed stadium. Natural nearly full size field; stadium holds 1,000 seats.
History: Our program began in 1994. Bridgeport NCAA Tournament around record in 1995. Conference Finalist once and semi-finalist twice in five years. Had 15 All-Conference players; 6 All-South players; 3 All-Americans, 2 All-Conference MVP's; 6 players graduated and playing professional in US and in Europe.
Achievements: Had 13 All-Conference players in four years of conference.
Coaching: Neal Bland, Head Coach, holds "A" License and played professional in Europe and in US. Originally he is from England.
Style of Play: Pass and move, very offensive, creative and imaginable, physically and strong and quick.

Women's Athletic Profile

Emory & Henry College, PO Box 4
Emory, VA 24327
Coach: Neal Bland
Email: Not Available

NCAA III
Wasps/Navy, White, Gold
Phone: (540) 949-6831
Fax: (540) 944-3673

Estimated # of Women's Soccer Scholarships: None
Conference: Old Dominion Athletic Conference
Program Profile: Game field with Bermuda grass and sprinkler system. Completely enclosed stadium. Natural grass and nearly full size field stadium that holds 1,000.
History: Started in 1994; biggest NCAA Tournament around record in 1995. Conference Finalist once and semi-finalist twice in five years.
Achievements: Has 15 All-Conference players, 6 All-South, 3 All-Americans, 2 Conference MVP's; 6 players graduated and playing professional in US and Europe.
Coaching: Neal Bland, Head Coach, he holds "A" License. He played professional in Europe and US. He is originally from England.
Style of Play: Pass and move, very effective, creative and imaginative, physically strong and quick.

Ferrum University

Academic Profile

Soccer Office
Ferrum, VA 24088

Phone:

Type: 4 Yr.,Private,Liberal Arts
Website: http://www.ferrum.edu
SAT/ACT/GPA: 820/17
Student/Faculty Ratio: 14:1
Undergraduate Enrollment: 1,200
Scholarships/Academic: Yes
Athletic: No
Expenses by: Year
In State: $ 16,000

Founded: 1913
Religion: Methodist
Housing: Yes
Male/Female Ratio: 5:4
Graduate Enrollment: N/A
Financial Aid: Yes
Out of State: $ 16,000

Specialty: Business, Environmental Science, Teacher Education
Degrees Conferred: BA, BS, BSW
Programs of Study: Accounting, Agriculture, Art, Biology, Business Administration, Chemistry, Computer Science, Criminal Justice, Environmental Science, Fine Arts, French, Liberal Arts, Physical Education, Mathematical Science, Medical Technology, Philosophy, Psychology, Religion

Men's Athletic Profile

Route 40 West, P.O. Box 1000
Ferrum, VA 24088
Coach: Tom Thatcher
Email: tthatcher@ferrum.edu

NCAA III
Panthers/Black, Gold
Phone: (540) 365-4490
Fax: (540) 365-4472

Estimated # of Men's Soccer Scholarships:
Conference: Dixie Conference
Program Profile: Ferrum plays a traditional fall season on a natural grass field that measures 120x75 yards. A separate practice field is used. A spring season of indoor, outdoor, small-side, and a full-side tournament play as well.
History: Our men's program was established in 1988. Coach Thatcher was hired full-time in 1991 and has progressively built the program into a highly competitive member of the tough Dixie Conference, The Virginia Intercollegiate Soccer Association as well as the NCAA South Region.
Achievements: ISAA All-American Scholar Athlete - Salvatore Fiorenza; VISA All-State - Emerson Umana, Will Cunningham, Patrick George.
Coaching: Tom Thatcher, Head Coach, entering his 12th season. Head Coach Tom Thatcher is a graduate of Rhode Island College and holds the NSCAA National Diploma. He served as an evaluator for the VA ODP program. He is also a member of USSF. Assistant Coach Mike Brizendine was a standout performer at James Madison University.

Roster In State: 12	**Out of State:** 10	**Out of Country:**
ODP State: 10	**Regional:**	**National:**
Walk-on/Other:	**Graduation %:** N/A	**Seniors on Team:** 2

Positions Needed: Goalkeeper, Sweeper, Forward, Midfield
Camp or Clinic Dates: July 2-7, 2000
Most Recent Record: 9-7-1
Schedule: Greensboro, Christopher Newport, Maryville, University of the South, Washington & Lee, NC Wesleyan, Lynchburg, Eastern Mennonite
Style of Play: At Ferrum, our desire is to play aggressive, attacking, and creative soccer. Possession is a top priority, working combinations, changing point of attack, and using second and third attackers. Defense is team oriented, using pressure on the ball, support, and anticipation off the ball.

Women's Athletic Profile

P.O. Box 1000
Ferrum, VA 24088
Coach: Emily Johnson
Email: ejohnson@ferrum.edu

NCAA III
Panthers/Black, Gold
Phone: (540) 365-5567
Fax: (540) 365-4226

Estimated # of Women's Soccer Scholarships: None
Conference: Dixie Intercollegiate Athletic Conference
Program Profile: Ferrum plays a traditional Fall season on a natural grass field that measures 120x70 yards. A Spring season of indoor and outdoor small-side and full-side tournament play is a part of the program as well.
History: Our women's program was established in 1990. Coach Thatcher was hired full time in 1991 and has progressively built the program into a highly competitive and respected member of the Dixie Conference and the NCAA South Region.
Achievements: Liz Adams was NSCAA South Region All-Academic 1st team in 1998; Regional All-American was Susan Sauter in 1995; GTE Academic All-American was Cynthia Rhinehatr.
Coaching: Tom Thatcher, Head Coach, entering his 11th season. He is a 1975 graduate of Rhode Island College and holds NSCAA National Diploma. He is also a member of USSF, and he serves also as a head coach of the Ferrum's men's program. Alan Green, Assistant Coach, beginning his second season at Ferrum having also coached at Frostburg State, Mankato State and University of North Alabama. He is a masters in Health and Physical Education from North Alabama.
Style of Play: At Ferrum, our desire is to play an aggressive, attacking and creative soccer. Possession is a top priority working on combination and switching the field, and using the second third attackers. Defense is team oriented using pressure on the ball, support and the anticipation off the ball.

George Mason University
Academic Profile

Fairfax, VA 22030
Phone: (703) 993-3200

Type: 4 Yr.,Public,Liberal Arts
Founded: 1972
Website: http://www.gmu.edu
Religion: Non-Affiliated
SAT/ACT/GPA: 1070/25/3.1
Housing: Yes
Student/Faculty Ratio: 17:1
Male/Female Ratio: 45:55
Undergraduate Enrollment: 15,262
Graduate Enrollment: 8,918
Scholarships/Academic: Yes **Athletic:** Yes
Financial Aid: Yes
Expenses by: Year **In State:** $9,708
Out of State: $18,552
Specialty: Business, Education, Communications, Physical Therapy
Degrees Conferred: Bachelors, Professional Masters, Doctoral
Programs of Study: 104 areas of study including: Accounting, Anthropology, Banking/Finance, Biology, Business, Chemistry, Computer, International, Journalism, Management, Marketing, Parks and Recreation, PreProfessional Programs

Men's Athletic Profile

4400 University Drive
Fairfax, VA 22030-4444
Coach: Gordon Bradley
Email: Not Available

NCAA I
Patriots/Green, Gold, White
Phone: (703) 993-3287
Fax: (703) 993-3239

Estimated # of Men's Soccer Scholarships: None
Conference: Colonial Athletic Association
Program Profile: George Mason is located in Fairfax, Virginia, thirty minutes outside Washington DC. GMU's stadium seats a capacity crowd of 5,000. The field is natural grass with a measurements of 115x75 yards. GMU has a unique blend of players consisting of Americans from primarily the east coast and southern United States as well as players from Europe, South America, and Africa. this is primarily due to coach Bradley's international experience and contacts as a professional coach.
History: In the 29-year history of George Mason soccer, the program has recorded of 289-178-54 for a winning percentage of .607. Gordon Bradley joined the program as a head coach in 1985 and immediately let the Patriots to a record of 18-4 and NCAA first-round victory over Virginia. since the inception of the Colonial athletic Association in 1984, George Mason has been the most dominant program in the conference with a league record of 69-20-12, and six shared or outright regular season titles in 14 years.
Achievements: In 1998, Rick Kotschlau, a 4-year starter was the 2nd pick in the 1st round of the MLS draft. Since his arrival at George Mason in 1985, he has seen 24 of his former players move on to play professionally or for their national teams. The team completed in the post-season NCAA Tournament 8 times since 1981. In 1996, won 1-0 at the University of Virginia before losing 2-1 to eventual national champion St. John's in the second round.
Coaching: Gordon Bradley is our Head Coach. He compiled a record of 156-81-34 in 13-year of coaching. He was considered the best among the seven coaches to lead the Patriots on the field. He guided the program to 12-8-2 record. In 1997 Distinguished Honoree at Third Annual Immigrant Achievement Awards. In 1996 - US National Soccer Hall of Fame Inductee and Inducted into New York Hall of Fame.
Style of Play: We play a possession style game and builds most of the attacks from the back. Defensively they play man on man marking with a sweeper.

Women's Athletic Profile

4400 University Dr., MS 3A5
Fairfax, VA 22030
Coach: Jac Cicala
Email: jcicala@gmu.edu

NCAA I
Patriots/Green, Gold
Phone: (703) 993-3295
Fax: (703) 993-3239

Estimated # of Women's Soccer Scholarships: None
Conference: Colonial Athletic Association
Program Profile: Play on natural grass, no lights but has bleachers seat for 5,000; tack surrounds field. Verti-drain system and an electronic seven-station irrigation system; 72 yards wide by 112 yards; 70% bluegrass and 30% rye.
History: Our program began in 1982 with an overall record of 216-103-35. NCAA Champions in 1985; NCAA Runner-Up in 1983 & 1993; has a record of 97-36-11 at home.
Achievements: Jac Cicala was named National Coach of the Year in 1993; 3-time All-American US National Team Goalkeeper Jaime Pagliarulo; Tammy Pearman All-American, US National Team; other All-Americans include Skye Eddy, Dana Hedin, Kim Maslin; 1998 Freshman All-American and CAA Rookie of the Year Katy Robertson.
Coaching: Jac Cicala, Head Coach, entering 8th year with a record of 90-45-15. He holds USSF "A" license, 1993 National Coach of the Year, led team to 1993 CAA Co-Champions, the languages first year giving award. He was a graduate of George Mason in 1975. Sue Vodicka, Assistant Coach, entering first year with the program. She was a graduate of George Mason University in 1986. Kim Maslin-Kammerdeiner, Assistant Coach, entering 6th year with the program. She was a graduate of George Mason University in 1998.
Style of Play: Varies depending on opponent.

Hampden - Sydney College

Academic Profile

Hampden - Sydney, VA 23943

Phone:

Type: 4 Yr.,Private,Liberal Arts,Pre-Engineering
Founded: 1776
Website: http://www.hsc.edu
Religion: Presbyterian
SAT/ACT/GPA: 1135/23/3.1
Housing: Yes
Student/Faculty Ratio: 13:1
Male/Female Ratio: All Male
Undergraduate Enrollment: 1000
Graduate Enrollment: N/A
Scholarships/Academic: Yes **Athletic:** No **Financial Aid:** Yes
Expenses by: Year **In State:** $ 23,029 **Out of State:** $ 23,029
Specialty: Liberal Arts
Degrees Conferred: BA, BS
Programs of Study: Biology, Chemistry, Classical Studies, Economics, Economics with Mathematics, English, Fine Arts, French, German, Greek, Greek and Latin, History, Humanities, InterScience, Latin, Management Economics, Mathematics, Mathematics with Computer Science, Philosophy, Physics, Political Science, Psychology, Religion, Religion and Philosophy, Spanish

Men's Athletic Profile

Kirby Fieldhouse, Soccer Office
Hampden-Sydney, VA 23943
Coach: Bert Molinary
Email: Bertm@HSU.EDU

NCAA III
Tigers/Maroon, Gray
Phone: (804) 223-6000
Fax: (804) 223-6346

Estimated # of Men's Soccer Scholarships: None
Conference: Old Dominion Athletic Conference
Program Profile: We have a beautiful stadium and Bermuda field with measurements of 120x80 yards. It has a seating capacity of 1,000. We have a fall and a spring season schedule. Our facilities include locker rooms and scoreboard.
History: The program was established in 1969. We attained a National ranking in 1997.
Achievements: Produced 1 All-American in 1994; 16 NSCAA All-South Atlantic players. Mike Melvin was drafted in the second round of the Premier Soccer Alliance draft in 1998. He was the only Division III player selected in the draft. Melvin was drafted by the Dallas Sidekicks. Don Hughes member of the Northern Virginia Royals A-League; Curtis player was a 1995 member of Columbia Heat (A-League).
Coaching: Bert Molinary, Head Coach, is chairman, NSCAA All-American Committee of South Atlantic Region. This is his third year here. He has an overall record of 38-20-2.
Style of Play: Attacking style, possession oriented.

Hollins College

Academic Profile

Phone:

Roanoke, VA 24020

Type: 4 Yr.,Private,Liberal Arts
Founded: 1842
Website: http://www.holins.edu
Religion: Non-Affiliated
SAT/ACT/GPA: Required
Housing: Yes
Student/Faculty Ratio: 9:1
Male/Female Ratio: Women
Undergraduate Enrollment: 867
Graduate Enrollment: 194
Scholarships/Academic: Yes **Athletic:** No **Financial Aid:** Yes
Expenses by: Year **In State:** $ 21,285 **Out of State:** $ 21,285
Degrees Conferred: BA, MA, MALS, MAT, CAS (Certificate of Advanced Studies)
Programs of Study: American Studies, Art, Biology, Chemistry, Classics, Communications, Economics, English, French, German, History, International Studies, Mathematics, Music, Philosophy, Physics, Political Science, Religion, Sociology, Spanish, Theatre

Women's Athletic Profile

Forest of Arden Way
Roanoke, VA 24020
Coach: Robert Hartman
Email: rhart12599@aol.com

NCAA III
Green, Gold
Phone: (540) 362-6476
Fax: (540) 362-6553

Estimated # of Women's Soccer Scholarships: None
Conference: Old Dominion Athletic Conference
Program Profile: Excellent facilities with a natural grass field, play a Fall season, surrounded by Moody Student Center.
History: One of the original members of the Old Dominion Athletic Conference. Runner-up to ODAC Champion in 1983.
Achievements: ODAC Co-Champions in 1982; 1 All-American; 8 All-ODAC; 3 players named ODAC All-Conference in 1990 and Coach of the Year in 1987.
Coaching: Head Coach- Robert Hartman, Assistant- Mike Renne
Roster in State: 4 **Out of State:** 18 **Out of Country:** 0
ODP State: 3 **Regional:** **National:**
Walk-on/Other: **Graduation %:** 100 **Seniors on Team:** 3
Positions Needed: ALL
Camp or Clinic Dates: Not Available
Most Recent Record: 4-10-0
Schedule: Lynchburg, Washington & Lee, Randolph-Macon, Va. Wesleyan, Eastern Mennonite

James Madison University

Academic Profile

Phone: (540) 568-6518

Harrisonburg, VA 22807

Type: 4 Yr.,Private,Liberal Arts
Founded: 1908
Website: http://www.jmu.edu
Religion: Non-Affiliated
SAT/ACT/GPA: 1175/3.4-3.5
Housing: Yes
Student/Faculty Ratio: 15:1
Male/Female Ratio: 45:55
Undergraduate Enrollment: 13,225
Graduate Enrollment: 723
Scholarships/Academic: Yes **Athletic:** Yes **Financial Aid:** Yes
Expenses by: Year **In State:** $ 9,408 **Out of State:** $ 15,014
Specialty: Liberal Arts
Degrees Conferred: BS, BA, MS, MA, MBA, MFA, EED

Programs of Study: Accounting, Anthropology, Art, Biology, Business, Communications, Chemistry, Computer Science, Dietetics, Economics, English, Finance, Foreign Languages, Grocery, Geology, Health Science, History, Integrated Science & Technology, International Affairs, International Business, Kinesiology, Management, Marketing, Mathematics, Media, Music, Nursing, Operations, Management, Physics, Philosophy & Religion, Political Science, Psychology, Public Administration, Social Science, Social Work, Sociology, Speech Communications, Theatre & Dance, Etc.

Men's Athletic Profile

MSC 2301; Athletics JMU
Harrisonburg, VA 22807
Coach: Dr. Tom Martin
Email: martintr@jmu.edu

NCAA I
Dukes/Purple, Gold
Phone: (540) 568-6518
Fax: (540) 568-6065

Estimated # of Men's Soccer Scholarships: variable
Conference: Colonial Athletic Association
Program Profile: We play in a stadium that has a 2,000 person capacity. The field has natural grass. We have very good facilities. We play both a fall and spring season. We have 19 regular season games, post season play and five spring dates.
History: We started in 1968. We went to the NCAA Tournaments in 1971, 1972, 1973, 1976, 1992, 1993, 1994, 1995 and 1996. We were NCAA Quarterfinalists in 1994 and 1995. We were Conference Tournament Champions in 1992, 1993 and 1994. Nationally ranked for the last 11 years
Achievements: 7 All-Americans, including four in the 1990's; Conference Player of the Year in 1972, 1974,1977, 1989, 1991, 1993 and 1994; Regional Coach of the Year in 1989 and 1995; Conference Coach of the Year in 1986, 1989 and 1993; State Coach of the Year in 1989, 1993, 1995, 1971 and 1972; Numerous alumni have played professionally; Kevin Knight is currently with MLS Metrostars.
Coaching: Dr. Tom Martin, Head Coach, has been head coach for eleven years. He has a USSF "A "License and an NSCAA Advanced National Diploma. He was National and Regional Coach of the Year. Tom Foley and Daniel Ensley are assistant coaches.

Roster In State: 15	**Out of State:** 13	**Out of Country:** 5-6
ODP State: 10-15	**Regional:** 8-9	**National:** 6
Walk-on/Other:	**Graduation %:** 90	**Seniors on Team:** 4

Positions Needed: 2 forwards, 2 MF, 2 defenders
Camp or Clinic Dates: 6/19-23, 7/9-13, 7/16-19
Most Recent Record: 11-7-1
Schedule: Virginia, St. Loves, URI, William & Mary, RCU
Style of Play: built around the players strengths and abilities

Women's Athletic Profile

305 Godwin Hall, MSC 2301
Harrisonburg, VA 22807
Coach: Dave Lombardo
Email: w-soccer@jmu.edu

NCAA I
Dukes/Purple, Gold, White
Phone: (540) 568-3452
Fax: (540) 568-6065

Estimated # of Women's Soccer Scholarships:
Conference: Colonial Athletic Association
Program Profile: We are one of the top 25 teams in the nation and we play in the fall. Our field has natural grass, lights and 1,900 seats. Our facilities include practice fields, game fields and support services. We have a personalized academic support and a strength and conditioning coach. We have an athletic training staff, an equipment staff and a sports media relations staff.
History: Our women's soccer program started in 1990. It has been in the Top 25 teams in the nation since 1991. We have been ranked 12th in the nation. We won the CAA Title in 1995. We went to the NCAA Tournament in 1995,1996,1997 and 1998. We advanced to the second round in 1998. We advanced to the Sweet 16 in 1995 and 1996.

Achievements: Coach of Year - Virginia Division I 1995-1996; Conference Coach in 1995; CAA Champions in 1995; All-Americans: Cathy Reid, Carrie Proost, Julie Revle, Kristi Palmacio, Sam Andersch,Therese Wolden, Lisa Cioffi; Canadian National Team: Tasha Ellis
Coaching: David Lombardo, Head Coach, started here in 1990. He coached at Keene State from 1981 to 1989. Assistant coach Carrie Proost started here in 1997. She was at VCU from 1995 to 1997. Assistant coach Jen Cuesta started here in 1998. Goalkeeper coach Greg Paynter started here in 1999.
Style of Play: Speed and possession.

Liberty University

Academic Profile

Lynchburg, VA 24502
Phone: (804) 582-2381

Type: 4 Yr.,Private,Liberal Arts
Founded: 1971
Website: http://www.liberty.edu
Religion: Non Affiliated
SAT/ACT/GPA:
Housing: Yes
Student/Faculty Ratio:
Male/Female Ratio:
Undergraduate Enrollment: 5200
Graduate Enrollment: n/a
Scholarships/Academic: Yes **Athletic:** Yes **Financial Aid:** Yes
Expenses by: Year **In State:** $14,900 **Out of State:** $14,900
Degrees Conferred: BA, MS, Ph.D., Religion
Programs of Study: Accounting, Advertising, Athletic Training, Biblical Studies, Biology, Business, Communication, Computer Science, Counseling, Elementary Education, English, Exercise Science & Fitness, Family & Consumer Sciences, Health Education, InterDisciplinary Studies, Journalism, Media Graphics, MultiDisciplinary Studies, Community Health Promotion, English, General Studies, Mathematics, Missions, Music, Nursing, Physical Education, Psychology, Philosophy, Physical Education, Psychology, Religion, Social Science, Sports Management, Theology

Men's Athletic Profile

1971 University Blvd.
Lynchburg, VA 24502
Coach: Jeff Alder
Email: jtalder@liberty.edu

NCAA I
Flames/Red, White, Blue
Phone: (804) 582-2381
Fax: (804) 582-2076

Estimated # of Men's Soccer Scholarships: Not Available
Conference: Big South Conference
Program Profile: Bermuda grass 120x75. Our out of conference schedule includes Virginia, Maryland, Wake Forest, Old Dominion. The Program caters to the Christian Student-Athlete that is looking for an environment to grow academically, athletically, socially, and spiritually.
History: Our soccer program began in 1975 with NCCAA , moved to NAIA (District 29 Champs) then moved to Division II NCAA (Visa Champs) and (6th in the nation) then became a member of the NCAA Division I (1994 Big South Runner-Up).
Achievements: Regular season Big South Champions 2 of last 3 years, Conference runner-up in 1998 and 1999. 2000-6 All-Big South Conference Players, 1999- 7 All Big South Conference players. 8 Liberty alumni are playing professionally.
Coaching: Jeff Alder is the Head Coach.
Roster In State: 2 **Out of State:** 22 **Out of Country:** 2
ODP State: 5 **Regional:** 1 **National:** 2
Walk-on/Other: **Graduation %:** N/A **Seniors on Team:** 4
Positions Needed: All
Camp or Clinic Dates: July 1-5 Overnight, Day camp July 30-August 2
Most Recent Record: 6-8-2
Schedule: Virginia, Maryland, Old Dominion, Wake Forest
Style of Play: Possession oriented style in a 3-5-2 or 4-4-2 system.

Women's Athletic Profile

1971 University Boulevard
Lynchburg, VA 24502
Coach: James Price
Email: jpricewsoc@aol.com

NCAA I
Lady Flames/Red, White, Blue
Phone: (804) 582-2768
Fax: (804) 582-2076

Estimated # of Women's Soccer Scholarships: None
Conference: Big South Conference
Program Profile: We have a developing Division I program. We have a Bermuda grass and natural bowl playing field. Our games are well attended.
History: We started in 1988. We had a part-time coach until 1997.
Achievements: Summer Abel - Rookie of the Year Big South Conference; Shannon Hutchinson - second team All-Conference Big South; Big South Conference Player of the Year in 1997 and 1998; 1998 All-Virginia first team-Christina Popotv.
Coaching: James Price, Head Coach, is a former Liberty goalkeeper. He played as a semi-pro with the Roanoke Wrath. He has an F.A. coaching badge. He worked with former schoolboys' forms in Swindon Town f.c., England. Jerry Lucido is assistant coach.
Style of Play: Counter attacking with great emphasis on wing play. Tough to break down and always looking to create a goal scoring chance.

Longwood College

Academic Profile

Farmville, VA 23909
Phone: 804-395-2057

Type: 4 Yr.,Public
Website: http://www.lwc.edu
SAT/ACT/GPA: N/A
Student/Faculty Ratio: N/A
Undergraduate Enrollment: 3900
Scholarships/Academic: Yes
Athletic: Yes
Expenses by: Year
In State: $8,655
Founded: 1839
Religion: Non-Affiliated
Housing: Yes
Male/Female Ratio: 33/67
Graduate Enrollment: N/A
Financial Aid: Yes
Out of State: $ 14,126
Specialty: Education, Business Administration
Degrees Conferred: BA, BS, MA, MS
Programs of Study: Anthropology, Art, Biology, Business Administration, Chemistry, Computer Science, Elementary Education, Economics, English, History, Liberal Arts, Math, Modern Languages, Music, Physical Education, Physics, Political Science, PreEngineering, Social Work, Sociology, PreTherapy, PreDentistry, PreMed

Men's Athletic Profile

201 High Street
Farmville, VA 23909
Coach: Todd Dyer
Email: tdyer@longwood.lwc.edu

NCAA II
Lancers/Navy, White
Phone: (804) 395-2794
Fax: (804) 395-2568

Estimated # of Men's Soccer Scholarships: N/A
Conference: Carolinas-Virginia Athletic Conference
Program Profile: The team will be playing on a new field in the fall of 1999 which is natural grass surface.
History: Our program began in 1977. There have been nine people chosen for the All-CVAC team, since Coach Dyer has been coaching the program, and four players selected as All-Region team members. Freshman, Andy Plum, was chosen as a Freshman Player of the Year this past season. He was also named All-Region and Freshman Athlete of the Year for Longwood.
Achievements: CVAC Regular season champs in 1997; #10 regional ranking in 1997.

Coaching: Todd Dyer, Head Coach, is entering his fourth season with the program. In three years, he boasts a 30-26-3 record and has led the men to one CVAC regular season championships in 1997. He graduated from Longwood in 1993. Former VISA All-Stars, All-Division in 1991 and 1992, and two-time captain.
Style of Play: Simple two-three touch, work it out of the back and get as many players involved in the attack as possible. Penetrate with a strong central midfielders. Possess at all cost; don't penetrate unless it is on.

Women's Athletic Profile

201 High Street
Farmville, VA 23909
Coach: Todd Dyer
Email: tdyer@longwood.lwc.edu

NCAA II
Lancers/Navy, White
Phone: (804) 395-2794
Fax: (804) 395-2568

Estimated # of Women's Soccer Scholarships: 2.28
Conference: Carolinas-Virginia Athletic Conference
Program Profile: NCAA II. Lancer Field. Natural Bermuda grass, Fall Championship season.
History: Our program began six years ago, and Coach Dyer boast a 58-29-3 record with the women's team. The women have taken second place in the CVAC Tournament for two years running. in their first year in the CVAC (1995), they went 14-2-2 and took second in their regular season. In 1998, the women were ranked at one time #24 nationally and #8 regionally. Overall record 86-40-5
Achievements: Coach Todd Dyer was named CVAC Coach of the Year in 1995; second place in CVAC Tournament in 1997 & 1998, 2nd place in Regular CVAC Season in 1995; numerous All-CVAC players in the years; 4 Total All-Region player (2 in 1995 and 2 in 1998); CVAC Freshman of the Year in 1995.
Coaching: Todd Dyer, Head Coach, Dyer is entering his sixth season as a head coach; He was a 1993 graduate from Longwood. He was a two-time All-Visa selection in 1991 & 1992 and a two-time captain, U-14 ODP Girls State team head coach. Alana Hill, Assistant Coach, a 1996 graduate from CVAC opponent Lees-McRae College in North Carolina; a two year All-Conference, 1 year All-Region and two-year co-captain.

Roster in State: 18	**Out of State:** 1	**Out of Country:** 0
ODP State: 5	**Regional:** 0	**National:** 0
Walk-on/Other: 0	**Graduation %:**	**Seniors on Team:** 4

Positions Needed: GK, Forward
Camp or Clinic Dates: Not Available
Most Recent Record: 14-5-1
Schedule: North Florida, Lynn College, Presbyterian, Belmont Abbey, Lee's McRae College
Style of Play: Versatile, everyone attacks and everyone defends.

Lynchburg College
Academic Profile

1501 Lakeside Drive
Lynchburg, VA 24501

Phone:

Type: 4 Yr.,Private,Liberal Arts		**Founded:** 1903
Website: http://www.lynchburg.edu		**Religion:** Disciple of Christ
SAT/ACT/GPA: 1010		**Housing:** Yes
Student/Faculty Ratio: 12:1		**Male/Female Ratio:** 30:70
Undergraduate Enrollment: 2,000		**Graduate Enrollment:** 450
Scholarships/Academic: Yes	**Athletic:** No	**Financial Aid:** Yes
Expenses by: Year	**In State:** $ 21,000	**Out of State:** $ 21,000

Degrees Conferred: BS, BA, MBA, MED
Programs of Study: Accounting, American Studies, Biology, Chemistry, Communications, Computer Science, English, Environmental Science, German, History, International Business, Marketing, Mathematics, Medical Laboratory Technology, Music, Nursing, Philosophy, Physics, Political Science, Psychology, Religion, Secondary Education, Social Science, Spanish, Special Education, Theatre Design

Men's Athletic Profile

Turner Gymnasium
Lynchburg, VA 24501
Coach: Dr. Bill Hayward
Email: hayward_w@mail.lynchburg.edu

NCAA III
Hornets/Crimson, Gray
Phone: (804) 544-8683
Fax: (804) 544-8365

Estimated # of Men's Soccer Scholarships: None
Conference: Old Dominion Athletic Conference
Program Profile: Program with a tradition of past success. We have a fine practice facility with a 120x70 field, 2 smaller practice fields. Our season begins in August and post season generally begins in October. Our game field is in the center of campus. A Bermuda/rye mixture provider a superb surface.
History: In 1954 Bill Shelleniberger introduced the game to Lynchburg. Upon his retirement in 1988 he posted a record of 371-167-48 for a .674 winning percentage. In addition, he posted 10 ODAC, 3 Mason-Dixon Conference, 8 Dixie Athletic, 8 VA State Championships. Shellenberger was introduced into the Soccer Hall of Fame in Oneonta NY in 1996.
Achievements: 10 ODAC Titles, 3 Mason Dixon Conference Titles, 8 Dixie Athletic Titles, 8 VA State Championships. In 1996 Coach Shellenberger inducted in National Soccer Hall of Fame, 2000 Johnathan Woug Honorable mention All-Conference.
Coaching: Bill Hayward is the Head Coach
Roster In State: 6 **Out of State:** 18 **Out of Country:** 1
Graduation %: 99% **Seniors on Team:** 3
Positions Needed: Postions not needed, we need technically proficient role players!
Most Recent Record: 5-10-1
Schedule: Elon University, Washington & Lee University, Roanoke College, VA Wesleyan College, Catawba College, Hampden-Sydney College, Randolph Macon College
Style of Play: We have a flexible system to fit our players. Generally play 4-4-2 with a sweeper. Love to counter attack, yet we are continually working to build out of the back. Possession is the key.

Women's Athletic Profile

1501 Lakeside Drive
Lynchburg, VA 24501
Coach: Todd Olsen
Email: olsen_t@mail.lynchburg.edu

NCAA III
Hornets/Crimson, Grey
Phone: (804) 522-8491
Fax: (804) 522-8495

Estimated # of Women's Soccer Scholarships: None
Conference: Old Dominion Athletic Conference
Program Profile: Field is located in the center of campus, play on a Bermuda grass. Play a Fall schedule and an indoor spring schedule.
History: Program began in 1987 and we have been Conference Champion 2 times out of the last 3 years and 3 consecutive NCAA Tournament Appearances.
Achievements: 1999 Regional Coach of the Year; 1999 Conference Coach of the Year; 1999 1 All-American; 5 All-South Players; 7 All-Conference
Coaching: Todd Olsen, Head Coach and Robert Travis is the Assistant Coach.
Roster in State: 12 **Out of State:** 12 **Out of Country:**
Walk-on/Other: **Graduation %:** 100 **Seniors on Team:** 9
Positions Needed: Centermid, Center Defense, Goalkeeper
Camp or Clinic Dates: Not Available
Most Recent Record: 20-2-0
Schedule: College of New Jersey, William Patterson, Emory University, Savannah College, Roanoke College
Style of Play: Direct- Attack oriented.

Mary Baldwin College
Academic Profile

Staunton, VA 24401

Phone: 540-887-7000

Type: 4 Yr.,Private,Liberal Arts
Website: http://www.mbc.edu
SAT/ACT/GPA: Varies
Student/Faculty Ratio: 11:1
Undergraduate Enrollment: 1387
Scholarships/Academic: Yes **Athletic:** No
Expenses by: Year **In State:** $23,360
Degrees Conferred: BA

Founded: 1842
Religion: Presbyterian
Housing: Yes
Male/Female Ratio: All Female
Graduate Enrollment: 64
Financial Aid: Yes
Out of State: $23,360

Programs of Study: Accounting, Advertising, Art, Art Administration, Asian Studies, BioChemistry, Biology, Business, Chemistry, Communications, Computer Science, Economics, English, French, History, Journalism, Management, Mathematics, Medical Technology, Political Science, Philosophy, Political Science, Psychology, Public Relations, Sociology, Spanish, Theatre

Women's Athletic Profile

Physical Activity Ctr, 128 Tams St.
Staunton, VA 24401
Coach: Teresa Somma
Email: vipersgo@hotmail.com

NCAA III
Fighting Squirrels/Yellow, Green
Phone: (540) 887-7185
Fax: (540) 887-7322

Estimated # of Women's Soccer Scholarships: None
Conference: Atlantic Women's Colleges Conference
Program Profile: One Field-natural 65x110, playing season fall 10 week program and home field natural grass.
History: Varsity program began fall 1995.
Achievements: AWCC Conference title 1996, Coach of the Year 1996.
Coaching: Teresa Somma Head Coach
Roster in State: 10 **Out of State:** 7 **Out of Country:** 2
Walk-on/Other: **Graduation %:** **Seniors on Team:** 3
Positions Needed: Goalkeeper
Camp or Clinic Dates: Not Available
Most Recent Record: 7-9-0
Schedule: Eastern Mennonite University, Bridgewater College, Hollins College, Randolph-Macon Woman's College, Sweet Briar College, Meredith College

Mary Washington College
Academic Profile

Fredericksburg, VA 22401

Phone: 540-654-1000

Type: 4 Yr.,Public,Liberal Arts
Website: http://www.mwc.edu
SAT/ACT/GPA: Open
Student/Faculty Ratio: 17:1
Undergraduate Enrollment: 3,000
Scholarships/Academic: Yes **Athletic:** No
Expenses by: Year **In State:** $ 9,552
Specialty: Liberal Arts & Sciences
Degrees Conferred: BA, BS, MFA

Founded: 1908
Religion: Non-Affiliated
Housing: Yes
Male/Female Ratio: 1:2
Graduate Enrollment: N/A
Financial Aid: Yes
Out of State: $ 15,076

Programs of Study: American Studies, Art, Biology, Business Administration, Chemistry, Classics, Computer Science, Dance, Dramatic Arts, Economics, English, Environmental Science, French, Earth Science, Geography, Geology, Historic Preservation, International Affairs, Mathematics, Music, Performing Arts, Philosophy, Physics, Political Science, Psychology, Sociology, Religion, Spanish

Men's Athletic Profile

1301 College Ave.
Fredericksburg, VA 22401
Coach: Roy Gdon
Email: rgordon@mwc.edu

NCAA III
Eagles/Navy, White
Phone: (540) 654-1875
Fax: (540) 654-1892

Estimated # of Men's Soccer Scholarships: N/A
Conference: Capital Athletic Conference
Program Profile: The team plays on natural Bermuda grass field that has a measurements of 120x74 with elevated bleacher seating for 800+; full size Bermuda grass practice field plus 100 yardsx60 yards secondary practice field - both located adjacent to game field.
History: The program started in 1977; record since it started was 254-136-29 includes eight NCAA National Tournament Appearances one as semi-finalist in 1997. Won 7 out of 8 Capital Athletic Conference Championships.
Achievements: Roy Gordon was named Coach of the Year five times in eight years and five times NSCAA Regional Coach of the Year; 5 players have achieve All-American status; 3 have played professionally (USISL).
Coaching: Roy Gordon, Head Coach, USSF "B" coaching license, NSCAA Advanced National Diploma, 28 years of coaching on college level. Mike Webb - Assistant Coach, former All-American at Indiana University of Pennsylvania. Chris Farrell - Assistant Coach, former player at MWC.
Style of Play: Possession: build from the back; quick counter attack on balls won in midfield.

Women's Athletic Profile

Athletic Dept.
Fredericksburg, VA 22401
Coach: Kurt Glaeser
Email: Not Available

NCAA III
Eagles/Navy, Gray, White
Phone: (540) 654-1875
Fax: (703) 899-4327

Estimated # of Women's Soccer Scholarships: None
Conference: Capital Athletic Conference

Marymount University

Academic Profile

Arlington, VA 22207-4299

Phone: 800-548-7638

Type: 4 Yr.,Private,Liberal Arts
Website: http://www.marymount.edu
SAT/ACT/GPA: 950/21
Student/Faculty Ratio: 14 :1
Undergraduate Enrollment: 2,000
Scholarships/Academic: Yes
Athletic: No
Expenses by: Year
In State: $ 19,900
Specialty: Nursing

Founded: 1950
Religion: Catholic
Housing: No
Male/Female Ratio: 25:75
Graduate Enrollment: 1,800
Financial Aid: Yes
Out of State: $ 19,900

Degrees Conferred: AA, AS, BA, BS, BSN, BBA, MA, MS, MBA, M.Ed.
Programs of Study: Accounting, Art, Banking and Finance, Biology, Business Administration, Communications, Computer Science, Criminal Justice, Economics, English, Environmental Science, Fashion Design, History, Human Resources, Liberal Arts, Management, Marketing, Mathematics, Nursing, Philosophy, Political Science, Psychology, Religion, Science, Theology and Religious Studies

Men's Athletic Profile

2807 N Glebe Rd
Arlington, VA 22207
Coach: Bob Meden
Email: Not Available

NCAA III
Saints/Royal Blue, White
Phone: (703) 284-1514
Fax: (703) 527-3684

Estimated # of Men's Soccer Scholarships: None
Conference: Capital Athletic Conference
Program Profile: The men's program is moving up on its tenth year of existence. We have seen a steady growth within the program. Each year our recruiting class is better and the player fit into our program. Our field is being renovated this Spring through summer (1997). It is a grass surface with 120x70 yards.
History: Program began in 1987 when the university went co-ed. Just in the last three seasons the program has made significant progress within our conference and region. 1997 finished the regular season in third place while advancing to conference semi-final for second year in a row.
Achievements: Coach of the Year in 1993 for Capital Athletic Conference.
Style of Play: We play a passing style of soccer defensively. We want to force opponents into mistakes and not allow their opportunities to get them into rhythm of play. Offensively, we like to build our attack using short indirect passing to set-up penetrating opportunities and get the ball to our target or get behind opponent's defense.

Women's Athletic Profile

2807 N Glebe Road
Arlington, VA 22207
Coach: Bob Meden
Email: robert.meden@marymount.edu

NCAA III
Saints/Royal Blue, White
Phone: (703) 284-1574
Fax: (703) 284-3859

Estimated # of Women's Soccer Scholarships: None
Conference: Capital Athletic Conference
Program Profile: Our practices and games are played on natural grass, both fields have lights for night games, practices, minimizing time-out of class. Traditionally season (fall) usually includes 20 games/scrimmages; non-traditional season (winter/spring) normally includes indoor and outdoor practices, several tournaments.
History: The program began varsity in 1985.
Achievements: Highest achieved national rank (19th) and regional rank (5th) in 1988. All-American's one member in 1988; South Regional Teams and 6 members in 1987, 1988, 1989, 1990, 1991 & 1993.
Coaching: Bob Meden is our Head Coach. He has coached the women's team during 1986,1987 and 1988, stepped aside to complete his doctorate and assume academic administration responsibilities, and returned to coaching again in 1998. He is a graduate of Kent State University (B.Arch and M.Arch) and the Catholic University of America (D.Arch). He also has previous coaching experience at Kent State University and Mount Vernon College.

Roster in State: 8	**Out of State:** 20	**Out of Country:** 0
ODP State: 12	**Regional:** 1	**National:** 0
Walk-on/Other: 0	**Graduation %:** 100	**Seniors on Team:** 2

Positions Needed: All positions
Camp or Clinic Dates: None planned
Most Recent Record: 5-13-1
Schedule: Mary Washington, Salisbury State, St. Mary's, Christopher Newport, Western Maryland, Frostburg State, York, Shenandoah, Catholic
Style of Play: Dependent primarily upon the strengths and weaknesses of the player personnel and the opposition's strengths and weaknesses. Willing to play an up-tempo attacking game when appropriate, but also comfortable with a deliberate passing game. Individual creativity is encouraged, but seeking primarily individual who are team-oriented players.

Old Dominion University

Academic Profile

Room 102
Norfolk, VA 23529
Phone: 757-683-3000

Type: 4 Yr.,Public
Founded: 1962
Website: http://www.odu.edu
Religion: Non-Affiliated
SAT/ACT/GPA: 850
Housing: Yes
Student/Faculty Ratio:
Male/Female Ratio:
Undergraduate Enrollment: 12,200
Graduate Enrollment: 5,800
Scholarships/Academic: Yes
Athletic: Yes
Financial Aid: Yes
Expenses by: Year
In State: Varies
Out of State: $ Same
Specialty: Biology, Prelaw, Sports Medicine, Exercise Science
Degrees Conferred: Bachelors, Masters, Doctorate
Programs of Study: Accounting, Allied Health, Banking/Finance, Biology, Business Education, Business Administration, Chemistry, Communications, Community Planning, Computer Science, Construction Technology, Consumer Service, Economics, Education, Electrical Engineering, English, Fine Arts, Geography, Health Education, History, Home Economics, Journalism, Management, Marketing, Math, Medical Laboratory Technology, Medical Records Administration, Music, Nursing, Physical Education, Political Science, PreLaw, Psychology, Social Science

Men's Athletic Profile

HPE Building, Rm. 103
Norfolk, VA 23529
Coach: Alan Dawson
Email: mwaite@odu.edu.com
NCAA I
Monarchs/Slate Blue/White
Phone: (757) 683-3607
Fax: (757) 683-5423

Estimated # of Men's Soccer Scholarships: 9.9
Conference: Colonial Athletic Conference
Program Profile: Fully enclosed stadium with bermuda grass, 4500 seating capacity. World Cup box style goals. Two game day locker rooms and a concession stand.
History: Program began in 1970. Overall record 268-185-59. NCAA Tournament appearances in 1989 & 1991. Sunbelt Champions in 1987. 1989, 1990. Colonial Athletic Conference Champions in 1991, 1999.
Coaching: Alan Dawson over 11 seasons in 160-50-13. Mark Waite and Justin Terranova are the assistant coaches.
Roster In State: 4
Out of State: 12
Out of Country: 5
ODP State: 10
Regional: 5
National: 2
Walk-on/Other: 2 Walk ons
Graduation %: 75
Seniors on Team: 4
Positions Needed: Striker and wide midfield
Camp or Clinic Dates: (757) 683-3022
Most Recent Record: 13-3-0
Schedule: UNC-Chapel Hill, Princeton, Georgetown, UNC-Greensboro, William and Mary, VCU, Richmond, American, UNC-Charlotte
Style of Play: Possession oriented team, prides itself in solid, organized defense (flat back four).

Women's Athletic Profile

H + PE Building Room 102
Norfolk, VA 23529
Coach: Joseph Pereira
Email: jpereiro@odu.edu
NCAA I
Monarchs/Navy Blue, Silver
Phone: (757) 683-5343
Fax: (757) 683-5423

Estimated # of Women's Soccer Scholarships:

Conference: Colonial Athletic Association
Program Profile: Four year old program; 4,000 fans stadium; season is in the fall; natural field, Bermuda playing surface.
History: 1994 marked the first year of the women's soccer program. Tied for the highest index of difficulty of schedule with Clemson University in 1994 and has a record of 8-10-1; 1996 is 7-11-2,
1997 9-9-1, 1998 11-7-0, 1999 11-9-0 and 2000 13-7-1.
Achievements: Coach of the Year 1998, Hall of Fame Methodist College 2000 200th win. 2000 CAA Player of the Year. CAA Players of the week, All-CAA (20), All-Mid Atlantic (6), All-American (1)
Coaching: Joe Pereira, Head Coach, 3rd year at ODU, former head coach at Methodist College, ODP Regional Staff; member of U-18, ODP staff member Women's U-16, Region III ODP Coach. Michael Hager and Ruth Keegan are the assistant coaches.
Roster in State: 12 | **Out of State:** 10 | **Out of Country:** 0
ODP State: 14 | **Regional:** 2 | **National:** 0
Walk-on/Other: 0 | **Graduation %:** 100 | **Seniors on Team:** 3
Positions Needed: Midfield
Camp or Clinic Dates: June 18-22, July 15-19 2001
Most Recent Record: 13-7-1
Schedule: Clemson, Duke, William & Mary, West Virginia, Richmond, James Madison
Style of Play: Build from the back, indirect.

Radford University

Academic Profile

Women's Soccer
Radford, VA 24141
Phone: 540-831-5128

Type: 4 Yr.,Public
Founded: 1910
Website: http://www.runet.edu
Religion: Non-Affiliated
SAT/ACT/GPA: 850
Housing: Yes
Student/Faculty Ratio: 16:1
Male/Female Ratio: 45:55
Undergraduate Enrollment: 8,146
Graduate Enrollment: 959
Scholarships/Academic: Yes | **Athletic:** Yes | **Financial Aid:** Yes
Expenses by: Year | **In State:** $ 7,458 | **Out of State:** $ 12,032
Specialty: Comprehensive, Committed Individualized
Degrees Conferred: BA, BS, Masters
Programs of Study: Business & Economics, Education & Human Development, Arts & Science, Nursing & Health Services, Visual & Performing Arts

Men's Athletic Profile

P.O. Box 6913
Radford, VA 24142
Coach: Spencer Smith
Email: s-smith@runet.edu
NCAA I
Highlanders/Red, Blue, White
Phone: (540) 831-5215
Fax: (540) 831-6095
Estimated # of Men's Soccer Scholarships: None
Conference: Big South Conference
Program Profile: Has a new soccer/track stadium opening in the year 2000. Bermuda grass with a measurements of 4,000, which has lights and state of the art facility.
History: Our program started in 1974. Radford University has been affiliated with Big South Conference since 1987. We have 3 Conference Championships. We have been ranked in South Atlantic Top Ten four of the last five years.
Achievements: The team produced 3 All-Americans, 1 Olympian, 1 MLS, 1 player in Peruvian 1st Division, 2 A-League player.

Coaching: Spencer Smith is our Head Coach. He enters his 5th year at Radford University. He was voted Big South Conference Coach of the Year in 1994. In his four years at Radford University, he has finished second twice and third once in the conference play. He has an NSCAA Advanced National Diploma and is currently with the Virginia State Team. Chris Barrett - Goalkeeper Coach.
Style of Play: The team play a 4-4-2 zonal system. Emphasis on possession and attacking.

Women's Athletic Profile

Box 6913, Women's Soccer
Radford, VA 24142
Coach: Ben Sohrabi
Email: bsohrabi@radford.edu

NCAA I
Highlanders/Red & White
Phone: (540) 831-5968
Fax: (540) 831-6095

Estimated # of Women's Soccer Scholarships: 7.5
Conference: Big South Conference
Program Profile: Dedmon Center Stadium is a natural grass field that seats 3,500 people. Our program has a rich tradition of soccer success that has participated in national tournaments and won conference titles. Facilities include a soccer stadium with a seating down on one side and the field is lighted. We have two advanced weight rooms, a new soccer field , a new track field and a new stadium built in 1999.
History: The Radford women's soccer program began in 1982 and went Division I in 1984. We received an at-large bid to the NCAA tournament in 1985 and an automatic bid in 1998. We had national tournament appearances and conference championships in 1998 with a record of 11-8-2.
Achievements: 1996 Big South Conference Freshman of the Year-Karen Dellavia; All-State first team- Jill McFarlane; Sue Williams was an All-American in1993; Conference titles 1993-1998; Kelly Moran All-Mid Atlantic 1997 & Amanda Lebo in 1998; Big South Conference Tournament MVP-Stephanie Rico, 1998.
Coaching: Ben Sohrabi, Head Coach, has been coaching for six years. He was a semi-professional player in 1990-1994 in the USISL. He managed the USISL Soccer Association "Nashville Metros Semi-professional" soccer for one year. He got his National Coaching License in 1996. Stephanie Rico is Assistant Coach.

Roster in State: 15 | **Out of State:** 9 | **Out of Country:** 1
ODP State: 24 | **Regional:** 1 | **National:** 1
Walk-on/Other: 0 | **Graduation %:** 100 | **Seniors on Team:** 5

Positions Needed: All
Camp or Clinic Dates: Not Available
Most Recent Record: 6-11-2
Schedule: Virginia Tech, ODU, UT Knoxville, East Carolina, Towson
Style of Play: Possession oriented attack. Team oriented 11 man high pressure defense. We build out of the back through the midfield with a short passing possession style game ultimately getting the back to our attacking players where we encourage creating a full attack style.

Randolph - Macon College

Academic Profile

Ashland, VA 23005
Phone: 804-752-7200

Type: 4 Yr.,Private,Liberal Arts
Website: http://www.rmc.edu
SAT/ACT/GPA: 1050/3.0
Student/Faculty Ratio: 12:1
Undergraduate Enrollment: 1,200
Scholarships/Academic: Yes | **Athletic:** No | **Financial Aid:** Yes
Expenses by: Year | **In State:** $ 22,000 | **Out of State:** $ 22,000
Specialty: Liberal Arts, Education
Degrees Conferred: BA, BS

Founded: 1830
Religion: Methodist
Housing: Yes
Male/Female Ratio: 50:50
Graduate Enrollment: N/A

Programs of Study: Accounting, Biology, Chemistry, Education, History, English, Business/Economics, Psychology, International Studies, Math, Political Science, Environmental Studies

Men's Athletic Profile

Patrick Street
Ashland, VA 23005
Coach: Helmut Werner
Email: hwerner@rmc.edu

NCAA III
Yellow Jackets/Lemon, Black
Phone: (804) 752-7299
Fax: (804) 752-7231

Estimated # of Men's Soccer Scholarships: None
Conference: ODAC
Program Profile: Usually one of the best in the region. Play a non-traditional season. Has a good Bermuda grass field and has a good student support.
History: Program began in 1957.
Achievements: Numerous state and conference championships; 9 Conference and State coach of the Year awards: 1 Regional Coach of the Year award; numerous All-American awards.
Coaching: Helmut Werner, Head Coach.
Style of Play: Very sound man-to-man defense, strong in the air. Often looking for the counter-attack. The team is known for its defense.

Women's Athletic Profile

103 E. Patrick Street
Ashland, VA 23005
Coach: David Burch
Email: dburch@rmc.edu

NCAA III
Yellow Jackets/Black, Yellow
Phone: (804) 752-3736
Fax: (804) 752-3748

Estimated # of Women's Soccer Scholarships: None
Conference: Old Dominion Athletic Conference (ODAC)
Program Profile: 120 x 70 Bermuda grass playing field, fall playing season. Very successful Division III program that plays in a competitive conference and is nationally recognized.
History: Program began in 1981 and has an overall record of 242-91-17, overall conference record 148-14-4, and 17 consecutive winning seasons.
Achievements: Twelve conference titles, 8 All-Americans, 11 ODAC Player-of the Year, 5 Coach of the Year Honors, 3 NCAA National Tournament Appearances.
Coaching: David Burch, Head Coach, 12 years college women's soccer experience, USSF "B" License, NSCAA Advanced National Diploma.

Roster in State: 5	**Out of State:** 17	**Out of Country:** 0
ODP State: 3	**Regional:** 0	**National:** 0
Walk-on/Other:	**Graduation %:** 100	**Seniors on Team:** 5

Positions Needed: Forward, midfield, goalkeeper
Camp or Clinic Dates: Not Available
Most Recent Record: 12-6-1
Schedule: Mary Washington, Lynchburg, North Carolina Wesleyan, Roanoke, Washington & Lee.
Style of Play: Attack oriented and ball possession.

Roanoke College

Academic Profile

Phone: (540) 375-2382

Salem, VA 24153-3794

Type: 4 Yr.,Private,Liberal Arts
Website: http://www2.Roanoke.edu

Founded: 1842
Religion: Evangelical Lutheran

SAT/ACT/GPA: 1100
Housing: Yes
Student/Faculty Ratio: 14:1
Male/Female Ratio: 2:1
Undergraduate Enrollment: 1,700
Graduate Enrollment: N/A
Scholarships/Academic: Yes
Athletic: No
Financial Aid: Yes
Expenses by: Year
In State: $ 21,935
Out of State: $ 21,935
Degrees Conferred: BS, BA, BBA
Programs of Study: Art, Biology, Chemistry, Criminal Justice, Economics, English, French, History, International Relations, Music, Philosophy, Physics, Political Science, Psychology, Religion, Sociology, Spanish, Theatre, Computer Science, Computer Information Systems, Health & Physical Education, Mathematics, Medical Technology, Sports Medicine

Men's Athletic Profile

221 College Lane
Salem, VA 24153
Coach: Scott Allison
Email: allison@roanoke.edu

NCAA III
Maroons/Maroon, White
Phone: (540) 375-2337
Fax: (540) 375-2382

Estimated # of Men's Soccer Scholarships: None
Conference: Old Dominion Athletic Conference
Program Profile: The home field is natural grass that seats 2,000. We enjoy a long tradition of outstanding teams.
History: The program began in 1947. It was a Division II power house in the late 1960's and early 1970's before becoming a Division III school.
Achievements: Conference Champs in 1968, 1969, 1970, 1985, 1988, 1993 & 1994. Scott Allison named 1993 UMBRO/NSCAA South Region Coach of the Year, All-South Atlantic in 1976-1998, All-ODAC in 1988-1998, Coach of the Year in 1985 & 1988, 12 All-Americans.
Coaching: Scott Allison, Head Coach, 12 season with the program, compiled a record of 135-84-14 (.609 winning percentage). NSCAA National Diploma, has coached the VA State ODP U-14 and U-18.
Roster In State: 10
Out of State: 14
Out of Country: 2
ODP State: 7
Regional: 1
National:
Walk-on/Other: 19
Graduation %: 90
Seniors on Team: 3
Positions Needed: Striker, Midfielder, Defender
Camp or Clinic Dates: June 19-23, 25-29
Most Recent Record: 8-9-2
Schedule: Mary Washington, Greensboro, Virginia Wesleyan, Eastern Mennonite, Christopher Newport, Washington and Lee, Methodist, Hamplen-Sydney, Randolph Macon, Maryville
Style of Play: Dependent on personnel. Preferably, we play indirect - emphasis on possession.

Women's Athletic Profile

221 College Lane
Salem, VA 24153
Coach: Phil Benne
Email: Not Available

NCAA III
Maroons/Maroon, White
Phone: (540) 375-2480
Fax: (540) 375-2382

Estimated # of Women's Soccer Scholarships: None
Conference: Old Dominion Athletic Conference (ODAC)
Program Profile: Year-round program with a 20-game Fall schedule and three Spring tournaments. Games are played at Elizabeth Campus that measures 120x80 yards, Bermuda grass, seating for 2,000.
History: Program began in 1985. Has been in the Conference Final 8 out of eleven years.
Achievements: Coach of the Year in 1990, 1992, and 1998; 1 All-American in 1992; Conference Champs in 1987 & 1990.
Coaching: Phil Benne, Head Coach, BA in 1986, MPS in 1989, NSCAA Advanced National Diploma.
Roster in State: 7
Out of State: 17
Out of Country: 0

ODP State: 5 **Regional:** 2 **National:** 0
Walk-on/Other: **Graduation %:** 90 **Seniors on Team:** 2
Positions Needed: 5-Defenders, Midfielders, Forward
Camp or Clinic Dates: Not Available
Most Recent Record: 13-7-2
Schedule: NCW, Lynchburg, Southwestern(TX) Maryville
Style of Play: play to our strength (speed up front or feet in the middle), 4-3-3, 4-4-2, 3-5-2. Make good decisions - attack in numbers up, look to build if we can.

Shenandoah University

Academic Profile

Phone: 800-432-2266

Winchester, VA 22601

Type: 4 Yr.,Private,
Founded: 1875
Website: http://www.su.edu
Religion: United Methodist
SAT/ACT/GPA: 1000/3.1
Housing: Yes
Student/Faculty Ratio: 10:1
Male/Female Ratio: N/A
Undergraduate Enrollment: 1300
Graduate Enrollment: 1000
Scholarships/Academic: Yes **Athletic:** No **Financial Aid:** Yes
Expenses by: Year **In State:** $23,300 **Out of State:** $23,300
Degrees Conferred: AS, BA, BS, BFA, BSM, MA, MS, MFA, MBA, Doctoral
Programs of Study: Accounting, Administration of Justice, American Studies, Arts and Sciences, Business Administration, Banking and Finance, Biology, Chemistry, Computer Information Systems, Computer Technology, Conservatory of Music, Dance, Education, English, Environmental Studies, History, Information Systems, Kinesiology, Marketing, Mass Communications, Music, Mathematics, Nursing, Occupational Therapy, Pharmacy, Philosophy, Physical Therapy, Political Science, Psychology, Religion, Respiratory Care, Sociology, Theatre

Men's Athletic Profile

1460 University Drive
Winchester, VA 22601
Coach: Rob Kulton
Email: rkulton@su.edu

NCAA III
Hornets/Red, White, M. Blue
Phone: (540) 665-4519
Fax: (540) 665-4934

Estimated # of Men's Soccer Scholarships: None
Conference: Dixie Intercollegiate Athletic Conference
Program Profile: The team plays on grass field. Our playing season is in the fall and in the spring. We share the facility with the women's soccer. Play at least one Division I team and in one tournament per year.
History: Program began in 1985. Previous coach was Court Smith which compiled a record of 75-56-12 from 1985 to 1991. Current coach is Rob Kulton which compiled a record of 64-57-3 from 1992 to the present. ESAC Champions in 1989.
Achievements: Our program has 1 All-American, 9 All-South Selections, 25 All-State Selections.
Coaching: Robert Kulton, Head Coach, is entering his 9th season with the program. He was a 1990 graduate of Shenandoah. He compiled a 64-57-3 in seven years. Rob Douglasr is the Assistant Coach.
Roster In State: 12 **Out of State:** 10 **Out of Country:** 0
ODP State: 5 **Regional:** 2 **National:**
Walk-on/Other: **Graduation %:** N/A **Seniors on Team:** 2
Positions Needed: Back, midfield
Most Recent Record: 4-9-2
Schedule: Greensboro, Christopher Newport, NC Wesleyan, Randolph Macon, Eastern Mennonite, Mary Wahington
Style of Play: Play an up-tempo and team is strong in the midfield and in the goal.

Women's Athletic Profile

1460 University Drive
Winchester, VA 22601
Coach: Lenny Paoletti
Email: lpaolett@su.edu

NCAA III
Hornets/Red, White, M. Blue
Phone: (540) 665-5538
Fax: (540) 665-4934

Estimated # of Women's Soccer Scholarships: None
Conference: Dixie Intercollegiate Athletic Conference
Program Profile: Dixie Conference member; play on newly resodded field. Playing season is the Fall and in the Spring.
History: The program began in 1991 with a record of 51-44-6 one losing season in the history; ranked in the South every year except in 1996.
Achievements: Has one Coach of the Year, one Conference Co-Champions, 2 All-Americans.
Coaching: Lenny Paolett, Head Coach, graduated from Western Carolina in 1994. She compiled a record of 30-31-1 in four seasons.

Roster in State: 10	**Out of State:** 8	**Out of Country:** 0
ODP State: 2	**Regional:** 1	**National:**
Walk-on/Other:	**Graduation %:**	**Seniors on Team:** 1

Positions Needed: Goal keeper, Midfield, forward
Camp or Clinic Dates: Not Available
Most Recent Record: 1-12-1
Schedule: NC Wesleyan, Christopher Newport, Ferrum, Villa Julie, VA Wesleyan, Methodist.
Style of Play: Counter attack-build from the back and control the play in the midfield.

Sweet Briar College

Academic Profile

Sweet Briar, VA 24595

Phone: (804) 381-6142

Type: 4 Yr.,Private,Liberal Arts		**Founded:** 1901
Website: http://www.sbc.edu		**Religion:** Non-Affiliated
SAT/ACT/GPA: 1170/24/3.5		**Housing:** Yes
Student/Faculty Ratio: 7:1		**Male/Female Ratio:** 100
Undergraduate Enrollment: 740		**Graduate Enrollment:** 0
Scholarships/Academic: Yes	**Athletic:** No	**Financial Aid:** Yes
Expenses by: Year	**In State:** $24,940	**Out of State:** $24,940

Specialty: Art History, Creative Writing, English, Mathematics, Sciences
Degrees Conferred: AB, BS
Programs of Study: Anthropology, Arts, Biochemistry, Computer Science, Creative Writing, Ecology, Economics, English, French, German, Greek, History, International Relations, Mathematics, Modern Language, Music, Philosophy, Political Science, Psychology, Religion, Social Science, Theater

Women's Athletic Profile

P.O. Box 87
Sweet Briar, VA 24595
Coach: Astrid Mel
Email: amel@sbc.edu

NCAA III
Vixens/White, Green
Phone: (804) 381-6291
Fax: (841) 381-6152

Estimated # of Women's Soccer Scholarships: None
Conference: Old Dominion Athletic Conference
Program Profile: Playing starts in August 28 through November 1st; has a one week pre-season try-outs, natural field, 15 game schedule includes minimal overnight.
History: The program began in 1980, institution now encouraging athletic success, increased recruiting and scouting - educational focus.

Achievements: 18 All-Conference selections, 1 All-South selection.
Style of Play: The team play - defensive game building to team attack, quick transition through midfield leading to early shots.

University of Richmond
Academic Profile

Phone:

Richmond, VA 23173

Type: 4 Yr.,Private,Liberal Arts
Founded: 1830
Website: http://www.richmond.edu
Religion: Non-Affiliated
SAT/ACT/GPA: 1250/27/3.4
Housing: Yes
Student/Faculty Ratio: 11:1
Male/Female Ratio: 1:1
Undergraduate Enrollment: 2,900
Graduate Enrollment: N/A
Scholarships/Academic: Yes **Athletic:** Yes **Financial Aid:** Yes
Expenses by: Year **In State:** $ 22,500 **Out of State:** $ 22,500
Specialty: Business, Leaderships, Arts & Sciences
Degrees Conferred: BA, BS, MA, MBA, JD
Programs of Study: Accounting, Arts, Biology, Business, Chemistry, Classics, Computer Science, Criminal Justice, Economics, Education, English, Finance, French, German, Journalism, Management, Mathematics, Music, Philosophy, Physical Education, Physics, Political Education, Psychology, Religion, Social Science

Men's Athletic Profile

28 W Hampton Way/Robin Center
Richmond, VA 23173
Coach: Jeff Gettler
Email: jgettler@richmond.edu

NCAA I
Spiders/Red, Blue
Phone: (804) 289-8357
Fax: (804) 289-8820

Estimated # of Men's Soccer Scholarships: TBA
Conference: Colonial Athletic Association
Program Profile: A Division I nationally ranked soccer team that is the 1998 Colonial Athletic Association Champion. Richmond plays on a natural Bermuda grass field inside a 5,000+ seated stadium. Richmond has hosted the NCAA men's soccer championships years in 1995-1998.
History: Varsity level sport since 1975, all-time record is 184-246-43; 1998 record was 14-7-2. The team won CAA champions two times including the 1998. Enter the CAA in 1985, 2 times earned NCAA tournament birth. Have earned national rankings three separate years. Presently at #24 wins in the 5th toughest schedule. 1998 year team GPA - 1 of 16 teams in the country over 3.0.
Achievements: Produced 2 NCC Tournament Appearances, 2 CAA Conference Champions, several All-Americans including, 2-time All-American Senior Peter Luzuch and Junior Craig Ziadic; several University of Richmond soccer alumni have played professional soccer.
Coaching: Jeff Gettler is Head Coach. Peter McEvoy is Assistant Coach.
Roster In State: 2 **Out of State:** 22 **Out of Country:** 1
ODP State: 7 **Regional:** 4 **National:** 1
Walk-on/Other: 2 **Graduation %:** 98 **Seniors on Team:** 6
Positions Needed: TBA
Camp or Clinic Dates: July 8-13, July 15-19 2001
Most Recent Record: 11-7-1
Schedule: Duke Univ. Bradley Univ. Rhode Island, Wake Forest, Seton Hall, Dayton, V.C.U
Style of Play: Possession oriented, attacking and pressure.

Women's Athletic Profile

The Robin Center, #217
Richmond, VA 23173
Coach: Peter Albright
Email: palbright@richmond.edu

NCAA I
Spiders/Red, Blue
Phone: (804) 287-6013
Fax: (804) 289-8820

Estimated # of Women's Soccer Scholarships:
Conference: Colonial Athletic Association Conference
Program Profile: Fast growing, extremely competitive program. We play in a 4,500 seat soccer/track natural grass complex in the middle of campus.
History: Our program began in 1996; first year record was 7-9-2, second year record was 13-8-0 and third year record was 13-7-1; lost in CAA Finals to William & Mary; RPI ranking in 1998 season (40).
Achievements: Jacklyn Raveia was named Regional All-American, Kristin Samuhel was named Freshman All-American.
Coaching: Peter Albrigh, Head Coach, USSF "A" License. Advanced National Diploma (NSCAA). Compiled a record of 169-86-24 and coached 13 All-Americans. Skye Eddy, Assistant Coach, former Division I All-American and MVP of the Final Four in 1993 (George Mason University), USSF "B" License.
Style of Play: Up-tempo transition style counter-attacking soccer. Strong defensive foundation.

University of Virginia

Academic Profile

Charlottesville, VA 22906

Phone: 804-924-0311

Type: 4 Yr.,Public,Liberal Arts,Engineering
Website: http://www.virginia.edu
SAT/ACT/GPA: 1150/3.5
Student/Faculty Ratio: 11:1
Undergraduate Enrollment: 12,500
Scholarships/Academic: Yes
Athletic: Yes
Expenses by: Year
In State: $ 9,900
Specialty: Strong Academics

Founded: 1819
Religion: Non-Affiliated
Housing: Yes
Male/Female Ratio: 48:52
Graduate Enrollment: 6,000
Financial Aid: Yes
Out of State: $ 20,800

Degrees Conferred: BA, BS, Masters, Ph.D., MD
Programs of Study: University has ten schools: College of Arts & Sciences, Graduate School of Arts & Sciences, School of Engineering and Applied Science, School of Architecture, School of Law, McIntire School of Commerce, Darden Graduate School of Business Administration, Curry School of Education, School of Medicine, School of Nursing

Men's Athletic Profile

P.O. Box 3785
Charlottesville, VA 22903
Coach: George Gelnovatch
Email: Not Available

NCAA I
Cavaliers/Orange, Blue, White
Phone: (804) 982-5710
Fax: (804) 982-4926

Estimated # of Men's Soccer Scholarships: None
Conference: Atlantic Coast Conference

Women's Athletic Profile

P.O. Box 400847
Charlottesville, VA 22906
Coach: Steve Swanson
Email:

NCAA I
Cavaliers/Orange, Blue
Phone: (804) 982-5711
Fax: (804) 982-4926

Estimated # of Women's Soccer Scholarships: 12
Conference: Atlantic Coast Conference
Program Profile: We have a top Division I program and our playing season is from August through December. Klockner Stadium has a field with a measurement of 120x80 yards and natural grass. We also have two practice fields that are natural grass and measure 120 x 65.
History: The program began in 1985 and we have made 10 NCAA Tournament appearances, 12 consecutive winning seasons and 12 NCAA Bids
Achievements: Won NSCAA 7 All-Americans; 5 Academic All-Americans; 2 Soccer Mvp's; numerous All-Region and All-ACC selections.
Coaching: Steve Swanson is our Head Coach and Roh Raab and Sue Eastman are the Assistant Coaches.
Roster in State: 9 **Out of State:** 16 **Out of Country:**
ODP State: 16 **Regional:** 12 **National:** 9
Walk-on/Other: 9 **Graduation %:** **Seniors on Team:** 6
Camp or Clinic Dates: June 25-29
Most Recent Record: 13-9-0
Schedule: UNC- Chapel Hill, Santa Clara, Stanford, Hartford, Clemson, Florida, William and Mary, Wake Forest
Style of Play: Attacking style with possession and combination play.

Virginia Commonwealth University

Academic Profile

Phone: 804-828-0100

Richmond, VA 23284

Type: 4 Yr.,Public
Founded: 1838
Website: http://www.vcu.edu
Religion: Non-Affiliated
SAT/ACT/GPA: Open
Housing: Yes
Student/Faculty Ratio: 13:1
Male/Female Ratio: 40:60
Undergraduate Enrollment: 12,527
Graduate Enrollment: 4,177
Scholarships/Academic: Yes **Athletic:** Yes **Financial Aid:** Yes
Expenses by: Year **In State:** $ 9,057 **Out of State:** $ 17,219
Degrees Conferred: AS, BA, BS, BFA, BSN, MA, MS, MBA, MFA, Ph.D.
Programs of Study: Accounting, Biology, Chemistry, Economics, Engineering, Finance, Marketing, Health, Occupational, Physical, Radiation, Real Estate, Safety and Risk, Science, Sociology, Urban, Anthropology, Art Education, Nursing, Criminal Justice, Dance, Design, Music, Psychology, Religion, Mathematics, Communications, Computer Science, Business Administration

Men's Athletic Profile

P.O. Box 842003
Richmond, VA 23284-2003
Coach: Tim O'Sullivan
Email: tvosulli@vcu.edu

NCAA I
Rams/Black, Gold
Phone: (804) 828-4839
Fax: (804) 828-9428

Estimated # of Men's Soccer Scholarships: 9
Conference: Colonial Athletic Association Conference
Program Profile: Sports Backer Stadium with a capacity of 3250 is located on Boulevard in Richmond, Va. Has a Bermuda grass playing surface.
History: The Men's program began in 1978. For the past 2 years, VCU has appeared in the NCAA tournament. The Rams won the CAAC Championship in 1997.
Achievements: 1998 Regular season CAAC title, 1998 Coach O'Sullivan was named coach of the year. The Rams have 16 former players who have become pros, including 5 current pros. 12 VCU players have played for the National Team. Ricardo Capilla was selected a 1998 All-American by College Soccer Weekly.

Coaching: Tim O'Sullivan is our Head Coach. He is entering 4th season at VCU after coaching at Richmond 12 seasons compiling a 115-108-25 record, 1990 CAA, State of Virginia Division I and NSCAA Division I South Atlantic Coach of the Year. Carlos Samoano and Ted Jones - Assistant Coaches.
Roster In State: 14 **Out of State:** 7 **Out of Country:** 1
Walk-on/Other: **Graduation %:** N/A **Seniors on Team:** 6
Most Recent Record: 7-9-2
Style of Play: Look to play the ball to feet rather than have forwards run on to long balls. The slow build-up style plays to their strengths.

Women's Athletic Profile

Athletic Department; VCU Box 2003
Richmond, VA 23284-2003
Coach: Denise Schilte
Email: DSCHILT@saturn.vcu.edu

NCAA I
Lady Rams/Black, Gold, White
Phone: (804) 828-7617
Fax: (804) 828-9428

Estimated # of Women's Soccer Scholarships: Varies
Conference: Colonial Athletic Association
Program Profile: The $5.5 million Sports Backers Stadium was completed in 1999. It includes an Olympic sized soccer field and seating for 3250.
History: Our program began in 1995.
Achievements: We have had numerous girls make All-Conference; 1 player got CAA Player of the Year in 1996 and she is now playing in Japan. All State honors.
Coaching: Denise Schilte is in her first year as Head Coach.
Roster in State: 10 **Out of State:** 6 **Out of Country:** 5
ODP State: 5 **Regional:** 2 **National:** 4
Walk-on/Other: **Graduation %:** **Seniors on Team:** 3
Positions Needed: ALL
Most Recent Record: 12-6-3
Schedule: William and Mary, James Madison, Richmond, George Mason, Navy, Old Dominion
Style of Play: Possession and hard working style of play.

Virginia Military Institute

Academic Profile

VMI
Lexington, VA 24450

Phone: 540-464-7000

Type: 4 Yr.,Public,Liberal Arts,Engineering **Founded:** 1839
Website: http://www.vmi.edu **Religion:** Military
SAT/ACT/GPA: 1100/22/3.2 **Housing:** Yes
Student/Faculty Ratio: 11:1 **Male/Female Ratio:** 24:1
Undergraduate Enrollment: 1,300 **Graduate Enrollment:** N/A
Scholarships/Academic: Yes **Athletic:** Yes **Financial Aid:** Yes
Expenses by: Year **In State:** $ 11,250 **Out of State:** $ 19,080
Specialty: Engineering, Sciences, Business, Economics
Degrees Conferred: BA, BS
Programs of Study: Mechanical Engineering, Civil Engineering, Electrical Engineering, Chemistry, Physics, Biology, Psychology, Modern Languages, English, History, Business and Economics, Computer Sciences, Modern Languages, International Studies

Men's Athletic Profile

Rt. 11 N. Cameron Hall
Lexington, VA 24450-0304
Coach: Stephen T. Ross
Email: Rosst@vmi.edu

NCAA I
Keydets/Red, White
Phone: (540) 464-7611
Fax: (540) 464-7790

Estimated # of Men's Soccer Scholarships: N/A
Conference: Southern Conference
Program Profile: Play on natural grass field in a beautiful Shenandoah Valley.
History: Became varsity sport in 1972.
Achievements: Southern Conference Player of the Year three of the last four years. Player to All-Southern Conference - Kevin Duhaine in 1996. 1998 graduate Rich Daughtridge was named All-South Atlantic, All-State, 1st team All-Conference.
Coaching: Stephen Ross, Head Coach, is starting his 11th year as a head coach. VMI Coach of the Year in 1990. Winningest coach in the school's history; four-year letterman for VMI; Captain in 1982 squad; Dan Sullivan - Assistant Coach, fourth year as an assistant coach. Played collegiately at James Madison University; keeper coach and recruiting coordinator.
Style of Play: 1-2 touch, aggressive man to man marking, high pressure.

Virginia Polytechnic Institute & State University

Academic Profile

Cassel Coliseum
Blacksburg, VA 24061-0502

Phone:

Type: 4 Yr.,Public,Liberal Arts,Engineering
Website: http://www.vt.edu
SAT/ACT/GPA: No minimum
Student/Faculty Ratio: 17:1
Undergraduate Enrollment: 19,496
Scholarships/Academic: Yes
Athletic: Yes
Expenses by: Year
In State: $ 7,407
Specialty: Business
Degrees Conferred: BA, BS, MS, MED, Ph.D., Ed
Programs of Study: Agronomy, Animal Husbandry, Business Management, Education, Home Economics, Engineering, Forestry and Wildlife, Physical Science, Social Science, Veterinary Medicine

Founded: 1872
Religion: Non-Affiliated
Housing: Yes
Male/Female Ratio: 59:41
Graduate Enrollment: 3,088
Financial Aid: Yes
Out of State: $ 14,059

Men's Athletic Profile

204 Cassell Coleseum
Blacksburg, VA 24061-0502
Coach: Jerry Cheynet
Email: msoccer$@vt.edu

NCAA I
Hokies/Maroon, Burnt Orange
Phone: (540) 231-5128
Fax: (540) 231-3613

Estimated # of Men's Soccer Scholarships: 4
Conference: Atlantic-10 Conference
Program Profile: Suffered the loss of positive field conditions due to heavy rain. The natural grass field was playable, but not in good condition. Tech recovered from a 1-8-2 start by winning seven out of their last nine games to post a 8-9-2 record on the year.
History: Tech started varsity soccer in 1972 and was taken over in 1974 by now head coach Jerry Cheynet. Cheynet has a 227-207-33 in his 27 years as Head Coach. Tech soccer left the Metro Conference in 1995 to join the Atlantic 10. Tech is a full member of the BIG EAST, with men's and women's soccer joining in 2001.
Achievements: Coach Jerry Cheynet was named Coach of the Year for Atlantic 10 Conference in 1997, regular season champs in 1997. 3 players named to All-South Atlantic team.

Coaching: Jerry Cheynet is our Head Coach. He is entering 24 years and compiled a record of 163-158-27. He graduated with a bachelor's degree in Physical Education in 1966 and received his Master's from KSU in 1967, head coach of the wrestling team since 1975 with a 182-152-6 record. He was named Atlantic 10 Conference Coach of the Year in 1997. Sam Gursal - Assistant Coach, second year certified as a coach, a referee, and an assessor, a master coach for the Olympic Development Program in Western Virginia; holds a NSCAA Regional and National, and Advanced Coaching Diploma, as well as National Youth License from the US Soccer Federation. Eric McClellan - Assistant Coach, third year, pursuing a maters degree in Business, earned a bachelor's degree in Finance in 1992; played professionally with Harrisburg Heat, a member of a National Professional Soccer League, currently playing professionally with the Washington Warthogs.
Roster In State: 14 **Out of State:** 14 **Out of Country:** 1
ODP State: 17 **Regional:** 3 **National:** 0
Walk-on/Other: 20 **Graduation %:** 95 **Seniors on Team:** 3
Positions Needed: Striker, Sweeper
Camp or Clinic Dates: June 18-22, July 22-26
Most Recent Record: 8-9-2
Schedule: South Carolina, William & Mary, UNC-Charlotte, James Madison Univ. Radford Univ.
Style of Play: Ball control, a 4-4-2 system, counter -attacks. Ball control with a short passing.

Women's Athletic Profile

364 Jamerson Athletic Ctr.
Blacksburg, VA 24061-0502
Coach: Sam Okpodu
Email: sokpodu@vt.edu

NCAA I
Hokies/Maroon, Burnt Orange
Phone: (540) 231-6423
Fax: (540) 231-3613

Estimated # of Women's Soccer Scholarships: None
Conference: Atlantic-10
Program Profile: We have a all playing season. Currently competing in the A-10 Conference. Tech plays at the Tech Soccer Field on natural grass.
History: The program began in 1993, finishing the season 6-10-1. From there the program continually grew.
Achievements: We have had several All-Conference players and Academic All-Conference players.
Coaching: Sam Okpodu is beginning his 7th season as the Hokie Head Coach. His overall record at Tech is 44-60-7. He played at NC State. Kim Stewart joined the staff in the spring of 1999.
Roster in State: 13 **Out of State:** 14 **Out of Country:** 1
Seniors on Team: 5
Positions Needed: Athletes
Camp or Clinic Dates: Not Available
Most Recent Record: 9-9-1

Virginia Wesleyan College

Academic Profile

Phone: (757) 455-3303

Norfolk/Virg. Beach, VA 23502

Type: 4 Yr.,Private,Liberal Arts **Founded:** 1961
Website: http://www.vwc.edu **Religion:** Methodist
SAT/ACT/GPA: 950/20/2.5 **Housing:** Yes
Student/Faculty Ratio: 1:14 **Male/Female Ratio:** 1:2
Undergraduate Enrollment: 1,600 **Graduate Enrollment:** N/A
Scholarships/Academic: Yes **Athletic:** No **Financial Aid:** Yes
Expenses by: Year **In State:** $ 17,500 **Out of State:** $ 19,500
Specialty: Business, Communications, Education

Degrees Conferred: BA, BS
Programs of Study: 35 different majors: most popular are Business, Communications, Education, Computer Science, PreLaw, Biology and Liberal Arts

Men's Athletic Profile

1584 Wesleyan Dr
Norfolk/Virginia Bea, VA 23502
Coach: Sonny A. Travis
Email: stravis@vwc.edu

NCAA III
Marlins/Navy, Silver
Phone: (757) 455-3387
Fax: (757) 461-2262

Estimated # of Men's Soccer Scholarships: None
Conference: Old Dominion Athletic Conference
Program Profile: Premier Program in NCAA III with top notch facilities. New stadium complete with a full-sized bermuda field, press box, permanent seating and Trinder Fieldhouse. The Trender Center is complete with locker rooms, meeting room, training room and offices.
History: Program began in 1969 and is now one of the premier soccer schools in NCAA III. Made 9 NCAA Tournament appearances in the past 10 seasons. Won six ODAC Championships in the 90's including 1999. Hosted the NCAA South Regional in 1999.
Achievements: Sonny Travis named Coach of the Year in the ODAC 5 times in the 90's, three-time All-South Region Coach of the Year and State of Virginia Coach of the Year 4 times. Nine All-Americans have come out of the program in the 90's. In 1992, VWC had the NCAA III Player of the Year.
Coaching: Head Coach, Sonny Travis has a USSF "A" license and has spent two years as a head coach at the USISL A League Level. Assistant Ryan Molloy, four year starter and three time All-South Region. Molloy was the leading scorer in the ODAC 1999. Eric von Hirsch , former goalkeeper at Rowan University (and Glassboro State), is the top Goalkeeper coach in the Hampton roads area.

Roster In State: 12	**Out of State:** 12	**Out of Country:** 0
ODP State: 10	**Regional:** 2	**National:** 0
Walk-on/Other: 0	**Graduation %:** 95	**Seniors on Team:** 5

Positions Needed: ALL
Camp or Clinic Dates: July 17-21, August 7-11
Most Recent Record: 13-7-1
Schedule: Rowan, Greensboro, Plymouth State, Hampden-Sydney, Roanoke, Mary Washington, Christopher Newport, Maryville, Allegheny, Randolph-Macon.
Style of Play: Ball possession with a short passing and counter attack. Numbers committed in the attack. Zonal defense.

Women's Athletic Profile

Wesleyan Drive
Norfolk, VA 23502-5599
Coach: Jeff Bowers
Email: marlin@vwc.edu

NCAA III
Marlins/Navy, Silver
Phone: (757) 455-3285
Fax: (757) 461-2262

Estimated # of Women's Soccer Scholarships: None
Conference: Old Dominion Athletic Conference
Program Profile: The Trinder Center is a state of the art facility including: team locker rooms, offices, training room, and Blue Marlin Room. Foster Field is a top notch Bermuda turf field with a brand new scoreboard, press box and stadium seating for 1,200.
History: Became NCAA varsity in 1985. We ranked as high as 15th nationally in 1995.
Achievements: 1995 3rd team All-American.
Seniors on Team: 2
Camp or Clinic Dates: August 2- 6

Most Recent Record: 8-10
Schedule: Mary Washington College, North Carolina Wesleyan, Washington Lee University, Lynchburg College, Roanoke College, Randolph and Macon College
Style of Play: We like to attack with numbers from our back. We have good speed up top and tend to play more of a direct style.

Washington and Lee University

Academic Profile

Lexington, VA 24450
Phone: 540-463-8400

Type: 4 Yr.,Private,Liberal Arts
Founded: 1749
Website: http://www.wlu.edu
Religion: Non-Affiliated
SAT/ACT/GPA: 1200
Housing: Yes
Student/Faculty Ratio: 10:1
Male/Female Ratio: 55:45
Undergraduate Enrollment: 1,700
Graduate Enrollment: 300
Scholarships/Academic: Yes
Athletic: No
Financial Aid: Yes
Expenses by: Year
In State: $ 21,970
Out of State: $ 21,970
Specialty: Law
Degrees Conferred: BA, BS, JD
Programs of Study: 40+ majors including Business & Management, Communications, Languages, Life Science, Physical Sciences, Psychology, Social Sciences

Men's Athletic Profile

P.O. Drawer 928
Lexington, VA 24450
Coach: Rolf Piranian
Email: Piranian r@wlu.edu
NCAA III
Generals/Blue, White
Phone: (540) 463-8685
Fax: (540) 463-8173

Estimated # of Men's Soccer Scholarships: None
Conference: Old Dominion Conference
Program Profile: We have an outstanding playing facility: Liberty Hall Field, prescription turf, 120x75 yards. We have an outstanding in season schedule, combined with a Winter season whom training and indoor with three weeks Spring practice.
History: Program began in 1947. State Champion in 1967, Conference Champions in 1986 & 1989. Overall record is 279-274-40. 2 NCAA Appearances, 2 All-Americans; team lost in conference in 1996.
Achievements: 2 NCAA Tournament appearances in 1965 & 1969; 56 All-Conference, 28 All-Regional, 1 All-American.
Coaching: Rolf Piranian, Head Coach, is entering his twenty second year. He holds a USSF "A" License and was five times Conference Coach of the Year. He's the School's all-time soccer coach. Rich Daughtridge, is the Assistant Coach.
Roster In State: 5
Out of State: 20
Out of Country:
Walk-on/Other:
Graduation %: 100
Seniors on Team: 5
Camp or Clinic Dates: Not Available
Most Recent Record: 9-8-
Style of Play: 4-4-2, man-to-man defense; ball control; play to win.

Women's Athletic Profile

P.O. Drawer 928
Lexington, VA 24450
Coach: Janine Hathorn
Email: hathornj@wlu.edu
NCAA III
Generals/Royal Blue, White
Phone: (540) 463-8668
Fax: (540) 463-8173

Estimated # of Women's Soccer Scholarships: None
Conference: Old Dominion Athletic Conference
Program Profile: W & L has produced a winning record in each of the last seven seasons and has had only four losing seasons. The home field is the Liberty Hall Fields which is overlooked by the Liberty Hall Ruins. A land mark from the University's beginning years as the Liberty Hall Academy in the mid-18th century. The playing surface in natural grass.
History: Soccer is one of W & L's oldest women's sports, starting in the spring of 1987, W & L's second year of co-education. W & L has reached at least the semifinal round of the ODAC tournament for 12 straight years.
Achievements: Jan Hathorn has been named ODAC Coach of the Year three times including last season. The generals have claimed the regular-season ODAC titles.
Coaching: Jan Hathorn has been the only head coach in school dating back to the programs inception in 1982. Her overall record stands at 129-88-9 (.594)

Roster in State: 3	**Out of State:** 19	**Out of Country:** 0
ODP State: 3	**Regional:** 1	**National:**
Walk-on/Other:	**Graduation %:** 100	**Seniors on Team:** 6

Positions Needed: Fullback, Goalkeeper
Camp or Clinic Dates: Not Available
Most Recent Record: 12-6-0
Schedule: Lynchburg, Roanoke, Carnegie MacLean, Emory, Eastern Mennonite
Style of Play: We like to play a faster pace, but I am pretty open to changing. The system to fit our different teams each season.

washington

WASHINGTON

SCHOOL	CITY	AFFILIATION	PAGE
Bellevue Community College	Renton	NJCAA	1176
Central Washington University	Ellensburg	NCAA II	1177
Eastern Washington University	Cheney	NCAA I	1178
Evergreen State College	Olympia	NAIA	1178
Gonzaga University	Spokane	NCAA I	1180
Northwest College	Kirkland	NAIA	1181
Pacific Lutheran University	Tacoma	NCAA III	1181
Seattle Pacific University	Seattle	NCAA II	1182
Seattle University	Seattle	NCAA III	1183
University of Puget Sound	Tacoma	NCAA III	1184
University of Washington	Seattle	NCAA I	1185
Washington State University	Pullman	NCAA I	1187
Western Washington University	Bellingham	NCAA II	1187
Whitman College	Walla Walla	NCAA III	1188
Whitworth College	Spokane	NCAA III/NAIA	1189

Bellevue Community College

Academic Profile

Bellevue, WA 98007-6484

Phone: 425-641-2222

Type: 2 Yr.,Public
Website: www.bcc.ctc.edu
SAT/ACT/GPA: Open
Student/Faculty Ratio: N/A
Undergraduate Enrollment: 20,000
Scholarships/Academic: Yes
Athletic: Yes
Expenses by: Per Hour
In State: $54/hour
Founded: 1965
Religion: Non-Affiliated
Housing: Yes
Male/Female Ratio: 44/56
Graduate Enrollment:
Financial Aid: Yes
Out of State: $209/hr
Degrees Conferred: 1,178 Associates
Programs of Study: Business Management, Computer/Information Sciences, Education, Engineering technologies, Health, Liberal Arts, Marketing, Parks & Recreation, Protective Services, Visual/performing arts

Men's Athletic Profile

3000 Landerholm Circle SE
Renton, WA 98058
Coach: Fred Thompson
Email: fthompso@bcc.ctc.edu

NJCAA
Helmsmen/Black, White
Phone: 425-564-3124
Fax: 425-564-3129

Estimated # of Men's Soccer Scholarships: 8
Conference: NWAACC
Program Profile: Stadium is natural surface and holds 500. We will be changing to Field truf within a year. Athletes have access to weight training facilities as well as indoor playing facilities.
History: Program began in 1974. Overall record is 248-108-59. Bellevue has been in the NEAACC Championship game 15 times winning 7 Championships.
Achievements: We have won 7 NWAACC Championships.
Coaching: Fred Thompson is our Head Coach. He has been successful at every level and age group of yout soccer through his time at Bellevue. An ODP State Coach, Fred is expecting to receive his USSF "A" license and makes it a point to always continue is knowledge as a coach. His playing experience as a collegiate, professional and international player brings an extra element to his teaching. Ramon Espinozq is the assistant coach and currently holds an USSF "C" License. He has been coaching club and High School for the past 11 years. Coach Espinoza is returning for his second season with BCC.
Roster In State: 14
Out of State: 0
Out of Country: 3
Walk-on/Other:
Graduation %: 100
Seniors on Team: 2 soph
Positions Needed: Keeper, Flank players both defending and attacking), striker
Camp or Clinic Dates: None
Most Recent Record: 11-4-4
Schedule: North Idaho, Edmonds CC, Highline CC, Tacoma CC, SW Oregon
Style of Play: Strong zonal defending allows the team to commit numbers to the attack. Tactically savvy players, who are always improving their technical ability and increasing the speed of play- makes for entertaining attack oriented soccer.

Women's Athletic Profile

3000 Landerholm Cir. S.E.
Bellevue, WA 98007
Coach: Ray Butler
Email: rbutler@bcc.ctc.edu

NJCAA
Helmswomen/Navy Blue, Red
Phone: (425) 864-2393
Fax: (425) 564-3129

Estimated # of Women's Soccer Scholarships: 8
Conference: North West Athletic Association of Community Colleges
Program Profile: Stadium is a natural surface with a seating capacity of 600. Will be changing to field turf within a year. Athletes have access to weight training facilities as well as indoor soccer training facilities.
History: The program began in 1999. Made the playoffs in the first year. Two year overall record is 11-16-4.
Coaching: Head Coach Ray Butler is a former College player, has 21 years of coaching experience. Assistant Coach Ramon Espinoza holds a "C" License and is entering first year with women's program.

Roster in State: 13	**Out of State:** 3	**Out of Country:** 2
Walk-on/Other: 0	**Graduation %:**	**Seniors on Team:**

Positions Needed: GK, Forwards, Attacking Mids, Defenders
Most Recent Record: 3-12-1
Schedule: North Idaho College, Edmonds CC, Columbia Basin College, Tacoma CC, Southwest Oregon College, Clark College
Style of Play: Basic system will be 4-4-2. Characterized by a flat back four with flexible attacking schemes.

Central Washington University

Academic Profile

Phone:

Ellensburg, WA 98926-7570

Type: 4 Yr.,Public		**Founded:** 1890
Website: http://www.central.edu		**Religion:** Non-Affiliated
SAT/ACT/GPA: 820/17		**Housing:** Yes
Student/Faculty Ratio: 22:1		**Male/Female Ratio:** 49:51
Undergraduate Enrollment: 8,304		**Graduate Enrollment:** 281
Scholarships/Academic: Yes	**Athletic:** Tuition waiver	**Financial Aid:** Yes
Expenses by: Year	**In State:** $ 10,018	**Out of State:** $ 16,204

Degrees Conferred: BA, BS, MA, MS
Programs of Study: Accounting, Actuarial Science, Anthropology, Banking & Finance, Biology, Broadcasting, Business Administration, Chemistry, Communications, Computer Science, Criminal Justice, Earth Science, Economics, Education, Engineering, Fine Arts, Geography, Geology, History, Psychology, Physics, Philosophy, Political Science

Women's Athletic Profile

401 East 8th Ave.
Ellensburg, WA 98926-7570
Coach: Michael Farrand
Email: farrandm@cwu.edu

NCAA II
Wildcats/Maroon/White
Phone: (509) 963-1939
Fax: (509) 963-2390

Estimated # of Women's Soccer Scholarships: 7
Conference: Greater Northwest Athletic Conference
Program Profile: CWU is home to 7500 students. A very good liberal arts University with men's and women' s sports. CWU opens a brand new soccer complex in 2001. All grass 75x115 field.
History: Program began in 1987. A overall record from 1987-1999 88-82-19
Achievements: 2 Conference Titles 1990, 1992.
Coaching: Michael Farrand has a USSF "A" License and a BA athletic training and physical education. 2 time Conference Coach of the Year, 4 time MVP Point Loma Nazarene Univ.

Roster in State: 20	**Out of State:** 0	**Out of Country:** 0
ODP State: 6	**Regional:** 1	**National:** 0
Walk-on/Other:	**Graduation %:**	**Seniors on Team:** 3

Positions Needed: Forwards, Midfield
Camp or Clinic Dates: Not Available
Most Recent Record: 12-6-1

Schedule: Idaho State, Gonzaga, Eastern Washington, Seattle Univ. Sonoma State, UC Davis, Western Washington, San Francisco State, Chico State, Western Oregon
Style of Play: Ball possession, zone defense, attacking from the back. Combination of German Defense and Dutch Attacking.

Eastern Washington University

Academic Profile

Cheney, WA 99004
Phone: 509-359-6200

Type: 4 Yr.,Public
Founded: 1882
Website: http://www.ewu.edu
Religion: Non-Affiliated
SAT/ACT/GPA: 720+
Housing: No
Student/Faculty Ratio: 20:1
Male/Female Ratio: 44:56
Undergraduate Enrollment: 6,990
Graduate Enrollment: 1,358
Scholarships/Academic: Yes **Athletic:** Yes
Financial Aid: Yes
Expenses by: Year **In State:** $ 7,360
Out of State: $ 11,872
Degrees Conferred: BA, BS, BFA, MA, MS, MBA, MFA, M.Ed.
Programs of Study: Contact school for programs of study.

Women's Athletic Profile

526 5th Street, Stop 66
Cheney, WA 99004
Coach: George Hageage
Email: george.hageage@mail.ewu.edu

NCAA I
Eagles/Red, White
Phone: (509) 359-7949
Fax: (509) 359-2828

Estimated # of Women's Soccer Scholarships: Fully Funded
Conference: Big Sky Conference
Program Profile: Fully funded D. I program. Play on grass and run both a varsity and developmental team.
History: Program began in `997 but did not play as a DI program until 1998. New coaching staff began in 2000. The 2000 year saw more wins than previous 2 years combined.
Achievements:
Coaching: Head Coach George Hageage. Assistant Coach Tamara Broulder Hageage.
Roster in State: 22 **Out of State:** 10 **Out of Country:** 2
ODP State: 5 **Regional:** 0 **National:** 0
Walk-on/Other: 0 **Graduation %:** **Seniors on Team:** 3
Most Recent Record: 7-11-0
Schedule: Univ. of Washington, Washington State, Montana, San Diego State, UNLV, Hawaii
Style of Play: Aggressive offensively and defensively. Possession ball while going forward as quickly and safely as possible.

Evergreen State College

Academic Profile

Olympia, WA 98501
Phone: 360-866-6000

Type: 4 Yr.,Public,Liberal Arts
Founded: 1972
Website: http://www.evergreen.edu
Religion: Non-Affiliated
SAT/ACT/GPA: Open
Housing: Yes
Student/Faculty Ratio: 25:1
Male/Female Ratio: 48:52
Undergraduate Enrollment: N/A
Graduate Enrollment: N/A
Scholarships/Academic: Yes **Athletic:** No
Financial Aid: Yes

Expenses by: Year **In State:** $ 8,437 **Out of State:** $ 15,100
Degrees Conferred: BA, BS, MA, MS, MPA, MES (Environmental Studies), MIT (Teaching Certificate)
Programs of Study: Agriculture, Arts, Biology, Chemistry, Communications, Economics, Education, Environmental Studies, Expressive Arts, History, Languages, MPI, Marine Science, Native American Studies, Philosophy, Physics, Psychology, Political Science, PreMed

Men's Athletic Profile

Evergreen Pkwy, CRC-213
Olympia, WA 98505
Coach: Scott Martin
Email: martinsc@evergreen.edu

NAIA
Geoducks/Forest, White
Phone: (360) 867-6521
Fax: (360) 867-6783

Estimated # of Men's Soccer Scholarships: To be determined
Conference: Cascade Collegiate Conference
Program Profile: We are currently in the early stages of rejuvenation of athletics at TESC. Our natural grass training and match fields are considered to be the best in our region. Pre-season training begins in mid-August with a rigorous regular season playing schedule that runs through the end of October. Our conference champion receives an automatic bid into the national playoffs. Our student-athletes are required to participate in a rigorous off-season training regimen.
History: Our program experienced a time of great success during the late 70's and 80's under the direction of Aaron Zoske. During this time, the program received numerous honors and prepared numerous players for the professional ranks. It is this level that we are committed to ance again to attain.
Achievements:
Coaching: Head Coach Scott Martin was formerly at the University of Wisconsin-Eau Claire where his teams received national ranking. Holds Advanced National Diploma and has worked with professional coaches from across USA and Europe.
Roster In State: 6 **Out of State:** 11 **Out of Country:** 0
ODP State: 3 **Regional:** 0 **National:** 0
Walk-on/Other: 0 **Graduation %:** 85 **Seniors on Team:** 4
Positions Needed: All
Camp or Clinic Dates: Not Available
Most Recent Record: 0-16-0
Schedule: Albertson, Seattle University, Concordia University, University of Puget Sound, Northwest College
Style of Play: We have begun our rebuilding process by looking to bring in players that bring with them a complete game. We look to play solid individual and group defense, control the tempo of the game in the midfield and use misdirection in the final third on our attack. Much of our style of play comes from the players.

Women's Athletic Profile

2700 Evergreen Park Drive
Olympia, WA 98505
Coach: Arlene McMahon
Email: mcmahona@evergreen.edu

NAIA
Geoducks/Forest, White
Phone: (360) 866-6538
Fax: (360) 866-6783

Estimated # of Women's Soccer Scholarships: Varies
Conference: Cascade Collegiate Conference
Program Profile: Play on a grass field with a seating capacity of 500. Playing season begins from September 1st through end of October.
History: 1980 will be the 19th intercollegiate season for the Geoducks. The 1996 season was the most successful in the history of the program as the team gained its first ever NAIA National Top 20 ranking (14th) and finished the season 12-8-0, the first winning record in the program's history.
Achievements: 1996 post-season awards were numerous. Camille Morgan was PNAC leading score with 26 goals and 6 assist for 38 points. Erica Brehm and Jean Teather were named to the PNAC All-Conference first team, Erica Brehm and Renee Mersing were named NAIA Scholar All-Americans.

Coaching: Arlene McMahon, Head Coach, will be entering her second season at the helm of the Geoducks program. She was the assistant coach the previous three years. McMahon played at the University of Washington and was a member of the West Team at the 1995 US Olympic Festival. Luise Frank - Assistant Coach.
Roster in State: 12 **Out of State:** 8 **Out of Country:** 0
ODP State: 8 **Regional:** 2 **National:** 0
Walk-on/Other: 10 **Graduation %:** 98 **Seniors on Team:** 2
Positions Needed: Forward, GK
Camp or Clinic Dates: Not Available
Most Recent Record: 3-14-1
Schedule: Simon Fraser, Central Washington, Western Washington, Concordia Univ. Western Baptist, Seattle Univ.
Style of Play: Mixture of possession and direct play.

Gonzaga University

Academic Profile

Spokane, WA 99258
Phone: (509) 323-6376

Type: 4 Yr.,Private,Liberal Arts,Engineering **Founded:** 1887
Website: http://www.gonzaga.edu **Religion:** Jesuit
SAT/ACT/GPA: 1000/3.2 **Housing:** Yes
Student/Faculty Ratio: 17:1 **Male/Female Ratio:** 48:52
Undergraduate Enrollment: 4,200 **Graduate Enrollment:** 1,300
Scholarships/Academic: Yes **Athletic:** Yes **Financial Aid:** Yes
Expenses by: Year **In State:** $ 22,160 **Out of State:** $ 22,160
Degrees Conferred: BA, BS, BBA, B.Ed., Bachelor of Education, BSE, Bachelor of General Studies, BSN, Juris Doctor
Programs of Study: For more information please contact the University Admission at 800-323-6572.

Men's Athletic Profile

502 E Boone Avenue
Spokane, WA 99258
Coach: Einar Tharinsson
Email: thorarin@gonzags.edu

NCAA I
Bulldogs/Blue, Red, White
Phone: (509) 323-4076
Fax: (509) 324-5730

Estimated # of Men's Soccer Scholarships: None
Conference: West Coast Conference
Program Profile: Year - round program with 20 fall matches, indoor training, and a spring season.
History: Our program began in 1989.
Achievements: 1997 Conference Co-Champs.
Coaching: Einar Thorarinsson, Head Coach. Dave Chattery - Assistant Coach.
Style of Play: Passing and quick counters.

Women's Athletic Profile

East 502 Boone Avenue
Spokane, WA 99258
Coach: Shannon Stiles
Email: Rgrennell@gonzaga.edu

NCAA I
Bulldogs/Zags/Blue, White, Red
Phone: (509) 328-4220
Fax: (509) 324-5787

Estimated # of Women's Soccer Scholarships: None
Conference: West Coast Conference
Program Profile: The playing season is fall on a natural grass field; stadium has 1,000 seated and 500 standing.
History: Team started in 1989. 1992-93 became a full-time varsity sport. 1993-94 became recognized member of West Coast Conference.

Achievements: All-League Honorable Mention
Style of Play: Depends on type of players we have at the time.

Northwest College
Academic Profile

P. O. Box 579
Kirkland, WA 98083-0579
Phone:

Type: 4 Yr.,Private,Liberal Arts
Founded: 1934
Website: http://www.nwcollege.edu
Religion: Assemblies of God
SAT/ACT/GPA: Open
Housing: Yes
Student/Faculty Ratio: 20:1
Male/Female Ratio: Not Avai
Undergraduate Enrollment: 800
Graduate Enrollment: N/A
Scholarships/Academic: Yes **Athletic:** Yes **Financial Aid:** Yes
Expenses by: Year **In State:** $ 12,500 **Out of State:**
Degrees Conferred: BA, AA
Programs of Study: Behavioral Sciences, Business, Interdisciplinary Studies, Teacher Education, Religion & Philosophy, Church Ministries

Men's Athletic Profile

5520 108th Ave. NE
Kirkland, WA 98083-0579
Coach: Dion Earl
Email: Not Available
NAIA
Eagles/Blue, Gold, White
Phone: (425) 889-4207
Fax: (425) 889-5823

Estimated # of Men's Soccer Scholarships: None
Conference: Cascade Conference
Program Profile: On campus grass practice facility; home games on astro-turf in 1,200 seat stadium.
History: Program has existed for 25 years. Completed first full year in the NAIA where all players are Christian.
Achievements: NCCAA West Regional Champions
Style of Play: We play possession soccer; we like attractive offensive - minded soccer with the purpose of creating goals.

Pacific Lutheran University
Academic Profile

Phone: (253) 535-7350
Tacoma, WA 98447

Type: 4 Yr.,Private,Liberal Arts
Founded: 1890
Website: http://www.plu.edu
Religion: Evangelical Lutheran
SAT/ACT/GPA: 1200/22
Housing: Yes
Student/Faculty Ratio: 16:1
Male/Female Ratio: 1:1.5
Undergraduate Enrollment: 3,000
Graduate Enrollment: 500
Scholarships/Academic: Yes **Athletic:** No **Financial Aid:** Yes
Expenses by: Year **In State:** $ 20,570 **Out of State:** $ 20,570
Specialty: Nursing, Business, Communications, Physical Education, Music
Degrees Conferred: BA, BS, BAE, BBA, BFA, BM, BME, BSN, BSPE
Programs of Study: Anthropology, Art, Biology, Chemistry, Chinese Studies, Classic, Communications, Computer Science, Earth Science, Economics, Education, English, French, German, Mathematics, Music, Philosophy, Physics, Political Science, Psychology, Religion, Social Work, Sociology, Accounting, Marketing, Management

Men's Athletic Profile

12180 Park Avenue
Tacoma, WA 98447
Coach: Joe Waters
Email: Not Available

NCAA III/NAIA
Lutes/Black, Gold
Phone: (206) 535-7495
Fax: (206 535-7584

Estimated # of Men's Soccer Scholarships: None
Conference: Northwest Conference of Independent Colleges
Program Profile: Playing season runs from September through early November. Grass field; travel to far away contest by van or bus. Mile Washington/Regional talent with an annual group of between 3-6 Scandinavian Student/Athletes.
History: National Tournament participant in 1992. Has a career record of 182-129-30 dating back to 1979.
Achievements: NAIA National Tournament Participant in 1992, Regional Qualified four times, two times champion, two 1st team All-Americans, one player currently in the Norwegian 1st Division.

Women's Athletic Profile

12180 Park Avenue
Tacoma, WA 98447
Coach: Sue Shinafelt Waters
Email: plusoccer@hotmail.com

NCAA III
Lutes/Black, Gold
Phone: (253) 535-7350
Fax: (253) 535-7584

Estimated # of Women's Soccer Scholarships: None
Conference: (NCIC) Northwest Conference of Independent Colleges
Program Profile: PLU plays on a natural grass field with portable bleachers for seating (no stadium). Practice late August and season Sept-early Nov.
History: Program began in 1981. Won 3 NAIA National Championship in 5 title match appearances, won 10 NCIC titles since 1981.
Achievements: NAIA National Title in 1988-89, 1991 (runner-up in 1990, 92), many conference titles, All-Americans, and former Coach Colleen Hacker is US National Team assistant Coach.
Coaching: Sue-Shinafelt Waters, Head Coach, high school experience, All-Conference player at Pacific Lutheran.
Roster in State: 11 **Out of State:** 8 **Out of Country:** 1
Walk-on/Other: **Graduation %:** 100 **Seniors on Team:** 4
Positions Needed: ALL
Camp or Clinic Dates: Not Available
Most Recent Record: 5-13-0

Seattle Pacific University

Academic Profile

Seattle, WA 98119
Phone: (206) 281-2941

Type: 4 Yr.,Private,Liberal Arts
Website: http://www.spu.edu
SAT/ACT/GPA: 1150/27/3.0
Student/Faculty Ratio: 17:1
Undergraduate Enrollment: 3,500
Scholarships/Academic: Yes **Athletic:** Yes
Expenses by: Year **In State:** $ 20,000
Specialty: Education, Business
Degrees Conferred: BA, BS, MA, Ph.D.

Founded: 1891
Religion: Protestant
Housing: Yes
Male/Female Ratio: 40:60
Graduate Enrollment: 1,500
Financial Aid: Yes
Out of State: $ 20,000

Programs of Study: Accounting, Arts, Biology, Business, Chemistry, Communications, Computer Science, Economics, Education, Engineering, English, Fine Arts, History, Liberal Arts, Mathematics, Music, Nursing, Philosophy, Physics, Political Science, Psychology, Religion, Science, Social Science, Theology

Men's Athletic Profile

3307 Third Avenue W
Seattle, WA 98119
Coach: Cliff McCrath
Email: cmccrath@spv.edu

NCAA II
Falcons/Maroon, White
Phone: (206) 281-2969
Fax: (206) 281-2266

Estimated # of Men's Soccer Scholarships: 6.0
Conference: Independent
Program Profile: Most successful program in Division II history with five NCAA championships. Has ten title game appearances and 25 play-off invitations. Extensive travel to all regions and home games played in new (1997) soccer-dedicated stadium with natural surface. Annually plays 2-3 games versus proven Division I programs. McCrath ranks #2 in collegiate coaching career wins, and the program regularly produces All-American and professional caliber players.
History: Three years after the program began in 1968, McCrath's team made the NCAA Tournament, and the Falcons have done so 24 of the last 26 years, making semi-final round in 1998. Falcon teams are very much representative of the local region, with the majority of players having graduated from high schools in western states. SPU has won NCAA Titles in 1978, 1983, 1985, 1986 and 1993.
Achievements: NCAA Champions in 1978, 1983, 1985, 1986 & 1993, playoffs Appearances in 1971-1981, 1983-1988, 1990-1998, McCrath National Coach of the Year in 1978, has 28 consecutive winning seasons, 16 All-Americans, 2 US National Team Selections, 36 formers players played in NASL, MISL, CISL, A-League or MLS.
Coaching: Cliff McCrath, Head Coach, ranks #2 in all time victories and has won NSCAA National Coach of the Year and Honors Awards, USSF "A" License. Chuck Seryra, & Bobby McLaughlin - Assistant Coaches.
Style of Play: Tough Defense, positive attack, great ball control and exciting to watch.

Women's Athletic Profile

3307 3rd Avenue W.
Seattle, WA 98119
Coach: TBD
Email: cmmcrath@spu.edu

NCAA II
Falcons/Maroon, White, Gold
Phone: (206) 281-2969
Fax: (206) 281-2266

Estimated # of Women's Soccer Scholarships: 2
Conference: PAC West
Program Profile: New program to begin play in Fall of 2001.

Seattle University
Academic Profile

Seattle, WA 98122

Phone: 206-296-6000

Type: 4 Yr.,Private,Liberal Arts,Engineering
Website: http://www.seattleu.edu
SAT/ACT/GPA: 1000/3.0
Student/Faculty Ratio: 13:1
Undergraduate Enrollment: 3,300
Scholarships/Academic: Yes **Athletic:** Yes
Expenses by: Year **In State:** $ 21,950
Degrees Conferred: BA, BS, MBA, MIT, Law School

Founded: 1891
Religion: Jesuit
Housing: Yes
Male/Female Ratio: 47:53
Graduate Enrollment: 1,000
Financial Aid: Yes
Out of State: $ 21,950

Programs of Study: Accounting, Arts, Bible Studies, Business, Chemistry, Communications, Computer Science, Dietetics, Economics, Education, Engineering, English, Fine Arts, Food Production & Science, History, Interdisciplinary Studies, Liberal Arts, Mathematics, Music, Nursing, Nutrition, Philosophy, Physical Fitness/Exercise Science, Physics, Political Science, Psychology, Recreation & Leisure, Religion, Science, Social Science, Special Education, Theatre, Theology

Men's Athletic Profile

Broadway & Madison
Seattle, WA 98122
Coach: Pete Fewing
Email: Not Available

NCAA III
Chieftains/Red, White
Phone: (206) 296-5498
Fax: (206) 296-2154

Estimated # of Men's Soccer Scholarships: 2,5 by 2002
Conference: Pacific Northwest Conference
Program Profile: The team plays in a nice grass with a measurements of 115x7. Has an average attendance of 400. Good fans, good atmosphere, and facility includes PA announcements, concession, etc..
History: Program began in 1967. Won National champions in 1997, Final Four in 1998, Regional Champions in 1997 & 1998, Regional Runner-Ups in 1996, 1995 & 1994. In the past three years has 10 All-Americans, 5 of them is 1st team, 8 Academic All-Americans; 5 players to senior bowl.
Achievements: Coach of the Year in 1997, Regional in 1991, 1997 & 1998, League Coach of the Year in 1991, 1997, & 1999. Tom Hardy was drafted #12 round by Kansas City.
Coaching: Peter Fewing, Head Coach, is entering his eleventh year as a head coach. Jeff Koch, Goalkeeper Coach, entering ten years with the program. Bill Colello, Assistant Coach, entering five years, alumni. Matt Potter, Assistant Coach, entering one with the program, alumni.
Style of Play: The team play a 4-4-2 attack via midfield; defenders get involved, possession, skillful organized.

Women's Athletic Profile

Broadway & Madison
Seattle, WA 98122
Coach: Julie Woodward
Email: Not Available

NCAA III
Cheiftains/Scarlet, White
Phone: (206) 296-5482
Fax: (206) 296-2154

Estimated # of Women's Soccer Scholarships: None
Conference: Northwest Conference of Independent Colleges
Program Profile: The home field is a natural grass.
History: The program began in 1985. Made NAIA Final Four in 1993.
Achievements: Numerous All-Americans

University of Puget Sound

Academic Profile

Phone: (253) 756-3412

Tacoma, WA 98416-0710

Type: 4 Yr.,Private,Liberal Arts
Website: http://www.ups.edu
SAT/ACT/GPA: 1000/3.0
Student/Faculty Ratio: 10:1
Undergraduate Enrollment: 2,800
Scholarships/Academic: Yes **Athletic:** No
Expenses by: Year **In State:** $ 25,000
Specialty: National Caliber Liberal Arts University

Founded: 1888
Religion: Non-Affiliated
Housing: Yes
Male/Female Ratio: .8:1
Graduate Enrollment: 100
Financial Aid: Yes
Out of State: $ 25,000

Degrees Conferred: BA, BS, MA, M.Ed
Programs of Study: Allied Health, Business & Management, Communications, Education, Letters & Literature, Life Sciences, Psychology, Social Sciences, Visual & Performing Arts

Men's Athletic Profile

1500 N Warner
Tacoma, WA 98416-0062
Coach: Reece Olney
Email: Not Available

NCAA III
Loggers/Green, Gold
Phone: 253-756-3586
Fax: 253-756-3634

Estimated # of Men's Soccer Scholarships: None
Conference: Northwest Conference
Program Profile: We have a separate training facility and game field. We do a twenty game season against top regional opponents to showcase and challenge players. Our home games are played at Baker Stadium, a natural grass pitch that is on campus and seats 3,000 spectators.
History: We began in 1985. We competed in the NAIA through 1998-1999. This will be our first year as NCAA III members. We had playoff appearances 2 of the last 3 years.
Achievements: 1998: 1 honorable mention All-American player; 1998: 1 All Region Pacific Northwest; 1998: 2 All-Conference 1st team, 1 2nd team player; 1998: 3 NSCAA All Region 2nd team Scholar Athletes
Coaching: Reece Olney, Head Coach, is a member of 1986 NCAA Division II National Championship team. He was an assistant coach at a four-year collegiate level. This is his second year at UPS with a record 19-19-2. Greg Ion, Assistant Coach, has 12 years as a professional player. He is a member of the 16 Canadian National Team. Adam White, Goalkeeper Coach, was All-Region Goalkeeper for 1992 and 1993.
Style of Play: Dependent on the talents available from each individual and determined yearly on what would be most successful for the team. Typically high level speed of play with 1 and 2 touch passing.

Women's Athletic Profile

1500 N Warner
Tacoma, WA 98416-0710
Coach: Randy Hanson
Email: Not Available

NCAA DIV III
Loggers/Green, Gold
Phone: (206) 756-3587
Fax: (206) 756-3634

Estimated # of Women's Soccer Scholarships: None
Conference: NCIC: National Conference of Independent Colleges
Program Profile: Play on campus on Baker Stadium which seats a 4,000 and has a natural grass pitch. Training facilities includes three fields; all natural grass and a state of the art weight training facility. Operational budget and athletic department support allows the program to strive forward with a goal of a national recognition.
History: Began in 1985 as a varsity program, NAIA National Appearances in 1985 and 1987.
Achievements: Four All-Conference members in 1996.
Coaching: Randy Hanson, Head Coach, entering fourth year, former player at University of Washington, ODP and State Instructional Staff Coach, Program Director of Premier Youth Soccer Club. Kelly Bendixen - Assistant and Goalkeeper Coach, former player at UPS. Katie Parks - Assistant Coach, NAIA All-American at UPS, former junior college coach.
Style of Play: Attacking - encourage attacking flair to organized sound defensive principles with ability to adapt to each opponent. Team's style of play will promote the strengths of its player.

University of Washington
Academic Profile

Phone: (206) 543-0432

Seattle, WA 98195-4080

Type: 4 Yr.,Public
Website: http://www.washington.edu

Founded: 1861
Religion: Non-Affiliated

SAT/ACT/GPA: NCAA Qualifier/3.6
Housing: Yes
Student/Faculty Ratio: 1:11
Male/Female Ratio: 50:50
Undergraduate Enrollment: 22,000
Graduate Enrollment: 13,000
Scholarships/Academic: Yes **Athletic:** Yes **Financial Aid:** Yes
Expenses by: Year **In State:** $ 11,500 **Out of State:** $ 19,500
Specialty: Social Sciences, Health Sciences, Engineering, Physical Science,
Degrees Conferred: BA, BS, BFA, MS, MA, MBA, MFA, Ph.D.
Programs of Study: Over 180 majors from which to chose.

Men's Athletic Profile

Box 355840
Seattle, WA 98195-5840
Coach: Dean Wurzberger
Email: askuwadm@washington.edu

NCAA I
Huskies/Purple, Gold
Phone: (206) 543-9686
Fax: (206) 685-1677

Estimated # of Men's Soccer Scholarships: None
Conference: Pacific Sports Federation, Pacific Ten Conference
Program Profile: The Husky Soccer Field holds 2,000, natural grass with a measurements of 72x118. Season begins September 1 and end mid-December including tournament finals.
History: Program began in 1968. Overall record is 356-125-59 which is .714 in winning percentage.
Achievements: 1992 MPSF Championship; 1996 Coach of the Year; drafted players by MLS were Jason Boyce, Joe Franchno, and Bill May.
Coaching: Dean Wurzberger, Head Coach. Nat Gonzalez - Full-time Assistant Coach, responsible for Goalkeeping. Jimmy Gabriel - Assistant Coach.
Style of Play: European midfield build-up with a South American Style around the goal area.

Women's Athletic Profile

Box 354080, Graves Annex
Seattle, WA 98195-5840
Coach: Lesle Gallimore
Email: lesleg@u.washington.edu

NCAA I
Huskies/Purple, Gold
Phone: (206) 685-3966
Fax: (206) 685-1677

Estimated # of Women's Soccer Scholarships: 4.5
Conference: Pacific 10 Conference
Program Profile: The Husky Soccer Field is natural grass with a measurement of 72x118; it is a permanent stadium with lights and seating capacity of 5,000 by year 2000. Play traditional season that starts August through December and non-traditional season from February through May.
History: Our program started in 1991 - 8 years old. Lesle Gallimore is the second head coach of the program. She took the team to the playoffs for four years.
Achievements: Lesle Gallimore was named 1994 West Coach of the Year; Katey Ward and Tara Bilanski were All-Americans. We have 2 current players on the US National Teams and one U-21 and one with a Full team.
Coaching: Lesle Gallimore, Head Coach. Amy Allman - Full-time Assistant Coach will do color commentary for NBC for 2000 Olympics in Sydney.
Roster in State: 14 **Out of State:** 11 **Out of Country:** 0
ODP State: 24 **Regional:** 16 **National:** 3
Walk-on/Other: 2 **Graduation %:** 98 **Seniors on Team:** 5
Positions Needed: Priority: I 1 Defender, 1-2 Forwards, 1 C. Mid
Camp or Clinic Dates: June 25-30, July 17-21
Most Recent Record: 8-8-2
Schedule: North Carolina, Brigham Young, UCLA, Stanford, USC, Portland, Nebraska, California, Northwestern, Arizona State
Style of Play: Organized team defense with skilled, ball-control possession. Emphasis on group attack, particularly from central midfield, outside back and forward combination.

Washington State University
Academic Profile

Pullman, WA 99164-0328
Phone: 509-335-3564

Type: 4 Yr.,Public
Website: http://www.wsu.edu/athletics
SAT/ACT/GPA: 700avg/17avg
Student/Faculty Ratio: 17:1
Undergraduate Enrollment: 16,000
Scholarships/Academic: Yes **Athletic:** Yes
Expenses by: Year **In State:** $ 7,900
Founded: 1890
Religion: Non-Affiliated
Housing: Yes
Male/Female Ratio: 53:47
Graduate Enrollment: 4,000
Financial Aid: Yes
Out of State: $ 13,000
Degrees Conferred: BA, BS, MA, MS, MBA
Programs of Study: Advertising, Animal, Anthropology, Banking/Finance, Biology, Chemistry, Communications, Computer, Criminal Justice, French, Geology, German, History, Horticulture, Hotel/Restaurant Management, Nursing, International, Parks/Recreation Management, PreProfessional Programs, Psychology, Pharmacy, Philosophy, Soil, Speech, Wildlife, Biology, Zoology

Women's Athletic Profile

PO Box 641602
Pullman, WA 99164-1602
Coach: Dan Tobias
Email: dan_tobias@wsu.edu
NCAA I
Cougars/Crimson, Grey
Phone: (509) 335-0306
Fax: (509) 335-5197

Estimated # of Women's Soccer Scholarships: 3
Conference: PAC-10
Program Profile: Top 25 Nationally and top 10 regionally in 2000. Member of the Pacific 10 Conference(rated #1 in the Nation). Soccer only Grass practice and game field (112x75 yards).
History: Program began in 1989. 1994 Earned spot in NCAA Playoffs. 1998 Best conference finish in school history (4-4-1). 2000 Earned spot in NCAA Playoffs;; best conference finish in school history (5-4-0).
Achievements: Academic All-American- Lindsey Jorgensen (99, 00). 1st team All-Pacific 10 Beka Dewitt (97-00). 2nd Team All-Pac 10, Lindsey Jorgenson (2000). 6 Honorable Mention All-Pac 10.
Coaching: Dan Tobias is 2 time Pac-10 Coach of the Year Nominee.
Roster in State: 13 **Out of State:** 6 **Out of Country:** 0
ODP State: 13 **Regional:** 4 **National:** 0
Walk-on/Other: 2 **Graduation %:** N/A **Seniors on Team:** 1
Positions Needed: Striker, Flanks
Camp or Clinic Dates: Not Available
Most Recent Record: 13-7-0
Schedule: UCLA, Washington, USC, Portland, Cal Berkeley, Stanford, Arizona State, Montana
Style of Play: Attacking, possession oriented.

Western Washington University
Academic Profile

Bellingham, WA 98225-6597
Phone: 360-650-3000

Type: 4 Yr.,Public,Liberal Arts
Website: http://www.wwu.edu
SAT/ACT/GPA: 1100
Student/Faculty Ratio: 21:1
Undergraduate Enrollment: 11,500
Founded: 1899
Religion: Non-Affiliated
Housing: Yes
Male/Female Ratio: 48:52
Graduate Enrollment: 750

Scholarships/Academic: Yes **Athletic:** Yes **Financial Aid:** Yes
Expenses by: Year **In State:** $ 10,325 **Out of State:** $ 16,508
Degrees Conferred: BA, BS, BFA, BM, MA, MS, MBA, M.Ed.
Programs of Study: Arts & Sciences, Business & Economics, Fine & Performing Arts, Environmental Studies, Education, Human Services, Liberal Arts

Men's Athletic Profile

516 High Street
Bellingham, WA 98225
Coach: Travis Connell and Todd Stauber
Email: todd.stauber@wwu.edu

NCAA II/NAIA
Vikings/Navy, White
Phone: (360) 650-3493
Fax: (360) 650-3495

Estimated # of Men's Soccer Scholarships: None
Conference: Pacific Northwest Athletic Conference
Program Profile: Became NCAA Division II in 1997-1998. Home field is Northwest Soccer Complex; grass field has a seating capacity of a 1,000. Field has a measurement of 120x70 yards, grass, and 65x110 astro turf practice facility. Varsity team has a physician and physiotherapy room. Full competitive season and Spring schedule include 20 annual in the Fall.
History: Began 1976, given varsity status in 1979.
Achievements: 6 Conference Titles, 1 Regional Championship, 18 previous All-Americans.
Style of Play: Possession style build-up with an emphasis on overlapping and switching the point of attack. Our style recognized all players involvement in the attack and defense. We believed in the individual skill development and functional training leading to the total player.

Women's Athletic Profile

516 High Street
Bellingham, WA 98225-9066
Coach: Derrek Falor
Email: cbfdrf@home

NCAA II
Vikings/Navy/White
Phone: (360) 650-6597
Fax: (360) 650-3495

Estimated # of Women's Soccer Scholarships: 5
Conference: Pacific West
Program Profile: Home field is Carver Field on campus with a seating capacity of 800. 110 x 70 grass playing surface. Team usually carries a playing roster of 22 players.
History: 1976 first year. 18 All-Americans throughout program history.
Coaching: Derek Falor is in his 6th year as Head Coach. Railene Thorsen is entering 2nd year as an assistant coach.
Roster in State: 22 **Out of State:** 4 **Out of Country:** 1
ODP State: 5 **Regional:** **National:**
Walk-on/Other: **Graduation %:** 99 **Seniors on Team:** 3
Positions Needed: Forward, outside midfield, goalkeeper
Camp or Clinic Dates: June 26-30, July 24-28
Most Recent Record: 9-9-2
Schedule: California Poly Pomona, Sonoma State, Univ. of California Davis, Seattle Univ, Idaho, Humboldt State, California State Dominguez
Style of Play: Possession with a focus on building out of the back. We believe in high pressure defense and inter changeable players and positions.

Whitman College
Academic Profile

Phone: (509) 521-5264

Walla Walla, WA 99362

Type: 4 Yr.,Private,Liberal Arts **Founded:** 1859
Website: http://www.whitman.edu **Religion:** Non-Affiliated

SAT/ACT/GPA: 1280/3.8
Student/Faculty Ratio: 10:1
Undergraduate Enrollment: 1,300
Scholarships/Academic: Yes **Athletic:** No
Expenses by: Year **In State:** $ 26,000+
Housing: Yes
Male/Female Ratio: 45:55
Graduate Enrollment: N/A
Financial Aid: Yes
Out of State: $ 26,000+
Specialty: Premed, Engineering, Economics, Art
Degrees Conferred: BA
Programs of Study: Anthropology, Asian Studies, Art, Biology, Chemistry, Computer Science, Dramatic Arts, Economics, English, Environmental Studies, Fine Arts, French, Geology, German, History, Mathematics, Music, Philosophy, Physics, Political Science, PreLaw, PreMed, Psychology, Social Science, Spanish, Theatre

Men's Athletic Profile

345 Boyer Avenue
Walla Walla, WA 99362
Coach: Mike Washington
Email: washingtonmj@whitman.edu
NCAA III
Missionaries/Blue, Yellow
Phone: (509) 527-5286
Fax: (509) 527-5960

Estimated # of Men's Soccer Scholarships: None
Conference: NWC
Program Profile: Our playing season is from September-November.
Coaching: Mike Washington, Head Coach, holds a USSF "A" License. He is a State and Regional Coach and an ODP State Coach.
Style of Play: Attacking and defending with numbers, high work rate, strong fitness base, 4-4-2 and 3-5-2 formation.

Women's Athletic Profile

345 Boyer Avenue
Walla Walla, WA 99362
Coach: Scott Shields
Email: shieldsp@whitman.edu
NCAA III/NAIA
Missionaries/Blue, Gold, White
Phone: (509) 527-5414
Fax: (509) 527-5960

Estimated # of Women's Soccer Scholarships: None
Conference: NWC
Program Profile: State of the Art weight room, new 3 field soccer complex.
One of the best programs in the conference, consistently finishing in the top four.
History: Program began in 1985.
Achievements: Coach of the Year - 1990, All-Americans
Coaching:
Roster in State: 10 **Out of State:** 14 **Out of Country:**
ODP State: 4 **Regional:** **National:**
Walk-on/Other: **Graduation %:** 100 **Seniors on Team:** 4
Positions Needed: Midfield, Forward
Camp or Clinic Dates: Not Available
Most Recent Record: 7-12
Style of Play: Controlled tempo, possession play.

Whitworth College

Academic Profile

Spokane, WA 99251
Phone:

Type: 4 Yr.,Private,Liberal Arts
Website: http://www.whitworth.edu
Founded: 1890
Religion: Presbyterian

SAT/ACT/GPA: 1160 avg.
Student/Faculty Ratio: 16.5:1
Undergraduate Enrollment: 1,500
Scholarships/Academic: Yes **Athletic:** Yes
Expenses by: Year **In State:** $ 19,824
Housing: Yes
Male/Female Ratio: 40:60
Graduate Enrollment: 300
Financial Aid: Yes
Out of State: $ 19,824
Degrees Conferred: BS, BA, M.Ed., MIT, MIM
Programs of Study: Accounting, Art, Liberal Studies, Biology, Business, Chemistry, Communications, Computer Science, Cross-Cultural Studies, Economics, Education, Engineering, English, French, History, Journalism, Math, Music, Philosophy, P.E., Physics, Political Studies, Psychology, Religion, Sociology, Spanish, Sports Medicine, Theatre

Men's Athletic Profile

Athletic Dept.
Spokane, WA 99251
Coach: Sean Bushey
Email: Not Available

NCAA III/NAIA
Pirates/Crimson, Black
Phone: (509) 466-1000x4385
Fax: (509) 466-3720

Estimated # of Men's Soccer Scholarships: None
Conference: Northwest Conference of Independent Colleges
Program Profile: An NAIA power, the team plays an exciting attacking style of soccer. All home games are played on grass in the Whitworth Pine Bowl, seats 1,500. NAIA men's soccer is a Fall sport.
History: Began in 1982 as an NAIA sport, conference titles and competed in NAIA District playoffs over 5 times.
Achievements: Steve Simmons was named 1995 NCIC Coach of the Year. Conference Players of the Year, and Honorable Mention All-Americans
Coaching: Head coach has USST 'A' License; has been on State & Regional ODP staffs; had successful USL coaching record; successful playing background
Roster In State: 14 **Out of State:** 18 **Out of Country:** 0
ODP State: 5-6 **Regional:** **National:**
Walk-on/Other: **Graduation %:** 95 **Seniors on Team:** 4
Positions Needed: Goalkeeper, Defenders, Midfielders, Forwards
Camp or Clinic Dates: Not Available
Most Recent Record: 9-8-2
Schedule: Willamette, University of Puget Sound, Pacific Lutheran, George Fox, Point Loma, MSU-Billings
Style of Play: Player have attacking freedom within the system of play.

Women's Athletic Profile

Athletic Dept.
Spokane, WA 99251
Coach: Sean Bushey
Email: Not Available

NCAA III/NAIA
Pirates/Crimson, Black
Phone: (509) 466-1000
Fax: (509) 466-3720

Estimated # of Women's Soccer Scholarships: None
Conference: Northwest Conference of Independent Colleges
Program Profile: The program is designed to allow student - athletes to pursue demanding academic tracks while still playing very competitive soccer. The training is functional in design, extensively using small - games to train all aspects of a players performance.
History: Soccer began as an official NAIA sport in 1989. Top 20 Nationally.
Achievements: Coach of the Year, All-Conference players, All-Americans
Style of Play: Team play is adaptable depending on an opponent. The team is effective at a quick counter attack, long through ball game to a tight highly controlled game. Common in Whitworth's style is a high pressure, hard tackling, team that is well organized and disciplined in its play.

west virginia

WEST VIRGINIA

SCHOOL	CITY	AFFILIATION	PAGE
Alderson - Broaddus College	Philippi	NCAA II	1192
Bethany College	Bethany	NCAA III	1192
Concord College	Athens	NCAA II	1193
Davis and Elkins College	Elkins	NCAA II	1195
Marshall University	Huntington	NCAA I	1195
Salem - Teikyo University	Salem	NCAA II	1196
Shepherd College	Shepherdstown	NCAA II	1197
University of Charleston	Charleston	NCAA II	1198
West Virginia University	Morgantown	NCAA I	1199
West Virginia Wesleyan College	Buckhannon	NCAA II	1200
Wheeling Jesuit College	Wheeling	NCAA II	1202

Alderson - Broaddus College

Academic Profile

Phone:

Philippi, WV 26416

Type: 4 Yr.,Private,Liberal Arts
Website: http://www.blue.ab.edu
SAT/ACT/GPA: 820/17
Student/Faculty Ratio: 13:1
Undergraduate Enrollment: 760
Scholarships/Academic: Yes **Athletic:** Yes
Expenses by: Year **In State:** $ 16,316
Founded: 1871
Religion: American Baptist
Housing: Yes
Male/Female Ratio: 40:60
Graduate Enrollment: 40
Financial Aid: Yes
Out of State: $ 16,316
Degrees Conferred: Associate, Bachelors
Programs of Study: Accounting, Applied Music, Biology, Business Administration, Christian Studies, Church Music, Communications, Computer Science, General Science, Education, Social Studies, Medical Technology, Environmental Science, History, Liberal Arts, Literature, Languages Art, Mathematics, Music Education, Political Science, Psychology, Nursing, Radiography, Secondary Education, Elementary Education, Biology, Chemistry, Physical Education, Sociology, Speech Communications, Business, General Studies, Natural Science, Sport Medicine, Writing, Theatre

Men's Athletic Profile

College Hill Road
Philippi, WV 26416
Coach: Dan Kelly
Email: Not Available
NCAA II
Battlers/Blue, White, Gold
Phone: (304) 457-6263
Fax: (304) 457-6239

Estimated # of Men's Soccer Scholarships: None
Conference: West Virginia Intercollegiate Athletic Conference
Program Profile: Beautiful natural grass field with a measurements of 120x80 yards, surrounded by hills. Vocal student body, 20-game Fall season, never missed playoffs. Nationally competitive.
History: Played in the National tournament in 1968, 1981, 1983, 7 1991; National Finalist in 1981 & 1991.
Achievements: 1994 All-Americans, Gary McCulloch and Academic All-Americans - Theo Stoev and Steve Free.
Style of Play: An attacking style emphasizing inter-play with a short passes. Defensively, play both high and low pressure, combination of zonal and man to man marking.

Bethany College

Academic Profile

Phone: (304) 829-7632

Bethany, WV 26032

Type: 4 Yr.,Private,Liberal Arts
Website: http://www.bethanywvnet.edu
SAT/ACT/GPA: 1000/23/2.8
Student/Faculty Ratio: 12:1
Undergraduate Enrollment: 800
Scholarships/Academic: Yes **Athletic:** No
Expenses by: Year **In State:** $ 24,696
Founded: 1840
Religion: Disciples of Christ
Housing: Yes
Male/Female Ratio: 55:45
Graduate Enrollment: 1-12
Financial Aid: Yes
Out of State: $ 24,696
Specialty: Communications, Education, Liberal, Physical Ed., PreLaw, PreMed
Degrees Conferred: BA, BS
Programs of Study: Biology, Business & Management, Chemistry, Communications, Computer Science, Economics, Education, Engineering, Environmental Science, Fine Arts, French, German, History, Journalism, Languages, Life Sciences, Mathematics, Philosophy, Physical Education, Physics, Political Science, PreDentistry, PreLaw, PreMed, Psychology, Public Administration, Religious Studies, Social Work, Sociology, Spanish, Sport Management

Men's Athletic Profile

201 Cramblet Hall
Bethany, WV 26032
Coach: John Cunningham
Email: j.cunningham@mail.bethany.wv.edu

NCAA III
Bison/Green, White
Phone: (304) 829-7632
Fax: (304) 829-7788

Estimated # of Men's Soccer Scholarships: None
Conference: President's Athletic Conference, ECAC
Program Profile: We have an excellent facilities Hoag Field has a sprinkler and drainage, 4 practice fields, a $ 4 million recreation center, a weight room and indoor facility and track.
History: Our Bethany Program began in 1969 - never had a losing season. We have 14 NCAA Tournament Appearances since 1980, a National Championship in 1994, National Finalist in 1982 and 27 Conference Championships.
Achievements: The program has 10 times Coach of the Year Awards; 27 Conference Titles; 50+ All-Americans, Dapper Dan Special Achievement Award.
Coaching: John Cunningham, Head Coach, has 31 years of soccer experience at collegiate level, traveled to Europe and holds a USSF and NSCAA. Frankie Taal, Assistant Coach, is experienced and excellent with players.
Style of Play: Possession with dynamic tactics and encouragement of individuality of players. Fitness and skill development are important. A combination of "Dutch", Germany and English Soccer.

Women's Athletic Profile

Hummel Memorial Fieldhouse
Bethany, WV 26032
Coach: Robert Clune
Email: rclune@mail.bethanywv.edu

NCAA III
Bison/Green, White
Phone: (304) 829-7269
Fax: (304) 829-7290

Estimated # of Women's Soccer Scholarships: None
Conference: President's Athletic Conference
Program Profile: Hoag Soccer Complex is rated best in the area; has a natural grass surface that seats 1,000 plus and is used for many NCAA playoffs.
History: Program began in 1987.
Achievements: PAC Conference Winners in 1992 & 1992. Produced 4 time conference Player of the Year.
Coaching: Robert Clune, Head Coach.
Roster in State: 3 **Out of State:** 17 **Out of Country:** 1
Walk-on/Other: **Graduation %:** 100 **Seniors on Team:** 3
Positions Needed: Forwards, Midfield
Camp or Clinic Dates: Not Available
Most Recent Record: 7-13-0
Schedule: Grove City, Westminster College, LaRoche College
Style of Play: Aggressive with a control, push the ball forward from the back.

Concord College
Academic Profile

Athens, WV 24712
Phone: (304) 384-5342

Type: 4 Yr.,Public,Liberal Arts
Website: http://www.concord.wvnet.edu
SAT/ACT/GPA: 820/17/2.0
Student/Faculty Ratio: 12:1
Undergraduate Enrollment: 2,700

Founded: 1871
Religion: Non-Affiliated
Housing: Yes
Male/Female Ratio: 2:1
Graduate Enrollment: N/A

Scholarships/Academic: Yes **Athletic:** Yes **Financial Aid:** Yes
Expenses by: Year **In State:** $ 6,238 **Out of State:** $ 9,103
Specialty: Education, Business, Social Work, Travel Management
Degrees Conferred: BS, BA, AA
Programs of Study: Business, Broadcasting, PreMed, Biology, Teacher Education, Psychology, Accounting, Communications, Travel Industry Management, Advertising & Graphic Design, Sport Management, Commercial Art, Marketing, Sciences

Men's Athletic Profile

P.O. Box 1000
Athens, WV 24712
Coach: Steve Barrett
Email: barretts@concord.edu

NCAA II
Mountain Lions/Maroon, Gray
Phone: (304) 384-5131
Fax: (304) 384-5117

Estimated # of Men's Soccer Scholarships: 4
Conference: WVIAC
Program Profile: Team plays on natural grass 110 x 75.
History: Program is 3 years old, started in 1998. Program is on verge with competing for conference championship.
Achievements: 2 All- Region.
Coaching: Steve Barrett, Head Coach, entering his 9th year of college coaching (95-82-5).
Roster In State: 4 **Out of State:** 10 **Out of Country:** 3
ODP State: 2 **Regional:** 2 **National:**
Walk-on/Other: **Graduation %:** N/A **Seniors on Team:** 1
Positions Needed: All Positions
Camp or Clinic Dates: July 10-14th
Most Recent Record: 4-14
Schedule: University of Charleston, West VA Wesleyan, Wheeling Jesuit, Tusculum, Longwood
Style of Play: Direct with high pressure defending.

Women's Athletic Profile

1000 Vermillion St.-Campus Box 77
Athens, WV 24712
Coach: Steve Barrett
Email: barrett@concord.edu

NCAA II
Mountain Lions/Maroon, Grey
Phone: (304) 384-5131
Fax: (304) 384-5117

Estimated # of Women's Soccer Scholarships: 4
Conference: WVIAC
Program Profile: We play on natural grass surface with bleachers in place.
History: Our program started in 1997 and is now looking to recruit heavily.
Achievements: We have had 1 All-Region player. We won 1st play-off game in 1999.
Coaching: Steve Barrett is our Head Coach. He came from England and has a nine years college coaching experience and will wins 100th game in 2000 season.
Roster in State: 10 **Out of State:** 4 **Out of Country:** 2
ODP State: 1 **Regional:** 0 **National:** 0
Positions Needed: All positions
Camp or Clinic Dates: July 13th - 17th, 2000
Most Recent Record: 2-12-0
Schedule: Ashland University, Wheeling Jesuit, West Virginia Wesleyan, Longwood, Tusculum, Limestone, Newberry
Style of Play: Direct style; mixing of high and low pressure defending.

Davis and Elkins College
Academic Profile

Phone: 304-637-1260

Elkins, WV 26241

Type: 4 Yr.,Private,Liberal Arts
Founded: 1904
Website: http://www.dne.wvnet.edu
Religion: Presbyterian
SAT/ACT/GPA: 820/18
Housing: Yes
Student/Faculty Ratio: 15:1
Male/Female Ratio: 50:50
Undergraduate Enrollment: 1,200
Graduate Enrollment: N/A
Scholarships/Academic: Yes **Athletic:** Yes **Financial Aid:** Yes
Expenses by: Year **In State:** $ 17,500 **Out of State:** $ 17,500
Specialty: Environmental Sciences, Business, Fine Arts
Degrees Conferred: AB, BS
Programs of Study: Arts, Fine Art, Biology, Environmental Science, Chemistry, Computer Science, Education, Nursing, Business Administration, Accounting, Management, Marketing, Communications, Political Science, Religion, Philosophy, Social Science, History, PreLaw, PreMed

Men's Athletic Profile

100 Sycamore St.
Elkins, WV 26241
Coach: Mark Stollesteimer
Email: Not Available

NCAA II
Senators/Red, White, Black
Phone: (304) 637-1388
Fax: (304) 637-1414

Estimated # of Men's Soccer Scholarships: None
Conference: West Virginia Intercollegiate Athletic Conference
Program Profile: Davis and Elkins College plays a regular Fall season on their home field of natural grass.
History: NAIA National Champs (1968 & 1970); National Tournament (1969, 1971, 1972, 1973, 1974, 1976, 1977, 1978 & 1980); NCAA Division II National Tournament (1983, 1984, 1985 & 1986).
Achievements: NAIA National Champions in 1968 & 1970.
Coaching: Mark Stollesteimer, Head Coach, first season was in 1996, former assistant at Davis and Elkins, played collegiate at University of Richmond.
Style of Play: Attacking with a freedom to create possession.

Marshall University
Academic Profile

Phone: (304)696-5408

Huntington, WV 25715

Type: 4 Yr.,Public
Founded: 1837
Website: http://www.herdzone.com
Religion: Non-Affiliated
SAT/ACT/GPA: 910192.0
Housing: Yes
Student/Faculty Ratio: 18:1
Male/Female Ratio: 45:55
Undergraduate Enrollment: 12,000
Graduate Enrollment: 4,000
Scholarships/Academic: Yes **Athletic:** Yes **Financial Aid:** Yes
Expenses by: Year **In State:** $10,000 **Out of State:** $14,000
Specialty: Liberal Arts
Degrees Conferred: AA, AAS, BA, BS, BFA, MA, MS, MBA
Programs of Study: Accounting, Arts, Athletic Training, Biological Science, Business, Chemistry, Communications, Dietetics, Exercise Science, Fine Arts, Finance, Forensic Science, Journalism, Labor Relations, Management, Marketing, Nursing, PreMed, Park Resources, Pathology, Public Relations, Speech.

Men's Athletic Profile

P.O. Box 1360
Huntington, WV 25715
Coach: Bob Gray
Email: martinez@marshall.edu

NCAA I
Thundering Herd/K Green,White
Phone: (304) 696-4569
Fax: (304) 696-2325

Estimated # of Men's Soccer Scholarships: 8
Conference: Mid-American Conference
Program Profile: NCAA Division I with a new stadium opened in 1996 season (natural turf with a capacity of 1,000). Marshall plays on a brand new soccer facility that boast a Bermuda grass surface. Practice field is adjacent to the playing field which is also grass. Our playing season runs from late August through the beginning of November.
History: Our program was started in 1979 in the Southern Conference and then changed to the MAC in 1997; Marshall has had a soccer program for twenty years.
Achievements: Bob Gray just recently inducted into the Hall of Fame; Tommy Greenwalt (Senior) 2nd team was named All-Region; players drafted into "A" League were Tommy Greenwalt (Lehigh Valley Storm); Hugo La Reservee and David Husband by Pittsburgh Riverhounds.
Coaching: Bob Gray, Head Coach, began coaching in 1977. He holds USSF "A" License and has recently been inducted into the NAIA Hall of Fame. Marty Martinez and Lawrence Fine - Assistant Coaches.
Style of Play: Controlled play starting with fall backs (playing around the back to find open inside or outside midfielders). Sometimes look for a target player up front!

Women's Athletic Profile

P.O. Box 1360
Huntington, WV 25715-1360
Coach: Teresa Patterson
Email: patterson@marshall.edu

NCAA I
Thundering Herd/Green, White
Phone: (304) 696-6388
Fax: (304) 696-2325

Estimated # of Women's Soccer Scholarships: 12
Conference: Mid-American Conference
Program Profile: Member of NCAA division I with a new lighted stadium opened in 1996. It is natural turf with a capacity of 1,000. Marshall plays in a brand new soccer stadium that boast a Bermuda grass surface. Practice field is also Bermuda grass and is adjacent to the game.
History: The program began in 1998.
Coaching: Teresa Patterson - Head Coach. Lawrence Fine and Liz Woodrow are Assistant Coaches.
Walk-on/Other: **Graduation %:** 98 **Seniors on Team:** 1
Positions Needed: Keeper, Forward, Outside Mids
Camp or Clinic Dates: Call for information
Most Recent Record: 8-10-1
Schedule: Kentucky, Xavier, Miami(OH)
Style of Play: Play a creative ball possession oriented team with an emphasis on disciplined team defending.

Salem - Teikyo University

Academic Profile

Salem, WV 26426

Phone: (304) 782-5252

Type: 4 Yr.,Private,Liberal Arts
Website: http://www.stulib.salem-teikyo.wvnet.edu
SAT/ACT/GPA: 17/2.0
Student/Faculty Ratio: 12:1
Undergraduate Enrollment: 650

Founded: 1888
Religion: Non-Affiliated
Housing: Yes
Male/Female Ratio: 60:40
Graduate Enrollment: 50

Scholarships/Academic: Yes **Athletic:** Yes **Financial Aid:** Yes
Expenses by: Year **In State:** $ 17,049 **Out of State:** $ 17,049
Specialty: International Business
Degrees Conferred: AA, AS, BA, AAS, BS, MA
Programs of Study: Accounting, Aeronautical Science, Airline Piloting Navigation, Biology, Equestrian Science, Broadcasting, Business Administration, Communications, Computer Science, Criminal Justice, Elementary Education, Engineering Technology, Industrial Engineering, Management, Marketing, Mathematics, Medical Laboratory Technology, Secondary Education

Men's Athletic Profile

223 W Main Street
Salem, WV 26426
Coach: Scott Fisher
Email: sfis792706@aol.com

NCAA II
Tigers/Forest, White, Black
Phone: (304) 782-5252
Fax: (304) 782-5516

Estimated # of Men's Soccer Scholarships: Yes
Conference: WVIAC
Program Profile: Has an on site locker room. Play on field that has a measurements of 74x115 natural grass and has a practice field also. Stadium has a seating capacity of 1,800.
History: Our program began in 1990.
Coaching: Scott M. Fischer, Head Coach. Steve Steel, Assistant Coach.
Style of Play: Indirect but will play whatever style best suits to the present team.

Shepherd College

Academic Profile

Shepherdstown, WV 25443

Phone:

Type: 4 Yr.,Public,Liberal Arts
Website: http://www.shepherd.wvnet.edu
SAT/ACT/GPA: 900/17/2.0
Student/Faculty Ratio: 15:1
Undergraduate Enrollment: 4,500
Founded: 1871
Religion: Non-Affiliated
Housing: Yes
Male/Female Ratio: 60:40
Graduate Enrollment: N/A
Scholarships/Academic: Yes **Athletic:** Yes **Financial Aid:** Yes
Expenses by: Year **In State:** $ 6,800 **Out of State:** $ 9,900
Degrees Conferred: AA, AS, AAS, BA, BS, BFA
Programs of Study: All located on wed page over 60 degrees offered.

Men's Athletic Profile

Butcher Athletic Ctr
Shepherdstown, WV 25443
Coach: Joseph Okoh
Email: jokoh@shepherd.edu

NCAA II
Rams/Blue, Gold
Phone: (304) 876-5481
Fax: (304) 876-3267

Estimated # of Men's Soccer Scholarships: None
Conference: West Virginia Intercollegiate Athletic Conference
Program Profile: The Rams Stadium is a natural grass that seats 2,000. Has a grass practice facility which is one mile off-campus. The off-season is indoor and spring schedule.

History: Our program is twelve years old; has five winning seasons out of past six years. Plays highly competitive Division II schedule.
Achievements: Several All-Conference players. Chris Doran All-Region selection. Mike Doran WVIAC Coach of the Year.
Style of Play: Based on player's strength; like to attack in numbers and defend as a unit.

Women's Athletic Profile

James Butcher Center
Shepherdstown, WV 25443-3210
Coach: Jen Wood
Email: jstorey@shepherd.edu

NCAA II
Rams/Blue, Gold, White
Phone: (304) 876-5144
Fax: (304) 876-3267

Estimated # of Women's Soccer Scholarships: None
Conference: West Virginia Intercollegiate Athletic Conference
Program Profile: Has 4,000-seat arena, full training facility, new program in the year 2000.
History: Will be a varsity team in the year 2000.
Achievements: New program.
Coaching: Jen Storey - Head Coach. Sue Bohrer is Assistant Coach.

University of Charleston

Academic Profile

Phone: 304-357-4800

Charleston, WV 25304

Type: 4 Yr.,Private,Liberal Arts
Website: http://www.uchaswv.edu
SAT/ACT/GPA: 820/18
Student/Faculty Ratio: 14:1
Undergraduate Enrollment: 1,500
Scholarships/Academic: Yes
Athletic: Yes
Expenses by: Year
In State: $ 16,000
Founded: 1888
Religion: Non-Affiliated
Housing: Yes
Male/Female Ratio: 1:3
Graduate Enrollment: 100
Financial Aid: Yes
Out of State: $ 16,000
Degrees Conferred: AA, AS, BA, BS, MBA, MHRM
Programs of Study: Art, Biology, Chemistry, Education, English, Environmental Science, History, Mathematics, Music, Mass Communication, Political Science, Psychology, Social Science, Sports Science, Sports Medicine, Paralegal Studies, Accounting, Business Administration, Computer Information Systems, Nursing, Radiology, PreProfessional

Men's Athletic Profile

2300 McCorkle Avenue, SE
Charleston, WV 25304
Coach: Marty Martinez
Email: Not Available

NCAA II
Golden Eagles/Maroon, Gold
Phone: (304) 357-4899
Fax: (304) 357-4989

Estimated # of Men's Soccer Scholarships: 6.5
Conference: West Virginia Intercollegiate Athletic Conference
Program Profile: Strong program in Division II conference; 17-2-1 record din 1996; has a great tradition. Very strong schedule; play on 115x75 yards natural grass enclosed field with a seating for 900. Field is lighted; soccer is main spectator sport in the fall semester - no football program!
History: Our program began in 1968. Previously member of NAIA, went NCAA Division II in 1995; two conference championships in the 90's; numerous All-Region and All-America selections; 1996 was most successful season in history of the program, despite playing its strongest schedule ever.

Achievements: 1991 Coach of the Year; 8 all-Americans; 11 Academic All-Americans; 3 Senior Bowl Appearances; 1993 Conference Player of the Year; 2 Conference Championships in four years; third in nation and first in region in 1996. Finalist in Conference in 2000.
Coaching: Marty Martinez Head Coach- assistant coach at Marhall University, USSF " A" License.
Roster In State: 4 **Out of State:** 2 **Out of Country:** 12
ODP State: 5 **Regional:** 0 **National:** 0
Walk-on/Other: 0 **Graduation %:** 74 **Seniors on Team:** 3
Positions Needed: ALL
Camp or Clinic Dates: June 11-15, July 16-20
Most Recent Record: 14-6-1
Schedule: WVU, Marshall University, Wheeling Jesuit College, Francis Marion Univ.
Style of Play: Pass and move controlled soccer.

Women's Athletic Profile

2300 MacCorkle Ave., SE
Charleston, WV 25304
Coach: Karen Pauley
Email: Not Available

NCAA II
Golden Eagles/Maroon, Gold
Phone: (304) 357-4819
Fax: (843) 953-8296

Estimated # of Women's Soccer Scholarships: None
Conference: WVIAC
Program Profile: Young program, improving each year. Play a very strong schedule. The program has grown with each recruiting class.
History: Program began in 1988. Has only had two coaches.
Achievements: Beth Converse - 1990 NAIA All-American Scholar Athlete; Mar Ann Arthur, Laura Lassman, Carrie Lutz were 1991 NAIA All-American Scholar Athletes; Andrea Griffith in 1993, 1994 NAIA All-American Scholar Athlete; Kasey Kruer - 1994 NAIA All-American Scholar Athlete; Staci LaPorte - 1994 NSCAA All-American second team.
Coaching: Karen Pauley, Head Coach, Masters in Physical Education, and Reading Education, Masters in Counseling.
Style of Play: We play aggressive defense, keep the score low.

West Virginia University

Academic Profile

Morgantown, WV 26507
Phone: (304) 293-4811

Type: 4 Yr.,Public,Engineering **Founded:** 1867
Website: http://www.wvu.edu **Religion:** Non-Affiliated
SAT/ACT/GPA: 950/20/2.25 **Housing:** Yes
Student/Faculty Ratio: 16:1 **Male/Female Ratio:** 2:1
Undergraduate Enrollment: 14,000 **Graduate Enrollment:** 9,000
Scholarships/Academic: Yes **Athletic:** Yes **Financial Aid:** Yes
Expenses by: Year **In State:** $ 7,714 **Out of State:** $ 12,898
Specialty: Health & Sciences, Physical Therapy, Education, Business, Engineering
Degrees Conferred: 166 Degrees
Programs of Study: College of Agriculture, Forestry Consumer Sciences, College of Business & Economics, College of Creative Arts, School of Dentistry, Arts & Sciences, Engineering, School of Medicine, Human Resources & Education, School of Journalism, Law, Nursing, Pharmacy, Physical Education, Social Work

Men's Athletic Profile

P.O. Box 807
Morgantown, WV 26507
Coach: Paul Marco
Email: pmarco@wvu.edu

NCAA I
Mountaineers/Blue, Gold
Phone: (304) 293-2300x548
Fax: (304) 293-2825

Estimated # of Men's Soccer Scholarships: 3-4
Conference: Big East Conference
Program Profile: We have a two-year old grass program stadium that measures 75x120 with adjoining training field. The stadium has lights and seats about 2,000. We have a brand new indoor training facility that measures 95x65 turf and a state-of-the-art weight room, with separate strength and conditioning staff. We have a traditional fall season. Out of season training is maximum NCAA allows.
History: Our program began in 1961; six NCAA Tournament Appearances; third in Big East Conference; 1998 Big East Tournament Quarterfinals.
Achievements: 10 former All-Americans; 19 All-Region players; 8 players currently playing professionally; 1992 Atlantic 10 Champions; 1998 big East Tournament Quarterfinals.
Coaching: Paul Marco, Head Coach, is entering his third season. He is on the NSCAA National Staff and has a NSCAA Advanced National Diploma. He is Director of Coaching at West Virginia and ODP Region I Staff. Chris Barrett, Assistant Coach, is entering his first year. He is the goalkeeper trainer, has a NSCAA Advanced National Diploma and is on the West Virginia ODP Staff.
Style of Play: Possession oriented, attacking style. Zonal defending with emphasis on transition into the attack.

Women's Athletic Profile

P.O. Box 0877
Morgantown, WV 26505
Coach: Nikki Izzo-Brown
Email: nizzo@wvo.edu

NCAA I
Mountaineers/Gold, Blue
Phone: (304) 293-2300
Fax: (304) 293-2525

Estimated # of Women's Soccer Scholarships: N/A
Conference: Big East Conference
Program Profile: The women's varsity program began in 1996 season. New grass soccer facility with an indoor complex astro turf. It is a full-sized soccer field with lights. We also have a lighted practice field. We are regionally ranked. We play a fall season and year round.
History: Our varsity program started in 1996. We finished fifth in the Big East out of 12 teams.
Achievements: Stacy Sollmann was All Big East Rookie team 1996, 1997,1998; Stacy Sollman was All Regional 1997; Vanessa Meppler was All Big East Rookie team in 1997; Katie Barnes was All Big East Rookie team 1998.
Coaching: Nicole Izzo, Head Coach, was an All-American in college. He has an Advanced National Diploma. He was Director of ODP in West Virginia and a West Virginia staff member. Jenn DePrez is assistant coach.

West Virginia Wesleyan College

Academic Profile

Buckhannon, WV 26201

Phone:

Type: 4 Yr.,Private,Liberal Arts
Website: http://www.wvwc.edu
SAT/ACT/GPA: 820/20/2.5
Student/Faculty Ratio: 15:1
Undergraduate Enrollment: 1,600
Founded: 1891
Religion: Methodist
Housing: Yes
Male/Female Ratio: 45:55
Graduate Enrollment: 100
Scholarships/Academic: Yes **Athletic:** Yes **Financial Aid:** Yes
Expenses by: Year **In State:** $ 21,225 **Out of State:** $ 21,225
Specialty: Liberal Arts, Business, Biology, Chemistry, Computer Information Sys.
Degrees Conferred: BA, MS, MBA
Programs of Study: Art, Accounting, Biology, Business Administration, Chemistry, Computer Information Systems, Computer Science, Communications Studies, Christian Education, Dramatic Arts, Economics, Education, English, Engineering, Physics, Environmental Science, Finance, History, International Studies, Management, Marketing, Mathematics, Music, Physical Education, Sports Medicine, Philosophy, Physics, Political Science, Psychology, Public Relations, Religion, Sociology, Nursing

Men's Athletic Profile

Box 1775 59 College Ave
Buchannon, WV 26201
Coach: Gavin Donaldson
Email: donaldson@wvwc.edu

NCAA II
Bobcats/Black, Orange
Phone: (304) 473-8195
Fax: (304) 473-8056

Estimated # of Men's Soccer Scholarships: Varies
Conference: WVIAC
Program Profile: We are a perennial Top 20 team. We play home games at Wood St. Soccer Complex which is 120x80 yards natural grass surface. Practice areas include full size grass field and indoor turf facility.
History: Our program began in 1961; 5 NAIA National Championships in 1984, 1985, 1990 & 1994; NCAA !! post-season last two years; 1997 ranked 7th in Final Poll.
Achievements: The program produced 5 NAIA National Championships in 1989, 1989, 1990, 1984, 1985 & 1994; 16 WVIAC Conference Championships including the last five years; 20 All-Americans, several All-South Atlantic Selections, several All-Conference Selections, WVIAC Coach of the Year in 1994, 1992 & 1997, NAIA NSCAA Coach of the Year in 1994.
Coaching: Gavin Donaldson is Head Coach. Jeff Cook, Assistant Coach, was named two-time National Championship winner, NAIA All-American; All-South Atlantic, All-Conference, Senior Bowl Participation and All-East team.
Style of Play: Generally, a physical, hard working mix of European and South American Play. Possession and attacking plays are emphasized.

Women's Athletic Profile

Box 1775 59 College Ave
Buckhannon, WV 26201
Coach: Anthony James
Email: james_a@wvwc.edu

NCAA II
Bobcats/Orange, Black
Phone: (304) 473-8101
Fax: (304) 473-5086

Estimated # of Women's Soccer Scholarships: 2
Conference: West Virginia Intercollegiate Athletic Conference
Program Profile: WVWC possesses a grass surface with bleachers to one side. We just completed a brand new practice surface for our student athletes. We play in the fall with a schedule of almost 23 games.
History: Our program has been in existence almost 10 years during that time, we have won approx. 130 games.
Achievements: We have also won 3 of the 4 conference titles, which have been played sine 1997. During that time we have produced numerous All-Americans both on the regional and national level. Our programs highlight was playing for the national championship in 1997 and receiving our highest national Ranking (2nd in the Country).
Coaching: Anthony James Head Women's Soccer Coach, we are presently performing a national search for an assistant.

Roster in State: 3	**Out of State:** 15	**Out of Country:** 2
ODP State: 4	**Regional:** 1	**National:** 0
Walk-on/Other: 0	**Graduation %:** 95	**Seniors on Team:** 8

Positions Needed: Defenders, Midfield
Camp or Clinic Dates: July 29- August 2
Most Recent Record: 14-9-0
Schedule: Northern Kentucky Univ. Lockhaven Univ. Mercyhurst Univ. Ashland Univ. Wheeling Jesuit Univ. Gannon Univ.
Style of Play: We rotate between 3-5-2 and 3-4-3. At the same time we emphasize a possession type game. It is a system built on speed. We encourage our players take on their opponents whenever, the opportunity presents itself.

Wheeling Jesuit College

Academic Profile

Phone: (304) 243-2365

Wheeling, WV 26003

Type: 4 Yr.,Private,Liberal Arts
Founded: 1954
Website: http://www.wju.edu
Religion: Catholic
SAT/ACT/GPA: 830/17/2.0
Housing: Yes
Student/Faculty Ratio: 12:1
Male/Female Ratio: 1:1.6
Undergraduate Enrollment: 1,329
Graduate Enrollment: 201
Scholarships/Academic: Yes **Athletic:** Yes **Financial Aid:** Yes
Expenses by: Year **In State:** $ 20,200 **Out of State:** $ 20,200
Specialty: Health Sciences, Business, Hi-Tech
Degrees Conferred: BS, BA, MS, MBA, MAAT
Programs of Study: Accounting, Biology, Chemistry, Computer Science, Criminal Justice, Engineering, Environmental Studies, French, History, International Business, Philosophy, Literature, Management, Marketing, Mathematics, Nuclear Medical Technology, Nursing, Physics, Political & Economic Philosophy, Political Science, Professional Writing, Psychology, Respiratory Therapy, Romance, Languages, Spanish, Teacher Prep, Technical Innovation, Theology & Religious Studies, Sports Management, PreMed, PreLaw, PreVeterinary, PreDental, PrePhysical Therapy, Master Degree Programs in Accountancy, Business Administration, Nursing, Applied Theology

Men's Athletic Profile

316 Washington Avenue
Wheeling, IL 26003
Coach: Jim Regan
Email: Jregan@wju.edu

NCAA II
Cardinals/Red, White
Phone: (304) 243-2365
Fax: (304) 243-2265

Estimated # of Men's Soccer Scholarships: 4
Conference: West Virginia Intercollegiate Athletic Conference
Program Profile: We play on a natural grass stadium field that measures 75x115 and has a lights, a 2,000 bleacher seats with press box and two practice fields.
History: Our program began in 1972. We are a consistent Division II Top 20 and produce All-Americans annually.
Achievements: Produced numerous All-Americans and Coach Jim Regan has been named Coach of the Year numerous times. Undefeated in regular season 18-0-0, NCAA D. II quarter-finalist.
Coaching: Jim Regan, Head Coach, was named Coach of the Year numerous times. Brian Cullen is the Assistant Coach.
Roster In State: 4 **Out of State:** 20 **Out of Country:** 5
ODP State: 2 **Regional:** 1 **National:** 0
Walk-on/Other: 0 **Graduation %:** 95 **Seniors on Team:** 4
Positions Needed: GK, Defenders, MF
Camp or Clinic Dates: Not Available
Most Recent Record: 20-2-0
Schedule: Mercyhurst, WV. Wesleyan, Ashland Univ. California Univ.
Style of Play: Very attacking oriented. In 2000 had leading scorer in nation, also were #1 NCAA II offensive team.

Women's Athletic Profile

316 Washington Avenue
Wheeling, WV 26003
Coach: Jim Regan
Email: jregan@wju.edu

NCAA II
Cardinals/Red, White
Phone: (304) 243-2365
Fax: (304) 243-2265

Estimated # of Women's Soccer Scholarships:
Conference: West Virginia Intercollegiate Athletic Conference
Program Profile: We play in a natural grass stadium field that measures 75 x 115 . The stadium has lights, 2,000 bleacher seats, a press box and two practice fields.
History: The women's soccer program began in 1988. In the early 1990's, we made three National Tournament appearances. We are consistently in the Top 20 nationally.
Achievements: All-Americans; Coach Regan -numerous Coach of the Year.
Coaching: Jim Regan is the Head Coach for the men's and women's soccer teams. Lee Hitchen is the Assistant Coach.

wisconsin

WISCONSIN

SCHOOL	CITY	AFFILIATION	PAGE
Beloit College	Beloit	NCAA III	1206
Cardinal Stritch University	Milwaukee	NAIA	1207
Carroll College	Waukesha	NCAA III	1208
Concordia University - Wisconsin	Mequon	NCAA III/NAIA	1209
Edgewood College	Madison	NCAA III	1210
Lakeland College	Sheboygan	NCAA III	1212
Lawrence University	Appleton	NCAA III	1213
Maranatha Baptist Bible College	Watertown	NCAA III/NAIA	1214
Marian College - Fond du Lac	Fond du Lac	NCAA III/NAIA	1215
Marquette University	Milwaukee	NCAA I	1216
Milwaukee School of Engineering	Milwaukee	NCAA III	1218
Mount Mary College	Milwaukee	NCAA III	1219
Mount Senario College	Lady Smith	NAIA	1219
Northland College	Ashland	NCAA III/NAIA	1221
Ripon College	Ripon	NCAA III	1222
Saint Norbert College	De Pere	NCAA III	1223
University of Wisconsin	Madison	NCAA I	1224
Univ of Wisconsin - Green Bay	Green Bay	NCAA I	1225
Univ of Wisconsin - La Crosse	La Crosse	NCAA III	1226
Univ of Wisconsin - Milwaukee	Milwaukee	NCAA I	1227
University of Wisconsin - Oshkosh	Oshkosh	NCAA III	1228
University of Wisconsin - Parkside	Kenosha	NCAA II	1229
Univ of Wisconsin - Platteville	Platteville	NCAA III	1230
Univ of Wisconsin - River Falls	River Falls	NCAA III	1231
Univ of Wisconsin - Stevens Point	Stevens Point	NCAA III	1232
University of Wisconsin - Stout	Menomonie	NCAA III	1233
University of Wisconsin - Superior	Superior	NCAA III	1234
Unive of Wisconsin - Whitewater	Whitewater	NCAA III	1234
Viterbo College	La Crosse	NAIA	1235
Wisconsin Lutheran College	Milwaukee	NCAA III	1236

STAR GOALKEEPER ACADEMY

"Daniel Gaspar's goalkeeper training method and professional attitude are of the highest standards. His preparation of the Portuguese National Team, as well as Sporting Lisbon has been very impressive. He has demonstrated to have a positive impact in our journey towards the 1994 World Cup qualification process. Dan Gaspar is qualified to train." professional teams in any international arena.
Professor Carlos Queiroz, US Soccer Project 2010 Consultant, Portugal National Teams, Sporting Lisbon, J League Grampus Eight, MLS Metrostars, United Arab Emirates National and Olympic Team, FIFA Technical Staff, 89 & 91 Youth World Cup Champions

"I've watched Dan Gaspar in clinics across the country, and that in itself is a testament to his value. He is in constant demand. It is no surprise. He has excellent presence when he instructs, he is enthusiastic, knowledgeable and worthy of your attention."
Anson Dorrance, Women's National Team Coach, World Cup Champions, University of North Carolina NCAA National Champions,

"Having worked with goalkeepers form youth to top international level, Dan's knowledge, experience and enthusiasm continues to make SGA a fantastic place to train, play and grow."
Glenn Myernick, MLS Head Coach Colorado Rapids, US Soccer National Staff

"As an international and US National Team Keeper, It's important that I be associated with the highest in quality goalkeeper education. That is why I fully endorse SGA."
Brad Friedel, US National Team, Liverpool, MLS Columbus Crew, UCLA National Champion & All American, Herman Trophy Winner

"A great teacher/coach with unquestioned knowledge, unlimited enthusiasm and the experience to properly train his students. If your looking for these qualities in an instructor, then Dan Gaspar is your man."
Coach John Rennie, Duke University National Champions

"Dan is one of the nation's leaders and true professionals in the art of goalkeeping. I unequivocally recommend him to any coach or keeper who wants to gain real insight into what goalkeeping is all about."

"Dan Gaspar is one of the finest teachers and motivators of goalkeepers in America. His enthusiasm is contagious, and his sincere commitment to excellence is unquestionable."
Coach Mike Berticelli, University of Notre Dame, NSCAA National Director of Coaching

"Goalkeepers trained by Dan Gaspar reflect his passion and dedication for the game-one can be assured of that."
Coach Sigi Schmid, MLS LA Galaxy, US National Team U20 Coach, UCLA National Champions, US Soccer National Staff

"Dan's use of imagery and relentless study of the art of goalkeeping qualifies him as one of the top teachers, if not trailblazer's in today's game. Indeed, I am a better coach because of the innovations he has given to goalkeeping training."
Coach Cliff McGrath, Seattle Pacific University National Champions, NSCAA Hall of Fame

"SGA is won of the top training environments I've been privileged to watch and the results are incredible."
Coach Ray Reid, University of Connecticut, Southern Connecticut National Champions

"Dan Gaspar is a goalkeeper expert who creates a wonderful learning environment. Dan is without doubt one of the leading goalkeeping coaches in America today and I recommend him with no hesitation."
Coach Bobby Clark, Stanford University, Former Dartmouth Coach and Scottish National Team Keeper

Beloit College

Academic Profile

Beloit, WI 53511
Phone: 800-356-0751

Type: 4 Yr.,Private,Liberal Arts
Founded: 1846
Website: http://www.stu.beloit.edu
Religion: Non-Affiliated
SAT/ACT/GPA: 1050-1200/25
Housing: Yes
Student/Faculty Ratio: 12:1
Male/Female Ratio: 40:60
Undergraduate Enrollment: 1,100
Graduate Enrollment: N/A
Scholarships/Academic: Yes
Athletic: No
Financial Aid: Yes
Expenses by: Year
In State: $ 24,096
Out of State: $ 24,096
Specialty: Various
Degrees Conferred: Ba, BS
Programs of Study: Art, Art History, Asian Studies, Biochemistry, Biology, Business & Management, Cell Biology, Chemistry, Communications, Comparative Literature, Computer Science, Creative Writing, Economics, Education, English, Environmental Biology, German, Journalism, Mathematics, Molecular Biology, Music, Philosophy, Physics, Political Science, PreDentistry, PreLaw, PreMed, Psychology, Religion, Social Science

Men's Athletic Profile

700 College Street
Beloit, WI 53511
Coach: Tim Schmiechen
Email: schmiech@beliot.edu

NCAA III
Buccaneers/Navy, Gold
Phone: (608) 363-2259
Fax: (608) 363-2044

Estimated # of Men's Soccer Scholarships: None
Conference: Midwest Conference
Program Profile: Very Successful program with new facilities and a new lighted stadium.
History: Better that a .500 winning percentage the last 7 years and have made it to the conference tournament 4 of the last 6 years. Regionally ranked the last 2 years.
Achievements: Coach of the year for the Conference in 1999 and Coach of the Year for state in 1996 and 1995.
Coaching: Tim Schmiechen, Head Coach, Beloit's first full time Men's Soccer Coach, former Ohio Wesleyan player where he was 3 time All-Mideast Region, 2 yr. captain, and helped the team to 4 straight NCAA tournaments, coach of the year in 1992
Roster In State: 5
Out of State: 15
Out of Country: 1
ODP State: 5
Regional:
National:
Walk-on/Other:
Graduation %: 100
Seniors on Team: 2
Positions Needed: Forward, midfield, Goalkeeper
Camp or Clinic Dates: Not Available
Most Recent Record: 9-7-2
Schedule: U. of Chicago, Gustavas Adalphas, U. W. Platteville, U. W. Oshkosh.
Style of Play: Attack, Attack, ATTACK!

Women's Athletic Profile

700 College Street
Beloit, WI 53511
Coach: Kristi Straub
Email: straubk@beloit.edu

NCAA III
Buccaneers/Navy, Gold
Phone: (608) 363-2398
Fax: (608) 363-2044

Estimated # of Women's Soccer Scholarships: None
Conference: Midwest Conference

Program Profile: Developing program, finished 10-7 last season and 6-8-1 this season, playing an improves schedule and most matches on the road. Season starts in August and finishes in October. Playing surface is natural turf- soccer complex is outstanding! Indoor playing facility on campus and also other indoor facilities within 20 minutes that team plays at in off-season.
History: First varsity season was in 1987 - won the Wisconsin state Championship that year. Built one of the stronger programs in the conference through the early 90's and fell on hard times with part time coaching in '94. Has been a rebuilding effort since '97 when full time coaching commitment was made and team finished 10-7 last season, tied for 3rd in the Midwest Conference. Still a young team, we look to take further steps forward next season and beyond.
Achievements: 1999 - Coaching Staff received Conference Coach of the Year Honors.
Coaching: Kristi Straub, Head Coach. Lisa D'Agostin and Kelly Unzicker are the Assistants.
ODP State: 1 **Regional:** **National:**
Walk-on/Other: **Graduation %:** 100 **Seniors on Team:** 2
Positions Needed: Keeper, Sweeper, Center-Mid
Camp or Clinic Dates: Call for details
Most Recent Record: 6-8-1
Schedule: Keene State, Smith College, Illinois Wesleyan, Lawrence, Grinnell, St. Norbert
Style of Play: Out of a 4-4-2 this season, we mixed things up, playing both direct and indirect. Great speed on the outside- and great ability in the air.

Cardinal Stritch College

Academic Profile

Milwaukee, WI 53217
Phone: (414) 410-4125

Type: 4 Yr.,Private,Liberal Arts
Founded: 1937
Website: http://www.stritch.edu
Religion: Roman Catholic
SAT/ACT/GPA: 20/2.5
Housing: Yes
Student/Faculty Ratio: 15:1
Male/Female Ratio: 40:60
Undergraduate Enrollment: 1,100
Graduate Enrollment: 4,400
Scholarships/Academic: Yes **Athletic:** Yes **Financial Aid:** Yes
Expenses by: Year **In State:** $ 15,400 **Out of State:** $ 15,400
Specialty: Liberal Arts
Degrees Conferred: AA, AS, BA, MA, MS, MBA, BS
Programs of Study: Accounting, Art, Biology, Business, Chemistry, Computer Science, Communications, Education, English, French, History Mathematics, Music, Nursing, Psychology, Public Relations, Sociology, Spanish, Special Education, Theatre

Men's Athletic Profile

6801 N Yates Road
Milwaukee, WI 53217
Coach: Pat Clemens
Email: soccoach@stritch.edu

NAIA
Crusaders/Maroon, Silver
Phone: (414) 410-4639
Fax: (414) 410-4127

Estimated # of Men's Soccer Scholarships: None
Conference: Chicagoland Collegiate Athletic Conference
Program Profile: The team plays on a natural grass field on campus. We have a one trip each season and play a year-long program.
History: Our program began in 1991.
Achievements: Jan Richard was named All-American now playing in the EISL Lake Michigan Conference in 1994.
Coaching: Pat Clemens, Head Coach, has a National license and over 21 year coaching experience. Rick Mobly and Tony Curatolo are the Assistant Coaches.
Roster In State: 6 **Out of State:** 7 **Out of Country:** 4

Walk-on/Other: **Graduation %:** **Seniors on Team:** 4
Positions Needed: Defenders and Forwards
Camp or Clinic Dates: Not Available
Most Recent Record: 4-14
Schedule: Carthage, Dominican, Mt. St. Clare, St. Xavier, Judson, Trinity International
Style of Play: Possession with a counter attack in the midfield.

Women's Athletic Profile

6801 N. Yates Rd.
Milwaukee, WI 53217
Coach: Pat Clemens
Email: soccoach@stritch.edu

NAIA
Crusaders/Maroon, Silver
Phone: (414) 410-4639
Fax: (414) 410-4127

Estimated # of Women's Soccer Scholarships:
Conference: Chicagoland Collegiate Athletic Conference
Program Profile: We play on a natural grass field on campus. We take one long trip each season. We have a year long program. A new gym under construction
History: We began in 1996. Our records are: 1996, 6-10; 1997, 7-13-1 and 1998, 14-6-1.
Achievements: Coach of the Year honors, Conference titles, All-Americans and drafted players
Coaching: Pat Clemens, Head Coach, is the new head coach. Kate Carpenter, Assistant Coach, is a nationally licensed coach who was the Olympic Development Administrator and State Coach for New Hampshire Soccer Association. Angela Balistreci is also Assistant Coach.
Roster in State: 9 **Out of State:** 7 **Out of Country:** 1
Walk-on/Other: **Graduation %:** **Seniors on Team:** 5
Positions Needed: Defenders and Forwards
Most Recent Record: 9-9
Schedule: Carthage, Mt. St. Clare, St. Xavier, Judson, Trinity International, Dominican
Style of Play: Possession, deliberate attack. Counter attack on change of possession in midfield.

Carroll College

Academic Profile

Phone: 262-547-1211

Waukesha, WI 53186

Type: 4 Yr.,Private,Liberal Arts
Founded: 1841
Website: http://www.cc.edu
Religion: Presbyterian Church
SAT/ACT/GPA: Required
Housing: Yes
Student/Faculty Ratio: 20:1
Male/Female Ratio: 1:2
Undergraduate Enrollment: 2,445
Graduate Enrollment: 80
Scholarships/Academic: Yes **Athletic:** No **Financial Aid:** Yes
Expenses by: Year **In State:** $ 18,140 **Out of State:** $ 18,140
Specialty: Biology, Business, Chemistry, Nursing, Physical Therapy
Degrees Conferred: BA, BS, BSMT, BSN, BS(Nursing), MS(Physical Therapy), M Ed
Programs of Study: Accounting, Art, Athletic Training, Biology, Business Administration, Chemistry, Coaching, Communication, Computer Science, Criminal Justice, Education (Early Childhood, Elementary, Secondary, Masters in Education), English, Environmental Science, Fitness Management, French, Geography, German, Graphic Communication, Health Science, History, Human Services, International Relations, Journalism. Land-use Planning, Marine Biology, Mathematics, Medical Technology, Music, Nursing, Photography, Physical Education, Physical Therapy, Physics, Politics, Public Administration, Psychology, Religious Studies, Sociology, Spanish, Theatre Arts, Women's Studies. PreProfessional (PreDental, PreEngineering, PreLaw, PreMedial, PreMinistry, PreVeterinary)

Men's Athletic Profile

100 N East Avenue
Waukesha, WI 53186
Coach: Rickey Mobley
Email: sama@carroll1.cc.edu

NCAA III
Pioneers/Orange, White
Phone: (414) 5247105
Fax: (414) 524-7376

Estimated # of Men's Soccer Scholarships: None
Conference: Midwest Collegiate Athletic Conference
Program Profile: Carroll plays a 16-game schedule against NCAA Division III teams from Wisconsin, Illinois and Iowa. Home field is the Van Male Stadium with a seating capacity of 4,200, a natural grass facility.
History: Men's soccer program began in 1992. Overall record is 42-62-5. Coach Mobley is entering his first season.
Coaching: Rickey Mobley enters his first season for the Pioneers.
Roster In State: 13 **Out of State:** 10 **Out of Country:**
Walk-on/Other: **Graduation %:** N/A **Seniors on Team:** 3
Camp or Clinic Dates: Not Available
Most Recent Record: 4-11-1
Schedule: UW-Whitewater, Carthage, Beliot, Ripon, St. Norbert, Lake Forest.
Style of Play: Offensively and defensively the men play a high pressure attacking style of soccer.

Women's Athletic Profile

100 North East Avenue
Waukesha, WI 53186
Coach: Carrie Storm
Email: sama@carroll1.cc.edu

NCAA III
Pioneers/Orange, White
Phone: (414) 524-7320
Fax: (414) 524-7376

Estimated # of Women's Soccer Scholarships: None
Conference: Midwest Conference
Program Profile: Playing season starts late August to November on a natural turf stadium, seats 4,000 located on campus. Competition begins first week in September. Sixteen game schedule with Conference Tournament.
History: Women's Soccer began here at Carroll College in 1993. We have an all-time record of 43-47-5 including winning seasons the past 3 years.
Achievements: Midwest Conference Champions in 1998.
Style of Play: Play for possession. Usually play 18-22 players per game. Outstanding defense works to move the ball up through the back. We are well-conditioned, respect our opponents and fear none.

Concordia University - Wisconsin

Academic Profile

Phone:

Mequon, WI 53097

Type: 4 Yr.,Private,Liberal Arts
Website: http://www.cuw.edu
SAT/ACT/GPA: 21+
Student/Faculty Ratio: 19:1
Undergraduate Enrollment: 3,833
Scholarships/Academic: Yes **Athletic:** No
Expenses by: Year **In State:** $ 17,250
Degrees Conferred: Associates, Masters, Bachelor

Founded: 1881
Religion: Lutheran Synod
Housing: Yes
Male/Female Ratio: 42:58
Graduate Enrollment: 708
Financial Aid: Yes
Out of State: $ 17,250

Programs of Study: Art, Accounting, Athletic Training, Biblical Languages, Biology, Business, Computer Science, Early Childhood, Economics, Elementary Education, English, Exercise Leadership, Exercise Physiology, Finance, Graphic Design, History, Humanities, Individualized Interior Design, Justice and Public Police, Lay Ministry, Management, Marketing Mass Communications, Mathematics, Missions, Music, Nursing, Occupational Therapy, Organizational Communications, Paralegal, Pastoral Ministry, Physical Education, Psychology, Radiological Technology, Secondary Education, Social Work, Spanish, Speech Communication, Telecasting, Theology

Men's Athletic Profile

12800 N Lake Shore Drive
Mequon, WI 53097-2402
Coach: Thomas Saleska
Email: tom.saleska@cuw.edu

NCAA III/NAIA
Falcons/Royal Blue, White
Phone: (414) 243-4258
Fax: (414) 243-4475

Estimated # of Men's Soccer Scholarships: None
Conference: Lake Michigan Conference
Program Profile: Program is located in strong Milwaukee area. Top contender for District 14 Championships and National Playoffs. Excellent indoor and outdoor playing and training areas with a natural grass surface.
History: Program began in 1984. Falcons were Conference Champs 1987, 1989-1992; District Playoffs 1986-1992; Runner-Up in 1986, 1987 & 1989.
Achievements: 2 NAIA Senior Bowl Selections, 3 All-Americans; there have been various All-Conference, All-District, Regional All-Stars, 3 Coach of the Year awards and 1993 captain signed by Milwaukee Wave.
Coaching: Thomas Saleska, Head Coach, 17 years of coaching experience from youth through college levels, one Coach of the Award, USSF Coaching License.
Style of Play: Total Soccer stressing ball controlled tempo, possession, short passing game. Attacking and defending with all players. Controlled tempo and pace, aggressive defensive play and attacking.

Women's Athletic Profile

12800 N Lake Shore Drive
Mequon, WI 53097-2402
Coach: Carey Halula
Email: Not Available

NCAA III/NAIA
Falcons/Blue, White
Phone: (414) 243-4385
Fax: (414) 243-4351

Did Not Return Profile

Edgewood College

Academic Profile

Phone:

Madison, WI 53711

Type: 4 Yr.,Private,Liberal Arts
Website: http://www.edgewood.edu
SAT/ACT/GPA: 850/18/2.5
Student/Faculty Ratio: 14:1
Undergraduate Enrollment: 1,000
Scholarships/Academic: Yes **Athletic:** No
Expenses by: Year **In State:** $ 14,000

Founded: 1927
Religion: Catholic
Housing: Yes
Male/Female Ratio: 1:3
Graduate Enrollment: 1,000
Financial Aid: Yes
Out of State: $ 14,000

Specialty: Arts, Business, Education, Nursing
Degrees Conferred: BS, BS, MBA, AA, MAE, MARS, MANA
Programs of Study: Accounting, Art, Art Therapy, Biology, Broad Fields Science, Business, Chemistry, Child Life, Computer Information Systems, Criminal Justice, CytoTechnology, Economics, Elementary Education, English, Graphic Design, History, International Relations, Mathematics, Music, Medical Technology, Nursing, Political Science, Psychology, Public Policy and Administration, Religion, Sociology, PreDentistry, PreLaw, PreMed, PrePharmacy, PreEngineering

Men's Athletic Profile

855 Woodrow Street
Madison, WI 53711
Coach: Tim Alexander
Email: talexander@edgewood.edu

NCAA III
Eagles/Black, Red, White
Phone: (608) 257-4861
Fax: (608) 257-1590

Estimated # of Men's Soccer Scholarships: None
Conference: Lake Michigan Conference
Program Profile: The Eagles are members of the NCAA Division III, as well as the Lake Michigan Conference. Edgewood plays all of their homes games at lighted, Breese Stevens Soccer Field, (grass playing surface, 3000 seat), home of the WIAA state soccer tournament. Coach Alexander has led the team for four seasons, steadily building a strong program from the ground up.
History: Program started in 1991 with a record of 1-10-2. 1994 was the most successful season in the four-year history of the program. They recorded a school-record ten victories and their 5-2-1 conference mark was their best in four seasons.
Achievements: The Eagles advanced to the finals of the LMC tournament in their inaugural year of the program. 1994-1995: 2 All-Lake Michigan Conference, 2 NAIA All-Great Lakes Region - Scott Mejia and Chris Schoenecker; 4 All-Lake Michigan Special Mention - Nate Brawner, Wally Jossart, Jeff Ornes, Nathan Selk; 1 All- Lake Michigan Honorable Mention: 1 Coach of the Year - Tim Alexander.
Coaching: Tim Alexander, Head Coach, 17 seasons, USSF 'B' License, 174-82-13 overall coaching record, 1974 and 1975 NJCAA first Team All-American (Forest Park CC, St. Louis, MO.) Scott Mejia - Assistant Coach.
Style of Play: Play a 4-4-2 or 4-3-3; attacking style. high pressure, quick passing style of play.

Women's Athletic Profile

855 Woodrow Street
Madison, WI 53711
Coach: Tim Alexander
Email: talexander@edgewood. edu

NCAA III
Eagles/Black, Red, White
Phone: (608) 663-3280
Fax: (608) 663-6703

Estimated # of Women's Soccer Scholarships: None
Conference: Lake Michigan Conference
Program Profile: We concentrate on defense but we do play a wide open attack. We have a tremendous training facility at Reddan Soccer Park and we play at Breese Stevens Soccer Field, located in downtown Madison, which is a grass stadium. The stadium is also used for the state- High School Tournament.
History: The team began in 1993. Since 1994 we have won 6 straight Lake Michigan Conference Championships and 4 Conference Tournament Championships and have played in 1 NCAA Tournament in 1999.
Achievements: 3 Coach of the Year; 6 Conference Title, 2 All-American.
Coaching: Tim Alexander, Head Coach, is going on to his nineteenth seasons and has a USSF"A" license. He was named two-time All-American. He has a 20 years of coaching experience with an overall coaching record of 309-148-21.
Roster in State: 18 **Out of State:** 1 **Out of Country:**
ODP State: 2
Seniors on Team: 1
Positions Needed: Forward, Midfield, Defense
Camp or Clinic Dates: Not Available
Most Recent Record: 17-4-2
Schedule: UW Stevens Point, Lawrence, Rockford, UW Oshkosh, Concordia, Ripon
Style of Play: Defense 1st and then attack wide with concentration on crosses from the dribble. We try to play up tempo and put the pressure on the opposing team.

Lakeland College

Academic Profile

Sheboygan, WI 53082-0359

Phone: (920) 565-1512

Type: 4 Yr.,Private,Liberal Arts
Website: http://www.lakeland.edu
SAT/ACT/GPA: 182.0
Student/Faculty Ratio: 15:1
Undergraduate Enrollment: 800
Scholarships/Academic: Yes
Athletic: No
Expenses by: Year
In State: $ 16,500
Specialty: Business and Education
Degrees Conferred: BA, MA

Founded: 1862
Religion:
Housing: Yes
Male/Female Ratio: 1:1
Graduate Enrollment:
Financial Aid: Yes
Out of State: $ 16,500

Programs of Study: Accounting, Anthropology, Art, Biology, Broad Field Social Science, Business Administration, Chemistry, Church Music, Criminal Justice, Communication, Computer Science, Early Childhood/Elementary Education, Coaching, Economics, Elementary/Middle School Education, English, English as a Second Language, Ethnic & Gender Studies, Exercise Science/Sports Studies, French, General Education, German, History, Hospitality Management, International Business, Japanese, Liberal Arts, Marketing, Mathematics, Philosophy, Physics, Political Science, Religion, Science, Secondary/Middle School Professional Sequence, Sociology, Spanish, Specialized Administration, Theatre and Speech, Writing, Athletic Training compromise 80% of students.

Men's Athletic Profile

P.O. Box 359
Sheboygan, WI 53082
Coach: Scott Mejia
Email: mejiasm@lakeland.edu

NCAA III
Muskies/Navy, Gold
Phone: (920) 565-1244
Fax: (920) 565-1399

Estimated # of Men's Soccer Scholarships: None
Conference: Lake Michigan Conference
Program Profile: An established program that competes in the Lake Michigan Conference. Our season is from early August through November with a limited spring season. Our field is the best in the conference, possibly best in the State of Wisconsin.
History: Our program was initiated in 1991; powerhouse in 1992 & 1993. Now the program is consistently in the top three in conference.
Achievements: The program produced 7 All-Conference players.
Coaching: Scot Mejia, Head Coach, is entering his first year with the program. Mike Heinen, Assistant Coach (graduate).
Positions Needed: Defender, Forwards
Most Recent Record: 8-13-1
Style of Play: We play a technically sound attacking style of soccer. We encourage players to get involved in the attack and that one on one situations are exploited.

Women's Athletic Profile

P.O. Box 359
Sheboygan, WI 53082-0359
Coach: Scott Mejia
Email: mejiasm@lakeland.edu

NCAA III
Muskies/Navy, Gold
Phone: (920) 565-1244
Fax: (920) 565-1399

Estimated # of Women's Soccer Scholarships: None
Conference: Lake Michigan Conference

Program Profile: A young program competing in the Lake Michigan Conference. We start in early August and continue through November. In the Spring, we have a limited season. Our fields are natural grass and probably use some of the best in the State of Wisconsin.
History: Began in 1994, has been building progressively since its inception. Had its best season ever in 1998.
Achievements: Has two All-Conference players.
Coaching: Scott Mejia, Head Coach. Mike Heinen, Assistant Coach (graduate).
Roster in State: 9 **Out of State:** 6 **Out of Country:** 0
Walk-on/Other: **Graduation %:** N/A **Seniors on Team:** 1
Positions Needed: Keeper, Defender, Forward
Camp or Clinic Dates: Call for details
Most Recent Record: 12-9-1
Style of Play: We play a technically sound attacking style of soccer. We encourage players to get involved in the attack and demand that one on one situations are exploited.

Lawrence University

Academic Profile

Phone:

Appleton, WI 54912-0599

Type: 4 Yr.,Private,Liberal Arts
Founded: 1847
Website: http://www.lawrence.edu
Religion: Non-Affiliated
SAT/ACT/GPA: Open
Housing: Yes
Student/Faculty Ratio: 11:1
Male/Female Ratio: 47:53
Undergraduate Enrollment: 1,350
Graduate Enrollment: N/A
Scholarships/Academic: Yes **Athletic:** No **Financial Aid:** Yes
Expenses by: Year **In State:** $ 21,054 **Out of State:** $ 21,054
Specialty: Liberal Arts, Education
Degrees Conferred: BA, BM
Programs of Study: Anthropology, Art History, Art Studio, Biology, Chemistry, Classics, Computer Science, Mathematics, East Asian Languages & Culture, Economics, English, French, Geology, German, Government, History, Mathematics, Music, Natural Science, Philosophy, Physics, Psychology, Religious Studies, Slavic, Spanish, Theatre & Drama, Business, PreLaw, PreMed, Engineering

Men's Athletic Profile

P.O Box 599, Alexander Gymnasium
Appleton, WI 54912
Coach: Blake Johnson
Email: blake.f.johnson@lawrence.edu

NCAA III
Vikings/Navy, White
Phone: (920) 832-7034
Fax: (920) 832-7349

Estimated # of Men's Soccer Scholarships: None
Conference: Midwest Conference
Program Profile: New Soccer park (2,000 natural grass), plus full training field and facility. Lawrence is a nationally ranked academic institution. Division 3 philosophy. 16 grame regular-season schedule, year-round weight training program for players, winter/spring training dates. School attracts student-athletes from all 50 states. Midwest Conference has 10 members, with conference tournament champion gaining automatic berth in NCAA regional tournament.
History: Men's program began in 1974. Second oldest program in Wisconsin varsity in 1982.
Achievements: Past NAIA Region3 Coach of the Year, UMAC Conference Coach of the Year, 3 NAIA All-Americans, 5 All-Region players, 10 All-Conference players, 2-year record 34-12. 1999 NAIA National Tournament.
Coaching: Blake Johnson brings a record of success to his first season at Lawrence University. Johnson comes to Lawrence from Mount Senario College, where he was the head men's coach from 1998-1999. Johnson compiled a 34-12 record at MSC and won the UMAC regular season and tournament titles both years, also capturing the Region 3 Championships, and playing in the 1999 NAIA National Tournament. Johnson has coached at the club, high school, ODP and college levels since 1983. He served as Assistant Coach at Bates College and at Maine-Farmington.

Roster In State: 7 **Out of State:** 8 **Out of Country:** 3
ODP State: **Regional:** **National:**
Walk-on/Other: 4 **Graduation %:** 85 **Seniors on Team:** 3
Positions Needed: 13 players
Camp or Clinic Dates: Not Available
Most Recent Record: 5-13
Schedule: Ripon College, Wisconsin-Whitewater, Edgewood College, Lake Forest College, Grinnell College, Wisconsin-Platteville, Beloit College, St. Norbert College.
Style of Play: Develop the individual to his maximum potential as a soccer player. I will recruit players who have played at a high standard with their club/high schools. We look for players who are comfortable playing with pressure, and who technically have composure with the ball. Collectively, the style is possession oriented, while emphasizing each player read the game to ensure decision is the best available. Defensively, we want to keep our shape playing combination of zone and individual marking in the middle to back thirds.

Women's Athletic Profile

1100 E. S. River Street, Alexander Gym
Appleton, WI 54912
Coach: Moria Ruhly
Email: moria.ruhly@lawrence.edu

NCAA III
Vikings/Navy, White
Phone: (920) 832-6974
Fax: (920) 832-7349

Estimated # of Women's Soccer Scholarships: None
Conference: Midwest Conference
Program Profile: Competitive program with a game and practice field. It is natural field with a bleacher seating. Playing season runs August - November.
History: Lawrence University Women's Soccer program began in 1982. It has been a varsity program since it inception.
Achievements: 2nd place in Conference last two years; 1998 Player of the Year- Megan Tiemann; Midwest Conference 1st and 2nd team All-Conference 1999-5 players and 1998 3 players.
Coaching: Moria Ruhly is our Head Coach and Kim Geise is our Assistant Coach and was a Goalie at Lawrence University.
Roster in State: 11 **Out of State:** 11 **Out of Country:**
Walk-on/Other: **Graduation %:** 100 **Seniors on Team:** 2
Positions Needed: Forwards, Midfielders
Camp or Clinic Dates: July 16-21
Most Recent Record: 11-6-1
Schedule: University of Chicago, St. Benedict, Grinnell College, Edgewood College, UW- Oshkosh, WU- Whitewater, St. Norbert College, Carroll College, St. Olaf, Aurora University
Style of Play: We play a controlled one-two style with some finesse up top for scoring. Most importantly, however, we play with incredible work effort, 100% all the time.

Maranatha Baptist Bible College

Academic Profile

Watertown, WI 53094

Phone:

Type: 4 Yr.,Private **Founded:** 1968
Website: Not Available **Religion:** Non-Affiliated
SAT/ACT/GPA: Open **Housing:** Yes
Student/Faculty Ratio: 20:1 **Male/Female Ratio:** 50:50
Undergraduate Enrollment: 475 **Graduate Enrollment:** 20
Scholarships/Academic: **Athletic:** **Financial Aid:**
Expenses by: Year **In State:** $ 8,000 **Out of State:** $ 8,000
Degrees Conferred: Bachelors, Masters

Programs of Study: Biblical Studies, Biblical Languages, Business, Early Childhood Education, Education, Elementary Education, Humanities, Liberal Arts, Management, Ministries, Music, Nursing, Physical Education, Religion, Secondary Education, Speech, Sports Administration, Theology

Men's Athletic Profile

745 West Main Street
Watertown, WI 53094
Coach: Ben Wright
Email: bwright@mbbc.edu

NCAA III/NAIA
Crusaders/Navy, Gold
Phone: (414) 261-9300
Fax: (414) 261-9109

Estimated # of Men's Soccer Scholarships: None
Conference: Lake Michigan Conference
Program Profile: Preseason begins late August, season continues through early November. competition is mostly NCAA Division III, with a few National Christian College Athletic Association opponents. Current facility is full-size game field with near regulation practice field. An additional regulation game/practice field is currently under construction
History: One of the oldest college programs in Wisconsin, began around 1970.
Joined Lake Michigan Conference in late 1980's.
Joined NCAA Division III in late 1990's.
Coaching: Head Coach Ben Wright: 3 years on coaching staff at MBBL, 1 year as head coach. Liftie college record 6-15.
Assistant coach Max Schuyler-1 year assistant at MBBL;played 4 years at MBBL in the 1970's; High school coach in Minneapolis & Chicago areas for 14 years
Assistant Coach Dave Teasdale: 1 year as assistant at MBBL; played 4 years at MBBL in late 1990's
Roster In State: 4 **Out of State:** 20 **Out of Country:** 1
ODP State: 1 **Regional:** **National:**
Walk-on/Other: **Graduation %:** N/A **Seniors on Team:** 2
Positions Needed: 4-5
Camp or Clinic Dates: August 7-11
Most Recent Record: 5-13-1
Schedule: Edgewood College, Ripon College, North Central, Northland Baptist Bible College, Concordia University, Milwaukee School of Engineering
Style of Play: 4-4-2 with sweeper/diamond midfield. We use some zonal principles in a marking backfield. We attempt to dominate ball control in the midfield to allow us to exploit the corners or attack with runners from the backfield.

Marian College - Fond du Lac
Academic Profile

Phone:

Fond Du Lac, WI 54935

Type: 4 Yr.,Private,Liberal Arts
Founded: 1936
Website: http://www.marian.edu
Religion: Catholic
SAT/ACT/GPA: 20
Housing: Yes
Student/Faculty Ratio: 15:1
Male/Female Ratio: 40:60
Undergraduate Enrollment: 1,800
Graduate Enrollment: 600
Scholarships/Academic: Yes **Athletic:** No **Financial Aid:** Yes
Expenses by: Year **In State:** $ 13,000 **Out of State:** $ 13,000
Specialty: Nursing
Degrees Conferred: BA, BS, BBA, BSEd, BSN, MA
Programs of Study: Accounting, Art, Biology, Business Administration, Chemistry, Communications, Criminal Justice, CytoTechnology, Education, English, Environmental Science, History, Human Development, Human Services, Liberal Arts, Management, Marketing, Mathematics, Medical Technology, Music, Nursing, PreDentistry, PreLaw, PreMed, PreVet, Psychology, Radiological Technology, Science, Social Science, Sport Administration

Men's Athletic Profile

45 S National Avenue
Fond du Lac, WI 54935
Coach: Craig Peltonen
Email: Not Available

NCAA III/NAIA
Sabres/Blue, White
Phone: (414) 923-7626
Fax: (414) 923-7154

Estimated # of Men's Soccer Scholarships: None
Conference: Lake Michigan Conference
Program Profile: Play some Div. I schools, High emphasis on Student/Athletes
Achievements: Conference Champs, Conference Coach of the Year, All American
Coaching: Craig Peltonen, Head Coach, USSF 'A' license, State and Regional ODP coach, many years playing experience
Style of Play: Ball Control, Passing, like to take the ball wide, and cross for goal scoring opportunity. Team Defense is important.

Women's Athletic Profile

45 S National Avenue
Fond du Lac, WI 54935
Coach: Craig Peltonen
Email: Not Available

NCAA III/NAIA
Sabres/Royal Blue, White
Phone: (414) 923-7626
Fax: (414) 923-8134

Estimated # of Women's Soccer Scholarships: None
Conference: Lake Michigan Conference
Program Profile: Excellent 120X72 grass field with adjacent to 110X70 grass practice field, additional space and adequate training facilities. Looking to develop a strong program.
History: Program began in 1989
Coaching: Craig Peltonen, Head Coach, Holds USSF 'A' License, state and regional ODP coach, many years playing experience at a major college and as a top amateur.
Style of Play: Emphasis on ball possession. We mix our styles up. At times we high pressure, and against other opponents we low pressure and counter-attack. Team defense is emphasized. We try to play a 3-5-2 committing different players forward.

Marquette University

Academic Profile

Phone: (800) 222-6544

Milwaukee, WI 53201-1881

Type: 4 Yr.,Private,Liberal Arts,Engineering
Website: http://www.marquette.edu
SAT/ACT/GPA: 1040/23
Student/Faculty Ratio: 15:1
Undergraduate Enrollment: 10,610
Scholarships/Academic: Yes **Athletic:** Yes
Expenses by: Year **In State:** $ 21,150

Founded: 1881
Religion: Catholic-Jesuit
Housing: Yes
Male/Female Ratio: 48:52
Graduate Enrollment: 3,500
Financial Aid: Yes
Out of State: $ 21,150

Specialty: Engineering, Physical Therapy, Business Administration, Nursing
Degrees Conferred: BA, MS, Law Degree, Ph.D., AA, BBE, BCE, BIE, BSN
Programs of Study: African-American Studies, Classical Languages, English, French, German, History, Philosophy, Spanish, Theology, BioChemistry, Biology, Chemistry, Physics, Computational Math, Computer Science, Mathematics & Statistics, Anthropology, Criminology, Political Science, Psychology, Social Work, Accounting, Finance, International Business, Advertising, Journalism, Public Relations, Theatre Arts, Elementary & Secondary Education, BioMedical Engineering, Civil & Environmental Engineering, Electrical and Computer Engineering, Mechanical Engineering, Physical Therapy, Speech Pathology and Audiology, Nursing, Industrial Engineering, Medical Laboratory Technology

Men's Athletic Profile

1532 W. Clybourn P.O. Box 1881
Milwaukee, WI 53201-1881
Coach: Steve Adlard
Email: musoccer@marquette.edu

NCAA I
Golden Eagles/Blue, Gold
Phone: (414) 288-3069
Fax: (414) 288-5282

Estimated # of Men's Soccer Scholarships: 9
Conference: Conference USA
Program Profile: Play on a natural grass full NCAA size with a seating capacity for 2,300. Playing season is the fall, next to campus complex, Valley Fields. First game is September 4th at Portland.
History: Program began in 1964. 17 winning seasons.
Achievements: 1997 NCAA Tournament Participant. Jim Welch (99) Keeper for US pro 40 Squad in "A" League
Coaching: Steve Adlard, Head Coach, Regional ODP Coach for Regions II and IV, FA and US coaching license, former international and Notts Forest player.
Roster In State: 11 **Out of State:** 17 **Out of Country:** 1
ODP State: 15 **Regional:** 8 **National:**
Walk-on/Other: **Graduation %:** N/A **Seniors on Team:** 4
Positions Needed: Goalkeeper
Camp or Clinic Dates: June 15-18, Last week in July
Most Recent Record: 9-11-1
Schedule: Portland, Washington, UAB, Creighton, UNC Charlotte, Cincinnati, Oakland, South Florida, St. Louis
Style of Play: Possession with a purpose, based on a sound defensive philosophy.

Women's Athletic Profile

P.O. Box 1881
Milwaukee, WI 53201-7414
Coach: Markus Roaders
Email: markus.roaders@marquette.edu

NCAA I
Golden Eagles/Navy, Gold
Phone: (414) 288-7271
Fax: (414) 288-5282

Estimated # of Women's Soccer Scholarships: 3
Conference: Conference USA
Program Profile: The facilities are second to none, and the field is the best in the Midwest. We have a grass field and a valley field, which is an artificial turf for practice and play. Facilities include: a light system, first aid, vending areas and a high security system. Our game field is natural grass, measures 120x78, is fully lit and has stands for 2,500 spectators.
History: Program began in 1993 1st year record was 6-10-2, 2nd year 7-7-4. Markus has been coach since 1996 and the records have improved. In 1999 the teams records was 16-7-2, in 2000 20-3-1.
Achievements: Won 1996 Coach of the Year in the Conference USA; multiple All-Conference members; Conference Player of the Year; Regional All-Americans; Academic All-Americans. 2000 C-USA Coach of the Year, Conference Champions and 2nd round in NCAA appearance in 2000.
Coaching: Markus Roeders, Head Coach, has a "B" coaching license. He is State Coach for the Wisconsin Olympic Development. He was captain for two years at Brevard Junior College. Frank Pelaez and Dano Holcomb are the assistant coaches.
Roster in State: 15 **Out of State:** 15 **Out of Country:** 0
ODP State: 24 **Regional:** 7 **National:** 0
Walk-on/Other: 6 **Graduation %:** 100 **Seniors on Team:** 5
Positions Needed: Forwards
Most Recent Record: 20-3-1
Schedule: BYU, UCLA, Wisconsin, C-USA
Style of Play: Very discipline defense, with defensive scoring power South American possession combined with German defense, very entertaining style with dangerous set plays.

Milwaukee School of Engineering

Academic Profile

Milwaukee, WI 53202-3109
Phone: 414-277-7300

Type: 4 Yr.,Private,Engineering
Founded: 1903
Website: http://www.msoe.edu
Religion: Non-Affiliated
SAT/ACT/GPA: Open
Housing: Yes
Student/Faculty Ratio: 15:1
Male/Female Ratio: 5:1
Undergraduate Enrollment: 2,500
Graduate Enrollment: 500
Scholarships/Academic: Yes **Athletic:** No **Financial Aid:** Yes
Expenses by: Year **In State:** $ 18,000 **Out of State:** $ 18,000
Specialty:
Degrees Conferred: 10 Engineering Majors, Business, Nursing
Programs of Study: Business & Management, Engineering, Engineering Technology, Nursing, Technical Communications

Men's Athletic Profile

1025 N Broadway
Milwaukee, WI 53202-3109
Coach: Jimmy Banks
Email: banks@msoe.edu

NCAA III
Raiders/Red, White, Black
Phone: (414) 277-7493
Fax: (414) 221-0610

Estimated # of Men's Soccer Scholarships: None
Conference: Lake Michigan Conference
Program Profile: Our program consists of a varsity and JV level teams. We participate in a seven team conference called the Lake Michigan Conference (LMC). Our home games are played at the Milwaukee Rampage Professional Stadium which seats 15,000 spectators. The practice location is at the Milwaukee Lake front, which is ten blocks of campus near the beach.
History: Program began in 1970's; initial success but struggle through 1987-1996. New focus, coaching and administration has turned things around. Had best finished last season kin over 10 years.
Achievements: Conference Coach of the Year in 1996; 2 All-District players in 1980's; 2 All-Midwest selections in 1997. 2000 LMC Coach of the Year.
Coaching: Head Coach former 1990 World Cup Player Jimmy Banks and now A licensed coach. Assistant Coach All-American Rolf Zersen
Roster In State: 22 **Out of State:** 18 **Out of Country:** 0
ODP State: 0 **Regional:** 0 **National:** 0
Walk-on/Other: 0 **Graduation %:** 100 **Seniors on Team:** 2
Positions Needed: 2 GK, 1 Forward, 1 Midfielder, 2 Backs
Camp or Clinic Dates: July 29-August 3
Most Recent Record: 7-5-0
Schedule: Puget Sound, St. Olaf, Marian, Millikin, North Park, Edgewood
Style of Play: MSOE plays a very technical, attacking style of play with hard working team defending from front to back in a zonal 4-4-2 formation.

Women's Athletic Profile

1025 N. Broadway
Milwaukee, WI 53202
Coach: Dave Siewert
Email: Siewert@msoe.edu

NCAA III
Raiders/Red, White
Phone: (414) 277-7148
Fax: (414) 277-7480

Estimated # of Women's Soccer Scholarships: None
Conference: Lake Michigan Conference
Program Profile: We have good NCAA 3 program at outstanding academic school, majors in engineering, nursing, business. Our season starts early September, last game late October. On campus field.
History: Our program started in 1995.
Achievements: We have had 2 All-Conference players in 1999.
Coaching: Dave Siewert is our Head Coach. He is entering first year with the program. Kevin Jacoby is our Assistant Coach.
Roster in State: 11 **Out of State:** 4 **Out of Country:** 0
Walk-on/Other: **Graduation %:** 100 **Seniors on Team:** 3/4
Positions Needed: Goalkeeper, Sweeper, Defender
Camp or Clinic Dates: Not Available
Most Recent Record: 3-15-0
Schedule: Edgewood, Concordia, Lakeland, Texas Lutheran, Marian

Mount Mary College

Academic Profile

Milwaukee, WI 53222 **Phone:** (414) 256-1220

Type: 4 Yr.,Private,Liberal Arts **Founded:** 1913
Website: http://www.mtmary.edu **Religion:** Catholic
SAT/ACT/GPA: 900/18/2.3 **Housing:** Yes
Student/Faculty Ratio: 14:1 **Male/Female Ratio:** Women
Undergraduate Enrollment: 1,100 **Graduate Enrollment:** 200
Scholarships/Academic: Yes **Athletic:** No **Financial Aid:** Yes
Expenses by: Year **In State:** $ 11,790 **Out of State:** $ 11,790-17,930
Specialty: Occupational Therapy, Design, Art, Education, Business, Social Work
Degrees Conferred: BS, BA, MS, MA
Programs of Study: Art, Art Therapy, Behavioral Science, Psychology, Biology, Accounting, Business Administration, Business Advertising, Business Management, Chemistry, Communications, Consumer Sciences, Hotel & Restaurant Management, Dietetics, Education, English, Fashion/Apparel Design, Fashion/Pattern Making, Merchandise Management, French, History, Mathematics, Music, Occupational Therapy, Philosophy, PreProfessional Programs, Public Relations, Social Work, Spanish, Theology, Religious Studies

Women's Athletic Profile

2900 N Menomonee River Pkwy **NCAA III**
Milwaukee, WI 53222 Crusaders/Royal Blue, White
Coach: TBA **Phone:** (414) 256-1220
Email: TBA **Fax:** (414) 256-0182
Estimated # of Women's Soccer Scholarships: None
Conference: Independent
Program Profile: Very scenic, grass field. Great Support from faculty, students and parents alike.
History: The program began as a club sport in 1993 and moved to varsity in 1994.
Achievements: All-Conference, Honorable Mention players.
Coaching: TBA

Mount Senario College

Academic Profile

Lady Smith, WI 54848 **Phone:** (715)532-5511x2260

Type: 4 Yr.,Private,Liberal Arts **Founded:** 1962
Website: www.mountsenario.edu **Religion:** Non-affiliated

SAT/ACT/GPA: Open18/2.0
Housing: Yes
Student/Faculty Ratio: 16/1
Male/Female Ratio: 2/1
Undergraduate Enrollment: 500
Graduate Enrollment: N/A
Scholarships/Academic: Yes
Athletic: No
Financial Aid: Yes
Expenses by: Year
In State: $16,990
Out of State: $16,990
Specialty: Education, Criminal Justice, Socail Work and Business
Degrees Conferred: AA, BA, BS
Programs of Study: Top 3: Education, Business, Criminal Justice

Men's Athletic Profile

1500 College Ave West
Lady Smith, WI 54848
Coach: Chris Currsn
Email: ccurran@mountsenario.edu
NAIA
Fighting Saints/Navy Blue, Gold
Phone: 715-532-5511x2280
Fax: 715-532-0371

Estimated # of Men's Soccer Scholarships: Not Available
Conference: Upper Midwest Athletic Conference
Program Profile: MSC has had success in soccer for a number of years with National Champions in 1979 in the NSC-CAA.
History:
Achievements: We have been udefeated in Conference play the last 2 seasons and have been ranked in the top 20 in the Nation. We have been at the NAIA National tournament the past 2 seasons.
Coaching: Chris Curran is the Head Coach and Derek Burton is the Assistant Coach.
Roster In State: 23
Out of State: 20
Out of Country: 20
Walk-on/Other:
Graduation %: 90
Seniors on Team: 6
Positions Needed: Keeper, Defenders, Forwards
Camp or Clinic Dates: August
Most Recent Record: 19-2-0
Schedule: Harris Stowe State, National American, John Brown, Aquinas, Oklahoma City, Walsh, Viterbo, University of Mary
Style of Play: Attacking-Flat back four.

Women's Athletic Profile

1500 College Avenue West
Ladysmith, WI 54848
Coach: Derek Burton
Email: dburton@mountsenario.edu
NAIA
Fighting Saints/Navy, Gold
Phone: (715) 532-5511
Fax: (715) 532-0371

Estimated # of Women's Soccer Scholarships: Unlimited Academic
Conference: Upper Midwest Athletic Conference, NAIA Region III
Program Profile: We share the school's on campus Sarkissian Soccer Complex with the men's program. The complex consists of a goal-equipped, training field that is 115x78. Both fields are of the highest quality Kentucky bluegrass, from the same seed that is used at Lambeu Field, home of the NFL's Green Bay Packers. All of the school's fields are maintained by our full-time grounds crew. The program has all of the most modern training equipment to help maximize our training efforts. The game field is equipped with international style goals. The complex is walking distance from the locker room facilities.
History: The women's program started in 1998 with a conference championship in its inaugural season. The program was started with upperclassmen and transfers who brought in vast experience. In 1999, the program had a difficult season due to mass injuries and the graduation of some upperclassmen. The program went on hiatus for the 2000 season, due to an institutional decision and the last minute decisions by a number of the school's top recruits. With the patience of the 6 returning players and a year of recruiting, we will be ready to jump right into the regional and national picture next season.

Achievements: Upper Midwest Athletic Conference Champions 1998, UMAC Player of the Year 1998, 6 All-Conference Players over the first 2 seasons. 2 former players have gone to play professionally in the first division in Sweden.
Coaching: Head Coach Derek Burton is a native of soccer-rich St. Louis and a former captain of D. I University of Arkansas. Drafted professionally by the EISL and a veteran of the USISL, Burton brings a host of playing experience of the highest level Coach Burton is a member of the NSCAA and the holder of a USSF "D" License, with a "C" License to come in the spring of 2001.
Roster in State: 1 **Out of State:** 3 **Out of Country:** 1
Walk-on/Other: 0 **Graduation %:** 100 **Seniors on Team:** 0
Positions Needed: Defense, Strikers
Camp or Clinic Dates: First two weeks in August
Most Recent Record: 2-16-0
Schedule: Northwestern College, Morehead State Univ. Aquinas College, National American U.
Style of Play: Play a possession game, building from the back. A lot of attacking from the wide positions, a 4-4-2 formation with a sweeper and a very attacking minded central midfielder. All of this with a team oriented attitude of defense first, all over the field, with the idea of counter attacking wide when ever possible. The team itself will be a melting pot of nationalities, Swedish, Caribbean, Canadian and of course American after a year of rebuilding the program.

Northland College

Academic Profile

Ashland, WI 54806
Phone: (715) 682-1224

Type: 4 Yr.,Private,Liberal Arts
Founded: 1892
Website: http://www.northland.edu
Religion: Church of Christ
SAT/ACT/GPA: 920/19
Housing: Yes
Student/Faculty Ratio: 16:1
Male/Female Ratio: 45:55
Undergraduate Enrollment: 900
Graduate Enrollment: N/A
Scholarships/Academic: Yes **Athletic:** No **Financial Aid:** Yes
Expenses by: Year **In State:** $ 17,715 **Out of State:** $ 17,715
Specialty: Environmental Education
Degrees Conferred: BA, BS
Programs of Study: Biology, Business Administration, Business Economics, Chemistry, Computer Science, Conflict and Peacemaking, Earth Sciences, Economics, Elementary Education, English, Environmental Studies, Fine Arts, Geology, History, Information Science, Management and Leadership, Mathematics, Meteorology , Music, Natural Resources, Occupational Therapy, Outdoor Education, Parks & Recreation, Physics, Policy Studies, Predental, PreLaw, PreMed, Psychology, Public Administration, Religion, Secondary Education, Social Science, Sociology and Writing.

Men's Athletic Profile

1411 Ellis Avenue
Ashland, WI 54806
Coach: Scott Mayfth
Email: Not Available

NCAA III/NAIA
Lumber Jacks/N. Blue, Orange
Phone: (715) 682-1245
Fax: (715) 682-1248

Estimated # of Men's Soccer Scholarships: None
Conference: Upper Midwest Athletic Conference
Program Profile: Joined UMAC Conference in 1998. Play on natural grass field. Playing season is in the Fall. Facilities include weight room, and pool.
History: Our program began in 1982 and was part of the National Small College Athletic Association, winning the National Championship in 1990. Joined NAIA in 1991 and is now complying for Division III. Still had a dual affiliation with NAIA.

Achievements: Coach of the Year in 1998, Conference Champions; 1998 was first year of conference, has one player drafted.

Ripon College

Academic Profile

Ripon, WI 54971-0248

Phone: (800) 947-4766

Type: 4 Yr.,Private,Liberal Arts
Founded: 1851
Website: http://www.ripon.edu
Religion: Non-Affiliated
SAT/ACT/GPA: 1140/24-25/3.20-3.30
Housing: Yes
Student/Faculty Ratio: 10:1
Male/Female Ratio: 50:50
Undergraduate Enrollment: 700
Graduate Enrollment: N/A
Scholarships/Academic: Yes **Athletic:** No
Financial Aid: Yes
Expenses by: Year **In State:** $ 22,640
Out of State: $ 22,640
Specialty: Economics, Education, Fine Arts, Liberal Arts, History, Politics
Degrees Conferred: BA
Programs of Study: Anthropology, Biology, Business Management, Chemistry, Computer Science, Economics, Educational Studies, English, Environmental Studies, Foreign Languages, French, German, Global Studies, History, Latin American Studies, Letters/Literature, Life Sciences, Mathematics, Music, Philosophy, Physical Education, Physical Sciences, Physics, Politics & Government, PreProfessional (Dentistry, Law, Medicine, Physical Therapy, Veterinary,), Psychology, Science, Self-Designed Majors, Sociology/Anthropology, Spanish, Speech Communication, Theatre

Men's Athletic Profile

300 Seward Street
Ripon, WI 54971
Coach: Bill Swartz
Email: swartzw@ripon.edu

NCAA III
Red Hawks/Red, White
Phone: (414) 748-8133
Fax: (414) 748-7386

Estimated # of Men's Soccer Scholarships: None
Conference: Midwest Collegiate Athletic Conference
Program Profile: 2 Natural grass fields, 120 x 80
History: Program began in 1972
Style of Play: Attacking with possession, all else depends on the players' strengths.

Women's Athletic Profile

300 Seward Street
Ripon, WI 54971
Coach: Rob Hartley
Email: Not Available

NCAA
Red Hawks/Red, White
Phone: (414) 748-8778
Fax: (414) 748-7386

Estimated # of Women's Soccer Scholarships: None
Conference: Midwest Conference
Program Profile: Two natural grass fields, 120X80. Brand new field (two years old); top facilities in the Midwest Conference for Soccer. Natural grass playing field which seats 1.000.
History: Program is approximately 15 years old. Two winning seasons for the last two years (10-6 & 8-7-1)

Saint Norbert College

Academic Profile

DePere, WI 54115

Phone:

Type: 4 Yr.,Private,Liberal Arts
Website: http://www.snc.edu
SAT/ACT/GPA: No requirements
Student/Faculty Ratio: 14:1
Undergraduate Enrollment: 2,050
Scholarships/Academic: Yes **Athletic:** No
Expenses by: Year **In State:** $ 19,700

Founded: 1898
Religion: Roman Catholic
Housing: Yes
Male/Female Ratio: 45:55
Graduate Enrollment: 25
Financial Aid: Yes
Out of State: $ 19,700

Specialty: International Business, Education
Degrees Conferred: BA, BS
Programs of Study: Biology, Business, Chemistry, Communications, International Studies, Business, Mathematics, PreDentistry, PreLaw, PreMed, Psychology, plus the usual Liberal Arts majors

Men's Athletic Profile

100 Grant Street
De Pere, WI 54115
Coach: Chad Johnson
Email: Not Available

NCAA III
Green Knights/Green, Gold
Phone: (920) 403-4077
Fax: (920) 403-3128

Estimated # of Men's Soccer Scholarships: None
Conference: Midwest Collegiate Athletic Conference
Program Profile: The men's soccer season starts in September and lasts through the end of October. They play at the Minohan Soccer Complex which is an all natural surface.
History: Our men's soccer program began in 1979, they joined the Midwest Conference in 1985. Since they joined the Midwest Conference in 1985 the team has maintained its 12 years conference winning record.
Achievements: Coach of the Year, All-Conference, All-State First Team, and All-Midwest First Team, NCAA III for more than 15 seasons, Conference Champions, Divisional Championships, the team has won three North Division Championships.
Style of Play: Attacking, disciplined style, overall system is designed to compliment the skills and abilities of our players.

Women's Athletic Profile

100 Grant St.
De Pere, WI 54115-2099
Coach: Chad Johnson
Email: admit@Mail.SNC.edu

NCAA III
Green Knights/Green, Gold
Phone: (920) 403-3148
Fax: (920) 403-4073

Estimated # of Women's Soccer Scholarships: None
Conference: Midwest Conference
Program Profile: Our women's soccer is a fall sport here. We play at the Minahan Soccer Complex, which is a natural playing surface. The Complex can hold 1,000 spectators.
History: The women's soccer program began in 1986. The team has an overall record of 120-60-10 and a Conference record of 92-18-7. The team has 6 Midwest Conference Titles, 2 North Division Titles and it has gained a playoff berth 12 of its 13 years of existence.
Achievements: 12 playoff berths; 6 Championship Titles; 40 First Team All-Midwest Conference Players.
Style of Play: Strong defense and player creativity on offense.

University of Wisconsin

Academic Profile

Phone:

Madison, WI 53711

Type: 4 Yr.,Public,Liberal Arts
Founded: 1849
Website: http://www.uwsa.edu
Religion: Non-Affiliated
SAT/ACT/GPA: 970+ Varies w/class rank
Housing: No
Student/Faculty Ratio: 12:1
Male/Female Ratio: 49:51
Undergraduate Enrollment: 28,900
Graduate Enrollment: 14,296
Scholarships/Academic: Yes **Athletic:** Yes **Financial Aid:** Yes
Expenses by: Year **In State:** $ 7,200 **Out of State:** $ 12,800
Degrees Conferred: BA, BS, MA, MS, MBA, Ph.D., JD, MD, PharmD, DVM
Programs of Study: Actuarial Science, Agribusiness, Business, Communications, Education, Engineering, Fine & Performing Arts, Health Science, Languages, Math & Science, PreProfessional, Teacher Education, Wildlife Management

Men's Athletic Profile

1440 Monroe Street
Madison, WI 53711
Coach: Kalekeni Banda
Email: kmb@athletics.wisc.edu

NCAA I
Badgers/Cardinal, White
Phone: (608) 262-7749
Fax: (608) 263-7849

Estimated # of Men's Soccer Scholarships: 9.9
Conference: Big Ten Conference
Program Profile: 1995 National Champions, Home field is natural grass (74 x 114), indoor facility (90 x 100), stadium fits 4,000 with bleachers and grass seating. Fall training begins mid-August and regular schedule concludes with Big Ten Championships mid-November. Spring season starts mid-February through late April with strength and conditioning during Januar6y through April
History: 19 years of varsity competition, program began in 1977 under Bill Redden who is still an associate coach. Launder has been the head coach since 1982. Wisconsin has finished in the top two in the region each of the past five years.
Achievements: Two recent A-League draftees.
Coaching: Head Coach, Kalekeni Banda. Assistant Coaches, David Laliberty and Michael Johnson.
Roster In State: 9 **Out of State:** 9 **Out of Country:** 7
ODP State: 4 **Regional:** **National:**
Walk-on/Other: **Graduation %:** 98 **Seniors on Team:** 4
Positions Needed: Midfielders
Camp or Clinic Dates: Day Camp June 5-9 & 26-30, Resident July 30-Aug. 3 & 6-10
Most Recent Record: 6-13-1
Schedule: Indiana, Penn State, Ohio State, Yale, Cincinnati
Style of Play: Possession oriented.

Women's Athletic Profile

1440 Monroe Street
Madison, WI 53711-2080
Coach: Dean Duerst
Email: Not Available

NCAA I
Badgers/Red, White
Phone: (608) 263-5493
Fax: (608) 263-7849

Estimated # of Women's Soccer Scholarships: None
Conference: Big Ten Conference

Program Profile: Practice field, game stadium and indoor facility
History: Program began in 1981.
Achievements: 1994 Big Ten Conference Tournament Champions.
Style of Play: Very fast team, which plays aggressive high pressure defense and emphasizes quick attacking play.

University of Wisconsin - Green Bay

Academic Profile

Green Bay, WI 54311
Phone: (920) 465-2573

Type: 4 Yr.,Public,Liberal Arts
Founded: 1965
Website: http://www.uwgb.edu
Religion: Non-Affiliated
SAT/ACT/GPA: Graduate top of class
Housing: Yes
Student/Faculty Ratio: 20:1
Male/Female Ratio: 1:1.6
Undergraduate Enrollment: 5,282
Graduate Enrollment: 137
Scholarships/Academic: Yes **Athletic:** Yes **Financial Aid:** Yes
Expenses by: Year **In State:** $ 7,194 **Out of State:** $ 13,979
Degrees Conferred: Bachelors
Programs of Study: Arts, Communication and the Arts, Communication Processes, English, French, German, History, Humanistic Studies, Music, Philosophy, Spanish, Theatre, Biology, Chemistry, Computer Science, Environmental Sciences, Environmental Policy & Planning, Political Science, Psychology, Human Development, Public Administration, Social Change & Development, Urban and Regional Studies, Business Administration, Education

Men's Athletic Profile

Phoenix Sports Ctr, 2420 Nicolet Dr.
Green Bay, WI 54311-7001
Coach: Simon Boddison
Email: boddisos@uwgb.edu

NCAA I
Phoenix/Red, Green, White
Phone: (920) 465-2145
Fax: (920) 465-2357

Estimated # of Men's Soccer Scholarships: N/A
Conference: Midwestern Collegiate Conference
Program Profile: 6 Practice Fields, 2 are lighted, natural grass fields, stadium is natural grass, is lighted, and holds 3,500 spectators. Team locker room for soccer only; swimming pool, weight room, training room facilities available
History: Program began in 1969 as an NAIA soccer program; in 1975 went to Division II status and qualified for the NCAA Division II Tournament in 1975, 1976, 1977, and 1978, finishing fourth nationally in 1975 and 1977. Program achieved highest national ranking in school history in 1992, #16, but was not selected to National Tournament. 1999, defeated 2 nationally ranked teams
Achievements: 10 players have played professionally, numerous All-Americans
Coaching: Simon Boddison, FA Preliminary Badge, USSF "B"
Quinn Ross, USSF "B"
Jesse Roberts, NSCAA Level II GK diploma, with distinction
Roster In State: 7 **Out of State:** 16 **Out of Country:**
ODP State: 5 **Regional:** **National:**
Walk-on/Other: **Graduation %:** N/A **Seniors on Team:** 4
Positions Needed: Defender, Goalkeeper, Striker
Camp or Clinic Dates: Loyola
Most Recent Record: 9-8-3
Schedule: Xavier, Marquette, UIC, Milwaukee, Redford
Style of Play: Attacking soccer with an emphasis on hard work by all 11 players to win the ball back. High-smart pressure from our forwards all the way back to our backs. Out work everyone!

Women's Athletic Profile

Phoenix Sports Ctr, 2420 Nicolet Dr.
Green Bay, WI 54311
Coach: Quinn Ross
Email: Not Available

NCAA I
Phoenix/Red, Green, White
Phone: (414) 465-2145
Fax: (414) 465-2357

Estimated # of Women's Soccer Scholarships: None
Conference: Midwestern Collegiate
Program Profile: 3 natural grass, 75 x 120, lighted fields equipped with underground sprinkler system and drainage titles, 2,00 capacity bleacher, concessions and restrooms. Stadium is used only for home soccer games.
History: Program began in 1987, NAIA finals in 1988, NCAA Division I in 1990
Achievements: All-Region and All-State
Coaching: Chad Johnson, Head Coach, member of the UW - Greenbay men's team, was MVP and led the team to a record of 13 wins, 4 losses and 2 ties.
Style of Play: Short passing, controlled.

University of Wisconsin - La Crosse

Academic Profile

La Crosse, WI 54601

Phone: 608-785-8000

Type: 4 Yr.,Public
Website: http://www.uwlax.edu
SAT/ACT/GPA: 21
Student/Faculty Ratio: 20:1
Undergraduate Enrollment: 8,000
Scholarships/Academic: Yes **Athletic:** No
Expenses by: Year **In State:** $ 5,173

Founded: 1909
Religion: Non-Affiliated
Housing: No
Male/Female Ratio: 45:55
Graduate Enrollment: 650
Financial Aid: Yes
Out of State: $ 10,308

Degrees Conferred: AA, AS, BA, BS, MS, MBA, MED
Programs of Study: Accounting, Archaeology, Art, Athletic Training, Biology, Business, Chemistry, Communications, Computer, Education, Finance, Geography, History, Liberal Arts, Marketing, Math, Medical, Philosophy, Physics, Political Science

Women's Athletic Profile

159 Mitchell Hall, 1725 State Street
La Crosse, WI 54601
Coach: Sara Burton
Email: burton.sara@uwlax.edu

NCAA III
Eagles/Maroon, Grey
Phone: (608) 785-6534
Fax: (608) 785-8674

Estimated # of Women's Soccer Scholarships: None
Conference: Wisconsin Intercollegiate Athletic Conference
Program Profile: Playing season begins in mid-August and goes thru early November. We have outstanding playing and practice facilities. We are the only varsity soccer team on campus so we do not have to compete for time or facilities in-season. The field is natural grass. We have quality indoor training facilities including a top-notch fieldhouse and strength center with allocated team times in the strength center.
History: The program gained varsity status in 1993. This program has been highly successful in its brief existence. UW-L won the conference title in 1996 and has consistently been a quality contender within the region.
Achievements: 1996 Conference Champions, 1996 Coach of the Year.
Coaching: Sara Burton is in her 7th season as head coach. She holds an Advanced National Diploma from the NSCAA. She has been coaching at the collegiate level since 1991.
Roster in State: 21 **Out of State:** 4 **Out of Country:** 0
ODP State: 8-10

Seniors on Team: 6
Positions Needed: Goalkeeper, midfielders, forwards, sweeper
Most Recent Record: 3-12-2
Schedule: UW-Stevens Point, Gustavus Adolphus, St. Thomas, Washington U. UW-Eau Claire
Style of Play: Possession play, with quick counter-attack.

University of Wisconsin - Milwaukee

Academic Profile

Milwaukee, WI 53201
Phone: (414) 229-3739

Type: 4 Yr.,Public,Liberal Arts
Founded: 1849
Website: http://www.uwm.edu
Religion: Non-Affiliated
SAT/ACT/GPA: Adequate/Upper half of class
Housing: Yes
Student/Faculty Ratio: 18:1
Male/Female Ratio: 45:55
Undergraduate Enrollment: 22,251
Graduate Enrollment: 5,500
Scholarships/Academic: Yes **Athletic:** Yes **Financial Aid:** Yes
Expenses by: Year **In State:** $ 7,136 **Out of State:** $ 15,026
Specialty: Business, Architecture, Education, Engineering, Fine Arts
Degrees Conferred: BA, BS, BFA, MA, MS, MBA, MFA, Ph.D.
Programs of Study: Accounting, Africology, Applied Mathematics, Architecture, Biological Aspects of Conservation, Civil Engineering, Communications, Computer Science (MIS), Dance, Education, Film, Finance, Geography, Electrical Engineering, Kinesiology, Marketing, Nursing, Psychology, Social Work, Theatre

Men's Athletic Profile

P.O. Box 413
Milwaukee, WI 53201
Coach: Louis Bennett
Email: looke@uwm.edu

NCAA I
Panthers/Gold, Black, White
Phone: (414) 229-5377
Fax: (414) 299-6759

Estimated # of Men's Soccer Scholarships: 9.9
Conference: Midwestern Collegiate Conference
Program Profile: On campus stadium, grass pitch, indoor facility, strong community support. Plan to move to new soccer complex. Traditional solid Division I program, 1997 MCC Champion, Engleman Field is natural grass located directly on campus and seats 2,500.
History: Program began in 1973. Three NCAA Tournament Appearances, numerous conference championships, only four losing seasons. 30 former Panthers have gone onto professional soccer and since 95 they have won a championship in every professional league this country has to offer.
Achievements: Louis Bennette was named MCC Coach of the Year in 1997; Conference Champions in 1997; MCC numerous past and current professional soccer players (USISL, A-League, MSL).
Coaching: Louis Bennett, Head Coach, was named MCC Coach of the Year in 1997. Stu Anderson and Jon Coleman - Assistant Coaches.
Roster In State: 12 **Out of State:** 9 **Out of Country:** 2
ODP State: 12 **Regional:** 1 **National:** 0
Walk-on/Other: 2 **Graduation %:** 64 **Seniors on Team:** 3
Positions Needed: ALL
Camp or Clinic Dates: June 11-15, June 18-22, July 30-Aug 3
Most Recent Record: 11-9-1
Schedule: UIC, Butler, Akron, Wisconsin, Marquette
Style of Play: Purposeful possession, focused on attack.

Women's Athletic Profile

P.O. Box 413
Milwaukee, WI 53201
Coach: Michael Moynihan
Email: moynihan@csd.uwm.edu

NCAA I
Panthers/Black, Gold, White
Phone: (414) 229-4593
Fax: (414) 229-6759

Estimated # of Women's Soccer Scholarships: 6
Conference: Midwestern Collegiate Conference
Program Profile: We are a Division I program with an all natural field and an indoor facilities.
History: We began our program in 1984. Our First NCAA appreance was in 1997 along with MCC Championship. We achieved begin national ranked in 1998 and in the top ten regional ranked for two seasons, '98 and '99. In 2000 we were MCC Champions with a 5-0 record.
Achievements: M. Maoynihan Co Coach of the Year 2000; Coach of the Year 1997; MCC Regular Season Championship 1997 and 2000; MCC Championsip tournament 1997; Lisa Krzykowski drafted to WUSA League; many All-Americans.
Coaching: Mike Moynihan, Head Coach, holds a USSF "A" License, Region II staff coach. David Nikolic and Crystalin Montgomery are our Assistant Coaches along with Stan Anderson as the Goalkeeper Coach.
Roster in State: 18 **Out of State:** 10 **Out of Country:** 1
ODP State: 15 **Regional:** 2 **National:**
Walk-on/Other: **Graduation %:** **Seniors on Team:** 5
Positions Needed: Defense, Outside Mid, Forward
Camp or Clinic Dates: July 5,6,7
Most Recent Record: 11-8-1
Schedule: Wisconsin, Marquette, Iowa, Tennesse, Vanderbuilt, Butler
Style of Play: Possession Build up. High pressure defense.

University of Wisconsin - Oshkosh

Academic Profile

Oshkosh, WI 54901
Phone: 920-424-0202

Type: 4 Yr.,Public
Founded: 1871
Website: http://www.uwosh.edu
Religion: Non-Affiliated
SAT/ACT/GPA: 1030/22
Housing: Yes
Student/Faculty Ratio: 19:1
Male/Female Ratio: 42/58
Undergraduate Enrollment: 9,171
Graduate Enrollment: 1,596
Scholarships/Academic: Yes **Athletic:** No **Financial Aid:** Yes
Expenses by: Year **In State:** $6,758 **Out of State:** $14,285
Degrees Conferred: BS, BA, MA, MS, MBA
Programs of Study: 49 Majors, 15 PreProfessional programs, 24 additional Minors; Art, Business and Management, Communications, Computer Science, Education, Health Sciences, Journalism, Nursing, Parks and Recreation, PreProfessional, Protective Services, Public Affairs, Social Science

Men's Athletic Profile

800 Algoma Blvd.
Oshkosh, WI 54901
Coach: Toby Bares
Email: bares@uwosh.edu

NCAA III
Titans/Black, Gold, White
Phone: (920) 424-1282
Fax: (920) 424-7445

Estimated # of Men's Soccer Scholarships: None
Conference: WIAC

Program Profile: Perennial NCAA Division III power; nationally ranked nine of the last eleven years; NCAA Tournament bids four of the last six years; field has a measurements of 120x75 and is natural grass adjacent to separate practice fields for men & women's teams.
History: Began in the fall of 1984. Went to its first NCAA bid in 1991, first NCAA Quarterfinalist Appearance in 1993 and first NCAA Final Four.
Achievements: 1994 NCAA III National Coach of the Year; 1994 NCAA III Midwest Region Coach of the Year; 6 State Coach of the Year Awards; 3 former players have played professionally.
Coaching: Toby Bares, Head Coach, WI ODP Coach. He compiled a record of 188-58-22 over the last 15 years of competition.
Roster In State: 25 **Out of State:** 3 **Out of Country:** 0
ODP State: 3 **Regional:** 0 **National:** 0
Walk-on/Other: **Graduation %:** N/A **Seniors on Team:** 7
Positions Needed: Forward, Keeper
Most Recent Record: 18-2-0
Schedule: Trinity, Wheaton, Wis-Whitewater
Style of Play: Disciplined, aggressive and exciting.

Women's Athletic Profile

Kolf Center, 800 Algoma Blvd.
Oshkosh, WI 54901-8683
Coach: Scott Haywood
Email: haywood@uwosh.edu
NCAA III
Titans/Black, Gold
Phone: (920) 424-1312
Fax: (920) 424-7445

Estimated # of Women's Soccer Scholarships:
Conference: Wisconsin Women's Intercollegiate Athletic Conference
Program Profile: Program began in 1993 All time record is 58-72-10. We play on natural grass and seating of 1000 capacity.
History: Placed fourth in the conference in 2000
Roster in State: 29 **Out of State:** 1 **Out of Country:** 1
ODP State: 5 **Regional:** 1 **National:** 0
Walk-on/Other: **Graduation %:** **Seniors on Team:** 0
Positions Needed: Forward
Camp or Clinic Dates: Not Available
Most Recent Record: 15-4-0
Schedule: Wis. Stevens Point, Wis. Eau Claire, Wis. Whitewater.
Style of Play: Aggressive and exciting.

University of Wisconsin - Parkside

Academic Profile

P. O. Box 2000
Kenosha, WI 53141
Phone: (414) 595-2412

Type: 4 Yr.,Public,Liberal Arts
Founded: 1960
Website: http://www.uwp.edu
Religion: Non-Affiliated
SAT/ACT/GPA: 900/18
Housing: Yes
Student/Faculty Ratio: 14:1
Male/Female Ratio: 45:55
Undergraduate Enrollment: 4,700
Graduate Enrollment: 300
Scholarships/Academic: Yes **Athletic:** Yes **Financial Aid:** Yes
Expenses by: Year **In State:** $ 7,700 **Out of State:** $ 13,800
Specialty: Business, Pre-Health
Degrees Conferred: BS, BA, MBA, MA
Programs of Study: Art, Biological Sciences, Business, Communications, Computer Science, Criminal Justice, Education, Music, Nursing, PreHealth, Psychology, Social Sciences

Men's Athletic Profile

900 Wood Road
Kenosha, WI 53141-2000
Coach: Rick Kilps
Email: Richard.kilps@uwp.edu

NCAA II
Rangers/Green, Black
Phone: (414) 595-2257
Fax: (414) 595-2225

Estimated # of Men's Soccer Scholarships: None
Conference: Great Lakes Valley Conference
Program Profile: play on 120x80 field, fenced, bleachers (eleven), press box, electronic scoreboard, team bench protected shelters, concession stand, and eight fields on campus.
History: Our program's 12 year record is 193-57-19.Origin was in 1969 - last 16 years winning record, last 14 years nationally ranked win 207, loss 61 and tie 20.
Achievements: Regional Coach of the Year two times; 27 All-Americans, 7 pros, one in 1990 World Cup with USA, one in US Concave Try with US Futsal team.
Coaching: Rick Kilps, Head Coach, USSF'A' Licensee. 21 years college head coach - never a losing record. Rick Vacca - Assistant Coach, NSCAA National Licensee. Former High School coach, 4 years at UWP. Brian Miller - Graduate Assistant Coach. Mike Guzaski - Goalkeeper Coach.
Style of Play: Possession, quick build up and quick counter.

Women's Athletic Profile

900 Wood Road, Box 2000
Kenosha, WI 53141
Coach: Oscar Suman
Email: Not Available

NCAA II
Rangers/Green, Black, White
Phone: (414) 595-2045
Fax: (414) 595-2225

Estimated # of Women's Soccer Scholarships:
Conference: Great Lakes Valley Conference
Program Profile: The Rangers have eight soccer fields, all natural grass. The varsity field seats 700.
History: The program began in 1994. 1996 first year coach.
Coaching: Oscar Suman, Head Coach, 1996 was his first season. USSF "A" License. PhD in Exercise Physiology.
Style of Play: Emphasis on ball possession. We mix our styles up. At times we high pressure, and against other opponents we low pressure and counter-attack. Team defense is emphasized. We try to play a 3-5-2 committing different players forward.

University of Wisconsin - Platteville

Academic Profile

Phone: 800-362-5515

Platteville, WI 53818-3099

Type: 4 Yr.,Public
Website: http://www.uwplatt.edu
SAT/ACT/GPA: Open
Student/Faculty Ratio: 20:1
Undergraduate Enrollment: 5,000
Scholarships/Academic: Yes
Athletic: No
Expenses by: Year
In State: $ Varies
Specialty: Engineering
Degrees Conferred: BA, MS, AS, BS

Founded: 1866
Religion: Non-Affiliated
Housing: Yes
Male/Female Ratio: 65:35
Graduate Enrollment: N/A
Financial Aid: Yes
Out of State: $ Varies

Programs of Study: Accounting, Agriculture, Art, Biology, Botany, Broadcasting, Business, Chemistry, Communications, Computer Science, Criminal Justice, Liberal Arts, Marketing, Mathematics, Economics, Education, Engineering, Geology, Geography, Philosophy, Physical Education

Men's Athletic Profile

1 University Plaza
Platteville, WI 53818-3099
Coach: Ray Smith
Email: smithra@uwplatt.edu

NCAA III
Pioneers/Royal, Orange, White
Phone: (608) 342-1578
Fax: (608) 342-1576

Estimated # of Men's Soccer Scholarships: 0
Conference: Independent
Program Profile: Our season is Mid August through early November. Indoor field, new weight room facilities, 2 outdoor natural grass fields.
History: Began in 1964 and is the oldest collegiate program in the State of Wisconsin.
Achievements: 1 3rd team All-American (plays for Milwaukee Wave). 1998-1st in State, 7th in the Region. 2 players play for the Rockford Raptors.
Coaching: Ray Smith is our Head Coach.
Schedule: UW-Oshkosh, Trinity, Washington, Luther College, Ripon, Beliot
Style of Play: Very tactical (Low pressure to high pressure) man marking.

Women's Athletic Profile

1 University Plaza
Platteville, WI 53818-3099
Coach: Craig Smith
Email: Smither@uwplatt.edu

NCAA III
Pioneers/Orange, Blue, White
Phone: (608) 342-1343
Fax: (608) 342-1576

Estimated # of Women's Soccer Scholarships: None
Conference: W.I.A.C.
Program Profile: Season- Sept.1 to October, field natural and have 3 proactive fields as well as an indoor field. State of the Art weight room facilities.
History: Began in 1990, now in it's 10th year.
Coaching: 1st year in the rebuilding process. Presently the USASA Midwest region women's select team administrator/asst. coach.
Roster in State: 13 **Out of State:** 1 **Out of Country:** 0
Positions Needed: All new coach rebuilding process
Most Recent Record: 4-16-0
Schedule: UW-Stevens Point, UW-Eau Claire, Concordia Univ. Luther College.
Style of Play: Very tactical, 11 on offense 11 on defense mixture of low pressure/high pressure. We play at all times with class and character.

University of Wisconsin - River Falls

Academic Profile

Phone: 715-425-3911

River Falls, WI 54022

Type: 4 Yr.,Public
Website: http://www.uwrf.edu
SAT/ACT/GPA: 900/22
Student/Faculty Ratio: 18:1
Undergraduate Enrollment: 4,800
Scholarships/Academic: Yes **Athletic:** No
Expenses by: Year **In State:** $ 5,200

Founded: 1874
Religion: Non-Affiliated
Housing: No
Male/Female Ratio: 45:55
Graduate Enrollment: 400
Financial Aid: Yes
Out of State: $ 9,900

Degrees Conferred: BA, BS, BFA, BME, BSW, MA
Programs of Study: Accounting, Agricultural, American Studies, Animal Science, Biological Science, Chemistry, Computer Science, Conservation, Early Childhood Education, Economics, Education, English, Food Services, Languages, Geology, Geography, History, Horticulture, Journalism, Land Use, Math, Music, Physical Science, Physics, Political Science, PreProfessional Programs, etc..

Women's Athletic Profile

410 South 3rd
River Falls, WI 54022
Coach: Jeff Hopkins
Email: Not Available

NCAA III
Falcons/Red, White
Phone: (715) 425-3900
Fax: (715) 425-4486

Did Not Return Profile

University of Wisconsin - Stevens Point

Academic Profile

Stevens Point, WI 54881

Phone: (715) 346-3626

Type: 4 Yr.,Public,Liberal Arts
Website: http://www.uwsp.edu
SAT/ACT/GPA: 18/2.3
Student/Faculty Ratio: 21:1
Undergraduate Enrollment: 8,500
Scholarships/Academic: Yes
Athletic: No
Expenses by: Year
In State: $ 3,000

Founded: 1894
Religion: Non-Affiliated
Housing: Yes
Male/Female Ratio: 1:1
Graduate Enrollment: N/A
Financial Aid: Yes
Out of State: $ 4,100

Degrees Conferred: AA, AS, BA, BS, MA, MS, MBA, Ph.D., JD
Programs of Study: Accounting, Anthropology, Art, Biology, Broadcasting, Business, Chemistry, Communications, Computer, Education, English, Fashion Merchandising, Fish/Game, Forestry, History, International, Liberal Arts, Math, Medical, Music, Natural Resources, PreProfessional Program, Psychology, Social Science, Speech, Theatre, Wildlife

Women's Athletic Profile

2100 Main Street
Stevens Point, WI 54481
Coach: Sheila Miech
Email: smeich@uwsp.edu

NCAA III
Pointers/Purple, Gold
Phone: (715) 346-2840
Fax: (715) 346-4415

Estimated # of Women's Soccer Scholarships: None
Conference: Wisconsin Women's Intercollegiate Athletic Conference
Program Profile: Played in NCAA III semi-finals last season (2000). Team plays one of the strongest schedules in D-III with seven games vs. top 15 opponents last season, including six conference champion teams. Take one trip every 2 years (past 2 have been to Texas).
History: Program began in 1987. Have 198-71-16 all-time record, including 63-0-2 all-time conference record. Have won 8 of 9 all-time conference titles and played in 7 of last 8 NCAA tournaments with 3 Elite Eight and one Final Four appearance.
Achievements: Have 3 first-team and 6 total All-Americans in past 9 seasons. Coach Shelia Miech has been WIAC and Central Region Coach of the Year 3 times each, including both last season. Have had 11 Conference Scholar Athletes 5 of last 9 years.
Coaching: Head Coach is Shelia Miech and she is assisted by Larry Leton.
Roster in State: 16
Out of State: 2
Out of Country: 0
Walk-on/Other:
Graduation %: N/A
Seniors on Team: 4

Positions Needed: Defense, Keeper
Most Recent Record: 22-5-0
Schedule: Wheaton, Macalester, St. Benedict, University of Chicago, St. Thomas, Wisconsin-Eau Claire, Gustavus Adolphus

University of Wisconsin - Stout

Academic Profile

Menomonie, WI 54751
Phone: (715) 232-1312

Type: 4 Yr.,Public,Engineering
Founded: 1891
Website: http://www.stout.edu
Religion: Non-Affiliated
SAT/ACT/GPA: 1000/22/3.0
Housing: Yes
Student/Faculty Ratio: 21:1
Male/Female Ratio: 51:49
Undergraduate Enrollment: 7,000
Graduate Enrollment: 1,000
Scholarships/Academic: Yes **Athletic:** No **Financial Aid:** Yes
Expenses by: Year **In State:** $ 5,880 **Out of State:** $ 12,160
Specialty: Early Childhood Education, Hospitality & Tourism
Degrees Conferred: BA, BS, MS, MA
Programs of Study: Apparel Design/Manufacturing, Applied Mathematics, Art, Art Education, Construction, Dietetics, Early Childhood Education, Family and Consumer Science Education, Foods Systems Technology, General Business Administration, Graphic Communications Management, Human Development & Family Studies, Industrial Technology, Manufacturing Engineering, Marketing Education, Packaging, Psychology, Retail Merchandising, Service Mangement, Technology, Telecommunications, Vocational

Women's Athletic Profile

245 Johnson Fieldhouse
Menomonie, WI 54751
Coach: Dave Morris
Email: morrisd@uwstout.edu

NCAA III
Blue Devils/Navy, White
Phone: (715) 232-1312
Fax: (715) 232-1684

Estimated # of Women's Soccer Scholarships: None
Conference: Wisconsin Women's Intercollegiate Athletic Conference
Program Profile: We will be moving to the Nelson Field in 2001, which is a women's soccer only stadium with a 120x80 grass field and 2,000 seating.
History: We are entering our 6th season.
Achievements: Coach Morris three time Coach of the Year; three players picked by the WPSC including All-WIAC selections.
Coaching: Dave Morris is our Head Coach, who is assisted by Sam Vang and Alyssa Halverson, the goalkeeper coach.
Roster in State: 14 **Out of State:** 14 **Out of Country:**
ODP State: 5 **Regional:** 2 **National:**
Walk-on/Other: 21 **Graduation %:** 100 **Seniors on Team:** 6
Positions Needed: All
Camp or Clinic Dates: July 5-7
Most Recent Record: 6-12-0
Schedule: Macalester, St. Mary's, St Thomas, Illinois Wesleyan, UW Steven's Point, UW Eau Claire
Style of Play: Tactically sophisticated, zonal approach that allows all our field players to be involved offensively.

University of Wisconsin - Superior

Academic Profile

Phone: (715) 394-8131

Superior, WI 54880

Type: 4 Yr.,Public,Liberal Arts
Founded: 1893
Website: http://www.super.edu
Religion: Non-Affiliated
SAT/ACT/GPA: 20/3.0
Housing: Yes
Student/Faculty Ratio: 4:1
Male/Female Ratio: 50:50
Undergraduate Enrollment: 2,500
Graduate Enrollment: 200
Scholarships/Academic: Yes
Athletic: No
Financial Aid: TAP
Expenses by: Year
In State: $ 2,334
Out of State: $ 7,470
Specialty: Education, Communications, Sociology, Music
Degrees Conferred: AA, BA, BFA, B.Mus., BME, BS, MA, MSEd, Specialist in Education
Programs of Study: Elementary Education, Music, Communications, Sociology, Criminal Justice, Business, Theatre, Physical Education, Human Performance Sciences, Health & Psychology

Women's Athletic Profile

Box 2000, Belknap & Catlin
Superior, WI 54880
Coach: Eryca Card
Email: enelson@staff.uwsuper.edu

NCAA III
Yellowjackets/Black, Old Gold
Phone: (715) 394-8023
Fax:

Estimated # of Women's Soccer Scholarships: N/A
Conference: WIAC
Program Profile: We will have a new facility in 2002. For the moment we are playing on a natural field stadium. Our program is in a re-developing stage.
Coaching: Eryca Card, Head Coach, is entering her first year as a head coach with the program. She served as an assistant coach and played with the Yellowjackets.
Roster in State: 10
Out of State: 2
Out of Country: 2
Walk-on/Other:
Graduation %:
Seniors on Team: 2
Positions Needed: All
Style of Play: Aggressive, first year of play with a new coach.

University of Wisconsin - Whitewater

Academic Profile

Phone: 262-472-1234

Whitewater, WI 53190

Type: 4 Yr.,Public
Founded: 1868
Website: http://www.uww.edu
Religion: Non-Affiliated
SAT/ACT/GPA: 21
Housing: Yes
Student/Faculty Ratio: 1:21
Male/Female Ratio: 45:55
Undergraduate Enrollment: 9,556
Graduate Enrollment: 1,122
Scholarships/Academic: Yes
Athletic: No
Financial Aid: Yes
Expenses by: Year
In State: $ 5,858
Out of State: $ 12,138
Specialty: Business, Education
Degrees Conferred: BA, BBA, BFA, BM, BS
Programs of Study: Arts, Business, Accounting, Marketing, Elementary Education, Various Secondary Education, Mathematics, Social Work, Management Computer Systems, Office Systems, English, History, Women's Studies, Physical Education

Men's Athletic Profile

121 Williams Center
Whitewater, WI 53190
Coach: Greg Henschel
Email: Not Available

NCAA III
Warhawks/Purple, White
Phone: (414) 472-1153
Fax: (414) 472-5656

Estimated # of Men's Soccer Scholarships: None
Conference: Wisconsin Intercollegiate Athletic Conference
Program Profile: Top 10 regionally ranked in 1998; excellent playing and training facilities. Men have their own training field 80x120 and separate on campus stadium for matches, which seats about 1,500. New $13 million dollar fieldhouse is under construction for increased indoor play.
History: Our program began in 1978. Very focused team in pursuit of Division III national championship in addition to team unity and highest level of play.
Achievements: Coach of the Year.
Coaching: Greg Hanschel, Head Coach. Robin Rameker, Assistant Coach.
Style of Play: Possession oriented style of play. Zonal defending tactics are typically used. Players on the field are given lots of freedom to take matches into their own hands.

Women's Athletic Profile

800 West Main Street
Whitewater, WI 53190
Coach: Greg Henschel
Email: kuffelM@uwwvnc.vww.edu

NCAA III
Warhawks/Purple, White
Phone: (414) 472-2265
Fax: (414) 472-2791

Estimated # of Women's Soccer Scholarships: None
Conference: WIAC
Program Profile: Our program is a model of a team. Our playing season is in the fall. We play in a natural game field and have natural practice fields.
History: Our program began in 1992 under Coach Carlos. In 1995, Matt Kuffel became the head coach of the program.
Achievements: All-American player in 1994-1995; WIAC Scholar Athlete in 1998
Style of Play: Controlled movement in a 4-4-2 formation with a wide field play.

Viterbo College

Academic Profile

Phone: 1-800-Viterbo

La Crosse, WI 54601

Type: 4 Yr.,Private,Liberal Arts
Website: http://www.viterbo.edu
SAT/ACT/GPA: 860/18/3.0
Student/Faculty Ratio: 16:1
Undergraduate Enrollment: 1,750
Scholarships/Academic: Yes **Athletic:** Yes
Expenses by: Year **In State:** $ 17,110

Founded: 1890
Religion: Catholic
Housing: Yes
Male/Female Ratio: 26:74
Graduate Enrollment: 300
Financial Aid: Yes
Out of State: $ 17,110

Degrees Conferred: BA, BS, MA, MS, MSN
Programs of Study: Biology, Business, Chemistry, Computer, Education, English, Fine Arts, Health Sciences, Humanities, Mathematics, Natural Sciences, Nursing, PreProfessional Programs (Dentistry, Medicine, Chemistry, Engineering, Pharmacy, Chiropractic, Law, Optometry) Psychology, Religious Studies, Social Science, Sociology

Men's Athletic Profile

815 South 9th Street
La Crosse, WI 54601
Coach: Michael Rahn
Email: MPRAHN@VITERBO.EDU

NAIA
V-Hawks/Cardinal , Silver
Phone: 608-796-3822
Fax: (608) 796-3818

Estimated # of Men's Soccer Scholarships: None
Conference: Midwest Classic Conference
Program Profile: Program has been consistently ranked in the top 20, brand new facility opening in the fall of 1998 with a stadium field and practice field. Team plays both fall and spring schedule.
History: Our program began in 1979. Has won five NAIA District 14 Championships, 3 Midwest Classic Conference Championships in six years, National Ranking seven out of the last nine years.
Achievements: Midwest Classic Conference Coach of the Year three times (1993, 1996 & 1997); NAIA District 14 Coach of the Year (1993), coached seven players who went on professionally, 17 All-Americans.
Style of Play: Possession oriented game with an emphasis on attacking as a team and defending as a team. Individually creativity and attacking philosophy.

Women's Athletic Profile

815 S 9th Street
La Crosse, WI 54601
Coach: Bruce Erickson
Email: Not Available

NAIA
V-Hawks/Cardinal, Silver
Phone: (608) 791-0391
Fax: (608) 791-0367

Estimated # of Women's Soccer Scholarships: None
Conference: Midwest Classic Conference
Program Profile: Program has great facilities, (76 x 110) and plays a comp. schedule
History: Our program began in 1995 without a prior club season
Achievements: N/A
Coaching: Bruce Erickson, Head Coach of the Year awards, 10 years, coaching experience, coaches both men and women and is the Athletic Director
Style of Play: Attacking soccer, possession oriented, looking for skillful and creative players with good distribution and ball control.

Wisconsin Lutheran College

Academic Profile

Phone:

Milwaukee, WI 53226

Type: 4 Yr.,Private,Liberal Arts
Website: http://www.wlc.edu
SAT/ACT/GPA: 20+/2.75
Student/Faculty Ratio: 12:1
Undergraduate Enrollment: 553
Scholarships/Academic: Yes **Athletic:** No
Expenses by: Year **In State:** $ 5,500

Founded: 1973
Religion: Lutheran
Housing: Yes
Male/Female Ratio: 45:55
Graduate Enrollment: N/A
Financial Aid: Yes
Out of State: $ 5,500

Degrees Conferred: BA, BS, Bachelor of Business Administration
Programs of Study: Art, Biology, Broad field Social Studies, Business Administration, Chemistry, Coaching, Communications, Communication Arts, Computer Information Systems, Education, English, Foreign Languages, History, Liberal Arts, Mathematics, Music, Philosophy, Pre-Law, Pre-Medicine, Pre-Nursing, Pre-Pharmacy, Psychology, Secondary Education, Spanish, Theatre, Theology

Men's Athletic Profile

88010 W. Bluemound Road
Milwaukee, WI 53226
Coach: Joe Luedke
Email: Not Available

NCAA III
Warriors/Forest Green, White
Phone: (414) 443-8808
Fax: (414) 443-8508

Estimated # of Men's Soccer Scholarships: None
Conference: Lake Michigan Conference
Program Profile: Natural grass off campus, stadium seats 1,000. goal is to be competitive program among the Lake Michigan Conference.
History: 1987 official program began, club prior to.
Achievements: Has 3 players from 1997-1998 team received conference honors.
Style of Play: Offensive minded.

Women's Athletic Profile

8800 W. Bluemound Rd.
Milwaukee, WI 53226
Coach: Brook Smith
Email: Not Available

NCAA III
Warriors/Forest Green, White
Phone: (414) 443-8701
Fax: (414) 443-8508

Estimated # of Women's Soccer Scholarships: None
Conference: Lake Michigan Conference
Program Profile: Fourth year of the program that has been successful and looking to improve. We play our home game at Uihlieu Field which is a natural surface. Play on a natural grass, off-campus, stadium has 1,000 seating. Goal is to be competitive among the Lake Michigan Conference.
History: The program began in 1995; 1996 we finished third in the Lake Michigan Conference and in 1997 we had a fourth place finish which is middle of the table.
Achievements: In 1996 we had an All-Midwest midfielder, this year we will return two All- Conference players.
Coaching: Tony Pierce, Head Coach, played college soccer at University of Connecticut. Won a NCAA Division I Championship in 1981. Played pro ball in the NSPL for ten years with the Milwaukee Wave. Now coaches with the Wisconsin ODP.
Style of Play: Possession game; European Style of play.

WYOMING

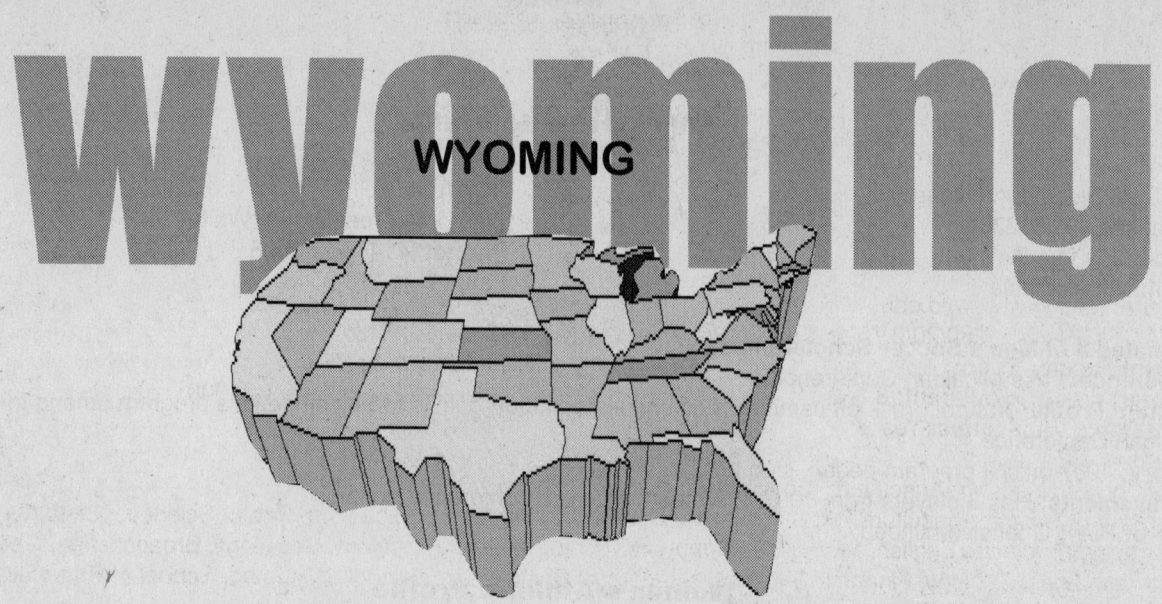

SCHOOL	CITY	AFFILIATION	PAGE
University of Wyoming	Laramie	NCAA I	1239

University of Wyoming
Academic Profile

Laramie, WY 87071

Phone: (307) 766-5507

Type: 4 Yr.,Public
Website: http://www.uwyo.edu
SAT/ACT/GPA: 810-960/20/2.75 or 3.0
Student/Faculty Ratio:
Undergraduate Enrollment: 8,806
Scholarships/Academic: Yes **Athletic:** Yes
Expenses by: **In State:** $ 7,948

Founded: 1886
Religion: Non-Affiliated
Housing: Yes
Male/Female Ratio:
Graduate Enrollment: 2,000
Financial Aid: Yes
Out of State: $ 12,336

Specialty: Engineering, Agriculture, Education, Science
Programs of Study: Agriculture, Art & Sciences, Business Education, Engineering, Health Sciences, Biology, Chemistry, Economics, English, Music, Philosophy, Psychology, History, Geology, Sociology, Broadcasting, Geography, Journalism, Math, Zoology, Finance, Chemical & Electrical Engineering, School of Nursing, School of Pharmacy, Exercise Science, Health Education

Women's Athletic Profile

Box 3414, University Station
Laramie, WY 82072
Coach: Anne B. Moore
Email: asmoore@uwuo.edu

NCAA I
Cowgirls/Brown, Gold
Phone: (307) 766-5507
Fax: (307) 766-5414

Estimated # of Women's Soccer Scholarships: 7/8
Conference: Western Athletic Conference
Program Profile: We play in a stadium with natural grass. There is a press box and about 500 seats. Our season is in the fall and the spring.
History: Our program started in 1995 and our total record is 8-66-0 but this year we have improved and the record for last year was 5-12-1.
Achievements: Two Second Team All-Conference Players
Coaching: Anne B.Moore, Head Coach, she started in 1999. Kim Murphy and Ileana Moschos are the Assistant Coaches.
Roster in State: 5 **Out of State:** 25 **Out of Country:**
ODP State: 20 **Regional:** **National:**
Walk-on/Other: **Graduation %:** 100 **Seniors on Team:** 5
Positions Needed: Goalkeeper, Center midfield, Forward
Camp or Clinic Dates: June 18-22, July 29- August 1,
Most Recent Record: 5-12-1
Schedule: BYU, San Diego State, Utah, Air Force, West Virginia, Sacramento State, Creighton, Pittsburgh
Style of Play: Attacking out of the back, switching fields diagonally, and zonal defense.

canada

CANADA

SCHOOL	CITY	AFFILIATION	PAGE
Simon Fraser University	Burnaby, BC	NAIA	1241
Trinity Western University	Langley	NCCAA	1242

Simon Fraser University
Academic Profile

Phone: 604-291-3224

Burnaby, BC, Cana V5A 1S6

Type: 4 Yr.,Public,
Website: http://www.sfu.ca
SAT/ACT/GPA: Open/3.0
Student/Faculty Ratio: 24:1
Undergraduate Enrollment: 15,000
Scholarships/Academic: Yes
Athletic: Yes
Expenses by: Year
In State: $ 6,300 Can
Specialty: Engineering
Founded: 1965
Religion: Non-Affiliated
Housing: Yes
Male/Female Ratio: 47:53
Graduate Enrollment: 3,000
Financial Aid: Yes
Out of State: $ 9,800 Can
Degrees Conferred: BA, BS, MA, MS, Ph.D., EdD
Programs of Study: Anthropology, Archaeology, BioChemistry, Biological Science, Business Administration, Canadian Studies, Criminology, Economics, Engineering Sciences, Geography, Liberal Arts, Mathematics, Philosophy, Physics, Political Science, Psychology, Statistics, Systems Science, Theatre

Men's Athletic Profile

8888 University Way
Burnaby, BC, CANA V5A 1S6
Coach: Keith Watts
Email: Not Available

NAIA
Clansmen/Red, Blue
Phone: (604) 291-3685
Fax: (604) 291-4922

Estimated # of Men's Soccer Scholarships: None
Conference: PNWCSC

Women's Athletic Profile

8888 University Way
Burnaby, B.C., CANA V5A 1S6
Coach: Shelley Howieson
Email: Not Available

NAIA
Clans/Red, White, Blue
Phone: (604) 291-3931
Fax: (604) 291-4922

Estimated # of Women's Soccer Scholarships: None
Conference: PNWAC
Program Profile: Home games played at Terry Fox Field located on campus and Coquitlam Town Center, which seats 1,000, both have grass turf. 20 game season begins early September, ends early November, followed by District, Area, & National Championships.
History: Program began in 1988.
Achievements: CSA Coach of the Year; 2 NAIA All - Americans; 6 All - Region; 4 NAIA Scholar Athletes.
Coaching: Shelley Howieson, Head Coach, Canadian Soccer Association Coach of the Year, started the women's program at SFU in 1988, holds CSA 'C' license.
Style of Play: Play through the midfield on the ground. Very direct attacking style of play - an adapted South American style.

Trinity Western University
Academic Profile

Phone: (604) 513-2065

Langley, BC V2Y 1Y1

Type: 4 Yr.,Private,Liberal Arts
Website: http://www.twu.ca.edu
SAT/ACT/GPA: 1065/22/2.5
Student/Faculty Ratio: 1:17
Undergraduate Enrollment: 2,700
Scholarships/Academic: Yes **Athletic:** Yes
Expenses by: Year **In State:** $ 10,590
Founded: 1962
Religion: Evangelical Church
Housing: Yes
Male/Female Ratio: 40:60
Graduate Enrollment: 2,700
Financial Aid: Yes
Out of State: $ 10,590
Specialty: 35 undergraduate majors; 14 graduate programs
Degrees Conferred: BSC, BA, BBA, B.Ed.., BSCN, BPE, MA, MC, MDivision, MLE
Programs of Study: Physical Education, Business Administration, Elementary and Secondary Education, Coaching (minor), Recreation (minor), Applied Math and Computer Science, Biblical Studies, Biology, Chemistry, Chemistry and Culture, Communications, Drama, English, Environmental Science, Fine Arts, Geography, History, International Relations & Studies, InterCultural, Religious Studies, Linguistics, Music, Natural and Applied Science, Nursing, Philosophy, Political Science, Psychology, Social Science, Counseling, Teaching English as a Secondary Languages

Men's Athletic Profile

7600 Glover Road
Langley, BC V2Y 1Y1
Coach: Alan Alderson
Email: Alderson@twu.ca

NCCAA
Spartans/Blue, Gold, White
Phone: (604) 513-2020 (2126)
Fax: (604) 513-2065

Estimated # of Men's Soccer Scholarships: 3 Full Ride
Conference: BCCAA
Program Profile: We are the Top Christian University program in Canada. We currently play in the CCAA and will be joining the CIUA (equivalent to NCAA Division I in the US), in the Fall of 2001. In preparation for the big jump, a brand new 80x120 yards, lighted stadium field, which will seat approximately 1,000, yearly increase in athletic scholarships and budget necessary to accommodate increase in air travel etc. We play both a fall and spring outdoor schedule.
History: Our soccer program began in early 1970's. Our most successful season was in 1989-1990 when TWU, finished 5th at the CCAA National Championships in Calgary Alberta. With a dramatic shift in favor of increasing the profile of program. The TWU Spartans will now be given the opportunity to be the top program in the country.
Achievements: Coach Alan Alderson has been Coach of the Year for the Conference region in three of his ten years as a head coach and was the National Coach of the Year this past season at his previous University in Indiana. Coach Alderson has also played three years of professional soccer, two in Canada and 1 in the US. He has worked with both the provincial and national team program in Canada.
Coaching: Alan Alderson, Head Coach, is returning to TWU after an extraordinary successful three year coaching at Indiana Wesleyan University when he won two times National titles in the NCCAA and finished a numerous Runner-Up in a third. He is assisted by Mike Shearan, a former player from Wheaton College, who is currently on staff with Athletic in Action.
Roster In State: 14 **Out of State:** 6 **Out of Country:** 1
ODP State: 5 **Regional:** **National:** 2
Walk-on/Other: **Graduation %:** High **Seniors on Team:** 0
Positions Needed: Forward, Outside Mid, Defender, Goalkeeper
Camp or Clinic Dates: TBA
Most Recent Record: 10-5-2
Style of Play: Very aggressive, hardworking and tenacious and defense. the lends itself to being direct an offence if we gain possession in middle or attacking third. Also very capable of playing attractive, possession oriented.

THE SPORT SOURCE

OFFICIAL ATHLETIC COLLEGE GUIDES

There are college Soccer programs that did not submit profiles prior to publication of the 4th edition of the ***Official Athletic College Guide: Soccer***. *THE SPORT SOURCE* will continue to encourage 100% participation by member colleges and universities. Please contact the National Collegiate Athletic Association (NCAA) for more information regarding their member institutions at (913) 339-1906, or visit the NCAA website at **http://www.ncaa.org**. You may contact the National Association of Intercollegiate Athletics (NAIA) for more information regarding their member institutions at (918) 494-8824, or visit the NAIA website at **http://www.naia.org**. For more information on the National Christian College Athletic Association (NCCAA) and their member institutions please call (765) 674-8401, or visit their website at **http://www.bright.net/~nccaa**.

PROGRAM AFFILITION LIST

COLLEGE PROFILE INDEX

ADDITIONAL RESOURCES

NCAA DIVISION I PROGRAMS

(Listed in the Soccer Athletic Guide)

SCHOOL	STATE
Alabama A & M University	AL
American University	DC
Appalachian State University	NC
Arizona State University	AZ
Auburn University	AL
Ball State University	IN
Baylor University	TX
Belmont University	TN
Boise State University	ID
Boston College	MA
Boston University	MA
Bowling Green State University	OH
Bradley University	IL
Brigham Young University	UT
Brown University	RI
Bucknell University	PA
Butler University	IN
California Polytechnic State	CA
California State University - Fresno	CA
California State Univ - Fullerton	CA
California State Univ- Sacramento	CA
California State U-Northridge	CA
Campbell University	NC
Canisius College	NY
Centenary College of Louisiana	LA
Central Connecticut State Univ	CT
Central Michigan University	MI
Charleston Southern University	SC
Citadel	SC
Clemson University	SC
Cleveland State University	OH
Coastal Carolina University	SC
Colgate University	NY
College of Charleston	SC
College of the Holy Cross	MA
College of William and Mary	VA
Colorado College	CO
Columbia University	NY
Cornell University	NY
Creighton University	NE
Dartmouth College	NH
Davidson College	NC
DePaul University	IL
Drake University	IA
Drexel University	PA
Drury University	MO
Duke University	NC
Duquesne University	PA
East Carolina University	NC
East Tennessee State University	TN

SCHOOL	STATE
Eastern Illinois University	IL
Eastern Michigan University	MI
Eastern Washington University	WA
Elon College	NC
Fairfield University	CT
Fairleigh Dickinson Univ- Teaneck	NJ
Florida Atlantic University	FL
Florida International University	FL
Florida State University	FL
Fordham University	NY
Furman University	SC
Gardner - Webb University	NC
George Mason University	VA
George Washington University	DC
Georgetown University	DC
Georgia Southern University	GA
Georgia State University	GA
Gonzaga University	WA
Hartwick College	NY
Harvard University	MA
High Point University	NC
Hofstra University	NY
Howard University	DC
Idaho State University	ID
Illinois State University	IL
Indiana State University	IN
Indiana University	IN
Indiana University - Purdue U	IN
Iona College	NY
Iowa State University	IA
Jacksonville State University	AL
Jacksonville University	FL
James Madison University	VA
La Salle University	PA
Lafayette College	PA
Lehigh University	PA
Liberty University	VA
Long Beach State University	CA
Long Island University - Brooklyn	NY
Louisiana State University	LA
Loyola College - Maryland	MD
Loyola Marymount University	CA
Loyola University - Chicago	IL
Manhattan College	NY
Marist College	NY
Marquette University	WI
Marshall University	WV
McNeese State University	LA
Mercer University	GA
Michigan State University	MI

NCAA DIVISION I PROGRAMS

(Listed in the Soccer Athletic Guide)

SCHOOL	STATE
Mississippi State University	MS
Monmouth University	NJ
Morehead State University	KY
Mount Saint Mary's College	MD
Murray State University	KY
Niagara University	NY
Nicholls State University	LA
North Carolina State University	NC
Northeastern University	MA
Northern Arizona University	AZ
Northern Illinois University	IL
Northwestern State University	LA
Northwestern University	IL
Oakland University	MI
Ohio State University	OH
Ohio University	OH
Oklahoma State University	OK
Old Dominion University	VA
Oral Roberts University	OK
Oregon State University	OR
Pennsylvania State University	PA
Pepperdine University	CA
Phila. College of Textiles & Science	PA
Portland State University	OR
Princeton University	NJ
Providence College	RI
Purdue University	IN
Radford University	VA
Rider University	NJ
Robert Morris College	PA
Rutgers - State Univ. of New Jersey	NJ
Saint Bonaventure University	NY
Saint Francis College - New York	NY
Saint Francis College	PA
Saint John's University	NY
Saint Joseph's University	PA
Saint Louis University	MO
Saint Mary's College	CA
Saint Peter's College	NJ
San Diego State University	CA
San Jose State University	CA
Santa Clara University	CA
Seton Hall University	NJ
Siena College	NY
Southeast Missouri State Univ	MO
Southeastern Louisiana University	LA
Southern Methodist University	TX
Southwest Missouri State University	MO
Stanford University	CA
Stephen F. Austin	TX

SCHOOL	STATE
Stetson University	FL
SUNY - Binghamton University	NY
SUNY - Stony Brook	NY
SUNYC - Oneonta	NY
Syracuse University	NY
Temple University	PA
Texas A & M University	TX
Texas Christian University	TX
Texas Tech University	TX
The University of Akron	OH
Towson University	MD
Troy State University	AL
Tulane University	LA
United States Air Force Academy	CO
United States Military Academy	NY
United States Naval Academy	MD
Univ of MO - Kansas City	MO
University at Albany	NY
University California - Irvine	CA
University California - Los Angeles	CA
University California- Santa Barbara	CA
University of Alabama	AL
University of Alabama - Birmingham	AL
University of Arizona	AZ
University of Arkansas - Fayetteville	AR
University of Arkansas - Little Rock	AR
University of California - Berkeley	CA
University of Central Florida	FL
University of Cincinnati	OH
University of Colorado - Boulder	CO
University of Connecticut	CT
University of Dayton	OH
University of Delaware	DE
University of Denver	CO
University of Detroit Mercy	MI
University of Evansville	IN
University of Findlay	OH
University of Florida	FL
University of Georgia	GA
University of Hartford	CT
University of Hawaii	HI
University of Houston	TX
University of Idaho	ID
University of IL - Chicago	IL
University of IL-Urbana-Campaign	IL
University of Iowa	IA
University of Kansas	KS
University of Kentucky	KY
University of Louisiana, Monroe	LA
University of Louisiana-Lafayette	LA

NCAA DIVISION I PROGRAMS
(Listed in the Soccer Athletic Guide)

SCHOOL	STATE
University of Louisville	KY
University of Maine	ME
University of Maryland	MD
Univ of Massachusetts - Amherst	MA
University of MD - Baltimore County	MD
University of Memphis	TN
University of Miami	FL
University of Michigan	MI
Univ of Minnesota - Twin Cities	MN
University of Missouri - Columbia	MO
University of Montana	MT
University of Nebraska - Lincoln	NE
University of Nevada - Las Vegas	NV
University of New Hampshire	NH
University of New Mexico	NM
Univ of North Carolina - Asheville	NC
Univ of North Carolina - Chapel Hill	NC
Univ of North Carolina - Charlotte	NC
Univ of North Carolina - Greensboro	NC
Univof North Carolina - Wilmington	NC
University of North Texas	TX
University of Notre Dame	IN
University of Oklahoma	OK
University of Oregon	OR
University of Pennsylvania	PA
University of Pittsburgh	PA
University of Portland	OR
University of Rhode Island	RI
University of Richmond	VA
University of San Diego	CA
University of San Francisco	CA
University of South Alabama	AL
University of South Carolina	SC
University of South Florida	FL
University of Southern California	CA
University of Southern Mississippi	MS
Univ of Tennessee - Chattanooga	TN
University of Tennessee - Knoxville	TN
University of Tennessee-Martin	TN
University of Texas - Austin	TX
University of Texas - Pan American	TX
University of Texas of El Paso	TX
University of the Pacific	CA
University of Toledo	OH
University of Tulsa	OK
University of Utah	UT
University of Vermont	VT
University of Virginia	VA
University of Washington	WA
University of Wisconsin	WI

SCHOOL	STATE
University of Wisconsin - Green Bay	WI
University of Wisconsin - Milwaukee	WI
University of Wyoming	WY
Utah State University	UT
Valparaiso University	IN
Vanderbilt University	TN
Villanova University	PA
Virginia Commonwealth University	VA
Virginia Military Institute	VA
Virginia Tech	VA
Wagner College	NY
Wake Forest University	NC
Washington State University	WA
Weber State University	UT
West Virginia University	WV
Western Carolina State University	NC
Western Illinois University	IL
Western Kentucky University	KY
Western Michigan University	MI
Winthrop University	SC
Wofford College	SC
Wright State University	OH
Xavier University	OH
Yale University	CT
Youngstown State University	OH

NCAA DIVISION II PROGRAMS

(Listed in the Soccer Athletic Guide)

SCHOOL	STATE
Adelphi University	NY
Alderson - Broaddus College	WV
American International College	MA
Anderson College	SC
Angelo State University	TX
Ashland University	OH
Assumption College	MA
Augusta State University	GA
Barry University	FL
Barton College	NC
Bellarmine College	KY
Belmont Abbey College	NC
Bentley College	MA
Bismarck State College	ND
Bloomsburg University	PA
Brigham Young U-Hawaii	HI
Bryant College	RI
California State Polytechnic	CA
California State U-Hayward	CA
California State U-Los Angeles	CA
California State Univ - Bakersfield	CA
California State University - Chico	CA
California State Univ - D. Hills	CA
California State U-San Bernardino	CA
California State U-Stanislaus	CA
California University	PA
Carson - Newman College	TN
Catawba College	NC
Central Missouri State University	MO
Central Washington University	WA
Christian Brothers University	TN
Clayton College & State University	GA
Coker College	SC
College of Notre Dame	CA
College of Saint Rose	NY
Colorado Christian University	CO
Colorado School of Mines	CO
Concord College	WV
Concordia College - New York	NY
Davis and Elkins College	WV
Dowling College	NY
East Central University	OK
East Stroudsburg University	PA
East Texas Baptist	TX
Eckerd College	FL
Erskine College	SC
Florida Institute of Technology	FL
Florida Southern College	FL
Fort Lewis College	CO
Francis Marion University	SC

SCHOOL	STATE
Franklin Pierce College	NH
Gannon University	PA
Grand Canyon University	AZ
Hillsdale College	MI
Humboldt State University	CA
Indiana University - Pennsylvania	PA
Indiana University - PU/Fort Wayne	IN
Jarvis Christian College	TX
Kentucky Wesleyan College	KY
Kutztown University	PA
Lander University	SC
Le Moyne College	NY
Lees - McRae College	NC
Lenoir - Rhyne College	NC
Lewis University	IL
Limestone College	SC
Lincoln Memorial College	TN
Lincoln University - Missouri	MO
Lock Haven University	PA
Long Island University - C.W. Post	NY
Long Island Univ - Southampton	NY
Longwood College	VA
Lynn University	FL
Mars Hill College	NC
Mercyhurst College	PA
Merrimack College	MA
Mesa State College	CO
Metropolitan State College - Denver	CO
Midwestern State University	TX
Millersville University	PA
Minnesota State University	MN
Minnesota State Univ-Moorhead	MN
Missouri Southern State College	MO
Molloy College	NY
Mount Olive College	NC
New Hampshire College	NH
New Mexico Highlands University	NM
New York Institute of Technology	NY
Newberry College	SC
North Dakota State University	ND
North Dakota State Univ - Fargo	ND
Northeastern State University	OK
Northern Kentucky University	KY
Northern Michigan University	MI
Northwest Missouri State University	MO
Northwood University	MI
Ouachita Baptist College	AR
Pace University	NY
Pfeiffer University	NC
Presbyterian College	SC

NCAA DIVISION II PROGRAMS PROGRAMS

(Listed in the Soccer Athletic Guide)

SCHOOL	STATE
PU - Johnstown	PA
Queens College	NC
Quincy University	IL
Quinnipiac College	CT
Regis University	CO
Rollins College	FL
Sacred Heart University	CT
Saint Andrews College	NC
Saint Anselm College	NH
Saint Cloud State University	MN
Saint Edward's University	TX
Saint Joseph's College	IN
Saint Leo University	FL
Saint Mary's University	TX
Saint Michael's College	VT
Salem - Teikyo University	WV
San Francisco State University	CA
Seattle Pacific University	WA
Shepherd College	WV
Shippensburg University	PA
Slippery Rock University	PA
Sonoma State University	CA
Southern Connecticut State Univ	CT
Southern Illinois Univ- Edwardsville	IL
Southwest Baptist University	MO
Southwest State University	MN
Southwestern Oklahoma State Univ	OK
Stonehill College	MA
Texas A &M University - Commerce	TX
Texas Wesleyan University	TX
Truman State University	MO
Tusculum College	TN
University California - Davis	CA
University of Alabama - Huntsville	AL
University of Bridgeport	CT
University of Central Arkansas	AR
University of Central Oklahoma	OK
University of Charleston	WV
University of CO-Colorado Springs	CO
University of Indianapolis	IN
Univ of Massachusetts - Lowell	MA
University of Minnesota - Duluth	MN
University of Minnesota - Morris	MN
University of Missouri - Rolla	MO
University of Missouri - St. Louis	MO
University of Nebraska - Omaha	NE
University of New Haven	CT
University of North Alabama	AL
Univof North Carolina - Pembroke	NC
University of North Florida	FL

SCHOOL	STATE
University of Northern Colorado	CO
University of South Carolina - Aiken	SC
University of Southern Colorado	CO
University of Southern Indiana	IN
University of Tampa	FL
University of the District of Col	DC
University of the Incarnate Word	TX
University of West Florida	FL
University of Wisconsin - Parkside	WI
USC - Spartanburg	SC
West Chester University	PA
West Texas A & M University	TX
West Virginia Wesleyan College	WV
Western Washington University	WA
Westminster College	PA
Wheeling Jesuit College	WV
Wingate University	NC

NCAA DIVISION III PROGRAMS

(Listed in the Soccer Athletic Guide)

SCHOOL	STATE
Adrian College	MI
Agnes Scott College	GA
Albertus Magnus College	CT
Albion College	MI
Albright College	PA
Alfred University	NY
Allegheny College	PA
Alma College	MI
Alvernia College	PA
Amherst College	MA
Anderson University	IN
Anna Maria College	MA
Arcadia College	PA
Augsburg College	MN
Augustana College	IL
Aurora University	IL
Austin College	TX
Averett College	VA
Babson College	MA
Baldwin - Wallace College	OH
Bard College	NY
Bates College	ME
Bates College	ME
Becker College	MA
Beloit College	WI
Benedictine University	IL
Bethany College	WV
Bethany College	WV
Bethel College	MN
Blackburn College	IL
Bluffton College	OH
Bowdoin College	ME
Brandeis University	MA
Bridgewater College	VA
Bridgewater State College	MA
Bryn Mawr College	PA
Buena Vista College	IA
Buffalo State College	NY
Cabrini College	PA
California Institute of Technology	CA
California Lutheran University	CA
Calvin College	MI
Capital University	OH
Carleton College	MN
Carnegie Mellon University	PA
Carroll College	WI
Case Western Reserve University	OH
Castleton State College	VT
Catholic University of America	DC
Centenary College - New Jersey	NJ

SCHOOL	STATE
Central College	IA
Centre College	KY
Chapman University	CA
Chowan College	NC
Christopher Newport University	VA
City College of New York	NY
Claremont - Mudd - Scripps	CA
Clark University	MA
Clarke College	IA
Clarkson University	NY
Coe College	IA
Colby - Sawyer College	NH
Colby College	ME
College of Mount Saint Vincent	NY
College of New Jersey	NJ
College of Notre Dame - Maryland	MD
College of Saint Benedict	MN
College of Saint Catherine	MN
College of Staten Island - CUNY	NY
College of Wooster	OH
Concordia College	MN
Concordia College - Moorhead	MN
Concordia University River Forest	ILL.
Connecticut College	CT
Cornell College	IA
Curry College	MA
Daniel Webster College	NH
Defiance College	OH
Delaware Valley College	PA
Denison University	OH
DePauw University	IN
DeSales University	PA
Dickinson College	PA
Drew University	NJ
Earlham College	IN
Eastern College	PA
Eastern Connecticut State Univ	CT
Eastern Mennonite College	VA
Eastern Nazarene College	MA
Edgewood College	WI
Elizabethtown College	PA
Elmhurst College	IL
Elmira College	NY
Elms College	MA
Emerson College	MA
Emory and Henry College	VA
Emory University	GA
Endicott College	MA
Eureka College	IL
Fairleigh Dickinson Univ - Madison	NJ

NCAA DIVISION III PROGRAMS

(Listed in the Soccer Athletic Guide)

SCHOOL	STATE
Ferrum College	VA
Fitchburg State College	MA
Fontbonne College	MO
Framingham State College	MA
Franklin and Marshall College	PA
Franklin College	IN
Frostburg State University	MD
Gallaudet University	DC
Geneseo State University	NY
George Fox University	OR
Gettysburg College	PA
Gordon College	MA
Goucher College	MD
Greensboro College	NC
Grinnell College	IA
Grove City College	PA
Guilford College	NC
Gustavus Adolphus College	MN
Gwynedd - Mercy College	PA
Hamilton College	NY
Hamline University	MN
Hampden - Sydney College	VA
Hanover College	IN
Hardin - Simmons University	TX
Harding University	AR
Haverford College	PA
Heidelberg College	OH
Hendrix College	AR
Hiram College	OH
Hobart College	NY
Hollins College	VA
Hope College	MI
Hunter College	NY
Illinois College	IL
Illinois Wesleyan University	IL
Ithaca College	NY
John Carroll University	OH
John Hopkins University	MD
Johnson & Wales University	RI
Johnson State College	VT
Juniata College	PA
Kalamazoo College	MI
Kean University	NJ
Keene State College	NH
Kenyon College	OH
Keuka College	NY
King's College	PA
Knox College	IL
La Roche College	PA
LaGrange College	GA

SCHOOL	STATE
Lake Erie College	OH
Lake Forest College	IL
Lakeland College	WI
Lawrence University	WI
Lebanon Valley College	PA
Lesley College	MA
LeTourneau University	TX
Lincoln University	PA
Linfield College	OR
Loras College	IA
Luther College	IA
Lycoming College	PA
Lynchburg College	VA
Macalester College	MN
MacMurray University	IL
Maine Maritime Academy	ME
Manchester College	IN
Manhattanville College	NY
Marietta College	OH
Mary Baldwin College	VA
Mary Washington College	VA
Marymount University	VA
Maryville College	TN
Maryville University	MO
Massachusetts College- Liberal Arts	MA
Mass Institute of Technology (MIT)	MA
Massachusetts Maritime Academy	MA
Medgar Evers College	NY
Menlo College	CA
Meredith College	NC
Messiah College	PA
Methodist College	NC
Middlebury College	VT
Millikin University	IL
Mills College	CA
Millsaps College	MS
Milwaukee School of Engineering	WI
Misericordia College	PA
Mississippi College	MS
Monmouth College	IL
Montclair State College	NJ
Moravian College	PA
Mount Holyoke College	MA
Mount Ida College	MA
Mount Mary College	WI
Mount Saint Mary College	NY
Mount Union College	OH
Muhlenberg College	PA
Muskingum College	OH
Nazareth College of Rochester	NY

NCAA DIVISION III PROGRAMS

(Listed in the Soccer Athletic Guide)

SCHOOL	STATE
Nebraska Wesleyan University	NE
New England College	NH
New Jersey City University	NJ
New Jersey Institute of Technology	NJ
New York University	NY
Nichols College	MA
North Carolina Wesleyan College	NC
North Central College	IL
North Park University	IL
Norwich University	VT
Oberlin College	OH
Occidental College	CA
Oglethorpe University	GA
Ohio Northern University	OH
Ohio Wesleyan University	OH
Olivet College	MI
Otterbein College	OH
Pacific Lutheran University	WA
Penn State Univ - Erie, Behrend	PA
Piedmont College	GA
Pine Manor College	MA
Plymouth State College	NH
Polytechnic University	NY
Pomona - Pitzer Colleges	CA
Pratt Institute	NY
Principia College	IL
Ramapo College of New Jersey	NJ
Randolph - Macon College	VA
Regis College	MA
Rensselaer Polytechnic Institute	NY
Rhode Island College	RI
Rhodes College	TN
Richard Stockton State College	NJ
Ripon College	WI
Roanoke College	VA
Rochester Institute of Technology	NY
Rockford College	IL
Roger Williams University	RI
Rose - Hulman Inst of Technology	IN
Rowan University	NJ
Russell Sage College	NY
Rutgers University - Camden	NJ
Rutgers University - Newark	NJ
Saint John Fisher College	NY
Saint John's University	MN
Saint Joseph's College	ME
Saint Joseph's College - New York	NY
Saint Lawrence University	NY
Saint Mary's College - Maryland	MD
Saint Mary's University - Minnesota	MN

SCHOOL	STATE
Saint Norbert College	WI
Saint Olaf College	MN
Salem State College	MA
Salisbury State University	MD
Salve Regina University	RI
Savannah College of Art & Design	GA
Schreiner College	TX
Seattle University	WA
Shenandoah University	VA
Simmons College	MA
Simpson College	IA
Skidmore College	NY
Smith College	MA
Southwestern University	TX
Springfield College	MA
Stephens College	MO
Stevens Institute of Technology	NJ
Suffolk University	MA
SUNY - Brockport	NY
SUNY - Buffalo College	NY
SUNY - New Paltz	NY
SUNY Maritime College	NY
SUNYC - Cortland	NY
SUNYC - Fredonia	NY
SUNYC - Old Westbury	NY
SUNYC - Oswego	NY
SUNYC - Plattsburgh	NY
SUNYC - Potsdam	NY
Susquehanna University	PA
Swarthmore College	PA
Sweet Briar College	VA
Theil College	PA
Thomas More College	KY
Trinity College - Connecticut	CT
Trinity University	TX
Tufts University	MA
Union College - New York	NY
U. S. Coast Guard Academy	CT
U. S. Merchant Marine Academy	NY
University California - San Diego	CA
University California - Santa Cruz	CA
University of Chicago	IL
University of Dallas	TX
University of La Verne	CA
University of Mary Hardin-Baylor	TX
Univ of Massachusetts - Boston	MA
Univ of Massachusetts - Dartmouth	MA
University of New England	ME
University of Pittsburgh - Bradford	PA
University of Puget Sound	WA

NCAA DIVISION III PROGRAMS

(Listed in the Soccer Athletic Guide)

SCHOOL	STATE
University of Redlands	CA
University of Rochester	NY
University of Saint Thomas	MN
University of Scranton	PA
University of Southern Maine	ME
University of Texas - Dallas	TX
University of the Ozarks	AR
University of the South	TN
Univ of Wisconsin - La Crosse	WI
Univ of Wisconsin - Oshkosh	WI
Univ of Wisconsin - Platteville	WI
Univ of Wisconsin - River Falls	WI
Univ of Wisconsin - Stevens Point	WI
Univ of Wisconsin - Stout	WI
Univ of Wisconsin - Superior	WI
Univ of Wisconsin - Whitewater	WI
UP - Greensburg	PA
Upper Iowa University	IA
Ursinus College	PA
Utica College - Syracuse	NY
Vassar College	NY
Villa Julie College	MD
Virginia Wesleyan College	VA
Wabash College	IN
Wartburg College	IA
Washington and Jefferson College	PA
Washington and Lee University	VA
Washington College	MD
Washington University - St. Louis	MO
Waynesburg College	PA
Webster University	MO
Wellesley College	MA
Wells College	NY
Wentworth Inst of Tech	MA
Wesley College	DE
Wesleyan College	GA
Wesleyan University	CT
Western Connecticut State U	CT
Western Maryland College	MD
Western New England College	MA
Westfield State College	MA
Westminster College	MO
Wheaton College	MA
Wheaton College - IL	IL
Whittier College	CA
Widener University	PA
Wilkes University	PA
Willamette University	OR
William Paterson University	NJ
William Penn University	IA
Williams College	MA
Wilmington College	OH
Wisconsin Lutheran College	WI
Wittenberg University	OH
Worcester Polytechnic Institute	MA
Worcester State College	MA
York College - CUNY	NY
York College - Pennsylvania	PA

NAIA PROGRAMS

(Listed in the Soccer Athletic Guide)

SCHOOL	STATE
Albertson College - Idaho	ID
Aquinas College	MI
Asbury College	KY
Auburn University - Montgomery	AL
Avila College	MO
Azusa Pacific University	CA
Baker University	KS
Bartlesville Wesleyan College	OK
Belhaven College	MS
Bellevue College	NE
Benedictine College	KS
Berea College	KY
Berry College	GA
Bethany College	KS
Bethel College	TN
Bethel College	IN
Bethel College	KS
Biola University	CA
Bloomfield College	NJ
Bluefield College	VA
Brescia College	KY
Brewton - Parker College	GA
Briar Cliff College	IA
Bryan College	TN
Caldwell College	NJ
California Baptist University	CA
Campbellsville University	KY
Cardinal Stritch University	WI
Carroll College	MT
Cedarville University	OH
Central Methodist College	MO
Christian Heritage College	CA
College of Saint Joseph - Vermont	VT
College of Saint Scholastica	MN
College of St. Mary	NE
College of the Southwest	NM
Columbia College	MO
Concordia College	MI
Concordia College - St. Paul	MN
Concordia University - Austin	TX
Concordia University - Irvine	CA
Concordia University - Portland	OR
Cornerstone College	MI
Covenant College	GA
Culver - Stockton College	MO
Cumberland College	KY
Cumberland University	TN
Dana College	NE
Doane College	NE
Dominican College-California	CA

SCHOOL	STATE
Dordt College	IA
Embry - Riddle University	FL
Evergreen State College	WA
Flagler College	FL
Fresno Pacific College	CA
Friends University	KS
Geneva College	PA
Georgetown College	KY
Georgian Court College	NJ
Goshen College	IN
Grace College	IN
Graceland University	IA
Grand View College	IA
Green Mountain College	VT
Harris Stowe State College	MO
Hasting College	NE
Holy Family College	PA
Hope International University	CA
Houghton College	NY
Huntingdon College	AL
Huntington College	IN
Huron University	SD
Husson College	ME
Indiana Institute of Technology	IN
Indiana Wesleyan University	IN
Iowa Wesleyan University	IA
Jamestown College	ND
John Brown University	AR
Judson College	IL
King College	TN
Lee University	TN
Life College	GA
Lindenwood University	MO
Lindsey Wilson College	KY
Loyola University - New Orleans	LA
Lyndon State College	VT
Madonna University	MI
Malone College	OH
Marian College	IN
Martin Methodist College	TN
Marycrest International University	IA
Master's College	CA
McKendree College	IL
McPherson College	KS
Midland Lutheran College	NE
Midway College	KY
Milligan College	TN
Missouri Baptist College	MO
Missouri Valley College	MO
Montana State University-Billings	MT

NAIA PROGRAMS

(Listed in the Soccer Athletic Guide)

SCHOOL	STATE
Montreat College	NC
Mount Marty College	SD
Mount Mercy College	IA
Mount Saint Clare College	IA
Mount Senario College	WI
Mount Vernon Nazarene College	OH
National American University	SD
Newman University	KS
N. Georgia College & State Univ	GA
Northwest College	WA
Northwest Nazarene University	ID
Northwestern College	MN
Notre Dame College	NH
Notre Dame College-Ohio	OH
Nyack College	NY
Ohio Dominican College	OH
Oklahoma Christian University	OK
Oklahoma City University	OK
Olivet Nazarene University	IL
Ottawa University	KS
Palm Beach Atlantic College	FL
Park University	MO
Point Loma Nazarene University	CA
Point Park College	PA
Purdue University Calumet	IN
Robert Morris College-Chicago	IL
Robert Morris College - Springfield	IL
Robert Wesleyan College	NY
Saint Ambrose University	IA
Saint Mary College	KS
Saint Thomas Aquinas College	NY
Saint Thomas University	FL
Saint Vincent College	PA
Saint Xavier University	IL
Seton Hill College	PA
Shawnee State University	OH
Siena Heights College	MI
Simon Fraser University	B.C.
Southern Nazarene University	OK
Southern Oregon University	OR
Southern Wesleyan University	SC
Southwestern College	KS
Spring Arbor College	MI
Spring Hill College	AL
St. Gregory's University	OK
Sterling College	KS
Taylor University	IN
Tennessee Wesleyan College	TN
Thomas University	GA
Transylvania University	KY
Tri - State University	IN
Trinity Christian College	IL
Union College	KY
University of IL-Springfield	IL
University of Maine - Presque Isle	ME
University of Maine-Machias	ME
University of Mary	ND
University of Mobile	AL
University of Rio Grande	OH
University of Saint Francis	IN
Univ of Science & Arts of Oklahoma	OK
University of Sioux Falls	SD
Vanguard U of S California	CA
Viterbo College	WI
Walsh University	OH
Warner Pacific College	OR
Wayne State College	NE
Webber College	FL
Western Baptist College	OR
Westminster C - SLC	UT
Westmont College	CA
William Carey College	MS
William Jewell College	MO
William Woods University	MO
York College - Nebraska	NE

NJCAA PROGRAMS

(Listed in the Soccer Athletic Guide)

SCHOOL	STATE
Andrew College	GA
Belleville Area College	IL
Bellevue Community College	WA
Cañada College	CA
Chesapeake College	MD
Danville Area College	IL
De Anza College	CA
Hill Junior College	TX
Itwamba Community College	MS
Kellogg Community College	MI
Lincoln College	IL
Mountian View College	TX
Newbury College	MA
Northern Oklahoma College-Enid	OK
North Idaho College	ID

NJCAA PROGRAMS
(Listed in the Soccer Athletic Guide)

SCHOOL	STATE
Phoenix College	AZ
Phoenix College	AZ
Richland College	TX
Spartanburg Methodist College	SC
Tyler Junior College	TX
Ventura College (Community)	CA
Yavapai College	AZ

DUAL AFFILIATIONS
(Listed in the Soccer Athletic Guide)

SCHOOL	STATE
Birmingham Southern College	AL
Cascade College	OR
Chatham College	PA
Columbia Union College	MD
Concordia University - Wisconsin	WI
Dallas Baptist University	TX
Dominican College	NY
Dominican University	IL
Goldey - Beacom College	DE
Greenville College	IL
Hawaii Pacific University	HI
Hilbert College	NY
Lambuth University	TN
Maranatha Baptist Bible College	WI
Marian College - Fond du Lac	WI
Northland College	WI
Nova Southeastern University	FL
Nyack College	NY
Pacific University	OR
Rivier College	NH
Rockhurst College	MO
Southern Vermont College	VT
Tabor College	KS
Teikyo Post University	CT
Texas Lutheran College	TX
Thomas College	ME
Tiffin University	OH
Trinity International University	IL
Union University	TN
University of Maine - Farmington	ME
University of Montevallo	AL
Whitman College	WA
Whitworth College	WA

INTERCOLLEGIATE PROGRAMS
(Listed in the Soccer Athletic Guide)

SCHOOL	STATE
Saint Mary-of-the-Woods College	IN
Trinity Western University	BC

index

Many college coaches sponsor summer soccer camps for boys and girls of all ages. The staff of a number of these camps consist of other college coaches, USSF State, Regional, and National Staff members and professional players.

The curriculum of these camps is designed to improve the serious soccer player's skills. They also provide the attending college coaches with an oppurtunity to take a personal look at a high school soccer player that they might not otherwise get to see. This helps both the coach and player during the recruiting process.

The following directory lists a few of the available camps and tournaments that are affiliated with the ***Official Athletic College Guide for Soccer*** and provide individuals and teams the opportunity to be seen by college coaches.

THE SPORT SOURCE'S

CAMP

AND

COLLEGE SHOWCASE TOURNAMENT DIRECTORY

Come join the WOLFPACK this summer for Soccer Camp!

We are gearing up for another summer of exciting soccer!

Coach George Tarantini, a former professional player and accomplished coach will be directing the camp for his thirteenth year. His goal is to share his vast knowledge of soccer with you personally! Coach Tarantini has proven that he has a remarkable ability to take a player and help him reach his full potential. Here is your chance to benefit from this!

The camp staffs have included players such as: Tab Ramos, 1990 and 1994 World Cup Team member; Henry Guiterrez, US National Team and Two-time ACC Player of the Year; and Dario Brose, 1992 Olympic Team Member and Three Time All-American.

All of these individuals are former NC State soccer players who benefited from George Tarantini's style of coaching.

NC State Soccer School Day Camp:

Two (2) Sessions
Ages 5 to 12 years old

NC State Soccer School:

Intensive Overnight Camp
Two (2) Sessions
Ages 11 to 18 years old

For a free brochure write or call:
NC State Soccer School
P.O. Box 5697· Raleigh, NC 27650
Phone: (919) 851-1627
Web-site: www.gopack.com
e-mail: george_tarantini@ncsu.edu

Best Camp Value
at 6 days, 5 nights
2001
CLEMSON
Soccer Academy
Residential
Camps
for young men
Directed by
Trevor Adair
Head Coach
Men's Soccer
Clemson University
Camp Dates 2001
Junior Elite Ages 10-13 June 22-24
Striker/ Goalkeeper Ages 10 & up June 22-24
Senior Elite Ages 14& up June 28-July 1
Advanced Ages 10 & up July 7-12
Advanced Ages 10 & up July 15-20
Advanced Ages 10 & up July 22-27
www.clemsonsocceracademy.com
email:info@clemsonsocceracademy.com
1-864-654-9300
105 Catawbah Rd. Clemson, SC 29631

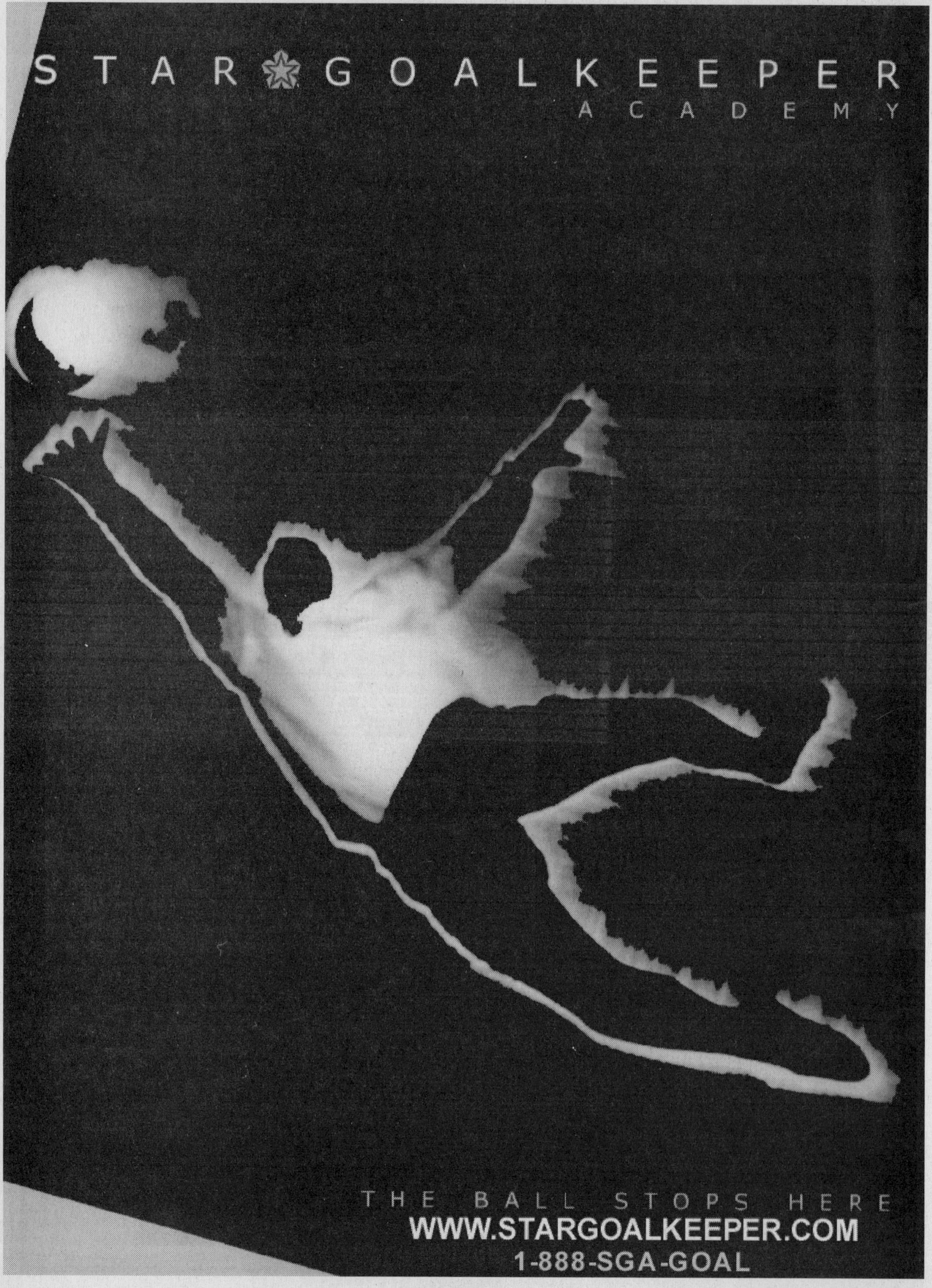
STAR GOALKEEPER
ACADEMY
THE BALL STOPS HERE
WWW.STARGOALKEEPER.COM
1-888-SGA-GOAL

SOUTHWEST MISSOURI
SOCCER SCHOOL
at Southwest Missouri State University
Directed by Jon Leamy (SMS Head Coach)
SOCCER
SMS
14
For complete information and a free brochure, call or write:
Southwest Missouri Soccer School
Boys Residential
Girls Residential
Boys Junior Residential
Girls Team Residential
Boys Team Residential
Special Goalkeepers Camp
SMS
417 836-5243
DIADORA

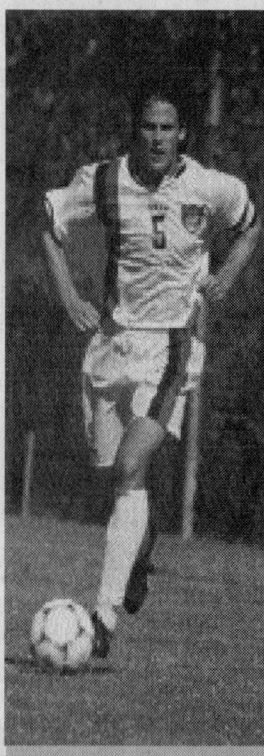

GOLDEN BEARS™

Golden Bear Soccer Camps For Boys 2001

Directed by
Head coach Kevin Grimes

Contact us now for a free brochure:

510-643-2267
calmsocc@uclink.berkeley.edu

Information & registration available online:

www.oski.org

Proud Sponsor of Cal Men's Soccer

Golden Bear Soccer Camps for Boys - directed by Head Coach Kevin Grimes

Advanced Players Camps
Resident and Commuter
June 24-28 Ages 11-19
July 8-12
July 28- August 1

Full Day Camps
June 25-29 Ages 9-18
July 9-13
July 30- August 3

Half Day Camps
June 25-29 Ages 5-11
July 9-13
July 30- August 3

Spring Break Camps
April 9-12 Ages 5-16
April 16-19

University of California at Berkeley
Intercollegiate Athletics & Recreational Sports

WOW!
WHAT AN EXPERIENCE!
ATM
10
TEXAS A&M SOCCER CAMP
TEXAS A&M SOCCER CAMP
CALL 979-862-3369
FOR MORE INFORMATION
-OR CHECK OUR WEBSITE-
http://sports.tamu.edu/sports/soccer

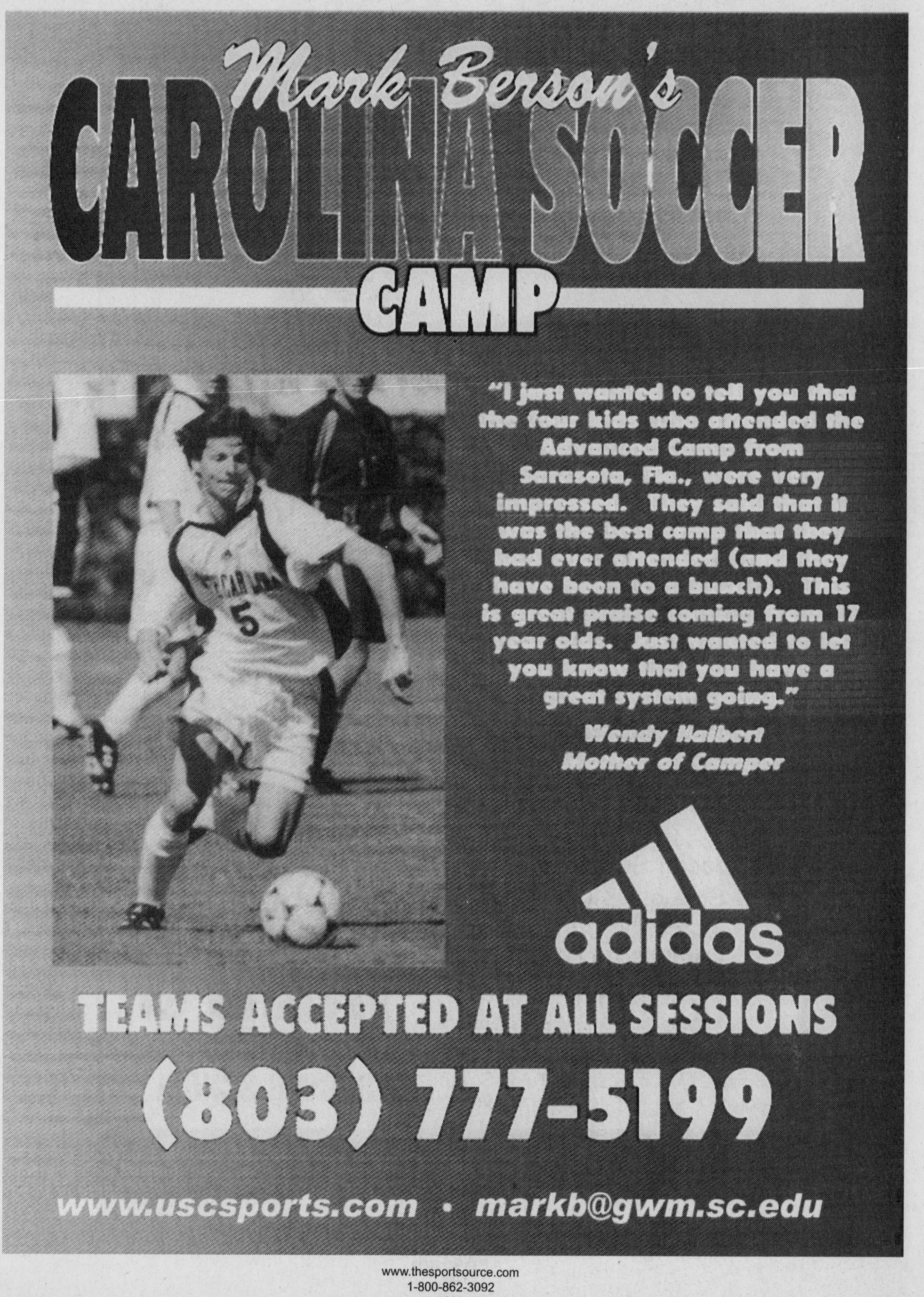
Mark Berson's
CAROLINA SOCCER
CAMP
"I just wanted to tell you that the four kids who attended the Advanced Camp from Sarasota, Fla., were very impressed. They said that it was the best camp that they had ever attended (and they have been to a bunch). This is great praise coming from 17 year olds. Just wanted to let you know that you have a great system going."
Wendy Halbert
Mother of Camper
adidas
TEAMS ACCEPTED AT ALL SESSIONS
(803) 777-5199
www.uscsports.com • markb@gwm.sc.edu

Like 10 College Camps in One!

THE DIFFERENCE

*** Coaches from different colleges from all across the country:**

-- Be *trained* by.

-- Be *seen* by.

adidas

Every year, MNSS brings staff from the finest universities, like
Tulsa, Creighton, Wake Forest, Drake, UNLV, Evansville, Oklahoma State, New Hampshire,Yale, Wisconsin-Milwaukee, UNC-Ashville, Texas Tech, and many more!

Write or call for July dates.

*** Age-specific, ability-specific sessions:**

-- High School/College Prep
(freshman - seniors)

-- Advanced Youth
(age 9 - 13 competitive)

(special requirements for entry into above)

-- Goalkeeping school at *every* session.

*** Special Subjects:**

-- Strength & Conditioning

-- Academic Counseling

-- Seminar on College Requirements

Write or call: Mac's National Soccer School, c/o University of Tulsa Soccer. 600 S. College, Tulsa, OK 74104-3189.

MAC'S NATIONAL SOCCER SCHOOL

FREE BROCHURE: 918.631.3595

BUFFALO Soccer Camp
Boy's and Girl's
Under the direction of Butch Lauffer
Head Men's & Women's Soccer Coach
West Texas A&M University
USSF National Staff Coach
1996-2000 Lone Star Coach of the Year
West Texas A&M University
Residential Day and Advanced Camps available for Summer 2001
~1997 NCAA Men's National Tournament Participants
~Finished in the top 2 in the Nation past 5 years
~One of only two men's teams in the State Of Texas
~1997 Women's Lone Star Conference Champions
~1996 Women's Lone Star Conference Champions
~2000 Men's Conference Champs
~2000 Men's Elite Eight Team
For a free brochure call
(806) 651-2678 or 2677

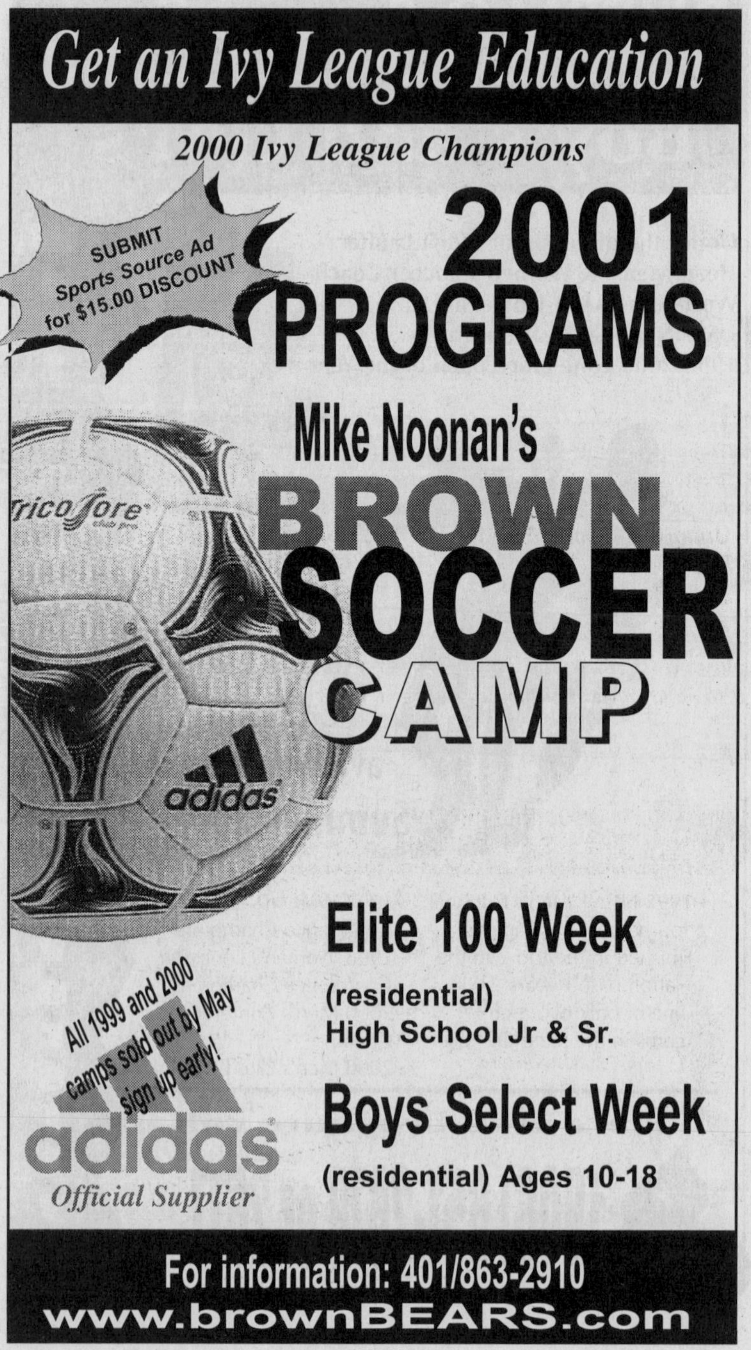
Get an Ivy League Education
2000 Ivy League Champions
SUBMIT Sports Source Ad for $15.00 DISCOUNT
2001 PROGRAMS
Mike Noonan's
BROWN SOCCER CAMP
Elite 100 Week
(residential)
High School Jr & Sr.
Boys Select Week
(residential) Ages 10-18
All 1999 and 2000 camps sold out by May sign up early!
adidas
Official Supplier
For information: 401/863-2910
www.brownBEARS.com

AMERICAN SOCCER PROGRAMS PRESENT

2000 Middle States Soccer Camp

for Boys And Girls Ages 8-18

Ursinus College - Collegeville, PA
Westtown School - Westtown, PA
Episcopal High School - Alexandria, VA
Goucher College - Baltimore, MD
St.Andrews School - Middletown, DE

- **7:1 Ratio Payer to Coaches**
- **Team Discounts**
- **Team & Pe-Season Training Camp**
- **All Girls Camp**
- **Uniform & Soccer Ball for Every Player**
- **Goalkeeper Training**
- **Advanced Player Camp**
- **Indoor & Small-Sided Competition**
- **Goalscoring/Specialized Goalkeeping Camp**
- **Written Evaluation on Every Player**

"I have experienced this camp from both sides of the spectrum - as a player and as a coach who sent a team there to train - and have found it to be a top-notch, training program. I highly recommend it!"

Michelle Shircliff - WAGS Administrator

"This is the best camp I have ever been to!"

Troy Stevenson - Jamison, PA

Write or call for our brochure & free camp video
P.O. Box 2835~Manassas, VA 20108~(703) 330-3423

Invest in Your Future wit American Soccer Programs

College Counseling Service

Richard Broad
- Former Men's Soccer Coach, George Mason University
- Athletic Counselor

Frank Damico
- Former Guidance Counselor Fairfax County (VA) Public Schools
- Academic Advisor

"Your College Counseling Service is as helpful as any high school guidance program"

Mr. William Helmsletter - Baltimore,MD

Let us help you find the college that is best for you!

For further information contact: **American Soccer Programs**
10510 Arrowood Street ~ Fairfax, VA 22032 ~ (703)764-0964

Come be a part of the Country's Premier Girls' Soccer Camp

KWIKGOAL

North Carolina Girls' Soccer Camp

"Where Champions are Trained"

Call: Toll-Free 1-800-394-1223 (24 hours a day)

North Carolina Girls' Soccer Camp
P.O. Box 4933
Chapel Hill, N.C. 27515

Website: www.ncgsc.com

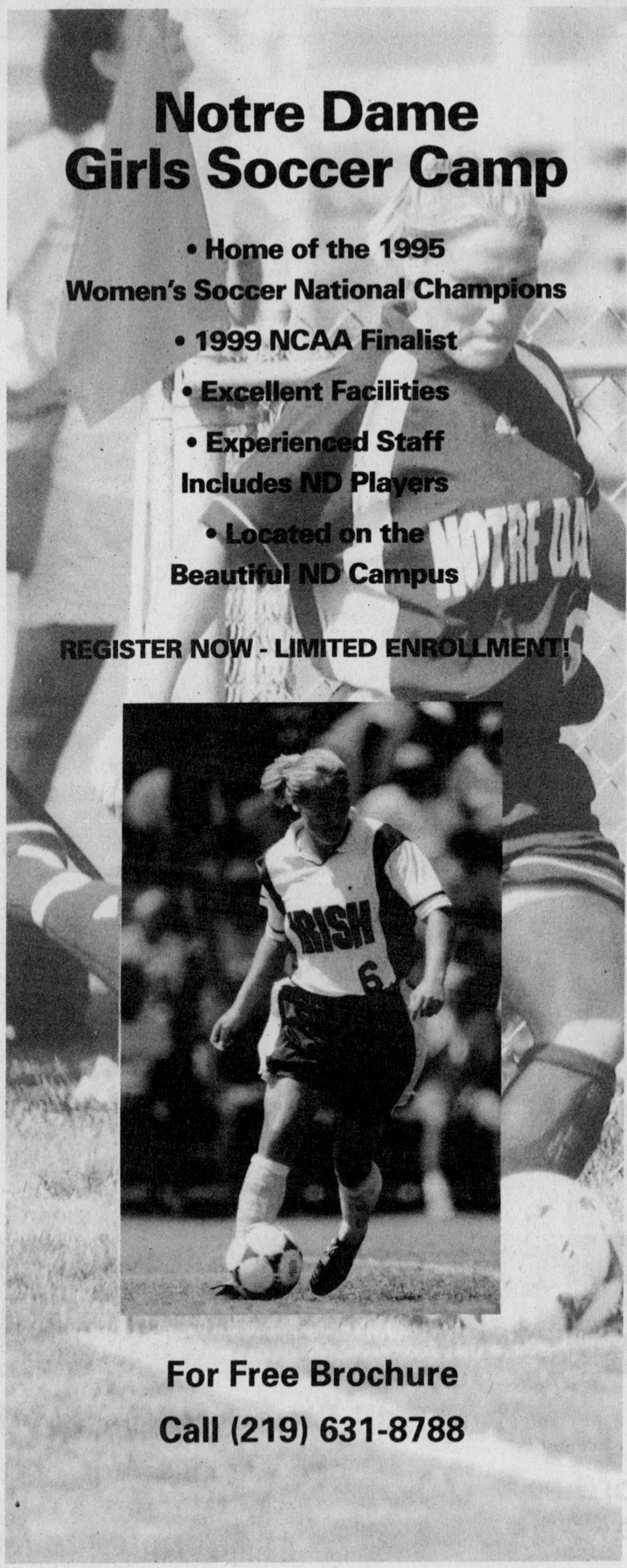
Notre Dame
Girls Soccer Camp
• Home of the 1995
Women's Soccer National Champions
• 1999 NCAA Finalist
• Excellent Facilities
• Experienced Staff
Includes ND Players
• Located on the
Beautiful ND Campus
REGISTER NOW - LIMITED ENROLLMENT!
IRISH
6
For Free Brochure
Call (219) 631-8788

STORM SOCCER CLUB

11th Annual

STORM SOCCER CLUB

JUNIOR / SENIOR SHOWCASE

November30th -December 2, 2001 Dallas, Texas

ELIGIBILITY

The Host Committee evaluates teams on the basis of strength of League competition, regional and state tournament championships. Other criteria being equal, preference is given to teams composed of primarily of high school seniors, representing the top soccer organizations in in the nation.

FORMAT

Each team will play (3) three eighty minute exhibition games scheduled in a two day time frame. The exhibition format allows players to perform at the highest level without the added pressure of playing for tournament results. All games will be at one location to allow the college coaches to observe the optimum amount of games.

COLLEGE REPRESENTATION

There will be representatives from many of the NCAA Div.I, II, III, NAIA, and NCJAA college programs. With **over 180 College Coaches** in attendance last year the opportunity to be identified for soccer scholarships and financial aide are obvious. This event is recognized by college coaches across the country as one of the premier college recruitment showcases.

COLLEGE REPRESENTATION

The Showcase provides a profile resume, which includes individual academic and athletic data. This information will be compiled in a team notebook and distributed to each university / college coach.

COLLEGE SEMINAR- " Plan for Success"

College Seminar - "Plan for Success" presentation will be conducted to answer many of the tough questions pertaining to the identification process, by the professional in the field. The Sport Source and College Coaches will tackle the questions that concern you most.

For a application or more information:

(972) 596-8726

www.stormsoccerclub.com

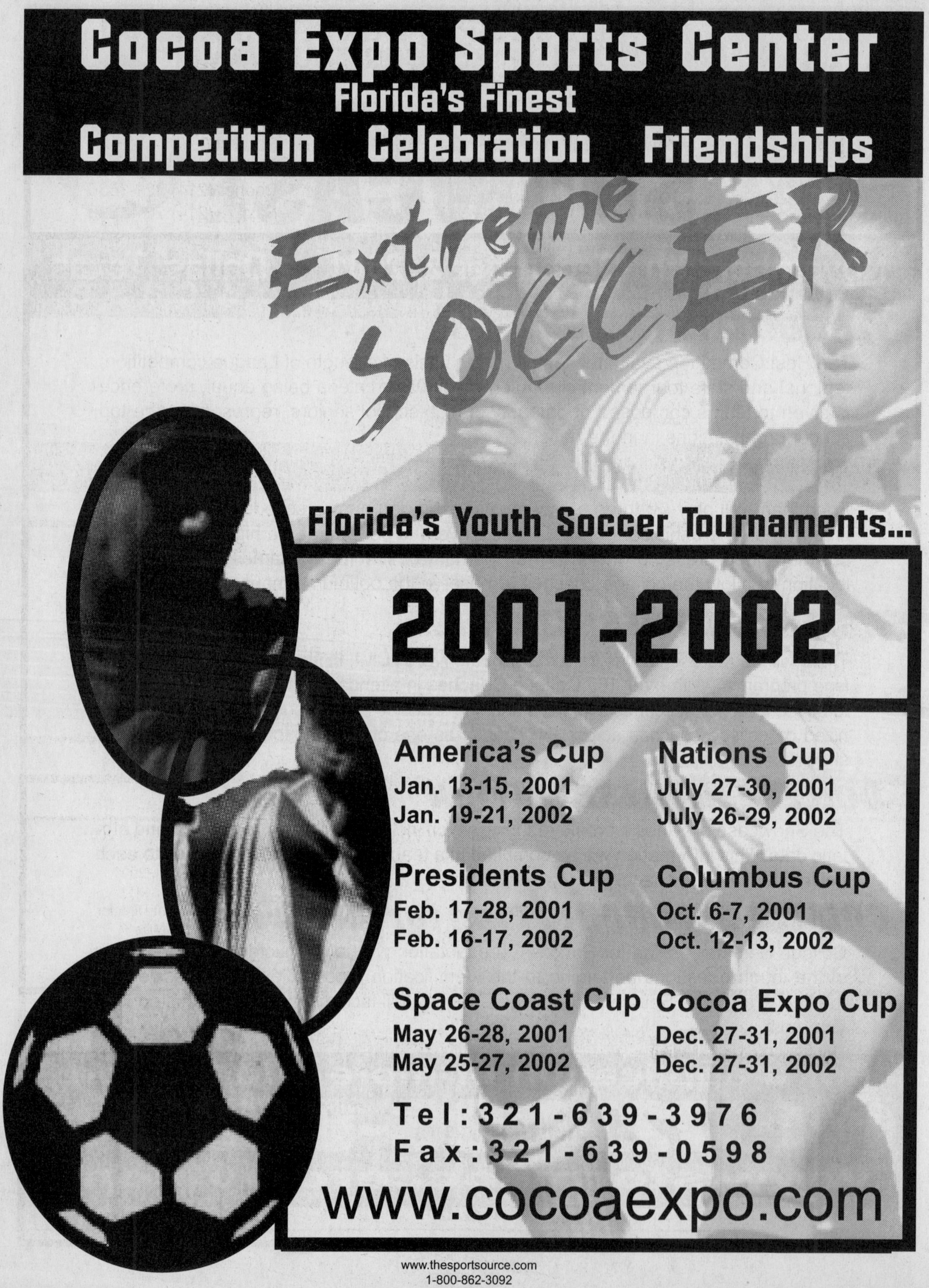
Cocoa Expo Sports Center
Florida's Finest
Competition Celebration Friendships
Extreme SOCCER
Florida's Youth Soccer Tournaments...
2001-2002
America's Cup
Jan. 13-15, 2001
Jan. 19-21, 2002
Nations Cup
July 27-30, 2001
July 26-29, 2002
Presidents Cup
Feb. 17-28, 2001
Feb. 16-17, 2002
Columbus Cup
Oct. 6-7, 2001
Oct. 12-13, 2002
Space Coast Cup
May 26-28, 2001
May 25-27, 2002
Cocoa Expo Cup
Dec. 27-31, 2001
Dec. 27-31, 2002
Tel: 321-639-3976
Fax: 321-639-0598
www.cocoaexpo.com

THE USA'S PREMIER INTERNATIONAL YOUTH SOCCER TOURNAMENT!

DALLAS CUP XXII
presented by FILA SOCCER

AGE GROUPS

SUPER GROUP:	Boys born August 1, 1981 & later
GROUP A:	Boys born August 1, 1982 & later
GROUP B:	Boys born August 1, 1983 & later
GROUP C:	Boys born August 1, 1984 & later
GROUP D:	Boys born August 1, 1986 & later
GROUP E:	Boys born August 1, 1988 & later

For more information contact:
Dallas Cup XXII
11551 Forest Central Dr.
Suite 260
Dallas, TX 76243
Phone: (214) 221-3636
Fax: (214) 221-4636

Junior / Senior Showcase

STORM SOCCER CLUB

- 16 Teams U-17 and U-19 boys
- 8 Teams U-17 and U-19 boys
- Each team plays 3 games
- Showcase Event held annually in the North Dallas area
- Over 200 college coaches representing NCAA Div. I, II, III, NAIA, NJCAA attended in 2000, more are expected in 2001!

Get in on the ground floor of the college recruiting season.
For application and information: www.stormsoccerclub.com

Spring Classic at DALLAS CUP XXII

Spring Classic At Dallas Cup

The Premier Showcase For Competitive Girls Soccer

U-11 August 1, 1989 & later	U-15 August 1, 1985 & later
U-12 August 1, 1988 & later	U-16 August 1, 1984 & later
U-13 August 1, 1987 & later	U-17 August 1, 1983 & later
U-14 August 1, 1986 & later	U-19 August 1, 1981 & later

Contact: Spring Classic ~6331 Waggoner Dr.~Dallas, TX 75230
Phone: (214) 891-0074 e-mail: helena2@msn.com

Plano Labor Day Invitational XXI

PLANO LABOR DAY INVITATIONAL

- U-11 to U-19 Boys & Girls
- 360 Teams Participating
- National, Regional & State Champions
- Multi-State Participation
- College Team Partcipation

(972) 422-7972

September 1st-3rd, 2001
Application Deadline
July 23th, 2001

Tournament Director
Jim Mills

e-mail: execdir@pysa.org

Rated One Of The Three Best Tournaments In The United States

SAN DIEGO SURF CUP
Presented by nike

For more info contact
San Diego Surf Cup Office
31-01 La Costa Ave,
Carlsbad, CA 92009

www.surfcup.com TOURNAMENT DATES
2001 Schedule

GIRLS CUP
NOV 23-25, 2001

U-10	U-15
U-11	U-16
U-12	U-17
U-13	U-19
U-14	Super Group

July 28-30
Boys & Girls

U-10	U-13
U-11	U-14
U-12	U-15

August 4-6
Boys & Girls

U-15	U-17
U-16	U-19
Super Group	

TOURNAMENT DIRECTORY

TEXAS LIGHTNING
EST. 1992

Texas Lightning Soccer Club

SHOWCASE

Sophomore-Junior-Senior

Tournament

www.texaslightning.com

4th Annual Showcase Event

Now in our fourth year of providing a excellent launching pad for the perspective collegiate student athlete looking to play at the next level.

Held Easter weekend in North Texas

At the request of college coaches, and with the permission of the Arlington Soccer Association games will be held at one site: Harold Patterson Soccer Complex, Arlington Texas.

U-16 thru U-19 Boys & Girls Club Teams

Boys and Girls teams will be accepted on basis of their level of competitiveness. The total number of teams will be limited to insure the coaches in attendance will be able to view the players in depth.

Teams play 3 games at high quality Soccer Complex

Our goal is to get as many of the participating youth players seen by college coaches as possible. Each team will play in a atmosphere that encourages the highest level of competition and sportsmanship.

Over 100 College coaches representing NCAA Div. I, II, III, NAIA and NJCAA in attendance in 2000, more to be expected in 2001!

Contact our Event Coordinator (Babette Haddox) for your reservations at:
Phone: (972) 263-3571
Fax: (972) 642-6963
Email: event@flash.net
Reply early to insure your reservation.

Sponsored by:
PUMA®

NDCCSA CLASSIC LEAGUE

Providing The Highest Level Of Boys Competitive Soccer In The DFW Metro Area For Over 30 Years.

Host for the
North America Memorial Day Cup
May 26-28, 2001

For Information Contact:
GARY ROBINSON-EXECUTIVE DIRECTOR
10707 PRESTON ROAD, DALLAS TX. 75230

High Level Tournament Competition For Boys & Girls U11 - U19

OFFICE 214 361-5345 **FAX 214 361-5413**

Email: robosoc@gte.net

NOMADS
SOCCER CLUB

Nomads Soccer Club 3rd Annual Memorial Tournament

May 25th, 26th, 27th, 2001

Please visit our website at nomadssc.com for other tournament information.
Or email us at nomadssc@yahoo.com

Coaches Showcase: March 17th, 18th, 19th, 23rd, 24th, 25th,30th, 31st April 1st, 2001

Thanksgiving Invitational: November 23rd, 24th, 25th 2001

I've LOST
my MAGIC BALL.
Please call me.
It Looks like this
SELECT
Some call it magic.
SELECT
www.selectsportamerica.com
The Official Match Ball For:
WUSA
www.wusaleague.com
CONCACAF
www.footballconfederation.com
USFF
U.S. FUTSAL
www.futsal.com
SELECT

NOKIA

is proud to join forces with
The National Youth Soccer Alliance
to provide scholarship funds for

A Financial Award for A Dedicated Scholar-Athlete

To apply for the
NOKIA / National Youth Soccer Alliance Scholarship,
Call toll-free (877) 276-2220
or apply by e-mail to editor@goalonline.com

NOKIA

Supporting Excellence in Soccer, in Education, in Life

12278 Scripps Summit Drive, San Diego, CA 92131

www.nokia.com

Nokia and *Connecting People* are either trademarks or registered trademarks of Nokia Corporation and/or its affiliates.

What others are are saying about...

"If you are a high school student who wants to play soccer in college, The Sport Source® is the most important resource available for you and your parents".

Cobi Jones
U.S. National Team

"The Sport Source® is the most comprehensive, and informative recruiting guide I have come accross. The information which can be obtained on each college or university and its athletic program is invaluable to any prospective student-athlete and his/her parents. A great investment in a future athletic and academic career."

Elmar Bolowich
Head Men's Coach- University of North Carolina

"What The Sport Source® provides for student-athletes should be required reading for every student who plans to play sports after high school. I recommend this guide above all others."

Robin Fraser
U.S. National Team

...the Official Athletic College Guide:Soccer!

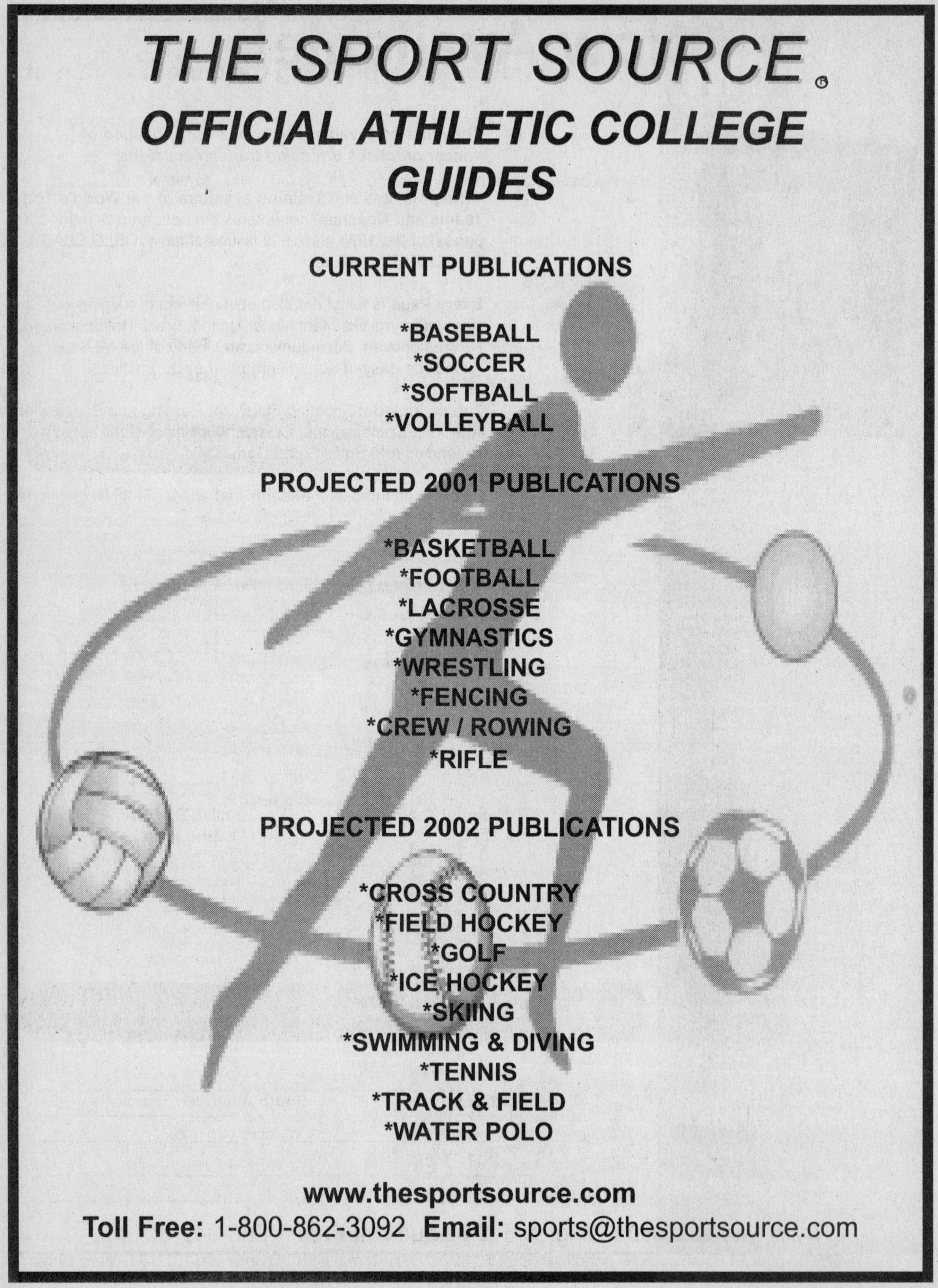
THE SPORT SOURCE ®
OFFICIAL ATHLETIC COLLEGE GUIDES
CURRENT PUBLICATIONS
*BASEBALL
*SOCCER
*SOFTBALL
*VOLLEYBALL
PROJECTED 2001 PUBLICATIONS
*BASKETBALL
*FOOTBALL
*LACROSSE
*GYMNASTICS
*WRESTLING
*FENCING
*CREW / ROWING
*RIFLE
PROJECTED 2002 PUBLICATIONS
*CROSS COUNTRY
*FIELD HOCKEY
*GOLF
*ICE HOCKEY
*SKIING
*SWIMMING & DIVING
*TENNIS
*TRACK & FIELD
*WATER POLO
www.thesportsource.com
Toll Free: 1-800-862-3092 Email: sports@thesportsource.com

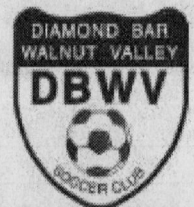

The Clubs of the CSL Premier League's 2000-2001 Season

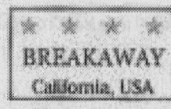

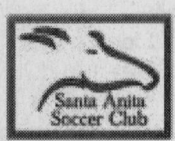

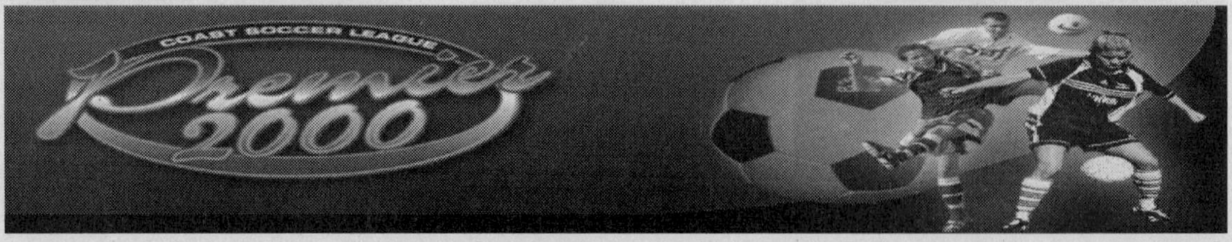

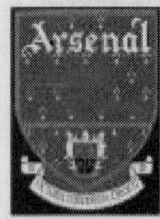

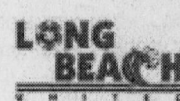

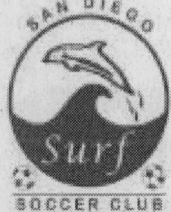

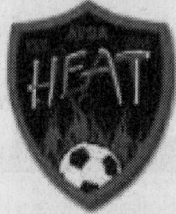

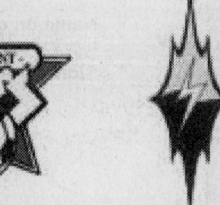

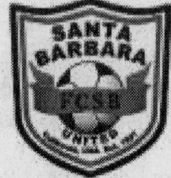

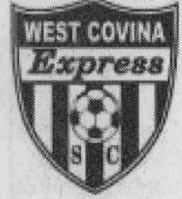

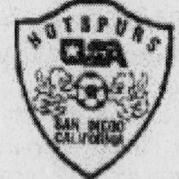

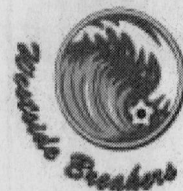

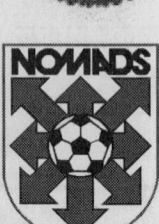

MESSAGE CSL PREMIER CHAIRMAN GARY SPARKS

The concept for the formation of the Coast Soccer Premier Leagues (CSL Premier League) is relatively simple: In order for truly great youth competition to become a reality, coaches, administrators, referees and players must all form a true partnership, each respecting the other, with a common goal of creating an atmosphere that will allow the players to do what they do best Play the Game.

The CSL Premier concept has been embraced by all those who participate in the CSL Premier League. Premier coaches have grasped the concept and are running with the ball. Games that need to be rescheduled due to recruiting trips are rescheduled between the respective coaches. Coaches control their sidelines. They take the responsibility to enforce Premier policy that referees, good or bad, are to be treated with respect and that all communication with a referee is to be between the coach and the referee.

The Referee Associations and their individual Premier referees have risen to the challenge as well and are working just as hard as the coaches to insure the games are won or lost on the field. Youth and Mentor Referees continue to provide a great surprise in their ability to grasp the significance of the Premier Leagues challenge and prove to be some of the best athletes on the field.

And CSL has committed to do its' part. CSL has leased two of the finest soccer complexes in Southern Calif. to host the Premier Games. CSL has created the Premier Magazine, the Premier League Website, fostered the development of Youth and Mentor Referees, and provide on site trainers to assist players to remain free from injury. And now, CSL introduces the CSL Premier League "Player Media Guide" in its' continuing efforts to promote the visibility of all CSL Premier League Players.

Each player has the ability to update their own home page at www.cslpremier.com as often as necessary to reflect their recent performances, both athletic and academic. We urge all coaches, scouts and recruiters to visit the Premier Games, watch our players and follow their careers. Coast Soccer League truly puts "The Best of the Best" on the pitch. The proof to this claim can clearly be demonstrated by the results of the 2000 MLS draft. Thirteen per cent (13%) of the 2000 draft consisted of CSL Players with six (6) out of twelve (12) first round selections coming from CSL.

This year, two (2) of our CSL Premier Leagues Champions, the So. Cal Blues Girls Under 16 and the Wolfpack Boys Under 18 made appearances at the Snicker's National Championship Finals. The So. Cal Blues took home the National Championship and the Wolfpack was a Finalist, losing a tough one in Shootouts. Excellent teams from excellent programs - that is what the CSL Premier Leagues is all about.

For every college coach who is planning a trip to our State, please do not hesitate to contact any member of the CSL Board of Directors or the CSL Premier Committee. We may easily be reached through the SCL Premier Website. We have made arrangements to accommodate you with our local sponsor hotels and will do everything possible to make your stay in Southern California enjoyable.

Very truly yours,

COAST SOCCER LEAGUE

By: **Gary L. Sparks**
Gary L. Sparks, CSL Premier Chairman

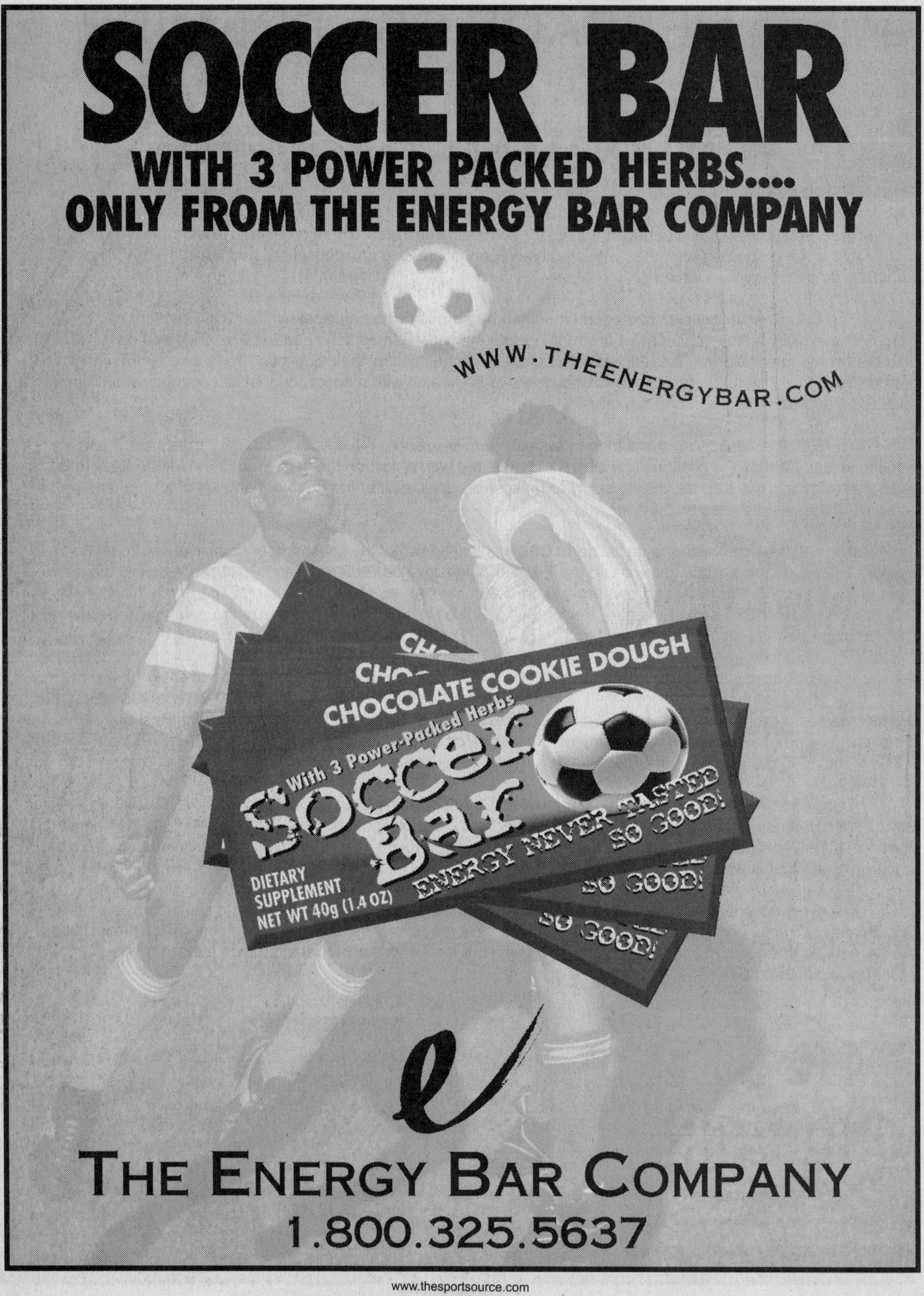
SOCCER BAR
WITH 3 POWER PACKED HERBS....
ONLY FROM THE ENERGY BAR COMPANY
WWW.THEENERGYBAR.COM
CHOCOLATE COOKIE DOUGH
With 3 Power-Packed Herbs
Soccer Bar
ENERGY NEVER TASTED SO GOOD!
DIETARY SUPPLEMENT
NET WT 40g (1.4 OZ)
THE ENERGY BAR COMPANY
1.800.325.5637

The Soccer St
TEAM SALES DIVISION • ALL MAJOR BRAN
13 YEARS EXPERIENCE!
PUMA
nike
adidas
• SOCCER COLLEGE GUIDES & WORKBOOKS
• FIELD EQUIPMENT
• RUGBY EQUIPMENT
• TEAM UNIFORMS
• REPLICA JERSEYS
• NFHS SOCCER BALLS
• EMBROIDERY & SILK SCREENING
SOCCER Stop
www.soccerstop.com
CALL OUR ORDER HOTLINE TOLL-FREE
1-888-220-8418

SOCCERPLUS
CAMPS
2001
GOALKEEPER
SCHOOL
FIELDPLAYER
ACADEMY
Presented by SoccerPlus and
Tony DiCicco, Head Coach of the
1996 USA Women s National
Team Olympic Champions and
1999 World Cup Champions
Call for a FREE Brochure
1-800 KEEPER 1
www.soccerpluscamps.com